THE
WRITERS
DIRECTORY
THIRTIETH EDITION

THE WRITERS DIRECTORY

THIRTIETH EDITION
VOLUME 5: R-U

Editor
Lisa Kumar

ST. JAMES PRESS
A part of Gale, Cengage Learning

GALE
CENGAGE Learning·

Detroit • New York • San Francisco • New Haven, Conn • Waterville, Maine • London

GALE
CENGAGE Learning·

Writers Directory, 30th Edition

Project Editor: Lisa Kumar

Editorial Support Services: Natasha Mikheyeva

Manufacturing: Rita Wimberley

© 2012 Gale, Cengage Learning

ALL RIGHTS RESERVED. No part of this work covered by the copyright herein may be reproduced, transmitted, stored, or used in any form or by any means graphic, electronic, or mechanical, including but not limited to photocopying, recording, scanning, digitizing, taping, Web distribution, information networks, or information storage and retrieval systems, except as permitted under Section 107 or 108 of the 1976 United States Copyright Act, without the prior written permission of the publisher.

This publication is a creative work fully protected by all applicable copyright laws, as well as by misappropriation, trade secret, unfair competition, and other applicable laws. The authors and editors of this work have added value to the underlying factual material herein through one or more of the following: unique and original selection, coordination, expression, arrangement, and classification of the information.

For product information and technology assistance, contact us at
Gale Customer Support, 1-800-877-4253.
For permission to use material from this text or product,
submit all requests online at **www.cengage.com/permissions.**
Further permissions questions can be emailed to
permissionrequest@cengage.com

While every effort has been made to ensure the reliability of the information presented in this publication, Gale, a part of Cengage Learning, does not guarantee the accuracy of the data contained herein. Gale accepts no payment for listing; and inclusion in the publication of any organization, agency, institution, publication, service, or individual does not imply endorsement of the editors or publisher. Errors brought to the attention of the publisher and verified to the satisfaction of the publisher will be corrected in future editions.

EDITORIAL DATA PRIVACY POLICY: Does this product contain information about you as an individual? If so, for more information about our editorial data privacy policies, please see our Privacy Statement at www.gale.cengage.com.

Gale
27500 Drake Rd.
Farmington Hills, MI, 48331-3535

ISBN-13: 978-1-4144-8712-0 (set)   ISBN-10: 1-4144-8712-6 (set)
ISBN-13: 978-1-4144-8713-7 (vol. 1)   ISBN-10: 1-4144-8713-4 (vol. 1)
ISBN-13: 978-1-4144-8714-4 (vol. 2)   ISBN-10: 1-4144-8714-2 (vol. 2)
ISBN-13: 978-1-4144-9901-7 (vol. 3)   ISBN-10: 1-4144-9901-9 (vol. 3)
ISBN-13: 978-1-4144-9902-4 (vol. 4)   ISBN-10: 1-4144-9902-7 (vol. 4)
ISBN-13: 978-1-4144-9903-1 (vol. 5)   ISBN-10: 1-4144-9903-5 (vol. 5)
ISBN-13: 978-1-4144-9904-8 (vol. 6)   ISBN-10: 1-4144-9904-3 (vol. 6)

ISSN 0084-2699

Printed in the United States of America
1 2 3 4 5   16 15 14 13 12

FD156

Contents

Preface

The Writers Directory is the newly revised and expanded thirtieth edition of this acclaimed reference work. It lists 26,615 writers—writing under 29,776 names—from all countries of the world who have had at least one work published in English.

The Directory is published in 6 individual volumes, with content divided as follows:

Volume 1: Lists entries from A-C
Volume 2: Lists entries from D-G
Volume 3: Lists entries from H-L
Volume 4: Lists entries from M-Q
Volume 5: Lists entries from R-U
Volume 6: Lists entries from V-Z, Obituaries, Index to Writing Categories, and Country of Citizenship Index

The Directory lists approximately 26,526 living writers of fiction and non-fiction who have published at least one full-length work in English. Listees run the gamut from the best-known, best selling authors of fiction and the most prominent non-fiction writers to those writers just embarking on their literary careers. The thirtieth edition includes nearly 1,000 writers whose listings have not appeared in a previous edition of The Writers Directory.

The **Obituaries** Section contains the entries for approximately 89 writers whose listings have appeared in previous editions of The Writers Directory and whose passing was made known to us in preparing this edition.

Compilation Methods

Selection of writers to appear in The Writers Directory is based primarily on reference value. Biographical and career information is researched for each writer, then a copy of the entry is sent to the writer for his or her approval and updates. By this process, the editors can assure comprehensive, current information. At the same time, entries in the previous edition were rigorously reviewed with an eye toward their current research value. As a result, some writers' entries have been retired to make way for those of new writers.

How to Read a Citation

Entries in The Writers Directory contain some or all of the following elements (please note that this is a sample entry for demonstration purposes only):

❚1❚ WILLIAMS, Mae. ❚2❚ (Allison May Williams) ❚3❚ Also writes as William Allison. ❚4❚ American (born Malta), ❚5❚ b. 1945. ❚6❚ **Genres:** Novels, Biography. ❚7❚ **Career:** Freelance writer. ❚8❚ **Publications:** Paris, L'amour, 1972; (ed.) Running through the Weeds, 1982; (as William Allison) Louis, My Love (biography), 1987; The Waves at My Back, 1997. ❚9❚ **Address:** 27500 Drake Rd., Farmington Hills, MI 48331U.S.A. ❚10❚ **Online address:** maewil@aol.com ❚11❚ Died 1997.

❚1❚ Name of writer with fuller name information in parentheses

❚2❚ Full name of writer if different from writing name or pseudonyms but not used for writing

❚3❚ Pseudonym information

❚4❚ Nationality—if birthplace is different from nationality, it will follow the nationality in parentheses

❚5❚ Birth year

❚6❚ Genres—corresponds to **Index to Writing Categories**

❚7❚ Brief career information

❚8❚ Publications: title, year of publication, pseudonym if used, special awards

❚9❚ Address

❚10❚ Online address and/or web site

❚11❚ Death notation and year (in **Obituaries** Section only)

Cross references appear in the following form:

To main entry in main section: **ALLISON, William**. See **WILLIAMS, Mae.**

From main section to main entry in **Obituaries** section: **WILLIAMS, Mae.** See Obituaries.

From pseudonym in main section to main entry in **Obituaries** section: **ALLISON, William.** See **WILLIAMS, Mae** in the Obituaries.

Writers (and cross references) are listed alphabetically by surname which are sorted letter-by-letter. In cases where surnames are identical, writers are listed first by surname, then by given and middle names, and finally by suffixes such as Jr., Sr., II, or III. Surnames beginning with a prefix (such as Du, Mac, or Van), however spaced, are listed alphabetically under the first letter of the prefix and treated as if there were no space. Other compound surnames, hyphenated names, and names with apostrophes are alphabetized as if there were no space or punctuation. Surnames beginning with Saint or St. appear after names beginning with Sains and before names beginning with Sainu.

Entries in the **Obituaries** Section follow the same style as those in the main entries with the addition of the notation *Died* and the death year (if known) at the end of the entry.

Features

The Writers Directory contains many features to enhance its usefulness:

Boldface Rubrics allow quick and easy scanning for specifics on genre, career, publication, and mailing and online addresses.

The Obituaries Section lists the entries for those writers whose listing appeared in previous editions of The Writers Directory and whose passing was made known to us in preparing this edition. Cross references have been provided in the main body of the Directory to those deceased writers.

Indexing

The Writers Directory includes two indexes. In the **Index to Writing Categories**, one can locate writers by the type of works they write. New categories are added to The Writers Directory as needed to reflect new topics of interest and to define a writer's body of work more accurately. The **Country of Citizenship Index** lists writers by their country of citizenship as provided by the writer. Users are advised that one writer with multiple citizenship may appear under one country grouping (e.g., Canada-England) while another with the same citizenships may appear under a different grouping (e.g., England-Canada) depending on how the writer submitted the information.

The **Index to Writing Categories and Country of Citizenship Index** can be found in Volume 6 of the Directory following the **Obituaries** Section.

Also Available in Electronic Formats

Licensing. *The Writers Directory* is available for licensing. The complete database is provided in a fielded format and is deliverable on such media as disk or CD-ROM. For more information, contact Gale's Business Development Group at 1-800-877-GALE, or visit us on our web site at gale. cengage. com.

Online. *The Writers Directory* is accessible as part of Gale's Biography in Context database, as well as through the Gale Biographies database (File GALBIO) through Lexis-Nexis. For more information on Biography in Context, visit us on our web site at gale.cengage.com. For more information on Gale Biographies, contact LexisNexis, P.O. Box 933, Dayton, OH 45401-0933; phone (937) 865-6800; toll- free: 800-227-4908.

Suggestions Welcome

Comments and suggestions from users of *The Writers Directory* on any aspect of the product as well as suggestions for writers to be included in a future edition are cordially invited. Please write:

The Editor

The Writers Directory

St. James Press

Gale, a part of Cengage Learning

27500 Drake Rd.

Farmington Hills, Michigan 48331-3535.

Entry in *The Writers Directory* is at the discretion of the editor.

Abbreviations Used In The Writers Directory

A

AB	Alberta
ABC	American Broadcasting Company
ACT	Australian Capital Territory
AK	Alaska
AL	Alabama
Apt.	Apartment
AR	Arkansas
Assn.	Association
Assoc.	Associate
Asst.	Assistant
Ave.	Avenue
AZ	Arizona

B

b.	born
BBC	British Broadcasting Corporation
BC	British Columbia
Beds.	Bedfordshire
Berks.	Berkshire
Bldg.	Building
Blvd.	Boulevard
Brig.	Brigadier
Bros.	Brothers
Bucks.	Buckinghamshire

C

CA	California
Cambs.	Cambridgeshire
Can.	Canada
Capt.	Captain
CBC	Canadian Broadcasting Company
CBS	Columbia Broadcasting System (US)
CIA	Central Intelligence Agency (US)
CO; co.	Colorado; Company; County
Co-ed.	Co-editor
Co-trans.	Co-translator
Col.	Colonel
Contrib.	Contributor; Contributing
Corp.	Corporation
CPA	Certified Public Accountant
Cres.	Crescent
CT; Ct.	Connecticut; Court

D

DC	District of Columbia
DE	Delaware
Dept.	Department
Derbys.	Derbyshire
Dir.	Director
Div.	Division
Dr.	Doctor; Drive

E

E.	East
Ed.	Editor; Edition
Exec.	Executive

F

FBI	Federal Bureau of Investigation (US)
FL	Florida
Ft.	Fort

G

GA	Georgia
Gen.	General
Glam.	Glamorgan
Glos.	Glouchestershire
Gov.	Governor
Govt.	Government

H

Hants.	Hampshire
HE	His Eminence; His/Her Excellency
Herts.	Hertfordshire
HI	Hawaii
HM	His/Her Majesty
HMS	His/Her Majesty's Ship; His/Her Majesty's Service
Hon.	Honorable; Honorary

I

IA	Iowa
ID	Idaho
IL	Illinois
IN	Indiana
Inc.	Incorporated
Inst.	Institute
Intl.	International

J

Jr.	Junior

K

KS	Kansas
KY	Kentucky

L

LA	Louisiana
Lab.	Laboratory
Lancs.	Lancashire
Leics.	Leicestershire
LI	Long Island
Lincs.	Lincolnshire
Lt.	Lieutenant
Ltd.	Limited

M

MA	Massachusetts
Mag.	Magazine
Maj.	Major
MB	Manitoba
MD	Maryland
ME	Maine
Mgr.	Manager
MI	Michigan
Middx.	Middlesex
MN	Minnesota
MO	Missouri
MP	Member of Parliament
MT; Mt.	Montana; Mount, Mountain

N

N.	North
NASA	National Aeronautics and Space Administration
NATO	North Atlantic Treaty Organization
NB	New Brunswick
NBC	National Broadcasting System (US)
NC	North Carolina
NE	North East
NF	Newfoundland
NH	New Hampshire
NJ	New Jersey
NL	Newfoundland and Labrador
NM	New Mexico
No.	Number

Northants.	Northamptonshire
Notts.	Nottinghamshire
nr.	Near
NS	Nova Scotia
NSW	New South Wales
NT	Northern Territory (Australia); Northwest Territories (Canada)
NU	Nunavut
NV	Nevada
NW	North West
NWT	Northwest Territories
NY	New York
NYC	New York City

O

OH	Ohio
OK	Oklahoma
ON	Ontario
OR	Oregon
Orch.	Orchestra
Org.	Organization
Oxon.	Oxfordshire

P

PA	Pennsylvania
PE, PEI	Prince Edward Island
PEN	Poets, Playwrights, Essayists, Editors, Novelists
Pl.	Place
PO	Post Office
Pres.	President
Prof.	Professor
Prog.	Program
Publrs.	Publishers
Publs.	Publications

Q

QC	Quebec
QLD	Queensland

R

Rd.	Road
Rep.	Representative
Rev. ed.	Revised edition
RI	Rhode Island
RR	Rural Route
Rte.	Route

S

S.	South
SA	South Australia
Salop.	Shropshire
SC	South Carolina
Sch.	School
SD	South Dakota
SE	South East
Sec	Secretary
SK	Saskatchewan
Soc.	Society
Sq.	Square
Sr.	Senior
St.	Saint; Street
Staffs.	Staffordshire
Ste.	Suite
Supt.	Superintendent
SW	South West

T

Tas.	Tasmania
Terr.	Terrace
TN	Tennessee
Trans.	Translator; Translation
Treas.	Treasurer
TX	Texas

U

UK	United Kingdom
UN	United Nations
Unesco	United Nations Educational, Scientific and Cultural Organization

Unicef	United Nations Children's Emergency Fund
Univ.	University
US;	USA United States, United States of America
USS	United States Ship; United States Service
USSR	Union of Soviet Socialist Republics
UT	Utah

V

VA	Virginia
VIC	Victoria
Vol(s).	Volume(s)
VT	Vermont

W

W.	West
WA	Washington; Western Australia
Warks.	Warwicks; Warwickshire
WHO	World Health Organization
WI	Wisconsin
Wilts.	Wiltshire
Worcs.	Worcestershire
WV	West Virginia
WY	Wyoming

Y

YM-YWHA	Young Men's-Young Women's Hebrew Association
YMCA	Young Men's Christian Association
Yorks.	Yorkshire
YWCA	Young Women's Christian Association
YT	Yukon Territory

R

R, Ji. *See* RENAUD, Jacques.

RA, Carol F. *See* LEWIS, Carol F. Ra.

RAAB, David. Israeli (born Israel), b. 1952?. Genres: Humanities, Trivia/Facts, Politics/Government, History, Social Commentary. Career: Raab & Co. (consulting firm), owner; University of Pennsylvania, faculty; Philadelphia College of Textiles and Science, faculty; Yeshiva University, Sy Syms School of Business, faculty; America Israel Chamber of Commerce, board director. Writer. Publications: Terror in Black September: The First Eyewitness Account of the Infamous 1970 Hijackings, 2007; Accountability to the People: Instituting Single-Member Electoral Districts for Israel's Knesset, 2007. Contributor to periodicals. Address: Palgrave Macmillan, 175 5th Ave., New York, NY 10010, U.S.A. Online address: davidraab@terrorinblackseptember.com

RAAD, Virginia. American (born United States), b. 1925. Genres: Music, Biography. Career: Teacher and writer. Publications: The Piano Sonority of Claude Debussy, 1994. Contributor to music journals. Address: 60 Terrace Ave., Salem, WV 26426-1116, U.S.A.

RAADSCHELDERS, Jos C. N. American/Dutch (born Netherlands), b. 1955. Genres: Politics/Government, Public/Social Administration, Social Sciences. Career: University of Leiden, assistant professor, 1983-92, associate professor of public administration, 1992-98; University of Oklahoma, Department of Political Science, assistant professor of public administration, 1998-2001, professor and Henry Bellmon chair of public service, 2000-11, adjunct professor; Public Administration Review, managing editor, 2006-11; The Ohio State University, John Glenn School of Public Affairs, interim associate director for academic affairs and research, professor, 2011-. Publications: Handbook of Administrative History, 1998; Church and State in Western Europe in an Administrative History Perspective (19th-20th Centuries), 2002; Government: A Public Administration Perspective, 2003; (ed.) Institutional Arrangements for Water Management in the 19th and 20th Centuries, 2005; (ed. with T.A.J. Toonen and F.M. van der Meer) The Civil Service in the 21st Century: Comparative Perspectives, 2007; (with B.R. Fry) Mastering Public Administration: From Max Weber to Dwight Waldo, 2008. UNTRANSLATED WORKS: Plaatselijke Bestuurlijke Ontwikkelingen: Een Historisch- Bestuurskundig Onderzoek in Vier Noord-Hollandse Gemeenten (title means: 'Local Government Administrative Development, 1600-1980: An Administrative History of Four North Holland Municipalities'), 1990; (with T.A.J. Toonen and F. Hendriks) Meso-Bestuurin Europees Perspectief: De (Randstad) Provincies uit de Pas? (title means: 'Meso-Government in European Perspective: The Randstad Provinces out of Touch?'), 1992; Lokale Bestuursgeschiedenis (title means: 'Local Government History'), 1992; De Vierde Macht: Ambtenaren in Nederland (title means: 'The Fourth Power: The Civil Service in the Netherlands'), 1992; (ed. with Toonen) Waterschappen in Nederland: Een Bestuurskundige Verkenningvan de Institutionele Ontwikkeling (title means: 'Waterboards in the Netherlands: An Administrative Science Exploration of the Institutional Development'), 1993; Tussen Markt en Overheid: Een Bestuursgeschiedenis vande Centrale Vereniging voor Ambulante Handel, 1921-1996 (title means: 'Between Market and Government: An Administrative History of the National Union for Itinerant

Trade'), 1996; (ed. with F.M. van der Meer) L'Entourage Administratif du Pouvoir Executif, 1998. Contributor of articles to journals. Address: John Glenn School of Public Affairs, The Ohio State University, 350c Page Hall, 1810 College Rd., Columbus, OH 43210-1336, U.S.A. Online address: raadschelders.1@osu.edu

RABALAIS, J. Wayne. American (born United States), b. 1944. Genres: Novels, Sciences, Technology, Engineering. Career: University of Florida, instructor in chemistry and physics, 1968; University of Uppsala, NATO postdoctoral fellow, 1970-71; University of Pittsburgh, assistant professor, 1971-75; University of Houston, Department of Chemistry, associate professor, 1975-79, associate chairman, 1978-82, professor of chemistry and physics, 1979-81, distinguished university chair professor, 1981-88, Hugh Roy and Lillie Cranz Cullen distinguished professor, 1988-, Cullen distinguished professor of chemistry and physics, 1988-, chairman, 2001-04, now professor emeritus, Physical Chemistry Division, chairman, 1990-95, Department of Physics, faculty, 1992-, Chemical Physics Program, chairman, 1994-; Center for Materials Chemistry, professor and chairman; Lamar University, Department of Chemistry and Biochemistry, distinguished professor of surface chemistry, 2004-. Writer. Publications: Principles of Ultraviolet Photoelectron Spectroscopy, 1977; (ed.) Low Energy Ion-Surface Interactions, 1994; Proceedings of the Twelfth International Workshop on Inelastic Ion-Surface Collisions, 1999; Principles and Applications of Ion Scattering Spectrometry: Surface Chemical and Structural Analysis, 2003. Contributor of articles to journals. Address: Department of Chemistry and Biochemistry, Lamar University, 122 Chemistry Bldg., 4400 MLK Blvd., PO Box 10022, Beaumont, TX 77710, U.S.A. Online address: wayne.rabalais@lamar.edu

RABAN, Jonathan. American/British (born England), b. 1942. Genres: Novels, Literary Criticism And History, Social Commentary, Travel/Exploration, Essays. Career: University College of Wales, lecturer in English literature, 1966-67; University of East Anglia, lecturer in English literature, 1967-69; writer, 1969-; Smith College, visiting lecturer, 1972. Publications: The Technique of Modern Fiction: Essay in Practical Criticism, 1968; Mark Twain: Huckleberry Finn, 1968; The Society of the Poem, 1971; Soft City, 1974; (ed. and intro.) Robert Lowell's Poems: A Selection, 1974; Arabia: A Journey through the Labyrinth, 1979; Old Glory: An American Voyage, 1981; Foreign Land: A Novel, 1985; Coasting, 1986 as Coasting: A Private Journey, 2003; For Love and Money: Writing, Reading, Travelling, 1969-1987, 1987 in US as For Love and Money: A Writing Life, 1969-1989, 1989; God, Man, and Mrs. Thatcher, 1989; Hunting Mister Heartbreak, 1990 in US as Hunting Mister Heartbreak: A Discovery of America, 1991; (ed.) The Oxford Book of the Sea, 1992; Bad Land: An American Romance, 1996; Old Glory: A Voyage Down the Mississippi, 1998; Passage to Juneau: A Sea and Its Meanings, 1999; (intro.) Pacific Northwest Landscape: A Painted History, 2001; Waxwings (novel), 2003; My Holy War: Dispatches from the Home Front, 2006; Surveillance, 2006; (with W.L. Lang) Here There Nowhere, 2007; Driving Home: An American Scrapbook, 2010; Driving Home: An American Journey, 2010. Contributor to periodicals. Address: Aitken & Stone Ltd., 29 Fernshaw Rd., London, GL SW10 0TG, England.

RABASA, George. American (born United States), b. 1941. Genres: Novels, Novellas/Short Stories. Career: Writer. Publications: 26 Minnesota Writers, 1995; Glass Houses (short story collection), 1996; Floating Kingdom: A Novel, 1997; The Cleansing, 2006; The Wonder Singer, 2008; Miss Entropia and the Adam Bomb, 2011. **Address:** Minneapolis, MN , U.S.A. **Online address:** garabasa@earthlink.net

RABASSA, Gregory. American (born United States), b. 1922. **Genres:** Poetry, Literary Criticism And History, Translations, Young Adult Fiction, Autobiography/Memoirs. **Career:** Columbia University, instructor in Spanish, 1947-52, associate, 1952-58, assistant professor, 1958-64, associate professor of Spanish and Portuguese, 1964-68; Odyssey Review, associate editor, 1961-64; City University of New York, Queens College, professor of romance languages, 1968-85, distinguished professor, 1985-. **Publications:** TRANSLATIONS: J. Cortazar, Hopscotch, 1966; C. Lispector, The Apple in the Dark, 1967; M. Asturias, Mulata in UK as Mulatta and Mr. Fly, 1967; A. Coutinho, An Introduction to Literature in Brazil, 1969; M. Asturias, Strong Wind, 1969; M. Mujica-Láinez, Bomarzo, 1969; M. Asturias, The Green Pope, 1971; G.G. Márquez, Leaf Storm and Other Stories, 1972; D. Trevisan, The Vampire of Coritiba, 1973; M. Asturias, The Eyes of the Interred, 1973; J.L. Lima, Paradiso, 1974; M.V. Llosa, Conversation in the Cathedral, 1975; J. Cortazar, A Manual for Manuel, 1978; D. Aguilera-Malta, Seven Serpents and Seven Moons, 1979; G.G. Marquez, In Evil Hour, 1979; J. Cortazar, A Change of Light and Other Stories, 1980; (and intro.) L.R. Sanchez, Macho Camacho's Beat, 1981; V. de Moraes, The Girl from Ipanêma, 1982; J. Benet, A Meditation, 1983; J. Cortazar, We Love Glenda So Much and Other Tales, 1983; G.G. Marquez, Chronicle of a Death Foretold, 1983; L. Valenzuela, The Lizard's Tail, 1983; J. Amado, Sea of Death, 1984; J. Cortazar, A Certain Lucas, 1984; (with B.J. Bernstein) G.G. Marquez, Collected Stories, 1984; J. Benet, Return to Región, 1985; O. França Jr., The Man in the Monkey Suit, 1986; J. Goytisolo, Marks of Identity, 1988; J. Amado, Captains of the Sands, 1988; J. Amado, Showdown, 1988; A.L. Antunes, Fado Alexandrino, 1990; J. Donoso, Taratuta and Still Life with Pipe, 1993; G.G. Márquez, One Hundred Years of Solitude, 1995; I. Vilar, A Message from God in the Atoimic Age, 1996; M. de Carvalho, A God Strolling in the Cool of the Evening, 1997; J.M.M. de Assis, The Posthumous Memoirs of Bras Cubas, 1997; J.M.M. de Assis, Quincas Borba, 1998; A.T. Torres, Dõna Ines vs. Oblivion: A Novel, 1999; (with J.S. Bernstein) G.G. Márquez, Collected Novellas, 1999; G.G. Marquez, The Autumn of the Patriarch, 1999; D. Ribeiro, The Brazilian People: The Formation and Meaning of Brazil, 2000; J. Cortázar, 62: A Model Kit, 2000; A.L. Antunes, The Return of the Caravels: A Novel, 2002; (and intro.) O. Lins, Avalovara, 2002; J de Melo, My World Is Not of This Kingdom, 2003; J. Zárate, Jail, 2003; J. Franco, Rosario Tijeras, 2003; G.G. Marquez, Innocent Erendira and Other Stories, 2005; J. Amado, the War of the Saints, 2005; G.G. Márquez, Innocent Erendira and Other Stories, 2005; M.V. Llosa, The Green House, 2005; J. Amado, War of the Saints, 2005; J. Goytisolo, Marks of Identity, 2007; J. Sarney, Saraminda: Black Desire in a Field of Gold, 2007; A.L. Antunes, What Can I Do When Everything's on Fire?, 2008; I. Vilar, The Ladie's Gallery: A Memoir of Family Secrets, 2009; J.M. Eça de Queirs, Correspondence of Fradique Mendes, 2010. OTHERS: O Negro na ficçäo brasileira, 1965; (intro.) The World of Translation, 1987; A Cloudy Day in Gray Minor (poetry), 1989; If This Be Treason: Translations and Its Dyscontents (memoir), 2005. **Address:** The Graduate Center, Queens College, City University of New York, 365 5th Ave., New York, NY 10016, U.S.A.

RABATÉ, Jean-Michel. American/French (born France), b. 1949. **Genres:** Literary Criticism And History, Mystery/Crime/Suspense. **Career:** University of Dijon, professor of English, 1980-92; University of Pennsylvania, School of Arts and Sciences, professor of English and comparative literature, 1992-, Vartan Gregorian professor in the humanities; Ulysse fin de siecle, (publishing house), co-chair; College International de Philosophie, program director; Journal of Modern Literature, managing editor, 2008-; American Academy of Arts and Science, fellow. **Publications:** (Comp.) Beckett avant Beckett, 1984; Joyce: Portrait de l'Auteur en Autre Lecteur, 1984; Language, Sexuality, and Ideology in Pound's Cantos, 1986; La Beauté Amère, Fragments d'Esthetiques, 1986; Maurice Darantiére: Les années vingt, 1988; (intro.) Lettres de Paris, 1988; Thomas Bernhard, 1991; James Joyce, Authorized Reader, 1991; Joyce upon the Void: The Genesis of Doubt, 1991; La Penultieme est Morte: Spectrographies de la Modernite, 1993, trans. as Ghosts of Modernity, 1996; James Joyce and the Politics of Egoism, 2001; Jacques Lacan: Psychoanalysis and the Subject of Literature, 2001; The Future of Theory, 2002; Tout dire ou ne rien dire, 2005; 1913: The Cradle of Modernism, 2007; Given, 1 Art 2 Crime: Modernity, Murder and Mass Culture, 2007; Ethics of the Lie, 2007; Given, 1/0 art 2/0 Crime, 2007. EDITOR: Ezra Pound: Je rassemble les membres d'Osiris, 1989; L'Ethique du Don: Derrida

et la Question du Don, 1992; Writing the Image after Roland Barthes, 1997; Jacques Lacan in America, 2000; The Cambridge Companion to Jacques Lacan, 2003; (with A. Levy) Of the Diagram: The Work of Marjorie Welish, 2003; Palgrave Advances in James Joyce Studies, 2004; (with A. Levy) William Anastasi's Pataphysical Society: Jarry, Joyce, Duchamp, and Cage, 2005; (with A. Levy) Ex-Cities, 2006. Contributor to periodicals. **Address:** Department of English, School of Arts & Sciences, University of Pennsylvania, Fisher-Bennett Hall 339, 3340 Walnut St., Philadelphia, PA 19104-6273, U.S.A. **Online address:** jmrabate@english.upenn.edu

RABB, Jonathan. American (born United States), b. 1964. **Genres:** Mystery/Crime/Suspense, Novels, Literary Criticism And History. **Career:** Columbia University, lecturer, 1992-95. Writer. **Publications:** NOVELS: The Overseer (thriller novel), 1998; The Book of Q (thriller novel), 2001. BERLIN TRILOGY SERIES: Rosa: A Novel, 2005; Shadow and Light, 2009; The Second Son, 2011. Contributor to periodicals. **Address:** 310 W 72nd St., New York, NY 10023-2675, U.S.A.

RABB, Margo. (M. E. Rabb). American (born United States), b. 1972?. **Genres:** Mystery/Crime/Suspense, Young Adult Fiction, Novels. **Career:** Author. **Publications:** MISSING PERSONS MYSTERY SERIES AS M.E. RABB: The Rose Queen, 2004; The Chocolate Lover, 2004; The Venetian Policeman, 2004; The Unsuspecting Gourmet, 2004. OTHERS: Midwest Writers' Resources, 1993; (co-author) Glimmer Train Stories, #33, 1999; Cures for Heartbreak, 2007. Contributor to periodicals. **Address:** c/o Author Mail, William Morris Agency, 1325 Ave. of the Americas, New York, NY 10019-6026, U.S.A. **Online address:** margo@margorabb.com

RABB, M. E. See **RABB, Margo.**

RABB, Theodore K. American/Czech (born Czech Republic), b. 1937. **Genres:** History, Art/Art History, Military/Defense/Arms Control, Intellectual History. **Career:** Stanford University, instructor in history, 1961-62; Northwestern University, instructor in history, 1962-63; Harvard University, assistant professor of history, 1963-67; Princeton University, associate professor, 1967-76, professor of history, 1976-2007, professor emeritus, 2007-; Johns Hopkins University, visiting associate professor, 1969; State University of New York, visiting associate professor, 1972-73. Writer and consultant. **Publications:** (Ed. and intro.) The Thirty Years' War: Problems of Motive, Extent and Effect, 1964, 2nd ed., 1981; Enterprise & Empire: Merchant and Gentry Investment in the Expansion of England, 1575-1630, 1967; The Struggle for Stability in Early Modern Europe, 1975; Climate and History: Studies in Interdisciplinary History, 1981; Renaissance Lives: Portraits of an Age, 1993, rev. ed., 2000; Origins of the Modern West: Essays and Sources in Renaissance & Early Modern European History, 1993; (co-author) The Western Experience, 6th ed., 1994, 8th ed., 2003; Jacobean Gentleman: Sir Edwin Sandys 1561-1629, 1998; Last Days of the Renaissance and the Path to Modernity, 2006; (trans. and intro.) H. Sachs, Sixteenth-century Book of Trades: das ständebuch, 2009; The Artist and the Warrior: Military History through the Eyes of the Masters, 2011. EDITOR: (with J.E. Segel) Action and Conviction in Early Modern Europe: Essays in Memory of E.H. Harbison, 1969; (with R.I. Rotberge) The Family in History: Interdisciplinary Essays, 1976; (with E.N. Suleiman) Making and Unmaking of Democracy: Lessons from History and World Politics, 2003; (with B. Hollinshead) I Wish I'd Been There II: Western History, 2008. CO-EDITOR: Marriage and Fertility: Studies in Interdisciplinary History, 1980; Industrialization and Urbanization: Studies in Interdisciplinary History, 1981; The New History, the 1980s and Beyond: Studies in Interdisciplinary History, 1982; Hunger and History: The Impact of Changing Food Production and Consumption Patterns on Society, 1985; Population and Economy: Population and History from the Traditional to the Modern World, 1986; Art and History: Images and Their Meaning, 1988; The Origin and Prevention of Major Wars, 1989. **Address:** Department of History, Princeton University, 129 Dickinson Hall, Princeton, NJ 08544, U.S.A. **Online address:** tkrabb@princeton.edu

RABE, Berniece (Louise). American (born United States), b. 1928. **Genres:** Children's Fiction, Picture/Board Books. **Career:** Teacher, 1963-76; Society of Midland Authors, board director; Off Campus Writers, board director; Fox Valley Writers, board director; Columbia College, instructor of creative writing. Writer. **Publications:** Rass, 1973; Two Peas in a Pod, 1974; Naomi, 1975; Can They See Me?, 1976; The Girl Who Had No Name, 1977; The Orphans, 1978; Who's Afraid?, 1980; The Balancing Girl, 1981; Margaret's Moves, 1987; A Smooth Move, 1987; Rehearsal for the Bigtime, 1988;

Where's Chimpy?, 1988; Tall Enough to Own the World, 1989; Magic Comes in Its Time, 1993; The First Christmas Candy Canes: A Legend, 1994; Hiding Mr. McMulty, 1997. Contributor to magazines. **Address:** McIntosh & Otis Inc., 353 Lexington Ave., New York, NY 10016, U.S.A. **Online address:** berniece@berniecerabe.com

RABE, Jean. (Jordan Gray). American (born United States), b. 1942?. **Genres:** Novels, Children's Fiction. **Career:** MechForce Quarterly, editor; TSR, game designer, 1987-. **Publications:** Cities of Mystery, 1989; Vale of the Mage, 1990; Red Magic, 1991; (with J. Lowder) The Jungles of Chult, 1993; Krynnspace, 1993; Swamplight, 1993; Secret of the Djinn, 1994; Night of the Tiger, 1995; (with T. Daniell) Maquesta Kar-Thon, 1995; The Dawning of a New Age, 1996; Book of Magecraft, 1996; Scoundrel's Folly, 1996; Sands of Deception, 1996; The Eve of the Maelstorm, 1997; (with P. McGilligan) The Day of the Tempest, 1997; The Silver Stair, 1998; Downfall, 2000; Betrayal, 2001; (ed. with M.H. Greenberg) Historical Hauntings, 2001; (ed. with M.H. Greenberg) Sol's Children, 2002; Redemption, 2002; (with J. Pack, M. Robertson and C. Stiles) Way of the Witch, 2002; The Lake of Death, 2004; The Finest Creation, 2004; The Finest Choice, 2005; (ed. with A. Norton) Renaissance Faire, 2005; (ed. with B.M. Thomsen) Furry Fantastic, 2006; The Finest Challenge, 2006; (ed. with A. Norton) Return to Quag Keep, 2006; (with J. Helfers) Aftershock, 2006; (with A. Norton) Taste of Magic, 2006; (ed. with M.H. Greenberg) Pandora's Closet, 2007; Fenzig's Fortune, 2007; (ed. with M.H. Greenberg) Time Twisters, 2007; (with F.L. Bailey) When the Husband is the Suspect, 2008; (with A. Norton) Dragon Mage, 2008; (ed. with S.D. Sullivan) Pirates of the Blue Kingdoms: Buxom Buccaneers, 2008; Goblin Nation, 2009; Eternal Journey, 2010. AS JORDAN GRAY: Stolen, 2010; Vanished, 2010; Unearthed, 2011; Submerged, 2011. **Address:** c/o Author Mail, Tor Forge, 175 5th Ave., New York, NY 10010-7703, U.S.A.

RABIE, Mohamed. American (born United States), b. 1940. **Genres:** International Relations/Current Affairs, Area Studies, Social Sciences. **Career:** South Texas College, assistant professor of economics, 1967-69; Texas Southern University, assistant professor of economics, 1968-70; Kuwait University, associate professor of economics, 1970-76; American University of Beirut, visiting professor, 1973; Arab Economists Corp., founder, 1973, chair, 1973-77; International Trade and Investment Inc., founder, 1977, president, 1977-82; Georgetown University, professor of economics, 1982-83; American University, professor of economics, 1984-86; Johns Hopkins University, School of Advanced International Studies, professor, 1984-85; Roots (nonprofit youth organization), president, 1986-87; Center for Educational Development, president, 1987-94; Erfurt University, International Academic Affairs, director, 1998-2000, academic advisor, 1999-2000; Al-Akhawayn University, professor of political and economic studies, 2001-. Writer. **Publications:** Hijrat al-Kifāyāt al-'ilmiyah, 1972; Isrā'il wa-al-qārrah al-Ifriqiyah: al-ab'ād wa-al-makhāṭir, 1986; Hijrah al-Yahūdiyah min Filasṭin al-muḥtallah' 1986; Al-Wajh al-ākhar lil-hazimah al-'Arabiyah, 1987; The Politics of Foreign Aid: U.S. Foreign Assistance and Aid to Israel, 1988; A Vision for the Transformation of the Middle East, 1990; Ṣun' al-siyāsah al-Amrīkīyah wa-al-'Arab, 1990; al-Ma'ūnāt al-Amrīkīyah li-Isrāil' 1990; The New World Order: A Perspective on the Post-Cold War Era, 1992; Conflict Resolution and the Middle East Peace Process, 1993; Riḥlah ma'a al-qalaq, 1994; Conflict Resolution and Ethnicity, 1994; The U.S.-PLO Dialogue, 1995; Ṣun' al-mustaqbal al-'Arabi: al-masirah al-tārikhiyah min al-qabaliyah ilá al-'wlamah, 2000; The Making of History, 2001; Kharif al-dhikrayāt: shi'r, 2006; Hurūb fi ayn al-shams: riwāyah, 2009. IN ARABIC: The Brain Drain, 1972; Economics and Society, 1973; The Geneva Conference and the Prospects for Peace, 1977; The Other Side of Arab Defeat, 1987; U.S. Foreign Assistance and Aid to Israel, 1990; The Making of American Foreign Policy, 1990; A Journey through Worry, 1994; The Making of the Arab Future, 2000; The Train of Time (poetry), 2001. Contributor to periodicals. **Address:** 7416 Helmsdale Rd., Bethesda, MD 20817, U.S.A. **Online address:** rabie1@aol.com

RABIEH, Linda R. American (born United States), b. 1969?. **Genres:** History, Philosophy. **Career:** Tufts University, Department of Political Science, lecturer; Harvard University, Program on Constitutional Government, fellow, 2002. Writer. **Publications:** Plato and the Virtue of Courage, 2006. **Address:** Department of Political Science, Tufts University, Eaton Hall, 3rd Fl., Medford, MA 02155, U.S.A. **Online address:** linda.rabieh@tufts.edu

RABIN, Robert L. American (born United States), b. 1939. **Genres:** Law. **Career:** University of Wisconsin, assistant professor of law, 1966-69, associate professor of law, 1969-70; Administrative Conference of the United States, consultant, 1970-72; Stanford University, Stanford Law School, associate professor of law, 1971-73, professor of law, 1973-84, A. Calder Mackay professor of law, 1984-, university fellow, 1982-85; Ford Foundation, Division of Resources and the Environment, consultant, 1971-81; U.S. Environmental Protection Agency, senior environmental fellow, 1979-80; Association of American Law Schools, Section on Administrative Law, chair, 1979-80; Center for Advanced Study in the Behavioral Sciences, fellow, 1982-83; ABA Action Commission to Improve the Tort Liability System, reporter, 1985-87; Harvard University, Harvard Law School, visiting professor, 1987-88; ALI Project on Compensation and Liability for Product and Process Injuries, associate reporter, 1988-91; Robert Wood Johnson Foundation, Tobacco Policy Research and Evaluation Program, program director, 1992-96, Substance Abuse Policy Research Program, senior program consultant, 1996-2002; New York University, New York University School of Law, visiting professor, 1999-2000, 2007-08; Yale Law School, China Law Center, consultant, 2002-07; Asia Foundation, advisor, 2005. **Publications:** Perspectives on tort Law, 1976, 4th ed., 1995; (ed.) Perspectives on the Administrative Process, 1979; (with M. Franklin) Tort Law and Alternatives: Cases and Materials, 1983, 9th ed., 2011; Real Property: Adaptable to Courses Utilizing Materials, 1984; (ed. with S.D. Sugarman) Smoking Policy: Law, Politics, and Culture, 1993; (ed. with S.D. Sugarman) Regulating Tobacco, 2001; (ed. with S.D. Sugarman) Torts Stories, 2003. Contributor of articles to journals. **Address:** Stanford Law School, Stanford University, Crown Quadrangle, 559 Nathan Abbott Way, Stanford, CA 94305-8610, U.S.A. **Online address:** rrabin@stanford.edu

RABINBACH, Anson (Gilbert). American (born United States), b. 1945. **Genres:** History, Politics/Government, Social Sciences. **Career:** University of Wisconsin, lecturer in history, 1972-73; Hampshire College, assistant professor of social science, 1973-83; Cooper Union, associate professor of history, 1983-96; Princeton University, premier journal of German studies, cofouder, 1974, Department of History, professor, 1996-. Writer. **Publications:** The Crisis of Austrian Socialism: From Red Vienna to Civil War, 1927-1934, 1983; The Human Motor: Energy, Fatigue, and the Origins Modernity, 1990; In the Shadow of Catastrophe: German Intellectuals Between Apocalypse and Enlightenment, 1997. EDITOR: The Austrian Socialist Experiment: Social Democracy and Austromarxism, 1918-1934, 1985; (with J. Zipes) Germans and Jews since the Holocaust: The Changing Situation in West Germany, 1986. Contributor to academic journals. **Address:** Department of History, Princeton University, 121 Dickinson Hall, Princeton, NJ 08544, U.S.A. **Online address:** rabin@princeton.edu

RABINOVITS, Dani. See **RABINOWITZ, Dan.**

RABINOWITZ, Alan. American (born United States), b. 1953. **Genres:** Natural History. **Career:** Wildlife Conservation Society, Science and Exploration Division, executive director; Panthera (nonprofit wildcat advocacy), president and chief executive officer. Writer. **Publications:** Jaguar: Struggle and Triumph in the Jungles of Belize, 1986 as Jaguar: One Man's Battle to Establish the World's First Jaguar Preserve, 1991, new ed. 2000; Chasing the Dragon's Tail: The Struggle to Save Thailand's Wild Cats, 1991; Wildlife Field Research and Conservation Training Manual, 1993; Beyond the Last Village: A Journey of Discovery in Asia's Forbidden Wilderness, 2001; (ed. with R. Woodroffe and S. Thirgood) People and Wildlife: Conflict or Coexistence?, 2005; Life in the Valley of Death: The Fight to Save Tigers in a Land of Guns, Gold, and Greed, 2008. Contributor to periodicals. **Address:** Panthera, 18th Fl., 8 W 40th St., New York, NY 10018, U.S.A.

RABINOWITZ, Dan. (Dani Rabinovits). Israeli (born Israel), b. 1954?. **Genres:** Local History/Rural Topics, International Relations/Current Affairs, Sociology. **Career:** Zukey David Field Study Center, instructor and chief instructor, 1975-79; World Heritage Status for Sinai, consultant, 1980; Society for the Protection of Nature in Israel, director of publications, 1983-85; Van-Leer Jerusalem Foundation, researcher, 1985-87; Hebrew University, Department of Sociology and Anthropology, lecturer and senior lecturer, 1991-2000; Israeli Anthropological Association, president, 1998-2001; Tel-Aviv University, Department of Sociology and Anthropology, senior lecturer, 2000-; University of Toronto, visiting professor, 2002. Freelance journalist and writer. **Publications:** (Ed. with A. Shaked) Spirit of the Earth, 1978; Mount Serbal Ecological Survey, 1978; Feiran Basin Ecological Survey, 1978; Nature Conservation in the Negev Mountains, 1979; Har Sirbal, 1979; Mount Serbal, 1979; Shemirat Teva Be-Har Ha- Negev, 1979; Nofe Pesagot Be-Har Mer-on: Tiyulim U-mishakim Le-khol Ha-mishpahah, 1985; Ruah Sinai, 1987; Spirit of Sinai, 1987; Shekspir Ba-g'ongel: al Mifgashim Ben-tarbutiyim, 1988; (ed.) Shakespeare in the Bush, 1988; 12 Mishpahot Be-Yisrael, 1988; (ed.) Voices in the Background: A Collection of Essays on the Arabs in Israel, 1994; (ed.) Five Voices: Arab Youth in Israel Speak about Their Lives and Culture, 1994; Overlooking Nazareth: The Ethnography of Exclusion in Galilee, 1997; Anthropology and the Palestinians, 1998; (contrib.) Border Identities, 1998; (contrib.) Ethnic Frontiers in Israel: Peripheral Development and Group Inequalities, 1998; (contrib.) Real-Time: The Al-Aqsa Intifada and the Israeli Left, 2001; (contrib.) Can the Israeli- Palestinian Conflict be Solved?, 2001; Ha-Dor Ha-zakuf, 2002; (with K. Abu-Baker) The Stand-Tall Generation, 2002; (with K. Abu-Baker) Coffins on Our Shoulders: The Experience of the Palestinian Citizens of Israel, 2005; (ed. with D. Monterescu) Mixed Towns, Trapped Communities: Historical Narratives, Spatial Dynamics, Gender Relations and Cultural Encounters in Palestinian-Israeli Towns, 2007; Hineh zeh ba: ketsad niśrod et shinui ha-aḳlim, 2009. Contributor to periodicals and journals. **Address:** Department of Sociology & Anthropology, Faculty of Social Sciences, Tel-Aviv University, Rm. 626, Naftaly Bldg., Ramant Aviv, Tel-Aviv, 69978, Israel. **Online address:** msdan@post.tau.ac.il

RABINOWITZ, Dorothy. American (born United States) **Genres:** Writing/Journalism, Law, History. **Career:** Wall Street Journal, editorial page writer and TV critic, 1990-96, critic-at-large (column), author, 1996-; Opinion Journal.com, author; New York University, English teacher; Pratt Institute, English teacher; WWOR-TV, news commentator. **Publications:** (With Y. Nielsen) Home Life; A Story of Old Age, 1971; The Other Jews; Portraits in Poverty, 1972; New Lives: Survivors of the Holocaust Living in America, 1976; About the Holocaust: What We Know and How We Know It, 1979; No Crueler Tyrannies: Accusation, False Witness, and Other Terrors of Our Times, 2003. Contributor to periodicals. **Address:** Wall Street Journal, 1 World Financial Ctr., 200 Liberty St., New York, NY 10281, U.S.A.

RABINYAN, Dorit. Israeli (born Israel), b. 1972?. **Genres:** Novels, Young Adult Fiction, History. **Career:** Am-Oved Publishers, staff. Writer. **Publications:** Ken, Ken, Ken: Shirim, 1991; Simṭat ha-shekediyot be-Omerig'an (novel), 1995; Persian Brides, 1998; ha-Ḥatunot shelanu, 1999; Strand of a Thousand Pearls, 2001; Our Weddings, 2001. **Address:** c/o Author Mail, Random House Publicity, 1745 Broadway, New York, NY 10019, U.S.A.

RABKIN, Jeremy. *See* **RABKIN, Jeremy A.**

RABKIN, Jeremy A. (Jeremy Rabkin). American (born United States), b. 1952. **Genres:** Law, Politics/Government. **Career:** Regulation, associate editor, 1978-80; Cornell University, instructor, 1980-82, professor of government, 1983-2007; Harvard University, visiting professor, 1993; George Mason University, professor of law, 2007-. Attorney and historian. **Publications:** (ed. with L.G. Crovitz) The Fettered Presidency: Legal Constraints on the Executive Branch, 1989; Judicial Compulsions: How Public Law Distorts Public Policy, 1989; Why Sovereignty Matters, 1998; The Case for Sovereignty: Why the World Should Welcome American Independence, 2004; Law without Nations? Why Constitutional Government Requires Sovereign States, 2005; (intro.) Jean Bodin, Six Books of the Republic, 2008. Contributor to books, periodicals and journals. **Address:** School of Law, George Mason University, Rm. 320, 3301 Fairfax Dr., Arlington, VA 22201-4426, U.S.A. **Online address:** jrabkin@gmu.edu

RABOTEAU, Albert J(ordy). American (born United States), b. 1943?. **Genres:** Theology/Religion, History. **Career:** Xavier University, instructor in theology; Yale University, teacher; University of California, teacher; Princeton University, visiting professor, 1982-, Graduate School, dean, 1992-93, Department of Religion, chair, 1987-92, Henry W. Putnam professor of religion, 1992-. Writer. **Publications:** God Struck Me Dead: Voices of Ex-Slaves, 1969; Slave Religion: The Invisible Institution in the Antebellum South, 1978; A Fire in the Bones: Reflections on African-American Religious History, 1995; (ed. with T.E. Fulop) African-American Religion: Interpretive Essays in History and Culture, 1997; African American-Religion, 1999; Canaan Land: A Religious History of African Americans, 2001; A Sorrowful Joy, 2002; (ed. with M.S. Copeland, L. Mosely) Uncommon Faithfulness: The Black Catholic Experience, 2009; (ed. with R. Alba and J. DeWind) Immigration and Religion in America: Comparative and Historical Perspectives, 2009.

Contributor to periodicals. **Address:** Department of Religion, Princeton University, 134 1879 Hall, Washington Rd., Princeton, NJ 08544, U.S.A. **Online address:** raboteau@princeton.edu

RABOY, Marc. Canadian/American (born United States), b. 1948. **Genres:** Communications/Media, Politics/Government. **Career:** Montreal Star, journalist, 1969-72; Canadian Broadcasting Corp., journalist, 1972-77; freelance journalist, 1972-86; Concordia University, professor, 1980-86; Laval University, associate professor, 1986-93; University of Montreal, professor, 1993; McGill University, Department of Art History and Communication Studies, professor, graduate director for communication studies, chair in ethics, media and communications, Beaverbrook chair in ethics, media and communications. Writer. **Publications:** Libérer la Communication: Médias et Mouvements Sociaux auQuébec, 1960-1980, 1983; Movements and Messages: Media and Radical Politics in Quebec, 1984; (ed.) Old Passions, New Visions: Social Movements and Political Activisim in Quebec, 1986; (ed. with P.A. Bruck) Communication For and Against Democracy, 1989; Missed Opportunities: The Story of Canada's Broadcasting Policy, 1990; (ed. with B. Dagenais) Media, Crisis, and Democracy: Mass Communication and The Disruption of Social Order, 1992; Développement Culturel et Mondialisation de l'économie: Un enjeu Démocratique, 1994; (ed.) Public Broadcasting for the 21st Century, 1995; Accès Inégal: Les canaux d'influence en radiodiffusion, 1995; (with D. Atkinson) Public Service Broadcasting: The Challenges of the Twenty-First Century, 1997; (ed.) Global Medial Policy in the New Millenium, 2002; (ed. with M.E. Price) Public Service Broadcasting in Transition: A Documentary Reader, 2002; (with N. Landry) Civil Society, Communication, and Global Governance: Issues From the World Summit on the Information Society, 2006; (ed. with F. Sauvageau) Le rôle de l'état dans la Gouvernance de la Radio diffusion, 2006; (co-author) Broadcasting, Voice and Accountability: A Public Interest Approach to Policy, Law and Regulation, 2008; (co-author) Media Divides: Communication Rights and the Right to Communicate in Canada, 2010; (with N. Landry and J. Shtern) Digital Solidarities, Communication Policy and Multi-stakeholder Global Governance: The Legacy of the World Summit on the Information Society, 2010; (ed. with R. Mansell) The Handbook of Global Media and Communication Policy, 2011. Contributor to periodicals. **Address:** Department of Art History & Communication Studies, McGill University, W-287 Arts, 853 Sherbrooke St. W, Montreal, QC H3A 2T6, Canada. **Online address:** marc.raboy@mcgill.ca

RABRENOVIC, Gordana. American (born United States), b. 1957?. **Genres:** Sociology, Sciences, History. **Career:** University of Belgrade, Department of Social Work and Social Policy, lecturer, 1982-84; State University of New York, Department of Sociology, teaching assistant, 1985-88, lecturer, 1988-90; Northeastern University, assistant professor of sociology, 1990-97, associate professor of sociology and education, 1997-, Center for Innovation in Urban Education, fellow, 1994-95, Human Service Program, co-director, 1997-98, Brudnick Center on Violence and Conflict, associate director, 1998-2007, director, 2007-; Radcliffe College, Graduate Consortium in Women's Studies, co-president, 1999-2001. **Publications:** The Community Builders: A Tale of Neighborhood Mobilization in Two Cities, 1996; (ed. with N. Kleniewski) Community Politics and Policy, vol. VII, 1999; The American Behavioral Scientist Special Issue on Hate Crimes and Ethnic Conflict, 2001; (with J. Levin) Why We Hate, 2004. Contributor to books and periodicals. **Address:** Department of Sociology and Anthropology, College of Arts & Sciences, Northeastern University, 571 Holmes Hall, 360 Huntington Ave., Boston, MA 02115, U.S.A. **Online address:** g.rabrenovic@neu.edu

RACHLEFF, Peter (J.). American (born United States), b. 1951. **Genres:** History, Organized Labor, Business/Trade/Industry. **Career:** Macalester College, Department of History, assistant professor, 1982-87, associate professor of history, 1987-95, professor of history, 1995-, chairman, 1997-2000, Cultural Pluralism Program, co-director, 1987-88; World Press Institute, adjunct faculty, 1988-2006; University of Minnesota, Labor Education Service, adjunct faculty, 1983-86; Metropolitan State University, community faculty, 1983-96, 2001-02; West Seventh Community Center, board director, 1984-86; University of St. Thomas, Center for Economic Education, faculty, 1989-99; North Minneapolis Community Center, board director, 1990; Hamline University, Graduate Liberal Studies Program, adjunct faculty, 1996-; Mellon Mays Undergraduate Fellowship Program, faculty director, 2000-; United Association for Labor Education, board director, 2005-09; Labor and Working Class History Association, board director, 2005-09; Working Class Studies Association, president, 2006-08; Australian National University, faculty. Writer. **Publications:** Root and Branch: The Rise of the Workers' Movements, 1975; Marxism and Council Communism, 1976; Black Labor in the South: Richmond, Virginia, 1865-1890, 1984 as Black Labor in Richmond, 1865-1890, 1989; Hard-Pressed in the Heartland: The Hormel Strike and the Future of the Labor Movement, 1993. Contributor of articles to books and periodicals. **Address:** Department of History, Macalester College, Rm. 306, Old Main Bldg., 1600 Grand Ave., St. Paul, MN 55105, U.S.A. **Online address:** rachleff@macalester.edu

RACHMAN, Stanley Jack. Canadian/South African (born South Africa), b. 1934?. **Genres:** Medicine/Health, Sciences, Sports/Fitness, Psychology. **Career:** University of the Witwatersrand, 1954-59; University of London, Institute of Psychiatry, lecturer, 1961-67, senior lecturer, 1967-73, reader, 1973-76, professor of abnormal psychology, 1976-; University of British Columbia, Vancouver, professor of psychology, 1983-, now professor emeritus. Writer. **Publications:** (Ed.) Critical Essays on Psychoanalysis, 1961; (with H.J. Eysenck) Causes and Cures of Neurosis, 1965; Phobias: Their Nature and Control, 1968; (with J. Teasdale) Aversion Therapy and the Behaviour Disorders, 1969; (with J. Bergold) Verhaltens therapie bei Phobein (title means: 'Behavioral Treatment of Phobias'), 1969, 3rd ed., 1972; Effects of Psychotherapy, 1971; (as Jack Durac) Wines, 1974; (as Jack Durac) The Art of Tasting, 1974; (as Jack Durac) A Matter of Taste, 1974; The Meanings of Fear, 1974; (with C. Philips) Psychology and Medicine, 1975; (ed.) Contributions to Medical Psychology, vol. I, 1977, vol. II, 1980; Fear and Courage, 1978, 2nd ed., 1990; (as Jack Durac) A Matter of Taste and Tasting, 1979; (with R. Hodgson) Obsessions and Compulsions, 1980; (with Philips) Psychology and Behavioral Medicine, 1980; (with G.T. Wilson) The Effects of Psychological Therapy, 1980; (ed.) The Expression of Emotions in Man and Animals, 1983; (ed. with J.D. Maser) Panic: Psychological Perspectives, 1988; (with P. de Silva) Obsessive-Compulsive Disorder: The Facts, 1992, 4th ed., 2009; (with de Silva) Panic Disorder, 1996, 3rd ed., 2010; (ed. with H.C. Philips) The Psychological Management of Chronic Pain: A Treatment Manual, 1996; (ed.) The Best of Behaviour Research and Therapy, 1997; Treatment of Obsessions, 2003; Anxiety, 2004; Fear of Contamination: Assessment and Treatment, 2006. **Address:** Department of Psychology, University of British Columbia, 2136 West Mall, Vancouver, BC V6T 1Z4, Canada. **Online address:** rachman@interchange.ubc.ca

RACINE, Philip N. American (born United States), b. 1941. **Genres:** Area Studies, History, Biography, Autobiography/Memoirs, Military/Defense/Arms Control. **Career:** Wofford College, faculty, 1969-, William R. Kenan Jr. professor of history, through 2009, now William R. Kenan Jr. professor emeritus, 2009-. Writer. **Publications:** Spartanburg County: A Pictorial History, 1980; Seeing Spartanburg: A History in Images, 1999. EDITOR: (and intro. with R. Harwell) The Fiery Trail: A Union Officer's Account of Sherman's Last Campaigns, 1986; (and intro.) Piedmont Farmer: The Journals of David Golightly Harris, 1855-1870, 1990; Unspoiled Heart: The Journal of Charles Mattocks of the 17th Maine, 1994; Gentlemen Merchants: A Charleston Family's Odyssey, 1828-1870, 2008. Contributor to journals. **Address:** Department of History, Wofford College, 429 N Church St., Spartanburg, SC 29303-3363, U.S.A. **Online address:** racinepn@wofford.edu

RACKHAM, Oliver. British (born England), b. 1939?. **Genres:** History, Botany, Natural History. **Career:** Cambridge University, Corpus Christi College, life fellow, Department of Plant Sciences, honorary professor of historical ecology, 2006-, master, 2007-08. Botanist, ecologist and writer. **Publications:** (Ed. with R. Bainbridge and G.C. Evans) Light as an Ecological Factor: A Symposium of the British Ecological Society, Cambridge, 30th March-1st April 1965, 1966; (co-ed.) Light as an Ecological Factor, II: The 16th Symposium of the British Ecological Society, 26-28 March, 1974, 1975; Hayley Wood: Its History and Ecology, 1975; Ancient Woodland: Its History, Vegetation and Uses in England, 1980, rev. ed., 2003; The History of the Countryside, 1986; The Ancient Woodland of England: The Woods of South-East Essex, 1986; The Last Forest: The Story of Hatfield Forest, 1989; (with J. Moody) The Making of the Cretan Landscape, 1996; The Illustrated History of the Countryside, 2000; (with A.T. Grove) The Nature of Mediterranean Europe: An Ecological History, 2001; Trees and Woodland in the British Landscape: The Complete History of Britain's Trees, Woods & Hedgerows, rev. ed., 2001; Treasures of Silver at Corpus Christi College, Cambridge, 2002; Woodlands, 2006. **Address:** Yale University Press, 302 Temple St., PO Box 209040, New Haven, CT 06511-8909, U.S.A. **Online address:** or10001@cam.ac.uk

RADANO, Ronald M. American (born United States), b. 1956. **Genres:** Music, Social Sciences, Human Relations/Parenting, Literary Criticism And History. **Career:** University of Wisconsin, visiting professor, 1989-90, assistant professor, 1990-95, associate professor of music and Afro-American studies, 1995-, professor of musicology and ethnomusicology; University of Pennsylvania, Center for the Study of Black Literature and Culture, Rockefeller Foundation, fellow, 1992-93; Smithsonian Institution, fellow, 1993-94; Guggenheim fellow, 1997. Writer. **Publications:** New Musical Figurations: Anthony Braxton's Cultural Critique, 1993; (ed. with P.V. Bohlman) Music and the Racial Imagination, 2000; Lying Up a Nation: Race and Black Music, 2003. Contributor to journals. **Address:** Departmentt of Afro-American Studies, University of Wisconsin, 4527 Mosse Humanities Bldg., 600 N Park St., Madison, WI 53706, U.S.A. **Online address:** rmradano@wisc.edu

RADAY, Sophia. American (born United States), b. 1964. **Genres:** Autobiography/Memoirs. **Career:** Literary Mama (online periodical), founding editor. **Publications:** Love in Condition Yellow: A Memoir of an Unlikely Marriage, 2009. Contributor to books. **Address:** Berkeley, CA, U.S.A. **Online address:** sophia@sophiaraday.com

RADCLIFFE, Timothy. British (born England), b. 1945. **Genres:** Theology/Religion, Adult Non-fiction. **Career:** Imperial College, chaplain, 1976-78; Blackfriars, teacher, 1978-88; English Province of the Order of Preachers, provincial, 1988-92; Conference of Major Religious Superiors of England and Wales, president, 1991-92; Order of Preachers, master, 1992-2001; Pontifical University of St. Thomas Aquinas, chancellor; University of St. Thomas, chancellor; University of Fribourg, theology faculty; Ecole Biblique, chancellor; Writer. **Publications:** (Ed. with F. Kerr) Multiple Echo: Explorations in Theology, 1979; Sing a New Song: The Christian Vocation, 1999; I Call You Friends, 2003; Seven Last Words, 2004; What Is the Point of Being a Christian?, 2005; (ed.) Just One Year: A Global Treasury of Prayer and Worship, 2007; Why Go to Church? The Drama of the Eucharist, 2008. **Address:** Blackfriars, St. Giles, Oxford, OX OX1 3LY, England. **Online address:** timothy.radcliffe@english.op.org

RADCLIFFE RICHARDS, Janet. British (born England), b. 1944. **Genres:** Environmental Sciences/Ecology, Ethics, Philosophy, Race Relations, Sciences, Social Commentary, Social Sciences, Women's Studies And Issues, Writing/Journalism, Biography. **Career:** University of Surrey, lecturer in philosophy, 1973-74; Oxford University, tutor in philosophy of science, 1973-78; University of Southampton, lecturer in philosophy, 1974-75; Open University, lecturer in philosophy, 1979-99; University of California, visiting professor, 1984; New York University, visiting faculty, 1986, 1988; University of San Diego Law School, director, 1995; University College London, reader in bioethics, Center for Bioethics, director, 1999-. Writer. **Publications:** The Sceptical Feminist: A Philosophical Enquiry, 1980, 2nd ed., 1994; Human Nature after Darwin, 2000. Contributor to periodicals. **Address:** Department of Primary Care & Population Sciences, Royal Free & University College Medical School, University College London, CHIME, 4th Level, Holborn Union Bldg., London, GL W1R 4HA, England. **Online address:** j.rr@chime.ucl.ac.uk

RADDEN, Jennifer H. American/Australian (born Australia), b. 1943. **Genres:** Philosophy, Essays. **Career:** University of Melbourne, tutor in philosophy, 1968-69; Tufts University, lecturer in philosophy, 1972-74; University of Massachusetts, lecturer, 1975-84, assistant professor, 1984-89, associate professor, 1990-97, acting chair, 1993, professor of philosophy, 1997-, chairperson, 2002-, Philosophy and Law Program of Study, director, 2002-05, Joint Major in Philosophy and Psychology, director, 1984-90, Major in Philosophy and Public Policy, director, 1987-90, 1992-, Public Policy Program, director, 1989-90; Society for Women in Philosophy, treasurer, 1986; Association for the Advancement of Philosophy and Psychiatry, president, 1997-2002; Massachusetts Institute of Technology Press, co-editor, 2004-. **Publications:** Madness and Reason, 1985; Divided Minds and Successive Selves: Ethical Issues in Disorders of Identity and Personality, 1996; Moody Minds Distempered: Essays on Melancholy and Depression, 2009; On Delusion, 2010; (with J.Z. Sadler) Virtuous Psychiatrist: Character Ethics in Psychiatric Practice, 2010. EDITOR: The Nature of Melancholy from Aristotle to Kristeva, 2000; Philosophy of Psychiatry: A Companion, 2004. Contributor to books and periodicals. **Address:** Department of Philosophy, University of Massachusetts, 05-018 Wheatley Bldg., 100 Morrissey Blvd., Boston, MA 02125, U.S.A. **Online address:** jennifer.radden@umb.edu

RADELET, Michael L. American (born United States), b. 1950. **Genres:**

Sociology, Bibliography. **Career:** Purdue University, Health Services Research and Training Program, fellow, 1974-77; University of Wisconsin, Department of Psychiatry, fellow, 1977-79; University of Florida, Department of Sociology, assistant professor, 1979-84, associate professor, 1984-93, professor of sociology, 1993-2001, chairman, 1996-2001; University of New Hampshire, fellow, 1990-91; University of Westminster, visiting professor, 1995-; University of Innsbruck, visiting professor, 1996, 1982; University of Colorado, Department of Sociology, professor, 2001-, associate chair, 2002-04, chair, 2004-. Writer. **Publications:** (With M. Vandiver) Capital Punishment in America: An Annotated Bibliography, 1988; (ed.) Facing the Death Penalty: Essays on a Cruel and Unusual Punishment, 1989; (with H.A. Bedau and C.E. Putnam) In Spite of Innocence: Erroneous Convictions in Capital Cases, 1992; (with K.S. Miller) Executing the Mentally Ill: The Criminal Justice System and the Case of Alvin Ford, 1993; (ed. and intro.) Final Exposure: Portraits from Death Row, 1996. Contributor to periodicals. **Address:** Department of Sociology, University of Colorado, 327 UCB, 219 Ketchum, Boulder, CO 80309-0327, U.S.A. **Online address:** michael.radelet@colorado.edu

RADER, Karen A. American (born United States), b. 1967. **Genres:** Sciences. **Career:** Massachusetts Institute of Technology, Mellon post-doctoral research fellow, 1994-95; Princeton University, Davis Center for Historical Studies, research fellow, 1996-97; Sarah Lawrence College, faculty, 1998-, Marilyn Simpson Chair of Science and Society, 1998-2006; Virginia Commonwealth University, Department of History, faculty, 2006, associate professor, director of the science, technology, and society initiative, Department of Women's Studies, affiliate faculty. Writer. **Publications:** Making Mice: Standardizing Animals for American Biomedical Research, 1900-1955, 2004. **Address:** Department of History, Virginia Commonwealth University, Rm. 201, Milhiser House, 916 W Franklin St., 811 and 813 S Cathedral Pl., PO Box 842001, Richmond, VA 23284-9081, U.S.A. **Online address:** karader@vcu.edu

RADFORD, Irene. Also writes as C. F. Bentley, P. R. Frost. American (born United States), b. 1950. **Genres:** Science Fiction/Fantasy, Novels. **Career:** Insurance Co. of North America, assistant underwriter, 1979-82; McLoughlin House Museum, assistant curator, 1985-89. **Publications:** The Glass Dragon, 1994; The Perfect Princess, 1995; The Loneliest Magician, 1996; The Dragon's Touchstone, 1997; The Last Battlemage, 1998; (contrib.) Olympus, 1998; The Renegade Dragon, 1999; Guardian of the Balance, 1999; Guardian of the Trust, 2000; The Wizard's Treasure, 2000; Treachery and Treason, 2000; Guardian of the Vision, 2001; The Hidden Dragon, 2002; Guardian of the Promise, 2003; The Dragon Circle, 2004; Little Red Riding Hood In the Big Bad City, 2004; Guardian of the Freedom, 2005; The Dragon's Revenge, 2005; (as P.R. Frost) Hounding the Moon, 2006; Moon in the Mirror, 2007; The Dragon Nimbus Novels, vol. I, 2007, vol. II, 2007, vol. III, 2008; Faery Moon, 2009. (as C.F. Bentley) Harmony, 2008; (contrib.) The Dimension Next Door, 2008; Enigma, 2009; Thistle Down, 2011; Chicory Up, 2012. **Address:** c/o Carol McCleary, Wilshire Literary Agency, 20 Barristers Walk, Dennis, MA 02638, U.S.A. **Online address:** ramblinphyl@hotmail.com

RADFORTH, Ian. Canadian (born Canada), b. 1952?. **Genres:** History, Travel/Exploration, Social Sciences. **Career:** University of Toronto, Department of History, professor, chair. Writer. **Publications:** Bushworkers and Bosses: Logging in Northern Ontario, 1900-1980, 1987; (ed. with L.S. MacDowell) Canadian Working Class History: Selected Readings, 1992, 3rd ed., 2006; (ed. with A. Greer) Colonial Leviathan: State Formation in Mid-Nineteenth-Century Canada, 1992; (contrib.) A Nation of Immigrants, 1998; (contrib.) Enemies Within: Italian and Other Internees in Canada and Abroad, 2000; Royal Spectacle: The 1860 Visit of the Prince of Wales to Canada and the United States, 2004. Contributor to periodicals. **Address:** Department of History, University of Toronto, UC 247, Sidney Smith Hall, Rm. 2074, 100 St. George St., Toronto, ON M5S 3G3, Canada. **Online address:** i.radforth@utoronto.ca

RADICK, Gregory M. American (born United States), b. 1970. **Genres:** Sciences, Reference. **Career:** University of Leeds, lecturer, 2000-06, senior lecturer, 2006-10, History and Philosophy of Science Division, chair, 2006-08, professor of history and philosophy of science, 2010-; British Journal for the History of Science, reviews editor, 2005-10. **Publications:** (Ed. with J. Hodge) The Cambridge Companion to Darwin, 2003, 2nd ed., 2009; (ed. with F. Penz and R. Howell) Space: In Science, Art, and Society, 2004; The Simian

Tongue: The Long Debate about Animal Language, 2007; (with M. Dixon) Darwin in Ilkley, 2009. Contributor to books. **Address:** University of Leeds, Leeds, WY LS2 9JT, England. **Online address:** g.m.radick@leeds.ac.uk

RADIN, Dean I. American (born United States), b. 1952. **Genres:** Psychology, Physics. **Career:** AT&T Bell Laboratories, staff; GTE Laboratories, staff; SRI Intl., staff; Interval Research Corp., staff; Princeton University, faculty; University of Edinburgh, faculty; Parapsychological Association, president, 1988, 1993, 1998, 2005; Society for Scientific Exploration, counselor; Boundary Institute, co-founder, 2001; Institute of Noetic Sciences, senior scientist, 2001-; Sonoma State University, Department of Psychology, adjunct faculty; Saybrook Graduate School, distinguished consulting faculty; University of Nevada, faculty. Writer. **Publications:** The Conscious Universe: The Scientific Truth of Psychic Phenomena, 1997; (foreword) Captain of My Ship, Master of My Soul: Living With Guidance, 2001; Entangled Minds: Extrasensory Experiences in a Quantum Reality, 2006. Contributor to journals. **Address:** Institute of Noetic Sciences, 101 San Antonio Rd., Petaluma, CA 94952-9524, U.S.A. **Online address:** dean@noetic.org

RADIN, Ruth Yaffe. American (born United States), b. 1938. **Genres:** Children's Fiction, History, Mystery/Crime/Suspense, Sociology. **Career:** Elementary school teacher, 1960-63; Congregation Keneseth, librarian, 1982-. Writer. **Publications:** A Winter Place, 1982; Tac's Island, 1986; Tac's Turn, 1987; High in the Mountains, 1989; Carver, 1990; All Joseph Wanted, 1991; From the Wooded Hill, 1993; Sky Bridges, and Other Poems, 1993; Morning Streets, 1993; Escape to the Forest: Based on a True Story of the Holocaust, 2000. **Address:** 1939 Weyhill Dr., Center Valley, PA 18034, U.S.A.

RADOSH, Daniel Lord. American (born United States), b. 1969. **Genres:** Young Adult Non-fiction. **Career:** New Youth Connections, entertainment editor, 1984-85; Below the Belt, editor-in-chief, 1988-91; Spy magazine, staff writer and editor, 1991-94; Freelance writer, 1992-; Transom, senior producer, 1995-97; Modern Humorist, senior editor, 2000-01; Week, contributing editor, 2002; Mode magazine, executive editor, 2003-; Radar, contributing editor, 2003-. **Publications:** Rapture Ready! Adventures in the Parallel Universe of Christian Pop Culture, 2008. Contributor to periodicals. **Address:** New York, NY, U.S.A. **Online address:** radosh@gmail.com

RADOVANOVIC, Ivan. /American (born United States), b. 1961?. **Genres:** History, Biography, Autobiography/Memoirs, Humanities. **Career:** Politica (newspaper), writer; Borba (daily newspaper), war reporter; Vreme (newspaper), war reporter; Dnevi Telegraf (daily newspaper), reporter, 1996; Evropljanin (weekly journal), assistant chief editor, 1997-99; Vecernje Novosti (daily newspaper), chief editor, 1999-; Media Center Belgrade, education coordinator, 1999-. **Publications:** Ništa, 1999; Kratka istorija života u mrtvom gradu, 2000; (with D. Bujosevic) Peti October: dvadeset i cetiri sata prevrata, 2001 as The Fall of Milosevic: The October Fifth Revolution, 2003. Contributor to periodicals. **Address:** c/o Author Mail, Palgrave Macmillan, 175 5th Ave., New York, NY 10010, U.S.A.

RADULESCU, Domnica. (Domnica Vera Maria Radulescu). American (born United States), b. 1961. **Genres:** Young Adult Non-fiction, Young Adult Fiction, History. **Career:** University of Chicago, lecturer in French, 1988-92; Washington and Lee University, assistant professor, 1992-98, associate professor, 1998-2003, professor, 2003-, Women's and Gender Studies Program, head. Writer. **Publications:** NONFICTION: André Malraux: The Farfelu as Expression of the Feminine and the Erotic, 1994; Sisters of Medea: The Tragic Heroine across Cultures, 2002; (and ed.) Realms of Exile: Nomadism, Diasporas, and Eastern European Voices, 2002; (ed. with V. Glajar) Vampirettes, Wretches, and Amazons: Western Representations of East European Women, 2004; The Theater of Teaching and the Lessons of Theater, 2005; Gypsies in European Literature and Culture, 2008; (ed. with E.C. Mayock) Feminist Activism in Academia: Essays on Personal, Political and Professional Change, 2010; FICTION: Train to Trieste, 2008; Women's Comedic Art as Social Revolution: Five Performers and the Lessons of Their Subversive Humor, 2012. **Address:** Department of Romance Languages, Washington and Lee University, 403A Tucker, 204 W Washington St., Lexington, VA 24450, U.S.A. **Online address:** radulescuvm@gmail.com

RADULESCU, Domnica Vera Maria. *See* **RADULESCU, Domnica.**

RADZIENDA, Tom. Thai (born Thailand), b. 1963. **Genres:** Poetry. **Career:** Writer. **Publications:** No More Pretty Pictures, 1998; A Promise for

Siam, 2002; Fire Dreams, 2005; Reiki: Palang Thammachart, 2011. **Address:** Reiki Thailand, Bangkok, 10260, Thailand. **Online address:** tomradzienda@gmail.com

RADZINSKIᴵᴵ, Ėdvard. See **RADZINSKY, Ėdvard (Stanislavovich).**

RADZINSKY, Ėdvard (Stanislavovich). (Ėdvard Radzinskiĭ). Russian (born Russia), b. 1936. **Genres:** Novels, Plays/Screenplays, Biography, History, Young Adult Fiction. **Career:** Rambler Media Group, chairman. Writer. **Publications:** AS ĖDVARD RADZINSKIĬ: Sto Chetyre Stranitsy Pro Liubov: Pesy, 1965; Snimaetsia Kino, 1966; Film Makers, 1968; Teatr, 1986; Gospodi Spasi i Usmiri Rossiiu: Nikolaĭ II, Zhizn Ismert, 1993; Vlastiteli Dum, 1993; Zagadki Istorii: Liubov v Galantnomveke, 1995; Zagadki Liubvi, 1996; (contrib.) Face of Russia-Rushes, 1996; I Sdelalas' Krov': Iz Tsikla Zagadki istorii, 1996; Nikolaĭ II: Zhizn i Smert, 1997; Gibel Galantnogoveka, 1998; Eshche Raz Pro Liubov, 1999; Kniazhna Tarakanova, 1999; Krovi Prizraki Russkoĭ Smuty, 1999; Parad Bogov, 1999; Proroki i Bezumtsy, 1999; Muchitel i Ten, 1999; Rasputin: Zhizn Ismert, 2000; Igry Pisateleĭ: Neizdannyĭ Bomarshe, 2001; Napoleon: Zhizn Posle Smerti, 2002; Na Rusi ot Uma Odno Gore, 2006; Aleksandr II, 2007; Moia Teatral Naia Zhizn, 2007; Vozhdi: Napoleon, Stalin, 2007; Tri Smerti, 2007; O Sebe, 2008; Tsàri: Aleksandr II, Nikolsi II, 2008; A Biography of Rasputin, forthcoming. Contributor to periodicals. **Address:** Union of Writers, 52 Ul Vorovskogo, Moscow, 121069, Russia. **Online address:** edvard@radzinski.ru

RAE, Ben. See **GRIFFITHS, Trevor.**

RAE, Hugh C(rawford). Also writes as Jessica Sterling, Robert Crawford, R. B. Houston, Stuart Stern, James Albany. Scottish (born Scotland), b. 1935. **Genres:** Novels, Mystery/Crime/Suspense, Romance/Historical, Plays/Screenplays, Young Adult Fiction. **Career:** John Smith & Son Ltd., assistant, 1952-65; full-time writer, 1965-; Scottish Association of Writers, president, 1970-77; University of Glasgow, lecturer in creative writing. **Publications:** NOVELS: Skinner, 1965; Vampire écossais, 1967; Night Pillow, 1967; A Few Small Bones, 1969; The House at Balnesmoor, 1969; The Interview, 1969; The Saturday Epic, 1970; The Marksman, 1971; The Shooting Gallery, 1972; The Rock Harvest, 1973; The Rookery: A Novel of the Victorian Underworld, 1974; Harkfast: The Making of the King, 1976; Sullivan, 1978; (ed.) Scottish Short Stories, 1978; The Travelling Soul, 1978; The Haunting at Waverley Falls, 1980; Privileged Strangers, 1982. CRIME AND MYSTERY: The Dear Ones, 1969; The Revenue Men, 1971; The Freezer, 1972; The Blue Evening Gone, 1980; The Gates of Midnight, 1982. FIGHTING SAGA OF SAS AS JAMES ALBANY: Warrior Caste, 1982; Mailed Fist, 1982; Deacon's Dagger, 1982; Colse Combat, 1983; Marching Fire, 1983; Last Bastion, 1984; Borneo Story, 1984. NOVELS AS ROBERT CRAWFORD: The Shroud Society, 1969; Cockleburr, 1969; Kiss the Boss Goodbye, 1970; The Badger's Daughter, 1971; Whip Hand, 1972. AS R.B. HOUSTON: Two for the Grave, 1972. AS STUART STERN: (with S. Ungar) The Minotaur Factor, 1977; The Poison Tree, 1978. HISTORICAL NOVELS AS JESSICA STERLING WITH P. CLOGHAN: The Spoiled Earth: A Novel, 1974; Strathmore, 1975; The Hiring Fair: A Novel, 1975; The Dresden Finch, 1976; Call Home the Heart, 1977; The Dark Pasture, 1978; The Deep Well at Noon, 1979; The Drums of Time, 1980; The Blue Evening Gone, 1982; The Gates of Midnight, 1983; Treasures on Earth, 1985. OTHERS AS JESSICA STERLING: Creature Comforts, 1986; Hearts of Gold, 1987; The Good Provider, 1988; The Asking Price, 1989; The Wise Child, 1990; The Welcome Light, 1991; Lantern for the Dark, 1992; The Haldanes, 1992; Shadows on the Shore, 1993; The Penny Wedding, 1994; The Marrying Kind, 1995; The Workhouse Girl, 1996; Masculinity, 1996; The Island Wife, 1997; The Wind from the Hills, 1998; Piper's Tune, 1999; Strawberry Season, 2000; Sisters Three, 2001; Shamrock Green, 2002; Wives at War, 2003; The Captive Heart, 2004; One True Love, 2005; Blessings in Disguise, 2006; The Fields of Fortune, 2008; A Kiss and a Promise, 2008; The Paradise Waltz, 2009; A Corner of the Heart, 2010. **Address:** Peters Fraser and Dunlop Group Ltd., Drury House, 34-43 Russell St., London, GL WC2B 5HA, England. **Online address:** hughsee@aol.com

RAEBURN, Antonia. British (born England), b. 1934. **Genres:** History, Women's Studies And Issues, Social Sciences, Art/Art History. **Career:** Hertfordshire Primary Schools, art and craft teacher, 1955-59; Holt Hall School, art director and head of art and craft department, 1959-62; Bath Academy of Art, lecturer, 1962-67; British Broadcasting Corp., art director, 1968; television researcher and art director, 1968-74; writer, 1974-. **Publications:** The Militant Suffragettes, 1973; The Sufragette View, 1976. Contributor to journals. **Address:** A.D. Peters & Company Ltd., 10 Buckingham St., London, GL WC2N 6BU, England.

RAEDER, Linda C. American (born United States), b. 1951. **Genres:** Philosophy, Biography. **Career:** Center for U.S. Studies, Civics Education fellow, 1999-2000; Palm Beach Atlantic University, assistant professor, associate professor of political science, 2001-. Writer. **Publications:** Marxism as Psychodrama, Humanitas, 1994; Education and the Free Society, 1997; The Liberalism/Conservatism of Burke and Hayek, 1999; Das Wesen der Zivilgesellschaft: Eine Amerikanische Perspektive, 2000; Mills Religion of Humanity, 2001; John Stuart Mill and the Religion of Humanity, 2002; Augustine and the Case for Limited Government, 2004; Edmund Burke: Old Whig, 2006; Liberalism and the Common Good, 2006; Voegelin on Gnosticism, Modernity and the Balance of Consciousness, 2007; Hayek on the Role of Reason in Human Affairs, 2008; F.A. Hayek: A Man of Measure, 2009. **Address:** Palm Beach Atlantic University, Rinker 1352, 901 S Flagler Dr., West Palm Beach, FL 33409, U.S.A. **Online address:** linda_raeder@pba.edu

RAFFEL, Keith. American (born United States), b. 1951?. **Genres:** Mystery/Crime/Suspense, Young Adult Non-fiction, E-books. **Career:** ROLM Corp., general manager, 1982-89; Echelon Corp., executive, 1990-96; UpShot Corp., founder, 1997-2003; Siebel Systems, vice president, 2003-06; Oracle Corp., vice president, 2006-07. Writer. **Publications:** SILICON VALLEY MYSTERY SERIES: Dot. Dead, 2006; Smasher, 2009; Drop by Drop, 2011. **Address:** c/o Josh Getzler, Writers House, 21 W 26th St., New York, NY 10010-1003, U.S.A. **Online address:** keith@keithraffel.com

RAFFI. (Raffi Cavoukian). Canadian/Egyptian (born Egypt), b. 1948. **Genres:** Children's Fiction, Songs/Lyrics And Libretti, Autobiography/Memoirs, Music. **Career:** Troubadour Music Inc., president. Singer and songwriter. **Publications:** The Life of a Children's Troubadour, 1999. RAFFI SONGS TO READ SERIES; PICTURE BOOK VERSIONS OF HIS SONGS: Down by the Bay, 1987; Shake My Sillies Out, 1987; One Light, One Sun, 1988; Wheels on the Bus, 1988; Tingalayo, 1989; Five Little Ducks, 1989; Everything Grows, 1987; Baby Beluga, 1990; Spider on the Floor, 1993. SONGBOOKS: The Raffi Singable Songbook, 1987; The Second Raffi Songbook, 1987; The Raffi Christmas Treasury, 1988; The Raffi Everything Grows Songbook, 1989; Raffi's Top Ten Songs to Read, 1995; Rise And Shine, 1996; This Little Light of Mine, 2004; If You're Happy And You Know It, 2005; Child Honouring, 2006. **Address:** Troubadour Music Inc., S3, C40, 610 Fernhill Rd., Mayne Island, BC V0N 2J0, Canada. **Online address:** music@troubadour-records.com

RAFTERY, Brian. American (born United States), b. 1976?. **Genres:** Art/Art History, Music, Autobiography/Memoirs. **Career:** Journalist. **Publications:** Don't Stop Believin': How Karaoke Conquered the World and Changed My Life, 2008. **Address:** Da Capo Press, 11 Cambridge Ctr., Cambridge, MA 02142, U.S.A. **Online address:** brianraftery@gmail.com

RAFUSE, Ethan S. American (born United States), b. 1968?. **Genres:** History. **Career:** Conservation, Environment and Historic Preservation Inc., research historian, 1993-94; Fort Ward Museum and Historic Site, museum aide, 1993-94; Johnson County Community College, lecturer, 1996-2001; University of Missouri, lecturer, 1997-2001; United States Military Academy, assistant professor of history, 2001-03; Maple Woods Community College, lecturer, 2004-; U.S. Army Command and General Staff College, associate professor, 2004-, professor. Writer. **Publications:** A Single Grand Victory: The First Campaign and Battle of Manassas, 2002; George Gordon Meade and the War in the East, 2003; (ed. and intro. with H. Hattaway) The Ongoing Civil War: New Versions of Old Stories, 2004; (ed.) The American Civil War, 2005; McClellan's War: The Failure of Moderation in the Struggle for the Union, 2005; Robert E. Lee and the Fall of the Confederacy, 1863-1865, 2008; Antietam, South Mountain, and Harpers Ferry: A Battlefield Guide, 2008; Stonewall Jackson, 2011. Contributor to journals. **Address:** Department of Military History, U.S. Army Command and General Staff College, Fort Leavenworth, KS 66027, U.S.A. **Online address:** ethan.rafuse@us.army.mil

RAGEN, Naomi. (N. T. Erline). Israeli/American (born United States), b. 1949. **Genres:** Novels, Plays/Screenplays, Writing/Journalism, Ghost Writer. **Career:** Israel Environmental Protection Service, publications editor, 1975-79; freelance writer, 1979-81; University of Santa Clara, director of development communications, 1981-82; San Jose Hospital Foundation, development coordinator, 1982-84; fiction writer, 1984-; Jerusalem Post, columnist, 1998-2001. **Publications:** Sipur Amerikai, 2001. NOVELS: Jephte's Daughter, 1988; Sotah, 1992; A Woman Under Suspicion, 1993; The Sacrifice of Tamar, 1994; The Ghost of Hannah Mendes, 1998; Chains Around the Grass, 2002; The Covenant, 2004; Women's Minyan, 2006; The Saturday Wife, 2007; The Tenth Song, 2010. EDITOR AS N.T. ERLINE: My Uncle the Netziv, 1988; Recollections: The Torah Temimah Recalls the Golden Age of European Jewry, 1989. Contributor to periodicals. **Address:** The Harry Walker Agency Inc., 355 Lexington Ave., 21st Fl., New York, NY 10017-6603, U.S.A. **Online address:** naomi@naomiragen.com

RAGONÉ, Heléna. American (born United States), b. 1955. **Genres:** Anthropology/Ethnology, Cultural/Ethnic Topics, Women's Studies And Issues, Technology. **Career:** University of Massachusetts, Department of Anthropology, lecturer in anthropology, 1992-, research associate; CBS-TV, consultant; ABC-TV, consultant; Spiegel Television, consultant. Writer. **Publications:** Surrogate Motherhood: Conception in the Heart, 1994; (ed. with L. Lamphere and P. Zavella) The Ethnography of Gender, Culture, and Practice, 1996; (ed. with L. Lamphere and P. Zavella) Situated Lives: Gender and Culture in Everyday Life, 1997; (ed. with S. Franklin) Reproducing Reproduction: Kinship, Power, and Technological Innovation, 1998; (ed. with F.W. Twine) Ideologies and Technologies of Motherhood: Race, Class, Sexuality, Nationalism, 2000; Completing Distant Kin: Gestational Surrogacy and Ovum Donation, forthcoming; Riding Danger: Women in Horse Culture, forthcoming; (ed. with L. Lamphere) A Companion to the Anthropology of Gender and Sexuality, forthcoming. Contributor to periodicals. **Address:** Department of Anthropology, University of Massachusetts, Rm. 00434, McCormack Hall, 100 Morrissey Blvd., 1st Fl., Boston, MA 02125-3393, U.S.A. **Online address:** helena.ragone@umb.edu

RAHAM, (R.) Gary. American (born United States), b. 1946. **Genres:** Writing/Journalism, Illustrations, Natural History, Young Adult Non-fiction, Science Fiction/Fantasy, Essays, Picture/Board Books. **Career:** Museum of Natural History, planetarium lecturer, 1965-68; high school science teacher, 1969-71; Citizen Printing Co., graphic designer and illustrator, 1971-98; Biostration (publishing company), founder, illustrator and writer, 1972-; Colorado State University, teacher of continuing education course, 1990, 1992, 1997; North Forty News, journalist and graphic designer, 2006-. **Publications:** SELF-ILLUSTRATED: Dinosaurs in the Garden: An Evolutionary Guide to Backyard Biology, 1988; Explorations in Backyard Biology: Drawing on Nature in the Classroom, 1996. OTHERS: Sillysaurs: The Dinosaurs That Could Have Been (coloring book of limericks), 1990; Explorations in Dinosaurs in the Garden, 1988; Teaching Science Fact with Science Fiction, 2004; Science Tutor: Chemistry, 2005; Science Tutor: Life Science, 2005; Jumpstarters for Science, 2005; Science Tutor: Earth & Space Science, 2006; Science Tutor: Physical Science, 2006; Jumpstarters for Life Science, 2008; Bugs That Kill, 2008; Fossils, 2008; Biodiversity and Food Chains, 2012. Contributor of articles to magazines. **Address:** Biostration, 3714 Grant Ave., PO Box 399, Wellington, CO 80549, U.S.A. **Online address:** grahambios@aol.com

RAHAMAN, Vashanti. American/Trinidadian (born Trinidad and Tobago), b. 1953. **Genres:** Children's Fiction, Human Relations/Parenting. **Career:** Trinidad and Tobago Teaching Service, secondary school teacher, 1977-83; Rolla First Presbyterian Church, chair, 1995-98. Writer. **Publications:** O Christmas Tree, 1996; Read for Me, Mama, 1997; A Little Salmon for Witness, 1997; Divali Rose, 2008. Contributor of stories and articles to children's magazines. **Address:** Boyds Mills Press, 815 Church St., Honesdale, PA 18431, U.S.A.

RAHE, Paul A. (Paul Anthony Rahe). American (born United States), b. 1948. **Genres:** History, Theology/Religion. **Career:** Yale University, Department of History, acting instructor, 1976-77, visiting professor, 1996-97; Cornell University, assistant professor of history, 1977-80; Franklin and Marshall College, Steinman assistant professor of classics and history, 1981-83; Crane-Rogers Foundation, board director, 1987-94 and 1997-2003, chair, 1998-2003; Institute of World Affairs, board director, 1991-94; The University of Tulsa, Department of History, assistant professor, 1983-91, associate professor, 1991-94, professor, 1994-2007, chair, 1994-98, First Seminar Program, director, 1990-92, Jay P. Walker professor of history, 1994-2007; Gaspar G. Bacon lecturer, 1996; Cambridge University, visiting research fellow, 1999; Thomas Aquinas College, E.L. Wiegand Visiting Lecturer, 1999-2000; St. John's College, E.L. Wiegand Visiting Lecturer, 1999-2000; Oxford University, visiting fellow, 2005-06; American Academy, Hans Arnhold Center, DaimlerChrysler Fellow, 2006; Hillsdale College, Department of History and Political Science, professor, 2007-, Western Heritage, Charles O. Lee and Louise K. Lee Chair; Bowling Green State University, visiting fellow, 2009. Writer. **Publications:** Republics Ancient and Modern: Classical Republicanism and the American Revolution, 1992, vol. I: The Ancient Regime in Classical Greece, 1994, vol. II: New Modes and Orders in Early Modern Political Thought, 1994, vol. III: Inventions of Prudence: Constituting the American Regime, 1994; (ed. with D.W. Carrithers and M.A. Mosher) Montesquieu's Science of Politics: Essays on The Spirit of Laws, 2001; (ed.) Machiavelli's Liberal Republic Legacy, 2006; Against Throne and Altar: Machiavelli and Political Theory Under the English Republic, 2008; Soft Despotism, Democracy's Drift: Montesquieu, Rousseau, Tocqueville and the Modern Prospect, 2009; Montesquieu and the Logic of Liberty: War, Religion, Commerce, Climate, Terrain, Technology, Uneasiness of Mind, the Spirit of Political Vigilance and the Foundations of the Modern Republic, 2009; The Spartan Way of War, forthcoming. Works appear in anthologies. Contributor of books to journals. **Address:** Department of History and Political Science, Hillsdale College, 33 E College St., Hillsdale, MI 49242, U.S.A. **Online address:** paul.rahe@hillsdale.edu

RAHE, Paul Anthony. See **RAHE, Paul A.**

RAHMAN, Matiur. Canadian/Indian (born India), b. 1940. **Genres:** Mathematics/Statistics, Engineering, Environmental Sciences/Ecology. **Career:** Jorhat Engineering College, lecturer in mathematics, 1964-66; University of London, Imperial College of Science and Technology, research fellow in mathematics, 1966-69, visiting professor, 1987-88; University of Windsor, research fellow and sessional lecturer in mathematics, 1969-73; University of Moncton, research fellow and assistant research professor of engineering, 1973-76; University of Manitoba, research associate in applied mathematics, 1976-77; National Research Council of Canada, Hydraulics Laboratory, assistant research officer and research associate, 1977-80; University of Ottawa, adjunct professor, 1977-80; Wessex Institute of Technology, director, 1980-, fellow, 2004-; Technical University of Nova Scotia, associate professor, 1980-87, professor of mathematics, 1987-97; University of London, visiting professor, 1987-88; Bedford Institute of Oceanography, adjunct scientist, 1988; Dalhousie University, adjunct professor, 1989-97, professor of engineering mathematics, 1997-2008, professor of applied mathematics, 1997, adjunct professor of computer science, 2010-. Writer. **Publications:** Hydrodynamics of Waves and Tides: With Applications, 1988; Ocean Wave Mechanics: Computational Fluid Dynamics, and Mathematical Modelling, 1990; Applied Differential Equations for Scientists and Engineers, vol. I: Ordinary Differential Equations, vol. II: Partial Differential Equations, 1991; Applied Complex Variables, 1992; (ed.) Ocean Waves Engineering, 1994; Water Waves: Relating Modern Theory to Engineering Applications, 1995; (ed.) Potential Flow of Fluids, 1995; (ed. with C.A. Brebbia) Advances in Fluid Mechanics Series, 60 vols., 1996-2010; (ed.) Laminar and Turbulent Boundary Layers, 1997; Complex Variables and Transform Calculus, 1997; Mathematical Methods, with Applications, 2000; (with I. Mulolani) Applied Vector Analysis, 2001, 2nd ed., 2008; (ed.) Instability of Flows, 2005; Applied Numerical Analysis, 2005; Integral Equations and Their Applications, 2007; Advanced Vector Analysis for Scientists and Engineers, 2007; Mechanics of Real Fluids, 2010; Applications of Fourier Transforms to Generalized Functions, 2010. EDITED WITH C.A. BREBBIA: Advances in Fluid Mechanics, 1996; Advances in Fluid Mechanics II, 1998; Advances in Fluid Mechanics III, 2000; Advances in Fluid Mechanics IV, 2002; Advances in Fluid Mechanics V, 2004; Advances in Fluid Mechanics VI, 2006; Advances in Fluid Mechanics VII, 2008; Advances in Fluid Mechanics VIII, 2010; Advances in Fluid Mechanics IX, 2012. Contributor to journals. **Address:** Dalhousie University, 6050 University Ave., Studley Campus, Halifax, NS B3H 1W5, Canada. **Online address:** matiur.rahman@dal.ca

RAI, Bali. British (born England), b. 1971?. **Genres:** Adult Non-fiction, Novels, Children's Fiction, Young Adult Non-fiction. **Career:** Writer. **Publications:** (Un)arranged Marriage, 2001; Dream On, 2002; The Crew, 2003; What's Your Problem?, 2003; Concrete Chips, 2004; Rani and Sukh, 2004; Two Timer, 2005; Dominoes: And Other Stories, 2005; The Whisper, 2005; Sold as Seen, 2005; What's Up?, 2005; Jugglin', 2006; Politics: Cutting Through the Crap, 2006; The Last Taboo, 2006; The Angel Collector, 2007; Revenge of the Number Two, 2007; Are You Kidding?, 2008; Starting Eleven, 2008; Missing!, 2008; Glory!, 2008; Stars!, 2008; City of Ghosts, 2009; Them and Us, 2009; The Gun, 2011; Killing Honour, 2011; Fire City, 2012. **Address:** c/o Author Mail, Random House Group Ltd., 20 Vauxhall Bridge Rd., London, GL SW1V 2SA, England.

RAIBMON, Paige Sylvia. Canadian (born Canada), b. 1971?. **Genres:** Social Sciences, History, Humanities. **Career:** Simon Fraser University, faculty; University of British Columbia, associate professor of history. Writer. **Publications:** (Contrib.) Seeing Nature through Gender, 2003; Authentic Indians: Episodes of Encounter from the Late-Nineteenth-Century Northwest Coast, 2005; (contrib.) New Histories for Old: Changing Perspectives on Canada's Native Pasts, 2007. Contributor to journals. **Address:** Department of History, University of British Columbia, Rm. 1220, Buchanan Twr., 1873 E Mall, Vancouver, BC V6T 1Z1, Canada. **Online address:** praibmon@mail.ubc.ca

RAICHLEN, Steven. American/Japanese (born Japan), b. 1953. **Genres:** Food And Wine. **Career:** La Varenne (cooking school), North American program coordinator; Cooking in Paradise (school), St. Barthelemy, founder; Boston Magazine, restaurant critic; Los Angeles Times Syndicate, syndicated columnist; Sante (healthy cooking magazine for physicians), editor; Barbecue University, television show host, 2003-. Cooking teacher and writer. **Publications:** Dining in-Boston, 1980; (ed.) Left Bank Celebrity Cookbook, 1982; Steven Raichlen's Guide to Boston Restaurants: Including Cape Cod, Suburbs and Surrounding Areas, 1983; A Taste of the Mountains Cooking School Cookbook, 1986; A Celebration of the Seasons: A Cook's Almanac, 1988; Boston's Best Restaurants: More than 100 Great Places to Eat In and Around the Hub, 1988; (ed. with C.D. Bates and E. Guiliano) The Best of Florida, 1991; Steven Raichlen's High-Flavor, Low-Fat Cooking, 1992; Miami Spice: The New Florida Cuisine, 1993; Steven Raichlen's High-Flavor, Low-Fat Vegetarian Cooking, 1995; The Caribbean Pantry Cookbook: Condiments and Seasonings from the Land of Spice and Sun, 1995; Steven Raichlen's High-Flavor, Low-Fat Chicken, 1996; Steven Raichlen's High-Flavor, Low-Fat Pasta, 1996; Steven Raichlen's High-Flavor, Low-Fat Appetizers, 1997; Steven Raichlen's High-Flavor, Low-Fat Desserts, 1997; Steven Raichlen's High-Flavor, Low-Fat Italian Cooking, 1997; The Barbecue! Bible, 1998; Steven Raichlen's Healthy Latin Cooking: 200 Sizzling Recipes from Mexico, Cuba, Caribbean, Brazil and Beyond, 1998; Jewish Cooking in America with Joan Nathan. Vegetarian-Who Knew?, 1998; Salud y sazón: 200 deliciosas recetas de la cocina de mamá: todas bajas en grasa, saly colesterol!, 1998; Steven Raichlen's High-Flavor, Low-Fat Mexican Cooking, 1999; Jewish Cooking in America with Joan Nathan Jewbano-Jewish Cuban Cuisine, 1999; Healthy Jewish Cooking, 2000; Barbecue Bible: Sauces, Rubs and Marinades, Bastes, Butters & Glazes, 2000; How to Grill, 2001; Jewish Celebrity Cookbook, 2001; Beer-can Chicken: And 74 Other Offbeat Recipes for the Grill, 2002; Steven Raichlen's BBQ USA: 425 Fiery Recipes From All Across America, 2003; Steven Raichlen's Big Flavor Cookbook: 445 Irresistible and Healthy Recipes from Around the World, 2003; Raichlen's Indoor! Grilling, 2004; Raichlen On Ribs, Ribs, Outrageous Ribs: 99 Top-Notch, Tasty, Truly Tempting Recipes Plus Slaws, Sauces, Baked Beans and More, 2006; Steven Raichlen's Planet Barbecue!: An Electrifying Journey Around the World's Barbecue Trail, 2010; Bold & Healthy Flavor, 2010. Contributor to periodicals. **Address:** Workman Publishing, 225 Varick St., New York, NY 10014, U.S.A. **Online address:** sraichlen@barbecuebible.com

RAIKES, Alison Mary. *See* MORGAN, Alison M.

RAIN, Patricia. American (born United States), b. 1943?. **Genres:** Food And Wine, How-to Books, Agriculture/Forestry, Sciences. **Career:** Freelance writer, 1970-; The Vanilla Co., owner, president, consultant; Smithsonian Institution, lecturer. **Publications:** The Artichoke Cookbook, 1985; Vanilla Cookbook, 1986; (ed.) Pea Soup Andersen's Scandinavian-American Cookbook, 1988; The Vanilla Chef, 2002; Vanilla: The Cultural History of the World's Most Popular Flavor and Fragrance, 2004. Contributor to periodicals. **Address:** The Vanilla Co., PO Box 3206, Santa Cruz, CA 95063, U.S.A. **Online address:** rain@vanilla.com

RAINBOLT, William. American (born United States), b. 1946. **Genres:** History, Novels. **Career:** Record-Chronicle, staff, 1964-69, 1974-75; Avalanche Journal, staff, 1964-69, 1974-75; Fort Worth Star-Telegram, staff, 1964-69, 1974-75; University of Missouri, lecturer in journalism, 1975-79; Rowan University, assistant professor of communication, 1979-84; University at Albany, lecturer in English, 1984-, director of journalism program, 1984-87, 1993, 1998, 1999-, associate professor; Siena College, part-time lecturer in journalism, adjunct faculty in English, 1990-93. **Publications:** The History of

Underground Communication in Russia since the Seventeenth Century, 1979; Moses Rose (novel), 1996. Contributor of articles to periodicals. **Address:** Department of English, University at Albany, 1400 Washington Ave., Albany, NY 12222, U.S.A. **Online address:** rainbolt@albany.edu

RAINE, Craig (Anthony). British (born England), b. 1944. **Genres:** Poetry, Essays, Young Adult Fiction, Literary Criticism And History. **Career:** Oxford University, Exeter College, lecturer, 1971-72; Lincoln College, lecturer, 1974-75; Christ Church, lecturer, 1976-79; New Review, books editor, 1977-78; Quarto, editor, 1979-80; New Statesman, poetry editor, 1981; Faber and Faber Publishers, poetry editor, 1981-91; New College, fellow, 1991-, lecturer in English, tutor, retired, 2010; Saint Anne's College, retired fellow; British Broadcasting Corp., broadcaster; Areté, publisher, 1999-, founder and editor. **Publications:** The Onion, Memory, 1978; A Martian Sends a Postcard Home, 1979; A Journey to Greece, 1979; A Free Translation, 1981; Rich, 1984; The Electrification of the Soviet Union, 1986; The Prophetic Book, 1988; 1953: A Version of Racine's Andromaque, 1990; Haydn and the Valve Trumpet, 1990; History: The Home Movie, 1994; Change, 1995; Clay: Whereabouts Unknown, 1996; In Defence of T.S. Eliot (essays), 2000; Collected Poems 1978-1999, 2000; A la recherche du temps perdu (poems), 2000; Heartbreak, 2010; How Snow Falls, 2011. EDITOR: A Choice of Kipling's Prose, 1987; Rudyard Kipling: Selected Poetry, 1992; New Writing 7, 1998; (intro.) Selected Stories of Rudyard Kipling, 2002; T.S. Eliot, 2006. Contributor to periodicals. **Address:** New College, Holywell St., Oxford, OX OX1 3BN, England. **Online address:** craig.raine@new.ox.ac.uk

RAINE, Jerry. British (born England), b. 1955. **Genres:** Mystery/Crime/Suspense, Novels. **Career:** Murder One Bookshop, assistant manager, 1988-. Writer. **Publications:** CRIME NOVELS: (with I. Mills) Punter's Handbook, 1992; Smalltime, 1996; Frankie Bosser Comes Home, 1999; Slaphead Chameleon, 2000; Small Change, 2001; Some Like it Cold, 2006. Contributor to periodicals. **Address:** Murder One Bookshop, 71-73 Charing Cross Rd., London, GL WC2 H0AA, England.

RAINER, Yvonne. American (born United States), b. 1934. **Genres:** Dance/Ballet, Film, Novels. **Career:** Judson Dance Theater, co-founder, 1962; New School for Social Research, teacher; California Institute of the Arts, teacher. Choreographer, filmmaker and writer. **Publications:** Work 1961-1973, 1974; The Films of Yvonne Rainer, 1989; A Woman Who-: Essays, Interviews, Scripts, 1999; Feelings are Facts: A Life, 2006. **Address:** 72 Franklin St., New York, NY 10013, U.S.A.

RAINEY, Gene Edward. American (born United States), b. 1934. **Genres:** International Relations/Current Affairs, Politics/Government. **Career:** Harding College, assistant professor of political science, 1960-62; American University, School of International Service, assistant dean, 1963-64, Graduate School, associate dean, 1964-66, assistant professor of international relations, 1965-66; Ohio State University, assistant professor of political science, 1966-69; University of North Carolina, associate professor, professor of political science, 1969-, head of department, professor emeritus of political science; Buncombe Co., Board of Commissioners, chairman, 1988-96; Our Next Generation Inc., president. Writer. **Publications:** (Ed.) Contemporary American Foreign Policy: The Official Voice, 1969; Patterns of American Foreign Policy, 1975. **Address:** Department of Political Science, University of North Carolina, 1 University Heights, Asheville, NC 28804, U.S.A. **Online address:** generainey@aol.com

RAINEY, Lawrence S. British (born England), b. 1954. **Genres:** Literary Criticism And History. **Career:** Yale University, assistant professor of English, associate professor of English, 1997-98; University of York, professor of English and chair of modernist English, 1998-, deputy head; Modernism/Modernity, founding editor. **Publications:** Ezra Pound and the Monument of Culture: Text, History and the Malatesta Cantos, 1991; (ed.) A Poem Containing History: Textual Studies in The Cantos, 1997; Institutions of Modernism: Literary Elites and Public Culture, 1998; (ed. and intro.) The Annotated Waste Land with Eliot's Contemporary Prose, 2005, 2nd ed., 2006; (ed.) Modernism: An Anthology, 2005; Revisiting The Waste Land, 2005; (ed.) Modernism: An Anthology, 2005; (ed. and trans.) Futurism: A Reader and Visual Repertory, 2008; (ed. with C. Poggi and L. Wittman) Futurism: An Anthology, 2009. **Address:** Department of English and Related Literature, University of York, L/D/202A, Heslington, York, NY YO10 5DD, England. **Online address:** lawrence.rainey@york.ac.uk

RAISIN, Ross. British (born England), b. 1979?. **Genres:** Novels. **Career:** Writer. **Publications:** God's Own Country in US as Out Backward (novel), 2008; Waterline, 2011. Contributor to periodicals. **Address:** Rogers, Coleridge & White Ltd., 20 Powis Mews, London, GL W11 1JN, England.

RAJADHYAKSHA, Ashish. Indian (born India), b. 1957. **Genres:** Art/Art History. **Career:** Centre for the Study of Culture and Society, senior fellow; Sir Ratan Tata Trust, program officer. Writer. **Publications:** Ritwik Ghatak: A Return to the Epic, 1982. (with P. Willemen) Encyclopaedia of Indian Cinema, 1995, rev. ed., 1999. (contrib. with K. Jain) Chaitanya Sambrani, Edge of Desire: Recent Art in India, 2005; (with S. Banerjee and S. Arvikara) Batacita Mahesa Elakuncavarasi, 2008; Indian Cinema in the Time of Celluloid: From Bollywood to the Emergency, 2009. Contributor to periodicals. **Online address:** ashish@cscsban.org

RAJAH, Susi. American/Australian (born Australia) **Genres:** Novels, Young Adult Non-fiction, Humor/Satire. **Career:** Novelist. **Publications:** NON-FICTION: (with A. Lang) How to Spot a Bastard by His Star Sign, 2002; (with A. Lang) I'm Not a Feminist, But..., 2003. NOVELS: The Gospel according to Sydney Welles, 2007; Heaven, 2007. **Address:** Bloomsbury Publishing, 175 5th Ave., New York, NY 10010-7703, U.S.A. **Online address:** hello@susirajah.com

RAJAN, Tilottama. Canadian/American (born United States), b. 1951. **Genres:** Poetry, Intellectual History, Literary Criticism And History. **Career:** University of Western Ontario, Huron College, assistant professor of English, 1977-80, professor of English and theory, 1990-, Center for Theory, director, 1995-2001, Canada Research chairman, 2001-, Distinguished University Professor; Queen's University, assistant professor, 1980-83, associate professor of English, 1983-85; University of Wisconsin, professor of English, 1984-90, H.I. Romnes chair, 1987-90. Writer. **Publications:** Myth in a Metal Mirror, 1967; Dark Interpreter: The Discourse of Romanticism, 1980; The Supplement of Reading: Figures of Understanding in Romantic Theory and Practice, 1990; Deconstruction and the Remainders of Phenomenology: Sartre, Derrida, Foucault, Baudrillard, 2002; Romantic Narrative: Shelley, Hays, Godwin, Wollstonecraft, 2010. EDITOR: (and intro. with D.L. Clark) Intersections: Nineteenth-Century Philosophy and Contemporary Theory, 1995; (with J.M. Wright) Romanticism, History and the Possibilities of Genre: Re-forming Literature, 1789-1837, 1998; Mary Shelley: Valperga or The Life and Adventures of Castruccio, Prince of Lucca, 1998; (with M.J. O'Driscoll) After Poststructuralism: Writing the Intellectual History of Theory, 2002; (with A. Plotnitsky) Idealism Without Absolutes: Philosophy and Romantic Culture, 2004. **Address:** Department of English, University of Western Ontario, 278 UC, 1151 Richmond St., London, ON N6A 3K7, Canada. **Online address:** trajan@uwo.ca

RAJIC, Negovan. Canadian (born Yugoslavia), b. 1923. **Genres:** Novels, Essays, Novellas/Short Stories, Literary Criticism And History. **Career:** Radio broadcaster, 1951-63; Ecole Polytechnique, research engineer in solid state physics laboratory, 1956-63; College of General and Professional Education of Three Rivers, professor of mathematics, 1969-86. Writer. **Publications:** Les Hommes-taupes (novel), 1978, trans. as The Mole Men, 1980; Propos d'un vieux radoteur (short story collection), 1982, trans. as The Master of Strappado, 1984; Sept Roses pour une boulangere: Recit, 1987, trans. as Seven Roses for a Baker, 1988; Service pénitentiaire national (short story collection), 1988, trans. as Shady Business, 1989; Ka drugoj obali zbogom, Beograde: Roman, 2002; To the Far Shore, 2006. Works appear in anthologies. **Address:** 300 Dunant, Three Rivers, QC G8Y 2W9, Canada. **Online address:** negovan.rajic@tr.cgocable.ca

RAJTAR, Steve. American (born United States), b. 1951. **Genres:** History, Local History/Rural Topics, Travel/Exploration. **Career:** Gearhiser and Peters, attorney, 1977-79; Matthias and Matthias, attorney, 1979-85; Central Florida, real estate lawyer; Florida Trail Association, activities leader. Writer. **Publications:** Hiking Trails, Eastern United States, 1995; Hiking Trails, Western United States, 1996; Indian War Sites: A Guidebook to Battlefields, Monuments and Memorials, 1999; (with F.E. Franks) War Monuments, Museums, and Library Collections of Twentieth Century Conflicts, 2002; Historic Hiking Trails: A Directory of over 900 Routes with Awards Available to Hikers, 2002; United States Holidays and Observances, 2003; Greenwood Cemetery Historical Trail, 2003; A Guide to Historic Orlando, 2006; (with K. Goodman) A Guide to Historic St. Augustine, Florida, 2007; The United States as Depicted On Its Postage Stamps, 2007; A Guide to Historic Tampa,

Florida, 2007; A Guide to Historic Lakeland, Florida, 2007; A Guide to Historic Gainesville, 2007; (with G.P. Rajtar) A Guide to Historic Winter Park, 2008; 101 Glimpses of Bartow, 2008; Historic Photos of Florida Tourist Attractions, 2008; Historic Photos of Gainesville, 2008; 101 Glimpses of Historic Micanopy, 2008; Historic Photos of the University of Florida, 2009; Historic Photos of Florida Ghost Towns, 2010; Remembering the University of Florida, 2010; Remembering Gainesville, 2010; Remembering Florida Tourist Attractions, 2010; (with G.P. Rajtar) Winter Park Chronicles, 2011. Contributor to periodicals. **Address:** 1063 Maitland Ctr. Commons, Ste. 100, Maitland, FL 32751, U.S.A. **Online address:** rajtar@aol.com

RAKE, Alan. British (born England), b. 1933. **Genres:** Travel/Exploration, Biography, Race Relations, History, Social Sciences. **Career:** Drum, correspondent, 1957-59, Africa Confidential, editor, 1963; Drum East Africa, editor, 1964-68; African Development, editor, 1969-77; African Business, editor, 1977-83; New African, editor, 1983-, now retired. **Publications:** Tom Mboya: Young Man of New Africa, 1962; (with J. Dickie) Who's Who in Africa: The Political, Military and Business Leaders of Africa, 1973; Travellers Guides to Africa, 1988; Who's Who in Africa: Leaders for the 1990s, 1992; One Hundred Great Africans, 1994; New African Yearbooks, rev. ed., 2000; African Leaders: Guiding the New Millenium, 2001. **Address:** 26 Campion Rd., London, GL SW15 6NW, England.

RAKE, Jody. (Jody Sullivan Rake). American (born United States), b. 1961. **Genres:** Children's Non-fiction, Young Adult Non-fiction. **Career:** Capstone Press, consultant, 1999; Freelance writer and proofreader, 1999-. **Publications:** UNDER NAME JODY SULLIVAN: Cheetahs: Spotted Speedster, 2003; Beavers: Big-toothed Builders, 2003; Deer: Graceful Grazers, 2003; Georgia, 2003; Hawaii, 2003; Parrotfish, 2006; Crabs, 2006; Sea Anemones, 2006; Sea Stars, 2006. UNDER NAME JODY SULLIVAN RAKE: Beagles, 2006; Dalmatians, 2006; Pugs, 2006; Saint Bernards, 2006; Rays, 2007; Sea Snakes, 2007; Sea Urchins, 2007; Sponges, 2007; Squids, 2007; Walruses, 2007; Eels, 2007; English Springer Spaniels, 2007; Jack Russell Terriers, 2007; Lobsters, 2007; Manatees, 2007; Puffer Fish, 2007; Sea Otters, 2008; Airedale Terriers, 2008; Boxers, 2008; Bulldogs, 2008; Collies, 2008; Mutts, 2008; Narwhal Whales Up Close, 2009; Proboscis Monkey, 2009; Frogfish, 2009; Killer Whales Up Close, 2009; Beluga Whales Up Close, 2009; Bottlenose Dolphins Up Close, 2009; Pumas: On the Hunt, 2010; Blue Whales Up Close, 2010; Hippos: In the Wild, 2010; Human Skeleton, 2010; Humpback Whales Up Close, 2010; Hyenas: On the Hunt, 2010; Polar Bears: On the Hunt, 2010; Bull Shark, 2011; Great White Shark, 2011; Hammerhead Shark, 2011; Mako Shark, 2011; Mystery of Whale Strandings: A Cause and Effect Investigation, 2011; Speed, Strength and Stealth: Animal Weapons and Defenses, 2012; Spines, Horns and Armor: Animal Weapons and Defenses, 2012; Why Bed Bugs Bite and Other Gross Facts About Bugs, 2012; Why Feet Smell and Other Gross Facts About Your Body, 2012; Why Rabbits Eat Poop and Other Gross Facts About Pets, 2012; Why Vampire Bats Suck Blood and Other Gross Facts About Animals, 2012. AS JODY RAKE: Meerkats, 2008; Pythons, 2008; Naked Mole-rat, 2009; Aye-aye, 2009. Contributor to periodicals. **Address:** 7813-60 Tommy Dr., Ste. 60, San Diego, CA 92119-1783, U.S.A. **Online address:** raked@sbcglobal.net

RAKE, Jody Sullivan. See **RAKE, Jody.**

RAKOFF, Alvin. British/Canadian (born Canada), b. 1927. **Genres:** Novels, Plays/Screenplays, Young Adult Fiction. **Career:** Journalist, 1949-53; freelance film and television director, 1952-; British Broadcasting Corp., writer, director and producer, 1953-57; Canadian Broadcasting Corp., Nascent Television, writer. **Publications:** NOVELS: & Gillian, 1996; Baldwin Street: A Novel, 2007. OTHER: Theatre: Too Marvelous for Words, 2002; Who is Sean Connery?, forthcoming. **Address:** 1 The Orchard, London, GL W4 1JZ, England. **Online address:** alvin@alvinrakoff.com

RALEIGH, Debbie. American (born United States), b. 1961. **Genres:** Romance/Historical, Horror, Novels, Young Adult Fiction. **Career:** Writer. **Publications:** ROMANCE NOVELS: Lord Carlton's Courtship, 2000; Spring Kittens Anthology, 2000; Lord Mumford's Minx, 2000; The Naughty Kitten, 2000; The Merry Cupids, 2001; A Bride for Lord Challmond, 2001; Valentine Rogues Anthology, 2001; A Bride for Lord Wickton, 2001; A Bride for Lord Brasleigh, 2001; Christmas Eve Kittens, 2001; Christmas Miracle, 2001; The Christmas Wish, 2001; The Valentine Wish, 2002; The Wedding Wish, 2002; Only with a Rogue, 2002; A Taste of Christmas Anthology, 2002; A Proper Marriage, 2002; One Night with Lucifer, 2002; The Elusive Bride,

2002; A Convenient Marriage, 2002; My Wedding Wish, 2002; A Scandalous Marriage, 2003; A Mother at Heart, 2003; Night of Seduction, 2003; My Lord Eternity, 2003; My Lord Vampire, 2003; The Bewitchment of Lord Dalford, 2003; My Lord Immortality, 2003; My Favorite Rogue, 2004; Miss Frazer's Adventure, 2005; The Wedding Clause, 2005; How to Marry a Duke, 2005; Some Like It Wicked, 2005; Highland Vampires, 2005; Some Like it Sinful, 2006; When Darkness Comes, 2007; Some Like it Brazen, 2007; Embrace the Darkness, 2007; Bedding the Baron, 2008; Darkness Everlasting, 2008; Darkness Revealed, 2009; Seducing the Viscount, 2009; Seduce Me by Christmas, 2009. **Address:** c/o Author Mail, Kensington Publishing Corp., 850 3rd Ave., New York, NY 10022, U.S.A. **Online address:** djral@marktwain.net

RALEIGH, Michael. American (born United States), b. 1947. **Genres:** Novels, Mystery/Crime/Suspense. **Career:** Truman Community College, instructor in English, Department of History, faculty, 1980-; De Paul University, part-time English teacher; Roosevelt University, part-time English teacher; Illinois Arts Council, fellow, 1984, 1985, 1986, 1989. Writer. **Publications:** PAUL WHELAN MYSTERIES: Death in Uptown, 1991; A Body in Belmont Harbor, 1993; The Maxwell Street Blues, 1994; A Killer on Argyle Street, 1995; The Riverview Murders, 1997. NOVELS: In the Castle of the Flynns: A Novel, 2002; The Blue Moon Circus: A Three-Ring Novel, 2003. Contributor to magazines. **Address:** Truman College, 1145 W Wilson Ave., Chicago, IL 60640, U.S.A. **Online address:** mraleigh@ccc.edu

RALLISON, Janette. (Sierra St. James). American (born United States), b. 1966. **Genres:** Novels. **Career:** Writer. **Publications:** YOUNG-ADULT NOVELS: Deep Blue Eyes and Other Lies, 1996; Dakota's Revenge, 1998; Playing the Field, 2002; All's Fair in Love, War, and High School, 2003; Life, Love and the Pursuit of Free Throws, 2004; Fame, Glory and Other Things on My To-Do List, 2005; It's a Mall World after All, 2006; How to Take the Ex out of Ex-Boyfriend, 2007; Revenge of the Cheerleaders, 2007; Can You Keep a Secret?, 2007; My Fair Godmother, 2009; Just One Wish, 2009; My Double Life, 2010; My Unfair Godmother, 2011. AS SIERRA ST. JAMES: Trial of the Heart, 1999; Masquerade, 2001; Time Riders, 2004; What the Doctor Ordered, 2004. **Address:** Walker & Co., 175 5th Ave., New York, NY 10010, U.S.A. **Online address:** jrallisonfans@yahoo.com

RALPH, James R. American (born United States), b. 1960. **Genres:** History, Civil Liberties/Human Rights, Sociology. **Career:** Middlebury College, assistant professor of history, 1989-96, associate professor of history, 1996-2005, professor of history, 2005-, William H. Rehnquist professor of American history and culture, 2006-, dean for faculty research and development, 2010-; De Montfort University, Fulbright fellow, 1994. Writer. **Publications:** Northern Protest: Martin Luther King, Jr., Chicago, and the Civil Rights Movement, 1993. **Address:** Department of History, Middlebury College, 106 Old Chapel Rd., Middlebury, VT 05753-6000, U.S.A. **Online address:** ralph@middlebury.edu

RAMADAN, Tariq. Swiss (born Switzerland), b. 1962. **Genres:** Theology/Religion, Biography, Autobiography/Memoirs, Humanities. **Career:** University of Oxford, St. Antony's College and Lokahi Foundation, visiting fellow, 2005-06, senior research fellow, 2006-, Faculty of Oriental Studies, professor; Erasmus University, visiting professor. Writer. **Publications:** Les Musulmans dans la laïcité: responsabilités et droits des musulmans dans les sociétés occidentales, 1994, 3rd ed., 2000; Islam, le face á face des civilisations, Quel projet pour quelle modernité?, 1995, 4th ed., 2001; Aux sources du renouveau musulman, 1998; (with J. Neirynck) Peut-on vivre avec l'islam, 1999; (with A. Gresh) Islam en Questions, 2000; Musulmans d'Occident et l'avenir de l'islam, 2003; Western Muslims and the Future of Islam, 2004; Muhammad: vie du prophète: les enseignements spirituels et contemporains, 2006; In the Footsteps of the Prophet: Lessons from the Life of Muhammad, 2007; Messenger: The Meanings of the Life of Muhammad, 2008; Islam, la réforme radicale: ethique et libération, 2008; Mon Intime Conviction, 2009; Radical Reform: Islamic Ethics and Liberation, 2009; Autre en nous: pour une philosophie du pluralisme: Essai, 2009; What I Believe, 2010; Quest for Meaning: Developing a Philosophy of Pluralism, 2010; Islam and the Arab Awakening, 2012. **Address:** European Studies Ctr., St. Antonys College, University of Oxford, 70 Woodstock Rd., Paris, 93200, France. **Online address:** office@tariqramadan.com

RAMAYA, Shona. American/Indian (born India) **Genres:** Novels, Novellas/Short Stories, Classics. **Career:** Hamilton College, assistant professor, 1993-96; Trinity College, writer-in-residence, 1996-2000; Catamaran, chief executive editor, 2000-. **Publications:** Flute, 1989; Beloved Mother, Queen of the Night, 1993; Operation Monsoon, 2003; Catamaran: South Asian American Writing, 2003. Contributor to periodicals. **Address:** c/o Susan Raihofer, David Black Literary Agency, 156 5th Ave., Ste. 608, New York, NY 10010-7789, U.S.A. **Online address:** shonaramaya@yahoo.com

RAMAZANI, Jahan. American (born United States), b. 1960. **Genres:** Poetry, Literary Criticism And History. **Career:** University of Virginia, assistant professor of English, 1988-94, professor of English, 1994-2001, Mayo NEH distinguished teaching professor of English, 2001-04, William R. Kenan Jr. professor of English, 2004-06, Edgar F. Shannon professor of English, 2006-, Department of English, chair, 2006-09. Writer. **Publications:** Yeats and the Poetry of Death: Elegy, Self-Elegy, and the Sublime, 1990; Poetry of Mourning: The Modern Elegy from Hardy to Heaney, 1994; The Hybrid Muse: Postcolonial Poetry in English, 2001; (ed. with R. Ellmann and R. O'Clair) The Norton Anthology of Modern and Contemporary Poetry, 3rd ed., 2003; (ed. with J. Stallworthy) The Twentieth Century and After, vol. F: The Norton Anthology of English Literature, 8th ed., 2006; A Transnational Poetics, 2009. **Address:** Department of English, University of Virginia, 219 Bryan Hall, PO Box 400121, Charlottesville, VA 22904, U.S.A. **Online address:** ramazani@virginia.edu

RAMBACH, Peggy. American (born United States), b. 1960?. **Genres:** Novels, Novellas/Short Stories. **Career:** University of New Hampshire, faculty, 1981-82; teacher, 1982-; Bradford College, faculty, 1982-85; Northern Essex Community College, faculty, 1986-88; University of Massachusetts, faculty, 1988-90, Lowell Writers, founder and director; Emerson College, faculty, 1990-98; Chatham University, Low-Residency M.F.A. Program in Creative Writing, faculty, 1998-; Brooks School, writer-in-residence; Hampstead Academy, faculty; Salem State College, Eastern Writers, interim director. **Publications:** When the Animals Leave (short stories), 1986; Fighting Gravity: A Novel, 2001. Contributor to journals and periodicals. **Address:** Chatham University, Woodland Rd., Pittsburgh, PA 15232, U.S.A. **Online address:** prambach@gmail.com

RAMBUSS, Richard. American (born United States) **Genres:** Novels, History. **Career:** Kenyon College, assistant professor of English, 1990-92; Tulane University, assistant professor of English, 1992-; Emory University, Department of English, director of graduate studies, associate professor, chair and professor, 1996-. Writer. **Publications:** Spenser's Secret Career, 1993; Closet Devotions, 1998. Work appears in anthologies. Contributor to scholarly journals. **Address:** Department of English, Emory University, N 302 Callaway Ctr., 537 Kilgo Cir., Atlanta, GA 30322, U.S.A. **Online address:** rrambus@emory.edu

RAMDIN, Ron(ald Andrew). British/Trinidadian (born Trinidad and Tobago), b. 1942. **Genres:** Novels, Area Studies, History, Biography. **Career:** British Library, staff, 1969-; British Broadcasting Corp., journalist, 1982-83. Educator and writer. **Publications:** From Chattel Slave to Wage Earner: A History of Trade Unionism in Trinidad and Tobago, 1982; (intro.) The Black Triangle: The People of the African Diaspora, 1985; The Making of the Black Working Class in Britain, 1987; Paul Robeson: The Man and His Mission, 1987; The West Indies, 1991; The Other Middle Passage, 1994; Re-Imaging Britain: Five Hundred Years of Black and Asian History, 1999; Arising from Bondage: A History of the Indo-Caribbean People, 2000; Rama's Voyage, 2004; Martin Luther King Jnr, 2004; Mary Seacole, 2005; The Griot's Tale, 2009; Isabella's Legacy: My Discovery of Spain, 2011; C.L.R. James, forthcoming. Contributor to books. **Address:** The British Library, St. Pancras, 96 Euston Rd., London, GL NW1 2DB, England. **Online address:** ron@ronramdin.com

RAMIREZ, Malin. American (born United States), b. 1974?. **Genres:** Young Adult Fiction, Novellas/Short Stories. **Career:** Writer and educator. **Publications:** Leti's Shoe Escandalo, Anthology Once Upon a Cuento, 2005; Estrella's Quinceanera, 2006; Sofi Mendoza's Guide to Getting Lost in Mexico, 2007; Quince Crashers, Anthology: 15 Candles, 2008; Border Town Book Series, 2012. **Address:** San Francisco, CA , U.S.A. **Online address:** malinalegria@gmail.com

RAMIREZ, Susan E(lizabeth). American (born United States), b. 1946. **Genres:** History, Anthropology/Ethnology, Area Studies, Theology/Religion, Business/Trade/Industry. **Career:** Ohio University, assistant professor of history, 1977-82, Latin American Studies Program, associate director, 1979-80; DePaul University, assistant professor, 1982-84, associate professor, 1984-89, professor of history, 1989-2003, Latin American Studies, co-director, 1984-95; Field Museum of Natural History, research fellow, 1982-86; Fulbright-Hayes fellow, 1978-79, 1993-94, 2000; Texas Christian University, AddRan College of Humanities and Social Sciences, Penrose professor of history and Latin American history, 2003-, Neville G. Penrose chair of history and Latin American studies. Writer. **Publications:** Provincial Patriarchs: Land Tenure and the Economics of Power in Colonial Peru, 1986; (ed.) Indian-Religious Relations in Colonial Spanish America, 1989; The World Upside Down: Cross-cultural Contact and Conflict in Sixteenth-Century Peru, 1996; To Feed and Be Fed: The Cosmological Bases of Authority and Identity in the Andes, 2005. Contributor to journals. **Address:** Department of History, Texas Christian University, 2800 S University Dr., PO Box 297260, Fort Worth, TX 76129-0001, U.S.A. **Online address:** s.ramirez@tcu.edu

RAMMOHAN, V. (V. Gowri Rammohan). Indian (born India), b. 1951. **Genres:** Biography, Autobiography/Memoirs, Language/Linguistics, Psychology. **Career:** Andhra University, research assistant, 1975-76, assistant professor, 1978-91, associate professor, 1991-2001, professor and chairman, 2001-. **Publications:** Tiruppavai, 1998; (ed.) New Frontiers of Human Science: A Festschrift for K. Ramakrishna Rao, 2002; Insight into the Lives and Works of the Musical Trinity: Tyagaraja, Muthuswamy Dikshitar and Syama Sastry, 2006. **Address:** Department of Psychology and Parapsychology, Colleges of Arts and Commerce, Andhra University, Visakhapatnam, AP 530 003, India. **Online address:** gowrisundari@yahoo.com

RAMMOHAN, V. Gowri. See **RAMMOHAN, V.**

RAMOS, Joseph R(afael). American/Chilean (born Chile), b. 1938. **Genres:** Economics. **Career:** Columbia University, instructor in international economics, 1967; University of Chile, co-teacher, 1968-69, Ford Foundation visiting professor, 1968-71, visiting professor, 1970-86, chair professor, 1971, professor of economics, 1999-2002, Faculty of Economics and Business, dean, 2002-06, professor, 2007-; Organization of American States, research fellow, 1971; FLACSO, researcher, 1971; International Labor Office, PRE-ALC, senior economist on employment policies for Latin America, 1972-81; ILADES, professor, 1982-86; ECLAC, Economic Development Division, deputy director, 1982-90, Division of Production and Management, director, 1992-98, senior economist and division chief; University of Notre Dame, Kellogg Institute, visiting fellow, 1985. Writer. **Publications:** Labor and Development in Latin America, 1970; Creación de empleos yabsorcion del adesempleo en Chile: La experiencia de 1971, 1972; Heterodoxical Interpretation of the Employment Problem in Latin America, 1973; (with E.F. Faivovich) Ciencia, tecnología y desarrollo en los países del Pacto andino: Una bibliografia comentada, 1974; Impacto de las inversiones públicas en el empleo en Panamá, 1976; Economics of Persistent Inflation, of Repressed Inflation, and of Hyperstagflation: Lessons from Inflation and Stabilisation in Chile, 1977; (with C. Kornevall) Employment Impact of Public Investments, 1977; Efectos del Código del trabajo sobre el empleo, la productividad, los costos y la inversión en Panamá, 1978; Concentración, difusión tecnológica restringida y empleo, 1978; Devolucion del Canal de Panama y su efecto sobre el empleo, 1980; Impacto ocupacional de la inversión pública en Bolivia, 1980; Políticas de empleo al alcance de los ministerios del trabajo, 1980; Empleo en la zafra azucarera dominicana, 1981; Desequilibrio externo y empleo en Brasil, 1982; Estabilizacion y liberalizacion economica en el Cono Sur, 1984; (co-author) External Debt in Latin America: Adjustment Policies and Renegotiation, 1985; Neoconservative Economics in the Southern Cone of Latin America, 1973-83, 1986; Mas allá de la economía, mas acá de la utopía, 1991; (ed.) Políticas de empleo e institucionalidad laboral para el siglo XXI, 2003; Flexibilidad laboral y empleo, 2007; El desarrollo exportador chileno, 2008. Contributor to journals. **Address:** Departamento de Economia, Universidad de Chile, Rm. 1406-A, Diagonal Paraguay 257, Santiago, 9783455, Chile. **Online address:** jramos@econ.uchile.cl

RAMOS, Luis Arturo. American/Mexican (born Mexico), b. 1947. **Genres:** Novellas/Short Stories, Novels, Literary Criticism And History. **Career:** University of Texas, assistant professor of languages and linguistics, Chicano Studies and Research Program, faculty, professor; Universidad Veracruzana, Editorial Universitaria (publishing house), director. Writer. **Publications:** SHORT STORY COLLECTIONS: Del Tiempo y Otros Lugares, 1979; Los Viejos Asesinos, 1981. NOVELS: Violeta-Perú, 1979; Intramuros, 1983; Este Era un Gato, 1988; La casa del ahorcado, 1993. OTHERS: (intro.) Acerca de literatura, 1979; Angela de Hoyos, a Critical Look: Lo Heroico y lo Antihe-

roico en su Poesía (literary criticism), 1979; Junto al Paisaje, 1984; Domingo Junto al paisaje, 1987; Melomanías: La Ritualizacíon del Universo (literary criticism), 1990; Blanca-Pluma, 1993; La Señora de la Fuente, 1995; Ciudad de arena, 1999; Mujer que quiso ser Dios, 2000; La noche en que desapareció la luna y otros cuentos, 2000; Cuentos casi completos, 2004; Argentinos no existen, 2005; Ricochet, o, los derechos de autor, 2007; Crónicas desde el país vecino, 2008; Mickey y sus amigos, 2010. Works appear in anthologies. **Address:** Department of Creative Writing, University of Texas, Rm. 415, Liberal Arts Bldg., 500 W University Ave., El Paso, TX 79968, U.S.A. **Online address:** laramos@utep.edu

RAMOS, Manuel. American (born United States), b. 1948. **Genres:** Law, Novels. **Career:** Colorado Legal Services, director of advocacy, 1975-78, 1980-; Continuing Legal Education, director, 1991-96, treasurer, 1995-96; Senior Support Services Inc., director, 1993-95; Metropolitan State College of Denve, part-time faculty, 1997-2003; Colorado Center on Law and Policy, board director, 1999-2003; Colorado Center of the American West, board director, 2000-03. Writer and attorney. **Publications:** The Ballad of Rocky Ruiz, 1993; The Ballad of Gato Guerrero, 1994; Blues for the Buffalo, 1997; Rights and Obligations: Colorado Landlord-Tenant Law: From the Perspective of a Tenant Advocate, 2002; Moony's Road to Hell, 2002; Brown-on-Brown, 2003; The Last Client of Luis Montez, 2004; King of the Chicanos, 2010. Contributor of articles to periodicals. **Address:** Colorado Legal Services, 1905 Sherman St., Ste. 400, Denver, CO 80203-1143, U.S.A. **Online address:** mrriter@aol.com

RAMPHAL, Shridath (Surendranath). British/Guyanese (born Guyana), b. 1928. **Genres:** International Relations/Current Affairs, Environmental Sciences/Ecology, Law, Humanities, Politics/Government, Sciences. **Career:** Government of Guyana, crown counsel, 1953-54, assistant, 1954-56, legal draftsman, 1956-58, attorney general, 1965-73, minister of state for external affairs, 1967-72, minister of foreign affairs, 1972-75, minister of justice, 1973-75; West Indies Federation, legal draftsman, 1958-59, solicitor-general, 1959-61, assistant attorney general, 1961-62; Commonwealth of Nations, secretary-general, 1975-90; United Nations General Assembly, vice president, 1968, 1973; United Nations Conference on Environment and Development, adviser to the secretary-general, 1992; Royal Commonwealth Society, vice president. Writer and public speaker. **Publications:** Safeguarding Human Rights, 1967; (contrib.) Friendship with Integrity, 1969; (contrib.) West Indian Nationhood, 1971; Charter's Mandate, 1971; Dialogue of Unity, 1971; The Laws of Guyana, rev. ed., 1973; Commonwealth in World Affairs, 1975; Keynote Address at the International Conference on Federalism, 1976; Keynote Address, 1976; One World to Share: Selected Speeches of the Commonwealth Secretary-General 1975-79, 1979; Options for the Caribbean, 1985; (with A. McIntyre and W.G. Demas) Caribbean Regionalism, 1987; Nkrumah and the Eighties, 1981; Our Country, The Planet: Forging a Partnership for Survival, 1992; Inseparable Humanity: An Anthology of Reflections of Shridath Ramphal, 1998; An End to Otherness: Commemorative Addresses by the Commonwealth Secretary-General, 1990; (ed. with S.W. Sinding) Population Growth and Environmental Issues, 1996. Contributor to periodicals. **Address:** 1 The Sutherlands, 188 Sutherland Ave., London, GL W9 1HR, England. **Online address:** ssramphal@msn.com

RAMPTON, Sheldon M. American (born United States), b. 1957. **Genres:** Documentaries/Reportage, History, Social Sciences. **Career:** Valley Times, reporter, 1985; Daily Register, reporter, 1984-86; Quick Quality Press, graphic artist, 1987-97; Wisconsin Coordinating Council on Nicaragua, outreach coordinator, 1992-; PR Watch, Center for Media and Democracy, editor, research director, through 2009. **Publications:** Friends in Deed, 1988; (with J.C. Stauber) Toxic Sludge Is Good for You, 1995; (with J. Stauber) Mad Cow U.S.A., 1997; (with J. Stauber) Trust Us, We're Experts!: How Industry Manipulates Science and Gambles with Your Future, 2001; (with J. Stauber) Weapons of Mass Deception: The Uses of Propaganda in Bush's War on Iraq, 2003; (with J. Stauber) Banana Republicans: How the Right Wing is Turning America into a One-Party State, 2004; (with J. Stauber) The Best War Ever: Lies, Damned Lies and the Mess in Iraq, 2006. **Address:** Center for Media and Democracy, 520 University Ave., Ste. 260, Madison, WI 53703, U.S.A. **Online address:** sheldon@execpc.com

RAMSAY, Caro. British/Scottish (born Scotland) **Genres:** Novels, Mystery/Crime/Suspense. **Career:** Physician and writer. **Publications:** Absolution (novel), 2007; Singing to the Dead, 2009; Dark Water, 2010. **Address:** Penguin Books Ltd., 80 Strand, London, GL WC2R 0RL, England. **Online address:** info@caroramsay.co.uk

RAMSAY, Frederick J. American (born United States) **Genres:** Theology/Religion. **Career:** Episcopal priest, 1971, now retired; University of Maryland, School of Medicine, faculty, researcher and instructor in anatomy, embryology, and histology and associate dean; WMAR-TV, news anchor. Writer. **Publications:** Artscape, 2004; Secrets, 2005; Impulse, 2006; Buffalo Mountain, 2007; Judas: The Gospel of Betrayal, 2007, 2nd ed., 2010; Stranger Room, 2008; Choker, 2009; Predators, 2009; Eye of the Virgin, 2010; Reapers, 2010; Rogue, 2011. **Address:** Poisoned Pen Press, 6962 E 1st Ave., Ste. 103, Scottsdale, AZ 85251, U.S.A. **Online address:** ramsaybooks@cox.net

RAMSAY, Jay. British (born England), b. 1958. **Genres:** Poetry, Translations. **Career:** Angels of Fire Collective, co-founder, performer, administrator, 1982-; Third Eye, editor, 1983-84; Directory of Social Change, assistant to the director, 1984; Think Green, assistant to the director, 1986; The Sacred Space of the Word, co-creator, 1988; Chrysalis-The Poet in You, teacher and project director, 1990-; St James' Church, poet-in-residence, 2005-06; Hawkwood College, tutor. **Publications:** Psychic Poetry: A Manifesto, 1985; Raw Spiritual: Selected Poems, 1980-1985, 1986; Trwyn Meditations, 1987; The White Poem, 1988; The Great Return, Books 1-3: The Opening, Knife in the Light: A Stage-Poem (and) The Hole, Books 4-5: In the Valley of Shadow: A Cine-Poem-Cum-Fantasy (and) Divinations, 1988; transmissions, 1989; (with G. Godbert) For Now, 1991; The Rain, the Rain, 1991; (co-trans.) Tao Te Ching, 1992; Improvisations, 1994; (trans.) I Ching, 1995; (trans. with M. Palmer) Kuan Yin, 1995; Meditations on the Unknown God, 1996; Psychic Poetry: A Manifesto, 1997; Alchemy the Art of Transformation, 1997; Kingdom of the Edge-New and Selected Poems, 1980-1998, 1999; Alchemy of the Invisible, 2001; After Rumi, 2002; The Message, 2002; Crucible of Love: The Alchemy of Passionate Relationships, 2004; Into the Further Reaches: An Anthology of Contemporary British Poetry, 2007; Out of Time: Poems 1998-2008, 2008; Anamnesis: The Remembering of Soul, 2008; The Poet in You, 2009; (with M. Palmer) Kuan Yin Chronicles: The Myths and Prophecies of the Chinese Goddess of Compassion, 2009. EDITOR: (with S. Paskin and J. Silver) Angels of Fire: An Anthology of Radical Poetry in the Eighties, 1986; Transformation: The Poetry of Spiritual Consciousness, 1988; Earth Ascending (anthology), 1997. **Address:** Chrysalis, 5 Oxford Terr., Uplands, Stroud, GC GL5 1TW, England. **Online address:** jay@ramsay3892.fsnet.co.uk

RAMSAY, Raylene. New Zealander (born New Zealand), b. 1945. **Genres:** Language/Linguistics, Women's Studies And Issues, Essays, Adult Nonfiction. **Career:** Pacific Conference of Churches, official interpreter, 1966; Universitéd'ete de Pau, teacher of English as a second language, 1972-74; Universitede Toulouse-le-Mirail, lecturer, 1972-74; Jesus College, Magdalene College, St. Johns, instructor, 1974-77; Bell School of Languages, teacher, 1976-77; Massey University, lecturer, 1977-81, senior lecturer, 1981-86; Noumea Summer Schools, teacher and administrator of New Caledonia summer schools, 1979-83; Tufts University, visiting assistant professor, 1986-87; Clark University, assistant professor, 1987-89; Simmons College, associate professor of French, 1989-94; Brown University, visiting lecturer, 1989; University of Auckland, professor of French, 1994-, School of European Languages and Literatures, head, 1997-2000. Writer and technical translator. **Publications:** Robbe-Grillet and Modernity: Science, Sexuality, and Subversion, 1992; The French New Autobiographies: Sarraute, Duras, Robbe-Grillet, 1996; (trans.) D. Gorode and N. Kurtovitch, To Tell the Truth, 1999; French Women in Politics: Writing Power, Paternal Legitimization, and Maternal Legacies, 2003; (trans. with D.Walker) Sharing as Custom Provides: Selected Poems of Déwé Gorodé, 2004; (ed.) Cultural Crossings: Negotiating Identities in Francophone and Anglophone Pacific Literature=À la croisée des Cultures: de la négociation des identités dans les littératures francophones et anglophones du Pacifique, 2010; (ed.) Nights of Storytelling: A Cultural History of Kanaky-New Caledonia, 2011; Between the Colonial and the Post Colonial. Hybridity in Contemporary French and Francophone Writing, forthcoming. Contributor to journals. **Address:** Department of French, University of Auckland, 14 A Symonds St., Arts 1 Bldg., Rm. 602, Level Level 6, Auckland, 1001, New Zealand. **Online address:** r.ramsay@auckland.ac.nz

RAMSDEN, Herbert. British (born England), b. 1927. **Genres:** Literary Criticism And History, Language/Linguistics, Romance/Historical. **Career:** Victoria University of Manchester (now University of Manchester), assistant lecturer, 1954-57, lecturer, 1957-61, professor of Spanish language and litera-

ture, 1961-82, emeritus professor of Hispanic studies, 1982-. Writer. **Publications:** An Essential Course in Modern Spanish, 1959; Weak-Pronoun Position in the Early Romance Languages, 1963; (ed. and intro.) La ruta de Don Quijote, 1966; Angel Genivet's Idearium Espanõl: A Critical Study, 1967; The 1898 Movement in Spain: Towards a Reinterpretation with Special Reference to En torno al casticismo and Idearium español, 1974; The Spanish Generation of 1898, 1974; (ed.) Bodas de sangre, 1980; Baroja, La busca, 1982; Pio Baroja: La busca 1903 to La busca 1904, 1982; (ed. and intro.) La casa de Bernarda Alba, 1983; (ed. and intro.) Romancero Gitano: Eighteen Commentaries, 1988. Contributor to journals. **Address:** University of Manchester, Oxford Rd., Manchester, GM M13 9PL, England.

RAMSEY, Doug(las K.). American (born United States), b. 1934. **Genres:** Novels, Music, Writing/Journalism, Biography, Essays. **Career:** Seattle Times, reporter and copy editor, 1956; Far East Network, manager, 1958-60; KIMA-TV, anchor and news director, 1960-61; KYW-TV, documentary producer, 1962; KOIN-TV, anchor and reporter, 1963; United Press International Television News, chief correspondent, 1973-74; Foundation for American Communications, vice president, 1983-84, senior vice president, 1984-99. **Publications:** (Ed. with D.E. Shaps) Journalism Ethics: Why Change?, 1986; The Corporate Warriors, 1987; Jazz Matters: Reflections on the Music and Some of Its Makers, 1989; (co-author) Soil Survey of Cortez Area, Colorado, Parts of Dolores and Montezuma Counties, 2003; (co-author) Take Five: The Public and Private Lives of Paul Desmond, 2005. Contributor to books. **Address:** 3714 W Chestnut Ave., Yakima, WA 98902, U.S.A. **Online address:** daramsey@charter.net

RAMSEY, Jarold. American (born United States), b. 1937. **Genres:** Plays/Screenplays, Poetry, Songs/Lyrics And Libretti, Mythology/Folklore, Novels. **Career:** University of Washington, faculty; University of Victoria, faculty; University of Rochester, instructor, 1965-66, assistant professor, 1966-71, associate professor, 1971-, professor of English, through 1995, professor emeritus, 1995-. Writer. **Publications:** The Space between Us, 1970; Love in an Earthquake, 1973; The Lodge of Shadows, (libretto), 1974; Dermographia, 1982; Reading the Fire: Essays in the Traditional Indian Literatures of the Far West, 1983, rev. ed., 1999; Hand-Shadows, 1989; (with D.Q. Ramsey) Piper of Cloone: Father Keegan and the early Gaelic revival, 2005. EDITOR: Coyote was Going There (anthology of Indian myths), 1977; Nehalem Tillamook Tales, 1990; (with S. Jones) The Stories We Tell: An Anthology of Oregon Folk Literature, 1994; New Era: Reflections on the Humans and Natural History of Central Oregon, 2003; (with L. Burlingame) In Beauty I Walk: The Literary Roots of Native American Writing, 2008. **Address:** Department of English, University of Rochester, 404 Morey Hall, PO Box 270451, Rochester, NY 14627-0451, U.S.A. **Online address:** jwr1937@madras.net

RAMSEY, Rebecca S. American (born United States), b. 1964?. **Genres:** History, Westerns/Adventure, Travel/Exploration, Reference. **Career:** Educator and writer. **Publications:** French by Heart: An American Family's Adventures in La Belle France, 2007. **Address:** c/o Nathan Bransford, Curtis Brown Ltd., 1750 Montgomery St., San Francisco, CA 94111, U.S.A. **Online address:** becky@rebeccasramsey.com

RAMSEY, William L. American (born United States), b. 1961. **Genres:** History. **Career:** Lander University, Department of History, associate professor and chair, 2008-; University of Idaho, faculty; Tulane University, faculty; State University of New York at Oswego, faculty. Writer and historian. **Publications:** The Yamasee War: A Study of Culture, Economy, and Conflict in the Colonial South, 2008. Contributor to periodicals. **Address:** SC , U.S.A. **Online address:** wramsey@lander.edu

RAMSEYER, Valerie. American (born United States) **Genres:** Theology/Religion. **Career:** Wellesley College, associate professor, director of medieval-renaissance studies. Educator and author of non-fiction. **Publications:** The Transformation of a Religious Landscape: Medieval Southern Italy, 850-1150, 2006. **Address:** 106 Central St., Wellesley, MA 02481-8203, U.S.A. **Online address:** vramseyer@wellesley.edu

RAMSLAND, Katherine. American (born United States), b. 1953. **Genres:** Novels, Mystery/Crime/Suspense, Horror, Science Fiction/Fantasy, Criminology/True Crime, Education, Food And Wine, Philosophy, Psychology, Biography, Sex. **Career:** Rutgers University, professor, 1980-95; DeSales University, assistant professor of forensic psychology, 2001-04, professor of forensic psychology, 2004-; Bard Clemente programs, director. Writer. **Publi-**

cations: Engaging the Immediate: Applying Kierkegaard's Theory of Indirect Communication to the Practice of Psychotherapy, 1989; Prism of the Night: A Biography of Anne Rice, 1991; The Art of Learning: A Self-help Manual for Students, 1992; The Vampire Companion: The Official Guide to Anne Rice's The Vampire Chronicles, 1993; The Witches Companion: The Official Guide to Anne Rice's Lives of the May Fair Witches, 1994; The Anne Rice Trivia Book, 1994; The Roquelaure Reader: A Companion to Anne Rice's Erotica, 1996; (ed.) The Anne Rice Reader, 1997; (with S. Ramsland) Quesadillas: Over 100 Fast, Fresh and Festive Recipes, 1997; Dean Koontz: A Writer's Biography, 1997; Piercing the Darkness: Undercover with Vampires in America Today, 1998; Bliss: Writing to Find Your True Self, 2000; Ghost: Investigating the Other Side, 2001; Cemetery Stories: Haunted Graveyards, Embalming Secrets and the Life of a Corpse After Death, 2001; The Forensic Science of C.S.I., 2001; The Criminal Mind: A Writer's Guide to Forensic Psychology, 2002; The Science of Vampires, 2002; (with G. McCrary) The Unknown Darkness: Profiling the Predators Among Us, 2003; The Science of Cold Case Files, 2004; Inside the Minds of Serial Killers: Why They Kill, 2006; (foreword) The Measure of Madness: Inside the Disturbed and Disturbing Criminal Mind, 2010. The Mind of a Murderer: Privileged Access to the Demons that Drive Extreme Violence, 2011; Snap, 2012. NOVELS: The Heat Seekers, 2002; The Blood Hunters, 2004; Human Predator: A Historical Chronicle of Serial Murder and Forensic Investigation, 2005; Inside the Minds of Mass Murderers: Why They Kill, 2005; Voice for the Dead: A Forensic Investigator's Pursuit of the Truth in the Grave, 2005; The C.S.I. Effect, 2006; Inside the Minds of Healthcare Serial Killers: Why They Kill, 2006; Beating The Devil's Game: A History of Forensic Science and Criminal Investigation, 2007; (with D. DeVito) Bethlehem Ghosts: Historical Hauntings In & Around Pennsylvania's Christmas City, 2007; True Stories of C.S.I.: The Real Crimes Behind the Best Episodes of the Popular TV Show, 2008; Murder in the Lehigh Valley, 2008; (with T. Burkey and K.M. Ramsland) Into The Devil's Den: How an FBI Informant Got inside the Aryan Nations and a Special Agent Got Him out Alive, 2008; (with P.N. McGrain) Inside the Minds of Sexual Predators, 2009; Forensic Psychology of Criminal Minds, 2009; (with H.C. Lee and E.M. Pagliaro) The Real World of a Forensic Scientist: Renowned Experts Reveal What it takes to Solve Crimes, 2009; Devil's Dozen: How Cutting-edge Forensics Took Down 12 Notorious Serial Killers, 2009. Contributor of articles to periodicals. Address: Department of Psychology, DeSales University, 2755 Station Ave., Center Valley, PA 18034, U.S.A. Online address: kmr0@desales.edu

RANA, Indi. See RANA, Indira Higham.

RANA, Indira Higham. (Indi Rana). Indian (born India), b. 1944. Genres: Children's Fiction, Novellas/Short Stories, Novels. Career: Harcourt Brace & World, art editor of school textbooks, 1965-66; Purnell and Sons, assistant and production manager, 1967-70; Paul Hamlyn Ltd., senior editor of children's trade books, 1970-71; Thomson Press Ltd., managing editor of children's trade books, 1976-80; Target Magazine, managing editor, 1976-80; researcher and writer, 1980-; Government of Nepal, secretary; Judicial Council Secretariat, secretary; Judicial Service Commission, secretary. Publications: AS INDI RANA: The Roller Birds of Rampur (novel for children), 1993. SELF-ILLUSTRATED: Favourite Stories from Sri Lanka, 1983; More Favourite Stories from Sri Lanka, 1983. OTHERS: (co-author) The Human Adventure, 1975; Beginners' Fun-to-Learn, 1979; (co-author) All Star Readers, 1983; Monkey See, Monkey Do, 1986; The Devil on Auntie's Shoulder (childrens' novel), 1986; The Devil in the Dustbin (novel for children), 1989. Address: B/G-1 Rosewood Apartments, Mayur Vihar Ph I Ext II, New Delhi, DH 110091, India.

RANA, J. See FORRESTER, Helen.

RANCE, Joseph. See HOYLE, Trevor.

RAND, Gloria. American (born United States), b. 1925. Genres: Picture/Board Books, Children's Non-fiction. Career: Writer. Publications: PICTURE BOOKS: Salty Dog, 1989; Salty Sails North, 1990; Salty Takes Off, 1991; Prince William, 1992; The Cabin Key, 1994; Aloha, Salty!, 1996; Willie Takes a Hike, 1996; Baby in a Basket, 1997; A Home for Spooky, 1998; Fighting for the Forest, 1999; (reteller) Sailing Home: A Story of a Childhood at Sea, 2001; Little Flower, 2002; Mary was a Little Lamb, 2004; A Pen Pal for Max, 2005. Address: 7621 SE 22nd St., Mercer Island, WA 98040, U.S.A.

RAND, Harry. American (born United States), b. 1947. Genres: Art/Art History, Poetry, Novels, Translations. Career: State University of New York-Buffalo, assistant professor of modern art and methodology, 1974-76; National Museum of American Art, Department of Twentieth-Century Painting and Sculpture, chair, 1978-84, curator, 1979-93, senior curator, 1993-96; National Academy of Science, consultant, 1984; Consanti Foundation, staff, 1989-; National Museum of American History, Division of Politics and Reform, curator, 1996-, senior curator. Writer. Publications: The Genius of American Painting, 1973; Seymour Lipton: Aspects of Sculpture, 1979; Arshile Gorky: The Implications of Symbols, 1981; (trans.) The Beginning of Things: Translations from Genesis, 1983; Louis Riback, the Late Paintings, 1984; (contrib.) Emilio Cruz: Recent Paintings and Drawings, 1984; The Martha Jackson Memorial Collection, 1985; Stokely Webster: Paintings Nineteen Twenty-Three to Nineteen Eighty-Four, 1985; Hundertwasser der Maler, 1986; Manet's Contemplation at the Gare Saint Lazare, 1987; (contrib.) Byron Browne: Paintings & Drawings from the 30's, 40's & 50's: April 5 through May 24, 1987, 1987; (contrib.) Lester Johnson: Selected Paintings, 1970-1986, 1987; Paul Manship, 1989; (co-author) Julian Stanczak: Decades of Light, edited by Robert J. Bertholf, 1990; Friedensreich Hundertwasser, 1991. POETRY: Color: Suite in Four Parts, 1993; The Clouds, 1996; (contrib.) William Scharf: Paintings, 1984-2000: The Phillips Collection, Washington, D.C. November 18, 2000-January 21, 2001, 2000. Contributor of articles and poems to periodicals. Address: National Museum of American History, Smithsonian Institution, Constitution Ave., 10th St. NW, PO Box 37012, Washington, DC 20013-7012, U.S.A. Online address: randh@si.edu

RAND, Jacki Thompson. American (born United States), b. 1956. Genres: Humanities. Career: University of Iowa, assistant professor of history and American Indian and native studies, 1998-; Jacobson Foundation, director; Smithsonian Institution, staff. Writer, historian, biographer and consultant. Publications: Wilma Mankiller, 1993; Kiowa Humanity and the Invasion of the State, 2008. Contributor to periodicals. Address: Department of History, University of Iowa, 280 Schaeffer Hall, Iowa City, IA 52242, U.S.A. Online address: jacki-rand@uiowa.edu

RANDALL, Adrian. British (born England), b. 1950. Genres: History. Career: University of Birmingham, lecturer, 1974-89, senior lecturer, 1989-, head of school of social sciences, 1991-97, chair in English social history, 1995-, dean of arts and social sciences, 2002-07, pro-vice chancellor for academic quality and students, 1995-. Writer and historian. Publications: Before the Luddites: Custom, Community, and Machinery in the English Woollen Industry, 1776-1809, 1991; Charities and Taxation, 1995; (ed. with A. Charlesworth) Markets, Market Culture, and Popular Protest in Eighteenth-Century Britain and Ireland, 1996; (ed. with A. Charlesworth and D. Gilberg) An Atlas of Industrial Protest in Britain, 1750-1990, 1996; (ed. with A. Charlesworth) Moral Economy and Popular Protest: Crowds, Conflicts, and Authority, 1999; Riotous Assemblies: Popular Protest in Hanoverian England, 2006. Address: England. Online address: a.j.randall@bham.ac.uk

RANDALL, Dale B(ertrand) J(onas). American (born United States), b. 1929. Genres: History, Literary Criticism And History, Theatre, Biography, Reference. Career: Rutgers University, assistant instructor in English, 1951-53; University of Pennsylvania, assistant instructor in English, 1953-57; Duke University, instructor, 1957-60, assistant professor, 1960-66, associate professor, 1966-70, Graduate School, assistant dean, 1967-70, associate dean, 1970-74, professor of English, 1970-99, professor emeritus of English and practice of drama, 1999-; Southeastern Institute of Medieval and Renaissance Studies, secretary, 1964-67, co-chairman, 1968-69, 1974-75, chairman, 1970-74, 1975-76. Writer. Publications: The Golden Tapestry: A Critical Survey of Non-Chivalric Spanish Fiction in English Translation 1543-1657, 1963; Joseph Conrad and Warrington Dawson: The Record of a Friendship, 1968; Jonson's Gypsies Unmasked: Background and Theme of The Gypsies Metamorphos'd, 1975; Gentle Flame: The Life and Verse of Dudley, Fourth Lord North (1602-1677), 1983; Theatres of Greatness: A Revisionary View of Ford's Perkin Warbeck, 1986; Winter Fruit: English Drama, 1642-1660, 1995. EDITOR: Medieval and Renaissance Studies, vol. VI, 1976, vol. VIII, 1979; (with G.W. Williams) Studies in the Continental Background of Renaissance English Literature: Essays Presented to John L. Lievsay, 1977; Soliloquy of a Farmer's Wife: The Diary of Annie Elliott Perrin, 1999; (with J.C. Boswell) Cervantes in Seventeenth-century England: The Tapestry Turned, 2009. Contributor to periodicals. Address: Department of English, Duke University, 0019 Trent Hall, 314 Allen Bldg., PO Box 90015, Durham, NC 27708, U.S.A. Online address: dbjandpr@acpub.duke.edu

RANDALL, Francis Ballard. American (born United States), b. 1931. **Genres:** Area Studies, History, Literary Criticism And History, Biography, Autobiography/Memoirs. **Career:** Amherst College, faculty, 1956-59; Columbia University, faculty, 1959-61, 1967-68; Sarah Lawrence College, professor history, 1961-2002, professor emeritus, 2002-. Writer. **Publications:** (Co-author) Essays in Russian and Soviet History, 1963; Stalin's Russia: An Historical Reconsideration, 1965; N.G. Chernyshevskii, 1967; Vissarion Belinskii, 1987; History Papers: A Teaching Life, 2000. **Address:** Sarah Lawrence College, 1 Mead Way, Bronxville, NY 10708, U.S.A.

RANDALL, John L(eslie). British (born England), b. 1933. **Genres:** Paranormal, Psychology, Sex, Social Work, Theology/Religion, Medicine/Health. **Career:** Oken High School, science master, 1958-62; Leamington College, tutor in biology, 1962-79; King Henry VIII School, teacher of biology, 1979-90. Writer. **Publications:** (Contrib.) New Directions in Parapsychology, 1974; Parapsychology and the Nature of Life, 1975; (contrib.) Surveys in Parapsychology, 1976; Tests for Extrasensory Perception and Psychokinesis, 1980; Psychokinesis: A Study of Paranormal Forces Through the Ages, 1982; (contrib.) Psychical Research: A Guide to Its History, Principles, and Practices, 1982; Childhood and Sexuality: A Radical Christian Approach, 1992. **Address:** Dorrance Publishing Company Inc., 701 Smithfield St., Ste. 301, Pittsburgh, PA 15222, U.S.A.

RANDALL, Lisa. American (born United States), b. 1962. **Genres:** Physics. **Career:** Harvard University, teaching assistant, 1984, Adams House physics tutor, 1984-87, assistant senior tutor, 1985-87, professor of physics, 2001-09, Frank B. Baird, Jr. professor of science, 2009-; University of California, president's fellow, 1987-89; Lawrence Berkeley Laboratory, postdoctoral fellow, 1989-90; Harvard Society of Fellows, junior fellow, 1990-91; Massachusetts Institute of Technology (MIT), assistant professor of physics, 1991-95, associate professor of physics, 1995-98, professor of physics, 1998-2001; Princeton University, professor of physics, 1998-2000; Radcliffe Institute Cosmology and Theoretical Astrophysics Cluster, chair, 2003. Writer. **Publications:** Warped Passages: Unraveling the Mysteries of the Universe's Hidden Dimensions, 2005; Knocking on Heaven's Door: How Physics and Scientific Thinking Illuminate the Universe and the Modern World, 2011. Contributer to articles. **Address:** Department of Physics, Harvard University, 17 Oxford St., Cambridge, MA 02138, U.S.A. **Online address:** randall@physics.harvard.edu

RANDALL, Margaret. American (born United States), b. 1936. **Genres:** Poetry, Politics/Government, Translations, Autobiography/Memoirs, Gay And Lesbian Issues, Essays, Photography. **Career:** Spanish Refugee Aid Inc., assistant, 1960-61; El Corno Emplumado, editor, 1962-69; Cuban Book Institute, editor and writer, 1969-75; freelance journalist and writer, 1976-80; Ministry of Culture, Managua, publicist, 1981-82; Foreign Press Center, staff, 1983; University of New Mexico, Department of American Studies and Women Studies Program, adjunct assistant professor, 1984-87; Trinity College, Department of English, visiting professor, 1987-94; University of Delaware, distinguished visiting professor, 1990-91; freelance writer, 1995-. **Publications:** Giant of Tears and Other Poems, 1959; Ecstasy Is a Number: Poem, 1961; Poems of the Glass, 1964; Small Sounds of the Bass Fiddle, 1964; October, 1965; 25 Stages of My Spine, 1967; Water I Slip into at Night: Poems, 1967; So Many Rooms Has a House, but One Roof, 1968; Getting Rid of Blue Plastic: Poems Old & New, 1968; Part of the Solution (miscellany): Portrait of a Revolutionary, 1973; This Great People Has Said Enough, and Has Begun to Move, 1973; Cuban Women Now: Interviews with Cuban Women, 1974; With Our Hands, 1974; Spirit of the People, 1975; Somos millones: Lavida de Doris María, combatiente nicaragüensa, 1977; Carlota: Prose and Poems from Havana, 1978; Inside the Nicaraguan Revolution, 1978; We, 1978; Reflections from Cuba, 1978; El pueblo no sólo es testigo: La historia de Dominga, 1979; (with A.A. Moreno) Sueños y realidadesde Guajiricantor, 1979; No se puede hacer la revolución sin nosotras, 1980; Todas estamos despiertas: Testimonios de la mujer nicaragüensede hoy, 1980; Women in Cuba: Twenty Years Later, 1981; Sandino's Daughters: Testimonies of Nicaraguan Women in Struggle, 1981, rev. ed., 1995; Testimonios, 1983; (comp.) Cristianos en la revolución: Del testimonio a la lucha, 1983; Christians in the Nicaraguan Revolution, 1983; Cristianos en la revolución nicaragüense: Del testimonio a la lucha, 1984; Ytambién digo mujer: Testimonio de la mujer nicaragüensa hoy, 2nd ed., 1984; Risking a Somersault in the Air: Conversations with Nicaraguan Writers, 1984; Women Brave in the Face of Danger: Photographs of, and Writings by Latin and North American Women, 1985; The Coming Home Poems, 1986; Albuquerque: Coming Back to the USA, 1986; This Is about

Incest, 1987; Memory Says Yes, 1988; Photographs by Margaret Randall: Image and Content in Differing Cultural Contexts, 1988; (with R. Hubbard) The Shape of Red: Insider/Outsider Reflections, 1988; Coming Home, 1990; Walking to the Edge: Essays of Resistance, 1991; River's Bend: A Decade of the Tunix Poetry Review, 1991; Dancing with the Doe (poems), 1992; Gathering Rage: The Failure of the 20th Century Revolutions to Develop a Feminist Agenda (essay), 1992; Sandino's Daughters Revisited: Feminism in Nicaragua, 1994; Our Voices, Our Lives: Stories of Women from Central America and the Caribbean, 1995; The Price You Pay: The Hidden Cost of Women's Relationship to Money, (essay), 1996; Hunger's Table: Women, Food and Politics (poems), 1997; Las Hijas de Sandino: Una Historia Abierta, 1999; Coming Up for Air, 2001; Where they Left You for Dead; Halfway Home, 2002; When I Look into the Mirror and See You: Women, Terror, and Resistance, 2003; Stones Witness, 2007; To Change the World: My Years in Cuba, 2009; Their Backs to the Sea: Poems and Photographs, 2009; My Town, 2010; First Laugh: Essays 2000-2009, 2011; Ruins, 2011; As if the Empty Chair, 2011; (intro.) Light that Puts an End to Dreams: New & Selected Poems, 2012. EDITOR: Los Hippies: Expression de Una Crises, 1968; Las Mujeres, 1970; La mujer cubana ahora, 1972; Poems from Latin America, 1973; La Gloria de Caballo Loco, 1973; Mujeres en la Revolución: Margaret Randall conversa con mujeres cubanas, 1978. TRANSLATOR: (and intro.) O.R. Castillo, Vámonos patria a caminar (title means: 'Let's Go!'), 1971; Inside These Living Songs: Fifteen New Cuban Poets, 1978; Breaking the Silences, 1981; T.B. Martinez, Carlos, the Dawn Is No Longer beyond Our Reach, 1984; (with E. Randall) D. Zamora, Clean Slate: New and Selected Poems, 1993. Contributor of articles to magazines. **Address:** 50 Cedar Hill Rd. NE, Albuquerque, NM 87122-1928, U.S.A. **Online address:** mrandall36@comcast.net

RANDALL, Robert. See **SILVERBERG, Robert.**

RANDALL, Rona. (Virginia Standage). British (born England), b. 1911?. **Genres:** Romance/Historical, How-to Books, Literary Criticism And History, Novels, Young Adult Fiction. **Career:** Writer. **Publications:** NOVELS: The Moon Returns, A Romance, 1942; Doctor Havelocks Wife, 1943; Rebel Wife, 1944; The Late Mrs Lane, 1946; The Howards of Saxondale, 1946; That Girl, Jennifer!, 1946; The Fleeting Hour, 1947; I Married a Doctor, A Romance, 1947, 2nd ed. as The Doctor Takes a Wife, 1947; The Street of the Singing Fountain, 1948; Shadows on the Sand, 1949; Delayed Harvest, 1950; Young Doctor Kenway, 1950; The Island Doctor, 1951; Bright Morning, A Romance, 1952; Girls in White in UK as Girls in White, A Romance, 1952; Young Sir Galahad, 1953; Journey to Love, 1953; Faith, Hope and Charity, 1954; The Merry Andrews, 1954; Desert Flower, 1955; Journey to Arcady, 1955; Leap in the Dark, a Romance, 1956; A Girl Called Ann, 1956; Runaway from Love, 1956; The Cedar Tree, 1957; The Doctor Falls in Love, 1958; Nurse Stacey Comes Aboard, 1958; Love and Dr Maynard, 1959; Enchanted Eden: A Romance, 1960; Sister at Sea: A Romance, 1960; Hotel De Luxe, 1961; Girl in Love, 1961; House Surgeon at Lukes, 1962; Walk into My Parlour, 1962, rev. ed. as Lyonhurst, 1977; Lab Nurse, 1962; The Silver Cord, 1963; The Willow Herb, 1965; Seven Days from Midnight, 1965; Arrogant Duke, 1966; Knights Keep, 1967; Broken Tapestry, 1969; The Witching Hour, 1970; Silent Thunder, 1971; Mountain of Fear, 1972; Time Remembered, Time Lost, 1973; Glenrannoch in US as The Midnight Walker, 1973; Dragonmede, 1974; Watchmans Stone, 1975; The Eagle at the Gate, 1977; Spiel der Leidenschaft: Roman, 1977; The Mating Dance, 1979; The Ladies of Hanover Square, 1981; (as Virginia Standage) Golden Rebel, 1981; Curtain Call, 1983; The Drayton Legacy, 1985; The Potters Niece, 1987; The Rival Potters, 1990; The Frozen Ceiling, 1999; The Tower Room, 2001; Sisters In Nursing, 2005. OTHERS: Jordan and the Holy Land, 1968; The Model Wife: Nineteenth Century Style, 1989; Writing Popular Fiction, 1992. **Address:** 10 Bishops Ct., Bishops Down Rd., Tunbridge Wells, KT TN4 8VL, England.

RANDALL, Willard Sterne. American (born United States), b. 1942. **Genres:** History, Biography, Humanities. **Career:** Pottstown Mercury, reporter, 1960-61; United States Corporation Co., legal writer and assistant manager, 1961-65; Mainland Journal, reporter, 1965-66; Philadelphia Bulletin, reporter, editor and feature writer, 1966-71; Philadelphia Magazine, editorial director, 1971-72; Time-Life News Service, correspondent, 1972-73; freelance writer, 1973-82; Princeton University, graduate fellow, 1982-4; University of Vermont, lecturer, 1984-91, visiting assistant professor, 1991-94; John Cabot University, visiting professor, 1994-; Champlain College, professor of history, 1998-; Ocean City Writers Workshop, founder and president; Ocean City Cultural Arts Center, vice president. **Publications:** The Proprietary House in Amboy, 1975; (ed. with D.R. Boldt) The Founding

City, 1976; (with S.D. Solomon) Building 6, 1977; A Little Revenge: Benjamin Franklin and His Son, 1984; Benedict Arnold: Patriot and Traitor, 1990; Thomas Jefferson: A Life, 1993; (with N.A. Nahra) American Lives, 1997; George Washington: A Life, 1997; (with N.A. Nahra) Forgotten Americans, 1998; (with N.A. Nahra) Thomas Chittenden's Town, 1998; Alexander Hamilton: A Life, 2003; Ethan Allen, His Life and Times, 2011. **Address:** Education & Human Services Division, Champlain College, 163 S Willard St., PO Box 34, Burlington, VT 05401, U.S.A. **Online address:** willnn@aol.com

RANDALL, William Lowell. Canadian (born Canada), b. 1950. **Genres:** Gerontology/Senior Issues, Psychology, Autobiography/Memoirs, Theology/Religion. **Career:** WGBH Educational Foundation, assistant business manager for special projects, 1972-73; Fraser Pulp and Paper Co., inventory cataloguer, 1978-79; United Church of Canada, minister, 1979-90; Seneca College of Applied Arts and Technology, English instructor, 1991-95; St. Bonaventure University, adjunct lecturer, 1992-94; University of New Brunswick, instructor in adult education, 1993, 1995, 2002; University of Toronto, part-time instructor, 1993; Brock University, seminar facilitator/site leader, 1993-95; St. Thomas University, Department of gerontology, visiting chair, 1995, research associate, 1996-2001, assistant professor, 2001-05, associate professor, 2005-10, professor, 2010-, Centre for Interdisciplinary Research on Narrative, director. Writer. **Publications:** Who Has Seen the Wind: Sermons from St. Paul's, 1988; The Stories We Are: An Essay on Self-Creation, 1995; (with G.M. Kenyon) Restorying Our Lives: Personal Growth through Autobiographical Reflection, 1997; (with G.M. Kenyon) Ordinary Wisdom: Biographical Aging and the Journey of Life, 2001; (with A.E. McKim) Reading Our Lives: The Poetics of Growing Old, 2008; (ed. with G. Kenyon and E. Bohlmeijer) Storying Later Life: Issues, Investigations, and Interventions in Narrative Gerontology, 2010. Contributor of articles to periodicals. **Address:** Department of Gerontology, St. Thomas University, 304 Brian Mulroney Hall, 51 Dineen Dr., Fredericton, NB E3B 5G3, Canada. **Online address:** brandall@stu.ca

RANDELL, Beverley. New Zealander (born New Zealand), b. 1931?. **Genres:** Children's Fiction, Children's Non-fiction, Young Adult Fiction, Young Adult Non-fiction, Picture/Board Books, Social Sciences. **Career:** Teacher, 1953-59; Price Milburn & Company Ltd., editor, 1962-84; writer, editor and consultant, 1984-92; Nelson Thomson Learning, curriculum materials consultant, 1992-. **Publications:** PM STORY READERS SERIES: Hedgehog Is Hungry, 1972; Cuckoo in the Nest, 1972; The Photo Book, 1972; The Lucky Dip, 1972; The Merry-go-round, 1972; No Breakfast for Tiger, 1972; The Lazy Pig, 1972; The Big Kick, 1972; Sausages, 1972; The Dodgems, 1972; Baby Lamb's First Drink, 1972; Bill's Treasure Hunt, 1972; Pussy and the Birds, 1972; Bill's Teddy Bear, 1972; Father Bear, 1972; Lizard Loses His Tail, 1972; Sticking Plaster, 1972; Up to the Moon, 1972; Blackberries, 1972; Back from the Moon, 1972; Sally's Beans, 1972; Mumps, 1972; Nicky's Monkeys, 1972; The Hungry Kitten, 1972; The Dog School, 1972; The New Baby, 1972; Bill's Dad, 1972; Little Bulldozer, 1972; Jane's Birthday, 1972; Jane Is a Teacher, 1972; Nicky Stays Home, 1972; Fishing, Sally's Bucket, 1972; The Helpful Helicopter, 1972; Hermit Crab, 1972; Honey for Baby Bear, 1972; Helping Mother, 1972; Christmas Eve, 1972; A Friend for Rabbit, 1972; Magpie's Baking Day, 1972; The Best Cake, 1972; The House in the Tree, 1972; Jean's Play House, 1972; Donald's Puppy, 1972; Baby Bear's Present, 1972; Locked Out, 1972; Seagull's Breakfast, 1972; Puppy Has a Bath, 1972; Jane's Car, 1972; Painting Pictures, 1972; Cows in the Garden, 1972; Garages, 1972; Sally at School, 1972; The Christmas Tree, 1972; The Naughty Ann, 1972; The Lion and the Rabbit, 1972; Off to Town, 1972; Donald Is Five, 1972; House Hunting, 1972; David and Brian, 1972; Mushrooms, 1972; Candle Light, 1972; The Dog in the Manger, 1972; The Lion and the Mouse, 1972; Pet Lambs, 1972; Here Comes the Bus, 1972; Show Day, 1972; Look at the Mess, 1972; My Baby Is a Lion, 1972; Dad Ties a Knot, 1972; The Little Red Bus, 1972; The Pictures, 1972; A Wet Morning, 1972; Going Swimming, 1972; The Fox Who Foxed, 1972; Bill's Tooth, 1972. METHUEN CAPTION BOOKS SERIES: Who Are You?, 1965, rev. ed., 1974; Where Are You Going?, 1965, rev. ed., 1974; Who Likes Flies?, 1965, rev. ed., 1974; Where Are the Children?, 1965, rev. ed., 1974; A Chair Is for Sitting, 1965, rev. ed., 1974; A Fire Is Hot, 1965, rev. ed., 1974; My Doll's House, 1965, rev. ed., 1974; Shopping, 1965, rev. ed., 1974; At School, 1965, rev. ed., 1974; The Road, 1965, rev. ed., 1974; A Birthday Book, 1965, rev. ed., 1974; Dinner Time, 1965, rev. ed., 1974; Susan Drew Herself, 1965, 2nd ed. as Susan's Drawing, 1974; Susan Drew a House, 1965, 2nd ed. as Susan's House, 1974; Peter Drew a Boat, 1965, 2nd ed. as Peter's Boat, 1974; Peter Drew a Train, 1965, 2nd ed. as Peter's Car, 1974; Funny Fishes, 1974;

Something Missing, 1974; The Rock Pool, 1974; Boats, 1974; The Street, 1974; Pockets, 1974; Putting Away, 1974; Pairs, 1974. TINY TALES SERIES: Wake up Father, 1965; Breakfast in Bed, 1965; Bedtime, 1965; Grandfather's Birthday, 1965; The Baby, 1965; Breakfast on the Farm, 1965; Planes, 1965; Ducks, 1965; Martin Teases Ann, 1965; Bread, 1965; Fireman Nicky, 1965; Where Are the Sunhats?, 1965; Puss Puss Puss, 1965; Brave Father Mouse, 1965; The Airport, 1965; Paul Is Father, 1965. PM COMMONWEALTH READERS SERIES: The Lambs, 1965; Run Rabbit Run, 1965; Tim Pretends, 1965; The Twins Can Draw, 1965; Big Dog and Little Kitten, 1965; Shopping after School, 1965; Sally's Dolls' House, 1965; Sally Is Sick, 1965; Tim Climbs a Tree, 1965; The Yellow Boat, 1965; Cracker Night, 1965; Sally Is Helpful, 1965; The Missing Cat, 1965; A Frock for a Party, 1965; The Night Train, 1965; The Barbecue, 1965. COUNTRY READERS SERIES: Boxes, 1968; Playing with the Girls, 1968; Simon's Lamb, 1968; Freshwater Crayfish, 1968; Shearing Time, 1968; Fun in the Hay, 1968; Wet and Muddy, 1968; The Pony, 1968; Janey's Hens, 1968; Janey's Bus Ride, 1968; Alan Goes Fishing, 1968. FELT BOOKS SERIES: Big and Little, 1969; My Toy Farm, 1969; Autumn Leaves, 1969; Christmas Cards, 1969; Cups and Saucers, 1969; Jugs, 1969; Our House, 1969; Can Plants Count?, 1969. INSTANT READERS SERIES: Me, 1970; My Family, 1970; My Family, 1970; Father, 1970; Big Sister, 1970; Big Brother, 1970; People We Know, 1971; After School, 1971; Pets, 1971; I Am Hungry, 1978; Homes, 1978; At School, 1978; Look at Me, 1978; Down the Stairs, 1978; Up on the Wall, 1978; Books, 1978; Helping, 1978; My Toy Farm, 1978; Where Is Ann?, 1978; Away They Went, 1978. THE MARK AND MEGBOOKS SERIES: Meg and the Windy Day, 1971; Meg and the Little Wooden Engine, 1971; Meg and the Cardboard Dolls' House, 1971; Meg and the 33 Oak Trees, 1971; Mark and the Half Birthday, 1971; Mark and the Trip to Hospital, 1971; The First Men on the Moon, 1971. CREATIVE WORKBOOKS: The Preparatory Book, 1970; The Red Book, 1970; The Yellow Book, 1970; The Blue Book, 1970; The Green Book, 1970; The Orange Book, 1970; The Turquoise Book, 1970; The Purple Workbook, 1970; The Gold Workbook, 1970. NUMBER STORY CAPTION BOOKS SERIES: Yellow Set, 1973; Red Set, 1973; Blue Set, 1973; Orange Set, 1973. ANIMAL BOOKS SERIES: Guinea Pigs, 1978; Horses, 1978; Goldfish, 1978; Cats, 1978; Dogs, 1978; Mice, 1978; Budgies, 1978; Hens, 1978; White Rabbits, 1978; Hares, 1978; Hedgehogs, 1978; Goats, 1978; Ducks and Drakes, 1978; Pigeons and Doves, 1978; Opossums, 1978; Fur Seals, 1978. READ ALONGS: Round the Year, 1979; It's Blowing, 1979; One Two, 1979; The Boat Race, 1979; One Big Dinosaur, 1979; Pop, Pop, Pop, 1979; Moon Shot, 1979; Tamsy and the Pirates, 1979; Red Hen and Sly Fox, 1979; Cowboy Danny, 1979. JOINING-IN BOOKS SERIES: At the Zoo, 1983; Australian Alphabet, 1983; Down by the Waterhole, 1983; Ten Small Koalas, 1983; A Day at the Beach, 1984; Sea Shells, 1984; Ten Little Swimming Crabs, 1984. RHYME AND RHYTHM SERIES: I Can Squeak, 1985; Stables Are for Horses, 1985; Tomatoes and Bricks, 1985; One Sun in the Sky, 1985. LOOK AND LISTEN SERIES: Set A: Follow the Leader, 1985; Set A: How Many Legs?, 1985; Set A: I'm Not, I'm Not, 1985; Set A: Where Can Pussy Sleep?, 1985; Set A: Where Are the Car Keys?, 1985; Set A: Where's Bear?, 1985; Set B: What's the Time, Mr. Wolf?, 1985; Set B: Who Wears This Hat?, 1985; Set B: Let's Go, 1985; Set B: Kitten Chased a Fly, 1985; Set B: Houses, 1985; Set B: Here's a House, 1985; Set C: The Race, 1985; Set C: Where Is Teddy's Head?, 1985; Set C: My Tower, 1985; Set C: James Is Hiding, 1985; Set C: I've Lost My Gumboot, 1985; Set C: Don't Splash Me, 1985. NEW PM STORY BOOKS SERIES: Tom Is Brave, 1993; Ben's Teddy Bear, 1993; Father Bear Goes Fishing, 1993; Ben's Treasure Hunt, 1993; Lucky Goes to Dog School, 1994; Ben's Dad, 1994; Baby Bear Goes Fishing, 1994; Fire! Fire!, 1994; Sally's Friends, 1994; Seagull Is Clever, 1994; Mushrooms for Dinner, 1994; Ben's Tooth, 1994; The Island Picnic, 1994; Tabby in the Tree, 1994; Brave Triceratops, 1994; The Clever Penguins, 1994; Pete Little, 1994; Mrs. Spider's Beautiful Web, 1994; Ten Little Garden Snails, 1994; Pepper's Adventure, 1994; The Waving Sheep, 1994. PM STARTERS ONE SERIES: Me, 1995; Mum, 1995; Dad, 1995; A House, 1995; Big Things, 1995; Little Things, 1995; Dressing-up, 1995; Playing, 1995; Pets, 1995; We Go Out, 1995; Time for Dinner, 1995; Animals at the Zoo, 1995; Mums and Dads, 1995; The Go-Karts, 1995; In the Trolley, 1995; Climbing, 1995; The Shopping Mall, 1995; Look at Me, 1995; The Way I Go to School, 1995; The Skier, 1995. PM STARTERS TWO SERIES: Cat and Mouse, 1995; Where Are the Babies?, 1995; Stop!, 1995; My Red Car, 1995; We Like Fish, 1995; The Pencil, 1995. CHILDREN'S BOOKS: John, the Mouse Who Learned to Read, 1969; Bowmar Primary Reading Series: Supplementary to All Basic Reading Series, 1969; Listening Skillbuilders, 1971; Phonic Blends, 1979; Singing Games, 1981; PM Alphabet Blends, 1995; PM Nonfiction, 1988; PM Tales and Plays, 1999; (with A. Smith and J.

Giles) PM Plus Starters, 1999; PM Plus Story Books, 2000. OTHERS: John the Mouse who Learned to Read, 1955; Baa Baa Black Sheep, 1968; Peter Is Awful, 1968; Janey and the Cows, 1968; The Island, 1968; Toss Helps the Boys, 1968; Patrick's Calf, 1968; Robin Joins the Cubs, 1968; Guide to the Ready to Read Series, and Supporting Books, 1971; A Crowded Thorndon Cottage: The Story of William and Sarah Randell and Their Ten Children, 1992; Guide to the PMs, 2000; (with A. Smith, J. Giles and E. Nelley) PM Benchmark Kits, 2000; Shaping the PM Story Books, 2000; Survivors in the Frozen North, 2002; The Man Who Rode A Tiger, 2002; Where Did Baby Bear Come From, 2003; Baby Bear's Real Name, 2003; When Dinosaurs Ruled the Earth, 2003; Balloons Go Pop!, 2006; Mother Bear's Scarf, 2006; Eggs and Dandelions, 2006; The Clever Jackals, 2006; (comp. with H. Price) Wellington at Work in the 1890s, 2009. **Address:** 24 Glasgow St., Kelburn, Wellington, 6012, New Zealand. **Online address:** randellprice@xtra.co.nz

RANDELL, Nigel. American/British (born England) **Genres:** Novels, Biography, History, Politics/Government. **Career:** Writer and documentary filmmaker. **Publications:** The White Headhunter: The Story of a Nineteenth-Century Sailor Who Survived a Heart of Darkness, 2003; The Bricklayer, the Boy and the Cannibal King. Contributor to periodicals. **Address:** c/o Author Mail, Carroll & Graf Publishers, 245 W 17th St., 11th Fl., New York, NY 10011-5379, U.S.A.

RANDI, James. (Randall Zwinge). American/Canadian (born Canada), b. 1928. **Genres:** Education, Paranormal, Sciences, Social Commentary, Reference, Archaeology/Antiquities. **Career:** WOR-Radio, host, 1966-67; SWIFT, editor; University of California, Regents lecturer, 1984; New York University, faculty; Brookdale Community College, faculty; magician, 1946-, now retired; James Randi Educational Foundation, founder, 1996. Writer. **Publications:** The Magic of Uri Geller, 1975, as The Truth about Uri Geller, 1982; (with B.R. Sugar) Houdini: His Life and Art, 1976; Flim-Flam!: The Truth about Unicorns, Parapsychology and Other Delusions, 1980; Test Your ESP Potential: A Complete Kit, 1982; The Faith Healers, 1987; The Magic World of the Amazing Randi, 1989; The Mask of Nostradamus, 1990; James Randi: Psychic Investigator, 1991; Conjuring, 1992; Encyclopedia of the Supernatural and the Occult, 1996; A Magician in the Laboratory, 2010; Wrong!, forthcoming. Contributor to journals. **Address:** James Randi Educational Foundation, 201 SE 12th St., Fort Lauderdale, FL 33316-1815, U.S.A. **Online address:** randi@randi.org

RANDLES, Jenny. British (born England), b. 1951. **Genres:** Paranormal, Sciences, Transportation. **Career:** Cheshire Middle School, teacher, 1972-74; Northern UFO News, editor, 1974-; British Rheumatism and Arthritis Charity, editor, 1979-82; British Telecom Network, writer and presenter of UFO call, a weekly telephone news and information service, 1988-; The New UFO logist magazine, co-founder, 1994; ITV Television, consultant for a news and information program on the paranormal, 1995; BBC TV documentary on UFOs, writer and presenter, 1996; Chicagos J. Allen Hynek Center for UFO Studies, consultant. **Publications:** (With P. Warrington) UFOs: A British Viewpoint, 1979; UFO Study: A Handbook For Enthusiasts, 1981; Alien Contact, 1982; UFO Reality: A Critical Look at the Physical Evidence, 1983; The Pennine UFO Mystery, 1983; (with B. Butler and D. Street) Sky Crash: A Cosmic Conspiracy, 1984, rev. ed., 1986; (with P. Warrington) Science and the UFOs, 1985; Beyond Explanation? Strange Experiences of Famous People, 1985; Sixth Sense: A Psychic Powers and Your Five Senses, 1987; The UFO Conspiracy: The First Forty Years, 1987; Abduction, 1988, rev. ed. as Alien Abductions, 1989; (with P. Hough) Death by Supernatural Causes?, 1988, 1989; Phantoms of the Soap Operas, 1989; Mind Monsters, 1990; (with P. Fuller) Crop Circles: The Mystery Solved, 1990, rev. ed., 1993; (with P. Hough) Scary Stories, 1991; From out of the Blue: The Facts in the UFO Cover-Up at Bentwaters NATO Air Base, 1991, rev. ed., 1993; (with P. Hough) Looking for the Aliens, 1992; UFOs and How to See Them, 1992, rev. ed., 1993; Aliens: The Real Story, 1993; (with P. Hough) Mysteries of the Mersey Valley, 1993; The Paranormal Year, 1993; (with P. Hough) The Afterlife: An Investigation into the Mysteries of Life after Death, 1994; (with P. Hough) Spontaneous Human Combustion, 1994; Alien Contacts & Abductions: The Real Story From the Other Side, 1994; Strange & Unexplained Mysteries of the 20th Century, 1994; Time Travel: Fact, Fiction and Possibility, 1994; (with P. Hough) Strange But True?, 1994; (with P.A. Hough) Worlds Best True UFO Stories, 1994; Star Children: The True Story of Alien Offspring Among Us, 1995; UFO Retrievals: The Recovery of Alien Spacecraft, 1995; The Paranormial Source Book, 1995; Life After Death, 1996; (with P. Hough) Complete Book of UFOs: An Investigation Into Alien Contacts & Encounters,

1996; Alien Contact: The First Fifty Years, 1997; Truth Behind Men in Black: Government Agents, or Visitors From Beyond, 1997; UFO Crash Landing? Friend or Foe?: The Full Story of the Rendlesham Forest Close Encounter, 1998; Truly Weird: Real-Life Cases of the Paranormal, 1998; (with P. Hough) Life After Death and the World Beyond: Investigating Heaven and the Spiritual Dimension, 1998; UFO!: Danger in the Air, 1999; Little Giant Encyclopedia of UFOs, 2000; Time Storms: Amazing Evidence for Time Warps, Space Rifts, and Time Travel, 2001; Psychic Detectives: The Mysterious Use of Paranormal Phenomena in Solving True Crimes, 2001; Breaking The Time Barrier: The Race to Build the First Time Machine, 2005. Contributor to journals, magazines and newspapers. Works appear in anthologies. **Address:** Sterling Publishing Company Inc., 387 Park Ave. S, New York, NY 10016, U.S.A. **Online address:** nufon@btinternet.com

RANDOLPH, Elizabeth. American (born United States), b. 1930. **Genres:** Animals/Pets, Humor/Satire, Children's Fiction. **Career:** Writer. **Publications:** Your Pet's Complete Record Book, 1977; (with Y. Omura and R.V. Overholser) Tofu-miso High Efficiency Diet, 1981; How to Be Your Cat's Best Friend, 1981; (ed. with W.J. Kay) The Complete Book of Dog Health, 1985; (with W.J. Kay) The Complete Book of Cat Health, 1985; (with G. Hamilton) How to Help Your Puppy Grow Up to Be a Wonderful Dog, 1987; The Basic Bird Book, 1989; The Basic Book of Fish Keeping, 1991; (with B. Dibra) Dog Training by Bash: The Tried and True Techniques of the Dog Trainer to the Stars, 1991; Rabbits and Other Furry Pets, 1992; (with B. Dibra) Teach Your Dog to Behave: Simple Solutions to Over 300 Common Dog Behavior Problems from A to Z, 1993; (ed.) PDR Nurse's Dictionary, 1994; (ed.) Community Response: Words are the Bugles of Social Change, 1995; The Veterinarians' Guide to Your Cat's Symptoms, 1999; The Veterinarians' Guide to Your Dog's Symptoms, 1999; (with B. Dibra) Cat Speak: How to Learn It, Speak It and, Use It to Have a Happy, Healthy, Well-Mannered Cat, 2001; (with B. Dibra and K. Brown) Your Dream Dog: A Guide to Choosing the Right Breed for You, 2003. Contributor to magazines. **Address:** Barbara Lowenstein, Barbara Lowenstein Associates Inc., 21 W 27th St., Ste. 601, New York, NY 10001, U.S.A. **Online address:** ehettich@aol.com

RANDOLPH, Ellen. See **RAWN, Melanie (Robin).**

RANDOLPH, Lewis A. American (born United States), b. 1952. **Genres:** History, Politics/Government. **Career:** Sinclair Community College, instructor in political science, 1975; Northern Kentucky University, counselor and academic advisor, 1977-79; Xavier University, lecturer in history, 1979; University of Delaware, assistant director of minority programming, 1979-84, lecturer in black American studies, 1980-81; Ohio University, assistant professor, 1990-2001, associate professor of political science, 2001-, professor, adjunct professor of community and development studies, 1993-, adjunct professor of American studies, 2002-, Center for Public and Environmental Affairs, faculty affiliate, 1995-, Contemporary Institute of History, faculty associate, 2000-; Ohio State University, visiting professor, 1992; Syracuse University, Maxwell School of Citizenship and Public Affairs, visiting professor, 1997, 1998. Writer and consultant. **Publications:** (Ed. with G.T. Tate) Dimensions of Black Conservatism in the United States: Made in America, 2002; (with G.T. Tate) Rights for a Season: The Politics of Race, Class, and Gender in Richmond, Virginia, 2003; (ed. with G.T. Tate) The Black Urban Community: From Dusk Till Dawn, 2006; (with R.E. Weems, Jr.) The Political and Historical Origins of Richard M. Nixon's Black Capitalism Initiative, 2007; (with R.E. Weems, Jr.) Business in Black and White: American Presidents & Black Entrepreneurs in the Twentieth Century, 2009. Contributor of articles to books and periodicals. **Address:** Department of Political Science, Ohio University, 266 Bentley Annex, Athens, OH 45701, U.S.A. **Online address:** lewisrandolph@msn.com

RANDOLPH, William. See **LINGEMAN, Richard.**

RANDSBORG, Klavs. Danish (born Denmark), b. 1944. **Genres:** Archaeology/Antiquities, History. **Career:** University of Copenhagen, lecturer, 1971, senior lecturer, 1971, reader, 1972-88, professor of archaeology, 1988-, research professor, 1990-, professor of world archaeology, 2003-; Washington University, visiting professor, 1975-76; University of Amsterdam, visiting professor, 1980-81; University of Frankfurt, visiting professor, 1989; University of Gothenburg, professor, 1989-92. Writer. **Publications:** The Viking Age in Denmark: The Formation of a State, 1980; (with R. Chapman and I. Kinnes) Archaeology of Death, 1981; The Making of Britain, 1984; (ed.) Birth of Europe: Archaeology and Social Development in the First Millennium A.D., 1989; The First Millennium A.D. in Europe and the Mediterranean: An Archaeological Essay, 1991; Le vie della preistoria, 1992; Barbarians, Classical Antiquity, and the Rise of Western Europe, Past and Present, 1992; Archaeology and the Man-Made Material Reality, 1992; Kivik: Archaeology and Iconography, 1993; Hjortspring: Warfare and Sacrifice between the Bronze Age and Rome, 1995; Absolute Chronology: Archaeological Europe 2, 500-500 B.C., 1996; Kephellénia: Archaeology and History, the Ancient Greek Cities, I-II, 2002; Inigo Jones and Christian IV, 2004. Contributor to journals. **Address:** Archaeological Division, SAXO-institute, University of Copenhagen, Njalsgade 80, Copenhagen, DK-2300, Denmark. **Online address:** randsb@hum.ku.dk

RANGOUSSIS, Steven. American (born United States), b. 1973. **Genres:** Novels, Plays/Screenplays. **Career:** L.A.S.T., instructor, 1992-96, 1999-; J. Fraser and Associates, marketing manager, 1998-99; BTI Exports, manager. Writer. **Publications:** Blood and the Imperial Purple (fiction), 1999. **Address:** Harris Literary Agency, PO Box 6023, San Diego, CA 92166, U.S.A. **Online address:** hesiodos@yahoo.com

RANIS, Gustav. American/German (born Germany), b. 1929. **Genres:** Economics. **Career:** Yale University, Sterling fellow, 1954-55, instructor in economics, 1956-57, assistant professor of economics, 1960-61, associate professor of economics, 1961-64, Economic Growth Center, associate director, 1961-64, professor of economics, 1964-82, assistant administrator for program and policy, 1965-67, director, 1967-75, 1992-93, Yale-Pakistan Project, director, 1970-71, Frank Altschul professor of international economics, 1982-2005, Yale Center for International and Area Studies, Henry R. Luce director, 1996-2004, Frank Altschul professor emeritus of international economics, 2005-; Pakistan Institute of Development Economics, joint director, 1958-61; The Ford Foundation, Overseas Development Program, economist, 1957-58; Brandeis University, trustee; U.S. Agency for International Development, assistant administrator, 1965-67; Institute for Advanced Study, fellow, 1993-94. Writer. **Publications:** (With J. Fei) Study of Planning Methodology with Special Reference to Pakistan's Second Five-Year Plan, 1960; Industrial Efficiency and Economic Growth: A Case Study of Karachi, 1961; Urban Consumer Expenditure and the Consumption Function, 1961; (with J. Fei) Development of the Labor Surplus Economy, 1964; The Gap between Rich and Poor Nations, 1972; (with J. Fei) Model of Growth and Employment in the Open Dualistic Economy: The Cases of Korea and Taiwan, 1973; (with J. Fei and S. Kuo) Growth with Equity: The Taiwan Case, 1979; (co-author) The Taiwan Success Story: Rapid Growth with Improved Distribution in the Republic of China 1952-1979, 1981; Comparative Technology Choice: The Indian and Japanese Cotton Textile Industries, 1988; (with F. Stewart and E. Angeles-Reyes) Linkages in Developing Economies: A Philippine Study, 1990; (with S.A. Mahmood) The Political Economy of Development Policy Change, 1992; Growth and Development from an Evolutionary Perspective, 1997. EDITOR: The U.S. and the Developing Economies, 1964; The Government and Economic Development, 1971; (with W. Beranek) Science, Technology and Economic Development: A Historical and Comparative Study, 1978; The Theory and Experience of Economic Development, 1982; Comparative Development Perspectives, 1984; Japan and the Developing Countries: A Comparative Analysis of Development Experience, 1985; (with T.P. Schultz) The State of Development Economics, 1988; Science and Technology: Lessons for Development Policy, 1990; Taiwan: From Developing to Mature Economy, 1992; En Route to Modern Economic Growth: Latin America in the 1990s, 1994; Japan and the United States in the Developing World, 1997; (with S. Hu and Y. Chu) Political Economy of Taiwan's Development into the 21st Century, 1999; (with S. Hu and Y. Chu) Essays in Memory of John C.H. Fei, 1999; (with L.K. Raut) Trade, Growth, and Development: Essays in Honor of Professor T.N. Srinivasan, 1999; (with S. Kosack) Growth and Human Development in Cuba's Transition, 2004; (with J.R. Vreeland and S. Kosack) Globalization and the Nation State: The Impact of the IMF and the World Bank, 2006; (with D.R. Cameron and A. Zinn) Globalization and Self Determination: Is the Nation State under Siege?, 2006. **Address:** Department of Economics, Yale University, Economic Growth Ctr., 27 Hillhouse Ave., PO Box 208269, New Haven, CT 06520-8269, U.S.A. **Online address:** gustav.ranis@yale.edu

RANKIN, H. D. See **RANKIN, Herbert David.**

RANKIN, Herbert David. (H. D. Rankin). British/Irish (born Ireland), b. 1931. **Genres:** Classics, Philosophy, Essays, Literary Criticism And History. **Career:** Monash University, foundation professor of classical studies, 1965-73; University of Southampton, professor of classics, 1973-88, professor of ancient philosophy, 1988-96, professor emeritus, 1996-. Writer. **Publications:** AS H.D. RANKIN: Plato and the Individual, 1964; Petronius the Artist: Essays on the Satyricon and Its Author, 1971; Pentheus and Plato: A Study in Social Disintegration: An Inaugural Lecture Delivered at the University 20 November, 1975, 1975; Archilochus of Paros, 1977; Sophists, Socratics and Cynics, 1983; Antisthenes Sokratikos, 1986; Celts and the Classical World, 1987. Contributor of articles to journals. **Address:** Department of Philosophy, School of Humanities, University of Southampton, Southampton, HM S017 1BJ, England.

RANKIN, Ian (James). (Jack Harvey). Scottish (born Scotland), b. 1960. **Genres:** Novels, Novellas/Short Stories, Mystery/Crime/Suspense, Graphic Novels. **Career:** Writer. **Publications:** INSPECTOR REBUS SERIES: Knots and Crosses, 1987; Hide and Seek: A John Rebus Mystery, 1990; Wolfman, 1992; Strip Jack, 1992; The Black Book, 1993; Mortal Causes, 1994; Let It Bleed: A John Rebus Mystery, 1995; Black and Blue, 1997; The Hanging Garden, 1998; Dead Souls, 1999; Death is Not the End, 1998; Set in Darkness, 2000; The Falls, 2001; Resurrection Men, 2002; A Question of Blood, 2003; Fleshmarket Close, 2004 in US as Fleshmarket Alley, 2005; The Naming of the Dead, 2006; Exit Music, 2008. NOVELS: The Flood, 1986; Watchman, 1988; Westwind, 1990; A Good Hanging and Other Stories (short stories), 1992; Beggars Banquet, 2002; Doors Open, 2008; Dark Entries, 2009; The Complaints, 2009; The Impossible Dead, 2011. OTHERS: Herbert in Motion: And Other Stories, 1997; Complete Short Stories, 2005; (with A.M. Smith and I. Welsh) One City, 2006; (co-author) Crimespotting, 2009; (co-author) Ox-Tales: Earth, 2009; (with A.M. Smith) The Book That Changed My Life, 2010. NOVELS AS JACK HARVEY: Witch Hunt, 1993; Bleeding Hearts, 1994; Blood Hunt, 1995. Contributor of articles to periodicals. Works appear in anthologies. **Address:** Dominick Abel Literary Agency, 146 W 82nd St., Ste. 1B, New York, NY 10024-5530, U.S.A.

RANKIN, Robert. Also writes as Robert Fleming Rankin. British (born England), b. 1949. **Genres:** Science Fiction/Fantasy, Novels, Novellas/Short Stories, Bibliography. **Career:** Writer. **Publications:** The Greatest Show Off Earth, 1994; The Garden of Unearthly Delights, 1995; The Most Amazing Man Who Ever Lived, 1995; A Dog Called Demolition, 1996; Sprout Mask Replica, 1997; Apocalypso, 1998; The Dance of the Voodoo Handbag, 1998; Sex and Drugs and Sausage Rolls, 1999; Snuff Fiction, 1999; Waiting for Godalming, 2000; Intrepid Coitions, 2000; Web Site Story, 2001; The Fandom of the Operator, 2001; The Hollow Chocolate Bunnies of the Apocalypse, 2002; The Witches of Chiswick, 2003; The Toyminator, 2006; The Da-Da-De-Da-Da Code, 2007; Necrophenia, 2008; Retromancer, 2009; The Japanese Devil Fish Girl and Other Unnatural Attractions, 2010; The Mechanical Messiah, 2011. THE BRENTFORD TRILOGY: The Antipope, 1981; The Brentford Triangle, 1982; East of Ealing, 1984; The Sprouts of Wrath, 1984; Nostradamus Ate My Hamster, 1996; The Brentford Chainstore Massacre, 1997; Knees Up Mother Earth, 2004; The Brightonomicon, 2005. ARMAGEDDON SERIES: Armageddon: The Musical, 1988; They Came and Ate Us, Armageddon II: The B-Movie, 1991; The Suburban Book of the Dead, Armageddon III: The Remake, 1992. HUGO RUNE SERIES: The Book of Ultimate Truths, 1993; Raiders of the Lost Car Park, 1994. Works appear in anthologies. **Address:** c/o Author Mail, Orion House, 5 Upper St., Martin's Ln., London, GL WC2H 9EA, England.

RANKIN, Robert Fleming. See **RANKIN, Robert.**

RANN, Sheila. American (born United States), b. 1952. **Genres:** Novels, Sports/Fitness, Young Adult Non-fiction. **Career:** Freelance writer, 1984-. **Publications:** The Broadway Workout (nonfiction), 1984; Anything for Love (novel), 1995. **Address:** 25 Ascan Ave., Forest Hills, NY 11375, U.S.A.

RANNEY, Joseph A. American (born United States), b. 1952. **Genres:** History, Law. **Career:** DeWitt, Ross, & Stevens, lawyer; Marquette University, adjunct professor of law; Legal Services of Northeastern Wisconsin, board director, 1982-88, treasurer, 1985-87, president, 1987-88; Exchange Center for Child Abuse Prevention, director; DeWitt Ross & Stevens S.C., partner. Historian and writer. **Publications:** Wisconsin's Legal History: An Article Series, 1998; Trusting Nothing to Providence: A History of Wisconsin's Legal System, 1999; In the Wake of Slavery: Civil War, Civil Rights and the Reconstruction of Southern Law, 2006. **Address:** Marquette University Law School, 1215 W Michigan St., PO Box 1881, Milwaukee, WI 53233, U.S.A. **Online address:** jar@dewittross.net

RANSOM, Harry Howe. American (born United States), b. 1922. **Genres:** International Relations/Current Affairs, Military/Defense/Arms Control, Politics/Government. **Career:** Princeton University, part-time instructor in politics, 1947-48; Vassar College, professor and instructor in political science, 1948-52; Michigan State University, assistant professor of political science, 1955; Harvard University, research associate, 1955-61; Vanderbilt University, associate professor of political science, 1961-64, professor of political science, 1964-87, chair of the department, 1969, professor emeritus of political science, 1987-. Writer. **Publications:** Central Intelligence and National Security, 1958, rev. ed. as The Intelligence Establishment, 1970; Can American Democracy Survive Cold War?, 1963; An American Foreign Policy Reader, 1965. Contributor of articles to journals. **Address:** Department of Political Science, Vanderbilt University, Commons Ctr., 230 Appleton Pl., PO Box 0505, Nashville, TN 37235, U.S.A.

RANSOM, Jane (Reavill). American (born United States), b. 1958. **Genres:** Novels, Poetry. **Career:** Cincinnati Enquirer, reporter, 1980; The Coloradoan, copy editor, 1981; San Juan Star, assistant editor, 1981-84; New York Daily News, national/international news editor, 1984-89; New York University, adjunct professor, 1991, 1997-2002; freelance writer, 1992-; Rutgers University, professor of creative writing, 1997-2002; writer and producer, 2003-; Saint Mary's College, distinguished poet-in-residence, 2004. **Publications:** Without Asking (poems), 1989; Bye-Bye (novel), 1997; Scene of the Crime: Poems, 1997. Contributor to books and periodicals. **Address:** Linda Chester Literary Agency, Rockefeller Ctr., 630 5th Ave., Ste. 2036, New York, NY 10111-0100, U.S.A. **Online address:** jane@janeransom.com

RANSTORP, Magnus. Swedish (born Sweden), b. 1965. **Genres:** International Relations/Current Affairs, Politics/Government, Social Sciences, Military/Defense/Arms Control. **Career:** Dagens Nyheter, foreign policy editorial writer; University of St. Andrews, Centre for the Study of Terrorism and Political Violence, director; Swedish National Defence College, Center for Asymmetric Threat Studies, research director; Swedish Institute of International Affairs, visiting fellow. **Publications:** Hizb'allah in Lebanon: The Politics of the Western Hostage Crisis, 1997; Mapping Terrorism Research: State of the Art, Gaps and Future Direction, 2006; (ed.) Understanding Violent Radicalisation: Terrorist and Jihadist Movements in Europe, 2009; (ed. with M. Normark) Unconventional Weapons and International Terrorism: Challenges and New Approaches, 2009. Contributor of articles to journals. **Address:** Centre for Asymmetric Threat Studies, Swedish National Defence College, Valhallavagen 117, PO Box 27805, Stockholm, 115 93, Sweden. **Online address:** magnus.ranstorp@fhs.se

RAO, Aruna P. American/Indian (born India), b. 1955. **Genres:** Area Studies, Women's Studies And Issues, Adult Non-fiction. **Career:** UNICEF, Program Division, research associate, 1979-80, consultant, 1981-82, Evaluation Section, consultant, 1982-83; Ford Foundation, Rural Poverty and Resources Division, consultant, 1983-84; Population Council, Asia regional coordinator for women and development, 1984-90; writer and consultant, 1990-; Association for Women's Rights in Development, president, 1998-2001; Gender at Work, director, co-founder and senior associate; CIVICUS, director, chair; U.S. Agency for International Development, consultant; NOVIB, consultant. **Publications:** EDITOR: Women's Studies International: Nairobi and Beyond, 1991; (with M.B. Anderson and C.A. Overholt) Gender Analysis in Development Planning: A Casebook, 1991; (with M.B. Anderson and C. Overholt) Gender Training and Development Planning: Learning from Experience, 1991; Reflections and Learnings, 1994. OTHER: (with R. Stuart and D. Kelleher) Gender at Work: Organizational Change for Equality, 1999. Works appear in anthologies. Contributor to periodicals. **Address:** 7400 Haddington Pl., House 61, Rd. 24, Gulshan, Bethesda, MD 20817, U.S.A. **Online address:** arao@genderatwork.org

RAO, J. N. K. Canadian/Indian (born India), b. 1937. **Genres:** Economics, Mathematics/Statistics, Sciences. **Career:** Iowa State University, assistant professor, 1961-63; Texas A&M University, associate professor, 1965-67, professor, 1967-69; University of Manitoba, professor, 1969-73; Carleton University, professor, 1973-2000; Carleton University, School of Mathematics and Statistics, distinguished research professor, professor emeritus, 2000-. Statistician and writer. **Publications:** (With V. Ramachandran) Comparison of the Separate and Combined Ratio Estimators, 1974; Unbiased Variance Estimation for Multistage Designs, 1975; (with D.R. Bellhouse) Systematic Sampling in the Presence of a Trend, 1975; (co-author) New Results in the Variate Difference Method, 1978; Sampling Designs Involving Unequal

Probabilities of Selection and Robust Estimation of a Finite Population Total, 1978; (with D. Krewski) Inference From Stratified Samples I: Large Sample Properties of the Linearization, Jackknife and Balanced Repeated Replication Methods, 1978; Estimating the Common Mean of Possibly Different Normal Populations: A Simulation Study, 1978; (co-ed.) Current Topics in Survey Sampling, 1981; Small Area Estimation, 2003. **Address:** School of Mathematics and Statistics, Carleton University, 1125 Colonel By Dr., Ottawa, ON K1S 5B6, Canada. **Online address:** jrao@math.carleton.ca

RAO, Saira. American (born United States), b. 1974. **Genres:** Novels. **Career:** WUSA-TV, television journalist and producer; WSVN-TV, television journalist and producer; Cleary Gottlieb Steen & Hamilton (law firm), legal associate; Third Circuit Court of Appeals, clerk, 2002. Novelist. **Publications:** Chambermaid, 2007. **Address:** Grove/Atlantic Inc., 841 Broadway, 4th Fl., New York, NY 10003-4704, U.S.A. **Online address:** saira@sairarao.com

RAO, Sirish. Indian (born India) **Genres:** Mythology/Folklore. **Career:** Tara Publishing, editor. **Publications:** Real Men Don't Pick Peonies: On an Alpine-Style Ascent, 1998; Leaf Life, 1998; The Tree Girl, 2001; Sophocles Antigone, 2001; An Ideal Boy: Charts from India, 2001; The Legend of the Fish, 2003; (with A. Ravishankar) One, Two, Tree!, 2003; Euripides The Bacchae, 2004; (with G. Wolf) Sophocles Oedipus the King, 2004; Euripides Hippolytos, 2006; (with G. Wolf) The Night Life of Trees, 2006; (with G. Wolf) That's How I See Things, 2007; The Nine Emotions of Indian Cinema Hoardings, 2007; The Old Animals Forest Band, 2008; (contrib.) The Flight of the Mermaid, 2009; (trans.) In the Land Of, 2009; (contrib.) The Circle of Fate, 2010. **Address:** Tara Books, Bldg Plot No. 9, CGE Colony, Kuppam Beach Rd., Chennai, TN 600 041, India. **Online address:** s.rao@kent.ac.uk

RAO, Srikumar S. American (born United States), b. 1951. **Genres:** Business/Trade/Industry. **Career:** Data Resources Inc., associate director of marketing research, 1978-80; City University of New York, Baruch College, assistant professor, 1983-85; Long Island University, Department of Marketing, associate professor, 1985, Louis and Johanna Vorzimer professor of marketing and chairman, 1991-; Columbia University, Graduate School of Business, adjunct professor; London Business School, adjunct professor; Continental Group, senior consultant. Writer. **Publications:** Are You Ready to Succeed? Unconventional Strategies for Achieving Personal Mastery in Business and Life, 2006. Contributor to periodicals. **Address:** 25 Shirley Ct., Commack, NY 11725, U.S.A. **Online address:** srikumarsrao@gmail.com

RAPALJE-BERGEN, Sarah. *See* TERPENING, Ron.

RAPF, Joanna E. American (born United States), b. 1941. **Genres:** Bibliography. **Career:** University of Oklahoma, professor of English, 1974-; Dartmouth College, visiting professor. Writer. **Publications:** (With G.L. Green) Buster Keaton: A Bio-Bibliography, 1995; (ed.) On the Waterfront, 2002; (ed.) Sidney Lumet: Interviews, 2005. Contributor to periodicals and anthologies. **Address:** Department of English, University of Oklahoma, Rm. 113, 760 Van Vleet Oval, Norman, OK 73019, U.S.A. **Online address:** jrapf@ou.edu

RAPHAEL, David Daiches. British (born England), b. 1916. **Genres:** Philosophy, Politics/Government, Social Sciences. **Career:** Oxford University, Oriel College, tutor in philosophy, 1940, All Souls College, visiting fellow, 1967-68; Ministry of Labour and National Service, assistant principal, principal, 1941-46; University of Otago, professor of philosophy, 1946-49; University of Glasgow, lecturer, 1949-51, senior lecturer, 1951-60, Edward Caird professor of political and social philosophy, 1960-70; Indiana University, Mahlon Powell lecturer in philosophy, 1959; Hebrew University, board governor, 1969-81, honorary governor, 1981-; University of Reading, professor of philosophy, 1970-73; International Association for Philosophy of Law and Social Philosophy, vice-president, 1971-; University of London, Imperial College, professor of philosophy, 1973-83, emeritus professor, 1983-, academic director of associated studies, 1973-80, head of department of humanities, 1980-83, senior research fellow, 1983-93, honorary fellow, 1987-; Aristotelian Society, president, 1974-75; United Kingdom Association for Legal and Social Philosophy, president, 1974-76; Johns Hopkins University, John Hinkley visiting professor of political science, 1984; Hamilton College, visiting professor of philosophy; University of Southern California, visiting professor of philosophy. Writer. **Publications:** The Moral Sense, 1947; Moral Judgement, 1955; The Paradox of Tragedy, 1960; Problems of Political Philosophy, 1970, 2nd ed., 1990; Hobbes: Morals and Politics, 1977; Justice and Liberty, 1980; Moral Philosophy, 1981, 2nd ed., 1994; Adam Smith, 1985;

(intro.) Wealth of Nations, 1991; Three Great Economists, 1997; Concepts of Justice, 2001; Impartial Spectator: Adam Smith's Moral Philosophy, 2007. EDITOR: Review of the Principal Questions in Morals, 1948; (and contrib.) Political Theory and the Rights of Man, 1967; British Moralists 1650-1800, 1969; (with A.L. Macfie) The Theory of Moral Sentiments, 1976, rev. ed., 1991; Lectures on Jurisprudence, 1978; Essays on Philosophical Subjects, 1980. Contributor to journals. **Address:** Imperial College, University of London, South Kensington Campus, London, GL SW7 2AZ, England.

RAPHAEL, Frederic (Michael). British/American (born United States), b. 1931. **Genres:** Novels, Plays/Screenplays, Biography, Translations, Novellas/Short Stories. **Career:** Sunday Times, fiction critic, 1962-65. Writer. **Publications:** Obbligato, 1956; The Earlsdon Way, 1958; The Limits of Love, 1960; A Wild Surmise, 1961; The Graduate Wife, 1962; The Trouble with England, 1962; Lindmann, 1963; Orchestra and Beginners, 1967; Like Men Betrayed, 1970; Who Were You with Last Night?, 1971; April, June and November, 1972; Richard's Things, 1973; (ed. and intro.) Bookmarks, 1975; California Times, 1975; The Glittering Prizes, 1976; Somerset Maugham and His World, 1976; (trans. with K. McLeish) The Poems of Catullus, 1978; (trans.) The Oresteia of Aeschylus, 1979; Sleeps Six (stories), 1979; Cracks in the Ice, 1979; (trans. with K. McLeish) The Serpent Son/Oresteia, 1979; Darling, 1980; (comp.) A List of Books, 1980; Oxbridge Blues (stories), 1981; Byron, 1982; Oxbridge Blues: And Other Stories, 1984; Heaven and Earth, 1985; Think of England, 1986; After the War, 1988; The Hidden I: A Myth Revised, 1990; (trans.) Complete Plays of Aeschylus, 1991; The Man in the Brooks Brothers Shirt, 1991; Of Gods and Men, 1993; A Double Life, 1993; The Latin Lover and Other Stories: 1994; France, the Four Seasons, 1994; Euripides' Medea (U.S. trans.), 1994; Old Scores, 1995; The Necessity of Anti-Semitism, 1997; Coast to Coast, 1999; Karl Popper, Historian, 1999; Eyes Wide Open: A Memoir of Stanley Kubrick, 1999; (with S. Kubrick) Eyes Wide shut: A Screenplay, 1999; (ed. with R. Monk) The Great Philosophers, 2000; Personal Terms: 1950-1960s, 2001; All His Sons: A Novella and Nine Stories, 2001; (trans.) The Satyricon of Petronius, 2001; The Benefits of Doubt (essays), 2003; A Spoilt Boy (autobiography), 2003; Cuts and Bruises: Personal Terms 3, 2006; Some Talk of Alexander, 2006; Fame and Fortune, 2007; Ticks and Crosses: Personal Terms 4, 2008; (trans.and intro.) P. Arbiter, Satyrica, 2009; Final Demands, 2010; Ifs and Buts: Personal Terms 5, 2011. **Address:** Rogers, Coleridge-White, 20 Powis Mews, London, GL W11 1JN, England.

RAPHAEL, Lev. American (born United States), b. 1954. **Genres:** Novels, Novellas/Short Stories, Mystery/Crime/Suspense, Literary Criticism And History, Psychology, Autobiography/Memoirs, Essays, Young Adult Non-fiction, Young Adult Non-fiction. **Career:** Fordham University, adjunct instructor, 1976-80; City University of New York, John Jay College of Criminal Justice, adjunct instructor, 1979; Michigan State University, instructor in education, 1983-85, assistant professor of American thought and language, 1985-88; Institute for Research on Teaching, Teacher Development and Organizational Change Project, intern, 1984-86; College of Education, associate editor, 1985-86; writer, 1988-. Consultant. **Publications:** (With G. Kaufman) The Dynamics of Power, 1983, rev. ed., 1991; Dancing on Tisha B'Av (short stories), 1990; (with G. Kaufman) Stick Up for Yourself! (young adult), 1990, (with G. Kaufman and P. Espeland) rev. ed., 1999; Edith Wharton's Prisoners of Shame: A New Perspective on Her Neglected Fiction, 1991; Winter Eyes, 1992; (with G. Kaufman) Coming Out of Shame, 1996; Journeys and Arrivals, 1996; Let's Get Criminal, 1996; The Edith Wharton Murders, 1997; The Death of a Constant Lover, 1999; Little Miss Evil, 2000; Burning Down the House, 2001; German Money, 2003; Tropic of Murder: A Nick Hoffman Mystery, 2004; Writing a Jewish Life: Memoirs, 2005; Secret Anniversaries of the Heart, 2006; Hot Rocks: A Nick Hoffman Mystery, 2007; My Germany, 2009. Contributor of articles to journals, magazines and newspapers. **Address:** c/o Sandra Dijkstra, Sandra Dijkstra Literary Agency, 1155 Camino Del Mar, PO Box 515, Del Mar, CA 92014-2605, U.S.A. **Online address:** levraphael@comcast.net

RAPOPORT, Nessa. American/Canadian (born Canada) **Genres:** Novels, Adult Non-fiction, Literary Criticism And History, Novellas/Short Stories, Theology/Religion. **Career:** Charles H. Revson Foundation, staff, 2005, senior program officer; Bantam Books, senior editor. Speaker. **Publications:** Preparing for Sabbath, 1981; (ed. with T. Solotaroff) Writing Our Way Home: Contemporary Stories by American Jewish Writers, 1992; A Woman's Book of Grieving, 1994; (ed. with T. Solotaroff) The Schocken Book of Contemporary Jewish Fiction, 1996; (foreword) Distant Sisters, 1996; (contrib.) Objects of the Spirit: Ritual and the Art of Tobi Kahn, 2004; House on the River: A

Summer Journey, 2004. Works appear in anthologies. **Address:** c/o Henry Dunow, Dunow, Carlson & Lerner Literary Agency Inc., 27 W 20th St., Ste. 1107, New York, NY 10011, U.S.A.

RAPOPORT, Sandra E. American (born United States), b. 1951. **Genres:** Theology/Religion. **Career:** Writer and lawyer. **Publications:** (With S.A. Tuchman) The Passions of the Matriarchs, 2004; (with S.A. Tuchman) Moses' Women, 2008. **Address:** 535 E 86th St., New York, NY 10028-7533, U.S.A.

RAPP, Anthony. American (born United States), b. 1971. **Genres:** Novels, Biography, Autobiography/Memoirs. **Career:** Writer. **Publications:** Without You: A Memoir of Love, Loss, and the Musical Rent (autobiography), 2006. **Address:** c/o David Buchalter, Greater Talent Network Inc., 437 5th Ave., New York, NY 10016, U.S.A.

RAPP, George Rip. See **RAPP, George (Robert).**

RAPP, George (Robert). (George Rip Rapp). American (born United States), b. 1930. **Genres:** Archaeology/Antiquities, Natural History, Sciences, Earth Sciences, Politics/Government. **Career:** South Dakota School of Mines and Technology, assistant professor, associate professor, 1957-65; University of Minnesota-Twin Cities, NSF Senior postdoctoral fellow, 1963-64, associate professor of geology and geophysics, 1965-75, director of undergraduate studies, 1965-71, Hellenic Institute of Oceanographic and Fishing Research, Division of Marine and Coastal Geology, founder, 1972-73, professor, 1972-85, College of Letters and Science, dean, 1975-83, Archaeometry Laboratory, director, 1975-85, archaeometric director, 1977-80, College of Science and Engineering, dean, 1984-89, professor of geology and archaeology, 1989-95, Regents professor of geoarchaeology, 1995-2003, Regents professor emeritus of geoarchaeology, 2003-; Sotira Kaminoudhia Excavation-Cyprus, co-director, 1983; Boston University, research professor of archaeology, 1988-. Writer. **Publications:** (With W.L. Roberts) Mineralogy of the Black Hills, 1965; (with D.T. Wallace) Guide to Mineral Collecting in Minnesota, 1966; (with N. Potter, Jr. and R.L. Bartels) Annotated Bibliography of 16-mm. Films Useful in College-Level Geology and Earth Science Courses, 1971; (co-author) The Evolving Earth, 1974, rev. ed., 1978; (ed. with C.F. Vondra) Hominid Sites: Their Geologic Settings, 1981; (contrib. with D.F. Overstreet and J.K. Huber) Archaeological Studies on the Southeast Wisconsin Uplands, 1992; (co-author) Determining Geologic Sources of Artifact Copper: Source Characterization Using Trace Element Patterns, 2000; Archaeomineralogy, 2002, 2nd ed., 2009. EDITOR: (With W.A. McDonald) The Minnesota Messenia Expedition: Reconstructing a Bronze Age Regional Environment, 1972; (ed. with W.L. Roberts and J. Weber, Jr.) Encyclopedia of Minerals, 1974, (with W.L. Roberts and T.J. Campbell) 2nd ed., 1989; (with S.E. Aschenbrenner) Excavations at Nichoria in Southwestern Greece, vol. I: Site Environs, Techniques, 1978; (with J.A. Gifford) Troy: The Archaeological Geology, 1982; (with J.A. Gifford) Archaeological Geology, 1985; (with Z. Herzog and O. Negbi) Excavations at Tel Michal, Israel, 1989; (with S.C. Mulholland) Phytolith Systematics: Emerging Issues, 1992; (with S. Swiny and E. Herscher) Sotira Kaminoudhia: An Early Bronze Age Site in Cyprus, 2002. AS George Rip Rapp: (with C.L. Hill) Geoarchaeology: The Earth-Science Approach to Archeology Interpretation, 1998, 2nd ed., 2006; (with R.D. Rothe and W.K. Miller) Pharaonic Inscriptions From the Southern Eastern Desert of Egypt, 2008. Contributor to periodicals. **Address:** Department of Geological Sciences, University of Minnesota, 206 RLB, 229 Heller Hall, 1114 Kirby Dr., Duluth, MN 55812-3036, U.S.A. **Online address:** grapp@d.umn.edu

RAPP, Rayna. (Rayna Rapp Reiter). American (born United States), b. 1946?. **Genres:** Women's Studies And Issues, Medicine/Health, Sciences, Politics/Government, Social Sciences. **Career:** New York University, College of Arts and Science, Department of Anthropology, professor of anthropology and associate chair. Writer. **Publications:** (As Rayna R. Reiter) Toward an Anthropology of Women, 1975; (ed. with S. Kruks and M.B. Young) Promissory Notes: Women in the Transition to Socialism, 1989; (ed. with J. Schneider) Articulating Hidden Histories: Exploring the Influence of Eric R. Wolf, 1995; (ed. with F.D. Ginsburg) Conceiving the New World Order: The Global Politics of Reproduction, 1995; Testing Women, Testing the Fetus: The Social Impact of Amniocentesis in America, 1999; (with D. Heath and K.S. Taussig) Genetic Citizenship, forthcoming. Works appear in anthologies. Contributor to periodicals. **Address:** Department of Anthropology, New York University, 507 Rufus D. Smith Hall, 25 Waverly Pl., New York, NY 10003-6701, U.S.A. **Online address:** rayna.rapp@nyu.edu

RAPP, Steven A. American (born United States), b. 1964. **Genres:** Sports/ Fitness, Social Commentary, Medicine/Health, Adult Non-fiction, Business/ Trade/Industry, Psychology. **Career:** United States Environmental Protection Agency, manager, 1989-, Air Enforcement Program, chief; Temple Beth David, teacher. Writer. **Publications:** Aleph-bet Yoga: Embodying the Hebrew Letters for Physical and Spiritual Well-being, 2002; (with S. Falk and D. Judson) The Jewish Pregnancy Book: A Resource for the Soul, Body and Mind During Pregnancy, Birth and the First Three Months, 2004. Contributor to books. **Address:** c/o Author Mail, Jewish Lights Publishing, Rte. 4, PO Box 237, Woodstock, VT 05091, U.S.A. **Online address:** rapp.steve@epa.gov

RAPPAPORT, Ann. American (born United States) **Genres:** Public/Social Administration, Social Work. **Career:** Massachusetts Department of Environmental Quality Engineering, Division of Hazardous Waste, deputy director and acting assistant director, 1981-84; Tufts University, Center for Environmental Management, associate director for research, 1984-88, senior environmental research analyst, 1988-92, Department of Civil and Environmental Engineering, faculty, 1992-97, School of Arts and Sciences, Department of Urban and Environmental Policy, lecturer, 1995-. Writer. **Publications:** (With M.F. Flaherty) Corporate Responses to Environmental Challenges: Initiatives by Multinational Management, 1992; Development and Transfer of Pollution Prevention Technology, 1993; (with S.H. Creighton) Degrees That Matter: Climate Change and the University, 2007. **Address:** Urban and Environmental Policy and Planning, Tufts University, 97 Talbot Ave., Medford, MA 02155, U.S.A. **Online address:** ann.rappaport@tufts.edu

RAPPAPORT, Doreen. American (born United States) **Genres:** Children's Non-fiction, Children's Fiction, Biography, Picture/Board Books. **Career:** Teacher of music and reading, 1961-68; teacher, 1965. Writer. **Publications:** NONFICTION: (with S. Kempler and M. Spirn) A Man Can Be, 1981; Escape from Slavery: Five Journeys to Freedom, 1991; Living Dangerously: American Women Who Risked Their Lives for Adventure, 1991; The Flight of Red Bird: The Life of Zitkala-S□a, 1997; Freedom River, 2000; Martin's Big Words: The Life of Dr. Martin Luther King, Jr., 2001; We Are the Many: A Picture Book of American Indians, 2002; No More! Stories and Songs of Slave Resistance, 2002; (with J. Verniero) Victory or Death! Stories of the American Revolution, 2003; Free at Last! Stories and Songs of Emancipation, 2004; John's Secret Dreams: The Life of John Lennon, 2004; The School Is Not White! A True Story of the Civil Rights Movement, 2005; In the Promised Land: Lives of Jewish Americans, 2005. BE THE JUDGE/BE THE JURY SERIES: NONFICTION: The Lizzie Borden Trial, 1992; The Sacco-Vanzetti Trial, 1992; The Alger Hiss Trial, 1993; Tinker vs. Des Moines: Student Rights on Trial, 1993. FICTION: But She's Still My Grandma!, 1982; Trouble at the Mines, 1987; The Boston Coffee Party, 1988; The Journey of Meng: A Chinese Legend, 1991; The Long-Haired Girl: A Chinese Legend, 1995; The New King, 1995; (with L. Callan) Dirt on Their Skirts: The Story of the Young Women Who Won the World Championship, 2000; The Secret Seder, 2003; Jack's Path of Courage: The Life of John F. Kennedy, 2010. OTHER: American Women: Their Lives in their Words: A Documentary History, 1990; Escape from Slavery: Five Journeys to Freedom, 1991; Year of the Paper Menorahs, 2000; Freedom Ship, 2006; Nobody Gonna Turn Me 'Round: Stories and Songs of the Civil Rights Movement, 2006; (with J. Verniero) United No More!: Stories of the Civil War, 2006; Eleanor's Big Words, 2007; Lady Liberty: A Biography, 2008; Abe's Honest Words: The Life of Abraham Lincoln, 2008; Eleanor, Quiet No More: The Life of Eleanor Roosevelt, 2009. Contributor to periodicals. **Address:** c/o Author Mail, HarperCollins Publishers, 10 E 53rd St., 7th Fl., New York, NY 10022-5244, U.S.A. **Online address:** rapabook@aol.com

RAPPAPORT, Helen. British (born England), b. 1947?. **Genres:** Biography, Women's Studies And Issues, History. **Career:** Writer and historian. **Publications:** NONFICTION: Joseph Stalin: A Biographical Companion, 1999; (ed. with S. Ratcliffe) The Little Oxford Dictionary of Quotations, 2001; Encyclopedia of Women Social Reformers, 2001; Queen Victoria: A Biographical Companion, 2003; No Place for Ladies: The Untold Story of Women in the Crimean War, 2007; Ekaterinburg: The Last Days of the Romanovs, 2008 in US as The Last Days of the Romanovs: Tragedy at Ekaterinburg, 2009; Conspirator: Lenin in Exile, 2009; Beautiful For Ever: Madame Rachel of Bond Street, 2010; A Magnificent Obsession: Victoria, Albert, and the Death That Changed the British Monarchy, 2012; Four Sisters, 2013; Capturing the Light, forthcoming. **Address:** c/o Charlie Viney, The Viney Agency, 23 Erlanger Rd., London, GL SE14 5TF, England. **Online address:** info@helenrappaport.com

RAPPAPORT, Nancy. American (born United States), b. 1959. **Genres:** Psychiatry. **Career:** Grade school teacher, 1983-84; Massachusetts General Hospital, intern in pediatrics, 1988-89, resident in adult psychiatry, 1989-92; Harvard Medical School, clinical fellow, 1990-95, clinical instructor, 1996-2002, instructor, 2002-04, assistant professor, 2004-; Cambridge City Hospital, fellow in child and adolescent psychiatry, 1992-95, attending psychiatrist and mental health director of teen health center, 1996-; Cambridge Public School System, attending child and adolescent psychiatrist, 1996-; Cambridge Superintendent and Cambridge High School, consultant, 1996-; Cambridge Health Alliance, Division of Child Psychiatry, Department of Psychiatry, director of school-based programs, 2001-. Writer. **Publications:** In Her Wake: A Child Psychiatrist Explores the Mystery of Her Mother's Suicide, 2009. **Address:** Department of Psychiatry, Cambridge Hospital, 1493 Cambridge St., Cambridge, MA 02139, U.S.A. **Online address:** nrappaport@nancyrappaport.com

RAPSON, Richard L. American (born United States), b. 1937. **Genres:** History, Intellectual History, Sex, Social Commentary, Social Sciences. **Career:** Amherst College, instructor of American studies, 1960-61; Stanford University, instructor of history, 1961-65, faculty resident, 1962-65, visiting professor, 1973-74; University of California, assistant professor, 1965-66; University of Hawaii, Department of History, assistant professor, 1966-68, associate professor, 1968-72, professor, 1972-, Humanities Programs, director, 1968-70, New College, founder and director, 1970-73. Writer. **Publications:** Britons View Americans: Travel Commentary, 1860-1935, 1971; (with S.B. Rapson) The Pursuit of Meaning: America, 1600 to 2000, 1977; Denials of Doubt: An Interpretation of American History, 1978; Fairly Lucky You Live Hawaii!: Cultural Pluralism in the Fiftieth State, 1980; American Yearnings: Love, Money, and Endless Possibility, 1988; (with E. Hatfield) Love, Sex, and Intimacy: Their Psychology, Biology, and History, 1993; (with E. Hatfield and J.T. Cacioppo) Emotional Contagion, 1994; (with E. Hatfield) Love and Sex: Cross-Cultural Perspectives, 1996; (with E. Hatfield) Rosie, 2000; (with E. Hatfield) Recovered Memories, 2003; (with E. Hatfield) Darwin's Law (with E. Hatfield), 2003; Deadly Wager (with E. Hatfield), 2004; Amazed by Life: Confessions of a Non-Religious Believer, 2004; (with E. Hatfield) Vengeance is Mine, 2005; (with E. Hatfield) Take Up Serpents, 2006; (with E. Hatfield) Hijacked, 2007; Magical Thinking and the Decline of America, 2007; (with E. Hatfield) Dangerous Characters, 2008; (with E. Hatfield) The G-String Murders, 2009. EDITOR: (and intro.) Individualism and Conformity in the American Character, 1967; (and intro.) The Cult of Youth in Middle-Class America, 1971; Major Interpretations of the American Past, 1971; (and contrib.) The Literature of History, 1971. Contributor to journals. **Address:** Department of History, University of Hawaii, B215 Sakamaki Hall, 2530 Dole St., Honolulu, HI 96822-2383, U.S.A. **Online address:** rapson@aol.com

RARICK, Ethan. American (born United States), b. 1964. **Genres:** History, Social Sciences, Politics/Government, Young Adult Non-fiction. **Career:** United Press Intl., journalist; Associated Press, journalist; Los Angeles Times, journalist; San Francisco Chronicle, journalist; University of California, Center on Politics, acting director, Institute of Governmental Studies, acting director of publications. Writer. **Publications:** California Rising: The Life and Times of Pat Brown, 2005; (ed.) California Votes: The 2006 Governor's Race, 2007; Desperate Passage: The Donner Party's Perilous Journey West, 2008. **Address:** Institute of Governmental Studies, University of California, 111 Moses Hall, MC 2370, Berkeley, CA 94720-2371, U.S.A. **Online address:** erarick@berkeley.edu

RASANAYAGAM, Angelo. Swiss/American (born United States) **Genres:** History, Politics/Government, Theology/Religion, Social Sciences. **Career:** United Nations High Commissioner for Refugees (UNHCR), director; Iran Government, chief of mission. Writer. **Publications:** Afghanistan: A Modern History: Monarchy, Despotism or Democracy?: The Problems of Governance in the Muslim Tradition, 2003. **Address:** c/o Author Mail, Palgrave Macmillan, 175 5th Ave., New York, NY 10010-7703, U.S.A.

RASH, Ron. American (born United States), b. 1953. **Genres:** Novels, Novellas/Short Stories, Poetry. **Career:** TriCounty Technical College, English instructor; Queens College, poetry instructor; Clemson University, instructor; University of Georgia, instructor; Western Carolina University, Appalachian Studies, John Parris distinguished professor, 2003-. Writer. **Publications:** The Night the New Jesus Fell to Earth and Other Stories from Cliffside, North Carolina, 1994; Eureka Mill, 1998; Among the Believers, 2000; Casualties, 2000; Raising the Dead (poetry collection), 2002; One Foot in Eden (novel),

2002; Saints at the River (novel), 2004; The World Made Straight (novel), 2006; Chemistry and Other Stories, 2007; Serena (novel), 2008; Burning Bright: Stories, 2010; Waking, 2011; The Cove, 2012. Contributor to periodicals. **Address:** Department of English, Western Carolina University, Coulter 402, Cullowhee, NC 28723, U.S.A. **Online address:** ronrash@email.wcu.edu

RASMUSSEN, Alis A. (Kate Elliott). American (born United States), b. 1958. **Genres:** Romance/Historical, Literary Criticism And History, Science Fiction/Fantasy. **Career:** British Broadcasting Corp., staff, 1978-79. Writer. **Publications:** AS ALIS A. RASMUSSEN: Highroad Trilogy, vol. I: A Passage of Stars, 1990, vol. II: Revolution's Shore, 1990, vol. III: The Price of Ransom, 1990. OTHERS: The Labyrinth Gate, 1988; Jaran, 1992; An Earthly Crown: The Sword of Heaven, 1993; His Conquering Sword: The Sword of Heaven, 1993; The Law of Becoming, 1994; (with M. Rawn and J. Roberson) The Golden Key, 1996; King's Dragon, 1997; Prince of Dogs, 1998; The Burning Stone, 1999; Child of Flame, 2000; The Gathering Storm, 2003; In the Ruins, 2005; Crown of Stars, 2006; Spirit Gate: Book One of Crossroads, 2006; Shadow Gate, 2008; Traitors' Gate, 2009; Cold Magic, 2010; Cold Steel, forthcoming. **Address:** c/o Russell Galen, Scovill Chichak Galen Literary Agency, 381 Park Ave. S, Ste. 1020, New York, NY 10016, U.S.A. **Online address:** kate.elliott@sff.net

RASO, Jack. American (born United States), b. 1954. **Genres:** Paranormal, Medicine/Health, Psychology, Theology/Religion. **Career:** City University of New York, adjunct college laboratory technician, 1986; Pratt Institute, visiting instructor, 1987; Wyckoff Heights Medical Center, graduate dietitian, 1987-90, assistant chief clinical dietitian, 1990-93; Brooklyn Center of Long Island University, assistant professor, 1989; Prometheus Books, editor, 1994-. **Publications:** Mystical Diets: Paranormal, Spiritual, and Occult Nutrition Practices, 1992; Alternative Health Care: A Comprehensive Guide: Natural Medicine, Hands-On Healing, Spiritualism, Occultism and Much More, 1994; The Dictionary of Metaphysical Healthcare: Alternative Medicine, Paranormal Healing, and Related Methods, 1996; The Dictionary of Metaphysical Healthcare, 1997. Contributor to books and periodicals. **Address:** 71-11 60th Ave., Maspeth, NY 11378-2908, U.S.A.

RATCLIFF, Carter. American (born United States), b. 1941. **Genres:** Poetry, Art/Art History, Biography, Photography. **Career:** St. Mark's Church, director of poetry workshop, 1969-70; New York Letter Monthly Column, columnist, 1969-79; Art News, associate editor, 1969-72; Art Intl., advisory editor, 1970-75; School of Visual Arts, lecturer, 1971-75; Philadelphia College of Art, lecturer, 1973; New York University, School of Continuing Education, lecturer, 1973-75; Art Spectrum, staff correspondent, 1975; Art in America Magazine, contributing editor, 1977-; Whitney Museum of American Art, lecturer. **Publications:** Painterly vs. Painted, 1971; Fever Coast (poetry), 1973; Deseo: An Adventure, 1973; Art Criticism: Other Minds, Other Eyes, 6 vols., 1974-75; Willem de Kooning, 1975; Robert Smithson, 1979; Rafael Ferrer, 1980; Lucas Samaras: Sittings, 1980; Illustration & Allegory: An Invitational Exhibition Curated by Carter Ratcliff, 1980; Joseph Cornell, 1980; Fernando Botero, 1980; Jean Dubuffet: Partitions 1980-1981, 1981; Psycho-Sites 1981, 1981; Lester John, Recent Paintings, 1981; Paul Rotterdam: Selected Paintings, 1972-1982, 1982; Salvador Dali, 1982; John Singer Sargent, 1982; Andy Warhol, 1983; (with C. Squires) Aperture, 91, 1983; Alex Katz: The Complete Prints, 1983; Give Me Tomorrow (poetry), 1983; Pressures of the Hand: Expressionist Impulses in Recent American Art, 1984; (contrib.) Robert Longo, 1985; Janet Fish: An Exhibition of Recent Paintings, 1985; Red Grooms, 1985; Frank Stella, 1985; Dramatis Personae, 5 vols., 1985-86; Jan Groth, 1986; Pat Steir: Paintings, 1986; Jorge Castillo: Drawing, Painting, Sculpture, 1986; Travel and Tourism: Bagpipes on the Shore, 3 vols., 1986-87; Gilbert & George: The Complete Pictures 1971-1985, 1987; Lynda Benglis and Keith Sonnier: A Ten Year Retrospective, 1977-1987, 1987; 60 Obras de Jacodo Borges: Museo de Asrte Contemporáneo International Rufino Tamayo, 1987; Dandyism and Abstraction, 1988; Michael Lucero: An Essay, 1988; Roy Lichtenstein, 1989; Socialist Surrealism: Komar and Melamid, 1989; Komar and Melamid, 1989; David Bowes: New Paintings, Cibachromes, 1984-1985, 1990; John Singer Sargent, 1990; Barnett Newman, 1991; Ralston Crawford and the Sea, 1991; Robert Stackhouse, 1991; Alex Katz: A Drawing Retrospective, 1991; (with R. Rosenblum) Gilbert and George: The Singing Sculpture, 1993; (ed. with M. Adjmi and G. Bertolo) Aldo Rossi: Drawings and Paintings, 1993; Jackson Pollock, 1994; Willem de Kooning, 1994; Ellsworth Kelly, 1996; The Fate of a Gesture: Jackson Pollock and Postwar American Art, 1996; Leon Polk Smith: American Painter, 1996; Robert Rahway Zakanitch: The Grand Dado Series, 1996; Francis Bacon, 1998; (with J.B. Ber-

gen) Gary T. Erbe: December 5, 1998-January 16, 1999, 1998; The Violet Hour: An Essay on Beauty, 1998; Eve Aschheim: Paintings and Drawings, 1999; Jackson Pollock's American Sublime, 1999; Richard Pousette-Dart: Painting to Paper, Black to White, 2000; Suzanne McClelland, Intersections and Interruptions: March 1-April 8, 2000, 2000; Out of the Box: The Reinvention of Art, 1965-1975, 2000; Joe Brainard's Quiet Dazzle, 2001; The Sublime Was Then: The Art of Barnett Newman, 2001; (contrib.) Joe Brainard: A Retrospective, 2001; (with A. Zajonc and S. Antonakos) The Magic of Light, 2001; William Blake: The People's Bard, 2001; Barnett Newman's Perennial Now, 2002; (with B. Curiger and P.J. Schneemann) Georgia O'Keeffe, 2003; (contrib.) Wade Schuman, 2004; (with R. Storr and I. Blazwick) Alex Katz, 2005; (contrib.) Thrown Rope, 2006; Hanaï in America, 2006; (foreword) Axial Stones: An Art of Precarious Balance, 2006; Donald Sultan: The Theater of the Object, 2008; (contrib.) Fletcher Benton: An American Artist, 2008; (contrib.) Waterway, 2009; (contrib.) Bernar Venet: l'hypothèse de la ligne droite, 2010; Albert Paley in the 21st Century, 2010; (with D. Anfam) Pousette-Dart: Predominantly White Paintings, 2010. Contributor to periodicals and journals. **Address:** Art in America, 575 Broadway, 5th Fl., New York, NY 10012-3227, U.S.A. **Online address:** carterratcliff@gmail.com

RATCLIFFE, Eric Hallam. British (born England), b. 1918. **Genres:** Science Fiction/Fantasy, Poetry, History, Biography, Essays, Reference, Literary Criticism And History, Novels, Autobiography/Memoirs, Politics/Government. **Career:** Ore Magazine, founder and editor, 1954-95. **Publications:** The Visitation, 1952; Little Pagan, 1955; The Ragnarok Rocket Bomb, 1957; Transitions, 1957; The Chronicle of the Green Man, 1960; Mist on My Eyes, 1961; Gleanings for a Daughter of Aeolus, 1968; Out of the Thickets (essays), 1969; Leo Poems, 1972; Warrior of the Icenian Queen, 1973; Romantic Acausalism (essays), 1974; Commius of the Atrebates: The Man and the Memory, 1975; Commius: The Man and the Memory: An Essay, 1975; Commius, 1976; A Sun-Red Mantle: Poems, 1976; The Great Arthurian Timeslip (history), 1978; Nightguard of the Quaternary, 1979; The Narrows and the Western Empire, 1981; (with V. Kembery) Sheila Ann Ratcliffe 1969-1983: A Biographical Memoir, 1984; Ballet Class, 1986; The French King, 1989; Leo Mysticus, 1989; The Infidelium, 1990; The Runner of the Seven Valleys, 1990; Hill 60, 1991; Scientary, 1991; The Ballad of Polly McPoo, 1991; Components of the Nation, 1992; Ghosts of the Quaternary, 1992; Advent, 1992; Kingdoms, 1992; Ark, 1992; The Golden Heart Man, 1993; Fire in the Bush (collected poems 1955-1992), 1993; The Caxton of Her Age: The Career and Family Background of Emily Faithfull (1835-95), 1993; William Ernest Henley: An Introduction, 1993; The Man in Green Combs, 1993; Winstanleys Walton 1694, 1994; Anthropos, 1995; Ratcliffes Megathesaurus: A Terminological Miscellany, 1995; Sholen: Memories of a Life by Hadrians Wall, 1996; The Millennium of the Magician, 1996; The Brussels Griffon, 1996; Strange Furlongs, 1996; (with W. Görtschacher) Veins of Gold: Ore, 1954-1995, 1997; Wellington: A Broad Front, 1998; Capabilities of the Alchemical Mind, 1999; Cosmologia, 2000; Loyal Women, 2000; On Bakers Level (science fiction poetry), 2002; The Divine Peter, 2002; No Jam in the Arsenal, 2003; Selected Long Poems, 2003; Desert Voices: A Tribute to Arul-ala the Syrian Poet, 2003. **Address:** 7 The Towers, Southgate, Stevenage, HF SG1 1HE, England. **Online address:** chessmaster@ntlworld.com

RATEY, John J(oseph). American (born United States), b. 1948. **Genres:** Psychology, Medicine/Health, Psychiatry, Human Relations/Parenting. **Career:** Massachusetts Mental Health Center, psychiatric attendant, 1970-71, psychiatric resident, 1977-80, chief resident in inpatient service, 1979-80, supervisor of residents, 1980-, assistant director of residency training, 1982-88; DARE Inc., halfway house parent, 1971-72; St. Francis General Hospital, rotating intern in neurology, 1976-77; Harvard Medical School, Chronic Care Program, clinical fellow, 1978-79, instructor, 1980-86, assistant clinical professor of psychiatry, 1986-, associate clinical professor of psychiatry; Clinton Child and Family Center, chief psychiatrist, 1978-82; New England Psychiatric Consultants, director, 1978-; Tufts University, assistant clinical professor, 1980-81; Medfield State Hospital, Developmental Disabilities Unit, clinical director, 1986-89, director of research, 1986-, acting executive medical director, 1989-91; Clinical Aggression Research Group, founder and developer, 1990. Writer. **Publications:** (Ed. and contrib.) Mental Retardation: Developing Pharmacotherapies, 1991; (ed. and contrib.) The Neuropsychiatry of Behavior Disorders, 1995; Shadow Syndromes, 1997; A User's Guide to the Brain: Perception, Behavior, ad the Four Theaters of the Brain, 2001; (with E. Hagerman) Spark: The Revolutionary New Science of Exercise and the Brain, 2008. WITH E. HALLOWELL: Answers to Distraction, 1994; Driven to Distraction: The Emotional Experience of ADD, 1994, rev. ed. as Driven to Distraction: Recognizing and Coping with Attention Deficit Disorder from Childhood through Adulthood, 1995; Attention Deficit Disorder, 1996; (with E.M. Hallowell) Delivered from Distraction: Getting the Most Out of Life with Attention Deficit Disorder, 2005. Contributor of articles to journals. **Address:** Psychiatry- Beth Israel-Deaconess Department, Harvard University, Mass Mental Health Ctr., 328 Broadway, Cambridge, MA 02139, U.S.A. **Online address:** john_ratey@hms.harvard.edu

RATH, Richard Cullen. American (born United States), b. 1969?. **Genres:** Adult Non-fiction, History, Humanities. **Career:** Oberlin College, visiting lecturer, 1998-99; Hamilton College, visiting lecturer, 1999-2000; New York University, visiting assistant professor, 2001; University of Hawaii, assistant professor of history, 2002-, associate professor of history. Writer. **Publications:** How Early America Sounded, 2003. **Address:** Department of History, University of Hawaii at Manoa, B203 Sakamaki, 2530 Dole St., Honolulu, HI 96822-2283, U.S.A. **Online address:** rrath@hawaii.edu

RATHBONE, Cristina. American/British (born England), b. 1966. **Genres:** Novels, Politics/Government, Social Sciences, Young Adult Non-fiction. **Career:** Ecclesia Ministries, associate minister; Episcopal Church, deacon. Journalist. **Publications:** On the Outside Looking In: A Year at an Inner-City High School, 1998; A World Apart: Women, Prison, and Life Behind Bars, 2005. **Address:** c/o Author Mail, Grove/Atlantic Monthly Press, 841 Broadway, 4th Fl., New York, NY 10003, U.S.A.

RATHBONE, Richard. Welsh/British (born England), b. 1942. **Genres:** Area Studies, Politics/Government, History. **Career:** University of London, Institute of Commonwealth Studies, lecturer, 1967-69, School of Oriental and African Studies, lecturer, 1969-85, senior lecturer, 1985-94, professor of history, 1994-2003, Emeritus professor, professorial research associate dean of graduate school, 1991-95, Centre for African Studies, chairman, 1994; Harvard University, W.E.B. Du Bois Institute, fellow, 1986; Princeton University, Shelby Cullom Davis fellow, 1990-91; University of Wales, honorary professor of history, 2003-; Aberystwyth University, honorary professor in history; Royal Historical Society, vice-president. Writer. **Publications:** Ghana: British Documents on the End of the Empire, 2 vols., 1992; Murder and Politics in Colonial Ghana, 1993; Nkrumah and the Chiefs, 2000; (with J. Parker) African History: A Very Short Introduction, 2007; Geschichte Afrikas, 2010. EDITOR: (with R. Moss) The Population Factor in African Studies, 1975; (with S. Marks) Industrialisation and Social Change in South Africa: African Class Formation, Culture, and Consciousness, 1870-1930, 1982; (with D. Killingray) Africa and the Second World War, 1986; (with D.C. O'Brien and J. Dunn) Contemporary West African States, 1989; Ghana, 1992; (with D. Anderson) Africa's Urban Past, 1999; Nkrumah and the Chiefs: The Politics of Chieftaincy in Ghana, 1951-60, 2000. Contributor to periodicals. **Address:** Department of History, University of Wales, Aberystwyth, Ceredigion, SY23 3DA, Wales. **Online address:** rar@aber.ac.uk

RATHBUN, Brian C. American (born United States), b. 1973. **Genres:** Adult Non-fiction, Politics/Government. **Career:** McGill University, assistant professor, 2004-06; Indiana University, assistant professor, 2006-08; Senator Evan Bayh (D-IN), legislative aide, 2003-04; University of Southern California, School of International Relations, assistant professor, 2008-, associate professor. Writer. **Publications:** Partisan Interventions: European Party Politics and Peace Enforcement in the Balkans, 2004; Trust in International Cooperation, 2011. **Address:** School of International Relations, University of Southern California, VKC 330, 3518 Trousdale Pkwy., Los Angeles, IN 90089-0043, U.S.A. **Online address:** brathbun@usc.edu

RATHJE, William (Laurens). American (born United States), b. 1945. **Genres:** Archaeology/Antiquities, Environmental Sciences/Ecology, Essays, Cartoons, Children's Fiction. **Career:** University of Arizona, Department of anthropology, assistant professor, 1971-76, associate professor, 1976-80, professor, 1980-, now professor emeritus; The Garbage Project, founder, 1972, director, 1973-; Stanford University, consulting associate; National Geographic-sponsored Cozumel Archaeological Project, director. Writer. **Publications:** (With M.B. Schiffer) Archaeology, 1982; (with V. Restrepo and G. Bernache) Demonios del consumo: basura y contaminación, 1991; (with C. Murphy) Rubbish!: The Archaeology of Garbage, 1992; (with R. Lilenfeld) Use Less Stuff: Environmental Solutions for Who We Really Are, 1998. Contributor of articles to journals. **Address:** School of Anthropology, University of Arizona, 1009 E S Campus Dr., Tucson, AZ 85721, U.S.A. **Online address:** rathjewl@tsaaol.com

RATHMANN, Peggy (Margaret Crosby). American (born United States), b. 1953. **Genres:** Children's Fiction, Illustrations, Children's Non-fiction, Animals/Pets. **Career:** Children's book writer and illustrator, 1991-. **Publications:** SELF-ILLUSTRATED: Ruby the Copycat, 1991; Good Night, Gorilla, 1994; Officer Buckle and Gloria, 1995; 10 Minutes till Bedtime, 1998; The Day the Babies Crawled Away, 2003; Buenas Noches, Gorila, 2004; 10 minutos y ala cama, 2005; How Many Lambies on Grammy's Jammies?, 2006. Contributor to periodicals. **Address:** c/o Author Mail, Putnam/Berkeley Publicity Department, 200 Madison Ave., New York, NY 10016, U.S.A.

RATHMELL, George W(esley). American (born United States), b. 1931. **Genres:** Education, Literary Criticism And History, Biography, Young Adult Non-fiction, Art/Art History. **Career:** Oakland Unified School District, teacher of English, 1958-87; University of California, Extension department, instructor in education, 1967-86; Santa Rosa Junior College, instructor in English, 1988-2000. Writer. **Publications:** Bench Marks in Reading: A Guide to Reading Instruction in the Second-Language Classroom, 1984; Realms of Gold: The Colorful Writers of San Francisco, 1850-1950, 1998; A Passport to Hell: The Mystery of Richard Realf, 2002. Contributor to periodicals. **Address:** PO Box 98, The Sea Ranch, CA 95497, U.S.A. **Online address:** gwr@mcn.org

RATHMELL, Neil. British (born England), b. 1947. **Genres:** Novels. **Career:** Teacher, 1968-88; Shropshire Education Authority, assistant adviser for English and drama, 1988-90, creative arts adviser, 1992-2004; Specialist Arts College, coordinator; Shropshire Visual Arts Trust, chairman; Pentabus Theatre Co., board director; Artists & Learning Information & Support Service, co-director; Belmont Arts Center, director. Writer and consultant. **Publications:** The Old School, 1976. **Address:** David Higham Associates Ltd., 5-8 Lower John St., Golden Sq., London, GL W1R 4HA, England. **Online address:** neil.rathmell@shropshire-cc.gov.uk

RATLIFF, Ben. American (born United States), b. 1968?. **Genres:** Music, Photography. **Career:** New York Times, jazz and pop critic, 1996-. Writer. **Publications:** Jazz: A Critic's Guide to the 100 Most Important Recordings, 2002; Coltrane: The Story of a Sound, 2007; The Jazz Ear: Conversations Over Music, 2008. Contributor to periodicals. **Address:** New York Times, 620 8th Ave., New York, NY 10018, U.S.A.

RATNER, Austin. American (born United States), b. 1972?. **Genres:** Novels. **Career:** Case School of Medicine, adjunct assistant professor. Writer. **Publications:** (With J. Seifter and D. Sloane) Concepts in Medical Physiology, 2005; The Jump Artist (novel), 2009. Contributor to magazines. **Address:** Anne Edelstein Literary Agency, 20 W 22nd St., Ste. 1603, New York, NY 10010, U.S.A. **Online address:** info@aeliterary.com

RATTO, Linda Lee. American (born United States), b. 1952. **Genres:** Children's Fiction, Human Relations/Parenting, Adult Non-fiction, Young Adult Non-fiction, Biography. **Career:** Education and Rehabilitation consultant, 1990; MINDmatters, chief executive officer, 1994-96; Avondale Estates, school principal, 1998-99; Eldercare, executive director, 2004-; Civil Services L.L.C., partner, 2006-; SNS Inc., co-founder, 2000-10. Writer. **Publications:** Coping with Being Physically Challenged, 1991; Coping with a Physically Challenged Brother or Sister, 1992; Where Dreams Come Ture, 2004; We Catch Them Falling, 2004; Perfection (young adult novel), 2004; (with D.L. Cunningham) Shift Your Life!, 2008; (with D.L. Cunningham) Holy Hostage, 2008; (with R.L. Wood) Lifeshift 2020, 2009. Contributor to magazines and newspapers. **Address:** 105 Wheaton Way, PO Box 622, Lake Pendleton, Tyrone, GA 30290-1854, U.S.A. **Online address:** ratto@mindspring.com

RAUCH, Bill. See **RAUCH, William.**

RAUCH, Jonathan (Charles). American (born United States), b. 1960. **Genres:** Politics/Government. **Career:** Winston-Salem Journal, education reporter, 1983-84; National Journal, budget and fiscal policy correspondent, 1984-87, economic policy correspondent 1987-89, contributing editor, senior writer, columnist, 1991-; American Enterprise Institute, visiting fellow, 1989-90; Economist, visiting writer, 1995; Brookings Institution, writer-in-residence, 1998-; National Journal, senior writer and columnist; The Atlantic Monthly, correspondent, contributing editor; Japan Society Leadership Program, fellow; Independent Gay Forum, vice president. **Publications:** The Outnation: A Search for the Soul of Japan, 1992; Kindly Inquisitors: The New Attacks on Free Thought, 1993; Demosclerosis: The Silent Killer of

American Government, 1994, rev. ed. as Government's End: Why Washington Stopped Working, 1999; (with R.E. Litan) American Finance for the 21st Century, 1997; Gay Marriage: Why it is Good for Gays, Good for Straights and Good for America, 2004. Contributor to periodicals. **Address:** National Journal Group Inc., The Watergate, 600 New Hampshire Ave. NW, Washington, DC 20037, U.S.A. **Online address:** jrauch@brookings.edu

RAUCH, William. (Bill Rauch). American (born United States), b. 1950. **Genres:** Autobiography/Memoirs, Politics/Government, Biography. **Career:** Judson Church Oral History Project, interviewer, 1975-77; Fire Island News, editor, 1977; New York City Mayor's Office, advance person, 1978-81, Koch for Governor Campaign, comptroller, 1981-82, assistant, 1982-83, press secretary, 1983-86; Henley Group, managing director, 1986-88; The Lowcountry Ledger, publisher, 1988-92; CoastNet, director, 1992-; Beaufort City, councilman, 1993-99, mayor, 1999-. **Publications:** WITH E.I. KOCH: Mayor, 1984; Politics, 1985. OTHER: (as Bill Rauch) Politicking: How to Get Elected, Take Action, and Make An Impact In Your Community, 2004. Contributor to books and periodicals. **Address:** 1605 North St., Beaufort, SC 29902, U.S.A.

RAUCHER, Herman. American (born United States), b. 1928. **Genres:** Novels, Plays/Screenplays, Young Adult Fiction. **Career:** 20th Century Fox, advertising writer, 1950-54; Walt Disney Studios, advertising writer, 1954-55. Calkins & Holden Inc., staff, 1956-57; Reach Mcclinton and Company Inc., vice president, creative director, 1963-64; Gardner, vice president, creative director, 1964-65; Benton & Bowles, consultant, 1965-67; writer, 1967-. **Publications:** Harold, a Comedy in Two Acts, 1963; Class of '44, 1973. NOVELS: Watermelon Man, 1970; Summer of '42, 1971; A Glimpse of Tiger, 1971; Ode to Billy Joe, 1975; There Should Have Been Castles, 1978; Maynard's House, 1980. **Address:** 66 Cat Rock Rd., Cos Cob, CT 06807-1707, U.S.A.

RAUDKIVI, A(rved) J(aan). New Zealander/Estonian (born Estonia), b. 1920. **Genres:** Engineering, Environmental Sciences/Ecology, Marine Sciences/Oceanography, Physics, Environmental Sciences/Ecology, Mathematics/Statistics. **Career:** New Zealand Ministry of Works, staff, 1950-55; University of Auckland, lecturer, senior lecturer, associate professor, 1956-69, professor, 1970-86, professor emeritus of civil and environmental engineering, 1986-; civil engineering consultant, 1986-; Technical University Braunschweig, visiting professor, 1986; Nanyang University of Technology, visiting professor, 1987; Schleswig Holstein, coordinator of coastal engineering researcher, 1988-94; Joint European Marine Science and Technology Program, scientific adviser, 1995-2001. Writer. **Publications:** Loose Boundary Hydraulics, 1967, 4th ed., 1998; (with R.A. Callander) Advanced Fluid Mechanics: An Introduction, 1975; (with R.A. Callander) Analysis of Groundwater Flow, 1976; Geschichtete Grundwasserströmungen, 1978; Hydrology: An Advanced Introduction to Hydrological Processes and Modelling, 1979; Grundlagen des Sedimenttransports, 1982; (with H.N.C. Breusers) Scouring, 1991; Sedimentation: Exclusion and Removal of Sediment from Diverted Water, 1993. **Address:** Auckland University, PO Box 92019, Auckland, 1142, New Zealand. **Online address:** a.raudkivi@auckland.ac.nz

RAUSE, Vince. American (born United States) **Genres:** Adult Non-fiction, Novels, Business/Trade/Industry. **Career:** Writer. **Publications:** Handy as I Wanna Be: A Novel with Tools, 1999; (with A. Newberg and E.G. D'Aquili) Why God Won't Go Away: Brain Science and the Biology of Belief, 2001; (with N. Parrado) Miracle in the Andes: 72 Days on the Mountain and My Long Trek Home, 2006; (with B. Strickland) Making The Impossible Possible: One Man's Blueprint For Unlocking Hidden Potential And Achieving The Extraordinary, 2007. Contributor to periodicals. **Address:** Ballantine Publishing Group, 1540 Broadway, New York, NY 10036, U.S.A.

RAUSING, Lisbet. See KOERNER, Lisbet.

RAUSING, Sigrid. British/Swedish (born Sweden), b. 1962. **Genres:** History, Autobiography/Memoirs. **Career:** Sigrid Rausing Trust, chair, 1995-; University College London, Department of Anthropology, fellow, 1997-98; Granta and Granta Books, publisher, 2005-; Portobello Books, publisher, 2005-. Writer. **Publications:** History, Memory and Identity in Post-Soviet Estonia: The End of a Collective Farm, 2004. Contributor of articles to journals and periodicals. **Address:** Sigrid Rausing Trust, Eardley House, 4 Uxbridge St., London, GL W8 7SY, England.

RAVAGE, Barbara. American (born United States) **Genres:** Adult Non-fiction, Biography. **Career:** Writer. **Publications:** George Westinghouse: A Genius for Invention, 1997; Rachel Carson: Protecting Our Environment, 1997; K.I.S.S. Guide to Weight Loss, 2001; The Everything Calorie Mini Book, 2002; The Everything Fat Gram Mini Book, 2002; The Everything Smart Nutrition Mini Book, 2002; Burn Unit: Saving Lives after the Flames, 2004; The GI Handbook: How the Glycemic Index Works, 2005. Contributor to periodicals. **Address:** c/o Author Mail, Da Capo Press, 11 Cambridge Ctr., Cambridge, MA 02142, U.S.A. **Online address:** barbara@barbararavage.com

RAVE, Tilmann. German (born Germany), b. 1974. **Genres:** Adult Non-fiction, Business/Trade/Industry, Economics, Transportation. **Career:** Administrator, 1995-2000; Wuppertal Institute for Climate, Environment and Energy, intern, 1998; Ifo Institute for Economic Research, intern, 1999-2000, research fellow, 2000-, economist. Writer. **Publications:** (With R. Arnott and R. Schob) Alleviating Urban Traffic Congestion, 2005; Umweltorientierte Subventionspolitik in Deutschland, 2005; Okonomische Auswirkungen Umweltpolitischer Regulierungen: Eine Machbarkeitsstudie vor dem Hintergrund der Anforderungen der Richtlinie 96/61/EG Uber die Integrierte Vermeidung und Verminderung von Umweltverschmutzungen (IVURichtlinie): Studie im Auftrag des Umweltbundesamtes, 2006; Assessment of Different Approaches to Implementation of the IPPC Directive and Their Impacts on Competitiveness: Some Evidence from the Steel and Glass Industry, 2007; Umweltbezogenes Subventionscontrolling: Studie im Suftrag des Umweltbundesamtes, 2010. Contributor to periodicals and journals. **Address:** Department of Environment, Regions, Transportation, Ifo Institute for Economic Research, Poschingerstrae 5, Munich, 81679, Germany. **Online address:** rave@ifo.de

RAVEL, Edeet. Canadian/Israeli (born Israel), b. 1955. **Genres:** Novels, Poetry. **Career:** McGill University, instructor in Jewish studies; Concordia University, instructor in creative writing; John Abbott College, instructor in English literature. Writer. **Publications:** Lovers: A Midrash (prose poems), 1994; Ten Thousand Lovers, 2003; Look for Me, 2004; Wall of Light (novel), 2005; The Saver, 2008; Your Sad Eyes and Unforgettable Mouth, 2008. PAULINE BTW SERIES: The Thrilling Life of Pauline de Lammermoor, 2007; The Mysterious Adventures of Pauline Bovary, 2007; The Secret Journey of Pauline Siddhartha, 2007; Held, 2011; The Last Rain, 2011. Works appear in anthologies. Contributor to periodicals. **Address:** Penguin Group, 90 Eglinton Ave. E, Ste. 700, Toronto, ON M4P 2Y3, Canada. **Online address:** edeet@wildmail.com

RAVELHOFER, Barbara. British (born England) **Genres:** Dance/Ballet. **Career:** Durham University, lecturer. Educator and author. **Publications:** (ed.) Louange de la danse (In Praise of the Dance), 2000; The Early Stuart Masque: Dance, Costume and Music, 2006; (ed. with T. Grant) English Historical Drama, 1500-1660: Forms outside the Canon, 2008. Contributor to books and periodicals. **Address:** Hallgarth House, 77 Hallgarth St., Durham, DH1 3AY, England. **Online address:** barbara.ravelhofer@durham.ac.uk

RAVEN, Daniel. See LAZUTA, Gene.

RAVENSDALE See Mosley, Nicholas.

RAVETZ, Alison. British (born England), b. 1930. **Genres:** Architecture, Homes/Gardens, Regional/Urban Planning, Urban Studies, Social Sciences, Sociology, Adult Non-fiction, History, History. **Career:** Teacher, 1951-68; University of Leeds, Quarry Hill Flats Project, research officer, 1968-71; Hull School of Architecture, teacher, 1971-75, research fellow and lecturer, 1975-80; Leeds Polytechnic, lecturer in home economics, 1981-84; The Housing Corp., monitoring officer, 1984-; Leeds Metropolitan University, professor, now professor emeritus. Writer. **Publications:** Model Estate: Planned Housing at Quarry Hill, Leeds, 1974; Remaking Cities: Contradictions of the Recent Urban Environment, 1980; The Government of Space: Town Planning in Modern Society, 1986; (with R. Turkington) The Place of Home: English Domestic Environments 1914-2000, 1995; Council Housing and Culture: The History of a Social Experiment, 2001. **Address:** Leeds Metropolitan University, 2 Great George St., City Ctr., Leeds, WY LS1 3HE, England.

RAVILIOUS, Robin. British (born England), b. 1944. **Genres:** Children's Fiction, Illustrations, Animals/Pets. **Career:** Newnham College, principals secretary. Illustrator and writer. **Publications:** FOR CHILDREN: (illus.) The Runaway Chick, 1987; (illus.) Two in a Pocket, 1991; Slowly Does It (in anthology: Crocodile Tears), 1997. FOR ADULTS: (with J. Ravilious) The Heart of the Country, 1980. Contributor to periodicals. **Address:** Gina Pollinger and Murray Pollinger, Literary Agents, 222 Old Brompton Rd., London, GL SW5 0BZ, England.

RAVITCH, Frank S. American (born United States), b. 1966. **Genres:** Law, Theology/Religion. **Career:** State University of New York, Buffalo School of Law, lecturer in law, 1994-96; University of Central Florida, assistant professor of legal studies and legal studies coordinator, 1996-98; Barry University School of Law, associate professor of law, 1999-2002; Syracuse University College of Law, visiting associate professor of law, 2001-02; Michigan State University, College of Law, associate professor of law, 2002-05, professor of law, 2002-, Granted Tenure, 2004. Writer. **Publications:** School Prayer and Discrimination: The Civil Rights of Religious Minorities and Dissenters, 1999; Law and Religion, a Reader: Cases, Concepts, and Theory, 2004, 2nd ed., 2008; Employment Discrimination Law: Problems, Cases, and Critical Perspectives, 2005; Masters of Illusion: The Supreme Court and the Religion Clauses, 2007; Marketing Creation: The Law and Intelligent Design, 2010. Contributor to periodicals. **Address:** College of Law, Michigan State University, 315 Law College Bldg., East Lansing, MI 48824-1300, U.S.A. **Online address:** fravitch@law.msu.edu

RAVITCH, Norman. American (born United States), b. 1936. **Genres:** History, Theology/Religion. **Career:** Philadelphia Museum College of Art, instructor in humanities, 1961-62; University of California, Riverside, assistant professor, 1962-67, associate professor, 1967-75, associate dean of humanities, 1970-75, professor of humanities, 1975-2001, professor emeritus, 2001-. Writer. **Publications:** Sword and Mitre: Government and Episcopate in France and England in the Age of Aristocracy, 1966; Christian Man, 1973; Classical Man, 1973; Modern Man, 1973; The Catholic Church and the French Nation, 1589-1989, 1990. **Address:** Department of History, University of California, 1212 HMNSS Bldg., 900 University Ave., Riverside, CA 92521, U.S.A. **Online address:** norman.ravitch@ucr.edu

RAVITZ, Abe (Carl). American (born United States), b. 1927. **Genres:** Intellectual History, Literary Criticism And History, Biography, Social Sciences. **Career:** Pennsylvania State University, assistant professor of English, 1953-58; Hiram College, professor of English, 1958-66; California State University, Department of English, chairman, 1966-80, professor of English, 1966-86, emeritus professor of English, 1986-. Writer. **Publications:** (Ed. with J.N. Primm) The Haywood Case: Materials for Analysis, 1960; Clarence Darrow and the American Literary Tradition, 1962; David Graham Phillips, 1966; The American Disinherited: A Profile in Fiction, 1970; (comp.) The Disinherited: Plays, 1974; Alfred Henry Lewis, 1978; Leane Zugsmith: Thunder on the Left, 1992; Rex Beach, 1994; Imitations of Life: Fannie Hurst's Gaslight Sonatas, 1997. Contributor of articles to journals. **Address:** Department of English, California State University, LCH E315, 1000 E Victoria St., Carson, CA 90747-0001, U.S.A.

RAVIV, Dan. American (born United States), b. 1954. **Genres:** International Relations/Current Affairs, Documentaries/Reportage. **Career:** Columbia Broadcasting System Radio, WEEI-AM, editor, 1974-76, CBS News, producer, 1976-78, Tel Aviv bureau staff, 1978-80, London bureau staff, 1980-92, Miami bureau staff, 1992-97, Washington national correspondent, 1997-, WCBS-AM, staff. **Publications:** WITH Y. MELMAN: Shutafut oyenet, 1987; Behind the Uprising: Israelis, Jordanians, and Palestinians, 1989; The Imperfect Spies, 1989; Every Spy a Prince: The Complete History of Israel's Intelligence Community, 1990; Meraglim lo Mushlamim, 1990; Jawāsīs al-mukhabarāt al- Isrā īlīyah, 1991; Friends in Deed: Inside the US-Israel Alliance, 1994; Shutafim Li-Devar ma Aśeh, 1994. OTHER: Comic Wars: How Two Tycoons Battled over the Marvel Comics Empire: And Both Lost, 2002. **Address:** CBS Radio News, 524 W 57th St., Ste. 1170, New York, NY 10019, U.S.A.

RAWLE, Graham. British (born England), b. 1955. **Genres:** Novels. **Career:** University of Brighton, lecturer on sequential design and illustration. Writer. **Publications:** Wonder Book of Fun, 1994; Diary of an Amateur Photographer, 1998; Woman's World: A Novel, 2008. LOST CONSONANTS SERIES: Lost Consonants, 1991; More Lost Consonants, 1992; Lost Consonants: No. 3, 1993; Lost Consonants: No. 4, 1994; Lost Consonants: No. 5, 1995; Lost Consonants: No. 6, 1996; Lost Consonants: No. 7, 1997; Lost Consonants: No. 8, 1998. **Address:** The Agy Ltd., 24 Pottery Ln., London, GL W11 4LZ, England. **Online address:** questions@grahamrawle.com

RAWLINGS, Helen. British (born England), b. 1955. **Genres:** Theology/Religion, History. **Career:** University of Leicester, lecturer, senior lecturer in Spanish and director of Spanish studies. Writer. **Publications:** Church, Religion and Society in Early Modern Spain, 2002; (contrib.) The Spanish Inquisition, 2005; Rhetoric and Reality in Early Modern Spain, 2006. Contributor to journals and periodicals. **Address:** School of Modern Languages, University of Leicester, University Rd., Leicester, LE LE1 7RH, England. **Online address:** h.rawlings@le.ac.uk

RAWN, Melanie (Robin). (Ellen Randolph). American (born United States), b. 1954. **Genres:** Science Fiction/Fantasy, Novels. **Career:** Writer. **Publications:** AS ELLEN RANDOLPH: The Rushden Legacy, 1985. FANTASY NOVELS: Knights of the Morningstar, 1994; (with J. Roberson and K. Elliot) The Golden Key, 1996; Spellbinder: A Love Story with Magical Interruptions, 2006; The Diviner, 2011. DRAGON PRINCE TRILOGY: Dragon Prince, 1988; The Star Scroll, 1989; Sunrunner's Fire, 1990. DRAGON STAR TRILOGY: Stronghold, 1990; The Dragon Token, 1992; Skybowl, 1993. EXILES TRILOGY: The Ruins of Ambrai, 1994; The Mageborn Traitor, 1997; Fire Raiser, 2009; The Captal's Tower, 2009. GLASS THORNS: Touchstone, 2012. **Address:** c/o Russell Galen, Scovil Chichak Galen Literary Agency Inc., 381 Park Ave. S, Ste. 1020, New York, NY 10016, U.S.A.

RAWSON, C. J. See **RAWSON, Claude Julien.**

RAWSON, Claude Julien. (C. J. Rawson). American (born United States), b. 1935. **Genres:** Literary Criticism And History. **Career:** University of Newcastle, lecturer in English, 1959-65; University of Warwick, lecturer, 1965-68, senior lecturer, 1968-71, professor of English, 1971-85, honorary professor of English, 1986-; British Society for 18th-Century Studies, president, 1974-75; Unwin Critical Library, general editor, 1974-; Modern Language Review and Yearbook of English Studies, editor, 1974-88; Yale Boswell Editions, general editor and chairman, 1989-2001; University of Illinois, George Sherburn professor of English, 1985-86; Yale University, George M. Bodman professor of English, 1991-96, Maynard Mack professor of English, 1996-; Cambridge Edition of the Works of Jonathan Swift, general editor, 2001-. **Publications:** Henry Fielding: Profiles in Literature, 1968; Gulliver and the Gentle Reader: Studies in Swift and Our Time, 1973; Order from Confusion Sprung: Studies in 18th Century Literature, 1985; Satire and Sentiment, 1660-1830, 1994, 2nd ed., 2000; (with H.B. Nisbet) Cambridge History of Literary Criticism, vol. IV: The Eighteenth Century, 1997; God, Gulliver and Genocide: Barbarism and European Imagination, 1492-1945, 2001. EDITOR: Focus Swift, 1971; Henry Fielding and the Augustan Ideal under Stress, 1972; Fielding: A Critical Anthology, 1973; Yeats and Anglo-Irish Literature: Studies by Peter Ure, 1974; The Character of Swift's Satire: A Revised Focus, 1982; English Satire and the Satiric Tradition, 1984; (with F.P. Lock) Complete Poems of Thomas Parnell, 1988; (with F.P. Lock) Collected Poems of Thomas Parnell, 1989; Jonathan Swift: A Collection of Critical Essays, 1994; (with A. Santesso) John Dryden (1631-1700): His Politics, His Plays and His Poets, 2004; (intro.) Gulliver's Travels, 2005; Cambridge Companion to Henry Fielding, 2007; Henry Fielding (1707-1754): Novelist, Playwright, Journalist, Magistrate: A Double Anniversary Tribute, 2008; Dryden, Pope, Johnson, Malone, 2010; Politics and Literature in the Age of Swift: English and Irish Perspectives, 2010; (with L. Higgins) Jonathan Swift: The Essential Writings: Authoritative Texts, Contexts, Criticism, 2010. **Address:** Department of English, Yale University, Rm. LC 303, 63 High St., PO Box 208302, New Haven, CT 06520-8302, U.S.A. **Online address:** claude.rawson@yale.edu

RAWSON, Jacob. American (born United States), b. 1983?. **Genres:** Travel/Exploration, Reference. **Career:** Writer. **Publications:** (With C. Legerton) Invisible China: A Journey through Ethnic Borderlands, 2009. **Address:** Chicago Review Press, 814 N Franklin St., Chicago, IL 60610, U.S.A. **Online address:** jtrawson@uw.edu

RAY, Brian Christopher. American (born United States), b. 1982. **Genres:** Novels. **Career:** Author. **Publications:** Through the Pale Door (novel), 2009. Contributor to magazines. **Address:** Greensboro, NC , U.S.A. **Online address:** ray822@hotmail.com

RAY, Daryll E. American (born United States), b. 1943. **Genres:** Agriculture/Forestry, Economics. **Career:** University of Tennessee, Blasingame professor of excellence, 1991-, Blasingame chair of excellence, Agricultural Policy Analysis Center, director. Writer. **Publications:** (With E.O. Heady) Simulated Effects of Alternative Policy and Economic Environments on

U.S. Agriculture, 1974; (with G.S. Collins) Statistics of Oklahoma Agriculture, 1975; Externalities in the Transformation of Agriculture, 1975; (with J.W. Richardson) Application of Optimal Control Techniques to Agricultural Policy Analysis, 1979; (with J.W. Richardson and J.N. Trapp) Illustrative Applications of Optimal Control Theory Techniques to Problems in Agricultural Economics, 1979; An Alternative Agricultural and Food Policy and the 1985 Farm Bill, 1985; (with M.R. Dicks and O.L. Walker) Estimated Impacts of Increased Planting. Flexibility, 1990; U.S. Agricultural Sector Models, 1993; An Analytical Database of U.S. Agriculture, 1993; (with R.K. Roberts, D.O. Mitchell and R.J. Schnatzer) His Impact on Agricultural Economics, 1994; (ed. with M.C. Hallberg and R.G.F. Spitze) Food, Agriculture and Rural Policy Into the Twenty-First Century, 1994; The 1995 Farm Bill: Policy Options and Consequences, 1995; (with K.J. Tiller and D.G.D.T. Ugarte) Rethinking U.S. Agricultural Policy, 2003. **Address:** Agricultural Policy Analysis Center, University of Tennessee, 309A Morgan Hall, Knoxville, TN 37996-4519, U.S.A. **Online address:** dray@utk.edu

RAY, David. American (born United States), b. 1932. **Genres:** Poetry, Novellas/Short Stories, Novels, Autobiography/Memoirs, Essays. **Career:** Cornell University, lecturer, 1960-64; Reed College, lecturer, 1964-66; University of Iowa, Writer's Workshop, lecturer, 1969-70; University of Missouri, professor of English, 1971-95, professor emeritus, 1995-; New Letters, editor, 1971-85. **Publications:** X-Rays, 1965; Dragging the Main, 1968; A Hill in Oklahoma, 1972; Gathering Firewood, 1974; Enough of Flying: Poems Inspired by the Ghazals of Ghalib, 1977; The Mulberries of Mingo and Other Stories, 1978; The Tramp's Cup, 1978; Farm in Calabria & Other Poems, 1979; The Touched Life: Poems, Selected and New, 1982; Not Far from the River, Translations from the Gatha Saptasati, 1983; (co-author) The Deepest Hunger (play), 1984; On Wednesday I Cleaned Out My Wallet, 1985; Elysium in the Halls of Hell: Poems about India, 1986; Sam's Book, 1987; Trinity for Sam Ray, 1988; The Maharani's New Wall and Other Poems, 1989; Wool Highways & Other Poems, 1993; Kangaroo Paws: Poems Written in Australia, 1994; Letter from Arizona to Dave Ignatow, 1998; Heart Stones: New and Selected Poems, 1998; Demons in the Diner: Poems, 1999; The Endless Search: A Memoir, 2003; One Thousand Years: Poems about the Holocaust, 2004; The Death of Sardanapalus and Other Poems of the Iraq Wars, 2004; David Ray: Greatest Hits 1960-2004, 2004; Music of Time: Selected and New Poems, 2006; When: Poems, 2007; After Tagore: Poems Inspired by Rabindranath Tagore, 2008. EDITOR: The Chicago Review Anthology, 1959; From the Hungarian Revolution, 1966; (with R. Bly) A Poetry Reading against the Vietnam War, 1966; (with R. Farnsworth) Richard Wright: Impressions and Perspectives, 1973; (with J. Salzman) The Jack Conroy Reader, 1979; From A to Z: 200 Contemporary American Poets, 1981; (intro.) Collected Poems of E.L. Mayo, 1981; (with A. Singh) India, An Anthology of Contemporary Writing, 1983; (with J. Ray) Fathers: A Collection of Poems, 1997; (with M. Rattee) Surfings: Selected Poems by Will Inman, 2005, Leaps of Hope and Fury: Poems by Will Inman, 2008; (with J. Ray) I Read You Green, Mother: poems by Will Inman, 2009. **Address:** 2033 E 10th St., Tucson, AZ 85719-5925, U.S.A. **Online address:** djray@gainbroadband.com

RAY, Jeanne. American (born United States), b. 1940?. **Genres:** Novels. **Career:** First Clinic, nurse. Writer. **Publications:** Julie and Romeo, 2000; Step-Ball-Change: A Novel, 2002; Eat Cake: A Novel, 2003; Julie and Romeo Get Lucky, 2005. **Address:** c/o Lisa Bankoff, International Creative Management, 730 5th Ave., New York, NY 10019, U.S.A.

RAY, Judy. (Suzanne Judy Ray). American/British (born England), b. 1939. **Genres:** Poetry, Autobiography/Memoirs. **Career:** Transition Magazine (Kampala, Uganda), Secretary, 1965-67; New Letters Magazine, associate editor, 1973-85; New Letters on the Air, co-producer, 1982-86; The Writers Place, executive director, 1992-95. Writer. **Publications:** Pebble Rings, 1980; The Jaipur Sketchbook: Impressions of India, 1991; Pigeons in the Chandeliers, 1993; Tangents, 2004; Sleeping in the Larder: Poems of a Sussex Childhood, 2005; Fishing in Green Waters, 2006; Greatest Hits: 1974-2008, 2008; To Fly Without Wings: Poems, 2009. EDITOR WITH D. RAY: New Asian Writing, 1979; Fathers: A Collection of Poems, 1997. **Address:** 2033 E 10th St., Tucson, AZ 85719-5925, U.S.A. **Online address:** jray@gainbroadband.com

RAY, Krishnendu. American/Indian (born India), b. 1962. **Genres:** History, Food And Wine. **Career:** Culinary Institute of America, faculty member and associate dean for curriculum development, 1996-2005; New York University, assistant professor of nutrition and food studies, 2005-. Writer. **Publications:**

The Migrant's Table: Meals and Memories in Bengali-American Households, 2004. Contributor to periodicals. **Address:** Steinhardt Sch of Culture, Edu, & Human Dev, New York University, 82 Washington Sq. E, New York, NY 10003-6680, U.S.A. **Online address:** krishnendu.ray@nyu.edu

RAY, Robert H. (Robert Henry Ray). American (born United States), b. 1940. **Genres:** Education, Literary Criticism And History, Poetry, Reference. **Career:** Baylor University, assistant professor, 1967-75, associate professor, 1975-85, professor of English literature, 1985-, English Department Graduate Program, director, 2000-. Writer. **Publications:** The Herbert Allusion Book: Allusions to George Herbert in the Seventeenth Century, 1986; A John Donne Companion, 1990; A George Herbert Companion, 1995; An Andrew Marvell Companion, 1998; (ed.) Approaches to Teaching Shakespeare's King Lear, 1986. Contributor to journals. **Address:** Department of English, Baylor University, Rm. 211 Carroll Science, PO Box 97406, Waco, TX 76798-7406, U.S.A. **Online address:** robert_ray@baylor.edu

RAY, Robert Henry. See **RAY, Robert H.**

RAY, Ruth E. American (born United States), b. 1954. **Genres:** Education, Humanities, Medicine/Health, Reference. **Career:** Wayne State University, professor of English and director of writing, Institute of Gerontology, faculty associate. Writer. **Publications:** The Practice of Theory: Teacher Research in Composition, 1993; (ed. with R. Cole and R. Kastenbaum) Handbook of the Humanities and Aging, 2nd ed., 2000; Beyond Nostalgia: Aging and Life-story Writing, 2000; Endnotes: An Intimate Look at the End of Life, 2008; (ed. with T.R. Cole and R. Kastenbaum) Guide to Humanistic Studies in Aging: What Does It Mean To Grow Old?, 2010; (ed. with T. Calasanti) Nobody's Burden, 2011; (with T.R. Cole) Aging and the Human Spirit, forthcoming. Contributor to books and journals. **Address:** Department of English, Wayne State University, 5057 Woodward, Ste. 10503.2, 4841 Cass Ave., Maccabees Bldg., 2155 Old Main, Detroit, MI 48202, U.S.A. **Online address:** ruth.ray@wayne.edu

RAY, Sandra King. See **KING, Cassandra.**

RAY, Sheila G(raham). (Sheila G. Bannister Ray). Welsh/British (born England), b. 1930?. **Genres:** Literary Criticism And History, Social Sciences, Young Adult Fiction. **Career:** West Riding of Yorkshire, librarian, 1952-68; City of Birmingham Polytechnic, senior lecturer in librarianship, 1968-83; Children's Literature Abstracts, associate editor, 1973-99; children's literature consultant, 1983-. **Publications:** Readers' Guide to Books on Attitudes and Adventure, 1965, 4th ed., 1974; Library Service to Schools, 1968, 3rd ed., 1982; Children's Fiction: A Handbook for Librarians, 1970, 1972; (with M. Barnes) Youth Library Work, 1976; Children's Librarianship, 1979; The Blyton Phenomenon: The Controversy Surrounding the World's Most Successful Children's Writer, 1982; (ed.) Montgomeryshire Memories, 1994; (ed. with P. Hunt) International Companion Encyclopedia of Children's Literature, 1996; (with S. Waring) Island to Abbey: Survival and Sanctuary in the Books of Elsie J. Oxenham, 1907 to 1959, 2006. **Address:** Tan-y-Capel, Bont Dolgadfan, Llanbrynmair, PW SY19 7BB, Wales.

RAY, Suzanne Judy. See **RAY, Judy.**

RAYFIELD, Donald. British (born England), b. 1942. **Genres:** History, Literary Criticism And History, Biography, Translations. **Career:** University of Queensland, lecturer in Russian, 1964-66; University of London, faculty, 1967-, Queen Mary College, lecturer, professor of Russian and Georgia, 1990-2005, professor emeritus, 2005-. Writer. **Publications:** (Intro. and trans.) O. Mandel'shtam, Chapter 42, by Nadezhda Mandel'shtam, 1973; Chekhov: The Evolution of His Art, 1975; (trans.) G. Tabidze, Ati Leksi, 1975; The Dream of Lhasa, 1976; (trans.) V. Pshavela, Three Poems, 1981; Confessions of Victor X, 1985; Cherry Orchard, 1994; The Chekhov Omnibus, 1994; Uncle Vania and the Wood Demon, 1994; The Literature of Georgia: A History, 1994, 2nd ed., 2000; Anton Chekhov-A Life, 1998; Understanding Chekhov, 1999; (contrib.) Dnevnik Alekseia Sergeevicha Suvorina, 1999; The Garnett Book of Russian Verse, 2000; Stalin and His Hangmen, 2004; (ed.) A Comprehensive Georgian-English Dictionary, 2006; (contrib.) Izbrannye stikhotvoreniia i poemy, 2008; (trans. and intro.) N. Gogol, Dead Souls, 2011. Contributor to journals. **Address:** School of Languages, Linguistics and Film, Queen Mary College, University of London, Mile End Rd., London, GL E1 4NS, England. **Online address:** d.rayfield@qmul.ac.uk

RAYMOND, Barbara Bisantz. American (born United States), b. 1947. **Genres:** History, Biography, Criminology/True Crime. **Career:** Sweet Home Junior High School, teacher, 1969-71; Maryvale Junior High School, teacher, 1971-77; Notre Dame College of Ohio, instructor, 1990-93; Academy of Court Reporting, instructor, 1999-2002; John Carroll University, instructor, 2000-02, College of Arts and Science, Tim Russert Department of Communication and Theatre Arts, part-time faculty. Writer. **Publications:** The Baby Thief: The Untold Story of Georgia Tann, the Baby Seller Who Corrupted Adoption, 2007. Contributor to periodicals. **Address:** Tim Russert Department of Communication & Theatre, Arts, John Carroll University, Rm. 51, O Malley Ctr., 20700 N Pk. Blvd., New York, OH 44118, U.S.A. **Online address:** braymond@babythief.com

RAYMOND, C. Elizabeth. American (born United States), b. 1953. **Genres:** History, Social Commentary, Local History/Rural Topics, Art/Art History, Business/Trade/Industry. **Career:** Nevada Historical Society, research associate, 1980-84; University of Nevada, assistant professor, 1984-91, associate professor of history, 1991-95, professor, 1995-. Writer. **Publications:** William Morris Stewart: A Guide to his Papers at the Nevada Historical Society, 1983; George Wingfield: Owner and Operator of Nevada, 1992; (contrib.) Stopping Time: A Rephotographic Survey of Lake Tahoe, 1992; (ed. with R.M. James) Comstock Women: The Making of a Mining Community, 1998; (with P. Goin) Changing Mines in America, 2004. **Address:** Department of History, University of Nevada, 208 Mack Social Sciences Bldg., 1664 N Virginia St., PO Box 0308, Reno, NV 89557-0037, U.S.A. **Online address:** raymond@unr.edu

RAYMOND, Jonathan. American (born United States), b. 1971?. **Genres:** Novels, Young Adult Fiction, Literary Criticism And History. **Career:** Plazm magazine, editor; The New School, teacher. **Publications:** The Half-Life, 2004; (with J. Kurland) Old Joy, 2004; Livability, 2009. Contributor to periodicals. **Address:** c/o Author Mail, Bloomsbury Publishing PLC, 38 Soho Sq., London, GL W1D 3HB, England.

RAYMOND, Patrick (Ernest). British (born England), b. 1924. **Genres:** Novels, Military/Defense/Arms Control, Young Adult Non-fiction. **Career:** Writer, 1977-. **Publications:** NOVELS: (with E. Raymond) Back to Humanity, 1945; A City of Scarlet and Gold, 1963; The Lordly Ones, 1966; The Sea Garden, 1970; The Last Soldier, 1974; A Matter of Assassination, 1977; The White War, 1978; The Grand Admiral, 1980; Daniel and Esther, 1989; The Maple Moon, 1990; Chika the Serb, 1994. **Address:** A. P. Watt Ltd., 20 John St., London, GL WC1N 2DR, England.

RAYNE, Sarah. See **WOOD, Bridget.**

RAYNER, Hugh. British (born England) **Genres:** Children's Fiction, Illustrations, Humor/Satire, Young Adult Fiction. **Career:** Land Registry, mapmaker. Writer. **Publications:** SELF-ILLUSTRATED PICTURE BOOKS AS SHOO RAYNER: Lamb Drover Jim: The Champion Sheepdog, 1988; Victoria: The Wednesday Market Bus, 1988; Gruesome Games, 1988; The Hardacres of Hardacre Farm, 1989; Harvest at Hardacre Farm, 1989; Santa's Diary, 1990; Games from the Twenty-First Century, 1990; Noah's ABC, 1992; Cat in a Flap, 1992; Hey Diddle Diddle and Other Mother Goose Rhymes (sequel to Cat in a Flap), 1995; Super Dad the Super Hero, 1999; Super Dad, 1999; Rock-a-Doodle-Do!, 2000; Treacle, Treacle, Little Tart, 2001; Craig M'Nure, 2002; Cash Crazy!, 2002; Dizzy DIY!, 2002. SELF-ILLUSTRATED JOKE BOOKS AS SHOO RAYNER: The Christmas Stocking Joke Book, 1989; My First Picture Joke Book, 1989; Ready Teddy Go!, 1991; The Fairy-Tale Joke Book, 1992; The Midnight Feast Joke Book, 1993; The Little Book of New Year's Resolutions, 1993; Shaggy Ghost Stories, 1997; The Little Book of Millennium Resolutions, 1999; The Pirate's Secret Joke Book, 1999. LYDIA SERIES SELF-ILLUSTRATED AS SHOO RAYNER: Lydia and Her Cat, 1988; Lydia at Home, 1988; Lydia Out and About, 1988; Lydia and Her Garden, 1994; Lydia at the Shops, 1994; Lydia and the Present, 1994; Lydia and the Letters, 1994; Lydia and the Ducks, 1994. VICTOR SERIES SELF-ILLUSTRATED AS SHOO RAYNER: Victor and the Sail-Kart, 1989; Victor and the Kite, 1989; Victor the Hero, 1989; Victor and the Martian, 1989; Victor and the Computer Cat, 1989; Victor the Champion, 1989. CYRIL'S CAT SERIES SELF-ILLUSTRATED AS SHOO RAYNER: Cyril's Cat, 1993; Charlie's Night Out, 1993; Cyril's Cat and the Big Surprise, 1993; Mouse Practice, 1996. JETS SERIES SELF-ILLUSTRATED AS SHOO RAYNER: Grandad's Concrete Garden, 1994; We Won the Lottery, 1996; Aunt Jinksie's Miracle Seeds, 1996; Boys Are Us, 1998. GINGER NINJA SERIES: SELF-ILLUSTRATED AS SHOO RAYNER: The Ginger Ninja, 1995; Return of Tiddles, 1995; Tiddle Strikes Back, 1995; Dance of the Apple Dumplings, 1996; St. Felix for the Cup!, 1996; World Cup Winners, 1997; Three's a Crowd, 1997. REX FILES SERIES SELF-ILLUSTRATED AS SHOO RAYNER: The Life-Snatcher, 1999; The Phantom Bantam, 1999; The Bermuda Triangle, 1999; The Shredder, 1999; The Frightened Forest, 1999; The Baa-Baa Club, 1999. ORCHARD CRUNCHIES: LITTLE HORRORS SERIES SELF-ILLUSTRATED AS SHOO RAYNER: The Pumpkin Man, 2001; The Swamp Man, 2001; The Spider Man, 2002; The Sand Man, 2002; The Shadow Man, 2003; The Snow Man, 2003; The Bone Man, 2003. DARK CLAW SERIES SELF-ILLUSTRATED AS SHOO RAYNER: Tunnel Mazers, 2002; Road Rage, 2002; Rat Trap, 2002; Breakout!, 2002; The Guiding Paw, 2002; The Black Hole, 2002. Illustrator of books by others. **Address:** c/o Author Mail, Hodder & Stoughton, Hodder Headline, 338 Euston Rd., London, GL NW1 3BH, England.

RAYNER, Mary (Yoma Grigson). British/Myanmar (born Myanmar), b. 1933. **Genres:** Children's Fiction, Cartoons, Illustrations. **Career:** Hammond Ltd., production assistant; Longmans, Green and Company Ltd., copywriter, 1959-62. Freelance writer and illustrator. **Publications:** SELF-ILLUSTRATED: Mr and Mrs Pig's Evening Out, 1976; The Rain Cloud: Story and Pictures, 1980; Mrs. Pig's Bulk Buy, 1981; Crocodarling, 1986; Oh, Paul!, 1989. OTHERS: The Witch-Finder, 1975; Garth Pig and the Icecream Lady, 1977; Mrs. Pig Gets Cross and Other Stories, 1987; Reilly, 1987; Rug, 1989; Marathon and Steve, 1989; Open Wide, 1990; The Echoing Green, 1992; Garth Pig Steals the Show, 1993; One by One: Garth Pig's Rain Song, 1994; Ten Pink Piglets: Garth Pig's Wall Song, 1994; Wicked William, 1996; Shark Sunday, 1997; The Small Good Wolf, 1997; Bathtime for Garth Pig, 1999; Benjamin Pig's Bad Day, 1999. **Address:** Chiseldon Cottage, May's Ln., Chiseldon, Swindon, WT SN4 0LQ, England. **Online address:** rayner.hawksley@virgin.net

RAYSIDE, David. Canadian (born Canada), b. 1947. **Genres:** Gay And Lesbian Issues, Politics/Government. **Career:** University of Toronto, Department of Political Science, assistant professor, 1974-79, associate professor, 1979-93, professor of political science, 1993-, graduate director and associate chair, 2002-05, Men's Forum, founder, 1989-94, University College, Canadian Studies Programme, coordinator, 1982-86, vice-principal, 1993-97, acting principal, 2001, graduate director and associate chair of political science, 2002-05, Mark S. Bonham Centre for Sexual Diversity Studies, director, 2004-08; Right to Privacy Foundation, secretary, 1981-91. Writer. **Publications:** A Small Town in Modern Times: Alexandria, Ontario, 1991; On the Fringe: Gays and Lesbians in Politics, 1998; Laboring for Rights: Unions and Sexual Diversity Across Nations, 1999; (ed. with G. Hunt) Equity, Diversity, and Canadian Labour, 2007; Queer Inclusions, Continental Divisions: Public Recognition of Sexual Diversity in Canada and the United States, 2008; (ed. with C. Wilcox) Faith, Politics, and Sexual Diversity in Canada and the United States, 2011. Contributor to books and periodicals. **Address:** Department of Political Science, University of Toronto, Rm. 158, 15 King's College Cir., Toronto, ON M5S 3H7, Canada. **Online address:** david.rayside@utoronto.ca

RAYSON, Hannie. Australian (born Australia), b. 1957. **Genres:** Plays/Screenplays. **Career:** Theatre Works, co-founder, writer and actor, 1981-83; The Mill Theatre, writer-in-residence, 1984; Playbox Theatre, writer-in-residence, 1985; LaTrobe University, writer-in-residence, 1987; Monash University, writer-in-residence, 1990; Victoria and Victorian College of the Arts, writer-in-residence, 1990. **Publications:** PLAYS: Mary, 1981; Room to Move (two-act play), 1985; Hotel Sorrento (two-act play), 1990; Falling From Grace, 1994; (with A. Bovell) Scenes from a Separation, 1995; Competitive Tenderness, 1996; Life after George (two-act play), 2000; Inheritance (two-act play), 2003; Two Brothers, 2005; The Glass Soldier, 2007; The Swimming Club, 2010. **Address:** HLA Management Theatrical Agency, 87 Pitt St., Redfern, PO Box 1536, Sydney, NW 2016, Australia.

RAZ, Aviad E. American (born United States) **Genres:** Psychology, Medicine/Health. **Career:** Ben-Gurion University of the Negev, Department of Sociology and Anthropology, senior lecturer in behavioral sciences, associate professor of sociology, Behavioral Sciences Program, director. Writer. **Publications:** Riding the Black Ship: Japan and Tokyo Disneyland, 1999; Emotions at Work: Normative Control, Organizations and Culture in Japan and America, 2002; The Gene and the Genie: Tradition, Medicalization and Genetic Counseling in a Bedouin Community in Israel, 2005; Community Genetics and Genetic Alliances: Eugenics, Carrier Testing and Networks of Risk, 2010. Contributor to periodicals. **Address:** Department of Behavioral

Sciences, Ben-Gurion University of the Negev, PO Box 653, Beer-Sheva, 84105, Israel. **Online address:** aviadraz@bgu.ac.il

RAZ, Hilda. American (born United States), b. 1938. **Genres:** Poetry, Essays, Autobiography/Memoirs, Young Adult Fiction. **Career:** Planned Parenthood League of Massachusetts, assistant director, 1960-62; Prairie Schooner, editorial assistant, 1969-72, contributing editor, 1972-75, poetry editor, 1976-, acting editor, 1980-81, 1985, editor-in-chief, 1987-2011; Association of Writers and Writing Programs, president; University of Nebraska, Department of English, associate professor, 1990-93, Luschei professor, 1993-2011, professor emeritus, 2011-, University of Nebraska Press, series editor, 2000-11; University of New Mexico Press, Mary Burritt Christiansen Poetry Series, editor, 2011-. **Publications:** What Is Good, 1988; The Bone Dish, 1989; Divine Honors, 1997; Trans, 2000; (with A.R. Link) What Becomes You, 2007; All Odd and Splendid, 2008; What Happens, 2009. EDITOR: The Prairie Schooner Anthology of Contemporary Jewish American Writing, 1998; Living on the Margins: Women Writers on Breast Cancer, 1999; (with K. Flaherty) Best of Prairie Schooner: Personal Essays, 2000; Best of Prairie Schooner: Fiction and Poetry, 2001; Loren Eiseley: Commentary, Biography and Remembrance, 2008. Contributor to journals. **Address:** 3 Vista del Sol, Placitas, NM 87043, U.S.A. **Online address:** hraz1@unl.edu

RAZ, Simḥah. *See* **RAZ, Simcha.**

RAZ, Simcha. (śimḥah Raz). Israeli/Palestinian (born Palestine), b. 1931. **Genres:** Theology/Religion, Biography, Autobiography/Memoirs. **Career:** World Hebrew Union, general director, 1960-78; Cape Board of Jewish Education, general director, 1978-82; Centre of Guidance for Public Libraries, assistant director, 1982-94. Writer. **Publications:** AS śIMḥAH RAZ: Pene Yisrael; Kovets Nivhòar Shel Sipurim Ketuvim Be-Ivrit Kalahve-menukedet, 1967; śiah Agadah, 1974; Ha-Hòolem-ha-lohòem, 1975; ye-ahavta, 1972; Al Bamotekha Hòalal: Hoveret Zikaronli-vene Shekhunat Bet-ha-Kerem vòi-Yefeh-Nof She-naflube-Milhòemet Yom-ha-Kipurim 734, 1976; Ish Tsadikò Hayah, 1976; Pitgeme Hòasidim, 1981; Judaism in a Nutshell: Basic Concepts and Terms, 1981; Hasidic Sayings (in Hebrew), 1981; Shaare Tefilah: Pirkehadrakhah La-mitpalel, 1981; The Legends of the Talmud, 3 vols., 1983; Agadot Hatalms, 1984; This World and the World to Come: Hasidic Legends, 1985; Gesher Tsar Meod: Imrot Rabi Nahòman Mi-Braslav, 1986; Hasidic Sayings of Rabbi Nachman of Breslav (in Hebrew), 1986; A Very Narrow Bridge: Saying of Rabbi Nahman of Breslau, 1987; Yerushalayim Le-dorvòa-dor: Pirkòe Agadah U-midrash, 1987; Jerusalem in Aggadah and Midrash (in Hebrew), 1987; Kokhav Ha-shaḥar: Imrot Rabi Menahòem Mendel Mi-Kòotskò, 1988; Hemyat Ha-lev: Tefilot Rabi Nahòmanmi-Braslav Vòe-talmidavò, 1990; Olam-ha-zeh, Olam-ha-ba: Sipure Hasidim, 1991; Agadot ha-Talmud, 1991; Malakhim ki-vene Adam: Ha-rav Avraham Yitshak Ha-Kohen Kuk, 1993; Angles As Human Beings (in Hebrew), 1993; Yahadut al Regelahat: Mu'sagim, Munahe Yesod U-minhagim, 1996; Tsadki Yesod Olam: Masekhet-hayav Shel Rabi Aryeh Levin, Yerid Ha-sefarim: Hafatsah Bil Adit, 1996; Kovetsha-Tsiyonut Ha-datit, 1997, 4th ed., 2001; Shiv Im Panim La-Torah, 5 vols., 1998; Hem-Yat Ha-lev: Prayers of Rabbi Nahmon of Breslau (in Hebrew), 1999; Sipure Tsadikim, 2000; Ma Aśe-Be-Rabi Yisrael Ba-alshem-tor, 2001; Kòovets Ha-Tsiyonut Ha-datit: Bi-melot Me Ah Shanahli-yesod Ha-Mizrahò, 2002; Rav Ha-kotel: Masekhet ḥayavò Shelha-Rav Me Ir Yehudah Gets, 2003; Helel Berosh Ki Nafal Erez, 2003; ḥakhme lev, 2004; Mitsyah Goreret Mitsyah: Taryag Mityot Ba-halakhahuva-agadah, 2007; Ohev Ve-ahuv: Rabi Levi Yitshak Mi-Berdits'ev, 2008; ha-Ne ehavim yeha-neimim: ha-aḥim Rabi Zusha ye-Rabi Elimelekh mi-Lizensk, 2009; Shabat u-mo ed be-ḥatsrot tsadikim, 2010. OTHERS: (ed.) The Sayings of Menahem Mendel of Kotsk, 1995; (ed.) Melodies From My Father's House: Hasidic Wisdom for the Heart and Soul, 1996. **Address:** 111 Uziel St., Bayet Vegan, Jerusalem, 96431, Israel.

RAZIN, Assaf. American/Israeli (born Israel), b. 1941. **Genres:** Economics, Business/Trade/Industry, History, Money/Finance. **Career:** University of Minnesota, assistant professor, 1969-70; Tel Aviv University, faculty, 1970-, Daniel and Grace Ross chair in international economics, 1980-93, Mario Henrique Simonsen professor of public economics, 1993-2005, professor emeritus, 2008-; University of Minnesota, visiting associate professor, 1971-74; University of Pennsylvania, department of economics, visiting professor, 1976, 1981; Northwestern University, Department of Economics, visiting professor, 1977-78; University of California-Berkeley, Department of Economics, visiting professor, 1979; Princeton University, Department of Economics, visiting professor, 1984; National Bureau of Economic Research, research associate, 1985-; University of Chicago, Department of Economics, visiting professor, 1986-87, 1991, 1995, 1997; Yale University, Department of Economics, visiting professorship, 1992, 2006; Center for Economic Policy Research, research fellow, 1992-; Harvard University, department of economics, visiting professor, 1998; Stanford University, department of economics, visiting professor, 1999-2001; Cornell University, The Friedman professor of international economics, 2001-; University of London, London School of Economics, visiting professor, 2006; University of Munich, visiting professor, 2007; European University Institute, visiting professor, 2008. Writer. **Publications:** (With E. Helpman) A Theory of International Trade under Uncertainty, 1978; (with J.A. Frenkel) Fiscal Policies, Debt and International Economic Interdependence, 1984; (with J.A. Frenkel) The International Transmission of Fiscal Expenditures and Budget Deficits in the World Economy, 1984; (with J.A. Frenkel) Fiscal Policies and Real Exchange Rates in the World Economy, 1986; (with M. Nerlove and E. Sadka) Household and Economy: Welfare Economics of Endogenous Fertility, 1987; (with Frenkel) Fiscal Policies and the World Economy: An Intertemporal Approach, 1987; (with J.A. Frenkel and E. Sadka) Internation Taxation, 1993; (with E. Sadka) The Economy of Modern Israel, 1994; (with E. Sadka) Population Economics, 1995; (with Sadka) Labor, Capital and Finance, 2002; (with E. Sadka) The Decline of the Welfare State, 2004; Foreign Direct Investment: Analysis of Aggregate Flows, 2007. **Address:** Department of Economics, Cornell University, Uris 422, Ithaca, NY 14853, U.S.A. **Online address:** razin@post.tau.ac.il

RAZZELL, Mary (Catherine). (Mary Nicol). Canadian (born Canada), b. 1930. **Genres:** Novels, Young Adult Fiction, Children's Non-fiction, History, Children's Fiction, Picture/Board Books, Theology/Religion. **Career:** Writer, 1979-; Grace Hospital, teacher. **Publications:** YOUNG ADULT FICTION: Snow Apples, 1984; Salmonberry Wine, 1987; Night Fires, 1990; White Wave, 1994; The Job, 1996; Smuggler's Moon, 1999; Haida Quest, 2002; Runaway at Sea, 2005; Turkey Weed, forthcoming. NONFICTION PICTURE BOOK: The Secret Code of DNA, 1986. OTHERS: (as Mary Nicol) St. Mary's Catholic Church: The First Fifty Years, 2000; A Local History, 2000. Contributor of articles to periodicals. **Address:** 3993 W 36th Ave., Vancouver, BC V6N 2S7, Canada. **Online address:** mcslinn@telus.net

READ, Anthony. British (born England), b. 1935. **Genres:** Plays/Screenplays, History, Military/Defense/Arms Control, Theatre, Biography, Politics/Government, Social Sciences. **Career:** C.P. Wakefield Advertising Ltd., advertising copywriter, 1954; Birlec Ltd., assistant publicity manager, 1956-58; Jonathan Cape Ltd., editor, 1958-60; Newman Neame Ltd., editor, 1960-63; BBC, producer and story editor, 1963-73; script editor, full-time writer, 1973-. **Publications:** The True Book About the Theatre, 1964; (with K. Bulmer) The Professionals: Where the Jungle Ends, 1978; (with D. Fisher) Operation Lucy: The Most Secret Spy Ring of the Second World War, 1980, 1981; Colonel Z (biography), 1983; (with D. Fisher) Colonel Z: The Life and Times of A Master of Spies, 1984; (with D. Fisher) Colonel Z: The Secret Life Of A Master of Spies, 1985; (with D. Fisher) The Deadly Embrace: Hitler, Stalin and The Nazi-Soviet Pact 1939-1941, 1988; (with D. Fisher) Kristallnacht: Unleashing The Holocaust, 1989; (with D. Fisher) Kristallnacht: The Nazi Night Of Terror, 1989; (with R. Bearse) Conspirator: The Untold Story of Tyler Kent, 1991; (with D. Fisher) The Fall of Berlin, 1992; Berlin Rising: The Biography of a City, 1994; (with D. Fisher) The Proudest Day: India's Long Road to Independence, 1998; Devil's Disciples: The Lives and Times of Hitler's Inner Circle, 2003; Devil's Disciples: Hitler's Inner Circle, 2004; World on Fire: 1919 and the Battle with Bolshevism, 2008. **Address:** David Higham Associates Ltd., 5-8 Lower John St., Golden Sq., London, GL W1F 9HA, England.

READ, Brian. (Brian Ahier Read). British (born England), b. 1927. **Genres:** Children's Fiction, Children's Non-fiction, Local History/Rural Topics, History. **Career:** Public health inspector, 1951-74; South Oxfordshire District Council, freelance writer, 1974-81; Jersey Society in London, freelance writer, 1987-2000. **Publications:** The Long Chase, 1963; The Empty Cottage, 1964; A Friend for Anna, 1964; Lucy and the Chinese Eggs, 1969; Healthy Cities, 1969; The Water Wheel, 1970; The Water We Use, 1973; Men of Iron, 1974; Building a House, 1977; How Your House Works, 1979; Underground, 1985; General Conway and His Jersey Temple, 1986; Jersey in London, 1994; No Cause for Panic, 1995; Henley Rural, 2004. **Address:** 50 St. Mark's Rd., Henley-on-Thames, OX RG9 1LW, England. **Online address:** writer@brianahier.demon.co.uk

READ, Brian Ahier. *See* **READ, Brian.**

READ, Christopher. British (born England), b. 1946. **Genres:** Theology/ Religion, History, Young Adult Non-fiction, Biography. **Career:** University of Warwick, lecturer, professor of history, 1973-. Writer. **Publications:** NONFICTION: Religion, Revolution and the Russian Intelligentsia, 1900-1912: The Vekhi Debate and Its Intellectual Background, 1979; Culture and Power in Revolutionary Russia: The Intelligentsia and the Transition from Tsarism to Communism, 1990; From Tsar to Soviets: The Russian People and Their Revolution, 1917-21, 1996; The Making and Breaking of the Soviet System: An Interpretation, 2001; (ed.) The Stalin Years: A Reader, 2003; Lenin: A Revolutionary Life, 2005. **Address:** Department of History, University of Warwick, Coventry, WM CV4 7AL, England. **Online address:** c.j.read@warwick.ac.uk

READ, David. American (born United States), b. 1956. **Genres:** Literary Criticism And History, Writing/Journalism, History, Poetry. **Career:** University of Missouri, Department of English, professor and chair, interim director of composition. Writer. **Publications:** Temperate Conquests: Spenser and the Spanish New World, 2000; New World, Known World: Shaping Knowledge in Early Anglo-American Writing, 2005. **Address:** Department of English, University of Missouri, 107 Tate Hall, Columbia, MO 65211-1500, U.S.A. **Online address:** readd@missouri.edu

READ, Miss. British (born England), b. 1913. **Genres:** Novels, Children's Fiction, Homes/Gardens. **Career:** Writer. **Publications:** Village School, 1955; Village Diary, 1957; Storm in the Village, 1958; Hobby Horse Cottage, 1958; Thrush Green, 1959; Fresh from the Country, 1960; Winter in Thrush Green, 1961; Miss Clare Remembers, 1962; Over the Gate, 1964; The Market Square, 1966; Village Christmas, 1966; The Howards of Caxley, 1967; The Fairacre Festival, 1968; Country Cooking, 1969; News from Thrush Green, 1970; Tiggy, 1971; Emily Davis, 1971; Tyler's Row, 1972; Christmas Mouse, 1973; Farther Afield, 1974; Hob and the Horse Bat, 1974; Battles at Thrush Green 1975; Animal Boy, 1975; No Holly for Miss Quinn, 1976; Village Affairs, 1977; Return to Thrush Green, 1978; The White Robin, 1979; Village Centenary, 1980; Gossip from Thrush Green, 1981; A Fortunate Grandchild, 1982; Affairs at Thrush Green, 1983; Summer at Fairacre, 1984; At Home in Thrush Green, 1985; Time Remembered, 1986; The School at Thrush Green, 1987; The World of Thrush Green, 1988; The English Vicarage Garden: Thirty Gardens of Beauty And Inspiration, 1988; Mrs. Pringle, 1989; Friends at Thrush Green, 1990; Changes at Fairacre, 1991; Celebration at Thrush Green, 1992; Miss Read's Country Cooking, 1992; Celebrations at Thrush Green, 1993; Farewell to Fairacre, 1993; Tales from Thrush Green, 1994; Tales From a Village School, 1994; A Year at Thrush Green, 1995; A Peaceful Retirement, 1996; The Villagers of Thrush Green, 1999; The Caxley Chronicles, 2007; Christmas at Fairacre, 2007; This Year at Thrush Green, 2009; Christmas at Thrush Green, 2009; Christmas with Miss Read, 2011. **Address:** Michael Joseph Ltd., 80 Strand, London, GL WC2R 0RL, England.

READ, Peter. Australian (born Australia), b. 1945?. **Genres:** Anthropology/Ethnology, History, Biography. **Career:** Link-Up Aboriginal Corp., cofounder, 1980, public officer, 1984-; Australian National University, National Centre for Indigenous Studies, deputy director, professor, 2005-; University of Sydney, Department of History, professor. Writer. **Publications:** A Hundred Years War: The Wiradjuri People and the State, 1988; Charles Perkins: A Biography, 1990, rev. ed., 2001; Responding to Global Warming: The Technology, Economics and Politics of Sustainable Energy, 1994; Returning to Nothing: The Meaning of Lost Places, 1996; A Rape of the Soul So Profound: The Return of the Stolen Generations, 1999; Belonging: Australians, Place and Aboriginal Ownership, 2000; Tripping Over Feathers: Scenes in the Life of Joy Janaka Wiradjuri Williams: A Narrative of the Stolen Generation, 2009. EDITOR: Down There with Me on the Cowra Mission: An Oral History of Erambie Aboriginal Reserve, Cowra, New South Wales, 1984; (with C. Edwards) The Lost Children: Thirteen Australians Taken from Their Aboriginal Families Tell of the Struggle to Find Their Natural Parents, 1989; (with J. Read) Long Time, Olden Time: Aboriginal Accounts of Northern Territory History, 1991; (with I. Donaldson and J. Walter) Shaping Lives: Reflections on Biography, 1992; (with V. Chapman) Terrible Hard Biscuits: A Reader in Aboriginal History, 1996; Settlement: A History of Australian Indigenous Housing, 2000; Haunted Earth, 2003. Contributor to periodicals. **Address:** Department of History, The University of Sydney, Rm. 813, Brennan Bldg., Sydney, NW 2006, Australia. **Online address:** peter.read@usyd.edu.au

READ, Piers Paul. British (born England), b. 1941. **Genres:** Novels, Plays/ Screenplays, Biography, Documentaries/Reportage, Novels. **Career:** Times Literary Supplement, sub-editor, 1964-65; writer, 1965-; Columbia University, adjunct professor or writing, 1980-. **Publications:** NOVELS: Game in Heaven with Tussy Marx, 1966; The Junkers, 1968; The Professor's Daughter, 1971; The Upstart, 1973; Polonaise, 1976; The Train Robbers, 1978; A Married Man, 1979; A Season in the West, 1988; On the Third Day, 1990; A Patriot in Berlin, 1995; The Patriot, 1996; Knights of the Cross, 1997; Alice in Exile, 2001; Death of a Pope, 2009; The Misogynist, 2010. DAN ROMAN SERIES: Monk Dawson, 1969; The Villa Golitsyn, 1981; The Free Frenchman, 1986. NONFICTION: Alive: The Story of the Andes Survivors, 1974; Quo Vadis?: Subversion of the Catholic Church, 1991; Ablaze: The Story of the Heroes and Victims of Chernobyl, 1993; The Templars: The Dramatic History of the Knights Templar, the Most Powerful Military Order of the Crusades, 1999; Alec Guinness: The Authorised Biography, 2003; Hell and Other Essays, 2006; Hell and Other Destinations: A Novelist's Reflections on This World and the Next, 2006; The Dreyfus Affair, 2012. Contributor to books and periodicals. **Address:** 50 Portland Rd., London, GL W11 4LG, England. **Online address:** piersread@dial.pipex.com

READ, Sylvia Joan. British (born England) **Genres:** Novels, Plays/Screenplays, Poetry. **Career:** Here and Now, co-editor, 1940-49; Theatre Roundabout Ltd., actress and scriptwriter, 1961-; Radius, director, 1977-80; Poets' Theatre Guild, lecturer, 2002. **Publications:** The Poetical Ark, 1946; Harvest, 1951; Burden of Blessing, 1952; A Cage of Arms, 1962; Travelling Actors, 1973; Poems, 1979; Singing Christmas, 1984; (with W. Fry) Christian Theatre, 1986; The Hill, 1991; Sharing a Grief, 1996. **Address:** Theatre Roundabout Ltd., 859 Finchley Rd., London, GL NW11 8LX, England.

READER, John. British (born England), b. 1937. **Genres:** Anthropology/ Ethnology, Environmental Sciences/Ecology, History. **Career:** Time Inc., photographer, 1969-73; University of London, honorary research fellow in anthropology; Royal Anthropological Institute, fellow. Writer. **Publications:** NONFICTION: (with H. Croze) Pyramids of Life: An Investigation of Nature's Fearful Symetry, 1977; (with H. Croze) Pyramids of Life: Illuminations of Nature's Fearful Symmetry, 1977, rev. ed., 2000; Missing Links: The Hunt for Earliest Man, 1981, 2nd ed., 1990; Kilimanjaro, 1982; The Rise of Life: The First 3.5 Billion Years, 1986; Mount Kenya, 1989; Man on Earth, 1998; Africa: A Biography of the Continent, 1998, rev. ed., 2007; Africa, 2001, rev. ed., 2007; Cities, 2004; Potato: A History of the Propitious Esculent, 2009; Missing Links: In Search of Human Origins, 2011. Contributor to periodicals. **Address:** 10 Albany Terr., Richmond, SR TW10 6DN, England. **Online address:** j.reader@blueyonder.co.uk

REAGIN, Nancy Ruth. American (born United States), b. 1960. **Genres:** History. **Career:** University of Texas, lecturer, 1989-90; Pace University, assistant professor, 1990-96, associate professor, 1996-2001, professor, 2002-07, professor of history and women's and gender studies, 2007-, chair, 2010-, Women's and Gender Studies Program, director, 2001-06, chair, 2006-07. Writer and historian. **Publications:** A German Women's Movement: Class and Gender in Hanover, 1880-1933, 1995; (ed. with K. O'Donnell and R. Bridenthal) The Heimat Abroad: The Boundaries of Germanness, 2005; Sweeping the German Nation: Domesticity and National Identity in Germany, 1870-1945, 2007; (ed.) Twilight & History, 2010. Contributor to books and periodicals. **Address:** Pace University, Rm. 1503, 41 Park Row, New York, NY 10038, U.S.A. **Online address:** nreagin@aol.com

REAL, Terrence. American (born United States), b. 1950?. **Genres:** Psychology, Social Sciences. **Career:** Family Institute, senior faculty; Meadows Institute, director of gender relations program; Smith College, School for Social Work, faculty; REAL Relational Solutions, founder; psychotherapist. Writer. **Publications:** I Don't Want to Talk About It: Overcoming the Secret Legacy of Male Depression, 1997; How Can I Get Through to You?: Reconnecting Men and Women, 2002; The New Rules of Marriage: What You Need to Know to Make Love Work, 2007. Contributor to periodicals. **Address:** REAL Relational Solutions, 754 Massachusetts Ave., Arlington, MA 02476, U.S.A.

REARDON-ANDERSON, James. American (born United States), b. 1944. **Genres:** History. **Career:** University of Michigan, faculty; Johns Hopkins University, School of Advanced International Studies, faculty; Inter-University Program for Chinese Language Studies, director, 1980-81, 1988; Columbia University, C.V. Starr East Asian Library, chief librarian, 1982-85; Georgetown University, faculty, 1985-, director of Asian studies, 1992-95, director of master of science in foreign service program, 2002-05, senior associate dean and director of undergraduate programs, School of Foreign Service, Sun Yat-Sen professor of Chinese studies, senior associate dean, 2005-, dean. Writer. **Publications:** Yenan and the Great Powers: The Origins of Chinese Communist Foreign Policy, 1944-1946, 1980; The Study of Change: Chemistry in China, 1840-1949, 1991; Pollution, Politics and Foreign Investment in Taiwan: The Lukang Rebellion, 1992; Grasslands and Grassland Sciences in Northern China, 1992; Reluctant Pioneers: China's Expansion Northward, 1644-1937, 2005. Contributor to periodicals. **Address:** School of Foreign Service, Georgetown University, A009E Liberal Arts & Sciences Bldg., Education City, PO Box 23689, Doha, 23689, Qatar. **Online address:** reardonj@georgetown.edu

REASONER, J. L. See **REASONER, Livia Jane Washburn.**

REASONER, Livia. See **WASHBURN, Livia J.**

REASONER, Livia Jane Washburn. Also writes as L. J. Washburn, Jim Austin, Livia James, J. L. Reasoner, Elizabeth Hallam. American (born United States), b. 1957?. **Genres:** Novellas/Short Stories, Mystery/Crime/Suspense, Romance/Historical, Science Fiction/Fantasy, Westerns/Adventure, History, Bibliography, Biography, Biography. **Career:** Writer. **Publications:** AS L.J. WASHBURN: Epitaph, 1987; Ghost River, 1988; Bandera Pass, 1989; Dead-Stick: A Lucas Hallam Mystery, 1989, rev. ed., 1992; The Black Moon, 1989; Wild Night, 1990; Dog Heavies, 1990; Riders of the Monte, 1990; Red River Ruse, 1991; A Peach of a Murder: A Fresh-Baked Mystery, 2006; The Gingerbread Bump-off: A Fresh-baked Mystery, 2011. WITH J. REASONER: Thunder Wagon, 1994; Wolf Shadow, 1994; Medicine Creek, 1995; Dark Trail, 1995; Judgment Day, 1995; The Wilderness Road, 1996; The Hunted, 1997; Wild Night: A Lucas Hallam Mystery, 1998; Tie a Black Ribbon, 2000. AS JIM AUSTIN: (with J.M. Reasoner) Fury, 1992; Blood Ransom, 1992; River War, 1993; Last Chance Canyon, 1994; Nevada Guns, 1995. AS LIVIA JAMES: (with J.M. Reasoner) The Emerald Land, 1983. AS J.L. REASONER: (with J.M. Reasoner) Rivers of Gold, 1995; The Healer's Road, 1995; Healer's Calling, 1996; Cossack Three Ponies, 1997. AS LIVIA REASONER: (with J. Reasoner) Lyron's Lament, 1995; Our Town, 1998; Murder By the Slice: A Fresh-baked Mystery, 2007; Christmas Cookie Killer: A Fresh-baked Mystery, 2008; Frankly My Dear, I'm Dead, 2008; Killer Crab Cakes: A Fresh-baked Mystery, 2009. AS ELIZABETH HALLAM: Haunting Hearts, 1998; Elizabeth Hallam, 1998; Magical Love, 1999; Alura's Wish, 1999; Time Passages, 2000; Yesterday's Flame, 2000. FORTHCOMING: For Whom the Funeral Bell Tolls; A Peck of Pickled Warlocks. **Address:** Kensington Publishing Corp., 119 W 40th St., New York, NY 10018, U.S.A. **Online address:** livia@flash.net

REAVEN, Gerald. (Gerald M. Reaven). American (born United States) **Genres:** Medicine/Health, How-to Books. **Career:** University of Chicago Hospital, intern, 1953-54; University of Michigan, residency in internal medicine, 1957-59; Stanford University School of Medicine, research fellow in medicine, 1954-55, research fellow, 1959-60, instructor, 1960-61, assistant professor, 1961-65, associate professor, 1965-70, professor of medicine, 1970-95, professor emeritus, 1995-, Division of Endocrinology and Metabolic Diseases, chief, 1974-79, General Clinical Research Center, director, 1974-90, Division of Gerontology, chief, 1977-90, Division of Endocrinology, Gerontology and Metabolism, chief, 1990-95; Yale University, visiting associate professor of medicine, 1967-68; Veterans Affairs Palo Alto Health Care System, Geriatric Research, Education and Clinical Center, director, 1977-95; Shaman Pharmaceuticals Inc., vice president of research, 1995-; National Diabetes Advisory Board, chair. Writer. **Publications:** Clinicians Guide to Non-Insulin-Dependent Diabetes Mellitus: Pathogenesis and Treatment, 1989; (ed. with A.C. Buck) Prostate Cancer: Questions and Answers, 1995; (ed. with A. Laws) Insulin Resistance: The Metabolic Syndrome X, 1999; (with T.K. Strom and B. Fox) Syndrome X: Overcoming the Silent Killer That Can Give You a Heart Attack, 2000; (ed. with T.K. Strom) Type 2 Diabetes: Questions and Answers, 2003. Contributor to periodicals. **Address:** Division of Cardiovascular Medicine, Stanford University, 300 Pasteur Dr., Stanford, CA 94305, U.S.A. **Online address:** greaven@cvmed.stanford.edu

REAVEN, Gerald M. See **REAVEN, Gerald.**

REAVIS, Dick J. American (born United States), b. 1945. **Genres:** History. **Career:** Texas Monthly, senior editor, 1981-90; Harvard University, Nieman fellow, 1989-90; San Antonio Light, journalist, 1991-92; Dallas Observer, contributor, 1992-93; San Antonio Express-News, journalist, 2000-04; North Carolina State University, Department of English, assistant professor, 2004-, associate professor. **Publications:** Without Documents, 1978; Conversations with Moctezuma: Ancient Shadows over Modern Life in Mexico, 1990; (trans.) Diary of an Undocumented Immigrant, 1991; Texas, 1995; The Ashes of Waco, 1998; (trans.) Diary of a Guerrilla, 1999; If White Kids Die: Memories of a Civil Rights Movement Volunteer, 2001; Catching Out: The Secret World of Day Laborers, 2010. **Address:** Department of English, North Carolina State University, 103 Tompkins Hall, PO Box 8105, Raleigh, NC 27695-8105, U.S.A. **Online address:** djreavis@social.chass.ncsu.edu

REAY, Barry. New Zealander/British/Australian (born Australia), b. 1950. **Genres:** History, Humanities, Gay And Lesbian Issues, Sex, Social Sciences, Local History/Rural Topics, Literary Criticism And History, Popular Culture, Urban Studies, Art/Art History, Cultural/Ethnic Topics. **Career:** South Australian College of Advanced Education, lecturer, 1979-81; University of Auckland, lecturer, 1982-, Keith Sinclair chair in history, associate dean of research. Writer. **Publications:** (With C. Hill and W. Lamont) The World of the Muggletonians, 1983; The Quakers and the English Revolution, 1985; The Last Rising of the Agricultural Labourers: Rural Life and Protest in Nineteenth-Century England, 1990; Microhistories: Demography, Society, and Culture in Rural England, 1800-1930, 1996; Popular Cultures in England, 1550-1750, 1998; Watching Hannah: Sexuality, Horror and Bodily De-Formation in Victorian England, 2001; Rural Englands: Labouring Lives in the Nineteenth Century, 2004; New York Hustlers: Masculinity and Sex in Modern America, 2010; (with K.M. Phillips) Sex before Sexuality: A Premodern History, 2011. EDITOR: (with J.F. McGregor) Radical Religion in the English Revolution, 1984; Popular Culture in Seventeenth-Century England, 1985; (with K.M. Phillips) Sexualities in History, 2002. **Address:** Department of History, University of Auckland, Rm. 33, 5 Wynyard St., PO Box 92019, Auckland, 1142, New Zealand. **Online address:** bg.reay@auckland.ac.nz

REBACK, Storms. American (born United States) **Genres:** Sports/Fitness, Humor/Satire. **Career:** Jackson Hole News, sports reporter and columnist. **Publications:** (With J. Grotenstein) All In: The (Almost) Entirely True Story of the World Series of Poker, 2005; Shuffle Up and Deal, 2005; (with S. Farha) Farha on Omaha: Expert Strategy for Beating Cash Games and Tournaments, 2007; The Last Showdown, forthcoming. **Address:** c/o Author Mail, Thomas Dunne Books, 175 5th Ave., New York, NY 10010, U.S.A.

REBEIN, Alyssa Chase. See **CHASE, Alyssa.**

REBER, Deborah. American (born United States), b. 1969. **Genres:** Young Adult Fiction, Young Adult Non-fiction. **Career:** Nickelodeon, program developer; Cartoon Network, program developer; freelance writer, 2003-. **Publications:** Run for Your Life: A Book for Beginning Women Runners, 2002; (with J. Canfield and M.V. Hansen) Chicken Soup for the Teenage Soul: The Real Deal: Friends: Best, Worst, Old, New, Lost, False, True, and More, 2005; (with J. Canfield and M.V. Hansen) Chicken Soup for the Teenage Soul: The Real Deal: School: Cliques, Classes, Clubs, and More, 2005; (with J. Canfield and M.V. Hansen) Chicken Soup for the Teenage Soul: The Real Deal: Challenges: Stories about Disses, Losses, Messes, Stresses, and More, 2006; In Their Shoes: Extraordinary Women Describe Their Amazing Careers, 2007; Chill: Stress-Reducing Techniques for a More Balanced, Peaceful You, 2008. "BLUE'S CLUES" SERIES; Weather Games with Blue!, 1999; Magenta and Me, 2000; Blue's Valentine's Day, 2000; My Favorite Letters, 2001; Meet My Family, 2001; My Pet Turtle, 2001; Blue's Egg Hunt, 2001; Blue's Memory Scrapbook, 2001; Blue's ABC Detective Game, 2002; Guess Who Loves Blue!, 2002; Magenta Gets Glasses, 2002; Louder Than Words, 2010; Language of Love, 2010. Contributor to periodicals. **Address:** 4509 Interlake Ave. N, PO Box 281, Seattle, WA 98103, U.S.A. **Online address:** deborah@deborahreber.com

RECH, Lindsay Faith. American (born United States), b. 1978. **Genres:** Women's Studies And Issues, Young Adult Fiction. **Career:** Writer. **Publications:** Losing It, 2003; Joyride, 2004; It Started With a Dare, 2010. **Address:** Harlequin Enterprises Ltd., 225 Duncan Mills Rd., 4th Fl., Don Mills, ON M3B 3K9, Canada. **Online address:** lindsay@lindsayfaithrech.com

RECHY, John (Francisco). American (born United States), b. 1934. **Genres:** Novels, Plays/Screenplays, Adult Non-fiction, Young Adult Non-fiction. **Career:** University of California-Los Angeles, faculty, 1976-77; University of California-Riverside, faculty, 1978; University of Southern California, Graduate Division, adjunct professor of creative writing, 1983-99, Master of

Professional Writing Program, part-time lecturer, 1983-. Writer. **Publications:** NOVELS: City of Night, 1963; Numbers, 1967; This Day's Death, 1969; The Vampires, 1971; The Fourth Angel, 1972, 2nd ed., 1983; Rushes: A Novel, 1979; Bodies and Souls: A Novel, 1983; Marilyn's Daughter: A Novel, 1988; The Miraculous Day of Amalia Gómez: A Novel, 1991; Our Lady of Babylon, 1996; The Coming of the Night: A Novel, 1999; The Life and Adventures of Lyle Clemens: A Novel, 2003. NON-FICTION: The Sexual Outlaw: A Documentary: A Non-Fiction Account, With Commentaries, of Three Days and Nights in the Sexual Underground, 1977, rev. ed., 1985; Beneath the Skin: The Collected Essays of John Rechy, 2004; About My Life and the Kept Woman: A Memoir, 2008. **Address:** Georges Borchardt Inc., 136 E 57th St., New York, NY 10022, U.S.A. **Online address:** contact@johnrechy.com

RECK, Andrew Joseph. American (born United States), b. 1927. **Genres:** Philosophy. **Career:** Yale University, instructor of philosophy, 1955-58; Tulane University, professor of philosophy, 1958-, Philosophy Department, chairman, 1969-89, Master of Liberal Arts Program, director, 1984-, emeritus professor; Fordham University, visiting professor, 1979; The Reader's Adviser, contributing editor, 1988-; History of Philosophy Quarterly, editor, 1992-98. **Publications:** Recent American Philosophy: Studies of Ten Representative Thinkers, 1964; (contrib.) Introduction to William James: An Essay and Selected Texts, 1967; William James et l'attitude pragmatiste. Présentation, choix de textes, 1967; New American Philosophers: An Exploration of Thought since World War II, 1968; Speculative Philosophy: A Study of Its Nature, Types, and Uses, 1972; (co-author) American Philosophers' Ideas of Ultimate Reality and Meaning, 1994. EDITOR: (intro.) Selected Writings, 1964, 1981; Knowledge and Value: Essays in Honor of Harold N. Lee, 1972. **Address:** Department of Philosophy, Tulane University, 6823 St. Charles Ave., New Orleans, LA 70118, U.S.A. **Online address:** areck@tulane.edu

REDCLIFT, Michael R. (M. R. Redclift). British (born England) **Genres:** Geography, Environmental Sciences/Ecology, Natural History. **Career:** Wye College, staff, 1973-97, professor of environmental sociology, 1987-97, ESRC Global Environmental Change Program, director, 1990-95; King's College, Department of Geography, professor of international environmental policy, 1999-, Environment, Society and Politics Research Group, head. Writer. **Publications:** (As M.R. Redclift) Agrarian Reform and Peasant Organization on the Ecuadorian Coast, 1978; Development Policymaking in Mexico: The Sistema Alimentario Mexicano (SAM), 1981; (with D. Goodman) From Peasant to Proletarian: Capitalist Development and Agrarian Transitions, 1982; Development and the Environmental Crisis: Red or Green Alternatives?, 1984; Sustainable Development: Exploring the Contradictions, 1987; (ed. with D. Goodman) The International Farm Crisis, 1989; (ed. with D. Goodman) Environment and Development in Latin America: The Politics of Sustainability, 1991; (with D. Goodman) Refashioning Nature: Food, Ecology, and Culture, 1991; (ed. with T. Benton) Social Theory and the Global Environment, 1994; (ed. with C. Sage) Strategies for Sustainable Development: Local Agendas for the Southern Hemisphere, 1994; (ed. with G. Woodgate) The Sociology of the Environment, 1995; (ed. with H.D. Haan and B. Kasimis) Sustainable Rural Development, 1997; (ed. with G. Woodgate) The International Handbook of Environmental Sociology, 1997, 2nd ed., 2010; (ed. with J.N. Lekakis and G.P. Zanias) Agriculture and World Trade Liberalisation: Socio-Environmental Perspectives on the Common Agricultural Policy, 1999; (ed.) Sustainability: Life Chances and Livelihoods, 2000; The Frontier Environment and Social Order: The Letters of Francis Codd from Upper Canada, 2000; (co-author) Social Environmental Research in the European Union: Research Networks and New Agendas, 2000; (ed. with E.A. Page) Human Security and the Environment: International Comparisons, 2002; Chewing Gum: The Fortunes of Taste, 2004; (ed.) Sustainability: Critical Concepts in the Social Sciences, 2005; (ed. with G. Woodgate) New Developments in Environmental Sociology, 2005; Frontiers: Histories of Civil Society and Nature, 2006; Wasted: Counting the Costs of Global Consumption, 2009; (ed. with M.K. Goodman and D. Goodman) Consuming Space: Placing Consumption in Perspective, 2010; (ed. with M. Pelling and D. Manuel-Navarrete) Climate Change and the Crisis of Capitalism, 2011. Works appear in anthologies. Contributor of articles to journals and periodicals. **Address:** Department of Geography, King's College, Strand, London, GL WC2R 2LS, England. **Online address:** michael.r.redclift@kcl.ac.uk

REDCLIFT, M. R. See **REDCLIFT, Michael R.**

REDDAWAY, Peter (Brian). American/British (born England), b. 1939. **Genres:** International Relations/Current Affairs, Politics/Government, Biography, Psychiatry, Young Adult Fiction, Children's Fiction, Social Sciences. **Career:** University of London, London School of Economics and Political Science, lecturer, 1965-72, senior lecturer in political science with special reference to Russia, 1972-; Kennan Institute for Advanced Russian Studies, director, 1986-89; George Washington University, professor of political science, 1989-2004, professor emeritus of political science and international Affairs, 2004-; British Broadcasting Corp., freelance broadcaster; Amnesty Intl., adviser. Writer. **Publications:** (Comp.) Soviet Short Stories: Sovetskie Rasskazy, 1963, vol. II, 1968; (ed. with L. Schapiro) Lenin: The Man, The Theorist, The Leader: A Reappraisal, 1967; (contrib.) Religion and The Search for New Ideals in the U.S.S.R., 1967, 2nd ed. 1987; (contrib.) U.S.S.R.: Dibattito nella Communita Cristiana, 1968; (contrib.) Rights and Wrongs: Some Essays on Human Rights, 1969; (ed., intro. and trans.) Uncensored Russia: The Human Rights Movement in the Soviet Union, 1972; (ed. and trans.) Uncensored Russia: Protest and Dissent in the Soviet Union; The Unofficial Moscow Journal A Chronicle of Current Events, 1972, (ed.) The Trial of Four, A Collection of Materials on the Case of Galanskov, Ginzburg, Dobrovolsky & Lashkova 1967-68, 1972; Forced Labor Camps in the U.S.S.R. Today; An Unrecognized Example of Modern Inhumanity, 1973; (with S. Bloch) Psychiatric Terror: How Soviet Psychiatry Is Used to Suppress Dissent, 1977; (with S. Bloch) Russia's Political Hospitals: The Abuse of Psychiatry in the Soviet Union, 1977; (ed. with T.H. Rigby and A. Brown) Authority, Power, and Policy in the USSR: Essays Dedicated to Leonard Schapiro, 1980; (with S. Bloch) Soviet Psychiatric Abuse: The Shadow Over World Psychiatry, 1984; (with D. Glinski) The Tragedy of Russia's Reforms: Market Bolshevism Against Democracy, 2001; (ed. with R.W. Orttung) The Dynamics of Russian Politics: Putin's Reform of Federal-Regional Relations, vol. I, 2003, vol.2, 2004; Will Putin Opt For Early Elections to the Duma and/or the Presidency?, 2006. Contributor to newspapers. **Address:** George Washington University, Rm. 412, 1957 E St. NW, Washington, DC 20052, U.S.A. **Online address:** reddaway@gwu.edu

REDDI, Rishi. American/Indian (born India) **Genres:** Novellas/Short Stories. **Career:** Massachusetts Department of Environmental Protection, attorney. Writer. **Publications:** Karma and Other Stories, 2007. **Address:** Lippincott Massie McQuilkin, 27 W. 20th St., Ste. 305, New York, NY 10011, U.S.A. **Online address:** rishi@rishireddi.net

REDDING, David A(sbury). American (born United States), b. 1923. **Genres:** Theology/Religion, Self Help, Children's Fiction. **Career:** Doylestown High School, teacher in English, 1947-49, Evangelical and Reformed Hungarian Church, preacher, 1950-52; First Presbyterian Church, minister, 1952-56, 1963-66; Glendale Presbyterian Church, minister, 1956-63; Tarkio College, writer-in-residence, 1966; Flagler Memorial Church, minister, 1968-74; Liberty Presbyterian Church, minister, 1974, senior minister, 1976, senior pastor emeritus. **Publications:** The Parables He Told, 1962; Psalms of David, 1963; The Miracles of Christ, 1964; If I Could Pray Again, 1965, rev. ed., 1975; New Immorality, 1967; The Couch and the Altar, 1968; What Is the Man?, 1970; Songs in the Night, 1970; Flagler and His Church, 1970; The Faith of Our Fathers, 1971; The Miracles and the Parables, 1971; Until You Bless Me, 1972; God Is Up to Something, 1972; Jesus Makes Me Laugh with Him: A Christian Statement on Humor, 1977; Lives He Touched, 1978; (ed.) The Prayers I Love, 1978; Before You Call, I Will Answer, 1985; Amazed by Grace, 1986; The Golden String, 1988; A Rose Will Grow Anywhere: Renewing Your Confidence That God Works All Things Together for Good, 1996; Liberty's Barn Church, 1996, 2nd ed., 2005; He Never Spoke Without A Parable: Your Neighbor, 2000; He Never Spoke Without A Parable: Your Father, 2001; Never Lose Heart, 2003; The Origin Of My Faith. Contributor of articles. **Address:** Starborne House, 1262 S State Rte. 257, Delaware, OH 43015, U.S.A. **Online address:** david@davidredding.com

REDDY, Maureen T. American (born United States), b. 1955. **Genres:** Literary Criticism And History, Autobiography/Memoirs, Essays, Politics/Government, Race Relations, Young Adult Fiction. **Career:** Haverford College, visiting assistant professor of English, 1985-87; Rhode Island College, Department of English, assistant professor of English and women's studies, 1987-92, associate professor, 1992-96, professor of English and women's studies, 1996-, Mary Tucker Thorp college professor, 2005-06, chair, 2006-, Women's Studies Program, director, 1988-95, 1996-99, faculty. Writer. **Publications:** Sisters in Crime: Feminism and the Crime Novel, 1988; Novel Mothering, 1990; (ed. with B.O. Daly) Narrating Mothers: Theorizing Maternal Subjectivities, 1991; Crossing the Color Line: Race, Parenting, and Culture, 1994; (ed. with M. Roth and A. Sheldon) Mother Journeys: Feminists

Write about Mothering, 1994; (ed.) Everyday Acts against Racism, 1996; (intro.) Mother Knot, 1997; (ed. with B. TuSmith) Race in the College Classroom: Pedagogy and Politics, 2002; Traces, Codes, and Clues: Reading Race in Crime Fiction, 2003. Contributor to periodicals. **Address:** Department of English, Rhode Island College, 263 Craig-Lee Hall, 600 Mount Pleasant Ave., Providence, RI 02908-1940, U.S.A. **Online address:** mreddy@ric.edu

REDFERN, Cameron S. *See* **HARTNETT, Sonya.**

REDFERN, Elizabeth. British (born England), b. 1950. **Genres:** Novels, Young Adult Fiction, Romance/Historical. **Career:** Novelist. **Publications:** The Music of the Spheres, 2001 in France as La Musique des Sphères, 2002; Auriel Rising, 2004. **Address:** c/o Author Mail, Penguin Group, G. P. Putnams Sons, 375 Hudson St., New York, NY 10014, U.S.A.

REDFIELD, James. American (born United States), b. 1950. **Genres:** Novels, Children's Fiction, How-to Books, Westerns/Adventure, Intellectual History, Philosophy, Young Adult Fiction, Theology/Religion, Theology/Religion. **Career:** Youth counselor and therapist, 1974-89; Satori Publishing, founder. Author, lecturer, counselor; screenwriter and film producer. **Publications:** The Celestine Prophecy: An Adventure (novel), 1993; (with C. Adrienne) The Celestine Prophecy: An Experiential Guide, 1995; The Tenth Insight: Holding the Vision (novel), 1996; (with Adrienne) The Tenth Insight: Holding the Vision: An Experiential Guide, 1996; The Celestine Prophecy: A Pocket Guide to the Nine Insights, 1996; La Pofecia Celestina, 1996; The Celestine Vision: Living the New Spiritual Awareness, 1997; The Celestine Insights: The Celestine Prophecy and the Tenth Insight, 1997; Tenth Insight: Holding the Vision: A Pocket Guide, 1997; (with D. Lillegard) The Song of Celestine (picture book), 1998; (intro.) The Purpose of Your Life: Finding Your Place in the World Using Synchronicity, Intuition and Uncommon Sense, 1998; The Secret of Shambhala: In Search of the Eleventh Insight (novel), 1999; (with L. Miller) Exploring the Zone, 2001; (foreword) Clearing for the Millennium, 2001; (with M. Murphy and S. Timbers) God and the Evolving Universe: The Next Step in Personal Evolution, 2002; The Celestine Prophecy: The Making of the Movie, 2005; Twelfth Insight: The Hour of Decision, 2011. **Address:** Grand Central Publishing, PO Box 8828, Boston, MA 02114, U.S.A. **Online address:** jamesredfield@celestinevision.com

REDFIELD, Marc. American (born United States), b. 1958. **Genres:** Politics/Government. **Career:** Universite de Geneve, Departement de langue et litterature anglaises, assistant professor, 1986-90; Claremont Graduate University, Department of English, assistant professor, 1990-96, associate professor, 1996-2001, chair, 2000-03, professorx, 2001-10, John D. and Lillian Maguire distinguished professor, 2002-, School of Arts and Humanities, interim dean, 2007-08, dean, 2008-10; Brown University, Department of English, professor of English and comparative literature, 2010-; London Graduate School, distinguished international fellow, 2010-. Writer. **Publications:** Phantom Formations: Aesthetic Ideology and the Bildungsroman, 1996; (ed. with J.F. Brodie) High Anxieties: Cultural Studies in Addiction, 2002; The Politics of Aesthetics: Nationalism, Gender, Romanticism, 2003; (ed.) Legacies of Paul De Man, 2007; Rhetoric of Terror: Reflections On 9/11 and The War on Terror, 2009; (contrib.) A Handbook to Romanticism Studies, 2011; Theory at Yale: Deconstruction in America, forthcoming; Romanticism, Aesthetics, and the Specter of Theory, forthcoming. Contributor of articles to periodicals. **Address:** Department of English, Brown University, 70 Brown St., PO Box 1852, Providence, RI 02912, U.S.A. **Online address:** marc_redfield@brown.edu

REDFORD, Donald B(ruce). American/Canadian (born Canada), b. 1934. **Genres:** Area Studies, History, Classics. **Career:** Brown University, lecturer, 1959-61; University of Toronto, assistant professor, 1962-65, associate professor, 1965-69, professor of Near Eastern studies, 1969-98; University of Pennsylvania, University Museum, Akhenaten Temple Project, consultant, 1971, director and research associate, 1972-76, visiting professor, 1995-96; Royal Ontario Museum, research associate, 1973-, visiting professor, 1995-96; Ben Gurion University of the Negeb, visiting professor, 1986; Pennsylvania State University, professor of classics and ancient Mediterranean studies, 1998-. Writer. **Publications:** History and Chronology of the Eighteenth Dynasty of Egypt, 1967; (ed. with J.W. Wevers) Essays on the Ancient Semitic World, 1970; A Study of the Biblical Story of Joseph (Genesis 37-50), 1970; (ed. with J.W. Wevers) Studies on the Ancient Palestinian World, 1972; (ed. with A.K. Grayson) Papyrus and Tablet, 1973; (contrib.) The Akhenaten Temple Project, vol. I, 1976, vol. II, 1988; Akhenaten: The Heretic King,

1984; Pharaonic King-Lists, Annals, and Day-Books: A Contribution to the Study of the Egyptian Sense of History, 1986; Egypt, Canaan, and Israel in Ancient Times, 1992; (contrib.) Aspects of Monotheism, 1997; (ed.) Oxford Encyclopedia of Ancient Egypt, 2001; (ed.) Ancient Gods Speak: A Guide to Egyptian Religion, 2002; The Wars in Syria and Palestine of Thutmose III, 2003; From Slave to Pharaoh: The Black Experience of Ancient Egypt, 2004; Excavations at Mendes, 2004; History of Ancient Egypt: Egyptian Civilization in Context, 2006; City of the Ram-man: The Story of Ancient Mendes, 2010. **Address:** Department of Classics and Ancient, Mediterranean Studies, Pennsylvania State University, 108 Weaver Bldg., University Park, PA 16802, U.S.A. **Online address:** dbr3@psu.edu

REDFORD, Kent H(ubbard). American/Taiwanese (born Taiwan), b. 1955. **Genres:** Sciences, Environmental Sciences/Ecology, Politics/Government. **Career:** Teton Science School, counselor, 1975; University of Florida, associate professor of Latin American studies and wildlife and range sciences, Program for Studies in Tropical Conservation, director, 1990-; The Nature Conservancy, director, 1992-97; Wildlife Conservation Society, staff, 1997-, vice president, director for biodiversity analysis and coordination, 2002-; Columbia University, adjunct professor. Writer and consultant. **Publications:** Adaptive Management: A Tool for Conservation Practitioners, 2001. EDITOR: (with J.F. Eisenberg) Advances in Neotropical Mammalogy, 1989; (with J.G. Robinson) Neotropical Wildlife Use and Conservation, 1991; (with C. Padoch) Conservation of Neotropical Forests: Building from Traditional Resource Use, 1992; (with J.F. Eisenberg) Mammals of the Neotropics, vol. II: The Southern Cone: Chile, Argentina, Uruguay and Paraguay, 1992; (with J.A. Mansour) Traditional Peoples and Biodiversity Conservation in Large Tropical Landscapes, 2006; (with K. Brandon and S.E. Sanderson) Parks in Peril, 1998. Contributor of articles and journals. **Address:** Columbia University, 116th St. and Broadway, New York, NY 10027, U.S.A. **Online address:** khredford@aol.com

REDHILL, Michael H. Canadian/American (born United States), b. 1966. **Genres:** Novels, Novellas/Short Stories, Plays/Screenplays, Poetry, Essays, Graphic Novels, Literary Criticism And History. **Career:** Yak, founder, 1984, editor-in-chief, 1986-90; writer, 1985-; Brick (literary journal), publisher and editor, 1998-; Tarragon Theatre, writer-in residence, 1993. **Publications:** (Coed.) Lost Classics, 2000; Martin Sloane (novel), 2001; Fidelity, 2003; Consolation, 2007. POETRY: Impromptu Feats of Balance, 1990; Lake Nora Arms, 1993; (ed. and intro.) Blues and True Concussions, 1996; Asphodel, 1997; Light-Crossing, 2001. PLAYS: Be Frank (one-act), 1991; Heretics (one-act), 1992; The Hanging Gardens of Willowdale, 1992; The Monkey Cage, 1993; Information for Visitors to Warsaw, 1993; Building Jerusalem, 2001; Goodness, 2005. Works appear in anthologies. Contributor to periodicals. **Address:** School of Continuing Studies, University of Toronto, 158 St. George St., Toronto, ON M5S 2V8, Canada. **Online address:** mredhill@interlog.com

REDICK, Robert V.S. American (born United States), b. 1967?. **Genres:** Science Fiction/Fantasy. **Career:** Clark University, International Development and Social Change Program, instructor. Writer. **Publications:** The Red Wolf Conspiracy, 2008. **Address:** MA , U.S.A. **Online address:** robertvsredick@gmail.com

REDINGER, Matthew A. American (born United States), b. 1962?. **Genres:** Theology/Religion, History. **Career:** Montana State University, Department of History, professor of history and chair, 1996-. Writer and historian. **Publications:** American Catholics and the Mexican Revolution, 1924-1936, 2005. **Address:** Department of History, Montana State University, 1500 University Dr., Billings, MT 59101-0298, U.S.A. **Online address:** mredinger@msubillings.edu

REDISH, Martin H. American (born United States), b. 1945. **Genres:** Law, Social Sciences. **Career:** Proskauer Rose Goetz & Mendelsohn, associate, 1970-71; University of Michigan, visiting professor of law, 1971-73, 1987-88; Northwestern University School of Law, assistant professor, 1973-76, associate professor, 1976-78, professor, 1978-90, Perkins-Bauer Teaching Professor of Law, 1982-83, Stanford Clinton Sr. Research Professor, 1988-89; Louis and Harriet Ancel Professor of Law and Public Policy, 1990-; Cornell University, visiting professor, 1987-88; Mayer, Brown, Rowe & Maw, special counsel; Center For Legal Studies, fellow. Writer, lawyer and consultant. **Publications:** Legislative Response to the Medical Malpractice Crisis: Constitutional Implications, 1977; The Constitutionality of Medical Malpractice Reform Legislation: A Supplemental Report, 1978; Federal Jurisdiction: Tensions in the Allocation of Judicial Power, 1980, 2nd ed., 1990; Federal Courts: Cases, Comments, and Questions, 1983, (with S. Sherry and J.E. Pfander) 7th ed., 2012; Freedom of Expression: A Critical Analysis, 1984; Federal Jurisdiction, 1985, 3rd ed. (with R.D. Freer), 2004; (with Barron, Dienes and McCormack) Constitutional Law, 3rd ed., 1987, 7th ed., 2006; (with R.L. Marcus and E.F. Sherman) Civil Procedure: A Modern Approach, 1989, 5th ed., 2009; The Federal Courts in the Political Order: Judicial Jurisdiction and American Political Theory, 1991; (with E.J. Brunet and M.A. Reiter) Summary Judgment: Federal Law and Practice, 1994, ((with E.J. Brunet) 3rd ed., 2006; The Constitution as Political Structure, 1995; (with L.S. Mullenix and G. Vairo) Understanding Federal Court Jurisdiction, 1999; Money Talks: Speech, Economic Power, and the Values of Democracy, 2001; The Logic of Persecution: Free Expression and the McCarthy Era, 2005; Wholesale Justice: Constitutional Democracy and the Problem of the Class Action Lawsuit, 2009. Contributor to periodicals. **Address:** Northwestern University School of Law, 357 E Chicago Ave., Chicago, IL 60611, U.S.A. **Online address:** m-redish@law.northwestern.edu

REDONNET, Marie. French (born France), b. 1948. **Genres:** Novels, Novellas/Short Stories, Plays/Screenplays, Poetry, Literary Criticism And History, Young Adult Non-fiction. **Career:** Conseil National de Recherche Scientifique (CNRS), associate; University of Paris III, associate. Writer. **Publications:** NOVELS: Splendid Hôtel, 1986; Forever Valley: Roman, 1986; Rose Mélie Rose, 1987; Candy Story: Roman, 1992; Nevermore: Roman, 1994; L'accord de Paix: Roman, 2000; Diego: Roman, 2005. PLAYS: Tir et Lir, 1988; Nosie Dip, 1989; Silsie, 1990; Seaside (one-act), 1992; Le Cirque Pandor, Suivi de, Fort Gambo, 1994. POEMS: Le Mort and Cie, 1985; (co-author) Dead Man and Company: Poems, 2003. STORIES: Doublures, 1986, Ville Rosa, 1996. CRITICISM: Jean Genet, le Poète Travesti: Portrait D'une Uvre, 1999. **Address:** Leaping Dog Press, PO Box 3316, San Jose, CA 95156-3316, U.S.A.

REDSAND, Anna. American (born United States), b. 1948?. **Genres:** Novels, Biography, Young Adult Non-fiction. **Career:** Cesar Chavez Community School, faculty in high school writing; Western Michigan University, faculty in english composition; University of California, Berkeley, Academic Talent Development Program, faculty in high school writing; University of New Mexico Honors Program, Outsider in Literature and Society, faculty. **Publications:** Viktor Frankl: A Life Worth Living, 2006; (co-author) Navajo Bilingual Bicultural Curriculum; Demons, Saints or Mortals: Exploring the Many Worlds of Missionaries, 2009; Too Soon the Thunder, forthcoming. **Address:** 2632 Indiana St. NE, Albuquerque, NM 87110, U.S.A. **Online address:** aredsand@yahoo.com

REDSHAW, Peggy A(nn). American (born United States), b. 1948?. **Genres:** History, Sciences. **Career:** St. Louis University, Medical School, postdoctoral fellow, 1974-77; Wilson College, assistant professor of biology, 1977-79; Austin College, assistant professor, associate professor, professor of biology, 1979-. Writer. **Publications:** (With E.H. Phillips and J.B. Lincecum) Science on the Texas Frontier: The Observations of Dr. Gideon Lincecum, 1997; (with J.B. Lincecum and E.H. Phillips) Gideon Lincecum's Sword: Civil War Letters from the Home Front, 2001. **Address:** Austin College, Moody Science 112C, Ste. 61565, 900 N Grand Ave., Sherman, TX 75090, U.S.A. **Online address:** predshaw@austincollege.edu

REDWOOD, John (Alan). British (born England), b. 1951. **Genres:** Economics, Money/Finance, Politics/Government, History, Theology/Religion. **Career:** All Souls College, fellow, 1972-87, 2003-05; Oxford Polytechnic, governor, 1974-77; Silverthorne School, board of governors, 1980-83; Prime Minister's Policy Unit, head, 1983-85; Norcros PLC, director, 1985; N.M. Rothschild & Sons, director, 1986; Parliament for Wokingham, member, 1987-, Parliamentary Under Secretary of State for Corporate Affairs, staff, 1989-90; Minister of State for Trade and Industry, staff, 1990-92; Minister of State for local government and inner cities, staff, 1992-; Shadow Secretary of State for Trade and Industry, 1997-99; Shadow Secretary of State for the Environment, Transport and the Regions, staff, 1999-2000; Middlesex University, Business School, visiting professor, 2000-; Shadow Secretary of State for Deregulation, staff, 2004-05; Economic Competitiveness Policy Group, chairman. Writer. **Publications:** (Contrib.) The Conservative Opportunity, 1976; Reason, Ridicule and Religion: The Age of Enlightenment in England, 1660-1750, 1976; (ed.) European Science in the Seventeenth Century, 1977; Public Enterprise in Crisis: The Future of the Nationalised Industries, 1980; (with J.V. Hatch) Value for Money Audits: New Thinking on the Nationalized Industries, 1980; (with M.Grylls) National Enterprise Board: A Case for Euthanasia, 1980; (with J.V. Hatch) Controlling Public Industries, 1982; Going for Broke: Gambling with Taxpayers' Money, 1984; Equity for Everyman, 1986; Rolling Back the Frontiers of the State, 1986; Popular Capitalism, 1988; Signals from a Railway Conference, 1988; The Popular Capitalist Manifesto, 1988; Can Growth and Greenery Be Reconciled?, 1989; The Democratic Revolution, 1989; Conservative Philosophy in Action, 1992; New Life for Old Cities, 1993; Our Currency, Our Country: The Dangers of European Monetary Union, 1997; The Death of Britain?: The U.K.'s Constitutional Crisis, 1999; Just Say No!: 100 Arguments Against the Euro, 2001; Stars & Strife: The Coming Conflicts Between the U.S.A. and the European Union, 2001; Third Way, Which Way?, 2002; Superpower Struggles: Mighty America, Faltering Europe, Rising Asia, 2005; I Want to Make a DifferenceBut I Don't Like Politics: The Crisis in Party Politics, 2006; After the Credit Crunch: No More Boom and Bust, 2009. **Address:** House of Commons, London, GL SW1A 0AA, England. **Online address:** john.redwood.mp@parliament.uk

REECE, Erik. American (born United States) **Genres:** Adult Non-fiction, Autobiography/Memoirs, Poetry, Natural History. **Career:** ORION Magazine, contributing editor; University of Kentucky, Department of English, faculty, 1997-, senior lecturer, writer-in-residence. **Publications:** My Muse Was Supposed to Meet Me Here, 1992; Lost Mountain: A Year in the Vanishing Wilderness: Radical Strip Mining and the Devastation of Appalachia, 2006; (ed.) Field Work: Modern Poems from Eastern Forests, 2008; American Gospel: On Family, History, and the Kingdom of God, 2009. Contributor to periodicals. **Address:** c/o Author Mail, The Wylie Agency, 250 W 57th St., Ste. 2114, New York, NY 10107, U.S.A. **Online address:** ereec0@pop.uky.edu

REED, Amy. American (born United States), b. 1979?. **Genres:** Novels. **Career:** Writer. **Publications:** Beautiful, 2009; Clean, 2011. Contributor to periodicals. **Address:** Oakland, CA , U.S.A. **Online address:** amy_lynn_reed@yahoo.com

REED, Bruce. American (born United States), b. 1963?. **Genres:** Politics/Government. **Career:** Senator Al Gore, chief speechwriter, 1985-89; Democratic Leadership Council, policy director, 1990-91, president, chief executive officer, 2001-, The New Democrat, founding editor; Clinton-Gore political campaign, deputy campaign manager for policy, 1992; Clinton White House, deputy assistant to the president for domestic policy, assistant to the president for policy planning, chief domestic policy advisor and director of the Domestic Policy Council; U.S. Vice President Joe Biden, chief of staff, 2011-; National Commission on Fiscal Responsibility and Reform, executive director, 2011. Writer. **Publications:** (With G. Williams) Denis Healey and the Policies of Power, 1971; (with R. Emanuel) The Plan: Big Ideas for America, 2006. **Address:** Democratic Leadership Council, 600 Pennsylvania Ave., SE, Ste. 400, Washington, DC 20003-4350, U.S.A.

REED, Christopher (G.). American (born United States), b. 1961. **Genres:** History, Gay And Lesbian Issues, Art/Art History. **Career:** University of Southern Maine, assistant professor of art history, 1991-96; Lake Forest College, assistant professor to associate professor of art history, 1996-2002; University of Memphis, Dorothy K. Hohenberg chair of excellence in art history, 2002-03; Pennsylvania State University, Department of English, associate professor of English and visual culture, 2003-11, professor of english and visual culture, 2011-. Writer. **Publications:** (Ed. and intro.) A Roger Fry Reader, 1996; (ed. and intro.) Not at Home: The Suppression of Domesticity in Modern Art and Architecture, 1996; Bloomsbury Rooms: Modernism, Subculture and Domesticity, 2004; (ed. with N.E. Green) Room of Their Own: The Bloomsbury Artists in American Collections, 2008; (trans. and intro.) Chrysanthème Papers: The Pink Notebook Of Madame Chrysanthème and Other Documents of French Japonisme, 2010; Art and Homosexuality: A History of Ideas, 2011; (with C. Castiglia) If Memory Serves: Gay Men, AIDS and the Promise of the Queer Past, 2012; Bachelor Japanists: Japanese Aesthetics and Western Masculinities, forthcoming. Contributor to books and periodicals. **Address:** Department of English, Pennsylvania State University, 220 Burrowes Bldg., University Park, PA 16802, U.S.A. **Online address:** cgr11@psu.edu

REED, Christopher Robert. American (born United States), b. 1942. **Genres:** History. **Career:** Sverdrup & Parcel, designer, 1970-72, project manager, 1976-79; Mayes, Sudderth & Etheredge, associate project engineer, 1973-76; Parsons Brinckerhoff, project manager, 1980-85; Post Buckley

Schuh and Jernigan Inc., associate, 1986-89; CRS Donohue and Associates Inc., manager, 1990-92; Virginia Department of Transportation, assistant distribution location and design engineer, 1992-95, distribution location and design engineer, 1995-98, program manager, 1998-2001, urban program manager, 2003; Michael Baker, Jr. Inc., vice president, 2001-03. Writer and designer. **Publications:** The Chicago NAACP and the Rise of Black Professional Leadership, 1910-1966, 1997. All the World Is Here! The Black Presence at White City, 2000. (with L. Palmer and P. Phillips) 3 Acres on the Lake: DuSable Park Proposal Project, 2003. Black Chicago's First Century, 1833-1900, 2005. **Address:** Roosevelt University, 430 S Michigan Ave., Chicago, IL 60605, U.S.A. **Online address:** creed@roosevelt.edu

REED, Dallas. *See* **PENDLETON, Thomas.**

REED, Ishmael. (Emmett Coleman). American (born United States), b. 1938. **Genres:** Novels, Poetry, Essays, Young Adult Non-fiction, Mystery/Crime/ Suspense, Humor/Satire. **Career:** Empire Star Weekly, staff writer, 1960-62; freelance writer, 1962-67; East Village Other, co-founder, 1965-; Advance, co-founder, 1965-; Yardbird Publishing Co., co-founder, 1971-, editorial director, 1971-75; Reed Cannon & Johnson Communications Co., co-founder, 1973-; Before Columbus Foundation, co-founder, 1976-; Quilt Mgazine, co-founder, 1980-; University of California, Regents Lecturer, 1988; Ishmael Reed Publishing Co., founder, Konch Magazine, founder and publisher, 1990-. **Publications:** The Free-lance Pallbearers, 1967; (as Emmett Coleman) The Rise, Fall, and ...? of Adam Clayton Powell, 1967; Yellow Back Radio Broke-down, 1969; Catechism of D Neoamerican Hoodoo Church (poetry), 1970; Mumbo Jumbo, 1972; Conjure: Selected Poems, 1963-1970, 1972; Chattanooga (poetry), 1973; The Last Days of Louisiana Red, 1974; Flight to Canada, 1976; A Secretary to the Spirits (poetry), 1978; Shrovetide in Old New Orleans (essays), 1978; God Made Alaska for the Indians (essays), 1982; The Terrible Twos (novel), 1982; Reckless Eyeballing, 1986; Writin' Is Fightin': Thirty-seven Years of Boxing on Paper (non-fiction), 1988, rev. ed. as Writing Is Fighting: Forty-three Years of Boxing on Paper, 1998; New and Collected Poems, 1988; The Terrible Threes (novel), 1989; Japanese by Spring, 1993; Airing Dirty Laundry, 1993; (intro.) Oakland Rhapsody: The Secret Soul of an American Downtown, 1995; The Reed Reader, 2000; Another Day at the Front: Dispatches from the Race War, 2002; Blues City: A Walk in Oakland, 2003; New and Collected Poems, 1964-2006, 2006; (intro.) Jitney, 2007; New and Collected Poems, 1964-2007, 2007; Mixing It Up: Taking on the Media Bullies and Other Reflections, 2008; The Plays, 2009; (intro.) Up from Slavery, 2010; Bigger than Boxing: Muhammad Ali, 2010; Barack Obama and the Jim Crow Media: The Return of the Nigger Breakers, 2010; Juice!, 2011; The Fighter and the Writer: Two American Stories, 2012. EDITOR: 19 Necromancers from Now, 1970; (with A. Young) Yardbird Lives!, 1978; Calafia: The California Poetry, 1979; (with A. Young) Quilt 2-3, 2 vols., 1981-82; (with K. Trueblood and S. Wong) The Before Columbus Foundation Fiction Anthology: Selections from the American Book Awards, 1980-1990, 1992; Multi America: Essays on Cultural Wars and Cultural Peace, 1997; From Totems to Hip-Hop, 2003; (with C. Blank) Pow Wow: Charting the Fault Lines in the American Experience: Short Fiction from Then to Now, 2009. Contributor to periodicals. **Address:** c/o Author Mail, Basic Books, 387 Park Ave. S, New York, NY 10016-8810, U.S.A.

REED, James. British (born England), b. 1922. **Genres:** Literary Criticism And History, Mythology/Folklore, Poetry, Language/Linguistics, History. **Career:** Bingley College, teacher, 1964-68, head of humanities, 1974-78. Writer. **Publications:** The Border Ballads, 1973; Sir Walter Scott: Landscape and Locality, 1980. EDITOR: Border Ballads: A Selection, 1991; Sir Walter Scott: Selected Poems, 1992. Contributor of articles to magazines. **Address:** 83 Raikes Rd., Skipton-in-Craven, NY BD23 1LS, England.

REED, John. American (born United States), b. 1969. **Genres:** Plays/Screenplays, History. **Career:** New School University, faculty. Writer. **Publications:** A Still Small Voice, 2000; Snowball's Chance, 2002; The Whole, 2005; All the World's a Grave: A New Play by William Shakespeare, 2008; Tales of Woe, 2010. Contributor to magazines. **Address:** New York, NY , U.S.A. **Online address:** alltheworldsagrave@gmail.com

REED, John Shelton. American (born United States), b. 1942. **Genres:** Area Studies, Social Commentary, Essays, Humor/Satire, Education. **Career:** Hebrew University of Jerusalem, American Studies and Sociology, Fulbright-Hays senior lecturer, 1973-74; Oxford University, St. Antony's College, senior associate, 1977-78; University of Cambridge, Pitt professor, 1996-97;

University of North Carolina, William R and Kenan Jr., professor of sociology, William R and Kenan Jr., professor emeritus, Howard Odum Institute for Research in Social Science, director. Writer. **Publications:** Enduring South: Subcultural Persistence in Mass Society, 1972; (with H.H. Hyman and C.R. Wright) Enduring Effects of Education, 1975; One South: An Ethnic Approach to Regional Culture, 1982; (ed. and intro. with D.J. Signal) Regionalism and the South: Selected Papers of Rupert Vance, 1982; Southerners, the Social Psychology of Sectionalism, 1983; (with M. Black) Perspectives on the American South, 1984; Southern Folk, Plain and Fancy, 1986; Whistling Dixie: Dispatches from the South, 1990; Surveying the South: Studies in Regional Sociology, 1993; My Tears Spoiled My Aim and Other Reflections on Southern Culture, 1993; Kicking Back: Further Dispatches from the South, 1995; Southern Humor, 1995; Glorious Battle: The Cultural Politics of Victorian Anglo-Catholicism, 1996; (with D.V. Reed) 1001 Things Everyone Should Know about the South, 1996; Minding the South, 2003; (ed. with D.V. Reed) Cornbread Nation 4: The Best Of Southern Food Writing, 2008; (with D.V. Reed and W. McKinney) Holy Smoke: The Big Book of North Carolina Barbecue, 2008. Contributor of articles to journals. **Address:** Department of Sociology, The University of North Carolina, 314-V Carolina Meadows, 155 Hamilton Hall, Chapel Hill, NC 27517, U.S.A. **Online address:** johnshelton@alum.mit.edu

REED, Linda. American (born United States), b. 1955. **Genres:** History, Adult Non-fiction. **Career:** Indiana University, associate instructor, 1980-81; Auburn University, assistant professor of history, 1985-87; University of North Carolina, assistant professor of history, 1987-89; University of Houston, assistant professor, 1988-91, associate professor of history, 1992-, African American Studies Program, director; Association of Black Women Historians, national director, 2001-03. Writer. **Publications:** Simple Decency and Common Sense: The Southern Conference Movement, 1938-1963, 1991; (ed.) Medications: A Guide for the Health Professions, 1992; (with K.T. Gottschang and A.F. Thurston) China Bound: A Guide to Academic Life and Work in the PRC, 1994; (ed. with D.C. Hine and W. King) We Specialize in the Wholly Impossible: A Reader in Black Women's History, 1995; Fannie Lou Hamer: A Mississippi Voice for American Democracy in Mississippi Women of Achievement, 2003; Fannie Lou Hamer, Biographical Entry in Notable American Women: A Biographical Dictionary Completing the Twentieth Century, 2004; From Freedom to Freedom: The Modern-Day Civil Rights Movement in Historical Perspective, forthcoming; George Liele: His Life and Legacy, forthcoming. Contributor to books and journals. **Address:** Department of History, University of Houston, 543 Agnes Arnold Hall, 4800 Calhoun Rd., Houston, TX 77204-3003, U.S.A. **Online address:** lreed@uh.edu

REED, Maureen G. (Maureen Gail Reed). Canadian (born Canada), b. 1961?. **Genres:** Novels, Education, Environmental Sciences/Ecology. **Career:** University of British Columbia, professor of geography, 1991-2000; University of Saskatchewan, professor of geography, 2000-, acting director, 2006-. Writer. **Publications:** Taking Stands: Gender and the Sustainability of Rural Communities, 2003; (with D. Draper) Our Environment: A Canadian Perspective, 4th ed., 2008. Contributor to journals. **Address:** College of Law, University of Saskatchewan, 15 Campus Dr., Saskatoon, SK S7N 5A6, Canada. **Online address:** m.reed@usask.ca

REED, Maureen Gail. *See* **REED, Maureen G.**

REED, Paula. American (born United States), b. 1962?. **Genres:** Romance/ Historical, Novels. **Career:** Columbine High School, teacher. Writer. **Publications:** For Her Love, 2004; Into His Arms, 2004; Nobody's Saint, 2005; Hester: The Missing Years of The Scarlet Letter: A Novel, 2010. **Address:** CO , U.S.A. **Online address:** paulareed@comcast.net

REED, Philip (Chandler). American (born United States), b. 1952. **Genres:** Adult Non-fiction, Plays/Screenplays, Mystery/Crime/Suspense, Ghost Writer, inspirational/Motivational Literature. **Career:** City News Bureau of Chicago, reporter, 1976-78; Sentinel Newspapers, reporter, 1978; Rocky Mountain News, reporter, 1978-82; Hollywood Drama-Logue, critic and columnist, 1982-90. **Publications:** (With A. Funt) Candidly, Allen Funt: A Million Smiles Later, 1994; (with T. Amberry) Free Throw: 7 Steps to Success at the Free Throw Line, 1996; Bird Dog, 1997; Low Rider, 1998; The Marquis de Fraud, 2001; Strategies for Smart Car Buyers, 2003; In Search of the Greatest Golf Swing, 2004. GHOST WRITER: Used Cars-How to Buy One, forthcoming; Lease Cars-How to Get One, forthcoming. Contributor to periodicals. **Address:** John Hawkins and Associates Inc., 71 W 23rd St., Ste. 1600, New York, NY 10010-4185, U.S.A. **Online address:** philreed@aol.com

REED, Ralph Eugene. American (born United States), b. 1961. **Genres:** Politics/Government, Novels. **Career:** College Republican National Committee, executive director, 1982-84; National College Republicans, president, 1983; Students for America, founder, 1984; Christian Coalition, executive director, 1989-97; Century Strategies (public relations and political consulting firm), founder and president, 1997-; Georgia Republican Party, chairman, 2001-03; George Bush Re-election Campaign, southeast regional campaign chairman, 2003-04. Writer, political strategist, public relations consultant, commentator, administrator and entrepreneur. **Publications:** Politically Incorrect: The Emerging Faith Factor in American Politics, 1994 as After the Revolution: How the Christian Coalition Is Impacting America, 1996; (intro.) Contract with the American Family: A Bold Plan, 1995; Active Faith: How Christians Are Changing the Soul of American Politics, 1996; Dark Horse (novel), 2008. Contributor to periodicals. **Address:** Century Strategies, 3235 Satellite Blvd., Ste. 575, Duluth, GA 30096-9017, U.S.A.

REED, T(erence) J(ames). (T. J. Reed). British (born England), b. 1937?. **Genres:** Literary Criticism And History, Translations. **Career:** Oxford University, Queen's College, fellow and tutor, St. John's College, lecturer in modern languages, 1963-88, Taylor professor of German language and literature and fellow, 1988-2004, Taylor professor emeritus of German language and literature, 2004-; Oxford German Studies, co-editor, 1965-; Oxford Magazine, editor, 1985-. **Publications:** Thomas Mann: The Uses of Tradition, 1974, 2nd ed., 1996; The Classical Centre: Goethe and Weimar 1775-1832, 1980; Klassische Mitte: Goethe und Weimar, 1775-1832, 1982; Goethe, 1984; (trans. and intro.) Deutschland, 1986, 2nd ed., 1997; Nobody's Master, 1990; Schiller, 1991; Death in Venice: Making and Unmaking a Master, 1994; Vital Necessity of Tolerance, 1995; Genesis: Some Episodes in Literary Creation, 1995; (trans. with D. Cram) Heinrich Heine: Poems, 1997; Humanpraxis Literatur: Essays um Goethe, 2001; Affirmative finding, 2004; Mehr Licht in Deutschland, 2009. EDITOR: Der Tod in Venedig, 1971, rev. ed., 1983; (trans. with D. Cram) Heinrich Heine, 1997; Selected Poems, 1999; (trans.) The Flight to Italy: Diary and Letters 1786-1788, 1999; (co-ed.) Poems, 2000; Frühe Erzählungen 1893-1912, 2004. **Address:** The Queen, University of Oxford, Wellington Sq., Oxford, OX OX1 4AW, England. **Online address:** jim.reed@queens.ox.ac.uk

REED, Thomas L. (Thomas Lloyd Reed). American (born United States), b. 1947. **Genres:** Literary Criticism And History, Poetry. **Career:** Dickinson College, professor of English literature. Writer. **Publications:** Middle English Debate Poetry and the aesthetics of Irresolution, 1990; The Transforming Draught: Jekyll and Hyde, Robert Louis Stevenson and the Victorian Alcohol Debate, 2006. **Address:** Department of English, Dickinson College, PO Box 1773, Carlisle, PA 17013-2896, U.S.A. **Online address:** reedt@dickinson.edu

REED, Thomas Lloyd. *See* **REED, Thomas L.**

REED, T. J. *See* **REED, T(erence) J(ames).**

REED-DANAHAY, Deborah. American (born United States), b. 1954?. **Genres:** Education. **Career:** University of Texas, faculty; Buffalo State College, faculty; State University of New York, professor, 2008-. Writer. **Publications:** Education and Identity in Rural France: The Politics of Schooling, 1996; (ed.) Auto/ethnography: Rewriting the Self and the Social, 1997; Locating Bourdieu, 2005; (ed. with C.B. Brettell) Citizenship, Political Engagement and Belonging: Immigrants in Europe and the United States, 2008. Contributor of articles to periodicals. **Online address:** der5@buffalo.edu

REEDER, Carolyn. American (born United States), b. 1937. **Genres:** Young Adult Fiction, History, Novels, Biography, Military/Defense/Arms Control, Young Adult Non-fiction. **Career:** Writer and educator. **Publications:** WITH J. REEDER: Shenandoah Heritage: The Story of the People Before the Park, 1978; Shenandoah Vestiges: What the Mountain People Left Behind, 1980; Shenandoah Secrets: The Story of the Park's Hidden Past, 1991; (contrib.) From a True Soldier and Son: The Civil War Letters of William C.H. Reeder, 2008. HISTORICAL NOVELS FOR CHILDREN: Shades of Gray, 1989; Grandpa's Mountain, 1991; Moonshiner's Son, 1993; Across the Lines, 1997; Foster's War, 1998; Captain Kate, 1999, 2nd ed., 2002; Before the Creeks Ran

Red, 2003; The Secret Project Notebook, 2005. **Address:** PO Box 419, Washington, VA 22747, U.S.A. **Online address:** reederbooks@juno.com

REEDER, Stephanie Owen. Australian (born Australia), b. 1951. **Genres:** Children's Fiction, Writing/Journalism, Literary Criticism And History, Children's Non-fiction, History. **Career:** Teacher, 1974-75; University of Canberra, tutor, 1981-82; National Library of Australia, librarian, 1983; Department of Parliamentary Services, editor, 1983-2006; freelance writer and illustrator, 2006-; Australian Catholic University, lecturer, 2009-11. **Publications:** (Ed. with B. Alderman) The Inside Story: Creating Children's Books, 1987; The Flaming Witch, 1997; Colour My World!, 2008; My Reading Journal, 2008; Lost! A True Tale from the Bush, 2009; I've Got a Feeling!, 2010; Feeling Fine!, 2011; The Vision Splendid, 2011; Amazing Grace: An Adventure at Sea, 2011; Dance Like a Pirate, 2012. Contributor to books, magazines and newspapers. **Address:** 10 Jensen St., Hughes, AC 2605, Australia. **Online address:** stephaniereeder@bigpond.com

REEHER, Grant. American (born United States), b. 1960. **Genres:** Politics/Government, Adult Non-fiction, Humanities. **Career:** Yale University, Department of Political Science, teaching fellow, 1986-89; Union College, Department of Political Science, visiting instructor, 1990-92; Syracuse University, Maxwell School of Citizenship and Public Affairs, Department of Political Science, assistant professor, 1992-98, associate professor, 1998-2008, professor of political science, director of undergraduate studies, 1988-2002, faculty coordinator, 2002-04, director of graduate studies, 2006-09, Alan K. Campbell Institute for Public Affairs, director, CNYSpeaks Project, co-director, 2008- , Politics and Media in Britain Program, director; University of Michigan, Robert Wood Johnson Foundation, health policy research fellow, 1995-97; United States Office of Personnel Management, Federal Executive Institute, Leadership for a Democratic Society Program, adjunct faculty, 1999; George Washington University, Graduate School of Political Management, Institute for Politics, Democracy & the Internet, visiting senior research fellow, 2004-05. Writer and scientist. **Publications:** (Ed. with I. Shapiro) Power, Inequality and Democratic Politics: Essays in Honor of Robert A. Dahl, 1988; Narratives of Justice: Legislators' Beliefs about Distributive Fairness, 1996; (ed. with J. Cammarano) Education for Citizenship: Ideas and Innovations in Political Learning, 1997; (ed. with M. Mariani) The Insider's Guide to Political Internships: What to Do Once You're in the Door, 2002; (with S. Davis and L. Elin) Click on Democracy: The Internet's Power to Change Political Apathy into Civic Action, 2002; First Person Political: Legislative Life and the Meaning of Public Service, 2006; (ed. with T. Newell and P. Ronayne) The Trusted Leader: Building the Relationships That Make Government Work, 2008, 2nd ed., 2011. Contributor to periodicals and journals. **Address:** Department of Political Science, Maxwell School of Citizenship & Public Affairs, Syracuse University, 313 Eggers Hall, Syracuse, NY 13244, U.S.A. **Online address:** gdreeher@maxwell.syr.edu

REEMAN, Douglas (Edward). (Alexander Kent). British (born England), b. 1924. **Genres:** Novels, Young Adult Fiction, Mystery/Crime/Suspense, Novellas/Short Stories. **Career:** Writer. **Publications:** A Prayer for the Ship, 1958; High Water, 1959; Send a Gunboat, 1960 as Escape from Santu, 1962; Dive in the Sun, 1961; The Hostile Shore, 1962; The Last Raider, 1963; With Blood and Iron, 1964; H.M.S. Saracen, 1965; Path of the Storm, 1966; The Deep Silence, 1967; The Pride and the Anguish, 1968; To Risks Unknown, 1969; The Greatest Enemy, 1970; Adventures in the High Seas: True Stories from Captain Bligh to the Nautilus, 1971; Against the Sea, 1971; Rendezvous-South Atlantic, 1972; Go in and Sink!, 1973; The Destroyers, 1974; Winged Escort, 1975; Surface with Daring, 1976; Strike from the Sea, 1978; A Ship Must Die, 1979; Torpedo Run, 1981; Badge of Glory, 1982; The First to Land, 1984; D-Day; A Personal Reminiscence, 1984; The Volunteers, 1985; (contrib.) Douglas Reeman Introduces Sea Captain's Tales, 1986; The Iron Pirate, 1986; In Danger's Hour, 1988; The White Guns, 1989; Killing Ground, 1991; The Horizon, 1993; Sunset, 1994; A Dawn Like Thunder, 1996; Battlecruiser, 1997; Dust on the Sea, 1999; For Valour, 2000; Twelve Seconds to Live, 2002; Knife Edge, 2004; The Glory Boys, 2008. AS ALEXANDER KENT: To Glory We Steer, 1968; Form Line of Battle!, 1969; Enemy in Sight, 1970; The Flag Captain, 1971; Sloop of War, 1972; Command a King's Ship, 1973; Signal-Close Action, 1975; Richard Bolitho: Midshipman, 1975; Passage to Mutiny, 1976; In Gallant Company, 1977; Midshipman Bolitho and the Avenger, 1978; The Inshore Squadron, 1978; Stand into Danger, 1980; A Tradition of Victory, 1981; Success to the Brave, 1983; Colours Aloft!, 1986; Honour This Day, 1987; With All Despatch, 1988; The Only Victor, 1990; Beyond the Reef, 1992; The Darkening Sea, 1993; For My Country's Freedom,

1995; Cross of St. George, 1996; Sword of Honour, 1998; Second to None, 1999; Relentless Pursuit, 2001; Man of War, 2003; Band of Brothers, 2005; The Complete Midshipman Bolitho, 2006; Heart of Oak, 2007; In the King's Name, 2011. **Address:** Peters Fraser and Dunlop, Drury House, 34-43 Russell St., London, GL WC2B 5HA, England.

REES, Brian. British/Australian (born Australia), b. 1929. **Genres:** Education, History, Biography, Reference. **Career:** Eton College, assistant master, 1952-63, house master, 1963-65; Merchant Taylors' School, headmaster, 1965-73; Charterhouse, headmaster, 1973-81; Rugby School, headmaster, 1981-84; University College of Buckingham, patron; Conference for Independent Further Education, patron and founder president; Headmasters' Conference, chair; Independent Schools Information Service, chair. Writer and broadcaster. **Publications:** (With P. Townsend) Personal, Family and Social Circumstances of Old People: Report of an Investigation Carried out in England in 1959 to Pilot a Future Cross-National Survey of Old Age, 1960; A Musical Peacemaker: The Life and Work of Sir Edward German, 1986; Camille Saint-Saens: A Life, 1999; Stowe: The History of A Public School, 1923-1989, 2008. EDITOR: History and Idealism: Essays, Addresses, and Letters, 1990. **Address:** Faber and Faber Ltd., Burnt Mill, Elizabeth Way, Harlow, EX CM20 2HX, England. **Online address:** reesflore@tiscali.uk

REES, Charles Roger. See REES, C. Roger.

REES, C. Roger. (Charles Roger Rees). American/British (born England), b. 1946. **Genres:** Sociology, Sports/Fitness. **Career:** Texas Christian University, assistant professor, 1980-83; Adelphi University, associate professor, 1983-92, professor of sociology and the social psychology of sport and physical education, 1992-; institutions of higher education, lecturer. Writer. **Publications:** (With A.W. Miracle, Jr.) Lessons of the Locker Room: The Myth of School Sports, 1994. EDITOR: (with A.O. Dunleavy and A.W. Miracle) Studies in the Sociology of Sport, 1982; (with A.W. Miracle) Sport and Social Theory, 1986; (with G.T. Barrette and R.S. Feingold) Sport Pedagogy: Myths, Models, and Methods, 1987. Work appears in anthologies. Contributor of articles to journals. **Address:** Department of Health Studies, Adelphi University, Rm. 24, Woodruff Hall, PO Box 701, Garden City, NY 11530, U.S.A. **Online address:** rees@adelphi.edu

REES, David. American (born United States), b. 1972. **Genres:** Humor/Satire, Cartoons, Picture/Board Books. **Career:** MNFTIU.CC, creator, 2000-. Writer and cartoonist. **Publications:** Get Your War On, 2002; My New Fighting Technique is Unstoppable, 2003; Get Your War On II, 2004; My New Filing Technique is Unstoppable, 2004; Get Your War On: The Definitive Account of the War on Terror, 2001-2008, 2008. CONTRIBUTOR: 411, Marvel Comics, 2003; Politically Inspired, 2003; Pictures and Words: New Comic Art and Narrative Illustration, 2005; Proud to Be Liberal, 2006; Ultimate Blogs: Masterworks from the Wild Web, 2008; Things I've Learned from Women Who've Dumped Me, 2008. Contributor to periodicals and journals. **Address:** c/o Kassie Evashevski, United Talent Agency, 9560 Wilshire Blvd., Ste. 500, Beverly Hills, CA 90212-2401, U.S.A. **Online address:** dr@mnftiu.cc

REES, Frank D. Australian (born Australia), b. 1950. **Genres:** Theology/Religion, Sociology. **Career:** Hobart Baptist Church, minister, 1973-80, 1983-90; University of Melbourne, Whitley College, Theological School, professor of systematic theology, 1991-, dean, principal, 2007-. Writer. **Publications:** (Ed.) Fair Dinkum Ministry: Stories of Authentic Australian Spirituality and Struggle, 1999; Wrestling with Doubt: Theological Reflections on the Journey of Faith, 2001. Contributor to books and periodicals. **Address:** Whitley College, University of Melbourne, 271 Royal Parade, Parkville, VI 3052, Australia. **Online address:** frees@whitley.unimelb.edu.au

REES, Matt Beynon. Welsh (born Wales), b. 1967?. **Genres:** Third World, History, Novels, Mystery/Crime/Suspense, Adult Non-fiction, Cultural/Ethnic Topics. **Career:** Scotsman, Middle East correspondent, 1996-98; Newsweek, Middle East correspondent, 1998-2000; Time, bureau chief, 2000-06, contributor, 2006-07; Global Post Jerusalem, correspondent, 2009-. Writer. **Publications:** (As Matt Rees) Cain's Field: Faith, Fratricide and Fear in the Middle East, 2004; The Collaborator of Bethlehem, 2007; A Grave in Gaza, 2008; (as Matt Rees) Saladin Murders: An Omar Yussef Novel, 2008; The Samaritan's Secret, 2009; The Fourth Assassin, 2010. **Address:** Jerusalem, Israel. **Online address:** mattbeynonrees@gmail.com

REES, Nigel (Thomas). British (born England), b. 1944. **Genres:** Reference, Language/Linguistics, Humor/Satire, Novels. **Career:** The Quote... Unquote Newsletter, publisher and editor, 1992-. Writer and broadcaster. **Publications:** Quote... Unquote, 1979; Graffiti 1, 1979; Graffiti Lives O.K., 1979; Quote Very Interesting ... But Stupid, 1980; Graffiti 3, 1981; Eavesdroppings, 1981; The Graffiti File, 1981; Graffiti 4, 1982; Slogans, 1982; Word of Mouth, 1983; The Nigel Rees Book of Slogans and Catchphrases, 1984; The Joy of Cliches, 1984; Sayings of the Century, 1984; The Gift of the Gab, 1985; (with V. Noble) A Who's Who of Nicknames, 1985; Graffiti 5, 1986; Nudge, Nudge, Wink, Wink: A Quote Book of Love and Sex, 1986; A Dictionary of Twentieth-Century Quotations, 1987; Why Do We Say ...?, 1987 as The Cassell Dictionary of Word and Phrase Origins, 1992 as Dictionary of Word and Phrase Origins, 1994 as Cassell's Dictionary of Word and Phrase Origins, 2002; The Newsmakers, 1987; Talent, 1988; A Family Matter, 1989; Why Do We Quote as The Phrase That Launched 1,000 Ships, 1991; Dictionary of Phrase and Allusion, 1991 as Dictionary of Phrase and Fable, 1993; Best Behaviour: A Complete Guide to Manners in the 1990s, 1992 as Guide to Good Manners, 1993 as Good Manners, 1994; Politically Correct Phrasebook, 1993; Epitaphs: Dictionary of Grave Epigrams and Memorial Eloquence, 1993; Dictionary of Modern Quotations, 1993; Letter Writing: A Guide to Personal and Professional Correspondence, 1994; Book of Humorous Anecdotes, 1994; Brewer's Quotations: A Phrase and Fable Dictionary, 1994; As We Say in Our House: A Book of Family Sayings, 1994; Dictionary of Jokes, 1995; Dictionary of Catchphrases, 1995; Brewer's Quotations: A Phrase and Fable Dictionary, 1995; Dictionary of Cliches, 1996; Dictionary of Slogans, 1997; Companion to Quotations, 1997 in US as Mark My Words, 2002; Dictionary of Humorous Quotations, 1998; The Cassell Dictionary of Anecdotes, 1999; Cassell's Movie Quotations, 2000; Cassell's Humorous Quotations, 2001; Oops, Pardon, Mrs Arden! An Embarrassment of Domestic Catchphrases, 2001; A Word in Your Shell-Like: 6,000 Curious and Everyday Phrases Explained, 2004; Cassell's Dictionary of Catchphrases, 2005; I Told You I Was Sick: A Grave Book of Curious Epitaphs, 2005; Brewer's Famous Quotations: 5,000 Quotations and the Stories behind Them, 2006; A Man about a Dog: 3,000 Figleaves of Speech, 2006; All Gong and No Dinner: 1,001 Homely Phrases and Curious Domestic Sayings, 2007; More Tea, Vicar?, 2009; Don't You Know There's a War On?, 2011. **Address:** 7 Hillgate Pl., London, GL W8 7SL, England. **Online address:** nigel.rees@btinternet.com

REESE, Ellen. (Ellen Rivoli Reese). American (born United States), b. 1969. **Genres:** History. **Career:** California State University, educator; University of California, associate professor of sociology. Writer and sociologist. **Publications:** Backlash against Welfare Mothers: Past and Present, 2005; (ed. with A.L. Cabezas and M. Waller) The Wages of Empire: Neoliberal Policies, Repression, and Women's Poverty, 2007; They Say Cut Back, We Say Fight Back! Welfare Activism in an Era of Retrenchment, 2011. Contributor to books, periodicals and journals. **Address:** University of California, 1217 Watkins Hall, Riverside, CA 92521, U.S.A. **Online address:** ellen.reese@ucr.edu

REESE, Ellen Rivoli. See REESE, Ellen.

REESE, James. American (born United States), b. 1964. **Genres:** Adult Non-fiction, Novels, Mystery/Crime/Suspense, Horror. **Career:** Writer. **Publications:** FICTION: HERCULINE TRILOGY: The Book of Shadows, 2002; The Book of Spirits, 2005; The Witchery, 2006. OTHERS: The Dracula Dossier, 2008; The Strange Case of Doctor Jekyll And Mademoiselle Odile, 2012. **Address:** c/o Author Mail, HarperCollins Publishers, 10 E 53rd St., 18th Fl., New York, NY 10022-5244, U.S.A. **Online address:** james@jamesreesebooks.com

REESE, Laura. American (born United States), b. 1950. **Genres:** Novels, Mystery/Crime/Suspense. **Career:** Writer, 1995-. **Publications:** Topping from Below (novel), 1995; Panic Snap (novel), 2000. **Address:** St. Martin's Press, 175 5th Ave., New York, NY 10010-7703, U.S.A.

REESE, Roger R(oi). American (born United States), b. 1959. **Genres:** History, Military/Defense/Arms Control. **Career:** Texas A&M University, assistant professor, 1990-96, associate professor of history, 1996-, professor of history. Writer. **Publications:** Stalin's Reluctant Soldiers: A Social History of the Red Army, 1925-1941, 1996; Soviet Military Experience: A History of the Soviet Army, 1917-1991, 2000; Red Commanders: A Social History of the Soviet Army Officer Corps, 1918-1991, 2005; (ed.) Russian Imperial Army, 1796-1917, 2006; Why Stalin's Soldiers Fought: The Red Army's Military Effectiveness in World War II, 2011. Contributor of articles to journals. Ad-

dress: Department of History, Texas A & M University, 109A, Glasscock Bldg., College Station, TX 77843, U.S.A. **Online address:** rreese@tamu.edu

REES-MOGG. (William Rees-Mogg). British (born England), b. 1928. **Genres:** Money/Finance, Politics/Government. **Career:** Financial Times, staff, 1952-55, chief lead writer, 1955-60, assistant editor, 1957-60; Sunday Times, city editor, 1960-61, political and economic editor, 1961-63, deputy editor, 1964-67; Times, editor, 1967-81; The Times Ltd., director, 1968-81; The Times Newspapers Ltd., director, 1978-81; British Broadcasting Corp., vice-chair of board of governors, 1981-86; Pickering and Chatto Ltd., owner, 1981-. **Publications:** AS WILLIAM REES-MOGG: Sir Anthony Eden, 1956; Liberty in 1984: The Conservative Approach to the Reform of Government, 1965; The Reigning Error: The Crisis of World Inflation, 1974; Democracy and the Value of Money: The Theory of Money from Locke to Keynes, 1977; An Humbler Heaven: The Beginnings of Hope (autobiography), 1977; How to Buy Rare Books: A Practical Guide to the Antiquarian Book Market, 1985; Picnics on Vesuvius: Steps Towards the Millennium, 1992; (ed.) Case for Gold, 2002; Memoirs, 2011. AS WILLIAM REES-MOGG WITH J.D. DAVIDSON: Blood in the Streets: Investment Profits in a World Gone Mad, 1987; The Great Reckoning: How the World Will Change in the Depression of the 1990s, 1991, rev. ed. as The Great Reckoning: Protect Yourself in the Coming Depression, 1993; The Sovereign Individual: How to Survive and Thrive During the Collapse of the Welfare State, 1997. **Address:** Pickering & Chatto Publishers, 21 Bloomsbury Way, London, GL WC1A 2TH, England.

REES-MOGG, William. *See* **REES-MOGG.**

REEVE, F(ranklin) D(olier). American (born United States), b. 1928. **Genres:** Novels, Novellas/Short Stories, Poetry, Literary Criticism And History, Translations. **Career:** Columbia University, instructor, assistant professor of Slavic languages, 1952-61; Wesleyan University, Department of Russian, associate professor and chairman, 1962-64, professor of Russian, 1964-66, adjunct professor, 1969-88, visiting professor, 1988, professor of letters, 1988-2002, professor of letters emeritus, 2002-, MFA Program in Poetry, core faculty, 2003-; Oxford University, visiting professor, 1964; Connecticut College, visiting professor, 1970; Yale University, visiting professor, 1972; Poetry Review, editor, 1982-84; Marlboro College, visiting professor, 1999; Pettee Memorial Library, trustee, 2001-; Vermont Center for the Arts, consultant. **Publications:** EDITOR and TRANSLATOR: Five Short Novels of Turgenev, 1961; Resurrection, 1963; An Anthology of Russian Plays, 2 vols., 1963; Great Soviet Short Stories, 1962; Contemporary Russian Drama, 1968; Garden: New and Selected Poetry and Prose, 1990; The Trouble with Reason, 1993; A. Borschchagovsky, The King and the Fool, 2001. LITERARY CRITICISM: Aleksandr Blok: Between Image and Idea, 1962; Robert Frost in Russia, 1964; On Some Scientific Concepts in Russian Poetry at the Turn of the Century, 1966; The Russian Novel, 1966; The White Monk: An Essay on Dostoevsky and Melville, 1989. POETRY: In the Silent Stones, 1968; The Blue Cat, 1972; Concrete Music, 1992; (ed. with J. Meek) After the Storm: Poems on the Persian Gulf War, 1992; The Moon and Other Failures, 1999; A World You Haven't Seen (poems), 2001; The Urban Stampede and Other Poems, 2001; The Return of the Blue Cat, 2005; The Blue Cat Walks the Earth, 2007; The Toy Soldier, 2007; The Puzzle Master and Other Poems, 2010. NOVELS: The Red Machines, 1968; Just over the Border, 1969; The Brother, 1971; White Colors, 1973. OTHERS: (ed. with W.J. Smith) An Arrow in the Wall: Selected Poetry and Prose, 1987; A Few Rounds of Old Maid (stories), 1995; My Sister Life, 2005; North River, 2006. **Address:** Wesleyan University, Wesleyan Sta., Middletown, CT 06459, U.S.A. **Online address:** freeve@wesleyan.edu

REEVES, Eileen Adair. American (born United States), b. 1956. **Genres:** Sciences, Translations, Art/Art History. **Career:** Princeton University, Department of Comparative Literature, professor, Program in European Cultural Studies, director. Writer. **Publications:** Painting the Heavens: Art and Science in the Age of Galileo, 1997; Galileo's Glassworks: The Telescope and the Mirror, 2008; (trans. and intro. with A. van Helden) G. Galilei and C. Scheiner, On Sunspots, 2010. **Address:** Department of Comparative Literature, Princeton University, 125 E Pyne, Princeton, NJ 08544, U.S.A. **Online address:** ereeves@princeton.edu

REEVES, Faye Couch. American (born United States), b. 1953. **Genres:** Theology/Religion, Novels, Plays/Screenplays. **Career:** KBHB Radio, copywriter, 1975-77; Burroughs Corp., account manager, 1977-79; Children's Day Out, teacher, 1980-88; freelance writer, 1988-. **Publications:** My Witness,

1989; Howie Merton and the Magic Dust, 1991; Birthday Wish Mystery, 1994; To Be Surprised by Love: Stories for Those Who Believe Faith Happens When You've Made Other Plans, 2000; Believe!: A Play with Traditional Christmas Music, 2006; Once an Angel, 2007; The Only Christmas Pageant in Town, 2007; Christmas in Comfort, 2008; Scraps: A Story of Fabric and Faith, 2008; On Christmas Day in the Morning: A Play with Tradition Christmas Music, 2009. Contributor to periodicals. **Address:** c/o Andrea Brown, Andrea Brown Literary Agency Inc., 1076 Eagle Dr., Salinas, CA 93905-4466, U.S.A.

REEVES, Marcus. American (born United States), b. 1969. **Genres:** Social Sciences. **Career:** Vibe magazine, staff. Writer. **Publications:** Somebody Scream! Rap Music's Rise to Prominence in the Aftershock of Black Power, 2008. Contributor to periodicals. **Address:** Brooklyn, NY , U.S.A. **Online address:** mreeves2020@gmail.com

REEVES, Thomas C. American (born United States), b. 1936. **Genres:** History, Biography, Theology/Religion. **Career:** Pacific Lutheran University, instructor in history, 1962-63; University of Colorado, assistant professor of history, 1966-70; University of Wisconsin, associate professor of history, 1970-73, professor of history, 1973-2001, retired, 2001; Wisconsin Policy Research Institute, senior fellow, 1992-2007; Wisconsin Association of Scholars, co-founder; American Catholic Historical Association, chairman, 2008. Writer. **Publications:** Freedom and the Foundation: The Fund for the Republic in the Era of McCarthyism, 1969; Gentleman Boss: The Life of Chester Alan Arthur, 1975; The Life and Times of Joe McCarthy, 1982; A Question of Character: A Life of John F. Kennedy, 1991; (intro.) James Lloyd Breck: Apostle of the Wilderness, 1992; The Empty Church: The Suicide of Liberal Christianity, 1996; Twentieth-Century America: A Brief History, 2000; America's Bishop: The Life and Times of Fulton J. Sheen, 2001; Distinguished Service: The Life of Wisconsin Governor Walter J. Kohler, Jr., 2006; (with J. Herrington and R. Oliver) A Guide to Authentic E-learning, 2010. EDITOR: Foundations under Fire, 1970; McCarthyism, 1973, 3rd ed. 1989; James De Koven, Anglican Saint, 1978; John F. Kennedy: The Man, the Politician, the President, 1990. Contributor to periodicals. **Address:** 15725 2 Mile Rd., Franksville, WI 53126-9607, U.S.A.

REEVES-STEVENS, Garfield. Canadian (born Canada), b. 1953?. **Genres:** Air/Space Topics, Novels, Young Adult Non-fiction, History, Adult Non-fiction, Sciences. **Career:** Novelist and television producer. **Publications:** NOVELS: Bloodshift, 1981; Dreamland, 1985; Children of the Shroud, 1987; Nighteyes, 1989; Dark Matter, 1990; (with J. Reeves-Stevens) Shifter, 1990; (with J. Reeves-Stevens) Nightfeeder, 1991; Alien Nation 1: The Day of Descent, 1993; (with J. Reeves-Stevens) Icefire, 1998; (with J. Reeves-Stevens) Quick Silver, 1999; (with J. Reeves-Stevens) Dark Hunter, 2003; (with J. Reeves-Stevens) Freefall, 2005; (with J. Reeves-Stevens) Search: A Novel of Forbidden History, 2010. STAR TREK SERIES: NOVELS WITH J. REEVES-STEVENS: Memory Prime, 1988; Prime Directive, 1990; Star Trek-Prime Directive, 1990; Star Trek: Federation, 1994; Star Trek World in Collision, 2003. NONFICTION: JUDITH REEVES-STEVENS: The Making of Star Trek: Deep Space Nine, 1994; The Art of Star Trek, 1995; Star Trek Phase II: The Lost Series, 1997; Star Trek the Next Generation-The Continuing Mission: A Tenth-Anniversary Tribute, 1998; (with B. Muirhead) Going to Mars: The Stories of the People behind NASAs Mars Missions Past Present and Future, 2004. CONTINUING ADVENTURES OF CAPTAIN KIRK SERIES: WITH WILLIAM SHATNER AND J. REEVES-STEVENS: Star Trek: The Ashes of Eden, 1995; Star Trek: The Return, 1996; Star Trek: Avenger, 1997; Star Trek: Spectre, 1998; Star Trek: Dark Victory, 1999; Star Trek: Preserver, 2000; Star Trek: Captains Peril, 2002; Star Trek: Captains Blood, 2003; Star Trek: Captain's Glory, 2006; Star Trek Academy. Collision Course, 2007. STARTREK DEEP SPACE NINE SERIES: NOVELS WITH JUDITH REEVES-STEVENS: The War of the Prophets, 2000; Inferno, 2000; The Fall of Terok Nor, 2000. **Address:** Martin Shapiro Management, 1010 Lexington Rd., Beverly Hills, CA 90210, U.S.A.

REGALBUTO, Robert J. Also writes as J. Robert Beagle. American (born United States), b. 1949. **Genres:** Travel/Exploration, History, Regional/Urban Planning. **Career:** Writer. **Publications:** (As J.R. Beagle) A Guide to Monastic Guest Houses (travel book), 1989, 4th ed., 2000; Weekend Walks in Historic New England: 45 Self-Guided Walking Tours in Cities, Towns, and Villages, 2003; Weekend Walks in the Historic Washington D.C. Region:

38 Self-Guided Walking Tours in the Capital and Five Surrounding States, 2004. **Address:** About Newport-Guided Tours, PO Box 1209, Newport, RI 02840, U.S.A.

REGALIA, Nanzi. *See* **COLLINS, Nancy A.**

REGAN, Dian Curtis. American (born United States), b. 1950. **Genres:** Young Adult Fiction, Children's Fiction, Science Fiction/Fantasy. **Career:** Hewlett Packard, staff, 1968-71; Colorado Interstate Gas Corp., staff, 1971-78; Denver Adams County School District 12, elementary school teacher, 1980-82; full-time author and speaker, 1982-; Society of Children's Book Writers and Illustrators, regional advisor, 1984-92. **Publications:** GHOST TWINS SERIES: Mystery of One Wish Pond, 1994; The Missing Moose Mystery, 1995; The Mystery of the Disappearing Dogs, 1995; The Haunted Campground Mystery, 1995; The Mystery at Hanover School, 1995; The Mystery of the Haunted Castle, 1995. YOUNG ADULT NOVELS: I've Got Your Number, 1986; The Perfect Age, 1987; Game of Survival, 1989; Jilly's Ghost, 1990; The Initiation, 1993; Princess Nevermore, 1995; Princess Nevermore, new ed., 2007; Cam's Quest, 2007. MIDDLE-GRADE NOVELS: The Kissing Contest, 1990; Liver Cookies, 1991; My Zombie Valentine, 1993; The Vampire Who Came for Christmas, 1993; Home for the Howlidays, 1994; Mystery at Kickingbird Lake, 1994; Mystery on Walrus Mountain, 1995; Monster of the Month Club, 1994; Monsters in the Attic, 1995; Fangs-giving, 1997; Monsters in Cyberspace, 1997; Monsters and My One True Love, 1998. CHAPTER BOOKS: The Class with the Summer Birthdays, 1991; The Curse of the Trouble Dolls, 1992; The Peppermint Race, 1994; The Friendship of Milly and Tug, 1999; The World According to Kaley, 2005; Cyberpals According to Kaley, 2006. ROCKY CAVE KIDS SERIES: The Dragon Stone, 2011. PICTURE BOOKS: Thirteen Hours of Halloween, 1993; Daddies, 1996; Mommies, 1996; Dear Dr. Sillybear, 1997; How Do You Know It's Halloween?, 2002; Eight Nights of Chanukah Lights, 2002; A Sparkly Christmas Eve, 2002; Chance, 2003; How Do You Know It's Easter? 2004; I Know God is Near, 2006; Peek-a-Boo Zoo, 2007; Nice Catch, 2008; Monster Baby, 2009; Barnyard Slam, 2009; The Snow Blew Inn, 2011. ANTHOLOGIES: New Year, New Love, 1996; Dirty Laundry, 1998; Shattered, 2002; Soul Searching, 2002; Period Pieces, 2003; What a Song Can Do, 2004; First Crossing, 2004; Unexpected, 2005; This Family is Driving Me Crazy, 2009. **Address:** 2250 N Rock Rd., Ste. 118-182, Wichita, KS 67226, U.S.A. **Online address:** dian@diancurtisregan.com

REGAN, Linda. British (born England), b. 1959. **Genres:** Novels, Mystery/Crime/Suspense, Young Adult Fiction. **Career:** Actress, 1970-2007. Writer. **Publications:** DI BANHAM AND SERGEANT ALISON GRAINGER CRIME SERIES: Behind You!, 2006; Passion Killers, 2007. NOVELS: Dead Like Her, 2009; Street Girls, 2012. OTHER: Brotherhood of Blades, 2011. **Address:** Andrew Manson Personal Management, 288 Munster Rd., London, GL SW6 6BQ, England. **Online address:** linda@lindareganonline.co.uk

REGAN, Milton C. American (born United States), b. 1952. **Genres:** Law, Politics/Government, Civil Liberties/Human Rights. **Career:** Community Development Block Grant Office, policy analyst, 1978-80; American Federation of State, County and Municipal Employees, economist in public policy, 1980-81; U.S. Court of Appeals for the District of Columbia, law clerk to Judge Ruth Bader Ginsburg, 1985-86; U.S. Supreme Court, law clerk to Justice William J. Brennan, Jr., 1986-87; David Polk and Wardwell, associate, 1987-90; Georgetown University, Georgetown University Law Center, associate professor, 1991-94, professor of law, 1994-, McDevitt professor of jurisprudence, Center for the Study of the Legal Profession, co-director, 2006-. Writer. **Publications:** (With E.C. Richardson) Resource Manual for Civil Litigation for Paralegals, 1992, 2nd ed., 1998; Family Law and the Pursuit of Intimacy, 1993; (ed. with A.L. Allen) Debating Democracy's Discontent, 1998; Alone Together: Law and the Meanings of Marriage, 1999; Eat What You Kill: The Fall of a Wall Street Lawyer, 2004; (with J.D. Bauman) Legal Ethics and Corporate Practice, 2005; (with J. Areen) Family Law: Cases and Materials, 2006. Works appear in anthologies. Contributor to journals. **Address:** Georgetown University Law Center, Georgetown University, Rm. 454, McDonough Hall, 600 New Jersey Ave. NW, Washington, DC 20001, U.S.A. **Online address:** regan@law.georgetown.edu

REGAN, Pamela C. American (born United States), b. 1966. **Genres:** Psychology. **Career:** California State University, Department of Psychology, assistant professor, 1996-99, associate professor of psychology, 1999-2003, professor of psychology, 2003-, Social Relations Lab, director. Writer. **Publications:** (With E. Berscheid) Lust: What We Know about Human Sexual Desire, 1999; The Mating Game: A Primer on Love, Sex, and Marriage, 2003, 2nd ed., 2008; (with E. Berscheid) The Psychology of Interpersonal Relationships, 2004; Close Relationships, 2011. **Address:** Department of Psychology, California State University, KH-D3071, 5151 State University Dr., Los Angeles, CA 90032-8227, U.S.A. **Online address:** pregan@calstatela.edu

REGAN, Stephen. British (born England), b. 1957. **Genres:** Literary Criticism And History, Social Sciences. **Career:** Oxford University, Ruskin College, tutor in literature, 1987-94; Open University-Milton Keynes, lecturer in literature, 1994-2000; University of London, Royal Holloway College, lecturer in English, 2000-04; University of Santiago de Compostela, visiting professor, 2004; Durham University, Department of English studies, professor, 2004-, head of department and chair of the board of studies; The North East Irish Culture Network, co-director; Jagiellonian University, visiting lecturer; Columbus State University, visiting lecturer. Writer. **Publications:** The Idea of the Beautiful in Late Victorian Literature: John Ruskin, Walter Pater, Oscar Wilde and the Poets of the Eighteen Nineties, 1983; Philip Larkin: The Critics Debate, 1992; Raymond William, 1995. EDITOR: George Meredith, 1988; Modern Love, 1989; The Year's Work in English Studies, 1991; The Year's Work in Critical and Cultural Theory, 1991; The Politics of Pleasure: Aesthetics and Cultural Theory, 1992; Philip Larkin: The New Casebook, 1997; The Eagleton Reader, 1998; The Nineteenth-Century Novel: A Critical Reader, 2001; Irish Writing: An Anthology of Irish Literature in English 1789-1939, 2004; (ed. with R.C. Allen) Irelands of the Mind: Memory and Identity in Modern Irish Culture, 2008. **Address:** Department of English Studies, Durham University, Rm. 001, Hallgarth House, Old Elvet, 77 Hallgarth St., Durham City, DU DH1 3AY, England. **Online address:** stephen.regan@durham.ac.uk

REGEHR, T(heodore) D. Canadian (born Canada), b. 1937. **Genres:** History, Social Commentary, Biography, Theology/Religion, Social Sciences, Business/Trade/Industry, Economics. **Career:** Public Archives of Canada, archivist, 1960-68; University of Saskatchewan, Department of History, professor, 1968-96, head, now professor emeritus; University of Calgary, Department of History, adjunct professor, 1996-. Writer. **Publications:** (Ed. and intro.) The Possibilities of Canada Are Truly Great: Memoirs, 1906-1924, 1971; The Canadian Northern Railway: Pioneer Road of the Northern Prairies, 1895-1918, 1976; Remembering Saskatchewan: A History of Rural Saskatchewan, 1979; For Everything a Season: A History of the Alexanderkrone Zentralschule, 1988; The Beauharnois Scandal, 1990; Mennonites in Canada, vol. III: 1939-1970: A People Transformed, 1996; Peace, Order and Good Government: Mennonites and Politics in Canada, 2000; Faith, Life and Witness in the Northwest, 1903-2003: Centennial History of the Northwest Mennonite Conference, 1903-2003, 2003; Generation of Vigilance: The Lives and Work of Johannes and Tina Harder, 2009. Contributor to books and journals. **Address:** Department of History, University of Saskatchewan, 721 Arts Bldg., 9 Campus Dr., Saskatoon, SK S7N 5A5, Canada. **Online address:** tregehr@ucalgary.ca

REGENSTREIF, S(amuel) Peter. American/Canadian (born Canada), b. 1936. **Genres:** Politics/Government, Social Sciences. **Career:** University of Rochester, research associate, 1961-63, assistant professor, professor, 1963-92, professor emeritus of political science and Canadian studies, 1992-. Writer. **Publications:** The Diefenbaker Interlude: Parties and Voting in Canada, an Interpretation, 1965. **Address:** Department of Political Science, University of Rochester, 335 Harkness Hall, Rochester, NY 14627-0146, U.S.A. **Online address:** peter.regenstreif@rochester.edu

REGER, Gary. American (born United States), b. 1954. **Genres:** Economics, Theology/Religion. **Career:** Trinity College, Department of History, assistant professor, 1987-93, associate professor, 1993-2000, professor, 2000-, Hobart professor of classical languages, 2011. Writer. **Publications:** Regionalism and Change in the Economy of Independent Delos, 314-167 B.C., 1994. **Address:** Department of History, Trinity College, Seabury N-044, 300 Summit St., PO Box 702550, Hartford, CT 06106-3100, U.S.A. **Online address:** gary.reger@trincoll.edu

REGER, James P. American (born United States), b. 1952. **Genres:** History, Young Adult Non-fiction, Biography, Civil Liberties/Human Rights, Military/Defense/Arms Control. **Career:** Teacher, 1985-. Writer. **Publications:** FOR YOUNG ADULTS: NONFICTION: (with J. McLennan and P.D. Muller) Topographic Map of Baltimore County, 1985; Earthquakes and Maryland,

1987; Topographic Map of Washington County, 1992; (ed. with D.K. Brezinski) Studies in Maryland Geology: In Commemoration of the Centennial of the Maryland Geological Survey, 1996; The Battle of Antietam, 1996; Customer Survey of Geologic Maps and Other Products and Services of the Maryland Geological Survey, 1997; Life in the South During the Civil War, 1997; The Rebuilding of Bosnia, 1997; Life Among the Indian Fighters, 1998; Civil War Generals of the Confederacy, 1999; Earthquakes in Maryland, 1999; Earthquake Hazard Maps for Maryland, 1999; Baptism at Bull Run, 2004. **Address:** 4703 Caminito Eva, San Diego, CA 92130-3402, U.S.A. **Online address:** jreb1@cox.net

REGINALD, Robert. Also writes as Boden Clarke, C. Everett Cooper, Boden Cooper, Michael Burgess, Miguel Alcalde. American/Japanese (born Japan), b. 1948. **Genres:** Novels, Mystery/Crime/Suspense, Science Fiction/ Fantasy, Genealogy/Heraldry, Literary Criticism And History, Bibliography, Reference. **Career:** California State University, periodicals librarian, 1970-75, assistant librarian, 1975-78, senior assistant librarian, 1978-81, associate librarian, 1981-84, chief cataloger, 1980-94, librarian, 1984-, head of technical services, 1994-2003, head of collection development, 1994-; Unicorn and Son, founder and publisher, 1970; Newcastle Publishing Co., editor, 1971-92; Borgo Press, co-founder, publisher and book editor, 1975-99; Arno Press, advisory editor, 1975-78; Millefleurs Information Services, owner and publisher, 2000-. **Publications:** Stella Nova, 1970; Cumulative Paperback Index, 1939-1959, 1973; Contemporary Science Fiction Authors, 1975; (ed.) Ancestral Voices, 1975; Alistair MacLean: The Key Is Fear, 1976; Ancient Hauntings, 1976; Phantasmagoria, 1976; R.I.P.: 5 Stories of the Supernatural, 1976; The Spectre Bridegroom and Other Horrors, 1976; John D. MacDonald and the Colorful World of Travis McGee, 1977; Things to Come, 1977; Dreamers of Dreams, 1978; King Solomon's Children, 1978; They, 1978; Worlds of Never, 1978; Science Fiction and Fantasy Literature, 1700-1974, 2 vols., 1979; Science Fiction and Fantasy Book Review, 1980; The Paperback Price Guide, 1980, vol. II, 1982; Science Fiction and Fantasy Awards, 1981; The Holy Grail Revealed, 1982; If J.F.K. Had Lived, 1982; Candle for Poland, 1982; Tempest in a Teapot, 1983; The Work of Julian May, 1985; Futurevisions, 1985; The Work of Bruce McAllister, 1985, rev. ed., 1986; (ed.) The Work of Charles Beaumont, 1986; (ed.) The Work of George Zebrowski, 1986, 3rd ed., 1996; Arms Control, Disarmament and Military Security Dictionary, 1989; Hancer's Price Guide to Paperback Books, 1990; Reginald's Science Fiction and Fantasy Awards, 1991, 3rd ed., 1993; Science Fiction and Fantasy Literature 1975-1991, 1992; Polemical Pulps, 1993; George Orwell's Guide through Hell, 1994; St. James Guide to Science Fiction Writers, 1996; BP 250, 1996; Xenograffiti, 1996; Codex Derynianus, 1998; Katydid and Other Critters, 2001; The DarkHaired Man, 2004; The Exiled Prince, 2004; Quaestiones, 2005; Trilobite Dreams or The Autodidact's Tale: A Romance of Autobiography, 2006; Invasion! or Earth vs. the Aliens: A Trilogy of Tales inspired by H.G. Wells's Classic SF Novel, War of the Worlds, 2007. EDITOR AS MIGUEL ALCALDE: Running from the Hunter: The Life and Works of Charles Beaumont, 1996. AS MICHAEL BURGESS: The House of the Burgesses, 1983, (with M.W. Burgess) 2nd ed., 1994; (with M.A. Burgess) The Wickizer Annals, 1983; A Guide to Science Fiction and Fantasy in the Library of Congress Classification Scheme, 1984, 2nd ed., 1988; (with J.M. Elliot) The Work of R. Reginald, 1985, 2nd ed., 1992; Mystery and Detective Fiction in the Library of Congress Classification Scheme, 1987; (with B.A. Ryan) Western Fiction in the Library of Congress Classification Scheme, 1988; (ed. with M.A. Burgess) California Ranchos, 1988, 2nd ed., 2007; (ed. with M.A. Burgess) To Kill or Not to Kill: Thoughts on Capital Punishment, 1990; The Trilemma of World Oil Politics, 1991; A Reference Guide to Science Fiction, Fantasy and Horror, 1992, 2nd ed., 2002; (with M.A. Burgess) The State and Province Vital Records Guide, 1993; (ed. with D.F. Mallett) Geo. Alec Effinger: From Entropy to Budayeen, 1993; Stalin: An Annotated Guide to Books in English, 1993; (ed. with D.F. Mallett) British Science Fiction Paperbacks and Magazines, 1949-1956, 1994, rev. ed., 1995; (ed.) Sermons in Science Fiction, 1994; CSUSB Faculty Authors, Composers and Playwrights, 1965-1995, 1996; (co-ed.) Viva California!: Four Accounts of Life in Early California, 1996; Reference Guide to Science Fiction, Fantasy and Horror, 2002; Eastern Orthodox Churches: Concise Histories with Chronological Checklists of their Primates, 2005; (with J.H. Vassilakos) Murder in Retrospect: A Selective Guide to Historical Mystery Fiction, 2005; (ed. with B.L. Petry) San Quentin: The Evolution of a California State Prison, 2005; (ed.) First Century Palestinian Judaism: An Annotated Guide to Works in English, 2007; (ed. with M.W. Burgess) California Ranchos: Patented Private Land Grants Listed by County, 2007. AS BODEN CLARKE: The Work of Jeffrey M. Elliot, 1984; Lords Temporal and Lords Spiritual, 1985, 2nd ed. (as Michael

Burgess), 1995; The Work of George Zebrowski, 1986, 3rd ed., 1996; (with J. Hopkins) The Work of William F. Nolan, 1988, 2nd ed., 1997; (ed.) The Work of Colin Wilson, 1989; (ed.) The Work of Chad Oliver, 1989; (ed.) The Work of Ross Rocklynne, 1989; (ed.) The Work of Ian Watson, 1989; (ed.) The Work of Reginald Bretnor, 1989; (ed.) The Work of Pamela Sargent, 1990, 2nd ed., 1996; The Work of Jack Dann, 1990; The Work of Charles Beaumont, 2nd ed., 1990; (ed.) The Work of Dean Ing, 1990; (ed.) The Work of Louis L'Amour, 1991; (ed.) The Work of Brian W. Aldiss, 1992; The Work of Katherine Kurtz, 1993; (ed.) The Work of Jack Vance, 1994; (ed.) The Work of Elizabeth Chater, 1994; (ed. with D.F. Mallett) The Work of William Eastlake, 1993; (ed.) The Work of William F. Temple, 1994; (ed. with D.F. Mallett) The Work of Gary Brandner, 1995; (ed.) The Work of Stephen King, 1996. AS C. EVERETT COOPER: Up Your Asteroid, 1977. AS LUCAS WEBB: The Attempted Assassination of John F. Kennedy, 1976. **Address:** PO Box 2845, San Bernardino, CA 92406, U.S.A. **Online address:** borgopr@gte.net

REGINSTER, Bernard. American (born United States) **Genres:** Philosophy. **Career:** Loyola Marymount University, assistant professor, 1992-94; Brown University, assistant professor of philosophy, 1994-2001, associate professor, 2001-07, professor of philosophy, 2007-, Pembroke Center, Chesler-Mallow senior faculty research fellow; Princeton University Center for Human Values, Laurance S. Rockefeller fellow, 1997-98. Writer. **Publications:** The Affirmation of Life: Nietzsche on Overcoming Nihilism, 2006. Contributor to periodicals. **Address:** Department of Philosophy, Brown University, 54 College St., PO Box 1918, Providence, RI 02912-9021, U.S.A. **Online address:** bernard_reginster@brown.edu

REGION, Oscar. See **TRIMPEY, John P.**

REGIS, Edward. American (born United States), b. 1944. **Genres:** Sciences, Adult Non-fiction, Essays, Technology, Biology. **Career:** Salisbury State College, assistant professor of philosophy, 1971-72; Howard University, assistant professor, 1972-76, associate professor of philosophy, 1976-87. Writer. **Publications:** AS ED REGIS: (contrib.) Intersteller Migration and the Human Experience, 1985; Who Got Einstein's Office? Eccentricity and Genius at the Institute for Advanced Study, 1987; Great Mambo Chicken and the Transhuman Condition: Science Slightly over the Edge, 1990; Nano: The Emerging Science of Nanotechnology: Remaking the World-Molecule by Molecule, 1995; Virus Ground Zero: Stalking the Killer Viruses with the Centers for Disease Control, 1996; The Biology of Doom: The History of America's Secret Germ Warfare Project, 1999; The Info Mesa: Science, Business and New Age Alchemy on the Santa Fe Plateau, 2003; What is Life?: Investigating the Nature of Life in the Age of Synthetic Biology, 2008. EDITOR: Gewirth's Ethical Rationalism: Critical Essays with a Reply by Alan Gewirth, 1984; Extraterrestrials: Science and Alien Intelligence, 1985. Contributor to periodicals. **Address:** Oxford University Press, 198 Madison Ave., New York, NY 10016, U.S.A. **Online address:** edregis@aol.com

REGIS, Helen A. American (born United States), b. 1965?. **Genres:** History, Humanities, Anthropology/Ethnology. **Career:** Louisiana State University, Department of Geography and Anthropology, associate professor. Writer. **Publications:** (With J.P. Bartkowski) Charitable Choices: Religion, Race and Poverty in the Post Welfare Era, 2003; Fulbe Voices: Marriage, Islam and Medicine in Northern Cameroon, 2003; (ed.) Caribbean and Southern: Transnational Perspectives on the U.S. South, 2006. Contributor of articles to periodicals. **Address:** Department of Geography and Anthropology, Louisiana State University, 135 Howe-Russell Geoscience Complex, Baton Rouge, LA 70803, U.S.A. **Online address:** hregis1@lsu.edu

REGNERUS, Mark D. American (born United States) **Genres:** Social Sciences, Self Help. **Career:** Carolina Population Center, research associate, 2000-01; Calvin College, assistant professor of sociology, Center for Social Research, director, 2001-02; University of Texas, assistant professor of sociology, 2002-07, Population Research Center, faculty research associate, 2002-, associate professor of sociology and religious studies, 2007-. Writer. **Publications:** (With C. Smith and M. Fritsch) Religion in the Lives of American Adolescents: A Review of the Literature, 2003; Forbidden Fruit: Sex and Religion in the Lives of American Teenagers, 2007; (with J. Uecker) Premarital Sex in America: How Young Americans Meet, Mate, and Think About Marrying, 2011. Contributor to periodicals and journals. **Address:** Department of Sociology, University of Texas, Rm. A1700, 1 University Sta., Austin, TX 78712-0118, U.S.A. **Online address:** regnerus@prc.utexas.edu

REGNERY, Alfred S. American (born United States), b. 1942. **Genres:** Law. **Career:** United States, senate staff, Department of Justice, deputy assistant attorney general for land and natural resources, 1981-82; Office of Juvenile Justice and Delinquency Prevention, administrator, 1982-86; Regnery Publishing Inc., chief executive officer, 1986-2003, publisher, president; The American Spectator, publisher, 2003-. Writer. **Publications:** (With R.J. Leighton) U.S. Direct Marketing Law: The Complete Handbook for Managers, 1993; Upstream: The Ascendance of American Conservatism, 2008. **Address:** The American Spectator, 1611 N Kent St., Ste. 901, Arlington, VA 22209, U.S.A.

REHDER, Ben. American (born United States) **Genres:** Advertising/Public Relations, Novels. **Career:** Freelance writer, 1991-. **Publications:** BLANCO COUNTY, TEXAS SERIES: Buck Fever, 2002; Bone Dry, 2003; Flat Crazy, 2004; Guilt Trip, 2005; Gun Shy, 2007; Holy Moly, 2008; Chicken Hanger, 2012. **Address:** c/o Author Mail, St. Martin's Press, 175 5th Ave., Fl. 21, New York, NY 10010-7703, U.S.A. **Online address:** benrehder@gmail.com

REHDER, William J. American (born United States), b. 1947?. **Genres:** Humor/Satire, Criminology/True Crime, Social Sciences, Adult Non-fiction. **Career:** Federal Bureau of Investigation, special agent, 1966-99. Writer. **Publications:** (With G. Dillow) Where the Money Is: True Tales from the Bank Robbery Capital of the World, 2003. **Address:** c/o Author Mail, W. W. Norton & Co., 500 5th Ave., New York, NY 10110, U.S.A.

REHG, William (Richard). American (born United States), b. 1952. **Genres:** Philosophy. **Career:** Wright-Patterson AFB, Aero-Space Research Labs, researcher, 1974-75; University of Colorado, technician, 1975-76; Rockhurst College, instructor, 1982-84; Northwestern University, teaching assistant, 1988-89; St. Louis University, assistant professor, 1992-97, associate professor of philosophy, 1998-2010, professor of philosophy, 2010-; Goethe-University, visiting professor, 2005; Loyola University, visiting professor, 2006; Saint Joseph's University, Philosophers in Jesuit Education, president, 2010-11. Writer. **Publications:** Insight and Solidarity: A Study in the Discourse Ethics of Jürgen Habermas, 1994; Cogent Science in Context: The Science Wars, Argumentation Theory and Habermas, 2009. TRANSLATOR: A. Honneth, Zwischenbetrachtungenim Prozess der Aufklärung: Jürgen Habermas zum 60, 1989; J. Habermas, Faktizität und Geltung: Beiträge zurDiskurstheorie des Rechts und des demokratischen Rechtsstaats, 1992. CO-EDITOR: Deliberative Democracy: Essays on Reason and Politics, 1997; Pluralism and the Pragmatic Turn: The Transformation of Critical Theory, 2001. **Address:** Department of Philosophy, St. Louis University, Humanities Bldg., 3800 Lindell Blvd., St. Louis, MO 63108, U.S.A. **Online address:** rehgsp@slu.edu

REIBETANZ, John. Canadian/American (born United States), b. 1944. **Genres:** Poetry, Literary Criticism And History, Young Adult Fiction. **Career:** University of Toronto, Victoria College, undergraduate instructor, graduate faculty, professor of English. Writer. **Publications:** The Lear World: A Study of King Lear in Its Dramatic Context, 1977; Ashbourn, 1986; Morning Watch, 1995; Midland Swimmer, 1996; Near Finisterre, 1996; Mining for Sun, 2000; Near Relations, 2005; Transformations, 2006. Works appear in anthologies. Contributor to periodicals. **Address:** Department of English, Victoria College, University of Toronto, 73 Queen's Park Cir. E, Toronto, ON M5S 1K7, Canada. **Online address:** john.reibetanz@utoronto.ca

REICH, Ali. See **KATZ, Bobbi.**

REICH, Christopher. American/Japanese (born Japan), b. 1961. **Genres:** Novels, Adult Non-fiction. **Career:** Union Bank of Switzerland, Mergers & Acquisitions, portfolio manager, staff, through 1991; Giorgio Beverley Hills Timepieces, chief executive officer, 1992-95. Novelist. **Publications:** Numbered Account, 1998; The Runner, 2000; The First Billion: A Novel, 2002; The Devil's Banker, 2003; The Patriot's Club, 2005; Rules of Deception, 2008; Rules of Vengeance, 2009; Rules of Betrayal, 2010. Contributor to periodicals. **Address:** 10602 Pickfair Dr., Austin, TX 78750, U.S.A. **Online address:** chreich@christopherreich.com

REICH, Eugenie Samuel. British/American (born United States), b. 1977?. **Genres:** Physics, Sciences. **Career:** British Broadcasting Corp. (BBC), researcher, 1999-2000; New Scientist, reporting intern, 2000, correspondent, 2001-02, features editor, 2002-05; freelance journalist, 2005-09; MIT Knight science journalism fellow, 2009-10; Nature, reporter, 2010-11, contributing correspondent, 2011-. **Publications:** Plastic Fantastic: How the Biggest Fraud in Physics Shook the Scientific World, 2009. Contributor to periodicals. **Address:** Cambridge, MA , U.S.A. **Online address:** eugenie.reich@gmail.com

REICH, Howard. American (born United States), b. 1954. **Genres:** Biography, Music, Autobiography/Memoirs, History. **Career:** Chicago Tribune, arts critic and jazz music critic, 1977-, staff, 1983-. Writer. **Publications:** Van Cliburn, 1993; (with W. Gaines) Jelly's Blues: The Life, Music and Redemption of Jelly Roll Morton, 2003; The First and Final Nightmare of Sonia Reich: A Son's Memoir, 2006; Let Freedom Swing: Collected Writings on Jazz, Blues, and Gospel, 2010. Contributor to journals. **Address:** Chicago Tribune, TT500, 435 N Michigan Ave., Chicago, IL 60611, U.S.A. **Online address:** hreich@tribune.com

REICH, Lee. American (born United States), b. 1947. **Genres:** Horticulture, Sciences. **Career:** U.S. Department of Agriculture, soil conservationist, 1977-79, Fruit Laboratory, research assistant, 1979-81; Cornell University, research associate, 1981-85; consultant and writer, 1984-; Ulster County Community College, department chairman and assistant professor of horticulture, 1987-89. **Publications:** Uncommon Fruits Worthy of Attention: A Gardener's Guide, 1991; A Northeast Gardener's Year, 1992; Fruits and Berries, 1996; Joy of Pruning, 1996; Growing Fruit in Your Backyard, 1996; The Pruning Book, 1997; Weedless Garden, 2001; Uncommon Fruits for Every Garden, 2004; Landscaping with Fruit, 2009. Contributor to magazines. **Address:** 387 Springtown Rd., New Paltz, NY 12561, U.S.A. **Online address:** garden@leereich.com

REICH, Robert B. (Robert Bernard Reich). American (born United States), b. 1946. **Genres:** Economics, Politics/Government, History, Social Sciences. **Career:** U.S. Department of Justice, assistant solicitor general, 1974-76; Federal Trade Commission, policy planning director, 1976-81; Harvard University, John F. Kennedy School of Government, professor of business and public policy, 1980-93; New Republic, contributing editor, 1982-93; U.S. Government, secretary of labor, 1993-97; Brandeis University, Maurice B. Hexter professor of social and economic policy, 1996-; University of California, Richard and Rhoda Goldman School of Public Policy, professor of public policy, chancellor's professor of public policy; PBS Television, host. **Publications:** (With I.C. Magaziner) Minding America's Business: The Decline and Rise of the American Economy, 1982; The Next American Frontier, 1983; An Industrial Policy for America: Is It Needed?, 1983; (with J.D. Donahue) New Deals: The Chrysler Revival and the American System, 1985; Tales of a New America, 1987, as Tales of a New America: The Anxious Liberal's Guide to the Future, 1988; (ed.) The Power of Public Ideas, 1988; Education and the Next Economy, 1988; The Resurgent Liberal: And Other Unfashionable Prophecies (essays), 1989; Public Management in a Democratic Society, 1990; The Work of Nations: Preparing Ourselves for 21st-Century Capitalism, 1991; The National JTPA Study: Title II-A Impacts on Earnings and Employment at 18 Months, 1993; American Competitiveness and American Brains, 1993; Locked in the Cabinet, 1997; The Future of Success, 2000; I'll Be Short: Essentials for a Decent Working Society, 2002; Reason: Why Liberals Will Win the Battle for America, 2004; Supercapitalism: The Transformation of Business, Democracy and Everyday Life, 2007; Aftershock: The Next Economy and America's Future, 2010. Contributor to periodicals. **Address:** Richard and Rhoda Goldman School of Public Policy, University of California, 203 GSPP Main, 2607 Hearst Ave., Berkeley, CA 94720-7320, U.S.A. **Online address:** bob@robertreich.org

REICH, Robert Bernard. See **REICH, Robert B.**

REICH, Simon (F.). American/British (born England), b. 1959. **Genres:** Economics. **Career:** University of Pittsburgh, assistant professor, 1987-92, associate professor, 1992-96, professor of political science, 1996-, Ford Institute for Human Security, director; U.S. Office of Technology Assessment, contractor, 1993-94; American Institute for Contemporary Studies, visiting fellow, 1995; Royal Institute of International Affairs, director of research and analysis, 2000-01; Rutgers University, professor of global affairs, The Division of Global Affairs, director, 2008; University of Minnesota, lecturer; Georgetown University, lecturer; University of California-San Diego, lecturer; University of California-Berkeley, lecturer. Writer. **Publications:** The Fruits of Fascism: Postwar Prosperity in Historical Perspective, 1990; (ed. with A.S. Markovits and M. Huelshoff) From Bundesrepublik to Deutschland: German Politics after Unification, 1993; (with W. Keller, C. Evans and others) Multinational Corporations and the National Interest: Playing by Different Rules, 1993; (with Keller, P. Doremus and L. Pauly) Multinationals and the U.S. Technology Base, 1994; (with A.S. Markovits) The German Predicament: Memory and Power in the New Europe, 1997; (with Keller, Pauly and Doremus) The Myth of the Global Corporation, 1998; Research Findings about Ford-Werke under the Nazi Regime, 2001; (ed. with H.R. Friman) Human Trafficking, Human Security, and the Balkans, 2007; (ed. with A.C. d'Appollonia) Immigration, Integration, and Security: America and Europe in Comparative Perspective, 2008; (ed. with A.C. d'Appollonia) Managing Ethnic Diversity After 9/11: Integration, Security, and Civil Liberties in Transatlantic Perspective, 2010; (ed. with S. Gates) Child Soldiers in the Age of Fractured States, 2010; Global Norms, American Sponsorship and the Emerging Patterns of World Politics, 2010. Contributor of articles to journals. **Address:** Ford Institute for Human Security, University of Pittsburgh, 3937 Wesley W Posvar Hall, 230 S Bouquet St., Pittsburgh, PA 15260, U.S.A. **Online address:** reichs@pitt.edu

REICHARDT, Mary R. American (born United States), b. 1956. **Genres:** Literary Criticism And History, Theology/Religion, Women's Studies And Issues, Young Adult Fiction. **Career:** University of St. Thomas, Department of Catholic Studies, associate professor, professor of catholic studies and literature, 1988-, Catholic Studies Master's Program, director, 2000-05, Catholic Studies in Rome Program, faculty director, 2000, 2004; consultant, 1992-. Writer. **Publications:** (Comp.) The Uncollected Stories of Mary Wilkins Freeman, 1992; A Web of Relationship: Women in the Short Stories of Mary Wilkins Freeman, 1992; (ed.) A Mary Wilkins Freeman Reader, 1997; Mary Wilkins Freeman: A Study of the Short Fiction, 1997; (ed.) Catholic Women Writers: A Bio-Bibliographical Sourcebook, 2001; Exploring Catholic Literature: A Companion and Resource Guide, 2003; (ed.) An Encyclopedia of Catholic Literature, 2 vols., 2004; (ed.) Scarlet Letter: With an Introduction and Contemporary Criticism, 2009; (ed.) Adventures of Huckleberry Finn: With an Introduction and Contemporary Criticism, 2009; (ed. with J. Pearce) Uncle Tom's Cabin, 2009; (ed. with J. Pearce) Study Guide for Adventures of Huckleberry Finn, 2009; (ed.) Between Human and Divine: The Catholic Vision in Contemporary Literature, 2010; (ed.) Moby-Dick, 2011. **Address:** Department of Catholic Studies, University of St. Thomas, 300 Sitzmann Hall, 2115 Summit Ave., St. Paul, MN 55105, U.S.A. **Online address:** mrreichardt@stthomas.edu

REICHE, Dietlof. German (born Germany), b. 1941. **Genres:** Novels. **Career:** Graphic designer, 1990-98; Hochschulinstitut für Ergonomie, staff. Writer. **Publications:** Freddy. Ein wildes Hamsterleben, 1998; Freddy. Ein Hamster lebt gefährlich, 1999; Freddy. Ein Hamster greift ein, 2000; Freddy und die Frettchen des Schreckens, 2001; Freddy. Ein Hamster ist verliebt, 2003. NOVELS: Der Bleisiegelfälscher: Dieser Roman spielt im Jahre 1613 in d. Freien Reichsstadt Nördlingen, 1977; Der verlorene Frühling: d. Geschichte von Louise Coith u.d. Lokomotivheizer Hannes Bühn, d. zum Barrikadenbauer wurde: Frankfurt 1848, 1979; Wie Spreu vor dem Wind, 1981; Geisterschiff, 2002; Zeit der Freiheit, 2003. **Address:** c/o Author Mail, Verlagsgruppe Beltz, PO Box 10 05 65, Weinheim, D-69445, Germany. **Online address:** dietlof.reiche@dreiche.de

REICHEL, Aaron I(srael). American (born United States), b. 1950. **Genres:** How-to Books, Law, Writing/Journalism, Theology/Religion, History, Business/Trade/Industry. **Career:** Prentice-Hall Inc., Legal Publishing Division, attorney and editor, 1977-89; Harry and Jane Fischel Foundation, board director, 1977-; New York Greater City Area, attorney at law, 1978-; West Side Institutional Synagogue, board director, 1987-; Warren, Gorham & Lamont, attorney editor, 1989-90; A. Edward Major Firm, associate, 1990-91; Allen L. Rothenberg Firm, associate, 1991-93. **Publications:** The Maverick Rabbi: Rabbi Herbert S. Goldstein and the Institutional Synagogue-A New Organizational Form, 1984, 2nd ed., 1986; (co-author) Style and Usage Manual, 1985; Back to the Past for Inspiration for the Future: West Side Institutional Synagogue Jubilee, 1937-1987, 1987; Fahrenheit 9-12: Rebuttal to Fahrenheit 9/11, 2004. EDITOR: The Yeshiva College Alumni Bulletin, 1974-78; Government Disclosure Service, 4 vols., 1978-83. EDITOR AND CONTRIBUTOR: The 1986 Jewish Directory and Almanac, 1985; (with A.S. Robinson) Prentice-Hall's Explanation of the Tax Reform Act of 1986, 1986; (with A.S. Robinson) A Complete Guide to the Tax Reform Act of 1986, 1986; The 1987-1988 Jewish Almanac, 1987; (co-author) Prentice-Hall's Explanation of the Technical and Miscellaneous Revenue Act of 1988, 1988. Contributor to periodicals. **Address:** Warren, Gorham & Lamont, 1 Penn Plz., New York, NY 10119, U.S.A.

REICHENBACH, Bruce. (Bruce R. Reichenbach). American (born United States), b. 1943. **Genres:** Philosophy. **Career:** Augsburg College, professor of philosophy, 1968-; Morija Theological Seminary, visiting professor, 1976-77; Juniata College, distinguished visiting professor of evangelical Christianity, 1985-86; Daystar University, visiting professor, 1998, 2005, 2007; Luther Theological Seminary, adjunct professor, 2000-; United International College, visiting professor of philosophy, 2009. Writer. **Publications:** AS BRUCE R. REICHENBACH: The Cosmological Argument: A Reassessment, 1972; Is Man the Phoenix?: A Study of Immortality, 1978; Evil and a Good God, 1982; The Law of Karma: A Philosophical Study, 1990; (co-author) Reason and Religious Belief, An Introduction to the Philosophy of Religion, 1991, 4th ed., 2009; (with V.E. Anderson) On Behalf of God: A Christian Ethic for Biology, 1995; Introduction to Critical Thinking, 2001; (co-author) Philosophy of Religion: Selected Readings, 4th ed., 2010. Contributor to journals and books. **Address:** Department of Philosophy, Augsburg College, 2211 Riverside Ave., PO Box 129, Minneapolis, MN 55440-0129, U.S.A. **Online address:** reichen@augsburg.edu

REICHENBACH, Bruce R. See **REICHENBACH, Bruce.**

REICHERT, Tom. American (born United States) **Genres:** History, Sex, Marketing, Popular Culture, Communications/Media. **Career:** Orange County Register, account executive, 1989-91; University of Arizona, Graduate Students in Communication Association, vice president, 1994-95; University of North Texas, College of Arts and Sciences, Department of Journalism, lecturer, 1996-98, assistant professor, 1998-2001; University of Alabama, College of Communication and Information Sciences, Department of Advertising and Public Relations, assistant professor, 2001-03, associate professor, 2003-04; University of Georgia, Grady College of Journalism and Mass Communication, Department of Advertising and Public Relations, associate professor, 2004-09, assistant department head, 2006-10, professor, 2009-, department head, 2010-. Writer. **Publications:** (With S.E. Morgan and T.R. Harrison) From Numbers to Words: Reporting Statistical Results for the Social Sciences, 2002; (ed. with J. Lambiase) Sex in Advertising: Perspectives on the Erotic Appeal, 2003; The Erotic History of Advertising, 2003; (ed. with J. Lambiase) Sex in Consumer Culture: The Erotic Content of Media and Marketing, 2006; (with M.A. Shaver) Make the Sale: How to Sell Media with Marketing, 2006; (ed.) Investigating the Use of Sex in Media Promotion and Advertising, 2007; Issues in American Advertising, vol. I: Sex, Politics and Viral Videos, 2007, (ed.) vol. II: Media, Society and a Changing World, 2008; (with W.R. Lane and K.W. King) Kleppner's Advertising Procedure, 2011. Contributor to books and periodicals. **Address:** Department of Advertising & Public Relations, Grady College of Journalism & Mass Communication, University of Georgia, Rm. 216, Journalism Bldg. 120 Hooper St., Athens, GA 30602, U.S.A. **Online address:** reichert@grady.uga.edu

REICHERTZ, Ronald R. Canadian/American (born United States), b. 1933. **Genres:** Poetry, Literary Criticism And History, How-to Books, Children's Fiction. **Career:** McGill University, professor of literature, 1965-96, retired, 1996. Writer. **Publications:** A Belated Lament for the Irish Giant (poems), 1987; The Making of the Alice Books: Lewis Carroll's Uses of Earlier Children's Literature, 1997. **Address:** 1970 Haro St., Vancouver, BC V6G 1H8, Canada.

REID, Alastair. American/Spanish/Scottish (born Scotland), b. 1926. **Genres:** Novels, Children's Fiction, Poetry, Essays, Translations, Young Adult Fiction, Reference. **Career:** Sarah Lawrence College, faculty, 1950-55; The New Yorker, staff writer and correspondent, 1959-; Columbia University, fellow, 1966; Association of American Colleges, lecturer, 1966, 1969; Latin American Studies, Antioch College, visiting professor, 1969-70; Latin American Literature, Oxford University, seminar instructor, 1972-73; Saint Andrews University, seminar instructor, 1972-73. Writer. **Publications:** To Lighten My House: Poems, 1953; I Will Tell You of a Town, 1955; Fairwater, 1956; A Balloon for a Blunderbuss, 1957; Allth, 1958; Ounce Dice Trice, 1958; (with B. Gill) Millionaires, 1959; Supposing, 1960; Oddments Inklings Omens Moments: Poems, 1959; A Ballon for a Blunderbuss, 1961; Passwords: Places, Poems, Preoccupations, 1963; To Be Alive, 1966; Uncle Timothy's Traviata, 1967; Discurso pronunciado con ocasión de la entrega del premio Nobel de literatura, 1971, 1972; Weathering: Poems and Translations, 1978; (ed. with E. Rodriguez Monegal) Borges: A Reader, 1981; Whereabouts: Notes on Being a Foreigner, 1987; Eternal Spain: The Spanish Rural Landscape, 1991; Ariel y Calibán: cró nicas de fútbol, 1994; An Alastair Reid Reader, 1995; Oases: Poems and Prose, 1997; Outside in: Selected Prose, 2008; Inside Out: Selected Poetry and Translations, 2008. TRANSLATOR:

(with A. Kerrigan) Mother Goose in Spanish, 1967; We Are Many, 1968; (with A. Kerrigan) J.L. Borges: A Personal Anthology, 1967; (with B. Belitt) A New Decade: Poems 1958-1967, 1968; Extravagaria, 1972; La Isla Azul, 1973; Sunday Sunday, 1973; P. Neruda, Fully Empowered, 1975; The Gold of the Tigers: Selected Later Poems: A Bilingual Edition, 1977; Don't Ask Me How the Time Goes By: Poems 1964-1968, 1978; Isla Negra, 1979; (with A. Horley) Legacies: Selected Poems, 1982; Suite Lirica: en homenaje a Wallace Stevens, 1982; Pablo Neruda: Absence and Presence, 1990; (with L. Clark) The Man Who Counted, 1993; F. Savater, Amador, 1994; On The Blue Shore of Silence: Poems of the Sea A La Orilla Azul Del Silencio, 2003; Antipodes, 2004; Intimacies, 2008. **Address:** The New Yorker, 4 Times Sq., New York, NY 10036, U.S.A.

REID, Andrew H. British/American (born United States), b. 1940?. **Genres:** Psychiatry, Medicine/Health. **Career:** Ninewells Hospital and Medical School, University Department of Psychiatry, honorary senior lecturer in psychiatry, 1972-2003; Dundee Psychiatric Services, consultant psychiatrist. Writer. **Publications:** The Psychiatry of Mental Handicap, 1982. **Address:** The Cottage, 36 Main St., Longforgan, Dundee, DD2 5ET, Scotland. **Online address:** margo.reid@btinternet.com

REID, Catherine. American (born United States), b. 1955?. **Genres:** Natural History, Gay And Lesbian Issues, Autobiography/Memoirs, Sex. **Career:** Warren Wilson College, Undergraduate Writing Program, faculty; Deerfield River Watershed Association, board secretary. Writer. **Publications:** (Ed. with H.K. Iglesias) Every Woman Ive Ever Loved: Lesbian Writers on Their Mothers, 1997; (ed. with H.K. Iglesias) His Hands His Tools His Sex His Dress: Lesbian Writers on Their Fathers, 2001; Coyote: Seeking the Hunter in Our Midst, 2004; Writing the Nature of Our Lives, forthcoming. Contributor to books. **Address:** Warren Wilson College, CPO 6192, 701 Warren Wilson Rd., PO Box 9000, Asheville, NC 28815-9000, U.S.A. **Online address:** creid@warren-wilson.edu

REID, Cindy. American (born United States), b. 1964?. **Genres:** Sports/Fitness. **Career:** US Golf Channel, staff; Tournament Players Club, director of instruction; Cindy Reid Golf Enterprises Ltd., chief executive officer; Cindy Reid Publishing House Ltd., chief executive officer. Writer. **Publications:** (With S. Eubanks) Cindy Reid's Ultimate Guide to Golf for Women, 2003; (with S. Eubanks) Get Yourself in Golf Shape: Year-Round Drills to Build a Strong, Flexible Swing, 2005. Contributor to periodicals. **Address:** Cindy Reid Golf Enterprise Ltd., 8th Fl. Gloucester Twr., 15 Queen's Rd., Central, 2, Hong Kong. **Online address:** crga@cindyreidgolf.com

REID, David. Scottish (born Scotland), b. 1940. **Genres:** Literary Criticism And History. **Career:** University of Salonica, lecturer in English, 1963-64; University of New Hampshire, instructor in English, 1964-66; University of British Columbia, lecturer in English, 1966-68; University of Stirling, lecturer in English studies, 1974-, now retired. Writer. **Publications:** (Ed.) The Party-Coloured Mind: Prose Relating to the Conflict of Church and State in Seventeenth Century Scotland, 1982; (ed. and intro.) Rob Stene's Dream, 1989; The Humanism of Milton's Paradise Lost, 1993; (ed.) David Hume of Godscroft's The History of the House of Douglas, 1996; The Metaphysical Poets, 2000; (ed.) David Hume of Godscroft's The History of the House of Angus, 2005. **Address:** 29A Snowdon Pl., Stirling, FK8 2JP, Scotland.

REID, Elwood. American (born United States) **Genres:** Novellas/Short Stories, Sports/Fitness, Young Adult Fiction, Mystery/Crime/Suspense, Social Sciences, Novels. **Career:** Novelist, screenwriter, carpenter and educator. **Publications:** If I Don't Six (novel), 1998; What Salmon Know (short stories), 1999; Midnight Sun (novel), 2000; D.B. (novel), 2004. Contributor of short stories to periodicals. **Address:** c/o Author Mail, Random House Inc., 1745 Broadway, New York, NY 10019, U.S.A.

REID, Harry M. American (born United States), b. 1939. **Genres:** Politics/Government. **Career:** State of Nevada, lieutenant governor, 1971-75; Nevada Gaming Commission, chair, 1977-81; U.S. Senate, senator, 1987-, minority whip, 1999-2001, 2003-05, majority whip, 2001-03, minority leader, 2005-07, majority leader, 2007-. Writer and politician. **Publications:** Searchlight: The Camp That Didn't Fail, 1998; The Good Fight: Hard Lessons from Searchlight to Washington, 2008. **Address:** 600 E William St., Ste. 302, Carson City, NV 89701, U.S.A.

REID, John P(hillip). American (born United States), b. 1930. **Genres:** History, Law, Biography, Politics/Government. **Career:** New York University School of Law, instructor, 1960-62, assistant professor, 1962-64, associate professor, 1964-66, professor of law, 1966-94, Russell D. Niles professor of law, 1994-2003, Russell D. Niles professor of law emeritus, 2003-. Writer. **Publications:** Chief Justice: The Judicial World of Charles Doe, 1967; An American Judge: Marmaduke Dent of West Virginia, 1968; A Law of Blood: The Primitive Law of the Cherokee Nation, 1970; A Better Kind of Hatchet: Law, Trade, and Diplomacy in the Cherokee Nation during the Early Years of European Contact, 1976; In a Defiant Stance: The Conditions of Law in Massachusetts Bay, the Irish Comparison; and the Coming of the American Revolution, 1977; In a Rebellious Spirit: The Argument of Facts, the Liberty Riot, and the Coming of the American Revolution, 1979; Law for the Elephant: Property and Social Behavior on the Overland Trail, 1980; In Defiance of the Law: The Standing-Army Controversy, the Two Constitutions, and the Coming of the American Revolution, 1981; (ed.) The Briefs of the American Revolution: Constitutional Arguments between Thomas Hutchinson, Governor of Massachusetts Bay, and James Bowdoin for the Council and John Adams for the House of Representatives, 1981; (with W.E. Nelson) Literature of American Legal History, 1985; Constitutional History of the American Revolution, vol. I: The Authority of Rights, 1986, vol. II: The Authority to Tax, 1987, vol. III: The Authority to Legislate, 1991, vol. IV: The Authority of Law, 1993; The Concept of Liberty in the Age of the American Revolution, 1988; The Concept of Representation in the Age of the American Revolution, 1989; Policing the Elephant: Crime, Punishment, and Social Behavior on the Overland Trail, 1997; Patterns of Vengeance: Crosscultural Homicide in the North American fur Trade, 1999; Contested Empire: Peter Skene Ogden and the Snake River Expeditions, 2002; Controlling the Law: Legal Politics in Early National New Hampshire, 2004; Rule of Law: The Jurisprudence of Liberty in the Seventeenth and Eighteenth Centuries, 2004; The Ancient Constitution and the Origins of Anglo-American Liberty, 2005; Legislating the Courts: Judicial Dependence in Early National New Hampshire, 2009; Forging a Fur Empire: Expeditions in the Snake River Country, 1809-1824, 2011. Contributor of articles to books and journals. **Address:** New York University School of Law, Rm. 401, 40 Washington Sq. S, New York, NY 10012-1005, U.S.A. **Online address:** john.reid@nyu.edu

REID, Julia. British (born England), b. 1974. **Genres:** Sciences, Reference. **Career:** University of Leeds, lecturer in Victorian literature. Writer. **Publications:** Robert Louis Stevenson, Science and the Fin de Siècle, 2006. Contributor to journals. **Address:** School of English, University of Leeds, Woodhouse Ln., Leeds, WY LS2 9JT, England. **Online address:** j.h.m.reid@leeds.ac.uk

REID, Loren. (Loren Dudley Reid). American (born United States), b. 1905. **Genres:** History, Speech/Rhetoric, Biography, Education. **Career:** Vermillion High School, teacher, 1927-29; University of Iowa, instructor, 1930-33; Westport High School, instructor, 1933-35; University of Missouri, Department of Speech and Dramatic Art, instructor, 1935-37, assistant professor, 1937-38, professor of speech, 1944-75, chairperson, 1947-52, 1966-67, professor emeritus, 1975-; Syracuse University, associate professor of speech and education, 1939-44; University of Maryland, visiting professor of German and English, 1952-53, 1960-61, visiting professor of English, 1955; University of Hawaii, Carnegie visiting professor, 1957. Writer. **Publications:** Charles James Fox: A Study of the Effectiveness of an Eighteenth Century Parliamentary Speaker, 1932; Course Book in Public Speaking, 1937, (with W.E. Gilman and B. Aly as Loren D. Reid) 2nd ed., 1939; Teaching Speech in the High School, 1952, 4th ed. as Teaching Speach, 1971; First Principles of Public Speaking, 1960, 2nd ed., 1962; (ed.) American Public Address: Studies in Honor of Albert Craig Baird, 1961; Speaking Well, 1962, 4th ed., 1982; Charles James Fox: A Man for the People, 1969; Hurry Home Wednesday: Growing Up in a Small Missouri Town, 1905-1921, 1978; Finally It's Friday: School and Work in Mid-America, 1921-1933, 1981; Speech Teacher: A Random Narrative, 1990; Professor on the Loose, 1992. Contributor of articles to journals. **Address:** Department of Communication, University of Missouri, 115 Switzler Hall, Columbia, MO 65211-2310, U.S.A.

REID, Loren Dudley. See REID, Loren.

REID, Richard M. Canadian (born Canada), b. 1943?. **Genres:** History. **Career:** University of Guelph, professor. Writer. **Publications:** (Ed.) The Upper Ottawa Valley to 1855: A Collection of Documents, 1990; Freedom for Themselves: North Carolina's Black Soldiers in the Civil War Era, 2008;

(ed.) Practicing Medicine in a Black Regiment: The Civil War Diary of Burt G. Wilder, 55th Massachusetts, 2010. **Address:** Canada. **Online address:** rreid@uoguelph.ca

REID, Robert Leonard. American (born United States), b. 1943. **Genres:** Natural History, Travel/Exploration. **Career:** Author and musician, 1975-; Riverdale Country School, teacher; Collegiate School, teacher; University of New Mexico, faculty; Western Nevada College, faculty. **Publications:** (Ed.) A Treasury of the Sierra Nevada, 1983; Mountains of the Great Blue Dream, 1991; America, New Mexico, 1998; Arctic Circle: Birth and Rebirth in the Land of the Caribou, 2009. **Address:** Carson City, NV , U.S.A. **Online address:** birdortree@charter.net

REID, Theresa. American (born United States) **Genres:** Autobiography/Memoirs. **Career:** American Professional Society on the Abuse of Children (APSAC), executive director, 1988-97; Chicago Children Advocacy Center, president of the board, 1999-2002; Journal of Interpersonal Violence, managing editor; APSAC Advisor, executive editor; APSAC Practice Guidelines, executive editor; Child Maltreatment, executive editor. **Publications:** Two Little Girls: A Memoir of Adoption, 2006. **Address:** Ann Arbor, MI , U.S.A. **Online address:** theresa@theresareidbooks.com

REID, T. R. British/American (born United States) **Genres:** Documentaries/Reportage, Medicine/Health, Sciences, History, Anthropology/Ethnology, Translations. **Career:** Washington Post, journalist, 1977-; National Geographic Radio, contributor; National Public Radio, contributor. **Publications:** Congressional Odyssey: The Saga of a Senate Bill, 1980; The Chip: How Two Americans Invented the Microchip and Launched a Revolution, 1984, rev. ed., 2001; Microchip: The Story of a Revolution and the Men Who Made it, 1985; Tomu no Me Tomu no Mimi: Nihonjin no Kigatsukanai Nippon no Sugata, 1994; Ski Japan!, 1994; (trans.) K. Inamori, For People-And for Profit: A Business Philosophy for the Twenty-first-Century, 1997; Confucius Lives Next Door: What Living in the East Teaches Us about Living in the West, 1999; United States of Europe: The New Superpower and the End of American Supremacy, 2004; Healing of America: A Global Quest for Better, Cheaper, and Fairer Health Care, 2009. **Address:** Washington Post, 1150 15th St. NW, Washington, DC 20071-0001, U.S.A.

REID, Van. American (born United States) **Genres:** Novels, Sports/Fitness, History. **Career:** Maine Coast Book Shop, assistant manager, 1991. Writer. **Publications:** MOOSEPATH LEAGUE SERIES: Cordelia Underwood, or, The Marvelous Beginnings of the Moosepath League, 1998; Mollie Peer or The Underground Adventure of the Moosepath League, 1999; Daniel Plainway, or, The Holiday Haunting of the Moosepath League, 2000; Peter Loon: A Novel, 2002; Mrs. Roberto or The Widowy Worries of the Moosepath League, 2003; Fiddler's Green or A Wedding, A Ball and the Singular Adventures of Sundry Moss, 2004. **Address:** Viking Penguin, 375 Hudson, New York, ME 10014, U.S.A. **Online address:** vanreid@midcoast.com

REIDEL, James. American (born United States), b. 1950?. **Genres:** Biography, Translations, Young Adult Fiction, Children's Fiction, Autobiography/Memoirs, Poetry. **Career:** Poet, translator and biographer. **Publications:** (Ed.) Limericks to Friends, 1985; (ed.) Reviews and Essays, 1936-55, 1988; (ed.) Fall Quarter, 1990; (with C. Skintik) Learning Macromedia Dreamweaver 3 & 4, 2001; Vanished Act: The Life and Art of Weldon Kees, 2003; (trans.) T. Bernhard, In Hora Mortis: Under the Iron of the Moon (poems), 2006; (ed. with C. Forché) Arrival, 2009; (ed. and intro.) Love is Like Park Avenue, 2009; (trans.) F. Werfel, Pale Blue Ink in a Lady's Hand: A Novel, 2011. Contributor to periodicals. **Address:** 3195 N Farmcrest Dr., Cincinnati, OH 45213-1111, U.S.A. **Online address:** jreidel@cinci.rr.com

REIKEN, Frederick. American (born United States), b. 1966. **Genres:** Novels, Young Adult Non-fiction. **Career:** Israeli Nature Reserves Authority, wildlife biologist, 1988-89; Cummington Community of the Arts, assistant director, 1992-93; Daily Hampshire Gazette, reporter, nature writer and columnist, 1992-98; Emerson College, assistant professor of writing and literature, director of the graduate program in writing. **Publications:** NOVELS: The Odd Sea, 1998; The Lost Legends of New Jersey, 2000; Ein Tag wie Kein Anderer, 2002; Day for Night, 2010. Contributor of articles to periodicals. **Address:** c/o Gail Hochman, Brandt & Hochman Literary Agents Inc., 1501 Broadway, New York, NY 10036, U.S.A.

REILLY, Bernard F. American (born United States), b. 1925. **Genres:** History, Novels, Military/Defense/Arms Control. **Career:** Villanova University, instructor, associate professor, 1955-71, professor of medieval history, 1972-, now professor emeritus; Pennsylvania University, Symposium in Medieval Studies, fellow, 1979-83; Library of Congress, Prints and Photographs Division, chief curator; Chicago Historical Society, Department of Research and Access, faculty, 1997-2001; Center for Research Libraries, president, 2001-. Writer. **Publications:** The Kingdom of León-Castilla Under Queen Urraca, 1109-1126, 1982; (ed. and contrib.) Santiago, Saint-Denis, and Saint Peter: Reception of the Roman Liturgy in León-Castile in 1080, 1985; The Kingdom of León-Castila Under King Alfonso VI, 1065-1109, 1988; The Contest of Christian and Muslim Spain, 1031-1157, 1992; The Medieval Spains, 1993; The Treasure of the Vanquished: A Novel of Visigothic Spain, 1994; The Secret of Santiago: A Novel of Medieval Spain, 1997; The Kingdom of León-Castila under King Alfonso VII, 1126-1157, 1998; Journey to Compostela: A Novel of Medieval Pilgrimage and Peril, 2001. Contributor of articles to journals. **Address:** Department of History, Villanova University, St. Augustine Ctr., Rm. 403, 800 Lancaster Ave., Villanova, PA 19085, U.S.A. **Online address:** breilly@crl.edu

REILLY, James. Canadian/American (born United States), b. 1954. **Genres:** History. **Career:** American University of Beirut, Department of History and Archaeology, instructor, 1979-80; University of Toronto, Department of Middle East and Islamic Studies, assistant professor, 1987-92, Department of Near and Middle Eastern Civilizations, associate professor, 1992-2003, chair, 2001-06, professor, 2003-. Writer. **Publications:** A Small Town in Syria: Ottoman Hama in the Eighteenth and Nineteenth Centuries, 2002. **Address:** Department of Near and, Middle Eastern Civilizations, University of Toronto, 4 Bancroft Ave., 2nd Fl., Toronto, ON M5S 1C1, Canada. **Online address:** james.reilly@utoronto.ca

REILLY, Kevin. American (born United States), b. 1941. **Genres:** History, Young Adult Non-fiction. **Career:** Raritan Valley Community College, professor of history, 1969-, humanities chair, 1988-92; Columbia University Teachers College, adjunct professor, 1988-89; Rutgers University, adjunct professor, 1991-92; Princeton University, visiting professor of history, 1992-94. Writer. **Publications:** The West and the World: A Topical History of Civilization, 1980, 2nd ed., 1988; (ed.) The Introductory History Course: Proceedings of the AHA Annapolis Conference on the Introductory History Course, 1984; World History, 1984, 4th ed., 1999; Readings in World Civilizations, 1988, 3rd ed., 1995; The West and the World: A History of Civilization from the Ancient World to 1700, 1997; (ed.) Worlds of History: A Comparative Reader, 2000, 4th ed., 2010; The West and the World: A History of Civilization from 1400 to the Present, 2002; Racism: A Global Reader, 2003. Contributor of books to periodicals. **Address:** Raritan Valley Community College, 118 Lamington Rd., Rm. S-319, Branchburg, NJ 08876, U.S.A. **Online address:** kreilly@raritanval.edu

REIMANN, Katya. American (born United States), b. 1965?. **Genres:** Science Fiction/Fantasy, Novels, Young Adult Fiction. **Career:** Freelance writer. **Publications:** FANTASY NOVELS CHRONICLES OF TIELMARK SERIES: Wind from a Foreign Sky, 1996; A Tremor in the Bitter Earth, 1998; Prince of Fire and Ashes, 2002; (with C. Wilder) Wanderer, 2004; Patternmaker, forthcoming; Pocketclock, forthcoming. **Address:** Tor Books, Tom Doherty Associates Inc., 175 5th Ave., New York, NY 10010, U.S.A. **Online address:** katyareimann@hotmail.com

REIN, Raanan. Israeli (born Israel), b. 1960. **Genres:** History. **Career:** IDF radio station, foreign news editor, 1979-82; Hadashot newspaper, commentaries on foreign affairs, 1982-84, foreign news editor, 1984-87; Estudios Interdisciplinarios de America Latina yel Caribe, associate editor, 1992-97; Tel Aviv University, Department of History, lecturer, 1992-96, senior lecturer, 1996-98, associate professor, 1998-2001, Institute of Latin American History and Culture, director, 2000-04, professor, 2001-, Wolf Foundation Fellow, 1992-94, vice rector; Zmanim, co-editor, 1995; University of Maryland, research fellow in history and at Latin American studies center, 1999-2000, Faculty of Humanities, chair, 2003-05, The S. Daniel Abraham Center for International and Regional Studies, head, 2004-, vice rector, 2005-, School of Communications, chair, 2007-, chair and board director, 2007-09, vice president, 2012-; Emory University, deans research professor, 2004; Latin American Jewish Studies Association, co-director. **Publications:** (Contrib.) La politica argentina, 1930- 1955, 1992; The FrancoPerónAlliance: Relations between Spain and Argentina, 1946-1955, 1993; Salvación de una dictadura, 1995; Betsel haShoah vehaInkvizitsyah, 1995; Franco, Israel y los judíos,

1996; In the Shadow of the Holocaust and the Inquisition: Israels Relations with Francoist Spain, 1995, rev. ed., 1997; (ed. with T. Medin) Society and Identity in Argentian: The European Context, 1997; Hòevrah vòezehutbeArgentòinah: Hahekòsher haEropi, 1997; Populizmyekarizmah, 1998; Populism and Charisma: Peróns Argentina, 1998; Mekòsikòo leahòar ha-mahpekhah: Hevrahu-fpolitòikòah, 1910-1952, 1999; Ha Fashizm lo yaavor: MilhemethaEzrahim biSefarad, 1936-1939, 2000; Argentina, Israel y los judíos: encuentros y des encuentros, mitos y realidades, 2001; Argenţinah, Yiśrael vehaYehudim, 2002; Argentina, Israel, and the Jews: Perón, the Eichmann Capture and After, 2002; (comp.) Transiciones de la dictadura a la democracia, 2005; (comp.) Primer Peronismo: de regreso a los comienzos, 2005; Juan Atilio Bramuglia: Bajola Sombra del liider: La segunda liinea de Liderazgo Peronista, 2006; Mi-hòuts LezziratHashevòarim: Sefarad Ba-meah haaśerim, 2007; Argentina, Israel y los judíos: de la partición de Palestina al caso Eichmann (1947-1962), 2007; (with orkhim and T. Groves) Miḫuts lezirat hasheyarim: Sefarad bameah haeśrim, 2007; In the Shadow of Peron: Juan Atilio Bramuglia and the Second Line of Argentinas Populist Movement, 2008; (comp.) Peronismo y prensa escrita: abordajes, miradas e interpretaciones nacionales y extranjeras, 2008; (co-author) Los estudios sobre el primer peronismo: aproximaciones desde el siglo XXI, 2009; (comp.) El retorno de Perón y el peronismo en la visión de la prensa nacional y extranjera, 2009; Argentine Jews or Jewish Argentines: Essays on Ethnicity, Identity, and Diaspora, 2010. EDITOR: (with T. Medin) Hevrah vezehut beArgenţinah: Haheksher haEropi, 1997; Spain and the Mediterranean since 1898, 1999; (ed. with T. Medin) Mexico since the Revolution, 1999; (with T. Medin) Meksiko leaḫar hamahpekhah: Hevrah u politikah, 1910-1952, 1999; (ed.) They Shall Not Pass: The Spanish Civil War, 2000; Argentina, Israel, y los Judiíos: Encuentros y Desencuentros, Mitos, y Realidades, 2001; Argentòinah, Yiśrael vòehaYehudim: Le-minhòalukòat Erets Yiśrael vead parashat Aikhman, 2002; Argentina, Israel, and the Jews: Peroón, the Eichmann Capture, and After, 2003; (ed. with C.H. Waisman) Spanish and Latin American Transitions to Democracy, 2005; (ed. with R. Sitman) El Primer Peronismo: De Regreso a los Comienzos, 2005; Jewish Identities in an Era of Globalization and Multiculturalism, 2007; Arabes y judíos en Iberoamérica: Similitudes, Diferencias y Tensiones Sobre el Trasfondode las tres Culturas, 2008; (with J. Lesser) Rethinking Jewish Latin AmericansLatin American Jews or Jewish Latin Americans, 2008. Contributor to periodicals. **Address:** Department of History, Tel Aviv University, Ramat Aviv, 69978, Israel. **Online address:** raanan@post.tau.ac.il

REINDERS, Eric. American (born United States), b. 1960. **Genres:** Theology/Religion, History. **Career:** Emory University, associate professor of religion, 1998-. Writer and historian. **Publications:** Borrowed Gods and Foreign Bodies: Christian Missionaries Imagine Chinese Religion, 2004. **Address:** Department of Religion, Emory University, S202 Callaway Memorial Ctr., 537 Kilgo Cir., PO Box 1535/002/1AA, Atlanta, GA 30322-1120, U.S.A. **Online address:** ereinde@emory.edu

REINERTSEN, Sarah. American (born United States), b. 1975. **Genres:** Biography, Medicine/Health. **Career:** Writer and motivational speaker. **Publications:** In a Single Bound: Losing My Leg, Finding Myself, and Training for Life, 2009. **Address:** U.S.A. **Online address:** prm@alwaystri.net

REINFELD, Linda M. American (born United States), b. 1940. **Genres:** Poetry, Literary Criticism And History, Translations, Humanities. **Career:** Monroe Community College, adjunct professor of English, 1982-2000; University of Buffalo, Millard Fillmore College, adjunct assistant professor of English, 1986-87; State University of New York College, adjunct assistant professor, 1992-93; Rochester Institute of Technology, College of Liberal Arts, department of language and literature, lecturer, 2000-, Department of English, creative writing coordinator, 2005-. Poet, writer. **Publications:** Language Poetry: Writing as Rescue, 1992; (trans. with T. Ishihara) Hyakunin Isshu: The Card Game of 100 Poems, 1996; (trans. with T. Ishihara) One Hundred Poets, One Hundred Poems, 1997. Contributor of articles to magazines. Works appear in anthologies. **Address:** Department of Language and Literature, College of Liberal Arts, Rochester Institute of Technology, 6-A106, Bldg. 6-2120, 92 Lomb Memorial Dr., Rochester, NY 14623-5604, U.S.A. **Online address:** lmrgla@rit.edu

REINGOLD, Dan. American (born United States), b. 1953?. **Genres:** Business/Trade/Industry. **Career:** Columbia University, Graduate School of Business, Columbia Institute for Tele-Information, project project director for telecom finance; Morgan Stanley, staff, 1989, managing director, telecom analyst; Credit Suisse First Boston, managing director, telecom analyst, through 2003;

Merrill Lynch, managing director, telecom analyst; MCI, financial executive. Writer. **Publications:** (With J. Reingold) Confessions of a Wall Street Analyst: A True Story of Inside Information and Corruption in the Stock Market, 2006. Contributor to periodicals. **Address:** c/o Author Mail, HarperCollins Publishers Inc., 10 E 53rd St., New York, NY 10022-5244, U.S.A. **Online address:** danreingold@wallstreetconfessions.com

REINHARDT, C. See **REINHARDT, Carsten.**

REINHARDT, Carsten. (C. Reinhardt). German (born Germany) **Genres:** Sciences, Adult Non-fiction. **Career:** Research Center on History and Philosophy of Science, research fellow, 1995; University of Regensburgh, instructor, 1996-97, assistant professor in history of science unit, 1997-2003, associate professor, 2003-05; Commission on the History of Modern Chemistry (IUHPS-DHS), executive officer, 1997-; Friedrich Schiller University, stand-in chair for history of science unit, 2005-06; Center for Interdisciplinary Studies, fellow, 2006-07; University of Bielefeld, Institute for Science and Technology Studies, professor, 2007-; University of Paris, Study Group on Methods of Sociological Analysis, visiting professor, 2008-09. Writer. **Publications:** (With R. Hahn) Scripta scientium: Gedruckte Und Ungedruckte Schriften Bedeutender Wissenschaftler: Eine Reihe von Verkaufskatalogen aus Den Sammlungen der Verfasser, 1993; (with G. Benz and R. Hahn) 100 Jahre Chemisch-Wissenschaftliches Laboratorium der Bayer AG in Wuppertal-Elberfeld, 1896-1996, 1996; (with A.S. Travis) Heinrich Caro and the Creation of Modern Chemical Industry, 2000; (ed. as C. Reinhardt) Chemical Sciences in the 20th Century: Bridging Boundaries, 2001; Shifting and Rearranging: Physical Methods and the Transformation of Modern Chemistry, 2006. **Address:** Institute of Science & Technology Studies, University of Bielefeld, Rm. U6-240, Universitatsstr 25, PO Box 10 01 31, Bielefeld, 33615, Germany. **Online address:** carsten.reinhardt@uni-bielefeld.de

REINHART, Peter. American (born United States), b. 1950. **Genres:** Food And Wine, Theology/Religion. **Career:** Root One Cafe, chef, 1971-74; Haven House Inc., youth counselor and house parent, 1975-77; Epiphany Journal, staff writer and associate editor, 1980-90; Brother Juniper's Cafe, partner and baker, 1986-89; Brother Juniper's Bakery, owner, manager, president and baker, 1989-; California Culinary Academy, full-time instructor, teacher, 1995-; Johnson and Wales University, faculty, 1999-. **Publications:** Brother Juniper's Bread Book: Slow Rise as Method and Metaphor, 1991; Sacramental Magic in a Small Town Cafe: Recipes and Stories from Brother Juniper's Cafe, 1994; Crust and Crumb: Master Formulas for Serious Bread Bakers, 1998; Bread upon the Waters: A Pilgrimage toward Self-Discovery and Spiritual Truth, 2000; The Bread Baker's Apprentice: Mastering the Art of Extraordinary Bread, 2001; American Pie: My Search for the Perfect Pizza, 2003; Brother Juniper's Bread Book: Slow Rise as Method and Metaphor, 2005; Peter Reinhart's Whole Grain Breads: New Techniques, Extraordinary Flavor, 2007; Peter Reinhart's Artisan Breads Every Day: Fast and Easy Recipes for World-class Breads, 2009. **Address:** Johnson and Wales University, 801 W Trade St., Charlotte, NC 28202, U.S.A. **Online address:** s.reinhart@prodigy.com

REINHARTZ, Adele. Canadian (born Canada), b. 1953?. **Genres:** History. **Career:** McMaster University, instructor, 1987; Wilfrid Laurier University, dean of graduate studies and research, 2002-05; University of Ottawa, professor, Department of Classics and Religious Studies, associate vice president of research, 2005-. Writer. **Publications:** The Word in the World: The Cosmological Tale in the Fourth Gospel, 1992; Why Ask My Name? Anonymity and Identity in Biblical Narrative, 1998; Befriending the Beloved Disciple: A Jewish Reading of the Gospel of John, 2001; (ed. with P. Fredricksen) Jesus, Judaism, and Christian Anti-Judaism: Reading the New Testament after the Holocaust, 2002; Scripture on the Silver Screen, 2003; Jesus of Hollywood, 2007; (ed.) Susan Haber, "They Shall Purify Themselves": Essays on Purity in Early Judaism, 2008; (ed. with W.O. McCready) Common Judaism: Explorations in Second-Temple Judaism, 2008. Contributor to books and periodicals. **Address:** epartment of Classics and Religious Studies, University of Ottawa,, Rm. 102, Arts Hall, 70 Laurier Ave. E, Ottawa, ON K1N 6N4, Canada.

REINSTEDT, Randall A. American (born United States), b. 1935. **Genres:** Area Studies, Paranormal, Marine Sciences/Oceanography, inspirational/Motivational Literature, History. **Career:** Writer, educator and historian. **Publications:** Dinosaur Dan, 1971; Gold in the Santa Lucias, 1973 as Monterey's Mother Lode, 1977; Ghosts, Bandits and Legends of Old Monterey Carmel, and Surrounding Areas, 1974, rev. ed., 1995; Shipwrecks and Sea Monsters of California's Central Coast, 1975; Tales, Treasures and Pirates of Old Monterey, 1976, rev. ed., 2005; Ghostly Tales and Mysterious Happenings of Old Monterey, 1977; (comp.) Where Have All the Sardines Gone?, 1978; Portraits of the Past, 1979; Mysterious Sea Monsters of California's Central Coast, 1979, rev. ed., 1993; Incredible Ghosts of Old Monterey's Hotel Del Monte, 1980; Incredible Ghosts of the Big Sur Coast, 1981, rev. ed., 2002; More Than Memories: History and Happenings of the Monterey Peninsula, 1985, rev. ed., 2001; Stagecoach Santa, 1986; The Monterey Peninsula: An Enchanted Land, 1987; Otters, Octopuses, and Odd Creatures of the Deep, 1987; The Strange Case of the Ghosts of the Robert Louis Stevenson House, 1988; One-Eyed Charley: The California Whip, 1990; Ghost Notes: Haunted Happenings on California's Historic Monterey Peninsula, 1991; Tales and Treasures of California's Missions, 1992; Tales and Treasures of the California Gold Rush, 1994; Lean John, California's Horseback Hero, 1996; Tales and Treasures of California's Ranchos, 1999; California Ghost Notes: Haunted Happenings throughout the Golden State, 2000; Ghosts and Mystery Along Old Monterey's Path of History, 2006; From Fisherman's Wharf to Steinbeck's Cannery Row: A Pictorial History of Monterey's Historic Waterfront and Its Famed Sardine Industry, 2009. **Address:** Ghost Town Publications, PO Box 5998, Carmel, CA 93921, U.S.A. **Online address:** ghtownpub@aol.com

REISMAN, Michael. American (born United States), b. 1972. **Genres:** Science Fiction/Fantasy, Horror, Mystery/Crime/Suspense. **Career:** Dreamworks Animation, script and story reader; Nickelodeon, script and story reader; Cartoon Network, script and story reader. Writer. **Publications:** Simon Bloom, the Gravity Keeper, 2008. Simon Bloom, the Octopus Effect, 2009. **Address:** Los Angeles, CA, U.S.A. **Online address:** michael@michaelreisman.com

REISS, Bob. *See* **BLACK, Ethan.**

REISS, Ed. *See* **REISS, Edward.**

REISS, Edward. (Ed Reiss). British (born England), b. 1964. **Genres:** Poetry, History, Intellectual History, International Relations/Current Affairs, Military/Defense/Arms Control, Politics/Government, Biography. **Career:** Writer. **Publications:** The Strategic Defense Initiative, 1992; An Original Introduction to Marx, 1995; Marx: A Clear Guide, 1997. **Address:** Flat 3, 24 Sherborne Rd., Bradford, WY BD7 1RB, England. **Online address:** a.e.reiss@bradford.ac.uk

REISS, Ira Leonard. American (born United States), b. 1925. **Genres:** Sex, Sociology. **Career:** Bowdoin College, professor of sociology, 1953-55; College of William and Mary, professor of sociology, 1955-59; Bard College, professor of sociology, 1959-61; University of Iowa, professor of sociology, 1961-69; University of Minnesota, professor of sociology, 1969-96, Family Study Center, director, 1969-74, professor emeritus of sociology, 1996-. Writer. **Publications:** Premarital Sexual Standards in America, 1960; The Social Context of Premarital Sexual Permissiveness, 1967; The Family Systems in America, 1971, 4th ed., 1988; Readings on the Family System, 1972; (with W. Burr, R. Hill and I. Nye) Contemporary Theories About the Family, vol. I-II, 1979; Journey into Sexuality: An Exploratory Voyage, 1986; (with H.M. Reiss) An End to Shame: Shaping Our Next Social Revolution, 1990; (with H.M. Reiss) Solving America's Sexual Crises, 1997; (with A. Ellis) At the Dawn of the Sexual Revolution: Reflections on a Dialogue, 2002; Insider's View of Sexual Science since Kinsey, 2006. **Address:** 5932 Medicine Lake Rd., Minneapolis, MN 55422-3328, U.S.A. **Online address:** irareiss@comcast.net

REISS, Kathryn. American (born United States), b. 1957. **Genres:** Novels, Mystery/Crime/Suspense, Children's Fiction, Young Adult Fiction. **Career:** Stuart Country Day School, director of foreign exchange, 1981-82; Europa (bookshop), bookstore manager, 1983-85; Princeton Public Library, assistant to children's librarian, 1983-85; Princeton Language Group, instructor, 1984-86; Princeton Young Women's Christian Association (YWCA), instructor, 1984-86; Trenton State College, Department of English, instructor, 1984-86; Princeton Arts Council, writer-in-residence, 1986; University of Michigan, Department of English, instructor, 1986-88; Mills College, Department of English, lecturer, 1989-95, 1997-2008, associate professor, 2008-. **Publications:** NOVELS: Time Windows, 1991; The Glass House People, 1992; Dreadful Sorry, 1993; Pale Phoenix, 1994; Dollhouse of the Dead, 1997; The Headless Bride, 1997; Rest in Peace, 1997; Paperquake, 1998; Riddle of the Prairie Bride, 2001; Paint by Magic, 2002; The Strange Case of Baby H, 2002; Sweet Miss Honeywell's Revenge, 2004; Blackthorn Winter, 2006; The Tangled Web, 2009; The Puzzle of the Paper Daughter: A Julie Mystery,

2010; The Silver Guitar: A Julie Mystery, 2011; A Bundle of Trouble: A Rebecca Mystery, 2011. Contributor of short stories and articles to periodicals. **Address:** Department of English, Mills College, Mills Hall 307, Oakland, CA 94613, U.S.A. **Online address:** kathryn@kathrynreiss.net

REISS, Mitchell. American (born United States), b. 1957. **Genres:** Military/Defense/Arms Control, Sciences. **Career:** International Institute for Strategic Studies, special assistant to the director, 1985; National Security Council, White House fellow and special assistant to national security adviser, 1988-89; Covington and Burling (law firm), associate, 1989-92; White House Fellows Alumni Association, board director, 1992-94; Business Executives for National Security, co-chair, 1993-95; Korean Peninsula Energy Development Organization, senior policy adviser and assistant executive director, 1995-; United States Department of State, director of policy planning, 2003-05; United States Special Envoy for Northern Ireland, ambassador, 2004; William and Mary Law School, vice provost for international affairs, professor of law and professor of government; U.S. Arms Control and Disarmament Agency, consultant; Lawrence Livermore National Laboratory, consultant; Los Alamos National Laboratory, consultant; Library of Congress, consultant; Ford Foundation, consultant; Cambridge Institute for Applied Research, senior associate; Center for Strategic and International Studies, senior associate. Writer. **Publications:** Without the Bomb: The Politics of Nuclear Nonproliferation, 1988; (ed. with R.S. Litwak) Nuclear Proliferation after the Cold War, 1994; Bridled Ambition: Why Countries Constrain Their Nuclear Capabilities, 1995; (ed. with C. Moon and M. Okonogi) Perry Report, The Missile Quagmire, and the North Korean Question: The Quest of New Alternatives, 2000; (ed. with K.M. Campbell and R.J. Einhorn) Nuclear Tipping Point: Why States Reconsider their Nuclear Choices, 2004. Contributor of articles and reviews to magazines and newspapers. **Address:** William & Mary Law School, 12th Fl., PO Box 8795, Williamsburg, VA 23187, U.S.A. **Online address:** reiss@wm.edu

REISS, Tom. American (born United States), b. 1964?. **Genres:** Politics/Government, Biography, History. **Career:** New York Times, political and cultural journalist; Wall Street Journal, political and cultural journalist; New Yorker, political and cultural journalist. **Publications:** (With I. Hasselbach) Führer-Ex: Memoirs of a Former Neo-Nazi, 1996; The Orientalist: Solving the Mystery of a Strange and Dangerous Life, 2005. **Address:** c/o Svetlana Katz, Janklow & Nesbit Associates, 445 Park Ave., 13th Fl., New York, NY 10022-2606, U.S.A. **Online address:** tom.theorientalist@gmail.com

REITER, Rayna Rapp. *See* **RAPP, Rayna.**

REITER, Victoria (Kelrich). Also writes as T. J. Hemings, Jacquine Delessert. American (born United States) **Genres:** Translations, Novels, Plays/Screenplays, Ghost Writer, Novellas/Short Stories, Mystery/Crime/Suspense. **Career:** Freelance writer. **Publications:** NOVELS: The Girl in the Gold Leather Dress, 1960; The Girl Who Had Everything, 1962; Casebook: Mymphomania, 1964; Charades, 1977. TRANSLATOR: Nana, 1979; Lola, 1984; Luna, 1985; Vida, 1985; Maryse Conde, Tree of Life, 1992. **Address:** c/o Eugene Winick, McIntosh & Otis Inc., 353 Lexington Ave., Fl. 15, New York, NY 10016, U.S.A.

REITMAN, Judith. American (born United States), b. 1951. **Genres:** Documentaries/Reportage, Animals/Pets, Criminology/True Crime. **Career:** The North Carolina Women's Prison Writing and Performance Project, founder and director; UNC School of Social Work, fellow. Freelance writer. **Publications:** Stolen for Profit: How the Medical Establishment is Funding a National Pet-Theft Conspiracy, 1992, Stolen for Profit, 1995; Blood Legacy: A True Story of Betrayal and Murder in Southampton, 1996; Bad Blood: Crisis in the American Red Cross, 1996; (comp.) American Proverbs, 2000. Contributor to periodicals. **Address:** Gelfman/Schneider Literary, 250 W 57th St., New York, NY 10021, U.S.A. **Online address:** jude.reitman@oxint.com

REITZ, Miriam. American/Canadian (born Canada), b. 1935. **Genres:** Social Work. **Career:** Elementary school teacher, 1955-58; Northwestern Memorial Hospital and Medical School, Family Institute of Chicago/Center for Family Studies, associate director of professional education, 1972-73, director of professional education, 1973-76, part-time staff, 1976-82, coordinator of consultation and community services, 1982-88; Northwestern University, faculty of psychiatry and behavioral sciences, 1975-91; Rocky Ridge Music Center Foundation, vice-president, 1989-; Institute for Clinical Social Work, faculty, 1990-. Writer. **Publications:** Model Building for Marital Assessment:

A Study of New Marriages on Systemic Dimensions, 1982; (with K.W. Watson) Adoption and the Family System: Strategies for Treatment, 1992. Contributor to periodicals. **Address:** Institute for Clinical Social Work, Robert Morris Ctr., 401 S State Street, Ste. 822, Chicago, IL 60605, U.S.A.

REIZBAUM, Marilyn. American (born United States) **Genres:** Literary Criticism And History, Essays. **Career:** Bowdoin College, professor of English, Harrison King McCann professor of English, Gay and Lesbian Studies Program, director. Writer. **Publications:** (Ed. with K.J. Devlin) Ulysses En-Gendered Perspectives: Eighteen New Essays on the Episodes, 1999; James Joyce's Judaic Other, 1999; Yiddish Modernisms: Red Emma Goldman, 2005; (ed. with L. McIlvanney) Ireland and Scotland: Culture and Society, 1700-2000, 2005; (contrib.) The Edinburgh Companion to Muriel Spark, 2010. Contributor to periodicals. **Address:** Department of English, Bowdoin College, 106 Massachusetts Hall, 8300 College Sta., Brunswick, ME 04011-8483, U.S.A. **Online address:** mreizbau@bowdoin.edu

REJAI, Mostafa. *See* Obituaries.

REJALI, Darius M. American (born United States), b. 1959. **Genres:** Area Studies, Young Adult Non-fiction, Politics/Government, Social Sciences. **Career:** McGill University, teaching assistant, 1982-85; lecturer, 1988; Union College, visiting assistant professor, 1988-89; Reed College, assistant professor, 1989-94, Department of Political Science, chair, 1993-95, 1996-2001, 2005, 2007-09, 2010-, associate professor of political science, 1994-2003, Hewlett Faculty/Student Grants in International and Comparative Policy Studies, co-chair, 1994-95, chair of division of history and social science, 1996-98, chair of international and comparative policy studies, 2000-01, professor, 2003-. Writer. **Publications:** NONFICTION: Torture and Modernity: Self, Society, and State in Modern Iran, 1994; Torture and Democracy, 2007; Approaches to Violence, 2008. Contributor to periodicals. **Address:** Department of Political Science, Reed College, 3203 SE Woodstock Blvd., Portland, OR 97202-8199, U.S.A. **Online address:** rejali@reed.edu

REKDAL, Paisley. American (born United States), b. 1970. **Genres:** Poetry. **Career:** University of Michigan, English Department, course assistant, 1994-95, English and Creative Writing Department, graduate student instructor, 1995-96, English Department, writing instructor, 1997-98, Sweetland Writing Center, writing instructor, 1998; Usok Girl's High School, English teacher, 1996-97; University of Wyoming, Department of English, assistant professor, 2000-03; University of Utah-Salt Lake City, Department of English, associate professor, 2003-; Goddard College, lecturer and associate professor, 2005-; University of Utah-Asia Center, associate professor. Writer. **Publications:** The Night My Mother Met Bruce Lee: Observations on Not Fitting In, 2000; Intimate: A Hybrid Memoir, 2011. POEMS: A Crash of Rhinos, 2000; Six Girls without Pants, 2002; The Invention of The Kaleidoscope, 2007; An American Family Photo Album, 2011; Animal Eye, 2012. **Address:** Department of English, University of Utah, Rm. 3500, 3403 LNCO, Langs & Communication Bldg., 255 S Central Campus Dr., Salt Lake City, UT 84112, U.S.A. **Online address:** paisleyr@english.utah.edu

RELYEA, Harold C. (Harold Clarence Relyea). American (born United States), b. 1944. **Genres:** Politics/Government, Young Adult Non-fiction. **Career:** Library of Congress, American national government for Congressional Research Service, specialist, 1971-. Writer. **Publications:** A Brief History of Emergency Powers in the United States, 1974; The Evolution and Organization of the Federal Intelligence Function: A Brief Overview, 1776-1975, 1976; (with L. Fisher) Presidential Staffing-A Brief Overview, 1978; (with L.S. Berman) The Presidency and Information Policy, 1981; Democracy-Toward an American Understanding: A Selected Reading List of Books, 1992; Silencing Science: National Security Controls and Scientific Communication, 1994; (with R.M. Nunno) Electronic Government and Electronic Signatures, 2000; Government at the Dawn of the 21st Century, 2001; (with C.V. Arja) The Vice Presidency of the United States: Evolution of the Modern Office, 2002; (with M.J.C. Riemann and H.B. Hogue) The National Performance Review, 2002; (with T.P. Carr) The Executive Branch, Creation and Reorganization, 2003; (with L.E. Halchin) Informing Congress: The Role of the Executive Branch in Times of War, 2003; Security Classified and Controlled Information, 2008. EDITOR: American Federal Government Printing and Publication Reform, 1980; (with T. Riley) Freedom of Information Trends in the Information Age, 1983; Striking a Balance: National Security and Scientific Freedom-First Discussions, 1985; (with C.R. McClure and P. Hernon) United States Government Information Policies: Views and Perspectives, 1989; (with McClure

and Hernon) Federal Information Policies in the 1990s, 1996; The Executive Office of the President, 1997; (co-ed.) United States Government Information: Policies and Sources, 2001; (with P. Hernon and R. Cullen) Comparative Perspectives on E-government, 2006. Contributor to articles. **Address:** Government & Finance Division, Congressional Research Service, Library of Congress, 101 Independence Ave. SE, Washington, DC 20540-7470, U.S.A. **Online address:** hrelyea@crs.loc.gov

RELYEA, Harold Clarence. *See* **RELYEA, Harold C.**

REMBER, John. American (born United States) **Genres:** Biography, Literary Criticism And History. **Career:** College of Idaho, professor of English, 1989, writer-at-large; Albertson College, associate professor of English, 1993-; Pacific University, faculty. Writer. **Publications:** Coyote in the Mountains, 1989; Cheerleaders from Gomorrah: Tales from the Lycra Archipelago, 1994; Memory Tricks: Memoirs of Place, 2002; Traplines: Coming Home to Sawtooth Valley, 2003; Mfa in A Box: A Why to Write Book, 2011. Contributor of articles to periodicals. **Address:** Department of English, Albertson College, 2112 Cleveland Blvd., Caldwell, ID 83605, U.S.A. **Online address:** john@johnrember.com

REMER, Gary. American (born United States), b. 1957. **Genres:** Politics/Government, Literary Criticism And History. **Career:** University of Judaism, lecturer, 1984-85; California State University, lecturer in political science, 1989-90; Tulane University, Department of Political Science, assistant professor, 1990-95, associate professor, 1995-. Writer. **Publications:** Humanism and the Rhetoric of Toleration, 1996. (co-ed.) Talking Democracy: Historical Perspectives on Rhetoric and Democracy, 2004. Contributor to books and periodicals. **Address:** Department of Political Science, Tulane University, 314 Norman Mayer Bldg., New Orleans, LA 70118-4929, U.S.A. **Online address:** gremer@tulane.edu

REMKIEWICZ, Frank. American (born United States), b. 1939. **Genres:** Illustrations, Humor/Satire, Children's Fiction. **Career:** Norcross Greeting Cards, staff illustrator, 1968-73. Freelance author and illustrator, 1973-92. **Publications:** SELF-ILLUSTRATED: The Last Time I Saw Harris, 1991; Greedy Anna, 1992; Final Exit for Cats: A Feline Suicide Guide, 1992; There's Only One Harris, 1993; Bone Stranger, 1994; Fiona Raps it Up, 1995; Twelve Days of Christmas in Florida, 2008; Gus Gets Scared, 2010; Gus Makes a Friend, 2011. **Address:** c/o Kendra Marcus, Bookstop Literary Agency, 67 Meadow View Rd., Orinda, CA 94563, U.S.A. **Online address:** info@remkiewicz.com

REMNICK, David (J.). American (born United States), b. 1958. **Genres:** Adult Non-fiction, Documentaries/Reportage, Autobiography/Memoirs. **Career:** Washington Post, reporter, 1982-88, correspondent in Moscow, 1988-92; New Yorker, staff writer, 1992-98; writer, 1998-. **Publications:** Lenin's Tomb: The Last Days of the Soviet Empire, 1993, rev. ed., 2004; The Devil Problem and Other True Stories, 1996; Resurrection: The Struggle for a New Russia, 1997, rev. ed. 1998; King of the World: Muhammad Ali and the Rise of an American Hero, 1998; Reporting: Writings From The New Yorker, 2006; The Bridge: The Life and Rise of Barack Obama, 2010; (intro.) Power: Photographs, 2011. EDITOR: (and intro.) The Second John McPhee Reader, 1996; Life Stories: Profiles from the New Yorker, 2000; The New Gilded Age: The New Yorker Looks at the Culture of Affluence, 2000; (with S. Choi) Wonderful Town: New York Stories from the New Yorker, 2001; (with H. Finder) Fierce Pajamas: An Anthology of Humor Writing from the New Yorker, 2001; The New Yorker Book of Food and Drink, 2007; Secret Ingredients: The New Yorker Book of Food and Drink, 2007; (with H. Finder) Disquiet, Please!: More Humor Writing from the New Yorker, 2008; And the Crowd Goes Wild: Sports Writing from the New Yorker, 2010; The Only Game in Town: Sportswriting from the New Yorker, 2010. INTRO.: The New Yorker Book of Business Cartoons, 1998; Part of Our Time: Some Ruins and Monuments of the Thirties, 1998; Theories of Everything: Selected, Collected and Health-Inspected Cartoons, 1978-2006, 2008. Contribution to periodicals. **Address:** c/o Author Mail, Knopf, 1745 Broadway, New York, NY 10019, U.S.A.

RENARD, John. American (born United States), b. 1944. **Genres:** Theology/Religion, History. **Career:** Saint Louis University, professor of theological studies, 1978-. Writer. **Publications:** In the Footsteps of Muhammad: Understanding the Islamic Experience, 1992; Islam and the Heroic Image: Themes in Literature and the Visual Arts, 1993; All the King's Falcons: Rumion Prophets and Revelation, 1994; Seven Doors to Islam: Spirituality and the Religious Life of Muslims, 1996; (ed.) Windows on the House of Islam: Muslim Sources on Spirituality and Religious Life, 1998; Responses to 101 Questions on Islam, 1998; Responses to 101 Questions on Buddhism, 1999; Responses to 101 Questions on Hinduism, 1999; 101 Questions and Answers on Confucianism, Daoism and Shinto, 2002; 101 Questions and Answers on Hinduism, 2002; 101 Questions and Answers on Islam, 2002; The Handy Religion Answer Book, 2002; Understanding the Islamic Experience, 2002; (trans. and intro.) Knowledge of God in Classical Sufism: Foundations of Islamic Mystical Theology, 2004; Historical Dictionary of Sufism, 2005; Friends of God: Islamic Images of Piety, Commitment and Servanthood, 2008; (ed.) Tales of God's Friends: Islamic Hagiography in Translation, 2009; Islam and Christianity: Theological Themes in Comparative Perspective, 2011. Contributor to periodicals and magazines. **Address:** 3800 Lindell Blvd, Saint Louis University, St. Louis, MO 63156, U.S.A. **Online address:** renard.john@gmail.com

RENAUD, Jacques. Also writes as Ji R, Elie-Pierre Ysrael. Canadian (born Canada), b. 1943. **Genres:** Novels, Translations. **Career:** Métro-Express, reporter, 1965-; Radio-Canada, journalist, researcher; Augsburg College, faculty of Roman language; Nuremberg College, faculty of Roman language. Writer. **Publications:** Electrodes, 1962; Le Cassé, 1964; En d'autres paysages, 1970; Le Fond pur de l'errance irradie, 1975; Le cassé et autres nouvelles, suivi de Le journal du cassé, 1977; Le Cycle du scorpion, 1979; La Colombe et la brisure éternité, 1979; L'Inde et le karma, 1979; Clandestine(s) ou la tradition du couchant, 1980; (with L. Cohen, C. Haeffely and M. Lachance) D'Ailies et d'îles, 1980; (as Elie-Pierre Ysrael) Arcane Seize, 1980; La Ville: Venus et la Mélancolie, 1981; (as Ji R.) Par la Main du soleil, Les Saisons du Saphir, 1981; La Nuit des temps, 1981; L'Escape du diable: nouvelles, 1989; La Constellation du bouc emissaire: clause derogatoire, loi 101 et prototo-talitarisme, 1993. **Address:** c/o Author Mail, Les Editions Balzac, 5000 rue Iberville, Ste. 328, Montreal, QC H2H 2M2, Canada.

RENAUER, Albin (J.). American (born United States), b. 1959. **Genres:** Law. **Career:** California Supreme Court, staff attorney, 1985-87; Nolo Press, editor, author and software developer, 1987-2004; Nolo.com, software development director, 1991-98, Web site information architect, designer, 1998-2001, webmaster, legal editor, author and information architect, 1998-2004; LegalConsumer.com (RelationalVision L.L.C.), owner, web developer and legal editor. **Publications:** (Ed.) Fight your Ticket, 1987; (with S. Elias and R. Leonard) How to File for Bankruptcy, 1989, 17th ed., 2011; (ed.) Law on the Net, 1997; (with E. Newman) Personal Record Keeper 5: Windows & Macintosh: Users' Manual, 5th ed., 1998; (with E. Newman) Willmaker8: Users' Manual, 2000. **Address:** RelationalVision L.L.C., PO Box 7571, Berkeley, CA 94707, U.S.A. **Online address:** albin@legalconsumer.com

RENAUX, Sigrid. Brazilian (born Brazil), b. 1938. **Genres:** Poetry, Literary Criticism And History, Translations, Young Adult Fiction. **Career:** Federal University of Parana, teacher of English, 1970-76, assistant professor, 1976-80, associate professor, 1980-88, School of Humanities, vice director, 1981-82, M.A. course in English, coordinator, 1983-85, professor of English, American and Canadian literature, 1988-95, senior professor, 1996-97; Uniandrade, professor of English and American literature, 2002, coordinator of B.A. course in letters, 2002. Writer. **Publications:** Do Mar e de Outras Coisas (poems in Portuguese and English), 1979; A Volta do Parafuso: Uma leitura semiótica, 1992; The Turn of the Screw: A Semiotic Reading, 1993. Contributor to journals and periodicals. **Address:** Rua Carmelo Rangel 680, Curitiba, PN 80440-050, Brazil. **Online address:** sigridrenaux@terra.com.br

RENCHER, Alvin C. American (born United States), b. 1934. **Genres:** Mathematics/Statistics, Education. **Career:** Brigham Young University, teaching assistant, 1959-61, instructor of mathematics, 1963-65, instructor, 1965-66, assistant professor, 1968-72, associate professor, 1972-77, professor of statistics, 1977-2000, department chairman, 1980-85, associate dean, 1985-92; Hercules Inc., statistician, 1961-63; Kennecott Copper Corp., statistician, 1969-. Writer. **Publications:** A Linear Regression Sequential Test Procedure, 1962; (co-author) Workprints in Translated Literature, 1982; Book of Mormon Authorship Chronology, 1986; Methods of Multivariate Analysis, 1995, 2nd ed., 2002; Multivariate Statistical Inference and Applications, 1998; Diskette, 1998; Linear Models in Statistics, 2000, 2nd ed., 2008; (co-author) SAS System for Linear Models, Fourth Edition + Linear Models in Statistics, Second Edition Set, 2008. Contributor to books. **Address:** c/o Publicity Director, Wiley Publishing Group, 605 3rd Ave., New York, NY 10158-0012, U.S.A.

RENDELL, Ruth. Also writes as Barbara Vine. British (born England), b.

1930. **Genres:** Novellas/Short Stories, Mystery/Crime/Suspense, Novels, Young Adult Non-fiction, inspirational/Motivational Literature, Young Adult Fiction. **Career:** Chigwell Times, reporter and sub-editor, 1948-52. **Publications:** To Fear a Painted Devil, 1965; Vanity Dies Hard, 1965 in US as In Sickness and in Health, 1966; The Secret House of Death, 1968; One Across, Two Down, 1971; The Face of Trespass, 1974; The Fallen Curtain and Other Stories, 1976; A Demon in My View, 1976; A Judgement in Stone, 1977; Make Death Love Me, 1979; Means of Evil and Other Stories, 1979; The Lake of Darkness, 1980; Master of the Moor, 1982; The Fever Tree and Other Stories, 1982; The Killing Doll, 1984; The Tree of Hands, 1984; The New Girl Friend and Other Stories, 1985; Live Flesh, 1986; Heartstones, 1987; Talking to Strange Men, 1987; Wexford: An Omnibus, 1987; A Warning to the Curious, 1987; The Bridesmaid, 1989; (with C. Ward) Undermining the Central Line, 1989; Ruth Rendell's Suffolk (non-fiction), 1989; Going Wrong, 1990; Ruth Rendell Mysteries: Three Inspector Wexford Mysteries as Seen on Television, 1990; (with H. Simpson) Unguarded Hours: Strawberry Tree/ Flesh and Grass, 1990; The Fifth Wexford Omnibus, 1991; Copper Peacock and Other Stories, 1992; The Crocodile Bird, 1993; Inspector Wexford, 1994; (ed. and intro.) The Reason Why, 1995; The Strawberry Tree, 1995; The Keys to the Street, 1996; Bloodlines (stories), 1996; A Dark Blue Perfume: And Other Stories, 1996; A Needle For the Devil: And Other Stories, 1996; Sight for Sore Eyes, 1999; Piranha to Scurfy and Other Stories, 2000; Demon in My View, 2000; Adam and Eve and Pinch Me: A Novel, 2001; Three Cases for Chief Inspector Wexford, 2002; Rottweiler: A Novel, 2003; Thirteen Steps Down: A Novel, 2004; The Thief, 2006; The Water's Lovely: A Novel, 2006; From Doon with Death, 2007; Collected Stories II, 2008; Portobello: A Novel, 2008; Tigerlily's Orchids, 2010; Vault, 2011; Saint Zita Society, 2012. INSPECTOR WEXFORD SERIES: Doon to Death, 1964; Wolf to the Slaughter, 1967; A New Lease of Death, 1967 in US as Sins of the Fathers, 1970; The Best Man to Die, 1969; A Guilty Thing Surprised, 1970; No More Dying Then, 1971; Murder Being Done Once, 1972; Some Lie and Some Die, 1973; Shake Hands for Ever, 1975; A Sleeping Life, 1978; Put on by Cunning in US as Death Notes, 1981; The Speaker of Mandarin, 1983; An Unkindness of Ravens, 1985; The Veiled One, 1988; Kissing the Gunner's Daughter, 1992; Simisola, 1994; Road Rage, 1997; Harm Done, 1999; Babes in the Wood, 2002; End in Tears, 2005; Not in the Flesh, 2007; The Monster in the Box, 2009. AS BARBARA VINE: A Dark Adapted Eye, 1986; A Fatal Inversion, 1987; The House of Stairs, 1988; Gallowglass, 1990; King Solomon's Carpet, 1991; Asta's Book, 1993; No Night Is Too Long, 1994; In the Time of His Prosperity, 1995; The Brimstone Wedding, 1995; The Chimney Sweeper's Boy, 1998; Grasshopper, 2000; The Blood Doctor, 2002; The Minotaur, 2005; The Birthday Present, 2008. Works appear in anthologies. **Address:** Peters Fraser & Dunlop Group Ltd., Drury House, 34-43 Russell St., London, GL WC2B 5HA, England.

RENDON, Armando B. American (born United States), b. 1939. **Genres:** Civil Liberties/Human Rights, International Relations/Current Affairs, Law, Social Sciences. **Career:** U.S. Commission on Civil Rights, deputy information officer, 1967-69; ATM Corp., vice-president, 1972-73; American University, associate professor, 1975-79; Latino Institute, director, 1975-; Spanish Educational Development Center, chair, 1977-; U.S. Bureau of Census, staff, 1979-88; Los Cerezos TV Co., president, 1980-82; Ollin and Associates Inc., president, 1983-; California Public Utilities Commission, public information officer, 1988. Writer. **Publications:** Chicano Manifesto, 1971; We Mutually Pledge, 1978; Ethnicity and U.S. Foreign Policy, 1981; The Treaty of Guadalupe Hidalgo, 1983. Contributor of articles to periodicals. **Address:** Ollin and Associates Inc., PO Box 9164, Berkeley, CA 94709, U.S.A. **Online address:** arendon@flash.net

RENDON, Marcie R. American/Indian (born India), b. 1952. **Genres:** Plays/Screenplays, Adult Non-fiction, Social Sciences. **Career:** Mentor, 1994-. Writer. **Publications:** (With V. RedHorse) Looks into the Night, 1995; Powwow Summer: A Family Celebrates the Circle of Life, 1996; (with C.W. Bellville) Farmers Market: Families Working Together, 2001. PLAYS: Bring the Children Home, 1996; Outside In, Outside Out, 1997; Songcatcher, 1998; Free Frybread, 1999; Rough Face Girl, 2001; (with A. Markusen) Native Artists: Livelihoods, Resources, Space, Gifts, 2009. Works appear in anthologies. Contributor to magazines and newspapers. **Address:** c/o Belleville, 308 Prince St., St. Paul, MN 55101, U.S.A. **Online address:** mrendon703@aol.com

RENEE, Janina. American (born United States), b. 1956. **Genres:** Paranormal, inspirational/Motivational Literature, Self Help. **Career:** Writer. **Publications:** Tarot Spells, 1990, rev. ed., 2000; Playful Magic, 1994; Tarot: Your

Everyday Guide: Practical Problem Solving and Everyday Advice, 2000; Tarot for a New Generation (for young adults), 2001; By Candlelight: Rites for Celebration, Blessing & Prayer, 2004. **Address:** c/o Author Mail, Llewellyn Worldwide Ltd., 2143 Wooddale Dr., Woodbury, MN 55125-2989, U.S.A. **Online address:** janinarenee@gmail.com

RENEHAN, Edward J(ohn). American (born United States), b. 1956. **Genres:** History, Biography, Essays. **Career:** Newbridge Book Clubs, director of computer publishing programs. Writer. **Publications:** John Burroughs: An American Naturalist (biography), 1992; 1001 Really Cool Web Sites, 1995; The Secret Six: The True Tale of the Men who Conspired with John Brown, 1995; 1001 Programming Resources, 1996; Net Worth: Creating and Maximizing Wealth with the Internet, 1996; Science on the Web: A Connoisseur's Guide to Over 500 of the Best, Most Useful, and Most Fun Science Websites, 1996; Great American Websites: An Online Discovery of a Hidden America, 1997; The Lion's Pride: Theodore Roosevelt and His Family in Peace and War, 1998; The Kennedys at War, 1937-1945, 2002; Dark Genius of Wall Street: The Misunderstood Life of Jay Gould, King of the Robber Barons, 2005; The Monroe Doctrine: The Cornerstone of American Foreign Policy, 2007; The Transcontinental Railroad: The Gateway to The West, 2007; Commodore: The Life of Cornelius Vanderbilt, 2007; Pope John Paul II, 2007; The Treaty of Paris: The Precursor to a New Nation, 2007. EDITOR: The Clearwater Songbook, 1980; A River View and Other Hudson Valley Essays, 1981. Contributor to periodicals. **Address:** c/o Chris Calhoun, Sterling-Lord Literistic Inc., 65 Bleecker St., New York, NY 10012, U.S.A. **Online address:** erenehan@yahoo.com

RENFIELD, Richard Lee. American (born United States), b. 1932. **Genres:** Education, Translations, History. **Career:** Institute for the Study of the USSR, translator, 1953-54; Educational Policies Commission, associate secretary, 1958-67; Communications Satellite Corp., Intelsat Affairs Department, interim, 1967-70; International Monetary Fund, reviser and translator, 1974-, assistant division chief, 1986-89, division chief, 1989-95. Writer. **Publications:** (Trans.) Winter Notes on Summer Impressions, 1955; If Teachers Were Free, 1969, 2nd rev. ed., 1972. Contributor to journals. **Address:** 2327 Senseney Ln., Falls Church, VA 22043, U.S.A. **Online address:** richard_renfield_ab53@post.harvard.edu

RENFREW, (Andrew) Colin. British (born England), b. 1937. **Genres:** Archaeology/Antiquities, History, Art/Art History. **Career:** University of Sheffield, lecturer, 1965-70, senior lecturer, 1970-72, reader in prehistory and archaeology, 1972; Southampton University, Department of Archaeology, professor of archaeology and head, 1972-81; Antiquity Trust, trustee, 1974-; Cambridge University, Disney professor of archaeology, 1981-2004, now emeritus Disney professor of archaeology, St. John's College, fellow, 1981-86, honorary fellow, 2005, Jesus College, master, 1986-97, honorary fellow, 1997, McDonald Institute for Archaeological Research, founding director, 1990-2004, senior fellow; National Academy of Sciences, foreign associate, 1996; World Archaeological Congress Taskforce on Looting, chair. Writer. **Publications:** (With J.D. Evans) Excavations at Saliagos near Antiparos, 1968; The Emergence of Civilisation, 1972; Before Civilisation, 1973; Investigations in Orkney, 1979; Problems in European Prehistory, 1979; Approaches to Social Archaeology, 1984; The Archaeology of Cult, 1985; Archaeology and Language, 1987; The Cycladic Spirit, 1991; (with P. Bahn) Archaeology: Theories, Methods and Practice, 1991, 5th ed., 2008; Loot, Legitimacy and Ownership, 2000; Figuring It Out, 2003; Traces of Ancestry, 2004; (with P. Bahn) Archaeology Essentials: Theories, Methods, and Practice, 2007; Excavations at Phylakopi in Melos, 1974-77, 2007; Prehistory: The Making of the Human Mind, 2007. EDITOR: The Explanation of Culture Change, 1973; British Prehistory: A New Outline, 1974; (with K.L. Cooke) Transformations: Mathematical Approaches to Culture Change, 1979; (with J.D. Evans and B. Cunliffe) Antiquity and Man: Essays in Honour of Glyn Daniel, 1981; (with M. Wagstaff) An Island Polity: The Archaeology of Exploitation in Melos, 1982; (with M.J. Rowlands and B.A. Segraves) Theory and Explanation in Archaeology, 1982; (with S. Shennan) Ranking, Resource, and Exchange: Aspects of the Archaeology of Early European Society, 1982; The Prehistory of Orkney, 1985; (with M. Gimbutas and E.S. Elster) Excavations at Sitagroi: A Prehistoric Village in Northeast Greece, 1986; (with J.F. Cherry) Peer Polity Interaction and Socio-Political Change, 1986; (with E.B.W. Zubrow) The Ancient Mind: Elements of Cognitive Archaeology, 1994; (with A. McMahon and L. Trask) Time Depth in Historical Linguistics, 2000; (with P. Bellwood) Examining the Farming/Language Dispersal Hypothesis, 2002; (with M. Levine and K. Boyle) Prehistoric Steppe Adaptation and the Horse,

2003; (with C. Gosden and E. DeMarrais) Substance, Memory, Display: Archaeology and Art, 2004; (with E. DeMarrais and C. Gosden) Rethinking Materiality: The Engagement of Mind with the Material World, 2004; (with P. Bahn) Archaeology: The Key Concepts, 2004; (with P. Forster) Phylogenetic Methods and the Prehistory of Languages, 2006; (co-ed.) Keros, Dhaskalio Kavos: The Investigations of 1987-88, 2007; (with I. Morley) Image and Imagination: A Global Prehistory of Figurative Representation, 2007; (with S. Matsumura and P. Forster) Simulations, Genetics and Human Prehistory, 2008; (with I. Morley) Becoming Human: Innovation in Prehistoric Material and Spiritual Culture, 2009; (with C. Frith and L. Malafouris) The Sapient Mind: Archaeology Meets Neuroscience, 2009; (with I. Morley) The Archaeology of Measurement: Comprehending Heaven, Earth and Time in Ancient Societies, 2010. Contributor to books and journals. **Address:** McDonald Institute for Archaeological Research, University of Cambridge, 3.2, West Bldg., Downing St., Cambridge, CB CB2 3ER, England. **Online address:** acr10@cam.ac.uk

RENGERT, George F. American (born United States), b. 1940. **Genres:** Criminology/True Crime, Geography. **Career:** Temple University, instructor, assistant professor of geography, 1970-78, associate professor of geography, 1978-83, associate professor of criminal justice, 1983-91, professor of criminal justice, 1991-, now professor emeritus. Writer. **Publications:** (With J. Wasilchick) Suburban Burglary: A Time and a Place for Everything, 1985; The Geography of Illegal Drugs, 1996; (with M.T. Mattson and K.D. Henderson) Campus Security: Situational Crime Prevention in High-Density Environments, 2001. EDITOR: (with S. Hakim) Crime Spillover, 1981; (with S. Hakim and R. Figlio) Metropolitan Crime Patterns, 1986; (with J. Wasilchick) Suburban Burglary: A Tale of Two Suburbs, 2000; (with J. Ratcliffe and S. Chakravorty) Policing Illegal Drug Markets: Geographic Approaches to Crime Reduction, 2005. (with E. Groff) Residential Burglary, 2011. Contributor to books and periodicals. **Address:** Department of Criminal Justice, Temple University, Philadelphia, PA 19122, U.S.A. **Online address:** grengert@temple.edu

RENKER, Elizabeth. American (born United States), b. 1961. **Genres:** Literary Criticism And History, Education, Poetry. **Career:** Johns Hopkins University, instructor in English, 1989-90; Smithsonian Institution, instructor, 1990; Ohio State University, assistant professor, 1991-97, associate professor of English, 1997-. **Publications:** Strike through the Mask: Herman Melville and the Scene of Writing, 1996; (intro.) Moby Dick, or The Whale, 1998; The Origins Of American Literature Studies: An Institutional History, 2007; Where is the American Department?: The Rise of American Literature Studies, 1865-1950, forthcoming; The Lost Era In American Poetry, forthcoming. Contributor to periodicals. **Address:** Department of English, Ohio State University, 511 Denney Hall, 164 W 17th Ave., Columbus, OH 43210, U.S.A. **Online address:** renker.1@osu.edu

RENNELL, Tony. British (born England) **Genres:** Business/Trade/Industry, Reference, History. **Career:** The Sunday Times, associate editor; Mail on Sunday, associate editor. **Publications:** (With B. Turner) When Daddy came Home: How Family Life Changed Forever in 1945, 1996; Last Days of Glory: The Death of Queen Victoria, 2000; (with J. Nichol) Last Escape: The Untold Story of Allied Prisoners of War in Germany, 1944-1945, 2002; (with J. Nichol) The Last Escape: The Untold Story of Allied Prisoners of War in Europe, 1944-1945, 2003; (with J. Nichol) Tail-End Charlies: The Last Battles of the Bomber War, 1944-45, 2004; (with J. Nichol) Medic: Saving Lives from Dunkirk to Afghanistan, 2009. **Address:** c/o Author Mail, Viking Children's Books, 375 Hudson St., New York, NY 10014, U.S.A. **Online address:** tonyrennell@compuserve.com

RENNIE, Bradford James. Canadian (born Canada), b. 1960. **Genres:** History, Politics/Government, Biography, Autobiography/Memoirs, Adult Non-fiction. **Career:** University of Victoria, instructor in history, 1996-98; University of Calgary, instructor in history, 1999-2000; University of Alberta, instructor in history, 2002; historian and writer, 2002-. **Publications:** The Rise of Agrarian Democracy: The United Farmers and Farm Women of Alberta, 1909-1921, 2000; (ed.) Alberta Premiers of the Twentieth Century, 2004. **Address:** 616 27th Ave. NW, Calgary, AB T2M 2J1, Canada.

RENNIE, Bryan S. British/Scottish (born Scotland), b. 1954. **Genres:** Theology/Religion, Philosophy. **Career:** Westminster College, professor, 1991-

, Department of Religion, History, Philosophy and Classics, chair and Vira I. Heinz professor of religion. Writer. **Publications:** Reconstructing Eliade: Making Sense of Religion, 1996; (ed.) Changing Religious Worlds: The Meaning and End of Mircea Eliade, 2000; (ed.) Mircea Eliade: A Critical Reader, 2006; (ed.) The International Eliade, 2007; (ed. with P.L. Tite) Religion, Terror and Violence: Religious Studies Perspectives, 2008. **Address:** Department of Religion, History, Philosophy and Cl, Westminster College, 319 S Market St., New Wilmington, PA 16172-0001, U.S.A. **Online address:** brennie@westminster.edu

RENNISON, Louise. British/American (born United States), b. 1951. **Genres:** Humor/Satire, Adult Non-fiction, Novels, Novellas/Short Stories, Mystery/Crime/Suspense. **Career:** British Broadcasting Corp., Radio-4, comedy columnist. Writer and comedian. **Publications:** Angus, Thongs and Full-Frontal Snogging: Confessions of Georgia Nicolson, 1999; It's OK, I'm Wearing Really Big Knickers!: Further Confessions by Georgia Nicolson, 2000 in US as On the Bright Side, I'm Now the Girlfriend of a Sex God: Further Confessions of Georgia Nicolson, 2001; Knocked out by My Nunga-Nungas, 2001; Dancing in My Nuddy-Pants, 2002; Further Confessions of Georgia Nicolson, 2004; Away Laughing on a Fast Camel, 2004; Then He Ate My Boy Entrancers: More Mad, Marvy Confessions of Georgia Nicolson, 2005; Startled by His Furry Shorts, 2006; Love is a Many Trousered Thing: Confessions of Georgia Nicolson, 2007; Fabbity-fab Journal, 2007; Georgia's Book of Wisdomosity, 2008; Stop in the Name of Pants!, 2008; Georgia Nicolson's Little Pink Book, 2009; Luuurve and Other Ramblings, 2009; Are These My Basoomas I See Before Me?: Final Confessions of Georgia Nicolson, 2009; Withering Tights, 2010; Fab Confessions of Georgia Nicolson, VII-X vols., 2011. Contributor to periodicals. **Address:** c/o Author Mail, Piccadilly Press, 5 Castle Rd., London, GL NW1 8PR, England.

RENSHAW, Corinne. Welsh (born Wales), b. 1929. **Genres:** Novels, Novellas/Short Stories. **Career:** Teacher, 1950-58; author, 1955-. **Publications:** Thalassine, 1971; The Shadow People, 1982; The Hand of Aquila Possett, 1993; The Sun House and Other Stories, 1996; High Water, 1999. Contributor of articles to journals. **Address:** Gomer Press Ltd., Llandysul Enterprise Pk., Llandysul, DY SA44 4JN, Wales.

RENSHON, Jonathan. American (born United States), b. 1982. **Genres:** Politics/Government, Social Sciences. **Career:** Author and scholar. **Publications:** Why Leaders Choose War: The Psychology of Prevention, 2006. Contributor to books and periodicals. **Address:** Harvard University, 1737 Cambridge St., Cambridge, MA 02138, U.S.A. **Online address:** jrenshon@fas.harvard.edu

RENTON, N(ick) E. Australian (born Australia), b. 1931. **Genres:** Money/Finance, Economics, How-to Books, Business/Trade/Industry. **Career:** Life Offices' Association of Australia, executive director, 1975-79; Life Insurance Federation of Australia, executive director, 1979-86; OFM Investment Group Ltd., director, 1987-2003, retired, 2003; Institute of Actuaries of Australia, fellow; Australian Shareholders' Association, founder. Writer. **Publications:** Guide for Meetings and Organizations: A Handy Reference Manual for Members of Clubs and Societies, 1961, 7th ed., Guide for Meetings and Organizations, 2 vols., 2000; Understanding Investment Property: A Handbook for Present and Potential Investors in the Australian Property Market, 1989, 4th ed., 2004; Understanding Managed Investments: A Handbook for Present and Potential Investors in Unit Trusts, Life Insurance and Superannuation, 1989; Understanding the Stock Exchange: A Handbook for Present and Potential Investors in Shares and Fixed-Interest Securities and a Primer on Other Common Forms of Investment, 1989, 4th ed., 2004; (ed.) Dictionary of Stock Exchange Terms, 1990; Compendium of Good Writing, 1990, 3rd ed., 2004; Metaphors: An Annotated Dictionary in US as Metaphorically Speaking: A Dictionary of 3800 Picturesque Idiomatic Expressions, 1990, 2nd ed., 1992; Understanding the Australian Economic Debate, 1990; Guide for Voluntary Associations, 5th ed., 1991; (with J. Gurney) Successful Clubs, 1995; Understanding Stockbrokers and Financial Advisers, 2001; Family Financial Affairs, 2001; Learn More About Shares, 2002; Learn More About Property, 2002; Renton's Understanding the Stock Exchange: The Essential Reference, 2004; Dictionary of Stock Exchange and Investment Terms, 2004, rev. ed., 2008; Public Relations: A Matter of Spin, 2004; Brain Teaser, 2006; The Wit and Wisdom of Money Experts, 2007; Reflections of A Business Rebel, 2007; Successful Public Relations, 2007; Australia Needs Tax Reform, 2008; Understanding Taxation for Investors, 2009. Contributor to periodicals. **Address:** 194 Kilby Rd., Kew East, VI 3102, Australia. **Online address:** ner@nickrenton.com

REPS, John W(illiam). American (born United States), b. 1921. **Genres:** Regional/Urban Planning, Art/Art History, History. **Career:** Cornell University, lecturer, 1948-50, associate professor, 1952-59, professor, 1960-87, professor emeritus of city and regional planning, 1987-, chair, 1952-64; Historic Urban Plans, owner and publisher, 1964-94; University of Georgia, distinguished Bicentennial visiting professor, 1985; Beijing University, visiting professor, 1988; Australian National University, visiting fellow, 1989. Writer. **Publications:** The Making of Urban America: A History of City Planning in the United States, 1965; Monumental Washington: The Planning and Development of the Capital Center, 1967; Town Planning in Frontier America, 1969; Tidewater Towns: City Planning in Colonial Virginia and Maryland, 1972; Cities on Stone, 1976; Cities of the American West: A History of Frontier Urban Planning, 1979; The Forgotten Frontier: Urban Planning in the American West before 1890, 1981; Panoramas of Promise: Pacific Northwest Cities and Towns on Nineteenth-Century Lithographs, 1984; Views and Viewmakers of Urban America: Lithographs of Towns and Cities in the United States and Canada, Notes on the Artists and Publishers, and a Union Catalog of their Work, 1825-1925, 1984; St. Louis Illustrated: Nineteenth-Century Engravings and Lithographs of a Mississippi River Metropolis, 1989; Washington on View: The Nation's Capital since 1790, 1991; Cities of the Mississippi: Nineteenth-Century Images of Urban Development, 1994; Canberra 1912, 1997; Bird's Eye Views: Historic Lithographs of North American Cities, 1998; John Caspar Wild: Painter and Printmaker of Nineteenth-Century Urban America, 2006. **Address:** Department of City & Regional Planning, Cornell University, 216 W Sibley Hall, Ithaca, NY 14853, U.S.A. **Online address:** jwr2@cornell.edu

RESÉNDEZ, Andrés. American/Mexican (born Mexico), b. 1970?. **Genres:** Politics/Government, History. **Career:** Editorial Clío, faculty, 1996-97; Yale University, visiting assistant professor of history, 1997-98; University of California, assistant professor, 1998-2005, associate professor of history, 2005-09, professor, 2009-; Cobblestone Publishing, consultant. Writer. **Publications:** (Co-author) Politica Exterior para un Mundo Nuevo: Mexico en el Nuevo Contexto Internacional, 1991; (with J.E. Pacheco) Cronica del 47, 1997; (contrib.) Continental Crossroads: Remapping U.S.-Mexico Borderlands History, 2004; (ed., trans. and intro.) A Texas Patriot on Trial in Mexico: Jose Antonio Navarro and the Texan Santa Fe Expedition, DeGolyer Library/William P. Clements Center for Southwest Studies, 2005; Changing National Identities at the Frontier: Texas and New Mexico, 1800-1850, 2005; (contrib.) The Divine Charter: Constitutionalism and Liberalism in Nineteenth-Century Mexico, 2005; (with R. Doak) California, 1542-1850, 2006; A Land So Strange: The Epic Journey of Cabeza de Vaca: The Extraordinary Tale of a Shipwrecked Spaniard Who Walked across America in the Sixteenth Century, 2007. Contributor to periodicals. **Address:** Department of History, University of California, 2216 Social Sciences and Humanities, Davis, CA 95616, U.S.A. **Online address:** aresendez@ucdavis.edu

RESIS, Albert. American (born United States), b. 1921. **Genres:** History, Military/Defense/Arms Control, Politics/Government, International Relations/Current Affairs, Biography, Autobiography/Memoirs. **Career:** Northern Illinois University, history faculty, 1964-92, professor emeritus, 1992-. Writer. **Publications:** Stalin, the Politburo and the Onset of the Cold War: 1945-1946, 1988; (ed. and intro.) Molotov Remembers: Inside Kremlin Politics: Conversations with Felix Chuev, 1993. **Address:** Department of History, Northern Illinois University, 1425 W Lincoln Hwy., DeKalb, IL 60115-2828, U.S.A. **Online address:** resis@niu.edu

RESNICK, Mike. American (born United States), b. 1942. **Genres:** Novellas/Short Stories, Science Fiction/Fantasy, Recreation, Sports/Fitness, Novels, Young Adult Non-fiction. **Career:** National Tattler, editor, 1965-66; freelance writer, 1966-; National Insider, editor, 1966-69; National Features Syndicate, editor; Oligarch Publishing, editor and publisher, 1969-70; Collie Cues Magazine, columnist, 1969-80; Briarwood Pet Motel, co-owner, 1976-93; Ben Bella Books, editor. **Publications:** GANYMEDE SERIES: The Goddess of Ganymede, 1968; Pursuit on Ganymede, 1968. FAR FUTURE HISTORY SERIES: Birthright: The Book of Man, 1982; Santiago: A Myth of the Far Future, 1980; The Dark Lady: A Romance of the Far Future, 1987. GALACTIC MIDWAY SERIES: Sideshow, 1982; The Three-legged Hootch Dancer, 1983; The Wild Alien Tamer, 1983; The Best Rootin' Tootin' Shootin' Gunslinger in the Whole Damned Galaxy, 1983. VELVET COMET SERIES:

Eros Ascending, 1984; Eros At Zenith, 1984; Eros Descending, 1985; Eros At Nadir, 1986; Tales Of The Velvet Comet, 2001. LUCIFER JONES SERIES: Adventures, 1985; Lucifer Jones, 1992; Exploits, 1993; Encounters, 1994; Hazards: The Chronicles of Lucifer Jones 1934-1938, 2009. FABLE OF TONIGHT SERIES: Stalking the Unicorn, 1987; Stalking the Vampire, 2008; Stalking the Dragon, 2009. GALACTIC COMEDY SERIES: Paradise: A Chronicle of a Distant World, 1989; Inferno: A Chronicle of a Distant World, 1993; Purgatory, 1993; Mike Resnick's The Galactic Comedy, 2003. ORACLE SERIES: Soothsayer, 1991; Oracle, 1992; Prophet, 1993. WIDOWMAKER SERIES: The Widowmaker, 1996; The Widowmaker Reborn, 1997; The Widowmaker Unleashed, 1998; Widowmakers, 1998; A Gathering Of Widowmakers, 2005. DRAGON AMERICA SERIES: Revolution, 2005. STARSHIP SERIES: Mutiny, 2005; Pirate, 2006; Mercenary, 2007; Rebel, 2008; Flagship, 2009. NOVELS: Redbeard, 1969; The Soul Eater, 1981; Walpurgis III, 1982; The Branch, 1984; Ivory: A Legend of Past and Future, 1988; Bully!, 1990; Second Contact, 1990; Kirinyaga, 1991; (with J.L. Chalker and G.A. Effinger) The Red Tape War, 1991; A Miracle of Rare Design: A Tragedy of Transcendence, 1994; (with B.N. Malzberg) Dog in the Manger, 1995; A Hunger in the Soul, 1998; Bwana, 1999; The Outpost, 2001; The Return of Santiago, 2003; Legends of Santiago, 2003; Lady with an Alien: An Encounter with Leonardo Da Vinci, 2005; A Club in Montmartre: An Encounter with Henri Toulouse-Lautrec, 2006; World Behind the Door: An Encounter with Salvador Dali, 2007; The Other Teddy Roosevelts, 2008; (with E. Flint) The Gods of Sagittarius, 2010; The Buntline Special, 2010; (with L. Robyn) Benchwarmer, 2010; The Doctor and the Kid, 2011; Doctor and the Rough Rider, 2012; (with J. McDevitt) The Cassandra Project, 2012. COLLECTIONS: Stalking the Wild Resnick, 1970; Unauthorized Autobiographies, 1981; Through Darkest Resnick with Gun and Camera, 1990; The Alien Heart, 1991; Pink Elephants and Hairy Toads, 1991; Will the Last Person To Leave the Planet Please Shut Off the Sun?, 1992; Solo Flights Through Shared Worlds, 1996; An Alien Land, 1997; Tales of the Galactic Midway, 1999; A Safari of the Mind, 1999; (with N. DiChario) Magic Feathers: The Mike And Nick Show, 2000; Hunting the Snark: And Other Short Novels, 2002; With a Little Help from My Friends, 2002; New Dreams for Old, 2006; Kilimanjaro: A Fable of Utopia, 2008; Shaka II, 2009; Dreamwish Beasts and Snarks, 2009; Blasphemy, 2010; The Hugo Stories, vol. I-II, 2010; (co-author) Untold Adventures: Dungeons & Dragons, 2011; Redchapel, 2011; Keepsakes, 2011; The Incarceration of Captain Nebula: And Other Lost Futures, 2012. FANTASTIC SERIES WITH M.H. GREENBERG: Dinosaur Fantastic, 1993; Witch Fantastic, 1994. NON-FICTION: Putting It Together: Turning Sow's Ear Drafts into Silk Purse Stories, 1985; Hunter's Choice: Thrilling True Stories, 1996; I Have This Nifty Idea: Now What Do I Do with It?, 2001; Once a Fan, 2002; The Science Fiction Professional: Seven Years of Ask Bwana Columns, 2002; Resnick at Large, 2003; New Voices in Science Fiction, 2003; (with J. Siclari) Worldcon Guest of Honor Speeches, 2006; History Revisited: Real Historians Debate the Best of Alternate History, 2007; (with J.D. Markham) History Revisited: The Great Battles: Eminent Historians Take On the Great Works of Alternative History, 2008; Always a Fan: True Stories from a Life in Science Fiction, 2009; (with B.N. Malzberg) The Business of Science Fiction: Two Insiders Discuss Writing and Publishing, 2010. Works appear in anthologies. Contributor to books and periodicals. **Address:** 10547 Tanagerhills Dr., Cincinnati, OH 45249-3637, U.S.A. **Online address:** mike-resnick@abooks.com

RESNICK, Rachel. American (born United States), b. 1964?. **Genres:** Novels, Autobiography/Memoirs, Literary Criticism And History. **Career:** University of California, writing instructor; Writers on Fire, founder and chief executive officer; Tin House Magazine, contributing editor. **Publications:** Go West Young F*cked-up Chick: A Novel of Separation, 1999; Love Junkie: A Memoir, 2008. Works appear in anthologies. Contributor to periodicals. **Address:** c/o Pilar Queen, McCormick & Williams, 37 W 20th St., New York, NY 10011, U.S.A. **Online address:** info@rachelresnick.com

RESSEGUIE, James L. American (born United States), b. 1945. **Genres:** Novels, Theology/Religion. **Career:** Winebrenner Theological Seminary, assistant professor, 1976-78, associate professor, 1979-83, professor of New Testament, dean of academic and student affairs/registrar, 1990-97, vice president of academic and student affairs, 1997-, director of master of arts; University of Iceland, Fulbright professor, 1990. Writer. **Publications:** Revelation Unsealed: A Narrative Critical Approach to John's Apocalypse, 1998; The Strange Gospel: Narrative Design and Point of View in John, 2001; Spiritual Landscape: Images of the Spiritual Life in the Gospel of Luke, 2004; Narrative Criticism of the New Testament: An Introduction, 2005. Contribu-

tor to books. **Address:** Winebrenner Theological Seminary, 950 N Main St., Findlay, OH 45840, U.S.A. **Online address:** resseguiej@mail.findlay.edu

RESTAK, Richard M(artin). American (born United States), b. 1942. **Genres:** Medicine/Health, Ethics, Sciences, Self Help. **Career:** St. Vincent's Hospital, intern, 1966-67; Mount Sinai Hospital, resident in psychiatry, 1967-68; Georgetown University Hospital, resident in psychiatry, 1968-69; George Washington University Hospital, resident in neurology, 1970-73, School of Medicine and Health Sciences, clinical professor of neurology; Georgetown University, clinical instructor, clinical associate professor of neurology and director of adult neurobehavioral center, 1975-; St. Elizabeth's Hospital, clinical faculty; Kenyon College, visiting lecturer; Ohio State University, visiting lecturer; Wright State University, visiting lecturer; National War College, visiting lecturer; University of Maryland, visiting lecturer; Loyola University of Chicago, visiting lecturer. Writer. **Publications:** Premeditated Man: Bioethics and the Control of Future Human Life, 1975, 2nd ed., 1977; The Brain: The Last Frontier: Explorations of the Human Mind and Our Future, 1979; The Self Seekers, 1982; The Brain, 1984; The Infant Mind, 1986; The Mind, 1988; The Brain has a Mind of Its Own: Insights from a Practicing Neurologist, 1991; The Modular Brain: How New Discoveries in Neuroscience are Answering Age-Old Questions about Memory, Free Will, Consciousness and Personal Identity, 1994; Receptors, 1994; Brainscapes, An Introduction to What Neuroscience has Learned about the Structure, Function and Abilities of The Brain, 1995; Older and Wiser: How to Maintain Peak Mental Ability for As Long As You Live, 1997, 2nd ed., 1998; (with D. Mohoney) The Longevity Strategy: How to Live to 100 Using the Brain-Body Connection, 1998; Mysteries of the Mind, 2000; Mozart's Brain and the Fighter Pilot, 2001; (with D. Grubin) The Secret Life of the Brain, 2001; The New Brain: How the Modern Age is Rewiring Your Mind, 2003; Poe's Heart and The Mountain Climber: Exploring the Effect of Anxiety on Our Brains and Our Culture, 2004; The Naked Brain: How the Emerging Neurosociety is Changing How we Live, Work and Love, 2006; Think Smart A Neuroscientist's Prescription for Improving your Brain's Performance, 2009; (with S. Kim) The Playful Brain: The Surprising Science of How Puzzles Improve Your Mind, 2010. **Address:** 1800 R St. NW, Washington, DC 20009, U.S.A. **Online address:** inquiries@richardrestak.com

RESTALL, Matthew. American/British (born England), b. 1964. **Genres:** History. **Career:** Southwestern University, assistant professor of Latin American history, 1993-95; Boston College, assistant professor of colonial Latin American history, 1995-98; Pennsylvania State University, associate professor of colonial Latin American history, 1998-2004, professor of colonial Latin American history, 2004-07, director of graduate studies in history, 2005-08, Edwin Erle Sparks professor of Latin American history, 2007-; Ethnohistory, editor, 2007-. **Publications:** Life and Death in a Maya Community: The Ixil Testaments of the 1760s, 1995; The Maya World: Yucatec Culture and Society, 1550-1850, 1997; (ed. with S. Kellogg and contrib.) Dead Giveaways: Indigenous Testaments of Colonial Mesoamerica and the Andes, 1998; Maya Conquistador, 1998; (ed. with U. Hostettler) Maya Survivalism, 2001; Seven Myths of the Spanish Conquest, 2003; (ed.) Beyond Black and Red: African-Native Relations in Colonial Latin America, 2005; (ed. and trans. with L. Sousa and K. Terraciano) Mesoamerican Voices: Native-Language Writings from Central Mexico, Oaxaca, Yucatan, and Guatemala, 2005; (with F. Asselbergs) Invading Guatemala: Spanish, Nahua, and Maya Accounts of the Conquest Wars, 2007; The Black Middle: Africans, Mayas, and Spaniards in Colonial Yucatan, 2009; (ed. with B. Vinson III) Black Mexico, 2009; (with A. Solari) 2012 and the End of the World: The Western Roots of the Maya Apocalypse, 2011. Contributor of articles to books and journals. **Address:** Department of History, Pennsylvania State University, Rm. 216, 108 Weaver Bldg., University Park, PA 16802, U.S.A. **Online address:** restall@psu.edu

RESTALL ORR, Emma. British (born England), b. 1965. **Genres:** Theology/Religion, Philosophy, Women's Studies And Issues. **Career:** Author and philosopher, 1987-; British Druid Order, priest and counselor, 1989-, joint chief, 1994-2002; The Druid Network, head, 2002-; Honouring the Ancient Dead, founder, 2004-. **Publications:** Spirits of the Sacred Grove, 1998; Thorson's Principles of Druidry, 1998; Ritual: A Guide to Life, Love and Inspiration, 2000; Druidry, 2000; Druid Priestess, 2001; A Druid Directory, 2001; Druidry: Rekindling the Sacred Flame, 2002; Living Druidry: Magical Spirituality for the Wild Soul, 2004; (ed. with L. de Angeles and T. van Dooren) Pagan Visions for a Sustainable Future, 2005; (with B. Melnyk) The Apple and The Thorn, 2007; Living With Honour: A Pagan Ethics, 2008; Kissing the Hag: The Dark Goddess and the Unacceptable Nature of Women, 2008.

Contributor to journals and periodicals. **Address:** The Druid Network, PO Box 3533, Whichford, Shipston-on-Stour, WW CV36 5YB, England. **Online address:** bobcat@druidnetwork.org

RETTSTATT, Chris. American (born United States), b. 1972. **Genres:** Graphic Novels, Science Fiction/Fantasy, Children's Fiction, Young Adult Fiction. **Career:** Highlights for Children (media company), director of digital dontent; Star Farm Productions (entertainment company), director of story development; Story Monk Studios (IP development studio), writer and creative consultant. **Publications:** KAIMIRA FANTASY SERIES: (with N. Ashland) The Sky Village, 2008; The Terrible Everything, 2010. **Address:** Chicago, IL , U.S.A. **Online address:** rettstatt@gmail.com

REUBEN, Bryan G. British (born England), b. 1934. **Genres:** Chemistry, Economics, Medicine/Health, Technology. **Career:** Brookhaven National Laboratory, postdoctoral fellow, 1958-60; Distillers Company Ltd., researcher, sales development executive, 1960-63; University of Surrey, lecturer, 1963-77; London South Bank University, reader, 1977-, professor of chemical technology, through 1997, professor emeritus, 1997-. Writer. **Publications:** (With M.L. Burstall) The Chemical Economy: A Guide to the Technology and Economics of the Chemical Industry, 1973; (with H.A. Wittcoff) Industrial Organic Chemicals in Perspective, vol. I: Raw Materials and Manufacture, vol. II: Technology, Manufacture, and Use, 1980; (with H.A. Wittcoff) Pharmaceutical Chemicals in Perspective, 1989; (with M.L. Burstall) Generic Pharmceuticals-The Threat, 1989; (with M.L. Burstall) Critics of the Pharmaceutical Industry, 1990; (with M.L. Burstall) Cost Containment in the European Pharmaceutical Market, 1992; (with I. Senior) Implications of the European Community's Proposed Policy for Self-Sufficiency in Plasma and Plasma Products, 1993; (with H.A. Wittcoff) Industrial Organic Chemicals, 1996, 2nd ed., 2003; (with M.L. Burstall) Outlook for the World Pharmaceutical Industry to 2010, 1999, 2nd ed. as Outlook for the World Pharmaceutical Industry to 2015, 2003; (with M.L. Burstall) Pharmaceutical R and D Productivity: The Path to Innovation, 2005; (with Marchant and Alcock) Bread: A Slice of History, 2008. Contributor to books and journals. **Address:** Department of Information Communications and Techn, London South Bank University, 90 London Rd., London, GL SE1 0AA, England. **Online address:** reubenbg@lsbu.ac.uk

REUBER, Grant L. Canadian (born Canada), b. 1927. **Genres:** Business/ Trade/Industry, Economics, Politics/Government. **Career:** Bank of Canada, economist, 1950-52; Government of Canada, Department of Finance, economist, 1955-57, deputy minister, 1979-80; University of Western Ontario, assistant professor, 1957-59, associate professor, 1959-62, professor of economics, 1962-69, chairman of department, 1963-69, dean of social sciences, 1969-74, vice president and provost, 1974-78, chancellor, 1988-92; Bank of Montreal, senior vice president and chief economist, 1978-79, executive vice-president, 1980-, deputy chairman, 1981-83, 1987-90, director, 1981-90, president and chief operating officer, 1983-87; Canada Deposit Insurance Corp., chairman, 1992-99; Sussex Circle, senior adviser and director, 1999-; C.D. Howe Institute, senior fellow. Writer. **Publications:** Growth and Changing Composition of Trade Between Canada and the United States, 1960; Britain's Export Trade with Canada, 1960; Canada-United States Trade: Its Growth and Changing Composition, 1960; (with R.J. Wonnacott) The Cost of Capital in Canada, 1961; Canada's Interest in the Trade Problems of Less-Developed Countries, 1964; The Objectives of Monetary Policy, 1964; (with R.G. Bodkin, E.P. Bond and T.R. Robinson) Price Stability and High Employment: The Options for Canadian Economic Policy, 1967; (with F. Roseman) The Take-Over of Canadian Firms 1945-61: An Empirical Analysis, 1969; (with R.E. Caves) Canadian Economic Policy and the Impact of International Capital Flows, 1969; Wage Determination in Canadian Manufacturing Industries, 1969; (co-author) Capital Transfers and Economic Policy: Canada 1951-62, 1970; (with H. Crookell, M. Emerson and G. Gallais-Hamonno) Private Foreign Investment in Development, 1973; (ed. with T.N. Guinsburg) Perspectives on the Social Sciences in Canada, 1974; Some Aspects of Private Direct Investment in Developing Countries, 1974; Canada's Political Economy, 1980. Contributor to journals. **Address:** Sussex Circle, 50 O'Connor St., Ste. 1424, Ottawa, ON K1P 6L2, Canada.

REULAND, Robert. American (born United States), b. 1963. **Genres:** Novels, Mystery/Crime/Suspense. **Career:** Brooklyn District Attorney's Office, Homicide Bureau, senior assistant district attorney, 1990-2001; Winthrop, Stimson, Putnam & Roberts, associate, 1990-93; Brown & Wood, associate, 1993-96. Writer. **Publications:** ANDREW GIOBBERTI SERIES: Hollow-

point: A Novel, 2001; Semiautomatic: A Novel, 2004. **Address:** c/o Jennifer Rudolph Walsh, William Morris Agency L.L.C., 1325 Ave. of the Americas, New York, NY 10019-6026, U.S.A. **Online address:** rob@robreuland.com

REUSCHE, Taylor McCafferty. Also writes as Barbara Taylor McCafferty, Taylor McCafferty, Tierney McClellan. American (born United States), b. 1946. **Genres:** Novels, Mystery/Crime/Suspense, Young Adult Fiction, Horror, Literary Criticism And History. **Career:** Schneider, DeMuth Advertising, art director, 1980-88. Writer. **Publications:** AS TAYLOR McCAFFERTY: HASKELL BLEVINS MYSTERY SERIES: Pet Peeves, 1990; Ruffled Feathers, 1992; Bed Bugs, 1993; Thin Skins, 1994; Hanky Panky, 1995; (contrib.) Canine Crimes, 1998; Funny Money, 2000. AS BARBARA TAYLOR Mc-CAFFERTY: BERT AND NAN TATUM MYSTERIES WITH B.T. HERALD: Double Murder, 1996; Double Exposure, 1997; Double Cross, 1998; Double Dealer, 2000; Double Date, 2001. AS TIERNEY McCLELLAN: SCHUYLER RIDGWAY MYSTERY SERIES: Heir Condition, 1995; Closing Statement, 1995; A Killing in Real Estate, 1996; Two-story Frame, 1997. Contributor to periodicals. **Address:** c/o Richard Parks, The Richard Parks Agency, 138 E 16th St., Ste. 5B, PO Box 693, New York, NY 10003-3561, U.S.A. **Online address:** barbara@mysterytwins.com

REUSS, Frederick. American/Ethiopian (born Ethiopia), b. 1960. **Genres:** Novels, Psychology. **Career:** Huffington Post, contributor. Writer. **Publications:** Horace Afoot, 1997; Henry of Atlantic City, 1999; The Wasties, 2002; Mohr, 2006; Geography of Secrets, 2010. **Address:** c/o Author Mail, Pantheon Books, 1540 Broadway, New York, NY 10036, U.S.A.

REUTER, Bjarne (B.). Danish (born Denmark), b. 1950. **Genres:** Plays/ Screenplays, Young Adult Fiction, Novels, Novellas/Short Stories, Mystery/ Crime/Suspense, Children's Fiction. **Career:** Teacher, 1975-80; writer, 1980-. **Publications:** Kidnapping, 1975; Slusernes kejser, 1978; Busters Verden (novel), 1978; Suzanne & Leonard, 1980; Kys stjernerne (novel), 1980; Knud, Otto & Carmen Rosita, 1981; Hvor regnbuen ender, 1982; Når Snerlen Blomstrer, 1983; Casanova, 1983; Da solen skulle saelges (retelling of a Chinese folk tale), 1985; Dag i Hector Hansens liv: Busters verden; Kom der lys i neonrøret, gutter?, 1984; Tro kopi, 1986; Månen over Bella Bio, 1988; Cubanske kabala, 1988; Buster's World, 1989; Skaeggede dame, 1989; Vi der valgte maelkevejen, 1989; Buster the Sheikh of Hope Street, 1991; Drengene fra Sankt Petri (novel), 1991; Drengene fra Sankt Petri, 1992; 7. a, 1992; Rem af huden: Roman, 1992; Korsıkanske Bisp, 1993; Johnny & The Hurrycanes: Roman, 1993; Boys from St. Petri, 1994; Langebro med tbende figurer, 1995; Ved profetens skaeg: Roman, 1996; Kaptajn Bimse & Kong Kylie, 1996; Fakiren fra Bilbao, 1997; En som Hodder, 1998; Willys fars bil, 1999; Under Kometens Hale, 1999; Mordet påLeon Culman: Roman, 1999; Prins Faisals Ring, 2000; Barolo Kvartetten, 2002; Kaptajn Bimse i Saltimbocca, 2002; Kaptajn Bimses jul, 2003; Ring of the Slave Prince, 2003; Halvvejen til Rafael, 2006; Skyggernes hus, 2007; [Fem]: Roman, 2008; Iranske Gartner: Roman, 2008; Den egyptische Tenor, 2009. **Address:** International Children Book Service, Skindergade 3 B, Copenhagen K, DK-1159, Denmark.

REUTER, Christoph. German (born Germany), b. 1968?. **Genres:** History. **Career:** Stern (magazine), reporter & international correspondent. Writer. **Publications:** (with I. Seebold) Medien und Meinungsfreiheit in Pal Astina Deutsches Orient-Institut (Hamburg, Germany), 2000; (trans.) Mein Leben ist eine Waffe (title means: 'My Life Is a Weapon: A Modern History of Suicide Bombing'), 2004.

RÉV, István. Hungarian (born Hungary), b. 1951?. **Genres:** History, Politics/ Government. **Career:** Hungarian Academy of Sciences, assistant research fellow, 1975-82, research fellow, 1981-85; Karl Marx University of Economics, scientific fellow, 1985-91; Budapest School of Economics, scientific research fellow and academic director, 1986-91; Central European University, Department of History and Political Science, professor, 1991-, Budapest College, director, 1991-94, academic pro-rector, 1994-95, Open Society Archive, founding academic director, 1994-97, director, 1997-; University of California, visiting faculty. Writer. **Publications:** Economic and Social History of Hungary in the Period of Socialism, 1990; Retroactive Justice: Prehistory of Post-Communism, 2005. Contributor to books and periodicals. **Address:** Department of History, Central European University, Nador u. 9, H-1051, Budapest, H-1051, Hungary. **Online address:** revist@ceu.hu

REVARD, Carter (Curtis). American (born United States), b. 1931. **Genres:** Poetry, Novellas/Short Stories, Essays, Autobiography/Memoirs,

Literary Criticism And History. **Career:** Amherst College, instructor, 1956-59, assistant professor of English, 1959-61; Washington University, assistant professor, 1961-66, associate professor, 1966-77, professor of English literature and language, 1977-97, professor emeritus, 1997-; Missouri Academy of Sciences, visiting linguist, 1965-67; System Development Corp., consultant to lexicography project, 1966-67, associate resident scientist, 1967-68; University of Tulsa, visiting professor of English, 1981; University of Oklahoma, visiting Sutton professor of humanities, 1989. Writer. **Publications:** My Right Hand Don't Leave Me No More (poetry), 1970; Ponca War Dancers (poetry), 1980; Cowboys and Indians, Christmas Shopping (poetry), 1992; An Eagle Nation (poetry), 1993; Family Matters/Tribal Affairs (essay, autobiography), 1998; Winning the Dust Bowl (poems, essays, autobiography), 2001; How The Songs Come Down (new and selected poems), 2005. Contributor to journals, books and periodicals. **Address:** Department of English, Washington University, St. Louis, MO 63130, U.S.A. **Online address:** ccrevard@artsci.wustl.edu

REVELLE, Jack B. American (born United States), b. 1935. **Genres:** Administration/Management, Information Science/Computers, Mathematics/Statistics. **Career:** General Dynamics, administrative assistant, 1970-71; consultant, 1971-72; University of Nebraska, chair of decision sciences program, 1972-77; Chapman University, School of Business and Management, founding dean, 1977-79; Ducommun Metals Co., manager of facilities and engineering, 1979-80; McDonnell Douglas Astronautics Co. (now Boeing Co.), head of facilities planning and technical specialist, 1980-81; Hughes Electronics Co., head of training and development for ground systems group, 1981-82, head of statistical services, 1982-85, senior statistician, 1985-86, manager of research and development for corporate human resources, 1986-88, chief statistician for corporate quality assurance staff, 1988-93, Raytheon Missile Systems, leader of continuous improvement, 1993-98; ReVelle Solutions L.L.C., consulting statistician, 1999-; GenCorp Aerojet, Center for Process Improvement, director; University of Southern California, faculty; University of Wisconsin, faculty; Institute of Industrial Engineers, regional vice president, senior vice president and treasurer, Aerospace and Defense Division, director. Writer. **Publications:** (With K.S. Brown) Quantitative Methods for Managerial Decisions, 1978; Safety Training Methods, 1980, (with J. Stephenson) 2nd ed. as Safety Training Methods: Practical Solutions for the Next Millennium, 1995; The Two-Day Statistician, 1984; The New Quality Technology, 1988; Policy Deployment, 1993; (with J.W. Moran) The Executive's Handbook on Quality Function Deployment, 1994; (with N.L. Frigon and H.K. Jackson) From Concept to Customer: The Practical Guide to Integrated Product and Process Development, and Business Process Re-engineering, 1995; (with J.W. Moran and C.A. Cox) The Quality Function Deployment Handbook, 1998; (with J.W. Moran and C.A. Cox) QFD Handbook, 1998; What Your Quality Guru Never Told You, 2000; (ed.) Manufacturing Handbook of Best Practices, 2002; Quality Essentials: A Reference Guide from A to Z, 2004; (with D.N. Margetts) Home Builder's Guide to Continuous Improvement: Schedule, Quality, Customer Satisfaction, Cost, and Safety, 2010. Contributor to books. **Address:** ReVelle Solutions L.L.C., PO Box 10315, Santa Ana, CA 92711-0315, U.S.A. **Online address:** info@revellesolutions.com

REVELS, Tracy J. American (born United States), b. 1963. **Genres:** History, Military/Defense/Arms Control. **Career:** Florida State University, teaching assistant, 1988-89, Gordon Rule instructor, 1989-90; Georgia Southern University, assistant professor, 1990-91; Wofford College, Department of History, assistant professor, 1991-97, associate professor, 1997-, department chair, 2008-. Writer. **Publications:** Watery Eden: A History of Wakulla Springs, 2002; Grander in Her Daughters: Florida's Women during the Civil War, 2004; Sunshine Paradise: A History of Florida Tourism, 2011. **Address:** Wofford College, 109 Old Main Bldg., 429 N Church St., Spartanburg, SC 29303-3663, U.S.A. **Online address:** revelstj@wofford.edu

REVIE, Linda Lee. Canadian (born Canada), b. 1962. **Genres:** Social Work, History. **Career:** University of Waterloo, part-time lecturer, 1997-2001; University of Guelph, lecturer, 1999-2005; St. Francis Xavier University, contract professor, 2005-06; Cape Breton University, lecturer, 2006-, assistant professor, professor. Writer. **Publications:** The Niagara Companion: Explorers, Artists, and Writers at the Falls, from Discovery through the Twentieth Century, 2003. Works appear in anthologies. Contributor to periodicals and journals. **Address:** Department of English, Cape Breton University, 1250 Grand Lake Rd., PO Box 5300, Sydney, NS B1P 6L2, Canada. **Online address:** linda_revie@cbu.ca

REX, John Arderne. British/South African (born South Africa), b. 1925. **Genres:** Race Relations, Sociology. **Career:** Leeds University, lecturer, 1949-62; University of Hull, visiting lecturer, 1960-61; Birmingham University, lecturer, 1962-64; University of Durham, professor, 1964-70; British Sociological Association, chairman, 1969-71; University of Warwick, professor of sociology, 1970-79, Centre for Research in Ethnic Relations, associate director, 1984-90, professor emeritus, 1990-; University of Toronto, visiting professor, 1974-75; American Journal of Sociology, consulting editor, 1974-76; University of Aston, Social Science Research Council's Research Unit on Ethnic Relations, director, visiting professor, 1979-84. Writer. **Publications:** Key Problems of Sociological Theory, 1961; (with R. Moore) Race Community and Conflict: A Study of Sparkbook, 1967; Race, Community and Conflict, 1967; Race Relations in Sociological Theory, 1970, 2nd ed., 1983; Race Colonialism and the City, 1973; Discovering Sociology, 1973; Sociology and the Demystification of the Modern World, 1974; (ed.) Approaches to Sociology, 1974; (with S. Tomlinson) Colonial Immigrants in a British City; A Class Analysis, 1979; (ed. with intro.) Apartheid and Social Research, 1981; Social Conflict: A Conceptual and Theoretical Analysis, 1981; (with M. Cross) Unemployment and Racial Conflict in the Inner City, 1982; Migrant Workers in Metropolitan Cities: Contributions to the First Workshop held in Birmingham on 23-25 June 1980, 1982; Concept of a Multi-cultural Society: A Lecture to Mark the Establishment of the Centre for Research in Ethnic Relations in the University Of Warwick, 1985; Race and Ethnicity, 1986; (with D. Mason) Theories of Race and Ethnic Relations, 1986; (ed. with D. Joly and C. Wilpert) Immigrant Associations in Europe, 1987; The Ghetto and The Underclass, 1988; Ethnic Identity and Ethnic Mobilisation in Britain, 1991; Knowledge and Passion, 1993; (ed. with B. Drury) Ethnic Mobilisation in a Multi-Cultural Europe, 1994; (with A. Binstock) Practical Algorithms for Programmers, 1995; Sociology of Ethnic Conflict, 1996; Ethnic Minorities in the Modern Nation State: Working Papers in the Theory of Multiculturalism and Political Integration, 1996; (with M. Guidginbu) The Ethnicity Reader: Nationalism, Multiculturalism and Migration, 1997, 2nd ed., 2010; (ed. with G. Sign) Governance in Multicultural Societies, 2004. Contributor to periodicals. **Address:** Center for Research in Ethnic Relations, University of Warwick, Coventry, CV4 7AL, England. **Online address:** j.rex@warwick.ac.uk

REX, Richard. British (born England), b. 1961. **Genres:** Theology/Religion. **Career:** Her Majesty's Treasury, administrative trainee, 1983-85; Cambridge University, St. John's College, research fellow, 1988-92, University Library, assistant under-librarian, 1992-95, faculty of divinity, lecturer, 1995-2002, senior lecturer, 2002-06, reader, 2006-, chair of faculty of divinity, 2006-, MPhil in Theology and Religious Studies, director, 2006-07, Queens' College, tutor, reader in reformation History, fellow, 1995-, director of studies in history, 2000-. Writer. **Publications:** The Theology of John Fisher, 1991; Henry VIII and the English Reformation, 1993, 2nd ed., 2006; (ed.) A Reformation Rhetoric: Thomas Swynnerton's The Tropes and Figures of Scripture, 1999; The Lollards, 2002; The Tudors, 2002, new ed., 2009; Elizabeth I, Fortune's Bastard: A Short Account of the Long Life of Elizabeth I, 2003, 2nd ed., 2009; (with P. Collinson and G. Stanton) Lady Margaret Beaufort and Her Professors of Divinity at Cambridge, 1502-1649, 2003. **Address:** Faculty of History, University of Cambridge, West Rd., Cambridge, CB CB3 9BS, England. **Online address:** rawr1@cam.ac.uk

REY, Bret. British (born England), b. 1918?. **Genres:** Westerns/Adventure, Novels, Young Adult Fiction. **Career:** Writer. **Publications:** Birth of a Gunman, 1985; Stranger in Town, 1987; Hold-Up, 1987; Ned Butler, Bounty Hunter, 1988; Railroad Robbers, 1988; Trouble Valley, 1989; The Killing Game, 1990; Arizona Ambush, 1990; Runaway, 1990; Arizona Breakout, 1990; Black Day in Woodville, 1991; Marshal without a Badge, 1991; Gunsmoke in a Colorado Canyon, 1991; Texas Pilgrim, 1992; Half-Way to Hell, 1992; The Devil Rode a Pinto, 1993; Guns and Gold, 1993; A Bullet for Darwen, 1993; Marshal Dick Blaine, 1994; Battle at Rocky Creek, 1994; Outlaw's Woman, 1995; West of the Brazos, 1995; Kill Conway, 1996; Colorado Conflict, 1997; Bullets in Buzzards Creek, 1997; A Killing in Horseshoe Bend, 1998. **Address:** Robert Hale Ltd., Clerkenwell House, 45/47 Clerkenwell Green, London, GL EC1R 0HT, England.

REY, Dennison. American (born United States), b. 1971. **Genres:** Novels, Horror, Literary Criticism And History. **Career:** Writer. **Publications:** Aware of My Hide, 2002; Torn: From the Shorts of Dennison Rey, 2005. **Address:** c/o Author Mail, Outskirts Press Inc., 10940 S Parker Rd., Ste. 515, Parker, CO 80134-7440, U.S.A. **Online address:** dennison@thesampsongallery.com

REYHNER, Jon (Allan). American (born United States), b. 1944. **Genres:** Cultural/Ethnic Topics, Education. **Career:** Chinle Junior High School, teacher, 1971-73; Fort Defiance Junior High School, social studies teacher, 1973-75; Navajo Public School, assistant principal, 1975-77; Wallace Public School, principal, 1977-78; Rocky Boy Public School, principal, 1978-80; Heart Butte Public School, principal/bilingual director, 1982-84; Havasupai School, chief administrator/principal/bilingual director, 1984-85; Eastern Montana College, assistant professor of education and Native American Studies, 1986-90; Rock Point Community School, assistant director of academics, 1988-89; Montana State University, associate professor of education, 1990-95; Northern Arizona University, associate professor of education, 1995-2002, professor of education, 2002-. Writer. **Publications:** (With H. Gilliland) Teaching the Native American, 1988; (with J. Eder) A History of Indian Education, 1989, 2nd ed., 1993; American Indian/Alaska Native Education, 1994; (with N. Francis) Language and Literacy Teaching for Indigenous Education: A Bilingual Approach, 2002. EDITOR/CO-EDITOR: (and contrib.) Teaching the Indian Child, 1986, 2nd ed., 1988; Autobiography of Mark Hanna, 1988; (and contrib.) Effective Language Education Practices and Native Language Survival, Native Language Issues, 1990; (with E.A.O. Coyote) Teepees Are Folded (poetry), 1991; (with R. Schaffer) Search for Identity, 1991; (and contrib.) Teaching American Indian Students, 1992; Partnerships in Education, 1997; Teaching Indigenous Languages, 1997; (co-ed.) Revitalizing Indigenous Languages, 1999; (co-ed.) Learn in Beauty, 2000; (with B. Burnaby) Indigenous Languages across the Community, 2002; (with N. Francis) Language and Literacy Teaching for Indigenous Education, 2002; Nurturing Native Languages, 2003; (with J. Eder) American Indian Education, 2004; Education and Language Restoration, 2006; (with L. Lockard) Indigenous Language Revitalization: Encouragement, Guidance & Lessons Learned, 2009; (with W.S. Gilbert and L. Lockard) Honoring Our Heritage: Culturally Appropriate Approaches for Teaching Indigenous Students, 2011. Works appear in anthologies. Contributor of articles to journals. **Address:** Northern Arizona University, PO Box 5774, Flagstaff, AZ 86011-0001, U.S.A. **Online address:** jon.reyhner@nau.edu

REYNALD, Lance M. American (born United States), b. 1970. **Genres:** Novels. **Career:** Writer. **Publications:** Pop Salvation (novel), 2009. **Address:** New York, NY , U.S.A. **Online address:** popsalvation09@gmail.com

REYNOLDS, Aaron. American (born United States), b. 1970. **Genres:** Graphic Novels, Picture/Board Books, Education. **Career:** Willow Creek Community Church, Promiseland (children's ministry), artistic director. Children's writer and consultant. **Publications:** The Nineteenth of Maquerk, 2005; Breaking Out of the Bungle Bird, 2005; Tale of the Poisonous Yuck Bugs, 2005; Chicks and Salsa, 2005; Buffalo Wings, 2007; The Fabulous Reinvention of Sunday School: Transformational Techniques for Reaching and Teaching Kids, 2007; Metal Man, 2008; Back of the Bus, 2009; Superhero School, 2009; Joey Fly, Private Eye in Creepy Crawly Crime, 2009. TIGER MOTH SERIES: GRAPHIC NOVELS: Tiger Moth, Insect Ninja, 2007; Tiger Moth and the Dragon Kite Contest, 2007; Tiger Moth: The Dung Beetle Bandits, 2007; Tiger Moth: The Fortune Cookies of Weevil, 2007; Tiger Moth: Kung Pow Chicken, 2008; Tiger Moth: The Pest Show on Earth, 2008. **Address:** Fox River Grove, IL , U.S.A. **Online address:** aaronreynolds@earthlink.net

REYNOLDS, Arlene. American (born United States), b. 1947. **Genres:** History, Military/Defense/Arms Control, Novels, Novellas/Short Stories. **Career:** Singer, 1986-88; Essex Institute, Eerie Events Program, staff, 1988-91; United States Civil War Center, associate. Writer. **Publications:** (Ed. and intro.) The Civil War Memories of Elizabeth Bacon Custer: Reconstructed from Her Diaries and Notes, 1994. Contributor to periodicals. **Address:** Company A Productions, PO Box 593, Lincoln City, OR 97367-0593, U.S.A.

REYNOLDS, Barrie (Gordon Robert). Australian/British (born England), b. 1932. **Genres:** Anthropology/Ethnology, Cultural/Ethnic Topics, Politics/Government, Philosophy, Social Sciences. **Career:** Rhodes-Livingstone Museum (now Livingston Museum), keeper of ethnography, 1955-64, director, 1964-66; Centennial Museum, chief curator, 1968-69; National Museums of Canada, chief ethnologist, 1969-75; James Cook University of North Queensland, professor of material culture, 1975-97; Council of Australian University Museums and Collections, president, 1992-95; University of West-

ern Sydney, adjunct professor, 1998-2000; Macquarie University, adjunct professor of museums and collections, 1998-2000. Writer. **Publications:** Magic, Divination and Witchcraft among the Barotse of Northern Rhodesia, 1963; The African, His Position in a Changing Society, 1963; Somalia Museum Development, 1966; The Material Culture of the Peoples of the Gwembe Valley, 1968; (contrib.) World Ceramics, 1968; Material Culture: A System of Communication, 1984. CO-AUTHOR: Cinderella Collections: University Museums and Collections in Australia, 1996; Transforming Cinderella Collections, 1998. EDITOR: The Fishing Devices of Central and Southern Africa, 1958; The Material Culture of the Ambo of Northern Rhodesia, 1964; (with M.A. Stott) Material Anthropology: Contemporary Approaches to Material Culture, 1987. Contributor to periodicals. **Address:** Prospect Cottage, 40-44 Hume Ave., Wentworth Falls, NW 2782, Australia. **Online address:** barrie.r@bigpond.net.au

REYNOLDS, Bill. American (born United States), b. 1945?. **Genres:** Sports/Fitness, Biography, Autobiography/Memoirs, Business/Trade/Industry, Economics, Self Help, History, Psychology, Psychology. **Career:** Providence Journal-Bulletin, columnist. writer. **Publications:** (With R. Pitino) Born to Coach: A Season with the New York Knicks, 1988; Big Hoops: A Season in the Big East Conference, 1989; Lost Summer: The 67 Red Sox and the Impossible Dream, 1992; Fall River Dreams: A Team's Quest for Glory, A Town's Search for Its Soul, 1994; Success is A Choice: Ten Steps to Overachieving in Business and Life, 1997; Glory Days: On Sports, Men and Dreams That Don't Die: Memoir, 1998; (with R. Pitino) Lead to Succeed: The Ten Traits of Great Leadership in Business and Life, 2000; Cousy: His Life, Career, and the Birth of Big-Time Basketball, 2005; 78: The Boston Red Sox, A Historic Game and A Divided City, 2009; Rise of A Dynasty: The 57 Celtics, the First Banner and the Dawning of A New America, 2010; (with C. Herren) Basketball Junkie: A Memoir, 2011. Contributor to books. **Address:** Providence Journal-Bulletin, Providence Journal Co., 75 Fountain St., Providence, RI 02902, U.S.A. **Online address:** breynold@projo.com

REYNOLDS, David. British (born England), b. 1952. **Genres:** History, International Relations/Current Affairs, Politics/Government, Local History/Rural Topics. **Career:** University of Cambridge, Gonville and Caius College, research fellow, 1978-80, 1981-83, Christ's College, fellow, 1983-, professor of international history, 2002-; Harvard University, visiting fellow, 1980-81; Nihon University, visiting professor, 1995; Sciences Po, visiting professor, 2011. Writer. **Publications:** The Creation of the Anglo-American Alliance, 1937-1941: A Study in Competitive Cooperation, 1982; Lord Lothian and Anglo-American Relations, 1939-1940, 1983; (with D. Dimbleby) An Ocean Apart: The Relationship between Britain and America in the Twentieth Century, 1988; Britannia Overruled: British Policy and World Power in the Twentieth Century, 1991, 2nd ed., 2000; Rich Relations: The American Occupation of Britain, 1942-1945, 1995; One World Divisible: A Global History since 1945, 2000; From Munich to Pearl Harbor: Roosevelt's America and the Origins of the Second World War, 2001; In Command of History: Churchill Fighting and Writing the Second World War, 2004; From World War to Cold War: Churchill, Roosevelt, and the International History of the 1940s, 2006; Summits: Six Meetings That Shaped the Twentieth Century, 2007; America, Empire of Liberty: A New History, 2009. EDITOR: (with W.F. Kimball and A.O. Chubarian) Allies at War: The Soviet, American and British Experience, 1939-1945, 1994; The Origins of the Cold War in Europe: International Perspectives, 1994; Christ's: A Cambridge College over Five Centuries, 2005; (with D.B. Woolner and W.F. Kimball) FDR's World: War, Peace and Legacies, 2008. **Address:** Christ's College, Cambridge, CB CB2 3BU, England. **Online address:** djr17@cam.ac.uk

REYNOLDS, Dee. British (born England) **Genres:** Adult Non-fiction. **Career:** Université de Paris IV, Sorbonne, Paris, France, lectrice, 1986-87; University of Manchester, Manchester, England, professor of French, 1998-; University of Lancaster, faculty; University of Warwick, faculty; University of Keele, faculty; University of Bristol, faculty. Writer. **Publications:** (Ed. with P. Florence) Feminist Subjects, Multi-Media: Cultural Methodologies, 1995; Symbolist Aesthetics and Early Abstract Art: Sites of Imaginary Space, 1995; Rhythmic Subjects: Uses of Energy in the Dances of Mary Wigman, Martha Graham, and Merce Cunningham, 2007. **Address:** School of Languages, Linguistics, & Cultures, University of Manchester, Oxford Rd., Manchester, GM M13 9PL, England. **Online address:** dee.reynolds@manchester.ac.uk

REYNOLDS, E. Bruce. American (born United States), b. 1947. **Genres:** History, Adult Non-fiction. **Career:** KOKO-AM, announcer, 1973-77; Daily

Star Journal, reporter, 1977-79; Chulalongkorn University, lecturer, 1979-82; San Jose State University, assistant professor, 1988-92, East Asian Regional Materials and Resources Center (EARMARC), director, 1990-, associate professor, 1992-98, Department of History, chair, 1995-99, professor of history, 1998-, advisor; East Asian Regional Materials and Resources Center, director, 1991. **Publications:** (Ed. with S. Chantavanich) Indochinese Refugees: Asylum and Resettlement, 1988; (ed. with C. Khamchoo) Thai-Japanese Relations in Historical Perspective, 1988; Thailand and Japan's Southern Advance, 1940-1945, 1994; (ed.) Japan in the Fascist Era, 2004; Thailand's Secret War: The Free Thai, OSS, and SOE during World War II, 2005. Contributor of articles to periodicals. **Address:** Department of History, San Jose State University, 140 Dudley Moorhead Hall, 1 Washington Sq., San Jose, CA 95192-0117, U.S.A. **Online address:** ereynold@email.sjsu.edu

REYNOLDS, Graham. British (born England), b. 1914. **Genres:** Art/Art History. **Career:** Victoria and Albert Museum, assistant keeper of prints and drawings, 1937-39, deputy keeper of paintings, 1945-59, Department of Prints, Drawings and Paintings, keeper, 1959-74; Ministry of Home Security, assistant principal, 1939-42, principal, 1942-45; Fitzwilliam Museum, honorary keeper of portrait miniatures, 1994-. Writer. **Publications:** Twentieth Century Drawings, 1946; (intro.) Paintings, 1947; Nicholas Hilliard and Isaac Oliver, 1947, 2nd ed., 1971; Nineteenth Century Drawings 1850-1900, 1949; Thomas Bewick, 1949; An Introduction to English Water-Colour Painting, 1950, rev. ed. as English Watercolors: An Introduction, 1988; Elizabethan and Jacobean Costume, 1951; English Portrait Miniatures, 1952, rev. ed., 1988; Painters of the Victorian Scene, 1953; Catalogue of the Constable Collection, Victoria and Albert Museum, 1960; Constable, the Natural Painter, 1965; Victorian Painting, 1966, rev. ed., 1987; The Engravings of S.W. Hayter, 1967; British Water-colours, 1968; The Etchings of Anthony Gross, 1969; Turner, 1969; (intro.) Starr Collection of Miniatures in the William Rockhill Nelson Gallery, 1971; A Concise History of Watercolours, 1971; Tudor & Jacobean Miniatures, 1973; (intro.) Sketch-Books of 1813-1814, 1973; Samuel Cooper's Pocket-book, 1975; Catalogue of Miniatures, 1980; Constable's England, 1983; The Later Paintings and Drawings of John Constable, 2 vols., 1984; Watercolors: A Concise History, 1985; (with G. Collier and H.L. Minton) Currents of Thought in American Social Psychology, 1991; The Early Paintings and Drawings of John Constable, 2 vols., 1996; (with K. Baetjer) European Miniatures in the Metropolitan Museum of Art, 1996; British Portrait Miniatures, 1998; Sixteenth and Seventeenth-Century Miniatures in the Collection of Her Majesty the Queen, 1999. EDITOR: Gastronomic Pleasures, 1950; Catalogue of Charles Dickens Centenary Exhibition, 1970; Constable with His Friends in 1806, 1981. **Address:** The Old Manse, Bradfield St. George, Bury St. Edmunds, SU IP30 0AZ, England.

REYNOLDS, Jan. British (born England), b. 1925. **Genres:** Art/Art History, Mystery/Crime/Suspense. **Career:** Writer, 1975-. **Publications:** The Williams Family of Painters, 1975; William Callow, 1980; Birket Foster, 1984. (with C. Lynxwiler and S. Gaskin) Down Home and Deadly: A Sleuthing Sisters Mystery, 2008; (with C. Lynxwiler and S. Gaskin) Drop Dead Diva: A Sleuthing Sisters Mystery, 2008; (with C. Lynxwiler and S. Gaskin) Death on a Deadline: A Sleuthing Sisters Mystery, 2008. Contributor to periodicals. **Address:** Lone Beech, Eaton Dr., Baslow, DB DE4 ISE, England.

REYNOLDS, Kevin. American (born United States), b. 1952. **Genres:** Plays/Screenplays, Film. **Career:** Writer. **Publications:** (With T.R. Price and D. Landau) Rapa Nui: The Easter Island Legend on Film, 1994. Contributor to periodicals. **Address:** William Morris Agency, 1 William Morris Pl., Beverly Hills, CA 90212, U.S.A.

REYNOLDS, Marjorie. American (born United States), b. 1944?. **Genres:** Novels, Mystery/Crime/Suspense. **Career:** Writer. **Publications:** The Starlite Drive-In (novel), 1997; The Civil Wars of Jonah Moran, 1999. **Address:** William Morrow & Co., 1350 Ave. of the Americas, New York, NY 10019-4702, U.S.A.

REYNOLDS, (Richard) Clay. American (born United States), b. 1949. **Genres:** Novels, Novellas/Short Stories, Literary Criticism And History, Essays, Young Adult Fiction. **Career:** University of Tulsa, graduate teaching fellow, 1974-77; Tulsa Junior College, instructor in English, 1977-78; Claremore College, instructor in English, 1977-78; Lamar University, associate professor of English, 1978-88; University of North Texas, professor/novelist-in-residence, 1988-92; Texas Association of Creative Writing Teachers, state officer, 1989-92; Center for Texas Studies, associate director, 1990-92; Vil-

lanova University, visiting professor/writer-in-residence, 1994; University of Texas at Dallas, professor of aesthetics and literature, 1998-, associate dean for undergraduate studies, 2001-, director of creative writing, College of Arts and Humanities, college master, 2001-; Western Writers of America, faculty. Freelance writer, and speaker. **Publications:** Stage Left: The Development of the American Social Drama in the Thirties, 1986; The Vigil, 1986, 3rd ed., 2002; Agatite, 1986; (ed.) Taking Stock: A Larry McMurtry Casebook, 1989; Franklin's Crossing, 1992; (with M. Schein) 100 Years of Heroes: A History of the Southwestern Exposition and Livestock Show, 1995; Players, 1997; Twenty Questions: Answers for the Aspiring Writer, 1998; (with H. Lundy) Let Us Prey, 1999; Monuments, 2000; The Tentmaker, 2002; Hoolian, A Love Story of the West, 2002; ARS Poetica: A Post-Modern Parable, 2003; Threading the Needle, 2003; Sandhill County lines: Stories, 2007; Of Snakes and Sex and Playing in the Rain, 2007; (ed. and intro.) The Hero of a Hundred Fights: Collected Stories From the Dime Novel King, From Buffalo Bill to Wild Bill Hickok, 2011. Contributor to periodicals. Works appear in anthologies. **Address:** School of Arts and Humanities, The University of Texas, JO31, PO Box 830688, Richardson, TX 75083-0688, U.S.A. **Online address:** clayr@utdallas.edu

REYNOLDS, Sheri. American (born United States), b. 1967. **Genres:** Novels, Young Adult Fiction. **Career:** Virginia Commonwealth University, part-time instructor of English, 1992-; Old Dominion University, associate professor, 1997-, Ruth and Perry Morgan chair of Southern literature, 1997-, director of creative writing; College of William and Mary, instructor; Davidson College, instructor. Writer. **Publications:** NOVELS: Bitterroot Landing, 1994; The Rapture of Canaan, 1995; A Gracious Plenty, 1997; Firefly Cloak, 2006; Sweet in-Between: A Novel, 2008. Contributor to periodicals. **Address:** Department of English, College of Arts and Letters, Old Dominion University, BAL 5010, Norfolk, VA 23529, U.S.A. **Online address:** sheri@sherireynolds.com

REYNOLDS, Thomas E. Canadian (born Canada), b. 1963. **Genres:** Philosophy, Theology/Religion. **Career:** St. Norbert College, faculty of religious studies; Victoria University, Emmanuel College, associate professor of theology. Writer and musician. **Publications:** The Broken Whole: Philosophical Steps toward a Theology of Global Solidarity, 2005; Vulnerable Communion: A Theology of Disability and Hospitality, 2008. Contributor to periodicals. **Address:** Emmanuel College, Victoria University, 73 Queen's Park Cres., Toronto, ON M5S 1K7, Canada. **Online address:** tom.reynolds@utoronto.ca

REZA, Yasmina. Spanish/French (born France), b. 1959. **Genres:** Plays/Screenplays, Novels. **Career:** Writer. **Publications:** PLAYS: Conversations après un enterrement, 1987; La Traverśe de l'hiver, 1989; L'homme du hasard, 1995; Art, 1996; Unexpected Man, 1998; Life x 3, 2000; Conversations after a Burial, 2000; Trois versions de la vie, 2000; Une pice espagnole, 2004; Pièce espagnole, 2004; Nulle Part, 2005; Dans la luge d'Arthur Schopenhauer, 2005; Plays One, 2005; Dieu du Carnage, 2007; Aube le Soir ou la Nuit, 2007; Dawn Dusk or Night, 2008; God of Carnage, 2008; Comment vous racontez la partie, 2011. NOVELS: Hammerklavier, 1997; Desolation, 2002; Adam Haberberg: Roman, 2003. Contributor to periodicals. **Address:** Casarotto Ramsay and Associates Ltd., Waverley House, 7-12 Noel St., London, GL W1F 8GQ, England.

REZITS, Joseph. American (born United States), b. 1925. **Genres:** Music, Biography, Autobiography/Memoirs. **Career:** Piano teacher, 1947-52; University of Illinois, instructor in music, 1953-57; Trenton State College, artist-in-residence, assistant professor of music and director of piano studies, 1957-62; Indiana University, assistant professor, 1962-66, associate professor, 1966-71, professor of music, 1971-90, professor emeritus of music, 1990-. Writer. **Publications:** Source Materials for Piano Techniques, 1965; Source Materials for Keyboard Skills, 1975; (with G. Deatsman) Pianist's Resource Guide: Piano Music in Print and Literature on the Pianistic Art, 1974; The Guitarist's Resource Guide, 1982; Beloved Tyranna: The Legend and Legacy of Isabelle Vengerova, 1995. Contributor to journals. **Address:** School of Music, Indiana University, 1201 E 3rd St., Bloomington, IN 47405, U.S.A. **Online address:** rezits@indiana.edu

RHEA, Gordon C. See RHEA, Gordon Campbell.

RHEA, Gordon Campbell. (Gordon C. Rhea). American (born United States), b. 1945. **Genres:** History, Military/Defense/Arms Control. **Career:** Law Offices of Barry Tarlow, associate, 1974-75; assistant U.S. attorney,

1976-82; Law Offices of Alkon, Rhea and Hart, partner, 1982-96; Richardson, Patrick, Westbrook & Brickman L.L.C., attorney; Gordon C. Rhea P.C., counsel, 2009-. Writer. **Publications:** (With C.R. Schenker and S.L. Urbanc) California Land Use Primer: A Legal Handbook for Environmentalists, 1973; The Battle of the Wilderness: May 5-6, 1864, 1994; The Battles of Wilderness & Spotsylvania, 1995; The Battle for Spotsylvania Court House and the Road to Yellow Tavern, May 7-12, 1864, 1997; To the North Anna River: Grant and Lee, May 13-25, 1864, 2000; Cold Harbor: Grant and Lee, May 26-June 3, 1864, 2002; Carrying the Flag: The Story of Private Charles Whilden, the Confederacy's Unlikely Hero, 2004; In the Footsteps of Grant and Lee: The Wildrness through Cold Harbor, 2007. **Address:** Law Offices of Richardson, Patrick, Westbrook &, Brickman L.L.C., 1037 Chuck Dawley Blvd., A Bldg., PO Box 1007, Mount Pleasant, SC 29465, U.S.A. **Online address:** grhea@rpwb.com

RHEIMS, Christine. *See* **ORBAN, Christine.**

RHEINGOLD, Howard (E.). American (born United States), b. 1947. **Genres:** Science Fiction/Fantasy, Information Science/Computers, Technology. **Career:** WELL, online host, 1985-; Whole Earth Review, editor; HotWired, founding executive editor, 1994; Electric Minds Inc., founder and chief exeutive officer, 1996-97; University of California, Berkeley School of Information, lecturer; Stanford University, Department of Communication, visiting lecturer. **Publications:** FICTION: Mama Liz Drinks Deep, 1973; Mama Liz Tastes Flesh, 1973; Secret Sisterhood, 1973; Jack Anderson against Dr. Tek!, 1974; War of the Gurus, 1974. OTHERS: (with H. Levine) Talking Tech: A Conversational Guide to Science and Technology, 1982; (with W. Harman) Higher Creativity: Liberating the Unconscious for Breakthrough Insights, 1984; Tools for Thought: The People and Ideas behind the Next Computer Revolution, 1985; (with B. Landreth) Out of the Inner Circle: A Hacker's Guide to Computer Security, 1985; (with H. Levine) The Cognitive Connection: Thought and Language in Man and Machine, 1987; Excursions to the Far Side of the Mind: A Book of Memes, 1988; They Have a Word for It: A Lighthearted Lexicon of Untranslatable Words and Phrases, 1988; (with S. LaBerge) Exploring the World of Lucid Dreaming, 1990; Virtual Reality, 1991; The Virtual Community: Homesteading on the Electronic Frontier, 1993, rev. ed., 2000; Smart Mobs: The Next Social Revolution, 2002. EDITOR: (with L. Benton) Ace It!: Use Your Computer to Improve Your Grades, 1984; (with L. Benton) The Everyone Can Build a Robot Book, 1984; Silicon Valley Guide to Financial Success in Software, 1984; The Millennium Whole Earth Catalog: Access to Tools and Ideas, 1994. Contributor to periodicals. **Address:** Keynote Speakers Inc., 425 Sherman Ave., Ste. 200, Palo Alto, CA 94306, U.S.A. **Online address:** howard@rheingold.com

RHOADS, Colleen. *See* **COBLE, Colleen.**

RHODES, Colin. Australian/British (born England), b. 1963. **Genres:** Art/Art History. **Career:** Loughborough College of Art and Design, faculty, 1991-98; Department of Contextual Studies, head, 1993-98; Loughborough University, reader, 1998-2003, School of Art and Design, director, 2002-06, professor of art history and theory, 2003-06; The University of Sydney, Sydney College of the Arts, dean and director, 2006-; The University of Sydney, chair, Division of Architecture and Creative Arts, 2010-. Writer. **Publications:** NONFICTION: Primitivism and Modern Art, 1994; Outsider Art: Spontaneous Alternatives, 2000; Ian Breakwell: Vocals, 2003. Contributor to books and periodicals. **Address:** Sydney College of the Arts, The University of Sydney, Locked Bag 15, Balmain Rd., Rozelle, NW 2039, Australia. **Online address:** colin.rhodes@sydney.edu.au

RHODES, Donna McKee. American (born United States), b. 1962. **Genres:** Theology/Religion, Novellas/Short Stories, Children's Fiction, Humanities. **Career:** Church of the Brethren, ordained minister; Stone Church of the Brethren, pastor of nurture; minister of nurture, 1989-; Elizabethtown College, Bethany Theological Seminary, Susquehanna Valley Ministry Center, Certificate and Continuing Education Programs, dean, director, 2001-06, executive director, 2006-. Writer. **Publications:** Little Stories for Little Children: A Worship Resource, 1995; More Little Stories for Little Children: A Worship Resource, 1997; Even More Little Stories for Little Children: A Worship Resource, 2000. **Address:** Susquehanna Valley Ministry Center, Elizabethtown College, 1 Alpha Dr., Elizabethtown, PA 17022-2290, U.S.A.

RHODES, Gary Don. American (born United States), b. 1972. **Genres:** History, Film, Autobiography/Memoirs. **Career:** University of Oklahoma, instructor, assistant professor of film and video studies, 1996-2005; Queens University, Northern Ireland, faculty, 2005. Writer. **Publications:** Lugosi: His Life in Films, on Stage, and in the Hearts of Horror Lovers, 1997; White Zombie: Anatomy of a Horror Film, 2001; (ed.) Horror at the Drive-In: Essays in Popular Americana, 2003; (ed. with J.P. Springer) Docufictions: Essays on the Intersection of Documentary and Fictional Filmmaking, 2006; (ed. with A. Webb) Alma Rubens, Silent Snowbird: Her Complete 1930 Memoir, with a New Biography and Filmography, 2006; (with R. Sheffield) Bela Lugosi: Dreams and Nightmares, 2007; (ed.) Stanley Kubrick: Essays on His Films and Legacy, 2008; (ed.) Edgar G. Ulmer: Detour on Poverty Row, 2008. **Address:** Belfast, Northern Ireland. **Online address:** gdrhodes@gmail.com

RHODES, Jane. American (born United States), b. 1955. **Genres:** Adult Non-fiction, History, Social Sciences. **Career:** State University of New York at Cortland, Department of Communication, assistant professor, 1985-91; Indiana University, School of Journalism, assistant professor, 1991-96; University of California, Department of Ethnic Studies, associate professor, 1999-2005, Department of Communication, associate professor, 1999-2005; Macalester College, Study of Race and Ethnicity, dean, Department of American studies, professor and chair, 2005-. Reporter, radio producer and writer. **Publications:** Mary Ann Shadd Cary: The Black Press and Protest in the Nineteenth Century, 1998; Framing the Black Panthers: The Spectacular Rise of a Black Power Icon, 2007. Contributor to periodicals. **Address:** Macalester College, Humanities 114a, 1600 Grand Ave., Saint Paul, MN 55105, U.S.A. **Online address:** rhodes@macalester.edu

RHODES, Jean E. American (born United States), b. 1961. **Genres:** Psychology. **Career:** University of Chicago, Medical School, clinical assistant professor, 1988-89; University of Illinois, assistant professor, 1989-95, associate professor, 1995- 99; Harvard University, visiting associate professor, 1999-2001; University of Massachusetts, associate professor, 2000-02, professor of psychology, 2002-; Research and Policy Council, National Mentoring Partnership, board director and chair. Writer. **Publications:** (With L.A. Jason) Preventing Substance Abuse among Children and Adolescents, 1988; (with F.H. Kanfer, S. Englund and C. Lennhoff) Helping Strategies for Mentors: A Guide to Working with Adolescents, 1995; Stand by Me: The Risks and Rewards of Mentoring Today's Youth, 2002; (ed. with P.M. Camic and L. Yardley) Qualitative Research in Psychology: Expanding Perspectives in Methodology and Design, 2003; (ed. with E.G. Clary) Mobilizing Adults for Positive Youth Development: Strategies for Closing the Gap between Beliefs and Behaviors, 2006; (with S. Boburg) Becoming Manny: Inside the Life of Baseball's Most Enigmatic Slugger, 2009. Contributor to books, journals and periodicals. **Address:** Department of Psychology, University of Massachusetts, 100 Morrissey Blvd., Boston, MA 02125, U.S.A. **Online address:** jean.rhodes@umb.edu

RHODES, Martha. American (born United States) **Genres:** Poetry. **Career:** The New School University, writing teacher; Emerson College, writing teacher; Four Way Books, co-founder, 1993-, director and founding editor, 2005-, vice president; University of California at Irvine, MFA Program, visiting professor, 2001; Readings on the Bowery, executive founding director; Sarah Lawrence College, faculty; Warren Wilson College, MFA Program for Writers, faculty. **Publications:** POETRY: At the Gate, 1995; Perfect Disappearance, 2000; Mother Quiet, 2004; The Beds, 2012. Contributor of articles to journals and magazines. **Address:** Four Way Books, PO Box 535, Village Sta., New York, NY 10014-0531, U.S.A. **Online address:** editors@fourwaybooks.com

RHODES, R. A. W. British/Australian (born Australia), b. 1944. **Genres:** Politics/Government, Public/Social Administration. **Career:** University of Birmingham, Institute of Local Government Studies, lecturer in public administration, 1970-75; University of Sussex, visiting fellow, 1973-75; University of the West Indies, visiting lecturer, 1976; University of Strathclyde, Department of Administration, lecturer, 1976-79; University of Essex, Department of Government, lecturer, 1979-87, reader, 1987-89, head of department, 1988-89; European Institute of Public Administration, visiting professor, 1985-89; University of York, professor of politics and head of department, 1989-94; University of Newcastle-upon-Tyne, professor of politics, 1994-2003, professor emeritus, 2003-; ESRCs Whitehall Research Programme, director, 1994-99; European University Institute, Jean Monnet visiting professor, 1995; Københavns Universitet, Institut for Statskundskab, adjungeret professor of political science, 1998-2003; Griffith University, School of Politics and Public Policy, adjunct professor of politics and public policy, 1999-2003, professor of governance and public policy, 2012-; Australia and New Zealand School of Government, research coordinator, 2003-04; Australian National University, professor of political science, 2003-06, Research School of Social Sciences, distinguished professor of political science, 2006-10, director, 2007-08; Academy of Social Sciences in Australia, fellow, 2004-; University of Tasmania, professor of government, 2008-; University of Melbourne, School of Social and Political Sciences, professorial fellow, 2010-11; University of Southampton, professor of government, 2012-. Writer. **Publications:** Public Administration and Policy Analysis, 1979; (co-author) Central-Local Government Relations: A Panel Report to the Research Initiatives Board, 1979; The National World of Local Government, 1986; Beyond Westminster and Whitehall: The Sub-Central Governments of Britain, 1988, rev. ed., 1992; Understanding Governance: Policy Networks, Governance, Reflexivity and Accountability, 1997; (with M. Bevir) Interpreting British Governance, 2003; (with M. Bevir) Governance Stories, 2006; (with P. Weller and J. Wanna) Comparing Westminster, 2009; (with M. Bevir) The State as Cultural Practice, 2010; Everyday Life in British Government, 2011. EDITOR: (with V. Wright) Tensions in the Territorial Politics of Western Europe, 1987; (with D. Marsh) Policy Networks in British Government, 1992; (with D. Marsh) Implementing Thatcherite Policies, 1992; (with P. Dunleavy) Prime Minister, Cabinet and Core Executive, 1995; (with H. Bakvis and P. Weller) The Hollow Crown: Countervailing Trends in Core Executives, 1997; (with B.G. Peters and V. Wright) Administering the Summit: Administration of the Core Executive in Developed Countries, 1999; British Government and Politics, 2 vols., 2000; Transforming British Government, 2 vols., 2000; United Kingdom, 2000; (with P. Weller) Mandarins or Valets?, 2000; (with P. Weller) The Changing World of Top Officials: Mandarins or Valets?, 2001; Decentralizing the Civil Service: From Unitary State of Differentiated Policy in the United Kingdom, 2003; (with S.A. Binder and B.A. Rockman) The Oxford Handbook of Political Institutions, 2006; (with P. Hart) Observing Government Elites, 2007; The Australian Study of Politics, 2009; Public Administration: 25 Years of Analysis and Debate, 2011. Contributor to periodicals. **Address:** Faculty of Social and Human Sciences, University of Southampton, University Rd., Southampton, HM SO17 1BJ, England. **Online address:** rod.rhodes@utas.edu.au

RHODES, Richard (Lee). American (born United States), b. 1937. **Genres:** Novels, History, Autobiography/Memoirs, Biography, Documentaries/Reportage, Sciences, Physics. **Career:** Newsweek, writer trainee, 1959; Radio Free Europe, staff assistant, 1960; Westminster College, instructor in English, 1960-61; Hallmark Cards Inc., book editing manager, 1962-70; Harper's, contributing editor, 1970-74; Kansas City Regional Council for Higher Education, writer-in-residence, 1972; Playboy, contributing editor, 1974-80; Rolling Stone, contributing editor, 1988-93; Massachusetts Institute of Technology, Defense and Arms Control Studies Program, visiting fellow, 1988-89; Alfred P. Sloan Foundation, advisor, 1990-; Stanford University, Center for International Security and Cooperation, affiliate, 2004-. Writer and journalist. **Publications:** (Ed. with B.H. Hall) Living in a Troubled World: Selections from the Writings of William C. Menninger, 1967; (with T.L. Friedman) Writing in an Era of Conflict, 1990; Nuclear Renewal: Common Sense about Energy, 1993; (intro.) Picturing the Bomb: Photographs from the Secret World of the Manhattan Project, 1995; (with G. Rhodes) Trying to Get Some Dignity: Stories of Triumph over Childhood Abuse, 1996; (with Alan and D. Brauer) ESO, rev. ed., 2001; Twilight of the Bombs: Recent Challenges, New Dangers and the Prospects for a World without Nuclear Weapons, 4 vols., 2010; Hedy's Folly: The Life and Breakthrough Inventions of Hedy Lamarr, the Most Beautiful Woman in the World, 2011. NON-FICTION: The Inland Ground: An Evocation of the American Middle West, 1970, rev. ed., 1991; The Ozarks, 1974; Looking for America: A Writer's Odyssey, 1979; The Making of the Atomic Bomb, 1987; (with L.W. Alvarez) Alvarez: The Adventures of a Physicist, 1987; National Book Critics Circle Award for Non-fiction, 1988; Farm: A Year in the Life of an American Farmer, 1989; A Hole in the World: An American Boyhood (autobiography), 1990; Making Love (autobiography), 1992; (ed. and intro.) The Los Alamos Primer: The First Lectures on How to Build an Atomic Bomb, 1992; How to Write, 1995; Dark Sun: The Making of the Hydrogen Bomb, 1995; Deadly Feasts: Tracking the Secrets of a Terrifying New Plague, 1997; (ed.) Visions of Technology (anthology), 1999; Why They Kill: The Discoveries of a Maverick Criminologist, 1999; Masters of Death: The SSEinsatzgruppen and the Invention of the Holocaust, 2002; John James Audubon: The Making of an American, 2004; (ed.) The Audubon Reader, 2006; Arsenals of Folly: Nuclear Weapons in the Cold War, 2007. NOVELS: The Ungodly, 1973; Holy Secrets, 1978; The Last Safari, 1980; Sons of Earth, 1981. **Address:** c/o Morton Janklow, Janklow & Nesbit Associates, 445 Park Ave., 13th Fl., New York, NY 10022-2606, U.S.A.

RHODES, Tricia McCary. American (born United States), b. 1952. **Genres:** Theology/Religion. **Career:** New Hope Church, co-founder, 1981-. Christian minister and writer. **Publications:** The Soul at Rest, 1996; Contemplating the Cross, 1998 as Contemplating the Cross: A 40-day Pilgrimage of Prayer, 2004; Taking Up Your Cross: The Incredible Gain of the Crucified Life, 2000; At the Name of Jesus: Meditations on the Exalted Christ, 2003; Intimate Intercession: The Sacred Joy of Praying for Others, 2005; Sacred Chaos: Spiritual Disciplines for the Life You Have, 2008. Contributor to periodicals. **Address:** The Soul at Rest, 10330 Carmel Mountain Rd., San Diego, CA 92129, U.S.A. **Online address:** soulatrest.rhodes@yahoo.com

RHODES-COURTER, Ashley Marie. American (born United States), b. 1985?. **Genres:** Autobiography/Memoirs, Young Adult Fiction, Children's Fiction, Biography. **Career:** Writer. **Publications:** Three Little Words: A Memoir, 2008. **Address:** Simon & Schuster Inc., 1230 Ave. of the Americas, New York, NY 10020, U.S.A. **Online address:** rhodesam@eckerd.edu

RHUE, Morton. *See* **STRASSER, Todd.**

RHYNE, Nancy. American (born United States), b. 1926. **Genres:** Children's Fiction, Young Adult Fiction, History, Mythology/Folklore, Travel/Exploration, Humanities. **Career:** Mecklenburg County Courthouse, Superior Court, deputy clerk; Kennedy, Covington, Lobdell & Hickman (attorneys), secretary to the senior partner; Davidson College, secretary to the vice-president. Writer. **Publications:** The Grand Strand: An Uncommon Guide to Myrtle Beach and Its Surroundings, 1981; Carolina Seashells, 1982; Tales of the South Carolina Low Country, 1982; More Tales of the South Carolina Low Country, 1984; Coastal Ghosts: Haunted Places from Wilmington, North Carolina to Savannah, Georgia, 1985; Murder in the Carolinas, 1988; Once upon a Time on a Plantation (juvenile), 1988; Plantation Tales, 1989; Carolina Seashells, 1989; More Murder in the Carolinas, 1990; Alice Flagg: The Ghost of the Hermitage, 1990; The South Carolina Lizard Man, 1992; Touring the Coastal South Carolina Backroads, 1992; Touring Coastal Georgia Backroads, 1994; The Jack-O-Lantern Ghost, 1996; The Ghost of John Henry Rutledge of Hampton Plantation, 1996; Southern Recipes & Legends, 1996; John Henry Rutledge: The Ghost of Hampton Plantation: A Parable, 1997; Chronicles of the South Carolina Sea Islands, 1998; (comp. and ed.) Voices of Carolina Slave Children, 1999; Slave Ghost Stores: Tales of Hags, Hants, Ghosts & Diamondback Rattlers, 2002; Low Country Voices: What Coastal Back Roads Folk Told Me of Ghosts, Sea Captains, and Charleston Jazzmen, 2003; (comp.) Before and After Freedom: WPA Narratives of Low country Folklore, 2005; Edisto Island: A Novel, 2006; Tales from the South Carolina Upstate: Where the Cotton and Peaches Grow, 2007; Crab Boys, 2007. **Address:** 405 Pinecrest Dr., Myrtle Beach, SC 29572, U.S.A. **Online address:** nancyrhyne@msn.com

RIACH, Alan. Scottish/New Zealander (born New Zealand), b. 1957. **Genres:** Poetry, Literary Criticism And History, Architecture. **Career:** Workers Education Association, course director and creative writing teacher, 1979-80; Foreign Language Study Programme, course director and teacher of English, 1981, 1982, 1983; Community Education, creative writing teacher, 1982; tutor in English literature, 1982-83; University of Waikato, School of Humanities, tutor, 1986-89, senior tutor, 1990, lecturer in English, 1990-94, faculty of arts and social sciences, pro-dean, senior lecturer and associate professor of English, 1995-2001; University of Glasgow, Department of Scottish Literature, reader in Scottish literature, 2001-, head, 2001-, professor of Scottish literature, 2003-. Writer. **Publications:** Hugh MacDiarmid's Epic Poetry, 1991; The Poetry of Hugh MacDiarmid, 1995; Stepping Westward, 2008. POEMS: (with P. McCarey) For What It Is, 1988; This Folding Map, 1990; An Open Return, 1991; First & Last Songs, 1995; From the Vision of Hell, 1998; Clearances, 2001; Representing Scotland in Literature, Popular Culture and Iconography: The Masks of the Modern Nation, 2005; Homecoming: New Poems 2001-2009, 2009. EDITOR: (with M. Williams) The Radical Imagination: Lectures and Talks by Wilson Harris, 1992; (with M. Grieve) Selected Poetry of Hugh MacDiarmid, 1992; Selected Prose of Hugh MacDiarmid, 1992; Scottish Eccentrics, 1993; Lucky Poet: The Autobiography of Hugh MacDiarmid, 1994; (and intro.) Contemporary Scottish Studies, 1995; (with A. Calder and G. Murray) Raucle Tongue, 3 vols., 1996-98; Albyn: Shorter Books and Monographs, 1996; (with R. Watson) Annals of the Five Senses and Other Stories, Sketches and Plays, 1999; (with Dorian Grieve and Owen Dudley Edwards) New Selected Letters, 2001; (J. Manson and D. Grieve) Revolutionary Art of the Future: Rediscovered Poems, 2003; (with L. Macdonald-Lewis and A. Moffat) Arts of Resistance: Poets, Portraits and Landscapes of Modern Scotland, 2008; (with I. Brown) Edinburgh Companion to Twentieth-century Scottish Literature, 2009. Contributor to books and periodicals. **Address:** Department of Scottish Literature, University of Glasgow, Rm. 307, 7 University Gardens, Glasgow, G12 8QH, Scotland. **Online address:** a.riach@scotlit.arts.gla.ac.uk

RIAHI-BELKAOUI, Ahmed. *See* **BELKAOUI, Ahmed R.**

RIBALOW, M(eir) Z(vi). American (born United States), b. 1948. **Genres:** Novels, Children's Fiction, Plays/Screenplays, Cultural/Ethnic Topics, Sports/Fitness. **Career:** New York Shakespeare Festival, Joseph Papp's Production Associate and head of script department, 1972-75; American Repertory Co., founder and producing director, 1976-78; Ithaca College, drama instructor, 1976-78; Fordham University, artist-in-residence, 1986-; New York University, Center for Advanced Technology, Jews in Sports Online, director for content; Playwrights Project, artistic director; Global Forum of Spiritual and Parliamentary Leaders on Human Survival, arts coordinator; Creative Coalition, board director and secretary, vice-president. Writer, script consultant and reader. **Publications:** Shrunken Heads, 1980; Raindance, 1985; (contrib.) Gallavanterna, 1988; (ed.) Plays from New River 1: Absence, 2011; Peanuts and Crackerjacks, 2012. NONFICTION WITH H.U. RIBALOW: Jewish Baseball Stars, 1984; The Jew in American Sports, 1985; Great Jewish Chess Champions, 1986. **Address:** 431 E 20th St., Ste. 4C, New York, NY 10010, U.S.A. **Online address:** mzr66@rcn.com

RIBOWSKY, Mark. American (born United States), b. 1951. **Genres:** Biography, History, Music, Literary Criticism And History. **Career:** TV Guide, staff writer, journalist and author. **Publications:** He's a Rebel: The Truth about Phil Spector-Rock and Roll's Legendary Madman, 1989; Slick: The Silver and Black Life of Al Davis, 1991; Don't Look Back: Satchel Paige on the Shadows of Baseball, 1994; Complete History of the Negro Leagues, 1884 to 1955, 1995; Power and the Darkness: The Life of Josh Gibson in the Shadows of the Game, 1996; Twice Golden: The Story of Michael Johnson and His Triumphs in Atlanta, 1997; Complete History of the Home Run, 2003; Josh Gibson: The Power and the Darkness, 2004; The Supremes: A Saga of Motown Dreams, Success, and Betrayal, 2009; Ain't Too Proud to Beg: The Troubled Lives and Enduring Soul of the Temptations, 2010; Signed, Sealed, and Delivered: The Soulful Journey of Stevie Wonder, 2010. Contributor to periodicals. **Address:** c/o Edward J. Acton, Acton, Leone, Hanson & Jaffee, PO Box 2080, New York, NY 10025-1552, U.S.A.

RICAPITO, Joseph V. American/Italian (born Italy), b. 1933. **Genres:** Poetry, Literary Criticism And History, Translations, Essays. **Career:** Pomona College, faculty, 1962-70; Indiana University, faculty, 1970-80; Louisiana State University, Department of Foreign Languages and Literatures, professor, 1980-, distinguished research master, 2002, Yenni distinguished professor and section head for Italian and Spanish, now professor emeritus, Development of Italian Studies, Joseph S. Yenni distinguished chair. Writer. **Publications:** (Ed.) La vida de Lazarillo de Tormes y de sus fortunas y adversidades, 1976; Bibliografía razonada y Anotada de las Obras Maestras de la Picaresca Española, 1980; (trans. and intro.) A. de Valdés, Dialogue of Mercury and Charon: English Translation of Diálogo de Mercurio y Carón, 1986; (ed.) Hispanic Studies in Honor of Joseph H. Silverman, 1990; Cervantes's Novelas Ejemplares: Between History and Creativity, 1996; Florentine Streets and Other Poems, 1997; Formalistic Aspects of Cervantes's Novelas Ejemplares, 1997; Consciousness and Truth in Don Quijote and Connected Essays, 2007; Fratelli, 2007; Second Wave, 2008. **Address:** Department of Foreign Languages and Literatures, Louisiana State University, 316 Hodges Hall, Baton Rouge, LA 70803-5306, U.S.A. **Online address:** ricapito@lsu.edu

RICARDO, Jack. American (born United States), b. 1940. **Genres:** Mystery/Crime/Suspense, Young Adult Fiction, Horror, Literary Criticism And History. **Career:** Michael's Thing, film critic, 1970. Writer. **Publications:** MYSTERIES: Death with Dignity, 1991; The Night G.A.A. Died: A Mystery, 1992. EDITOR: Leathermen Speak Out: An Anthology on Leathersex, 1991; Leathermen Speak Out II, 1993. **Address:** Lyle Steele and Company Ltd., 511 E 73rd St., Ste. 6, New York, NY 10021-4000, U.S.A.

RICCI, Nino. Canadian/Italian (born Italy), b. 1959. **Genres:** Novels, History. **Career:** Ogun State Education Board, secondary school teacher, 1981-83; Concordia University, teacher of creative writing, 1987-88; Humber School for Writers, teacher, 1991-2009; York University, Mariano Elia chairman, 1999-2000; University of Windsor, writer-in-residence, 2005-06; Assumption University, chairman of religion and arts, 2005-06; John Carroll University, chairman in literary studies, 2008; Bridgewater State College, Killam professor in Canadian studies, 2009; Kitchener Public Library, writer-in-residence, 2009; Colorado College, Maclean distinguished visiting professor, 2011. **Publications:** Lives of the Saints in US as The Book of Saints, 1991; In A Glass House, 1993; Where She Has Gone, 1997; Testament, 2002; Roots and Frontiers, 2003; The Origin of Species, 2008; Pierre Elliott Trudeau, 2009. Contributor to books and periodicals. **Address:** c/o Writers Union of Canada, 90 Richmond St., E Ste. 200, Toronto, ON M5C 1P1, Canada. **Online address:** nino@ninoricci.com

RICCIO, Dolores Stewart. American (born United States) **Genres:** Food And Wine. **Career:** Editorial director and writer. **Publications:** (with O. Riccio) The Weighing Game & How to Win It, Without Getting Sick or Going Broke, 1974; Superfoods: 300 Recipes for Foods That Heal Body and Mind, 1992; Superfoods for Women: 300 Recipes That Fulfill Your Special Nutritional Needs, 1996; 366 Delicious Ways to Cook Pasta with Vegetables, 1997; Superfoods for Life: 250 Anti-aging Recipes for Foods That Keep You Feeling Fit and Fabulous, 1998; Antioxidant Power: 366 Delicious Recipes for Great Health and Long Life, 1999. WITH JOAN BINGHAM: Make It Yourself: A Consumer's Guide to Cutting Household Costs, 1978; The Energy Crunch Cookbook, 1979; The Complete All-in-the- Oven Cookbook, 1981; The Smart Shopper's Guide to Food Buying and Preparation, 1982; The Versatile Vegetable Cookbook, 1983; Rodale's Sensational Desserts, 1985; Haunted Houses U.S.A., 1989; More Haunted Houses, 1991. CIRCLE OF FIVE SERIES-AS DOLORES STEWART RICCIO: Circle of Five, 2003; Charmed Circle, 2003; The Divine Circle of Ladies Making Mischief, 2005; Ladies Courting Trouble, 2006. **Address:** Duxbury, MA , U.S.A. **Online address:** doloresriccio@comcast.net

RICCIOTTI, Hope. American (born United States), b. 1963. **Genres:** Medicine/Health, Food And Wine. **Career:** Harvard University, Harvard Medical School, Beth Israel Deaconess Medical Center, associate professor of obstetrics, gynecology, and reproductive biology, Department of Obstetrics and Gynecology, vice chair for medical education, residency program director, director of women's health theme; Dimock Community Health Center, clinical director of obstetrics and gynecology. Writer. **Publications:** (With V. Connelly) The Pregnancy Cookbook, 1996, rev. ed. 2002; (with V. Connelly) The Menopause Cookbook: How to Eat Now and for the Rest of Your Life, 1999; (with V. Connelly) The Breast Cancer Prevention Cookbook, 2002; (with V. Connelly) The Healthy Family Cookbook, 2004; (with V. Connelly) I'm Pregnant! Now What Do I Eat?, 2007; (with M.D. Spencer) Real Life Body Book: A Young Woman's Complete Guide to Health and Wellness, 2010. **Address:** Beth Israel Deaconess Medical Center, Harvard Medical School, Harvard University, 330 Brookline Ave., Boston, MA 02215, U.S.A. **Online address:** hricciot@bidmc.harvard.edu

RICE, Andrew. American (born United States), b. 1975. **Genres:** History. **Career:** Institute of Current World Affairs (nonprofit), fellow, 2002-04; Conde Nast Portfolio, contributing editor; New York Times Magazine, contributing writer; Philadelphia Inquirer, staff; New York Observer, staff. **Publications:** The Teeth May Smile but the Heart Does Not Forget: Murder and Memory in Uganda, 2009. Contributor to periodicals. **Address:** Brooklyn, NY , U.S.A. **Online address:** andrewrice75@yahoo.com

RICE, Anne. Also writes as A. N. Roquelaure. American (born United States), b. 1941. **Genres:** Novels. **Career:** San Francisco State University, professor. Writer. **Publications:** Interview with the Vampire: A Novel, 1976; The Feast of All Saints, 1979; Cry to Heaven, 1982; The Vampire Lestat, 1985; Belinda: A Novel, 1986; The Queen of the Damned, 1988; The Mummy, or Ramses the Damned: A Novel, 1989; Witching Hour: A Novel, 1990; Tale of the Body Thief, 1992; Lasher: A Novel, 1993; Taltos: Lives of the Mayfair Witches, 1994; Memnoch the Devil, 1995; Servant of the Bones, 1996; Violin, 1997; Pandora: New Tales of the Vampires, 1998; The Vampire Armand, 1998; Vittorio, the Vampire: New Tales of the Vampires, 1999; Merrick: A Novel, 2000; Blood and Gold or, the Story of Marius, 2001; Vittorio the Vampire, 2001; Blackwood Farm, 2002; The Vampire Chronicles Collection, 2002; Blood Canticle, 2003; Christ the Lord: Out of Egypt: A Novel, 2005; Called Out of Darkness: A Spiritual Confession, 2008; Christ the Lord: The Road to Cana: A Novel, 2008; Angel Time, 2009; Of Love and Evil: The Songs of the Seraphim, A Novel, 2010. Christ the Lord: The Kingdom of Heaven, forthcoming. AS A.N. ROQUELAURE: The Claiming of Sleeping

Beauty, 1999; Beauty's Punishment, 1999; Beauty's Release, 1999. **Address:** Random House, 1745 Broadway, New York, NY 10019, U.S.A. **Online address:** anneobrienrice@mac.com

RICE, Bebe Faas. American (born United States), b. 1932. **Genres:** Children's Fiction, Novels, Horror. **Career:** Writer. **Publications:** THE GIRLS FROM MISS MINSHAM'S SERIES: Boy Crazy, 1988; Spring Break, 1988; Winter Madness, 1990. OTHERS: My Sister, My Sorrow, 1991; Class Trip, 1993; Love You to Death, 1994; The Year the Wolves Came, 1994; Class Trip II, 1994; The Listeners, 1996; Music from the Dead, 1997; With Flame and Sword, 2001; The Place at the Edge of the Earth, 2002; The Hoar Apple Tree, forthcoming. DOOMSDAY MALL SERIES: The Dollhouse, 1995; The Hunt, 1995; The Beast, 1995; The Witch, 1996; The Vampire, 1996; The Jungle, 1996. Contributor to periodicals. **Address:** 46898 Grissom St., Potomac Falls, VA 20165-3591, U.S.A. **Online address:** rice2@falconsresidents.org

RICE, Condi. *See* **RICE, Condoleezza.**

RICE, Condoleezza. (Condi Rice). American (born United States), b. 1954. **Genres:** Area Studies, International Relations/Current Affairs, Autobiography/Memoirs. **Career:** U.S. Department of State, intern, 1977, secretary of state, 2005-09; Rand Corp., intern, 1980; Stanford University, assistant professor, 1981-87, associate professor, 1987-93, professor of political science, 1993-99, Center for International Security and Arms Control, assistant director, 1981-86, Institute for International Studies, member of executive committee, 1988-89, 1991-93, senior fellow of the institute, 1991-94, provost of the university, 1993-99; Hoover Institution on War, Revolution, and Peace, national fellow, 1985-86; Council on Foreign Relations, international affairs fellow, 1986-87; University of Michigan, visiting lecturer, 1988; National Security Council, director of soviet and east european affairs, 1989-90, senior director for soviet affairs, 1990-91; special assistant to the president for national security affairs, 1990-91; Howard University, Patricia Roberts Harris distinguished visitor, 1991; national security advisor, 2001-05, secretary of state, 2005-09; Chevron Corp., board of director; Joint Chiefs of Staff, consultant; ABC News, consultant. Writer. **Publications:** Uncertain Allegiance: The Soviet Union and the Czechoslovak Army, 1984; (ed. with A. Dallin) The Gorbachev Era, 1986; (with P. Zelikow) Germany Unified and Europe Transformed: A Study in Statecraft, 1995; (contrib.) Busi haengjŏngbu ŭi Hanbando rip ot ŭ, 2001; Extraordinary, Ordinary People: A Memoir of Family, 2010; Condoleezza Rice: A Memoir of My Extraordinary, Ordinary Family and Me, 2010. Contributor to books and journals. **Address:** Hoover Institution, Stanford University, 2201 C St. NW, Washington, DC 20520, U.S.A.

RICE, Earle. American (born United States), b. 1928. **Genres:** Novels, Young Adult Fiction, History, Law, Military/Defense/Arms Control, Young Adult Non-fiction. **Career:** Technical writer and senior design engineer; freelance writer, 1993-. **Publications:** FICTION: Tiger, Lion, Hawk, 1977; The Animals, 1979; Death Angel, 1981; The Gringo Dies at Dawn, 1993. SPORTS FICTION: Fear on Ice, 1981; More Than Macho, 1981. NONFICTION: The Cuban Revolution, 1995; The Battle of Belleau Wood, 1996; The Battle of Britain, 1996; The Battle of Midway, 1996; The Inchon Invasion, 1996; The Attack on Pearl Harbor, 1997; The Tet Offensive, 1997; The Nuremberg Trials, 1997; The Salem Witch Trials, 1997; The O.J. Simpson Trial, 1997; The Final Solution, 1997; Nazi War Criminals, 1997; Life among the Great Plains Indians, 1998; Life during the Crusades, 1998; The Battle of the Little Bighorn, 1998; Life during the Middle Ages, 1998; Kamikazes, 1999; Strategic Battles in Europe, 2000; Strategic Battles in the Pacific, 2000; The Third Reich, 2000; The Cold War, 2000; The Bombing of Pearl Harbor, 2001; Normandy, 2002; The First Battle of the Marne, 2002; Gettysburg, 2002; Claire Chennault, Flying Tiger, 2002; Manfred von Richthofen, the Red Baron, 2002; Sir Francis Drake, 2002; Point of No Return: Tonkin Gulf and the Vietnam War, 2002; George S. Patton, 2003; Erwin J.E. Rommel, 2003; Douglas MacArthur, 2003; Korea 1950, 2003; Alexandra David-Neel: Explorer at the Roof of the World, 2004; Ulysses S. Grant: Defender of the Union, 2005; Robert E. Lee: First Soldier of the Confederacy, 2005; Empire in the East: The Story of Genghis Khan, 2005; U.S. Army and Military Careers, 2006; Adolf Hitler and Nazi Germany, 2006; Life and Times of Sir Walter Raleigh, 2007; Life and Times of John Cabot, 2007; Overview of the Persian Gulf War, 1990, 2008; Life and Times of the Brothers Custer: Galloping to Glory, 2008; Life and Times of Leif Eriksson, 2008; Canaletto, 2008; A Brief Political and Geographic History of Latin America: Where are Gran Colombia, La Plata, and Dutch Guiana, 2008; Blitzkrieg! Hitler's Lightning War, 2008; Overview of the Korean War, 2009; Life and Times of Erik the Red,

2009; FDR and the New Deal, 2010; Life and Times of Eleanor of Aquitaine, 2010; Life and Times of Clovis, King of the Franks, 2010; Life and Times of Attila the Hun, 2010. ADAPTOR: Dracula, 1995; All Quiet on the Western Front, 1995; The Grapes of Wrath, 1996. **Address:** PO Box 2131, Julian, CA 92036-2131, U.S.A. **Online address:** ericejr@sbcglobal.net

RICE, Graham. British (born England), b. 1950. **Genres:** Horticulture, Homes/Gardens. **Career:** The Observer, gardening columnist; London Evening Standard, gardening correspondent, 1996-; National Newspaper, columnist; Lecturer and writer. **Publications:** Pruning, 1982; A Handbook of Annuals and Bedding Plants, 1986; Gardening for Beginners, 1986; The Gardening Handbook 1987; Plants for Problem Places, 1988; Perfect Plants, 1990; (with C. Lloyd) Garden Flowers from Seed, 1991; The Complete Small Garden, 1992; Herbaceous Perennials. 1992; Bedding Plants, 1993; (with E. Strangman) The Gardener's Guide to Growing Hellebores, 1993; (with C. Lloyd) Garden Flowers from Seed, 1994; (with K.N. Sanecki) Gardening with Flowers, 1994; Hardy Perennials, 1995; The Complete Book of Perennials, 1996; The Planting Planner, 1996; Discovering Annuals, 1999; Hellebores, 2002; The Sweet Pea Book, 2003; Ultimate Book of Small Gardens 2004; All-in-One Garden 2006; American Horticultural Society's Encyclopedia of Perennials 2006; Royal Horticultural Society's Encyclopedia of Perennials 2006; Planting The Dry Shade Garden: The Best Plants For The Toughest Spot in Your Garden, 2011. Contributor to periodicals. **Address:** c/o Author Mail, Sterling Publishing Co., 387 Park Ave. S, New York, NY 10016, U.S.A. **Online address:** graham@grahamrice.com

RICE, Hugo. *See* **HOUGHTON, Eric.**

RICE, Linda Lightsey. American (born United States), b. 1950?. **Genres:** Novels, Mystery/Crime/Suspense, Autobiography/Memoirs. **Career:** Novelist. College of St. Catherine, adjunct associate professor; University of Tennessee, writing instructor; Loft Center, Inroads Writing Program, mentor; Lenoir Rhyne University, writer-in-residence. **Publications:** NOVELS: Southern Exposure, 1991; The Thistle Man, forthcoming. OTHERS: This Half-Mad Dance, forthcoming. **Address:** Doubleday, 1540 Broadway, New York, NY 10036, U.S.A. **Online address:** llr@lindalightseyrice.com

RICE, Luanne. American (born United States), b. 1955. **Genres:** Novels, Romance/Historical. **Career:** Writer, 1986-. **Publications:** NOVELS: Angels All over Town, 1986; Crazy in Love, 1988; Stone Heart, 1990; Secrets of Paris, 1991; Blue Moon, 1993; Home Fires, 1995; Cloud Nine, 1999; Follow the Stars Home, 2000; Dream Country, 2001; Firefly Beach, 2001; Safe Harbor, 2002; True Blue, 2002; Summer Light, 2002; The Perfect Summer, 2003; The Secret Hour, 2003; Silver Bells: A Holiday Tale, 2004; Dance with Me, 2004; Beach Girls, 2004; Summer of Roses, 2005; Summer's Child, 2005; Sandcastles, 2006; The Edge of Winter, 2007; What Matters Most, 2007; Light of the Moon, 2008; (with J. Monninger) The Letters, 2008; Last Kiss, 2008; The Geometry of Sisters, 2009; Deep Blue Sea for Beginners, 2009; The Silver Boat, 2011. Contributor to periodicals. **Address:** c/o Andrea Cirillo, Jane Rotrosen Agency, 318 E 51st St., New York, NY 10022, U.S.A.

RICE, Michael. British (born England), b. 1928. **Genres:** Anthropology/Ethnology, Archaeology/Antiquities, History, Mythology/Folklore, Humanities. **Career:** British Commonwealth and Foreign Governments, consultant, 1955-; Institute of Public Relations, fellow, 1975. Writer. **Publications:** Understanding the Arab Case, 1967; The Temple Complex at Barbar, Bahrain, 1983; (ed. and intro.) Dilmun Discovered: The First Hundred Years of the Archaeology of Bahrain, 1984; Search for the Paradise Land: The Archaeology of Bahrain and the Arabian Gulf, 1984; (ed. with K.A. Khalifa) Bahrain through the Ages, vol. I, The Archaeology, 1986, vol. II, The History, 1983; Egypt's Making: A Study of the Origins of the Egyptian State 5000-2000 B.C., 1990, 2nd ed., 2003; The Archaeology of the Arabian Gulf, 1994; False Inheritance: Israel in Palestine and the Search for a Solution, 1994; Egypt's Legacy: The Archetypes of Western Civilization, 1997; The Power of the Bull, 1998; Who's Who in Ancient Egypt, 1999; (ed. with S. MacDonald) Consuming Ancient Egypt, 2003; Swifter than the Arrow: The Golden Hunting Hounds of Ancient Egypt, 2006. **Address:** Odsey House, Baldock Rd., Odsey, HW SG7 6SD, England.

RICE, Prudence M. American (born United States), b. 1947. **Genres:** Social Sciences, Politics/Government, Astronomy. **Career:** University of Florida, faculty; Southern Illinois University, Department of Anthropology, faculty, 1991-, professor of anthropology, head of department, 1993-99, now professor emeritus, Office of Research and Development Administration, director, associate vice chancellor for research, Graduate School, associate dean; Illinois Groundwater Consortium, director; University of Illinois, extension service and farm research station, director. Writer. **Publications:** (Comp. with M.E. Saffer) Analysis, Technical and Ethnographic Approaches to Pottery Production and Use, 1982; (ed.) Pots and Potters: Current Approaches in Ceramic Archaeology, 1984; (ed. with A.F. Chase) The Lowland Maya Postclassic, 1985; Macanché Island, El Petén, Guatemala: Excavations, Pottery, and Artifacts, 1987; (ed. with R.J. Sharer) Maya Ceramics: Papers from the 1985 Maya Ceramic Conference, 1987; Pottery Analysis: A Sourcebook, 1987; (ed.) The Prehistory & History of Ceramic Kilns, 1997; (ed. with A.A. Demarest and D.S. Rice) The Terminal Classic in the Maya Lowlands: Collapse, Transition, and Transformation, 2004; Maya Political Science: Time, Astronomy, and the Cosmos, 2004; Maya Calendar Origins: Monuments, Mythistory, and the Materialization of Time, 2007; (ed. with D.S. Rice) The Kowoj: Identity, Migration, and Geopolitics in Late Postclassic Petén, Guatemala, 2009; Vintage Moquegua, 2012. Contributor to journals. **Address:** Department of Anthropology, Southern Illinois University, 3525 Faner Hall, 1000 Faner Dr., Carbondale, IL 62901-4502, U.S.A. **Online address:** price@siu.edu

RICE, Stephen P. American (born United States), b. 1963. **Genres:** Social Sciences, History, Sociology. **Career:** Ramapo College, associate professor of American studies, 1996-, professor of American studies. Writer. **Publications:** Minding the Machine: Languages of Class in Early Industrial America, 2004. Contributor to periodicals. **Address:** Ramapo College, 505 Ramapo Valley Rd., Mahwah, NJ 07430, U.S.A. **Online address:** srice@ramapo.edu

RICE, Zoe. American (born United States), b. 1977?. **Genres:** Novels, Literary Criticism And History. **Career:** Writer. **Publications:** Pick Me Up, 2006. Contributor to periodicals. **Address:** New York, NY , U.S.A. **Online address:** zhrice@gmail.com

RICH, Adrienne (Cecile). American (born United States), b. 1929. **Genres:** Poetry, Women's Studies And Issues, Essays, Literary Criticism And History, History, Translations. **Career:** YM-YWHA Poetry Center, conductor of workshop, 1966-67; Swarthmore College, visiting lecturer, 1967-69; Columbia University, Graduate School of the Arts, adjunct professor in writing division, 1967-69; City University of New York, City College, SEEK English Program, lecturer, 1968-70, instructor in creative writing program, 1970-71, assistant professor of English, 1971-72, 1974-75; Brandeis University, Fannie Hurst visiting professor of creative literature, 1972-73; Bryn Mawr College, Lucy Martin Donnelly fellow, 1975; Rutgers University, Douglass College, professor of English, 1976-78; Cornell University, A.D. White professor-at-large, 1982-85; Scripps College, Clark lecturer and distinguished visiting professor, 1983, 1984; San Jose State University, visiting professor, 1984-96; Pacific Oaks College, Burgess lecturer, 1986; Stanford University, professor of English and feminist studies, 1986-92; University of Chicago, Marjorie Kovler visiting fellow, 1989; The National Writers' Voice Project, national director, 1992-. Writer. **Publications:** Ariadne: A Play in Three Acts, and Poems, 1939; A Change of World, 1951; Poems, 1952; The Diamond Cutters, and Other Poems, 1955; Snapshots of a Daughter-in-Law: Poems, 1954-1962, 1963; Necessities of Life: Poems, 1962-1965, 1966; Selected Poems, 1967; Leaflets: Poems, 1965-1968, 1969; (trans. with A. Ahmad and W. Stafford) M.A. Ghalib, Poems, 1969; The Will to Change: Poems, 1968-1970, 1971; Diving into the Wreck: Poems, 1971-72, 1973; (trans.) M. Insingel, Reflections, 1973; Poems: Selected and New, 1950-74, 1974; Of Woman Born: Motherhood As Experience and Institution, 1976; Twenty-one Love Poems, 1977; The Meaning of Our Love for Women is What we Have Constantly to Expand, 1977; Pieces, 1977; Women and Honor: Some Notes on Lying, 1977; The Dream of a Common Language: Poems, 1974-1977, 1978; On Lies, Secrets, and Silence: Selected Prose, 1966-78, 1979; Compulsory Heterosexuality and Lesbian Existence, 1981; A Wild Patience Has Taken Me This Far: Poems, 1978-1981, 1981; Sources, 1983; The Fact of a Doorframe: Poems Selected and New, 1950-1984, 1984; Your Native Land, Your Life, 1986; Blood, Bread, and Poetry: Selected Prose, 1979-1985, 1986; Time's Power: Poems, 1985-1988, 1989; An Atlas of the Difficult World: Poems, 1988-1991, 1991; (contrib.) Birth of the Age of Woman, 1991; Collected Early Poems, 1950-1970, 1993; What is Found There: Notebooks on Poetry and Politics, 1993; Dark Fields of the Republic: Poems, 1991-1995, 1995; Selected Poems, 1950-1995, 1996; Midnight Salvage: Poems, 1995-1998, 1999; Fox: Poems, 1998-2000, 2001; Arts of the Possible: Essays and Conversations, 2001; Fact of a Doorframe: Selected Poems, 1950-2001, 2002; (ed.) Selected Poems, 2004; The School among the Ruins: Poems, 2000-2004, 2004; Telephone

Ringing in the Labyrinth: Poems, 2004-2006, 2007; Poetry & Commitment: An Essay, 2007; Human Eye: Essays on Art in Society, 1997-2008, 2009; Tonight No Poetry will Serve: Poems, 2007-2010, 2011. Contributor to books and periodicals. **Address:** W. W. Norton & Company Inc., 500 5th Ave., New York, NY 10110-0002, U.S.A.

RICH, Elaine Sommers. American (born United States), b. 1926. **Genres:** Children's Fiction, Poetry, Women's Studies And Issues, Biography, Young Adult Fiction, Theology/Religion. **Career:** Goshen College, instructor in speech and English, 1947-49, 1950-53; Mennonite Publishing House, staff, 1950; Bethel College, instructor in speech, 1953-66; International Christian University, lecturer, 1971-78; Bluffton College, advisor to international students, 1979-89, Institute for Learning in Retirement, moderator of courses, 1991-; University of Findlay, adjunct professor, 1986-95; Mennonite Weekly Review, columnist. **Publications:** (Ed.) Breaking Bread Together, 1958; Hannah Elizabeth, 1964; Tomorrow, Tomorrow, Tomorrow, 1966; Am I This Countryside?, 1980; Mennonite Women: A Story of God's Faithfulness, 1683-1983, 1983; Spiritual Elegance: A Biography of Pauline Krehbiel Raid, 1987; (comp.) Prayers for Everyday, 1990; (ed.) Walking Together in Faith: The Central District Conference, 1957-1990, 1993; Pondered in Her Heart: Hannah's Book, Inside and Outside, 1998. Contributor to periodicals. **Address:** 112 S Spring St., Bluffton, OH 45817-1112, U.S.A.

RICH, Francine Poppo. American (born United States), b. 1967. **Genres:** Children's Fiction, Children's Non-fiction, Literary Criticism And History. **Career:** Blue Marlin Publications, founder. Writer. **Publications:** Why Can't I Spray Today: A Pee Wee Pipes Adventure, 1999; Pee Wee Pipes and the Wing Thing, 2000; Small, not Tall, 2001; Mama, Can Armadillos Swim?, 2004; Larry Bird: The Boy from French Lick, 2009. **Address:** Blue Marlin Publications, 823 Aberdeen Rd., West Bay Shore, NY 11706, U.S.A. **Online address:** abigmarlin@optonline.net

RICH, Ivana B. See **BAILEY-WILLIAMS, Nicole.**

RICH, Nathaniel. American (born United States), b. 1980. **Genres:** Novels, History, Film, Novellas/Short Stories, Literary Criticism And History, Essays, Translations. **Career:** The Paris Review, fiction editor. **Publications:** San Francisco Noir: The City in Film Noir from 1940 to the Present, 2005; The Mayor's Tongue (novel), 2008. Contributor to magazines. **Address:** NY , U.S.A. **Online address:** nathaniel@nathanielrich.com

RICH, Simon. American (born United States), b. 1984?. **Genres:** Novels, Humor/Satire. **Career:** Writer. **Publications:** Ant Farm: And Other Desperate Situations, 2007; Free Range Chickens, 2008; Elliot Allagash (novel), 2010. Contributor to periodicals. **Address:** Levine Greenberg Literary Agency, 307 7th Ave., Ste. 2407, New York, NY 10001, U.S.A.

RICH, Susan. (Susan Beth Rich). American (born United States), b. 1959. **Genres:** Poetry. **Career:** Highline Community College, faculty; Antioch University M.F.A. Program, faculty; Floating Bridge Press, editor; Boston Center for Adult Education, program administrator, 1986-87; Harvard Institute for Development, research assistant, 1987; Oxfam America, policy assistant, 1988; Amnesty Intl., program coordinator, 1989. **Publications:** The Cartographer's Tongue: Poems of the World, 2000; Cures Include Travel, Poems, 2006; The Alchemist's Kitchen, 2010; The Alchemist's Kitchen, Finalist for the Foreword Prize, 2010. Contributor to journals. Works appear in anthologies. **Address:** PO Box 16035, Seattle, WA 98116, U.S.A. **Online address:** susan@susanrich.net

RICH, Susan Beth. See **RICH, Susan.**

RICH, Thomas H(ewitt). American/Australian (born Australia), b. 1941. **Genres:** Zoology, Autobiography/Memoirs, Sciences. **Career:** University of California, paleontology technician, 1961-63, Radiation Laboratory, computer programmer, 1964-67; American Museum of Natural History, leader, 1968-70, scientific assistant in vertebrate paleontology and collector of mammalian fossil remains, 1971-73; Ohio State University, field assistant, 1970; Museum Victoria, curator, 1974-97, senior curator of vertebrate paleontology, 1997-; Monash University, honorary research associate in earth sciences, 1995-. Writer. **Publications:** Deltatheridia, Carnivora and Condylarthra (Mammalia) of the Early Eocene, 1971; (with D.L. Rasmussen) New North American Erinaceine Hedgehogs (Mammalia: Insectivora), 1973; Origin and History of the Erinaceinae and Brachyericinae (Mammalia, Insectivora) in North

America, 1981; (with P.V. Rich and M.A. Fenton) The Fossil Book, 1989; (co-ed.) Vertebrate Palaeontology of Australasia, 1991; (with P.V. Rich) Wildlife of Gondwana, 1993, rev. ed. as Wildlife of Gondwana: Dinosaurs and Other Vertebrates from the Ancient Supercontinent, 1999; (with P.V. Rich) Australia's Lost World, 1996; (co-author) The Fossil Hunter's Guide, 1997; (with P.V. Rich, L. Rich and T. Rich) Australia's Ancient Backboned Animals, 1997; (co-author) Australia's Dinosaurs, 1997; (co-author) Australia's Ancient Birds, 1997; (co-author) Diprotodon and Its Relatives, 1997; (ed. with P. Vickers-Rich and Y. Tomida) Proceedings of the Second Gondwana Dinosaur Symposium, 1999; (with P.V. Rich) The Dinosaurs of Darkness, 2000; Polar Dinosaurs of Australia, 2007; (with P.V. Rich and T. Rich) A Century of Australian Dinosaurs, 2003; (with P. Trusler and P. Vickers-Rich) The Artist and the Scientists: Bringing Prehistory to Life, 2010. Contributor to books and magazines. **Address:** Museum Victoria, PO Box 666, Melbourne, VI 3001, Australia. **Online address:** trich@museum.vic.gov.au

RICHARD, Adrienne. American (born United States), b. 1921. **Genres:** Novels, Medicine/Health, Mystery/Crime/Suspense, Sports/Fitness, Social Sciences. **Career:** Writer. **Publications:** NOVELS: Pistol, 1969; The Accomplice, 1973; Wings, 1974; Into the Road, 1976. OTHER: (with J. Reiter) Epilepsy: A New Approach, 1990, rev. ed., 1995. Contributor of articles to journals, magazines and newspapers. **Address:** 45 Chiltern Rd., Weston, MA 02493-2716, U.S.A.

RICHARD, Carl J(ohn). American (born United States), b. 1962. **Genres:** History. **Career:** University of Texas, visiting assistant professor of history, 1988-89; University of Southern Mississippi, assistant professor of history, 1989-91; University of Louisiana, professor of history, 1991-. Writer. **Publications:** The Founders and the Classics: Greece, Rome and the American Enlightenment, 1994; The Louisiana Purchase, 1995; Twelve Greeks and Romans Who Changed the World, 2003; The Battle for the American Mind: A Brief History of a Nation's Thought, 2004; Greeks and Romans Bearing Gifts: How the Ancients Inspired the Founding Fathers, 2008; The Golden Age of the Classics in America: Greece, Rome and the Antebellum United States, 2009; Why We're all Romans: The Roman Contribution to the Western World, 2010. Contributor to periodicals. **Address:** Department of History, University of Louisiana at Lafayette, Lafayette, LA 70504-2531, U.S.A. **Online address:** richard_carl@hotmail.com

RICHARD, Cliff. (Harry Roger Webb). British/Indian (born India), b. 1940. **Genres:** Theology/Religion, Autobiography/Memoirs, Biography, Music. **Career:** Arora International Hotel, co-owner, 2004-; singer, actor and writer. **Publications:** The Way I See It Now, 1973; Which one's Cliff?, 1977; Single-Minded, 1988; Mine for Ever, 1989; Cliff Richard-The Biography, 1993; My Life, My Way, 2008. **Address:** The Sir Cliff Richard Charitable Trust, PO Box 46C, Esher, SR KT10 ORB, England.

RICHARD, T. Dawn. American (born United States) **Genres:** Mystery/Crime/Suspense, Young Adult Non-fiction. **Career:** U.S. Air Force, instructor and curriculum developer. Educator and writer. **Publications:** MAY LIST MYSTERY SERIES: Death for Dessert, 2003; Digging Up Otis, 2005; A Wrinkle in Crime, 2007; Par for the Corpse, 2011. **Address:** WA , U.S.A. **Online address:** tdawnrichard@gmail.com

RICHARD-ALLERDYCE, Diane. American (born United States), b. 1958. **Genres:** Literary Criticism And History, History, Psychology, Biography, Autobiography/Memoirs. **Career:** Lynn University, instructor, 1985-88, assistant professor, 1988-93, associate professor, 1993-98, department head, 1994-2001, professor of English, 1998-2002, coordinator of honors program, 1993-2001, adjunct faculty, 2002-; Florida Atlantic University, adjunct faculty member, 1988-89, 1992; Toussaint L'Ouverture High School for Arts and Social Justice, co-founder and chief academic officer, 2002-, principal. Writer. **Publications:** Anais Nin and the Remaking of Self: Gender, Modernism, and Narrative Identity, 1998. Works appear in anthologies. Contributor of articles to books and periodicals. **Address:** Toussaint L'Ouverture High School, 777 E Atlantic Ave., Ste. 242, Delray Beach, FL 33483, U.S.A. **Online address:** drichardallerdyce@lynn.edu

RICHARDS, Alayna. See POSNER, Richard.

RICHARDS, Amelia M. (Amy Richards). American (born United States), b. 1970. **Genres:** Design, Social Sciences, Women's Studies And Issues. **Career:** Third Wave Foundation, co-founder; Soapbox (lecture agency), co-

founder; Ms. Foundation, consultant; Feminist.com, board director. Writer. **Publications:** AS AMY RICHARDS: (with J. Baumgardner) Manifesta: Young Women, Feminism, and the Future, 2000; (with J. Baumgardner) Grassroots: A Field Guide for Feminist Activism, 2005; Opting In: Having a Child without Losing Yourself, 2008; (with J. Baumgardner) Recipe-tested: An Idea Bank for Activists, forthcoming. Contributor to books and periodicals. **Address:** c/o Author Mail, Farrar, Straus & Giroux, 18 W 18th St., New York, NY 10011, U.S.A.

RICHARDS, Amy. See RICHARDS, Amelia M.

RICHARDS, David A. J. American (born United States), b. 1944. **Genres:** Law, Politics/Government, Essays. **Career:** Harvard University, lecturer in general education, 1968-71; Cleary, Gottlieb, Steen & Hamilton, associate, 1971-74; Fordham University, associate professor of law, 1974-77; Barnard College, visiting associate professor of philosophy, 1974-77; New York University, program for study of law, philosophy and social theory, associate professor of law, 1977-79, professor of law and director, 1979-94, Edwin D. Webb professor of law, 1994-; American Society for Political and Legal Philosophy, vice president, 1984; Harvard Law School, shikes lecturer, 1998; Law School's internationally distinguished Program for the Study of Law, Philosophy and Social Theory, founder. Writer. **Publications:** A Theory of Reasons for Action, 1971; The Moral Criticism of Law, 1977; Sex, Drugs, Death, and the Law: An Essay on Human Rights and Overcriminalization, 1982; Toleration and the Constitution, 1986; Foundations of American Constitutionalism, 1989; Conscience and the Constitution: History, Theory, and Law of the Reconstruction Amendments, 1993; Women, Gays, and the Constitution: The Grounds for Feminism and Gay Rights in Culture and Law, 1998; Free Speech and the Politics of Identity, 1999; Identity and the Case for Gay Rights: Race, Gender, Religion as Analogies, 1999; Italian American: The Racializing of an Ethnic Identity, 1999; Tragic Manhood and Democracy: Verdi's Voice and the Power of Musical Art, 2004; Disarming Manhood: Roots of Ethical Resistance, 2005; The Case for Gay Rights: From Bowers to Lawrence and Beyond, 2005; Patriarchal Religion, Sexuality, and Gender: A Critique of New Natural Law, 2007; The Sodomy Cases: Bowers v. Hardwick and Lawrence v. Texas, 2009; The Deepening Darkness: Patriarchy, Resistance, and Democracy's Future, 2009; Fundamentalism in American Religion and Law: Patriarchy as Threat to Democracy, 2010. **Address:** New York University School of Law, Vanderbilt Hall, 40 Washington Sq. S, Ste. 421, New York, NY 10012-1066, U.S.A. **Online address:** david.richards@nyu.edu

RICHARDS, David P. American (born United States), b. 1950. **Genres:** Art/Art History, Self Help. **Career:** Writer. **Publications:** How to Discover Your Personal Painting Style, 1995; Color Sense, 2000. Contributor to books. **Address:** North Light Books, 1507 Dana Ave., Cincinnati, OH 45207, U.S.A. **Online address:** dprichardsart@hotmail.com

RICHARDS, Dusty. American (born United States), b. 1937. **Genres:** Young Adult Fiction, Novels, Young Adult Non-fiction. **Career:** Teacher, 1960-61; farmer, 1961-63; Tyson Foods, management staff, 1963-96; KFAY-TV, farm director, 1977-96, television anchor, 1990-96; Ozark Electric Cooperative, board director, 1985-, chairman; fiction writer, 1996-; Rodeo of the Ozarks, director; Ozark Creative Writers Conference, director. **Publications:** Noble's Way, 1992; From Hell to Breakfast, 1994; By the Cut of Your Clothes, 1995; Fiction Writer's Guide: A Guide to Writing Fiction That Sells, 1998; The Lawless Land, 2000; Servant of the Law, 2000; Rancher's Law, 2001; The Natural, 2002; The Abilene Trail: A Ralph Compton Novel, 2003; Waltzing With Tumbleweeds, 2004; Deuces Wild, 2004; Aces High, 2004; Trail to Fort Smith: A Ralph Compton Novel, 2004; The Ogallala Trail: A Ralph Compton Novel, 2005; Horse Creek Incident, 2006; Comanche Moon, 2006; There Comes a Time, 2006; Trail to Cottonwood Falls: A Ralph Compton Novel, 2007; Montana Revenge, 2007; The Sundown Chaser, 2009; (with P. Fielding) Two Foxy Holiday Hens and One Big Rooster, 2009; Texas Blood Feud, 2009; Writing the West with Dusty Richards and Friends, 2010; Wulf's Tracks, 2010; (with R. Compton) North to the Salt Fork, 2010; Between Hell and Texas: A Byrnes Family Ranch Novel, 2011. **Address:** 21319 Perry Rd., Springdale, AR 72762, U.S.A. **Online address:** dustyrichards@cox.net

RICHARDS, Emilie. American (born United States), b. 1948?. **Genres:** Romance/Historical, Mystery/Crime/Suspense. **Career:** Author. **Publications:** Brendan's Song, 1985; Sweet Georgia Gal, 1985; Gilding the Lily, 1985; The Unmasking, 1985; Lady of the Night, 1986; Something So Right, 1986; Sweet Sea Spirit, 1986; Angel and the Saint, 1986; Sweet Mockingbird's,

1986; Good Time Man, 1986; Sweet Mountain Magic, 1986; Season of Miracles, 1986; Bayou Midnight, 1987; Aloha Always, 1987; Sweet Homecoming, 1987; Outback Nights, 1987; From Glowing Embers, 1987; Smoke Screen, 1988; All the Right Reasons, 1988; A Classic Encounter, 1988; Rainbow Fire, 1989; Out of the Ashes, 1989; Island Glory, 1989; Runaway, 1990; (with J. Greene and K. Keast) Birds, Bees and Babies, 1990; The Way Back Home, 1990; Fugitive, 1990; Labor Dispute, 1990; All Those Years Ago, 1991; Desert Shadows, 1991; Twilight Shadows, 1991; From a Distance, 1992; One Perfect Rose, 1992; Somewhere Out There, 1993; Dragonslayer: American Heroes, 1993; The Trouble with Joe, 1994; Duncan's Lady, 1995; Ian Ross's Woman, 1995; Macdougall's Darling, 1995; Woman without a Name, 1996; Once More with Feeling, 1996; Iron Lace, 1996; Rising Tides, 1997; Mail-Order Matty, 1997; Twice upon a Time, 1997; (with J. Blake) Southern Gentlemen, 1998; (co-author) A Mother's Gift, 1998; Beautiful Lies, 1999; One Moment Past Midnight, 1999; Whiskey Island, 2000; Fox River, 2001; Prospect Street, 2002; (with A. Leigh and P. Moreland) To the One I Love, 2003; (with F. Michaels and S. Woods) Maybe this Time, 2003; The Parting Glass, 2003; Wedding Ring, 2004; Endless Chain, 2005; Blessed is the Busybody, 2005; A Mother's Touch, 2005; Let There be Suspects, 2006; Lover's Knot, 2006; Touching Stars, 2007; Beware False Profits, 2007; Sister's Choice, 2008; A Lie for a Lie, 2009; Happiness Key, 2009; Fortunate Harbor, 2010; Sunset Bridge, 2011. Works appear in anthologies. **Address:** The Axelrod Agency, 55 Main St., PO Box 357, Chatham, NY 12037, U.S.A. **Online address:** info@emilierichards.com

RICHARDS, Eric. Australian/Welsh (born Wales), b. 1940. **Genres:** Demography, History, Writing/Journalism, Biography. **Career:** University of Adelaide, lecturer in economics, 1964-67; University of Stirling, lecturer in history, 1967-72; Flinders University, lecturer, reader, 1971-74, professor of history, 1975-, department head; University of Glasgow, senior visiting research fellow, 1975; University of Warwick, visiting research fellow, 1981; Australian National University, Research School of Social Sciences, Institute of Advance Studies, visiting fellow, 1989-90, 2001, 2002-05, F.B. Smith lecturer, 1999, research affiliate, 2002-05; University of London, Birkbeck College, visiting professor, 1994, King's College, Menzies Australian Studies Centre, visiting professor, 2003; University of Otago, Bamforth lecturer, 1998; University of Cardiff, visiting professor, 2001; Case Western Reserve University, adjunct professor of history, 2004. Writer. **Publications:** The Leviathan of Wealth: The Sutherland Fortune in the Industrial Revolution, 1973; The Last Scottish Food Riots, 1982; A History of the Highland Clearances, vol. I: Agrarian Transformation and the Evictions, 1746-1886, 1982, vol. II: Emigration, Protest, Reasons, 1985; (ed.) The Flinders History of South Australia, 1986; (with M. Clough) Cromartie: Highland Life, 1650-1914, 1989; (with R. Reid and D. Fitzpatrick) Visible Immigrants, vol. I: Neglected Sources for the History of Australian Immigration, 1989, (ed.) vol. II: Poor Australian Immigrants in the Nineteenth Century, 1991, vol. IV: Visible Women: Female Immigrants in Colonial Australia, 1995, vol. V: The Australian Immigrant in the 20th Century, 1998, vol. VI: Speaking to Immigrants: Oral Testimony and the History of Australian Immigration, 2002; Patrick Sellar and the Highland Clearances: Homicide, Eviction, and the Price of Progress, 1999; The Highland Clearances: People, Landlords, and Rural Turmoil, 2000; (ed.) Speaking to Immigrants: Oral Testimony and the History of Australian Immigration, 2002; Australian Journal of Irish Studies, 2002; New Zealand Books, 2003; Britannia's Children: Emigration from England, Scotland, Wales and Ireland since 1600, 2004; Debating the Highland Clearances, 2007; Australian Journal of Irish Studies, 2008; Destination Australia: Migration to Australia since 1901, 2008; The British Diaspora, 1600-2000, forthcoming. Contributor to books and journals. **Address:** Department of History, Faculty of Social Sciences, Flinders University, 217, Social Sciences S, PO Box 2100, Adelaide, SA 5001, Australia. **Online address:** eric.richards@flinders.edu.au

RICHARDS, Eugene. American (born United States), b. 1944. **Genres:** Local History/Rural Topics, Adult Non-fiction, Photography. **Career:** Vista, staff; Art Institute of Boston, instructor of photography, 1974-76; Union College, instructor, 1977; Maine Photo Workshop, artist-in-residence, 1977-78; International Center of Photography, artist-in-residence, 1978-79; Magnum Photos, staff, 1978-, 2002-; Many Voices, co-director. Writer and director. **Publications:** Few Comforts or Surprises: The Arkansas Delta, 1973; Dorchester Days, 1978, 2nd ed., 2000; 50 Hours: The Birth of Henry Harry, 1983; (with D. Lynch) Exploding into Life, 1986; Below the Line: Living Poor in America, 1987; The Knife and Gun Club: Scenes from an Emergency Room, 1989; (with E.Barnes and Danny.J) Cocaine True, Cocaine Blue, 1994; Americans We: Photographs and Notes, 1994; Eugene Richards, 1997; Eugene

Richards: 55, 2001; Stepping through the Ashes, 2002; The Fat Baby: Stories, 2004; Procession of them, 2008; The Blue Room, 2008; War is Personal: A Chronicle of the Human Cost of the Iraq War, 2010. Contributor to books and periodicals. **Address:** c/o Author Mail, Aperture Foundation, 20 E 23rd St., New York, NY 10010, U.S.A. **Online address:** richardseugene@aol.com

RICHARDS, Jean. American (born United States), b. 1940. **Genres:** Children's Fiction, Young Adult Fiction, Young Adult Non-fiction, Children's Non-fiction, Animals/Pets. **Career:** Writer. **Publications:** (Reteller) God's Gift, 1993; (reteller) The First Olympic Games: A Gruesome Greek Myth with a Happy Ending, 2000; A Fruit Is a Suitcase for Seeds, 2002; How the Elephant Got Its Trunk: A Retelling of the Rudyard Kipling Tale, 2003. **Address:** 25 Washington Sq. N, New York, NY 10011-9108, U.S.A. **Online address:** nonsequito@earthlink.net

RICHARDS, Jeffrey H. (Jeffrey Hamilton Richards). American (born United States), b. 1948. **Genres:** Cultural/Ethnic Topics, Plays/Screenplays, History. **Career:** University of North Carolina, faculty; Duke University, faculty; Old Dominion University, Eminent Professor of Literature and head of department. Writer. **Publications:** (ed.) An Introduction to Film Criticism: Prepared for English 42 and Christopher Brookhouse and Howard Harper, 3rd ed., 1977; Theater Enough: American Culture and the Metaphor of the World Stage, 1607-1789, 1991; Mercy Otis Warren, 1995; (ed. and intro.) Early American Drama, 1997; (ed.) Anna Cora Ogden Mowatt Ritchie, Mimic Life; or, Before and Behind the Curtain, 2000; (ed. and intro.) Early Plays, 2001; Drama, Theatre, and Identity in the American New Republic, 2005; (ed. with S.M. Harris) Mercy Otis Warren: Selected Letters, 2009. Contributor of articles to books and journals. **Address:** Department of English, Old Dominion University, Norfolk, VA 23529-0086, U.S.A. **Online address:** jhrichar@odu.edu

RICHARDS, Jeffrey Hamilton. See **RICHARDS, Jeffrey H.**

RICHARDS, Judith M. Australian (born Australia), b. 1938?. **Genres:** Biography, History. **Career:** La Trobe University, senior lecturer in history, History Program, honorary research associate. Historian and writer. **Publications:** Mary Tudor, 2008. Contributor to books and journals. **Address:** History Program, La Trobe University, Melbourne, VI 3086, Australia. **Online address:** j.richards@latrobe.edu.au

RICHARDS, Lawrence. American (born United States), b. 1959. **Genres:** Business/Trade/Industry, Economics. **Career:** Miami University, instructor. Writer. **Publications:** Union-Free America: Workers and Antiunion Culture, 2008. Contributor to books. **Address:** Miami University, Rm. 208, Johnston Hall, Middletown Campus, Oxford, OH 45056, U.S.A. **Online address:** richarl@muohio.edu

RICHARDS, Leigh. See **KING, Laurie R.**

RICHARDS, Linda L. Canadian (born Canada), b. 1960?. **Genres:** Mystery/Crime/Suspense, Novels. **Career:** January Magazine, editor and co-founder; The Rap Sheet, contributor; Simon Fraser University, faculty. **Publications:** Web Graphics for Dummies, 1997; Teach Yourself Photoshop 4 for Macintosh and Windows, 1997; Teach Yourself Photoshop 5 and 5.5, 1999; MADELINE CARTER SERIES NOVELS: Mad Money, 2004; The Next Ex, 2005; Calculated Loss, 2006; KITTY PANGBORN SERIES MYSTERY NOVELS: Death Was the Other Woman, 2008; Death Was in the Picture, 2009. **Address:** 101-1001 W Broadway, Ste. 192, Vancouver, BC V6H 4E4, Canada. **Online address:** linda@lindalrichards.com

RICHARDS, Matt. American (born United States), b. 1968. **Genres:** How-to Books, Adult Non-fiction, Homes/Gardens, Sciences. **Career:** Backcountry Buckskin, director, 1988-; teacher, 1990-. Writer. **Publications:** SELF-ILLUSTRATOR: Deerskins into Buckskins: How to Tan with Natural Materials: A Field Guide for Hunters and Gatherers, 1997. Contributor to periodicals. **Address:** 3303 Dick George Rd., Cave Junction, OR 97523, U.S.A. **Online address:** matt@braintan.com

RICHARDS, Scott. See **CARD, Orson Scott.**

RICHARDS, Serena. See **CARROLL, Susan.**

RICHARDSON, Anne. See **ROIPHE, Anne Richardson.**

RICHARDSON, Bonham C. American (born United States), b. 1939. **Genres:** Environmental Sciences/Ecology, Geography, History. **Career:** General Electric Co., financial trainee, 1963-64; California State College, assistant professor of geography, 1970-72; Rutgers University, assistant professor of geography, 1972-77; Virginia Polytechnic Institute and State University, associate professor, 1977-85, professor of geography, 1985-, now professor emeritus; University of the West Indies, visiting research fellow, 1981-82; University of London, visiting lecturer, 1986-87. Writer. **Publications:** Caribbean Migrants: Environment and Human Survival on St. Kitts and Nevis, 1983; Panama Money in Barbados, 1900-1920, 1985; The Caribbean in the Wider World, 1492-1992: A Regional Geography, 1992; Economy and Environment in the Caribbean: Barbados and the Windwards in the Late 1800s, 1997; South and the Caribbean: Essays and Commentaries, 2001; Igniting the Caribbean's Past: Fire in British West Indian History, 2004. Works appear in anthologies. **Address:** Department of Geography, Virginia Polytechnic Institute, 115 Major Williams Hall, PO Box 0115, Blacksburg, VA 24061-0115, U.S.A. **Online address:** borichar@vt.edu

RICHARDSON, Brian W. American/Canadian (born Canada), b. 1966?. **Genres:** Travel/Exploration, History, Biography. **Career:** Bolen Books, clerk, 1980-91; University of Victoria, Computer Store, sales and support staff, 1991-92; University of Hawaii, College of Social Sciences, computer support, 1993-2002, Marine Option Program, newsletter editor, 1999-2004, Globalization Research Center, computer support, 2000-02, Windward Community College, reference librarian, 2002-, instructor, dean of academic affairs of division II; Hawaii State Capitol, legislative assistant, 1996. **Publications:** Longitude and Empire: How Captain Cook's Voyages Changed the World, 2005. Contributor to periodicals. **Address:** Windward Community College, Hale Alaka'i, 121D, 45-720 Kea'ahala Rd., Kaneohe, HI 96744-3528, U.S.A. **Online address:** richards@hawaii.edu

RICHARDSON, David (Horsfall Stuart). British (born England), b. 1942?. **Genres:** Environmental Sciences/Ecology, Botany, Biology, History, Children's Fiction. **Career:** Trinity College, professor of botany; Saint Mary's University, dean of science, through 2006, now retired. Writer. **Publications:** The Vanishing Lichens: Their History, Biology and Importance, 1974; The Biology of Mosses, 1981; (ed.) Biological Indicators of Pollution: Proceedings of a Seminar, 24-25 February 1986, 1987; Pollution Monitoring with Lichens, 1992. **Address:** Richmond Publishing Company Ltd., The Cottage, Allerds Rd., Slough, BR SL2 3TJ, England. **Online address:** david.richardson@stmarys.ca

RICHARDSON, G. B. See **RICHARDSON, George Barclay.**

RICHARDSON, George Barclay. (G. B. Richardson). British (born England), b. 1924. **Genres:** Economics, Philosophy. **Career:** United Kingdom Atomic Energy Authority, economic advisor, 1968-74; Oxford University, Oxford University Press, secretary to the delegates and chief executive, 1974-88, Corpus Christi College, honorary fellow, 1987, pro-vice-chancellor, 1988-94, now retired, St. John's College, honorary fellow, 1989, Keble College, faculty, warden, 1989-94, honorary fellow, 1994, now retired. Writer. **Publications:** Information and Investment: A Study in the Working of the Competitive Economy, 1961, 2nd ed., 1990; Economic Theory, 1964; The Economics of Imperfect Knowledge, 1998; (ed. with N.J. Foss and B.J. Loasby) Economic Organization, Capabilities and Co-Ordination, 1998. **Address:** University of Oxford, Saint Giles, Oxford, OX OX1 3JP, England. **Online address:** george.richardson@keb.ox.ac.uk

RICHARDSON, Heather Cox. American (born United States), b. 1962?. **Genres:** History. **Career:** Massachusetts Institute of Technology, instructor, 1993-2002; Harvard University, Charles Warren Center fellow, 1998-99; University of Massachusetts, Department of History, professor of history; The Boston College, Department of History, professor. Writer and consultant. **Publications:** The Greatest Nation of the Earth: Republican Economic Policies during the Civil War, 1997; The Death of Reconstruction: Race, Labor and Politics in the Post-Civil War North, 1865-1901, 2001; (contrib. and intro.) The South since the War: As Shown by Fourteen Weeks of Travel and Observation in Georgia and the Carolinas, 2004; West from Appomattox: The Reconstruction of America after the Civil War, 2007; Wounded Knee: Party Politics and the Road to an American Massacre, 2010. **Address:** Department of History, College of Humanities and Fine Arts, University of Massachusetts, Herter Hall, 300 Massachusetts Ave., Amherst, MA 01003-9312, U.S.A. **Online address:** heather.richardson@bc.edu

RICHARDSON, James T. American (born United States), b. 1941. **Genres:** Sociology, Theology/Religion. **Career:** Texas Tech University, Department Sociology, instructor, 1965-66; University of Nevada, Department of Sociology, assistant professor, 1968-71, associate professor, 1971-77, professor, 1977-88, professor of sociology and judicial studies, 1988-, Center for Justice Studies, director; London School of Economics, Department of Sociology, departmental visitor, 1974-75; Washoe County Democratic Party, chair, 1977-79; Catholic University, Department of Psychology of Culture and Religion, Fulbright fellow, 1981; Litigation Technologies Inc., partner. Writer. **Publications:** With A. Brady) Basic Programming Language, 1973; (ed.) Conversion Careers, 1978; (with M. Stewart and R. Simmonds) Organized Miracles, 1979; (ed. with D. Bromley) The Brainwashing/Deprogramming Controversy, 1983; (ed.) Money and Power in the New Religions, 1988; (ed. with J. Best and D. Bromley) The Satanism Scare, 1991; (ed. with J.A. Beckford) Challenging Religion, 2003; (ed.) Regulating Religion: Case Studies from Around the Globe, 2004. **Address:** Grant Sawyer Center for Justice Studies, University of Nevada, PO Box 313, Reno, NV 89557, U.S.A. **Online address:** jtr@unr.edu

RICHARDSON, Justin. American (born United States), b. 1963. **Genres:** Human Relations/Parenting, Animals/Pets. **Career:** Columbia University, Center for Psychoanalytic Training and Research, assistant professor of psychiatry; Cornell University, assistant professor of psychiatry. Writer. **Publications:** (With M.A. Schuster) Everything You Never Wanted Your Kids to Know about Sex, (but Were Afraid They'd Ask): The Secrets to Surviving Your Child's Sexual Development from Birth to the Teens, 2003; (with P. Parnell) And Tango Makes Three, 2005; (with P. Parnell) Christian, the Hugging Lion, 2010. **Address:** Center for Psychoanalytic Training and Research, Columbia University, 21 W 12th St., Ste. A, New York, NY 10011, U.S.A. **Online address:** jr195@columbia.edu

RICHARDSON, Mark. British (born England), b. 1962. **Genres:** Theology/Religion, Philosophy, Human Relations/Parenting. **Career:** Ottawa Citizen, senior feature writer, 1986-94; Care Canada and Care Intl., media relations officer, 1990; WTN, producer, 1996-97; Toronto Star, writer, editor and columnist, 1998-2003, Wheels section, editor, 2003-. **Publications:** Zen and Now: On the Trail of Robert Pirsig and Zen and the Art of Motorcycle Maintenance, 2008. Contributor of journalism. **Address:** Toronto Star, 5 th fl., 1 Yonge St., Toronto, ON M5E 1E6, Canada. **Online address:** mark@zenandnow.org

RICHARDSON, Mark. American (born United States), b. 1963?. **Genres:** Literary Criticism And History. **Career:** Doshisha University, Department of English, Faculty of Letters, faculty researcher. Writer and critic. **Publications:** (Ed. with R. Poirier) Robert Frost: Collected Poems, Prose, and Plays, 1995; The Ordeal of Robert Frost: The Poet and His Poetics, 1997; (contrib.) Two Poems By Robert Frost Recently Discovered, 2006; (ed.) The Collected Prose of Robert Frost, 2007. **Address:** University of Illinois Press, 1325 S Oak St., Champaign, IL 61820-6903, U.S.A. **Online address:** marksrichardson@mac.com

RICHARDSON, Midge Turk. (Midge Turk). American (born United States), b. 1930. **Genres:** Children's Non-fiction, Autobiography/Memoirs, Biography. **Career:** New York University, assistant dean, 1966-67; Glamour Magazine, college editor, 1967-74; CO-ED Magazine, editor-in-chief and editorial director, 1974-75; Seventeen Magazine, executive editor, 1975-79, editor-in-chief, 1979-, now retired. **Publications:** AS MIDGE TURK: The Buried Life: A Nun's Journey, 1971; Gordon Parks: A Biography, 1971. **Address:** Sterling Lord Agency, 660 Madison Ave., New York, NY 10021, U.S.A.

RICHARDSON, Miles. American (born United States), b. 1932. **Genres:** Anthropology/Ethnology, Social Sciences. **Career:** Indiana State College (now Indiana University of Pennsylvania), assistant professor, 1963-64, associate professor of anthropology, 1964-65; Louisiana State University, assistant professor, 1965-69, associate professor, 1969-71, professor of anthropology, 1971-, chair of department, 1969-72, Doris Z. Stone distinguished professor in Latin American studies, now professor emeritus. Writer. **Publications:** (With B. Bode) Urban and Societal Features of Popular Medicine in Puntarenas, Costa Rica, 1969; San Pedro, Colombia: Small Town in a Developing Society, 1970; (ed.) The Human Mirror: Material and Spatial Images of Man, 1974; (ed.) Place: Experience and Symbol, 1984; (ed. with M.C. Webb) The Burden of Being Civilized: An Anthropological Perspective on the Discontents of Civilization, 1986; Cry Lonesome and Other Accounts of the Anthropologist's Project, 1990; Being-in-Christ and Putting Death in

Its Place: An Anthropologist's Account of Christian Performance in Spanish America and the American South, 2003; (ed. with D.W. Davis) Coastal Zone: Papers in Honor of H. Jesse Walker, 2004; (ed. with D. Lindenfeld) Beyond Conversion and Syncretism: Indigenous Encounters with Missionary Christianity, 1800-2000, 2012. Contributor of articles to journals. **Address:** Department of Geography and Anthropology, Louisiana State University, 227 Howe-Russell Geoscience Complex, Baton Rouge, LA 70803, U.S.A. **Online address:** gamile@lsu.edu

RICHARDSON, Nigel. British (born England), b. 1957?. **Genres:** Young Adult Fiction, Novels, Travel/Exploration. **Career:** Daily Telegraph, deputy travel editor; novelist; journalist. **Publications:** Breakfast in Brighton, 1998; Dog Days in Soho: One Man's Adventures in 1950s Bohemia, 2000; (contrib.) Jon Nicholson, A1: Portrait of a Road, 2000; (with N. Richardson) Britain's Best Drives, 2009. FICTION: The Wrong Hands, 2005; The Rope Ladder, 2007. Contributor to Periodicals. **Address:** c/o Clare Alexander, Aitken Alexander Associates, 18-21 Cavaye Pl., London, GL SW10 9PT, England.

RICHARDSON, Paul. Spanish/American (born United States), b. 1963?. **Genres:** Animals/Pets, Travel/Exploration, Food And Wine, Reference. **Career:** Wine Magazine, journalist; Taste, staff. **Publications:** Not Part of the Package: A Year in Ibiza, 1993; Our Lady of the Sewers: And Other Adventures in Deep Spain, 1999; Cornucopia: A Gastronomic Tour of Britain, 2000; Indulgence: Around the World in Search of Chocolate, 2002; (contrib.) Barcelona: Authentic Recipes Celebrating the Foods of the World, 2004; Foods of The World Barcelona, 2005; A Late Dinner: Discovering the Food of Spain, 2007. Contributor to periodicals. **Address:** Bloomsbury Publishing PLC, 36 Soho Sq., London, GL W1D 3QY, England.

RICHARDSON, Peter. American (born United States), b. 1959. **Genres:** Education, Literary Criticism And History. **Career:** University of North Texas, professor; Public Policy Institute of California, communications analyst; San Francisco State University, professor; PoliPointPress, editorial director. Writer. **Publications:** (Ed. with R. Abcarian and M. Klotz) Literature: Reading and Writing, the Human Experience, 7th ed., 1998, 2nd ed., 2002; Style: A Pragmatic Approach, 1998, 2nd ed., 2002; School Finance and California's Master Plan for Education, 2001; School Budgets and Student Achievement in California: The Principal's Perspective, 2004; American Prophet: The Life & Work of Carey McWilliams, 2005; A Bomb in Every Issue: How the Short, Unruly Life of Ramparts Magazine Changed America, 2009. Contributor to periodicals. **Address:** San Francisco State University, 1600 Holloway Ave., San Francisco, CA 94132-1740, U.S.A. **Online address:** peter_richardson@comcast.net

RICHARDSON, R. C. British (born England), b. 1944. **Genres:** History. **Career:** Thames Polytechnic, lecturer, senior lecturer, 1968-77; King Alfred's University College (now The University of Winchester), Department of History, head, 1977-98, professor, 1993, head of research, 1998-, Graduate Centre, head, through 2001, director of international relations, 2001-, professor emeritus of history, 2007-. Writer. **Publications:** Puritanism in North-West England: A Regional Study of the Diocese of Chester to 1642, 1972; (with W.H. Chaloner) British Economic and Social History: A Bibliographical Guide, 1976, 3rd ed., 1996; The Debate on the English Revolution, 1977, 3rd ed., 1998; (with T.B. James) The Urban Experience: English, Scottish and Welsh Towns, 1450-1700, 1983; (with G.M. Ridden) Freedom and the English Revolution, 1986; The Study of History: A Bibliographical Guide, 1988, 2nd ed., 2000; Town and Countryside in the English Revolution, 1992; Images of Oliver Cromwell, 1993; The English Civil Wars: Local Aspects, 1997; (ed.) The Changing Face of English Local History, 2000; Household Servants in Early Modern England, 2010. **Address:** Department of History, University of Winchester, Winchester, HM SO22 4NR, England. **Online address:** roger.richardson@winchester.ac.uk

RICHARDSON, Richard Judson. American (born United States), b. 1935. **Genres:** Politics/Government. **Career:** Tulane University, graduate teaching assistant, 1960-62, instructor, arts and science faculty, 1962-65; Western Michigan University, assistant professor, 1965-67, associate professor, 1967-69; University of Hawaii, associate professor of political science, 1967-68; Hawaii State Constitutional Convention, consultant, 1967-68; University of North Carolina, Department of Political Science, associate professor, 1968-72, professor, 1973-77, associate chair, 1973, department chairman, 1975-80, 1985-90, Burton Craig professor, 1977-2000, university provost, vice chancellor, 1995-2000; Institute for Research in Social Science, research associate, 1969-. Writer. **Publications:** Orleans Parish Offices; Notes on a City-Parish

Consolidation, 1961; (with K.N. Vines) The Politics of Federal Courts: Lower Courts in the United States, 1970; Trial of Traffic Cases in Hawaii, 1970; (co-author) Perspectives on the Legal Justice System, Public Attitudes and Criminal Victimization, 1972; (with N.D. Walker) Public Attitudes Toward the Police, 1974; (co-author) The Politics of American Democracy, 1977, 7th ed., 1981. **Address:** Department of Political Science, University of North Carolina, 361 Hamilton Hall, CB 3265, Chapel Hill, NC 27599-3265, U.S.A.

RICHARDSON, Riché. American (born United States), b. 1971?. **Genres:** Literary Criticism And History. **Career:** Spelman College, Comprehensive Writing Program, writing tutor, 1990-93; Duke University, Department of English, teaching assistant, 1995, research assistant, 1996-98; University of California, Department of English, assistant professor of literature, 1998-2005, associate professor, 2005-08; Cornell University, Africana Studies and Research Center, associate professor of African American literature, 2008-. Writer. **Publications:** Black Masculinity and the U.S. South: From Uncle Tom to Gangsta, 2007; Black Femininity, Global South: Visualizing the Politics of Race, forthcoming; Slim: Black Body Politics and an Eating Disorder in Reverse, forthcoming. **Address:** Africana Studies and Research Center, Cornell University, 310 Triphammer Rd., Ithaca, NY 14850, U.S.A. **Online address:** rdr83@cornell.edu

RICHARDSON, Robert. British (born England), b. 1940. **Genres:** Mystery/Crime/Suspense, Local History/Rural Topics, Novels. **Career:** Daily Mail, copy editor, 1966-72; Welwyn and Hatfield Times, editor, 1973-82; Hertsfordshire Advertiser, editor, 1982-87. **Publications:** MYSTERY NOVELS: AUGUSTUS MALTRAVERS SERIES: The Latimer Mercy, 1985; Bellringer Street, 1988; The Book of the Dead, 1989; The Dying of the Light, 1990; Sleeping in the Blood, 1991 in US as Murder in Waiting, 1991; The Lazarus Tree, 1992. OTHER MYSTERY NOVELS: The Hand of Strange Children, 1993; Significant Others, 1995; Victims, 1997. OTHERS: The Book of Hatfield: A Portrait of the Town, 1978, 2nd ed., 1988; Yesterday's Town, 1986; (ed. with W. Pratt) Homage to Imagism, 1992. **Address:** Gregory & Co., 3 Barb Mews, Hammersmith, London, GL W6 7PA, England.

RICHARDSON, Robert Galloway. British (born England), b. 1926. **Genres:** History, Medicine/Health, Sciences, Biography. **Career:** West Kent General Hospital, house physician and surgeon, 1951-52; Eaton Hall Officer Cadet School, medical officer, 1952-54; Butterworth & Co., medical editor, 1955-63; Medical News, assistant editor, 1963-65, features editor, 1965-67; Abbottempo, editor, 1967-72, consultant medical editor, 1972-; Spectrum Intl., editor, 1974-; International Medicine, consultant editor, 1979-. **Publications:** The Surgeon's Tale, 1958, rev. ed. as The Surgeon's Tale: The Story of Modern Surgery, 1964, rev. ed. as Surgery: Old and New Frontiers, 1969; (intro.) Modern Trends in Cardiac Surgery, 1960; The Surgeon's Heart: A History of Cardiac Surgery, 1969 as The Scalpel and the Heart, 1970, rev. ed. as Heart and Scalpel, 2001; (ed.) The Second World Conference on Smoking and Health: The Proceedings of a Conference Organized by the Health Education Council at Imperial College, London, 20 to 24 September 1971, 1972; The Menopause: A Neglected Crisis, 1973; (ed.) The Fetus at Risk, 1973; The Abominable Stoma: A Historical Survey of the Artificial Anus, 1973; The Hairs of Your Head Are Numbered, 1974; Larrey: Surgeon to Napoleon's Imperial Guard, 1974, rev. ed., 2000; Blood: A Very Special Juice, 1974; (ed.) Nurse Sarah Anne: With Florence Nightingale at Scutari, 1977; (ed.) Round-Table Discussion on Gentamicin and Tobramycin, 1978; (ed.) Practical Problems in Rheumatology, 1980; (ed.) Pulmonary and Circulation Abnormalities in Chronic Obstructive Airways Disease: An Evaluation of Pirbuterol, 1983; (ed.) The Rheumatological Disease Process: Focus on Piroxicam, 1984; Medicine through the Ages with Dr Baldassare, 1999. **Address:** Apple Tree Cottage, French St., Westerham, KT TN16 1PW, England.

RICHBURG, Keith B(ernard). American (born United States), b. 1958. **Genres:** Documentaries/Reportage. **Career:** Washington Post, Metropolitan staff, 1980-83, national staff, 1983-86, Southeast Asian bureau chief, 1986-90, Africa bureau chief, 1991-95, Hong Kong and Southeast Asia bureau chief, 1995-2000, Paris bureau chief, 2000-07, New York bureau chief, 2007-; East-West Center, journalist-in-residence, 1990-91. Writer. **Publications:** Out of America: A Black Man Confronts Africa, 1997. **Address:** The Washington Post, New York Bureau, 251 W 57th St., 12 Fl., New York, NY 10019, U.S.A. **Online address:** richburgk@washpost.com

RICHEMONT, Enid. Welsh/British (born England), b. 1940. **Genres:** Young Adult Fiction, Children's Fiction, Novellas/Short Stories, Picture/

Board Books, Novels, Plays/Screenplays. **Career:** Rudolf Steiner School for Disturbed Children, teacher, 1960-62; children's author and writing professional, 1990-. **Publications:** The Time Tree, 1990; The Glass Bird, 1990; My Mother's Daughter, 1990; The Game, 1990; The Magic Skateboard, 1992; Wolfsong, 1992; Kachunka!, 1992; Gemma and the Beetle People, 1994; Twice Times Danger, 1995; The Dream Dog, 1996; The Stone That Grew, 1996; To Summon a Spirit, 1999; The Enchanted Village, 1999; Jamie and the Whippersnapper, 2000; For Maritsa, With Love, 2001; Plop City, 2006; Jack The Fearless, 2006; Double Dragons, 2007; Billy and the Wizard, 2008; Sticky Vickie, 2008; Wow! 366, 2008; (with K. Waldek) Big Purple Wonderbook, 2009; Brownilocks and the Three Bowls of Cornflakes, 2010; Pirates of the Storm, 2010. **Address:** c/o Sophie Hicks, Ed Victor Ltd., 6 Bayley St., Bedford Sq., London, GL WC1B 3HB, England. **Online address:** enid@enidrichemont.org.uk

RICHERSON, Peter J. American (born United States), b. 1943. **Genres:** Earth Sciences, Cultural/Ethnic Topics, Environmental Sciences/Ecology, History. **Career:** University of California-Davis, researcher, 1969-71, assistant professor, 1971-77, associate professor, 1977-83, professor, 1983-2006, Institute of Ecology, associate director, 1977-80, director, 1983-90, Department of Environmental Science and Policy, distinguished professor, 2006-; University of California-Berkeley, Energy and Resources Program, visiting professor, 1977-78; Duke University, Forestry and Environmental Studies, visiting professor, 1984; University of Bielefeld, Center for Interdisciplinary Studies, Neurosciences Institute, visiting fellow, 1984; Rockefeller University, Neurosciences Institute, visiting fellow, 1984; Society for Human Ecology, president, 1994-95; Human Behavior and Evolution Society, treasurer, 1999-2005; University of Exeter, visiting professor, 2004; California Academy of Sciences, fellow, 2006; Davis Faculty Association, board director. Writer. **Publications:** NONFICTION: (ed. with C.R. Goldman and J. McEvoy III) Environmental Quality and Water Development, 1973; (ed. with J. McEvoy III) Human Ecology: An Environmental Approach, 1976; (with R. Boyd) Culture and the Evolutionary Process, 1985; (with R. Boyd) Not by Genes Alone: How Culture Transformed Human Evolution, 2005; (with R. Boyd) The Origin and Evolution of Cultures, 2005. Contributor to periodicals. **Address:** Department of Environmental Science & Policy, University of California, 3146A Wickson Hall, 1 Shields Ave., Davis, CA 95616, U.S.A. **Online address:** pjricherson@ucdavis.edu

RICHETTI, John J. American (born United States), b. 1938. **Genres:** Literary Criticism And History, History, Geography. **Career:** New York University, faculty; St. John's University, instructor, 1961-64, assistant professor of English, 1964-65; Columbia University, lecturer, 1967-68, assistant professor of English, 1968-70; Rutgers University, associate professor, 1970-75, professor, 1975-87; University of Pennsylvania, Leonard Sugarman professor, A.M. Rosenthal professor of English, 1987-, A.M. Rosenthal professor emeritus of English, Department of English, chair, 1991-95, 2000-02. Writer. **Publications:** Popular Fiction before Richardson: Narrative Patterns 1700-1739, 1969; Defoe's Narratives: Situations and Structures, 1975; Philosophical Writing: Locke, Berkeley, Hume, 1983; Daniel Defoe, 1987; The Columbia History of the British Novel, 1994; (ed.) Cambridge Companion to the British Novel, 1996; (ed.) Hamlet, 1998; English Novel in History, 1700-1780, 1999; The Novel in History: 1700-1780, 1999; (ed. and intro.) Robinson Crusoe, 2001; The Life of Daniel Defoe: A Critical Biography, 2005; (ed.) The Cambridge History of English Literature: 1660-1780, 2005; (ed.) History of Jemmy and Jenny Jessamy, 2005; (ed.) Cambridge Companion to Daniel Defoe, 2008. **Address:** Department of English, University of Pennsylvania, Fisher-Bennett Hall, 3340 Walnut St., Philadelphia, PA 19104, U.S.A. **Online address:** jrichett@english.upenn.edu

RICHIE, Donald. Japanese/American (born United States), b. 1924. **Genres:** Novels, Anthropology/Ethnology, Film, Literary Criticism And History, Travel/Exploration, Young Adult Fiction. **Career:** Pacific Stars and Stripes, civilian staff writer, 1947-49; Saturday Review of Literature, arts critic, 1950-51; Japan Times, film critic, 1953-69, literary critic, 1972-, art critic, 1973-; Waseda University, lecturer in American literature, 1954-59; Nation, arts critic, 1959-61; UniJapan Film, advisor, 1963; New York Museum of Modern Art, curator of film, 1968-73; Newsweek, arts critic, 1973-76; University of Michigan, Toyota chair, 1993. **Publications:** This Scorching Earth, 1956; Where are the Victors?: A Novel, 1956, rev. ed., 1986; The Land and People of Japan, 1958; (with J.L. Anderson) The Japanese Film: Art and Industry, 1959, rev. ed., 1982; Japanese Movies, 1961; (trans.) Six Kabuki Plays, 1963; The Films of Akira Kurosawa, 1965, 3rd ed., 1996; The Japa-

nese Movie: An Illustrated History, 1966, rev. ed., 1982; The Erotic Gods, 1966; (ed. with M. Weatherby) Masters' Book of Ikebana: Background and Principles of Japanese Flower Arrangement, 1966; Irezumi, 1966; Art Des Fleurs Au Japon, Hier Et Aujourd'hui, 1967; Nihonno Dentō, 1967; (ed. and intro.) Ikiru: A Film, 1968; Companions of the Holiday: A Novel, 1968; (ed.) Rashomon: A Film, 1969; George Stevens: An American Romantic, 1970; The Inland Sea, 1971; Japanese Cinema: Film Style and National Character, 1971; Focus on Rashomon, 1972; Three Modern Kyogen, 1972; (ed.) Film: The Museum of Modern Art Department of Film Circulating Programs, 1973; Ozu: The Man and His Films, 1974; Tien ying I shu, 1975; (ed. and trans. with E. Klestadt) Y. Ozu, Tokyo Story, 1977; Introducing Japan, 1978; (ed. with M. Hyoe) A Hundred More Things Japanese, 1980; The Japanese Tattoo, 1980; Kyōto hakken, 1981; Some Aspects of Japanese Popular Culture, 1981; Zen Inklings: Some Stories, Fables, Parables, and Sermons, 1982; Notes for a Study of Shohei Imamura, 1983; A Taste of Japan: Food Fact and Fable: What the People Eat: Customs and Etiquette, 1984; Viewing Film, 1985; Introducing Tokyo, 1987; A Lateral View: Essays on Contemporary Japan, 1987; Different People, 1987; (contrib.) Prints of Marian Korn: A Catalogue Raisonné, 1988; Tokyo Nights, 1988; Japanese Cinema: An Introduction, 1990; A Lateral View: Essays on Culture and Style in Contemporary Japan, 1992; The Honorable Visitors, 1994; (with A. Georges) The Temples of Kyoto, 1995; Partial Views, 1995; (ed. and intro.) Lafcadio Hearns' Japan: An Anthology of his Writings on the Country and Its People, 1997; Ricercar Fur Donald Richie, 1997; Tokyo: A View of the City, 1999; The Memoirs of the Warrior Kumagai: A Historical Novel, 1999; Words, Ideas, and Ambiguities: Four Perspectives on Translating from the Japanese, 2000; A Hundred Years of Japanese Film: A Concise History, with a Selective Guide to Videos and DVDs, 2001; The Donald Richie Reader: 50 Years of Writing on Japan, 2001; Japanese Literature Reviewed, 2003; The Image Factory: Fads and Fashions in Japan, 2003; Japan Journals, 1947-2004, 2004; (foreword and afterword) The Scarlet Gang of Asakusa, 2005; A Tractate on Japanese Aesthetics, 2007; Travels in the East, 2008; Tokyo: Megacity, 2010; Viewed Sideways: Essays on Culture and Style in Contemporary Japan, 2011. Contributor to periodicals and newspapers. **Address:** Stone Bridge Press, PO Box 8208, Berkeley, CA 94707, U.S.A.

RICHLER, Daniel. British/Canadian (born Canada), b. 1956. **Genres:** Novels, Young Adult Fiction. **Career:** CHOM-FM, presenter and critic, 1977-; CJCL, presenter and critic; CFNY-FM, The Edge, presenter and critic; CITY-TV, The New Music, co-host and producer, 1985; The Journal, chief arts correspondent, 1987, 1988; Canadian Broadcasting Corp., CBC Radio, cultural commentator, The Journal, chief arts correspondent, 1988, pop culture commentator; TV-Ontario, executive producer for adult arts and host of Imprint, 1988-; City TV, producer and host; CBC Newsworld, show host; Book Television Channel, editor-in-chief; BookTelevision, editor-in-chief; ChumCity, editor-in-chief/executive producer, 2001. **Publications:** Kicking Tomorrow (novel), 1991. **Address:** Speakers' Spotlight, 179 John St., Ste. 302, Toronto, ON M5T 1X4, Canada. **Online address:** danielr@citytv.com

RICHLER, Nancy. Canadian (born Canada), b. 1957?. **Genres:** Novels. **Career:** Novelist. **Publications:** NOVELS: Throwaway Angels, 1996; Your Mouth Is Lovely, 2002; The Imposter Bride, 2012. Contributor to journals. **Address:** c/o Dean Cooke, The Cooke Agency, 278 Bloor St. E, Ste. 305, Toronto, ON M4W 3M4, Canada. **Online address:** richrise@telus.net

RICHMAN, Irwin. American (born United States), b. 1937. **Genres:** Art/Art History, History, Homes/Gardens, Local History/Rural Topics, Reference. **Career:** Pennsylvania Historical and Museum Commission, historian, 1961-65; William Penn Memorial Museum (now State Museum of Pennsylvania), curator of science, industry and technology, 1965-68; Pennsylvania State University, Capital College, professor of American studies and history, 1968-2003, emeritus professor, 2003-; Bard College, Parents Leadership Council, president, 1996-2006; Landis Valley Museum, Heirloom Seed Project, director of research and development, 2004-. Writer. **Publications:** (With D.H. Kent) Pennsylvania and the Federal Constitution, 1964; Historical Manuscript Depositories in Pennsylvania, 1965; Penn Pictures, 1965; The Brightest Ornament, 1967; Pennsylvania's Architecture, 1969, rev. ed., 1997; Pennsylvania's Decorative Arts in the Age of Handcraft, 1978; Pennsylvania's Painters, 1983; Borscht Belt Bungalows: Memories of Catskill Summers, 1998; Catskill Postcards, 1999; Pennsylvania German Arts: More Than Hearts, Parrots, and Crowns, 2001; Hudson River from New York City to Albany, 2001; Sullivan County: Borscht Belt, 2001; Catskill Hotels, 2003; German Architecture in America: Folkhouse, Bauhaus, Your House, 2003; The Pennsylvania Dutch

Country, 2004; Catskills, 2006; Hudson River, the (SOA), 2006; Pennsylvania German Farms, Gardens, and Seeds: Landis Valley in Four Centuries, 2007; Lancaster County, Pennsylvania, Postcards: Featuring the Collection of the Landis Valley Museum, 2008; Seed Art: The Package Made Me Buy It, 2008; Landis Family: A Pennsylvania German Family Album, 2008; Holidays and Other Weird Events, 2009; (with M.B. Emery) Yesterday's Farm Tools & Equipment, 2010. Contributor of articles to periodicals. **Address:** Landis Valley Museum, 2451 Kissel Hill Rd., Lancaster, PA 17604, U.S.A. **Online address:** msr1@psu.edu

RICHMAN, Jana. American (born United States), b. 1956. **Genres:** Novels. **Career:** Writer, journalist and accountant. **Publications:** Riding in the Shadow of Saints: A Woman's Story of Motorcycling the Mormon Trail, 2005; The Last Cowgirl (novel), 2008. **Address:** Salt Lake City, UT , U.S.A. **Online address:** lastcowgirl@comcast.net

RICHMAN, Kenneth A. American (born United States), b. 1966. **Genres:** Medicine/Health. **Career:** Haverford College, special assistant to the dean of college, through 1989; Educational Testing Service, assistant examiner and content specialist, 1996-97; Kalamazoo College, assistant professor of philosophy, 1997-2001; Bryn Mawr College, assistant professor, 2000-04; Interactivity Foundation, fellow, 2001-03; Massachusetts College of Pharmacy and Health Sciences, associate professor of philosophy and health care ethics, 2004-, professor of health care ethics, Institutional Review Board, chair, 2006-, Medical Humanities Interest Group, vice-chair; Boston University, visiting faculty, 2007; Harvard Universtiy, Dana Farber-Harvard Cancer Center, faculty. Writer. **Publications:** (Co-ed.) Current Moral and Social Issues, 1996; (ed. with R. Read) The New Hume Debate, 2000, rev. ed., 2007; Ethics and the Metaphysics of Medicine: Reflections on Health and Beneficence, 2004. Contributor of articles to books and periodicals. **Address:** School of Arts and Sciences, Massachusetts College of Pharmacy and, Health Sciences, Rm. F217, 179 Longwood Ave., Boston, MA 02115-5896, U.S.A. **Online address:** kenneth.richman@mcphs.edu

RICHMOND, Anthony Henry. Canadian/British (born England), b. 1925. **Genres:** Demography, Social Sciences, Race Relations, Sociology. **Career:** University of Edinburgh, lecturer, 1952-63; University of British Columbia, visiting Canada council research fellow, 1960-61; Bristol College of Science and Technology, reader, 1963-65; York University, professor of sociology, 1965-89, York IBR (now Institute for Social Research) 1979-82, F.R.S.C. Professor Emeritus of Sociology, 1989-, Centre for Refugee Studies, through 2007. Writer. **Publications:** Colour Prejudice in Britain: A Study of West Indian Workers in Liverpool, 1941-1951, 1954; The Colour Problem: A Study of Racial Relations, 1955, rev. ed., 1961; Post-War Immigrants in Canada, 1967; (ed.) Readings in Race and Ethnic Relations, 1972; Ethnic Residential Segregation in Metropolitan Toronto, 1972; (with S. Ziegler) Characteristics of Italian Householders in Metropolitan Toronto, 1972; (with B. Neumann and R. Mezoff) Immigrant Integration and Urban Renewal in Toronto, 1973; Migration and Race Relations in an English City: A Study in Bristol, 1973; Aspects of the Absorption and Adaptation of Immigrants, 1974; Certains Aspects de l'intégration et de l'adaptation des Immigrants, 1974; (ed. with D. Kubát) Internal Migration: The New World and the Third World, 1976; (with W.E. Kalbach) Degré d'adaptation des Immigrants et leurs descendants: étude analytique du recensement, 1980; (with W.E. Kalbach) Factors in the Adjustment of Immigrants and Their Descendants, 1980; (ed.) After the Referenda: The Future of Ethnic Nationalism in Britain and Canada, 1981; (with J. Clodman) Immigration and Unemployment, 1982; (ed. with F. Richmond) Immigrants in Canada and Australia, 1984; Immigration and Ethnic Conflict, 1988; (ed. with J. Dumas) Caribbean Immigrants: A Demo-Economic Analysis, 1989; Global Apartheid: Refugees, Racism and the New World Order, 1994. Contributor to journals. **Address:** Department of Sociology, York University, 329 York Ln., 4700 Keele St., Toronto, ON M3J 1P3, Canada. **Online address:** richmond@yorku.ca

RICHMOND, Hugh Macrae. British (born England), b. 1932. **Genres:** Literary Criticism And History, Theatre, Humor/Satire, Bibliography, Young Adult Fiction. **Career:** Lycee Jean Perrin, assistant in English, 1954-55; University of California, Department of English, assistant/associate professor, 1957-68, professor, 1968-94, Shakespeare Program, director, 1973-, chancellor's adviser for educational development, 1983-96, professor emeritus of English, 1994-; Shakespeare Globe, Education Division, director, 1995-99. Writer. **Publications:** The School of Love: The Evolution of the Stuart Love Lyric, 1964; Shakespeare's Political Plays, 1967; Shakespeare's Sexual

Comedy, 1971; Renaissance Landscapes: English Lyrics in a European Tradition, 1973; The Christian Revolutionary: John Milton, 1974; Puritans and Libertines: Anglo-French Literary Relations in the Reformation, 1981; King Richard III, 1989; John Milton's Drama of Paradise Lost, 1991; King Henry VIII, 1994; Critical Bibliographies of A Dictionary of Shakespeare's Theatre, 2002; Shakespeare's Theatre: A Dictionary of His Stage Context, 2002. EDITOR: First Part of the History of King Henry the Fourth, 1967; Shakespeare's Henry VIII, 1971; (with J. Halio) Shakespearean Illuminations: Essays in Honor of Marvin Rosenberg, 1998; Shakespeare and the Renaissance Stage to 1616: Shakespearean Stage History 1616 to 1998: An Annotated Bibliography of Shakespeare Studies, 1576-1998, 1999; Critical Essays on Shakespeare's Richard III, 1999. **Address:** Department of English, University of California, 322 Wheeler Hall, Berkeley, CA 94720, U.S.A. **Online address:** hmr@berkeley.edu

RICHMOND, Michelle. American (born United States), b. 1970. **Genres:** Novels, Mystery/Crime/Suspense. **Career:** University of Miami, James Michener fellow; University of San Francisco, faculty; California College of the Arts, teacher in the MFA writing program; St. Marys College, writer-in-residence; Bowling Green State University, visiting writer; Authors Guild, executive council. **Publications:** The Girl in the Fall-Away Dress: Stories, 2001; Dream of the Blue Room (novel), 2003; The Year of Fog (novel), 2007; No One You Know (novel), 2008. Contributor of stories and essays to periodicals. **Address:** c/o Valerie Borchardt, Georges Borchardt Inc., 136 E 57th St., New York, NY 10022, U.S.A. **Online address:** fogtalk@gmail.com

RICHMOND, Peter. American (born United States), b. 1953. **Genres:** Sports/Fitness, Music. **Career:** Miami Herald, reporter, 1983-89; National Sports Daily, staff writer, 1989-91; Gentleman's Quarterly, special correspondent and staff writer, 1992-; Indian Mountain School, teacher. **Publications:** Baseball: The Perfect Game, 1992; Ballpark: Camden Yards and the Building of an American Dream, 1993; My Father's War: A Son's Journey, 1996; Fever: The Life and Music of Miss Peggy Lee, 2006; (with F. Gifford) Glory Game: How the 1958 NFL Championship Changed Football Forever, 2008; Badasses: the Legend of Snake, Foo, Dr. Death, and John Madden's Oakland Raiders, 2010. Works appear in anthologies. Contributor to periodicals. **Address:** PO Box 958, Millerton, NY 12546-0958, U.S.A. **Online address:** pcterrichmond@journalist.com

RICHMOND, Robin. British/American (born United States), b. 1951. **Genres:** Art/Art History, Communications/Media, Children's Fiction, Biography. **Career:** Teacher, 1977-85; British Broadcasting Corp. (BBC), regular broadcaster, Radio 3 and 4 and World Service, regular broadcaster; Camberwell School of Art, visiting professor, 1982-85; University of London, lecturer, 1983-85, lecturer; University of California, visiting professor, 1984-85; Yale University, Morse College, artist-in-residence, 2005; First Financial Credit Union, regional operations manager, vice president of marketing; Santel Credit Union, vice president of marketing and quality service; SensCom Inc., executive vice president of marketing and strategic alliances, senior vice president of business development; Marketing Association of Credit Unions, chairman. Writer and artist. **Publications:** Michelangelo and the Creation of the Sistine Chapel, 1992; Introducing Michelangelo, 1992; The Story in a Picture, vol. I: Children in Art, 1992, vol. II: Animals in Art, 1993; Frida Kahlo in Mexico: Painters & Places, 1994; Credit Union Branding: Winning Strategies for Marketers, 1999; The Storm Tree, 2006; Brand Marketing: Winning Strategies for Credit Union Marketers. Contributor to periodicals. **Address:** 20 Calabria Rd., London, GL N5 1JA, England. **Online address:** robin@calabria.fsnet.co.uk

RICHTEL, Matt. (Theron Heir). American (born United States), b. 1966. **Genres:** Humor/Satire, Technology, Horror, Novels. **Career:** The Times, writer, 1996-2000; The New York Times, San Francisco Bureau, technology reporter, 2000-. **Publications:** AS THERON HEIR: (with D. Bell) Rudy Park: The People Must Be Wired, 2003; (with D. Bell) Peace, Love & Lattes: A Rudy Park Collection, 2004. OTHERS: Hooked: A Thriller About Love and Other Addictions, 2007; Devil's Plaything, 2011. **Address:** Poisoned Pen Press, 6962 E 1st Ave., Ste. 103, Scottsdale, AZ 85251, U.S.A. **Online address:** mattrichtel@gmail.com

RICHTER, Daniel K(arl). American (born United States), b. 1954. **Genres:** Cultural/Ethnic Topics, History, Social Sciences, Literary Criticism And

History. **Career:** Seton Hall University, adjunct instructor in history, 1979; Columbia University, instructor in history, 1981, visiting professor of history, 2000; Pace University, adjunct instructor in social sciences, 1981-82; Millersville State College, instructor in history, 1982-83; College of William and Mary, assistant professor of history, 1983-85; Dickinson College, assistant professor, 1985-91, associate professor of history, 1991-97, professor, 1997-99; Ethnohistory, associate editor, 1986-90; University of East Anglia, Fulbright exchange lecturer, 1992-93; University of Pennsylvania, professor of history, 1999-, Roy F. and Jeannette P. Nichols professor of American history, McNeil Center for Early American Studies, Richard S. Dunn director, 2000-. Writer. **Publications:** (Ed. with J.H. Merrell and contrib.) Beyond the Covenant Chain: The Iroquois and Their Neighbors in Indian North America, 1600-1800, 1987, rev. ed., 2003; The Ordeal of the Longhouse: The Peoples of the Iroquois League in the Era of European Colonization, 1992; Facing East from Indian Country: A Native History of Early America, 2001; (ed. with W.A. Pencak) Friends and Enemies in Penns Woods: Indians, Colonists, and the Racial Construction of Pennsylvania, 2004; Native Americans Pennsylvania, 2005; Before the Revolution: Americas Ancient Pasts, 2011. Contributor to books and journals. **Address:** Department of History, University of Pennsylvania, College Hall 309C, Philadelphia, PA 19104, U.S.A. **Online address:** drichter@history.upenn.edu

RICHTER, Gregory C. American (born United States), b. 1955. **Genres:** Translations, Literary Criticism And History, Music, Poetry. **Career:** World Translation Inc., programmer for computer-based Russian-English and German-English translation systems, 1982-83; Northeast Missouri State University, assistant professor, 1983-87, associate professor of linguistics, Russian, and German, 1987-; Truman State University, assistant professor, 1983, professor of linguistics, Russian and German, 1983-; U.S./U.S.S.R. Educator Encounter, lecturer, 1987; Guangzhou Institute of Foreign Languages, lecturer, 1990-92. Writer. **Publications:** TRANSLATOR: O. Rank, The Incest Theme in Literature and Legend: Fundamentals of a Psychology of Literary Creation, 1992; Rank, Psychology and Soul-Belief, 1994; Laozi, The Gate of All Marvelous Things: A Guide to Reading the Tao Te Ching, 1998; (and intro.) Albert Giraud, Albert Giraud's Pierrot Lunaire, 1998; (with E.J. Lieberman) O. Rank, The Myth of The Birth of the Hero: A Psychological Exploration of Myth, 2004. Contributor of articles to periodicals. **Address:** Department of English and Linguistics, Truman State University, 310 McClain Hall, 100 E Normal, PO Box 323, Kirksville, MO 63501, U.S.A. **Online address:** grichter@truman.edu

RICHTER, Harvena. *See* Obituaries.

RICHTER, Jutta. German (born Germany), b. 1955?. **Genres:** Novels, Children's Fiction. **Career:** Writer. **Publications:** Popcorn und Sternbenbanner: Tagebuch einer Austauschschülerin, 1975; Dad Geraniengefängis (novel), 1980; Die Puppermütter, 1980; HerrOska und das Zirr, 1998; Der Hund mit dem gelben Herzen oder die Geschichte vom Gegenteil, 1998; Es lebte ein Kind auf den Bäumen, 1999; Der Tag, als ich lernte die Spinnen zu zähmen, 2000; Hinter dem Bahnhof lieght das Meer, 2001; Annabella Klimperauge, 2002; An einemgroszen stillen see, 2003; Hechtsommer, 2004; Sommer und Bär Eine Liebesgeschichte, 2006; Die Katze oder Wie ich die Ewigkeit verloren habe, 2006; All das w'nsch ich dir, 2007; The Cat: Or, How I Lost Eternity, 2007; Der Anfang Von Allem, 2008; Beyond the Station Lies the Sea, 2009; The Sky is A Laugh, 2009; When I Was Mary, 2010; Forest Witches and Magic Socks, 2010. **Address:** Castle Westerwinkel, Ash Mountain, D 59387, Germany. **Online address:** post@juttarichter.de

RICHTER, Roland Suso. American/German (born Germany), b. 1961. **Genres:** Plays/Screenplays, Novels. **Career:** Film director, producer and writer. **Publications:** Sara Amerika, 1999. Contributor to periodicals. **Address:** c/o Dimension Films/Miramax Films, 375 Greenwich St., New York, NY 10013, U.S.A.

RICKARDS, John. (Sean Cregan). American/British (born England), b. 1978. **Genres:** Mystery/Crime/Suspense, Young Adult Fiction, Literary Criticism And History. **Career:** Writer. **Publications:** ALEX ROURKE SERIES: Winters End, 2003; The Touch of Ghosts, 2004; The Darkness Inside, 2007; Burial Ground, 2008. OTHERS: Dublin Noir, 2006; (as Sean Cregan) The Levels, 2010; Fuck Noir. Contributor to periodicals. **Address:** c/o Author Mail, Carlisle and Co., 260 W 39th St., 6th Fl., New York, NY 10018, U.S.A. **Online address:** namelesshorror@gmail.com

RICKELS, Laurence A. American (born United States), b. 1954. **Genres:** Area Studies, Humor/Satire, Psychology. **Career:** University of Dusseldorf, lecturer of German studies, 1980-81; University of California at Santa Barbara, assistant professor of German and comparative literature, 1981-86, associate professor of German and comparative literature, 1986-90, department chair, 1989-95, professor of German and comparative literature, 1990-, acting department chair, 2001-02; State Academy of Fine Arts in Karlsruhe, professor of art and theory, 2011-. Writer. **Publications:** Aberrations of Mourning: Writing on German Crypts, 1988; Derunbetrauerbare Tod, 1989; Gottfried Keller's Jugenddramen, 1990; The Case of California, 1991; (with E.A. Brown) Lari Pittman Drawings, 1996; The Vampire Lectures, 1999; Nazi Psychoanalysis, vol. I: Only Psychoanalysis Won the War, vol. II: Crypto Fetishism, vol. III: Psy Fi, 2002; David Deutsch, 2004; Vampirismus Vorlesungen, 2007; Ulrike Ottinger Eine Autobiografie des Kinos, 2007; Ulrike Ottinger. The Autobiography of Art Cinema, 2008; The Devil Notebooks, 2008; I Think I Am. Philip K. Dick, 2010. EDITOR: Die Jugenddramen, 1989; Looking after Nietzsche, 1990; Poetry, Poetics, Translation, 1994; Acting Out in Groups, 1999; Die Kindheit ueberleben, 2004. **Address:** Department of Germanic, Slavic, and Semitic, Studies, University of California, 6206 Phelps Hall, Santa Barbara, CA 93106-4130, U.S.A. **Online address:** rickels@gss.ucsb.edu

RICKMAN, Hans Peter. British/Czech (born Czech Republic), b. 1918. **Genres:** Intellectual History, Philosophy, Social Sciences. **Career:** University of Hull, staff tutor in philosophy and psychology, 1949-61; City University, senior lecturer, 1961-67, reader, 1967-82, visiting professor of philosophy, 1982, now professor emeritus. Writer. **Publications:** Meaning in History: Dilthey's Thought on History and Society in US as Pattern and Meaning in History, 1961; Preface to Philosophy, 1964; Living with Technology, 1967; Understanding and the Human Studies, 1967; (ed., trans. and intro.) W. Dilthey, Selected Writings, 1976; Wilhelm Dilthey: Pioneer of the Human Studies, 1979; The Adventure of Reason: The Uses of Philosophy in Sociology, 1983; Change, 1985; British Universities, 1987; Dilthey Today: A Critical Appraisal of the Contemporary Relevance of his Work, 1988; Haunted by History (suspense novel), 1995; Paper Chase (suspense novel), 1995; Philosophy Today, 1996; Philosophy in Literature, 1996; The Challenge of Philosophy, 2000; Riddle of the Sphinx: Interpreting the Human World, 2004. Contributor to Encyclopedia of Philosophy. **Address:** 12 Fitzroy Ct., 57 Shepherds Hill, London, GL N6 5RD, England.

RICKMAN, Philip. Also writes as Thom Madley. British (born England) **Genres:** Mystery/Crime/Suspense, Novels, Horror, Children's Fiction. **Career:** Novelist and journalist. **Publications:** (With G. Nown) Mysterious Lancashire: Legends and Ley-Lines of Lancelot's Shire, 1977; (with G. Nown) Mysterious Derbyshire, 1977; Mysterious Cheshire, 1980; Curfew, 1993; Crybbe, 1993; December, 1994; The Man in the Moss, 1994; Candlenight, 1995; The Chalice, 1997; (as Will Kingdom) The Cold Calling, 1998; The Wine of Angels, 1998; Midwinter of the Spirit, 1998; A Crown of Lights, 2001; (as Will Kingdom) Mean Spirit, 2001; The Cure of Souls, 2001; The Lamp of the Wicked, 2002; The Prayer of the Night Shepherd, 2004; The Smile of a Ghost, 2005; The Remains of an Altar, 2006; The Fabric of Sin: Merrily Watkins Mysteries, 2007; To Dream of the Dead, 2008; (with J. Mason) Merrily's Border: The Marches Share Their Secrets, 2009; The Bones of Avalon, 2010. AS THOM MADLEY: Marco's Pendulum, 2006; Marco and the Blade of Night, 2007. **Address:** c/o Author Mail, Johnson and Alcock, Clerkenwell House, London, GL EC1R 0HT, England. **Online address:** rickmans@exorcizing.demon.co.uk

RICKS, Christopher. American/British (born England), b. 1933. **Genres:** Literary Criticism And History. **Career:** Balliol College, research fellow, 1957; Oxford University, Worcester College, lecturer, 1958-68, fellow, professor of poetry, 2004-10; Stanford University, visiting professor, 1965; University of California, visiting professor, 1965; Smith College, visiting professor, 1967; University of Bristol, professor of English, 1968-75; Harvard University, visiting professor, 1971; Wesleyan University, visiting professor, 1974; Cambridge University, professor, 1975-86; Brandeis University, visiting professor, 1977, 1981, 1984; Boston University, professor of English, 1986-97, N.E.H. distinguished teaching professor, 1994-97, professor of the humanities, 1997-, William M. and Sara B. Warren professor of the humanities, Boston Editorial Institute, co-director, 1999-; American Academy of Arts and Sciences, fellow; British Academy, fellow; Tennyson Society, vice president. Writer. **Publications:** Milton's Grand Style, 1963; Tennyson, 1972; Keats and Embarrassment, 1974; The Force of Poetry, 1984; T.S. Eliot and Prejudice, 1988; Beckett's Dying Words: The Clarendon Lectures, 1990,

1993; Essays in Appreciation, 1996; Allusion to the Poets, 2002; Reviewery, 2002; Dylan's Visions of Sin, 2003; Decisions and Revisions in T.S. Eliot, 2003; True Friendship: Geoffrey Hill, Anthony Hecht, and Robert Lowell under the Sign of Eliot and Pound, 2010. EDITOR: Dissertation upon English Typographical Founders and Foundries, 1962; (and intro.) Poems and Critics: An Anthology of Poetry and Criticism from Shakespeare to Hardy, 1966; A.E. Housman: A Collection of Critical Essays, 1968; Milton's Paradise Lost, and Paradise Regained, 1968; Poems of Tennyson, 1969, rev. ed. as Tennyson: A Selected Edition, 2007; English Poetry and Prose 1540-1674, 1970; (and intro.) The Brownings: Letters and Poetry, 1970; English Poetry and Prose, 1540-1674, 1970; English Drama to 1710, 1971; Selected Criticism of Matthew Arnold, 1972; (and intro.) A Collection of Poems by Alfred Tennyson, 1972; Keats and Embarrassment, 1974; Geoffrey Hill and The Tongue's Atrocities: The W.D. Thomas Memorial Lecture Delivered at the College on February 15th, 1978, 1978; (with L. Michaels) The State of the Language, 1980; Force of Poetry, 1984; (with A. Day) Tennyson, The Harvard Manuscripts, Loose Papers, 1987; The New Oxford Book of Victorian Verse, 1987; A.E. Housman: Collected Poetry and Selected Prose, 1987; (with A. Day) Tennyson, the Manuscripts and Proofs at the Tennyson Research Centre, 1989; (with A. Day) Tennyson Archive, 1989; (with A. Day) Tennyson, the manuscripts at the University Library, Cambridge, 1991; Golden Treasury of the Best Songs and Lyrical Poems in the English Language, 1991; The Faber Book of America, 1992; (with A. Day) Tennyson, The Manuscripts at the Victoria and Albert Museum, the Princeton University Library, and the University Of Virginia Library, 1992; (with A. Day) Tennyson, The Manuscripts at the Fitzwilliam Museum, the Bodleian Library of Oxford University, and the Sterling Library of the University of London, 1992; T.S. Eliot: Inventions of the March Hare: Poems, 1909-1917, 1996; The Oxford Book of English Verse, 1999; Selected Poems of James Henry, 2002; New and Selected Poems, 2005; (ed.) Joining Music with Reason: 34 Poets, British and American, Oxford 2004-2009, 2010. Contributor of articles to periodicals and journals. **Address:** Editorial Institute, Boston University, 143 Bay State Rd., Boston, MA 02215-1719, U.S.A. **Online address:** cricks@bu.edu

RICKS, James. Australian (born Australia), b. 1975?. **Genres:** Documentaries/Reportage, Young Adult Fiction, Literary Criticism And History. **Career:** Writer. **Publications:** Eleven Months in Bunbury, 1997. **Address:** Allen & Unwin, PO Box 8500, St. Leonards, NW 1590, Australia.

RIDD, Stephen (John). British (born England), b. 1948. **Genres:** History, Young Adult Non-fiction, Education. **Career:** Teacher; Ipswich High School, examination officer. Writer. **Publications:** (Ed. and intro.) Julius Caesar in Gaul and Britain, 1995. **Address:** Merton, 4 Warren Heath Rd., Ipswich, Suffolk, SU IP3 8TD, England.

RIDDELL, Peter G. Australian/British (born England), b. 1951. **Genres:** Humanities, History, Theology/Religion, Language/Linguistics, International Relations/Current Affairs, Social Commentary. **Career:** Canberra College of Advanced Education, tutor, 1985; University of New England, IPB-Australia Project, senior lecturer, 1985-88; Hebrew University of Jerusalem, research fellow, 1988-90; International Development Program of Australian Universities and Colleges, senior manager, 1990-93; World Vision Australia, regional manager, 1993-95; London School of Theology, senior lecturer, professor of Islamic studies, 1996-2007; Melbourne School of Theology, Center for the Study of Islam and Other Faiths, professorial dean, 2008-. Writer. **Publications:** Transferring a Tradition: Abd al-Rauf al-Singkili's Rendering into Malay of the Jalalayn Commentary, 1990; Reading Technical English, 1990; Islam: Essays on Scripture Thought and Society: A Festschrift in Honour of Anthony H. Johns, 1997; Islam and the Malay-Indonesian World: Transmission and Responses, 2001; Islam in Context: Past Present and Future, 2003; Christians and Muslims: Pressures and Potential in a Post 9/11 World, 2004; Angels and Demons: Perspectives and Practice in Diverse Religious Traditions, 2007; (intro.) Moslem Women, 2009; Talking Points in Christian-Muslim Relations into the 21st Century, 2012. **Address:** Centre for the Study of Islam and Other Faiths, Melbourne School of Theology, 5 Burwood Hwy., Wantirna, VI 3152, Australia. **Online address:** peter_riddell@yahoo.com

RIDDELL, Roger C. British (born England), b. 1947. **Genres:** Social Sciences, Sociology. **Career:** Saint Ignatius College, secondary school teacher, 1965-66; University of Zimbabwe, Department of Economics, research assistant, 1973-74, part-time lecturer, 1981-83; Catholic Institute of International Relations, research officer, 1977-80; Presidential Commission of Inquiry into Prices, Incomes and Conditions of Service, chair, 1980-81; Confederation of Zimbabwe Industries, chief economist, 1981-83; Overseas Development Institute, senior research fellow, 1984-99; Christian Aid, international director, 1999-2004; Oxford Policy Management, faculty, non-executive director and independent consultant, 2004-; Policy Practice Ltd., principal, 2004-; African Development Bank's Study on Economic Integration in Southern Africa, senior consultant, 1993. Writer. **Publications:** (With V.S. Cubitt) The Urban Poverty Datum Line in Rhodesia: A Study of the Minimum Consumption Needs of Families, 1974; (with P.S. Harris) The Poverty Datum Line as a Wage Fixing Standard: An Application to Rhodesia, 1975; Alternatives to Poverty, 1977; The Land Question, 1978; The Land Problem in Rhodesia: Alternatives for the Future, 1978; (with J. Gilmurray and D. Sanders) The Struggle for Health, 1979; Alternative Development Strategies for Zimbabwe, Centre for Applied Social Sciences, 1980; Education for Employment, 1980; Economic Sanctions and the South African Agricultural Sector, 1981; Foreign Aid Reconsidered, 1987; (co-author) Manufacturing Africa: Performance & Prospects of Seven Countries in Sub-Saharan Africa, 1990; (with L. Cockcroft) Foreign Direct Investment in Sub-Saharan Africa, 1991; Zimbabwe to 1996: At the Heart of a Growing Region, 1992; (co-author) Strengthening the Partnership: Evaluation of the Finnish NGO Support Programme, 1994; (co-author) Non-Governmental Organizations and Rural Poverty Alleviation, 1995; Does Foreign Aid Really Work?, 2007. **Address:** Policy Practice, 33 Southdown Ave., Brighton, BN1 6EH, England. **Online address:** roger.riddell@thepolicypractice.com

RIDDLE, Jean. See **WEIHS, Jean (Riddle).**

RIDDLE, Paxton. American (born United States), b. 1949. **Genres:** Novels, History, Race Relations. **Career:** Novelist, copy editor and musician. **Publications:** HISTORICALS/WOMEN'S FICTION: Lost River, 1999; The Education of Ruby Loonfoot, 2002. Contributor to periodicals. **Address:** 26 Pin Oak Dr., Phoenixville, PA 19460-1145, U.S.A. **Online address:** pax@riddle.net

RIDDLES, Libby. American (born United States), b. 1956. **Genres:** Travel/Exploration, Novels, History. **Career:** Author and lecturer, 1985-; dog racer; television commentator. **Publications:** (With T. Jones) Race across Alaska: First Woman to Win the Iditarod Tells Her Story, 1988; (with S. Gill) Danger, the Dog Yard Cat, 1992; Storm Run, 1996 as Storm Run: The Story of the First Woman to Win the Iditarod Sled Dog Race, 2002. **Address:** PO Box 15253, Fritz Creck, AK 99603, U.S.A.

RIDE, W. D. L. Australian/British (born England), b. 1926. **Genres:** Natural History, Zoology, Earth Sciences. **Career:** Oxford University, Department of Zoology and Comparative Anatomy, departmental demonstrator in vertebrate zoology, 1954-55; Brasenose College, Hulme lecturer in zoology, 1955-57; Western Australian Museum, director, 1957-75; University of Western Australia, reader-in-zoology, 1957; Australian Biological Resources Study, director, 1975-80; Canberra College of Advanced Education, fellow in life sciences, 1980-82, School of Applied Science, head, 1982-87, principal, 1987, retired, 1987; Australian National University, Department of Geology, visiting fellow, 1988-2002. Writer. **Publications:** (Ed. with A.J. Fraser) The Results of an Expedition to Bernier and Dorre Islands, Shark Bay, Western Australia, in July 1959, 1962; Report on the Aboriginal Engravings and Flora and Fauna of Depuch Island, Western Australia, 1964; A Guide to the Native Mammals of Australia, 1970; (with J.A. Mahoney) Index to the Genera and Species of Fossil Mammalia Described from Australia and New Guinea between 1838 and 1968, 1975; (ed. with R.H. Groves) Species at Risk: Research in Australia, 1982; (co-ed.) International Code of Zoological Nomenclature, 3rd ed., 1985, 4th ed., 1999; (ed. with T. Younes) Biological Nomenclature Today, 1986. Contributor of articles to journals. **Address:** 35/67 Macgregor St., Deakin, AC 2600, Australia. **Online address:** dride@webone.com.au

RIDGWAY, John M. British (born England), b. 1938. **Genres:** Children's Non-fiction, Recreation, Travel/Exploration, Autobiography/Memoirs, Biography, Young Adult Fiction, Education, Reference, Reference. **Career:** John Ridgway School of Adventure, proprietor, 1968-. Writer. **Publications:** (With C. Blyth) A Fighting Chance, 1966; Journey to Ardmore, 1971; Amazon Journey: From the Source to the Sea, 1972; Cockleshell Journey: The Adventures of Three Men and a Girl, 1974; Gino Watkins, 1974; Storm Passage, 1975; The Sinatrafile, 1977; Scientific Illustration, 1978; (with M.C. Ridgway) Round the World with Ridgway, 1978; (with A. Briggs) Round the World Non-Stop, 1985; Road to Elizabeth: A Quest in the Mountains of Peru, 1986; Road to Osambre: A Daring Adventure in the High Country of Peru, 1987;

Flood Tide, 1988; (co-author) Rick Mason, The Agent, 1989; Judge Dredd: The Dead Man, 1991; (co-author) John Constantine: Hellblazer: Original Sins, 1992; Tommy Dorsey, Frank Sinatra The Song Is You, 1994; (with M. Christine and R. Ridgway) Then We Sailed Away, 1996; Michael Moorcock's Multiverse, 1999; (co-author) Chiller, 2001. Contributor to periodicals. **Address:** c/o Marie Christine Ridgway, Ardmore, Rhiconich by Lairg, Sutherland, IV27 4RB, Scotland. **Online address:** j.ridgway@btinternet.com

RIDGWAY, Keith. British/Irish (born Ireland), b. 1965. **Genres:** Novels, Novellas/Short Stories, Literary Criticism And History. **Career:** Writer. **Publications:** STORIES: Horses, 1997; Standard Time, 2001. NOVELS: The Long Falling, 1998; The Parts, 2003; Animals, 2006. Contributor of periodicals. **Address:** c/o David Miller, Rogers Coleridge and White Ltd., 20 Powis Mews, London, GL W11 IJN, England. **Online address:** info@keithridgway.com

RIDINGTON, Robin. Canadian/American (born United States), b. 1939. **Genres:** Novellas/Short Stories, Anthropology/Ethnology. **Career:** Virtual Museum of Canada, ethnographer and project consultant, 1964-; University of British Columbia, assistant professor, 1967-79, associate professor, 1979-84, professor of anthropology, 1989-95, professor emeritus, 1995-. Writer. **Publications:** Swan People: A Study of the Dunne-Za Prophet Dance, 1978; (with J. Ridington) People of the Trail: How the Northern Forest Indians Lived, 1978; (with J. Ridington) People of the Longhouse: How the Iroquois People Lived, 1982; Trail to Heaven: Knowledge and Narrative in a Northern Native Community, 1988; Little Bit Know Something: Stories in a Language of Anthropology, 1990; Blessing for a Long Time: The Sacred Pole of the Omaha Tribe, 1997; (with J. Ridington) When You Sing It Now, Just Like New: First Nations Poetics, Voices, and Representations, 2006; The Poets Don't Write Sonnets Anymore, 2008. Contributor to journals. **Address:** Department of Anthropology, University of British Columbia, 6303 NW Marine Dr., Vancouver, BC V6T 1Z1, Canada. **Online address:** doctorzogo@gmail.com

RIDLEY, Elizabeth J(ayne). American (born United States), b. 1966. **Genres:** Novels, Mystery/Crime/Suspense, Plays/Screenplays. **Career:** Author, 1993-2010; Writer's Digest School, writing instructor, 1998-2003; Writer's Digest Criticism Service, freelance critiquer, 1999-2004; The Writer's Midwife, founder and director, 2001-; Advanced Self-Publishing Books, freelance ghostwriter, 2002-05; Get Published, associate, 2003-05; Authors Team, associate, 2005-06. **Publications:** NOVELS: Throwing Roses, 1993; The Remarkable Journey of Miss Tranby Quirke, 1996; Rainey's Lament, 1999; Dear Mr. Carson, 2006; Brutus on the Basepaths, forthcoming. OTHER: In Pursuit of Gloom: A Tongue-In-Cheek Guide to Scandinavia's Most Depressing Tourist Destinations, forthcoming. **Address:** The Writer's Midwife, PO Box 1391, Brookfield, WI 53008-1391, U.S.A. **Online address:** ejridley@earthlink.net

RIDLEY, Jane. British (born England), b. 1953. **Genres:** History, Biography, Architecture. **Career:** University of Buckingham, lecturer, 1979-94, senior lecturer in history, 1994-2002, reader in history, 2002-07, senior tutor, 2003-, professor of history, 2007-. Writer. **Publications:** Fox Hunting, 1990; Young Disraeli, 1995; The Architect and His Wife: A Life of Edwin Lutyens, 2002; Edwin Lutyens: His Life, His Wife, His Work, 2003; Bertie: A Life of Edward VII, 2012. EDITOR: (with C. Percy) Letters of Edwin Lutyens, 1985; Letters of A.J. Balfour and Lady Elcho, 1992. Contributor to periodicals. **Address:** Department of Economics & International Studies, University of Buckingham, Hunter St., Buckingham, BK MK18 1EG, England. **Online address:** jane.ridley@buckingham.ac.uk

RIDLEY, Matt(hew White). British (born England), b. 1958. **Genres:** Politics/Government, Medicine/Health. **Career:** Economist, science correspondent, 1983-84, science and technology editor, 1984-87, Washington correspondent, 1987-89, American editor, 1990-92; Daily Telegraph, science correspondent, 1992-, columnist, 1996-2000; Sunday Telegraph, freelance journalist, 1992-, columnist, 1993-96; Northern Investors, director, 1994-2007; Northern Rock P.L.C., director, 1994-2007, deputy chairman, chair, 2004-07; International Center for Life, chair, 1996-2003; Northern 2 Venture Capital Trust, chair, 1999-2008; Cold Spring Harbor Laboratory, visiting professor; International Centre for Life, founding chairman, 1996-2003. **Publications:** Warts and All: The Men Who Would Be Bush, 1989; The Red Queen: Sex and the Evolution of Human Nature, 1994; Down to Earth: A Contrarian View of Environmental Problems, 1995; Down to Earth II: Combating Environmental Myths, 1996; Origins of Virtue, 1996; Origins of Virtue: Human Instincts and the Evolution of Cooperation, 1997; Disease, 1997; Genome The Autobiography of a Species in Twenty-Three Chapters, 1999; (ed.) The Best American Science Writing 2002, 2002; Nature Via Nurture: Genes, Experience and What Makes Us Human, 2003; Francis Crick: Discoverer of the Genetic Code, 2006; The Rational Optimist: How Prosperity Evolves, 2010. Contributor to periodicals. **Address:** 10 Clifton Gardens, London, GL W9 1DT, England. **Online address:** mattridley@4thestate.co.uk

RIDLEY, Philip. British (born England), b. 1967. **Genres:** Children's Fiction, Novels, Plays/Screenplays, Young Adult Fiction, Novellas/Short Stories. **Career:** Writer and director. **Publications:** NOVELS: Crocodilia, 1988; In the Eyes of Mr. Fury, 1989; Dakota of the White Flats, 1989; Mercedes Ice, 1989; Krindlekrax, 1991; Meteorite Spoon, 1994; Kasper in the Glitter, 1994; Scribbleboy, 1997; ZinderZunder, 1998; Vinegar Street, 2000; Mighty Fizz Chilla, 2002; Zip's Apollo, 2005. COLLECTIONS: Flamingoes in Orbit, 1990; Philip Ridley Plays, vol. I: Pitchfork Disney/Fastest Clock in the Universe/Ghost from a Perfect Place, 1997; The American Dreams: Reflecting Skin/Passion of Darkly Noon, 1997; Two Plays for Young People: Fairytaleheart/Sparkleshark, 1998; (with P. Goetzee) Brokenville/The Pilgrimage, 2001. PLAYS: The Pitchfork Disney, 1991; The Fastest Clock in the Universe, 1992; Ghost from a Perfect Place, 1994; Apocalyptica, 1996; The Krays, 1997; Sparkleshark, 2000; Vincent River, 2000; Daffodil Scissors, 2004; Mercury Fur, 2005; Leaves of Glass, 2007; Piranha Heights, 2008; Ridley Plays 2, 2009; Moonfleece, 2010. OTHER: Tender Napalm, 2011. **Address:** c/o Rod Hall, The Rod Hall Agency Ltd., Fairgate House, 78 New Oxford St., 6th Fl., London, GL WC1A 1HB, England.

RIDLEY, Ronald T(homas). Australian (born Australia), b. 1940. **Genres:** History, Biography, Archaeology/Antiquities, Translations. **Career:** University of Sydney, Department of History, teaching fellow, 1962-64, St. Andrew's College, resident tutor, 1963-64; University of Melbourne, The School of Historical and Philosophical Studies, Department of History, lecturer, 1965-73, senior lecturer, 1974-81, reader, 1982-96, personal chair, 1997-2005, fellow and professor emeritus, 2006-. Writer. **Publications:** The Unification of Egypt, 1973; (trans.) Zosimus, New History, 1982; Gibbon's Complement: Louis de Beaufort, 1986; A History of Rome: A Documented Analysis, 1987; The Historical Observations of Jacob Perizonius, 1991; The Eagle and the Spade: The Archaeology of Rome during the Napoleonic Era, 1992; Jessie Webb, A Memoir, 1994; Melbourne's Monuments, 1996; Napoleon's Proconsul in Egypt: The Life and Times of Bernardino Drovetti, 1998; Infancy of Historiography, 1998; The Pope's Archaeologist: The Life and Times of Carlo Fea, 2000; (ed.) Diary of a Vice-Chancellor, 2002; The Emperor's Retrospect: Augustus' Res Gestae in Epigraphy, Historiography and Commentary, 2003. **Address:** The School of Historical and Philosophical Studies, University of Melbourne, East Wing, Old Quad, 150 Bldg., Ground Fl., Parkville, VI 3010, Australia. **Online address:** r.ridley@unimelb.edu.au

RIDLON, Florence. (Florence V. Ridlon). American (born United States), b. 1946?. **Genres:** Biography, Autobiography/Memoirs, Women's Studies And Issues, History. **Career:** University of North Texas, Department of Journalism, writer-in- residence. Sociologist and biographer. **Publications:** A Fallen Angel: The Status Insularity of the Female, 1988; A Black Physician's Struggle for Civil Rights: Edward C. Mazique, M.D., 2005. **Address:** Department of Journalism, University of North Texas, 1155 Union Cir., Ste. 311277, Denton, TX 76203-5017, U.S.A.

RIDLON, Florence V. See **RIDLON, Florence.**

RIDPATH, Michael. British (born England), b. 1961. **Genres:** Mystery/Crime/Suspense, Young Adult Fiction. **Career:** Saudi International Bank, credit analyst to bond trader, 1982-91; Apax Partners, staff, 1991-94; Standard and Poor, managing director; International Centre for Financial Regulation, chief executive; The Crime Writers Association, vice chair. Writer. **Publications:** NOVELS: Free to Trade, 1995; Trading Reality, 1997; The Marketmaker, 1998; Final Venture, 2000; The Predator, 2001; Fatal Error, 2003; On the Edge, 2005; See No Evil, 2006; Where the Shadows Lie, 2010; 66 North, 2011; Meltwater, 2012; Edge of Nowhere, 2012. **Address:** c/o Carole Blake, Blake Friedmann Literary Agency Ltd., 122 Arlington Rd., London, GL NW1 7HP, England. **Online address:** comments@michaelridpath.com

RIEDE, David G(eorge). American (born United States), b. 1951. **Genres:** Literary Criticism And History, Poetry, Young Adult Fiction. **Career:** University of Virginia, lecturer in English, 1976-77; University of Rochester, assistant professor, 1977-82; Ohio State University, Department of English, associate professor of English, 1982-85, professor, 1985-. Writer. **Publications:** Swinburne: A Study of Romantic Mythmaking, 1978; Dante Gabriel Rossetti and the Limits of Victorian Vision, 1983; Matthew Arnold and the Betrayal of Language, 1988; Oracles and Hierophants: Constructions of Romantic Authority, 1991; Dante Gabriel Rossetti Revisited, 1992; (ed.) Critical Essays on Dante Gabriel Rossetti, 1992; Allegories of One's Own Mind: Melancholy in Victorian Poetry, 2005. Contributor to journals. **Address:** Department of English, Ohio State University, 544 Denney Hall, 164 W 17th Ave., Columbus, OH 43210-1326, U.S.A. **Online address:** riede.1@osu.edu

RIEDER, Jonathan. American (born United States), b. 1948. **Genres:** History, Biography. **Career:** Yale University, faculty; Barnard College, Department of Sociology, professor, 1990-, chair, 1990-2003, Barnards Civic Engagement Program, director; CommonQuest: The Magazine of Black-Jewish Relations, founding co-editor, 1995-2001; New York Times Sunday Book Review, contributor; New Republic, contributing editor. Writer. **Publications:** Canarsie: The Jews and Italians of Brooklyn against Liberalism, 1985; The Fractious Nation? Unity and Division in Contemporary American Life, 2003; The Word of the Lord Is upon Me: The Righteous Performance of Martin Luther King, Jr., 2008. Contributor to periodicals. **Address:** Department of Sociology, Barnard College, 322C Milbank, Knox Hall, 606 W 122nd St., PO Box 9649, New York, NY 10027, U.S.A. **Online address:** jrieder@barnard.edu

RIEDLING, Ann Marlow. American (born United States), b. 1952. **Genres:** Librarianship, Education, Adult Non-fiction. **Career:** Northeast Georgia Cooperative Educational Service Agency, resource library media specialist, 1974-80; University of Louisville, media production coordinator, 1980-82; New Albany Public Library, director of circulation, 1982-84; New Albany High School, school library media specialist, 1984-93; Jefferson County Public Schools, school library media specialist, 1993-96; Spalding University, Department of library and information science, chair, associate professor, 1996-2003, Online School Library and Information Science Program, director; Teacher Librarian Journal, column writer, 2002-04; Syllabus Journal, case study writer, 2002-04; WordWizard Online Editing Co., president, 2003-06; DigitalEel Web Publishing Co., web editor, 2003-07; EditAvenue.com, online editor, 2003-06; Saint Leo University, Graduate School of Education, associate professor and director of Online MAT, 2003-06; Kentucky School for the Blind, assistive technology library media specialist, 2006-07; Mansfield University, Library and Instructional Technology, associate professor, 2006-08, adjunct online instructor, 2006-08; University of South Florida, School of Library and Information Science, visiting professor, 2007-08, associate professor, 2008-; American Research Center in Cairo, consultant. Writer. **Publications:** Reference Skills for the School Library Media Specialist: Tools and Tips, 2000, 2nd ed., 2005; Catalog It!: A Guide to Cataloging School Library Materials, 2006; Learning to Learn: A Guide to Becoming Information Literate in the 21st Century, 2002; Helping Teachers Teach: School Library Media Specialists Role, 3rd ed., 2003; How We Became Camels, 2004; Information Literacy: What Does It Look Like in the School Library Media Center?, 2004; Internet Sources on Each U.S. State, 2005; Educators as Writers: Publishing for Personal and Professional Development, 2006; Learning to Learn: A Guide to Becoming Information Literate in the 21st Century, 2nd ed., 2006; An Educators Guide to Information Literacy: What Every High School Senior Needs to Know, 2007. **Address:** School Library and Information Science, University of South Florida, Rm. 2032, 4202 E Fowler, CIS 1040, Tampa, FL 33620-7800, U.S.A. **Online address:** ariedlin@cas.usf.edu

RIEFF, David Sontag. American (born United States), b. 1952. **Genres:** Urban Studies, Humanities, Military/Defense/Arms Control, Autobiography/Memoirs. **Career:** New York University, New York Institute for Humanities, director of publications, 1977-78, fellow, 1980-, program director, 1980-85; Farrar, Straus & Giroux Inc., senior editor, 1978-89; City University of New York, visiting professor in creative writing, 1985-86; freelance writer, 1989-; Skidmore College, Empire State Summer Writing Program, writing faculty, 1990-95; New School for Social Research, World Policy Institute, senior fellow; The New Republic Magazine, contributing editor; Salmagundi Magazine, columnist; Susan Sontag Foundation, president. **Publications:** (With S. DeLano) Texas Boots, 1981; (ed.) Humanities in Review, 1982; Going to Miami: Exiles, Tourists, and Refugees in the New America, 1987; Los Angeles: Capital of the Third World, 1991; Notes on the Ottoman Legacy: Written in a Time of War, 1993; The Exile: Cuba in the Heart of Miami, 1993; Slaughterhouse: Bosnia and the Failure of the West, 1995; (ed. with R. Gutman) Crimes of War: What the Public Should Know, 1999, (with R. Gutman and

A. Dworkin) 2nd ed., 2007; Bed for the Night: Humanitarianism in Crisis, 2002; At the Point of a Gun: Democratic Dreams and Armed Intervention, 2005; (with J. Ribas) Demonstration Drawings, 2008; Swimming in a Sea of Death: A Son's Memoir, 2008; (ed.) Reborn: Journals and Notebooks, 1947-1963, 2008. Contributor to periodicals. **Address:** Susan Sontag Foundation, 76 Franklin St., Ste. 3, New York, NY 10013-3444, U.S.A. **Online address:** davidrieff@compuserve.com

RIEGER, Bernhard. British (born England), b. 1967?. **Genres:** Social Sciences, History. **Career:** University College London, Department of History, lecturer, senior lecturer; International University of Bremen, staff. Historian and author. **Publications:** (Ed. with M.J. Daunton) Meanings of Modernity: Britain in the Age of Imperialism and World Wars, 2001; Technology and the Culture of Modernity in Britain and Germany, 1890-1945, 2005; (ed. with F. Kiessling) Mit dem Wandel leben: Neuorientierungund Tradition in der Bundesrepublik der 1950er und 60er Jahre, 2011. Contributor of articles to periodicals. **Address:** Department of History, University College London, 401, 23 Gordon Sq., Gower St., London, GL WC1E 6BT, England. **Online address:** b.rieger@ucl.ac.uk

RIEHECKY, Janet Ellen. American (born United States), b. 1953. **Genres:** Children's Non-fiction, Novels, Children's Fiction, Young Adult Fiction, Young Adult Non-fiction. **Career:** Blue Mound High School, English speech instructor, 1977-80; West Chicago Community High School, English instructor, 1984-86; The Child's World Publishing Co., editor and writer, 1987-90; speaker and freelance writer, 1990-; Judson University, adjunct professor of writing, 2004-. **Publications:** Sharing, 1988; Tyrannosaurus, 1988; Polka-dot Puppys Walk: A Book about Sequences, 1988; Polka-Dot Puppy's Visitor: A Book about Opposites, 1988; The Old Sandman, 1988; The Vain Little Mouse, 1988; Tom Thumb, 1988; Thumbelina, 1988; Sinbad the Sailor, 1988; Stegosaurus, 1988; Peter Pan, 1988; Responsibility, 1988; Hansel and Gretel, 1988; Alice in Wonderland, 1988; Triceratops, 1988; Till Eulenspiegels Merry Pranks, 1988; Apatosaurus, 1988; Allosaurus, 1988; Ali Baba and the Forty Thieves, 1988; The Princess and the Pea, 1988; Thank You, 1989; Please, 1989; May I?, 1989; I'm Sorry, 1989; Excuse Me, 1989; Haunted Houses, 1989; UFOs, 1989; After You, 1989; Anatosaurus, 1989; Brachiosaurus, 1989; Iguanodon, 1989; Maiasaura, 1989; Good Sportsmanship, 1990; Saltasaurus, 1990; Cooperation, 1990; What Plants Give Us: The Gift of Life, 1990; Robots: Here They Come!, 1990; Saving the Forests: A Rabbits Story, 1990; Snow: When Will It Fall?, 1990; Carefulness, 1990; Diplodocus, 1991; Parasaurolophus, 1991; Oviraptor 1991; Ornithomimus, 1991; Compsognathus, 1991; Discovering Dinosaurs, 1991; Ankylosaurus, 1991; Megalosaurus, 1991; Protoceratops, 1991; Pachycephalosaurus, 1991; Dinosaur Relatives, 1991; Hypsilophodon, 1991; Deinonychus, 1991; Carolina Herrera: International Fashion Designer, 1991; Coelophysis, 1991; Troodon, 1991; Baryonyx, 1991; Little Lady's Adventure in Alphabet Town, 1992; Walrus's Adventure in Alphabet Town, 1992; Jack and Jill's Adventure in Alphabet Town, 1992; Cinco de Mayo, 1993; Kwanzaa, 1993; Japanese Boy's Festival, 1994; St. Patrick's Day, 1994; The Mystery of the UFO, 1996; The Mystery of the Missing Money, 1996; Television, 1996; Velociraptor: The Swift Hunter, 1998; Tyrannosaurus: The Tyrant Lizard, 1998; Triceratops: The Horned Dinosaur, 1998; Stegosaurus: The Plated Dinosaur, 1998; China, 1999; A Ticket to China, 1999; Sweden, 2001; George Lucas; An Unauthorized Biography, 2001; Greece, 2001; (with V.J. Weber) The Siege of the Alamo, 2002; Indonesia, 2002; Nicaragua, 2002; The Plymouth Colony, 2002; The Emancipation Proclamation, 2002; (with M. Knowlton) The Settling of Jamestown, 2002; The Wampanoag: The People of the First Light, 2003; The Osage, 2003; The Cree Tribe, 2003; Benjamin Franklin, 2003; Daniel Boone, 2003; (with S. Crewe) The Settling of St. Augustine, 2003; William McKinley: Americas 25th President, 2004; Ulysses S. Grant: Americas 18th President, 2004; Citizenship, 2005; Cooperation, 2005; Respect, 2005; Pteranodon, 2006; Iguanodonte, 2006; Megalodon, 2006; (with K. O'Hern) Battle of the Alamo, 2006; Giganotosaurus, 2007; Giant Ground Sloths, 2007; Tigre dientes de sable, 2008; Tigre de Tasmania, 2008; Tasmanian Tiger, 2008; Sabertooth Cat, 2008; Oso de las cavernas, 2008; Cave Bear, 2008; Komodo Dragons, 2009; Giant Rhinoceros, 2009; Great White Sharks: On the Hunt, 2009; Cobras: On the Hunt, 2009; Scorpions: On the Hunt, 2010; Killer Whales: On the Hunt, 2010. **Address:** 657 Shenandoah Trl., Elgin, IL 60123, U.S.A. **Online address:** jr@janetriehecky.com

RIELAGE, Dale C. American (born United States), b. 1970?. **Genres:** Military/Defense/Arms Control, History. **Career:** Writer. **Publications:** Russian

Supply Efforts in America during the First World War, 2002. **Address:** c/o Author Mail, McFarland and Company Inc., 960 NC Hwy 88 W, PO Box 611, Jefferson, NC 28640, U.S.A.

RIES, Laura. American (born United States), b. 1971?. **Genres:** Advertising/Public Relations, Marketing, Business/Trade/Industry, Economics. **Career:** TBWA Advertising, account executive, 1993-94; Ries & Ries, president, marketing consultant and strategist, 1994-. Writer. **Publications:** (With A. Ries) The 22 Immutable Laws of Branding: How to Build a Product or Service into a World-Class Brand, 1998; (with A. Ries) The 11 Immutable Laws of Internet Branding, 2000; The Fall of Advertising and the Rise of PR, 2002; (with A. Ries) The Origin of Brands: Discover the Natural Laws of Product Innovation and Business Survival, 2004; (with A. Ries) War In The Boardroom: Why Left-brain Management And Right-brain Marketing Don't See Eye-to-eye and What To Do About It, 2009; Visual Hammer, 2011. **Address:** Ries & Ries, 2195 River Cliff Dr., Roswell, GA 30076, U.S.A. **Online address:** lauraries@ries.com

RIESENBERG, Peter N. American (born United States), b. 1925. **Genres:** History, Cultural/Ethnic Topics, Politics/Government. **Career:** Rutgers University, instructor in history, 1953-54; Swarthmore College, assistant professor of history, 1954-60; Washington University, assistant professor, professor of history, 1960-93, professor emeritus of history, 1993-; National Taiwan University, visiting professor, 1993; Bowdoin College, adjunct professor of history, 1995-96. Writer. **Publications:** Inalienability of Sovereignty in Medieval Political Thought, 1955; (with J.H. Mundy) The Medieval Town, 1958; Traditions of the Western World, 1980; Citizenship in the Western Tradition: Plato to Rousseau, 1992; A History of Citizenship: Sparta to Washington, 2002. OTHER: (ed. with J. Agresto) The Humanist as Citizen, 1981. **Address:** Washington University, 1 Brookings Dr., PO Box 1070, St. Louis, MO 63130-4862, U.S.A.

RIESNER, Rainer. German (born Germany), b. 1950. **Genres:** Archaeology/Antiquities, Theology/Religion. **Career:** University of Tubingen, New Testament studies, lecturer. Writer. **Publications:** Formen gemeinsamen Lebens im Neuen Testament und heute, 1977; (contrib.) Jesus, der Christus: 8 Aufsätze, 1978; Jesus als Lehrer, 1981, 3rd ed., 1988; (co-author) Jesus, Qumran und der Vatiken, 1993, trans. as Jesus, Qumran, and the Vatican, 1994; Die Frühzeit des Apostels Paulus: Studien zur Chronologie, Missionsstrategie und Theologie, 1994; Paul's Early Period, 1998; Essenes and Urgemeinde, 1998; Der Ursprung der Jesus-Oberireferung, 2002; Bethanien jenseits des Jordan: Topographie und Theologie im Johannes-Evangelium, 2002; (co-author) Judäa: Geschichte, Exegese, Archoälogie, 2003; (ed.) Paths of the Messiah and Sites of the Early Church from Galilee to Jerusalem: Jesus and Jewish Christianity in Light of Archaeological Discoveries, 2010; (co-author) Blutzeuge: Tod und Grab des Petrus in Rom, 2010. **Address:** University of Tubingen, Wilhelmstrabe 7, Tubingen, 72074, Germany.

RIESS, Jana. American (born United States), b. 1969. **Genres:** Writing/Journalism. **Career:** Publishers Weekly, religious book review editor, 1999-2008; Westminster John Knox Press, acquisitions editor; Miami University, professor of religion and American studies. **Publications:** The Spiritual Traveler: Boston and New England: A Guide to Sacred Sites and Peaceful Places, 2002; What Would Buffy Do?: The Vampire Slayer as Spiritual Guide, 2004; (with C.K. Bigelow) Mormonism for Dummies, 2005; (with M. Ogilbee) American Pilgrimage: Sacred Journeys and Spiritual Destinations, 2006; (comp. and ed.) God is in the Manger: Reflections on Advent and Christmas, 2010; Flunking Sainthood: A Year of Breaking the Sabbath, Forgetting to Pray, and Still Loving My Neighbor, 2011. Contributor of periodicals. **Address:** DeChant-Hughes & Associates Inc., 1440 N Kingsbury St., Chicago, IL 60642, U.S.A.

RIFBJERG, Klaus (Thorvald). Danish (born Denmark), b. 1931. **Genres:** Plays/Screenplays, Novels, Poetry. **Career:** Film director, 1955-57; Information, literary critic, 1955-57; Politiken, literary critic, 1959-65; Vindrosen, editor-in-chief, 1959-63; Gyldendal Publishers, literary director, 1984-92, board director, 1992-; Laererhojskole, professor of aesthetics, 1986. **Publications:** NOVELS: Den kroniske uskyld, 1958; (with J. Jensen) Hva' skal vi lave; revykomedie, 1963; Operaelskeren, 1966; Arkivet, 1967; Lonni og Karl, 1968; Anna (jeg) Anna, 1969; Marts 1970, 1970; Leif den lykkelige junior, 1971; Lena Jorgensen Klintevej 2650 Hvidovre, 1971; Brevet til Gerda, 1972; R.R. Gyldendal, 1972; Spinatfuglene, 1973; Dilettanterne, 1973; Du skal ikke v're ked af det, Amalia. En pamflet-roman, 1974; En hugorm i solen, 1974; Vejen ad hvilken, 1975; Tak for turen, 1975; Kiks, 1976; Twist, 1976; Et bort-

vendt ansigt, 1977; Drengene, 1977; Tango eller syv osmotiske fortllinger, 1978; Dobbeltgnger eller Den korte, inderlige men fuldstndig sande beretning om Klaus Rifbjergs liv, 1978; Joker, 1979; Voksdugshjertet, 1979; Det sorte hul, 1980; De hellige aber, 1981; Jus, og/eller, Den gyldne middelvej, 1982; Hvad sker der i kvarteret, 1983; En Omvej til klosteret, 1983; Patience eller Kortene pa bordet, 1983; Falsk forar, 1984; Harlekin skelet: en pantomime roman, 1985; Som man behager, 1986; Engel, 1987; Det ville gl'de: en skj'lmeroman, 1989; Rapsodi i blat, 1991; Divertimento i mol: roman, 1996; Billedet: roman, 1998; Huset, eller hvad der gjorde storst indtryk pa mig i det tyvende arhundrede, 2000; Nansen og Johansen: et vintereventyr, 2002; Tidsmaskinen: en rutsjebaneforers bekendelser, 2002; Esbern: Roman, 2005; Det gælder om at holde balancen: noveller og essays fra dengang til i dag, 2006; Hvordan har vi det så i dag?: kroniker i Politiken 1957-2006, 2006; Naturlig Forklaring, 2006; Hovedløs: Roman, 2007; (co-author) Fiktionens åbenhed: samtaler med 11 danske forfattere, 2008; Huse, 2008; Dagstelegrafen: Roman, 2009; Knastorre digte= Strohtrockene Gedichte, 2009; Saa kom en haeslig, 2010; Skiftespor: Roman, 2010; Så kom en hæslig jæger: essays og historier om jagt, 2010; Jordbær: Roman, 2011. POETRY: Under vejr med mig selv, 1956; Efterkrig, 1957; Konfrontation, 1960; Camouflage, 1961; Voliere: et Fuglekor pa femogtyve Stemmer, 1962; Portrt, 1963; Amagerdigte, 1965; Faedrelandssange, 1967; I skyttens tegn. Digte i udvalg 1956-67, 1970; Mytologi. Digte, 1970; Scener fra det daglige liv, 1973; 25 desperate digte, 1974; Stranden, 1974; Den sondag: digte, 1975; Spring, 1977; Livsfrisen: Fixérbillede med satyr, 1979; Spansk motiv, 1981; Landet Atlantis: digte, 1982; Det svaevende trae, 1984; Udenfor har vinden lagt sig, 1984; Digte, 1986; Byens Tvelys, 1987; Septembersang, 1988; Bjerget i himlen, 1991; Krigen: en digtcyklus, 1992; (with T. Sorensen and P. Laugesen) Tuschrejse, 1994; Kandestedersuiten: et digt, 1994; Leksikon: digte, 1996; Terrains vagues, 1998. CHILDREN'S BOOKS: Kesses krig, 1981; Linda og baronen, 1989; Da Oscar blev tosset, 1990; Det ved jeg da godt!, 1990; Den hemmelige kilde, 1991; Hjemve, 1993. Contributor to periodicals. **Address:** Gyldendal Publishers, 3 Klareboderne, Copenhagen, 1001, Denmark. **Online address:** inge-rif@terra.es

RIFKIN, Shepard. *See* Obituaries.

RIGBY, Nigel. British (born England) **Genres:** Intellectual History. **Career:** National Maritime Museum, staff, 1996-, head of research. Historian and writer. **Publications:** (Ed. with H.J. Booth) Modernism and Empire, 2000; (with P.V. Merwe) Captain Cook in the Pacific, 2002; (ed. with H.V. Brown and M. Lincoln) The Worlds of the East India Company, 2002; (ed. with D. Killingray and M. Lincoln) Maritime Empires: British Imperial Maritime Trade in the Nineteenth Century, 2004; (ed. with G. Clifton) Treasures of the National Maritime Museum, 2004; (with P.V. Merwe and G. Williams) Pioneers of the Pacific: Voyages of Exploration, 1787-1810, 2005. **Address:** National Maritime Museum, Romney Rd., Greenwich, GL SE10 9NF, England.

RIGBY, Sue. *See* **RIGBY, Susan.**

RIGBY, Susan. Also writes as Sue Rigby. Scottish/British (born England), b. 1965. **Genres:** Earth Sciences, Geography, Natural History, Sciences, Biology, Earth Sciences. **Career:** Cambridge University, junior research fellow, 1990-92; University of Leicester, lecturer, 1992-95; University of Edinburgh, School of Geosciences, senior lecturer in geosciences, 1995-, Grant Institute, head, 2005-, assistant principal. Writer. **Publications:** The Mitchell Beazley Guide to Rocks, Minerals, and Gemstones, 1991; Caves (juvenile), 1994; Eyewitness Guide to Rocks, Minerals, and Gemstones, 1995; (as Sue Fuller) Rocks & Minerals, 1995, 2nd ed., 2003; (as Sue Rigby) Fossils: The Story of Life, 1997; (with P. Kipping) The Speech-language Pathologist's Guide to Managing the New Medicare, 2000; (as Sue Fuller with C. Maynard) 1001 Facts about Rocks and Minerals, 2003; (as Sue Rigby with C. Milsom) Fossils at a Glance, 2004, 2nd ed., 2010. **Address:** Grant Institute, School of Geosciences, University of Edinburgh, Rm. 329a, The King's Bldg., W Mains Rd., Edinburgh, EH9 3JW, Scotland. **Online address:** sue.rigby@ed.ac.uk

RIGG, Sharon. *See* **CREECH, Sharon.**

RIGGS, Cynthia. American (born United States), b. 1931. **Genres:** Mystery/Crime/Suspense, Novels. **Career:** Freelance writer, 1953-64; Smithsonian Oceanographic Sorting Center, museum aide, 1964-65; Ocean Science News, associate editor, 1965-67; U.S. Congress, press secretary for congressman Hastings Keith, 1967; Marine Tech Society Journal, managing editor, 1967-71; MTS Memo, editor, 1967-71; National Geographic Society, freelance writer, editor, researcher, 1971-75; Petroleum Today, editor, 1972-84; AAA Tour Books, managing editor, 1984-86; Cleveland House, proprietor. Writer, 1998-. **Publications:** MARTHA'S VINEYARD MYSTERY SERIES: Deadly Nightshade, 2001; The Cranefly Orchid Murders, 2002; The Cemetery Yew, 2003; Jack in the Pulpit, 2004; The Paperwhite Narcissus, 2005; Indian Pipes, 2006; Shooting Star: A Martha's Vineyard Mystery, 2007; Death and Honesty, 2009; Touch-Me-Not, 2010; The Bee Balm Murders, 2011; Victoria Trumbull's Secrets of Martha's Vineyard, 2011. **Address:** PO Box 3041, West Tisbury, MA 02575, U.S.A. **Online address:** cynthia@cynthiariggs.com

RIGGS, Jack C. American (born United States), b. 1954. **Genres:** Novels. **Career:** Harvard University, School of Education, research assistant, 1980; Home Box Office (HBO), story analyst; Georgia Perimeter College, associate professor of English, Writer's Institute, writer-in-residence. **Publications:** When the Finch Rises (novel), 2003; The Fireman's Wife (novel), 2008. Contributor to periodicals. **Address:** Writers Institute at Georgia Perimeter College, Clarkston Campus, 555 North Indian Creek Dr., Clarkston, GA 30021-2396, U.S.A. **Online address:** jriggs@gpc.edu

RIGGS, Paula Detmer. American (born United States), b. 1944. **Genres:** Romance/Historical, Young Adult Fiction, Literary Criticism And History. **Career:** Freelance writer, 1986-; San Diego State University, writing faculty; Long Beach State University, writing faculty; Irvine State University, writing faculty. **Publications:** MATERNITY ROW: Mummy by Surprise, 1997; Daddy by Choice, 2000; Daddy with a Badge, 2001. NOVELS: Beautiful Dreamer, 1986; Fantasy Man, 1987; Tender Offer, 1989; A Lasting Promise, 1990; Forgotten Dream, 1990; Rough Passage, 1991; Silent Impact, 1991; Paroled!, 1992; Suspicious Minds, 1988; Firebrand, 1993; A Man of Honor, 1993; Once Upon a Wedding, 1993; No Easy Way Out, 1994; Murdock's Family, 1994; Daddy by Accident, 1997; Baby by Design, 1997; Taming the Night, 1998; The Parent Plan, 1998; Once More a Family, 1999; Never Walk Alone, 2003. OTHERS: Desperate Measures, 1988; Full Circle, 1989; The Bachelor Party, 1995; A High Price to Pay, 1995; Her Secret, His Child, 1996. **Address:** Silhouette Books, Harlequin Books, Steeple Hill Books, 233 Broadway, Ste. 1001, 300 E 42nd St., New York, NY 10279-1001, U.S.A. **Online address:** pdriggs@wizzards.net

RIGGS, Robert E(dwon). American (born United States), b. 1927. **Genres:** International Relations/Current Affairs, Law, Politics/Government. **Career:** Brigham Young University Law School, instructor, assistant professor of political science, 1955-60, professor of law, 1975-92, professor emeritus, 1992-; Columbia University, Ruckefeller research fellow, 1957-58; University of Arizona, Bureau of Business and Public Research, research specialist, 1960-63; private practice of law, 1963-64; University of Minnesota, associate professor, 1964-68, professor, 1968-75; mayor of Golden Valley, 1972-75. Writer. **Publications:** Laws Affecting Planning: Arizona, Pima County, 1952; Politics in the United Nations: A Study of United States Influence in the General Assembly, 1958; The Movement for Administrative Reorganization in Arizona, 1961; Arizona State Personnel Policies, 1962; Vox Populi: The Battle of 103, 1964; (with J.C. Plano) Forging World Order: The Politics of International Organization, 1967; US/UN: Foreign Policy and International Organization, 1971; (with J.C. Plano) Dictionary of Political Analysis, 1973, 2nd ed., 1982; (with J.C. Plano and H. Robin), 1982; (with J.C. Plano and others) Political Science Dictionary, 1973; (with I.J. Mykletun) Beyond Functionalism, 1979; (with L. Ziring and J.C. Plano) The United Nations: International Organization and World Politics, 1988, 4th ed., 2005. **Address:** J. Reuben Clark Law School, Brigham Young University, 492 W 75 North, Orem, UT 84057, U.S.A. **Online address:** roberteriggs@comcast.net

RIGGS, Stephanie. American (born United States), b. 1964. **Genres:** Self Help. **Career:** KHGI, assignment reporter and morning anchor, 1987-88; KSEE/KNTV, news anchor and reporter, 1987-92; KOVR, news anchor and reporter, 1992-94; WKRC, news anchor and reporter, 1994-96; KCNC, news anchor and reporter, 1996-2002. **Publications:** Never Sell Yourself Short, 2001. Contributor to periodicals. **Address:** 1044 Lincoln St., Denver, CO 80203, U.S.A.

RIGGS, Webster. American (born United States), b. 1934. **Genres:** Medicine/Health, Philosophy, Psychology, Sports/Fitness. **Career:** Methodist Hospital, resident in radiology, 1961-64; University of Tennessee, professor of radiology, 1964-; Boston Children's Hospital, fellow in pediatric radiology, 1965; Le Bonheur Children's Hospital, pediatric radiologist, 1968-; American Board of Radiology, examiner; Baptist Memorial Hospital, staff. Writer.

Publications: Pediatric Chest Roentgenology: Recognizing the Abnormal, 1979; The You You Don't Know: Covert Influences on Your Behavior, 1997; Satan and Science Are Bunk: Confronting Postmodern Reality, forthcoming. Contributor to books and journals. **Address:** 3438 Central Ave., Memphis, TN 38111, U.S.A.

RIGGSBY, Andrew M. American (born United States) **Genres:** History, Criminology/True Crime. **Career:** University of Texas, associate professor of classics. Writer. **Publications:** Crime and Community in Ciceronian Rome, 1999; Caesar in Gaul and Rome: War in Words, 2006. **Address:** Department of Classics, University of Texas, C3400, 1 University Sta., Austin, TX 78712-0308, U.S.A. **Online address:** ariggsby@mail.utexas.edu

RIGHTMIRE, G. Philip. American (born United States), b. 1942. **Genres:** Anthropology/Ethnology, Natural History. **Career:** Binghamton University, State University of New York, assistant professor, 1969-73, associate professor, 1973-82, professor of anthropology, 1982-2002, distinguished professor, 2002-09; University of Stockholm, Osteological Research Laboratory, fellow, 1973; University of Cape Town, visiting lecturer, 1975-76; Harvard University, Peabody Museum, Department of Anthropology, research associate, 2006-09, Department of Human Evolutionary Biology, faculty affiliate and research associate, 2009-. Writer. **Publications:** The Evolution of Homo erectus: Comparative Anatomical Studies of an Extinct Human Species, 1990. Contributor to periodicals. **Address:** Department of Human Evolutionary Biology, Peabody Museum, Harvard University, Cambridge, MA 02138, U.S.A. **Online address:** gprightm@fas.harvard.edu

RIGHTON, Caroline. British (born England), b. 1958. **Genres:** Economics, Self Help. **Career:** The West Briton, junior reporter; Cornish Guardian, junior reporter; Falmouth Packet, staff, 1977-79; The Seafood Restaurant, chef, 1979-81; Carrick and West Cornwall Review, proprietor and publisher, 1980-82; BBC Radio, senior producer, 1982-84; Popular Craft, columnist and associate editor, 1997-98; Family Circle Magazine, columnist, 1997; Really Vital Television Ltd., producer. **Publications:** The Life Audit: A Step-By-Step Guide to Taking Stock, Gaining Control and Creating the Life You Want, 2004. **Address:** The Life Audit, PO Box 73, Thurlestone, Kingsbridge, DN TZ7 3WZ, England. **Online address:** caroline@thelifeaudit.com

RIKER, H. Jay. See **KEITH, William H(enry).**

RILEY, Carroll L. American (born United States), b. 1923. **Genres:** Anthropology/Ethnology, Archaeology/Antiquities, History, Politics/Government, Social Sciences. **Career:** U.S. Department of Justice, consultant to Lands Division, 1952-53; University of Colorado, instructor in anthropology, 1953-54; University of North Carolina, assistant professor of anthropology, 1954-55; Southern Illinois University, curator of physical anthropology museum, 1955-61, assistant professor, 1955-60, associate professor, 1960-67, professor, 1967-86, Department of Anthropology, co-director of graduate studies, 1970-72, director of graduate studies, 1978-79, 1983-84, 1985-87, director, 1972-74, associate director, 1974-77, professor of anthropology, 1974-86, University Museum, curator, 1978, distinguished professor of anthropology, 1986-87, distinguished professor emeritus, 1987-; Museum of New Mexico, Lab of Anthropology, research associate, 1987-90, adjunct professor, 1990-; Camino Real Museum project, director, 1995-. Writer. **Publications:** The Origins of Civilization, 1969; (with J.C. Kelley) Pre-Columbian Contact with Nuclear America, 1969; (co-author) Coras, Huicholes y Tepehuanes, 1972; Historical and Cultural Dictionary of Saudi Arabia, 1972; Salish and Chimakuam-Speaking Indians of the Puget Sound Basin of Washington, 1973; Ethnological Field Investigation and Analysis of Historical Material Relative to Group Distribution and Utilization of Natural Resources among Puget Sound Indians in Washington, 1974; The Frontier People: The Greater Southwest in the Protohistoric Period, 1982, rev. ed., 1987; Rio del Norte: People of the Upper Rio Grande from Earliest Times to the Pueblo Revolt, 1995; (with C.L. Riley) Bandelier: The Life and Adventures of Adolph Bandelier, 1996; The Kachina and the Cross: Indians and Spaniards in the Early Southwest, 1999; Becoming Aztlan: Mesoamerican Influence in the Greater Southwest, AD 1200-1500, 2005; Troubled Century: Native Americans and Spaniards in the Seventeenth Century Southwest, forthcoming. EDITOR: (with C.H. Lange) Southwestern Journals of Adolph F. Bandelier 1880-1882, 1966; (with W.W. Taylor) American Historical Anthropology: Essays in Honor of Leslie Spier, 1967; (co-ed.) Man Across the Sea: Problems of Pre-Columbian Contacts, 1971, 3rd ed., 1976; (with B.C. Hedrick and J.C. Kelley) The North Mexican Frontier, 1971; (with B.C. Hedrick and J.C. Kelley) The Classic Southwest,

1973; (with B.C. Hedrick and J.C. Kelley) The Mesoamerican Southwest: Readings in Archeology, Ethnohistory and Ethnology, 1973; (with B.C. Hedrick) The Journey of the Vaca Party: A Translation of the Joint Report of Alvar Nunez Cabeza de Vaca and His Companions as Reproduced in Oviedo de Valdes, with the Spanish Text, University Museum Studies, 1974; Makah Indians of Western Washington: A Study of Group Distribution, Political Organization and Concepts of Land Use, 1976; (with B.C. Hedrick) Documents Ancillary to the Vaca Journey, 1976; Sixteenth Century Trade in the Greater Southwest, 1976; (with B.C. Hedrick) Across the Chichimec Sea: Papers in Honor of J. Charles Kelley, 1978; New Frontiers in the Archaeology and Ethnohistory of the Greater Southwest in the Protohistoric Period, 1980; (ed. with J.A. Jones) A Zuni Life: A Pubelo Indian In Two Words, 1998; (with C.F. Schaafsma) The Casas Grandes World, 1998. **Address:** 1106 6th St., Las Vegas, NM 87701, U.S.A. **Online address:** criley@newmexico.com

RILEY, Charles A. American (born United States), b. 1958. **Genres:** Art/Art History, Business/Trade/Industry, Economics, Design. **Career:** WE magazine, editor-in-chief; WE Media, co-founder; International Center for Corporate Accountability Inc., director of communications; City University of New York, Baruch College, Weissman School of Arts and Sciences, associate professor, professor. **Publications:** (Ed. with O. Robinson and R. Freeman) Arts in the World Economy: Public Policy and Private Philanthropy for a Global Cultural Community, 1994; Color Codes: Modern Theories of Color in Philosophy, Painting and Architecture, Literature, Music, and Psychology, 1995; Small Business, Big Politics: What Entrepreneurs Need to Know to Use Their Growing Political Power, 1995; (ed. with J.M. Schuster and J. de Monchaux) Preserving the Built Heritage: Tools for Implementation, 1997; Saints of Modern Art: The Ascetic Ideal in Contemporary Painting, Sculpture, Architecture, Music, Dance, Literature, and Philosophy, 1998; High-access Home: Design and Decoration for Barrier-free Living, 1999; Aristocracy and the Modern Imagination, 2001; Art of Peter Max, 2002; Ben Schonzeit Paintings, 2002; Sacred Sister, 2003; Jazz Age in France, 2004; Disability and the Media: Prescriptions for Change, 2005; Disability and Business: Best Practices and Strategies for Inclusion, 2006; Surrealism: Dreams on Canvas, 2007; (with P. Kaplan) Arthur Carter: Sculptures, Drawings, and Paintings, 2009; Art at Lincoln Center: The Public Art and List Print and Poster Collections, 2009; (contrib.) Associated American Artists: Catalogue Raisonne, 1934-2000, 2010. **Address:** Department of English, Bernard M. Baruch College, City Univ of NY, 6-244, Vertical Campus, 17 Lexington Ave., Rm. 6-244, New York, NY 10010, U.S.A. **Online address:** charles_riley@baruch.cuny.edu

RILEY, Helene M. (Helene M. Kastinger Riley). American/Austrian (born Austria), b. 1939. **Genres:** Antiques/Furnishings. **Career:** Rice University, instructor, 1971; Kemper Insurance, staff, 1971; Yale University, assistant professor, 1975-78, associate professor, 1979-85, Summer Language Institute, head, 1979-81, Davenport College, fellow; Washington State University, associate professor, 1979-85, Department of Foreign Languages, chair, 1981-; Clemson University, associate professor, through 1985, professor of German, 1985-95, alumni distinguished professor of German, 1995-, Department of Languages, head, 1985-86; The Germanic Notes and Reviews, editor. **Publications:** Idee und Gestaltung: Das konfigurative Strukturprinzip in der Kurzprosa Achim von Arnims, 1977; Ludwig Achim von Arnims Jugend und Reisejahre: e. Beitr. zur Biographie mit unbekannten Breifzeugnissen, 1978; Achim von Arnim in Selbstzeugnissen und Bilddokumenten, 1979; Romain Rolland, 1979; Das Bild der Antike in der deutschen Romantik, 1981; Virginia Woolf, 1983; Clemens Brentano, 1985; Die weibliche Muse: sechs Essays über künstlerisch schaffende Frauen der Goethezeit, 1986; Ludwig Achim von Arnim. Erstdrucke und Unbekanntes, 1988; Max Weber, 1991; Michael Kalteisen: Ein Deutscher in South Carolina, 1995; Hildegard von Bingen, 1997; Clemson University, 2002. Contributor of articles to periodicals. **Address:** Department of Languages, Clemson University, 510 Strode Twr., PO Box 340535, Clemson, SC 29634-0535, U.S.A. **Online address:** rhelene@clemson.edu

RILEY, Helene M. Kastinger. See **RILEY, Helene M.**

RILEY, James A. American (born United States), b. 1939. **Genres:** Sports/Fitness, Biography, Reference, History, Autobiography/Memoirs. **Career:** Negro Leagues Baseball Museum, director of research. Writer. **Publications:** The All-Time All-Stars of Black Baseball, 1983; Dandy, Day, and the Devil, 1987; (with R.W. Speer) The Hundred Years of Chet Hoff: A Special Tribute to His Life and Baseball Career & A Celebration of His 100th Birthday, May 8th, 1991, 1991; The Biographical Encyclopedia of the Negro Baseball Leagues, 1994; Buck Leonard: The Black Lou Gehrig, 1995; Monte Irvin: Nice Guys Finish First, 1996; The Negro Leagues, 1997; (ed.) Barnstorming to Heaven: Syd Pollock and His Great Black Teams, 2006. Contributor to books and to baseball magazines. **Address:** PO Box 1122, Holly Springs, GA 30142-1122, U.S.A. **Online address:** tkpublish@aol.com

RILEY, James C. American (born United States), b. 1943. **Genres:** History, Medicine/Health, Money/Finance, Economics, Social Sciences. **Career:** University of Houston, instructor, 1970-71, assistant professor, 1971-73, associate professor of history, 1973-75; Indiana University, Department of History, assistant professor, 1975-78, associate professor, 1978-83, professor of history, 1983-2002, distinguished professor emeritus, 2002-, University Graduate School, College of Arts and Sciences, adjunct professor of philanthropic studies; University of Amsterdam, 1976; University of Illinois, Summer Research Laboratory on Russia and Eastern Europe, research associate, 1979; Catholic University of Louvain, visiting fellow, 1983; Netherlands Institute for Advanced Study, visiting fellow, 1985-86; Australian National University, visiting fellow, 1989. Writer. **Publications:** (Ed.) Dutch Investment and American Finance, 1780-1805, 2 vols., 1977; International Government Finance and the Amsterdam Capital Market, 1740-1815, 1980; Population Thought in the Age of the Demographic Revolution, 1985; The Seven Years War and the Old Regime in France: The Economic and Financial Toll, 1986; The Eighteenth-Century Campaign to Avoid Disease, 1987; Sickness, Recovery, and Death: A History and Forecast of Ill Health, 1989; Sick, not Dead: The Health of British Workingmen During the Mortality Decline, 1997; Rising Life Expectancy: A Global History, 2001; Poverty and Life Expectancy: The Jamaica Paradox, 2005; Low Income, Social Growth, and Good Health: A History of Twelve Countries, 2008. **Address:** Department of History, Indiana University, 742 Ballantine Hall, 1020 E Kirkwood Ave., Bloomington, IN 47405-7103, U.S.A. **Online address:** rileyj@indiana.edu

RILEY, Jess. American (born United States), b. 1974. **Genres:** Novels, Psychology. **Career:** Writer. **Publications:** Driving Sideways: A Novel, 2008. **Address:** Random House Inc., 1745 Broadway, New York, NY 10019, U.S.A. **Online address:** jess@jessriley.com

RILEY, Joan. British/Jamaican (born Jamaica), b. 1958. **Genres:** Novels, Adult Non-fiction, Romance/Historical, Literary Criticism And History. **Career:** Drug Advice and Research Office, researcher, 1983-85; CALC, action researcher, 1985-87; freelance drug adviser and consultant, 1989. Writer. **Publications:** The Unbecoming, 1985; Waiting in the Twilight, 1987; Romance, 1988; A Kindness to the Children, 1992; (ed. with B. Wood) Leave to Stay: Stories of Exile and Belonging, 1996. **Address:** c/o Anthony Harwood, Curtis Brown Ltd., 162-164 Regent St., London, GL W1R 5TB, England.

RILEY, Madeleine (Veronica). British (born England), b. 1933. **Genres:** Novels, Young Adult Fiction. **Career:** Writer. **Publications:** A Spot Bigger Than God, 1966; Brought to Bed, 1968; Diary for Two, 1969; An Ideal Friend, 1977. **Address:** David Higham Associates, 5-8 Lower John St., Golden Sq., London, GL W1F 9HA, England. **Online address:** madeleine@themanorhouse.fg.co.uk

RILEY, Martin. British (born England), b. 1948. **Genres:** Songs/Lyrics And Libretti, Science Fiction/Fantasy, Children's Fiction, Plays/Screenplays, Young Adult Fiction. **Career:** Countesthorpe Community College, teacher, 1972-75; Carnegie College, part-time lecturer, 1976-87; Trinity College, part-time lecturer, 1976-87; All Saints Colleges, part-time lecturer, 1976-87; National Festival of Youth Theatres, part-time lecturer, 1976-87; Stainbeck School, part-time lecturer, 1976-87; Collegiate College, part-time lecturer, 1976-87; Local Brew Song and Dance Co., founder, writer, director and performer, 1977-80; Leeds Drama Therapy Group, founder and developer, 1980. **Publications:** FOR CHILDREN BASED ON RILEY'S TELEPLAYS: Gruey, 1988; Gruey 2, 1989; Boggart Sandwich, 1989; Kevin's Cousins, 1992; (with J. Coombes) Kevin and Co., 1992; Tales from the Edge of the World, 1992; (with J. Coombes) Wilderness Edge, 1992; The Canterbury Tales: Geoffrey Chaucer, 1998. **Address:** c/o John Rush, Sheil Land Associates Ltd., 43 Doughty St., London, GL WC1N 2LF, England.

RILEY, Sam G. American (born United States), b. 1939?. **Genres:** Writing/Journalism, Biography. **Career:** Temple University, assistant professor of journalism, 1970-73; Georgia Southern University, associate professor of journalism, 1973-81; Virginia Polytechnic Institute and State University, professor of communication, 1981-. Writer. **Publications:** Magazines of the American South, 1986; GR8 PL8S: The Best of America's Vanity Plates, 1991; Biographical Dictionary of American Newspaper Columnists, 1995; The American Newspaper Columnist, 1998; African Americans in the Media: An Encyclopedia, 2 vols., 2007; Star Struck: An Encyclopedia of Celebrity Culture, 2010. EDITOR: Dictionary of Literary Biography, vol. VII3: American Magazine Journalists, 1741-1850, 1988; American Magazine Journalists, 1850-1900, 1989; Dictionary of Literary Biography, vol. VII9: American Magazine Journalists, 1850-1900, 1989; American Magazine Journalists, 1900-1960, 1990; (ed. with G.W. Selnow) Regional Interest Magazines of the United States, 1991; Corporate Magazines of the United State, 1992; Consumer Magazines of the British Isles, 1993; The Best of the Rest: Non-Syndicated Newspaper Columnists Select Their Best Work, 1993; American Magazine Journalists, 1900-1960, 1994. COMPILER: Index to Southern Periodicals, 1986; (with G.W. Selnow) Index to City and Regional Magazines, 1989; African Americans in the Media Today, 2 vols., 2007; Star Struck: An Encyclopedia of Celebrity Culture, 2010. **Address:** Department of Communication, Virginia Polytechnic Institute, 103 Shanks Hall, Blacksburg, VA 24061, U.S.A. **Online address:** sriley@vt.edu

RIMLER, Walter. American (born United States), b. 1946. **Genres:** Music, Novellas/Short Stories, Biography, Autobiography/Memoirs, Bibliography, Art/Art History. **Career:** Rimler and Associates, co-owner. Writer. **Publications:** Not Fade Away: A Comparison of Jazz Age With Rock Era Pop Song Composers, 1984; A Gershwin Companion: A Critical Inventory and Discography, 1916-1984, 1991; A Cole Porter Discography, 1995; Death in D-Minor, 1999; Beatle Rhett and Other Stories, 2000; George Gershwin: An Intimate Portrait, 2009. Contributor of stories to literary magazines. **Address:** Rimler and Associates, 253 26th Ave., San Francisco, CA 94121, U.S.A. **Online address:** wlr@crl.com

RIMMINGTON, Gerald Thorneycroft. British (born England), b. 1930. **Genres:** Social Sciences, Education. **Career:** Geography master, 1951-59; Union College, lecturer in geography, 1959-60; Ministry of Education, district education officer, 1961-63; Acadia University, assistant professor of education, 1963-65, associate professor of education, 1965-67; Brandon University, faculty of education, associate professor of education and dean, 1967-73; Mount Allison University, professor of education and head of department of education, 1973-81; Diocese of Peterborough, rector of Paston, 1981-86; vicar of Cosby and Diocesan director of continuing ministerial education, 1986-90; Diocese of Leicester, rector of Barwell with Stapleton and Potters Marston, 1990-95, retired, 1995; University of Leicester, Centre for the History of Religious and Political Pluralism, honorary visiting fellow. Writer. **Publications:** (With J.G. Pike) Malawi: A Geographical Study, 1965; (co-author) Yarmouth County Study: A Preliminary Socio-Economic Assessment, 1965; (co-author) The Resources of the Shubenacadie-Stewiacke Area of Nova Scotia: A Socio-Economic Study, 1966; (with L.M. Logan) Social Studies: A Creative Direction, 1969; (with R.D. Traill and L.M. Logan) Teaching the Social Sciences, 1972; Education, Politics and Society in Leicester 1833-1903, 1978; The Comprehensive School Issue in Leicester 1945-74, 1984; The Education of Maladjusted Children in Leicester 1892-1974, 1985; Your 100 Prayers for School and Church, 1986; The Rise and Fall of Elected School Boards in England, 1986; Your Assembly in School 1984, 1988; (with A. McWhirr) Gallowtree Gate Congregational Chapel, Leicester, 1823-1921, 1999; Bishop Cyril Bardsley and the Diocese of Leicester, 1927-1940, 1999. Contributor of articles to journals. **Address:** 7 Beechings Close, Countesthorpe, Leicester, LE LE8 5PA, England.

RIMPOCHE, Gelek. See GELEK, Ngawang.

RIMSTEAD, Roxanne L. Canadian (born Canada), b. 1953. **Genres:** Literary Criticism And History, Women's Studies And Issues, Social Sciences, Politics/Government, History. **Career:** McGill University, assistant professor, 1995-98; Universite de Sherbrooke, assistant professor, 1999-2002, associate professor, 2002-, professor. Writer. **Publications:** Remnants of Nation: On Poverty Narratives by Women, 2001; (co-ed.) Beyond Comparison, 2005. Contributor to books and periodicals. **Address:** Departement des lettres et communications, Faculte des lettres et sciences humaines, Universite de Sherbrooke, 2500 boulevard de l'Université, Sherbrooke, QC J1K 2R1, Canada. **Online address:** roxanne.rimstead@usherbrooke.ca

RINALDI, Ann. American (born United States), b. 1934. **Genres:** Young Adult Fiction, Novels, Romance/Historical. **Career:** Somerset Messenger Gazette, columnist, 1969-70; Trentonian, columnist, feature writer and editorial writer, 1970-91. Educator. **Publications:** YOUNG ADULT FICTION: Term Paper, 1979; Promises Are for Keeping, 1982; But in the Fall I'm Leaving, 1985; Time Enough for Drums, 1986; The Good Side of My Heart, 1987; The Last Silk Dress, 1988; A Ride into Morning: The Story of Tempe Wick, 1991; Wolf by the Ears, 1991; A Break with Charity: A Story about the Salem Witch Trials, 1992; In My Father's House, 1992; The Fifth of March: A Story of the Boston Massacre, 1993; A Stitch in Time, 1994; Finishing Becca: The Story of Peggy Shippen and Benedict Arnold, 1994; The Secret of Sarah Revere, 1995; Broken Days, 1995; Hang a Thousand Trees with Ribbons: The Story of Phillis Wheatley, 1996; The Blue Door, 1996; Keep Smiling Through, 1996; Mine Eyes Have Seen, 1997; Nightflower, 1997; An Acquaintance with Darkness, 1997; The Second Bend in the River, 1997; Cast Two Shadows, 1998; Ameila's War, 1999; My Heart is on the Ground, 1999; The Coffin Quilt, 1999; The Journal of Jasper Jonathan Pierce, 2000; The Education of Mary, 2000; The Staircase, 2000; The Girl in Blue, 2001; Numbering All the Bones, 2002; Taking Liberty, 2002; Millicent's Gift, 2002; Ride into Morning, 2003; Or Give Me Death, 2003; The Secret of Sarah Revere, 2003; Mutiny's Daughter, 2004; Brooklyn Rose, 2005; Sarah's Ground, 2005; Nine Days a Queen: The Short Life and Reign of Lady Jane Grey, 2005; Color of Fire: A Novel, 2005; Unlikely Friendship: A Novel of Mary Todd Lincoln and Elizabeth Keckley, 2007; Ever-After Bird, 2007; Come Juneteenth, 2007; Redheaded Princess: A Novel, 2008; Letter Writer: A Novel, 2008; Juliet's Moon, 2008; My Vicksburg, 2009; Leigh Ann's Civil War: A Novel, 2009; Last Full Measure, 2010; Family Greene: A Novel, 2010. **Address:** 302 Miller Ave., Somerville, NJ 08876, U.S.A. **Online address:** info@annrinaldi.net

RINDER, Lenore. American (born United States), b. 1949. **Genres:** Novels, Art/Art History. **Career:** University of Wisconsin, taught film, painting and animation, 1981-88; Warner Cable/Community Television, video production and public access training, 1992-. Educator, filmmaker and writer. **Publications:** A Big Mistake, 1994; (with P. Moschea) Star's Circus Parade, 2000; Tiger Tail and Fat & Thin, forthcoming. Contributor to periodicals. **Address:** 1652 S 36th St., Milwaukee, WI 53215-1829, U.S.A.

RINDERLE, Walter. American (born United States), b. 1940. **Genres:** Anthropology/Ethnology, Classics, Economics, History, Local History/Rural Topics, Medicine/Health, Speech/Rhetoric, Regional/Urban Planning, Regional/Urban Planning. **Career:** Vincennes University, instructor, 1969-71, adjunct professor, 1989-93; Saint Mary's College, instructor, 1974-84; College of the Holy Cross, instructor, 1985-87; University of Southern Indiana, instructor, 1993-98; Indiana State University, instructor, 1999-, Department of Communication, lecturer, Department of History, lecturer. Writer. **Publications:** (With B. Norling) The Nazi Impact on a German Village, 1992; Two Hundred Years of Catholic Education in Knox County, Indiana, 1792-1992, 1993. **Address:** Department of History, Indiana State University, 621 Chestnut St., Terre Haute, IN 47809, U.S.A.

RINDO, Ron(ald J.). American (born United States), b. 1959. **Genres:** Novellas/Short Stories, Novels, Young Adult Fiction, Romance/Historical. **Career:** Birmingham-Southern College, assistant professor of English, 1989-92; University of Wisconsin, Department of English, associate professor, 1992-, chair; Council for Wisconsin Writers Inc., board director. Writer. **Publications:** Suburban Metaphysics and Other Stories, 1990; Secrets Men Keep, 1995; Love in an Expanding Universe: Stories, 2005. Works appear in anthologies. Contributor to books. **Address:** Department of English, University of Wisconsin, Radford 201, Algoma Blvd., Oshkosh, WI 54901, U.S.A. **Online address:** rindo@uwosh.edu

RINEHART, Steven. American (born United States) **Genres:** Novellas/Short Stories, Novels, Young Adult Fiction. **Career:** Writer and teacher. **Publications:** Kick in the Head: Stories, 2000; Built in a Day: A Novel, 2003. Contributor to magazines. **Address:** c/o Publicity Director, Doubleday, 1540 Broadway, New York, NY 10036, U.S.A.

RING, Jennifer. American (born United States), b. 1948. **Genres:** Politics/Government, Race Relations, Social Commentary, Sports/Fitness, Women's Studies And Issues, Social Sciences. **Career:** Columbia University, assistant professor of political science, 1979-80; University of California, lecturer in political science, 1981-85; Stanford University, lecturer in political science, 1981-85; University of South Carolina, associate professor of government and international studies, 1989-97; University of Nevada, professor, 1997-. Writer. **Publications:** Modern Political Theory and Contemporary Feminism: A Dialectical Analysis, 1991; The Political Consequences of Thinking: Gender and Judaism in the Work of Hannah Arendt, 1997; Stolen Bases: Why American Girls Don't Play Baseball, 2009. Contributor to books. **Address:** Department of Political Science, University of Nevada, 227 Mack Social Science, PO Box 046, Reno, NV 89557-0042, U.S.A. **Online address:** jring@unr.edu

RING, Nancy G. American (born United States), b. 1956. **Genres:** Art/Art History, Biography, Autobiography/Memoirs. **Career:** Montalvo Center for the Arts, resident artist, 1987; Zebra Art Gallery, artist-in-residence, 1988; Skidmore College, resident artist, 1988; Djerassi Foundation, artist-in-residence, 1989; Far Brook School, art educator, 2004-. Writer. **Publications:** New Drawing in America (exhibition catalog), 1982; Walking on Walnuts, 1996. Contributor to periodicals. **Address:** Dumont-Landis Fine Art Inc., Deer Park Dr., Ste. H-2, Princeton Corporation Plz., Monmouth Junction, NJ 08852, U.S.A.

RING, Victoria A. American (born United States), b. 1958. **Genres:** Business/Trade/Industry. **Career:** Graphico Publishing, typesetter and designer, 1988-99; Fifty State Notary, owner, 2001-. Writer. **Publications:** My Homemade Business, 2004; Notary Signing Agent, 2004; How to Start a Bankruptcy Forms Processing Service, 2004; How to Start, Operate and Market a Freelance Notary Signing Agent Business, 2004; Best of the Notary News, vol. I, 2004; From Author to Publisher to Profit, 2005; Virtual Bankruptcy Assistant Training Workbook, 2006; How to Start a Virtual Bankruptcy Assistant Service, 2006; Foreclosure Mediation Training Guide, 2007; How to Self-Publish Your Own Book and Kiss Your Publisher and Agent Goodbye, forthcoming. **Address:** Colorado Bankruptcy Training, 1670 E Cheyenne Mountain Blvd., Ste. F257, Colorado Springs, CO 80906, U.S.A. **Online address:** victoria@50statenotary.com

RINGGOLD, Faith. American (born United States), b. 1930. **Genres:** Children's Fiction. **Career:** Teacher, 1955-73; Purdue University, lecturer, 1977; University of Massachusetts, lecturer, 1980; Rutgers University, lecturer, 1981; Occidental College, lecturer, 1984; University of California, professor of art, 1984-2002, professor emeritus, 2002-; Long Island University, lecturer, 1986; Mills College, lecturer, 1987; Museum of Modern Art, performance artist, 1988; Baltimore Museum of Art, performance artist, 1988; San Diego Museum, performance artist, 1990; De Pauw University, lecturer, 1989; University of West Florida, lecturer, 1989; Washington and Lee University, lecturer, 1991; Museum of African American Art, performance artist, 1991; Atlantic Center for the Arts, lecturer, 1992; Faith Ringgold Inc., chief executive officer. Writer. **Publications:** CHILDREN'S BOOKS (and illustrator): Tar Beach, 1991; Aunt Harriet's Underground Railroad in the Sky, 1992; Dinner at Aunt Connie's House, 1993; My Dream of Martin Luther King, 1995; Bonjour, Lonnie, 1996; The Invisible Princess, 1999; 3 Tar Beach Board Books, 2000. OTHER: French Collection=La Collection Franca¸ise, 1992; (with L. Freeman and N. Roucher) Talking to Faith Ringgold, 1996; We Flew over the Bridge: The Memoirs of Faith Ringgold, 1995; If a Bus Could Talk: The Story of Rosa Parks, 1999; Cassie's Colorful Day, 1999; Counting to Tar Beach, 1999; Cassie's Word Quilt, 2002; O Holy Night, 2004; (with C.R. Holton) Faith Ringgold: A View from the Studio, 2004; The Three Witches, 2006; Bronzeville Boys and Girls, 2007; Henry Ossawa Tanner, 2011. Contributor to periodicals. **Address:** Faith Ringgold Inc., 127 Jones Rd., Englewood, NJ 07631, U.S.A. **Online address:** ringgoldfaith@aol.com

RINGO, John. American (born United States), b. 1963. **Genres:** Science Fiction/Fantasy, Novels. **Career:** Writer. **Publications:** POSLEEN WAR SERIES: A Hymn Before Battle, 2000; Gust Front, 2001; When the Devil Dances, 2002; Hell's Faire, 2003; (with M.Z. Williamson) The Hero, 2004; (with J. Cochrane) Cally's War, 2004; (with T. Kratman) Watch on the Rhine, 2005; (with T. Kratman) Yellow Eyes, 2007; (with J. Cochrane) Sister Time, 2007; (with J. Cochrane) Honor of the Clan, 2009; Eye of the Storm, 2009; (with T. Kratman) The Tuloriad, 2009. EMPIRE OF MAN SERIES WITH D. WEBER: March Upcountry, 2001; March to the Sea, 2001; March to the Stars, 2003; We Few, 2005. COUNCIL WARS SERIES: There Will Be Dragons, 2003; Emerald Sea, 2004; Against the Tide, 2005; East of the Sun, West of the Moon, 2006. LOOKING GLASS SERIES: Into the Looking Glass, 2005; (with T.S. Taylor) Vorpal Blade, 2007; (with T.S. Taylor) Manxome Foe, 2008; (with T.S. Taylor) Claws That Catch, 2008. PALADIN OF SHADOWS SERIES: Ghost, 2005; Kildar, 2006; Choosers of the Slain, 2006; Unto the Breach, 2006; A Deeper Blue, 2007. NOVELS: (with L. Evans) The Road to Damascus, 2004; (with T.S. Taylor) Von Neumann's War, 2006; Princess of

Wands, 2006; The Last Centurion, 2008; (ed. with B.M. Thomsen) Citizens, 2010; Live Free or Die, 2010; Citadel, 2011; The Hot Gate, 2011; (with J.L. Nyle, S.M. Stirling and H. Turtledove) Exiled, 2011. **Address:** c/o Author Mail, Baen Books, PO Box 1403, Riverdale, NY 10471, U.S.A. **Online address:** abn1508@mindspring.com

RINGQUIST, Evan J. American (born United States), b. 1962. **Genres:** Politics/Government, Social Sciences. **Career:** Texas Tech University, Department of Political Science and the Center for Public Service, assistant professor, 1990-93; Florida State University, Department of Political Science, assistant professor, 1993-96, associate professor, 1996-2000, professor, 2000-01; Indiana University, School of Public and Environmental Affairs, professor, 2002-, Department of Political Science, faculty affiliate, West European Studies, faculty affiliate, Programs in Public Affairs and Public Policy, director, 2008-. Writer. **Publications:** Environmental Protection at the State Level: Politics and Progress in Controlling Pollution, 1993; (with M.A. Eisner and J. Worsham) Contemporary Regulatory Policy, 2000, 2nd ed., 2006. Contributor to books and political science journals. **Address:** School of Public and Environmental Affairs, Indiana University, SPEA Rm. 223, 1315 E 10th St., Bloomington, IN 47405, U.S.A. **Online address:** eringqui@indiana.edu

RINGWALD, Christopher D. American (born United States), b. 1956. **Genres:** Theology/Religion, Humanities. **Career:** Advocates for Human Potential Inc., senior writer; Times Union, reporter; The Sage Colleges, adjunct faculty, Faith and Society Project, director. Writer. **Publications:** Faith in Words: Ten Writers Reflect on the Spirituality of Their Profession, 1997; Aux sources du renouveau musulman, un siècle de réformisme islamique, 1998; Jewish Farming Communities of Northeastern New York, 1998; Muslims in France, 1999; To Be a European Muslim, 1999; Entre l'homme et son coeur, 2000; Islam, The West and the Challenges of Modernity, 2000, 2nd ed., 2004; (with A. Gresh) L'Islam en questions, 2000; The Soul of Recovery: Uncovering the Spiritual Dimension in the Treatment of Addictions, 2002; Dar ash-shahada, l'Occident, espace du témoignage, 2002; De l'Islam, 2002; Jihad, violence guerre et paix en islam, Tawhid (Lyon, France), 2002; La foi, la voie, la résistance, 2002; Musulmans d'Occident, construire et contribuer, 2002; Globalisation, Muslim Resistances, 2003; Les Musulmans d'Occident et l'avenir de l'Islam, 2003; Muhammad: vie du prophète: les enseignements spirituels et contemporains, 2006; A Day Apart: How Jews, Christians, and Muslims Find Faith, Freedom, and Joy on the Sabbath, 2007. **Address:** The Sage Colleges, 140 New Scotland Ave., Albany, NY 12208-3423, U.S.A. **Online address:** ringwc@sage.edu

RINPOCHE, Khandro. Indian (born India), b. 1968. **Genres:** History, Theology/Religion. **Career:** Lotus Garden Retreat Center, teacher; Western World, teacher; Nunnery in India, director; Buddhist nun and writer. **Publications:** This Precious Life: Tibetan Buddhist Teachings on the Path to Enlightenment, 2003. Contributor to periodicals. **Address:** c/o Author Mail, Shambhala Publications Inc., Horticultural Hall, 300 Massachusetts Ave., Boston, MA 02115, U.S.A.

RINZLER, Carol Ann. American (born United States), b. 1937. **Genres:** Food And Wine, Medicine/Health, Self Help, How-to Books. **Career:** Writer. **Publications:** The Book of Chocolate, 1977; Cosmetics: What the Ads Don't Tell You, 1977; The Signet Book of Yogurt, 1978; The Consumer's Brand Name Guide to Household Products, 1979; The Dictionary of Medical Folklore, 1980; Strictly Female: An Evaluation of Brand Name Health and Hygiene Products for Women, 1981; The Children's Medicine Chest, 1984; The Safe Pregnancy Book, 1984; What to Use Instead: A Handbook of Practical Substitutes, 1987; The Complete Book of Food: A Nutritional, Medical and Culinary Guide, 1987, 2nd ed., 2009; The Complete Book of Herbs, Spices and Condiments, 1990; Are You at Risk?: How to Identify and Reduce Your Risk for More Than 100 Diseases and Medical Conditions, 1991; Feed a Cold, Starve a Fever, 1991; Estrogen and Breast Cancer, a Warning to Women, 1993; The Women's Health Products Handbook, 1997; Nutrition for Dummies, 1997, 5th ed., 2011; (with L. Fishher) Healthy Eating on-the-go For Dummies, 1997; The Healing Power of Soy: The Enlightened Person's Guide to Nature's Surprising Wonder Food, 1998; Weight Loss Kit for Dummies, 2001; (with M.W. Graf) Controlling Cholesterol for Dummies, 2002; (with K. DeVault) Heartburn & Reflux for Dummies, 2004; The Encyclopedia of Cosmetic and Plastic Surgery, 2009; New Complete Book of Food: A Nutritional, Medical and Culinary Guide, 2009; Encyclopedia of Dental and Oral Health, 2010. **Address:** c/o Phyllis Westberg, Harold Ober Associates Inc., 425 Madison Ave., New York, NY 10017, U.S.A.

RIO, Michel. French (born France), b. 1945. **Genres:** Novels, Essays, Plays/Screenplays. **Career:** Writer. **Publications:** IN FRENCH: NOVELS: Accidents Siliceux Dans Le Crétacé Du Bassin Vocontien (sud-est de la France): Contribution à L'étude De La Silicification Des Formations Calcaires, 1982; Mélancolie Nord, 1982; Le Perchoir Du Perroquet, 1983; Alizés, 1984; Les Jungles Pensives: Roman, 1985; Archipel: Roman, 1987; Merlin: Roman, 1989; Faux Pas: Roman, 1991; Tlacuilo: Roman, 1992; Le Principe D'incertitude: Roman, 1993; Manhattan Terminus: Roman, 1995; La Statue de La Liberté: Roman, 1997; La Mort: Une Enquête De Francis Malone, 1998; Morgane, 1999; Arthur, 2001; La Remise Au Monde: Roman, 2002; La Terre Gaste: Roman, 2003; Lecond'abime, 2003. PLAYS: Baleine Pied-de-poule, 1990; L'Ouroboros: Théâtre, 1993; Transatlantique, 2002; Script, 2002; Sans Songer à Mal: Une Enquête De Francis Malone: Roman, 2004. OTHERS: Rêve De Logique: Essais Critiques (essays), 1992; Merlin, Le Faiseur De Rois, 2006; Malone, Tome 1, 2007; Coupe Réglée: Une Non-enquête De Francis Malone, 2009; Vazaha sans terre: Roman, 2011. **Address:** c/o Author Mail, Editions du Seuil, 27 rue Jacob, Paris, 75261, France.

RIORDAN, James (William). British (born England), b. 1936. **Genres:** Children's Fiction, Area Studies, Dance/Ballet, International Relations/Current Affairs, Sports/Fitness, Children's Non-fiction, Adult Non-fiction, Novels, Translations, Young Adult Fiction. **Career:** British Railways, clerk, 1956-57; Progress Publisher, senior translator, 1962-65; Portsmouth Polytechnic, lecturer in Russian, 1965-69; University of Bradford, senior lecturer and reader in Russian studies, 1971-89; University of Surrey, head of linguistic and international studies, 1989-, professor of Russian studies and head of the department, professor emeritus in communist studies, 2002-; University of Stirling, professor in sports studies, visiting professor, through 2006; St. Edmund's Catholic School, governor, link governor for English department and library; University of Worcester, visiting professor in sports studies, 2006-. Writer. **Publications:** FOR CHILDREN: (with E. Colwell) Little Grey Neck: A Russian Folktale, 1975; Beauty and the Beast, 1979; Sleeping Beauty, 1979; The Three Magic Gifts, 1980; The Secret Castle, 1980; Flight into Danger, 1980; Changing Shapes, 1982; The Little Humpback Horse, 1983; Peter and the Wolf, 1986; The Wild Swans, 1987; (reteller) Pinocchio, 1988; Babes in the Wood, 1989; The Snowmaiden, 1989; Thumbelina, 1990; Gulliver's Travel, 1992; (comp.) A Book of Narnians: The Lion, the Witch and the Others, 1994; My G-r-r-reat Uncle Tiger, 1995; The Barnyard Band: A Story from the Brothers Grimm, 1996; Grace the Pirate, 1996; The Twelve Labors of Hercules, 1997; Little Bunny Bobkin, 1998; (reteller) King Arthur, 1998; The Coming of Night: A Yoruba Tale from West Africa, 1999; The Story of Martin Luther King (biography), 2001; The Story of Nelson Mandela (biography), 2001; Match of Death, 2002; Boxcar Molly: A Story from the Great Depression, 2002; The Enemy: A Story from World War II, 2002; (reteller) Great Expectations, 2002; (with B. Myers) Enemy closes in, 2009; (with B. Myers) On the Run, 2009. COLLECTIONS FOR CHILDREN: Mistress of the Copper Mountain (folk tales), 1975; Tales from Central Russia: Russian Tales, vol. I, 1977; Tales from Tartary: Russian Tales, vol. II, 1978; A World of Fairy Tales, 1981; A World of Folk Tales, 1981; Tales of King Arthur, 1982; Tales from the Arabian Nights, 1983; The Boy Who Turned into a Goat, 1983; Petrushka and Other Tales from the Ballet, 1984; Stories from the Ballet, 1984, rev. ed. as Favorite Stories of the Ballet, 1984; (trans.) The Twelve Months: Fairy Tales by Soviet Writers, 1984; The Woman in the Moon, and Other Tales of Forgotten Heroines, 1985; A World of Myths and Legends, 1985; (trans.) Russian Gypsy Tales, 1986; (with B.R. Lewis) An Illustrated Treasury of Myths and Legends, 1987; The Sun Maiden and the Crescent Moon: Siberian Folk Tales, 1989; Korean Folk-tales, 1994; (ed.) A Treasury of Irish Stories, 1995; (comp.) Stories from the Sea, 1996; (ed.) The Songs My Paddle Sings: Native American Legends, 1996; (ed.) Young Oxford Book of Football Stories, 1999; (ed.) Young Oxford Book of Sports Stories, 2000; (ed.) Young Oxford Book of War Stories, 2000; (reteller) Russian Folk-Tales, 2000; The Storytelling Star: Tales of the Sun, Moon, and Stars, 2000. NON FICTION: (ed.) New Soviet Legislation on Marriage and the Family, 1973; Sport in Soviet Society: Development of Sport and Physical Education in Russia and the USSR, 1977; (ed.) Sport under Communism: The USSR, Czechoslovakia, the G.D.R., China, Cuba, 1978, rev. ed., 1981; Soviet Sport: Background to the Olympics, 1980; The Soviet Union: The Land and Its Peoples, 1987; Folktales of the British Isles, 1987; Eastern Europe: The Land and Their Peoples, 1987; (ed.) Soviet Education: The Gifted and the Handicapped, 1988; (ed.) Soviet Youth Culture, 1989; Soviet Youth Problems, 1989; Sports, Politics and Communism, 1991; (ed. and trans. with S. Bridger) Dear Comrade Editor: Readers' Letters to the Soviet Press under Perestroika, 1992; (ed.) Soviet Social Reality in the Mirror of Glasnost, 1992; (with V. Peppard) Playing Politics: Soviet Sport Diplomacy to 1992, 1993; (ed. with I.S. Kon) Sex and Russian Society, 1993, rev. ed. as The Sexual Revolution in Russia: From the Age of the Czars to Today, 1995; Russia and the Commonwealth of Independent States, 1993, rev. ed., 1999; (ed. with C. Williams and I. Ilynsky) Young People in Post-Communist Russia and Eastern Europe, 1995; (ed. with P. Mitev) Europe, the Young, the Balkans, 1996; (ed. with A. Krüger) The Story of Worker Sport, 1996; Dhá shaothar déag Earcail, 1997; (ed., trans. and intro.) Memories of the Dispossessed: Descendants of Kulak Families Tell Their Stories, 1998; (ed. with P. Arnaud) Sport and International Politics: The Impact of Fascism and Communism on Sport, 1998; (ed. with P. Arnaud) Sport et Relations Internationales (1900-1941): les démocraties face au fascisme et au nazisme, 1998; (ed. with R. Jones) Sport and Physical Education in China, 1999; (ed. with A. Krüger) The International Politics of Sport in the 20th Century, 1999; (ed. with A. Krüger) European Cultures in Sport: Examining the Nations and Regions, 2003; Jason and the Golden Fleece, 2003; (comp. with A. Krüger and T. Terret) Histoire du sport en Europe, 2004; Escape from War, 2005; Comrade Jim, 2009. NOVELS: Mistress of the Copper Mountain, 1970; Sweet Clarinet, 1998; The Prisoner, 1999; When the Guns Fall Silent, 2000; War Song, 2001; Boxcar Molly: A Story from the Great Depression, 2002. OTHER: (trans.) Lion and the Puppy, 2012. **Address:** St. Edmund's Catholic School, Arundel St., Portsmouth, HM PO1 1RX, England. **Online address:** jim@riordanj.freeserve.co.uk

RIORDAN, Rick. American (born United States), b. 1964. **Genres:** Mystery/Crime/Suspense, Young Adult Fiction. **Career:** Teacher, 1990-98. Writer. **Publications:** Big Red Tequila, 1997; The Widower's Two-Step, 1998; The Last King of Texas, 2000; The Devil Went Down to Austin, 2001; Cold Springs, 2003; Southtown, 2004; Mission Road, 2005; Lightning Thief, 2005; Sea of Monsters, 2006; Titan's Curse, 2007; Rebel Island, 2007; Battle of the Labyrinth, 2008; Maze of Bones, 2008; (ed. with L. Wilson) Demigods and Monsters, 2008; Demigod Files, 2009; Last Olympian, 2009; Lost Hero, 2010; Red Pyramid, 2010; Lightning Thief: The Graphic Novel, 2010; The Son of Neptune, 2011; (with P. Lerangis and G. Korman) Vespers Rising, 2011; The Throne of Fire, 2011. Contributor to magazines. **Address:** Hyperion Books for Children, 114 5th Ave., New York, NY 10011-5690, U.S.A. **Online address:** rick@rickriordan.com

RIORDAN, Teresa. American (born United States) **Genres:** Novels, Fashion/Costume. **Career:** Knight Science Journalism, fellow, 2000-01; New York Times, patents columnist, invention columnist. Writer. **Publications:** Inventing Beauty: A History of the Innovations That Have Made Us Beautiful, 2004. Contributor of articles to periodicals. **Address:** PO Box 11305, Takoma Park, MD 20913, U.S.A. **Online address:** tr@inventingbeauty.com

RIORDAN, Timothy B. American (born United States), b. 1952. **Genres:** History, Archaeology/Antiquities. **Career:** Historic St. Mary's City, chief archaeologist. Writer. **Publications:** (With W.H. Adams and S.D Smith) Archaeological Investigations at Waverly Ferry, Clay Co., Mississippi: Mitigation Interim Report, 1980; (contrib.) Silas D. Hurry, 'Once the Metropolis of Maryland': The History and Archaeology of Maryland's First Capital, 2001; The Plundering Time: Maryland and the English Civil War, 1645-1646, 2003; Prince of Quacks: The Notorious Life of Dr. Francis Tumblety, Charlatan and Jack the Ripper Suspect, 2009. Contributor to periodicals. **Address:** Historic St. Mary's City, PO Box 39, Saint Marys City, MD 20686, U.S.A.

RIORDON, Michael. Canadian (born Canada), b. 1944. **Genres:** Mystery/Crime/Suspense, Plays/Screenplays, Gay And Lesbian Issues, Social Sciences, History, Adult Non-fiction. **Career:** Freelance writer and film director, 1964-. **Publications:** The First Stone: Homosexuality and the United Church (nonfiction), 1990; Out Our Way: Gay and Lesbian Life in the Country (nonfiction), 1996; Eating Fire: Family Life, on the Queer Side, 2001; Unauthorized Biography of the World: Oral History on the Front Lines, 2004. **Address:** c/o Jan Whitford, Lucinda Vardey Agency, 297 Seaton St., Toronto, ON M5A 2T6, Canada. **Online address:** books@michaelriordon.net

RIOS, Julian. French/Spanish (born Spain), b. 1941. **Genres:** Novels, Translations, Young Adult Fiction. **Career:** Editor and author, 1970-; Editorial Fundamentos, Espiral Magazine, founder, 1974. **Publications:** (With O. Paz) Solo a dos voces, 1973, rev. ed., 1999; (co-author) Guillermo Cabrera Infante, 1974; (with O. Paz) Teatro de signos, 1974; Babel de una noche de San Juan, 1983; Larva (novel), 1983, trans. as (with R.A. Francis and S.J. Levine) Larva: Midsummer Night's Babel, 1990; Poundemonium: homenaje a Ezra Pound (novel), 1986, rev. ed. as Poundemonium: Larva, 1989; Impresiones de Kitaj: La novela pintada, 1989; La vida sexual de las palabras, 1991; Las Tentaciones de Antonio Saura, 1991; Retrato de Antonio Saura, 1991; (with E. Arroyo) Ulises ilustrado, 1991; (with E. Arroyo) Sombreros para Alicia, 1993; Kitaj: Pictures and Conversations, 1994, 1st ed., 1997; Album de Babel, 1995; Amores que atan, o, Belles lettres (a novel), 1995; Epifanias sin fin, 1996; Monstruario (novel), 1999; Nuevos sombreros para Alicia, 2001; (contrib.) En el taller de Miró, 2005; Larva y otras noches de Babel: antológa, 2007; Cortejo de sombras: la novela de Tamoga, 2007; Quijote e hijos: una genealóga literaria, 2008; Puente de Alma, 2009; The House of Ulysses: A Novel, 2010; Procession of Shadows, 2011. Contributor to books. **Address:** Carmen Balcells Agencia Literaria S.A., Diagonal 580, Barcelona, 08021, Spain.

RIPLEY, Catherine. Canadian (born Canada), b. 1957. **Genres:** Children's Non-fiction, Animals/Pets. **Career:** Cricket Magazine, editorial assistant, associate editor, 1979-81; Chickadee Magazine, editorial assistant, editor, 1982-91; Canadian Museum of Nature Publishing Division, Global Biodiversity, managing editor, 1992-. Writer. **Publications:** Night and Day, 1985; The Polka Dot Door Activity Book, 1987; Two Dozen Dinosaurs: A First Book of Dinosaur Facts, Mysteries, Games and Fun, 1991; Why Is Soap So Slippery? and Other Bathtime Questions, 1995; Do the Doors Open by Magic? and Other Supermarket Questions, 1995; Why Do Stars Twinkle? And Other Nighttime Questions, 1996; Why Is the Sky Blue? And Other Outdoor Questions, 1997; Why Does Popcorn Pop? And Other Kitchen Questions, 1997; Why Do Cows Moo? And Other Farmyard Questions, 1998; Why?: The Best Ever Question and Answer Book About Nature, Science and the World, 2001; Great Math Ideas, 2008; How?: The Most Awesome Question and Answer Book About Nature, Animals, People, Places and You!, 2012. COMPILER AND EDITOR: Kitchen Fun, 1988; Outdoor Fun, 1989; Party Fun, 1989; (with M. Baillie) The Anti-boredom Book, 1999. Contributor to periodicals. **Address:** c/o Publicity Director, Greey de Pencier Books, OWL Communications, 179 John St., Ste. 500, Toronto, ON M5T 3G5, Canada. **Online address:** catherine.ripley@epsb.ca

RIPLEY, Randall. (Randall B. Ripley). American (born United States), b. 1938. **Genres:** Politics/Government, Public/Social Administration, Social Sciences. **Career:** Harvard University, teaching fellow, 1960-62; Brookings Institution, research fellow, 1962-63, research assistant, 1963-64, research associate, 1964-67; Ohio State University, Department of Political Science, associate professor, 1967-69, professor, 1969-2005, chairman, 1969-91, College of Social and Behavioral Sciences, dean, 1992-2004, emeritus professor, 2005-. Writer. **Publications:** Party Whip Organizations in the United States House of Representatives, 1964; (with C.O. Jones) Role of Political Parties in Congress; a Bibliography and Research Guide, 1966; Party Leaders in the House of Representatives, 1967; Majority Party Leadership in Congress, 1969; Power in the Senate, 1969; The Politics of Economic and Human Resource Development, 1972; (co-author) Structure, Environment, and Policy Actions: Exploring a Model of Policy-Making, 1973; American National Government and Public Policy, 1974; Congress, 1975, 4th ed., 1988; (with G.A. Franklin) Congress, The Bureaucracy, and Public Policy, 1976, 5th ed. 1991; Policy Research and the Clinical Relationship, 1977; (with R.H. Davidson and S.C. Patterson) A More Perfect Union, 1979, 4th ed. 1989; (with G.A. Franklin) Bureaucracy and Policy Implementation, 1982, 2nd as Policy Implementation and Bureaucracy, 1986; (with G.A. Franklin) CETA: Politics and Policy 1973-1982, 1984; Policy Analysis in Political Science, 1985; (with S.C. Patterson and R.H. Davidson) More Perfect Union: Introduction to American Government, 1989; (with E.E. Slotnick) Readings in American Government and Politics, 1989, 3rd ed., 1999; (co-author) American Labor Unions in the Electoral Arena, 2001. EDITOR: Public Policies and Their Politics, 1966; (with T.J. Lowi) Legislative Politics U.S.A., 3rd ed., 1973; (with G.A. Franklin) Policy-Making in the Federal Executive Branch, 1975; (with G.A. Franklin) National Government and Policy in the United States, 1977; (with J.M. Lindsay) Congress Resurgent: Foreign and Defense Policy on Capitol Hill, 1993; (with J.M. Lindsay) U.S. Foreign Policy after the Cold War, 1997. **Address:** Department of Political Science, Ohio State University, 2116 Derby Hall, 154 N Oval Mall, Columbus, OH 43210, U.S.A. **Online address:** ripley.1@osu.edu

RIPLEY, Randall B. See **RIPLEY, Randall.**

RIPPE, James M. American (born United States), b. 1947. **Genres:** Medicine/Health, Sports/Fitness. **Career:** Alpha House Inc., founder and executive director, 1969-73; Credence House Inc., founder and executive director, 1970-74; Radcliffe Pottery Studio, director, 1970-74; Harvard School of Public Health, research assistant, 1975-76; University of Massachusetts-Worcester, Medical Center, Department of Cardiology, research associate, 1978-79, medical director of cardiac rehabilitation, 1981-85, instructor of medicine and fellow in cardiovascular medicine, 1981-83, Cardiac Catheterization Laboratory, attending physician, 1983-93, Medical School, assistant professor of medicine, 1983-88, associate professor of medicine, 1988-93, director of exercise physiology and nutrition laboratory, 1983-93, Journal of Intensive Care Medicine, editor-in-chief, 1985-; Harvard Medical School, clinical fellow in medicine, 1979-81; Massachusetts General Hospital, intern in internal medicine, 1979-80, resident in internal medicine, 1980-81; University of Massachusetts-Amherst, Department of Exercise Science, adjunct professor of exercise science, 1984-; Center for Clinical and Lifestyle Research (now Rippe Lifestyle Institute), director, 1988-; Medicine, Exercise, Nutrition and Health, editor-in-chief, 1990-95; Leaps & Bounds, medical and child development director, 1991-94; Television Food Network, medical editor, 1993-97; Tufts University, School of Medicine, associate professor of medicine, 1994-; Discovery Zone, medical and child development director, 1994-96; Interdisciplinary Council on Lifestyle and Obesity Management, chairman, 1996-99; Nutrition in Clinical Care, founding editor, 1997-98; Florida Hospital, founder and director, 1998-2008; University of Central Florida, adjunct faculty, 2003-, professor of biomedical sciences, 2005-, Center for Lifestyle Medicine, chairman, 2005-; University of South Florida, College of Medicine, affiliate associate professor of medicine, 2003-; American Journal of Lifestyle Medicine, editor-in-chief, 2006-; Rippe Health Evaluation, founder and director, 2008-; Orlando Regional Healthcare, Lifestyle Medicine Initiative, director, 2008-11. **Publications:** (With J.S. Alpert) Manual of Cardiovascular Diagnosis and Therapy, 1980, 4th ed., 1996; (ed. with M. Csete) Manual of Intensive Care Medicine, 1983, 4th ed., 2005; (R. Sweetgall and F.I. Katch) Fitness Walking, 1985; (co-ed.) Intensive Care Medicine, 1985, 6th ed., 2007; The Sports Performance Factors, 1986; (with A. Kashiwa) Fitness Walking for Women, 1987; (with A. Ulene) Ulene's Fitness Walking Book, 1988; Starting Your Personal Fitness Program, 1988; Walking for Health and Fitness, 1988; (with A. Ward and K. Dougherty) The Rockport Walking Program, 1989; Dr. James M. Rippes Fit for Success: Proven Strategies for Executive Health, 1989; (with A. Ward) Dr. James M. Rippe's Complete Book of Fitness Walking, 1989; (with P. Amend) The Exercise Exchange Program, 1992; The Polar Fat Free and Fit Forever Program, 1994; (co-ed.) Procedures and Techniques in Intensive Care Medicine, 1995, 4th ed., 2007; Fit over Forty: A Revolutionary Plan to Achieve Lifelong Physical and Spiritual Health and Well-Being, 1996; (ed. with R.S. Irwin and F.B. Cerra) Irwin and Rippe's Intensive Care Medicine, 4th ed., 1999, (ed. with R.S. Irwin) 6th ed., 2008; (ed.) Lifestyle Medicine, 1999; The Healthy Heart for Dummies, 2000; (with A.G. Myrdal, A.H. Kirkpatrick and M.A. Waite) The Healthy Heart Cookbook for Dummies, 2000; (ed. with J.T. Dwyer) Lifestyle Nutrition, 2001; (with S. McCarthy and M.A. Waite) The Joint Health Prescription: 8 Weeks to Stronger, Healthier, Younger Joints, 2001; (co-author) Lifestyle Obesity Management, 2003; Heart Disease for Dummies, 2004; (with W. Watchers) Weight Loss That Lasts: Break through the 10 Big Diet Myths, 2005; (ed. with R.S. Irwin and C.H. Linden) Manual of Overdoses and Poisonings, 2005; High Performance Health: 10 Real-Life Solutions to Redefine your Health and Revolutionize your Life, 2007; Your Plan for a Balanced Life, 2008; (ed. with T.J. Angelopoulos) Obesity: Prevention and Treatment, 2012; (ed.) Encyclopedia of Lifestyle Medicine and Health, 2012. Contributor to periodicals. **Address:** Rippe Lifestyle Institute, 21 N Quinsigamond Ave., Shrewsbury, MA 01545-2400, U.S.A.

RIPPLEY, LaVern J. American (born United States), b. 1935. **Genres:** History, Humanities, Language/Linguistics, Literary Criticism And History, Local History/Rural Topics, Translations, Art/Art History, Photography, Photography. **Career:** Ohio Wesleyan University, instructor, 1964-65, assistant professor of German, 1965-67; St. Olaf College, associate professor, 1967-71, professor of German, 1971-, chair of department, 1967-74, 1992-2000; Yearbook of German-American Studies, co-editor, 1981-. **Publications:** The Columbus Germans, 1968; Of German Ways, 1970; (trans. and ed.) N. Mohr, Excursion through America, 1973; (trans. and ed. with A. Bauer) R. Sallet, Russian-German Settlements in the United States, 1974; The German-Americans, 1976; (ed. and intro. and bibliography) H. Kloss, Research Possibilities in the German-American Field, 1980; (ed.) The Autobiography of Theodore F. Straub, 1981; The Immigrant Experience in Wisconsin, 1985; (with R.H.

Schmeissner) German Place Names in Minnesota: Deutsche Ortsnamen in Minnesota, 1989; German-Bohemian Roots of the Whoopee John Wilfahrt Dance Band, 1992; (trans. and adapted) W.P. Adams, German-Americans: An Ethnic Experience, 1993; (with J. Reppmann) Hans Reimer Claussen, 1804-1894: eine Lebensskizze: A Sketch of His Life, 1994; German-Bohemians: The Quiet Immigrants, 1995; (ed. with E. Reichmann and J. Nagler) Emigration and Settlement Patterns of German Communities in North America, 1995; Noble Women, Restless Men: The Rippley (Rieple, Ripley, Ripli, Rippli) Family in Wisconsin, North Dakota, Minnesota and Montana, 1996; Waumandee, Wisconsin, 1860-1960: An Affectionate Portrait, 2003; The Chemnitzer Concertina: A History and an Accolade, 2006. Contributor of articles to periodicals. **Address:** Department of German, St. Olaf College, Rm. 338, Tomson Hall, 1520 St., Olaf Ave., Northfield, MN 55057, U.S.A. **Online address:** rippleyl@stolaf.edu

RIPS, Michael. American (born United States), b. 1954?. **Genres:** Mystery/Crime/Suspense, Law, Autobiography/Memoirs, History. **Career:** US Supreme Court, clerk; Steptoe & Johnson L.L.P., Department of Litigation, special counsel. Writer. **Publications:** Pasquale's Nose: Idle Days in an Italian Town, 2001; The Face of a Naked Lady: An Omaha Family Mystery, 2005. **Address:** The Marsh Agency, 11 Dover St., London, GL W1S 4LJ, England. **Online address:** mrips@steptoe.com

RISCHIN, Moses. American (born United States), b. 1925. **Genres:** Cultural/Ethnic Topics, History, Biography, Theology/Religion, Essays. **Career:** City University of New York, Brooklyn College, lecturer, 1949-53; Brandeis University, instructor, 1953-54; New School for Social Research, lecturer, 1955-58; Institute of Human Relations, American Jewish Committee, research associate, 1956-58; Long Island University, assistant professor of history, 1958-59; Radcliffe College, Notable American Women, assistant editor, 1959-60; University of California, lecturer, 1962-64; San Francisco State University, faculty, 1964-, professor of history, professor emeritus, 2002-; University of Uppsala, Fulbright-Hays lecturer, 1969; Western Jewish History Center of the Magnes Museum, director, 1967-; Northern Illinois University Press, American Minority History Series, editor, 1973-; Center for the Study of Democratic Institutions, consultant; California Council for the Humanities, consultant; Harvard Encyclopedia for American Ethnic Groups, consultant. **Publications:** An Inventory of American Jewish History, 1954; Our Own Kind: Voting by Race, Creed or National Origin, 1960; The Promised City: New York's Jews 1870-1914, 1962; The American Gospel of Success: Individualism and Beyond, 1965; The Jews and Pluralism: Toward an American Freedom Symphony, 1980; (contrib.) An Inventory of Promises: Essays on American Jewish History in Honor of Moses Rischin, 1995. EDITOR: The Spirit of the Ghetto, 1967; (with S.J. Hurwitz) Liberal in Two Worlds: Essays of Solomon F. Bloom, 1968; Concentration Camps U.S.A., 1971; Bonds of Loyalty, 1974; The Abolitionists, 1974; Modern Jewish Experience series, 59 vols., 1975; First Majority, Last Minority, 1976; Immigration and the American Tradition, 1976; The Jews of the West: The Metropolitan Years, 1979; (with W.M. Brinner) Like All the Nations? The Life and Legacy of Judah L. Magnes, 1982; (and intro.) Grandma Never Lived in America: The New Journalism of Abraham Cahan, 1985; (and intro.) The Jews of North America, 1987; (with R. Asher) The Jewish Legacy and the German Conscience, 1991; (with J. Livingston) Jews of the American West, 1991; (with J. Sarna) American Jewish Civilization Series, 1991. Contributor to books. **Address:** Department of History, San Francisco State University, 1600 Holloway Ave., San Francisco, CA 94132-1722, U.S.A. **Online address:** mrischin@sfsu.edu

RISE, Eric W. American (born United States), b. 1963. **Genres:** Criminology/True Crime, History, Law. **Career:** University of Delaware, Department of Sociology and Criminal Justice, assistant professor, 1992-97, University faculty senator, 1994-96, 2004-, associate chair, 1997-, associate professor, 1997-, professor of sociology and criminal justice; American Journal of Legal History, associate editor. **Publications:** (With K.L. Hall) From Local Courts to National Tribunals: The Federal District Courts of Florida, 1821-1990, 1991; The Martinsville Seven: Race, Rape and Capital Punishment, 1995; The Supreme Court of Florida and Its Predecessor Courts, 1821-1917, 1997. **Address:** Department of Sociology & Criminal Justice, University of Delaware, 342 Smith Hall, Newark, DE 19716, U.S.A. **Online address:** erise@udel.edu

RISEBERO, Bill. British (born England), b. 1938. **Genres:** Architecture, Urban Studies, History. **Career:** Chamberlain Group, Department of Architects, junior assistant, 1957-59; Richard and Margaret Finch, assistant architect, 1963-65; Hugh Wilson and Lewis Womersley, architect and planning assistant, 1965-70; Chapman Taylor Partners, architect, 1970-73; Local Government, architect, planner, 1973-88; City of Westminster, assistant group planning officer, 1973-74; teacher, 1974-88; Railway Lands Project, principal assistant planner, 1974-80; Catholic University, faculty, 1977-78; University of East London, professor, 1988-, senior research fellow; University of the Arts, teacher; New York University-London, faculty; Polytechnic of the South Bank, faculty; Polytechnic of Central London, faculty; Polytechnic of North London, faculty; Nalgo (local government employees' union), trade union officer; Central Saint Martins College of Art and Design, faculty; Syracuse University, London Program, faculty. Writer. **Publications:** The Story of Western Architecture, 1979, 3rd ed., 2001; Modern Architecture and Design: An Alternative History, 1982; Fantastic Form: Architecture and Planning Today, 1992. **Address:** New York University, 6 Bedford Sq., London, GL WC1B 3RA, England.

RITCHIE, Daniel E. American (born United States), b. 1955. **Genres:** Literary Criticism And History, Philosophy, History. **Career:** National Review, editorial assistant, 1975; Courier-Journal, reporter, 1978; Daily Enterprise, reporter, 1978-79; Bethel College, professor of English, 1985-, department head, 1988-91, Humanities Program, director. **Publications:** Reconstructing Literature in an Ideological Age: A Biblical Poetics and Literary Studies from Milton to Burke, 1996; The Fullness of Knowing: Modernity and Postmodernity from Defoe to Gadamer, 2010. EDITOR: Edmund Burke: Appraisals and Applications, 1990; Further Reflections on the Revolution in France by Edmund Burke, 1992. Contributor of articles to books and periodicals. **Address:** Department of English, Bethel College, Rm. AC317, 3900 Bethel Dr., PO Box 86, St. Paul, MN 55112-6999, U.S.A. **Online address:** d-ritchie@bethel.edu

RITCHIE, Harry. Scottish (born Scotland), b. 1958. **Genres:** Essays, Novellas/Short Stories, Autobiography/Memoirs, Literary Criticism And History, Travel/Exploration, Novels, Young Adult Non-fiction, Young Adult Fiction, Young Adult Fiction. **Career:** Sunday Times, deputy literary editor, 1988-92, literary editor, 1993-95. **Publications:** Success Stories: Literature And the Media in England, 1950-59, 1988; Here We Go: A Summer on the Costa del Sol, 1993; The Last Pink Bits, 1997; (ed.) New Scottish Writing, 1996; (ed.) Acid Plaid: New Scottish Writing, 1997; Friday Night Club, 2002; Third Party, 2006. **Address:** c/o Rachel Calder, Tessa Sayle Agency, 11 Jubilee Pl., London, GL SW3 3TE, England.

RITCHIE, James A. American (born United States), b. 1953. **Genres:** Westerns/Adventure. **Career:** Writer. **Publications:** WESTERNS: Over on the Lonesome Side, 1991; The Payback, 1992; Kerrigan, 1993; The Last Free Range, 1995; The Wagon Wars, 1997. Contributor to journals. **Address:** c/o Alison J. Picard, PO Box 2000, Cotuit, MA 02635-2000, U.S.A. **Online address:** Jamesaritchie@yahoo.com

RITCHIE, Pamela E. Canadian (born Canada), b. 1971?. **Genres:** Politics/Government, History, Bibliography. **Career:** TannerRitchie Publishing, vice president, co-founder and partner. Writer. **Publications:** Mary of Guise in Scotland, 1548-1560: A Political Career, 2002; (contrib.) Bibliographical Dictionary of Scottish Women, 2006. **Address:** TannerRitchie Publishing, 357 Delaware Ave., Burlington, ON L7R 3B4, Canada. **Online address:** pamela@tannerritchie.com

RITER, Tim. American (born United States), b. 1948?. **Genres:** History, Theology/Religion, Psychology. **Career:** Hope International University, writing teacher, adjunct assistant professor of communication; Linfield Christian School, writing teacher; Azusa Pacific University, teacher of communications. Pastor and writer. **Publications:** Deep Down: Character Change through the Fruit of the Spirit, 1995; A Passionate Pursuit of God: How Knowing God Transforms Your Life, 1999; Twelve Lies You Hear about the Holy Spirit, 2004; Twelve Lies You Hear in Church, 2004; (with D. Timms) Just Leave God Out of It: Cultural Compromises we Make, 2004; Strong Enough to Be a Man: Reclaiming God's Plan for Masculinity, 2005; Twelve Lies Wives Tell Their Husbands, 2005; Twelve Lies Husbands Tell Their Wives, 2005; Not a Safe God: Wrestling with the Difficult Teachings of Jesus, 2006. **Address:** Hope International University, 2500 E Nutwood Ave., Fullerton, CA 92831, U.S.A.

RITTER, Gretchen. American (born United States) **Genres:** Social Sciences. **Career:** University of Texas, associate professor of government, Center for Women's and Gender Studies, director; Princeton University, faculty; Harvard Law School, faculty. Educator and author. **Publications:** Goldbugs and Greenbacks: The Antimonopoly Tradition and the Politics of Finance in America, 1865-1896, 1997; The Constitution as Social Design: Gender and Civic Membership in the American Constitutional Order, 2006. Contributor of articles to journals. **Address:** Garamond Agency Inc., 12 Horton St., Newburyport, MA 01950, U.S.A. **Online address:** ritterg@mail.utexas.edu

RITTERHOUSE, Jennifer. (Jennifer Lynn Ritterhouse). American (born United States), b. 1970. **Genres:** History, Social Sciences. **Career:** University of North Carolina, Southern Oral History Program, Publicity and Media Relations, research assistant, 1999; Duke University, Center for Documentary Studies, research associate, 1999-2000; Utah State University, Department of History, assistant professor, 2000-06, associate professor, 2006-. Writer. **Publications:** (ed. and intro.) The Desegregated Heart: A Virginian's Stand in Time of Transition, 2001; (co-ed.) Remembering Jim Crow: African Americans Tell about Life in the Segregated South: A Collection of Oral History Interviews from Behind the Veil, 2001; Growing Up Jim Crow: How Black and White Southern Children Learned Race, 2006. Contributor to journals and periodicals. **Address:** Department of History, Utah State University, Main 323, Logan, UT 84322-0710, U.S.A. **Online address:** jennifer.ritterhouse@usu.edu

RITTERHOUSE, Jennifer Lynn. *See* **RITTERHOUSE, Jennifer.**

RITTHALER, Shelly. American (born United States), b. 1955. **Genres:** Children's Fiction, Young Adult Fiction, History, Literary Criticism And History. **Career:** Eastern Wyoming College, teacher in creative writing; University of Wyoming, trustee. Writer. **Publications:** FOR CHILDREN: Dinosaurs for Lunch, 1993; Dinosaurs Wild, 1994; Dinosaurs Alive, 1994. YOUNG ADULT NOVELS: Heart of Hills, 1996; With Love, Amanda, 1997. OTHER: Weston County-The First 100 Years, 1989; The Ginger Jar (essays), 1990; Through the Cooperation of People-Fifty Years of Service: Tri-County Electric Association: The First Fifty Years, 1995. Contributor to periodicals. **Address:** PO Box 160, Upton, WY 82730-0160, U.S.A.

RITVO, Harriet. American (born United States), b. 1946. **Genres:** History, Animals/Pets, Natural History. **Career:** Harvard University, teaching fellow in history, literature and English, 1971-75; University of Massachusetts, lecturer in English, 1974-75; Boston University, Office of Sponsored Research, assistant director, 1975-76; American Academy of Arts and Sciences, staff associate, 1976-79, editor, 1977-79; Massachusetts Institute of Technology, Humanities Department, lecturer, 1979-80, School of Humanities and Social Science, assistant, 1979-80, Writing Program, assistant director, 1980-81, assistant professor, 1980-85, associate professor, 1985-91, professor of history, 1991-95, associate dean, 1992-95, Arthur J. Conner professor of history, 1995-, head, 1999-2006. Writer. **Publications:** The Diminishing Countryside: Studies In Georgic Fiction, 1800-1875, 1975; The Animal Estate: The English and Other Creatures in the Victorian Age, 1987; (ed. with J. Arac) Macropolitics of Nineteenth-Century Literature: Nationalism, Exoticism, Imperialism, 1991; (co-author) An English Arcadia: Landscape and Architecture in Britain and America, 1992; (with T.L. Lott and R. Platt) Next of Kin: Looking at the Great Apes: James Balog, Walton Ford, Sean Landers, Jean Lowe, Richard Ross, Daisy Youngblood, 1995; The Platypus and the Mermaid, and Other Figments of the Classifying Imagination, 1997; (foreword) The Variation of Animals and Plants Under Domestication, 1998; Dawn of Green: Manchester, Thirlmere, and Modern Environmentalism, 2009; Noble Cows and Hybrid Zebras: Essays on Animals and History, 2010. **Address:** Department of History, Massachusetts Institute of Technology, Bldg. E51-287, 77 Massachusetts Ave., Cambridge, MA 02139, U.S.A. **Online address:** ritvo@mit.edu

RIVARD, David. American (born United States), b. 1953. **Genres:** Poetry. **Career:** Santa Clara University, Department of English, lecturer, 1985-86; Tufts University, Department of English, lecturer, 1987-2008; Sarah Lawrence College, visiting professor, 1996-97; Vermont College, teacher for Writing Program, faculty, 1989-99, 2005; Harvard Review, poetry editor, 1995-2000; University of New Hampshire, Department of English, associate professor, 2008-, professor. Writer. **Publications:** POETRY: Torque, 1988; Wise Poison, 1996; Bewitched Playground, 2000; Sugartown, 2006; The Insubordinate Powers of A Glamorous Day, 2011; Otherwise Elsewhere, 2011. Contributor to periodicals. **Address:** Department of English, University of New Hampshire, 207 Hamilton Smith Hall, Durham, NH 03824-3574, U.S.A. **Online address:** david.rivard@unh.edu

RIVARD, Robert. American (born United States), b. 1952. **Genres:** Novels, Mystery/Crime/Suspense. **Career:** Brownsville Herald, sports reporter; Cor-

pus Christi Caller Times, news reporter; 1970; Dallas Times Herald, news reporter, 1980-83; Newsweek Magazine, Central American bureau chief, chief of correspondent, 1983-89, senior editor; San Antonio Light, reporter, 1989-93; San Antonio Express-News, reporter, 1993-94, managing editor, 1994-97, editor and executive vice president of news, 1997-; Inter American Press Association, director. **Publications:** Trail of Feathers: Searching for Philip True: A Reporter's Murder in Mexico and His Editor's Search for Justice, 2005. **Address:** San Antonio Express-News, 301 Ave. E, San Antonio, TX 78205, U.S.A. **Online address:** bob@robertrivard.com

RIVAS, Manuel. Spanish (born Spain), b. 1957?. **Genres:** Novels, Novellas/Short Stories, Poetry. **Career:** Luzes de Galicia magazine, director and editor. **Publications:** Libro do entroido, 1979; (with X. Seoane) Anisia e outras sombras (title means: 'Anisia and Other Shadows'), 1981; Balada nas praias do Oeste, 1985; Mohicania (poetry), 1987; Galicia, el bonsáiatlántico: Descripción del antiguo reino del oeste (journalism), 1989, rev. ed., 1994; Ningún cisne, 1989; Unmillón de vacas (short stories; title means: 'A Million Cows'), 1990; No mellor país do mundo, 1991; Os comedores de patacas, 1991; Toxos eflores, 1992; Millón de vaques, 1993; En sanvaje compañía, 1994; En salvaje compañía, 1994; Costa da Morte Blues, 1995; Que me queres, amor?, 1995; El pueblode la noche, 1997; El periodismo esun cuento, 1997; El lápiz del carpintero (novel), 1999, trans. as The Carpenter's Pencil, 2001; El secreto de la tierra, 1999; Ella, malditaalma, 1999; Lapis do carpinteiro, 1999; (with X. Estéves) Compostela, vanguardia y sosiego, 2000; Butterfly's Tongue, 2000; Mandos paíños, 2000; Vermeer's Milkmaid: And Other Stories, 2001; Llamadas perdidas, 2002; In the Wilderness, 2003; Espía no reino de Galicia, 2004; Espía en el reino de Galicia, 2005; O Heroe, 2005; Libros arden mal, 2006; Grouchos, 2008; A cuerpo abierto, 2008; Desaparicion da neve = la desaparicio de la neu, elurraren urtzea, la desaparicoin de la nieve/Manuel vas, 2009; Episodios galegos: tempos de esperpento, 2009; Todo é silencio, 2010; Books Burn Badly, 2010; In the Wilderness, 2011. Contributor to periodicals. **Address:** c/o Author Mail, Overlook Press, 1 Overlook Dr., Woodstock, NY 12498, U.S.A.

RIVAS, Mim Eichler. American (born United States) **Genres:** Novels. **Career:** Writer. **Publications:** (With J. Stallone) Starpower: An Astrological Guide to Supersuccess, 1989; (with R.G. Singleton and B. Brown) Berry, Me and Motown: The Untold Story, 1990; How to Sell Your Idea to Hollywood, 1991; Angels along the Way: My Life with Help from Above, 1998; (with A.W. Fisher) Finding Fish: A Memoir, 2001; Beautiful Jim Key: The Lost History of a Horse and a Man Who Changed the World, 2005; (with C. Gardner and Q. Troupe) The Pursuit of Happyness, 2006; (with C. Gardner) Start Where You Are: Life Lessons in Getting from Where You Are to Where You Want To Be, 2009; (with D. Phelps) A Mother for all Seasons, 2009; (with C. Robinson) A Game of Character: A Family Journey from Chicago's Southside to the Ivy League and Beyond, 2010; (with S. Stoute) The Tanning of America: How Hip-Hop Created a Culture that Rewrote the Rules of the New Economy, 2011; (with A. Quiñones-Hinojosa) Becoming Dr. Q, 2011. **Address:** Elizabeth Kaplan Literary Agency, 80 5th Ave., Ste. 1101, New York, NY 10011, U.S.A. **Online address:** mim@bringbackkindness.com

RIVENBARK, Celia. American (born United States) **Genres:** Novels, Adult Non-fiction. **Career:** Sun News, news reporter and freelance columnist; Wallace, reporter and photographer; Morning Star, reporter and photographer; Enterprise, reporter and photographer; Wilmington, reporter and photographer. **Publications:** Bless Your Heart, Tramp, 2000; We're Just Like You, Only Prettier: Confessions of a Tarnished Southern Belle, 2004; Stop Dressing Your Six-Year-Old Like a Skank: And Other Words of Delicate Southern Wisdom, 2006; Belle Weather, Mostly Sunny with a Chance of Scattered Hissy Fits, 2008; You Can't Drink All Day If You Don't Start in the Morning, 2009; You Don't Sweat Much for a Fat Girl: Observations on Life from the Shallow End of the Pool, 2011. Contributor to periodicals. **Address:** Sun News, PO Box 406, Myrtle Beach, SC 29578, U.S.A. **Online address:** celiariven@aol.com

RIVERA, Eléna. American/Mexican (born Mexico) **Genres:** Poetry, Translations. **Career:** Brown University, instructor in learning community, 1996-98, lead encoder and text editor for university web site, 1999; New York University, adjunct associate professor, 2001-; New School for Social Research, instructor, 2001-04; Bard College, Institute for Writing and Thinking, faculty, 2002-. Writer. **Publications:** Fugitive (poetry), 1992; The Artist as a Young

Woman (poetry), 1993; In the Bed of the Press (poetry), 1993; The Wait; or Homer's Penelope (poetry), 1994; Wale or The Corse (poetry), 1994; (co-ed.) Facts and Fictions: A Millennial Celebration, 1999; Unknowne Land (poetry), 2000; Suggestions at Every Turn, 2005; Disturbances in the Ocean of Air, 2005; Mistakes, Accidents and the Want of Liberty, 2006; In Respect of Distance, 2007; (trans.) I.B. Howald, Secret of Breath, 2008. Works appear in anthologies. Contributor to periodicals. **Address:** School of Continuing and Professional Studies, New York University, Rm. 201, 7 E 12th St., Ste. 923, New York, NY 10003, U.S.A. **Online address:** rivera@bard.edu

RIVERBEND. Iraqi (born Iraq), b. 1979?. **Genres:** Novels, History, Social Sciences, Humanities. **Career:** Writer and computer programmer. **Publications:** Baghdad Burning: Girl Blog from Iraq, 2005; Baghdad Burning II: More Girl Blog from Iraq, 2006. Contributor to periodicals. **Address:** c/o Author Mail, The Feminist Press, City University of New York, The Graduate Ctr., 365 5th Ave., Ste. 5406, New York, NY 10016, U.S.A. **Online address:** baghdad.burning@gmail.com

RIVERS, Francine (Sandra). American (born United States), b. 1947. **Genres:** Novels, Novellas/Short Stories, Romance/Historical, Young Adult Fiction. **Career:** Pleasanton Times, reporter, 1967; Transinternational Airlines, stewardess, 1969; California Lung Association, secretary, 1970-73; Alameda Naval Air Station, preschool teacher, 1974-77; freelance writer, 1977-. **Publications:** NOVELS: Kathleen, 1979; Sycamore Hill, 1981; Rebel in His Arms, 1981; This Golden Valley, 1983; Sarina, 1983; An Echo in the Darkness, 1994; As Sure as the Dawn, 1995; The Scarlet Thread, 1996; The Atonement Child, 1997; The Last Sin Eater, 1998; Leota's Garden, 1999; Priest: A Novella, 2004; Prince, 2005; Warrior: A Novella, 2005; Prophet: A Novella, 2006; Scribe: A Novella, 2007. ROMANCE NOVELS: Hearts Divided, 1983; Heart in Hiding, 1984; Pagan Heart, 1985; A Fire in the Heart, 1987; Redeeming Love, 1991. HISTORICAL NOVELS: Not So Wild a Dream, 1985; A Voice in the Wind, 1993. STORIES: Unveiled, 2000; Unashamed, 2000; Unshaken, 2001; Unspoken, 2001; Unafraid, 2001. OTHERS: Shoe Box: A Christmas Story, 1999; And the Shofar Blew, 2003; (with S.R. Coibion) Bible Stories for Growing Kids, 2007, trans. as Historias bíblicas para niños, 2008; Lineage of Grace: Five Stories of Unlikely Women who Changed Eternity, 2009; Her Daughter's Dream, 2010; El sueño de su hija, 2010; Her Mother's Hope, 2010. **Address:** c/o Jane Jordan Browne, Browne & Miller Literary Associates, 410 S Michigan Ave., Ste. 460, Chicago, IL 60605-1495, U.S.A.

RIVERS, Karen. Canadian (born Canada), b. 1970. **Genres:** Novellas/Short Stories. **Career:** Writer. **Publications:** The Tree Tattoo, 1999; Dream Water, 1999; Waiting to Dive, 2001; Surviving Sam, 2001; You Be Me: Friendship in the Lives of Teen Girls, 2002; The Gold Diggers Club, 2002; The Healing Time of Hickeys, 2002; Cure for Crushes, 2005; The Quirky Girls' Guide to Rest Stops and Road Trips, 2006; Barely Hanging On, 2007; X in Flight, 2007; The Actual Total Truth, 2007; Miss Kiss., 2007; Y in the Shadows, 2008; What Z Sees, 2008; What is Real, 2011; The Encyclopedia of Me, 2012. Works appear in anthologies. **Address:** FinePrint Literary Management, 240 W 35th St., Ste. 500, New York, NY 10001-2506, U.S.A. **Online address:** karen@karenrivers.com

RIVERS, Larry E. American (born United States), b. 1950?. **Genres:** Theology/Religion, Social Sciences, History. **Career:** Florida A&M University, professor of history, administrator, College of Arts and Sciences, dean, 2002-06; Fort Valley State University, president, 2006-; Florida Southern College, Lawton M. Chiles Center for Florida History, advisor. Writer. **Publications:** (Contrib.) The African American Heritage of Florida, 1995; (contrib.) Florida's Heritage of Diversity, 1997; Slavery in Florida: Territorial Days to Emancipation, 2000; (with C. Brown, Jr.) Laborers in the Vineyard of the Lord: The Beginnings of the AME Church in Florida, 1865- 1895, 2001; (ed. with R. Mathews and C. Brown, Jr.) Lays in Summer Lands, 2002; (with C. Brown, Jr.) For a Great and Grand Purpose: The Beginnings of the AMEZ Church in Florida, 1864- 1905, 2004; (ed. with C. Brown, Jr.) Varieties of Women's Experiences, 2009. Contributor of articles to periodicals. **Address:** Fort Valley State University, 1005 State University Dr., Fort Valley, GA 31030-4313, U.S.A.

RIVERS, Reggie. American (born United States), b. 1968. **Genres:** Novels, Mystery/Crime/Suspense, Young Adult Non-fiction. **Career:** San Antonio Light, obituary writer, 1985; Rocky Mountain News, weekly sports columnist, 1991-99; KOA-AM, radio talk show host, 1997-99; KHOW-AM, radio show host, 1999-2002; Denver Post, editorial columnist; Pro Football Week-ly, columnist; KCNC Channel 4, Countdown to Kickoff, co-host; American Broadcasting Corp., College Football Division, analyst. Writer and athlete. **Publications:** (With V. Johnson) The Vance: The Beginning & the End, 1994; Power Shift, 2000; 4th and Fixed, 2004; My Wife's Boyfriend: And Our Feud with the Highlands Ranch Homeowners Association, 2006; The Colony: A Political Tale, 2009. **Address:** c/o Author Mail, Sourcebooks Inc., 1935 Brookdale Rd., Ste. 139, Naperville, IL 60563-2773, U.S.A. **Online address:** reggierivers2002@yahoo.com

RIVIERE, Jim (E.). American (born United States), b. 1953. **Genres:** Sciences, Medicine/Health, Environmental Sciences/Ecology. **Career:** North Carolina State University, College of Veterinary Medicine, Center for Chemical Toxicology Research and Pharmacokinetics, director, 1981-, Department of Population Health and Pathobiology, Burroughs Wellcome Fund distinguished professor of pharmacology, 1981-, alumni distinguished graduate professor, 2010-. Writer. **Publications:** (With A.L. Craigmill and S.F. Sundlof) Handbook of Comparative Pharmacokinetics and Residues of Veterinary Antimicrobials, 1991; (with A.L. Craigmill and S.F. Sundlof) Handbook of Comparative Pharmacokinetics and Residues of Veterinary Therapeutic Drugs, 1994; (with A.L. Craigmill and S.F. Sundlof) Handbook of Comparative Veterinary Pharmacokinetics and Residues of Pesticides and Environmental Contaminants, 1995; Comparative Pharmacokinetics: Principles, Techniques, and Applications, 1999, 2nd ed., 2011; Chemical Food Safety, 2002; (ed.) Dermal Absorption Models in Toxicology and Pharmacology, 2005; (with A.L. Craigmill and A.I. Webb) Tabulation of FARAD Comparative and Veterinary Pharmacokinetic Data, 2006; (ed.) Biological Concepts and Techniques in Toxicology: An Integrated Approach, 2006; (ed. with M.G. Papich and H.R. Adams) Veterinary Pharmacology and Therapeutics, 9th ed., 2009. **Address:** Department of Population Health and Pathobiology, North Carolina State University, Rm. D-332, Main Bldg., 1060 William Moore Dr., PO BOX 8401, Raleigh, NC 27607, U.S.A. **Online address:** jim_riviere@ncsu.edu

RIVIÈRE, William. British/Italian (born Italy), b. 1954. **Genres:** Novels, Young Adult Fiction, History. **Career:** University of Verona, faculty, 1980-84; Osaka Gakuin University, faculty, 1985-89; University of Urbino, faculty, 1990-, professor of modern English literature, 1999-; Royal Society of Literature, fellow, 2000. Writer. **Publications:** Watercolour Sky, 1990; A Venetian Theory of Heaven, 1992; Eros and Psyche, 1994; Borneo Fire, 1995; Echoes of War, 1997; Kate Caterina, 2001; By the Grand Canal, 2004. **Address:** Peters, Fraser & Dunlop, Drury House, 34-43 Russell St., London, GL WC2B 5HA, England. **Online address:** ahardman@pfd.co.uk

RIVKIN, Steve. American (born United States), b. 1947. **Genres:** Marketing, Business/Trade/Industry. **Career:** Iron Age magazine, associate editor; Financial Marketing Abstracts, co-founder and editor; International Utilities Corp., staff; Trout & Ries Inc., executive vice president; Rivkin & Associates L.L.C., founder, 1989; Estes Park Institute, faculty, Health Communications & Marketing Strategy, senior fellow; Volunteers in Medicine Institute, board director. **Publications:** (With J. Trout) The New Positioning: The Latest on the World's Number-One Business Strategy, 1995; (with H. Greeley) To the Point: Effective Communications for the Medical Staff, 1996; (with J. Trout) The Power of Simplicity: A Management Guide to Cutting through the Nonsense and Doing Things Right, 1999; (with J. Trout) Differentiate or Die: Survival in Our Era of Killer Competition, 2000, 2nd ed., 2008; (with F. Seitel) IdeaWise: How to Transform Your Ideas into Tomorrows Innovations, 2002; (with F. Sutherland) The Making of a Name: The Inside Story of the Brands We Buy, 2004; (with J. Trout) Repositioning: Marketing in an Era of Competition, Change and Crisis, 2010. Contributor to periodicals. **Address:** Rivkin & Associates L.L.C., 233 Rock Rd., Ste. 130, PO Box 188, Glen Rock, NJ 07452, U.S.A. **Online address:** steve@rivkin.net

RIVLIN, Gary. American (born United States), b. 1958. **Genres:** Politics/Government. **Career:** Chicago Reader, staff writer, 1985-89; Conta Costa Times, reporter, 1990-91; East Bay Express, staff writer, 1990-96, executive editor, 1998-99; freelance writer, 1995-98, 2002-03; The Industry Standard, senior writer and editor, 2000-01; Wired Magazine, contributing editor, 2001-04; New York Times, technical reporter, 2004-. **Publications:** Fire on the Prairie: Chicago's Harold Washington and the Politics of Race, 1992; Drive-By, 1995; The Plot to Get Bill Gates: An Irreverent Investigation of the World's Richest Man-and the People Who Hate Him, 1999; The Godfather of Silicon Valley: Ron Conway and the Fall of the Dot-Coms, 2002; Broke, USA: From Pawnshops to Poverty, Inc. - How the Working Poor Became Big Business,

2010. **Address:** Elizabeth Kaplan Literary Agency, 80 5th Ave., Ste. 1101, New York, NY 10011, U.S.A. **Online address:** grivlin@garyrivlin.com

RIVLIN, Paul Anthony. Israeli/British (born England), b. 1952. **Genres:** Economics, History, Business/Trade/Industry. **Career:** University of London, part-time lecturer, 1978-79; Jerusalem Institute of Management, faculty, 1985-87; Bank Hapoalim, Planning and Budgeting Department of International Division, staff, 1988-89; Middle East Economics, managing editor, 1989-; Tel Aviv University, Moshe Dayan Center for Middle East and African Studies, fellow, 1995-; Lloyds Bank Intl., staff; International Institute for Strategic Studies, staff. **Publications:** Liberalization of the Egyptian Economy: An Examination of the Decision-Making Process, 1981; The Dynamics of Economic Policy Making in Egypt, 1985; The Israeli Economy, 1992; (with E. Ziser) Syria: Domestic Political Stress and Globalization, 1999; Economic Policy and Performance in the Arab World, 2001; Political Stability in Arab States: Economic Causes and Consequences, 2004; Arab Economies in the Twenty-First Century, 2009; Israeli Economy from the Foundation of the State Through the 21st Century, 2010. Works appear in anthologies. **Address:** The Moshe Dayan Center, for Middle Eastern and African Studies, Tel Aviv University, Ramat Aviv, 69978, Israel. **Online address:** privlin@post.tau.ac.il

RIZZO, Margaret. American (born United States) **Genres:** Education, Librarianship, Literary Criticism And History. **Career:** Burnt Hills-Ballston Lake Central Schools, Richard H. O'Rourke Middle School, school library media specialist, 1972-, K-12 Library Department, department head, 1999-; Schenectady County Community College, adjunct instructor in English, 1981-2000. Writer. **Publications:** WITH R. JWEID: The Library-Classroom Partnership: Teaching Library Media Skills in Middle and Junior High Schools, 1988, 2nd ed., 1998; Building Character through Literature: A Guide for Middle School Readers, 2001; Building Character through Multicultural Literature: A Guide for Middle School Readers, 2004. OTHERS: (with J. Brown) Building Character Through Community Service: Strategies to Implement the Missing Element in Education, 2006; (with J. Newman) Sara's Rocking Chair, forthcoming. **Address:** Richard H. O'Rourke Middle School, Burnt Hills-Ballston Lake Central Schools, 173 Lakehill Rd., Burnt Hills, NY 12027, U.S.A. **Online address:** mrizzo@bhbl.org

ROACH, Archie. Australian (born Australia), b. 1956?. **Genres:** Songs/Lyrics And Libretti, Picture/Board Books. **Career:** Writer and composer. **Publications:** You Have the Power, 1994; Took the Children Away, 2009. **Address:** Festival Mushroom Records, 27 Dudley St., West Melbourne, VI 3003, Australia. **Online address:** jmas16@bigpond.com

ROACH, Catherine M. American/Canadian (born Canada), b. 1965?. **Genres:** Environmental Sciences/Ecology, Sex, Social Sciences, Biography, Autobiography/Memoirs. **Career:** University of Alabama, New College, faculty, 1998-2005, professor, Department of Religious Studies, assistant professor of religious studies, associate professor, 2004-, graduate adjunct faculty women's studies. Writer. **Publications:** Mother/Nature: Popular Culture and Environmental Ethics, 2002; Stripping, Sex and Popular Culture, 2007. **Address:** Department of Religious Studies, University of Alabama, 101F Carmichael Hall, Tuscaloosa, AL 35487, U.S.A. **Online address:** croach@nc.ua.edu

ROADS, Michael J. Australian/British (born England), b. 1937. **Genres:** Environmental Sciences/Ecology. **Career:** Writer, 1976-. **Publications:** A Guide to Organic Gardening in Australia, 1976; A Guide to Organic Living in Australia, 1977; Talking with Nature: Sharing the Energies and Trees, Plants, Birds and Earth, 1987; The Natural Magic of Mulch, 1989; Journey into Nature: A Spiritual Adventure, 1990; Simple Is Powerful: Anecdotes for a Complex World, 1992, rev. ed. as A Glimpse of Something Greater, 2011; Journey into Oneness: A Spiritual Odyssey, 1994; Into a Timeless Realm, 1995; Getting There: A Novel, 1998; The Magic Formula: It Works!, 2003; (co-author) More than Money, True Prosperity: A Wholistic Guide to Having it All, 2004; Through the Eyes of Love: Journeying with Pan, 2008; Conscious Gardening, 2008. **Address:** PO Box 778, Nambour, QL 4560, Australia. **Online address:** roadsway@optusnet.com.au

ROAHEN, Sara. American (born United States), b. 1970?. **Genres:** Food And Wine. **Career:** Gambit Weekly, restaurant critic. Writer and oral historian. **Publications:** Gumbo Tales: Finding My Place at the New Orleans Table, 2008. Works appear in anthologies. Contributor to periodicals. **Address:** c/o

Esmond Harmsworth, Zachary Shuster Harmsworth L.L.C., 535 Boylston St., 11th Fl., Boston, MA 02116, U.S.A. **Online address:** mothgirl@earthlink.net

ROARK, Dallas M. American (born United States), b. 1931. **Genres:** Intellectual History, Philosophy, Theology/Religion, Biography. **Career:** Baptist Church, pastor, 1956-60; Wayland Baptist College, instructor, 1960-63, assistant professor, 1963-65, associate professor of religion, 1965-66; Emporia State University, Department of Social Sciences, professor of philosophy, 1966-2001, emeritus professor of philosophy, 2001-. Writer. **Publications:** (Ed.) The Wayland Lectures, 1962; The Christian Faith, 1969; Dietrich Bonhoeffer, 1972; Introduction to Philosophy, 1979. Contributor to journals. **Address:** Department of Social Sciences, Emporia State University, 411 Plumb Hall, 1200 Commercial St., PO Box 4032, Emporia, KS 66801-5057, U.S.A.

ROBARDS, Elizabeth. *See* **THOMPSON, Nancy Robards.**

ROBB, B. R. (Bruce Robb Steinberg). American (born United States), b. 1958. **Genres:** Novels, Mystery/Crime/Suspense, Young Adult Fiction. **Career:** Bruce Steinberg Law Office P.C., attorney, 1987-. Freelance writer. **Publications:** (As Bruce Steinberg) The Widow's Son, 2001; River Ghosts, 2008. **Address:** Bruce Steinberg Law Office, 428 S Batavia Ave., Batavia, IL 60510, U.S.A. **Online address:** steinberglaw@aol.com

ROBB, Candace. American (born United States), b. 1950. **Genres:** Mystery/Crime/Suspense, Literary Criticism And History. **Career:** American Airlines, reservation sales agent, 1973-74; University of Cincinnati, instructor; 1974-78; Pan Am Base Services, technical writer, 1979-80; University of Washington, Applied Physics Laboratory, editor of research publications, 1980-93; University of Washington Extension, creative writing instructor, 1996-98. **Publications:** OWEN ARCHER MYSTERIES: Apothecary Rose: A Medieval Mystery, 1993; The Lady Chapel, 1994; The Nun's Tale, 1995; The King's Bishop, 1996; The Riddle of St. Leonard's, 1997; A Gift of Sanctuary, 1998; A Spy for the Redeemer, 2002; The Cross-legged Knight, 2003; The Guilt of Innocents, 2007; A Vigil of Spies, 2008. OTHERS: A Trust Betrayed: First Chapter of Margaret Kerr of Perth, 2001; The Fire in the Flint, 2003; A Cruel Courtship, 2004. **Address:** PO Box 15902, Seattle, WA 98115-0902, U.S.A.

ROBB, Christina. American (born United States), b. 1946. **Genres:** Psychology, Adult Non-fiction, Medicine/Health. **Career:** Boston Globe, cultural reporter and book critic, staff writer, through 1992; Harvard University, Bunting Institute, researcher. **Publications:** This Changes Everything: The Relational Revolution in Psychology, 2006. **Address:** Farrar, Straus and Giroux Book Publishers, 19 Union Sq. W, New York, NY 10003, U.S.A. **Online address:** christina@christinarobb.com

ROBB, Daniel. American (born United States), b. 1965?. **Genres:** Autobiography/Memoirs, Homes/Gardens, Sports/Fitness. **Career:** Writer, political consultant and educator. **Publications:** Crossing the Water: Eighteen Months on an Island Working with Troubled Boys: A Teacher's Memoir, 2001; Sloop: Restoring My Family's Wooden Sailboat: An Adventure in Old-fashioned Values, 2008. **Address:** Woods Hole, MA , U.S.A. **Online address:** sloop2008@gmail.com

ROBB, David L. American (born United States) **Genres:** Film, Politics/Government, History, Humor/Satire. **Career:** Daily Variety, labor and legal reporter; Hollywood Reporter, labor and legal reporter. **Publications:** Operation Hollywood: How the Pentagon Shapes and Censors the Movies, 2004; Shrink and the Gumshoe: Nixon, Kennedy and the Secret History of the 1960 Election, 2010. Contributor to periodicals. **Address:** c/o Author Mail, Prometheus Books, 59 John Glenn Dr., Amherst, NY 14228-2197, U.S.A.

ROBB, George. American (born United States), b. 1964. **Genres:** History. **Career:** St. Bonaventure University, teacher; William Paterson University, associate professor of history. Writer. **Publications:** White-Collar Crime in Modern England: Financial Fraud and Business Morality, 1845-1929, 1992; (ed. with N. Erber) Disorder in the Court: Trials and Sexual Conflict at the Turn of the Century, 1999; British Culture and the First World War, 2002; Why Not?, 2005. **Address:** Department of History, William Paterson University, 300 Pompton Rd., Wayne, NJ 07470, U.S.A. **Online address:** robbg@wpunj.edu

ROBB, James Harding. New Zealander (born New Zealand), b. 1920.

Genres: Sociology, Social Sciences. **Career:** Victoria University of Wellington, junior lecturer in psychology, 1947, lecturer, senior lecturer, 1954-64, associate professor, 1965-66, professor, 1966-86, Social Administration and Sociology, head, 1971-, professor emeritus, 1986-; Family Discussion Bureau (casework agency), caseworker, 1949-50; Tavistock Institute of Human Relations, research associate, 1950-54. Writer. **Publications:** Working Class Anti-Semite: A Psychological Study in a London Borough, 1954; (co-author) Social Casework in Marital Problems, 1955; (with A. Somerset) Report to Masterton: Results of a Social Survey, 1957; Social Science and Social Welfare, 1966; (co-author) The City of Porirua: The Results of a Survey, 1969; Life and Death of Official Social Research in New Zealand, 1987; The Emergence of Social Theory, 2001. Contributor to journals. **Address:** Victoria University of Wellington, PO Box 196, Wellington, 6006, New Zealand. **Online address:** jim.robb@paradise.net.nz

ROBB, J. D. *See* **ROBERTS, Nora.**

ROBB, JoAnn. *See* **ROSS, JoAnn.**

ROBB, Peter. British/New Zealander (born New Zealand), b. 1945. **Genres:** Area Studies, History, Essays, Politics/Government, Economics, Law, Cultural/Ethnic Topics. **Career:** Victoria University, junior lecturer, 1967; University of London, School of Oriental and African Studies, Department of History, lecturer, 1971-, research professor of the history of India, head, pro-director, through 2008, Centre of South Asian Studies, chair. Writer. **Publications:** The Government of India and Reform: Policies Towards Politics and the Constitution, 1916-1921, 1976; The Evolution of British Policy Towards Indian Politics, 1880-1920: Essays on Colonial Attitudes, Imperial Strategies, and Bihar, 1992; Ancient Rights and Future Comfort: Bihar, the Bengal Tenancy Act of 1885, and British Rule in India, 1997; Clash of Cultures?, 1998; A History of India, 2002, 2nd ed., 2011; Peasants, Political Economy, and Law, 2007; Liberalism, Modernity, and the Nation, 2007. EDITOR: (with D. Taylor) Rule, Protest, Identity: Aspects of Modern South Asia, 1978; Rural India: Land, Power, and Society Under British Rule, 1983; Rural South Asia: Linkages, Change, and Development, 1983; Dalit Movements and the Meanings of Labour in India, 1993; (with D. Arnold) Institutions and Ideologies: A SOAS South Asia Reader, 1993; (with K.N. Chaudhuri and A. Powell) Society and Ideology: Essays in South Asian History Presented to Professor K.A. Ballhatchet, 1993; (with K.N. Malik) India and Britain: Recent Past and Present Challenges, 1994; The Concept of Race in South Asia, 1995; Meanings of Agriculture: Essays in South Asian History and Economics, 1996; (with K. Sugihara and H. Yanagisawa) Local Agrarian Societies in Colonial India: Japanese Perspectives, 1996. Contributor to journals and periodicals. **Address:** Department of History, University of London, Rm. 4411, College Bldg., Thornhaugh St., Russell Sq., London, GL WC1H 0XG, England. **Online address:** pr4@soas.ac.uk

ROBB, Peter. Australian (born Australia), b. 1946?. **Genres:** Documentaries/Reportage, Biography, Art/Art History, Food And Wine, Travel/Exploration. **Career:** Victoria University of Wellington, junior lecturer in history, 1967; London University, School of Oriental and African Studies, lecturer, 1971-; University of Melbourne, teacher; University of Oulu, teacher; Istituto Universitario, teacher. Writer. **Publications:** Midnight in Sicily, 1996; Midnight in Sicily: On Art, Food, History, Travel, and La Cosa Nostra, 1998; Pig's Blood and Other Fluids, 1999; M: The Man Who Became Caravaggio, 2000; Death in Brazil: A Book of Omissions, 2004. Contributor to journals and periodicals. **Address:** c/o Author Mail, Duffy & Snellgrove, PO Box 177, Potts Point, NW 1335, Australia. **Online address:** pr4@soas.ac.uk

ROBBERS, James E. American (born United States), b. 1934. **Genres:** Medicine/Health, Sports/Fitness, Sciences. **Career:** University of Houston, assistant professor, 1964-66; Purdue University, assistant professor, professor emeritus of pharmacognosy, 1967-; Journal of Natural Products, editor, 1983-93. Licensed pharmacist and writer. **Publications:** (With L.R. Brady and V.E. Tyler) Pharmacognosy, 7th ed., 1976, 9th ed., 1988; (with M.K. Speedie and V.E. Tyler) Pharmacognosy and Pharmacobiotechnology, 1996; (with V.E. Tyler) Tyler's Herbs of Choice: The Therapeutic Use of Phytomedicinals, 1999, 3rd ed., 2009. **Address:** College of Pharmacy, Nursing and Health Sciences, Purdue University, 575 Stadium Mall Dr., West Lafayette, IN 47907-2091, U.S.A.

ROBBIN, Tony. American (born United States), b. 1943. **Genres:** Art/Art History, Young Adult Fiction, Architecture, Technology. **Career:** Artist and writer. **Publications:** Fourfield: Computers, Art and the Fourth Dimension, 1992; Engineering a New Architecture, 1996; Shadows of Reality: The Fourth Dimension in Relativity, Cubism and Modern Thought, 2006. Contributor to periodicals. **Address:** Robin Straus Agency Inc., 229 E 79th St., New York, NY 10021, U.S.A. **Online address:** tonyrobbin@att.net

ROBBINS, Bruce. American (born United States), b. 1949. **Genres:** Literary Criticism And History, Humanities, Social Commentary. **Career:** University of Geneva, assistant, 1976-81; University of Lausanne, maitre-assistant, 1981-83; University Rutgers, State University of New Jersey, professor of English, 1984-2000, Social Text, co-editor, 1988-2000; Columbia University, Old Dominion foundation professor in the humanities. **Publications:** The Servant's Hand: English Fiction from Below, 1986; Secular Vocations: Intellectuals, Professionalism, Culture, 1993; Feeling Global: Internationalism in Distress, 1999; Upward Mobility and the Common Good: Toward a Literary History of the Welfare State, 2007; Perpetual War: Cosmopolitanism from the Viewpoint of Violence, 2012. EDITOR: Intellectuals: Aesthetics, Politics, Academics, 1990; The Phantom Public Sphere, 1993; (with P. Cheah) Cosmopolitics: Thinking and Feeling beyond the Nation, 1998; (with D. Palumbo-Liu and N. Tanoukhi) Immanuel Wallerstein and the Problem of the World, 2011. **Address:** Department of English, Columbia University, 605 Philosophy Hall, 2960 Broadway, New York, NY 10027-6902, U.S.A. **Online address:** bwr2001@columbia.edu

ROBBINS, Hollis. American (born United States), b. 1963?. **Genres:** Public/Social Administration. **Career:** Millsaps College, assistant professor of English, 2004-06; Princeton University, visiting research collaborator, 2003-04; Harvard University, W.E.B. DuBois Center for African and African American Research, Black Periodical Literature Project, director/managing editor, adviser, 2003-06; John Hopkins University, Peabody Institute, Department of Humanities, faculty, 2006-, professor. **Publications:** (Ed. with H.L. Gates, Jr.) In Search of Hannah Crafts: Critical Essays on The Bondwoman's Narrative, 2004; (ed. and intro. with H.L. Gates, Jr.) The Annotated Uncle Tom's Cabin, 2007; (ed. with P. Garret) Selected Works of William Wells Brown, 2006; Post Office Stories: Communication, Circulation, and the Structure of Narrative Literature, 2006; (ed. with H.L. Gates and intro.) Iola Leroy, or, Shadows Uplifted, 2010. **Address:** Peabody Institute, The Johns Hopkins University, 1 E Mount Vernon Pl., Baltimore, MD 21202, U.S.A. **Online address:** hrobbins@jhu.edu

ROBBINS, James S. American (born United States), b. 1962?. **Genres:** Romance/Historical, Military/Defense/Arms Control. **Career:** National Defense University, professor of international relations, 2000-; Trinity Washington University, director of intelligence center, 2007-, Master of Arts in International Security Studies, program chair, 2008-; Office of the Secretary of Defense, special assistant; Tufts University, Fletcher School of Law and Diplomacy, assistant professor of diplomacy; U.S. Marine Corps Command and Staff College, associate professor of international relations and course director for military operations other than war; Boston University, instructor; Bentley College, instructor; Washington Times, senior editorial writer for foreign affairs; National Review, contributing editor. Political commentator, historian, broadcaster and foreign policy consultant. **Publications:** Last in Their Class: Custer, Pickett, and the Goats of West Point, 2006; This Time We Win: Revisiting the Tet Offensive, 2010. Contributor to books, newspapers and periodicals. **Online address:** author@lastintheirclass.com

ROBBINS, JoAnn. *See* **ROSS, JoAnn.**

ROBBINS, Kay. *See* **HOOPER, Kay.**

ROBBINS, Lawrence H. American (born United States), b. 1938. **Genres:** Anthropology/Ethnology, Archaeology/Antiquities. **Career:** University of California, lecturer, 1964; University of Maryland, lecturer, 1965; University of Utah, assistant professor, 1967-68; Michigan State University, Department of Anthropology, assistant professor, 1968, 1971, associate professor, 1972-76, professor of anthropology, 1977-, chair, 1992-95, African Studies Center, core faculty, Consortium for Archaeological Research Center, coordinator, Michigan State University Museum, adjunct curator; University of Nairobi, visiting research associate, 1969-70; National Museums of Kenya, visiting research associate, 1974-75; British Institute, visiting research associate, 1974-75; University of Botswana, visiting lecturer, 1982-83. Writer. **Publications:** Archaeology of Turkana District, 1970; The Lothagam Site: A Late Stone Age Fishing Settlement in the Lake Rudolph Basin, Kenya, 1974;

(with J.L. Angel, T.W. Phenice and B.M. Lynch) Late Stone Age Fisherman of Lothagam Kenya, 1980; Lopoy, a Late Stone Age Fishing and Pastoralist Settlement West of Lake Turkana, Kenya, 1980; The Archaeologist's Eye: Great Discoveries, Missing Links, and Ancient Treasures, 1989 in US as Stones, Bones, and Ancient Cities: Great Discoveries in Archaeology and the Search for Human Origins, 1990. Contributor to journals. Works appear in anthologies. **Address:** Department of Anthropology, Michigan State University, 355 Baker Hall, East Lansing, MI 48824-1118, U.S.A. **Online address:** lrobbins@msu.edu

ROBBINS, Rogene A. American (born United States), b. 1957. **Genres:** Crafts, Reference. **Career:** Parkview Learning Center, qualified mental retardation professional, 1990-91; Crafty Lady, co-owner and designer, 1992-93; fabric artist, 1994-. Writer. **Publications:** (With R.O. Robbins) Creating a Successful Craft Business, 2003. **Address:** c/o Author Mail, Allworth Press, 307 W 36th St., 11th Fl., New York, NY 10018, U.S.A. **Online address:** quiltnart@yahoo.com

ROBBINS, Tom. American (born United States), b. 1936. **Genres:** Novels, Biography, inspirational/Motivational Literature, Young Adult Fiction. **Career:** Richmond Times-Dispatch, copy editor, 1960-62; Seattle Times, copyeditor, 1962-63; Seattle Post-Intelligencer, copy editor, 1962-63; Seattle Magazine, reviewer and art critic, 1964-68. **Publications:** Guy Anderson, 1965; Another Roadside Attraction, 1971; Even Cowgirls Get the Blues, 1976; Still Life with Woodpecker, 1980; Jitterbug Perfume, 1984; Skinny Legs and All, 1990; Half Asleep in Frog Pajamas, 1994; Fierce Invalids Home from Hot Climates, 2000; Villa Incognito, 2003; Wild Ducks Flying Backward: The Short Writings of Tom Robbins, 2005; (foreword) Natural Skagit, 2008; B is for Beer, 2009; Conversations with Tom Robbins, 2011. **Address:** c/o Phoebe Larmore, 228 Main St., Venice, CA 90291-5201, U.S.A.

ROBENALT, James David. American (born United States), b. 1956. **Genres:** History, Mystery/Crime/Suspense. **Career:** Thomson Hine L.L.P., lawyer, 1981-89, partner, 1989-; National Institute of Trial Advocacy, instructor. Writer. **Publications:** Linking Rings: William W. Durbin and the Magic and Mystery of America, 2004; The Harding Affair: Love and Espionage during the Great War, 2009. **Address:** Thompson Hine L.L.P., 3900 Key Ctr., 127 Public Sq., Cleveland, OH 44114-1291, U.S.A. **Online address:** jim.robenalt@thompsonhine.com

ROBERSON, Houston Bryan. American (born United States) **Genres:** Theology/Religion, History. **Career:** Sewanee: The University of the South, professor. Writer and educator. **Publications:** (ed. and contrib. with J.B. Armstrong) Teaching the American Civil Rights Movement: Freedom's Bittersweet Song, 2002; Fighting the Good Fight: The Story of the Dexter Avenue King Memorial Baptist Church, 1865- 1977, 2005. **Address:** Department of History, Sewanee: The University of the South, 735 University Ave., Sewanee, TN 37383-1000, U.S.A. **Online address:** hroberso@sewanee.edu

ROBERT, Dana L. American (born United States), b. 1956. **Genres:** Theology/Religion, History. **Career:** History teacher, 1978; Yale University, instructor, 1982; Boston University, assistant professor, 1984-90, associate professor, 1990-97, professor of international mission, 1997-, Center for Global Christianity and Mission, co-director; Gordon-Conwell Theological School, lecturer, 1992. Writer. **Publications:** Arthur Tappan Pierson and Evangelical Movements, 1988; American Women in Mission: A Social History of Their Thought and Practice, 1997; (co-author) Christianity: A Social and Cultural History, 2nd ed., 1997; Evangelism as the Heart of Mission, 1998; (ed.) Gospel Bearers, Gender Barriers: Missionary Women in the 20th Century, 2002; Occupy until I Come: A.T. Pierson and the Evangelization of the World, 2003; (ed.) African Christian Outreach, vol. II: Mission Churches, 2003; (ed.) Frontiers of African Christianity, 2003; (ed.) Converting Colonialism, 2008; Christian Mission: How Christianity Became a World Religion, 2009; Joy to the World! Mission in the Age of Global Christianity, 2010. Contributor to books and periodicals. **Address:** School of Theology, Boston University, 745 Commonwealth Ave., Boston, MA 02215, U.S.A. **Online address:** drobdan@bu.edu

ROBERTS, Adam. British (born England) **Genres:** History, Young Adult Non-fiction, Politics/Government. **Career:** The Economist, Foreign Department, intern, 1998, writer on foreign affairs, 1998-2001, Southern Africa correspondent, 2001-05, news editor, 2006-10, South Asia Bureau, chief and correspondent, 2010-. **Publications:** (Ed. with H. Holland) From Jo'burg to Jozi: Stories about Africa's Infamous City, 2002; (ed. with J. Thloloe) Soweto Inside Out: Stories about Africa's Famous Township, 2004; The Wonga Coup: Guns, Thugs, and a Ruthless Determination to Create Mayhem in an Oil-Rich Corner of Africa, 2006. **Address:** The Economist, PO Box 471, Haywards Heath, WS RH16 3GY, England. **Online address:** adamroberts36@btinternet.com

ROBERTS, Alasdair Scott. American/Canadian (born Canada) **Genres:** Politics/Government, Economics. **Career:** Queens University, lecturer, 1990-93, associate director, 1993-95, School of Policy Studies, assistant professor, 1993-96; University of Southern California. visiting associate professor, 1996-97; Georgetown University, visiting fellow, 1996-97; Syracuse University, Maxwell School of Citizenship and Public Affairs, associate professor, 1996-2001, Campbell Public Affairs Institute, director, 2001-06, professor, 2007-08; University College, School of Public Policy, Constitution Unit, honorary senior research fellow, 2005-; National Academy of Public Administration, fellow, 2007-; Institute for National Security and Counterterrorism, research associate, 2007-; Suffolk University Law School, Rappaport Center, Jerome L Rappaport professor of law and public policy, 2008-. Writer. **Publications:** Blacked Out: Government Secrecy in the Information Age, 2006; The Collapse of Fortress Bush: The Crisis of Authority in American Government, 2008; The Logic of Discipline: Global Capitalism and The Architecture of Government, 2010; The First Great Depression: Economic Crisis And Political Disorder In The United States, 1837-1848, 2012. Contributor to books. **Address:** Suffolk University Law School, Rm. 210C, 120 Tremont St., Boston, MA 02108-4977, U.S.A. **Online address:** alasdair.roberts@gmail.com

ROBERTS, Alvin. American (born United States), b. 1930. **Genres:** Novels, History, Young Adult Fiction, Social Sciences, Education. **Career:** Department of Children and Family Services, rehabilitation teacher and supervisor, 1963-80; Bureau of Blind Services, regional administrator, 1980-84, area supervisor, 1987-2000; regional supervisor, regional administrator; Illinois Visually Handicapped Institute, superintendent, 1984-87; Illinois Bureau of Blind Service, quality assurance administrator, 2000-; Mid-America Conference of Rehabilitation Teachers, president. Writer. **Publications:** Psychosocial Rehabilitation of the Blind, 1973; Tavern Tales (fiction), 1993; Coping with Blindness (fiction), 1998; Bar Stool Fiction, 2001. Contributor to periodicals. **Address:** Office of Rehabilitation, 309 E Jackson, Carbondale, IL 62901, U.S.A.

ROBERTS, Bertram. See **ROBERTS, Brian.**

ROBERTS, Brian. (Bertram Roberts). British (born England), b. 1930. **Genres:** History, Biography, Autobiography/Memoirs, Biography. **Career:** Educator, 1958-67. Writer. **Publications:** Ladies in the Veld, 1965; Cecil Rhodes and the Princess, 1969; Churchills in Africa, 1970; The Diamond Magnates, 1972; The Zulu Kings, 1974; Kimberley: Turbulent City, 1976; The Mad Bad Line: The Family of Lord Alfred Douglas, 1981; Randolph: A Study of Churchill's Son, 1984; Cecil Rhodes: Flawed Colossus, 1987; Those Bloody Women: Three Heroines of the Boer War, 1991. Contributor to magazines. **Address:** John Farquharson Ltd., 250 West 57th St., Ste. 1914, New York, NY 10107, U.S.A.

ROBERTS, Callum. British (born England), b. 1962. **Genres:** Marine Sciences/Oceanography, History, Natural History, Sciences, Zoology. **Career:** York University, professor of marine conservation biology; Harvard University, Hrdy visiting professor of conservation biology. WWF-UK, ambassador; Save Our Seas Foundation, scientific advisor. Writer. **Publications:** (With C. Sheppard and A. Price) Marine Ecology of the Arabian Region, 1992; (ed. with N.V.C. Polunin) Reef Fisheries, 1996; The Unnatural History of the Sea, 2007. **Address:** Department of Environment, University of York, Heslington, York, NY YO10 5DD, England. **Online address:** callum.roberts@york.ac.uk

ROBERTS, Charles E. American (born United States), b. 1953. **Genres:** Sciences, Geography, Biology. **Career:** Florida Atlantic University, Department Of Geosciences, associate professor and graduate program chair. Writer. **Publications:** (With E.J. Petuch) The Geology of the Everglades and Adjacent Areas, 2007. Contributor to journals and periodicals. **Address:** Department Of Geosciences, Florida Atlantic University, PS 348. 777 Glades Rd., Boca Raton, FL 33431-6424, U.S.A. **Online address:** croberts@fau.edu

ROBERTS, Cokie. (Corinne Boggs Roberts). American (born United States), b. 1943. **Genres:** Communications/Media, Human Relations/Parenting. **Career:** WRC-TV, assistant producer, Meeting of the Minds, television anchor,

1964-66; Insider's Newsletter, editor and correspondent, 1967; WNEW-TV, producer, 1968; KNBC-TV, producer, 1969-74; CBS News, reporter, 1974-77; National Public Radio, congressional correspondent to news analyst, 1978-, contributing senior news analyst, senior news analyst; WETA-TV (PBS), anchor, 1981-84; MacNeil-Lehrcr Newshour, correspondent, 1984-88; ABC News, political commentator, chief congressional analyst, 1988-, This Week, commentator, 1992-96, co-anchor, 1996-; George Washington University, Shapiro professor of media and public Affairs, 1997-. **Publications:** NONFICTION: We Are Our Mothers' Daughters, 1998, rev. ed., 2009; (with S. Roberts) From This Day Forward, 2000; Founding Mothers: The Women Who Raised Our Nation, 2004; Ladies of Liberty: The Women Who Shaped Our Nation, 2008; (co-author) This is NPR, 2010; (with S. Roberts) Our Haggadah, 2011. OTHER: (contrib.) The Theodore H. White Lecture with Cokie Roberts, 1994. Contributor to periodicals. **Address:** ABC News, 1717 DeSales St. NW, Washington, DC 20036, U.S.A.

ROBERTS, Corinne Boggs. *See* **ROBERTS, Cokie.**

ROBERTS, Daniel Sanjiv. Irish/British/Indian (born India), b. 1965. **Genres:** Literary Criticism And History. **Career:** Loyola College, assistant professor, 1987-88; Orient Longman, assistant editor, 1996; University of Manchester, research fellow, 1996-99; Queen's University, lecturer in English, 1999-, reader in romanticism and Indian literature in English. **Publications:** Revisionary Gleam: De Quincey, Coleridge, and The High Romantic Argument, 2000; (ed.) The Works of Thomas De Quincey, vol. XIX: Autobiographic Sketches, 2003; (ed.) Robert Southey: Poetical Works, 1793-1810, vol. IV: The Curse of Kehama, 2004; (ed. with R. Morrison) Thomas De Quincey: New Theoretical and Critical Directions, 2008. Contributor to periodicals. **Address:** School of English, Queen's University, 2 University Sq., University Rd., Belfast, AT BT7 1NN, Northern Ireland. **Online address:** d.s.roberts@qub.ac.uk

ROBERTS, Denys (Tudor Emil). British (born England), b. 1923. **Genres:** Novels, Humor/Satire, Mystery/Crime/Suspense, Biography, History. **Career:** Attorney-general, 1960-62; solicitor-general of of Gibralter, 1962-66; attorney-general of Hong Kong, 1966-73; colonial secretary of Hong Kong, 1973-78; chief secretary, 1976, Supreme Court of Hong Kong, chief justice, 1979-88; chief justice of Brunei Darussalam, 1978-2001; Court of Appeal for Bermuda, president, 1988-93, now retired. Writer. **Publications:** Smuggler's Circuit, 1954; Beds and Roses, 1956; Thc Elwood Wager, 1957; The Bones of the Wajingas, 1959; How to Dispense with Lawyers, 1964; Doing Them Justice, 1987; I'll Do Better Next Time, 1995; Yes Sir, But, 2000; Another Disaster: Hong Kong Sketches, 2006. **Address:** Leithen Lodge, Innerleithen, Pebblesshire, BR EH44 6NW, Scotland. **Online address:** roberts.leithen@btinternet.com

ROBERTS, D(erek) H. *See* **ROBERTS, Derek Harry.**

ROBERTS, Derek Harry. (D(erek) H. Roberts). British (born England), b. 1931. **Genres:** Antiques/Furnishings, Medicine/Health, Engineering. **Career:** Institute of Dental Surgery, Eastman Dental Hospital, honorary lecturer; Derek Roberts Fine Antique clocks, owner, 1968-. Writer. **Publications:** (With J. Sowray) Local Analgesia in Dentistry, 1970, 3rd ed., 1987; Fixed Bridge Prostheses, 1970; (ed. with F.J. Harty) Restorative Procedures for the Practicing Dentist, 1970; Precision Pendulum Clocks, 1986; British Skeleton Clocks, 1987; Continental and American Skeleton Clocks, 1989; Collector's Guide to Clocks, 1990; British Longcase Clocks, 1992; Carriage Clocks, 1993; Mystery, Novelty and Fantasy Clock, 1998; Precision Pendulum Clocks, vol. I: The Quest for Accurate Timekeeping, 2003, vol. II: English Precision Pendulum Clocks, 2003, vol. III: Precision Pendulum Clocks: France, Germany, America and Recent Advancements, 2004. **Address:** Derek Roberts Antiques, 25 Shipbourne Rd., PO Box 117, Tonbridge, KT TN10 3DN, England. **Online address:** drclocks@clara.net

ROBERTS, Diane. American (born United States), b. 1937?. **Genres:** Novels, Children's Fiction, Literary Criticism And History, Humor/Satire. **Career:** Writer and puppeteer. **Publications:** Made You Look, 2003; Puppet Pandemonium, 2006. **Address:** Yearling Books, 1745 Broadway 10th Fl., New York, NY 10019, U.S.A. **Online address:** draccoon@aol.com

ROBERTS, (Edward) Adam. British (born England), b. 1940. **Genres:** International Relations/Current Affairs, Politics/Government. **Career:** Peace News Ltd., assistant editor, 1962-65; University of London, London School of Economics, Noel Buxton fellow in international relations, 1965-68, lecturer in international relations, 1968-81, honorary fellow, 1997-; Oxford University, St. Antony's College, Alastair Buchan reader in international relations and professorial fellow, 1981-86, Centre for International Studies, Department of Politics and International Relations, senior research fellow, Montague Burton professor of international relations, 1986-2007, now emeritus professor of international relations, Balliol College, now emeritus fellow; British Academy, fellow, 1990, president, 2009-; Order of St. Michael and St. George, knight commander, 2002. **Publications:** (Trans. with A. Lieven) End of a War: Indochina 1954; (co-author) Civilian Defence, 1964; (with A. Carter and D. Hoggett) Non-Violent Action, Theory and Practice, 1966, rev. ed., 1970; (ed.) The Strategy of Civilian Defence: Non-Violent Resistance to Aggression, 1967; (ed.) Civilian Resistance as a National Defense, Non-Violent Action Against Aggression, 1968; (with P. Windsor) Czechoslovakia 1968; Reform, Repression and Resistance, 1969; Nations in Arms: The Theory and Practice of Territorial Defence, 1976, rev. ed., 1986; (ed. with R. Guelff) Documents on the Laws of War, 1982, 3rd ed., 2000; (with F. Newman and B. Joergensen) Academic Freedom under Israeli Military Occupation, 1984; (ed. with B. Kingsbury) United Nations, Divided World, 1988, 2nd ed., 1993; (ed. with H. Bull and B. Kingsbury) Hugo Grotius and International Relations, 1990; Civil Resistance in the East European and Soviet Revolutions, 1991; Presiding Over a Divided World: Changing UN Roles, 1945-1993, 1994; Humanitarian Action in War, 1996; (co-author) Los desafíos de la acción humanitaria, 1999; al-Iḥtilāl al-Amrīkī lil-'Irāq, 2005; (with D.Zaum) Selective Security: War and the United Nations Security Council Since 1945, 2008; (ed. with G.M. Ash) Civil Resistance and Power Politics, 2009. **Address:** Department of Politics & International Relations, Balliol College, Oxford University, Broad St., Oxford, OX OX1 3BJ, England.

ROBERTS, Elizabeth. British (born England), b. 1944. **Genres:** International Relations/Current Affairs, Politics/Government, History, Humanities. **Career:** South Wales Echo, reporter, 1965-66; Watford Evening Echo, women's editor; Sunday Times, reporter, 1969; teacher, 1976; Cooper Estates Ltd., director, 1978-, president, 1985-90. **Publications:** Focus on the Soviet Union, 1988, rev. ed. as Focus on Russia and the Republics, 1992; Glasnost, the Gorbachev Revolution, 1989; Europe 1992, 1990, rev. ed. as The New Europe, After Maastricht and Beyond, 1993; (trans.) Armenian Tragedy: An Eye-Witness Account of Human Conflict and Natural Disaster in Armenia and Azerbaijan, 1990; (trans. with J. Roberts) The Soviet Mafia, 1991; Georgia, Armenia, and Azerbaijan, 1992; Belarus, Ukraine and Moldova, 1992; Strong Enough for Two, 1993; (ed. with A. Shukman) Christianity for the Twenty-first Century: The Life and Work of Alexander Men, 1996; Realm of the Black Mountain: A History of Montenegro, 2007; Diary of a Young Capitalist, forthcoming. Contributor to newspapers and periodicals. **Address:** Rosemary Sandberg Ltd., 6 Bayley St., London, GL WC1B 3HE, England.

ROBERTS, Francis X. American (born United States), b. 1932. **Genres:** Poetry, Bibliography, Librarianship, Literary Criticism And History, Intellectual History, Humanities, History. **Career:** Teacher, 1959-61, 1963-66; Tanzanian Government, education officer, 1961-63; Emerson College, library assistant, 1966-67; Veterans Administration Hospital, librarian, 1967-68; Leeds Polytechnic, lecturer, 1968-75; Makerere University, lecturer, 1972; Gippsland Institute of Advanced Education, lecturer, 1975-79; California State College, librarian, 1979-80; State University of New York, Medical School, administrative assistant, 1982-84, reference librarian and bibliographer, 1985-86; Marlboro College, library director, 1986-87; University of Northern Colorado, professor of library science, 1987-97. Writer. **Publications:** POETRY: Feathers and Anvils, 1989; At Length, 1990; Vitae Summa Brevis, 1991; Miscellanea, 1992; Ballad of the Entry-Level Librarian, 1993; Poems for the Kids, 1997; Roundelay and Other Poems, 1998. OTHERS: Sixteenth-Century English Humanist Educational Theories and Their Influence on the Development of the American College Curriculum, 1990; (comp. with C.D. Rhine) James A. Michener: A Checklist of His Works, with a Selected, Annotated Bibliography, 1995; Fifty Years of Poetic Experiments, 2008. Contributor to books and periodicals. **Address:** 2316 W 15th St., Apt. 401, Greeley, CO 80634-6459, U.S.A. **Online address:** fraober32@aol.com

ROBERTS, Geoffrey. (Geoffrey Charles Roberts). Irish/British (born England), b. 1952. **Genres:** Military/Defense/Arms Control, History, Young Adult Non-fiction. **Career:** University College Cork, professor of history.

Writer. **Publications:** NONFICTION: The Unholy Alliance: Stalin's Pact with Hitler, 1989; The Soviet Union and the Origins of the Second World War: Russo-German Relations and the Road to War, 1933-1941, 1995; The Soviet Union in World Politics: Coexistence, Revolution, and Cold War, 1945-1991, 1999; (ed. with B. Girvin) Ireland and the Second World War: Politics, Society and Remembrance, 2000; (ed.) The History and Narrative Reader, 2001; Victory at Stalingrad: The Battle That Changed History, 2002; Stalin's Wars: From World War to Cold War, 1939-1953, 2006. **Address:** Department of History, University College Cork, Tyrconnell, Off College Rd., Cork, CK 1, Ireland. **Online address:** g.roberts@ucc.ie

ROBERTS, Geoffrey Charles. *See* **ROBERTS, Geoffrey.**

ROBERTS, Gregory David. Australian (born Australia), b. 1952. **Genres:** Novels, Young Adult Fiction. **Career:** Sydney Morning Herald, columnist. **Publications:** Shantaram, 2003. Contributor of articles to journals. **Address:** Scribe Publications, 595 Drummond St., Carlton North, VI 3054, Australia. **Online address:** shantaram@shantaram.com

ROBERTS, Iolo Francis. British (born England), b. 1925. **Genres:** Chemistry, Education, Adult Non-fiction. **Career:** Raine's Foundation School for Boys, chemistry master, 1947-50; Sir Thomas Jones School, senior science master, 1950-56; Flintshire Technical College, lecturer in chemistry, 1956-62; Keele University, lecturer, 1962-70, senior lecturer in education, 1970-82, fellow, 1982-, senior warden. Writer. **Publications:** (With L.M. Cantor) Further Education in England and Wales, 1969, 1972; Crystals and Their Structures, 1974; (with L.M. Cantor) Further Education Today: A Critical Review, 1979, 3rd ed., 1986; (with L.M. Cantor and B. Pratley) A Guide to Further Education in England and Wales, 1995. **Address:** University of Keele, Keele, ST ST5 5BG, England.

ROBERTS, J(ames) Deotis. American (born United States), b. 1927. **Genres:** Civil Liberties/Human Rights, Cultural/Ethnic Topics, Human Relations/Parenting, Philosophy, Politics/Government, Race Relations, Theology/Religion, Third World, Urban Studies. **Career:** Baptist church, pastor, 1948-50; Georgia Baptist College, dean of religion, 1952-53; Shaw University, assistant professor of philosophy and religion, 1953-55, associate professor of philosophy and religion, 1957-58; Howard University, Divinity School, professor of systematic theology, 1958-80; Catholic University of America, visiting professor, 1968-69, 1970-72; Swarthmore College, visiting professor, 1969-70; Wesley Theological Seminary, visiting professor, 1970-71; University of Virginia, visiting professor, 1971-72; Virginia Union University, School of Theology, dean, 1973-; Journal of Religious Thought, editor, 1974-80; Claremont Theological Seminary, visiting professor, 1978; Interdenominational Theological Center, president and distinguished professor, 1980-84; Emory University and Columbia Theological Seminary, Candler School of Theology, adjunct professor, 1983-84; Eastern Baptist Theological Seminary, distinguished professor of philosophical theology, 1984-; Foundation for Religious and Educational Exchanges, founder, 1984-94; George Mason University, commonwealth professor of philosophy and religious studies, 1986-88; University of Edinburgh, New College, honorary professor, 1994; Yale University, Divinity School, visiting professor, 1996; Duke Divinity School, research professor of Christian theology, 1998-2001. **Publications:** Faith and Reason in Pascal, Bergson and James, 1962; From Puritanism to Platonism in 17th Century England, 1969; Liberation and Reconciliation: A Black Theology, 1971; (ed. with J. Gardner) Quest for a Black Theology, 1971; Extending Redemption and Reconciliation, 1973; A Black Political Theology, 1974; Christian Beliefs, 1976; Roots of a Black Future: Family and Church, 1980; Black Theology Today: Liberation and Contextualization, 1983; Black Theology in Dialogue, 1987; Philosophical Introduction to Theology, 1991; Prophethood of Black Believers, 1994; Liberation and Reconciliation, 1994, 2nd ed., 2003; Christian Beliefs, 2000; Africentric Christianity: A Theological Appraisal for Ministry, 2000; Dietrich Bonhoeffer and Martin Luther King Jr.: Speaking Truth to Power, 2005. **Address:** Virginia Union University, School of Theology, 1500 N Lombardy St., Richmond, VA 23220, U.S.A.

ROBERTS, Jennifer L. American (born United States), b. 1969?. **Genres:** History, Art/Art History, Photography. **Career:** Harvard University, assistant professor, 2002-07, Gardner Cowles associate professor of history of art and architecture, 2007-. Writer and educator. **Publications:** Mirror-Travels: Robert Smithson and History, 2004; (co-author) American Encounters: Art, History and Cultural Identity (textbook), 2007. **Address:** Sackler Museum 507, Harvard University, 485 Broadway, Cambridge, MA 02138, U.S.A. **Online address:** roberts6@fas.harvard.edu

ROBERTS, Jon H. American (born United States), b. 1947. **Genres:** History, Education, Sciences. **Career:** Wisconsin Institute for Research in the Humanities, Woodrow Wilson fellow, 1969; Harvard University, assistant professor of history, 1980-85, Charles Warren Center for American History, fellow; University of Wisconsin, assistant professor of history, 1985-88, associate professor of history, 1988-95, professor of history, 1995-2001, director of American studies, 1986-88, University Honors Program, director, 1990-92, Institute for Research in the Humanities, system fellow, 1993-94; Isis, advisory editor, 1993-95; History of Psychology, consulting editor, 1997-2009; Boston University, professor of history, 2001-, Tomorrow Foundation professor of American intellectual history, 2007-, director of graduate studies, 2003-04, 2005-07. **Publications:** Darwinism and the Divine in America: Protestant Intellectuals and Organic Evolution, 1859-1900, 1988; (with J. Turner) The Sacred and the Secular University, 2000. **Address:** Department of History, Boston University, Rm. 406, 226 Bay State Rd., Boston, MA 02215, U.S.A. **Online address:** roberts1@bu.edu

ROBERTS, Katherine. British (born England), b. 1962. **Genres:** Science Fiction/Fantasy, Novels, Children's Fiction. **Career:** GEC Measurements, engineering mathematician, 1984-87; MPSI Systems, analyst programmer, 1987-89; writer, 1999-. **Publications:** NOVELS: Spell Wars, 2000; Spellfall, 2000; I am the Great Horse, 2006. ECHORIUM SERIES: Song Quest, 1999; Crystal Mask, 2001; Dark Quetzal, 2003. SEVEN FABULOUS WONDERS SERIES: The Great Pyramid Robbery, 2001; The Babylon Game, 2002; The Amazon Temple Quest, 2002; The Mausoleum Murder, 2003; The Olympic Conspiracy, 2004; The Colossus Crisis, 2005; The Cleopatra Curse, 2006. PENDRAGON LEGACY: Sword of Light, 2012. COLLECTION: Magical Horses, 2009. **Address:** c/o Jill Hughes, Maggie Noach Literary Agency, Manor Farm, Aubourn, Lincoln, LI LN5 9DX, England. **Online address:** author@katherineroberts.co.uk

ROBERTS, Ken. Canadian (born Canada), b. 1946?. **Genres:** Children's Fiction. **Career:** Hamilton Public Library, chief librarian, through 2011; University of British Columbia, faculty; Simon Fraser University, faculty; University of Lethbridge, faculty; Vancouver School Board, storyteller-in-residence. Writer. **Publications:** FICTION, Crazy Ideas, 1984., Pop Bottles, 1987., Hiccup Champion of the World, 1988. (with L. Castellarin) Spike, 1988 as Degrassi Junior High: Spike, 2006. (with L. Castellarin) Stephanie Kaye, 1988 as Degrassi Junior High: Stephanie Kaye, 2006; Nothing Wright, 1991; Past Tense, 1994. NONFICTION, Exploring Altona with Rachel, Photographs by Chuck Heath, 1986; Exploring Vancouver with Francisco, Photographs by Chuck Heath, 1986; Exploring Red Deer with Paula, Photographs by Chuck Heath, 1986; Exploring Regina with Jarrod, Photographs by Chuck Heath, 1986; Exploring Kentville with Billy, Photographs by Chuck Heath, 1986; Freedom within Boundaries: A Scrapbook of Ideas for Fostering Story Creation Skills in Young People, 1987; Pre-school Storytimes, 1987; Jacques Cartier, 1988. Contributor to periodicals. **Address:** Hamilton Public Library, 55 York Blvd., Hamilton, ON L8N 4E4, Canada. **Online address:** robetshpl@me.com

ROBERTS, Kristina LaFerne. (Zane). American (born United States), b. 1967?. **Genres:** Novels, Sex. **Career:** Strebor Books International L.L.C., founder and publisher, 1999-2005; Zanes Endeavors Books and Gifts, owner; Zane Entertainment (film production company), partner, 2005-. Writer. **Publications:** AS ZANE: The Sex Chronicles: Shattering the Myth (short stories), 1999; Addicted, 2001; Shame on It All, 2001; Gettin' Buck Wild: Sex Chronicles II, 2002; The Heat Seekers, 2002; Of Royal Blood, 2002; Nervous, 2003; The Sisters of APF: The Indoctrination of Soror Ride Dick, 2003; Skyscraper, 2003; (ed.) Afterburn, 2005; Breaking the Cycle, 2005; Love is Never Painless, 2006; Caramel Flava, 2006; Dear G-Spot: Straight Talk about Sex and Love, 2007; (ed.) (co-author) Another Time, Another Place, 2008; Zane's Sex Chronicles, 2008; Head Bangers: An APF Sexcapade, 2009; Total Eclipse of the Heart, 2010; Hot Box, 2010. **Address:** c/o Author Mail, Atria Books/Simon & Schuster, 1230 Ave. of the Americas, New York, NY 10020, U.S.A. **Online address:** zane@eroticanoir.com

ROBERTS, Leigh. *See* **SMITH, Lora Roberts.**

ROBERTS, Madge Thornall. American (born United States), b. 1929.

Genres: History, Young Adult Fiction, Biography. **Career:** San Antonio Independent School District, elementary school teacher, 1950-72; Northside Independent School District, elementary school teacher, 1972-90; Cobblestones (children's magazine), contributing editor. **Publications:** A Child's View of Texas History from A to Z, 1979; Star of Destiny: The Private Life of Sam and Margaret Houston, 1993; (ed.) The Personal Correspondence of Sam Houston, vol. I: 1839-1845, 1996, vol. II: 1846-1848, 1997, vol. III: 1848-1852, 1999. Contributor to periodicals. **Address:** University of North Texas Press, Bain Hall 101, 1820 Highland St., PO Box 311336, Denton, TX 76203-3856, U.S.A.

ROBERTS, Nancy N(orma). American (born United States), b. 1957. **Genres:** Translations, History, Young Adult Fiction. **Career:** Indiana University, associate instructor in English, 1980-81, instructor in Arabic, 1991-93; American University, instructor in English, 1981-82; Kuwait University, College of Commerce, instructor of English, 1982-87; Earlham College, instructor in English, 1988-90; ALal-Bayt University, instructor in English, 1994-97; Mitchell Translations, translator from Arabic to English, 1994; Federal Broadcasting Information Service, translator, 1998-99, 2000; freelance translator, 1999-. Writer. **Publications:** TRANSLATOR: Beirut '75 (novel), 1995; Beirut Nightmares (novel), 1997; M.S.R. al-Buti, The Jurisprudence of the Prophetic Biography, 2001, 2nd ed. as Jurisprudence of the Prophetic Biography and a Brief History of Rightly Guided Caliphs, 2008; M.S.R. al-Buti, Women: Between the Tyranny of the Western System and the Mercy of the Divine Law, 2002; (and intro. and contrib.) Subtle Blessings in the Saintly Lives of Abū al-'Abbās al-Mursī and his Master Abu al-Ḥasan al-Shādhilī, the Founders of the Shādhilī order/Laṭāif al-minan, 2005; The Night of the First Billion, 2005; Islamic Jurisprudence According to the Four Orthodox Schools, forthcoming. Contributor to periodicals. **Address:** AL al-Bayt University, PO Box 130029, Mafraq, 25113, Jordan. **Online address:** batoula@go.com.jo

ROBERTS, Nora. Also writes as Sarah Hardesty, J. D. Robb. American (born United States), b. 1950. **Genres:** Novels, Romance/Historical, Novellas/Short Stories. **Career:** Wheeler & Korpeck, legal secretary, 1968-70; Hecht Co., clerk, 1970-72; R&R Lighting, secretary, 1972-75. Full-time writer, 1979-. **Publications:** IRISH HEARTS SERIES: Irish Thoroughbred, 1981; Irish Rose, 1988; Irish Hearts (omnibus), 2000; Irish Rebel, 2000. BANNION FAMILY SERIES: Reflections, 1983; Dance of Dreams, 1983; Reflections and Dreams (omnibus), 2001. NIGHT TALES SERIES: Night Shift, 1990; Night Shadow, 1991; Nightshade, 1993; Night Smoke, 1994; Night Shield, 2000; Night Tales (omnibus), 2000. MACGREGOR SERIES: Playing the Odds, 1985; Tempting Fate, 1985; All the Possibilities, 1985; One Man's Art, 1985; For Now, Forever, 1987; Rebellion, 1988; In From the Cold, in Historical Christmas Stories 1990; Serena-Caine (omnibus), 1998; The Winning Hand, 1998; The MacGregor Grooms, 1998; Alan-Grant (omnibus), 1999; Daniel-Ian (omnibus), 1999; The Perfect Neighbor, 1999; Robert-Cybil (omnibus), 2007. GREAT CHEFS SERIES: Summer Desserts, 1985; Lessons Learned, 1986. CELEBRITY MAGAZINE SERIES: Second Nature, 1985; One Summer, 1986. CORDINA'S ROYAL FAMILY SERIES: Affaire Royale, 1986; Command Performance, 1987; The Playboy Prince, 1987; Cordina's Crown Jewel, 2002; Bennett-Camilla (omnibus), 2007. D.C. DETECTIVES SERIES: Sacred Sins, 1987; Brazen Virtue, 1988. O'HURLEY SERIES: The Last Honest Woman, 1988; Dance to the Piper, 1988; Skin Deep, 1988; Without a Trace, 1990; Born O'Hurley (omnibus), 2002; O'Hurley's Return (omnibus), 2005. TIME AND AGAIN SERIES: Time Was, 1989; Times Change, 1989; Time and Again (omnibus), 2001. STANISLASKI FAMILY SERIES: Taming Natasha, 1990; Luring a Lady, 1991; Falling for Rachel, 1993; Convincing Alex, 1994; The Stanislaski Sisters (omnibus), 1997; Waiting for Nick, 1997; The Stanislaski Brothers, 2000; Considering Kate, 2001. CALHOUN WOMEN SERIES: Courting Catherine, 1991; A Man for Amanda, 1991; For the Love of Lilah, 1991; Suzanna's Surrender, 1991; Catherine and Amanda (omnibus), 1996; Megan's Mate, 1996; Lilah and Suzanna (omnibus), 1998; Catherine, Amanda and Lilah (omnibus), 2005; Suzanna and Megan (omnibus), 2005; The Calhouns (omnibus), 2006. DONOVAN LEGACY SERIES: Captivated, 1992; Entranced, 1992; Charmed, 1992; The Donovan Legacy (omnibus), 1999; Enchanted, 1999. MACKADE BROTHERS: The Return of Rafe MacKade, 1995; The Pride of Jared MacKade, 1995; The Heart of Devin MacKade, 1996; The Fall of Shane MacKade, 1996; The Mackade Brothers: Devin and Shane (omnibus), 2004; The Mackade Brothers: Rafe and Jared (omnibus), 2004. DREAM TRILOGY SERIRES: Daring to Dream, 1996; Holding the Dream, 1996; Finding the Dream, 1997; Lovers and Dreamers (omnibus), 2005. CHESAPEAKE BAY SERIES: Sea Swept, 1997; Rising Tides, 1998; Inner Harbor, 1998; Nora Roberts Boxed Set (om-

nibus), 2000; Chesapeake Blue, 2002; The Quinn Brothers Trilogy (omnibus), 2002; The Lives and Loves of Four Brothers on the Windswept Shores of the Chesapeake Bay (omnibus), 2004; The Quinn Legacy (omnibus), 2006. STARS OF MITHRA SERIES: Hidden Star, 1997; Captive Star, 1997; Secret Star, 1998. IRISH GALLAGHER'S SERIES: Jewels of the Sun, 1999; Tears of the Moon, 2000; Heart of the Sea, 2000. THREE SISTERS ISLAND SERIES: Dance Upon the Air, 2001; Heaven and Earth, 2001; Face the Fire, 2002. KEY SERIES: Key of Light, 2003; Key of Knowledge, 2003; Key of Valor, 2003. IN THE GARDEN SERIES: Blue Dahlia, 2004; Black Rose, 2005; Red Lily, 2005. CIRCLE TRILOGY: Morrigan's Cross, 2006; Dance of the Gods, 2006; Valley of Silence, 2006. SIGN OF SEVEN TRILOGY: Blood Brothers, 2007; The Hollow, 2008; The Pagan Stone, 2008. BRIDE QUARTET SERIES: Vision in White, 2009; Bed of Roses, 2009; Savor the Moment, 2010; Happy Ever After, 2010. OMNIBUS: Silhouette Christmas Stories: Home For Christmas/Let it Snow/ Starbright /Under the Mistletoe, 1986; (co-author) Silhouette Summer Sizzlers, 1989; (co-author) Historical Christmas Stories 1990: In From The Cold/Miracle of the Heart/Christmas at Bitter Creek, 1990; Once More With Feeling/Song of the West, 1991; (co-author) Jingle Bells, Wedding Bells, 1994; A Special Love: Best Mistake/Baby Machine/Cullen's Child, 1995; From the Heart, 1996; (co-author) Forever Mine, 1998; (co-author) Once Upon A Castle, 1998; (co-author) Once Upon A Star, 1999; (co-author) Once Upon A Dream, 2000; (co-author) Take This Man, 2000; Three Complete Novels: Honest Illusions/Private Scandals/Hidden Riches, 2000; True Betrayals/Montana Sky/Sanctuary, 2001; (co-author) Once Upon A Rose, 2001; (co-author) Once Upon a Kiss, 2002; Going Home, 2002; Table for Two, 2002; Dangerous, 2002; A Little Magic, 2002; Summer Pleasures, 2002; Nora Roberts Collection: Homeport/The Reef/River's End, 2002; Truly Madly Manhattan: Local Hero/Dual Image, 2003; Engaging the Enemy, 2003; Mysterious, 2003; Love by Design, 2003; (co-author) Once Upon a Midnight, 2003; Suspicious, 2003; Less of a Stranger/The Best Mistake, 2004; A Little Fate, 2004; With Open Arms, 2004; (co-author) Moon Shadows, 2004; Winner Takes All, 2004; Reunion, 2004; The Gift: Home For Christmas/All I want for Christmas, 2004; Carolina Moon/The Villa/Three Fates, 2004; Nora Roberts Collection 5: Midnight Bayou/Chesapeake Blue/Birthright, 2004; Winner Take All, 2004; Two of a Kind, 2005; Rules of Play, 2005; By My Side: From This Day/Temptation, 2006; Dream Makers: Untamed/Less Of A Stranger, 2006; The Electrifying Trilogy Box Set, 2006; Irish Dreams: Irish Rebel/Sullivan's Woman, 2007; Treasures: Secret Star/Treasures Lost, Treasures Found, 2008; Falling for Rachel/Convincing Alex, 2008; Summer Delights, 2008. NOVELS: The Heart's Victory, 1982; Search For Love, 1982; Song of the West, 1982; Blithe Images, 1982; Island of Flowers, 1982; Once More With Feeling, 1983; This Magic Moment, 1983; Tonight and Always, 1983; Untamed, 1983; Her Mother's Keeper, 1983; From This Day, 1983; Endings and Beginnings, 1984; A Matter of Choice, 1984; Rules of the Game, 1984; Storm Warning, 1984; Promise Me Tomorrow, 1984; Opposites Attract, 1984; First Impressions, 1984; Sullivan's Woman, 1984; The Law is a Lady, 1984; Less of a Stranger, 1984; Night Moves, 1985; The Right Path, 1985; Boundary Lines, 1985; Dual Image, 1985; Partners, 1985; The Art of Deception, 1986; Treasures Lost, Treasures Found, 1986; Risky Business, 1986; A Will and a Way, 1986; Hot Ice, 1987; Local Hero, 1987; Mind Over Matter, 1987; Temptation, 1987; Name of the Game, 1988; Loving Jack, 1988; Sweet Revenge, 1988; Best Laid Plans, 1989; Impulse, 1989; Gabriel's Angel, 1989; The Welcoming, 1989; Lawless, 1989; Public Secrets, 1990; Carnal Innocence, 1991; Genuine Lies, 1991; Unfinished Business, 1992; Honest Illusions, 1992; Divine Evil, 1992; Private Scandals, 1993; Birds, Bees and Babies, 1994; Hidden Riches, 1994; True Betrayals, 1995; Sanctuary, 1996; Montana Sky, 1996; Home port, 1998; The Reef, 1998; River's End, 1999; Carolina Moon, 2000; Midnight Bayou, 2001; The Villa, 2001; Three Fates, 2002; Birthright, 2003; Northern Lights, 2004; Blue Smoke, 2005; Angels Fall, 2006; High Noon, 2007; Tribute, 2008; Black Hills, 2009; Hot Rocks, 2010; The Search, 2010; Chasing Fire, 2011; Ever After, 2011; The Witness, 2012. OTHERS: Home for Christmas, 1986; Spellbound, 2005; Christmas Angels, 2007. IN DEATH SERIES AS J.D. ROBB: Naked in Death, 1995; Glory in Death, 1995; Immortal in Death, 1996; Rapture in Death, 1996; Ceremony In Death, 1997; Vengeance in Death, 1997; Holiday in Death, 1998; Conspiracy in Death, 1999; Loyalty in Death, 1999; Witness in Death, 2000; Judgment in Death, 2000; Betrayal in Death, 2001; Seduction in Death, 2001; Reunion In Death, 2002; Purity in Death, 2002; Portrait in Death, 2003; Remember When, 2003; Imitation in Death, 2003; Divided in Death, 2004; Visions in Death, 2004; Survivor in Death, 2005; Origin in Death, 2005; Memory in Death, 2006; Born in Death, 2006; Innocent in Death, 2007; Creation in Death, 2007; Strangers in Death, 2008; Salvation In Death, 2008; The Lost, 2009; Promises in Death, 2009; Kindred in

Death, 2009; Fantasy in Death, 2010; Indulgence in Death, 2010; Treachery in Death, 2011; Celebrity in Death, 2012. OTHERS AS J.D. ROBB: Midnight In Death, 1998; (co-author) Naked Came the Phoenix, 2001; Haunted In Death, 2006; Interlude In Death, 2006; Eternity in Death, 2007; Ritual in Death, 2008; Missing In Death, 2009; Possession in Death, 2010; (co-author) The Other Side, 2010; New York to Dallas, 2011. IN DEATH OMNIBUS: In Death Three-Book Set, 2003; Three in Death, 2008; In Death: The First Cases, 2009. AS SARAH HARDESTY: CONCANNON SISTERS TRILOGY: Born in Fire, 1994; Born in Ice, 1995; Born in Shame, 1995; Irish Born (omnibus), 1996. INN BOONSBORO TRILOGY: The Next Always, 2011; The Last Boyfriend, 2012; The Perfect Hope, 2012. **Address:** c/o Amy Berkower, Writers House Inc., 21 W 26th St., New York, NY 10010-1003, U.S.A. **Online address:** readers@noraroberts.com

ROBERTS, Paul. (Paul Edward Roberts). American (born United States), b. 1961. **Genres:** Business/Trade/Industry, Food And Wine, Young Adult Non-fiction, Economics, Social Sciences, Earth Sciences. **Career:** Journalist, 1983-. Broadcaster, educator and public speaker. **Publications:** The End of Oil: On the Edge of a Perilous New World, 2004; The End of Food, 2008. Contributor to periodicals, magazines and newspapers. **Address:** Houghton Mifflin Harcourt Publishing Co., 215 Park Ave. South, New York, NY 10003, U.S.A. **Online address:** proberts@nwi.net

ROBERTS, Paul Edward. See **ROBERTS, Paul.**

ROBERTS, Paul William. Canadian/Welsh (born Wales), b. 1950. **Genres:** Novels, Travel/Exploration. **Career:** Bangalore University, faculty; British Broadcasting Corp., television producer; Canadian Broadcasting Corp., television producer; Citytv, television producer. Freelance writer. **Publications:** River in the Desert: Modern Travels in Ancient Egypt, 1993, rev. ed., 2005; Empire of the Soul: Some Journeys in India, 1994; The Palace of Fears (novel), 1994; In Search of the Birth of Jesus: The Real Journey of the Magi, 1995, rev. ed. as Journey of the Magi: Travels in Search of the Birth of Jesus, 2006; The Demonic Comedy: Some Detours in the Baghdad of Saddam Hussein, 1997; (with N. Snider) Smokescreen: One Man Against the Underworld, 2001; A War Against Truth: An Intimate Account of the Invasion of Iraq, 2004; A War Against Truth: Behind the Lines in the Invasion of Iraq, 2004; Homeland: A Novel, 2006. Contributor to periodicals. **Address:** I.B.Tauris & Company Ltd., 6 Salem Rd., London, GL W2 4BU, England. **Online address:** paulwmroberts@rogers.com

ROBERTS, Philip J. American (born United States), b. 1948. **Genres:** History, Law, Economics, Military/Defense/Arms Control. **Career:** Private practice of law, 1977-79, 1984-85; State of Wyoming, historian, 1979-84; Annals of Wyoming: The Wyoming History Journal, editor, 1979-82, 1995-98, 1999-2002; Capitol Times, co-publisher, 1981-84; University of Wyoming, associate professor of history, 1990-; State of Wyoming, gubernatorial candidate, 1998; Albany County Democratic Party, chair, 1998-2000, 2002-04; American Bar Association Central European and Eurasian Law Initiative, law liaison, 2003-04. **Publications:** (Ed.) More Buffalo Bones: Stories from Wyoming's Past, 1982; (with D.L. Roberts and S.L. Roberts) Wyoming Almanac, 1989, rev. ed., 2010; (as P. Roberts) A Penny for the Governor, A Dollar for Uncle Sam: Income Taxation in Washington, 2002; (ed., as P. Roberts) Readings in Wyoming History, 5th ed., 2009; (ed., as P. Roberts) Wyoming Blue Book, 2009. **Address:** Department of History, University of Wyoming, Rm. 3198, 1000 E University Ave., Laramie, WY 82071, U.S.A. **Online address:** philr@uwyo.edu

ROBERTS, Priscilla. British (born England), b. 1955. **Genres:** History. **Career:** University of Hong Kong, lecturer in history, 1984-2006, associate professor, 2006-, research grant co-ordinator; Northeastern University, adjunct professor, 2002. Writer. **Publications:** (Ed. and intro.) Sino-American Relations in the Twentieth Century, 1991; (ed.) Window on the Forbidden City: The Beijing Diaries of David Bruce, 1973-1974, 2001; (ed.) Behind the Bamboo Curtain: China, Vietnam, and the World beyond Asia, 2006. **Address:** Department of History, University of Hong Kong, Rm. MB165, Pokfulam Rd., 1, Hong Kong. **Online address:** proberts@hkucc.hku.hk

ROBERTS, (Ray) Clayton. American/Chinese (born China), b. 1923. **Genres:** History, Philosophy. **Career:** Ohio State University, instructor, 1952-56, assistant professor, 1956-61, associate professor, 1961-66, professor of history, 1966-91, professor emeritus, 1991-; Columbus Figure Skating Club, president, 1970-72. Writer. **Publications:** The Growth of Responsible Government in Stuart England, 1966; (with D. Roberts) A History of England, vol. I, 1980, (with D. Roberts and D.R. Bisson) 5th ed., 2009; Schemes and Undertakings: A Study of English Politics in the Seventeenth Century, 1985; The Logic of Historical Explanation, 1996; The Struggle for the Sceptre: A Study of Politics in Eighteenth Century Britain, forthcoming. Contributor to journals. **Address:** Department of History, Ohio State University, 106 Dulles Hall, 230 W 17th Ave., Columbus, OH 43210-1361, U.S.A. **Online address:** roberts.26@osu.edu

ROBERTS, Russell D. American (born United States), b. 1954?. **Genres:** Economics, Business/Trade/Industry. **Career:** University of Rochester, instructor; Stanford University, instructor; University of California, instructor; Washington University, Weidenbaum Center on the Economy, Government, and Public Policy, John M. Olin senior fellow, John M. Olin School of Business, Center for Experiential Learning, founding director; George Mason University, Department of Economics, professor of economics, Department of Global Affairs, faculty; Library of Economics and Liberty, associate editor. **Publications:** The Choice: A Fable of Free Trade and Protectionism, 1994, 3rd ed., 2007; The Invisible Heart: An Economic Romance, 2001; The Price of Everything: A Parable of Possibility and Prosperity, 2008; The Economic Cosmos: A Conversation on Why the Ordinary Is Extraordinary, forthcoming. **Address:** Department of Economics, George Mason University, MSN 3G4, 332 Enterprise Hall, 3rd Fl., 4400 University Dr., Fairfax, VA 22030-4444, U.S.A. **Online address:** rrobert2@gmu.edu

ROBERTS, Sally. See **JONES, Sally Roberts.**

ROBERTS, Tansy Rayner. Australian (born Australia), b. 1978. **Genres:** Novels, Young Adult Fiction. **Career:** Andromeda Spaceways Inflight Magazine, co-founding member. Writer. **Publications:** NOVELS: Splashdance Silver, 1998; Liquid Gold, 1999; The Glamoured Girl, 1999; Hobgoblin Boots, 2004; Soapy Ballads, 2005; Seacastle: Lost Shimmaron, 2007; Siren Beat/Roadkill, 2009; Power and Majesty, 2010; Saturnalia, 2010; The Shattered City, 2011; Love and Romanpunk, 2011. Contributor to magazines. **Address:** c/o Author Mail, Random House Australia Ltd., 100 Pacific Hwy., Level 3, Sydney, NW 2060, Australia. **Online address:** creaturecourt@gmail.com

ROBERTS, Yvonne. British (born England), b. 1948. **Genres:** Novels, Human Relations/Parenting, Social Commentary, Psychology, Young Adult Non-fiction, Theology/Religion. **Career:** University of Exeter, Department of Modern Languages, honorary university fellow; writer, 1990-. **Publications:** Man Enough: Men of Thirty-Five Speak Out, 1984; Animal Heroes, 1990; Mad about Women (nonfiction), 1994; Every Woman Deserves an Adventure (novel), 1994; The Trouble with Single Women (novel), 1998; Jean-Antoine de Baif and the Valois Court, 2000; A History of Insects (nonfiction), 2001; Shake!, 2004; Where Did Our Love Go: Reviving A Marriage in Twelve Months, 2006. **Address:** c/o Jacqueline Korn, David Higham Associates Ltd., 5-8 Lower John St., Golden Sq., London, GL W1R 4HA, England. **Online address:** y.c.roberts@ex.ac.uk

ROBERTSON, Barbara Anne. Canadian (born Canada), b. 1931. **Genres:** Biography, History, Poetry, Social Sciences, Autobiography/Memoirs. **Career:** Queen's University, tutor in Canadian history, 1955-. Writer. **Publications:** (Comp. with M.A. Downie) The Wind Has Wings: Poems from Canada, 1968; Sir Wilfrid Laurier: The Great Conciliator, 1971; (with M.A. Downie) The Well-Filled Cupboard, 1987; Laurier as Sir Wilfrid Laurier: The Great Conciliator, 2nd ed., 1991. EDITOR: (with M.A. Downie) Doctor Dwarf and Other Poems for Children by A.M. Klein, 1990; (intro. with F.W. Gibson) Ottawa at War: The Grant Dexter Memoranda, 1939-1945, 1994. **Address:** 52 Florence St., Kingston, ON K7M 1Y6, Canada.

ROBERTSON, C(harles) K(evin). American (born United States), b. 1964. **Genres:** Novels, Theology/Religion, Autobiography/Memoirs. **Career:** St. John's Episcopal Church, priest-in-charge, 1993-96; Church of England, priest-in-residence, 1996-99; St. Stephen's Episcopal Church, rector, 1999-2004; Georgia College and State University, adjunct professor of communications, 1999-2004; Film Clips Spirit of America Inc., executive director, 2002-07; Episcopal Diocese of Arizona, canon to the ordinary, 2004-07; Episcopal Church Center, canon to the presiding bishop, 2007-; General Theological Seminary, distinguished visiting professor, 2009-. Writer. **Publications:** The Kerygma of Billy Graham, 1987; Conflict in Corinth: Redefining the System, 2001; (ed.) Religion As Entertainment, 2002; (ed.) A Living Heritage: St. Stephen's Episcopal Church, 1841-1907, 2003; (ed.) Religion & Alcohol:

Sobering Thoughts, 2004; (ed.) Religion & Sexuality: Passionate Debates, 2006; Transforming Stewardship, 2009; (ed. with B.J. Oropeza and D.C. Mohrmann) Jesus and Paul: Global Perspectives, 2010; Conversations with Scripture: The Acts of the Apostles, 2010; A Dangerous Dozen, 2010. Contributor to periodicals. **Address:** Episcopal Church Center, 815 2nd Ave., New York, NY 10017, U.S.A. **Online address:** crobertson@episcopalchurch.org

ROBERTSON, Deborah. American/Australian (born Australia), b. 1959?. **Genres:** Novels, Novellas/Short Stories, History. **Career:** Murdoch University, Department of English and Comparative Literature, lecturer. Writer. **Publications:** Proudflesh, 1997; Careless, 2007. Contributor of stories and articles. **Address:** Division of Arts, School of Social Sciences & Humanities, Murdoch University, Fremantle, WA 6150, Australia. **Online address:** d.robertson@murdoch.edu.au

ROBERTSON, Elspeth. *See* **ELLISON, Joan Audrey.**

ROBERTSON, Ian (Campbell). French/Japanese (born Japan), b. 1928. **Genres:** History, Military/Defense/Arms Control, Travel/Exploration, Biography. **Career:** Writer, 1962-. **Publications:** Los Curiosos Impertinentes: Viajeros Ingleses por Espana, 1760-1855, 1975, 2nd ed., 1988; Paris and Environs, 1977; Cyprus, 1981, (with B.M. Donagh) 4th ed., 1998; Portugal, 1982, 4th ed., 1996; France, 1984; (with M. Aguilar) Jewish Spain, a Guide, 1984; Portugal: A Traveller's Guide, 1992; Wellington at War in the Peninsula, 1808-1814: An Overview and Guide, 2000; Paris and Versailles, 10th ed., 2001; Wellington Invades France: The Final Phase of the Peninsular War, 1813-1814, 2003; Richard Ford: Hispanophile, Connoisseur and Critic, 1796-1858, 2004; Commanding Presence: Wellington in the Peninsula, 1808-1814: Logistics, Strategy, Survival, 2008. EDITOR: Wellington in the Peninsula, 1962; Handbook for Spain, 1966; Spain: The Country, Her History and Culture, 1970; Journey from London to Genoa, 1970; Blue Guides, Spain, 3rd ed., 1975; Spain, the Mainland, 1975; The Loire Valley, Normandy, Brittany, 4th ed., 1978; Ireland, 4th ed., 1979, 6th ed., 1992; Austria, 1985, 3rd ed., 1992; Travels in Spain, 1989; Switzerland, 5th ed., 1992; (with L.C. Taylor and contrib.) Portugal: A Companion History, 1997; The Private Journal of Judge-Advocate, 2nd ed., 2000; Gatherings from Spain, 2000; The Subaltern: The Diaries of George Greig During the Peninsular War, 2001; A Traveller's History of Portugal, 2002. **Address:** 2 rue Dieudonné, Arles, 13200, France.

ROBERTSON, James I. American (born United States), b. 1930. **Genres:** History, Bibliography, Essays. **Career:** University of Iowa, editor of civil war history, 1959-61; U.S. Civil War Centennial Commission, executive director, 1961-65; George Washington University, associate professorial lecturer, 1962-65; University of Montana, associate professor of history, 1965-67; Virginia Polytechnic Institute and State University, Department of History, professor, 1967-76, C.P. Miles professor, 1976-, chairman, 1969-76, Alumni distinguished professor, 1991-, Virginia Center for Civil War Studies, executive director. **Publications:** Virginia, 1861-1865: Iron Gate to the Confederacy, 1961; (contrib.) The Diary of Dolly Lunt Burge, 1962; The Stonewall Brigade, 1963; The Civil War: A Student Handbook, 1963; The Sack of Lawrence: What Price Glory?, 1963; (comp.) Civil War History: Cumulative Index, 1955-1959, 1963; The Concise Illustrated History of the Civil War, 1971; (comp.) An Index Guide to the Southern Historical Society Papers, 1876-1959, 1980; (with B.S. Wills) Civil War Sites in Virginia, 1981, rev. ed., 2011; 4th Virginia Infantry, 1982; 18th Virginia Infantry, 1984; Tenting Tonite: The Soldiers Life, 1984; General A.P. Hill: The Story of a Confederate Warrior, 1987; Soldiers Blue and Gray, 1988, rev. ed., 1998; Civil War Virginia: Battleground for a Nation, 1991; Civil War: America Becomes One Nation, 1992; The Civil Wars Common Soldier, 1994; Jackson & Lee: Legends in Gray, the Paintings of Mort Kunstler, 1995; Stonewall Jackson: The Man, the Soldier, the Legend, 1997; (contrib.) The Confederate Spirit: Valor, Sacrifice and Honor, 2000; Standing Like a Stone Wall: The Life of General Thomas J. Jackson, 2001; Gods and Generals: The Paintings of MortKünstler, 2002; Robert E. Lee: Virginian Soldier, American Citizen, 2005; (contrib.) For Us the Living, 2010; The Untold Civil War, 2011; (contrib.) Hearts Touched by Fire, 2011. EDITOR: (author of foreword) A Confederate Girls Diary, 1960; (and intro.) From Manassas to Appomattox: Memoirs of the Civil War in America, 1960; (and intro.) Four Years with General Lee, 1962; Diary, 1962; One of Jacksons Foot Cavalry, 1965; The Civil War Letters of General Robert McAllister, 1965; (with A. Nevins and B.I. Wiley) Civil War Books: A Critical Bibliography, 1967; Four Years in the Stonewall Brigade, 1972; (with R. McMurry) Rank and File: Civil War Essays in Honor of Bell Irvin Wiley, 1977; Proceedings of the Advisory Council of the State of Virginia,

April 21-June 19, 1861, 1977; (ed. with J.H. Segars) Bell Irvin Wiley Reader, 2001; Soldier of Southwestern Virginia: The Civil War Letters of Captain John Preston Sheffey, 2004; (co-ed.) Virginia at War, 1861, 2005; Robert E. Lee: Virginian Soldier, American Citizen, 2005; (with W.C. Davis) Virginia at War, 1861, 2005; (with W.C. Davis) Virginia at War, 1865, 2005; (with W.C. Davis) Virginia at War, 1862, 2007; (with W.C. Davis) Virginia at War, 1864, 2009. Contributor to periodicals. **Address:** Department of History, Virginia Polytechnic Institute, and State University, 437 Major Williams, Blacksburg, VA 24061-0117, U.S.A. **Online address:** jircw@vt.edu

ROBERTSON, Janet (E.). American (born United States), b. 1935. **Genres:** Local History/Rural Topics, Photography, Recreation, Biography, Westerns/Adventure, Adult Non-fiction, Westerns/Adventure. **Career:** Norsk Ltd., salesperson, 1969-71; Leanin' Tree, typist, 1974; Omnibus Company Inc., secretary, 1975; Universities Space Research Association, secretary to program director, 1975-76; Words and Pictures, founder, writer and photographer, 1978-; William Allen White Cottage, artist-in-residence, 1984; Colorado Authors League, 1990; Rocky Mountain National Park, president of associates board, 1994-. **Publications:** The Front Rangers, 1970; Liberalism in South Africa, 1948-63, 1971; Magnificent Mountain Women: Adventures in the Colorado Rockies, 1990, rev. ed., 2003; Day Hikes on the Colorado Trail, 1991; Oscar's Spots, 1993; Betsy Cowles Partridge: Mountaineer (biography), 1998. Contributor to encyclopedias. **Address:** University of Nebraska Press, 1111 Lincoln Mall, Lincoln, NE 68588-0630, U.S.A. **Online address:** jan@robsoft.com

ROBERTSON, Joel C. American (born United States), b. 1952. **Genres:** Self Help, Medicine/Health. **Career:** Gladwin Hospital, director of clinical services, Regional Health Center, director; Robertson Institute, owner and president, 1991-; Bay Medical Center, director of chemical dependency, Robertson Research Institute, president and founder, 2002; Robertson Intl., president; Robertson Global Health Solutions, chairman and chief executive officer. Writer. **Publications:** Help Yourself: A Revolutionary Alternative Recovery Program, 1992; Kids Don't Want to Use Drugs, 1992; Help Yourself: Love Yourself, Non-Diet Weight Loss Plan, 1992; Crises Response Planning: Managing a Crisis in the School Family, 1995; Aftercare: Dealing With Death, 1995; Peak Performance Living, 1996; Natural Prozac, 1997; Crises Response Planning: A Procedure Manual for Schools, 1998. Contributor to books and periodicals. **Address:** Robertson Research Institute, 4215 Fashion Square Blvd., Ste. 3, Saginaw, MI 48603, U.S.A. **Online address:** peakperformance@worldnet.att.net

ROBERTSON, Leslie A. Canadian (born Canada), b. 1962?. **Genres:** History. **Career:** University of Windsor, assistant professor. Writer. **Publications:** Imagining Difference: Legend, Curse and Spectacle in a Canadian Mining Town, 2005; (ed. with D. Culhane) In Plain Sight: Reflections on Life in Downtown Eastside Vancouver, 2005. **Address:** Department of Sociology and Anthropology, University of Windsor, Windsor, ON N9B 3P4, Canada. **Online address:** rleslie@uwindsor.ca

ROBERTSON, Robin. British/Scottish (born Scotland), b. 1955. **Genres:** Poetry, Novels. **Career:** Penguin Books, assistant fiction editor, 1978-85; Secker & Warburg, editorial director, 1985-93; Jonathan Cape, deputy publishing director and poetry editor, 1993-; Annaghmakerrig Residency, deputy publishing director and poetry editor, 1993-94; Writers Room, first writer-in-residence, 1999; Grand Street, contributing editor. **Publications:** Camera Obscura, 1996; A Painted Field, 1998, Slow Air, 2002; (ed.) Mortification: Writer's Stories of Their Public Shame, 2004; (trans.) T. Transtr̈omer, Deleted World, 2006; Swithering, 2006; (ed.) Love Poet, Carpenter: Michael Longley at Seventy, 2009; Wrecking Light, 2010. Works appear in anthologies. Contributor to journals and periodicals. **Address:** c/o Jonathan Cape, 20 Vauxhall Bridge Rd., London, GL SW1V 2SA, England.

ROBERTSON Q.C., Geoffrey R. British/Australian (born Australia), b. 1946. **Genres:** Law. **Career:** Middle Temple, barrister, 1973-; Supreme Court of South Wales, barrister, 1977-; University of New South Wales, visiting fellow, 1977; University of Warwick, visiting fellow, 1980-81; Inquiry into Press Council, chairperson, 1982-83; Federal Attorney General's Department, barrister, 1984-; Queen's Counsel, staff, 1988; Doughty Street Chambers, founder and head, 1990-; Supreme Court of Antigua, barrister, 1990-; Supreme Court of Trinidad, barrister, 1992-; Supreme Court of Malawi, barrister, 1995-; University of London, visiting fellow, 1998-; UN Special Court for War Crimes in Sierra Leone, appeal judge, 2002-, president, 2002-04. Writer. **Publications:** The Trials of Oz, 1972; Whose Conspiracy?, 1974; Reluctant Judas: The Life and Death of the Special Branch Informer, Kenneth Lennon, 1976; Obscenity: An Account of Censorship Laws and Their Enforcement in England and Wales, 1979; People Against the Press: An Enquiry into the Press Council, 1983; (with A.G.L. Nicol) Media Law: The Rights of Journalists and Broadcasters, 1984, 5th ed., 2005; Hypotheticals, 1986; Does Dracula Have AIDS?, 1987; Blood on the Wattle, 1988; Freedom, the Individual and The Law, 1989, 8th ed., 1993; Geoffrey Robertson's Hypotheticals, 1991; What Kind of Constitution?, 1991; (intro.) The Trial of Lady Chatterly, 1992; Cure for the British Disease: Freedom of Information, 1993; The Justice Game, 1998; Crimes Against Humanity: The Struggle for Global Justice, 1999, 3rd ed., 2006; Justice and Revenge: International Law After Tuesday 11th September 2001, 2002; The Tyrannicide Brief in US as Tyrannicide Brief: Story of the Man who Sent Charles I to the Scaffold, 2005; (foreword) Time for Change: Australia in the 21st Century, 2006; Geoffrey Robertson Presents the Levellers: The Putney Debates, 2008; The Statute of Liberty, 2009. **Address:** Doughty Street Chambers, 53-54 Doughty St., London, GL WC1N 2LS, England. **Online address:** g.robertson@doughtystreet.co.uk

ROBESON, Paul. American (born United States), b. 1927. **Genres:** Social Commentary, Essays, Biography, Art/Art History. **Career:** School of Industrial Technology, teacher of electronics and power engineering, 1949-53; Othello Associates, chief executive officer, 1953-56; Plenum Press, translator, 1953-57; International Physical Index, editor, 1957-72, publisher, 1973-81; freelance translator, 1971-89; American Program Bureau, lecturer, 1979-89; Allerton Press, translator and consultant, 1982-91; WNET-TV, host, 1986; WBAI-FM Radio, host; Program Corporation of America, lecturer, 1990-92. **Publications:** Paul Robeson, Jr. Speaks to America, 1993; The Undiscovered Paul Robeson: An Artist's Journey, 1898-1939, 2001; A Black Way of Seeing: From Liberty to Freedom, 2006. Contributor to periodicals. **Address:** c/o Lawrence Jordan, 345 W 121st St., New York, NY 10027, U.S.A. **Online address:** maparobe@aol.com

ROBIE, Bill. (William A. Robie). American (born United States), b. 1947. **Genres:** Air/Space Topics, History, Military/Defense/Arms Control. **Career:** Actor, 1972-90; University of Maryland, adjunct teacher of U.S. History, 1990-. Writer. **Publications:** For the Greatest Achievement: A History of the Aero Club of America and the National Aeronautic Association, 1993. **Address:** University of Maryland, 621 West Lombard St., Baltimore, MD 21201-1627, U.S.A.

ROBIE, William A. See **ROBIE, Bill.**

ROBIN, Corey. American (born United States), b. 1967?. **Genres:** Politics/Government, Young Adult Non-fiction, History, Philosophy, Social Sciences. **Career:** Yale University, instructor and teaching assistant, 1991-99; Brooklyn College, Department of Political Science, assistant professor, 1999-2005, associate professor, 2005-. Writer. **Publications:** Fear: The History of a Political Idea, 2004; The Reactionary Mind: Conservatism From Edmund Burke To Sarah Palin, 2011; (with E. Schrecker) The American Way of Repression, forthcoming; On Counterrevolution, forthcoming. **Address:** Department of Political Science, Brooklyn College, City University of New York, 3405 James Hall, 2900 Bedford Ave., Brooklyn, NY 11210, U.S.A. **Online address:** crobin@brooklyn.cuny.edu

ROBINETTE, Joseph A. American (born United States), b. 1939. **Genres:** Plays/Screenplays. **Career:** University of Oregon, lecturer; University of Maryland, lecturer; Rowan University, professor of theatre, 1971-, now retired. Writer. **Publications:** PLAYS: (with T. Tierney) The Fabulous Fable Factory (musical), 1975; Mr. Herman and the Cave Company (musical), 1977; The Princess, the Poet, and the Little Gray Man (musical), 1978; Showdown at the Sugar Cane Saloon (musical), 1979; Once upon a Shoe, 1979; Charlotte's Web, 1979; Planet of the Perfectly Awful People, 1979; Get Bill Shakespeare Off the Stage, 1980; Oh, Brother!, 1980; Up the Ivory Tower, 1981; Legend of the Sun Child (musical), 1981; The Paper Chase (2-act), 1981; Ashes, Ashes, All Fall Down (with music), 1982; Kiddledywinks! (musical), 1983; Melissa and the Magic Nutcracker (musical), 1983; A Rose for Emily, 1983; Beanstalk!: A Musical Play for Children's Theatre, 1985; Penny and the Magic Medallion: A One-Act Musical for Children, 1987; Penny and the Anne of Green Gables, 1989; The Lion, the Witch and the Wardrobe, 1989; Dorothy Meets Alice (musical), 1990; The Trial of Goldilocks, 1990; ABC

(America before Columbus), 1991; The Phantom of the Opera: Based upon the Novel by Gaston Leroux, 1991; Stuart Little, 1991; The Trumpet of the Swan, 1992; The Adventures of Peter Rabbit and His Friends, 1994; The Littlest Angel (musical), 1994; The Jungle Book, 1994; Anne of Avonlea, 1997; The Trial of the Big Bad Wolf, 1999; Humpty Dumpty is Missing, 2001; Just So Stories, 2001; Chocolate War, 2001; Sarah, Plain and Tall, 2002; Chanticleer and the Fox, 2003; (with S.F. Asher and K.R. Brown) 125 Original Audition Monologues, 2003; The Day the Rooster Didn't Crow, 2003; Agatha Raisin and the Quiche of Death, 2004; Open House at Hightower U.: A Semi-Serious Comedy in One Act, 2008. **Address:** Richwood-Harrisonville Rd., Richwood, NJ 08074, U.S.A.

ROBINS, Glenn. American (born United States) **Genres:** Biography, Theology/Religion. **Career:** University of Southern Mississippi, visiting assistant professor, 19992000; Brewton-Parker College, assistant professor, 2000-01; Georgia Southwestern State University, associate professor, 2001-. Writer and educator. **Publications:** The Bishop of the Old South: The Ministry and Civil War Legacy of Leonidas Polk, 2006. Contributor of journals. **Address:** Department of History & Political Science, College of Arts & Sciences, Georgia Southwestern State University, 800 Wheatley St., Americus, GA 31709, U.S.A. **Online address:** grobins@gsw.edu

ROBINS, Madeleine E. American (born United States), b. 1953. **Genres:** Novels, Novellas/Short Stories, Young Adult Fiction, Children's Fiction. **Career:** Harvard University, Graduate School of Design, faculty, through 1981; Tor Books, freelance writer, 1990, assistant, editor, 1991-98; freelance writer, 1998-; Book View Cafe, founding member. **Publications:** Althea, 1977; My Dear Jenny, 1981; The Heiress Companion (short stories), 1981; Lady John, 1982; The Spanish Marriage, 1984; The Stone War, 1999; Daredevil: The Cutting Edge, 1999; Point of Honour, 2003; Petty Treason: A Sarah Tolerance Mystery, 2004; (ed.) Lace and Blade 2, 2009; The Sleeping Partner, 2011. **Address:** c/o Author Mail, Tor Books, 175 5th Ave., New York, NY 10010, U.S.A. **Online address:** madrobins@earthlink.net

ROBINS, Patricia. See **LORRIMER, Claire.**

ROBINS, Robert S. American (born United States), b. 1938. **Genres:** Education, Politics/Government, Psychology. **Career:** Tulane University, professor of political science, 1965-, deputy provost, 1991-; Oxford University, St. Antony's College, senior associate, 1972-73, 1978-79; Tavistock Clinic, visiting scientist, 1987-88, 1994. **Publications:** Political Institutionalization and the Integration of Elites, 1976; (ed.) Psychopathology and Political Leadership, 1977; (with J.M. Post) When Illness Strikes the Leader: The Dilemma of the Captive King, 1993; (with J.M. Post) Political Paranoia: The Psychopolitics of Hatred, 1997. Contributor to journals. **Address:** Office of the Provost, Tulane University, 200 Gibson Hall, 6823 St., Charles Ave., New Orleans, LA 70118, U.S.A. **Online address:** robins@mailhost.tcs.tulane.edu

ROBINS, Sari. American (born United States) **Genres:** Novels, Young Adult Non-fiction, Romance/Historical. **Career:** Delta Air Lines, tax attorney; SEASON Magazine, staff; Atlanta Woman Magazine, staff; CHAI Magazine, staff; POINTS NORTH Magazine, staff; The Jewish Times, staff; LILITH Magazine, staff; The Northside Neighbor, staff; writer, 2000-. **Publications:** Her Scandalous Intentions, 2002; All Men Are Rogues, 2003. ANDERSEN HALL SERIES: One Wicked Night, 2004; More Than a Scandal, 2004; What to Wear to a Seduction, 2006; When Seducing a Spy, 2007; The Governess Wears Scarlet, 2008. Contributor to magazines. **Address:** c/o Author Mail, HarperCollins Publishers, 10 E 53rd St., 11th Fl., New York, NY 10022, U.S.A. **Online address:** sari@sarirobins.com

ROBINSON, Alex. See **ROBINSON, Wayne Alexander.**

ROBINSON, Andrew. British (born England), b. 1957. **Genres:** Novellas/Short Stories, Archaeology/Antiquities, Art/Art History, Earth Sciences, Film, History, Language/Linguistics, Literary Criticism And History, Physics, Biography, Psychology. **Career:** Macmillan Publishers, staff, 1979-82; Granada Television, staff, 1983-88; Brian Lapping Associates, staff, 1989-90; The Times Higher Education Supplement, literary editor, 1994-2006; Cambridge University, Wolfson College, visiting fellow, 2006-10; Royal Asiatic Society, fellow. **Publications:** (Intro.) The Coasts of India, 1987; Maharaja: The Spectacular Heritage of Princely India, 1988; Satyajit Ray: The Inner Eye, 1989, 2nd ed., 2004; The Art of Rabindranath Tagore, 1989; (with S. Berthon) The Shape of the World: The Mapping and Discovery of the Earth,

1991; Earthshock: Hurricanes, Volcanoes, Earthquakes, Tornadoes and Other Forces of Nature, 1993, rev. ed., 2002; (with K. Dutta) Rabindranath Tagore: The Myriad-Minded Man, 1995; The Story of Writing: Alphabets, Hieroglyphs and Pictograms, 1995, rev. ed. 2007; (trans. with K. Dutta) R. Tagore, The Post Office, 1996; Lost Languages: The Enigma of the World's Undeciphered Scripts, 2002, rev. ed. 2009; The Man Who Deciphered Linear B: The Story of Michael Ventris, 2002; (with N. Ghosh) Satyajit Ray: A Vision of Cinema, 2005; Einstein: A Hundred Years of Relativity, 2005; The Last Man Who Knew Everything: Thomas Young, the Anonymous Polymath Who Proved Newton Wrong, Explained How We See, Cured the Sick and Deciphered the Rosetta Stone, Among Other Feats of Genius, 2006; The Story of Measurement, 2007; Writing and Script: A Very Short Introduction, 2009; Sudden Genius? The Gradual Path to Creative Breakthroughs, 2010; Genius: A Very Short Introduction, 2011; The Apu Trilogy: Satyajit Ray and the Making of an Epic, 2011. EDITOR: (with K. Dutta): (trans.) Noon in Calcutta: Short Stories from Bengal, 1992; Selected Letters of Rabindranath Tagore, 1997. **Address:** 13 Lonsdale Sq., London, GL N1 1EN, England. **Online address:** andrew.robinson33@virgin.net

ROBINSON, Chuck. American (born United States), b. 1950. **Genres:** Marine Sciences/Oceanography, Environmental Sciences/Ecology, Sciences. **Career:** Park Chevrolet Inc., assistant service manager, 1969-76; Spring Lake Heights Fire Department, secretary, 1982-83; Old Squan Village Publishing, owner and manager, 1994-. Writer. **Publications:** WITH D. ROBINSON: The Art of Shelling: A Complete Guide to Finding Shells and Other Beach Collectibles at Shelling Locations from Florida to Maine, 1995, 3rd ed., 2008; Treasure for Our Sand Castle (juvenile), 1997. **Address:** Old Squan Village Publishing, 18 Willow Way, Manasquan, NJ 08736, U.S.A.

ROBINSON, Cynthia. American (born United States), b. 1958. **Genres:** Novels. **Career:** University of San Francisco, fiction writing teacher. Writer. **Publications:** The Dog Park Club (novel), 2010. Works appear in anthologies. **Address:** San Francisco, CA , U.S.A. **Online address:** maxbravo@cynthiarobinsonauthor.com

ROBINSON, David L. American (born United States), b. 1963. **Genres:** Mystery/Crime/Suspense, Young Adult Fiction. **Career:** Royal Wholesalers, business manager, 1987-90; Business Development Associates, marketing consultant, 2000-02; Chicago State University, adjunct faculty, 2002-. Writer. **Publications:** Emotional Deception: Every Persons Weakness, 2004. **Address:** Platinum One Publishing, 21 W 551 North Ave., Ste. 132, Lombard, IL 60148, U.S.A.

ROBINSON, Debbie. American (born United States), b. 1958. **Genres:** Marine Sciences/Oceanography, Social Sciences. **Career:** Jersey Shore Medical Center, community caseworker, 1980-82; New Jersey Easter Seal Society, rehabilitation supervisor, 1983-84, Second Step Program, manager, 1984-86, director of rehabilitation services, 1986-89; Ocean County College, Project CAREER/Customized Training, director, 1989-, Business Education and Training, director, 1989-2006, Continuing and Professional Education, director, 2007-; Lakewood Chamber of Commerce, board director, 1993-96. Writer. **Publications:** (With C. Robinson) The Art of Shelling: A Complete Guide to Finding Shells and Other Beach Collectibles at Shelling Locations from Florida to Maine, 1995, 3rd ed., 2008; (with C. Robinson) Treasure for Our Sand Castle (juvenile), 1997. **Address:** Old Squan Village Publishing, 18 Willow Way, Manasquan, NJ 08736-2835, U.S.A. **Online address:** drobinson@ocean.edu

ROBINSON, Eden. Canadian (born Canada), b. 1968. **Genres:** Novels, Novellas/Short Stories. **Career:** Writer. **Publications:** Traplines, 1996; Monkey Beach, 2000; Blood Sports, 2006; The Sasquatch at Home: Traditional Protocols & Modern Storytelling, 2011. Contributor to periodicals. **Address:** Henry Holt & Company Inc., 175 5th Ave., New York, NY 10010, U.S.A.

ROBINSON, Frank M(alcolm). American (born United States), b. 1926. **Genres:** Science Fiction/Fantasy, Novellas/Short Stories, Mystery/Crime/Suspense, Art/Art History, History, Picture/Board Books, Photography. **Career:** Family Weekly, assistant editor, 1955-56; Science Digest, assistant editor, 1956-59; Rogue magazine, editor, 1959-65; Cavalier, managing editor, 1965-66; Censorship Today, editor, 1967; Playboy Magazine, staff writer, 1969-73; freelance writer, 1973-; Ziff-Davis Publishing Co., office boy. **Publications:** The Power, 1956, 2nd ed., 2000; (ed. with E. Kemp) The Truth about Vietnam: Report on the U.S. Senate Hearings, 1966; (ed. with N. Lehrman) Sex American Style, 1971; (with T.N. Scortia) The Glass Inferno, 1974; (contrib.) Towering Inferno, 1974; (with T.N. Scortia) The Prometheus Crisis, 1975; (with T.N. Scortia) The Nightmare Factor, 1978; (with T.N. Scortia) The Gold Crew, 1980; A Life in the Day of, and Other Stories, 1980; (with J.F. Levin) The Great Divide, 1982, rev. ed., 2004; (with T.N. Scortia) Blow-Out!, 1987; The Dark beyond the Stars, 1991; (with P. Hull) Death of a Marionette, 1995; (with L. Davidson) Pulp Culture: The Art of Fiction Magazines, 1998; Waiting, 1999; Science Fiction of the 20th Century: An Illustrated History, 1999; Art of Imagination: 20th Century Visions of Science Fiction, Horror, and Fantasy, 2002; (co-author) Through my Glasses, Darkly: Science Fiction Stories by Frank M. Robinson, 2003; Donor, 2004; Incredible Pulps: A Gallery of Fiction Magazine Art, 2006. **Address:** TOR Books, 175 5th Ave., New York, NY 10010, U.S.A.

ROBINSON, H(enry) Basil. Canadian/British (born England), b. 1919. **Genres:** History, Young Adult Fiction, Social Sciences. **Career:** Canadian Department of External Affairs, foreign service officer, 1945-56, Middle East Division, head, 1956-57, liaison officer with the prime minister's office, 1957-62, Canadian embassy, deputy head of mission, 1962-64, assistant undersecretary, 1964-67, deputy undersecretary, 1967-69, Department of Indian Affairs and Northern Development, deputy minister, 1970-74, undersecretary 1974-77, Northern Pipeline Agency, commissioner, 1977-78, special adviser to undersecretary of state for external affairs, 1979-81; consultant and writer, 1981-96. **Publications:** Diefenbaker's World: A Populist in Foreign Affairs, 1989; This Family Robinson, 1996. **Address:** 17 Mariposa Ave., Ottawa, ON K1M 0T9, Canada.

ROBINSON, Holly. American (born United States), b. 1955. **Genres:** Autobiography/Memoirs. **Career:** University of Massachusetts, Medical Center, science and health writer; Ladies' Home Journal, contributing editor; Parents Magazine, contributing editor; Northeastern University, adjunct faculty. **Publications:** The Gerbil Farmer's Daughter: A Memoir, 2009. Contributor to periodicals. **Address:** MA , U.S.A. **Online address:** holly@authorhollyrobinson.com

ROBINSON, Jennifer L. American (born United States), b. 1976. **Genres:** Young Adult Non-fiction, History. **Career:** University of Utah, Center for Public Policy and Administration, research associate and associate director. Writer. **Publications:** (with D. McCool and S.M. Olson) Native Vote: American Indians, the Voting Rights Act and the Right to Vote (nonfiction), 2007. **Address:** University of Utah Public Relations, 201 Presidents Cir., Ste. 308, Salt Lake City, UT 84112, U.S.A. **Online address:** robinson@cppa.utah.edu

ROBINSON, Jeremy. American (born United States), b. 1974. **Genres:** Novels, Illustrations. **Career:** Breakneck Books, founder. Author and illustrator. **Publications:** SELF-ILLUSTRATED: (with T. Mungovan) The Screenplay Workbook: The Writing before the Writing (nonfiction), 2003. OTHERS: Raising the Past (novel), 2006; POD People: Beating the Print-on-Demand Stigma (nonfiction), 2006; The Didymus Contingency (novel), 2007; Antarktos Rising (novel), 2008; Kronos (novel), 2009; Pulse (novel), 2009; Instinct: A Chess Team Adventure (novel), 2010. **Address:** Trident Media Group, 41 Madison Ave., 36th Fl., New York, NY 10010, U.S.A. **Online address:** info@jeremyrobinsononline.com

ROBINSON, Julian. British (born England), b. 1931. **Genres:** Anthropology/Ethnology, Fash Ion/Costume. **Career:** Child actor, 1944-49; freelance writer and consultant, 1985-; Julian Robinson and Associates (designers), owner and designer; Royal College of Art, fellow; Hornsey College of Art (now Middlesex University), head of fashion and textile studies; Sydney College of the Arts (now University of Sydney), founding professor and head of department of fashion, textiles, interior design and graphics; University of California, lecturer; American College, lecturer; Hong Kong College of Technology, lecturer; Church of God International Offices, director. **Publications:** (With R. Robinson) Odhams Fashion and Dressmaking, 1962; (with R. Robinson) Streamlined Dressmaking, 1966; (with R. Robinson) Streamlined Sewing for Fun, 1971; (with R. Robinson) Streamlined Decorative Sewing, 1971; (with R. Robinson) Streamlined Curtains and Covers, 1971; Instant Dressmaking: The Three-in-One Guide, 1973; The Art of Dressmaking and Tailoring; The Penguin Book of Sewing, 1973; Fashion in the Forties, 1976, as Fashion in the '40s, 1980; The Golden Age of Style, 1976; Fashion in the '30s, 1978; The Brilliance of Art Deco, 1988; Body Packaging: A Guide to

Human Sexual Display, 1988; The Quest for Human Beauty: An Illustrated History, 1998; The Fine Art of Fashion: An Illustrated History, 1989; Grand Chic: Art Deco Fashion Illustration; An Encyclopedia of Human Aesthetics: Fashion, Beauty, Body Arts, 2004; Nuevos realismos, 1957-1962, 2010. Contributor to magazines. **Address:** Church of God International Offices, 2490 Keith St., PO Box 2430, Cleveland, TN 37320, U.S.A. **Online address:** jrbodyarts@yahoo.com.au

ROBINSON, Ken. American/British (born England), b. 1950. **Genres:** Education, Theatre. **Career:** National Curriculum Council, The Arts School Project, director, 1985-89; University of Warwick, professor, 1989-2001, professor emeritus, 2001-. Writer and consultant. **Publications:** (With L. McGregor and M. Tate) Learning through Drama: Report of the Schools Council Drama Teaching Project (10-16), Goldsmiths' College, University of London, 1977; (ed.) Exploring Theatre and Education, 1980; (ed.) The Arts and Higher Education, 1982; Culture, Creativity and the Young: Developing Public Policy, 1999; Out of Our Minds: Learning to Be Creative, 2001; (with L. Aronica) The Element: How Finding Your Passion Changes Everything, 2009. **Address:** Los Angeles, CA , U.S.A. **Online address:** info@sirkenrobinson.com

ROBINSON, Leah Ruth. American (born United States), b. 1951. **Genres:** Mystery/Crime/Suspense, Medicine/Health, Young Adult Fiction. **Career:** St. Luke's-Roosevelt Hospital Center, Emergency Department, staff; Lenox Hill Hospital, basic life support instructor. Writer. **Publications:** DR. EVELYN SUTCLIFFE SERIES: Blood Run, 1988; First Cut, 1997; Unnatural Causes, 1999. Contributor to periodicals. **Address:** The Karpfinger Agency, 357 W 20th St., New York, NY 10011-3379, U.S.A. **Online address:** author@leahruthrobinson.com

ROBINSON, Lee. (Lee M. Robinson). American (born United States), b. 1948. **Genres:** Novels, Poetry, Novellas/Short Stories, History. **Career:** Family Court, lawyer, 1975-; The University of Texas, Health Science Center-San Antonio, Center for Medical Humanities and Ethics, faculty associate, 1998-. Writer. **Publications:** Gateway, 1996; Hearsay, 2004; Creed, 2009. Contributor to periodicals. **Address:** Center for Medical Humanities & Ethics, Health Science Ctr., University of Texas, 7703 Floyd Curl Dr., PO Box 7730, San Antonio, TX 78229-3901, U.S.A. **Online address:** leemrob9@aol.com

ROBINSON, Lee M. See **ROBINSON, Lee.**

ROBINSON, Lynda S(uzanne). American (born United States), b. 1951. **Genres:** Mystery/Crime/Suspense, Romance/Historical. **Career:** Educator and writer. **Publications:** HISTORICAL ROMANCE NOVELS AS SUZANNE ROBINSON: Heart of the Falcon, 1990; Lady Gallant, 1992; Lady Hellfire, 1992; Lady Defiant, 1993; Lady Valiant, 1993; Lady Dangerous, 1994; Lord of the Dragon, 1995; Lord of Enchantment, 1995; The Engagement, 1996; The Rescue, 1998; The Treasure, 1999; Just before Midnight, 2000; The Legend, 2001; Never Trust a Lady, 2003. MYSTERY NOVELS: Murder in the Place of Anubis, 1994; Murder at the God's Gate, 1995; Murder at the Feast of Rejoicing, 1996; Eater of Souls, 1997; Drinker of Blood, 1998; Slayer of Gods, 2001. **Address:** Cherry Weiner Literary Agency, 28 Kipling Way, Manalapan, NJ 07726, U.S.A. **Online address:** lynda@meren.com

ROBINSON, Marguerite S(tern). American (born United States), b. 1935. **Genres:** Anthropology/Ethnology, Money/Finance, Politics/Government. **Career:** Cambridge University, National Science Foundation fellow, 1966; Brandeis University, lecturer, 1964-65, Department of Anthropology, assistant professor, 1965-72, associate professor, 1972-78, professor of anthropology, 1978-85, College of Arts and Sciences, dean, 1973-75; Harvard University, research fellow in ethnology of India, 1969, fellow, 1980-85, Harvard Institute for International Development, faculty, 1978-, Institute fellow, 1985-2000, Institute fellow emeritus, 2000; National Institutes of Health Project, project officer, 1971-72; consultant, 2000-. Writer. **Publications:** (Contrib.) Cambridge Papers in Social Anthropology, 1968; (contrib.) Structuralism: A Reader, 1970; Political Structure in a Changing Sinhalese Village, 1975; Local Politics, The Law of the Fishes: Development Through Political Change in Medak District, Andhra Pradesh, 1988; (with O. Sugianto and S. Purnomo) Pembiayaan Pertanian Pedesaan: Bunga Rampai, 1993; The Micro finance Revolution, vol. I: Sustainable Finance for the Poor, 2001, vol. II: Lessons from Indonesia, 2002, vol. III: Regional Analyses and Global Trends, 2006, vol. IV: The Emerging Industry, 2007. **Address:** Harvard University, Massachusetts Hall, Cambridge, MA 02138, U.S.A. **Online address:** mrobinso1@aol.com

ROBINSON, Michael F. (Michael Frederick Robinson). American (born United States), b. 1966. **Genres:** Cultural/Ethnic Topics. **Career:** University of Hartford, assistant professor of history, 2002-; University of Southern Maine, Osher Map Library, guest curator. Writer, historian and educator. **Publications:** The Coldest Crucible: Arctic Exploration and American Culture, 2006. **Address:** 316 Hillyer Hall, 200 Bloomfield Ave., West Hartford, CT 06117, U.S.A. **Online address:** microbins@hartford.edu

ROBINSON, Michael Frederick. See **ROBINSON, Michael F.**

ROBINSON, Paul H. American (born United States), b. 1948. **Genres:** Law, Criminology/True Crime. **Career:** Rutgers University, law faculty, 1977-93; Northwestern University, Law School, law faculty, 1993-98, Edna and Ednyfed Williams professor of law, 2000-; University of Michigan, visiting professor, 1998-99; University of Pennsylvania, Law School, Colin S. Diver professor of law. Writer. **Publications:** Criminal Law Defenses, 1984; Fundamentals of Criminal Law, 1988; Justice, Liability and Blame: Community Views and the Criminal Law, 1995; Structure and Function in Criminal Law, 1997; Criminal Law, 1997; Would You Convict? Seventeen Cases That Challenged the Law, 1999; Criminal Law Case Studies, 2000; Law Without Justice: Why Criminal Law Doesn't Give People What They Deserve, 2005; Criminal Law: Case Studies and Controversies, 2005, 2nd ed., 2008; Distributive Principles of Criminal Law: Who Should be Punished, How Much?, 2008; (ed. with S.P. Garvey and K.K. Ferzen) Criminal Law Conversations, 2010. **Address:** Law School, University of Pennsylvania, 3400 Chestnut St., Philadelphia, PA 19104-6204, U.S.A. **Online address:** phr@law.upenn.edu

ROBINSON, Peter (Mark). Also writes as Jazz Voyd Johnson, Charles Floyd Johnson, Chas Floyd Johnson. American (born United States), b. 1957. **Genres:** Adult Non-fiction, Biography, Essays, Social Sciences. **Career:** The White House, chief speechwriter to vice-president George Bush, 1982-83, special assistant and speechwriter to president Ronald Reagan, 1983-88; Fox Television, reporter; The News Corporation Ltd., press secretary to chairman, assistant and political counsel to Rupert Murdoch, Gulf War commentator and producer of news segments for Fox television affiliates, 1990-91; Securities and Exchange Commission, Office of Public Affairs, Policy Evaluation and Research, director, 1991-93; The Dartmouth, reporter, columnist and editor; Stanford University, Hoover Institution (public policy research center), fellow, 1993-, research fellow, Hoover Digest, editor; Dartmouth College, trustee, 2005. **Publications:** School Days: An Essay on the Hoover Institution Conference Choice and Vouchers-the Future of American Education?, 1993; Snapshots from Hell: The Making of an MBA, 1994; (ed.) Can Congress Be Fixed (and is it Broken)?: Five Essays on Congressional Reform, 1995; It's My Party: A Republican's Messy Love Affair with the GOP, 2000; How Ronald Reagan Changed My Life, 2003. Contributor of articles to periodicals. **Address:** Hoover Institution, 434 Galvez Mall, Stanford, CA 94305-6010, U.S.A.

ROBINSON, Phyllis C(umins). American (born United States), b. 1924. **Genres:** Regional/Urban Planning, History, Biography, Autobiography/Memoirs. **Career:** Manhattan Community Board No. 8, chair, 1960-63; Yorkville Civic Council, president, 1963-67; New York City Department of Parks, Recreation and Cultural Affairs, staff, 1965-74, deputy commissioner of cultural affairs, 1971-74; Lenox Hill Neighborhood Association, director, 1968-; New York City Parks Council, director, 1976-85; Book-of-the-Month Club, senior editor and reader, 1985-97; United Neighborhood House of New York, vice president. Writer. **Publications:** (With A. Heckscher) Open Spaces: The Life of American Cities, 1977; (with A. Heckscher) When LaGuardia Was Mayor: New York's Legendary Years, 1978; Willa: The Life of Willa Cather, 1983; (ed.) The Shyp of Fooles, 1983. **Address:** 530 E 90th St., New York, NY 10128, U.S.A. **Online address:** crob530@aol.com

ROBINSON, Roxana (Barry). American (born United States), b. 1946. **Genres:** Novels, Novellas/Short Stories, Biography, Mystery/Crime/Suspense, Young Adult Fiction. **Career:** Sotheby-Parke-Bernet, assistant head of American painting department, 1970-74; Terry Dintenfass Gallery, exhibition director, 1974-75; freelance writer, 1976-; Katonah Gallery, board director, 1984-; Wesleyan University, teacher, 1997-, 2002-03; Bennington College, teacher; University of Southern Indiana, teacher; George Mason University, teacher; Hunter College, MFA Program, teacher. **Publications:** Summer Light, 1987; Georgia O'Keeffe: A Life, 1989; A Glimpse of Scarlet and Other Stories, 1991; (intro.) A Matter of Prejudice and other Stories, 1992; Asking for Love and Other Stories, 1996; This is My Daughter: A Novel, 1998;

Sweetwater: A Novel, 2003; A Perfect Stranger: And Other Stories, 2005; (intro.) The New York Stories of Edith Wharton, 2007; Cost, 2008. Contributor of articles to magazines and newspapers. **Address:** c/o Lynn Nesbit, Janklow and Nesbit Associates, 445 Park Ave., New York, NY 10022-2606, U.S.A.

ROBINSON, Spider. Canadian/American (born United States), b. 1948. **Genres:** Novels, Novellas/Short Stories, Science Fiction/Fantasy, Writing/Journalism, Essays, Humor/Satire, Literary Criticism And History, Young Adult Fiction, Young Adult Fiction. **Career:** Long Island Review, realty editor, 1972-73; freelance writer, 1973-; Galaxy magazine, book reviewer, 1975-77; Writers Federation of Nova Scotia, chairman, 1981-83; Clarion Michigan State University, Science Fiction Writers Workshop, instructor, 1989; Toronto Globe and Mail, columnist, 1995-. **Publications:** Telempath, 1976; Callahan's Crosstime Saloon (short stories), 1978; (with J. Robinson) Stardance, 1979, 2nd ed., 1996; Antinomy (short stories), 1980; (ed.) The Best of All Possible Worlds, 1980; Mindkiller, 1982; Melancholy Elephants (short stories), 1985; Night of Power, 1985; Callahan's Secret (short stories), 1986; Tales from the Planet Earth, 1986; Time Pressure, 1987; Callahan and Company (short stories), 1989; Callahan's Lady, 1989; Copyright Violation, 1990; True Minds, 1990; (with J. Robinson) Starseed; 1991; (ed.) Kill the Editor, 1991; Lady Slings the Booze, 1992; Callahan's Touch, 1993; Off the Wall at Callahan's, 1994; Starmind, 1995; Callahan's Legacy, 1996; Lifehouse, 1997; Callahan Chronicals, 1997; User friendly, 1998; Callahan's Key, 2000; Time Travelers Strictly Cash (short stories), 2001; By Any Other Name, 2001; The Free Lunch, 2001; God is an Iron and Other Stories, 2002; Callahan's Con, 2003; The Crazy Years (essays), 2004; Very Bad Deaths, 2004; (with J. Robinson) The Stardance Trilogy, 2006; Variable Star, 2006; The Lifehouse Trilogy, 2007; Very Hard Choices, 2008. Contributor to books. **Address:** c/o Eleanor Wood, Spectrum Literary Agency, 320 Central Park W, Ste. 1-D, New York, NY 10025, U.S.A. **Online address:** spiderweb@shaw.ca

ROBINSON, V. Gene. American (born United States), b. 1947. **Genres:** Theology/Religion. **Career:** Christ Church, curate, 1973-75; Province 1, youth ministries coordinator, 1978-85; Episcopal Province New England, executive secretary, 1983-2003; Episcopal Diocese, New Hampshire, canon to the ordinary, 1988-2003, bishop co-adjutor, 2003-04; Bishop Diocesan, bishop co-adjutor, 2004. Writer. **Publications:** In the Eye of the Storm: Swept to the Center by God, 2008. **Address:** Diocese of New Hampshire, The Episcopal Church, Diocesan House, 63 Green St., Concord, NH 03301, U.S.A. **Online address:** grinnh@aol.com

ROBINSON, Wayne Alexander. (Alex Robinson). American (born United States), b. 1969. **Genres:** Graphic Novels. **Career:** Independent cartoonist and graphic novelist, 1994-. Writer. **Publications:** AS ALEX ROBINSON: Box Office Poison, 2001; BOP!, 2003; Tricked, 2005; Lower Regions, 2007; Too Cool to Be Forgotten, 2008; (adaptor) A Kidnapped Santa Claus, 2009. Contributor to books. **Address:** Top Shelf Productions, PO Box 1282, Marietta, GA 30061-1282, U.S.A. **Online address:** comicbookalex@aol.com

ROBISHEAUX, Thomas. American (born United States), b. 1951. **Genres:** History, Translations, Young Adult Non-fiction. **Career:** University of Tennessee, assistant professor, 1981-83; Duke University, assistant professor, 1983-89, associate professor, 1989-2009, professor of history, 2009-. Writer. **Publications:** NONFICTION: Rural Society and the Search for Order in Early Modern Germany, 1989; (trans.) A.E. Imhof, Lost Worlds: How Our European Ancestors Coped with Everyday Life and Why Life Is So Hard Today, 1996; The Last Witch of Langenburg: Murder in a German Village, 2009. Contributor of articles to periodicals. **Address:** U.S.A. **Online address:** trobish@duke.edu

ROBISON, John Elder. American (born United States), b. 1957?. **Genres:** Biography, Autobiography/Memoirs, Psychology, Self Help. **Career:** KISS, special effect designer, 1970; Milton Bradley, toy and game design engineer; JE Robison Service Company Inc., founder; writer, 2006-. **Publications:** Look Me in the Eye: My Life with Asperger's (memoir), 2007; Be Different, Adventures of a Free Range Aspergian, 2011; (foreword) Gravity Pulls You In, 2011; (foreword) Unstuck and On Target, 2011. **Address:** J E Robison Service Co., 347 Page Blvd., Springfield, MA 01104, U.S.A. **Online address:** john@johnrobison.com

ROBLES, Harold E. Dutch/American (born United States), b. 1948. **Genres:** Children's Non-fiction, Biography, Humanities. **Career:** Albert Schweitzer Center, founder and president, 1973-81; International Albert Schweitzer Or-

ganization, secretary general, 1975-81; Albert Schweitzer Institute for the Humanities, founder and president, 1984-98, now president emeritus; Albert Schweitzer Institute Press, founder and president, 1994-96; International Trust for Children's Health Care, president, 1995-; Medical Knowledge Institute, chairman and president, 1999-. Writer. **Publications:** (With J.M. van Veen) Albert Schweitzer, 1975; (ed.) International Albert Schweitzer Symposium, 1979; (comp.) Reverence for Life: The Words of Albert Schweitzer, 1993; Albert Schweitzer: An Adventurer for Humanity, 1994. Contributor to journals. **Address:** Medical Knowledge Institute, PO Box 332, Oostvoorne, 3233 ZG, Netherlands. **Online address:** hrobles@infomki.org

ROBOTHAM, Michael. Australian (born Australia), b. 1960. **Genres:** Novels, Criminology/True Crime. **Career:** The Mail on Sunday, senior feature writer, 1986-92; freelance writer, 1992-; ghostwriter, 1993-; Sun, reporter. **Publications:** NOVELS: The Suspect, 2005; Lost, 2005 as The Drowning Man, 2006; Night Ferry, 2007; Shatter, 2008; Bombproof, 2009; Bleed for Me, 2010; The Wreckage, 2011; Say You're Sorry, 2012. **Address:** c/o Mark Lucas, Lucas Alexander Whitley Ltd., 14 Vernon St., London, GL W14 0RJ, England. **Online address:** michael@michaelrobotham.com

ROBSON, Brian Turnbull. British (born England), b. 1939. **Genres:** Geography, Urban Studies, Business/Trade/Industry, Economics, Politics/Government, Social Sciences. **Career:** University College of Wales, lecturer, 1964-67; Cambridge University, lecturer in geography, 1967-77, Fitzwilliam College, fellow and admissions tutor, 1967-77; The University of Manchester, professor of geography, 1977-, now professor emeritus, Centre for Urban Policy Studies, director. Writer. **Publications:** Urban Analysis: A Study of City Structure with Special Reference to Sunderland, 1969; Urban Growth: An Approach, 1973; Urban Social Areas, 1975; (ed.) Houses and People in the City, 1976; (ed.) Man's Impact on Past Environments, 1976; (ed.) Geographical Agenda for a Changing World, 1982; Where is the North?, 1985; (ed.) Managing the City: The Aims And Impacts Of Urban Policy, 1987; Those Inner Cities: Reconciling the Economic and Social Aims of Urban Policy, 1988; Assessing the Impact of Urban Policy, 1994; A Matrix of Deprivation in English Local Authorities, 1995; (with Bradford and Tomlinson) Updating and Revising the Index of Local Deprivation, 1998; (with J.A. Peck and A. Holden) Regional Agencies and Area-based Regeneration, 2000; (co-author) The State of English Cities, 2000. **Address:** Department of Geography, School of Environment and Development, University of Manchester, 1.036 Arthur Lewis Bldg., PO Box 88, Manchester, GM M60 1QD, England. **Online address:** brian.robson@manchester.ac.uk

ROBSON, Derek Ian. (D. I. Robson). Australian/British (born England), b. 1935. **Genres:** Education, History, Social Sciences. **Career:** Teacher, 1958-59; Victorian Ministry of Education, assistant teacher, 1959-69, senior teacher, 1970-77, deputy principal, 1978-82, principal, 1983-89; Fawkner High School, head of history faculty, 1961-69; Royal Melbourne Institute of Technology, correspondence lecturer in British history, 1965-70; Blackburn South High School, head of history faculty, 1969-; Staff Development Journal, editor, 1974. **Publications:** A Student's British History, 1964; A Student's Asian History, 1968; Indonesia: A Brief Survey, 1968; (co-author) The Use of Sources, 1969; (co-author) Evaluation, 1974; (ed.) Studies in Administration, 19 vols., 1977-93; Junior Technical Education: The First Century, 1988; The Level Coordinator, 1991. **Address:** 2 Apple Ct., Burwood E, Melbourne, VI 3151, Australia.

ROBSON, D. I. See **ROBSON, Derek Ian.**

ROBSON, Lloyd. Welsh/British (born England), b. 1969?. **Genres:** Poetry. **Career:** Writer and broadcaster. **Publications:** Cardiff Cut (poetry and prose), 2001; Bbboing! & Associated Weirdness, or, Somebody Stole My Ritalin, 2003; Oh Dad! A Search for Robert Mitchum, 2008. Work appears in anthology. **Address:** Cardiff, Wales. **Online address:** web@lloydrobson.co.uk

ROBSON, Lucia St. Clair. American (born United States), b. 1942. **Genres:** Novels, Romance/Historical, Westerns/Adventure. **Career:** Teacher, 1966-68, 1969-71; Hialeah Public Library, librarian, 1968-69; Fort Jackson Library, librarian, 1971-72; Anne Arundel County Public Library, librarian, 1975-81; Writer, 1982-. **Publications:** Ride the Wind: The Story of Cynthia Ann Parker and the Last Days of the Comanche, 1982; Walk in My Soul, 1985; Light a Distant Fire, 1988; The Tokaido Road, 1991; Mary's Land, 1995; Fearless: A

Novel of Sarah Bowman, 1998; Ghost Warrior: Lozen of the Apaches, 2002; Shadow Patriots, 2005; Last Train from Cuernavaca, 2010. **Address:** PO Box 682, Arnold, MD 21012, U.S.A. **Online address:** looshr@aol.com

ROBSON, Roy R(aymond). American (born United States), b. 1963. **Genres:** History, Theology/Religion. **Career:** Boston College, adjunct assistant professor of history, 1992-94; Harvard University, Davis Center for Russian and Eurasian Studies, fellow, 1992-95; Fayetteville State University, assistant professor of history, 1994-97; University of the Sciences, assistant professor of history, 1997-2000, associate professor, 2000-06, professor, 2006-, Honors Program, director; Symposion, editor, 2004-08; Northern Illinois University Press, Orthodox Christian Studies Series, editor, 2008-. **Publications:** Old Believers in Modern Russia, 1995; Solovki: The Story of Russia Told through Its Most Remarkable Islands, 2004; Think World Religions, 2010. Contributor of articles to books and periodicals. **Address:** Department of Humanities, University of the Sciences, 600 S 43rd St., Philadelphia, PA 19104-4495, U.S.A. **Online address:** r.robson@usciences.edu

ROCHA, Luis Miguel. Portuguese (born Portugal), b. 1976. **Genres:** Theology/Religion, Mystery/Crime/Suspense, History. **Career:** Writer. **Publications:** VATICAN THRILLER SERIES: The Holy Bullet, 2009. **Address:** c/o Maru de Montserrat, International Editors' Co., Provenza, 276, 1R, Barcelona, 08008, Spain. **Online address:** info@luismiguelrocha.com

ROCHARD, Henri. See **CHARLIER, Roger Henri.**

ROCHBERG, Francesca. Also writes as Francesca Halton. American (born United States), b. 1952?. **Genres:** History, Translations, Young Adult Fiction. **Career:** University of California, professor of history, Near Eastern Studies, Catherine and William L. Magistretti distinguished professor of Near Eastern studies, Center for Ideas and Society, fellow, 2004; University of Notre Dame, professor; Universität Tübingen, fellow; Yale University, fellow in history; University of North Carolina, Michael Polanyi visiting lecturer in the history and philosophy of natural science, 1996. Writer and historian. **Publications:** Aspects of Babylonian Celestial Divination, 1980; (as Francesca Halton with C. Fagg) Atlas of the Ancient World, 1981; (trans. as Francesca Rochberg-Halton) G. Rochberg, Songs of Inanna and Dumuzi, for Contralto and Piano, 1983; (ed. as Francesca Rochberg-Halton) Language, Literature and History: Philological and Historical Studies Presented to Erica Reiner, 1987; Babylonian Horoscopes, 1998; The Heavenly Writing: Divination, Horoscopy, and Astronomy in Mesopotamian Culture, 2004; In the Path of the Moon: Babylonian Celestial Divination and Its Legacy, 2010. **Address:** Department of Near Eastern Studies, University of California, 262 Barrows Hall, Berkeley, CA 94720-1940, U.S.A. **Online address:** rochberg@berkeley.edu

ROCHE, Alex F. American/Australian (born Australia), b. 1921. **Genres:** Medicine/Health. **Career:** University of Melbourne, Department of Anatomy, senior demonstrator, 1949-57, lecturer, 1950-51, faculty, 1952-61, Child Growth Study, director, 1954-68; Wright State University, faculty, 1968-, Fels professor of obstetrics and gynecology, 1977-90, Department of Community Health, head, 1984-92, Wright State University School of Medicine, Fels professor of community health and pediatrics, 1990-, now Fels professor emeritus of community health abd pediatrics, University professor, 1990-95; Fels Research Institute, senior scientist; Human Biology Council, president, 1980-81; Journal of Human Ecology, editor-in-chief, 1993; Royal Australasian College of Physicians, fellow. **Publications:** Manual of Anthropometric Studies for Latin America and the Caribbean, 1973; (with H. Wainer and D. Thissen) Predicting Adult Stature for Individuals, 1975; (with H. Wainer and D. Thissen) Skeletal Maturity: The Knee Joint as a Biological Indicator, 1975; (with R.M. Malina) Manual of Physical Status and Performance in Childhood, vol. I: Physical Status, vol. II: Physical Performance, 1983; Osteoporosis: Current Concepts, 1987; (with W.C. Chumlea and D. Thissen) Assessing the Skeletal Maturity of the Hand-Wrist: FELS Method, 1988; Growth, Maturation, and Body Composition: The Fels Longitudinal Study, 1929-1991, 1992; Man-Environment Relationship: In Honour of Prof. Alex F. Roche, 2000; (with S. Sun) Human Growth: Assessment and Interpretation, 2003. EDITOR: (with F. Falkner) Nutrition and Malnutrition: Identification and Measurement, 1974; (with F.E. Johnston and C. Susanne) Human Physical Growth and Maturation: Methodologies and Factors, 1980; Body-Composition Assessments in Youth and Adults, 1985; The Gastrointestinal Response to Injury, Starvation, and Enteral Nutrition, 1987; (with T.G. Lohman and R. Martorell) Anthropometric Standardization Reference Manual, 1988; Prevention of Adult Atherosclerosis during Childhood, 1988; The Role of Nutrients

in Cancer Treatment, 1991; Short-Chain Fatty Acids: Metabolism and Clinical Importance, 1991; Cytokines in Critical Illness, 1992; Nutritional Essentiality: A Changing Paradigm, 1993; Human Body Composition, 1996. Contributor to journals. **Address:** Wright State University School of Medicine, 3640 Colonel Glenn Highway, Dayton, OH 45435, U.S.A. **Online address:** alex.roche@wright.edu

ROCHE, Denis (Mary). American (born United States), b. 1967. **Genres:** Illustrations, Children's Fiction, Animals/Pets, Art/Art History. **Career:** Author and illustrator. **Publications:** FOR CHILDREN SELF-ILLUSTRATED: Loo-Loo, Boo, and Art You Can Do, 1996; Only One Ollie, 1997; Ollie All Over, 1997; Brave Georgie Goat: 3 Little Stories About Growing Up, 1997; Art Around the World!: Loo-Loo, Boo, and More Art You Can Do, 1998; Oodles to Do With Loo-Loo and Boo: The Collected Art Adventures, 2001; Little Pig Is Capable, 2002; Mim, Gym, and June, 2003; The Best Class Picture Ever!, 2003. Illustrator of books by others. Contributor to periodicals. **Address:** 245 Chestnut St., Cambridge, MA 02139, U.S.A.

ROCHE, Mark W. (Mark William Roche). American (born United States), b. 1956. **Genres:** Philosophy, Education, Reference. **Career:** Ohio State University, assistant professor, 1984-90, associate professor of Germanic languages and literature, 1990-96, department chair, 1991-96; Technical University of Dresden, visiting professor, 1994; Wake Forest University, distinguished visiting lecturer, 1995; University of Notre Dame, Reverend Edmund P. Joyce C.S.C. professor of German language and literature and professor of philosophy, 1996-, department chair, 1996-97, College of Arts and Letters, I.A. O'Shaughnessy dean, 1997-2008. Writer. **Publications:** AS MARK WILLIAM ROCHE: Dynamic Stillness: Philosophical Conceptions of Ruhe in Schiller, Hoelderlin, Buechner, and Heine, 1987; Gottfried Benn's Static Poetry: Aesthetic and Intellectual-Historical Interpretations, 1991; Tragedy and Comedy: A Systematic Study and a Critique of Hegel, 1998; Die Moral der Kunst. Ueber Literatur und Ethik, 2002; The Intellectual Appeal of Catholicism and the Idea of a Catholic University, 2003; Why Literature Matters in the Twenty-first Century, 2004; Why Choose the Liberal Arts?, 2010. Contributor to periodicals. **Address:** Department of German, University of Notre Dame, 318 O'Shaughnessy Hall, Notre Dame, IN 46556-5639, U.S.A. **Online address:** mroche@nd.edu

ROCHE, Mark William. See **ROCHE, Mark W.**

ROCHMAN, Hazel. American/South African (born South Africa), b. 1938. **Genres:** Librarianship, Literary Criticism And History, Young Adult Fiction, Cultural/Ethnic Topics. **Career:** Journalist, through 1963; American Library Association, assistant editor, senior editor and book reviewer for booklist, 1984-2003, contributing editor, 2003-, now retired. **Publications:** Tales of Love and Terror: Booktalking the Classics, Old and New, 1987; Against Borders: Promoting Books for a Multicultural World, 1993. EDITOR: Somehow Tenderness Survives: Stories of Southern Africa, 1988; (comp. with D.Z. McCampbell) Who Do You Think You Are?: Stories of Friends and Enemies, 1993; (comp. with D. McCampbell) Bearing Witness: Stories of the Holocaust, 1995; (comp. with D.Z. McCampbell) Leaving Home: Stories, 1997. Contributor to periodicals. **Address:** The American Library Association, 50 E Huron St., Chicago, IL 60611, U.S.A. **Online address:** hrochman@ala.org

ROCK, Dr. See **BORDOWITZ, Hank.**

ROCK, Howard B. American (born United States), b. 1944. **Genres:** History, Social Sciences. **Career:** Florida International University, Department of History, assistant professor, 1973-79, associate professor, 1979-90, chair of department of history, 1983-89, professor of history, 1990-, now professor emeritus, Faculty Senate, chair, 1999-2003. Writer. **Publications:** Artisans of the New Republic, 1979; (ed.) The New York City Artisan 1789-1825: A Documentary History, 1989; (ed. with P. Gilfe) Keepers of the Revolution: The Workers of New York City in the Early Republic, 1992; (ed. with P. Gilje and R. Asher) American Artisans: Crafting Social Identity, 1750-1850, 1995; (with D.D. Moore) Cityscapes: A History of New York in Images, 2001. **Address:** Department of History, Modesto A. Maidique Campus, Florida International University, DM 397, Miami, FL 33199, U.S.A. **Online address:** rockh@fiu.edu

ROCKEFELLER, Barbara Bellows. See **BELLOWS, Barbara L(awrence).**

ROCKLAND, Michael Aaron. American (born United States), b. 1935. **Genres:** Novels, Area Studies, Film, History, Social Commentary, Writing/ Journalism, Translations. **Career:** U.S. Embassies in Argentina and Spain, assistant cultural attache, 1961-68; State of New Jersey, executive assistant to the chancellor of higher education, 1968-69; Rutgers University, dean, 1969-72, Department of American Studies, professor, 1972-; New Jersey Monthly, contributing editor; PBS-TV, New Jersey News, producer. **Publications:** Sarmiento's Travels in the United States in 1847, 1970; (ed.) America in the Fifties and Sixties: Julian Marias on the United States, 1972; The American Jewish Experience in Literature, 1975; Homes on Wheels, 1980; (co-author) Looking for America on the New Jersey Turnpike, 1989; A Bliss Case, 1989; Que Tiene America de'Americano?, 1992; Snowshoeing through Sewers, 1994; What's American about American Things?, 1996; Popular Culture: Or, Why Study Trash?, 1998; (co-author) The Jews of New Jersey: A Pictorial History, 2001; The George Washington Bridge: Poetry in Steel, 2008; Stones, 2009; An American in Franco Spain, 2010. **Address:** Department of American Studies, Rutgers University, Ruth Adams Bldg., Rm. 024, Douglass Campus, 131 George St., New Brunswick, NJ 08901-1414, U.S.A. **Online address:** rockland@rci.rutgers.edu

ROCKLIN, Joanne. American (born United States), b. 1946. **Genres:** Children's Fiction, Writing/Journalism. **Career:** Devonshire Elementary School, teacher, 1968-72; Burbank Child Guidance Clinic, psychotherapist, 1984-87; Omega Center for Mental Health, psychotherapist, 1984-92; West Valley Center for Educational Therapy, psycho-diagnostic assessor, 1987; University of Southern California, writer-in-residence, 1995. **Publications:** CHILDREN'S FICTION: Sonia Begonia, 1986; Dear Baby, 1988; Jace the Ace, 1990; Discovering Martha, 1991; For Your Eyes Only!, 1997; Strudel Stories, 1999; The Very Best Hanukkah Gift, 1999; One Day and One Amazing Morning on Orange Street, 2011. FIRST READERS: Three Smart Pals, 1994; How Much is that Guinea Pig in the Window?, 1995; The Case of the Missing Birthday Party, 1997; One Hungry Cat, 1997; Not Enough Room, 1998; The Case of the Backyard Treasure, 1998; Jake and the Copycats, 1998; The Case of the Shrunken Allowance, 1999; Just Add Fun!, 1999; The Incredibly Awesome Box, 2000; This Book is Haunted, 2002. OTHER: (with N.S. Levinson) Getting High in Natural Ways: An Infobook for Young People of All Ages (nonfiction), 1986 as Feeling Great: Reaching Out to Life, Reaching In to Yourself-Without Drugs, 1992; Musical Chairs and Dancing Bears (picture book), 1993. Contributor of articles to publications. **Address:** c/o Ruth Cohen, PO Box 2244, La Jolla, CA 92038-2244, U.S.A. **Online address:** jrocklin@aol.com

ROCKS, Burton. American (born United States), b. 1972. **Genres:** Autobiography/Memoirs, Sports/Fitness. **Career:** Freelance sports writer and producer. **Publications:** (With C. King) A King's Legacy: The Clyde King Story, 1999; (with B. Feller) Bob Feller's Little Black Book of Baseball Wisdom, 2001; (with A. North) The Long and the Short of It, 2002; (with P. O'Neill) Me and My Dad: A Baseball Memoir, 2003; (with J. Klugman and G. Marshall) Tony and Me: A Story of Friendship, 2005; (with C. Erskine) What I Learned From Jackie Robinson: A Teammate's Reflections on and off the Field, 2005; (with B. Feller) Bob Feller's Little Blue Book of Baseball Wisdom, 2009; (with S. Lyons) Psycho 100: Baseball's Most Outrageous Moments, 2009. **Address:** The Literary Group, 330 W 38th St., Ste. 408, New York, NY 10018, U.S.A.

ROCKS, Misako. *See* **TAKASHIMA, Misako.**

ROCKWELL, Anne (Foote). American (born United States), b. 1934. **Genres:** Children's Fiction, Children's Non-fiction, Novellas/Short Stories, Illustrations, Education, Young Adult Fiction, Social Commentary. **Career:** Silver Burdett Publishers, Production Department, staff, 1952; Young & Rubicam (advertising agency), art-buying secretary, 1953; Goldwater Memorial Hospital, assistant recreation leader, 1954-56. Author and illustrator. **Publications:** SELF-ILLUSTRATED CHILDREN'S BOOKS: Paul and Arthur Search for the Egg, 1964; Gypsy Girl's Best Shoes, 1966; Sally's Caterpillar, 1966; Filippo's Dome: Brunelleschi and the Cathedral of Florence, 1967; The Stolen Necklace: A Picture Story from India, 1968; Glass, Stones, and Crown: The Abbé Suger and the Building of St. Denis, 1968; The Good Llama: A Picture Story from Peru, 1968; Temple on a Hill: The Building of the Parthenon, 1968; The Wonderful Eggs of Furicchia: A Picture Story from Italy, 1968; (comp.) Savez-vous Planter Les Choux? and Other French Songs, 1968; When the Drum Sang: An African Folktale, 1970; (adapter) The Monkey's Whiskers: A Brazilian Folktale, 1971; El Toro Pinto and Other Songs in

Spanish, 1971; Paintbrush and Peacepipe: The Story of George Catlin, 1971; Tuhurahura and the Whale, 1971; What Bobolino Knew, 1971; The Dancing Stars: An Iroquois Legend, 1972; Paul and Arthur and the Little Explorer, 1972; The Awful Mess, 1973; The Boy Who Drew Sheep, 1973; Games (and How to Play Them), 1973; Befana: A Christmas Story, 1974; Gift for a Gift, 1974; The Gollywhopper Egg, 1974; The Story Snail, 1974; Big Boss, 1975; No More Work, 1976; I Like the Library, 1977; A Bear, a Bobcat, and Three Ghosts, 1977; Albert B. Cub and Zebra: An Alphabet Storybook, 1977; Willy Runs Away, 1978; Timothy Todd's Good Things Are Gone, 1978; Gogo's Pay Day, 1978; Gogo's Car Breaks Down, 1978; Buster and the Bogeyman, 1978; The Girl with a Donkey Tail, 1979; The Bump in the Night, 1979; Walking Shoes, 1980; Honk Honk!, 1980; Henry the Cat and the Big Sneeze, 1980; Gray Goose and Gander and Other Mother Goose Rhymes, 1980; When We Grow Up, 1981; Up a Tall Tree, 1981; Thump Thump Thump!, 1981; Boats, 1982; The Mother Goose Cookie-Candy Book, 1983; Cars, 1984; Trucks, 1984; In Our House, 1985; Planes, 1985; First Comes Spring, 1985; The Three Sillies and Ten Other Stories to Read Aloud, 1986; Big Wheels, 1986; Fire Engines, 1986; Things That Go, 1986; At Night, Crowell, 1986; At the Playground, 1986; In the Morning, 1986; In the Rain, 1986; Come to Town, 1987; Bear Child's Book of Hours, 1987; Bikes, 1987; Handy Hank Will Fix It, 1988; Hugo at the Window, 1988; Things to Play With, 1988; Puss in Boots and Other Stories, 1988; Trains, 1988; My Spring Robin, 1989; On Our Vacation, 1989; Bear Child's Book of Special Days, 1989; Willy Can Count, 1989; Hugo at the Park, 1990; When Hugo Went to School, 1990; Root-a-Toot-Toot, 1991; What We Like, 1992; Mr. Panda's Painting, Macmillan, 1993; The Robber Baby: Stories from the Greek Myths, 1994; The Way to Captain Yankee's, 1994; Ducklings and Pollywogs, 1994; (with D. Brion) Space Vehicles, 1994; The Storm, 1994; No! No! No!, 1995; Sweet Potato Pie, 1996; The One-eyed Giant and Other Monsters from the Greek Myths, 1996; I Fly, 1997; Once upon a Time This Morning, 1997; Romulus and Remus, 1997; Our Earth, 1998; One Bean, 1998; Our Stars, 1999; Ferryboat Ride!, 1999; Bumblebee, Bumblebee, Do You Know Me?: A Garden Guessing Game, 1999; Long Ago Yesterday, 1999; Pumpkin Day, Pumpkin Night, 1999; The Boy Who Wouldn't Obey: A Mayan Legend, 2000; Only Passing Through: The Story of Sojourner Truth, 2000; Welcome to Kindergarten, 2001; The Prince Who Ran Away: The Story of Gautama Buddha, 2001; Morgan Plays Soccer, 2001; Growing Like Me, 2001; Bugs Are Insects, 2001; They Called Her Molly Pitcher, 2002; My Pet Hamster, 2002; Becoming Butterflies, 2002; Katie Catz Makes a Splash, 2003; Two Blue Jays, 2003; Seba the Scribe: A Story of Ancient Egypt, 2003; At the Firehouse, 2003; Four Seasons Make a Year, 2004; Chip and the Karate Kick, 2004; Little Shark, 2005; Honey in a Hive, 2005; Good Morning, Digger, 2005; At the Train Station, 2005; Brendan and Belinda and the Slam Dunk, 2007. WITH H. ROCKWELL: SELF-ILLUSTRATED: Olly's Polliwogs, 1970; Molly's Woodland Garden, 1971; The Toolbox, 1971; Machines, 1972; Thruway, 1972; Toad, 1972; Head to Toe, 1973; Blackout, 1979; The Supermarket, 1979; Out to Sea, 1980; My Barber, 1981; Happy Birthday to Me, 1981; I Play in My Room, 1981; Can I Help?, 1982; How My Garden Grew, 1982; I Love My Pets, 1982; Sick in Bed, 1982; The Night We Slept Outside, 1983; My Back Yard, 1984; When I Go Visiting, 1984; Nice and Clean, 1984; My Baby-sitter, 1985; The Emergency Room, 1985 in UK as Going to Casualty, 1987; At the Beach, 1987; The First Snowfall, 1987. OTHERS: Our Garage Sale, 1984; Apples and Pumpkins, 1989; Our Yard Is Full of Birds, 1992; Pots and Pans, 1993; Show and Tell Day, 1997; Halloween Day, 1997; Thanksgiving Day, 1999; Valentine's Day, 1999; Career Day, 2000; What Good Are Alligators?, 2000; Valentine's Day, 2001; 100 School Days, 2002; Mother's Day, 2004; Father's Day, 2005; Whoo! Whoo! Goes the Train, 2005; Why are the Ice Caps Melting?: The Dangers of Global Warming, 2006; Who Lives in an Alligator Hole?, 2006; Here Comes the Night, 2006; Backyard Bear, 2006; Presidents' Day, 2008; My Preschool, 2008; Clouds, 2008; What's So Bad About Gasoline?: Fossil Fuels and What They Do, 2009; Big George: How a Shy Boy Became President Washington, 2009; St. Patrick's Day, 2010; At the Supermarket, 2010; First Day of School, 2010; Hey, Charleston!, 2011. Illustrator of books by others. **Address:** c/o Michael Bourret, Dystel & Goderich Literary Management, 1 Union Sq. W, New York, NY 10003-3303, U.S.A. **Online address:** info@annerockwell.com

ROCKWELL, Theodore. American (born United States), b. 1922. **Genres:** Engineering, Technology. **Career:** Princeton Engineer, co-founder, 1941; Atomic Bomb Project, process improvement engineer, 1944-49; U.S. Atomic Energy Commission, Nuclear Technology Division, director, 1949-54; Admiral Rickover's Nuclear Power Program, technical director, 1954-64; U.S. Navy, Nuclear Technology Division, director, 1949-54; MPR Associates

Inc. (engineering firm), co-founder, 1964, principal officer, 1964-87; Johns Hopkins University, Center for Foreign Policy Research, research associate, 1965-68; Atomic Industrial Forum, chair of reactor safety task force, 1966-72; Radiation Science and Health Inc., founder and director. Freelance writer, 1988-. **Publications:** (Ed.) The Reactor Shielding Design Manual, 1956; (co-author) The Shippingport Pressurized Water Reactor, 1958; Zashchita iàdernykh reaktorov, 1958; (co-author) Arms Control Agreements: Designs for Verification, 1968; The Rickover Effect: How One Man Made a Difference, 1992, 4th ed., 2002; Rickover Effect: The Inside Story of How Adm. Hyman Rickover Built the Nuclear Navy, 1995; Creating the New World: Stories and Images from the Dawn of the Atomic Age, 2003; The Virtual Librarian: A Tale of Alternative Realities, 2007. Contributor to journals and periodicals. **Address:** 3403 Woolsey Dr., Chevy Chase, MD 20815, U.S.A. **Online address:** tedrock@starpower.net

RODDA, Emily. Also writes as Mary-Anne Dickinson, Jennifer Rowe. Australian (born Australia), b. 1948. **Genres:** Children's Fiction, Young Adult Fiction, Novels, Picture/Board Books. **Career:** Full-time writer, 1994-; Angus & Robertson Publishers, editor and publisher; Australian Women's Weekly, editor. **Publications:** FOR CHILDREN: Something Special, 1984; Pigs Might Fly, 1986 in US as The Pigs Are Flying, 1988; The Best-Kept Secret, 1988; Finders Keepers, 1990; Crumbs!, 1990; The Timekeeper, 1992; Rowan of Rin, 1993; Rowan and the Travelers, 1994; Power and Glory, 1994; Yay!, 1996; Rowan and the Keeper of the Crystal, 1996; (with K. Rowe) Dirty Tricks, 1997; Game Plan, 1998; Bob the Builder & the Elves, 1998; Fuzz, the Famous Fly, 1999; The Julia Tapes, 1999; Deep Freeze, 1999; Rowan and the Zebak, 1999; The Secret Enemy, 1999; Forests of Silence, 2000; Return to Del, 2001; Bob and the House Elves, 2001; Green Fingers, 2001; Where Do You Hide Two Elephants?, 2001; Shifting Sands, 2001; Valley of the Lost, 2001; City of the Rats, 2001; Dread Mountain, 2001; Lake of Tears, 2001; Maze of the Beast, 2001; Cavern of the Fear, 2002; (contrib.) Deltora Book of Monsters, 2002; Isle of Illusion, 2002; Shadowlands, 2002; Charm Bracelet, 2003; Flower Fairies, 2003; Last Fairy-Apple Tree, 2003; Rowan and the Ice-Creepers, 2003; Third Wish, 2003; Dragon's Nest, 2004; Isle of the Dead, 2004; Magic Key, 2004; Shadowgate, 2004; Unicorn, 2004; (with M. McBride) How to Draw Deltora Monsters, 2005; Beware the Gingerbread House, 2005; Ghost of Raven Hill, 2005; Sister of the South, 2005; Star Cloak, 2005; Water Sprites, 2005; Dead End, 2006; (with K. Applegate and K. Lasky) Fantastic Tales for Boys, 2006; (with R. Sexton) Deep Secrets, 2006; Peskie Spell, 2006; Rainbow Wand, 2006; Tales of Deltora, 2006; Enter the Realm, 2007; The Key to Rondo, 2007; The Wizard of Rondo, 2008. AS JENNIFER ROWE: The Commonsense International Cookery Book, 1978; Eating Well in Later Life, 1982; Grim Pickings, 1988; Murder by the Book, 1989; Death in Store, 1991; The Makeover Murders, 1992; Stranglehold, 1993; Lamb to the Slaughter, 1996; Deadline, 1997 in US as Suspect, 1999; Something Wicked, 1998; Angela's Mandrake and Other Feisty Fables, 1999; Fairy Tales for Grown-ups, 2002. TEEN POWER INC. SERIES: The Secret of Banyan Bay, 1994; The Sorcerer's Apprentice, 1994; The Bad Dog Mystery, 1994; Beware the Gingerbread House, 1994; Cry of the Cat, 1994; The Disappearing TV Star, 1994; The Ghost of Raven Hill, 1994; Green for Danger, 1994; Poison Pen, 1994; Breaking Point, 1994; Nowhere to Run, 1995; Crime in the Picture, 1995; The Case of Crazy Claude, 1995; Fear in Fashion, 1995; Dangerous Game, 1995; Danger in Rhyme, 1995; The Missing Millionaire, 1995; Haunted House, 1995; Cry Wolf, 1996; Photo Finish, 1996; Stage Fright, 1996; St. Elmo's Fire, 1996; Bad Apples, 1996; The War of the Work Demons, 1997; Hit or Miss, 1998; Hot Pursuit, 1998. SQUEAK STREET STORIES: Fee-Fee's Holiday, 2007; Old Bun and the Burglar, 2007; One-shoe's Wishes, 2007; Pink-Paw's Painting, 2007. **Address:** Omnibus Books, 52 Fullarton Rd., Norwood, SA 5067, Australia.

RODDAM, Franc(is George). British (born England), b. 1946. **Genres:** Plays/Screenplays, Film, Art/Art History. **Career:** Ziji Publishing, founder and chairman. Director, documentary maker, producer and writer. **Publications:** (With D. Waddell) The Auf Wiedersehen Pet Story: That's Living Alright, 2003. **Address:** Union Pictures Ltd., 36 Marshall St., London, GL W1F 7EY, England.

RODDEN, John (Gallagher). American/Irish (born Ireland), b. 1956. **Genres:** Communications/Media, Cultural/Ethnic Topics, Education, Literary Criticism And History, Speech/Rhetoric. **Career:** University of Virginia, assistant professor of rhetoric, 1985-89; University of Texas, assistant professor of rhetoric, 1989-93, adjunct assistant professor. Writer. **Publications:** The Politics of Literary Reputation: The Making and Claiming of St. George

Orwell, 1989; (ed.) Lionel Trilling and the Critics, 1999; (ed.) Conversations with Isabel Allende, 1999; (ed.) Understanding Animal Farm: A Student Casebook to Issues, Sources and Historical Documents, 1999; Performing the Literary Interview: How Writers Craft Their Public Selves, 2001; Textbook Reds: Schoolbooks, Ideology, and Eastern German Identity, 2001; (trans.) To Light a Candle: Memoirs of Ruth Pfau, 2001; Repainting the Little Red Schoolhouse: A History of Eastern German Education, 1945-95, 2002; George Orwell: The Politics of Literary Reputation, 2002; Scenes from an Afterlife: The Legacy of George Orwell, 2003; (ed.) Conversations with Isabel Allende, 2004; (ed. with T. Cushman) George Orwell: Into the Twenty-First Century, 2004; (ed. and intro.) Irving Howe and the Critics: Celebrations and Attacks, 2005; (ed.) The Worlds of Irving Howe: The Critical Legacy, 2005; Textbook Reds: Schoolbooks, Ideology and Eastern German Identity, 2006; Every Intellectual's Big Brother: George Orwell's Literary Siblings, 2006; (ed.) Cambridge Companion to George Orwell, 2007; Walls that Remain: Eastern and Western Germans since Reunification, 2008; Dialectics, Dogmas and Dissent: Stories from East German Victims of Human Rights Abuse, 2009; (ed. with E. Goffman) Politics and the Intellectual: Conversations with Irving Howe, 2009; (ed.) Isabel Allende, 2011; Unexamined Orwel, 2011. **Address:** 2502 Nueces St., Austin, TX 78705, U.S.A. **Online address:** jgr@mail.utexas.edu

RODDICK, Alan. (Alan Melven Roddick). New Zealander/British (born England), b. 1937. **Genres:** Poetry, Literary Criticism And History. **Career:** New Zealand Broadcasting Corp., Radio Poetry Program, staff, 1968-69, 1973-74; Estate of Charles Brasch, literary executor, 1973-; public health dentist, now retired; New Zealand Dental Journal, editor, 2003-07; Anna and John Caselberg Charitable Trust, treasurer. **Publications:** The Eye Corrects: Poems 1955-1965, 1967; (ed.) Home Ground: Poems, 1974; Allen Curnow, 1981; (ed.) Collected Poems, 1984. **Address:** Anna & John Caselberg Charitable Trust, PO Box 71, Portobello, Dunedin, 9048, New Zealand. **Online address:** alan.roddick@clear.net.nz

RODDICK, Alan Melven. See **RODDICK, Alan.**

RODGER, N. A. M. British/New Zealander (born New Zealand), b. 1949. **Genres:** Military/Defense/Arms Control, History, Politics/Government, Biography, Autobiography/Memoirs, Essays. **Career:** Public Record Office, assistant keeper, 1974-91; National Maritime Museum, Anderson fellow, 1992-2000; University of Exeter, professor of naval history, 2003-08; University of Oxford, All Souls College, senior research fellow, 2008-. Writer. **Publications:** The Admiralty, 1979; Articles of War: The Statutes Which Governed Our Fighting Navies, 1661, 1749, and 1886, 1982; Naval Records for Genealogists, 1984; The Wooden World: An Anatomy of the Georgian Navy, 1986; The Armada in the Public Records, 1988; Naval Records for Genealogists, 1988; (ed. with G.J.A. Raven and M.C.F. van Drunen) Navies and Armies: The Anglo-Dutch Relationship in War and Peace, 1688-1988, 1990; The Insatiable Earl: A Life of John Montagu, Fourth Earl of Sandwich, 1718-1792, 1993; (ed.) Naval Power in the Twentieth Century, 1996; The Safeguard of the Sea: A Naval History of Britain, 660-1649, 1998; The Command of the Ocean: A Naval History of Britain, 1649-1815, 2005; (ed. with R. Cock) Guide to the Naval Records in the National Archives of the UK, 2006, 2nd. ed., 2008; Essays in Naval History, from Medieval to Modern, 2009. Contributor to periodicals. **Address:** University of Oxford, All Souls College, High St., Oxford, OX OX1 4AL, England. **Online address:** nicholas.rodger@all-souls.ox.ac.uk

RODGER, Richard. British (born England), b. 1947?. **Genres:** History, Bibliography, Sociology, Social Sciences, Economics. **Career:** University of Liverpool, lecturer in economic and social history, 1971-79; University of Leicester, lecturer, 1979-88, senior lecturer in economic and social history, 1988-, professor of urban history, honorary visiting professor, East Midlands Oral History Archive, director; Centre for Urban History, director; University of Kansas, associate professor, 1982-83, 1987, Center for the Humanities, visiting research fellow, 1986-87; Urban History, editor, 1987-2007; Trinity College, visiting professor, 1990, professor of urban history; University of Edinburgh, professor of economic and social history, 2007. **Publications:** (Comp. with D.H. Aldcroft) A Bibliography of European Economic and Social History, 1984, 2nd ed., 1993; Housing in Urban Britain, 1780-1914: Class, Capitalism, and Construction, 1989; (with L. McKenna) The Economic History Review Index, Second Series, vols. XXIV-XLII, 1971-1989, 1991; Research in Urban History, 1993; Research in Urban History, 1994; Housing in Urban Britain 1780-1914, 1995; A Consolidated Bibliography of Urban History, 1996, 2nd ed., 1999; (with I. Backouche and D. Menjot) L'Histoire

Urbaine en France: Guide Bibliographique, 1998; Housing the People, 1999; The Transformation of Edinburgh, 2001. EDITOR: Scottish Housing in the Twentieth Century, 1989; European Urban History: Prospect and Retrospect, 1993; (with R.J. Morris) The Victorian City: A Reader in British Urban History, 1820-1914, 1993; (with D. Reeder, D.N. Nash, and P. Jones) Leicester in the Twentieth Century, 1993; (with R. Colls) Cities of Ideas: Civil Society and Urban Governance in Britain, 1800-2000: Essays in Honour of David Reeder, 2004; (with J. Herbert) Testimonies of the City: Identity, Community and Change in a Contemporary Urban World, 2007; (with G. Massard-Guilbaud) Environmental and Social Justice in the City, 2011. **Address:** Department of Economic and Social History, University of Leicester, University Rd., Leicester, LE1 7RH, England. **Online address:** rgr@le.ac.uk

RODGERS, Alan (Paul). American (born United States), b. 1959?. **Genres:** Novels, Novellas/Short Stories, Literary Criticism And History, Young Adult Fiction, Science Fiction/Fantasy. **Career:** Writer. **Publications:** NOVELS: Blood of the Children, 1989; New Life for the Dead, 1990; Fire, 1990; Night, 1991; Pandora, 1994; The Bear Who Found Christmas, 1994; Bone Music, 1995; Night Cry, 1995; Her Misbegotten Son, 1996; Menace: Battle Mountain, 2000; Ghosts Who Cannot Sleep, 2000. OTHERS: Alien Love, 2002; The River of Our Destiny, 2002. Works appear in anthologies. **Address:** Bantam Books, Random House Inc., 1745 Broadway, New York, NY 10019-4368, U.S.A. **Online address:** alanrodg@aol.com

RODGERS, Audrey T(ropauer). American (born United States), b. 1923. **Genres:** Literary Criticism And History, Women's Studies And Issues, Reference. **Career:** Educator and writer, 1956-; Pennsylvania State University, director of women's studies, 1980-84, professor of English, through 1994, professor emeritus of English, 1994-; University of Rome, visiting professor, 1988; University of Wisconsin, faculty. **Publications:** The Universal Drum: Dance Imagery in the Poetry of Eliot, Crane, Roethke, and Williams, 1979; Virgin and Whore: The Image of Women in the Poetry of William Carlos Williams, 1987; Denise Levertov: The Poetry of Engagement, 1993. Contributor to books and periodicals. **Address:** Department of English, Pennsylvania State University, 117 Burrowes Bldg., 417 Old Main, University Park, PA 16802-6200, U.S.A.

RODGERS, Eamonn. Irish (born Ireland), b. 1941. **Genres:** Literary Criticism And History, History, Social Sciences. **Career:** Trinity College, lecturer in Spanish, 1964-89; University of Strathclyde, professor of Spanish and Latin American studies, 1990-2004; now professor emeritus. Writer. **Publications:** Pérez Galdós Miau, 1978; From Enlightenment to Realism: The Novels of Galdós, 1870-1887, 1987; (ed. with V. Rodgers) Encyclopedia of Contemporary Spanish Culture, 1999. Contributor to journals. **Address:** Department of Modern Languages, University of Strathclyde, 16 Richmond St., Glasgow, G1 1XQ, Scotland. **Online address:** e.rodgers@strath.ac.uk

RODGERS, Eugene. American (born United States), b. 1939. **Genres:** Air/Space Topics, Travel/Exploration, Sciences, Reference. **Career:** University of Wisconsin-Madison, research assistant in science writing, 1961-63; U.S. Antarctic Research Program, public information officer, 1963-65; freelance writer, 1965-67; Westinghouse Electric Corp., director of science public relations, 1967-75; Atomic Industrial Forum (now U.S. Council for Energy Awareness), editor, 1975; Energy Research and Development Administration (now Department of Energy), speech writer, 1976; International Business Machines Corp., speech writer, 1977-79; United Technologies Corp., speech writer, 1979-82; Virginia Power, senior writer, 1983-87; Electric RD and D (newsletter), editor and publisher, 1987-88; freelance writer, 1988-. **Publications:** Beyond the Barrier: The Story of Byrd's First Expedition to Antarctica, 1990; Flying High: The Story of Boeing and the Rise of the Jetliner Industry, 1996. **Address:** 2621 Ellesmere Dr., Midlothian, VA 23113-3939, U.S.A.

RODGERS, Frank. Scottish (born Scotland), b. 1944?. **Genres:** Children's Fiction, Illustrations, Animals/Pets, Young Adult Fiction, Science Fiction/Fantasy, Humor/Satire. **Career:** Glasgow School of Art, art teacher, through 1987. Illustrator and author, 1987-. **Publications:** Think of Magic, 1986; Bumps in the Night, 1996; The Ghost in the Telly, 1999; Billy the Brave Puppy, 2000; Pirate Penguins, 2006. YOUNG ADULT NOVELS: The Drowning Boy, 1992; Eyetooth, 2003; Battle for Eyetooth, 2005. SELF-ILLUSTRATED: Who's Afraid of the Ghost Train?, 1988; A Is for Aaargh!, 1989; The Bunk-Bed Bus, 1989; The Summertime Christmas Present, 1989, as Ricky's Summertime Christmas Present, 1991; Cartoon Fun, 1990; Doodle Dog 1990; The Intergalactic Kitchen, 1990; Animal Art, 1991; Can Piggles Do It?, 1991;

I Can't Get to Sleep!, 1991; The Intergalactic Kitchen Goes Prehistoric, 1991; Looking after Your First Monster, 1991; B Is for Book!, 1992; Comic Fun, 1992; Ricky, Zedex, and the Spooks, 1992; Millie's Letter, 1993; Teachers... or Creatures?, 1993; The Ship-Shape Shop, 1993; The Intergalactic Kitchen Sinks, 1995; Count Drawcula's Cartoon Fun, 1995; The Pirate and the Pig, 1996; Rattle and Hum: Robot Detectives, 1996; Rattle and Hum in Double Trouble, 1997; Gorilla Granny, 1997; Cartoon Tips, 1997; Mac and the Big Feet, 1998; The Witch's Dog, 1998; The Witch's Dog at the School of Spells, 1998; The Witch's Dog and the Magic Cake, 1999; Mr. Croc's Walk, 1999; Mr Croc's Clock, 1999; Mr Croc's Silly Sock, 1999; What Mr Croc Forgot, 1999; My Rat Is a Hero, 1999; My Rat Is an Alien, 1999; My Rat Is a Teacher, 1999; My Rat Is a Cowboy, 1999; The Witch's Dog and the Crystal Ball, 2000; The Witch's Dog and the Flying Carpet, 2001; The Robodog, 2001; The Robodog and the Big Dig, 2002; The Witch's Dog and the Ice-Cream Wizard, 2002; The Robodog Superhero, 2002; What Mr. Croc Forgot, 2007; Mr. Croc's Silly Sock, 2007; Mr. Croc Rocks, 2008; The Nostrils of Neptune, 2008; The Witch's Dog and the Treasure Map, 2008; Sherlock Mr Croc, 2010. MY FIRST MONSTER SERIES: Hairy Monster in I Spy Scary Monsters, 1993; Short-Horned Monster in Best Noise in the World, 1993; Ring-Tailed Monster in Save Our Swamp, 1993; Curley-Top Monster in Rocky Rolly Party, 1993; Furry Monster in Seaside Surprise, 1994; Long-Horned Monster in the Spooky Wooo, 1994; Spotted Monsters in Here Come the Clowns, 1994; The Monsters in Birthday Mud Hunt, 1994. THE LITTLE T SERIES: Little T and Lizard the Wizard, 2006; Little T and the Crown Jewels, 2007; Little T and the Dragon's Tooth, 2007; Little T and the Royal Roar, 2007. THE CHILLS SERIES: Head for Trouble, 2002; Haunted Treasure, 2002. **Address:** Caroline Sheldon Literary Agency, 71 Hillgate Pl., London, GL W8 7SS, England.

RODGERS, Marion Elizabeth. American/Chilean (born Chile), b. 1958?. **Genres:** Biography, Adult Non-fiction, History, Literary Criticism And History, Reference. **Career:** Writer. **Publications:** NONFICTION: (ed.) Mencken and Sara: A Life in Letters; The Private Correspondence of H.L. Mencken and Sara Haardt, 1987; (ed.) The Impossible H.L. Mencken: A Selection of His Best Newspaper Stories, 1991; Mencken: The American Iconoclast, 2005; (intro.) Notes on Democracy, 2009. **Address:** c/o Author Mail, Oxford University Press, 198 Madison Ave., New York, NY 10016, U.S.A.

RODGERS, Peter. Australian (born Australia), b. 1946?. **Genres:** History, Writing/Journalism, Politics/Government. **Career:** Australian Department of Foreign Affairs and Trade, ambassador, 1970-78, 1983-98. Journalist and consultant on foreign affairs, defense and trade. **Publications:** The Domestic and Foreign Press in Indonesia: Free but Responsible?, 1982; The Prison of Memory, 1999; Herzl's Nightmare: One Land, Two Peoples, 2005; Arabian Plights: The Future Middle East, 2009; (ed.) Nanoscience and Technology: A Collection of Reviews from Nature Journals, 2010. COntributor to periodicals. **Address:** Australia.

RODIN, Robert L. American (born United States) **Genres:** Novels, Young Adult Fiction, Psychology. **Career:** Writer. **Publications:** Articles of Faith, 1998. Contributor to periodicals. **Address:** St. Martins Press, 175 5th Ave., 14th Fl., New York, NY 10010, U.S.A.

RÖDL, Sebastian. Swiss/German (born Germany), b. 1967. **Genres:** Adult Non-fiction, Psychology. **Career:** University of Leipzig, assistant professor, 1999-2004; New School University, visiting professor, 2002; University of Pittsburgh, Department of Philosophy, visiting assistant professor, 2003-04, associate professor, 2004-05, visiting professor, 2006; University of Chicago, visiting professor, 2004, distinguished visiting professor, 2010; University of Basel, professor of philosophy, 2005-; University of Amiens, visiting professor, 2006. Writer and philosopher. **Publications:** Selbstbezug Und Normativität, 1998; Kategorien Des Zeitlichen: Eine Untersuchung Der Formen Des Endlichen Verstandes, 2005; Self-Consciousness, 2007. **Address:** Department of Philosophy, University of Basel, Rm. 12, Nadelberg 6-8, Basel, 4051, Switzerland. **Online address:** sebastian.roedl@unibas.ch

RODNEY, William. Canadian (born Canada), b. 1923. **Genres:** History, Politics/Government, Biography, Sociology. **Career:** Government of Canada, research officer, 1953-58, 1961-62; Royal Roads Military College (now Royal Roads University), assistant professor, 1962-65, associate professor, 1965-68, professor of European history, Canadian history and economic and political geography, 1969-89, professor emeritus, 1989-, dean of arts. Writer. **Publications:** Soldiers of the International: A History of the Communist Party of Canada, 1919-1929, 1968; Kootenai Brown: His Life and Times, 1839-1916, 1969, 2nd ed., 1998; Joe Boyle: King of the Klondike, 1974; (with C.E. Rolfs) Cauldrons in the Cosmos: Nuclear Astrophysics, 1988; Kootenai Brown: Canada's Unknown Frontiersman, 1996; Deadly Mission: Canadian Airmen over Nuremberg, March 30th/31st, 1944, 2001. Contributor to books and Journals. **Address:** 308 Denison Rd., Victoria, BC V8S 4K3, Canada.

RODRIGUE, George. American (born United States), b. 1944. **Genres:** Animals/Pets. **Career:** Blue Dog Relief Charitable Organization, founder, 2001. Writer and artist. **Publications:** The Cajuns of George Rodrigue, 1976; Blue Dog, 1994; Blue Dog Man, 1999; A Blue Dog Christmas, 2000; Blue Dog Love, 2001; Why Is Blue Dog Blue? A Tale of Colors, 2001; The Art of George Rodrigue, 2003; Blue Dog Speaks, 2008; Are You Blue Dog's Friend?, 2009. **Address:** U.S.A. **Online address:** info@georgerodrigue.com

RODRIGUES DOS SANTOS, Jose. Portuguese/Mozambiquian (born Mozambique), b. 1964?. **Genres:** Novels. **Career:** Journalist, lecturer, news broadcaster and novelist. **Publications:** O Sétimo Selo, 2007; A Ilha das Trevas, 7th ed., 2008; A Vida num Sopro, 3rd ed., 2008; O Codex 632, 2008; A Filha do Capitão; A Fórmula de Deus. **Address:** Portugal. **Online address:** jrsnovels@gmail.com

RODRIGUEZ, Alejo. American (born United States), b. 1941. **Genres:** Children's Non-fiction, Poetry, Language/Linguistics, Young Adult Fiction, Reference. **Career:** Columbia Broadcasting System Inc. (CBS), production supervisor. Writer. **Publications:** Life Experiences, 1988; Simple Poems: Looking at Life through a Broken Glass, 1990; Hey! What Kind of World is This?, 1992; I'm Tired of Being Quiet, 1994; It's Tough Being a Kid These Days, 1995. **Address:** Rm. 3E12, 530 W 57th St., New York, NY 10019, U.S.A.

RODRIGUEZ, Alfred. American (born United States), b. 1932. **Genres:** Literary Criticism And History, Language/Linguistics, Translations, Novellas/Short Stories. **Career:** Rutgers University, professor of Spanish, 1959-69; University of Wisconsin, professor of Spanish, 1969-72; University of New Mexico, professor of Spanish, 1972-97, now professor emeritus. Writer. **Publications:** An Introduction to the Episodios Nacionales of Galdos, 1967; (with W. Rosenthal) Modern Spanish essay, 1969; Estudios sobre la novela de Galdós, 1978; (trans. with M. Encinias) Gaspar Perez de Villagra, Historia de la Nueva Mexico, 1610, 1992. NOVELS: De perros y personas, 1985; Negro pelo en pluma, 1985; Estas tierras, 1987; Ella, 1992; Echoes, 2000; In Rerum Natura, 2001; Plus Ultra, 2001. **Address:** Department of Spanish and Portuguese, University of New Mexico, Rm. 235, Ortega Hall, MSC03 2100, 1 University of New Mexico, Albuquerque, NM 87131-0001, U.S.A.

RODRÍGUEZ, Andrés. American (born United States), b. 1955. **Genres:** Poetry, Literary Criticism And History, Bibliography, Writing/Journalism, Travel/Exploration. **Career:** Stanford University, collection development specialist at foreign language library, 1984-86; University of Arizona, adjunct lecturer in humanities, 1990-91; William Jewell College, instructor in English, 1993; Rockhurst College, visiting professor of English, 1994; University of Missouri, writing tutor, 1994-96, adjunct lecturer in English, 1997-99; University of Kansas, adjunct lecturer in English, 2000-01; University of New Mexico, lecturer in Chicano studies, 2001-02; freelance writer and editor, 2002-. **Publications:** COMPILED WITH R.G. TRUJILLO: Current Bibliography of Chicano Literature: Creative and Critical Writings through 1984, 1984; Literatura Chicana: A Comprehensive Bibliography, 1980-June 1984, 1984; Literatura Chicana: Creative and Critical Writings Through 1984, 1985. OTHERS: Book of the Heart: The Poetics, Letters, and Life of John Keats, 1993; Night Song (poems), 1994. FORTHCOMING: The Nets and Other Poems; The Spirits of Prayer and Ruin: On Poetry and Poetics; The Whole Codex: Selected Poems of Jose Roberto Cea; Traveling in the Family. Contributor to periodicals. Works appear in anthologies. **Address:** 3203 Central St., Kansas City, MO 64111-1322, U.S.A.

RODRIGUEZ, Clara E. American (born United States), b. 1944?. **Genres:** Politics/Government, Autobiography/Memoirs, Social Sciences, Young Adult Non-fiction. **Career:** Centro Colombo-Americano, instructor in English, 1965; New York Urban Coalition, staff associate in housing, 1969; Washington University, instructor, 1970-71; City University of New York, Graduate Center, Centro de Estudios Puertorriqueños, research associate, 1973; Herbert H. Lehman College, Department of Puerto Rican Studies, head, Sociology Department, associate, 1974-76; Fordham University, dean of general stud-

ies, Pre-Health Professions Program, project director, 1976-81, College at Lincoln Center, professor of sociology, associate chair, 1981-. Writer. **Publications:** The Ethnic Queue in the United States: The Case of Puerto Ricans, 1974; Puerto Ricans: Born in the USA, 1989; Latin Looks: Latina and Latino Images in the Media, 1997; Changing Race: The Latinos, the Census, and the History of Ethnicity in the United States, 2000; Heroes, Lovers, and Others: The Story of Latinos in Hollywood, 2004; (with A.L. Greco and R.M. Wharton) Culture and Commerce of Publishing in the 21st Century, 2007. EDITOR: (with V.S. Korrol and O. Alers) The Puerto Rican Struggle: Essays on Survival in the United States, 1980; (with E. Melendez and J.B. Figueroa and contrib.) Hispanics in the Labor Force: Issues and Policies, 1991; (with Korrol) Historical Perspectives on Puerto Rican Survival in the United States, 1996. Contributor of articles to books and journals. **Address:** Lincoln Center Campus, Fordham University, Lowenstein 916B, 113 W 60th St., New York, NY 10023, U.S.A. **Online address:** crodriguez@fordham.edu

RODRIGUEZ, Gregory. American (born United States) **Genres:** Social Sciences, History, Race Relations. **Career:** Arizona State University, Center for Social Cohesion, director; Los Angeles Times, op-ed columnist. Consultant. **Publications:** Mongrels, Bastards, Orphans and Vagabonds: Mexican Immigration and the Future of Race in America, 2007. Contributor to periodicals. **Address:** Los Angeles, CA , U.S.A. **Online address:** rodriguez@newamerica.net

RODRIGUEZ, Ileana. American (born United States), b. 1939. **Genres:** Social Commentary, History, Translations. **Career:** University of Minnesota, Department of Spanish and Portuguese, assistant professor, 1975-79, associate professor, 1980-85; Universidad Nacional Autónoma de Managua, visiting professor, 1983-85; Ohio State University, Department of Spanish and Portuguese, associate professor, 1992-99, professor of literatures and cultures of Latin America, 1999-, distinguished professor of humanities, 2004-. Writer and consultant. **Publications:** (Ed. with W.L. Rowe) Marxism and New Left Ideology, 1977; (comp. with M. Zimmerman) Cultural Creation in Modern Society, 1977; (ed. with M. Zimmerman) Process of Unity in Caribbean Society: Ideologies and Literature, 1983; Primer inventario del invasor, 1984; (with R.L. Acevedo and M.R. Morales) Literatura y crisis en Centroamérica: Ponencias, 1986; Registradas en la historia: 10 años del quehacer feminista en Nicaragua, 1990; (and trans. with R. Carr) House/Garden/Nation: Space, Gender, and Ethnicity in Post-colonial Latin American Literatures by Women, 1994; (and trans. with R. Carr) Women, Guerrillas, and Love: Understanding War in Central America, 1996; (ed.) The Latin American Subaltern Studies Reader, 2001; (ed.) Convergencia de tiempos: Estudios subalternos/contextos Latinoamericanos estado, cultura, subalternidad, 2001; Cánones literarios masculinos y relecturas transculturales: Lostrans-femenino/masculine/queer, 2002; Transatlantic Topographies: Islands, Highlands, Jungles, 2004; (contrib.) Postcolonialidades históricas, 2008; (ed. with M. Szurmuk) Memoria y ciudadanía, 2008; Liberalism at Its Limits: Crime and Terror in the Latin American Cultural Text, 2009; (ed. with J. Martínez) Estudios transatlánticos postcoloniales, 2010; (contrib.) Máscaras, 2011; Identidades regionales, forthcoming; Debates de Campo, forthcoming. **Address:** Department Spanish & Portuguese, Ohio State University, 244 Hagerty Hall, 1775 College Rd., Columbus, OH 43210-1229, U.S.A. **Online address:** rodriguez.89@osu.edu

RODRIGUEZ, Jarbel A. American (born United States), b. 1971. **Genres:** History, Theology/Religion. **Career:** San Francisco State University, assistant professor, 2001-07, graduate co-ordinator, associate professor, 2007-. Writer, educator and historian. **Publications:** Captives & Their Saviors in the Medieval Crown of Aragon, 2007; (with T.R. Getz and R.J. Hoffman) Exchanges: A Global History Reader, 2008. **Address:** Department of History, San Francisco State University, 1600 Holloway Ave., San Francisco, CA 94132, U.S.A.

RODRIGUEZ, Judith (Green). Australian (born Australia), b. 1936. **Genres:** Plays/Screenplays, Poetry, Songs/Lyrics And Libretti, Translations. **Career:** Fairholme Presbyterian Girls' College, resident teacher, 1958; University of Queensland, Department of External Studies, lecturer, 1959-60; University of the West Indies, lecturer in English, 1963-65; Saint Giles School of English, lecturer, 1965-66; Saint Mary's College of Education, lecturer, 1966-68, lecturer, 1969-76, senior lecturer, 1977-85; La Trobe University, lecturer, senior lecturer in English, 1969-85; Sydney Morning Herald, writer of poetry column, 1984-86; Macquarie University, lecturer, 1985; Western Australian Institute of Technology, visiting fellow, 1986; Macarthur Institute of Higher Education, lecturer in English, 1987; Royal Melbourne Institute of

Technology, Foundations of Professional Writing, lecturer, 1988-89; Ormond College, writer-in-residence, 1988-89; Deakin University, senior lecturer in literature and professional writing, 1989-2003; Victoria College, lecturer, 1989-; Penguin Books, poetry consultant, 1989-97; University of Madras, visiting fellow, 2000-04; Council of Adult Education, lecturer, 2004-. **Publications:** (With D. Malouf, D. Maynard and R. Hall) Four Poets, 1962; Nu-Plastik Fanfare Red and Other Poems, 1973; Water Life, 1976; Shadow on Glass, 1978; Mudcrab at Gambaro's, 1980; Witch Heart, 1982; (co-author) Mrs. Noah and the Minoan Queen, 1983; (with V. Pauli) Noela Hjorth, 1984; (A. Taylor) Poems Selected from the Australian's 20th Anniversary Competition, 1985; Floridian Poems, 1986; The House by Water: New and Selected Poems, 1988; (ed. with J. Rankin) Collected Poems, 1990; The Cold, 1992; (trans.) J. Vanegas, Your Good Colombian Friend, 1994; Terror! Poems, 2002; Manatee, 2007. **Address:** 18 Churchill St., Mont Albert, VI 3127, Australia. **Online address:** rodju@tpg.com.au

RODRIGUEZ, Julia. (Julia E. Rodriguez). American (born United States), b. 1967?. **Genres:** Sciences, Medicine/Health, History. **Career:** University of Vermont, Department of History, predissertation fellow, 1997-98; Colby College, faculty teaching fellow, 1998-99; University of New Hampshire, assistant professor, 1999-2006, associate professor of history and women's studies, 2006-; National Science Foundation, grant reviewer, 2002. Writer. **Publications:** (contrib.) Argentina on the Couch: Psychiatry and the State in Argentina, 2003; Civilizing Argentina: Science, Medicine, and the Modern State, 2006. Contributor to books and periodicals. **Address:** Department of History and Women's Studies, University of New Hampshire, 203 Huddleston Hall, Durham, NH 03824, U.S.A. **Online address:** juliar@cisunix.unh.edu

RODRIGUEZ, Julia E. See **RODRIGUEZ, Julia.**

RODRIGUEZ, Junius P. American (born United States), b. 1957. **Genres:** History. **Career:** Central Lafourche High School, teacher, 1979-88; Alexander City Junior College, adjunct instructor, 1988; Auburn University, graduate teaching assistant, 1988-92; Central Alabama Community College, adjunct instructor, 1989; Troy State University, adjunct instructor, 1989-90; Southern Union State Junior College, adjunct instructor, 1989-92; Eureka College, assistant professor of history, 1992-97, associate professor of history, 1997-. Writer. **Publications:** (Ed.) The Historical Encyclopedia of World Slavery, 1997; The Chronology of World Slavery, 1999; (ed.) The Louisiana Purchase: A Historical and Geographical Encyclopedia, 2002; (ed.) Slavery in the United States: A Social, Political and Historical Encyclopedia, 2007; (ed.) Encyclopedia of Slave Resistance and Rebellion, 2007; (ed.) Encyclopedia of Emancipation and Abolition in the Transatlantic World, 2007. (ed.) Slavery in the Modern World: A History of Political, Social, and Economic Oppression, 2011. **Address:** Eureka College, 300 E College Ave., Eureka, IL 61530, U.S.A. **Online address:** jrodrig@eureka.edu

RODRIGUEZ, Luis J. American (born United States), b. 1954. **Genres:** Poetry, Autobiography/Memoirs. **Career:** Bienvenidos Community Center, director, 1972; Eastern Group Publications, photographer and reporter, 1980; reporter, 1980-85; American Federation of State, County, and Municipal Employees (AFL-CIO), public affairs associate, 1982-85; Chismearte, publisher and editor, 1982-85; Latino Writers Association, director and publisher, 1982-85; Trade Union Public Affairs, associate, 1982-85; People's Tribune, editor, 1985-88; WMAQ-AM, part-time news writer, 1989-92; Tia Chucha Press, founder and director, 1989-; Shakespeare and Co., writer-in-residence, 1991; Mosaic Multicultural Foundation, elder and teacher, 1993-; North Carolina's Word Wide, writer-in-residence, 2000. **Publications:** Always Running: La Vida Loca, Gang Days in L.A. (memoir), 1994; Hearts and Hands: Creating Community in Violent Times (nonfiction), 2001; The Republic of East LA: Stories (fiction), 2002; Music of the Mill, 2005; It Calls You Back, 2011. POETRY: Poems across the Pavement, 1989; The Concrete River, 1991; Trochemoche, 1998; My Nature is Hunger, 2005. FOR CHILDREN: America Is Her Name, 1998; It Doesn't Have to Be This Way, 1999. Contributor to periodicals. Works appears in anthologies. **Address:** Tia Chucha Press, 13197-A Gladstone Ave., 12 Western Ave., Sylmar, CA 91342, U.S.A. **Online address:** luis@luisjrodriguez.com

RODRIGUEZ, Manuel. (Spain Rodriguez). American (born United States), b. 1940. **Genres:** Graphic Novels, Literary Criticism And History. **Career:** The East Village, editor; United Cartoon Workers of America, founder. **Publications:** SELF-ILLUSTRATED GRAPHIC NOVELS AS SPAIN RODRIGUEZ: Trashman Lives!: The Collected Stories from 1968 to 1985, 1989;

(with S. Bright) She: Anthology of Big Bitch, 1993; My True Story, 1994. Contributor to periodicals. **Address:** c/o Author Mail, Word-Play Publications, 300 Montgomery St., Ste. 800, San Francisco, CA 94104, U.S.A. **Online address:** spainrodriguez@comcast.net

RODRIGUEZ, Spain. See **RODRIGUEZ, Manuel.**

ROE, Caroline. (Medora Sale). Canadian (born Canada), b. 1937?. **Genres:** Novels, Mystery/Crime/Suspense, Romance/Historical. **Career:** Novelist. **Publications:** CHRONICLES OF ISAAC OF GIRONA SERIES: HISTORICAL MYSTERY NOVELS: Remedy for Treason, 1998; Cure for a Charlatan, 1999; An Antidote for Avarice, 1999; Solace for a Sinner, 2000; A Potion for a Widow, 2001; A Draught for a Dead Man, 2002; A Poultice for a Healer, 2003; A Consolation for an Exile, 2004. DETECTIVE NOVELS AS MEDORA SALE: Murder on the Run, 1986; Murder in Focus, 1989; Murder in a Good Cause, 1990; Sleep of the Innocent, 1991; Pursued by Shadows, 1992; Short Cut to Santa Fe, 1994. NOVEL: The Spider Bites, 2010. Contributor to periodicals. **Address:** 243 Dewhust Blvd. N, Toronto, ON M4J 3K4, Canada. **Online address:** harry.roe072@sympatico.ca

ROE, JoAnn. American (born United States), b. 1926?. **Genres:** Children's Fiction, History, How-to Books, Travel/Exploration. **Career:** John Freiburg Advertising Agency, copywriter, 1945-46; Guest Informant, advertising writer, 1946-47; JoAnn Roe Advertising Agency, owner, 1948-52; freelance public relations and magazine writer, 1952-64; Skyhaven Inc., public relations manager, 1964-66; Northwestern Technology Inc., secretary and treasurer, 1967-70; IGM Communications, secretary and treasurer, 1974-80, public relations manager, 1980-84; freelance writer, 1984-. **Publications:** The North Cascadians, 1980; The Real Old West, 1981; Frank Matsura, Frontier Photographer, 1981; F.S. Matsura, 1983; The Columbia River: A Historical Travel Guide, 1992; Ghost Towns and Mining Camps, 1994; Ghost Camps & Boom Towns, 1995; Stevens Pass: The Story of Railroading and Recreation in the North Cascades, 1995, rev. ed., 2002; Seattle Uncovered, 1996; The North Cascades Highway: Washington's Popular and Scenic Pass, 1997; Ranald MacDonald: Pacific Rim Adventurer, 1997; Sister Cities, 2003; Blakely Island in Time, 2005; San Juan Islands: Into the 21st Century, 2011. CHILDREN'S BOOKS: Castaway Cat, 1984; Fisherman Cat, 1988; Alaska Cat, 1990; Samurai Cat, 1993. Contributor of articles to magazines and newspapers. **Address:** 3467 Pinehurst Ct., Bellingham, WA 98225, U.S.A. **Online address:** joroe@joannroe.com

ROE, Nicholas. Scottish/British (born England), b. 1955. **Genres:** Literary Criticism And History, Biography, Autobiography/Memoirs, Humanities. **Career:** Queens University, lecturer in English, 1982-85; University of St. Andrews, Scotland, lecturer, professor of English, 1985-; University of Sao Paulo, Department of English, visiting professor, 1989; Romanticism, editor; Coleridge Summer Conference, academic director. **Publications:** (Ed. with R. Gravil and L. Newlyn) Coleridge's Imagination: Essays in Memory of Pete Laver, 1985; Wordsworth and Coleridge: The Radical Years, 1985; The Politics of Nature: Wordsworth and Some Contemporaries, 1992, 2nd rev. ed., 2002; (ed.) William Wordsworth, Selected Poetry, 1992; (ed.) Keats and History, 1995; John Keats and the Culture of Dissent, 1997; (ed.) Samuel Taylor Coleridge and the Sciences of Life, 2001; (ed.) Leigh Hunt: Life, Poetics, Politics, 2003; (ed.) Romanticism: An Oxford Guide, 2005; Fiery Heart: The First Life of Leigh Hunt, 2005; (ed.) English Romantic Writers and the West Country, 2010. **Address:** School of English, University of St. Andrews, 42 Castle House, 16 The Scores, St. Andrews, FF KY16 9AX, Scotland. **Online address:** nhr@st-andrews.ac.uk

ROE, Sue. British (born England), b. 1956?. **Genres:** Biography, Autobiography/Memoirs, Novels, Poetry, Literary Criticism And History, Young Adult Fiction. **Career:** University of East Anglia, lecturer in creative writing; University of Sussex, Centre for Community Engagement, associate tutor and lecturer in creative studies, senior lecturer in continuing education. Writer. **Publications:** Estella, Her Expectations (novel), 1982; (ed.) Women Reading Women's Writing, 1987; Writing and Gender: Virginia Woolf's Writing Practice, 1990; (ed. and intro.) Jacob's Room, 1992; (co-author) The Semi-Transparent Envelope: Women Writing-Feminism and Fiction, 1994; The Spitfire Factory (poems), 1998; (ed. with S. Sellers) The Cambridge Companion to Virginia Woolf, 2000; Gwen John: A Painter's Life, 2001; The Private Lives of the Impressionists, 2006. Contributor to periodicals. **Address:** Centre for Community Engagement, University of Sussex, 4B19 Mantell Bldg., Sussex House, Falmer, Brighton, ES BN1 9RF, England. **Online address:** s.m.roe@sussex.ac.uk

ROE, Sue (Lynn). American (born United States), b. 1956?. **Genres:** Essays, Novels, Social Commentary, Adult Non-fiction, Literary Criticism And History, Reference. **Career:** Nevada Evening Journal, writer, 1978-79; Time-Republican, editor, 1978-98, freelance writer, 1980-; Marshalltown Community College, instructor, 1985; Marshalltown School District Newsletter, editor, 1993-98; Elim Children's Center, president, 1994-98; Iowa Valley Community College, District Marketing and Communications Services, supervisor, 1999-; University of East Anglia, lecturer in creative writing; University of Sussex, Centre for Continuing Education, lecturer in continuing education, senior lecturer, Centre for Community Engagement, associate tutor and lecturer in creative studies. **Publications:** Estella, Her Expectations: A Novel, 1982; (ed.) Women Reading Women's Writing, 1987; Writing and Gender: Virginia Woolf's Writing Practice, 1990; (ed. and intro.) Jacob's Room, 1992; (co-author) The Semi-Transparent Envelope: Women Writing-Feminism and Fiction, 1994; (ed. with S.Sellers) The Cambridge Companion to Virginia Woolf, 2000; Gwen John: A Painter's Life, 2001; The Private Lives of the Impressionists, 2006. **Address:** Centre for Continuing Education, The Sussex Institute, University of Sussex, Essex House Eh 232 C, Brighton, ES BN1 9QQ, England. **Online address:** s.m.roe@sussex.ac.uk

ROEDIGER, David R(andall). American (born United States), b. 1952. **Genres:** History, Cultural/Ethnic Topics, Essays, Race Relations. **Career:** Students for a Democratic Society, president, 1970; Workers Defense, vice-chairperson, 1978-80; Yale University, Frederick Douglass Papers, assistant editor, 1979-80; Northwestern University, lecturer in history, 1980-81, Mellon assistant professor, 1981-83, assistant professor, 1984-85; American Council of Learned Societies, fellow, 1983-84; Exxon Educational Foundation, fellow, 1983-84; University of Missouri-Columbia, assistant professor, associate professor, 1985-92, professor of history, 1992-94; Charles H. Kerr Publishing Co., president of board of directors, 1992-; University of Minnesota, professor of history, 1995-2000, American Studies Program, chairman, 1996-2000; University of Illinois, professor of history, Kendrick C. Babcock professor, Kendrick C. Babcock chairman of history and Afro-American studies, 2000-, Center on Democracy in a Multiracial Society, director. Writer. **Publications:** (Ed. and intro.) Dreams and Dynamite: Selected Poems, 1985; (ed. with F. Rosemont) Hay market Scrapbook, 1986; (with P.S. Foner) Our Own Time: A History of American Labor and the Working Day, 1989; (ed. with P. Boanes) Haymarket Heritage: The Memoirs of Irving S. Abrams, 1989; The Wages of Whiteness: Race and the Making of the American Working Class, 1991, rev. ed., 2007; (ed.) Fellow Worker: The Life of Fred W. Thompson, 1993; Towards the Abolition of Whiteness: Essays on Race, Politics, and Working Class History, 1994; (ed. and intro.) Black on White: Black Writers on What It Means to Be White, 1998; (ed. with M.H. Blatt) The Meaning of Slavery in the North, 1998; (ed. and intro.) Labor Struggles in the Deep South and Other Writings, 2000; (ed. and intro.) John Brown, 2001; Colored White: Transcending the Racial Past, 2002; Whiteness, a Wayward Construction, 2003; Working Toward Whiteness: How America's Immigrants Became White: The Strange Journey from Ellis Island to the Suburbs, 2005; History Against Misery, 2005; (ed.) The Best American History Essays 2008, 2008; How Race Survived U.S. History: From Settlement and Slavery to the Obama Phenomenon, 2008; (with E.D. Esch) Production of Difference: Race And The Management of U.S. Labor, 2012. Contributor to history journals and other magazines. **Address:** Department of History, University of Illinois at Urbana-Champaign, 304 Gregory Hall, 810 S Wright St., Urbana, IL 61801, U.S.A. **Online address:** droedige@illinois.edu

ROEHRIG, Catharine H. American (born United States), b. 1949. **Genres:** Archaeology/Antiquities, Children's Non-fiction, Art/Art History. **Career:** University of California, research assistant, 1979-85, teaching assistant, 1982-85, Berkeley Theban Mapping Project, assistant director, 1980-88; Museum of Fine Arts, research assistant, 1985-88; Metropolitan Museum of Art, Department of Egyptian Art, curator, 1989-, associate curator of Egyptian art. Writer. **Publications:** (With S. D'Auria and P. Lacovara) Mummies and Magic: An Introduction to Egyptian Funerary Beliefs, 1988; Fun with Hieroglyphs, 1990; Explorers and Artists in the Valley of the Kings, 2002; Life along the Nile: Three Egyptians of Ancient Thebes, 2002; (ed. with R. Dreyfus and C.A. Keller) Hatshepsut, from Queen to Pharaoh, 2005. **Address:** Department of Egyptian Art, Metropolitan Museum of Art, 1000 5th Ave., New York, NY 10028-0198, U.S.A. **Online address:** catharine.roehrig@metmusuem.org

ROESCH, Mattox. American (born United States), b. 1977?. **Genres:** Young Adult Fiction. **Career:** Writer. **Publications:** Sometimes We're Always Real Same-Same, 2009. **Address:** Unalakleet, AR , U.S.A. **Online address:** mattox@mattoxroesch.com

ROESKE, Paulette. American (born United States), b. 1945. **Genres:** Poetry, Novellas/Short Stories, Young Adult Fiction, Young Adult Non-fiction. **Career:** Harper High School, English teacher, 1968-69; College of Lake County, professor of English, 1969-2001, professor emeritus, 2001-, Reading Series, founder and director, 1983-2001; Willow Review, founder and editor, 1983-; Christ Church College, professor, 1995-2002, professor emeritus, 2002-; University of Southern Indiana, professor of creative writing, 2002-03; Harlaxton College, poet-in-residence, 2003. **Publications:** Breathing Under Water: Poems, 1988; The Body Can Ascend No Higher (chapbook), 1992; Divine Attention: Poems, 1995; Anvil, Clock & Last, 2001; Bridge of Sighs: A Novella and Stories (fiction), 2002; (ed.) Climate Controlled. Works appear in anthologies. Contributor of articles to periodicals. **Address:** Department of English, College of Lake County, 19351 W Washington St., Ste. B237, Grayslake, IL 60030-1198, U.S.A. **Online address:** pauletteroeske@usi.edu

ROESSNER, Michaela. American (born United States), b. 1950. **Genres:** Novels, Science Fiction/Fantasy, Novellas/Short Stories, Education. **Career:** Locus (magazine), assistant editor, 1980-81; Western State College of Colorado, MFA in Creative Writing Program, creative writing instructor; Gotham Writers' Workshop, creative writing instructor. **Publications:** NOVELS: Walkabout Woman (fantasy), 1988; Vanishing Point, 1993; The Stars Dispose, 1997; The Stars Compel, 1999; Inside Outside, 2004. OTHER: The Escape Artist, 1996. Works appear in anthologies. Contributor to periodicals. **Address:** c/o Merrilee Heifetz, Writers House Inc., 21 W 26th St., New York, NY 10010-1003, U.S.A. **Online address:** mroessner@bnis.net

ROGAN, Johnny. British (born England), b. 1953. **Genres:** Music, Biography, Art/Art History, Autobiography/Memoirs. **Career:** Writer, 1981-. **Publications:** Timeless Flight: The Definitive Biography of The Byrds, 1981, rev. ed., 1990; Roxy Music: Style with Substance, 1982; Neil Young: Here We Are in the Years, 1982; Van Morrison: A Portrait of the Artist in US as Van Morrison: The Great Deception, 1984; The Kinks: The Sound and the Fury in US as The Kinks: A Mental Institution, 1984; Wham!: The Death of a Supergroup, 1987; Starmakers and Svengalis: The History of British Pop Management, 1988; The Football Managers, 1989; (ed.) The Guinness Encyclopaedia of Popular Music, 1992; Morrissey and Marr: The Severed Alliance, 1993; The Smiths: The Visual Documentary, 1994; The Complete Guide to the Music of the Smiths and Morrissey/Marr, 1995; The Complete Guide to the Music of Neil Young, 1996; Crosby, Stills, Nash and Young: The Visual Documentary, 1996; The Complete Guide to the Music of John Lennon, 1997; The Byrds: Timeless Flight Revisited-The Sequel, 1997; The Complete Guide to the Music of Crosby, Stills, Nash and Young, 1998; The Complete Guide to the Music of the Kinks, 1998; Neil Young: Zero to Sixty-A Critical Biography, 2000; Van Morrison: No Surrender, 2005. Works appears in anthologies. **Address:** Music Sales Corp., 8/9 Frith St., London, GL W1V 5TZ, England.

ROGAN, Josh. *See* **MATHESON, Richard (Burton).**

ROGER, Philippe. French (born France), b. 1949?. **Genres:** Intellectual History, Essays, Literary Criticism And History. **Career:** Yale University, assistant, 1972-73; Lycée Claude-Bernard, stage d'agrégation, 1973-74; Lycée Polyvalent de Vernon, professor of humanities, 1974-76; New York University, Institute of French Studies, deputy director, 1978-81, associate professor, 1981-84, professor of French and chair of eighteenth-century studies, 1985-, global distinguished professor of French; Centre National de la Recherche Scientifique (French National Center for Scientific Research), research program director, 1985-; école des Hautes études en Sciences Sociales, professor of French and director of studies; University of Virginia, professor of French; Critique, editor. **Publications:** Sade: La Philosophie dans le pressoir, 1976; (ed. with M. Camus) Sade, Ecrire la crise, 1983; Roland Barthes, roman, 1986, new ed. as Livre de Poche, 1990; (ed. with J.C. Bonnet) La Legende de la Revolution au XXe siecle: De Gance A Renoir, de Romain Rolland A Claude Simon, 1988; (ed.) L'Homme des Lumi Eres: De Paris A Petersbourg: Actes du colloque international (automne 1992), 1995; (ed.) Biblioteca Europea, 1995; (ed. with R. Morrissey) L'encyclopedie: du reseau au livre et du livre au reseau, 2001; L'ennemi americain: Genealogie de l'antiam ericanisme franais, 2002; (ed. with J. Dagen) Un Siecle de deux cents ans? Les XVIIe et XVIIIe siecles: Continuites et discontinuites, 2004.

CONTRIBUTOR: Language and Rhetoric of the Revolution, 1990; Sade and the Narrative of Transgression, 1995; Writing the Image after Roland Barthes, 1997; Erotikon: Essays on Eros, Ancient and Modern, 2005. Contributor to periodicals and journals. **Address:** EHESS, 190-198 avenue de France, Paris, 75244, France. **Online address:** roger@ehess.fr

ROGERS, Annie G. American (born United States) **Genres:** Psychiatry, Psychology. **Career:** Harvard University, assistant professor of human development and psychology; Hampshire College, associate professor of clinical psychology, professor of psychoanalysis and clinical psychology. Writer. **Publications:** (Ed. with C. Gilligan and D.L. Tolman) Women, Girls, and Psychotherapy: Reframing Resistance (nonfiction), 1991; A Shining Affliction: A Story of Harm and Healing in Psychotherapy, 1995; Unsayable: The Hidden Language of Trauma, 2006. **Address:** Hampshire College, FPH 217, 893 West St., Amherst, MA 01002, U.S.A. **Online address:** agrss@hampshire.edu

ROGERS, Bettye. American (born United States), b. 1934?. **Genres:** Local History/Rural Topics, Children's Non-fiction, Children's Fiction, Animals/Pets. **Career:** East Texas State University, associate professor, 1963-69; Texas Tech University, associate professor, 1970-88; South Plains Teacher Education Center, director and executive secretary, 1974-87; Texas Co-operative Teacher Center Network, president, treasurer, executive secretary, 1980-86. Writer. **Publications:** Prairie Dog Town, 1993; Paul Wylie from Cowboy to Cowboy Artist, 1998. Contributor to magazines. **Address:** 16 E Canyon View Dr., Ransom Canyon, TX 79366, U.S.A.

ROGERS, Cindy. American (born United States), b. 1950. **Genres:** Children's Fiction, Theology/Religion. **Career:** Fargo public schools, junior high teacher, 1984-90; McDonald Montessori School, substitute teacher, 1994-95; Institute of Children's Literature (correspondence school), writing instructor, 1995-. **Publications:** Noah and the Arkettes, 1994; A Family for Casey, 1995; (with M. Keefer and C. Mishica) Surprising Stories: 3 Fun-to-Read-Aloud Stories with a Message, 1999; (with S. Dardis) As I Journey on: Meditations for those Facing Death, 2000; Word Magic for Writers, 2004; Prairie Spirits, forthcoming. Contributor to periodicals. **Address:** 1090 82nd St. E, Inver Grove Heights, MN 55077-3826, U.S.A.

ROGERS, Colin D(arlington). British (born England), b. 1936. **Genres:** Genealogy/Heraldry, Local History/Rural Topics, Genealogy/Heraldry, Self Help, Human Relations/Parenting, History, Psychology. **Career:** Teacher at a grammar school, 1959-66; Didsbury College of Education, lecturer, 1966-77; Manchester Polytechnic, lecturer, 1977-91; Manchester Metropolitan University, head of overseas liaison, 1991-2000; Rogers and Rogers (consultants on locating missing beneficiaries), partner; Suzy Lamplugh Trust, consultant. Writer. **Publications:** Lancashire Population Crisis of 1623, 1975; A Social Psychology of Schooling: The Expectancy Process, 1982; Tracing Your English Ancestors, 1983 in UK as The Family Tree Detective, rev. ed., 1997; The Family Tree Detective: A Manual for Analyzing and Solving Genealogical Problems in England and Wales, 1538 to the Present Day, 1983, 2nd ed., 1985; Tracing Missing Persons: An introduction to Agencies, Methods and Sources in England and Wales, 1986; Tracing Your English Ancestors: A Manual for Analysing and Solving Genealogical Problems, 1538 to the Present, 1989; (with J. Gibson) Electoral Registers since 1832 and Burgess Rolls, 2nd ed., 1990; (with J. Gibson) Pollbooks, c. 1696-1872: A Directory to Holdings in Great Britain, 1990, 3rd ed., 1998; (with J.H. Smith) Local Family History in England, 1991; Coroners' Records in England and Wales, 1992, 2nd ed., 1998; (with J. Gibson) Coroner's Records in England and Wales, 1992; (with J.H. Smith) Poor Law Union Records, 1993; (ed.) The Registers of St. James's, George Street, Manchester: Baptisms and Burials, 1788-1837, 1993; The Surname Detective: Investigating Surname Distribution in England, 1066 to the Present Day, 1995; The Family Tree Detective: Tracing Your Ancestors in England and Wales, 1997, 4th ed., 2009; (ed.) Registers of St. Luke's Chapel, Heywood, 2006. **Address:** Ebenezer Chapel, 121 Old Rd., Tintwistle, Glossop, DB SK13 1JZ, England. **Online address:** rogerses@aol.com

ROGERS, Deborah D(ee). American (born United States), b. 1953?. **Genres:** Literary Criticism And History, Women's Studies And Issues, Biography, Essays, Bibliography, Art/Art History. **Career:** University of Maine, assistant professor, 1982-89, associate professor, 1990-96, professor of English, 1996-. Writer. **Publications:** Bookseller as Rogue: John Almon and the Politics of Eighteenth-Century Publishing, 1986; (ed.) The Critical Response to Ann Radcliffe, 1994; (ed. and intro.) Two Gothic Classics by Women, 1995; Ann Radcliffe: A Bio-Bibliography, 1996; The Matrophobic Gothic and Its Legacy: Sacrificing Mothers in the Novel and in Popular Culture, 2007. **Address:** Department of English, University of Maine, Rm. 403A, 5752 Neville Hall, Orono, ME 04469-5752, U.S.A. **Online address:** drogers@maine.edu

ROGERS, Douglas. American/Zimbabwean (born Zimbabwe), b. 1968. **Genres:** Autobiography/Memoirs. **Career:** Writer and educator. **Publications:** The Last Resort: A Memoir of Zimbabwe, 2009. Contributor to periodicals. **Address:** c/o Susan Golomb, Susan Golomb Literary Agency, 875 Ave. of the Americas, Ste. 2303, New York, NY 10001, U.S.A. **Online address:** douglas@douglasrogers.org

ROGERS, Franklin Robert. American (born United States), b. 1921. **Genres:** Literary Criticism And History, History, Novels. **Career:** Fresno State College, instructor, 1950-51; Merced Union High School, teacher, 1952-54; University of California-Berkeley, teaching assistant, 1956-58; University of Wisconsin-Milwaukee, instructor, 1958-60, assistant professor of American literature, 1960-63; University of California-Davis, visiting assistant professor, 1963-64; San Jose State University, associate professor, 1964-, professor, 1967-87, professor emeritus of English, 1987-; University of Lyon, Fulbright professor in American literature, 1966-67, visiting professor of American literature, 1969-71; University of Paris, visiting professor of American literature, 1975-76; Institut des Hautes Etudes Scientifiques, lecturer, 1976; Kyoto American Studies Summer Seminar, lecturer, 1986. Writer. **Publications:** Mark Twain's Burlesque Patterns, as seen in the Novels and Narratives, 1855-1885, 1960; The Pattern for Mark Twain's Roughing It, 1961; (intro.) Roughing It, 1972; (with M. Rogers) Painting and Poetry: Form, Metaphor, and the Language of Literature, 1985; (with M. Rogers) Occidental Ideographs: Image, Sequence, and Literary History, 1991; When the Fight was Done: A Novel of the Maratha Wars, 2003; Blood Feud in Paradise, the Course of Conflict in Kashmir, 2002; Moonlight Sonata, 2010; Dewdrop on the Lotus, 2011. EDITOR: Simon Wheeler, Detective, 1963; (intro.) Mark Twain's Satires and Burlesques, 1967. **Address:** 206 Woodland Ridge, Los Gatos, CA 95033, U.S.A. **Online address:** franklin.rogers@sjsu.edu

ROGERS, Hal. See **SIRIMARCO, Elizabeth.**

ROGERS, Heather. American (born United States), b. 1970?. **Genres:** Recreation, Environmental Sciences/Ecology. **Career:** Writer and journalist. **Publications:** Gone Tomorrow: The Hidden Life of Garbage, 2005; Green Gone Wrong: How Our Economy is Undermining the Environmental Revolution, 2010. **Address:** c/o Author Mail, The New Press, 38 Greene St., 4th Fl., New York, NY 10013, U.S.A. **Online address:** hrogers@gonetomorrow.org

ROGERS, Katharine M. American (born United States), b. 1932. **Genres:** Literary Criticism And History, Animals/Pets. **Career:** Skidmore College, instructor in English, 1954-55; Cornell University, instructor in English, 1955-57; City University of New York, Brooklyn College, Department of English, instructor, 1958-64, assistant professor, 1965-70, associate professor, 1971-73, professor of English, 1974-89, professor emeritus, 1989-, doctoral faculty, 1972-89. Writer. **Publications:** The Troublesome Helpmate: A History of Misogyny in Literature, 1966; William Wycherley, 1972; Feminism in Eighteenth-century England, 1982; Frances Burney: The World of Female Difficulties, 1990; The Cat and the Human Imagination: Feline Images from Bast to Garfield, 1997; L. Frank Baum: Creator of Oz, 2002; First Friend: A History of Dogs and Humans, 2005; Cat, 2006. EDITOR: Selected Poems of Anne Finch, Countess of Winchilsea, 1979; Before Their Time, 1979; The Signet Classic Book of Eighteenth and Nineteenth Century British Drama, 1979; (and intro.) Selected Writings of Samuel Johnson, 1981; (with W. McCarthy) The Meridian Anthology of Early Women Writers, 1987; The Meridian Anthology of Early American Women Writers, 1991; Meridian Anthology of Restoration and Eighteenth-Century Plays by Women, 1994. Contributor of articles to journals. **Address:** Department of English, Brooklyn College, City University of New York, Rm. 2308, Boylan Hall, 2900 Bedford Ave., Brooklyn, NY 11210, U.S.A. **Online address:** katharinerogers@earthlink.net

ROGERS, Keith. See **HARRIS, Marion (Rose).**

ROGERS, Pat. American/British (born England), b. 1938. **Genres:** Literary Criticism And History, Biography, Language/Linguistics. **Career:** Sidney Sussex College, fellow, 1964-69; University of London, King's College, lecturer, 1969-73, School of Advanced Study, visiting professorial fellow, 2010; British Society for Eighteenth-Century Studies, secretary, 1972-74, president, 1982-84; University College of North Wales, professor of English, 1973-76;

University of Bristol, professor of English, 1977-86; Johnson Society of Lichfield, president, 1982-83; University of South Florida, DeBartolo chair in the liberal arts, 1986-, distinguished university professor. Writer. **Publications:** Grub Street: Studies in a Subculture, 1972, rev. ed. as Hacks and Dunces, 1980; The Augustan Vision, 1974; An Introduction to Pope, 1975; Henry Fielding: A Biography, 1979; Robinson Crusoe, 1979; Literature and Popular Culture in the Eighteenth Century, 1985; Eighteenth-Century Encounters: Studies in Literature and Society in the Age of Walpole, 1985; Samuel Johnson, 1993; Essays on Pope, 1993; Selected Poems of Alexander Pope, 1994; Johnson and Boswell: The Transit of Caledonia, 1995; The Samuel Johnson Encyclopedia, 1996; The Text of Great Britain: Theme and Design in Defoe's Tour, 1997; Symbolic Design of Windsor-Forest: Iconography, Pageant, and Prophecy in Pope's Early Work, 2004; The Alexander Pope Encyclopedia, 2004; Pope and the Destiny of the Stuarts: History, Politics, and Mythology in the Age of Queen Anne, 2005; (with P. Baines) Edmund Curll, Bookseller, 2007; (with J. Ferrarp and P. Baines) Wiley-Blackwell Encyclopedia of Eighteenth-Century Writers and Writing, 1660-1789, 2011; Documenting Eighteenth-Century Satire, forthcoming; Alexander Pope: A Political Biography, forthcoming. EDITOR: (intro.) A Tour Through the Whole Island of Great Britain, 1971; A Tour Through Great Britain, 1989; Defoe: The Critical Heritage, 1972; The Eighteenth Century, 1978; Jonathan Swift: Complete Poems, 1983; The Oxford Illustrated History of English Literature, 1987; (with G.S. Rousseau) Enduring Legacy: Alexander Pope Tercentenary Essays, 1988; (intro.) Discourses, 1992; (co-ed.) The Blackwell Companion to the Enlightenment, 1992; Outline of English Literature, 1992, 2nd ed., 1998; Selected Poems of Jonathan Swift, 1993; The Oxford Authors: Pope, 1993; Jonston and Boswell in Scotland: A Journey to the Hebrides, 1993; Moll Flanders by Daniel Defoe, 1994; Persuasion by Jane Austen, 1994; Vanity Fair by W.M. Thackeray, 1997; (intro.) Selected Poetry, 1998; (with R. Hewitt) Orthodoxy and Heresy in Eighteenth-Century Society: Essays from the DeBartolo Conference, 2002; The Oxford Dictionary of National Biography, 2004; Letters, Life, and Works of John Oldmixon: Politics and Professional Authorship in Early Hanoverian England, 2005; (intro.) Major Works, 2006; Pride and Prejudice, 2006; (contrib.) Cambridge Companion to Alexander Pope, 2007; (with L. Runge) Producing the Eighteen-Century Book, forthcoming. Contributor to journals and periodicals. **Address:** Department of English, University of South Florida, CPR303, 4202 E Fowler Ave., Tampa, FL 33620-5550, U.S.A. **Online address:** rogersp@usf.edu

ROGERS, Rebecca Elizabeth. American (born United States), b. 1959. **Genres:** Novels. **Career:** University of Iowa, assistant professor of history, 1989-94, associate professor, 1994; Universite Paris, professor of the history of education, 2006-. Writer. **Publications:** Les Demoiselles de la Legion d'Honneur: Les Maisons d'education de la Legion d'Honneur au XIXe Siecle, 1992; La Mixite dans l'education: Enjeux Passes et Presents, 2004; From the Salon to the Schoolroom: Educating Bourgeois Girls in Nineteenth-Century France, 2005. **Address:** Ctr. de recherche sur les liens sociaux, Universite Paris 5, Rene Descartes, 45, rue des Saints-Peres, Paris, 75270, France.

ROGERS, Richard. British/Italian (born Italy), b. 1933. **Genres:** Architecture. **Career:** Skidmore, Owings and Merrill, architect, 1962-63; Team 4, architect and co-founder, 1963-67; Rogers Stirk Harbour & Partners LLP, chairman; KK Rogers Stirk Harbour Partners, chairman; Rogers Stirk Harbour & Partners SL, chairman; RSHP Australia Pty Ltd, director. Writer. **Publications:** (With R. Legorreta, F. Maki and R. Meier) Architecture, Shaping the Future: A Symposium and Exhibition, 1990; Architecture: A Modern View, 1990; (with M. Fisher) A New London, 1992; Richard Rogers: Partnership: Works and Projects, 1996; Cities for a Small Planet, 1997; Richard Rogers: Architecture of the Future, 2006. CONTRIBUTOR: Norman Foster: Team 4 and Foster Associates: Buildings and Projects, 1989; Towards an Urban Renaissance, 1999; Richard Rogers: Complete Works, 1999; Richard Rogers: Centre Pompidou, 2011. **Address:** Faber and Faber Ltd., 3 Queen Sq., London, GL WC1N 3AU, England.

ROGERS, Robert F. American (born United States), b. 1930. **Genres:** Local History/Rural Topics. **Career:** U.S. Department of State, foreign service officer, 1956-70; consultant, 1973-77; University of Guam, professor of political science, 1977-94; Guam Commission on Self-Determination, executive director, 1984-86; writer, 1994-. **Publications:** (Co-author) Guam's Political Status: Military, Airline, and Energy Aspects of Change, 1980; Guam's Search for Commonwealth Status, 1984; Guam Commission on Self-Determination,

1985-86, 1986; Guam's Commonwealth Effort, 1987-1988, 1988; Destiny's Landfall: A History of Guam, 1995. Contributor to periodicals. **Address:** University of Hawaii Press, 2840 Kolowalu St., Honolulu, HI 96822, U.S.A.

ROGERS, Rosemary. American/Sri Lankan (born Sri Lanka), b. 1932. **Genres:** Romance/Historical, Novels, Literary Criticism And History, Young Adult Fiction, History. **Career:** Associated Newspapers of Ceylon Ltd., writer of features and public affairs information, 1959-62; Travis Air Force Base, secretary in billeting office, 1964-69; Solano County Parks Department, secretary, 1969-74; Fairfield Daily Republic, part-time reporter. **Publications:** NOVELS: The Wildest Heart, 1974; The Crowd Pleasers, 1978; The Insiders, 1979; Love Play, 1981; Surrender to Love, 1982; The Wanton, 1985; (with S. Kelly) Saints Preserve Us!: Everything You Need to Know about Every Saint, You'll Ever Need, 1993; The Tea Planter's Bride, 1995; A Dangerous Man, 1996; (with S. Kelly) Who in Hell: A Guide to the Whole Damned Bunch, 1996; Midnight Lady, 1997; (with L. Stasi) Boomer Babes: A Woman's Guide to the New Middle Ages, 1998; All I Desire, 1998; In Your Arms, 1999; (with S. Kelly) How to Be Irish Even if You Already Are, 1999; A Reckless Encounter, 2001; (with S. Kelly) Birthday Book of Saints: Your Powerful Personal Patrons of Every Blessed Day of the Year, 2001; Jewel of My Heart, 2004; (with C.E. Bode and N.R. Michlin) Mother-Daughter Movies: 101 Films to See Together, 2004; Sapphire, 2005; A Daring Passion, 2007; Scandalous Deception, 2008; Bound by Love, 2009; Scoundrel's Honor, 2010. MORGAN/CHALLENGER SERIES: Sweet Savage Love, 1974; Dark Fires, 1975; Wicked Loving Lies, 1976; Bound by Desire, 1988; Lost Love, Last Love, 1980; Savage Desire, 2000. LOGAN DUOLOGY: An Honorable Man, 2002; Return to Me, 2003. OTHER: Bride for a Night, 2011. Contributor to magazines. **Address:** Villard Books, Random House Publishing Group, 1745 Broadway, 18th Fl., New York, NY 10019-4368, U.S.A.

ROGLER, Lloyd Henry. American/Puerto Rican (born Puerto Rico), b. 1930. **Genres:** Anthropology/Ethnology, Psychiatry, Sociology, Psychology, Human Relations/Parenting. **Career:** University of Iowa City, instructor in sociology, 1955-57; University of Puerto Rico, School of Medicine and College of Social Sciences, assistant professor, lecturer of department of psychiatry, Social Sciences Research Center, research associate, 1957-60, visiting professor in the behavioral sciences, 1971-72; Yale University, Department of Sociology, lecturer, 1960-62, assistant professor, 1962-64, Latin American Studies, associate chairman, Latin American Studies Undergraduate Program, director, 1964-65, associate professor, 1964-68, visiting professor, 1990-91; Case Western Reserve University, professor of sociology, 1968-74; Fordham University, Albert Schweitzer professor in the humanities, 1974-2002, Hispanic Research Center, director, 1977-90, Albert Schweitzer professor emeritus, 2002-; Albert Einstein College of Medicine Bronx, visiting professor of psychiatry, 1990-91; New York University Bellevue Medical Center, visiting professor of department of psychiatry, 1992-93; Yale University School of Medicine Genetic Epidemiology Research Unit, consultant, 1997; Columbia University, Mailman School of Public Health, Sociomedical Sciences Division, visiting professor, 2000, School of Social Work, visiting professor, 2001-02. Writer. **Publications:** (With A.B. Hollingshead) Trapped: Families and Schizophrenia, 1965, 2nd ed., 1975; Migrant in the City: The Life of a Puerto Rican Action Group, 1972; (with I.A. Canino and B.F. Earley) The Puerto Rican Child in New York City: Stress and Mental Health, 1980; (with A. Farber) Unitas-Hispanic and Black Children in a Healing Community, 1981; (co-author) A Conceptual Framework for Mental Health Research on Hispanic Populations, 1983; (with G. Costantino and Robert G. Malgady) Cuento Therapy: Folktales As a Culturally Sensitive Psychotherapy for Puerto Rican Children, 1985; (with R.G. Malgady and O. Rodriguez) Hispanics and Mental Health: A Framework for Research, 1989; Barrio Professors: Tales of Naturalistic Research, 2008. **Address:** Department of Sociology & Anthropology, Fordham University, Rose Hill Campus, 403E Dealy Hall, Bronx, NY 10458, U.S.A. **Online address:** rogler@fordham.edu

ROGOVOY, Seth. American (born United States), b. 1960?. **Genres:** Poetry, Music. **Career:** Berkshire Eagle, rock and jazz music critic; Berkshire Living, editor-in-chief; Berkshire Business Quarterly, editor-in-chief; Berkshire Living Home+Garden, editor-in-chief; Living.com, editor-in-chief; Berkshire Daily, editor-in-chief; South Berkshire Minyan, founder and lay leader, 2003-06. **Publications:** The Essential Klezmer: A Music Lover's Guide to Jewish Roots and Soul Music, from the Old World to the Jazz Age to the Downtown Avant-Garde, 2000; Bob Dylan: Prophet, Mystic, Poet, 2009. Contributor to periodicals. **Address:** Great Barrington, MA , U.S.A. **Online address:** seth@rogovoy.com

ROGOW, Roberta. American (born United States), b. 1942. **Genres:** Mystery/Crime/Suspense, Science Fiction/Fantasy. **Career:** Paterson Free Public Library, librarian, 1971-82; Other Worlds Books, editor, publisher and owner, 1978-95; Ridgefield Public Library, children's librarian, 1982-87; Union Free Public Library, children's librarian, 1987-2008; Grip, editor. **Publications:** Trexindex: An Index to Star Trek Fanzines, 1976; Future Speak: A Fan's Guide to the Language of Science Fiction, 1991; The Problem of the Missing Miss, 1998; The Problem of the Spiteful Spiritualist, 1999; The Problem of the Missing Hoyden, 1999; The Problem of the Evil Editor, 2000; The Problem of the Surly Servant, 2001; The Guilty Client, 2009; The Root of the Matter, 2010. **Address:** 1755-A Manor Dr., Irvington, NJ 07111, U.S.A. **Online address:** rogowr@aol.com

ROGOW, Zack. American (born United States), b. 1952. **Genres:** Poetry, Translations, Novels. **Career:** Sweet Ch'i Press, managing editor, 1983-87, substitute teacher, 1986-89; Benemann Translation Center, production coordinator, 1989-92; San Francisco State University, Poetry Center, managing director, 1992, M.A. Writing Program, teacher, 1995-; University of California, Graduate School of Education, editor and teacher, 1993-; University of San Francisco, lecturer in creative writing, 1995-99; California College of the Arts, senior adjunct professor of writing, 2002-; University of Alaska, Department of Creative Writing and Literary Arts, associate faculty. Writer. **Publications:** POETRY: Glimmerings, 1979; Make It Last, 1983; A Preview of the Dream, 1985; The Selfsame Planet, 1999; Greatest Hits: 1979-2001, 2002; Number before Infinity: Poems, 2008. OTHERS: Oranges, 1988; (ed.) The Face of Poetry, 2005. TRANSLATOR: M. Jacob, The Dice Cup, 1979; (cotrans.) M. Sachs, The Kiss, 1992; (with B. Zavatsky) A. Breton, Earthlight, 1993; A. Breton, Arcanum 17: With Apertures, Grafted to the End, 1994; G. Sand, Horace, 1995; Colette, Green Wheat: A Novel, 2004. Works appear in anthologies. Contributor to magazines and periodicals. **Address:** Department of Creative Writing and Literary Arts, University of Alaska, Administration 270, 3211 Providence Dr., Anchorage, AK 99508-4614, U.S.A. **Online address:** afzr@uaa.alaska.edu

ROHAN, Michael Scott. British/Scottish (born Scotland), b. 1951. **Genres:** Science Fiction/Fantasy, Adult Non-fiction, Novels, Young Adult Non-fiction, Natural History. **Career:** London Times, columnist; Asgard, owner. **Publications:** FANTASY NOVELS: (with A.J. Scott) Fantastic People, 1980; (with A.J. Scott) The Ice King, 1986 in US as Burial Rites, 1987; (with A.J. Scott) A Spell of Empire: The Horns of Tartarus, 1992; The Lord of Middle Air, 1994. WINTER OF THE WORLD SERIES: The Anvil of Ice, 1986; The Forge in the Forest, 1987; The Hammer of the Sun, 1988; The Castle of the Winds, 1998; The Singer and the Sea, 1999; Shadow of the Seer, 2001. SPIRAL SERIES: Chase the Morning, 1990; The Gates of Noon, 1992; Cloud Castles, 1993; Maxie's Demon, 1997. NONFICTION: (with A.J. Scott) The Hammer and the Cross, 1980; First Byte: Choosing and Using a Home Computer, 1983; (with A.J. Scott and P. Gardner) The BBC Micro Add-On Guide, 1985; The Classical Video Guide, 1994. SCIENCE-FICTION NOVELS: Run to the Stars, 1982. Works appear in anthologies. Contributor of articles to magazines and newspapers. **Address:** Maggie Noach Literary Agency, 7 Peacock Yard, Iliffe St., London, GL SE17 3LH, England. **Online address:** mike.scott.rohan@asgard.zetnet.co.uk

ROHDE, David S. (David Stephenson Rohde). American (born United States), b. 1967. **Genres:** International Relations/Current Affairs, Politics/Government, Adult Non-fiction. **Career:** American Broadcasting Companies Inc., production assistant, 1990-91, 1993; freelance reporter, 1991-92; Philadelphia Inquirer, suburban correspondent, 1993-94; Christian Science Monitor, national reporter and editor, 1994; foreign correspondent, 1994-96; New York Times, reporter, 1997-, investigative journalist; Times, head of South Asia bureau, co-chief, 2002-04. **Publications:** A Safe Area: Srebrenica, Europe's Worst Massacre Since the Second World War, 1997; Endgame: The Betrayal and Fall of Srebrenica, Europe's Worst Massacre Since World War II, 1997; (intro.) After the Fall: Srebrenica Survivors in St. Louis, 2000; (foreword) Evil Doesn't Live Here: Posters from the Bosnian War, 2001; (with K. Mulvihill) Rope and a Prayer: A Kidnapping from Two Sides, 2010. **Address:** The New York Times, 229 W 43rd St., New York, NY 10036, U.S.A.

ROHDE, David Stephenson. See **ROHDE, David S.**

ROHMER, Richard. Canadian (born Canada), b. 1924. **Genres:** Science Fiction/Fantasy, Environmental Sciences/Ecology, Military/Defense/Arms Control, Biography, Adult Non-fiction, Young Adult Fiction. **Career:** Lang,

Michener & Cranston, partner, through 1959; Royal Commission on Book Publishing, chairman, 1970-72, counsel, 1975-77; University of Windsor, chancellor, 1978-89, 1996-97, chancellor emeritus, 1997-; Standard Broadcasting Ltd., director; Northern and Central Gas, chairman; Mediacom Inc., chairman; NewVR/TV of Barrie, on-air commentator; Toronto Sun newspaper, military editor; Ontario Provincial Police, honorary chief superintendent, 2001, honorary deputy commissioner, 2006; Toronto Emergency Medical Service, honorary chief, 2002; Commander of the Order of Military Merit; Rohmer & Fenn, co-founder; ADR Chamber, mediator and arbitrator; Order of Canada, officer; Don Mills Foundation, founder. **Publications:** FICTION: Ultimatum, 1973; Exxoneration, 1974; Exodus U.K., 1975; Separation, 1976; Balls!, 1979; Periscope Red, 1980; Separation Two, 1981; Retaliation, 1982; Triad, 1982; Starmageddon, 1986; Rommel and Patton, 1986; Red Arctic, 1989; John A's Crusade, 1995; Death by Deficit: A 2001 Novel, 1995; Caged Eagle: A Novel, 2002; Borehole, 2003; Ultimatum 2, 2007. NONFICTION: The Green North, 1970; Practice and Procedure Before the Ontario Highway Transport Board Report, 1972; The Arctic Imperative: An Overview of the Energy Crisis, 1973; E.P. Taylor (biography), 1978; Patton's Gap: An Account of the Battle of Normandy, 1944, 1981; How to Write a Best Seller, 1984; Massacre 747: The Story of Korean Air Lines Flight 007, 1984; Mustangs Over Normandy, 1997; The Golden Phoenix: The Biography of Peter Munk, 1997; HMS Raleigh on the Rocks, 2003; Memoires, 2004. OTHERS: Hour of the Fox, 1988; Generally Speaking, 2004. **Address:** RailCore Press Inc., PO Box 34, Collingwood, ON L9Y 3Z4, Canada. **Online address:** generalrohmer@georgian.net

ROHNER, Ronald P. American (born United States), b. 1935. **Genres:** Anthropology/Ethnology, Cultural/Ethnic Topics, Human Relations/Parenting, Psychology, Social Sciences, Sociology, Bibliography. **Career:** University of Connecticut, assistant professor of anthropology, 1964-67, associate professor, 1967-75, professor 1975-96, Ronald and Nancy Rohner Center, director, 1981-, professor emeritus of family studies and anthropology, 1996-; Ronald and Nancy Rohner Center for the Study of Interpersonal Acceptance and Rejection, Department of Human Development and Family Studies, director, 1981-. Writer. **Publications:** The People of Gilford: A Contemporary Kwakiutl Village, 1967; The Ethnography of Franz Boas: Letters and Diaries of Franz Boas Written on the Northwest Coast, 1886-1931, 1969; (with E.C. Bettauer) The Kwakiutl Indians of British Columbia, 1970; They Love Me, They Love Me Not: A Worldwide Study of the Effects of Parental Acceptance and Rejection, 1975; (with C.C. Nielson) Parental Acceptance and Rejection: A Review and Annotated Bibliography of Research and Theory, 2 vols., 1978; (with E.C. Rohner) Worldwide Tests of Parental Acceptance-Rejection Theory, 1980; Handbook for the Study of Parental Acceptance and Rejection, 1980, 4th ed., 2005; The Warmth Dimension: Foundations of Parental Acceptance-Rejection Theory, 1986; (with M. Chaki-Sircar) Women and Children in a Bengali Village, 1988. **Address:** Ronald & Nancy Rohner Center, University of Connecticut, U-2058 Human Development & Family Studies, Storrs, CT 06269-2058, U.S.A. **Online address:** r.rohner@uconn.edu

ROHRBOUGH, Malcolm Justin. American (born United States), b. 1932. **Genres:** History, Law, Politics/Government. **Career:** Princeton University, instructor in history, 1962-64; University of Iowa, Department of History, assistant professor, 1964-68, associate professor, 1968-71, professor of history, 1971-2008, professor emeritus, 2008-. Writer. **Publications:** The Land Office Business: The Settlement and Administration of American Public Lands, 1789-1837, 1968; The Trans-Appalachian Frontier: People, Societies, and Institutions, 1775-1850, 1978, 3rd ed., 2008; Aspen: The History of a Silver-Mining Town, 1879-1893, 1986; Days of Gold: The California Gold Rush and the American Nation, 1997. **Address:** Department of History, University of Iowa, 280 Schaeffer Hall, Iowa City, IA 52242-1409, U.S.A. **Online address:** malcolm-rohrbough@uiowa.edu

ROHRER, Scott. See **ROHRER, S. Scott.**

ROHRER, S. Scott. (Scott Rohrer). American (born United States), b. 1957. **Genres:** Theology/Religion, Social Sciences. **Career:** National Journal, copy desk chief, 2006-. Writer, journalist and historian. **Publications:** Hope's Promise: Religion and Acculturation in the Southern Backcountry, 2005; Wandering Souls: Protestant Migrations in America, 1630-1865, 2010. **Address:** National Journal, 600 New Hampshire Ave. NW, Washington, DC 20037, U.S.A. **Online address:** srohrer@nationaljournal.com

ROIPHE, Anne Richardson. (Anne Richardson). American (born United

States), b. 1935. **Genres:** Novels, Psychology, Young Adult Non-fiction. **Career:** New York Observer, columnist, 1997-2002. Writer. **Publications:** (As Anne Richardson) Digging Out, 1967; Up the Sandbox!, 1970; Long Division, 1972; Torch Song, 1977; Generation without Memory: A Jewish Journey in Christian America, 1981; (with H. Roiphe) Your Child's Mind: The Complete Book of Infant and Child Mental Health Care, 1985; Loving Kindness, 1987; A Season for Healing: Reflections on the Holocaust, 1988; The Pursuit of Happiness, 1991; If You Knew Me, 1993; Fruitful: A Real Mother in the Modern World, 1996; 1185 Park Avenue: A Memoir, 1999; For Rabbit, with Love and Squalor: An American Read, 2000; Married: A Fine Predicament, 2002; Secrets of the City, 2003; Water From The Well: Sarah, Rebekah, Rachel, and Leah, 2006; An Imperfect Lens, 2006; Epilogue: A Memoir, 2008; Art and Madness: A Memoir of Love Without Reason, 2011. **Address:** 107 W 86th St., New York, NY 10024, U.S.A.

ROIPHE, Katie. American (born United States), b. 1968. **Genres:** Women's Studies And Issues, Sex, Novels, Young Adult Non-fiction. **Career:** New York University, Arthur L. Carter Journalism Institute, Department of Journalism, assistant professor and assistant director of the cultural criticism and reporting program, professor of journalism, 2007-. Writer. **Publications:** NOVELS: Last Night in Paradise: Sex and Morals at the Century's End, 1997; Still She Haunts Me, 2001. NON-FICTION: The Morning After: Sex, Fear, and Feminism on Campus, 1993; Uncommon Arrangements: Seven Portraits of Married Life in London Literary Circles, 1910-1939, 2007; In Praise of Messy Lives, 2012. Contributor to periodicals. **Address:** Arthur L. Carter Journalism Institute, New York University, 20 Cooper Sq., 6th Fl., New York, NY 10003-7112, U.S.A. **Online address:** katie.roiphe@nyu.edu

ROLDE, Neil. American (born United States), b. 1931. **Genres:** Area Studies, History, Money/Finance, Travel/Exploration, Biography, Novels, Romance/Historical, Young Adult Fiction, Young Adult Fiction. **Career:** State of Maine, assistant, 1967-75; Tilbury House, owner. Writer. **Publications:** York Is Living History, 1976; Sir William Pepperrell of Colonial New England, 1982; Rio Grande do Norte: The Story of Maine's Partner State in Brazil: What It's Like, What Its Past has Been, and What are Its Ties to Maine, 1984; So You Think You Know Maine, 1984; Maine: A Narrative History, 1990; Your Money or Your Health: America's Cruel, Bureaucratic, and Horrendously Expensive Health Care System: How it Got that Way and What to Do About It, 1992; An Illustrated History of Maine, 1995; The Baxters of Maine: Downeast Visionaries, 1997; The Interrupted Forest: A History of Maine's Wildlands, 2001; Unsettled Past, Unsettled Future: The Story of Maine Indians, 2004; Continental Liar from the State of Maine: James G. Blaine, 2006; Maine: Downeast and Different: An Illustrated History, 2006; Irenic Theology: A Study of Some Antitheses in Religious Thought, 2008; Maine In the World: Stories of Some of Those from Here Who Went Away, 2009; O. Murray Carr: A Novel, 2010. **Address:** 3 Old Seabury Rd., Sewalls Hl, PO Box 304, York, ME 03909, U.S.A.

ROLEY, Brian Ascalon. American (born United States), b. 1966?. **Genres:** Novels, Novellas/Short Stories. **Career:** Cornell University, lecturer; Epoch Magazine, associate editor; Miami University, Department of English, assistant professor, associate professor of English and creative writing, Miami University Press, faculty. Writer. **Publications:** American Son: A Novel, 2001. Contributor of articles to books and periodicals. **Address:** Department of English, Miami University, 328 Bachelor Hall, 501 E High St., Oxford, OH 45056-1846, U.S.A. **Online address:** brianroley@gmail.com

ROLLE, Andrew. (Andrew Frank Rolle). American (born United States), b. 1922. **Genres:** History, Biography. **Career:** U.S. Department of State, vice-consult, 1945-48; Pacific Historical Review, editorial associate, 1951-52; Occidental College, instructor, 1952-53, assistant professor, 1953-57, associate professor, 1957-62, professor of history, 1962-65, Robert Glass Cleland professor of American history, 1965-88, Robert Glass Cleland professor emeritus of American history, 1988-; American Studies Association, president, 1958; consultant, 1966-68; Southern California Psychoanalytic Institute, clinical associate, 1972-76. Writer. **Publications:** Riviera Path, 1946; An American in California: The Biography of William Heath Davis, 1822-1909, 1956; The Road to Virginia City, 1960, 2nd ed., 1990; (with A. Nevins and I. Stone) Lincoln: A Contemporary Portrait, 1962; Occidental College: The First Seventy-Five Years, 1887-1962, 1962; California: A History, 1963, (with A. Verge) 7th ed., 2008; The Lost Cause: Confederate Exiles in Mexico, 1965, 2nd ed., 1993; California: A Students' Guide to Localized History, 1965; (with J.S. Gaines) The Golden State: A History of California, 1965, 4th ed. as The Gold-

en State: California History and Government, 2000; Los Angeles: A Students' Guide to Localized History, 1965; The Immigrant Upraised: Italian Adventurers and Colonists in an Expanding America, 1968; The American Italians: Their History and Culture, 1972; (co-author) Essays and Assays: California History Reconsidered, 1973; The Italian Americans: Troubled Roots, 1980; Los Angeles: From Pueblo to City of the Future, 1982, 2nd ed., 1995; Occidental College: A Centennial History, 1887-1987, 1986; John Charles Frémont: Character as Destiny, 1991; Henry Mayo Newhall and His Times, A California Legacy, 1991; Westward the Immigrants: Italian Adventurers and Colonists in an Expanding America, 1999. EDITOR: Helen Hunt Jackson's A Century of Dishonor: The Early Crusade for Indian Reform, 1965; Alfred Robinson's Life in California, 1970. **Address:** Department of History, Occidental College, Swan Hall, 1600 Campus Rd., Ste. M-13, Los Angeles, CA 90041-3314, U.S.A.

ROLLE, Andrew Frank. See **ROLLE, Andrew.**

ROLLIN, Roger B. American (born United States), b. 1930. **Genres:** Communications/Media, Literary Criticism And History, Essays, Politics/Government. **Career:** Franklin and Marshall College, instructor, 1959-60, assistant professor, 1960-65, faculty research grant, 1965; associate professor, 1965-72, professor of English, 1972-75; Clemson University, William James Lemon professor of literature, 1975-95, now William James Lemon professor emeritus of literature. Writer. **Publications:** Robert Herrick, 1966, rev. ed., 1992. EDITOR: Hero/Anti-Hero, 1973; (with J.M. Patrick) Trust to Good Verses: Herrick Tercentenary Essays, 1978; The Americanization of the Global Village: Essays in Comparative Popular Culture, 1989. Contributor to books. **Address:** Department of English, Clemson University, Clemson, SC 29634, U.S.A. **Online address:** nerrick@innovz.net

ROLLINS, Alden M(ilton). American (born United States), b. 1946. **Genres:** Genealogy/Heraldry, History, Bibliography, Reference. **Career:** University of Alaska, instructor, 1973-77, assistant professor, 1977-81, associate professor, 1981-91, professor, 1991-99, professor emeritus of library science, 1999-, librarian. Writer. **Publications:** (Comp.) Census Alaska, 1978; The Anchorage Documents File, 1978; (ed. with T.P. Chang) The Anchorage Times Obituaries Index, 1979; The Fall of Rome: A Reference Guide, 1983; Rome in the Fourth Century A.D.: An Annotated Bibliography with Historical Overview, 1991; Vermont Warnings Out, vol. I, 1995, vol. II, 1997; Rollins Family in the New Hampshire Provincial Deeds, 1655-1771, 1997; (comp.) Vermont Religious Certificates, 2003. **Address:** Consortium Library, University of Alaska Anchorage, 3211 Providence Dr., Anchorage, AK 99508, U.S.A. **Online address:** afamr@uaa.alaska.edu

ROLLINS, David A. Australian (born Australia), b. 1958. **Genres:** Novels. **Career:** Writer. **Publications:** TOM WILKES SERIES: Rogue Element, 2002; Sword of Allah, 2004. VIN COOPER SERIES: A Knife Edge, 2006; The Death Trust, 2007; Hard Rain, 2008; Ghost Watch, 2010. STAND ALONE BOOK: The Zero Option, 2009. **Address:** c/o Ian Drury, Sheil Land, 52 Doughty St., London, GL WC1N 2LS, United Kingdom. **Online address:** drollins1@mac.com

ROLLINS, Wayne Gilbert. American (born United States), b. 1929. **Genres:** Theology/Religion. **Career:** United Church of Christ, ordained minister; Princeton University, instructor in religion, 1958-59; Wellesley College, assistant professor of biblical history, 1959-66; Hartford Seminary Foundation, associate professor of biblical studies, 1966-74; Colgate-Rochester Divinity School, visiting professor, 1968; Yale University, visiting lecturer, 1968-69; Cambridge University, researcher, 1970; Mount Holyoke College, visiting lecturer, 1972; Assumption College, professor of biblical studies, now professor emeritus of biblical studies, Ecumenical Institute, director, 1974-99, coordinator of graduate program in religious studies, 1974-; College of the Holy Cross, visiting lecturer, 1976-77; Society of Biblical Literature, Psychology and Biblical Studies Section, founder and chairman, 1990-2000; Hartford Seminary, adjunct professor of scripture, 1999-. Writer. **Publications:** The Gospels: Portraits of Christ, 1963; Jung and the Bible, 1983; Soul and Psyche: The Bible in Psychological Perspective, 1999; (ed. with J.H. Ellens) Psychology and the Bible: A New Way to Read the Scriptures, 4 vols., 2004; (ed. with D.A. Kille) Psychological Insight into the Bible: Texts and Readings, 2007. Contributor of articles to journals. **Address:** Hartford Seminary, 77 Sherman St., Hartford, CT 06105-6203, U.S.A. **Online address:** wrollins@worldnet.att.net

ROLSTON, Steve. Canadian (born Canada), b. 1978?. **Genres:** Graphic Novels. **Career:** A.k.a. Cartoon, storyboard artist; Barking Bullfrog Cartoon Co., storyboard artist; Vancouver Institute of Media Arts, instructor in comic-book art. Writer, illustrator, animator and comic artist. **Publications:** SELF-ILLUSTRATED: One Bad Day (graphic novel), 2003. **Address:** PO Box 93570, Vancouver, BC V6E 4L7, Canada. **Online address:** steve@steverolston.com

ROMACK, Janice Reed. (Janice LeNoir). American (born United States), b. 1941. **Genres:** Romance/Historical, Children's Fiction. **Career:** John F. Kennedy Space Center, resource coordinator, 1983-. Writer. **Publications:** The Glass Jar, 1994; The Fury Friend, forthcoming; A New Family, forthcoming. **Address:** Chameleon Enterprise, PO Box 3902, Cocoa, FL 32924, U.S.A. **Online address:** JLenoir268@aol.com

ROMAN, Peter. American (born United States), b. 1941. **Genres:** Politics/Government, History. **Career:** Northern Illinois University, professor of political science, 1967-69; Guardian, journalist, 1969-71; City University of New York, Hostos Community College, professor of behavioral and social sciences, 1971-, coordinator of social sciences, Graduate School and Undergraduate Center, professor of political science, 2000-; Institute for Theoretical History, editorial associate, 1979-82; Bildner Center for Western Hemisphere Studies, fellow, Bildner Center Cuba Program, faculty advisor. **Publications:** People's Power: Cuba's Experience with Representative Government, 1999, rev. ed., 2003; Representative Government in Socialist Cuba, forthcoming. Contributor of articles and reviews to periodicals. **Address:** Department of Behavioral & Social Sciences, Hostos Community College, City University of New York, B-326, 500 Grand Concourse, Bronx, NY 10451, U.S.A. **Online address:** proman@hostos.cuny.edu

ROMANELLI, Giandomenico. Italian (born Italy), b. 1945. **Genres:** Art/Art History, History. **Career:** University Institute of Architecture, professor of history of architecture, 1978-88; Civic Museums of Venice, director, 1979-; Center for Arts and Culture City of Venice, director, 2000-. Writer. **Publications:** Ottant'anni Di Architettuta e Allestimenti Alla Biennale Di Venezia, 1976; Venezia Ottocento: Materiali Per Una Storia Architettonica eUrbanistica Della Citta Nel Secolo XIX, 1977; Venezia Vienna: Il Mito Della Cultura Veneziana Nell'Europa Asburgica, 1983; Museo Correr, 1984; (with G. Bellavitis) Venezia, 1985; (with F. Pedrocco) Ca' Rezzonico, 1986; (with G. Pavanello) Palazzo Grassi: Storia, architettura, Decorazioni Dell'ultimo Palazzo Veneziano, 1986; Venezia Ottocento: l'architettura, l'urbanistica, 1988; Tra Gotico e Neogotico: Palazzo Cavalli Franchetti a San Vidal, 2nd ed., 1990; Ca' Pesaro: La Galleria D'arte Moderna, Introduzione Alle Raccolte, 1991; (with A. Mariuz and G. Pavanello) Pietro Longhi, 1993; Ca' Corner della Ca' Grana: Architettura e Committenza Nella Venezia Del Cinquecento, 1993; Palazzo Ziani: Storia, Architettura, Decorazioni, 1994; Tintoretto, le Scuola grande di San Rocco, 1994; Palladio, 1995; Venezia Quarantotto: Episodi, Luoghi E Protagonisti Di Una Rivoluzione 1848-49, 1998; Palazzo Ducale: Storia e restauri, 2004; Doge's Palace in Venice, 2005; Dogana Da Mar, 2010. EDITOR: (with G. Pavanello) Canova, 1992. **Address:** c/o Electa, Via Trentacoste 7, Milan, 20134, Italy.

ROMANO, Christy Carlson. American (born United States), b. 1984. **Genres:** Children's Fiction. **Career:** Writer and actor. **Publications:** Grace's Turn, 2006. **Address:** Los Angeles, CA , U.S.A.

ROMANO, Dennis. American (born United States), b. 1951?. **Genres:** History. **Career:** Carthage College, visiting assistant professor of history, 1982-83; University of Mississippi, assistant professor of history, 1984-87; National Endowment for the Humanities, Division of Research Programs, program officer, 1986-87; Syracuse University, assistant professor of history, 1987-91, associate professor of history, 1991-97, Dr. Walter Montgomery and Marian Gruber professor of history (Maxwell School), 2009-; Venice International University, Summer Humanities Institute, lecturer, 2001- 02. Writer. **Publications:** Patricians and Popolani: The Social Foundations of the Venetian Renaissance State, 1987; Housecraft and Statecraft: Domestic Service in Renaissance Venice, 1400-1600, 1996; (ed. and intro. with J. Martin) Venice Reconsidered: The History and Civilization of an Italian City-State, 1297-1797, 2000; The Likeness of Venice: A Life of Doge Francesco Foscari, 1373-1457, 2007. Contributor to books and periodicals. **Address:** Maxwell School of Syracuse University, 200 Eggers Hall, Syracuse, NY 13244-1020, U.S.A. **Online address:** dromano@maxwell.syr.edu

ROMANO, Louis. (Louis G. Romano). American (born United States), b. 1921. **Genres:** Children's Fiction, Children's Non-fiction, Education, Young Adult Non-fiction, Politics/Government, Theology/Religion, Social Sciences. **Career:** Shorewood Public Schools, teacher, 1944-54, assistant superintendent and director of instruction, 1954-64; Wilmette Public Schools, superintendent, 1964-66; Michigan State University, College of Education, Department of Educational Administration, associate professor of education, 1966-71, professor of administration and higher education, 1971-, now professor emeritus; Michigan Association of Middle School Educators, executive director, 1975-; Michigan Middle School Journal, editor. **Publications:** (Co-author) A Guide to Successful Parent-Teacher Conferences, 1964; Challenge to the Fives, 1965; (with A.L. Hamachek) Focus on Parent-Teacher Conferences, 1984; (with W. Powell) Evaluative Criteria for a Middle School, 1988. WITH N.P. GEORGIADY: Exploring Wisconsin, 1957, rev. ed., 1970; Gertie the Duck, 1959; Anden Agda, 1959; Anden Gertrud, 1959; Trudi La Cane, 1960; Tulita La Patita, 1960; This Is a Department Store, 1962; Our Country's Flag, 1963; Our National Anthem, 1963; Quack, die Ente, 1965; Wisconsin Indians, 1966; Wisconsin Women, 1966; Wisconsin Men, 1966; Wisconsin Historical Sights, 1966; Events in the Life of Thomas Jefferson, 1966; Know about Money, 1966; Know about Banks, 1966; The Ironclads, 1966; The Boston Tea Party, 1966; Illinois Indians, 1967; Illinois Women, 1967; Illinois Men, 1967; Illinois Historical Sights, 1967; Michigan Indians, 1967; Michigan Women, 1967; Michigan Men, 1967; Michigan Historical Sights, 1967; Indiana Indians, 1968; Indiana Women, Indiana Men, 1968; Indiana Historical Sights, 1968; The History of the Nation's Capitol, 1968; Monuments and Memorials in Our Nation's Capitol, 1968; Famous People in the Early History of Our Capitol, 1968; Important Buildings in Our Nation's Capitol, 1968; (ed. with J.G. Heald) Selected Readings on General Supervision, 1970; Introduction to the Defenders, 1973; Pope, 1973; Tecumseh, 1973; King Philip, 1973; (ed. with J.E. Heald) The Middle School, 1973; (co-ed.) The Management of Educational Personnel: Readings on the Administration of Human Resources, 1973, rev. ed., 1976; Know about Airports, 1975; Know about Shopping Centers, 1975; Know about Computers, 1975; Know about Skyscrapers, 1975; Know about Assembly Lines, 1975; Know about Highways, 1975; Know about Stamp Collecting, 1975; (ed. with J.E. Heald) A Guide to an Effective Middle School, 1984; Focus on Censorship in the Middle School, 1985; Focus on Successful Characteristics of a Middle School, 1992; Focus on Study Habits in School, 1994; Focus on Study Habits at Home for Middle School Students, 1994; (ed. with J.E. Heald) Building an Effective Middle School, 1994. **Address:** Department of Educational Administration, College of Education, Michigan State University, 418 Erickson Hall, East Lansing, MI 48824-1034, U.S.A.

ROMANO, Louis G. See **ROMANO, Louis.**

ROMANO, Ray. American (born United States), b. 1957. **Genres:** Mystery/Crime/Suspense, Young Adult Fiction, Children's Fiction, Humor/Satire, Photography. **Career:** Actor, comedian and writer. **Publications:** Everything and a Kite: A Book of Comic Observations, 1998; (with P. Rosenthal) Everybody Loves Raymond: Our Family Album, 2004; (with R. Romano and R. Romano) Raymie, Dickie and the Bean: Why I Love and Hate My Brothers, 2005. **Address:** c/o Everybody Loves Raymond, Talk Productions, Warner Bros Studios, Warner Blvd., Burbank, CA 91522, U.S.A. **Online address:** ray@rayromano.com

ROMANO, Tony. American/Italian (born Italy), b. 1957. **Genres:** Novels, Young Adult Fiction. **Career:** William Fremd High School, teacher of English and psychology. Writer. **Publications:** (With F.B. McMahon and J.W. McMahon) Psychology and You, 1990, 2nd ed., 1995; When the World Was Young (novel), 2007; (with G. Anderson) Expository Composition: Discovering Your Voice, 2008; If You Eat, You Never Die: Chicago Tales, 2009. Contributor to periodicals. **Address:** Marly Rusoff & Associates Inc., PO Box 524, Bronxville, NY 10708, U.S.A. **Online address:** tonyromano2@comcast.net

ROMANO-LAX, Andromeda. American (born United States), b. 1970. **Genres:** Natural History, Novels, Travel/Exploration, Young Adult Non-fiction. **Career:** Freelance journalist; travel writer. **Publications:** Sea Kayaking in Baja, 1993; Walking Southeast Alaska: Scenic Walks and Easy Hikes for Inside Passage Travelers, 1997; How to Rent a Public Cabin in Southcentral Alaska: Access and Adventures for Hikers, Kayakers, Anglers, and More, 1999; Adventure Kayaking: Baja, 2001; Alaska's Kenai Peninsula: A

Traveler's Guide, 2001; Searching for Steinbeck's Sea of Cortez: A Makeshift Expedition along Baja's Desert Coast (memoir), 2002; (ed. with B. Sherwonit and E. Bielawski) Alaska: True Stories, 2003; Kenai Fjords National Park, 2004; Chugach National Forest: Legacy of Land, Sea, and Sky, 2007; The Spanish Bow (novel), 2007; Denali National Park and Preserve, 2009; Tongass National Forest: A Temperate Rainforest in Transition, 2011. Contributor to periodicals. **Address:** c/o Michelle Blankenship, Harcourt Inc., 15 E 26th St., 15th Fl., New York, NY 10010, U.S.A. **Online address:** andromeda@romanolax.com

ROMBS, Ronnie J. American (born United States), b. 1972. **Genres:** Young Adult Fiction. **Career:** St. Joseph Seminary College, assistant professor of theology; Washington Theological Union, assistant professor; University of Dallas, associate professor of theology. Writer. **Publications:** (Contrib.) Exodus, Leviticus, Numbers, Deuteronomy, 2001; Saint Augustine and the Fall of the Soul: Beyond O'Connell and His Critics, 2006; (ed. with A.Y. Hwang) Tradition and the Rule of Faith in the Early Church: Essays in Honor of Joseph T. Lienhard, S.J., 2011. Contributor of articles to journals. **Address:** Washington Theological Union, 6896 Laurel St. NW, Washington, DC 20012, U.S.A. **Online address:** rrombs@udallas.edu

ROME, Elaine. *See* BARBIERI, Elaine.

ROME, Margaret. British (born England) **Genres:** Romance/Historical, Novels, Young Adult Fiction. **Career:** Writer. **Publications:** The Lottery for Matthew Devlin, 1968; The Marriage of Caroline Lindsay, 1968; A Chance to Win, 1969; Flower of the Marsh, 1969; Man of Fire, 1970; Bird of Paradise, 1970; Chateau of Flowers, 1971; The Girl at Eagles' Mount, 1971; The Girl At Eagles' Point, 1971; Bride of the Rif, 1972; Island of Pearls, 1973; The Bartered Bride, 1973; Palace of the Hawk, 1974; Valley of Paradise, 1975, 2nd ed., 1990; Cove of Promises, 1975; The Girl at Dane's Dyke, 1975; Adam's Rib, 1976; Bride of Zarco, 1976; Lion of Venice, 1977, 2nd ed., 1983; The Thistle and the Rose, 1977; Son of Adam, 1978; Castle of the Fountains, 1979; Champagne Spring, 1979; Isle of Calypso, 1979; Maid of the Border, 1979; Marriage by Capture, 1980; Miss High and Mighty, 1980; The Wild Man, 1980; Second-Best Bride, 1981; King of Kielder, 1981; Castle in Spain, 1981, 2nd ed., 1986; King Kielder, 1981; Rapture of the Deep, 1982; Valley of Gentians, 1982, 2nd ed., 1987; Bay of Angels, 1983, 2nd ed., 1989; Castle of the Lion, 1983; Lord of the Land, 1983, 2nd ed., 1990; Bride by Contract, 1984; Pagan Gold, 1985. **Address:** Harlequin Mills & Boon Ltd., Eton House, 18-24 Paradise Rd., Richmond, SR TW9 1SR, England.

ROMER, (Louis) John. American/Italian/British (born England), b. 1941. **Genres:** Archaeology/Antiquities, History, Biography. **Career:** University of Chicago, faculty, 1966-68; lecturer in the history of art, 1968-72; British Institute in Teheran, Epigraphic artist, 1972; German Archaeological Institute in Cairo, Epigraphic artist, 1972-73; Oriental Institute Epigraphic Survey, artist, 1973-77; Brooklyn Museum, archaeologist, field director, 1977-79; Theban Foundation, founder, president, 1979-. Writer. **Publications:** Valley of the Kings, 1981; Romer's Egypt, 1982 in US as People of the Nile, 1982; Ancient Lives: Story of the Pharaoh's Tombmakers, 1984; Ancient Lives: Daily Life in Egypt of the Pharaohs, 1984; Testament: Bible and History, 1988; (with E. Romer) The Rape of Tutankham, 1993; Valley of the Kings: Exploring the Tombs of the Pharaohs, 1994; (with E. Romer) The Seven Wonders of the World: A History of the Modern Imagination, 1995; Great Excavations: John Romer's History of Archaeology, 2000; History of Archaeology, 2001; The Great Pyramid: Ancient Egypt Revisited, 2007. **Address:** Theban Foundation, 2134 Allston Way, Berkeley, CA 94704, U.S.A.

ROMERIL, John. Australian (born Australia), b. 1945. **Genres:** Plays/Screenplays, Literary Criticism And History, History. **Career:** Australian Performing Group, founding member, 1970-81; Western Australian Institute of Technology, writer-in-residence, 1977; University of Newcastle, writer-in-residence, 1978; Flinders University, writer-in-residence, 1984; Matthew J. Cody, artist-in-residence, 1985; National University of Singapore, writer-in-residence, 1986-87; Australian National Playwrights Centre, chairman, 1998; Victorian Arts Centre, artist-in-residence. **Publications:** Two Plays, 1971; Rearguard Action, 1971; The Magnetic Martian, 1971; Hackett Gets Ahead, 1972; He Can Swagger Sitting Down, 1972; I Don't Know Who to Feel Sorry For, 1973; The Floating World: With Notes on the Yellow Peril and Comment from Allan Ashbolt, Katharine Brisbane and the Official History of Australia in the Second World War, 1975, rev. ed., 1982; The Accidental Poke, 1977; Bastardy, 1982; 6 of the Best, 1984; (with T. Robertson) Waltzing Matilda: A

National Pantomime with Tomato Sauce, 1984; The Kelly Dance, 1986; (co-author) Legends, 1986; Koori Radio, 1987; Top End, 1988; Lost Weekend, 1989; Definitely Not the Last, 1989; Love Suicides, 1997; Miss Tanaka, 2001; Damage: A Collection of Plays, 2010. **Address:** Bryson Agency Australia Pty Ltd., Flinders Ln., PO Box 226, Melbourne, VI 8009, Australia.

ROMERO, George A. American (born United States), b. 1940. **Genres:** Novels, Plays/Screenplays, Horror. **Career:** Latent Image (a production company), founder; Laurel Productions (film production company), founder, 1973-; film director. Writer. **Publications:** (With S. Sparrow) Martin: A Novel, 1977; (with S. Sparrow) Dawn of the Dead, 1978. **Address:** Gersh Agency, 232 N Cannon Dr., Ste. 202, Beverly Hills, CA 90210, U.S.A.

ROMM, Robin. American (born United States), b. 1975. **Genres:** Young Adult Fiction, Novellas/Short Stories. **Career:** College of Santa Fe, assistant professor of creative writing and literature; New Mexico State University, MFA Program, faculty. Writer. **Publications:** The Mother Garden (short stories), 2007; Mercy Papers: A Memoir of Three Weeks, 2009. Contributor to periodicals. **Address:** c/o Aisha Cloud, Scribner Publicity, 1230 Ave. of the Americas, New York, NY 10020, U.S.A. **Online address:** robinromm@gmail.com

RONAN, Frank. Irish (born Ireland), b. 1963. **Genres:** Novels, Novellas/Short Stories, Young Adult Fiction, Human Relations/Parenting. **Career:** IBM, staff; Kodak, staff; Enviorovantage, business manager, 2004-09. Writer. **Publications:** The Men Who Loved Evelyn Cotton, 1989; A Picnic in Eden, 1992; The Better Angel, 1992; Dixie Chicken, 1994; (ed.) In My Garden, 1994; Lovely, 1996; Handsome Men Are Slightly Sunburnt, 1996; Home, 2002. Contributor to periodicals. **Address:** c/o Deborah Rogers, Rogers, Coleridge & White Ltd., 20 Powis Mews, London, GL W11 1JN, England. **Online address:** a@frankronan.com

RONELL, Avital. American/Czech (born Czech Republic), b. 1956. **Genres:** Language/Linguistics, Literary Criticism And History, Writing/Journalism, Young Adult Fiction. **Career:** University of California, associate professor, professor of comparative literature, 1986-95; New York University, professor of German, English and comparative literature, 1995-, Department of Germanic Languages and Literature, chair, 1995-2005; European Graduate School, professor of philosophy. Writer. **Publications:** Dictations: On Haunted Writing, 1986; The Telephone Book: Technology, Schizophrenia, Electric Speech, 1989; Crack Wars: Literature, Addiction, Mania, 1992; Finitude's Score: Essays for the End of the Millennium, 1994; (contrib.) 13 Alumni Artists, 2000; Stupidity, 2002; Test Drive, 2005; (ed. with A. Scholder and C. Harryman) Lust for Life: On The Writings of Kathy Acker, 2006; American Philo, 2006; Ṭipshut, 2006; (ed. with D. Davis) UberReader, 2007; (contrib.) Field is Lethal, 2011. Contributor of articles to periodicals. **Address:** Department of Germanic Languages and Literature, New York University, Rm. 319, 19 University Pl., 736 Broadway, New York, NY 10003-4556, U.S.A. **Online address:** avital.ronell@nyu.edu

RONK, Martha C(lare). American (born United States), b. 1940. **Genres:** Novellas/Short Stories, Poetry. **Career:** North Carolina College, lecturer; Tufts University, assistant professor, 1967-71; Immaculate Heart College, coordinator of curriculum, 1972-80; University of Southern California, part-time teacher, 1978-79; Occidental College, professor of English and creative writing, 1980-, Irma and Jay Price Professor of English; The New Review, editor; Littoral Books, editor; Colorado University, faculty; Otis College of Art and Design, faculty; Naropa University Summer Writing Program, faculty. **Publications:** POETRY: Desire in LA, 1990; Desert Geometries, 1992; State of Mind, 1995; Eyetrouble, 1998; Recent Terrains: Terraforming the American West (poetry), 2000; Displeasures of the Table (nonfiction), 2000; (ed. with P. Vangelisti) Place as Purpose: Poetry from the Western States, vol. I, 2002; Why/Why Not, 2003; In a Landscape of Having to Repeat, 2004; Vertigo, (poetry), 2007; Glass Grapes: Stories, 2008. Works appear in anthologies. Contributor of articles to periodicals. **Address:** Department of English, Occidental College, 1600 Campus Rd., Swan N 204, Los Angeles, CA 90041, U.S.A. **Online address:** ronk@oxy.edu

ROODENBURG, Herman. Dutch (born Netherlands), b. 1951?. **Genres:** Cultural/Ethnic Topics, History, Humor/Satire. **Career:** University of Amsterdam, Sociological Institute, educator, 1981-82; Criminological Institute, VU University Amsterdam, educator, 1983-87; Meertens Institute of the Royal Dutch Academy of Sciences, researcher, 1987-2000, department head,

2004-, researcher in ethnology; Katholieke Universiteit Leuven, Lueven, professor, 2002-. Writer. **Publications:** WORKS IN ENGLISH: (ed. with J. Bremmer) A Cultural History of Gesture, 1992; (ed. with J. Bremmer) A Cultural History of Humour: From Antiquity to the Present Day, 1997; (ed. with R.R. Bendix) Managing Ethnicity: Perspectives from Folklore Studies, History and Anthropology, 2000; (with P.C. Spierenburg) Social Control in Europe, 2 vols., 2004; The Eloquence of the Body: Perspectives on Gesture in the Dutch Republic, 2004; Cultural Exchange in Early Modern Europe, vol. IV: Forging European Identities, 1400-1700, 2007; (ed. with P.J. Margry) Reframing Dutch Culture: Between Otherness and Authenticity, 2007; (ed. with A. Lehmann) Body and Embodiment in Netherlandish Art, 2008. WORKS IN DUTCH: Soete minne en helsche boosheit: seksuele voorstellingen in Nederland, 1300-1850, 1988; Onder Censuur: de kerkelijke tucht in de gereformeerde gemeente van Amsterdam, 1578-1700, 1990; Misdaad, zoen en straf: aspekten van de middeleeuwse strafrechtsgeschiedenis in de Nederlanden, 1991; Volkscultuur: een inleiding in de Nederlandse etnologie, 2000; (with L.P. Grijp) Blues en balladen: Alan Lomax en Ate Doornbosch, twee muzikale veldwerkers, 2005. Contributor to journals and periodicals. **Address:** Meertens Institute, PO Box 94264, Amsterdam, 1090 GG, Netherlands. **Online address:** herman.roodenburg@meertens.knaw.nl

ROODMAN, David Malin. American (born United States), b. 1968. **Genres:** Business/Trade/Industry. **Career:** Microsoft Corp., summer software engineer, 1988; Worldwatch Institute, staff researcher, 1993-94, research associate, 1995-97, senior researcher, 1997; Center for Global Development, research fellow, senior fellow, Commitment to Development Index Project, architect and manager, 2002-. Writer. **Publications:** (Contrib.) Arabic Translations of Works by U.S. Authors, 1992; (N.K. Lenssen) Building Revolution: How Ecology and Health Concerns are Transforming Construction, 1995; Paying the Piper: Subsidies, Politics, and the Environment, 1996; Getting the Signals Right: Tax Reform to Protect the Environment and the Economy, 1997; The Natural Wealth of Nations: Harnessing the Market for the Environment, 1998; Still Waiting for the Jubilee: Pragmatic Solutions for the Third World Debt Crisis, 2001. Contributor to periodicals and journals. **Address:** Center for Global Development, 1800 Massachusetts Ave. NW, 3rd Fl., Washington, DC 20036-1806, U.S.A. **Online address:** droodman@cgdev.org

ROOK, Tony. British (born England), b. 1932. **Genres:** Mystery/Crime/Suspense, Archaeology/Antiquities, History. **Career:** George Wimpey and Company Ltd., Department of Building and Civil Engineering Research and Development, deputy head, 1957-60; Chalk Line and Allied Industries Research Association, Department of Building and Civil Engineering Research and Development, deputy head, 1960-63; Sherrardswood School, senior science teacher, 1963-73; Hertfordshire Archaeological Review, editor; Lockleys Archaeological Trust, education officer. Freelance archaeologist and author. **Publications:** Roman Villa, 1973; Roman Legionary, 1974; Strange Mansion (novel), 1974; Pompeiian House, 1978; Roman Bath House, 1978; The Labrador Trust, 1983; A History of Hertfordshire, 1984; Of Local Interest, 1986; Welwyn Roman Baths, 1988; (with V. Scott) County Maps and Histories-Hertfordshire, 1989; Roman Baths in Britain, 1992; Before the Railway Came, 1994. Contributor to magazines. **Address:** Old Rectory, 23 Mill Ln., Welwyn, HF AL6 9EU, England. **Online address:** tony.rook@virgin.net

ROOKE, L. See ROOKE, Leon.

ROOKE, Leon. (L. Rooke). Canadian/American (born United States), b. 1934. **Genres:** Novels, Novellas/Short Stories, Plays/Screenplays, Literary Criticism And History. **Career:** University of North Carolina, writer-in-residence, 1965-66; University of Victoria, lecturer in creative writing, 1971-72, visiting professor, 1980-81; Southwest Minnesota State College, writer-in-residence, 1975-76; University of Toronto, writer-in-residence, 1984-85; University of Western Ontario, writer-in-residence, 1990-91. **Publications:** SHORT STORIES: Last One Home Sleeps in the Yellow Bed, 1968; Vault, 1973; The Love Parlour: Stories, 1977; The Broad Back of the Angel, 1977; Cry Evil, 1980; Death Suite, 1981; The Birth Control King of Upper Volta, 1982; Sing Me No More Love Songs, I'll Say You No Prayers, 1984; A Bolt of White Cloth, 1984; How I Saved the Province, 1989; The Happiness of Others, 1991; Who Do You Love?, 1992; Oh!: Twenty Seven Stories, 1997; Painting the Dog: The Best Stories of Leon Rooke, 2001; Beautiful Wife: The Best Stories of Leon Rooke, 2005; Hitting the Charts: Selected Stories, 2006; Pope and Her Lady, 2010. NOVELS: Fat Woman, 1981; The Magician in Love, 1981; Shakespeare's Dog: A Novel, 1983; A Good Baby, 1990; Who Goes There, 1998; The Fall of Gravity: A Novel, 2000; Hot Poppies, 2005, Last

Shot: A Novella and Eleven Stories, 2009. PLAYS: Krokodile, 1973; Sword Play, 1974; The Good Baby, 1987; Evening Meeting of the Club of Suicide, 1991. EDITOR WITH JOHN METCALF: 81: Best Canadian Stories, 1981; 82: Best Canadian Stories, 1982; The New Press Anthology: Best Canadian Short Fiction, 1984; The Macmillan Anthology One, 1988; The Macmillan Anthology Two, 1989. Contributor to periodicals. **Address:** c/o Liz Darhansoff, Darhansoff & Verrill Literary Agents, Rm. 802, 236 W 26th St., New York, NY 10001-6736, U.S.A.

ROOKS, Judith P. (Judith Pence Rooks). American (born United States), b. 1941. **Genres:** History, Medicine/Health, Women's Studies And Issues, Sciences, Adult Non-fiction, Sociology. **Career:** King County Hospital, staff nurse, 1963-64; Sacred Heart Hospital, staff nurse, 1964; National Institutes of Health, staff nurse at clinical center, 1965; San Jose State College (now University), assistant professor of nursing, 1967-69; Centers for Disease Control and Prevention, epidemiologist, 1970-78; Oregon Health Sciences University, assistant professor of obstetrics and gynecology, 1978-79; U.S. Department of Health and Human Services, expert for office of population affairs and office of the surgeon general, 1979-80; Frontier Nursing Service, academic faculty for school of midwifery and family nursing, 1993-95; Western Consortium for Public Health, associate of pacific institute for women's health, 1993-2001; New York Academy of Medicine/Maternity Center Association, Evidence-Based Symposium on the Nature and Management of Labor Pain, director, 1999-2002. Writer. **Publications:** (Contrib.) Estrogens in the Environment, 1980; (ed. with J.E. Haas and contrib.) Nurse-Midwifery in America: A Report of the American College of Nurse-Midwives Foundation, 1986; Midwifery and Childbirth in America, 1997. Contributor to books and periodicals. **Address:** 2706 SW English Ct., Portland, OR 97201, U.S.A. **Online address:** jprooks1@attbi.com

ROOKS, Judith Pence. See ROOKS, Judith P.

ROOKS, Noliwe M. American (born United States), b. 1963?. **Genres:** Women's Studies And Issues, History, Cultural/Ethnic Topics, Humanities, Social Sciences. **Career:** Princeton University, Centre of African-American Studies Program, associate director. Writer. **Publications:** (Ed.) Paris Connections: African American Artists in Paris, 1920-1975, 1992; Hair Raising: Beauty, Culture and African American Women, 1996; Ladies Pages: African American Women's Magazines and the Culture That Made Them, 2004; (ed.) Black Women's Studies: A Reader, 2005; White Money/Black Power: The Surprising History of African American Studies and the Crisis of Race in Higher Education, 2006. **Address:** Program in African-American Studies, Princeton University, 112 Dickinson Hall, Stanhope Hall, Princeton, NJ 08544, U.S.A. **Online address:** nrooks@princeton.edu

ROOKSBY, Rikky. British (born England), b. 1958. **Genres:** Music, Literary Criticism And History, Poetry, Young Adult Fiction. **Career:** University College, tutor, 1980-85; St. Michael's Hall, tutor, 1985-; Oxford University, Department of Continuing Education, tutor. Guitar teacher and music writer. **Publications:** (Ed. with N. Shrimpton) The Whole Music of Passion: New Essays on Swinburne, Scolar (England), 1993; A.C. Swinburne: A Poet's Life, 1997; How to Write Songs on Guitar, 2000; Inside Classic Rock Tracks: Songwriting and Recording Secrets of 100 Great Songs from 1960 to the Present Day, 2001; The Complete Rock & Pop Guitar Player, 2006. Contributor of articles and periodicals. **Address:** Department for Continuing Education, St. Michael's Hall, Shoe Ln., 1 Wellington Sq., Oxford, OX 0X1 2DP, England.

ROONEY, Andy. See Obituaries.

ROONEY, Jennie. British (born England), b. 1980?. **Genres:** Young Adult Fiction. **Career:** Writer and lawyer. **Publications:** Inside the Whale, 2008; The Opposite of Falling, 2011. Contributor to periodicals. **Address:** Aitken Alexander Associates, 18-21 Cavaye Pl., London, GL SW10 9PT, England.

ROONEY, Lucy. British (born England), b. 1926?. **Genres:** Theology/Religion. **Career:** Sisters of Notre Dame de Namur, staff, 1947; teacher, 1950-58; All Souls School, principal, 1958-62; Notre Dame College of Education, lecturer in teacher training and arts and crafts, 1964-69; Convent of Notre Dame, administrative staff, 1969-75; Congregation of Notre Dame, assistant archivist, 1976-79; writer, 1979-. **Publications:** WITH ROBERT FARICY: Mary Queen of Peace: Is the Mother of God Appearing in Medjugorje?, 1984; Medjugorje Up Close: Mary Speaks to the World, 1986 in UK as Medjugorje Unfolds; The Contemplative Way of Prayer: Deepening Your Life with God,

1986; Medjugorje Journal: Mary Speaks to the World, 1987; Lord Teach Us to Pray, 1987; Lord Jesus, Teach Me to Pray: A Seven Week Course in Personal Prayer, 1988; Medjugorje Retreat, 1989; Our Lady Comes to Scottsdale: Is It Authentic?, 1991; Return to God: The Scottsdale Message, 1993; Medjugorje Unfolds in Peace and in War, 1994; Knowing Jesus in the World: Prayer with Teilhard De Chardin, 1996; Your Wounds I Will Heal: Prayer for Inner Healing, 1999; Praying with Mary: Contemplating Scripture at Her Side, 2002. **Address:** Sisters of Notre Dame, 266 Woolton Rd., Childwall, Liverpool, MS L16 8NF, England.

ROOP, Connie. American (born United States), b. 1951. **Genres:** Children's Fiction, Children's Non-fiction, Biography, Picture/Board Books. **Career:** Appleton Area School District, science teacher, 1973-; Lady Hawkins School, fulbright exchange teacher, 1976-77; D.C. Heath Co., consultant, 1986-87; Duquesne University, workshop coordinator, 1986-. Writer. **Publications:** WITH P. ROOP: Space Out!, 1984; Go Hog Wild!, 1984; Out to Lunch!, 1984; Keep the Lights Burning, Abbie, 1985; Buttons for General Washington, 1986; Stick out Your Tongue!, 1986; Going Buggy!, 1986; Let's Celebrate!, 1986; The Extinction of the Dinosaurs, 1987; Mysteries of the Solar System, 1987; Poltergeists, 1987; We Sought Refuge Here, 1987; Snips the Tinker, 1988; Seasons of the Cranes, 1989; Stonehenge, 1989; (ed.) I, Columbus, 1990; One Earth, a Multitude of Creatures, 1992; Ahyoka and the Talking Leaves, 1992; Discovering Nonfiction Series: Sea Creatures, The Solar System, Flowering Plants, Insects and Spiders, Dinosaurs, 1992; (ed.) Off the Map: The Journals of Lewis and Clark, 1993; (ed.) Capturing Nature: The Art and Writings of Audubon, 1993; Goodbye for Today, 1995; Mary Jemison, 1995; The Pilgrims' Voices, 1995; Small Deer and the Buffalo Jump, 1996; David Farragut, 1996; Westward Ho! Ho! Ho!, 1996; Let's Celebrate Halloween, 1997; Let's Celebrate Christmas, 1997; Walk on the Wild Side!, 1997; Grace's Letter to Lincoln, 1998; Brazil, 1998; China, 1998, rev. ed., 2008; A City Album, 1998; Egypt, 1998; Greece, 1998; A Home Album, 1998; If You Lived with the Cherokee, 1998; India, 1998; Israel, 1998; Japan, 1998; Martin Luther King Jr., 1998; Susan B. Anthony, 1998; Vietnam, 1998, rev. ed., 2009; A Town, 1999; A Suburb, 1999; A City, 1999; A School Album, 1999; Let's Celebrate Valentine's Day, 1999; Girl of the Shining Mountains, 1999; A Farming Town, 1999; A Farm Album, 1999; Let's Celebrate Thanksgiving, 1999; Whales and Dolphins, 2000; An Eye for an Eye, 2000; Christopher Columbus, 2000; Benjamin Franklin, 2000; Escape from the Ice, 2001; Let's Celebrate Earth Day, 2001; Let's Celebrate Presidents' Day, 2001; Octopus under the Sea, 2001; Up to the Challenge, 2001; Sew What, Betsy Ross?, 2001; Let's Split Logs, Abe Lincoln!, 2002; Let's Play Soldier, George Washington!, 2002; Good-bye for Today, 2002; California Gold Rush, 2002; Starfish: Stars of the Sea, 2002; Take Command, Captain Farragut!, 2002; Let's Celebrate St. Patrick's Day, 2003; Turn on the Light, Thomas Edison!, 2003; Let's Fly Wilbur and Orville!, 2003; Go Fly a kite, Ben Franklin!, 2003; Over in the Rain Forest, 2003; Sacagawea: Girl of the Shining Mountains, 2003; Millions of Monarchs, 2003; Louisiana Purchase, 2004; Holiday Howlers: Jokes for Punny Parties, 2004; Let's Ride, Paul Revere!, 2004; Let's Drive, Henry Ford!, 2004; Let's Dream, Martin Luther King, Jr.!, 2004; Give Me a Sign, Helen Keller!, 2004; (with D.L. Burns) Backyard Beasties: Jokes to Snake You Smile, 2004; The Declaration of Independence, 2005; Thank You, Squanto!, 2005; Going to Yellowstone, 2005; Take a Giant Leap, Neil Armstrong!, 2005; Explore the Midwest, 2006; Explore the West, 2006; Tales of Famous Americans, 2007; River Roads West: America's First Highways, 2007; Who Cracked the Liberty Bell?, 2007; Did Pilgrims Really Wear Black and White?, 2007; Who Conducted the Underground Railroad?: And Other Questions about the Path to Freedom, 2008; A Visit to Egypt, 2008; Visit to Brazil, 2008; Visit to Japan, 2008; Visit to India, 2008; Top-secret Adventure of John Darragh, Revolutionary War Spy, 2010; Stormy Adventure of Abbie Burgess, Lighthouse Keeper, 2010; Tales Of Famous Heroes, 2010; Baby Dolphin's First Day, 2011. IN THEIR OWN WORDS SERIES: Betsy Ross, 2001; Sojourner Truth, 2002; Sitting Bull, 2002. IN MY OWN WORDS SERIES: (ed. with P. Roop) The Diary of Joseph Plumb, 2001; (ed. with P. Roop) Diary of John Wesley Powell, 2001; (ed. with P. Roop) The Diary of David R. Leeper, 2001; (ed. with P. Roop) Diary of Joseph Plumb Martin, a Revolutionary War Soldier, 2001; (ed. with P. Roop) The Diary of Mary Jemison, 2001. **Address:** 2601 N Union St., Appleton, WI 54911-2141, U.S.A.

ROOP, Peter. (Peter Geiger Roop). American (born United States), b. 1951. **Genres:** Children's Fiction, Education, Children's Non-fiction, Biography, Travel/Exploration, Politics/Government. **Career:** Appleton Area School District, teacher, 1973-99; Kingston County Primary School, Fulbright exchange teacher, 1976-77; University of Wisconsin, instructor, 1983-84; Uni-

versity of Wisconsin, School of the Arts-Rhinelander, instructor, 1986-87; Heath Co., consultant, 1986-87; Duquesne University, workshop coordinator, 1986-99; Learning Magazine, teacher consultant, 1988-99; Booklinks Magazine, educational consultant. Writer. **Publications:** The Cry of the Conch, 1984; Little Blaze and the Buffalo Jump, 1984; Siskimi, 1984; Natosi, 1984; (with R.R. McCown and M. Driscoll) Educational Psychology and Classroom Practice: A Partnership, 1992, (with R. McCown and M. Driscoll) 2nd ed. as Educational Psychology: A Learning-centered Approach to Classroom Practice, 1996. WITH C. ROOP: Space Out!, 1984; Go Hog Wild, 1984; Out to Lunch!, 1984; Keep the Lights Burning, Abbie, 1985; Buttons for General Washington, 1986; Stick Out Your Tongue! Jokes about Doctors and Patients, 1986; Going Buggy! Jokes about Insects, 1986; Let's Celebrate! Jokes about Holidays, 1986; Dinosaurs: Opposing Viewpoints, 1988; The Solar System: Opposing Viewpoints, 1988; Poltergeists: Opposing Viewpoints, 1988; Stonehenge, 1989; Seasons of the Cranes, 1989; Snips the Tinker, 1990; I, Columbus, 1990; Ahyoka and the Talking Leaves, 1992; One Earth: A Multitude of Creatures, 1992; (ed.) Off the Map, 1993; Capturing Nature, 1993; Pilgrims' Voices, 1995; Mary Jemison, 1995; The Buffalo Jump, 1996; Let's Celebrate Christmas, 1997; Let's Celebrate Halloween, 1997; Westward Ho! Ho! Ho!, 1998; Walk on the Wild Side!, 1998; Sacajawea, 1999; Goodbye for Today, 2000; An Eye for an Eye, 2000; Whales and Dolphins, 2000; Christopher Columbus, 2000; Benjamin Franklin, 2000; (ed.) The Diary of Mary Jemison, Captured by the Indians, 2001; (ed.) The Diary of David R. Leeper: Rushing for Gold, 2001; (ed.) The Diary of Joseph Plumb Martin, a Revolutionary War Soldier, 2001; Take Command, Captain Farragut!, 2001; Let's Celebrate Presidents' Day, 2001; The Diary of John Wesley Powell: Conquering the Grand Canyon, 2001; Starfish, 2001; Betsy Ross, 2001; Escape from the Ice: Shackleton and the Endurance, 2001; Let's Celebrate Earth Day, 2001; Octopus Uder the Sea, 2001; Sitting Bull, 2001; California Gold Rush, 2002; Let's Play Soldier, George Washington!, 2002; Let's Split Logs, Abe Lincoln!, 2002; Sew What, Betsy Ross?, 2002; Sojourner Truth, 2002; Millions of Monarchs, 2003; Over in the Rain Forest, 2003; Go Fly a Kite, Ben Franklin!, 2003; Let's Celebrate St. Patrick's Day, 2003; Let's Fly, Wilbur and Orville!, 2003; Turn On the Light, Thomas Edison!, 2003; (and D.L. Burns) Backyard Beasties: Jokes to Snake You Smile, 2004; Give Me a Sign, Helen Keller!, 2004; Holiday Howlers: Jokes for Punny Parties, 2004; Let's Dream, Martin Luther King, Jr.!, 2004; Let's Drive, Henry Ford!, 2004; Let's Ride, Paul Revere, 2004; The Louisiana Purchase, 2004; Going to Yellowstone, 2005; Take a Giant Leap, Neil Armstrong!, 2005; Take a Stand, Rosa Parks, 2005; Thank You, Squanto!, 2005; Lead Us to Freedom, Harriet Tubman!, 2006; Explore the West, 2006; Explore the Midwest, 2006; Who Cracked the Liberty Bell?: And Other Questions about the American Revolution, 2007; Did Pilgrims Really Wear Black and White?: And Other Questions about Colonial Times, 2007; Tales of Famous Americans, 2007; River Roads West: America's First Highways, 2007; Who Conducted the Underground Railroad?: And Other Questions about the Path to Freedom, 2008; Baby Dolphin's First Day, 2011; Stormy Adventure of Abbie Burgess, Lighthouse Keeper, 2011; Top-secret Adventure of John Darragh, Revolutionary War Spy, 2011. ACCELERATED READER BOOKS WITH C. ROOP: A Visit to China, 1998, rev. ed. as China, 2008; A Visit to Egypt, 1998, rev. ed., 2008; A Visit to Greece, 1998; A Visit to Brazil, 1998; A Visit to Israel, 1998; A Visit to India, 1998, rev. ed., 2008; A Visit to Vietnam, 1998, rev. ed. as Vietnam, 2009; A Visit to Japan, 1998, rev. ed., 2008; Long Ago and Today-Schools, 1998; Long Ago and Today-Homes, 1998; Long Ago and Today-Farms, 1998; Long Ago and Today-Cities, 1998; Walk around a Farming Town, 1998; Walk Around a City, 1998; Walk Around a Small Town, 1998; Walk Around a Suburb, 1998. Contributor of articles to periodicals. **Address:** Millbrook Press Inc., 2 Old New Milford Rd., Brookfield, CT 06804-2426, U.S.A. **Online address:** peterroop@aol.com

ROOP, Peter Geiger. *See* **ROOP, Peter.**

ROORBACH, Bill. American (born United States), b. 1953. **Genres:** Novels, Novellas/Short Stories, Autobiography/Memoirs, Essays, Young Adult Fiction. **Career:** Columbia (A Magazine of Poetry and Prose), fiction editor; University of Maine, assistant professor, associate professor of English, 1991-95, retired, 2001; Ohio State University, assistant professor, 1995-98, associate professor, 1998-2001, retired, 2001; full time writer, 2001-; College of the Holy Cross, Jenks Chair in Contemporary American Letters, 2004-09; Ithaca College, distinguished visiting writer, 2006. **Publications:** Summers with Juliet (memoir), 1992; Turning toward Home, 1993; The Quotable Moose, 1994; Writing Life Stories, 1998, 2nd ed. as Writing Life Stories: How to Make Memories into Memoirs, Ideas into Essays and Life into Literature, 2008; (ed.) Contemporary Creative Nonfiction (anthology), 2000; Big Bend (short stories), 2001; The Smallest Color (novel), 2001; Into Woods: Essays, 2002; (with R. Kimber and W. McNair) A Place on Water: Essays, 2004; Temple Stream: A Rural Odyssey, 2004; A Healing Touch, 2009; The High Side, 2012. Works appear in anthologies. **Address:** c/o Betsy Lerner, The Gernert Co., 136 E 57th St., New York, NY 10022, U.S.A. **Online address:** bill@billroorbach.com

ROOS, Johan. Danish/Swedish (born Sweden), b. 1961. **Genres:** Administration/Management, Business/Trade/Industry. **Career:** University of Pennsylvania, Wharton School, research associate, 1988-90, William H. Wurster Center for Multinational Management Studies, research fellow, 1988-90; Norwegian School of Management, assistant professor, associate professor, 1990-94, Norwegian Institute for Marketing, fellow; International Institute for Management Development, professor of strategy and general management, 1995-2000; Imagination Lab Foundation, managing director, 2000-06; école Polytechnique Fédérale de Lausanne, visiting professor, 2006-07, 2008-09; Eidgenössische Technische Hochschule Zürich, visiting professor, 2006-07, 2008-09; Stockholm School of Economics, Bo Rydin and SCA professor of business administration, 2007-09; Copenhagen Business School, professor, 2009-; Swiss-based Imagination Lab Foundation, managing director. Writer. **Publications:** (Ed. with P. Lorange) The Challenge of Cooperative Ventures, 1987; (with Lorange) Strategic Alliances: Formation, Implementation and Evolution, 1992; (ed. with Lorange, B. Chakravarthy and A. Van de Ven and contrib.) Implementing Strategic Processes: Learning, Change, and Cooperation, 1993; (with G. von Krogh) Samarbeidsstrategier: Allianser og Oppkjop, 1993; (with G. Roos and von Krogh) Strategi, 1994; (ed. and contrib.) European Case Book on Cooperative Strategies, 1994; (with G. Yip and von Krogh) Global Strategi, 1994; (with von Krogh) Organizational Epistemology: A Treatise, 1994; (co-author) Strategizing, 1994; (ed. with G. von Krogh) Managing Knowledge: Perspectives on Cooperation and Competition, 1996; (with G.V. Krogh and P.S. Bronn) Managing Strategy Processes in Emergent Industries: The Case of Media Firms, 1996; (co-author) Intellectual Capital: Navigating in the New Business Landscape, 1998; (ed. with G.V. Krogh and D. Kleine) Knowing in Firms: Understanding, Managing and Measuring Knowledge, 1998; (with M. Lissack) The Next Common Sense: An E-Manager's Guide to Mastering Complexity, 2000; (with M. Roos) Thinking from Within: A Hands-on Strategy Practice, 2006; (with M. Statler) Everyday Strategic Preparedness: The Role of Practical Wisdom in Organizations, 2007. Contributor to journals. **Address:** Copenhagen Business School, Solbjergs Plads 3, Frederiksberg, 2000, Denmark. **Online address:** johan.roos@cbs.dk

ROOS, Murphre. See **Norris, Ken.**

ROOSE, Kevin. American (born United States), b. 1987. **Genres:** Theology/Religion, Biography, Autobiography/Memoirs, Education. **Career:** College Hill Independent, staff writer; Brown Daily Herald, columnist; The New York Times, business reporter. **Publications:** The Unlikely Disciple: A Sinner's Semester at America's Holiest University, 2009. Contributor to periodicals. **Address:** The New York Times, 620 8th Ave., 5th Fl., New York, NY 10018, U.S.A. **Online address:** kevin@kevinroose.com

ROOSE-EVANS, James. British (born England), b. 1927. **Genres:** Children's Fiction, Plays/Screenplays, Theatre, Biography, Photography. **Career:** Maddermarket Theatre, artistic director, 1954-55; Juilliard School of Music, faculty, 1955-56; Royal Academy of Dramatic Art, staff and judge, 1957-62; Hampstead Theatre Club, founder, 1959-, artistic director, 1959-71; Pitlochry Festival Theatre, artistic director, 1960; Stage Two, founder and director, 1969-; National Union of Students Drama Festival, adjudicator, 1970; National Drama Festival of Zambia, adjudicator, 1973; Bleddfa Trust-Centre for Caring and the Arts in Mid-Wales, founder and chairman, 1974-; Middlesex, reader in drama, 1979-; Ohio State University, distinguished visiting fellow, 1991-92; The Bleddfa Trust, founder and chairman. Freelance theatre director and writer. **Publications:** Directing a Play, 1968; Experimental Theatre from Stanislavsky to Today, 1970, 4th ed., 1989; The Adventures of Odd and Elsewhere, 1971; The Secret of the Seven Bright Shiners: An Odd and Elsewhere Story, 1972; Odd and the Great Bear, 1973; Elsewhere and the Gathering of the Clowns, 1974; The Return of the Great Bear: An Odd and Elsewhere Story, 1975; The Secret of Tippity-Witchit, 1975; The Female Messiah (radio documentary), 1975; Actor Training 2, 1976; The Lost Treasure of Wales: An Odd and Elsewhere Story, 1977; London Theatre: From the Globe to the National, 1977; Topsy and Ted, (radio play), 1977; Acrobats of God (TV documentary), 1977; Pride of Players (dramatic anthology), 1978; The Third Adam (radio documentary), 1978; A Well-Conducted Theatre (ra-

dio documentary), 1979; Lady Managers (TV documentary), 1980; 84 Charing Cross Road (play), 1983; Odd to the Rescue, 1983; Experimental Theatre from Stanislavsky to Peter Brook, 1984; Cook a Story, 1986; Inner Journey, Outer Journey: Finding a Spiritual Centre in Everyday Life, 1987, rev. ed., 1998; Re Joyce! (play), 1988; The Inner Stage, 1990; Passages of the Soul, 1994; Cider with Rosie by Laurie Lee: A Stage Adaptation, 1994; One Foot on the Stage (biography), 1996; The Christ Mouse, 2005; What Is Spirituality?, 2005; Opening Doors and Windows: A Memoir in Four Acts, 2009. EDITOR: Darling Ma: Letters to Her Mother, 1932-1944, 1988; The Time of My Life: The Wartime Journals of Joyce Grenfell, 1989; The Cook-a-Story, 2005; Contributor to periodicals. **Address:** Sheil Land Associates Ltd., 52 Doughty St., London, GL WC1N 2LS, England.

ROOSEVELT, Lucky. See **ROOSEVELT, Selwa.**

ROOSEVELT, Selwa. (Lucky Roosevelt). American (born United States), b. 1929. **Genres:** International Relations/Current Affairs, Politics/Government, Autobiography/Memoirs. **Career:** Kingsport Times, reporter, 1946-50; Washington Star, columnist, 1954-58; Washington Post, feature writer, 1967-68; contributing editor, 1974-81; U.S. Government, chief of protocol, Reagan Administration, ambassador, 1982-89; Mediterranean Quarterly, senior editor, 1995-. **Publications:** Keeper of the Gate: An Intimate View of American Diplomacy in the Reagan Years, 1990. **Address:** The Colonnade, 2801 New Mexico Ave. NW, Apt. 724, Washington, DC 20007, U.S.A.

ROOT, Deborah. Canadian/American (born United States), b. 1953. **Genres:** Art/Art History, Social Sciences, Photography, Human Relations/Parenting. **Career:** Ontario College of Art, course director, 1991-96; University of Toronto, faculty of architecture and landscape architecture. Writer. **Publications:** Cannibal Culture: Art, Appropriation, and the Commodification of Difference, 1996; (with W. Ra'ad) Entangled Territories: Imagining the Orient, 1998; Letters of Transit, forthcoming. Contributor to periodicals. **Address:** Fuse Magazine, 454-401 Richmond St. W, Ste. 454, Toronto, ON M5V 3A8, Canada. **Online address:** droot@web.net

ROOT, Hilton L. American (born United States), b. 1951. **Genres:** Politics/Government, Economics, History, International Relations/Current Affairs. **Career:** University of Pennsylvania, Department of History, assistant professor, 1985-88, Janice and Julian Bers assistant professor in the social sciences, 1988-91; Stanford University, associate professor of public policy, 1995-98, Hoover Institution, senior research fellow, 1992-98, Initiative on Economic Growth and Democracy, director, 1996-98; Milken Institute, director and senior fellow of global studies, 1998-2001, senior fellow, 2002-03; United States Department of the Treasury, senior advisor, 2001-02; Pitzer College, Freeman Fellow and visiting professor of economics, 2003-06; Claremont Graduate University, senior research fellow, 2006-; George Mason University, School of Public Policy, professor of public policy, 2006-. Writer. **Publications:** Peasants and King in Burgundy: Agrarian Foundations of French Absolutism, 1987; The Fountain of Privilege: Political Foundations of Markets in Old Regime France and England, 1994; Has China Lost Its Way?: Getting Stuck in Transition, 1995; Small Countries, Big Lessons: Governance and the Rise of Asia, 1996; (with J.E. Campos) The Key to the Asian Miracle: Making Shared Growth Credible, 1996; India, Asia's Next Tiger?, 1998; (ed. with B.B. de Mesquita) Governing for Prosperity, 2000; Capital and Collusion: The Political Logic of Global Economic Development, 2006; Alliance Curse: How America Lost the Third World, 2008. Contributor to books, periodicals and journals. **Address:** School of Public Policy, George Mason University, 3401 Fairfax Dr., PO Box 3B1, Arlington, VA 22201-4411, U.S.A. **Online address:** hroot2@gmu.edu

ROOT, Phyllis. American (born United States), b. 1949. **Genres:** Children's Fiction. **Career:** Norwich University, Vermont College, Fine Arts in Writing for Children Program, instructor, 2002-; University of Minnesota, Practical Scholar Program, faculty; Hamline University, MFA Writing for Children Program, teacher, instructor and faculty advisor. Writer. **Publications:** Hidden Places, 1983; (with C.A. Marron) Gretchen's Grandma, 1983; (with C.A. Marron) Just One of the Family 1984; (with C.A. Marron) No Place for a Pig, 1984; My Cousin Charlie, 1984; Moon Tiger, 1985; Soup for Supper, 1986; Great Basin, 1988; Glacier, 1989; Galápagos, 1989; The Old Red Rocking Chair, 1992; The Listening Silence, 1992; Coyote and the Magic Words, 1993; Sam Who Was Swallowed by a Shark, 1994; Contrary Bear, 1996; Aunt Nancy and Old Man Trouble, 1996; Mrs. Potter's Pig, 1996; One Windy Wednesday, 1996; The Hungry Monster, 1996; Rosie's Fiddle, 1997;

What Baby Wants, 1998; One Duck Stuck: A Mucky Ducky Counting Book, 1998; Aunt Nancy and Cousin Lazybones, 1998; Turnover Tuesday, 1998; Grandmother Winter, 1999; Here Comes Tabby Cat, 2000; Hey, Tabby Cat!, 2000; Meow Monday, 2000; Foggy Friday, 2000; Kiss the Cow!, 2000; All for the Newborn Baby, 2000; Rattletrap Car, 2001; Soggy Saturday, 2001; Big Momma Makes the World, 2002; Oliver Finds His Way, 2002; (with M. Edwards) What's That Noise?, 2002; Mouse Goes Out, 2002; Mouse Has Fun, 2002; The Name Quilt, 2003; Ten Sleepy Sheep, 2004; Baby Ducklings, 2004; Baby Bunnies, 2004; If You Want to See a Caribou, 2004; Gladys on the Go: In Which She Finds Her Destiny, 2004; Quack!, 2004; Hot Flash Gal, 2004; Who Said Boo?, 2005; Ask Gladys: Household Hints for Gals on the Go, 2005; Dear Hot Flash Gal: Every Answer to a Gal's Every Question, 2005; Hop!, 2005; The House that Jill Built, 2005; Looking for a Moose, 2006; Lucia and the Light, 2006; Aunt Nancy and the Bothersome Visitors, 2007; Flip! Flap! Fly!, 2009; (with M. Cordell) Toot Toot Zoom!, 2009; (with H. Craig) Thirsty Thursday, 2009; Paula Bunyan, 2009; Creak! Said the Bed, 2010; Lilly and the Pirates, 2010; Big Belching Bog, 2010; Scrawny Cat, 2011. Contributor to periodicals. **Address:** Farrar, Straus & Giroux, 18 W 18th St., New York, NY 10011, U.S.A. **Online address:** rootx005@umn.edu

ROOT, William Pitt. American (born United States), b. 1941. **Genres:** Novellas/Short Stories, Poetry, Translations. **Career:** Rock State College, instructor in English, 1967; Michigan State University, assistant professor of writing, 1967-68; Amherst College, visiting writer, 1971; Wichita State University, visiting writer, 1976, distinguished writer-in-residence; University of Southwestern Louisiana, visiting writer, 1976; University of Montana, visiting writer, 1977-78, 1980-81, 1983-84; Interlochen Arts Academy, visiting writer, 1979; Hunter College, professor, 1986-2005; Pacific Lutheran University, visiting writer, 1990-, distinguished writer-in-residence; poet laureate, 1997-2002. **Publications:** The Storm and Other Poems, 1969; Striking the Dark Air for Music, 1973; The Port of Galveston, 1974; Journey South: A Poem, 1977; Coot and Other Characters: Poems New and Familiar, 1977; Fireclock, 1981; Reasons for Going It on Foot, 1981; In the World's Common Grasses, 1981; Faultdancing, 1986; Trace Elements from a Recurring Kingdom: The First Five Books, 1994; A Beauty Warrior: Bruce's Book, 2005; Storm and Other Poems, 2005; White Boots: New and Selected Poems of the West, 2006. EDITOR: What a World, What a World!: Poetry by Young People in Galveston Schools, 1974; Timesoup (poetry), 1980. **Address:** 154 Concho Cir., Bayfield, CO 81122, U.S.A. **Online address:** wprpoet@attglobal.net

ROOT-BERNSTEIN, Michèle. American (born United States), b. 1953. **Genres:** Adult Non-fiction, Intellectual History, Psychology, Essays, Poetry. **Career:** Pinecrest Elementary School, writer-in-residence, 1993-95; Michigan State University, Department of History, visiting assistant professor, 1994; Kennedy Center, teaching artist, 2004-; Michigan State University, Department of Theatre, faculty, 2005-, adjunct assistant professor. **Publications:** Boulevard Theater and Revolution in Eighteenth-Century Paris (Theater and Dramatic Studies, no. 22), 1984; (with R. Root-Bernstein) Honey, Mud, Maggots and Other Medical Marvels: The Science Behind Folk Remedies and Old Wives' Tales, 1997; (with R. Root-Bernstein) Sparks of Genius: The Thirteen Thinking Tools of the World's Most Creative People, 1999. Contributor to periodicals. **Address:** Department of Theatre, Michigan State University, 113 Auditorium, East Lansing, MI 48824, U.S.A. **Online address:** rootber3@msu.edu

ROOT-BERNSTEIN, Robert Scott. American (born United States), b. 1953. **Genres:** Biology, Education, Medicine/Health, Sciences, Art/Art history, Essays. **Career:** Salk Institute for Biological Studies, post-doctoral fellow, 1981-83; research associate, 1981-85; Veterans Administration Hospital, research associate, 1985-87; University of California, visiting associate professor, 1987; Michigan State University, MacArthur fellow, 1981-86, assistant professor, 1987-89, associate professor, 1989-95, professor of physiology, 1996-. Writer. **Publications:** The Ionists: Founding Physical Chemistry, 1872-1890, 1981; Discovering: Inventing and Solving Problems at the Frontiers of Scientific Knowledge, 1989; Rethinking AIDS: The Tragic Cost of Premature Consensus, 1993; Honey, Maggots, Mud and Other Modern Medicines, 1997; Sparks of Genius: The Thirteen Thinking Tools of the World's Most Creative People, 1999. Contributor of essays to periodicals. **Address:** Department of Physiology, Michigan State University, 2174 Biomedical & Physical Sciences Bldg., East Lansing, MI 48824, U.S.A. **Online address:** rootbern@msu.edu

ROPES, Linda Brubaker. American (born United States), b. 1942. **Genres:**

Medicine/Health. **Career:** Creative Ink (writing service), owner, 1981-. Writer. **Publications:** The Health Care Crisis in America: A Reference Handbook, 1991. **Address:** 500 Creekside Ct., Golden, CO 80403-1903, U.S.A.

ROQUELAURE, A. N. See **RICE, Anne.**

RORBY, Ginny. American (born United States), b. 1944. **Genres:** Young Adult Fiction, Novels. **Career:** National Airlines (later Pan American Airways), flight attendant, 1966-89, now retired; Mendocino Coast Audubon Soceity, president; Point Cabrillo Lightkeepers Association, president; College of the Redwoods, faculty. Writer. **Publications:** Dolphin Sky (juvenile novel), 1996; Hurt Go Happy, 2006; Outside of a Horse: A Novel, 2010; Lost in a River of Grass, 2011. **Address:** Barbara S. Kouts Literary Agency, PO Box 560, Bellport, NY 11713, U.S.A. **Online address:** ginnyrorby@mcn.org

RORIPAUGH, Robert (Alan). American (born United States), b. 1930. **Genres:** Novels, Novellas/Short Stories, Poetry, Young Adult Fiction. **Career:** University of Wyoming, College of Arts and Sciences, Department of English, instructor, 1958-62, assistant professor, 1962-67, associate professor, 1967-72, professor, 1972-93, professor emeritus, 1993-; Wyoming poet laureate, 1995-2002. Writer. **Publications:** A Fever for Living (novel), 1961; Honor Thy Father (novel), 1963; Learn to Love the Haze: Poems, 1976; (contrib.) Historic Ranches of Wyoming, 1986; The Ranch: Wyoming Poetry, 2001; The Legend of Billy Jenks and Other Wyoming Stories, 2007. Contributor to periodicals. **Address:** Department of English, University of Wyoming, 1000 E University Ave., Laramie, WY 82071, U.S.A.

RORTY, Amélie Oksenberg. American/Belgian (born Belgium), b. 1932. **Genres:** Intellectual History, Philosophy, Essays. **Career:** Wheaton College, instructor, assistant professor, 1957-61, assistant professor of philosophy, 1959-61; Rutgers University, assistant professor, distinguished professor, 1961-88, associate professor, 1965-72, professor of philosophy, 1972-88; Barnard College, visiting assistant professor, 1962-63; Princeton University, visiting assistant professor, 1962-63; Haverford College, visiting associate professor, 1968-69; Center for Advanced Study in the Behavioral Sciences, fellow, 1969-70; King's College, research fellow, 1971-73; University of Illinois, visiting professor, 1981-82; Boston University, Philosophy Department, visiting professor, 1984-86, 2008-09, 2009-10; Radcliffe College, Matina Horner distinguished visiting professor, 1986-91; Brandeis University, visiting Hannah Obermannn professor, 1986-89, professor of the history of ideas, 1995-2003; Tufts University, visiting Hannah Obermann professor, 1987-88; Harvard University, Harvard Graduate School of Education, visiting professor, 1993-95, Harvard Medical School, lecturer in social medicine, 2002-, visiting professor, 2004-07, professor, 2007-; Mt. Holyoke College, professor of philosophy, 1993-95; Yale University, visiting Orick professor, 2003-04. Writer. **Publications:** EDITOR: Pragmatic Philosophy, 1966; (ed.) Modern Studies in Philosophy, 1967, 33 vols., 1966; The Identities of Persons, 1977; (ed.) Major Thinkers, 5 vols., 1978; Explaining Emotions, 1979; Essays on Aristotle's Ethics, 1980; Essays on Descartes' Meditations, 1986; (with B.P. McLaughlin) Perspectives on Self Deception, 1988; (with O. Flanagan) Identity, Character and Morality: Essays in Moral Psychology, 1990; Essays on Aristotle's Poetics, 1990; (with M. Nussbaum) Essays on Aristotle's Philosophy of Mind, 1992; Essays on Aristotle's Rhetoric, 1996; Philosophers on Education, 1998; The Many Faces of Evil, 2001; The Many Faces of Philosophy, 2003; (ed. with J. Schmidt) Kant's Idea for a Universal History with a Cosmopolitan Aim: A Critical Guide, 2009. OTHER: Mind in Action: Essays in the Philosophy of Mind, 1988. Contributor to journals. **Address:** Department of Global Health and Social Medicine, Harvard Medical School, 641 Huntington Ave., Boston, MA 02215, U.S.A. **Online address:** amelie_rorty@hms.harvard.edu

ROSALER, Robert C. American (born United States), b. 1920. **Genres:** Engineering, Business/Trade/Industry, Administration/Management, Technology. **Career:** Writer. **Publications:** EDITOR: Standard Handbook of Plant Engineering, 1983, 3rd ed., 2002; Plant Engineering Reference Guide, 1987; (with N.R. Grimm) Handbook of HVAC Design, 1990, 2nd ed. as HVAC Systems and Components Handbook, 1998. OTHERS: Industrial Maintenance Reference Guide, 1987; HVAC Maintenance and Operations Handbook, 1998; HVAC Handbook, 2004. **Address:** 232 Silver Creek Cir., Santa Rosa, CA 95409, U.S.A.

ROSAND, David. American (born United States), b. 1938. **Genres:** Art/Art History, Architecture. **Career:** Columbia University, instructor, 1964-67, assistant professor, 1967-69, associate professor, 1969-73, professor of art history, 1973, Meyer Schapiro professor of art history, 1964-, Department of Art History and Archeology, chairman, Art Humanities, director. Writer. **Publications:** (Ed. with M. Muraro) Tiziano e la Silografia Veneziana del Cinquecento, 1976; (with M. Muraro) Titian and the Venetian Woodcut: A Loan Exhibition, 1976; Titian, 1978; Painting in Cinquecento Venice: Titian, Veronese, Tintoretto, 1982; (ed. with A.W. Lowenthal and J. Walsh) Rubens and His Circle: Studies, 1982; (ed.) Titian: His World and His Legacy, 1982; (ed. with R.W. Hanning) Castiglione: The Ideal and the Real in Renaissance Culture, 1983; (ed.) Interpretazioni Veneziane: Studi di Storia Dell'artein Onore di Michelangelo Muraro, 1984; The Meaning of the Mark: Leonardo and Titian, 1988; (co-author) Places of Delight: The Pastoral Landscape, 1988; (ed.) Robert Motherwell on Paper: Drawings, Prings, Collages, 1997; Painting in Sixteenth-Century Venice: Titian, Veronese, Tintoretto, 1997; Myths of Venice: The Figuration of a State, 2001; Drawing Acts: Studies in Graphic Expression and Representation, 2002; Invention of Painting in America, 2004; (intro.) Titian: Materiality, Likeness, Istoria, 2007; Edward Koren: Lhe Capricious Line, 2010. **Address:** Department of Art History and Archaeology, Columbia University, 906 Schermerhorn Hall, 1190 Amsterdam Ave., New York, NY 10027, U.S.A. **Online address:** dr17@columbia.edu

ROSCHELLE, Anne R. American (born United States) **Genres:** Novels, Politics/Government. **Career:** State University of New York, associate professor, Department of sociology, chair; University of San Francisco, faculty associate. Writer. **Publications:** No More kin: Exploring Race, Class, and Gender in Family Networks, 1997; The Tattered Web of Kinship: Black White Differences in Social Support in a Puerto Rican Community, 2002; In The New Politics of Race: From DuBois to the 21st Century, 2002; In Urban Fortunes, 2003; (with T. Wright) Shaping the Future City Through Gentrification and Social Exclusion: Spatial Policing and Homeless Activist Responses in the San Francisco Bay Area. Contributor to periodicals. **Address:** Department of Sociology, State University of New York, 75 S Manheim Blvd., New Paltz, NY 12561, U.S.A.

ROSCO, Jerry. American (born United States), b. 1953. **Genres:** Biography. **Career:** Gannett Newspapers, reporter; Mavety Magazines, associate editor, 1989-94; Mandate magazine, managing editor, 2004-09; Scholastic Inc., copywriter. **Publications:** (Ed. with R. Phelps) Continual Lessons: The Journals of Glenway Wescott, 1937-55, 1990; Glenway Wescott Personally: A Biography, 2002; (ed.) Last Journals, 1956-84, forthcoming; (ed.) A Visit to Priapus and Other Stories, forthcoming. Works appear in anthologies. Contributor to periodicals and journals. **Address:** 51 Bond St., New York, NY 10012, U.S.A. **Online address:** jerry_rosco@hotmail.com

ROSCOE, Patrick. Canadian/Spanish (born Spain), b. 1965. **Genres:** Novels, Novellas/Short Stories, Songs/Lyrics And Libretti, Essays, Young Adult Non-fiction. **Career:** Writer. **Publications:** NOVELS: Beneath the Western Slopes, 1987; Birthmarks, 1990; God's Peculiar Care, 1991; Love Is Starving for Itself, 1994; The Lost Oasis, 1995; The Truth about Love, 2001; The Reincarnation of Linda Lopez, 2003; How Much the Heart Can Hold, 2003; The History of a Hopeful Heart, 2008; The Lonely Dream: A Manifesto, forthcoming. Contributor to magazines. **Address:** 3495 Cambie St., Ste. 542, Vancouver, BC V5Z 4R3, Canada. **Online address:** roscoepatrick@hotmail.com

ROSCOE, Will. American (born United States), b. 1955. **Genres:** Gay And Lesbian Issues, Cultural/Ethnic Topics, Social Sciences. **Career:** Will Roscoe Instructional Design, educational design consultant, 1980-88; Van Waveren Foundation, fellow, 1987, 1991; University of California Extensions-Berkeley, instructor in training development, 1989 and 1990; University of California-Santa Cruz, lecturer in anthropology, 1991; Stanford University, staff development and training specialist at university libraries, 1992-93, Jing Lyman Lecturer, 1993; San Francisco State University, Center for Education and Research in Sexuality, research associate, 1992-, lecturer, assistant professor of anthropology, 1993-94; University of California-Berkeley, lecturer in Native American studies, 1994-97, visiting lecturer in American studies, 1995-96; California Institute of Integral Studies, adjunct faculty in anthropology, 1997, 1999. Writer. **Publications:** (With H. Hay) A Blessing from Wovoka, 1988; The Zuni Man-Woman, 1991; (ed.) Queer Spirits: A Gay Men's Myth Book, 1995; Changing Ones: Third and Fourth Genders in Native North America, 1998; Jesus and the Shamanic Tradition of Same-Sex Love, 2004. EDITOR: Living The Spirit: A Gay American Indian Anthology, 1988; Radically Gay: Gay Liberation in the Words of Its Founder, 1996; (with S.O. Murray) Islamic Homosexualities: Culture, History, and Literature, 1996; (with S.O. Murray)

Boy-Wives and Female Husbands: Studies in African Homosexualities, 1998. Contributor of articles and journals to books. **Address:** c/o Charlotte Sheedy, Sheedy Literary Agency Inc., 65 Bleecker St., Fl. 12, New York, NY 10012, U.S.A. **Online address:** wroscoe@sfsu.edu

ROSE, Alison (C.). American (born United States), b. 1944?. **Genres:** Autobiography/Memoirs, Biography. **Career:** Writer. **Publications:** Better than Sane: Tales from a Dangling Girl, 2004. Contributor to periodicals. **Address:** c/o Author Mail, Random House Inc., 1745 Broadway, New York, NY 10019, U.S.A.

ROSE, Andrew (Wyness). British (born England), b. 1944. **Genres:** Criminology/True Crime, Homes/Gardens. **Career:** Barrister, 1968-88. Writer. **Publications:** Stinie: Murder on the Common, 1985; The Collector's All-Colour Guide to Toy Soldiers: A Record of the World's Miniature Armies, From 1850 to the Present Day, 1985; Scandal at the Savoy, 1991. **Address:** c/o The Society of Authors, 84 Drayton Gardens, London, GL SW10 9SB, England. **Online address:** andrewroseauthor@gmail.com

ROSE, David. British (born England), b. 1959. **Genres:** Biography, Criminology/True Crime, Humanities, History. **Career:** Time Out Magazine, reporter, 1981; Observer, home affairs correspondent; Guardian, staff, 1984; BBC, staff; Mail on Sunday, special investigations writer; Vanity Fair, writer, 2001, investigative journalist and contributing editor, 2002-. **Publications:** (With R. Gregson) Beneath the Mountains: Exploring the Deep Caves of Asturias, 1987; Climate of Fear: Blakelock Murder and the Tottenham Three, 1992; In the Name of the Law: The Collapse of Criminal Justice, 1996; Guildford and District, 2000; (with E. Douglas) Regions of the Heart: The Triumph and Tragedy of Alison Hargreaves, 2000; Guildford: Our Town: Uncovering the Stories Behind the Facts, 2001; The Poupart Family in the Borough of Twickenham, 1874-1936, 2002; Guildford & Villages: Then and Now, 2003; Guantánamo: The War on Human Rights, 2004; The Big Eddy Club: The Stocking Stranglings and Southern Justice, 2007. **Address:** Vanity Fair, Vogue House, 1-2 Hanover Sq., London, GL W1S 1JU, England.

ROSE, Elisabeth. Australian (born Australia), b. 1951?. **Genres:** Novels, Romance/Historical, Music, Human Relations/Parenting. **Career:** Writer, musician and educator. **Publications:** The Right Chord, 2007; Strings Attached, 2008; Coming Home, 2008; Outback Hero, 2009; Stuck, 2009; The Tangled Web, 2010: Instant Family 2010; The Wedding Party, 2011. **Address:** Canberra, AC , Australia. **Online address:** lis@elisabethrose.com.au

ROSE, Emilie. *See* **CHILD, Maureen.**

ROSE, Karen. American (born United States), b. 1964. **Genres:** Novels, Mystery/Crime/Suspense. **Career:** Novelist and educator. **Publications:** Don't Tell, 2003; Have You Seen Her?, 2004; I'm Watching You, 2004; (with A. Solomon and C. Cassidy) Hot Pursuit, 2005; Nothing to Fear, 2005; You Can't Hide, 2006; Count to Ten, 2007; Die for Me, 2007; Scream for Me, 2008; Kill for Me, 2009; I Can See You, 2009; Silent Scream, 2010; You Belong to Me, 2011; No One Left to Tell, 2012. **Address:** New American Library, 375 Hudson St., New York, NY 10014-3657, U.S.A. **Online address:** karen@karenrosebooks.com

ROSE, Kenneth (Vivian). British (born England), b. 1924. **Genres:** History, Biography, Autobiography/Memoirs. **Career:** Eton College, assistant master, 1948; Daily Telegraph, editorial staff, 1952-60; Sunday Telegraph, columnist, 1961-. **Publications:** Superior Person: A Portrait of Curzon and His Circle in Late Victorian England, 1969 as Curzon: A Most Superior Person, 1985; The Later Cecils, 1975; King George V, 1983; Kings, Queens & Courtiers: Intimate Portraits of the Royal House of Windsor from Its Foundation to the Present Day in US as Who's Who in the Royal House of Windsor, 1985; Elusive Rothschild: The Life of Victor, Third Baron, 2003. Contributor to books. **Address:** Sunday Telegraph, 111 Buckingham Palace Rd., London, GL SW1W 0DT, England.

ROSE, Melody. American (born United States), b. 1966. **Genres:** Politics/Government, Medicine/Health. **Career:** Portland State University, Department of Political Science, associate professor and chair, vice provost for academic programs and instruction, Center for Women, Politics, & Policy, founder and director. Writer. **Publications:** Safe, Legal and Unavailable? Abortion Politics in the United States, 2007; Abortion: A Documentary and Reference Guide, 2008; (with R.G. Lawrence) Hillary Clinton's Race for the

White House: Gender Politics and the Media on the Campaign Trail, 2010. **Address:** Portland State University, PO Box 751, Portland, OR 97207-0751, U.S.A. **Online address:** rosem@pdx.edu

ROSE, Michael. British (born England), b. 1940?. **Genres:** Politics/Government, History. **Career:** British Army, commissioned to the Coldstream Guards, 1964; Special Air Service, staff; 22nd Special Air Service Regiment, commander, 1979-82; United Nations forces, commander, 1994-95. Writer. **Publications:** Fighting for Peace: Bosnia 1994, 1998; Washington's War: The American War of Independence to the Iraq Insurgency, 2007. **Address:** Celebrity Speakers Ltd., 90 High St., Burnham, SL1 7JT, England.

ROSE, Michael R. American/German (born Germany), b. 1955. **Genres:** Sciences, Biology, Environmental Sciences/Ecology. **Career:** University of Wisconsin, Laboratory of Genetics, NATO science fellow, 1979-81; Dalhousie University, assistant professor of biology, 1981-85, associate professor of biology, 1985-88; University of California, School of Biological Sciences, Department of Ecology and Evolutionary Biology, associate professor of biology, 1986-90, professor of biology, 1990-, Intercampus Research Program on Experimental Evolution, director, 2004-05, Network for Experimental Research on Evolution, director, 2006-, The Rose Laboratory, principal investigator. Writer, evolutionary biologist and researcher. **Publications:** Quantitative Ecological Theory: An Introduction to Basic Models, 1987; Evolutionary Biology of Aging, 1991; (ed. with C.E. Finch) Genetics and Evolution of Aging, 1994; (ed. with G.V. Lauder) Adaptation, 1996; Darwin's Spectre: Evolutionary Biology in the Modern World, 1998; (with H.B. Passananti and M. Matos) Methuselah Flies: A Case Study in the Evolution of Aging, 2004; The Long Tomorrow: How Advances in Evolutionary Biology Can Help Us Postpone Aging, 2005; (with L.D. Mueller) Evolution and Ecology of the Organism, 2006; (ed. with T. Garland, Jr.) Experimental Evolution: Concepts, Methods, and Applications of Selection Experiments, 2009; (with L.D. Mueller and C.L. Rauser) Does Aging Stop?, 2011. Contributor to periodicals. **Address:** Department of Ecology and Evolutionary Biology, School of Biological Sciences, University of California, PO Box 2525, Irvine, CA 92697-2525, U.S.A. **Online address:** mrrose@uci.edu

ROSE, Mike. American (born United States), b. 1944?. **Genres:** Education, Literary Criticism And History. **Career:** University of California, Graduate School of Education and Information Studies, Social Research Methodology Division, Department of Education, professor of social research methodology and associate director of writing programs. Writer. **Publications:** Writer's Block: The Cognitive Dimension, 1984; (ed.) When a Writer Can't Write: Studies in Writer's Block and Other Composing-Process Problems, 1985; (ed. with E.R. Kintgen and B.M. Kroll) Perspectives on Literacy, 1988; Lives on the Boundary: The Struggles and Achievements of America's Underprepared, 1989, rev. ed. as Lives on the Boundary: A Moving Account of the Struggles and Achievements of America's Educationally Unprepared, 2005; (with M. Kiniry) Critical Strategies for Academic Writing: Cases, Assignments, and Readings, 1990, 3rd ed. as Critical Strategies for Academic Thinking and Writing: A Text with Readings, 1998; Possible Lives: The Promise of Public Education in America, 1995; (ed. with E.R. Kintgen, E. Cushman and B.M. Kroll) Literacy: A Critical Sourcebook, 2001; The Mind at Work: Valuing the Intelligence of the American Worker, 2004; Open Language: Selected Writing on Literacy, Learning, and Opportunity, 2006; Why School?: Reclaiming Education for All of Us, 2009. Contributor to periodicals and journals. **Address:** School of Education and Information Studies, University of California, 2005D Moore Hall, 405 Hilgard Ave., PO Box 951521, Los Angeles, CA 90095-1521, U.S.A. **Online address:** mrose@gseis.ucla.edu

ROSE, M. L. See **MCLAREY, Myra.**

ROSE, Nikolas S. British (born England), b. 1947?. **Genres:** Philosophy, Sociology. **Career:** University of London, Goldsmiths College, professor; London School of Economics, James Martin White professor of sociology, BIOS Centre for the Study of Bioscience, Biomedicine, Biotechnology and Society, director, 2003-; Economy and Society, managing editor, 1996-2004; History of the Present Research Network, co-ordinator; Writer, educator and psychologist. **Publications:** Ten Therapeutic Playgroups: a Preliminary Study of the Children Attending and Their Families, 1973; The Psychological Complex: Psychology, Politics and Society in England, 1869-1939, 1985; Governing the Soul: The Shaping of the Private Self, 1990; Inventing Our Selves: Psychology, Power and Personhood, 1996; Powers of Freedom: Reframing Political Thought, 1999; (as Nikolas Rose) The Politics of Life Itself: Biomedicine,

Power and Subjectivity in the Twenty-first Century, 2006. EDITOR: (with P. Miller) The Power of Psychiatry, 1986; (with A. Barry and T. Osborne) Foucault and Political Reason: Liberalism, Neo-liberalism and Rationalities of Government, 1996; (with E.F. Isin and T. Osborne) Governing Cities: Liberalism, Neoliberalism, Advanced Liberalism, 1998; (with P. Rabinow) The Essential Foucault: Selections from Essential Works of Foucault, 1954-1984, 2003. Contributor of articles to journals and books. **Address:** Department of Sociology, London School of Economics, Houghton St., London, WC2A 2AE, England. **Online address:** n.rose@lse.ac.uk

ROSE, Norman Anthony. Israeli/British (born England), b. 1934. **Genres:** History, International Relations/Current Affairs, Biography. **Career:** The Weizmann Letters, senior research editor, 1968-70; Hebrew University, lecturer, 1971-74, senior lecturer, 1974-78, associate professor, 1978-82, Chaim Weizmann professor of international relations, 1982-2003, now professor emeritus, 2003-; Royal Historical Society, fellow. **Publications:** The Gentile Zionists: A Study in Anglo-Zionist Diplomacy 1929-39, 1973; Vansittart: Study of a Diplomat, 1978; Lewis Namier and Zionism, 1980; Chaim Weizmann: A Biography, 1986; Churchill: An Unruly Life, 1994; Churchill: The Unruly Giant, 1995; The Cliveden Set: Portrait of an Exclusive Fraternity, 2000; Harold Nicolson, 2005; A Senseless, Squalid War: Voices from Palestine, 1945-1948, 2009. EDITOR: Baffy: The Diaries of Blanche Dugdale 1936-1947, 1973; The Letters of Chaim Weizmann Jan. 1939-June 1940, 1980; From Palmerston to Balfour: Collected Essays of Meyir Verete, 1992. **Address:** Department of International Relations, Hebrew University, Mount Scopus, Jerusalem, 91905, Israel. **Online address:** msrose@mscc.huji.ac.il

ROSE, Paul. British (born England), b. 1951?. **Genres:** Natural History. **Career:** British Broadcasting Corp., television presenter; British Antarctic Survey, Rothera Research Station, base commander. Writer and explorer. **Publications:** (With A. Laking) Oceans: Exploring the Hidden Depths of the Underwater World, 2008. **Address:** c/o Rosemary Scoular, United Agents, 12-26 Lexington St., London, GL W1F OLE, England.

ROSE, Paul (Bernard). British (born England), b. 1935. **Genres:** History, Law, Politics/Government, Social Sciences, Criminology/True Crime, Philosophy. **Career:** Cooperative Union Ltd., legal adviser, 1957-60; Salford University, lecturer, 1960-62; practicing barrister, 1963-89; deputy circuit judge, 1975-88; H.M. Coroner, staff, 1988-2001; Manchester Left Club, chairman. Writer. **Publications:** Law Relating to Industrial and Provident Societies, 1962; Weights and Measures Law, 1964; The Manchester Martyrs, 1970; The Moonies Unmasked, 1981; History of the Fenian in England, 1980; The Westminster Treadmill, 1980; Backbencher's Dilemma, 1981; (with P. Quinlivan) The Fenians in England, 1865-1872: A Sense of Insecurity, 1982. Contributor to journals and newspapers. **Address:** Lynnden, 70 Amersham Rd., Chalfont St. Peter, BK SL9 0PB, England. **Online address:** ari2612@aol.com

ROSE, Peter I(saac). American (born United States), b. 1933. **Genres:** Cultural/Ethnic Topics, Race Relations, Sociology, Travel/Exploration, Autobiography/Memoirs. **Career:** Goucher College, instructor, 1958-60; Smith College, assistant professor, 1960-63, associate professor, 1963-67, professor, 1967-73, Sophia Smith professor of sociology and anthropology, 1973-2003, American Studies Diploma Program, director, 1975-2003, Sophia Smith professor emeritus, 2003-, Kahn Liberal Arts Institute, senior fellow, 2000-; University of Leicester, visiting professor, 1964-65, Fulbright professor; Random House Publishers, consulting editor, 1965-80; University of Massachusetts, graduate faculty, 1965; Wesleyan University, visiting professor, 1966-67; Social Problems, associate editor, 1967-70; Yale University, visiting professor, 1969; Flinders University, visiting professor, 1970; Clark University, visiting professor, 1970-71; Time-Life Books, editorial consultant, 1972-77; Harvard University, visiting professor, 1983-84; Journal of Refugee Studies, associate editor, 1987-91; University of Vienna, visiting professor, 2004. **Publications:** They and We, 1964, 6th ed., 2006; The Study of Society, 1967, 4th ed., 1977; The Subject Is Race, 1968; Many Peoples, One Nations, 1973; (with M. Glazer and P.M. Glazer) Sociology: Inquiring into Society, 1977, 3rd ed., 1988; Strangers in Their Midst, 1977; Mainstream and Margins, 1983; Tempest-Tost, 1997; Guest Appearances and Other Travels in Time and Space, 2003. EDITOR: The Ghetto and Beyond (essays), 1969; Americans from Africa, vol. I: Slavery and Its Aftermath, 1970, vol. II: Old Memories, New Moods, 1970; Nation of Nations, 1972; Seeing Ourselves, 1972, 2nd ed., 1975; (with S. Rothman and W.J. Wilson) Through Different Eyes, 1973; Views from Abroad, 1978; Socialization and the Life Cycle, 1979; Working with Refugees, 1986; Interminority Affairs in the U.S., 1993; Professorial

Passions, 1997; Guest Appearances and Other Travels in Time and Space, 2003, The Disappeared, 2005; Dispossessed: An Anatomy of Exile, 2005; With Few Reservations, 2010. **Address:** Department of Sociology, Smith College, Lilly Hall B04, Northampton, MA 01063, U.S.A. **Online address:** prose@smith.edu

ROSE, Phyllis. American (born United States), b. 1942. **Genres:** Literary Criticism And History, Women's Studies And Issues, Autobiography/Memoirs, Biography, Essays, Human Relations/Parenting, Young Adult Fiction. **Career:** Harvard University, teaching fellow, 1966-67; Yale University, acting instructor, 1969; Wesleyan University, assistant professor, 1969-76, associate professor, 1976-82, professor of English, 1982-2005, professor emeritus, 2005-; University of California, visiting professor, 1981-82. Writer. **Publications:** Woman of Letters: A Life of Virginia Woolf, 1978; Parallel Lives: Five Victorian Marriages, 1983; Writing of Women: Essays in a Renaissance (literary criticism), 1985; Jazz Cleopatra: Josephine Baker in Her Time, 1989; Never Say Goodbye: Essays, 1990; (ed.) The Norton Book of Women's Lives, 1993; Year of Reading Proust: A Memoir in Real Time, 1997; (contrib.) Julia Margaret Cameron's Women, 1998; (intro.) May Stevens, 2005. **Address:** Georges Borchardt Inc., 136 E 57th St., New York, NY 10022-2707, U.S.A. **Online address:** prose@wesleyan.edu

ROSE, Richard. American (born United States), b. 1933. **Genres:** International Relations/Current Affairs, Politics/Government. **Career:** St. Louis Post-Dispatch, reporter, 1955-57; University of Manchester, lecturer in government, 1961-66; University of Strathclyde, professor of politics, 1966-76, Centre for the Study of Public Policy, director, 1976-2005, professor of public policy, 1982-; Stanford University, fellow, 1967; Woodrow Wilson Center, fellow, 1974; Brookings Institution, fellow, 1976; European University Institute, visiting professor, 1977-78, 2011-; American Enterprise Institute, fellow, 1980; International Monetary Fund, fellow, 1984; Journal of Public Policy, editor, 1985-; Johns Hopkins University, Hinkley professor, 1987; Wissenschaftszentrum, visiting professor, 1988-90; British Academy, fellow, 1992; University of Oxford, Oxford Internet Institute, senior fellow, Nuffield College, associate, 2003-05; University of Aberdeen, Centre for the Study of Public Policy, director, 2005-, professor of politics, 2005-. **Publications:** (With D.E. Butler) The British General Election of 1959, 1960; (with M. Abrams) Must Labour Lose?, 1960; Politics in England, 1964, 5th ed., 1989; Influencing Voters: A Study of Campaign Rationality, 1967; Class and Party Divisions: Britain as a Test Case, 1968; People in Politics, 1970; The United Kingdom as a Multi-National State, 1970; Governing without Consensus, 1971; (with T.T. Mackie) International Almanac of Electoral History, 1974, 3rd ed., 1991; The Problem of Party Government, 1975; Northern Ireland: Time of Choice, 1976; Managing Presidential Objectives, 1976; Ordinary People in Extraordinary Economic Circumstances, 1977; What Is Governing?: Purpose and Policy in Washington, 1978; From Steady State to Fluid State: The Unity of the Kingdom Today, 1978; (co-author) Elections without Choice, 1978; (with P. Mair and I. McAllister) Is There a Concurring Majority about Northern Ireland?, 1978; (with G. Peters) The Juggernaut of Incrementalism: A Comparative Perspective on the Growth of Public Policy, 1978; (with G. Peters) Can Government Go Bankrupt?, 1978; Towards Normality: Public Opinion Polls in the 1979 Election, 1979; (with I. McAllister and R. Parry) United Kingdom Rankings: The Territorial Dimension in Social Indicators, 1979; (co-author) Britain: Progress and Decline, 1980; (co-author) Presidents and Prime Ministers, 1980; Do Parties Make a Difference?, 1980; (with I. McAllister) United Kingdom Facts, 1982; (co-author) The Territorial Dimension in United Kingdom Politics, 1982; (co-author) Fiscal Stress in Cities, 1982; Understanding the United Kingdom, 1982; (with I. McAllister) The Nationwide Competition for Votes, 1984; Understanding Big Government, 1984; (with T. Karran) Inertia or Incrementalism?: A Long-Term View of the Growth of Government, 1984; National Pride: Cross-National Surveys, 1984; (with I. McAllister) European Parliament Constituencies in Britain in 1984, 1984; (with T.T. Mackie) Do Parties Persist or Disappear?: The Big Tradeoff Facing Organizations, 1984; Public Employment in Western Nations, 1985; (with I. McAllister) Voters Begin to Choose, 1986; (with R. Shiratori) Welfare State East and West, 1986; (with D. Van Mechelen) Patterns of Parliamentary Legislation, 1986; Ministers and Ministries, 1987; (with T. Karran) Taxation by Political Inertia, 1987; The Postmodern President, 1988, 2nd ed., 1991; Ordinary People in Public Policy, 1989; Prime Ministers in Parliamentary Democracies, 1990; Evaluating the Presidency: A Positive-and-Normative Approach, 1990; (co-author) Training without Trainers?, 1990; (with I. McAllister) The Loyalties of Voters: A Lifetime Learning Model, 1990; Lesson-Drawing in Public Policy, 1993; (with P. Davies) Inheritance in Public

Policy: Change without Choice in Britain, 1994; What Is Europe?: A Dynamic Perspective, 1996; (with S. White and I. McAllister) How Russia Votes, 1997; (with W. Mishler and C. Haerpfer) Democracy and Its Alternatives: Understanding Post-Communist Societies, 1998; International Encyclopedia of Elections, 2000; The Prime Minister in a Shrinking World, 2001; (with N. Munro) Elections without Order: Russia's Challenge to Vladimir Putin, 2002; (with N. Munro) Elections and Parties in New European Democracies, 2003; Learning from Comparative Public Policy: a Practical Guide, 2005; (with N. Munro and W. Mishler) Russia Transformed: Developing Popular Support for a New Regime, 2006; Political Behaviour in Time and Space, 2006; Internet Diffusion in Russia: A Model of a Laggard Catching Up, 2006; Understanding Post-Communist Transformation: A Bottom Up Approach, 2009; (with W. Mishler and N. Munro) Popular Support for an Undemocratic Regime: The Changing Views of Russians, 2011. EDITOR: Studies in British Politics: A Reader in Political Sociology, 1966, 3rd ed., 1976; Policy-making in Britain, 1969; The Polls and the 1970; Election, 1970; (with M. Dogan) European Politics: A Reader, 1971; Electoral Behavior: A Comparative Handbook, 1973; Lessons from America: An Exploration, 1974; The Management of Urban Change in Britain and Germany, 1974; The Dynamics of Public Policy: A Comparative Policy, 1976; (with J. Wiatr) Comparing Public Policies, 1977; (with D. Kavanagh) New Trends in British Politics, 1977; Challenge to Governance, 1980; Electoral Participation, 1980. **Address:** School of Social Science, University of Aberdeen, Edward Wright Bldg., Aberdeen, AB24 3QY, Scotland. **Online address:** prof_r_rose@yahoo.co.uk

ROSE, Steven. British (born England), b. 1938. **Genres:** Biology, Sciences, Natural History. **Career:** Open University, professor of biology, neurobiologist, Brain Research Group, head, 1969-99, professor emeritus, 1999-; Australian National University, visiting professor; Harvard University, visiting professor; University of Minnesota, visiting professor; San Francisco Exploratorium, visiting professor; Academica Sinica, visiting professor; University College, Department of Anatomy, visiting professor, Developmental Biology, visiting professor; Gresham College, joint professor of physick, now professor emeritus of physick. Writer. **Publications:** The Chemistry of Life, 1966, 2nd ed., 1979; (with H. Rose) Science and Society, 1969; The Conscious Brain, 1973, rev. ed., 1988; (with R.C. Lewontin and L.J. Kamin) Not in Our Genes: Biology, Ideology, and Human Nature, 1984; (with S. Murphy and A. Hay) No Fire, No Thunder, 1984; Molecules and Minds: Essays on Biology and the Social Order, 1987, rev. ed., 1991; (with R.C. Lewontin and L.J. Kamin) Not in Our Genes: Biology, The Making of Memory: From Molecules to Mind, 1993; (with M. Rolph) Brain Box, 1997; Lifelines: Biology Beyond Determinism, 1998; Lifelines: Life Beyond the Gene, 2003; The Future of the Brain: The Promise and Perils of Tomorrow's Neuroscience, 2005; The 21st-century Brain: Explaining, Mending and Manipulating the Mind, 2005. EDITOR: (with Z. Lodin) Macromolecules and the Function of the Neuron; Proceedings, 1968; C.B.W., 1968; (with N. Chalmers and R. Crawley) The Biological Bases of Behaviour, 1971; (ed. with L.L. Iversen and B. Pearce) Biochemistry and Mental Illness, 1973; (with H. Rose) Radicalisation of Science, 1976; (with H. Rose) Political Economy of Science, 1976; (with H. Rose) Ideology of/in the Natural Sciences, 1980; Against Biological Determinism, 1982; Towards a Liberatory Biology, 1982; (with L. Appignanesi) Science and Beyond, 1986; From Brains to Consciousness?: Essays on the New Sciences of the Mind, 1998; (with H. Rose) Alas, Poor Darwin, 2000; (with D. Rees) The New Brain Sciences: Perils and Prospects, 2004; (with P. McGarr and intro.) The Richness of Life: The Essential Stephen Jay Gould, 2006. **Address:** Department of Life Sciences, The Open University, PO Box 197, Milton Keynes, BK MK7 6AA, England. **Online address:** s.p.r.rose@open.ac.uk

ROSE, Tricia. American (born United States) **Genres:** Sex, Race Relations, Social Sciences. **Career:** New York University, assistant professor of history and Africana studies, through 2002; University of California, professor of American studies, 2002-, department chair, 2003-; Brown University, professor of Africana Studies, chair. Writer. **Publications:** Black Noise: Rap Music and Black Culture in Contemporary America, 1994; (ed. with A. Ross) Microphone Fiends: Youth Music and Youth Culture, 1994; (comp.) Longing to Tell: Black Women Talk about Sexuality and Intimacy, 2003; Hip Hop Wars: What We Talk about When We Talk about Hip Hop, 2008. Contributor to books. **Address:** Department of Africana Studies, Brown University, 115 Angell St., PO Box 1904, Providence, RI 02912, U.S.A. **Online address:** tricia_rose@brown.edu

ROSEGRANT, Susan. American (born United States), b. 1954. **Genres:**

Business/Trade/Industry, Young Adult Non-fiction, Biography, History. **Career:** Business Week, correspondent, 1982-84; freelance writer, 1984-90; Harvard University, Harvard Business School, writer, 1990-93, Kennedy School of Government, case writer, 1993-2007; University of Michigan, Residential College, lecturer creative writing, 2007-. **Publications:** (With D. Lampe) Route 128: Lessons from Boston's High-Tech Community, 1992; AT&T: The Dallas Works, 1992; Gulf Crisis: Building a Coalition for War, 1994; Carrots, Sticks, and Question Marks: Negotiating the North Korean Nuclear Crisis, 1995; A Seamless Transition: United States and United Nations Operations in Somalia, 1992-1993, 1996; Getting to Dayton: Negotiating an End to the War in Bosnia, 1996; Banana Wars: Challenges to the European Union's Banana Regime, 1999; The Flawed Emergency Response to the 1992 Los Angeles Riots, 2000; Testing the Reach of International Law: The Effort to Extradite General Augusto Pinochet to Spain, 2000; (with M. Watkins) Breakthrough International Negotiation: How Great Negotiators Transformed the World's Toughest Post-Cold War Conflicts, 2001; The Shootings at Columbine High School: Responding to a New Kind of Terrorism, 2001; Standing up for Steel: The U.S. Government Response to Steel Industry and Union Efforts to Win Protection from Imports (1998-2001), 2002. **Address:** Residential College, University of Michigan, 135 Greene, E Quadrangle, 701 E University, Ann Arbor, MI 48109-1245, U.S.A. **Online address:** rosegran@umich.edu

ROSELL, Steven A. Canadian (born Canada) **Genres:** Politics/Government, Education, Law. **Career:** Viewpoint Learning Inc., president and co-founder; Meridian International Institute, president. Writer. **Publications:** (Co-author and ed.) Governing in an Information Society, 1992; (co-author) Changing Maps: Governing in a World of Rapid Change, 1995; Renewing Governance: Governing by Learning in the Information Age, 1999. **Address:** Viewpoint Learning Inc., 4660 La Jolla Village Dr., Ste. 700, San Diego, CA 92122, U.S.A. **Online address:** srosell@viewpointlearning.com

ROSELLE, Mike. American (born United States), b. 1954?. **Genres:** Social Sciences. **Career:** Earth First! (an activist organization), co-founder, 1980; Greenpeace, forest campaign coordinator, 1986-90, rapid response team director, 1990-98; Ruckus Society (an activist organization), co-founder, 1995. Writer and memoirist. **Publications:** (With J. Mahan) Tree Spiker: From Earth First! to Lowbagging: My Struggles in Radical Environmental Action, 2009. **Address:** Missoula, MT , U.S.A. **Online address:** roselle@lowbagger.org

ROSEMURGY, Catie. American (born United States), b. 1969. **Genres:** Poetry. **Career:** Northwest Missouri State University, assistant professor of English; College of New Jersey, Department of English, assistant professor of creative writing, associate professor. Writer. **Publications:** My Favorite Apocalypse: Poems, 2001; The Stranger Manual: Poems, 2010. Works appear in anthologies. **Address:** Department of English, College of New Jersey, 129 Bliss Hall, 2000 Pennington Rd., PO Box 7718, Ewing, NJ 08628, U.S.A. **Online address:** rose@tcnj.edu

ROSEN, David J. American (born United States) **Genres:** Young Adult Fiction, Novels, Literary Criticism And History. **Career:** MTV, advertising director, producer. Writer. **Publications:** I Just Want My Pants Back (novel), 2007; What's That Job and How the Hell Do I Get It?: The Inside Scoop on More Than 50 Cool Jobs from People Who Actually Have Them, 2008. Contributor to magazines. **Address:** Broadway Books, 1745 Broadway, New York, NY 10019, U.S.A. **Online address:** rosen@ijustwantmypantsback.com

ROSEN, James. American (born United States), b. 1960. **Genres:** Novels. **Career:** WWOR-TV, associate producer; Columbia Broadcasting System Inc, researcher and managing editor; Fox Broadcasting Co., Washington correspondent, 1999-. Journalist and news researcher. **Publications:** The Strong Man: John Mitchell and the Secrets of Watergate, 2008. Contributor to books and periodicals. **Address:** Writers' Representatives L.L.C., 116 W 14th St., 11th Fl., New York, NY 10011-7305, U.S.A.

ROSEN, Jeffrey. American (born United States), b. 1964. **Genres:** Law, Young Adult Non-fiction. **Career:** The New Republic, legal affairs editor, 1992-; George Washington University, Law School, associate professor, 1997-2003, professor of law, 2004-; New Yorker, staff writer, 1997-99; The Brookings Institution, nonresident senior fellow, 2008-. **Publications:** The Unwanted Gaze: The Destruction of Privacy in America, 2000; The Naked Crowd: Reclaiming Security and Freedom in an Anxious Age, 2004; The Most Democratic Branch: How the Courts Serve America, 2006; Supreme Court: The Personalities and Rivalries that Defined America, 2007; (ed. with

B. Wittes) Constitution 3.0: Freedom and Technological Change, 2011; Louis Brandeis: An Interpretative Biography, forthcoming. **Address:** Law School, George Washington University, 2000 H St. NW, Washington, DC 20052, U.S.A. **Online address:** jrosen@law.gwu.edu

ROSEN, Leora N(adine). American/South African (born South Africa), b. 1950. **Genres:** Psychology, Social Commentary, Adult Non-fiction, Military/Defense/Arms Control. **Career:** University of the Witwatersrand, lecturer in social anthropology, 1974-75; New York State Psychiatric Institute, research assistant in lithium clinic, 1977-78, research assistant in child psychiatry, 1978; Psychiatric Institutes of Washington, research assistant, 1981-85; Walter Reed Army Institute of Research, department of military psychiatry, research social scientist, 1985-98; National Institute of Justice, Social Science Program, manager, Violence and Victimization Research Division, social science analyst, 1998-. Writer. **Publications:** (With M. Etlin) The Hostage Child: Sex Abuse Allegations in Custody Disputes, 1996; (ed. with J.A. Martin and L.R. Sparacino) The Military Family: A Practice Guide for Human Service Providers, 2000. Contributor to professional journals. **Address:** U.S. Department of Justice, National Institute of Justice, 810 7th St. NW., 8th Fl., Washington, DC 20531, U.S.A. **Online address:** leora.rosen@usdoj.gov

ROSEN, Louis H. American (born United States), b. 1955. **Genres:** Novels, Music, History. **Career:** New York University, adjunct assistant professor of arts. Composer, lyricist, librettist and author. **Publications:** The Ugly Duckling, 1984; Book of the Night, 1991; A Child's Garden, 1996; The South Side: The Racial Transformation of an American Neighborhood, 1998. **Address:** School of Continuing and Professional Studies, New York University, Rm. 201, 145 4th Ave., New York, NY 10003-4906, U.S.A.

ROSEN, Michael J(oel). American (born United States), b. 1954. **Genres:** Novels, Children's Fiction, Poetry, Animals/Pets, Young Adult Fiction, Novellas/Short Stories, Humor/Satire, Illustrations, Picture/Board Books. **Career:** Leo Yassenoff Jewish Center, director, program coordinator, administrator of children's services, 1973-78; Ohio State University, instructor, 1978-84, lecturer, 1983, 1985; freelance illustrator and designer, 1981-; Thurber House, literary director, 1983-; Jefferson Center for Learning and the Arts, design consultant, 1982-. Writer and illustrator. **Publications:** A Drink at the Mirage (poems), 1985; Elijah's Angel (juvenile), 1992; The Company of Cats, 1992; Kids' Best Dog Book, 1993; The Greatest Table (children's), 1994; Bonesy and Isabel, 1994; All Eyes on the Pond, 1994; A School for Pompey Walker (children's), 1995; Penn: The Stories of Gordon Penn (poetry), 1996; Purr... Children's Book Illustrators Brag about Their Cats, 1996; Telling Things (poetry), 1997; The Genius of James Thurber (anthology), 1997; The Heart is Big Enough: Five Stories (children's), 1997; Winter Stripes (picture book), 1997; The Dog Who Walked with God, 1998; Avalanche, 1998; With a Dog like That, A Kid Like Me, 2000; Our Eight Nights of Hanukkah, 2000; Blessing of the Animals, 2000; ChaseR: A Novel in E-Mails, 2002; (with S. Reiss) Midnight Snacks: 150 Easy and Enticing Alternatives to Standing by the Freezer Eating Ice Cream with a Spoon, 2002; (with S. Reiss) Midnight Snacks, 2002; Cooking from the Heart: 100 Great American Chefs Share Recipes They Cherish, 2003; Baking from the Heart: Our Nation's Best Bakers Share Cherished Recipes for the Great American Bake Sale, 2004; The 60-Second Encyclopedia, 2005; Fishing with Dad: Lessons of Love and Lure from Father to Son, 2005; Three Feet Small, 2005; Balls!, 2006; Drive in the Country, 2007; Don't Shoot!, 2007; Our Farm: Four Seasons with Five Kids on One Family's Farm, 2008; Balls!: Round 2, 2008; (with B. Kassoy) No Dribbling the Squid: Octopush, Shin Kicking, Elephant Polo and Other Oddball Sports, 2009; The Cuckoo's Haiku and Other Birding Poems, 2009; Cuckoo's Haiku, 2009; Night of the Pumpkinheads, 2011; The Hound Dog's Haiku and Other Poems for Dog Lovers, 2011. EDITOR: Collecting Himself: James Thurber on Writing and Writers, Humor and Himself, 1989; The Company of Dogs: 21 Stories by Contemporary Masters, 1990; Home (writings and drawings by contemporary children's authors), 1991; SPEAK! Children's Book Illustrators Brag about Their Dogs, 1993; The Company of Animals, 1993; People Have More Fun Than Anybody: A Centennial Collection of James Thurber's Works, 1994; Dog People: Portraits of Canine Companionship (anthology), 1995; Food Fight: Poets Join the Fight against Hunger with Poems to Favorite Foods, 1996; Horse People: Writers and Artists on the Horses They Love, 1998; My Bug: For Everyone who Owned, Loved, or Shared a VW Beetle, 1999; Mirth of a Nation: The Best Contemporary Humor, 2000; 21st Century Dog: A Visionary Compendium, 2000; The Dog Department, 2001; Chanukah Lights Everywhere, 2001; 101 Damnations: The Humorist's Tour of Personal Hells, 2002; More Mirth of a Nation: The Best Contemporary Humor, 2002;

May Contain Nuts: A Very Loose Canon of American Humor, 2004; Dogs We Love, 2008. SELF-ILLUSTRATED: 50 Odd Jobs, 1988; The Kids' Book of Fishing, 1991. Works appear in anthologies. **Address:** c/o Author Mail, HarperCollins Publisher, 10 E 53rd St., 7th Fl., New York, NY 10022, U.S.A.

ROSEN, Michael (Wayne). British (born England), b. 1946. **Genres:** Novellas/Short Stories, Children's Fiction, Plays/Screenplays, Poetry, Humor/Satire. **Career:** Freelance writer and broadcaster, 1982-; University of London, visiting professor of children's literature. **Publications:** CHILDREN'S FICTION: Once There Was a King Who Promised He Would Never Chop Anybody's Head Off, 1976; The Bakerloo Flea, 1979; Nasty!, 1982, rev. ed., 1984; Hairy Tales and Nursery Crimes, 1984; How to Get out of the Bath and Other Problems, 1984; Under the Bed, 1986; Smelly Jelly Smelly Fish (miscellany), 1986; Hard-Boiled Legs, 1987; You're Thinking about Doughnuts, 1987; Spollyollytiddlydiddlyitis, 1987, as Down at the Doctors, 1987; Norma and the Washing Machine, 1988; Beep Beep!: Here Come-The Horribles!, 1988; The Class Two Monster, 1989; We're Going on a Bear Hunt, 1989; The Golem of Old Prague (stories), 1990; The Royal Huddle, 1990; The Royal Muddle (stories), 1990; Clever Cakes (stories), 1991; The Deadman Tapes, 1991; Burping Bertha, 1993; Songbird Story, 1993; Moving, 1993; Dad's Fig Bar, 1994; The Arabian Frights and Other Gories, 1994; Off the Wall, 1994; The Old Woman and the Pumpkin, 1994; Lisa's Letter, 1994; Even Stevens, F.C., 1995; This Is Our House, 1996; Snore, 1998; Rover, 1999; Mission Ziffoid, 1999; Lovely Old Roly, 2001; William Shakespeare, 2001; Two European Tales, 2001; Zoomababy: And the Mission to Mars, 2001; Bear's Day Out, 2007. CHILDREN'S POETRY: Mind Your Own Business, 1974; (with R. McGough) You Tell Me, 1979; Wouldn't You Like to Know, 1981; You Can't Catch Me!, 1981; I See a Voice (on poetry), 1981; (ed. with S. Steele) Inky Pinky Ponky, 1982; Quick, Let's Get Out of Here, 1983; Bloody L.I.A.R.S, 1984; Don't Put Mustard in the Custard, 1985; When Did You Last Wash Your Feet?, 1986; The Hypnotiser, 1988; Freckly Feet and Itchy Knees, 1990; Never Mind!, 1990; Who Drew on the Baby's Head?, 1991; Mind the Gap, 1992; Nuts about Nuts, 1993; You Are, Aren't You?, 1993; The Best of Michael Rosen, 1995; Michael Rosen's ABC, 1996; The Zoo at Night, 1996; The Skin of Your Back, 1996; You Wait till I'm Older Than You, 1996; Michael Rosen's Book of Nonsense, 1997; Tea in the Sugar Bowl: Potato in My Shoe, 1997; Lunch Boxes Don't Fly, 1999; Even More Nonsense, 2000; Centrally Heated Knickers, 2000; Uncle Billy Being Silly, 2001; Carrying the Elephant, 2002; No Breathing in Class, 2002. EDITOR: (with D. Jackson) Speaking to You (for children), 1984; Poetry, 1985; Kingfisher Book of Children's Poetry, 1985; (with J. Griffiths) That'd Be Telling (stories), 1986; A Spider Bought a Bicycle (for children), 1987; A Spider Bought a Bicycle, and Other Poems for Young Children, 1987; Kingfisher Book of Funny Stories, 1988; Experiences, 1989; Tell Tales, 1989; Culture Shock, 1990; Dirty Ditties, 1990; Stories from Overseas/Histoires d'outre-mer (folk tales), 1990; Give Me Shelter, 1991; Mini Beasties, 1991 as Itsy-Bitsy Beasties, 1992; Vulgar Verses, 1991; (with D. Widgery) The Chatto Book of Dissent, 1991; A World of Poetry, 1991; Rude Rhymes, 1992; South and North, East and West, The Oxfam Book of Children's Stories, 1992; Action Replay, 1993; Poems for the Very Young, 1993; A Different Story: Poems from the Past, 1994; Pilly Soems, as Michael Rosen's Book of Very Silly Poems, 1994; The Penguin of Childhood, 1994; Rude Rhymes II, 1994; Penguin Book of Childhood, 1994; Walking the Bridge of Your Nose, 1995; (with M. Barrs) A Year with Poetry, 1997; A Different Story, 1997; Classic Poetry, 1998; Night-Night Knight, 1998; Funny Stories, 2004; Poems for the Very Young, 2004; Ribticklers: Funny Stories, 2007. RETELLING OF FOLK TALES: A Cat and Mouse Story, 1982; The Wicked Tricks of Till Owlyglass, 1989; Little Rabbit Foo Foo, 1990; How the Animals Got Their Colours, 1991; How the Giraffe Got Such a Long Neck, 1993; Crow and Hawk, 1995. OTHER: Backbone, 1968; Did I Hear You Write?, 1987; (with Q. Blake) Spollyollydiddlytiddlyitis, 1987; Silly Stories (jokes), 1988; Goodies and Daddies, An A-Z Guide to Fatherhood, 1991; (ed.) Sonsense Nongs (song book), 1992; (with J. Burridge) Treasure Islands II, 1993; Rap with Rosen, 1995; Figgy Roll, 1995; (ed.) The Secret Life of Schools, 1997; (with S. Elmes) Word of Mouth, 2002; Howler, 2004; (with J. Ray) Shakespeare's Romeo & Juliet, 2004; Dickens: His Work and his World, 2005; Fantastically Funny Stories, 2005; Michael Rosen's Sad Book, 2005; Totally Wonderful Miss Plumberry, 2006; Fighters for Life, 2007; Red Ted and the Lost Things, 2009; I'm Number One, 2009; Bear Flies High, 2009; Michael's Big Book of Bad Things, 2009; Tiny Little Fly, 2010; All About Me, 2010; Roald Dahl Biography, 2011; Bananas in My Ears, 2011; Dear Fairy Godmother, 2011; Even My Ears are Smiling, 2011;

Chanukah Lights, 2011; Hairy Tales and Nursery Crimes and Arabian Frights and Other Gories, 2011. Contributor to periodicals. **Address:** Peter, Fraser & Dunlop Group Ltd., Drury House, 34-43 Russell St., London, GL WC2B 5HA, England. **Online address:** michael@michaelrosen.co.uk

ROSEN, Robert H. American (born United States), b. 1955. **Genres:** Human Relations/Parenting, Psychiatry, Business/Trade/Industry, Psychology. **Career:** George Washington University, assistant clinical professor of psychiatry, 1984-85; Healthy Companies Institute, president, 1986-90; Healthy Companies Intl., chairman, founder and chief executive officer, 1987-, author and speaker, 1991-2008; University of Virginia, Darden School Business, Batten fellow. **Publications:** Healthy Companies: A Human Resources Approach, 1986; (with L. Berger) The Healthy Company: Eight Strategies for Developing People, Productivity, and Profits, 1991; (with P. Brown) Leading People: Transforming Business from the Inside Out, 1996; (co-author) Global Literacy: Lessons on Business Leadership and National Cultures: A Landmark Study of Ceos From 28 Countries, 2000; Just Enough Anxiety: The Hidden Driver of Business Success, 2008; (with J. Liedtka and R. Wiltbank) Cracking the Growth Code, 2009; (with J. Liedtka and R. Wiltbank) The Catalyst: How You Can Become an Extraordinary Growth Leader, 2009. Contributor to magazines and newspapers. **Address:** Healthy Companies Intl., 2101 Wilson Blvd., Ste. 1002, Arlington, VA 22201-3062, U.S.A. **Online address:** bob.rosen@healthycompanies.com

ROSEN, Selina. American (born United States), b. 1960. **Genres:** Novels, Young Adult Non-fiction, Horror. **Career:** Yard Dog Press, founder, Writer and educator. **Publications:** HOST SERIES: Host, 1997; Fright Eater, 1998, 2nd ed., 2007; Gang Approval, 1999, 2nd ed., 2008; Sword Masters, 2007; Chains of Redemption, 2008; Jabone's Sword, 2010. FANTASY, HORROR AND SCIENCE FICTION NOVELS AND NOVELLAS: Queen of Denial, 1999; The Boat Man (novella), 1999; The Bubba Chronicles; Chains of Freedom, 2001; Hammer Town, 2002, 2nd ed., 2006; Chains of Destruction, 2002; Recycled (sequel to Queen of Denial), 2003; Fire & Ice, 2003; Reruns, 2004; Material Things (novella), 2004; Strange Robby, 2006; (with L.J. Underwood) Bad Lands: A Holmes & Storm Mystery, 2007; Bad City, 2012. EDITOR: Stories That Won't Make Your Parents Hurl, 2000; Bubbas of the Apocalypse, 2001; More Stories That Won't Make Your Parents Hurl, 2002; Four Bubbas of the Apocalypse, 2003; Shadows in Green, 2004; International House of Bubbas, 2005; Houston: We've Got Bubbas!, 2007; The Best of the Bubbas of the Apocalypse, 2008; A Bubba In Time Saves None, 2009. SHORT FICTION: Marion Zimmer Bradley's Sword & Sorcery; Thieves' World; Chicks in Chain Mail; Witch Way to the Mall; Space Sirens, 2009. **Address:** Yard Dog Press, 710 W. Redbud Ln., Alma, AR 72921, U.S.A. **Online address:** selinarosen@cox.net

ROSEN, Stanley Howard. American (born United States), b. 1929. **Genres:** Poetry, Philosophy. **Career:** Pennsylvania State University, instructor, 1956-58, assistant professor, 1958-63, associate professor, 1963-66, professor of philosophy, 1966-94, Evan Pugh professor, Institute for Arts and Humanistic Studies, fellow, 1972-; Metaphysical Society of America, president, 1991; Boston University, professor of philosophy, 1994-, university professor, 1999-, Borden Parker Bowne professor of philosophy, now professor emeritus. Writer. **Publications:** Death in Egypt (poetry), 1950; Plato's Symposium, 1968, 2nd ed., 1987; Nihilism: A Philosophical Essay, 1969; G.W.F. Hegel: An Introduction to the Science of Wisdom, 1974; The Limits of Analysis, 1980; Plato's Sophist: The Drama of Original and Image, 1983; Hermeneutics as Politics, 1987, 2nd ed., 2003; The Quarrel between Philosophy and Poetry, 1988; The Ancients and the Moderns, 1989; The Question of Being, 1993; Plato's Statesman: The Web of Politics, 1995; The Mask of Enlightenment, 1995, 2nd ed., 2004; Metaphysics in Ordinary Language, 1999; (ed.) Examined Life: Readings From Western Philosophy From Plato To Kant, 2000; Elusiveness of The Ordinary: Studies in the Possibility of Philosophy, 2002; Question of Being: A Reversal of Heidegger, 2002; Ancients and the Moderns: Rethinking Modernity, 2002; Plato's Statesman: The Web of Politics, 2002; Plato's Republic: A Study, 2005; La production platonicienne, 2005. **Address:** Department of Philosophy, Boston University, STH 640A, 745 Commonwealth Ave., Boston, MA 02215, U.S.A. **Online address:** srosen@bu.edu

ROSEN, William S. American (born United States), b. 1955. **Genres:** History. **Career:** Macmillan, senior executive, publisher and editor; Free Press, senior executive, publisher and editor; Simon & Schuster, senior executive, publisher and editor. **Publications:** Justinian's Flea: Plague, Empire, and the Birth of Europe, 2007; The Most Powerful Idea in the World: A Story of Steam, Industry, and Invention, 2010. **Address:** Princeton, NJ , U.S.A. **Online address:** bill@justiniansflea.com

ROSENAK, Chuck. American (born United States), b. 1927. **Genres:** Art/Art History, Mythology/Folklore, Literary Criticism And History. **Career:** Rosenak & Rosenak (law firm), partner, 1956-62; Small Business Administration, litigator, 1963-84; Los Caminitos Homeowners Association, board director, 1984-90, president, 1985-86; photographer, writer and art consultant, 1984-. **Publications:** WITH J. ROSENAK: Museum of American Folk Art Encyclopedia of Twentieth-Century American Folk Art and Artists, 1990; The People Speak: Navajo Folk Art, 1994, 3rd ed. as Navajo Folk Art, 2008; Contemporary American Folk Art: A Collector's Guide, 1996; The Saint Makers: Contemporary Santeras Y Santeros, 1998. Contributor to periodicals. **Address:** PO Box 549, Tesuque, NM 87574, U.S.A.

ROSENAK, Jan(ice M.). American (born United States), b. 1930. **Genres:** Art/Art History, Biography, History, Photography. **Career:** Rosenak and Rosenak, attorney, 1956-62; Interstate Commerce Commission, Bureau of Rates and Practices, attorney, 1963-66, commissioner's staff, 1966-72, administrative law judge, 1972-74, Office of Proceedings, deputy director, senior executive service, legislative counsel, 1981-84, Office of Legislative and Governmental Affairs, director, 1984; Senate Commerce Committee, transportation counsel, 1979-81; transportation consultant and writer, 1986-; Homeowners Association, director, 1990-. **Publications:** WITH C. ROSENAK: Museum of American Folk Art Encyclopedia of Twentieth-Century American Folk Art and Artists, 1990; The People Speak: Contemporary Navajo Folk Art, 1994; Contemporary American Folk Art: A Collector's Guide, 1996; Navajo Folk Art: The People Speak, 1998, 3rd ed., 2008; The Saint Makers: Contemporary Sainteras Y Santeros, 1998. Contributor to journals. **Address:** PO Box 549, Tesuque, NM 87574, U.S.A.

ROSENAU, Pauline Vaillancourt. (Pauline Marie Vaillancourt). American/Canadian (born Canada), b. 1943. **Genres:** Medicine/Health, Politics/Government, Social Sciences. **Career:** McGill University, assistant professor, 1969-73; University of Ottawa, visiting professor, 1972; University of Quebec, professor, 1973-93; University of Haute, visiting professor, 1984-85; University of California, visiting professor, 1988; University of Southern California, Center for International Studies, adjunct fellow, 1989; University of Texas, School of Public Health, Houston Health Science Center, professor of management and policy studies and health policy, 1993-. Writer. **Publications:** The Political Socialization of Young People, 1972; Post-Modernism and the Social Sciences: Insights, Inroads and Intrusions, 1992; (ed. and contrib.) Health Reform in the Nineties, 1994; (ed.) Health Care Reform in the Nineties, 1994; (ed. and contrib.) Public/Private Policy Partnerships, 2000; The Competition Paradigm: America's Romance with Contest, Conflict and Commerce, 2003. AS PAULINE MARIE VAILLANCOURT: (ed.) Quebec and the Parti Quebecois, 1979; (co-author) Sondage politique et politiques des sondages au Quebec, 1979; When Marxists Do Research, 1986. Contributor to books and journals. **Address:** School of Public Health, University of Texas, RAS 915-E, 1200 Herman Pressler, PO Box 20186, Houston, TX 77030, U.S.A. **Online address:** pauline.rosenau@uth.tmc.edu

ROSENBAUM, Benjamin. Swiss/American (born United States), b. 1969. **Genres:** Young Adult Fiction, Novellas/Short Stories. **Career:** Digital Addiction, co-founder. Writer and computer programmer. **Publications:** Other Cities (chapbook), 2003; The Ant King and Other Stories, 2008. Works appear in anthologies. Contributor to periodicals. **Address:** Basel, Switzerland. **Online address:** info@benjaminrosenbaum.com

ROSENBERG, Gerald N. American (born United States), b. 1954?. **Genres:** Reference. **Career:** Australian National University, Research School of Social Sciences, visiting fellow, 1995-96; Xiamen University Law School, Fulbright professor, 2003-04; Northwestern University School of Law, Jack N. Pritzker distinguished visiting professor of law; University of Chicago, associate professor of political science and lecturer in law; Yale University, faculty. Writer. **Publications:** The Hollow Hope: Can Courts Bring about Social Change?, 1991, 2nd ed., 2008. Contributor to books. **Address:** University of Chicago, 5828 S University Ave., 406 Pick Hall, Chicago, IL 60637, U.S.A. **Online address:** g-rosenberg@uchicago.edu

ROSENBERG, Howard. American (born United States), b. 1938. **Genres:** Reference, Young Adult Non-fiction. **Career:** University of Southern California, Annenberg School of Communication, faculty, School of Cinematic Arts, faculty; White Bear Press, editor; Moline Dispatch, reporter. Television critic and writer. **Publications:** Not So Prime Time: Chasing the Trivial on American Television, 2004; (with C.S. Feldman) No Time to Think: The Menace of Media Speed and the 24-Hour News Cycle, 2008. **Address:** School of Cinematic Arts, University of Southern California, SCA 465, University Pk., Los Angeles, CA 90089-2211, U.S.A. **Online address:** hrsnbrg@yahoo.co

ROSENBERG, Joel C. American (born United States), b. 1967. **Genres:** Novels, Young Adult Non-fiction, Theology/Religion, Politics/Government. **Career:** Joshua Fund (a nonprofit charitable and educational organization), founder and president. Writer, consultant and public speaker. **Publications:** Epicenter: How the Current Rumblings in the Middle East Will Change Your World (nonfiction), 2006; Epicenter Study Guide (nonfiction), 2008; Inside the Revolution: How the Followers of Jihad, Jefferson, and Jesus are Battling to Dominate the Middle East and Transform the World (nonfiction), 2009; Tehran Initiative, 2011. JON BENNETT AND ERIN MCCOY SERIES: NOVELS: The Last Jihad, 2002; The Last Days, 2003; The Ezekiel Option, 2005; The Copper Scroll, 2006; Dead Heat, 2008; Twelfth Imam, 2010. **Address:** c/o Scott Miller, Trident Media Group, 41 Madison Ave., New York, NY 10010, U.S.A.

ROSENBERG, John D(avid). American (born United States), b. 1929. **Genres:** Literary Criticism And History, Poetry, Young Adult Fiction. **Career:** Harvard University, faculty; Columbia University, instructor, 1953-54, assistant professor, 1962-65, associate professor, 1966-67, William Peterfield Trent professor of English, 1967-, now William Peterfield Trent professor emeritus of English; City University of New York, City College, instructor, 1954-62; Princeton University, visiting professor, 1978; Cambridge University, visiting fellow, 1969; University of British Columbia, faculty. Writer. **Publications:** The Darkening Glass: A Portrait of Ruskin's Genius, 1961; The Fall of Camelot: A Study of Tennyson's Idylls of the King, 1973; Carlyle and the Burden of History, 1985; Elegy For an Age: The Presence of the Past in Victorian Literature, 2005. EDITOR: The Genius of John Ruskin: Selections from His Writing, 1963; (and intro.) Selected Poetry and Prose, 1968; (and intro.) The Poems of Alfred, Lord Tennyson, 1975; Ruskin on Art, Architecture and Society: Selected Writings, 1998. **Address:** Department of English, Columbia University, B2-3 Heyman Ctr., 1150 Amsterdam Ave., New York, NY 10027, U.S.A. **Online address:** jdr6@columbia.edu

ROSENBERG, Liz. American (born United States), b. 1958. **Genres:** Poetry, Novels, Young Adult Fiction, Novellas/Short Stories, Essays, Children's Fiction. **Career:** State University of New York at Binghamton, professor of English, 1979-; Manuscript magazine, editor, 1980-87; Hollins University, Hamilton College, Bennington College, visiting professor; Colgate University, NEH chair. Writer. **Publications:** Angel Poems, 1984; The Fire Music (poems), 1986; Adelaide and the Night Train, 1989; Window, Mirror, Moon, 1990; The Scrap Doll, 1992; Monster Mama, 1993; Children of Paradise (poems), 1993; Carousel, 1995; Heart and Soul (novel), 1996; The Invisible Ladder (poetry anthology), 1996; Moonbathing, 1996; Grandmother and the Runaway Shadow, 1996; Big and Little Alphabet, 1997; Eli and Uncle Dawn, 1997; (ed.) Earth Shattering Poems, 1998; I Did it Anyway, 1998; Silence in the Mountains, 1999; On Christmas Eve, 2000; (ed.) Light-Gathering Poems, 2000; (ed.) Roots & Flowers: Poets and Poems on Family, 2001; These Happy Eyes (prose poems), 2001; Eli's Night-Light, 2001; Seventeen: A Novel in Prose Poems, 2002; We Wanted You, 2002; This is the Wind, 2008; Lily Poems, 2008; Demon Love, 2008; I Did it Anyway, 2009; Home Repair, 2009; Noody, 2010; Tyrannosaurus Dad, 2011. Contributor to periodicals. **Address:** Department of English, State University of New York, PO Box 6000, Binghamton, NY 13902-6000, U.S.A. **Online address:** lrosenb@binghamton.edu

ROSENBERG, Nathan. American (born United States), b. 1927. **Genres:** Economics, Money/Finance, Business/Trade/Industry. **Career:** Indiana University, lecturer, 1955-57; University of Pennsylvania, assistant professor, 1957-61; Purdue University, associate professor, 1961-64, professor, 1964-67; Harvard University, visiting professor, 1967-69; University of Wisconsin, professor, 1969-74; Stanford University, professor of economics, 1974-, department chair, Fairleigh S. Dickinson Jr. professor of public policy, now Fairleigh S. Dickinson Jr. professor of public policy emeritus; University of Cambridge, Pitt professor of American history and institutions, 1989; National Bureau of Economic Research, director; UN Institute for New Technology, chairman. Writer. **Publications:** Economic Planning in the British Building

Industry, 1945-1949, 1960; Enfield Arsenal in Theory and History, 1966; Technology and American Economic Growth, 1972; Perspectives on Technology, 1976; Transfer of Technology, Opportunities and Problems, 1977; (with W.G. Vincenti) The Britannia Bridge: The Generation and Diffusion of Technical Knowledge, 1978; Inside the Black Box: Technology and Economics, 1982; Perspectives on Technology, 1985; (with L.E. Birdzell) How the West Grew Rich: The Economic Transformation of the Industrial World, 1986; On Technology Blending, 1986; (with D.C. Mowery) Technology and the Pursuit of Economic Growth, 1989; Exploring the Black Box: Technology, Economics, and History, 1994; Emergence of Economic Ideas: Essays in the History of Economics, 1994; (with D.C. Mowery) Paths of Innovation Technological Change in the 20th Century, 1998; Schumpeter and the Endogeneity of Technology: Some American Perspectives, 2000; (with M. Henrekson) Akademiskt entreprenörskap: universitet och näringsliv i samverkan, 2000. EDITOR: (and intro.) The American System of Manufactures, 1969; The Economics of Technological Change: Selected Readings, 1971; (with C. Frischtak) International Technology Transfer: Concepts, Measures, and Comparisons, 1985; (with R. Landau) The Positive Sum Strategy: Harnessing Technology for Economic Growth, 1986; (with R. Landau and D.C. Mowery) Technology and the Wealth of Nations, 1992; (with A. Arora and R. Landau) Chemicals and Long Term Economic Growth: Insights from the Chemical Industry, 1998; Studies on Science and the Innovation Process: Selected Works, 2010. **Address:** Department of Economics, Stanford University, Rm. 337, Ralph Landau Bldg., 579 Serra Mall, Stanford, CA 94305, U.S.A. **Online address:** nate@stanford.edu

ROSENBERG, Robert Alan. American (born United States), b. 1970?. **Genres:** Novels, History. **Career:** White Mountain Apache Reservation, teacher, 1996-98; teacher, 1999-2001; Bucknell University, assistant professor of English. Writer. **Publications:** This is not Civilization, 2004. **Address:** Bucknell University, 12 Bucknell Hall, Lewisburg, PA 17837, U.S.A. **Online address:** robert.rosenberg@bucknell.edu

ROSENBERG, Saralee. American (born United States), b. 1955. **Genres:** Travel/Exploration, Human Relations/Parenting, Women's Studies And Issues, Humor/Satire. **Career:** Writer. **Publications:** Destination Florida: The Guide to a Successful Relocation, 1989; (with L. Rosenberg) 50 Fabulous Places to Retire in America, 1991; (with L. Rosenberg) 50 Fabulous Places to Raise Your Family, 1993; (with L. Rosenberg) Lee and Saralee Rosenberg's 50 Fabulous Places to Raise Your Family, 1996; A Little Help from Above, 2003; Claire Voyant, 2004; Fate and Ms. Fortune, 2006; Dear Neighbor, Drop Dead, 2008. Contributor to magazines. **Address:** Cornerstone Literary, 4525 Wilshire Blvd., Ste. 208, Los Angeles, CA 90010, U.S.A. **Online address:** saralee@saraleerosenberg.com

ROSENBLATT, Jason P. American (born United States), b. 1941. **Genres:** Literary Criticism And History. **Career:** University of Pennsylvania, assistant professor of English, 1968-74; Swarthmore College, visiting lecturer in English literature, 1972-73; Georgetown University, assistant professor of English, 1974-76, associate professor of English, 1976-83, professor of English, 1983-, chair, 2008-09; University of New Hampshire, lecturer of department of German and Russian, 1973-74; University of Wisconsin, department of Slavic languages and literatures, assistant professor, 1980-87, associate professor, 1987-90; Massachusetts Institute of Technology, visiting associate professor, foreign languages and literatures, literature, 1990-94; Boston College, Department of Slavic and Eastern Languages, associate professor, 1994-, chair, 2002-05; professor of Slavic studies, 2003-, undergraduate program director, 2006-. Writer. **Publications:** (Ed. with J.C. Sitterson Jr.) Not in Heaven: Coherence and Complexity in Biblical Narrative, 1991; Torah and Law in Paradise Lost, 1994; Renaissance England's Chief Rabbi: John Selden, 2006; John Milton's Selected Poetry and Prose, 2009. Contributor to journals. **Address:** Department of English, Georgetown University, 306 New North Bldg., PO Box 571131, Washington, DC 20057-1131, U.S.A. **Online address:** rosenblj@gunet.georgetown.edu

ROSENBLATT, Joe. See **ROSENBLATT, Joseph.**

ROSENBLATT, Joseph. (Joe Rosenblatt). Canadian (born Canada), b. 1933. **Genres:** Poetry. **Career:** Canadian Pacific Railway, railway worker, 1958-65; Jewish Dialogue, editor, 1970-83; University of Western Ontario, writer-in-residence, 1979-80; University of Victoria, visiting lecturer, 1980;

Malahat Review, associate editor, 1980-82; University of Victoria, Extension Department, writer-in-residence, 1981; League of Canadian Poets, president, 1983-85; Saskatoon Public Library, writer-in-residence, 1985; University of Rome, writer-in-residence, 1987; University of Bologna, writer-in-residence, 1987; Porcupine's Quill, literary consultant; Blackfish Press, literary consultant; McClelland and Stewart Ltd., literary consultant; Oolichan Books, literary consultant. **Publications:** Voyage of the Mood, 1963; The LSD Leacock: Poems, 1966. AS JOE ROSENBLATT: Winter of the Luna Moth, 1968; (contrib.) How Do I Love Thee: Sixty Poets of Canada (and Quebec) Select and Introduce Their Favourite Poems From Their Own Work, 1970; Greenbaum, 1971; The Bumble-bee Dithyramb, 1972; The Blind Photographer, 1973; Dream Craters, 1974; Virgins & Vampires 1975; Top Soil, 1976; Doctor Anaconda's Solar Fun Club, 1977; Loosely Tied Hands, 1978; Snake Oil, 1978; The Sleeping Lady, 1979; Tommy Fry and the Ant Colony, 1979; Brides of the Stream, 1983; Poetry Hotel: Selected Poems, 1963-1985, 1985; Escape from the Glue Factory: A Memoir of a Paranormal Toronto Childhood in the Late Forties, 1985; The Kissing Goldfish of Siam, 1989; Gridi nel Buio, 1990; Beds & Consenting Dreamers, 1994; A Tentacled Mother, 1995; Joe Rosenblatt Reader, 1995; Madre Tentacolare, 1995; The Voluptuous Gardener: The Collected Art and Writing of Joe Rosenblatt, 1973-1996, 1996; Parrot Fever, 2002; Le Perroquet Facheux, 2002; Deliriodi Pappagallo, 2003; The Lunatic Muse, 2007; (with C. Owen) Dog, 2008; (with C. Owen) Dark Fish & Other Infernos: Epistles and Poems, 2011. **Address:** 221 Elizabeth, Qualicum Beach, BC V9K 1G8, Canada. **Online address:** rosenblatt@bcsupernet.com

ROSENBLOOM, Joseph R. American (born United States), b. 1928. **Genres:** History, Theology/Religion, Biography. **Career:** University of Kentucky, Department of Ancient Languages and Literature, instructor, 1956-61; Washington University, adjunct professor of classics, 1961-; Temple Emanuel, rabbi, 1961-, rabbi emeritus, 2009-. Writer. **Publications:** Biographical Dictionary of Early American Jewry: Colonial Times through 1800, 1960; The Dead Sea Isaiah Scroll: A Literary Analysis; A Living Faith, 1970; Conversion to Judaism: From the Biblical Period to the Present, 1978. Contributor to journals. **Address:** Temple Emanuel, 12166 Conway Rd., St. Louis, MO 63141, U.S.A. **Online address:** rabbiJoe@testl.org

ROSENBLUM, Nancy L. American (born United States), b. 1947. **Genres:** Politics/Government, Social Sciences. **Career:** Harvard University, Henry LaBarre Jayne Assistant professor, 1973-77, associate professor, 1977-80, visiting professor, 1985, Harvard Law School, liberal arts fellow, 1992-93, Senator Joseph Clark professor of ethics in politics and government, 2001-, Centre for Ethics and Professions, faculty fellow, 2003-04, Edmond J. Safar Foundation Centre for Ethics, associate faculty, 2004-, chair, 2004-10; Brown University, professor, 1980-, Department of Political Science, professor, 1985-2001, chair person, 1989-95; Henry Merritt Wriston professor, 1997-2001; Radcliffe College, Bunting Institute, fellow, 1988-89; Steven Robert Initiative for the Study of Values, founder and director, 1998-2000. Writer. **Publications:** Bentham's Theory of the Modern State, 1978; Another Liberalism: Romanticism and the Reconstruction of Liberal Thought, 1987; Liberalism and the Moral Life, 1989; Membership and Morals: The Personal Uses of Pluralism in America, 1998; (co-author) Nature and History in American Political Development: A Debate, 2006; On the Side of the Angels: An Appreciation of Parties and Partisanship, 2008. EDITOR: Political Writings, 1996; Obligations of Citizenship and Demands of Faith: Religious Accommodation in Pluralist Democracies, 2000; (intro.) Breaking the Cycles of Hatred: Memory, Law and Repair, 2002; (with R.C. Post) Civil Society and Government, 2002. **Address:** Department of Government, Harvard University, 1737 Cambridge St., CGIS Knafel Bldg. 437, PO Box 1844, Cambridge, MA 02138, U.S.A. **Online address:** nrosenblum@gov.harvard.edu

ROSENFELD, Dina. (Dina Herman Rosenfeld). American (born United States), b. 1962. **Genres:** Children's Fiction, Young Adult Fiction, Theology/Religion, Food And Wine. **Career:** Yeshiva Achei Tmimim, preschool teacher, 1981-83; Beth Rivka Academy, preschool teacher, 1983-84; Hachai Publishing, editor-in-chief; freelance author and editor, 1984-. **Publications:** (As Dina Herman Rosenfeld) The Very Best Place for a Penny, 1984; (as Dina Herman Rosenfeld) A Tree Full of Mitzvos, 1985; Tiny Treasures: The Wonderful World of a Jewish Child, 1988; All about Us, 1989, 2nd ed., 2009; A Little Boy Named Avram, 1989; (ed.) Little leaf, 1989; Labels for Laibel, 1990; Kind Little Rivka, 1991; Yossi and Laibel Hot on the Trail, 1991; Why the Moon Only Glows, 1992; Peanut Butter and Jelly for Shabbos, 1995; Dovid the Little Shepherd, 1996; The Very Best Book, 1997; Yossi and Laibel On the Ball, 1998; A Little Girl Named Miriam, 2001; Get Well Soon, 2001;

Where Does Food Come From?, 2002; How in the World Does Bread Come From the Earth?, 2002; Five Alive!: My Yom Tov Five Senses, 2003; Kedves kicsi Rebeka, 2006; King in the Field, 2008; Yossi & Laibel Learn to Share, 2010. Works appear in anthologies. **Address:** 555 Crown St., Ste. 2a, Brooklyn, NY 11213, U.S.A.

ROSENFELD, Dina Herman. See **ROSENFELD, Dina.**

ROSENFELD, Nancy (G.). American (born United States), b. 1941. **Genres:** Adult Non-fiction, Literary Criticism And History, Sports/Fitness. **Career:** Chicago Action for Soviet Jewry, volunteer, 1981-; Jewish Community Centers of Chicago, director of outreach program for Russian Jewish immigrants, 1988-89. Writer. **Publications:** Unfinished Journey, 1993; (with D.W. Bolen) Just as Much a Woman: Your Personal Guide to Hysterectomy and Beyond, 1999; (co-author) New Hope for People with Bipolar Disorder, 2000; (with M. Stern) The Human Satan in Seventeenth-Century English Literature: From Milton to Rochester, 2008. **Address:** 88 Greenbriar Dr. E, Deerfield, IL 60015, U.S.A.

ROSENFELD, Richard N. American (born United States), b. 1941?. **Genres:** Writing/Journalism, History. **Career:** Yale University, Timothy Dwight College, independent researcher and associate fellow; American Antiquarian Society, councillor. Writer. **Publications:** American Aurora: A Democratic-Republican Returns: The Suppressed History of Our Nation's Beginnings and the Heroic Newspaper That Tried to Report It, 1997. Contributor to periodicals. **Address:** Timothy Dwight College, Yale University, 345 Temple St., New Haven, CT 06520, U.S.A. **Online address:** richard.rosenfeld@yale.edu

ROSENFELD, Stephanie. American (born United States), b. 1968?. **Genres:** Civil Liberties/Human Rights, Business/Trade/Industry, Young Adult Fiction. **Career:** Institute for Food and Development Policy, faculty. Author. **Publications:** (With W. Bello) Dragons in Distress: Asia's Miracle Economies in Crisis, 1990; What About the Love Part?, 2002; Massachussetts, California, Timbuktu, 2003. **Address:** 81 North St., Salt Lake City, UT 84103, U.S.A.

ROSENFIELD, Israel. American (born United States), b. 1939. **Genres:** Biology, Philosophy, Psychiatry, Psychology, Graphic Novels. **Career:** City University of New York, Queens College, assistant professor of political science, 1966-70, assistant professor, 1970-75, associate professor, 1975-85, John Jay College of Criminal Justice, professor of history, 1986-; Princeton University visiting lecturer, 1966-69. **Publications:** Freud: Character and Consciousness: A Study of Freud's Theory of Unconscious Motives, 1970; (with E. Ziff and B. van Loon) DNA for Beginners, 1983; The Brain for Beginners, 1985; The Invention of Memory: A New View of the Brain, 1988; The Strange, Familiar and Forgotten: An Anatomy of Consciousness, 1992; Freud's Megalomania, 2000; (with E. Ziff and B. van Loon) DNA: A Graphic Guide to the Molecule that Shook the World, 2011. Contributor to books. **Address:** Department of History, John Jay College of Criminal Justice, City University of New York, Rm. 4311N, 899 10th Ave., New York, NY 10019, U.S.A. **Online address:** irosenfield@jjay.cuny.edu

ROSENGARTEN, David. American (born United States), b. 1950. **Genres:** Food And Wine. **Career:** Food Network, taste program host, 1994-; Gourmet Magazine, restaurant critic and contributing editor, 1995-99; The Rosengarten Report, publisher and editor-in-chief; Skidmore College, assistant professor of theater. **Publications:** (With J. Wesson) Red Wine with Fish: The New Art of Matching Wine with Food, 1989; (with J. Dean and G. DeLuca) The Dean & DeLuca Cookbook, 1996; Taste: One Palate's Journey Through the World's Greatest Dishes, 1998; It's All American Food: The Best Recipes for More than 400 New American Classics, 2003; David Rosengarten Entertains: Fabulous Parties for Food Lovers, 2005. **Address:** Food Network, 1177 Ave. of the Americas, New York, NY 10036, U.S.A.

ROSENGREN, John. American (born United States) **Genres:** Adult Non-fiction, Biography, Autobiography/Memoirs. **Career:** University of Minnesota, faculty; Loft Literary Center, faculty. Freelance journalist and author. **Publications:** Life Is Just a Party: Portrait of a Teenage Partier, 1989; Meeting Christ in Teens: Startling Moments of Grace, 2002; Blades of Glory: The True Story of a Young Team Bred to Win, 2003; Big Book Unplugged: A Guide to Alcoholics Anonymous, 2003; (with E. Tuaolo) Alone in the Trenches: My Life As a Gay Player in the NFL (biography), 2006; Hammerin Hank, George

Almighty and the Say Hey Kid: The Year that Changed Baseball Forever, 2008. Contributor to periodicals. **Address:** c/o Author Mail, Sourcebooks Inc., 1935 Brookdale Rd., Ste. 139, Naperville, IL 60563, U.S.A. **Online address:** john@johnrosengren.net

ROSENKRANTZ, Gerald. See **AZRIEL, Yakov.**

ROSENKRANZ, E. Joshua. American (born United States), b. 1961. **Genres:** Law, Young Adult Non-fiction, Politics/Government, Social Sciences. **Career:** U.S. Court of Appeals for the District of Columbia Circuit, law clerk, 1986-87; Supreme Court of the United States, law clerk, 1987-88; Office of the Appellate Defender, founding attorney-in-charge, 1988-96, vice-president, 1988-92, president and chief executive officer, 1992-96; New York University, Brennan Center for Justice, founding president and executive director, 1994-; Orrick, Herrington & Sutcliffe L.L.P., partner; Heller Ehrman L.L.P., partner. Writer. **Publications:** A Practitioner's Guide to Harmless Error, 1991; (with M. Gimpel) A Guide to Criminal Appeals, 1995; Voter Choice '96: A Fifty-State Report Card on the Presidential Elections, 1996; (with R. Winger) What Choice Do We Have?, 1997; (ed. with B. Schwartz) Reason and Passion: Justice Brennan's Enduring Influence, 1997; Buckley Stops Here: Loosening the Judicial Stranglehold on Campaign Finance Reform Report, 1998; (ed.) If Buckley Fell: A First Amendment Blueprint for Regulating Money in Politics, 1999. Contributor to periodicals. **Address:** Orrick, Herrington & Sutcliffe L.L.P., 51 W 52nd St., New York, NY 10019-6142, U.S.A. **Online address:** jrosenkranz@orrick.com

ROSENKRANZ, Ze'ev. Australian/Austrian/Israeli (born Israel), b. 1961. **Genres:** Biography, Autobiography/Memoirs, History, Physics. **Career:** Hebrew University of Jerusalem, Albert Einstein Archives, curator, 1989-2003; California Institute of Technology, Einstein Papers Project, senior editor, 2002-. **Publications:** Albert through the Looking-Glass: The Personal Papers of Albert Einstein, 1998; The Einstein Scrapbook, 2002; Albert Einstein: privat und ganz persoenlich, 2004; (co-ed.) The Collected Papers of Albert Einstein, vol. X: The Berlin Years: Correspondence, May-December 1920 and Supplementary Correspondence, 1909-1920, 2005, vol. XII: The Berlin Years: Correspondence, January-December 1921, 2009; Einstein Before Israel: Zionist Icon or Iconoclast?, 2011. **Address:** Einstein Papers Project, California Institute of Technology, M-C 20-7, Pasadena, CA 91125, U.S.A. **Online address:** zeev@einstein.caltech.edu

ROSENMEYER, Patricia A. American (born United States), b. 1958. **Genres:** Classics, Education. **Career:** Princeton University, Department of Classics, assistant in instruction, 1984-85; University of Michigan, visiting instructor, 1986-87, assistant professor of classical studies, 1987-90; Yale University, Department of Classics, assistant professor, 1990-93, associate professor, 1993-96, director of undergraduate studies in classics, 1994-96; University of Wisconsin, Department of Classics, associate professor, 1997-2001, professor, 2001-. Writer. **Publications:** The Poetics of Imitation: Anacreon and the Anacreontic Tradition, 1992; Ancient Epistolary Fictions: The Letter in Greek Literature, 2001. Contributor to journals. Works appear in anthologies. **Address:** Department of Classics, University of Wisconsin, 966 Van Hise Hall, 1220 Linden Dr., Madison, WI 53706, U.S.A. **Online address:** prosenme@facstaff.wisc.edu

ROSENSON, Beth A. American (born United States) **Genres:** Politics/Government, Adult Non-fiction. **Career:** University of Florida, Department of Political Science, assistant professor, associate professor. Writer. **Publications:** The Shadowlands of Conduct: Ethics and State Politics, 2005. Contributor of articles to journals. **Address:** Department of Political Science, University of Florida, 202 Anderson Hall, PO Box 117325, Gainesville, FL 32611-7325, U.S.A. **Online address:** rosenson@polisci.ufl.edu

ROSENSTIEL, Tom. American (born United States), b. 1956. **Genres:** Business/Trade/Industry, Politics/Government, Adult Non-fiction, Reference. **Career:** Jack Anderson's Washington Merry Go Round column, columnist, reporter, 1978-79; Peninsula Times Tribune, business editor and reporter, 1980-83; Los Angeles Times, media critic, Washington correspondent, business writer to national media and political correspondent, 1983-95; Project for Excellence in Journalism, founder, 1997, editor, principal author, director; Newsweek Magazine, chief congressional correspondent. **Publications:** Strange Bedfellows: How Television and the Candidates Changed American Politics, 1992, 1993; The Beat Goes On: President Clinton's First Year with the Media, 1994; (with B. Kovach) Warp Speed: America in the Age of Mixed

Media, 1999; (with B. Kovach) The Elements of Journalism: What Newspeople Should Know and the Public Should Expect, 2001, rev. ed., 2007; (ed. with A.S. Mitchell) Thinking Clearly: Cases in Journalistic Decision-Making: Teaching Notes, 2003; (co-author) We Interrupt this Newscast: How to Improve Local News and Win Ratings, Too, 2007; (with B. Kovach) Blur: How to know What's True in the Age of Information Overload, 2010. Contributor to books. **Address:** Project for Excellence in Journalism, 1615 L St. NW 700, Washington, DC 20036, U.S.A.

ROSENTHAL, Chuck P. American (born United States), b. 1951. **Genres:** Young Adult Fiction. **Career:** Loyola Marymount University, professor. Writer. **Publications:** Loop's Progress, 1986; Experiments with Life and Deaf, 1987; Loop's End, 1992; Elena of the Stars, 1995; Jack Kerouac's Avatar Angel: His Last Novel, 2001; My Mistress, Humanity, 2002; Never Let Me Go, 2004; The Heart of Mars, 2007; Are We Not There Yet? Travels in Nepal, North India, and Bhutan, 2009. **Address:** Department of English, Loyola Marymount University, 1 LMU Dr., Ste. 3800, Los Angeles, CA 90045-2659, U.S.A. **Online address:** crosenth@lmu.edu

ROSENTHAL, Debra J. American (born United States), b. 1964. **Genres:** Literary Criticism And History, Young Adult Fiction. **Career:** John Carroll University, assistant professor of English, 1998-, associate professor, professor of American literature, director of graduate program; Oxford University, visiting fellow, 2005-06; Writer. **Publications:** (Ed. with D.S. Reynolds) The Serpent in the Cup: Temperance in American Literature, 1997; (ed. with M. Kaup) Mixing Race, Mixing Culture: Inter-American Literary Dialogues, 2002; (ed.) Routledge Literary Sourcebook on Harriet Beecher Stowe's Uncle Tom's Cabin, 2003; Race Mixture in Nineteenth-Century U.S. and Spanish American Fictions: Gender, Culture, and Nation Building, 2004; (ed.) Harriet Beecher Stowe's Uncle Tom's Cabin: A Sourcebook, 2004. **Address:** Department of English, John Carroll University, OC 223, 20700 N Park Blvd., University Heights, OH 44118, U.S.A. **Online address:** drosenthal@jcu.edu

ROSENTHAL, Donald B. American (born United States), b. 1937. **Genres:** Politics/Government. **Career:** State University of New York, assistant professor, 1964-68, associate professor, 1968-72, professor of political science, 1972-, now professor emeritus; Rockefeller Institute of Government, senior fellow, 1983. Writer. **Publications:** (With R.L. Crain and E. Katz) The Politics of Community Conflict, 1969; The Limited Elite: Politics and Government in Two Indian Cities, 1970; (with M. Kesselman) Local Power and Comparative Politics, 1974; (ed.) The City in Indian Politics, 1976; The Expansive Elite: District Politics and State Policy-making in India, 1977; Sticking-Points and Ploys in Federal-Local Relations, 1979; (ed.) Urban Revitalization, 1980; Urban Housing and Neighborhood Revitalization: Turning a Federal Program into Local Projects, 1988. **Address:** Department of Political Science, State University of New York, 520 Park Hall, Buffalo, NY 14260, U.S.A. **Online address:** dbr@acsu.buffalo.edu

ROSENTHAL, Elizabeth J. American (born United States), b. 1960?. **Genres:** Music. **Career:** Writer, biographer and attorney. **Publications:** His Song: The Musical Journey of Elton John, 2001; Birdwatcher: The Life of Roger Tory Peterson, 2008. **Address:** Burlington, NJ , U.S.A. **Online address:** ejrose@aol.com

ROSENTHAL, Judy. American (born United States) **Genres:** Anthropology/Ethnology, Cultural/Ethnic Topics, Adult Non-fiction. **Career:** University of Michigan-Flint, associate professor of anthropology, professor. Writer. **Publications:** Possession, Ecstasy and Law in Ewe Voodoo, 1998; Foreign Spirits Inside the Family-Vodu Home on the Ex-slave Coast, 2004; Contributor to journals. **Address:** Department of Anthropology, University of Michigan, 522 French Hall, 303 E Kearsley St., Flint, MI 48502-2186, U.S.A. **Online address:** jvros@umflint.edu

ROSENTHAL, Ken S. American (born United States), b. 1951. **Genres:** Medicine/Health, Biology, Medicine/Health. **Career:** Northeastern Ohio Universities, Colleges of Medicine and Pharmacy, professor of microbiology and immunology, 1979-. Writer and researcher. **Publications:** Ace the Boards Microbiology, 1996; Medical Microbiology, 1990, 6th ed., 2009; Rapid Review Microbiology and Immunology, 2002, 3rd ed., 2010; Review of Medical Microbiology, 2005; Medical Microbiology and Immunology Flash Cards, 2006. Contributor to journals. **Address:** Colleges of Medicine and Pharmacy, Northeastern Ohio Universities, 4209 State Rte. 44, PO Box 95, Rootstown, OH 44272-0095, U.S.A. **Online address:** ksr@neoucom.edu

ROSENTHAL, Lucy (Gabrielle). American (born United States) **Genres:** Novels, Novellas/Short Stories, Plays/Screenplays, Literary Criticism And History. **Career:** Radiology, assistant editor, 1955-57; University of Iowa, Writers Workshop, admissions staff, 1965-68; Book-of-the-Month Club, editor, 1973-74, senior editorial adviser, 1979-87; New York University, adjunct professor, 1986; Sarah Lawrence College, faculty in writing, 1996-; Columbia University, School of General Studies, lecturer of writing program, 1990-96, adjunct associate professor, 1996-. **Publications:** The Ticket Out, 1983; (ed. and intro.) Great American Love Stories, 1988; (ed. and intro.) World Treasury of Love Stories, 1995; (ed. and intro.) The Eloquent Short Story: Varieties of Narration, 2004. Contributor to periodicals. **Address:** Department of Writing, Sarah Lawrence College, 1 Mead Way, Bronxville, NY 10708, U.S.A. **Online address:** lrosenth@sarahlawrence.edu

ROSENTHAL, Nan. American (born United States), b. 1937. **Genres:** Art/Art History. **Career:** University of California, assistant professor of art history, 1971-77, associate professor, 1977-84, professor, 1985-86, Department of Art History, chair, 1976-80; National Gallery of Art, curator of 20th-century art, 1985-92, now emeritus curator of 20th-century art; Metropolitan Museum of Art, Department of 20th Century Art, consultant, senior consultant, 1993-2008, now emeritus senior curator of modern art; Fordham University, Lincoln Center, visiting professor of art history, 1981, 1985; Princeton University, visiting lecturer in visual arts, 1985, 1988, 1992; Princeton University, visiting lecturer in visual arts, 1985, 1988, 1992; New York University, Institute of Fine Arts, Lila Acheson Wallace visiting professor of fine arts, 1996, 2000. Writer. **Publications:** Painting From 1850 to the Present, 1976; George Rickey, 1977; (with R.E. Fine, M. Prather and A.M. Zorn) The Drawings of Jasper Johns, 1990; (with K. Baetjer and L.M. Messinger) The Jackson Pollock Sketchbooks in the Metropolitan Museum of Art, 1997; Anselm Kiefer: Works on Paper in the Metropolitan Museum of Art, 1998; Terry Winters: Printed Works, 2001; (ed. with G. Tinterow and L.M. Messinger) Abstract Expressionism and Other Modern Works: The Muriel Kallis Steinberg Newman Collection in the Metropolitan Museum of Art, 2007; (contrib.) Jasper Johns: Gray, 2007. Contributor to books. **Address:** Metropolitan Museum of Art, 1000 5th Ave., New York, NY 10028-0198, U.S.A.

ROSENTHAL, Naomi B(raun). American (born United States), b. 1940. **Genres:** Women's Studies And Issues. **Career:** State University of New York, Stony Brook University, Department of Political Science, secretary, 1964-65, technical assistant at library, 1966-68, visiting assistant professor, 1972-73, research associate professor, 1980-97, research associate, 1981-87, visiting professor, 1997-; University of Sussex, tutor, 1973; State University of New York, instructor, 1975-76, assistant professor, 1976-82, associate professor, 1982-90, professor of American studies, 1990-, chair of American studies, 1985-87; National Endowment for the Humanities, fellow, 1980, 1995-96; Village Cinema, founder and co-chair, 1985-92; Old Westbury Foundation, board director, 1991-92; Port Jefferson Free Library, vice president, 2000-. Writer. **Publications:** Spinster Tales and Womanly Possibilities, 2002. EDITOR: Services for Women on Long Island: A Directory, 1985; Women's Record, 4th ed., 1991. Contributor to books and periodicals. **Address:** Department of Sociology, Stony Brook University, Rm. SBS S-408, Stony Brook, NY 11794-4356, U.S.A. **Online address:** naorosenthal@notes.cc.sunysb.edu

ROSENTHAL, T(homas) G(abriel). American (born United States), b. 1935?. **Genres:** Art/Art History, Military/Defense/Arms Control, Philosophy. **Career:** Secker & Warburg (publishing house), managing director, 1971-84; Heinemann and Secker, chairman, 1981-84; Institute of Contemporary Arts, chairman. Journalist. **Publications:** European Art History, 1960; American Fiction Since 1900, 1961; The Artist and War in the Twentieth Century, 1967; The Art of Jack B. Yeats, 1993; Sidney Nolan, 2002; Paula Rego: The Complete Graphic Work, 2003; (intro.) Josef Albers: Formulation: Articulation, 2006. Contributor to books and journals. **Address:** c/o Author Mail, Thames & Hudson Inc., 500 5th Ave., New York, NY 10110-0002, U.S.A.

ROSES, Lorraine Elena. American (born United States), b. 1943. **Genres:** Literary Criticism And History, Translations, Race Relations. **Career:** Boston University, assistant professor, 1975-77; Wellesley College, Spanish Department, professor, 1977-, now professor emeritus, chair, director of Latin American studies, 1992-, Luella LaMer Slaner professor of Latin American studies, 2001-05, Luella LaMer Slaner chair of Latin American studies, 2001-; Mary Ingraham Bunting Institute (now Radcliffe Institute), fellow in literature, 1998-99; Harvard University, Du Bois Institute, Sheila Biddle Ford fellow, 2005. Writer. **Publications:** Voices of the Storyteller: Cuba's Lino Novas Calvo, 1986; (with R.E. Randolph) Harlem Renaissance and Beyond: Literary Biographies of 100 Black Women Writers, 19-1945, 1990; (ed. with R.E. Randolph) Harlem's Glory: Black Women Writing, 1900-1950, 1996. **Address:** 63 Columbus St., Newton, MA 02461, U.S.A. **Online address:** lroses@wellesley.edu

ROSHWALD, Aviel. American (born United States), b. 1962. **Genres:** History. **Career:** University of Massachusetts, visiting lecturer, 1988-89; Pomona College, visiting assistant professor of history, 1989-91; Georgetown University, Department of History, assistant professor of history, 1991-97, associate professor of history, 1997-2001, professor of history, 2001-, acting chair, 2006-07, chair, 2009-12, MA Studies, International and Comparative History Program director, Master of Arts in Global, director, 2007-09, director of global history, 2008-09. Writer. **Publications:** Estranged Bedfellows: Britain and France in the Middle East during the Second World War, 1990; (ed. with R. Stites) European Culture in the Great War: The Arts, Entertainment and Propaganda, 1914-1948, 1999; Ethnic Nationalism and the Fall of Empires: Central Europe, Russia and the Middle East, 1914-1923, 2001; The Endurance of Nationalism: Ancient Roots and Modern Dilemmas, 2006. **Address:** Department of History, Georgetown University, 601 Intercultural Ctr., 3700 O St. NW, PO Box 571035, Washington, DC 20057-1035, U.S.A. **Online address:** roshwaav@georgetown.edu

ROSHWALD, Mordecai. American/Polish (born Poland), b. 1921. **Genres:** Novels, Science Fiction/Fantasy, Philosophy, Politics/Government, Sociology, Theology/Religion, Sciences, Science Fiction/Fantasy, Science Fiction/Fantasy. **Career:** Hebrew University, lecturer in political theory, 1951-55; University of Minnesota, assistant professor, 1957-60, associate professor, 1960-72, professor of humanities, 1972-84, now professor emeritus of humanities; Israel Technological Institute, visiting associate professor, 1963-64; University of Bath, visiting professor, 1966. Writer. **Publications:** Humanizm le-maaseh, 1945; Adam Ve-hoinukho, 1954; The Education of Man (in Hebrew), 1954; Humanism in Practice: A Blue-Print for a Better World, 1955; Level 7 (novel), 1959; A Small Armageddon (novel), 1962; (with M. Roshwald) Moses: Leader, Prophet, Man, The Story of Moses and his Image Through the Ages, 1969; Modern Technology: The Promise and the Menace, 1997; The Transient and the Absolute: An Interpretation of the Human Condition and of Human Endeavor, 1999; Liberty: Its Meaning and Scope, 2000; The Half-Truths by Which We Live, 2006; Dreams and Nightmares: Science and Technology in Myth and Fiction, 2008. **Address:** 8811 Colesville Rd., Ste. 502, Silver Spring, MD 20910-4332, U.S.A. **Online address:** roshwald@netscape.com

ROSIERS, Annécie. *See* HUSTON, Nancy.

ROSIS, Brendan. *See* TILLY, Chris.

ROSKAMP, Karl Wilhelm. American/German (born Germany), b. 1923. **Genres:** Economics, Essays. **Career:** Massachusetts Institute of Technology, Center for International Studies, research assistant, 1955-56; Brandeis University, visiting assistant professor of economics, 1959-60; Wayne State University, associate professor, 1960-65; professor, 1965-88, professor emeritus of economics, 1988-, Academy of Scholars, president, 1989-91; University of Paris II, associate professor, 1977-83, 1986-87; International Institute of Public Finance, vice-president, 1978, president, 1984-87. Writer. **Publications:** (With W.F. Stolper) Industrial Production in Soviet Germany, 1956; (with W.F. Stolper) The Structure of the East German Economy, 1960; Capital Formation in West Germany, 1965; (ed.) Verzeichnis ausgewählter laufender Literatur über die Volkswirtschaft der Deutschen Demokratischen Republik, 1967; Die Amerikanische Wirtschaft: Eine Einfuehrung, 1975; The American Economy 1929-1970, 1977; (ed.) Public Choice and Public Finance, 1978; (ed. with F. Forte) Reforms of Tax Systems, 1979; (co-ed.) Public Finance and Economic Growth, 1981; (ed. with D. Bietl and W.F. Stolper) Public Finance and Economic Growth=Finances Publiques et croissance économique: Proceedings of the 37th Congress of the International Institute of Public Finance, Tokyo, 1981, 1983; (with J. Wiseman and H.V.H. Hanusch) Staat und politische Ökonomie heute: Horst Claus Recktenwald zum 65. Geburtstag=Public Sector and Political Economy Today: Essays in Honour of Horst Claus Recktenwald, 1985; (co-ed.) Public Finance and the Performance of Enterprises, 1987; (ed.) International Institute of Public Finance: Semicentennial 1937 to 1987, 1987; (ed. with M. Neumann) Public Finance and Performance of Enterprises=Finances Publiques et Performance des Entreprises: Proceedings

of the 43rd Congress of the International Institute of Public Finance, Paris, 1987, 1989. **Address:** Department of Economics, Wayne State University, 2074 FAB, 656 W Kirby, Detroit, MI 48202, U.S.A.

ROSLUND, Anders. Swedish (born Sweden), b. 1961?. **Genres:** Young Adult Fiction, Mystery/Crime/Suspense, Social Sciences. **Career:** Culture News, founder and head; Aktuellt, editor-in-chief; Rapport (Swedish television station), editor-in-chief. **Publications:** WITH B. HELLSTRÖM: Beast, 2005; Flickan Under Gatan, 2008; Tre Sekunder, 2009; EWERT GRENS AND SVEN SUNDKVIST THRILLER SERIES: The Satisfaction of Edward Finnegan, 2006; Box 21, 2007; The Girl below the Street, 2007; The Vault, 2008; Three Seconds, 2010. **Address:** Salomonsson Agency, Svartensgatan 4, Stockholm, 116 20, Sweden. **Online address:** info@roslund-hellstrom.se

ROSMAN, Katherine. American (born United States), b. 1972?. **Genres:** Biography. **Career:** Wall Street Journal, reporter, 2004-. Writer. **Publications:** If You Knew Suzy: A Mother, a Daughter, a Reporter's Notebook, 2010. Contributor to periodicals. **Address:** c/o Kate Lee, International Creative Management, 825 8th Ave., New York, NY 10019, U.S.A. **Online address:** katie@katherinerosman.com

ROSMAN, Steven M(ichael). American (born United States), b. 1956. **Genres:** Children's Fiction, Mythology/Folklore, Theology/Religion, Young Adult Fiction, Human Relations/Parenting. **Career:** Jewish Family Congregation, rabbi, 1982-; New York University, School of Continuing Education lecturer, 1987-88, School of Education adjunct instructor, 1989; Vassar College, associate Jewish chaplain, 1987-88; Academy for Jewish Studies, lecturer, 1991-92. Writer. **Publications:** Sidrah Stories: A Torah Companion, 1989; (with P. Schram) Eight Tales for Eight Nights: Stories for Chanukah, 1990; Deena the Damselfly, 1992; (with K. Olitzky and D. Kasakove) When Your Jewish Child Asks You Why: Answers for Tough Questions, 1993; The Twenty-two Gates to the Garden, 1994; Spiritual Parenting: A Sourcebook for Parents and Teachers, 1994; The Bird of Paradise and Other Sabbath Stories, 1994; Jewish Healing Wisdom, 1997; Jewish Parenting Wisdom, 1997. Contributor to journals. **Address:** 34 Lewis Ln., Port Washington, NY 11050-2512, U.S.A.

ROSNER, Bob. American (born United States), b. 1956. **Genres:** Administration/Management, Business/Trade/Industry, inspirational/Motivational Literature. **Career:** Smoking Policy Institute, executive director, 1982-93; United Way of King County, deputy chairperson, 1993-94; Workingwounded. com Inc., chairperson and shop steward, 1995-; Giraffe Project, chairperson and board director. Writer. **Publications:** Working Wounded: Advice That Adds Insight to Injury, 1998; (with A. Halcrow and A.S. Levins) The Boss's Survival Guide, 2001; (with A. Halcrow and A.S. Levins) Gray Matters: The Workplace Survival Guide, 2004; (with A. Halcrow) Boss's Survival Guide: Workplace 911 For The Toughest Problems Today's Managers Face, 2010. **Address:** Workingwounded.com Inc., 9187 Mandus Olson Rd. NE, Bainbridge Island, WA 98110-1529, U.S.A. **Online address:** bob@workingwounded.com

ROSNER, Elizabeth J. American (born United States), b. 1959. **Genres:** Novels, Poetry, Young Adult Fiction, Novellas/Short Stories. **Career:** Contra Costa College, professor of English, 1992-2000. Writer. **Publications:** Gravity (poetry), 1998; The Speed of Light: A Novel, 2001; Blue Nude: A Novel, 2006; Under My Skin, forthcoming. Contributor to periodicals. Works appear in anthologies. **Address:** c/o Joëlle Delbourgo, Joëlle Delbourgo Associates Inc., 101 Park St., 3rd Fl., Montclair, NJ 07042, U.S.A. **Online address:** elizabeth@elizabethrosner.com

ROSNER, Lisa. American (born United States), b. 1958. **Genres:** Information Science/Computers, Reference. **Career:** Richard Stockton College, professor of history, 1987-. Writer. **Publications:** Medical Education in the Age of Improvement: Edinburgh Students and Apprentices, 1720-1826, 1991; First Look at Quattro Pro 2.0/3.0, 1992; (with J. Shuman) Using Quattro Pro 2.0/3.0, 1993; First Look at Quattro Pro for Windows, 1993; Quick Success: Word Perfect 6.0 for Windows, 1995; Quick Success: Windows 3.1, 1995; Quick Success: Microsoft Word 6.0 for Windows, 1995; Quick Success: DOS 6.2, 1995; Quick Success: dBase 5.0 for Windows, 1996; Quick Success: Lotus 1-2-3 Release 4 for DOS, 1996; Quick Success: Lotus 1-2-3 Release 5 for DOS, 1996; Quick Success: Paradox 5.0 for Windows, 1996; The Most Beautiful Man in Existence: The Scandalous Life of Alexander Lesassier, 1999; Quick Success. Lotus 1-2-3 Release 5 for Windows, 1996; (with J. Theibault)

A Short History of Europe, 1600-1815: Search for a Reasonable World, 2000; The Anatomy Murders: Being the True and Spectacular History of Edinburgh's Notorious Burke and Hare, and of the Man of Science Who Abetted Them in the Commission of Their Most Heinous Crimes, 2009. EDITOR: (with A. Stroup) Directory of Women in the History of Science, Technology, and Medicine, 1991; Chronology of Science: From Stonehenge to the Human Genome Project, 2002; The Technological Fix: How People Use Technology to Create and Solve Problems, 2004; (with M.E. Bowden and M. Gapp) Joseph Priestley: Radical Thinker, 2005. **Address:** Historical Studies Program, Richard Stockton College, B114, Main Stockton Campus, PO Box 195, Pomona, NJ 08240-0195, U.S.A. **Online address:** rosnerl@stockton.edu

ROSS, Adam Thayer. American (born United States), b. 1967. **Genres:** Young Adult Fiction. **Career:** Nashville Scene, feature writer and editor, 1999-2003; Harpeth Hall School, writer-in-residence, 2004-. Actor. **Publications:** Mr. Peanut, 2010. Contributor to periodicals. **Address:** c/o Mark Kessler, Susanna Lea Associates, 331 W 20th St., New York, NY 10011, U.S.A.

ROSS, Alex. American (born United States), b. 1968?. **Genres:** Music. **Career:** New York Times, music critic, 1992-96; New Yorker, music critic, 1996-. Writer. **Publications:** The Rest Is Noise: Listening to the Twentieth Century, 2007; Listen to This, 2010; (ed. with D. Carr) Best Music Writing 2011, 2011. Contributor to periodicals. **Address:** c/o Tina Bennett, Janklow & Nesbit Associates, 445 Park Ave., New York, NY 10022, U.S.A.

ROSS, Angus. Also writes as Henry Marlin. British (born England), b. 1927. **Genres:** Mystery/Crime/Suspense, Westerns/Adventure, Biography, History, Autobiography/Memoirs, Business/Trade/Industry, Literary Criticism And History. **Career:** D.C. Thomson, sales manager, 1952-71; writer, 1971-. **Publications:** The Manchester Thing, 1970; The Huddersfield Job, 1971; The London Assignment, 1972; The Dunfermline Affair, 1973; The Bradford Business, 1974; The Amsterdam Diversion, 1974; The Leeds Fiasco, 1975; The Edinburgh Exercise, 1975; The Ampurias Exchange, 1977; The Aberdeen Conundrum, 1977; Congleton Lark, 1979; Burgos Contract, 1979; The Hamburg Switch, 1980; The Menwith Tangle, 1982; The Darlington Jaunt, 1983; The Greenham Plot, 1984; Bad April, 1984; Manchester Connection, 1984; The Luxembourg Run, 1985; (with A. Dicks) Famous Fighting Planes (nonfiction), 1985; The Tyneside Ultimatum, 1988; Classic Sailing Ships (non-fiction), 1988; A Bad April, 1989; Doom Indigo, 1989; The Leipzig Manuscript, 1990; John Worsley's War (biography), 1991; The Last One, 1992; The Deep Purple Fall, 1992. Contributor to periodicals. **Address:** Viking Publicity, 375 Hudson St., New York, NY 10014-3658, U.S.A.

ROSS, Becki L. Canadian (born Canada), b. 1959. **Genres:** Gay And Lesbian Issues, Sociology, Women's Studies And Issues. **Career:** Toronto Centre for Lesbian and Gay Studies, co-chair, 1992-94; University of British Columbia, assistant professor of anthropology, sociology and women's studies, 1995-, associate professor of sociology, Women's and Gender Studies, chair. Writer. **Publications:** The House That Jill Built: A Lesbian Nation in Formation, 1995; (with B. Cossman, S. Bell and L. Gotell) Bad Attitude/s: Feminism, Pornography, and the Butler Decision, 1996; Burlesque West: Showgirls, Sex, and Sin in Postwar Vancouver, 2009. Contributor to periodicals. **Address:** Department of Anthropology and Sociology, University of British Columbia, Rm. AnSo 3119, WMST 10, 6303 NW Marine Dr., Vancouver, BC V6T 1Z1, Canada. **Online address:** becki@interchange.ubc.ca

ROSS, Bernard L. See FOLLETT, Ken(neth Martin).

ROSS, Catherine. See BEATY, Betty (Smith).

ROSS, Cecily. Canadian (born Canada) **Genres:** Food And Wine, Biography. **Career:** Globe and Mail, senior editor, 1996-2009. Journalist. **Publications:** Love in the Time of Cholesterol: A Memoir with Recipes, 2006. Contributor to magazines. **Address:** c/o Author Mail, The McGraw-Hill Companies, PO Box 182604, Columbus, OH 43272, U.S.A. **Online address:** cecily.ross@gmail.com

ROSS, Charles L(ouis). American (born United States), b. 1945. **Genres:** Literary Criticism And History, Women's Studies And Issues. **Career:** University of Virginia, assistant professor of English, 1973-78; University of Hartford, Guggenheim fellow, 1978-79, professor of English, 1979-, Humanities Research Center, director, 2006-. Writer. **Publications:** The Composition of The Rainbow and Women in Love: A History, 1979; Women in Love: A

Novel of Mythic Realism, 1991; (ed. with D. Jackson) Editing D.H. Lawrence: New Versions of a Modern Author, 1995. Contributor to journals. **Address:** Department of English, University of Hartford, 212J Auerbach Bldg., 200 Bloomfield Ave., West Hartford, CT 06117, U.S.A. **Online address:** chross@mail.hartford.edu

ROSS, Deborah J. See WHEELER, Deborah (Jean Ross).

ROSS, Dennis. American (born United States), b. 1948. **Genres:** International Relations/Current Affairs, Local History/Rural Topics. **Career:** Pentagon, Office of Net Assessment, deputy director, 1982-84; Berkeley-Stanford program on Soviet international behavior, executive director, 1984-86; National Security Council, Near East and South Asian Affairs, director, 1986-88; U.S. Department of State, director of policy planning, 1988-92, coordinator of Middle East, 1997-2001; Kol Shalom Synagogue, co-founder, 2002; Washington Institute for Near East Policy, counselor and Ziegler distinguished fellow; Fox News Channel, foreign affairs analyst; Persian Gulf, special adviser. Writer. **Publications:** (Intro.) 1999 Soref Symposium: The Barak Victory: Implications for Israel, The Peace Process, and U.S. Policy, 1999; The Missing Peace: The Inside Story of the Fight for Middle East Peace, 2004; (contrib.) Al-Qaeda's Armies: Middle East Affiliate Groups & the Next Generation of Terror, 2005; Statecraft: And How to Restore America's Standing in the World, 2008; (with D. Makovsky) Myths, Illusions and Peace: Finding A New Direction for America in The Middle East, 2009. Contributor to periodicals. **Address:** Washington Institute for Near East Policy, 1828 L St. NW, Ste. 1050, Washington, DC 20036, U.S.A. **Online address:** dennisr@washingtoninstitute.org

ROSS, Dorothy. American (born United States), b. 1936. **Genres:** History. **Career:** Cornell University Medical College, Payne Whitney Clinic, fellow in history and psychiatry, 1965-67; George Washington University, Department of Psychology, research associate, 1967-68; Princeton University, assistant professor of history, 1972-78, Philip and Beulah Rollins bicentennial preceptor, 1973-76; University of Virginia, associate professor, professor of history, 1978-90; Johns Hopkins University, Arthur O. Lovejoy professor of history, 1990-2007, professor emeritus, 2007-, Department of History, chair, 1993-96; Center for Advanced Study in the Behavioral Sciences, fellow, 1992-93; Woodrow Wilson Center, fellow, 1996-97, senior scholar, 2010-. Writer. **Publications:** G. Stanley Hall: The Psychologist as Prophet, 1972; The Origins of American Social Science, 1991; (ed.) Modernist Impulses in the Human Sciences, 1870-1930, 1994; The Modern Social Sciences, 2003. Works appear in anthologies. Contributor to periodicals. **Address:** Department of History, Johns Hopkins University, 3400 N Charles St., Baltimore, MD 21218, U.S.A. **Online address:** dottross@comcast.net

ROSS, Ellen. American (born United States), b. 1942. **Genres:** Women's Studies And Issues, Travel/Exploration, History. **Career:** Connecticut College, instructor, assistant professor, 1971-76; Ramapo College, School of Social Science and Human Services, assistant professor, professor of history and women's studies, 1976-; National Endowment for the Humanities, fellow, 1989-90. Writer. **Publications:** Love and Toil: Motherhood in Outcast London, 1870-1918, 1993; (ed. and intro.) Slum Travelers: Ladies and London Poverty, 1860-1920, 2007. Contributor to periodicals. **Address:** School of Social Science and Human Servcies, Ramapo College, G-221, 505 Ramapo Valley Rd., Mahwah, NJ 07430-1623, U.S.A. **Online address:** eross@ramapo.edu

ROSS, Erin. See TALLMAN, Shirley.

ROSS, Ian Campbell. British (born England), b. 1950. **Genres:** Literary Criticism And History, History. **Career:** University of Birmingham, lecturer in English literature, 1975-77, lecturer in modern English, 1977-87; Trinity College, fellow, senior lecturer, 1987-2000, associate professor of English, 2000-08, professor of eighteenth-century studies, 2008-, Centre for Irish-Scottish and Comparative Studies, co-director, School of English, director of research, Eighteenth-Century Ireland Society/Cumann éireann san Ochtú Céad Déag, co-founder, Eighteenth-Century Ireland/Iris an dá chultúr, co-founder of journal and co-editor, Eighteenth-Century Literature Research Network, founder and convenor. Writer. **Publications:** Swift's Ireland, 1983; Umbria: A Cultural History, 1996; Laurence Sterne: A Life, 2001. EDITOR: (and intro.) The Life and Opinions of Tristram Shandy, Gentleman, 1983, rev. ed., 2009; Public Virtue, Public Love: The Early Years of the Dublin Lying-in Hospital, the Rotunda, 1986; (with A. Douglas and P. Kelly) Locating Swift:

Essays from Dublin on the 250th Anniversary of the Death of Jonathan Swift, 1667-1745, 1998; (and intro.) The Europeans, 2000. (trans. and intro.) Gian Gaspare Napolitanto, To War with The Black Watch, 2007; (and intro.) Vertue Rewarded; Or, the Irish Princess, 2010; (with A. Douglas and A. Markey) Irish Tales, or, Instructive Histories for the Happy Conduct of Life, 2010; (and intro. with A. Douglas) Triumph of Prudence Over Passion, or, The History of Miss Mortimer and Miss Fitzgerald, 2011. **Address:** School of English, Trinity College, University of Dublin, Dublin, 2, Ireland. **Online address:** icross@tcd.ie

ROSS, James R(odman). American (born United States), b. 1950. **Genres:** Documentaries/Reportage. **Career:** Washington Star, reporting intern, 1971; Hartford Courant, reporter and bureau chief, 1972-80; University of Connecticut, instructor in journalism, 1980-81, associate professor of journalism, 1986-88, 1988-94; University of Pittsburgh, assistant professor of writing, 1982-86; Pittsburgh Post Gazette, copy editor, 1983-86; Shanghai Foreign Languages Institute, visiting journalism professor, 1985-86, Fulbright professor in Ecuador; Northeastern University, associate professor of journalism, 1988-, Stotsky professor of Jewish historical and cultural studies, 2002-05, School of Journalism, graduate coordinator, 2002-; Nanjing University, Fulbright lecturer. **Publications:** Escape to Shanghai: A Jewish Community in China, 1994; Caught in a Tornado: A Chinese American Woman Survives the Cultural Revolution, 1994; Fragile Branches: Travels through the Jewish Diaspora, 2000. Contributor of articles to periodicals. **Address:** School of Journalism, Northeastern University, 102 Lake Hall, 360 Huntington Ave., Boston, MA 02115, U.S.A. **Online address:** rossinsky@msn.com

ROSS, JoAnn. Also writes as JoAnn Robb, JoAnn Robbins. American (born United States) **Genres:** Novels, Romance/Historical, Novellas/Short Stories. **Career:** Writer. **Publications:** ROMANCE NOVELS: (as JoAnn Robbins) A Winning Season, 1983; Love Thy Neighbor, 1985; Stormy Courtship, 1985; Duskfire, 1985; Risky Pleasure (companion to Duskfire), 1985; Without Precedent, 1986; A Hero At Heart, 1986; Bait and Switch, 1986; Hot on the Trail, 1987; Worth Waiting For, 1988; Spirit of Love, 1988; In a Class by Himself, 1988; Wilde 'n' Wonderful, 1988; Eve's Choice, 1988; Murphy's Law, 1989; Secret Sins, 1990; Tangled Hearts, 1991; Tangled Lives, 1991; Private Pleasures, 1992; Dark Desires, 1992; The Knight in Shining Armor, 1992; Lovestorm, 1993; Angel of Desire, 1994; Scandals, 1994; The Return of Caine O'Halloran, 1994; Legacy of Lies, 1995; I Do, I Do For Now, 1996; It Happened One Week, 1996; No Regrets, 1997; 1-800-HERO, 1998; Hunk of the Month, 1998; Mackenzie's Woman, 1999; Homeplace, 1999; Far Harbor, 2000; Confessions, 2003; Southern Comforts, 2004; (with N. Warren and E.C. Sheedy) Bayou Bad Boys, 2005; Blaze, 2005; Impulse, 2006; No Safe Place, 2007; Crossfire: A High Risk Novel, 2008; Freefall: A High Risk Novel, 2008; Shattered, 2009; Breakpoint: A High Risk Novel, 2009; The Homecoming, 2010; Bodyguards in Bed, 2011; One Summer, 2011; On Lavendar Lane, 2012. LUCKY PENNY SERIES: Magic in the Night, 1986; Playing For Keeps, 1987; Tempting Fate, 1987. MONTACROIX ROYAL FAMILY SERIES: Guarded Moments, 1990; The Prince and the Showgirl, 1993; The Outlaw, 1996. CASTLE MOUNTAIN SERIES: Starcrossed Lovers, 1993; Moonstruck Lovers, 1993; Thirty Nights, 2001. KNIGHTS OF NEW ORLEANS SERIES: Private Passions, 1995; Roarke: The Adventurer, 1997; Shayne: The Pretender, 1997; Michael: The Defender, 1997. BACHELOR ARMS SERIES: Never a Bride, 1995; For Richer, For Poorer, 1995; Three Grooms and a Wedding, 1995. MEN OF WHISKEY RIVER SERIES: Ambushed, 1996; Wanted!, 1996; Untamed, 1996. CASTLELOUGH IRISH SERIES: Fair Haven, 2000; Legends Lake, 2001; A Woman's Heart, 2002. CALLAHAN BROTHERS SERIES: Blue Bayou, 2002; River Road, 2002; Magnolia Moon, 2003. STEWART SISTERS SERIES: Out of the Mist, 2003; Out of the Blue, 2004; Out of the Storm, 2004. ROMANCE NOVELS AS JOANN ROBB: Stardust and Diamonds, 1983; Dreamlover, 1984; Tender Betrayal (Dreamlover) sequel, 1984; Sterling Deceptions, 1984; A Secure Arrangement, 1984; Touch the Sun, 1984; Wolfe's Prey, 1985; A Dangerous Passion, 1985; Promises to Keep, 1985; High Stakes Affair, 1986. **Address:** Penguin Group Inc., 375 Hudson St., New York, NY 10014, U.S.A. **Online address:** joann@joannross.com

ROSS, Jonathan. See ROSSITER, John.

ROSS, Kent. American (born United States), b. 1956?. **Genres:** Children's Fiction, Young Adult Fiction, Travel/Exploration, Romance/Historical. **Career:** University Church of Christ, minister. Writer. **Publications:** (With A. Ross and C. Ross) Whistle Punk (middle-level historical fiction), 1994; (with A. Ross) Cemetery Quilt (picture book), 1995; (with A. Ross) The Copper Lady (early reader), 1997; (with A. Ross) Jezebel's Spooky Spot, 1998. **Address:** 230 Malvern Rd., Arkadelphia, AR 71923-9628, U.S.A.

ROSS, Lawrence C. American (born United States), b. 1967?. **Genres:** Education, Art/Art History, History, Social Sciences, Literary Criticism And History. **Career:** Avalon Catering, president; RBG Online, president; "Black Web" column, columnist, 1995; Rap Sheet magazine, managing editor, 1997. **Publications:** The Divine Nine: The History of African American Fraternities and Sororities, 2000; The Ways of Black Folks: A Year in the Life of a People, 2003; Friends with Benefits, 2005; Money Shot: The Wild Days and Lonely Nights Inside the Black Porn Industry, 2007; Skin Game, 2007. Contributor to periiodicals. **Address:** c/o Manie Barron, Menza Barron Literary Agency, 1170 Broadway, Ste. 807, New York, NY 10001, U.S.A. **Online address:** alpha1906@gmail.com

ROSS, Michael Elsohn. American (born United States), b. 1952. **Genres:** Children's Non-fiction, Anthropology/Ethnology. **Career:** National Park Service, ranger, 1976-77; Yosemite Association, Yosemite National Park, naturalist, 1977-; Mariposa County Schools, teacher, 1981-84; Life Lab Science Program, curriculum developer, 1988-92; El Portal Child Development Center, chair, 1990-91. Illustrator and writer. **Publications:** Cycles, Cycles, Cycles, 1979; What Makes Everything Go?, 1979; (with D. Gaines and B. Shearin) Mono Lake Color and Learn Book, 1981; Easy Day Hikes in Yosemite, 1985; Faces in All Kinds of Places, 1986; The Yosemite Fun Book, 1987; Become a Bird and Fly, 1992; Great Explorations, 1992; Earth Is Home, 1992; Changes Around Us, 1992; The World of Small: Nature Explorations with a Hand Lens, 1993; The Happy Camper Handbook, 1994; Sandbox Scientist, 1995; Rolypolyology, 1996; Wormology, 1996; Cricketology, 1996; Snailology, 1996; Ladybugology, 1997; Caterpillarology, 1997; Bird Watching with Margaret Morse Nice, 1997; Wildlife Watching with Charles Eastman, 1997; Flower Watching with Alice Eastwood, 1997; Bugwatching with Charles Henry Turner, 1997; A Kid's Golden Gate!, 1997; Fish Watching with Eugenie Clark, 2000; Millipedeology, 2000; Exploring the Earth with John Wesley Powell, 2000; Spiderology, 2000; Exploring the Earth Exploring with John Wesley Powell, 2000; Pond Watching with Ann Morgan, 2000; Nature Art with Chiura Obata, 2000; Children of Northern Ireland, 2000; Children of Ireland, 2001; Children of Puerto Rico, 2001; Earth Cycles, 2001; Life Cycles, 2001; Body Cycles, 2002; Re-cycles, 2002; Mexican Christmas, 2002; Toy Lab, 2002; Junk Lab, 2002; Kitchen Lab, 2002; The Indoor Zoo, 2003; Salvador Dali and the Surrealists, 2003; Snug as a Bug, 2004; What's the Matter in Mr. Whisker's Room?, 2004; Baby Bear Isn't Hungry, 2006; Mama's Milk, 2007; Play with Me, 2009; Yosemite Trivia, 2011. **Address:** PO Box 295, El Portal, CA 95318, U.S.A. **Online address:** meross@att.net

ROSS, Oakland. Canadian (born Canada), b. 1952?. **Genres:** Novellas/Short Stories, Essays, Social Sciences. **Career:** Globe and Mail, foreign correspondent; The Toronto Star, feature writer, columnist, middle east bureau chief. **Publications:** Guerrilla Beach, 1994; A Fire on the Mountains: Exploring the Human Spirit from Mexico to Madagascar, 1995; The Dark Virgin, 2001. Contributor to periodicals. **Address:** The Toronto Star, 1 Younge St., 5th Fl., Toronto, ON M5E 1E6, Canada. **Online address:** oakland_ross@mac.com

ROSS, Rosetta E. American (born United States) **Genres:** Theology/Religion, History. **Career:** Writer. **Publications:** Witnessing and Testifying: Black Women, Religion, and Civil Rights, 2003; (co-author) Career Guide for Racial and Ethnic Minority Faculty in Religion, 2006. **Address:** Department of Philosophy and Religious Studies, Spelman College, 427 Cosby, 350 Spelman Ln. SW, Atlanta, GA 30314-4399, U.S.A. **Online address:** rross@spelman.edu

ROSS, Stephen M. American (born United States), b. 1943. **Genres:** Literary Criticism And History, Writing/Journalism. **Career:** Purdue University, assistant professor of English, 1970-77; United States Naval Academy, assistant professor, 1977-81, associate professor, 1981-86, professor of English, 1987; University of Geneva, lecturer, 1985; Universite de Strasbourg, associate professor, 1985; National Endowment for the Humanities, Summer Seminars for College Teachers, program officer, 1988-90, Division of Fellowships and Seminars, deputy, 1990-94, Office of Challenge Grants, director, 1994-. Writer. **Publications:** Fiction's Inexhaustible Voice: Speech and Writing in Faulkner, 1989; (with N. Polk) Reading Faulkner: The Sound and the Fury, 1996; (ed. with C.A. Kolmerten and J.B. Wittenberg) Unflinching Gaze: Morrison and Faulkner Re-Envisioned, 1997. Contributor of articles to books and periodicals. **Address:** Office of Challenge Grants, National Endowment for the Humanities, 1100 Pennsylvania Ave. NW, Washington, DC 20506, U.S.A. **Online address:** sross@neh.gov

ROSS, Stewart. British (born England), b. 1947. **Genres:** Children's Nonfiction, History. **Career:** Trinity College, teacher, 1965-66; Exeter University, assistant tutor, 1970-72; University of Riyadh, lecturer, 1972-74; King's School, master/housemaster, 1974-78; Rollins College, lecturer, 1979-89; full-time writer, 1989-; I.C.E.S. La Roche-sur-Yon, lecturer, 1995-97. **Publications:** NONFICTION: Columbus and the Age of Exploration, 1985; Chaucer and the Middle Ages, 1985; A Medieval Serf, 1985; Pepys and the Stuarts, 1985; A Saxon Farmer, 1985; A Victorian Factory Worker, 1985; Dickens and the Victorians, 1986; Spotlight on Medieval Europe, 1986; The Ancient Britons, 1987; Lloyd George and the First World War, 1987; Spotlight on the Stuarts, 1987; Spotlight on the Victorians, 1987; Winston Churchill and the Second World War, 1987; The Ancient World, 1990; Britain between the Wars, 1990; The Home Front, 1990; Elizabethan Life, 1991; The Nineteen Eighties, 1991; Europe, 1992; Racism in the Third Reich, 1992; Battle of Little Bighorn, 1993; Britain at War 1914-1918, 1993; Gunfight at O.K. Corral, 1993; Propaganda, 1993; Wild Bill Hickok and Calamity Jane, 1993; World Leaders, 1993; Wounded Knee, 1993; Cavaliers and Roundheads, 1994; Shakespeare and Macbeth: The Story behind the Play, 1994; Britain since 1930, 1995; Ancient Greece: Greek Theatre, 1996; Ancient Greece: The Original Olympics, 1996; And Then-: A History of the World in 128 Pages, 1996; Beware the King! The Story of Anne Boleyn and King Henry VIII, 1996; Down with the Romans: The Tragic Tale of Queen Boudicca, 1996; Charlotte Bronte and Jane Eyre, 1997; Gods and Giants: Myths of Northern Europe, 1997; Warriors & Witches, 1997; Dragons and Demons: Myths of China, Japan and India, 1998; Monsters and Magic, 1998; Oxford Children's Book of the 20th Century: A Concise Guide to a Century of Contrast and Change, 1998; Spirits and Sorcerers, 1998; Mark Twain and Huckleberry Finn, 1999; Daily Life, 1999; The Original Olympics, 1999; Greek Theatre, 1999; Vikings, 2000; The War in Kosovo, 2000; Assassination in Sarajevo: The Trigger for World War I, 2001, rev. ed., 2006; The American Revolution, 2001; The Industrial Revolution, 2001; Leaders of World War II, 2001; The Fall of the Bastille: Revolution in France, 2001; Alexander Graham Bell, 2001; The Story of Anne Frank, 2001; The Story of Mother Teresa, 2001; The Story of Ludwig van Beethoven, 2002; The Star Houses: A Story from the Holocaust, 2002; Only a Matter of Time: A Story From Kosovo, 2002; The Causes of the Cold War, 2002; The Technology of World War I, 2003; The Russian Revolution, 2003; Michael Faraday, 2003; Leonardo da Vinci, 2003; Leaders of World War I, 2003; The French Revolution, 2003; The Causes of World War I, 2003; World War I, 2004; Wolfgang Amadeus Mozart, 2004; William Shakespeare: Poet and Playwright, 2004; Monarchs, 2004; The Collapse of Communism, 2004; The Battle of the Somme, 2004. HOW THEY LIVED SERIES: A Family in World War II, 1985; An Edwardian Household, 1986; A Crusading Knight, 1986; A Roman Centurion, 1985; A Soldier in World War I, 1987. POLITICS TODAY SERIES: The Alliance Parties, 1986; The Conservative Party, 1986; The House of Commons, 1986; The House of Lords, 1986; The Labour Party, 1986; The Prime Minister, 1986; The Cabinet and Government, 1987; Elections, 1987; The European Parliament and the European Community, 1987; Local Government, 1987; The Monarchy, 1987; Trade Unions and Pressure Groups, 1987. WITNESS HISTORY SERIES: China since 1945, 1988; Toward European Unity, 1989; The Origins of World War I, 1989; The Russian Revolution, 1989; The United Nations, 1989; War in the Trenches, 1990; The USSR under Stalin, 1991; Witness to History: the Arab-Israeli Conflict, 2004. STARTING HISTORY SERIES: Food We Ate, 1991; How We Travelled, 1991; What We Wore, 1991; Where We Lived, 1991; Our Environment, 1992; Our Family, 1992; Our Health, 1992; Our Holidays, 1992; Our Schools, 1992; Shopping, 1992. FACT OR FICTION SERIES: Spies and Traitors, 1995; Pirates: The Story of Buccaneers, Brigands, Corsairs and Their Piracy on the High Seas from the Spanish Main to the China Sea, 1995; Cowboys: A Journey down the Long, Lonely Cattle Trail in Search of the Hard-Riding, Gun-Slinging Cowhands of the Old West, 1995; Bandits and Outlaws: The Truth about Outlaws, Highwaymen, Smugglers and Robbers from the Bandit Gangs of Ancient China to the Desperados of Today, 1995; Conquerors and Explorers, 1996; Secret Societies, 1996; Knights, 1996; Witches, 1996; Beasts, 1997; Monsters of the Deep, 1997. CAUSES AND CONSEQUENCES SERIES: Causes and Consequences of the Arab-Israeli Conflict, 1996; Causes and Consequences of the Rise of Japan and the Pacific Rim, 1996; Causes and Consequences of World War II, 1996; Causes and Consequences of the Great Depression, 1998; Causes and Consequences of World War I, 1998. FOR ADULTS-NONFICTION: Monarchs of Scotland,

1990; Scottish Castles, 1990; Ancient Scotland, 1991; History in Hiding: The Story of Britain's Secret Passages and Hiding Places, 1991; The Stewart Dynasty, 1993. FICTION: One Crowded Hour, 1994; Beneath Another Sun, 1994. COMING ALIVE SERIES: Long Live Mary, Queen of Scots, 1998; Athens Is Saved!: The First Marathon, 1998; Find King Alfred!, 1999. OTHERS: The Last Clarinet (libretto), 1995; Admiral Sir Francis Bridgeman, 1998; Ancient Egyptians, 2003; Art and Architecture, 2004; Egypt in Spectacular Cross-Section, 2005; Ancient China, 2006; Tales of the Dead: Ancient Rome, 2005; The British Monarchy from Henry VIII, 2005; Pirates, Plants And Plunder!, 2005; Dear Mum, I Miss You!, 2006; Down with the Romans, 2006; Curse of the Crocodile God, 2007; Greed, Seeds and Slavery, 2007; Instruments of Death, 2007; Price of Victory, 2007; Ancient Greece Daily Life, 2007; Terror Trail, 2007; Ancient Greece Entertainment, 2007; Higher, Further, Faster: Is Technology Improving Sport?, 2008; Please Help, Miss Nightingale!, 2008; Look Around a Shakespearean Theater, 2008; What If the Bomb Goes Off?, 2008; Ice Age, 2009; Medieval Europe, 2010; Moon, 2010; Understand The Israeli-Palestinian Conflict, 2010; Understand the Middle East, 2010; Hiroshima, 2011; Into the Unknown, 2011; (with J. Woodward) Pearl Harbor, 2011; Sports Technology, 2012. EDITOR: The First World War, 1989; The Second World War, 1989. **Address:** c/o James Wills, Watson Little Ltd., 48-56 Bayham Pl., London, GL NW1 0EU, England. **Online address:** words@stewartross.com

ROSS, Stewart Halsey. *See* Obituaries.

ROSS, Stuart. Canadian (born Canada), b. 1959. **Genres:** Poetry, Novels. **Career:** Writer and educator. **Publications:** FICTION: (with M. Laba) The Pig Sleeps, 1991; (with G. Barwin) The Mud Game: A Novel, 1995; Henry Kafka & Other Stories, 1997; Confessions of a Small Press Racketeer, 2005. POETRY: The Thing in Exile, 1975; The Inspiration Cha-Cha, 1996; Farmer Gloomy's New Hybrid, 1999; Razovsky at Peace, 2001; Hey, Crumbling Balcony! Poems New & Selected, 2003; (ed.) Surreal Estate: 13 Canadian Poets under the Influence, 2004; Robots at Night, 2005; I Cut My Finger, 2007; Dead Cars in Managua, 2008; Buying Cigarettes for the Dog, 2009; (ed.) Why are You So Long and Sweet?: Collected Long Poems, 2010; (ed. with S. Brockwell) Rogue Stimulus: The Stephen Harper Holiday Anthology for a Prorogued Parliament Edition, 2010; Snowball, Dragonfly, Jew, 2011. Contributor to periodicals. **Address:** ECW PRESS, 2120 Queen St. E, Ste. 200, Toronto, ON M4E 1E2, Canada. **Online address:** hunkamooga@sympatico.ca

ROSS, Tony. British (born England), b. 1938. **Genres:** Children's Fiction, Illustrations, Human Relations/Parenting. **Career:** Smith Kline & French Pharmaceuticals, graphic designer, 1962-64; Brunnings Advertising, art director, 1964-65; Manchester Polytechnic, lecturer in illustration, 1965-72, senior lecturer in illustration, 1972-85; writer and illustrator, 1985-. **Publications:** SELF-ILLUSTRATED: Tales from Mr. Toffy's Circus: Big Ethel, Blodwen, Bop, Mr. Toffy, Samuel, Tiger Hary, 6 vols., 1973; Goldilocks and the Three Bears, 1976; Hugo and the Man Who Stole Colors, 1977; Hugo and the Wicked Winter, 1977; Norman and Flop Meet the Toy Bandit, 1977; Hugo and Oddsock, 1978; The Greedy Little Cobber, 1979; The True Story of Mother Goose and Her Son Jack, 1979; Jack and the Beanstalk, 1980; Hugo and the Ministry of Holidays, 1980 in US as Hugo and the Bureau of Holidays, 1982; Puss in Boots: The Story of a Sneaky Cat, 1981; Naughty Nigel, 1982 in US as Naughty Nicky, 1983; Jack the Giantkiller, 1983; The Three Pigs, 1983; I'm Coming to Get You, 1984; Towser and Sadie's Birthday, 1984; Towser and the Terrible Thing, 1984; Towser and the Water Rats, 1984; Lazy Jack, 1985; The Boy Who Cried Wolf, 1985; I Want My Potty, 1986; Towser and the Haunted House, 1987; Towser and the Funny Face, 1987; Towser and the Magic Apple, 1987; Oscar Got the Blame, 1987; Super Dooper Jezebel, 1988; I Want a Cat, 1988; The Treasure of Cozy Cove, or, The Voyage of the Kipper, 1989; Hansel and Gretel, 1989; The Happy Rag in US as The Happy Blanket, 1990; Mrs. Goat and Her Seven Little Kids, 1990; This Old Man: A Musical Counting Book, 1990; Going Green: A Kid's Handbook to Saving the Planet, 1990; Don't Do That!, 1991; A Fairy Tale, 1991; Big Bad Barney Bear, 1992; I Want to Be, 1993; Eventful Years: A Tribute to the Royal Air Force, 1918-1993, 1993; Weather, 1994; Pets, 1994; Bedtime, 1995; Shapes, 1995; Towser and Towser's Party, 1995; Towser and the Monster Egg, 1995; I Want My Dinner, 1995; Furry Tales: A Bumper Book of Ten Favourite Animal Tales, 1999; I Want a Sister, 1999; Wash Your Hands!, 2000; I Want My Dummy, 2001; I Want My Tooth, 2002; Centipede's 100 Shoes, 2002; I Don't Want to Go to Bed!, 2004; I Want My Pacifier, 2004; I Want My Mom!, 2004; I Want a Friend, 2005; I Want My Present, 2005; Is It Because?, 2005; (with I. Whybrow) Badness for Beginners: A Little Wolf and Smellybreff Adventure,

2005; (with J. Willis) Killer Gorilla, 2005; (with J. Willis) Misery Moo, 2005; Say Please, 2005; (with I. Whybrow) What's The Time, Little Wolf?: Another Little Wolf and Smellybreff Adventure, 2006; I Want to Go Home!, 2006; I Want My Light On!, 2007; (with Z. Ross) Nicky, 2007; (with J. Willis) Cottonball Colin, 2008; (and ed.) Three Little Kittens and Other Favorite Nursery Rhymes, 2009; I Want Two Birthdays!, 2010; (with J. Willis) Caterpillar Dreams, 2010; Victor, 2011; I Want a Party!, 2011; I Want to do It Myself!, 2011; I Want to Win!, 2012. Illustrator of books by others. **Address:** Andersen Press Ltd., 20 Vauxhall Bridge Rd., London, GL SW1V 2SA, England.

ROSSANT, Colette. American/French (born France), b. 1932?. **Genres:** Food And Wine, inspirational/Motivational Literature, International Relations/Current Affairs, Third World. **Career:** St. Anne's Episcopal School, Language Department, chair; New York Magazine, underground gourmet writer, 1979-; McCalls, food and design editor, 1982-; America Entertains, founder, 1984-; New York Daily News, columnist, 1993-; Hofstra University, instructor in French. **Publications:** Cooking with Colette, 1975; (with J.H. Herman) A Mostly French Food Processor Cookbook, 1977, rev. ed., 1983; Colette Rossant's After-Five Gourmet, 1981; Colette's Slim Cuisine, 1983; Colette's Japanese Cuisine, 1985; New Kosher Cooking, 1986; (with M. Melendez) Vegetables: The Art of Growing, Cooking, and Keeping the New American Harvest, 1991; Memories of a Lost Egypt: A Memoir with Recipes, 1999; Apricots on the Nile, 2002; Return to Paris: A Memoir, 2003; The World In My Kitchen: The Adventures Of A (Mostly) French Woman In New York, 2006. Contributor to periodicals. **Address:** c/o Gloria Loomis, Watkins/Loomis Agency Inc., 133 E 35th St., Ste. 1, PO Box 20925, New York, NY 10016, U.S.A. **Online address:** colette@coletterossant.com

ROSSEN, Jake. American (born United States) **Genres:** Novels. **Career:** Freelance writer. **Publications:** Superman vs. Hollywood: How Fiendish Producers, Devious Directors and Warring Writers Grounded an American Icon, 2008. **Address:** Binghamton, NY , U.S.A. **Online address:** jrossen@sherdog.com

ROSSER, Sue V(ilhauer). American (born United States), b. 1947. **Genres:** Women's Studies And Issues, Education, Social Sciences, Reference. **Career:** University of Wisconsin, post-doctoral fellow, 1973-76, lecturer, 1976, visiting professor, 1976-86; Mary Baldwin College, assistant professor, 1976-83, associate professor, 1983-86, Division of Theoretical and Natural Sciences, coordinator, 1983-84; Towson State University, consultant, 1984-85; Duke University, consultant, 1985; Randolph Macon Women's College, consultant, 1985; Appalachian State University, consultant, 1986; University of California, consultant, 1986; University of South Carolina, associate professor, 1986-90, director of women's studies, 1986-95, professor of family and preventive medicine, 1990-95; Southern Illinois University, consultant, 1987; Virginia Polytechnic and State University, consultant, 1987; University of Georgia, consultant, 1988; University of Maine, consultant, 1988; University of Oklahoma, consultant, 1989; University of North Carolina, consultant, 1989; Smith College, consultant, 1990; University of Nevada, consultant, 1991; North Carolina Wesleyan College, consultant, 1993; University of Minnesota, consultant, 1993; University of Wisconsin System, visiting distinguished professor, 1993; University of Florida, Center for Women's Studies and Gender Research, director, professor of anthropology, 1995-99; Georgia Institute of Technology, Ivan Allen College, dean, 1999-, School of Public Policy, professor, 1999-, School of History, Technology and Society, adjunct professor of biology, 1999-, professor, 1999-, Ivan Allen Dean's chair of liberal arts and technology, 2005-. Writer. **Publications:** Teaching Science and Health from a Feminist Perspective: A Practical Guide, 1986; (ed. and contrib.) Feminist Approaches to Science, 1986; Feminism Within the Science and Health Care Professions: Overcoming Resistance, 1988; Female-Friendly Science: Applying Women's Studies Methods and Theories to Attract Students to Science, 1990; (contrib.) The Nobel Prize Winners: Physiology and Medicine, 1991; Biology & Feminism: A Dynamic Interaction, 1992; (contrib. with J. Altekruse) The Knowledge Explosion, 1992; Women's Health: Missing from U.S. Medicine, 1994; (ed.) Teaching the Majority: Breaking the Gender Barrier in Science, Mathematics, and Engineering, 1995; Re-Engineering Female Friendly Science, 1997; Women, Science, and Society: The Crucial Union, 2000; Science Glass Ceiling: Academic Women Scientists and the Struggle to Succeed, 2004; (ed. with M.F. Fox and D.G. Johnson) Women, Gender, and Technology, 2006; (ed.) Women, Science, and Myth: Gender Beliefs from Antiquity to the Present, 2008; (ed.) Diversity and Women's Health, 2009;

People Friendly Medicine, forthcoming. Contributor of articles to books and periodicals. **Address:** Ivan Allen College of Liberal Arts, Georgia Institute of Technology, 781 Marietta St., Atlanta, GA 30332-0525, U.S.A. **Online address:** sue.rosser@iac.gatech.edu

ROSSI, Hozy (Joe). American (born United States), b. 1965?. **Genres:** Novels, Literary Criticism And History, Young Adult Fiction. **Career:** KHET, producer and writer; Manoa Center for Oral History, field interviewer; eNature.com, news producer. **Publications:** Appointment with Il Duce, 2001. Contributor of poetry to anthologies. **Address:** 1045 Sansome St., Ste. 304, San Francisco, CA 94111, U.S.A.

ROSSI, John V. American (born United States), b. 1955. **Genres:** Animals/Pets, Zoology. **Career:** Blanding Animal Hospital, veterinarian, 1986-94; Baywood Animal Hospital, veterinarian, 1994-; Jacksonville University, professor of vertebrate biology, 1994-95; North American Snake Institute, director; Jacksonville Museum of Science and History, consulting veterinarian; St. Augustine Alligator Farm, consulting veterinarian; Jacksonville Herpetological Society, co-founder; Riverside Animal Hospital, veterinarian. Writer. **Publications:** Snakes of the United States and Canada: Keeping Them Healthy in Captivity, vol. I: Eastern Area, 1992, vol. II: Western Area, 1994; (with R. Rossi) What's Wrong With My Snake?, 1996, new ed., 2006; (with R. Rossi) Snakes of the United States and Canada: Natural History and Care in Captivity, 2001. Contributor to periodicals. **Address:** Riverside Animal Hospital, 2641 Park St., Jacksonville, FL 32204-4519, U.S.A. **Online address:** rossi@rossidvm.com

ROSSI, Roxanne. American (born United States), b. 1962. **Genres:** Animals/Pets, Zoology, Natural History, Biology. **Career:** North American Snake Institute, curator. Writer. **Publications:** Snakes of the United States and Canada: Keeping Them Healthy in Captivity, 1992, vol. II: Western Area, 1994; (with J.V. Rossi) What's Wrong With My Snake?, 1996, new ed., 2006; (with J.V. Rossi) Snakes of the United States and Canada: Natural History and Care in Captivity, 2003. **Address:** 10023 Belle Rive Blvd., Ste. 1118, Jacksonville, FL 32256-9579, U.S.A.

ROSSING, Barbara. American (born United States) **Genres:** Theology/Religion, Education, Reference. **Career:** Lutheran School of Theology, associate professor of New Testament, 1994-2001, professor, 2001-; American Lutheran Church, Global Mission Interpretation, assistant and acting director; Holden Village Retreat Center, pastor; Harvard University, Divinity School, chaplain. Writer. **Publications:** The Choice between Two Cities: Whore, Bride and Empire in the Apocalypse, 1999; The Rapture Exposed: The Message of Hope in the Book of Revelation, 2004. Contributor to books and periodicals. **Address:** Lutheran School of Theology, 1100 E 55th St., Chicago, IL 60615, U.S.A. **Online address:** brossing@lstc.edu

ROSSIO, Terry. American (born United States), b. 1960. **Genres:** Novels, Young Adult Fiction. **Career:** Scheherazade Productions, co-owner; Wordplay, co-founder; screenwriter; producer. **Publications:** (Co-author) The Mask of Zorro: A Novelization, 1998. **Address:** Brian Siberell, Creative Artists Agency, 9830 Wilshire Blvd., Beverly Hills, CA 90212-1825, U.S.A.

ROSSITER, John. (Jonathan Ross). British (born England), b. 1916. **Genres:** Mystery/Crime/Suspense, Young Adult Fiction, Novels. **Career:** Wiltshire Constabulary, detective chief superintendent, 1939-69; Wiltshire Courier, columnist, 1963-64. **Publications:** The Murder Makers, 1970; The Deadly Green, 1970; The Victims, 1971; A Rope for General Dietz, 1972; The Manipulators, 1973; The Villains, 1974; The Golden Virgin in US as The Deadly Gold, 1975; The Man Who Came Back (non-mystery novel), 1978; Dark Flight (non-mystery novel), 1981; Andropov Deception, 1984; (as John R. Rossiter) Measurement for the Social Sciences, 2010; Like Niobe, All Tears, forthcoming. AS JONATHAN ROSS: The Blood Running Cold, 1968; Diminished by Death, 1968; Dead at First Hand, 1969; The Deadest Thing You Ever Saw, 1969; Here Lies Nancy Frail, 1972; The Burning of Billy Toober, 1974; I Know What It's Like to Die, 1976; A Rattling of Old Bones, 1979; Dark Blue and Dangerous, 1981; Death's Head, 1982; Dead Eye, 1983; Dropped Dead, 1984; Burial Deferred, 1985; Fate Accomplished, 1987; Sudden Departures, 1988; A Time for Dying, 1989; Daphne Dead and Done For, 1990; Murder Be Hanged, 1993; The Body of a Woman, 1994; None the Worse for a Hanging, 1995; Murder! Murder! Burning Bright, 1996; This Too, Too Sullied Flesh, 1997. **Address:** 3 Leighton Home Farm Ct., Wellhead Ln., Westbury, WT BA13 3PT, England.

ROSSITER, John. *See* **CROZIER, Brian.**

ROSS-MACDONALD, Malcolm (John). Also writes as Malcolm Macdonald, M. R. O'Donnell. British/Irish (born Ireland), b. 1932. **Genres:** Novels, Plays/Screenplays, Sciences. **Career:** Umeå University, teacher in English, 1958-61; Folkuniversitet, lecturer, 1959-61; Aldus Books Ltd., caption writer, executive editor, 1961-65; Hornsey College of Art, visiting lecturer, 1966-69. **Publications:** The Big Waves, 1962; (ed.) Spare Part Surgery, 1968; (with Longmore) Machines in Medicine, 1969; (with K. Coppard and B. Cooper) Guide to the Orient and Pacific, 1970; (with Longmore) The Heart, 1971; The World Wildlife Guide, 1971; Beyond the Horizon, 1971; Kristina's Winter, 1972; Conditional People, 1973; Every Living Thing, 1973; Doors Doors Doors, 1974; Life in the Future, 1974; World from Rough Stones, 1974; The Origin of Johnny, 1975; Crissy's Family in US as The Trevarton Inheritance, 1996; Like a Diamond, 1999. AS MALCOLM MACDONALD: The Rich Are with You Always, 1976; Sons of Fortune, 1978; Abigail, 1979; The Dukes, 1981; Goldeneye, 1982; Tessa d'Arblay, 1983; For They ShallInherit in UK as In Love and War, 1984; On a Far Wild Shore in UK as Mistress of Pallas, 1986; The Silver Highways, 1987; Honour and Obey in UK as The Sky with Diamonds, 1988; A Notorious Woman, 1988; His Father's Son, 1989; An Innocent Woman, 1989; Hell Hath No Fury, 1990; A Woman Alone, 1990; The Captain's Wives, 1991; A Woman Possessed, 1992; To the End of Her Days, 1994; All Desires Known, 1994; Dancing on Snowflakes, 1994; Kernow & Daughter, 1996; Tomorrow's Tide, 1996; The Carringtons of Helston, 1997; Tamsin Harte, 2000; Rose of Nancemellin, 2001. AS M.R. O'DONNELL: A Woman Scorned, 1991; For I Have Sinned, 1995. **Address:** David Higham Association Ltd., 5-8 Lower John St., Golden Sq., London, GL W1R 4HA, England.

ROSSMAN, C. L. American (born United States), b. 1946. **Genres:** Science Fiction/Fantasy, Military/Defense/Arms Control. **Career:** Dearborn Press and Guide, education editor; HRD and Associates, marketing staff; Eton Senior Center, developer and director; Dearborn Times-Herald, city news editor, 1975-77; Manistee News Advocate, bureau chief, 1997-99. Journalist and writer. **Publications:** Renegade the Hunter, 2003; Renegade: The Warrior, 2006; The Mission to Earth: A Tale of the Hunters, 2009. **Address:** c/o Author Mail, 1stBooks Library, AuthorHouse, 1663 Liberty Dr., Ste. 200, Bloomington, IN 47403, U.S.A. **Online address:** kahnie@msn.com

ROSSMAN, Jeffrey J. American (born United States), b. 1965. **Genres:** Business/Trade/Industry, History. **Career:** University of Virginia, associate professor, director of undergraduate studies and director of distinguished majors program, 1999-, Soviet Film Study Group, coordinator, 2000-02, Page-Barbour Interdisciplinary Initiative on Ethnic Cleansing and Forced Deportation, co-director, 2009-, Center for Russian, East European and Eurasian Studies, director, 2012-. Writer. **Publications:** Worker Resistance under Stalin: Class and Revolution on the Shop Floor, 2005. **Address:** Corcoran Department of History, University of Virginia, 385 Nau Hall, South Lawn, 1540 Jefferson Park Ave., PO Box 400180, Charlottesville, VA 22904, U.S.A. **Online address:** jrossman@virginia.edu

ROSSMAN, Vadim. American/Russian (born Russia), b. 1964. **Genres:** Novels, History, Social Sciences. **Career:** University of Texas, instructor, 1993-2000; General Motors Co., financial analyst, 2000-; Broadwing Communications, senior business analyst, 2000-01; Micromark Labs, senior marketing analyst, 2002-; Deloitte & Touche, consultant. Writer. **Publications:** Russian Intellectual Antisemitism in the Post-Communist Era, 2002. Works appear in anthologies. Contributor of articles to periodicals. **Address:** 12410 Alameda Trace Cir., Apt. 2331, Austin, TX 78727-6337, U.S.A. **Online address:** vjrossman@yahoo.com

ROSSOL, Monona. American (born United States), b. 1936. **Genres:** Engineering, Art/Art History, Theatre, Medicine/Health, Crafts. **Career:** Bjorksten Research Laboratory, research chemist, 1959-60; University of Wisconsin-Madison, instructor in integrated liberal studies and ceramics, 1961-62, project assistant in civil engineering, 1964-67; City University of New York, Herbert H. Lehman College, ceramics teacher, 1964-80; Henry Street Settlement House, ceramics teacher, 1964-80; Greenwich House Pottery, ceramics teacher, 1964-80; Center for Occupational Hazards (now Center for Safety in the Arts), co-founder, 1977, director of information, 1977-87, president, 1980-86; Arts, Crafts and Theatre Safety Inc., founder and president, 1987-. Writer. **Publications:** Stage Fright: Health and Safety in the Theater, 1986, 2nd ed., 1991; The Artist's Complete Health and Safety Guide: Everything You Need to Know about Art Materials to Make Your Workplace Safe and Comply with United States and Canadian Right-to-Know Laws, 1990, 3rd ed., 2001; Safety Training Manual: Our Right-to-Know Program, 1991; (with S.D. Shaw) Overexposure: Health Hazards in Photography, 2nd ed., 1991; (with B. Bartlett) Danger! Artists at Work: A Guide to Occupational Hazards and Precautions for Arts Workers and Teachers, 1991, 2nd ed., 1996; Keeping Clay Work Safe and Legal, 1993, 2nd ed., 1996; The Health & Safety Guide for Film, TV & Theater, 2000; Artist's Complete Health and Safety Guide, 2001. Contributor to periodicals. **Address:** Arts, Crafts and Theater Safety Inc., 181 Thompson St., Ste. 23, New York, NY 10012-2586, U.S.A. **Online address:** 75054.2542@compuserve.com

ROSSUM, Ralph A. (Ralph Arthur Rossum). American (born United States), b. 1946?. **Genres:** Administration/Management, Politics/Government, Law. **Career:** Chicago City Colleges, instructor in behavioral sciences, 1970-71; Grinnell College, instructor in political science, 1972-73; Memphis State University, assistant professor, 1973-77, associate professor of political science, 1977-80; Loyola University, associate professor of political science, 1980-83, associate dean of graduate school, 1981-83; National Endowment for the Humanities, review panelist, 1984-; National Institute of Justice, review panelist, 1985-; University of Aix-Marseilles Law School, visiting instructor, 1987; Hampden-Sydney College, professor of political science and president, 1991-92; Claremont McKenna College, Alice Tweed Tuohy Professor of Government and Ethics, 1984-88, vice president and dean of faculty, 1988-91, visiting professor, 1992-93, Henry Salvatori Professor of Political Philosophy and American Constitutionalism, 1994-, Henry Salvatori Center for the Study of Freedom in the Modern World, director, 1984-89, Rose Institute of State and Local Government, director, 2000-; University of Redlands, Fletcher Jones Professor of American Politics, 1993-94; American Academy of Liberal Education, staff, 1994-, chair, 1997-2008; Commission on the Bicentennial of the United States Constitution, review panelist; St. Martin's Press, manuscript reviewer; Prentice-Hall, manuscript reviewer; University of California Press, manuscript reviewer. Writer. **Publications:** (ed. with A.E. Bent) Urban Administration: Management, Politics, and Change, 1976; (with A.E. Bent) Police, Criminal Justice, and the Community, 1976; The Politics of the Criminal Justice System: An Organizational Analysis, 1978; Reverse Discrimination: The Constitutional Debate, 1980; (ed. with G.L. McDowell) The American Founding: Politics, Statesmanship, and the Constitution, 1981; (with G.A. Tarr) American Constitutional Law: Cases and Interpretation, 2 vols., 1983, 8th ed., 2009; (with B.J. Koller and C.P. Manfredi) Juvenile Justice Reform: A Model for the States, 1987; Congressional Control of the Judiciary: The Article III Option, 1988; Federalism, the Supreme Court, and the Seventeenth Amendment: The Irony of Constitutional Democracy, 2001; Antonin Scalia's Jurisprudence: Text and Tradition, 2006. Contributor to books, journals and periodicals. **Address:** Claremont McKenna College, 850 Columbia Ave., Claremont, CA 91711-3901, U.S.A. **Online address:** ralph.rossum@claremontmckenna.edu

ROSSUM, Ralph Arthur. *See* **ROSSUM, Ralph A.**

ROSTKER, Bernard D. American (born United States), b. 1944. **Genres:** Military/Defense/Arms Control, History. **Career:** Office of the Assistant Secretary of Defense for Systems Analysis, economist, 1968-70; RAND Corp., research economist, 1970-72, program director for Manpower Personnel and Training Program, 1972-77, Arroyo Center, associate director and deputy director of the U.S. Army Studies and Analysis Center, 1984-90, Defense Manpower Research Center, director, 1990-94, senior fellow; U.S. Navy, principal deputy assistant secretary of Manpower and Reserve Affairs, 1977-79, director of Selective Service, 1979-81, Center for Naval Analyses, director of Navy management program, 1981-83; Systems Research and Applications Corp., Systems Management Division, director, 1983-84; U.S. Navy, assistant secretary for Manpower and Reserve Affairs, 1994-98, special assistant to the deputy secretary for Gulf War illnesses; Under Secretary of the Army, 1998-2000; Under Secretary of Defense for Personnel and Readiness, 2000. Writer. **Publications:** The Personnel Structure and Posture of the Air National Guard and the Air Force Reserve, 1973; (with R. Shishko) The Air Reserve Forces and the Economics of Secondary Labor Market Participation, 1973; Air Reserve Forces Personnel Study, 1973; (co-author) The Defense Officer Personnel Management Act of 1980: A Retrospective Assessment, 1993; Total Force Planning, Personnel Costs and the Supply of New Reservists: A Report Prepared for United States Air Force Project RAND, 1974; The Air Reserve Forces and the All-Volunteer Force, a Statement before the Defense Manpower Commission, 1975; (with D. Greenberg and A. Lipson) Incentive Pay in the Civil Service: The Case of the California Job Agent, 1975; An Evaluation-Management Information System for Vocational Rehabilitation, 1975; Depleted Uranium: A Case Study of Good and Evil, 2002; (with G. Kauvar and R. Shaver) Safer Skies: Baggage Screening and Beyond-with Supporting Analyses, 2002; I Want You! The Evolution of the All-Volunteer Force, 2006; (with W.M. Hix and J.M. Wilson) Recruitment and Retention: Lessons for the New Orleans Police Department, 2007; America Goes to War: Managing the Force during Times of Stress and Uncertainty, 2007; (co-author) Evaluation of the New York City Police Department Firearm Training and Firearm-Discharge Review Process, 2008. Contributor to books. **Address:** Special Assistant on Gulf War Illnesses, 4 Skyline Pl., Ste. 901, 5113 Leesburg Pke., Falls Church, VA 22041, U.S.A. **Online address:** bernard_rostker@rand.org

ROSTKOWSKI, Margaret I. American (born United States), b. 1945. **Genres:** Young Adult Fiction, Novels, Sports/Fitness. **Career:** Washington Junior High School, reading teacher, 1974-84; Mount Ogden Middle School, teacher of English and French, 1979-84; Ogden High School, teacher of English and writing, 1984-. Writer. **Publications:** NOVELS: After the Dancing Days, 1982; The Best of Friends, 1989; Moon Dancer, 1995. **Address:** c/o Ruth Cohen, PO Box 7626, Menlo Park, CA 94026-7626, U.S.A. **Online address:** rostkowskim@m.ogden.k12.ut.us

ROSTON, Murray. British/Israeli (born Israel), b. 1928. **Genres:** Art/Art History, Literary Criticism And History, Theatre, Intellectual History. **Career:** Bar-Ilan University, faculty, 1956-, professor of English literature; University of California, adjunct professor of English literature, 1999-. Writer. **Publications:** Prophet and Poet: The Bible and the Growth of Romanticism, 1965; Biblical Drama in England from the Middle Ages to the Present Day, 1968; The Soul of Wit: A Study of John Donne, 1974; Milton and the Baroque, 1980; Sixteenth-Century English Literature, 1982; Renaissance Perspectives in Literature and the Visual Arts, 1987; Changing Perspectives in Literature and the Visual Arts 1650-1820, 1990; Victorian Contexts: Literature and the Visual Arts, 1996; Modernist Patterns: In Literature and the Visual Arts, 1999; The Search for Selfhood in Modern Literature, 2001; Graham Greene's Narratives Strategies, 2006; Tradition and Subversion in Renaissance Literature, 2008; The Comic Mode in English Literature, 2011. **Address:** Department of English, Bar-Ilan University, Ramat-Gan, 52900, Israel. **Online address:** murrayroston@gmail.com

ROTELLO, Gabriel. American (born United States), b. 1953. **Genres:** Gay And Lesbian Issues, Medicine/Health, Social Commentary, Documentaries/Reportage, Environmental Sciences/Ecology. **Career:** OutWeek Magazine, co-founder, editor-in-chief, 1989-91; Newsday, columnist, 1992-95. Journalist, producer and director. **Publications:** Sexual Ecology: AIDS and the Destiny of Gay Men, 1997. Contributor to books and periodicals. **Address:** 1036 S Hudson Ave., Los Angeles, CA 90019, U.S.A. **Online address:** grotello@gmail.com

ROTENBERG, Marc. American (born United States), b. 1960. **Genres:** Law, Technology, Communications/Media. **Career:** Public Interest Registry, chair; Georgetown University, adjunct professor of law, Electronic Privacy Information Center (EPIC), president and director, 1994-; Stanford Law School, Stanford Law Review, articles editor; Stanford Public Interest Law Foundation (SPILF), research assistant and president. Writer. **Publications:** (Ed. with P.E. Arge) Technology and Privacy: The New Landscape, 1997; The Privacy Law Sourcebook: United States Law, International Law and Recent Developments, 1998; Privacy in America: The New Challenge, 1999; (with D.J. Solove and P.M. Schwartz) Information Privacy Law, 2003, 2nd ed., 2006; (with D.J. Solove and P.M. Schwartz) Privacy, Information and Technology, 2006; (co-author) Privacy and Human Rights: An International Survey of Privacy Laws and Developments, 2007; (co-author) Litigation Under the Federal Open Government Laws 2006, 2007. **Address:** Electronic Privacy Information Ctr., 1718 Connecticut Ave. NW, Ste. 200, Washington, DC 20009, U.S.A. **Online address:** rotenberg@epic.org

ROTENBERG, Robert. Canadian (born Canada), b. 1953. **Genres:** Novels. **Career:** Passion, The Magazine of Paris, managing editor, 1980; TO, Magazine of Toronto, founder, publisher and editor, 1982-88; Rotenberg, Shidlowski and Jesin (a legal firm), co-founder, partner and attorney, 1990; Canadian Broadcasting Corp. (CBC), film executive, radio journalist and producer. **Publications:** Old City Hall, 2009; Guilty Plea, 2011. **Address:** c/o Victoria Skurnick, Levine Greenberg Literary Agency, 307 7th Ave., Ste. 2407, New York, NY 10001, U.S.A. **Online address:** info@robertrotenberg.com

ROTH, Darlene R(ebecca). American (born United States), b. 1941. **Genres:** Archaeology/Antiquities, Architecture, Local History/Rural Topics, History. **Career:** Emory University, lecturer, 1974-82; History Group Inc., principal, 1976-82; D. Roth and Associates, principal, 1982-90; Atlanta History Center, associate; Delta Air Lines, Delta Air Transport Heritage Museum, director. Writer. **Publications:** (Comp. with V. Shadron) Women's Records, a Preliminary Guide, 1978; (with L.E. Shaw) Atlanta Women from Myth to Modern Times: A Century of History, 1980; (ed.) The Atlanta Exposition Cookbook, 1980; Architecture, Archaeology, and Landscapes: Resources for Historic Preservation in Unincorporated Cobb County, Georgia, 1988; Matronage: Patterns in Women's Organizations, Atlanta, Georgia, 1890-1940, 1994; (with A. Ambrose) Metropolitan Frontiers: A Short History of Atlanta, 1996; Greater Atlanta: A Shared Destiny, 2000; (ed. with J. Kemph) Piedmont Park: Celebrating Atlanta's Common Ground, 2004. **Address:** Atlanta History Center, 130 W Paces Ferry Rd. NW, Atlanta, GA 30305-1366, U.S.A.

ROTH, Eric. American (born United States), b. 1945. **Genres:** Biography, Sports/Fitness. **Career:** Writer. **Publications:** Ali: The Movie and the Man, 2001. Contributor to periodicals. **Address:** Creative Artists Agency, 9830 Wilshire Blvd., Beverly Hills, CA 90212-1804, U.S.A.

ROTH, Gerhard (Jurgen). Austrian (born Austria), b. 1942. **Genres:** Novels, Autobiography/Memoirs, Essays. **Career:** Graz Center for Statistics, computer operator, manager, 1966-77; freelance writer, 1978-; photographer. **Publications:** OTHER FICTION: NOVELS: Die Autobiographie des Albert Einstein, 1972; Der Wille zur Krankheit, 1973; Der Grosse Horizont: Roman, 1974; Ein Neuer Morgen: Roman, 1976; Winterreise, 1978; Circus Saluti, 1981; Die Vergessenen, 1986; Bild-Sprache: Osterreichische Malerei Nach 1945, 1992; Der See, 1995; (with B. Hunziker and M. Grüninger) Fristen von A-Z: Die Wichtigsten Fristen Aus ZGB, or und SchKG, 1997; Der Plan, 1998; The Lake, 1999; The Story of Darkness, 1999; Der Berg: Roman, 2000; Der Strom, 2002; Labyrinth: Roman, 2005; Das Alphabet Der Zeit, 2007. STORIES: Der Ausbruch des Ersten Weltkriegs und Andere Romane, 1972. FICTION: DIE ARCHIVE DES SCHWEIGENS SERIES: Der Stille Ozean: Roman, 1980; Landlaufiger Tod: Roman, 1984; Am Abgrund, 1986; Der Untersuchungsrichter: Die Geschichte eines Entwurfs, 1988; Im Tiefen österreich (photographs), 1990; Die Geschichte der Dunkelheit: Ein Bericht, 1991; Reise in Das Innere von Wien, 1991. NONFICTION: (with K.R. Mueller and P. Turrini) Bruno Kreisky, 1981; Grenzland, 1981; Ueber Bienen, 1989; über Bilder: österreichische Malerei Nach 1945: Ausder Sammlung der Zentralsparkasse, 1990; (with E. Horandner) Von Bienen und Imkern. von Wachs und vom Honig, 1993. OTHERS: Lichtenberg, 1973; (ed.) Kritik der Verhaltensforschung, 1974; Herr Mantel und Herr Hemd (for children), 1974; Menschen Bilder Marionetten (collected works), 1979; Schönenen Bilder beim Trabrennen, 1982; Das Töeten des Bussards, 1982; Dorfchronik zum Landlaufiger Tod, 1984; Gerhard Roth: Materialien zu Die Archive des Schweigens, 1992; Gerhard Roth: Orkus: im Schattenreich der Zeichen, 2003; Will to Sickness, 2006; Die Stadt, 2009; Gespräche mit Gerhard Roth: das Frühwerk bis zum Landläufigen Tod, 2009. **Address:** Am Heumarkt 714137, Wien, N030, Austria.

ROTH, Klaus. German (born Germany), b. 1939. **Genres:** Bibliography, Anthropology/Ethnology. **Career:** University of Muenster, assistant professor, 1976-82; University of Munich, professor, 1982-; University of California, visiting professor, 1988, 1991. Writer. **Publications:** Ehebruchschwaenke in Liedform: Eine Untersuchung zur deutschundenglischsprachigen Schwankballade, 1977; (with H. Mannheims) Probate Inventories: An International Bibliography, 1984; Slike u glavama: Ogledio narodnoj kulturi u jugoistocnoj Evropi (in Serbian), 2000. EDITOR: Entdeckung Balkan: Jugoslawien, Griechenland, Bulgarien; Land und Menschenzwischen Adria, ägäis und Schwarzem Meer, 1987; Handwerk im Mittelund Südosteuropa: Mobilität, Vermittlung und Wandel im Handwerk des 18. bis 20. Jahrhunderts, 1987; Southeast European Folk Culture in the Modern Era, 1992; (and comp. with G. Wolf) South Slavic Folk Culture: Bibliography of Literature in English, German, and French on Bosnian-Hercegovinian, Bulgarian, Macedonian, Montenegrin, and Serbian Folk Culture, 1993; Suedosteuropäische Popularliteratur im 19. und 20. Jahrhunders, 1993; (and trans.) Typenverzeichnis der bulgarischen Volksmärchen, 1995; (with H. Gerndt) Gesamtregister der Zeitschriftfuer Volkskunde Jahrgang 1-90, 1891-1994, 1996; Mit der Differenz leben: Europäsche Ethnologie und Interkulturelle Kommunikation, 1996; (with F.D. Grimm) Das Dorf in Südosteuropa zwischen Tradition und Umbruch, 1997; Radost Ivanova: Folklore of the Change: Folk Culture in Post-Socialist Bulgaria, 1999; (with R. Alsheimer and A. Moosmüller) Lokale Kulturen in einer globalisierenden Welt: Perspektiven auf interkulturelle Spannungsfelder, 2000; Nachbarschaft: Interkulturelle Beziehungen zwischen Deutschen, Polen und Tschechen, 2001. Contributor of articles and reviews to academic journals. **Address:** Institut für Volkskunde/European Ethnology, Ludwig-Maximilians-Universität, Ludweigstr. 25, Munich, D-80539, Germany. **Online address:** k.roth@lrz.uni-muenchen.de

ROTH, Lorna. (Lorna Frances Roth). Canadian (born Canada), b. 1947?. **Genres:** Literary Criticism And History, Art/Art History, Photography. **Career:** Teacher, 1968-73; cross-cultural communications and education consultant, 1977-93; Concordia University, Department of Communications, lecturer, 1992-94, assistant professor of communication studies and chair, 1994-. Writer and media historian. **Publications:** Something New in the Air: The Story of First Peoples Television Broadcasting in Canada, 2005. Contributor to books, periodicals and journals. **Address:** Department of Communication Studies, Concordia University, 7141 Sherbrooke W, Montreal, QC H4B 1R6, Canada. **Online address:** l.roth@sympatico.ca

ROTH, Lorna Frances. *See* **ROTH, Lorna.**

ROTH, Louise Marie. American/Canadian (born Canada), b. 1970?. **Genres:** Sociology. **Career:** University of Arizona, Department of Sociology, assistant professor, 2000-07, associate professor of sociology, 2007-, faculty coordinator, 2000-09, sociology brown bag colloquium coordinator, 2002-03. Writer. **Publications:** Selling Women Short: Gender Inequality on Wall Street, 2006. Works appear in anthologies. Contributor to periodicals. **Address:** Department of Sociology, University of Arizona, 433 Social Sciences Bldg., 1145 SE Campus Dr., PO Box 210027, Tucson, AZ 85721-0027, U.S.A. **Online address:** lroth@email.arizona.edu

ROTH, Norman. American (born United States), b. 1938. **Genres:** Cultural/Ethnic Topics, Literary Criticism And History, Theology/Religion, History, Intellectual History, Literary Criticism And History, Theology/Religion. **Career:** University of Wisconsin-Madison, Department of Hebrew and Semitic Studies, assistant professor, associate professor, 1976-90, professor, 1990-, now professor emeritus. Writer. **Publications:** Maimonides: Essays and Texts, 1985; Jews, Visigoths and Muslims in Medieval Spain: Cooperation and Conflict, 1994; Conversos, the Inquisition and Expulsion of the Jews from Spain, 1995, rev. ed., 2002; (ed.) Medieval Jewish Civilization: An Encyclopedia, 2002; Daily Life of the Jews in the Middle Ages, 2005; Dictionary of Iberian Jewish and Converso Authors, 2007. **Address:** Department of Hebrew & Semitic Studies, University of Wisconsin, Rm. 1352, Van Hise Hall, 1220 Linden Dr., Madison, WI 53706, U.S.A. **Online address:** ndroth@wisc.edu

ROTH, Philip. American (born United States), b. 1933. **Genres:** Novels, Essays, Young Adult Non-fiction, Novellas/Short Stories. **Career:** The Nation, film critic; University of Chicago, instructor, 1956-58; University of Iowa, visiting lecturer, 1960-62; Princeton University, writer-in-residence, 1962-64; University of Pennsylvania, faculty, writer-in-residence, 1965-80, retired, 1991; State University of New York, visiting lecturer, 1967-68; City University of New York, Hunter College, distinguished professor, 1989-92. **Publications:** Goodbye, Columbus and Five Short Stories, 1959; Letting Go, 1962; When She was Good, 1967; Portnoy's Complaint, 1969; On the Air: A Long Story, 1970; Our Gang: Starring Tricky and His Friends, 1971; The Breast, 1972; The Great American Novel, 1973; My Life As a Man, 1974; Reading Myself and Others, 1975; The Professor of Desire, 1977; The Ghost Writer, 1979; A Philip Roth Reader, 1980; Novotny's Pain, 1980; Zuckerman Unbound, 1981; The Anatomy Lesson, 1983; Zuckerman Bound: A Trilogy and Epilogue 1979-1985 in UK as The Prague Orgy, 1985; American West's Acid Rain Test, 1985; The Counterlife, 1986; The Facts: A Novelist's Autobiography, 1988; Deception: A Novel, 1990; Patrimony: A True Story, 1991; Conversations with Philip Roth, 1992; Conversion of the Jews, 1992; Operation Shylock: A Confession, 1993; Werner Pfeiffer: Endangered Species, 1994; Sabbath's Theater, 1995; American Pastoral, 1997; I Married a Communist, 1998; The Human Stain, 2000; The Dying Animal, 2001; Shop Talk: A Writer and His Colleagues and their Work, 2001; The Plot Against America, 2004; Novels & Stories, 1959-1962, 2005; Novels, 1967-1972, 2005; Novels, 1973-1977, 2006; Everyman, 2006; Exit Ghost, 2007; Novels & Other Narratives, 1986-1991, 2008; Indignation, 2008; The Humbling, 2009; Nemesis, 2010; Novels, 1993-1995, 2010; (with V. Hage) A Writer at Work, 2011; Philip Roth: The American Trilogy, 2011; Notes for My Biographer, 2012. Works

appear in anthologies. Contributor of articles to periodicals. **Address:** c/o Jeffrey Posternak, The Wylie Agency, 250 W 57th St., Ste. 2114, New York, NY 10107-2199, U.S.A.

ROTH, Randolph Anthony. American (born United States), b. 1951?. **Genres:** History. **Career:** Ohio State University, professor of history and sociology, Historical Violence Database, co-founder and co-director. Historian and writer. **Publications:** The Democratic Dilemma: Religion, Reform, and the Social Order in the Connecticut River Valley of Vermont, 1791-1850, 1987; American Homicide, 2009. Contributor to books and journals. **Address:** Department of History, Ohio State University, 165 Dulles Hall, 230 W 17th Ave., Columbus, OH 43210, U.S.A. **Online address:** roth.5@osu.edu

ROTHENBERG, David. American (born United States), b. 1962. **Genres:** Mystery/Crime/Suspense, Novels. **Career:** New Jersey Institute of Technology, Department of Humanities, assistant professor, associate professor, professor of philosophy; Antioch New England Graduate School, adjunct professor, 1990-91; Banff Centre for Arts, artist-in-residence, 1991; Babson College, adjunct professor, 1992; Artemis Ensemble, founder. Writer. **Publications:** Walking with the Trees: Twelve Hikes in and around Fairfield County, 1978; (trans.) A. Naess, Ecology, Community, and Lifestyle: Outline of an Ecosophy, 1989; Arne Nass: gjør det vondt å tenke?, 1992; Hand's End: Technology and the Limits of Nature, 1993; (ed. with P. Reed) Wisdom in the Open Air: The Norwegian Roots of Deep Ecology, 1993; Is It Painful to Think?: Conversations with Arne Naess, 1993; (ed.) Wild Ideas, 1995; (ed. with M. Ulvaeus) The New Earth Reader: The Best of Terra Nova, 1999; (ed. with E. Katz and A. Light) Beneath the Surface: Critical Essays in the Philosophy of Deep Ecology, 2000; (ed. with M. Tobias and J.P. Fitzgerald) Parliament of Minds: Philosophy for a New Millennium, 2000; Blue Cliff Record: A Poetic Echo, 2001; (ed. with M. Ulvaeus) Writing on Water, 2001; (ed. with M. Ulvaeus) The Book of Music and Nature: An Anthology of Sounds Words Thoughts, 2001; (ed. with M. Ulvaeus) The World and the Wild, 2001; Always the Mountains, 2002; Sudden Music: Improvisation Sound Nature, 2002; (ed. with W.J. Pryor) Writing on Air, 2003; (ed. with W.J. Pryor) Writing the Future: Progress and Evolution, 2004; (ed. with W.J. Pryor) Writing the World: On Globalization, 2005; Why Birds Sing: A Journey into the Mystery of Bird Song, 2005; Thousand Mile Song: Whale Music in a Sea of Sound, 2008; Survival of the Beautiful, 2011. **Address:** Department of Humanities, New Jersey Institute of Technology, Rm. 317 Cullimore, University Heights, Newark, NJ 07102, U.S.A. **Online address:** info@thousandmilesong.com

ROTHENBERG, Jerome. American (born United States), b. 1931. **Genres:** Poetry, Translations. **Career:** Hawk's Well Press, founding publisher, 1958-65; City College of New York, instructor, 1959-60; Mannes College of Music, lecturer in English, 1961-70; University of California, regents professor, 1971; New School for Social Research, visiting lecturer in anthropology, 1971-72; University of Wisconsin, visiting professor, 1974-75; San Diego State University, visiting professor, 1976-77; University of California, visiting professor, 1977-79, 1980-84; University of California, visiting professor, 1980; University of Southern California, distinguished Aerol Arnold chair in English, 1983; University of Oklahoma, visiting professor, 1985; State University of New York, professor of English, 1986-88; New York State Writers Institute, distinguished writer-in-residence, 1986; University of California, San Diego, professor of visual arts and literature, 1988-, now professor emeritus. **Publications:** White Sun Black Sun, 1960; The Seven Hells of the Jigoku Zoshi, 1962; Sightings I-IX, 1964; The Gorky Poems, 1966; Between: Poems 1960-1963, 1967; Conversations, 1968; Sightings and Red Easy Color, 1968; Poems 1964-1967, 1968; Poland/1931, 1969, rev. ed., 1974; A Book of Testimony, 1971; Poems for the Game of Silence, 1971; Esther K. Comes to America, 1973; A Seneca Journal I: A Poem of Beavers, 1973, rev. ed., 1978; The Cards, 1974; The Pirke and the Pearl, 1975; The Notebooks, 1976; Seneca Journal: Midwinter, and The Serpent, 2 vols., 1975-77; A Big Jewish Book, 1977; Narratives and Real Theatre Pieces, 1978; Poemes pour le jeu dusilence, 1978; Numbers and Letters, 1979; Vienna Blood, 1980; Pre-Faces, 1981; Poems for the Society of Mystic Animals, 1982; Altar Pieces, 1982; That Dada Strain, 1983; 15 Flower World Variations, 1984; (with E. Mottram and G. Selerie) The Riverside Interviews, 1984; A Merz Sonata, 1986; New Selected Poems, 1986; Khurbn and Other Poems, 1989; Further Sightings and Conversations, 1989; The Lorca Variations 1-8, 1990; Apres le jeu da silence, 1991; Gematria, 1993; The Lorca Variations (complete), 1993; An Oracle for Delfi, 1995; Seedings and Other Poems, 1996; Pictures of the Crucifixion and Other Poems, 1996; Paris Elegies and Improvisations, 1998; (with I. Tyson) Delights/Delices & Other Gematria, 1998; A Paradise of Poets, 1999; The Case for Memory, 2001; Livre de Temoignage, 2002; Un Cruel Nirvana, 2002; A Book of Witness, 2003; A Book of Concealments, 2004; 25 Caprichos: After Goya, 2004; (with S. Bee) The Burning Babe & Other Poems 2005; China Notes and The Treasures of Dunhuang, 2006; Triptych, 2007; Three Poems after Images by Nancy Tobin, 2007; A Second Book of Concealments, 2007; Poetics & Polemics, 2008; Gematria Complete, 2009; Concelments and Caprichos, 2010. TRANSLATOR: (ed.) New Young German Poets, 1959; R. Hochhuth, The Deputy, 1965; The Flight of Quetzalcoatl, 1967; (with M. Hamburger) H.M. Enzensberger, Poems for People Who Don't Read Poems, 1968; E. Gomringer, The Book of Hours and Constellations, 1968; The 17 Horse-Songs of Frank Mitchell: X-XIII, 1970; (with H. Lenowitz) Gematria 27, 1977; 4 Lorca Suites, 1989; (with P. Joris) K. Schwitters, Poems Performance Pieces Proses Plays Poetics, 1993; (with M. Sovak) V. Nezval, Antilyrik & Other Poems, 2001; F. Garcia Lorca, Suites, 2001; (with P. Joris) P. Picasso, The Burial of the Count of Orgaz & Other Poems, 2004; Writing Through: Translations & Variations, 2004. EDITOR: Ritual: A Book of Primitive Rites and Events, 1966; Technicians of the Sacred: A Range of Poetries from Africa, America, Asia and Oceania, 1968, 2nd ed., 1985; Shaking the Pumpkin: Traditional Poetry of the Indian North Americas, 1972, rev. ed. 1986; (with G. Quasha) America a Prophecy: New Reading of American Poetry from Pre-Columbian Times to the Present, 1973; Revolution of the World: A New Gathering of American Avant Garde Poetry 1914-1945, 1974; (with M. Benamou) Ethnopoetics: A First International Symposium, 1976; (with H. Lenowitz and C. Doria) A Big Jewish Book, 1978, rev. ed. (with H. Lenowitz) as Exiled in the Word, Port, 1989; (with D. Rothenberg) Symposium of the Whole, 1982; (with D. Rothenberg) Symposium of the Whole: A Range of Discourse Toward an Ethnopoetics, Berkeley, 1983; Exiled in the Word, 1989; (with P. Joris) Poems for the Millennium: The University of California Book of Modern & Postmodern Poetry, vol. I, 1995, vol. II, 1998; (with D. Guss) The Book, Spiritual Instrument, 1996; (with S. Clay) A Book of the Book: Some Works and Projections about the Book and Writing, 2000; Maria Sabina Selections, 2003; (with J.C. Robinson) Poems for the Millennium, vol. III, 2009. Address: New Directions Publishers, 80 8th Ave., New York, NY 10011, U.S.A. Online address: jrothenberg@cox.net

ROTHFUSS, Pat J. American (born United States), b. 1973. Genres: Novels. Career: University of Wisconsin, instructor in English and fencing. Writer. Publications: Your Annotated, Illustrated College Survival Guide, 2005; The Name of the Wind, 2007; The Adventures of the Princess and Mr. Whiffle: the Thing Beneath the Bed, 2010; The Wise Man's Fear, 2011. Contributor to periodicals. Address: Department of English, University of Wisconsin, CCC 318, 2100 Main St., Stevens Point, WI 54481-3897, U.S.A. Online address: prothfus@uwsp.edu

ROTH-HANO, Renée. American/French (born France), b. 1931. Genres: Autobiography/Memoirs, Young Adult Fiction. Career: Renault Inc., bilingual secretary, salesperson and assistant section chief, 1959-62; Telcolab Corp., bilingual secretary, 1963-66; French-American Chamber of Commerce, assistant, 1966-67; Manhattan Veterans Administration Medical Center, psychiatric social worker, 1969-92; New York University, School of Social Work, adjunct professor of social work, 1992-2009, retired, 2009. Writer. Publications: Touch Wood: A Girlhood in Occupied France, 1988; Safe Harbors, 1993; (with S. Morgenthaler) A Demain a New York: Je Porterai Votre Echarpe, 2003; 13 North-Irregulars, forthcoming. Contributor to periodicals. Address: 315 E 72nd St., New York, NY 10021-4638, U.S.A. Online address: reneeroth@juno.com

ROTHKOPF, David J. American (born United States), b. 1955. Genres: Economics, Business/Trade/Industry, Money/Finance, Politics/Government. Career: Office of Congressman Stephen J. Solarz, press secretary, 1979-80; Tilley, Marlieb & Alan, senior vice president, 1980-82; Financial World (magazine), vice president, 1984-85; Institutional Investor Inc., vice president of publications, 1985-87; Global Money Management Forum, editor, 1986-87; Global Capital Markets Forum, editor, 1986-87; International Media Partners Inc., chair, chief executive officer, 1987-93; CEO International Strategies, editor-in-chief, 1989-93; World Market Outlook, staff, 1991-93; National Convention News, staff, 1991; U.S. Department of Commerce, deputy undersecretary of commerce for international trade policy development, 1993-95, acting undersecretary of commerce for international trade policy development, 1995-96; Kissinger Associates Inc., managing director, 1996-; Columbia University, faculty in international relations, 1996; Carnegie Endowment for International Peace, visiting associate, 1996; Intellibridge Corp., chair and chief executive officer; Garten Rothkopf (advisory firm), president

and chief executive officer. Publications: (With C.Z. Rothkopf) The Common Market: Uniting the European Community, 1977; The Price of Peace: Emergency Economic Intervention and U.S. Foreign Policy, 1998; (ed. with S. Purcell) Cuba: The Contours of Change, 2000; Running the World: The Inside Story of the National Security Council and the Architects of American Power, 2005; Superclass: The Global Power Elite and the World They are Making, 2008. Contributor to periodicals. Address: Kissinger Associates Inc., 350 Park Ave., New York, NY 10022-6022, U.S.A. Online address: drothkopf@ceip.org

ROTHMAN, David J. American (born United States), b. 1937. Genres: Civil Liberties/Human Rights, Criminology/True Crime, History, Medicine/Health. Career: Columbia University, assistant professor, 1964-67, associate professor, 1967-70, professor of history, 1971-, Bernard Schoenberg professor of social medicine, 1982-, Center for the Study of Society and Medicine, director, 1982-, Center for Medicine as a Profession, director; Harvard University, Center for the Study of History of Liberty in America, fellow, 1965-66; Hebrew University, Fulbright professor, 1968-69, Samuel Paley lecturer, 1977; State University of New York, School of Criminal Justice, visiting Pinkerton professor, 1973-74; Mental Health Law Project, board director, 1973-80, 1982-; Project on Community Alternatives, co-director, 1978-82. Writer. Publications: Politics and Power: The United States Senate, 1869-1901, 1966; The Discovery of the Asylum, 1971, rev. ed., 2002; (co-author) Doing Good: The Limits of Benevolence, 1978; Incarceration and Its Alternatives in 20th Century America, 1979; Conscience and Convenience: The asylum and its Alternatives in Progressive America, 1980. rev. ed., 2002; (with S.M. Rothman) The Willowbrook Wars, 1984; Strangers at the Bedside: A History of How Law and Bioethics Transformed Medical Decision-Making, 1991, 2nd ed. 2003; (with A. Neier) Prison Conditions in India, 1991; (with S. Powers and S. Rothman) Hollywood's America: Social and Political Themes in Motion Pictures, 1996; Beginnings Count: The Technological Imperative on American Health Care, 1997; (with S.M. Rothman) The Pursuit of Perfection: The Promise and Perils of Medical Enhancement, 2003; (with S.M. Rothman) Trust is Not Enough: Bringing Human Rights to Medicine, 2006. EDITOR: (with N. Harris and S. Thernstrom) American History, 1969; (with N. Harris and S. Thernstorm) The History of the United States: Source Readings, 2 vols., 1969; (with S.M. Rothman) On Their Own: The Poor in Modern America, 1972; (with S.M. Rothman) The Sources of the American Social Tradition, 1975; The World of the Adams Chronicles, 1976; (with S.M. Rothman and G. Brown) The Family, 1978; (with S. Wheeler) Social History and Social Policy, 1981; (with S.M. Rothman) Children's Hospitals in the Progressive Era, 1987; (with S.M. Rothman) Consumers' League of New York, 1987; (with S.M. Rothman) Divorce: The First Debates, 1987; (with S.M. Rothman) The Dangers of Education, 1987; (with S.M. Rothman) Low Wages and Great Sins, 1987; (with S.M. Rothman) National Congress of Mothers, 1987; (with S.M. Rothman) Women in Prison, 1834-1928, 1987; (with S.M. Rothman) Risks for the Single Woman in the City, 1987; (with S.M. Rothman) Maternal Mortality in New York City and Philadelphia, 1931-1933, 1987; (with S. Marcus and S.A. Kiceluk) Medicine and Western Civilization, 1995; (with N. Morris) The Oxford History of the Prison: The Practice of Punishment in Western Society, 1995; The Geography of Hope: Poets of the Colorado Western Slope, 2000; (with H.L. Rosenthal) What Do We Owe Each Other?: Rights and Obligations in Contemporary American Society, 2008; (with D. Blumenthal) Medical Professionalism in the New Information Age, 2010. Address: Department of History, Columbia University, 622 W 168th St., Ste. 15-25, PO Box 2510, New York, NY 10032, U.S.A. Online address: djr5@columbia.edu

ROTHMAN, William. American (born United States), b. 1944. Genres: Film, Humanities, Essays, Philosophy, Plays/Screenplays, Popular Culture, History, Humor/Satire, Humor/Satire. Career: University of Miami, School of Communication, professor of motion picture and video-film, 1991-; KB Productions Inc., vice president. Writer. Publications: Hitchcock-The Murderous Gaze, 1982; The I of the Camera: Essay in Flims Criticism, History and Aesthethics, 1988, 2nd ed., 2004; The Taste for Beauty: Writings of Eric Rohmer, 1990; Documentary Film Classics, 1997; (with M. Keane) Reading Cavell's The World Viewed: A Philosophical Perspective on Film, 2000; (ed. and intro.) Cavell on Film and Video, 2005; (ed.) Jean Rouch: A Celebration of Life and Film, Schena Editore and Presses de l'Universite de Paris-Sorbonne, 2007; (ed.) Three Documentary Filmmakers: Errol Morris, Ross McElwee, Jean Rouch, 2009. Address: School of Communication,

University of Miami, 5100 Brunson Dr., Frances L. Wolfson Bldg. 4009, PO Box 248127, Coral Gables, FL 33146-2105, U.S.A. **Online address:** rothman@miami.edu

ROTHSTEIN, Hy S. American (born United States) **Genres:** Military/Defense/Arms Control, History, International Relations/Current Affairs. **Career:** Armed Forces, military advisor, 1987-89; Graduate School of Operational and Information Sciences, senior service fellow, 1994-95, senior lecturer, 2002-; Joint Special Operations Command, chief of plans and exercises, 1995-98; U.S. Army John F. Kennedy Special Warfare Center, director of concept developments, 1999. Writer. **Publications:** Afghanistan and the Troubled Future of Unconventional Warfare, 2006. **Address:** Graduate School of Operational and Information, Sciences, Department of Defense Analysis, Monterey, CA 93943, U.S.A. **Online address:** hsrothst@nps.edu

ROTHSTEIN, Robert L. American (born United States), b. 1936. **Genres:** Politics/Government, Economics. **Career:** Columbia University, instructor in political science, 1964-66, Institute of War and Peace Studies, Carnegie fellow, 1970-71, visiting professor, 1977, 1978, 1979; Johns Hopkins University, assistant professor, associate professor of political science, 1967-74; Colgate University, Department of Political Science, Harvey Picker professor of international relations, International Relations Program, director, Harvey Picker professor emeritus of international relations; Washington Foreign Policy Research Institute, research associate, 1968-69; Rockefeller Foundation Program, fellow, 1975-77; University of Baroda, Ford Foundation, lecturer, 1991, consultant, distinguished visiting professor, 1989, 1991; U.S. Institute of Peace, Jennings Randolph fellow, 1991-92; Hebrew University of Jerusalem, Rebecca Meyerhoff memorial lecturer, 1995; Organization for Economic Cooperation and Development, consultant; Carnegie Foundation, fellow; Social Science Research Council, fellow. Writer. **Publications:** Alliances and Small Powers, 1968; Planning, Prediction, and Policymaking in Foreign Affairs, 1972; The Weak in the World of the Strong: The Developing Countries in the International System, 1977; Global Bargaining: UNCTAD and the Quest for a New International Economic Order, 1979; The Third World and U.S. Foreign Policy: Cooperation and Conflict in the 1980s, 1981; Sri Lankan Peace Process: Lessons from the Middle East and Northern Ireland, 2003; (with D.D. Perlmutter) Challenge of Climate Change: Which Way Now?, 2010. EDITOR: The Evolution of Theory in International Relations: Essays in Honor of William T.R. Fox, 1991; (with E. Kaufman and S.B. Abed) Democracy, Peace, and the Israeli-Palestinian Conflict, 1993; After the Peace: Resistance and Reconciliation, 1999; (with M. Ma'oz and K. Shikaki) Israeli-Palestinian Peace Process: Oslo and the Lessons of Failure: Perspectives, Predicaments and Prospects, 2002. Contributor of articles to books and journals. **Address:** Department of Political Science, Colgate University, 13 Oak Dr., Hamilton, NY 13346-1338, U.S.A. **Online address:** rrothstein@colgate.edu

ROTHSTEIN, Sam. *See* **ROTHSTEIN, Samuel.**

ROTHSTEIN, Samuel. (Sam Rothstein). Canadian/Russian (born Russia), b. 1921. **Genres:** Librarianship. **Career:** University of California, principal library assistant, 1947; University of British Columbia, School of Library, Archival and Information Studies, junior librarian, 1947-48, head of acquisitions, 1948-51, assistant university librarian, 1954-59, associate university librarian, 1959-61, acting university librarian and founding director, 1961-62, professor of library science, 1962-, director of school of librarianship, 1962-70, director and professor of librarianship, 1970-86, professor emeritus, 1986-; Science Secretariat of Canada, consultant, 1969; University of Toronto, visiting professor, 1970, librarian-in-residence, 1979; Vancouver Jewish Community Centre, president, 1972-; Hebrew University, visiting professor, 1973; Vancouver Public Library Trust, president, 1987-88; Vancouver Combined Jewish Appeal, divisional chairman, 1992-95. Writer. **Publications:** The Development of Reference Services, 1955; (co-ed.) As We Remember It, 1970; (co-author) The Library-The University, 1972; (co-author) Rothstein on Reference- With Some Help from Friends, 1989. **Address:** School of Librarianship, University of British Columbia, Vancouver, BC V6T 1Z1, Canada.

ROTHWELL, Victor Howard. British/Scottish (born Scotland), b. 1945. **Genres:** History, Politics/Government, Biography, Autobiography/Memoirs. **Career:** University of Exeter, tutor in history, 1969-70; University of Edinburgh, School of History, Classics and Archaeology, lecturer in history, 1970-, reader, 1989-, honorary fellow. Writer. **Publications:** British War Aims and Peace Diplomacy, 1914-1918, 1971; Britain and the Cold War, 1941-1947, 1982; Anthony Eden: A Political Biography, 1931-57, 1992; The Origins of the Second World War, 2001; The War Aims in the Second World War: The War Aims of the Major Belligerents 1939-1945, 2005. **Address:** School of History, Classics and Archaeology, University of Edinburgh, Rm. 1M.30, William Robertson Bldg., 4 Doorway, Old Medical School, Teviot Pl., Edinburgh, BR EH8 9AG, Scotland. **Online address:** victor_rothwell@yahoo.co.uk

ROTHWELL, William J. American (born United States), b. 1951. **Genres:** Administration/Management, Business/Trade/Industry, Economics, Technology. **Career:** Illinois Department of Personnel, staff development specialist, 1979; Illinois Office of the Auditor General, special services officer and training director, 1979-87; Sangamon State University, lecturer, 1983-85; R&K Consultants, senior associate, 1987-88; Franklin Life Insurance Co., assistant vice-president and director of management development, 1987-93; Illinois State University, lecturer, 1988; University of Oklahoma, consultant, 1990-91; Pennsylvania State University, College of Education, Department of Adult Education, Instructional Systems, and Workforce Education and Development, associate professor of human resource development, 1993-97, professor of human resource development, 1997-, Department of Learning and Performance Systems, Workforce Education and Development Program, professor-in-charge, 2003-06; Rothwell & Associates Inc., president, 1993-; The Rothwell Partnership, vice president, 1999-. Writer. **Publications:** (With H.J. Sred) The American Society for Training and Development Reference Guide to Professional Training Roles and Competencies, 2 vols., 1987, 2nd ed., 1992; (with H.C. Kazanas) Strategic Human Resources Planning and Management, 1988; (with H.C. Kazanas) Strategic Human Resource Development, 1989; (with D. Brandenburg) The Workplace Literacy Primer: An Action Manual for Training and Development Professionals, 1990; (with H.C. Kazanas) Mastering the Instructional Design Process: A Systematic Approach, 1992, 4th ed., 2008; (with H.C. Kazanas) The Complete AMA Guide to Management Development, 1993; (with H.C. Kazanas) Planning and Managing Human Resources: Strategic Planning for Personnel Management, rev. ed., 1994; (with H.C. Kazanas) Human Resource Development: A Strategic Approach, rev. ed., 1994; (with H.C. Kazanas) Improving On-the-Job Training: How to Establish and Operatea Comprehensive OJT Program, 1994, 2nd ed., 2004; Effective Succession Planning: Ensuring Leadership Continuity and Building Talent from Within, 1994, 4th ed., 2010; (contrib.) In Action: Needs Assessment, 1995; Beyond Training and Development: State-of-the Art Strategies for Enhancing Human Performance, 1996, 2nd ed. as Beyond Training and Development: The Groundbreaking Classic on Human Performance Enhancement, 2005; (with P. Cookson) Beyond Instruction: Comprehensive Program Planning for Business and Education, 1997; (with R.K. Prescott and M.W. Taylor) The Strategic Human Resource Leader: How to Prepare Your Organization for the Six Key Trends Shaping the Future, 1998; The Action Learning Guidebook: A Real-Time Strategy for Problem Solving, Training Design and Employee Development, 1999; Workplace Learning and Performance Roles: The Intervention Selector, Designer and Developer, and Implementor, 2000; Workplace Learning and Performance Roles: The Evaluator, 2000; (with C.K. Hohne and S.B. King) Human Performance Improvement: Building Practitioner Competence, 2000, 2nd ed., 2007; Workplace Learning and Performance Roles: The Analyst, 2000; The Competency Toolkit, 2 vols., 2000; Workplace Learning and Performance Roles: The Manager and the Change Leader, 2001; (with S.B. King and M. King) The Complete Guide to Training Delivery: A Competency-Based Approach, 2001; The Workplace Learner: How to Align Training Initiatives with Individual Learning Competencies, 2002; (with W.E. Donahue and J.E. Park) Creating In-House Sales Training and Development Programs: A Competency-Based Approach to Building Sales Ability, 2002; (with J.A. Benkowski) Building Effective Technical Training: How to Develop Hard Skills within Organizations, 2002; (with J.E. Lindholm and W.G. Wallick) What CEOs Expect from Corporate Training: Building Workplace Learning and Performance Initiatives that Advance Organizational Goals, 2003; Career Planning and Succession Management: Developing Your Organization's Talent for Today and Tomorrow, 2005; (co-author) The Handbook of Training Technologies, 2006; (with B. Powers) Instructor Excellence: Mastering the Delivery of Training, 2nd ed., 2007; (with R.D. Cecil) Next Generation Management Development: The Complete Guide and Resource, 2007; (with J.M. Graber) Competency-Based Training Basics, 2010; Invaluable Knowledge: Securing Your Company's Technical Expertise, 2011; Lean But Agile: Rethink Workforce Planning and Gain a True Competitive Edge, 2012. TRAINING PACKAGES: The Right-to-Know Workshop, 1989; The Strategic Planning Workshop, 1989; The Structured On-the-Job Training Workshop, 2 vols., 1989; The Employee Discipline Workshop, 2 vols., 1990; The Employee Selection Workshop, 2 vols., 1990; The Self-Directed On-the-Job Learning Workshop, 1996; (with R.K. Prescott and M.W. Taylor) Human

Resource Transformation: Demonstrating Strategic Leadership in the Face of Future Trends, 2008; Adult Learning Basics, 2008; (co-author) Working Longer: New Strategies for Managing, Training, and Retaining Older Employees, 2008; Manager's Guide to Maximizing Employee Potential: Quick and Easy Strategies to Develop Talent Every Day, 2010. EDITOR AND CONTRIBUTOR: (with H. Sred) The Workforce of the Eighties: Developing the Critical Resource, 1983; (with R. Sullivan and G.N. McLean) Practicing Organization Development: A Guide for Consultants, 1995, (co-ed.) 3rd ed. as Practicing Organization Development: A Guide for Leading Change, 2010; The Emerging Issues in Human Resource Development Sourcebook, 1995; The ASTD Models for Human Performance Improvement: Roles, Competencies, Outputs, 1997; (with D. DuBois) Improving Performance in Organizations: Eleven Case Studies from the Real World of Training, 1998; Linking HRD Programs with Organizational Strategy, 1998; (with P.E. Gerity and E.A. Gaertner) Linking Training to Performance, 2004; (with P.E. Gerity) Linking Workforce Development to Economic Development: A Casebook for Community Colleges, 2008; (with J. Alexander and M. Bernhard) Cases in Government Succession Planning, 2008; Encyclopedia of Human Resource Management, 2012. Contributor to journals. **Address:** Department of Learning and Performance Systems, Pennsylvania State University, 310 B Keller Bldg., University Park, PA 16802, U.S.A. **Online address:** wrj9@psu.edu

ROTNER, Shelley. American (born United States), b. 1951. **Genres:** Children's Fiction, Children's Non-fiction, Illustrations, Picture/Board Books. **Career:** Freelance photographer, 1975-; Aggasiz Community School District, photography instructor, 1975; Learning Guild, photography instructor, 1975-76; Lincoln Community School System, photography instructor, 1975-76; International Center of Photography, assistant photography instructor, 1977; Bank Street School for Children, photography instructor, 1977-78; United Nations Photo Library, photo researcher, 1977-78; International Center of Photography, curatorial assistant, 1977-78; UNICEF, photographer, 1979-; The American Museum of Natural History, photography instructor, 1979. Writer. **Publications:** (With M.N. Allen) Changes, 1991; (with K. Kreisler) Nature Spy, 1992; (with K. Kreisler) Ocean Day, 1993; (with K. Kreisler) Citybook, 1994; (with K. Kreisler) Faces, 1994; Wheels Around, 1995; Action Alphabet, 1995; Colors around Us, 1996; (with J.P. Hellums) Hold the Anchovies: A Book about Pizza, 1996; (with S.M. Kelly) Lots of Moms, 1996; (with S.M. Kelly) Lots of Dads, 1997; (with R. Olivo) Close, Closer, Closest, 1997; Boats Afloat, 1998; About Twins, 1999; (with C. García) Pick a Pet, 1999; (with S.M. Kelly) About Twins, 1999; (with S. Calcagnino) Body Book, 2000; (with S.M. Kelly) Feeling Thankful, 2000; (with S.M. Kelly) A.D.D. Book for Kids, 2000; Parts, 2001; (with S.M. Kelly) What Can you Do?: A Book About Discovering What You Do Well, 2001; (with S.M. Kelly) Lots of Grandparents, 2001; (with S.M. Kelly) Good-Byes, 2002; (with S.M. Kelly) Something's Different, 2002; Lots of F, 2003; (with K. Kreisler) Everybody Works, 2003; (with G. Goss) Where Does Food Come From?, 2006; Senses at the Seashore, 2006; (with S.M. Kelly) Many Ways: How Families Practice their Beliefs and Religions, 2006; (with A.L. Woodhull) Every Season, 2007; (with S.M. Kelly) De Muchas Maneras: Cómo las Familias Practican sus Creencias y Religiones, 2007; Senses in the City, 2008; Senses on the Farm, 2009; (with S. Rotner) Shades of People, 2009; (with D. deGroat) Dogs Don't Brush Their Teeth!, 2009; (with A. Woodhull) The Buzz on Bees: Why are They Disappearing?, 2010; (with A. Goldbas) Home, 2011; (with S.M. Kelly) I'm Adopted!, 2011; (with S.M. Kelly) Being Adopted, 2011; Body Actions, 2012; Homer, 2012. **Address:** 64 Old Lyme Rd., Chappaqua, NY 10514, U.S.A. **Online address:** shellro243@aol.com

ROTTER, Andrew J. American (born United States), b. 1953. **Genres:** History, Military/Defense/Arms Control. **Career:** Stanford University, instructor, 1979; California State University, visiting assistant professor, 1980-81; St. Mary's College, assistant professor, 1981-84; Vanderbilt University, assistant professor, 1987-88; Colgate University, visiting assistant professor, 1986-87, assistant professor, 1988-90, associate professor, 1990-98, professor, 1998-2006, Charles A. Dana professor of history, 2006-. Writer and historian. **Publications:** The Path to Vietnam: Origins of the American Commitment to Southeast Asia, 1987; (ed.) Light at the End of the Tunnel: A Vietnam War Anthology, 1991, 3rd ed., 2010; Comrades at Odds: The United States and India, 1947-1964, 2000; Hiroshima: The World's Bomb, 2008. Contributor to periodicals and journals. **Address:** Department of History, Colgate University, 13 Oak Dr., Hamilton, NY 13346-1382, U.S.A. **Online address:** arotter@colgate.edu

ROTTER, Gabe. American (born United States), b. 1978. **Genres:** Nov-

els, Literary Criticism And History. **Career:** Chris Carter's Ten Thirteen Productions, director of development. Producer, novelist and screenwriter. **Publications:** Duck Duck Wally (novel), 2007; The Human Bobby (novel), 2010. Contributor to periodicals. **Address:** The Jud Laghi Agency L.L.C., 708 3rd Ave., 16th Fl., New York, NY 10017, U.S.A. **Online address:** gaberotter@gmail.com

ROTTER, Jeffrey. American (born United States), b. 1968. **Genres:** Novels. **Career:** Writer. **Publications:** The Unknown Knowns: A Novel, 2009. **Address:** Brooklyn, NY , U.S.A. **Online address:** cityofnautika@gmail.com

ROTTMANN, Erik. (Erik J. Rottmann). American (born United States) **Genres:** Theology/Religion. **Career:** Grace Lutheran Church, pastor, 1997-; Good News Journal, staff writer. **Publications:** (With E. Grube and R. Hartwig) To All Eternity: The Essential Teachings of Christianity, 2002; Barabbas Goes Free: The Story of the Release of Barabbas, Matthew 27: 15-26, Mark 15: 6-15, Luke 23: 13-25, and John 18: 20 for Children, 2003; A Meal for Many: the Story of the Feeding of the 5, 000, Matthew 14: 13-21, Mark 6: 30-44, Luke 9: 10-17, John 6: 1-13, 2003; Timothy Joins Paul, 2004; Follow Me: Peter Lays Down His Net; An Easter Story, 2004; (ed.) Guide Me Ever: 365 Classic Devotions from Portals of Prayer, 2005; Jesus, My Good Shepherd, 2005; Food: A Theme throughout Scripture (Fusion bible study), 2006; Timothy, Titus, Philemon, 2006; The Easter Victory: The Story of Easter, Matthew 26-28 for Children, 2006; His Name is John, 2007; Rahab's Red Thread, 2009; Fruit of the Spirit: Galatians 5: 22-23 for Children, 2010. **Address:** Grace Lutheran Church, 403 S Burke St., Versailles, MO 65084-1368, U.S.A. **Online address:** echo-romeo@sbcglobal.net

ROTTMANN, Erik J. See **ROTTMANN, Erik.**

ROTUNDO, Louis C. American/Israeli (born Israel), b. 1949. **Genres:** History, Military/Defense/Arms Control, Engineering, Technology, Astronomy. **Career:** Valencia Community College, instructor in federal government, 1977; U.S. Senator Lawton Chiles, staff assistant, 1977-80; Florida Ocean Thermal Energy Consortium, deputy director, 1980-82; Florida Solar Energy Center, special assistant, 1980-84; University of Central Florida, special assistant, 1984-87; Central Intelligence Agency, consultant on active deceptive measures, 1985; Rotundo and Associates, private consultant, 1987-, principal; Combat Studies Institute, visiting lecturer in Soviet studies; U.S. Army War College Foundation, advanced research fellow. Writer. **Publications:** (Ed.) Battle for Stalingrad: The 1943 Soviet General Staff Study, 1989; Forgotten Dawn: The X-1 at Pinecastle, 1990; Into the Unknown: The X-1 Story, 1994. Contributor to newspapers and publications. **Address:** 302 Pinestraw Cir., Altamonte Springs, FL 32714, U.S.A. **Online address:** lcr5002@aol.com

ROUBINI, Nouriel. American/Turkish (born Turkey), b. 1959. **Genres:** Politics/Government, Economics. **Career:** National Bureau of Economic Research, faculty research fellow, 1988-; International Monetary Fund, visiting economist and consultant, 1988-2003; Yale University, assistant professor, 1988-93, associate professor, 1993-95; Center for Economic Policy Research, research fellow, 1991-; World Bank, consultant, 1995-98; New York University, Stern School of Business, associate professor, 1995-; Journal of Development Economics, associate editor, 1995-2000; Journal of International Economics, associate editor, 1997-2001; White House Council of Economic Advisers, senior economist for international affairs, 1998-99; U.S. Treasury Department, Office of Policy Development and Review, director, 1999-2000, Undersecretary for International Affairs, senior advisor, 2000-01; Roubini Global Economics, creator, editor and manager. **Publications:** (With A. Alesina and G. Cohen) Political Cycles and the Macroeconomy, 1997; (with B. Setser) Bailouts or Bail-ins? Responding to Financial Crises in Emerging Economies, 2004; (ed. with M. Uzan) New International Financial Architecture, 2005; (with S. Mihm) Crisis Economics: A Crash Course in the Future of Finance, 2010. **Address:** Department of Economics, Stern School of Business, New York University, KMC 7-83, 44 W 4th St., New York, NY 10012, U.S.A. **Online address:** nroubini@stern.nyu.edu

ROUDINESCO, Elisabeth. French (born France), b. 1944. **Genres:** Psychology, History. **Career:** Universite de Paris VII, professor of history, director of research of history department, 1992-; L'Ecole des Hautes Etudes en Sciences Sociales, minister of conferences, 1992-96; University of Paris I, director of studies, 2001-09; Société Internationale d'Histoire de la Psychiatrie et de la Psychanalyse, president; Middlesex University, visiting professor, 2006-. Writer and psychoanalyst. **Publications:** Initiation à la Linguistique générale, 1967; Un Discours Auréel: Théorie de L'inconscient et Politique de la Psychanalyse, 1973; L'inconscient et ses Lettres, 1975; Pour Une Politique de La Psychanalyse, 1977; (with H. Deluy) La Psychanalyse mére et Chienne, 1979; La Bataille de Cent Ans: Histoire de la Psychanalyse en France, 2vols., 1982; Théroigne de Méricourt, Une Femmemélancolique Sous la Révolution, 1989; Madness and Revolution: The Lives and Legends of Theroigne de Mericourt, 1992; Penser la Folie: Essais sur Michel Foucault, 1992; Jacques Lacan: Esquisse d'une Vie, Histoire d'un Système de Pensée, 1993; Généalogies, 1994; Pourquoi la Psychanalyse?, 1999; (with M. Plon) Dictionnaire de la Psychanalyse, 1997; Autour des Etudes Surl'hystérie: Vienne 1985, 1998; Actualité de Georges Canguilhem: le normal et le Pathologique: Actes du Xe Colloque de la Société internationale D'histoire de la Psychiatrie et de la Psychanalyse, 1998; Edipe à Vincennes: Séminaire 69, 1999; Pourquoi la Psychanalyse?, 1999; Analyse, l'archive, 2001; De Quoi Demain-: Dialogue, 2001; Familleen désordre, 2002; (with J. Derrida) For What Tomorrow: A Dialogue, 2004; Patient, le Thérapeute et l'état, 2004; Philosophes Dans Latourmente, 2005; La Part Obscure de Nous-mêmes - Une Histoire Despervers, 2007; Philosophy in Turbulent Times: Canguilhem, Sartre, Foucault, Althusser, Deleuze, Derrida, 2008; Our Dark Side, a History of Perversion, 2009; Mais Pourquoi tant de haine?, 2010. Contributor to periodicals. **Address:** c/o Olivier Betourne, Artheme Fayard, 75 rue des Saints-Peres, Paris, 75006, France.

ROUGEAU, Remy. American (born United States), b. 1948?. **Genres:** Novels, Theology/Religion. **Career:** Trappist monk, 1968-79; benedictine monk, 1983-. Writer. **Publications:** All We Know of Heaven, 2001; (intro.) The Diary of a Country Priest, 2002. Contributor to periodicals. **Address:** c/o Author Mail, Houghton Mifflin Co., 222 Berkeley St., 9th Fl., Boston, MA 02116, U.S.A.

ROUGH, Bonnie J. American (born United States), b. 1979?. **Genres:** Autobiography/Memoirs. **Career:** Loft Literary Center, faculty; Birth Doula; Versal (English-language literary journal), fiction editor. **Publications:** Carrier: Untangling the Danger in My DNA (memoir), 2010. Contributor to books and periodicals. **Address:** c/o Michelle Brower, Folio Literary Management, 505 8th Ave., Ste. 603, New York, NY 10018, U.S.A. **Online address:** bjr@bonniejrough.com

ROUGHGARDEN, Tim. American (born United States) **Genres:** Young Adult Fiction, Information Science/Computers. **Career:** Stanford University, Department of computer science, assistant professor, associate professor; radio station KZSU, host. Writer. **Publications:** Selfish Routing and the Price of Anarchy, 2005; (ed. with N. Nisan, E. Tardos and V.V. Vazirani) Algorithmic Game Theory, 2007. Contributor to books. **Address:** Department of Computer Science, Stanford University, 462 Gates Bldg., 353 Serra Mall, Stanford, CA 94305, U.S.A. **Online address:** tim@cs.stanford.edu

ROUNDS, David. American (born United States), b. 1942. **Genres:** Children's Fiction, Music, Theology/Religion, Novels. **Career:** Teacher and writer, 1964-. **Publications:** Coalitions, 1970; Celebrisi's Journey: A Novel, 1976; Cannonball River Tales (children's stories), 1992; Perfecting a Piece of the World: Arthur Imperatore and the Blue-Collar Aristocrats of A-P-A, 1993; (with L. Quartet) The Four and the One: In Praise of String Quartets, 1999. **Address:** The Spieler Agency, 154 W 57th St., Ste. 135, New York, NY 10019, U.S.A.

ROUNTREE, Owen. *See* **KITTREDGE, William.**

ROUS, Stephen N. (Stephen Norman Rous). American (born United States), b. 1931. **Genres:** Medicine/Health. **Career:** Michigan State University, professor of surgery, urology, 1972-75; Medical University of South Carolina, professor of urology, 1975-88; Dartmouth Medical School, professor of urological surgery, 1988-2001; Brown University, School of Medicine, clinical professor of surgery, urology, 2005-. Writer. **Publications:** Understanding Urology, 1973; Urology in Primary Care, 1976; Urology: A Core Textbook, 1985, 2nd ed., 1996; The Prostate Book: Sound Advice on Symptoms and Treatment, 1988, rev. ed., 2001; (with H.B. Zobel) Doctors and the Law: Defendants and Expert Witnesses, 1993; (with P.I. Ellsworth) Little Black Book of Urology, 2001. EDITOR: Stone Disease: Diagnosis and Management, 1987; Urology Annual, 11 vols., 1987-97. **Address:** 421 Bellevue Ave., Ste. 2A, Newport, RI 02840, U.S.A. **Online address:** stephen.n.rous@dartmouth.edu

ROUS, Stephen Norman. *See* **ROUS, Stephen N.**

ROUSE, Anne (Barrett). British/American (born United States), b. 1954. **Genres:** Poetry. **Career:** Prince of Wales Hospital, student nurse, 1979-82; St. Luke's Hospital, staff nurse, 1982-86; Islington Mind, project director, 1986-, director, 1992-95; writer, 1995-; University of Glasgow, Royal Literary Fund, visiting fellow, 2000-02, associate fellow, 2001-02, project fellow, 2002-03; St Mary's University College, fellow, 2004-05; Courtauld Institute of Art, fellow, 2007-08; Mind The Mental Health Charity, nurse and director of local branch. **Publications:** POETRY: Sunset Grill, 1993; Timing, 1997; The School of Night, 2004; The Upshot: New and Selected Poems, 2008; The Divided, 2008. Contributor to periodicals. **Address:** Bloodaxe Books, PO Box 1SN, Highgreen, Tarset, Newcastle upon Tyne, NM NE99 15N, England. **Online address:** rouseanne@hotmail.com

ROUSE, Mary A(mes). American (born United States), b. 1934. **Genres:** History, Literary Criticism And History. **Career:** Teacher, 1955-56, 1957-58, 1960-61; University of California, Viator, managing editor, Center for Medieval and Renaissance Studies, faculty, 1976-99, now retired; Yale University, visiting Beinecke professor, 2009. **Publications:** WITH R.H. ROUSE: Preachers, Florilegia and Sermons: Studies on the Manipulus Florum of Thomas of Ireland, 1979; Cartolai, Illuminators and Printers in Fifteenth-Century Italy: The Evidence of the Ripoli Press, 1988; Authentic Witnesses: Approaches to Medieval Texts and Manuscripts, 1991; Manuscripts and Their Makers: Commercial Book Producers in Medieval Paris, 1200-1500, 2000. EDITOR: (with W.M. Newman) Charters of St-Fursy of Péronne, 1977; (with R.H. Rouse and intro.) Registrum Anglie de Libris Doctorum et Auctorum Veterum, 1991; (with R.H. Rouse) Henry of Kirkestede, Catalogus de libris autenticis et apocrifis, 2004. Works appear in anthologies. Contributor to journals. **Address:** 11444 Berwick St., Los Angeles, CA 90049, U.S.A. **Online address:** rouse@history.ucla.edu

ROUSE, Wade. American (born United States), b. 1965?. **Genres:** Autobiography/Memoirs, Humor/Satire, Gay And Lesbian Issues, Adult Non-fiction, Essays. **Career:** Author and humorist. **Publications:** America's Boy (memoir), 2006; Confessions of a Prep School Mommy Handler (memoir), 2007; At Least in the City Someone Would Hear Me Scream: Misadventures in Search of the Simple Life (memoir), 2009; It's All Relative: Two Families, Three Dogs, 34 Holidays and 50 Boxes of Wine (memoir), 2011; (ed.) I'm Not The Biggest Bitch in This Relationship, 2011. Contributor to magazines, periodicals and newspapers. **Address:** c/o Wendy Sherman, Wendy Sherman Associates Inc., 27 W 24th St., Ste. 700B, New York, NY 10010, U.S.A. **Online address:** wade@waderouse.com

ROUSSEAU, George S. American (born United States), b. 1941. **Genres:** Intellectual History, Literary Criticism And History. **Career:** Princeton University, Osgood fellow in English literature, 1965-66; Harvard University, instructor in English literature, 1966-68; University of California, professor of English, 1968-75, professor of eighteenth-century studies, 1975-94; senior Fulbright research professor, 1983; University of Aberdeen, Thomas Reid Institute, Regious professor of English and director, 1994-; De Montfort University, research professor of humanities, now professor emeritus; Oxford University, faculty of modern history. Writer. **Publications:** (With M.H. Nicolson) This Long Disease My Life: Alexander Pope and the Sciences, 1968; Goldsmith: The Critical Heritage, 1974; Oliver Goldsmith: The Critical Heritage, 1974; The Renaissance Man in the Eighteenth Century, 1978; The Letters and Papers of Sir John Hill, 1982; Tobias Smollett: Essays of Two Decades, 1982; Enlightenment Borders: Pre and Post-Modern Discourses: Medical, Scientific, 1991; Perilous Enlightenment: Pre and Post-Modern Discourses: Sexual, Historical, 1991; Enlightenment Crossings: Pre and Post-Modern Discourses: Anthropological, 1991; (co-author) Hysteria Beyond Freud, 1993; Nervous Acts: Essays on Literature, Culture and Sensibility, 2004. EDITOR/CO-EDITOR: Hypochondriasis, 1969; Twentieth-Century Interpretations of The Rape of the Lock, 1969; (with E. Rothstein) The Augustan Milieu: Essays Presented to Louis A. Landa, 1970; (with P.G. Boucé) Tobias Smollett: Bicentennial Essays Presented to Lewis M. Knapp, 1971; Organic Form: The Life of an Idea, 1972; (with N. Rudenstine) English Poetic Satire: Wyatt to Byron, 1972; (with R. Porter) The Ferment of Knowledge: Studies in the Historiography of Eighteenth-Century Science, 1980; Literature and Science, 1985; Sexual Underworlds of the Enlightenment, 1987; (with P. Rogers) The Enduring Legacy: Alexander Pope Tercentenary Essays, 1988; (with R. Porter) Exoticism in the Enlightenment, 1988; Languages of Psyche: Mind and Body in Enlightenment Thought: Clark Library Lectures 1985-1986, 1989; Hysteria beyond Freud, 1993; (with R. Porter) Gout: The Patrician Malady, 1998; Framing and Imagining Disease in Cultural History, 2003; Nervous

Acts: Essays On Literature, Culture and Sensibility, 2004; (ed. with K. Borris) The Sciences of Homosexuality in Early Modern Europe, 2008; Notorious Sir John Hill, 2012. Contributor of articles to periodicals. **Address:** De Montfort University, 52 1/2 Gateway St., Leicester, LE LE1 9BH, United Kingdom. **Online address:** george.rousseau@magdalen.oxford.ac.uk

ROUTH, Francis John. British (born England), b. 1927. **Genres:** Music. **Career:** Battersea College of Technology, instructor, 1959-66; Redcliffe Concerts of British, founder and artistic director, 1963-; Morley College, faculty, 1970. Freelance writer and composer. **Publications:** Playing the Organ, 1958; Teach Yourself the Organ, 1958; Contemporary Music, 1968; Sonatina, for Organ, 1969; (ed.) The Patronage and Presentation of Contemporary Music, 1970; The Manger Throne, 1970; Contemporary British Music, 1972; Lumen Christi, 1972; Dialogue, for Violin and Orchestra, 1972; Early English Organ Music, 1973; Aeterne Rex Altissime, 1973; Early English Organ Music from the Middle Ages to 1837, 1973; Stravinsky, 1974; (with I. Bruce, D. Castillejo, C. Cornford and C. Gosford) Patronage of the Creative Artist, 1974; Gloria tibi Trinitatis, 1976; Spring Night, 1977; Annual Register (contributor on music), 1980-; (ed.) Overture in E, 2001. Contributor to books. **Address:** 68 Barrowgate Rd., Chiswick, London, GL W4 4QU, England. **Online address:** redcliffe@frouth.freeserve.co.uk

ROUTLEY, (Bernarra) Jane. (Rebecca Locksley). American/Australian (born Australia), b. 1962. **Genres:** Science Fiction/Fantasy, Novels, Young Adult Fiction. **Career:** Librarian, 1986-91; writer, 1991-. **Publications:** Mage Heart (fantasy novel), 1996; Fire Angels, 1998; Aramaya, 1999. AS REBECCA LOCKSLEY: The Three Sisters, 2004. **Address:** c/o James Frenkel, James Frenkel & Associates, 415 S Randall Ave., Madison, WI 53715-1512, U.S.A.

ROWAN, Diedre. See **WILLIAMS, Jeanne.**

ROWAN, Roy. American (born United States), b. 1920. **Genres:** Documentaries/Reportage, History, Biography, Self Help. **Career:** Time Inc., staff, 1948-71, national affairs editor of Life, 1959-61, assistant managing editor, 1961-77; On The Sound Magazine, editor; Seascape Publications, founder, 1970; Fortune Magazine, senior writer, 1977-85. **Publications:** The Four Days of Mayaguez, 1975; The Intuitive Manager, 1986; (co-ed.) A Day in the Life of Italy, 1990; Powerful People: From Mao to Now, 1996; (with B. Janis) First Dogs, 1997; Surfcaster's Quest: Seeking Stripers, Blues and Solitude at the Edge of the Surging Sea, 1999; Solomon Starbucks Striper: A Fish Story about Following Your Dreams, 2003; Chasing the Dragon: A Veteran Journalist's Firsthand Account of the 1949 Chinese Revolution, 2004; Throwing Bullets: A Tale of Two Pitchers Chasing a Dream, 2006; Never Too Late: A 90-Year-Old's Pursuit of a Whirlwind Life, 2011. Contributor to magazines. **Address:** c/o Carol Mann, Carol Mann Agency, 55 5th Ave., New York, NY 10003, U.S.A. **Online address:** rowanroy1@aol.com

ROWBOTHAM, Sheila. British (born England), b. 1943. **Genres:** History, Politics/Government, Women's Studies And Issues. **Career:** Workers Educational Association, teacher; Black Dwarf newspaper, staff; University of Amsterdam, visiting professor, 1981-83; Greater London Council, research officer, 1983-86; London University, Extra Mural lecturer; World Institute for Development Economics Research, consultant research adviser; United Nations University, consultant, 1987-91; Manchester University, Sociology Department, Simon Research Fellow, 1993-94, professor. Freelance writer and journalist. **Publications:** Women's Liberation & the New Politics, 1971; Women, Resistance and Revolution, 1972; Woman's Consciousness, Man's World, 1973; Hidden from History: 300 Years of Women's Oppression and the Fight Against It, 1973, 3rd ed., 1977; A New World for Women, 1977; (with J. Weeks) Socialism and the New Life, 1977; (with J. McCrindle) Dutiful Daughters, 1977; Persona Donna, 1978; (with L. Segal and H. Wainwright) Beyond the Fragments, 1981, trans. as Nach dem Scherbengerich: über das Verhältnis von Feminismus und Sozialismus, 1993; Dreams and Dilemmas: Collected Writings, 1983; Friends of Alice Wheeldon, 1986; The Past Is before Us: Feminism in Action from the Late 1960's, 1989; Women in Movement Feminism and Social Action, 1992; Homeworkers Worldwide, 1993; (with S. Mitter) Dignity and Daily Bread, 1994; (with S. Mitter) Women Encounter Technology, 1995; A Century of Women, 1999; Threads through Time: Essays in History and Autobiography, 1999; Promise of a Dream: Remembering the Sixties, 2000; (ed. with S. Linkogle) Women Resist Globalization, 2001; (with H. Beynon) Looking at Class, 2002; Edward Carpenter: A Life of Liberty and Love, 2008; Dreamers of a New Day: Women Who

Invented the Twentieth Century, 2010; (contrib.) A Vindication of the Rights of Woman, 2010. Contributor to periodicals. **Address:** School of Social Science, University of Manchester, Arthur Lewis Bldg., Oxford Rd., Manchester, M13 9PL, England. **Online address:** sheila.rowbotham@manchester.ac.uk

ROWE, C(hristopher) J(ames). British (born England), b. 1944. **Genres:** Classics, Philosophy, Translations, History, Ethics. **Career:** University of Bristol, assistant lecturer, 1968-72, lecturer, 1972-82, senior lecturer, 1982-85, reader in classics, 1985-89, professor of ancient philosophy and Greek, 1989-91, Henry Overton Wills professor of Greek, 1991-95, head of department, 1989-93; University of Edinburgh, Institute for Advanced Studies in the Humanities, visiting fellow, 1972; Center for Hellenic Studies, junior fellow, 1974-75; Local Community Schools, manager, governor, 1979-89; University of Wisconsin, Solmsen Fellow, 1994-95; University of Durham, Department of Classics and Ancient History, professor of Greek, 1996-2009, head of the department, 2004-08, professor emeritus, 2009-. Writer. **Publications:** The Eudemian and Nicomachean Ethics: A Study in the Development of Aristotle's Thought, 1971; An Introduction to Greek Ethics, 1976; Essential Hesiod, 1978; Philosophers in Context: Plato, 1984; (trans.) Plato: Phaedrus, 1986; (ed.) Phaedo, 1993; Reading the Statesman: Proceedings of the III Symposium Platonicum, 1995; Plato: Statesman, 1995; Plato: Symposium, 1999; (trans. and intro.) Stateman, 1999; (ed. with M. Schofield) Cambridge History of Greek and Roman Political Thought, 2000; (trans.) Aristotle, Nicomachean Ethics, 2002; (ed. with J. Annas) New Perspective on Plato, Modern and Ancient, 2002; An Easier Yoke, 2003; (with T. Penner) Plato's Lysis, 2004; Plato and the Art of Philosophical Writing, 2007. Contributor to periodicals. **Address:** Department of Classics and Ancient History, University of Durham, 38 N Bailey, Durham, DU DH1 3EU, England. **Online address:** c.j.rowe@durham.ac.uk

ROWE, Jennifer. See **RODDA, Emily.**

ROWE, Lee Pelham. (Lee Pelham Cooper). American (born United States), b. 1926. **Genres:** Children's Fiction, Children's Non-fiction. **Career:** Cooper-Leedy Realtors, real estate broker; Falmouth High School, teacher of Spanish and English, 1948-50; Harris Elementary School, librarian, 1950-51; Maury Elementary School, librarian, 1951-60; Cooper's Furniture, vice president; Washington-Lee Savings and Loan, director; UCLA Anderson School of Management, Department of Marketing, faculty, 1969, chair, 1988-91, now professor emeritus, 2004-, Management in the Arts Program, director; Cooper Realty of Fredericksburg, broker; Strategic Data Corp., founder, 1999-. Writer. **Publications:** AS LEE COOPER: Fun with Spanish, 1960; (with C.B. McIntosh) Fun with French, 1963; (with L. Beretta and M. Greene) Fun with Italian, 1964; Fun with German, 1965; More Fun with Spanish, 1967; Five Fables from France, 1970; The Pirate of Puerto Rico, 1972; Space Jam, 1996; Midlife Startup: Lessons from Venturing out of the Ivory Tower, 2004. SELF-ILLUSTRATED: The Chinese Language for Beginners, 1971. **Address:** Department of Marketing, UCLA Anderson School of Management, 110 Westwood Plz., PO Box 951481, Los Angeles, CA 90095-1481, U.S.A. **Online address:** lee.cooper@anderson.ucla.edu

ROWE, Melanie. See **BROWNING, Pamela.**

ROWE, Rosemary. See **AITKEN, Rosemary.**

ROWELL, Douglas Geoffrey. British (born England), b. 1943. **Genres:** History, Theology/Religion, Cultural/Ethnic Topics. **Career:** Church of England, ordained minister, 1968; Oxford University, New College, assistant chaplain, 1968-72; Keble College, chaplain fellow, 1972-94, emeritus fellow, 1994-; Chichester Cathedral, canon, 1981-2001; Anglo-Oriental Orthodox International Forum, co-chair, 1996-; Bishop Suffragan of Basingstoke, 1994-2001; Churches Group on Funeral Service at Cemeteries and Crematoria, chair, 1997-; bishop of Gibraltar in Europe, 2001-; Cathedral of the Holy Trinity, bishop, 2001-. Writer. **Publications:** Hell and the Victorians: A Study of the Nineteenth-century Theological Controversies Concerning Eternal Punishment and the Future Life, 1974; The Liturgy of Christian Burial: An Introductory Survey of the Historical Development of Christian Burial Rites, 1977; The Vision Glorious: Themes and Personalities of the Catholic Revival in Anglicanism, 1983; (with J. Chilcott-Monk) The Nails and the Cross: Entering into the Mysteries of the Passion, 2003; (with J. Chilcott-Monk) Come, Lord Jesus!: Daily Readings for Advent, Christmas, and Epiphany, 2003; The Vision Glorious, 2007; (intro.) Two Essays on Biblical and On Ecclesiastical Miracles, 2010. EDITOR: (with B.E. Juel-Jensen) Rock-Hewn

Churches of Eastern Tigray: An Account of the Oxford University Expedition to Ethiopia, 1974, 1975; Tradition Renewed: The Oxford Movement Conference Papers, 1986; To the Church of England: Essays and Papers and the Preface to Crockford's Clerical Directory 1987-88, 1988; (contrib.) Confession and Absolution, 1990; The English Religious Tradition and the Genius of Anglicanism, 1992; (with M. Dudley) The Oil of Gladness: Anointing in the Christian Tradition, 1993; (with K. Stevenson and R. Williams) Love's Redeeming Work: The Anglican Quest for Holiness, 2001; (with C. Hall) The Gestures of God: Explorations in Sacramentality, 2004. Contributor to journals. **Address:** c/o Author Mail, Continuum International Publishing Group Inc., 15 E 26th St., New York, NY 10010, U.S.A. **Online address:** bishop@dioceseineurope.org.uk

ROWEN, Michelle. (Michelle Maddox). Canadian (born Canada), b. 1971. **Genres:** Romance/Historical, Young Adult Fiction, Sex. **Career:** Graphic designer and writer. **Publications:** NOVELS: Bitten & Smitten, 2006; Angel with Attitude, 2006; Fanged & Fabulous, 2007; Lady & the Vamp, 2008; Stakes & Stilettos, 2009; Tall, Dark & Fangsome, 2009. OTHERS: Bewitched, Bothered & Be Vampyred, 2005; Hot Spell, 2009; The Mammoth Book of Paranormal Romance, 2009; Reign or Shine, 2009; Reign Check, 2010; Kiss Me Deadly, 2010; (as Michelle Maddox) Countdown, 2008; (as Michelle Maddox) The Mammoth Book of Time Travel Romance, 2009. FORTHCOMING: The Demon in Me, 2010; Touch and Go, 2010; Something Wicked, 2010; That Old Black Magic, 2011; Nightshade, 2011; Primal, 2011; Bloodlust, 2011; Inevitable, 2011; Familiar, 2011; Vampire Academy: The Ultimate Guide, 2011. **Address:** c/o Jim McCarthy, Dystel & Goderich Literary Management, 1 Union Sq. W, Ste. 904, New York, NY 10003, U.S.A. **Online address:** michelle@michellerowen.com

ROWER, Ann. American (born United States), b. 1938?. **Genres:** Adult Non-fiction, Novels, Young Adult Fiction, Gay And Lesbian Issues. **Career:** School of Visual Arts, faculty. Writer. **Publications:** If You're a Girl, 1990; Armed Response, 1996; Baby, 2002; Lee & Elaine, 2002. Contributor to periodicals. **Address:** School of Visual Arts, 209 E 23rd St., New York, NY 10010-3901, U.S.A.

ROWETT, Helen (Graham Quiller). British (born England), b. 1915?. **Genres:** Biology, Zoology, Local History/Rural Topics, Archaeology/Antiquities, Architecture, Education, Sciences, Sports/Fitness, Sports/Fitness. **Career:** Plymouth Polytechnic, lecturer in zoology, 1944-67, senior lecturer, 1968-73, principal lecturer in educational technology, 1973-76, now retired. Writer. **Publications:** Dissection Guides 1957; The Rat as a Small Mammal, 1957, 3rd ed., 1974; Histology and Embryology, 1962; Guide to Dissection, 1962; Basic Anatomy and Physiology, 1966, 4th ed. 1999; Two Moors Way, 1976, 6th ed., 1999; Roundabout Family Rambling, 1995. **Address:** 3 Manor Pk., Dousland, Yelverton, DN PL20 6LX, England.

ROWH, Mark. (Mark C. Rowh). American (born United States), b. 1952. **Genres:** Young Adult Non-fiction, Administration/Management, Business/Trade/Industry. **Career:** Parkersburg Community College, assistant to the president, 1975-78; Bluefield State College, assistant to the president and director of community relations, 1978-82, director of continuing education, 1979-85, executive assistant to the president, 1982-85; Tazewell (Virginia) High School, writer-in-residence, 1983; Greenville Technical College, director of planning and grants, 1985-88, associate vice president for institutional development, 1988-89; New River Community College, NRCC Educational Foundation, director of institutional advancement, 1989-, vice president for planning and advancement, executive director. Writer and consultant. **Publications:** (With M. Hartman) The One Person Manager, 1984; The Small Shop in Resource Development, 1985; Opportunities in Drafting Careers, 1986; Coping with Stress in College, 1989; Opportunities in Welding Careers, 1990; Opportunities in Metalworking Careers, 1991, rev. ed., 2008; Drafting Careers, 1991; Opportunities in Waste Management and Recycling Careers, 1992; Winning Government Grants and Contracts for your Small Business, 1992; Opportunities in Electronics Careers, 1992, rev. ed., 2007; Opportunities in Warehousing Careers, 1993; Welding Careers, 1994; Opportunities in Electronic Careers, 1994; Careers for Crafty People and Other Dexterous Types, 1994, 3rd ed., 2006; How to Improve Your Grammar and Usage, 1994; How to Write Dynamic Business Proposals, 1994; Opportunities in Installation and Repair Careers, 1994; Crafts, 1996; Slam Dunk Cover Letters, 1997, 2nd ed., 2005; Opportunities in Religious Service Careers, 1998; W.E.B. Du Bois: Champion of Civil Rights, 1999; Great Jobs for Political Science Majors, 1999, 2nd ed., 2004; Great Jobs for Chemistry Majors, 1999, 2nd

ed., 2006; Opportunities in Fund-Raising Careers, 2001; Opportunities in Educational Support Careers, 2001; Opportunities in Technical Sales Careers, 2002; Thurgood Marshall: Civil Rights Attorney and Supreme Court Justice, 2002; Careers in Real Estate, 2003; Great Jobs for Computer Science Majors, 2003; (as Mark C. Rowh) Community College Companion: Everything You Wanted to Know About Succeeding in a Two-Year School, 2011. Contributor to magazines. **Address:** NRCC Educational Foundation, New River Community College, 5251 College Dr., PO Box 1127, Dublin, VA 24084-1127, U.S.A. **Online address:** mrowh@nr.edu

ROWH, Mark C. See **ROWH, Mark.**

ROWLAND, Arthur Ray. American (born United States), b. 1930. **Genres:** History, Librarianship, Bibliography, Business/Trade/Industry, Administration/Management. **Career:** Georgia State College (now University) Library, circulation librarian, 1952-53; Armstrong College of Savannah (now Armstrong State College), librarian, 1954-56; Auburn University Library, head of circulation department, 1956-58; Jacksonville University, librarian and associate professor, 1958-61; Augusta College, librarian and associate professor, 1961-76, librarian and professor of library science, 1976-91; University of Georgia-Augusta, lecturer, 1962-66, University System of Georgia, chairman, 1969-71. Writer. **Publications:** (Contrib.) Library Services for Junior Colleges, 1964; A Bibliography of the Writings on Georgia History, 1965, (with J.E. Dorsey) rev. ed., 1978; A Guide to the Study of Augusta and Richmond County, 1967; (with H. Callahan) Yesterday's Augusta, 1976; The Librarian and Reference Service, 1977; (with M.F. Fogleman) Reese Library Genealogical Resources, 1988; Goodman Cousins, 1988; Index to City Directories of Augusta, Georgia, 1841-79, 1991; Seeking Mary Ann, My Fair Grandmother: The Huguenots, Connecting Deveaux, Fair, Bessant and Rowland Families, 1994, 2nd ed. as Ancestors of Mary Ann Fair: First Wife of Peter G. Bessent of Charleston, South Carolina, 2000; The Bessent Family of Georgia Descendants of Abraham Bessent and Peter Bessent, 1995; Distant Cousins, 1995; Descendants of Wiley Reeves of York County, 1996, rev. ed., 1999; Rowland-Huckaby and Goodman-Reeves-Williams-Huckaby Connections: With Descendants of John Huckaby, 1996; Augusta Imprints: A Checklist, 1789-1860, 1998; Ancestors of David Jackson, 1998; Ancestors of Elizabeth Proctor in Virginia and England, 1998; Ancestors of Martha (Patsey) Whitehead in Virginia and North Carolina with Connections to the Rowland Family in Georgia, 1998; Ancestors of Rachael Hines Lewis with Rowland Family Connections: The Lewis Family of Greene County, Georgia, Christ's Church Parish, Middlesex County, Virginia, England and Wales, 1998; Atkinson Family in Virginia: With Connections to Gwaltney, Marriott, Flake (Flack), Williamson, Holleman and Allen Families: Some Ancestors of the Rowland Family, 1998; Augusta Imprints: A Checklist, 1786-1860, 1998; Rowland Family of Virginia, North Carolina, Georgia and Beyond: Including John Rowland (Immigrant in 1635) in James City County and Surry County, Virginia and His Descendants in Franklin County, North Carolina Including Jesse Rowland and Frederick Rowland, 1998; Ancestors of Rhoda Atkinson in Georgia, North Carolina and Virginia: With Rowland Connections in Georgia, 1999; Wiley Reeves: His Descendants and Ancestors from England to Virginia, North Carolina, South Carolina and Jasper, Fayette and Spalding Counties, Georgia: With Connections to Goodman and Rowland Families, 1999; Williams Family: Descendants of Moses Williams and Chaney Huckaby in Oglethorpe, Fayette and Spalding Counties, Georgia and beyond, 1999; Printing in Washington, Georgia, Wilkes County: With a Checklist of Nineteeth (Sic) Century Imprints and the Early Printers-Alexander McMillian, David P. Hillhouse, Sarah Hillhouse, Michael J. Kappel, John K.M. Charlton, 2000; Rowland Family in Georgia: Frederick Rowland, 1753-1826, Hiram Rowland, 1772-1845, William Rowland, 1797-1867 and their Children in Greene County, Georgia, 2000; Some Head Family Connections: to Reeves, Goodman, Ponder, Barfield, Smith and Black Cousins from Virginia to Fayette and Spalding counties, Georgia and beyond, 2000; Goodman Family of North Carolina and Georgia and Their Cherokee Indian Heritage: In Monroe, Fayette, Spalding and Henry Counties, Georgia and Beyond, 2000; Hillhouse Family of Washington, Georgia, Wilkes County: Printers to the State of Georgia, 2000; Jacob Martin: Physician, Huguenot, of Charleston, South Carolina: His Ancestors and Descendants Through the DeVeaux, Fair and Bessent Families of South Carolina with Connections to the Roosevelt Family and Rowland Family of Georgia, 2000; John Gensel of Charleston, South Carolina: With Origins in Germany and Pennsylvania: With Connections to the Fair, Fyfer (Jeyser, Physer), Bessent, and Rowland Families, 2000; Mississippi Branch of the Rowland Family: Descendants of Andrew Rowland and His Two Sons, Baldwin Rowland and Michael Rowland: With Connections to the

Traylor and Northen Families in Georgia and the Littrell and Denney Families in Kentucky, 2000; Mrs. Kreitner (Barbara Swint Fyfer Boomer Kreitner): Another Lost Grandmother of Charleston, South Carolina: Swint, Fyfer (Physer, Jeyser), Boomer (Bohnar), Kreitner and Gensel of Germany and South Carolina: With Some Connections To Fair and Bessent Families, 2000; Printing in Louisville, Georgia, 1798-1816: A Checklist: Printers D. Clarke, Ambrose Day, James Hely, Alexander M'Millian, George Wheeler, A. Wright, 2000; Albert Walter Rowland, 1830-1882: Teacher, Preacher, Farmer, Minister, Methodist Episcopal Church, Emory College Class of 1850, Ancestor of the Rowland Family of Greene, Newton, Fayette, Spalding, Henry Counties in Georgia and Beyond, 2000; Ancestors and Connections of Dunbar Rowland of Mississippi, 2000; Ancestors of Mary Ann Fair: First Wife of Peter G. Bessent of Charleston, South Carolina, 2000; Berou Family of France and Charleston, South Carolina: The Early Generations Connecting to Maulard, Poitevin, Postell, Trezevant and de Bourdeaux Families, 2000; Bessent Family: Including Edwards and Meredith Family Origins With Connection to the Rowland Family, from England, Barbados, South Carolina, North Carolina, Georgia, Florida and Beyond, 2000; Chambers Family of York County, South Carolina and Fayette and Spalding Counties, Georgia and Beyond, 2000; Connections to the DeVeaux Family of Charleston, South Carolina and Beyond: Eberson, Palmer, Bellinger, Splatt, Bulloch and Roosevelt Families: The Early Generations, 2000; De Bourdeaux Family of France, England and Charleston, South Carolina and Beyond: With Connections to De Veaux, Poitevin, Fair, Bessent and Rowland Families, 2000; Printing in Milledgeville, Georgia: With a Preliminary Checklist Of Nineteenth Century Imprints 1807-1860, 2002; Preliminary Checklist of Georgia Imprints, 1763-1860, Using the WPA Files and Other Sources, 2003; Printers, of Augusta, Georgia, 1786-1900: Including Publishers and Others of the Eighteenth and Nineteenth Centuries, 2003; Preliminary Checklist of Penfield, Georgia imprints, 1840-1856, using the WPA Files and Other Sources, 2003; Grocers, Butchers, Bakers, and Others in the Food Business in Augusta, Georgia: From the Augusta City Directories 1841-1879, 2004; New Look at the Postells: Chronicle of a Southern Family: Connections to the Poitevin and DeVeaux Families, 2004; Name Index to Augusta, Georgia City Directories, 1880-1901, 2005; 1890 Census of Augusta and Richmond County, Georgia: A Substitute Data from Augusta City Directories for 1888, 1889 and 1891, 2005; Business Directories of Augusta, Georgia, 1841-1901: From the Augusta City Directories: With a Name Index, 2005; Citizens of Augusta and Richmond County, Georgia during the Civil War, 1860-1865, 2005; Brides and Grooms Marriages Licenses and Certificates of Richmond County, Georgia, 2005; Village of Summerville: Listing of Citizens from U.S. Census Records 1880-1910, 2006; Women in Business in Augusta, Georgia: Richmond County, 1841-1901, from the Augusta City Directories, 2006; Soldiers and Families at the Augusta Arsenal, Augusta, Georgia: After the War from U.S. Census Records, 1870-1930, 2006; Ecclesiastical Index to Names in Augusta, Georgia with a Listing of Churches, Clergymen and Other Religious Leaders and a Bibliography of Sources for Studying Churches and Church History in Augusta, Georgia, 1736-1901, 2006; Citizens of North Augusta in Aiken County, South Carolina: From the U.S. Census Records, 1910-1930, 2006; Some Medical Professionals in Augusta, Georgia, 1736-1941: A Name Index of Physicians, Nurses, Dentists, Druggists and Others, 2006; Hephzibah, Georgia in Richmond County, 2006; China and Immigrants to Augusta and Richmond County, Georgia: From United States Census Record 1870, 1880, 1900, 1910, 1920, 1930, 2006; Color: Black or Mulatto in Richmond County, Georgia: Free Persons of Color, Listed in the 1850 and 1860 Federal Census Records: An African American Research Aid, 2006; Slave Owners in the City of Augusta and Richmond County, Georgia: From U.S. Census for 1850 and 1860, 2006; Foreign Born Citizens in Augusta and Richmond County, Georgia: Extracted from the United States Federal Census for 1850 and 1860, 2006; Boarding Houses, Furnished Rooms, and Hotels: Including Proprietors, Owners, Operators, and Managers in Augusta, Georgia, 2007; Classified Business Directory: Business Owners, Managers and Professionals in Augusta, Georgia, including North Augusta, SC, 2007; List of Prisoners in Penitentiary, Convict Camps, Chain Gangs, and Jails in Georgia: Including a List of Guards, Jailers, Sheriffs, and Others: From 1880 Federal Census Records, 2007; McPherson Barracks, List of Solider in 1880 from U.S. Census Records, 1880, 2007; Bankers, Cashiers, Tellers, and Other Officers in Banks of Augusta, Georgia during the Nineteenth and Twentieth Centuries, 2008; Ancestors in Columbia County, Georgia found in the United States Census Records, 2008; Name Index to Names Changed Legally in Georgia, 2008; Cross References to Personal Surnames in Augusta, Richmond County, Georgia Records, from the Series Published by the Augusta Genealogical Society and RR Books, 2008; Public Buildings in Augusta, Georgia: Including Office Build-

ings, Halls and Meeting Places, Government Facilities and Hotels, 2008; (with J.T. Rowland) Teachers, Principals, Presidents, Librarians and Other Administrators in Augusta and Richmond County, Georgia, 1783-1960, 2009; Index to Marriage Licenses of Richmond County, Georgia, 2009; (with J.T. Rowland) Is This Your Alma Mater?, 2010; (with J.T. Rowland) Georgia Imprints, 1861-1876, Using the WPA Files and Other Sources, 2010. Contributor of articles to books. **Address:** 17th St., Ste. 1503, Augusta, GA 30901-1328, U.S.A. **Online address:** rrow999@aol.com

ROWLAND, Peter Kenneth. British (born England), b. 1938. **Genres:** Novels, History, Biography, Reference, Literary Criticism And History, Humanities. **Career:** Greater London Council, Highways and Transportation Department, administrative officer, 1962-74, Public Health Engineering Department, administrative officer, 1974, retired, 1998. Writer. **Publications:** The Last Liberal Governments, The Promised Land, 1905-1910, 1968; Unfinished Business 1911-1914, 1971; Lloyd George, 1975; David Lloyd George: A Biography, 1976; The Disappearance of Edwin Drood, 1991; The Life and Times of Thomas Day, 1748-1789: English Philanthropist and Author: Virtue almost Personified, 1996; Just Stylish, 1998; Raffles and His Creator: The Life and Works of E.W. Hornung, 1999; What's Where in the Saturday Books: A Comprehensive Guide and Index, 2002; The Unobtrusive Miss Hawker: The Life and Works of Lanoe Falconer, Late Victorian Novelist and Short Story Writer, 1848-1908, 2009; Dickensian Digressions: The Hunter, the Haunter and the Haunted, 2010. EDITOR: The History of England in the Eighteenth Century, 1980; Macaulay's History of England from 1485 to 1685, 1985; (comp.) My Early Times, 1997; (and intro.) Collected Stories of Lanoe Falconer, 2010. **Address:** 18 Corbett Rd., London, GL E11 2LD, England. **Online address:** prow792188@aol.com

ROWLANDS, Mark. American/Welsh (born Wales), b. 1962. **Genres:** Adult Non-fiction, Philosophy, Social Sciences, Sciences. **Career:** University of Manchester, Department of Philosophy, graduate tutor, 1985-86; Oxford University, Jesus College, assistant tutor, 1987-88; University of Alabama, Department of Philosophy, assistant professor, 1988-95, associate professor, 1994-95; University College Cork, lecturer in philosophy, 1995-2002; University of Iceland, Socrates visiting fellow, 1998; University of London, Birkbeck College, visiting lecturer, 2001; University of Turku, visiting research professor, 2002; University of Exeter, Department of Sociology and Philosophy, Centre for the Philosophy of the Social Sciences, director, reader in Philosophy, 2002-04; University of Hertfordshire, School of Humanities, professor of mental and moral philosophy, 2004-06; Macquarie University, visiting research fellow, 2004; University of Miami, Department of Philosophy, professor, 2007-. Writer. **Publications:** Supervenience and Materialism, 1995; Animal Rights: A Philosophical Defense, 1998, 2nd ed. as Animal Rights: Moral Theory and Practice, 2009; The Body in Mind: Understanding Cognitive Processes, 1999; The Environmental Crisis: Understanding the Value of Nature, 2000; The Nature of Consciousness, 2001; Animals Like Us, 2002; Externalism: Putting Mind and World Back Together Again, 2003; The Philosopher at the End of the Universe, 2003; Philosophy of Psychology, 2004; Everything I Know I Learned from TV, 2004; Body Language: Representation in Action, 2006; The Philosopher and the Wolf: Lessons from the Wild on Love, Death and Happiness, 2008; Fame, 2008; The New Science of the Mind: From Extended Mind to Embodied Phenomenology, 2010. **Address:** Department of Philosophy, University of Miami, Rm. 710, Ashe Bldg., 1252 Memorial Dr., Coral Gables, FL 33124-4670, U.S.A. **Online address:** mrowlands@mail.as.miami.edu

ROWLEY, Charles K(ershaw). American/British (born England), b. 1939. **Genres:** Economics. **Career:** University of Nottingham, lecturer in industrial economics, 1962-65; University of Kent, lecturer in economics, 1965-69, senior lecturer in economics, 1969-70; Columbia University, research associate, 1967; University of York, Social Science Research Council, senior research fellow, 1968-69, reader in economic and social statistics, 1970-72; University of Newcastle upon Tyne, David Dale professor of economics and head of department, 1972-83, Centre for Research in Public and Industrial Economics, director, 1974-83, dean of the faculty of social sciences, 1978-81, 1983; Virginia Polytechnic Institute and State University, Public Choice Center, research associate, 1974, 1979; Emory University, Legal Institute for Economists, visiting fellow, 1982; Oxford University, Wolfson College, Centre for Socio-Legal Studies, visiting research fellow, 1984-86; George Mason University, professor of economics, 1984-99, Duncan Black professor of economics, Center for Study of Public Choice, editorial and program director, 1984-86, research associater, 1984-86, senior research fellow, 1984-96, dean of the graduate school and director of university research, 1986-88, associate editorial director, 1986-87, senior research associate, 1987-, director of graduate studies in economics, 1991-93, politics and the law at the James M. Buchanan Center, Program in Economics, director; Locke Institute, general director, 1989-; Royal Swedish Academy of Sciences, consultant. Writer. **Publications:** The British Monopolies Commission, 1966; Steel and Public Policy, 1971; Antitrust and Economic Efficiency, 1973; (with A.T. Peacock) Welfare Economics: A Liberal Restatement, 1975; (with G.K. Yarrow) The Evolution of Concentration in the United Kingdom Cement Industry, 1978; (with B. Beavis and M. Walker) A Study of Effluent Discharges in the River Tees, 1979; Frihet, Rattvisa, Effektivitet, 1979; (with C. Mulley, M. Walker and J. Whittaker) The Use of Roll-On/Roll-Off Vessels for Moving Freight via Coastal Waters within the United Kingdom, 1982; (with C. Mulley and J. Whittaker) The Use of Roll-On/Roll-Off Vessels for Moving Freight Between the Ports of Tees and Harwich, 1983; (with C. Mulley and J. Whittaker) The Use of RollOn/Roll-Off Vessels for Moving Freight Between the Ports of Tees and London, 1983; (with A.I. Ogus) Prepayments and Insolvency, 1984; The Right to Justice: The Political Economy of Legal Services in the United States 1992; Liberty and the State, 1993; (with W. Thorbeclu and R. Wagner) Trade Protection in the United States, 1995. EDITOR AND AUTHOR OF INTRODUCTION: Public Choice Theory, vol. I: Homo Economicus in the Political Marketplace, vol. II: The Characteristics of Political Equilibrium, vol. III: The Separation of Powers and Constitutional Political Economy, 1993; Social Choice Theory, vol. I: The Aggregation of Preferences, vol. II: Utilitarian and Contractarian Goals, vol. III: Social Justice and Classical Liberal Goals, 1993; The Political Economy of the Minimal State, 1996; Virginia Political Economy, 2004; Calculus of Consent: Logical Foundations of Constitutional Democracy, 2004; (with F. Schneider) Encyclopedia of Public Choice, 2004; Social Dilemma: Of Autocracy, Revolution, Coup d'Etat, and War, 2005; Economics and Politics of Wealth Redistribution, 2005; Economics of Politics, 2005; Law and Economics, 2005; Organization of Inquiry, 2005; Rent-Seeking Society, 2005; Bureaucracy, 2005; Economics without Frontiers, 2006; James M. Buchanan: Political Economist and Economic Philosopher, forthcoming. EDITOR AND CONTRIBUTOR: Readings in Industrial Economics, vol. I: Theoretical Foundations, vol. II: Private Enterprise and State Intervention, 1972; (with J.M. Buchanan and R.D. Tollison) Deficits, 1987; Democracy and Public Choice: Essays in Honor of G. Tullock, 1987; (with R.D. Tollison and G. Tullock) The Political Economy of Rent Seeking, 1988; Property Rights and the Limits of Democracy, 1993; (with F. Schneider and R.D. Tollison) The Next Twenty Years of Public Choice, 1993, The Political Economy of the Minimal State, 1996; Classical Liberalism and Civil Society, 1997; Constitutional Political Economy in a Public Choice Perspective, 1997; (with W.F. Shughart II and R.D. Tollison) The Economics of Budget Deficits, 2002; Encyclopedia of Public Choice, 2002; (with F. Parisi) Origins of Law and Economics: Essays by the Founding Fathers, 2005; (with F.G. Schneider) Readings in Public Choice and Constitutional Political Economy, 2008. Works appear in anthologies. Contributor of articles to journals. **Address:** Department of Economics, George Mason University, Enterprise Hall 348, 4400 University Dr., 3G4, Fairfax, VA 22030-4444, U.S.A. **Online address:** crowley@gmu.edu

ROWLING, J(oanne) K. Scottish/British (born England), b. 1965. **Genres:** Science Fiction/Fantasy, Children's Fiction, Young Adult Fiction, Mystery/Crime/Suspense, Sciences, Novels, Mystery/Crime/Suspense. **Career:** Author of books for children, 1987-. Teacher. **Publications:** Harry Potter and the Philosopher's Stone, 1997 in US as Harry Potter and the Sorcerers Stone, 1998; Harry Potter and the Chamber of Secrets, 1998; Harry Potter and the Prisoner of Azkaban, 1999; Harry Potter and the Goblet of Fire, 2000; (as Newt Scamander) Fantastic Beasts and Where to Find Them, 2001; (with K. Whisp) Quidditch Through the Ages, 2001; Harry Potter and the Order of the Phoenix, 2003; Harry Potter and the Half-Blood Prince, 2005; Harry Potter and the Deathly Hallows, 2007; (and intro.) The Tales of Beedle the Bard, 2008. **Address:** c/o Author Mail, Scholastic Inc., 557 Broadway, New York, NY 10012-3962, U.S.A.

ROWLINSON, Matthew. Canadian (born Canada), b. 1956. **Genres:** Literary Criticism And History. **Career:** Dartmouth College, associate professor of English, 1984-; University of Western Ontario, associate professor of English, University College, faculty. Writer. **Publications:** Tennyson's Fixations: Psychoanalysis and the Topics of the Early Poetry, 1994; Real Money and Romanticism, 2010; Real Money: Money, Materiality and the Literary Com-

modity in Nineteenth Century Britain, forthcoming; The Social Meanings of Blood in Victorian England, forthcoming. **Address:** Department of English, University of Western Ontario, UC 266, London, ON N6A 3K7, Canada. **Online address:** mrowlins@uwo.ca

ROWNTREE, Derek. British (born England), b. 1936?. **Genres:** Administration/Management, Education, Information Science/Computers, Mathematics/Statistics. **Career:** U.S. Industries (G.B.) Ltd., Educational Materials, editor-in-chief, 1961-66; Brighton College of Education, senior lecturer in programmed learning, 1967-70; Open University, Institute of Educational Technology, professor of educational development, retired, 2001. Writer and consultant. **Publications:** Basic Statistics, 16 vols., 1964-72; Basically Branching: A Handbook for Programmers, 1966; Learn How to Study, 1970, 4th ed., 1988; Educational Technology in Curriculum Development, 1974; Assessing Students: How Shall We Know Them?, 1977; A Dictionary of Education, 1981; Statistics without Tears: A Primer for Non-Mathematicians, 1981; Developing Courses for Students, 1981; Probability Without Tears, 1984; Do You Really Need a Home Computer?, 1985; Teaching Through Self-instruction: A Practical Handbook for Course Developers, 1986, rev. ed. as Teaching Through Self-instruction: How to Develop Open Learning Materials, 1990; How to Manage Your Boss, 1989; Exploring Open and Distance Learning, 1992; Preparing Materials for Open, Distance and Flexible Learning, 1994; Teaching with Audio in Open and Distance Learning, 1994; The Manager's Book of Checklists, 1996, 4th ed. as Brilliant Checklists for Managers, 2011. **Address:** Pearson Education, 1 Lake St., Upper Saddle River, NJ 07458, U.S.A.

ROWSE, Sharon. Canadian (born Canada) **Genres:** Mystery/Crime/Suspense, Novels. **Career:** Novelist, 2007'. **Publications:** The Silk Train Murder: A Mystery of the Klondike (novel), 2007. **Address:** Vancouver, BC , Canada. **Online address:** sharon@sharonrowsc.com

ROWSON, Pauline. British (born England) **Genres:** Novels, How-to Books. **Career:** Writer, 1998-. **Publications:** EASY STEP BY STEP GUIDES SERIES: Easy Step by Step Guide to Telemarketing, Cold Calling, Appointment Making: How to Win More Business through the Phone, 1999; Easy Step by Step Guide to Marketing, 2000; Easy Step by Step Guide to Successful Selling, 2000; Easy Step by Step Guide to Being Positive and Staying Positive (Even When the Going Gets Tough), 2002, rev. ed., 2007; Easy Step by Step Guide to Fundraising for Your School: How to Raise Money for Your School, 2005; Easy Step by Step Guide to Communicating with More Confidence: How to Influence and Persuade People, 2005, rev. ed., 2007; Easy Step by Step Guide to Publishing and Promoting Your Book, 2006; Are Your Customers Being Served?: How to Boost Profits by Delivering Exceptional Customer Service, 2007. MYSTERY NOVELS: In Cold Daylight, 2006; Tide of Death, 2006; In for the Kill, 2007; Deadly Waters, 2007; The Suffocating Sea, 2008. OTHERS: Dead Man's Wharf, 2009; Blood on the Sand, 2010; Footsteps on the Shore, 2011; A Killing Coast, 2012. **Address:** Severn House Publishers Ltd., 9-15 High St., Sutton, SR SM1 1DF, England. **Online address:** pauline@rowmark.co.uk

ROY, Alexander. American (born United States), b. 1971. **Genres:** Sports/Fitness. **Career:** Europe by Car, president, 1997-; Polizei 144, president, 2000-; Chrome Productions, host, 2006; Gravid Films, producer, 2009; Gizmodo, automotive technology columnist; Jalopnik, automotive technology columnist. Writer and philanthropist. **Publications:** The Driver: My Dangerous Pursuit of Speed and Truth in the Outlaw Racing World, 2007. **Address:** HarperEntertainment, 10 E 53rd St., New York, NY 10022, U.S.A. **Online address:** alex@teampolizei.com

ROY, Archibald Edmiston. *See* **ROY, Archie E.**

ROY, Archie E. (Archibald Edmiston Roy). Scottish (born Scotland), b. 1924. **Genres:** Novels, Astronomy, Paranormal. **Career:** Shawlands Academy, science teacher, 1954-58; University of Glasgow, lecturer, 1958-66, senior lecturer, 1966-73, reader, 1973-77, professor of astronomy, 1977-89, professor emeritus of astronomy, 1989-, honorary senior research fellow; Vistas in Astronomy, co-editor, 1983-; Scottish Society for Psychical Research, founding president; Society for Psychical Research, president. **Publications:** Great Moments in Astronomy, 1963; The Foundations of Astrodynamics, 1965; Deadlight, 1968; (trans.) T. de Galiana, Concise Encyclopedia of Astronautics, 1968; The Curtained Sleep, 1969; All Evil Shed Away, 1970; Sable Night, 1973; The Dark Host, 1976; (with D. Clarke) Astronomy: Principles and Practice, 1977, 4th ed., 2003; (with D. Clarke) Astronomy, Structure of the Universe, 1977, 3rd ed., 1989; Orbital Motion, 1978, 4th ed., 2005; Devil in the Darkness, 1978; A Sense of Something Strange, 1990; Archives of the Mind, 1996. EDITOR: Long-Term Dynamical Behaviour of Natural and Artificial N-Body Systems, 1988; Predictability, Stability, and Chaos in N-body Dynamical Systems, 1991; (with B.A. Steves) From Newton to Chaos: Modern Techniques for Understanding and Coping with Chaos in N-Body Dynamical Systems, 1995; (with B.A. Steves) Dynamics of Small Bodies in the Solar System: A Major Key to Solar System Studies, 1999. **Address:** School of Physics and Astronomy, University of Glasgow, Rm. 605, Kelvin Bldg., Glasgow, G12 8QQ, Scotland. **Online address:** archie@astro.gla.ac.uk

ROY, Arundhati. (Suzanna Arundhati Roy). Indian (born India), b. 1961. **Genres:** Novels, Politics/Government, Social Commentary, Essays. **Career:** Actor; screenwriter. **Publications:** The God of Small Things (novel), 1997; The End of Imagination, 1998; The Greater Common Good, 1999; The Cost of Living, 1999; Power Politics: The Reincarnation of Rumpelstiltskin, 2001; The Algebra of Infinite Justice, 2002; In Which Annie Gives it those Ones: The Original Screenplay, 2003; War Talk, 2003; Ordinary Person's Guide to Empire, 2004; Public Power in the Age of Empire, 2004; (co-ed.) Mumbai, 2004; (intro.) 13 December, A Reader: The Strange Case of the Attack on the Indian Parliament, 2006; The Shape of the Beast, 2008; Field Notes on Democracy: Listening to Grasshoppers, 2009; Walking With The Comrades, 2011; Broken Republic, 2011; Kashmir, 2011. Contributor to periodicals. **Address:** Random House, 1745 Broadway, Ste. B-1, New York, NY 10019-4305, U.S.A.

ROY, Donald H. American (born United States), b. 1944. **Genres:** Politics/Government, Intellectual History, Social Commentary, Philosophy, Social Sciences. **Career:** Carroll College, assistant professor of political Science, 1978-82; Dallas Chamber of Commerce, director of research, 1984-87; Jefferson Community College, assistant professor of political science, 1987-89; Ferris State University, associate professor of political science, 1989-. Writer. **Publications:** Dialogues in American Politics, 1993; Public Policy Dialogues, 1994; The Reuniting of America: Eleven Multicultural Dialogues, 1996; The Dialogic Resurgence of Public Intellectuals, 2001; State Governments: Institutions and Issues, 2005; Women and Children First: The Horrible Hartford Circus Fire, 2008. **Address:** Department of Social Sciences, College of Arts and Sciences, Ferris State University, 2092 ASC, 820 Campus Dr., Big Rapids, MI 49307, U.S.A. **Online address:** royd@ferris.edu

ROY, F. Hampton. American (born United States), b. 1937. **Genres:** Local History/Rural Topics, Medicine/Health. **Career:** U.S. Army, Madigan General Hospital, staff, 1967-69; University of Arkansas, assistant professor of ophthalmology, 1969-74, associate clinical professor of ophthalmology, 1974-; Arkansas Cataract Center, physician, through 1974. Writer. **Publications:** Ocular Differential Diagnosis, 1972, 6th ed., 1997; Practical Management of Eye Problems: Glaucoma, Strabismus, Visual Fields, 1975; Current Ocular Therapy, 1980, 5th ed., 1995; Intraocular Lenses, 1981; (with E.C. Perry) Light in the Shadows, 1982; Charles L. Thompson and Associates: Arkansas architects 1885-1938, 1982; Charles L. Thompson and Associates: Arkansas Architects, 1886-1937, 1984; (with C. Witsell) How We Lived: Little Rock as an American City, 1984; Greater Little Rock, One in a Million: A Photographic Journal, 1984; Ocular Syndromes and Systemic Diseases, 1985, 3rd ed., 2002; (with C. Russell) The Encyclopedia of Aging and the Elderly, 1992; (ed.) Master Techniques in Ophthalmic Surgery, 1995; (ed. with D. Singh and R.J. Fugo) Ocular Applications of the Fugo Blade, 2010. Works appear in anthologies. Contributor to journals. **Address:** 1 St Vincent Cir., Ste. 360, Little Rock, AR 72205, U.S.A. **Online address:** hamproy@aristotle.net

ROY, Jacqueline. British (born England), b. 1954. **Genres:** Novels, Children's Fiction, Young Adult Fiction. **Career:** Manchester Metropolitan University, lecturer, 1992, senior lecturer in English and creative writing. Novelist. **Publications:** (Ed.) No Black Sparrows: A Vivid Portrait of Jamaica in the 1930s, 1989; Soul Daddy, 1990; King Sugar, 1993; Fat Chance, 1994; A Daughter Like Me, 1996; Playing It Cool, 1997; The Fat Lady Sings, 2000; Benjy's Ghost, 2004. **Address:** Department of English, Manchester Metropolitan University, Rm. 414, Geoffrey Manton Bldg., Rosamond St. W, Manchester, GM M15 6LL, England. **Online address:** j.roy@mmu.ac.uk

ROY, James Charles. American (born United States), b. 1945. **Genres:** History, Reference, Travel/Exploration. **Career:** Time Inc., staff journalist, 1967-70; Allagash Group, editor, 1970-72; writer, 1972-. Photographer. **Publications:** The Road Wet, the Wind Close: Celtic Ireland, 1986; Islands of Storm=Eileán annraidh (bilingual Gaelic and English), 1991; (ed. with J.L. Pethica) To the Land of the Free from This Island of Slaves: Henry Stratford Persse's Letters from Galway to America, 1821-1832, 1998; The Vanished Kingdom: Travels through the History of Prussia, 1999; The Fields of Athenry: A Journey through Irish History, 2001; The Back of Beyond: A Search for the Soul of Ireland, 2002. Contributor to newspapers and periodicals. **Address:** PO Box 641, Newburyport, MA 01950, U.S.A. **Online address:** jvroy@attbi.com

ROY, James (Henry Barstow). (J. H. B. Roy). British (born England), b. 1922?. **Genres:** Agriculture/Forestry, Medicine/Health, Animals/Pets, Administration/Management, Sciences. **Career:** National Institute for Research in Dairying, agricultural research worker, 1949-85. Writer. **Publications:** (As J.H.B. Roy) The Calf, vol. I: Its Management, Feeding and Health, 1955, 5th ed., 1990, vol. II: Nutrition and Health, 1970. **Address:** Bruncketts, The St., Mortimer, Reading, BR RG7 3PE, England.

ROY, J. H. B. See ROY, James (Henry Barstow).

ROY, Lucinda (H.). American/British (born England), b. 1955. **Genres:** Novels, Poetry. **Career:** Virginia Tech University, Outreach, Curriculum and Diversity, associate dean, 1994-96, Gloria D. Smith professor of black studies, 1995-97, alumni distinguished professor in English, 1997-, associate professor of English, Creative Writing Program, director, chair, 2002-06. Writer and educator. **Publications:** POETRY: Wailing the Dead to Sleep, 1988; The Humming Birds, 1995. NOVELS: Lady Moses, 1998; The Hotel Alleluia, 2000; No Right to Remain Silent: The Tragedy at Virginia Tech, 2009. Contributor to periodicals. **Address:** Department of English, Virginia Tech University, Shanks Hall, 309 Williams Hall, 323 Shanks, PO Box 0112, Blacksburg, VA 24061-0112, U.S.A. **Online address:** lroy@vt.edu

ROY, Olivier. Italian/French (born France), b. 1949. **Genres:** Theology/Religion. **Career:** Teacher, 1973-81; French Foreign Ministry (Center for Analysis and Forecast), consultant, 1984-2009; United Nations Office for Coordinating Relief in Afghanistan (UNOCA), consultant, 1988; CNRS (French National Center for Scientific Research), research director, lecturer, senior researcher, 1985-; Organization for Security and Cooperation in Europe (OSCE), representative to Tajikistan, 1993-94, OSCE Mission for Tajikistan, head, 1994; Berkeley University, Department of Political Sciences, visiting professor, 2008-09; European University Institute, professor, director of the mediterranean programme 2009-. Writer. **Publications:** Leibniz et la Chine, 1972; (ed. with A. Brigot) Guerre d'Afghanistan: intervention soviétique et résistance, 1985; Afghanistan: islam et modernité politique, 1985; Islam and Resistance in Afghanistan, 1986; échec de l'islam politique, 1992; (with F. Adelkhah and J. Bayart) Thermidor en Iran, 1993; Failure of Political Islam, 1994; Généalogie de l'islamisme, 1995; Afghanistan: From Holy War to Civil War, 1995; La nouvelle Asie centrale, ou, La fabrication des nations, 1997; Vers un islam européen, 1999; (with F. Khosrokhavar) Iran: comment sortir d'une révolution religieuse, 1999; New Central Asia: The Creation of Nations, 2000; (with M.A. Zahab) Réseaux islamiques: la connexion afghano-pakistanaise, 2002; Islam Mondialisé, 2002; Globalised Islam: The Search for a New Ummah, 2002; Les Illusions du 11 septembre: le débat stratégique face au terrorisme, 2002; La Turquie aujourd'hui: un pays europen?, 2004; Afghanistan: la difficile reconstruction d'un etat, 2004; (with M.A. Zahab) Islamist Networks: The Afghan-Pakistan Connection, 2004; Laïcité face à l'islam, 2005; (ed.) Turkey Today: A European Country?, 2005; Islamische Weg nach Westen: Globalisierung, Entwurzelung und Radikalisierung, 2006; Secularism Confronts Islam, 2007; (with A. Sfeir) Columbia World Dictionary of Islamism, 2007; Croissant Et Le Chaos, 2007; Politics of Chaos in the Middle East, 2008; La sainte ignorance: le temps de la religion sans culture, 2008; Holy Ignorance: When Religion and Culture Part Ways, 2010. Contributor to periodicals. **Address:** Department of Political and Social Sciences, European University Institute, Convento-SD, SD019, Badia Fiesolana - Via dei Roccettini 9, San Domenico, I-50014, Italy. **Online address:** olivier.roy@eui.eu

ROY, Suzanna Arundhati. See ROY, Arundhati.

ROYAL, Priscilla. American (born United States), b. 1944. **Genres:** Mystery/Crime/Suspense, Novels. **Career:** Writer. **Publications:** MEDIEVAL MYSTERY SERIES: Wine of Violence, 2003; Tyrant of the Mind, 2004; Sorrow Without End, 2006; Justice for the Damned, 2007, Forsaken Soul, 2008, Chambers of Death, 2009; Valley of Dry Bones, 2010; Killing Season, 2011. NOVEL: Favas Can Be Fatal, 2006. **Address:** Poisoned Pen Press, 6962 E 1st Ave., Ste. 103, Scottsdale, AZ 85251-4337, U.S.A. **Online address:** tynprior@aol.com

ROYAL, Robert. American (born United States), b. 1949?. **Genres:** Literary Criticism And History, History, Social Sciences, Politics/Government, Theology/Religion, Philosophy. **Career:** Prospect Magazine, editor-in-chief, 1980-82; Ethics and Public Policy Center, vice-president; Faith Reason Institute, president; Brown University, instructor; Rhode Island College, instructor; Catholic University, instructor; Catholic Thing, editor-in-chief. **Publications:** 1492 and All That: Political Manipulations of History, 1992; (trans. with R. Papini) The Christian Democrat International, 1997; Dante Alighieri: Divine Comedy, Divine Spirituality, 1999; The Virgin and the Dynamo: Use and Abuse of Religion in Environmental Debates, 1999; The Catholic Martyrs of the Twentieth Century: A Comprehensive World History, 2000; (trans. with J. Torrell) Saint Thomas Aquinas, vol. I: The Person and His Work, rev. ed., 2005; The Popes Army: 500 Years of the Papal Swiss Guard, 2006; The God That Did Not Fail: How Religion Built and Sustains the West, 2006; (trans. with Y.R.M. Simon) Ethiopian Campaign and French Political Thought, 2009. EDITOR: (with M. Falcoff) Crisis and Opportunity: U.S. Policy in Central America and the Caribbean: Thirty Essays by Statesmen, Scholars, Religious Leaders, and Journalists, 1984; Challenge and Response: Critiques of the Catholic Bishops Draft Letter on the U.S. Economy, 1987; (with M. Falcoff) The Continuing Crisis: U.S. Policy in Central America and the Caribbean: Thirty Essays by Statesmen, Scholars, Religious Leaders, and Journalists, 1987; (with G. Weigel) A Century of Catholic Social Thought: Essays on Rerum Novarum and Nine Other Key Documents, 1991; (with V. Nemoianu) The Hospitable Canon: Essays on Literary Play, Scholarly Choice, and Popular Pressures, 1991; (with V. Nemoianu) Play, Literature, Religion: Essays in Cultural Intertextuality, 1992; (with G. Weigel) Building the Free Society: Democracy, Capitalism, and Catholic Social Teaching, 1993; Jacques Maritain and the Jews, 1994; Reinventing the American People: Unity and Diversity Today, 1995. Contributor to periodicals. **Address:** Faith Reason Institute, 1100 G St. NW, Ste. 450, Washington, DC 20005, U.S.A. **Online address:** royal@frinstitute.org

ROYAL, Rosamond. *See* **HINES, Jeanne.**

ROYBAL, Laura (Husby). American (born United States), b. 1956. **Genres:** Children's Fiction, Young Adult Fiction. **Career:** Writer. **Publications:** Billy, 1994. Contributor to periodicals. **Address:** PO Box 218, Pecos, NM 87552, U.S.A.

ROYLE, Nicholas. British (born England), b. 1957. **Genres:** Literary Criticism And History. **Career:** University of Tampere, teacher of literature, 1987-92, associate professor of English and American literature, 1989-92; University of Stirling, reader in English studies, 1992-99, teacher of theories of literature, 1992-99; University of Sussex, professor of English, 1999-. Writer. **Publications:** Telepathy and Literature: Essays on the Reading Mind, 1991; (ed.) Afterwords, 1992; (with A. Bennett) Elizabeth Bowen and the Dissolution of the Novel: Still Lives, 1994; After Derrida, 1995; (with A. Bennett) An Introduction to Literature, Criticism and Theory, 1995, 4th ed., 2009; E.M. Forster, 1999; (ed.) Deconstructions: A User's Guide, 2000; The Uncanny, 2003; Jacques Derrida, 2003; How to Read Shakespeare, 2005; In Memory of Jacques Derrida, 2009; Quilt, 2010. **Address:** Department of English, University of Sussex, Arts Bldg. B338, Sussex House, Falmer, ES BN1 9QN, England. **Online address:** n.w.o.royle@sussex.ac.uk

ROYTE, Elizabeth. American (born United States), b. 1960?. **Genres:** Sciences, Natural History, Regional/Urban Planning, Travel/Exploration, Environmental Sciences/Ecology. **Career:** The Nation, intern; GEO, assistant editor. Freelance journalist. **Publications:** The Tapir's Morning Bath: Mysteries of the Tropical Rain Forest and the Scientists Who Are Trying to Solve Them, 2001; Garbage Land: On the Secret Trail of Trash, 2005; Bottlemania: How Water Went on Sale and Why We Bought It, 2008. Contributor to periodicals and magazines. **Address:** c/o Author Mail, Little Brown and Co., 1271 Ave. of the Americas, New York, NY 10020, U.S.A. **Online address:** eroyte@yahoo.com

ROZAN, S. J. American (born United States), b. 1950?. **Genres:** Mystery/Crime/Suspense. **Career:** Writer and architect. **Publications:** China Trade, 1994; Concourse, 1995; Mandarin Plaid, 1996; No Colder Place, 1997; A Bitter Feast, 1998; A Tale About a Tiger, 1998; Stone Quarry, 1999; The Grift of the Magi: A Christmas Story, 2000; Reflecting the Sky, 2001; Winter and Night, 2002; Absent Friends, 2004; In This Rain, 2007; Bronx Noir, 2007; Shanghai Moon, 2009; (ed. with J. Santlofer) Dark End of the Street: New Noir Stories, 2010; Trail of Blood, 2010; On the Line: A Bill Smith/Lydia Chin Novel, 2010; Ghost Hero, 2011. Contributor to periodicals. **Address:** c/o Steven Axelrod, The Axelrod Agency, 49 Main St., PO Box 357, Chatham, NY 12037, U.S.A. **Online address:** sjrozan@sjrozan.com

ROZBICKI, Michal J. American/Polish (born Poland), b. 1946. **Genres:** History, Education, Biography, Autobiography/Memoirs, Social Sciences. **Career:** University of Warsaw, assistant professor, 1976-84, associate professor of history, 1984-90, American Studies Center, head, 1987-90; Indiana University-Bloomington, visiting associate professor of history and associate director of Polish Studies Center, 1990-92; Saint Louis University, Department of History, assistant professor, 1992-97, associate professor, 1997-, department chair. Writer. **Publications:** Samuel Hartlib, z dziejów polsko-angielskich zwiazków kulturalnychw XVII wieku, 1980; The Transformation of English Cultural Ethos in Colonial America: Maryland, 1634-1720, 1988; Od kolonizacji do secesji: Historia Stanów Zjednoczonych Ameryki do 1860 roku, 1990; (ed.) European and American Constitutionalism in the Eighteenth Century, 1990; Narodziny Narodu: Historia Stanów Zjednoczonych Ameryki do 1861 Roku, 1991; (co-ed.) A Selection of Sources on the History and Culture of the United States of America: From Colonization to 1945, 1994; The Complete Colonial Gentleman: Cultural Legitimacy in Plantation America, 1998; Culture and Liberty in the Age of the American Revolution, 2011; (ed. with G. O. Ndege) Cross-Cultural History and the Domestication of Otherness, 2012. **Address:** Department of History, St. Louis University, 3800 Lindell Blvd., PO Box 56907, St. Louis, MO 63108, U.S.A. **Online address:** rozbicmj@slu.edu

ROZELL, Mark J. American (born United States), b. 1959. **Genres:** Politics/Government, Biography, Autobiography/Memoirs, Theology/Religion. **Career:** Mary Washington College, assistant professor, 1986-90, associate professor of political science, 1991-95; American University, associate professor of political science, 1995-98; The Catholic University of America, ordinary professor of politics, 1999-2004, department chair, 2002-04; George Mason University, professor of public policy, 2004-. Writer. **Publications:** The Press and the Carter Presidency, 1989; (ed. with J.F. Pontuso) American Conservative Opinion Leaders, 1990; The Press and the Ford Presidency, 1992; Executive Privilege: The Dilemma of Secrecy and Democratic Accountability, 1994, rev. ed. as Executive Privilege: Presidential Power, Secrecy, and Accountability, 2002, 3rd ed., 2010; (ed. with C. Wilcox) God at the Grass Roots: The Christian Right in the 1994 Elections, 1995; The Press and the Bush Presidency, 1996; In Contempt of Congress: Postwar Press Coverage on Capitol Hill, 1996; Second Coming: The New Christian Right in Virginia Politics, 1996 (ed. with W.D. Pederson) and the FDR Modern Presidency: Leadership and Legacy, 1997 (ed. with C. Wilcox) God has the Grass Roots, 1996: The Christian Right in the American Elections, 1997; (ed. with C.S. Bullock III) The New Politics of the Old South: An Introduction to Southern Politics, 1998, 4th ed., 2010; (with C. Wilcox) Interest Groups in American Campaigns: The New Face of Electioneering, 1999, (with M. Franz and C. Wilcox) 3rd ed., 2012; (contrib.) Patriot Sage: George Washington and the American Political Tradition, 1999; (ed. with C. Wilcox) The Clinton Scandal and the Future of American Government, 2000; (ed. with J.C. Green and C. Wilcox) Prayers in the Precincts: The Christian Right in the 1998 Elections, 2000; (ed. with W.D. Pederson and F.J. Williams) George Washington and the Origins of the American Presidency, 2000; (ed. with E. Fishman and W.D. Pederson) George Washington: Foundation of Presidential Leadership and Character, 2001; (ed. with J.K. White) Contemporary Readings in American History, 2002; (ed.) Media Power, Media Politics, 2003, (with J.D. Mayer) 2nd ed., 2008; (ed. with J.C. Green and C. Wilcox) The Christian Right in American Politics: Marching to the Millennium, 2003; (with R.J. Barilleaux) Power and Prudence: The Presidency of George HW Bush, 2004; (ed. with G.L. Gregg, II) Considering the Bush Presidency, 2004; (ed. with J.C. Green and C. Wilcox) Values Campaign?: The Christian Right and the 2004 Elections, 2006; (ed. with G. Whitney) Religion and the American Presidency, 2007, (ed. with G. Whitney) 2nd ed., 2012; (ed. with G. Whitney) Religion and the Bush Presidency, 2007; (ed. with K.E. Heyer and M.A. Genovese) Catholics and Politics: The Dynamic Tension between Faith and Power, 2008;

(ed. with G. Whitney) Testing the Limits: George W. Bush and the Imperial Presidency, 2009; (ed. with M.A. Hamilton) Fundamentalism, Politics, and the Law, 2010; (ed. with C.S. Bullock, III) The Oxford Handbook of Southern Politics, 2012; (with M.A. Sollenberger) The President's Czars, 2012. Contributor to periodicals. **Address:** School of Public Policy, George Mason University, 3351 Fairfax Dr., MS 3B1, Arlington, VA 22201, U.S.A. **Online address:** mrozell@gmu.edu

ROZENBERG, Joshua. British (born England), b. 1950. **Genres:** Law, Politics/Government. **Career:** British Broadcasting Corp., journalist, 1975, legal affairs correspondent, 1985-97, legal and constitutional affairs correspondent, 1997-2000; Daily Telegraph, legal editor, 2000-08, legal author and commentator, 2008-. **Publications:** (With N. Watkins) Your Rights and the Law, 1986; The Case for the Crown: The Inside Story of the Director of Public Prosecutions, 1987; The Search for Justice: An Anatomy of the Law, 1994; Trial of Strength: The Battle between Ministers and Judges over Who Makes the Law, 1998; Privacy and the Press, 2004. **Address:** BCM Rozenberg, London, GL WC1N 3XX, England. **Online address:** joshua@rozenberg.net

ROZO, Marco Antonio Palacios. Mexican/Colombian (born Colombia), b. 1944. **Genres:** Novels. **Career:** National University of Colombia, researcher, 1970-72, rector, 1984-88, 2003-05; University of London, Institute of Latin American Studies, research fellow, 1977-78; Colegio de Mexico, Center for International Studies, research professor, 1978-82, professor of Latin American history and director, general academic coordinator, Center for Historical Studies, research professor; Colombia Institute for the Promotion of Higher Educacaion, director general, 1989-90; Duke University, McWane distinguished visiting professor, 1991-92; Oxford University, St. Antony's College, senior associate, 1991-94; Autonomous University of Barcelona, Department of Economics and Institutions Economics, visiting professor, 1992-94; University of Los Angels, Faculty of Management, professor, 2003. Writer. **Publications:** NONFICTION: El Populismo en Colombia, 1971; El cafe en Colombia, 1850-1970: una historia economica, social y politica, 1979, rev. ed., 2009; Colombia no alineada: memoria de un foro y declaraciOn de Nueva Delhi, 1983, 1983; La Unidad Nacional en America Latina: del regionalismo a ja nacionalidad, 1983; La delgada corteza de nuestra civilizacion, 1986; Estado y clases sociales en Colombia, 1986; Entre la legitimidad y la violencia: Colombia 1875-1994, 1995; Parabola del liberalismo, 1999; Aventuras y desventuras de la paz cuatrienal, 1999; De populistas, mandarines y violencias: luchas por el poder, 1999; La clase mas ruidosa y otros ensayos sobre politica e historia, 2002; (with F. Safford) Colombia: Fragmented Land, Divided Society, 2002; Populistas: el poder de las palabras: estudios de politica, 2011. **Address:** Avenida Toluca 1047, Casa 35, Col. Olivar de los Padres, Mexico City, 01700, Mexico. **Online address:** mpalacios@colmex.mx

RUBENS, Jim M. American (born United States), b. 1950. **Genres:** History, inspirational/Motivational Literature. **Career:** New Hampshire republican state senator, 1994-98; Union of Concerned Scientists, consultant. Writer, entrepreneur and politician. **Publications:** OverSuccess: Healing the American Obsession with Wealth, Fame, Power, and Perfection, 2009. **Address:** Hanover, NH , U.S.A. **Online address:** jimrubens@aol.com

RUBENSTEIN, Richard Lowell. American (born United States), b. 1924. **Genres:** History, Politics/Government, Psychology, Theology/Religion, Autobiography/Memoirs, Essays, Young Adult Non-fiction. **Career:** B'nai B'rith Hillel Foundation, assistant director, 1956, director, 1958-70; Harvard University, chaplain, 1956; University of Pittsburgh, chaplain, 1958-70, Department of Humanities, adjunct professor, 1964-70, Charles E. Merrill Lecturer, through 1969; Florida State University, professor, 1970-77, distinguished professor of religion, 1977-95, Center for Study of Southern Religion, director, professor emeritus of religion, 1995-; Yale University, National Humanities Institute, fellow, 1976-77; Washington Institute for Values in Public Policy, president, 1982-85; University of Bridgeport, president and professor of religion, 1995-99, distinguished professor of religion, Center for Holocaust and Genocide Studies, director, president emeritus, 1999-; Carnegie Mellon University, chaplain; Duquesne University, chaplain. **Publications:** After Auschwitz, 1966; The Religious Imagination, 1968; Morality and Eros, 1970; My Brother Paul, 1972; Power Struggle (autobiography), 1974; The Cunning of History, 1975; The Age of Triage: Fear and Hope in an Overcrowded World, 1983; Lessons of Grenada and the Ethics of Military Intervention, 1984; (with J.K. Roth) Approaches to Auschwitz: The Holocaust and its Legacy, 1987, 2nd ed., 2003; After Auschwitz: History, Theology and Contemporary Judaism, 1992; (contrib.) What Kind of God?, 1995; Jihad and Genocide, 2010.

EDITOR: Modernization: The Humanist Response to Its Promise and Problems, 1982; The Dissolving Alliance: The United States and the Future of Europe, 1987; Spirit Matters: The Worldwide Impact of Religion on Contemporary Politics, 1987; (with J.K. Roth) Politics of Latin American Liberation Theology: The Challenge to U.S. Public Policy, 1988. **Address:** c/o George Borchardt, 145 E 52nd St., New York, CT 10022, U.S.A. **Online address:** president@bridgeport.edu

RUBIN, Adam. American (born United States) **Genres:** Novels. **Career:** New York Daily News, beat writer for the New York Mets, 2003-. **Publications:** Pedro, Carlos, and Omar: The Story of a Season in the Big Apple and the Pursuit of Baseball's Top Latino Stars, 2006, rev. ed. as Pedro, Carlos (and Carlos) and Omar: The Rebirth of the New York Mets, 2006. **Address:** Long Beach, NY , U.S.A. **Online address:** arubin@nydailynews.com

RUBIN, Barnett R(ichard). American (born United States), b. 1950. **Genres:** Area Studies, International Relations/Current Affairs. **Career:** Amnesty International USA, founder and chair, 1981-89; Yale University, assistant professor of political science, 1982-89; United States Institute of Peace, peace fellow, 1989-90; Columbia University, associate professor of political science and director, 1990-96, Center for the Study of Central Asia, director, 1992-95, Project on Political Order and Conflict in the Former Soviet Union, director, 1994-96; Council on Foreign Relations, senior fellow, 1994-2000, Center for Preventive Action, director, 1994-2000, Peace and Conflict Studies, director, 1994-2000; Conflict Prevention and Peace Forum, founder and deputy chair, 2000-, chair; New York University, Center on International Cooperation, project co-ordinator, director of studies and senior fellow, 2000-. Writer. **Publications:** Feudal Revolt and State-Building: The 1938 Sikar Agitation in Jaipur, 1983; (with J. Laber) Tears, Blood, and Cries: Human Rights in Afghanistan since the Invasion, 1979-1984, 1984; To Die in Afghanistan, 1985; Cycles of Violence: Human Rights in Sri Lanka since the Indo-Sri Lanka Agreement, 1987; (with J. Laber) Nation is Dying: Afghanistan under the Soviets, 1979-87, 1988; The Search for Peace in Afghanistan: From Buffer State to Failed State, 1995; The Fragmentation of Afghanistan: State Formation and Collapse in the International System, 1995, 2nd ed., 2002; (ed.) Toward Comprehensive Peace in Southeast Europe: Conflict Prevention in the South Balkans, 1996; (ed.) Cases and Strategies for Preventive Action, 1998; (with P.M. Lewis and P.T. Robinson) Stabilizing Nigeria: Sanctions, Incentives, and Support for Civil Society, 1998; (ed. with J. Snyder) Post-Soviet Political Order: Conflict and State Building, 1998; (with N. Lubin) Calming the Ferghana Valley: Development and Dialogue in the Heart of Central Asia, 1999; Blood on the Doorstep: The Politics of Preventive Action, 2002; Afghanistan's Uncertain Transition from Turmoil to Normalcy, 2006. Works appear in anthologies. Contributor of articles to journals. **Address:** Center on International Cooperation, New York University, 726 Broadway, Ste. 543, New York, NY 10003, U.S.A. **Online address:** barnett.rubin@nyu.edu

RUBIN, Barry. Israeli/American (born United States), b. 1950. **Genres:** Area Studies, Civil Liberties/Human Rights, International Relations/Current Affairs, History, Politics/Government. **Career:** Georgetown University, Center for Strategic and International Studies, senior research fellow in Middle East studies, 1978-85, School of Foreign Service, professorial lecturer, 1978-; Johns Hopkins University, School of Advanced International Studies, visiting professor, 1983; Orkand Corp., senior analyst, 1986-90, Foreign Policy Institute, senior fellow, 1986-93; Washington Institute for Near East Policy, senior fellow, 1988-91, visiting fellow, 2007; Hebrew University, Truman Center, senior fellow, 1989-, Rotheberg School, staff, 1994-95; Tel Aviv University, Fulbright fellow, 1990-91; Haifa University, Fulbright fellow, 1990-91, Jewish-Arab Center, senior fellow, 1994-; Bar-Ilan University, staff, 1995-96, BESA Center, senior fellow, 1994-96; Global Research in International Affairs (GLORIA) Center, ICD Global Research, director, 2001-, Middle East Review of International Affairs (MERIA) Journal, editor, Lauder School of Government and Diplomacy, research director, 2001-; The American University, Seymour and Lillian Abensohn visiting professor, 2005-06; Turkish Studies Journal, editor; Interdisciplinary Center, professor; PajamasMedia, columnist. **Publications:** International News and the American Media, 1977; How Others Report Us: America in the Foreign Press, 1979; Paved with Good Intentions: The American Experience and Iran, 1980; The Great Powers in the Middle East, 1941-1947: The Road to the Cold War, 1980; (with O. Greene) London after the Bomb, 1982; The Arab States and the Palestine Conflict, 1981; Secrets of State: The State Department and the Struggle Over U.S. Foreign Policy, 1985; Modern Dictators: Third World Coup Makers, Strongmen, and Populist Tyrants, 1987; Istanbul Intrigues, 1989; The PLO's New Policy:

Evolution Until Victory?, 1989; (trans.) L. Chukovskaya, Conversations with Akhmatova, vol. I: 1938-1941, 1990; Islamic Fundamentalism in Egyptian Politics, 1990; Cauldron of Turmoil: America in the Middle East, 1992; Assimilation and Its Discontents, 1995; Essays on the Middle East's New Era, 1997; The Transformation of Palestinian Politics, 1999; The Region at the Center of the World, 2001; America and Its Allies, 2001; Contemporary Islamist Movements in the Middle East, 2001; (with J.C. Rubin) Why September 11?, 2002; The Tragedy of the Middle East, 2002; (with J.C. Rubin) Yasir Arafat: A Political Biography, 2003; (with J.C. Rubin) Hating America: A History, 2004; The Long War for Freedom: The Arab Struggle for Democracy in the Middle East, 2006; Iranian Revolution and the Resurgence of Islam, 2007; Middle East in the Age of Uncertainty, 1991-present, 2007; Truth about Syria, 2007; (with J.C. Rubin) Chronologies of Modern Terrorism, 2008; History of Islam, 2010; Israel, 2011. EDITOR: (with E.P. Spiro) Human Rights and U.S. Foreign Policy, 1979; (with W. Laqueur) The Human Rights Reader, 1979, rev. ed., 1990; The Israel-Arab Reader: A Documentary History of the Middle East Conflict, 1984, (with W. Laqueur) 7th ed., 2008; (with R.S. Leiken) The Central American Crisis Reader, 1987; The Politics of Terrorism: Terror as a State and Revolutionary Strategy, 1989; The Politics of Terrorism: Counterterrorist Policies, 1990; The Politics of Counterterrorism: The Ordeal of Democratic States, 1990; (with I.S. Lustick) Critical Essays on Israeli Society, Politics and Culture, vol. II, 1991; (co-editor) Gulfwatch Anthology: August 30, 1990-March 28, 1991: The Day-by-day Analysis of the Gulf Crisis by the Scholars and Associates of the Washington Institute, 1991; Terrorism and Politics, 1991; (with A. Baram) Iraq's Road to War, 1993; From War to Peace, 1973-1993, 1994; Revolution until Victory, 1994; Turkish Foreign Policy, 2000; (with K. Kirisci) Turkey in World Politics: An Emerging Multiregional Power, 2001; (with T. Keaney) U.S. Allies in a Changing World, 2001; Efficient Use of Limited Water Resources: Making Israel a Model State, 2 001; (ed. with J.C. Rubin) Anti-American Terrorism and the Middle East: A Documentary Reader, 2002; (ed. with T.A. Keaney) Armed Forces in the Middle East: Politics and Strategy, 2002; Crisis in the Contemporary Persian Gulf, 2002; (with M. Heper) Political Parties in Turkey, 2002; Revolutionaries and Reformers: Contemporary Islamist Movements in the Middle East, 2003; (with A. Çarkoğlu) Turkey and the European Union: Domestic Politics, Economic Integration, and International Dynamics, 2003; (with Z. Öniş) The Turkish Economy in Crisis, 2003; (with A. Çarkoglu) Greek-Turkish Relations in an Era of Détente, 2004; (with A. Çarkoğlu) Religion and Politics in Turkey, 2006; Political Islam: Critical Concepts in Islamic Studies, 2007; Lebanon: Liberation, Conflict, and Crisis, 2009; Conflict and Insurgency in the Contemporary Middle East, 2009; Muslim Brotherhood: The Organization and Policies of a Global Islamist Movement, 2010; West and the Middle East: Critical Concepts in Political Science, 2010; Guide to Islamist Movements, 2010; Middle East, 2012; Security and Stability in the Middle East, 2012. Contributor to magazines, periodicals and journals. **Address:** Global Research in International Affairs (GLORIA), Center, PO Box 167, Herzliya, 46150, Israel. **Online address:** profbarryrubin@yahoo.com

RUBIN, Bruce Joel. American (born United States), b. 1943. **Genres:** Plays/Screenplays, Art/Art History, Photography. **Career:** National Broadcasting Co. (NBC-TV), assistant film editor in news department; Whitney Museum, curator of film department. **Publications:** (With R. Statzel and P.F. Messina) Brainstorm, 1983; Deadly Friend, 1986; Jacob's Ladder, 1990; (with M. Tolkin) Deep Impact, 1996; Stuart Little 2, 2002. Contributor to books. **Address:** Sanford-Gross & Associates, 1015 Gayley Ave., Ste. 301, Los Angeles, CA 90024, U.S.A. **Online address:** bjrclass@aol.com

RUBIN, Charles. American (born United States), b. 1953. **Genres:** Information Science/Computers, Technology. **Career:** Waterside Associates, partner; Personal Computing Magazine, editor, 1983-; Macintosh Business Review, executive editor; Internet Research Group, industry analyst; Gallagher Public Relations, senior strategist; Gallagher Group Communications, partner and senior strategist; Story Public Relations, staff. Writer and consultant. **Publications:** The Endless Apple: How to Maintain State-of-the-Art Performance on your Apple II and IIe, 1984; (with M. McCarthy) Thinking Small: The Buyer's Guide to Portable Computers, 1984; Appleworks: Boosting Your Business with Integrated Software, 1985, 2nd ed., 1987; Appleworks: The Microsoft Desktop Dictionary and Cross-Reference Guide, 1986; Microsoft Works on the Apple Macintosh, 1986, 2nd ed. as Microsoft Works for the Apple Macintosh, 1989; (with B. Calica) Macintosh Hard Disk Management, 1988, 2nd ed., 1989; The Macintosh Bible, What Do I Do Now? Book: What to Do Instead of Panicking, 1990, 2nd ed., 1991; Running Microsoft Works, 1990, 2nd ed. as Running Microsoft Works for the PC, 1993; The Macintosh

Bible Guide to System 7: The Most Dramatic Changes Ever in the Mac's System Software, 1991; The Macintosh Bible Guide to FileMaker Pro: All You Need to Know to Manage Your Files Quickly and Efficiently, 1991, 2nd ed., 1993; The Macintosh Bible Guide to System 7.1, 1992; Running Microsoft Works 3 for the Apple Macintosh, 1993; The Little Book of Computer Wisdom: How to Make Friends with Your PC or Mac, 1995; The Macintosh Bible Guide to ClarisWorks 3, 1995; The Macintosh Bible Guide to ClarisWorks 4, 1995; (with J.C. Levinson) Guerrilla Marketing Online: The Entrepreneur's Guide to Earning Profits on the Internet, 1995, 2nd ed., 1997; (with J.C. Levinson) Guerrilla Marketing Online Weapons: 100 Low-Cost, High-Impact Weapons for Online Profits and Prosperity, 1996; The Macintosh Bible Guide to FileMaker Pro 3, 1996; (with D. Parssinen) Managing Your Business with QuickBooks 6, 1998; Running Microsoft Word 2000, 1999. Contributor of articles to periodicals. **Address:** Story Public Relations, PO Box 642429, San Francisco, CA 94164-2429, U.S.A. **Online address:** charlie@storypr.com

RUBIN, Gretchen (Craft). American (born United States), b. 1966?. **Genres:** Biography, Business/Trade/Industry, Economics, Self Help, Autobiography/Memoirs. **Career:** Yale University, instructor, Yale Law School, instructor, Yale School of Management, instructor, Yale Law Journal, editor-in-chief; U.S. Supreme Court Justice Sandra Day O'Connor, clerk; Federal Communications Commissions chairman Reed Hundt, chief advisor; Skadden, summer associate; Arps, associate; Slate, associate; Meagher & Flom, associate; Davis Polk and Wardwell, associate. Writer. **Publications:** Power, Money, Fame, Sex: A User's Guide, 2000; Forty Ways to Look at Winston Churchill: A Brief Account of a Long Life, 2003; Forty Ways to Look at JFK, 2005; Profane Waste, 2006; Happiness Project: Or Why I Spent a Year Trying to Sing in the Morning, Clean My Closets, Fight Right, Read Aristotle and Generally have More Fun, 2009; Happier at Home: Kiss More, Jump More, Abandon A Project, Read Samuel Johnson and My Other Experiments in the Practice of Everyday Life, 2012. **Address:** c/o Author Mail, Ballantine, Random House, 201 E 50th St., New York, NY 10022, U.S.A. **Online address:** grubin@gretchenrubin.com

RUBIN, Hyman. American (born United States), b. 1971. **Genres:** History, Politics/Government, Race Relations. **Career:** Columbia College, assistant professor, associate professor of history, 1999-. Writer and historian. **Publications:** South Carolina Scalawags, 2006. **Address:** Department of History and Political Science, Columbia College, 1301 Columbia College Dr., Columbia, SC 29203-5949, U.S.A. **Online address:** hrubin@colacoll.edu

RUBIN, Joan Shelley. American (born United States), b. 1947. **Genres:** Cultural/Ethnic Topics, Intellectual History, History. **Career:** Yale University, instructor in American studies and history, 1974-76; McMaster University, assistant professor of history, 1976-77; University of Western Ontario, assistant professor of history, 1977-79; State University of New York College, assistant professor, 1979-85, associate professor of American studies and history, 1985-93; University of Rochester, professor of history, 1995-. Writer. **Publications:** Constance Rourke and American Culture, 1980; The Making of Middlebrow Culture, 1992; Songs of Ourselves: The Uses of Poetry in America, 2007; (ed. with D.P. Nord and M. Schudson) Enduring Book: Print Culture in Postwar America, 2009. Contributor to periodicals and journals. **Address:** Department of History, University of Rochester, 365 Rush Rhees Library, Rochester, NY 14627-0070, U.S.A. **Online address:** joan.rubin@rochester.edu

RUBIN, Jordan. American (born United States), b. 1975?. **Genres:** Medicine/Health, Food And Wine, Sciences. **Career:** Garden of Life, founder and chief executive officer, 1998-. Nutritionist, health consultant and writer. **Publications:** Patient Heal Thyself: A Remarkable Health Program Combining Ancient Wisdom with Groundbreaking Clinical Research, 2003; The Maker's Diet, 2004; (with D. Remedios) The Great Physician's Rx for Health and Wellness, 2005; The Maker's Diet Shopper's Guide, 2005; The Maker's Diet: Daily Reminders, 2006; (with N. Rubin and P. Wilson) Great Physician's Rx for Women's Health, 2006; Perfect Weight Shopping and Dining Out Guide, 2008; (with B. Bulwer) Perfect Weight America, 2008; (with B. Bulwer) Perfect Weight Canada, 2008; (with F. Blair) Great Physician's Rx for Children's Health, 2008; (with B. Bulwer) Perfect Weight South Africa, 2008; Maker's Diet for Weight Loss, 2009; (foreword) Healing Code, 2010. WITH J. BRASCO: Restoring Your Digestive Health: How the Guts and Glory Program Can Transform Your Life, 2003; Great Physician's Rx for Colds and Flu, 2006; Great Physician's Rx for a Healthy Heart, 2006; Great Physician's Rx for Diabetes, 2006; Great Physician's Rx for Weight Loss, 2006; Great Physician's Rx for Irritable Bowel Syndrome, 2006; Great Physician's Rx for Cancer,

2006; Great Physician's RX for High Blood Pressure, 2007; Great Physician's Rx for Heartburn and Acid Reflux, 2007; Great Physician's Rx for High Cholesterol, 2007; Great Physician's RX for Depression and Anxiety, 2007; Great Physician's RX for Chronic Fatigue and Fibromyalgia, 2007; Great Physician's RX for Arthritis, 2007. **Address:** Garden of Life, 5500 Village Blvd., Ste. 202, West Palm Beach, FL 33407, U.S.A.

RUBIN, Larry (Jerome). American (born United States), b. 1930. **Genres:** Novels, Poetry, Literary Criticism And History, Young Adult Fiction. **Career:** Georgia Institute of Technology, instructor, 1956-58, assistant professor, 1958-65, associate professor, 1965-73, professor of English, 1973-99, professor emeritus of English, 1999-; Jagiellonian University, visiting professor, 1961-62; University of Bergen, visiting professor, 1966-67; Free University of West Berlin, visiting professor, 1969-70; University of Innsbruck, visiting professor, 1971-72. Writer. **Publications:** The World's Old Way, 1962; Lanced in Light, 1967; All My Mirrors Lie, 1975; Unanswered Calls: A Book of Poems, 1997. **Address:** Department of English, Georgia Institute of Technology, Atlanta, GA 30333, U.S.A.

RUBIN, Rose M. American (born United States), b. 1939?. **Genres:** Economics, Adult Non-fiction, Business/Trade/Industry. **Career:** University of Michigan, teaching assistant, 1963-64; Kansas State University, instructor in economics, 1967-68; State of Kansas, Office of Economic Analysis, economist, 1969-70; Mississippi State University, assistant professor of economics, 1970-77; University of North Texas, assistant professor, 1977-84, associate professor, 1984-90, professor of economics, 1990-94, special assistant, 1993-94; Johns Hopkins University, Robert Wood Johnson Foundation fellow, 1986-87; Brookings Institution, visiting fellow, 1987; University of Memphis, Fogelman College of Business and Economics, professor of economics, 1994-2009, head of department, 1994-96, research fellow, professor emeritus, 2009-. Writer. **Publications:** (Contrib.) Great Ideas for Teaching Economics, 1992; (with B.J. Riney) Working Wives and Dual-Earner Families, 1994; (with M.L. Nieswiadomy) Expenditures of Older Americans, 1997; (contrib.) Women and Aging: A Research Guide, 1997; (contrib.) Contemporary Nursing: Issues, Trends and Management, forthcoming. Contributor to journals. **Address:** Department of Economics, University of Memphis, FAB315, 303 Administration Bldg., Memphis, TN 38152, U.S.A. **Online address:** rmrubin@memphis.edu

RUBIN, Susan Goldman. American (born United States), b. 1939. **Genres:** Children's Fiction, Young Adult Fiction, Children's Non-fiction, Biography, Illustrations. **Career:** Freelance writer, 1975-78; California State University, Department of Continuing Education, instructor, 1977-86; University of California, Extension School Writer's Program, instructor, 1986-; Designers West, editorial assistant, 1991-92. **Publications:** SELF-ILLUSTRATED: Grandma Is Somebody Special, 1976; Cousins Are Special, 1978; Grandpa and Me Together, 1980. OTHERS: Walk with Danger, 1986; The Black Orchid, 1988; Emily Good As Gold, 1993; The Rainbow Fields, 1993, 2nd ed., 1995; Frank Lloyd Wright, 1994; The Whiz Kids Plugged In, 1997; Emily in Love, 1997; The Whiz Kids Take Off!, 1997; Toilets, Toasters and Telephones, 1998; Margaret Bourke-White: Her Pictures were Her Life, 1999; Fireflies in the Dark: The Story of Fried Dicker-Brande is and the Children of Terezin, 2000; There Goes the Neighborhood, 2001; The Yellow House: Vincent van Gogh and Paul Gauguin Side by Side, 2001; Steven Spielberg: Crazy for Movies, 2002; Degas and the Dance: The Painter and the Petits Rats, Perfecting Their Art, 2002; Searching for Anne Frank: Letters from Amsterdam to Iowa, 2003; Art Against the Odds: From Slave Quilts to Prison Paintings, 2004; Lchayim!: To Jewish Life in America!, 2004; The Flag with Fifty-Six Stars: A Gift from the Survivors of Mauthausen, 2005; Andy Warhol: Pop Art Painter, 2006; (with E. Weissberger) The Cat with the Yellow Star: Coming of Age in Terezin, 2006; Edward Hopper: Painter of Light and Shadow, 2007; Delicious: The Life and Art of Wayne Thiebaud, 2007; Haym Salomon: American Patriot, 2007; Counting with Wayne Thiebaud, 2007; Andy Warhols Colors, 2007; Whaam!: The Life and Art of Roy Lichtenstein, 2008; Matisse Dance for Joy, 2008; Georgia Okeeffes Seasons, 2008; Simon Wiesenthal: He Never Forgot, 2009; Magritte's Imagination, 2009; Anne Frank Case: Simon Wiesenthals Search for the Truth, 2009; Jacob Lawrence in the City, 2009; Breaking the Rules: What is Contemporary Art?, 2010; Wideness and Wonder: The Life and Art of Georgia Okeeffe, 2010; Irena Sendler and the Children of the Warsaw Ghetto, 2011; Jean Lafitte: The Pirate Who Saved America, 2011; Music Was It: Young Leonard Bernstein, 2011. Contributor to periodicals. **Address:** c/o George M. Nicholson, Sterling Lord Literistic Inc., 65 Bleecker St., New York, NY 10012, U.S.A. **Online address:** susanrubin@yahoo.com

RUBIN-DORSKY, Jeffrey. American (born United States), b. 1947. **Genres:** Literary Criticism And History, Essays, Young Adult Fiction, Children's Fiction, Medicine/Health, Humanities, Psychology. **Career:** University of California, professor of English, 1980-88; University of Colorado, professor of English, 1988-, now professor emeritus. Writer. **Publications:** Adrift in the Old World: The Psychological Pilgrimage of Washington Irving, 1988; (ed. with S.F. Fishkin) People of the Book: Thirty Scholars Reflect on Their Jewish Identity, 1996; (afterword) The Man That Corrupted Hadleyburg and Other Stories and Essays, 1997; (ed.) The Other Romance: Re/Viewing an American Genre, 1998; Philip Roth and Woody Allen: The Loyal Opposition, 1999. **Address:** Department of English, University of Colorado, 1420 Austin Bluffs Pkwy., Colorado Springs, CO 80933, U.S.A. **Online address:** jrubin-d@cyberclass.uccs.edu

RUBINETTI, Donald. American (born United States), b. 1947. **Genres:** Children's Fiction, Animals/Pets. **Career:** South Junior High School, teacher, 1974; North Junior High School, teacher, 1976-83; North Arlington High School, teacher, 1979-80; Bloomfield High School, teacher, 1980-83; Whippany Park High School, teacher, 1983-86; New Jersey Commission for the Blind and Visually Impaired, teacher, 1985-; Franklin Avenue Middle School, teacher, 1986-; Montclair State College, adjunct instructor, 1986-. Writer. **Publications:** Cappy the Lonely Camel, 1996. **Address:** Franklin Lakes Public Schools, Pulis Ave., Franklin Lakes, NJ 07417-2708, U.S.A.

RUBINO, Anna. American (born United States), b. 1955. **Genres:** Biography, Technology, Autobiography/Memoirs, Writing/Journalism. **Career:** Petroleum Intelligence Weekly, reporter, 1980; Columbia Broadcasting System Inc., director of publications; Government Research Corp., staff analyst; OTR Global, investigative reporter, 2002-. **Publications:** Queen of the Oil Club: The Intrepid Wanda Jablonski and the Power of Information, 2008. **Address:** c/o Lisa Adams, The Garamond Agency Inc., 12 Horton St., Newburyport, MA 01950, U.S.A. **Online address:** anna@annarubino.com

RUBINOFF, M. Lionel. Canadian (born Canada), b. 1930. **Genres:** Environmental Sciences/Ecology, Philosophy, Social Commentary, Social Sciences, Theology/Religion, Politics/Government. **Career:** University of Toronto, instructor, 1957-58; York University, lecturer, 1960-63, assistant professor, 1963-68, associate professor, 1968-70, professor of social sciences and philosophy, 1970-71; Canadian Broadcasting Corp., freelance radio and television writer, broadcaster, 1964-; Trent University, professor of philosophy, 1971-96, vice-dean arts and sciences, 1980-85, Department of Philosophy, chairman, 1991-96, professor emeritus, 1996-; Peterborough Regional Health Centre, medical coordinator, 2006-. **Publications:** The Pornography of Power, 1968; Collingwood and the Reform of Metaphysics, 1970; The Dialectic of Work and Labour in the Ontology of Man, 1971; Violence and the Retreat from Reason, 1974; Auschwitz and the Theology of Holocaust, 1974; Nationalism and Celebration, 1975; Vico and the Verification of Historical Interpretation, 1976; Auschwitz and the Pathology of Jew-Hatred, 1976; Technology and the Crisis of Rationality, 1977; The Metaphysics of Technology and the Crisis of Rationality, 1978; In Nomine Diaboli, 1978; On Theorizing Human Conduct, 1979; Hymn to Apollo, 1981; Utopianism and the Eschatology of Violence, 1981; Multiculturalism and the Metaphysics of Pluralism, 1982; Beyond the Domination of Nature, 1985; Obligations to Future Generations, 1988; Technology and the Conserver Society, 1990; Historicity and Point of View, 1991; History and Human Nature: Reflections on R.G. Collingwood, 1991; The Editing of Collingwood's Manuscripts, 1992; Jewish Identity and the Challenge of Auschwitz, 1993; The Relation between Philosophy and History in the Thought of Benedetto Croce and R.G. Collingwood, 1996; F.H. Bradley and the Presuppositions of Critical History, 1996; Politics, Ethics, Ecology, 1997; Capitalism, Ethics and Ecology, 2000; The World is Your Body, 2004. EDITOR: (and intro.) The Presuppositions of Critical History, 1968; Faith and Reason: Essays in the Philosophy of Religion, 1968; Tradition and Revolution, 1971; Objectivity, Method, and Point of View: Essays in the Philosophy of History, 1991. Contributor of articles. **Address:** Department of Philosophy, Trent University, Peterborough, ON K9J 7C6, Canada. **Online address:** lrubinoff@trentu.ca

RUBINSKY, Holley. Canadian/American (born United States), b. 1943. **Genres:** Novellas/Short Stories, inspirational/Motivational Literature. **Career:** University of Toronto, School of Continuing Studies, instructor, 1988-90. Writer. **Publications:** (Co-ed.) The Event Horizon: Essays on Hope, Sexuality, Social Space, and Media(tion) in Art, 1987; Rapid Transits and Other Stories, 1991; At First I Hope for Rescue, 1997, 3rd ed., 1999; (ed.)

The Journey Prize Anthology Ten, 1999; Beyond This Point, 2006. Contributor to magazines and journals. **Address:** McClelland & Stewart Ltd., 75 Sherbourne St., 5th Fl., Toronto, ON M5A 2P9, Canada. **Online address:** holley@holleyrubinsky.com

RUBINSTEIN, Gillian (Margaret Hanson). (Lian Hearn). Australian/British (born England), b. 1942. **Genres:** Children's Fiction, Young Adult Fiction, Plays/Screenplays. **Career:** London School of Economics, research assistant, 1964-65; Greater London Council, administrative officer, 1965-66; Tom Stacey Ltd., editor, 1969-71; freelance journalist and film critic, 1971-74; freelance writer, 1986-; Magpie Theatre, writer-in-residence, 1989; English School Foundation School, writer-in-residence, 1998. **Publications:** Space Demons, 1986; Melanie and the Night Animal, 1988; Answers to Brut, 1988; Beyond the Labyrinth, 1988; Melanie and the Night Animal, 1988; Skymaze, 1989; Flashback: The Amazing Adventures of a Film Horse, 1990; At Ardilla, 1991; Dog In, Cat Out, 1991; Squawk and Screech, 1991; Galax-Arena, 1992; Keep Me Company, 1992; Mr. Plunkett's Pool, 1992; The Giant's Tooth, 1993; Foxspell, 1994; Peanut the Ponyrat, 1995; Jake and Pete, 1995; Shinkei, 1996; Sharon Keep Your Hair On, 1996; Annie's Brother's Suit, 1996; Witch Music, 1996; Jake & Pete & the Stray Dogs, 1997; Under the Cat's Eye, 1997; Each Beach, 1998; Hooray for the Kafe Karaoke, 1998; Pure Chance, 1998; The Pirate's Ship, 1998; The Fairy's Wings, 1998; The Mermaid of Bondi Beach, 1999; Jake & Pete and the Catrowbats, 1999; Ducky's Nest, 1999; Jake & Pete & the Magpies' Wedding, 2000; Prue Theroux: The Cool Librarian, 2001; Terra-Farma, 2001; The Whale's Child, 2002. AS LIAN HEARN: Across the Nightingale Floor, 2002; Grass for His Pillow, 2003; Brilliance of the Moon, 2004; Lord Fujiwara's Treasures, 2005; The Way Through The Snow, 2005; The Harsh Cry of the Heron, 2006; Battle for Marnyama, 2006; Scars of Victory, 2006; Heaven's Net Is Wide: The First Tale of the Otori, 2007; Blossoms and Shadows, 2011. **Address:** Jenny Darling & Associates, PO Box 413, Toorak, VI 3142, Australia.

RUBINSTEIN, Helge. British/German (born Germany), b. 1929. **Genres:** Self Help, Food And Wine, Medicine/Health, Reference. **Career:** London Marriage Guidance Council, chair, 1977-82; Ben's Cookies, founder, 1984-. Writer. **Publications:** (With S. Bush) Penguin Freezer Cookbook, 1976; (with S. Bush) Ices Galore, 1977; French Cookery, 1979; The Chocolate Book, 1981 in US as The Ultimate Chocolate Cake and 110 Other Chocolate Indulgences, 1983; Provincial French cooking, 1983; (with J. Largesse) Fitness Over Forty: A Woman's Guide to Exercise, Health and Emotional Wellbeing, 1986; (ed.) The Oxford Book of Marriage, 1990. **Address:** Ben's Cookies, 39 Leadenhall Market, London, GL EC3V 1LT, England.

RUBINSTEIN, Hilary (Harold). British (born England), b. 1926. **Genres:** Travel/Exploration, Adult Non-fiction, Recreation, Medicine/Health, Psychology. **Career:** Victor Gollancz Ltd., editor, 1950-54, editorial director, 1954-58, assisting managing director, 1958-63; The Observer newspaper, special features editor, 1963-64; The Observer Magazine, deputy editor, 1964-65; AP Watt Ltd., director, 1965-82, chairman and managing director, 1982-92; Hilary Rubinstein Books Ltd., managing director, 1992-. **Publications:** (And ed.) The Complete Insomniac in US as Insomniacs of the World, Goodnight: A Bedside Book, 1974; (ed.) The Good Hotel Guide, 1978 in US as Europe's Wonderful Little Hotels and Inns, 1990; Hotels and Inns: An Anthology, 1984. **Address:** Hilary Rubinstein Books Ltd., 32 Ladbroke Grove, London, GL W11 3BQ, England. **Online address:** hrubinstein@beeb.net

RUBINSTEIN, Isaak. Israeli/Russian (born Russia), b. 1949. **Genres:** Physics. **Career:** Latvian State University, senior assistant, 1971-73, engineer and mathematician, 1973-74; University of Cambridge, Department of Applied Mathematics and Theoretical Physics, senior visitor, 1978; Massachusetts Institute of Technology, Department of Mechanical Engineering, postdoctoral fellow, 1978-79, research associate, 1978-79; Weizmann Institute of Science, postdoctoral research fellow, 1979-81, senior researcher, 1981-85, associate professor of mathematics, 1985-88; Stanford University, Department of Mathematics, research associate, 1986-87; Ben Gurion University of the Negev, Jacob Blaustein Institute for Desert Research, associate professor, 1988-91, professor of mathematics, 1991-. Writer. **Publications:** Electro-Diffusion of Ions, 1990; (with L. Rubinstein) Partial Differential Equations in Classical Mathematical Physics, 1993. **Address:** Jacob Blaustein Institute for Desert Research, Ben Gurion University, Sede Boqer Campus, Midreshet Ben-Gurion, Beersheva, 84990, Israel. **Online address:** robinst@math.cs.bgu.ac.il

RUBINSTEIN, Ruth P. American/Israeli (born Israel) **Genres:** Fash Ion/ Costume, Social Sciences, Adult Non-fiction. **Career:** Fashion Institute of Technology, assistant professor, associate professor of sociology, 1970-. Writer. **Publications:** Dress Codes: Meanings and Messages in American Culture, 1995, 2nd ed., 2001; Society's Child: Identity Clothing and Style, 2000. **Address:** Fashion Institute of Technology, 7th Ave., 227 W 27th St., New York, NY 10001, U.S.A. **Online address:** ruth_rubinstein@fitnyc.edu

RUBIO, Gwyn Hyman. American (born United States), b. 1949. **Genres:** Novellas/Short Stories, Young Adult Fiction. **Career:** Writer, 1986-. **Publications:** NOVEL: Icy Sparks, 1998; The Woodsman's Daughter, 2005; Sharing Power (short stories). Contributor to literary journals. **Address:** 130 Lorraine Ct., Berea, KY 40403, U.S.A.

RUBRIGHT, Lynn. American (born United States), b. 1936?. **Genres:** Novels, Mythology/Folklore. **Career:** Webster University, teacher, 1971-, assistant professor, associate professor, now professor emeritus; Metro Theatre Circus (now Metro Theater Company), co-founder, 1973; St. Louis Storytelling Festival, co-founder, 1975; Northwestern University, visiting professor of drama; Drake University, visiting professor of drama; Des Moines University, visiting professor of drama; University of Alaska, visiting professor of drama. Writer. **Publications:** (With L. Ulmer and R. Kronberg) For the Bible Tells Me So: Bible Story-Plays with Puppets, 1979; Rabbit's Tale, and Other Native American Myths and Legends, 1987; Beyond the Beanstalk: Interdisciplinary Learning through Storytelling, 1996; Mama's Window, 2005. **Address:** c/o Author Mail, Lee & Low Books, 95 Madison Ave., Ste. 1205, New York, NY 10016, U.S.A. **Online address:** lynntells@aol.com

RUBY, Jay. American (born United States), b. 1935. **Genres:** Archaeology/ Antiquities, Anthropology/Ethnology, Biography, Cultural/Ethnic Topics, Photography. **Career:** University of California-Los Angeles, survey archaeologist, 1962-64, Sudanese Nubian Project, staff archaeologist, 1962-63; University of California-Santa Barbara, lecturer in anthropology, 1964-65; University of California-Davis, lecturer in anthropology, 1965-67; Temple University, Department of Anthropology, instructor, 1967-69, assistant professor, 1969-70, associate professor of anthropology, 1977-90, professor, now professor emeritus, Center for Visual Communication, president and director of conferences on visual anthropology, 1968-80; Rutgers University, visiting professor, 1971; University of Pennsylvania, visiting professor, 1972-74; Princeton University, visiting professor, 1976; Pennsylvania State University, Psychological Cinema Register, editor, 1989-90. **Publications:** (Ed. and contrib.) A Crack in the Mirror: Reflexive Perspectives in Anthropology, 1982; (ed.) Robert J. Flaherty: A Biography, 1983; (ed. with M. Taureg) Visual Explorations of the World: Selected Papers from the International Conference on Visual Communication, 1987; (ed. with L. Gross and J.S. Katz) Image Ethics: The Moral Rights of Subjects in Photographs, Film and Television, 1988; (ed.) Cinema of John Marshall, 1993; Secure the Shadow: Death and Photography in America, 1995; The World of Francis Cooper: Nineteenth Century Pennsylvania Photographer, 1999; The Photographic World of Francis Cooper: Not A Bad Shot, 1999; (with L.A. Ries) Directory of Pennsylvania Photographers, 1839-1900, 1999; Picturing Culture: Explorations of Film & Anthropology, 2000; (ed. with L. Gross and J.S. Katz) Image Ethics in the Digital Age, 2003; (ed. with M. Banks) Made to be Seen: Perspectives on the History of Visual Anthropology, 2011. Contributor to journals. **Address:** 8 4th St., Mifflintown, PA 17059, U.S.A. **Online address:** ruby@temple.edu

RUBY, Lois. American (born United States), b. 1942. **Genres:** Children's Fiction, Young Adult Fiction. **Career:** Dallas Public Library, young adult librarian, 1965-67; University of Missouri, art and music librarian, 1967-68; Temple Emanu-El, synagogue librarian, 1974-2003; educator, 1985-. Writer. **Publications:** YOUNG ADULT FICTION: Arriving at a Place You've Never Left, 1977; What Do You Do in Quicksand?, 1979; Two Truths in My Pocket (short stories), 1982; This Old Man, 1984; Pig-Out Inn, 1987; Miriam's Well, 1993; Skin Deep, 1994; Steal Away Home, 1994; Soon Be Free, 2000; Swindletop, 2000; The Moxie Kid, 2001; Anita Diamant's The Red Tent, 2003; Journey to Jamestown, 2005; Shanghai Shadows, 2006; Secret of Laurel Oaks, 2008. **Address:** c/o Susan Cohen, The Writers House, 21 W 26th St., New York, NY 10010, U.S.A. **Online address:** loisruby@comcast.net

RUBY, Robert H. (Robert Holmes Ruby). American (born United States), b. 1921. **Genres:** History, Transportation, Biography, Social Sciences, Young Adult Non-fiction. **Career:** Physician, 1955-; Moses Lake Museum, chairman of board, 1958-68; Moses Lake Public Library, chairman of board, 1959-71; Grant County Historical Society, board director, 1962-72; Washington

Library Trustees Association, president, 1967-69; Washington Library Association, director, 1971-73. Writer. **Publications:** The Oglala Sioux, Warriors in Transition, 1955. WITH J.A. BROWN: Half-Sun on the Columbia: A Biography of Chief Moses, 1965; The Spokane Indians, Children of the Sun, 1970; The Cayuse Indians: Imperial Tribesmen of Old Oregon, 1972; Ferryboats on the Columbia River, lthe Bridges and Dams, 1974; The Chinook Indians: Traders of the Lower Columbia River, 1976; Myron Eells and the Puget Sound Indians, 1976; Indians of the Pacific Northwest: A History, 1981; A Guide to the Indian Tribes of the Pacific Northwest, 1986; Dreamer-Prophets of the Columbia Plateau: Smohalla and Skolaskin, 1989; The Highland Runners A Tale of the O'kanogan, 1992; Indian Slavery in the Pacific Northwest, 1993; Half-Sun on the Columbia: A Biography of Chief Moses, 1995; John Slocum and the Indian Shaker Church, 1996; Esther Ross Stillaguamish Champion, 2001; Cayuse Indians: Imperial Tribesmen of Old Oregon, 2005; Spokane Indians: Children of the Sun, 2006; Doctor among the Oglala Sioux Tribe, 2010; Oglala Sioux: Warriors in Transition, 2010; A Guide to the Indian Tribes of the Pacific Northwest, 2010. **Address:** 1022 Ivy St., Moses Lake, WA 98837, U.S.A.

RUBY, Robert Holmes. *See* **RUBY, Robert H.**

RUCHELMAN, Leonard I. American (born United States), b. 1933. **Genres:** Politics/Government, Public/Social Administration, Urban Studies, Law, Humanities, Technology. **Career:** West Virginia University, visiting assistant professor of political science, 1962-64; Alfred University, assistant professor, 1964-67, associate professor of political science, 1967-69, chairman of department, 1968-69; Lehigh University, associate professor of government, 1969-, director of urban studies, 1972-75; Old Dominion University, College of Business and Public Administration, Department of Urban Studies and Public Administration, professor and chair, 1975-81, now professor emeritus, William B. Spong chair of management, 2001-. Writer. **Publications:** (Ed.) Big City Mayors: The Crisis in Urban Politics, 1970; Political Careers: Recruitment Through the Legislature, 1970; (ed.) Who Rules the Police?, 1973; Police Politics: A Comparative Study of Three Cities, 1974; World Trade Center: Politics and Policies of Skyscraper Development, 1977; A Workbook in Program Design for Public Managers, 1985; A Workbook in Redesigning Public Services, 1989; Cities in the Third Wave: The Technological Transformation of Urban America, 2000, 2nd ed., 2007. Contributor of articles to periodicals. **Address:** College of Business & Public Administration, Old Dominion University, 2093 Constant Hall, 5115 Hampton Blvd., Norfolk, VA 23529, U.S.A. **Online address:** lruchelm@odu.edu

RUCKER, Mike. American (born United States), b. 1940?. **Genres:** Children's Fiction, Literary Criticism And History. **Career:** Caterpillar Inc., service representative and supervisor, 1963-; Peoria Academy of Science, director. **Publications:** Terry the Tractor, 1993; Terry and the Bully, 1994; Terry the Athlete, 1995; Terry and the Super Powerful Fuel, 1996; Terry and the Elephant, 1997; Terry and the Ecological Disaster, 1998; Terry and the High Tech Dozing System, 1999; Terry and the South Pole Breakdown, 2000; Terry the Smoke Jumper, 2001; Terry and the Wild Well Blowout, 2002; Terry and Beaver Dam Fiasco, 2003; Terry and the Trouble with Trash, 2004; Terry and the Obsolete Locomotive, 2005; Terry and the Earthquake, 2006; Terry and the Martians, 2007; Terry and the Sunken Submarine, 2008; Terry and the Dinosaurs, 2009. **Address:** 1003 W Centennial Dr., Peoria, IL 61614-2828, U.S.A. **Online address:** mikruc@aol.com

RUCKER, Patrick Michael. American (born United States), b. 1974. **Genres:** Classics, Adult Non-fiction. **Career:** Freelance journalist. **Publications:** This Troubled Land: Voices from Northern Ireland on the Front Lines of Peace, 2002. Contributor to periodicals. **Address:** c/o Gail Ross, Gail Ross Literary Agency L.L.C., 1666 Connecticut Ave., 5th Fl., Washington, DC 20009-1039, U.S.A. **Online address:** patrick_rucker@hotmail.com

RUCKER, Rudolf von Bitter. *See* **RUCKER, Rudy.**

RUCKER, Rudy. (Rudolf von Bitter Rucker). American (born United States), b. 1946. **Genres:** Novellas/Short Stories, Science Fiction/Fantasy, Poetry, Sciences. **Career:** State University of New York, faculty, 1972-78; University of Heidelberg, faculty, 1978-80; Randolph-Macon Woman's College, associate professor of mathematics, 1980-82; San Jose State University, professor of computer science, 1986-2004, professor emeritus, 2004-. Writer. **Publications:** SCIENCE FICTION NOVELS: White Light, 1980; Spacetime Donuts, 1981, rev. ed, 2009; Software, 1982; The Sex Sphere, 1983, rev. ed.,

2009; Master of Space and Time, 1984; The Secret of Life, 1985; Wetware, 1988; The Hollow Earth: The Narrative of Mason Algiers Reynolds of Virginia, 1990; The Hacker and the Arts, 1995; Freeware, 1997; Saucer Wisdom, 1999; Realware, 2000; Spaceland, 2002; Frek and the Elixir, 2004. HISTORICAL NOVELS: As Above, So Below: A Novel of Peter Bruegel, 2002; Mathematicians in Love, 2006. STORY AND ESSAY COLLECTIONS: The Fifty-Seventh Franz Kafka, 1983; Transreal!, 1990; Seek!, 1999; Gnarl!, 2000. OTHER: Geometry, Relativity, and the Fourth Dimension, 1977; Infinity and the Mind: The Science and the Philosophy of the Infinite, 1982; (ed.) Speculations on the Fourth Dimension: Selected Writings of Charles H. Hinton, 1983; Light Fuse and Get Away (poetry), 1983; The Fourth Dimension: Toward a Geometry of Higher Reality, 1984; Mind Tools: The Five Levels of Mathematical Reality, 1987; (ed.) Mathenauts: Tales of Mathematical Wonder, 1987; All the Visions (memoir), 1991; (ed. with R.U. Sirius and Q. Mu) Mondo 2000: A User's Guide to the New Edge, 1992; Artificial Life Lab, 1994; Live Robots: 2 in 1 Volume of Software/Wetware, 1994; Software Engineering and Computer Games (textbook), 2003; The Lifebox, the Seashell, and the Soul: What Gnarly Computation Taught Me About Ultimate Reality, the Meaning of Life, and How To Be Happy, 2005; Postsingular, 2007; Mad Professor: The Uncollected Short Stories, 2007; Hylozoic, 2009; (contrib.) Year's Best SF 14, 2009; The Ware Tetralogy, 2010; Nested Scrolls: A Memoir, 2011; Jim and the Flims, 2011. **Address:** San Jose State University, 1 Washington Sq., San Jose, CA 95192, U.S.A. **Online address:** rucker@cs.sjsu.edu

RUCKER, Walter C. American (born United States), b. 1970?. **Genres:** History, Cultural/Ethnic Topics. **Career:** San Bernardino Valley College, Department of History, instructor, 1996-99; State University of West Georgia, Department of History, assistant professor, 1999-2000; University of Nebraska, Department of History, assistant professor, 2000-03, Institute for Ethnic Studies, assistant professor, 2000-03; Ohio State University, Department of African American and African Studies, assistant professor, 2003-06, associate professor, 2006-11, director of undergraduate studies, 2010-11; University of North Carolina, Department of African and Afro-American Studies, associate professor and associate chair, 2011-. Writer. **Publications:** The River Flows On: Black Resistance, Culture, and Identity Formation in Early America, 2006; (ed. with J.N. Upton) Encyclopedia of American Race Riots, 2007; (ed. with L. Alexander) The Encyclopedia of African American History, 2010. **Address:** Department of African and Afro-American Studies, University of North Carolina, 107 Battle Hall, PO Box 3395, Chapel Hill, NC 27599-3395, U.S.A. **Online address:** wrucker@email.unc.edu

RUCKLEY, Brian. British/Scottish (born Scotland) **Genres:** History. **Career:** Freelance environmental consultant, 2003-. Writer. **Publications:** Winterbirth, 2007; Bloodheir, 2008. Contributor of articles to periodicals. **Address:** c/o Tina Betts, Andrew Mann Ltd., 1 Old Compton St., London, W1D 5JA, England. **Online address:** brian@brianruckley.com

RUDD, Anthony. Chinese/British (born England), b. 1963. **Genres:** Philosophy. **Career:** Layer, 1988-92; University of Bristol, Department of Philosophy, teaching assistant, 1993-99; University of Hertfordshire, lecturer, 1999-2001, visiting senior lecturer, 2007-08; Saint Olaf College, assistant professor, 2001-07, associate professor, 2008-, professor. Writer. **Publications:** Kierkegaard and the Limits of the Ethical, 1993; (ed. with J. Davenport) Kierkegaard after MacIntyre: Essays on Freedom, Narrative, and Virtue, 2001; Expressing the World: Skepticism, Wittgenstein and Heidegger, 2003. **Address:** Department of Philosophy, St. Olaf College, Holland Hall 504, 1520 St. Olaf Ave., Northfield, MN 55057, U.S.A. **Online address:** rudd@stolaf.edu

RUDDELL, Deborah. American (born United States), b. 1949?. **Genres:** Poetry, Natural History, Children's Non-fiction, Children's Fiction, Picture/Board Books, Animals/Pets. **Career:** Writer, educator and artist. **Publications:** Today at the Bluebird Cafe: A Branchful of Birds, 2007; A Whiff of Pine, a Hint of Skunk: A Forest of Poems, 2009; Who Said Coo?, 2010. Contributor to periodicals. **Address:** Peoria, IL , U.S.A. **Online address:** druddell@deborahruddell.com

RUDDICK, Nicholas. Canadian/British (born England), b. 1952. **Genres:** Literary Criticism And History, Science Fiction/Fantasy, Film. **Career:** McMaster University, part-time lecturer in English, 1979-80; Brock University, instructor in English, 1980; University of New Brunswick, assistant professor of English, 1980-81; University of Manitoba, assistant professor of English, 1981-82; University of Regina, professor of English, 1982-, Humanities Research Institute, director, 2003-08. Writer. **Publications:** Christopher Priest, 1989; British Science Fiction: A Chronology, 1478-1990, 1992; Ultimate Island: On the Nature of British Science Fiction, 1993; The Fire in the Stone: Prehistoric Fiction from Charles Darwin to Jean M. Auel, 2009. EDITOR: State of the Fantastic: Studies in the Theory and Practice of Fantastic Literature and Film, 1992; H.G. Wells, The Time Machine, 2001; I. Donnelly, Caesar's Column, 2003; G. Allen, The Woman Who Did, 2004; J. London, The Call of the Wild, 2009. Work represented in anthologies. Contributor of to journals. **Address:** Department of English, University of Regina, 3737 Wascana Pkwy., Regina, SK S4S 0A2, Canada. **Online address:** nicholas.ruddick@uregina.ca

RUDDIMAN, William F. American (born United States), b. 1943. **Genres:** Environmental Sciences/Ecology, Sciences. **Career:** U.S. Naval Oceanographic Offics, senior scientist, oceanographer, 1969-76; Columbia University, Lamont-Doherty Earth Observatory, senior research scientist, 1976-83, associate director, 1982-86, Doherty senior research scientist, 1983-92; University of Virginia, Department of Environmental Sciences, professor, 1991-2001, department chair, 1993-96, now professor emeritus. **Publications:** (Ed.) Tectonic Uplift and Climate Change, 1997; Plows, Plagues and Petroleum: How Humans Took Control of Climate, 2005; Earth's Climate, 2001, 2nd ed., 2007. **Address:** Department of Environmental Sciences, University of Virginia, Clark Hall, 291 McCormick Rd., PO Box 400123, Charlottesville, VA 22904-4123, U.S.A. **Online address:** wfr5c@virginia.edu

RUDDOCK, Ted. Scottish/Irish (born Ireland), b. 1930. **Genres:** Architecture, Engineering, History, Biography. **Career:** Joseph Mallagh and Son, engineer, 1954-58; Belfast College of Technology, senior lecturer in building, 1958-60; University of Science and Technology, senior lecturer in civil engineering, 1960-65; Commonwealth Scientific and Industrial Research Organization, affiliated, 1964; University of Edinburgh, senior lecturer in architecture, head of department and honorary fellow, 1966-2004; California Polytechnic State University, affiliated, 1986. Consulting engineer, historian and writer. **Publications:** Fabrics and Meshes in Roads: State of the Art, 1977, 3rd ed., 1983; Arch Bridges and Their Builders, 1735-1835, 1979. EDITOR/CO-EDITOR: Travels in the Colonies in 1773-1775: Described in the Letters of William Mylne, 1993; Masonry Bridges, Viaducts and Aqueducts, 2000; (and contrib.) Biographical Dictionary of Civil Engineers, vol. I: 1500-1830, 2002, vol. II: 1830-1890, 2008. **Address:** 20 Lennox St., Edinburgh, EH4 1QA, Scotland.

RUDGLEY, Richard. British (born England), b. 1961?. **Genres:** Anthropology/Ethnology, History, Social Sciences. **Career:** Pitt Rivers Museum, anthropologist; University of Oxford, Institute of Social and Cultural Anthropology, anthropologist; Royal Geographical Society, fellow. Writer. **Publications:** The Alchemy of Culture: Intoxicants in Society, 1993; Essential Substances: A Cultural History of Intoxicants in Society, 1993; The Encyclopedia of Psychoactive Substances, 1998; The Lost Civilizations of the Stone Age, 1999; Wildest Dreams: An Anthology of Drug-Related Literature, 2001; Barbarians: Secrets of the Dark Ages, 2002. Contributor to periodicals. **Address:** Pitt River Museum, School of Anthropology & Museum Ethnography, S Parks Rd., Oxford, OX OX1 3PP, England.

RUDIAK-GOULD, Peter. British/American (born United States), b. 1983?. **Genres:** Autobiography/Memoirs. **Career:** Teacher, 2003-04; University of Tromsø, researcher. Writer. **Publications:** Practical Marshallese (language manual), 2004; Surviving Paradise: One Year on a Disappearing Island (memoir), 2009; The Fallen Palm: Climate Change and Culture Change in the Marshall Islands (master's thesis), 2009. Contributor to periodicals. **Address:** c/o Andy Ross, Andy Ross Literary Agency, 767 Santa Ray Ave., Oakland, CA 94610, U.S.A. **Online address:** peterrg@gmail.com

RUDKIN, (James) David. British/American (born United States), b. 1936. **Genres:** Plays/Screenplays, Translations, Photography. **Career:** Royal Signals, cipher operator, 1955-57; County High School, assistant master of Latin, Greek and music, 1961-64. Writer. **Publications:** PLAYS: Afore Night Come, 1963; (with U. Nyssen) Radikales Theater, 1969; The Grace of Todd, 1969; Cries from Casement as His Bones are Brought to Dublin, 1974; Penda's Fen, 1975; Ashes, 1977; Hippolytus: A Version, 1980; The Triumph of Death, 1981; The Saxon Shore, 1986. BOOKS: Vampyr, 2005. TRANSLATOR: Schoenberg, Moses and Aaron, 1965; The Persians, 1965; Euripides, 1975; Peer Gynt, 1983; Death Watch, 1987; The Maids, 1987; Rosmersholm,

1990, new ed., 1997; When We Dead Waken, 1990. **Address:** Casarotto Ramsay & Associates Ltd., Waverley House, 7-12 Noel St., London, GL W1F 8GQ, England.

RUDOLF, Anthony. British (born England), b. 1942. **Genres:** Poetry, Literary Criticism And History, Autobiography/Memoirs, Essays, Translations, Biography, Novels. **Career:** British Travel Association, junior executive, 1964-66; English and French teacher, 1967-68; Menard Press, co-founder and editor, 1969-; Stand magazine, editor, 1969-72; London bookshops, co-proprietor, 1969-71; European Judaism, literary editor, 1970-72, Jewish Quarterly, managing editor, 1972-75; London Metropolitan University, visiting lecturer in arts and humanities, 2000-03; University of Hertfordshire, fellow, 2003-08; University of Westminster, fellow, 2005-08. **Publications:** (Trans.) Selected Poems of Yves Bonnefoy, 1968; The Manifold Circle, 1971; (trans.) A. Novac, The Soup Complex, 1972; (ed. with R. Burns) An Octave for Octavio Paz, 1972; Dinas Bran: Welsh, Englyn by Taliesin o Eifion, 1820-1876, 1974; (ed.) Edmund Jabes Bibliography, 1974; (trans.) Tyorkin and The Stovemakers: Selected Verse and Prose of Alexander Tvardovsky, 1974; (trans.) F. Basch, Relative Creatures: Victorian Women in Society and the Novel, 1974; (contrib.) Boxes, Stairs & Whistle Time, 1975; The Same River Twice, 1976; (contrib.) The Storm: The Tragedy of Sinai, 1976; (trans. with D. Weissbort) E. Vinokurov, The War Is Over, 1976; (ed.) Poems from Shakespeare IV, 1976; (trans.) E. Jabes, A Share of Ink, 1979; (ed. with H. Schwartz) Voices Within the Ark: The Modern Jewish Poets, 1980; After the Dream: Poems 1964-1979, 1980; (co-ed.) For David Gascoyne on His Sixty-fifth Birthday: 10 October, 1981, 1981; From Poetry to Politics: The Menard Press, 1969-1984, 1984; (trans.) Y. Bonnefoy, Things Dying, Things Newborn: Selected Poems, 1985; (trans.) Balzac, The Unknown Masterpiece, 1988; At An Uncertain Hour: Primo Levis War Against Oblivion, 1990; (trans., ed. and intro.) I'm Not Even a Grown-Up: The Diary of Jerzy Feliks Urman, 1991; Wine from Two Glasses: Trust and Mistrust in Language, 1991; (ed. and trans.) C. Cigee, Flow Tide: Selected Poetry and Prose, 1992; (ed.) Sage Eye: The Aesthetic Passion of Jonathan Griffin: A Celebration in Poetry and Prose, 1992; Mandorla, 1994; (trans.) Y. Bonnefoy Traite du piomistre, 1995; Poets Voice II, 1995; Blood from the Sky, 1995; Simonovic Poems, 1995; (ed. with J. Naughton) New and Selected Poems, 1995; (ed.) Theme & Version: Plath & Ronsard, 1995; Engraved in Flesh: Piotr Rawicz and His Novel Blood from the Sky, 1996; (trans.) Ifigenija Simonovic, Striking Root, 1996; The Arithmetic of Memory, 1999; (with C. Wiggins) Kitaj in the Aura of Cézanne and Other Masters, 2001; Chants de labsence=Songs of Absence, 2007; Zigzag, 2010. Contributor to books. Works appear in anthologies. **Address:** Menard Press, 8 The Oaks, Woodside Ave., London, GL N12 8AR, England. **Online address:** rudolf@menardpress.co.uk

RUDOLPH, Christopher. American (born United States), b. 1966?. **Genres:** Politics/Government, Social Sciences. **Career:** University of Southern California, professor; University of California, professor; Georgetown University, professor; American University, professor. Writer. **Publications:** National Security and Immigration: Policy Development in the United States and Western Europe since 1945, 2006. Contributor of articles to journals. **Address:** School of International Service, American University, 4400 Massachusetts Ave. NW, Washington, DC 20016-8071, U.S.A. **Online address:** crudolph@american.edu

RUDOLPH, Kurt. German (born Germany), b. 1929. **Genres:** Theology/Religion. **Career:** University of Leipzig, research assistant, 1954-60, lecturer, 1961, professor of religious studies, 1963-, Religious History Institute, associate professor, 1970-84; University of Toronto, Centre of Religious Studies, visiting professor, 1980-81; University of Chicago, Divinity School, distinguished visiting professor and Haskell lecturer on comparative religion, 1983-84; University of California, professor of religious studies, 1984-86; University of Marburg, associate professor of religious History, 1986-94; Harvard Divinity School, visiting professor, 1986-87. Writer. **Publications:** Bindungen des Eigentums: eine rechtsvergleichende Studie, 1960; Die Mandaeer I: Das Mandaerproblem, 1960; Die Mandaeer II: Der Kult, 1961; Die Religionsgeschichte und der Universitaet Leupzig und die Entwicklung der Religionswissenschaft, 1961; Theogonie, Kosmogonie und Anthropogenie in den mandaeischen Schriften, 1965; (with M. Höfner) Die Religionen Altsyriens, Altarabiens und der Mandäer, 1970; (contrib.) Zur Sprache und Literatur der Mandäer, 1976; Die Gnosis, 1977, 2nd ed., 1980; Mandaeism, 1978; Wellhausen als Arabist (biography), 1983; Historical Fundamentals and the Study of Religions, 1985; Geschichte und Probleme der Religionswissenschaft, 1992; Gnosis und Speätantike Religionsgeschichte: Gesammelte Aufseatze, 1996; (contrib.) Religionswissenschaft in Konsequenz, 2000. EDITOR: (with E. Walter) W. Baetke, Kleine Schriften: Geschichte, Recht u. Religion in germ. Schrifttum, 1973; Gnosis und Gnostizismus, 1975; (and trans.) Der Mandäische Diwan der Fleusse, 1982; (with G. Rinschede) Beiträge zur Religion/Umwelt-Forschung: erster Tagungsband des Interdisziplinearen Symposiums in Eichsteatt, 5-8 Mai 1988, 1989; (with B. Kytzler and J. Reupke) Eduard Norden (1868-1941): ein Deutscher Gelehrter Jeudischer Herkunft, 1994. Contributor of articles to books and journals. **Address:** Ringstrasse 9, Leipzig, D-04209, Germany.

RUDRUM, Alan (William). British/Canadian (born Canada), b. 1932. **Genres:** Literary Criticism And History, Intellectual History, Humanities, Law. **Career:** Adelaide University, lecturer in English, 1958-64, Queen's University, lecturer in English, 1964-66; University of California, assistant professor of English, 1966-68; Kent State University, professor, 1968-69; Simon Fraser University, professor of English, 1969-98, professor emeritus, 1998-. Writer. **Publications:** (Ed. with P. Dixon) Selected Poems of Samuel Johnson and Oliver Goldsmith, 1965; Milton's Paradise Lost: A Critical Commentary, 1966; A Critical Commentary on Milton's Comus and Shorter Poems, 1967; (ed.) Modern Judgements on Milton, 1968; A Critical Commentary on Milton's Samson Agonistes, 1969; (ed.) Complete Poems of Henry Vaughan, 1976; Writers of Wales: Henry Vaughan, 1981; (ed.) The Works of Thomas Vaughan, 1984; Essential Articles for the Study of Henry Vaughan, 1987; (ed. with J. Black and H.F. Nelson) The Broadway Anthology of Seventeenth Century Verse and Prose, 2000. **Address:** 718 Sticks Allison Rd. W, S-14 C-27 RR1, Galiano Island, BC V0N 1P0, Canada. **Online address:** alanrudrum@gmail.com

RUDWICK, Martin J.S. American/British (born England), b. 1932?. **Genres:** History, Sciences. **Career:** University of California, Department of History, professor of history, now professor emeritus. Writer. **Publications:** Living and Fossil Brachiopods, 1970; The Meaning of Fossils: Episodes in the History of Palaeontology, 1972, 3rd ed., 1985; The Great Devonian Controversy: The Shaping of Scientific Knowledge Among Gentlemanly Specialists, 1985; Scenes from Deep Time: Early Pictorial Representations of the Prehistoric World, 1992; Georges Cuvier, Fossil Bones, and Geological Catastrophes: New Translations and Interpretations of the Primary Texts, 1997; The New Science of Geology: Studies in the Earth Sciences in the Age of Revolution, 2004; Lyell and Darwin, Geologists: Studies in the Earth Sciences in the Age of Reform, 2005; Bursting the Limits of Time: The Reconstruction of Geohistory in the Age of Revolution, 2005; Worlds Before Adam: The Reconstruction of Geohistory in the Age of Reform, 2008. **Address:** Department of History, University of California, 9500 Gilman Dr., La Jolla, CA 92093-0104, U.S.A. **Online address:** mjsr100@cam.ac.uk

RUDY, Jarrett. Canadian (born Canada), b. 1970?. **Genres:** Young Adult Non-fiction. **Career:** McGill University, professor of history and director of Quebec Studies Program. Writer. **Publications:** The Freedom to Smoke: Tobacco Consumption and Identity, 2005. **Address:** Department of History, McGill University, 855 Sherbrooke W, Montreal, QC H3A 2T7, Canada. **Online address:** jarrett.rudy@mcgill.ca

RUDY, Jason R. American (born United States), b. 1975?. **Genres:** Poetry, Literary Criticism And History. **Career:** University of Maryland, Department of English, associate professor. Writer. **Publications:** Electric Meters: Victorian Physiological Poetics, 2009. Contributor to periodicals and journals. **Address:** Department of English, University of Maryland, College Park, MD 20742, U.S.A. **Online address:** jrrudy@umd.edu

RUDY, Kathy. (M. Kathy Rudy). American (born United States), b. 1956. **Genres:** Ethics, Theology/Religion. **Career:** Princeton University, Center for the Study of American Religion, visiting research fellow, 1993-94; Duke University, Women's Studies Program, assistant professor of the practice of ethics and women's studies, 1994-2000, associate professor of ethics and women's studies, 2000-. Writer. **Publications:** The Politics of Representing Jesus: Jacques Derrida and John Howard Yoder, 1989; Beyond Pro-Life and Pro-Choice: Moral Diversity in the Abortion Debate, 1996; Sex and the Church: Gender, Homosexuality, and the Transformation of Christian Ethics, 1997; Loving Animals: Toward a New Animal Advocacy, 2011; (as M.K. Rudy) Culture and Connection in Animal Advocacy, forthcoming; (as M.K. Rudy) Making Meat, Science, Ethics, and the Local Farm, forthcoming. Contributor

of articles to books and periodicals. **Address:** Department of Women Studies, Duke University, 210 E Duke Bldg., PO Box 90760, Durham, NC 27708-0760, U.S.A. **Online address:** krudy@acpub.duke.edu

RUDY, M. Kathy. *See* **RUDY, Kathy.**

RUDY, Susan Arlene. (Susan Rudy Dorscht). Canadian (born Canada), b. 1961. **Genres:** Literary Criticism And History. **Career:** University of Calgary, assistant professor, 1988-93, associate professor, 1993-99, professor of English, 1999-, department chair, 2003-; Association for Canadian and Quebec Literatures, president, 1994-96; Canadian Association of Chairs of English, president, 2007, 2008. Writer. **Publications:** (As Susan Rudy Dorscht) Women, Reading, Kroetsch: Telling the Difference, 1991; (ed. with N. Brossard and intro.) Fluid Arguments (essays), 2005; (with P. Butling) Poets' Talk: Interviews with Marie Annharte Baker, Dionne Brand, Jeff Derksen, Daphne Marlatt, Robert Kroetsch, Erin Moure, and Fred Wah, 2005; (with P. Butling) Writing in Our Time: Canada's Radical Poetries in English (1957-2003), 2005. Contributor to books. **Address:** Department of English, University of Calgary, 2500 University Dr. NW, Calgary, AB T2N 1Z3, Canada. **Online address:** srudy@ucalgary.ca

RUE, Leonard Lee. American (born United States), b. 1926. **Genres:** Natural History, Animals/Pets, Natural History, Sciences, Zoology, Travel/Exploration, Reference. **Career:** Leonard Rue Enterprises, founder; Red Hawk Outdoors Inc., consultant; Leonard Rue Video Productions Inc., producer; Outdoor Channel, producer, 2003; Leonard Lee Rue Enterprises, president. Writer. **Publications:** Animals in Motion, 1956; Tracks and Tracking, 1956; (with D. Knight) American Animals, 1961; (contrib.) World of the White-Tailed Deer, 1962; (contrib.) World of the Beaver, 1963; (contrib.) New Jersey Out-of-Doors, 1964; (contrib.) World of the Raccoon, 1964; Cottontail, 1965; (with J. Bailey) Our Wild Animals, 1965; (contrib.) Pictorial Guide to the Mammals of North America, 1967; Sportsman's Guide to Game Animals, 1968; (contrib.) The World of the Red Fox, 1969; Pictorial Guide to Birds of North America, 1970; The World of the Ruffed Grouse, 1973; Game Birds of North America, 1973; The Deer of North America, 1978; Furbearing Animals of North America, 1981; When Your Deer Is Down, 1981; (with J. Fischl) After Your Deer is Down: The Care and Handling of All Big Game, 1981; Complete Guide to Game Animals, 2nd ed., 1981; (co-author) White-Tailed Deer, 1984; How I Photograph Wildlife and Nature, 1984; (with W. Owen) Meet the Opossum, Moose, Beaver, 3 vols., 1984-86; (co-author) The Outdoor Life Deer Hunters Encyclopedia, 1985; (with W. Owen) Meet the Moose, 1985; (with W. Owen) Meet the Beaver, 1986; Leonard Lee Rue III's Whitetails, 1991; Leonard Lee Rue III's Whitetails, 1991; Birds of Prey, 1993; Wolves, 1993; Alligator and Crocodiles, Elephants, 1994; (with L. Rue Jr.) Photographing Animals in the Wild, 1996; How to Photograph Animals in the Wild, 1996; Leonard Lee Rue III's Way of the Whitetail, 2000; The Deer Hunter's Encyclopedia, 2000; The Deer Hunter's Illustrated Dictionary, 2001; (and contrib.) Beavers, 2002; Encyclopedia of Deer of the World, 2003; Leonard Lee Rue III's Deer Hunting Tips and Techniques, 2007. Contributor of articles to books. **Address:** Leonard Rue Video Productions Inc., 138 Millbrook Rd., Blairstown, NJ 07825-9534, U.S.A. **Online address:** ruevideo@erols.com

RUE, Loyal D. American (born United States), b. 1944. **Genres:** Philosophy, Young Adult Non-fiction. **Career:** University of Hartford, instructor of philosophy, 1972-73; Luther College, assistant professor, 1974-82, associate professor, 1982-90, professor of religion and philosophy, 1990-, HEW TRIO Programs, director, 1974-76, Luther College Study Centre, director, 1977-78, 2001-02, registrar, 1979-85, interim vice president, 1982; University of Durham, visiting fellow, 1985-86; Harvard University, senior fellow, 1997-98. Writer. **Publications:** Amythia: Crisis in the Natural History of Western Culture, 1989; (ed. with A. Loades) Contemporary Classics in Philosophy of Religion, 1991; By the Grace of Guile: The Role of Deception in Natural History and Human Affairs, 1994; Everybody's Story: Wising Up to the Epic of Evolution, 2000; Religion is Not About God: How Spiritual Traditions Nurture Our Biological Nature and What to Expect When They Fail, 2005; Nature is Enough: Religious Naturalism and the Meaning of Life, 2011. Contributor of articles to periodicals. **Address:** Department of Religion & Philosophy, Luther College, 013 Ockham House, 700 College Dr., Decorah, IA 52101-1041, U.S.A. **Online address:** rueloyal@luther.edu

RUEDY, John. American (born United States), b. 1927. **Genres:** History, Third World, Young Adult Non-fiction, Humanities. **Career:** Georgetown University, assistant professor, associate professor, 1965-92, professor of history, 1992-, Program of Arab Studies, head, 1975-88, now professor emeritus; Johns Hopkins University, School for Advanced International Studies, professorial lecturer, 1968-75; U.S. Defense Intelligence Agency, lecturer, 1972-; U.S. Foreign Service Institute, lecturer, 1974-84, 1991-, Advanced Area Studies Seminar on Northern Africa, chairperson, 1984-91. Writer. **Publications:** Land Policy in Colonial Algeria, 1967; (with S.A. Marshall) On Call: Principles and Protocols, 1989, 4th ed., 2004; Modern Algeria: The Origins and Development of a Nation, 1992, 2nd ed., 2005; (ed. and contrib.) Islamism and Secularism in North Africa, 1994. Contributor to books and journals. **Address:** Department of History, Georgetown University, Rm. 225, Intercultural Center Bldg., 37th O St. NW, PO Box 571035, Washington, DC 20057-1035, U.S.A. **Online address:** ruedyj@georgetown.edu

RUEF, John Samuel. American (born United States), b. 1927. **Genres:** Theology/Religion, Race Relations, Cultural/Ethnic Topics. **Career:** Episcopal Parish, vicar, 1950-54; Berkeley Divinity School, professor of New Testament, 1960-71; Episcopal Church, associate rector, 1971-72; Diocese of Western New York, director of lay studies, 1972-74; Nashotah House, dean, 1974-85, president; Chatham Hall, chaplain. Writer. **Publications:** Understanding the Gospels, 1963; The Gospels and the Teachings of Jesus: An Introduction for Laymen, 1967; Paul's First Letter to Corinth, 1971; The New Testament and the Sacraments of the Church, 1973. **Address:** Nashotah House, 2777 Mission Rd., Nashotah, WI 53058-9793, U.S.A. **Online address:** revruef@gamewood.net

RUEFLE, Mary. American (born United States), b. 1952?. **Genres:** Novels, Poetry, Young Adult Fiction. **Career:** Vermont College of Fine Arts, MFA Program, professor; University of Iowa, Writers' Workshop, visiting faculty. Poet and essayist. **Publications:** POETRY: Memling's Veil, 1982; Life without Speaking, 1987; The Adamant, 1989; Cold Pluto, 1996; Post Meridian, 1999; Apparition Hill, 2001; Among the Musk Ox People, 2002; Tristimania, 2003; A Little White Shadow, 2006; Indeed I was Pleased with the World, 2007; Go Home and Go To Bed, 2007; Most of It, 2008; Selected Poems, 2010. **Address:** c/o Author Mail, Wave Books, 1938 Fairview Ave. E, Ste. 201, Seattle, WA 98102-3650, U.S.A.

RUELL, Patrick. See **HILL, Reginald (Charles).**

RUELLE, Karen Gray. American (born United States), b. 1957. **Genres:** Illustrations, Ghost Writer. **Career:** Library Journal, assistant editor, 1980-83; Publishers Weekly, associate editor, 1983-85; English-Speaking Union, librarian, 1985-90. **Publications:** Seventy-five Fun Things to Make and Do by Yourself, 1993; The Book of Baths, 1997; The Book of Breakfasts, 1997; The Book of Bedtimes, 1997; (with D.D. DeSaix) Hidden on the Mountain: Stories of Children Sheltered from the Nazis in Le Chambon, 2007; The Tree, 2008; (with D.D. DeSaix) The Grand Mosque of Paris: A Story of How Muslims Saved Jews During the Holocaust, 2008. SELF-ILLUSTRATED: Bark Park, 2007. SELF- ILLUSTRATED: HARRY AND EMILY SERIES: The Monster in Harry's Backyard, 1999; The Thanksgiving Beast Feast, 1999; Snow Valentines, 2000; Spookier Than a Ghost, 2001; April Fool!, 2002; Easy as Apple Pie, 2002; The Crunchy, Munchy Christmas Tree, 2003; Mother's Day Mess, 2003; Just in Time for New Year's!, 2004; Easter Egg Disaster, 2004; Great Groundhogs!, 2006; Dear Tooth Fairy, 2006. Contributor of articles to books and journals. **Address:** Kirchoff/Wohlberg Inc., 866 United Nations Plz., Ste. 525, New York, NY 10017, U.S.A.

RUEMMLER, John D(avid). (Courtney Bishop). American (born United States), b. 1948. **Genres:** Novels, History. **Career:** Volunteers in Service to America, teen crisis counselor, 1972-; Teen Center, supervisor, 1972-73; writer, 1980-; Iron Crown Enterprises, writer and editor, 1983-90; Writer's Digest School, writing instructor, 1990-; Institute of Children's Literature, writing instructor, 1990-. **Publications:** (With S.T. Hitchcock and P.C. Fenlon, Jr.) Mirkwood, 1981; Rangers of the North, 1982; Night of the Nazgul, 1985; Rescue in Mirkwood, 1986; (ed.) Death at Appledore Towers, 1987; (as Courtney Bishop) Brothers in Arms, 1988; (ed.) Norek: Intrigue in a City-State of Jaiman, 1990; Smoke on the Water: A Novel of Jamestown and the Powhatans, 1992; Hitler Does Hollywood. **Address:** 1611 Jamestown Dr., Charlottesville, VA 22901-3039, U.S.A.

RUEPP, Krista. German (born Germany), b. 1947. **Genres:** Children's Fiction, Animals/Pets. **Career:** WDR-School TV, teacher, 1973-83; AAR-Pharma GMBH, marketing and advertising director, 1984. Writer. **Publications:** Midnight Rider, 1995; Horses in the Fog, 1997; Horelwinj: An di ünhiamelk ridjer am madernaacht, 1998; The Sea Pony, 2001; Winter Pony, 2002; Runaway Pony, 2005; Anna's Prince, 2006; Island Friends, forthcoming; Winter Pony II, forthcoming. **Address:** Remscheiderstrasse 210, Remscheid, 42855, Germany. **Online address:** reupp@aar.de

RUESCHEMEYER, Dietrich. American (born United States), b. 1930. **Genres:** Politics/Government, Sociology. **Career:** University of Cologne, Sociological Research Institute, research assistant, 1953-55, Seminar for Sociology, research assistant, 1956-62; Dartmouth College, assistant professor, 1962-63; University of Toronto, assistant professor, 1963-65, associate professor of sociology, 1965-66; Brown University, associate professor, 1966-71, professor of sociology, 1971-, department head, 1975-79, Center for the Comparative Study of Development, director, 1989-97, Watson Institute for International Studies, Research Program in Political Economy and Development, director, 1997-2002, Asa Messer professor, 1995-98, Charles C. Tillinghast Jr. professor of international studies, 1998-2000, professor emeritus of sociology and Charles C. Tillinghast Jr. professor emeritus of international studies, 2000-. Writer. **Publications:** Lawyers and Their Society, 1973; Power and the Division of Labor, 1986; (with E.H. Stephens and J. Stephens) Capitalist Development and Democracy, 1992; Usable Theory: Analytic Tools for Social and Political Research, 2009. EDITOR: (with P. Evans and T. Skocpol) Bringing the State Back In, 1985; (with P. Evans and E.H. Stephens) States versus Markets in the World System, 1985; (with L. Putterman) State and Market in Development: Synergy or Rivalry?, 1992; (with T. Skocpol) State, Social Knowledge and the Origins of Modern Social Policy, 1996; (with M. Rueschemeyer and B. Wittrock) Participation and Democracy East and West: Comparisons and Interpretation, 1998; (with J. Mahoney) Comparative Historical Analysis in the Social Sciences, 2003; States and Development: Historical Antecedents of Stagnation and Advance, 2005; Globalization and the Future of the Welfare State, 2005. IN GERMAN: Anwaltschaft und Gesellschaft, 1976. EDITOR IN GERMAN: (with R. Koenig and E.K. Scheuch) Das Interview: Formen, Technik, Auswertung, 2nd ed., 1957; (and trans. with B. Heister) T. Parsons, Beitraege zur soziologischen Theorie, 1964. **Address:** Department of Sociology, Brown University, PO Box 1916, Providence, RI 02912, U.S.A. **Online address:** dietrich_rueschemeyer@brown.edu

RUFIN, Jean Christophe. French (born France), b. 1952. **Genres:** Adult Non-fiction. **Career:** Senegal, ambassador of France, 2007-10; Action Against Hunger, founder; Médecins Sans Frontières, co-founder. Physician and writer. **Publications:** L'evolution fixe: Principes d'évolutique générale, 1981; Lepiege: quand l'aide humanitaire remplace la guerre, 1986; L'empire et les nouveaux barbares, 1991; La dictature libérale: le secret de latoutepuissance des democraties au 20e siecle, 1994; Economie des guerres civiles, 1996; L'Abyssin: relation des extraordinaires voyages de Jean-Baptiste Poncet, ambassadeur du Negus auprès de Sa Majeste Louis XIV: roman, 1997; Sauver Ispahan: Roman, 1998; Les causes perdues, 1999; Rouge Brésil, 2001; Empire et les nouveaux barbares, 2001; Globalia: Roman, 2003; La Salamandre: Roman, 2005; (intro.) Ras Tafari, Haïlé Sélassié, 2006; Parfum d'Adam: (roman), 2007; Un léopard sur le garrot: chroniques d'un médecin nomade, 2008; (intro.) France en Afrique, 2009; Katiba, 2010. **Address:** c/o Author Mail, Editions Gallimard, 5 rue Sebastien-Bottin, Paris, 75328, France.

RUFUS, Anneli S. American (born United States), b. 1959. **Genres:** Art/Art History, History, How-to Books, Local History/Rural Topics. **Career:** East Bay Express, literary editor. Journalist. **Publications:** The World Holiday Book: Celebrations for Every Day of the Year, 1994; Magnificent Corpses: Searching through Europe for St. Peter's Head, St. Chiara's Heart, St. Stephen's Hand, and Other Saints' Relics, 1999; Party of One: The Loners' Manifesto, 2003; Farewell Chronicles: How We Really Respond to Death, 2005; Stuck: Why We Can't (Or Won't) Move On, 2008. WITH K. LAWSON: Europe Off the Wall: A Guide to Unusual Sights, 1988; America Off the Wall: The West Coast: A Guide to Unusual Sights, 1989; Goddess Sites, Europe: Discover Places Where the Goddess Has Been Celebrated and Worshiped throughout Time, 1991; Weird Europe: A Guide to Bizarre, Macabre, and Just Plain Weird Sights, 1999; California Babylon: A Guide to Sites of Scandal, Mayhem and Celluloid in the Golden State, 2000; Scavengers' Manifesto, 2009. Contributor to books. **Address:** c/o Author Mail, Marlowe & Co., 161 William St., 16th Fl., New York, NY 10038, U.S.A. **Online address:** anneli@annelirufus.com

RUGELEY, Terry. American (born United States), b. 1956. **Genres:** Autobiography/Memoirs, Travel/Exploration, Biography, History, Translations. **Career:** University of Oklahoma, Department of History, assistant professor of history, 1992-, Professor, presidential professor of Latin American history, 2007-, director of graduate studies, acting departmental chair, acting director, 2010-; Southwest Council of Latin American Studies, president. Writer. **Publications:** Yucatán's Maya Peasantry and the Origins of the Caste War, 1996; Of Wonders and Wise Men: Religion and Popular Cultures in Southeast Mexico, 1800-1876, 2001; (ed.) Maya Wars: Ethnographic Accounts from Nineteenth-Century Yucatán, 2001; (ed. and trans.) Alone in Mexico: The Astonishing Travels of Karl Heller, 1845-1848, 2007; Rebellion Now and Forever: Mayas, Hispanics and Caste War Violence in Yucatán, 1800-1880, 2009; The River People in Flood Time: Tabasco and the Mexican Civil Wars, forthcoming; The Town at the Edge of the World, forthcoming; (ed. with B. Fallaw) Forced Marches, forthcoming. **Address:** Department of History, University of Oklahoma, Rm. 403A, 455 W Lindsey St., Norman, OK 73019, U.S.A. **Online address:** trugeley@ou.edu

RUGG, Linda (Haverty). American (born United States), b. 1957. **Genres:** Adult Non-fiction, Picture/Board Books, History, Photography, Autobiography/Memoirs. **Career:** Ohio State University, associate professor of German and Swedish, 1989-99; Brigham Young University, visiting professor, 1993-94; University of California, visiting professor, 1998, Scandinavian Studies Department, associate professor, 1999-, chair. Writer. **Publications:** Picturing Ourselves: Photography and Autobiography, 1997; (trans.) R. Swartz, Room Service: Reports from Eastern Europe (journalism and travel literature), 1998; (trans.) H.M. Enzensberger, Zig-Zag (cultural essays), 1998; The Auteur's Autograph: Cinematic Auteurism and Autobiography, forthcoming. **Address:** Department of Scandinavian, University of California, 6406 Dwinelle Hall 2-5355, Berkeley, CA 94720, U.S.A. **Online address:** rugg@berkeley.edu

RUGGLES, Lucy. *See* **WILLIAMS, Kathryn.**

RUHL, Sarah. American (born United States), b. 1974?. **Genres:** Plays/Screenplays, Sex. **Career:** Millay Colony, resident artist; Ragdale Foundation, resident artist; Ucross Foundation, resident artist. Writer and teacher. **Publications:** The Clean House and Other Plays, 2006; Dead Man's Cell Phone, 2008; Eurydice, 2008; In the Next Room, 2010; Passion Play, 2010. **Address:** Bret Adams Ltd., 448 W 44th St., New York, NY 10036-5220, U.S.A.

RUIN, Hans. Swedish/Finnish (born Finland), b. 1961?. **Genres:** History, Philosophy. **Career:** Stockholm University, research assistant, director of theoretical philosophy, 1994; Södertörns University College, professor, 1999-; Nordic Society for Phenomenology, co-founder. Writer. **Publications:** Enigmatic Origins: Tracing the Theme of Historicity through Heideggers Works, 1994; (ed. with A. Orlowski) Fenomenolgiska perspektiv: Studier i Husserls och Heideggers filosofi, 1996; (with H. Rehnberg) Herakleitos Fragment, 1998; (ed. with D. Zanhavi and S. Heinämaa) Metaphysics Facticity Interpretation: Phenomenology in the Nordic Countries, 2003. Contributor to books. **Address:** Department of Culture and Communication Philosophy, Södertö University, Rm PD216 Primus, Marinens väg 30, Huddinge, 141 89, Sweden. **Online address:** hans.ruin@sh.se

RULE, Ann. (Andy Stack). American (born United States), b. 1935. **Genres:** Mystery/Crime/Suspense, Novels, Criminology/True Crime, Travel/Exploration, inspirational/Motivational Literature. **Career:** Writer and police officer. **Publications:** NONFICTION: Beautiful Seattle, 1979 as Beautiful America's Seattle, 1989; The Stranger beside Me, 1980, rev. ed., 2000; Small Sacrifices: A True Story of Passion and Murder, 1987; If You Really Loved Me: A True Story of Desire and Murder, 1991; Everything She Ever Wanted: A True Story of Obsessive Love, Murder, and Betrayal, 1992; Dead by Sunset: Perfect Husband, Perfect Killer?, 1995; Bitter Harvest: A Woman's Fury, a Mother's Sacrifice, 1997; And Never Let Her Go: Thomas Capano, the Deadly Seducer, 1999; Every Breath You Take: A True Story of Obsessive Revenge and Murder, 2001; Heart Full of Lies: A True Story of Desire and Death, 2003; Without Pity: Ann Rule's Most Dangerous Killers, 2003; Green River, Running Red: The Real Story of the Green River Killer, America's Deadliest Serial Murderer, 2004; No Regrets, 2006; Too Late to Say Goodbye: A True Story of Murder and Betrayal, 2007; Smoke, Mirrors, and Murder, 2008; Mortal Danger, 2008; But I Trusted You, 2009; In the Still of the Night: The Strange Death of Ronda Reynolds, 2010; Don't Look Behind You, 2011. ANN RULE'S CRIME FILES SERIES: A Rose for Her Grave: And Other True Cases, 1993; You Belong to Me: And Other True Cases, 1994; A Fever

in the Heart and Other True Cases, 1996; In the Name of Love: And Other True Cases, 1998; The End of the Dream: The Golden Boy Who Never Grew Up and Other True Cases, 1999; A Rage to Kill and Other True Cases, 1999; Empty Promises: And Other True Cases, 2001; Last Dance, Last Chance and Other True Cases, 2003; Kiss Me, Kill Me, and Other True Cases, 2004; Worth More Dead: And Other True Cases, 2005. TRUE CRIME ANNALS AS ANDY STACK: Lust Killer, 1983; Want-Ad Killer, 1983; The 1-5 Killer, 1984. OTHER: Possession: A Novel, 1983. Contributor to periodicals. **Address:** The Foley Literary Agency, 34 E 38 St., New York, NY 10016, U.S.A. **Online address:** annrule@annrules.com

RULON, Philip Reed. American (born United States), b. 1934. **Genres:** History, Biography, Autobiography/Memoirs, Literary Criticism And History, Social Sciences. **Career:** Oklahoma State University, instructor in history, 1964-67; Northern Arizona University, faculty, 1967-, assistant professor of history, Research Center for Excellence in Education, director, 1967-, associate professor, 1971-80, professor of history, 1980-98, professor emeritus, 1998-. Writer and consultant. **Publications:** Oklahoma State University Since 1890, 1975; Compassionate Samaritan: The Life of Lyndon Baines Johnson, 1981; (with W.H. Lyon) Speaking Out: An Oral History of the American Past, 2 vols., 1981; (ed.) Letters from the Hill Country: The Correspondence Between Rebekah and Lyndon Baines Johnson, 1983; (ed.) Navajo Trader, 1986; (ed.) Keeping Christmas: The Celebration of an American Holiday, 1990; (with R. Jenson and W. Lyon) Great Speeches in American History, 1990; (ed. with W.J. Close, Sr.) Many Faces of Zane Grey, 1993. **Address:** Department of History, Northern Arizona University, Rm. 201, Liberal Arts Bldg., Ste. 18, PO Box 6023, Flagstaff, AZ 86011-6023, U.S.A.

RUMBAUT, Hendle. American (born United States), b. 1949. **Genres:** Adult Non-fiction. **Career:** Austin Public Library, Marketing and Public Information Division, public information specialist, 1974-; Permanent Press/Second Chance Publishing, copy editor, 1991-; photographer. **Publications:** Dove Dream, 1994. Contributor to periodicals. **Address:** Austin Public Library, 800 Guadalupe St., Austin, TX 78701, U.S.A.

RUMENS, Carol. British (born England), b. 1944. **Genres:** Novels, Poetry, Literary Criticism And History. **Career:** Freelance reviewer and journalist, 1963-; Heinemann Educational Books, publicity assistant, 1974-77; advertising copywriter, 1977-81; Quarto, poetry editor, 1982-84; University of Kent, creative writing fellow, 1983-85; Literary Review, poetry editor, 1984-88; Queen's University, writer-in-residence, 1991-93, creative writing tutor, 1995-98; University College Cork, poet-in-residence, 1994; University of Stockholm, poet-in-residence, 1999; University of Bangor, visiting professor of creative writing, 2000-05, 2006-; University of Hull, Philip Larkin Centre for Poetry and Creative Writing, director, 2005-06, visiting professor in creative writing, 2009-. **Publications:** Strange Girl in Bright Colours, 1973; A Necklace of Mirrors, 1978; Unplayed Music, 1981; Scenes from the Gingerbread House, 1982; Star Whisper, 1983; Direct Dialling, 1985; (ed.) Making for the Open: The Chatto Book of Post-Feminist Poetry 1964-1984, 1985; (ed.) Slipping Glimpses: The Poetry Book Society 1985 Anthology, 1985; Jean Rhys: A Critical Study, 1985; Icons, Waves, 1986; Selected Poems, 1987; Plato Park (novel), 1987; The Greening of the Snow Beach, 1988; From Berlin to Heaven, 1989; (ed.) The Bloodaxe Book of Women Poets, 1990; (ed.) New Women Poets, 1990; Thinking of Skins: New & Selected Poems, 1993; Best China Sky, 1995; Two Women Dancing: New and Selected Poems, 1995; Witch's Manuscript: For Soprano and Brass Quintet, 1997; The Miracle Diet, 1998; Holding Pattern, 1998; Hex, 2002; Selected Poems: 1968-2004, 2004; Self into Song: Newcastle, 2006; Writing Poetry, 2006; Blind Spots, 2008; De Chirico's Threads, 2010; Dracula Presses Save, forthcoming. TRANSLATOR: Irina Ratushinskaya (title means: 'Pencil Letter'), 1988; The Poetry of Perestroika, 1990; Yevgenii Rein: Selected Poems, 2001. **Address:** Bloodaxe Books Ltd., PO Box 1SN, Newcastle upon Tyne, NM NE99 1RP, England. **Online address:** c.rumens@tesco.net

RUMER, Boris. (Boris Z. Rumer). American/Russian (born Russia) **Genres:** Economics, International Relations/Current Affairs, Business/Trade/Industry. **Career:** National Institute of the Construction Industry, Department of Economics and Investment, head, 1964-77; Industrial Executive Training Institute, adjunct professor, 1970-77; Harvard University, research associate, 1979-, Davis Center for Russian and Eurasian Studies, fellow, 1979-, associate. Writer and consultant. **Publications:** Current Problems in the Industrialization of Siberia, 1984; (as Boris Z. Rumer) Investment and Reindustrialization in the Soviet Economy, 1984; (as Boris Z. Rumer) Soviet

Steel: The Challenge of Industrial Modernization in the USSR, 1989; (contrib.) The Impoverished Superpower: Perestroika and the Burden of Soviet Military Spending, 1989; (as Boris Z. Rumer) Soviet Central Asia: A Tragic Experiment, 1989. EDITOR: Central Asia in Transition: Dilemmas of Political and Economic Development, 1996; (with S. Zhukov) Central Asia: The Challenges of Independence, 1998; Central Asia and the New Global Economy, 2000; Central Asia: A Gathering Storm?, 2002; Central Asia at the End of the Transition, 2005. Contributor to books and periodicals. **Address:** Davis Center for Russian and Eurasian Studies, Harvard University, Rm. S301, 1730 Cambridge St., Cambridge, MA 02138, U.S.A. **Online address:** borisrumer@gmail.com

RUMER, Boris Z. *See* **RUMER, Boris.**

RUMMEL, Jack. American (born United States), b. 1950. **Genres:** Novels, Biography, History, Young Adult Fiction, Children's Fiction. **Career:** Writer and editor. **Publications:** Langston Hughes (juvenile), 1988; Muhammad Ali (juvenile), 1988; Malcolm X (juvenile), 1989, rev. ed. as Malcolm X: Civil Rights Leader, 2012; The U.S. Marine Corps, 1990; Mexico (juvenile), 1990; Robert Oppenheimer: Dark Prince (juvenile), 1992; (with M. Rebennack) Under a Hoodoo Moon: The Life of Dr. John the Night Tripper (autobiography), 1994; Philadelphia (juvenile), 1995; Frida Kahlo: A Spiritual Biography, 2000; (ed.) Lonesome Whistle, 2002; African-American Social Leaders and Activists, 2003, rev. ed., 2011. Contributor to magazines. **Address:** 1316 West St., Silver City, NM 88061, U.S.A.

RUMMEL-HUDSON, Robert. American (born United States), b. 1967. **Genres:** Human Relations/Parenting, Biography, Autobiography/Memoirs. **Career:** University of Texas, School of Architecture, current coordinator of communications. Writer. **Publications:** Schuyler's Monster: A Father's Journey with His Wordless Daughter (memoir), 2008. **Address:** Sarah Jane Freymann, 59 W 71st St., 9B, New York, NY 10023, U.S.A. **Online address:** robert@schuylersmonster.com

RUMPF, Eva Augustin. American (born United States), b. 1939. **Genres:** Novels, Young Adult Fiction. **Career:** Writer, 1974-; Milwaukee Journal, reporter, 1976-80; Marquette University, instructor in journalism, 1977-80, 1990-93, adjunct faculty, 1990, adjunct assistant professor, 1993-95; Curative Rehabilitation Center, publications editor, 1980-81; De Paul Hospital, director of public relations, director of advertising and marketing, 1981-83; Mayor's Office-Milwaukee, director of communication, 1983-87; consultant, 1990-93; Texas Christian University, director of student publications, journalism instructor and student media advisor, 1995-2000; University of Wisconsin-Milwaukee, instructor, 2004-. **Publications:** (With B.J. Grottkau) Till Divorce Do Us Part: A Practical Guide for Women in Troubled Marriages, 1996; Prot U, 2004. Contributor of articles to magazines and newspapers. **Address:** c/o Author Mail, Glenridge Publishing Ltd., 19923 E Long Ave., Centennial, CO 80016-1969, U.S.A. **Online address:** berumpf@milwpc.com

RUMSTUCKLE, Cornelius. *See* **BRENNAN, J(ames) H(erbert).**

RUMSTUCKLE, Cornelius. *See* **BRENNAN, Herbie.**

RUNCIE, James. Scottish/British (born England), b. 1959. **Genres:** Novels. **Career:** Writer and filmmaker. **Publications:** NOVELS: The Discovery of Chocolate, 2001; The Colour of Heaven, 2003; Canvey Island, 2008; East Fortune, 2009. Contributor to periodicals. **Address:** c/o David Godwin, David Godwin Associates, 55 Monmouth St., London, GL WC2H 9DG, England. **Online address:** james@jamesruncie.com

RUNCO, Mark A. American (born United States), b. 1957. **Genres:** Psychology, History. **Career:** University of Hawaii-Hilo, professor of psychology, 1983-87; California State University, professor of child development, 1987-; American Psychological Association, president; Creativity Research Journal, editor. **Publications:** Divergent Thinking, 1991; Creativity Research Handbook, 1997; Creativity: Theories and Themes: Research, Development and Practice, 2007. EDITOR AND CONTRIBUTOR: (with R.S. Albert) Theories of Creativity, 1990, rev. ed., 2001; (with M.P. Shaw) Creativity and Affect, 1994; Problem Finding, Problem Solving and Creativity, 1994; Creativity Research Handbook, 3 vols., 1997, 2nd ed., 2001; (with R. Richards) Eminent Creativity, Everyday Creativity, and Health, 1997; (with S. Pritzker) Encyclopedia of Creativity, 1999; Critical Creative Processes, 2001; (with S. Moger and T. Rickards) The Routledge Companion to Creativity, 2008.

Contributor to books and periodicals. **Address:** Department of Psychology, Child and Adolecent Studies, California State University, EC 650, Fullerton, CA 92834, U.S.A. **Online address:** runco@fullerton.edu

RUNYON, Randolph Paul. American (born United States), b. 1947. **Genres:** Literary Criticism And History. **Career:** Case Western Reserve University, assistant professor of French, 1974-76; Miami University, assistant professor, 1977-82, associate professor, 1982-87, professor of French, 1987-, Department. Honors, French Minors and Thematic Sequences, advisor, university carillonneur. Writer. **Publications:** Fowles/Irving/Barthes: Canonical Variations on an Apocryphal Theme, 1981; The Braided Dream: Robert Penn Warren's Late Poetry, 1990; The Taciturn Text: The Fiction of Robert Penn Warren, 1990; Reading Raymond Carver, 1992; Delia Webster and the Underground Railroad, 1996; In La Fontaine's Labyrinth: A Thread through the Fables, 2000; The Art of the Persian Letters: Unlocking Montesquieu's Secret Chain, 2005; Ghostly Parallels: Robert Penn Warren and the Lyric Poetic Sequence, 2006; (ed. and trans.) La Fontaine's Complete Tales in Verse, 2009; Intratextual Baudelaire: The Sequential Fabric of the Fleurs du mal and Spleen de Paris, 2010. **Address:** Department of French and Italian, Miami University, 216 Irvin Hall, 501 E High St., Oxford, OH 45056, U.S.A. **Online address:** runyonr@muohio.edu

RUOFF, A. LaVonne Brown. American (born United States), b. 1930. **Genres:** Literary Criticism And History, Young Adult Non-fiction, Bibliography, History. **Career:** University of Illinois, instructor in English, 1956-57, assistant professor, 1966-69, associate professor, 1969-81, professor of English, 1981-94, professor emeritus, 1994-; Roosevelt University, instructor, 1961-62, assistant professor of English, 1962-66; Newberry Library, D'Arcy McNickle Center for American Indian History, interim director, 1999-2000. Writer. **Publications:** (Ed. and intro.) The Moccasin Maker, 1987; American Indian Literatures: An Introduction, Bibliographic Review, and Selected Bibliogrpahy, 1990; (ed. with J.W. Ward, Jr.) Redefining American Literary History, 1990; Literatures of the American Indian, 1991; (ed.) Wynema: A Child of the Forest, 1997; (ed. with D.B. Smith) Life, Letters and Speeches, 1997; (ed.) From the Deep Woods to Civilization and Excerpts from Indian Boyhood, 2001. Contributor to books and periodicals. **Address:** 761 Highview Ave., Glen Ellyn, IL 60137-5559, U.S.A. **Online address:** lruoff@uic.edu

RUOKANEN, Miikka. Finnish (born Finland), b. 1953. **Genres:** Theology/Religion, Cultural/Ethnic Topics. **Career:** Minister of the (Lutheran) Church of Finland, 1977-; Univerity of Helsinki, docent, 1983-93, professor of dogmatics (systematic theology), 1993-, responsible for discipline; Thomas Mass, co-founder, 1988; visiting professor, Russia, 1993-; Fudan University, advisory professor, 2004-; Nanjing Union Theological Seminary, visiting professor, 2004-. Writer. **Publications:** Ihmiskäsitys vapausrangaistuksen täytäntöönpanoa Koskevassa lainsäädännössä Suomessa 1889-1980, 1981; Hermeneutics as an Ecumenical Method: In the Theology of Gerhard Ebeling, 1982; Luther in Finnland: Der Einfluss der Theologie Martin Luthers inFinnland und finnische Beiträge zur Lutherforschung, 1984; Doctrina divinitus Inspirata: Martin Luther's Position in the Ecumenical Problem of Biblical Inspiration, 1985; Hermeneutica moderna: teologinen Hermeneutiikka historiallis-kriittisen raamatuntutkimuksen aikakaudella, 1987; The Catholic Doctrine of Non-Christian Religions: According to the Second Vatican Council, 1992; Theology of Social Life in Augustine's De Civitate Dei, 1993; Milloin maailma loppuu, 1999; (ed. with P. Huang) Christianity and Chinese Culture: A Sino-Nordic Conference on Chinese Conrextual Theology (August 13-17, 2003, Lapland, Finland), 2004; (ed. with S. Bevans) Studies in Systematic Theology, 2008; Truth and Context: Models of Christianity in Asia, forthcoming. **Address:** Department of Systematic Theology, University of Helsinki, Aleksanterinkatu 7, 6th Fl., PO Box 33, Helsinki, 00014, Finland. **Online address:** miikka.ruokanen@helsinki.fi

RUOTSILA, Markku. Finnish (born Finland), b. 1969?. **Genres:** History, Theology/Religion, Intellectual History, International Relations/Current Affairs. **Career:** University of Helsinki, adjunct professor of American church history; University of Tampere, adjunct professor of American and British history; New York University, visiting fellow; University of Oxford, Rothermere American Institute, visiting fellow; The Academy of Finland, researcher. Writer and historian. **Publications:** British and American Anticommunism before the Cold War, 2001; Churchill ja Suomi: Winston Churchillin Suomea koskeva ajattelu ja toiminta, 2002; Churchill and Finland: A Study in Anticommunism and Geopolitics, 2005; John Spargo and American Socialism, 2006; The Origins of Christian Anti-Internationalism: Conservative Evangelicals and the League of Nations, 2008; Yhdysvaltain kristillinen oikeisto, 2008. Contributor to periodicals. **Address:** Department of Church History, University of Helsinki, 7 Aleksanterinkatu, Helsinki, 00014, Finland. **Online address:** markkuruotsila@hotmail.com

RUPP, Joyce. American (born United States), b. 1943. **Genres:** inspirational/ Motivational Literature, Poetry, Novellas/Short Stories. **Career:** The Institute of Compassionate Presence, co-director; Archdiocese of Omaha, vocation director. Writer. **Publications:** Fresh Bread and Other Gifts of Spiritual Nourishment, 1985; Praying Our Goodbyes, 1988; The Star in My Heart: Experiencing Sophia, 1990; May I Have This Dance?, 1992; Little Pieces of Light: Darkness and Personal Growth, 1994; Dear Heart, Come Home: The Path of Midlife Spirituality, 1996; The Cup of Our Life: A Guide for Spiritual Growth, 1997; Your Sorrow Is My Sorrow: Hope and Strength in Times of Suffering, 1999; (with J. Hutchison) May I Walk You Home?: Courage and Comfort for Caregivers of the Very Ill (stories and prayers), 1999; Prayers to Sophia, 2000; Out of the Ordinary: Prayers, Poems, and Reflections for Every Season, 2000; Inviting God In: Scriptural Reflections and Prayers Throughout the Year, 2001; The Cosmic Dance: An Invitation to Experience Our Oneness, 2002; Rest Your Dreams on a Little Twig (poems), 2003; Star in My Heart: Experiencing Sophia, Inner Wisdom, 2004; Prayers to Sophia, 2004; Walk in a Relaxed Manner: Life Lessons from the Camino, 2005; The Circle of Life: The Heart's Journey through the Seasons, 2005; Prayer, 2007; Open the Door: A Journey to the True Self, 2008; God's Enduring Presence, 2008; (co-author) With Grateful Hearts, 2010; (comp. with J. Hutchison) Now that you've Gone Home: Courage and Comfort for Times of Grief, 2009; Fragments of Your Ancient Name, 2011. CARENOTES SERIES (booklets): Walking With God Through Grief and Loss, 1989; Growing Through Failure, 1990; Believing in Your Own Inner Goodness, 1991; When a Loved One Has a Stroke, 1991; Recovering After a Mastectomy, 1991. OTHER BOOKLETS: Following Jesus, 1993; With All My Heart, 1995; I Place My Trust in You: Prayers in Times of Suffering, 2000. Contributor to periodicals. **Address:** Ave Maria Press Inc., PO Box 428, Notre Dame, IN 46556-0428, U.S.A.

RUPP, Richard H. American (born United States), b. 1934. **Genres:** Novels, Biography, Literary Criticism And History. **Career:** Gilmour Academy, instructor, 1957-58; Georgetown University, assistant professor, 1961-68; University of Miami, assistant professor, 1968-72; City University of New York, Brooklyn College, associate professor, 1972-74; Indiana State University, faculty; Appalachian State University, Graduate School, dean, 1975-79, associate professor, 1978-81, professor, 1981-, now professor emeritus. Writer. **Publications:** Celebration in Postwar American Fiction 1945-67, 1970; Getting through College: A Guidebook to Help You Get Into, Pay for, Survive, Pass, Graduate from the College of Your Choice, 1984; Unity (novel), 1999; (intro.) Ireland Standing Firm and Eamon de Valera: A Memoir, 2002. EDITOR: (and intro.) The Marble Faun or The Romance of Monte Beni, 1971; Critics on Whitman, 1972; Critics on Emily Dickinson, 1972; Epic Perspectives, 1990; Writing About Literature, 1995; Allegiance, forthcoming. Contributor of articles to journals. **Address:** Appalachian State University, PO Box 32068, Boone, NC 28608, U.S.A. **Online address:** rupprh@appstate.edu

RUSCH, Elizabeth. American (born United States), b. 1966. **Genres:** Natural History, Air/Space Topics, Sports/Fitness, Picture/Board Books. **Career:** Teacher Magazine, managing editor; PointsBeyond.com, editor-in-chief; Attic Writers' Workshop, faculty; Child and Fit Pregnancy Magazine, contributing editor. Freelance magazine writer. **Publications:** Generation Fix: Young Ideas for a Better World, 2002; The Planet Hunter: How Astronomer Mike Brown's Search for the 10th Planet Shook Up the Solar System, 2007; A Day with No Crayons, 2007; Will It Blow?: Become a Volcano Detective at Mount St. Helens, 2007; Girls' Tennis: Conquering the Court, 2007; For the Love of Music: The Remarkable Story of Maria Anna Mozart, 2011; Mighty Mars Rovers: The Incredible Adventures of Spirit and Opportunity, 2012; Volcano Rising, 2013. Contributor to books and periodicals. **Address:** c/o Kelly Sonnack, Andrea Brown Literary Agency, 1076 Eagle Dr., Salinas, CA 93905, U.S.A. **Online address:** author@elizabethrusch.com

RUSCH, Kristine Kathryn. (Sandy Schofield). American (born United States), b. 1960. **Genres:** Science Fiction/Fantasy, Literary Criticism And History, Writing/Journalism, Novels. **Career:** WORT Radio, reporter, 1980-86, news director, 1983-86; Shire Frame Shop & Galleries, owner, 1981-84; William C. Brown Publishers, editorial assistant, 1984; Pulphouse Publishing, co-founder, 1987-, editor, 1987-91; Magazine of Fantasy & Science Fiction, editor, 1991-97. Writer. **Publications:** PULPHOUSE ANTHOLOGIES:

Pulphouse, the Hardback Magazine: Issues One and Two, 1988; Pulphouse, the Hardback Magazine: Issues Three, Four and Five, 1989; Pulphouse, the Hardback Magazine: Issues Six, Seven, Eight and Nine, 1990; Pulphouse, the Hardback Magazine: Issues Ten and Eleven, 1991; The Best of Pulphouse: The Hardback Magazine, 1991. NOVELS: The Gallery of His Dreams (short novel), 1991; The White Mists of Power. 1991; (with K.J. Anderson) Afterimage, 1992; (as Sandy Schofield with D.W. Smith) Star Trek: Deep Space Nine: The Big Game, 1993; Traitors, 1993; Heart Readers, 1993; Facade, 1993; Alien Influences, 1994; Sins of the Blood, 1994; (with D.W. Smith) Star Trek: Voyager: The Escape, 1995; (as Sandy Schofield with D.W. Smith) Aliens: Rogue, 1995; The Fey: The Sacrifice, 1995; The Fey: Changeling, 1996; (with D.W. Smith) Star Trek: Deep Space Nine: The Long Night, 1996; (with D.W. Smith) Star Trek: Klingon!, 1996; (with D.W. Smith) Star Trek: Rings of Tautee, 1996; (with D.W. Smith) Star Trek: The Next Generation: Invasion! Soldiers of Fear, 1996; The Devil's Churn, 1996; Star Wars: The New Rebellion, 1996; The Sacrifice: The First Book of the Fey, 1996; The Fey: The Rival, 1997; (as Sandy Schofield with D.W. Smith) Quantum Leap: The Loch Ness Monster, 1997; (with D.W. Smith) Star Trek: Day of Honor-Book Four, 1997; (as Kris Rusch) Hitler's Angel, 1997; The Fey: The Resistance, 1998; The Fey: Victory, 1998; (with D.W. Smith and N.K. Hoffman) Star Trek: Voyager: Echoes, in Press; X-men: A Novelization, 2000; Paloma: A Retrieval Artist Novel, 2006. WITH DEAN WESLEY SMITH: Tenth Planet, 1999; Oblivion, 2000; Shadow, 2001; Stories For an Enchanted Afternoon, 2001; No Good Deed, 2001; Little Green Men, 2002. OTHER: (ed. with D.W. Smith) Science Fiction Writers of America Handbook: The Professional Writer's Guide to Writing Professionally, 1990; (ed. with E.L. Ferman) The Best From Fantasy & Science Fiction: A 45th Anniversary Anthology, 1994; Echoes, 1998; Black King, 2000; (with D.W. Smith) Final Assault, 2000; (with D.W. Smith) Thin Air, 2000; Little Miracles and Other Tales of Murder, 2001; Retrieval Artist and Other Stories, 2002; Disappeared: A Retrieval Artist Novel, 2002; Extremes, 2003; (as Kathryn Wesley) Salem Witch Trials, 2003; Fantasy Life, 2003; Consequences, 2004; Buried Deep, 2005; Creating Criminal Masterminds, 2006; Cheez Whiz and the Future: Battlestar Galactica and Me, 2006; Losing Dolly, 2006; Crunchers, 2006; Recovery Man: A Retrieval Artist Novel, 2007; Diving into the Wreck, 2009; Recovering Apollo 8 and Other Stories, 2010; Crossing Over, 2010; Hitler's Angel: A Novel, 2010; The One That Got Away, 2010; The Amazing Quizmo, 2010; The Assassin's Dagger, 2010; Broken Windchimes, 2010; Coolhunting, 2010; Cowboy Grace, 2010; Destiny: A Story of the Fey, 2010; Details, 2010; Discovery, 2010; Domestic Magic, 2010; Dragon's Tooth, 2010; Flower Fairies, 2010; Going Native, 2010; Jury Duty, 2010; The Moorhead House, 2010; Paparazzi of Dreams, 2010; Patriotic Gestures, 2010; The Poop Thief, 2010; Pudgygate, 2010; Say Hello to My Little Friend, 2010; The Secret Lives of Cats, 2010; Spinning, 2010; The Spires of Denon, 2010; Stomping Mad, 2010; Victims, 2010; What Fluffy Knew, 2010; What the Monster Saw, 2010; Unknown Baby Girl, 2011; Blind, 2011; The Death of Davy Moss: A Love Story, 2011; June Sixteenth at Anna's, 2011; City of Ruins, 2011; Anniversary Day, 2011; Duplicate Effort: A Retrieval Artist, 2011; Recovery Man: A Retrieval Artist, 2011; Utterly Charming, 2011; Boneyards, 2012; Assassins in Love: Assassins Guild, 2012. Contributor to periodicals. **Address:** c/o Merrilee Heifetz, Writers House, 21 W 26th St., New York, NY 10010, U.S.A. **Online address:** kris@kristinekathrynrusch.com

RUSH, Christopher. Scottish (born Scotland), b. 1944. **Genres:** Novels, Novellas/Short Stories, Plays/Screenplays, Poetry, Autobiography/Memoirs, Biography, History. **Career:** Teacher, 1970-72; George Watson's College, assistant principal English teacher, 1972-99. Writer. **Publications:** Peace Comes Dropping Slow, 1983; A Resurrection of a Kind, 1984; Twelvemonth and a Day, 1986; Two Christmas Stories, 1988; Into the Ebb: A New Collection of East Neuk Stories, 1989; Venus Peter, 1989; Where the Clock Stands Still: A Portrait of the East Neuk of Fife, 1990; With Sharp Compassion: Norman Dott, Freeman Surgeon of Edinburgh, 1990; Venus Peter Saves the Whale, 1992; Last Lesson of the Afternoon: A Satire, 1994; Will: The Autobiography of Mr. W.S., 2004; To Travel Hopefully: Footsteps in the French Cévennes, 2005; Hellfire and Herring: A Childhood Remembered, 2007; (trans. with A.K. Rush) Yury Tynyanov, Young Pushkin: A Novel, 2007; Sex, Lies and Shakespeare, 2009; Aunt Epp's Guide for Life, 2010. Contributor of magazines. **Address:** East Cottage, Newton of Wormiston, FF KY10 3XH, Scotland.

RUSHDIE, Salman. Indian (born India), b. 1947. **Genres:** Novels, Novellas/ Short Stories, Plays/Screenplays, Essays, Travel/Exploration, Young Adult Non-fiction, Children's Fiction. **Career:** Fringe Theatre, actor, 1968-69; freelance advertising copywriter, 1970-73, 1976-80; writer, 1975-; Massachusetts Institute of Technology, honorary visiting professor of the humanities, 1993; PEN American Center, staff, 2004-06; Emory University, distinguished writer-in-residence, 2006-, university distinguished professor. **Publications:** Grimus: A Novel, 1975; Midnight's Children, 1980; Shame, 1983; The Jaguar Smile: A Nicaraguan Journey, 1987; The Satanic Verses, 1988; Haroun and the Sea of Stories, 1990; In Good Faith, 1990; Imaginary Homelands: Essays and Criticism 1981-1991, 1991; The Wizard of Oz, 1992; (intro.) Soldiers Three and In Black and White, 1993; The Rushdie Letters: Freedom to Speak, Freedom to Write, 1993; East, West (short stories), 1994; The Moor's Last Sigh, 1995; (ed. with E. West) Vintage Book of Indian Writing, 1947-1997, 1997; (ed. with E. West) Mirrorwork: 50 Years Of Indian Writing, 1947-1997, 1997; The Ground Beneath Her Feet: A Novel, 1999; Fury: A Novel, 2001; Woede, 2001; Step across This Line: Collected Nonfiction 1992-2002, 2002; Shalimar the Clown: A Novel, 2005; Careless Masters, 2007; Parallelville, 2007; The Enchantress of Florence: A Novel, 2008; (intro.) Best American Short Stories 2008, 2008; Luka and the Fire of Life: A Novel, 2010; Birds of Prey: Seven Sardonic Stories, 2010; Joseph Anton, 2012. Contributor to magazines and newspapers. **Address:** The Wylie Agency Ltd., 17 Bedford Sq., London, GL WC1B 3JA, England.

RUSHFIELD, Richard. American (born United States) **Genres:** Novels. **Career:** Monkey Zero, co-founder, 1998-; Arena Magazine, columnist, 2000-02; Los Angeles Times, entertainment editor, 2005-09; Gawker, west coast editor, 2009; The Daily Beast, entertainment columnist; Vanity Fair, contributing editor. Journalist. **Publications:** On Spec: A Novel of Young Hollywood, 2000; Don't Follow Me, I'm Lost: A Memoir of Hampshire College in the Twilight of the '80s, 2009; (contrib.) Reality Matters: 19 Writers Come Clean About the Shows We Can't Stop Watching, 2010; American Idol: The Untold Story, 2011. Contributor to periodicals. **Address:** Hyperion Books, 114 5th Ave., New York, NY 10011, U.S.A. **Online address:** rr@richardrushfield.com

RUSHING, Josh. American (born United States), b. 1972. **Genres:** Social Commentary, Trivia/Facts, Third World, History, Social Sciences. **Career:** Al Jazeera, programme presenter and correspondent, 2005-. **Publications:** (With S. Elder) Mission Al Jazeera: Build a Bridge, Seek the Truth, Change the World, 2007. **Address:** Palgrave Macmillan Ltd., 175 5th Ave., New York, NY 10010-7703, U.S.A. **Online address:** onceamarine@joshrushing.com

RUSHKOFF, Douglas. American (born United States), b. 1961. **Genres:** Popular Culture, Documentaries/Reportage, Technology. **Career:** The New School, professor of media; New York University, adjunct assistant professor of communications, professor of communications; Esalen Institute, instructor; Banff Center for the Arts, instructor. Writer and film producer. **Publications:** (With P. Wells) Free Rides: How to Get High without Drugs, 1991, as Stoned Free: How to Get High Without Drugs, 1995; Cyberia: Life in the Trenches of Hyperspace, 1994; The Gen X Reader, 1994; Media Virus!: Hidden Agendas in Popular Culture, 1994, rev. ed., 1996; Cyber Taror, 1994; Children of Chaos: Surviving the End of the World as We Know It, 1995; Playing the Future: How Kids' Culture Can Teach Us to Thrive in an Age of Chaos, 1996; Ecstasy Club: A Novel, 1997; Playing the Future: What We Can Learn from Digital Kids, 1999; Coercion: Why We Listen to What They Say, 1999; Bull, 2001; Exit Strategy, 2001; Nothing Sacred: The Truth about Judaism, 2003; Open Source Democracy: How Online Communication is Changing Offline Politics, 2003; Club Zero-G: A Graphic Novel, 2004; The Persuaders, 2004; Get Back in the Box: Innovation from the Inside Out, 2005; ScreenAgers: Lessons in Chaos from Digital Kids, 2006; Testament, 2007; Life Inc: How the World became a Corporation and How to Take It Back, 2009; Program or Be Programmed, 2010; A.D.D: Adolescent Demo Division, 2012. **Address:** New York University, 721 Broadway, 4th Fl., 1325 Ave. of the Americas, New York, NY 10003, U.S.A. **Online address:** rushkoff@rushkoff.com

RUSHTON, Julian (Gordon). British (born England), b. 1941. **Genres:** Literary Criticism And History, Music. **Career:** University of East Anglia, lecturer in music, 1968-74; Cambridge University, King's College, lecturer in music and fellow, 1974-81; University of Leeds, professor of music, 1982-2005, professor emeritus, 2005-, head of department, director of research and tutor. Writer. **Publications:** EDITOR: Berlioz: Huit scenes de Faust, 1971; Berlioz: La damnation de Faust, vol. I, 1979, vol. II, 1986; Berlioz: Choral Music, 1991; Potter: Symphony in G Minor, 2001; (with D.M. Grimley) The Cambridge Companion to Elgar, 2004; (with R.E. Cowgill) Europe, Empire and Spectacle in Nineteenth-century British Music, 2006; (with J.P.E. Harper-Scott) Elgar Studies, 2007; Elgar: Music for String Orchestra, 2011. OTH-

ERS: W.A. Mozart: Don Giovanni, 1981; W.A. Mozart: Idomeneo, 1981; The Musical Language of Berlioz, 1983; Classical Music, A Concise History, 1986; Berlioz: Romeo et Juliette, 1994; Elgar: Enigma Variations, 1999; The Music of Berlioz, 2001; Mozart, An Extraordinary Life, 2005; Mozart (The Master Musicians), 2006; The New Grove Guide to Mozart's Operas, 2007; Coffee with Mozart, 2007. Contributor of articles to books and periodicals. **Address:** School of Music, University of Leeds, Leeds, WY LS2 9JT, England. **Online address:** j.g.rushton@leeds.ac.uk

RUSI, Alpo M. Finnish (born Finland), b. 1949. **Genres:** Politics/Government, Architecture, Social Sciences, History. **Career:** Finnish Ministry for Foreign Affairs, attache, 1973-75, vice consultant, 1975-76, secretary, 1977-79, first secretary in political department, 1980-81, Finnish mission to the United Nations, counselor, 1983-86, counselor in political department and head of section on research and planning, 1987-90, director of research and planning, 1990, director of Nordic and other western states, 1991, deputy chief of embassy in Bonn, 1992-93, ambassador, 1993-94, security adviser to the president of Finland, 1994-; Center of War, Peace and the News, associate, 1985-; University of Tampere, adjunct professor, 1986-; Institute of East-West Studies, resident fellow, 1988-89; University of Helsinki, adjunct professor, 1994-; Republic to Brussels, Office of the President, deputy special coordinator, 1999; University of Lapland, professor of international policy, 2000-03. Writer. **Publications:** (With J. Kuisma) Avaus äärikeskustaan, 1980; Lehdistösensuuri jatkosodassa: sanan valvonta sodankäynnin välineenä 1941-1944, 1982; After the Cold War: Europe's New Political Architecture, 1991; Dangerous Peace: New Rivalry in World Politics, 1997; Myrskyjen Aika, 2004; Tiitisen Lista, 2011. **Address:** Office of the President, Republic of Finland, Mariankatu 2, Helsinki, 00170, Finland. **Online address:** arusi@kolumbus.fi

RUSKAN, John. American (born United States) **Genres:** Self Help, Psychology, Philosophy. **Career:** Writer, psychologist and musician. **Publications:** Emotional Clearing: Releasing Negative Feelings and Awakening Unconditional Happiness, 1993; Between the Moon and the Walking: An Excursion into Emotion and Art, 1998; Emotion and Art, 2012. **Address:** c/o John Ruskan, R. Wyler and Co., 147 West 22 St., Ste. 5S, New York, NY 10011, U.S.A. **Online address:** jrusk@emclear.com

RUSS, Daniel. American (born United States), b. 1949?. **Genres:** Theology/Religion. **Career:** Trinity Christian Academy, headmaster, 1994-2002; Gordon College, Christians in the Visual Arts, executive director, 2002-03, Dallas Institute of Humanities and Culture, managing director; Studies in Leadership program, founder; Center for Christian Studies, director; Trinity Forum, Children of Prometheus: Technology and the Good Life curriculum, project director, Provocations journal, editor. **Publications:** Flesh-and-Blood Jesus: Learning to Be Fully Human from the Son of Man, 2008. Contributor to books. **Address:** Danvers, MA , U.S.A. **Online address:** dan.russ@gordon.edu

RUSSELL, Alan. American (born United States), b. 1956. **Genres:** Mystery/Crime/Suspense, Novels, Young Adult Fiction, Humor/Satire. **Career:** Writer. **Publications:** No Sign of Murder, 1990; The Forest Prime Evil, 1992; The Hotel Detective, 1994; The Fat Innkeeper, 1995; Multiple Wounds, 1996; Shame: A Novel, 1998; Exposure, 2002; Political Suicide, 2003; (with K. Kuhlken) Road Kill: Mystery Authors on the Book Signing Circuit, 2003. **Address:** Mysterious Galaxy Bookstore, 7051 Clairemont Mesa Blvd., Ste. 302, San Diego, CA 92111, U.S.A. **Online address:** alanruss@alanrussell.net

RUSSELL, Catherine. Canadian (born Canada), b. 1959. **Genres:** Film. **Career:** New York University, instructor, 1987; Queen's University, lecturer, 1988-90; Concordia University, assistant professor, 1990-94, associate professor, 1995-2004, professor of film studies, 2004-; Canadian Journal of Film Studies, co-editor. **Publications:** Narrative Mortality: Death, Closure, and New Wave Cinemas, 1995; Experimental Ethnography, 1999; (ed. with A. Gaudreault and P. Véronneau) Le cinématographe, nouvelle technologie du XXe siècle, 2004; The Cinema of Naruse Mikio: Women and Japanese Modernity, 2008; Classical Japanese Cinema Revisited, 2011. Contributor to books and periodicals. **Address:** Concordia University, 1455 de Maisonneuve Blvd. W, Montreal, QC H3G 1M8, Canada. **Online address:** crus@alcor.concordia.ca

RUSSELL, Cheryl. American/German (born Germany), b. 1953. **Genres:** Documentaries/Reportage, Philosophy, Sociology, Anthropology/Ethnology, Business/Trade/Industry, Economics. **Career:** American Demographics, editor-in-chief, 1984-90, contributing editor, 1995-; Money, contributing editor,

1990-91; Age Wave, executive editor, 1992-94; New Strategist Publications, editor-in-chief, 1993-, editorial director; Boomer Report, executive editor, 1996-98; American Demographics Magazine, editor-in-chief. **Publications:** 100 Predictions for the Baby Boom: The Next Fifty Years, 1982; The Master Trend: How the Baby Boom Generation Is Reshaping America, 1993; (with M. Ambry) The Official Guide to American Incomes: A Comprehensive Look at How Much Americans Have to Spend: With a Special Section on Discretionary Income, 1993; The Official Guide to Racial and Ethnic Diversity, 1996; The Mid-Youth Market: Baby Boomers in Their Peak Earning and Spending Years, 1996; Racial and Ethnic Diversity: Asians, Blacks, Hispanics, Native Americans and Whites, 1998, 4th ed., 2002; Americans and Their Homes: Demographics of Homeownership, 1998, 2nd ed., 2005; (with S. Mitchell) Best Customers: Demographics of Consumer Demand, 1999, 2nd ed., 2001; The Baby Boom: Americans Aged 35 to 54, 1999, 3rd ed., 2001; Demographics of the U.S.: Trends and Projections, 2000; (contrib.) American Incomes, 2001; Bet You Didn't Know: Hundreds of Intriguing Facts About Living in the USA, 2008. **Address:** New Strategist Publications Inc., 120 W State St., 4th Fl., PO Box 242, Ithaca, NY 14850, U.S.A. **Online address:** cher@newstrategist.com

RUSSELL, Dick. American (born United States), b. 1947. **Genres:** Adult Non-fiction, Politics/Government. **Career:** Topeka Capital-Journal (newspaper), sports and feature writer, columnist, 1965-72; Sports Illustrated (magazine), reporter, 1969-70; TV Guide (magazine), 1977-79. Freelance journalist, 1980-. **Publications:** NONFICTION: The Man Who Knew Too Much: Hired to Kill Oswald and Prevent the Assassination of JFK: Richard Case Nagell, 1992; Black Genius and the American Experience, 1998; Eye of the Whale: Epic Passage from Baja to Siberia, 2001; Striper Wars: An American Fish Story, 2005; On the Trail of the JFK Assassins: A Groundbreaking Look at America's Most Infamous Conspiracy, 2008; (with J. Ventura) Don't Start the Revolution Without Me!: From the Minnesota Governor's Mansion to the Baja Outback: Reflections and Revisionings, 2008; Black Genius: Inspirational Portraits of America's Black Leaders, 2009; (with J. Ventura) American Conspiracies: Lies, Lies and More Dirty Lies that the Government Tells Us, 2010; (with J. Ventura) 63 Documents the Government Doesn't Want You To Read, 2011; Life and Ideas of James Hillman, 2012. Contributor to periodicals. **Address:** c/o Sarah Jane Freymann, Stepping Stone Literary Agency Inc., 59 W 71st St., New York, NY 10023-4111, U.S.A. **Online address:** dickrusl@aol.com

RUSSELL, Helen Ross. American (born United States), b. 1915. **Genres:** Children's Non-fiction, Education, Autobiography/Memoirs, Environmental Sciences/Ecology, Art/Art History. **Career:** Teacher, 1935-46; Cornell University, Nature Study department, staff; Massachusetts State College (now Fitchburg State College), professor of biology, 1949-66, chair of science department, 1951-56, dean of studies, 1956-66; Wave Hill Center for Environmental Studies, science consultant, part-time science consultant and director, 1966-70; Manhattan Country School, science consultant, 1970-. Writer. **Publications:** City Critters, 1969, rev. ed., 1975; True Book of Buds, 1970; Clarion the Killdeer, 1970; Winter Search Party, 1971; Winter: A Field Trip Guide, 1972; Small Worlds: A Field Trip Guide, 1972; Soil: A Field Trip Guide, 1972; The True Book of Springtime Tree Seeds, 1972; Ten Minute Field Trips, Using the School Grounds for Environmental Studies (teacher's book), 1973, rev. ed., 1998; Water: A Field Trip Guide, 1973; Earth the Great Recycler, 1973; Foraging for Dinner, 1975; Wave Hill Trail Guide, 1978; (with D. Fitzgerald and B. Devans) Teachers Guide: Eastern Woodland and Plains Indians of the American Museum of Natural History, 1988; Interpreters Manual, Bugs and Other Insects, 1989; (ed.) First Nations People: Teaching about Native American Culture and Environment, 1994; Journey through the 20th Century (memoir), 2002; Dandelion, Flower of the Sun, 2005. **Address:** 44 College Dr., Jersey City, NJ 07305, U.S.A. **Online address:** rrussell14@juno.com

RUSSELL, Jan Jarboe. American (born United States), b. 1951?. **Genres:** Biography. **Career:** San Antonio Express-News, columnist, 1981-85, 2000-; King Features, columnist, 2001-; Texas Monthly, contributing editor, writer-at-large; Linda Pace Foundation, founder, 2003, vice president, interim executive director; University of Texas, visiting lecturer. Writer and educator. **Publications:** (With K. Diehl) Cisneros: Portrait of a New American, 1985; (with M. Langford and C. Smith) San Antonio: A Cultural Tapestry, 1998; Lady Bird: A Biography of Mrs. Johnson, 1999; (co-author) Dreaming Red: Creating ArtPace, 2003; (ed. and intro.) They Lived to Tell the Tale: True Stories of Modern Adventure from the Legendary Explorers Club, 2008. Contributor

to books. **Address:** San Antonio Express-News, 301 Ave. E, PO Box 2171, San Antonio, TX 78205, U.S.A. **Online address:** jjarboe@express-news.net

RUSSELL, Jeffrey Burton. American (born United States), b. 1934. **Genres:** History, Theology/Religion, Bibliography. **Career:** University of New Mexico, assistant professor of history, 1960-61; Harvard University, Society of Fellows, junior fellow, 1961-62; University of California-Riverside, assistant professor, 1962-65, associate professor, 1965-69, professor of medieval and religious history, 1969-75, Graduate Division, associate dean, 1967-75, Religious Studies Program, chair, 1972-73; University of Notre Dame, Michael P. Grace professor of Medieval studies, 1975-79, Medieval Institute, director, 1975-79; University of California at Santa Barbara, Sacramento, graduate dean, 1977-79; University of California at Santa Barbara, professor of medieval and church history, 1979, professor of history and religious studies, 1994-, now professor emeritus; Pacifica Graduate Institute, adjunct professor, 1994-. Writer. **Publications:** Dissent and Reform in the Early Middle Ages, 1965; (co-author) The Transformation of the Roman World, 1966; Medieval Civilization, 1968; A History of Medieval Christianity: Prophecy and Order, 1968; (ed.) Religious Dissent in the Middle Ages, 1971; Witchcraft in the Middle Ages, 1972; The Devil: Perceptions of Evil from Antiquity to Primitive Christianity, 1977; (with B. Alexander) A History of Witchcraft: Sorcerers, Heretics and Pagans, 1980, 2nd ed., 2007; (with C.T. Berkhout) Medieval Heresies: A Bibliography 1960-1979, 1981; Satan: The Early Christian Tradition, 1981; Lucifer, the Devil in the Middle Ages, 1984; Mephistopheles: The Devil in the Modern World, 1986; The Prince of Darkness: Radical, Evil and the Power of Good in History, 1988; (trans.) Ruga in aevis (title means: 'A Wrinkle in Time'), 1990; Inventing the Flat Earth: Columbus and the Historians, 1991; Dissent and Order in the Middle Ages: The Search for Legitimate Authority, 1992; A History of Heaven: The Singing Silence, 1997; Life of the Jura Fathers: The Life and Rule of the Holy Fathers Romanus, Lupicinus, and Eugendus, Abbots of the Monasteries in the Jura Mountains, 1999; (foreword) Henry I, 2001; Paradise Mislaid: How We Lost Heaven-and How We can Regain It, 2006. Contributor to periodicals. **Address:** Department of History, University of California, 552 University Rd., Santa Barbara, CA 93106, U.S.A. **Online address:** russell@humanitas.ucsb.edu

RUSSELL, Jeremy (Longmore). British (born England), b. 1935. **Genres:** Environmental Sciences/Ecology, International Relations/Current Affairs, Travel/Exploration, Reference. **Career:** Shell International Chemical Co., staff, 1959-63; Shell International Petroleum Company Ltd., staff, 1963-81, manager for relations with the U.S.S.R., 1968-79, public affairs division manager for international affairs and government relations, 1979-81, manager of group planning for business environment, 1983-; Royal Institute of International Affairs, research fellow, 1974-75; Harvard University, Energy and Environmental Policy Center, visiting research fellow, 1981-82; Nature Conservancy Council, industry adviser. Writer. **Publications:** Energy as a Factor in Soviet Foreign Policy, 1976; Geopolitics of Natural Gas, 1983; Environmental Issues in Eastern Europe: Setting an Agenda, 1990; Energy and Environmental Conflicts in East/Central Europe: The Case of Power Generation, 1991; (ed.) Mind Training like the Rays of the Sun, 1992; Dharamsala, Tibetan Refuge, 2000; (trans. with G.L. Jordhen and L.C. Ganchenpa) Stages of Meditation, 2001; (contrib.) Norbulingka: The First Ten Years of An Adventure, 2006. **Address:** Shell International Petroleum Company Ltd., Shell-Mex House, Strand, London, GL WC2, England.

RUSSELL, Kenneth Victor. British (born England), b. 1929. **Genres:** Criminology/True Crime, Law, Local History/Rural Topics, Sociology, Theology/Religion, History. **Career:** Deputy headmaster, 1957-59, 1961-63; Leicester College of Education, senior lecturer in education, 1963-76; Leicester Polytechnic Law School, principal lecturer, 1976-; Anstey Scene, editor, 2003-. Writer. **Publications:** (With J.D. Tooke) Learning to Give, 1967; (contrib.) Religious Studies, 1970; (with J.D. Tooke) Crime Is Our Business, 1973; (with J.D. Tooke) Projects in Religious Education, 1974; Complaints against the Police: A Sociological View, 1976, 3rd ed., 1985; Police Acts 1964 and 1976: Complaints against the Police Which Are Withdrawn, 1986; (with R. MacKay) Psychiatry and the Criminal Process, 1986; (with R. MacKay) Psychiatric Disorders and the Criminal Process, 1987; (with R. Lilly) The Electronic Monitoring of Offenders, 1989; Glenfield: Life and Times Remembered, 1994; Glenfield: More Lives and Times, 1996; Glenfield: Lives and Times in Pictures, 1998; Glenfield: More Lives and Times in Pictures, 2001. Contributor to newspapers. **Address:** Cedar House, Leicester Rd., Leicester, LE LE3 8BZ, England.

RUSSELL, Martin (James). Also writes as James Arney. British (born England), b. 1934. **Genres:** Mystery/Crime/Suspense, Young Adult Fiction, Literary Criticism And History. **Career:** Kentish Times, reporter, 1951-58; Royal Air Force, staff, 1955-57; Croydon Advertiser, reporter and sub-editor, 1958-73. **Publications:** No Through Road, 1965; No Return Ticket, 1966; Danger Money, 1968; Hunt to a Kill, 1969; Deadline, 1971; Advisory Service, 1971; Concrete Evidence, 1972; Double Hit, 1973; Crime Wave, 1974; Phantom Holiday, 1974; The Client, 1975; Murder by the Mile, 1975; Double Deal, 1976; Mr. T., 1977; Man Without a Name, 1977; Dial Death, 1977; Daylight Robbery, 1978; (with S.I. Pettersson) Labyrinten, 1978; A Dangerous Place to Dwell, 1978; Touchdown, 1979; Death Fuse, 1980; Catspaw, 1980; Backlash, 1981; Rainblast, 1982; All Part of the Service, 1982; The Search for Sara, 1983; A Domestic Affair, 1984; Censor, 1984; The Darker Side of Death, 1985; Prime Target, 1985; Unwelcome Audience, 1986; Dead Heat, 1986; The Second Time is Easy, 1987; House Arrest, 1988; Dummy Run, 1989; Mystery Lady, 1992; Leisure Pursuit, 1993. **Address:** 15 Breckonmead, Wanstead Rd., Bromley, KT BRI 3BW, England.

RUSSELL, Mary D(oria). American (born United States), b. 1950. **Genres:** Novels, Science Fiction/Fantasy, Theology/Religion, Mystery/Crime/Suspense. **Career:** Law Enforcement Agencies, forensic consultant, 1979-85; Case Western Reserve University, School of Dentistry, Department of Oral Biology, prosector and special lecturer, 1983, clinical instructor, 1984-86, Department of Anthropology, adjunct professor, 1986; North Coast Technical Writing, proprietor, 1986-92. Writer. **Publications:** NOVELS: The Sparrow, 1996; Children of God, 1998; Thread of Grace, 2005; Dreamers of the Day, 2008; Eight to Five, Against, 2011; Doc: A Novel, 2011. Contributor to periodicals. **Address:** Jane Dystel Literary Management, 1 Union Sq. W, New York, NY 10003, U.S.A. **Online address:** mdrussell@literati.net

RUSSELL, Norman H. *See* Obituaries.

RUSSELL, Paul. American (born United States), b. 1956. **Genres:** Novels, Gay And Lesbian Issues, Biography, Romance/Historical. **Career:** Vassar College, professor of English, 1983-. Writer. **Publications:** NOVELS: The Salt Point, 1990; Boys of Life, 1991; Sea of Tranquillity, 1994; The Coming Storm, 1999; War Against Animals, 2003; The Unreal Life of Sergey Nabokov, 2011. NONFICTION: The Gay 100: A Ranking of the Most Influential Gay Men and Lesbians, Past and Present, 1995. Contributor to magazines. **Address:** Vassar College, 124 Raymond Ave., PO Box 215, Poughkeepsie, NY 12604-0215, U.S.A. **Online address:** russell@vassar.edu

RUSSELL, Richard L. American (born United States), b. 1961. **Genres:** History, Young Adult Non-fiction. **Career:** National Defense University, Department of Defense, Near East-South Asia Center for Strategic Studies, professor of national security affairs; University of California, instructor; George Washington University, instructor; University of Virginia, instructor; Central Intelligence Agency (CIA), political-military analyst and security analyst; Georgetown University, Edmund A. Walsh School of Foreign Service, Institute for the Study of Diplomacy, adjunct associate professor and research associate. Writer. **Publications:** George F. Kennan's Strategic Thought: The Making of an American Political Realist, 1999; Weapons Proliferation and War in the Greater Middle East: Strategic Contest, 2005; Sharpening Strategic Intelligence: Why the CIA Gets It Wrong and What Needs to Be Done to Get It Right, 2007; Iran's Nuclear Program: Security Implications for The Uae and The Gulf Region, 2009. Contributor to books. **Address:** Near East South Asia Center for Strategic Studies, National Defense University, 2100 2nd St. SW, Ste. 4308, Washington, DC 20593, U.S.A. **Online address:** russellr@ndu.edu

RUSSELL, Rinaldina. American/Italian (born Italy), b. 1934?. **Genres:** Literary Criticism And History, Philosophy, Translations, Language/Linguistics. **Career:** Columbia University, instructor, 1967-68; Barnard College, instructor, 1968-71; City University of New York, Queens College, assistant professor, 1971-79, associate professor, 1979-85, professor of European languages and literatures, 1985-2003, now professor emeritus, Italian Program, coordinator, 1986-88, 1992-. Writer. **Publications:** Tre Versanti della Poesia Stilnovistica: Guinizzelli, Cavalcanti, Dante, 1973; Generi Poetici Medievali: Modelli e Funzioni Letterarie, 1982. EDITOR: (and contrib.) Italian Women Writers: A Bio-Bibliographical SourceBook, 1994; (trans. with B. Merry and intro.) T. d'Aragona, Dialogue on the Infinity of Love, 1997; (and contrib.) Feminist Encyclopedia of Italian Literature, 1997; (and trans.) Sister Maria Celeste's Letters to Her Father, Galileo, 2001; (and trans.) M. Sarrocchi, Scanderbeide: The Heroic Deeds of George Scanderbeg, King of Epirus,

2006. Contributor to periodicals. **Address:** Queens College, City University of New York, 6530 Kissena Blvd., New York, NY 10019-1142, U.S.A. **Online address:** rinaldina_russell@qc.edu

RUSSELL, Ronald. Scottish/British (born England), b. 1924. **Genres:** Archaeology/Antiquities, Area Studies, Art/Art History, Medicine/Health, Paranormal, Psychology, Travel/Exploration, Theology/Religion, Theology/Religion. **Career:** Monmouth School, Head of English, 1956-70; University of Cambridge, Local Examinations Syndicate, moderator and examiner, 1969-89; Soham Grammar School, head of English, 1971; City of Ely College, head of English, 1972-85, senior teacher, 1973-85, director of studies, 1973-. Writer. **Publications:** Lost Canals of England and Wales, 1971; Waterside Pubs, 1974; Discovering Lost Canals, 1975; (with J. Boyes) Canals of Eastern England, 1977; Rivers, 1978; Guide to British Topographical Prints, 1979; Lost Canals and Waterways of Britain, 1982; Discovering Antique Prints, 1982, rev. ed., 2001; Cambridgeshire and Cambridge, 1988; Swimming for Life, 1989; The Country Canal, 1991; The Vast Enquiring Soul, 2000; Journey of Robert Monroe: From Out-of-Body Explorer to Consciousness Pioneer, 2007. EDITOR: Walking Canals, 1984; Using the Whole Brain, 1993; Focusing the Whole Brain: Transforming Your Life with Hemispheric Synchronization, 2004. **Address:** Greenhead House, New Galloway, New Galloway, DG7 3RN, Scotland. **Online address:** rrussell@tiscali.co.uk

RUSSELL, Roy. British (born England), b. 1918. **Genres:** Plays/Screenplays, Documentaries/Reportage, Novels, Humor/Satire. **Career:** Midland Bank Ltd., Overseas Branch, bank officer, 1946-58; Wyndsor Recording Co., general manager, 1958-63; writer, 1963-. **Publications:** Return to Bedlam, A Comedy in Three Acts, 1947; Sawdust and Shuttlecocks, a Comedy in One Act, 1947; Rope Enough, a Play, 1949; A Family at War: Towards Victory (novel), 1972; Women on View: A Play, 1973. **Address:** Harvey Unna & Stephen Durbridge Ltd., 24 Pottery Ln., Holland Pk., London, GL W11 4LZ, England.

RUSSELL, Sharman Apt. American (born United States), b. 1954. **Genres:** Adult Non-fiction, Natural History, Sciences, Archaeology/Antiquities. **Career:** El Paso Times, stringer, 1981; Western New Mexico University, instructor in developmental writing, 1981-, Department of Humanities, professor; Antioch University, faculty in MFA writing program; Alimento para el Nino, founder and director; Upper Gila Watershed Association, president. Writer. **Publications:** (With S. Berry) Built to Last: An Architectural History of Silver City, New Mexico, 1986; Frederick Douglass, 1987; Songs of the Fluteplayer: Seasons of Life in the Southwest, 1991; Kill the Cowboy: A Battle of Mythology in the New West, 1993; The Humpbacked Fluteplayer, 1994; When the Land Was Young: Reflections on American Archaeology, 1996; The Last Matriarch, 2000; Anatomy of a Rose: The Secret Life of Flowers, 2001; Obsession with Butterflies: Our Long Love Affair with a Singular Insect, 2003; Hunger: An Unnatural History, 2005; Standing in the Light: My Life as a Pantheist, 2008. Contributor of essays and articles to periodicals. **Address:** Department of Humanities, Western New Mexico University, Light Hall 207, PO Box 680, Silver City, NM 88062, U.S.A. **Online address:** sharman@sharmanaptrussell.com

RUSSELL, Sharon A. American (born United States), b. 1941. **Genres:** Film, Literary Criticism And History, Communications/Media, Science Fiction/Fantasy. **Career:** Northwestern University, speaker, 1980-; Howard University, exchange speaker, 1994-; Indiana State University, professor of communication and women's studies, now retired. Writer. **Publications:** CONTRIBUTOR: The Mysteries of Africa, 1991; It's a Print, 1994; First in a Series, 1995; Planks of Reason, 1984. OTHERS: Semiotics and Lighting: A Study of Six Modern French Cameramen, 1981; Stephen King: A Critical Companion, 1996; Guide to African Cinema, 1998; Revisiting Stephen King: A Critical Companion, 2002. Contributor to books and periodicals. **Address:** Department of Communications, Indiana State University, 200 N 7th St., Erickson Hall, Terre Haute, IN 47809, U.S.A. **Online address:** cmrusse@ruby.indstate.edu

RUSSELL, Sheldon. American (born United States), b. 1942. **Genres:** History. **Career:** University of Central Oklahoma, professor emeritus, 2000-; University of Louisville. co-owner. Writer. **Publications:** Empire, 1993; The Savage Trail, 1998; Requiem at Dawn, 2000; Dreams to Dust: A Tale of the Oklahoma Land Rush, 2006; The Yard Dog, 2009. Contributor to periodicals. **Address:** Guthrie, OK , U.S.A. **Online address:** sheldon@sheldonrussell.com

RUSSELL, Willy. British (born England), b. 1947. **Genres:** Plays/Screenplays. **Career:** Manchester Polytechnic, fellow of creative writing, 1977-78; Liverpool Playhouse, associate director, 1981-83. **Publications:** PLAYS: Breezeblock Park, 1978; Break In, 1978; One for the Road, 1980, rev. ed., 1985; Educating Rita: A Comedy, 1980, rev. ed., 1986; I Read the News Today, 1982, 2nd ed., 1987; Stags and Hens: A Comedy, 1985; Blood Brothers, 1983, 2nd ed., 1996; Our Day Out: A Play, 1984; Stags and Hens: A Comedy, 1985; Shirley Valentine, 1986; Blood Brothers: Two Plays and Musical, 1986; Our Day Out and Other Plays, 1987; (intro.) Plays, 1996. OTHER AS WILLY RUSSELL: Sam O'Shankar: A Liverpool Tale, 1978; The Wrong Boy, 2000; Hoovering The Moon, 2003. **Address:** Casarotto Ramsay Ltd., National House, 60-66 Wardour St., London, GL W1V 3HP, England.

RUSSELL-BROWN, Katheryn. American (born United States), b. 1961. **Genres:** Criminology/True Crime. **Career:** Alabama State University, assistant professor, 1987-89; Howard University, instructor, 1991; University of Maryland, assistant professor, 1992-98, associate professor, 1998-2003, director of undergraduate studies, 1998-2002; University of Florida, Levin College of Law, Chesterfield Smith professor of law and director of center for study of race and race relations, 2003-. Writer and lawyer. **Publications:** The Color of Crime: Racial Hoaxes, White Fear, Black Protectionism, Police Harassment, and Other Macroaggressions, 1998, 2nd ed., 2009; (comp. with H.L. Pfeifer and J.L. Jones) Race and Crime: An Annotated Bibliography, 2000; (ed. with D. Milovanovic) Petit Apartheid in the U.S. Criminal Justice System, 2001; Underground Codes: Race, Crime, and Related Fires, 2004; Protecting Our Own: Race, Crime, and African Americans, 2006. **Address:** Levin College of Law, University of Florida, PO Box 117625, Gainesville, FL 32611-7620, U.S.A. **Online address:** russellbrownk@law.ufl.edu

RUSSELL TAYLOR, Elisabeth. British (born England), b. 1930. **Genres:** Novels, Novellas/Short Stories, Children's Fiction, Homes/Gardens, Travel/Exploration, Young Adult Fiction. **Career:** Assicurazion General, translator of legal documents, 1953-55; freelance journalist, 1957-; British Broadcasting Corp., journalist, broadcaster on domestic, sociological and social subjects, 1963-65; London University, lecturer in English and European fiction, 1981-89; The Times, journalist; The Observer, journalist; New Library World, journalist; Medical News, journalist; Amateur Gardening, journalist; Living, journalist; Queen, journalist; Library Association Record, journalist; Daily Telegraph, journalist; Sunday Times, journalist. **Publications:** CHILDREN'S FICTION: The Gifts of the Tarns, 1977; Tales from Barleymill, 1978; The Loadstone, 1978; Turkey in the Middle, 1983. OTHERS: Wish You Were Here (travel), 1976; London Lifelines, 1977; The Potted Garden, 1980; The Diabetic Cookbook, 1981; Marcel Proust and His Contexts: A Critical Bibliography of English Language Scholarship, 1981; (intro.) In a Summer Season, 2000; ADULT FICTION: Swann Song, 1988; Divide and Rule, 1989; Tomorrow, 1991; Mother Country, 1992; Pillion Riders, 1993; I Is Another, 1995; Present Fears, 1996; Will Dolores Come to Tea?, 2000. **Address:** c/o Margaret Hanbury, The Hanbury Agency, 28 Moreton St., London, GL SW1V 2PE, England.

RUSSETT, Bruce Martin. American (born United States), b. 1935. **Genres:** International Relations/Current Affairs, Military/Defense/Arms Control, Politics/Government. **Career:** Massachusetts Institute of Technology, instructor, 1961-62; Yale University, assistant professor, 1962-66, associate professor, 1966-68, professor, 1968-85, director of graduate studies in political science, 1970-72, International Relations, director of graduate studies, 1974-79, Dean Acheson professor of international relations and political science, 1985-, Department of Political Science, chair, 1990-96, United Nations Studies, director, 1993-2006; Columbia University, visiting professor, 1965; University of Michigan, visiting research political scientist, 1965-66; Universite Libre de Bruxelles, visiting professor, 1969-70; Journal of Conflict Resolution, editor, 1972-2009; University of North Carolina, visiting professor, 1979-80; Netherlands Institute for Advanced Study, fellow, 1984; Tel Aviv University, visiting professor of political science, 1989; University of Tokyo Law School, visiting professor, 1996; Harvard University, visiting professor of government, 2001; Richardson Institute, visiting professor; U.S. Department of Energy, consultant; United Nations Centre for Disarmament, consultant. **Publications:** The Economic Impact of German Rearmament, 1957; Community and Contention: Britain and America in the Twentieth Century, 1963; (contrib.) World Handbook of Political and Social Indicators, 1964; (with H. Alker) World Politics in the General Assembly, 1965; Trends in World Politics, 1965; The Asia Rimland as a Region for Containing China, 1966; Homogeneous Regions, 1966; (with C.C. Cooper) Major Proposals for Arms Control in Europe: A

Review, 1966; Arms Control in Europe: Proposals and Political Constraints, 1967; International Regions and the International System: A Study In Political Ecology, 1967; (with J.D. Singer and M. Small) National Political Units in the Twentieth Century: A Standardized List, 1968; What Price Vigilance? The Burdens of National Defense, 1970; No Clear and Present Danger, 1972; Power and Community in World Politics, 1974; (with E.C. Hanson) Interest and Ideology: The Foreign Beliefs Of American Businessmen, 1975; (intro. with B. Blair) Progress in Arms Control?, 1979; (with H. Starr and D. Kinsella) World Politics: The Menu of Choice, 1981, 9th ed., 2009; The Prisoners of Insecurity: Nuclear Deterrence, the Arms Race, and Arms Control, 1983; Controlling the Sword: The Democratic Governance of National Security, 1990; Grasping the Democratic Peace: Principles for a Post-Cold War World, 1993; (with J.R. Oneal) Triangulating Peace: Democracy, Interdependence, and International Organizations, 2001; Hegemony and Democracy, 2011. EDITOR: Economic Theories of International Politics, 1968; Peace, War, and Numbers, 1972; (with A. Stepan) Military Force and American Society, 1973; (with R. Merritt) From National Development to Global Community, 1981; (with F. Chernoff) Arms Control and the Arms Race: Readings From Scientific American, 1985; (with H. Starr and R. Stoll) Choices in World Politics, 1989; Esoteric Evidence on the Democracies Rarely Fight Each Other? Phenomenon, 1992; The Once and Future Security Council, 1997; (with F. Oakley) Governance, Accountability, and the Future of the Catholic Church, 2004; (with A. Mintz) New Directions for International Relations: Confronting the Method-of-Analysis Problem, 2004; Purpose and Policy in the Global Community, 2006; (ed.) International Security and Conflict, 2008. Contributor to journals. **Address:** Department of Political Science, Yale University, Rm. 101, Rosenkranz Hall, 115 Prospect St., PO Box 208301, New Haven, CT 06520-8301, U.S.A. **Online address:** bruce.russett@yale.edu

RUSSO, Elena. American/Italian (born Italy), b. 1958?. **Genres:** History, Politics/Government, Novels. **Career:** Princeton University, teaching assistant, 1982-87; Wellesley College, assistant professor, 1987-89; Yale University, assistant professor, 1989-94, associate professor, 1994-96; University of Virginia, associate professor, 1996-2000; Stanford University, visiting associate professor, 1999-2000; Johns Hopkins University, professor, 2000-. Writer. **Publications:** Incisori ferraresi nelle stampe del Museo Schifanoia dal XVII al XIX secolo, 1990; Maestri incisori del XVI secolo nelle stampe del Museo Schifanoia, 1993; (with S. Gesú) Le Madonie, cinema ad alte quote, 1995; Skeptical Selves: Empiricism and Modernity in the French Novel, 1996; (ed.) Exploring the Conversible World: Test and Sociability from the Classical Age to the Enlightenment, 1997; La cour et la ville de la littérature classique aux lumières: L'invention de soi, 2002; Styles of Enlightenment: Taste, Politics and Authorship in Eighteenth-Century France, 2007. Contributor of articles to periodicals and journals. **Address:** Department of German & Romance Languages & Lit, Johns Hopkins University, Gilman Hall 330, 3400 N Charles St., Baltimore, MD 21218-2608, U.S.A. **Online address:** erusso@jhu.edu

RUSSO, John (A.). American (born United States), b. 1939?. **Genres:** Novels, Film, Graphic Novels, Young Adult Non-fiction. **Career:** John Russo's Movie Academy, lead instructor. Writer, director and producer. **Publications:** Return of the Living Dead, 1978; The Majorettes, 1979; Midnight, 1980; Limb to Limb, 1981; Bloodsisters, 1982; Black Cat: A Novel of Terror, 1982; The Awakening, 1983; Day Care, 1985; The Complete Night of the Living Dead Filmbook, 1985; Inhuman, 1986; Scare Tactics: The Art, Craft, and Trade Secrets of Writing, Producing, and Directing Chillers and Thrillers, 1986; Voodoo Dawn, 1987; The Filmmaker's Guide to Producing Low Budget Independent Motion Pictures, 1987; Living Things, 1988; (with G. Romero) Day of the Dead, 1988; Making Movies: The Inside Guide to Independent Movie Production, 1989; How to Make and Market Your Own Feature Movie for $10000 or Less, 1994; Hell's Creation, 1995; (with D. Verma) Escape of the Living Dead, 2006; (with D. Verma) Escape Of The Living Dead: Resurrected, 2008; (co-author) Holiday of the Dead, 2011. **Address:** Barclay House Books, 35-19 215 Pl., Bayside, NY 11361-1725, U.S.A.

RUSSO, Marisabina. American (born United States), b. 1950. **Genres:** Children's Fiction, Picture/Board Books, Illustrations, Novels, Young Adult Fiction. **Career:** Writer. **Publications:** The Line up Book, 1986; Why Do Grown-ups Have All the Fun?, 1987; The Big Fat Worm, 1987; Only Six More Days, 1988; Waiting for Hannah, 1989; Where Is Ben?, 1990; A Visit to Oma, 1991; Alex Is My Friend, 1992; Trade-in-Mother, 1993; Time to Wake Up, 1994; I Don't Want to Go Back to School, 1994; Grandpa Abe, 1996; Under the Table, 1997; When Mama Gets Home, 1998; Hannah's Baby Sister, 1998; Mama Talks too Much, 1999; The Big Brown Box, 2000; Come

Back, Hannah!, 2001; House of Sports, 2002; The Trouble with Baby, 2003; Always Remember Me: How One Family Survived World War II, 2005; The Bunnies are Not in Their Beds, 2007; A Portrait of Pia, 2007; Very Big Bunny, 2010; I Will Come Back for You: A Family in Hiding During World War II, 2011. SELF-ILLUSTRATED: Peter is just a Baby, 2012. Illustrator of books by others. **Address:** Greenwillow Books, HarperCollins Publishers Inc., 10 E 53rd St., New York, NY 10022, U.S.A. **Online address:** marisabinarusso@marisabinarusso.com

RUSSO, Thomas A. American (born United States), b. 1932. **Genres:** Antiques/Furnishings, History, Crafts, Reference. **Career:** Delaware Office Equipment Company Inc., founder and president, 1976-; Remington Rand, Kansas City, typewriter salesman; Remington Rand, Philadelphia, branch manager. Writer. **Publications:** Office Collectibles: 100 Years of Business Technology, 2000; Antique Office Machines: 600 Years of Calculating Devices, 2001; Mechanical Typewriters: Their History, Value, and Legacy, 2002. **Address:** Delaware Office Equipment Company Inc., 1200 Philadelphia Pike, Ste. 1, Wilmington, DE 19809, U.S.A.

RUST, Elissa Minor. American (born United States), b. 1977?. **Genres:** Young Adult Fiction, Humanities. **Career:** Portland Community College, faculty. Writer. **Publications:** The Prisoner Pear: Stories from the Lake, 2005. Contributor to periodicals. **Address:** Brickhouse Literary Agency, 80 5th Ave., Ste. 1101, New York, NY 10011, U.S.A.

RUST, Graham (Redgrave). British (born England), b. 1942. **Genres:** Art/Art History, Design, Architecture. **Career:** Time Inc., Architectural Forum, assistant to art director, 1962-63; Woodberry Forest School, artist-in-residence, 1967-68. **Publications:** The Painted House, 1988; Decorative Designs: Over 100 ideas for Painted Interiors, Furniture, and Decorated Objects, 1996; Needlepoint Designs, 1998; The Painted Ceiling: Over 100 Original Designs and Details, 2001; Revisiting the Painted House: More than 100 New Designs for Mural and Trompe l'oeil Decoration, 2005. Illustrator of books. **Address:** Old Rectory, Somerton, Bury St. Edmunds, SU IP29 4ND, England.

RUST, H. Lee. American (born United States), b. 1940. **Genres:** Business/Trade/Industry, Money/Finance. **Career:** Corporate finance consultant, 1978-; Florida Corporate Finance, owner. Writer. **Publications:** Jobsearch: The Complete Manual for Jobseekers, 1979, rev. ed., 1991; Let's Buy a Company: How to Accelerate Growth through Acquisitions, 2006. **Address:** Florida Corporate Finance, 1509 Oak Tree Ct., Apopka, FL 32712, U.S.A. **Online address:** author@letsbuyacompany.com

RUSTICI, Craig M. (Craig Michael Rustici). American (born United States), b. 1964. **Genres:** History. **Career:** Lafayette College, visiting instructor, 1991-92; Hofstra University, Department of English, assistant professor, 1992-98, associate professor of English, 1998-, director of writing center, 1998-2005, Distinguished Faculty Lecturer, 2001; University of Chicago, Norman Maclean Lector, 2000; New York State Speaker in the Humanities, 2003-05. Writer. **Publications:** The Afterlife of Pope Joan: Deploying the Popess Legend in Early Modern England, 2006. Contributor to books, periodicals and journals. **Address:** Department of English, Hofstra University, 209 Calkins Hall, Hempstead, NY 11549, U.S.A. **Online address:** craig.m.rustici@hofstra.edu

RUSTICI, Craig Michael. See RUSTICI, Craig M.

RUSTON, Sharon. British (born England), b. 1972. **Genres:** Medicine/Health. **Career:** University of Wales, lecturer of English literature; Keele University, senior lecturer of English, director of the media, communications and culture program. Writer and educator. **Publications:** The Influence and Anxiety of the British Romantics: Spectres of Romanticism, 1999; Shelley and Vitality, 2005; Romanticism, 2007. Contributor of articles to periodicals. **Address:** Keele University, Keele, ST ST5 5BG, England. **Online address:** s.ruston@engl.keele.ac.uk

RUTAN, J. Scott. American (born United States), b. 1940. **Genres:** Psychiatry, Psychology, Medicine/Health, Social Sciences. **Career:** Harvard Medical School, associate professor of clinical psychiatry, 1973-; Boston Institute for Psychotherapy, co-founder, executive director and senior faculty; Massachusetts General Hospital, staff psychologist, Center for Group Psychotherapy, founder. Writer. **Publications:** (With W.N. Stone) Psychodynamic Group Psychotherapy, 1984, (with W.N. Stone and J.J. Shay) 4th ed., 2007; (ed.)

Psychotherapy for the 1990s, 1992. **Address:** Massachusetts General Hospital, WACC 8, 15 Parkman St., Boston, MA 02114-3117, U.S.A.

RUTGERS, Leonard Victor. Dutch (born Netherlands), b. 1964. **Genres:** History. **Career:** Royal Dutch Academy of Arts and Sciences, research fellow, 1993-98; Roman Jewish Catacombs Project, director; Sepphoris Regional Project, staff; University of Utrecht, faculty of theology 1998-2003, Department of History and Art History, professor, chair in late antiquity 2003-. Writer. **Publications:** The Jews in Late Ancient Rome: Evidence of Cultural Interaction in the Roman Diaspora, 1995; The Hidden Heritage of Diaspora Judaism, 1998; Subterranean Rome: In Search of the Roots of Christianity in the Catacombs of the Eternal City, 2000, trans. as Onderaards Rome: een speurtocht naar de wortels van het Christendom in de catacomben van de Eeuwige Stad, 2000; (ed.) What Athens Has to Do with Jerusalem: Essays on Classical, Jewish, and Early Christian Art and Archaeology in Honor of Gideon Foerster, 2002; Making Myths: Jews in Early Christian Identity Formation, 2009. **Address:** Department of History and Art History, University of Utrecht, Drift 10, Utrecht, 3512 BS, Netherlands. **Online address:** l.v.rutgers@uu.nl

RUTHCHILD, Rochelle Goldberg. (Sarah Matilsky). American (born United States), b. 1940. **Genres:** History, Bibliography, Women's Studies And Issues, Gay And Lesbian Issues. **Career:** Goddard College, Goddard-Cambridge Graduate Program in Social Change, faculty, 1974-78, core faculty for graduate program, 1979-81; Harvard University, Union Institute and University, Davis Center for Russian and Eurasian Studies, center associate, 1979-, Harvard Summer School, program director and faculty, Vermont College, professor of graduate studies, 2001-07, professor emeritus of graduate studies, 2007-; Norwich University, assistant professor, associate professor, 1981-87, professor of graduate studies, 1988-2001, Russian School, director, 1988-95. Writer. **Publications:** (Ed. as Sarah Matilsky) Women and Russia: Feminist Writings from the Soviet Union, 1984; Women in Russia and the Soviet Union: An Annotated Bibliography, 1994; Equality and Revolution: Women's Rights in the Russian Empire, 1905-1917, 2010. FORTHCOMING: A History of the Cambridge Women's Center; Family History and Memoir. **Address:** Davis Center for Russian and Eurasian Studies, Harvard University, 1730 Cambridge St., Cambridge, MA 02138-4317, U.S.A. **Online address:** ruthchil@yahoo.com

RUTHERDALE, Robert. Canadian (born Canada), b. 1956?. **Genres:** Military/Defense/Arms Control, History, Social Sciences. **Career:** Trent University, instructor; Memorial University of Newfoundland, instructor; University of Northern British Columbia, instructor; University of British Columbia, instructor; Algoma University, associate professor of history, Division of Humanities, chair. Writer and historian. **Publications:** Hometown Horizons: Local Responses to Canada's Great War, 2004; (ed. with M. Fahrni) Creating Postwar Canada: Community, Diversity, and Dissent, 1945-75, 2008. Contributor to books and journals. **Address:** Department of History and Philosophy, Algoma University, Rm. 406, Shingwauk Hall, 1520 Queen St. E, Sault Ste. Marie, ON P6A 2G4, Canada. **Online address:** rutherdale@algomau.ca

RUTHERFURD, Edward. (Francis Edward Wintle). British (born England), b. 1948?. **Genres:** Novels, Romance/Historical. **Career:** Writer. **Publications:** HISTORICAL NOVELS: Sarum: The Novel of England, 1987; Russka: The Novel of Russia, 1991; London, 1996; The Forest, 2000; Dublin: Foundation, 2001 in US as The Princes of Ireland, 2004; Ireland: Awakening in US as The Rebels of Ireland: The Dublin Saga, 2006; New York, 2009. **Address:** c/o Gill Coleridge, Rogers, Coleridge & White Ltd., 20 Powis Mews, London, GL W11 1JN, England.

RUTKOSKI, Marie. American (born United States), b. 1977. **Genres:** Children's Fiction. **Career:** Harvard University, lecturer, 2006-; Brooklyn College, assistant professor of English. Writer. **Publications:** KRONOS CHRONICLES: The Cabinet of Wonders, 2008; The Celestial Globe, 2009. **Address:** Brooklyn College, 2157 Boylan Hall, 900 Bedford Ave., Brooklyn, NY 11210, U.S.A. **Online address:** marie@marierutkoski.com

RUTLAND, Suzanne D. Australian (born Australia), b. 1946. **Genres:** Theology/Religion, History. **Career:** B'nei Akiva Youth Movement, leader, 1965-67; high school teacher, 1970-74, 1976-78; University of Sydney, Department of Hebrew, Biblical and Jewish Studies, lecturer in Jewish education, 1990-96, senior lecturer in Jewish civilization, 1997-2004, chair, 1999-, associate professor, 2004-, professor; Association for Jewish Studies Journal, Sydney editor, 1991-; Jewish Educators' Network, honorary secretary, 1995-97; Australian Association for Jewish Studies, editor, 1995-97, 1999-2001; Joint Authority for Jewish/Zionist Education in the Diaspora, National Advisory Council for Australia, co-chair, 1995-98; International School for Holocaust Studies, Australian academic representative to seminar for educators from abroad, 1998-; Shalom Institute, Melton Adult Education Program, academic chair, 2001, 2002-07. **Publications:** Seventy Five Years: The History of a Jewish Newspaper, 1970; (contrib.) New South Wales Jewish Community, 2nd ed., 1978; Edge of the Diaspora: Two Centuries of Jewish Settlements in Australia, 1988, rev. ed., 2001; Pages of History: A Century of the Australian Jewish Press, 1995; (with S. Caplan) With One Voice: A History of the New South Wales Jewish Board of Deputies, 1998; Jewish Life Down Under: The Flowering of Australian Jewry, 2001; If You Will It, It Is No Dream: The Moriah Story 1943-2003, 2003; The Jews in Australia, 2005; Triumph of the Jewish Spirit: 40 Years of the Jewish Communal Appeal, 2007; (with S. Rood) Nationality Stateless: Destination Australia, 2008. **Address:** Department of Hebrew, Biblical and Jewish Studies, University of Sydney, Rm. 618, A18 Brennan-MacCallum Bldg., Sydney, NW 2006, Australia. **Online address:** suzanne.rutland@sydney.edu.au

RUTLEDGE, Ian. British (born England) **Genres:** History. **Career:** University of Sheffield, teacher of energy economics, 1985-2003; University of London, Department of Economics and Sociology, faculty; British Coal Corp., staff; Sheffield Energy & Resources Information Services (an energy economics consultancy and publishing business), partner, 1989-. Writer. **Publications:** (ed. with K. Duncan) Land and Labour in Latin America: Essays on the Development of Agrarian Capitalism in the Nineteenth and Twentieth Centuries, 1977; Cambio agrario e integraciOn: el desarrollo del capitalismo en jujuy, 1550- 1960, 1987; Addicted to Oil: America's Relentless Drive for Energy Security, 2005. Contributor of articles to journals. **Online address:** idr@seris.co.uk

RUTLEDGE, Leigh W. American (born United States), b. 1957. **Genres:** Humor/Satire, Essays, Gay And Lesbian Issues, Novels, Poetry, History, Animals/Pets, Young Adult Fiction, Young Adult Fiction. **Career:** Writer, 1976-. **Publications:** The Gay Book of Lists, 1987, 3rd ed., 2003; (comp.) Unnatural Quotations: A Compendium of Quotations By, For or About Gay People, 1988; The Gay Fireside Companion, 1989; The Gay Decades: From Stonewall to the Present: The People and Events that Shaped Gay Lives, 1992; (comp.) Excuses, Excuses: A Compendium of Rationalizations, Alibis, Denials, Extenuating Circumstances and Outright Lies (humor), 1992; (with R.E. Donley) The Left-Hander's Guide to Life, 1992; A Cat's Little Instruction Book (humor), 1993; It Seemed Like a Good Idea at the Time: A Book of Brilliant Ideas We Wish We'd Never Had (humor), 1994; Cat Love Letters: Collected Correspondence of Cats in Love (novella), 1994; Dear Tabby (humor), 1995; Diary of a Cat: True Confessions and Lifelong Observations of a Well-Adjusted House Cat (novel), 1995; When My Grandmother Was a Child (history), 1996; The New Gay Book of Lists, 1996; If People Were Cats (poems), 1997; Would I Lie to You?: A Medley of Famous Fibs, Devious Deceptions and Barefaced Lies, 1998; (comp.) Nice Girls Don't Wear Cha-Cha Heels! (humor), 1999; The Lighthouse, the Cat and the Sea: A Tropical Tale (novel), 1999; The Left-Hander's Book of Days, 1999; (ed. with G.P. Hancock) Too Much of a Good Thing: Quotes You Can't Get Enough Of, 2000; Gay Friends, 2001; The Left Hander's Guide to Life: A Witty and Informative Tour of the World According to Southpaws, 2002; Celebrated Left-Handers, 2003. Works appear in anthologies. Contributor of articles to periodicals. **Address:** c/o Jennifer Walsh, Virginia Barber Literary Agency, 101 5th Ave., 11th Fl., New York, NY 10003, U.S.A.

RUTSALA, Vern A. American (born United States), b. 1934. **Genres:** Poetry, Novels. **Career:** Hubbub, editor, 1985; Lewis & Clark College, staff, 1961-, professor of English, through 2004, professor emeritus of English, 2004-; University of Minnesota, visiting professor, 1968-69; Bowling Green State University, visiting professor, 1970; Redlands University, writer-in-residence, 1979; University of Idaho, visiting professor, 1988. **Publications:** The Window: Poems, 1964; Small Songs: A Sequence of Poems, 1969; The Harmful State, 1971; (ed.) British Poetry 1972, 1972; Laments, 1975; The Journey Begins, 1976; Paragraphs, 1978; The New Life, 1978; Walking Home from the Icehouse, 1981; The Mystery of Lost Shoes, 1984; Backtracking, 1985; Ruined Cities, 1987; Selected Poems, 1991; Little-Known Sports, 1994; Vern Rutsala: Greates Hits: 1964-2002, 2002; The Moment's Equation, 2004; A Handbook for Writers: New and Selected Prose Poems, 2004; How We Spent

Our Time, 2006. Works appears in anthologies. Contributor to periodicals. **Address:** Department of English, Lewis & Clark College, 0615 SW Palatine Hill Rd., MSC 58, Portland, OR 97219, U.S.A.

RUTTER, Jeremy B. (Jeremy Bentham Rutter). American (born United States), b. 1946. **Genres:** Archaeology/Antiquities, Art/Art History, Classics, History. **Career:** University of California, Department of Classics, visiting assistant professor, 1975-76; Dartmouth College, Department of Classics, assistant professor, 1976-81, associate professor, 1981-87, professor, 1987-, chairman, 1992-98, 2003-06, Sherman Fairchild professor of the humanities, 2001-; History Book Club, reader, 1987-. **Publications:** (With S.H. Rutter) The Transition to Mycenaean: A Stratified Middle Helladic II to Late Helladic IIA Pottery Wequence from Ayios Stephanos in Lakonia, 1976; Ceramic Change in the Aegean Early Bronze Age: The Kastri group, Lefkandi I and Lerna IV: A Theory Concerning the Origin of Early Helladic III Ceramics, 1979; The Pottery of Lerna IV, 1995; (ed. with A. Cohen) Constructions of Childhood in Ancient Greece and Italy, 2007. **Address:** Department of Classics, Dartmouth College, 310 Reed Hall, Hanover, NH 03755, U.S.A. **Online address:** jeremy.b.rutter@dartmouth.edu

RUTTER, Jeremy Bentham. *See* **RUTTER, Jeremy B.**

RUTTER, Michael (Llewellyn). British/Lebanese (born Lebanon), b. 1933. **Genres:** Psychiatry, Psychology, Medicine/Health, Education, Sports/Fitness. **Career:** Bethlem Royal and Maudsley Hospital, registrar, 1958-61, senior registrar, 1961, Medical Research Council Social Psychiatry Research Unit, scientific staff, 1962-65, honorary consultant child psychiatrist, 1966-; University of London, King's College London, Institute of Psychiatry, Social, Genetic and Developmental Psychiatry Centre (MRC), senior lecturer, 1965-68, reader, 1968-73, professor of child psychiatry, 1973-, professor of developmental psychopathology, 1998-, Department of Child and Adolescent Psychiatry, head; Center for Advanced Study in the Behavioral Sciences, fellow, 1979-80; Medical Research Council, Child Psychiatry Unit, honorary director, 1984-98; Social, Genetic and Developmental Psychiatry Research Center, honorary director, 1994-98. Writer. **Publications:** Children of Sick Parents: An Environmental and Psychiatric Study, 1966; (with P. Graham and W. Yule) A Neuropsychiatric Study in Childhood, 1970; Maternal Deprivation Reassessed, 1972, 2nd ed., 1981; The Qualities of Mothering: Maternal Deprivation Reassessed, 1974; (with D. Shaffer and M. Shepherd) A Multi-Axial Classification of Child Psychiatric Disorders, 1975; Helping Troubled Children, 1975; (with N. Madge) Cycles of Disadvantage: A Review of Research, 1976; (with B. Maughan and P. Mortimer) Fifteen Thousand Hours: Secondary Schools and Their Effects on Children, 1979; Changing Youth in a Changing Society: Patterns of Adolescent Development and Disorder, 1980; Scientific Foundations of Developmental Psychiatry, 1980; A Measure of Our Values: Goals and Dilemmas in the Upbringing of Children, 1983; (with H. Giller) Juvenile Delinquency: Trends and Perspectives, 1984; (with P. Howlin) Treatment of Autistic Children, 1987; (with W. Yule) Language Development and Disorders, 1987; (with D. Quinton) Parenting Breakdown: The Making and Breaking of Inter-generational Links, 1988; (with M. Rutter) Developing Minds: Challenge and Continuity across the Lifespan, 1993; (with H. Giller and A. Hagell) Antisocial Behavior by Young People, 1998; Genes and Behavior: Nature-Nurture Interplay Explained, 2006. EDITOR: (with J. Tizard and K. Whitmore) Education, Health, and Behaviour, 1970; (with J. Tizard and K. Whitmore) Education, Health, and Behaviour; Psychological and Medical Study of Childhood Development, 1970; Infantile Autism: Concepts, Characteristics, and Treatment, 1971; (with J.A.M. Martin) The Child with Delayed Speech, 1972; (with L.A. Hersov) Child Psychiatry: Modern Approaches, 1976, 2nd ed. as Child and Adolescent Psychiatry: Modern Approaches, 1985, (with E. Taylor) 4th ed., 2002; (with E. Schopler) Autism: A Reappraisal of Concepts and Treatment, 1978; Scientific Foundation of Developmental Psychiatry, 1980; (with N. Garmezy) Stress, Coping, and Development in Children, 1983; Developmental Neuropsychiatry, 1983; (with R.R. Jones) Lead versus Health: Sources and Effects of Low Level Lead Exposure, 1983; (with C. Izard and P. Read) Depression in Young People: Developmental and Clinical Perspectives, 1986; Developmental Psychiatry, 1987; (with A.H. Tuma and I.S. Lann) Assessment and Diagnosis in Child Psychopathology, 1988; Studies of Psychosocial Risk: The Power of Longitudinal Data, 1988; (with L. Robins) Straight and Devious Pathways from Childhood to Adulthood, 1990; (with P. Casaer) Biological Risk Factors for Psychosocial Disorders, 1991; (with D.F. Hay) Development through Life: A Handbook for Clinicians, 1994; (with R. Haggerty, L. Sherrod and N. Garmezy) Stress, Risk, and Resilience in Children and Adolescents: Processes,

Mechanisms, and Interventions, 1994; Psychosocial Disturbances in Young People: Challenges for Prevention, 1995; (with D. Smith) Psychosocial Disorders in Young People: Time Trends and Their Causes, 1995; (with M. Tienda) Ethnicity and Causal Mechanisms, 2005; (co-ed.) Rutter's Child and Adolescent Psychiatry, 2008; (with K.A. Dodge) Gene-environment Interactions in Developmental Psychopathology, 2011. **Address:** Social, Genetic & Developmental Psychiatry Center, Institute of Psychiatry, King's College London, De Crespigny Pk., PO Box 80, London, GL SE5 8AF, England. **Online address:** j.wickham@iop.kcl.ac.uk

RUTTER, Virginia Beane. American (born United States) **Genres:** Psychology, Human Relations/Parenting, Women's Studies And Issues. **Career:** C.G. Jung Institute, psychotherapist and Jungian analyst. Educator and writer. **Publications:** Woman Changing Woman: Feminine Psychology Re-conceived through Myth and Experience, 1993; Celebrating Girls: Nurturing and Empowering Our Daughters, 1996; (foreword) 200 Ways to Raise a Girl's Self-Esteem: An Indespensable Guide for Parents, Teachers & Other Concerned Caregivers, 1999; Embracing Persephone: How to Be the Mother You Want For the Daughter You Cherish, 2000; (ed. with T. Krisch and T. Singer) Initiation: The Living Reality of an Archetype, 2007. **Address:** The C.G. Jung Institute of San Francisco, 205 Camino Alto Ct., Ste. 240, Mill Valley, CA 94941, U.S.A.

RUURS, Margriet. Canadian/Dutch (born Netherlands), b. 1952. **Genres:** Children's Fiction, Adult Non-fiction, Children's Non-fiction. **Career:** Between the Covers, Bed & Breakfast, owner; Kidswwwrite, editor. **Publications:** Apenkinderen, 1982; (trans.) J. Viorst, Alexander and the Terrible, Horrible, No Good, Very Bad Day, 1985; Fireweed, 1986; The R.C.M.P, 1992; Big Little Dog, 1992; On The Write Track, 1993; Spectacular Spiders, 1993; A Mountain Alphabet, 1996; Emma and the Coyote, 1999; Emma's Eggs, 1999; The Power of Poems: Teaching the Joy of Writing Poetry, 2000; Emma's Cold Day, 2001; Virtual Maniac: Silly and Serious Poems for Kids, 2001; Logan's Lake, 2001; When We Go Camping, 2001; A Pacific Alphabet, 2001; Wild Babies, 2003; Ms. Bee's Magical Bookcase, 2004; Animal Alphabed, 2005; My Librarian is a Camel: How Books are bought to Children around the World, 2005; No Dogs Allowed, 2005; Me and Martha Black, 2005; Wake Up, Henry Rooster!, 2006; Emma at the Fair, 2007; In My Backyard, 2007; My School in the Rain Forest: How Children Attend School Around the World, 2009; Amazing Animals, 2011; Power of Poems: Writing Activities that Teach and Inspire, 2011. **Address:** Maupin House Publishing Inc., 2416 NW 71st Pl., Gainesville, FL 32653, U.S.A. **Online address:** margriet@margrietruurs.com

RUYSLINCK, Ward. Belgian (born Belgium), b. 1929. **Genres:** Novels, Biography. **Career:** Royal Academies for Science and the Arts of Belgium, president, 1985. Writer. **Publications:** Fanaal in de mist; het epos van een paria, 1956; De ontaarde slapers (novel), 1957, trans. as The Deadbeats, 1968 as The Depraved Sleepers, 1978; Wierook en tranen (novel), 1958; De madonna met de buil, 1959; Hat dal van Hinnom (novel), 1961; De stille zomer, 1962; Het reservaat (novel), 1964; De Paardevleeseters (stories and radio play), 1965; Oeroude vijver, 1966; Golden Ophelia (novel), 1966, trans. as Golden Ophelia, 1975; Het reservaat (novel), 1967, trans. as The Reservation, 1978; Het ledikant van Lady Cant, 1968; De Karakoliers, 1969; De Apokatastasis of het Apocriefe boek van Galax Niksen, 1970; Neozoisch, Parapoetische montages, 1971; De heksenkring, 1972; Uitspraken in opspraak, 1972; De verliefde akela, 1973; Het ganzenbord, 1974; In naam van de beesten (nonfiction), 1976; De sloper in het slakkehuis, 1977; Valentijn van Uytvanck: tekenaar zonder vaderland (nonfiction), 1977; Depraved Sleepers and Golden Ophelia, 1978; Reservation: A Novel, 1978; Op toernee met Leopold Sondag, 1978; Alle verhalen, 1979; Wurgtechnieken, 1980; De boze droom het medeleven, 1982; Leegstaande huizen: Verhalen, 1983; Open beeldboek (nonfiction): verzamelde opstellen over plastische kunsten, 1983; De uilen van Minerva, 1985; Stille waters, 1987; IJlings naar nergens: ontboezemingen aan een boezemvriend, 1989; Profiel, Ward Ruyslinck (biography), 1992; (with M. Lo Cascio) Speeltuin, 1992; De claim van de duivel: Roman, 1993; Geboortehuis, 1995; Bovenste trede, 1997; Traumachia: Roman, 1999. Contributor to periodicals. **Address:** Standaard Uitgevery NV, Belgielei 147A, Antwerp, B-2018, Belgium. **Online address:** monika.macken@yucom.be

RYAN, Barbara. Singaporean (born Singapore), b. 1958?. **Genres:** Literary Criticism And History, History. **Career:** University of Missouri, Department of English and Black Studies, assistant professor; National University of Singapore, Scholars Program, assistant professor. Writer. **Publications:** (Ed. with A.M. Thomas) Reading Acts: U.S. Readers' Interactions with Literature,

1800-1950, 2002; Love, Wages, Slavery: The Literature of Servitude in the United States, 2006. Contributor to journals. **Address:** University Scholars Programme, National University of Singapore, 02-04 Lobe, Cinnamon S Learn, 18 College Avenue E, Singapore, 138593, Singapore. **Online address:** usprbt@nus.edu.sg

RYAN, Craig. American (born United States), b. 1953. **Genres:** Air/Space Topics, History, Travel/Exploration. **Career:** Portland State University, adjunct professor; Sequent Computer Systems, software engineering manager. Writer. **Publications:** The Pre-Astronauts: Manned Ballooning on the Threshold of Space (history), 1995; Magnificent Failure: Free Fall from the Edge of Space (biography), 2003; What We did to Weinstein, 2005; Happy Savages, 2008; (with J. Kittinger) Come Up and Get Me: An Autobiography of Colonel Joe Kittinger, 2010. TRAVEL BOOKS: (contrb.) Beautiful New Mexico, 1979; (contrib.) Beautiful New York, 1979; (contrib.) Beauty of New York, 1989. **Address:** c/o Albert Zuckerman, Writers House, 21 W 26th St., New York, NY 10010-1003, U.S.A. **Online address:** ryan@sequent.com

RYAN, Donald P. American (born United States), b. 1957?. **Genres:** Travel/ Exploration, History, Archaeology/Antiquities. **Career:** Kon-Tiki Museum, research associate; Valley of the Kings Preservation Project, director, 1993; Pyramides de Guimar Excavations, field director, 1997-2000; Digital Epigraphy Project, director, 2004; Pacific Lutheran University, Valley of the Kings Project, director, 1989-91, 2005-, faculty fellow. Writer. **Publications:** The Complete Idiot's Guide to Biblical Mysteries, 2000; The Complete Idiot's Guide to Ancient Egypt, 2002; The Complete Idiot's Guide to the World of the Bible, 2003; The Everything Family Guide to Hawaii, 2004; (ed.) A Shattered Visage Lies': Nineteenth Century Poetry Inspired by Ancient Egypt, 2007; Egypt 1250 BC: A Traveler's Companion, 2010; Beneath the Sands of Egypt: Adventures of an Unconventional Archaeologist, 2010. Contributor to books and periodicals. **Address:** Division of Humanities, Pacific Lutheran University, Tacoma, WA 98447, U.S.A. **Online address:** ryandp@plu.edu

RYAN, Frank. British/Irish (born Ireland), b. 1944. **Genres:** Novels, Science Fiction/Fantasy, Medicine/Health, Biology, History, Philosophy, Sciences, Mathematics/Statistics. **Career:** Northern General Hospital, Department of Gastroenterology, director, emeritus consultant physician, Nutrition Institute, consultant advisor and lecturer; Sheffield Health Authority/PCT, medical advisor, 1992-; Sheffield University, Department of Animal and Plant Sciences, honorary research fellow, 2007-; Royal College of Physicians, fellow, 1985; Royal Society of Medicine, sectional editor. **Publications:** NOVELS: Sweet Summer, 1987; Tiger, Tiger, 1989; Goodbye Baby Blue, 1990; The Sundered World, 1999; Taking Care of Harry, 2001; The Doomsday Genie, 2007. NONFICTION: The Eskimo Diet, 1990; Tuberculosis: The Greatest Story Never Told: The Search for the Cure and the New Global Threat, 1992; The Forgotten Plague: How the Battle against Tuberculosis was Won and Lost, 1993; Virus X: Tracking the New Killer Plagues, 1997; (ed.) Darwin's Impact: The Social Evolution in America, 1880-1920, 2001; (ed.) Darwinism and Theology in America, 1850-1930, 2002; Darwin's Blind Spot: Evolution beyond Natural Selection, 2002; The Brain Food Diet, 2007; Virolution, 2009; Mystery of Metamorphosis: A Scientific Detective Story, 2011. **Address:** FPR-Books Ltd., PO Box 1436, Sheffield, SY S17 3XP, England. **Online address:** frankryan@fprbooks.com

RYAN, Gig (Elizabeth). Australian (born Australia), b. 1956. **Genres:** Poetry, Songs/Lyrics And Libretti. **Career:** The Age, poetry editor, 1998-. Musician. **Publications:** POETRY: The Division of Anger: Poems, 1980; Manners of an Astronaut, 1984; The Last Interior, 1986; Excavation, 1990; Research, 1998; Pure and Applied, 1998; Heroic Money, 2001. OTHER: New and Selected Poems, 2011. **Address:** The Age, 655 Collins St., PO Box 257, Melbourne, VI 3008, Australia.

RYAN, Halford (Ross). American (born United States), b. 1943. **Genres:** Communications/Media, History, Education. **Career:** Washington and Lee University, instructor, faculty, 1970-, professor of English and speech, 1984-2010, retired, 2010. Writer. **Publications:** Persuasive Advocacy: Cases for Argumentation and Debate, 1985; Franklin D. Roosevelt's Rhetorical Presidency, 1988; Harry Emerson Fosdick: Persuasive Preacher, 1989; Henry Ward Beecher: Peripatetic Preacher, 1990; Classical Communication for the Contemporary Communicator, 1992; Harry S. Truman: Presidential Rhetoric, 1992; The Inaugural Addresses of Twentieth-Century American Presidents, 1993; U.S. Presidents as Orators, 1995. EDITOR: (ed.) American Rhetoric from Roosevelt to Reagan, 1983, 3rd ed. as Contemporary American Public

Discourse, 1992; (with B.K. Duffy) American Orators before 1900: Critical Studies and Sources, 1987; (with B.K. Duffy) American Orators of the Twentieth Century: Critical Studies and Sources, 1987; Oratorical Encounters: Selected Studies and Sources on Twentieth-Century Political Accusations and Apologies, 1988. Contributor to periodicals. **Address:** 16 Grey Dove Rd., Lexington, VA 24450, U.S.A. **Online address:** ryanh@wlu.edu

RYAN, James G(ilbert). American (born United States), b. 1947. **Genres:** History, Biography. **Career:** Drexel University, adjunct assistant professor, 1982-85, visiting assistant professor of history and politics, 1985; Temple University, adjunct assistant professor of political science, 1985-87; Muhlenberg College, visiting assistant professor of political science, 1987-90; Texas A&M University, assistant professor, 1990-96, associate professor of history, 1996-2004, professor, 2004-; Russian Center for the Preservation and Study of Documents of Recent History, researcher, 1993. Writer. **Publications:** Earl Browder: The Failure of American Communism, 1997, 2nd ed., 2005; (ed. with L. Schlup) Historical Dictionary of the Gilded Age, 2003; (ed. with L. Schlup) Historical Dictionary of the 1940s, 2006. Contributor of articles to journals. **Address:** Department of General Academics, Texas A&M University, CLB 123A, Mitchell Campus, Galveston, TX 77551, U.S.A. **Online address:** ryanj@tamug.edu

RYAN, Kate Moira. See MOIRA, Kate.

RYAN, Kay. American (born United States), b. 1945. **Genres:** Poetry. **Career:** Library of Congress, 16th poet laureate consultant in poetry, 2008-10; College of Marin in Kentfield, part-time remedial English teacher. Writer. **Publications:** Dragon Acts to Dragon Ends, 1983; Strangely Marked Metal: Poems, 1985; Flamingo Watching: Poems, 1994; Elephant Rocks, 1996; Say Uncle: Poems, 2000; Believe It or Not!, 2002; The Niagara River: Poems, 2005; Best of It: New and Selected Poems, 2010. Contributor to books. Works appear in anthologies. **Address:** Steven Barclay Agency, 12 Western Ave., Petaluma, CA 94952, U.S.A. **Online address:** kayryan@earthlink.net

RYAN, Margaret. American (born United States), b. 1950. **Genres:** How-to Books, Young Adult Non-fiction, Poetry. **Career:** Ryan Business Writing, speechwriter and owner, 1976-; New York State Poets in Public Service, teacher, 1987-91; 92nd Street Y, Poetry 60 Program, teacher. **Publications:** So, You Have to Give a Speech!, 1987; Figure Skating, 1987; How to Read and Write Poems, 1991; How to Give a Speech, 1994; How to Write a Poem, 1996; Extraordinary Oral Presentations, 2005; Extraordinary Poetry Writing, 2006. POETRY: Filling Out a Life, 1982; Black Raspberries, 1988. Contributor to periodicals. **Address:** 250 W 104th St., Ste. 63, New York, NY 10025, U.S.A.

RYAN, Mark Dermot. British (born England), b. 1962?. **Genres:** Information Science/Computers, Sciences, Technology. **Career:** University of Birmingham, School of Computer Science, professor of computer security, EPSRC College, faculty, 2006-09, leadership fellow. Writer. **Publications:** (Ed. with G. Burn and S. Gay) Theory and Formal Methods: Proceedings of the First Imperial College Department of Computing Workshop on Theory and Formal Methods, Isle of Thorns Conference Centre, Chelwood Gate, Sussex, UK, 29-31 March 1993, 1993; (with M. Huth) Logic in Computer Science: Modelling and Reasoning about Systems, 2000, 2nd ed., 2004; (ed. with S. Gilmore) Language Constructs for Describing Features: Proceedings of the FIREworks Workshop, 2001; (ed. with L. Chen and G. Wang) Information and Communications Security: 10th International Conference, ICICS 2008, Birmingham, UK, October 20-22, 2008: Proceedings, 2008. **Address:** School of Computer Science, University of Birmingham, Birmingham, WM B15 2TT, England. **Online address:** m.d.ryan@cs.bham.ac.uk

RYAN, Olivia. See NORTON, Sheila.

RYAN, Pam Muñoz. American (born United States), b. 1951. **Genres:** Children's Fiction, Children's Non-fiction, Novels, Animals/Pets. **Career:** Writer. **Publications:** Snow White, 1999; Becoming Naomi Leon, 2004; (contrib.) Our House, 2005; Nacho and Lolita, 2005; There was no Snow on Christmas Eve, 2005; Paint the Wind, 2007; Our California, 2008; NOVELS: Riding Freedom, 1998; Esperanza Rising, 2000. FOR CHILDREN: One Hundred is a Family, 1994; (with J. Pallotta) The Crayon Counting Book, 1996; The Flag We Love, 1996; The Crayon Counting Board Book, 1997; Armadillos Sleep in Dugouts: And Other Places Animals Live, 1997; Pinky is a Baby Mouse: And Other Baby Animal Names, 1997; California, Aquí Vamos!,

1997, trans. as California, Here We Come!, 1997; Amelia and Eleanor Go for a Ride: Based on a True Story, 1999; Hello, Ocean, 2001; Mice and Beans, 2001; Mud is Cake, 2002; How Do You Raise a Raisin?, 2002; When Marian Sang: The True Recital of Marian Anderson, 2002; A Box of Friends, 2002; Hello Ocean/Hola Mar, 2003; Neruda: A Novel, 2010; Dreamer, 2010; Tony Baloney, 2011. DOUG SERIES: Doug Counts Down, 1998; Disney's Doug's Treasure Hunt, 1998; Funnie Family Vacation, 1999. Contributor to books and periodicals. **Address:** Scholastic Inc., 557 Broadway, New York, NY 10012-3999, U.S.A. **Online address:** pmunozryan@aol.com

RYAN, Patrick. (P. E. Ryan). American (born United States), b. 1965?. **Genres:** Novels, Children's Fiction, Social Sciences. **Career:** Granta Magazine, editor. **Publications:** Send Me, 2006; Gemini Bites, 2011. AS P.E. RYAN: Saints of Augustine, 2007; In Mike We Trust, 2009. **Address:** c/o Author Mail, Dial Press, 1745 Broadway, New York, NY 10019, U.S.A.

RYAN, P. E. See RYAN, Patrick.

RYAN, Peter Allen. Australian (born Australia), b. 1923. **Genres:** Writing/Journalism, Autobiography/Memoirs, Biography, History, Military/Defense/Arms Control. **Career:** United Service Publicity Proprietary Ltd., director, 1953-57; Imperial Chemical Industries of Australia and New Zealand Ltd., manager of public relations, 1957-61; University of Melbourne, assistant, 1962; Melbourne University Press, director, 1962-89. Writer. **Publications:** Fear Drive My Feet, 1959; The Preparation of Manuscripts, 1966; Redmond Barry, 1972, 2nd ed. as Redmond Barry: A Colonial Life, 1813-1880, 1980; (ed.) Encyclopaedia of Papua and New Guinea, 1972; William Macmahon Ball: A Memoir, 1990; Black Bonanza: A Landslide of Gold, 1991; (contrib.) Chance Encounters, 1992; Lines of Fire, 1997; Brief Lives, 2004. Contributor to magazines. **Address:** PO Box 319, Flemington, VI 3031, Australia.

RYAN, Rachel. See BROWN, Sandra.

RYAN, Trish. American (born United States), b. 1969?. **Genres:** Autobiography/Memoirs. **Career:** Writer and lawyer. **Publications:** (With B. Holmes and D. Gibson) A National Minimum Data Set for Home and Community Care, 1999; He Loves Me, He Loves Me Not: A Memoir of Finding, Faith, Hope, and Happily Ever After, 2008. **Address:** Cambridge, MA , U.S.A. **Online address:** trishryanonline@gmail.com

RYANG, Sonia. American/Japanese (born Japan), b. 1960?. **Genres:** Anthropology/Ethnology. **Career:** University of Newcastle upon Tyne, lecturer in Japanese, 1987-88; University of Adelaide, Center for Asian Studies, lecturer in Asian studies, 1988-89; Australian National University, Research School of Pacific and Asian Studies, research fellow in anthropology, 1995-97; Johns Hopkins University, assistant professor of anthropology, 1997-2000, associate professor of anthropology, 2000-06; University of Iowa, associate professor of anthropology and international studies, 2006-10, professor of anthropology and international studies, 2010-, Center for Asian and Pacific Studies, director, 2008-, Office of Executive Vice President and Provost, faculty fellow, 2009, C. Maxwell and Elizabeth M. Stanley Family and Korea Foundation chair of Korean studies, 2010-. Writer. **Publications:** North Koreans in Japan: Language, Ideology and Identity, 1997; (ed.) Koreans in Japan: Critical Voices from the Margin, 2000; Japan and National Anthropology: A Critique, 2004; Love in Modern Japan: Its Estrangement from Self, Sex, and Society, 2006; Writing Selves in Diaspora: Ethnography of Autobiographics of Korean Women in Japan and the US, 2008; (ed.) North Korea: Toward a Better Understanding, 2008; (ed. with J. Lie) Diaspora Without Homeland: Being Korean in Japan, 2009; Reading North Korea: An Ethnological Inquiry, 2011. **Address:** Department of Anthropology, University of Iowa, 215 Macbride Hall, 3400 N Charles St., Iowa City, IA 52242-1322, U.S.A. **Online address:** sonia-ryang@uiowa.edu

RYBCZYNSKI, Witold. American/Canadian/Scottish (born Scotland), b. 1943. **Genres:** Architecture, Homes/Gardens, Urban Studies. **Career:** Edouard Fiset, architect; Moshe Safdie, architect; Luis Villa, architect; Schoenauer & Desnoyers, architect, 1967-71; McGill University, research associate, 1973-75, assistant professor, 1975-80, associate professor, 1980-86, professor, 1986-93; United Nations, consultant, 1976; International Development Research Center, consultant, 1977; World Bank, consultant, 1978; Banco de Mexico, consultant, 1980; writer, 1980-; University of Pennsylvania, Meyerson professor of urbanism, 1993-. **Publications:** Paper Heroes: A Review of Appropriate Technology, 1980; Taming the Tiger: The Struggle to Control

Technology, 1983; Home: A Short History of An Idea, 1986; The Most Beautiful House in the World, 1989; Waiting for the Weekend, 1991; Paper Heroes: Appropriate Technology: Panacea or Pipe Dream?, 1991; Looking Around: A Journey through Architecture, 1993; A Place for Art: The Architecture of the National Gallery of Canada, 1993; City Life: Urban Expectations in a New World, 1995; A Clearing in the Distance: Frederick Law Olmsted and America in the Nineteenth Century, 1999; One Good Turn: A Natural History of the Screwdriver and the Screw, 2000; The Look of Architecture, 2001; The Perfect House: A Journey with the Renaissance Master Andrea Palladio, 2002; (intro.) Robert A.M. Stern: Houses and Gardens, 2005; (with L. Olin) Vizcaya: An American Villa and Its Makers, 2007; Last Harvest: How a Cornfield Became New Daleville: Real Estate Development in America from George Washington to the Builders of the Twenty-First Century, and Why We Live in Houses Anyway, 2007; My Two Polish Grandfathers: And Other Essays on the Imaginative Life, 2009; Makeshift Metropolis: Ideas about Cities, 2010; The Biography of a Building: How Robert Sainsbury and Norman Foster Built a Great Museum, 2011. Contributor to periodicals. **Address:** 7801 Lincoln Dr., Philadelphia, PA 19118, U.S.A. **Online address:** rybczyns@design.upenn.edu

RYBOLT, Thomas R. American (born United States), b. 1954. **Genres:** Young Adult Non-fiction, Sciences, How-to Books, Self Help, Children's Non-fiction, Physics, Chemistry, Environmental Sciences/Ecology, Environmental Sciences/Ecology. **Career:** University of Tennessee, Department of Chemistry, assistant professor, 1981-86, associate professor, 1986-, department head, 2010-, UC Foundation professor of chemistry. Writer. **Publications:** SCIENCE FOR YOUNG ADULTS: (with L.M. Rybolt) Science Fair Success with Scents, Aromas, and Smells, 2002; (with R.C. Mebane) Environmental Science Fair Projects Using Water, Feathers, Sunlight, Balloons, and More, 2005; (with R. Gardner and M. Goodstein) Ace Your Physical Science Project: Great Science Fair Ideas, 2010; (with S. Tocci and R. Gardner) Ace Your Food Science Project: Great Science Fair Ideas, 2010. SCIENCE FOR YOUNG ADULTS WITH ROBERT C. MEBANE: Adventures with Atoms and Molecules: Chemistry Experiments for Young People, 1985; Adventures with Atoms and Molecules Book II: More Chemistry Experiments for Young People, 1987; Adventures with Atoms and Molecules Book III, 1990; Environmental Experiments about Water, 1993; Environmental Experiments about Air, 1993; Environmental Experiments about Life, 1993; Environmental Experiments about Land, 1993; Environmental Experiments about Renewable Energy, 1994; Adventures with Atoms and Molecules, vol. V: Chemistry Experiments for Young People, 1995; Air & Other Gases, 1995; (with R.C. Mebane) Metals, 1995; Plastics & Polymers, 1995; Salts & Solids, 1995; Water & Other Liquids, 1995. FICTION: (as Tom Rybolt) Forbidden Light, 2004; Soda Pop Science Projects: Experiments with Carbonated Soft Drinks, 2004; (with R.C. Mebane) Environmental Science Fair Projects, Revised and Expanded using the Scientific Method, 2010. Contributor to periodicals. **Address:** Department of Chemistry, University of Tennessee, 318A Grote, 615 McCallie Ave., Chattanooga, TN 37403, U.S.A. **Online address:** tom-rybolt@utc.edu

RYCHLAK, Joseph F(rank). American (born United States), b. 1928. **Genres:** Philosophy, Psychology, Social Sciences. **Career:** Florida State University, assistant professor of psychology, 1957-58; American Telephone & Telegraph Corp., research consultant, 1957-82; Washington State University, assistant professor of psychology, 1958-61; Saint Louis University, associate professor of psychology, 1961-65, professor, 1965-69; Purdue University, professor of psychology, 1969-83; Loyola University of Chicago, Maude C. Clarke professor of humanistic psychology, 1983-99, Maude C. Clarke emeritus professor, 1999-; Journal of Mind and Behavior, associate editor. **Publications:** A Philosophy of Science for Personality Theory, 1968, 2nd ed., 1981; Introduction to Personality and Psychotherapy: A Theory-Construction Approach, 1973, 2nd ed., 1981; Dialectic: Humanistic Rationale for Behavior and Development, 1976; The Psychology of Rigorous Humanism, 1977, 2nd ed., 1987; Discovering Free Will and Personal Responsibility, 1979; Personality and Life-Style of Young Male Managers: A Logical Learning Theory Analysis, 1982; (with N. Cameron) Personality and Development: A Dynamic Approach, 1985; Artificial Intelligence and Human Reason: A Teleological Critique, 1991; Logical Learning Theory: A Human Teleology and Its Empirical Support, 1994; In Defense of Human Consciousness, 1997; The Human Image in Postmodern America, 2003. **Address:** Department of Psychology, Loyola University Chicago, 6525 N Sheridan Rd., Chicago, IL 60626, U.S.A.

RYCHLAK, Ronald (J.). American (born United States), b. 1957. **Genres:** Law, History. **Career:** United States Court of Appeals, judicial law clerk, 1983-84; Jenner & Block, General Litigation Department, associate, 1984-87; University of Mississippi, School of Law, assistant professor, 1987-, professor of law, associate dean for academic affairs, Mississippi defense lawyers association professor of law; Central and East European Law Initiative, consultant, 1997-2003. Writer. **Publications:** Real and Demonstrative Evidence: Applications and Theory, 1995, 2nd ed., 2003; Hitler, the War, and the Pope, 2000, rev. ed., 2010; (with R. Jarvis) Gaming Law: Cases and Materials, 2003; Courting the Yankees: Legal Essays on the Bronx Bombers, vol. XII: Unlucky Numbers: Betting on, Against, and With the Yankees, 2003; The Pius War, 2004; (with M.M. Harrold) Mississippi Criminal Trial Practice, 2004; Trial by Fury: Restoring the Common Good in Tort Litigation, 2004; Righteous Gentiles: How Pius XII and the Catholic Church Saved Half a Million Jews from the Nazis, 2005; (with D.W. Case) Environmental Law, 2010. Contributor to books, journals and periodicals. **Address:** School of Law, University of Mississippi, Rm. 541, Robert C. Khayat Law Ctr., PO Box 1848, University, MS 38677, U.S.A. **Online address:** rrychlak@olemiss.edu

RYCZEK, William J. American (born United States), b. 1953. **Genres:** Sports/Fitness, History. **Career:** Barclays American Business Credit Inc., national marketing manager, vice president, 1979-87; University of Hartford, adjunct professor of finance, 1985-93; Liberty Bank, senior vice president and timeshare manager, 1988-2002, chief lending officer, through 2002; Colebrook Financial Co., principal, 2003-. Writer. **Publications:** Blackguards and Red Stockings, 1992; When Johnny Came Sliding Home, 1998; Crash of the Titans: The Early Years of the New York Jets and the AFL, 2000, rev. ed. 2009; Amazin' Mets, 1962-1969, 2008; Yankees in the Early 1960s, 2008; Baseball's First Inning: A History of the National Pastime Through the Civil War, 2009. **Address:** Colebrook Financial Co., 100 Riverview Ctr., Ste. 203, Middletown, CT 06457, U.S.A. **Online address:** bryczek@colebrookfinancial.com

RYDELL, Katy. American (born United States), b. 1942. **Genres:** Children's Fiction. **Career:** California State University, instructor; Stories, editor and publisher, 1987-2002; Long Beach Public Library, storyteller-in-residence, 1992-98; Storytelling Association of Alta California, storyline contributor, 1997-2005; California State University, instructor, 1997-. **Publications:** Wind Says Good Night, 1994; (ed.) A Beginner's Guide to Storytelling, 2003. Contributor to periodicals. **Address:** 12600 Woodbine St., Los Angeles, CA 90066, U.S.A. **Online address:** Katy@katyrydell.com

RYDEN, Hope. American (born United States) **Genres:** Children's Fiction, Adult Non-fiction, Animals/Pets, Botany, Children's Non-fiction, Natural History, Young Adult Non-fiction, Photography, Photography. **Career:** Drew Associates, film producer, 1960-64; Hope Ryden Productions, film producer, writer and director, 1965; American Broadcasting Corp., feature producer for ABC-TV evening news, 1966-68. Writer and photographer. **Publications:** SELF-ILLUSTRATOR: America's Last Wild Horses (for adults), 1970, rev. ed., 1990; The Wild Colt: The Life of a Young Mustang, 1972; God's Dog: A Celebration of the The North American Coyote (for adults), 1975; The Little Deer of Florida Keys, 1978, rev. ed., 1986; Bobcat Year (for adults), 1981; Bobcat, 1983; America's Bald Eagle, 1985; Wild Animals of America ABC, 1988; Lily Pond: Four Years with a Family of Beavers (for adults), 1989; Your Cat's Wild Cousins, 1991; The Raggedy Red Squirrel, 1992; Your Dog's Wild Cousins, 1994; Joey: The Story of a Baby Kangaroo, 1994; Out of the Wild: The Story of Domesticated Animals, 1995; ABC of Crawlers and Flyers, 1996; Wild Horses I Have Known, 1999; Wildflowers around the Year, 2001. OTHERS: Mustangs: A Return to the Wild, 1972; The Wild Pups: The True Story of a Coyote Family, 1975; The Beaver, 1986; Wild Animals of Africa ABC, 1989; Backyard Rescue, 1994; Wild Horse Summer, 1997. Contributor of articles to periodicals. **Address:** N.S. Bienstock Inc., 250 W 57th St., Ste. 333, New York, NY 10107, U.S.A. **Online address:** hope@hoperyden.com

RYDER, Joanne (Rose). American (born United States), b. 1946. **Genres:** Children's Fiction, Animals/Pets, Education, Poetry, Young Adult Fiction, Natural History, Sciences. **Career:** Harper & Row Publishers Inc., editor, 1970-80; writer, 1980-. Educator. **Publications:** Simon Underground, 1976; Fireflies, 1977; A Wet and Sandy Day, 1977; Fog in the Meadow, 1979; (with H.S. Feinberg) Snail in the Woods, 1979; The Spiders Dance, 1981; Beach Party, 1982; The Snail's Spell, 1982; C-3PO's Book about Robots, 1983; The Evening Walk, 1985; Inside Turtle's Shell, and Other Poems of the Field, 1985; The Night Flight, 1985; Old Friends, New Friends, 1986; Animals in the Woods, 1987; Chipmunk Song, 1987; Hardie Gramatky's Little Toot, 1988; My Little Golden Book about Cats, 1988; Puppies Are Special Friends,

1988; Step into the Night, 1988; Animals in the Wild, 1989; Catching the Wind, 1989; A Christmas Carol, 1989; Mockingbird Morning, 1989; Under the Moon, 1989; Where Butterflies Grow, 1989; White Bear, Ice Bear, 1989; Lizard in the Sun, 1990; Under Your Feet, 1990; The Bear on the Moon, 1991; Hello, Tree!, 1991; When the Woods Hum, 1991; Winter Whale, 1991; Dancers in the Garden, 1992; Turtle Time, 1992; First Grade Elves, 1993; Sea Elf, 1993; First Grade Ladybugs, 1993; Hello, First Grade, 1993; First Grade Valentines, 1993; The Goodbye Walk, 1993; One Small Fish, 1993; Walt Disney's Bambi, 1993; Walt Disney's Bambi's Forest, 1993; A House by the Sea, 1994; My Father's Hands, 1994; First Grade Elves, 1994; Without Words, 1995; Bears out There, 1995; Night Gliders, 1996; Earthdance, 1996; Jaguar in the Rain Forest, 1996; Shark in the Sea, 1997; Pondwater Faces, 1997; Winter White, 1997; Tyrannosaurus Alive, 1999; Tyrannosaurus Time, 1999; Rainbow Wings, 2000; Each Living Thing, 2000; Fawn in the Grass, 2001; Little Panda: The World Welcomes Hua Mei at the San Diego Zoo, 2001; The Waterfall's Gift, 2001; Mouse Tail Moon, 2002; Big Bear Ball, 2002; Come Along, Kitten, 2003; Wild Birds, 2003; (with M. Sweet) Won't You Be My Kissaroo?, 2004; Bear of My Heart, 2006; My Mother's Voice, 2006; A Pair of Polar Bears: Twin Cubs Find a Home at the San Diego Zoo, 2006; (with M. Sweet) Won't You Be My Hugaroo?, 2006; Dance by the Light of the Moon, 2007; Toad by the Road: A Year in the Life of These Amazing Amphibians, 2007; Panda Kindergarten, 2009. Contributor to periodicals. **Address:** William Morrow and Company Inc., 1350 Ave. of the Americas, New York, NY 10019-4702, U.S.A.

RYDER, Pamela. *See* **LAMB, Nancy.**

RYDER, Thom. *See* **HARVEY, John.**

RYDILL, Jessica. British (born England), b. 1959?. **Genres:** Novels, Novellas/Short Stories. **Career:** The Write Fantastic, founding member, 2005-. Writer. **Publications:** Children of the Shaman, 2001; The Glass Mountain, 2002; (co-author) Anniversaries: The Write Fantastic, 2010; Malarat, forthcoming. **Address:** c/o Author Mail, Time Warner Books, Brettenham House, Lancaster Pl., London, GL WC2E 7EN, England. **Online address:** landseer@shamansland.com

RYKEN, Leland. American (born United States), b. 1942. **Genres:** Literary Criticism And History, Theology/Religion. **Career:** Wheaton College, faculty, 1968-, professor of English, Clyde S. Kilby professor of English. Writer. **Publications:** The Apocalyptic Vision in Paradise Lost, 1970; The Literature of the Bible, 1974; Triumphs of the Imagination: Literature in Christian Perspective, 1979; (ed.) The Christian Imagination: Essays on Literature and the Arts, 1981; (ed. with J.H. Sims) Milton and Scriptural Tradition: The Bible into Poetry, 1984; (ed. and comp.) The New Testament in Literary Criticism, 1984; How to Read the Bible as Literature, 1984; Windows to the World, 1985; Culture in Christian Perspective, 1986; Worldly Saints: The Puritans as They Really Were, 1986; Words of Delight: A Literary Introduction to the Bible, 1987, 2nd ed., 1992; Words of Life: A Literary Introduction to the New Testament, 1987; Work and Leisure in Christian Perspective, 1987; Effective Bible Teaching, 1988; The Liberated Imagination, 1989; Realms of Gold: The Classics in Christian Perspective, 1991; (ed. C. Walhout) Contemporary Literary Theory: A Christian Appraisal, 1991; (ed. with T. Longman III) A Complete Literary Guide to the Bible, 1993; The Discerning Reader: Christian Perspectives on Literature and Theory, 1995; Redeeming the Time: A Christian Approach to Work and Leisure, 1995; (co-aed.) A Dictionary of Biblical Imagery, 1998; The Christian Imagination: The Practice of Faith in Literature and Writing, 2002; The Word of God in English: Criteria for Excellence in Bible Translation, 2002; Bible Translation Differences: Criteria For Excellence In Reading and Choosing a Bible Translation, 2004; (with M.L. Mead) A Reader's Guide through the Wardrobe: Exploring C.S. Lewis's Classic Story, 2005; Ryken's Bible Handbook, 2005; (ed. with P.G. Ryken) Literary Study Bible: ESV Containing the Old and New Testaments, 2007; (ed. with T.A. Wilson) Preach the Word: Essays on Expository Preaching in Honor of R. Kent Hughes, 2007; (with M.L. Mead) Reader's Guide to Caspian: A Journey into C.S. Lewis's Narnia, 2008; Understanding English Bible Translation: The Case for an Essentially Literal Approach, 2009; Legacy of The King James Bible: Celebrating 400 Years of the Most Influential English Translation, 2011; ESV and the English Bible Legacy, 2011; (with T. Wilson and P. Ryken) Pastors in the Classics: Timeless Lessons on Life and Ministry from World Literature, 2012. **Address:** Department of English, Wheaton College, 315 Blanchard Hall, 501 College Ave., Wheaton, IL 60187-5593, U.S.A. **Online address:** leland.ryken@wheaton.edu

RYKWERT, Joseph. American/Polish (born Poland), b. 1926. **Genres:** Architecture, Art/Art History, Adult Non-fiction, Poetry, Anthropology/Ethnology, History, Essays. **Career:** Firm of E. Maxwell Fry & Jane Drew, architect, 1947; Richard Sheppard and Partners, architect, 1947-48; Hammersmith School of Arts and Crafts, studio master and lecturer in the history of architecture, 1952-53; Hochschule für Gestaltung, visiting lecturer, 1958-60; Royal College of Art, librarian and tutor in history of architecture, 1961-67; University of Essex, professor of art, 1967-79, head of department, 1967-70; Princeton University, visiting professor, 1971, 1977; University of Paris, visiting professor, 1974, 1976; Cooper Union, Andrew Mellon visiting professor, 1977; Ecole Polytechnique Federale de Lausanne, visiting professor, 1979-80; Cambridge University, Darwin College, Slade professor of fine arts and visiting fellow, 1979-80, reader in architecture, 1981-87; Harvard University, visiting professor, 1980; University of Palermo, visiting professor, 1981; National Gallery of Art, Center for Advanced Studies in the Visual Arts, senior fellow, 1981; University of Louvain, visiting professor, 1982; Columbia University, George Lurcy Professor, 1986; University of Pennsylvania, Paul Philippe Cret professor, 1988-, now Paul Philippe Cret professor emeritus of architecture, chair of doctoral program in architecture, professor of art history, now professor emeritus of art history; Delft Polytechnic, lecturer; York University, lecturer; Carnegie-Mellon University, lecturer; Massachusetts Institute of Technology, lecturer; University of Naples, lecturer and reader in architecture. **Publications:** The Golden House, 1947; (contrib.) Image of Tomorrow, 1953; (ed.) Ten Books on Architecture, 1955; The Idea of a Town: The Anthropology of Urban Form in Rome, Italy, and the Ancient World, 1963; Church Building, 1966; On the Early Pictures of Giorgio de Chirico: A Poem, 1969; On Adam's House in Paradise: The Idea of the Primitive Hut in Architectural History, 1972, 2nd ed., 1981; (ed.) A. Loos, Parole nel Vuoto, 1972; (ed.) Parole nel Vuoto, 1972; G. B. Nolli's Plan of Rome, 1977; (ed. with H. Beck) Leonis Baptiste Alberti, 1979; The First Moderns: Architects of the Eighteenth Century, 1980; The Necessity of Artifice (collected essays), 1982; (co-author) Palermo: La Memoria Costruita, 1982; (with A. Rykwert) Robert and James Adam: The Men and the Style, 1985; (trans.) Alberti, On the Art of Building, 1988; (ed. with A. Engel) Leon Battista Alberti, 1994; Gregotti Associati, 1995; The Dancing Column, 1996; (with K. Frampton) Architect, vol. III, 1998; The Palladian Ideal, 1999; The Seduction of Place: The City in The Twenty-first Century, 2000 as Seduction of Place: The History and Future of the City, 2002; (contrib.) Visionary Clients for New Architecture, 2000; The Villa: From Ancient to Modern, 2000; (intro. with H. Ciriani) Miguel Angel Roca, 1990-2000, 2000; Louis Kahn, 2001; (contrib.) Body and Building: Essays on the Changing Relation of Body and Architecture, 2002; (contrib.) Richard Meier, Architect: 2000/2004, 2004; (ed. with T. Atkin) Structure and Meaning in Human Settlements, 2005; (contrib.) Grotta House by Richard Meier, 2007; Judicious Eye: Architecture Against the Other Arts, 2008. Contributor of articles to books, journals and magazines. **Address:** Department of the History of Art, University of Pennsylvania, Elliot and Roslyn Jaffe History of Art Bldg., 3405 Woodland Walk, Philadelphia, PA 19104-6208, U.S.A. **Online address:** rykwert@design.upenn.edu

RYLANDS, Jane Turner. Italian (born Italy), b. 1939?. **Genres:** Novellas/Short Stories, Young Adult Fiction. **Career:** University of Maryland, European Division, teacher of English. Writer. **Publications:** SHORT STORIES: Venetian Stories, 2003; Across the Bridge of Sighs: More Venetian Stories, 2005. **Address:** c/o Author Mail, Pantheon Books, 1745 Broadway, New York, NY 10019, U.S.A.

RYLANDS, Philip. British/Italian (born Italy), b. 1950. **Genres:** Art/Art History. **Career:** Peggy Guggenheim Collection, administrator, 1979-86, deputy director, 1986-2000, director, 2000-; University of Virginia, School of Architecture, adjunct distinguished professor, 1998-99; New York University, faculty; University of Maryland, Overseas Division, faculty. Writer. **Publications:** (Ed. with A. Clarke) The Church of the Madonna dell'Orto: Restoring Venice, 1977; Palma il Vecchio: L'Opera Completa, 1988; Palma Vecchio, 1992; (with E.D. Martino) Flying the Flag for Art: The United States and the Venice Biennale, 1895-1991, 1993; (ed.) Pablo Picasso: L'atelier, 1996; (ed.) Umberto Boccioni: Dinamismo di un Cavallo in Corsa & Case, 1996; (ed.) Stuart Davis, 1997; (ed.) Licht und Schatten Linie, The Timeless Eye: Opere su Carta Della Collezione Jan e Marie-Ann Krugier-Poniatowski, 1999; Richard Pousette-Dart, 2007. Contributor of articles to periodicals. **Address:** Peggy Guggenheim Collection, 701 Dorsoduro, Venice, 30123, Italy. **Online address:** director@guggenheim-venice.it

RYLANT, Cynthia. American (born United States), b. 1954. **Genres:** Children's Fiction, Novellas/Short Stories, Children's Non-fiction, Picture/Board Books, Sciences, Natural History, Animals/Pets, Humor/Satire, Humor/Satire. **Career:** Marshall University, part-time English instructor, 1979-80; Akron Public Library, childrens librarian, 1983; University of Akron, part-time English lecturer, 1983-84; Northeastern Ohio Universities, Colleges of Medicine and Pharmacy, part-time lecturer, 1991-. Writer. **Publications:** SELF-ILLUSTRATED: Dog Heaven, 1995. OTHERS: When I Was Young in the Mountains, 1982; Miss Maggie, 1983: This Year's Garden, 1984; Waiting to Waltz: A Childhood (verse), 1984; A Blue-Eyed Daisy in UK as Some Year for Ellie, 1985; The Relatives Came, 1985; Every Living Thing (stories), 1985; A Fine White Dust, 1986; Night in the Country, 1986; Birthday Presents, 1987; Children of Christmas: Stories for the Season, 1987 in UK as Silver Packages: An Appalachian Christmas Story, 1997; All I See, 1988; A Kindness, 1988; But I'll Be Back Again: An Album, 1989; Mr. Griggs' Work, 1989; Soda Jerk (verse), 1990; A Couple of Kooks and Other Stories About Love (stories), 1990; Appalachia: The Voices of Sleeping Birds, 1991; Best Wishes, 1992; An Angel for Solomon Singer, 1992; Missing May, 1992; The Dreamer, 1993; I Had Seen Castles, 1993; The Everyday Books, 5 vols., 1993; Something Permanent, 1994; The Van Gogh Cafe, 1995; Gooseberry Park, 1995; The Old Woman Who Named Things, 1996; Whales, 1996; Bookshop Dog, 1996; Margaret, Frank and Andy: Three Writers' Stories, 1996; Blue Hill Meadows, 1997; Poppleton, 1997; Poppleton and Friends, 1997; Cat Heaven, 1997; Blue Hill Meadows and the Much-Loved Dog, 1997; Scarecrow, 1998; Bear Day, 1998; Tulip Sees America, 1998; Poppleton Everyday, 1998; Poppleton Forever, 1998; Bird House, 1998; Islander, 1998; Bless Us All, 1998; A Little Shopping, 1998; In Aunt Lucy's Kitchen, 1998; Bunny Bungalow, 1999; Cookie-Store Cat, 1999; Poppleton in Spring, 1999; Cobble Street Cousins: Some Good News, 1999; Cobble Street Cousins: Special Gifts, 1999; Poppleton in Fall, 1999; Give Me Grace: A Child's Daybook of Prayers, 1999; Heavenly Village, 1999; Poppleton Through and Through, 2000; Wonderful Happens, 2000; Thimbleberry Stories, 2000; In November, 2000; Poppleton Has Fun, 2000; Little Whistle's Dinner Party, 2001; Tickytacky Doll, 2001; Little Whistle, 2001; The Great Gracie Chase, 2001; Poppleton in Winter, 2001; Summer Party, 2001; Good Morning Sweetie Pie, and Other Poems for Little Children, 2001; Old Town in the Green Groves: The Lost Little House Years, 2002; Let's Go Home: The Wonderful Things About a House, 2002; Wedding Flowers, 2002; Christmas in the Country, 2002; Little Whistle's Medicine, 2002; Old Town in the Green Groves, 2002; God Went to Beauty School, 2003; Moonlight: The Halloween Cat, 2003; Little Whistle's Christmas, 2003; Long Night Moon, 2004; Boris, 2005; If You'll be My Valentine, 2005; Miracles in Motion, 2005; Puppies and Piggies, 2005; Stars will Still Shine, 2005; The Journey: Stories of Migration, 2006; Ludie's Life, 2006; Alligator Boy, 2007; Annie and Snowball and the Dress-up Birthday: The First Book of their Adventures, 2007; Annie and Snowball and the Prettiest House, 2007; (reteller) Walt Disney: Cinderella, 2007; The World of Horror, 2007; Annie and Snowball and the Pink Surprise, 2008; Annie and Snowball and the Teacup Club: The Third Book of Their Adventures, 2008; Baby Face: A Book of Love For Baby, 2008; Snow, 2008; Hansel and Gretel, 2008; Annie and Snowball and the Cozy Nest, 2009; Annie and Snowball and the Shining Star, 2009; All in a Day, 2009; The Beautiful Stories of Life: Six Greeks Myths, Retold, 2009; Annie and Snowball and the Magical House, 2010; Annie and Snowball and the Wintry Freeze, 2010; Annie and Snowball and the Book Bugs Club, 2011; Annie and Snowball and the Thankful Friends, 2011; Annie and Snowball and the Grandmother Night, 2012; Annie and Snowball and the Surprise Day, 2012. BROWNIE & PEARL SERIES: Step Out, 2009; Get Dolled Up, 2010; See the Sights, 2010; Grab a Bite, 2011; Hit the Hay, 2011; Take a Dip, 2011; Go for a Spin, 2012; Make Good, 2012. MR. PUTTER AND TABBY SERIES: Walk the Dog, 1994; Bake the Cake, 1994; Pour the Tea, 1994; Pick the Pears, 1995; Fly the Plane, 1997; Row the Boat, 1997; Toot the Horn, 1998; Take the Train, 1998; Paint the Porch, 2000; Feed the Fish, 2001; Catch the Cold, 2002; Stir the Soup, 2003; Write the Book, 2004; Make a Wish, 2005; Spin the Yarn, 2006; See the Stars, 2007; Run the Race, 2008; Spill the Beans, 2009; Drop the Ball, 2010; Clear the Decks, 2010; Ring the Bell, 2011; Dance the Dance, 2012. THE HIGH-RISE PRIVATE EYES SERIES: The Case of the Climbing Cat, 2000; The Case of the Missing Monkey, 2000; The Case of the Puzzling Possum, 2001; The Case of the Troublesome Turtle, 2001; The Case of the Sleepy Sloth, 2002; The Case of the Fidgety Fox, 2003; The Case of the Baffled Bear, 2004; The Case of the Desperate Duck, 2005. HENRY AND MUDGE SERIES: Henry and Mudge: The First Book of their Adventures, 1987; Henry and Mudge in Puddle Trouble: The Second Book of their Adventures, 1987; Henry and Mudge in the Green Time: The Third Book of their Adventures, 1987; Henry and Mudge under the Yellow Moon: The Fourth Book of Their Adventures, 1987; Henry and Mudge in the Sparkle Days: The Fifth Book of their Adventures, 1988; Henry and Mudge and the Forever Sea: The Sixth Book of their Adventures, 1989; Henry and Mudge Get the Cold Shivers: The Seventh Book of Their Adventures, 1989; Henry and Mudge and the Happy Cat: The Eighth Book of Their Adventures, 1990; Henry and Mudge and the Bedtime Thumps: The Ninth Book of Their Adventures, 1991; Henry and Mudge Take the Big Test, 1991; Henry and Mudge and the Long Weekend: The Eleventh Book of Their Adventures, 1992; Henry and Mudge and the Wild Wind: The Twelfth Book of Their Adventures, 1992; Henry and Mudge and the Careful Cousin: The Thirteenth Book of Their Adventures, 1994; Henry and Mudge and the Best Day of All: The Fourteenth Book of Their Adventures, 1995; Henry and Mudge in the Family Trees: The Fifteenth Book of Their Adventures, 1997; Henry and Mudge he Sneaky Crackers: The Sixteenth Book of Their Adventures, 1998; The Starry Night: The Seventeenth Book of Their Adventures, 1998; Annie's Good Move: The Eighteenth Book of Their Adventures, 1998; The Snowman Plan: The Nineteenth Book of Their Adventures, 1999; Annie's Perfect Pet: The Twentieth Book of Their Adventures, 2000; The Tall Tree House: The Twenty-first Book of Their Adventures, 2002; Mrs. Hooper's House: The Twenty-second Book of Their Adventures, 2003; The Wild Goose Chase: The Twenty-third Book of Their Adventures, 2003; The Funny Lunch: The Twenty-fourth Book of Their Adventures, 2004; A Very Merry Christmas: The Twenty-fifth Book of Their Adventures, 2004; The Great Grandpas: The Twenty-sixth Book of Their Adventures, 2005; The Tumbling Trip: The Twenty-seventh Book of Their Adventures, 2005; The Big Sleepover: The Twenty-eighth Book of Their Adventures, 2006. LIGHTHOUSE FAMILY SERIES: The Eagle, 2002; The Storm, 2002; The Whale, 2003; The Octopus, 2005; The Turtle, 2005. PUPPY MUDGE SERIES: Takes a Bath, 2002; Has a Snack, 2003; Finds a Friend, 2004; Loves His Blanket, 2004; Wants To Play, 2005. Contributor to periodicals. **Address:** Simon & Schuster Inc., 1230 Ave. of the Americas, New York, NY 10020, U.S.A.

RYLE, Anthony. British (born England), b. 1927?. **Genres:** Psychiatry, Psychology, Medicine/Health. **Career:** Caversham Centre Group Practice, general medical practitioner, 1952-64; University of Sussex, University Health Service, director, 1964-79, senior research fellow, 1979-; St. Thomas Hospital, consultant psychotherapist, 1983-92; Guy's Hospital, Munro Clinic, United Medical and Dental Schools, emeritus consultant psychotherapist. Writer. **Publications:** Neurosis in the Ordinary Family: A Psychiatric Survey, 1967; Student Casualties, 1969; Frames and Cages: The Repertory Grid Approach to Human Understanding, 1975; Psychotherapy: A Cognitive Integration of Theory and Practice, 1982; Cognitive Analytic Therapy: Active Participation in Change: A New Integration in Brief Psychotherapy, 1990; (ed.) Cognitive Analytic Therapy: Developments in Theory and Practice, 1995; Cognitive Analytic Therapy and Borderline Personality Disorder: The Model and the Method, 1997; (with I.B. Kerr) Introducing Cognitive Analytic Therapy: Principles and Practice, 2002. Contributor to journals and periodicals. **Address:** CAT Office, Munro Clinic, Guy's Hospital, 66 Snowsfields, London, GL SE1 3SS, England.

RYLE, Michael. British (born England), b. 1927. **Genres:** Politics/Government. **Career:** Writer, 1989-. Educator. **Publications:** (With J.A.G. Griffith and M.A.J. Wheeler-Booth) Parliament: Functions, Practice and Procedures, 1989. EDITOR: (with S.A. Walkland) The Commons in the Seventies, 1977; (with S.A. Walkland) The Commons Today, 1981; (with P.G. Richards) The Commons Under Scrutiny, 1988. Contributor to books, political science journals and periodicals. **Address:** Jasmine Cottage, Winsford, Minehead, SM TA24 7JE, England. **Online address:** michaelryle@tiscali.co.uk

RYMPH, Catherine E. American (born United States) **Genres:** Women's Studies And Issues, Social Sciences, Adult Non-fiction. **Career:** University of Iowa, instructor; University of Greifswald, fulbright lecturer; University of Missouri, associate professor of history, 2000-. Writer. **Publications:** Republican Women: Feminism and Conservatism from Suffrage Through the Rise of the New Right, 2006. **Address:** Department of History, College of Arts and Science, University of Missouri, 315 Read Hall, Columbia, MO 65211-7500, U.S.A. **Online address:** rymphc@missouri.edu

S

SAAL, Jocelyn. *See* SACHS, Judith.

SAARI, Carolyn. American (born United States), b. 1939. **Genres:** Social Work. **Career:** Bryn Mawr College, field instructor, 1967-68; Smith College, field instructor, 1968-71, 1973-77, research advisor of master's program, 1973-77, associate dean, 1977-78, research advisor of doctoral program, 1977-82, coordinator of field advisor of master's and doctoral programs, 1977-79, professor, 1977-91; Yale Psychiatric Institute, instructor and assistant chief social worker, 1969-71, School of Medicine, instructor and co-director of social work, 1974-77; State University of New York at Albany, instructor, 1973-74; Loyola University of Chicago, professor, 1980-, School of Social Work, director of doctoral program, 1986-87, now chair of social work, professor emerita; Children's Memorial Hospital, Department of Social Work, case consultant, 1987-91; Institute for Clinical Social Work, professor of social work, 1984-92. Writer. **Publications:** Clinical Social Work Treatment: How Does It Work?, 1986; The Creation of Meaning in Clinical Social Work, 1991; The Environment: Its Role in Psychosocial Functioning and Psychotherapy, 2002. Contributor to periodicals. **Address:** School of Social Work, Loyola University of Chicago, 820 N Michigan Ave., Lewis Towers 847, Chicago, IL 60611, U.S.A.

SABAN, Cheryl (Lynn). American (born United States), b. 1951. **Genres:** Novels, Children's Fiction, Plays/Screenplays, Adult Non-fiction, Human Relations/Parenting. **Career:** Saban Entertainment, personal secretary, head of toy development, director, 1986-87; A Child's Room, owner, 1988-92; Fox Television, staff writer, 1993-. **Publications:** Miracle Child: Genetic Mother, Surrogate Womb, 1993; Griffin's Play Group, 1995; Griffin's Busy Day, 1995; Griffin's Shopping, 1995; Griffin's Shopping Trip, 1995; Griffin's Day at the Zoo, 1995; Griffin Busy Day, 1996; Sins of the Mother (suspense novel), 1997; 50 Ways to Save Our Children: Small, Medium & Big Ways You Can Change a Child's Life, 2002; Recipe for a Good Marriage, 2005; Recipe for Good Parenting: Words of Wisdom for Parents of All Ages, from Parents of All Ages, 2007; New Mother's Survival Guide, 2008; What Is Your Self-Worth?: A Woman's Guide to Validation, 2009. **Address:** Hay House Inc., PO Box 5100, Carlsbad, CA 92018-5100, U.S.A. **Online address:** info@whatisyourselfworth.com

SABAR, Ariel. American (born United States), b. 1971?. **Genres:** Autobiography/Memoirs, Adult Non-fiction, Essays, Urban Studies, Design, Biography. **Career:** Providence Journal, staff writer; Baltimore Sun, staff writer; Christian Science Monitor, national correspondent; New York Times Magazine, journalist; Washington Monthly, journalist; Boston Globe, journalist. **Publications:** My Father's Paradise: A Son's Search for His Jewish Past in Kurdish Iraq (memoir), 2008; Heart of the City: Nine Stories of Love and Serendipity on the Streets of New York (narrative nonfiction), 2011. Contributor to magazines and newspapers. **Address:** Washington, DC , U.S.A. **Online address:** wd@arielsabar.com

SABATINE, Jean A. American (born United States), b. 1941. **Genres:** Dance/Ballet, Theatre, Photography. **Career:** Illinois State University, teacher of dance and movement, 1967-69; Wayne State University, teacher of movement, 1969-71, Jazz Dance Theatre, founder, 1970; Pennsylvania State University, coordinator of dance and movement, 1972-80, Jazz Dance Theatre, founder, 1974; University of Connecticut, Dramatic Arts in Movement and Dance, professor, 1980-, Movement/Dance Area, head, 1980-, Jazz Dance Theatre, founder, 1980. Writer. **Publications:** Techniques and Styles of Jazz Dance, 1969; (with D. Hodge) The Actor's Image: Movement Training for the Stage and Screen, 1983; Movement Training for the Stage and Screen: The Organic Connection, Mind, Spirit, Body, 1995; Jazz Dance: The Road Travelled the Road ahead: Jean Sebatine's Theatre Jazz Dance Technique, forthcoming. **Address:** Department of Dramatic Arts, University of Connecticut, 802 Bolton Rd., Ste. 1127, Storrs Mansfield, CT 06269-1127, U.S.A. **Online address:** jean.sabatine@uconn.edu

SABATINI, Sandra. Canadian (born Canada), b. 1959. **Genres:** Novellas/Short Stories, Novels. **Career:** University of Guelph for Literature and the Modern World, graduate teaching assistantship, 1994; University of Waterloo, graduate teaching assistantship, 1995-96; St. Jerome's University, sessional instructor, 1996-. Writer. **Publications:** The One with the News, 2000; Making Babies: Infants in Canadian Fiction, 2004; The Dolphins at Sainte-Marie, 2006; Dante's War, 2009; Theft, forthcoming. Contributor to periodicals. Works appear in anthologies. **Address:** Department of English, University of Waterloo, Hagey Hall of Humanities Bldg., Waterloo, ON N2L 3G1, Canada. **Online address:** sandy_sabatini@yahoo.com

SABATO, Haim. Egyptian (born Egypt), b. 1952?. **Genres:** Autobiography/Memoirs, Young Adult Fiction. **Career:** Rabbi and novelist. **Publications:** Minḥat Aharon: me'asaf Torani le-zikhro shel ha-Rav, Aharon Shuyeḳah, 1980; Emet me-erets titsmaḥ/Truth Shall Spring from the Earth, 1997; Ahavat Torah/Love of Torah, 2000; Te um Kavanot, 1999; Ke-af ape shaḥar: ma aseh be-Ezra Siman Ṭov, 2005; Be-or panekha: iyunim be-sugyot min ha-Talmud, 2005; Ani le-dodi, 2005; Dawning of the Day: A Jerusalem Tale, 2006; Bo i ha-ruaḥ, 2008; From the Four Winds, 2010. **Address:** c/o Author Mail, Toby Press, PO Box 8531, New Milford, CT 06776-8531, U.S.A.

SABBAGH, Marwan Noel. American (born United States), b. 1965. **Genres:** Medicine/Health. **Career:** Good Samaritan Hospital, intern, 1991-92; Baylor College of Medicine, resident, 1992-95; University of California, fellow, 1995-97, staff physician, 1995, attending physician, 1995, assistant professor, 1997; Alvarado Hospital, associate director of neuroscience, 1997; Sun Health Research Institute, Cleo Roberts Center for Clinical Research, consultant, director of clinical research, 1999-; Arizona Alzheimer's Disease Core Center, co-director; Banner Health/St. Joseph's Geriatric Fellowship Program, clinical instructor; Mayo Clinic Scottsdale, Department of Neurology, visiting scientist; Midwestern University, adjunct professor; Arizona State University, adjunct professor. Writer and geriatric neurologist. **Publications:** The Alzheimer's Answer: Reduce Your Risk and Keep Your Brain Healthy, 2008. Contributor to journals. **Address:** Sun Health Research Institute, 10515 W Santa Fe Dr., Sun City, AZ 85351-3020, U.S.A. **Online address:** marwan.sabbagh@sunhealth.org

SABIN, Roger (John). British (born England), b. 1961. **Genres:** Literary Criticism And History, Novels, History. **Career:** University of the Arts London, Central Saint Martins College of Art and Design, lecturer, 1995-, senior lecturer, reader in popular culture; University of London, Birkbeck College, lecturer; freelance journalist, 1986-; Middlesex University, visiting lecturer; London College of Printing and Distributive Trades, visiting lecturer; London School of Journalism, visiting lecturer; Intellect, consulting editor. **Publications:** Adult Comics: An Introduction, 1993; (with M. Barker) The Lasting of the Mohicans: History of an American Myth, 1995; Comics, Comix, and Graphic Novels: A History of Comic Art, 1996. EDITOR: Punk Rock: So What?: The Cultural Legacy of Punk, 1999; (with T. Triggs) Below Critical Radar: Fanzines and Alternative Comics from 1976 to Now, 2000; (contrib.) Splat, Boom, Pow!: The Influence of Cartoons in Contemporary Art, 2003. Work appears in anthologies. Contributor to journals. **Address:** Central Saint Martins College of Art and Design, University of the Arts London, Southampton Row, London, GL WC1B 4AP, England. **Online address:** r.sabin@csm.arts.ac.uk

SABLE, Martin Howard. American (born United States), b. 1924. **Genres:** Area Studies, Librarianship, Bibliography, Reference, History, Business/Trade/Industry. **Career:** Northeastern University, staff librarian and bibliographer, 1959-63; Harvard University, bibliographer, 1962-63; California State College (now California State University), Office of Latin America Studies, language librarian, 1963-64; Los Angeles County Library, reference librarian, 1964-65; University of California, Latin American Center, research associate, 1965-68; Encyclopedia Americana, advisory editor on Latin America, 1967-; University of Wisconsin, School of Information Studies, associate professor, 1968-72, professor, 1972-; Hebrew University, Graduate Library School, visiting professor, 1972-73; International Library Review, reference librarian, 1987-. Writer. **Publications:** A Selective Bibliography in Science and Engineering, 1964; Master Directory of Latin America, 1965; Periodicals for Latin American Economic Development, Trade and Finance: An Annotated Bibliography, 1965; A Guide to Latin American Studies, 1967; UFO Guide 1947-1967, 1967; Communism in Latin America, an International Bibliography: 1900-1945, 1960-67, 1968; A Bio-Bibliography of the Kennedy Family, 1969; Latin American Agriculture: A Bibliography, 1970; Latin American Studies in the Non-Western World and Eastern Europe, 1970; Latin American Urbanization: A Guide to the Literature, Organizations, and Personnel, 1971; International and Area Studies Librarianship, 1973; The Guerrilla Movement in Latin America since 1950: A Bibliography, 1977; Latin American Jewry: A Research Guide, 1978; Exobiology: A Research Guide, 1978; A Guide to Nonprint Materials for Latin American Studies, 1979; The Latin American Studies Directory, 1981; A Bibliography of the Future, 1981; The Protection of the Library: An International Bibliography, 1984; Industrial Espionage and Trade Secrets: An International Bibliography, 1985; Warfare and the Library: An International Bibliography, 1986; Research Guides to the Humanities, Social Sciences, Sciences, and Technology: An Annotated Bibliography of Guides to Library Resources and Usage, Arranged by Subject or Discipline of Coverage, 1986; Holocaust Studies: A Directory and Bibliography of Bibliographies, 1987; Mexican and Mexican-American Agricultural Labor in the United States: An International Bibliography, 1987; The Northwest Ordinance of 1787: An Interdisciplinary Bibliography, 1987; A Guide to the Writings of Pioneer Latinamericanists of the United States, 1989; Maquiladoras: Assembly and Manufacturing Plants on United States-Mexican Border: An International Guide, 1989; Columbus, Marrano Discoverer from Majorca: In Honor of the 500th Anniversary of the Discovery of America by Columbus, 1992, 1992; (with R.A. Sauers) William Francis Bartlett: Biography of a Union General in the Civil War, 2009; Gen. William F. Bartlett: Hero and Healer, forthcoming. Contributor to periodicals. **Address:** University of Wisconsin, 2200 E Kenwood Blvd., PO Box 413, Milwaukee, WI 53201, U.S.A.

SABLEMAN, Mark (Stephen). American (born United States), b. 1951. **Genres:** Communications/Media, Law. **Career:** Clearwater Sun, reporter and editor, 1973-76; Washington Post, reporter, 1977; Reuben and Proctor (law firm), associate, 1979-86, Thompson Coburn L.L.P. (law firm), associate, 1986-88, partner, 1989-; Webster University, adjunct professor, 1992-98; Washington University, School of Law, adjunct professor, 2001-. **Publications:** More Speech, Not Less: Communications Law in the Information Age, 1997. Contributor to journals. **Address:** Thompson Coburn L.L.P., 1 US Bank Plz., St. Louis, MO 63101-1611, U.S.A. **Online address:** msableman@thompsoncoburn.com

SABUDA, Robert (James). American (born United States), b. 1965. **Genres:** Children's Fiction, Children's Non-fiction, Illustrations, Picture/Board Books. **Career:** Pratt Institute, associate professor; Children's book author and illustrator, 1988-. **Publications:** SELF-ILLUSTRATED: (reteller) Saint Valentine, 1992; Tutankhamen's Gift, 1994; Arthur and the Sword, 1995; The Adventures of Providence Traveler, 1503: Uh-oh, Leonardo!, 2002.

OTHERS: The Knight's Castle: A Pop-up Book, 1994; A Christmas Alphabet (pop-up book), 1994; The Mummy's Tomb: A Pop-up Book, 1994; Cookie Count: A Tasty Pop-up, 1997; ABC Disney, 1998; Movable Mother Goose, 1999; The Blizzard's Robe, 1999; (with M. Reinhart) Young Naturalist's Pop-up Handbook Butterflies, 2001; (with M. Reinhart) Young Naturalist's Pop-up Handbook Beetles, 2001; Alice's Adventures in Wonderland, 2003; (contrib.) America the Beautiful, 2004; (with M. Reinhart) Encyclopedia Prehistorica Dinosaurs, 2005; (with M. Reinhart) Encyclopedia Prehistorica Sharks and Other Sea Monsters, 2006; The 12 Days of Christmas, 2006; (contrib.) Sabuda and Reinhart Present Castle, 2006; Winter in White: A Mini Pop-up Treat, 2007; (with M. Reinhart) Mega-beasts, 2007; Peter Pan: A Pop-Up Adaptation Of JM Barrie's Original Tale, 2008; (with M. Reinhart) Fairies and Magical Creatures, 2008; (with T. DePaola and M. Reinhart) Brava, Strega Nona!, 2008; Abc Disney: Anniversary Edition, 2009; (with M. Reinhart) Gods & Heroes, 2010; Beauty & the Beast, 2010; (with M. Reinhart) Encyclopedia Mythologica: Dragons and Monsters Pop-Up, 2011; Chanukah Lights, 2011. Illustrator of books by others. **Address:** Dunham Literary Inc., 156 5th Ave., Ste. 625, New York, NY 10010-7002, U.S.A. **Online address:** robert.sabuda@robertsabuda.com

SACHS, Jeffrey D. American (born United States), b. 1954. **Genres:** Economics, Novels. **Career:** Harvard University, assistant professor, 1980-82, associate professor, 1982-83, professor of economics, 1983-2002, Galen L. Stone professor of international trade and director of center for international development; Columbia University, Earth Institute, director, 2002-, Quetelet professor of sustainable development, professor of health policy and management; Unites Nations Millennium Project, director, 2002-06; Millennium Promise Alliance Inc., president and co-founder; Broadband Commission for Digital Development, commissioner, 2010-. Writer. **Publications:** (With M. Bruno) Macroeconomic Adjustment with Import Price Shocks: Real and Monetary Aspects, 1979; Theoretical Issues in International Borrowing, 1984; (with M. Bruno) Economics of Worldwide Stagflation, 1985; New Approaches to the Latin-American Debt Crisis, 1989; Developing Country Debt and the Economic Performance, 1989; Efficient Debt Reduction, 1989; Que se piensa en el exterior de la political económica Venezolana, 1989; (ed.) Developing Country Debt and the World Economy, 1989; Developing Country Debt and Economic Performance, 1989; Social Conflict and Populist Policies in Latin America, 1990; (with C.E. Paredes) Perus Path to Recovery: A Plan for Economic Stabilization and Growth, 1991; Global Linkages: Macroeconomic Interdependence and Cooperation in the World Economy, 1991; Poland's Jump to the Market Economy, 1993; (with F. Larrain) Macroeconomics in the Global Economy, 1993; (ed. with O.J. Blanchard and K.A. Froot) The Transition in Eastern Europe, 1994; (ed. with W.T. Woo and S. Parker) Economics in Transition: Comparing Asia and Eastern Europe, 1997; (ed. with K. Pistor) The Rule of Law and Economic Reform in Russia, 1997; The Global Competitiveness Report 1998, 1998; The Africa Competitiveness Report 1998, 1998; The Asia Competitiveness Report 1999, 1999; (ed. with A. Varshney and N. Bajpai) India in the Era of Economic Reforms, 1999; The Global Competitiveness Report 1999, 1999; (co-ed.) The Role of Law and Legal Institutions in Asian Economic Development: 1960-1995, 1999; The Global Competitiveness Report 2000, 2000; (ed. with W.T. Woo and K. Schwab) The Asian Financial Crisis: Lessons for a Resilient Asia, 2000; The Africa Competitiveness Report 2000/2001, 2001; Macroeonomics and Health: Investing in Health for Economic Development, 2001; The Latin-American Competitiveness Report 2001-2002, 2002; Global Public Goods for Health: The Report of Working Group Two of the Commission on Macroeconomics and Health, 2002; The Global Competitiveness Report 2001-2002, 2002; (foreword) Economics Development and the Division of Labor, 2003; Investing in Development: A Practical Plan to Achieve the Millennium Development Goals, 2005; (co-author) Propriedade intelectual e desenvolvimento, 2005; The End of Poverty: Economic Possibilities for Our Time, 2005; (ed. with M. Humphreys and J.E. Stiglitz) Escaping the Resource Curse, 2007; (ed. with M. Humphreys and J.E. Stiglitz) Escaping the Resource Curse, 2007; Common Wealth: Economics for a Crowded Planet, 2008; (with N. Bajpai and R.H. Dholakia) Improving Access and Efficiency in Public Health Services: Mid-term Evaluation of India's National Rural Health Mission, 2010; Price of Civilization: American Values and the Return to Prosperity, 2011. **Address:** The Earth Institute, Columbia University, 405 Low Library, 535 W 116th St., PO Box 4335, New York, NY 10027, U.S.A. **Online address:** sachs@columbia.edu

SACHS, Judith. Also writes as Antonia Saxon, Jennifer Sarasin, Petra Diamond, Jocelyn Saal. American (born United States), b. 1947. **Genres:** Novels, Romance/Historical, Medicine/Health, Self Help, Sex, Adult Non-fiction, Psychology, Social Sciences, Social Sciences. **Career:** The Magazine, editorial assistant, 1969-70; Saturday Review Press, assistant, associate editor, 1970-73; Arbor House Publishing Co., managing editor, 1973; Delacorte Press, senior editor, 1973-77; Hawthorn Books, senior editor, 1977-79; writer, 1979-; Trenton State College, adjunct professor of health and physical education, 1994-; Human Resource Development Institute of New Jersey, adjunct faculty teaching stress management and mid-life issues, 1999-2000; Intellitecs, product spokesperson; Chesebrough-Ponds, product spokesperson; Proctor & Gamble, product spokesperson; HealthAnswers, writer, 2000-01; SimStar/Rosetta Marketing Group, writer and behavioral marketer, 2001-04; breastcancer.org, writer, 2004-05; ParentingTeensNetwork, editorial director, 2005-08; Harte-Hanks, writer, 2009-09; Evokeinteraction, associate creative director, 2010-. **Publications:** AS JOCELYN SAAL: Dance of Love, 1982; Trusting Hearts, 1982; Running Mates, 1983; On Thin Ice, 1983. AS JENNIFER SARASIN: Spring Love, 1983; The Hidden Room, 1984; Splitting, 1985; Cheating, 1985; Living It Up, 1986; Over, 1987; Together Again, 1987; Acting Up, 1988; Getting Serious, 1988. WITH A. BRUNO AS ANTONIA SAXON: Paradiso, 1983; Just Another Friday Night, 1984. AS PETRA DIAMOND: Confidentially Yours, 1984; Night of a Thousand Stars, 1985; Play It Again, Sam, 1986. OTHER: (as Rebecca Diamond) Summer Romance, 1982; (as Emily Chase) The Big Crush, 1984; (as Emily Chase) With Friends like That, 1985; Rites of Spring, 1988; What Women Can Do about Chronic Endometriosis, 1990; What Women Should Know about Menopause, 1990; What You Can Do about Osteoporosis, 1991; (with A. Mollen) Dr. Mollen's Anti-Aging Diet: The Breakthrough Program for Easy Weight Loss and Longevity, 1991; (with P. Sinaikin) After the Fast, 1992; (with M. Schwartzman) The Anxious Parent, 1993; (with P. Sinaikin) Fat Madness: How to Stop the Diet Cycle and Achieve Permanent Well-Being, 1994; (with L. Domash) Wanna Be My Friend?: How to Strengthen Your Child's Social Skills, 1994; The Healing Power of Sex, 1994; When Someone You Love Has AIDS: A Caregivers Guide, 1995; (with E. Ross) Healing the Female Heart, 1995; Natural Medicine for Heart Disease, 1996; (with B. Burch) Natural Healing for the Pregnant Woman, 1997; (with K.A. Hutchinson) What Every Woman Should Know about Estrogen: Natural and Traditional Therapies for a Longer, Healthier Life, 1997; Nature's Prozac, 1997; Reflexology: An A-to-Z Guide to Pressure-Point Healing, 1997; The Natural Healing Guide to Heat Disease, 1997; Break the Stress Cycle: 10 Steps to Reducing Stress for Women, 1998; (with R.J. Paulson) Rewinding Your Biological Clock: Motherhood Late in Life, 1998; Sensual Rejuvenation: Maintaining Sexual Vigor Through Midlife and Beyond, 1999; Twenty-Minute Vacations, 2001; (with S. Leiblum) Naked Woman: Uncovering Female Sexuality, 2001; Getting the Sex You Want: A Woman's Guide to Becoming Proud, Passionate, and Pleased in Bed, 2002. **Address:** 904 S Front St., Philadelphia, PA 19147, U.S.A. **Online address:** judithsachs@mac.com

SACHS, Marilyn (Stickle). American (born United States), b. 1927. **Genres:** Children's Fiction, Young Adult Fiction, Novels, Novellas/Short Stories. **Career:** Brooklyn Public Library, children's librarian, 1949-60; San Francisco Public Library, part-time children's librarian, 1961-67. Writer. **Publications:** Amy Moves In, 1964; Laura's Luck, 1965; Amy and Laura, 1966; Veronica Ganz, 1968; Peter and Veronica, 1969; Marv, 1970; The Bears' House, 1971, rev. ed., 1987; Reading between the Lines, 1971; The Truth about Mary Rose, 1973; A Pocket Full of Seeds, 1973; Matt's Mitt, 1975; Dorrie's Book, 1975; A December Tale, 1976; A Secret Friend, 1978; A Summer's Lease, 1979; Bus Ride, 1980; Class Pictures, 1980; Fleet-footed Florence, 1981; Hello Wrong Number, 1981; Beach Towels, 1982; Call Me Ruth, 1982; Fourteen, 1983; The Fat Girl, 1984, 2nd ed., 2007; Thunderbird, 1985; Underdog, 1985; Baby Sister, 1986; Almost Fifteen, 1987; Fran Ellen's House, 1987; Sisters and Friends, 1988; Just Like a Friend, 1989; At the Sound of the Beep, 1990; (ed. with A. Durell) The Big Book for Peace, 1990; Circles, 1991; What My Sister Remembered, 1992; Thirteen Going on Seven, 1993; Ghosts in the Family, 1995; The Golden Gate Murders, 1995; Another Day, 1997; The Surprise Party, 1998; JoJo & Winnie: Sister Stories, 1999; JoJo & Winnie Again: More Sister Stories, 2000; Four Ugly Cats in Apartment 3D, 2002; Lost in America, 2005; First Impressions, 2006. Contributor to periodicals. **Address:** 733 31st Ave., San Francisco, CA 94121-3523, U.S.A. **Online address:** marilynsachs@marilynsachs.com

SACHS, Mendel. American (born United States), b. 1927. **Genres:** Philosophy, Physics, Sciences, History. **Career:** University of California, Radiation Laboratory, theoretical physicist, 1954-56; Lockheed Missiles and Space Laboratory, senior scientist, 1956-61; San Jose State College, assistant pro-

fessor of physics, 1957-61; McGill University, research professor of physics, 1961-62; Boston University, associate professor of physics, 1962-66; State University of New York, University at Buffalo, professor, 1966-97, professor emeritus of physics, 1997-. Writer. **Publications:** Solid State Theory, 1963; The Search for a Theory of Matter, 1971; The Field Concept in Contemporary Science, 1973; Ideas of the Theory of Relativity: General Implications from Physics to Problems of Society, 1974; Ideas of Matter: From Ancient Times to Bohr and Einstein, 1981; General Relativity and Matter: A Spinor Field Theory from Fermis to Light-Years, 1982; Quantum Mechanics from General Relativity: An Approximation for a Theory of Inertia, 1986; Einstein versus Bohr: The Continuing Controversies in Physics, 1988; Relativity in Our Time: From Physics to Human Relations, 1993; Dialogues on Modern Physics, 1998; Quantum Mechanics and Gravity, 2004; Concepts of Modern Physics: The Haifa Lectures, 2007; Physics of the Universe, 2010. **Address:** Department of Physics, University at Buffalo, State University of New York, 239 Fronczak Hall, Buffalo, NY 14260, U.S.A. **Online address:** msachs@buffalo.edu

SACHS, Murray. American/Canadian (born Canada), b. 1924. **Genres:** Humanities, Language/Linguistics, Literary Criticism And History, Translations. **Career:** University of California, instructor in French, 1948-50; University of Detroit, lecturer in French, 1951-52; Williams College, assistant professor, 1954-60; Brandeis University, Department of Romance and Comparative Literature, assistant professor, 1960-61, associate professor, 1961-66, professor, 1966-96, chairman, 1981-84, professor emeritus of French and comparative literature, 1996-. Writer. **Publications:** (Ed. with E.M. and R.B. Grant) French Stories, Plays and Poetry, 1959; The Career of Alphonse Daudet, 1965; (ed.) The French Short Story in the Nineteenth Century, 1969; Anatole France: The Short Stories, 1974. Contributor of articles to periodicals. **Address:** Department of Romance & Comparative Literature, Brandeis University, 415 South St., Golding, 12, PO Box 024, Waltham, MA 02453, U.S.A. **Online address:** sachs@brandeis.edu

SACHS, Robert. American (born United States), b. 1952. **Genres:** Medicine/Health. **Career:** Diamond Way Ayurveda, co-director, 1995-. Writer and radio host. **Publications:** Rebirth into Pure Land, 1994; Health for Life: Secrets of Tibetan Ayurveda, 1995; Perfect Endings: A Conscious Approach to Dying and Death, 1998; Nine Star Ki: Your Astrological Companion to Feng Shui, 2001; Tibetan Ayurveda: Health Secrets from the Roof of the World, 2001; The Passionate Buddha: Wisdom on Intimacy and Enduring Love, 2002; The Buddha at War, 2006; The Wisdom of the Buddhist Masters: Common and Uncommon Sense, 2008. **Address:** Diamond Way Ayurveda, PO Box 13753, San Luis Obispo, CA 93406, U.S.A. **Online address:** passion8@earthlink.net

SACHS, Wolfgang. German (born Germany), b. 1946. **Genres:** Environmental Sciences/Ecology, Third World, Social Sciences. **Career:** Technical University of Berlin, assistant professor, 1975-80, research fellow, 1980-84; Society for International Development, co-editor, 1984-87; Pennsylvania State University, visiting professor, 1987-90; Institute for Cultural Studies, fellow, 1990-93; Wuppertal Institute for Climate, Environment and Energy, senior research fellow, 1993-, The President's Research Unit, project coordinator, Berlin Office, head, 2009-; Greenpeace Germany, chair, 1993-2001; Intergovernmental Panel on Climate Change, lead author, 1999-2001; University of Kassel, Department of Social Sciences, honorary professor, 2007-; Schumacher College, lecturer. Writer. **Publications:** Schulzwang und soziale Kontrolle: Argumente für e. Entschulung d. Lernens, 1976; Liebe zum Automobil: ein Rückblick in die Geschichte unserer Wünsche, 1984; Zur Archäologie der Entwicklungsidee: (acht essays), 1992; (ed.) The Development Dictionary: A Guide to Knowledge as Power, 1992; (ed.) Global Ecology: A New Arena of Political Conflict, 1993; Planet Dialectics: Explorations in Environment and Development, 1999; Nach uns die Zukunft: der globale Konflikt um Gerechtigkeit und Ökologie, 2003; (with T. Sintarius) Fair Future: Resource Conflicts, Security and Global Justice, 2007; (ed. with T. Sintarius) Slow Trade-Sound Farming, 2007; Zukunftsfähiges Deutschland in einer globalisierten Welt, 2008. **Address:** Wuppertal Institute for Climate, Environment and, Energy, ProjektZentrum Berlin der Stiftung Mercator, Neue Promenade 6, Berlin, 10178, Germany. **Online address:** wolfgang.sachs@wupperinst.org

SACK, Allen L. American (born United States), b. 1945. **Genres:** Sports/Fitness. **Career:** University of New Haven, Department of Sociology, assistant professor, 1974-80, associate professor, 1980-86, professor, 1986-91, professor of management, 1991-, Department of Sociology and Social Welfare, head, 1983-86, Arts and Science Honors Program, director, 1987-91, university ombudsman, 1988-91; Management of Sport Industries Program, coordinator, 1991-2001, Institute for Sports Management, School of Business, director, 2006-; Center for Athletes Rights and Education, project director, 1981-83; University of Connecticut, adjunct professor, 1996-2000. Writer. **Publications:** (With E.J. Staurowsky) College Athletes for Hire: The Evolution and Legacy of the NCAA's Amateur Myth, 1998; Counterfeit Amateurs: An Athlete's Journey Through the Sixties to the Age of Academic Capitalism, 2008. Contributor of articles to books, journals. **Address:** Department of Management, University of New Haven, M112, 300 Boston Post Rd., West Haven, CT 06516, U.S.A. **Online address:** asack@newhaven.edu

SACKETT, Jeffrey. American (born United States), b. 1949?. **Genres:** Novels, Horror. **Career:** Dowling College, Department of History, adjunct associate professor; Suffolk Community College, Department of History, adjunct associate professor. Writer. **Publications:** NOVELS: Stolen Souls, 1987; Candlemas Eve, 1988; Blood of the Impaler, 1989; Mark of the Werewolf, 1990; The Demon, 1991. **Address:** c/o Author Mail, Bantam Dell Books, 1745 Broadway, 10th Fl., New York, NY 10019-4368, U.S.A.

SACKMAN, Douglas Cazaux. American (born United States), b. 1968. **Genres:** History. **Career:** University of California, instructor, 1995, lecturer, 1997-98; California State University, instructor, 1996; Oberlin College, visiting assistant professor of history, 1998-2000; University of Puget Sound, assistant professor of history, 2000-; Longman Press, consultant; Claremont Children's Museum, consultant. Writer. **Publications:** Orange Empire: California and the Fruits of Eden, 2005; (ed.) A Companion to American Environmental History, 2010; Wild Men: Ishi and Kroeber in the Wilderness of Modern America, 2010. Contributor to books, journals and periodicals. **Address:** University of Puget Sound, 1500 Warner St., PO Box 1033, Tacoma, WA 98416, U.S.A. **Online address:** dsackman@ups.edu

SACKNOFF, Scott. American (born United States), b. 1967. **Genres:** Business/Trade/Industry, Sciences. **Career:** International Space Business Council, president; SPADE Defense Index, index manager; ITT, General Dynamics, Department of Defense, NASA, FMR/Fidelity Investments, consultant. Writer. **Publications:** (ed.) United States Space Directory, 1995; (with L. David) The Space Publications Guide to Space Careers, 1998; (ed.) In Their Own Words: Conversations with the Astronauts and Men Who Led America's Journey into Space and to the Moon, 2003. **Address:** SPADE Defense Index, 1725 I St. NW, Ste. 300, Washington, DC 20006, U.S.A.

SACKS, David Harris. American (born United States), b. 1942. **Genres:** History, Humanities. **Career:** University of Massachusetts at Boston, lecturer, 1977-79; Harvard University, lecturer and tutor, 1978-86; Reed College, assistant professor, 1986-89, associate professor of history and humanities, 1989-93, professor, 1993-2003, Richard F Scholz professor of history and humanities, 2003-, chair; Folger Shakespeare Library, National Endowment for the Humanities long-term fellow, 1989-90; Yale University, visiting professor of history, 1998-99; Woodrow Wilson Center, fellow, 1992-93; Guggenheim, fellow, 1992-93. Writer. **Publications:** Trade, Society and Politics in Bristol, 1500-1640, 2 vol., 1985; The Widening Gate: Bristol and the Atlantic Economy, 1450-1700, 1991. EDITOR: (with D.R. Kelley) The Historical Imagination in Early Modern Britain: History, Rhetoric and Fiction, 1500-1800, 1997; (ed. and intro.) Utopia, 1999. Works appear in anthologies. **Address:** Department of History, Reed College, 206A Eliot Hall, 3203 SE Woodstock Blvd., Portland, OR 97202, U.S.A. **Online address:** dsacks@reed.edu

SACKS, Howard L. American (born United States), b. 1949. **Genres:** Music, Cultural/Ethnic Topics, Art/Art History, Local History/Rural Topics. **Career:** Kenyon College, professor of sociology, 1975-, Department of Anthropology/Sociology, chair, 1990-, Rural Life Center, director, senior advisor to the president; National Council for the Traditional Arts, associate director, 1982-83. **Publications:** Seems Like Romance to Me, 1985; (with J.R. Sacks) Way up North in Dixie: A Black Family's Claim to the Confederate Anthem, 1993, 2nd ed., 2003; (co-author) Catching Stories: A Practical Guide to Oral History, 2009. Contributor of articles to periodicals. **Address:** Department of Anthropology/Sociology, Kenyon College, Treleaven House 201, Ralston House, Gambier, OH 43022, U.S.A. **Online address:** sacksh@kenyon.edu

SACKS, Oliver (Wolf). British (born England), b. 1933. **Genres:** Medicine/Health, Anthropology/Ethnology, Psychology, Adult Non-fiction. **Career:** Middlesex Hospital, intern in medicine, surgery and neurology, 1958-60; Mt. Zion Hospital, research assistant, 1960-61, rotating intern, 1961-62; University of California, resident in neurology and neuropathology, 1962-65; Yeshiva University, Albert Einstein College of Medicine, fellow in neurochemistry and neuropathology, 1965-66, instructor in neurology, 1966-75, assistant professor of neurology, 1975-78, associate professor of neurology, 1978-85, clinical professor of neurology, 1985-2007; Montefiore Hospital, Headache Unit, consulting neurologist, 1966-68; Bronx Psychiatric Center, consulting neurologist, 1966-91; Beth Abraham Hospital, consulting neurologist, 1966-2007; Little Sisters of the Poor, consulting neurologist, 1972-; Bronx Developmental Services, consulting neurologist, 1974-76; University of California-Santa Cruz, Cowell College, visiting professor, 1987; New York University, School of Medicine, adjunct professor of psychiatry, 1992-2007; Comprehensive Epilepsy Center, consulting neurologist, 1999-2007; Columbia University, Medical Center, professor of neurology and psychiatry, 2007-, artist, 2007-. Writer. **Publications:** Migraine, 1970, rev. ed., 1999; Awakenings, 1973; A Leg to Stand On, 1984; The Man Who Mistook His Wife for a Hat And Other Clinical Tales, 1985; Seeing Voices: A Journey into the World of the Deaf, 1989, rev. ed., 1991; An Anthropologist on Mars: Seven Paradoxical Tales, 1995; The Island of the Colorblind, 1996; Uncle Tungsten: Memories of A Chemical Boyhood, 2001; Oaxaca Journal, 2002; Musicophilia: Tales Of Music And The Brain, 2007, rev. ed., 2008; The Mind's Eye, 2010; Hallucinations, 2012. Contributor to books and journals. **Address:** 2 Horatio St., Apt. 3G, New York, NY 10014-1638, U.S.A. **Online address:** mail@oliversacks.com

SACKS, Steven. American (born United States), b. 1968. **Genres:** Human Relations/Parenting, Self Help. **Career:** Promotions.com, director of customer acquisition marketing; MetLife Insurance, product manager; Mate Map Enterprises, founder; Bank of America, consultant. Writer. **Publications:** The Mate Map: The Right Tool for Choosing the Right Mate, 2002. Contributor to periodicals. **Address:** Mate Map Enterprises, 1289 N Fordham Blvd., Ste. 349, Chapel Hill, NC 27514-6110, U.S.A. **Online address:** steven@matemap.com

SACRE, Antonio. American (born United States), b. 1968. **Genres:** Children's Fiction, Plays/Screenplays, Theatre, Mythology/Folklore, Race Relations, Humor/Satire. **Career:** Writer, Storyteller, performance artist and artist-in-residence. **Publications:** The Barking Mouse, 2003; Noche Buena: A Christmas Story, 2010; Mango in the Hand: A Story Told Through Proverbs, 2011. **Address:** PO Box 3444, Hollywood, CA 90078-3444, U.S.A. **Online address:** asacre@earthlink.net

SADDLEMYER, (Eleanor) Ann. Canadian (born Canada), b. 1932. **Genres:** Literary Criticism And History, Theatre, Women's Studies And Issues, Biography. **Career:** University of Victoria, professor of English, 1968-71, visiting professor, 1995-; Victoria College, professor of English, 1971-; Colin Smythe Ltd., director, 1971-; University of Toronto, Graduate Drama Centre, director, 1972-77, acting director, 1985-86; Theatre History in Canada, co-editor, 1978-86; Massey College, master, 1988-95, master emerita, 1995-. **Publications:** (Co-author) The World of W.B. Yeats, 1965; In Defence of Lady Gregory, Playwright, 1966; Synge and Modern Comedy, 1968, Theatre Business: The Correspondence of the First Abbey Theatre Directors, 1982; The Collected Letters of J.M. Synge, vol. I, 1983, vol. II, 1984; Becoming George: The Life of Mrs. W.B. Yeats, 2002. EDITOR: The Plays of J.M. Synge: Books One and Two, 1968; J.M. Synge: Plays, 1969; The Plays of Lady Gregory, Books I-IV, 1970; A Selection of Letters from J.M. Synge to W.B. Yeats and Lady Gregory, 1971; Letters to Molly: J.M. Synge to Maire O'Neill, 1971; (co-ed.) Lady Gregory Fifty Years After, 1987; Early Stages: Essays on Theatre in Ontario 1800-1914, 1990; J.M. Synge: The Playboy of the Western World and Other Plays, 1995; (co-ed.) Later Stages: Essays on Ontario Theatre from WWI to the 1970s, 1997; W.B. Yeats and George Yeats: The Letters, 2011. **Address:** 10876 Madrona Dr., North Saanich, BC V8L 5N9, Canada. **Online address:** saddlemy@uvic.ca

SADDLER, Allen. Also writes as K. Allen Saddler. British (born England), b. 1923. **Genres:** Novels, Children's Fiction, Plays/Screenplays, Theatre, Young Adult Fiction. **Career:** The Guardian, West Country theatre critic, 1972-. Writer. **Publications:** AS K. ALLEN SADDLER: The Great Brain Robbery, 1965; Gilt Edge, 1966; Talking Turkey, 1968; Betty, 1974. JUVENILES AS ALLEN SADDLER: The Clockwork Monster, 1981; Mr. Whizz, 1982; Smudger's Seaside Spectacular, 1986; The Relay Race, 1986; Jerry and the Monsters, 1986; Smudger's Saturday Special, 1988; Jerry and the Inventions, 1988. THE KING AND QUEEN SERIES: The Archery Contest, 1982; The King Gets Fit, 1982; The King and the Invisible Dwarf, 1983; The

Fishing Competition, 1983; The King at Christmas, 1983; The Queen's Painting, 1983; Bless 'Em All, 2007; Long and the Short, 2008. CHILDREN: The King and Queen series, 1982; Smudger's Seaside Spectacular, 1986; Jerry and the Monsters, 1986; The Relay Race, 1986; Smudger's Saturday Special, 1988; Jerry and the Inventions, 1988; Sam's Swop Shop, 1993. OTHERS: Daddy Good, forthcoming. Contributor to periodicals. **Address:** Serafina Clarke, 98 Tunis Rd., London, GL W12 7EY, England. **Online address:** allen@stjohnshall.eclipse.co.uk

SADDLER, Joseph Robert. American/Barbadian (born Barbados), b. 1958. **Genres:** Music. **Career:** The Chris Rock Show, Home Box Office Network (HBO), music director. Writer. **Publications:** (With D. Ritz) The Adventures of Grandmaster Flash: My Life, My Beats, 2008. **Address:** Grandmaster Flash Enterprises, 00 Johnson Ave., Ste. E-7, Bohemia, NY 11716, U.S.A.

SADDLER, K. Allen. *See* **SADDLER, Allen.**

SADER, Emir. Brazilian (born Brazil), b. 1943. **Genres:** Politics/Government, Sociology. **Career:** University of Paris, professor of politics, 1968, 1971, 1973; University of Sao Paulo, professor of philosophy, 1969-70, professor of sociology, 1983-, now professor emeritus; University of Chile, professor of sociology, 1973-76; Institute of Brazilian Studies, 1987-88; State University of Rio de Janeiro, Department of Social Policy, professor, 1993-2009, Department of History, teacher, 2009-, Laboratory of Public Policies, coordinator, 2000-, director and principal investigator; Latin American Sociology, president, 1997-99; Latin American Council of Social Sciences, executive secretary, 2006-09, 2009-. Writer. **Publications:** POLITICAL ANALYSES: Estado e política em Marx, 1983; A Revoluacao Cubana, 1985; E agora, PT?: caráter e identidade, 1986; (with M.I. Bierrenbach and C.P. Figueiredo) Fogo no pavilhão: uma proposta de liberdade para o menor, 1987; Movimentos sociais na transição democrática, 1987; Transição no Brasil: da ditadura à democracia?, 1991; (with K. Silverstein) Without Fear of Being Happy, 1991; Amazônia: as raízes da destruição, 1991; Governar para todos: uma avaliação da gestão Luiza Erundina, 1992; Chile 1810-1980, 1992; O Socialismo na America Latina, 1992; (with C. Benjamim) 1994: Ideias Para uma Alternativa de Esquerda a Crise Brasileira, 1993; (with H. Salem) As Tribos do Mal, 1995; O Anjo Torto, 1995; (co-author) Pos-Neoliberalismo, 1995; (co-ed.) No Fio da Navalha, 1996; (co-ed.) O Brasil do Real, 1996; Cartas al Che, 1997; (comp. with P. Gentili) La Trama del Neoliberalismo, 1999; Pós-Neoliberalismo II, 1999; 7 Pecados do Capital, 2000; Contraversões: civilização ou barbárie na virada do século, 2000; (comp.) El Ajuste Estructural en America Latina, 2001; (with M.C. Tavares and E. Jorge) Globalização e socialismo, 2001; Seculo IX-Uma Biografia nao Autorisada, 2002; A Vingança da História, 2003, 2nd ed., 2007; Crisis hegemónicas en tiempos imperiales, 2004; (co-ed.) Hegemonías y emancipaciones en el siglo XXI, 2004; Perspectivas, 2005; Posneoliberalismo en América Latina, 2008; (ed. with H. Aboites and P. Gentili) Reforma universitaria, 2008; (co-author) Estado, sociedade e formação profissional em saúde, 2008; Nova toupeira: Os caminhos da esquerda latino-americana, 2009. **Address:** Universidade do Estado do Rio de Janeiro, Rua Sao Francisco Xavier, 524, 1 andar Bloco F, Marcana, Rio de Janeiro, RJ 20550-013, Brazil. **Online address:** emir@lpp-uerj.net

SADICK, Neil (S.). American (born United States), b. 1951. **Genres:** How-to Books, Medicine/Health, Sports/Fitness. **Career:** State University of New York Downstate Medical Center, intern in internal medicine, 1977-78; North Shore University Hospital, resident in internal medicine, 1978-80, director of pediatric dermatology clinic, director of dermatology/immunology clinic; Memorial Sloane Kettering Medical Center, resident in internal medicine, 1978-80, resident in dermatology, 1980-82; Cornell Medical Center, New York Hospital, resident in dermatology, 1980-82, chief resident, 1982-83; Cornell University, Weill Cornell Medical College, assistant clinical professor, 1990, associate clinical professor 1997-2002, clinical professor of dermatology, 2002-, Scott Clinical professor of dermatology; Dermatology Foundation, vice-chair of leadership society, 1992; Sadick Aesthetic Surgery and Dermatology, physician, medical director and owner; Sadick Research Group, director; Cosmetic Surgery Foundation, president; Christian Dior Beauty, global medical advisor; Womens Dermatologic Society, board director; American Academy of Cosmetic Surgery, board director; American Society of Dermatologic Surgery, board director; American Society of Cosmetic and Laser Surgeons, treasurer; American College of Phlebology, president. Writer. **Publications:** HIV in Infants and Pregnant Women, 1989; (co-author) Your Hair: Helping to Keep It: Treatment and Prevention of Hair Loss for Men and Women, 1991; (ed.) The Eleventh Congress of the International Union of Phlebology, 1992; (co-author) Infectious Diseases in Dermatology, 1992; (co-author) Cutaneous Manifestations of Retrovirus Diseases, 1992; Dermatology Clinics, 1997; Infectious Diseases, 1999; Manual of Sclerotherapy, 2000; (ed.) Augmentation Fillers, 2010; (co-ed.) Illustrated Manual of Injectable Fillers: A Technical Guide to the Volumetric Approach to Whole Body Rejuvenation, 2011; (with S. Marshall and A. Dinkes) The New Natural: Your Ultimate Guide To Cutting-Edge Age Reversal, 2011. Contributor to journals. **Address:** Sadick Aesthetic Surgery & Dermatology, 911 Park Ave., New York, NY 10075, U.S.A. **Online address:** nssderm@sadickdermatology.com

SADIQ, Nazneen. Canadian/Pakistani (born Pakistan), b. 1944. **Genres:** Young Adult Fiction, Westerns/Adventure. **Career:** Liberal and York View, featurist, 1977-78; Newsline, freelance correspondent, 1983-96; writer, 1985-; Globe and Mail, freelance writer and book reviewer, 1989-92. **Publications:** YOUNG ADULT FICTION: Camels Can Make You Homesick: And Other Stories (Time of Our Lives), 1985; Heartbreak High (Junior High Novels), 1988; Lucy, 1989. ADULT FICTION: Ice Bangles, 1988; Chopin People, 1994. **Address:** Lugus Publications, 215-28 Industrial St, East York, ON M4G 1Y9, Canada.

SADLER, Amy. British (born England), b. 1924?. **Genres:** Westerns/Adventure, Young Adult Fiction, Literary Criticism And History. **Career:** Union for Marine Engineers for West Coast Ports, medical insurance adjuster, 1955-58; Australian Trade Commission, secretary, 1958; United Engineers, secretary, 1960-61; Southern Pacific Railroad, secretary, 1961-63; Heating Engineering, secretary, 1976-78, secretary, 1979-85; part-time writer, 1985-. **Publications:** California Their Aim, 1988; Stop-Off at Wichita, 1989; Showdown at Mesa Verde, 1990; Striker Hits Pay-Dirt, 1990; Feuding at Dutchman's Creek, 1990; Night of the Rope, 1991; No Place to Die, 1991; The Night Rider, 1992; The Sons of Batt Coltrain, 1992; A Man of Texas, 1993; Heartbreak Valley, 1993; One Year at Yuma, 1994; Luck Is Where You Find It, 1994; Last Hanging at Fallstown, 1995; Bracken's Nightmare, 1995; Bandoleros Along the Nueces, 1996; The Final Showdown, 1997; Santiago, 1997; Dead Is for Ever, 1997; The Protectors, 1999. **Address:** 4 Hillside Cres., Skipton, NY BD23 2LE, England.

SADLIER, Darlene J. American (born United States), b. 1950. **Genres:** Literary Criticism And History, Women's Studies And Issues. **Career:** Kent State University, visiting lecturer, 1977-78; Indiana University, visiting assistant professor, 1978-79, assistant professor, 1979-85, associate professor, 1985-91, professor of Spanish and Portuguese, 1991-, adjunct professor of women's studies, Portuguese Program, director; Midwest Modern Language Association, president, 1985-86. Writer. **Publications:** Imagery and Theme in the Poetry of Cecília Meireles: A Study of Mar Absoluto, 1983; Cecília Meireles e João Alphonsus, 1984; The Question of How: Women Writers and New Portuguese Literature, 1989; (ed. and trans.) One Hundred Years after Tomorrow: Brazilian Women's Fiction in the Twentieth Century, 1992; Introduction to Fernando Pessoa: Modernism and the Paradoxes of Authorship, 1998; Nelson Pereira dos Santos, 2003; Brazil Imagined: 1500 to the Present, 2008; (ed. and intro.) Latin American Melodrama: Passion, Pathos, and Entertainment, 2009. Contributor of articles, reviews, and translations to periodicals. **Address:** Department of Spanish & Portuguese, Indiana University-Bloomington, Ballantine Hall 806, 1020 E Kirkwood, Bloomington, IN 47405, U.S.A. **Online address:** sadlier@indiana.edu

SADOWSKY, Jonathan Hal. American (born United States), b. 1962?. **Genres:** History. **Career:** Case Western Reserve University, assistant professor of history, 1993-98, associate professor of history, 1999-, Dr. Theodore J. Castele associate professor of medical history and chair, adjunct associate professor of global health and diseases, 1999-, Dr. Theodore J. Castele professor of the history of medicine, 2000-, College Scholars Program, director, 2001-06, chair, 2006-. Writer. **Publications:** Imperial Bedlam: Institutions of Madness in Colonial Southwest Nigeria, 1999. **Address:** Department of History, Case Western Reserve University, 11201 Euclid Ave., Cleveland, OH 44106, U.S.A. **Online address:** jonathan.sadowsky@case.edu

SADRI, Ahmad. American/Iranian (born Iran), b. 1953. **Genres:** Sociology, History. **Career:** Tehran Planing and Budget Organization, research assistant, 1975-78; Tehran College of Educators, lecturer in sociology, 1975-78; Abu-Reihan University, lecturer, 1977-78; Farabi University, lecturer, 1977-78; William Paterson College, lecturer in sociology, 1980-81; CRITICA (interdisciplinary studies forum), founder and organizer, 1982-87; Kean College, lecturer in sociology, 1986-88; New School for Social Research, Department of Sociology, student advisor, 1987-89; International Journal of Politics, Culture and Society, associate editor, 1988-93; Lake Forest College, assistant professor, 1988-94, associate professor of sociology, 1994-2000, professor of sociology, 2002-, James P. Gorter professor of Islamic world studies, Department of Sociology and Anthropology, chair, 2001-; Allameh Tabatabaie University, visiting professor, 1992; University of Tehran, visiting professor, 1992; Tarbiat Modarres University, visiting professor, 1993. Writer. **Publications:** Max Weber's Sociology of Intellectuals, 1992, 2nd ed., 1994; (trans. and ed. with M. Sadri) Reason, Freedom and Democracy in Islam: Essential Writings of Abdolkarim Soroush, 2000; (trans.) Saddam City, 2004. Contributor to books and journals. **Address:** Department of Sociology and Anthropology, Lake Forest College, 555 N Sheridan Rd., Lake Forest, IL 60045, U.S.A. **Online address:** sadri@lakeforest.edu

SAENZ, Benjamin Alire. American (born United States), b. 1954. **Genres:** Poetry, Novels, Novellas/Short Stories, Young Adult Fiction. **Career:** Catholic priest; University of Texas, faculty of creative writing, MFA Creative Writing Program, director. Writer. **Publications:** Calendar of Dust (poetry), 1991; Flowers for the Broken (short stories), 1992; Carry Me Like Water (novel), 1995; Dark and Perfect Angels (poetry), 1995; The House of Forgetting (novel), 1997; A Gift from Papá Diego, 1998; Elegies in Blue: Poems, 2002; Sammy & Juliana in Hollywood, 2004; In Perfect Light: A Novel, 2005; Dreaming the End of War, 2006; Names On a Map: A Novel, 2008; He Forgot to Say Good-Bye, 2008; A Perfect Season for Dreaming, 2008; Last Night I Sang to the Monster: A Novel, 2009; Dog Who Loved Tortillas=La perrita que le encantaban las tortillas, 2009; (intro.) Native, 2010; Book of What Remains, 2010; Aristotle and Dante Discover the Secrets of the Universe, 2012. Contributor to periodicals. **Address:** Department of Creative Writing, University of Texas, Liberal Arts 415, 500 W University Ave., El Paso, TX 79968, U.S.A. **Online address:** bsaenz@utep.edu

SAENZ, Gil. American (born United States), b. 1941. **Genres:** Poetry, Young Adult Fiction. **Career:** Depressive Bipolar Support Association, president; Detroit Federal Executive Board, vice president, president, through 2004; Poetry Society of Michigan, treasurer, 2005-. Writer. **Publications:** Colorful Impressions, 1993; Moments in Time, 1995; Dreaming of Love, 1999; Poems of Life, 2001; Spaces in Between: A Collection of Poems, 2002; (comp. and ed.) The Other Side of Darkness: MDDA Anthology, 2003. Works appears in anthologies. **Address:** Poetry Society of Michigan, PO Box 614, Allen Park, MI 48101-0614, U.S.A. **Online address:** gilbertsaenz@comcast.net

SÆTERØY, John Arne. (Jason). French/Norwegian (born Norway), b. 1965. **Genres:** Novels, Criminology/True Crime. **Career:** Writer. **Publications:** AS JASON: Hey, Wait, 2001; SHHHH!, 2002; The Iron Wagon, 2003; Why Are You Doing This?, 2004; You Can't Get There from Here, 2004; Tell Me Something, 2004; (co-author) Rosetta: A Comics Anthology, vol. II, 2004; The Left Bank Gang, 2006; The Living and the Dead, 2007; I Killed Adolf Hitler, 2007; The Last Musketeer, 2008. **Address:** Fantagraphics Books, 7563 Lake City Way NE, Seattle, WA 98115, U.S.A. **Online address:** info@employe-du-moi.org

SAFDIE, Moshe. Canadian/Israeli (born Israel), b. 1938. **Genres:** Architecture, Urban Studies. **Career:** H.P.D. Van Ginkle and Associates, architects and planners, 1961-62; Louis I. Kahn, architect, 1962-63; Canadian Corp. For the 1967 World Exposition, staff, 1963-64; Moshe Safdie and Associates, principal, 1964-; Canadian Corp., section head, architect and planner, 1967; McGill University, visiting professor of architecture, 1970; Yale University, Charlotte Shepherd Davenport professor of architecture, 1971-72; Ben Gurion University, Desert Research Institute, professor of architecture and director of desert architecture and environment department, 1975-78; Harvard University, Urban Design Program, director, 1978-84, Ian Woodner professor of architecture and urban design, 1984-89. Writer. **Publications:** Habitat: Moshe Safdie Interviewed by John Gray, 1967; Beyond Habitat, 1970; For Everyone a Garden, 1974; Form & Purpose: Is the Emperor Naked?, 1982; Collective Significance, 1984; The Harvard Jerusalem Studio: Urban Designs for the Holy City, 1986; Jerusalem: The Future of the Past, 1988; The Language and Medium of Architecture: Lecture Delivered at Harvard Graduate School of Design, 1989; Jean-Noël Desmarais Pavilion: The Architects of the Montreal Museum of Fine Arts, Desnoyers, M, 1991; Moshe Safdie, Architect, 1992; Moshe Safdie: Buildings and Projects, 1967-1992, 1996; (with W. Kohn) The City after the Automobile: An Architect's Vision, 1997; Yad Vashem: Moshe Safdie-The Architecture of Memory, 2006; (ed. with R.H. Solomon) Peace

Building, 2011. Contributer to periodicals. **Address:** Moshe Safdie and Associates, 100 Properzi Way, Somerville, MA 02143, U.S.A. **Online address:** safdieb@msafdie.com

SAFERSTEIN, Dan. American (born United States) **Genres:** Novels, Human Relations/Parenting, Biography. **Career:** Clinical psychologist, consultant and author. **Publications:** Love for the Living: Meditations on the Meaning of Marriage and Life, 2000; Win or Lose: A Guide to Sports, 2005; Strength in You: A Student-Athlete's Guide to Competition and Life, 2006. Contributor to periodicals. **Address:** c/o Author Mail, Hyperion Books, 77 W 66th St., 11th Fl., New York, NY 10023-6201, U.S.A. **Online address:** dansaferstein@earthlink.net

SAFFER, Barbara. American/German (born Germany) **Genres:** Education, Children's Fiction, Science Fiction/Fantasy, Medicine/Health, Young Adult Fiction, Reference, Travel/Exploration. **Career:** Writer. **Publications:** ABC Science Riddles, 2001; Polar Exploration Adventures, 2001; Mexico, 2002; Kenya, 2002; Jesse James, 2002; Henry Hudson: Ill-fated Explorer of North America's Coast, 2002; The California Gold Rush, 2003; Life on the Reservation, 2003; Harry S. Truman, 2003; Smallpox, 2003; Anthrax, 2004; Measles and Rubella, 2005. GIFTED AND TALENTED SERIES: Science Questions and Answers: The Human Body, for Ages Six to Eight, 1998; Science Questions and Answers: The Ocean, for Ages 6-8, 1998; Science Experiments, for Ages 6-8, 1999; Science Questions and Answers: Dinosaurs, for Ages Six to Eight, 2000; Kitchen Science Experiments, for Ages 6-8, 2000; Backyard Science Experiments, for Ages 6-8, 2000. Contributor of articles to magazines. **Address:** Lucent Books, 10911 Technology Pl., San Diego, CA 92127, U.S.A. **Online address:** barbsaffer1@aol.com

SAFFLE, Michael. American (born United States), b. 1946. **Genres:** Music, Humanities, Film. **Career:** Stanford University, instructor in music and humanities, 1977-78; Virginia Polytechnic Institute and State University, assistant professor of music and humanities, 1978-83, associate professor, 1984-93, Department of Religion and Culture, professor of music and humanities, 1993-; University of Helsinki, bicentennial Fulbright distinguished professor. Writer. **Publications:** Franz Liszt: A Guide to Research, 1991, 2nd ed., 2004, 3rd ed., 2009; Liszt in Germany, 1840-1845: A Study in Sources, Documents and the History of Reception, 1994; (ed.) New Light on Liszt and His Music: Essays in Honor of Alan Walker's 65th Birthday, 1997; (ed. and intro.) The Symphonic Poems of Franz Liszt, 1997; (ed.) Music and Culture in America, 1861-1918, 1998; (ed.) Liszt and His World: Proceedings of the International Liszt Conference held at Virginia Polytechnic Institute and State University, 20-23 May 1993, 1998; (ed.) Perspectives in American Music, 1900-1950, 2000; (ed. with J.R. Heintze) Reflections on American Music: The Twentieth Century and the New Millennium, 2000; (ed. with D.W. Mosser and E.W. Sullivan) Puzzles in Paper: Concepts in Historical Watermarks: Essays from the International Conference on the History, Function and Study of Watermarks, Roanoke, Virginia, 2000; Richard Wagner: A Guide to Research, 2002, 2nd ed., 2010; (ed.) Liszt and the Birth of Modern Europe: Music as a Mirror of Religious, Political, Cultural and Aesthetic Transformations: Proceedings of the International Conference held at the Villa Serbelloni, Bellagio (Como) 14-18 December 1998, 2003; Franz Liszt: A Research and Information Guide, 2009; Richard Wagner: A Research and Information Guide, 2010; (ed. with J.C. Tibbetts and C. McKinney) Liszt: A Chorus of Voices / Essays, Interviews, and Reminiscences, 2011. **Address:** Department of Religion and Culture, Virginia Polytech Inst and State University, 243 Ln. Hall, Blacksburg, VA 24061, U.S.A. **Online address:** msaffle@vt.edu

SAFINA, Carl. American (born United States), b. 1955. **Genres:** Environmental Sciences/Ecology, Natural History. **Career:** National Audubon Society, founder, Living Oceans Program, head, 1990-; Yale University, visiting professor, School of Forestry and Environmental Studies, adjunct professor; Blue Ocean Institute, co-founder, president, 2003-; Stony Brook University, adjunct professor, School of Marine and Atmospheric Sciences, professor; World Wildlife Fund, fellow. Writer. **Publications:** Song for the Blue Ocean: Encounters along the World's Coasts and beneath the Seas (nonfiction), 1998; (with M. Lee and S. Iudicello) Seafood Lovers Almanac, 2000; Eye of the Albatross: Visions of Hope and Survival, 2002; Voyage of the Turtle: In Pursuit of the Earth's Last Dinosaur, 2006; View from Lazy Point: A Natural Year in an Unnatural World, 2010; A Sea in Flames: The Deepwater Horizon Oil Blowout, 2011. Contributor of articles to periodicals. **Address:** Blue Ocean Institute, 250 Lawrence Hill Rd., Cold Spring Harbor, NY 11724, U.S.A. **Online address:** csafina@blueoceaninstitute.org

SAFIR, Howard. American (born United States), b. 1941. **Genres:** Law, Politics/Government. **Career:** Federal Bureau of Narcotics, special agent, 1965-70, deputy chief of special projects, 1970-72, assistant regional director, 1972-74, special assistant for organized crime, 1974-75, chief of special enforcement programs, 1975-76, deputy regional director, 1976-77, assistant director, 1977-79; Southeast Asia Interdiction Program, national coordinator of special operations, 1971; U.S. Marshals Service, chief of witness security division, 1979-81, associate director for operations; U.N. General Assembly, operational director of security force for foreign delegations, 1979-89; assistant director of operations, 1979-84, associate director of operations, 1984-90; Interpol General Assembly, delegate, 1981-88; Presidential Task Force on Victims of Crime, director of security, 1982; Warrant Apprehension Narcotic Team Program, director, 1989; Safir Associates Ltd., president, 1990-96; New York City Fire Department, commissioner, 1994-96; New York City Police Department, commissioner, 1996-2000; Safir Rosetti, Omnicon Group Inc. (security consulting firm), partner, chairman and chief executive officer, 2001-; Document Security Systems Inc., advisor; GVI Security Solutions Inc., chairman; Verint Systems Inc., director, 2002-; November Group Ltd., director and chief executive officer, 2003-; Bio-key International Inc., strategic advisor of business development and strategic initiatives, 2004-; ChoicePoint Inc., consultant; GlobalOptions Group Inc., Security Consulting & Investigations Unit, chief executive officer, 2006-; Bode Technology Group Inc., 2007-; Implant Sciences Corp., director; LexisNexis Special Services Inc., director; Drug Enforcement Administration, assistant director. Writer. **Publications:** Expert Report of Howard Safir, 2002; Rebuttal Report of Howard Safir & Daniel Nigro, 2002; (with E. Whitman) Security: Policing Your Homeland, Your City, Yourself, 2003. **Address:** Verint Systems Inc., 330 S Service Rd., Melville, NY 11747, U.S.A. **Online address:** hasafir@safirrosetti.com

SAFRANSKY, Sy. American (born United States), b. 1945. **Genres:** Adult Non-fiction, Education. **Career:** The Sun Magazine, founder and editor, 1974-. **Publications:** The Sun, 1975; (ed.) A Bell Ringing in the Empty Sky: The Best of the Sun, 1985; (ed.) Sunbeams: A Book of Quotations, 1990; Four in the Morning: Essays, 1993; (ed.) Stubborn Light: A Collection of Writings from the Second Decade of the Sun, 2000; (co-ed.) The Mysterious Life of the Heart: Writing from The Sun About Passion, Longing and Love, 2009; (ed. with T. McKee and A. Snee) Paper Lanterns: More Quotations from the Back Pages of the Sun, 2010. **Address:** The Sun Magazine, 107 N Robertson St., Chapel Hill, NC 27516, U.S.A.

SAGALYN, Lynne B. American (born United States), b. 1947. **Genres:** Money/Finance, Urban Studies, Economics. **Career:** Rutgers University, Center for Urban Policy Research, research associate, 1971-72; Massachusetts Institute of Technology, postdoctoral fellow and instructor, 1980, assistant professor, 1980-84, 1986-87, class of 1922 assistant professor, 1984-86, Department of Urban Studies and Planning, associate professor of planning and real estate development, 1987-91; Cambridge Young Women's Christian Association, vice president of board of directors, 1988-; Lincoln Institute of Land Policy, research associate, 1988-89, faculty associate, 1994-98; Columbia University, visiting professor of business, 1991-92, 2007-08, Graduate School of Business, professor, 1992-2003, Earle W. Kazis and Benjamin Schore professor of real estate, 2008-, MBA Real Estate Program, coordinator, 1992-98, Earle W. Kazis and Benjamin Schore director, 1998-2003, Paul Milstein Center for Real Estate, director, 1998-2003, 2008-; Weimer School for Advanced Studies in Real Estate and Land Economics, Homer Hoyt Institute for Advanced Studies in Real Estate and Land Economics, fellow, 1992-93, faculty, 1993-; United Dominion Realty Trust, director, 1996-; University of Pennsylvania, School of Design, professor of real estate development and planning, 2004-08; Massachusetts Industrial Finance Agency, consultant; New York City Public Development Corp., consultant; New York School, Chancellor's Commission on the Capital Plan, director. Writer. **Publications:** (With G. Sternlieb and R.W. Burchell) The Affluent Suburb: Princeton, 1971; (ed. with G. Sternlieb) Housing: An Annual Anthology, 1970-1971, 1972; (with G. Sternlieb) Zoning and Housing Costs: The Impact of Land-Use Controls on Housing Price, 1973; (with B.J. Frieden) Downtown, Inc.: How America Rebuilds Cities, 1989; Cases in Real Estate Finance and Investment, 1999; Times Square Roulette: Remaking the City Icon, 2001. Contributor to journals. **Address:** Graduate School of Business, Columbia University, 816 Uris, 3022 Broadway, New York, NY 10027, U.S.A. **Online address:** lbs4@columbia.edu

SAGASTIZABAL, Patricia. Argentine (born Argentina), b. 1953. **Genres:** Novels, Language/Linguistics, Mystery/Crime/Suspense. **Career:** Writer and

lawyer. **Publications:** En Nombre de Dios: la cruzada de un jesuita en tierra americana, 1997; Un Secreto Para Julia, 1999; La colección del Führer, 2009; Estados Mentales; La Cantante De Tango. **Address:** Guillermo Schavelzon Literary Agency, Rodriguez Peña 2067, 3A, Buenos Aires, 1021, Argentina.

SAGE, Angie. American/British (born England), b. 1952. **Genres:** Novels, Young Adult Fiction, Children's Fiction. **Career:** Writer. **Publications:** Monkeys in the Jungle, 1989; (with C. Sage) The Trouble with Babies, 1989; (with C. Sage) Happy Baby, 1990; (with C. Sage) Sleepy Baby, 1990; (with C. Sage) That's Mine, That's Yours, 1991; (illus.) Stack-a-Car: Read the Books! Make the Toy!, 1999; Give a Little Love: Stories of Love and Friendship, 2001; Magyk, 2005; Flyte, 2006; Physik, 2007; Queste, 2008; Magykal Papers, 2009; Syren, 2009; Darke, 2011. SELF-ILLUSTRATED: In My Home, 1997; On the Move, 1997; Molly and the Birthday Party, 2001; Molly at the Dentist, 2001; Say Hello: To Children all Over the World, 2004. **Address:** Katherine Tegen Books, 1350 Ave. of the Americas, New York, NY 10019, U.S.A. **Online address:** harperchildrens@harpercollins.com

SAGER, Mike. American (born United States), b. 1956. **Genres:** Novels. **Career:** Rolling Stone, contributing editor; GQ, writer-at-large; Esquire Magazine, writer-at-large; Washington Post, staff writer; University of California, Periera visiting writer. **Publications:** Scary Monsters and Super Freaks: Stories of Sex, Drugs, Rock 'n' Roll, and Murder (collection), 2003; Revenge of the Donut Boys: True Stories of Lust, Fame, Survival and Multiple Personality (collection), 2007; Deviant Behavior: A Novel of Sex, Drugs, Fatherhood, and Crystal Skulls, 2008; Wounded Warriors: Those for Whom the War Never Ends, 2008; (with V. Neil) Tattoos & Tequila: To Hell and Back with One of Rock's Most Notorious Frontmen, 2010. Works appear in anthologies. Contributor to periodicals. **Address:** Da Capo Press, 1094 Flex Dr., Jackson, TN 38301-5070, U.S.A. **Online address:** info@mikesager.com

SAHGAL, Nayantara (Pandit). Indian (born India), b. 1927. **Genres:** Novels, History, Autobiography/Memoirs, Travel/Exploration. **Career:** Southern Methodist University, writer-in-residence, 1973, 1977; Colorado University, lecturer, 1979; Woodrow Wilson Center, fellow, 1981-82; National Humanities Center, fellow, 1983-84. **Publications:** Prison and Chocolate Cake, 1954; A Time to Be Happy, 1958; From Fear Set Free, 1962; This Time of Morning, 1965; Storm in Chandigarh, 1969; History of the Freedom Movement, 1970; (with C. Mehta and R. Dar) Sunlight Surrounds You, 1970; The Day in Shadow, 1971; A Voice for Freedom, 1977; A Situation in New Delhi, 1977; Indira Gandhi's Emergence and Style, 1978; Rich Like Us, 1985; Plans for Departure, 1985; Mistaken Identity, 1988; Indira Gandhi: Her Road to Power, 1982; Relationship, 1994; Point of View, 1997; Microcosms of Modern India, 1998; Before Freedom: Nehru's Letters to His Sister 1909-1947, 2000; Lesser Breeds, 2003; Jawaharlal Nehru, 2010. Contributor to newspapers and magazines. **Address:** 181-B Rajpur Rd., Uttaranchal, Dehra Dun, UP 248009, India.

SAHLINS, Peter. American (born United States), b. 1957. **Genres:** History. **Career:** Harvard University, instructor in history, 1985-86; Princeton University, Center for Advanced Study, research assistant, 1986-87; Columbia University, lecturer, 1987-88; Yale University, assistant professor, 1988-89; University of California-Berkeley, Department of History, assistant professor, 1989-92, associate professor, 1992-97, professor, 1997-, vice-chair, 2000-02, Gaspar de Portola Catalan Studies Program, faculty, 1990-96, French Cultural Studies Program, director, 1990-94, Iberian Studies Program, director, 1992-94, Center for Western European Studies, faculty, 1994-98; France-Berkeley Fund, executive director, 1994-2002; Maastricht University, visiting professor, 1996-2002; ACLS Collaborative Research Network, co-director, 1998-2004; École des Hautes Études en Sciences Sociales, visiting professor, 1999; University of California-Paris, director, 2002-05; Social Science Research Council, Academic Programs, director, 2006-08. Writer. **Publications:** Boundaries: The Making of France and Spain in the Pyrenees, 1989; Fronteres i Dentitas: La Formací d'Espanya i Franca a la Cerdanya, s. XVII-XIX, 1993; Forest Rites: The War of the Demoiselles in Nineteenth-Century France, 1994; (with J. Dubost) Et Si On Faisait Payer Les Etrangers? Louis XIV, Les Immigrs et Quelques Autres, 1999; Unnaturally French: Foreign Citizens in the Old Regime and After, 2004. **Address:** Department of History, University of California, 3214 Dwinelle Hall, Berkeley, CA 94720-2550, U.S.A. **Online address:** sahlins@berkeley.edu

SAIL, Lawrence (Richard). British (born England), b. 1942. **Genres:** Poetry, Essays, Autobiography/Memoirs, Young Adult Fiction. **Career:** Greater

London Council, administrative officer, 1964-65; Lenana School, head of modern languages, 1966-70; Millfield School, teacher, 1973-74; Blundell's School, teacher, 1976-80, visiting writer, 1980-81; South West Review, editor, 1980-85; Exeter School, teacher, 1982-91; freelance writer, 1991-; Cheltenham Festival of Literature, programme director, 1991, co-director, 1999. **Publications:** POETRY: Opposite Views, 1974; The Drowned River, 1978; The Kingdom of Atlas, 1980; Devotions, 1987; Aquamarine, 1988; Out of Land: New and Selected Poems, 1992; Building into Air, 1995; The World Returning, 2002; Eye-Baby, 2006. EDITOR: South West Review: A Celebration, 1985; First and Always: Poems for the Great Ormond Street Children's Hospital, 1989; 100 Voices: A Century of County Councils, 1989; (with K. Crossley-Holland) The New Exeter Book of Riddles, 1999; (with K. Crossley-Holland) Light Unlocked: Christmas Card Poems, 2005. OTHERS: Cross-Currents: Essays, 2005; Sift: Memories of Childhood, 2010; Waking Dreams, 2010; Songs of the Darkness, 2010. Contributor to periodicals. **Address:** Richmond Villa, 7 Wonford Rd., Exeter, DN EX2 4LF, England.

SAILLANT, John. (John Daniel Saillant). American (born United States), b. 1957. **Genres:** History, Cultural/Ethnic Topics. **Career:** Omohundro Institute of Early American History and Culture, moderator, 1994-; Brown University, Leadership Alliance Early Identification Program, mentor, 1996, Department of History and Program in Afro-American Studies, visiting professor; Western Michigan University, director of graduate fields in early American history and African American history and religion, 1997-, lecturer, associate professor, professor of English, Department of History, professor of history, Department of Comparative Religion, faculty; Michigan Department of Education and the Michigan Department of Treasury, Secondary School Social Science, consultant, 2000-. Writer. **Publications:** NONFICTION: (ed.) Afro-Virginian History and Culture, 1999; (ed. and intro. with J. Brooks) Face Zion Forward: First Writers of the Black Atlantic, 1785-1798, 2002; Black Puritan, Black Republican: The Life and Thought of Lemuel Haynes, 1753-1833, 2003. Contributor of articles to journals. **Address:** Department of English, Western Michigan University, 918 Sprau Twr., 1903 W Michigan Ave., Kalamazoo, MI 49008-5331, U.S.A. **Online address:** john.saillant@wmich.edu

SAILLANT, John Daniel. See **SAILLANT, John.**

SAILLE, Davydd Ap. See **SEALS, David.**

SAINI, B(alwant) S(ingh). Australian/Indian (born India), b. 1930. **Genres:** Architecture, Education, Reference. **Career:** Delhi School of Planning and Architecture, senior lecturer in architecture, 1956-59; University of Melbourne, senior lecturer, 1959-68, reader in architecture, 1968-72; University of Queensland, professor of architecture, 1972-95, now professor emeritus. Writer. **Publications:** Architecture in Tropical Australia, 1970; Building Environment: An Illustrated Analysis of Problems in Hot Dry Lands, 1973; Evaluation of Housing Standards in Tropical Australia, 1975; Building in Hot Dry Climates, 1980; (with R. Joyce) The Australian House, 1982. **Address:** Department of Architecture, University of Queensland, St. Lucia, Brisbane, QL 4072, Australia. **Online address:** b.saini@uq.edu.au

SAINSBURY, Maurice Joseph. Australian (born Australia), b. 1927. **Genres:** Psychiatry. **Career:** Psychiatric, 1957-62; St. Clements Hospital, senior house officer, 1957-58; Claybury Hospital, senior house officer, 1958-59, psychiatric registrar, 1959-60; North Middlesex Hospital, senior registrar in psychiatry, 1961-62; North Ryde Psychiatric Centre, psychiatrist and deputy medical superintendent, 1962-68; New South Wales Institute of Psychiatry, director, 1968-83; New South Wales Nurse Registration Board, chief examiner in psychiatric medicine, 1969-71; Sydney Hospital, honorary psychiatrist, 1971-77; Australian Army Office, consultant psychiatrist, 1976-86; Royal Australian and New Zealand College of Psychiatrists, president, 1976, fellow; New South Wales Department of Health, Mental Health Services, senior specialist, 1983-87; Aftercare Association of N.S.W., president, 1983-95; Royal Commission into Deep Sleep Therapy, consultant psychiatrist, 1988-90. Writer. **Publications:** Key to Psychiatry: A Textbook for Students, 1974, (with L.G. Lambeth) 4th ed., 1988; (contrib.) Acupuncture: A Report to the National Health and Medical Research Council, 1974. Contributor to journals. **Address:** 3 Bimbil Pl., Killara, NW 2071, Australia. **Online address:** msainsbury@ozemail.com.au

SAINT, Andrew (John). British (born England), b. 1946. **Genres:** Architecture, Biography, Local History/Rural Topics, Urban Studies. **Career:** University of Essex, part-time lecturer in art history, 1971-74; English Heri-

tage, Survey of London, architectural editor, 1974-86, general editor, 2006-; Historic Buildings and Monuments Commission, London Division, historian, 1986-95; University of Cambridge, Department of Architecture, professor, 1995-2006. **Publications:** St. Antony's College: A History of Its Buildings and Site, 1973; Richard Norman Shaw, 1976, rev. ed., 2010; The Image of the Architect, 1983; Towards a Social Architecture: The Role of School-Building in Post-war England, 1987; (with S. Barson) A Farewell to Fleet Street, 1988; (ed.) Politics and the People of London: The London County Council, 1889-1965, 1989; (with E. Harwood) Exploring England's Heritage, 1992; (with G. Darley) The Chronicles of London, 1994; (ed. with C. Brooks) The Victorian Church: Architecture and Society, 1995; (intro.) London Suburbs, 1999; (ed. with M. Echenique) Cities for the New Millennium, 2001; (co-ed.) St. Paul's: The Cathedral Church of London, 604-2004, 2004; Architect and Engineer: A Study in Sibling Rivalry, 2008. Contributor to magazines. **Address:** Survey of London, English Heritage, 1 Waterhouse Sq., 138-142 Holborn, London, GL EC1N 2ST, England. **Online address:** ajs61@cam.ac.uk

SAINT-LAURENT, Justine. See **GARDON, Anne.**

SAJDAK, Bruce T. American (born United States), b. 1945. **Genres:** Literary Criticism And History, Bibliography, Language/Linguistics, Young Adult Non-fiction. **Career:** University of Houston, Victoria Campus, humanities librarian, 1975-77; University of Maryland, reference librarian, 1977-80; Smith College, reference librarian, 1980-, Department of English, library liaison. Writer. **Publications:** (Ed.) Shakespeare Index: An Annotated Bibliography of Critical Articles on the Plays, 1959-1983, 1992; (foreword) Shakespeare and Minorities: An Annotated Bibliography, 1970-2000, 2001; (ed. with J.R. Kelly) Annual Bibliography of English Language and Literature for 2002, 2003. **Address:** Neilson Library, X2967, Smith College, Northampton, MA 01063, U.S.A. **Online address:** bsajdak@email.smith.edu

SAKAMOTO, Kerri. Canadian (born Canada), b. 1959. **Genres:** Novels, Plays/Screenplays, Novellas/Short Stories, Art/Art History, Young Adult Fiction. **Career:** Writer. **Publications:** James Luna: Indian Legends, 1, 1993; The Electrical Field (novel), 1998; (ed. with H. Lee) Like Mangoes in July: The Work and Writing of Richard Fung, 2002; One Hundred Million Hearts, 2003; (with R.W. Hill) Human Measure: Kazuo Nakamura, 2004; Fille du kamikaze: Roman, 2004. Contributor to periodicals. **Address:** W. W. Norton & Company Inc., 500 5th Ave., New York, NY 10110, U.S.A.

SAKAMOTO, Yoshikazu. Japanese/American (born United States), b. 1927. **Genres:** International Relations/Current Affairs, Military/Defense/Arms Control, Social Sciences, Law. **Career:** University of Tokyo, research fellow in history of European political thought and international politics, 1951-54, associate professor, 1954-64, professor of international politics, 1964-88, professor emeritus, 1988-; Meiji Gakuin University, professor of peace and world order studies, 1988-93, International Peace Research Institute, deputy director; International Christian University, Peace Research Institute, senior research fellow, 1993-96. Writer. **Publications:** Korea as a World Order Issue, 1978; (ed. with E. Jahn) Elements of World Instability, 1981; Gunshuku no seijigaku, 1982; Kakujidai no kokusai seiji, 1982; (with N. Kazuji) Jichitai no kokusai kōryū: hirakareta chihō o mezashite, 1983; (with M. Shigekazu) Hendōsuru Ajia kokusai seiji, 1984; (with R.E. Wōo) Nihon senryō no kenkyu, 1987; Chikyū jidai no kokusai seiji, 1990; (with O. Kazuo) Chikyū minshu shugi no jōken: shita kara no minshuka o mezashite, 1991; Sōtaika no jidai, 1997; Kaku to ningen, 1999; (with K. Yōichi and Y. Yoshio) Rekishi kyōkasho nani ga mondai ka: tettei kenshō &QA, 2001; (co-author) Sengo 60-nen o toinaosu, 2005. EDITOR: (with R.E. Ward) Democratizing Japan: The Allied Occupation, 1987; Strategic Doctrines and Their Alternatives, 1987; Asia, Militarization and Regional Conflict, 1988; The Emperor System as a Japan Problem, 1989; Global Transformation: Challenges to the State System, 1994; (with A. Clesse and R. Cooper) International System after the Collapse of the East-West Order, 1994. Works appear in anthologies. Contributor to journals. **Address:** University of Tokyo, 7-3-1 Hongo Bunkyo-ku, Tokyo, 113-0033, Japan.

SAKNUSSEMM, Kris. Australian/American (born United States), b. 1961. **Genres:** Novels, Humor/Satire, Young Adult Fiction. **Career:** Vardoger, head. Writer, painter, sculptor and advertiser. **Publications:** Zanesville, 2005; Private Midnight, 2009; Enigmatic Pilot, 2011. Contributor to books and periodicals. **Address:** c/o Matthew Bialer, Sanford J. Greenburg and Associates, 55 5th Ave., 15th Fl., New York, NY 10003, U.S.A.

SAKS, Mike. British (born England), b. 1952. **Genres:** Sociology, Medicine/Health, How-to Books. **Career:** Leicester Polytechnic (now De Montfort University), lecturer in sociology, senior lecturer, 1978-88, Department of Health and Community Studies, head, 1989-93, School of Health and Life Sciences, professor and head, 1993-94, School of Health and Community Studies, professor and head, 1994-, Faculty of Health and Community Studies, dean; University of Lincoln, professor, senior pro-vice chancellor, 2002-10; University Campus Suffolk, provost and chief executive officer, 2009-; Institute of Directors, fellow; University of Essex, visiting chair; University of Lincoln, visiting chair. Writer. **Publications:** Professions and the Public Interest: Medical Power, Altruism and Alternative Medicine, 1995; Orthodox and Alternative Medicine: Politics, Professionalization and Health Care, 2003. EDITOR: Alternative Medicine in Britain, 1992; (with T. Johnson and G. Larkin) Health Professions and the State in Europe, 1995; (with I. Hellberg and C. Benoit) Professional Identities in Transition, 1999; (with M. Williams and B. Hancock) Developing Research in Primary Care, 2000; (co-ed.) Complementary and Alternative Medicine: Challenge and Change, 2000; (with J. Allsop) Regulating the Health Professions, 2002; (with J. Allsop) Researching Health: Qualitative, Quantitative and Mixed Methods, 2007; (with E. Kuhlmann) Rethinking Professional Governance: International Directions in Healthcare, 2008. Contributor to journals. **Address:** University Campus Suffolk, Waterfront Bldg., Neptune Quay, Ipswich, SU IP4 1QJ, England. **Online address:** msaks@lincoln.ac.uk

SAKURAI, Gail. American (born United States), b. 1952. **Genres:** Children's Fiction, Children's Non-fiction, Sciences, Astronomy. **Career:** Writer. **Publications:** FOR CHILDREN: Peach Boy: A Japanese Legend, 1993; Mae Jemison: Space Scientist, 1995; The Liberty Bell, 1996; Stephen Hawking: Understanding the Universe, 1996; The Jamestown Colony, 1997; Paul Revere, 1997; The Louisiana Purchase, 1998; The Library of Congress, 1998; Asian-Americans in the Old West, 2000; The Thirteen Colonies, 2000; Juan Ponce de León, 2001; Japanese American Internment Camps, 2002. **Address:** c/o Author Mail, Houghton Mifflin, 222 Berkeley St., Boston, MA 02116-3764, U.S.A.

SALAITA, Steven. American (born United States), b. 1975. **Genres:** Race Relations, Cultural/Ethnic Topics, Politics/Government. **Career:** University of Wisconsin, assistant professor of English; Virginia Tech, assistant professor of English, associate professor of English. Writer. **Publications:** Anti-Arab Racism in the USA: Where It Comes from and What It Means for Politics Today, 2006; The Holy Land in Transit: Colonialism and the Quest for Canaan, 2006; Arab American Literary Fictions, Cultures and Politics, 2006. **Address:** Department of English, Virginia Tech, 201 Shanks Hall, Blacksburg, VA 24061, U.S.A. **Online address:** salaita@vt.edu

SALAK, Kira. American (born United States), b. 1971. **Genres:** Novels. **Career:** National Geographic Adventure, contributing editor. **Publications:** Four Corners: A Journey into the Heart of Papua New Guinea, 2003; The Cruelest Journey: Six Hundred Miles to Timbuktu, 2004; The White Mary (novel), 2008. Works appears in anthologies. **Address:** c/o Aaron Priest, Aaron Priest Literary Agency, 703 3rd Ave., 23rd Fl., New York, NY 10017, U.S.A. **Online address:** tinyhippos@kirasalak.com

SALAM, Reihan. American (born United States), b. 1979. **Genres:** Politics/Government, History. **Career:** Council on Foreign Relations, research associate; National Broadcasting Company Inc. (NBC), associate news producer; New York Times, junior editor; The New Republic, reporter; The Atlantic, associate editor; Forbes.com, columnist; New America Foundation, fellow. Journalist. **Publications:** (With R. Douthat) Grand New Party: How Republicans Can Win the Working Class and Save the American Dream, 2008. Contributor to newspapers and magazines. **Address:** Washington, DC , U.S.A. **Online address:** reihan@gmail.com

SALAMAN, Nicholas. British (born England), b. 1936. **Genres:** Novels, Young Adult Fiction, Children's Fiction, Mystery/Crime/Suspense. **Career:** London Herb & Spice Company Ltd., director and partner, 1978-; freelance author, 1981-; My First Books, director and partner, 1984-; Salaman Mallet Ltd., director and partner, 1994-. **Publications:** JUVENILES: Once Upon a Time - My First Watch from Timex, 1983; Clean Away!: My First Toothbrush from Wisdom, 1984; Quick on the Draw: My First Crayons, from Platignum, 1984; A Pocketful of Beams: My First Torch from Duracell, 1984; Write Away!: My First Pen from Platignum, 1984. OTHERS: The Frights, 1981; Dangerous Pursuits: A Novel, 1983; Falling Apart: A Novel, 1986; Forces

of Nature, 1989; The Grimace, 1991; The Garden of Earthly Delights, 1993; Rogue Female, 1995; A State of Shock, 1996. Contributor to periodicals. **Address:** Salaman Mallet Ltd., 40-42 Lexington St., London, GL W1F 0LN, England.

SALAMON, Julie. American (born United States), b. 1953. **Genres:** Film, Writing/Journalism, Novels. **Career:** Wall Street Journal, reporter and film critic, 1978-83, weekly columnist, 1983-; New York Times, culture writer, 2000-; New York University, Tisch School of the Arts, adjunct professor; British Retail Consortium, chair. **Publications:** White Lies, 1987; The Devil's Candy, 1991; The Net of Dreams, 1996; The Christmas Tree, 1996; Facing the Wind: A True Story of Tragedy and Reconciliation, 2001; Rambam's Ladder, 2003; Hospital: Man, Woman, Birth, Death, Infinity, Plus Red Tape, Bad Behavior, Money, God, and Diversity on Steroids, 2008; Wendy and the Lost Boys: The Uncommon Life of Wendy Wasserstein, 2011. Works appear in anthologies. **Address:** New York Times, 229 W 43rd St., New York, NY 10036-3913, U.S.A. **Online address:** info@juliesalamon.com

SALAMON, Sonya. American (born United States), b. 1939. **Genres:** Anthropology/Ethnology, Sociology. **Career:** University of Illinois, Department of Human and Community Development, assistant professor, 1974-80, associate professor, 1980-87, Center for Advanced Study, associate, 1981-82, graduate program in human development and family studies, coordinator, 1981-88, 1991-93, affiliate in anthropology, 1984-, affiliate in agricultural economics, 1986-, professor of family studies, 1987-95, professor of community studies, 1995-2006, professor emeritus, 2006-; University of Texas, School of Economic, Political and Policy Sciences, research professor of sociology, 2007-. Writer. **Publications:** Prairie Patrimony: Family, Farming, and Community in the Midwest, 1992; Newcomers to Old Towns: Suburbanization of the Heartland, 2003. **Address:** School of Economic, Political & Policy Sciences, University of Texas, GR31, 800 W Campbell Rd., PO Box 830688, Richardson, TX 75080-3021, U.S.A. **Online address:** ssalamon@utdallas.edu

ŠALAMUN, Tomaž. American/Slovenian/Croatian (born Croatia), b. 1941. **Genres:** Poetry, Translations. **Career:** Modern Gallery, assistant curator, 1968-70; Academy of Fine Arts, assistant professor, 1970-73; poet and writer, 1973-; Yaddo, writer-in-residence, 1973-74, 1979, 1986, 1989; MacDowell Colony, writer-in-residence, 1986; University of Tennessee, teacher of workshop class, 1987-88, 1996; Karoly Foundation, writer-in-residence, 1987; Vermont College, visiting writer, 1988; Slovenian Cultural Attache, consult, 1996-97; Maisons des escrivains ctrangers, writer-in-residence, 1996; Civitella Ranieri, writer-in-residence, 1997; University of Alabama, visiting professor, 1999; University of Massachusetts, visiting professor, 2001; University of Georgia, visiting professor, 2003; University of Pittsburgh, visiting professor, 2005-07; Columbia University, Fulbright fellow; Consulate General of Slovenia, cultural attache; University of Richmond, visiting professor in creative writing and distinguished writer-in-residence, 2008; James A. Michener Center for Writers, visiting faculty, 2011. **Publications:** Poker, 1966, 1989; Namen Pelerine, 1968; Romanje za Marusko, 1971; Bela Itaka, 1972; Amerika, 1972; Arena, 1973; English Turbines: Twenty One Poems (English), 1973; Snow, 1973; Sokol, 1974; Imre, 1975; Druidi, 1975; Praznik, 1976; Zvezde, 1977; Metoda Angela, 1978; Po Sledeh Divjadi, 1979; Zgodovina Svetlobe je Oranzna, 1979; (with S. Makarovic and N. Grafenauer) Pesmi, 1979; Maske, 1980; Balada za Metko Krasovec, 1981; Analogije Svetlobe, 1982; Glas, 1983; Sonet o Mleku, 1984; Soy Realidad, 1985; Ljubljanska Pomlad, 1986; Mera Casa, 1987; Ziva Rana, Zivi Sok, 1988; The Selected Poems of Tomaz Salamun, 1988; Otrok in Jelen, 1990; The Shepherd, The Hunter, 1992; Hiša Markova, 1992; Glagoli Sonca: Izbrane Pesmi, 1993; Ambra, 1995; Poemes Choisis, 1995; The Four Questions of Melancholy: New and Selected Poems (English), 1997; črni labod, 1997; Knjiga za mojega brata, 1997; Morje, 1999; Gozd in Kelihi, 2000; Feast, 2000; Table, Litera, 2001; Od tam, 2003; Z Arhilohom po Kikladih, 2004; Sončni voz, 2005; Row, 2006; Book for My Brother, 2006; Sinji stolp, 2007; (and trans. with B. Henry) Woods and Chalices, 2008; (and co-trans.) There's the Hand and There's the Arid Chair, 2009; Mrzle pravljice, 2009; Ko vdre senca, 2010; (and trans. with M. Biggins) The Blue Tower, 2011. Contributor of articles to periodicals. Works appear in anthologies. **Address:** The James A. Michener Center for Writers, 702 E Dean Keeton St., Austin, TX 78705, U.S.A. **Online address:** metka.krasovec@siol.net

SALANT, James. American (born United States), b. 1984. **Genres:** Biography, Psychology, Autobiography/Memoirs. **Career:** Comprehensive Educational Resources, office manager, 2005-07. Writer. **Publications:** Leaving

Dirty Jersey: A Crystal Meth Memoir, 2007. **Address:** Paul Bresnick Literary Agency, 115 W 29th St., 3rd Fl., New York, NY 10001-5080, U.S.A.

SALAZAR, Carles. Spanish (born Spain), b. 1961. **Genres:** Anthropology/ Ethnology, Natural History, Social Sciences. **Career:** University of Barcelona, lecturer, 1994-95; University of Lleida, lecturer in social anthropology, 1994-, senior lecturer in social anthropology, professor of anthropology, Department of Art History and Social History, faculty. Writer. **Publications:** A Sentimental Economy: Commodity and Community in Rural Ireland, 1996; De la Razón y Sus Descontentos: Indagaciones en la Historia de Laantropología, 1996; Anthropology and Sexual Morality: A Theoretical Investigation, 2006; (ed. with J. Edwards) European Kinship in the Age of Biotechnology, 2009. **Address:** Department of Social History, University of Lleida, 1 Victor Sivrana, Lleida, 25003, Spain. **Online address:** salazar@trivium.gh.ub.es

SALAZAR, Dixie. (Dixie Lane). American/Spanish (born Spain), b. 1947. **Genres:** Poetry, Novels. **Career:** Corcoran State Prison, poetry instructor, 1990-; Fresno Adult School, parenting instructor, 1992-; Chowchilla Women's Prison, art instructor, 1992-95; California State University, lecturer in writing, 1994-; Valley State Prison for Women, poetry instructor. Writer, photographer and painter. **Publications:** (As Dixie Lane) Hotel Fresno (poems) 1988; Limbo: A Novel (fiction), 1995; Reincarnation of the Commonplace (poetry), 1999; Blood Mysteries, 2003; Flamenco Hips and Red Mud Feet, 2010; Altar for Escaped Voices, 2012. **Address:** 704 E Brown Ave., Fresno, CA 93704, U.S.A. **Online address:** dsalazar@csufresno.edu

SALDANA, Rene. American (born United States) **Genres:** Novels, Young Adult Non-fiction. **Career:** University of Texas, assistant professor of English; Texas Tech University, assistant professor of language and literacy, 2006-. Writer. **Publications:** The Jumping Tree, 2001; Finding Our Way, 2003; The Whole Sky Full of Stars, 2007; The Case of the Pen Gone Missing: A Mickey Rangel Mystery, 2009; A Good Long Way, 2010. Contributor to periodicals. **Address:** College of Education, Texas Tech University, PO Box 41071, Lubbock, TX 79409-1071, U.S.A. **Online address:** rene.saldana@ttu.edu

SALE, J. Kirkpatrick. See SALE, Kirkpatrick.

SALE, Kirkpatrick. (J. Kirkpatrick Sale). American (born United States), b. 1937. **Genres:** Social Commentary, Environmental Sciences/Ecology, History, Sciences, Social Sciences, Anthropology/Ethnology, Archaeology/ Antiquities. **Career:** New Leader, associate editor, 1959-61; San Francisco Chronicle, foreign correspondent, 1961-62; Chicago Tribune, foreign correspondent, 1961-62; University of Ghana, lecturer in history, 1963-65; New York Times Magazine, editor, 1965-68; Board of E.F. Schumacher Society, member, 1980-; Nation, contributing editor, 1986-; Cornell Daily Sun, editor. **Publications:** SDS, 1973; Power Shift: The Rise of the Southern Rim and Its Challenge to the Eastern Establishment, 1975; Human Scale, 1980, 2nd ed., 1982; Dwellers in the Land: The Bioregional Vision, 1985; The Conquest of Paradise: Christopher Columbus and the Columbian Legacy, 1990; The Green Revolution: The American Environmental Movement, 1962-92, 1993; Rebels against the Future: The Luddites and Their War on the Industrial Revolution: Lessons for the Computer Age, 1995; The Fire of His Genius: Robert Fulton and the American Dream, 2001; After Eden: The Evolution of Human Domination, 2006. **Address:** 153 E Mountain Rd., Cold Spring, NY 10516, U.S.A.

SALE, Medora. See ROE, Caroline.

SALEEM, Hiner. French/Iraqi (born Iraq), b. 1964. **Genres:** Novels, Biography. **Career:** Writer, director, composer, producer and filmmaker. **Publications:** Le fusil de mon père: Récit, 2004. **Address:** c/o Author Mail, Farrar, Straus & Giroux, 19 Union Sq. W, New York, NY 10003, U.S.A.

SALER, Benson. American (born United States), b. 1930. **Genres:** Adult Non-fiction. **Career:** University of Connecticut, faculty, 1963; Society for the Anthropology of Religion, president, 1997; Brandeis University, professor of anthropology, professor emeritus of anthropology, 2000-; Hebrew University of Jerusalem, Sir Isaac Wolfson visiting professor. Writer. **Publications:** Conceptualizing Religion: Immanent Anthropologists, Transcendent Natives, and Unbounded Categories, 1993; (with C.A. Ziegler and C.B. Moore) UFO Crash at Roswell: The Genesis of a Modern Myth, 1997; Understanding Religion: Selected Essays, 2009; Contributor to books and journals. **Address:**

Department of Anthropology, Brandeis University, Brown 221, 415 South St., PO Box 549110, Waltham, MA 02453-9110, U.S.A. **Online address:** saler@brandeis.edu

SALERNO, Beth A. American (born United States) **Genres:** History, Reference, Social Sciences. **Career:** St. Anselm College, Department of History, associate professor, 2000-. Writer. **Publications:** Sister Societies: Women's Antislavery Organizations in Antebellum America, 2005. Contributor of articles to journals. **Address:** Department of History, St. Anselm College, 308 Joseph House, 100 Saint Anselm Dr., Manchester, NH 03102-1308, U.S.A. **Online address:** bsalerno@anselm.edu

SALIBA, George. American (born United States), b. 1939. **Genres:** Area Studies, Theology/Religion. **Career:** Harvard University, Center for Middle East Studies, research fellow, 1974-76; New York University, visiting assistant professor, 1976-79; Columbia University, visiting assistant professor, 1977-78, assistant professor, 1979-84, associate professor, 1984-90, Department of Middle East and Asian Languages and Cultures, professor of Arabic and Islamic science, 1991-, chairperson, 1990-93; Institute for Advanced Study, O. Neugebauer fellow, 1988-89; Princeton University, visiting fellow, 1985-86; American University in Cairo, distinguished visiting professor, 1994. Writer. **Publications:** (With S. Gibbs) Planispheric Astrolabes From the National Museum of American History, 1984; (trans.) The Crisis of the Abbāsid Caliphate, 1985; Tārīkh ilm al-falak al-Arabī: Muayyad al-Dīn al-Urḍ ī, al-mutawaffā sanat 664 H/1266 M, Kitāb al-hayah, 1990; A History of Arabic Astronomy: Planetary Theories During the Golden Age of Islam, 1994; Al-Fikr al-ilmī al-Arabī: nashatuhu wa-Taṭawwuruh, 1998; Rethinking the Roots of Modern Science: Arabic Manuscripts in European Libraries, 1999; Islamic Science and the Making of the European Renaissance, 2007. EDITOR: (D.A. King) From Deferent to Equant: A Volume of Studies in the History of Science in the Ancient and Medieval Near East in Honor of E.S. Kennedy, 1987; (intro.) The Astronomical Work of Mu'ayyad al-Din al-'Urdi (d. 1266): A Thirteenth Century Reform of Ptolemaic Astronomy, 1990. Contributor of articles to books and journals. **Address:** Department of Middle East/Asian Language, Columbia University, Rm. 312, 606 W 122nd St., 604 Kent Hall, PO Box 3942, New York, NY 10027, U.S.A. **Online address:** gsaliba@columbia.edu

SALIERS, Emily. American (born United States), b. 1963. **Genres:** Novels, Music. **Career:** Amy Ray, staff, 1983-; Watershed Restaurant, co-owner; Flying Biscuit Cafe, co-founder. Writer. **Publications:** (Contrib.) Heart and Soul: New Songs from Ally McBeal, 1999; The Road to Bliss, 2003; (with D. Saliers) A Song to Sing, a Life to Live: Reflections on Music as Spiritual Practice, RECORD ALBUMS WRITER WITH AMY RAY AS THE INDIGO GIRLS: Early 45, 1985; Indigo Girls, 1985; Strange Fire, 1989; Indigo Girls, 2004; Nomads Indians Saints, 1990; Rites of Passage, 1992; Swamp Ophelia, 1994; 1200 Curfews, 1995; Shaming of the Sun, 1997; Come On Now Social, 1999; Retrospective, 2000; Become You, 2002; All That We Let In, 2004; Rarities, 2005; Despite Our Differences, 2006. **Address:** Russell Carter Artist Management, 567 Ralph McGill Blvd. NE, Atlanta, GA 30312, U.S.A. **Online address:** igfan@rcam.com

SALINGER, Michael. American (born United States), b. 1962. **Genres:** Poetry. **Career:** Poetry Slam Inc., consultant; Nova Lizard (performance troupe), founder, director; Playhouse Square Foundation, chief facilitator of teen writing and performance program. Writer and artist. **Publications:** (With S. Holbrook) Outspoken! How to Improve Writing and Speaking Skills through Poetry Performance, 2006; Well Defined: Vocabulary in Rhyme, 2009. POETRY: Big Machines and Wheeled Things, 1986; Rizz, 1988; Sunday Morning, 1999; Neon, 2002; (ed. with R. Gibson and L. Anderton) From Page to Stage and Back Again: National Poetry Slam 2003 (anthology), 2004; They Call It Fishing Not Catching, 2004; Stingray, 2007. Contributor to periodicals and journals. **Address:** 7326 Presley Ave., Mentor, OH 44060, U.S.A. **Online address:** salinger@ameritech.net

SALISBURY, Frank B(oyer). American (born United States), b. 1926. **Genres:** Biology, Botany, Theology/Religion, Air/Space Topics, Environmental Sciences/Ecology, Horticulture, Sciences, Agriculture/Forestry, Agriculture/Forestry. **Career:** Boyart Studio, photographer, 1949-50; Pomona College, assistant professor of botany, 1954-55; Colorado State University, assistant professor of plant physiology, 1955-61, professor of plant physiology, 1961-66, Research Foundation, board trustee, 1959-62; National Science Foundation, senior postdoctoral fellow, 1962-63; Utah State University, professor of plant physiology, 1966-68, head of plant science, 1966-70, professor of botany, 1968-97, professor emeritus, 1997-; U.S. Atomic Energy Commission (now U.S. Department of Energy), technical representative in plant physiology, 1973-74; Hebrew University of Jerusalem, Lady Davis fellow, 1983. Writer. **Publications:** The Flowering Process, 1963; (with R.V. Parke) Vascular Plants: Form and Function, 1964, 2nd ed., 1970; Truth by Reason and by Revelation, 1965; (with C.W. Ross) Plant Physiology, 1969, 4th ed., 1992; The Biology of Flowering, 1971; (with W.A. Jensen) Botany, 1972, 2nd ed., 1984; The Utah UFO Display: A Biologist's Report, 1974, (with J.J. Hicks) 2nd ed. as The Utah UFO Display: A Scientist's Report, 2010; The Creation, 1976; (co-author) Biology, 1977; (contrib.) Analysis of Growth and Development of Xanthium, 1990; (ed.) Units, Symbols, and Terminology for Plant Physiology, 1996; The Case for Divine Design, 2006; (ed.) Geochemistry and The Biosphere, 2007. Contributor of articles to periodicals. **Address:** Department of Plants, Soils and Climate, Utah State University, 322C Agricultural Science, 1400 Old Main Hill, Logan, UT 84322-1400, U.S.A. **Online address:** franksals@aol.com

SALISBURY, John. See CAUTE, (John) David.

SALISBURY, Joyce E(llen). American (born United States), b. 1944. **Genres:** History, Sex, Theology/Religion, Social Sciences. **Career:** Middlesex Community College, adjunct teacher of history, 1975-76; Rutgers University, adjunct teacher of history, 1976; American School of Madrid, instructor, 1978; University of Wisconsin, assistant professor, 1981-85, associate professor, 1985-90, Frankenthall professor of history and humanistic studies, 1990-2005, Frankenthall professor emeritus of history and humanistic studies, 2005-, director of international education, 1989-2000, director of introduction to college, 1990-99, History Program, chair, 1999-2001, associate dean of liberal arts and sciences, 2003-05. Writer. **Publications:** Iberian Popular Religion, 600 B.C. to 700 A.D.: Celts, Romans, and Visigoths, 1985; Medieval Sexuality: A Research Guide, 1990; Church Fathers, Independent Virgins, 1991; The Beast Within: Animals in the Middle Ages, 1994, 2nd ed., 2010; Perpetua's Passion: Death and Memory of a Young Roman Woman, 1997; (with D. Sherman) The West in the World: A Mid-Length Narrative History, 2000, 4th ed., 2011; Encyclopedia of Women in the Ancient World, 2001; The Blood of Martyrs: Unintended Consequences of Ancient Violence, 2004. EDITOR: Sex in the Middle Ages, 1991; The Medieval World of Nature: A Book of Essays, 1993; Greenwood Encyclopedia of Daily Life: A Tour Through History from Ancient Times to the Present, 2004; Greenwood Encyclopedia of Global Medieval Life and Culture, 2009; (W.D. Sherman) West, 2011. **Address:** 985 N Broadway, Apt. 74, De Pere, WI 54115, U.S.A. **Online address:** salisbuj@uwgb.edu

SALISBURY, Mike. British (born England), b. 1942. **Genres:** Natural History, Travel/Exploration. **Career:** Horticultural Engineering, service manager and director, 1963-71; BBC-TV, Science Department, researcher; Natural History Unit, writer and producer, 1971-, retired, 2006. **Publications:** (With H. Miles) Kingdom of the Ice Bear: A Portrait of the Arctic, 1986; Arctic Expedition, 1989. Contributor to journals and periodicals. Works appear in anthologies. **Address:** Natural History Unit, BBC-TV, Whiteladies Rd., Bristol, GL BS8 2LR, England.

SALITAN, Laurie P. American (born United States) **Genres:** Politics/Government, Social Sciences. **Career:** Johns Hopkins University, Department of Political Science, assistant professor, 1987-94, Undergraduate Program in Political Science, director, 1990-92, specialist in Soviet politics; New York University, Graduate School of Arts and Science, Department of Politics, adjunct associate professor, 2009-. Writer. **Publications:** Politics and Nationality in Contemporary Soviet Jewish Emigration, 1968-89, 1992. **Address:** Department of Politics, New York University, Rm. 303, 19 W 4th St., 2nd Fl., New York, NY 10012, U.S.A. **Online address:** laurie.salitan@nyu.edu

SALLENAVE, Daniele. French (born France), b. 1940. **Genres:** Novels, Translations. **Career:** University of Paris X Nanterre, lecturer of literature and film history, 1968-2001; France Culture, weekly column, 2009-. Writer and educator. **Publications:** Paysage De Ruines Avec Personages, 1975; Digraphe: Theéorie; Numéro Special Francis Ponge, 1976; Le Voyage d'Amsterdam; Ou Les Règlesde La Conversation, 1977; Les Portes De Gubbio, 1980; Si Par Une Nuitdhiver Un Voyageur, 1981; Un Printemps Froid: Récits, 1983; Rome Avec Danile Sallenave, 1986; Un Si Grande âge: Une Exposition, 1986; La Vie fantôme, 1986; Conversations Conjugales, 1987; Adieu: Récit, 1987; Les éreuves De Lart: Essai, 1988; Visages Secretsregards

Discrets: Parcours Photographique Dans La DGA, 1990; Lethéâtre Des Idées, 1991; Le Don Des Morts: Sur Lalittérature, 1991; Villes Et Villes, 1991; Passages De Lest: Carnetsde Voyages 1990-1991, 1992; Vilnius, Riga, Tallinn, 1992; Les Trois Minudedu Diable: Roman, 1994; Le Principe De Ruine, 1994; Letres Mortes: Delenseignement Des Lettres En Général Et De La Culture Générale En Particulier, 1995; Sarajevo Légende(s), 1996; Viol: Six Entretiens Quelques Lettres Et Une Conversation Finale, 1997; Aquoi Set La Littérature?: Entretien Avec Philippe Petit, 1997; Lamazone Du Grand Dieu, 1997; Carnet De Route En Palestine Occupée: Gaza-Cisjordanie Novembre 1997, 1998; Entretien, 2000; Un Bagagepoétique Pour Le 3e Millénaire: Entretiens, 2001; Nos Amours De La France: République Identités Régions: Entretien Avec Phillipe Petit, 2002; Damour: Récit, 2002; Dieu.com, 2004; La Fraga, 2005; Quand Même, 2006; Castor De Guerre, 2008; Nous, On N'aime Pas Lire, 2009; La vie éi claircie, 2010. **Address:** c/o Author Mail, éditions Gallimard, 5 rue Sébastien-Bottin, Paris, 75328, France.

SALLIS, James. American (born United States), b. 1944. **Genres:** Novellas/Short Stories, Mystery/Crime/Suspense, Science Fiction/Fantasy, Poetry, Cultural/Ethnic Topics, Literary Criticism And History, Music, Translations, Translations. **Career:** Novelist, critic, biographer, musicologist and translator. **Publications:** NOVELS: The Long-Legged Fly, 1992; Moth, 1993; Black Hornet, 1994; Renderings, 1995; The Eye of the Cricket, 1997; Bluebottle, 1999; Ghost of a Flea, 2001; Cypress Grove, 2003; Drive, 2005. SHORT STORIES: A Few Last Words (science fiction), 1970; Limits of the Sensible World, 1994; A City Equal to My Desire, 2004. NONFICTION: The Guitar Players, 1981; Difficult Lives, 1993; Chester Himes: A Life, 2001. OTHER: (trans.) R. Queneau, Saint Glinglin, 1993. EDITOR: The War Book, 1969; The Shores Beneath, 1970; Jazz Guitars: An Anthology, 1984; The Guitar in Jazz, 1996; Ash of Stars: On the Writing of Samuel R. Delany, 1996; Time's Hammers: Collected Stories, 2000; Sorrow's Kitchen (poems), 2001; A James Sallis Reader, 2005: Cripple Creek (novel), 2006; Salt River (novel), 2007; Potato Tree (stories), 2007; What You Have Left: The Turner Trilogy (novels), 2008; The Killer Is Dying (novel), 2011. **Address:** 1534 E Earll Dr., Phoenix, AZ 85014, U.S.A. **Online address:** jimsallis@aol.com

SALLIS, John C(leveland). American (born United States), b. 1938. **Genres:** Philosophy. **Career:** University of the South, instructor in philosophy, 1964-66; Duquesne University, Department of Philosophy, associate professor, 1966-70, professor of philosophy, 1970-83, chairman, 1978-83; Loyola University of Chicago, Arthur J. Schmitt professor of philosophy, 1983-90, Continental Philosophy Program, director, 1985-88; Vanderbilt University, W. Alton Jones professor of philosophy, 1990-95; Pennsylvania State University, liberal arts professor of philosophy, 1996-2000, Edwin Erle Sparks professor of philosophy, 2000-05; Boston College, Frederick J. Adelmann S.J. professor of philosophy, 2005-. Writer. **Publications:** Introduction to the Techniques of Symbolic Logic, 1966; Heidegger and the Path of Thinking, 1970; Phenomenology and the Return to Beginnings, 1973; Being and Logos: The Way of Platonic Dialogue, 1975, 3rd ed., 1996; The Gathering of Reason, 1980, 2nd ed., 2005; Delimitations: Phenomenology and the End of Metaphysics, 1986; Spacings of Reason and Imagination in Texts of Kant, Fichte, Hegel, 1987; Echoes: After Heidegger, 1990; Crossings: Nietzsche and the Space of Tragedy, 1991; Stone, 1994; Double Truth, 1995; Shades-Of Painting at the Limit, 1998; Chorology: On Beginning in Plato's Timaeus, 1999; Force of Imagination: The Sense of the Elemental, 2000; (with D. Eccher) Paladino: Una Monografia: Paladino: A Monograph, 2001; On Translation, 2002; Platonic Legacies, 2004; Topographies, 2006; The Verge of Philosophy, 2007; Trans Figurements: On the True Sense of Art, 2008. EDITOR: Radical Phenomenology: Essays in Honor of Martin Heidegger, 1978; Studies in Phenomenology and the Human Sciences, 1979; (with K. Maly) Heraclitean Fragments: A Companion Volume to the Heidegger/Fink Seminar on Heraclitus, 1980; Merleau-Ponty, Perception, Structure, Language: A Collection of Essays, 1981; Philosophy and Archaic Experience: Essays in Honor of Edward G. Ballard, 1982; Husserl and Contemporary Thought, 1983; (with H.J. Silverman and T.M. Seebohm) Continental Philosophy in America, 1983; Deconstruction and Philosophy: The Texts of Jacques Derrida, 1987; (with G. Moneta and J. Taminiaux) The Collegium Phaenomenologicum: The First Ten Years, 1988; Reading Heidegger: Commemorations, 1993; (with J. Russon) Retracing the Platonic Text, 2000; (with C.E. Scott) Interrogating the Tradition: Hermeneutics and the History of Philosophy, 2000; (co-ed.) Heidegger-Jahrbuch II: Heidegger und Nietzsche, 2005. OTHERS: Recondite Image, 1991; Ombre del Tempo: I Covoni di Monet, 1992; Very Ancient Memories, 2000; La mirada de las cosas: el arte como provocacion, 2008. Contributor of articles to journals. **Address:** Department of Philosophy, Boston College, Rm. 392, 21 Campanella Way, 140 Commonwealth Ave., Chestnut Hill, MA 02467-3806, U.S.A. **Online address:** sallis@bc.edu

SALMANSOHN, Karen. American (born United States), b. 1960. **Genres:** Novels, Humor/Satire, Self Help, Illustrations. **Career:** Freelance writer and columnist. **Publications:** SELF-ILLUSTRATED: How to Change Your Entire Life by Doing Absolutely Nothing: 10 Do-Nothing Relaxation Exercises to Calm You Down Quickly So You Can Speed Forward Faster, 2003. OTHERS: 50 Percent Off: A Novel, 1993; How to Make Your Man Behave in 21 Days or Less, Using the Secrets of Professional Dog Trainers, 1994; How to Succeed in Business without a Penis: Secrets and Strategies for the Working Woman, 1996; Whip Your Career into Submission: The 30-Day Plan to Transform Yourself from a Job Slave into the Master of Your Destiny, 1998; Even God is Single: So Stop Giving Me A Hard Time, 2000; How to be Happy, Dammit: A Cynic's Guide to Spiritual Happiness, 2001; One Puppy, Three Tales, 2001; Oh, and Another Thing, 2001; I Don't Need to Have Children, I Date Them: 23 Child Psychology Techniques to Use on Boys of All Ages, 2001; Wherever I Go, There I Am, 2002; Mr. Right When You Need Him, 2002; How to Speak Fluent Lovey Dovey in 11 Languages in 24 Hours, 2002; The Clitourist: A Guide to One of the Hottest Spots on Earth, 2002; 7 Lively Sins: How to Enjoy Your Life, Dammit, 2003; Art, 2003; Quickie Stickies: 100 Pick-Me-Ups for When You're Feeling Unglued, 2003; Hot Mama: How to Have a Babe and Be a Babe, 2003; Good Karma: In a Box, 2003; 8 Minute Guts Builder: A Portable Coach to Pump Up Your Courage, 2004; Mama Sutra, 2004; Enough, Dammit: The Cynic's Guide to Finally Getting What You Want Out of Life, 2004; Fashion, 2005; Gut: How to Think from Your Middle to Get to the Top, 2006; Ballsy: 99 Ways to Grow a Bigger Pair and Score Extreme Business Success, 2006; Girl wonders, 2007; Bounce Back Book: When Life Throws You Curve Balls, Hit Them Out of the Park: How to Thrive in the Face of Adversity, Setbacks and Losses, 2007; Prince Harming Syndrome: Break Bad Relationship Patterns for Good, 2009; Hollywood Intuition, 2009. **Address:** c/o Lydia Wills, Writers & Artists Agency, 19 W 44th St., Ste. 1000, New York, NY 10036, U.S.A. **Online address:** karen@notsalmon.com

SALMON, Jacqueline L. American (born United States), b. 1957. **Genres:** How-to Books, Human Relations/Parenting, Psychiatry, Psychology, Young Adult Non-fiction. **Career:** Peninsula Times-Tribune, editor, 1982-83; San Jose Mercury News, editor, 1983-87; Washington Post, reporter, 1987-, staff writer; Pew Charitable Trusts, senior officer. **Publications:** NON-FICTION: (with S.I. Greenspan) Playground Politics: Understanding the Emotional Life of Your School-Age Child, 1993; (with S.I. Greenspan) The Challenging Child: Understanding, Raising, and Enjoying the Five Difficult Types of Children, 1995; Arsenal, 2000; (with S.I. Greenspan) The Four-Thirds Solution: Solving the Childcare Crisis in America Today, 2001. **Address:** The Washington Post, 1150 15th St. NW, Washington, DC 20071, U.S.A. **Online address:** jls.salmon@gmail.com

SALMOND, Amiria. See HENARE, Amiria J.M.

SALMOND, Anne. See SALMOND, Mary Anne.

SALMOND, Mary Anne. (Anne Salmond). New Zealander (born New Zealand), b. 1945. **Genres:** Anthropology/Ethnology, Language/Linguistics. **Career:** University of Auckland, junior lecturer, 1967, part-time lecturer, 1968, lecturer, 1971-75, senior lecturer, 1976-88, associate professor, 1989-91, professor of Maori studies and social anthropology, 1991-, distinguished professor, 2002-; Cambridge University, lecturer, 1981; Alexander Turnbull Library, founder lecturer, 1992; Museum of New Zealand, board director, 1992; National Maritime Museum, Caird fellow, 2004; Australian National University, Cross-cultural Research Centre, visiting fellow, 2004; École des Haute Études, visiting professor, 2006; New Zealand Academy of the Humanities, founding fellow, 2007; British Academy, fellow, 2008; U.S. National Academy of Sciences, foreign associate, 2009. Writer. **Publications:** AS ANNE SALMOND: A Generative Syntax of Luangiua, 1974; A Luangiua (Ontong Java) Word List, 1975; Hui: A Study of Maori Ceremonial Gatherings, 1975; (contrib.) Amiria: The Life Story of a Maori Woman, 1976 as For Better, for Worse, 1979; (contrib.) Eruera: The Teachings of a Maori Elder, 1980; (ed.) Early Eyewitness Accounts of Maori Life, vol. I: Extracts of the Journals of the Ship St. Jean Baptiste, 1769, 1982, vol. II: Extracts from Journals Relating to the Visit to New Zealand in May-July 1772 of the French Ships the Mascarin and the Marquis de Castries, 1985, vols. III-IV: Extracts from New

Zealand Journals Written on Ships under the Command of d'Entrecasteaux and Duperry, 1783 and 1824, 1986; Two Worlds: First Meetings between Maori and Europeans, 1642-1772, 1991; Between Worlds: Early Exchanges Between Maori and Europeans, 1773-1815, 1997; Trial of the Cannibal Dog: The Remarkable Story of Captain Cook's Encounters in the South Seas, 2003; Aphrodite's Island: The European Discovery of Tahiti, 2009; Bligh: William Bligh in the South Seas, 2011. Works appear in anthologies. Contributor to journals and newspapers. **Address:** University Of Auckland, Human Sciences Bldg., Levels 7 and 8, 10 Symonds St., Auckland, 1010, New Zealand. **Online address:** a.salmond@auckland.ac.nz

SALOFF, Jamie L. American (born United States), b. 1960. **Genres:** Medicine/Health, inspirational/Motivational Literature, Self Help, Art/Art History, Education, Philosophy. **Career:** Author, speaker, minister and book designer. **Publications:** (With T. Saloff) The Collector's Encyclopedia of Cowan Pottery: Identification & Values, 1993; The Publishing Center: How to Create a Successful Publishing Center in Your School, Church, or Other Community Group, 1996; Transformational Healing: Five Surprisingly Simple Keys Designed to Redirect Your Life toward Wellness, Purpose, and Prosperity, 2005; Prayer Superchargers: The How to Pray Book for People Who Need Answers in Today's Troubled Times, 2010; The Wisdom of Emotional Healing: Renowned Psychics Andrew Jackson Davis and Phineas P. Quimby Reveal Mind Body Healing Secrets for Clairvoyants, Spiritualists, and Energy Healers, 2010. **Address:** Saloff Enterprises, PO Box 339, Edinboro, PA 16412, U.S.A. **Online address:** info@saloff.com

SALOMON, Frank. American (born United States), b. 1946. **Genres:** Politics/Government, Anthropology/Ethnology. **Career:** University of Illinois, Center for Latin American and Caribbean Studies and Department of Anthropology, visiting lecturer, 1976-78, visiting assistant professor, 1978- 82; University of Wisconsin, Department of Anthropology, assistant professor, 1982-84, associate professor, 1984-91, research associate, 1987-94, professor, 1991-2006, chair, 1991-94, John V. Murra professor of anthropology, 2006-. Writer. **Publications:** Native Lords of Quito in the Age of the Incas: The Political Economy of North-Andean Chiefdoms, 1986; (ed. with H.O. Skar) Natives and Neighbors in South America: Anthropological Essays, 1987; (with M.M. Carrera) Historia y cultura popular de Zámbiza, 1990; Reproducción y transformación de las sociedades andinas, siglos xvi-xx: simposio auspiciado por el Social Science Research Council, 1991; (trans. and ed. with G.L. Urioste) The Huarochirí Manuscript: A Testament of Ancient and Colonial Andean Religion, 1991; (with J.A.G. Gil) La visita personal de indios: ritual político y creación del indio en los andes coloniales, 1996; The Cambridge History of the Native Peoples of the Americas, vol. III, 1999; The Cord Keepers: Khipus and Cultural Life in a Peruvian Village, 2004; (with S. Hyland) Graphic Pluralism: Native American Systems of Inscription and the Colonial Situation, 2010; (with M. Niño-Murcia) The Lettered Mountain: A Peruvian Village's Way With Writing, 2011; The Sacred Precinct of Rapaz, Peru: Temple, Khipu, and Storehouse, forthcoming. **Address:** Department of Anthropology, University of Wisconsin, 5240 Sewell Social Sciences Bldg., 1180 Observatory Dr., Madison, WI 53706-1393, U.S.A. **Online address:** fsalomon@wisc.edu

SALSI, Lynn. American (born United States), b. 1947. **Genres:** Children's Fiction, Education, Local History/Rural Topics, Mythology/Folklore, History. **Career:** Creative Concepts, president, 1984-98; North Carolina Youth Touring Theater, drama educator, 1992-2000; Barnes and Noble, community relations manager, 1999-2001; Guilford Technical Community College, teacher, 2000-, on-line English instructor, 2007-; freelance writer, 2001-; Randolph Community College, teacher, 2002-04. Writer. **Publications:** Carteret County, 1999; (with R. Hicks) The Jack Tales, 2000; (with F. Eubanks) The Crystal Coast, 2000; (with F. Eubanks) Craven County, 2001; (with B. Salsi) Guilford County, North Carolina: Heart of the Piedmont, 2001; Columbia, SC, A Southern Capital, 2003; (with F. Eubanks) Portsmouth Island Outer Banks Treasure, 2004; The North Carolina Imagination Box, 2004; Young Ray Hicks Learns the Jack Tales, 2005; (with B. Sulsi) North Carolina State University, 2005; Greensboro, 2007; Voices from the North Carolina Mountains: Appalachian Oral Histories, 2007; Life and Times of Ray Hicks: Keeper of the Jack Tales, 2008; Firefight, forthcoming; Appalachian Jack Tales, forthcoming. **Address:** 3103 Henderson Rd., Greensboro, NC 27410, U.S.A. **Online address:** bsalsi@tiad.rr.com

SALTER, David F. American (born United States), b. 1961. **Genres:** Business/Trade/Industry, Sports/Fitness. **Career:** Blue Cross/Blue Shield, communications specialist, 1987-88; March of Dimes, community director, 1989-90; Ramapo College, assistant director of public relations, 1990-94; York College of Pennsylvania, director of public relations, 1994-. Writer. **Publications:** Blueprint for Success: An In-Depth Analysis of NCAA Division III Athletics, and Why it Should be the Model for Intercollegiate Reform, 1993; Crashing the Old Boys' Network: The Tragedies and Triumphs of Girls and Women in Sports, 1996; Dear Daughter, I Forgot Some Things, 2004. **Address:** York College of Pennsylvania, Rm. STU-130, York, PA 17405-7199, U.S.A. **Online address:** dsalter@ycp.edu

SALTER, Mary Jo. American (born United States), b. 1954. **Genres:** Children's Fiction, Poetry. **Career:** The Atlantic Monthly, staff editor, 1978-80; Harvard University, instructor in expository writing, 1978-79; Asahi Culture Center, instructor in English, 1980-83; Robert Frost Place, poet-in-residence, 1981; Mount Holyoke College, lecturer in English, 1985-95, Emily Dickinson lecturer in the humanities, 1995-2001, Emily Dickinson senior lecturer in the humanities, 2001-07; The New Republic, poetry editor, 1992-95; Poetry Society of America, vice president, 1995-2007; Johns Hopkins University, The Writing Seminars, professor, 2007-, Andrew W. Mellon professor in the humanities, co-chair, Graduate Studies, director. **Publications:** Henry Purcell in Japan: Poems, 1985; Unfinished Painting: Poems, 1989; The Moon Comes Home (children's fiction), 1989; Sunday Skaters: Poems, 1994; (ed. with M. Ferguson and J. Stallworthy) Norton Anthology of Poetry, 4th ed., 1996, 5th ed., 2005; A Kiss in Space: Poems, 1999; Open Shutters: Poems, 2003; A Phone Call to the Future: New and Selected Poems, 2008; (ed.) Selected Poems, 2010. Contributor of articles to periodicals. **Address:** The Writing Seminars, Johns Hopkins University, 081 Gilman Hall, 3400 N Charles St., Baltimore, MD 21218, U.S.A. **Online address:** mjsalter@jhu.edu

SALUTIN, Rick. Canadian (born Canada), b. 1942. **Genres:** Plays/Screenplays, Novels, History, Biography. **Career:** Playwright, 1967-; This Magazine, columnist, 1975-, contributing editor; University of Toronto, University College, Canadian Studies Programme, lecturer, 1978-; Toronto Life, columnist. 1985-; Globe and Mail, editor and columnist, 1991-99, op-ed columnist, through 2010; Ryerson University, Maclean Hunter chair in ethics in communication, 1993-95; Toronto Star, columnist, 2011-. **Publications:** William Lyon Mackenzie and the Canadian Revolution, 1975; (with M. Soupcoff and G. Dunford) Good Buy, Canada!, 1975; (with T.P. Muraille) 1837: William Lyon Mackenzie and the Canadian Revolution, 1976; (with K. Dryden) Les Canadiens (play), 1977; Kent Rowley, the Organizer: A Canadian Union Life, 1980; The False Messiah (play), 1981; Marginal Notes: Challenges to the Mainstream, 1984; (with R. Donegan) Spadina Avenue, 1985; A Man of Little Faith, 1988; Waiting for Democracy: A Citizen's Journal, 1989; Living in a Dark Age, 1991; The Age of Improv: A Political Novel of the Future, 1995; The Womanizer: A Man of His Time, 2002. Contributor to periodicals. **Address:** University College, University of Toronto, 15 King's College Cir., Toronto, ON M5S 3H7, Canada. **Online address:** ricksalutin@ca.inter.net

SALVATORE, R(obert) A(nthony). American (born United States), b. 1959. **Genres:** Science Fiction/Fantasy, Young Adult Non-fiction, Novels, Graphic Novels, Novellas/Short Stories. **Career:** Fantasy writer. **Publications:** FORGOTTEN REALMS SERIES: The Crystal Shard, 1988; Streams of Silver, 1989; The Halfling's Gem, 1990; Homeland, 1990; Exile, 1990; Sojourn, 1991; Canticle, 1991; In Sylvan Shadows, 1992; The Legacy, 1992; Night Masks, 1992; The Fallen Fortress, 1993; Starless Night, 1993; The Chaos Curse, 1994; Siege of Darkness, 1994; Passage to Dawn, 1996; The Dark Elf Trilogy, 1998; The Silent Blade, 1998; The Spine of the World, 1999; The Cleric Quintet, 1999; The Icewind Dale Trilogy, 2001; Legacy of the Drow, 2001; The Thousand Orcs, 2002; The Lone Drow, 2003; The Two Swords, 2004; Paths of Darkness Collector's Edition, 2004; Siege of Darkness, 2006. SPEARWIELDER'S TALE SERIES: The Woods out Back, 1993; The Dragon's Dagger, 1994; Dragonslayer's Return, 1995; Spearwielder's Tale, 2004; (co-author) Dragons: Worlds Afire, 2006. CRIMSON SHADOW TRILOGY: The Sword of Bedwyr, 1995; Luthien's Gamble, 1996; The Dragon King, 1996. DEMON WARS SERIES: The Demon Awakens, 1997; The Demon Spirit, 1997; The Demon Apostle, 1999; Mortalis, 2000; Ascendance, 2001; Transcendence, 2002; Immortalis, 2003; Crimson Shadow, 2006. THE SELLSWORDS SERIES: Servant of the Shard, 2000; Promise of the Witch-King: The Sellswords, 2006; Road of the Patriarch: The Sellswords, 2006; The Orc King, 2007. OTHERS: Echoes of the Fourth Magic, 1990; Tarzan: The Epic Adventures, 1997; The Witch's Daughter, 1999; The New Jedi Order: Vector Prime, 1999; Bastion of Darkness, 2000; Sea of Swords, 2001; Star Wars: Attack of the Clones, 2002; The Highwayman, 2007; Star Wars:

The Prequel Trilogy, 2007; Hunter's Blades Trilogy, 2007; (with G. Salvatore) Stowaway, 2008; Legend of Drizzt Collector's Edition, 2008; Pirate King, 2008; Spooks, 2008; Ancient, 2008; (with G. Salvatore) Shadowmask, 2009; Ghost King, 2009; Dame, 2009; (with G. Salvatore) The Sentinels, 2010; The Bear, 2010; The Sellswords, 2010; Gauntlgrym, 2010; Transitions Gift Set, 2011; The Legend of Drizzt Collector's Edition, Book IV, 2011; Neverwinter Wood, 2011; How to Write a Damn Good Fight Scene, 2011; Charon's Claw, 2012; The Dark Elf of Leominster, 2012; Kingdoms of Amalur: Reckoning, 2012. Contributor to periodicals. **Address:** 776 Warren Ave., Brockton, MA 02301-6456, U.S.A.

SALWAK, Dale (Francis). American (born United States), b. 1947. **Genres:** Literary Criticism And History, Autobiography/Memoirs, Bibliography, Biography, Young Adult Fiction, Poetry. **Career:** Magic Carpet, publisher, 1962-70; magician, 1965-; Purdue University, Department of Agricultural Information, assistant editor, 1966-69; University of Southern California, instructor, 1972-73; Citrus College, instructor, professor of English, 1973-; Stars of Magic, producer, 1974-; Chavez College of Manual Dexterity and Prestidigitation, West Coast Division, owner, director, teacher, 1978-; Borgo Press, Reader's Guides to Mystery and Detective Writers and Contemporary Writers Series, editor, 1985-; Magic Club of America, founder. **Publications:** Kingsley Amis: A Reference Guide, 1978; John Braine and John Wain: A Reference Guide, 1980; John Wain, 1981; A.J. Cronin: A Reference Guide, 1982; Literary Voices: Interviews with Britain's Angry Young Men, 1984; Carl Sandburg: A Reference Guide, 1988; Mystery Voices: Interviews with British Crime Writers, 1991; Barbara Pym: A Reference Guide, 1991; Kingsley Amis: Modern Novelist, 1992; Faith in the Family, 2001; Teaching Life: Letters from a Life in Literature, 2008. EDITOR: The Life and Work of Barbara Pym, 1987; Philip Larkin: The Man and His Work, 1989; Kingsley Amis in Life and Letters, 1991; David Lodge: How Far Can You Go?, 1991; (with P.D. Seldis) Dragons & Martinis: The Skewed Realism of John Cheever, 1993; Anne Tyler as Novelist, 1994; Christopher Hampton: An Introduction to His Plays, 1994; (with D.F. Mallett) Roald Dahl: From the Gremlins to the Chocolate Factory, 1994; (and intro.) The Wonders of Solitude, 1995; The Literary Biography: Problems and Solutions, 1996; Drawn into the Circle of Its Repetitions: Paul Auster's New York Trilogy, 1996; The Words of Christ, 1996; The Wisdom of Judaism, 1997; The Power of Prayer, 1998; A Passion for Books, 1999; Living with a Writer, 2004; Afterword, 2011. Contributor of articles to books and periodicals. **Address:** Chavez Studio of Magic, PO Box 8054, La Verne, CA 91750, U.S.A. **Online address:** dsalwak@citruscollege.edu

SALWAY, Peter. British (born England), b. 1932. **Genres:** History, Literary Criticism And History, Archaeology/Antiquities. **Career:** University of Durham, research fellow, 1956-57; Cambridge University, Sidney Sussex College, fellow, 1957-64; University of Bristol, fellow, 1964-65; Oxford University, All Souls College, fellow, 1965-69; Open University, regional director, 1970-86, professor of history and archaeology, 1983-89, professor emeritus, 1991-. Writer. **Publications:** The Frontier People of Roman Britain, 1965; (ed.) Roman Archaeology and Art: Essays and Studies, 1969; Roman Britain, 1981; The Oxford Illustrated History of Roman Britain, 1993; A History of Roman Britain, 1997; Roman Britain: A Very Short Introduction, 2000; (ed.) Roman Era: The British Isles, 55 BC-AD 410, 2002; (ed. with A. Crossley and T. Hassall) William Morris's Kelmscott: Landscape and History, 2007; (co-ed.) New Dictionary of National Biography, forthcoming. Contributor of articles and journals. **Address:** Department of Classical Studies, Faculty of Arts, The Open University, Walton Hall, Milton Keynes, BK MK7 6AA, United Kingdom.

SALWEN, Hannah. American (born United States), b. 1993?. **Genres:** Biography, Autobiography/Memoirs. **Career:** Writer and lawyer. **Publications:** (With K. Salwen) The Power of Half: One Family's Decision to Stop Taking and Start Giving Back, 2010. **Address:** Atlanta, GA, U.S.A. **Online address:** admin@thepowerofhalf.com

SALWEN, Kevin. American (born United States), b. 1959?. **Genres:** Biography. **Career:** Wall Street Journal, writer and editor; Motto Media (magazine company), co-creator. Entrepreneur. **Publications:** (With H. Salwen) The Power of Half: One Family's Decision to Stop Taking and Start Giving Back, 2010. Contributor to periodicals. **Address:** Atlanta, GA, U.S.A. **Online address:** admin@thepowerofhalf.com

SALWOLKE, Scott. American (born United States), b. 1964. **Genres:** Film. **Career:** Area Residential Care, vocational instructor, 1989; Ad Hoc Marketing Inc., consultant. Writer. **Publications:** Nicholas Roeg: Film by Film, 1993; The Films of Michael Powell and the Archers, 1997. **Address:** Ad Hoc Marketing Inc., 1435 Mt. Pleasant St., Dubuque, IA 52001-4235, U.S.A. **Online address:** salwolke@adhocmarketing.com

SALWOOD, F. K. *See* **KILWORTH, Garry.**

SALYER, Lucy E. American (born United States), b. 1956. **Genres:** History, Law. **Career:** University of California, research assistant, 1981-85, teaching assistant, 1983-86; Federal Litigation Assessment Project, U.S. District Court for the Northern District of California, research coordinator, 1985; University of New Hampshire, associate professor of history, 1989-, Center for the Humanities, Gustafsen fellow, 1996-97. Writer. **Publications:** (Contrib.) Entry Denied: Exclusion and the Chinese Community in America, 1882-1943, 1991; (contrib.) Asian Immigrants and American Law: Historical and Contemporary Perspectives, 1994; Laws Harsh as Tigers: Chinese Immigrants and the Shaping of Modern Immigration Law, 1995. Contributor to books and journals. **Address:** Department of History, Horton Social Science Ctr., University of New Hampshire, 409 Horton Social Science Ctr., Durham, NH 03824, U.S.A. **Online address:** fsa@cisunix.unh.edu

SALZBERG, Allen. American (born United States), b. 1953. **Genres:** Animals/Pets, Children's Non-fiction, Environmental Sciences/Ecology, Zoology, Natural History. **Career:** Freelance publicist, 1982-; OMNI Magazine, contributing writer, 1985-95; writer, 1975-; HerpDigest, publisher and editor, 2000-. **Publications:** (With A. Baskin-Salzberg) Predators, 1991; (with A. Baskin-Salzberg) Flightless Birds, 1993; (with A. Baskin-Salzberg) Turtles, 1996. Contributor to magazines. **Address:** c/o Wendy Lipkind, Wendy Lipkind Agency, 165 E 66th St., New York, NY 10021, U.S.A. **Online address:** asalzberg@herpdigest.org

SALZBERG, Sharon. American (born United States), b. 1952?. **Genres:** inspirational/Motivational Literature, Young Adult Non-fiction, Theology/Religion. **Career:** Insight Meditation Society, Barre Center for Buddhist Studies, and Forest Refuge, co-founder; Oprah's O Magazine, editor. Educator. **Publications:** Lovingkindness: The Revolutionary Art of Happiness, 1995; A Heart as Wide as the World: Living with Mindfulness, Wisdom, and Compassion, 1997; (ed.) Voices of Insight, 1999; Faith: Trusting Your Own Deepest Experience, 2002; Force of Kindness: Change Your Life with Love & Compassion, 2005; Kindness Handbook: A Practical Companion, 2008; The Force of Kindness: Change Your Life with Love and Compassion, 2010; Real Happiness: The Power of Meditation a 28-day Program, 2011; (with D. Gia and N.D. Nhiên) Tú vô lượng tâm. Contributor to books. **Address:** Insight Meditation Society, 1230 Pleasant St., Barre, MA 01005, U.S.A. **Online address:** sharon@sharonsalzberg.com

SALZMAN, Eva Frances. British/American (born United States), b. 1960. **Genres:** Novels, Novellas/Short Stories, Plays/Screenplays, Poetry, Songs/Lyrics And Libretti, Writing/Journalism, Young Adult Fiction, Literary Criticism And History, Literary Criticism And History. **Career:** Springhill Prison, writer-in-residence, 1994-96; The Printer's Devil Magazine, co-editor; Long Island University, adjunct professor; Poetry Society, instructor of poetry class, 2001-. **Publications:** Bargain with the Watchman, 1997; Double Crossing: New and Selected Poems, 2004. POEMS: The English Earthquake, 1992; After Verlaine; The Buddhas of Bamiyan; Brooklyn Bridge. Contributor to periodicals. Works appear in anthologies. **Address:** 68 Fairfax Rd., London, GL N8 0NG, England. **Online address:** evasalzman@writersartists.net

SALZMAN, Michele Renee. American (born United States), b. 1952. **Genres:** History. **Career:** Swarthmore College, classics lecturer, 1980; Columbia University, visiting assistant professor of classics, 1980-82; Boston University, assistant professor of classics, 1982-90, associate professor, 1990-95; University of California, associate professor of history, 1995-2000, multicampus research group, 1999, history department chair, 1999-2000, professor, 2000-. Writer. **Publications:** On Roman Time: The Codex-Calendar of 354 and the Rhythms of Urban Life in Late Antiquity, 1990; The Making of a Christian Aristocracy: Social and Religious Change in the Western Roman Empire, 2002. **Address:** Department of History, University of California, 1212 Humanities & Social Sciences Bldg., Riverside, CA 92521, U.S.A. **Online address:** michele.salzman@ucr.edu

SALZMAN, Neil. (Neil V. Salzman). American (born United States), b. 1940. **Genres:** Biography. **Career:** Fairleigh Dickinson University, instruc-

tor, 1970-75, assistant professor, 1975-80, associate professor, 1980-91, professor of history and political science, 1991-; New Jersey Department of Education's Holocaust, consultant. Writer and public speaker. **Publications:** (Ed. with W. Cummins) The World of Newton: An Anthology of Readings, 1984; (as Neil V. Salzman) Reform and Revolution: The Life and Times of Raymond Robins, 1991; Fifth Jewish Currents Reader: 1986-1996, 1998; (ed. as Neil V. Salzman) Russia in War and Revolution: General William V. Judson's Accounts from Petrograd, 1917-1918, 1998. Works appear in anthologies. Contributor of articles to periodicals. **Address:** Department of Political Science, Fairleigh Dickinson University, Mansion 34A, 285 Madison Ave., Madison, NJ 07940, U.S.A. **Online address:** grnsalzman@worldnet.att.net

SALZMAN, Neil V. *See* **SALZMAN, Neil.**

SAMAR, Vincent J(oseph). American (born United States), b. 1953. **Genres:** Law, Gay And Lesbian Issues, Philosophy. **Career:** City of Syracuse, law clerk to corporation counsel, 1977; U.S. District Court for the Northern District of New York, special summer clerk, 1980, law clerk, 1980-84; Roosevelt University, lecturer, 1982-84; St. Xavier College, lecturer in philosophy, 1982-84; Foss, Schuman, Drake & Barnard, law clerk, 1983-85; Loyola University of Chicago, lecturer in philosophy, 1984-89, visiting assistant professor, 1989-90, adjunct professor of philosophy, 1990-, adjunct professor of political science, 2008-; Coffield, Ungaretti, Harris & Slavin, law clerk, 1985-86; Burke, Griffin, Chomicz & Wienkie, law clerk, 1986; private practice of law in Chicago, 1986-; IIT Chicago/Kent College of Law, adjunct professor of law, 1990-; Oakton Community College, adjunct professor of philosophy, 2000-; St. Xavier University, adjunct professor of criminal justice, 2003-. Writer. **Publications:** The Right to Privacy: Gays, Lesbians, and the Constitution, 1991; Justifying Judgment: Practicing Law and Philosophy, 1998; (ed.) Gay Rights Movement, 2001. Contributor to books and periodicals. **Address:** Department of Philosophy, Loyola University Chicago, 6525 N Sheridan Rd., Chicago, IL 60626, U.S.A. **Online address:** vsamar@luc.edu

SAMBROOK, A(rthur) J(ames). (James Sambrook). British (born England), b. 1931. **Genres:** Literary Criticism And History, Biography, History, Essays, Poetry, Language/Linguistics. **Career:** St. David's College, lecturer in English, 1957-64; University of Southampton, lecturer, 1964-71, senior lecturer in English, 1971-75, reader, 1975-81, professor, 1981-92, emeritus professor of English, 1992-; Newberry Library, visiting research fellow, 1969; Folger Shakespeare Library, visiting research fellow, 1974, 1982; Oxford University, Magdalen College, visiting research fellow, 1984, St. John's College, visiting research fellow, 1985; Australian National University, Humanities Research Centre, visiting research fellow, 1988. Writer. **Publications:** (Intro.) The Scribleriad (anonymous, 1742) The Difference Between Verbal and Practical Virtue (1742), 1967. AS JAMES SAMBROOK: A Poet Hidden: The Life of Richard Watson Dixon, 1833-1900, 1962; William Cobbett: An Author Guide, 1973; English Pastoral Poetry, 1983; The Eighteenth Century: The Intellectual and Cultural Context of English Literature, 1700-1789, 1986, 2nd ed., 1993; James Thomson, 1700-1748: A Life, 1991; With the Rank and Pay of a Sapper, 1998; (co-author) William Collins, 2009. EDITOR AS JAMES SAMBROOK: The Seasons and the Castle of Indolence, 1972, 3rd ed., 1987; (and intro.) Pre-Raphaelitism: A Collection of Critical Essays, 1974; (and intro.) The Seasons, 1981; Liberty, the Castle of Indolence and Other Poems, 1986; The Task and Selected Other Poems, 1994. Contributor of articles to books and journals. **Address:** University of Southampton, University Rd., Southampton, HM SO17 1BJ, England.

SAMBROOK, James. *See* **SAMBROOK, A(rthur) J(ames).**

SAMMON, Paul M. American (born United States), b. 1949?. **Genres:** Film, Horror, Young Adult Non-fiction, Novellas/Short Stories, Mystery/Crime/Suspense, Literary Criticism And History. **Career:** The Los Angeles Times, writer; The American Cinematographer, writer. Film publicist. **Publications:** The Christmas Carol Trivia Book: Everything You Ever Wanted to Know About Every Version of the Dickens Classic, 1994; Future Noir: The Making of Blade Runner, 1996; The Making of Starship Troopers, 1997; The Complete Aliens Companion, 1998; Ridley Scott, 1999; Conan the Phenomenon, 2007. EDITOR: Splatter-Punks: Extreme Horror, 1990; Splatterpunks II: Over the Edge, 1994; The King Is Dead: Tales of Elvis Postmortem, 1994. **Address:** c/o Author Mail, HarperCollins Inc., 10 E 53rd St., 7th Fl., New York, NY 10022, U.S.A.

SAMPLES, John Curtis. American (born United States), b. 1956?. **Genres:**

Politics/Government. **Career:** Twentieth Century Fund, vice president; Georgetown University Press, director; Cato Institute Center for Representative Government, director; Johns Hopkins University, adjunct professor. Educator and writer. **Publications:** Three Myths about Voter Turnout in the United States, 2004; The Fallacy of Campaign Finance Reform, 2006; (with A. Simoni) La corsa più lunga: Obama vs McCaine: Due visioni, una nazione, 2008. EDITOR (and contrib.) James Madison and the Future of Limited Government, 2002; Welfare for Politicians? Taxpayer Financing of Campaigns, 2005; (with C. Edwards) The Republican Revolution 10 Years Later: Smaller Government or Business as Usual?, 2005; (with M.P. McDonald) The Marketplace of Democracy: Electoral Competition and American Politics, 2006; Contributor of articles to journals. **Address:** Cato Institute, 1000 Massachusetts Ave. NW, Washington, DC 20001-5403, U.S.A. **Online address:** jsamples@cato.org

SAMPSELL, Kevin. American (born United States), b. 1967. **Genres:** Autobiography/Memoirs, Novellas/Short Stories. **Career:** Future Tense Books, founder, 1990-; Powell's Books, fiction curator. Writer. **Publications:** (Ed.) The Insomniac Reader: Stories of the Night, 2005; Creamy Bullets (stories), 2008; A Common Pornography: A Memoir, 2010. Contributor to magazines. **Address:** Portland, OR , U.S.A. **Online address:** futuretense@q7.com

SAMPSON, Catherine. British (born England), b. 1962?. **Genres:** Novels, Mystery/Crime/Suspense, Young Adult Fiction. **Career:** British Broadcasting Corp., Monitoring Service, journalist; The Times, journalist and Beijing correspondent, 1988. Writer and educator. **Publications:** Falling off Air, 2004; Out of Mind, 2005; The Pool of Unease, 2007; The Slaughter Pavilion, 2008. Contributor to periodicals. **Address:** c/o Author Mail, Mysterious Press, 1271 Ave. of the Americas, New York, NY 10020, U.S.A.

SAMPSON, Curt. American (born United States), b. 1952. **Genres:** Sports/Fitness, Recreation, Biography, History, Autobiography/Memoirs. **Career:** Writer. **Publications:** The Eternal Summer: Palmer, Nicklaus and Hogan in 1960, Golf's Golden Year, 1992; Texas Golf Legends, 1993; Full Court Pressure: A Tumultuous Season with Coach Karl and the Seattle Sonics, 1995; Hogan, 1996; The Masters: Golf, Money and Power in Augusta, Georgia, 1998; (with S. Elkington) Five Fundamentals: Steve Elkington Reveals the Secrets of the Best Swing in Golf, 1998; Royal and Ancient: Blood, Sweat and Fear at the British Open, 2000; Chasing Tiger, 2002; Lost Masters: Grace and Disgrace in '68, 2005; Slam: Bobby Jones and The Price of Glory, 2005; Golf Dads: Fathers, Sons and the Greatest Game, 2008. **Address:** Houghton Mifflin Company, 222 Berkeley St., Boston, MA 02116, U.S.A. **Online address:** msampson@joimail.com

SAMPSON, Edward E. American (born United States), b. 1934. **Genres:** Psychology, Social Sciences, Sociology. **Career:** University of California, assistant professor, 1960-66, associate professor of psychology, 1966-70; Brunel University, lecturer, 1970-71; Clark University, visiting professor, 1971-72, professor of sociology and psychology, 1971-82, department chairman; California State University, Wright Institute, dean, 1982-86, professor of psychology, 1986-, now professor emeritus of psychology. Writer. **Publications:** (Ed.) Approaches, Contexts, and Problems of Social Psychology, 1964; (co-author) Student Activism and Protest, 1970; Social Psychology and Contemporary Society, 1971, 2nd ed., 1976; Ego at the Threshold, 1975; Group Process for the Health Professions, 1977, 3rd ed., 1990; Introducing Social Psychology, 1980; Justice and the Critique of Pure Psychology, 1983; Social Worlds, Personal Lives, 1991; Celebrating the Other: A Dialogic Account of Human Nature, 1993; Dealing with Differences: An Introduction to the Social Psychology of Prejudice, 1999; Not in Control: A Different Place for Humanity in the World, forthcoming. **Address:** 1150 Sterling Ave., Berkeley, CA 94708, U.S.A.

SAMPSON, Geoffrey (Richard). British (born England), b. 1944. **Genres:** Information Science/Computers, Philosophy, Politics/Government, Language/Linguistics. **Career:** Queen's College, fellow, 1969-72; London School of Economics, lecturer, 1972-74; University of Lancaster, lecturer, 1974-76, reader, 1976-84; University of Leeds, professor of linguistics, 1985-90; University of Sussex, Department of Informatics, reader, 1991, department chairman, 1993-96, professor, 1999-2009, professor emeritus, 2009-; Centre for Advanced Software Applications, director, 1991-96; freelance writer, 2009-. **Publications:** Stratificational Grammar: A Definition and an Example, 1970; Chomskyan Linguistics: Aims, Achievements and Prospects, 1974; The Form of Language, 1975; Liberty and Language, 1979; Making

Sense, 1980; Schools of Linguistics, 1980; An End to Allegiance: Individual Freedom And The New Politics, 1984; Writing Systems: A Linguistic Introduction, 1985; (with R. Garside and G. Leech) The Computational Analysis of English: A Corpus-Based Approach, 1987; English for the Computer: The SUSANNE Corpus and Analytic Scheme, 1995; Evolutionary Language Understanding, 1996; Educating Eve: The Language Instinct Debate, 1997, rev. ed., 2005; Empirical Linguistics, 2001; Brissac and Its Mediaeval Seigneurs, 2002; e.biz: The Anatomy of Electronic Business, 2003; (ed. with D. McCarthy) Corpus Linguistics: Readings in a Widening Discipline, 2004; Love Songs of Early China, 2006; Electronic Business, 2008; (ed. with D. Gil and P. Trudgill) Language Complexity as an Evolving Variable, 2009; Law for Computing Students, 2009; Perl for Beginners, 2010. **Address:** School of Informatics, University of Sussex, Falmer, Brighton, ES BN1 9QJ, England. **Online address:** sampson@cantab.net

SAMPSON, Michael. (Michael R. Sampson). American (born United States), b. 1952. **Genres:** Children's Fiction, Education. **Career:** Commerce Independent School District, teacher, 1974-76; University of Arizona, Department of Reading, instructor, 1977-79; East Texas University, assistant professor, 1979-83, associate professor, 1983-87; The International Institute of Literacy Learning, executive director, 1980-; Texas A&M University, professor, 1987-2004, department head, 1994-97; University of South Florida, associate professor, 2007-10; Southern Connecticut State University, School of Education, dean, 2010-. Writer. **Publications:** FOR CHILDREN: The Football That Won, 1996; (with M.B. Sampson) Star of the Circus, 1997. FOR ADULTS: (ed.) The Pursuit of Literacy: Early Reading and Writing, 1986; Experiences for Literacy, 1990; (with M.B. Sampson and R. van Allen) Pathways to Literacy: A Meaning-Centered Perspective, 1991, 2nd ed. as Pathways to Literacy: Process Transactions, 1995; (with T.V. Rasinski and M.B. Sampson) Total Literacy: Reading, Writing, and Learning, 2003. WITH B. MARTIN, JR.: Si Won's Victory, 1996; Yummy Tum Tee, 1996; Swish!, 1997; Adam, Adam, What Do You See?, 2000; Little Squeegy Bug, 2001; Little Granny Quarterback, 2001; Rock it, Sock it, Number Line, 2001; Trick or Treat?, 2002; I Pledge Allegiance, 2002; Caddie, the Golf Dog, 2002; Chicka Chicka 1, 2, 3, 2004; (and with B. Martin) Chicken Chuck, 2005; I Love Our Earth, 2006; Kitty Cat, Kitty Cat, are you Waking Up?, 2008; (ed.) Bill Martin Jr. Big Book of Poetry, 2008; Kitty Cat, Kitty Cat, Are You Going to Sleep?, 2011. Contributor of articles to periodicals and journals. **Address:** Southern Connecticut State University, 501 Crescent St., New Haven, CT 06515, U.S.A. **Online address:** michaelrsampson@mac.com

SAMPSON, Michael R. See **SAMPSON, Michael.**

SAMS, Ferrol. (William Sims). American (born United States), b. 1922. **Genres:** Novels, Novellas/Short Stories, Adult Non-fiction. **Career:** Physician in private practice, 1951-2006; Emory University, instructor in creative writing, 1991-. **Publications:** Run with the Horsemen (novel), 1982; The Whisper of the River (novel), 1984; The Widow's Mite and Other Stories (short stories), 1987; The Passing: Perspectives of Rural America (nonfiction), 1988; Christmas Gift! (nonfiction), 1989; When All the World was Young (novel), 1992; Epiphany: Stories, 1994; Down Town: The Journal of James Aloysius Holcombe, Jr. for Ephraim Holcombe Mookinfoos, 2007. Contributor to periodicals. **Address:** Emory University, 201 Dowman Dr., Atlanta, GA 30322, U.S.A.

SAMSON, Suzanne M. American (born United States), b. 1959?. **Genres:** Animals/Pets, Horticulture, Children's Fiction, Natural History, Picture/Board Books, Children's Non-fiction. **Career:** Glenshire Elementary School, teacher. Writer. **Publications:** Fairy Dusters and Blazing Stars: Exploring Wildflowers with Children, 1994; Sea Dragons and Rainbow Runners: Exploring Fish with Children, 1995; Tumblebugs and Hairy Bears: Exploring Insects with Children, 1996; Roadrunners and Sandwich Terns: Exploring Birds with Children, 1997. **Address:** Glenshire Elementary School, 10990 Dorchester Dr., Truckee, CA 96161-1537, U.S.A.

SAMUELS, Cynthia K(alish). American (born United States), b. 1946. **Genres:** Politics/Government, Young Adult Non-fiction. **Career:** Columbia Broadcasting System Inc. (CBS), CBS News, researcher, 1973-74, assistant foreign editor, 1974-76, New York Bureau, assistant chief, 1976-80; National Broadcasting Company Inc., NBC News, producer and writer, 1980-84, political producer, 1984-88, planning and political producer, 1988-89; Whittle Communications, Channel One, vice president and executive producer, 1988-91, executive vice president of programming and development, 1991-;

National Public Radio, senior nutritional editor, 1999-; Cobblestone Associates L.L.P., partner; Care2.com Inc., causes managing editor. **Publications:** It's a Free Country!: A Young Person's Guide to Politics & Elections, 1988. **Address:** Care2.com Inc., 275 Shoreline Dr., Ste. 300, Redwood City, CA 94065-1490, U.S.A. **Online address:** csamuels@cobblestone-associates.com

SAMUELS, David. American (born United States), b. 1967?. **Genres:** Politics/Government, Social Sciences. **Career:** University of Minnesota, Benjamin E. Lippincott assistant professor, 1998-2003, Benjamin E. Lippincott associate professor, 2003-; Centro de Estudos da Cultura Contemporanea, visiting scholar, 1996-97; Fundacao GetUlio Vargas, visiting scholar, 2001-02; Latin American Studies Association, Political Institutions Section, chair, 2003-04; Comparative Political Studies, editorial board member, 2005-. **Publications:** Ambition, Federalism and Legislative Politics in Brazil, 2003; (ed. with A.P. Montero) Decentralization and Democracy in Latin America, 2004. Contributor of articles to periodicals. **Address:** Department of Political Science, University of Minnesota, 1414 Social Sciences Bldg., 267 19th Ave. S, Minneapolis, MN 55455, U.S.A. **Online address:** dsamuels@umn.edu

SAMUELS, Richard J. American (born United States), b. 1951. **Genres:** Politics/Government, Technology, Cultural/Ethnic Topics, History. **Career:** Massachusetts Institute of Technology, Industrial Liaison Program, faculty consultant, 1980-83, Center for Energy Policy Research, research associate, 1980-86, Department of Political Science, assistant professor, 1980-84, associate professor, 1984-90, Mitsui Career Development associate professor of contemporary technology, 1984-86, associate department head, 1989-92, head, 1992-97, director, 1992-97, Ford international professor of political science, 1992-, Japan Science and Technology Program, founding director, 1981-, Center for International Studies, director, 2000-; RAND Corp., adjunct staff, 2009-11. Writer, political scientist and administrator. **Publications:** (Ed.) Political Generations and Political Development (meeting proceedings), 1977; (ed. with R.B. Gillmor) Japanese Scientific and Technical Information in the United States: Workshop Proceedings, 1983; The Politics of Regional Policy in Japan: Localities Incorporated?, 1983; (ed. with R.A. Morse) Getting America Ready for Japanese Science and Technology, 1985; The Business of the Japanese State: Energy Markets in Comparative and Historical Perspective, 1987; (ed. with M. Weiner) The Political Culture of Foreign Area and International Studies: Essays in Honor of Lucian W. Pye, 1992; Rich Nation, Strong Army: National Security and the Technological Transformation of Japan, 1994; (ed. with W.W. Keller) Crisis and Innovation in Asian Technology, 2003; Machiavelli's Children: Leaders and Their Legacies in Italy and Japan, 2003; (with J.P. Boyd) Nine Lives?: The Politics of Constitutional Reform in Japan, 2005; (ed.) Encyclopedia of United States National Security, 2006; Securing Japan: Tokyo's Grand Strategy and the Future of East Asia, 2007. Contributor to magazines and periodicals. **Address:** Department of Political Science, Massachusetts Institute of Technology, Rm. E40-455, 77 Massachusetts Ave., 30 Wadsworth St., Cambridge, MA 02139, U.S.A. **Online address:** samuels@mit.edu

SAMUELS, Shirley. American (born United States), b. 1957. **Genres:** Literary Criticism And History, Women's Studies And Issues. **Career:** Princeton University, assistant professor of English, 1985-86; Cornell University, assistant professor, 1986-92, associate professor of English, 1992-98, professor of English and American studies, 1998-, Women's Studies Program, director, 1996-2000, acting chair, 2005-06, History of Art, chair, 2006-, Flora Rose House professor and dean, 2009-, graduate faculty; University of Delaware, H. Fletcher Brown professor of the humanities, 2000-01. Writer. **Publications:** (Ed.) The Culture of Sentiment: Race, Gender, and Sentimentality in Nineteenth-Century America, 1992; Romances of the Republic: Women, the Family and Violence in the Literature of the Early American Nation, 1996; (ed.) Companion to American Fiction, 1780-1865, 2004; Facing America: Iconography and the Civil War, 2004; (ed. with J. Parini) The Wadsworth Themes in American Literature Series, 1800-1865, 2009; Reading the American Novel, 1780-1865, 2011; (ed.) Companion to Abraham Lincoln, 2011; A History of American Literature, 1783-1865, 2012. **Address:** Department of English, Cornell University, 257 Goldwin Smith Hall, Ithaca, NY 14853, U.S.A. **Online address:** srs8@cornell.edu

SAMUELS, Warren J(oseph). *See* Obituaries.

SAMUELSON, Robert J(acob). American (born United States), b. 1945. **Genres:** Essays, Local History/Rural Topics, Social Sciences. **Career:** Washington Post, reporter, 1969-73; freelance reporter, 1973-76, columnist, 1984-;

National Journal, reporter and columnist, 1976-84; Newsweek, contributing editor and columnist, 1984-. **Publications:** The Numbskull Factor: The Decline of Common Sense in America, 1993; The Good Life and Its Discontents: The American Dream in the Age of Entitlement, 1945-1995, 1995; Untruth: Why the Conventional Wisdom is (Almost Always) Wrong, 2001; Great Inflation and its Aftermath: The Transformation of America's Economy, Politics, and Society, 2008; The Great Inflation and Its Aftermath: The Past and Future of American Affluence, 2008, rev. ed., 2010. Contributor to periodicals. **Address:** Washington Post, 1150 15th St. NW, Washington, DC 20071, U.S.A.

SANCHEZ, Alex. American/Mexican (born Mexico), b. 1957?. **Genres:** Young Adult Fiction, Gay And Lesbian Issues. **Career:** Writer and public speaker. **Publications:** Rainbow Boys, 2001; Rainbow High, 2003; So Hard to Say, 2004; Rainbow Road, 2005; Getting It, 2006; The God Box, 2007; Bait, 2009; Boyfriends with Girlfriends, 2011. **Address:** c/o Miriam Altshuler, Miriam Altshuler Literary Agency, 53 Old Post Rd. N, Red Hook, NY 12571, U.S.A. **Online address:** alex@alexsanchez.com

SANCHEZ, Ivan William. American (born United States), b. 1972. **Genres:** Autobiography/Memoirs, Biography. **Career:** Writer, memoirist, biographer, advocate and motivational speaker. **Publications:** Next Stop: Growing Up Wild-Style in the Bronx (memoir), 2008; (with L. Cedeno) It's Just Begun: The Epic Journey of DJ Disco Wiz, Hip Hop's First Latino DJ, 2009. Contributor to newspapers and periodicals. **Address:** c/o Jenoyne Adams, Levine Greenberg Literary Agency, 307 7th Ave., Ste. 2407, New York, NY 10001, U.S.A.

SANCHEZ, Lavinia. *See* **ELMSLIE, Kenward.**

SANCHEZ, Patrick. American (born United States), b. 1970. **Genres:** Novels, Humor/Satire. **Career:** Value Options Managed Healthcare Co., representative, director of proposals, 1993-. Writer. **Publications:** Girlfriends, 2001; The Way It Is, 2003; Tight, 2006; Once Upon a Nervous Breakdown, 2007. **Address:** c/o Deborah Schneider, 250 W 57th St., New York, NY 10107-0001, U.S.A. **Online address:** patrick@erols.com

SANCHEZ, Sonia. American (born United States), b. 1934. **Genres:** Children's Fiction, Plays/Screenplays, Poetry, Young Adult Fiction, Women's Studies And Issues. **Career:** Downtown Community School, instructor, 1965-67; San Francisco State College, instructor, 1966-68; University of Pittsburg, assistant professor, 1969-70; Rutgers University, assistant professor, 1970-71; City University of New York, Manhattan Community College, assistant professor of black literature and creative writing teacher of writing, 1971-73, City College, teacher of creative writing, 1972; Amherst College, associate professor, 1972-73; University of Pennsylvania, faculty, 1976-77; American Poetry Review, columnist, 1977-78; Temple University, associate professor of English, 1977-79, professor of English, 1979, professor emeritus, 1999-, Provost's Office, faculty fellow, 1986-87, presidential fellow, 1987-88, Laura H. Carnell professor of English, Laura H. Carnell chair of English, through 1999, poet-in-residence; Philadelphia Daily News, columnist, 1982-83; Spelman College, distinguished poet-in-residence, 1988-89; University of Delaware, distinguished minority fellow; Tulane University, Sophie Newcomb College, Zale writer-in-residence; Black Scholar, contributing editor; The Journal of African Studies, contributing editor. **Publications:** POETRY: Home Coming: Poems, 1969; We a BaddDDD People, 1970; Liberation Poems, 1971; Ima Talken Bout The Nation of Islam, 1971; A Blues Book for Blue Black Magical Women, 1973; Love Poems, 1973; A Blues Book for Blue Black Magical Women, 1974; I've Been a Woman: New and Selected Poems, 1980; Homegirls and Hand Grenades: Poems, 1984; Under a Soprano Sky: Poems, 1987; Shake Down Memory and Continuous Fire, 1991; Wounded in the House of a Friend, 1995; Does Your House Have Lions?, 1997; Like the Singing Coming off the Drums: Love Poems, 1998; Shake Loose My Skin: New and Selected Poems, 1999; Ash, 2001; Bum Rush the Page: A Def Poetry Jam, 2001; Morning Haiku, 2010. CHILDREN BOOKS: It's a New Day: Poems for Young Brothas and Sistuhs, 1971; The Adventures of Fathead, Smallhead, and Squarehead, 1973; A Sound Investment and Other Stories, 1979. OTHER: (ed. and intro.) Living at the Epicenter, 1995; (contrib.) Black Panther, 2007; I'm Black When I'm Singing, I'm Blue When I Ain't and Other Plays, 2010. Works appear in anthologies. **Address:** Beacon Press, 25 Beacon St., Boston, MA 02108, U.S.A.

SANCHEZ-EPPLER, Karen. American (born United States), b. 1959. **Genres:** History, Literary Criticism And History, Education, Humanities. **Ca-**

reer: Yale University, visiting professor, 1996. Amherst College, Department of English, professor of English and American studies; Journal for the History of Childhood and Youth, founding editor. **Publications:** Touching Liberty: Abolition, Feminism, and the Politics of the Body, 1993; Dependent States: The Child's Part in Nineteenth-Century American Culture, 2005; The Unpublished Republic: Manuscript Cultures of the Mid-Nineteenth-Century U.S., forthcoming; In the Archives of Childhood: Personal and Historical Pasts, forthcoming. Contributor to periodicals. **Address:** Department of English, Amherst College, 1 Johnson Chapel, 101 Morgan Hall, PO Box 2234, Amherst, MA 01002-5000, U.S.A. **Online address:** kjsanchezepp@amherst.edu

SÁNCHEZ-WALSH, Arlene M. American (born United States), b. 1966. **Genres:** Sociology. **Career:** California Baptist University, Department of History, adjunct professor, 1998-99; Chaffey College, Department of History, adjunct professor, 1998-99; University of Southern California, Center for Religion and Civic Culture, program director of immigrant studies and research assistant, 1999-2000; Association of Vineyard Churches, consultant, 1999-; DePaul University, assistant professor, 2000-05; Azusa Pacific University, Graduate School of Theology, associate professor of church history and Latino church studies, 2005-, Department of Ministry, chair; Emory University, Lilly Fellow, 2006; Fuller Theological Seminary, visiting associate professor, 2006-. Writer. **Publications:** Latino Pentecostal Identity: Evangelical Faith, Self, and Society, 2003. Contributor of articles to journals and books. **Address:** Graduate School of Theology, Azusa Pacific University, Ronald 150, Ronald Bldg., CLAS Ste., E Campus, 701 E Foothill Blvd., PO Box 7000, Azusa, CA 91702-2606, U.S.A. **Online address:** asanchez-walsh@apu.edu

SANDAY, Peggy Reeves. American (born United States), b. 1937. **Genres:** Anthropology/Ethnology, Sex, Ethics, Local History/Rural Topics. **Career:** Carnegie-Mellon University, School of Urban and Public Affairs, assistant professor of anthropology and urban affairs, 1969-72; University of Pennsylvania, Department of Anthropology, associate professor, 1972-85, professor of anthropology, 1985-2001, professor emeritus of anthropology, 2001-, School of Arts and Sciences, R. Jean Brownlee endowed term chair, 2001-06. Writer. **Publications:** (Ed.) Anthropology and the Public Interest: Fieldwork and Theory, 1976; Female Power and Male Dominance: On the Origins of Sexual Inequality, 1981; Divine Hunger: Cannibalism as a Cultural System, 1986; (ed. with R.G. Goodenough) Beyond the Second Sex: New Directions in the Anthropology of Gender, 1990; Fraternity Gang Rape: Sex, Brotherhood, and Privilege on Campus, 1990, 2nd ed., 2007; A Woman Scorned: Acquaintance Rape on Trial, 1996; Women at the Center: Life in a Modern Matriarchy, 2002; Aboriginal Paintings of the Wolfe Creek Crater: Track of the Rainbow Serpent, 2007. **Address:** Department of Anthropology, University of Pennsylvania, 325 University Museum, 3260 South St., Philadelphia, PA 19104-6398, U.S.A. **Online address:** psanday@sas.upenn.edu

SANDBURG, Helga. American (born United States), b. 1918. **Genres:** Novels, Novellas/Short Stories, Children's Fiction, Young Adult Fiction, Poetry. **Career:** Library of Congress, Manuscripts Division and Keeper of the Collections, secretary, 1952-56; Freelance writer, 1957-; Woodrow Wilson Foundation, administrative assistant, 1958-59; W. Colston Leigh Lecture Bureau Inc., lecturer, 1960-64; U.S. Department of State, Bureau of Cultural and Educational Affairs, lecturer, 1961. **Publications:** The Wheel of Earth, 1958; Measure My Love, 1959; The Owl's Roost, 1962; Blueberry, 1963; Sweet Music: A Book of Family Reminiscence and Song, 1963; Joel and the Wild Goose, 1963; (contrib.) Uninhibited Treasury of Erotic Poetry, 1963; Gingerbread, 1964; Bo and the Old Donkey, 1965; The Unicorns, 1965; (contrib.) Wide Horizons, 1966; The Wizard's Child, 1967; (with G. Crile, Jr.) Above and Below, 1969; Anna and the Baby Buzzard, 1970; To a New Husband, 1970; Children and Lovers: 15 Stories, 1976; A Great and Glorious Romance: The Story of Carl Sandburg and Lilian Steichen, 1978; Where Love Begins, 1989; The Age of the Flower: Poems, 1994. Contributor of articles to magazines. **Address:** 2060 Kent Rd., Cleveland Heights, OH 44106-3339, U.S.A. **Online address:** helgacrile@aol.com

SANDEL, Michael J. American (born United States), b. 1953. **Genres:** Philosophy, Adult Non-fiction, Social Sciences. **Career:** Harvard University, instructor in political philosophy, 1980-99, professor, 1999-, Anne T. and Robert M. Bass professor of government; Oxford University, visiting lecturer, 1998; Sorbonne, visiting professor, 2001. Writer. **Publications:** NONFICTION: Liberalism and the Limits of Justice, 1982, 2nd ed., 1998; (ed.) Liberalism and Its Critics, 1984; Democracy's Discontent: America in Search of a Public Philosophy, 1996; Public Philosophy: Essays on Morality in Politics,

2005; The Case Against Perfection: Ethics In The Age Of Genetic Engineering, 2007; (ed.) Justice: A Reader, 2007; Justice: What's The Right Thing To Do?, 2010; What Money Can't Buy: The Moral Limits of Markets, 2012. **Address:** Department of Government, Harvard University, 1737 Cambridge St., 432 CGIS Knafel Bldg., Cambridge, MA 02138, U.S.A. **Online address:** msandel@gov.harvard.edu

SANDER, Heather L. Canadian (born Canada), b. 1947. **Genres:** Young Adult Non-fiction, Animals/Pets, Social Sciences. **Career:** Victoria School District, elementary school councilor, 1987-. Writer. **Publications:** Robbie Packford: Alien Monster, 2003; Make Mine with Everything, 2004; Whatever Happened to My Dog Cuddles?, 2004. **Address:** c/o Author Mail, Orca Book Publishers Ltd., PO Box 5626, Sta. B, Victoria, BC V8R 6S4, Canada. **Online address:** gandh.sander@shaw.ca

SANDERLIN, George. (George William Sanderlin). American (born United States), b. 1915. **Genres:** History, Biography, Writing/Journalism, Education, Children's Non-fiction, Translations, Travel/Exploration. **Career:** University of Maine, associate professor of English, 1938-55; San Diego State University, professor of English, 1954-83, emeritus professor of English, 1983-. Writer. **Publications:** (As George William Sanderlin) The Influence of Milton and Wordsworth on the Early Victorian Sonnet: A Portion of the Sonnet in English Literature, 1800-1850, 1938; College Reading, 1953, 2nd ed., 1958; St. Jerome and the Bible, 1961; (with J.I. Brown) Effective Writing and Reading, 1962; St. Gregory the Great, Consul of God, 1964; Eastward to India, Vasco da Gama's Voyage, 1965; Effective Writing, 1966; (comp.) 1776: Journals of American Independence, 1968; (comp.) The Sea-Dragon, Journals of Francis Drake's Voyage around the World, 1969; Benjamin Franklin as Others Saw Him, 1971; The Settlement of California, 1972; A Hoop to the Barrel: The Making of the American Constitution, 1974; Washington Irving: As Others Saw Him, 1975; Mark Twain: As Others Saw Him, 1978. EDITOR: First Around the World, a Journal of Magellan's Voyage, 1964; Across the Ocean Sea, a Journal of Columbus's Voyage, 1966; (and trans.) Bartolomé de Las Casas: A Selection of His Writings, 1971; (and trans.) Witness: Writings of Bartolomé de las Casas, 1992. Contributor to periodicals and journals. **Address:** Orbis Books, PO Box 302, Maryknoll, NY 10545-0302, U.S.A.

SANDERLIN, George William. *See* **SANDERLIN, George.**

SANDERS, Alan J. K. British (born England), b. 1937. **Genres:** Reference, International Relations/Current Affairs, Military/Defense/Arms Control, Language/Linguistics, Politics/Government, Institutions/Organizations. **Career:** British Broadcasting Corp., Russian monitor and editor, 1961-90, Hong Kong Office, manager, 1971-75; University of London, London School of Oriental and African Studies, lecturer in Mongolian studies, 1991-95. **Publications:** The People's Republic of Mongolia: A General Reference Guide, 1968; Mongolia: Politics, Economy, and Society, 1987; (with J. Bat-Ireedui) Mongolian Phrasebook, 1995; Historical Dictionary of Mongolia, 1996, 3rd ed., 2010; (with J. Bat-Ireedui) Colloquial Mongolian, 1999. Contributor to books and periodicals. **Address:** 29 Cardinal Close, Reading, BR RG4 8BZ, England. **Online address:** alan.sanders@fsmail.net

SANDERS, Andrew. British (born England), b. 1946. **Genres:** Literary Criticism And History, Politics/Government, History. **Career:** University of Leeds, lecturer in English, 1971-72; University of Sussex, lecturer in English, 1972-73; University of London, Birkbeck College, lecturer, 1973-89, reader in modern English literature, 1989-; Dickens House Museum, Board of Trustees, chairperson, 1992-. Writer. **Publications:** St. Augustine of Canterbury, Highgate: A Short History of the Church, 1975; The Victorian Historical Novel, 1840-1880, 1978; Charles Dickens, Resurrectionist, 1982; A Companion to A Tale of Two Cities, 1988; The Short Oxford History of English Literature, 1994, 3rd ed., 2004; Anthony Trollope, 1998; Dickens and the Spirit of the Age, 1999; Charles Dickens's London, 2010. EDITOR: (and intro.) Romola, 1980; (intro.) Sylvia's Lovers, 1982; (intro.) Memoirs of Barry Lyndon, Esq., 1984; (intro.) A Tale of Two Cities, 1989; (co-ed.) Studies in Eighteenth and Nineteenth Century Literature, 1992; Bleak House, 1994; (intro.) Newcomes: Memoirs of a Most Respectable Family, 1995; (intro.) Tom Brown's Schooldays, 1999; (intro.) Dombey and Son, 2002; Great Victorian Lives: An Era in Obituaries, 2007. Works appears in anthologies. **Address:** Department of English, Birkbeck College, University of London, Malet St., London, GL WC1E 7HX, England.

SANDERS, Arlene. American (born United States) **Genres:** Adult Non-fiction, Novellas/Short Stories, Literary Criticism And History. **Career:** Writer. **Publications:** Tiger Burning Bright (short story collection), 2008. Contributor to periodicals and journals. **Address:** Jefferson Press L.L.C., 808 Scenic Hwy., Lookout Mountain, TN 37350-1418, U.S.A. **Online address:** arlenesanders@dellmail.com

SANDERS, Arthur. American (born United States), b. 1955. **Genres:** Politics/Government, Medicine/Health, Social Commentary, Ethics. **Career:** Hamilton College, Department of Government, assistant professor of political science, 1982-90, Washington Program, director, 1983; United Way of Greater Utica, consultant, 1989-90; Drake University, assistant professor, 1990-93, associate professor, 1993-2002, University Senate, president, 2002-03, professor, 2002-, department chair, 2004-, The Ellis And Nelle Levitt professor of politics, Drake's Honors Program, director, 2000-, associate provost; ICPSR, official representative, 1991-; WHO-Radio, election analyst, 1996, 1998, 2000, 2002. Writer. **Publications:** Making Sense of Politics, 1990; Victory: How a Progressive Democratic Party Can Win and Govern, 1992; (ed. with K.V. Iserson and D.R. Mathieu) Ethics in Emergency Medicine, 1995; (ed.) Emergency Care of the Elder Person, 1996; Prime Time Politics, 2002; Losing Control: Presidential Elections and the Decline of Democracy, 2007. Contributor to journals. **Address:** Department of Politics, Drake University, 212 Meredith Hall, 2507 University Ave., Des Moines, IA 50311-4505, U.S.A. **Online address:** arthur.sanders@drake.edu

SANDERS, Bill. American (born United States), b. 1951. **Genres:** Young Adult Non-fiction, Children's Non-fiction, Theology/Religion. **Career:** Writer, 1968-; Big Brothers of America, trainer, 1970-; speaker, 1978-; United Way, trainer, 1980-82; Youth for Christ, board director, 1983-86. **Publications:** FOR YOUNG ADULTS: Tough Turf, 1986; Almost Everything Teens Want Parents to Know, 1987; Outtakes: Devotions for Guys, 1988; Outtakes: Devotions for Girls, 1988; Goalposts: Devotions for Guys, 1990; Goalposts: Devotions for Girls, 1990; Life, Sex, and Everything in Between, 1991; School Daze, 1992; Stand Tall, 1992; Stand Up, 1993; Stand Out, 1994; Straight Talk for Girls, 1995; Straight Talk for Guys, 1995; What Your Kids Are Up to and in For, 1996; Seize the Moment, Not Your Teen: The Art of Opportunity Parenting, 1997. **Address:** 14681 N Barton Lake Dr., Vicksburg, MS 49097, U.S.A. **Online address:** billspeaks@billspeaks.com

SANDERS, Charles W. American (born United States), b. 1947?. **Genres:** Adult Non-fiction, Military/Defense/Arms Control, History. **Career:** Kansas State University, Department of History, instructor, 2000-02, assistant professor, 2001-05, associate professor of history, 2005-. Writer. **Publications:** While in the Hands of the Enemy: Military Prisons of the Civil War, 2005; Brawlers for Liberty: A Social History of the Battle of New Orleans, forthcoming. **Address:** Department of History, Kansas State University, 316 Eisenhower Hall, Manhattan, KS 66506-1002, U.S.A. **Online address:** chassan@ksu.edu

SANDERS, Clinton R. (Tolen S. Lateef). American (born United States), b. 1944. **Genres:** Sociology, Social Sciences. **Career:** Northwestern University, Department of Sociology, instructor in sociology, 1966-67, instructor, 1967-68, Meddill School of Journalism, Urban Journalism Program, research assistant, 1969; University of Chicago, Epidemiology Unit of Illinois Drug Abuse Program, director of field research, 1970-71; Loyola University of Chicago, lecturer in guidance and counseling, 1971-72; Alternatives Inc., director of research and evaluation, 1971-73; Temple University, Department of Sociology, assistant professor, 1973-76, Press, co-editor, 1996-; Pacific Institute for Research and Evaluation, consultant, 1974-79; University of Connecticut, Department of Sociology, assistant professor, 1976-79, associate professor, 1979-91, professor of sociology, 1991-; Sexual Assault Crisis Service, consultant, 1977; Qualitative Sociology, book review editor, 1977-83; Journal of Popular Culture, editor, 1982; Yale University, visiting faculty fellow, 1983-84; Hartford Environmental and Health Policy Group, evaluation specialist, 1984-86; Marketplace Exchange, associate editor, 1986-90; Research Department Child and Family Services, consultant, 1987; Tattoo Advocate, editorial consultant, 1988-90; Journal of Contemporary Ethnography, associate editor, 1989-; Tufts University, Center for Animals and Public Policy, associate, 1990-, faculty, 1995-; Graduate School of the Union Institute, adjunct professor, 1992-98; Society for the Study of Symbolic Interaction, associate editor and vice president, 1994-95, president, 2002-03; Society and Animals, co-editor, 1996, associate editor, 2001-. **Publications:** (With E. Afterman) Drugs and Your Life, 1974; Customizing the Body: The Art and Culture of Tattooing, 1989, (with D.A. Vail) 2nd ed., 2008; (with A. Arluke) Regard-

ing Animals, 1996; Understanding Dogs: Living and Working with Canine Companions, 1999. EDITOR: Marginal Conventions: Popular Culture, the Mass Media and Social Deviance, 1990; (ed. with J. Ferrell) Cultural Criminology, 1995; (ed. with A. Arluke) Between the Species, 2009. Work appears in anthologies. Contributor of articles to journals. **Address:** Department of Sociology, University of Connecticut, 221 Manchester Hall, 344 Mansfield Rd., Storrs, CT 06269, U.S.A. **Online address:** clinton.sanders@uconn.edu

SANDERS, David. (David Scott Sanders). American (born United States), b. 1926?. **Genres:** Literary Criticism And History, Bibliography, Young Adult Fiction, Essays. **Career:** Harvey Mudd College, faculty, 1959, Department of Humanities and Social Sciences, staff, 1959-70, department chairman, 1973-77, professor of English, 1977-85, Miller professor of humanities, 1985-91, professor emeritus of English, 1991-; Clarkson College, Department of Humanities, chairman, 1970-73. Writer. **Publications:** John Hersey, 1967; (ed.) Studies in U.S.A. (essays), 1972; John Dos Passos: A Comprehensive Bibliography, 1987; John Hersey Revisited, 1991. **Address:** Harvey Mudd College, 301 Platt Blvd., Claremont, CA 91711-5901, U.S.A.

SANDERS, David Scott. See **SANDERS, David.**

SANDERS, Ed(ward). American (born United States), b. 1939. **Genres:** Novels, Poetry, Music, Social Commentary. **Career:** Fuck You, A Magazine of the Arts, founder, editor and publisher, 1962-65; Peace Eye Bookstore, owner, 1964-70; The Wordsworth Journal, bi-weekly newspaper, publisher, 1965-2003; Bard College, visiting professor of language and literature, 1979, 1983; New York State Writers Institute, writer-in-residence, 2000, 2003. **Publications:** (Ed.) Poems for Marilyn, 1962; Poem from Jail, 1963; (ed.) Despair: Poems to Come Down By King Lord-Queen Freak, 1964; (ed.) Bugger: An Anthology, 1964; The Toe-Queen: Poems, 1964; A Valorium Edition of the Entire Extant Works of Thales! New York, 1964; Banana: An Anthology of Banana-Erotic Poems, 1965; (ed. with K. Weaver and B. Klein) The Fugs Song Book, 1965; The Complete Sex Poems of Ed Sanders, 1965; Peace Eye, 1965, rev. ed., 1967; Fuck God in the Ass, 1967; Shards of God, 1970; The Family: The Story of Charles Manson's Dune Buggy Attack Battalion, 1971, rev. ed., 2002; (with A. Hoffman and J. Rubin) Vote, 1972; Egyptian Hieroglyphics, 1973; Tales of Beatnik Glory, 1975; Investigative Poetry, 1976; 20,000 A.D., 1976; Love and the Falling Iron, 1977; Fame and Love in New York, 1980; The Party, 1980; The Cutting Prow, 1981; The Z-D Generation, 1982; Thirsting for Peace in a Raging Century: Selected Poems 1961-1985, 1987, rev. ed., 2009; Hymn to Maple Syrup and Other Poems, 1985; Poems for Robin, 1987; The Ocean ãtude and Other Poems, 1990; Creativity and the Self-Fulfilled Bard, 1992; Hymn to the Rebel Cafe, 1993; Chekhov, a Biography in Verse, 1995; 1968 A History in Verse, 1997; America, A History in Verse, vol. I: 1900-1939, 2000, vol. II: 1940-1961, 2001, vol. III: 1962-1970, 2004; The Poetry and Life of Allen Ginsberg, 2000; Poems for New Orleans, 2004; Let's not Keep Fighting the Trojan War: New and Selected Poems, 1986-2009, 2009; Fug You: An Informal History of the Peace Eye Bookstore, the Fuck You Press, the Fugs, and Counterculture in the Lower East Side, 2011. **Address:** PO Box 729, Woodstock, NY 12498, U.S.A.

SANDERS, Eve Rachele. American (born United States) **Genres:** Literary Criticism And History. **Career:** Concordia University, assistant professor of English; University of California, faculty; Washington University, faculty. Writer. **Publications:** Gender and Literacy on Stage in Early Modern England, 1998. **Address:** Department of English, Concordia University, Rm. 501, 1400 Maisonneuve Blvd. W, Montreal, QC H3G 1M8, Canada.

SANDERS, James. American (born United States), b. 1955?. **Genres:** Architecture. **Career:** New York Times, contributor; Center for Urban Experience, direcor and writer; A New School University, faculty. Architect, author and filmmaker. **Publications:** (With R. Burns) New York: An Illustrated History, 1999; Celluloid Skyline: New York and the Movies, 2001; Scenes From the City: Filmmaking in New York, 1966-2006, 2006. Contributor to periodicals. **Address:** Center for Urban Experience, 45 Lispenard St. 7E, New York, NY 10013, U.S.A. **Online address:** sanders@speakeasy.org

SANDERS, John H. American (born United States), b. 1941. **Genres:** Economics, Business/Trade/Industry. **Career:** Tennessee Valley Authority, Regional Development Office, staff, 1967-; Federal University of Ceara, Ford Foundation visiting professor, 1973-74; Centro Internacional de Agricultura Tropical, agricultural economist in bean program, 1976-81; Purdue University, associate professor, professor of agricultural economics, 1983-; University of Evora, project coordinator, 1981-83; Purdue Farming Systems Project, technical coordinator, 1983-85; INTSORMIL Project, director, 1985-; Journal of Production Agriculture, associate editor, 1986-90; Intergovernmental Authority for Development (IGAD), project leader, 1999-2000; Writer. **Publications:** Avaliaçao da introduçao de nova tecnologia para pequenos e médios agricultores sob condiçoes de risco; o Seridó do Rio Grande do Norte, 1975; (with B.I. Shapiro and S. Ramaswamy) The Economics of Agricultural Technology in Semiarid Sub-Saharan Africa, 1996. Contributor of books to journals. **Address:** Department of Agricultural Economics, Purdue University, 609 Krannert, 403 W State St., West Lafayette, IN 47907-2056, U.S.A. **Online address:** jsander1@purdue.edu

SANDERS, Katrina M. American (born United States), b. 1965. **Genres:** History, Young Adult Non-fiction, Education. **Career:** Public school teacher, 1988-93; University of Iowa, postdoctoral fellow, 1997-, assistant professor; Indiana University, minority faculty fellow, 1997. Writer. **Publications:** Intelligent and Effective Direction: The Fisk University Race Relations Institute and the Struggle for Civil Rights, 1944-1969, 2005. Contributor to books, journals and periodicals. **Address:** College of Education, University of Iowa, 428 N Lindquist Ctr., Iowa City, IA 52242-1529, U.S.A.

SANDERS, Lisa. American (born United States), b. 1956. **Genres:** Medicine/Health, Food And Wine. **Career:** Columbia Broadcasting System, news producer; National Broadcasting Co., news producer; Yale University, School of Medicine, assistant clinical professor of medicine, Primary Care Internal Medicine Residency Program, clinician educator. Writer and physician. **Publications:** The Perfect Fit Diet: Combine What Science Knows about Weight Loss with What You Know about Yourself, 2004; The Perfect Fit Diet: How to Lose Weight, Keep It Off, and Still Eat the Foods You Love, 2006; Every Patient Tells a Story: Medical Mysteries and the Art of Diagnosis, 2009. Contributor to magazines. **Address:** School of Medicine, Yale University, PO Box 208025, New Haven, CT 06520-8025, U.S.A. **Online address:** lisa.sanders@yale.edu

SANDERS, Peter (Basil). British (born England), b. 1938. **Genres:** History, Race Relations, Translations, Biography. **Career:** Lesotho, administrative officer, 1961-66; Ministry of Defence, officer, 1971-73; Race Relations Board, principal conciliation officer, 1973-74, deputy chief officer, 1974-77; Commission for Racial Equality, director, 1977-88, chief executive, 1988-93. Writer. **Publications:** Moshweshwe of Lesotho, 1971; Moshoeshoe, Chief of the Sotho, 1975; The Simple Annals: The History of an Essex and East End Family, 1989; The Last of the Queen's Men: A Lesotho Experience, 2000; (with C. Murray) Medicine Murder in Colonial Lesotho: The Anatomy of a Moral Crisis, 2005. EDITOR: (trans. with M. Damane) Lithoko: Sotho Praise Poems, 1974; (with T. Blackstone and B. Parekh) Race Relations in Britain: A Developing Agenda, 1998. Contributor to Journal. **Address:** The Old Post Office, High St., Widdington, Saffron Walden, EX CB11 3SG, England.

SANDERS, Scott Loring. American (born United States), b. 1970. **Genres:** Novels, Young Adult Fiction. **Career:** Verizon, sales consultant, 1998-2003. Writer. **Publications:** The Hanging Woods: A Novel, 2008; Gray Baby: A Novel, 2009. Contributor to books and periodicals. **Address:** c/o Scott Miller, Trident Media Group, 41 Madison Ave., 36th Fl., New York, NY 10010, U.S.A. **Online address:** contact@scottloringsanders.com

SANDERS, Tony. American (born United States), b. 1957?. **Genres:** Poetry, Literary Criticism And History. **Career:** Fairfield University, lecturer in English. Poet. **Publications:** Partial Eclipse: A Book of Poetry, 1994; Transit Authority: Poems, 2000; Warning Track, 2004. Contributor to periodicals. **Address:** Department of English, Fairfield University, 1073 N Benson Rd., Fairfield, CT 06430-5195, U.S.A.

SANDFORD, John. (John (Roswell) Camp). American (born United States), b. 1944. **Genres:** Novels, Mystery/Crime/Suspense, Adult Non-fiction, Medicine/Health, Horror, Young Adult Fiction. **Career:** Writer, 1966-; Cape Girardeau Southeast Missourian, reporter, 1968-70; Miami Herald, reporter, 1971-78; St. Paul Pioneer Press, reporter and columnist, 1978-90. **Publications:** PREY SERIES: Rules of Prey, 1989; Shadow Prey, 1990; Eyes of Prey, 1991; Silent Prey, 1992; Winter Prey, 1993; Night Prey, 1994; Mind Prey, 1995; Sudden Prey, 1996; Secret Prey, 1998; Certain Prey, 1999; Easy Prey, 2000; Chosen Prey, 2001; Mortal Prey, 2002; Naked Prey, 2003; Hidden Prey, 2004; Broken Prey, 2005; Invisible Prey, 2007; Phantom Prey, 2008; Wicked prey, 2009; Storm Prey, 2010; Buried Prey, 2011. KIDD SERIES: The Fool's

Run, 1989; (as John Camp) The Empress File, 1991; The Devil's Code, 2000; The Hanged Man's Song, 2003. OTHERS: (as John Camp) The Eye and the Heart: The Watercolors of John Stuart Ingle, 1988; (as John Camp) Plastic Surgery: The Kindest Cuts (nonfiction), 1989; The Night Crew, 1997; Dead Watch, 2006; Dark of the Moon, 2007; Heat Lightning, 2008; Rough Country, 2009; Bad Blood, 2010; Shock Wave, 2011. **Address:** c/o Esther Newberg, International Creative Management, 730 5th Ave., New York, NY 10019, U.S.A. **Online address:** js@johnsandford.org

SANDILANDS, Al P. (A. P. Sandilands). Canadian (born Canada), b. 1946?. **Genres:** Environmental Sciences/Ecology. **Career:** Gray Owl Environmental Inc., senior ecologist & principal. Ecologist, environmental consultant and writer. **Publications:** Birds of Ontario: Habitat Requirements, Limiting Factors and Status, 2005. **Online address:** grayowlenvironmental@sympatico.ca

SANDILANDS, A. P. *See* **SANDILANDS, Al P.**

SANDLER, Ellen. American (born United States) **Genres:** Adult Nonfiction, Film, Communications/Media. **Career:** University of California, Extension Writers Program, instructor in film and television writing; The New School, instructor in television writing; Herbert Berghof Playwrights Foundation, instructor in television writing; Sandler Ink, founder and owner. Writer, producer and consultant. **Publications:** The TV Writer's Workbook: A Creative Approach to Television Scripts, 2007. **Address:** Random House, 1745 Broadway, 3rd Fl., New York, NY 10019, U.S.A. **Online address:** sandlerinkinfo@gmail.com

SANDLER, Irving (Harry). American (born United States), b. 1925. **Genres:** Art/Art History, Autobiography/Memoirs, Literary Criticism And History. **Career:** Tanager Gallery, director, 1956-59; Art News, senior critic, 1956-62; New York Post, art critic, 1961-64; New York University, instructor in art history, 1960-71; State University of New York, Purchase College, professor of art history, 1972-2001, professor emeritus, 2001-; Pratt Institute, faculty; New York University, faculty. Writer. **Publications:** (With E.C. Goossen and R. Goldwater) Three American Sculptors, 1959; (contrib.) School of New York: Some Younger Artists, 1960; Paul Burlin, 1962; (contrib.) American Sculpture of the Sixties, 1967; The Triumph of American Painting: A History of Abstract Expressionism, 1970; (ed. with B. Berkson) Alex Katz, 1971; (contrib.) Contemporary Art, 1942-1972: Collection of the Albright-Knox Art Gallery, 1973; (contrib.) New Ideas invArt Education, 1973; (contrib.) The Hirshhorn Museum and Sculpture Garden, 1974; Adolph Gottlieb paintings, 1945-1974, 1977; The New York School: Painters and Sculptors of the Fifties, 1978; (contrib.) Images of the Self: 1979 Arts Month, Hampshire College Gallery, February 19 -March 14, 1979, 1979; (with B. Davis) Shape of Space: The Sculpture of George Sugarman, 1981; Twenty Artists: Yale School of Art, 1950-1970, 1981; Concepts in Construction: 1910-1980, 1982; Mark Rothko: Paintings 1948-1969, 1983; Al Held, 1984; (ed. with A. Newman) Defining Modern Art: Selected Writings of Alfred H. Barr, Jr., 1986; American Art of the 1960s, 1988; (with C. Goodman and C. Greenberg) Hans Hofmann, 1990; Mark di Suvero at Storm King Art Center, 1996; Art of the Postmodern Era: From the Late 1960s to the Early 1990s, 1996; Alex Katz: A Retrospective, 1998; Natvar Bhavsar: Painting and the Reality of Color, 1998; Antonakos, 1999; The Fields of David Smith (memoir), 1999; The Collector As Patron in the Twentieth Century: May 2 Through July 31, 2000, 2000; Sweeper-up After Artists: A Memoir, 2003; Judy Pfaff, 2003; Angelo Ippolito, a Retrospective Exhibition: Binghamton University Art Museum, November 22, 2003 through January 10, 2004 (essay), 2004; (with T. Hanrahan and J. Kastner) Socrates Sculpture Park (essay), 2006; Abstract Expressionism and the American Experience: A Reevaluation, 2009; (with I. Sandler and K. Wilkin) American Vanguards, 2011. **Address:** School of the Arts, Purchase College, State University of New York, 735 Anderson Hill Rd., Purchase, NY 10577, U.S.A.

SANDLER, Kevin S. American (born United States), b. 1969. **Genres:** Film. **Career:** Indiana State University, lecturer in speech, 1994-95; University of Michigan-Dearborn, adjunct lecturer in speech, 1995-96; American College in London, lecturer in television studies, 1996; University of Michigan-Ann Arbor, lecturer in film studies, 1997-99; University of Arizona, Department of Media Arts, assistant professor of media industries, associate professor, Film and Media Studies Program, associate director and the director of internships. Writer. **Publications:** FILM AND CULTURAL STUDIES: (ed.) Reading the Rabbit, 1998; (ed. with G. Studlar) Titanic: Anatomy of a Blockbuster, 1999; Naked Truth: Why Hollywood Doesn't Make X-rated Movies, 2007; Animation, Conglomeration, Convergence, forthcoming; The Shield, forthcoming. Works appear in anthologies. Contributor to journals. **Address:** Deparment of Media Arts, University of Arizona, Rm. 220, Marshall Bldg., 845 N Park Ave., PO Box 210158, Tucson, AZ 85721-0158, U.S.A. **Online address:** kevin.sandler@asu.edu

SANDLER, Lauren. American (born United States) **Genres:** Theology/Religion. **Career:** National Public Radio, reporter and producer; Salon.com, life editor; New York University, journalism teacher; Assignment Zero, editor. **Publications:** Righteous: Dispatches from the Evangelical Youth Movement, 2006. Contributor to periodicals. **Address:** Viking Press, 375 Hudson St., New York, NY 10014-3658, U.S.A. **Online address:** laurenosandler@gmail.com

SANDLER, Merton. British (born England), b. 1926. **Genres:** Medicine/Health, Sciences. **Career:** Junior specialist in pathology, 1951-53; Brompton Hospital, research fellow in in clinical pathology, 1953-54; Royal Free Hospital School of Medicine, lecturer in chemical pathology, 1955-58; Queen Charlotte's Maternity Hospital, consultant chemical pathologist, 1958-91; University of London, Royal Postgraduate Medical School, Institute of Obstetrics and Gynaecology, professor, 1973-91, professor emeritus, 1991-; British Journal of Pharmacology, editor, 1974-8; Clinical Science, editor, 1975-77; Journal of Psychiatric Research, editor-in-chief, 1982-92; University of New Mexico, visiting professor, 1983; Chicago Medical School, visiting professor, 1984; University of South Florida, visiting professor, 1988; Imperial College, professor; Association for Post-Natal Illness, president. Writer. **Publications:** (Ed. with E. Costa) Monoamine Oxidases - New Vistas, 1972; (ed. with E. Costa and G.L. Gessa) Serotonin: New Vistas, 1974; (ed. with G.L. Gessa) Sexual Behavior: Pharmacology and Biochemistry, 1975; (ed. with E. Usdin) Trace Amines and the Brain, 1976; (ed.) Mental Illness in Pregnancy and the Puerperium, 1978; (ed.) The Psychopharmacology of Aggression, 1979; (ed.) Enzyme Inhibitors as Drugs, 1980; (ed.) Amniotic Fluid and Its Clinical Significance, 1981; (ed.) The Psychopharmacology of Alcohol, 1980; The Psychopathology of Anticonvulsants, 1981; (ed. with S.L. Jeffcoate) Progress Towards a Male Contraceptive, 1982; (ed.) Psychopharmacology of Anticonvulsants, 1982; (ed. with T. Silverstone) Psychopharmacology and Food, 1985; (ed.) Drug Dependence and Emotional Behavior, 1986; (ed. with C. Feuerstein and B. Scatton) Neurotransmitter Interactions in the Basal Ganglia, 1987; (ed. with A. Dahlström and R.H. Belmaker) Progress in Catecholamine Research, 1988; (ed. with H.J. Smith) Design of Enzyme Inhibitors as Drugs, 1989; (ed. with G. Collins) Migraine: A Spectrum of Ideas, 1990; (ed. with A. Coppen and S. Harnett) 5-Hydroxytryptamine and Psychiatry, 1991; Nervous Laughter, 1991; Monoamine Oxidase: Basic and Clinical Aspects, 1993; Design of Enzyme Inhibitors as Drugs, vol. I, 1989, vol. II, 1994; Migraine: Pharmacology and Genetics, 1996; (ed. with R. Pinder) Wine: A Scientific Exploration, 2002. **Address:** Association for Post-Natal Illness, 145 Dawes Rd., Fulham, London, GL SW6 7EB, England. **Online address:** m.sandler@imperial.ac.uk

SANDMAN, Peter (Mark). American (born United States), b. 1945. **Genres:** Communications/Media, Environmental Sciences/Ecology, Writing/Journalism, Education, Reference. **Career:** Freelance writer, 1966-; Toronto Star, reporter, 1966; Time, stringer, 1966-67; Stanford University, instructor, 1968-70; California State College, Hayward (California State University), instructor in journalism, 1970; Magazine, senior editor, 1970; Ohio State University, Department of journalism, assistant professor, 1971-72; Apartment Ideas, contributing editor, 1971-75; University of Michigan, assistant professor, 1972-75, associate professor, 1975-77, ECRP, director, 1986-92; American College of Physicians, consultant on communications, 1976-79; Ithaca College, adjunct professor, 1976; Cousteau Society, consultant on communications, 1977-76; U.S. Department of Agriculture, Cooperative Extension Service, specialist in communications, 1977-86; Rutgers University, associate professor, 1977-83, professor of journalism, 1983-94, Graduate Program in Public Health, adjunct professor, 1986-2004, Environmental Communication Research Program, founder and director, 1986-92, Department of Human Ecology, adjunct professor, 1994-2004; Holt, Rinehart and Winston, consulting editor, 1978-81; New Jersey Campaign for a Nuclear Weapons Freeze, communications coordinator, 1982-85; Random House, consulting editor, 1982-89; McGraw-Hill, consulting editor, 1989-96; U.S. Environmental Protection Agency, Office of Policy Analysis, consultant on risk communication, 1986-88; Robert Wood Johnson Medical School, Department of Environmental and Community Medicine, adjunct professor, 1987-; Clark University, George Perkins Marsh Institute, research professor, 1994-; National Center for Food Protection and Defense, Department of Homeland Security, principal

investigator, 2004-; University of Minnesota, Center for Infectious Disease Research and Policy, CIDRAP Business Source Weekly Briefing, deputy editor, 2006-. **Publications:** Where the Girls Are, 1967; (with D.R. Goldenson) How to Succeed in Business Before Graduating, 1968; The Unabashed Career Guide, 1969; Students and the Law, 1971; (with D.M. Rubin and D.B. Sachsman) Media: An Introductory Analysis of American Mass Communications, 1972; (co-author) Emerging Issues in Environmental Education, 1974; (with J. Myer and J.B. Garry) Writing about Wildlife, 1974; (co-author) Report on the Accident at Three Mile Island, 1980; Green Acres in the 1980's: Meeting New Jersey's Needs for Open Space and Recreation, 1983; (with C.S. Klompus and B.G. Yarrison) Scientific and Technical Writing, 1985; (with N.D. Weinstein and M.L. Klotz) Public Response to the Risk from Radon, 1987; (with D.B. Sachsman and M.R. Greenberg) The Environmental News Source, 1987; (co-author) Environmental Risk and the Press, 1987; (with B.J. Hance and C. Chess) Improving Dialogue with Communities, 1988; (co-author) Directory of New Jersey Environmental Risk Education Efforts, 1988; (with P. Slovic and V.T. Covello) Risk Communication, Risk Statistics and Risk Comparisons: A Manual For Plant Managers, 1988; (with M. Kline and C. Chess) Evaluating Risk Communication Programs: A Catalogue of Quick and Easy Feedback Methods, 1989; (with C. Chess and B.J. Hance) Planning Dialogue with Communities: A Risk Communication Workbook, 1989; (with C. Chess and S.K. Long) Making Technical Assistance Grants Work, 1990; (with C. Chess and B.J. Hance) Industry Risk Communication Manual: Improving Dialogue with Communities, 1990; Responding to Community Outrage: Strategies For Effective Risk Communication, 1993. EDITOR: Business Careers After College, 1966; Five Hundred Back-to-Work Ideas for Housewives, 1970; From Campus Coed to Working Woman, 1970; (with F. Philpot) Three Months to Earn, 1970; The Independent Teenager, 1970; Not Quite Ready to Retire, 1970; Careers After High School, 1970; (with D.M. Rubin and D.B. Sachsman) Media Casebook: An Introductory Reader in American Mass Communications, 1972; (with B.G. Yarrison) Source Book of Educational and Training Resources in Agriculture, Home Economics and Natural Resources of Institutions on the Title XII Registry, 1979; (with D.B. Sachsman and M.R. Greenberg) Environmental Reporter's Handbook, 1988; (with C. Chess and A. Saville) Environmental Risk Communication Notebook for State Health Agencies, 1990; (with B. West and M.R. Greenberg) The Reporter's Environmental Handbook, 1998. **Address:** 59 Ridgeview Rd., Princeton, NJ 08540-7601, U.S.A. **Online address:** peter@psandman.com

SANDOR, Marjorie. American (born United States) **Genres:** Novellas/Short Stories, Autobiography/Memoirs. **Career:** University of Florida, professor, 1988-94; Oregon State University, professor in literature and creative writing, 1994-, associate professor of English, professor of English, MFA Creative Writing, director. Writer. **Publications:** A Night of Music: Stories, 1989; The Night Gardener, 1999; Portrait of My Mother, Who Posed Nude in Wartime: Stories, 2003; Late Interiors: A Life Under Construction, 2011. Works appear in anthologies. Contributor of articles to periodicals. **Address:** Department of English, Oregon State University, 314 Moreland Hall, Corvallis, OR 97331, U.S.A. **Online address:** msandor@oregonstate.edu

SANDOZ, (George) Ellis. American (born United States), b. 1931. **Genres:** Intellectual History, Philosophy, Politics/Government. **Career:** Louisiana Polytechnic Institute, instructor, 1959-60, assistant professor, 1960-66, associate professor, 1966-67, professor of political science, 1967-68, Center for International Studies, director, 1966-68; East Texas State University, Political Science Department, professor and head, 1968-78; Louisiana State University, Department of political science, professor, 1978-98, chairman, 1980-81, Eric Voegelin Institute for American Renaissance Studies, director, 1987-, Hermann Moyse Jr. distinguished professor, 1998-. Writer. **Publications:** Political Apocalypse: A Study of Dostoevsky's Grand Inquisitor, 1971, 2nd ed., 2000; Conceived in Liberty: American Individual Rights Today, 1978; The Voegelinian Revolution: A Biographical Introduction, 1981, 2nd ed., 2000; A Government of Laws: Political Theory, Religion and the American Founding, 1990; The Roots of Liberty: Magna Carta, Ancient Constitution, and the Anglo-American Tradition of Rule of Law, 1993; The Politics of Truth and Other Untimely Essays: The Crisis of Civic Consciousness, 1999; Order and History, 2000; Philosophy, Literature and Politics, 2005; Republicanism, Religion, and the Soul of America, 2006. EDITOR/CO-EDITOR: A Tide of Discontent: The 1980 Elections and Their Meaning, 1981; Eric Voegelin's Thought: A Critical Appraisal, 1982; Election 84: Landslide without a Mandate?, 1985; Autobiographical Reflections, 1989, rev. ed., 2006; Published Essays, 1965-1985, 1990; (ed.) The Collected Works of Eric Voegelin, 24 vols., 1989-2005; Political Sermons of the American Founding, 1730-1805,

1991; Eric Voegelin's Significance for the Modern Mind, 1991; Index to Political Sermons of the American Founding Era, 1730-1805, 1997. **Address:** Eric Voegelin Institute for, American Renaissance Studies, Louisiana State University, 240 Stubbs Hall, Baton Rouge, LA 70803-5466, U.S.A. **Online address:** esandoz@lsu.edu

SANDS, Lynsay. Canadian (born Canada) **Genres:** Romance/Historical, Novels. **Career:** Novelist. **Publications:** The Deed, 1997; The Key, 1999; The Switch, 1999; Sweet Revenge, 2000; Always, 2000; Misteltoe and Magic, 2000; Bliss, 2001; Lady Pirate, 2001; Wish List, 2001; Reluctant Reformer, 2002; What She Wants, 2002; The Loving Daylights, 2003; Single White Vampire, 2003; Tall Dark and Hungry, 2004; The Eternal Highlander, 2004; The Chase, 2004; Love Bites, 2004; A Quick Bite, 2005; The Perfect Wife, 2005; Love Is Blind, 2006; A Bite to Remember, 2006; The Brat, 2007; Bite Me If You Can, 2007; Devil of the Highlands, 2008; The Accidental Vampire, 2008; Vampires Are Forever, 2008; Vampire, Interrupted, 2008; The Rogue Hunter, 2008; The Immortal Hunter, 2009; The Renegade Hunter, 2009; Bitten By Cupid, 2010; Taming The Highland Bride, 2010; The Hellion & The Highlander, 2010; Born To Bite, 2010; Hungry For You, 2010; The Countess, 2011; The Heiress, 2011; The Reluctant Vampire, 2011. **Address:** Avon Books, Harper Collins Publishers, 10 E 53rd St., New York, NY 10022-5299, U.S.A. **Online address:** lynsay@lynsaysands.net

SANDS, Philippe. British (born England), b. 1960. **Genres:** Law, Environmental Sciences/Ecology, History. **Career:** St. Catharine's College, research fellow, 1984-88; King's College, lecturer in law, 1988-93; London University School of Oriental and African Studies, lecturer in international law, 1993-97, reader in international law, 1997; University College, Centre on International Courts and Tribunals, director, 1994; Matrix Chambers, barrister and Queen's Counsel; Foundation for International and Environmental Law and Development, co-founder, 1990, director, 1990-97; University College London, professor of law, 2002-; New York University, visiting professor of law. Writer. **Publications:** (Ed. and intro.) Chernobyl, Law and Communication: Transboundary Nuclear Air Pollution, the Legal Materials, 1988; (ed. with J. Verhoeven and M. Bruce) The Antarctic Environment and International Law, 1992; (ed.) Greening International Law, 1994; (ed. with R. Tarasofsky and M. Weiss) Documents in International Environment Law, (ed. with P. Galizzi) 2nd ed., 1994; (ed. with R.G. Tarasofsky) Documents in European Community Environmental Law, 1995; (ed. with R. Mackenzie and Y. Shany) Manual on International Courts and Tribunals, 1999; (ed. with L. Boisson de Chazournes) International Law, the International Court of Justice, and Nuclear Weapons, 1999; (ed. with D. Bethlehem and J. Crawford) International Environmental Law Reports, 1999; (ed. with R.L. Revesz and R.B. Stewart) Environmental Law, the Economy, and Sustainable Development: The United States, the European Union, and the International Community, 2000; (with P. Klein) Principles of International Environmental Law, 2nd ed., 2003; (ed. with M. Lattimer) Justice for Crimes against Humanity, 2003; (ed.) From Nuremberg to the Hague: The Future of International Criminal Justice, 2003; Lawless World: America and the Making and Breaking of Global Rules from FDR's Atlantic Charter to George W. Bush's Illegal War, 2005; Torture Team, 2008; Bowett's Law of International Institutions, 6th ed., 2010; (with P. Klein); (co-author) Manual on Intrenational Courts and Tribunals, 2nd ed., 2010. **Address:** Faculty of Laws, University College London, Bentham House, Endsleigh Gardens, London, GL WC1H 0EG, England. **Online address:** p.sands@ucl.ac.uk

SANDSTROM, Alan R(ussell). American (born United States), b. 1945. **Genres:** Anthropology/Ethnology, Social Sciences, History. **Career:** Southeast Missouri State University, instructor in anthropology, 1974-75; Indiana-Purdue University, Department of Anthropology, assistant professor, 1975-82, associate professor, 1982-93, professor, 1993-2009, coordinator of anthropology program, 1982-2002, chair, 2002-09, professor emeritus of anthropology, 2009-. Writer. **Publications:** Image of Disease: Medical Practices of Nahua Indians of the Huasteca, 1978; Traditional Curing and Crop Fertility Rituals Among Otomi Indians of the Sierra de Puebla, Mexico: The Lopez Manuscripts, 1981; (with P.E. Sandstrom) Traditional Papermaking and Paper Cult Figures of Mexico, 1986; Corn Is Our Blood: Culture and Ethnic Identity in a Contemporary Aztec Indian Village, 1991; (ed. with J.W. Dow) Holy Saints and Fiery Preachers: The Anthropology of Protestantism in Mexico and Central America, 2001; (ed. with B.R. Huber) Mesoamerican Healers, 2001; (ed. with E.H.G. Valencia) Native Peoples of the Gulf Coast of Mexico, 2005; Ethnic Identity in Nahua Mesoamerica, 2008. **Address:** Department of Anthropology, Indiana-Purdue University, 2101 Coliseum Blvd. E, Fort Wayne, IN 46805, U.S.A. **Online address:** sandstro@ipfw.edu

SANDSTROM, Eve K. Also writes as JoAnna Carl, Elizabeth Storm. American (born United States), b. 1936. **Genres:** Mystery/Crime/Suspense, Novels. **Career:** The Lawton Constitution, reporter, editor and columnist, 1960-62, 1976-98; writer, 1991-. **Publications:** NOVELS: (as Elizabeth Storm) Firing Line, 1988; Death Down Home, 1990; The Devil Down Home: A Sam and Nicky Titus Mystery, 1991; The Down Home Heifer Heist: A Sam and Nicky Titus Mystery, 1993; The Violence Beat, 1997; The Homicide Report, 1998; The Smoking Gun: A Nell Matthews Mystery, 2000. AS JOANNA CARL: The Chocolate Cat Caper, 2002; The Chocolate Bear Burglary, 2002; The Chocolate Frog Frame-Up, 2003; The Chocolate Puppy Puzzle, 2004; The Chocolate Mouse Trap, 2005; The Chocolate Bridal Bash, 2006; The Chocolate Jewel Case, 2007; The Chocolate Snowman Murders, 2008; The Chocolate Cupid Killings, 2009; The Chocolate Pirate Plot, 2010; The Chocolate Castle Clue, 2011. Contributor to periodicals. **Address:** Mystery Writers of America, 17 E 47th St., 6th Fl., New York, NY 10017-1920, U.S.A. **Online address:** joanna@joannacarl.com

SANDU, Gabriel. French/Finnish/Romanian (born Romania), b. 1954. **Genres:** Language/Linguistics, Philosophy. **Career:** Academy of Finland, researcher, 1986-; University of Helsinki, Department of Philosophy, docent in philosophy, 1992-, professor, 1998-; Institute of the History and Philosophy of Science and Technology, research director, 2004-08; University of Paris 1, Department of Philosophy, professor of philosophy, 2008-. Writer. **Publications:** (With J. Hintikka) On the Methodology of Linguistics: A Case Study, 1991; (with A.L. Mann and M. Sevenster) Independence-friendly Logic: A Game-Theoretic Approach, 2011. Contributor to journals. Works appear in anthologies. **Address:** Department of Philosophy, University of Paris 1, 13, rue du Four, Pleinlaan, Paris, 75006, France. **Online address:** gabriel.sandu@univ-paris1.fr

SANDWEISS, Martha A(nn). American (born United States), b. 1954. **Genres:** Photography, History, Biography. **Career:** National Portrait Gallery, research fellow, 1975-76; Strawbery Banke Inc., National Trust for Historic Preservation, intern, 1977; Yale-New Haven Teachers' Institute, instructor in colonial American material culture, 1978; Amon Carter Museum, curator of photographs, 1979-86, adjunct curator, 1987-89; Princeton University, Eberhard L. Faber memorial lecturer, 1988, professor of history, 2009-10; Amherst College, director of Mead Art Museum, 1989-, adjunct associate professor of fine arts and American studies, 1989-94, associate professor of American studies, 1994-, professor of American studies and history; Yale University, Howard R. Lamar Center, Beinecke senior research fellow, 2004-05; University of Arizona, lecturer; Wesleyan University, lecturer. Writer. **Publications:** Pictures from an Expedition: Early Views of the American West, 1978; Carlotta Corpron: Designer with Light (book and video tape), 1980; Masterworks of American Photography: The Amon Carter Museum Collection, 1982; Laura Gilpin: An Enduring Grace (book and documentary film), 1986; (with P. Stewart and B.W. Huseman) Eyewitness to War: Prints and Daguerreotypes of the Mexican War, 1846-1848, 1989; (contrib.) Perpetual Mirage, 1996; Print the Legend: Photography and the American West, 2002; Passing Strange: A Gilded Age Tale of Love and Deception Across the Color Line, 2009. EDITOR: (with R. Flukinger and A.W. Tucker) Historic Texas: A Photographic Portrait, 1985; (with A.W. Tucker and R. Flukinger) Contemporary Texas: A Photographic Portrait, 1985; (and author of forward) Eliot Porter, 1987; (intro.) Denizens of the Desert: A Tale in Word and Picture of Life Among the Navaho Indians, 1988; Photography in Nineteenth-Century America, 1991; (with C.A. Milner II and C.A. O'Connor) Oxford History of the American West, 1994; (co-ed.) Language As Object: Emily Dickinson and Contemporary Art, 1997. **Address:** Amherst College, 101 Morgan Hall, AC Ste. 2225, Amherst, MA 01002-5000, U.S.A. **Online address:** mas@marthaasandweiss.com

SANDY, Stephen. American (born United States), b. 1934. **Genres:** Poetry, Literary Criticism And History, Translations, Young Adult Fiction. **Career:** Harvard University, instructor in English, 1963-67, visiting professor, 1986; University of Tokyo, visiting Fulbright professor of English, 1967-68; Brown University, visiting assistant professor of English, 1968-69; University of Rhode Island, lecturer in English, 1969; Bennington College, staff of literature faculty, 1969-2000, emeritus, 2000-, chair of the literature and languages division, 1972-73, 1985; Chautauqua Institution, director of poetry workshops, 1975, 1977; Johnson State College, director of poetry workshops, 1976-77. Writer. **Publications:** The Austin Tower, 1975; The Raveling of the

Novel: Studies in Romantic Fiction from Walpole to Scott, 1980; (contrib.) Dictionary of Literary Biography Yearbook: 1985, 1986; The Breakers Pound, 1989. TRANSLATOR: LVIII: To Caelius, 1969; Seneca, A Cloak for Hercules, 1994; The Second Law, 1994; Aeschylus, Seven against Thebes, 1998. POETRY: The Norway Spruce, 1964; Stresses in the Peaceable Kingdom: Poems, 1967; Home Again, Looking Around, 1968; Spring Clear, 1969; A Dissolve, 1970; Light in the Spring Poplars, 1970; Jerome, 1971; Roofs, 1971; Soaking, 1971; Elegy, 1972; Phrases, 1972; Can, 1973; One Section from Revolutions, 1973; From Freestone, 1975; Freestone: Sections 25 and 26, 1977; Arch, 1977; Chapter and Verse, 1982; Riding to Greylock, 1983; Man in the Open Air, 1988; Thanksgiving over the Water, 1992; Gulf Memo, 1993; The Thread, 1998; Black Box, 1999; Surface Impressions, 2002; Weathers Permitting, 2005; Netsuke Days, 2009; Overlook: Poems, 2010. POETRY CHAPBOOKS: Caroms, 1960; Mary Baldwin, 1962; The Destruction of Bullfinch's House, 1964; Wild Ducks, 1965; Japanese Room, 1969; The Difficulty, 1975; Landscapes, 1975; End of the Picaro, 1977; The Hawthorne Effect, 1980; After the Hunt, 1982; Flight of Steps, 1982; To a Mantis, 1987; The Epoch, 1990. Contributor to periodicals. Works appear in anthologies. **Address:** Department of English, Bennington College, 1 College Dr., Bennington, VT 05201-6003, U.S.A. **Online address:** sandys@bennington.edu

SANDYS, Celia. (Celia Mary Sandys). British (born England), b. 1943. **Genres:** Biography. **Career:** Writer. **Publications:** From Winston with Love and Kisses: The Young Churchill, 1994, as The Young Churchill: The Early Years of Winston Churchill, 1995; Churchill Wanted Dead or Alive, 2001; Churchill, 2003; Chasing Churchill: The Travels With Winston Churchill by his Granddaughter, 2003; (with J. Littman) We Shall Not Fail: The Inspiring Leadership of Winston Churchill, 2003; Chasing Churchill: The Travels of Winston Churchill, 2003; Churchill: The Book of the Museum, 2005. Contributor to periodicals. **Address:** Penguin Putnam Inc., 405 Murray Hill Pkwy., East Rutherford, NJ 07073-2136, U.S.A. **Online address:** info@celiasandys.com

SANDYS, Celia Mary. See **SANDYS, Celia.**

SANECKI, Kay Naylor. British (born England), b. 1922?. **Genres:** Homes/Gardens, Horticulture, Biography, Bibliography, Sciences. **Career:** Writer, 1955-. Educator. **Publications:** Wild and Garden Herbs, 1956; (with D.G. Hewer) Practical Herb Growing, 1969; Discovering English Gardens, 1969; Discovering Herbs, 1970, 5th ed., 1993; Humphry Repton, 1974; The Complete Book of Herbs, 1974; Old Garden Tools, 1979; The Fragrant Garden, 1981; Fragrant and Aromatic Plants, 1983, 2nd ed., 1993; The Book of Herbs, 1985; The Scented Garden, 1985; Spices, 1985; A Short History of Studley College, 1990; The History of the English Herb Garden, 1992; Herb Gardens, 1994; (with G. Rice) Gardening with Flowers, 1994; Ashridge: A Living History, 1996; Growing & Using Herbs, 1998. EDITOR: Tenth Anniversary Handbook, 1967; Discovering Period Gardens, 1970; Gardening for the Disabled, 1971; Discovering Flower Arrangement, 1971; (and contrib.) What is That Flower, 1974. Contributor to books. **Address:** Sterling Publishing Company Inc., 387 Park Ave. S, New York, NY 10016, U.S.A.

SANER, Reg(inald Anthony). American (born United States), b. 1931. **Genres:** Poetry, Essays, Young Adult Non-fiction, Theology/Religion. **Career:** Freelance photographer, 1952-56; Montgomery Publishing Co., photographer and writer, 1956; University of Colorado, assistant instructor of English, 1956-60, instructor of English, 1961-62, assistant professor of English, 1962-67, associate professor of English, 1967-72, professor of English, 1973-, now professor emeritus, Creative Writing Program, co-founder. **Publications:** POETRY: Climbing into the Roots, 1976; So This Is the Map, 1981; Essay on Air, 1984; Red Letters, 1989. OTHERS: The Four-Cornered Falcon: Essays on the Interior West and the Natural Scene, 1993, rev. ed., 1994; Reaching Keet Seel: Ruin's Echo and the Anasazi, 1998; The Dawn Collector: On My Way to the Natural World, 2005; Living Large in Nature: A Writer's Idea of Creationism, 2010. **Address:** Department of English, University of Colorado, Rm. 226, Hellems 101, Boulder, CO 80309-0226, U.S.A. **Online address:** saner@colorado.edu

SANFORD, Kathleen (D.). American (born United States), b. 1952. **Genres:** Administration/Management, Economics. **Career:** Eden Hospital, surgical supervisor, 1979-80; St. Joseph Hospital, clinical coordinator, 1980-83; Harrison Memorial Hospital, vice-president for nursing, 1983-, administrator, 2001-; U.S. Pacific Lutheran University, affiliated faculty, 1995-; University of Washington, affiliated faculty, 1996-; St. Catherine University, Catholic

Health Initiatives, senior vice president and chief nursing officer; Leadership Kitsap, president, 2001-. Writer. **Publications:** Leading with Love: How Women and Men Can Transform Their Organizations through Maternalistic Management, 1998. Contributor to magazines. **Address:** Harrison Memorial Hospital, 2520 Cherry Ave., Bremerton, WA 98310, U.S.A. **Online address:** kathleensanford@hmh.westsound.net

SANFORD, Richard. American (born United States), b. 1950. **Genres:** Plays/Screenplays, Horror, Novels, Young Adult Non-fiction. **Career:** Synapse Software, electronic novels, project manager, 1984-86; Broderbund Software, project manager, 1986-87; freelance technical writer, 1987-91; Boeing Co., technical writer, 1991-; Pomegranate Foundation, Art of Citizenship Program, artist-in-residence. **Publications:** The Calling (horror novel), 1990; The Troubador (play), 1991; Roadkill (horror novel), 1995. **Address:** c/o Teresa Chris Literary Agency, 16 Castellain Mansions, Castellain Rd., London, GL W9 1HA, England.

SANGALLI, Arturo. Argentine (born Argentina), b. 1940. **Genres:** Novels, Mathematics/Statistics, Information Science/Computers. **Career:** Writer and mathematician. **Publications:** The Importance of Being Fuzzy: And Other Insights from the Border between Math and Computers, 1998; Pythagoras' Revenge: A Mathematical Mystery (novel), 2009. Contributor to magazines. **Address:** Argentina. **Online address:** asangall@hotmail.com

SANJEK, David. See Obituaries.

SANKAR, Andrea (Patrice). American (born United States), b. 1948. **Genres:** Gerontology/Senior Issues, Medicine/Health, Race Relations, Sciences, Adult Non-fiction, Self Help, Politics/Government. **Career:** Health care consultant in Ann Arbor, 1982-89; Wayne State University, associate professor of anthropology, 1989-, professor and chair. Writer. **Publications:** (Contrib. with B. Frank) I Eat, Therefore I Am: The Guide to Bars & Restaurants in Ann Arbor, 1980; The Identification and Reporting of Abuse: A Training Manual, 1988; (ed. with J. Gubrium) The Home Care Experience, 1990; Dying at Home: A Guide for Family Caregivers, 1991, rev. ed., 1999; (ed. with Gubrium) Qualitative Research in Gerontology, 1994; (with R. McCoy) Living and Dying in Detroit s HIV Epidemic, forthcoming. Contributor to journals. **Address:** Department of Anthropology, Wayne State University, 3043 FAB, 906 W Warren Ave., Detroit, MI 48202, U.S.A. **Online address:** asankar@wayne.edu

SAN MARTIN, Mario Valdés. See **VALDÉS, Mario J.**

SANNA, Ellyn. Also writes as Rae Simons, Ben Preston. American (born United States), b. 1957. **Genres:** inspirational/Motivational Literature, Novels, Young Adult Non-fiction, Children's Non-fiction, Natural History, Environmental Sciences/Ecology. **Career:** Teacher, 1982-88; freelance editor, 1986-; Women's Groups, leader of retreats, 1997-; Harding House Publishing Service Inc., owner and editor-in-chief, 2001-07, executive editor, 2001-. **Publications:** Motherhood: A Spiritual Journey, 1997; (ed.) The Riches of Bunyan, 1998; (ed.) The Practice of the Presence of God, 1998; (comp.) A Mother's Love is Forever: Collected Stories and Quotations, 1998; God's Hall of Fame, 1998; (comp.) Forever Sisters, 1999; (comp.) WWJD, 1999; (and comp.) 101 Holiday Gift Ideas, 1999; (comp.) Favorite Christmas Traditions, 1999; (comp.) Holiday Cookies and Desserts, 1999; (comp.) Angels, Messengers of Hope, 1999; Romance, 1999; (comp.) 101 Family Activities for the Holidays, 1999; A Mother's Heart, 1999; (comp.) Feast, 1999; Mary, Mother of Jesus, 1999; Keep It Simple: Finding Peace in a Hectic World, 1999; (comp.) Friends, 1999; (intro.) Religious Affections, 1999; Coffee Talk: A Celebration of Good Coffee and Great Friends, 1999; Baby Love, 1999; The One I Love: Inspirational Thoughts on Love and Devotion, 1999; (comp.) The Language of the Heart, 1999; A Union of Hearts: Celebrating the Beauty of Love, 2000; Just the Girls: A Celebration of Mothers and Daughters, 2000; Good Job!: I'm Proud of You, 2000; The Miracles of Jesus, 2000; The Parables of Jesus, 2000; Something Borrowed, Something Blue: A Celebration of Your Wedding Day, 2000; Still the One: A Celebration of a Journey Shared, 2000; By the Water: A Collection of Prayers for Everyday, 2000; The Language of the Heart, 2000; (comp.) A Beacon of Hope: Reflecting the Light of Christ, 2000; (comp.) An Invitation to Tea: A Celebration on Tea & Good Friends, 2000; (comp.) Happy Birthday: A Celebration of You, 2000; A Simple Christmas: Keeping Joy in Your Holiday Celebrations, 2000; A Sampler of Christmas Wisdom, 2000; 101 Advent Activities for Kids, 2000; (ed.) A Leever Daily Disciples Study Guide, 2000; (comp.) Always A Friend, 2000;

Now You're a Graduate, 2000; 101 Simple Holiday Craft Ideas, 2000; (comp.) 101 Favorite Holiday Recipes, 2000; 101 Easy Supper Ideas: A Smorgasbord of Recipes and Inspiration for Busy Moms, 2001; (comp.) A Heart of Purest Gold, 2001; (ed.) The Christian Bed and Breakfast, 2001; Jesus is the Reason for the Season, 2002; Merry Christmas, 2002; Silent Night, 2002; Touching God: Experiencing Metaphors for the Divine, 2002; (with V.R. Gommer) Wise Men Still Seek Him Today, 2002; Career Assessments and Their Meanings, 2003; Special Education Teacher, 2003; Childcare Worker, 2003; Nolan Ryan, 2003; Mothers are Forever, 2003; Dieting in Real Life: 101 Tips and Inspiration for a Healthier You, 2003; Firefighters' Folklore, 2003; Folk Customs, 2003; Folk Festivals, 2003; Folk Religion, 2003; Folk Tales and Legends, 2003; Food Folklore, 2003; Homeland Security Officer, 2003; Mexico: Facts and Figures, 2003; Ethnic Folklore, 2003; (with J. Libal) Politician, 2003; (with S. Brinkerhoff) Family Folklore, 2003; Mothers Are Forever: Enduring Bonds of Love, 2003; Potawatomi, 2004; (comp.) African American, 2005; (comp.) Louisiana, 2005; (comp.) American Indian, 2005; The Expanding United States: The Rise of Nationalism, 1812-1820, 2005; Thanksgiving, 2005; Women in the World of China, 2005; America's Unhealthy Lifestyle: Supersize It!, 2006; (with W. Hunter) Canada's Modern-Day First Nations: Nunavut and Evolving Relationships, 2006; The Gift of Hope: In the Wake of the 2004 Tsunami and the 2005 Hurricanes, 2006; Latino Folklore and Culture: Stories of Family, Traditions of Pride, 2006; Mexican Americans' Role in the United States: A History of Pride, A Future of Hope, 2006; Nature's Wrath: Surviving Natural Disasters, 2009; Those Who Remain: What It Means to be a Survivor, 2009; We Shall All be Free: Survivors of Racism, 2009; (comp.) Power of Positive Parenting, 2011; (with C. Smith and R. Phillips) Women of the Bible, 2011. AS RAE SIMONS: The Quiet Heart, 1995; Against That Day, 1995; The Refuge, 1996; Things You Can't See Can Make You Sick, 2009; Pollution Can Make You Sick!, 2009; Malnutrition & Kids, 2009; Kids & Diabetes, 2009; Nutrition & Poverty, 2009; Cancer & Kids, 2009; Bugs Can Make You Sick!, 2009; Immunizations: Saving Lives, 2009; AIDS & HIV: The Facts for Kids, 2009; You & the Environment, 2009; Why Can't I Breathe? Kids & Asthma, 2009; What Causes Allergies?, 2009; AIDS & Poverty, 2009. AS BEN PRESTON: (comp.) A Strong Hand to Hold: A Celebration of Fatherhood, 1999. **Address:** Harding House Publishing Service Inc., 220 Front St., Vestal, NY 13850-1514, U.S.A. **Online address:** info@hardinghousepages.com

SANNEH, Lamin. (Lamin O. Sanneh). American/Gambian (born Gambia) **Genres:** History, Theology/Religion. **Career:** Centre for the Study of Islam and Christianity, tutor, 1969-71; University of Ghana, lecturer, 1975-78; University of Aberdeen, lecturer, 1978-81; Journal of Religion in Africa, co-editor, 1979-84; Harvard University, visiting lecturer, 1981-82, Center for the Study of World Religions, assistant professor, associate professor, 1981-89; Yale University, Divinity School, D. Willis James professor of missions and world christianity, 1989-, Department of History, professor of history, 1989-, Trumbull College, fellow, 1989-; University of London, School of Oriental and African Studies, honorary professional research fellow, 1997-; The Christian Century, editor-at-large. **Publications:** (As Lamin O. Sanneh) Jakhanke: The History of an Islamic Clerical People of the Senegambia, 1979; West African Christianity: The Religious Impact, 1983; The Jakhanke Muslim Clerics: A Religious and Historical Study of Islam in Senegambia, 1989; Translating the Message: The Missionary Impact on Culture, 1989, 2nd ed., 2009; Encountering the West: Christianity and the Global Cultural Process: The African Dimension, 1993; The Crown and the Turban: Muslims and West African Pluralism, 1996; Piety and Power: Muslims and Christians in West Africa, 1996; Religion and the Variety of Culture: A Study in Origin and Practice, 1996; (with L. Newbigin and J. Taylor) Faith and Power: Christianity and Islam in Secular Britain, 1998; Abolitionists Abroad: American Blacks and the Making of Modern West Africa, 1999; Whose Religion Is Christianity?: The Gospel Beyond the West, 2003; (ed. with J.A. Carpenter) The Changing Face of Christianity: Africa, the West, and the World, 2005; Disciples of All Nations: Pillars of World Christianity, 2008. Contributor of articles to books and periodicals. **Address:** Yale University, Divinity School, 409 Prospect St., New Haven, CT 06511, U.S.A. **Online address:** lamin.sanneh@yale.edu

SANNEH, Lamin O. *See* **SANNEH, Lamin.**

SANSOM, C. J. Also writes as The Medieval Murderers. British/Scottish (born Scotland), b. 1952?. **Genres:** Novels, Young Adult Fiction. **Career:** Attorney and fiction writer. **Publications:** Dissolution, 2003; Dark Fire, 2004; Sovereign, 2006; Winter in Madrid, 2006; Revelation, 2008; Heartstone, 2010. AS THE MEDIEVAL MURDERERS: (co-author) The Tainted

Relic, 2005; (co-author) Sword of Shame, 2006; (co-author) House of Shadows, 2007; (co-author) The Lost Prophecies, 2008; (co-author) King Arthur's Bones, 2009; (co-author) The Sacred Stone, 2010; (co-author) Hill of Bones, 2011; The First Murder, 2012. **Address:** c/o Author Mail, Viking Press, Penguin USA, 375 Hudson St., New York, NY 10014-3658, U.S.A.

SANSOM, Peter. British (born England), b. 1958. **Genres:** Poetry. **Career:** North, editor, 1985-; Ampersand (copy writing agency), partner, 1989-; Huddersfield University, professor of poetry; Leeds University, fellow in creative writing; Prudential, poet; Poetry Business, director, The North Magazine, editor, Smith/Doorstop Books, editor. **Publications:** On the Pennine Way, 1987; Making Maps, 1989; Everything You've Heard Is True, 1990; Writing Poems, 1994; January, 1994; Talk Sense, 1997; Point of Sale, 2000; The Last Place on Earth, 2006; Selected Poems, 2010. **Address:** Poetry Business, Bank St. Arts, 32-40 Bank St., Sheffield, SY S1 2DS, England.

SANT, Thomas. American (born United States), b. 1948. **Genres:** Novels, Business/Trade/Industry, Marketing, Technology. **Career:** University of Cincinnati, instructor in English, 1975-78; freelance writer and trainer, 1978-; The Sant Corp., founder; Hyde Park Partners, co-founder. **Publications:** The Amazing Adventures of Albert and His Flying Machine, 1990; Persuasive Business Proposals: Writing to Win Customers, Clients and Contracts, 1992, 2nd ed., 2004; The Giants of Sales: What Dale Carnegie, John Patterson, Elmer Wheeler and Joe Girard Can Teach You About Real Sales Success, 2006; The Language of Success: Business Writing that Informs, Persuades and Gets Results, 2008. **Address:** Qvidian, 10260 Alliance Rd., Ste. 210, Cincinnati, OH 45242, U.S.A.

SANT CASSIA, Paul. British (born England), b. 1954. **Genres:** Anthropology/Ethnology. **Career:** Cambridge University, Christ's College, research fellow, 1981-85, University Museum of Archeology and Anthropology, lecturer and museum curator, 1985-90; Trinity College, director of studies in social anthropology, 1985-; Selwyn College, director of studies in social anthropology, 1986-; University of Durham, lecturer, 1991-2001, reader in anthropology, 2002-, professor, Department of Anthropology, honorary research fellow; Australian Institute of Multicultural Affairs, consultant, 1982-83, research fellow, 1992-94; University of Malta, visiting professor, 1992-94, anthropology coordinator. Writer. **Publications:** (With C. Bada) The Making of the Modern Greek Family: Marriage and Exchange in Nineteenth-Century Athens, 1992; Bodies of Evidence: Burial, Memory, and the Recovery of Missing Persons in Cyprus, 2005; Défis et Les Peurs: Entre Europe et Méditerranée, 2005; (ed. with T. Fabre) Between Europe and the Mediterranean: The Challenges and the Fears, 2007. Contributor to books. **Address:** Department of Anthropology, University of Durham, Dawson Bldg., South Rd., Durham, DH1 3LE, England. **Online address:** paul.sant-cassia@durham.ac.uk

SANTE, Luc. Belgian (born Belgium), b. 1954. **Genres:** Adult Non-fiction. **Career:** Strand Book Store, clerk, 1976-79; New York Review of Books, mail clerk and editorial assistant, 1980-84; Sports Illustrated, proofreader, 1987-90; Columbia University, School of the Arts, adjunct assistant professor of writing, 1994-97; New School, associate professor of writing, 1999; Bard College, visiting professor of writing and photography, 1999-. Freelance journalist and critic. **Publications:** Low Life: Lures and Snares of Old New York, 1991; Evidence, 1992; The Factory of Facts, 1998; (ed. with M.H. Pierson) O.K. You Mugs: Writers on Movie Actors, 1999; Walker Evans, 2001; Kill All Your Darlings: Pieces 1990-2005, 2007; (trans. and ed.) F. Fénéon, Novels in Three Lines, 2007; Folk Photography. 2009. **Address:** Bard College, PO Box 5000, Annandale, NY 12504, U.S.A. **Online address:** lucsante@gmail.com

SANTIAGO, Fabiola. American/Cuban (born Cuba), b. 1959?. **Genres:** Novels. **Career:** Miami Herald, features writer, 1980-. **Publications:** Fifteen Candles: 15 Tales of Taffeta, Hairspray, Drunk Uncles and Other Quinceañera Stories (includes The Year of Dreaming: A Tale of Two Quinceañeras), 2007; Reclaiming Paris (novel), 2008; The Empty Nest: 31 Parents Tell the Truth about Relationships, Love and Freedom after the Kids Fly the Coop (includes The Science of Ghost Hunting), 2008. **Address:** Miami Herald, 1 Herald Pl., Miami, FL 33132, U.S.A.

SANTLOFER, Jonathan. American (born United States), b. 1946. **Genres:** Mystery/Crime/Suspense, Novels. **Career:** Jersey City State College, instructor of studio and art history, 1974-80; New School for Social Research, teacher of art history, 1976; Columbia University, instructor of drawing and painting, 1988-90; writer, 1990-; Vermont Studio Center, instructor and resident artist, 1991; Lacoste School of the Arts, instructor of drawing and painting, 1992. **Publications:** Jonathan Santlofer, Paintings, 1986; The Death Artist: A Novel of Suspense, 2002; Color Blind, 2004; The Killing Art: A Novel of Suspense, 2005; (contrib.) Reiner Leist, 2006; Anatomy of Fear, 2007; The Murder Notebook: A Novel of Visual Suspense, 2008; (ed. with S.J. Rozan) The Dark End of the Street: New Stories of Sex and Crime by Today's Top Authors, 2010; (co-author) No Rest for the Dead, 2011. Contributor to periodicals and journals. **Address:** James Graham & Sons, 32 E 67th St., New York, NY 10065, U.S.A. **Online address:** jsantlofer@hotmail.com

SANTORO, Michael A(nthony). American/Canadian (born Canada), b. 1954. **Genres:** Economics. **Career:** Webster and Sheffield (law firm), associate, 1981-85; BioTechnica International Inc., general counsel, 1985-87; Finevest Services Inc. (now Interlaken Capital), general counsel, 1987-89; Harvard University, John F. Kennedy School of Government, adjunct lecturer, 1990-, teaching fellow; Harvard Business School, research associate, 1990-; University of Hong Kong, Fulbright fellow, 1993-94; Rutgers University, Business Environment Department, assistant professor, 1996-2003, associate professor, 2003-, professor of management and global business. Writer. **Publications:** Profits and Principles: Global Capitalism and Human Rights in China, 2000; (ed. with T.M. Gorrie) Ethics and the Pharmaceutical Industry, 2005; China 2020: How Western Business Can-and Should-Influence Social and Political Change in the Coming Decade, 2009. Contributor to periodicals. **Address:** Department of International Business &, Business Environment, Rutgers Business School, Rutgers University, Newark Campus, 111 Washington St., Newark, NJ 07102, U.S.A. **Online address:** msantoro@andromeda.rutgers.edu

SANTOS, Michael Wayne. American (born United States), b. 1956. **Genres:** History. **Career:** Carnegie-Mellon University, instructor in history, 1983-84, Teaching Center's Summer Program, director; Lynchburg College, assistant professor of history, professor of history, 1984-, Center for the History and Culture of Central Virginia, director, 1984-, LCSR program, director; Greater Lynchburg Habitat for Humanity, board director, 1988; Lynchburg Historical Foundation, board director, 1999-2000; Mystic Seaport Museum, visiting researcher; Fire Fighters Museum of Central Virginia, vice president of board of directors, 2002-. Writer. **Publications:** Caught in Irons: North Atlantic Fishermen in the Last Days of Sail, 2002; A Beacon through the Years: A History of Lynchburg College 1903-2003, 2005. Contributor to books and periodicals. **Address:** Center for the History, Lynchburg College, 505 Brevard, 1501 Lakeside Dr., Lynchburg, VA 24501, U.S.A. **Online address:** santos@lynchburg.edu

SANTOS, Sherod. American (born United States), b. 1948. **Genres:** Poetry, Essays, Literary Criticism And History, Translations, Theatre. **Career:** University of Missouri, professor of English, 1983-2006; Robert Frost House, poet-in-residence, 1984; University of California, visiting professor, 1989-90; Poet's House in Belfast, poet-in-residence, 1990-97. Poet and translator. **Publications:** Accidental Weather (poetry), 1982; The Southern Reaches (poetry), 1989; The City of Women (poetry), 1993; The Pilot Star Elegies (poetry), 1998; A Poetry of Two Minds (essays), 2000; The Perishing (poetry), 2003; Greek Lyric Poetry, 2005; The Intricated Soul: Selected Poems, 2010. **Address:** Department of English, University of Missouri, 107 Tate Hall, Columbia, MO 65211, U.S.A. **Online address:** santoss@missouri.edu

SANTOSUOSSO, Antonio. Canadian/Italian (born Italy), b. 1936. **Genres:** History. **Career:** University of Western Ontario, lecturer, 1971-72, assistant professor, 1972-74, associate professor, 1974-81, professor of history, 1981-, now emeritus; The Newcomers, Nielsen-Ferns, television consultant, 1976-80. Writer. **Publications:** The Bibliography of Giovanni Della Casa: Books, Readers and Critics, 1537-1975, 1979; Vita di Giovanni Della Casa, 1979; Soldiers, Citizens, and the Symbols of War: From Classical Greece to Republican Rome, 500-167 B.C., 1997; Storming the Heavens: Soldiers, Emperors, and Civilians in the Roman Empire, 2001; Barbarians, Marauders, and Infidels: The Ways of Medieval Warfare, 2004. Contributor to journals. **Address:** Department of History, University of Western Ontario, Rm. 4328, Social Science Ctr., London, ON N6A 5C2, Canada.

SAPERSTEIN, David. American (born United States), b. 1937. **Genres:** Novels, Mystery/Crime/Suspense, Science Fiction/Fantasy, Plays/Screenplays, Songs/Lyrics And Libretti. **Career:** Columbia Broadcasting System Inc. (CBS-TV), reporter, 1957-58; Thomas Craven Film Corp., producer and director of documentaries, 1958-62; Skyline Films Inc., vice president and owner, 1962-82, founder, producer and director of films, 1963-89; Ebbets Field Productions Ltd., affiliate, 1980-, president. Writer. **Publications:** (Comp. with S.R. Brown) Proclaim Liberty: A Jewish Guide to the Nation's Capital: Historic Places and People, 1976; (ed.) Preventing the Nuclear Holocaust: A Jewish Response, 1983. NOVELS: Cocoon, 1985; Fatal Reunion, 1987; Metamorphosis: The Cocoon Story Continues: A Novel, 1988; The Red Devil, 1989; (with A. Vorspan) Tough Choices: Jewish Perspectives on Social Justice, 1992; Fune-a-Rama, 1995; (with A. Vorspan) Jewish Dimensions of Social Justice: Tough Moral Choices of Our Time, 1998; Dark Again, 1999; Green Devil: The Book of Belail, 2004; (with G. Samerjan) A Christmas Visitor, 2004; (with G. Samerjan) A Christmas Passage, 2008; (with J. J. Rush) A Christmas Gift, 2009. **Address:** Susan Schulman Literary Agency, 454 W 44th St., New York, NY 10036-5205, U.S.A.

SAPINSLEY, Barbara. American (born United States), b. 1918?. **Genres:** History, Adult Non-fiction, Psychology, Social Sciences, Medicine/Health. **Career:** CBS, television documentaries, scriptwriter; ABC, television documentaries, writer and producer; Newsweek's, Department of Business News, researcher. **Publications:** From Kaiser to Hitler: The Life and Death of a Democracy, 1919-1933, 1968; Taxes (for young adults), 1986; The Private War of Mrs. Packard, 1991. Contributor to periodicals. **Address:** 331 E 71st St., New York, NY 10021, U.S.A.

SAPOLSKY, Robert M. American (born United States), b. 1957. **Genres:** Biology, Medicine/Health, Essays. **Career:** Stanford University, School of Medicine, John A. and Cynthia Fry Gunn professor of biological sciences and neurology, 1987-, School of Humanities and Sciences, professor of neurology and neurological sciences, School of Neurosurgery, professor; National Museums of Kenya, research associate. Writer, primatologist, biologist and neurologist. **Publications:** Stress, the Aging Brain and the Mechanisms of Neuron Death, 1992; Why Zebras Don't Get Ulcers: A Guide to Stress, 1994 as Why Zebras Don't Get Ulcers: An Updated Guide to Stress, Stress-Related Diseases and Coping, 1998, 3rd ed., 2004; The Trouble with Testosterone: And Other Essays on the Biology of the Human Predicament, 1997; A Primate's Memoir, 2001; Monkeyluv: And Other Essays on Our Lives as Animals, 2005. Contributor to periodicals. **Address:** Department of Biological Sciences, Stanford University, Gilbert Hall, PO Box 5020, Stanford, CA 94305-5020, U.S.A. **Online address:** sapolsky@stanford.edu

SARAF, Sujit. Indian/American (born United States), b. 1969?. **Genres:** Novels. **Career:** Indian Institute of Technology, assistant professor; Lockheed Martin, research scientist. Naatak (a theater and film company), co-founder & artistic director, 1995. Writer. **Publications:** Limbo (novel), 1994; The Peacock Throne (novel), 2007. **Address:** c/o Isobel Dixon, Blake Friedmann Literary, Film & TV Agency, 122 Arlington Rd., London, NW1 7HP, England. **Online address:** sujitsaraf@hotmail.com

SARAH, Edith. (Edith Sarah Stein). American (born United States), b. 1921. **Genres:** Human Relations/Parenting, Biography. **Career:** Beth Israel Hospital, assistant in public relations, 1960-66; Jewish Community Center, social worker, 1970-71; Action for Boston Community Development, community organizer and administrator, Foster Grandparent Program, director, 1970-92; cart-time instructor in women's studies, 1976-83; Lesley College, instructor; Radcliffe College, instructor. Writer. **Publications:** (As Edith Sarah Stein) A Time for Every Purpose: Life Stories of Foster Grandparents, 1994. Contributor to books and periodicals. **Address:** 615 Washington St., Brookline, MA 02446, U.S.A.

SARASIN, Jennifer. *See* SACHS, Judith.

SARDI, Jan. Australian (born Australia), b. 1953?. **Genres:** Plays/Screenplays, Art/Art History. **Career:** Writer. **Publications:** (With C. Cannon) Street Hero, 1984; (with S. Hicks) Shine, 1997; Love's Brother, 2003. **Address:** William Morris Agency, 1 William Morris Pl., Beverly Hills, CA 90212, U.S.A.

SARDONE, Susan B(reslow). *See* BRESLOW, Susan.

SAREWITZ, Daniel (R.). American (born United States), b. 1955. **Genres:** Sciences. **Career:** Foster Miller Associates, staff engineer, 1978-80; Cornell University, Department of Geological Sciences, research assistant, 1981-85, postdoctoral research associate and lecturer in geological sciences, 1986-89; U.S. House of Representatives, congressional, Office of Representative George E. Brown, Jr., science fellow, 1989-90; House of Representatives

Committee on Science, Space and Technology, congressional science consultant, 1989-93; freelance writer, 1993-95; Geological Society of America, Institute for Environmental Education, director, 1995-98; Carlton College, lecturer, 1997; Columbia University, Center for Science, Policy and Outcomes, director, 1998-2003; America's Institute for Environmental Education, director; Arizona State University, Consortium for Science, Policy and Outcomes, director, School of Life Sciences and School of Sustainability, professor of science and society, Center for Nanotechnology in Society, associate director. Writer. **Publications:** Frontiers of Illusion: Science, Technology and the Politics of Progress, 1996; (ed. with R.A. Pielki and R. Byerly) Prediction: Science, Decision Making and The Future of Nature, 2000; (ed. with A. Lightman and C. Desser) Living With the Genie: Essays on Technology and the Quest for Human Mastery, 2003; (ed. with D.H. Guston) Shaping Science and Technology Policy: The Next Generation of Research, 2006; (with B.R. Allenby) The Techno-Human Condition, 2011. Contributor to journals. **Address:** Consortium for Science, Policy & Outcomes, Arizona State University, 427 E Tyler Mall, PO Box 4701, Tempe, AZ 85287, U.S.A. **Online address:** daniel.sarewitz@asu.edu

SARFOH, Joseph A. See SARFOH, Kwadwo A.

SARFOH, Kwadwo A. (Joseph A. Sarfoh). American/Ghanaian (born Ghana), b. 1936. **Genres:** Geography, Area Studies, Technology, Engineering. **Career:** University of Science and Technology, lecturer, 1966-72; Tennessee Technological University, visiting professor, 1976-77; State University of New York, assistant professor, 1980-90, associate professor of African studies, 1990-, chair of department, 1993-2001. Writer. **Publications:** (Comp.) Population, Urbanization and Rural Settlement in Ghana: A Bibliographical Survey, 1987; Hydropower Development in West Africa: A Study in Resource Development, 1990; (comp.) Energy in the Development of West Africa: A Selected Annotated Bibliography, 1992. **Address:** Department of Africana Studies, State University of New York, Business Administration 118C, 1400 Washington Ave., Albany, NY 12222, U.S.A. **Online address:** ksarfoh@albany.edu

SARGENT, Inge. Austrian (born Austria), b. 1932. **Genres:** Autobiography/Memoirs, Biography. **Career:** Maternity and Child Welfare Society and Birthing Center, president, 1954-62; Foundation School, founder, 1959, director, 1959-62; Royal Thai Embassy, interpreter and secretary, 1964-66; Centennial Junior High School, teacher of German and European literature, 1970-75; Fairview High School, teacher of German language and European literature, 1975-89; writer, 1989-. **Publications:** Twilight Over Burma: My Life as a Shan Princess, 1994. **Address:** University of Hawaii Press, 2840 Kolowalu St., Honolulu, HI 96822-1888, U.S.A.

SARGENT, Lyman Tower. American (born United States), b. 1940. **Genres:** Literary Criticism And History, Politics/Government, Bibliography, History. **Career:** University of Wyoming, instructor, 1964-65; University of Missouri, Department of Political Science, assistant professor 1965-70, chairman, 1969-71, 1975-78, 1992-97, associate professor, 1970-75, professor, 1975-2005, professor emeritus 2005-, Political Science Laboratory, director, 1968-69; University of Exeter, visiting professor, 1978-79, 1983-84; Utopian Studies, editor, 1990-; University of East Anglia, visiting professor; London School of Economics and Political Science, visiting professor; Victoria University of Wellington, visiting professor; University of Oxford, Centre for Political Ideologies, research fellow. **Publications:** Contemporary Political Ideologies: A Comparative Analysis, 1969, 14th ed., 2009; (with T.A. Zant) Techniques of Political Analysis, 1970; New Left Thought, 1972; British and American Utopian Literature, 1516-1975, 1979; British and American Utopian Literature, 1516-1985, 1988; Contemporary Political Ideologies: A Reader, 1990; New Zealand Intentional Communities, 1997; New Zealand Utopian Literature, 1997; (with L. Sargisson) Living in Utopia: New Zealand's Intentional Communities, 2004; Utopianism: A Very Short Introduction, 2010. EDITOR: Consent, 1979; Extremism in America: A Reader, 1995; Political Thought in the United States: A Documentary History, 1997; (with G. Claeys) The Utopia Reader, 1999; (with R. Schaer) Utopie: La Quête de la Société Idéale en Occident, 2000; (with R. Schaer and G. Claeys) Utopia: The Search for the Ideal Society in the Western World, 2000. Contributor to journals and periodicals. **Address:** Department of Political Science, University of Missouri, 347 SSB, 1 University Blvd., St. Louis, MO 63121-4400, U.S.A. **Online address:** lyman.sargent@umsl.edu

SARGENT, Pamela. American (born United States), b. 1948. **Genres:** Novellas/Short Stories, Romance/Historical, Science Fiction/Fantasy, Young Adult Fiction, History, Literary Criticism And History, Women's Studies And Issues, Essays, Essays. **Career:** Honigsbaums, sales clerk and model, 1964-65; Endicott Coil Company Inc., staff, 1965; Towne Distributors, sales clerk, 1965; State University of New York, Library Cataloging Department, typist, 1965-66, teaching assistant in philosophy, 1969-71; Webster Paper Co., office worker, 1969; freelance writer, 1971-; Commission on Independent Colleges and Universities, administrative assistant, 2005-. **Publications:** SCIENCE FICTION FOR ADULTS: Cloned Lives, 1976; Starshadows (short stories), 1977; The Sudden Star, 1979 in UK as The White Death, 1980; Watchstar, 1980; The Golden Space, 1982; The Alien Upstairs, 1983; The Mountain Cage (chapbook), 1983; The Shore of Women, 1986; The Best of Pamela Sargent (short stories), 1987; Firebrands: The Heroines of Science Fiction and Fantasy, 1998; Behind the Eyes of Dreamers and Other Short Novels, 2002; The Mountain Cage and Other Stories, 2002; (with G. Zebrowski) Garth of Izar, 2003; Eye of Flame: Fantasies Five Star, 2003; Thumbprints, 2004. VENUS SERIES: Venus of Dreams, 1986; Venus of Shadows, 1988; Child of Venus, 2001. STAR TREK SERIES WITH G. ZEBROWSKI: A Fury Scorned, 1996; Heart of the Sun, 1997; Across the Universe, 1999. FOR CHILDREN AND YOUNG ADULTS: Earthseed, 1983; Eye of the Comet, 1984; Homesmind, 1984; Alien Child, 1988; Farseed, 2007; Seed Seeker, 2010. EDITOR: (and intro.) Women of Wonder: Science Fiction Stories by Women about Women, 1975; (and intro.) Bio-Futures: Science Fiction Stories about Biological Metamorphosis, 1976; (and intro.) More Women of Wonder: Science Fiction Novelettes by Women about Women, 1976; (and intro.) The New Women of Wonder: Recent Science Fiction Stories by Women about Women, 1978; (with I. Watson) Afterlives: Stories about Life after Death, 1986; (and intro.) Women of Wonder: The Classic Years-Science Fiction by Women from the 1940s to the 1970s, 1995; (and intro.) Women of Wonder: The Contemporary Years-Science Fiction by Women from the 1970s to the 1990s, 1995; Nebula Awards 29: SFWA's Choices for the Best Science Fiction and Fantasy of the Year, 1995; Beneath the Red Star: Studies on International Science Fiction, 1996; Nebula Awards 30: SFWA's Choices for the Best Science Fiction and Fantasy of the Year, 1996; Nebula Awards 31: SFWA's Choices for the Best Science Fiction and Fantasy of the Year, 1997; Conqueror Fantastic, 2004. OTHERS: Ruler of the Sky: A Novel of Genghis Khan, (fiction), 1993; Climb the Wind: A Novel of Another America (fiction), 1999. Works appear in anthologies. Contributor to books, magazines and periodicals. **Address:** Richard Curtis Associates Inc., 171 E 74th St., 2nd Fl., New York, NY 10021, U.S.A. **Online address:** pamsargent@gmail.com

SARGENT, Ted H. Canadian (born Canada), b. 1973?. **Genres:** Technology. **Career:** University of Toronto, Department of Electrical and Computer Engineering, professor, 1998-, Nortel Junior professor of emerging technologies, 1998-, Nortel junior chair in emerging technologies, Canada research chair in nanotechnology; Massachusetts Institute of Technology Microphotonics Center, visiting professor of nanotechnology; InVisage Technologies, founder and chief technology officer; American Association for the Advancement of Science, fellow; Institute of Electrical and Electronics Engineers, fellow. Writer. **Publications:** The Lateral Current Injection Laser: Theory, Design, Fabrication, 1998; The Dance of Molecules: How Nanotechnology is Changing Our Lives, 2005. Contributor to periodicals. **Address:** Department of Electrical and Computer Engineerin, University of Toronto, Galbraith Bldg., Rm. GB447, 10 King's College Rd., Toronto, ON M5S 3G4, Canada. **Online address:** ted.sargent@utoronto.ca

SARKODIE-MENSAH, Kwasi. American/Ghanaian (born Ghana), b. 1955. **Genres:** Adult Non-fiction, Librarianship, Education. **Career:** Teacher of French and English, 1979-82; Redco Co., translator and interpreter, 1979; Frontiers in Human Resources, trainee aide, 1983-84; Xavier University of Louisiana, head of public services, 1986-89, acting director of university library, 1987, instructor in French; Southern University, French teacher, 1988-89; Northeastern University, library instruction coordinator, 1989-92; Boston College, O'Neill Library, chief reference librarian, 1992-95, manager of instructional services, 1992-, Benjamin E. Mayes mentor, 1995-, College of Advancing Studies, faculty, 1996-. Writer. **Publications:** (With B. Rapple) Research in the Electronic Age: How to Distinguish between Good and Bad Data, 1999; (ed.) Reference Services for the Adult Learner: Challenging Issues for the Traditional and Technological Era, 2000; (ed.) Helping the Difficult Library Patron: New Approaches to Examining and Resolving a Long-standing and Ongoing Problem, 2002; (ed.) Managing the Twenty-First Century Reference Department: Challenges and Prospects, 2003; Plagiarism and the International Student, 2010. Contributor to books and periodicals.

Works appear in anthologies. **Address:** O'Neill Library, Boston College, Rm. 312, 140 Commonwealth Ave., Chestnut Hill, MA 02467, U.S.A. **Online address:** sarkodik@bc.edu

SARNA, Igal. Israeli (born Israel), b. 1952?. **Genres:** Documentaries/Reportage. **Career:** Israeli Army, Yom Kippur War, tank commander, 1973; Yediot Aharonot, reporter. Journalist. **Publications:** Yonah Valakh: Biyografyah, 1993; Tsayad ha-zikaron, 1997; Chasseur de mémoire: Roman, 2000; Makom shel osher, 2000; Man Who Fell into a Puddle, 2002 in UK as Broken Promises: Israeli Lives, 2003; Muzungu: The Story of the Airplane that Crashed on the Moon-Mountains, 2003; Shitafon, 2005; 'Ed medinah, 2007; Yad 'anugah, 2008. Contributor to newspapers. **Address:** Publicity Department, Random House, 1745 Broadway, New York, NY 10019, U.S.A.

SARNA, Jonathan D(aniel). American (born United States), b. 1955. **Genres:** History, Theology/Religion, Bibliography, Biography. **Career:** American Jewish Historical Society, Hebrew Free Loan Association fellow, 1974-75, chair, 1992-95; Hebrew Union College-Jewish Institute of Religion, visiting lecturer, 1979-80, assistant professor, 1980-84, associate professor, 1984-88, professor of American Jewish history, 1988-90; Center for the Study of the American Jewish Experience, academic adviser, 1981-84, director, 1984-89; University of Cincinnati Hillel Foundation, board director, 1981-86; American Jewish Experience Curriculum Project, director, 1982-90; University of Cincinnati, visiting assistant professor of Judaic studies, 1983-84; Cincinnati Council for Soviet Jews, director, 1986-; Hebrew University, visiting associate professor, 1986-87, visiting professor, 2001-02; Brandeis University, Joseph H and Belle R. Braun professor of American Jewish history, 1990-, department chair, 1992-95, 1998-2001, Hornstein Program for Jewish Professional Leadership, director, 2006-09; Boston Jewish History Project, director, 1992-95; Jewish Telegraphic Agency, board director, 2003-; National Museum of American Jewish History, chief historian. Writer. **Publications:** Jacksonian Jew: The Two Worlds of Mordecai Noah, 1981; (with A.S. Korros) American Synagogue History: A Bibliography and State-of-the Field Survey, 1988; (with N H. Klein) The Jews of Cincinnati, 1989; JPS: The Americanization of Jewish Culture, 1989; American Jews and Church-State Relations: The Search for Equal Footing, 1989; (with J. Liss) Yahadut Amerika: An Annotated Bibliography of Publications in Hebrew, 1991; A Great Awakening: The Transformation That Shaped Twentieth-Century American Judaism and Its Implications for Today, 1995; The American Jewish Community's Crisis of Confidence, 1996; American Judaism in Historical Perspective, 2003; American Judaism: A History, 2004; (with J.B. Krasner) The History of the Jewish People: A Story of Tradition and Change, 2006; Time to Every Purpose: Letters to a Young Jew, 2008. EDITOR: Jews in New Haven, 1978; (and trans.) People Walk on Their Heads: Moses Weinberger's Jews and Judaism in New York, 1982; (co-ed.) Jews and the Founding of the Republic, 1985; (and intro.) The American Jewish Experience: A Reader, 1986, 2nd ed., 1997; (with H.D. Shapiro) Ethnic Diversity and Civic Identity: Patterns of Conflict and Cohesion in Cincinnati since 1820, 1992; (with L. Gartner and M. Shazar) Yehude Artsot-Ha-Berit, 1992; (with D.J. Elazar and R.G. Monson) A Double Bond: The Constitutional Documents of American Jewry, 1992; (and foreword) Observing America's Jews: Selected Writing of Marshall Sklare, 1993; America: The Jewish Experience, 1994; (with E. Smith) The Jews of Boston: Essays on the Occasion of the Centenary (1895-1995) of the Combined Jewish Philanthropies of Greater Boston, 1995; (with D.G. Dalin) Religion and State in the American Jewish Experience: A Documentary History, 1997; (with M.A. Raider and R.W. Zweig) Abba Hillel Silver and American Zionism, 1997; Minority Faiths and the American Protestant Mainstream, 1998; (with P.S. Nadell) Women and American Judaism: Historical Perspectives, 2001; (with E. Lederhandler) America and Zion: Essays and Papers in Memory of Moshe Davis, 2002; (with A. Mittleman and R. Licht) Jews and the American Public Square: Debating Religion and Republic, 2002; (with A. Mittleman and R. Licht) Jewish Polity and American Civil Society: Communal Agencies and Religious Movements in the American Public Square, 2002; (with A. Mendelsohn) Jews and the Civil War: A Reader, 2010; (with P.S. Nadell and L.J. Sussman) New Essays in American Jewish History, 2010; (ed. with E.P. Fishbane) Jewish Renaissance and Revival in America: Essays in Memory of Leah Levitz Fishbane, 2011; When General Grant Expelled the Jews, 2012. Contributor to periodicals. **Address:** Department of Near Eastern & Judaic Studies, Brandeis University, 415 South St., Waltham, MA 02453, U.S.A. **Online address:** sarna@brandeis.edu

SARNO, Ronald Anthony. American (born United States), b. 1941. **Genres:** Communications/Media, History, Sex, Theology/Religion, Law, Education. **Career:** Parochial High School, teacher of English and religion, 1966-69; Sacred Heart Messenger, assistant editor, 1967; National Conference of Christians and Jews, facilitator for high school human relations workshops, 1968-71; St. Peter's College, lecturer on mass media, 1970; National Jesuit News, contributing editor, 1971-72; St. Ignatius Retreat House, associate director, 1972-75; St. John's University, lecturer on New Testament, 1975; St. Joseph's Hospital and Medical Center, administrative assistant in department of pediatrics, 1976-79; Mountainview Medical Associates, administrator, 1980-82; Caldwell College, chief development officer, 1982-83; Family Dynamics Inc., director of development and public relations, 1983-86; Memorial Sloan Kettering Cancer Center, administrative manager, 1986-88; Belair Klein and Evans, manager, 1988-89; Attorney Dennis J. Cummins, Junior Esq., Fair Lawn attorney, 1991-93; Law Office of Burger & Sarno, attorney, 1995-; Entertainment and Mass Media Law Journal, staff; Law Office of Joseph Massood, senior associate, 2008-09; Sarno & DeFelice L.L.C., senior partner, 2009-. Writer. **Publications:** Achieving Sexual Maturity: A Guide to Christian Morality for Young People, 1969; Let Us Proclaim the Mystery of Faith, 1970; The People of Hope, 1971; The Story of Hope: The Nation, The Man, The Kingdom, 1972; Prayers for Modern, Urban, Uptight Man, 1974; (co-ed.) Liturgical Handbook for CLCs, 1974; The Cruel Caesars: Their Impact on the Early Church, 1976; David and Bathsheba, 1977; (with L.F. Badia) Morality, How to Live it Today: Contemporary Moral Issues in the Catholic Church, with an Introduction to Traditional Doctrine and Principles, 1980; Using Media in Religious Education, 1987. Contributor to journals. **Address:** Sarno & DeFelice L.L.C., 235 W 23rd St., 5th Fl., New York, NY 10011-2302, U.S.A. **Online address:** rsarno@dumann.com

SARNOFF, Irving. American (born United States), b. 1922. **Genres:** Social Commentary, Psychology, Sex, Social Commentary, Human Relations/Parenting, Social Sciences, Photography. **Career:** University of Michigan, student health service, mental hygienist and senior psychologist, 1951-54; Yale University, assistant professor of psychology, 1955-60; Western Reserve University, School of Applied Social Sciences, professor of psychology and social work and director of the research center, 1960-62; New York University, professor of psychology, 1962-92, now professor emeritus; Encyclopedia Britannica, staff, 1968-88. Writer. **Publications:** (Contrib.) Public Opinion and Propaganda, 1954; Personality Dynamics and Development, 1962; Society with Tears, 1966; (contrib.) Theories of Cognitive Consistency: A Sourcebook, 1968; Testing Freudian Concepts: An Experimental Social Approach, 1971; (with S. Sarnoff) Sexual Excitement/Sexual Peace: The Place of Masturbation in Adult Relationships, 1979; (with S. Sarnoff) Love-Centered Marriage in a Self-Centered World, 1989; (with S. Sarnoff) Intimate Creativity: Partners in Love and Art, 2002. Contributor of articles to journals. **Address:** Department of Psychology, New York University, 6 Washington Pl., New York, NY 10003, U.S.A. **Online address:** is3@nyu.edu

SAROTTE, Mary Elise. American (born United States), b. 1968. **Genres:** History. **Career:** University of Southern California, professor of international relations; University of Cambridge, professor; British Broadcasting Co. (BBC), political commentator; Cable News Network (CNN) Intl., political commentator, Sky News, political commentator; Time, journalist; Die Zeit, journalist; Economist, journalist. Writer, political scientist and broadcaster. **Publications:** (As M.E. Sarotte) Dealing with the Devil: East Germany, Détente and Ostpolitik, 1969-1973, 2001; German Military Reform and European Security, 2001; 1989: The Struggle to Create Post-Cold War Europe, 2009. **Address:** College of Letters, Arts and Sciences, University of Southern California, 3551 Trousdale Pkwy., VKC 330, Los Angeles, CA 90089-4012, U.S.A. **Online address:** sarotte@usc.edu

SAROYAN, Aram. American (born United States), b. 1943. **Genres:** Novels, Plays/Screenplays, Poetry, Biography, Young Adult Fiction. **Career:** Lines magazine, publisher and founding editor, 1964-67; Telegraph Books, editor, 1971-72; University of California, faculty, 1988-94; University of Southern California, Master of Professional Writing Program, faculty, 1996. **Publications:** (With J. Caldwell and R. Kolmar) Poems, 1963; In, 1964; Top, 1965; Works, 1966; Sled Hill Voices, 1966; Coffee Coffee, 1967; Aram Saroyan, 1968; Pages, 1969; Words and Photographs, 1970; The Beatles, 1970; 5 Mini-Books, 1971; Cloth: An Electric Novel, 1971; The Rest, 1971; Poems, 1972; (with V. Bockris) By Airmail, 1972; The Bolinas Book, 1974; Marijuana and Me, 1974; The Street: An Autobiographical Novel, 1974; O My Generation and Other Poems, 1976; Genesis Angels: The Saga of Lew Welch and the Beat Generation, 1979; Last Rites: The Death of William Saroyan, 1982; William Saroyan, 1983; Trio: Gloria Vanderbilt, Carol Matthau, Oona

Chaplin, 1985; The Romantic: A Novel, 1988; Kahlil Gibran: Paintings & Drawings, 1905-1930, 1989; Friends in the World: The Education of a Writer, 1992; Gurgen Hanikyani Datavarut'yan Patmakanĕ, 1992; Rancho Mirage: An American Tragedy of Manners, Madness and Murder, 1993; (ed.) Selected Poems, 1994; Day and Night: Bolinas Poems 1972-1981, 1998; Beatles, 2000; Starting Out in the Sixties: Selected Essays, 2001; Artists in Trouble: Novels and Stories, 2001; Complete Minimal Poems, 2007; The Lake Matters: Notes About Writing and Life, 2009; Door to the River: Essays and Reviews from the 1960s into the Digital Age, 2009. Contributor to periodicals. **Address:** 5482 Village Green, Los Angeles, CA 90016, U.S.A. **Online address:** information@aramsaroyan.com

SARRIS, Greg. American (born United States), b. 1952. **Genres:** Novels, Adult Non-fiction, Sociology, History, Social Sciences. **Career:** University of California, professor of English, 1989-99; Federated Indians of Graton Rancheria, chief, 1993-95; Word for Word Theater Co., chair, 1995-; Loyola Marymount University, Fletcher Jones professor of English and chair, 2000-05; Sonoma State University, Graton Rancheria chair, 2005-; Turner Broadcasting System, consultant. Writer. **Publications:** Keeping Slug Woman Alive: A Holistic Approach to American Indian Texts, 1993; Mabel McKay: Weaving the Dream, 1994; (ed. and contrib.) The Sound of Rattles and Clappers: A Collection of New California Indian Writing, 1994; Grand Avenue, 1994; Watermelon Nights: A Novel, 1998; (ed. with C.A. Jacobs and J.R. Giles) Approaches to Teaching the Works of Louise Erdrich, 2004; The Last Human Bear: Her True Life Story, 2007. **Address:** Frederick Hill Bonnie Nadell Inc., 1842 Union St., San Francisco, CA 94123, U.S.A.

SARRIS, Jonathan Dean. American (born United States), b. 1967. **Genres:** History, Military/Defense/Arms Control, Social Sciences. **Career:** North Carolina Wesleyan College, associate professor of history. Writer. **Publications:** A Separate Civil War: Communities in Conflict in the Mountain South, 2006. **Address:** Department of History, North Carolina Wesleyan College, 3400 N Wesleyan Blvd., Rocky Mount, NC 27804-9906, U.S.A. **Online address:** jdsarris@ncwc.edu

SARTI, Raffaella. Italian (born Italy), b. 1963. **Genres:** Cultural/Ethnic Topics. **Career:** University of Bologna, professor of social history, 2006-07, professor of women's and gender history, 2007-08; University of Urbino, researcher and professor of early modern history, 2002-; University of Vienna, Kathe-Leichter Gastprofessorin, visiting professor, 2006-07; Genesis, editor. **Publications:** Vita di casa: Abitare, mangiare, vestire nell'Europa moderna, 1999; Europe at Home: Family and Material Culture, 1500-1800, 2002; Nubili e celibi tra scelta e costrizione: Secoli XVI-XX, 2006. **Address:** Faculty of Political Sciences, Instituto Storico-Politico, 4 Piazza Gherardi, Urbino PU, 61029, Italy. **Online address:** r.sarti@unibo.it

SARTI, Ron. American (born United States), b. 1947?. **Genres:** Science Fiction/Fantasy, Novels, History. **Career:** Writer and educator. **Publications:** FANTASY NOVELS: The Chronicles of Scar, 1996; Legacy of the Ancients: Book Two of the Chronicles of Scar, 1997; The Lanterns of God: Book Three of the Chronicles of Scar, 1998. **Address:** c/o Donald Maass, Donald Maass Literary Agency, 121 W 27th St., Ste. 801, New York, NY 10001, U.S.A.

SARTORI, Anne E. American (born United States), b. 1966?. **Genres:** Adult Non-fiction, Politics/Government. **Career:** University of Wisconsin, instructor, honorary fellow, 1997, assistant professor of political science, 1997-99; World Politics, associate editor, 1999-2007; Princeton University, assistant professor of politics, 2000-07, Charles G. Osgood preceptor, 2003-07; Northwestern University, associate professor of political science and (by courtesy) of managerial economics and decision sciences, 2007-. Writer. **Publications:** Deterrence by Diplomacy, 2005. **Address:** Department of Political Science, Weinberg College of Arts and Sciences, Northwestern University, Scott Hall, 601 University Pl., Evanston, IL 60208, U.S.A. **Online address:** a-sartori@northwestern.edu

SARTRE, Maurice. French (born France), b. 1944. **Genres:** History, Adult Non-fiction, Humanities. **Career:** University of Clermont-Ferrand, assistant professor of Greek history, 1969-78; Université François Rabelais, professor of ancient history, 1978-, dean of faculty of human sciences, 1980-83, professor emeritus of ancient history; University of Damascus, professor of French civilization, 1970-72; Institut Français d'Archéologie du Proche Orient, staff, 1973-74; Institut Universitaire de France, staff, 1998-; UMR, Antenna Tours, director. Writer. **Publications:** Trois etudes sur l'Arabie romaine et byzantine,

1982; Bostra: Des origines A l'Islam, 1985; Inscriptions grecques et latines de la Syrie, t. 13: Bostra, 1985; L'Orient romain: Provinces et sociétés provincialés en Méditerranée orientale d'Auguste aux Sévères (31 avant J.-C.-235 apres J.-C.), 1991; Inscriptions grecques et latines de la Jordanie, t. 4: Petra et la Nabatene meridionale, 1993; L'asie mineure et l'Anatolie, d'Alexandre A Diocl Etien: IVe s. av. J.-C.-IIIe s. ap. J.C., 1995; Le Haut-Empire romain: Les Provinces orientales, 1998; D'Alexandre À Zénobie: Histoire du Levant antique, IVe siècle avant J.-C.-IIIe siècle après J.-C., 2001; La Syrie antique, 2002; L'Anatolie hell Enistique: De l'Egee au Caucase, 2003, 2nd ed., 2004; Histoires grecques, 2006; (with A. Sartre-Fauriat) Palmyre, la cite des caravanes, 2008; (with A. Sartre-Fauriat and P. Brun) Dictionnaire Du Monde Grec Antique, 2009; Histoires Grecques: Snapshots from Antiquity, 2009. Contributor to periodicals. **Address:** Département d'histoire, Université Franois-Rabelais, 3 Rue des Tanneurs, Tours, BP 4103, France.

SARTWELL, Crispin. American (born United States), b. 1958. **Genres:** Philosophy, History, Autobiography/Memoirs, Essays. **Career:** Vanderbilt University, assistant professor of philosophy, 1989-93; University of Alabama, assistant professor of philosophy, 1993-97; Pennsylvania State University, The Capitol College, associate professor of humanities, 1997-2000; Maryland Institute College of Art, chair of humanities and sciences, 2000-; Dickinson College, visiting associate professor of political science. Writer. **Publications:** (Co-ed.) The Blackwell Companion to Aesthetics, 1992; The Art of Living: Aesthetics of the Ordinary in World Spiritual Tradition, 1995; Obscenity, Anarchy, Reality, 1996; (ed. with P. Lamarque and D.E. Cooper) Aesthetics: The Classic Readings in Aesthetics, 1997; (ed. with N. Zack and L. Shrage) Race, Class, Gender, and Sexuality: The Big Questions, 1998; Act like You Know: African-American Autobiography and White Identity, 1998; End of Story: Toward an Annihilation of Language and History, 2000; Extreme Virtue: Truth and Leadership in Five Great American Lives, 2003; Six Names of Beauty, 2004; (ed. with S. Presley) Exquisite Rebel: The Essays of Voltairine de Cleyre: Feminist, Anarchist, Genius, 2005; Against the State: An Introduction to Anarchist Political Theory, 2008; Political Aesthetics, 2010; (ed. and intro.) The Practical Anarchist: Writings of Josiah Warren, 2011; Knowledge Without Justification. Forthcoming. **Address:** Department of Humanities and Science, Maryland Institute College of Art, 1300 Mt. Royal Ave., Baltimore, MD 21217-4191, U.S.A. **Online address:** c.sartwell@verizon.net

SARVAS, Mark. American (born United States), b. 1964. **Genres:** Novels, Psychology, Humor/Satire. **Career:** Literary critic and newspaper editor. **Publications:** Harry, Revised (novel), 2008. Contributor to journals. **Address:** c/o Simon Lipskar, Writers House, 21 W 26th St., New York, NY 10010-1003, U.S.A. **Online address:** sarvas@gmail.com

SASLOW, James M(axwell). American (born United States), b. 1947. **Genres:** Art/Art History, Literary Criticism And History, Gay And Lesbian Issues, Sex. **Career:** Advocate, New York arts editor, 1978-85; Vassar College, assistant professor of art history, 1984-86; Columbia University, assistant professor, 1986-87; Queens College, Graduate Center of the City University of New York, associate professor of art history, 1987-97, professor, 1997-; Smith College, Kennedy visiting professor, 2004; Renaissance Art and Theater, professor. **Publications:** Ganymede in the Renaissance: Homosexuality in Art and Society, 1986; The Poetry of Michelangelo: An Annotated Translation, 1991; (ed.) Bibliography of Gay and Lesbian Art, 1994; The Medici Wedding of 1589: Florentine Festival as Theatrum Mundi, 1996; Pictures and Passions: A History of Homosexuality in the Visual Arts, 1999. **Address:** Queens College, City University of New York, Klapper 167, 65-30 Kissena Blvd., Flushing, NY 11367-1597, U.S.A. **Online address:** james_saslow@qc.edu

SASS, Stephen L. American (born United States), b. 1940. **Genres:** History, Sciences, Art/Art History. **Career:** Technische Hogeschool, postdoctoral research associate, 1966-67; Cornell University, assistant professor, 1967-73, associate professor, 1973-79, professor of materials science and engineering, 1979-2008, professor emeritus, 2008-; University of London, visiting scientist, 1975; Max-Planck-Institute, visiting scientist, 1980-81. Writer. **Publications:** The Substance of Civilization: Materials and Human History from the Stone Age to the Age of Silicon, 1998. Contributor to journals. **Address:** Department of Materials Science and Engineering, Cornell University, 214 Bard Hall, 113 Thurston, Ithaca, NY 14853-1501, U.S.A. **Online address:** sls7@cornell.edu

SASSEN, Saskia. American/Dutch (born Netherlands), b. 1949. **Genres:**

International Relations/Current Affairs, Money/Finance, Regional/Urban Planning, Social Commentary, Third World, Sociology. **Career:** City University of New York, assistant professor, 1976-80, associate professor, 1980-85, professor, 1985-; Columbia University, professor of urban planning, 1985-98, department head, 1987-91, Robert S. Lynd professor of sociology, 2007-; University of Chicago, professor, Ralph Lewis professor of sociology, 1993-97; Social Science Research Council, Committee on Information Technology, chair, 2000-; London School of Economics and Social Policy, Department of Sociology, centennial visiting professor; Harvard University, Center for International Affairs, post-doctoral fellow; United Nations University, Institute of Advanced Studies, project director. Writer. **Publications:** Exporting Capital and Importing Labor: The Role of Caribbean Migration to New York City, 1981; The Mobility of Capital and Labor, 1988; The Global City: New York, London, Tokyo, 1991, 2nd ed., 2001; Cities in a World Economy, 1994, 4th ed., 2012; Losing Control? Sovereignty in an Age of Globalization, 1996; De-facto Transnationalizing of Immigration Policy, 1996; Globalization and Its Discontents, 1998; Guests and Aliens, 1999; (ed.) Global Networks, Linked Cities, 2002; Las ciudades Latinoamericanas en el nuevo (des)orden mundial, 2004; (ed. with R. Latham) Digital Formations: IT and New Architectures in the Global Realm, 2005; Territory, Authority and Rights, 2006; Sociology of Globalization, 2007; (ed.) Deciphering the Global: Its Scales, Spaces and Subjects, 2007; Immigration Policy in a World Economy: From National Crisis to Multilateral Management, forthcoming. Contributor to journals. **Address:** Department of Sociology, Columbia University, 713 Knox Hall, 1180 Amsterdam Ave., 606 W 122nd St., PO Box 9649, New York, NY 10027, U.S.A. **Online address:** sjs2@columbia.edu

SASSER, Charles W(ayne). (Mike Martell). American (born United States), b. 1942. **Genres:** Novels, Novellas/Short Stories, Mystery/Crime/Suspense, Agriculture/Forestry, Military/Defense/Arms Control, Autobiography/Memoirs. **Career:** U.S. Navy, staff, 1960-64; Whidbey Approach, editor, 1962-64; U.S. Army, staff, 1965-83; Miami Police Department, officer, 1965-68; Tulsa Police Department, homicide detective, 1969-79; Law Enforcement News, associate editor, 1969-82; Tulsa Jr. College, instructor in sociology and director of criminal justice department, 1975-78; Keystone Sportsman, managing editor, 1975-76; Police Journal, associate editor, 1975-80; American Christian College, Criminal Justice Department, director, 1975-78; Keystone Crossroad Historical Society, president, 1975; National Association for Crime Victims Rights, board director, 1978; photographer and freelance writer, 1979-; Cedar Press Publishing Co., president, 1981-; Military Police Co., sergeant, 1991; Oklahoma Criminal Justice Educators Association, founding member. **Publications:** The Girl Scout Murders, 1989; (with C. Roberts) The Walking Dead, 1989; (with C. Roberts) One Shot-One Kill, 1990; Homicide!, 1990; Shoot to Kill, 1994; Always a Warrior, 1994; (with M.W. Sasser) Last American Heros, 1994; In Cold Blood: Oklahoma's Most Notorious Murders, 1994; Smoke Jumpers, 1996; (with R. Boehm) First Seal, 1998; (with D. Evans) Platoon Medic, 1998; (with M.W. Sasser) Fire Cops, 1998; At Large, 1998; (with N. Cobb) Arctic Homestead, 2000; (with R. Alexander) Taking Fire, 2001; Raider, 2002; The Encyclopedia of Navy Seals, 2002; Raider: The True Story of the Legendary Soldier Who Performed more POW Raids than Any Other American in History, 2002; Magic Steps to Writing Success, 2003; (with R. Hildreth) Hill 488, 2003; (with C. Roberts) Crosshairs on the Kill Zone, 2004; Going Bonkers, 2004; Patton's Panthers, 2005; At Large: The Life and Crimes of Randolph Franklin Dial, 2006; Final Option, 2007; God in the Foxhole: Inspiring True Stories of Miracles on the Battlefield, 2008; Hitler's A-Bomb, 2008; The Foxy Hens Meet a Romantic Adventurer, 2010. NOVELS: No Gentle Streets, 1984; The 100th Kill, 1992; (as Mike Martell) Operation No Man's Land, 2000; Liberty City, 2000; The Return, 2001; Encyclopedia of the Navy Seals, 2002; Dark Planet, 2004; At large: the Life and Crimes of Randolph Franklin Dial, 2006; OSS Commando: Final Option, 2007; None Left Behind: The 10th Mountain Division and the Triangle of Death, 2009; (with M.T. Martin) Predator: The Remote-Control Air War over Iraq and Afghanistan: A Pilot's Story, 2010. DETACHMENT DELTA SERIES: Punitive Strike, 2002; Operation Iron Weed, 2003; Operation Deep Steel, 2003; Operation Aces Wild, 2005; Operation Cold Dawn, 2005. Work appears in anthologies. Contributor of articles and short stories to magazines. **Address:** 14406-D E 23rd Pl., Tulsa, OK 74134, U.S.A. **Online address:** charlessas@msn.com

SASSO, Sandy Eisenberg. American (born United States), b. 1947. **Genres:** Children's Fiction, Theology/Religion, Biography. **Career:** Jewish Reconstructionist Foundation, research associate, 1974-76; Manhattan Reconstructionist Havurah, rabbi, 1974-77; Congregation Beth-El Zedeck, rabbi, 1977-;

Butler University, Department of Religion, lecturer in religious studies, 1996, adjunct professor, 1996-; Indianapolis Star, columnist, 1998-; Christian Theological Seminary, lecturer in literature and religion. Writer. **Publications:** FOR CHILDREN: God's Paintbrush, 1992; In God's Name, 1994; But God Remembered, 1995; A Prayer for the Earth, 1996 as Naamah, Noah's Wife, 2002; God in Between, 1998; For Heaven's Sake, 1999; (with D. Schmidt) God's Paintbrush, 1999; God Said Amen, 2000; Cain and Abel, 2001; Adam and Eve's First Sunset, 2003; Abuelita's Secret Matzahs, 2005; Butterflies Under Our Hats, 2006; I am God's Paintbrush, 2009. FOR ADULTS: When Your Children Ask, 2001; Tell Me a Story about God: Teaching about God and Spirituality, 2002; I Am Jewish, Personal Reflections Inspired by the Last Words of Daniel Pearl, 2004; Affixing Our Name to the Holy Narrative, 2004; Las Matzas Secretas de Abuelita, 2005; Kol Hanoar: The Voice of Children, 2005; God's Echo: Exploring Scripture with Midrash, 2007; Children, Childhood, and Religious Ethics: Jewish, Christian, and Muslim Perspectives-Children's Spirituality in the Jewish Narrative Tradition, forthcoming. EDITOR: Crossing Boundaries in Faith Traditions, 2001; Urban Tapestry, Indianapolis Stories, 2002; Breaking Silence, Keeping Silence, 2002; Religious Perspective on Spirituality in Childhood and Adolescence, 2005. Contributor to books and periodicals. **Address:** Congregation Beth-El Zedeck, 600 W 70th St., Indianapolis, IN 46260, U.S.A. **Online address:** ssasso@bez613.org

SASSOON, Donald. British/Egyptian (born Egypt), b. 1946. **Genres:** Politics/Government, History, Social Sciences. **Career:** Pennsylvania State University, State College, teaching assistant, 1969-71; Walbrook College, faculty, 1971-72; Hillcroft College, faculty, 1975-79; University of London, Queen Mary College, lecturer in history, 1979-80, reader in history, 1989-97, professor of comparative European history, 1997-, Centre for the Study of the History of Political Thought, associate researcher, Westfield College, lecturer in history, 1980-89, reader in history, 1989-97, Birbeck College, visiting professor, 1985-88, 1994-95; Nuffield Social Science, research fellow, 1997-98; University of Trento, visiting professor, 1999; New York University, Remarque Institute, senior research fellow, 2000; Maison des Sciences de l'Homme, senior research fellow, 2002. Writer. **Publications:** (Ed.) Italian Communists Speak for Themselves, 1978; (ed. and intro.) On Gramsci, and Other Writings, 1979; Strategy of the Italian Communist Party, 1981; Contemporary Italy: Politics, Economy, and Society since 1945, 1986, 2nd ed. as Contemporary Italy: Economy, Society, and Politics since 1945, 1997; One Hundred Years of Socialism, 1996; (ed.) Looking Left, 1997; (co-author) New European Left, 1999; Mona Lisa: The History of the World's Most Famous Painting, 2001; Becoming Mona Lisa: The Making of a Global Icon, 2001; Leonardo and the Mona Lisa Story, 2006; Culture of the Europeans, 2006; Mussolini and the Rise of Fascism, 2007. **Address:** Queen Mary College, University of London, 3.13 Arts Two, Mile End Rd., London, GL E1 4NS, England. **Online address:** d.sassoon@qmul.ac.uk

SATERSTROM, Selah. American (born United States), b. 1974. **Genres:** Novels. **Career:** University of Denver, creative writing instructor; Slab Projects, co-curator. Writer. **Publications:** The Pink Institution (novel), 2004; The Meat and Spirit Plan (novel), 2007. **Address:** University of Denver, 2199 S University Blvd., Denver, CO 80208, U.S.A. **Online address:** selahann@aol.com

SATHASIVAM, Kanishkan. American/Sri Lankan (born Sri Lanka) **Genres:** Novels, International Relations/Current Affairs, Politics/Government. **Career:** Texas A&M University, assistant lecturer, 1998-2000; Carleton College, visiting assistant professor, 2000-02; Salem State College, associate professor of political science and department chair, 2002. Writer. **Publications:** Uneasy Neighbors: India, Pakistan, and U.S. Foreign Policy, 2005; Keeping Up with the Joneses: Modeling Arms Races as Multi-State System Processes, 2009. Writer. **Address:** Salem State College, 352 Lafayette St., Salem, MA 01970, U.S.A. **Online address:** kanishkan.sathasivam@salemstate.edu

SATHRE, Vivian. American (born United States), b. 1952. **Genres:** Children's Fiction, Novels, Young Adult Fiction. **Career:** Children's book writer, 1987-; Renton Technical College, instructor in creative writing, 1990-91; artist, 2004-; art teacher, 2010-11. **Publications:** FOR CHILDREN: Carnival Time, 1992; J.B. Wigglebottom and the Parade of Pets (novel), 1993; Mouse Chase, 1995; Three Kind Mice, 1997; On Grandpa's Farm, 1997; Leroy Potts Meets the McCrooks, 1997; Slender Ella and Her Fairy Hogfather, 1999. WISHBONE: THE EARLY YEARS SERIES: Hansel and Gretel, 1999; The Brave Little Tailor, 2000. WISHBONE SERIES: Digging up the Past, 1997; Dog Days of the West, 1998; Dog Overboard!, 1998; Stage Invader, 1999.

Contributor to periodicals. **Address:** 63693 E Whispering Tree Ln., Tucson, AZ 85739, U.S.A. **Online address:** vsathre@msn.com

SATO, Hiroaki. American/Taiwanese (born Taiwan), b. 1942. **Genres:** Poetry, Translations. **Career:** Japan External Trade Organization (JETRO), staff, 1969-, associate director, 1980-84, deputy director, 1984-, director of research and planning, 1991-, senior research fellow, 2005-; Haiku Society of America, president, 1979-81; St. Andrews Presbyterian College, adjunct professor of Japanese letters, 1985-91; University of Massachusetts Amherst, adjunct faculty, 1998-; California State Library, American Haiku Archives, honorary curator, 2006-07. Writer. **Publications:** One Hundred Frogs, 1983; The Sword and the Mind, 1985; Eigo Haiku (title means: 'Haiku in English'), 1987; That First Time, 1988; Manhattan Culture School (collected columns), 1990; Manhattan Bungaku Mampo (essays), 1992; America Hon'yaku Musha Shugyo (essays), 1993; Legends of the Samurai, 1994; Nani ga yakusenai ka (title means: 'What Can't Be Translated'), 1994; The Village Beyond: Poems of Nobuko Kimura, 2002; Santoka, 2002; Howling at the Moon: Poems and Prose of Hagiwara Sakutaro, 2002; My Friend Hitler and Other Plays of Yukio Mishima, 2002. TRANSLATIONS: Poems of Princess Shikishi, 1973; Ten Japanese Poets, 1973; Spring and Asura: Poems of Kenji Miyazawa, 1973; Anthology of Modern Japanese Poets, 1973; Mutsuo Takahashi: Poems of a Penisist, 1975; Lilac Garden: Poems of Minoru Yoshioka, 1976; Howling at the Moon: Poems of Hagiwara Sakutaro, 1978; See You Soon: Poems of Taeko Tomioka, 1979; Chieko and Other Poems of Takamura Kotaro, 1980; M. Takahashi, A Bunch of Keys: Selected Poems, 1984; (and intro.) A Future of Ice: Poems and Stories of a Japanese Buddhist, 1989; G. Yoshimasu, Osiris: The God of Stone, 1989; M. Young, Legal Systems of Japan and the United States and Their Social Implications, 1989; J. Ashbery, A Wave, 1991; A Brief History of Imbecility: Poetry and Prose of Takamura Kotaro, 1992; Mutsuo Takahashi: Sleeping Sinning Falling, 1992; (and intro.) String of Beads: Complete Poems of Princess Shikishi, 1993; Right under the Big Sky, I Don't Wear a Hat: The Haiku and Prose of Hosai Ozaki, 1993; Basho's Narrow Road, 1996; Voice Garden: Poems of Mutsuo Takahashi, 1996; (and intro.) Breeze through Bamboo: Kanshi of Ema Saiko, 1997; Y. Mishima, Silk and Insight, 1998; Talk to a Stone, 1998; R. Koyanagi, Rabbit of the Nether World, 1999; Not a Metaphor: Poems of Kazue Shinkawa, 1999; The Girl Who Turned into Tea: Poems of Minako Nagashima, 2000; Howling at the Moon and Blue, 2001; Grass and Tree Cairn, 2002; Village Beyond: Poems of Nobuko Kimura, 2002; My friend Hitler and Other Plays of Mishima Yukio, 2002; Runners in the Margins: Poems, 2003; Toward Meaning: Poems of Kikuo Takano, 2004; (and intro.) Japanese Women Poets: An Anthology, 2008. EDITOR AND TRANSLATOR WITH B. WATSON: From the Country of Eight Islands: An Anthology of Japanese Poetry, 1981; (with D. Burleigh) Autumn Stone in the woods, 1997; (and intro.) Miyazawa Kenji: Selections, 2007. Contributor of articles to periodicals. **Address:** Japan External Trade Organization, 1221 Ave. of the Americas, McGraw Hill Bldg., 42nd Fl., New York, NY 10020, U.S.A. **Online address:** hironan@ix.netcom.com

SATTER, Ellyn. American (born United States), b. 1942. **Genres:** Food And Wine, Human Relations/Parenting, Medicine/Health, Psychology, Adult Nonfiction, Sports/Fitness. **Career:** University of Wisconsin Hospitals, clinical dietitian, 1964-65; Jackson Medical Clinic, clinical dietitian, 1967-82, Nutrition Center, clinical dietitian and director, 1967-81, psychiatry department, psychotherapist, 1981-85, clinical social worker, 1982-; Community Memorial Hospital, clinical nutrition consultant, 1973-78; independent consultant, author and trainer, 1979-; Family Therapy Center of Madison, psychotherapist and specialist in eating disorders, 1985-2002; Ellyn Satter Associates, owner and director, 1992-; Ellyn Satter Institute, owner and director, 2002-. **Publications:** Child of Mine: Feeding with Love and Good Sense, 1983; Parent and Child, 1985; How to Get Your Kid to Eat-But Not Too Much, 1987; Secrets of Feeding a Healthy Family, 1999; Your Child's Weight, Helping Without Harming, 2005. Contributor to books and periodicals. **Address:** Ellyn Satter Associates, 4226 Mandan Cres., Madison, WI 53711, U.S.A. **Online address:** info@ellynsatter.com

SATTER, Robert. American (born United States), b. 1919. **Genres:** Law, Essays. **Career:** Ritter and Satter Law Firm, partner, 1952-61; Satter and Fleischmann Law Firm, partner, 1961-75; Hartford Community Council, president, 1964-65; general counsel for Democratic majority of the Connecticut Legislature, 1967-75; Superior Court of Connecticut, judge, 1975-, senior judge; Connecticut School of Law, adjunct professor, 1976-. Writer. **Publications:** Doing Justice: A Trial Judge at Work, 1990; A Path in the Law, 1996; The Furniture of My Mind: Collected Essays, 1999; Under the Gold Dome:

An Insider's Look at the Connecticut Legislator, 2004, 2nd ed., 2009. Contributor to periodicals. **Address:** Superior Court, 95 Washington St., Hartford, CT 06106, U.S.A. **Online address:** bsatter@att.net

SAUDER, Robert A(lden). American (born United States), b. 1943. **Genres:** Geography, Local History/Rural Topics, History. **Career:** University of New Orleans, instructor, 1970-71, 1972-74, assistant professor, 1974-81, associate professor, 1981-89, Department of Geography and Anthropology, head, 1981-84, professor of geography, 1989-2001, professor emeritus, 2001-. Writer. **Publications:** The Lost Frontier: Water Diversion in the Growth and Destruction of Owens Valley Agriculture, 1994; The Yuma Reclamation Project: Irrigation, Indian Allotment, and Settlement Along the Lower Colorado River, 2009. EDITOR and CONTRIBUTOR: (with R.H. Kessel) A Field Guidebook for Louisiana, 1978; (with K. Frantz) Ethnic Persistence and Change in Europe and America: Traces in Landscape and Society, 1995. Contributor of articles to journals. **Address:** Department of Geography, University of New Orleans, New Orleans, LA 70148, U.S.A. **Online address:** rasauder@earthlink.net

SAUER, Elizabeth M. Canadian (born Canada), b. 1964. **Genres:** Literary Criticism And History, Language/Linguistics. **Career:** Brock University, assistant professor, 1991-95, associate professor, 1995-99, professor of English, 1999-. Writer. **Publications:** Barbarous Dissonance and Images of Voice in Milton's Epics, 1996; Paper-Contestations and Textual Communities in England, 1640-1675, 2005. EDITOR AND CONTRIBUTOR: (with J. Lungstrum) Agonistics: Arenas of Creative Contest, 1997; (with B. Rajan) Milton and the Imperial Vision, 1999; (with J. Andersen) Books and Readers in Early Modern England: Material Studies, 2002; (with J. Andersen) Literature and Religion in Early Modern England, 2003; (with H. Ostovich) Reading Early Modern Women: An Anthology of Texts in Manuscript and Print, 1550-1700, 2004; (with B. Rajan) Imperialisms: Historical and Literary Investigations 1500-1900, 2004; Milton and the Climates of Reading: Essays, 2006; (with S. Achinstein) Milton and Toleration, 2007; (with J.M. Wright) Reading the Nation in English Literature: A Critical Reader, 2010; (with P.C. Herman) The New Milton Criticism, 2012; Milton's Defences: The Oxford Handbook of Literature and the English Revolution, forthcoming; Milton, Toleration and Reformation Nationhood, forthcoming. Contributor to books and periodicals. **Address:** Department of English Language and Literature, Brock University, GLN 135, 500 Glenridge Ave., St. Catharines, ON L2S 3A1, Canada. **Online address:** esauer@brocku.ca

SAUERS, Michael P(atrick). American (born United States), b. 1970. **Genres:** Technology, Communications/Media, Information Science/Computers, Social Sciences. **Career:** Bibliographical Center for Research (library services cooperative), internet trainer, 1997-; Nebraska Library Commission, technology innovation librarian. Writer. **Publications:** Using Microsoft Outlook 2000: Internet E-Mail, Scheduling & Contact Management, 2000; Microsoft Front Page 2000: Advanced Topics, 2000; Using the Internet as a Reference Tool: A How-to-Do-It Manual for Librarians, 2001; (with R.A. Wyke) XHTML Essentials, 2001; Using Microsoft Outlook: A How-to-Do-It Manual And CD-ROM Tutorial, 2001; A Collector's Guide to Dean Koontz, 2003; (with L.E. Alcorn) The Neal-Schuman Directory of Management Software for Public Access Computers, 2003; XHTML and CSS Essentials for Library Web Design, 2004; Blogging and RSS: A Librarian's Guide, 2006, 2nd ed., 2010; Searching 2.0, 2009. Contributor to periodicals. **Address:** Bibliographical Center for Research, 14394 E Evans Ave., Aurora, CO 80014-1478, U.S.A. **Online address:** msauers@bcr.org

SAUERS, Richard A(llen). American (born United States), b. 1954. **Genres:** History. **Career:** Harrisburg Area Community College, teacher; 1983-91; Butternut and Blue Press, editor, 1992-; Soldiers and Sailors Memorial Hall, museum curator, 1997-; Susquehanna University, teacher; Pennsylvania State University, teacher; Lebanon Valley College, teacher. Historian and consultant. **Publications:** (Comp.) The Gettysburg Campaign, June 3-August 1, 1863: A Comprehensive, Selectively Annotated Bibliography, 1982; Advance the Colors! Pennsylvania Civil War Battleflags, 2 vols., 1987-91; A Caspian Sea of Ink: The Meade-Sickles Controversy, 1989; (with W.D. Gorges) The Battle of New Bern and Related Sites in Craven County, North Carolina, 1861-1865, 1994; To Care for Him Who Has Borne the Battle: Research Guide to Civil War Material in the National Tribune, vol. I: 1877-1884, 1995; (with A. Sauers) Research Secrets of a Civil War Historian, 1995; A Succession of Honorable Victories: The Burnside Expedition in North Carolina, 1996; (with M.F. Graham and G. Skoch) The Blue and the Gray, 1996; Pennsylvania in the Spanish-American War: A Commemorative Look Back, 1998; (ed.) Fighting Them Over: How the Veterans Remembered Gettysburg in the Pages of the National Tribune, 1998; How to do Civil War Research, 2000; (ed.) The Civil War Journal of Colonel William J. Bolton: 51st Pennsylvania, April 20, 1861-August 2, 1865, 2000; (ed.) Bloody 85th: The Letters of Milton McJunkin, a Western Pennsylvania Soldier in the Civil War, 2000; (with P. Tomasak) Ricketts' Battery: A History of Battery F, 1st Pennsylvania Light Artillery, 2001; Meade: Victor of Gettysburg, 2003; Guide to Civil War Philadelphia, 2003; Gettysburg: The Meade-Sickles Controversy, 2003; America's Battlegrounds: Walk in the Footsteps of America's Bravest, 2005; (with M.H. Sable) William Francis Bartlett: Biography of a Union General in the Civil War, 2009; Nationalism, 2009; Expansionism, 2010; (with M.L. Huffines) Lewisburg, 2010. Contributor of articles and reviews to periodicals. **Address:** Soldiers & Sailors Memorial Hall, 4141 5th Ave., Pittsburgh, PA 15213, U.S.A.

SAUL, John Ralston. Canadian (born Canada), b. 1947. **Genres:** Novels, Philosophy, Social Commentary. **Career:** Gainsborough Publications, correspondant, 1972-75; Chapel Land, director general and administrator, 1972-75; Petro-Canada, special assistant to the chairman, 1976-78; Film Five Inc., president, 1978-82; International PEN, The Canadian Centre, secretary, 1987-89, vice president, 1989-90, president, 1990-92, 2009; Institute for Canadian Citizenship, co-chair; Le francais pour l'avenir/French for the Future, founder and honorary chair; LaFontaine-Baldwin symposium, founder and chair. **Publications:** NOVELS: Mort d'un général: Roman, 1977; The Birds of Prey, 1977; Baraka, 1985; The Next Best Thing, 1986; The Paradise Eater, 1988; De Si Bons Américains, 1994. NON-FICTION: Voltaire's Bastards: The Dictatorship of Reason in the West, 1992; The Doubter's Companion: A Dictionary of Aggressive Common Sense, 1994; The Unconscious Civilization, 1995; Reflections of a Siamese Twin: Canada at the End of the Twentieth Century, 1997; (co-author) Do We Care?: Renewing Canada's Commitment to Health: Proceedings of the First Directions for Canadian Health Care Conference, 1999; On Equilibrium: Six Qualities of the New Humanism, 2001; (with A. Dubuc and G. Erasmus) Dialogue on Democracy in Canada, 2002; The Collapse of Globalism and the Reinvention of the World, 2005; Joseph Howe and the Battle for Freedom of Speech, 2006; A Fair Country: Telling Truths about Canada, 2008; OTHERS: Le Citoyen dans un cul-de-sac?: Anatomie d'une société en crise, 1996; Louis-Hippolyte LaFontaine and Robert Baldwin, 2010. **Address:** c/o Natasha Daneman, Westwood Creative Artists, 94 Harbord St., Toronto, ON M5S 1G6, Canada.

SAULNIER, Beth. (Elizabeth Bloom). American (born United States), b. 1969. **Genres:** Mystery/Crime/Suspense. **Career:** Vassar College, editor-in-chief; Cornell Magazine, contributing editor, associate editor and staff writer; Weill Cornell Medical College Magazine, editor; Ithaca Journal, film critic, 1992-, movie reviewer and columnist. **Publications:** ALEX BERNIER MYSTERY SERIES: Reliable Sources, 1999; Distemper, 2000; The Fourth Wall, 2001; Bad Seed: An Alex Bernier Mystery, 2002; Ecstasy, 2003. OTHERS: (as Elizabeth Bloom) See Isabelle Run, 2005; (as Elizabeth Bloom) The Mortician's Daughter, 2006. Contributor to periodicals. **Address:** Ithaca Journal, 123 W State St., Ithaca, NY 14850, U.S.A.

SAULNIER, Karen Luczak. American (born United States), b. 1940. **Genres:** Children's Fiction, Education, Language/Linguistics, Reference. **Career:** Clarke School for the Deaf, teacher, 1963-65; Gallaudet University, assistant professor, 1965-73, Center for Studies in Education and Human Development, researcher, 1974-. Writer. **Publications:** SIGNED ENGLISH SERIES: I Want to Be a Farmer, 1972; My Animal Book, 1973; Mealtime at the Zoo, 1973; Spring Is Green, 1973; Tommy's Day, 1973; Baby's Animal Book, 1974; A Book about Me, 1974; Count and Color, 1974; The Holiday Book, 1974; Mouse's Christmas Eve, 1974; My Toy Book, 1974; Questions and More Questions, 1974; All by Myself, 1975; I Am a Kitten, 1975; The Things I Like to Do, 1975; With My Legs, 1975; At Night: A First Book of Prepositions, 1976; Circus Time, 1976; The Clock Book, 1976; Firefighter Brown, 1976; Oliver in the City, 1976; The Pet Shop, 1976; Policeman Jones, 1976. ADAPTOR: SIGNED ENGLISH SERIES: (with H. Bornstein) Goldilocks and the Three Bears, 1972; Hansel and Gretel, 1972; The Three Little Pigs, 1972; (with H. Bornstein) The Night before Christmas, 1973; Songs in Signed English, 1973; The Three Little Kittens, 1973; (with H. Bornstein) Little Red Riding Hood, 1990; (with H. Bornstein) Nursery Rhymes from Mother Goose, 1992. WITH H. BORNSTEIN: (and L. Hamilton) The Basic Preschool Signed English Dictionary, 1973; (and L. Hamilton) The Signed English Dictionary for Preschool and Elementary Levels, 1975; (ed. with L.

Hamilton) The Comprehensive Signed English Dictionary, 1983; The Signed English Starter, 1984 as Signing: Signed English: A Basic Guide, 1986; The Signed English School Book, 1987. OTHER WITH H. BORNSTEIN AND L. HAMILTON: Guide to the Selection and Use of the Teaching Aids of the Signed English System, 1976; Signed English for the Residence Hall, 1979; Signed English: A Guide to Its Components and Materials, 1983. OTHERS: (contrib.) Signed English for the Classroom, 1975. **Address:** Gallaudet University, 800 Florida Ave. NE, Washington, DC 20002, U.S.A.

SAUM, Karen. American/Panamanian (born Panama), b. 1935. **Genres:** Novellas/Short Stories, Mystery/Crime/Suspense, Children's Fiction, Novels, Gay And Lesbian Issues. **Career:** City University of New York, Brooklyn College, lecturer in history, 1964-67, Manhattan Community College, instructor in history, 1967-68; University of Maine-Augusta, assistant professor of history, 1970-74; William Shakespeare Co., office manager, 1979-80; State Employment and Training Council, policy development coordinator, 1980-81; Homeworkers Organized for More Employment Inc., Rural Education Program, director, 1981-, Outreach Program, director, 1982-85, Learning Center, director, 1985-86; Vermont College, adjunct professor, 1981-85; University of Maine, visiting lecturer, 1985; College of the Atlantic, visiting lecturer, 1986. Writer. **Publications:** MYSTERY NOVELS: Murder Is Relative, 1990; Murder Is Germane: A Brigid Donovan Mystery, 1991; Murder Is Material: A Brigid Donovan Mystery, 1994; I Never Read Thoreau: A Mystery Novel, 1996. OTHERS: The Adventures of Max Pine (children's), 1997; El Valle and Other Jessica Stories about Growing Up in Panama, 2003; A Midsummer Night's Dream, 2004; Take the Cash, 2007. **Address:** Homeworkers Organized for More Employment Inc., PO Box 10, Orland, ME 04472, U.S.A. **Online address:** karen.saum@stanfordalumni.org

SAUMS, Mary. American (born United States) **Genres:** Social Sciences, Novels, Humor/Satire. **Career:** Author. **Publications:** WILLI TAFT SERIES: Midnight Hour, 2000; The Valley of Jewels, 2001; When the Last Magnolia Weeps, 2004. OTHERS: Thistle and Twigg (novel), 2007; Mighty Old Bones, 2008. Contributor to books. **Address:** St. Martin's Press, Publicity Department, 175 5th Ave., New York, NY 10010, U.S.A. **Online address:** marysaums@hotmail.com

SAUNDERS, Ann Loreille. (Ann Cox-Johnson). British (born England), b. 1930. **Genres:** Archaeology/Antiquities, Architecture, History, Essays, Biography, Reference. **Career:** Lambeth Palace, deputy librarian, 1952-55; British Museum, assistant keeper, 1955-56; St. Marylebone Public Library, archivist, 1956-63; Journal of the British Archaeological Association, sub-editor, 1964-75; Costume, editor, 1967-2008, editor emeritus, 2008-; London Topographical Record, editor, 1975-; Richardson College, lecturer in history. **Publications:** Regent's Park, 1969, 2nd ed., 1981; London North of the Thames, Except the City and Westminster, 1972; London, the City and Westminster, new ed., 1975; The Regent's Park Villas, 1981; Art Historian's Guide to the Greater London Area, 1982; The Art and Architecture of London: An Illustrated Guide, 1984, 2nd ed., 1988; (ed. with H. Hobhouse) Good and Proper Materials, 1989; (ed.) Facsimiles of the Ordnance Surveyors' Drawings of the London Area, 1799-1808, 1991; The Royal Exchange, 1991; (ed.) The Mercers' Company 1579-1959, 1994; (ed. and contrib.) Major Volume on Royal Exchange, 1997; St Paul's: The Story of the Cathedral, 2001; (with M. Davies) The History of the Merchant Taylors' Company, 2004; Historic Views of London: From the Collection of B.E.C. Howarth-Loomes, 2008. AS ANN COX-JOHNSON: (ed.) Handlist to the Ashbridge Collection on the History and Topography of St. Marylebone, 1959; John Bacon, R.A. 1740-1799, 1961; (comp.) Handlist of Painters, Sculptors and Architects Associated with St. Marylebone, 1760-1900, 1963. **Address:** Costume Society, 28 Eburne Rd., London, GL N7 6AU, England.

SAUNDERS, Fiona. See **JONES, Allan Frewin.**

SAUNDERS, Gail. Bahamian (born Bahamas), b. 1944. **Genres:** Local History/Rural Topics, Cultural/Ethnic Topics, Civil Liberties/Human Rights, Social Sciences, Reference. **Career:** History teacher, 1967-68; Department of Archives, staff, 1969-, chief archivist, 1980-83, director, 1983-2004; Ministry of Education, public records officer, 1970-71, archivist, 1971-80; United Nations Educational, Scientific and Cultural Organization (UNESCO) consultant, 1979, 1982, 1994; Government of Dominica, consultant on preservation of dominican record and national archives, 2001. Writer. **Publications:** (With E.A. Carson) Guide to the Records of the Bahamas, 1973; (with D. Cartwright) Historic Nassau, 1980; Bahamian Loyalists and Their Slaves,

1983; Slavery in the Bahamas, 1648-1838, 1985; The Bahamas: A Family of Islands, 1988, 2nd ed., 1993; Bahamian Society After Emancipation: Essays in Nineteenth and Early Twentieth Century Bahamian History, 1990; (with P. Cash and S. Gordon) Sources of Bahamian History, 1991; (with M. Craton) Islanders in the Stream: A History of the Bahamian People, vol. I, 1992, vol. II, 1998; Bahamas: A Family of Islands, 1993; Bahamian Society after Emancipation, 1994; Social Life in the Bahamas, 1880s-1920s, 1996; Nassau's Historic Landmarks, 2001; (ed.) Cultural Perspectives, 2003, 2003; (ed. with W.K. Jones) Bahamas: Independence and Beyond, 2004; (with P.M. Williams) Conflict, Controversy and Control, 2006. **Address:** Department of Archives, Mackey and Shirley St., PO Box SS 6341, Nassau, 78073, Bahamas. **Online address:** saunders@batelnet.bs

SAUNDERS, George W. American (born United States), b. 1958. **Genres:** Military/Defense/Arms Control, Literary Criticism And History. **Career:** Radian Intl. (environmental engineering firm), technical writer and geophysical engineer, 1989-96; Siena College, adjunct professor, 1989; Saint John Fisher College, adjunct professor, 1990-95; Syracuse University, visiting professor, 1996-97, assistant professor of creative writing, 1997-, professor. **Publications:** Civil War Land in Bad Decline, 1996; Pastoralia: Stories, 2000; The Very Persistent Gappers of Frip, 2000; The Brief and Frightening Reign of Phil, 2005; In Persuasion Nation: Stories, 2006; The Braindead Megaphone, 2007. **Address:** Department of English, Syracuse University, 212 Tolley, Syracuse, NY 13244, U.S.A. **Online address:** gwsaunde@syr.edu

SAUNDERS, James Robert. American (born United States), b. 1953. **Genres:** Literary Criticism And History, Essays, History. **Career:** University of Virginia, resident advisor, 1973-74, instructor, 1973-74, 1980-82, Afro American and African Studies Program, student coordinator, 1980-81; Central National Bank, management trainee, 1978; Department of Welfare, research analyst, 1979; Vinegar Hill Oral History Project, director, 1980; Mary Washington College, lecturer, 1981-82; University of Michigan, academic advisor, 1984-85; Washtenaw County Community College, instructor, 1984; University of Toledo, instructor, 1985-86, assistant professor, 1986-90, faculty research fellow, 1988, 1990, 1995, associate professor, 1990-96, professor of English, 1996-97; Purdue University, Department of English, professor, 1997-. Writer. **Publications:** The Wayward Preacher in the Literature of African American Women (literary criticism), 1995; Tightrope Walk: Identity, Survival and the Corporate World in African American Literature (literary criticism), 1997; (with R.N. Shackelford) Urban Renewal and the End of Black Culture in Charlottesville, Virginia: An Oral History of Vinegar Hill, 1998; (with R.N. Shackelford) The Dorothy West Martha's Vineyard: Stories, Essays and Reminiscences by Dorothy West Writing in the Vineyard Gazette, 2001; (with M.R. Saunders) Black Winning Jockeys in the Kentucky Derby, 2003. Contributor to books and periodicals. **Address:** Department of English, Purdue University, Heavilon 330B, 500 Oval Dr., West Lafayette, IN 47907-2038, U.S.A. **Online address:** saunderj@purdue.edu

SAUNDERS, Jean (Innes). Also writes as Sally Blake, Jean Innes, Rowena Summers, Rachel Moore, Jodi Nicol. British (born England), b. 1932. **Genres:** Novels, Romance/Historical, Children's Fiction, Writing/Journalism, Natural History, Young Adult Fiction, Adult Non-fiction. **Career:** Medical Research Council, assay laboratory assistant, 1948-54; writer, 1965-. **Publications:** NOVELS: The Fugitives, 1974; Only Yesterday, 1975; Nightmare, 1977; The Tender Trap, 1977; Roses All the Way, 1978; The Tally-Man, 1979; Lady of the Manor, 1979; Cobden's Cottage, 1979; Rainbow's End, 1979; Anchor Man, 1980; Dangerous Enchantment, 1980; The Kissing Time, 1982; The Spider's Web, 1982; The Language of Love, 1983; Taste the Wine, 1983; Love's Sweet Music, 1983; Partners in Love, 1984; Scarlet Rebel, 1985; Golden Destiny, 1986; All in the April Morning, 1989; The Bannister Girls, 1990; To Love and Honour, 1992; With This Ring, 1993; Journey's End, 1996; Wives, Friends and Lovers, 1996; A Different Kind of Love, 1998; Thicker Than Water, 1999; Illusions, 2000; Deadly Suspicions, 2001; A Perfect Marriage, 2002; Unforgettable, 2003; Village Fate, 2011; Writing Romantic Fiction, 2011. NON-FICTION: Gelatine Home Cooking Secrets, 1977; The Craft of Writing Romance, 1986, rev. ed., 2000; Writing Step by Step, 1988; How to Create Fictional Characters, 1992; How to Research Your Novel, 1993; How to Write Realistic Dialogue, 1994; How to Plot Your Novel, 1999; Successful Novel Plotting, 2009; Writing Dialogue, 2011; Creating Fictional Characters, 2011. AS SALLY BLAKE: The Devil's Kiss, 1981; Moonlight Mirage, 1982; Outback Woman, 1990; Lady of Spain, 1990; Far Distant Shores, 1991; A Royal Summer, 1992; House of Secrets, 1993; Marrying for Love, 1997; A Gentleman's Masquerade, 1999. AS JEAN INNES:

Ashton's Folly, 1975; Sands of Lamanna, 1975; The Golden God, 1975; The Whispering Dark, 1975; White Blooms of Yarrow; Boskelly's Bride, 1976; The Wishing Stone, 1976; The Dark Stranger, 1979; Silver Lady, 1981; Scent of Jasmine, 1982; Enchanted Island, 1982; Legacy of Love, 1982; Seeker of Dreams, 1983; Buccaneer's Bride, 1989; Dream Lover, 1990; Golden Captive, 1991; Secret Touch, 1992; Tropical Fire, 1992; (co-author) A Bride's Desire, 1994; Beloved, 1996; Jewel, 1998. AS ROWENA SUMMERS: Blackmaddie, 1980; The Savage Moon, 1982; The Sweet Red Earth, 1983; Willow Harvest, 1984; Killigrew Clay, 1986; Clay Country, 1987; Family Ties, 1988; Velvet Dawn, 1991; Angel of the Evening, 1992; Ellie's Island, 1993; Bargain Bride, 1993; Hidden Currents, 1994; Woman of Property, 1994; Family Shadows, 1995; A Safe Haven, 1996; Primmy's Daughter, 1998; White Rivers, 1998; September Morning, 1999; A Brighter Tomorrow, 2000; Taking Heart, 2000; Daisy's War, 2001; The Caldwell Girls, 2001; Dreams of Peace, 2002; This Girl, 2004; Shelter From the Storm, 2005; Monday's Child, 2005; Blackthorn Cottage, 2006; Chasing Rainbows, 2009; Pot of Gold, 2009. AS JODI NICOL: Silken Chains, 1997. AS RACHEL MOORE: The Soldier's Wife, 2004; The Farmer's Wife, 2005; A Cornish Maid, 2006; Prodigal Daughter, 2007; Days to Remember, 2009; Summer of Love, 2010. **Address:** Severn House Publishers Inc., 110 E 59th St., 22th Fl., New York, NY 10022, U.S.A.

SAUNDERS, Max. British (born England), b. 1957. **Genres:** Biography, Essays, Literary Criticism And History. **Career:** Cambridge University, Selwyn College, research fellow, 1983-88, college lecturer, 1988-89; University of London, King's College, lecturer, 1989-97, reader in English, 1997-2000, professor of English, 2000-. Writer. **Publications:** Ford Madox Ford (biography): A Dual Life, vol. I: The World before the War, vol. II: The After-War World, 1996; (ed.) Ford: Selected Poems, 1997; (ed.) Ford: War Prose, 1999; (ed. with R. Stang) Critical Essays, 2002; (ed. with K. Carabine) Inter-relations: Conrad, James, Ford and Others, 2003; (ed.) Ford, Some Do Not Autobiografiction and the Forms of Modern Literature, 2010. **Address:** Department of English, King's College, University of London, The Strand, London, GL WC2R 2LS, England. **Online address:** max.saunders@kcl.ac.uk

SAUNDERS, Nicholas J. (Nick Saunders). British (born England), b. 1953?. **Genres:** History. **Career:** University College London, faculty, 2006-, reader in anthropology, honorary research fellow; University of Bristol, Archaeology and Anthropology Department, tutor, programme director, 2007, professor; University of Mexico, faculty; University of the West Indies, faculty. Writer and archaeologist. **Publications:** (Ed. with O. de Montmollin) Recent Studies in Pre-Columbian Archaeology, 1988; People of the Jaguar: The Living Spirit of Ancient America, 1989; The Cult of the Cat, 1991; The Jaguars of Culture: Symbolizing Humanity in Pre-Columbian and Amerindian Societies, 1991; (ed.) Ancient America: Contributions to New World Archaeology, 1992; (ed. with C.L.N. Ruggles) Astronomies and Cultures: Papers Derived from the Third Oxford International Symposium on Archaeoastronomy, St. Andrews, U.K., September 1990, 1993; Animal Spirits, 1995; (ed.) Icons of Power: Feline Symbolism in the Americas, 1998; The Incas, 2000; Trench Art: A Brief History & Guide, 1914-1939, 2001; Trench Art: Materialities and Memories of War, 2003; (ed.) Matters of Conflict: Material Culture, Memory and the First World War, 2004; Ancient Americas: The Great Civilizations, 2004; Peoples of the Caribbean: An Encyclopedia of Archeology and Traditional Culture, 2005; (as Nick Saunders) The Inca City of Cuzco, 2005; (with T. Allan) The Aztec Empire, 2005; The Life of Julius Caesar, 2006; The Life of Alexander the Great, 2006; Alexander's Tomb: The Two Thousand Year Obsession to Find the Lost Conqueror, 2006; The Life of Anne Frank, 2006; Ancient Americas: Maya, Aztec, Inka & Beyond, 2006; Killing Time: Archaeology and the First World War, 2007; Perseus and Medusa, 2007; The Twelve Labours of Hercules, 2007; Pandora's Box, 2007; Academies and Trust Schools: Where do Universities Fit In?, 2009; (ed. with P. Cornish) Contested Objects: Material Memories of the Great War, 2009. **Address:** Department of Archaeology & Anthropology, University of Bristol, 43 Woodland Rd., Bristol, BS8 1UU, England. **Online address:** nicholas.saunders@bris.ac.uk

SAUNDERS, Nick. See SAUNDERS, Nicholas J.

SAUNDERS, Steven. See JONES, Allan Frewin.

SAUNT, Claudio. American (born United States), b. 1967. **Genres:** History, Politics/Government, Social Sciences, History. **Career:** St. Philip's Archaeological Project, assistant director, 1993; Columbia University, lecturer, 1996-98; University of Georgia, assistant professor, associate professor of history, 1998-, now professor, Richard B. Russell professor in American history; Institute of Native American Studies, associate director. Writer and educator. **Publications:** A New Order of Things: Property, Power and the Transformation of the Creek Indians, 1733-1816, 1999; Black, White and Indian: Race and the Unmaking of an American Family, 2005. Contributor to books and periodicals. **Address:** Department of History, University of Georgia, LeConte Hall, Athens, GA 30602-1602, U.S.A. **Online address:** csaunt@uga.edu

SAURO, Christy W. American (born United States), b. 1949. **Genres:** History, Military/Defense/Arms Control. **Career:** U.S. Marines, sergeant, 1967-73. Writer. **Publications:** The Twins Platoon: An Epic Story of Young Marines at War in Vietnam, 2006. Contributor to periodicals. **Address:** North Branch, MN , U.S.A. **Online address:** csaurojr@msn.com

SAUTER, Doris Elaine. American (born United States) **Genres:** Novels, Medicine/Health, Science Fiction/Fantasy. **Career:** Writer. **Publications:** (Ed. with G. Lee) What If Our World Is Their Heaven?: The Final Conversations of Philip K. Dick, 2000; Cure That Cold! Fight That Flu!, 2005. **Address:** Overlook Press, 1 Overlook Dr., Woodstock, NY 12498, U.S.A.

SAUVAIN, Philip Arthur. British (born England), b. 1933. **Genres:** Children's Non-fiction, Environmental Sciences/Ecology, Geography, History, Humanities, Natural History, Communications/Media. **Career:** Steyning Grammar School, Department of Geography, head, 1957-61; Penistone Grammar School, Department of Geography, head, 1961-63; James Graham College, senior lecturer in geography, 1963-68; Charlotte Mason College of Education, Department of Environmental Studies, head, 1968-74; writer, 1974-. **Publications:** A Map Reading Companion, 1961; A Geographical Field Study Companion, 1964; Exploring at Home, 1966; Exploring Britain, 1966; Exploring the World, 1967; Hulton's Practical Geography, vol. IV, 1969-72; Facts, Maps and Places, 1970; Discovery, vol. VI, 1970; Lively History, vol. VI, 1970-72; Man and Environment, 1971; The Great Wall of China, 1972; The First Men on the Moon, 1972; A First Look at Maps, 1973; Exploring the World of Man, vol. X, 1973-77; Breakaway, vol. VIII, 1973-76; Environment Books, vol. I, 1974, vol. II, 1978; Looking around Town and Country, 1975; A First Look at Winds (Dinosaurs, Discoveries, Rain, Ice and Snow), vol. V, 1975-78; Imagining the Past: First Series, vol. VI, 1976, Second Series, vol. VI, 1979; Looking Back, 1977; Discoveries and Inventions before the Age of Steam, 1977; Macmillan Local Studies Kit, 1979; Looking around Cards, 1979; Certificate Mapwork, 1980; The British Isles, 1980; Story of Britain series, vol. IV, 1980; Science Discussion Pictures, 1981; Britain's Living Heritage, 1982; History of Britain, vol. IV, 1982; Theatre, 1983; Macmillan Junior Geography, vol. IV, 1983; Hulton New Geographies, vol. V, 1983; History Map Books, vol. II, 1983; Hulton New Histories, vol. V, 1984-85; France and the French, 1985; European and World History 1815-1919, 1985; Modern World History 1919 Onwards, 1985; How History Began, 1985; About Castles and Crusaders, 1986; What to Look For, vol. IV, 1986; British Economic and Social History, vol. II, 1987; Wind and Water Power, 1987; Wood and Coal, 1987; Carrying Energy, 1987; Oil and Natural Gas, 1987; GCSE History Companions, vol. IV, 1988; Mine, 1988; Airport, 1988; Ship, 1988; Skills for Geography, 1989; The Modern World 1914-1980, 1989; Skyscrapers, 1990; Roads, 1990; Tunnels, 1990; Old World, 1991; Work, 1991; Holidays and Pastimes, 1991; Changing World, 1992; Over 1, 600 Years Ago: In the Roman Empire, 1992; Over 2,000 Years Ago: In Ancient Greece, 1992; The Era of the Second World War, 1993; Expanding World, 1993; Robert Scott in the Antarctic, 1993; Over 3,000 Years Ago: In Ancient Egypt, 1993; Over 450 Years Ago: In the New World, 1993; Communication, 1994; The Tudors and Stuarts, 1995; Key Themes of the Twentieth Century, 1996; Germany in the Twentieth Century, 1997; Vietnam, 1997; Easter, 1997; Exploring the Past: Expanding World, 2004; (with N. Shepley and S. Archer) Skills for Standard Grade History, 2004; People with Problems, 2004; Focus on World History: Nazi Germany, 2004. GREAT BATTLES AND SIEGES SERIES: Hastings, 1992; El Alamein, 1992; Midway, 1993; Waterloo, 1993. HISTORY DETECTIVE SERIES: In Ancient Greece, 1992; In the Roman Empire, 1992; In Ancient Egypt, 1993; In the New World, 1993. THE WAY IT WORKS SERIES: Air, 1992; Water, 1992; Motion, 1992. TARGET GEOGRAPHY SERIES: Big Book, 1994; Near and Far, 1994; Look Around, 1994; Using the Land, 1994; Maps and Places, 1994; At Home and Abroad, 1994; Around the World, 1994; At Home and in Britain, 1994; About Our World, 1994; Our Earth, 1994; Key Stage 3: Book 1, 1995; Teacher's Guide: Key Stages 1 and 2, 1995. BRITAIN SINCE 1930 SERIES: Life at Home, 1995; Life at Work, 1995; Leisure Time, 1996; The Advance of Technology, 1996. FAMOUS LIVES SERIES: Kings and Queens, 1996; Saints, 1996. GEOGRAPHY DETECTIVE SERIES: Rivers and Valleys, 1996; Mountains, 1996; Rain Forests, 1996; Oceans, 1996. Contributor of articles to periodicals. **Address:** 70 Finborough Rd., Stowmarket, SU IP14 1PU, England.

SAVAGE, Allan Maurice. Canadian (born Canada), b. 1946. **Genres:** Theology/Religion, Philosophy. **Career:** Roman Catholic Diocese of Thunder Bay, priest, 1982-; Adult Faith Office, director; University of Winnipeg, lecturer in theology; Lakehead Psychiatric Hospital, chaplain; Regional Health Sciences Centre, chaplain. St Patricks Church, pastor. Writer. **Publications:** A Phenomenological Understanding of Certain Liturgical Texts: The Anglican Collects for Advent and the Roman Catholic Collects for Lent, 2001; (as Allan M. Savage with S.W. Nicholl) Faith, Hope and Charity As Character Traits in Adler's Individual Psychology: With Related Essays in Spirituality and Phenomenology, 2003; (as Allan M. Savage with G. Drazenovich) Reflections on the Interior Life: Critical Insights from William Gladstone and George Tyrrell, 2006; A Contemporary Understanding of Religious Belief Within Mental Health, 2007; The Ecology: A New to You View-An Orthodox Theological Ecology, 2008; Dehellenization and Dr Dewart Revisited-A First Person Philosophical Reflection, 2009; Phenomenological Philosophy: and Reconstruction in Western Theism, 2010. **Address:** St Patricks Church, 1145 de Salaberry Ave., Quebec City, ON G1R 2V6, Canada. **Online address:** savagea@tbaytel.net

SAVAGE, Charlie. American (born United States), b. 1975?. **Genres:** Politics/Government, History. **Career:** Miami Herald, reporter, 1999-2003; Boston Globe, reporter, 2003-08; New York Times, reporter, 2008-, correspondent. **Publications:** Takeover: The Return of the Imperial Presidency and the Subversion of American Democracy, 2007. **Address:** Back Bay Books, 237 Park Ave, New York, NY 10017, U.S.A. **Online address:** charlie.savage@gmail.com

SAVAGE, Felicity. Japanese/American (born United States), b. 1975. **Genres:** Science Fiction/Fantasy, Biography, Young Adult Fiction. **Career:** Writer. **Publications:** SCIENCE-FICTION NOVELS: EVER SERIES: The War in the Waste, 1997; The Daemon in the Machine, 1998; A Trickster in the Ashes, 1998. GARDEN OF SALT SERIES: Humility Garden: An Unfinished Biography, 1994; Delta City, 1995. **Address:** HarperPrism, 10 E 53rd St., New York, NY 10022, U.S.A.

SAVAGE, Georgia. Australian (born Australia) **Genres:** Novels, Novellas/Short Stories, Literary Criticism And History, Young Adult Fiction. **Career:** Writer. **Publications:** Slate and Me and Blanche McBride, 1983; The Estuary, 1987; The House Tibet, 1991; The Tournament, 1993; Ceremony at Lang Nho, 1994. Work appears in anthologies. Contributor to periodicals. **Address:** Hickson & Associates, PO Box 271, Woollahra, NW 2025, Australia.

SAVAGE, Jeff. American (born United States), b. 1961. **Genres:** Sports/Fitness, Biography, Adult Non-fiction, Children's Non-fiction. **Career:** San Diego Union-Tribune, sportswriter, reporter, 1984-92; children's author, 1993-. **Publications:** SPORTS GREAT SERIES: Sports Great Jim Abbott, 1993; Sports Great Karl Malone, 1995; Sports Great Brett Favre, 1998; Sports Great Juwan Howard, 1999. TAKING PART SERIES: Kristi Yamaguchi: Pure Gold, 1993; Whitney Houston, 1998. SPORTS REPORTS SERIES: Cal Ripken, Jr.: Star Shortstop, 1994; Thurman Thomas: Star Running Back, 1994; Deion Sanders: Star Athlete, 1996; Emmitt Smith: Star Running Back, 1996; Junior Seau: Star Linebacker, 1997. WORKING OUT SERIES: Aerobics, 1995; Karate, 1995; Running, 1995; Weight Lifting, 1995. TRAILBLAZERS OF THE WILD WEST SERIES: Cowboys and Cow Towns of the Wild West, 1995; Gold Miners of the Wild West, 1995; Gunfighters of the Wild West, 1995; Pioneering Women of the Wild West, 1995; Pony Express Riders of the Wild West, 1995; Scouts of the Wild West, 1995. THE ACHIEVERS SERIES: Julie Krone: Unstoppable Jockey, 1996; Andre Agassi: Reaching the Top Again, 1997; Barry Bonds: Mr. Excitement, 1997; Grant Hill: Humble Hotshot, 1997; Mike Piazza: Hard-Hitting Catcher, 1997; Tiger Woods: King of the Course, 1997; Paul Kariya: Hockey Magician, 1998; Eric Lindros: Center of Attention, forthcoming; Mia Hamm: Soccer Superstar, forthcoming. RACE CAR LEGENDS SERIES: Motorcycles, 1997. ACTION EVENTS SERIES: Demolition Derby, 1997; Drag Racing, 1997; Monster Trucks, 1997; Mud Racing, 1997; Supercross Motorcycle Racing, 1997; Truck and Tractor Pullers, 1997. FUNDAMENTAL SPORTS SERIES: Fundamental Strength Training, 1998. SPORTS TOP 10 SERIES: Top 10 Basketball Point Guards, 1997; Top 10 Basketball Power Forwards, 1997; Top 10 Football Sackers, 1997; Top

10 Professional Football Coaches, 1998; Top 10 Aggressive Inline Skaters, 1999; Top 10 Heisman Trophy Winners, 1999. SPORTS ISSUES SERIES: A Sure Thing? Sports and Gambling, 1997. OTHERS: Demolition Derby, 1995; Monster Truck Wars, 1995; Mud Racing, 1995; Truck and Tractor Pulling, 1995; A Career in Professional Sports, 1996; Careers in Sports, 1996; In-Line Skating Basics, 1996; Motocross Cycles, 1996; Racing Cars, 1996; Wrestling Basics, 1996; Monster Trucks, 1997; Mike Piazza: Hard-Hitting Catcher, 1997; Junior Seau: Star linebacker, 1997; Andre Agassi: Reaching the Top, Again, 1997; Truck and Tractor Pullers, 1997; Top 10 Football Sackers, 1997; Top 10 Professional Football Coaches, 1998; Whitney Houston, 1998; Paul Kariya, Hockey Magician, 1998; Fundamental Strength Training, 1998; Eric Lindros: High-Flying Center, 1998; Y2K, 1999; Top 10 in-Line Skaters, 1999; Top 10 Heisman Trophy Winners, 1999; Sports Great Juwan Howard, 1999; Mark McGwire, Home Run King, 1999; Julie Foudy: Soccer Superstar, 1999; Home Run Kings, 1999; Drew Bledsoe, Cool Quarterback, 1999; Top 10 Sports Bloopers and who Made Them, 2000; Top 10 Physically Challenged Athletes, 2000; Terrell Davis: TD, 2000; Super Cross Motorcycle Racing, 2000; Sports Great Stephon Marbury, 2000; Sports Great Ken Griffey, Jr, 2000; Sammy Sosa, héRoe De Los Jonrones, 2000; Mud Racing, 2000; Monster Trucks, 2000; Kobe Bryant: Basketball Big Shot, 2000, rev. ed., 2011; Jeff Gordon: Racing's Superstar, 2000, rev. ed., 2007; Drag Racing, 2000; Demolition Derby, 2000; Truck and Tractor Pullers, 2000; Top 10 Women's Sports Legends, 2001; Top 10 Women's Basketball Stars, 2001; Top 10 African-American Men's Athletes, 2001; Sports Great Rebecca Lobo, 2001; Peyton Manning: Precision Passer, 2001, rev. ed., 2008; Sports Great Vince Carter, 2002; Barry Bonds: Record Breaker, 2002; World's Fastest Stock Cars, 2003; World's Fastest Pro Stock Trucks, 2003; Go-Karts, 2003; Stunt Planes, 2003; South Dakota, 2003; Mountain Bikes, 2003; Maryland, 2003; Ichiro Suzuki, 2003, rev. ed., 2007; Georgia, 2003; Demolition Derby Cars, 2003; California: A My Report Links.com Book, 2003; Tiger Woods, 2003, rev. ed., 2010; Play-by-Play Football, 2004; Barry Bonds, 2004, rev. ed., 2008; Rally Cars, 2004; ATVs, 2004; Hydroplane Boats, 2004; Yao Ming, 2005, rev. ed., 2009; X Games: Skateboarding's Greatest Event, 2005; Vert skating: Mastering The Ramp, 2005; Sammy Sosa, 2005; Street Skating: Grinds and Grabs, 2005; Tony Hawk: Skateboarding Legend, 2005; Annika Sorenstam, 2005; Carly Patterson, 2005; Lisa Leslie: Slam Dunk Queen, 2005; Dale Earnhardt, Jr., 2006, rev. ed., 2009; David Ortiz, 2006, rev. ed., 2010; Freddy Adu, 2006; LeBron James, 2006, rev. ed., 2012; Michael Vick, 2006, rev. ed., 2012; Thrill Rides!: All About Roller Coasters, 2006, Tom Brady, 2006, rev. ed., 2009; Travis Pastrana, 2006; Dave Mirra, 2007; Dallas Friday, 2007; Danica Patrick, 2007, rev. ed., 2010; Michelle Wie, 2007; Albert Pujols, 2007; Steve Nash, 2007; Dwyane Wade, 2007; Oscar De la Hoya: The Golden Boy, 2007; Muhammad Ali: The Greatest, 2007; David Beckham, 2008; Maria Sharapova, 2008; Ryan Howard, 2008, rev. ed., 2012; James Stewart, 2008; Roger Federer, 2009; Sidney Crosby, 2009; Eli Manning, 2009, rev. ed., 2013; Josh Hamilton, 2009; Brian Urlacher, 2010; LaDainian Tomlinson, 2010; Chris Paul, 2010; Tim Duncan, 2010; Choppers, 2010; Monster Trucks, 2010; Dwight Howard, 2011; Adrian Peterson, 2011; Tuner Cars, 2011; Roy Halladay, 2011; Tony Romo, 2011; Top 25 Hockey Skills, Tips, and Tricks, 2011; Brett Favre, 2011; Drew Brees, 2011, rev. ed., 2013; Alex Ovechkin, 2012; Mark Sanchez, 2012; Top 25 Soccer Skills, Tips, and Tricks, 2012; Aaron Rodgers, 2012; Tim Lincecum, 2012; Fearless Scouts, 2012; Maya Moore, 2012; Top 25 Gymnastics Skills, Tips, and Tricks, 2012; Tito Ortiz, 2012; American Cowboys, 2012; Pioneering Women, 2012; Daring Pony Express Riders, 2012; Calvin Johnson, 2012; Kevin Durant, 2012; Prince Fielder, 2012; Quick-Draw Gunfighters, 2012; Rugged Gold Miners, 2012; Tim Tebow, 2013. **Address:** Savage Books, 2740 Aberdeen Ln., El Dorado Hills, CA 95762-5667, U.S.A. **Online address:** jeff@jeffsavage.com

SAVAGE, Kirk. American (born United States), b. 1958. **Genres:** Art/Art History, History. **Career:** University of Pittsburgh, Department of History of Art and Architecture, assistant professor, 1990-98, associate professor, 1998-, professor, chair, 2004-; College of William and Mary, visiting assistant professor, 1991-93. Writer. **Publications:** Standing Soldiers, Kneeling Slaves: Race, War and Monument in Nineteenth-Century America, 1997; Monument Wars: Washington, D.C., The National Mall, and The Transformation of the Memorial Landscape, 2009. **Address:** Department of History, University of Pittsburgh, 104 Frick Fine Arts, Pittsburgh, PA 15260, U.S.A. **Online address:** ksa@pitt.edu

SAVAGE, (Maria) Ania. American/Ukranian (born Ukraine), b. 1941. **Genres:** Autobiography/Memoirs, Travel/Exploration. **Career:** Journal-News, reporter, 1964-66, legislative correspondent and political reporter,

1966-68; Record, reporter, 1968-70, environmental reporter, 1970-72; freelance editor, 1972-; Kyiv State University, journalism instructor, 1991; University of Denver, lecturer in media, film and journalism studies, lecturer in mass communication, advisor to student newspaper; Time-Life Books, staff; Gannett Syndicate, staff; Rocky Mountain News, staff. **Publications:** (Ed.) The Colorado Mountain Club Pocket Guide to the Colorado 14ers, 1997; Return to Ukraine, 2000; Walkin' the Dog, Denver (hiking guide), 2001; (trans.) M.S. Pyskir, Thousands of Roads: A Memoir of a Young Woman's Life in the Ukrainian Underground During and After World War II, 2001; Best Hikes With Dogs Colorado, 2005. Contributor to periodicals. **Address:** Department of Media, Film & Journalism Studies, University of Denver, Rm. 122A, 2490 S Gaylord St., Denver, CO 80208, U.S.A. **Online address:** asavage@du.edu

SAVAGE, Roz. British (born England), b. 1967. **Genres:** Natural History. **Career:** Writer, motivational speaker, environmental advocate and consultant. **Publications:** Rowing the Atlantic: Lessons Learned on the Open Ocean, 2009. **Address:** Simon & Schuster, 1230 Ave. of the Americas, 11th Fl., New York, NY 10020, U.S.A.

SAVAGE, Sean J. American (born United States), b. 1964. **Genres:** Politics/Government, History, Law, International Relations/Current Affairs, Social Sciences. **Career:** Curry College, lecturer, 1987; Regis College, lecturer, 1989-90; Saint Mary's College, assistant professor, 1990-96, associate professor of political science, 1996-2006, professor 2006-. Radio, TV commentator and writer. **Publications:** Roosevelt: The Party Leader, 1932-1945, 1991; Truman and the Democratic Party, 1997; JFK, LBJ, and the Democratic Party, 2004. Contributor to books and journals. **Address:** Department of Political Science, St. Mary's College, Spes Unica 247, Notre Dame, IN 46556, U.S.A. **Online address:** ssavage@saintmarys.edu

SAVAGE, Tom. (T. J. Phillips). American (born United States), b. 1948. **Genres:** Novels, Mystery/Crime/Suspense, Literary Criticism And History, Young Adult Fiction. **Career:** Writer. **Publications:** Precipice, 1994; (as T.J. Phillips) Dance of the Mongoose, 1995; Valentine, 1996; (as T.J. Phillips) Woman in the Dark, 1997; The Inheritance, 1998; Scavenger, 2000. Contributor to periodicals. **Address:** Berkley Publishing, 375 Hudson St., New York, NY 10014-3658, U.S.A.

SAVARD, Jeannine. American (born United States), b. 1950. **Genres:** Novels, Poetry. **Career:** United States Air Force Base, teaching assistant, 1972; Big Cross Street School, teacher, 1973; Queensbury Middle School, teacher, 1973; Kenilworth School, part-time instructor, 1975-76; Seton High School, instructor, 1976-78; Deerfield School for the Emotionally Handicapped, instructor, 1979; University of New Hampshire, graduate teaching assistant, 1979-80; The Loft Press, consulting editor, 1982; Arizona State University, College of Liberal Arts and Sciences, Department of English, Creative Writing Program, lecturer, 1983-85, faculty associate, 1985-88, assistant professor, 1989-96, associate professor of English, 1996-. **Publications:** Snow Water Cove, 1988; Trumpeter, 1993; My Hand upon Your Name, 2005; Accounted For: Poems, 2011. **Address:** Department of English, Arizona State University, Rm. 315A, 851 S Cady Mall, PO Box 870302, Tempe, AZ 85287-0302, U.S.A. **Online address:** jeannine.savard@asu.edu

SAVARIN, Julian Jay. British (born England) **Genres:** Novels, Mystery/Crime/Suspense, Young Adult Fiction. **Career:** Writer and musician. **Publications:** NOVELS: Arena, 1979; Waterhole, 1982; Lynx, 1984; Wolf Run, 1984; Gunship, 1985; Windshear, 1985; Naja, 1987; Hammerhead, 1987; Red Gunship, 1988; The Quiraing List, 1988; Trophy, 1989; Villiger, 1991; Target Down!, 1991; Pale Flyer, 1994; The Queensland File, 1994; Typhoon Strike, 1996; Horsemen in the Shadows, 1996; Strike Eagle, 1997; Norwegian Fire, 1998; Starfire, 2000. OTHERS: Waiters on the Dance, 1976; Beyond the Outer Mirr, 1976; The Archives of Haven, 1976; MacAllister's Run, 1995; MacAllister's Task, 1997; A Cold Rain in Berlin, 2002; Romeo Summer, 2003; Winter and the General, 2003; Hunters Rain, 2004; A Hot Day in May, 2004; Summer of the Eagle, 2005; Seasons of Change, 2005; The Other Side of Eden, 2006; Sunset and the Major, 2007. **Address:** Severn House Publishers Ltd., 9-15 High St., Sutton, SR SM1 1DF, England.

SAVIANO, Roberto. Italian (born Italy), b. 1979. **Genres:** Translations. **Career:** L'espresso and La Repubblica, journalist. **Publications:** Gomorra: Viaggio nell'impero economico e nel sogno di dominio della camorra, 2006 in US as Gomorrah, 2007; (co-author) A occhi aperti: le nuove voci della narrativa italiana raccontano la realtaà, 2008; (co-author) Sei fuori posto: storie italiane, 2010; (co-author) Vieni via con me, 2011. Contributor to periodicals. **Address:** Naples, Italy.

SAVILLE, Andrew. *See* **TAYLOR, Andrew (John Robert).**

SAVILLE, Diana. British (born England), b. 1943. **Genres:** Novels, Design, Homes/Gardens, Romance/Historical, Literary Criticism And History. **Career:** A.D. Peters, literary agent, 1970-74; writer, 1974-; BBC-TV, researcher; British Foreign Office, researcher. **Publications:** NOVELS: The Marriage Bed, 1996; The Honey Makers, 1997; The Hawk Dancer, 1997. OTHER: The Observer's Book of British Gardens, 1982; Walled Gardens: Their Planting and Design, 1982; The Illustrated Garden Planter, 1986; Gardens for Small Country Houses, 1988; Colour, 1992; (ed. and intro.) Green and Pleasant Land: A Thousand Years of Poetry (anthology of poems and paintings), 1993; Walls and Screens, 1994. Contributor to magazines and newspapers. **Address:** Sterling Lord Literistic Inc., 65 Bleecker St., New York, NY 10012, U.S.A.

SAVIR, Uri. Israeli/American (born United States), b. 1953. **Genres:** International Relations/Current Affairs. **Career:** Israel's Embassy in Ottawa, communication and press officer, 1980-83; Office of Foreign Minister, director, 1986-88; Israel's consul general, 1988-92; Ministry of Foreign Affairs, director general, 1993-96, general manager and administrator; Peres Center for Peace, founder, 1996, director general, 1996-99, president, 1999-, head; Glocal Forum, president, 2001-; Shimon Peres, director; Oslo Accords, chief negotiator. Writer. **Publications:** Process: 1, 100 Days That Changed the Middle East, 1998; ha-Tahalikh: Me-haḥore ha-ḳelim shel Hakhráah Hisṭorit, 1998; Mar Yiśre'eli bi-veḥirot 2006, 2006; ḳodem Shalom: Modernizatsyah Shel Tahalikhe Shalom, 2007; Peace First: A New Model to End Ear, 2008. **Address:** Random House, 201 East 50th St., New York, NY 10022, U.S.A.

SAVITZKAYA, Eugne. Belgian (born Belgium), b. 1955. **Genres:** Novels, Young Adult Fiction, Poetry. **Career:** Writer. **Publications:** Le Coeur de Schiste, 1974; Rue Obscure, 1975; Mongolie Plaine Sale, 1976; L'Empire, 1976; Mentir: Roman, 1977; Un jeune homme trop gors, 1978; La traversée de lAfrique, 1979; Les Couleurs de Boucheries: Poèmes, 1980; La Disparition de Maman, 1982; Les Morts Sentent Bon, 1983; Veulerie, 1984; Quatorze cataclysmes, 1985; Bufo Bufo Bufo, 1986; Capolican: Un Secret de Fabrication, 1987; Sang de Chien, 1988; La Folie Originelle, 1991; Marin Mon Coeur, 1992; Mongolie Plaine Sale; L'Empire; Rue obscure, 1993; Alain le Bras, 1993; En Vie, 1994; Jérôme Bosch & Eugène Savitzkaya, 1994; Ecorces: Jean-Dominique Burton, 1994; Cochon Farci, 1996; Ketelslegers, 1997; Mamouze, 1998; Cénotaphe: pomes inédits-1973, 1998; Saperlotte!, 1998; Fou civil, 1999; Célébration d'un mariage improbable et illimité, 2002; Exquise Louise: Roman, 2003; Rules of Solitude, 2004; Fou Trop Poli, 2005. **Address:** Quale Press L.L.C., 93 Main St., Ste. 2, PO Box 511, Florence, MA 01062, U.S.A.

SAVREN, Shelley. American (born United States), b. 1949. **Genres:** Poetry. **Career:** Gavilan College, part-time teacher, 1975; San Diego Community College District, part-time teacher, 1976; University of California, extension teacher, 1976; Southwestern College, part-time teacher, 1989-92; Oxnard College, professor of English, 1992-. Writer. **Publications:** Gathering My Belongings, 1983; Photo Album, 1987; The Common Fire, 2004. Contributor to magazines. **Address:** Oxnard College, 4000 S Rose Ave., Oxnard, CA 93033-6699, U.S.A. **Online address:** ssavren@vcccd.edu

SAWATSKY, John. Canadian (born Canada), b. 1948. **Genres:** Writing/Journalism, Biography, Politics/Government, Social Sciences. **Career:** Vancouver Sun, reporter, 1970-74, Ottawa correspondent; British Columbia Petroleum Corp., research coordinator, 1974-75; Vancouver Sun, parliamentary correspondent, 1975-79; freelance journalist and author, 1979-; University of Regina, professor, 1984-85; Carleton University, sessional lecturer, 1985-89, adjunct professor, 1990-; Canadian Broadcasting Corp., consultant, 1991-; ESPN, director of talent development, senior director of talent development, 2004-, trainer. **Publications:** Men in the Shadows: The RCMP Security Service, 1980; For Services Rendered: Leslie James Bennett and the RCMP Security Service (biography), 1982; Gouzenko: The Untold Story (biography), 1984; The Insiders: Government, Business, and the Lobbyists (politics), 1987 as The Insiders: Power, Money and Secrets in Ottawa, 1989; Mulroney: The Politics of Ambition, 1991. Contributor to periodicals. **Address:** School of Journalism and Communication, Carleton University, 346 St. Patricks, 1125 Colonel By Dr., Ottawa, ON K1S 5B6, Canada.

SAWREY, Robert D. American (born United States), b. 1948. **Genres:** History, Young Adult Fiction. **Career:** Monarch Machine Tool Co., corporate archivist and historian, 1977-79; West Virginia University, visiting assistant professor of history, 1979-80; Marshall University, assistant professor, 1980-85, associate professor, 1985-90, professor of American history, 1990-. Writer. **Publications:** Dubious Victory: The Reconstruction Debate in Ohio, 1992; Our Spiritual Home: A History of Enslow Park Presbyterian Church, 1949-1999, 2000. **Address:** Department of History, Marshall University, 124 Harris Hall, 1 John Marshall Dr., Huntington, WV 25755, U.S.A. **Online address:** sawrey@marshall.edu

SAWYER, Cheryl. New Zealander (born New Zealand), b. 1947?. **Genres:** Young Adult Fiction, Cultural/Ethnic Topics, Science Fiction/Fantasy. **Career:** University of Auckland, French language and literature, faculty. Writer and publisher. **Publications:** La Créole, 1998; Rebel, 2000; Siren, 2005; The Chase, 2005; The Code of Love, 2006; The Winter Prince, 2007; The Propagation of Fire, forthcoming; Farewell Cavaliers, forthcoming. **Address:** Nelson Literary Agency, 1732 Wazee St., Ste. 207, Denver, CO 80202, U.S.A. **Online address:** cheryl@cherylsawyer.com

SAWYER, (Frederick) Don(ald). Canadian/American (born United States), b. 1947. **Genres:** Children's Fiction, Education, Young Adult Fiction, Adult Non-fiction, Novels, Humor/Satire, Reference, Politics/Government, Politics/Government. **Career:** Musgrave Harbour, high school teacher, 1970-72; Michigan State University, Institute for International Studies in Education, research assistant, 1972-73; high school teacher in Lytton, 1973-75; Spallumcheen Indian Band, Adult Basic Education Program, coordinating teacher, 1976-78; Simon Fraser University, faculty associate in charge of North Okanagan Native Teacher Education Program, 1978-80, instructor, 1981-82; Okanagan University College, Salmon Arm Centre, instructor in adult basic education, 1980-88, ABE department chair, 1993-2000, developer and coordinator of West African development projects, International Development Institute, director, 2000-04; Ministry of Advanced Education and Job Training, curriculum project leader, 1983-84, 1986; Native Adult Education Resource Centre, Salmon Arm, curriculum director, 1988-93; Northern Education Services Associates, principal, 1993-; Workplace ABE program, developer and coordinator, 1996-; AUCC West Africa Rural Development Centre, trainer for African facilitators on several education programs and coordinator, 1999. Writer. **Publications:** Tomorrow Is School and I Am Sick to the Heart Thinking about It, 1979, as Tomorrow Is School, 1984; (comp. with H. Green) The NESA Bibliography for Native American Studies, 1983; (with H. Green) NESA Activities Handbook for Native and Multicultural Classrooms, vol. I, 1984, vol. II (with A. Napoleon), 1990, vol. III (with W. Lundberg), 1993; Where the Rivers Meet, 1988; Donna Meets Coyote, 1988; Miss Haack Stories, 1990; Running, 1991; Adventures with Miss Flint, 1993; The Buckle, Crocodiles & Rivers, Frozen Tears, The Buckle, 1997; Grampa & The Four Brothers: A Modern Adaptation of a Traditional Salish Story, 1998; More Adventures with Miss Flint, 2000. Contributor to magazines. **Address:** Northern Education Services Associates, PO Box 2653, Salmon Arm, BC V1E 4R5, Canada. **Online address:** donsawyer@telus.net

SAWYER, Kathy. American (born United States) **Genres:** Air/Space Topics, Astronomy, Sciences, Geography. **Career:** Tennessean, feature writer; Washington Post, reporter, 1986-2003. **Publications:** The Rock from Mars: A Detective Story on Two Planets, 2006. Contributor to periodicals. **Address:** c/o Author Mail, Random House Inc., 1745 Broadway, New York, NY 10019-4368, U.S.A. **Online address:** kathy@kathysawyer.com

SAWYER, Keith. (Robert Keith Sawyer). American (born United States), b. 1960?. **Genres:** Adult Non-fiction. **Career:** General Computer Corp., project manager and video game designer, 1982-84; Kenan Systems Corp. (information technology management), principal manager, 1984-90, consultant, 1991-93; University of Chicago, lecturer, 1993-94; University of California, postdoctoral fellow in developmental research, 1995-96; Washington University, Department of Education, assistant professor, 1996-2003, associate professor, 2003-, Department Of Psychology, adjunct associate professor, 1997-, professor of psychology and education, Philosophy-Neuroscience-Psychology Program, affiliated professor, 1997-, Social Thought and Analysis Program, affiliated professor, 1997-2006, Olin School of Business, adjunct associate professor, 2007-; Culpeper Consulting Group, senior consultant, 1994-95; Central Institute for the Deaf, affiliated professor, 1999-; Savannah College of Art & Design, visiting professor, 2010; University of Exeter, honorary visiting professor, 2010-. Writer. **Publications:** Pretend Play as Improvisation:

Conversation in the Preschool Classroom, 1997; (ed.) Creativity in Performance, 1997; Creating Conversations: Improvisation in Everyday Discourse, 2001; Creativity and Development, 2003; Group Creativity: Music, Theater, Collaboration, 2003; Improvised Dialogues: Emergence and Creativity in Conversation, 2003; Social Emergence: Societies as Complex Systems, 2005; (ed.) The Cambridge Handbook of the Learning Sciences, 2006; Explaining Creativity: The Science of Human Innovation, 2006, 2nd ed., 2012; Group Genius: The Creative Power of Collaboration, 2007. CONTRIBUTOR: Innovative Applications of Artificial Intelligence, 1989; Sociological Studies of Children, vol. VII, 1995; Encyclopedia of Creativity, 1999; Critical Creative Processes, 2003; Faces of the Muse, 2005; Encyclopedia of Social Theory, 2006; Cambridge Handbook of the Learning Sciences, 2006; Play and Literacy in Early Childhood: Research from Multiple Perspectives, 2007; The Sage Handbook of Social Science Methodology, 2007; (ed.) Structure and Improvisation in Creative Teaching, 2011. Contributor to books, periodicals and journals. **Address:** Department of Education, Washington University, 140 Seigle Hall, 1 Brookings Dr., PO Box 1183, St. Louis, MO 63130, U.S.A. **Online address:** ksawyer@wustl.edu

SAWYER, Kem Knapp. American (born United States), b. 1953. **Genres:** Children's Fiction, Young Adult Fiction, Children's Non-fiction, Young Adult Non-fiction. **Career:** Corcoran College of Art & Design, faculty advisor, writing teacher; Design Information Alliance, board director. Educator and writer. **Publications:** The National Foundation on the Arts and the Humanities, 1989; The U.S. Arms Control and Disarmament Agency, 1990; Lucretia Mott: Friend of Justice, 1991, 2nd ed., 1998; Marjory Stoneman Douglas: Guardian of the Everglades, 1994; Refugees: Seeking a Safe Haven, 1995; The Underground Railroad in American History, 1997; (ed.) Irish Americans, 1998; Freedom Calls: Journey of a Slave Girl, 2001; Anne Frank, 2004; Eleanor Roosevelt, 2006; Abigail Adams, 2009; Harriet Tubman, 2010; Champion of Freedom: Nelson Mandela, 2011; The Amazing Underground Railroad, 2012; Champion of Freedom: Mohandas Gandhi, 2012. **Address:** Corcoran College of Art & Design, 1801 35th St. NW, Washington, DC 20007, U.S.A. **Online address:** kemsawyer@clevelandpark.com

SAWYER, Mary R. American (born United States), b. 1944. **Genres:** Theology/Religion, Sociology, Social Sciences, History. **Career:** Iowa State University, assistant professor, 1986-92, associate professor of religious studies, 1992-, professor-in-charge, professor of philosophy and religious studies. Writer. **Publications:** Black Ecumenism: Implementing the Demands of Justice, 1994; The Church on the Margins: Living Christian Community, 2003; (ed. with R. Moore and A.B. Pinn) Peoples Temple and Black Religion in America, 2004. **Address:** Religious Studies Program, Department of Philosophy and Religious Studies, Iowa State University, 413 Catt Hall, Ames, IA 50011, U.S.A. **Online address:** sawyerm@iastate.edu

SAWYER, Ralph D. American (born United States) **Genres:** History, Popular Culture, Military/Defense/Arms Control, Translations. **Career:** Sawyer Strategic Consultants, president; University of Massachusetts, senior research fellow, 2003-07; Centre for Military and Strategic Studies, fellow, 2003-. Writer. **Publications:** (With P. Townsend) The Ancient World: A Reading and Writing Approach, 1983; (trans. and intro. with M.C. Sawyer) The Seven Military Classics of Ancient China, 1993; (trans. and intro. with M.C. Sawyer) Sunzi, The Art of War, 1994; (trans. and intro. with M.C. Sawyer) Ling Ch'i Ching: A Classic Chinese Oracle, 1995; (trans. and intro. with M.C. Sawyer) Sun Pin Military Methods, 1995; (trans. and intro. with M.C. Sawyer) The Art of the Warrior: Leadership and Strategy from the Chinese Military Classics: With Selections from the Seven Military Classics of Ancient China and Sun Pin's Military Methods, 1996; (trans. and intro. with M.C. Sawyer) Sunzi, The Complete Art of War, 1996; (trans. and intro. with M.C. Sawyer) One Hundred Unorthodox Strategies: Battle and Tactics of Chinese Warfare, 1996; (trans. and intro. with M.C. Sawyer) Unorthodox Strategies for the Everyday Warrior, 1996; (trans. and intro. with M.C. Sawyer) Shang LU, The Six Secret Teachings on the Way of Strategy, 1997; (with M.C. Sawyer) The Tao of Spycraft: Intelligence Theory and Practice in Traditional China, 1998; (trans. and intro. with M.C. Sawyer) The Tao of Peace: Lessons from Ancient China on the Dynamics of Conflict, 1999; (with M.C. Sawyer) Fire and Water: The Art of Incendiary and Aquatic Warfare in China, 2004; (with M.C. Sawyer) Sunzi, The Essential Art of War, 2005; (with M.C. Sawyer) The Tao of Deception: Unorthodox Warfare in Historic and Modern China, 2007; Ancient Chinese Warfare, 2011. **Address:** PO Box 56, Orleans, MA 02653, U.S.A. **Online address:** sawyer@ralphsawyer.com

SAWYER, Robert J(ames). Canadian/American (born United States), b. 1960. **Genres:** Science Fiction/Fantasy, Mystery/Crime/Suspense, Novels. **Career:** Ryerson Polytechnical Institute, teaching assistant, 1982-83; Canadian Broadcasting Corp. (CBC), freelance radio documentary writer and narrator, 1984-; Discovery Channel, monthly columnist, 1997-98; ScienceFACTion, weekly syndicated radio columnist, 2002-; Robert J. Sawyer Books, editor, 2004-; Supernatural Investigator, host 17-part series Vision TV, 2009; FlashForward, consultant ABC TV show, 2009-10. **Publications:** SCIENCE FICTION: Golden Fleece, 1990, rev. ed., 1999; Far-Seer, 1992, rev. ed., 2004; Fossil Hunter, 1993, rev. ed., 2005; Foreigner, 1994, rev. ed., 2005; End of an Era, 1994, rev. ed., 2001; (ed. with C. Clink) Early Harvest Magazine: Young Adult Collection of Short Stories and Poetry, 1994; The Terminal Experiment, 1995; Starplex, 1996; Frameshift, 1997; Illegal Alien, 1997; (ed. with C. Clink) Tesseracts 6: The Annual Anthology of New Canadian Speculative Fiction, 1997; Factoring Humanity, 1998, rev. ed., 2004; (ed. with D. Skene-Melvin) Crossing the Line: Canadian Mysteries with a Fantastic Twist, 1998; Flash Forward, 1999, rev. ed., 2009; Calculating God, 2000; (ed. with P. Sellers) Over the Edge: The Crime Writers of Canada Anthology, 2000; Iterations, 2002; Hominids, 2002; Humans, 2003; Hybrids, 2003; Mindscan, 2005; (ed. with D. Gerrold) Boarding The Enterprise: Transporters, Tribbles, and The Vulcan Death Grip In Gene Roddenberry's Star Trek, 2006; Rollback, 2007; Identity Theft and Other Stories, 2008; (ed.) Distant Early Warnings: Canada's Best Science Fiction, 2009; Wake, 2009; Watch, 2010; Wonder, 2011; Triggers, 2012. **Address:** Red Deer Press, 195 Allstate Parkway, Markham, ON L3R 4T8, Canada. **Online address:** sawyer@sfwriter.com

SAWYER, Robert Keith. See **SAWYER, Keith.**

SAWYER, Roger. British (born England), b. 1931. **Genres:** Civil Liberties/Human Rights, History, Race Relations, Cultural/Ethnic Topics, Politics/Government, Women's Studies And Issues, Biography. **Career:** Forton House Preparatory School, assistant master, 1950-52; Blue Coat School, housemaster, 1958-60; Bembridge Preparatory School, deputy head, 1960-77, headmaster, 1977-83; University of London, examiner in English, 1965-; Royal Life Saving Society, chairman of Isle, 1978; writer, 1983-. **Publications:** Casement: The Flawed Hero, 1984; Slavery in the Twentieth Century, 1986; Children Enslaved, 1988; The Island from Within, 1990; We are but Women: Women in Ireland's History, 1993; (ed.) Roger Casement's Diaries 1910: The Black and the White, 1997. Contributor of articles to periodicals. **Address:** Routledge, 7625 Empire Dr., Florence, KY 41042-2919, U.S.A.

SAWYER, Suzana. American (born United States), b. 1961. **Genres:** History, Business/Trade/Industry, Sociology, Politics/Government. **Career:** University of California, Department of Anthropology, associate professor; United Nations Research Institute for Social Development, project leader, 2006-. Writer. **Publications:** Crude Chronicles: Indigenous Politics, Multinational Oil and Neoliberalism in Ecuador, 2004; (with E.T. Gomez) Transnational Governmentality and Resource Extraction: Indigenous Peoples, Multinational Corporations, Multilateral Institutions and the State, 2008. Contributor to books. **Address:** Department of Anthropology, University of California, 317 Young Hall, 1 Shields Ave., Davis, CA 95616-8522, U.S.A. **Online address:** smsawyer@ucdavis.edu

SAWYER-LAUCANNO, Christopher. American (born United States), b. 1951. **Genres:** Poetry, Business/Trade/Industry, Language/Linguistics, Literary Criticism And History, Biography, Translations. **Career:** Human Factors Research Inc., field researcher, 1973-74; Brandeis University, part-time instructor in French and Spanish, 1974-77; Dean Jr. College, instructor in foreign languages and English, 1977-80; Time-Life Educational Systems Co., staff writer, 1980-82; Meiji Gakuin University, part-time instructor in English and linguistics, 1981-82; Massachusetts Institute of Technology, lecturer in foreign languages and literature, 1982-90, Program in Writing and Humanistic Studies, writer-in-residence, 1991-2006, retired, 2006; Naropa Institute Summer Writing Program, writer-in-residence, 1989; McCann-Erickson, advertising copywriter; Overseas Research and Development Inc., consultant; Laboratory Technologies Corp., consultant. Freelance technical translator. **Publications:** (Ed.) On Wind and Wave: Poems by Children, 1970; English for Daily Living, 1980; Imaginative Situations, 1980; English Skills Development Course, 2 vols., 1981; Ongoing English, vol. I, A Basic Course, vol. II, An Intermediate Course, 1981; English Communication Workshop, 1981; Yamaha Technical Training Course, 1982; Cases in International Business, 1982; Curso Tecnico Basico, 1982; A Glossary of Business English, 1983; Case Studies in International Management, 1985; An Invisible Spectator: A

Biography of Paul Bowles, 1989; The Continual Pilgrimage: American Writers in Paris, 1944-1960, 1992; The World's Words: A Semiotic Reading of Joyce and Rabelais, 1993; Les Mots Anglais, 2001; E.E. Cummings: A Biography, 2004. CONTRIBUTOR: Learning to Use Black: Painted Poems, 1987; Simulation, Gaming and Language Learning, 1990. TRANSLATOR: The Destruction of the Jaguar, 1987; Barbarous Nights: Legends and the Little Theater, 1992; Concerning the Angels, 1995; The Life of Lazarillo de Tormes, 1997; Demons and Spirits: Contemporary Chol Mayan Chants and Incantations, 1997; (with M. Polizzotti) M. Ray, B. Peret and L. Aragon, 1929, 1996; The Incident, 1998. Contributor of articles to books and periodicals. **Address:** Roslyn Targ Literary Agency, 105 W 13th St., New York, NY 10011, U.S.A. **Online address:** csl@mit.edu

SAX, Boria. American (born United States), b. 1949. **Genres:** Humanities, Mythology/Folklore, History, Language/Linguistics, Intellectual History. **Career:** Pace University, adjunct professor of German, 1982-92; American Online, faculty, 1996-2000; Mercy College, instructor in English and philosophy, 1985-, adjunct professor of English, 1986-, Center for Independent Learning, coordinator, 1993-99, director of online research and development, 1999-2006; New York Botanical Garden, instructor, 1997-; Metropolitan University, faculty, 1999-2002; University of Illinois, adjunct faculty, 2005-; Sing Sing Prison, college instructor, 2005-; Berkeley College, adjunct faculty, 2006-09. **Publications:** The Romantic Heritage of Marxism: A Study of East German Love Poetry, 1987; The Frog King: On Legends, Fables, Fairy Tales, and Anecdotes of Animals, 1990; The Parliament of Animals: Anecdotes and Legends from Books of Natural History, 1775-1900, 1992; Sir Gawain and the Green Knight, 1996; Thomas Mann's Death in Venice, 1996; William Faulkner's The Sound and the Fury, 1996; The Serpent and the Swan: The Animal Bride in Folklore and Literature, 1998; (ed. and trans. with I. von Tannenberg) L. Rathenow, The Fantastic, Ordinary World of Lutz Rathenow: Poems, Plays, and Stories, 2000; Animals in the Third Reich: Pets, Scapegoats, and the Holocaust, 2000; The Mythical Zoo: An Encyclopedia of Animals in World Myth, Legend, and Literature, 2001; Crow, 2003; City of Ravens: The True Story of the Legendary Birds in the Tower of London, 2011; The Raven and the Sun: Poems and Stories, 2011. **Address:** Department of Civic and Cultural Studies, Mercy College, 555 Broadway, Dobbs Ferry, NY 10522, U.S.A. **Online address:** bsax@mercy.edu

SAXON, Antonia. See SACHS, Judith.

SAXTON, Josephine (Howard). British (born England), b. 1935. **Genres:** Science Fiction/Fantasy, Novellas/Short Stories, Homes/Gardens, Novels, Women's Studies And Issues, Horticulture. **Career:** Writer. **Publications:** The Hieros Gamos of Sam and An Smith, 1969; Vector for Seven: Or The Weltanschaung of Mrs. Amelia Mortimer and Friends, 1970; The Group Feast, 1971; The Travails of Jane Saint, 1980; The Power of Time, 1985; Little Tours of Hell: Tales of Food and Holidays, 1986; The Queen of the States, 1986; The Travails of Jane Saint and Other Stories, 1986; (with J. Russ) Woman Space: Future and Fantasy Stories and Art by Women, 1986; Jane Saint and the Backlash: The Further Travails of Jane Saint, with The Consciousness Machine, 1989; Gardening down a Rabbit Hole, 1996, vol. II, forthcoming. Contributor to periodicals. Works appear in anthologies. **Address:** 12 Plymouth Pl., Leamington Spa, WW CV31 1HN, England.

SAXTON, Judith. See TURNER, Judith.

SAY, Allen. American/Japanese (born Japan), b. 1937. **Genres:** Children's Fiction. **Career:** EIZO Press, publisher, 1968; commercial photographer and illustrator, 1969-. Writer. **Publications:** FOR CHILDREN: Dr. Smith's Safari, 1972; Once under the Cherry Blossom Tree: An Old Japanese Tale, 1974; The Feast of Lanterns, 1976; The Bicycle Man, 1982; A River Dream, 1988; The Lost Lake, 1989; El Chino, 1990; Tree of Cranes, 1991; Grandfather's Journey, 1993; Stranger in the Mirror, 1995; Emma's Rug, 1996; Allison, 1997. FOR YOUNG ADULTS: The Ink-Keeper's Apprentice, 1979. OTHER: Tea with Milk, 1999; Sign Painter, 2000; Home of the Brave, 2002; Music for Alice, 2004; Kamishibai Man, 2005; Erika-San, 2009; The Boy in the Garden, 2010; Drawing from Memory, 2011. Contributor to periodicals. Illustrator of books by others. **Address:** c/o Author Mail, Houghton Mifflin Co., 222 Berkeley St., Boston, MA 02116, U.S.A.

SAYER, Ian (Keith Terence). British (born England), b. 1945. **Genres:** Military/Defense/Arms Control, History, Biography. **Career:** Sayer Transport Group, managing director, 1967-79; International Parcels Express Co.

(IPEC), director, 1979-83; Worldwide Autographs Ltd., director, 1979-89; Ian Sayer Transport Consultants, director, 1983-88; Citylink Transport Holdings Ltd., director, 1984-87; Northern Ireland Airports Ltd., director, 1988-94; FRX International Ltd., managing director, 1988-98. Writer. **Publications:** WITH D. BOTTING: Nazi Gold, 1984; America's Secret Army: The Untold Story of the Counter Intelligence Corps, 1989; Hitler's Last General: The Case against Wilhelm Mohnke, 1989; (ed.) Hitler's Bastard: Through Hell and Back in Nazi Germany and Stalin's Russia, 2003; Hitler and Women: The Love Life of Adolf Hitler, 2004; Women Who Knew Hitler: The Private Life of Adolf Hitler, 2004. Contributor to periodicals and newspapers. **Address:** Westerlands, Sherbourne Dr., Sunningdale, BR SL5 0LG, England. **Online address:** ian@sayer.net

SAYER, Mandy Jane. Australian (born Australia), b. 1963. **Genres:** Novels, Novellas/Short Stories, Plays/Screenplays, Autobiography/Memoirs, Essays, Biography, Young Adult Fiction, Children's Fiction, Children's Fiction. **Career:** The Bill Evans Dance Co., dancer, 1987-89. Writer. **Publications:** NOVELS: Mood Indigo, 1989; Blind Luck, 1993; The Cross, 1995. OTHERS: Dreamtime Alice: A Memoir, 1998; (ed. with L. Nowra) In the Gutter-Looking at the Stars: A Literary Adventure through Kings Cross, 2000; 15 Kinds of Desire (stories), 2001; Velocity: A Memoir, 2005; (ed.) Australian Long Story, 2009; Love in the Years of Lunacy, 2011. Contributor to periodicals. **Address:** c/o Gaby Naher, Naher Agency, PO Box 249, Paddington, NW 2021, Australia. **Online address:** sayerm@ozemail.com.au

SAYERS, Janet. British (born England), b. 1945. **Genres:** Psychiatry, Psychology. **Career:** Tavistock Clinic, clinical psychologist, 1968-70; St. Augustine's Hospital, clinical psychologist, 1970-71; Child Guidance Clinic, educational psychologist, 1971-73; University of Colorado, Manual High Program, lecturer; University of Kent at Canterbury, lecturer in psychology, 1974-92, professor of psychoanalytic psychology, 1992-; Canterbury and Thanet Health Authority, senior clinical psychologist, 1986-; Cossington Road Clinic, senior clinical psychologist, 1986-; Mount Hollyoke College, Department of Psychology, research associate, 2007-. Writer. **Publications:** Biological Politics: Feminist and Anti-Feminist Perspectives, 1982; Sexual Contradictions: Psychology, Psychoanalysis, and Feminism, 1986; (ed. with M. Evans and N. Redclift) Engels Revisited, 1987: New Feminist Essays; (ed.) V. Klein, The Feminine Character, 1990; Mothers of Psychoanalysis, 1991; (ed. with M.Tremaine) Vision and the reality: Equal Employment Opportunities in the New Zealand Workplace, 1994; The Man Who Never Was: Freudian Tales of Women and Their Men, 1995; Boy Crazy: Remembering Adolescence, Therapies and Dreams, 1998; Kleinians: Psychoanalysis Inside Out, 2000; (ed. with J.S. Williams) Revisioning Duras: Film, Race, Sex, 2000; Divine Therapy: Love, Mysticism and Psychoanalysis, 2003; Freud's Art: Psychoanalysis Retold, 2007. **Address:** School of Social Policy, Sociology and Social, Research, University of Kent, Cornwallis NE, Canterbury, KT CT2 7NF, England. **Online address:** j.v.sayers@kent.ac.uk

SAYERS, Kari. American (born United States), b. 1941. **Genres:** Novellas/Short Stories. **Career:** Marymount College, assistant professor of English, 1986, associate professor, professor. Writer. **Publications:** Views and Values: Diverse Readings on Universal Themes, 1996, 3rd ed., 2005. **Address:** Department of English, Marymount College, 30800 Palos Verdes Dr. E, Rancho Palos Verdes, CA 90275-6299, U.S.A. **Online address:** ksayers@marymountpv.edu

SAYERS, Valerie. American (born United States), b. 1952. **Genres:** Novels, Women's Studies And Issues, Literary Criticism And History. **Career:** University of Notre Dame, professor of English, 1993-. Writer. **Publications:** Due East, 1987; How I Got Him Back, or, Under the Cold Moon's Shine, 1989; Who Do You Love?, 1991; The Distance Between Us, 1994; Brain Fever, 1996. Contributor to periodicals. **Address:** Department of English, University of Notre Dame, 356 O'Shaughnessy Hall, Notre Dame, IN 46556-5639, U.S.A. **Online address:** vsayers@nd.edu

SAYLOR, Steven W(arren). (Aaron Travis). American (born United States), b. 1956. **Genres:** Novellas/Short Stories, Mystery/Crime/Suspense, Novels, Young Adult Fiction, Romance/Historical. **Career:** Fiction editor and literary agent. **Publications:** MYSTERY NOVELS: ROMA SUB ROSA SERIES: Roman Blood, 1991; Arms of Nemesis, 1992; Catilina's Riddle, 1993; The Venus Throw, 1995; Murder on the Appian Way, 1996; House of the Vestals: The Investigations of Gordianus the Finder, 1997; Rubicon, 1999; Last Seen in Massilia, 2000; A Mist of Prophecies, 2002; Judgment of Caesar: A Novel of Ancient Rome, 2004; A Gladiator Dies Only Once: The Further Investigations of Gordianus the Finder, 2005; The Triumph of Caesar, 2008. NOVELS: A Twist at the End: A Novel of O. Henry, 2000; Have You Seen Dawn?, 2003; Roma: The Novel of Ancient Rome, 2007; Empire: The Novel of Imperial Rome, 2010. AS AARON TRAVIS: All-Stud, 1969; Beast of Burden, 1993; Big Shots, 1993; Slaves of the Empire (novel), 1985; Exposed, 1993; In the Blood, 1995; (with C. Caldwell) Tag Team Studs: Wrestling Tales, 1997; (with C. Caldwell) Jock Studs, 1998. **Address:** St. Martin's Press, 175 5th Ave., New York, NY 10010, U.S.A. **Online address:** steven@stevensaylor.com

SAYRAFIEZADEH, Said. American (born United States), b. 1968?. **Genres:** Autobiography/Memoirs. **Career:** Writer. **Publications:** When Skateboards Will Be Free: A Memoir, 2009. **Address:** New York, NY , U.S.A. **Online address:** sayrafiezadeh@gmail.com

SAYRE, Gordon M. American/Swedish (born Sweden), b. 1964. **Genres:** Literary Criticism And History, History. **Career:** Université de Paris VII, Institut Charles V, reader, 1991-92; University of Oregon, Department of English, assistant professor of English, 1993-99, library representative, 1995-2009, associate professor of English, 1999-2006, Graduate Program, job search advisor, 2001-03, director of graduate studies, 2004-06, professor of English, 2006-, University Senate, vice president, 2006-07, president, 2007-08. Writer. **Publications:** Les Sauvages Américains, 1997; (ed.) American Captivity Narratives, 2000; The Indian Chief as Tragic Hero: Native Resistance and the Literatures of America, from Moctezuma to Tecumseh, 2005; (ed. with C. Zecher and S. Dawdy) Dumont de Montigny: Regards sur le monde atlantique, 2008. **Address:** Department of English, University of Oregon, PLC 472, 1286 University of Oregon, 1415 Kincaid St., Eugene, OR 97403, U.S.A. **Online address:** gsayre@uoregon.edu

SAYRE, Shay. American (born United States), b. 1942. **Genres:** Communications/Media, Marketing, Social Commentary, Novellas/Short Stories, Popular Culture, Travel/Exploration, Gerontology/Senior Issues, Photography, Photography. **Career:** Stoorza Communications, account manager, 1975-77; Young and Rubicam Advertising, account executive, 1977-80; San Diego Symphony, marketing director, 1980-82; Menlo College, associate dean of admissions, 1985-87; San Jose State University, associate professor of journalism and mass communication, 1986-92; San Francisco State University, visiting professor of business, 1987-88; California State University, associate professor, 1992-98, coordinator of advertising concentration, 1995-2000; professor of communications, 1998-2009, coordinator of graduate program, 2001-06, professor emeritus, 2009-; Emerson College, visiting professor, 1997-2009. Writer. **Publications:** (With D.A. Horne) Earth, Wind, Fire, and Water: Perspectives on Natural Disaster, 1996; Qualitative Methods for Marketplace Research, 2001; Campaign Planner, 2nd ed., 2002; Entertainment & Society: Audiences, Trends, and Impacts, 2002; Campaign Planner for Integrated Brand Communications, 2005; Entertainment Marketing Prentice Hall, 2008; Entertainment & Society, 2nd ed., 2010; Entertainment Promotion and Communication, 2010. Contributor to books and periodicals. **Address:** California State University, 800 N State College Blvd., Fullerton, CA 92831-3599, U.S.A. **Online address:** shaysayre@cox.net

SCAGLIONE, Aldo. American/Italian (born Italy), b. 1925. **Genres:** Language/Linguistics, Literary Criticism And History, Bibliography, Art/Art History, Essays. **Career:** University of Toulouse, lecturer, 1949-51; University of Chicago, instructor in Italian, 1951-52; University of California, instructor in Italian, 1952-63, professor of Italian, 1963-68; Yale University, visiting professor, 1965-66; University of North Carolina, W.R. Kenan professor of romance languages and comparative literature, 1968-87; City University of New York, professor, 1971-72; University of Wisconsin, Institute for Research in the Humanities, H. Johnson research professor, 1981-82; New York University, Department of Italian, Erich Maria Remarque professor of literature, 1987-, now professor emeritus. Writer. **Publications:** Nature and Love in the Late Middle Ages: An Essay on the Cultural Context of the Decameron, 1963; Ars Grammatica: A Bibliographic Survey, Two Essays on the Grammar of the Latin and Italian Subjunctive, and A Note on the Ablative Absolute, 1970; The Classical Theory of Composition from Its Origins to the Present, 1972; (intro.) The Order of Words in the Ancient Languages Compared With That of the Modern Languages, 1978; The Theory of German Word Order, 1981; Komponierte Prosa von derAntike bis zur Gegenwart, 2 vols., 1981; The Liberal Arts and the Jesuit College System, 1986; Knights at Court: Courtliness, Chivalry and Courtesy in Germany, France and Italy, 1991; Essays on the Arts of Discourse: Linguistics, Rhetoric, Poetics, 1998. EDITOR:

Orlando Innamorato, Amorum Libri, 1951, rev. ed., 1963; Francis Petrarch, Six Centuries Later: A Symposium, 1975; Ariosto 1974 in America: atti del Congresso ariostesco, dicembre 1974, Casa italiana della Columbia University, 1976; The Emergence of National Languages, 1984; (co-ed.) Dante and the Encyclopedia of Arts and Sciences, 1987; (with G.D. Scipio) The Divine Comedy and the Encyclopedia of Arts and Sciences: Acta of the International Dante Symposium, 13-16 November 1983, Hunter College, New York, 1988; The Image of the Baroque, 1995. Contributor of articles to periodicals. **Address:** Department of Italian Studies, New York University, Casa Italiana Zerilli-Marimò, 24 W 12th St., New York, NY 10011-8604, U.S.A. **Online address:** aldo.scaglione@nyu.edu

SCALAPINO, Robert Anthony. See Obituaries.

SCALES, Barbara. American (born United States), b. 1926. **Genres:** Theatre, Sex, Anthropology/Ethnology, Art/Art History, Communications/Media, Cultural/Ethnic Topics, Education, Environmental Sciences/Ecology, Language/Linguistics, Sociology. **Career:** School teacher, 1970-75; Allston Way Mural Arts Project, designer and coordinator, 1974; University of California, instructor in education, Harold E. Jones Child Study Center, head teacher, 1975-90, administrator, 1991-93; Uriarte Project, co-founder and director, 1985; San Francisco State University, part-time faculty, 1989-; Mills College, part-time faculty; Children's Media Laboratory, consultant. Writer. **Publications:** Looking at Children's Play: A Bridge between Theory and Practice, 1987. EDITOR: (with M. Almy, A. Nicolopoulou and S. Ervin-Tripp) Play and the Social Context of Development in Early Care and Education, 1991; (with P. Monighan-Nourot, J. Van Hoorn and K.A. Alward) Play at the Center of the Curriculum, 1992, (with J. Van Hoorn and P. Monighan-Nourot) 5th ed., 2011. Contributor to books. **Address:** Harold E. Jones Child Study Center, Institute of Human Development, University of California, 2425 Atherton, Berkeley, CA 94705, U.S.A. **Online address:** bscales@uclink4.berkeley.edu

SCALES-TRENT, Judy. American (born United States), b. 1940. **Genres:** Politics/Government, Race Relations, Biography, Autobiography/Memoirs. **Career:** Oberlin College Peace Corps Training Program, French teacher, 1962-68; Office of Decisions and Interpretations, Equal Employment Opportunity Commission, supervisory attorney and attorney, 1973-76, special assistant, 1977-79, special assistant, 1979-80, attorney for appellate division, 1980-84; Catholic University Law School, adjunct faculty, 1983; State University of New York, Buffalo Law School, professor of law, 1984-, now professor emeritus; National Conference of Black Lawyers, co- chair of women's rights section, 1985-86; National Women and the Law Association, director, 1987-91; Society of American Law Teachers, governor, 1992-95; St. Mary's University School of law, visiting professor of law, 1994. Writer, poet and professor of law. **Publications:** (With R.V. Friedenberg) Political Campaign Communication: Principles and Practices, 1983, 4th ed., 2000; Notes of a White Black Woman: Race, Color, and Community, 1995. Works appear in anthologies. Contributor to books, periodicals and essays. **Address:** University at Buffalo Law School, State University of New York, 317 O'Brian Hall, North Campus, Buffalo, NY 14260-1100, U.S.A. **Online address:** scalest@buffalo.edu

SCALETTA, Kurtis. American (born United States), b. 1968. **Genres:** Children's Fiction. **Career:** Writer. **Publications:** Mudville, 2009; Mamba Point, 2010. Contributor of stories to magazines. **Address:** PO Box 22151, Minneapolis, MN 55422, U.S.A. **Online address:** kurtis@kurtisscaletta.com

SCALIA, Antonin. American (born United States), b. 1936. **Genres:** Law, Social Commentary, Essays. **Career:** Jones, Day, Cockley and Reavis (law firm), associate, 1961-67; University of Virginia Law School, associate professor, 1967-70, professor, 1970-74; Office of Telecommunications Policy, Executive Office of the President, general counsel, 1971-72; Administrative Conference of U.S., chairman, 1972-74; U.S. Office of Legal Counsel, Department of Justice, assistant attorney general, 1974-77; University of Chicago, professor of law, 1977-82; Georgetown Law Center, visiting professor, 1977; Regulation Magazine, editor, 1979-82; Stanford Law School, visiting professor, 1980-81; U.S. Court of Appeals for DC circuit, judge, 1982-86; U.S. Supreme Court, associate justice, 1986-. Writer. **Publications:** A Matter of Interpretation: Federal Courts and the Law: An Essay, 1997; Scalia Dissents: Writings of the Supreme Court's Wittiest, Most Outspoken Justice, 2004; Opinions of Justice Antonin Scalia: The Caustic Conservative, 2004; Mullahs of the West: Judges as Authoritative Expositors Of The Natural

Law?, 2005; (with B.A. Garner) Making Your Case: The Art of Persuading Judges, 2008. **Address:** U.S. Supreme Court, Supreme Court Bldg., 1 1st St. NE, Washington, DC 20543-0002, U.S.A.

SCALMER, Sean. Australian (born Australia) **Genres:** Local History/Rural Topics, Politics/Government, Social Commentary, History, Social Sciences, Civil Liberties/Human Rights. **Career:** Macquarie University, research fellow, 1998-2004, lecturer, 2004-06, visiting fellow; University of Melbourne, faculty, 2007-, senior lecturer, associate professor. Writer. **Publications:** Dissent Events: Protest, the Media, and the Political Gimmick in Australia, 2002; (with S. Maddison) Activist Wisdom: Practical Knowledge and Creative Tension in Social Movements, 2006; (ed. with S. Macintyre) What If? Australian History as It Might Have Been, 2006; The Little History of Australian Unionism, 2006. Contributor to journals. **Address:** Department of History, University of Melbourne, Rm. 311 W, John Hedley Bldg., Melbourne, VI 3010, Australia. **Online address:** sscalmer@unimelb.edu.au

SCAMMELL, Michael. American/British (born England), b. 1935. **Genres:** Literary Criticism And History, Biography, Area Studies, Translations. **Career:** Ljubljana University, lecturer in English, 1958-59; Hunter College, lecturer in Russian, 1961-62; freelance writer, 1962-70; British Broadcasting Corp., language supervisor and program assistant, 1965-67; Index on Censorship, editor, 1971-80; Writers and Scholars Educational Trust, director, 1971-80; Columbia University, School of the Arts, professor of writing division. **Publications:** NONFICTION: Blue Guide to Yugoslavia, 1969; (contrib.) Handbook to East Europe, 1970; Alexander Solzhenitsyn, 1971; Solzhenitsyn: A Biography, 1984. EDITOR: (and intro.) Russia's Other Writers, 1970, as Russia's Other Writers: Selections from Samizdat Literature, 1971; (and intro.) Unofficial Art from the Soviet Union, 1977; (and intro.) The Solzhenitsyn Files: Secret Soviet Documents Reveal One Man's Fight against the Monolith, 1995; Koestler: The Literary and Political Odyssey of a Twentieth Century Skeptic, 2009. TRANSLATOR: K. Fedin, Cities and Years, 1962, rev. ed., 1993; F. Dostoevsky, Crime and Punishment, 1963; The Gift, 1963; V.V. Nabokov, The Defense: A Novel, 1964, rev. ed., 1990; Childhood, Boyhood and Youth, 1964; My Testimony, 1969; (ed. and intro.) E.Kocbek, Nothing is Lost: Selected Poems, 2004. OTHERS: Letteratura Contemporanea Nell'Europa Dell'Est, 1977. Contributor to periodicals. **Address:** Writing Program, School of the Arts, Columbia University, 415 Dodge Hall, PO Box 1804, 2960 Broadway, New York, NY 10027, U.S.A. **Online address:** mscammell1@gmail.com

SCANLON, Bill. American (born United States), b. 1956. **Genres:** Novels, Biography, Autobiography/Memoirs, Sports/Fitness. **Career:** Boulder Daily Camera, business editor; Denver Rocky Mountain News, science writer; ATP Tour, board directors; Dallas Youth Foundation, founder. **Publications:** (With S. Long and C. Long) Bad News for McEnroe: Blood, Sweat, and Backhands with John, Jimmy, Ilie, Ivan, Bjorn, and Vitas, 2004. Contributor to periodicals. **Address:** c/o Author Mail, St. Martins Press, 175 5th Ave., New York, NY 10010, U.S.A. **Online address:** bill_scanlon@ziffdavis.com

SCANLON, Jennifer. American (born United States), b. 1958. **Genres:** Biography, Women's Studies And Issues, History. **Career:** Bowdoin College, William R. Kenan Jr. professor of the humanities in gender and women's studies, Gender and Women's Studies Program, director. Writer. **Publications:** Inarticulate Longings: The Ladies Home Journal, Gender, and the Promises of Consumer Culture, 1995; (with S. Cosner) American Women Historians, 1700s-1990s: A Biographical Dictionary, 1996; (ed.) Significant Contemporary American Feminists: A Biographical Sourcebook, 1999; (ed.) The Gender and Consumer Culture Reader, 2000; Bad Girls Go Everywhere: The Life of Helen Gurley Brown, 2009. **Address:** Bowdoin College, 5000 College Sta., Brunswick, ME 04011, U.S.A. **Online address:** jscanlon@bowdoin.edu

SCANNELL, Christy. American (born United States), b. 1967. **Genres:** Novels. **Career:** Christian Communicator, staff; Rainbow Publishers/Legacy Press, editorial director, 1996-2005; Grossmont College, journalism instructor, 2007-09, The Summit (student newspaper), advisor; San Diego Metropolitan (business magazine), associate editor; North Park News (community newspaper), associate editor; San Diego Uptown News, senior editor. **Publications:** SECRETS OF LULU'S CAFE SERIES: NOVELS WITH G. KOLBABA: Desperate Pastors' Wives, 2007; A Matter of Wife and Death, 2008; Katt's in the Cradle, 2009. **Address:** PO Box 16196, San Diego, CA 92176, U.S.A.

SCARBOROUGH, Vernon L(ee). American (born United States), b. 1950. **Genres:** Anthropology/Ethnology, Archaeology/Antiquities. **Career:** University of Oregon, student excavator, 1970-, excavator and laboratory assistant, 1973-; Bureau of Land Management-Dillon, archaeologist, 1974-; Eastern New Mexico University, excavator, 1975-; Bureau of Land Management-Boulder, archaeologist, 1975-; Southern Methodist University-New Mexico, research archaeologist, 1975-, Fort Burgwin Research Center, instructor in archaeological field methods, 1980-; Southern Methodist University-Texas, laboratory archaeologist, 1976-77; University of Khartoum, lecturer of archaeology, 1981-82, Archaeological Field School, director, 1982-; University of Texas, lecturer of anthropology, 1982-83, Archaeological Field School, director, 1983-, instructor of anthropology, 1983-, 1986-87, Meyer Pithouse Project, director, 1983-85; University of Alabama, instructor of anthropology, 1983-; University of Peshawar, Fulbright lecturer of archaeology, 1986-, Fulbright Program, investigator, 1986-; University of Cincinnati, Department of Anthropology, assistant professor, 1988-92, associate professor, 1992-99, department head, 2008-10, distinguished research professor, 2010-, Charles Phelps Taft professor, 2010-; Ancient Maya Water Management Project-Guatemala, director, 1991-; Ancient Maya Water Management Project-Belize, director, 1992-, 1994-. Consultant and writer. **Publications:** Archeological and Historical Survey in the West Dillon and Tendoy Mountain Planning Units of Beaverhead County, Southwestern Montana, 1974; Archaeology at Cerros, Belize, Central America: The Settlement System in a Late Preclassic Maya Community, vol. III, 1991; The Flow of Power: Ancient Water Systems and Landscapes, 2003. EDITOR: (with D.R. Wilcox) The Mesoamerican Ballgame, 1991; (with B.L. Isaac and contrib.) Economic Aspects of Water Management in the Prehispanic New World, 1993; (with F. Valdez, Jr. and N. Dunning) Heterarchy, Political Economy and the Ancient Maya: The Three Rivers Region of the East-Central Yucatán Peninsula, 2003; Catalyst for Ideas: Anthropological Archaeology and the Legacy of Douglas Schwartz, 2005; (with J.E. Clark) Political Economy of Ancient Mesoamerica: Transformations During the Formative and Classic Periods, 2007. Works appears in anthologies. Contributor of articles and journals. **Address:** Department of Anthropology, University of Cincinnati, 452 Braunstein Hall, PO Box 380, Cincinnati, OH 45221, U.S.A. **Online address:** vernon.scarborough@uc.edu

SCARBOROUGH, William Kauffman. American (born United States), b. 1933. **Genres:** History. **Career:** Millsaps College, assistant professor of history, 1961-63; Northeast Louisiana University, assistant professor of history, 1963-64; University of Southern Mississippi, associate professor, 1964-76, professor of history, 1976-2009, chairman, 1980-90, Charles W. Moorman distinguished alumni professor in the humanities, 1996-98, professor emeritus, 2009-. Writer. **Publications:** The Overseer: Plantation Management in the Old South, 1966; (ed.) The Diary of Edmund Ruffin, vol. I: Toward Independence, 1972, vol. II: The Years of Hope, 1976, vol. III: A Dream Shattered, 1989; Masters of the Big House: Elite Slaveholders of the Mid-nineteenth Century South, 2003; The Allstons of Chicora Wood: Wealth, Honor, and Gentility in the South Carolina Lowcountry, 2011. **Address:** Department of History, University of Southern Mississippi, 409 Liberal Arts Bldg., 118 College Dr., Ste. 5047, Hattiesburg, MS 39406, U.S.A. **Online address:** william.scarborough@usm.edu

SCARF, Maggie. American (born United States), b. 1932. **Genres:** Psychiatry, Psychology, Geography, Sciences. **Career:** The New Republic magazine, contributing editor, 1978-; Yale University, Jonathan Edwards College, associate fellow, 1979, 1981, 1983-, writer-in-residence, Bush Center in Child Development, senior fellow, Whitney Humanities Center, visiting fellow, 2005-; Self Magazine, contributing editor, 1990-. **Publications:** Meet Benjamin Franklin, 1968; Antarctica: Exploring the Frozen Continent, 1970; Body, Mind, Behavior, 1976; Unfinished Business: Pressure Points in the Lives of Women, 1980; Intimate Partners: Patterns in Love and Marriage, 1987; Intimate Worlds: Life Inside the Family, 1995; Secrets, Lies, Betrayals: How the Body Holds the Secrets of a Life and How to Unlock Them, 2004; September Songs: The Good News about Marriage in the Later Years, 2008. **Address:** Whitney Humanities Center, Yale University, 53 Wall St., New Haven, CT 06520, U.S.A. **Online address:** maggie@maggiescarf.com

SCARFE, Allan John. Australian (born Australia), b. 1931. **Genres:** Novels, Biography, Race Relations, Third World, History, Social Sciences. **Career:** Victorian Education Department, teacher, 1948-56, 1958-60, 1963-; Buckinghamshire Education Authority, secondary teacher, 1956-58; Sawa Seva Sangh (Gandhian movement), teacher and social worker, 1960-63. Writer. **Publications:** NOVELS: A Corpse in Calcutta, 2000. WITH W. SCARFE:

(contrib.) Reflections, 1965; A Mouthful of Petals, 1967; Tiger on a Rein: Report on the Bihar Famine, 1969; People of India: A Sourcebook for Asian Studies, 1972; The Black Australians, 1974; Victims or Bludgers? Case Studies in Poverty in Australia, 1974, 2nd ed. as Victims or Bludgers? A Poverty Inquiry for Schools, 1981; J.P., His Biography, 1975, rev. ed., 1998; (co-ed.) Labor's Titan: The Story of Percy Brookfield 1878-1921, 1983; (comp.) All That Grief: Migrant Recollections of Greek Resistance to Facism 1941-1949, 1994; Remembering Jayaprakash, 1997; No Taste for Carnage: Alex Sheppard: A Portrait, 1913-1997, 1998; Left of Centre: The Story of Gilbert Giles Roper, 1905-1974, forthcoming. Contributor to periodicals. **Address:** 8 Bostock St., Warrnambool, VI 3280, Australia.

SCARFE, Wendy (Elizabeth). Australian (born Australia), b. 1933. **Genres:** Novels, Poetry, Race Relations, Third World, Biography, Young Adult Fiction, Young Adult Non-fiction. **Career:** Melbourne Church of England Girls' Grammar School, resident mistress, 1954; Victorian Education Department, secondary teacher, 1955-56, 1958-60; Buckinghamshire Education Authority, secondary teacher, 1956-58; Sawa Seva Sangh (Gandhian movement), teacher, 1960-63; Community Aid Abroad, branch president, 1966-68. Writer. **Publications:** POETRY: Shadow and Flowers (poetry), 1964; (with J.R. Keith) Dragonflies and Edges (poetry), 2004. NOVELS: The Lotus Throne, 1976; Neither Here nor There, 1984; Laura My Alter Ego, 1988; The Day They Shot Edward, 1991, rev. ed., 2003; Miranda, 1998; Fishing for Strawberries, 2001; Jerusha Braddon, Painter, 2005. WITH A.J. SCARFE: A Mouthful of Petals, 1967; Tiger on a Rein, 1969; People of India, 1972; The Black Australians, 1974; Victims or Bludgers? Case Studies in Poverty in Australia, 1974; J.P., His Biography, 1975, rev. ed., 1998; Victims or Bludgers? A Poverty Inquiry for Schools, 1981; Labor's Titan: The Story of Percy Brookfield, 1878-1921, 1983; All That Grief: Migrant Recollections of Greek Resistance to Facism, 1941-1949, 1994; Remembering Jayaprakash, 1997; No Taste for Carnage: Alex Sheppard, A Portrait, 1913-1997, 1998. **Address:** 8 Bostock St., Warrnambool, VI 3280, Australia.

SCARGILL, David Ian. British (born England), b. 1935. **Genres:** Geography, Travel/Exploration, History, Essays. **Career:** Oxford University, departmental demonstrator, 1959-64, St. Edmund Hall, fellow, 1962-, lecturer in geography, 1964-. Writer. **Publications:** Economic Geography of France, 1968; (ed.) Problem Regions of Europe, 1972; The Dordogne Region of France, 1974; (ed. with C.G. Smith) Oxford and Its Region: Geographical Essays, 1975; The Form of Cities, 1979; (with A.G. Crosby) Oxford and Its Countryside, 1982; Urban France, 1983; (with K.E. Scargill) Containing the City: The Role of Oxford's Green Belt, 1994. Contributor to journals. **Address:** Centre for the Environment, School of Geography and the Environment, Oxford University, Dyson Perrins Bldg., South Parks Rd., Oxford, OX OX1 3QY, England.

SCARLETT, Elizabeth. (Elizabeth A. Scarlett). American (born United States), b. 1961. **Genres:** Film, Literary Criticism And History, Travel/Exploration. **Career:** University of Virginia, assistant professor of Spanish, 1991-, sesquicentennial fellow, 1995; University of Seville, visiting assistant professor of English, 1988-89; Charlottesville Public Access Cable Television, production assistant, 1995-96; State University of New York, assistant professor, 1997-2000, associate professor, 2000-. Writer. **Publications:** Under Construction: The Body in Spanish Novels, 1994. EDITOR: Let's Go: Spain, Portugal and Morocco, 1988; Let's Go: Mexico, 1988; (ed. with H.B. Wescott) Convergencias Hispanicas: Selected Proceedings And Other Essays On Spanish And Latin American Literature, Film, And Linguistics, 2001. Contributor of articles to periodicals. **Address:** Department of Romance Languages and Literatures, State University of New York, 929 Clemens Hall, Buffalo, NY 14260, U.S.A. **Online address:** scarlett@buffalo.edu

SCARLETT, Elizabeth A. *See* **SCARLETT, Elizabeth.**

SCARPACI, Sherry. American (born United States) **Genres:** Mystery/Crime/Suspense. **Career:** Women's World magazine, freelance writer; Linear Electric, freelance writer. **Publications:** Lullaby, Five Star, 2007. Contributor to magazines. **Address:** Chicago, IL , U.S.A. **Online address:** sherryscarpaci@yahoo.com

SCARR, Deryck (Antony). Australian/British (born England), b. 1939. **Genres:** Humanities, History, Social Sciences, Sociology. **Career:** Australian National University, research fellow, 1964-68, fellow, 1968-71, senior fellow in Pacific history, 1971-97, acting head of department, 1973-74, now pro-

fessor emeritis; University of Adelaide, visiting senior lecturer, 1980, 1989. Writer. **Publications:** Fragments of Empire: A History of the Western Pacific High Commission, 1877-1914, 1967; The Majesty of Colour: A Life of Sir John Bates Thurston, vol. I: I, the Very Bayonet, 1973, vol. II: Viceroy of the Pacific, 1980; More Pacific Islands Portraits, 1978; Ratu Sukuna: Soldier, Statesman, Man of Two Worlds, 1980; Fiji, the Three Legged Stool: Selected Writings of Ratu Sir Lala Sukuna, 1982; Fiji: A Short History, 1984; The Fiji: Politics of Illusion, The Military Coups in Fiji, 1988; Kingdoms of the Reefs: The History of the Pacific Islands, 1990; Slaving and Slavery in the Indian Ocean, 1998; Seychelles since 1770: A Slave and Post-slavery Society, 1999; A History of the Pacific Islands: Passages through Tropical Time, 2001; Tuimacilai: A Life of Ratu Sir Kamisese Mara, 2008. EDITOR: A Cruize in a Queensland Labour Vessel to the South Seas, 1968; (with J.W. Davidson) Pacific Islands Portraits, 1970; More Pacific Islands Portraits, 1979; (with N. Gunson and J. Terrell) Echoes of Pacific War, 1998. **Address:** Australian National University, Ellery Crescent, Acton, AC 2601, Australia. **Online address:** dscarr@pcug.org.au

SCARRY, Elaine (Margaret). American (born United States), b. 1946. **Genres:** Medicine/Health, Psychology, Social Sciences, Essays. **Career:** University of Pennsylvania, assistant professor, 1974-79, associate professor of English, 1979-87; Harvard University, professor of English and American literature and language, 1988-, Walter M. Cabot professor of aesthetics and the general theory of value. Writer. **Publications:** (Contrib.) Literary Monographs, 1975; (contrib.) Essays in Numerical Criticism of Medieval Literature, 1980; The Body in Pain: The Making and Unmaking of the World, 1985; (ed.) Literature and the Body: Essays on Populations and Persons, 1988; (ed.) Fin-de-siècle: English Poetry in 1590, 1690, 1790, 1890, 1990; Resisting Representation, 1994; (ed.) Fins-de-siècle, 1995; Making Mental Pictures Fly, 1998; Dreaming by the Book, 1999; On Beauty and Being Just, 1999; (contrib.) Who Defended the Country?, 2003; Rule of Law, Misrule of Men, 2010; Thinking in an Emergency, 2011. Contributor to books and periodicals. **Address:** Department of English, Harvard University, 273 Barker Ctr., 12 Quincy St., Cambridge, MA 02138, U.S.A.

SCARRY, Huck. Swiss/American (born United States), b. 1953. **Genres:** Illustrations, Picture/Board Books, Reference. **Career:** McGraw-Hill Book Co., book designer, 1976; Swiss Watch and Jewelry Journal, designer, 1977-79; writer and illustrator, 1979-. **Publications:** SELF-ILLUSTRATED FOR CHILDREN: Huck Scarry's Steam Train Journey, 1979; On Wheels, 1980; Huck Scarry's Steam Train Press-Outs, 1980; On the Road: A Panorama of Early Automobiles, 1981; Voyage En Peniche, 1981; Life on a Barge: A Sketchbook, 1982; Voyage En Ballon, 1982; Balloon Trip: A Sketchbook, 1983; La Nostraterra, 1982; Our Earth, 1984; Aboard on a Fishing Boat, 1983; Looking Into the Middle Ages, 1984; Lo Sai Come Si Vola?, 1984; Things That Fly, 1986; Lo Sai Come Si Naviga?, 1985; Things That Sail?, 1986; Lo Sai Come Si Viaggia?, 1985; Things That Go, 1986; Aboard a Steam Locomotive, 1987; Pompieri, Pompieri, 1989; If I Were a Fireman, 1989; Diario Toscano, 1998; Richard Scarry's Father Cat's Christmas Tree, 2003. ART BOOKS: Diano Venziano, 1993 in US as Huck Scarry's Venice Sketchbook, 1994; Richard Scarry's a Day at the Airport, 2001; A Day at the Fire Station, 2003; A Day at the Police Station, 2004. Illustrator of books by R.M. Peyton, M.J. Shapiro. **Address:** Birkenweg, Gstaad, 3780, Switzerland.

SCARTH, Alwyn. American (born United States) **Genres:** Geography, Biography, Sciences, Earth Sciences. **Career:** University of Dundee, lecturer in geography, professor. Geologist and author. **Publications:** Volcanoes: An Introduction, 1994; Vulcan's Fury: Man against the Volcano, 1999; (with J. Tanguy) Volcanoes of Europe, 2001; La Catastrophe: The Eruption of Mount Pelee, the Worst Volcanic Eruption of the Twentieth Century, 2002; Savage Earth: The Dramatic Story of Volcanoes and Earthquakes, 2002; Vesuvius: A Biography, 2009. **Address:** c/o Author Mail, Oxford University Press, 2001 Evans Rd., Cary, NC 27513, U.S.A.

SCATES, Shelby. American (born United States), b. 1931. **Genres:** History, Politics/Government, Local History/Rural Topics, Autobiography/Memoirs. **Career:** International News Service, news reporter, 1956-58; United Press Intl., reporter, 1958-59; Associated Press, reporter, 1959-64; Seattle Post-Intelligencer, columnist and reporter, 1966-91. **Publications:** Sea First: The Story of Seattle First National Bank, 1968; War and Politics by Other Means: A Journalist's Memoir, 1997; Warren G. Magnuson and the Shaping of Twentieth-Century America, 1999; Maurice Rosenblatt and the Fall of Joseph McCarthy, 2006. **Address:** 5203 SW Jacobsen Rd., Seattle, WA 98116, U.S.A.

SCERRI, Eric R. British (born England), b. 1953. **Genres:** Chemistry, Philosophy. **Career:** Chemistry tutor, 1980-85; Abbey Tutorial College, senior tutor, 1985-91; Richmond College, professor, 1991-93; London School of Economics, postdoctoral fellow, 1993-95; California Institute of Technology, postdoctoral fellow, 1995-97; Bradley University, assistant professor, 1997-98; Purdue University, visiting professor, 1998-99; University of California, lecturer in chemistry. Writer. **Publications:** (ed. with D. Baird and L. McIntyre) Philosophy of Chemistry: Synthesis of a New Discipline, 2006; The Periodic Table: Its Story and Its Significance, 2007; Collected Papers on Philosophy of Chemistry, 2008. **Address:** Department of Chemistry & Biochemistry, 607 Charles E. Young Dr. E, Los Angeles, CA 90095-1569, U.S.A. **Online address:** scerri@chem.ucla.edu

SCHAAFSMA, David. American (born United States), b. 1953. **Genres:** Education, Social Sciences. **Career:** Holland Christian High School, Department of English, teacher, 1975-77; Hudsonville Unity Christian High School, Department of English, teacher, 1977-81; Grand Valley State University, Department of English, teacher, 1981-85, Department of Humanities, teacher, 1981-85; University of Michigan, instructor in English and education, 1985-90; Dewey Center Community Writing Center, director, 1988-91; University of Wisconsin, assistant professor of English and education, 1990-95; Wisconsin Writing Project, director, 1992-95; Write for Your Life, director, 1992-98; Columbia University, Teachers College, assistant professor of English and education, 1995-99; University of Illinois, Department of English, associate professor of English education, 1999-, director. Writer. **Publications:** (Co-author) Language and Reflection: An Integrated Approach to Teaching Literacy, 1992; Eating on the Street: Teaching Literacy in a Multicultural Society, 1993; (with C. Fleischer) Literacy and Democracy: Teacher Research and Composition Studies in Pursuit of Habitable Spaces: Further Conversations from the Students of Jay Robinson, 1998; Narrative Inquiry in English Education, 2011; Jane Addams, Hull-House and the Call to Education, forthcoming. Contributor to books and periodicals. **Address:** Department of English, University of Illinois, 601 S Morgan St., PO Box 162, University Hall, Ste. 1904, Chicago, IL 60607-7120, U.S.A. **Online address:** schaafl@uic.edu

SCHABAS, Margaret. Canadian/American (born United States), b. 1954. **Genres:** Economics, Politics/Government, History. **Career:** Michigan State University, visiting assistant professor, 1983-84; University of Michigan, instructor, 1985; University of Colorado, visiting assistant professor, 1985-87; Harvard University, visiting assistant professor, 1987-88; University of Wisconsin, assistant professor, 1987-91; Madison Symphony Orchestra, oboist, 1988-90; York University, professor, 1991-2001; California Institute of Technology, Humanities and Social Sciences Division, visiting assistant professor, 1992; University of British Columbia, Department of Philosophy, professor, 2001, head, 2004-. Writer and historian. **Publications:** A World Ruled by Number: William Stanley Jevons and the Rise of Mathematical Economics, 1990; (ed. with N.D. Marchi) Oeconomies in the Age of Newton, 2003; The Natural Origins of Economics, 2005; (ed. with C. Wennerlind) David Hume's Political Economy, 2007. Contributor of articles to books, periodicals and journals. **Address:** Department of Philosophy, University of British Columbia, E370, 1866 E Mall, Vancouver, BC V6T 1Z1, Canada. **Online address:** mschabas@interchange.ubc.ca

SCHACHT, Richard. American (born United States), b. 1941. **Genres:** Philosophy, Anthropology/Ethnology, Essays. **Career:** University of Illinois, assistant professor, 1967-71, associate professor, 1971-80, chair of department, 1979-91, professor of philosophy, 1980-, professor of criticism and interpretive theory, 1981-, Jubilee professor of liberal arts and sciences, 1990-, College of Liberal Arts and Sciences, interim dean, 1994, now professor emeritus; University of Oregon, visiting professor, 1969; University of Pittsburgh, visiting professor, 1973; University of Michigan, visiting professor, 1979. Writer. **Publications:** Alienation, 1970; Hegel and After: Studies in Continental Philosophy between Kant and Sartre, 1975; Nietzsche, 1983; Classical Modern Philosophers: Descartes to Kant, 1984; (ed. and intro.) Nietzsche Selections, 1993; (ed.) Nietzsche, Genealogy, Morality: Essays on Nietzsche's Genealogy of Morals, 1994; The Future of Alienation, 1994; Making Sense of Nietzsche: Reflections Timely and Untimely, 1995; (ed.) Human, All Too Human, 1996; (ed.) Nietzche's Postmoralism: Eessays on Nietzsche's Prelude to Philosophy's Future, 2001; (with P. Kitcher) Finding an Ending: Reflections on Wagner's Ring, 2004; (ed. with J. Conant) Norton Anthology of Western Philosophy, 2009. FORTHCOMING: (ed.) On Human Nature: Readings in Philosophical Anthropology; The Interpretive Tradition, vol. V.

Address: Department of Philosophy, University of Illinois, 201A Greg Hall, 810 S Wright St., PO Box 468, Urbana, IL 61801, U.S.A. **Online address:** rschacht@uiuc.edu

SCHACTER, Daniel L. American (born United States), b. 1952. **Genres:** Psychology, Biography, Sciences. **Career:** Oxford University, Department of Experimental Psychology, visiting researcher, 1978; University of Toronto, research associate and assistant professor of psychology, 1981-87; University of Arizona, Department of Psychology, associate professor, 1987-89, professor, 1989-91; Harvard University, professor of psychology, 1991-95, chair of department, 1995-2005, William R. Kenan, Jr. professor of psychology, 2002-; Annual Review of Psychology, associate editor, 1998-; University College London, Institute for Cognitive Neuroscience, visiting professor, 1999; Perspectives on Psychological Science, associate editor, 2005-07. **Publications:** Stranger behind the Engram: Theories of Memory and the Psychology of Science, 1982; Searching for Memory: The Brain, the Mind and the Past, 1996; Forgotten Ideas, Neglected Pioneers: Richard Semon and the Story of Memory, 2001; The Seven Sins of Memory: How the Mind Forgets and Remembers, 2001; How the Mind Forgets and Remembers: The Seven Sins of Memory, 2003. EDITOR: (with R.R. Bootzin and J.F. Kihlstrom) Sleep and Cognition, 1990; (with G.P. Prigatano) Awareness of Deficit after Brain Injury: Theoretical and Clinical Aspects, 1991; (with E. Tulving) Memory Systems 1994, 1994; Memory Distortion: How Minds, Brains and Societies Reconstruct the Past, 1995; (with L.R. Squire) Biological and Psychological Perspectives on Memory and Memory Disorders, 1997; The Cognitive Neuropsychology of False Memories, 1999; (with E. Scarry) Memory, Brain and Belief, 2000; (with L.R. Squire) Neuropsychology of Memory, 3rd ed., 2002; (with D.T. Gilbert and D.M. Wegner) Psychology, 2007, 2nd ed., 2010; (with D.T. Gilbert and D.M. Wegner) Introducing Psychology, 2009. Contributor to journals and periodicals. **Address:** Department of Psychology, Harvard University, William James Hall, 33 Kirkland St., Cambridge, MA 02138, U.S.A. **Online address:** dls@wjh.harvard.edu

SCHAECHTER, Elio. (Moselio Schaechter). American/Italian (born Italy), b. 1928. **Genres:** Biology. **Career:** Tufts University, School of Medicine, faculty member, 1962-95, distinguished professor, 1987, emeritus, 1995-; American Academy of Microbiology, fellow, 1974-; Association of Medical School Microbiology and Immunology Chairs, president, 1984-85; American Society for Microbiology, president, 1985-86; TV Microbial Literacy Project, scientific advisor, 1993-99; San Diego State University, Department of Biology, adjunct professor emeritus; ASM News, Editorial Board, chairman, 1999-. **Publications:** In the Company of Mushrooms: A Biologist's Tale, 1997. AS MOSELIO SCHAECHTER: (co-ed.) Molecular biology of bacterial growth, 1985; (co-ed.) Mechanisms of Microbial Disease, 1989, 4th ed., 2007; (with F.C. Neidhardt and J.L. Ingraham) Physiology of the Bacterial Cell: A Molecular Approach, 1990; (ed.) Desk Encyclopedia of Microbiology, 2004; (with F.C. Neidhardt and J.L. Ingraham) Microbe, 2006; Eukaryotic Microbes, 2012. **Address:** Department of Biology, San Diego State University, 5500 Campanile Dr., San Diego, CA 92182, U.S.A. **Online address:** mschaech@sunstroke.sdsu.edu

SCHAECHTER, Moselio. *See* **SCHAECHTER, Elio.**

SCHAEF, Anne Wilson. American (born United States), b. 1934. **Genres:** Cultural/Ethnic Topics, Humanities, inspirational/Motivational Literature, Medicine/Health, Philosophy, Social Commentary, Women's Studies And Issues, Psychology, Psychology. **Career:** Bellevue Hospital, clinical intern, 1960-61; St. Louis Hospital, Youth Center, supervising psychologist, 1964-66; Alton State Hospital, Youth Center, clinical director, 1966-68; National Training Laboratories, black trainer program, director, 1968-70; Women's Institute for Alternative Psychotherapy, co-founder and director, 1974-78; Illinois Department of Mental Health, consultant; Royal Commission on the Status of Women in Canada, consultant; University of California, Neuropsychiatric Institute, consultant. Writer, psychologist and psychotherapist and educator. **Publications:** Women's Reality: An Emerging Female System in a White Male Society, 1981, 3rd ed., 1992; When Society Becomes an Addict, 1987; (with D. Fassel) The Addictive Organization, 1988; Escape from Intimacy: Untangling the Love Addictions, Sex, Romance, Relationships, 1989; Meditations for Women Who Do Too Much, 1990, rev. ed., 2004; Laugh, I Thought I'd Die, If I Didn't: Meditations on Healing Through Humor, 1990; Beyond Therapy, Beyond Science: A New Model for Healing the Whole Person, 1992; Native Wisdom for White Minds: Daily Reflections Inspired by the Native Peoples of the World, 1995; Meditations for People Who (May) Worry

Too Much, 1996; Co-Dependence: Misunderstood, Mistreated, 1986; Living in Process: Basic Truths for Living the Path of the Soul, 1998; Meditations for Living in Balance: Daily Solutions for People Who Do Too Much, 2000. Contributor to journals. **Address:** 8 Wild Tiger Ln., Boulder, CO 80302, U.S.A.

SCHAEFER, Claudia. (Claudia Schaefer-Rodriguez). American (born United States), b. 1949. **Genres:** Area Studies, Cultural/Ethnic Topics, Gay And Lesbian Issues, Literary Criticism And History, Third World, Social Sciences. **Career:** University of Rochester, assistant professor, 1977-85, Susan B. Anthony Center for Gender and Womens Studies, associate, 1984-, associate professor, 1985-94, director of comparative literature program, 1991-93, professor of Spanish and comparative literature, 1994-, Rush Rhees professor, department chair, Graduate Studies, associate chair. Writer. **Publications:** Juan Goytisolo: Del Realismo Critico a la Utopia, 1984; Textured Lives: Women, Art and Representation in Modern Mexico, 1992; (intro.) City of Kings, 1993; Danger Zones: Homosexuality, National Identity and Mexican Culture, 1996; Bored to Distraction: Cinema of Excess in End-of-the-Century Mexico and Spain, 2003; Frida Kahlo: A Biography, 2009. Contributor to periodicals. **Address:** Department of Modern Languages and Cultures, University of Rochester, 408 Lattimore, 500 Wilson Blvd., PO Box 270082, Rochester, NY 14627, U.S.A. **Online address:** claudia.schaefer@rochester.edu

SCHAEFER, David Lewis. American (born United States), b. 1943. **Genres:** Administration/Management, Politics/Government, Philosophy. **Career:** College of the Holy Cross, professor of political science. Writer. **Publications:** Justice or Tyranny? A Critique of John Rawls's A Theory of Justice, 1979; (ed.) The New Egalitarianism: Questions and Challenges, 1979; (ed. with R.R. Schaefer) The Statesman, 1988, rev. ed., 1992; The Political Philosophy of Montaigne, 1990; (ed. with P.A. Lawler and R.M. Schaefer) Active Duty: Public Administration as Democratic Statesmanship, 1998; (ed.) Freedom over Servitude: Montaigne, La Boetie, and On Voluntary Servitude, 1998; Illiberal Justice: John Rawls vs. the American Political Tradition, 2007. Contributor to periodicals. **Address:** Department of Political Science, College of the Holy Cross, Fenwick 306, PO Box 101A, Worcester, MA 01610, U.S.A. **Online address:** dschaefe@holycross.edu

SCHAEFER, Eric. (Eric P. Schaefer). American (born United States), b. 1959?. **Genres:** Film, Art/Art History, Social Commentary. **Career:** Emerson College, Department of Visual and Media Arts, associate professor, 1992-, associate chair, 1996. Writer. **Publications:** Bold! Daring! Shocking! True!: A History of Exploitation Films, 1919-1959, 1999; Massacre of Pleasure: A History of Sexploitation Films, 1960-1979, forthcoming. **Address:** Department of Visual and Media Arts, Emerson College, 120 Boylston St., Boston, MA 02116-4624, U.S.A. **Online address:** eric_schaefer@emerson.edu

SCHAEFER, Eric P. See **SCHAEFER, Eric.**

SCHAEFER, Lola M. American (born United States), b. 1950. **Genres:** Children's Fiction, Children's Non-fiction, Picture/Board Books, Adult Nonfiction, Food And Wine, Medicine/Health, Animals/Pets, Biography, Biography. **Career:** St. Jude Elementary, seventh grade teacher, 1973-76; J.E. Ober Elementary, kindergarten teacher, 1983-84; McKenney-Harrison, elementary teacher, 1984-88; McIntosh Elementary, elementary teacher, 1988-. Writer and consultant. **Publications:** FOR CHILDREN: Out of the Night, 1995; Candlelight Service, 1995; Turtle Nest, 1996; Zap!, 1998; Models, 2000; What Grows from a Tree?, 2000; This Is the Sunflower, 2000; This Is the Rain, 2001; Pick, Pull, Snap!: Where Once a Flower Bloomed, 2003; What's Up, What's Down?, 2002; Arrowhawk, 2004; Loose Tooth, 2004; A River Flows, 2004; Boo Who?, 2009; Please Pass the Manners, 2009; Easter Surprises, 2009; Frankie Stein Starts School, 2010; Happy Halloween, Mittens, 2010. FAMILIES SERIES: Fathers, 1999, rev. ed., 2008; Mothers, 1999, rev. ed., 2008; Grandfathers, 1999, rev. ed., 2008; Grandmothers, 1999, rev. ed., 2008; Sisters, 1999, rev. ed., 2008; Brothers, 1999, rev. ed., 2008; Cousins, 1999, rev. ed., 2008; Uncles, 1999, rev. ed., 2008; Aunts, 1999, rev. ed., 2008; Family Pets, 1999, rev. ed., 2008. OCEAN LIFE SERIES: Crabs, 1999; Corals, 1999; Octopuses, 1999; Parrotfish, 1999; Sea Anemones, 1999; Sea Horses, 1999; Sea Stars, 1999; Sea Urchins, 1999. HONEY BEES SERIES: Honey Bees, 1999; Honey Bees and Flowers, 1999; Honey Bees and Hives, 1999; Honey Bees and Honey, 1999. FALL FUN SERIES: Costumes, 1999; Jack-o-Lanterns, 1999; Scarecrows, 1999; Masks, 1999; A Snowy Day, 2000; A Rainy Day, 2000; A Windy Day, 2000; A Hot Day, 2000; A Cold Day, 2000; A Sunny Day, 2000. TRANSPORTATION LIBRARY SERIES: Airplanes, 2000; Tow Trucks, 2000; Tractor Trailers, 2000; Tugboats, 2000;

Barges, 2000; Cable Cars, 2000; Ferries, 2000; Airplanes, 2000; Bicycles, 2000. HELPERS IN OUR COMMUNITY SERIES: We Need Dentists, 2000; We Need Doctors, 2000; We Need Farmers, 2000; We Need Fire Fighters, 2000; We Need Mail Carriers, 2000; We Need Nurses, 2000; We Need Police Officers, 2000; We Need Veterinarians, 2000. WHO WORKS HERE? SERIES: Hospital, 2000; Dental Office, 2000; Airport, 2000; Construction Site, 2000; Police Station, 2000; Supermarket, 2000; Car Dealership, 2001; Courthouse, 2001; Fast-Food Restaurant, 2001; Fire Station, 2001; Library, 2001; Zoo, 2001. HOLIDAYS AND CELEBRATIONS SERIES: Chinese New Year, 2001; Hanukkah, 2001; Kwanzaa, 2001; Cinco de Mayo, 2001. UNDERSTANDING DIFFERENCES SERIES: Some Kids Are Blind, 2001, rev. ed., 2008; Some Kids Are Deaf, 2001, rev. ed., 2008; Some Kids Use Wheelchairs, 2001, rev. ed., 2008; Some Kids Wear Leg Braces, 2001, rev. ed., 2008. FAMOUS AMERICANS SERIES: Abraham Lincoln, 1998; Martin Luther King, Jr., 1999; CesarChavez, 1999; George Washington, 1999. THE WAY THINGS MOVE SERIES: Back and Forth, 2000; Push and Pull, 2000; Zigzag Movement, 2000; Vibrations, 2000; Circular Movement, 2000; Start and Stop, 2000. FAMOUS PEOPLE IN TRANSPORTATION SERIES: The Wright Brothers, 2000; Henry Ford, 2000; Robert Fulton, 2000; Robert Goddard, 2000. ANIMAL KINGDOM SERIES: What Is a Mammal?, 2001; What Is a Reptile?, 2001; What Is an Amphibian?, 2001; WhatIs an Insect?, 2001; What Is a Fish?, 2001; What Is a Bird?, 2001. WILDWORLD OF ANIMALS SERIES: Frogs: Leaping Amphibians, 2001; Sharks: Hunters of the Deep, 2001; Spiders: Spinners and Trappers, 2001; Wolves: Life inthe Pack, 2001; Rhinos: Horn-Faced Chargers, 2002; Zebras: StripedGrass-Grazers, 2002; Giraffes: Long-Necked Leaf Eaters, 2002; Leopards: Spotted Hunters, 2002. FIRST BIOGRAPHIES SERIES: Christopher Columbus, 2002; Frederick Douglass, 2002; Rosa Parks, 2002; Pocahontas, 2002; Thomas Edison, 2003; Clara Barton, 2003; Jackie Robinson, 2003; Amelia Earhart, 2003; Alexander Graham Bell, 2003; Johnny Appleseed, 2003; Booker T. Washington, 2003; Mother Teresa, 2003; (with W.S. Schaefer) Albert Einstein, 2003. HOME FOR ME SERIES: Apartment, 2002; House, 2003; Houseboat, 2003; Mobile Home, 2003; Homes ABC, 2003. OOEY-GOOEY ANIMALS SERIES: Earthworms, 2002; Jellyfish, 2002; Leeches, 2002; Newts, 2002; Sea Anemones, 2002; Slugs, 2002; Ooey-Gooey Animals 123, 2002. MUSTY-CRUSTY ANIMALS SERIES: Lobsters, 2002; Crayfish, 2002; Barnacles, 2002; Horseshoe Crabs, 2002; Sea Horses, 2002; Medusa, 2002; Hermit Crabs, 2002; Musty-Crusty Animals 123, 2002; Musty-Crusty Animals ABC, 2002. SYMBOLS OF FREEDOM SERIES: Mount Rushmore, 2002; The U.S. Capitol, 2002; The Washington Monument, 2002; The Pledge of Allegiance, 2002. TINY-SPINY ANIMALS SERIES: Tiny-Spiny Animals 123, 2003; Tiny-Spiny Animals ABC, 2003; Sea Urchins, 2003; Horned Toad, 2003; Porcupine, 2003; Echidna, 2003. IT'S MY BODY SERIES: It's My Body ABC, 2003; My Head, 2003; My Neck and Shoulders, 2003; Body Pairs, 2003; Arms, Elbows, Hands, and Fingers, 2003; Legs, Knees, Feet, and Toes, 2003; Hair, 2003. WHEELS, WINGS, AND WATER SERIES: Wheels, Wings, and Water ABC, 2003; Shapes to Go, 2003; Trains, 2003; Boats, 2003; Aircraft, 2003; Bicycles, 2003. NON-FICTION: FOR ADULTS: Teaching Young Writers, 2001; Ten Writing Lessons for the Overhead, 2002; Writing Lessons for the Overhead: Grades 5 and Up, 2003; Writing Lessons For the Overhead, Grade 1, 2006; Writing Lessons for the Overhead, Grades 2-3, 2006; Writing Lessons for the Interactive Whiteboard, 2009; Writing Lessons for the Overhead: Responding to Literature, Grades 3-6, 2009. OTHERS: Homes 123, 2003; Las ardillas, 2004; Deer, 2004; Lizards, 2004; Echidnas, 2004; Horned Toads, 2004; Javelinas, 2004; Squirrels, 2004; Roadrunners, 2004; Armadillos, 2004; Elarmadillo, 2004; El correcaminos, 2004; (with W. Schaefer) Marie Curie, 2005; (with W. Schaefer) Jane Goodall, 2005; (with W. Schaefer) Florence Nightingale, 2005; (with T. Schaefer) The Pentagon, 2005; (with T. Schaefer) Snacks, 2006; (with T. Schaefer) Breakfast, 2006; (with T. Schaefer) Lunch, 2006; (with T. Schaefer) Dinner, 2006; (with T. Schaefer) Independence Hall, 2006; (with T. Schaefer) Arlington National Cemetery, 2006; (with T. Schaefer) The Franklin Delano Roosevelt Memorial, 2006; (with T. Schaefer) The Thomas Jefferson Memorial, 2006; The Alamo, 2006; (with T. Schaefer) The Vietnam Veterans Memorial, 2006; (with T. Schaefer) The National World War II Memorial, 2006; Toolbox Twins, 2006; Mittens, 2006; An Island Grows, 2006; What is Big, Big, Big?, 2007; Follow Me, Mittens, 2007; Frankie Stein, 2007; What is Good for You?, 2007; Milk, 2008; (with H. Miller) Look Behind!: Tales Of Animal Ends, 2008; Meat And Protein, 2008; Vegetables, 2008; Oils, 2008; Grains, 2008; What's that, Mittens?, 2008; Fruits, 2008; Please Pass the Manners! Mealtime Tips for Everyone, 2009; Guess Who?, 2009; Just One Bite, 2010; Algunos niños son ciegos, 2010; Algunos niños usan sillas de ruedas, 2010; Algunos niños son sordos, 2010; Mittens, Where is Max?, 2011; Semitrucks, 2011; Semitrucks in

Action, 2012; Airplanes in action, 2012; One Special Day, 2012; Tow Trucks in Action, 2012; Swamp Chomp, 2013. **Address:** 4924 CR 7, Garrett, IN 46738-9713, U.S.A. **Online address:** lola@lolaschaefer.com

SCHAEFER, William D. American (born United States), b. 1928. **Genres:** Novellas/Short Stories, Biography, Education. **Career:** University of California, assistant professor to associate professor, 1962-70, professor of English, 1970-, chair of department, 1969-71, executive vice-chancellor of the university, 1978-87, now professor emeritus; Modern Language Association, executive director, 1971-78; New York University, visiting professor, 1973; Columbia University, adjunct professor, 1974. Writer. **Publications:** James Thomson (B.V.): Beyond The City, 1965; (ed.) The Speedy Extinction of Evil and Misery: Selected Prose of James Thomson (B.V.), 1967; Education Without Compromise: From Chaos to Coherence in Higher Education, 1990. Contributor to journals. **Address:** Department of English, University of California, 149 Humanities Bldg., PO Box 951530, Los Angeles, CA 90095-1530, U.S.A. **Online address:** wllmschaefer@yahoo.com

SCHAEFER-RODRIGUEZ, Claudia. *See* **SCHAEFER, Claudia.**

SCHAEFFER, Mark. American (born United States), b. 1956. **Genres:** Children's Fiction, Plays/Screenplays, Librarianship, Education, Communications/Media, How-to Books. **Career:** Visual Education Corp., associate producer, 1978-79, project director, 1979-84; freelance writer and audiovisual producer, 1984-2003; author, 1991-; Princeton Mime Co., founder; San Francisco State University, faculty, University of San Francisco, faculty; Golden Gate University, Center for Electronic Arts, faculty; Chabot College, digital media instructor, 2003-. **Publications:** Library Displays Handbook, 1990; (with A. Persidsky) Macromedia Director MX for Windows and Macintosh, 2003; (with A. Persidsky) Macromedia Director MX 2004 for Windows and Macintosh, 2004; Adobe Flash CS3 Professional How-Tos: 100 Essential Techniques, 2008; Adobe Flash CS4 Professional How-Tos: 100 Essential Techniques, 2009. **Address:** School of the Arts, Chabot College, Rm. 1115, 25555 Hesperian Blvd., Hayward, CA 94545, U.S.A. **Online address:** mark@roseavenue.com

SCHAERF, Carlo. Italian (born Italy), b. 1935. **Genres:** Military/Defense/Arms Control, Physics, Politics/Government. **Career:** University of Rome-Rome, National Institute for Nuclear Physics, research associate, 1958-60; Stanford University, High Energy Physics Laboratory, research associate, 1960-63; Nuclear Energy Commission, Frascati National Laboratory, research associate and project director, 1963-73; International School on Disarmament and Research on Conflicts, co-founder, 1966, director, 1970, president; University of Rome-La Sapienza, professor of physics, 1973-81, Institute of Physics, director, 1975-80; University of Rome-Tor Vergata, professor of physics, 1981-. Writer. **Publications:** EDITOR: (with F. Barnaby) Disarmament and Arms Control, 1972; (with D. Carlton) The Dynamics of the Arms Race, 1975; (with D. Carlton) International Terrorism and World Security, 1975; (with D. Carlton) Arms Control and Technological Innovation, 1977; International School on Electro and Photonuclear Reactions II: Proceedings of the International School on Electro and Photonuclear Reactions, 1977; (with S. Costa) Photonuclear Reactions, 2 vols., 1977; Perspectives of Fundamental Physics, 1979; (with W. Bertozzi and S. Costa) Electron and Pion Interactions with Nuclei at Intermediate Energies, 2 vols., 1980; (with D. Carlton) Contemporary Terror: Studies in Sub-State Violence, 1981; (with D. Carlton) The Arms Race in the 1980s, 1982; (with D. Carlton) The Hazards of the International Energy Crisis: Studies of The Coming Struggle For Energy and Strategic Raw Materials, 1982; (with R. Bergere and S. Costa) Intermediate Energy Nuclear Physics, 1982; (with D. Carlton) South-Eastern Europe after Tito: A Powder-Keg for the 1980s?, 1983; (with D. Carlton) Reassessing Arms Control: Studies in Disarmament and Conflicts, 1984; (with D. Carlton) The Arms Race in the Era of Star Wars: Studies in Disarmament and Conflicts, 1988; (with B.H. Reid and D. Carlton) New Technologies and the Arms Race, 1989; (with D. Carlton) Perspectives on the Arms Race, 1989; (with D. Carlton) The Arms Race in an Era of Negotiations, 1991; (with D. Carlton) Reducing Nuclear Arsenals, 1991; (with D. Carlton and Longo) Space and Nuclear Weaponry in the 1990s, 1992. OTHER: (with D. Carlton) Controlling the International Transfer of Weaponry and Related Technology, 1995. **Address:** Dipartimento di Fisica, Universita' di Roma, Tor Vergata, via della Ricerca Scientifica 1, Rome, 00133, Italy. **Online address:** schaerf@roma2.infn.it

SCHAFER, Elisabeth. American (born United States), b. 1945. **Genres:**

Food And Wine, Medicine/Health. **Career:** Pennsylvania State University, instructor in English, 1968-70; Iowa State University, instructor in English, 1970-71, assistant professor, 1980-86, associate professor, 1986-94, Food Science and Human Nutrition, professor, 1994-, extension nutrition specialist, 1980-, now emeritus; Hebei Agricultural University, teacher, 1986; Latvian Academy of Sports Pedagogy, research collaborator and trainer, 1992; University of Glasgow, lecturer, 1997; Nutrition Coalition, president, 1989-90; Des Moines Science Center, consultant. Writer. **Publications:** (With J.L. Miller) Lunches to Go: Brown-Bagging It, 1991; (with J.L. Miller) Vegetable Desserts: Beyond Carrot Cake and Pumpkin Pie, 1998; Die offene Seite der Schrift: J.D. und H.C. coôte aà côte, 2008. Contributor to books and journals. **Address:** Department of Food Science andHuman Nutrition, Iowa State University, 2312 Food Sciences Bldg., Ames, IA 50011, U.S.A. **Online address:** eschafer@iastate.edu

SCHAFFER, Frederic Charles. American (born United States), b. 1961. **Genres:** Politics/Government. **Career:** University of Massachusetts, Department of Political Science, associate professor of political science and director of graduate program. Writer. **Publications:** Democracy in Translation: Understanding Politics in an Unfamiliar Culture, 1998; (ed.) Elections for Sale: The Causes and Consequences of Vote Buying, 2007; The Hidden Costs of Clean Election Reform, 2008. **Address:** Department of Political Science, University of Massachusetts, 324 Thompson Hall, 200 Hicks Way, Amherst, MA 01003, U.S.A. **Online address:** schaffer@polsci.umass.edu

SCHAFFERT, Timothy. American (born United States) **Genres:** Novels, Young Adult Fiction. **Career:** Omaha Pulp, editor; Reader, editor; Omaha Lit Fest, founder and director; University of Nebraska, Department of English, lecturer. **Publications:** The Phantom Limbs of the Rollow Sisters, 2002; The Singing and Dancing Daughters of God, 2005; Devils in the Sugar Shop, 2007; The Coffins of Little Hope, 2011. Works appear in anthologies. Contributor to periodicals. **Address:** c/o Author Mail, Unbridled Books, 2000 Wadsworth Blvd., Ste. 195, Lakewood, CO 80214, U.S.A. **Online address:** timothy@omahalitfest.com

SCHAFFNER, Bradley L(ewis). American (born United States), b. 1959. **Genres:** Bibliography, Librarianship. **Career:** Indiana University, library assistant, 1985-86, instructor in history, 1985-89, Slavic copy cataloger, 1986-89; University of Kansas, librarian, Russian and East Slavic studies bibliographer, Slavic Department, head and head of international programs, 1989-2004; Emporia State University, School of Library and Information Management, adjunct professor, 2000-; Harvard University, Harvard College Library, Widener Library, Slavic Division, head, 2004-. Writer. **Publications:** Bibliography of the Soviet Union, Its Predecessors and Successors, 1995; (ed. with G.C. Ference) Books, Bibliographies and Pugs: A Festschrift to Honor Murlin Croucher, 2006. Contributor to books and periodicals. **Address:** Slavic Division, Widener Library, Harvard College Library, Harvard University, Cambridge, MA 02138, U.S.A. **Online address:** bschaffn@fas.harvard.edu

SCHAIN, Martin A. American (born United States), b. 1940. **Genres:** Politics/Government, Social Sciences. **Career:** New York University, Department of Politics, faculty, 1966-, director of undergraduate studies, 1974-75, 1978-79, 1986-87, 1988-90, director of graduate studies, 1975-77, 1979-81, 1982-85, professor of politics, 1986-, director of placement, 1994-95; Center for European Studies, associate director, 1990-93, director, 1993-2005, Dialogues-Islam and the West, academic advisor, 2006-07; School of Law, Straus and Emile Noel senior fellow, 2010-11; New York Consortium for European Studies, co-director, 1993-2005; European Union Center of New York, co-director, 1998-2004. Writer. **Publications:** European Society and Politics: Britain France and Germany, 1976; French Politics and Public Policy, 1980; French Communism and Local Power: Urban Politics and Political Change, 1985; (with H.W. Ehrmann) Politics in France, 1992; Politics of Immigration in France, Britain, and the United States: A Comparative Study, 2008. EDITOR: (with P.G. Cerny) Socialism the State and Public Policy in France, 1985; (with M. Baldwin-Edwards) The Politics of Immigration in Western Europe, 1994; (with J.T.S. Keller) Chirac's Challenge: Liberalization Europeanization and Malaise in France, 1996; (with H. Chapman and M. Kesselman) A Century of Organized Labor in France: A Union Movement for the Twenty-first Century?, 1998; The Marshall Plan: Fifty Years After, 2001; (with A. Zolberg and P. Hossay) Shadows over Europe: The Development and Impact of the Extreme Right in Western Europe, 2002; (with M. Berezin) Europe without Borders: Remapping Territory Citizenship and Identity in a Transnational Age, 2003; (with A. Menon) The U.S. and E.U. in Comparative

Perspective, 2006. **Address:** Department of Politics, New York University, Rm. 206, 19 W 4th St., New York, NY 10012-1119, U.S.A. **Online address:** martin.schain@nyu.edu

SCHAKEL, Peter J. American (born United States), b. 1941. **Genres:** Poetry, History. **Career:** University of Nebraska, faculty; Hope College, faculty, 1969-, professor of English, Peter C. and Emajean Cook professor of English, 1984-. Writer. **Publications:** The Poetry of Jonathan Swift: Allusion and the Development of a Poetic Style, 1978; Reading with the Heart: The Way into Narnia, 1979; Reason and Imagination in C.S. Lewis: A Study of Till We Have Faces, 1984; (with J. Ridl) Approaching Poetry: Perspectives and Responses, 1997; Imagination and the Arts in C.S. Lewis: Journeying to Narnia and Other Worlds, 2002; (with J. Ridl) Approaching Literature in the 21st Century: Fiction, Poetry, Drama, 2005, 3rd ed. as Approaching Literature: Reading + Thinking + Writing, 2012; The Way into Narnia: A Reader's Guide, 2005; Is Your Lord Large Enough?: How C.S. Lewis Expands Our View of God, 2008. EDITOR: The Longing for a Form: Essays on the Fiction of C.S. Lewis, 1977; (with C.A. Huttar) Word and Story in C.S. Lewis, 1991; Critical Approaches to Teaching Swift, 1992; (with C.A. Huttar) The Rhetoric of Vision: Essays on Charles Williams, 1996; (with H.D. Weinbrot and S.E. Karian) Eighteenth-Century Contexts: Historical Inquiries in Honor of Phillip Harth, 2001; (with J. Ridl) 250 Poems: A Portable Anthology, 2003, 2nd ed., 2009. Contributor to journals. **Address:** Department of English, Hope College, 126 E 10th St., Holland, MI 49423, U.S.A. **Online address:** schakel@hope.edu

SCHALL, Lucy. American (born United States), b. 1946. **Genres:** Education. **Career:** Allegheny College, teacher, 1970-78, 1985, now retired. Writer. **Publications:** Booktalks Plus: Motivating Teens to Read, 2001; Booktalks and More: Motivating Teens to Read, 2003; Teen Genre Connections: From Booktalking to Booklearning, 2005; Booktalks and Beyond: Promoting Great Genre Reads to Teens, 2007; Genre Talks for Teens: Booktalks and More for Every Teen Reading Interest, 2009; Value-Packed Booktalks: Genre Talks and More for Teen Readers, 2011. Contributor to periodicals. **Address:** c/o Author Mail, Libraries Unlimited Inc., PO Box 6633, Englewood, CO 80155-6633, U.S.A.

SCHALLER, George B(eals). American/German (born Germany), b. 1933. **Genres:** Zoology, Animals/Pets, Biology, Young Adult Fiction. **Career:** Stanford University, Center for Advanced Study in the Behavioral Sciences, Department of Behavioral Sciences, fellow, 1962-63; Johns Hopkins University, research associate, assistant professor, 1963-66; The Wildlife Conservation Society, director for science, 1966-, senior conservationist; Rockefeller University, research associate, 1966-72, adjunct associate professor; New York Zoological Society, research associate and zoologist, 1966-79, Animal Research and Conservation Center, director, 1979-88; New York Zoological Society, International Conservation Program, director, 1979-88; Panthera Corp., vice president, 2008-; American Museum of Natural History, research associate; East China Normal University, adjunct associate professor; Peking University, adjunct associate professor. Writer. **Publications:** (With B. Kessel) Birds of the Upper Sheenjek Valley, Northeastern Alaska, 1960; The Mountain Gorilla: Ecology and Behavior, 1963; The Year of the Gorilla, 1964; The Deer and the Tiger: A Study of Wildlife in India, 1967; An chez les gorilles, 1967; Year of the Gorilla: An Exploration, 1967; God Pod Znakom Gorilly, 1968; (with M.E. Selsam) The Tiger: Its Life in the Wild (juvenile), 1969; The Serengeti Lion: A Study of Predator-Prey Relations, 1972; Serengeti: A Kingdom of Predators, 1972; Golden Shadows, Flying Hooves: With a New Afterword, 1973; Mountain Monarchs: Wild Sheep and Goats of the Himalaya, 1977; (with K. Schaller) V Vonders of Lions, 1977; Stones of Silence: Journeys in the Himalaya, 1980; (with J.B. Wexo and C.R. Schroeder) The Giant Pandas of Wolong, 1985; Stones of Silence: Journeys in the Himalaya, 1988; (contrib.) Gorilla, 1989; The Last Panda, 1993; Tibet's Hidden Wilderness: Wildlife and Nomads of the Chang Tang Reserve, 1997; Wildlife of the Tibetan Steppe, 1998; (with E.S. Vrba) Antelopes, Deer, and Relatives: Fossil Record, Behavioral Ecology, Systematics, and Conservation, 2000; Giant Pandas in the Wild, 2002; Naturalist and Other Beasts: Tales from a Life in the Field, 2007; Year of the Gorilla: With a New Postscript, 2009; (foreword) Chinese Alligator: Ecology, Behavior, Conservation and Culture, 2010. Contributor of articles to journals and magazines. **Address:** Panthera Corp., 8 W 40th St., 18th Fl., New York, NY 10018, U.S.A.

SCHALLER, Lyle E(dwin). American (born United States), b. 1923?. **Genres:** Urban Studies, Theology/Religion, History. **Career:** City of Madison, city planner, 1951-54; pastor of Methodist churches, 1955-60; ordained Methodist minister, 1957; Regional Church Planning Office, church planner and director, 1960-68; Garrett Theological Seminary, professor, 1968-71; Center for Parish Development, director, 1969; Yokefellow Institute, parish consultant, 1971-93; Religious Research Association, H. Paul Douglass lecturer, 1974. Writer. **Publications:** Planning for Protestantism in Urban America, 1965; Community Organization: Conflict and Reconciliation, 1966; Churches' War on Poverty, 1967; The Local Church Looks to the Future, 1968; The Impact of the Future, 1969; Parish Planning, 1971; The Change Agent, 1972; The Pastor and the People, 1973, rev. ed., 1986; The Decision-Makers, 1974; Hey, That's Our Church!, 1975; (with C.A. Tidwell) Creative Church Administration, 1975; Understanding Tomorrow, 1976; Survival Tactics in the Parish, 1977; Assimilating New Members, 1978; Effective Church Planning, 1979; The Multiple Staff and the Larger Church, 1980; Activating the Passive Church, 1981; The Small Church Is Different!, 1982; (ed.) Women as Pastors, 1982; Growing Plans, 1983; Looking in the Mirror: Self-Appraisal in the Local Church, 1984; The Church Looks in a Mirror, 1984; The Middle-Sized Church, 1985; Getting Things Done, 1986; It's a Different World, 1987; The Senior Minister, 1988; 44 Ways to Increase Church Attendance, 1988; 44 Ways to Expand the Financial Base of Your Congregation, 1989; Reflections of a Contrarian, 1989; 44 Ways to Revitalize the Women's Organization, 1990; Choices for Churches, 1990; Create Your Own Future, 1991; 44 Questions For Church Planters, 1991; Seven-day-a-week Church, 1992; 44 Ways to Expand the Teaching Ministry of Your Church, 1992; (ed.) Center City Churches: The New Urban Frontier, 1993; Strategies for Change, 1993; 44 Steps Up off the Plateau, 1993; 21 Bridges to the 21st Century, 1994; (ed.) Put Your Best Foot Forward: How to Minister from Your Strength, 1994; Innovations in Ministry, 1994; The Small Membership Church, 1994; The New Reformation, 1995; (with R. Frazee) Comeback Congregation: New Life for a Troubled Ministry, 1995; (with H. Edington) Downtown Church: The Heart of the City, 1996; Tattered Trust, 1996; The Interventionist, 1997; 44 Questions for Congregational Self-Evaluation, 1998; Discontinuity and Hope, 1999; (with R.L. Dunagin) Beyond These Walls: Building The Church in a Built-Out Neighborhood, 1999; The Very Large Church, 2000; The Evolution of the American Public High School, 2000; What Have We Learned?, 2001; New Context for Ministry: The Impact of the New Economy on Your Church, 2002; From Geography to Affinity: How Congregations can Learn from One Another, 2003; Small Congregation, Big Potential: Ministry in the Small Membership Church, 2003; Ice Cube is Melting: What is Really at Risk in United Methodism?, 2004; Mainline Turnaround: Strategies for Congregations and Denominations, 2005; From Cooperation to Competition: Change, Choice, and Conflict in the Congregation, 2006. **Address:** 530 N Brainard St., Naperville, IL 60563, U.S.A.

SCHAMA, Simon (Michael). American/British (born England). b. 1945. **Genres:** History. **Career:** Christs College, Cambridge University, director of studies in history, 1966-76, honorary fellow; Oxford University, Brasenose College, tutor in history and lecturer, 1976-80; Harvard University, Erasmus lecturer in the civilization of the Netherlands, 1978, professor of history, Mellon professor of social sciences and senior associate, Center for European Studies, faculty, 1980-93; University of Columbia, university professor of art history and history, 1994-; The New Yorker Magazine, art critic, 1995-98. Writer. **Publications:** (Ed. with E. Homberger and W. Janeway) The Cambridge Mind: Ninety Years of the Cambridge Review, 1879-1969, 1970, 2nd ed., 1971; Patriots and Liberators: Revolution in the Netherlands 1780-1813, 1977; Two Rothschilds and the Land of Israel, 1978; Bet Rotòshildvòe-Erets-Yiśrael: mifalam shel Edmond vòe-Gaims Rotòshildba-Arets, 1980; Affluence and Anxiety: A Social Interpretation of Dutch Culture in Its Golden Age, 1983; The Embarrassment of Riches: An Interpretation of Dutch Culture in the Golden Age, 1987; Citizens: A Chronicle of the French Revolution, 1989; Dead Certainties: Unwarranted Speculations, 1992; Landscape and Memory, 1995; (contrib.) Jews, America, 1996; Rembrants Eyes, 1999; A History of Britain: At the Edge of the World? 3000 BC-AD 1603, 2000; History of Britain: The Fate of Empire, 1776-2000, vol. III, 2003; (contrib.) Cy Twombly in der Eremitage, 2003; (with R. Barthes) Cy Twombly: Fifty Years of Works on Paper, 2004; Cy Twombly: Cinquante Années de Dessins, 2004; (with P. Moorehouse and C. Wiggins) John Virtue: London Paintings, 2005; Rough Crossings: Britain, the Slaves and the American Revolution, 2006; Simon Schamas Power of Art, 2006; Rough Crossings: Britain, The Slaves and the American Revolution, 2006; American Future: A History, 2008; (contrib.) Anselm Kiefer: Karfunkelfee, The Fertile Crescent, 2009; Scribble: Writings on Ice Cream, Obama, Churchill and My Mother, 2010; Scribble, Scribble,

Scribble, 2010. Contributor of articles to magazines and newspapers. **Address:** Department of History, Columbia University, 522 Fayerweather Hall, 1190 Amsterdam Ave., New York, NY 10027, U.S.A. **Online address:** sms53@columbia.edu

SCHANK, Roger C(arl). American (born United States), b. 1946. **Genres:** Information Science/Computers, Education. **Career:** Semiotics Group, engineer and scientist, 1966-68; Stanford University, research associate in computer science, 1968-69, assistant professor of linguistics and computer science, 1969-73; Institute for Semantics and Cognition, research fellow, 1973-74; Yale University, associate professor, 1974-76, professor of computer science and psychology, 1976-89, Yale Artificial Intelligence Project, director, 1974-89, Department of Computer Science, chairman, 1980-85; Cognitive Systems Inc., president, 1981-83, chairman of board, 1983-88; Compu-Teach Inc., president, 1982-84, chairman, 1984-88; Northwestern University, The Institute for the Learning Science, John Evans professor of computer science, education and psychology, director, 1989-; Cognitive Arts Corp., founder, chairman and chief technology officer, 1995-; Carnegie Mellon West, chief education officer, 2001-04; Socratic Arts, president and chief executive officer, 2002-; Trump University, chief learning officer, 2004-10. Writer. **Publications:** (Ed. with K.M. Colby) Computer Models of Thought and Language, 1973; (ed. with B. Nash-Webber) Proceedings of the Conference on Theoretical Issues in Natural Language Processing, 1975; Conceptual Information Processing, 1975; (with R.P. Abelson) Scripts, Plans, Goals and Understanding: An Inquiry into Human Knowledge Structures, 1977; (ed. with C.K. Riesbeck) Inside Computer Understanding: Five Programs Plus Miniatures, 1981; Reading and Understanding: Teaching from the Perspective of Artificial Intelligence, 1982; Dynamic Memory: A Theory of Reminding and Learning in Computers and People, 1982; (with P.G. Childers) The Cognitive Computer: On Language, Learning and Artificial Intelligence, 1984; Explanation Patterns: Understanding Mechanically and Creatively, 1986; (with P.G. Childers) The Creative Attitude: Learning to Ask and Answer the Right Questions, 1988; (with C.K. Riesbeck) Inside Case-Based Reasoning, 1989; Tell Me a Story: A New Look at Real and Artificial Memory, 1990; The Connoisseur's Guide to the Mind: How We Think, How We Learn and What it Means to be Intelligent, 1991; (ed. with E. Langer) Beliefs, Reasoning and Decision Making: Psycho-Logic in Honor of Bob Abelson, 1994; (with A. Kass and C.K. Riesbeck) Inside Case-Based Explanation, 1994; (with C. Cleary) Engines for Education, 1995; Tell Me a Story: Narrative and Intelligence, 1995; (ed.) Computer in Classe: Le Nouvo Technologie Nella Scuola, 1997; Virtual Learning: A Revolutionary Approach to Building a Highly Skilled Workforce, 1997; Inside Multi-media Case-Based Instruction, 1998; Dynamic Memory Revisited, 1999; Coloring Outside the Lines: Raising a Smarter Kid by Breaking All the Rules, 2000; Scrooge Meets Dick and Jane, 2001; Designing World Class E-Learning: How IBM, GE, Harvard Business School and Columbia University are Succeeding at E-Learning, 2002; Making Minds Less Well Educated than Our Own, 2004; Lessons in Learning, E-Learning and Training: Perspectives and Guidance for the Enlightened Trainer, 2005; Future of Decision Making, 2010; Teaching Minds, 2011. CONTRIBUTOR: Natural Language Processing, 1972; Representation and Understanding: Studies in Cognitive Science, 1975; The Nature of Human Memory, 1976; Thinking Reading in Cognitive Science, 1977; Machine Intelligence 8, 1977; Pattern-Directed Inference Systems, 1978; Recent Advances in the Psychology of Language: Formal and Experimental Approaches, 1978; Human and Artificial Intelligence, 1978; Studies in the Perception of Language, 1978; Applied Natural Language Processing, 1987. Contributor to books and journals. **Address:** Socratic Arts, 3 Longview Dr., Holmdel, NJ 07733, U.S.A. **Online address:** roger@socraticarts.com

SCHAPIRO, Barbara. American (born United States), b. 1952. **Genres:** Literary Criticism And History, Psychology, Literary Criticism And History. **Career:** Boston University, assistant professor of humanities, 1979-83, Metropolitan College, master lecturer, 1980-84; Harvard University, lecturer in history and literature, 1983-87; Rhode Island College, assistant professor, 1987-91, professor of English and director of graduate studies, 1991-. Writer. **Publications:** The Romantic Mother: Narcissistic Patterns in Romantic Poetry, 1983; (ed. with L. Layton) Narcissism and the Text: Studies in Literature and the Psychology of Self, 1986; Literature and the Relational Self, 1994; D.H. Lawrence and the Paradoxes of Psychic Life, 1999. Works appear in anthologies. Contributor of articles to journals. **Address:** Department of English, Rhode Island College, 355 Craig-Lee Hall, 600 Mount Pleasant Ave., Providence, RI 02908-1991, U.S.A. **Online address:** bschapiro@ric.edu

SCHARF, Michael P(aul). American (born United States), b. 1963. **Genres:** International Relations/Current Affairs, Law. **Career:** U.S. Court of Appeals (11th circuit), judicial clerk, 1988-89; U.S. Department of State, Office Legal Adviser, attorney-adviser, 1989-93; Georgetown University Law Center, adjunct professor of law, 1992-93, New England School of Law, professor of international law, 1993-, Center for International Law and Policy, director, 1993-2002; New England School of Law, assistant professor, 1993-95, associate professor, 1995-97, professor of international law, 1995-2002; Public International Law and Policy Group, co-founder, vice chairman, managing director, 1995-; Australian National University, visiting professor of international law, 2001; Case Western Reserve University School of Law, professor of international law, 2002-, Frederick K. Cox International Law Center, director, 2003-, Summer Institute for Global Justice, director, 2002-, John Deaver Drinko-Baker and Hostetler professor of law, Henry T. King War Crimes Research Office, founder, director; Public International Law & Policy Group, co-founder; Summer Institute for Global Justice in Utrecht, director. Writer. **Publications:** (With V. Morris) An Insider's Guide to the International Criminal Tribunal for the Former Yugoslavia: A Documentary History and Analysis, 1995; (with J. Paust) International Criminal Law, 1996, 3rd ed., 2007; Balkan Justice: The Story Behind the First International War Crimes Trial Since Nuremberg, 1997; (with Morris) The International Criminal Tribunal for Rwanda, 1998; The Law of International Organizations: Problems and Materials, 2001, 2nd ed., 2007; (with W. Schabas) Slobodan Milosevic on Trial: A Companion, 2002; (with P. Williams) Peace with Justice: War Crimes and Accountability in the Former Yugoslavia, 2002; (comp. with G.S. McNeal) Saddam on Trial: Understanding and Debating the Iraqi High Tribunal, 2006; (ed. with L.N. Sadat) Theory and Practice of International Criminal Law: Essays in Honor of M. Cherif Bassiouni, 2008; (with M.A. Newton) Enemy of the State: The Trial and Execution of Saddam Hussein, 2008; (ed. with J.M. Willem and S.E. Radin) Criminal Jurisdiction 100 Years After the 1907 Hague Peace Conference, 2009; (with P.R. Williams) Shaping Foreign Policy in Times of Crisis: The Role of International Law and the State Department Legal Adviser, 2010; Henry T. King, Jr., 2011. **Address:** School of Law, Case Western Reserve University, 11075 East Blvd., Cleveland, OH 44106, U.S.A. **Online address:** mps17@case.edu

SCHARRER, Erica. American (born United States) **Genres:** Psychology, Communications/Media. **Career:** River Reporter newspaper, stringer reporter, 1992; WDNH-FM, news director, 1992; WWCC-AM, news director, 1992; WGGY-FM, copy writer, 1993; WKRZ-FM, copy writer, 1993; WILK-AM, copy writer, 1993; WCGR-AM, disc jockey, 1994; Syracuse University, research assistant, 1995-98; State University of New York, Department Of Communication, assistant professor, 1998-99, faculty director, 1998-99; University of Massachusetts, Department Of Communication, assistant professor, 1999-2005, associate professor, 2005-. Writer. **Publications:** (With G.A. Comstock) Television: What's On, Who's Watching, and What It Means, 1999; (with G.A. Comstock) The Psychology of Media and Politics, 2005; (with G.A. Comstock) Media and the American Child, 2007. Contributor to journals and publications. **Address:** Department of Communication, University of Massachusetts, 309 Machmer Hall, 240 Hicks Way, Amherst, MA 01003-9278, U.S.A. **Online address:** scharrer@comm.umass.edu

SCHATZKER, Mark. Canadian (born Canada), b. 1974?. **Genres:** Food And Wine. **Career:** Globe and Mail, columnist. **Publications:** Steak: One Man's Search for the World's Tastiest Piece of Beef, 2010. **Address:** Toronto, ON , Canada. **Online address:** steakthebook@gmail.com

SCHATZKIN, Paul. American (born United States) **Genres:** Adult Non-fiction, Biography, Autobiography/Memoirs. **Career:** American Broadcasting Co. (ABC)-TV, videotape editor; Cohesion Arts, founder. Writer. **Publications:** The Boy Who Invented Television: A Story of Inspiration, Persistence and Quiet Passion, 2002. Contributor to periodicals. **Address:** c/o Author Mail, TeamCom L.L.C., PO Box 1251, Burtonsville, MD 20866-0651, U.S.A. **Online address:** webcon06@49chevy.com

SCHECK, Florian A. German (born Germany), b. 1936. **Genres:** Novels. **Career:** Weizmann Institute of Science, visiting scientist, 1964-66; University of Heidelberg, university assistant, 1967-68; CERN (European Organization for Nuclear Research), research fellow, 1968-70; ETH Zurich, titular professor, 1970-76; Johannes Gutenberg-University, professor, 1976-2005, professor emeritus, 2005-; Weizmann Institute of Science, 1973. Writer. **Publications:** NONFICTION: Leptons, Hadrons, and Nuclei, 1983, rev. ed., Electroweak and Strong Interactions: An Introduction to Theoretical Particle Physics, with Fifty-nine Figures, Eighty Exercises, and Solutions, 1996; Mechanik: Von den Newtonschen gesetzen zum determinstischen chaos, 2005; (ed. with S. Ciulli, F. Scheck, and W. Thirring) Rigorous Methods in Particle Physics, 1990; (ed. with H. Upmeier and W. Werner) Noncommutative Geometry and the Standard Model of Elementary Particle Physics, 2002; Quantum Physics, 2007. Contributor to professional journals. **Address:** Institute for Physics, Johannes Gutenberg-University, Mainz, D-55099, Germany. **Online address:** scheck@thep.physik.uni-mainz.de

SCHECK, Raffael. American/German (born Germany), b. 1960. **Genres:** Politics/Government, History, Young Adult Non-fiction. **Career:** University of Zürich, tutor, 1983-86; Brandeis University, research and teaching assistant, 1989-92; Bowdoin College, visiting assistant professor of modern European history, 1993-94; Colby College, assistant professor 1994-99, associate professor, 1999-2006, professor of modern European history, 2006-, chair of history department, 2000-03, 2005-. Writer. **Publications:** NONFICTION: Alfred Von Tirpitz and German Right-Wing Politics, 1914-1930, 1998; Mothers of the Nation: Right-Wing Women in Weimar Germany, 2003; Hitler's African Victims: The German Army Massacres of Black French Soldiers in 1940, 2006; Germany, 1871-1945: A Concise History, 2008. **Address:** Department of History, Colby College, Waterville, ME 04901-8853, U.S.A. **Online address:** rmscheck@colby.edu

SCHECTER, Barnet. American (born United States) **Genres:** Architecture, Biography. **Career:** Walker & Co., independent historian, 1999-; New York Academy of History, fellow. Writer. **Publications:** (Co-author) Back in the USSR: An American Family Returns to Moscow, 1989; The Battle for New York: The City at the Heart of the American Revolution, 2002; Devil's Own Work: The Civil War Draft Riots and the Fight to Reconstruct America, 2005; George Washington's America: A Biography Through His Maps, 2010. Contributor to books and magazines. **Address:** c/o Author Mail, Walker Books, 175 5th Ave., New York, NY 10010, U.S.A.

SCHECTER, Darrow. British (born England), b. 1961. **Genres:** Politics/Government, Industrial Relations, International Relations/Current Affairs, History. **Career:** Oxford University, Brasenose College, tutor, 1986-87; St. Anne's College, tutor, 1988-89; Ecole Nationale des Sciences Politiques, lecturer in English and American studies, 1989-90; University of Sussex, lecturer in European studies, 1990-, School of Humanities, Art History and Humanities, reader. Writer. **Publications:** Gramsci and the Theory of Industrial Democracy, 1991; (with R. Bellamy) Gramsci and the Italian State, 1993; Radical Theories: Paths Beyond Marxism and Social Democracy, 1994; I can Read about Planets, 1996; Sovereign States or Political Communities, 1999; Beyond Hegemony: Towards a New Philosophy of Political Legitimacy, 2005; The History of the Left from Marx to the Present: Theoretical Perspectives, 2007; Critique of Instrumental Reason from Weber to Habermas, 2010. Contributor of articles to periodicals. **Address:** School of European Studies, University of Sussex, Arts A A165, Sussex House, Brighton, ES BN21 9QN, England. **Online address:** d.schecter@sussex.ac.uk

SCHEELE, Roy. American (born United States), b. 1942?. **Genres:** Poetry, Literary Criticism And History. **Career:** University of Tennessee, instructor in English, 1966-68; City Library of Lincoln, research librarian, 1969-70; Theodor Heuss Gymnasium, instructor in English, 1974-75; Nebraska Arts Council, poet, 1976-85; Creighton University, lecturer in classics, 1977-79; University of Nebraska, visiting instructor in classics, 1980-81; Doane College, instructor of English as a second language, 1982-90, poet-in-residence, 1990-, associate professor of English. Writer. **Publications:** (Ed.) Bestiary, 1973; Grams and Epigrams, 1973; Accompanied, 1974; Noticing, 1979; (with N.D. Anderson and G. Tremblay) Close to Home: Poems, 1981; The Sea-Ocean, 1981; Pointing out the Sky: Poems, 1985; The Voice We Call Human, 1991; To See How It Tallies, 1995; Short Suite: Short Poems, 1997; Keeping the Horses, 1998; From the Ground Up: Thirty Sonnets, 2000; No Music, No Poem: Interviews with W.R. Moses and W.D. Snodgrass, 2001; A Far Allegiance, 2010. **Address:** Doane College, Perry Campus Ctr., 1014 Boswell Ave., Crete, NE 68333, U.S.A. **Online address:** roy.scheele@doane.edu

SCHEERES, Julia. American (born United States), b. 1967. **Genres:** Children's Non-fiction, Novels. **Career:** Journalist. **Publications:** Jesus Land: A Memoir, 2005 in UK as Another Hour on a Sunday Morning, 2006; A Thousand Lives: The Untold Story of Faith, Deception and the Fight to Survive Jonestown, 2011. Contributor to periodicals. **Address:** Judi Farkas Management, 116 N Mansfield Ave., Los Angeles, CA 90036, U.S.A. **Online address:** julia@juliascheeres.com

SCHEESE, Donald. American (born United States), b. 1954. **Genres:** Environmental Sciences/Ecology, History, Literary Criticism And History. **Career:** Gustavus Adolphus College, associate professor of English, 1992, Environmental Studies Program, director, 1997-, professor of English and environmental studies. Writer. **Publications:** Nature Writing: The Pastoral Impulse in America, 1996; Mountains of Memory: A Fire Lookout's Life in the River of No Return Wilderness, 2001; Stories of Stone: Representations of the Anasazi in Art and Literature, forthcoming. Contributor to periodicals and books. **Address:** Department of English, Gustavus Adolphus College, Ogden P. Confer Hall, 310, 800 W College Ave., Saint Peter, MN 56082, U.S.A. **Online address:** dscheese@gustavus.edu

SCHEFFER, Kathy J(ean). American (born United States), b. 1955. **Genres:** Medicine/Health, Sciences. **Career:** Piqua Memorial Hospital, Medical-Surgical Unit, assistant charge nurse, 1976-78; Lakewood General Hospital, staff nurse, 1978; Tacoma General Hospital, float pool staff nurse, 1979-80, short-stay acting head nurse, 1980-82, radiology charge nurse and clinical coordinator, 1982-, clinical manager imaging services, Nurse Resource Department, clinical manager; Tacoma Community College, lecturer, 1997. Writer. **Publications:** (With R.S. Tobin) Better X-ray Interpretation: A Handbook for Health Care Professionals, 1997. Contributor to journals. **Address:** Tacoma General Hospital, 315 Martin Luther King Jr Way, Tacoma, WA 98405-4234, U.S.A.

SCHEFFLER, Ursel. German (born Germany), b. 1938. **Genres:** Children's Fiction, Picture/Board Books. **Career:** Author, 1975-. **Publications:** FOR CHILDREN: Spatzen brauchen keinen Schirm, 1984; Kraehverbot fuer Kasimir, 1986; Der Riesenapfel, 1988; Stop Your Crowing, Kasimir!, 1988; Der schlaue Fuchs Rinaldo, 1992; Der schlaue Fuchs Rinaldo plant neue Tricks, 1993; Alle nannten ihn Tomate; Sonnen-Jan/Regen-Jan; Der schlaue Fuchs Rinaldo und der Pizza Koenig, 1994; Sun Jack & Rain Jack, 1994; Rinaldo on the Run, 1995. KOMMISSAR KUGELBLITZ SERIES FOR CHILDREN: Die rote Socke, 1982; Die orangefarbene Maske, 1982; Der gelbe Koffer, 1982; Der gruene Papagei, 1983; Das blaue Zimmer, 1983; Der lila Leierkasten, 1983; Der schwarze Geist, 1986; Das rosa Nilpferd, 1987; Die schneeweisse Katze, 1988; Der goldene Drache, 1990; Der Jade-Elefant, 1992; Der Fall Koralle, 1993. LESELOEWEN SERIES FOR CHILDREN: Leseloewen: Zirkusgeschichten, 1980; Leseloewen: Weihnachtsgeschichten, 1984; Leseloewen: Ostergeschichten, 1986; Leseloewen: Maerchenkueche, 1986; Leseloewen: Der Kater im Theater, 1988; Leseloewen: Feriengeschichten, 1991. OTHER: Auf dem Markt, 1980; Hier bin ich zu Hause, 1983; Ein Tag in unserer Stadt, 1986; Aetze, das Tintenmonster, 1986; Das ABC-Monster, 1987; Das Zahlenmonster, 1988; Aetze, das Hosentaschenmonster, 1990; Die Wunschkiste, 1990; Uexe, der Fischstaebchentroll, 1990; Piratenlissy, 1990; Ach, du dicker Weihnachtsmann, 1991; Das neue Hamburger Sagenbuch: Ein Spaziergang durch die Stadtgeschichte, 1991; Adventskalendergeschichten (Christmas stories), 1991; Dinosaurus Klex: Die schwimmende Insel, 1991; Lucy und die Vampire, 1991; Lucy und Dr. Acula, 1992; Dinosaurus Klex: Die Reise nach Gondwana, 1992; Geschichten von der Maus fuer die Katz (short stories), 1992; Als David den Goliath besiegte (Old Testament stories), 1992; Die Hexe Alexa, 1992; Oma Paloma, 1992; Hallo, lieber Uexe!, 1992; Prinzessin Knallerbse, 1993; Aetze, das Rucksackmonster, 1993; Die baerenstarke Anna, 1993; Die baerenstarke Anna zieht um, 1994; Neues von der Hexe Alexa, 1994; Jeff und Molly: Geschichten zum Mutmachen, 1994; Aetze, das Zirkusmonster, 1995; Die baerenstarke Anna: Der Schulauszug, 1995; Nelli, das Quatschmonster, 1995; Who has Time for Little Bear?, 1998; Taking Care of Sister Bear, 1999; Bleib Mein Freund, kleiner Bär!: eine Geschichte, 1999; Tikitonga, 2010. Contributor to periodicals. **Address:** Diekkamp 45G, Hamburg, 22359, Germany. **Online address:** ursel.scheffler@hanse.net

SCHEFT, Bill. American (born United States), b. 1957. **Genres:** Novels, Recreation. **Career:** Albany Times-Union, sportswriter, 1979-80; stand-up comedian, 1980-91; CBS Broadcasting Inc., Late Night with David Letterman, monologue writer, 1991-92, Late Show with David Letterman, monologue writer, 1993-; ESPN Magazine, columnist, 2000-02; Sports Illustrated, columnist, 2002-05. **Publications:** The Ringer: A Novel, 2002; Time Won't Let Me, 2005; The Best of The Show: A Classic Collection of Wit and Wisdom,

2005; Everything Hurts: A Novel, 2009. Contributor to periodicals. **Address:** Late Show With David Letterman, CBS Broadcasting Inc., 1697 Broadway, New York, NY 10019, U.S.A. **Online address:** billscheft@yahoo.com

SCHEIBER, Harry N. American (born United States), b. 1935?. **Genres:** History, Law, Politics/Government, Agriculture/Forestry, Economics, Social Sciences. **Career:** Cornell University, teaching fellow, 1958-59; Dartmouth College, instructor to professor of history, 1960-71, Dartmouth Center for the Study of Social Change, founding director, 1968-70; University of California-San Diego, professor of history, 1971-80; Agricultural History Society, president, 1977-78; University of California-Berkeley, professor of law and history, 1980-91, Jurisprudence and Social Policy Program, chair, 1982-84, 1990-93, 1996-99, associate dean of law, 1990-93, 1996-99, Stefan A. Riesenfeld chair professor of law and history, 1991-, Faculty Senate, vice chair, 1993-94, chair, 1994-95, Center for the Study of Social Change, director, 2000-01, Center for the Study of Law and Society, faculty associate, acting director, 2000-02, Sho Sato Program in Japanese and U.S. Law, co-director, Institute for Legal Research, director; Rockefeller Foundation, fellow, 1980-81; University of California Humanities Research Institute, fellow, 1988; California Sea Grant Program, coordinator of marine affairs, 1988-2000; Uppsala University, visiting research professor of law, 1995; California Supreme Court History Society, vice president, 1998-99; DiTella University, honorary professor, 1999; Law of the Sea Institute, co-director, 2000-; Earl Warren Legal Institute, director, 2002-; American Society of Legal History, president, 2003-05; History of American Economy Series, Johnson Reprint, co-editor. **Publications:** The Wilson Administration and Civil Liberties, 1917-1921, 1960; (co-author) America: Purpose and Power, 1965; The Condition of American Federalism, 1966; Ohio Canal Era, A Case Study of Government and the Economy, 1820-1861, 1969; (contrib.) The Frontier in American Development, 1969; (co-author) Law in American History, 1972; (contrib.) The Supreme Court and Individual Liberties, 1975; (with J. Shideler) Agriculture in the Development of the Far West, 1975; (with H.G. Vatter and H.U. Faulkner) American Economic History: A Comprehensive Revision of the Earlier Work by Harold Underwood Faulkner, 1976; Perspectives on Federalism: Papers from the First Berkeley Seminar on Federalism, 1987; (co-author) Technology, the Economy and Society, 1987; Abbot-Downing and the Concord Coach, 1989; Inter-Allied Conflicts and Ocean Law, 1945-54, 2001. EDITOR: United States Economic History, 1964; The Old Northwest, 1969; (with L.M. Friedman) American Law and the Constitutional Order: Historical Perspectives, 1978, rev. ed., 1988; Federalism in Perspective, 1987; Federalism: Studies in History, Law and Policy, 1988; (with M.M. Feeley and T. Correl) Power Divided: Essays on the Theory and Practice of Federalism, 1989; Federalism and the Judicial Mind: Essays on American Constitutional Law and Politics, 1992; North American and Comparative Federalism: Essays for the 1990s, 1992; (with L.M. Friedman) Legal Cultures and the Legal Profession, 1996; The State and Freedom of Contract, 1998; Law of the Sea: The Common Heritage and Emerging Challenges, 2000; (with D.D. Caron) Bringing New Law to Ocean Waters, 2004; Earl Warren and the Warren Court: The Legacy in American and Foreign Law, 2007; (with L. Mayali) Emerging Concepts of Rights in Japanese Law, 2007; (with L. Mayali) Japanese Family Law in Comparative Perspective, 2009; (with D.D. Caron) The Oceans in the Nuclear Age: Legacies and Risks, 2010. **Address:** School of Law, University of California, 442 Boalt Hall, Berkeley, CA 94720-7200, U.S.A. **Online address:** hscheiber@law.berkeley.edu

SCHEIL, Andrew P. American (born United States), b. 1968. **Genres:** Theology/Religion, Literary Criticism And History, Sociology, Anthropology/Ethnology. **Career:** University of Toronto, Open fellow, 1990-95; Saint Joseph College, adjunct professor of English, 1996-99; University of Hartford, adjunct professor of English, 1997-98; Ohio State University, visiting assistant professor of English, 1999-2000; University of Connecticut, visiting assistant professor of English, 2000-01; Harvard University, lecturer and tutor in history and literature, 2001-04, school lecturer, 2001-05, Freshman Seminar Program, lecturer, 2003-04, Department of English and American literature, research associate, 2004-05; Boston University, College of Arts and Sciences Writing Program, lecturer, 2004-05; University of Minnesota, assistant professor, 2005-07, associate professor, 2007-, McKnight presidential fellow, 2007-10; University of Wisconsin, Institute for Research in the Humanities, Solmsen fellow, 2008-09. Writer. **Publications:** The Footsteps of Israel: Understanding Jews in Anglo-Saxon England, 2004. Contributor to periodicals. **Address:** Department of English, University of Minnesota, 207 Lind Hall, 207 Church St. SE, Minneapolis, MN 55455, U.S.A. **Online address:** ascheil@umn.edu

SCHEIL, Katherine West. American (born United States), b. 1966. **Genres:** Humor/Satire, History. **Career:** St. Joseph College, assistant professor of English, 1995-99; University of Rhode Island, assistant professor, 1999-2003, associate professor of English, 2003-05, director, 2004-05; University of Minnesota, visiting associate professor, 2005-06, associate professor of English, 2006-. Writer. **Publications:** The Taste of the Town: Shakespearean Comedy and the Early Eighteenth-Century Theatre, 2003. **Address:** Department of English, University of Minnesota, 210G Lind Hall, 207 Church St. SE, Minneapolis, MI 55455-0134, U.S.A. **Online address:** kscheil@umn.edu

SCHEIN, Elyse. American (born United States), b. 1969. **Genres:** Biography, Autobiography/Memoirs, Women's Studies And Issues. **Career:** Writer and educator. **Publications:** (With P. Bernstein) Identical Strangers: A Memoir of Twins Separated and Reunited, 2007. Contributor to journals and periodicals. **Address:** c/o Peter Steinberg, Steinberg Agency, 47 E 19th St., 3rd Fl., New York, NY 10001, U.S.A. **Online address:** elyse@elyseschein.com

SCHEINDLIN, Raymond P. American (born United States), b. 1940. **Genres:** Literary Criticism And History, History, Songs/Lyrics And Libretti, Education, Humanities. **Career:** McGill University, assistant professor of Jewish studies, 1969-72; Cornell University, assistant professor of Hebrew language, 1972-74; Jewish Theological Seminary of America, associate professor, 1974-85, professor of medieval Hebrew literature, 1985-, Department of Jewish Literature, head, 1977-79, 1981-83, 1990-93, provost, 1984-88, Genesis Seminar, leader, 1992-97, Shalom Spiegel Institute of Medieval Hebrew Poetry, director; New York University, visiting associate professor, 1975-76; Kane Street Synagogue, rabbi, 1979-82; Oxford University, Centre for Postgraduate Hebrew Studies, senior associate fellow, 1989-; University of Pennsylvania, Center for Judaic Studies, fellow, 1993-. Writer. **Publications:** Form and Structure in the Poetry of Al-Mu'tamid Ibn Abbād, 1974; 201 Arabic Verbs: Fully Conjugated in All the Forms, 1978; Miriam and the Angel of Death (opera libretto), 1984; (comp.) Wine, Women & Death: Medieval Hebrew Poems on the Good Life, 1986; Loves' Wounded: Two Songs for Baritone and Orchestra, 1987; (comp. and trans.) The Gazelle: Medieval Hebrew Poems on God, Israel and the Soul, 1991; (trans.) Ismar Elbogen, Jewish Liturgy in Its Historical Development, 1993; (trans.) The Psalm of the Distant Dove: Canticle for Mezzo-Soprano and Piano (cantata), 1995; (trans. and intro.) The Book of Job, 1998; A Short History of the Jewish People: From Legendary Times to Modern Statehood, 1998; (ed. with M.R. Menocal and M. Sells) The Literature of Al-Andalus, as The Cambridge History of Arabic Literature: Al-Andalus, 2000; The Song of the Distant Dove: Judah Halevi's Pilgrimage, 2007; (ed. with M. Rand) Studies in Arabic and Hebrew letters, 2007; 501 Arabic Verbs: Fully Conjugated in all the Aspects in a New, Easy-to-Learn Format, Alphabetically Arranged, 2007. Contributor of articles to journals and books. **Address:** Jewish Theological Seminary of America, 607 Brush, 3080 Broadway, New York, NY 10027, U.S.A. **Online address:** rascheindlin@jtsa.edu

SCHELL, Jim. American (born United States), b. 1936. **Genres:** Business/Trade/Industry, Industrial Relations. **Career:** Kings Court, president, 1968-75; General Sports, founder and chief executive officer, 1970-81, Opportunity Knocks, founder and chief executive officer, 1996-; City Club of Central Oregon, co-founder; Partnership to End Poverty, director of development. Writer. **Publications:** The Brass-Tacks Entrepreneur, 1993; Small Business Management Guide: Advice from the Brass-Tacks Entrepreneur, 1994; Winning Together: How Small Business Employees Can Help Themselves and Their Companies, Grow and Succeed, 1994; Entrepreneur Magazine: Small Business Answer Book: Solutions to the 101 Most Common Small Business Problems, 1996; (with E. Tyson) Small Business for Dummies, 1998, 3rd ed., 2008; Understanding Your Financial Statements, 2002; There Oughta Be a Law, 2003. **Address:** Partnership to End Poverty, PO Box 147, Redmond, OR 97756, U.S.A. **Online address:** jim@partnershiptoendpoverty.org

SCHELL, Orville. See **SCHELL, Orville (Hickok).**

SCHELL, Orville (Hickok). (Orville Schell). American (born United States), b. 1940. **Genres:** Environmental Sciences/Ecology, International Relations/Current Affairs, Social Commentary. **Career:** Atlantic, correspondent, 1962-64; Look, correspondent, 1962-64; New York Review of Books, correspondent, 1962-64; Newsweek, correspondent, 1962-64; New Yorker, correspondent, 1962-64; Harper's, correspondent, 1962-64; Boston Globe, correspondent, 1962-64; San Francisco Chronicle, correspondent, 1962-64; The Bay Area Institute, co-director, 1968-71; Pacific News Service, founder and editor-in-chief, 1970-71; University of California, Center for Chinese Studies, research associate, 1986, Graduate School of Journalism, regents' lecturer, 1990, professor, dean, 1996-2007, professor emeritus, 2007-; Chico State University, visiting distinguished professor, 1987; NBC Nightly News, consultant, 1987, commentator, 1989; ABC Nightline, consultant, 1989; CBC News, consultant, 1995; Project Syndicate China column, editor, 2000-; University of Southern California, Center on Communication Leadership, Annenberg School of Communications, senior fellow, 2007-; Center on U.S.-China Relations, Arthur Ross director, 2007-, Columbia University, Weatherhead East Asian Instituted, fellow. **Publications:** AS ORVILLE SCHELL: (Ed. and intro. with H.F. Schurmann) The China Reader, vol. I: The Decline of the Last Dynasty and the Origins of Modern China, vol. II: Republican China: Nationalism, War and the Rise of Communism, vol. III: Communist China: Revolutionary Reconstruction and International Confrontation, 1968; (ed. with F. Crews) Starting Over: A College Reader, 1970; (with J. Esherick) Modern China: The Making of a New Society, from 1839 to the Present, 1972; Modern China: The Story of a Revolution, 1972; The Town That Fought to Save Itself, 1976; China: In the People's Republic, 1977 in US as In the People's Republic: An American's First-Hand View of Living and Working in China, 1978; Brown, 1978; Watch Out for the Foreign Guests!: China Encounters the West, 1981; Modern Meat, 1984; To Get Rich Is Glorious: China in the 1980's, 1984; Discos and Democracy: China in the Throes of Reform, 1988; Mandate of Heaven: A New Generation of Entrepreneurs, Dissidents, Bohemians and Technocrats Lay Claim to China's Future, 1994; (ed. and intro. with D. Shambaugh) The China Reader: The Reform Era, 1999; Virtual Tibet: Searching for Shangri-la from the Himalayas to Hollywood, 2000; Tibet Since 1950: Silence, Prison or Exile, 2000; Empire: Impressions of China, 2004. Contributor to periodicals. **Address:** Graduate School of Journalism, University of California at Berkeley, 121 N Gate Hall, Ste. 5860, Rm. 140A, Berkeley, CA 94720-5860, U.S.A. **Online address:** schell@uclink.berkeley.edu

SCHELLENBERG, Betty A. Canadian (born Canada) **Genres:** Novels, Social Sciences, Young Adult Fiction. **Career:** Simon Fraser University, Department of English, assistant professor of English, 1991-97, associate professor of English, 1997-2006, professor of English, 2006-. Writer. **Publications:** The Conversational Circle: Re-Reading the English Novel, 1740-1775, 1996; (ed. with P. Budra) Part Two: Reflections on the Sequel, 1998; (ed. with N. Pohl) Reconsidering the Bluestockings, 2003; Professionalization of Women Writers in Eighteenth-century Britain, 2005. **Address:** Department of English, Simon Fraser University, AQ 6132, 8888 University Dr., Burnaby, BC V5A 1S6, Canada. **Online address:** schellen@sfu.ca

SCHELLING, Andrew. American (born United States), b. 1953. **Genres:** Poetry, Translations. **Career:** Naropa University, associate professor of writing and poetics, professor, 1990-; Jack Kerouac School of Disembodied Poetics, chairperson 1993-96; Deer Park Institute, faculty. Writer. **Publications:** POETRY: Claw Moraine (chapbook), 1987; Ktaadn's Lamp (chapbook), 1991; Moon Is a Piece of Tea (chapbook), 1993; Old Growth: Selected Poems and Notebooks, 1986-1994, 1995; The Road to Ocosingo, 1998; Tea Shack Interior: New and Selected Poetry, 2002; Wild Form, Savage Grammar, 2003; Erotic Love Poems from India, 2004; Dropping the Bow: Poems of Ancient India, 2008; From the Arapaho Songbook, 2011. ESSAYS: Twilight Speech, 1993; The India Book, 1993; Two Immortals, 1994; The Kavyayantra Press: A Brief History, 1993-1997, 1997; The Handful of Seeds: Three and a Half Essays, 1999; Wild Form, Savage Grammar, 2003. TRANSLATOR: Dropping the Bow: Poems from Ancient India, 1991; For Love of the Dark One: Songs of Mirabai, 1993, rev. ed., 1998; (with A. Waldman) Songs of the Sons and Daughters of Buddha (poems), 1996; The Cane Groves of Narmada River: Erotic Poems from Old India, 1998. OTHER: Old Tale Road, 2008. EDITOR: (with A. Waldman) Disembodied Poetics: Annals of the Jack Kerouac School, 1994; Wisdom Anthology of North American Buddhist Poetry, 2005; Old Tale Road, 2008. Works appear in anthologies. Contributor to periodicals. **Address:** Writing & Poetics, Naropa University, 2130 Arapahoe Ave., Boulder, CO 80302-6697, U.S.A. **Online address:** schell@ecentral.com

SCHELLING, Thomas C. American (born United States), b. 1921. **Genres:** Economics, International Relations/Current Affairs, Social Sciences, Essays. **Career:** U.S. Bureau of the Budget, economist, 1945-46; Economic Cooperation Administration Mission to Denmark, economist, 1948-49; Office of the Special Representative, economist, 1949-50; The White House and Executive Office of the President, staff, 1951-53; Yale University, associate professor, professor of economics, 1953-58; RAND Corp., adjunct fellow, 1956-2002,

researcher, 1958, economist, 1958-59; Harvard University, professor of economics, 1958-90, John F. Kennedy School of Government, faculty, 1969-90, Lucius N. Littauer professor of political economy, 1974-90, professor emeritus of political economy, 1990-; Institute for the Study of Smoking Behavior and Policy, director, 1984-90; University of Maryland, School of Public Policy, distinguished professor of economics and public affairs, 1990-2003, distinguished university professor emeritus, 2003-; New England Complex Systems Institute, co-faculty. Writer. **Publications:** National Income Behavior, 1951; International Cost-Sharing Arrangements, 1955; International Economics, 1958; The Strategy of Conflict, 1960; (with M.H. Halperin) Strategy and Arms Control, 1961; Stability of Total Disarmament, 1961; Arms and Influence, 1966; La Diplomazia della Violenza, 1968; Planning-programming-Budgeting: PPBS and Foreign Affairs: Memorandum Prepared at the Request of the Subcommittee on National Security and International Operations of the Committee on Government Operations, 1968; Models of Segregation, 1969; Micromotives and Macrobehavior, 1978, new ed., 2006; Thinking through the Energy Problem, 1979; (ed.) Incentives for Environmental Protection, 1983; Choice and Consequence, 1984; (ed. with A. Clesse) The Western Community and the Gorbachev Challenge, 1989; Bargaining, Communication and Limited War, 1993; Costs and Benefits of Greenhouse Gas Reduction, 1998; Strategies of Commitment and Other Essays, 2006; Organising to Cope with Global Warming, 2009. **Address:** Maryland School of Public Policy, University of Maryland, 2101 Van Munching Hall, College Park, MD 20742, U.S.A. **Online address:** tschelli@umd.edu

SCHEN, Claire S. American (born United States) **Genres:** History, Social Work, Humanities, Social Sciences. **Career:** The State University of New York, University at Buffalo, Department of History, associate professor; Journal of British Studies, editor. **Publications:** Charity and Lay Piety in Reformation London, 1500-1620, 2002. **Address:** Department of History, University at Buffalo, State University of New York, 577 Park Hall, Buffalo, NY 14260-4100, U.S.A. **Online address:** cschen@buffalo.edu

SCHENCK, Hilbert. American (born United States), b. 1926. **Genres:** Science Fiction/Fantasy, Engineering, Sports/Fitness, Novellas/Short Stories. **Career:** Pratt and Whitney Aircraft, test engineer, 1952-56; Clarkson College, assistant professor, professor, 1956-66; University of Rhode Island, professor, 1966-83, Scuba Safety Project, director, 1968-80. Writer. **Publications:** SCIENCE FICTION: Wave Rider (short stories), 1980; At the Eye of the Ocean (novel), 1980; A Rose for Armageddon (novel), 1982; Chronosequence (novel), 1988; Steam Bird, 1988. OTHER: (with H. Kendall) Shallow Water Diving for Pleasure and Profit, 1950; (with H. Kendall) Underwater Photography, 1954; (with H. Kendall) Shallow Water Diving and Spearfishing, 1954; Skin Diver's and Spearfisherman's Guide to American Waters, 1955; Heat Transfer Engineering, 1959; (with R. Kenyon) Thermodynamics, 1961; Fortran Methods in Heat Flow, 1963; Theories of Engineering Experimentation, 1963, 3rd ed. 1979; An Interdisciplinary Laboratory to Teach Experimentation: Final Report, 1963; An Introduction to the Engineering Research Project, 1968; Case Studies in Experimental Engineering: A Programmed Approach (text book) McGraw-Hill, 1970; (ed.) Introduction to Ocean Engineering, 1975. **Address:** 343 Delano Rd., Marion, MA 02738, U.S.A.

SCHENDEL, Dan. (Dan E. Schendel). American (born United States), b. 1934. **Genres:** Business/Trade/Industry, Administration/Management, Industrial Relations, Mathematics/Statistics. **Career:** Purdue University, Krannert Graduate School of Management, professor of business, 1965-, director of business opportunity program, 1969-71, past director of executive education programs, Blake Family endowed chair emeritus in strategic management; University of Michigan, William Davidson visiting professor of business administration, 1988-89; University of Chicago, visiting professor, 1990-91; Strategic Management Journal, founding editor; Strategic Entrepreneurship Journal, founding editor. **Publications:** Needs and Developments in Policy Curricula at the Ph.D. Level, 1975; Designing Strategic Planning Systems, 1977. CO-AUTHOR: Can Corporate Strategy be Modelled?, 1975; Corporate Turnaround Strategies, 1975; Simultaneous Equation Model of Corporate Strategy, 1976; Strategy Formulation: Analytical Concepts, 1978; Divided Loyalties: Whistle Blowing at BART, 1980; Empirical Analysis of Strategy Types, 1982; Development of the Strategic Management Field: Some Accomplishments and Challenges, 1983; Performance Differences Among Strategic Group Members, 1986; Strategic Group Formation and Performance: The Case of the U.S. Pharmaceutical Industry, 1963-1982, 1986. AS DAN E. SCHENDEL: (with A.C. Cooper and K.J. Hatten) Strategic Model of the U.S. Brewing Industry, 1952-1971, 1976; (with K.J. Hatten) Heterogeneity within an Industry: Firm Conduct in the U.S. Brewing Industry, 1952-1971, 1976; (ed. with C.W. Hofer) Strategic Management: A New View of Business Policy and Planning, 1979; (ed. with R.P. Rumelt and D.J. Teece) Fundamental Issues in Strategy: A Research Agenda for the 1990s, 1994. Contributor to journals. **Address:** Krannert Graduate School of Management, Purdue University, 403 W State St., West Lafayette, IN 47907-2056, U.S.A. **Online address:** schendel@purdue.edu

SCHENDEL, Dan E. *See* **Schendel, Dan.**

SCHENKEN, Suzanne O'Dea. American (born United States), b. 1950. **Genres:** Politics/Government, Biography, History. **Career:** Writer. **Publications:** Legislators and Politicians: Iowa's Women Lawmakers, 1995; From Suffrage to the Senate: An Encyclopedia of American Women in Politics, 1999, 2nd ed., 2006. **Address:** 567 Cape Rd., McKinleyville, CA 95519, U.S.A. **Online address:** suzodea@mac.com

SCHENKER, Dona. American (born United States), b. 1947. **Genres:** Children's Fiction, Young Adult Fiction, Novels. **Career:** Children's librarian, 1972-76; kindergarten teacher. Writer. **Publications:** Throw a Hungry Loop (for young adults), 1990; Fearsome's Hero, 1994; The Secret Circle, 1998. **Address:** 802 E El Prado, San Antonio, TX 78212, U.S.A. **Online address:** dschen1@aol.com

SCHENKKAN, Robert (Frederic). American (born United States), b. 1953. **Genres:** Plays/Screenplays, Literary Criticism And History, Young Adult Fiction. **Career:** Writer. **Publications:** Heaven on Earth, 1992; Final Passages, 1993; Four One-act Plays, 1993; Conversations with the Spanish Lady and Other One-Act Plays, 1993; The Kentucky Cycle, 1995; The Dream Thief, 1999; The Marriage of Miss Hollywood and King Neptune, 2004; Handler, 2004. Contributor to periodicals. **Address:** c/o Bill Craver, Writers & Artists, 19 W 44th St., Ste. 1000, New York, NY 10036, U.S.A.

SCHERER, Marcia J. (Marcia Joslyn Scherer). American (born United States), b. 1948. **Genres:** Communications/Media. **Career:** Institute for Matching Person & Technology, president & director; University of Rochester Medical Center, professor of physical medicine and rehabilitation. Academic, administrator and writer. **Publications:** Communication in the Human Services: A Guide to Therapeutic Journalism, 1980; Living in the State of Stuck: How Technologies Affect the Lives of People with Disabilities, 1993, 4th ed., 2005; (ed. with L.A. Cushman) Psychological Assessment in Medical Rehabilitation, 1995; (ed. with J.C. Galvin) Evaluating, Selecting and Using Appropriate Assistive Technology, 1996; Assistive Technology: Matching Device and Consumer for Successful Rehabilitation, 2002; Connecting to Learn: Educational and Assistive Technology for People with Disabilities, 2004; (with D. de Jonge and S. Rodger) Assistive Technology in the Workplace, 2007. **Address:** Institute for Matching Person & Technology, 486 Lake Rd., Webster, NY 14580, U.S.A. **Online address:** impt97@aol.com

SCHERER, Marcia Joslyn. *See* **SCHERER, Marcia J.**

SCHERER, Migael. American (born United States), b. 1947. **Genres:** Adult Non-fiction, Communications/Media, Travel/Exploration, Biography, Social Sciences. **Career:** Seattle School District, Nathan Hale High School, teacher, 1970-81, Aki Kurose Middle School Academy, development coach, 2004-; freelance writer and consultant, 1981-83, 1988-; University of Washington, Academic Computer Center, technical writer and instructor, 1981-83, Department of Communications, lecturer, Dart Center for Journalism and Trauma, teacher and consultant, 1992-, Dart Award for Excellence in Reporting on Victims of Violence, director, 1999-; University of Alaska, Computerized Office Occupations Program, grant coordinator, 1984-85, visiting instructor, 1985-86, lecturer and microlab instruction technician, 1986-87, Alaska Public Affairs Journal, technical editor, 1985-87. **Publications:** Still Loved by the Sun: A Rape Survivor's Journal, 1992; A Cruising Guide to Puget Sound: Olympia to Port Angeles, Including the San Juans, 1995, 2nd ed. as A Cruising Guide to Puget Sound and the San Juan Islands: Olympia to Port Angeles, 2004; Sailing to Simplicity: Life Lessons Learned at Sea, 1999; Back Under Sail: Recovering the Spirit of Adventure, 2003. **Address:** c/o Elizabeth Wales, Wales Literary Agency Inc., PO Box 9426, Seattle, WA 98109, U.S.A.

SCHERF, Kathleen D. Canadian (born Canada), b. 1960. **Genres:** Literary Criticism And History, Cultural/Ethnic Topics, Poetry, Young Adult Non-fiction. **Career:** University of British Columbia, sessional lecturer, 1988; University of New Brunswick, assistant professor, 1989-92, associate professor, 1992-96, coordinator of drama, 1992, sexual harassment advisor, associate dean of arts, 1995, professor of English, 1996; Studies in Canadian Literature, editor, 1989-96; University of Calgary, dean of faculty of communication and culture, 1999-. **Publications:** (Ed. and intro.) The Collected Poetry of Malcolm Lowry, 1992; (with D.L. Macdonald) The Collected Fiction of John Polidori, 1994; (ed. and intro. with D.L. MacDonald) Vampyre and Ernestus Berchtold or The Modern Oedipus, 1994; (ed. with D.L. Macdonald) Frankenstein: The 1818 Text, 1994, 2nd ed., 1999; The Canadian Handbook for Writers, 1995; (ed. with D.L. Macdonald) A Vindication of the Rights of Men, 1997; (ed. with D.L. MacDonald) Monk: A Romance, 2004. Contributor to journals and magazines. **Address:** Faculty of Communication & Culture, University of Calgary, 2500 University Dr. NW, Calgary, AB T2N 1N4, Canada. **Online address:** kath@ucalgary.ca

SCHERMBRUCKER, Bill. (William Gerald Schermbrucker). Canadian (born Canada), b. 1938. **Genres:** Novellas/Short Stories, Novels, Education. **Career:** Teacher, 1959-64; University of East Africa, part-time lecturer, 1963-64; Capilano College, instructor in English, 1968-2001, Humanities Division, chair, 1970-71, department coordinator, 1974-75, instructor emeritus, 2000-; Genessee Community College, lecturer, 1972-73; The Capilano Review, editor, 1977-82; The Banff Center, faculty. Writer. **Publications:** FICTION: Chameleon and Other Stories, 1983; Mimosa (novel), 1988; Motortherapy, and Other Stories, 1993. OTHER: The Aims and Strategies of Good Writing (textbook), 1976; (ed.) Readings for Canadian Writing Students, 1976, rev. ed. as The Capilano Reader, 1984, 4th ed., 1993. Contributor to periodicals. **Address:** Capilano University, 2055 Purcell Way, North Vancouver, BC V7J 3H5, Canada. **Online address:** bscherm@capcollege.bc.ca

SCHERMBRUCKER, William Gerald. *See* **SCHERMBRUCKER, Bill.**

SCHEUER, Jeffrey. American (born United States), b. 1953. **Genres:** Education, Social Sciences. **Career:** Freie Universität, lecturer; New York University, lecturer; Chester Fund, board director; Symphony Space, board director; University Settlement, board director, 1986-90; Loka Institute, board director, 1999-2003; New York University, adjunct professor, 2003. Writer. **Publications:** The Sound Bite Society: Television and the American Mind, 1999 as The Sound Bite Society: How Television Helps the Right and Hurts the Left, 2001; The Big Picture: Why Democracies Need Journalistic Excellence, 2008. Contributor to books, magazines and periodicals. **Address:** U.S.A. **Online address:** jscheuer1@aol.com

SCHEVILL, Margot Blum. American (born United States), b. 1931. **Genres:** Anthropology/Ethnology, History, Adult Non-fiction, Crafts, Art/Art History, Antiques/Furnishings. **Career:** New Music Ensemble of Providence, founder, 1968, manager, 1968-84; Brown University, research associate, publicity liaison, Haffenreffer Museum of Anthropology, exhibition developer, 1982-91, assistant curator of public programming and exhibition development, 1987-91; University of California, Hearst Museum of Anthropology, senior museum scientist, 1988-92, textile consultant, 1993-98; California College of Arts and Crafts, visiting lecturer, 1993; University of California, visiting lecturer, 1994; San Francisco Airport Museums, curator, 1998-2003; Fiber Scene, researcher. Writer. **Publications:** Evolution in Textile Design from the Highlands of Guatemala: Seventeen Male Tzutes, or Headdresses, from Chichicastenango in the Collections of the Lowie Museum of Anthropology, University of California, Berkeley, 1985; Costume as Communication: Ethnographic Costumes and Textiles from Middle America and the Central Andes of South America in the Collections of the Haffenreffer Museum of Anthropology, Brown University, Bristol, Rhode Island, 1986; Maya Textiles of Guatemala: The Gustavus A. Eisen Collection, 1902, The Hearst Museum of Anthropology, the University of California at Berkeley, 1993; (intro.) Yurok-Karok Basket Weavers, 1995; (reteller) The Pollen Path, 1998. EDITOR AND CONTRIBUTOR: (with J.C. Berlo and E.B. Dwyer) Textile Traditions of Mesoamerica and the Andes: An Anthology, 1991; The Maya Textile Tradition, 1997. Contributor to books and journals. **Address:** FiberScene, 2443 Fillmore St., Ste. 364, San Francisco, CA 94115, U.S.A. **Online address:** mschevill@aol.com

SCHEWE, Phillip F. American (born United States), b. 1950. **Genres:** Physics, Sciences. **Career:** American Institute of Physics, senior science writer, 1979-, director of public information, chief science writer. **Publications:** (Ed. with R.J. Barish) Glossary of Terms Used in Medical Physics, 1984; The

Grid: A Journey through the Heart of Our Electrified World, 2007. **Address:** American Institute of Physics, 1 Physics Ellipse, College Park, MD 20740-3843, U.S.A. **Online address:** pschewe@aip.org

SCHIAPPA, (Anthony) Edward. American (born United States), b. 1954. **Genres:** Speech/Rhetoric. **Career:** Kansas State University, instructor, 1985-88, assistant professor, 1989-90; Purdue University, assistant professor, 1990-93, associate professor of communications and director, 1993-95, School of Liberal Arts, senator; Rhetoric Society of America, board director, 1993-95; University of Minnesota, associate professor, 1995-99, professor, 1999-, department chair, 2005-; Argumentation and Advocacy, editor. Writer. **Publications:** Protagoras and Logos: A Study in Greek Philosophy and Rhetoric, 1991, 2nd ed., 2003; The Beginnings of Rhetorical Theory in Classical Greece, 1999; Defining Reality: Definitions and the Politics of Meaning, 2003; Beyond Representational Correctness: Rethinking Criticism of Popular Media, 2008; (with J. Nordin) Keeping Faith With Reason, 2009; (with D.M. Timmerman) Disciplining Discourse: The Emergence of Terms of Art in Rhetorical Theory in Classical Greece, 2010; (with D.M. Timmerman) Classical Greek Rhetorical Theory and the Disciplining of Discourse, 2010; Making Sense of It All: Constitutive Interpretation, forthcoming. EDITOR: Landmarks in Classical Rhetoric, 1993; Warranting Assent: Case Studies in Argument Evaluation, 1995. **Address:** Department of Communication Studies, University of Minnesota, 225 Ford Hall, 224 Church St. SE, Minneapolis, MN 55455-0427, U.S.A. **Online address:** schiappa@umn.edu

SCHIAVONE, Giuseppe. Italian (born Italy), b. 1938. **Genres:** Politics/Government, Business/Trade/Industry, Economics, Law. **Career:** General Confederation of Italian Industry, Department of Economic and Statistical Studies, officer, 1962-73; University of Catania, professor of international organization, 1973-; Institute of European Studies, School of Postgraduate Studies, president and director of scientific research; Italian National School of Public Administration, International and European Union Area, head; Institut Robert Schuman pour l'Europe, president; Italian Ministry of Foreign Affairs, expert; United Nations Development Program, consultant; lecturer at public and private institutions. Writer. **Publications:** (Contrib.) La Programmazione concertata francese, 1965; Il principio di non-discriminazione nei rapporti commerciali internazionali, 1966; Il Comecon, 1967; Scambi Est-Ovest: problemi e prospettive, 1971; (contrib.) Nigeria, 1976; (contrib.) Ecuador, 1977; Comecon: cooperazione e integrazione fra le economie dei paesi socialisti, 1979; The Institutions of Comecon, 1981; International Organizations: A Dictionary and Directory, 1983, 7th ed., 2008; Winstanley: il profeta della rivoluzione inglese, 1991; (co-author) L'Utopia nella storia: la Rivoluzione inglese, 1992; (co-author) La democrazia diretta: un progetto politico per la società di giustizia, 1997; Scritti massonici di Ernesto Nathan, 1998; Democrazia e modernità: l'apporto dell'utopia, 2001. EDITOR: East-West Relations: Prospects for the 1980s, 1982; Western Europe and South-East Asia: Cooperation or Competition?, 1989. Work represented in anthologies. Contributor to academic journals. **Address:** Faculty of Political Science, University of Catania, Catania, 1, Italy.

SCHICKLER, David. American (born United States), b. 1969. **Genres:** Novellas/Short Stories, Novels, Romance/Historical. **Career:** The Harley School, teacher, 1994-. Writer. **Publications:** Kissing in Manhattan, 2001; Sweet and Vicious, 2004. Contributor to periodicals. **Address:** c/o Theresa Zoro, Bantam Dell Publishing Group, 1745 Broadway, New York, NY 10019-4368, U.S.A. **Online address:** david@davidschickler.com

SCHIER, Steven E. American (born United States), b. 1952. **Genres:** Politics/Government, Business/Trade/Industry, Economics. **Career:** University of Wisconsin, teaching assistant, 1975-77, State Legislative Internship Program, director, 1977-78; Wittenberg College, assistant professor, 1978-81; Carleton College, Department of Political Science, assistant professor, 1981-87, associate professor, 1987-93, professor, 1997, Political Economy Concentration, coordinator, 1983-92, Summer Teaching Institute, instructor, 1987-2000, department chair, 1995-2001, 2003, Dorothy H. and Edward C. Congdon professor of political science, 1997-; KSTP Television, political analyst, 1983-2010; M.E. Sharpe, consulting editor. **Publications:** The Rules of the Game: Democratic National Convention Delegate Selection in Iowa and Wisconsin, 1980; Political Economy in Western Democracies, 1985; A Decade of Deficits: Congressional Thought and Fiscal Action, 1992; (with S.E. Frantzich) Congress: Games and Strategies, 1995, 2nd ed., 2003; (with T.J. Penny) Payment Due: A Nation of Debt a Generation in Trouble, 1996; By Invitation Only: The Rise of Exclusive Politics in the United States, 2000; (ed.)

The Postmodern Presidency: Bill Clinton's Legacy in U.S. Politics, 2000; You Call This an Election?: Americas Peculiar Democracy, 2003; (ed.) High Risk and Big Ambition: The Presidency of George W. Bush, 2004; (ed. and contrib.) Making Big Waves: The George W. Bush Legacy in U.S. Politics, 2008; Raising the Stakes: The Controversial Presidency of George W. Bush, 2008; (ed. with J.M. Box-Steffensmeier) The American Elections of 2008, 2009; Panorama of a Presidency: How George W. Bush Acquired and Spent His Political Capital, 2009; (ed.) Ambition and Division: Legacies of the George W. Bush Presidency, 2009; (with N. Polsby, A. Wildavsky and D. Hopkins) Presidential Elections: Strategies and Structure of American Politics, 13th ed., 2012; (ed. and contrib.) A Transformative Presidency? Barack Obama in the White House, 2012. Contributor to periodicals. **Address:** Department of Political Science, Carleton College, Willis Hall 414, 1 N College St., Northfield, MN 55057, U.S.A. **Online address:** sschier@carleton.edu

SCHIFF, Isaac. American/Canadian (born Canada), b. 1944. **Genres:** Medicine/Health. **Career:** Montreal General Hospital, rotating intern, 1968-69, resident in medicine, 1969-71; Boston Hospital for Women, resident in obstetrics and gynecology, 1971-73, fellow in reproductive endocrinology, 1974-76, assistant obstetrician and gynecologist, 1974-76, instructor in obstetrics and gynecology, 1974-78, Menopause Clinic, founder, 1976; New England Medical Center, resident in surgery, 1974; Brigham and Women's Hospital, obstetrician and gynecologist, 1976-, associate director of reproductive endocrinology, 1980-86, director, 1986-88; Harvard University Medical School, assistant professor, 1978-81, associate professor, 1981-88, Joe Vincent Meigs professor of gynecology, 1988-; Massachusetts General Hospital, chief of Vincent Memorial Gynecology Service, 1988-93; North American Menopause Society, president, 1992; Vincent Memorial Obstetrics and Gynecology Service, chief, 1993-; Menopause journal, editor-in-chief; North American Menopause Society, president; ACOG's Task Force on Hormone Therapy, chairman; NAMS professional journal, editor-in-chief; Domestic Violence Task Force, co-chairperson, 1995-; Dana-Farber Cancer Institute, consultant; National Institute on Aging, consultant; American Medical Association, consultant; American College of Obstetricians and Gynecologists, fellow; Society of Andrology, fellow; American Fertility Society, fellow; Endocrine Society, fellow; Society for Gynecologic Investigation, fellow; Society of Reproductive Surgeons, fellow; Association of Gynecology and Obstetrics, fellow; Royal College of Surgeons, fellow; Obstetrical Society of Boston, vice-president, 1994-96, president, 1996-. **Publications:** (With A.B. Parson) The Massachusetts General Hospital Guide to Menopause: What It Is, How to Treat It, How to Cope With It, 1996; (with A.B. Parson) Menopause: The Most Comprehensive, Up-to-date Information Available to Help You Understand this Stage of Life, Make the Right Treatment Choices, and Cope Effectively, 1996. EDITOR: (with R.L. Barbieri) Reproductive Endocrine Therapeutics, 1988; (with C.B. Hammond and F.P. Haseltine) Menopause: Evaluation, Treatment, and Health Concerns, 1989; (with S. Smith) Modern Management of Premenstrual Syndrome, 1993; (co-ed.) Primary Care of Women, 1995; Contributor to books. **Address:** Department of Obstetrics & Gynecology, Massachusetts General Hospital, 55 Fruit St., VBK-113, Boston, MA 02114-2696, U.S.A. **Online address:** schiffi@a1.mgh.harvard.edu

SCHIFF, James A(ndrew). American (born United States), b. 1958. **Genres:** Literary Criticism And History, Essays, Education, History. **Career:** University of Cincinnati, Department of English, adjunct assistant professor, 1997-2000, assistant professor, 2000-06, associate professor, 2006-; Duke University, editor; The John Updike Review, editor; Community Learning Center Center Institute, editor; Mercantile Library, editor; WCET-TV, editor; The Seven Hill School, editor. **Publications:** Updike's Version: Rewriting The Scarlet Letter, 1992; Understanding Reynolds Price, 1996; John Updike Revisited, 1998; (ed.) Critical Essays on Reynolds Price, 1998; (ed.) Updike in Cincinnati: A Literary Performance, 2007. Contributor to periodicals. **Address:** Department of English, University of Cincinnati, 229C McMicken Hall, PO Box 69, Cincinnati, OH 45221-0069, U.S.A. **Online address:** james.schiff@uc.edu

SCHIFF, Nancy Rica. American (born United States), b. 1945. **Genres:** Photography, Humor/Satire. **Career:** Photographer and writer. **Publications:** (Contrib.) A Celebration of the 80s: Portraits, 1983; Odd Jobs: Portraits of Unusual Occupations, 2002; Odder Jobs: More Portraits of Unusual Occupations, 2006. Contributor to periodicals. **Address:** 24 W 30th St., New York, NY 10001-4410, U.S.A. **Online address:** mail@nancyricaschiff.com

SCHIFF, Robyn. American (born United States), b. 1973. **Genres:** Poetry. **Career:** University of Iowa, associate professor, professor and director of undergraduate creative writing. Writer. **Publications:** Worth (poems), 2002; Revolver (poems), 2008. Contributor to books. **Address:** Department of English, The University of Iowa, 358 EPB, 308 English Philosophy Bldg., Iowa City, IA 52242-1492, U.S.A. **Online address:** robyn-schiff@uiowa.edu

SCHIFFER, James (M.). American (born United States), b. 1948. **Genres:** Literary Criticism And History, Plays/Screenplays, Mystery/Crime/Suspense, Essays. **Career:** St. Lawrence University, visiting assistant professor of English, 1978-80; Blackburn College, assistant professor of English, 1980-85; Hampden-Sydney College, Department of English, assistant professor, 1985-89, associate professor, 1989-95, chair, 1991-94, 1998-2000, director of rhetoric program, 1994-97, Elliott associate professor, 1995-96, William W. Elliott professor of English, 1996-2000; State University of New York, Press, consultant, 1993, College of Liberal Arts and Sciences, dean, 2008-; Northern Michigan University, Department of English, professor and head, 2000-08; Michigan Association of Departments of English, president.Writer. **Publications:** (With S. Schiffer as Susan James) Foul Deeds (mystery novel), 1989; Richard Stern, 1993; (ed.) Shakespeare's Sonnets: Critical Essays, 1999; (ed.) Twelfth Night: New Critical Essays, 2011. Contributor to books and periodicals. **Address:** State University of New York, 1 Hawk Dr., New Paltz, NY 12561-2447, U.S.A. **Online address:** jschiffe@nmu.edu

SCHIFFERDECKER, Kathryn M. American (born United States), b. 1968. **Genres:** Theology/Religion. **Career:** Evangelical Lutheran Church of America, ordained, 2001; Luther Seminary, adjunct instructor, 2005, assistant professor of Old Testament, 2006-. Writer and ordained minister. **Publications:** Out of the Whirlwind: Creation Theology in the Book of Job, 2008. Contributor to books and journals. **Address:** Luther Seminary, 1456 Branston St., St. Paul, MN 55108, U.S.A. **Online address:** kschiffer@luthersem.edu

SCHILLER, Lawrence. (Lawrence Julian Schiller). American (born United States), b. 1936. **Genres:** Mystery/Crime/Suspense, Adult Non-fiction, Social Sciences. **Career:** Writer. **Publications:** Scavengers and Critics of The Warren Report; The Endless Paradox, 1967; (with S. Atkins) Killing of Sharon Tate, 1970; (with J. Willworth) American Tragedy: The Uncensored Story of the Simpson Defense, 1996; Perfect Murder, Perfect Town, 1999; Into the Mirror: The Life of Master Spy Robert P. Hanssen, 2002; Cape Max Court House, 2002. **Address:** International Creative Management Inc., 10250 Constellation Blvd., Los Angeles, CA 90067, U.S.A. **Online address:** lschiller@klscomm.com

SCHILLER, Lawrence Julian. See **SCHILLER, Lawrence.**

SCHILLING, Mark R. Japanese/American (born United States), b. 1949. **Genres:** Communications/Media, Film, Local History/Rural Topics, Politics/Government, Sports/Fitness, Translations, Travel/Exploration, Reference, Reference. **Career:** Japan Times, film reviewer, 1989-; Screen Intl., Japan correspondent, 1990-2005; Variety, Japan correspondent, 2005-. Writer. **Publications:** Jesse: Sumo Superstar, 1985; (trans.) M. Sato, The Shogun's Gold, 1991; Sumo: A Fan's Guide, 1994; The Encyclopedia of Japanese Pop Culture, 1997; Tokyo after Dark, 1998; Contemporary Japanese Film, 1999; (trans. and intro.) Princess Mononoke: The Art and Making of Japan's Most Popular Film of All Time, 1999; (contrib.) Japan Pop, 2000; (contrib.) Ichikawa Kon, 2001; The Yakuza Movie Book: A Guide to Japanese Gangster Films, 2003; No Borders, No Limits: The Cinema of Nikkatsu Action, 2007; Nudes! Guns! Ghots! The Sensational Films of Shintoho, 2010. **Address:** 3-12-23 Chuo-Cho, Higashi, Kurume-shi, Tokyo, 203-0054, Japan. **Online address:** schill@gol.com

SCHILLING, Peter. American (born United States), b. 1968?. **Genres:** Novels, Sports/Fitness. **Career:** MudvilleMagazine.com, editor. **Publications:** The End of Baseball (novel), 2008. **Address:** c/o Dana Kaye, Kaye Publicity, 5412 N Clark St., Ste. 213, Chicago, IL 60640, U.S.A. **Online address:** peter@mudvillemagazine.com

SCHIMPF, Ann L. See **LINNEA, Ann.**

SCHIMPFF, Jill Wagner. American (born United States), b. 1945. **Genres:** Language/Linguistics, Education, Reference. **Career:** Teacher, 1969-73; Stockholm Peace Research Institute, English editor, 1973-74; Junior High School, English teacher, 1975-78; Claremont Colleges, Community Friends

of International Students, president, 1975-2000; University of California, instructor in English as a second language (ESL), 1978-79; Pitzer College, instructor in English as a second language (ESL), 1979-2000; Schimpff's Confectionery, co-owner, 1990-. Writer. **Publications:** The Oxford Picture Dictionary of American English: Intermediate Workbook, 1981; The Open Sesame Picture Dictionary, 1982; The Open Sesame Picture Dictionary Activity Book, 1988; The New Oxford Picture Dictionary: Intermediate Workbook, 1988. Works appear in anthologies. Contributor to periodicals. **Address:** Schimpff's Confectionery, 347 Spring St., Jeffersonville, IN 47130-3449, U.S.A. **Online address:** info@schimpffs.com

SCHINE, Cathleen. American (born United States), b. 1953?. **Genres:** Novels, Film, Travel/Exploration, Romance/Historical. **Career:** Writer. **Publications:** NOVELS: Alice in Bed: A Novel, 1983; To the Birdhouse, 1990; Rameau's Niece, 1993; The Love Letter, 1995; The Evolution of Jane, 1998; She is Me: A Novel, 2003; The New Yorkers, 2007; Three Weissmanns of Westport, 2010. Contributor of articles to periodicals. **Address:** Molly Friedrich, The Friedrich Agency, 136 E 57th St., 19th Fl., New York, NY 10022, U.S.A.

SCHINTO, Jeanne. American (born United States), b. 1951. **Genres:** Adult Non-fiction, Cultural/Ethnic Topics, History, Photography, Novels. **Career:** Brooks School, English teacher, 1992-98; San Diego Weekly Reader, columnist and contributor, 1998-. **Publications:** Shadow Bands (stories), 1988; Children of Men (novel), 1991; Huddle Fever: Living in the Immigrant City (non-fiction), 1995. EDITOR: (intro.) The Literary Dog: Great Contemporary Dog Stories, 1990; Show Me a Hero: Great Contemporary Stories about Sports, 1995; Virtually Now: Stories of Science, Technology and the Future, 1996. **Address:** 53 Poor St., Andover, MA 01810-2501, U.S.A.

SCHIOPPA, Fiorella Kostoris Padoa. Belgian/Italian (born Italy), b. 1945. **Genres:** Economics, Business/Trade/Industry. **Career:** University of Rome, associate professor, 1977-80, professor, 1989-; University of Trieste, professor, 1980-83; Postgraduate School of Public Administration, professor, 1984-89; Italian National Research Council, chief, 1985-87, 1992-; Centre for Economic Policy Research, Public Policy Programme, research fellow, 1989-, professor of economics, 1989-; Oxford University, Nuffield College, Jemolo Fellow, 1992; Institute for Economic Studies and Analyses, president, 1999-2003; Foundation Nationale des Sciences Politiques, visiting professor, 2000-01; College of Europe, Department of European Economic Studies, visiting professor, professor, 2002-, University and Research, Research Programming of the Ministry of Education, technical secretariat, 2003-, School of Economics, professor of political economics; International Monetary Fund, consultant; Organization for Economic Cooperation and Development, consultant. Writer. **Publications:** IN ENGLISH: (ed.) Mismatch and Labour Mobility, 1991; Italy: The Sheltered Economy: Structural Problems of the Italian Economy, 1993; Excesses and Limits of the Public Sector in the Italian Economy: The Ongoing Reform, 1996; (ed.) Principles of Mutual Recognition in the European Integration Process, 2005; (ed. with J. Fitoussi) Report on the State of the European Union, 2005. IN ITALIAN: Scuola e Classi Sociali, 1974; La Forza Lavoro Femminile, 1977; (with T. Padoa-Schioppa) Agenda e Nonagenda: Limiti e Crisi Della Politica Economica, 1984; (ed. with T. Padoa-Schioppa) Reddito, Interesse, Inflazione, 1987; L'Economia Sotto Tutela: Problema Strutturali Dell'intervento Pubblico in Italia, 1990; (ed.) Squilibri Erigidita Nelmercato Del Lavoro Italiano: Rilevanza Quantitativa e Proposte Correttive, 1992; (ed.) Struttua di Mercato e Regolamentazione del Tresporto aereo, 1995; (with G. De Arcangelis) Esercizi di Micro e Macroeconomia, 1995; (ed.) Pensioni e Risanamento Della Finanza Pubblica, 1996; (with F. Modigliani) Sostenibilità e Solvibilità del Debito Pubblico in Italia: Il Conto Dei Flussi e Degli Stock Della Pubblica Amministrazione a Livello Nazionale e Regionale, 1998. **Address:** European Economic Studies Department, College of Europe, 11 Dijver, Bologna, 8000, Belgium. **Online address:** presidente@isae.it

SCHIPPER, Mineke. See **SCHIPPER DE LEEUW, W. J. J.**

SCHIPPER DE LEEUW, W. J. J. (Mineke Schipper). Dutch (born Netherlands), b. 1938. **Genres:** Novels, Anthropology/Ethnology, Cultural/Ethnic Topics, Humanities, Literary Criticism And History, Race Relations, Theatre. **Career:** Universite Nationale du Zaire, lecturer in arts, 1964-68, 1970-72; radio program maker, 1972-76; Netherlands PEN Centre, secretary, 1976-82; Amsterdam Free University, senior lecturer, associate professor, 1977-88, professor of intercultural studies and comparative literature, through 1993; Leiden University, senior lecturer, professor of intercultural studies and comparative literature, 1993-, chair of intercultural literary studies, head of the department of literary theory and comparative literature; Intercultural Study of Literature and Society, head of research program. Writer. **Publications:** Le Blanc et l'Occident au miroir du roman negro-africain de langue francaise, 1973; Le Blanc vu d'Afrique, 1973; Text and Context in Africa, 1977; Toneel en maatschappij in Afrika, 1977, trans. as Theatre and Society in Africa, 1982; Realisme: De illusie van werkelijkheid in literatuur, 1979; De tovertam en andere oude verhalen uit Zaire, 1979; Het zwarte paradijs: Afrikaanse scheppingsmythen, 1980; Afrikaanse letterkunde, 1983; Theatre et Societe en Afrique Dakar/Abidjan/Lome, 1984; Boeken van zwarte schrijvers, 1987; Onsterfelijke roem: het epos in verschillende culturen, 1989; Beyond the Boundaries: African Literature and Literary Theory, 1989; (with W.L. Idema and H.M. Leyten) White and Black, 1990; (with P. Schmitz) Ik is anders: Autobiografie in verschillende culturen, 1991; Een goede vrouw is zonder hoofd: Europese spreekwoorden en zegswijzen over vrouwen, 1993; (with Idema and P.H. Schrijvers) Mijn naam is Haas: dierenverhalen in verschillende culturen, 1993; Conrads River (novel), 1994; Een vrouw is als de aarde, 1995; De boomstam en de krokodil, 1995; (with S. Gupta) Een wenkbrauw als een wilgenblad, 1995; (with W.L. Idema and P.H. Schrijvers) Bezweren en betoveren Magie en literatuur wereldwijd, 1995; (with S. Cohn) De rib uit zijn lijf (title means: 'The Rib from His Body'), 1996; De zieleneters (title means: 'The Soul Eaters'), 1997; Imagining Insiders: Africa and the Question of Belonging, 1999; Never Marry a Woman with Big Feet: Women in Proverbs from around the World, 2003; Vogel Valt Vogel Vliegt, 2007. EDITOR: Ongehoorde woorden, 1984, trans. as Unheard Words, 1985; Source of All Evil, 1991; (with Y. Hubin and Guangxi) Epics and Heroes in China's Minority Cultures, 2004; (with M.J. Geller) Imagining Creation, 2008; (with Ye Shuxian and Yin Hubin) Chinas Creation and Origin Myths: Cross-Cultural Explorations in Oral and Written Traditions, 2011. Works appear in anthologies. Contributor to journals and periodicals. **Address:** Department of Literary Theory, Leiden University, Rm. 203B, PO Box 9515, Leiden, 2300 RA, Netherlands. **Online address:** w.j.j.schipper@hum.leidenuniv.nl

SCHISGAL, Murray. American (born United States), b. 1926. **Genres:** Plays/Screenplays, Novels, Documentaries/Reportage, Young Adult Fiction. **Career:** Musician, 1947-50; teacher, 1955-59. Writer. **Publications:** Ducks and Lovers, 1961; Knit One, Purl Two, 1963; The Typist and the Tiger, 1963; Fragments, Windows and Other Plays, 1965; The Love Song of Barney Kempinski, 1966; Luv, 1966; The Tiger Makes Out, 1967; Jimmy Shine, 1969; The Chinese and Dr. Fish, 1970; Ducks and Lovers, 1972; An American Millionaire, 1974; All Over Town, 1974; Natasha Kovolina Pipshinsky, 1976; The Pushcart Peddlers, The Flatulist and Other Plays, 1980; The Days and Nights of a French Horn Player, 1980; Luv and Other Plays, 1983; Twice around the Park, 1983; Tootsie, 1984; Closet Madness and Other Plays, 1984; Popkins, 1984, rev. ed., 1990; Jealousy and There Are No Sacher Tortes in Our Society!, 1985; The New Yorkers, 1985; The Rabbi and the Toyota Dealer, 1985; Old Wine in a New Bottle, 1987; Road Show, 1987; Man Dangling, 1988; Oatmeal and Kisses, 1990; The Songs of War, 1992; Extensions, 1992; 74 Georgia Avenue, 1992; The Japanese Foreign Trade Minister, 1992; Circus Life, 1992; Sexaholics and Other Plays, 1995; The Artist and the Model, 1996; An Occasion for Celebration, 1997; Play Time, 1997; Fifty Years Ago, 1998; First Love, 1998; Mentors, 1998; Angel Wings, 1998; The Man Who Couldn't Stop Crying, 1999; Bob, 1999; We Are Family, 2000; Regret, 2002; Seize the Moment, 2002. **Address:** Punch Productions, 11661 San Vicente Blvd., Ste. 222, Los Angeles, CA 90049-5110, U.S.A. **Online address:** murrays@punch21.com

SCHLESIER, Karl H. American/German (born Germany), b. 1927. **Genres:** Anthropology/Ethnology, Archaeology/Antiquities, Social Sciences, Natural History, Young Adult Fiction, History. **Career:** University of Kansas, faculty; Wichita State University, professor of anthropology, now professor emeritus. Writer and anthropologist. **Publications:** The Archaeology of Sedna Creek, 1971; The Wolves of Heaven: Cheyenne Shamanism, Ceremonies and Prehistoric Origins, 1987; (ed.) Plains Indians, A.D. 500-1500: The Archaeological Past of Historic Groups, 1994; Josanie's War: A Chiricahua Apache Novel, 1998; Trail of the Red Butterfly, 2007; Aurora Crossing, 2008. Contributor to journals. **Address:** Wichita State University, 1845 Fairmount St., Wichita, KS 67260, U.S.A.

SCHLESINGER, Allen B(rian). American (born United States), b. 1924. **Genres:** Biology, Sciences. **Career:** Creighton University, professor of biology, 1952-2000, professor emeritus of developmental biology, 2000-. Writer. **Publications:** Explaining Life, 1994. **Address:** Department of Biology, Creighton University, 2500 California Plz., Omaha, NE 68178, U.S.A. **Online address:** aschles@creighton.edu

SCHLESINGER, Benjamin. Canadian/German (born Germany), b. 1928. **Genres:** Human Relations/Parenting, Social Sciences, Bibliography, Essays, Medicine/Health. **Career:** Jewish Immigrant Aid Society, social worker, 1947-51; Children's Aid Society, social worker, 1953-56; Merrill-Palmer Institute, intern in psychotherapy, 1956-57; Aloka World Assembly of Youth, faculty, 1959-60; University of Toronto, Factor-Inwentash Faculty of Social Work, assistant professor, 1960-64, associate professor of social work, 1965-94, professor emeritus, 1994-; University of the West Indies, visiting professor, 1967; University of Western Australia, visiting lecturer, 1971-72; University of Aukland, visiting professor, 1978-79. Writer. **Publications:** The Multi-Problem Family, 1963, 3rd ed., 1970; Poverty in Canada and the United States, 1966; The One-Parent Family, 1969, 4th ed., 1978; The Jewish Family, 1971; The Single-Parent Family in Australia: Some Facts and Figures, 1972; Families: A Canadian Perspective, 1972; Family Planning in Canada: A Source Book, 1974; Child Abuse in Canada, 1977; Families: Canada, 1979; One in Ten: The One-Parent Family in Canada, 1979; Sexual Abuse of Children: A Resource Guide and Annotated Bibliography, 1982; Remarriage: A Review and Annotated Bibliography, 1983; Canadian Family Studies: A Selected, Annotated Bibliography, 1970-1982, 1983; The One-Parent Family in the 1980's, 1985; Jewish Family Issues: A Resource Guide, 1987; (with R.A. Schlesinger) Canadian Families: A Resource Guide, 1988; (with R.A. Schlesinger) Canadian Families in Transition, 1992; (with S. Kingsmill) The Family Squeeze: Surviving the Sandwich Generation, 1998; Canadian Families: 1900-2000: A Bibliography, 2000; (with R.A. Schlesinger) Jewish Families: Introduction and Annotated Bibliography, 2000. EDITOR: The Chatelaine Guide to Marriage, 1975; Sexual Behavior in Canada: Patterns and Problems, 1977; Sexual Abuse of Children in the 1980's: Ten Essays and an Annotated Bibliography, 1986; (and comp. with R. Schlesinger) Abuse of the Elderly: Issues and Annotated Bibliography, 1988. **Address:** Factor-Inwentash Faculty of Social Work, University of Toronto, 246 Bloor St. W, Toronto, ON M5S 1V4, Canada.

SCHLESSINGER, Laura. American (born United States), b. 1947. **Genres:** How-to Books, Psychology, Human Relations/Parenting, Young Adult Fiction. **Career:** KFI-AM Radio, host, 1990-; University of Southern California, instructor in physiology and human sexuality; Pepperdine University, adjunct professor; Dr. Laura Schlessinger Foundation, founder; Premier Radio Network, host. Writer. **Publications:** Ten Stupid Things Women Do to Mess up Their Lives, 1995; How Could You Do That?!: The Abdication of Character, Courage and Conscience, 1996; Ten Stupid Things Men Do to Mess up Their Lives, 1997; (with R.S. Vogel) Ten Commandments: The Significance of God's Laws in Everyday Life, 1998; Damsels, Dragons and Regular Guys, 2000; Good People Where You Fit In, 2000; Ten Commandments, Do They Still Count, 2000; Parenthood by Proxy: Don't Have Them if You Won't Raise Them, 2000; (foreword) Coming out Straight: Understanding and Healing Homosexuality, 2000; Ten Stupid Things Couples do to Mess up Their Relationships, 2001; Ten Stupid Things Parents Do to Mess up Their Kids, 2002. FOR CHILDREN: (with M. Lambert) Why do You Love Me?, 1999; But I Waaannt It!, 2000; Cope with It!, 2000; I Hate My Life!, 2001; Growing up Is Hard, 2001; Dr. Laura Schlessinger's Where is God?, 2003; Woman Power: Transform Your Man, Your Marriage, Your Life, 2004; The Proper Care and Feeding of Husbands, 2004; Larry King live. CNN, 2004; Bad Childhood-Good Life: How to Blossom and Thrive in Spite of an Unhappy Childhood, 2006; The Proper Care and Feeding of Marriage, 2007; Stop Whining, Start Living, 2008; In Praise of Stay-at-Home Moms, 2009; Surviving a Shark Attack (on Land): Overcoming Betrayal and Dealing with Revenge, 2011. Contributor to periodicals. **Address:** Premier Radio Network, 15260 Ventura Blvd., Ste. 500, 5th Fl., Sherman Oaks, CA 91403, U.S.A.

SCHLINK, Bernhard. German (born Germany), b. 1944. **Genres:** Novels, Novellas/Short Stories, Law. **Career:** Rheinische Friedrich Wilhelm University, professor, 1982-91; Constitutional Court of Northrhine-Westfalia, justice, 1988-2006; J.W. Goethe University, professor, 1991-92; Humboldt University, professor, 1992-; St. Anne's College, honorary fellow, 2009-. Writer and consultant. **Publications:** NONFICTION: Abwägung im Verfassungsrecht (thesis), 1976; Die Amtshilfe: Ein Beitrag zu einer Lehre von der Gewaltenteilung in der Verwaltung, 1982; (with B. Pieroth) Grundrechte. Staatsrecht II, 1985, 27th ed., 2011; (ed. with A.J. Jacobson) Weimar: A Jurisprudence of Crisis, 2000; (with B. Pieroth and M. Kniesel) Polizei-und Ordnungsrecht, 2002, 6th ed., 2011; Vergewisserungen, 2002; Vergangenheitsschuld, 2007; Gedanken üeber das Schreiben, 2011. NOVELS: (with W. Popp) Selbs Justiz, 1987; Die gordische Schleife, 1988; Selbs Betrug, 1992; Der Vorleser, 1995; Selbs Mord, 2001; Die Heimkehr, 2006; Das Wochende, 2008. SHORT STORIES: Liebesfluchten, 2000; Sommerlüegen, 2010. **Address:** Law School, Humboldt University, Unter den Linden 6, Berlin, D-10099, Germany. **Online address:** schlink@rewi.hu-berlin.de

SCHLITZ, Laura Amy. American (born United States) **Genres:** Young Adult Fiction, Novels, History, Plays/Screenplays. **Career:** Park School, lower school librarian. Writer. **Publications:** A Drowned Maiden's Hair: A Melodrama, 2006; The Hero Schliemann: The Dreamer Who Dug for Troy, 2006; Good Masters! Sweet Ladies! Voices from a Medieval Village, 2007; Night Fairy, 2010. **Address:** Park School, 2425 Old Court Rd., PO Box 8200, Baltimore, MD 21208, U.S.A. **Online address:** lschlitz@parkschool.net

SCHLOSBERG, Suzanne. American (born United States), b. 1971?. **Genres:** Humor/Satire, Sports/Fitness, Medicine/Health, Travel/Exploration, Reference. **Career:** Shape, contributing editor. **Publications:** (With L. Neporent) Fitness for Dummies, 1996; Kathy Smith's Fitness Makeover: A Ten-Week Guide to Exercise and Nutrition That Will Change Your Life, 1997; (with L. Neporent and S. Archer) Weight Training for Dummies, 1997, 3rd ed., 2006; Fitness for Travelers: The Ultimate Workout Guide for the Road, 2002; The Curse of the Singles Table: A True Story of 1001 Nights without Sex, 2004; (with L. Neporent) The Fat-free Truth: 240 Real Answers to the Fitness and Weight-Loss Questions You Wonder about Most, 2005; The Ultimate Workout Log, 2005; The Essential Fertility Log: An Organizer and Record Keeper to Help You Get Pregnant, 2007; (with L. Neporent) The Active Woman's Pregnancy Log, 2008; (with C. Sass) The Ultimate Diet Log, 2009; (with S.B. Shea) The Essential Breastfeeding Log, 2009; (with S. Quessenberry) The Good Neighbor Cookbook, 2011. **Address:** c/o Author Mail, Warner Books, 1271 Ave. of the Americas, New York, NY 10020, U.S.A. **Online address:** suzanne@suzanneschlosberg.com

SCHMAHMANN, David. American/South African (born South Africa), b. 1953. **Genres:** Novels, Law, Adult Non-fiction, Mystery/Crime/Suspense. **Career:** Nutter, McClennen & Fish (law firm), senior partner, 1979-2001; Schmahmann Realty L.L.C., principal. Writer. **Publications:** Empire Settings, 2001; Nibble & Kuhn, 2009; The Double Life of Alfred Buber, 2011; Ivory from Paradise, 2011. **Address:** Schmahmann Realty L.L.C., 1577 Beacon St., Brookline, MA 02446, U.S.A. **Online address:** david@davidschmahmann.com

SCHMANDT, Jurgen. American/Vietnamese/German (born Germany), b. 1929. **Genres:** Environmental Sciences/Ecology, Organized Labor, Public/Social Administration, Education. **Career:** University of Bonn, faculty; Organization for Economic Cooperation and Development (OECD), staff; Harvard University, faculty; U.S. Environmental Protection Agency, staff; University of Texas, Lyndon Baines Johnson School of Public Affairs, professor of public affairs, 1971-, now professor emeritus of public affairs; Houston Advanced Research Center, Mitchell Center for Sustainable Development, director, 1986-2002, HARC distinguished fellow. Writer. **Publications:** (Co-ed.) Nutrition Policy in Transition, 1980; (ed. with H. Roderick) Acid Rain and Friendly Neighbors: The Policy Dispute Between Canada and the United States, 1985, (with H. Roderick and J. Clarkson) rev. ed., 1988; (ed. with R. Wilson) Promoting High-Technology Industry: Initiatives and Policies for State Governments, 1987; (with E.T. Smerdon and J. Clarkson) State Water Policies: A Study of Six States, 1988; (ed. with F.D. Bean and S. Weintraub) Mexican and Central American Population and U.S. Immigration Policy, 1989; (ed. with F. Williams and R.H. Wilson) Telecommunications Policy and Economic Development: The New State Role, 1989; (ed. with R. Wilson) Growth Policy in the Age of High Technology: The Role of Regions and States, 1990; (co-ed.) New Urban Infrastructure: Cities and Telecommunications, 1990; (co-ed.) Telecommunications and Rural Development: A Study of Private and Public Sector Innovation, 1991; (ed. with J. Clarkson) The Regions and Global Warming: Impacts and Response Strategies, 1992; (ed. with G.R. North and J. Clarkson) The Impact of Global Warming on Texas: A Report of the Task Force on Climate Change in Texas, 1995, 2nd ed., 2011; (comp. with A.R. Magalhães) The Road to Sustainable Development: A Guide for Non-governmental Organizations, 1998; (comp. with C. Stolp and G. Ward) Scarce Water: Doing More with Less in the Lower Rio Grande: A Research Project, 1998; (with C. Stolp, G. Ward and L. Rhodes) Navigating the Waters of the Paso del Norte: A People's Guide, 1999; (ed. with C.H. Ward) Sustainable Development: The Challenge of Transition,

2000; (co-ed.) Explorando las Aguas del Paso del Norte: Una Guia Para la Gente, 2000; George Mitchell and the Idea of Sustainability, 2010. Works appear in anthologies. **Address:** Houston Advanced Research Center, 4800 Research Forest Dr., The Woodlands, TX 77381-4142, U.S.A. **Online address:** jschmandt@harc.edu

SCHMEISER, Douglas A. Canadian (born Canada), b. 1934. **Genres:** Civil Liberties/Human Rights, Criminology/True Crime, Law, Politics/Government. **Career:** University of Saskatchewan, special lecturer in law, 1956-57, assistant professor, 1961-64, associate professor, 1964-68, professor, 1968-95, director of graduate legal studies, 1969-74, dean of law, 1974-77, professor emeritus, 1995-; lawyer, 1958-61. Writer. **Publications:** Civil Liberties in Canada, 1964; Cases and Comments on Criminal Law, 1966, 4th ed., 1981; Cases On Canadian Civil Liberties, 1971; Délinquance Chez Lesautochtones Et La Loi, 1974; The Native Offender and the Law, 1974; Criminal Law: Cases and Comments, 3rd ed., 1977; Report on the Law Reform Commission of Tanzania and the Law Review Commission of Zanzibar, 1994; (with W.H. McConnell) The Independence of Provincial Court Judges: A Public Trust, 1996. **Address:** College of Law, University of Saskatchewan, Rm. 106 Law, 15 Campus Dr., Saskatoon, SK S7N 5A6, Canada.

SCHMID, Walter Thomas. American (born United States), b. 1946. **Genres:** Literary Criticism And History, Philosophy, Ethics. **Career:** Yale University, instructor, 1976-77; University of Hartford, instructor, 1977-78; Valparaiso University, lecturer, 1978; Grinnell College, assistant professor, 1979; University of North Carolina, faculty, 1979-91, professor, 1991-. Writer. **Publications:** On Manly Courage: A Study of Plato's Laches, 1992; Plato's Charmides and the Socratic Ideal of Rationality, 1998. **Address:** Department of Philosophy & Religion, University of North Carolina, 263 Bear Hall, 601 S College Rd., Wilmington, NC 28403-3297, U.S.A. **Online address:** schmidt@uncw.edu

SCHMID, W. George. See **SCHMID, Wolfram George.**

SCHMID, Wolfram George. (W. George Schmid). American/German (born Germany), b. 1930. **Genres:** Agriculture/Forestry, Botany, Design, Earth Sciences, Environmental Sciences/Ecology, Homes/Gardens, Horticulture, Natural History, Sciences, Reference. **Career:** Architect of practiced architecture and landscape architecture, 1952-64; forest products engineering and silviculture, 1964-92; American Hosta Society, director and historian, 1984-; Georgia Hosta Society, founder, 1984. Writer. **Publications:** The Genus Hosta: Giboshi Zoku, 1991; An Encyclopedia of Shade Perennials, 2002; Timber Press Pocket Guide to Shade Perennials, 2005. Contributor to magazines. **Address:** 4417 Goodfellows Ct., Tucker, GA 30084-2710, U.S.A. **Online address:** hostahill@bellsouth.net

SCHMIDLE, Nicholas. American (born United States), b. 1978?. **Genres:** History. **Career:** Journalist. **Publications:** To Live or to Perish Forever: Two Tumultuous Years in Pakistan, 2009. Contributor to periodicals. **Address:** Washington, DC , U.S.A. **Online address:** nickschmidle@gmail.com

SCHMIDT, Arthur. American (born United States), b. 1943. **Genres:** Area Studies, Essays, Social Sciences. **Career:** Temple University, instructor, 1971-73, assistant professor, 1973-83, associate professor of history, 1983-95, professor, 1995-. Writer. **Publications:** (Contrib.) Two Essays on Neglected Aspects of the Economic History of the Mexican Revolution, 1977; The Social and Economic Effect of Railroads in Puebla and Veracruz, Mexico, 1867-1911, 1987; (trans. and foreword with A. Camacho de Schmidt) E. Poniatowska, Nothing, Nobody: Voices of the Mexico City Earthquake, 1995; (ed. and intro.) El Salvador in the Eighties: Counterinsurgency and Revolution, 1996; (ed. and trans. with A. Camacho de Schmidt)Surviving Mexico's Dirty War: A Political Prisoner's Memoir, 2007. Contributor of articles to books and periodicals. **Address:** Department of History, Temple University, Gladfelter Hall 9th Fl., 1115 W Berks St., Philadelphia, PA 19122, U.S.A. **Online address:** arturo@temple.edu

SCHMIDT, Benno Charles. American (born United States), b. 1942. **Genres:** Education, History, Law. **Career:** U.S. Supreme Court, law clerk, 1966-67; U.S. Department of Justice, Assistant Attorney General's Office of Legal Counsel, special assistant, 1967-69; Columbia University, Harlan Fiske Stone, professor of constitutional law, 1969-86, dean of law school, 1984-86; National Humanities Center, director, 1985-; Yale University, university president and professor of law, 1986-92; Edison Schools, CEO, 1992-, chairman, 1997-2007, vice-chairman-2007-. Writer. **Publications:** Frankfurter Amts- und Zunfturkunden bis zum Jahre 1612, 1968; Legal Gambling in New York: A Discussion of Numbers and Sports Betting, 1972; Freedom of the Press versus Public Access, 1974; (with A.M. Bickel) The Judiciary and Responsible Government, 1910-1921, 1985. **Address:** Edison Schools, 521 5th Ave. 11th Fl, New York, NY 10175, U.S.A.

SCHMIDT, C. A. American (born United States) **Genres:** Novels. **Career:** Journalist and educator. **Publications:** Useful Fools (young- adult novel), 2007. Contributor to periodicals. **Online address:** emailme@caschmidt.com

SCHMIDT, Elizabeth. American (born United States), b. 1955. **Genres:** History, Women's Studies And Issues. **Career:** Macalester College, visiting assistant professor, 1987-90; University of Minnesota, adjunct assistant professor, 1988; University of Conakry, Fulbright professor, 1990-91; Loyola University Maryland, Department of History, assistant professor, 1990-95, associate professor, 1995-2000, chair, 1995-98, professor, 2000-. Writer. **Publications:** Decoding Corporate Camouflage: U.S. Business Support for Apartheid, 1980; (with J. Blewett and P. Henriot) Religious Private Voluntary Organizations and the Question of Government Funding, 1981; One Step in the Wrong Direction: An Analysis of the Sullivan Principles as a Strategy for Opposing Apartheid, 1985; Ideology, Economics, and the Social Control of Women in Southern Rhodesia, 1910-1939: Paper, 1986; South Africa Sanctions Fact Sheet: Lessons from Rhodesia, 1986; Seminar Paper on Women, Agriculture, and Social Change in Southern Rhodesia, 1898-1934: With Special Reference to the Goromonzi District, 1986; Peasants, Traders, and Wives: Shona Women in the History of Zimbabwe, 1870-1939, 1992; Mobilizing the Masses: Gender, Ethnicity, and Class in the Nationalist Movement in Guinea, 1939-1958, 2005; Cold War and Decolonization in Guinea, 1946-1958, 2007. Contributor to books and journals. **Address:** Department of History, Loyola University Maryland, Humanities 313, 4501 N Charles St., Baltimore, MD 21210, U.S.A. **Online address:** eschmidt@loyola.edu

SCHMIDT, Gary D. American (born United States), b. 1957. **Genres:** Children's Fiction, Children's Non-fiction, Literary Criticism And History, Biography, Adult Non-fiction, Novels. **Career:** Calvin College, professor of English, 1985-, department head, 1991-97. Writer. **Publications:** FOR CHILDREN: John Bunyan's Pilgrim's Progress, 1994; Robert Frost, 1994; The Sin Eater (novel), 1996; (ed. with D.R. Hettinga) British Children's Writers, 1914-1960, 1996; The Blessing of the Lord, 1997; William Bradford: Pilgrim of Answerable Courage, 1997; Anson's Way, 1999; Saint Ciaran: The Tale of a Saint of Ireland, 2000; Straw into Gold, 2001; Mara's Stories, 2001; The Wonders of Donal O'Donnell, 2002; The Great Stone Face, 2002; Lizzie Bright and the Buckminster Boy, 2004; First Boy, 2005; (with L. Kushner) In God's Hands, 2005; The Wednesday Wars, 2007; Trouble, 2008. FOR ADULTS: Supplementary Essays for College Writers, 1988; Robert McCloskey, 1990; Hugh Lofting, 1992; Katherine Paterson, 1994; The Iconography of the Mouth of Hell: Eighth-Century Britain to the Fifteenth Century, 1995; Robert Lawson, 1997; (with C. Winters) Edging the Boundaries of Children's Literature, 2001; A Passionate Usefulness: The Life and Literary Labors of Hannah Adams, 2004. EDITOR: (with C.F. Otten) The Voice of the Narrator in Children's Literature: Insights From Writers and Critics, 1989; (with D.R. Hettinga) Sitting at the Feet of the Past: Retelling the North American Folktale for Children, 1992; (with W.J. Vande Kopple) Communities of Discourse: The Rhetoric of Disciplines, 1993; (with F.S. Bolin and B. Bagert) The Blackbirch Treasury of American Poetry, 2001; (reteller) Pilgrim's Progress, 2008; Emmaus Readers: Listening for God in Contemporary Fiction, 2008. SPIRITUAL BIOGRAPHY OF THE SEASON SERIES: (ed. with S.M. Felch) Winter: 2003; (ed. with S.M. Felch) Autumn, 2004; (ed. with S.M. Felch) Summer, 2005; (ed. with S.M. Felch) Spring, 2006. OTHERS: Okay for Now, 2011; (with D. Diaz) Martíne Porres, 2012. Contributor to books. **Address:** Department of English, Calvin College, CFAC 287, 1795 Knollcrest Cir., 3201 Burton SE, Grand Rapids, MI 49546, U.S.A. **Online address:** schg@calvin.edu

SCHMIDT, Heidi. (Heidi Jon Schmidt). American (born United States) **Genres:** Novellas/Short Stories, Novels, Literary Criticism And History. **Career:** Fine Arts Work Center, fellow, 1982-83, 1985-86, teacher. Writer. **Publications:** AS HEIDI JON SCHMIDT: The Rose Thieves, 1990; Darling?, 2001; The Bride of Catastrophe, 2003; The House on Oyster Creek, 2010. Contributor to books and periodicals. **Address:** Fine Arts Work Center, 24 Pearl St., Provincetown, MA 02657, U.S.A.

SCHMIDT, Heidi Jon. See **SCHMIDT, Heidi.**

SCHMIDT, Karl H. American (born United States), b. 1955. **Genres:** Human Relations/Parenting, Adult Non-fiction, Medicine/Health, Romance/ Historical, Psychology. **Career:** Writer and entrepreneur. **Publications:** Marriage Mediator: The Street Smart Guide to a Successful Marriage, 1998; Parenting, forthcoming. **Address:** OnTrack Publishing, 2377 Gold Meadow Way, Gold River, CA 95670, U.S.A.

SCHMIDT, Leigh Eric. American (born United States), b. 1961. **Genres:** Cultural/Ethnic Topics, History, Theology/Religion. **Career:** Stanford University, Mellon fellow, 1987-88; University of Oregon, assistant professor, 1988-89; Drew University, assistant professor of church history, 1989-94, associate professor of church history, 1994; Princeton University, Department of Religion, professor, Agate Brown and George L. Collord professor of religion, department chair, Graduate Studies, director, 1995-2009; Harvard University, Harvard Divinity School, Charles Warren professor of the history of religion in America, 2009-11; Washington University, Edward Mallinckrodt distinguished university professor, 2011-. Writer. **Publications:** Holy Fairs: Scottish Communions and American Revivals in the Early Modern Period, 1989, 2nd ed., 2001; Consumer Rites: The Buying and Selling of American Holidays, 1995; Hearing Things: Religion, Illusion, and the American Enlightenment, 2000; (with E.S. Gaustad) Religious History of America, 2002; Restless Souls: The Making of American Spirituality, 2005; (ed. with L.F. Maffly-Kipp and M. Valeri) Practicing Protestants: Histories of Christian Life in America, 1630-1965, 2006; Heaven's Bride: The Unprintable Life of Ida C. Craddock, American Mystic, Scholar, Sexologist, Martyr, and Madwoman, 2010. Contributor to periodicals. **Address:** John C. Danforth Center on Religion & Politics, Washington University, 1 Brookings Dr., PO Box 1066, St. Louis, MO 63130, U.S.A. **Online address:** lschmidt@hds.harvard.edu

SCHMIDT, Michael (Norton). British/Mexican (born Mexico), b. 1947. **Genres:** Novels, Poetry, Literary Criticism And History, Translations. **Career:** Carcanet Press Ltd., founder and editorial director, 1969-; University of Manchester, part-time lecturer, 1971-84, Gulbenkian fellow in poetry, 1972-75; PN Review, general editor, 1972-; Poetry Centre, director, 1984-98, lecturer, 1984-94, senior lecturer, 1994-98; Literary Periodical Poetry Nation, editor, 1984; Manchester Metropolitan University, founder and director of the Writing School, 1998-2005, professor of English, 2000-05; University of Glasgow, convener of the writing M. Litt program, professor of poetry, 2006-; John Rylands University Library, Modern Literature Archive project, co-founder and director. **Publications:** POEMS: Black Buildings, 1969; Desert of Lions, 1972; It Was My Tree, 1972; My Brother Gloucester: New Poems, 1976; A Change of Affairs, 1978; Choosing a Guest: New and Selected Poems, 1983; The Love of Strangers, 1988; Selected Poems, 1972-1997, 1999; New and Collected Poems, 2009. EDITOR: (with G. Lindop) British Poetry Since 1960: A Critical Survey, 1972; Ten English Poets: An Anthology, 1976; The Avoidance of Literature: Collected Essays, 1978; A Reader's Guide to Fifty Modern British Poets, 1979; Eleven British Poets: An Anthology, 1980; (with P. Jones) British Poetry since 1970: A Critical Survey, 1980; Seven Contemporary Poets of Britain and Ireland: An Anthology, 1983; (trans. with E. Kissam) Poems of the Aztec Peoples, 1983; A Calendar of Modern Poetry, 1994; New Poetries, 1994; (with A. Niven) Enigmas and Arrivals: An Anthology of Commonwealth Writing, 1997; (with N. Rennison) Poets on Poets, 1997; New Poetries II: An Anthology, 1999; Twentieth-Century Poetry in English, 1999; New Poetries III, 2002; New Collected Poems, 2002; The Great Modern Poets, 2006; New Poetries IV, 2007. OTHER: Bedlam and the Oakwood: Essays on Various Fiction, 1970; (trans. and intro. with E. Kissam) Flower and Song: Poems of the Aztec Peoples, 1977; An Introduction to Fifty British Poets, 1300-1900, 1979; The Colonist, 1980 in US as Green Island, 1982; A Reader's Guide to Fifty British Poets, 1300-1900, 1980; (trans.) O. Paz, On Poets and Others, 1986; The Dresden Gate, 1987; Reading Modern Poetry (criticism), 1989; Lives of the Poets, 1999; The Story of Poetry, 2001; The First Poets: Lives of the Ancient Greek Poets, 2004; The Resurrection of the Body, 2007; The Story of Poetry III: From Pope to Burns, 2007; (with R. Maslen) The Shakespeare Handbook, 2008. **Address:** Carcanet Press Ltd., Alliance House, 30 Cross St., Manchester, GM M2 7AP, England. **Online address:** schmidt@carcanet.co.uk

SCHMIDT, Peter. American (born United States), b. 1964. **Genres:** Adult Non-fiction, Education, History, Social Sciences, Law. **Career:** Chronicle of Higher Education, senior writer; Education Week, reporter. **Publications:** Color and Money: How Rich White Kids Are Winning the War over College Affirmative Action, 2007. **Address:** Chronicle of Higher Education, 7th Fl., 1255 23rd St. NW, Washington, DC 20001-3179, U.S.A.

SCHMIDT, Samuel. Mexican/American (born United States), b. 1950. **Genres:** Politics/Government, Translations, History. **Career:** Colegio Monte Sinai, teacher of Jewish history, 1969; Universidad Nacional Autonoma de Mexico, associate professor of political science, 1975-93, professor of socio-economics, 1981-84; Universidad Autonoma de Nuevo Leon, teacher, 1980; Universidad de Guadalajara, teacher, 1984; Mexican Department of Education, national research scientist, 1985-90; University of California, visiting researcher, 1985-87, research associate in Program on Mexico, 1986-, visiting associate professor, 1988, 1991; San Diego State University, visiting associate professor, 1989-90; Universidad Autonoma de Baja California, visiting professor, 1989-91; University of Texas, El Paso, associate professor, 1991-98, Center for Inter-American and Border Studies, director, 1991-; Universityersidad Autonoma de Ciudad Juarez, professor, 1998-, colegio de Chihuahua, Center for North American studies, director. Writer. **Publications:** (Trans. and intro.) A General Model of Planning, 1980; El Deterioro del Presidencialismo Mexicano: Los Años de Luis Echeverria, 1986; La autonomia relativa del estado (title means: 'The Relative Autonomy of the State'), 1988; (ed. with J.W. Wilke and M. Esparza) Estudios Cuantitativos sobre la Historia de México, 1988; (ed.) Yehezkel, Dror, Enfrentando el futuro (title means: 'Facing the Future'), 1990; Humor enserio: Análisis del Chiste Político en México, 1996; Antologiadel Chiste Politico, 1996; El Mexicano es es su propio enemigo, 1996; (ed.) United States-Mexico Border Environmental Directory 1996/DirectorioAmbiental Fronterizo Mexico-Estados Unidos 1996, 1997; Amenaza y Oportunidad, 1997; En Busca de la Decisión: La Industria Maquiladoraen Ciudad Juárez, 1998; México Encadeuado: El Legado de Zedillo ylos Retos de Fox, 2001; Nueva crisis de México, 2003; Los Grandes Problema Nacionale, 2003; Grandes Problemas Nacionales: Versión SigloXXI, 2003; Fox a Mitad del Camino, 2004; Las Grandes Soluciones Nacionales: Propuestas Para una Agenda Nacional, 2005; México- La Nueva Gobernabilidad: una Reflexión Para Tiempos de Turbulencia, 2005; (with J.G. Mendieta) Estudios sobre la red política de México, 2005; (contrib.) México visto desde lejos, 2007; (with A.H. Andújar) Pensar Iberoamérica, 2009. Works appear in anthologies. **Address:** Department of Social Sciences, Universityersidad Autonoma de Ciudad Juarez, 312 Benedict Hall, Ciudad Juarez, 79968, Mexico. **Online address:** sschmidt@uacj.mx

SCHMIDT, Sarah. Israeli/American (born United States), b. 1934. **Genres:** Biography, Autobiography/Memoirs. **Career:** University of Maryland, lecturer in American studies, 1974-78; Institute for Jewish Policy Planning and Research, associate director, 1978-79; Holocaust Memorial Council, deputy director, 1979-81; Rockland Community College, Israel Office, director, 1985-88; Tel Aviv University, senior lecturer, 1994-; Hebrew University of Jerusalem, Rothberg International School, senior lecturer, 1995-. Writer. **Publications:** Horace M. Kallen: Prophet of American Zionism, 1995. Contributor to periodicals. **Address:** Rothberg International School, Hebrew University of Jerusalem, Boyar Bldg., Mount Scopus, Jerusalem, 91905, Israel. **Online address:** slschmid@post.tau.ac.il

SCHMIDT, Stanley (Albert). American (born United States), b. 1944. **Genres:** Novels, Novellas/Short Stories, Science Fiction/Fantasy, Children's Fiction, Sciences, Writing/Journalism, Essays, History, History. **Career:** Heidelberg College, assistant professor of physics, 1969-78; Davis Publications Inc., Analog Science Fiction and Fact, editor, 1978-. **Publications:** Newton and the Quasi-Apple, 1975; The Sins of the Fathers, 1976; Lifeboat Earth, 1978; Tweedlioop, 1986; Aliens and Alien Societies, 1995; Which Way to the Future: Selected Essays from Analog, 2001; Argonaut (novel), 2002; Generation Gap and Other Stories, 2002; Coming Convergence: Surprising Ways Diverse Technologies Interact to Shape Our World and Change the Future, 2008. EDITOR: Analog's Golden Anniversary Anthology, 1980; Analog's Children of the Future, 1982; Analog's Lighter Side, 1982; War and Peace: Possible Futures from Analog, 1984; Analog: Writer's Choice, 1983; Aliens from Analog, 1983; From Mind to Mind: Tales of Communication from Analog, 1984; Analog's Expanding Universe, 1986; Analog Essays on Science, 1990; (with R. Zubrin) Islands in the Sky: Bold New Ideas for Colonizing Space, 1996; (with G. Dozois) Roads Not Taken: Tales of Alternate History, 1998. Contributor of articles to magazines. **Address:** c/o Eleanor Wood, Spectrum Literary Agency, 320 Central Pk. W, Ste. 1-D, New York, NY 10025, U.S.A.

SCHMIDT, Ulf. British (born England), b. 1967. **Genres:** Medicine/Health, History. **Career:** University of Kent, senior lecturer in modern history; Porton Down Project, principal investigator. Writer. **Publications:** Medical Films, Ethics, and Euthanasia in Nazi Germany: The History of Medical Research and Teaching Films of the Reich Office for Educational Films-Reich Institute for Films in Science and Education, 1933-1945, 2002; Justice at Nuremberg: Leo Alexander and the Nazi Doctors' Trial, 2004; (ed. with A. Frewer) Standards der Forschung: Historische Entwicklung und ethische Grundlagen klinischer Studien, 2007; (ed. with A. Frewer) History and Theory of Human Experimentation: The Declaration of Helsinki and Modern Medical Ethics, 2007; Karl Brandt: The Nazi Doctor: Medicine and Power in the Third Reich, 2008. Contributor to books, periodicals and journals. **Address:** England. **Online address:** u.i.schmidt@kent.ac.uk

SCHMIDT, Vivien A. (Vivien Ann Schmidt). American (born United States), b. 1949. **Genres:** Politics/Government, History. **Career:** University of Massachusetts, instructor, 1979-81, assistant professor, 1981-87, associate professor, 1987-93, professor of management, 1993-96, professor of political science, 1996-98; University of Massachusetts, European Studies program, director, 1993-98, Center for Democracy and Development, McCormack Institute, director, 1994-98; University of Lille, visiting professor, 1995-96; Boston University, professor of international relations and director of Center for International Relations, 1998-, Jean Monnet Professor of European Integration, 2001-; Max Planck Institute for the Study of Societies, visiting professor, 1998-99; European Union Institute, Florence, visiting professor, 1999-2000; Institute d'Etudes Politiques, visiting professor, 2000-05; Nuffield College, Oxford University, Fulbright fellow, 2001-02; Institute for Advanced Studies, visiting professor, 2003; Free University of Brussels and Louvain, Franqui Interuniversity Chair for Foreign Scholars, 2007; Center for the Study of Politics (CEVIPOF), Sciences Po, visiting researcher; Harvard University, Center for European Studies, faculty affiliate. Writer, political scientist and consultant. **Publications:** Democratizing France: The Political and Administrative History of Decentralization, 1990; From State to Market? The Transformation of French Business and Government, 1996; (ed. with F.W. Scharpf) Welfare and Work in the Open Economy, 2000; The Futures of European Capitalism, 2002; Public Discourse and Welfare State Reform: The Social Democratic Experience, 2005; Democracy in Europe: The EU and National Polities, 2006. Contributor to books, periodicals and journals. **Address:** Department of International Relations, Boston University, 152 Bay State Rd., Boston, MA 02215, U.S.A. **Online address:** vschmidt@bu.edu

SCHMIDT, Vivien Ann. *See* **SCHMIDT, Vivien A.**

SCHMIDT, Winsor C. American (born United States), b. 1949. **Genres:** Adult Non-fiction, Law, Gerontology/Senior Issues, Civil Liberties/Human Rights, Social Sciences, Psychology, Public/Social Administration, Medicine/Health, Politics/Government, Social Work. **Career:** Florida State University, associate professor of public administration, 1976-86; University of Virginia, School of Law, mental health law fellow, 1983-84; University of Memphis, professor of political science, 1986-98, Center of Health Services Research, director; Pace University School of Law, associate professor, 1989-90; Washington State University, Department of Health Policy and Administration, chair and professor, 1998-2009; University of Louisville, School of Medicine, endowed chair, professor of psychiatry and behavioral sciences and professor of family and geniatric medicine, 2009-, School of Public Health and Information Sciences, professor of health management and health sciences, 2009-. Writer and attorney. **Publications:** Legal Issues in Compensating Victims of Violent Crime, 1976. NONFICTION: (with K. Miller, W. Bell and E. New) Public Guardianship and the Elderly, 1981; (ed.) Guardianship: Court of Last Resort for the Elderly and Disabled, 1995; (co-author) Public Guardianship: In the Best Interests of Incapacitated People?, 2010. Contributor to journals. **Address:** Department of Family and Geriatric Medicine, School of Medicine, University of Louisville, Med Ctr. 1, 501 E Broadway, Ste. 240, Louisville, KY 40202, U.S.A. **Online address:** wcschm01@louisville.edu

SCHMIECHEN, Peter. American (born United States), b. 1938. **Genres:** Theology/Religion, Humanities. **Career:** United Church of Christ, ordained minister, 1962; United Church of Christ, pastor, 1962-65; United Church of Christ, staff member, Biennial Emphasis Committee on Urbanization and the Church, 1965-66; Elmhurst College, instructor, professor of theology and religion, 1966-85, dean of the college, 1975-85; United Church of Christ, Council for Higher Education, member, 1975-; Lancaster Theological Seminary, professor of theology and president of seminary, 1985-; United Church of Christ, chairperson, 1989-93. Writer. **Publications:** The Gift and the Promise: Becoming What We Are in Christ, 1989; Christ the Reconciler: A Theology for Opposites, Differences and Enemies, 1996; Saving Power: Theories of Atonement and Forms of the Church, 2005. Contributor to journals and magazines. **Address:** Lancaster Theological Seminary, 555 W James St., Lancaster, PA 17603, U.S.A.

SCHMIEDING, Holger. British/German (born Germany), b. 1958. **Genres:** Economics, Business/Trade/Industry. **Career:** Westfaelische Nachrichten, journalist, 1976-78; Kiel Institute of World Economics, economist, assistant to the president and head of the research group, 1986-92; International Monetary Fund, desk economist, economist, senior economist, 1993; Bank of America-Merrill Lynch, senior economist, 1993-97, chief economist; Merrill Lynch, senior strategist and chief economist, 1998-2001; Bank of America, chief economist, managing director and head of European economics, 2002- ; Berenberg Bank, chief economist. **Publications:** Lending Stability to Europe's Emerging Market Economies: On the Potential Importance of the EC and the ECU for Central and Eastern Europe, 1992; (with H. Giersch and K. Paqué) The Fading Miracle: Four Decades of Market Economy in Germany, 1992, rev. ed., 1994; Europe after Maastricht, 1993. **Address:** Berenberg Bank, 60 Threadneedle St., London, EC2R 8HP, England. **Online address:** holger_schmieding@ml.com

SCHMIT, Patricia Brady. *See* **BRADY, Patricia.**

SCHMITZ, Cecilia M. American (born United States), b. 1960. **Genres:** Medicine/Health, Bibliography, Social Sciences, Reference, Self Help. **Career:** Texas A&M University, microforms cataloger, 1987-88; Auburn University, social science cataloger, 1988-, librarian. Writer. **Publications:** (With R.A. Gray) The Gift of Life-Organ and Tissue Transplantation: An Introduction to Issues and Information Sources, 1993; (with R.A. Gray) Smoking-The Health Consequences of Tobacco Use: An Annotated Bibliography with an Analytical Introduction, 1995; (with R.A. Gray) Alcoholism: The Health and Social Consequences of Alcohol Use, 1998. Contributor to books and periodicals. **Address:** Cataloging Department, Auburn University, 231 Mell St., Auburn, AL 36849, U.S.A. **Online address:** schmice@auburn.edu

SCHMITZ, Dennis. American (born United States), b. 1937. **Genres:** Poetry, Literary Criticism And History. **Career:** Illinois Institute of Technology, instructor in English, 1961-62; University of Wisconsin, instructor in English, 1962-66; California State University, assistant professor, 1966-70, poet-in-residence, 1966-, associate professor of English, 1970-74, professor of English, 1974-2003, professor emeritus, 2003-. Writer. **Publications:** We Weep for Our Strangeness, 1969; Double Exposures, 1971; Goodwill, Inc., 1976; String, 1980; Singing, 1985; Eden: Poems, 1989; About Night: Selected and New Poems, 1993; (ed. with V. Weinberg) Sacramento Anthology: One Hundred Poems, 2001; Truth Squad, 2002. Contributor to periodicals. **Address:** Department of English, California State University, 6000 J St., Sacramento, CA 95819-6076, U.S.A.

SCHMOOKLER, Andrew Bard. American (born United States), b. 1946. **Genres:** Social Sciences, History, Anthropology/Ethnology, Sociology, Military/Defense/Arms Control. **Career:** Prescott College, assistant professor of contemporary events, 1973-75; Center for Strategic and International Studies, research associate, 1980-82; Public Agenda Foundation, senior research associate for nuclear defense issues, 1983-84; Search for a Common Ground, senior policy adviser, 1985-94; Albuquerque Academy, teacher of American studies and writing, 2002-04; University of Montana, presidential lecturer; Woodrow Wilson International Center for Scholars, presidential lecturer. Author and host. **Publications:** The Parable of the Tribes: The Problem of Power in Social Evolution, 1984, 2nd ed., 1995; Out of Weakness: Healing the Wounds That Drive Us to War, 1988; Sowings and Reapings: The Cycling of Good and Evil in the Human System, 1989; The Illusion of Choice: How the Market System Shapes Our Destiny, 1993; Fool's Gold: The Fate of Values in a World of Goods, 1993; Living Posthumously: Confronting the Loss of Vital Powers, 1997; Debating the Good Society: A Quest to Bridge America's Moral Divide, 1999. **Address:** 1855 Tramway Terr., Loop NE, Albuquerque, NM 87122, U.S.A. **Online address:** schmoore@shentel.net

SCHNAKENBERG, Robert. American (born United States), b. 1969. **Genres:** Children's Fiction. **Career:** Grand Herring Creative Services, owner. Writer. **Publications:** Scottie Pippen: Reluctant Superstar, 1997; Teammates: Karl Malone and John Stockton, 1998; The Encyclopedia Shatnerica, 1998; Martin Brodeur, 1999; Derek Jeter, Surefire Shortstop, 1999; Kobe Bryant, 1999; Cynthia Cooper, 2001; Mia Hamm, 2001; (ed.) Distory: A Treasury of Historical Insults, 2004; The Central Division: The Atlanta Hawks, the Chi-cago Bulls, the Cleveland Cavaliers, the Detroit Pistons, the Indiana Pacers, the Milwaukee Bucks, the New Orleans Hornets, and the Toronto Raptors, 2004; (with J. Gigliotti) The Southeast Division, 2006; The Central Division, 2006; (with J. Gigliotti) The Atlantic Division, 2006; (with J. Walters) The Southwest Division, 2006; Sci-Fi Baby Names: 500 Out-of-this-World Baby Names, from Anakin to Zardoz, 2007; Christopher Walken A to Z: The Man, the Movies, the Legend, 2008; Secret Lives of Great Authors: What Your Teachers Never Told You about Famous Novelists, Poets, and Playwrights, 2008; Secret Lives of the Supreme Court: What Your Teachers Never Told You about America's Legendary Justices, 2009; Old Man Drinks: Recipes, Advice, and Barstool Wisdom, 2010; DC Comics: The 75th Anniversary Poster Book, 2010; The Underground Baseball Encyclopedia: Baseball Stuff You Never Needed to Know and Can Certainly Live Without, 2010; Secret Lives of Great Filmmakers: What Your Teachers Never Told You about the World's Greatest Directors, 2010. Contributor to books and periodicals. **Address:** Brooklyn, NY , U.S.A. **Online address:** robertschnakenberg@gmail.com

SCHNEIDER, Barbara. American (born United States), b. 1946. **Genres:** Education, Sociology. **Career:** Teacher, 1967-73; National Louis University, Foster McGaw Graduate School, adjunct professor, 1975-76; Northwestern University, School of Education, associate dean for research and development, assistant professor, 1980-87; University of Chicago, Ogburn-Stouffer Center for the Study of Population and Social lOrganization, research associate, 1987-2005, professor of sociology, 1999-2005, National Opinion Research Center, research associate, 1987-2007, senior social scientist, 1991-2005, senior fellow, 2005-, Population Research Center, research associate, 1995-2007, Center on Advancing Research and Communication in STEM, principal investigator, 2008-, university faculty research associate, 2005-, research associate professor; Educational Evaluation and Policy Analysis, editor, 2000-03; American Sociological Association, chair, 2002-03; Michigan State University, College of Education, John A. Hannah distinguished university professor, and John A. Hannah chair, 2005-, Department of Sociology, John A. Hannah distinguished university professor, 2005-. **Publications:** (Ed. with J.S. Coleman) Parents, their Children, and Schools, 1993; (ed. with P.W. Cookson, Jr.) Transforming Schools, 1995; (co-author) Redesigning American Education, 1997; (ed. with K. Borman) Adolescent Years: Social Influences and Educational Challenges, The 97th Yearbook of the National Society for the Study of Education, 1998; (with D. Stevenson) The Ambitious Generation: America's Teenagers, Motivated but Directionless, 1999; (with M. Csikszentmihalyi) Becoming Adult: How Teenagers Prepare for the World of Work, 2000; (with A.S. Bryk) Trust in Schools: A Core Resource for Improvement, 2002; (ed. with L.V. Hedges) The Social Organization of Schooling, 2005; (ed. with L.J. Waite) Being Together, Working Apart: Dual-Career Families and the Work-life Balance, 2005; (ed. with S. McDonald) Scale-up in Education, 2007; Estimating Causal Effects using Experimental and Observational Designs, 2007; (ed. with G. Sykes, D.N. Plank and T.G. Ford) Handbook of Education Policy Research, 2009; (ed. with K. Christensen) Workplace Flexibility: Realigning 20th-century Jobs for a 21st-century Workforce, 2010. **Address:** Department of Sociology, Michigan State University, 516B Erickson Hall, East Lansing, MI 48824-1111, U.S.A. **Online address:** bschneid@msu.edu

SCHNEIDER, Ben Ross. American (born United States), b. 1920. **Genres:** Literary Criticism And History, Politics/Government, Business/Trade/Industry, Information Science/Computers. **Career:** University of Cincinnati, instructor in English, 1947-48; University of Colorado, instructor in English, 1950-54; Oregon State College (now Oregon State University), instructor in English, 1954-55; Lawrence University, professor of English, 1955-83, now professor emeritus of English. Writer. **Publications:** Wordsworth Portraits: A Biographical Catalogue, 1950; Wordsworth's Cambridge Education, 1957; (with H.K. Tjossem) Themes and Research Papers, 1962; The Ethos of Restoration Comedy, 1971; Travels in Computerland: Or, Incompatabilities and Interfaces: A Full and True Account of the Implementation of the London Stage Information Bank, 1974; (contrib.) The London Stage, 1660-1800, 1978; (comp. and intro.) Index to The London Stage, 1660-1800, 1979; My Personal Computer and Other Family Crises, 1984; Politics Within the State: Elite Bureaucrats and Industrial Policy in Authoritarian Brazil, 1991; (ed. with S. Maxfield) Business and the State in Developing Countries, 1997; (trans.) The Stoic Legacy to the Renaissance, forthcoming. Contributor to journals. **Address:** Lawrence University, 115 S Drew St., PO Box 599, Appleton, WI 54911, U.S.A. **Online address:** ben.r.schneider@lawrence.edu

SCHNEIDER, Deborah Lucas. American (born United States), b. 1943.

Genres: Translations, History, Social Sciences. **Career:** Harvard (alumni publication), contributing editor, 1996-. Writer. **Publications:** TRANSLATOR: A. Borbely, Secrets of Sleep, 1986; L. Ciompi, The Psyche and Schizophrenia, 1988; I. Mueller, Hitler's Justice: The Courts of the Third Reich, 1991; A. Mitgutsch, Jacob (novel), 1991; K. Wolff, Kurt Wolff: A Portrait in Essays and Letters, 1991; H. Stern, The Last Hunt (novella), 1993; U.K. Preuss, Constitutional Revolution: The Link between Constitutionalism and Progress, 1995; S. Oettermann, The Panorama: History of a Mass Medium, 1997; C. Habicht, Athens from Alexander to Antony, 1997; P. Zanker, Pompeii: Public and Private Life, 1998; H. Schulze, Germany: A New History, 1998; The Age of Augustus, 2003; (with J. Bernard) Priestblock 25487: A Memoir of Dachau, 2008. OTHER: (with F. Fleischmann) Women's Studies and Literature: neun Beiträge aus der Erlanger Amerikanistik, 1987. **Address:** Harvard Magazine, 7 Ware St., Cambridge, MA 02138, U.S.A.

SCHNEIDER, Elisa. *See* **KLEVEN, Elisa.**

SCHNEIDER, Fred B. American (born United States), b. 1953. **Genres:** Mathematics/Statistics, Information Science/Computers, Education. **Career:** Cornell University, Department of Computer Science, assistant professor, 1978-84, associate professor, 1984-93, professor of computer science, 1993-, AFRL/Cornell Information Assurance Institute, director, 2000-08, Samuel B. Eckert professor of computer science, 2009-; University of Tromso, professor-at-large, 1996-; Microsoft, co-chair, 2003-; Griffiss Institute, chief scientist, 2003-04, board director, science advisor; NST TRUST Science and Technology Center, chief scientist, 2005-. Writer. **Publications:** (With D. Gries) A Logical Approach to Discrete Math, 1993; On Concurrent Programming, 1997; (ed.) Trust in Cyberspace, 1999; (co-author) Using External Security Monitors to Secure BGP, forthcoming. Contributor to books and journals. **Address:** Department of Computer Science, Cornell University, 4115C Upson Hall, Ithaca, NY 14853, U.S.A. **Online address:** fbs@cs.cornell.edu

SCHNEIDER, Gregory L. American (born United States), b. 1965. **Genres:** History. **Career:** Emporia State University, professor of history, 1998-; Flint Hills Center for Public Policy, consultant. Writer and historian. **Publications:** Cadres for Conservatism: Young Americans for Freedom and the Rise of the Contemporary Right, 1999; (ed.) Conservatism in America since 1930: A Reader, 2003; (ed. and intro.) Equality, Decadence, and Modernity: The Collected Essays of Stephen J. Tonsor, 2005; The Conservative Century: From Reaction to Revolution, 2009. **Address:** Department of Social Sciences, Emporia State University, 1200 Commercial St., Emporia, KS 66801, U.S.A. **Online address:** gschneid@emporia.edu

SCHNEIDER, Helga. Italian/German (born Germany), b. 1937. **Genres:** Novels, Autobiography/Memoirs, Biography. **Career:** Writer and educator. **Publications:** La Bambola Decapitata: Una Sindrome Incestuosa, 1993; Porta di Brandeburgo, 1997; Stelle di Cannella, 2002; L'albero di Goethe, 2004; Let Me Go, 2004; Io, Piccola Ospite del Führer, 2006; The Bonfire of Berlin, 2006. **Address:** Walker Co., 104 5th Ave., New York, NY 10011, U.S.A.

SCHNEIDER, Karen. American (born United States), b. 1948. **Genres:** Literary Criticism And History, Film. **Career:** Colorado State University, graduate teaching assistant, 1980-82; Indiana University, associate instructor, 1984-89, Groups Program, assistant coordinator, 1989-90, adjunct professor of English, 1991-92; Western Kentucky University, assistant professor of English, 1992-97, associate professor of English 1997-2003, full professor 2003-. Writer. **Publications:** Loving Arms: British Women Writing the Second World War, 1996. Contributor to books and academic journals. **Address:** Department of English, Western Kentucky University, Rm. 100B, Cherry Hall, 1626 Ogden Way, 1906 College Heights Blvd., Ste. 11086, Bowling Green, KY 42101-1086, U.S.A. **Online address:** karen.schneider@wku.edu

SCHNEIDER, Mindy. American (born United States), b. 1961?. **Genres:** Young Adult Fiction, Autobiography/Memoirs. **Career:** Los Angeles Department of Recreation and Parks, staff. Writer. **Publications:** Not a Happy Camper: A Memoir, 2007. Work appears in anthologies. **Address:** c/o Dan Lazar, Writers House, 21 W 26th St., New York, NY 10010, U.S.A.

SCHNEIDER, Richard J. American (born United States), b. 1945. **Genres:** Humanities, Biography, How-to Books, Essays. **Career:** High school English teacher, 1969-70; Ventura College, instructor in English, 1972; Atlantic Christian College (now Barton College), professor of English, 1973-86, department chair, 1979-84, Center for Professional Development, director,

1985-86; Wartburg College, professor of English, 1986-, department chair, 1986-94, Slife professor of humanities, 1994-, chair of faculty council, 1999-2001; University of Northern Iowa, lecturer, 1987; University of Edinburgh, lecturer, 2001. Writer. **Publications:** Henry David Thoreau, 1987; (ed.) Approaches to Teaching Thoreau's Walden and Other Works, 1996; A Teacher's Guide to Walden, 1997; (ed.) Thoreau's Sense of Place: Essays in American Environmental Writing, 2000; (ed.) Henry David Thoreau: A Documentary Volume, 2004. Contributor to books and periodicals. **Address:** Department of English & Modern Languages, Wartburg College, 321 Luther Hall, 100 Wartburg Blvd., Waverly, IA 50677, U.S.A. **Online address:** richard.schneider@wartburg.edu

SCHNEIDER, Robert. American (born United States), b. 1933. **Genres:** Children's Fiction, Young Adult Fiction, History, Literary Criticism And History. **Career:** University of Minnesota, instructor, 1958-59; College of Wooster, instructor, 1959-61; Northern Illinois University, assistant professor, 1961-65, associate professor, 1965-73, professor of history, 1973-98, now professor emeritus. Writer. **Publications:** Five Novelists of the Progressive Era, 1965; Novelist to a Generation: The Life and Thought of Winston Churchill, 1976. Contributor to journals. **Address:** Department of History, Northern Illinois University, Zulauf Hall 715, DeKalb, IL 60115-2854, U.S.A. **Online address:** schneider@niu.edu

SCHNEIDER, Robyn. American (born United States), b. 1986. **Genres:** Young Adult Fiction, Novels, Education. **Career:** Writer and producer. **Publications:** NOVELS: Better Than Yesterday, 2007; The Social Climber's Guide to High School, 2007. **Address:** c/o Bernadette Cruz, Simon & Schuster Inc., 1230 Ave. of the Americas, 11th Fl., New York, NY 10020-1513, U.S.A. **Online address:** robynschneider@yahoo.com

SCHNEIDER, Stuart L. American (born United States), b. 1950. **Genres:** Photography, Paranormal, Earth Sciences, Antiques/Furnishings. **Career:** Writer and attorney. **Publications:** (With R.B. Etter) Collecting and Valuing Early Fountain Pens, 1980; (with R.B. Etter) Halley's Comet: Memories of 1910, 1985; (with G. Fischler) Fountain Pens and Pencils: The Golden Age of Writing Instruments, 1990, 3rd ed., 2008; (with G. Fischler) The Book of Fountain Pens and Pencils, 1992; Collecting the Space Race, 1993; (with G. Fischler) The Illustrated Guide to Antique Writing Instruments, 1994, 3rd ed., 2000; Halloween in America, 1995, 2nd ed., 2011; Collecting Flashlights: With Value Guide, 1996; (with G. Fischler) Cigarette Lighters, 1996; Collecting Lincoln, 1997; (with H. Gostony) The Incredible Ball Point Pen: A Comprehensive History and Price Guide, 1998; Collecting Picture and Photo Frames, 1998; (with I. Pilossof) The Handbook of Vintage Cigarette Lighters, 1999; Ronson's Art Metal Works, 2000; (with B. Zalkin) Halloween Costumes and Other Treats, 2001; (with I. Pilossof) The Golden Age of Cigarette Lighters, 2004; Collecting Fluorescent Minerals, 2004, 2nd ed., 2011; The World of Fluorescent Minerals, 2006; Ghosts in the Cemetery: A Pictorial Study, 2008; Ghosts in the Cemetery II: Farther Afield, 2010. **Address:** 820 Kinderkamack Rd., River Edge, NJ 07661-2324, U.S.A. **Online address:** stuart@wordcraft.net

SCHNEIDER, Thomas E. American (born United States), b. 1963?. **Genres:** Politics/Government, History. **Career:** Bowdoin College, visiting assistant professor, 2007; Boston University, faculty of political science. Political scientist and writer. **Publications:** Lincoln's Defense of Politics: The Public Man and His Opponents in the Crisis over Slavery, 2006. Contributor to journals. **Address:** Bowdoin College, Brunswick, ME 04011, U.S.A. **Online address:** tschneid@bowdoin.edu

SCHNEIDERMAN, David. Canadian (born Canada), b. 1958. **Genres:** Law, Politics/Government, History, Business/Trade/Industry. **Career:** Davis and Co. (barristers and solicitors), associate, 1984-86; Canadian Civil Liberties Association, research director, 1987-89; University of Alberta, Centre for Constitutional Studies, executive director, 1989-99; University of Toronto, associate professor of law, 1999-, professor of law and political science; Constitutional Forum Constitutionnel, founding editor; Review of Constitutional Studies, founding editor-in-chief; Georgetown University Law Center, visiting associate professor of law. Writer. **Publications:** EDITOR: Conversations Among Friends: Proceedings of an Interdisciplinary Conference on Women and Constitutional Reform: Conversations entre amies, 1991; Freedom of Expression and the Charter, 1991; (co-ed.) Social Justice and the Constitution: Perspectives on a Social Union for Canada, 1992; (with R.C. Macleod) Police Powers in Canada: The Evolution and Practice of Authority, 1993; (with K. Sutherland) Charting the Consequences: The Impact of Charter Rights on

Canadian Law and Politics, 1997; The Quebec Decision: Perspectives on the Supreme Court Ruling on Secession, 1999. OTHERS: (with F. Sauvageau and D. Taras) The Last Word: Media Coverage of the Supreme Court of Canada, 2006; Constitutionalizing Economic Globalization: Investment Rules and Democracy's Promise, 2008. **Address:** Faculty of Law, University of Toronto, 78 Queen's Pk., Toronto, ON M5S 2C5, Canada. **Online address:** david.schneiderman@utoronto.ca

SCHNIEDEWIND, William M. American (born United States), b. 1962. **Genres:** Theology/Religion. **Career:** Hebrew University, Bible Project, research associate, 1985-86; Jerusalem University College, instructor, 1992-94; Albright Institute of Archaeological Research, fellow, 1992-94, secretary; University of California, Department of Biblical Studies and Northwest Semitic Languages, assistant professor, 1994-99, associate professor, 1999-2003, professor, 2003-, Department of Near-Eastern Languages and Cultures, chair, Kershaw Chair of Ancient Eastern Mediterranean Studies, Qumran Visualization Project, director, Jaffa Cultural Heritage Project, associate director. Writer. **Publications:** The Word of God in Transition: From Prophet to Exegete in the Second Temple Period, 1995; Society and the Promise to David: The Reception History of 2 Samuel 7: 1-17, 1999; How the Bible Became a Book: The Textualization of Ancient Israel, 2004; (with J.H. Hunt) A Primer on Ugaritic: Language, Culture, and Literature, 2007. Contributor to books. **Address:** Department of Near Eastern Languages & Culture, University of California, 380 Humanities, Los Angeles, CA 90095-1511, U.S.A. **Online address:** williams@humnet.ucla.edu

SCHNITTER, Jane T. American (born United States), b. 1958. **Genres:** Novellas/Short Stories, Children's Fiction, Sciences. **Career:** Mark Twain Elementary PTA, president, 1994-96. Writer. **Publications:** William Is My Brother, 1991; Let Me Explain: A Story about Donor Insemination, 1995. **Address:** 614 Valley Forge Ct., Westerville, OH 43081, U.S.A.

SCHNITTER, Nicholas J. Swiss/Italian (born Italy), b. 1927. **Genres:** Engineering, Technology, Mathematics/Statistics. **Career:** Motor-Columbus (consulting engineers), dam engineer, 1952-68, chief engineer, 1969-72, vice president, 1973-87, retired, 1988. Writer. **Publications:** Bibliographie Suisse Des Barrages Réservoirs: Swiss Bibliography on Storage Dams, 1980; (with D. Vischer) Drei Schweizer Wasserbauer: Conradin Zschokke (1842-1918), Eugen Meyer-Peter (1883-1969), Gerold Schnitter, 1900-1987, 1991; Geschichte Des Wasserbaus in Der Schweiz (title means: 'A History of Hydraulic Engineering in Switzerland'), 1992; A History of Dams: The Useful Pyramids, 1994. Contributor of articles to journals. **Address:** Fleinerweg 4, Zurich, CH-8044, Switzerland.

SCHNUR, Steven. American (born United States), b. 1952. **Genres:** Novels, Children's Fiction, Ghost Writer, Theology/Religion, Autobiography/Memoirs, Humor/Satire, Novellas/Short Stories. **Career:** City University of New York, Bernard M. Baruch College, instructor, 1977; Union of American Hebrew Congregations, editor, 1981-92; Sarah Lawrence College, Writing Institute, faculty, 1990-; Mercy College, adjunct professor, 1991-92; Reform Judaism Magazine, literary editor, 1994-99. **Publications:** The Narrowest Bar Mitzvah, 1986; The Return of Morris Schumsky, 1987; Daddy's Home!: Reflections of a Family Man, 1990, rev. ed. as Father's Day, 1991; Hannah and Cyclops, 1990; This Thing Called Love: Thoughts of an Out-of-Step Romantic, 1992; The Shadow Children, 1994; The Tie Man's Miracle: A Chanukah Tale, 1995; Beyond Providence, 1996; The Koufax Dilemma, 1997; Autumn: An Alphabet Acrostic, 1997; Spring: An Alphabet Acrostic, 1999; Night Lights, 2000; Spring Thaw, 2000; Summer: An Alphabet Acrostic, 2001; Winter: An Alphabet Acrostic, 2002; 9/11, 2002; (ed.) Henry David's House, 2002; Mrs. Popham's Library, 2003; Sanctuary, 2003. Contributor to periodicals. **Address:** 19 Montrose Rd., Scarsdale, NY 10583, U.S.A.

SCHNURNBERGER, Lynn. (Lynn Edelman Schnurnberger). American (born United States), b. 1950?. **Genres:** Novels, Young Adult Non-fiction, Art/Art History, Sports/Fitness, Human Relations/Parenting. **Career:** New York Metropolitan Museum of Art, special consultant; Foster Pride, founder and executive director. Journalist. **Publications:** (As Lynn Edelman Schnurnberger) Kings, Queens, Knights, and Jesters: Making Medieval Costumes, 1978; (as Lynn Edelman Schnurnberger) Star Trek, the Motion Picture, Make-Your-Own Costume Book, 1979; (as Lynn Edelman Schnurnberger) A World of Dolls That You Can Make, 1982; Kids Love New York!, 1984; Let There Be Clothes: 40, 000 Years of Fashion, 1991; (with J. Kaplan) The Botox Diaries, 2004; (with J. Kaplan) Mine Are Spectacular!, 2005; (with

J. Kaplan) The Men I Didn't Marry: A Novel, 2006; The Best Laid Plans: A Novel, 2011. Contributor to periodicals. **Address:** c/o Author Mail, Random House Inc., 1745 Broadway, New York, NY 10019, U.S.A. **Online address:** lynn@lynnschnurnberger.com

SCHNURNBERGER, Lynn Edelman. *See* **SCHNURNBERGER, Lynn.**

SCHOEMER, Karen. American (born United States), b. 1965?. **Genres:** Music, Art/Art History, History. **Career:** Newsweek, pop music critic; Spin magazine, senior editor. Music critic and writer. **Publications:** Great Pretenders: My Strange Love Affair with '50s Pop Music, 2006. Contributor to anthologies and periodicals. **Address:** c/o Author Mail, Simon & Schuster, 1230 Ave. of the Americas, New York, NY 10020, U.S.A.

SCHOEMPERLEN, Diane. Canadian (born Canada), b. 1954. **Genres:** Novels, Novellas/Short Stories, Romance/Historical. **Career:** St. Lawrence College, instructor in creative writing, 1987-91; Kingston School of Writing, instructor, 1987-93; University of Toronto, Writers Workshop, instructor, 1992. Writer. **Publications:** Double Exposures, 1984; Frogs & Other Stories, 1986; Hockey Night in Canada, 1987; Man of My Dreams: Stories, 1990; In the Language of Love: A Novel in 100 Chapters, 1994; Vital Signs: New Women Writers in Canada, 1997; Forms of Devotion, 1998; Our Lady of the Lost and Found: A Novel, 2001; Red Plaid Shirt: Stories, New & Selected, 2002; Names of the Dead: An Elegy for the Victims of September 11, 2004; At a Loss for Words, 2008; Love in the Time of Cliches. Contributor to periodicals. Works appear in anthologies. **Address:** c/o Bella Pomer, Bella Pomer Agency Inc., 22 Shallmar Blvd., PH 2, Toronto, ON M5N 2Z8, Canada.

SCHOEN, Lawrence M. American (born United States), b. 1959?. **Genres:** Novels. **Career:** Klingon Language Institute (nonprofit), founder and director, 1992-; Paper Golem, publisher. Educator and writer. **Publications:** NOVELS: (as Klingon Language Institute) The Klingon Hamlet, 2000; Buffalito Destiny, 2009. ANTHOLOGIES: (ed. with M. Livingstone) Prime Codex: The Hungry Edge of Speculative Fiction, 2007; (ed. with A. Dorrance) Alembical, 2008; (ed. with A. Dorrance) Alembical 2, 2010. OTHERS: Buffalogic, Inc.: Tales of the Amazing Conroy No. 1 (collection), 2003; Buffalogenesis: Tales of the Amazing Conroy, #2 (collection), 2006; Buffalogistics: Tales of the Amazing Conroy #3 (collection), 2008. **Address:** Philadelphia, PA , U.S.A. **Online address:** lmschoen@noblefusion.com

SCHOEN, Robert. American (born United States), b. 1946. **Genres:** Theology/Religion. **Career:** Author, musician and optometrist. **Publications:** (With S.H. Preston and N. Keyfitz) Causes of Death, 1972; (with M. Collins) Mortality by Cause: Life Tables for California, 1950-1970, 1973; (with W.L. Urton) Marital Status Life Tables for Sweden, 1979; (ed. with D. Landman) Population, Theory and Policy, 1982; Modeling Multigroup Populations, 1988; What I Wish My Christian Friends Knew About Judaism, 2004; Dynamic Population Models, 2006. **Address:** AEI Speakers Bureau, 214 Lincoln St., Ste. 113, Boston, MA 02134, U.S.A. **Online address:** robert@robertschoen.com

SCHOENBERG, Robert J. American (born United States), b. 1933. **Genres:** Adult Non-fiction, Ghost Writer. **Career:** Esquire Inc., subscription direct mail staff, 1958-59; Hearst Magazine Corp., subscription direct mail staff, 1959-60; Batten, Barton, Durstine and Osborn, staff, 1960-71; Bowes Co., staff, 1971-74; freelance writer, 1971-. **Publications:** The Art of Being a Boss, 1978; Geneen, 1985; Mr. Capone, 1992. **Address:** c/o Don Congdon Associates, 156 5th Ave., Ste. 625, New York, NY 10010-7002, U.S.A. **Online address:** rjschoen9@dslextreme.com

SCHOENBROD, David. American (born United States), b. 1942. **Genres:** Law. **Career:** U.S. Senator for Vice President Hubert H. Humphrey, intern and staff, 1962, 1963, 1965; U.S. Court of Appeals, lawyer, 1968-69; Bedford-Stuyvesant Restoration/D&S Corp., director of program development, 1969-71; Association of the Bar of the City of New York, Special Committee On Electric Power And The Environment, staff attorney, 1971-72; Natural Resources Defense Council Inc., senior staff attorney, 1972-79; New York University School of Law, associate professor, 1979-83; New York Law School, associate professor, 1984-85, professor, 1985-2006, trustee professor of law, 2006-; Cato Institute, senior fellow, 2006-07; Breaking the Logjam Project, co-leader, 2006-. Writer. **Publications:** (Co-author) Electricity and the Environment, 1972; (co-author) A New Direction in Transit, 1978; (co-author) Remedies: Public and Private, 1990, 5th ed., forthcoming; Power without Responsibility: How Congress Abuses the People through Delegation, 1993;

(with R. Sandler) Democracy by Decree: What Happens When Courts Run Government, 2003; Saving Our Environment from Washington: How Congress Grabs Power, Shirks Responsibility and Shortchanges the People, 2005. (with R.B. Stewart and K.M. Wyman) Breaking the Logjam: Environmental Protection that will Work, 2010. Contributor of articles to journals. **Address:** New York Law School, SW913, 185 West Broadway, New York, NY 10013, U.S.A. **Online address:** dschoenbrod@nyls.edu

SCHOENEWOLF, Gerald. American (born United States), b. 1941. **Genres:** Psychology, Plays/Screenplays. **Career:** Living Center Films, founder and director, 1979-, producer, writer, director, composer, 2004-; Community Guidance Service, staff therapist, 1984-87; New School, adjunct associate professor, 1994-96; New York Institute of Technology, adjunct associate professor, 1997-; Hunter College, adjunct assistant professor, 1999-2001; Borough of Manhattan Community College, adjunct assistant professor, 2001-; Brooklyn College, adjunct assistant professor, 2006. **Publications:** (With R.C. Robertiello) 101 Common Therapeutic Blunders: Countertransference and Counterresistance in Psychotherapy, 1987; 101 Therapeutic Successes: Overcoming Transference and Resistance in Psychotherapy, 1989; Sexual Animosity Between Men and Women, 1989; Turning Points in Analytic Therapy: The Classic Cases, 1990; Turning Points in Analytic Therapy: From Winnicott to Kernberg, 1990; The Art of Hating, 1991; Jennifer and Her Selves, 1991; Counter Resistance: The Therapist's Interference with the Therapeutic Process, 1993; Erotic Games: Bringing Intimacy and Passion Back into Sex and Relationships, 1995; The Couple Who Fell in Hate And Other Tales of Eclectic Psychotherapy, 1996; The Dictionary of Dream Interpretation, 1997; The Couples Guide to Erotic Games: Bringing Intimacy and Passion Back into Sex and Relationships, 1998; The Way According to Lao Tzu, Chuang Tzu, and Seng Tsan, 2000; Psychotherapy with People in the Arts: Nurturing Creativity, 2002; 111 Common Therapeutic Blunders, 2005; The Couples' Guide to Erotic Games: Get Intimate, Be Passionate, Have Fun, 2006; A Way You'll Never Be, 2009; Flugelhorn's Flight: Or, Kidnapped by Babes from Outer Space, 2009; Holding On and Letting Go: Poems and Drawings, 2010; A Man's Life, 2010, An Ordinary Lunacy, 2010. Contributor of articles to periodicals. **Address:** Living Center Films, 207 E 15th St., 1H, New York, NY 10003-3733, U.S.A. **Online address:** gfswolf@hotmail.com

SCHOENFELD, Bruce. American (born United States) **Genres:** Sports/Fitness, History, Travel/Exploration, Reference. **Career:** Tennis Magazine, contributing editor; Street & Smith's Sports Business Journal, contributor. Sportswriter. **Publications:** The Last Serious Thing: A Season at the Bullfights, 1992; The Match: Althea Gibson and Angela Buxton: How Two Outsiders-One Black, the Other Jewish-Forged a Friendship and Made Sports History, 2004. **Address:** c/o Author Mail, Simon & Schuster Inc., 1230 Ave. of the Americas, New York, NY 10020-1513, U.S.A.

SCHOENFELDT, Beth. American (born United States) **Genres:** Business/Trade/Industry, Economics. **Career:** FLOinc, creator; Ladies Who Launch, co-founder, Ladies Who Launch Incubator Program, creator. Writer. **Publications:** WITH V. COLLIGAN AND A. SWIFT: Ladies Who Launch: Embracing Entrepreneurship & Creativity as a Lifestyle, 2007; Ladies Who Launch: An Innovative Program that Will Help You Get Your Dreams off the Ground, 2008. **Address:** Ladies Who Launch, 265 W 37th St., 7th Fl., New York, NY 10018, U.S.A. **Online address:** beth@ladieswholaunch.com

SCHOENHALS, Michael. Swedish (born Sweden) **Genres:** History. **Career:** Lund University, Centre for Languages and Literature, senior lecturer, professor of modern Chinese society, Institute for Security and Development Policy, senior research fellow, senior lecturer; University of British Columbia, Institute of Asian Research, visiting professor, 2004-05. Writer. **Publications:** Saltationist Socialism: Mao Zedong and the Great Leap Forward 1958, 1987; Doing Things with Words in Chinese Politics: Five Studies, 1992; (ed.) China's Cultural Revolution, 1966-1969: Not a Dinner Party, 1996; (with R. MacFarquhar) Mao's Last Revolution, 2006; (with X. Guo) Cadres and Discourse in the People's Republic of China, 2007. **Address:** Centre for Languages and Literature, Chinese, Lund University, PO Box 713, Lund, 220 07, Sweden. **Online address:** mschoenhals@silkroadstudies.org

SCHOESER, Mary. British/American (born United States), b. 1950. **Genres:** Art/Art History, Fash Ion/Costume, Crafts, Design, Reference. **Career:** Freelance researcher, exhibition organizer and lecturer, 1978-; Christie's South Kensington, staff, 1980-82; Warner Fabrics, archivist, 1982-90. Writer. **Publications:** Marianne Straub, 1984; Twentieth-Century Fabrics and Wallpaper,

1986; Printed Handkerchiefs, 1988; (with C. Rufey) English and American Textiles from 1790 to the Present, Thames and Hudson, 1989. French Textiles, 1760-1960, 1991. Why Jumpers are Woolly, Why T-Shirts Are Cotton, Why Leggings Are Lycra, Why Textiles Can Fly, 1994; International Textile Design, 1995; Factfile: Weaving, Spinning and Dyeing, 1997; More is More: An Antidote to Minimalism, 2001; World Textiles: A Concise History, 2003; (with C. Stevens) Chintz, 2004; Silk, 2007; Rozanne Hawksley, 2009; Sanderson: The Essence of English Decoration, 2010; V&A Pattern: Boxed Set iv, 2012; V&A pattern: Heal's, 2012, V&A Pattern: Sanderson, 2012. **Address:** Coggeshall, 25 East St., Essex, CO6 1SH, England. **Online address:** schoeser@aol.com

SCHOFFMAN, Nachum. Israeli/American (born United States), b. 1930. **Genres:** Literary Criticism And History, Music, Photography. **Career:** Piano soloist and accompanist, 1955-71; Seminar Hakibbutzim, school for music teachers, teacher, 1965-71; Rubin Academy of Music, teacher, 1973-76; Hebrew University, teacher, 1973-78; Ben-Gurion University of the Negev, Department of Foreign Literatures and Linguistics, senior lecturer, 1980-2000; Isreal Radio, lecturer and performer. Writer. **Publications:** From Chords to Simultaneities: Chordal Indeterminacy and the Failure of Serialism, 1990; There Is No Truer Truth: The Musical Aspect of Browning's Poetry, 1991. EDITOR: Israel Studies in Musicology, vol. VI, 1996. Contributor of articles to journals. **Address:** Kibbutz Kisufim, D. N. Negev, 85130, Israel. **Online address:** schof@netvision.net.il

SCHOFIELD, Brian. British (born England), b. 1975?. **Genres:** History. **Career:** Writer. **Publications:** Selling Your Father's Bones: The Epic Fate of the American West, 2008 in US as Selling Your Father's Bones: America's 140-year War against the Nez Perce Tribe, 2009. Contributor of articles to periodicals. **Address:** Brighton, ES , England. **Online address:** briantschofield@yahoo.co.uk

SCHOFIELD, Carey. British (born England), b. 1955. **Genres:** Military/Defense/Arms Control, History. **Career:** Heron House Publishing Co., researcher, 1976-78; Clare college, reader of English and theology. Journalist. **Publications:** Mesrine: The Life and Death of a Supercrook, 1980; Jagger, 1985; (ed.) Russia at War, 1941-45, 1987; Inside the Soviet Army, 1991; The Russian Elite: Inside Spetsnaz and the Airborne Forces, 1993; Ireland in Old Photographs, 1994. Contributor to periodicals. **Address:** The Reform Club, 104 Pall Mall, London, GL SW1Y 5EW, England. **Online address:** mail@careyschofield.co.uk

SCHOFIELD, John A. British (born England), b. 1948. **Genres:** Archaeology/Antiquities, History, Intellectual History, Architecture. **Career:** Museum of London, archaeologist, 1974-98, curator of architecture, 1998-2008; City of London Archaeological Trust, secretary, 1991-; archaeologist and architectural historian, 2008-. Writer. **Publications:** The Building of London from the Conquest to the Great Fire, 1984, 3rd ed., 2003; The London Surveys of Ralph Treswell, 1987; (with A. Vince) Medieval Towns, 1994, 2nd ed., 2003; Medieval London Houses, 1995, rev. ed., 2003; (with R. Lea) Holy Trinity Priory, 2005; St. Paul's Cathedral before Wren, 2011; London 1100-1600, 2011. Contributor of articles to periodicals. **Address:** GL , England. **Online address:** john@jschd.demon.co.uk

SCHOFIELD, Robert E(dwin). American (born United States), b. 1923. **Genres:** Intellectual History. **Career:** Fercleve Corporation and Clinton Labs, research associate, 1944-46; Knolls Atomic Power Laboratory, General Electric Co., research associate, 1948-51; University of Kansas, assistant professor, 1955-, associate professor, through 1959; Case Institute of Technology, associate professor, 1960-72; Case Western Reserve University, Lynn Thorndike professor, 1972-79; Iowa State University, Program in History of Technology and Science, director, professor of history, 1979-93, emeritus professor, 1993-. Writer. **Publications:** Lunar Society of Birmingham: A Social History of Provincial Science and Industry in Eighteenth-Century England, 1963; (ed.) Scientific Autobiography of Joseph Priestley, 1733-1804, 1966; Mechanism and Materialism: British Natural Philosophy in An Age of Reason, 1970; (ed. with W.C. Williams) Man & Nature: An Introduction to the Humanities in Science, 1971; (ed. with I.B. Cohen) Isaac Newton's Papers and Letters on Natural Philosophy and Related Documents, 2nd ed., 1978; (with D.G.C. Allan) Stephen Hales: Scientist and Philanthropist, 1980; (with E.N. Hiebert and A.J. Ihde) Joseph Priestley, Scientist, Theologian and Metaphysician, 1980; The Enlightenment of Joseph Priestley: A Study of his Life and Work from 1733 to 1773, 1997; Enlightened of Joseph Priestley: A

Study of His Life and Work from 1773 to 1804, 2004. Contributor of articles to periodicals. **Address:** Department of History, Iowa State University, Ames, IA 50011, U.S.A.

SCHOFIELD, Sandy. *See* **RUSCH, Kristine Kathryn.**

SCHOLEFIELD, Alan (A. T.). (Lee Jordan). British/South African (born South Africa), b. 1931. **Genres:** Novels, Plays/Screenplays, History. **Career:** Cape Argus, journalist, 1952-53; Sydney Morning Herald, London staff, 1954-55, 1959-60; Cape Times, journalist, 1957-59; Scotsman, defense correspondent, 1960-61; writer, 1961-. **Publications:** A View of Vultures, 1966; Great Elephant, 1967; The Eagles of Malice, 1968; Wild Dog Running, 1970; The Young Masters, 1971; The Hammer of God, 1973; Lion in the Evening, 1974; The Dark Kingdoms: The Impact of White Civilization on Three Great African Monarchies (history), 1975; The Alpha Raid, 1976; Venom, 1977; Point of Honour, 1979; Berlin Blind, 1980; The Human Zero, 1981; The Stone Flower, 1982; The Sea Cave, 1984; Fire in the Ice, 1984; King of the Golden Valley, 1985; The Last Safari, 1987; The Lost Giants, 1989; Dirty Weekend, 1991; (ed. with S. Dunn) Beneath the Wide Wide Heaven: Poetry of the Environment From Antiquity to the Present, 1991; Loyalties, 1991; (ed. with S. Dunn) Poetry for the Earth, 1992; Thief Taker, 1992; Never Die In January, 1993; Night Child, 1993; Threats & Menaces: A Macrae and Silver Novel, 1994; Don't be a Nice Girl, 1994; Buried Treasure, 1995; Burn Out, 1995; Night Moves, 1996; Bad Timing, 1997; The Drowning Mark, 1997. AS LEE JORDAN: Cat's Eyes, 1981; Criss Cross, 1984; The Deadly Side of the Square, 1988; The Toy Cupboard, 1989; Chain Reaction, 1989; Starlight Memories, 2002. **Address:** Greene & Heaton Ltd., 37 Goldhawk Rd., London, GL W12 8QQ, England.

SCHOLES, Ken. American (born United States), b. 1968. **Genres:** Young Adult Fiction. **Career:** Writer. **Publications:** Long Walks, Last Flights and Other Strange Journeys (short fiction), 2008. PSALMS OF ISAAK SAGA SERIES: Lamentation, 2009; Canticle, 2009. Contributor to magazines. Works appear in anthologies. **Address:** c/o Jennifer Jackson, Donald Maass Literary Agency, 121 W 27th St., Ste. 801, New York, NY 10001, U.S.A. **Online address:** ken@kenscholes.com

SCHOLEY, Arthur (Edward). British (born England), b. 1932. **Genres:** Children's Fiction, Plays/Screenplays, Songs/Lyrics And Libretti, Classics, Education, Humanities, Mythology/Folklore, Philosophy, Theology/Religion. **Career:** Writer. **Publications:** (With D. Swann) The Song of Caedmon, 1971; Christmas Plays and Ideas for Worship, 1973; The Discontented Dervishes, 1977; Wunschvogel: eine Geschichte, 1978; Sallinka and the Golden Bird, 1978; Twelve Tales for a Christmas Night, 1978; (with D. Swann) Wacky and His Fuddlejig, 1978; (with D. Swann) Singalive, 1978; (with R. Chamberlain) Herod and the Rooster, 1979; The Dickens Christmas Carol Show, 1979; (with D. Swann) Baboushka, 1979; (with D. Swann) Candletree, 1981; Five Plays for Christmas, 1981; Four Plays about People, 1983; Martin the Cobbler, 1983; The Hosanna Kids, 1985; Magda and the Christmas Rose, 1988; Make a Model Crib, 1988; Who'll Be Brother Donkey?, 1992; (with D. Swann) Brendan A-hoy!, 1994; (with K. Bradley) The Journey of the Christmas Creatures, 1999; The Paragon Parrot, 2002; The Scarab and the Frog, forthcoming. **Address:** Anchorage Press Plays, PO Box 2901, Louisville, KY 40201-2901, U.S.A. **Online address:** scholey@arthurscholey.co.uk

SCHOLZ-WILLIAMS, Gerhild. *See* **WILLIAMS, Gerhild Scholz.**

SCHONE, Robin. American (born United States), b. 1954?. **Genres:** History, Women's Studies And Issues, Romance/Historical, Novels, Literary Criticism And History. **Career:** Author. **Publications:** Awaken, My Love, 1995; The Lady's Tutor, 1999; (with T. Devine, S. Johnson and B. Small) Captivated, 1999; (with T. Devine, S. Johnson and B. Small) Fascinated, 2000; The Lover, 2000; Gabriel's Woman, 2001; Scandalous Lovers, 2007; (with C. Dain, A. James and S. Walker) Private Places, 2008; Cry for Passion, 2009. **Address:** PO Box 72725, Roselle, IL 60172, U.S.A. **Online address:** robin@robinschone.com

SCHOR, Esther H. American (born United States) **Genres:** Poetry, Humanities, Adult Non-fiction, Language/Linguistics. **Career:** Princeton University, professor of English, 1986-; Tufts University, faculty; Columbia University, Barnard College, faculty. Writer. **Publications:** (Ed. with P.C. Hoy II and R.D. Yanni) Women's Voices: Visions and Perspectives, 1990; (ed. with A.A. Fisch and A.K. Mellor) The Other Mary Shelley: Beyond Frankenstein, 1993;

Bearing the Dead: The British Culture of Mourning from the Enlightenment to Victoria, 1994; The Hills of Holland (poems), 2002; (ed.) The Cambridge Companion to Mary Shelley, 2003; Emma Lazarus, 2006; Strange Nursery: New and Selected Poems, 2012. Contributor to periodicals. **Address:** Department of English, Princeton University, 22 McCosh Hall, Princeton, NJ 08544, U.S.A. **Online address:** eschor@princeton.edu

SCHOR, Juliet B. American (born United States), b. 1955. **Genres:** Business/Trade/Industry, Economics, Money/Finance. **Career:** University of Massachusetts, teaching fellow, 1976-79; South End Press, founder and editor, 1977-79; Center for Popular Economics, founder and staff economist, 1978-90; Brookings Institution, research fellow, 1980-81; Williams College, assistant professor of economics, 1981-83; Columbia University, Barnard College, assistant professor of economics, 1983-84; Harvard University, assistant professor of economics, 1984-89, associate professor of economics, 1989-92, senior lecturer in economics and director of studies in women's studies, 1992-96, 1997-2001, Center for European Studies, research affiliate, 1986-91, Harvard Graduate School of Education, Harvard Graduate School of Education, faculty, 2001-; United Nations, World Institute for Development Economics Research (WIDER), Project on Global Macropolicy, research advisor, 1985-92; Zeta Magazine, economic columnist, 1987-91; University of Tilburg, professor in economics of leisure studies, 1995-2001; Commercial Alert, board director, 2004-09; Center for a New American Dream, founding member and secretary, 1995-2007, co-chair, 2007-10; Boston College, professor of sociology, 2001-, department chair, 2005-08. Writer. **Publications:** (With D. Cantor) Tunnel Vision: Labor, the World Economy, and Central America, 1987; (with G.A. Epstein) Macropolicy in the Rise and Fall of the Golden Age, 1988; The Overworked American: The Unexpected Decline of Leisure, 1991; The Overspent American: Upscaling, Downshifting, and the New Consumer, 1998; Sustainable Economy for the 21st Century, 1998; The Overspent American: Why We Want What We Don't Need, 1999; Born to Buy: The Commercialized Child and the New Consumer Culture, 2004; Plenitude: The New Economics of True Wealth, 2010. EDITOR: (with S.A. Marglin) The Golden Age of Capitalism: Reinterpreting the Postwar Experience, 1990; (with T. Banuri) Financial Openness and National Policy Autonomy: Opportunities and Constraints, 1992; (with J. You) Capital, the State, and Labour: A Global Perspective, 1995; (with D.B. Holt) Consumer Society Reader, 2000; (with B. Taylor) Sustainable Planet: Solutions for the Twenty-First Century, 2002. Contributor of articles to books and journals. **Address:** Department of Sociology, Boston College, 519 McGuinn Hall, 140 Commonwealth Ave., Chestnut Hill, MA 02467, U.S.A. **Online address:** juliet.schor@bc.edu

SCHOR, Mira. American (born United States), b. 1950. **Genres:** Art/Art History, Politics/Government. **Career:** Parsons The New School for Design, associate teaching professor; Nova Scotia College of Art and Design, faculty, 1974-78, State University of New York, faculty, 1983-85; Sarah Lawrence College, faculty, 1991-94, Rhode Island School of Design, faculty, 1999- 2000, Vermont College, faculty; Maine College of Art low-residency programs, faculty; School of Visual Arts, faculty. Writer. **Publications:** Wet: On Painting, Feminism, and Art Culture, 1997; (with J. Tully) Sarah Wells, 2000; (ed. with S. Bee) M/E/A/N/I/N/G: An Anthology of Artists' Writings, Theory, and Criticism, 2000; (ed.) The Extreme of the Middle: Writings of Jack Tworkov, 2009; A Decade of Negative Thinking: Essays on Art, Politics, and Daily Life, 2009. Contributor to periodicals. **Online address:** miraschor@yahoo.com

SCHORSCH, Laurence. American (born United States), b. 1960. **Genres:** Children's Fiction, Children's Non-fiction, Mystery/Crime/Suspense, Young Adult Fiction. **Career:** Writer. **Publications:** RETELLER: Noah's Ark, 1992; The Story of Joseph, 1992; David and Goliath, 1992; The Story of Jonah, 1992. EDITOR: The Real Mother Goose Book of Christmas Carols, 1993; Evil Tales of Evil Things, 1993; Tales of the Living Dead, 1994. JUVENILE: Grandma's Visit, 1990; Mr. Boffin, 1993; The AAA Children's Atlas, 1994; Biggest and Smallest, 1994; Medal of Honor, 1994. **Address:** c/o Kathy Berger, 868 Sheridan Rd., Ste. 100, Evanston, IL 60202-1473, U.S.A.

SCHOTT, John R. American (born United States), b. 1951. **Genres:** Sciences, Earth Sciences, Engineering. **Career:** Rochester Institute of Technology, Chester F. Carlson Center for Imaging Science, professor of imaging science, Fredrick and Anna B. Weidman chaired professor, Digital Image and Remote Sensing Laboratory, director. Writer. **Publications:** Remote Sensing: The Image Chain Approach, 1997, 2nd ed., 2007; Fundamentals of Polarimetric Remote Sensing, 2009. **Address:** Rochester Institute of Technology, Chester F. Carlson Center for Imaging Science, 54 Lomb Memorial Dr., Rochester, NY 14623-5604, U.S.A. **Online address:** schott@cis.rit.edu

SCHOTT, Penelope Scambly. American (born United States), b. 1942. **Genres:** Novels, Poetry. **Career:** Rutgers University, Douglass College, assistant professor, 1971-78, professor of English; Thomas Edison State College, consultant, 1975-, faculty; Somerset County College, assistant professor and coordinator of accelerated programs, 1978-83; Educational Testing Service, associate research scientist, 1983-87; Raritan Valley Community College, professor of English. Writer. **Publications:** POETRY: My Grandparents Were Married for Sixty-five Years, 1977; These Are My Same Hands, 1989; The Perfect Mother, 1994; Wave Amplitude in the Mona Passage, 1998; Penelope: The Story of the Half-Scalped Woman, 1999; The Pest Maiden: A Story of Lobotomy, 2004; Almost Learning to Live in this World, 2004; Baiting the Void, 2005; May the Generations Die in the Right Order, 2007; A is for Anne: Mistress Hutchinson Disturbs the Commonwealth, 2007; Six Lips, 2010; Crow Mercies, 2010. OTHER: A Little Ignorance, 1986. Contributor of articles to journals and magazines. **Address:** 507 NW Skyline Crest Rd., Portland, OR 97229-6828, U.S.A. **Online address:** penelopeschott@comcast.net

SCHOUVALOFF, Alexander. British (born England), b. 1934. **Genres:** Novels, Dance/Ballet, Theatre, Music, Art/Art History, Photography, Fashion/Costume, Humor/Satire, Humor/Satire. **Career:** H.M. Tennent, manager, 1959-64; Central Office of Information, information officer, 1964; Edinburgh Festival, assistant director, 1965-67; North West Arts Association, founding director, 1967-74; Victoria and Albert Museum, Theatre Museum, founding curator, 1974-89; London Archives of the Dance, trustee, 1976-. Writer. **Publications:** (Ed.) Place for the Arts, 1970; The Summer of the Bullshine Boys (novel), 1979; (with V. Borovsky) Stravinsky on Stage, 1982; (contrib.) A Month in the Country: An Exhibition Presented by the Theatre Museum, Victoria and Albert Museum and Arranged in Conjunction with April FitzLyon, 1983; The Thyssen-Bornemisza Catalogue of Theatre and Ballet Designs, 1987; The Theatre Museum, 1987; Set and Costume Designs for Ballet and Theater, 1987; Theatre on Paper, 1990; Léon Bakst: The Theatre Art, 1991; The Art of Ballets Russes: The Serge Lifar Collection of Theater Designs, Costumes and Paintings at the Wadsworth Atheneum, Hartford, Connecticut, 1997. **Address:** 10 Avondale Park Gardens, London, GL W11 4PR, England. **Online address:** schouvaloff@clara.co.uk

SCHRAG, Ariel. American (born United States), b. 1979?. **Genres:** Education, Cartoons. **Career:** The New School, Graphic Novel Workshop, teacher, 2004. Writer, illustrator and cartoonist. **Publications:** (ed.) Stuck in the Middle: Seventeen Comics from an Unpleasant Age, 2007. HIGH SCHOOL COMIC CHRONICLES SERIES: Awkward and Definition: The High School Comic Chronicles of Ariel Schrag, 2008; Potential: The High School Comic Chronicles of Ariel Schrag, 2008; Likewise: The High School Comic Chronicles of Ariel Schrag, 2009. **Address:** Los Angeles, CA , U.S.A. **Online address:** arielschrag@hotmail.com

SCHRAGER, Sam(uel Alan). American (born United States) **Genres:** Adult Non-fiction, Law, Mystery/Crime/Suspense. **Career:** Evergreen State College, instructor in cultural and community studies. Writer and folklorist. **Publications:** The Trial Lawyer's Art, 1999. **Address:** Evergreen State College, Lab II 3273, 2700 Evergreen Pkwy. NW, Olympia, WA 98505, U.S.A. **Online address:** schrages@evergreen.edu

SCHRAMM, Carl J. American (born United States) **Genres:** Social Sciences. **Career:** Johns Hopkins Center for Health Care Finance and Management, founder & director, 1980-87; Johns Hopkins University, Health Policy Management, professor; Health Insurance Association of America, director; Fortis (now Assurant), executive vice president, 1992-96; HCIA Inc., founder; Patient Choice Health Care, founder, 1999; Ewing Marion Kauffman Foundation, president & CEO, 2002-; Greenspring Advisors consulting, founder; 21st Century Economic Advisory Committee, U.S. Department of Commerce's Measuring Innovation, chair, 2007; National Academy of Science, Institute of Medicine, Robert Wood Johnson Health Policy fellow; University of Virginia, Darden School, Batten fellow; New York Academy of Medicine, fellow; American University, Kogod School of Business, entrepreneur-in-residence. Scholar, writer, speaker and foundation executive. **Publications:** United States Strategies for World Hunger, 1976; (ed.) Alcoholism and Its Treatment in Industry, 1977; (with W. Mandell and J. Archer) Workers Who Drink: Their Treatment in an Industrial Setting, 1978; (ed.) Health Care and Its Costs, 1987; The Entrepreneurial Imperative: How America's Economic Miracle Will Reshape the World (and Change Your Life), 2006; (foreword) Brent Bowers, If at First You Don't Succeed: The Eight Patterns of Highly Effective Entrepreneurs, 2006; (with W.J. Baumol and R.E. Litan) Good Capitalism, Bad Capitalism and the Economics of Growth and Prosperity, 2007. Contributor to periodicals and journals. **Address:** Ewing Marion Kauffman Foundation, 4801 Rockhill Rd., Kansas City, MO 64110, U.S.A.

SCHRAMM, Laurier L. Canadian (born Canada), b. 1954. **Genres:** Engineering, Sciences, Technology, Chemistry. **Career:** Syncrude Canada Ltd., senior research scientist, 1980-88; Petroleum Recovery Institute, president and chief executive officer, 1988-2000; University of Calgary, adjunct professor of chemistry, 1991-2001, adjunct professor of chemical and petroleum engineering, 2001-; Alberta Research Council, vice-president for energy, 2000-01; Saskatchewan Research Council, president and chief executive officer, 2001-. Writer. **Publications:** The Language of Colloid and Interface Science: A Dictionary of Terms, 1993; Dictionary of Colloid and Interface Science, 2001; Emulsions, Foams, and Suspensions, Fundamentals and Applications, 2005; Dictionary of Nanotechnology, Colloid and Interface Science, 2008. EDITOR AND CONTRIBUTOR: Emulsions: Fundamentals and Applications in the Petroleum Industry, 1992; Foams: Fundamentals and Applications in the Petroleum Industry, 1994; Suspensions: Fundamentals and Applications in the Petroleum Industry, 1995; Surfactants: Fundamentals and Applications in the Petroleum Industry, 2000. Contributor to journals. **Address:** Saskatchewan Research Council, 125-15 Innovation Blvd., Saskatoon, SK S7N 2X8, Canada. **Online address:** schramm@src.sk.ca

SCHRECK, Harley Carl. American (born United States), b. 1948. **Genres:** Anthropology/Ethnology, Gerontology/Senior Issues, Urban Studies, Children's Fiction, Philosophy. **Career:** World Vision Intl., researcher, 1984-88; Westmont College, instructor, 1986; Fuller Theological Seminary, School of World Missions, adjunct professor, 1986-88; Southern California College, adjunct professor, 1987; Bethel University, professor of anthropology, 1988-, Gerontology Program, Masters of Arts, program director, co-chairperson. Writer. **Publications:** (Ed. with D. Barrett) Clarifying the Task, 1987; The Elderly in America: Volunteerism and Neighborhood in Seattle, 1996; Community and Caring: Older Persons, Intergenerational Relations, and Change in an Urban Community, 2000. Contributor of articles to periodicals and magazines. **Address:** Department of Anthropology and Sociology, Bethel University, 3900 Bethel Dr., PO Box 24, St. Paul, MN 55112-6999, U.S.A. **Online address:** schhar@bethel.edu

SCHRECKER, Judie. American (born United States), b. 1954. **Genres:** Children's Fiction, Animals/Pets, Young Adult Fiction. **Career:** Federal Bureau of Investigation (F.B.I.), personnel assistant and research analyst, 1972-79; Highland School, teacher assistant, 1989-; Laurel Rescue Squad, emergency medical technician. Writer and educator. **Publications:** FOR CHILDREN: The Pet Shop Mouse, 1994; Santa's New Reindeer, 1996. **Address:** 2336 Ferndown Ln., Keswick, VA 22947-9191, U.S.A. **Online address:** chopperschreck@yahoo.com

SCHREFER, Eliot. American (born United States), b. 1978. **Genres:** Young Adult Non-fiction, Novels. **Career:** Writer and Educator. **Publications:** Glamorous Disasters, 2006; The New Kid, 2007; Hack the SAT: A Private SAT Tutor Spills the Secret Strategies and Sneaky Shortcuts That Can Raise Your Score Hundreds of Points, 2008; School for Dangerous Girls, 2009; The Deadly Sister, 2010; Geek Fantasy Novel, 2011. **Address:** c/o Richard Pine, Inkwell Management, 521 5th Ave., 26th Fl., New York, NY 10175, U.S.A. **Online address:** eliot@eliotschrefer.com

SCHREIBER, Joseph. American (born United States), b. 1969. **Genres:** Novels, Plays/Screenplays, Novellas/Short Stories, Travel/Exploration, Reference. **Career:** Writer. **Publications:** Next of Kin (novel), 1994; Martha's Vineyard & Nantucket, 1997. **Address:** c/o Claire Smith, Harold Ober Associates, 425 Madison Ave., New York, NY 10017, U.S.A.

SCHREIBER, Le Anne. American (born United States), b. 1945. **Genres:** Autobiography/Memoirs, Intellectual History, Essays, Natural History, Writing/Journalism, Autobiography/Memoirs, Essays. **Career:** Harvard University, teaching fellow, 1971-74; Time, staff writer, 1974-76; Women Sports Magazine, editor-in-chief, 1976-78; The New York Times, Sports Department, assistant editor, 1978, sports editor, 1978-80, assistant book review editor, 1980-82, deputy book review editor, 1982-84; independent journalist and writer, 1984-; State University of New York, University at Albany, Department of English, associate professor, writer-in-residence; Columbia University, Graduate Writing Department, faculty; National Book Critics Circle, board director. **Publications:** Midstream: The Story of a Mother's Death and a Daughter's Renewal, 1990; Light Years: A Memoir, 1996. Contributor to periodicals. **Address:** Department of English, University at Albany, State University of New York, Humanities 350, 1400 Washington Ave., Albany, NY 12222-0100, U.S.A.

SCHREIBER, Roy E. American (born United States), b. 1941. **Genres:** History, Biography, Autobiography/Memoirs, Military/Defense/Arms Control. **Career:** University of London, Institute of Historical Research, fellow, 1966-67; Upsala College, professor of history, 1967-68; Indiana University at South Bend, professor of history, 1968-2005, professor emeritus, 2005-; Journal of British Studies, referee, 1980; Canadian Journal of History, referee, 1981. Writer and speaker. **Publications:** The Political Career of Sir Robert Naunton, 1589-1635 (monograph), 1981; The First Carlisle: Sir James Hay, First Earl of Carlisle, 1580-1636, as Courtier, Diplomat and Entrepreneur, 1984; The Fortunate Adversities of William Bligh, 1991. EDITOR: (with P. Scherer) Hardinge of Penshurst: A Study in the Old Diplomacy, 1980; (with Scherer) A Protestant in Purgatory: Richard Whately, Archbishop of Dublin, 1981; Fragmenta Regalia: Observations on the Late Queene Elizabeth, Her Times and Favorites, 2002; Captain Bligh's Second Chance: An Eyewitness Account of His Return to the South Seas, 2007. Contributor to periodicals. **Address:** Department of History, Indiana University at South Bend, 1700 Mishawaka Ave., PO Box 7111, South Bend, IN 46634-7111, U.S.A. **Online address:** rschreib@jusb.edu

SCHREIBER, Terry. American (born United States), b. 1937. **Genres:** Film. **Career:** T. Schreiber Studio & Theatre, owner, artistic director and teacher, 1969-; American Theatre Wing, staff. Writer. **Publications:** (With M.B. Barber) Acting: Advanced Techniques for the Actor, Director, and Teacher, 2005. **Address:** T. Schreiber Studio & Theatre, 151 W 26th St., 7th Fl., New York, NY 10001-6810, U.S.A. **Online address:** info@tschreiber.org

SCHREIBMAN, Laura. (Laura Ellen Schreibman). American (born United States) **Genres:** Psychology, Race Relations, Medicine/Health. **Career:** University of California, faculty, 1983-, distinguished professor, principal investigator, Autism Research Program, director. Writer and psychologist. **Publications:** Autism, 1988; The Science and Fiction of Autism, 2005. Contributor to periodicals. **Address:** Department of Psychology, University of California, 9500 Gilman Dr., PO Box 0109, La Jolla, CA 92093-5004, U.S.A. **Online address:** lschreibman@ucsd.edu

SCHREIBMAN, Laura Ellen. *See* **SCHREIBMAN, Laura.**

SCHREINER, Samuel (Agnew). American (born United States), b. 1921. **Genres:** Novels, Documentaries/Reportage, Adult Non-fiction, Biography, Autobiography/Memoirs, Self Help, Philosophy. **Career:** U.S. Army, Office of Strategic Services, cryptographer, 1942-45; McKeesport Daily News, reporter, 1946; Pittsburgh Sun-Telegraph, reporter, 1946-51; Parade Magazine, writer and assistant managing editor, 1951-55; Reader's Digest, associate editor, 1955-68, senior editor, 1968-74, staff writer, 1975-85; Schreiner Associates, president; Darien Library Association, secretary; writer, 1974-. **Publications:** Urban Planning and Public Opinion, 1942; Thine is The Glory, 1975; Pleasant Places, 1977; The Condensed World of the Reader's Digest, 1977; Angelica, 1978; The Possessors and the Possessed, 1980; The Van Alens, 1981; A Place Called Princeton, 1984; The Trials of Mrs. Lincoln, 1987; Cycles, 1990; Mayday! Mayday!, 1990; (with E. Alvarez, Jr.) Code of Conduct, 1991; Henry Clay Frick: The Gospel of Greed, 1995; The Passionate Beechers: A Family Saga of Sanctity and Scandal that Changed America, 2003; Concord Quartet: Alcott, Emerson, Hawthorne, Thoreau and the Friendship that Freed the American Mind, 2006; World According to Cycles: How Recurring Forces can Predict the Future and Change Your Life, 2009. **Address:** 137 Hollow Tree Ridge, Apt. 1213, Darien, CT 06820-5045, U.S.A. **Online address:** sasmoon@aol.com

SCHRIFT, Alan D. American (born United States), b. 1955. **Genres:** Philosophy, Intellectual History, Humanities, Translations, Reference. **Career:** Purdue University, Department Of Philosophy, fellow, 1978-79, graduate instructor, 1980-82, visiting assistant professor, 1983-85; Indiana University, Department Of Philosophy, adjunct assistant professor, 1984; Grinnell College, assistant professor, 1987-92, associate professor, 1992-98, professor, 1998-2006, F. Wendell Miller professor of philosophy, 2006-, department chair, 1994-2000, 2003-07, 2008-12; Center for the Humanities, founding director, 1999-2007; Clarkson University, visiting assistant professor, 1985-87; Katholieke Universiteit, Institute of Philosophy, faculty, 1994. Writer. **Publications:** (Ed. with G.L. Ormiston) The Hermeneutic Tradition: From Ast to Ricoeur, 1990; Nietzsche and the Question of Interpretation: Between Hermeneutics and Deconstruction, 1990; (ed. with G.L. Ormiston) Transforming the Hermeneutic Context: From Nietzsche to Nancy, 1990; Nietzsche's French Legacy: A Genealogy of Poststructuralism, 1995; (ed.) The Logic of the Gift: Toward an Ethic of Generosity, 1997; (ed.) Why Nietzsche Still? Reflections on Drama, Culture, Politics, 2000; (ed.) Modernity and the Problem of Evil, 2005; Twentieth-Century French Philosophy: Key Themes and Thinkers, 2006; (ed.) The History of Continental Philosophy, 8 vols., 2010; (ed.) The Complete Works of Friedrich Nietzsche, 17 vols., 2011. Contributor of articles to journals. **Address:** Department of Philosophy, Grinnell College, PO Box 805, Grinnell, IA 50112, U.S.A. **Online address:** schrift@grinnell.edu

SCHRIJVERS, Peter. Belgian (born Belgium), b. 1963. **Genres:** History, Adult Non-fiction. **Career:** Brussels Royal Military Academy, research assistant, 1989-90; Catholic University of Louvain, visiting lecturer, 1994-95; Institut Universitaire de Hautes Etudes Internationales, Geneva, Switzerland, lecturer, 1997-2001; University of Antwerp, visiting lecturer, 2003-04; University of New South Wales, School of History and Philosophy, senior lecturer, 2004-. Writer. **Publications:** The Crash of Ruin: American Combat Soldiers in Europe during World War II, 1998; The GI War Against Japan: American Soldiers in Asia and the Pacific During World War II, 2002, rev. ed. as Bloody Pacific: American Soldiers at War with Japan, 2010; The Unknown Dead: Civilians in the Battle of the Bulge, 2005; Wreed als ijs: het lot van de burgers in de Slag om de Ardennen, 2004; Liberators: The Allies and Belgian Society, 1944-1945, 2009. **Address:** School of History & Philosophy, University of New South Wales, Rm. No 358-Morven Brown Bldg., Sydney, NW 2052, Australia. **Online address:** p.schrijvers@unsw.edu.au

SCHROCK, Kathleen. American (born United States), b. 1957. **Genres:** Education. **Career:** Morristown Township Public Library, children's and audiovisual librarian, 1981-83; Timberlane Regional High School, library media specialist, 1983-84; University of Maryland, circulation department head, 1984-86, Education Library, assistant director, 1986-87; Cape Cod Museum of Natural History, librarian, 1987-90, library director; Museum of Natural History, librarian, 1987-90; NH Wixon Middle School, library media specialist, 1990-97; Dennis-Yarmouth Regional School District, library media specialist, 1990-97, technology coordinator, 1997-2001; Technology Pathfinders for Teachers and Administrators, editorial consultant, 1997-2004; Cape Cod School Technology Facilitators, chair, 1998-; Creative Classroom Magazine, columnist, 1999-; Short Circuits E-Newsletter, columnist, 1999-; Linworth Publishing, columnist, 2001-; Nauset Public Schools, administrator and director for technology, 2001-; International Society for Technology in Education, board director, 2004-06; Wilkes University, faculty; Mt. Wachusett Community College, reference librarian; Northeast Document Conservation Center, preservation microfilm inspector. **Publications:** Evaluating Internet Web Sites: An Educators Guide, 1997; (with S. Hixson) Beginner's Handbook: Developing Web Pages for School and Classroom, 1998; (with M. Frazel) Microsoft Publisher for Every Day of the School Year, 1998; (with M. Frazel) Inquiring Educators Want to Know: TeacherQuests for Today's Teachers, 2000; (ed.) The Technology Connection: Building a Successful Library Media Program, 2000; (with J. Wahlers and M. Watkins) Writing and Researching Books Using the Computer, 2001. **Address:** Nauset Public Schools, 78 Eldredge Pkwy., Orleans, MA 02653, U.S.A. **Online address:** kathy@kathyschrock.net

SCHROEDER, Alan. American (born United States), b. 1961. **Genres:** Children's Fiction, Young Adult Non-fiction, Biography, Picture/Board Books, Children's Non-fiction, Travel/Exploration. **Career:** Writer. **Publications:** PICTURE BOOKS: Ragtime Tumpie, 1989; The Stone Lion, 1994; Lily and the Wooden Bowl, 1994; Carolina Shout!, 1995; Minty: A Story of Young Harriet Tubman, 1996; Satchmo's Blues, 1996, rev. ed. as Satchmo's Blues: Louis Armstrong's Centennial Celebration!, 1999; Smoky Mountain Rose: An Appalachian Cinderella, 1997; The Tale of Willie Monroe, 1999; In Her Hands: The Story of Sculptor Augusta Savage, 2009; A is for Almanac: A Ben Franklin ABC, forthcoming. YOUNG ADULT BIOGRAPHIES: Josephine Baker, 1991; Jack London, 1992; Booker T. Washington, 1992; James Dean, 1994; Charlie Chaplin: The Beauty of Silence, 1997; (with A. Beier) Booker T. Washington: Educator and Racial Spokesman, 2005; Josephine Baker: Entertainer, 2006; Ben Franklin: His Wit and Wisdom from A to Z, 2011; Baby Flo: Florence Mills Lights Up The Stage, 2012. Contributor to periodicals. **Address:** 1225 College Ave., Alameda, CA 94501, U.S.A. **Online address:** salan446@aol.com

SCHROEDER, Gerald L. Israeli (born Israel) **Genres:** Sciences, Theology/Religion. **Career:** Massachusetts Institute of Technology, researcher and instructor, faculty of physics; Weizmann Institute of Science, Volcani Research Institute, researcher and instructor; Aish Hatorah College for Jewish Studies, researcher and instructor, Discovery Seminar, lecturer; U.S. Atomic Energy Commission, consultant. Writer. **Publications:** Genesis and the Big Bang: The Discovery of Harmony between Modern Science and the Bible, 1990; The Science of God: The Convergence of Scientific and Biblical Wisdom, 1997; The Hidden Face of God: How Science Reveals the Ultimate Truth, 2001; God According to God: A Physicist Proves We've Been Wrong about God All Along, 2009. Contributor of articles to journals. **Address:** Hahish 5, Jerusalem, 93223, Israel. **Online address:** gerald_schroeder@alum.mit.edu

SCHROEDER, Joy A. American (born United States), b. 1963. **Genres:** Theology/Religion, Humanities. **Career:** St. Mark Lutheran Church, assistant pastor, 1990-94; Gloria Dei Lutheran Church, assistant pastor, 1995-97; Luther College, assistant professor of religion, 1999-2000; Capital University, Bergener professor of theology and religion, 2000-; Trinity Lutheran Seminary, Bergener professor of theology and religion, 2000-, assistant professor of church history, 2000-06, associate professor of church history, 2006-, acting director of graduate studies, 2008-09. Writer. **Publications:** Dinah's Lament: The Biblical Legacy of Sexual Violence in Christian Interpretation, 2007. Contributor of articles to periodicals and journals. **Address:** Trinity Lutheran Seminary, 2199 E Main St., Columbus, OH 43209, U.S.A. **Online address:** jschroed@capital.edu

SCHROEDER, Lucinda Delaney. American/Filipino (born Philippines), b. 1952?. **Genres:** Young Adult Fiction, Biography, Law. **Career:** U.S. Fish and Wildlife Service, Law Enforcement Division, special agent, 1974-2004, retired, 2004. Writer. **Publications:** A Hunt for Justice: The True Story of a Woman Undercover Wildlife Agent, 2006. **Address:** Lyons Press, 246 Goose Ln., PO Box 480, Guilford, CT 06437-2186, U.S.A. **Online address:** lucinda@lucindaschroeder.com

SCHROEDER-LEIN, Glenna R(uth). American (born United States), b. 1951. **Genres:** History, Social Sciences, Biography, Military/Defense/Arms Control. **Career:** Southwest Museum, archivist and library assistant, 1977-81; World Vision, photograph librarian, 1982-84; University of Tennessee, assistant editor of Andrew Johnson Papers Project, 1990-2000, adjunct instructor in history, 1993-2000; Washington College, visiting assistant professor, 1990; Lincoln Memorial University, visiting professor, 2000; Papers of Abraham Lincoln, assistant editor, 2001-03; Abraham Lincoln Presidential Library, manuscript librarian. **Publications:** Confederate Hospitals on the Move: Samuel H. Stout and the Army of Tennessee, 1994; (with R. Zuczek) Andrew Johnson: A Biographical Companion, 2001; Encyclopedia of Civil War Medicine, 2008. Contributor of articles and reviews to history journals. **Address:** 2605 S Chase Dr., Springfield, IL 62704, U.S.A.

SCHRYER, Frans J(ozsef). Canadian (born Canada), b. 1946. **Genres:** Anthropology/Ethnology, History, Social Sciences, Theology/Religion. **Career:** University of Guelph, assistant professor, 1974-80, associate professor, 1980-90, professor of sociology and anthropology, 1990-, Graduate Programs in Sociology and Anthropology, coordinator, graduate coordinator for collaborative international development studies, 1997-2000; Colegio de Postgraduados, visiting lecturer, 1981; York University, Centre for Research on Latin America and the Caribbean, Mexico Project, director, 1981-86, visiting lecturer, 1987; Centre for Research and Documentation on Latin America, visiting researcher, 1988; Yale University, Centre for Agrarian Studies, fellow, 1994-95. **Publications:** Faccionalismo y Patronazgo del PRI en un Municipio de la Huasteca Hidalguense, 1976; The Rancheros of Pisaflores: The Case History of a Peasant Bourgeoisie in Twentieth-Century Mexico, 1980; Ethnicity and Class Conflict in Rural Mexico, 1990; The Netherlandic Presence in Ontario: Pillars, Class, and Dutch Ethnicity, 1998; Native Peoples of Central Mexico since Independance, in the Cambridge History of the Native Peoples of the Americans, 1999. CONTRIBUTOR: A House Divided 1984; Region, State, and Capitalism in Mexico, 1989; Pilgrimage in Latin America, 1991; The Indian in Latin American History: Resistance, Resilience, and Acculturation, 1993. Contributor of articles to journals. **Address:** Deparment of Sociol-

ogy and Anthropology, University of Guelph, MacKinnon Bldg., Ste. 626, Guelph, ON N1G 2W1, Canada. **Online address:** fschryer@uoguelph.ca

SCHUBEL, Vernon James. American (born United States) **Genres:** Theology/Religion. **Career:** University of California, Urdu Language Program in Pakistan, member, 1981-82; American Institute of Pakistan Studies, fellow, 1983; James Madison University, instructor in philosophy and religion, 1984; Central Michigan University, assistant professor of religion, 1984-87; Miami University, lecturer, 1987; National Council of U.S.-Arab Relations, Malone fellow in Egypt, 1988; Kenyon College, assistant professor, associate professor of religion, 1988-, head of department, 1992-94, chair; University of Washington, lecturer, 1990. Writer. **Publications:** Religious Performance in Contemporary Islam: Shi'i Devotional Rituals in South Asia, 1993. Works appear in anthologies. Contributor of articles to periodicals. **Address:** Department of Religious Studies, Kenyon College, Ascension Hall, 202 College-Park St., Gambier, OH 43022, U.S.A. **Online address:** schubel@kenyon.edu

SCHUBERT, Frank N. American (born United States), b. 1943. **Genres:** History, Military/Defense/Arms Control, Social Sciences, Young Adult Nonfiction. **Career:** U.S. Department of Defense, U.S. Army, officer, 1965-68, Center of Military History, historian, 1973-75, 1990-93, Army Corps of Engineers, historian, 1977-90, Joint Chiefs of Staff, chairman, 1993-2003, now retired; Schubert Flint Public Affairs, founder and president, 2003-; Goddard Claussen Porter Novelli, partner. Writer. **Publications:** Soldiers of the American Revolution: A Sketchbook, 1976; Vanguard of Expansion: Army Engineers in the Trans-Mississippi West, 1819-1879, 1980; (intro.) Explorer on the Northern Plains: Lieutenant Gouverneur K. Warren's Preliminary Report of Explorations in Nebraska and Dakota in the Years 1855-'56-'57, 1981; Interviews with Colonel William W. Badger, 1983; Building Air Bases in the Negev: The U.S. Army Corps of Engineers in Israel, 1979-1982, 1992; Buffalo Soldiers, Braves, and the Brass: The Story of Fort Robinson, Nebraska, 1993; Mobilization: The U.S. Army in World War II, 1994; Outpost of the Sioux Wars, 1995; Black Valor: Buffalo Soldiers and the Medal of Honor, 1866-1917, 1997; Lieutenant General Ernest Graves, 1997; Open House Collection, 2000. EDITOR: (and intro.) March to South Pass: Lieutenant William B. Franklin's Journal of the Kearny Expedition of 1845, 1979; The Nation Builders: A Sesquicentennial History of the Corps of Topographical Engineers, 1838-1863, 1988; (with T.L. Kraus) The Whirlwind War: The United States Army in Operations Desert Shield and Desert Storm, 1994; (and comp.) On the Trail of the Buffalo Soldier, 1995; Voices of the Buffalo Soldier, 2003; The Occupation of Bosnia and Herzegovina in 1878, 2005. Contributor to books. Contributor of articles to books and periodicals. **Address:** Schubert Flint Public Affairs, 1415 L St., Ste. 1250, Sacramento, CA 95814-3972, U.S.A. **Online address:** frank@schubertflintpa.com

SCHUBERT, Leda. American (born United States), b. 1950?. **Genres:** Children's Fiction. **Career:** Cabot School, librarian, 1980-84; Kellogg-Hubbard Library, children's librarian, 1984-85; Vermont Department of Education, school library consultant, 1986-2003; Vermont College of Fine Arts, MFA Program, core faculty. Writer. **Publications:** Winnie All Day Long, 2000; Winnie Plays Ball, 2000; Here Comes Darrell, 2005; Ballet of the Elephants, 2006; Donna and the Robbers, 2007; Feeding the Sheep, 2010; Reading to Peanut, 2011; Princess of Borscht, 2011; Monsieur Marceau, 2012. **Address:** Vermont College of Fine Arts, 36 College St., Montpelier, VT 05602-3145, U.S.A. **Online address:** leda@ledaschubert.com

SCHUDSON, Charles B(enjamin). American (born United States), b. 1950. **Genres:** Law. **Career:** Fulbright-Hayes fellow, 1974; Milwaukee County, assistant district attorney, 1975-82; Offices of the U.S. Attorney of the Eastern District of Wisconsin, attorney general of Wisconsin and district attorney of Milwaukee county, Medicaid Fraud Investigations and Prosecutions, coordinator, 1976-79; Eastern District of Wisconsin, special assistant U.S. attorney, 1977-79; Wisconsin attorney general, special assistant, 1978-79; University of Wisconsin-Milwaukee, instructor in criminal justice, 1978-86; Circuit Court of Wisconsin, Milwaukee County, judge, 1982-92; National Council of Juvenile and Family Court Judges, faculty, 1984-2007; National Judicial College, faculty, 1984-2007; Wisconsin Court of Appeals, judge, 1992-2004; University of Wisconsin Law School, adjunct professor, 1999-; von Briesen & Roper, S.C., senior counsel, 2004-06; Wisconsin Reserve Judge, 2004-; Bjorklunden Seminars, faculty, 2004-; La Causa Inc., legal counsel, 2005-; Keynote Seminars, president, 2006-; Marquette University, adjunct professor of law, 2007-; writer. **Publications:** (With B.W. Dziech) On Trial: America's Courts and Their Treatment of Sexually Abused Children, 1989, 2nd ed., 1991. Contributor to journals and periodicals. **Address:** University of Wisconsin Law School, 975 Bascom Mall, Madison, WI 53706-1399, U.S.A. **Online address:** highroad@wi.rr.com

SCHUELER, G(eorge) F(rederick). American (born United States), b. 1944. **Genres:** Philosophy, Adult Non-fiction, Psychology. **Career:** University of New Mexico, assistant professor, 1971-79, associate professor, 1979-90, professor of philosophy, 1990-2007, Philosophy Department, chair, 1996-2000; Oxford University, professor, 1977-78, 1984-85, 1991-92; University of Delaware, professor and chair of philosophy, 2007-. Writer. **Publications:** (Ed.) Guidebook to Publishing in Philosophy, 2nd ed., 1986; The Idea of a Reason for Acting: A Philosophical Argument, 1989; Desire: Its Role in Practical Reason and the Explanation of Action, 1995; Reasons and Purposes: Human Rationality and the Teleological Explanation of Action, 2003. Contributor to journals. **Address:** Department of Philosophy, University of Delaware, Rm. 101B, 24 Kent Way, Newark, DE 19716, U.S.A. **Online address:** schueler@udel.edu

SCHUITEN, François Louis Marie. Also writes as Robert Louis Marie de la Barque, Schuiten Peeters. Belgian (born Belgium), b. 1956. **Genres:** Humor/Satire, Mystery/Crime/Suspense. **Career:** Scenographer, columnist and writer. **Publications:** AS SCHUITEN PEETERS: Aux médianes de Cymbiola, 1980; Carapaces, 1981; Le Rail, 1982; (with B. Peeters) Les Murailles de Samaris, 1983; (with B. Peeters) La fiévre d'Urbicande, 1985; (with L. Schuiten) Zara, 1985; Le Mystre d'Urbicande, 1985; (with B. Peeters) L'archiviste, 1987; La Tovr, 1987; La route d'Armilia, 1988; Encyclopédie des transports présents et venir by Axel Wappendorf, 1988; Plagiat!, 1989; Le musée A. Desombres, 1990; Nogegon, 1990; Dolors, 1991; Brüsel, 1992; Lecho des cités, 1993; Souvenirs de léternel présent, 1993; Mary la penchée, 1995; Le guide des cités, 1996; L'aventure des images de la bande dessinée au multimédia, 1996; L'enfant penchée, 1996; L'ombre dun homme, 1999; Voyages en utopie, 2000; (with B. Peeters) Brüsel, 2001; (with L. Schuiten) NogegoN, 2000; (with L. Schuiten) Zara, 2001; (with L. Schuiten) Carapaces, 2001; (with B. Peeters) La frontire invisible, 2002; The Book of Schuiten, 2004; Maison Autrique, 2004. **Address:** Casterman Editions, Rue Royal 132, Ste. 2, Brussels, 1000, Belgium.

SCHULENBERG, David. (David Louis Schulenberg). American (born United States), b. 1955. **Genres:** Music. **Career:** State University of New York, lecturer, 1982; University of Virginia, visiting assistant professor, 1983; Baruch College of City University of New York, visiting assistant professor, 1986; Columbia University, assistant professor, 1987-89; University of Texas, lecturer, 1990; University of North Carolina, assistant professor, 1992-99; Duke University, visiting assistant professor, 1995-97; University of South Dakota, research associate, 1999-2001, visiting assistant professor, 2000; University of Notre Dame, visiting assistant professor, 2000-01; Wagner College, Department of Music, professor and chair, 2001-, The Juilliard School, historical performance faculty, 2010-. Writer. **Publications:** The Instrumental Music of C.P.E. Bach, 1984; The Keyboard Music of J.S. Bach, 1992, 2nd ed., 2006; Music of the Baroque, 2001, 2nd ed., 2008; The Music of Wilhelm Friedemann Bach, 2010. EDITOR: Bach Perspectives, vol. IV, 1999; C.P.E. Bach: The Complete Works, 3 vols.. Contributor of articles to journals. **Address:** Department of Music, Wagner College, 1 Campus Rd., Staten Island, NY 10301, U.S.A. **Online address:** dschulen@wagner.edu

SCHULENBERG, David Louis. *See* **SCHULENBERG, David.**

SCHULER, Douglas. American (born United States), b. 1954?. **Genres:** Information Science/Computers, Social Commentary, Sociology. **Career:** Evergreen State College, instructor; Computer Professionals for Social Responsibility, chair; Seattle Community Network, founding member. Computer network specialist, consultant and writer. **Publications:** New Community Networks: Wired for Change, 1996; Liberating Voices: A Pattern Language for Communication Revolution, 2008. EDITOR: (with J.P. Jacky) Directions and Implications of Advanced Computing, 1989; (with A. Namioka) Participatory Design: Principles and Practices, 1993; (with P.E. Agre) Reinventing Technology, Rediscovering Community, 1997; (with C. Page) Community Space and Cyberspace, 1997; (with P. Day) Shaping the Network Society: The New Role of Civil Society in Cyberspace, 2003; (with P. Day) Community Practice in the Network Society: Local Action, Global Interaction, 2004; Online Communities and Social Computing, 2007. Contributor to periodicals. **Address:** Evergreen State College, 2700 Evergreen Pkwy. NW, Olympia, WA 98505, U.S.A. **Online address:** douglas@scn.org

SCHULKIN, Jay. American (born United States), b. 1952. **Genres:** Medicine/Health, Sports/Fitness. **Career:** Georgetown University, research professor of physiology, biophysics and neuroscience. Writer. **Publications:** (ed.) Preoperative Events: Their Effects on Behavior following Brain Damage, 1989; Sodium Hunger: The Search for a Salty Taste, 1991; The Pursuit of Inquiry, 1992; (ed.) Hormonally Induced Changes in Mind and Brain, 1993; The Delicate Balance: Decision-Making, Rights, and Nature, 1996; (ed. with L.A. Schmidt) Extreme Fear, Shyness, and Social Phobia: Origins, Biological Mechanisms, and Clinical Outcomes, 1999; The Neuroendocrine Regulation of Behavior, 1999; Roots of Social Sensibility and Neural Function, 2000; Calcium Hunger: Behavioral and Biological Regulation, 2001; Rethinking Homeostasis: Allostatic Regulation in Physiology and Pathophysiology, 2003; (ed.) Allostasis, Homeostasis and the Costs of Physiological Adaptation, 2004; Bodily Sensibility: Intelligent Action, 2004; (ed. with M.L. Power) Birth, Distress, and Disease: Placental-Brain Interactions, 2005; Curt Richter: A Life in the Laboratory, 2005; Effort: A Behavioral Neuroscience Perspective on the Will, 2007; Medical Decisions, Estrogen and Aging, 2008; (with M.L. Power) The Evolution of Obesity, 2009; Cognitive Adaptation: A Pragmatist Perspective, 2009. **Address:** Department of Physiology, Georgetown University, Basic Sciences Bldg., Washington, DC 20057, U.S.A. **Online address:** jschulkin@acog.org

SCHULLER, Gunther. American (born United States), b. 1925. **Genres:** Music. **Career:** Cincinnati Symphony, principal horn, 1943-45; Metropolitan Opera Orchestra, principal horn, 1945-59, musical composer, 1959-67; jazz, french horn player, 1949-50; Manhattan School of Music, teacher, 1950-63; Berkshire Music Centre, acting head, 1963-65, Department of Composition, head, artistic director, 1964-84; Yale University, associate professor of music, 1964-67; New England Conservatory of Music, president, 1967-77; Margun Music Inc., founder and editor, 1975-; GM Recordings Inc., founder, 1981-; Modern Jazz Society, founder; Smithsonian Jazz Masterworks Orchestra, co-director; Composer, conductor, jazz historian and author. **Publications:** Horn Technique, 1962; Early Jazz: Its Roots and Musical Development, 1968; Musings: The Musical Worlds of Gunther Schuller, 1985; The Swing Era: The Development of Jazz, 1930-1945, 1988; The Compleat Conductor, 1997; Grand Concerto: For Percussion and Keyboards, 2005. Contributor to periodicals. **Address:** GM Recordings Inc., 167 Dudley Rd., Newton Centre, MA 02459, U.S.A.

SCHULMAN, Arlene. American (born United States), b. 1961. **Genres:** Adult Non-fiction, Children's Non-fiction, Criminology/True Crime, Biography, Documentaries/Reportage. **Career:** Ohio State University, School of Journalism, visiting professor, 1996; James Thurber House Writing Camp, instructor, 1996; Columbus Dispatch, writing coach, 1996; New York City Public Schools, artist and writer-in-residence, 1997-2001; Hunter College, Continuing Education, instructor, 2003-. **Publications:** SELF-ILLUSTRATED: The Prizefighters: An Intimate Look at Champions and Contenders, 1994; Carmine's Story: A Book about a Boy Living with AIDS, 1997; T.J.'s Story: A Book about a Boy Who Is Blind, 1998; 23rd Precinct: The Job, 2001; Cop on the Beat: Officer Steven Mayfield in New York City, 2002. OTHERS: Muhammad Ali: Champion, 1996; Robert F. Kennedy: Promise for the Future, 1998. **Address:** Lerner Publishing Group, 1251 Washington Ave. N, Minneapolis, MN 55401, U.S.A. **Online address:** arlenetheauthor@aol.com

SCHULMAN, Audrey. American/Canadian (born Canada), b. 1963. **Genres:** Novels, Young Adult Fiction. **Career:** Grassroots activist and writer. **Publications:** NOVELS: The Cage, 1994; Swimming With Jonah, 1999; A House Named Brazil, 2000. **Address:** c/o Richard Parks, The Richard Parks Agency, 138 E 16th St., Ste. 5B, PO Box 693, New York, NY 10003-3561, U.S.A. **Online address:** audrey@audreyschulman.com

SCHULMAN, Ivan A(lbert). American (born United States), b. 1931. **Genres:** Literary Criticism And History, Novels. **Career:** Washington University, assistant professor, 1959-62, associate professor, 1962-64, professor of Spanish, 1964-68, professor Spanish American literature, 1968-70, Latin American Studies Program, founder and chairman, 1962-64, Summer Language Institute, director, 1963, Department of Romance Languages, chairman, 1965-69; State University of New York, professor of Spanish, 1970-71, professor of Spanish American literature, 1970-73, Department of Romance Languages, chairman, 1970-71, Department of Hispanic Languages and Literatures, chairman, 1971-73; University of Florida, graduate research professor of Latin American literatures, 1973-80, Center for Latin American Studies, director, 1977-80; Wayne State University, professor of Spanish, 1980-85; University of Illinois, professor of Spanish and comparative literature, 1985-96, head of department of Spanish, Italian and Portuguese, 1985-92, professor emeritus, 1996-; Florida Atlantic University, professor of Hispanic studies; University of South Florida, research associate. Writer. **Publications:** Simbolo y color en la obra de Jose Marti, 1960, 2nd ed., 1970; (with M.P. Gonzalez) Esquema ideologico de Jose Marti, 1961; Genesis del modernismo: Marti, Najera, Silva, Casal, 1966, 2nd ed., 1968; Marti, Casal y el modernismo, 1969; El modernismo hispanoamericano, 1969; (with R. Gullon and G. Sobejano) Antonio Machado, 1976; (with V.A. Chamberlin) La Revista ilustrada de Nueva York, 1976; (with E.P. Garfield) Poesia Modernista hispanoamericana y espanola, 1986, 2nd ed., 1999; (co-author) Nuevos asedios al modernismo, 1987; Relectures Martianas: narracion y nacion, 1994. EDITOR: (contrib.) Coloquio sobre la novela hispanoamericana, 1967; (with M.P. Gonzalez) Dario y el modernismo, 1969, 2nd ed., 1974; Versos libres, 1970; Autobiografia de un esclavo, 1975; (intro.) Cecilia Valdes (novel), 1981; (intro.) Ismaelillo, Versos libres, Versos sencillos, 1982; (with E.P. Garfield) Literatura Colonial Hispanoamericana, 1990; (with E.P. Garfield) Contextos, 1991; El Proyecto Inconcluso: La Vigencia del Modernismo, 2002. **Address:** Department of Spanish, Italian & Portuguese, University of Illinois, 707 S Mathews, Urbana, IL 61801, U.S.A. **Online address:** ischulman@earthlink.net

SCHULMAN, Michael D. American (born United States), b. 1948. **Genres:** Sociology, Medicine/Health, Anthropology/Ethnology. **Career:** North Carolina State University, Department of Sociology and Anthropology, William Neal Reynolds professor, 1977-, and alumni distinguished graduate professor; Rural Sociology, editor, 2008-11. **Publications:** (With J. Leiter) Hanging by a Thread: Social Change in Southern Textiles, 1991; (ed. with W.W. Falk and A.R. Tickamyer) Communities of Work: Rural Restructuring in Local and Global Contexts, 2003. Contributor to journals. **Address:** Department of Sociology & Anthropology, North Carolina State University, 1911 Bldg. 333b, PO Box 8107, Raleigh, NC 27695-8107, U.S.A. **Online address:** michael_schulman@ncsu.edu

SCHULTZ, Celia E. American (born United States), b. 1971?. **Genres:** Theology/Religion, Women's Studies And Issues, History. **Career:** Johns Hopkins University, faculty; Pennsylvania State University, faculty; Bryn Mawr College, faculty; Yale University, associate professor of classics, 2001-. Writer. **Publications:** (Ed. with P.B. Harvey) Religion in Republican Italy, 2006; Women's Religious Activity in the Roman Republic, 2006. Contributor to journals. **Address:** Department of Classics, Yale University, 344 College St., PO Box 208266, New Haven, CT 06520-8266, U.S.A. **Online address:** celia.schultz@yale.edu

SCHULTZ, (Reynolds) Bart(on). American (born United States), b. 1951. **Genres:** Social Sciences, Ethics, Politics/Government, Biography, Essays. **Career:** University of Chicago, faculty, 1987-, lecturer in social sciences, 1989-, Division of the Humanities, Department of Philosophy, senior lecturer, Civic Knowledge Project, director, executive director, Graham School of General Studies, special coordinator; Intellex Corp., general editor. Writer. **Publications:** (Ed.) Essays on Henry Sidgwick, 1992; Henry Sidgwick, Eye of the Universe: An Intellectual Biography, 2004; (ed. with G. Varouxakis) Utilitarianism and Empire, 2005. Contributor to professional journals. **Address:** Department of Philosophy, Division of the Humanities, University of Chicago, Edelstone Bldg. 133, 6030 S Ellis Ave., Chicago, IL 60637-1404, U.S.A. **Online address:** rschultz@uchicago.edu

SCHULTZ, Susan M. American (born United States), b. 1958. **Genres:** Poetry, Literary Criticism And History. **Career:** University of Hawaii, professor of English; Tinfish Press, editor, 1995-. Poet and critic. **Publications:** (Ed.) The Tribe of John: Ashbery and Contemporary Poetry, 1995; Aleatory Allegories, 2000; Memory Cards & Adoption Papers, 2001; And Then Something Happened, 2004; A Poetics of Impasse in Modern and Contemporary American Poetry, 2005; Dementia Blog, 2008; (ed. with A. Finch) Multiformalisms: A Postmodern Poetics of Form, 2009; Memory Cards: 2010-2011 Series, 2011. **Address:** Department of English, University of Hawaii, 214 Kuykendall, 1733 Donaghho Rd., Honolulu, HI 96822, U.S.A. **Online address:** sschultz@hawaii.edu

SCHULTZE, Quentin J(ames). American (born United States), b. 1952. **Genres:** Communications/Media. **Career:** Drake University, professor, 1978-82; Calvin College, professor of communication arts and sciences, 1982-, Arthur H. DeKruyter chair. Writer, consultant and speaker. **Publica-**

tions: Television: Manna from Hollywood?, 1986; (ed.) American Evangelicals and the Mass Media: Perspectives on the Relationship between American Evangelicals and the Mass Media, 1990; Televangelism and American Culture: The Business of Popular Religion, 1991; (co-author) Dancing in the Dark: Youth, Popular Culture and the Electronic Media, 1991; Redeeming Television: How TV Changes Christians-How Christians Can Change TV, 1992; (with B. Schultze) The Best Family Videos: For the Discriminating Viewer, 1994; Winning Your Kids Back from the Media, 1994; Internet for Christians: Everything You Need to Start Cruising the Net Today, 1995, rev. ed., 1998; Communicating for Life: Christian Stewardship in Community and Media, 2000; Habits of the High-Tech Heart: Living Virtuously in the Information Age, 2002; Christianity and the Mass Media in America: Towarda Democratic Accommodation, 2003; High-Tech Worship?: Using Presentational Technologies Wisely, 2004; Here I Am: Now What on Earth Should I be Doing?, 2005; Essential Guide to Public Speaking: Serving Your Audience With Faith, Skill and Virtue, 2006; (with A.H. DeKruyter) Suburban Church: Practical Advice for Authentic Ministry, 2008; (ed. with R.H. Woods) Understanding Evangelical Media, 2008; (with B.J. Kim) How to Write Powerful College Student Resumes & Cover Letters, 2010; (with L. Vander Meer) Recovering from Churchism: How to Renew, Grow, and Celebrate Your Church; Resume 101: A Student and Recent Grad Guide, 2012. Contributor of articles to periodicals. **Address:** CAS-DeVos Communication Center, Calvin College, 1810 E Beltline SE, Grand Rapids, MI 49546-5951, U.S.A. **Online address:** schu@calvin.edu

SCHULZ, William F(rederick). American (born United States), b. 1949. **Genres:** Civil Liberties/Human Rights, Politics/Government. **Career:** First Parish Unitarian Universalist, minister, 1975-78; Unitarian Universalist Association of Congregations, staff, 1978-93, president, 1985-93; Amnesty International USA, executive director, 1994-2006; Center for American Progress, senior fellow; The New School, adjunct professor of international relations; Unitarian Universalist Service Committee, president and chief executive officer. Writer. **Publications:** Finding Time and Other Delicacies, 1992; In Our Own Best Interest: How Defending Human Rights Benefits Us All, 2001; Making the Manifesto: The Birth of Religious Humanism, 2002; Tainted Legacy: 9/11 and the Ruin of Human Rights, 2003. EDITOR: (and intro.) Transforming Words: Six Essays on Preaching, 1984, 2nd ed., 1996; The Unitarian Universalist Pocket Guide, 2nd ed., 1993; (and intro.) The Phenomenon of Torture: Readings and Commentary, 2007; Future of Human Rights: U.S. Policy for a New Era, 2008. Contributor to periodicals. **Address:** Center for American Progress, 1333 H St. NW, 10th Fl., Washington, DC 20005, U.S.A. **Online address:** bschulz@americanprogress.org

SCHULZE, Dallas. (Dallas Hamlin). American (born United States) **Genres:** Romance/Historical, inspirational/Motivational Literature, Novels. **Career:** Author. **Publications:** ROMANCE NOVELS: Moment to Moment, 1986; Mackenzie's Lady, 1986; Stormwalker, 1987; Tell Me a Story, 1988; Lost and Found, 1988; Donovan's Promise, 1988; So Much Love, 1988; The Morning After, 1989; Together Always, 1989; Of Dreams and Magic, 1989; The Vow, 1990; Saturday's Child, 1990; A Summer to Come Home, 1990; Rafferty's Choice, 1991; The Baby Bargain, 1991; A Practical Marriage, 1991; Everything but Marriage, 1991; Charity's Angel, 1992; A Christmas Marriage, 1992; Strong Arms of the Lion, 1992; Temptation's Price, 1992; Angel and the Bad Man, 1992; The Hell-Raiser, 1992; Secondhand Husband, 1993; Strong Arms of the Law, 1993; A Very Convenient Marriage, 1994; Michael's Father, 1994; Snow Bride, 1994; The Way Home, 1994; Another Man's Wife, 1995; Gunfighter's Bride, 1995; Short Straw Bride, 1996; Together Always, 1996; Addie and the Renegade, 1996; Rafferty's Choice, 1997; Home to Eden, 1997; Tessa's Child, 1997; The Marriage, 1998; Summer Dreams, 1999; Sleeping Beauty, 1999; Loving Jessie, 2001; Lovers & Other Strangers, 2002; The Substitute Wife, 2003; (with M. Ferrarella) California Christmas, 2004; Somewhere Past Forever, 2004; (with R. Lee) Breaking Through, 2004. ROMANCE NOVELS AS DALLAS HAMLIN: Desperate Yearning, 1984; Another Eden, 1985; Surrender to a Stranger, 1986; Prisoner in His Arms, 1987. Works appear in anthologies. Contributor to books and periodicals. **Address:** Harlequin Enterprises Ltd., PO Box 5190, Buffalo, NY 14240-5190, U.S.A. **Online address:** dallas@dallasschulze.com

SCHULZE, Franz. American (born United States), b. 1927. **Genres:** Architecture, Art/Art History. **Career:** Lake Forest College, Department of Art, Hollender professor, 1974-91, head, Hollender professor emeritus, 1991; Purdue University, instructor of art, 1950-52; University of Chicago, lecturer in humanities, 1952-53; Chicago Sun-Times, art critic, 1978-85; University of

Oregon, professor of historic preservation; Musuem of Modern Art, senior deputy director of curatorial affairs. Writer. **Publications:** Art, Architecture and Civilization, 1968; Fantastic Images: Chicago Art since 1945, 1971; (with O.W. Grube and P.C. Pran) 100 Years of Architecture in Chicago: Continuity of Structure and Form, 1976; (with L. Brock) Stealing is My Game, 1976; Mies van der Rohe: Interior Spaces, 1982; Mies van der Rohe: A Critical Biography, 1985; (intro.) Mies van der Rohe Archive, 1986; The University Club of Chicago, 1987; (intro.) Buildings and Projects of Lohan Associates 1978-1993, 1993; Philip Johnson: Life and Work, 1994; The Farnsworth House, 1997; (with R. Cowler and A.H. Miller) 30 miles North: A History of Lake Forest College, Its Town, and Its City of Chicago, 2000; (contrib.) Mies van der Rohe im Nachkriegsdeutschland, 2001; Illinois Institute of Technology: The Campus Guide: An Architectural Tour, 2005. EDITOR: Mies van der Rohe: Critical Essays, 1989; (with K. Harrington) Chicago's Famous Buildings, 1993, 5th ed., 2003; The Mies van der Rohe Archive, vol. VII-XX, 1993. **Address:** Department of Art, Lake Forest College, 872 N Moor Rd., Lake Forest, IL 60045, U.S.A. **Online address:** schulze@lfc.edu

SCHULZE, Ingo. German (born Germany), b. 1962. **Genres:** Novellas/Short Stories. **Career:** State Theater, acting editor, 1988-90; Altenburger Weekly, co-founder, 1990-92; Gazette, co-founder, 1990-92. **Publications:** 33 Augenblicke des Glücks, 1995; Simple Storys, 1998; (with H. Penndorf) Von Nasen, Faxen und Ariadnefäden: Zeichnungen und Fax-Briefe, 2000; (intro.) Barbara Klemm: Künstler porträts, 2004; Neue Leben: die Jugend Enrico Türmers in Briefen und Prosa, 2005; Handy: dreizehn Geschichten in alter Manier, 2007; Adam und Evelyn, 2008; Tausend Geschichten sind nicht genug, 2008; Der Herr Augustin, 2008; Was wollen wir?, 2009; Orangen und Engel, 2010. Contributor to periodicals. **Address:** c/o Carsten Sommerfeldt, 207 Greifswalder Strabe, Berlin, 10405, Germany.

SCHUMACHER, Evelyn A(nn). American (born United States), b. 1919. **Genres:** Theology/Religion. **Career:** School teacher, 1941-54, 1961-62; Holy Family College (now Silver Lake College of the Holy Family), teacher of theology, 1968-70; Saint Francis House of Prayer, retreat director, 1988-. Writer. **Publications:** Pray with the Psalmist, 1980; Covenant Love, 1981; Presence through the Word, 1983; An Undivided Heart: John Paul II on the Deeper Realities of the Consecrated Life, 2002; Holiness: The Heart of Renewal, 2005; To Whom Shall We Go? (meditations). Contributor to magazines. **Address:** Holy Family Convent, 2409 S Alverno Rd., Manitowoc, WI 54220, U.S.A. **Online address:** sevelynann@hotmail.com

SCHUMACHER, Jim. American (born United States), b. 1955?. **Genres:** Medicine/Health. **Career:** Vermont district offices of Congressman Bernie Sanders, director; State of Vermont, deputy state auditor. Lawyer and writer. **Publications:** (With D. Bookchin) The Virus and the Vaccine: The True Story of a Cancer-Causing Monkey Virus, Contaminated Polio Vaccine, and the Millions of Americans Exposed, 2004. Contributor to periodicals. **Address:** c/o Author Mail, St. Martins Press, 175 5th Ave., New York, NY 10010, U.S.A. **Online address:** author@thevirusandthevaccine.com

SCHUMACHER, John N(orbert). Filipino/American (born United States), b. 1927. **Genres:** History, Social Commentary, Theology/Religion, Bibliography, Essays. **Career:** San Jose Seminary, instructor in Latin and English, 1951-54, dean of men, 1951-54, 1965-66; Ateneo de Manila University, professor of history, 1965-77, Loyola School of Theology, professor of history, 1965-, now professor emeritus; San Carlos Seminary, lecturer, 1973-83; Regional Major Seminary of Mindanao, lecturer, 1977, 1979; Entered Societas Jesu (Society of Jesus; Jesuits), ordained Roman Catholic priest. Writer. **Publications:** (With N.P. Cushner) Burgos and The Cavite Mutiny, 1969; Father Jose Burgos, Priest and Nationalist, 1972, rev. ed. as Father Jose Burgos: A Documentary History with Spanish Documents and Their Translation, 1999; The Propaganda Movement, 1880-1895: The Creators of a Filipino Consciousness, the Makers of Revolution, 1973, rev. ed., 1997; (ed.) Philippine National Retrospective Bibliography, 1523-1699, 1974; (with H. de la Costa) Church and State: The Philippine Experience, 1978; (with H. de la Costa) The Filipino Clergy: Historical Studies and Future Perspectives, 1978; Readings in Philippine Church History, 1979, rev. ed., 1987; The Revolutionary Clergy: The Filipino Clergy and the Nationalist Movement, 1850-1903, 1981; The Making of a Nation: Essays on Nineteenth-Century Filipino Nationalism, 1991; Reform and Revolution, vol. V: Kasaysayan: The Story of the Filipino People, 1998; Growth and Decline: Essays on Philippine church His-

tory, 2009. Contributor to journals. **Address:** Department of History, Loyola School of Theology, Ateneo de Manila University, PO Box 240, Quezon City, 1144, Philippines. **Online address:** jns@admu.edu.ph

SCHUMACHER, Julie. American (born United States), b. 1958. **Genres:** Novels, Novellas/Short Stories, Children's Fiction. **Career:** P.W. Communications, associate editor, 1983-85; Epoch (magazine), fiction editor, 1985; Cornell University, lecturer in English, 1985-88; University of Minnesota, associate professor of English, professor of English, Creative Writing Program, director. **Publications:** The Body Is Water, 1995; An Explanation for Chaos, 1997; Grass Angel, 2004; The Chain Letter, 2005; The Book of One Hundred Truths, 2006; Black Box, 2008. Contributor to periodicals. **Address:** Department of English, University of Minnesota, 207 Lind Hall, 207 Church St. SE, Minneapolis, MN 55455, U.S.A. **Online address:** schum003@umn.edu

SCHUMACHER, Linda H. American (born United States) **Genres:** Business/Trade/Industry, Economics. **Career:** Schumacher Consulting Inc., founder and president, 1998-; Penn State University, adjunct professor; Pittsburgh Chapter of Project Management Institute, vice president, 2004-09; PMCenters USA, instructor. Writer and consultant. **Publications:** Ready, Set, Succeed!: How Successful Projects Triumph over Business as Usual, 2004. **Address:** Schumacher Consulting Inc., 5317 Ellsworth Ave., Pittsburgh, PA 15232-1423, U.S.A. **Online address:** linda@adminhelpnow.com

SCHUMACHER, Michael. American (born United States), b. 1950. **Genres:** Biography, Autobiography/Memoirs. **Career:** Writer. **Publications:** Reasons to Believe: New Voices in American Fiction, 1988; Creative Conversations: The Writer's Guide to Conducting Interviews, 1990; Dharma Lion: A Critical Biography of Allen Ginsberg, 1992; Crossroads: The Life and Music of Eric Clapton, 1995; There But for Fortune: The Life of Phil Ochs, 1996; Francis Ford Coppola: A Filmmaker's Life, 1999; Family Business: Selected Letters between a Father and Son, 2001; Mighty Fitz: The Sinking of the Edmund Fitzgerald, 2005; Mr. Basketball: George Mikan, the Minneapolis Lakers, and the Birth of the NBA, 2007; Wreck of the Carl D.: A True Story of Loss, Survival, and Rescue at Sea, 2008; (ed. with H.Helin and H. Schuldt) CASCOM: Intelligent Service Coordination in the Semantic Web, 2008; Will Eisner: A Dreamer's Life in Comics, 2010. **Address:** c/o Author Mail, Citadel Press/Kensington Publishing, 850 3rd Ave., New York, NY 10022, U.S.A.

SCHUMAKER, Paul. American (born United States), b. 1946. **Genres:** Politics/Government, Social Sciences. **Career:** University of Kansas, assistant professor, 1972-78, associate professor, 1978-90, professor of political science, 1990-, department head, 1981-85, 1998-2003, Division of Government, director, 1984-85, Western Civilization Program, lecturer, 1990-92, distinguished lecturer, 1995-98. Writer. **Publications:** (With R. Getter and T. Clark) Policy Responsiveness and Fiscal Strain in Fifty-One American Communities: A Manual for Studying City Politics Using the NORC Permanent Community Sample, 1979, rev. ed., 1983; Critical Pluralism, Democratic Performance, and Community Power, 1991; (with D. Kiel and T. Heilke) Great Ideas/Grand Schemes: Political Ideologies in the 19th and 20th Centuries, 1996; (comp., ed. and intro. with T. Heilke and D. Kiel) Ideological Voices: An Anthology in Modern Political Ideas, 1997; (with B. Loomis) Choosing a President: The Electoral College and Beyond, 2001; (co-author) From Ideologies to Public Philosophies: An Introduction to Political Theory, 2008; The Political Theory Reader, 2010. Contributor to journals. **Address:** Department of Political Science, University of Kansas, 1541 Lilac Ln., 504 Blake Hall, Lawrence, KS 66045-3177, U.S.A. **Online address:** schu@ku.edu

SCHUMAKER, Ward. American (born United States), b. 1943. **Genres:** Children's Fiction, Illustrations, Autobiography/Memoirs. **Career:** Writer. **Publications:** SELF-ILLUSTRATED: All My Best Friends Are Animals Address Book, 1991; Dance!, 1996; Sing a Song of Circus, 1997; In My Garden: A Counting Book, 2000. OTHER: (contrib.) Deux cuisines en Provence: Two Kitchens in Provence, 1999; (contrib.) Toddler Two-step, 2000; (contrib.) Paris, France: A Memoir, 2000. Illustrator of books by others. Contributor to periodicals. **Address:** 466 Green St., San Francisco, CA 94133-4067, U.S.A. **Online address:** ward@warddraw.com

SCHUMAN, Michael A. American (born United States), b. 1953. **Genres:** Travel/Exploration, Young Adult Non-fiction, Biography, Children's Nonfiction. **Career:** The Baseball Bulletin, correspondent and staff writer, 1975-79; Building News Inc., staff writer, 1978-79; Yankee Books, Division of Yankee Magazine, editor and writer, 1979-82. Self-employed writer, 1983-.

Publications: Favorite Daytrips in New England, 1982, 4th ed., 1987; New England's Special Places, 1986, 2nd ed. as New England's Special Places: Easy Outings to Historic Villages, Working Museums, Presidential Homes, Castles, and Other Year-Round Attractions, 1990; New York State's Special Places, 1988; The Four Season Guide to New England, 1991; Cape Cod and the Islands, 1992; 52 New York Weekends, 1994, 2nd ed., 1999; Elie Wiesel: Voice from the Holocaust, 1994; Eleanor Roosevelt: First Lady and Humanitarian, 1995; Bill Cosby: Actor and Comedian, 1995; Franklin D. Roosevelt: The Four-Term President, 1996; 52 Connecticut and Rhode Island Weekends, 1996, 2nd ed., 1999; Martin Luther King, Jr.: Leader for Civil Rights, 1996; Theodore Roosevelt, 1997; Harry S. Truman, 1997, rev. ed., 2003; Richard M. Nixon, 1998, rev. ed., 2003; Lyndon B. Johnson, 1998; Bill Clinton, 1999, rev. ed., 2003; Alexander Graham Bell: Inventor and Teacher, 1999; Delaware, 2000, (with M. Richards) 2nd ed., 2009; Mayan and Aztec Mythology, 2001; Charles M. Schulz: Cartoonist and Creator of Peanuts, 2002; George H.W. Bush, 2002; Bob Dylan: The Life and Times of an American Icon, 2003; Ulysses S. Grant, 2004; Bosnia and Herzegovina, 2004; Croatia, 2004; Serbia and Montenegro, 2004; Halle Berry: Beauty is Not Just Physical, 2006; Will Smith: I Like Blending a Message with Comedy, 2006; Bill Gates: Computer Mogul and Philanthropist, 2008; Louis Armstrong: Jazz Is Played From the Heart, 2008; Barack Obama: We Are One People, 2008, rev. ed., 2009; Frederick Douglass: Truth is of No Color, 2009; Miracle: The Epic Story of Asia's Quest for Wealth, 2009; Jim Thorpe: There's No Such Thing as Can't, 2009; Adam Sandler: Celebrity with Heart, 2010; Led Zeppelin: Legendary Rock Band, 2010; Angelina Jolie: Celebrity with Heart, 2010; Tina Fey, 2010; Scarlett Johansson, 2011; Robert Pattinson: Shining Star, 2011; Rihanna: Music Megastar, 2011; Maya and Aztec Mythology Rocks!, 2011; Adam Sandler: Celebrity With Heart, 2011; Halle Berry: A Biography of an Oscar-winning Actress, 2012; Will Smith: A Biography of Rapper Turned Movie Star, 2012; Write Science Fiction in 5 Simple Steps, 2012. **Address:** 33 Shadow Ln., Keene, NH 03431-5223, U.S.A. **Online address:** mschuman@ne.rr.com

SCHUMER, Fran. American (born United States), b. 1953. **Genres:** Business/Trade/Industry, Biography. **Career:** City University, instructor, 1979-81; William Paterson College, journalism instructor, associate professor, 1988-89; Charlotte Observer, reporter; Boston Globe, editor; City College of the City University of New York, editor; New York magazine, columnist; New York Times, columnist; New Jersey section, columnist. **Publications:** (With M. Cunningham) Powerplay: What Really Happened at Bendix, 1984; Most Likely to Succeed: Six Women from Harvard and What Became of Them, 1986. Contributor to periodicals. **Address:** Sterling Lord Agency, 65 Blumer St., New York, NY 10012, U.S.A. **Online address:** frannyrs@aol.com

SCHUPACK, Deborah. American (born United States) **Genres:** Novels, Young Adult Non-fiction, Literary Criticism And History. **Career:** Yale University, teacher of writing and English literature; Vermont College, teacher of writing and English literature; New School University, teacher of writing and English literature. Writer. **Publications:** Between Friends, 2002; Love Lessons, 2002; Secrets of Success, 2002; The Boy on the Bus, 2003; The Opposition Leader's Husband, 2008; Sylvan Street, 2010. Contributor to periodicals. **Address:** c/o Maria Massie, Lippincott Massie McQuilkin, 27 W 20th St., Ste. 305, New York, NY 10011-3731, U.S.A.

SCHUSKY, Ernest L. American (born United States), b. 1931. **Genres:** Novels, Agriculture/Forestry, Anthropology/Ethnology, Archaeology/Antiquities, Race Relations, Social Sciences, History. **Career:** South Dakota State University, instructor in sociology, 1958-60; Southern Illinois University, Department of Anthropology, assistant professor, 1960-64, associate professor, 1964-69, professor of anthropology, 1969-93, professor emeritus of anthropology, 1993-, Graduate Program in Behavioral Science, director, 1977; Seoul National University, Fulbright professor, 1982. Writer. **Publications:** Politics and Planning in a Dakota Indian Community: A Case Study of Views on Termination and Plans for Rehabilitation on the Lower Brule Reservation in South Dakota, 1959; (with V.D. Malan) Dakota Indian community: An Analysis of the Non-Ranching Population on the Pine Ridge Reservation, 1962; A Manual for Kingship Analysis, 1965, 2d ed., 1983; (with T.P. Culbert) Introducing Culture, 1967, 4th ed., 1987; The Right to Be Indian, 1970; Variation in Kinship, 1974; The Study of Cultural Anthropology, 1975; The Forgotten Sioux: An Ethnohistory of the Lower Brule Reservation, 1975; (ed.) The Political Organization of Native North Americans, 1980; Introduction to Social Science, 1981; Culture and Agriculture: An Ecological Introduction to Traditional and Modern Farming Systems, 1989; (with S.G. Denny) Ancient Splendor of Prehistoric Cahokia, 1992; Journey to the Sun, 2001; Ride

the Whirlwind, 2004; Return to Beauty (novel), 2009; Too Many Miracles: A Novel, 2012. **Address:** Department of Anthropology, Southern Illinois University, PO Box 1451, Edwardsville, IL 62026-1451, U.S.A. **Online address:** eschusky@aol.com

SCHUSTER, Marilyn R. American (born United States), b. 1943. **Genres:** Literary Criticism And History, Women's Studies And Issues, Language/Linguistics. **Career:** Smith College, professor of French, 1971-99, Program for Study of Women and Gender, professor, 1999-2009, Andrew W. Mellon professor in the humanities, provost and dean of faculty, 2009-. Writer. **Publications:** Marguerite Duras Revisited, 1993; Passionate Communities: Reading Lesbian Resistance in Jane Rule's Fiction, 1999. EDITOR: (with S.R. Van Dyne) Women's Place in the Academy: Transforming the Liberal Arts Curriculum, 1985. **Address:** Office of the Provost & Dean of the Faculty, Smith College, College Hall 206, Northampton, MA 01063, U.S.A. **Online address:** mschuste@smith.edu

SCHUTT, Christine. American (born United States), b. 1948. **Genres:** Novels, Novellas/Short Stories. **Career:** Nightingale-Bamford School, middle-school English teacher; NOON, senior editor; Barnard College, faculty; Bennington College, faculty; Columbia University, faculty; Hollins University, faculty; Sarah Lawrence College, faculty; University of Massachusetts, faculty; University of California, faculty. Educator. **Publications:** Nightwork (stories), 1996; Florida (novel), 2004; A Day, a Night, Another Day, Summer (short stories), 2005; All Souls (novel), 2008. **Address:** The Nightingale-Bamford School, 20 E 92nd St., New York, NY 10128, U.S.A. **Online address:** cs@christineschutt.com

SCHUTTE, Anne Jacobson. American (born United States), b. 1940. **Genres:** History, Translations. **Career:** Lawrence University, instructor, 1966-69, assistant professor, 1971-77, chair of history department, 1976-79, 1989-91, associate professor, 1977-85, professor of history, 1985-91; University of Virginia, professor of history, 1992-2006. Writer and historian. **Publications:** Pier Paolo Vergerio: The Making of an Italian Reformer, 1977; Printed Italian Vernacular Religious Books, 1465-1550: A Finding List, 1983; (ed.) Autobiografia di una santa mancata, 1990; (trans.) F. Tomizza, Heavenly Supper: The Story of Maria Janis, 1991; (ed. and trans.) C. Ferrazzi, Autobiography of an Aspiring Saint, 1996; (co-ed) Tempi e spazi di vita femminile tra medioevo ed eta moderna, 1999; Aspiring Saints: Pretense of Holiness, Inquisition, and Gender in the Republic of Venice, 1618-1750, 2001; (co-ed.) Time, Space, and Women's Lives in Early Modern Europe, 2001; By Force and Fear: Taking and Breaking Monastic Vows in Early Modern Europe, 2011. Works appear in anthologies. Contributor of articles to journals. **Address:** Cannaregio 3314/e, Venezia, 30121, Italy. **Online address:** ajs5w@virginia.edu

SCHWAB, George M. American (born United States), b. 1961. **Genres:** Adult Non-fiction, Theology/Religion. **Career:** Associate Reformed Presbyterian Church, ordained minister; Erskine College, Erskine Theological Seminary, assistant professor of Old Testament, associate professor of Old Testament, professor of Old Testament. Writer. **Publications:** Cultivating the Vineyard: Studies in the Song of Solomon, 1997; The Song of Songs Cautionary Message Concerning Human Love, 2002; Hope in the Midst of a Hostile World: The Gospel According to Daniel, 2006; Right in Their Own Eyes: The Gospel According To Judges, 2011. **Address:** Erskine Theological Seminary, Erskine College, PO Box 668, Due West, SC 29639-0668, U.S.A. **Online address:** schwab@erskine.edu

SCHWANTES, Carlos A(rnaldo). American (born United States), b. 1945. **Genres:** Area Studies, Local History/Rural Topics, Transportation. **Career:** University of Michigan, teaching fellow, 1968; Walla Walla College, instructor, professor of history, 1969-86; University of Oregon, visiting lecturer, 1981; University of Idaho, associate professor, 1984-87, acting chair, 1987-88, professor, 1987-2002; American Orient Express Railway Co., train lecturer, 1995; University of Missouri, Saint Louis Mercantile Library endowed professor of transportation studies and the West, 2001-; American Historical Association, president, 1999-2000. Writer. **Publications:** Radical Heritage: Labor, Socialism and Reform in Washington and British Columbia, 1885-1917, 1979; Coxey's Army: An American Odyssey, 1985; (ed. with G.T. Edwards) Experiences in a Promised Land: Essays in Pacific Northwest History, 1986; (ed.) The Pacific Northwest in World War II, 1986; The Pacific Northwest: An Interpretive History, 1989, 2nd ed., 1996; In Mountain Shadows: A History of Idaho, 1991; In Mountain Shadows: A History of Idaho, 1991;

(ed. with T. Vaughan) Bisbee: Urban Outpost on the Frontier, 1992; Railroad Signatures across the Pacific Northwest, 1993; Hard Traveling: A Portrait of Worklife in the New Northwest, 1994; (ed. with E. Pickett) Encounters with a Distant Land: Exploration and the Great Northwest, 1994; So Incredibly Idaho!: Seven Landscapes That Define the Gem State, 1996; Long Day's Journey: The Steamboat and Stagecoach Era across the Northern West, 1999; Columbia River: Gateway to the West, 2000; Vision and Enterprise: Exploring the History of Phelps Dodge Corporation, 2000; Going Places: Transportation Redefines the Twentieth-Century West, 2003; (with J.P. Ronda) West the Railroads Made, 2008; Just One Restless Rider: Reflections on Trains and Travel, 2009. **Address:** Ctr. for Transportation Studies, University of Missouri, 1 University Blvd., 154 University Ctr., St. Louis, MO 63121-4499, U.S.A. **Online address:** schwantesc@umsl.edu

SCHWARCZ, Vera. American/Romanian (born Romania), b. 1947. **Genres:** Poetry, Area Studies. **Career:** Stanford University, history instructor, 1973; Wesleyan University, lecturer, 1975-77, assistant professor, 1977-83, associate professor, 1983-88, East Asian Studies Program, chair, 1982-84, 1985-88, 1994-96, professor, Mansfield Freeman professor of East Asian studies, 1988-, Freeman Center for East Asian Studies, director, 1987-88, 1998-99, Department of History, chair, 2000-02, professor of history, Jewish & Israel Studies Program, faculty; Chinese Academy of Social Sciences, International Institute of Chinese Culture, faculty, 1989; Hebrew University, visiting professor, 1996-97; Beijing University, faculty. Writer. **Publications:** Long Road Home: A China Journal, 1984; Chinese Enlightenment: Intellectuals and the Legacy of the May Fourth Movement of 1919, 1986; Zhongguo qi meng yun dong, 1989; Time for Telling Truth is Running Out: Conversations with Zhang Shenfu, 1992; Bridge Across Broken Time: Chinese and Jewish Cultural Memory, 1998; Fresh Word for a Jaded World, 2000; A Scoop of Light: Poems, 2000; In the Garden of Memory, 2004; Truth is Woven, 2005; Place and Memory in the Singing Crane Garden, 2008; Chisel of Remembrance: Poems, 2009; Brief Rest in the Garden of Flourishing Grace, 2009. Contributor to periodicals. **Address:** Department of History, Wesleyan University, 303 Public Affairs Ctr., 238 Church St., Middletown, CT 06459-0002, U.S.A. **Online address:** vschwarcz@wesleyan.edu

SCHWARTAU, Winn. American (born United States), b. 1952. **Genres:** Novels, Information Science/Computers, Adult Non-fiction, Technology. **Career:** Kaypro, vice president of marketing, 1981-85; American Computer Security Industries Inc., president, 1984-90; Interpact Inc., executive director and president, 1990; Security Awareness Co., president, chief executive officer and founder, 1990-; Mobile Application Development Partners L.L.C., chairman and board of director; Trusted Learning Corp., founder and chief executive officer; InfowarCon, founder; SCIPP Intl., founder. Writer. **Publications:** Terminal Compromise (novel), 1992; Cyber Christ I and II, 1994; Information Warfare: Chaos On the Electronic Superhighway, 1994, 2nd ed. as Information Warfare: Cyberterrorism-Protecting Your Personal Security in the Electronic Age, 1996; Cyber War I, 1996; (with C. Goggans) The Complete Internet Business Toolkit, 1996; Cyber War II, 1998; The Cyber Wars, 1998; Time Based Security, 1999; Cybershock: Surviving Hackers, Phreakers, Identity Thieves, Internet Terrorists and Weapons of Mass Disruption, 2000; Internet & Computer Ethics for Kids, 2001; Pearl Harbor Dot Com, 2002; Advanced Time Based Security, forthcoming; Beyond Information Warfare, forthcoming; Information Warfare: 2007, forthcoming. Contributor to periodicals. **Address:** Peter Miller and Associates, 220 W 19th St., New York, FL 10011, U.S.A. **Online address:** winn@alwayschaos.com

SCHWARTZ, Adam. American (born United States), b. 1965. **Genres:** Biography, Young Adult Fiction, History. **Career:** Christendom College, associate professor of history. Writer. **Publications:** The Third Spring: G.K. Chesterton, Graham Greene, Christopher Dawson and David Jones, 2005. Contributor to books and periodicals. **Address:** Department of History, Christendom College, 134 Christendom Dr., Front Royal, VA 22630, U.S.A. **Online address:** ajmschwartz@yahoo.com

SCHWARTZ, David B. American (born United States), b. 1948. **Genres:** Public/Social Administration, Psychology. **Career:** Pennsylvania Developmental Disabilities Planning Council, executive director, 1983-92. Writer and mental health counselor. **Publications:** Crossing the River: Creating a Conceptual Revolution in Community and Disability, 1992; Who Cares?: Rediscovering Community, 1997. **Address:** 1212 Trumansburg Rd., PO Box 6681, Ithaca, NY 14850-1314, U.S.A. **Online address:** jflutezoo@pa.net

SCHWARTZ, E(arl) A(lbert). American (born United States), b. 1942?. **Genres:** History. **Career:** The Associated Press, news writer, 1971-73, photo editor, 1973-75; Canby Herald, editor, 1975-78; Multnomah Athletic Club, publications director, 1978-79; Print Production Center, manager, 1979-84; KCYX-AM, news director, 1984; Statesman-Journal, correspondent, 1984-87; University of Missouri-Columbia, Department of English, teaching assistant, 1987-88, Department of history, teaching assistant, 1988-91, graduate instructor, 1991; California State University, associate professor of history, 1991-2010. **Publications:** The Rogue River Indian War and Its Aftermath, 1850-1980, 1997. **Address:** Department of History, California State University, Rm. 26, Markstein Hall, 333 S Twin Oaks Valley Rd., San Marcos, CA 92096, U.S.A. **Online address:** schwartz@csusm.edu

SCHWARTZ, Elliott S. American (born United States), b. 1936. **Genres:** Music, History. **Career:** University of Massachusetts, instructor in music, 1960-64; Bowdoin College, assistant professor, 1964-70, associate professor, 1970-75, Robert K. Beckwith professor of music, 1975-, department chair, 1975-87, Robert K. Beckwith professor of music emeritus; Trinity College of Music, visiting lecturer, 1967; University of California-Santa Barbara, College of Creative Studies, visiting lecturer, 1970, 1973, 1974; British Broadcasting Corp., composer, 1972, 1974, 1978, 1983; University of California-Center for Music Experiment, visiting lecturer, 1978-79; American Society of University Composers (now Society of Composers Inc.), chairman, 1983-88; Ohio State University, distinguished university visiting professorship, 1985-86; College Music Society, president, 1989-90; Robinson College, visiting professor, 1993-94, 1999; American Music Center, vice-president; Maine Composers Forum, president; Maine Arts Council, music panelist; University of the Pacific, visiting composer; University of Minnesota, visiting composer; College of William & Mary, visiting composer. Writer. **Publications:** The Symphonies of Ralph Vaughan Williams, 1964; (ed. with B. Childs) Contemporary Composers on Contemporary Music, 1967, rev. ed., 1998; Electronic Music: A Listener's Guide, 1973, rev. ed., 1975; Music: Ways of Listening, 1982; (with D. Godfrey) Music Since 1945: Issues, Materials, Literature, 1993. **Address:** Bowdoin College, 4500 College Sta., Brunswick, ME 04011-3338, U.S.A. **Online address:** elliott@schwartzmusic.com

SCHWARTZ, Evan I. American (born United States) **Genres:** Business/Trade/Industry, Biography, Philosophy, Literary Criticism And History. **Career:** Business Week, editor. Journalist. **Publications:** Webonomics: Nine Essential Principles for Growing Your Business on the World Wide Web, 1997; Digital Darwinism: 7 Breakthrough Business Strategies for Surviving in the Cutthroat Web Economy, 1999; The Last Lone Inventor: A Tale of Genius, Deceit and the Birth of Television, 2002; Juice: The Creative Fuel that Drives Today's World-Class Inventors, 2004; Finding Oz: How L. Frank Baum Discovered the Great American Story, 2009. Contributor to periodicals. **Address:** c/o Author Mail, HarperCollins, 1350 Ave. of the Americas, New York, NY 10019, U.S.A.

SCHWARTZ, Gary (David). Dutch/American (born United States), b. 1940. **Genres:** Art/Art History, Novels. **Career:** Freelance translator, 1966-86; Meulenhoff Intl., editor, 1967-70; Rijksbureau voor Kunsthistorische Documentatie, staff, 1968-70; Collectors Editions, outside editor, 1970-72; Junius Press, partner, 1971-75; Uitgeverij Gary Schwartz, founder and operator, 1971-88; Menil Foundation, Image of the Black in Western Art, consultant, 1985-86; SDU (former Dutch Government Publishing Office), publisher, 1988-92; University of California, Regents Lecturer, 1989-90; Harvard University, Leventritt Lecturer, 1989-90; CODART International Council of Curators of Dutch and Flemish Art, director, 1998-2005, webmaster, 2005-09; Netherlands Institute for Advanced Study in the Humanities and Social Sciences, fellow-in-residence, 2009-10. **Publications:** Rembrandt: All the Etchings Reproduced in True Size, 1977; Rembrandt, zijn leven, zijn schilderijen: een nieuwe biografie, 1984, trans. as Rembrandt: His Life, His Paintings: A New Biography with All Accessible Paintings Illustrated in Colour, 1985; The Dutch World of Painting: Vancouver Art Gallery, April 6-June 29, 1986, 1986; (with M.J. Bok) Pieter Saenredam: de schilder in zijn tijd, 1989, trans. as Pieter Saenredam: The Painter and His Time, 1989; Rembrandt: His Life, His Paintings, 1991; Rembrandt: First Impressions, 1992, rev. ed., 2009; Dutch Kills (novel), 1994; Bets and Scams: A Novel of the Art World, 1996; Hieronymus Bosch: First Impressions, 1997; The Night Watch, 2002; The Rembrandt Book, 2006. EDITOR: Rembrandt Paintings, 1968; (and trans.) J.B. de la Faille, The Works of Vincent van Gogh, 1970; Complete Etchings of Rembrandt: Reproduced in Original Size, 1994; Jacob van Campen: het klassieke ideaal in de Gouden Eeuw, 1995. Contributor to periodicals. **Address:** Herengracht 22, Maarssen, 3601AM, Netherlands. **Online address:** gary.schwartz@xs4all.nl

SCHWARTZ, Gary E. American (born United States), b. 1944. **Genres:** Medicine/Health, Psychology, Adult Non-fiction. **Career:** Harvard University, assistant professor of psychology, 1971-75; University of British Columbia, visiting associate professor of psychology, 1975-76; Yale University, School of Medicine, assistant professor of psychiatry, 1976-79, associate professor, professor of psychology and psychiatry, 1980-87, Yale Psychophysiology Center, director, 1976-88, Yale Behavioral Medicine Clinic, co-director, 1976-88; University of California, Medical School, visiting associate professor of psychiatry, 1976; University of Arizona, Human Energy Systems Laboratory, Psychology, Medicine, Neurology, Psychiatry and Surgery, professor and director, 1988-, Department of Psychology, Human Energy Systems Laboratory, VERITAS Research Program, director. Writer. **Publications:** (With S.M. Weiss) Proceedings of the Yale Conference on Behavioral Medicine, February 4-6, 1977, 1977; (with L.G.S. Russek) The Living Energy Universe: A Fundamental Discovery That Transforms Science and Medicine, 1999; (with S. Smith and L.G.S. Russek) The Afterlife Codes: Searching for Evidence of the Survival of the Soul, 2000; (with W.L. Simon) The Afterlife Experiments: Breakthrough Scientific Evidence of Life after Death, 2002; (with W.L. Simon) Truth about Medium: Extraordinary Experiments with the Real Allison DuBois of NBC's Medium and Other Remarkable Psychics, 2005; (with W.L. Simon) G.O.D. Experiments: How Science is Discovering God in Everything, Including Us, 2006; (with W.L. Simon) The Energy Healing Experiments: Science Reveals Our Natural Power to Heal, 2007; Sacred Promise: How Science is Discovering Spirit's Collaboration with Us in Our Daily Lives, 2011; (foreword) Love Eternal, 2011. EDITOR: (with D. Shapiro) Consciousness and Self-Regulation: Advances in Research, vol. I, 1976; (with J. Beatty) Biofeedback, Theory and Research, 1977; (with L. White and B. Tursky) Placebo: Theory, Research and Mechanisms, 1985. **Address:** Department of Psychology, University of Arizona, Rm. 324, 1503 E University Blvd., PO Box 210068, Tucson, AZ 85721, U.S.A. **Online address:** gschwart@u.arizona.edu

SCHWARTZ, Jeffrey H. American (born United States), b. 1948. **Genres:** Zoology, Animals/Pets, Sciences. **Career:** University of Pittsburgh, professor of anthropology, history and philosophy of science; American Museum of Natural History, Department of Anthropology, research associate; Carnegie Museum of Natural History, Department of Vertebrate Paleontology, research associate; World Academy of Art and Science, president, 2007-; writer. **Publications:** (With I. Tattersall) Craniodental Morphology and the Systematics of the Malagasy Lemurs (Primates Prosimii), 1974; (with L. Krishtalka) The Lower Antemolar Teeth of Litolestes Ignotus a Late Paleocene Erinaceid (Mammalia Insectivora), 1976; (with I. Tattersall) The Phylogenetic Relationships of Adapidae (Primates Lemuriformes), 1979; (with I. Tattersall) A Revision of the European Eocene Primate Genus Protoadapis and Some Allied Forms, 1983; The Red Ape: Orang-utans and Human Origins, 1987, rev. ed., 2005; (ed.) Orang-utan Biology, 1988; What the Bones Tell Us, 1993; (co-author) A Diverse Hominoid Fauna from the Late Middle Pleistocene Breccia Cave of Tham Khuyen Socialist Republic of Vietnam, 1994; Skeleton Keys: An Introduction to Human Skeletal Morphology Development and Analysis, 1995, 2nd ed., 2007; Sudden Origins: Fossils Genes and the Emergence of Species, 1999; (with I. Tattersall) Extinct Humans, 2000; The Human Fossil Record, 2001. **Address:** Department of Anthropology, University of Pittsburgh, 3134 WWPH, Pittsburgh, PA 15213, U.S.A. **Online address:** jhs@pitt.edu

SCHWARTZ, Joan. American (born United States), b. 1938. **Genres:** Food And Wine, Cultural/Ethnic Topics. **Career:** University of Chicago Press, editorial assistant, 1961; Columbia University Press, assistant editor, 1961-62; Macmillan, assistant editor, 1962-63; Free Press, assistant editor, 1963-66; freelance editor, 1966-83. **Publications:** (With M. London) The Mitchel London's Gracie Mansion Cookbook, 1989; (with D. Liederman) David's Delicious Weight-Loss Program: Conquering Compulsive Eating & Lowering Cholesterol, 1990, rev. ed. as David's Lose Weight Permanently, Reduce Your Cholesterol, and Still Eat 97 Percent of the Food You Love Diet, 1991; (with M.U. Randelman) Memories of a Cuban Kitchen, 1992; (with A. Bouterin) Cooking Provence: Four Generations of Traditions and Recipes, 1994; (with B. Flay) Bobby Flay's Bold American Food: More than 200 Revolutionary Recipes, 1994; (with D. Ponzek) French Food, American Accent: Debra Ponzek's Spirited Cuisine, 1996; (with B. Flay) From My Kitchen to Your Table, 1998; (with B. Flay) Bobby Flay's Boy Meets Grill: With More Than 125 Bold New Recipes, 1999; (with J. Patraker) The Greenmarket Cookbook: Recipes, Tips and Lore from the World Famous Urban Farmer's Market, 2000; Macaroni and Cheese: 52 Recipes from Simple to Sublime, 2001; (with M. Kenney) Matthew Kenney's Big City Cooking: Recipes for a Fast-Paced World, 2003; Meat and Potatoes: 52 Recipes, from Simple to Sublime, 2003; The Comfort Food Cookbook: Macaroni & Cheese, Meat & Potatoes: 104 Recipes, from Simple to Sublime, 2006. **Address:** Dystel & Goderich Literary Management, 1 Union Sq. W, Ste. 904, New York, NY 10003, U.S.A.

SCHWARTZ, John Burnham. American (born United States), b. 1965. **Genres:** Novels. **Career:** Harvard University, faculty; University of Iowa, Writers' Workshop, faculty; Sarah Lawrence College, faculty. Writer. **Publications:** NOVELS: Bicycle Days, 1989; Reservation Road, 1998; Claire Marvel, 2002; The Commoner, 2008; Northwest Corner, 2011. Contributor to periodicals. **Address:** c/o Amanda Urban, International Creative Management, 825 8th Ave., New York, NY 10019-7416, U.S.A. **Online address:** jbs@johnburnhamschwartz.com

SCHWARTZ, Joyce R. American (born United States), b. 1950. **Genres:** Adult Non-fiction, Autobiography/Memoirs, Politics/Government, History. **Career:** University of Michigan, laboratory assistant in physiology, 1972-73; National Museum of Natural History, docent, 1976-; Murch Elementary School, science lab instructor, 1982-84; Calvert Marine Museum, intern, 1983; Somerset Elementary School, science lab aide, 1986-87; Sidwell Friends Middle School, substitute science teacher, 1989-; I Have a Dream Foundation, science teacher, 1989; Business Enterprise, mathematics instructor, 1992. Writer. **Publications:** WITH E.R. BUTTS: May Chinn: The Best Medicine, 1995; Eugenie Clark: Adventures of a Shark Scientist, 2000; Carl Sagan, 2001; Fidel Castro, 2005. Contributor to journals and periodicals. **Address:** 106 Hesketh St., Chevy Chase, MD 20815-4223, U.S.A. **Online address:** jr.schwartz@verizon.net

SCHWARTZ, Kessel. American (born United States), b. 1920. **Genres:** Literary Criticism And History, History. **Career:** University of Missouri, assistant instructor, 1940-42; Hofstra University, instructor in Spanish, 1949-50; State Department, director of cultural centers, 1946-48; Hamilton College, instructor, 1950-51; Colby College, instructor, 1951-53; University of Vermont, assistant professor, 1953-57; University of Arkansas, professor and chairman, 1957-62; University of Miami, Department of Foreign Languages, professor, 1962-90, chairman, 1962-64, 1973-83, director of graduate studies, 1964-65, 1983-90, now professor of modern languages emeritus; Hispania, associate editor, 1965-84; University of North Carolina, visiting professor, 1966-67. **Publications:** The Contemporary Novel of Ecuador, 1953; (with J. Chaplin) Los Hermanos Penitentes, 1958; (with R. Chandler) A New History of Spanish Literature, 1961, rev. ed., 1991; (intro.) Fiestas, 1964; (with R.E. Chandler) A New Anthology of Spanish Literature, 2 vols., 1967; Introduction to Modern Spanish Literature: An Anthology of Fiction, Poetry and Essay, 1968; Vicente Aleixandre, 1970; The Meaning of Existence in Contemporary Hispanic Literature, 1970; Juan Goytisolo, 1970; A New History of Spanish American Fiction, 2 vols., 1972; Studies on Twentieth-Century Spanish and Spanish-American Literature, 1983. Contributor to periodicals. **Address:** Department of Foreign Languages, University of Miami, Coral Gables, FL 33124, U.S.A.

SCHWARTZ, Lynne Sharon. American (born United States), b. 1939. **Genres:** Novels, Novellas/Short Stories, Poetry, Essays, Humor/Satire, Translations. **Career:** City University of New York, Hunter College, lecturer, 1970-75; University of Iowa Writers' Workshop, visiting lecturer, 1982-83; Washington University, visiting writer-in-residence, 1996-98; Bennington College, faculty, 2002-. Writer. **Publications:** NOVELS: Rough Strife, 1980; Balancing Acts, 1981; Disturbances in the Field, 1983; The Accounting, 1983; Leaving Brooklyn, 1989; The Fatigue Artist, 1995; In the Family Way: An Urban Comedy, 1999; The Writing on the Wall, 2005; Not Now, Voyager, 2009. STORIES: Acquainted with the Night and Other Stories, 1984; The Melting Pot and Other Subversive Stories, 1987; A Lynne Sharon Schwartz Reader: Selected Prose and Poetry, 1992; Referred Pain and Other Stories, 2004. OTHER: We Are Talking about Homes: A Great University Against Its Neighbors, 1985; The Four Questions, 1989; (trans.) L. Millu, Smoke over Birkenau, 1993; Ruined by Reading: A Life in Books, 1996; Only Connect (essays), 1999; Face to Face: A Reader in the World, 2000; (trans.) Natalia Ginzburg, Essays. English. Selections (title means: 'A Place to Live: Selected Essays of Natalia Ginzburg'), 2002; In Solitary (poems), 2002; (trans.) Silvana Gandolfi, ldabra, la tartaruga che amava Shakespeare English (title means: 'Aldabra, or, The Tortoise Who Loved Shakespeare'), 2004; (ed.) The Emergence of Memory: Conversations with W.G. Sebald, 2007; See You in the Dark, 2011. **Address:** c/o Sterling Lord Literistic Inc., 65 Bleecker St., New York, NY 10012, U.S.A. **Online address:** lynne@lynnesharonschwartz.com

SCHWARTZ, Marie Jenkins. American (born United States), b. 1946. **Genres:** History. **Career:** University of Rhode Island, assistant professor of history, 1995-2000, associate professor, 2000-05, professor, 2005-, chair, Center for the Humanities, executive director, 2000-07, affiliated faculty in African-American studies; Brown University, John Nicholas Brown Center for the Study of American Civilization, fellow, 1998. Writer. **Publications:** Born in Bondage: Growing Up Enslaved in the Antebellum South, 2000; Birthing a Slave: Motherhood and Medicine in the Antebellum South, 2006; Slaves in the First Families: The Washingtons, Jeffersons, and Madisons, forthcoming. Contributor to books and periodicals. **Address:** Department of History, University of Rhode Island, 207 Tucker House, 80 Upper College Rd., Ste. 3, Kingston, RI 02881, U.S.A. **Online address:** schwartz@uri.edu

SCHWARTZ, Mel. American (born United States), b. 1950. **Genres:** Sex, Social Sciences. **Career:** Writer, psychotherapist, educator and speaker. **Publications:** The Art of Intimacy, the Pleasure of Passion: A Journey into Soulful Relationships, 1999; A Shift of Mind: Reframing the Way We Think, forthcoming. **Address:** 177 Post Rd. W, Westport, CT 06880, U.S.A. **Online address:** mel@melschwartz.com

SCHWARTZ, Richard A(lan). American (born United States), b. 1951. **Genres:** Film, History, Politics/Government, Reference, Novels, Literary Criticism And History. **Career:** Indiana University Northwest, adjunct professor, 1975-77; University of Miami, adjunct professor, 1977-78; New England Telephone Co., computer programmer, 1978-79; Florida International University, adjunct instructor, 1978, Department of English, assistant professor, 1979-85, associate professor, 1985-98, professor, 1998-2009, director of graduate studies in literature, 2008-09, Institute for Public Policy, associate director 1989-90, Honors College, fellow, 1997-2002, director of film certificate program, 2000-09, professor emeritus, 2010; University of Palermo, lecturer, 1985-86. Writer. **Publications:** The Cold War Reference Guide: A General History and Annotated Chronology with Selected Biographies, 1997; Cold War Culture: Media and the Arts, 1945-1990, 1997; Encyclopedia of the Persian Gulf War, 1998; Woody: From Antz to Zelig: A Reference Guide to Woody Allen's Creative Work, 1964-1998, 2000; The Films of Ridley Scott, 2001; The 1950s, 2002; 1990s, 2006; The Conflicted Liberal, a Novel, 2006. Contributor of articles to periodicals. **Address:** 8030 SW 97 St., Miami, FL 33156, U.S.A. **Online address:** ras1951@bellsouth.net

SCHWARTZ, Samuel M. American/Canadian (born Canada), b. 1929. **Genres:** How-to Books, Medicine/Health. **Career:** George Washington University, associate professor of medicinal chemistry, 1956-64; National Institutes of Health, National Cancer Institute, research grants program officer, 1964, Division of Research Grants, Medicinal Chemistry Study Section, executive secretary, 1964-68, Referral Office, assignment officer, chief, 1968-71, National Eye Institute, associate director, Scientific Programs Branch, chief, 1971-73, National Heart, Lung and Blood Institute, Scientific Review, associate director, 1972-78, Division of Research Grants, associate director, 1978-83, National Institute of Arthritis, Diabetes, Digestive and Kidney Diseases and the Division of Research Grants, special assistant to the director, 1983-88; Professional and Scientific Associates, scientific director, 1988-91; Peer Review Associates Inc., scientific director and president, 1991-; NIH study section, executive secretary. Writer and consultant. **Publications:** (With M.E. Friedman) A Guide to NIH Grant Programs, 1992. **Address:** Peer Review Associates Inc., 4620 N Park Ave., Ste. 708E, Chevy Chase, MD 20815-4557, U.S.A. **Online address:** smssam@aol.com

SCHWARTZ, Sanford. American (born United States), b. 1948. **Genres:** Theology/Religion. **Career:** Pennsylvania State University, associate professor of English. Writer. **Publications:** The Matrix of Modernism: Pound, Eliot and Early Twentieth-Century Thought, 1985; C.S. Lewis on the Final Frontier: Science and the Supernatural in the Space Trilogy, 2009. **Address:** Department of English, Pennsylvania State University, 24 Burrowes Bldg., University Park, PA 16802, U.S.A. **Online address:** sxs8@psu.edu

SCHWARTZ, Sheila R. (Sheila (Ruth) Schwartz). American (born United

States), b. 1929. **Genres:** Novels, Education, Young Adult Non-fiction, Documentaries/Reportage, Human Relations/Parenting. **Career:** Hofstra University, lecturer, 1958-60; City College of New York, instructor, 1962-63; State University College, professor, 1963-, now professor emeritus. Writer. **Publications:** (With G.H. Reuben) How People Lived in Ancient Greece and Rome, 1967; (with N.L. Schwartz) How People Live in Mexico, 1969; Teaching the Humanities: Selected Readings, 1970; Earth in Transit, 1977; Like Mother, Like Me, 1978; Growing Up Guilty, 1978; Teaching Adolescent Literature: A Humanistic Approach, 1978; The Solid Gold Circle, 1980; The Hollywood Writers' Wars, 1982; One Day You'll Go, 1982; Jealousy, 1982; Sorority, 1987; Bigger is Better, 1987; The Most Popular Girl, 1988; The Little Terrorist, 2001. Contributor to periodicals. **Address:** 15 W 72nd St., Apt. 5J, New York, NY 10023-3424, U.S.A. **Online address:** sheila@sheilaschwartz.com

SCHWARTZ, Sheila (Ruth). *See* **SCHWARTZ, Sheila R.**

SCHWARTZ, Shuly Rubin. American (born United States), b. 1953?. **Genres:** Theology/Religion. **Career:** Jewish Theological Seminary, Irving Lehrman research associate professor of American Jewish history, 1993-, Albert A. List College of Jewish Studies, dean, 1993-. Writer and historian. **Publications:** The Emergence of Jewish Scholarship in America: The Publication of the Jewish Encyclopedia, 1991; The Rabbi's Wife: The Rebbetzin in American Jewish Life, 2006. **Address:** U.S.A. **Online address:** shschwartz@jtsa.edu

SCHWARTZ, Stephen (Alfred). (S. Solsona). American (born United States), b. 1948. **Genres:** History, Politics/Government, International Relations/Current Affairs, Travel/Exploration. **Career:** City of San Francisco Magazine, staff writer, 1975; ReSearch Publications, staff writer, 1977-81; The Alarm, editor, 1980-83; Pacific Shipper Weekly, senior editor, 1981-84; Sailors Union of the Pacific, historian, 1983-86; Institute for Contemporary Studies, senior editor and fellow, 1984-89; U.S. Institute of Peace, research associate, 1988; San Francisco Chronicle, staff writer and editor, 1989-99. **Publications:** (Trans.) Antinarcissus, 1969; Hidden Locks, 1972; A Sleepwalker's Guide to San Francisco, 1983; Brotherhood of the Sea: A History of the Sailors' Union of the Pacific, 1885-1985, 1986; (ed.) The Transition from Authoritarianism to Democracy in the Hispanic World, 1986; (with V. Alba) Spanish Marxism versus Soviet Communism: A History of the P.O.U.M., 1988; Heaven's Descent, 1990; A Strange Silence: The Emergence of Democracy in Nicaragua, 1992; Incidentes de la Vida de Benjamin Peret con Anotaciones Sobre el Comunismo de G. Munis, 1994; From West to East: California and the Making of the American Mind, 1998; Intellectuals and Assassins: Writings at the End of Soviet Communism, 2000; Kosovo: Background to a War, 2000; Nepoštena komedija 20 stoljeća: A Dishonest 20th Century Comedy, 2000; Two Faces of Islam: The House of Sa'ud from Tradition to Terror, 2002; Sarajevo Rose: A Balkan Jewish Notebook, 2005; Is It Good for the Jews?: The Crisis of America's Israel Lobby, 2006; Other Islam: Sufism and the Road to Global Harmony, 2008; Islami tjetër: sufizmi dhe rrëfimi për respektin, 2009; (with V. Alba) Spanish Marxism Versus Soviet Communism: A History of the P.O.U.M. in the Spanish Civil War, 2009; AS S. SOLSONA: Incidents from the Life of Benjamin Peret, 1981. Contributor to books and periodicals. **Address:** San Francisco Chronicle, 901 Mission St., San Francisco, CA 94103, U.S.A.

SCHWARTZ, Sunny. American (born United States), b. 1954. **Genres:** Law, Social Sciences. **Career:** San Francisco Sheriff's Department, legal counsel to the sheriff and law intern, 1980-87, program administrator, 1990-. Writer. **Publications:** (With D. Boodell) Dreams from the Monster Factory: A Tale of Prison, Redemption and One Woman's Fight to Restore Justice to All, 2009. **Address:** c/o Priscilla Gilman, Janklow and Nesbit, 445 Park Ave., New York, NY 10022, U.S.A. **Online address:** sunny@sunnyschwartz.com

SCHWARTZ, Virginia Frances. Canadian (born Canada), b. 1950. **Genres:** Young Adult Fiction. **Career:** Nurse, 1975-88; elementary school teacher, 1988-. **Publications:** YOUNG ADULT HISTORICAL FICTION: Send One Angel Down, 2000; If I Just Had Two Wings, 2001; Messenger, 2002; Initiation, 2003; Der Weg nach Norden, 2003; 4 Kids in 5E & 1 Crazy Year, 2006; Crossing to Freedom, 2010. **Address:** c/o Author Mail, Holiday House Inc., 425 Madison Ave., New York, NY 10017, U.S.A. **Online address:** virginiafschwartz@yahoo.com

SCHWARTZ-NOBEL, Loretta. American (born United States) **Genres:** Adult Non-fiction, Social Sciences. **Career:** Journalist. **Publications:** Starving in the Shadow of Plenty, 1981; Engaged to Murder: The Inside Story of the Main Line Murders, 1987; (with M.B. Whitehead) A Mother's Story: The Truth About the Baby M Case, 1989; The Baby Swap Conspiracy: The Shocking Truth Behind the Florida Case of Two Babies Switched at Birth, 1993; Forsaking All Others: The Real Betty Broderick Story: Including Prison Interviews, 1993; The Journey, 2001; Growing Up Empty: The Hunger Epidemic in America, 2002; Growing Up Empty: How Federal Policies Are Starving America's Children, 2003; Poisoned Nation: Pollution, Greed, and The Rise Of Deadly Epidemics, 2007. **Address:** c/o Author Mail, HarperCollins Publishers, 10 E 53rd St., New York, NY 10022, U.S.A. **Online address:** askloretta@lorettaschwartznobel.com

SCHWARZ, Adam. Singaporean/American (born United States), b. 1961. **Genres:** Area Studies, Politics/Government, Biography, Autobiography/Memoirs. **Career:** Banco Roberts, Investment Banking Division, analyst, 1983-85; Columbia Journal of World Business, managing editor, 1985-87; Jakarta Post, journalist, 1987-88; freelance journalist, 1988-89; Far Eastern Economic Review, correspondent, 1989-92, assistant editor, 1993-94, correspondent, 1994, bureau chief, 1995-96; Murdoch University, Asia Research Centre, visiting fellow, 1992-93; McKinsey Global Institute, staff, 2001-, director of communications, Mckinsey Global Institute, senior fellow. **Publications:** A Nation in Waiting: Indonesia in the 1990s, 1994, 2nd ed., 2000; (co-ed.) Politics of Post-Suharto Indonesia, 1999; Indonesia: The 2004 Election and Beyond, 2004. Contributor to periodicals. **Address:** McKinsey Global Institute, 3 Temasek Ave., 18/F Centennial Twr., Singapore, 039190, Singapore. **Online address:** adam_schwarz@mckinsey.com

SCHWARZ, Arturo (Samuele). Italian/Egyptian (born Egypt), b. 1924. **Genres:** Art/Art History, Poetry, Essays. **Career:** Culture (bookshop), owner and manager, 1946-48; Gallery Schwarz (publishing house, bookshop, and gallery), owner and manager, 1952-75; essayist, poet, art historian and curator, 1960-. **Publications:** Avant Que le Coq ne Chante, 1951; Il Reale Assoluto, 1964; (with W. Hopps and U. Linde) Marcel Duchamp, 1964; The Large Glass and Related Works, 1967; (intro.) Notes and projects for the Large Glass, 1969; (ed.) The Complete Works of Marcel Duchamp, 1969, rev. ed., 1997; Man Ray, 60 anni di libertà, 60 ans de libertés, 60 years of liberties, 1971; Marcel Duchamp: 66 Creative Years, 1972; New York Dada: Duchamp, Man Ray, Picabia, 1973; Almanacco Dada: Antologia Letteraria-Artistica, 1976; Man Ray: The Rigour of Imagination, 1977; André Breton, Trotsky et L'Anarchie, 1977; Pieces of Dreams, 1977; L'Immaginazione Alchemica, 1980; L'Arte dell'Amore in India e in Nepal: La Dimensione Alchemica del Mito di Siva, 1980; Anarchia e Creatività, 1981; Il culto della donnanella tradizione Indiana, 1983; Introduzione all'alchimia Indiana, 1984; Claudio Parmiggiani, 1985; Arte e Alchimia, 1986; If I Forget Thee (poems), 1994; La luce dell'amore, 1994; Marsel Dushan, 1994; Canuti, 1996; L'avventura surrealista: Amore e rivoluzione, anche, 1997; Fabio De Sanctis: La Memoria del Viaggio, trans. as Fabio De Sanctis: The Memory of the Journey, 1997; Cabbalà e Alchimia: Saggiosugli Archetipi comuni, 1999, trans. as Kabbalah and Alchemy: An Essay on Common Archetypes, 2000; ha-Hedpes veha-shir, 2000; Dreaming with Open Eyes: The Vera, Silvia and Arturo Schwarz Collection of Dada and Surrealist Art, 2000; Love at First Sight: The Vera, Silvia and Arturo Schwarz Collection of Israeli Art, 2001; (ed.) Chi non ha interesse a far la pace in Israele?, 2001; Enzo Cucchi: Un Opera Senza Fine in Divenire, 2001; Konrad Klaphech Ovvero la Dimensione Sapienziale Della Pricisione, 2002; (ed.) Max Ernst e i suoi amici surrealisti, 2002; Mordekhai Ardon: tsiv e ha-zeman, 2003; Mordecai Ardon: The Colors of Time, 2003; Scultura Italiana 1960-2004, 2004; Tatslume deyoḳna'ot, 2005; (ed.) Marcel Duchamp: una collezione italiana, 2006; Marcel Duchamp: An Italian Israele: Arte Contemporanea, 2007; Israele, 2007; Alik Cavaliere: poeta, filosofo, umanista e scultore, anche (quasi una biografia), 2008; Donna e l'amore Al Tempo dei Miti: la Valenza Iniziatica ed Erotica del femminile, 2009; (ed.) Dada e surrealismo riscoperti, 2009; Sam Havadtoi, 2010; Una poesia per ogni giorno della settimana di Linda, 2011. **Address:** Via M Giuriati 17, Milan, 20129, Italy.

SCHWARZ, Daniel R(oger). American (born United States), b. 1941. **Genres:** Poetry, Humanities, Literary Criticism And History, Cultural/Ethnic Topics, History, Intellectual History. **Career:** Cornell University, assistant professor, 1968-74, associate professor, 1974-80, professor of English, 1980-, director of undergraduate study in English, 1976-80, Stephe H. Weiss presidential fellow, 1999-, Frederic J. Whiton professor of English literature, 2007-; University of Arkansas, Cooper professor, 1988; University of Hawaii, citizen's chair in literature, 1992-93. Writer. **Publications:** Disraeli's Fiction,

1979; Conrad, Almayer's Folly to Under Western Eyes, 1980; Conrad's Fiction, 1980; Conrad: The Later Fiction, 1982; Humanistic Heritage: Critical Theories of the English Novel from James to Hillis Miller, 1986; Reading Joyce's Ulysses, 1987; The Transformation of the English Novel, 1890-1930, 1989, rev. ed., 1995; The Case for a Humanistic Poetics, 1991; Narrative and Representation in Wallace Stevens, 1993; Reconfiguring Modernism: Explorations in the Relationship between Modern Art and Modern Literature, 1997; Reconfiguring Modernism, 1997; Secret Sharer, 1997; Imagining the Holocaust, 1999; Rereading Conrad, 2001; Broadway Boogie Woogie: Damon Runyon and the Making of New York City Culture, 2003; Reading the Modern British and Irish Novel, 1890-1930, 2005; In Defense of Reading: Teaching Literature in the Twenty-First Century, 2008; Endtimes?: Crisis and Turmoil at New York Times, 1999-2009, 2011. EDITOR: James Joyce's The Dead: A Case Study in Contemporary Criticism, 1993; Dead: Complete, Authoritative Text with Biographical and Historical Contexts, Critical History, and Essays from Five Contemporary Critical Perspectives, 1994; (with J. Carlisle) Narrative and Culture, 1994; Joseph Conrad's The Secret Sharer: A Case Study in Contemporary Criticism, 1997; Disraeli's Early Novels, 6 vols., 2004; Guys and Dolls and other Writings, 2008. **Address:** Department of English, Cornell University, 242 Goldwin Smith Hall, Ithaca, NY 14853, U.S.A. **Online address:** drs6@cornell.edu

SCHWARZ, Frederick A. O. American (born United States), b. 1935. **Genres:** Biography, Autobiography/Memoirs, History, Politics/Government. **Career:** Harvard University, Law Review, editor; Government of Nigeria, assistant commissioner for law revision; Cravath, Swaine & Moore LLP, litigation partner, 1969-75, 1976-82, 1986-2003; New York City Government, corporation counsel, 1982-86; New York City Revision Commission, chair, 1989; New York University, School of Law, Brennan Center for Justice, chief counsel, 2002-; New York City Campaign Finance Board, chairman, 2003-08; Commission on Safety and Abuse in America's Prisons, commissioner; Vera Institute of Justice, chairman; Natural Resources Defense Council, chairman. **Publications:** (With H.H. Marshall) The Laws of Northern Nigeria: In Force on the 1st Day of October, 1963, rev. ed., 1965; Nigeria: The Tribes, the Nation, or the Race: The Politics of Independence, 1965; (with A.Z. Huq) Unchecked and Unbalanced: Presidential Power in a Time of Terror, 2007. **Address:** Brennan Center for Justice, School of Law, New York University, 161 6th Ave., 12th Fl., New York, NY 10013, U.S.A. **Online address:** fschwarz@cravath.com

SCHWARZ, Henry G. American (born United States), b. 1928. **Genres:** History, Politics/Government, Language/Linguistics, Local History/Rural Topics, Adult Non-fiction. **Career:** University of the Philippines, Fulbright professor, 1964-65; University of Washington, Far Eastern Institute, assistant professor, 1965-69; Western Washington University, Center for East Asian Studies, professor, 1969-94, Studies on East Asia, editor, 1971-, professor emeritus, 1994-. Writer. **Publications:** Leadership Patterns in China's Frontier Regions, 1964; China: Three Facets of a Giant, 1966; The Great Proletarian Cultural Revolution, 1966; Liu Shao-ch'i and People's War: A Report on the Creation of Base Areas in 1938, 1969; (contrib.) Understanding Modern China, 1969; Chinese Policies Towards Minorities: An Essay and Document, 1971; Mongolian Short Stories, 1974; Bibliotheca Mongolica, 1978; (ed.) Studies on Mongolia: Proceedings of the First North American Conference on Mongolian Studies, Center for East Asian Studies, 1979; (ed.) Reminiscences, 1983; The Minorities of Northern China: A Survey, 1984; (ed.) Chinese Medicine on the Golden Mountain: An Interpretive Guide, 1984; Mongolian Publications at Western Washington University, 1984; An Uyghur-English Dictionary, 1992; Mongolia and the Mongols: Holdings at Western Washington University, 1992; (contrib.) Opuscula Altaica: Essays Presented in Honor of Henry Schwarz, 1994; (contrib.) Essays on Mongolia, China and Japan: Politics, Economics and Lessons of Development, 1996; Mongolia and the World, 2000; (co-author) Mongolian Historical Writings From 1200 to 1700, 2nd ed., 2002; (ed.) Mongolian Culture and Society in the Age of Globalization, 2006. **Address:** Center for East Asian Studies, Western Washington University, 516 High St., Bellingham, WA 98225-9057, U.S.A. **Online address:** schwarz@cc.wwu.edu

SCHWARZ, Jan. Danish (born Denmark), b. 1954?. **Genres:** Novels, Biography. **Career:** Royal Library, Department of Oriental and Judaic Studies, research librarian, 1990-91; University of Pennsylvania, German Department, lecturer, 1994-95; Gratz College, lecturer, 1997-98; University of Illinois, Department of Germanic Languages and Literatures, Sheldon Drobny assistant professor of Yiddish and Hebrew languages and literatures, 1998-2002; University of Chicago, visiting lecturer, 2003-04, lecturer, 2004- 06, senior lecturer, 2006-09; Northwestern University, adjunct lecturer, 2003-04, lecturer in Jewish studies and German, 2004-05; University of Miami, Sue and Leonard Miller Center for Contemporary Judaic Studies, research fellow, 2005-06. Writer. **Publications:** (Ed.) The Golden Chain: An Anthology of Yiddish Literature, 1993; (with R. Lillian) The Yiddish Teacher, 2005; Imagining Lives: Autobiographical Fiction of Yiddish Writers, 2005; The Last of a Great Generation: Yiddish Writing After The Holocaust, forthcoming. Contributor to books. **Address:** Department of Germanic Studies, University of Chicago, 511 Foster Hall, 1130 E 59th St., Chicago, IL 60637, U.S.A. **Online address:** schwarzj@uchicago.edu

SCHWARZ, John E. American (born United States), b. 1939?. **Genres:** Politics/Government, Adult Non-fiction. **Career:** University of Minnesota, political science faculty, 1966; University of Arizona, professor of political science, 1970-, chair of faculty, 1995-97, now professor emeritus; Demos, distinguished senior fellow. Writer and political scientist. **Publications:** (With L.E. Shaw) The United States Congress in Comparative Perspective, 1976; America's Hidden Success: A Reassessment of Twenty Years of Public Policy, 1983, as America's Hidden Success: A Reassessment of Public Policy from Kennedy to Reagan, 1988; (with T.J. Volgy) The Forgotten Americans, 1992; Illusions of Opportunity: The American Dream in Question, 1997; Freedom Reclaimed: Rediscovering the American Vision, 2005. Contributor to periodicals. **Address:** Department of Political Science, University of Arizona, Rm. 329, Social Sciences Bldg., PO Box 210027, Tucson, AZ 85721-0027, U.S.A. **Online address:** jes@email.arizona.edu

SCHWARZ, Philip J. American (born United States), b. 1940. **Genres:** History. **Career:** Virginia Commonwealth University, professor of history, now professor emeritus. Writer. **Publications:** Jarring Interests: New York's Boundary Makers, 1664-1776, 1979; Twice Condemned: Slaves and the Criminal Laws of Virginia, 1988; Slave Laws in Virginia, 1996; Migrants against Slavery: Virginians and the Nation, 2001. **Address:** Department of History, Virginia Commonwealth University, 813 S Cathedral Pl., PO Box 842001, Richmond, VA 23284, U.S.A. **Online address:** pjschwar@vcu.edu

SCHWARZ, Robin. American (born United States) **Genres:** Novels. **Career:** J. Walter Thompson-New York, creative director/writer and senior vice president, 1981-95; J. Walter Thompson-Paris, creative director, 1995-96; The Kaplan Thaler Group, creative director/writer, 1997-2008. **Publications:** Night Swimming, 2004. **Address:** c/o Author Mail, Warner Books, 1271 Ave. of the Americas, New York, NY 10020, U.S.A. **Online address:** blueskies7772003@yahoo.com

SCHWARZBEIN, Diana. American (born United States), b. 1960?. **Genres:** How-to Books, Medicine/Health, Military/Defense/Arms Control, Food And Wine. **Career:** Schwarzbein Principle Institute, founder and physician, 1993-. Health expert and writer. **Publications:** (With N. Deville and E.J. Jaffe) The Schwarzbein Principle Vegetarian Cookbook, 1999; (with N. Deville) The Schwarzbein Principle: The Truth about Losing Weight Being Healthy and Feeling Younger, 1999; (with N. Deville and E.J. Jaffe) The Schwarzbein Principle Cookbook, 1999; (with M. Brown) The Schwarzbein Principle II: The Transition: A Regeneration Process to Prevent and Reverse Accelerated Aging, 2002; The Schwarzbein Principle: The Program: Losing Weight the Healthy Way: An Easy Five-step No-nonsense Approach, 2004. Contributor to periodicals. **Address:** The Schwarzbein Institute, 350 S Hope Ave., Bldg. A, Ste. 102, Santa Barbara, CA 93105, U.S.A.

SCHWEBER, Howard. American (born United States), b. 1961. **Genres:** Business/Trade/Industry, Money/Finance. **Career:** University of Wisconsin, associate professor of political science, legal studies and law, 1999-, Wisconsin Center for the Study of Liberal Democracy, board director. Writer. **Publications:** Speech, Conduct & the First Amendment, 2003; The Creation of American Common Law, 1850-1880: Technology, Politics and the Construction of Citizenship, 2004; The Language of Liberal Constitutionalism, 2007. Contributor to books and periodicals. **Address:** Department of Political Science, University of Wisconsin, 1050 Bascom Mall, 110 North Hall, Madison, WI 53706, U.S.A. **Online address:** schweber@polisci.wisc.edu

SCHWEDLER, Jillian. American (born United States), b. 1966. **Genres:** Popular Culture, Politics/Government. **Career:** University of Maryland, Department Of Government and Politics, assistant professor, 2000-; Middle East Research and Information Project, chair of the board of directors; Univer-

sity of Massachusetts, Department of Political Science, associate professor of political science; Arab Archives Institute, senior research fellow. Writer. **Publications:** (Ed.) Toward Civil Society in the Middle East? A Primer, 1995; (ed.) Islamist Movements in Jordan, 1997; (ed. with D.J. Gerner) Understanding the Contemporary Middle East, 2004, 3rd ed., 2008; Faith in Moderation: Islamist Parties in Jordan and Yemen, 2006; (ed. with L. Khalili) Policing and Prisons in The Middle East: Formations of Coercion, 2010. Contributor to journals. **Address:** Department of Government & Politics, University of Maryland, 3140 Tydings Hall, College Park, MD 20742-7215, U.S.A. **Online address:** jschwedler@gvpt.umd.edu

SCHWEGEL, Theresa. American (born United States), b. 1975. **Genres:** Novels, Mystery/Crime/Suspense. **Career:** Writer. **Publications:** Officer Down, 2005; Probable Cause, 2007; Person of Interest, 2007; Last Known Address, 2009; Some Beasts, forthcoming; The Interrupter, forthcoming. **Address:** Minotaur Books, 175 Fifth Ave., 18th Fl., New York, NY 10010-7703, U.S.A. **Online address:** theresa@theresaschwegel.com

SCHWEICKART, Patrocinio P. Filipino (born Philippines), b. 1942. **Genres:** Adult Non-fiction, Education, Literary Criticism And History, Women's Studies And Issues. **Career:** University of New Hampshire, assistant professor, 1979-85, associate professor, 1985, professor of English, 1985-98; NWSA Journal, editor, 1990-97; Purdue University, Department of English and Women's Studies, professor, 1998-. Writer. **Publications:** (Ed. with E.A. Flynn and contrib.) Gender and Reading: Essays on Readers, Texts, and Contexts, 1985; Reading Ourselves: Toward a Feminist Theory of Reading; Engendering Critical Discourse, 1987; Reading, Teaching, and the Ethic of Care, 1990; What Are We Doing? What Do We Want? Who Are We? Comprehending the Subject of Feminism, 1995; (ed. with E.A. Flynn) Reading Sites: Social Difference and Reader Response, 2004; (with E. Flynn) Reading Sites: Gender, Race, Class, Ethnicity, Sexual Orientation, forthcoming. Works appear in anthologies. **Address:** Department of English and Women's Studies, Purdue University, Heavilon 327C, West Lafayette, IN 47907, U.S.A. **Online address:** pschweic@purdue.edu

SCHWEIKART, Larry E. American (born United States), b. 1951. **Genres:** Money/Finance, History. **Career:** Arizona State University, research assistant, 1977-78; Brophy College Preparatory, history instructor, 1979-81; University of California, teaching assistant, 1981-82; University of Wisconsin, instructor, 1984-85; University of Dayton, assistant professor, 1985-88, associate professor, 1988-95, professor of U.S. History, 1995-. Writer. **Publications:** A History of Banking in Arizona, 1982; (with D.D. Dalgleish) Trident, 1984; (ed.) Banking in the West, 1984; That Quality Image: The History of Continental Bank, 1987; Banking in the American South from the Age of Jackson to Reconstruction, 1987; Banking and Finance to 1913, 1990; (ed.) Banking and Finance, 1913-1989, 1990; (with L.P. Doti) Banking in the American West: From the Gold Rush to Deregulation, 1991; (with L.P. Doti) California Bankers, 1848-1993, 1994; The Hypersonic Revolution: Case Studies in the History of Hypersonic Technology, 1998; The Entrepreneurial Adventure: A History of Business in the United States, 2000; (with B.J. Birzer) The American West, 2003; (with M. Allen) A Patriot's History of the United States: From Columbus's Great Discovery to the War on Terror, 2004; America's Victories: Why the U.S. Wins Wars and Will Win the War on Terror, 2006; 48 Liberal Lies about American History (That You Probably Learned in School), 2008; (with L.P. Doti) American Entrepreneur, 2009; Seven Svents that Made America America: And Proved that the Founding Fathers Were Right all Along, 2010; (comp. with D. Dougherty and M. Allen) Patriot's History Reader: Essential Documents for Every American, 2011; What Would the Founders Say?: A Patriot's Answers to America's Most Pressing Problems, 2011. Contributor to books, periodicals and journals. **Address:** Department of History, University of Dayton, 300 College Pk., Dayton, OH 45469-1450, U.S.A. **Online address:** schweikart@erinet.com

SCHWEIKART, Larry (Earl). American (born United States), b. 1951. **Genres:** Money/Finance, Ghost Writer, History, Military/Defense/Arms Control, Social Commentary, Music. **Career:** Arizona State University, research assistant, 1977-78; Brophy College Preparatory, history teacher, 1979-81, 1982-84; University of California, U.S. history, American business, teaching assistant, 1981-82; UCSB graduate fellow history, 1982-83; University of Wisconsin, U.S. History, Business History Center, instructor in history, 1984-85; University of Dayton, assistant professor, associate professor of history, 1985-95, professor of history, 1995-; Discover the Past Inc. (historical consultants), president, 1988-94. Writer. **Publications:** A History of Banking in Arizona, 1982; (with D.D. Dalgleish) Trident, 1984; Banking in the American South from the Age of Jackson to Reconstruction, 1987; That Quality Image: The History of Continental Bank, 1987; (with J.G. Sproat) Making Change: South Carolina Banking in the Twentieth Century, 1990; (with L.P. Doti) Banking in the American West from Gold Rush to Deregulation, 1991; (with Doti) California Bankers, 1991; Hypersonic Revolution: Case Studies in the History of Hypersonic Technology, 1998; The Quest for the Orbital Jet: The National Aerospace Plane, 1999; The Entrepreunerial Adventure: A History of Business in the United States, 1999; Marriage of Steel: The Life and Times of William and Peggy Verity, 2000; (with M. Allen) Patriot's History of the United States: From Columbus's Great Discovery to the War on Terror, 2004; America's Victories: Why the U.S. Wins Wars and Will Win the War on Terror, 2006; September Day, 2006; 48 Liberal Lies About American History, 2008; Halsey's Bluff, 2008; American Entrepreneur, 2009; Seven Events that Made America America, 2010; (comp. with D. Dougherty and M. Allen) Patriot's History Reader: Essential Documents for Every American, 2011; What Would the Founders Say?: A Patriot's Answers to America's Most Pressing Problems, 2011. EDITOR: Banking in the West: A Collection of Essays, 1984; Banking and Finance, to 1913, 1990; Banking and Finance, 1913-1989, 1990. **Address:** Department of History, University of Dayton, 300 College Pk., Dayton, OH 45469-1450, U.S.A. **Online address:** larry.schweikart@notes.udayton.edu

SCHWEIZER, Karl W. American/German (born Germany), b. 1946. **Genres:** Criminology/True Crime, History, International Relations/Current Affairs, Military/Defense/Arms Control, Adult Non-fiction, Law. **Career:** Bishop's University, professor of history, 1976-88; London School of Economics, academic visitor, 1986-87, 1994; Darwin College, visiting fellow, 1986-87, 1994, senior research associate, 2003; Rutgers University, New Jersey Institute of Technology, chairman of humanities, 1988-93, 2000-03, Division of Social Science, professor, 1993-, Center for Global Change, faculty, 1997-, Federated Department of History, professor, 2007-; Yale University, visiting professor, 1994-95; Princeton University, visiting professor, 1994; Cambridge University, visiting professor, 1994. Writer. **Publications:** (Coauthor) The Origins of War in Early Modern Europe, 1987; England, Prussia, and the Seven Years War: Studies in Alliance Policies and Diplomacy, 1989; (with J.W. Osborne) Cobbett in His Times, 1990; Frederick the Great, William Pitt, and Lord Bute: The Anglo-Prussian Alliance, 1756-1763, 1991; Lord Chatham, 1993; William Pitt, Earl of Chatham, 1708-1778: A Bibliography, 1993; Francois De Callières: Diplomat and Man of Letters, 1645-1717, 1995; War, Politics and Diplomacy: The Anglo-Prussian Alliance, 1756-1763, 2001; Seeds of Evil: The Gray-Snyder Murder Case, 2001; Politics, Diplomats and the Press, 2002; Statesmen, Diplomats, and the Press: Essays on 18th Century Britain, 2002; (with M. Schumann) Seven Years War: A Transatlantic History, 2008; (foreword) The Entrapment of the Poor into Involuntary Labor: Understanding the Worldwide Practice of Modern-Day Slavery, 2008. EDITOR: (with P.D. Brown) Memoranda on State of Affairs, 1759-1762: The Devonshire Diary, 1982; (with H.M.A. Keens-Soper) The Art of Diplomacy, 1983; (with J. Black and contrib.) Essays in European History, 1648-1815, 1985; (ed.) Lord Bute: Essays in Re-interpretation, 1988; (ed. with J. Black) Politics and the Press in Hanoverian Britain, 1989; (ed. and intro.) Herbert Butterfield: Essays on the History of Science, 1998; (ed. and intro.) In Defence of Australia's Constitutional Monarchy, 2003; (with P. Sharp) The International Thought of Herbert Butterfield, 2007. Contributor to books. **Address:** Federated Department of History, New Jersey Institute of Technology, Rm. 308, Cullimore Hall, University Heights, Newark, NJ 07102-1982, U.S.A.

SCHWELLER, Randall. American (born United States), b. 1958?. **Genres:** Politics/Government, History, Military/Defense/Arms Control. **Career:** Ohio State University, Department of Political Science, associate professor, 1999-2006, professor, 2006-. Writer. **Publications:** Deadly Imbalances: Tripolarity and Hitler's Strategy of World Conquest, 1998; Unanswered Threats: Political Constraints on the Balance of Power, 2006. Contributor of articles to books and journals. **Address:** Department of Political Science, Ohio State University, 2106 Derby Hall, 154 N Oval Mall, Columbus, OH 43210-1330, U.S.A. **Online address:** schweller.2@osu.edu

SCHYFFERT, Bea. (Bea Uusma Schyffert). Swedish (born Sweden), b. 1966. **Genres:** Children's Fiction. **Career:** Children's book illustrator and writer. **Publications:** (As Bea Uusma Schyffert) Astronauten Som Inte Fick Landa, 2000. Illustrator of books by others. **Address:** c/o Author Mail, Chronicle Books, 680 2nd St., San Francisco, CA 94107, U.S.A.

SCHYFFERT, Bea Uusma. See SCHYFFERT, Bea.

SCIABARRA, Chris Matthew. American (born United States), b. 1960. **Genres:** Intellectual History, Social Sciences, Adult Non-fiction. **Career:** Writer. **Publications:** Ayn Rand: The Russian Radical, 1995; Marx, Hayek, and Utopia, 1995; Total Freedom: Toward a Dialectical Libertarianism, 2000; A History of Dialectical Thinking, forthcoming. EDITOR: (with M.R. Gladstein) Feminist Interpretations of Ayn Rand, 1999; The Journal of Ayn Rand Studies, 1999. **Address:** 1840 W 5th St., Brooklyn, NY 11223, U.S.A.

SCIESZKA, Jon. American (born United States), b. 1954. **Genres:** Children's Fiction, Picture/Board Books, Animals/Pets, Young Adult Non-fiction. **Career:** Manhattan Day School, teacher, 1980; Guys Read Literacy Program, founder. Writer. **Publications:** CHILDREN'S BOOKS: Computer Challenges: Atari, 1985; The True Story of the Three Little Pigs, 1989; The Frog Prince Continued, 1991; Knights of the Kitchen Table, 1991; The Not-So-Jolly Roger, 1991; The Good, the Bad, and the Goofy, 1992; The Stinky Cheese Man and Other Fairly Stupid Tales, 1992; Your Mother Was a Neanderthal, 1993; The Book That Jack Wrote, 1994; Math Curse, 1995; 2095, 1995; Tut, Tut, 1996; Squids Will Be Squids: Fresh Morals, Beastly Fables, 1998; Summer Reading is Killing Me!, 1998; It's All Greek to Me, 1999; Road Atlas, 1999; See You Later, Gladiator, 2000; Baloney, Henry P., 2001; Sam Samurai, 2001; Hey Kid, Want to Buy a Bridge?, 2002; Viking It & Liking It, 2002; Me oh Maya!, 2003; Da Wild, da Crazy, da Vinci, 2004; (with L. Smith) Science Verse, 2004; (ed.) Guys Write for Guys Read, 2005; Oh Say, I Can't See, 2005; Seen Art?, 2005; Marco? Polo!, 2006; Nightmare on Joe's Street, 2006; The Seven Blunders Of The World, 2006; Lewis and Clark ... and Jodie, Freddi, and Samantha, 2006; You Can't, But Genghis Khan, 2006; What's So Great About Peter?, 2007; Wushu Were Here, 2007; Birdman or Birdbrain?, 2007; Cowboy and Octopus, 2007; Harem Scare'em, 2007; The High and The Flighty, 2007; Meet You at Waterloo, 2007; Plaid To The Bone, 2007; South Pole or Bust (An Egg), 2007; Pete's Party, 2008; Melvin Might?, 2008; Smash! Crash!, 2008; Snow Trucking!, 2008; Zoom! Boom! Bully, 2008; Truckery Rhymes, 2009; The Ultimate Guide, 2009; I Think I Can't, 2009; Kat's Mystery Gift, 2009; The Spooky Tire, 2009; Uh-oh Max, 2009; Robot Zot!, 2009; Melvin's Valentine, 2009; Trucksgiving, 2010; Dizzy Izzy, 2010; Welcome to Trucktown, 2010; (ed. and intro.) Guys Read: Funny Business, 2010; Garage Tales, 2010; The Great Truck Rescue, 2010; (with F. Sedita) SPHDZ, 2010; Trucks Line Up, 2011; Kat's Maps, 2011; Trucktown Treasury, 2011; (with F. Sedita) Spaceheadz Save the World, 2011; (ed. and of intro.) Thriller, 2011. **Address:** Penguin Group Inc., 375 Hudson St., New York, NY 10014-3657, U.S.A. **Online address:** guysread@aol.com

SCIPES, Kim. (Steven Scipes). American (born United States), b. 1951. **Genres:** Organized Labor, Area Studies, International Relations/Current Affairs, Third World, Sociology, Military/Defense/Arms Control. **Career:** International Labour Reports, North American representative, 1984-89; Purdue University-North Central, Department of Social Sciences, assistant professor of sociology, associate professor of sociology. Writer. **Publications:** KMU: Building Genuine Trade Unionism in the Philippines, 1980-1994, 1996; AFL-CIO's Secret War against Developing Country Workers: Solidarity or Sabotage?, 2010. **Address:** Department of Social Sciences, Purdue University-North Central, Schwarz Hall 210D, 1401 S US Hwy. 421, Westville, IN 46391-9542, U.S.A. **Online address:** kscipes@pnc.edu

SCIPES, Steven. See SCIPES, Kim.

SCIUTTO, Jim. British/American (born United States), b. 1970?. **Genres:** Theology/Religion. **Career:** Asia Business News, Hong Kong correspondent; American Broadcasting Corp. (ABC), ABC News, correspondent, anchor and senior foreign correspondent, 1998-. **Publications:** Against Us: The New Face of America's Enemies in the Muslim World, 2008. **Address:** London, GL , England. **Online address:** jim@jimsciutto.com

SCOFIELD, Martin (Paul). British (born England), b. 1945. **Genres:** Literary Criticism And History. **Career:** University of Southampton, assistant lecturer in English, 1968-69; University of Kent, School of English, lecturer, 1969-93, senior lecturer, 1993-2009; University of Massachusetts, faculty, 1974-75. Writer. **Publications:** The Ghosts of Hamlet: The Play and Modern Writers, 1980; T.S. Eliot: The Poems, 1988; Cambridge Introduction to the American Short Story, 2006. Contributor to professional journals. **Address:** School of English, Rutherford College, University of Kent, Canterbury, KT CT2 7NX, England. **Online address:** m.p.scofield@kent.ac.uk

SCOFIELD, Sandra (Jean). American (born United States), b. 1943. **Genres:** Novels, Autobiography/Memoirs. **Career:** Southern Oregon State College, assistant professor of education, 1979-80, adjunct professor of English, 1991-; Seattle Pacific University, faculty, 2006-; Pine Manor College, MFA in Creative Writing Program, faculty. Writer. **Publications:** NOVELS: Gringa, 1989; Beyond Deserving, 1991; Walking Dunes, 1992; More Than Allies, 1993; Opal on Dry Ground, 1994; A Chance to See Egypt, 1996; Plain Seeing, 1997; Occasions of Sin: A Memoir, 2004; (ed.) Children of the Dust: An Okie Family Story, 2006; Scene Book: A Primer for the Fiction Writer, 2007; (contrib.) As a Farm Woman Thinks, 2010. Contributor of articles to periodicals. Works appear in anthologies. **Address:** MFA in Creative Writing Program, Pine Manor College, 400 Heath St., Chestnut Hill, MA 02467-2332, U.S.A. **Online address:** ssandra@prodigy.net

SCOPPETTONE, Sandra. (Jack Early). American (born United States), b. 1936. **Genres:** Mystery/Crime/Suspense, Children's Fiction, Plays/Screenplays, Young Adult Fiction, Novels. **Career:** Full-time professional writer. **Publications:** FOR ANYONE: Suzuki Beane, (with L. Fitzhugh), 1961. FOR YOUNG ADULTS NOVELS: Trying Hard to Hear You, 1974, 2nd ed., 1996; The Late Great Me, 1976; Happy Endings are all Alike, 1978; Long Time Between Kisses, 1982; Playing Murder, 1985; FOR ADULTS NOVELS: Some Unknown Person, 1977; Such Nice People, 1980; Innocent Bystanders, 1983. LAUREN LAURANO DETECTIVE SERIES: Everything You Have Is Mine, 1991; I'll Be Leaving You Always, 1993; My Sweet Untraceable You, 1994; Let's Face the Music and Die, 1996; Gonna Take a Homicidal Journey, 1999; Beautiful Rage, 2004; This Dame for Hire, 2005; Too Damn Hot, 2006. NOVELS AS JACK EARLY: A Creative Kind of Killer, 1984; Razzamatazz, 1985; Donato & Daughter, 1988. PLAYS: Three One-Act Plays, 1964; One-Act Play, 1965; Two One-Act Plays, 1968; Home Again, Home Again Jiggity Jig, 1969; Two One-Act Plays, 1970; Something for Kitty Genovese, 1971; Stuck, 1972; A Little Bit Like Murder, 1973; The Inspector of Stairs, 1975. FOR CHILDREN FICTION. (with L. Fitzhugh) Bang Bang You're Dead, 1969. OTHER: Too Darn Hot, 2006. **Address:** 124 Hickory Ave., Southold, NY 11971, U.S.A. **Online address:** sandrasc@optonline.net

SCOT-BERNARD, P. See BERNARD, Patricia.

SCOTCH, Allison Winn. American (born United States), b. 1970. **Genres:** Young Adult Non-fiction, Psychiatry. **Career:** Writer. **Publications:** The Department of Lost & Found, 2007; Time of My Life: A Novel, 2009; The One That I Want: A Novel, 2010; The Song Remains the Same, 2012. **Address:** c/o Elisabeth Weed, Weed Literary, 55 E 65th St., Ste. 4E, New York, NY 10065, U.S.A. **Online address:** allison@allisonwinn.com

SCOTCHIE, Joseph. American (born United States), b. 1956. **Genres:** Novels, Biography, Politics/Government, Autobiography/Memoirs. **Career:** Asheville-Buncombe Technical Community College, teacher, 1985-86; teacher, 1986-87; National Mortgage News, editor, 1990-93; Anton Community Newspapers, editor, 1994-. **Publications:** Memoirs of an Old Virginian: Robert E. Lee Remembers The Civil War Years: A Play, 1993; (ed.) The Vision of Richard Weaver, 1995; Barbarians in the Saddle: An Intellectual Biography of Richard M. Weaver, 1997; (ed.) The Paleoconservatives: New Voices of the Old Right, 1999; Thomas Wolfe Revisited, 2001; Revolt from the Heartland: The Struggle for an Authentic Conservatism, 2002; Street Corner Conservative: Patrick J. Buchanan and His Times, 2003. **Address:** c/o Author Mail, Transaction Publishers, Rutgers University, 35 Berrue Cir., Piscataway, NJ 08854-8042, U.S.A.

SCOTLAND, Jay. See JAKES, John.

SCOTT, Alan (B.). American (born United States), b. 1957. **Genres:** History, Theology/Religion, Philosophy. **Career:** North Carolina State University, professor, 1987-88; Flanders Baptist and Community Church, minister, 1988-91, 1993-; Barnard College, professor, 1991-92. Writer. **Publications:** Origen and the Life of the Stars: A History of an Idea, 1991. **Address:** 138 Boston Post Rd., East Lyme, CT 06333-1606, U.S.A.

SCOTT, Amanda. (Lynne Scott-Drennan). American (born United States), b. 1944. **Genres:** Romance/Historical, Novels, Mystery/Crime/Suspense. **Career:** CA School System, teacher, 1968-71. Writer. **Publications:** The Fugitive Heiress, 1980; The Kidnapped Bride, 1983; The Indomitable Miss Harris, 1983; Ravenwood's Lady, 1984; An Affair of Honor, 1984; Lady Hawk's Folly, 1985; The Battling Bluestocking, 1985; Lady Escapade, 1986;

Lord Abberley's Nemesis, 1986; Mistress of the Hunt, 1987; Lady Meriel's Duty, 1987; Lady Brittany's Choice, 1988; Lord Greyfalcon's Reward, 1988; The Madcap Marchioness, 1989; The Dauntless Miss Wingrave, 1989; Lord Lyford's Secret, 1990; Border Bride, 1990, rev. ed., 2001; The Bath Quadrille, 1991; Bath Charade, 1991; The Bath Eccentric's Son, 1992; The Forthright Lady Gillian, 1992; The Rose at Twilight, 1993; The Fickle Fortune Hunter, 1993; The Bawdy Bride, 1995; Highland Fling, 1995; Dangerous Games, 1996; Dangerous Angles, 1997; Highland Secrets, 1997; Highland Treasure, 1998; Highland Spirits, 1999; Dangerous Lady, 1999; Border Fire, 2000; Dangerous Illusions, 2001; Border Storm, 2001; Highland Princess, 2004; Lord of the Isles, 2005; Prince of Danger, 2005; Lady's Choice, 2006; Knight's Treasure, 2007; King of Storms, 2007; Border Lass, 2008; Border Wedding, 2008; Tamed by a Laird, 2009; Border Moonlight, 2009; Seduced by a Rogue, 2010; Tempted by a Warrior, 2010; Highland Master, 2011; Highland Hero, 2011. SECRET CLAN SERIES: Abducted Heiress, 2001; Hidden Heiress, 2002; Highland Bride, 2003; Reiver's Bride, 2003. AS LYNNE SCOTT-DRENNAN: Omaha City Architecture, 1977; Summer Sandcastle, 1984; Sweet Thunder, 1987; The Tycoon's Daughter, 1988. **Address:** 137 Rambling Dr., PO Box 1644, Folsom, CA 95630, U.S.A. **Online address:** amandascott@att.net

SCOTT, Amoret (Scudamore). See SCOTT, Amoret (Tanner).

SCOTT, Amoret (Tanner). (Amoret (Scudamore) Scott). British/Canadian (born Canada), b. 1930. **Genres:** Antiques/Furnishings, Food And Wine, Recreation, Biography, Reference, History, Travel/Exploration. **Career:** Ephemera Society, founding member; Parrot Society, founding member. Writer. **Publications:** WITH C. SCOTT: A-Z of Antique Collecting, 1963; Collecting Bygones, 1964; Dummy Board Figures, 1966; Tobacco and the Collector, 1966; Collecting, 1967; Antiques as an Investment, 1967; Discovering Staffordshire Figures, 1969; Discovering Smoking Antiques, 1970; Treasures in Your Attic, 1971; Discovering Stately Homes, 1973; Wellington, 1973; Hedgerow Harvest, 1979; Parrots, 1982; Staffordshire Figures, 1993; Smoking Antiques, 1981, 1996; (ed.) The Encyclopedia of Ephemera, 2000. OTHERS: Portobello Passport, 1968; (comp.) A Murmur of Bees, 1980. **Address:** The Footprint, Padworth Common, Reading, BR RG7 4QG, England.

SCOTT, Aurelia C. American (born United States), b. 1956. **Genres:** Documentaries/Reportage, Novels, Essays, History. **Career:** Portland Trails, president emeritus. Writer. **Publications:** Otherwise Normal People: Inside the Thorny World of Competitive Rose Gardening, 2007. Contributor to periodicals. **Address:** Algonquin Books, PO Box 2225, Chapel Hill, NC 27515-2225, U.S.A. **Online address:** aurelia@aureliacscott.com

SCOTT, Darieck. American (born United States), b. 1964. **Genres:** Novels. **Career:** Stanford University, instructor Freshman English, 1993, Program in Culture, Ideas and Values, instructor, 1996-97, Introduction to the Humanities Program, teaching fellow, 1998-99; University of San Francisco, Master of Arts in Writing Program, instructor, 1997-98; University of Texas, Department of English, assistant professor, 1999-2003; University of California, assistant professor of English, 2003-. Writer. **Publications:** Traitor to the Race (novel), 1995; (ed.) Best Black Gay Erotica, 2005; Hex: A Novel of Love Spells, 2007; Extravagant Abjection, 2010. Works appear in anthologies. Contributor to periodicals. **Address:** Department of English, University of California, 2607 South Hall, Santa Barbara, CA 93106-3170, U.S.A. **Online address:** dbscott@english.ucsb.edu

SCOTT, David A. (David Alexander Scott). Canadian (born Canada), b. 1949. **Genres:** Documentaries/Reportage, Cultural/Ethnic Topics. **Career:** Writer. **Publications:** (As David Alexander Scott) Pornography, its Effects on the Family, Community, and Culture, 1985; Behind the G-String: An Exploration of the Stripper's Image, Her Person and Her Meaning, 1997; Living the Authentic Life, 1998. Contributor to periodicals. **Address:** 700 Chilco St., Ste. 304, Vancouver, BC V6G 2R1, Canada. **Online address:** dscott777@telus.net

SCOTT, David Alexander. See SCOTT, David A.

SCOTT, David L. (David Lindsay Scott). British (born England), b. 1920?. **Genres:** Medicine/Health. **Career:** County Hospital, Department of Anaesthesia, head, 1950-60; Whiston Hospital, staff, 1961-85; retired consultant anaesthetist. Writer. **Publications:** (Ed. with A.N. Exton-Smith) Vitamins in the Elderly, 1968; Modern Hospital Hypnosis: Especially for Anaesthetists, 1974. **Address:** Ravelstone, Manley Rd., Manley, CH WA6 9ED, England.

SCOTT, David Lindsay. *See* **SCOTT, David L.**

SCOTT, David L(ogan). American (born United States), b. 1942. **Genres:** Money/Finance, Travel/Exploration, Business/Trade/Industry, Economics. **Career:** Florida Southern College, professor of business administration; Valdosta State University, professor of finance, through 2007, professor emeritus of finance, 2007-. Writer. **Publications:** Pollution in the Electric Power Industry, 1973; Financing the Growth of Electric Utilities, 1975; Traveling and Camping in the National Park Areas, 3 vols., 1978-79, (with K. Scott) as Guide to the National Park Areas: Western States, 2 vols., 2004; Finance, 1979; Security Investments, 1981; Stretching Your Income: 101 Ways to Help You Cope with Inflation, 1982; The Investor's Guide to Discount Brokers, 1983; (with K. Moore) Fundamentals of the Time Value of Money, 1984; Dictionary of Accounting, 1985; Wall Street Words, 1988, 3rd ed., 2003; Understanding and Managing Investment Risk and Return, 1990; Investing in Tax-Saving Municipal Bonds, 1991; The Elvis Quiz Book, 1991; How Wall Street Works, 1992, rev. ed., 1999; The Guide to Personal Budgeting, 1992, 2nd ed., 1995; Municipal Bonds: The Basics and Beyond, 1992; The Guide to Investing in Bonds, 1993, 2nd ed., 1997; The Guide to Investing in Common Stocks, 1993, 2nd ed., 1995; The Guide to Investing in Mutual Funds, 1993, 2nd ed., 1996; The Guide to Buying Insurance, 1994; The Guide to Managing Credit, 1994; The Guide to Tax-Saving Investing, 1995; The Guide to Investing for Current Income: How to Build Your Wealth by Mastering the Basic Strategies, 1995; The Guide to Saving Money, 1996; W.K. The Ultimate Elvis Quiz Book, 1999; How Stocks Work, 2001; David Scott's Guide to Investing in Bonds, 2004; Guide to the National Park Areas: Eastern States, 2004; David Scott's Guide to Investing in Mutual Funds, 2004; David Scott's Guide to Investing in Common Stocks, 2005; David Scott's Guide to Managing Credit and Debt, 2005; (with K. Scott) The Complete Guide to National Park Lodges, 6th ed., 2009; The American Heritage Dictionary of Business Terms, 2009. **Address:** College of Business Administration, Valdosta State University, Rm. 214, Pound Hall, Valdosta, GA 31698, U.S.A. **Online address:** dlscott@valdosta.edu

SCOTT, D(onald) F. *See* **SCOTT, Donald Fletcher.**

SCOTT, Donald Fletcher. (D(onald) F. Scott). British (born England), b. 1930. **Genres:** Medicine/Health, Psychology, Sciences, Medicine/Health. **Career:** Maudsley Hospital, senior registrar, 1963-65; Mayo Clinic, research assistant, 1965-66; London Hospital, consultant electroencephalographer, 1967-. Writer. **Publications:** (Intro. with B. Dodd) Neurological and Neurosurgical Nursing, 1966; About Epilepsy, 1969, 3rd ed. 1982; The Psychology of Work, 1970; Fire and Fire Raisers, 1974; (with C. Braschler) Estimation of Industry Labor Income Multipliers for County Groupings in Missouri, 1975; The Psychology of Fire, 1975; Understanding EEG: An Introduction to Electroencephalography, 1976; Coping with Suicide, 1989; Beating Job Burnout, 1989; The History of Epileptic Therapy: An Account of How Medication was Developed, 1993. **Address:** 3 Weigall Rd., Lee, London, GL SE12 8HE, England.

SCOTT, Elizabeth. American (born United States), b. 1972?. **Genres:** Novels. **Career:** Writer. **Publications:** Bloom, Simon, 2007; Perfect You, 2008; Stealing Heaven, 2008; Living Dead Girl, 2008; Something, Maybe, 2009; Love You, Hate You, Miss You, 2009; Grace, 2010; The Unwritten Rule, 2010; Miracle, 2010. **Address:** PO Box 638, Manassas Park, VA 20111, U.S.A. **Online address:** elizabeth@elizabethwrites.com

SCOTT, Elizabeth S. American (born United States), b. 1945?. **Genres:** Law. **Career:** University of Virginia, Forensic Psychiatry Clinic, Institute of Law, Psychiatry and Public Policy, legal director, 1979-87, associate professor, 1988-91, professor, 1992-2006, Class of 1962 Professor of Law, 2001-06, Center for Children, Families and the Law, founder and co-director; Columbia School of Law, visiting professor, 1987-88, 2001-02, 2003, 2005, Harold R. Medina professor of law, 2006. Writer. **Publications:** (Co-author) Family Law: Cases, Text, Problems, 4th ed., 2004; (with S. Davis, W. Wadlington and C. Whitebread) Children and the Legal System, 4th ed., 2008; (with L. Steinberg) Rethinking Juvenile Justice, 2008. **Address:** Columbia Law School, Columbia University, Rm. 715 Jerome Greene Hall, 435 W 116th St., PO Box D-3, New York, NY 10027, U.S.A. **Online address:** es2054@columbia.edu

SCOTT, Eugenie Carol. American (born United States), b. 1945. **Genres:** Novels. **Career:** University of Kentucky, assistant professor of anthropology, 1974-82; University of California, postdoctoral fellow, 1983-84; University of Colorado, assistant professor of anthropology, 1984-86; National Center for Science Education, executive director and publisher, 1987-; Bookwatch Reviews, publisher, 1988-92; Biological Sciences Curriculum Study, director, 1993-99. Writer. **Publications:** Evolution vs. Creationism: An Introduction, 2004, 2nd ed., 2009; (ed. with G. Branch) Not in Our Classrooms: Why Intelligent Design is Wrong for Our Schools, 2006. **Address:** National Center for Science Education, 420 40th St., Ste. 2, Oakland, CA 94609-2509, U.S.A. **Online address:** scott@ncse.com

SCOTT, Frank. American/British (born England), b. 1942?. **Genres:** Music. **Career:** Roots & Rhythm, co-owner and general manager, 1978-. Writer. **Publications:** (Co-author) The Down Home Guide to the Blues, 1991; (co-author) The Roots & Rhythm Guide to Rock, 1993. **Address:** Roots & Rhythm, PO Box 837, El Cerrito, CA 94530-0837, U.S.A. **Online address:** roots@toast.net

SCOTT, Grant F. American (born United States), b. 1961. **Genres:** Literary Criticism And History, Biography. **Career:** Muhlenberg College, Department of English, associate professor, 1989-95, professor, 1995-, head, 2007-, Donald B. Hoffman research fellow, 2000-01; European Romantic Review, co-editor. **Publications:** The Sculpted Word: Keats, Ekphrasis and the Visual Arts, 1994; (ed.) Selected Letters of John Keats, 2002; (ed.) Joseph Severn: Letters and Memoirs, 2005; (ed.) New Letters from Charles Brown to Joseph Severn, 2007. Contributor of articles to periodicals. **Address:** Department of English, Muhlenberg College, 277 Center for the Arts, 2400 Chew St., Allentown, PA 18104, U.S.A. **Online address:** scott@muhlenberg.edu

SCOTT, Jill. Canadian (born Canada), b. 1968. **Genres:** Psychology. **Career:** Carleton University, School of Comparative Literature, lecturer, 1996-97; York University, Program in German, lecturer, 1998-99; University of Toronto, Department of German, lecturer, 1998-99, assistant professor, 2000-01; University of Chicago, SSHRC postdoctoral fellow, 1999-2000; Queen's University, Department of German, associate professor, 2001-, undergraduate chair of German, 2004-05, 2007-10, coordinator of linguistics, 2009-10; Department of Gender Studies, faculty, 2010-, head, 2010-11, Department of Languages, Literatures and Cultures, undergraduate chair, 2011-, Department of Languages, Literatures and Cultures, acting associate associate head, 2011-. **Publications:** Electra after Freud: Myth and Culture, 2005; Poetics of Forgiveness: Cultural Responses to Loss and Wrongdoing, 2010. Contributor of articles to periodicals. **Address:** Department Of Languages, Literatures and Cultures, Queen's University, 406 Kingston Hall, 103 Stuart St., 103 Stuart St., Kingston, ON K7L 3Z2, Canada. **Online address:** jill.scott@queensu.ca

SCOTT, Joan Wallach. American (born United States), b. 1941. **Genres:** Politics/Government, History. **Career:** University of Illinois, assistant professor, 1970-72; Northwestern University, assistant professor, 1972-74; University of North Carolina, assistant professor, 1974-77, professor, 1977-80; Brown University, Nancy Duke Lewis university professor and professor of history, 1980-85; Institute for Advanced Study, professor of social science, 1985-, Harold F. Linder professor, 2000-; Brown University, Pembroke Center for Teaching and Research on Women, founding director. Writer, social scientist, gender theorist and historian. **Publications:** The Glassworkers of Carmaux: French Craftsmen and Political Action in a Nineteenth-Century City, 1974; (with L.A. Tilly) Women, Work, and Family, 1978; (comp. with B. Tierney) Western Societies: A Documentary History, 1984; Gender and the Politics of History, 1988, rev. ed., 1999; (ed. as Joan W. Scott with J.K. Conway and S. Borque) Learning about Women: Gender, Politics and Power, 1989; (ed. with J. Butler) Feminists Theorize the Political, 1992; (ed.) Love and Politics in Wartime: Letters to My Wife, 1943-45, 1992; Only Paradoxes to Offer: French Feminists and the Rights of Man, 1996; (ed.) Feminism and History, 1996; (ed. with C. Kaplan and D. Keates) Transitions, Environments, Translations: Feminisms in International Politics, 1997; (ed. with D. Keates) Schools of Thought: Twenty-five Years of Interpretive Social Science, 2001; (ed. with D. Keates) Going Public: Feminism and the Shifting Boundaries of the Private Sphere, 2004; Parité! Sexual Equality and the Crisis of French Universalism, 2005; The Politics of the Veil, 2007; (ed.) Women's Studies on the Edge, 2008. **Address:** Institute for Advanced Study, Einstein Dr., Princeton, NJ 08540, U.S.A. **Online address:** jws@ias.edu

SCOTT, John Beldon. American (born United States), b. 1946. **Genres:** Architecture, Art/Art History. **Career:** Rutgers University, instructor, 1979; University of Pennsylvania, lecturer, 1981-82; University of Iowa, School of Art and Art History, assistant professor, associate professor, 1982-98, professor, 1998-, Elizabeth M. Stanley professor of the arts, 2004-; Princeton University, Robert Janson-La Palme visiting professor in art and archaeology, 2007. Writer. **Publications:** Images of Nepotism: The Painted Ceilings of Palazzo Barberini, 1991; Architecture for the Shroud: Relic and Ritual in Turin, 2003; (with R.P. Lehnertz) The University of Iowa Guide to Campus Architecture, 2006. Contributor to books and periodicals. **Address:** University of Iowa, School of Art and Art History, W612B SSH, 141 N Riverside Dr., 150 Art Bldg. W, Iowa City, IA 52242, U.S.A. **Online address:** jb-scott@uiowa.edu

SCOTT, John T. American (born United States), b. 1963?. **Genres:** Translations, Philosophy. **Career:** University of Chicago, Department of Political Science, Grodzins Prize lecturer, 1991-92; Loyola University, visiting assistant professor of political science, 1992-93; Dartmouth College, visiting assistant professor of government, 1993-94; University of Houston, assistant professor of political science, 1994-2000; University of California, Department of Political Science, associate professor, 2000-05, professor, 2005-, director of undergraduate studies, 2001-03, director of graduate studies, 2006-08, 2003-05, chair, 2010-. Writer. **Publications:** (Ed. and trans.) J. Rousseau, Essay on the Origin of Languages and Writings Related to Music, 1998; (ed.) Critical Assessments of Leading Political Philosophers, 2006; (ed. with O. Mostefai) Rousseau and l'Infâme: Religion, Toleration and Fanaticism in the Age of Enlightenment, 2009; (with R. Zaretsky) The Philosophers' Quarrel: Rousseau, Hume and the Limits of Human Understanding, 2009. Contributor to journals and periodicals. **Address:** Department of Political Science, University of California, 683 Kerr Hall, 1 Shields Ave., Davis, CA 95616, U.S.A. **Online address:** jtscott@ucdavis.edu

SCOTT, Jonathan. New Zealander (born New Zealand), b. 1958. **Genres:** History, Biography, Politics/Government, Cultural/Ethnic Topics, Essays. **Career:** Cambridge University, research fellow of Magdalene College, 1985-87; Victoria University of Wellington, lecturer in history, 1987-88; University of Sheffield, lecturer in history, 1989-91; Cambridge University, Downing College, fellow, director of studies in history, 1991-2001; University of Pittsburgh, Caroll Amundson professor of British history, 2001-09; University of Auckland, professor of history, 2009-. Writer. **Publications:** Algernon Sidney and the English Republic, 1623-1677, 1988; (contrib.) The Politics of Religion in Restoration England, 1990; Algernon Sidney and the Restoration Crisis, 1677-1683, 1991; (contrib.) Political Discourse in Early Modern Britain, 1993; Harry's Absence: Looking for My Father on the Mountain, 1997, 2nd ed., 2000; England's Troubles: Seventeenth-Century English Political Instability in European Perspective, 2000; Commonwealth Principles: Republican Writing of the English Revolution, 2004; (ed. with John Morrow) Liberty, Authority, Formality: Political Ideas and Culture, 1600-1900: Essays in Honour of Colin Davis, 2008; When the Waves Ruled Britannia: Geography and Political Identities, 1500-1800, 2011. Contributor to books. **Address:** Department of History, University of Auckland, 7 Wynyard St., Rm. 44, Auckland, 1010, New Zealand. **Online address:** jonathan.scott@auckland.ac.nz

SCOTT, Kay W. (Kay Woelfel Scott). American (born United States) **Genres:** Travel/Exploration, How-to Books, Transportation. **Career:** Travel writer. **Publications:** (With D.L. Scott as Kay Woelfel Scott) Traveling and Camping in the National Park Areas: Mid-America, 1978; (with D.L. Scott as Kay Woelfel Scott) Traveling and Camping in the National Park Areas: Western States, 1978; (with D.L. Scott as Kay Woelfel Scott) Traveling and Camping in the National Park Areas: Eastern States, 1979; The Complete Guide to the National Park Lodges, 5th ed., 2006; (with D.L. Scott) Guide to the National Park Areas: Eastern States, 8th ed., 2004; Guide to the National Park Areas: Western States, 8th ed., 2004. **Address:** 2605 N Sherwood Dr., Valdosta, GA 31602-2136, U.S.A. **Online address:** woelfelscott@excite.com

SCOTT, Kay Woelfel. See **SCOTT, Kay W.**

SCOTT, Kim. Australian (born Australia), b. 1957?. **Genres:** Novels. **Career:** Curtin University, Curtin Health Innovation Research Institute, Aboriginal Health and Education Research Unit, associate professor, School of Media, Culture & Creative Arts, Faculty of Humanities, professor of writing. Writer. **Publications:** True Country, 1993; Benang: From the Heart, 1999; The Dredgersaurus, 2001; (with H. Brown) Kayang & Me, 2005; Lost, 2006; That Deadman Dance, 2010; (ed. with R. Thackrah and J. Winch) Indigenous Australian health and cultures, 2011. Works appear in anthologies. Contribu-

tor to journals. **Address:** Fremantle Art Centre Press, PO Box 158, North Fremantle, WA 6159, Australia. **Online address:** k.scott@curtin.edu.au

SCOTT, Leonard B. American/German (born Germany), b. 1948. **Genres:** Westerns/Adventure, Novels, Mystery/Crime/Suspense. **Career:** Writer. **Publications:** MILITARY/ACTION ADVENTURE NOVELS: Charlie Mike, 1985; The Last Run, 1987; The Battle of Hill 875, Dak to Vietnam 1967, 1988; The Hill, 1989, rev. ed. 1995; The Expendables, 1991; The Iron Men, 1993; Duty Bound, 1995; Forged in Honor, 1995; Solemn Duty, 1997. **Address:** 1808 Canary Dr., Edmond, OK 73034, U.S.A.

SCOTT, Manda. (M. C. Scott). Scottish/British (born England) **Genres:** Romance/Historical, Mystery/Crime/Suspense, Novels. **Career:** Writer, veterinary surgeon and equine neonatologist. **Publications:** KELLEN STEWART SERIES: Hen's Teeth, 1996; Night Mares, 1998; Stronger than Death, 1999. NOVELS: No Good Deed, 2001; Absolution, 2005; The Crystal Skull, 2008. BOUDICA SERIES: Dreaming the Eagle, 2003; Dreaming the Bull, 2004; Dreaming the Hound, 2005; Dreaming the Serpent Spear, 2006. AS M.C. SCOTT ROME SERIES: The Emperor's Spy, 2010; The Coming of the King, 2011; The Eagle of the Twelfth, 2012. **Address:** c/o Author Mail, Delacorte/ Dell Publishing, 1540 Broadway, New York, NY 10036, U.S.A. **Online address:** manda@mandascott.co.uk

SCOTT, Margaret (Allan Bennett). New Zealander (born New Zealand), b. 1928?. **Genres:** Literary Criticism And History, Autobiography/Memoirs, Young Adult Fiction, Women's Studies And Issues. **Career:** Children's Service Center, social worker, 1952-54; Alexander Turnbull Library, librarian, 1967-73. Writer. **Publications:** (With V. O'Sullivan) The Collected Letters of Katherine Mansfield, vol. I: 1903-17, 1984, vol. II: 1918-19, 1987, vol. III: 1919-20, 1993, vol. IV: 1920-21, 1996, vol. V: 1922, 2008; (ed.) The Katherine Mansfield Notebooks, vol. II, 1997; Recollecting Mansfield: A Memoir, 2001; (intro.) Charles Brasch in Egypt, 2007. Contributor to periodicals. **Address:** 13 Purau Ave., R.D. Diamond Harbour, Christchurch, 8013, New Zealand. **Online address:** scottma@xtra.co.nz

SCOTT, M. C. See **SCOTT, Manda.**

SCOTT, Melissa. American (born United States), b. 1960. **Genres:** Science Fiction/Fantasy, Novels, Adult Non-fiction. **Career:** Writer. **Publications:** SCIENCE FICTION NOVELS: Territorial Rights, 1984; The Game Beyond, 1984; A Choice of Destinies, 1986; The Kindly Ones, 1987; (with L.A. Barnett) The Armor of Light, 1988; Mighty Good Road, 1990; Dreamships, 1992; Burning Bright, 1993; Trouble and Her Friends, 1994; Proud Helios, 1994; Shadow Man, 1995; Night Sky Mine, 1996; Dreaming Metal, 1997; Shapes of their Hearts, 1998; The Jazz, 2000. ROADS OF HEAVEN TRILOGY: Five-Twelfths of Heaven, 1985; Silence in Solitude, 1986; The Empress of Earth, 1987. OTHERS: (with L.A. Barnett) Point of Hopes, 1995; Conceiving the Heavens: Creating the Science-Fiction Novel (nonfiction), 1997; The Garden, 1997; (with L.A. Barnett) Point of Dreams, 2001; (with J. Graham) Homecoming, 2010. **Address:** c/o Richard Curtis, Richard Curtis Associates Inc., 171 E 74th St., 2nd Fl., New York, NY 10021-3221, U.S.A. **Online address:** mes@pointsman.net

SCOTT, Michael. (Anna Dillon). Irish (born Ireland), b. 1959. **Genres:** Novels. **Career:** Writer, 1982-; Tyrone Productions, Department of Drama, head. **Publications:** Irish Folk and Fairy Tales, vol. II, 1983, vol. III, 1984; The Song of the Children of Lir, 1983; A Celtic Odyssey: The Voyage of Maildun, 1985; The Last of the Fianna, 1987; Navigator: The Voyage of Saint Brendan, 1988; The Quest of the Sons, 1988; Green and Golden Tales: Irish Fairytales, 1988; Irish Folk and Fairy Tales Omnibus, 1989; Irish Hero Tales, 1989; Banshee, 1990; Saint Patrick, 1990; The Story of Ireland, 1990; The River Gods, 1991; Image, 1991; The Seven Treasures: The Quest of the Sons of Tuireann, 1992; Irish Myths and Legends, 1992; The Piper's Ring, 1992; Reflection, 1992; Lottery, 1993; Gemini Game, 1993; Imp, 1993; Irish Ghosts and Hauntings, 1994; Fungie and the Magical Kingdom, 1994; Magical Irish Folk Tales, 1995; (with M. Llywelyn) Ireland: A Graphic History, 1995; The Hallows, 1995; Vampyre, 1995; Wolf Moon, 1995; Nineteen Railway Street, 1996; (with M. Llewellyn) Etruscans: Beloved of the Gods (Beloved of the Gods series), 2000; (with A. Shimerman) The Merchant Prince, 2000; The Quiz Master, 2004; The Alchemyst: The Secrets of the Immortal Nicholas Flamel, 2007; (with A. Barbeau) Vampyres of Hollywood, 2008; The Magician: The Secrets of the Immortal Nicholas Flamel, 2008; The Sorceress: The Secrets of the Immortal Nicholas Flamel, 2009; The Necromancer: The Secrets of the Immortal Nicholas Flamel, 2010; (with C. Freedman) The Thirteen Hallows, 2011; The Warlock, 2011; The Enchantress, 2012. TALES FROM THE LAND OF ERIN SERIES: A Bright Enchantment, 1985; A Golden Dream, 1985; A Silver Wish, 1985; Tales from the Land of Erin, 1985. TALES OF THE BARD SERIES: Magician's Law, Sphere 1987; Demon's Law, 1988; Death's Law, 1989; The Culai Heritage, 2001. DE DANNAN TALES SERIES: Windlord, 1991; Earthlord, 1992; Firelord, 1994. OTHER WORLD SERIES: October Moon, 1992; House of the Dead, 1993. ARCANA SERIES: (with M. Llywelyn) Silver Hand, 1995; (with M. Llywelyn) Silverlight, 1996. NONFICTION: (ed.) Hall's Ireland: Mr. & Mrs. Hall's Tour of 1840, 1984; (ed.) An Irish Herbal: The Botanalogia Universalis Hibernica, 1986; Celtic Wisdom for Business, 2001; The Book of Celtic Wisdom: Poems, Proverbs and Blessings, 2002. AS ANNA DILLON: Seasons, 1988; Another Time, Another Season, 1989; Season's End, 1990; Lies, 1998; The Affair, 2004; Consequences, 2005; Closure, 2007. AS MIKE SCOTT: Judith and the Traveler, 1991; Judith and Spider, 1992; Good Enough for Judith, 1994; (with A. Scott) Engen Afrikatourism Guide, 1998; (with A. Compton and H. Fielding) Supporting Numeracy, 2007. **Address:** Delacorte Press Books for Young Readers, 1745 Broadway, New York, NY 10019, U.S.A. **Online address:** michaeldillonscott@gmail.com

SCOTT, Nina M. American/German (born Germany), b. 1937. **Genres:** Literary Criticism And History, Translations, Social Sciences, Local History/ Rural Topics. **Career:** University of Massachusetts, professor of Spanish, 1968-, adjunct professor of comparative literature, graduate program director, emeritus; University of Freiburg, visiting professor, 1983-84; University of Buenos Aires, senior lecturer, 1987; New England Council of Latin American Studies, vice president, 1993-94, president, 1994-95. Writer. **Publications:** Language, Humor and Myth in the Frontier Novels of the Americas: Wister, Guiraldes and Amado, 1983. EDITOR: (with A. Horno-Delgado, E. Ortega and N.S. Sternbach) Breaking Boundaries: Latina Writing and Critical Readings, 1989; (with F.J. Cevallos-Candau, J.A. Cole and N. Suarez-Arauz) Coded Encounters: Writing, Gender and Ethnicity in Colonial Latin America, 1994; (trans. and intro.) Madres del verbo/Mothers of the Word, 1999. TRANSLATOR: G.G. de Avellaneda, Sab; Autobiography, 1993; K.A. Myers, Fernández de Oviedo's Chronicle of America: A New History for a New World, 2007. Contributor to periodicals. **Address:** University of Massachusetts, PO Box 33945, Amherst, MA 01003-3945, U.S.A. **Online address:** nmscott@spanport.umass.edu

SCOTT, P(aul) H(enderson). Scottish (born Scotland), b. 1920. **Genres:** History, International Relations/Current Affairs, Politics/Government, Biography, Literary Criticism And History, Social Sciences, Anthropology/Ethnology. **Career:** Control Commission for Germany, Quadripartite Committee, staff, 1947-50; British Diplomatic Service, staff, 1950-80, foreign office staff, 1950-53, secretary, 1953-59, United Nations Department, assistant head, 1959-62; Canadian National Defence College, affiliate, 1964-65; International Institute for Strategic Studies, research associate, 1975-76; Dundee University, rector, 1989-92. Writer. **Publications:** 1707: The Union of Scotland and England, 1979; Walter Scott and Scotland, 1981; John Galt, 1985; In Bed with an Elephant, 1985; Cultural Independence, 1989; The Thinking Nation, 1989; Towards Independence: Essays on Scotland, 1991; Andrew Fletcher and the Treaty of Union, 1992; Scotland in Europe, 1992; Defoe in Edinburgh and Other Papers, 1995; Scotland: An Unwon Cause, 1997; Still in Bed with an Elephant, 1998; The Boasted Advantages, 1999; A Twentieth Century Life, 2002; Scotland Resurgent, 2003; Union of 1707: Why and How?, 2006. EDITOR: (with A.C. Davis) The Age of MacDiarmid, 1980; Sir Walter Scott's Letters of Malachi Malagrowther, 1981; Andrew Fletcher's United and Separate Parliaments, 1982; (with G. Bruce) A Scottish Postbag: Eight Centuries of Scottish Letters, 1986, rev. ed., 2002; (with A.C. Davis) Policy for the Arts: A Selection of AdCAS Papers, 1991; Scotland: A Concise Cultural History, 1993; Scotland's Ruine, 1995; The Saltoun Papers, 2003. Contributor to periodicals. Works appears in anthologies. **Address:** 33 Drumsheugh Gardens, Edinburgh, EH3 7RN, Scotland. **Online address:** scott.fiori@virgin.net

SCOTT, Peter. British (born England), b. 1946?. **Genres:** Education, Sciences, Reference. **Career:** Times Educational Supplement, reporter, news editor, 1967-69; Times, reporter, 1969-71, leader writer, 1974-76; Times Higher Education Supplement, deputy editor, 1971-73, editor, 1976-92; University of Leeds, professor of education, 1992-97, pro-vice-chancellor for external affairs, 1995-97, vice-chairman, Centre for Policy Studies in Education, director, 1992-97; Kingston University, vice-chancellor, 1997-2010; University of London, Institute of Education, professor of higher education studies. **Publications:** Introduction to 3-manifolds, 1975; Strategies for Post-secondary Education, 1976; Future of Higher Education, 1979; The Crisis of the University, 1984; Knowledge and Nation, 1990; (co-author) The New Production of Knowledge: The Dynamics of Science and Research in Contemporary Societies, 1994; The Meanings of Mass Higher Education, 1995; (with C. Bargh and D. Smith) Governing Universities: Changing the Culture?, 1996; (ed.) The Globalization of Higher Education, 1998; (ed.) Higher Education Reformed, 2000; (with H. Novotny and M. Gibbons) Rethinking Justice: Knowledge and the Public in an Age of Uncertainty, 2001. **Address:** Institute of Education, University of London, 829A, 20 Bedford Way, London, GL WC1H 0AL, England. **Online address:** p.scott@ioe.ac.uk

SCOTT, (Robert James) Munroe. Canadian (born Canada), b. 1927. **Genres:** Novels, Plays/Screenplays, Young Adult Non-fiction, Biography. **Career:** Crawley Films Ltd., staff writer, 1950-57; freelance writer, 1957-. **Publications:** African Manhunt: A Layman's-Eye View of the Umbundu People of Angola (Portuguese West Africa), 1959; Wu-Feng, 1974; McClure, vol. I: The China Years (biography), 1977, vol. II: The Years of Challenge (biography), 1979; Devil's Petition: A Folk Play in Two Acts, 1982; Shylock's Treasure, 1982; Waltz for a Pagan Drum (novel), 1988; From Nation to Colony (political essays), 1988; Oh, Vulgar Wind (non-fiction), 1994; The Carving of Canada (non-fiction), 1999; The Liberators (novel), 2001; Always an Updraft (auto-biography), 2006. **Address:** 1457 Sherwood Cres., Peterborough, ON K9J 6T6, Canada. **Online address:** munscott@sympatico.ca

SCOTT, Robyn. British (born England), b. 1981. **Genres:** Biography, Autobiography/Memoirs, Women's Studies And Issues. **Career:** Writer. **Publications:** Twenty Chickens for a Saddle: The Story of an African Childhood, 2008. Contributor to periodicals. **Address:** c/o David Godwin, David Godwin Associates, 55 Monmouth St., London, GL WC2H 9DG, England.

SCOTT, Roy Vernon. American (born United States), b. 1927. **Genres:** Agriculture/Forestry, History. **Career:** University of Southwestern Louisiana, assistant professor, 1957-58; Business History Foundation, research associate, 1958-59, 1963-64; University of Missouri, visiting assistant professor, 1959-60; Mississippi State University, assistant professor, 1960-62, associate professor, 1962-64, professor of history, 1964-98, William L. Giles distinguished professor, 1978-98, distinguished professor emeritus, 1998-. Writer. **Publications:** The Agrarian Movement in Illinois, 1880-1896, 1962; The Reluctant Farmer: The Rise of Agricultural Extension to 1914, 1971; (with J.G. Shoalmire) The Public Career of Cully A. Cobb: A Study in Agricultural Leadership, 1973; (ed. with G.L. Robson, Jr.) Southern Agriculture since the Civil War: A Symposium, 1979; Railroad Development Programs in the Twentieth Century, 1985; (with R.W. Hidy and others) The Great Northern Railway: A History, 1988; Eugene B. Ferris and Agricultural Science in the Lower South, 1991; (with S. Vance) Wal-Mart: A History of Sam Walton's Retail Phenomenon, 1994; (with C. Lowery) Old Main: Images of a Legend, 1995; (co-author) The Great Northern Railway: A History, 2004; (with D.S. Nordin) From Prairie Farmer to Entrepreneur: The Transformation of Midwestern Agriculture, 2005; Change in America's Heartland: Farming and Farm Life in the Middle West, 1900-1975, forthcoming. **Address:** Department of History, Mississippi State University, 214 Allen Hall, Mississippi State, MS 39762, U.S.A. **Online address:** royvandjaneb@aol.com

SCOTT, Sophronia. American (born United States), b. 1966?. **Genres:** How-to Books. **Career:** Time Magazine, staff, 1988-95; People Magazine, writer, style watch editor and senior entertainment editor of Teen People, 1995-2003; Creative Coaching Plans, founder and coach, 2003-; Done For You Writing and Publishing Co., executive editor. **Publications:** All I Need to Get By, 2004; Doing Business By The Book: How To Craft A Crowd-pleasing Book And Attract More Clients And Speaking Engagements Than You Ever Thought Possible, 2008; How the Fierce Handle Fear: Secrets to Succeeding in Challenging Times, 2010; A Family of Widows, forthcoming. Contributor to periodicals. **Address:** The Book Sistah, 261 S Main St., Ste. 319, Newtown, CT 06470-2746, U.S.A. **Online address:** coachsoph@creativecoachingplans.com

SCOTT, Tom. Scottish (born Scotland), b. 1947. **Genres:** Economics. **Career:** University of St. Andrews, Reformation Studies Institute, professor. Writer. **Publications:** Regional Identity and Economic Change: The Upper Rhine, 1450-1600, 1997; (ed.) The Peasantries of Europe from the Fourteenth to the Eighteenth Centuries, 1998; Society and Economy in Germany, 1300-1600, 2002; Town, Country, and Regions in Reformation Germany, 2005. **Address:** School of History, University of St. Andrews, St. Katharine's Lodge, The Scores, St. Andrews, FF KY16 9AR, Scotland. **Online address:** ts30@st-andrews.ac.uk

SCOTT, Trevor. American (born United States) **Genres:** Mystery/Crime/Suspense. **Career:** Writer. **Publications:** NOVELS: Nottinghamshire, 1995; Hypershot, 2001; Strong Conviction, 2002; The Dawn of Midnight, 2003; Boom Town, 2006; Vital Force, 2006; Global Shot, 2007; Rise of the Order, 2007; Burst of Sound, 2008; The Cold Edge, 2008; Duluthians, 2011; Shadows of Berlin, 2011. JAKE ADAMS SERIES: Fatal Network, 1998; Extreme Faction, 1999; The Dolomite Solution, 2000; Drifting Back, 2010. **Address:** c/o Author Mail, Salvo Press, 61428 Elder Ridge St., Bend, OR 97702, U.S.A. **Online address:** scott@trevorscott.com

SCOTT, Whitney S. American (born United States), b. 1945. **Genres:** Novels, Mystery/Crime/Suspense, Romance/Historical, Poetry, Food And Wine, Literary Criticism And History, Social Sciences. **Career:** Foote, Cone and Belding Communications Inc., advertising researcher, 1974-84; Prairie State College, adjunct professor of business and creative writing, 1990-; St. Xavier University, adjunct professor, 1991-97; Columbia College, adjunct professor, 2000-; DeVry Institute of Technology, adjunct professor, 2000-. Writer. **Publications:** Listen to the Moon (poems), 1988; In the Field, 1989; Dancing to the End of the Shining Bar (novel), 1994; Scratching it Out, forthcoming. EDITOR: Words against the Shifting Seasons: Women Speak on Breast Cancer, 1994; Prairie Hearts, 1996; Alternatives, 1997; Freedom's Just Another Word, 1998; Feathers, Fins and Fur, 1999; Earth Beneath, Sky Beyond, 2000; A Kiss Is Still a Kiss, 2001; Take Two-They're Small, 2002; Family Gatherings, 2003; Things That Go Bump in the Night, 2004; Falling in Love Again, 2005; Vacations: the Good, the Bad & Ugly, 2006; A Walk Through My Garden, 2007. Contributor of articles to periodicals. **Address:** Outrider Press Inc., 937 Patricia Ln., Crete, IL 60417-1375, U.S.A. **Online address:** outriderpr@aol.com

SCOTT-CLARK, Cathy. British (born England), b. 1965?. **Genres:** History, Business/Trade/Industry, Social Sciences. **Career:** Sunday Times, education correspondent, 1995, foreign correspondent; Sun Alliance, libel insurance underwriter. Freelance writer, photographer and broadcaster. **Publications:** WITH A. LEVY: The Stone of Heaven: Unearthing the Secret History of Imperial Green Jade, 2001; Amber Room: The Fate of the World's Greatest Lost Treasure, 2004; Deception: Pakistan, the United States and the Secret Trade in Nuclear Weapons, 2007. Contributor to periodicals. **Address:** c/o Helen Oldfield, Guardian Weekend, 119 Farringdon Rd., London, GL EC1R 3ER, England. **Online address:** cathy@secrets-and-lies.co.uk

SCOTT-DRENNAN, Lynne. See SCOTT, Amanda.

SCOVELL, Brian (Souter). British (born England), b. 1935. **Genres:** Sports/Fitness, Biography. **Career:** Daily Mail, sportswriter, 1960-2000; freelance writer, 2000-. **Publications:** (With J. Clarke) Everything That's Cricket: The West Indies Tour 1966, 1966; (with N. Burtenshaw) Whose Side Are You on, Ref?, 1974; (with D. Bird) Not Out, 1978; (intro. and ed.) Diary of a Season: Lawrie McMenemy's Account of the 1978-9 Season as Manager of Southampton Football Club, 1979; (with T. Brooking) Trevor Brooking, 1981; (with B. Robson) Time on the Grass, 1982; Ken Barrington: A Tribute, 1982; (with B. Nicholson) Glory, Glory, 1984; (with T. Neill) Revelations of the Football Manager, 1985; (with D. Howe) The Handbook of Soccer, 1988; (with G. Sobers) Sobers: Twenty Years at the Top, 1988; (with B. Lara) Beating the Field, 1995; Dickie: A Tribute to Umpire Dickie Bird, 1996; Chelsea Azzurri, 1997; (with C. Walcott) Sixty Years on the Back Foot: The Cricketing Life of Sir Clyde Walcott, 1999; Football Gentry: The Cobbold Brothers, 2005; The England Managers: The Impossible Job, 2006; 19-90 Jim Laker, 2006; Brian Lara: Cricket's Troubled Genius, 2007; Bill Nicholson: Football's Perfectionist, 2010; Thank You Hermann Goering: The Life of a Sports Writer, 2010. **Address:** 84 Widmore Rd., Bromley, KT BR1 3BD, England.

SCOVILLE, James Griffin. American (born United States), b. 1940. **Genres:** Economics, Industrial Relations, Business/Trade/Industry. **Career:** Harvard University, instructor, 1964-65, assistant professor of economics, 1966-69; International Labor Office, economist, 1965-66; University of Illinois, associate professor, 1969-75, professor of economics and labor and industrial relations, 1975-79; University of Minnesota, Industrial Relations Center, director, 1979-82, Center for Human Resources and Labor Studies, professor of industrial relations, 1979-, professor emeritus of industrial relations, director of graduate studies, 1990-97, Graduate School, now emeritus; U.S. Department of Labor, consultant. Writer. **Publications:** The Job Content of the U.S. Economy, 1940-70, 1970; (ed.) Perspectives on Poverty and Income Distribution, 1971; Manpower and Occupational Analysis: Concepts and Measurements, 1972; (ed. with A. Sturmthal) The International Labor Movement in Transition, 1973; (with T. Nyamadzabo) Report on the Impact of Minimum Wages in Botswana, 1988; (ed.) Status Influences in Third World Labor Markets: Gender, Caste and Custom, 1991; (ed. with J.W. Budd) The Ethics of Human Resources and Industrial Relations, 2005. **Address:** Carlson School of Management, University of Minnesota, Industrial Relations Ctr., 3-289 CarlSMgmt, 321 19th Ave. S, Minneapolis, MN 55455, U.S.A. **Online address:** scovi001@umn.edu

SCREECH, M(ichael) A(ndrew). British (born England), b. 1926. **Genres:** Intellectual History, Literary Criticism And History, Theology/Religion, Bibliography, Translations. **Career:** University College London, undergraduate, assistant, 1947-51, fellow; University of Birmingham, lecturer, 1951-58, senior lecturer, 1959-61; University of London, reader, 1961-66, personal chair of French, 1966-71, Fielden professor of French language and literature, 1971-84; University of Western Ontario, visiting professor, 1964-65; State University of New York at Albany, visiting professor, 1968-69; University of Wisconsin, Institute for Research in the Humanities, Johnson professor, 1978-79; Oxford University, visiting fellow, 1981-; All Souls College, senior research fellow, 1984-93, Zaharoff lecturer, 1988, professor emeritus, 1993-, chaplain and fellow, 2001-03, emeritus fellow; University of Regina, Edmund Campion lecturer, 1985-; University of North Carolina at Chapel Hill, Wiley visiting professor, 1986-; College de France, professor, 1989-; University of Paris IV, associate professor, 1990-; Wolfson College, extraordinary fellow, 1993-2001. Writer. **Publications:** The Rabelaisian Marriage: Aspects of Rabelais's Religion, Ethics & Comic Philosophy, 1958, rev. ed., 1991; L'Evangélisme de Rabelais, 1959, rev. ed., 1991; (ed.) Le Tiers Livre, 1964; Tiers Livrede Pantagruel, 1964; épistres & évangiles pour les cinquante and deux Sepmaines de l'an, 1964; Les epistres et évangiles de Lefèvred'Etaples, 1964; (with J. Jollife) Les Regrets et Autres oeuvrespoétiques, 1966; Marot évangéliquei, 1967; Invention Etimitation, 1968; Aspects of Rabelais's Christian Comedy, 1968; (ed. with R.M. Calder) Rabelais, Gargantua, 1970; Pantagruéline Prognostication Pour l'an 1533 Avec Les Almanachs Pour les Ans 1533, 1535 et 1541, La Grande et Vraye Pronostication Nouvelle de 1544, 1974; Erasmus: Ecstasy and the Praise of Folly, 1980, rev. ed., 1991; Rabelais, 1982, rev. ed., 1991; Montaigne and Melancholy: The Wisdom of the Essays, 1983, rev. ed., 1991; (ed. and trans.) Michel de Montaigne, An Apology for Raymond Sebond, 1987; (with S. Rawles) A New Rabelais Bibliography: Editions before 1626, 1987; Looking at Rabelais, 1988; (ed. with A. Reeve) Erasmus' Annotations on the New Testament: Acts, Romans, First and Second Corinthians: Facsimile of the Final Latin Text, with All Earlier Variants, 1990; Rabelais and the Challenge of the Gospel: Evangelism, Reformation, Dissent, 1992; Some Renaissance Studies: Selected Articles 1951-1991 with a Bibliography, 1992; (trans., ed. and intro.) Michel de Montaigne: The Complete Essays, 1993; Clément Marot: A Renaissance Poet Discovers the Gospel, 1993; (trans. and intro.) Essays: A Selection, 1993; Clément Marot: A Renaissance Poet Discovers the Gospel: Lutheranism, Fabrism and Calvinism in the Royal Courts of France and of Navarre and in the Ducal Court of Ferrara, 1994; (ed. and intro.) Doctrina at Politia Ecclesiae Anglicanae: An Anglican Summa: Facsimile with Variants of the Text of 1617, 1995; Laughter at the Foot of the Cross, 1997, 2nd ed., 1999; Montaigne's Annotated Copy of Lucretius: A Transcription and Study of the Manuscript, Notes and Pen-marks, 1998. Contributor to journals. **Address:** All Souls College, Oxford, OX OX1 4AL, England. **Online address:** michael.screech@all-souls.ox.ac.uk

SCRIBBLER See Hollingsworth, Mary.

SCRIVENER, Michael (Henry). American (born United States), b. 1948. **Genres:** Literary Criticism And History. **Career:** Wayne State University, assistant professor, 1976-82, associate professor of English, 1982-93, professor of English, 1992-. Writer. **Publications:** Radical Shelley: The Philosophical Anarchism and Utopian Thought of Percy Bysshe Shelley, 1982; (ed.) Poetry and Reform: Periodical Verse from the English Democratic Press 1792-1824, 1992; Seditious Allegories: John Thelwall and Jacobin Writing, 2001; (ed. with F. Felsenstein) Incle and Yarico and The Incas: Two Plays, 2006; Cosmopolitan Ideal in the Age of Revolution and Reaction, 1776-1832, 2007; Jewish Representation in British Literature 1780-1840: After Ahylock, 2011.

Address: Department of English, Wayne State University, 9201.2, 5057 Woodward, 4841 Cass Ave., 2155 Old Main, Detroit, MI 48201, U.S.A. **Online address:** michael.scrivener@wayne.edu

SCRUTON, Roger. American/British (born England), b. 1944. **Genres:** Novellas/Short Stories, Architecture, Philosophy, Politics/Government. **Career:** Peterhouse, research fellow, 1969-71; University of London, Birkbeck College, lecturer in philosophy, 1971-79, reader, 1979-85, professor of aesthetics, 1985-92, visiting professor of philosophy, 1995-; freelance writer, 1974-; Salisbury Review, editor, 1982-2001; Claridge Press Ltd., founder and director, 1987-2004; Central European Consulting Ltd., co-founder and director, 1989-2004; Boston University, professor of philosophy and university professor, 1992-95; Horsell's Farm Enterprises, co-founder and consultant, 1999-; Institute for the Psychological Sciences, research professor, 2005-; Princeton University, visiting professor; Stanford University, visiting professor; Universite catholique de Louvain, visiting professor; University of Guelph, visiting professor; University of Waterloo, visiting professor; Wits University, visiting professor; Cambridge University, visiting professor. **Publications:** (Co-author) Morality and Moral Reasoning, 1971; Art and Imagination: A Study in the Philosophy of Mind, 1974; The Aesthetics of Architecture, 1979; The Meaning of Conservatism, 1980, 3rd ed., 2000; Fortnight's Anger, 1981; From Descartes to Wittgenstein: A Short History of Modern Philosophy, 1981, 2nd ed., 2002; The Politics of Culture, 1981; A Dictionary of Political Thought, 1982, rd ed., 2007; Kant, 1983, rev. ed., 2001; The Aesthetic Understanding: Essays in the Philosophy of Art and Culture, 1983, rev. ed. 1997; (co-author) Karol Szymanowski in seiner Zeit, 1984; (with F. Brennan and J. Hyde) Land Rights and Legitimacy: Three Views, 1985; Untimely Tracts, 1985; Sexual Desire: A Philosophical Investigation in US as Sexual Desire: A Moral Philosophy of the Erotic, 1986; Thinkers of the New Left, 1986; A Land Held Hostage: Lebanon and the West, 1987; Spinoza, 1988, rev. ed., 2002; (ed. and intro.) Conservative Thoughts: Essays from the Salisbury Review, 1988; (ed. and intro.) Conservative Thinkers: Essays from The Salisbury Review, 1988; The Philosopher on Dover Beach, 1989; Francesca, 1991; A Dove Descending and Other Stories, 1991; (ed. and intro.) Conservative Texts: An Anthology, 1991; Xanthippic Dialogues: A Philosophical Fiction, 1993; Modern Philosophy: A Survey, 1994; The Classical Vernacular: Architechural Principles in the Age of Nihilism, 1995; Animal Rights and Wrongs, 1996, 3rd ed., 2000; An Intelligent Person's Guide to Philosophy, 1996; The Aesthetics of Music, 1997; On Hunting, 1998; An Intelligent Person's Guide to Modern Culture, 2000; (trans.) Perictione in Colophon, 2000; England: An Elegy, 2000; Meaning of Conservatism, 2001; The West and the Rest: Globalization and Terrorism Threat, 2002; News from Somewhere: On Setting, 2004; Death-Devoted Heart: Sex and the Sacred in Wagner's Tristan and Isolde, 2004; Philosophy: Principles and Problems, 2005; Modern Culture, 2005; Gentle Regrets: Thoughts from a Life, 2005; A Political Philosophy, 2006; Palgrave Macmillan Dictionary of Political Thought, 2007; Culture Counts: Faith and Feeling in a World Besieged, 2007; I Drink Therefore I Am, 2009; Understanding Music, 2009; Beauty, 2009; (ed.) Liberty and Civilization, 2010; Uses of Pessimism and the Danger of False Hope, 2010; (with V. Meelberg and M.J.M. Hoondert) Meer Dan Ontspanning Alleen: Over het Belang van muziek, 2010. **Address:** Institute for the Psychological Sciences, 2001 Jefferson Davis Hwy., Ste. 511, Haymarket, Arlington, VA 22202, U.S.A. **Online address:** rogerscruton@mac.com

SCULLE, Keith A. American (born United States), b. 1941. **Genres:** Environmental Sciences/Ecology, History. **Career:** Illinois Historic Preservation Agency, head of research and education; University of Illinois, adjunct professor; University of Illinois, Urbana-Champaign, professor of geography. Writer. **Publications:** (With J.A. Jakle) The Gas Station in America, 1994; (with J.A. Jakle and J.S. Rogers) The Motel in America, 1996; (with J.A. Jakle) Fast Food: Roadside Restaurants in the Automobile Age, 1999; (with J.A. Jakle) Lots of Parking: Land Use in a Car Culture, 2004; (with J.A. Jakle) Signs in America's Auto Age: Signatures of Landscape and Place, 2004; (with J.A. Jakle) Motoring: The Highway Experience in America, 2008; (with J.A. Jakle) America's Main Street Hotels: Transiency and Community in the Early Auto Age, 2009; (with J.A. Jakle) Remembering Roadside America: Preserving the Recent Past as Landscape and Place, 2011. Contributor to periodicals. **Address:** University of Tennessee Press, 110 Conference Ctr., 600 Henley St., Knoxville, TN 37996, U.S.A. **Online address:** keith.sculle@illinois.gov

SCULLY, Helen. American (born United States), b. 1977. **Genres:** Novels.

Career: Barcelona Metropolitan, art columnist, 2001. Writer. **Publications:** In the Hope of Rising Again, 2004. Contributor to periodicals. **Address:** c/o Author Mail, Penguin Group, 375 Hudson St., New York, NY 10014, U.S.A.

SCULLY, James (Joseph). American (born United States), b. 1937. **Genres:** Literary Criticism And History, Translations, Poetry, Theatre. **Career:** Rutgers University, instructor in English, 1963-64; University of Connecticut, assistant professor, 1965-67; associate professor, 1968-74; professor of English, 1975-92, emeritus professor, 1992-; Hartford Street Academy, teacher, 1969; University of Massachusetts, visiting writer, 1973. **Publications:** Modern Poetics, 1965, rev. ed. as Modern Poets On Modern Poetry, 1966; The Marches: A Book of Poems, 1967; Communications between Grandin Conover and James Scully, 1970; Avenue of the Americas, 1971; Santiago Poems, 1975, 2nd ed., 1982; (trans. with C.J. Herington) Prometheus Bound, Aeschylus, 1975; (trans. with M.A. Proser) Quechua Peoples Poetry, 1976; Scrap Book: Poems, 1977; (trans. with M. Proser and A. Scully) De Repente/ All of a Sudden, by Teresa de Jesus, 1979; May Day, 1980; (ed. and trans. with A. Scully) Poetry and Militancy in Latin America, 1981; Apollo Helmet, 1983; Line Break: Poetry as Social Practice, 1988; Raging Beauty: Selected Poems, 1994; Donatello's Version: Poems, 2007; Angel in Flames, 2011. **Address:** Department of English, University of Connecticut, 215 Glenbrook Rd., Ste. 4025, Storrs, CT 06269-4025, U.S.A.

SCULLY, Matthew. American (born United States), b. 1959. **Genres:** Animals/Pets, Social Sciences. **Career:** Special assistant and senior speechwriter to President George W. Bush, 2001-04; National Review magazine, literary editor. **Publications:** Dominion: The Power of Man, the Suffering of Animals and the Call to Mercy, 2002. Contributor to periodicals. **Address:** St. Martin's Press, 175 5th Ave., New York, NY 10010-7703, U.S.A.

SCULLY, Pamela (Frederika). American/South African (born South Africa), b. 1962. **Genres:** History, Biography. **Career:** University of Cape Town, lecturer, 1986-92; Georgia State University, lecturer, 1991; Kenyon College, visiting instructor, 1992-93, assistant professor of history, 1993-; University of Cincinnati, Taft Memorial Fund lecturer, 1995; National Endowment for the Humanities, fellow, 1995-96; Case Western Reserve University, lecturer, 1997; Emory University, director and director of undergraduate studies, associate professor of women's studies and African studies. Writer. **Publications:** Bouquet of Freedom: Social and Economic Relations in the Stellenbosch District, South Africa, 1870-1900, 1990; Liberating the Family? Gender and British Slave Emancipation in the Rural Western Cape, South Africa, 1823-1853, 1997; (ed. with D. Paton) Gender and Slave Emancipation in the Atlantic World, 2005; (with C.C. Crais) Sara Baartman and the Hottentot Venus: A Ghost Story and a Biography, 2009. Contributor to books and periodicals. **Address:** Department of Women's Studies, Emory University, 128 Candler Library, Atlanta, GA 30322, U.S.A. **Online address:** pamella.scully@emory.edu

SCULLY, Vincent. American (born United States), b. 1920. **Genres:** Architecture, Art/Art History. **Career:** Yale University, instructor, 1947, professor, 1961-91, senior faculty fellow, 1962-63, Sterling professor of history of art, through 1991, Sterling professor emeritus of the history of art, 1991-; Brown University, Howard Foundation fellow, 1956; Morse College, master, 1969-75; University of Miami, distinguished visiting professor, 1992; California Institute of Technology, Mellon visiting professor, 1995. Writer. **Publications:** (Co-author) The Architectural Heritage of Newport, Rhode Island, 1640-1915, 1952, 2nd ed., 1982; The Shingle Style, 1955; Frank Lloyd Wright, 1960; Modern Architecture: The Architecture of Democracy, 1961; Louis I. Kahn, 1962; The Earth, the Temple, and the Gods: Greek Sacred Architecture, 1962, rev. ed., 1979; American Architecture and Urbanism, 1969, rev. ed., 1988; Pueblo Architecture of the Southwest, 1971; The Shingle Style Today: Or the Historian's Revenge, 1974; Pueblo: Mountain, Village, Dance, 1975, 2nd ed., 1989; (co-author) Robert Stern, 1981; Studies and Executed Buildings by Frank Lloyd Wright, 1986; The Villas of Palladio, 1986; New World Visions of Household Gods and Sacred Places: American Art and the Metropolitan Museum, 1650-1914, 1988; The Architecture of the American Summer: The Flowering of the Shingle Style, 1989; (co-author) The Architecture of Robert Venturi, 1989; (co-author) The Great Dinosaur Mural at Yale: The Age of Reptiles, 1990; Architecture: The Natural and the Manmade, 1991; (co-author) Between Two Towers: The Architecture of the School of Miami, 1996; Louis I. Kahn, 2000; Modern Architecture and Other

Essays, 2003. **Address:** Department of History of Art, Yale University, 56 High St., PO Box 208272, New Haven, CT 06520, U.S.A. **Online address:** vincent.scully@yale.edu

SCUPHAM, (John) Peter. British (born England), b. 1933. **Genres:** Poetry. **Career:** Skegness Grammar School, teacher in English, 1957-61; St. Christopher School, Department of English, head, 1961-; Mandeville Press, co-founder and proprietor, 1974-. Writer. **Publications:** The Small Containers, 1972; The Snowing Globe, 1972; Children Dancing, 1972; The Nondescript, 1973; The Gift, 1973; Prehistories, 1975; The Hinterland, 1977; A Mandeville Troika, 1977; Natura, 1978; Megaliths And Water: Andy Christians Drawings, 1978; Summer Palaces, 1980; Transformation Scenes: A Sequence of Five Poems, 1982; Winter Quarters, 1983; Out Late, 1986; The Air Show, 1988; Under the Barrage, 1988; Watching the Perseids, 1990; Selected Poems, 1972-1990, 1990; The Ark, 1994; Night Watch, 1999; Collected Poems, 2002; (ed. and intro.) Ovid's Metamorphoses: A Selection, 2005; Borrowed Landscapes, 2011. WITH J. MOLE: Christmas Past, 1981; Christmas Games, 1983; Christmas Visits, 1985; Christmas Emblems, 1986; Christmas Fables, 1987; Christmas Gifts, 1988; Christmas Books, 1989; Christmas Boxes, 1990. **Address:** c/o Carcanet Press, Alliance House, 30 Cross St., 4th Fl., Manchester, NF M2 7AQ, England. **Online address:** goodman@dircon.co.uk

S.D., Trav. American (born United States), b. 1965. **Genres:** Novels, Humor/Satire. **Career:** American Vaudeville Theater, director; Mountebanks, founder. Writer, producer and comedian. **Publications:** No Applause-Just Throw Money: The Book That Made Vaudeville Famous: A High-class, Refined Entertainment, 2005. Contributor to periodicals. **Address:** 650 Leonard St., Brooklyn, NY 11222, U.S.A.

SEABRIGHT, Paul. French/British (born England), b. 1958. **Genres:** Economics, Business/Trade/Industry. **Career:** All Souls College, fellow, 1980-94, Prize fellow, 1982-87; Churchill College, teaching fellow, 1986-87; Economic Policy, assistant editor, 1988-94, managing editor, 2000-; University of Cambridge, assistant director of research, 1988-99, reader in economics, 1999-2001; CEPR, research fellow, 1989-; Université Libre de Bruxelles, Ganshof van der Meersch visiting chair, 1997-98; école Polytechnique, assistant professor, 1998-2003; College of Europe, lecturer in economics, 1998-99; Université Toulouse I, professor of economics, 2000-; McMaster University, Hooker distinguished visiting professor, 2006; European Bank for Reconstruction and Development, consultant; World Bank, consultant; United Nations, consultant; European Commission, consultant. Writer. **Publications:** (With D. Neven and R. Nuttall) Merger in Daylight: The Economics and Politics of European Merger Control, 1993; (contrib.) The Quality of Life, 1993; (with J. Crémer and A. Estache) The Decentralization of Public Services: Lessons from the Theory of the Firm, 1994; (with D. Neven, E. Fox and J. Fingleton) Competition Policy and the Tranformation of Central Europe, 1996; (with D. Neven and P. Papandropoulos) Trawling for Minnows: European Competition Policy and Agreements between Firms, 1998; (ed.) The Vanishing Rouble: Barter Networks and Non-monetary Transactions in Post-Soviet Societies, 2000; The Company of Strangers: A Natural History of Economic Life, 2004, rev. ed., 2010; (contrib.) Globalization, Culture and the Limits of the Market, 2004; (ed. with J. von Hagen) The Economic Regulation of Broadcasting Markets: Evolving Technology and the Challenges for Policy, 2007; (contrib.) The Political Economy of Antitrust, 2007. Contributor to periodicals. **Address:** Institut d'Economie Industrielle, Université de Toulouse-1, Manufacture des Tabacs, 21, Allée de Brienne, Toulouse, 31000, France. **Online address:** seabrigh@cict.fr

SEABROOK, John M. American (born United States), b. 1959. **Genres:** Marketing, Biography, Autobiography/Memoirs, Novellas/Short Stories. **Career:** Manhattan Inc. (business journal), staff, 1983-; New Yorker, staff writer, 1993-; Princeton University, visiting Robbins professor of writing; Nassau Weekly, literary editor. **Publications:** Deeper: My Two-Year Odyssey in Cyberspace, 1997; Nobrow: The Culture of Marketing the Marketing of Culture, 2000; Flash of Genius: And Other True Stories of Invention, 2008. Contributor to periodicals. **Address:** c/o Author Mail, Vintage Publicity, 1745 Broadway, New York, NY 10019, U.S.A. **Online address:** jmseabrook@gmail.com

SEABROOK, Mike. French/British (born England), b. 1950. **Genres:** Autobiography/Memoirs, Sports/Fitness, Novels, Biography, Music, Information Science/Computers, Essays. **Career:** Police officer, 1971-74; advertising copywriter, 1975-78; computer software technical writer, 1978-89; writer, 1989-. **Publications:** Quick Singles (cricket essays), 1986; Coppers: An In-

side View of the British Police, 1987; Unnatural Relations (novel), 1989; Fine Glances (cricket essays), 1990; Conduct Unbecoming (novel), 1991; Out of Bounds (novel), 1992; (ed. with P. Alliss) One Over Par (golf essays), 1992; Max: The Life and Music of Peter Maxwell Davies, 1994; (ed. with G. Armytage) Turf Accounts (racing essays), 1994; (ed. with S. Barnes) Nice Tries: A Collection of New Rugby Writing, 1995. Contributor to magazines. **Address:** La Ferme du Laurier, Goux les Usiers, 25520, France.

SEAFORD, Richard. British (born England) **Genres:** Art/Art History, Philosophy. **Career:** University of Exeter, Department of Classics and Ancient History, professor of classics and ancient history and head. Writer. **Publications:** Pompeii, 1978; (intro.) Cyclops, 1984; Reciprocity and Ritual: Homer and Tragedy in the Developing City-State, 1994; Bacchae, 1996; (ed. with C. Gill and N. Postlethwaite) Reciprocity in Ancient Greece, 1998; Money and the Early Greek Mind: Homer, Philosophy, Tragedy, 2004; Dionysos, 2006; Cosmology and the Polis: The Social Construction of Space and Time in the Tragedies of Aeschylus, 2012. Contributor to periodicals and journals. **Address:** Department of Classics & Ancient History, University of Exeter, Amory Bldg., Rennes Dr., Exeter, DN EX4 4RJ, England. **Online address:** r.a.s.seaford@exeter.ac.uk

SEAGRAVE, Sterling. American (born United States), b. 1937. **Genres:** Military/Defense/Arms Control, History, Mystery/Crime/Suspense, Social Sciences. **Career:** Merchant seaman; reporter and columnist, 1959-67; Time (magazine), stringer, 1962; Washington Post, reporter, assistant foreign news editor, 1962-65; freelance journalist, 1965-72; St. Petersburg Times, feature editor, foreign news editor, 1973-75; Time-Life Books, editor and writer, 1975-80; writer, 1980-. **Publications:** Yellow Rain: A Journey Through the Terror of Chemical Warfare, 1981; Soldiers of Fortune, 1981; The Soong Dynasty 1985; The Marcos Dynasty, 1988; (with P. Seagrave) Dragon Lady: The Life and Legend of the Last Empress of China, 1992; Lords of the Rim: The Invisible Empire of the Overseas Chinese, 1995; (with P. Seagrave) The Yamato Dynasty: The Secret History of Japan's Imperial Family, 1999; (with P. Seagrave) Gold Warriors: America's Secret Recovery of Yamashita's Gold, 2003; (with P. Seagrave) Huang jin wu shi: er zhan Riben lue duo Ya Zhou ju e huang jin hei mu, 2005. **Address:** c/o Robert Gottlieb, William Morris Agency, 1325 Ave. of the Americas, New York, NY 10019, U.S.A.

SEAGRAVES, Donny Bailey. American (born United States), b. 1951. **Genres:** Children's Fiction. **Career:** Junebug Books (online used and rare-book dealer), owner and operator. Journalist and freelance writer. **Publications:** Gone from These Woods, 2009. Contributor to periodicals. **Address:** PO Box 556, Winterville, GA 30683, U.S.A. **Online address:** donnyseagraves@gmail.com

SEALE, Alan. American (born United States), b. 1955. **Genres:** Self Help, inspirational/Motivational Literature. **Career:** Center for Transformational Presence, founder, principal coach and director. Writer. **Publications:** On Becoming a Twenty-First Century Mystic: Pathways to Intuitive Living, 1997; Intuitive Living: A Sacred Path, 2001; Soul Mission or Life Vision: Recognize Your True Gifts and Make Your Mark in the World, 2003; Manifestation Wheel: A Practical Process for Creating Miracles, 2008; The Power of Your Presence, 2009; Create a World That Works: Tools for Personal and Global Transformation, 2011. **Address:** PO Box 18471, Rochester, NY 14618, U.S.A. **Online address:** info@alanseale.com

SEALE, William. American (born United States), b. 1939. **Genres:** Architecture, History, Biography, Autobiography/Memoirs. **Career:** Lamar State College of Technology (now Lamar University), assistant professor of history, 1965-69; Historic Columbia Foundation, director, 1969-71; freelance writer, 1971-73; National Park Service and White House Historical Association, staff, 1973-77; historian and restorationist, 1977-; George C. Marshall International Center, architectural historian. Writer. **Publications:** Texas Riverman, 1966, 2nd ed., 2009; San Augustine in the Texas Republic, 1969; Sam Houston's Wife, 1970; Texas in Our Time, 1971; The Tasteful Interlude: American Interiors Through the Camera's Eye, 1860-1917, 1975, 2nd ed., 1981; (with H.R. Hitchcock) Temples of Democracy: The State Capitols of the USA, 1976; Courthouse, 1978; Recreating the Historic House Interior, 1978; (intro.) The Kentucky Governor's Mansion, 1984; The President's House, 1986, 2nd ed., 2008; Virginia's Executive Mansion: A History, 1988; The White House: The History of an American Idea, 1992; Of Houses and Time, 1992; (contrib.) Domestic Views, 1992; (with E. Ostendorf) Domes of America, 1994; Michigan's Capitol, 1995; The White House Garden, 1996; A Guide to Historic

Alexandria, 2000; (ed.) White House: Actors and Observers, 2002. **Address:** George C. Marshall International Center, 217 Edwards Ferry Rd., Leesburg, VA 20176, U.S.A. **Online address:** oeconomy@aol.com

SEALS, David. (Davydd Ap Saille). American (born United States), b. 1947. **Genres:** Novels, Plays/Screenplays, Poetry, Young Adult Fiction, Adult Non-fiction. **Career:** Freelance journalist, 1967-; Sky and Sage Books, publisher; League of Indigenous Sovereign Nations, ambassador. Actor, producer and director. **Publications:** NOVELS: The Powwow Highway, 1979; Sweet Medicine, 1992. AS DAVYDD AP SAILLE: Thunder Nation (novel), 1990, rev. ed., 1996; Third Eye Theatre (novel), 1991; The Poetic College: Essays and Poems on Literature and Society, 1989-1991, 1992; Crazy Horse, 1994; (contrib.) The Seventh Generation: Images of the Lakota Today, 1998. OTHER: Abduction at Roswell, 2008. Contributor to periodicals. **Address:** University of Arizona Press, Main Library Bldg., 5th Fl., 1510 E University Blvd., PO Box 210055, Tucson, AZ 85721-0055, U.S.A.

SEALY, I(rwin) Allan. Indian (born India), b. 1951. **Genres:** Novels, Travel/Exploration, Adult Non-fiction, Romance/Historical. **Career:** Writer and educator. **Publications:** The Trotter-Nama: A Chronicle (novel), 1988; Hero: A Fable (novel), 1990; From Yukon to Yucatan: A Western Journey, 1994; The Everest Hotel: A Calendar, 1998; Brainfever Bird, 2003; Red: An Alphabet, 2006. **Address:** A. P. Watt Ltd., 20 John St., London, GL WC1N 2DR, England.

SEAMAN, Ann Rowe. American (born United States), b. 1946?. **Genres:** Biography, Literary Criticism And History, Autobiography/Memoirs. **Career:** University of Southern California, public relations director, editor; Los Angeles County Natural History Museum, freelance editor; TERRA, editor. Journalist. **Publications:** Swaggart: An Unauthorized Biography of an American Evangelist, 1999; America's Most Hated Woman: The Life and Gruesome Death of Madalyn Murray O'Hair, 2005. **Address:** c/o Author Mail, Continuum International Publishing Group, 15 E 26th St., Ste. 1703, New York, NY 10010-1505, U.S.A. **Online address:** annseaman@gmail.com

SEAMAN, Gerald Roberts. British (born England), b. 1934. **Genres:** Music, Bibliography, Biography. **Career:** Nottingham Training College, lecturer in music, 1962-64; University of Western Australia, temporary lecturer in music, 1964-65; University of Auckland, senior lecturer, 1965-69, associate professor of musicology, 1970-98, acting head of department, 1978, professor of musicology; St. Antony's College, senior associate, 1980; Oxford University, Department for Continuing Education, part-time lecturer, 1998-, tutor; University of Liverpool, associate lecturer, 1999; University of Surrey, associate lecturer, 1999-2000; Birmingham Conservatoire, research coordinator, 2001-02, research fellow, 2002-03, visiting lecturer, 2004-. Writer. **Publications:** History of Russian Music, vol. I, 1967; (comp. with D. Freed) Orchestral Scores, 1978, 2nd ed., 1984; Nikolai Andreevich Rimsky-Korsakov: A Guide to Research, 1988. **Address:** University of Oxford, Rewley House, 1 Wellington Sq., Oxford, OX OX1 2JA, England. **Online address:** gerald.seaman@conted.ox.ac.uk

SEAMAN, P. David. American (born United States), b. 1932. **Genres:** Language/Linguistics, Humanities, Anthropology/Ethnology, History. **Career:** Asbury College, instructor, 1957-65, professor of languages and head of division of languages, 1965-67; Northern Arizona University, associate professor, 1967-70, professor of linguistics, 1970-94, professor emeritus, 1994-, NDEA English as a Second Language Institute, staff, 1968, National Science Foundation Summer Linguistics Institute, founder and director, 1968-73; Arizona Academy of Science, Anthropology Section, head, 1968-69; University of Athens, senior Fulbright lecturer, 1969-70; U.S. Educational Foundation in Greece, English Language Program in Greece, head, 1969-70; Native Americans and sociolinguistics, lecturer. Writer. **Publications:** Modern Greek and American English in Contact, 1972; Hopi Dictionary: Hopi-English, English-Hopi, Grammatical Appendix, 1985, rev. ed., 1996; The A.F. Whiting Collection: User Guide and Index, 1993; Bootstraps and Blessings: From Poverty to Success, 2004; From Greece with Love: A True Account, 2011. EDITOR: (with S. Weber) Havasupai Habitat: A.F. Whiting's Ethnography of a Traditional Indian Culture, 1985; Born a Chief: The Nineteenth Century Hopi Boyhood of Edmund Nequatewa, 1993; A Mosaic from Broken Glass, 2006. TRANSLATOR: K. Farantakis, The Leaden-Sky Years of World War II: Diary Notes of a Schoolboy in Occupied Crete, 2004. Contributor of ar-

ticles to journals. **Address:** Department of Anthropology, Northern Arizona University, PO Box 15200, Flagstaff, AZ 86011, U.S.A. **Online address:** pdseaman@gmail.com

SEARCY, David. American (born United States), b. 1946?. **Genres:** Novels, Horror. **Career:** Southern Methodist University, teacher of English; Interstate Batteries, staff. Writer. **Publications:** Peter Rabbit's Trick, 1980; Ordinary Horror, 2001; Last Things, 2002; Santa Claus, forthcoming. Contributor to periodicals. **Address:** Viking Press, 375 Hudson St., New York, NY 10014-3657, U.S.A.

SEARING, Donald D. American (born United States), b. 1942. **Genres:** Adult Non-fiction, Politics/Government. **Career:** University of North Carolina, Burton Craige professor of political science, acting director. Writer. **Publications:** Westminster's World: Understanding Political Roles, 1994. **Address:** Department of Political Science, University of North Carolina, 361 Hamilton Hall, Ste. 3265, Chapel Hill, NC 27599-3265, U.S.A.

SEARLE, Elizabeth. American (born United States), b. 1962. **Genres:** Novels, Novellas/Short Stories, Literary Criticism And History. **Career:** Oberlin College, adjunct lecturer in fiction writing, 1983-84; New Haven Regional Center, special education teacher and caretaker for mentally handicapped adults, 1985-86; Groden Center, special education reading assistant, 1986-87; Brown University, adjunct lecturer in fiction writing, 1988-89; Suffolk University, instructor in composition, 1990-91; University of Massachusetts, instructor, 1990-92, visiting writer, 2007-08; Emerson College, instructor in fiction writing, 1991-; University of Southern Maine, instructor of fiction writing, 2002-. Writer. **Publications:** My Body to You (stories), 1993; A Four-Sided Bed (novel), 1998; Celebrities in Disgrace: A Novella and Stories, 2001; Girl Held in Home, 2011. Contributor to periodicals. **Address:** c/o John Talbot, Talbot Fortune Agency L.L.C., 180 E Prospect Ave., Ste. 188, Mamaroneck, NY 10543, U.S.A. **Online address:** e.searle@comcast.net

SEARLE, G(eoffrey) R(ussell). British (born England), b. 1940. **Genres:** History, Politics/Government, Social Commentary, Adult Non-fiction, Economics, Social Sciences, Business/Trade/Industry. **Career:** University of East Anglia, lecturer, 1965-81, senior lecturer, 1981-93, professor of modern British history, 1993-2001, professor emeritus of history, 2001-. Writer. **Publications:** The Quest for National Efficiency: A Study in British Politics and Political Thought, 1899-1914, 1971, rev. ed., 1990; Efficiency and Empire, 1973; Eugenics and Politics in Britain, 1900-1914, 1976; Corruption in British Politics, 1895-1930, 1987; The Liberal Party: Triumph and Disintegration, 1886-1929, 1992, rev. ed., 2001; Entrepreneurial Politics in Mid-Victorian Britain, 1993; Country before Party: Coalition and the Idea of National Government in Modern Britain, 1885-1987, 1995; Morality and Market in Victorian Britain, 1998; New England?: Peace and War, 1886-1918, 2004. **Address:** Centre of East Anglian Studies, University of East Anglia, 4.32 Arts Bldg., Norwich Research Pk., Norwich, NF NR4 7TJ, England. **Online address:** g.searle@uea.ac.uk

SEARLE, John R(ogers). American (born United States), b. 1932. **Genres:** Philosophy, History. **Career:** University of Wisconsin, faculty; Oxford University, lecturer in philosophy, 1956-59; University of California, assistant professor, 1959-64, associate professor, 1964-67, Willis S. and Marion Slusser professor of the philosophy of mind and language, 1966-, professor, 1967-, special assistant to the chancellor, 1965-67, chair of philosophy department, 1973-75; Brasenose College, visiting fellow, 1967-68. Writer. **Publications:** Speech Acts: An Essay in the Philosophy of Language, 1969; The Campus War, 1971; Expression and Meaning: Studies in the Theory of Speech Acts, 1979; Intentionality: An Essay in the Philosophy of Mind, 1983; Meaning: Protocol of the Forty Fourth Colloquy, 3 October 1982, 1983; Minds, Brains, and Science, 1984; (with D. Vanderveken) Foundations of Illocutionary Logic, 1985; John Searle and His Critics, 1991; The Rediscovery of The Mind, 1992; Searle on Conversation, 1992; The Construction of Social Reality, 1995; The Mystery of Consciousness, 1997; Mind, Language and Society, Philosophy in the Real World, 1998; Rationality in Action, 2001; Consciousness and Language, 2002; Mind: A Brief Introduction, 2004; Freedom and Neurobiology: Reflections on Free Will, Language, and Political Power, 2007; Philosophy in a New Century: Selected Essays, 2008; Making the Social World: The Structure of Human Civilization, 2010. EDITOR: The Philosophy of Language, 1971; (ed. with F. Kiefer and M. Bierwisch) Speech Act Theory and Pragmatics, 1980. **Address:** Department of Philosophy, University of California, 148 Moses Hall, Ste. 2390, Berkeley, CA 94720-2390, U.S.A.

SEARLE, Ronald (William Fordham). *See* Obituaries.

SEARLES, P. D(avid). American (born United States), b. 1933. **Genres:** Documentaries/Reportage, Biography, Autobiography/Memoirs, History. **Career:** Business executive, 1958-69, 1980-90; U.S. Peace Corps, country director, 1971-74, deputy director, 1974-76; National Endowment for the Arts, assistant chairman and deputy chairman, 1976-80. Educator and writer. **Publications:** A College for Appalachia: Alice Lloyd on Caney Creek, 1995; The Peace Corps Experience: Challenge and Change, 1969-1976, 1997. **Address:** 1907 Littlewood Dr., Owensboro, KY 42301, U.S.A. **Online address:** jan133@aol.com

SEARLS, David. American (born United States), b. 1947. **Genres:** Business/Trade/Industry. **Career:** Matzner Newspapers, editor, 1970-71; Hodskins, Simone & Searls Inc., partner and vice president, 1976-98; The Searls Group, co-founder, 1978-; Linux Journal, senior editor, 1999-; Harvard University, Berkman Center for Internet & Society, fellow, fellow alumnus, 2006-10; University of California, Center for Information Technology and Society, fellow. **Publications:** (With C. Locke, D. Weinberger and R. Levine) The Cluetrain Manifesto: The End of Business as Usual, 2000. Contributor to periodicals. **Address:** Linux Journal, PO Box 55549, Seattle, WA 98155-0549, U.S.A. **Online address:** doc@searls.com

SEARLS, Hank. Also writes as Lee Costigan. American (born United States), b. 1922. **Genres:** Novels, Science Fiction/Fantasy, Plays/Screenplays, Biography, Mystery/Crime/Suspense. **Career:** Hughes Aircraft, writer, 1955-56; Douglas Aircraft, writer, 1956-57; Warner Brothers, writer, 1959; freelance writer, 1959-. **Publications:** NOVELS: The Big X, 1959; The Crowded Sky, 1960; The Astronaut, 1962; The Pilgrim Project, 1964; The Hero Ship, 1969; The Lost Prince: Young Joe, The Forgotten Kennedy, The Story of the Oldest Brother, 1969; Pentagon, 1971; Overboard, 1977; Jaws 2, 1978; Firewind, 1981; Sounding, 1982; Blood Song, 1984; Kataki, 1987; Jaws: The Revenge, 1987; The Adventures of Mike Blair: A Dime Detective Book, 1988; The Penetrators, 1988; Altitude Zero, 1991. AS LEE COSTIGAN: NOVELS: Never Kill a Cop, 1959; The New Breed, 1962; The Hard Sell, 1964; The Deceivers, 1967. **Address:** Scovil Galen Ghosh Literary Agency Inc., 276 5th Ave., Ste. 708, New York, NY 10001-4509, U.S.A. **Online address:** hanksearls@harbornet.com

SEARS, David O('Keefe). American (born United States), b. 1935. **Genres:** Politics/Government, Psychology, Social Sciences. **Career:** University of California-Los Angeles, Department of Social Psychology, assistant professor, 1961-67, associate professor, 1967-71, professor, 1971-, dean of social sciences, 1983-92, Institute for Social Science Research, director, distinguished professor; Harvard University, visiting lecturer, 1967-68; University of California-Berkeley, Brookings Institution, fellow, Center for Advanced Study, Guggenheim Fellow; Society for the Advancement of Socio-Economics, president, 1992; International Society of Political Psychology, president, 1994. Writer. **Publications:** (With R.E. Lane) Public Opinion, 1964; Los Angeles Riot Study, 1967; (with J.L. Freedman and J.M. Carlsmith) Social Psychology, 1970, 12th ed., 2006; (with J. Sidanius and L. Bobo) Racialized Politics, 1970, 10th ed., 2000; Racial Tensions and Voting in Los Angeles, 1971; (ed. with Freedman and Carlsmith) Readings in Social Psychology, 1971; (with J.B. McConahay) The Politics of Violence, 1973; (with J. Citrin) Tax Revolt: Something for Nothing in California, 1982; (ed. with R. Lau) Political Cognition: The Nineteenth Annual Carnegie Symposium on Cognition, 1986; (with L. Huddy and R. Jervis) Oxford Handbook of Political Psychology, 2003; (with M. Tesler) Obama's Race: The 2008 Election and the Dream of a Post-Racial America, 2010. **Address:** Department of Psychology, University of California, Franz Hall 5445B, 405 Hilgard Ave., Los Angeles, CA 90095-1563, U.S.A. **Online address:** sears@psych.ucla.edu

SEARS, James T(homas). American/Spanish (born Spain), b. 1951. **Genres:** Education, Gay And Lesbian Issues, Sex, Social Commentary, Adult Non-fiction, History, Cultural/Ethnic Topics, Local History/Rural Topics, Sociology, Women's Studies And Issues, Reference. **Career:** Trinity University, visiting instructor, 1983-84; University of South Carolina, assistant professor, 1984-89, associate professor, 1989-93, professor of curriculum studies, 1993-2005, South Carolina Policy Center, senior research associate, 1989-92, retired, 2005; Far West Laboratory, research associate, 1986; ONE Institute, research fellow, 1997; Harvard University, visiting professor, 2001; Journal of Gay and Lesbian Issues in Education, editor; Pennsylvania State University, faculty, 2006-08. **Publications:** (With J. Dan Marshall and A. Otis-Wilborn) Teacher Education Policies and Programs: Implementing Reform Proposals of the 1980s, 1988; Growing Up Gay in the South: Race, Gender, and Journeys of the Spirit, 1991; (with J.D. Marshall and A. Otis-Wilborn) When Best Doesn't Equal Good: Educational Reform and Teacher Recruitment: A Longitudinal Study, 1994; Bound by Diversity, 1994; Lonely Hunters: An Oral History of Lesbian and Gay Southern Life, 1948-1968, 1997; Curriculum, Religion, and Public Education: Conversations For an Enlarging Public Square, 1998; (with J.D. Marshall and W. Schubert) Turning Points in Curriculum: A Contemporary American Memoir, 2000; Rebels, Rubyfruit & Rhinestones: Queering Space in the Stonewall South, 2001; Democratic Curriculum Theory & Practice: Retrieving Public Spaces, 2001; Gay, Lesbian & Transgender Issues in Education: Programs, Policies, & Practices, 2005; Youth, Education, and Sexualities: An International Encyclopedia, 2005; Behind The Mask of The Mattachine: The Hal Call Chronicles And The Early Movement For Homosexual Emancipation, 2006; The Modern World/Twentieth & Twenty-First Centuries, vol. VI, 2008; Edwin and John: A Southern Gay Couples Half Century Journey Together, 2009. EDITOR AND CONTRIBUTOR: (with J.D. Marshall) Teaching and Thinking about Curriculum: Critical Inquiries, 1990, rev. ed., 2001; Sexuality and the Curriculum: The Politics and Practices of Sexuality Education, 1992; (with W.L. Williams) Overcoming Heterosexism and Homophobia: Strategies That Work, 1997; Curriculum, Religion, and Public Education: Conversations for an Enlarging Public Square, 1998; (with D. Epstein) A Dangerous Knowing: Sexual Pedagogies and Popular Culture, 1999; Queering Elementary Education: Advancing the Dialogue about Sexualities and Schooling, 1999; (with K. Sloan) Democratic Curriculum Theory & Practice, 2001; (with R. Gaztambibe) Curriculum Work as Public Moral Enterprise, 2004; Youth, Education, and Sexualities: An International Encyclopedia, 2005; Gay, Lesbian, and Transgender Issues in Education: Programs, Policies, and Practices, 2005; Homophobic Bullying, 2006; Growing Older: The Millennial LGBTs, 2007. Contributor to books, journals and magazines. **Address:** Routledge Publishing, 270 Madison Ave., New York, NY 10016-0601, U.S.A. **Online address:** islandauthor@gmail.com

SEARS, Joe. American (born United States), b. 1949. **Genres:** Plays/Screenplays. **Career:** San Antonio Mental Health Units, preventive mental health specialist in drama and art. Writer. **Publications:** PLAYS: (with J. Williams and E. Howard) Greater Tuna, 1982; Eddie Lee, Eddie Lee (a one-act play), 1993; (with J. Williams and E. Howard) Tuna Christmas, 1996; (with J. Williams and E. Howard) Tuna does Vegas, 2010. **Address:** 1202 College St., Austin, TX 78704, U.S.A.

SEARS, Richard. American (born United States) **Genres:** Mystery/Crime/Suspense, Novels, Young Adult Fiction. **Career:** Writer. **Publications:** First Born (novel), 2000; Last Day (novel), 2001. **Address:** c/o Tom Doherty, Tom Doherty Associates L.L.C., 175 5th Ave., New York, NY 10010, U.S.A.

SEARS, William P. American (born United States), b. 1939. **Genres:** Human Relations/Parenting, Medicine/Health, Sports/Fitness. **Career:** Harvard University, Children's Hospital, intern; University of Toronto, Hospital for Sick Children, resident in pediatrics, associate professor of pediatrics and associate ward chief of newborn nursery; University of Southern California, assistant clinical professor of pediatrics; University of California, School of Medicine, associate clinical professor of pediatrics; America Online, co-creator (weekly online parenting program-Parent Soup); Sears Family Pediatrics, physician. Writer and consultant. **Publications:** Creative Parenting: How to Use the New Continuum Concept to Raise Children Successfully from Birth through Adolescence, 1982, rev. ed. as Creative Parenting: How to Use the Attachment Parenting Concept to Raise Children Successfully from Birth through Adolescence, 1987; Christian Parenting and Child Care, 1985, rev. ed. as Parenting and Child Care: A Guide for Christian Parents, 1993; Nighttime Parenting: How to Get Your Baby and Child to Sleep, 1985, rev. ed., 1999; (with M. Sears) The Fussy Baby: How to Bring Out the Best in Your High Need Child, 1985, rev. ed., 2002; Becoming a Father: How to Nurture and Enjoy Your Family, 1986, rev. ed., 2003; Growing Together: A Parent's Guide to Baby's First Year, 1987; Safe and Healthy: A Parent's Guide to Children's Illnesses and Accidents, 1989; (with M. Sears) The Ministry of Parenting Your Baby, 1990; (with M. Sears) Preparing for Your New Baby, 1991; (with M. Sears) 300 Questions New Parents Ask: About Pregnancy, Childbirth, and Infant & Child Care, 1991; (with M. Sears) Keys to Breast Feeding, 1991; Keys to Becoming a Father, 1991; Keys to Calming the Fussy Baby, 1991;

Keys to Preparing & Caring for Your Newborn, 1991; (with M. Sears) The Baby Book: Everything You Need to Know About Your Baby-from Birth to Age Two, 1993, (co-author) 2nd ed., 2003; (with M. Sears) The Birth Book: Everything You Need to Know to Have a Safe and Satisfying Birth, 1994; (with M. Sears) The New Baby Planner, 1994; Christian Parenting Answers: A Reference Book for Parents of Children Ages 0 to 5, 1994; (with M. Sears) The Discipline Book: Everything You Need to Know to Have A Better-Behaved Child-From Birth to Age Ten, 1995; (with M. Sears) 25 Things Every New Mother Should Know, 1995; SIDS: A Parent's Guide to Understanding and Preventing Sudden Infant Death Syndrome, 1995; (with M. Sears) Parenting the Fussy Baby and High-Need Child: Everything You Need to Know from Birth to Age Five, 1996; (with M. Sears and L.H. Holt) The Pregnancy Book: A Month by Month Guide, 1997; (with M. Sears) The Complete Book of Christian Parenting & Child Care: A Medical & Moral Guide to Raising Happy, Healthy Children, 1997; (with L. Thompson) The A.D.D. Book: New Understandings, New Approaches to Parenting Your Child, 1998; (with M. Sears) The Growing Years, 1998; (with M. Sears) Now That Baby is Home, 1998; (with M. Sears) So You're Going to be a Parent, 1998; (with M. Sears) The Family Nutrition Book: Everything You Need to Know About Feeding Your Children-from Birth Through Adolescence; 1999; (with M. Sears) The Breastfeeding Book: Everything You Need to Know About Nursing Your Child from Birth Through Weaning, 2000; (with M. Sears and C.W.Kelly) What Baby Needs, 2001; (with M. Sears) The Attachment Parenting Book: A Commonsense Guide to Understanding and Nurturing Your Baby, 2001; (with M. Sears and C.W. Kelly) Baby on the Way, 2001; (with M. Sears) Feeding The Picky Eater: America's Foremost Baby and Childcare Experts Answer the Most Frequently Asked Questions, 2001; (with M. Sears) The First Three Months: America's Foremost Baby and Childcare Experts Answer the Most Frequently Asked Questions; 2001; (with M. Sears) How to Get Your Baby to Sleep: America's Foremost Baby and Childcare Experts Answer the Most Frequently Asked Questions; 2001; (with M. Sears) Keeping Your Baby Healthy, 2001; (with M. Sears and C.W. Kelly) Eat Healthy, Feel Great, 2002; (with M. Sears and E. Pantley) The Successful Child: What Parents Can Do to Help Kids Turn Out Well, 2002; (with M. Sears and C.W. Kelly) You Can Go to the Potty, 2002; (with P. Sears and S. Foy) Dr. Sears' LEAN Kids: A Total Health Program for Children Ages 6-12, 2003; (co-author) The Premature Baby Book: Everything You Need to Know About Your Premature Baby from Birth to Age One, 2004; (co-author) The Baby Sleep Book: The Complete Guide to a Good Night's Rest for the Whole Family, 2005; (co-author) The Healthiest Kid in the Neighborhood: Ten Ways to Get Your Family on the Right Nutritional Track, 2006; The NDD Book: How Nutrition Deficit Disorder Affects your Child's Learning, Behavior, and Health, and What You Can Do About it-Without Drugs, 2009; (with M. Sears) Prime-Time Health: A Scientifically Proven Plan for feeling Young and Living Longer, 2010; (contrib.) The Autism Book, 2010; (co-author) Portable Pediatrician: Everything You Need to Know About Your Child's Health, 2011. Contributor to books. **Address:** Sears Family Pediatrics, 26933 Camino De Estrella, Ste. A, Capistrano Beach, CA 92624-1680, U.S.A. **Online address:** drsears@askdrsears.com

SEASKULL, Cecil. See CASTELLUCCI, Cecil.

SEATON, J(erome) P. American (born United States), b. 1941. **Genres:** Poetry, Philosophy, Translations. **Career:** University of North Carolina, professor of Chinese and Asian studies, 1968-, now professor emeritus. Writer. **Publications:** (With A. Tobias and J.H. Sanford) The View from Cold Mountain, 1982; (with J.M. Cryer) Bright Moon, Perching Bird, 1988; Love and Time: Poems of Ou-yang Hsiu, 1989; (ed. with D. Maloney) A Drifting Boat: An Anthology of Chinese Zen Poetry, 1994; I Don't Bow to Buddhas: Selected Poems of Yuan Mei, 1997; (with U.K. Le Guin) The Tao Te Ching of Lao Tzu, 1997; Bright Moon, White Cloud, 2011. TRANSLATOR: (and intro.) The Wine of Endless Life (poems), 1978, 2nd ed., 1985; (with D.W. Riggs) Francois Cheng, Chinese Poetic Writing, 1982; (with S. Hamill) The Essential Teaching of Chuang Tzu, 1998; (and ed. with S. Hamill) Poetry of Zen, 2004; (and ed.) Shambhala Anthology of Chinese Poetry, 2006; Cold Mountain Poems: Zen Poems of Han Shan, Shih Te, and Wang Fan-chih, 2009. Works appear in anthologies. Contributor of articles to magazines. **Address:** Department of Asian Studies, University of North Carolina, 124 New W, Chapel Hill, NC 27599, U.S.A. **Online address:** jpseaton@email.unc.edu

SEAY, James. American (born United States), b. 1939. **Genres:** Poetry, Documentaries/Reportage, Adult Non-fiction. **Career:** Virginia Military Institute, instructor of English, 1966-68; University of Virginia School of General Studies, instructor of English, 1967; University of Alabama, assistant professor of English, 1968-71; Vanderbilt University, assistant professor of English, 1971-74; University of North Carolina, lecturer in English, 1974-89, Creative Writing Program, director, 1987-97, associate professor of English, 1989-94, professor of English, 1994-, Bowman and Gordon Gray professor, 1996-99. Writer. **Publications:** POETRY: Let Not Your Hart, 1970; Water Tables, 1974; Where Our Voices Broke Off, 1978; Said There Was Somebody Talking to Him through the Air Conditioner, 1985; The Light as They Found It, 1990; Open Field, Understory: New and Selected Poems, 1997. Contributor to periodicals. Works appear in anthologies. **Address:** Department of English & Comparitive Literature, University of North Carolina, Chapel Hill, NC 27514, U.S.A. **Online address:** jseay@email.unc.edu

SEAY, Jody. American (born United States), b. 1949. **Genres:** Mystery/Crime/Suspense, Novels, Young Adult Fiction. **Career:** Writer, 1986-. **Publications:** The Second Coming of Curly Red, 1999. Contributor to periodicals. **Address:** PO Box 82213, Portland, OR 97282-0213, U.S.A. **Online address:** jodybobfromtexas@yahoo.com

SEBANC, Mark. Canadian (born Canada), b. 1953. **Genres:** Science Fiction/Fantasy, Translations. **Career:** Toronto School Board, archivist and librarian; Stoneharp Press, co-founder. Writer and translator. **Publications:** (Trans.) H. de Lubac, Medieval Exegesis, 1998. FANTASY NOVELS: Flight to Hollow Mountain, 1996; (with J.G. Anderson) The Stoneholding, 2004; (with J.G. Anderson) Darkling Fields of Arvon, 2010. **Address:** Ottawa Valley, ON , Canada. **Online address:** contact@stoneharp.com

SEBASTIAN, Lee. See SILVERBERG, Robert.

SEBASTIAN, Margaret. See GLADSTONE, Arthur M.

SEBBAR, Leïla. French (born France), b. 1941. **Genres:** Novels, Novellas/Short Stories, Essays, Adult Non-fiction. **Career:** Writer. **Publications:** On tue les petites filles, 1978; Le Pédophile et la maman: L'amour des enfants, 1980; Fatima, ou, Les Algériennes au square: récit, 1981; (with N. Huston) Lettres parisiennes: Autopsie de l'exil (correspondance), 1986; Le Négresse à l'enfant (short stories), 1990; (with N. Huston) Une Enfance d'ailleurs, 1993; (contrib.) Mémoire de Kabylie: Scénes de la vie traditionelle, 1937-1939, 1994; Le Jeune Fille au balcon, 1996; (ed.) Une Enfance algérienne (essays), 1997; Soldats, 1999; Silence on the Shores, 2000; (ed.) Algerian Childhood: A Collection of Autobiographical Narratives, 2001; (with J. Belorgey) Femmes d'Afrique du nord: Cartes postales, 1885-1930, 2002; Marguerite, 2002; Je ne parle pas la langue de mon père: récit, 2003; Mes Algéries, 2004; Mes Algéries en France, 2004; Journal de mes Algéries en France, 2005; Femmes au bain, 2006; Métro: instantanés, 2007; Peintre et son modèle, 2007; Seine was red: Paris, October 1961, 2008; Voyage en Algéries autour de ma chambre: Abécédaire, 2008. NOVELS: Shérazade: 17 ans, brune, frisée, les yeux verts: Roman, 1982; Parle mon fils, parle à ta mère, 1984; Le Chinois vert d'Afrique, 1984; Les Carnets de Shérazade, 1985; J.H. cherche âme sur, 1987; Le Fou de Shérazade, 1991; Le Silence des rives, 1993; Sept Filles, 2003; Zizou l'algérien, 2005; Ravin de la femme sauvage, 2007; (contrib.) C'éetait leur France, 2007; Une femmea à sa fenêtre, 2010. Contributor to periodicals. **Address:** c/o Author Mail, Editions du Seuil, 25 bd Romain Rolland, Paris, 75014, France. **Online address:** cnetter1@swarthmore.edu

SEBELL, Mark Henry. American (born United States) **Genres:** Business/Trade/Industry, Economics, Administration/Management. **Career:** Colgate-Palmolive New Ventures Group, brand manager, 1974-; Richardson-Vicks, brand manager; Carter-Wallace, brand manager; Synetics Inc. (problem-solving training firm), managing partner, 1986-; Creative Realities Inc. (consulting firm), founder and chief executive officer, 1988-; Synectics, staff. Writer. **Publications:** (With J. Yocum) Ban the Humorous Bazooka, 2001. **Address:** Creative Realities Inc., 8 Faneuil Hall Marketplace, Boston, MA 02109, U.S.A. **Online address:** mark@creativerealities.com

SEBLEY, Frances Rae. See JEFFS, Rae.

SECRETAN, Lance H. K. Canadian (born Canada), b. 1939. **Genres:** Business/Trade/Industry, inspirational/Motivational Literature, Philosophy, Sciences, Ethics, Public/Social Administration, Marketing, Self Help, Self Help. **Career:** Office Overload, sales manager, 1960-67; Manpower Ltd., chief executive officer, 1967-81; The Secretan Center Inc., founder and chief executive officer, 1972-; McMaster University, faculty, 1980-85, visiting professor of entrepreneurship; York University, faculty, 1985-, visiting professor of entrepreneurship; writer and consultant, 1989-. **Publications:** How to Be an Effective Secretary, 1972; From Guns to Butter, 1981; Managerial Moxie: A Basic Strategy for the Corporate Trenches, 1986; The Masterclass: Modern Fables for Working and Living, 1988; The Way of the Tiger: Gentle Wisdom for Turbulent Times, 1989; Living the Moment: A Sacred Journey, 1992; Managerial Moxie: The 8 Proven Steps to Empowering Employees and Super Charging Your Company, 1993; Reclaiming Higher Ground: Creating Organizations that Inspire the Soul, 1996; Inspirational Leadership: Destiny, Calling and Cause, 1999; Spirit @ Work Cards: Bringing Spirit & Values to Work, 2002; Inspire: What Great Leaders Do, 2004; ONE: The Art and Practice of Conscious Leadership, 2006; The Spark, the Flame and the Torch: Inspire Self, Inspire Others, Inspire the World, 2010. **Address:** 1177 Cataract Rd., Caledon, ON L7K 1P2, Canada. **Online address:** lance@secretan.com

SECUNDA, Victoria (H.). American (born United States), b. 1939. **Genres:** Biography, Adult Non-fiction, Psychology, Self Help, Medicine/Health. **Career:** Newsweek, administrative assistant and researcher, 1962-64; Columbia Broadcasting System News, researcher, 1964-68; Public Broadcasting Service, associate producer, 1968-69; The Patent Trader, columnist, 1970-74; Reader's Digest, editor, 1975-77; Gannett Newspapers, columnist, 1977-84. **Publications:** NONFICTION: (co-author) Good Housekeeping Women's Almanac, 1977; Bei Mir Bist Du Schöen: The Life of Sholom Secunda (biography), 1982; By Youth Possessed: The Denial of Age in America, 1984; (with T.A. Warschaw) Winning with Kids: How to Negotiate with Your Baby Bully, Kid Tyrant, Loner, Saint, Underdog or Winner so They Love Themselves and You, Too, 1988; When You and Your Mother Can't Be Friends: Resolving the Most Complicated Relationship of Your Life, 1990; Women and Their Fathers: The Sexual and Romantic Impact of the First Man in Your Life, 1992; When Madness Comes Home: Help and Hope for the Children, Siblings and Partners of the Mentally Ill, 1997; Losing Your Parents, Finding Your Self: The Defining Turning Point of Adult Life, 2000. Contributor to periodicals. **Address:** c/o Elaine Markson, Elaine Markson Agency, 44 Greenwich Ave., New York, NY 10011, U.S.A.

SEDAITIS, Judith B. American (born United States) **Genres:** Area Studies, Sociology, Business/Trade/Industry, History. **Career:** Columbia University, W. Averell Harriman Institute, fellow, 1991-93; Stanford University, Sloan Management Foundation Study on Outsourcing Computer Services, research associate and associate director, 1994-97; Social Science Research Council, Eurasia Program, director, 1997-. Writer. **Publications:** (Ed. with J. Butterfield) Perestroika from Below: Social Movements in the Soviet Union, 1991; (contrib.) Legacies, Linkages, and Localities: The Social-Embeddedness of Market Transformations in Eastern Europe, 1996; (ed.) Commercializing High Technologies: East and West, 1997; (with V.S. Vardys) Lithuania: A Rebel Nation, 1997. Contributor to journals. **Address:** Eurasia Program, Social Science Research Council, 1 Pierrepont Plz., 15th Fl., Brooklyn, NY 11201, U.S.A.

SEDARIS, Amy. American (born United States), b. 1961. **Genres:** Plays/Screenplays, Novels, Humor/Satire. **Career:** Writer and actor. **Publications:** PLAYS WITH D. SEDARIS: The Book of Liz, 2002. OTHERS: (with P. Dinello and S. Colbert) Wigfield: The Can-Do Town That Just May Not (novel), 2003; I Like You: Hospitality Under the Influence, 2006; (contrib.) Home Studio Home, Providence, RI, 2008; Simple Times: Crafts for Poor People, 2010. **Address:** c/o Author Mail, Hyperion Books, 77 W 66th St., 11th Fl., New York, NY 10023, U.S.A.

SEDARIS, David. American (born United States), b. 1957. **Genres:** Novellas/Short Stories, Essays, Plays/Screenplays, Novels, Humor/Satire. **Career:** Art Institute of Chicago, teacher. Writer. **Publications:** AUTOBIOGRAPHICAL ESSAYS: Origins of the Under Class and Other Stories, 1992; Barrel Fever, 1994; Holidays on Ice, 1997, 2nd ed., 2008; Naked, 1997; Me Talk Pretty One Day, 2000; Dress Your Family in Corduroy and Denim, 2004. PLAYS: Jamboree, 1991; Stump the Host, 1993; One Woman Shoe, 1995; (with J. Mantello) The Santa Land Diaries, 1996 as Santa Land Diaries and Seasons Greetings: Two Plays, 1998; (with A. Sedaris) Incident at Cobbler's Knob, 1997; (with A. Sedaris) The Book of Liz, 2002; When You are Engulfed in Flames, 2008. COMEDY ALBUMS: Barrel Fever and Other Stories, 2001. OTHER: (ed. and intro.) Children Playing before a Statue of Hercules, 2005; Squirrel Seeks Chipmunk, 2010. Contributor to periodicals. **Address:** Steven Barclay Agency, 12 Western Ave., Petaluma, CA 94952, U.S.A.

SEDDON, Andrew M. American/British (born England), b. 1959. **Genres:** Novellas/Short Stories, Science Fiction/Fantasy, Adult Non-fiction, History, Medicine/Health, Travel/Exploration. **Career:** Wheeling Hospital, intern and resident, 1985-88; private practice, 1989-90; Billings Clinic, staff physician, 1990-; Christian Library Journal, editor, 1998-2003, The Christian Communicator, editor, 1998-2000. Writer. **Publications:** Red Planet Rising, 1995; Imperial Legions: A Novel, 2000; (with N. Kennedy-Jones and G. Kennedy-Jones) Walking with the Celtic Saints: A Devotional, 2004. Works appear in anthologies. Contributor to books and periodicals. **Address:** Billings Clinic, 2825 8th Ave. N Billings, Billings, MT 59101, U.S.A. **Online address:** aseddon@billingsclinic.org

SEDGWICK, Fred. British/Irish (born Ireland), b. 1945. **Genres:** Poetry, Education. **Career:** Swing Gate First School, head teacher, 1975-81, Bramford Primary School, teacher, 1981-84; Downing Primary School, teacher, 1984-90; Open University, tutor, 1986-88; writer, 1990-. **Publications:** POETRY: Really in the Dark, 1976; The Garden, 1977; (with J. Cotton and F. Downie) A Berkhamsted Three, 1978; Details, 1980; From Another Part of the Island, 1981; A Garland for William Cowper, 1984; The Living Daylights, 1986; Falernian, 1987; (with J. Cotton) Hey!, 1990; The Biggest Riddle in the World, as Two by Two, 1990; Lies, 1991; Pizza Curry Fish and Chips, 1994; Fifty, 1995; Blind Date (for children), 1997; (with J. Cotton) The Ammonite's Revenge, 2000; Moving House (for children), 2003; Stone and Other Poems, 2004. EDITOR: This Way, That Way, 1989; Collins Primary Poetry, 1994; Jenny Kissed Me, 2000; Will There Really Be a Morning?: Life, a Guide, 2002. OTHER: Here Comes the Assembly Man: A Year in the Life of a Primary School, 1989; Lighting Up Time: On Children's Writing, 1990; The Expressive Arts, 1993; Drawing to Learn, 1993; Personal, Social and Moral Education, 1994; (with D. Sedgwick) Art across the Curriculum, 1995; Read My Mind: Young Children, Poetry and Learning, 1994; (with D. Sedgwick) Learning Together: Enhance Your Child's Creativity, 1996; Thinking about Literacy, 1999; Shakespeare and the Young Writer, 1999; Writing to Learn, 2000; Themes for Poetry, 2000; Forms of Poetry, 2000; Teaching Literacy: A Creative Approach, 2001; Enabling Children's Learning through Drawing, 2002; Teaching Poetry, 2003; How to Write Poetry and Get It Published, 2002; How to Teach with a Hangover: A Practical Guide to Overcoming Classroom Crises, 2005; 100 Ideas for Assemblies: Primary Edition, 2006; 101 Essential Lists for Primary Teachers, 2006; 100 Ideas for Developing Thinking in the Primary School, 2008; So You Want to be a Teacher?, 2008; Where Words Come From: A Dictionary Of Word Origins, 2009; 100 Ideas for Teaching Literacy, 2010; Inspiring Children to Read and Write For Pleasure: Using Literature To Inspire Literacy Learning For Ages 8-12, 2011; Resources for Teaching Shakespeare 11-16, 2011. **Address:** 52 Melbourne Rd., Ipswich, SU IP4 5PP, England. **Online address:** fred.sedgwick@btinternet.com

SEDIA, E. See SEDIA, Ekaterina.

SEDIA, Ekaterina. (E. Sedia). American/Russian (born Russia) **Genres:** Novels, Literary Criticism And History. **Career:** Writer. **Publications:** (As E. Sedia) According to Crow (novel), 2005; (ed. with E.J. McFadden as E. Sedia) Jigsaw Nation: Science Fiction Stories of Secession (anthology), 2006; The Secret History of Moscow (novel), 2007; (ed.) Paper Cities: The Anthology of Urban Fantasy, 2008; The Alchemy of Stone (novel), 2008; The House of Discarded Dreams, 2010; Heart of Iron, 2011. Works appear in anthologies. **Address:** New York, NY , U.S.A. **Online address:** katsedia@hotmail.com

SEDLEY, Kate. See CLARKE, Brenda.

SED-RAJNA, Gabrielle. French/Hungarian (born Hungary), b. 1927. **Genres:** Art/Art History, Translations. **Career:** Centre National de la Recherche Scientifique, Institut de Recherche et d'Histoire des Textes, Hebrew Department, head, 1962-93, professor. Writer. **Publications:** Commentaire Sur la Liturgie Quotidienne: Introduction, Traduction Annotée et Glossaire Des Termes Techniques Par, 1974; L'Art Juif, 1975; (ed. with B. Narkiss) Iconographical Index of Hebrew Illuminated Manuscripts, vol. I: Paris-Jerusalem, 1976, (ed. with B. Narkiss) vol. II: Paris-Munich, 1981, (ed. with B. Narkiss) vol. III: Jerusalem, 1983, vol. IV (with B. Narkiss): Les Manuscrits Enlumines de la Collection Kaufmann de Budapest, 1988; Ancient Jewish Art: East and West, 1985; (intro.) The Lisbon Bible, 1482: British Library Or. 2626, 1988; The Kaufmann Haggadah, 1990; Jewish Art, 1997. UNTRANSLATED WORKS: Manuscrits Hebreux de Lisbonne, 1970; Azriel de Gerone: Commentaire sur le Liturgie Quotidienne, 1974; L'Art Juif, Orient et Occident, 1975; A Maimuni Kodex: Moóse Má jmunitorveiny koìdexe, a budapesti Misnè Tóra legszebb lapjai, 1980; La Mahzor Enlumine: Les Voies de Formation d'un Programme Iconographique, 1983; Codex Maimuni: Moses Maimonides' Code of Law, 1984; L'Art Juif, 1985; La Bible Hebraique, 1987; (ed.) Rashi, 1040-1990: Hommage á Ephraim E. Urbach: Congrés Européen des études juives, 1993; Les Manuscrits Hebreux Enlumines des Bibliotheques de France, 1994; Juedische Kunst, 1997; La Bible: Texte de la Bible de Jérusalem: enluminures du VIe au XIIe siécle, 1998; L'ABCdaire du judaïsme, 2000. TRANSLATOR: L. Ginzberg, Les legendes des Juifs, vol. I, 1997, vol. II, 1998, vol. III, 2002, vol. IV-VI, forthcoming. **Address:** 1 rue d'Alencon, Paris, 75015, France.

SEE, Carolyn. Also writes as Monica Highland. American (born United States), b. 1934. **Genres:** Novels, Young Adult Fiction, Young Adult Nonfiction. **Career:** Loyola University of Los Angeles, associate professor, professor of English, 1970-85; Los Angeles Times, book reviewer, 1981-93; University of California, Department of English, visiting professor, 1986-89, adjunct professor of English, 1989-, professor of literature, now professor emeritus; Newsday, book reviewer, 1990-92; Washington Post, book reviewer, 1993-. Journalist. **Publications:** The Rest Is Done with Mirrors, 1970; Blue Money, 1973; Mothers, Daughters, 1977; Rhine Maidens, 1981; Golden Days, 1987; Literary Exiles & Refugees in Los Angeles, 1988; Making History, 1991; (with J. Espey) Two Schools of Thought: Some Tales of Learning and Romance, 1991; Dreaming: Hard Luck and Good Times in America, 1995; The Handyman, 1999; Making a Literary Life: Advice for Writers and Other Dreamers, 2002; There will Never be Another You: A Novel, 2006. AS MONICA HIGHLAND: Lotus Land, 1983; 110 Shanghai Road, 1986; Greetings from Southern California, 1988. Contributor to magazines. **Address:** Department of English, University of California, 149 Humanities Bldg., PO Box 951530, Los Angeles, CA 90095-1530, U.S.A. **Online address:** csee@ucla.edu

SEED, David. British (born England), b. 1946. **Genres:** Literary Criticism And History, Science Fiction/Fantasy, Film, History, Psychology, Novels, Travel/Exploration. **Career:** University of Liverpool, reader in English, 1976-94, Science Fiction Texts and Studies, general editor, 1994-2000, professor of American literature, 2000-. Writer. **Publications:** Stream Runner, 1979; The Fictional Labyrinths of Thomas Pynchon, 1988; The Fiction of Joseph Heller: Against the Grain, 1988; The Fiction of Joseph Heller: Against the Grain, 1989; Rudolph Wurlitzer: American Novelist and Screenwriter, 1991; James Joyce's A Portrait of the Artist as a Young Man, 1992; American Science Fiction and the Cold War: Literature and Film, 1999; Brainwashing: A Study in Cold War Demonology, 2002; Brainwashing: The Fictions of Mind Control: A Study of Novels and Films Since World War II, 2004; Cinematic Fictions, 2009. EDITOR: (intro.) The Handling of Words and Other Studies in Literary Psychology, 1992; Anticipations: Essays on Early Science Fiction and Its Precursors, 1995; Joseph Conrad and Ford Madox Ford, the Inheritors, 1999; Imagining Apocalypse: Studies in Cultural Crisis, 2000; (with A. Sawyer) Speaking Science Fiction: Dialogues and Interpretations, 2000; (and foreword) Level 7, 2004; The Yearbook of English Studies, vol. XXXIV: Nineteenth-Century Travel Writing, 2004; (and intro.) Coming Race, 2005; Companion to Science Fiction, 2005; Literature and the Visual Media: Essays and Studies, 2005; The Yearbook of English Studies, vol. 37 II: Science Fiction, 2007; (with S. Castillo) Travel and Empire, 2009; Companion to Twentieth-century United States Fiction, 2010; Science Fiction: A Very Short Introduction, 2011. Contributor to books and articles in journals. **Address:** Department of English, University of Liverpool, Liverpool, MS L69 3BX, England. **Online address:** dseed@liverpool.ac.uk

SEED, Jenny. South African (born South Africa), b. 1930. **Genres:** Children's Fiction, History, Romance/Historical, Young Adult Fiction, Mythology/Folklore. **Career:** South Africa Government, Department of Roads, Department of Town Planning, draftsman, 1947-53; freelance writer, 1965-. **Publications:** FICTION: The Dancing Mule, 1964; The Always-Late Train, 1965; Small House, Big Garden, 1965; Peter the Gardener, 1966; Tombi's Song, 1966 in US as Ntombi's Song, 1989; To the Rescue, 1966; Stop Those Children!, 1966; Timothy and Tinker, 1967; The River Man, 1968; The Voice of the Great Elephant, 1968; Canvas City, 1968; Prince of the Bay, 1970, 2nd ed., 1989; Vengeance of the Zulu King, 1970; The Broken Spear, 1972; The Red Dust Soldiers, 1972; The Great Thirst, 1973; Warriors on the Hills, 1975; The Unknown Land, 1976; Strangers in the Land, 1977; The Year One, 1981; The Policeman's Button, 1981; Gold Dust, 1982; The New Fire, 1983; The 59 Cats, 1983; The Shell, 1983; The Sad Cat, 1984; The Karoo Hen, 1984; The Disappearing Rabbit, 1984; Big Boy's Work, 1984; The Spy Hill, 1984; The Lost Prince, 1985; Day of the Dragon, 1985; Bouncy Lizzie, 1985; The

Strange Blackbird, 1986; The Far-Away Valley, 1987; The Christmas Bells, 1987; Place among the Stones, 1987; The Station-Master's Hen, 1987; The Corner Cat, 1987; Hurry, Hurry, Sibusiso, 1988; The Big Pumpkin, 1989; Stowaway to Nowhere, 1990; Nobody's Cat, 1990; The Wind's Song, 1991; The Hungry People, 1992; Old Grandfather Mantis: Tales of the San, 1992; Tom's Garden, 1992; A Time to Scatter Stones, 1993; Eyes of a Toad, 1993; Run, Run, White Hen, 1994; Lucky Boy, 1995; The Strange Large Egg, 1996; Phuthuma, Phuthuma, Sibusiso!, 1996. FOLKTALES: Kulumi the Brave: A Zulu Tale, 1970; The Sly Green Lizard, 1973; The Bushman's Dream: African Tales of the Creation, 1975. Contributor to periodicals. **Address:** 10 Pioneer Cres., Northdene, KwaZulu-Natal, 4093, South Africa.

SEELYE, John. See SEELYE, John (Douglas).

SEELYE, John (Douglas). (John Seelye). American (born United States), b. 1931. **Genres:** Novels, Film, Literary Criticism And History. **Career:** University of California, associate professor of English, 1960-65; University of Connecticut, associate professor, 1966-71, professor of English, 1971-74; New Republic, contributing editor, 1971-79; University of North Carolina, alumni professor of English, 1974-84, distinguished alumni service professor; American Literature, member of editorial board, 1974-78; Penguin Books, consulting editor, 1979-; University of Florida, graduate research professor of American literature, 1984-. **Publications:** (Intro.) Rachel Dyer, 1964; The True Adventures of Huckleberry Finn, 1970, 2nd ed., 1987; Melville: The Ironic Diagram, 1970; The Kid, 1972; Dirty Tricks, or, Nick Noxin's Natural Nobility, 1974; Prophetic Waters: The River in Early American Life and Literature, 1977; Mark Twain in the Movies: A Meditation with Pictures, 1977; Beautiful Machine: Rivers and the Republican Plan: 1755-1825, 1991; Memory's Nation: The Place of Plymouth Rock, 1998; War Games: Richard Harding Davis and the New Imperialism, 2003; Jane Eyre's American Daughters: From The Wide, Wide World to Anne of Green Gables, 2005; (intro.) Captains Courageous, 2005; Two Years before the Mast: A Personal Narrative, 2009; (intro.) The Call of the Wild and White Fang, 2010. EDITOR: Arthur Gordon Pym, Benito Cereno, and Related Writings, 1967; Etchings of a Whaling Cruise, 1968; The Adventures of Huckleberry Finn, 1985; The Adventures of Tom Sawyer, 1986; The Virginian, 1988; Yankee Drover: Being the Unpretending Life of Asa Sheldon, 1988; Life on the Mississippi, 1990; Tarzan of the Apes, 1990; (and intro.) The Swiss Family Robinson, 1991; Stories of the Old West: Tales of the Mining Camp, 1994; Treasure Island, 1999; (and intro.) On to the Alamo: Col. Crockett's Exploits and Adventures in Texas, 2003. **Address:** University of Florida, 4328 Turlington Hall, PO Box 117310, Gainesville, FL 32611-7310, U.S.A. **Online address:** jseelye@english.ufl.edu

SEESE, June Akers. American (born United States), b. 1935. **Genres:** Novels, Novellas/Short Stories, Young Adult Fiction, Literary Criticism And History. **Career:** Detroit Public Schools, secondary English teacher, 1960-68; Uptown/On the Town, associate producer, 1987-92; Spelman College Continuing Education Program, instructor, 1989; Callanwolde Fine Arts Center, instructor, 1991. Writer. **Publications:** NOVELS: What Waiting Really Means, 1990; Is This What Other Women Feel Too?, 1991; James Mason and the Walk-in Closet and Collected Stories, 1994; Some Things Are Better Left to Saxophones, 2007. Contributor to periodicals. **Address:** c/o Robin Rue, Writers House, 21 W 26th St., New York, NY 10010, U.S.A.

SEFTON, Catherine. See WADDELL, Martin.

SEGAL, Harriet. American (born United States), b. 1931. **Genres:** Novels, Young Adult Fiction, Social Sciences. **Career:** McCann-Erickson Inc., assistant account executive and copywriter, 1954-55; art buyer, 1955-57; Albert-Frank-Guenther Law, assistant account executive and copywriter, 1958-60; Show Magazine, assistant art director and photography editor, 1960-61; U.S. Information Service, writer and editor, 1962-63; freelance editor, 1963-80; Greenburgh Independent, staff reporter and feature writer, 1969-72; Children's School of Science, director, 1973-83; Plenum Press, Chorionic Gonadotropin, managing editor, 1979; Blythedale Children's Hospital, writer and videotape producer; novelist, 1980. **Publications:** Susquehanna, 1984 in UK as On Flows the River, 1985; Catch the Wind, 1987; Shadow Mountain, 1990; The Skylark's Song, 1994; Northern Lights, forthcoming. **Address:** c/o Ellen Levine, Ellen Levine Literary Agency Inc., 15 E 26th St., New York, NY 10010, U.S.A.

SEGAL, Howard P. American (born United States), b. 1948. **Genres:** Technology, Politics/Government, History, Business/Trade/Industry, Theology/Religion. **Career:** Franklin and Marshall College, visiting instructor in history, 1975; University of Cincinnati, lecturer of history, 1975-76; Dalhousie University, lecturer of history, 1976-77; University of Michigan, assistant professor of history, 1978-83; Eastern Michigan University, adjunct assistant professor of history, 1983-84; Harvard University, lecturer of history of science, 1984-86; University of Maine, assistant professor, 1986-88, associate professor, 1988-92, professor of history, 1992-96, Bird and Bird professor of history, 1996-, Adelaide and Alan Bird professor, College of Engineering, Technology and Society Project, associate director, 1986-88, director, 1988-. Writer. **Publications:** Technological Utopianism in American Culture, 1985; (with A.I. Marcus) Technology in America: A Brief History, 1989, 2nd ed., 1999; Future Imperfect: The Mixed Blessings of Technology in America, 1994; (ed. with Y. Ezrahi and E. Mendelsohn) Technology, Pessimism, and Postmodernism, 1994; (intro.) Life in a Technocracy: What it Might be Like, 1996; Recasting the Machine Age: Henry Ford's Village Industries, 2005; Technology and Utopia, 2006; Utopias: A Brief History from Ancient Writings to Virtual Communities, 2012; The Wave of the Future: High-Tech Utopias, forthcoming. Contributor to journals, magazines and newspapers. **Address:** Department of History, University of Maine, 200 B Stevens Hall, Orono, ME 04469-5774, U.S.A. **Online address:** howard.segal@umit.maine.edu

SEGAL, Jeffrey A. American (born United States), b. 1956. **Genres:** Law, Politics/Government. **Career:** New York State Assembly, legislative aide, 1978; Michigan State University, Department of Political Science, teaching assistant, 1978-82, research assistant, 1980-81; Department of Housing and Urban Development, program analyst, 1979; U.S. Department of Labor, Vocational Exploration and Development Program, program analyst, 1980; Stony Brook University, Department of Political Science, assistant professor, 1982-87, associate professor, 1987-92, professor, 1992-2004, department chair, 2004-, distinguished professor, 2004-; Northwestern University, Law and Social Sciences Program, fellow, 1988-89; New York University, School of Law, Hauser Global Law School Program, global research fellow, 2003-04; State University of New York, distinguished professor, 2004-. Writer. **Publications:** (With A.I. Abramowitz) Senate Elections, 1992; (with H.J. Spaeth) The Supreme Court and the Attitudinal Model, 1993; (with H.J. Spaeth) Majority Rule or Minority Will: Adherence to Precedent on the U.S. Supreme Court, 1999; (with H.J. Spaeth) The Supreme Court and the Attitudinal Model Revisited, 2002; (with H.J. Spaeth, T.G. Walker and L. Epstein) The Supreme Court Compendium: Data, Decisions, and Developments, 3rd ed., 2003, 4th ed., 2007; (with H.J. Spaeth and S.C. Benesh) The Supreme Court in the American Legal System, 2005; (with L. Epstein) Advice and Consent: The Politics of Judicial Appointments, 2005; (with J. Geer and W. Schiller) Gateways to Democracy, 2011; (with J. Geer, W. Schiller and D. Glenncross) Gateways to Democracy: The Essentials, 2011. Contributor to journals and periodicals. **Address:** Department of Political Science, Stony Brook University, Stony Brook, NY 11794-4392, U.S.A. **Online address:** jeffrey.segal@stonybrook.edu

SEGAL, Jerome M. American (born United States), b. 1943?. **Genres:** Natural History, Economics. **Career:** U.S. Agency for International Development, coordinator for the Near East, senior advisor for agency planning, 1979-; Jewish Peace Lobby, founder and president, 1989-; University of Pennsylvania, faculty of philosophy; University of Maryland, Institute for Philosophy and Public Policy, research associate, affiliate professor. Writer. **Publications:** Creating the Palestinian State: A Strategy for Peace, 1989; Agency and Alienation: A Theory of Human Presence, 1991; Strategic Choices Facing Palestinians in the Negotiations, 1993; Is Jerusalem Negotiable?, 1997; Graceful Simplicity: Toward a Philosophy and Politics of Simple Living, 1999; (co-author) Negotiating Jerusalem, 2000; Joseph's Bones: Understanding the Struggle between God and Mankind in the Bible, 2007; Agency, Illusion, and Well-Being: Essays in Moral Psychology and Philosophical Economics, 2009. Contributor to periodicals. **Address:** Maryland School of Public Policy, University of Maryland, 2101 Van Munching Hall, College Park, MD 20742, U.S.A. **Online address:** jsegal@umd.edu

SEGAL, Julia (Clare). British (born England), b. 1950. **Genres:** Medicine/Health, Psychology. **Career:** University of London, Queen Elizabeth College, tutor, 1973-75; Central Middlesex Hospital, Multiple Sclerosis Unit, research counselor, 1985-; Willesden Community Hospital, staff. Writer. **Publications:** Phantasy in Everyday Life, 1985; Melanie Klein: Key Figures in Counseling and Psychotherapy, 1992, 2nd ed., 2004; (with J. Simkins) Helping Children with Ill or Disabled Parents, 1996; Phantasy, 2000. Contributor

to books and periodicals. **Address:** Brent NHS Primary Care Trust, Willesden Community Hospital, Robson Ave., Willesden Green, London, GL NW2 4NA, England. **Online address:** juliasegal@mscounselling.com

SEGAL, Lore. (Lore Groszmann). American/Austrian (born Austria), b. 1928. **Genres:** Novels, Children's Fiction, Essays, Translations, Young Adult Fiction. **Career:** Columbia University, professor of creative writing, 1969-78; Bennington College, visiting professor, 1973; Princeton University, visiting professor, 1974-77; Sarah Lawrence College, visiting professor, 1975-76; University of Illinois-Chicago, professor of English, 1978-92; Ohio State University, professor of English, 1991-96, professor emeritus, 1996-; Bryn Mawr College, lecturer, 2001-02. Writer. **Publications:** Other People's Houses: A Novel, 1964; Tell Me a Mitzi, 1970; All the Way Home, 1973; Tell Me: A Trudy, 1977; Lucinella: Novel, 1976; The Church Mice Adrift, 1976; The Story of Old Mrs. Brubeck and How She Looked for Trouble and Where She Found Him, 1981; Her First American: A Novel, 1985; The Story of Mrs. Lovewright and Purrless Her Cat, 1985; (with L. Baskin) The Book of Adam to Moses, 1987; The Story of King Saul and King David; 1991; (contrib.) Into the Arms of Strangers: Stories of the Kindertransport, 2000; Morris the Artist, 2003; Why Mole Shouted and Other Stories, 2004; More Mole Stories and Little Gopher, Too, 2005; Shakespeare's Kitchen: Stories, 2007. TRANSLATOR: (with W.D. Snodgrass) Gallows Songs, 1967; (with M. Sendak and ed.) The Juniper Tree and Other Tales from Grimm, 1973, rev. ed., 2003; The Bear and the Kingbird, 1979. Contributor to periodicals. **Address:** Department of English, Ohio State University, 535 Denney Hall, 164 W 17th Ave., Columbus, OH 43210-1326, U.S.A. **Online address:** lore@usa.net

SEGAL, Lynne. British/Australian (born Australia), b. 1943. **Genres:** Psychology, Human Relations/Parenting, Women's Studies And Issues, Humanities, Sex, Politics/Government, Biography, Social Sciences, Social Sciences. **Career:** University of London, Birkbeck College, Department of English and Humanities, faculty, 2004-05, Department of Psychosocial Studies, anniversary professor of psychology and gender studies, 1999-, faculty, 2004-05, tutor. Writer. **Publications:** (With S. Rowbotham and H. Wainwright) Beyond the Fragments: Feminism and the Making of Socialism, 1981; What Is to Be Done about the Family?, 1983; Is the Future Female?: Troubled Thoughts on Contemporary Feminism, 1988; Slow Motion: Changing Masculinities, Changing Men, 1990, rev. ed., 2006; (ed. with M. McIntosh) Sex Exposed: Sexuality and the Pornography Debate, 1992; Straight Sex: Rethinking the Politics of Pleasure, 1994; (ed.) New Sexual Agendas, 1997; Why Feminism?: Gender, Psychology, Politics, 1999; Making Trouble: Life and Politics, 2007. **Address:** Department of Psychosocial Studies, Birkbeck College, University of London, Rm. 651, Extension Bldg., Malet St., London, GL WC1E 7HX, England. **Online address:** l.segal@bbk.ac.uk

SEGAL, Susan. American (born United States), b. 1956?. **Genres:** Novels, Young Adult Fiction, Literary Criticism And History. **Career:** University of Southern California, teacher; University of California, teacher. Writer. **Publications:** Aria: A Novel, 2001. Contributor of short stories to periodicals. **Address:** c/o Bridge Works Publishing, 221 Bridge Ln., PO Box 1798, Bridgehampton, NY 11932-1798, U.S.A.

SEGER, Linda. American (born United States), b. 1971?. **Genres:** History. **Career:** Grand Canyon College, assistant professor, 1969-71; McPherson College, assistant professor, 1976-77; University of LaVerne, assistant professor; script consultant and entrepreneur, 1981; Colorado College, instructor, 1993. Screenwriter, director and theologian. **Publications:** Making a Good Script Great, 1987, 3rd ed., 2010; Creating Unforgettable Characters, 1990; The Art of Adaptation: Turning Fact and Fiction into Film, 1992; (with E.J. Whetmore) From Script to Screen: The Collaborative Art of Filmmaking, 1994, 2nd ed., 2004; When Women Call the Shots: The Developing Power and Influence of Women in Television and Film, 1996; Making a Good Writer Great: A Creativity Workbook for Screenwriters, 1999; Web Thinking: Connecting, Not Competing, for Success, 2002; Advanced Screenwriting: Raising Your Script to the Academy Award Level, 2003; Jesus Rode a Donkey: Why Republicans Don't Have the Corner on Christ, 2006; And the Best reteller Award Goes To-Sideways, Shakespeare in Love, Crash: Learning from the Winners, 2008; Making a Good Script Great, 2010; Writing Subtext: What Lies Beneath, 2011. Contributor to periodicals. **Address:** 4705 Hagerman Ave., Cascade, CO 80809, U.S.A. **Online address:** lsseger@aol.com

SEGHERS, Jan. See ALTENBURG, Matthias.

SEGRÈ, Gino. American/Italian (born Italy), b. 1938?. **Genres:** Physics, Adult Non-fiction. **Career:** C.E.R.N, research associate, 1963-65; University of California, staff, 1965-67; University of Pennsylvania, professor of physics and astronomy, 1967-, department chair, 1987-92, now emeritus; National Science Foundation, director of theoretical physics; Alfred P. Sloan Foundation, director of theoretical physics; Guggenheim Foundation, director of theoretical physics. Writer. **Publications:** A Matter of Degrees: What Temperature Reveals about the Past and Future of Our Species, Planet, and Universe, 2002; Faust in Copenhagen: A Struggle for the Soul of Physics, 2007; Ordinary Geniuses: Max Delbrück, George Gamow, and the Origins of Genomics and Big Bang Cosmology, 2011. Contributor to professional journals. **Address:** Department of Physics & Astronomy, University of Pennsylvania, 2N1, David Rittenhouse Laboratory, 209 S 33rd St., Philadelphia, PA 19104-6396, U.S.A. **Online address:** segre@dept.physics.upenn.edu

SEGRE, Roberto. Brazilian/Italian (born Italy), b. 1934. **Genres:** Architecture, Urban Studies. **Career:** University of Buenos Aires, assistant professor, 1957-62, graduate in architecture, 1960; University of Havana, professor, 1963-94; Superior Polytechnic Institute, head of department of architectural history, chair, 1970-94; University of Guadalajara, visiting professor, 1981; Columbia University, visiting professor, 1982; University of Santo Domingo, honorary professor, 1985; Virginia Polytechnic Institute, visiting professor, 1985, 1987; Ricardo Palma University, honorary professor, 1987; University of Sao Paulo, postgraduate professor, 1989; University of Zulia, postgraduate professor, 1989, 1992; Superior Technical School of Barcelona, postgraduate professor, 1993; University of Paris, Institute of Urbanism, postgraduate professor, 1993; Catholic University of Salta, honorary professor, 1993; Major University of San Andres, honorary professor, 1993; Rice University, Craig Francis Cullinan professor of architecture, Craig Francis Cullinan chair of architecture, 1995-96; Federal University of Rio de Janeiro, visiting professor, 1994-99, professor of architecture, 2000-, Department of Graduate Course in Urbanism, chairman, 2002-; Miami University, visiting critic, 1997; Regional Institute of Urban Studies, board director. Writer. **Publications:** IN ENGLISH: (with M. Coyula and J. Scarpaci) Havana: Two Faces of the Antillean Metropolis, 1997, rev. ed., 2002; (contrib.) Oscar Niemeyer: 100 years, 100 works, 2007. OTHERS: Diez Anos de arquitectura en Cuba revolucionaria, 1970; Cuba: Arquitectura de la Revolucion, 1970; Las Estructuras Ambientales en America Latina, 1977; (with F. Salinas) La Progettazione Ambientale nell'era della Industrializzazione, 1980; (with J. Rallo) Introduccion Historica a las Estructuras Urbanas y Territoriales de Cuba, 1519-1959, 1980; La vivienda en Cuba en el siglo XX, 1980; (with R.L. Rangel) Architettura e Territorio nell'America Latina, 1982; Arquitectura, Historia, y Revolucion, 1982; (with E. Cardenas) Critica Arquitectonica, Colegio de Arquitectos de Ecuador, 1984; La Vivienda en Cuba: Republica y Revolucion, 1985; Historia de la Arquitectura y del Urbanismo Modernos: Paises Desarrollados, Capitalismo y Socialismo, 1985; (with Rangel) Arquitectura y Sociedad en America Latina, 1986; (with Rangel) Caos Urbano y Nuevas Tendencias en la Arquitectura Latinoamericana, 1986; (with R.L. Rangel) Tendencias arquitectónicas y caos urbano en Am, 1986; Arquitectura e Urbanismo da Revolucao Cubana, 1987; Arquitectura y urbanismo modernos, 1988; Arquitectura y urbanismo de la revolución cubana, 1989; America Latina dim de Milenio, 1990; Lectura Critica del Entorno Cubano, 1991; La Plaza de Armas de La Habana, 1995; Historia del Arte y la Arquitectura Barroca Europea, 1995; Ruy Othake, 1999; America Latina fin de Milenio, 1999; Miguel Angel Roca, 1990-2000, 2000; Arquitectura en la ciudad de La Habana, 2000; Jõo Diniz: Arquiteturas, 2002; Arquitetura Brasileira Contemporânea, 2003; Indio da Costa, 2003; Brasil: Jovens Arquitetos, 2004; Rio de Janeiro: guia de arquitetura contempornea, 2005; Ruy Ohtake: edificio hoteleiros, 2005; Casas brasileiras=Brazilian Houses, 2006; Gustavo Penna: Expominas Centro de Feiras e Exposições de Minas Gerais, 2007; Gustavo Penna, 2009; Tributo a Niemeyer, 2009; Tributo a Niemeyer, 2009; Museus brasileiros, 2010; Arquitetura+arte+cidade, 2010. EDITOR: Transformacion Urbana en Cuba: La Habana, 1974; America Latina en Su Arquitectura, 1975, trans. as Latin America in Its Architecture, 1982. Contributor to journals. **Address:** Federal University of Rio de Janeiro, Rio de Janeiro, 21941-972, Brazil. **Online address:** bobsegre@acd.ufrj.br

SEGRIFF, Larry. American (born United States), b. 1960. **Genres:** Science Fiction/Fantasy, Young Adult Fiction, Mystery/Crime/Suspense. **Career:** TeknoBooks, vice-president, 1994-. Consultant and writer. **Publications:** NOVELS: Spacer Dreams (science fiction), 1995; (with W.R. Forstchen) The Four Magics (fantasy), 1996; Alien Dreams (science fiction), 1997; Wizardspawn, 2003; Nightmare Logic, 2004. OTHER: (with S. Perry) Tom Clancy's Net Force: State of War, 2003; (with S. Perry) Tom Clancy's Net Force: Changing of the Guard, 2004; (with S. Perry) Tom Clancy's Net Force: Springboard, 2005; (with S. Perry) Tom Clancy's Net Force: The Archimedes Effect (2006). ANTHOLOGIES EDITED WITH M.H. GREENBERG SCIENCE FICTION: Future Net, 1996; (and E. Gorman) An Anthology of Angels, 1996; First Contact, 1997; Battle Magic (fantasy), 1998; Spell Fantastic, 2000; Guardsmen of Tomorrow, 2000; Far Frontiers, 2000; Past Imperfect, 2001; Silicon Dreams, 2001; Future Wars, 2003. MYSTERY: (ed. with M.H. Greenberg and E. Gorman) Cat Crimes for the Holidays, 1995; Murder Most Irish, 1996; Cat Crimes through Time, 1998; (ed. with M.H. Greenberg and E. Gorman) Murder Most Feline, 2001. NONFICTION: (ed. with M.H. Greenberg, J.L. Breen and E. Gorman) The Fine Art of Murder, 1993. OTHERS: (contrib.) Noir 13, 2010. **Address:** Tekno-Books, PO Box 8296, Green Bay, WI 54308, U.S.A. **Online address:** lsegriff@new.rr.com

SEGUIN, Marilyn W(eymouth). American (born United States), b. 1951. **Genres:** Children's Fiction, Young Adult Fiction, Education, History, Writing/Journalism, Biography, Autobiography/Memoirs. **Career:** The University of Akron, Department of Mass Media Communication, part-time instructor, 1977-89; Kent State University, Department of English, part-time instructor, 1987-90, lecturer in English, 1990-2000, NTT faculty, 2000-. Freelance writer. **Publications:** FOR CHILDREN: Song of Courage, Song of Freedom: The Story of Mary Campbell, Held Captive in Ohio by the Delaware Indians from 1759-1764, 1993; The Bell Keeper: The Story of Sophia and the Massacre of the Indians at Gnadenhutten, Ohio, in 1782 (historical fiction), 1995; Silver Ribbon Skinny: The Towpath Adventures of Skinny Nye, a Muleskinner on the Ohio and Erie Canal, 1884, (historical fiction), 1996; Dogs of War: And Stories of Other Beasts of Battle in the Civil War, 1998; Where Duty Calls: The Story of Sarah Emma Edmonds, Soldier and Spy in the Union Army (historical fiction), 1999; One Eternal Winter: The Story of What Happened at Donner Pass, Winter of 1846-47, (historical fiction), 2001; The Freedom Stairs: The Story of Adam Lowry Rankin, Underground Railroad Conductor, 2004; Gilbert Van Zandt: The Story of Civil War Drummer Boy and His Pony, 2006; (ed.) No Ordinary Lives: Four 19th Century Teenage Diaries, 2009. OTHERS: The Perfect Portfolio for Artists and Writers: How to Put Together a Creative Book that Sells, 1991; Teaching Middle Graders to Use Process Writing Skills: Strategies, Techniques, and Activities, 1994; Images of America: Cuyahoga Falls, 2000; (S. Seguin) Cuyahoga Falls, 2000; Gilbert VanZandt-The Story of a Civil War Drummer Boy and his Pony, Fannie Lee, 2006; No Ordinary Lives-Four 19th Century Teenage Diaries, 2009; Writing Historical Fiction: Digital Age Advice, 2011. **Address:** Department of English, Kent State University, 206D Satterfield Hall, Kent, OH 44242, U.S.A. **Online address:** mseguin@kent.edu

SEGUN, Mabel D. Also writes as Mabel Jolaoso, Mabel Imoukhuede, Dorothy Okanima. Nigerian (born Nigeria), b. 1930. **Genres:** Novellas/Short Stories, Children's Fiction, Poetry, Food And Wine, Autobiography/Memoirs, Essays, Young Adult Fiction, Picture/Board Books, Picture/Board Books. **Career:** Teacher, 1953-59; Western Nigeria Legislature, Hansard editor, 1958-61; Western Nigeria Ministry of Information, information officer, 1961-63; Lintas Ltd., copywriter, 1964; Silver Burdett, trainee editor, 1965, Harper & Row, trainee editor, 1966; Modern Woman, editor, 1966-67, Franklin Book Programmes, 1967; Federal Ministry of Education, Broadcasting Unit, education officer, 1967-68, head, 1969-70; National Technical Teachers College, Department of English and Social Studies, head, 1971-79, acting vice-principal, 1978-79; UNESCO, deputy permanent delegate of Nigeria, 1979-81, acting permanent delegate, 1981; chief federal inspector of education, 1981-82; University of Ibadan, Institute of African Studies, senior research fellow, 1982-89; Children's Literature Documentation and Research Centre, director, 1990-2003; Edo College, faculty; Nigerian Book Development Council, secretary. **Publications:** Friends, Nigerians, Countrymen (essays), 1977 in Nigeria as Sorry, No Vacancy, 1985; Conflict and Other Poems, 1986; (ed.) Illustrating for Children, 1988; Ping Pong: 25 Years of Table Tennis, 1989; The Surrender and Other Stories, 1995; Rhapsody: A Celebration of Nigerian Cooking and Food Culture, 2005. FOR CHILDREN: My Father's Daughter (autobiography), 1965; (ed. with N. Grant) Under the Mango Tree (poetry), 2 vols., 1980; Youth Day Parade, 1983; Olu and the Broken Statue, 1985; My Mother's Daughter (autobiography), 1987; The First Corn (picture book), 1989; The Twins and the Tree Spirits (picture book), 1991; Readers' Theatre: Twelve Plays for Young People, 2007. **Address:** 2 Alade Sonubi St., PO Box 3262, Surulere, LG 00234, Nigeria. **Online address:** mabelsegun@yahoo.com

SEHENE, Benjamin. French/Canadian (born Canada), b. 1959?. **Genres:**

Humanities, Local History/Rural Topics, Politics/Government, History. **Career:** Writer. **Publications:** (With L. Couvreur-Schiffer) Le Piège ethnique, 1999; Le Feu sous la soutane: Un prêtre au coeur du génocide rwandais, 2005. **Address:** 9 passage Dagorno, Paris, 75020, France. **Online address:** contact@benjaminsehene.com

SEIB, Gerald. American (born United States), b. 1956. **Genres:** Politics/ Government, History, International Relations/Current Affairs. **Career:** Wall Street Journal, staff, 1978-, assistant managing editor, executive Washington reporter, Washington bureau chief, 1980-, political editor, 1992-, deputy bureau chief, 1997-, White House reporter and diplomatic correspondent; University of Kansas, Daily Kansan, editor. **Publications:** (With J. Harwood) Pennsylvania Avenue: Profiles in Backroom Power, 2008. **Address:** The Wall Street Journal, 1211 Ave. of the Americas, New York, NY 10036, U.S.A. **Online address:** jerry.seib@wsj.com

SEIDEL, Frederick (Lewis). American (born United States), b. 1936. **Genres:** Poetry. **Career:** Paris Review, Paris editor, 1960-61, advisory editor, 1962-; poet, 1963-; Rutgers University, visiting lecturer, 1964-. **Publications:** POEMS: Final Solutions, 1963; Sunrise, 1980; Men and Women: New and Selected Poems, 1984; These Days: New Poems, 1989; Poems 1959-1979, 1989; My Tokyo, 1993; Going Fast, 1998; The Cosmos Poems, 2000; Poems 1959-2009, 2009. OTHERS: Life on Earth, 2001; Area Code 212, 2002; Selected Poems, 2006; Ooga-Booga, 2006; Nice Weather, 2012. **Address:** 251 W 92nd St., New York, NY 10025, U.S.A.

SEIDEL, George Joseph. American (born United States), b. 1932. **Genres:** Philosophy. **Career:** Saint Martin's University (formerly St. Martin's College), Department of Philosophy, chairman, 1962-, professor. Writer. **Publications:** Martin Heidegger and the Pre-Socratics: An Introduction to His Thought, 1964; Crisis of Creativity, 1966; A Contemporary Approach to Classical Metaphysics, 1969; Being, Nothing and God: A Philosophy of Appearance, 1970; Activity and Ground: Fichte, Schelling, and Hegel, 1976; Fichte's Wissenschaftslehre of 1794: A Commentary on Part 1, 1993; Angels, 1995; Knowledge as Sexual Metaphor, 2000; Toward a Hermeneutics of Spirit, 2000. **Address:** Department of Philosophy, Saint Martin's University, Rm. 373, Old Main, 5000 Abbey Way SE, Lacey, WA 98503-7500, U.S.A. **Online address:** gseidel@stmartin.edu

SEIDEL, Ross. Canadian (born Canada) **Genres:** Novels, Picture/Board Books, Young Adult Fiction. **Career:** Teacher and writer. **Publications:** Le Retour Des Rats, 1995, trans. as The Rats Came Back, 1995. **Address:** 6 Gilchrist Pl., St. Albert, AB T8N 2M3, Canada.

SEIDENSTICKER, John. American (born United States), b. 1944. **Genres:** Animals/Pets, Natural History, Young Adult Non-fiction. **Career:** Smithsonian-Nepal Tiger Ecology Project, founding principal investigator, 1972-74; Smithsonian Institution, research associate, 1973-76; Smithsonian National Zoological Park, visiting scientist, 1975-76, 1979, wildlife ecologist, 1980-84, assistant curator, 1984-86, Department of Mammalogy, associate curator, 1986-89, curator of mammals, 1989-2000, senior curator and curator of mammals, 2000-03, Conservation and Research Center, senior scientist, 2003-. Writer and conservation biologist. **Publications:** NONFICTION: The Javan Tiger and the Meru-Betiri Reserve: A Plan for Management, 1980; Managing Elephant Depredation in Agricultural and Forestry Projects, 1984; (with S. Lumpkin) Cats and Wild Cats, 1996; Tigers, 1996; (ed. with S. Christie and P. Jackson) Riding the Tiger: Tiger Conservation in Human-Dominated Landscapes, 1999; (with S. Lumpkin) Smithsonian Book of Giant Pandas, 2002 as Giant Pandas, 2007; (with S. Lumpkin) Cats: Smithsonian Answer Book, 2004 as Cats: Smithsonian Q&A: The Ultimate Question and Answer Book, 2006; (with S. Lumpkin) Predators, 2007; (with S. Lumpkin) Rabbits: The Animal Answer Guide, 2011. Contributor to periodicals. **Address:** Biological Research Center, Smithsonian's National Zoological Park, 3001 Connecticut Ave., NW, Washington, DC 20008-2537, U.S.A. **Online address:** jseidensticker@nzp.si.edu

SEIDL, Amy. American (born United States), b. 1965. **Genres:** Sciences. **Career:** Living Future Foundation, associate director, 2005-08; University of Vermont, faculty, 2000-02; Middlebury College, faculty, 2002-05. Ecologist and writer. **Publications:** Early Spring: An Ecologist and Her Children Wake to a Warming World, 2009. Contributor to journals and periodicals. **Address:** Huntington, VT , U.S.A. **Online address:** amy@amyseidl.com

SEIDLER, Ann. American (born United States), b. 1925. **Genres:** Children's Fiction, Speech/Rhetoric. **Career:** Punahau School, teacher of speech and drama, 1946-47; National Hospital for Speech Disorders, speech consultant, 1949-51; Mountainside Hospital, speech consultant, 1953-54; Cedar Grove Board of Education, speech consultant, 1954-62; Montclair State College, associate professor of speech, professor of speech, 1967-, professor emeritus, 1997-. Writer. **Publications:** (With J. Slepian) Magic Arthur and the Giant, 1964; (with J. Slepian) The Cock Who Couldn't Crow, 1964; (with J. Slepian) Roaring Dragon of RedRose, 1964; (with J. Slepian) Alfie and the Dream Machine, 1964; (with J. Slepian) Mr. Sipple and the Naughty Princes, 1964; Lester and the Sea Master, 1964; (with J. Slepian) The Best Invention of All, 1967; (with J. Slepian) The Silly Listening Book, 1967; (with J. Slepian) Ding Dong Bing Bong, 1967; (with J. Slepian) The Hungry Thing, 1967; (with J. Slepian) An Ear Is to Hear, 1967; (with J. Slepian) Bendemolena, 1967; (co-author) Make Yourself Clear, 1974; The Cat Who Wore a Pot on Her Head, 1981; (with D.B. Bianchi) Voice And Diction Fitness: A Comprehensive Approach, 1988; (with J. Slepian) The Hungry Thing Returns, 1990; (with J. Slepian) The Hungry Thing Goes to a Restaurant, 1992. **Address:** Department of Drama & Speech, Montclair State College, 1 Normal Ave., Montclair, NJ 07043-1624, U.S.A.

SEIDMAN, Hugh. American (born United States), b. 1940. **Genres:** Poetry. **Career:** Nassau County Board of Cooperative Educational Services, lecturer at in-service seminars for elementary and secondary school teachers, 1969-70; Yale University, visiting poet, 1971, 1973; Columbia University, faculty; New School, faculty; City University of New York, City College, poet-in-residence, 1972-75; Wilkes College, poet-in-residence, 1975; University of Wisconsin, faculty; College of William and Mary, faculty. **Publications:** Collecting Evidence, 1970; Blood Lord, 1974; Throne/Falcon/Eye: Poems, 1982; People Live, They Have Lives: Poems, 1992; Selected Poems, 1965-1995, 1995; 12 Views of Freetown, 1 View of Bumbuna, 2002; Somebody Stand Up and Sing, 2005. EDITOR: (with R. Zarro) Westbeth Poets, 1971; (with F. Whyatt) Equal Time, 1972. Contributor to periodicals. **Address:** 463 W St., Apt. H960, New York, NY 10014, U.S.A. **Online address:** email@hughseidman.com

SEIDMAN, Louis Michael. American (born United States), b. 1947. **Genres:** Social Sciences, Law. **Career:** Georgetown University, Law School, Carmack Waterhouse professor of constitutional law, 1976-; D.C. Public Defender Service, staff attorney, through 1976. Writer. **Publications:** (With M.V. Tushnet) Remnants of Belief: Contemporary Constitutional Issues, 1996; Great and Extraordinary Occasions: Developing Guidelines for Constitutional Change, 1999; Our Unsettled Constitution: A New Defense of Constitutionalism and Judicial Review, 2001; Constitutional Law: Equal Protection of the Laws, 2003; Silence and Freedom, Stanford Law and Politics, 2007. Contributor to books and journals. **Address:** Georgetown University Law Ctr., McDonough 495, 600 New Jersey Ave. NW, Washington, DC 20001, U.S.A. **Online address:** seidman@law.georgetown.edu

SEIDMAN, Michael. American (born United States), b. 1950. **Genres:** History, Politics/Government. **Career:** University of North Carolina, Department of History, professor, 1990-. Writer. **Publications:** Workers against Work: Labor in Barcelona and Paris During the Popular Fronts, 1991; Republic of Egos: A Social History of the Spanish Civil War, 2002; Imaginary Revolution: Parisian Students and Workers in 1968, 2004; The Victorious Counterrevolution: The Nationalist Effort in the Spanish Civil War, 2011. **Address:** Department of History, University of North Carolina, Morton Hall 231, 601 S College Rd., Wilmington, NC 28403-3297, U.S.A. **Online address:** seidmanm@uncw.edu

SEIFE, Charles. American (born United States) **Genres:** Documentaries/ Reportage, Sciences, Adult Non-fiction, Biography. **Career:** Freelance journalist, 1994-97; The Economist, Richard Casement Intern, 1995; Scientific American, news intern, 1995-96; writer, 1997-; New Scientist, U.S. correspondent, 1997-2000; Science Magazine, writer, 2000-; New York University, Department of Journalism, associate professor. **Publications:** Zero: The Biography of a Dangerous Idea, 2000; Alpha and Omega: The Search for the Beginning and End of the Universe, 2003; New Law: How the Science of Information is Changing Our Universe, 2005; Decoding the Universe: How the New Science of Information is Explaining Everything in the Cosmos, From Our Brains to Black Holes, 2006; Sun In A Bottle: The Strange History Of Fusion And The Science Of Wishful Thinking, 2008; Proofiness: The Dark Arts of Mathematical Deception, 2010. **Address:** Arthur L. Carter Institute of Journalism, Neqw York University, 20 Cooper Sq., 6th Fl., New York, NY 10003, U.S.A. **Online address:** charles.seife@nyu.edu

SEIFERLE, Rebecca. American (born United States), b. 1951. **Genres:** Poetry, Translations, Literary Criticism And History. **Career:** Navajo Academy, librarian and substitute teacher of English, 1988-89; San Juan Community College, instructor in English, 1991-; The Drunken Boat (Internet magazine), editor, publisher, web designer and founder, 2000-; Brandeis University, poet-in-residence. Writer. **Publications:** POETRY: The Ripped-Out Seam, 1993; The Music We Dance To, 1999; Bitters, 2001; Wild Tongue, 2007. TRANSLATOR: C. Vallejo, Trilce (poetry), 1992; The Black Heralds (poetry), 2003. Contributor to periodicals. Works appear in anthologies. **Address:** 5602 Tarry Terr., Farmington, NM 87402, U.S.A. **Online address:** seiferle@thedrunkenboat.com

SEIFERT, Lewis C. American (born United States), b. 1962. **Genres:** Cultural/Ethnic Topics. **Career:** Brown University, assistant professor, 1989-96, associate professor, 1996-2009, professor of French studies, 2009-, Program in Renaissance Studies, director, 1992-94, Program in Renaissance and Early Modern Studies, director, 1996-98. Writer. **Publications:** Fairy Tales, Sexuality, and Gender in France, 1690-1715: Nostalgic Utopias, 1996; (ed. with T.W. Reeser) Entre Hommes: French and Francophone Masculinities in Culture and Theory, 2008; Manning the Margins: Masculinity and Writing in Seventeenth-Century France, 2009. Contributor of articles to journals and periodicals. **Address:** Brown University, 21 Brown St., Annmary Brown Memorial, PO Box 1905, St. Providence, RI 02912, U.S.A. **Online address:** seifert@brown.edu

SEIFRID, Thomas. American (born United States), b. 1956. **Genres:** Area Studies, Cultural/Ethnic Topics, Literary Criticism And History, Humanities. **Career:** Reed College, assistant professor of Russian and the humanities, 1982-85, chair of Russian department, 1983-85; University of Southern California, Department of Slavic Languages and Literatures, assistant professor of Slavic, 1985-91, associate professor of Slavic, 1991-2005, department chair, 1991-2000, 2007-, professor of Slavic, 2005-, supervisor of German program, 2008-09. Writer. **Publications:** Andrei Platonov: Uncertainties of Spirit, 1992; The Word Made Self: Russian Writings on Language, 1860-1930, 2005; Companion to Andrei Platonov's The Foundation Pit, 2009. Works appear in anthologies. Contributor of articles to journals. **Address:** Department of Slavic Languages and Literatures, University of Southern California, 255 Taper Hall of the Humanities, Los Angeles, CA 90089-4353, U.S.A. **Online address:** seifrid@usc.edu

SEIGEL, Catharine F. American (born United States), b. 1933. **Genres:** Literary Criticism And History, Young Adult Fiction. **Career:** State University of New York, assistant professor of English, 1957-59; Catholic University of America Press, assistant editor, 1959-60; Catholic University of America, instructor in English, 1960-65; University of Rhode Island, lecturer, 1966-75; Rhode Island School of Design, professor of English, 1975-, department head, 1983-90, now professor emeritus. **Publications:** The Fictive World of Conrad Aiken: A Celebration of Consciousness, 1992. Contributor to books and periodicals. **Address:** Department of English, Rhode Island School of Design, 2 College St., Providence, RI 02903-2784, U.S.A. **Online address:** cseigel@risd.edu

SEIHO *See* **Sullivan, M(ichael) J(ustin).**

SEITZ, Rebeca. American (born United States), b. 1977?. **Genres:** Novels. **Career:** West Bow, publicist; Glass Road Public Relations, president and founder, 2005-, publicist. Writer. **Publications:** Prints Charming (novel), 2007; Sisters, Ink (novel), 2008; Coming Unglued, 2008; Perfect Piece, 2009; Scrapping Plans, 2009. **Address:** Glass Road Public Relations, 7926 State Rte. 166 E, Fulton, KY 42041, U.S.A. **Online address:** rebeca@glassroadpr.com

SEKARAN, Shanthi. British/American (born United States), b. 1977. **Genres:** Novels. **Career:** Writer. **Publications:** The Prayer Room: A Novel, 2008. Contributor to books. Works appear in anthologies. **Address:** England. **Online address:** theprayeroom@gmail.com

SEKLER, Eduard F(ranz). American/Austrian (born Austria), b. 1920. **Genres:** Architecture, Urban Studies, Essays. **Career:** Vienna Technical University, teaching and research assistant, 1945-53, lecturer, 1953, professor extra ordinarius, 1960; architect in Vienna, 1946-; Harvard University, visiting professor, 1955-56, associate professor, 1956-60, professor of architecture, 1960-70, Carpenter Center for the Visual Arts, Osgood Hooker professor of visual arts, 1970-91, professor emeritus, 1991-, director, 1966-76, Department of Visual and Environmental Studies, chairman, 1972-73, acting chairman, 1975. Writer. **Publications:** Annus Mirabilis: Zeitgemaesse Gedanken Zu Einer Wiederaufbauplanung Der Vergangenheit (title means: 'Timely Thoughts on a Reconstruction Plan of the Past'), 1951; Das Punkthaus im Europaeischen Wohnungsbau (title means: 'Pointhouses in European Housing'), 1952; Wren and His Place in European Architecture, 1956; Proportion: Measure of Order, 1965; (contrib.) Structure in Art and in Science, 1965; (contrib.) The Fine Arts and the University, 1965; (contrib.) Essays in the History of Architecture Presented to Rudolf Wittkower, 1967; (co-author) Kathmandu Valley: The Preservation of Physical Environment and Cultural Heritage: Protective Inventory, 1975; (contrib.) Perspectives on Vision, 1976; (with W. Curtis) Le Corbusier at Work: The Genesis of the Carpenter Center for the Visual Arts, 1978; Proposal for the Urbanistic Conservation of Patan Durbar Square, 1980; Josef Hoffmann: Das Architektonische Werk, 1982; Josef Hoffman: The Architectural Work, 1985; Architecture and the Flow of Time, 1988; (contrib.) Bauwerk und die Stadt, 1994; Form, Modernism and History: Essays in Honor of Eduard Sekler, 1997; (co-author) Das Semperdepot, 1997. EDITOR: Historic Urban Spaces vol. I-IV, 1962-71; (contrib.) Bauhaus: A Teaching Idea, 1967; (contrib.) Form from Process: The Thonet Chair, 1967; (contrib.) Master Plan for the Conservation of the Cultural Heritage in the Kathmandu Valley, 1977. Contributor to journals and periodicals. **Address:** Department of Architecture, Graduate School of Design, Harvard University, Frances Loeb Library, 203 Gund Hall, 48 Quincy St., Cambridge, MA 02138, U.S.A.

SELAK, Joy H. American (born United States), b. 1947. **Genres:** Medicine/Health, Novels. **Career:** School teacher, 1969-73; Arizona State University, instructor, 1973-80; Arizona State Department of Education, curriculum specialist, 1975-80; Smith Barney, financial consultant, 1981-92; Conejo Women in Business, director, 1985-89; San Juan Island WA Community Foundation, director and board president, 1997-2000; A Legacy of Giving, founder and vice-chair, 2006-09, consultant, 2011; ZACH Theatre, board president and chair, 2004-. Author and speaker. **Publications:** (With S.S. Overman) You Don't LOOK Sick!: Living Well with Invisible Chronic Illness, 2005; Informa Health, 2nd ed., forthcoming. **Address:** 1200 Barton Creek Blvd., Austin, TX 78735, U.S.A. **Online address:** joy@joywrites.com

SELBOURNE, David. British (born England), b. 1937. **Genres:** Plays/Screenplays, Politics/Government, Social Commentary, Ethics, Theology/Religion, History, Translations. **Career:** University of Chicago Law School, British Commonwealth fellow; Ruskin College, faculty. Writer. **Publications:** The Play of William Cooper and Edmund Dew-Nevett, 1968; The Two-Backed Beast, 1969; Dorabella, 1970; Samson and Alison Mary Fagan, 1971; The Damned, 1971; Class Play, 1973; Brook's Dream: The Politics of Theatre, 1974; What's Acting, and Think of a Story, Quickly!, 1977; An Eye to India, 1977; An Eye to China, 1978; Through the Indian Looking-Glass: Selected Articles on India, 1976-1980, 1982; The Making of a Midsummer Night's Dream: An Eye-witness Account of Peter Brooks Production from First Rehearsal to First Night, 1982; Against Socialist Illusion: A Radical Argument, 1984; Left Behind: Journeys into British Politics, 1987; Death of the Dark Hero: Eastern Europe, 1987-1990, 1990; The Spirit of the Age: An Account of Our Times, 1993; Not an Englishman: Conversations with Lord Goodman, 1993; The Principle of Duty: An Essay on the Foundations of the Civic Order, 1994; Moral Evasion, 1999; Losing Battle with Islam, 2005. EDITOR: In Theory and in Practice: Essays on the Politics of Jayaprakash Narayan, 1985; A Doctor's Life, 1989; (and trans.) J. d'Ancona, The City of Light, 1997. Contributor to journals. **Address:** c/o Christopher Sinclair-Stevenson, Sinclair-Stevenson Ltd., 3 S Terr., London, GL SW7 2TB, England. **Online address:** selbourne@info-net.it

SELCER, Richard F. American (born United States), b. 1950. **Genres:** Criminology/True Crime, History, Local History/Rural Topics, Biography, Horror. **Career:** Tarrant County College, adjunct professor, 1977-; Cottey College, academic dean, 1982-83; Dallas County Community College, adjunct professor, 1984-; Collin County Community College, adjunct faculty, 1986-89; International Christian University, visiting professor, 1987-; Northlake College, faculty; Cedar Valley College, professor of history. Writer. **Publications:** Hell's Half Acre: The Life and Legend of a Red-Light District, 1991; (contrib.) The Fort That Became a City, 1995; Lee vs. Pickett: Two Divided by War, 1998; (with D. Bowser, N. Hamilton and C. Parsons and ed. and comp.) Legendary Watering Holes: The Saloons that Made Texas Famous, 2004; Almanac of American Life Series: The Civil War Years, 2003; Cops and Cowboys, 2004; Fort Worth: A Texas Original!, 2004; Civil War America, 1850 to 1875, 2006; Fort Worth Characters, 2009; (with K.S. Foster) Written in Blood: The History of Fort Worth's Fallen Lawmen, 2010. Contributor to periodicals. **Address:** Cedar Valley College, 3030 N Dallas Ave., Lancaster, TX 75134-3705, U.S.A.

SELDON, Lynn. American (born United States), b. 1961. **Genres:** Travel/Exploration, Food And Wine, Photography, Recreation, Transportation, Reference. **Career:** Freelance travel writer and photographer, 1986-. **Publications:** Country Roads of Virginia: Drives, Day Trips, and Weekend Excursions, 1994, 2nd ed., 1999; Country Roads of Maryland and Delaware: Drives, Day Trips, and Weekend Excursions, 1994, 2nd ed., 1999; Virginia Outdoor Activity Guide, 1994; 52 Virginia Weekends: Great Getaways and Adventures for Every Season, 1996, 2nd ed., 2000; Virgin Islands Dive Travel Guide, 1996; Quick Escapes Florida: 29 Weekend Escapes in and Around the Sunshine State, 1997, 2nd ed., 2000; Hidden Bahamas, 1997; Country Roads of West Virginia: Drives, Day Trips, and Weekend Excursions, 1998. Contributor to periodicals. **Address:** 3516 E Pelican Dr., Oak Island, NC 28465, U.S.A. **Online address:** lynn@lynnseldon.com

SELESHANKO, Kristina. (Kristina Harris). American (born United States), b. 1971. **Genres:** History, Music, Popular Culture, Food And Wine, E-books, Writing/Journalism, Songs/Lyrics And Libretti, Antiques/Furnishings, Crafts, Homes/Gardens, Art/Art History. **Career:** Crains New York Business, sales associate; Gourmet, research librarian; Costume Society of Americas national newsletter, editor. Author. **Publications:** Vintage Fashion Collector: Collected Articles, 1994; Vintage and Edwardian Fashions for Women 1840-1919, 1995, 2nd ed., 2002; Fifty-Nine Authentic Turn-of-the-Century Fashion Patterns, 1995; Home Pattern Company 1914 Fashions Catalog, 1995; Vintage Fashions for Women: 1920s-1940s, 1996; Vintage Fashions for Women: 1950s 60s, 1997; The Child in Fashion 1750-1920, 1999; Collectors Guide to Vintage Fashions: Identification and Values, 1999; Authentic Victorian Dressmaking Techniques, 1999; Authentic Victorian Fashion Patterns: A Complete Lady's Wardrobe, 2000; Turn-of-the-Century Fashion Patterns and Tailoring Techniques, 2000; Victorian Fashion in America: 264 Vintage Photographs, 2003; Carry Me over the Threshold: A Christian Guide to Wedding Traditions, 2005; 60 Civil War Era Fashion Patterns, 2008; Historic English Costumes and How to Make Them, 2009. **Address:** 1205 S 8th St., Cottage Grove, OR 97424, U.S.A. **Online address:** kriswrite@aol.com

SELF, Nancy Starr. See **LINDISFARNE-TAPPER, Nancy.**

SELF, Robert O. American (born United States), b. 1968?. **Genres:** History, Race Relations, Military/Defense/Arms Control. **Career:** University of Wisconsin, assistant professor of history and urban studies, 2002-04; Brown University, assistant professor, 2004-06, associate professor of history, 2006-. Writer. **Publications:** American Babylon: Race and the Struggle for Postwar Oakland, 2003. Contributor of articles to books and periodicals. **Address:** Department of History, Brown University, 79 Brown St., PO Box N, Providence, RI 02912, U.S.A. **Online address:** robert_self@brown.edu

SELF, Will. British (born England), b. 1961. **Genres:** Novels, Novellas/Short Stories, History. **Career:** Writer. **Publications:** Slump, 1985; The Quantity Theory of Insanity (short stories), 1991; Cock & Bull (two novellas), 1992; My Idea of Fun: A Cautionary Tale (novel), 1994; Grey Area (short stories), 1994; Quantity Theory, 1995; Junk Mail (collected journalism), 1995; The Rock of Crack as Big as the Ritz, 1995; Scale, 1995; The Sweet Smell of Psychosis (novella), 1996; Cybersex, 1996; A Story for Europe, 1996; Great Apes, 1997; The Mammoth Book of New Erotica, 1998; Tough, Tough Toys for Tough, Tough Boys, 1999; (co-author) Nicola Hicks, 1999; (with H. Marks and K. Kesey) The Idler: For Those Who Live to Loaf, 1999; How the Dead Live, 2000; (with D. Gamble) Perfidious Man, 2000; Sore Sites, 2000; (co-author) Spacebomb: Martin Richardson Holographics-1980-2000, 2000; (with S. Levinson) Antony Gormley: Some of the Facts, 2001; Feeding Frenzy, 2002; Dorian: An Imitation, 2003; Dr. Mukti and Other Tales of Woe, 2004; The Book of Dave, 2006; Psychogeography: Disentangling the Modern Conundrum of Psyche and Place, 2007; Liver, 2008; The Butt: An Exit Strategy, 2008; (intro.) The Undivided Self, 2010; Walking to Hollywood, 2010. Contributor of articles to periodicals. **Address:** c/o Tracy Bohan, The Wylie Agency Ltd., 17 Bedford Sq., London, GL WC1B 3JA, England.

SELFORS, Suzanne. American (born United States), b. 1963?. **Genres:** Novels. **Career:** Writer. **Publications:** To Catch a Mermaid, 2007; Saving Juliet, 2008; Fortune's Magic Farm, 2009; Coffeehouse Angel, 2009. **Address:** Michael Bourret, Dystel & Goderich Literary Management, PO Box 10414, Bainbridge Island, WA 98110, U.S.A. **Online address:** mail@suzanneselfors.com

SELGIN, George. American/Italian (born Italy), b. 1957. **Genres:** Economics. **Career:** George Mason University, assistant professor, 1985-88; University of Hong Kong, lecturer, 1988-89; University of Georgia, assistant professor, 1989-95, associate professor, 1995-2001, professor, 2001-; West Virginia University, professor, 2008-09; Independent Institute, research fellow; Cato Institute, senior fellow. Writer and researcher. **Publications:** The Theory of Free Banking: Money Supply under Competitive Note Issue, 1988; Bank Deregulation and Monetary Order, 1996; Less Than Zero: The Case for a Falling Price Level in a Growing Economy, 1997; (ed. and intro.) The Fluttering Veil: Essays on Monetary Disequilibrium, 1997; Good Money: Birmingham Button Makers, the Royal Mint, and the Beginnings of Modern Coinage, 1775- 1821, 2008. Contributor to journals. **Address:** Terry College of Business, University of Georgia, Athens, GA 30602-6254, U.S.A. **Online address:** selgin@uga.edu

SELGIN, Peter. American (born United States), b. 1957. **Genres:** Novels. **Career:** Georgia College and State University, visiting professor, 2009-10; Alimentum: The Literature of Food, editor; Gotham Writers Workshop, faculty; Montclair State University, faculty; Yeshiva University, faculty; Manhattanville College, faculty; New York University, faculty; Mercantile Library Center for Fiction, faculty; Western Connecticut State University, M.F.A. program, faculty; St. Lawrence University, Viebranz distinguished visiting professor of creative writing. Writer and visual artist. **Publications:** S.S. Gigantic across the Atlantic: The Story of the World's Biggest Ocean Liner Ever! and Its Disastrous Maiden Voyage, Based on a True Story, 1999; By Cunning & Craft: Sound Advice and Practical Wisdom for Fiction Writers, 2007; Drowning Lessons: Stories, 2008; Life Goes to the Movies (novel), 2009; 179 Ways to Save a Novel: Matters of Vital Concern to Fiction Writers, 2009; The Man Who Lived Alone, 2010; Confessions of a Left-Handed Man: An Artist's Memoir, 2011. Works appear in anthologies. Contributor to periodicals. **Address:** New York, NY , U.S.A. **Online address:** peter@pcterselgin.com

SELIG, Robert L. American (born United States), b. 1932. **Genres:** Biography, Literary Criticism And History, Young Adult Fiction. **Career:** Queens College of the City University of New York, instructor in English, 1961-67; Purdue University-Calumet, assistant professor, 1967-72, associate professor, 1972-81, professor of English, 1981-. Writer. **Publications:** Elizabeth Gaskell: A Reference Guide, 1977; George Gissing, 1983, rev. ed., 1995; Time and Anthony Powell: A Critical Study, 1991; (ed. and intro.) George Gissing, Lost Stories From America: Five Signed Stories Never Before Reprinted, A Sixth Signed Story, and Seven Recent Attributions, 1992. **Address:** Department of English and Philosophy, Purdue University, CLO Rm. 282, 2200 169th St., Hammond, IN 46323-2094, U.S.A. **Online address:** maureen911@aol.com

SELIGMAN, Craig. American (born United States) **Genres:** Novels, Biography, Art/Art History, Young Adult Fiction, History. **Career:** Bloomberg News, critic. Writer. **Publications:** Sontag and Kael: Opposites Attract Me, 2004; Marine Vet Returns to Vietnam with Nosy Journalist, 2007. **Address:** c/o Author Mail, Counterpoint Press, 841 Broadway, 4th Fl., New York, NY 10003-8802, U.S.A. **Online address:** cseligman@bloomberg.net

SELIGMAN, Martin E. P. American (born United States), b. 1942. **Genres:** Psychology, Self Help, Education, Sciences, Reference. **Career:** Cornell University, assistant professor of psychology, 1967-70; University of Pennsylvania, Department of Psychology, visiting associate professor, 1970-71, associate professor, 1972-76, professor, 1976-, director of clinical training program, 1980-94, Bob and Arlene Kogod term professor, 1992-99, Robert A. Fox leadership professor, 1999-2009, Positive Psychology Center, director, 2004-, Zellerbach Family professor, 2009-; University of London, Institute of Psychiatry, visiting fellow, 1975; Foresight Inc., Scientific Board, chairman, 1984-, director; American Psychological Association, president, 1993-95, 1999; University of Wales, Department of Psychology, honorary professor of psychology, 1997-, John Templeton Foundation, program director, 1999-2002. Writer. **Publications:** (Comp.) Biological Boundaries of Learning, 1972; Helplessness: On Depression, Development and Death, 1975; (ed. with J.D. Maser) Psychopathology: Experimental Models, 1977; (with J. Garber)

Human Helplessness: Theory and Applications, 1980; (with D.L. Rosenhan) Abnormal Psychology, 1984, 4th ed., 2001; Learned Optimism, 1991; (with C. Peterson and S.F. Maier) Learned Helplessness: A Theory for the Age of Personal Control, 1993; What You Can Change and What You Can't, 1994; (ed. with G.M. Buchanan) Explanatory Style, 1995; The Optimistic Child, 1995; (with D.L. Rosenhan) Abnormality, 1998; (ed. with D. Chirot) Ethnopolitical Warfare: Causes, Consequences and Possible Solutions, 2001; Authentic Happiness: Using the New Positive Psychology to Realize Your Potential for Lasting Fulfillment, 2002; (with C. Peterson) Character Strengths and Virtues: A Handbook and Classification, 2004; (with E. Diener) Beyond Money: Toward an Economy of Well-being, 2004; Flourish: A Visionary New Understanding of Happiness and Well-being, 2011. **Address:** Positive Psychology Ctr., University of Pennsylvania, Rm. 205, 3701 Market St., Ste. 200, Philadelphia, PA 19104, U.S.A. **Online address:** seligman@psych.upenn.edu

SELIGSON, Susan. American (born United States) **Genres:** Children's Fiction, Reference, Travel/Exploration. **Career:** Journalist. **Publications:** Going with the Grain: A Wandering Bread Lover Takes a Bite out of Life, 2002; Stacked: A 32DDD Reports from the Front, 2007. CHILDREN'S BOOKS: (with H. Schneider) Amos: The Story of an Old Dog and His Couch, 1987; The Amazing Amos and the Greatest Couch on Earth, 1989; (with H. Schneider) Amos, Ahoy! A Couch Adventure on Land and Sea, 1990; Amos Camps Out: A Couch Adventure in the Woods, 1992. **Address:** Simon & Schuster Inc., 1230 Ave. of the Americas, New York, NY 10020, U.S.A.

SELIY, Shauna. American (born United States), b. 1970?. **Genres:** Novels, Young Adult Fiction. **Career:** St. Albans School, writer-in-residence, 2003-04; Northwestern University, Department of English, artist-in-residence. **Publications:** When We Get There (novel), 2007. Contributor to periodicals. **Address:** The Wylie Agency, 250 W 57th St., Ste. 2114, New York, NY 10107-2199, U.S.A. **Online address:** s-seliy@northwestern.edu

SELLARS, Jane. British (born England), b. 1951. **Genres:** Plays/Screenplays, Art/Art History, Women's Studies And Issues, Autobiography/Memoirs, Photography. **Career:** Walker Art Gallery, education officer, 1980-89; Bronte Parsonage Museum, director, 1989-96; Harewood House, principal curator, 1996-2001; freelance art and museums consultant, 2001-03; Harrogate Arts and Museums, curator of art, 2003-. Writer. **Publications:** Women's Works: Paintings, Drawings, Prints, and Sculpture by Women Artists in the Permanent Collection, 1988; (with C. Alexander) The Art of the Brontës, 1995; Writers' Lives: Charlotte Bronte, 1997. Contributor to magazines. **Address:** The Mercer Art Gallery, Swan Rd., Keighley, Harrowgate, NY HG1 2SA, England.

SELLERBERG, Ann Mari. Swedish (born Sweden), b. 1943. **Genres:** Economics, Money/Finance, Sociology. **Career:** University of Lund, professor of sociology. Writer. **Publications:** Kvinnorna på den svenska arbetsmarknaden under 1900-talet, En sociologisk analys av kvinnornas underordnade position i arbetslivet, 1973; Women in the Swedish Labour Market in the Twentieth Century, 1973; Konsumtionenes Sociologi, 1978; Avstånd och Attraktion: Om modets växlingar, 1987; A Blend of Contradictions: Georg Simmel in Theory and Practice, 1994. Contributor to periodicals. **Address:** Department of Sociology, University of Lund, Rm. 418, Paradisgatan 2, PO Box 117, Lund, S-22100, Sweden. **Online address:** ann_mari.sellerberg@soc.lu.se

SELLERS, Alexandra. British/Canadian (born Canada) **Genres:** Romance/Historical, Animals/Pets, Language/Linguistics, Humor/Satire, Young Adult Fiction, Novels. **Career:** Writer, 1980-. **Publications:** NOVELS: The Indifferent Heart, 1981; Captive of Desire, 1982; Fire in the Wind, 1982; Season of Storms, 1983; The Forever Kind, 1984; The Real Man, 1984; The Male Chauvinist, 1985; The Old Flame, 1986; Best of Friends, 1990; The Man Next Door, 1991; A Gentleman and a Scholar, 1993; The Vagabond, 1994; Dearest Enemy, 1995; Roughneck, 1995; A Nice Girl Like You, 1996; Not Without a Wife!, 1997; Shotgun Wedding, 1997; How to Speak Cat: The Essential Primer of Cat Language, 1998; Wife on Demand, 1998; Born Royal, 2001. SONS OF THE DESERT SERIES: Bride of the Sheikh, 1997; Sheikh's Ransom, 1999; The Solitary Sheikh, 1999; Beloved Sheikh, 1999; Sheikh's Temptation, 2000; Sheikh's Honour, 2000; Sheikh's Woman, 2001; Sheikh's Castaway, 2004; The Ice Maiden's Sheikh, 2004; The Fierce and Tender Sheikh, 2005; Sheikh's Betrayal, 2009. OCCUPATION, VENABLES SERIES: Occupation, Millionaire, 1998; Occupation, Casanova, 1999. SONS OF THE DESERT: THE SULTANS: The Sultan's Heir, 2001; Undercover Sultan, 2001; Sleeping with the Sultan, 2001; The Playboy Sheikh, 2002. OTHERS: (with P. More-

land) One Hundred Per Cent Male, 2001; (with M. Child) Secret Child, 2002; (with M. Child) Up Close and Passionate, 2002; (with G. Dayton) Seduced by the Sheikh, 2002; (with F. Brand and S. Mallery) Sheikhs of Summer, 2002; (with A.M. Winston) The Playboy Sheikh/Billionaire Bachelors: Stone, 2002; (with K. Brant and L. Worth) Captured Hearts/The Greek Tycoon's Baby/ Sophie's Sheikh/Spring Fling 2003; (with B. Young) Sheikh's Desire, 2003; (with S. Mallery) Desert Heat, 2005; (with K. Gold) Princes of the Desert, 2005; (with S. Mallery) The Sheikh's Captive, 2006; Sophie's Sheikh, 2006; (with L. Gordon and M. Reid) Desert Princes, 2007; (with S. Mallery) Possessed by the Sheikh, 2007; (with S. Mallery) Surrender to the Sheikh, 2007; (with C. Grace and M. Reid) At the Sheikh's Command: Sleeping with the Sultan/Sheikh's Chosen Wife/Taming the Sheikh, 2008; (with P. Jordan and L. Wright) Chosen by the Sheikh, 2010; (with L. Fielding and S. Stephens) Rescued by the Sheikh, 2010; (with B. McMahon and A. West) The Sheikh's Cinderella, 2010. **Address:** PO Box 9449, London, GL NW3 2WH, England.

SELLERS, Christopher C. American (born United States), b. 1958. **Genres:** Medicine/Health, Environmental Sciences/Ecology. **Career:** Rutgers University, assistant professor of history, 1992-98; State University of New York, associate professor of history, 1998-. Writer. **Publications:** Hazards of the Job: From Industrial Disease to Environmental Health Science, 1997; (ed. with J. Melling) Dangerous Trade: Industrial Hazards and Globalization in the Twentieth Century, 2007; (ed. with J. Melling) Dangerous Trade: Histories of Industrial Hazard Across a Globalizing World, 2011; Crabgrass Crucible: Suburban Nature and the Rise of Environmentalism in Twentieth-Century America, 2012; Unsettling Ground: Sprawl, Nature and Environmentalism in Post-WWII America, forthcoming; Green in Black and White: Environmentalism and Suburbanizing in Post-WWII Atlanta, forthcoming. **Address:** Department of History, State University of New York, N301A Social and Behavioral Sciences Bldg., 3rd Fl., Stony Brook, NY 11794-4348, U.S.A. **Online address:** csellers@notes.cc.sunysb.edu

SELLERS, Heather (Laurie). American (born United States), b. 1964. **Genres:** Poetry, Novels, Writing/Journalism, Children's Fiction. **Career:** University of Texas, assistant professor of English, 1992-95; Hope College, Department of English, associate professor of English, professor, 1995-; St. Lawrence University, Viebranz visiting professor of creative writing, 2001-03. Writer. **Publications:** Georgia Under Water (novel), 2001; Spike & Cubby's Ice Cream Island Adventure, 2004. POETRY: Your Whole Life: Poems, 1994; Drinking Girls and Their Dresses: Poems, 2002; The Boys I Borrow, 2007. NON FICTION: Page After Page: Discover the Confidence and Passion You Need to Start Writing and Keep Writing (No Matter What!), 2005; Chapter After Chapter: Discover the Dedication and Focus You Need to Write the Book of Your Dreams, 2007; The Best Creative Nonfiction, 2007; The Practice of Creative Writing: A Guide for Students, 2008, 2nd ed., 2012; The Nighttime Novelist, 2010; Face First: A Memoir, 2010; You don't Look Like Anyone I Know, 2010. Works appear in anthologies. Contributor to magazines. **Address:** Department of English, Hope College, Lubbers Hall, 126 E 10th St., Holland, MI 49423-9000, U.S.A. **Online address:** sellers@hope.edu

SELLERS, John. American (born United States), b. 1970?. **Genres:** Autobiography/Memoirs, Novels. **Career:** The Atlantic Monthly, writer; The Believer, writer; The New York Times, writer; Time Out New York, TV editor. **Publications:** PCAT, Preparation for the Pop-Culture Aptitude Test: Rad '80s Version, 1998; Arcade Fever: The Fan's Guide to the Golden Age of Video Games, 2001; Perfect from Now On: How Indie Rock Saved My Life (memoir), 2007; The Old Man and the Swamp, 2011. **Address:** Simon & Schuster Inc., 1230 Ave. of the Americas, 17th Fl., New York, NY 10020, U.S.A. **Online address:** perfectbook@verizon.net

SELLERS-GARCIA, Sylvia. American (born United States), b. 1975?. **Genres:** Young Adult Fiction. **Career:** Harper's, staff; New Yorker, staff. Novelist. **Publications:** When the Ground Turns in Its Sleep, 2007. **Address:** c/o Dorian Karchmar, William Morris Agency, 1325 Ave. of the Americas, New York, NY 10019, U.S.A. **Online address:** sylvia@sellersgarcia.com

SELLIN, Christine Petra. American (born United States), b. 1961. **Genres:** Literary Criticism And History, Theology/Religion. **Career:** California Lutheran University, assistant professor of art history. Writer. **Publications:** Fractured Families and Rebel Maidservants: The Biblical Hagar in Seventeenth-Century Dutch Art and Literature, 2006; (with R. Mellinkoff)

From Unholy to Holy: The Four Female Ancestors of Christ according to the Gospel of Matthew, 2009. **Address:** California Lutheran University, 60 W Olsen Rd., Thousand Oaks, CA 91360-2700, U.S.A. **Online address:** csellin@callutheran.edu

SELLIN, Eric. American (born United States), b. 1933. **Genres:** Poetry, Literary Criticism And History. **Career:** Pennsylvania Literary Review, editor, 1954-55; University of Bordeaux, American literature, lecturer, 1956-57; Clark University, instructor of French, 1958-59; University of Pennsylvania, lecturer in creative writing, 1960-62; Temple University, instructor, 1962-65, assistant professor, 1965-67, associate professor, 1967-70, professor of French, 1970-91, Department of French and Italian, chairman, 1970-73; University of Algiers, American literature, Fulbright-Hays lecturer, 1968-69; American Association for the Study of Dada and Surrealism, vice president, 1970-76; University of Dakar, American literature, Fulbright-Hays lecturer, 1978-79; CELFAN Review, founder and editor, 1981-2001; Center for the Study of the Francophone Literature of North Africa, founder, 1981; Africana Journal, editor, 1983-87; Tulane University, professor of French and Francophone literatures, 1991-2001, professor emeritus, 2001-. **Publications:** Night Voyage, 1964; The Dramatic Concepts of Antonin Artaud, 1968; Trees at First Light, 1973; Tanker Poems, 1973; Borne kilométrique, 1973; As-Shamsu, 1973; Valéry, Stevens, and the Cartesian Dilemma, 1975; The Inner Game of Soccer, 1976; Soccer Basics, 1977; Marginalia: Poems, 1979; Crepuscule prolonge a El Biar, 1982; Nightfall over Lubumbashi, 1982; Night Foundering, 1985; Dead of Noon, 1992; Reflections on the Aesthetics of Futurism, Dadaism, and Surrealism, 1993. **Address:** Tulane University, 6823 St. Charles Ave., New Orleans, LA 70118, U.S.A. **Online address:** sellin@mailhost.tcs.tulane.edu

SELMAN, Robyn. American (born United States), b. 1959. **Genres:** Poetry, Photography, Young Adult Fiction. **Career:** Producer of commercial photography, 2000-. Writer and photographer. **Publications:** Directions to My House (poems), 1995; (ed.) Gold Book's Eye on People Photography 3, 1995. Works appear in anthologies. Contributor to periodicals. **Address:** University of Pittsburgh Press, 3400 Forbes Ave., Eureka Bldg., 5th Fl., Pittsburgh, PA 15260, U.S.A.

SELMANOVIC, Samir. American/Yugoslav (born United States), b. 1965. **Genres:** Theology/Religion. **Career:** Faith House Manhattan, founder; CrossWalk Church, founder; Citylights, director. Writer. **Publications:** It's Really All about God: Reflections of a Muslim Atheist Jewish Christian, 2009. Contributor to books. **Address:** New York, NY , U.S.A. **Online address:** samir@faithhousemanhattan.org

SELTZER, David. American (born United States), b. 1940?. **Genres:** Plays/Screenplays, Horror, Young Adult Fiction. **Career:** Director, producer and novelist. **Publications:** The Omen, 1976; Prophecy, 1979. **Address:** Creative Artists Agency, 9830 Wilshire Blvd., Beverly Hills, CA 90212-1825, U.S.A.

SELTZER, Leon F(rancis). American (born United States), b. 1940. **Genres:** Literary Criticism And History, Psychology, Psychiatry, Medicine/Health. **Career:** Queens College of the City University of New York, assistant professor of English, 1967-70, professor of English; Cleveland State University, associate professor of English, 1970-78. Writer. **Publications:** The Vision of Melville and Conrad: A Comparative Study, 1970; Paradoxical Strategies in Psychotherapy: A Comprehensive Overview and Guidebook, 1986. **Address:** 14195 Mango Dr., Del Mar, CA 92014-2924, U.S.A. **Online address:** lseltzer@san.rr.com

SELTZER, Mark. American (born United States), b. 1951?. **Genres:** Criminology/True Crime, Novels, Young Adult Fiction, Social Sciences, Art/Art History. **Career:** Humbolt University, chair of American studies, through 2001; University of California, Evan Frankel chair in English and American literature, 2001-, professor, 2001-; Cornell University, professor of English. Writer. **Publications:** Henry James and the Art of Power, 1984; Bodies and Machines, 1992; Serial Killers: Death and Life in America's Wound Culture, 1998; True Crime: Observations on Violence and Modernity, 2007. **Address:** Department of English, University of California, 180 Humanities Bldg., PO Box 951530, Los Angeles, CA 90095-1530, U.S.A. **Online address:** mseltzer@humnet.ucla.edu

SELVADURAI, Shyam. Canadian/Sri Lankan (born Sri Lanka), b. 1965.

Genres: Novels, Young Adult Fiction, Novellas/Short Stories. **Career:** Novelist, essayist and writer. **Publications:** Funny Boy: A Novel in Six Stories, 1994; Cinnamon Gardens, 1998; Swimming in the Monsoon Sea, 2005; (ed.) Story-Wallah: Short Fiction from South Asian Writers, 2005; The Hungry Ghosts, 2012. **Address:** William Morrow & Company Inc., 1350 Ave. of the Americas, New York, NY 10019, U.S.A.

SELVIDGE, Marla J(ean). American (born United States), b. 1948. **Genres:** Theology/Religion, Women's Studies And Issues. **Career:** John Wesley College, assistant professor of religion, 1973-74; Thalhimers, personnel director and senior executive, 1974-76; Center for Reformation Research, research assistant, 1976-77; St. Louis University, College of Arts and Sciences, director of evening division, 1977-80, lecturer, 1978-80; Carthage College, assistant professor of religion, 1980-81; University of Dayton, assistant professor of religious studies, 1981-83; Converse College, assistant professor of religion, 1983-87, Department of Religion and Philosophy, chair, 1984-85; Marist College, assistant professor of religious studies and philosophy, 1989-90; Central Missouri State University, associate professor, 1990-94, director of Center for Religious Studies, 1990-, professor of religious studies, 1994-; American Schools of Oriental Research, vice president and board director, 1997-. Writer. **Publications:** (Ed.) Fundamentalism Today: What Makes It So Attractive?, 1984; Daughters of Jerusalem, 1987; Woman, Cult, and Miracle Recital, 1990; Discovering Women, 1995; Notorious Voices: The Roots of Feminist Biblical Interpretation, 1996; Women, Violence and the Bible, 1996; Notorious Voices: A Reader, 1997; The New Testament: A Timeless Book for All Peoples, 1999; Exploring the New Testament, 2003; (with A.P. Davis) Women Nobel Peace Prize Winners, 2006. Contributor of articles to journals. **Address:** Center for Religious Studies, Central Missouri State University, Wood Bldg., Rm 124, Martin 118, Warrensburg, MO 64093, U.S.A. **Online address:** selvidge@ucmo.edu

SELVIN, Joel. American (born United States), b. 1950. **Genres:** Music, Biography. **Career:** San Francisco Chronicle, columnist, 1972-; San Francisco State University, lecturer, 1975-91. Writer. **Publications:** Ricky Nelson: Idol for a Generation, 1990; Monterey Pop: June 16-18, 1967, 1992; Photopass: The Rock & Roll Photography of Randy Bachman, 1994; Summer of Love: The Inside Story of LSD, Rock & Roll, and High Times in the Wild West, 1994, 2nd ed., 1999; San Francisco, the Musical History Tour: A Guide to over 200 of the Bay Area's Most Memorable Music Sites, 1996; Sly and the Family Stone: An Oral History, 1998; (P. Grushkin) Treasures of the Hard Rock Cafe: The Official Guide to the Hard Rock Cafe Memorabilia Collection, 2001; (intro.) Jim Marshall: Proof, 2004; Smart Ass, 2011; (with S. Hagar) Red: My Uncensored Life in Rock, 2011. **Address:** c/o Frank Weimann, 262 Central Pk. W, Ste. 1H, New York, NY 10024, U.S.A. **Online address:** joelselvin@aol.com

SELZ, Peter. American/German (born Germany), b. 1919. **Genres:** Art/Art History. **Career:** University of Chicago, instructor, 1949-53; Institute of Design, assistant professor of art history and head of art education department, 1949-55; Pomona College, chair of art department and director of art gallery, 1955-58; Museum of Modern Art, department of painting and sculpture exhibitions, curator, 1958-65, chief curator; University of California, University Art Museum, founding director, 1965-73, professor of art history, 1965-88, professor emeritus, 1988-; Hebrew University of Jerusalem, Zaks professor, 1976; City University of New York, visiting professor, 1987. Writer. **Publications:** German Expressionist Painting, 1957; New Images of Man, 1959; Art Nouveau, 1960, rev. ed. (ed. with M. Constantine), 1975; Mark Rothko, 1961; 15 Polish Painters, 1961; The Work of Jean Dubuffet, 1962; Emil Nolde, 1963; Max Beckmann, 1964; (intro.) Alberto Giacometti, 1965; Seven Decades, 1895-1965, Crosscurrents in Modern Art, 1966; Directions in Kinetic Sculpture, 1966; Funk, 1967; (contrib.) Theories of Modern Art, 1968; (ed.) Harold Paris: The California Years, 1972; Ferdinand Hodler, 1972; Sam Francis, 1975, rev. ed., 1982; (with T.C. Blaisdell) The American Presidency in Political Cartoons, 1776-19762, 1976; 2 Jahrzehnte Amerikanische Malerei 1920-1940, 1979; Art in a Turbulent Era, 1985; Art in Our Times, 1981; Chillida, 1986; Dramas of Human Encounter: The Work of Bedri Baykam, 1986; (with F. Licht and Balzarotti) Congdon, 1992; Max Beckmann: The Self Portraits, 1992; Bruce Beasley, 1994; William Congdon, 1995; (comp.) Dimitri Hadzi, 1996; (contrib.) Richard Lindner, 1996; (ed.) Theories and Documents of Contemporary Art, 1996; Beyond the Mainstream, 1997; (with A.F. Janson) Barbara Chase-Riboud, 1999; Il Maestro E L'allievo, 2001; Nathan Oliveira, 2002; Monet to Matisse, 2004; Art of Engagement: Visual Politics in California and Beyond, 2005; Raimonds Staprans, 2005; (with C.

Chattopadhyay and D. Ghirado) Fletcher Benton: The Kinetic Years, 2008; Rudolf Bauer: Works on Paper, 2010. **Address:** Department of History of Art, University of California, 416 Doe Library, Ste. 6020, Berkeley, CA 94720-6021, U.S.A.

SELZER, Adam. American (born United States), b. 1980?. **Genres:** Novels, How-to Books. **Career:** Writer. **Publications:** How to Get Suspended and Influence People, 2007; Pirates of the Retail Wasteland, 2008; I Put a Spell on You, 2008; Lost and Found, 2009. Contributor to books. **Address:** Chicago, IL , U.S.A. **Online address:** adam.selzer@gmail.com

SELZER, Jack. American (born United States) **Genres:** Literary Criticism And History, Humanities. **Career:** Pennsylvania State University, Department of English, assistant professor, 1978-85, associate professor, 1985-96, professor, 1996-, College of the Liberal Arts, associate dean, 2005-09, Paterno Fellows Program, Barry Director, 2009-, director of composition, director of graduate studies in English. Writer. **Publications:** Conversations: Readings for Writing, 1991; (ed.) Understanding Scientific Prose, 1993; Kenneth Burke in Greenwich Village: Conversing with the Moderns, 1915-1931, 1996; (ed. with S. Crowley) Rhetorical Bodies: Toward a Material Rhetoric, 1999; (with L. Faigley) Good Reasons: Designing and Writing Effective Arguments, 2000, 4th ed., 2008; (with L. Faigley) Good Reasons with Contemporary Arguments: Reading, Designing and Writing Effective Arguments, 2001, 5th ed., 2012; (intro. with M.S. Morrisson) Tambour, 2002; (comp.) Argument in America: Essential Issues, Essential Texts, 2004; (with A. George) Kenneth Burke in the 1930s, 2007; (comp. with D.D. Carpini) Conversations: Readings for Writing, 2009, 8th ed., 2012; (with L. Faigley) Little Argument, 2009; Good Reasons: Researching and Writing Effective Arguments, 2012. **Address:** Deans Office, College of the Liberal Arts, Pennsylvania State University, 15 Burrowes Bldg., University Park, PA 16802, U.S.A. **Online address:** jselzer@psu.edu

SEMAAN, Khalil I. H. American/Syrian (born Syrian Arab Republic), b. 1920. **Genres:** Language/Linguistics, Humanities, Third World, History. **Career:** New York University, lecturer in Semitic languages, 1955-56; Columbia University, lecturer in Arabic, 1957; University of California, assistant professor of Oriental languages, 1957-59; Library of Congress, reference librarian, 1960-62; Afro-Asian Research Institute, director, 1962-64; Binghamton University, State University of New York, assistant professor, 1965-70, associate professor, 1966-70, professor of Arabic, 1970, now professor emeritus of Arabic; Harvard University, professor, 1966. Writer. **Publications:** Ash-Shafiis Risalah: Basic Ideas, 1961; (trans.) Arabic phonetics: IbnSīnā's Risālah On The Points of Articulation of The Speech-Sounds, 1963; Linguistics in the Middle Ages: Phonetic Studies in Early Islam, 1968; (trans.) Salā Abd al-abūr, Ma'sat at-Hallaj (title means: 'Murder in Baghdad'), 1972; Yahud al-bilad al-Islamiyyah, 1987. EDITOR: Islam and the Medieval West: Aspects of Intercultural Relations, 1980; The Crusades: Other Experiences, Alternate Perspectives: Selected Proceedings From the 32nd annual CEMERS Conference, 2003. Contributor of articles to journals. **Address:** Department of Classical and Near Eastern Studies, Binghamton University, State University of New York, 713 Country Club Rd., Vestal, NY 13850-3911, U.S.A. **Online address:** ksemaan@binghamton.edu

SEMANS, Anne. American (born United States) **Genres:** Sex, Psychology. **Career:** Good Vibrations, catalog marketing manager, 1986-99; Annabelle Inc., writer, 1990-; Libida, ecommerce manager, 1999-2002; Babeland L.L.C., director of marketing, 2004-, marketing manager. **Publications:** (With C. Winks) The Good Vibrations Guide to Sex, 1994, 3rd ed., 2002; (ed. with C. Winks) Sex Toy Tales, 1998; (with C. Winks) The Woman's Guide to Sex on the Web, 1999; (with C. Winks) The Mother's Guide to Sex: Enjoying Your Sexuality through All Stages of Motherhood, 2001; The Many Joys of Sex Toys: The Ultimate How-To Handbook for Couples and Singles, 2004; (with C. Winks) Sexy Mamas: Keeping Your Sex Life Alive While Raising Kids, 2004. **Address:** Babeland L.L.C., 94 Rivington St., New York, NY 10002, U.S.A. **Online address:** comments@anneandcathy.com

SEMCHYSHYN, Stefan. American (born United States), b. 1940. **Genres:** Medicine/Health, Human Relations/Parenting, Sports/Fitness. **Career:** University of Toronto, intern and resident in obstetrics and gynecology, 1971-75; Ohio State University, research associate and fellow in maternal-fetal medicine, 1976-78, clinical instructor, 1976-77, assistant professor of medicine, 1977-78; Texas Tech University, associate professor of medicine and attending physician at Health Sciences Center, 1978-79; University of Illinois-

Chicago, associate professor of clinical obstetrics and gynecology, 1979-81; Robert Wood Johnson Medical School, associate professor of obstetrics and gynecology, 1983-88; Seton Hall University, School of Graduate Medical Education, associate professor of obstetrics and gynecology, 1989-. Writer. **Publications:** (With C. Colman) How to Prevent Miscarriage and Other Crises of Pregnancy, 1989; Diabetes and Pregnancy, 1994; Prematurity Prevention, 1995; Making Every Pregnancy Count, Saving Lives and Dollars, 1998. **Address:** c/o Richard Curtis, Richard Curtis Associates Inc., 171 E 74th St., 2nd Fl., New York, NY 10021, U.S.A. **Online address:** drsem@aol.com

SEMLER, Ricardo. American/Brazilian (born Brazil), b. 1959?. **Genres:** Administration/Management, Biography, Business/Trade/Industry, Economics, Autobiography/Memoirs. **Career:** Semco S.A., counselor and co-owner, 1980-, chief executive officer, president. Writer. **Publications:** Virando a própria mesa, 1988, trans. as Maverick: Embrulhando o peixe, 1991; The Success Story Behind the World's Most Unusual Workplace, 1993; The Seven-Day Weekend: Changing the Way Work Works, 2004. Contributor to periodicals. **Address:** International Creative Management, 40 W 57th St., New York, NY 10019, U.S.A.

SEMMES, Clovis E. American (born United States), b. 1949. **Genres:** History, Sociology, Reference. **Career:** Malcolm X College, teacher, 1974; Olive-Harvey College, teacher, 1976; Roosevelt University, teacher, 1976, 1977; University of Illinois, visiting lecturer, 1976-79, assistant professor of black studies, 1979-86, acting director of black studies, 1980-82; Northeastern Illinois University, teacher, 1986; Northwestern University, assistant director of admissions and coordinator of admissions and financial aid for minority students, 1986-88, LEAD Program, operations director, 1987-88; Eastern Michigan University, associate professor, 1988-93, professor of African-American studies, 1993-, now professor emeritus; Regal Theater Foundation, consultant; University of Missouri, Department of Sociology, professor, Black Studies Program, visiting professor of black studies, professor and director. Writer. **Publications:** Cultural Hegemony and African American Development, 1992; Racism, Health, and Post-Industrialism: A Theory of African-American Health, 1996; (comp.) Roots of Afrocentric Thought: A Reference Guide to Negro Digest/Black World, 1961-1976, 1998; Regal Theater and Black Culture, 2006. Contributor of articles to books and journals. **Address:** Department of Sociology, University of Missouri, Rm. 304, Haag Hall, 5100 Rockhill Rd., Kansas City, MO 64110-2499, U.S.A. **Online address:** semmesc@umkc.edu

SEMPLE, Andrea. British (born England), b. 1975?. **Genres:** Civil Liberties/Human Rights, Young Adult Fiction. **Career:** Writer and freelance journalist. **Publications:** (With M. Haig) The Internet Job Search Handbook, 2001. NOVELS: The Ex-Factor, 2002; The Make-Up Girl, 2004; The Man from Perfect, 2005; (co-author) Leeds Stories 2, 2005. Contributor to periodicals. **Address:** The Marsh Agency, 50 Albemarle St., London, GL W1S 4BD, England. **Online address:** andrea@andreasemple.com

SEMPLE, Maria. American (born United States), b. 1964. **Genres:** Novels. **Career:** Writer. **Publications:** This One Is Mine (novel), 2010. **Address:** Seattle, WA , U.S.A. **Online address:** maria@mariasemple.com

SEMRUD-CLIKEMAN, Margaret (Elaine). American (born United States), b. 1950. **Genres:** Psychiatry. **Career:** Psychologist for public schools, 1974-86; University of Georgia, Center for Clinical and Developmental Neuropsychology, associate director, 1988-89; Jasper County Schools, school psychology intern, 1989-90; Massachusetts General Hospital, psychology intern, 1989-91, postdoctoral fellow in neuroscience, 1990-91; University of Washington, assistant professor of educational psychology, 1991-95; University of Minnesota, assistant professor of neurology, 1995-97; Leech Lake Reservation, Fetal Alcohol Project, affiliate, 1995-97; University of Texas, associate professor of educational psychology, 1997-; Children's Hospital of Austin, consulting pediatric neuropsychologist, 1999-; Michigan State University, professor of psychology and psychiatry. Writer. **Publications:** Child and Adolescent Therapy, 1995; (with P.A.T. Ellison) Child Neuropsychology: Assessment and Interventions for Neurodevelopmental Disorders, 1997; Traumatic Brain Injury in Children and Adolescents: Assessment and Intervention, 2001; Social Competence in Children, 2007; (with L.A. Guli and A.D. Wilkinson) Scip: Social Compence Intervention Program, 2008. **Address:** Department of Psychiatry, Michigan State University, 321 W Fee Hall, East Lansing, MI 48824-1316, U.S.A. **Online address:** semrudcl@msu.edu

SEMYONOV, Moshe. Armenian/Israeli (born Israel), b. 1946. **Genres:** Sociology, Social Sciences, Women's Studies And Issues, Economics. **Career:** University of Nebraska, Department of Sociology, Visiting Happold Assistant Professor, 1978-79, assistant professor, 1979-82, associate professor, 1982-86; University of Haifa, Department of Sociology, lecturer, 1980-82, senior lecturer, 1982-86; University of Illinois-Chicago, Department of Sociology, professor of sociology, 1987-, interim head, 2003-05; Tel Aviv University, Department of Sociology, senior lecturer, 1986, associate professor, 1987, professor of sociology and labor studies, 1991-, Bernard and Audre Rapoport chair in the sociology of labor, 2005-, Institute for Social Research, director, 1988-90, Department of Sociology and Anthropology, chair, 1990-93, Golda Meir Institute for Social and Labor Research, director, 1993-98, dean and Gershon H. Gordon faculty of social sciences, 1998-2002, Institute for Diplomacy and Regional Cooperation, director, 2005-08. Writer. **Publications:** WITH N. LEWIN-EPSTEIN: Economic Development, Investment Dependence, and the Rise of Services in Less Developed Nations, 1984; Hewers of Wood and Drawers of Water: Noncitizen Arabs in the Israeli Labor Market, 1987; Modernization and Subordination: Arab Women in the Israeli Labor Force, 1991; Gender and the Ethnic Enclave Labor Market: A Study of Arabs in the Israeli Labor Force, 1991; Arabs in the Israeli Economy, 1993; Arvim be-Yisráel be-shuk ha-'avodah, 1994; (ed.) Stratification in Israel: Class, Ethnicity, and Gender, 2004; (ed. with A. Markus) Immigration and Nation Building: Australia and Israel Compared, 2010. OTHER: Hishtalvut 'olim be-shuḳ ha-'avodah, 1995. **Address:** Department of Sociology, University of Illinois, 4173 BSB, 1007 W Harrison St., Chicago, IL 60607-7140, U.S.A. **Online address:** semyonov@uic.edu

SEN, Zekai. Turkish (born Turkey), b. 1947. **Genres:** Meteorology/Atmospheric Sciences. **Career:** Istanbul Technical University, professor of meteorology, 1992-; City of Istanbul, chief consultant for water resources management. Writer. **Publications:** Applied Hydrogeology for Scientists and Engineers, 1995; (ed.) Türkiye'dc kuraklýk ve su kaynaklarýmýz, 2001; (ed.) İklim değişkliği ve Türkiye su Kaynaklarina etkisi, 2002; (co-auhtor) Sinir aşan sularimiz, 2002; (ed.) I Türkiye Yerel Yönetimler Su Sorunlari Kongresi: 3-5 Haziran 2002, İstanbul: bildiri kitabi, 2002; (ed. with S. Sirdass) Suyumuzun Geleceği veTürkiye Su Politikalari, 2003; Ortadoğu'da su sorunlu Bereketli Hilal ve Turkiye, 2006; Solar Energy Fundamentals and Modeling Techniques: Atmosphere, Environment, Climate Change and Renewable Energy, 2008; Wadi Hydrology, 2008; Spatial Modeling Principles in Earth Sciences, 2009; Fuzzy Logic and Hydrological Modeling, 2010. **Address:** Faculty of Aeronautics and Astronautics, Istanbul Technical University, Rm. 221, ITU Hydraulics Lab, Maslak, Istanbul, 80626, Turkey. **Online address:** zsen@itu.edu.tr

SENATE, Melissa. American (born United States) **Genres:** Novels. **Career:** Silhouette Books, senior editor. **Publications:** NOVELS: See Jane Date, 2001; Starring You and Me, 2002; The Solomon Sisters Wise Up, 2003; Whose Wedding is It Anyway?, 2004; Un Novio Para Jane, 2004; Miss Ex-Girlfriend Pageant, 2005; 005-Nos Reves Les Plus Fous, 2005; The Breakup Club, 2006; Theodora Twist, 2006; Love You To Death, 2007; Questions to Ask Before Marrying, 2008; Secret of Joy, 2009; The Mosts, 2010; The Love Goddess' Cooking School, 2010. **Address:** c/o Kim Witherspoon, InkWell Management, 521 5th Ave., 26th Fl., New York, NY 10175, U.S.A. **Online address:** melissasenate@yahoo.com

SENDAK, Maurice. American (born United States), b. 1928. **Genres:** Novellas/Short Stories, Children's Fiction, Essays, Illustrations, Picture/Board Books, Animals/Pets, Humor/Satire, Science Fiction/Fantasy, Science Fiction/Fantasy. **Career:** Timely Service, window display artist, 1946; F.A.O. Schwartz, display artist, 1948-51; writer and illustrator of children's books, 1951-; The Night Kitchen, co-founder and artistic director, 1990-; Yale University, Parsons School of Design, instructor. **Publications:** Kenny's Window, 1956; Very Far Away, 1957; The Acrobat, 1959; The Sign on Rosie's Door, 1960; The Nutshell Library, 1962; Alligators All Around: An Alphabet, 1962; Chicken Soup with Rice: A Book of Months, 1962; Where the Wild Things Are, 1963; Hector Protector, and As I Went Over the Water, 1965; Higglety Pigglety Pop! Or, There Must Be More to Life, 1967; In the Night Kitchen, 1970; Fantasy Sketches, 1970; Ten Little Rabbits: A Counting Book with Mino the Magician, 1970; Pictures by Maurice Sendak, 1971; Really Rosie: Starring the Nutshell Kids, 1975; (with M. Margolis) Some Swell Pup: Or Are You Sure You Want a Dog?, 1976; Seven Little Monsters, 1977; Outside Over There, 1981; Collection of Books, Posters, and Original Drawings, 1984; Really Rosie: A New Musical, 1985; Posters, 1986; Caldecott & Co.:

Notes on Books & Pictures (essays), 1988; We Are All in the Dumps with Jack and Guy, 1993; Sendak in Asia: Exhibition and Sale of Original Artwork, 1996; (with E.H. Minarik) Little Bear's Egg, 2002; Bumble Ardy, 2004; (with A. Yorinks and M. Reinhart) Mommy?, 2006. OTHERS: (ed. and intro.) Maxfield Parrish Poster Book, 1974; (ed.) The Disney Poster Book, 1977; (intro.) Babar's Anniversary Album, 1981; (intro.) Masterworks of Children's Literature, 1984; (intro.) Victorian Color Picture Books, 1985; (foreword) Winsor McCay: His Life and Art, 1987; (intro.) Mickey Mouse Movie Stories, 1988; Maurice Sendak Book and Poster Package: Wild Things, 1991; Maurice Sendak's Christmas Mystery, 1995; (co-author) Worlds of Childhood: The Art and Craft of Writing for Children, 1998; (co-author) Harper Collins Treasury of Picture Book Classics, 2002; Making Mischief, 2009. Illustrator of books by others. **Address:** HarperCollins Children's Books, 10 E 53rd St., New York, NY 10022-5244, U.S.A.

SENDER BARAYON, Ramon. American/Spanish (born Spain), b. 1934. **Genres:** Novels, Adult Non-fiction, Young Adult Non-fiction. **Career:** San Francisco Tape Music Center, co-founder and co-director, 1962-65; Peregrine Foundation, founder. Writer and composer, 1966-. **Publications:** (With A.B. Laurel) Being of the Sun (nonfiction), 1973; The Morning Star Scrapbook, 1976; Zero Weather (novel), 1980; A Death in Zamora (nonfiction), 1989. **Address:** Peregrine Foundation, PO Box 460141, San Francisco, CA 94146-0141, U.S.A. **Online address:** rabar@mindspring.com

SENIE, Harriet F. American (born United States), b. 1943. **Genres:** Art/Art History, Adult Non-fiction, History. **Career:** Moore College of Art, instructor, 1974-75; Hunter College, adjunct professor, 1974-78; Adelphi University, instructor, 1976-79; New York Post, art critic, 1978-79; State University of New York, Amelie A. Wallace Gallery, director, 1978-82, assistant professor of art history, 1979-82; State University of New York, Council of Gallery and Exhibition Directors, vice president, 1979-82; Princeton University, Art Museum, associate director, 1982-85; Art news, art critic, 1986-87; City College of New York, Museum Studies Program, director, professor of art history, 1986-; City University of New York, Graduate Center, visiting professor, 1994-96, professor of contemporary American art, 1997-; Carnegie-Mellon University, visiting distinguished professor, 2000. Writer. **Publications:** Dangerous Precedent? The Tilted Arc Controversy, 2001. CONTRIBUTOR: The Memorial Redefined, 1989; Contemporary Public Sculpture: Tradition, Transformation, and Controversy, 1992; (ed. with S. Webster) Critical Issues in Public Art: Content, Context and Controversy, 1992; Encyclopedia of New York City, 1995; Memory and Oblivion: Acts of the XXIXth International Congress of the History of Art, 1999; Complex Identities: Jewish Consciousness and Modern Art, 2000. **Address:** City College of New York Graduate Center, City University of New York, 365 5th Ave., New York, NY 10016, U.S.A. **Online address:** hsenie@ccny.cuny.edu

SENIOR, Michael. Welsh (born Wales), b. 1940. **Genres:** Plays/Screenplays, Geography, History, Travel/Exploration, Biography. **Career:** Writer. **Publications:** Portrait of North Wales, 1973; Portrait of South Wales, 1974; Greece and Its Myths, 1978; Tropical Lands, 1979; Myths of Britain, 1979; (contrib.) Heroes and Heroines, 1980; (ed. and intro.) Tales of King Arthur, 1980; Life and Times of Richard II, 1981; The Conwy Valley and Its Long History, 1984; Illustrated Who's Who in Mythology, 1985; The Crossing of the Conwy, 1991; Gods and Heroes in North Wales, 1993; North Wales in the Making, 1994, new ed. as North Wales in the Making: A Guide to the Area's Early History, 2003; Figures in a Landscape: A Guide To The Great Historical Characters Of North Wales, 1997; Did Lewis Carroll Visit Llandudno?, 2000; Llys Helig and the Myth of Lost Lands, 2002; Back from Catraeth, Poems, 2002; The Standing Stones of North-Western Wales, 2003; Did Prince Madog Discover America?, 2004; No Finer Courage, 2004; Hillforts of Northern Wales, 2005; Cromlechs and Cairns, 2006; This Is Where You Live, 2007; Faithful Hound, 2009; Eryri, 2011. Contributor of articles to magazines and newspapers. **Address:** David Higham Associates Ltd., 5-8 Lower John St., Golden Sq., London, GL W1F 9HA, England.

SENIOR, Olive (Marjorie). Canadian/Jamaican (born Jamaica), b. 1941. **Genres:** Novellas/Short Stories, Poetry, Area Studies, Young Adult Non-fiction. **Career:** Daily Gleaner newspaper, reporter and sub-editor; Jamaica Information Service, information officer, 1967-69; Jamaica Chamber of Commerce, public relations officer, 1969-71; JCC Journal, editor, 1969-71; Institute of Social and Economic Research, University of the West Indies, publications editor, 1972-77; Social and Economic Studies, editor, 1972-77; teacher in communications, publishing consultant and speech writer, Jamaica,

1977-82; Institute of Jamaica Publications, managing editor, 1982-89; Jamaica Journal, freelance writer, researcher, editor, 1982-89; University of the West Indies, Cave visiting lecturer and writer-in-residence, 1990; Caribbean Writers Summer Institute, University of Miami, director of fiction workshop, 1994, 1995; St. Lawrence University, Dana visiting professor of creative writing, 1994-95; University of Calgary, writer-in-residence, 1998-99; Humber College, Humber School for Writers, faculty, 1998-. **Publications:** POETRY: Talking of Trees, 1985; Gardening in the Tropics, 1994; Over the Roofs of the World, 2005. SHORT STORIES: Summer Lightning and Other Stories, 1986; Arrival of the Snake-Woman, 1989; (co-author) Quartet, 1994; Discerner of Hearts, 1995. OTHER: The Message is Change: A Perspective on the 1972 General Election, 1972; Pop Story Gi Mi (4 booklets on Jamaican heritage for schools), 1973; A-Z of Jamaican Heritage, 1983; Working Miracles: Women's Lives in the English-Speaking Caribbean, 1991; (intro.) Jamaica: Portraits, 1955-1998, 1998; Encyclopedia of Jamaican Heritage, 2003; Shell, 2007. **Address:** c/o Katherine Fausset, Aragi Inc., 143 W 27th St., Ste. 4F, New York, NY 10001, U.S.A.

SENIOR, W(illiam) A. American (born United States), b. 1953. **Genres:** Literary Criticism And History, Young Adult Fiction. **Career:** University of Notre Dame, graduate teaching assistant, 1977-83; Broward Community College (now Broward College), associate professor of English, 1983-, associate dean; Southern Association Accreditation Team, honors program director, 1998-2001. Writer. **Publications:** Variations on the Fantasy Tradition: Stephen R. Donaldson's Chronicles of Thomas Covenant, 1995. Contributor to books and magazines. **Address:** 361 W Tropical Way, Plantation, FL 33317-3328, U.S.A. **Online address:** wsenior@broward.edu

SENN, Bryan. American (born United States), b. 1962. **Genres:** Film, Horror, Art/Art History, Photography. **Career:** University of Washington, Harborview Medical Center, psychometrist, 1985-87; Children's Hospital and Medical Center, psychometrist, 1988-. Writer. **Publications:** (With J. Johnson) Fantastic Cinema Subject Guide: A Topical Index to 2500 Horror, Science Fiction, and Fantasy Films, 1992; Golden Horrors: An Illustrated Critical Filmography of Terror Cinema, 1931-1939, 1996; Drums of Terror: Voodoo in the Cinema, 1998; 365 Silver Screams: A Calendar of Horrors, 2005; A Year of Fear: A Day-by-Day Guide to 366 Horror Films, 2007; (with M. Clark) Sixties Shockers: A Critical Filmography of Horror Cinema, 1960-1969, 2011. Works appear in anthologies. Contributor to periodicals. **Address:** 12526 SE 188th Pl., Renton, WA 98058, U.S.A.

SENNA, Danzy. American (born United States), b. 1970. **Genres:** Novels, Young Adult Non-fiction, Literary Criticism And History. **Career:** Newsweek, researcher and reporter, 1992-94; American Benefactor, contributing editor, 1996-97; Sarah Lawrence College, visiting writer; College of the Holy Cross, Jenks chair in contemporary American letters, 2000-02, teacher in writing and literature. **Publications:** Caucasia (novel), 1997; Symptomatic: A Novel, 2004; Where did You Sleep Last Night?: A Personal History, 2009; You are Free: Stories, 2011. Contributor to books and periodicals. **Address:** c/o Amanda Urban, International Creative Management Inc., 40 W 57th St., New York, NY 10019-4001, U.S.A.

SENNETT, Frank (Ronald). American (born United States), b. 1968. **Genres:** Writing/Journalism, Novels, Mystery/Crime/Suspense, Education, Reference. **Career:** Chicago Convention and Tourism Bureau, public relations consultant, 1988-; Relax, assistant editor and columnist, 1990-91; Slip-up.com, editor; NewCity.com, editor; University of California, humor writing instructor; Time Out Chicago, editor-in-chief and president, 2008-. **Publications:** It Takes Two: Wise Words and Quotable Quips on the Attraction of Opposites, 2002; Teacher of the Year: More than 400 Quotes of Insight, Inspiration and Motivation from America's Greatest Teachers, 2002; Nash, Rambler (novel), 2003; (ed.) 400 Quotable Quotes from the World's Leading Educators, 2004; Nash, Metropolitan (novel), 2004; 101 Stunts for Principals to Inspire Student Achievement, 2005; FUNdraising: 50 Proven Strategies for Successful School Fundraisers, 2008. Contributor to periodicals. **Address:** Time Out Chicago, 247 S State St., 17th Fl., Chicago, IL 60604, U.S.A. **Online address:** frank@franksennett.com

SENNETT, Richard. American (born United States), b. 1943. **Genres:** History, Sociology. **Career:** New York University, university professor of the humanities, professor of history and sociology, 1969-; London School of Economics, Centennial professor of sociology, 1998-, now emeritus; New York Institute for the Humanities, founder. Writer. **Publications:** Families Against the City: Middle Class Homes of Industrial Chicago 1872-1890, 1970; The Uses of Disorder, 1970; (with J. Cobb) The Hidden Injuries of Class, 1972; The Fall of Public Man, 1977; (co-author) Beyond the Crisis Society, 1977; Authority, 1980; The Frog Who Dared to Croak, 1982; An Evening of Brahms, 1984; Pala is Royal, 1987; The Conscience of the Eye, 1990; Flesh and Stone, 1994; (contrib.) Thomas Struth, Strangers and Friends, Photographs, 1986-1992, 1994; The Corrosion of Character, 1998; (with D. Libeskind, J.P. Reemtsma and S. Carp) Alles Kunst?, 2001; Respect in a World of Inequality, 2003; Culture of the New Capitalism, 2006; Craftsman, 2008. EDITOR: (with S. Thernstrom and contrib.) Nineteenth-Century Cities, 1969; (and contrib.) Classic Essays on the Culture of Cities, 1969; Classic Essays on the Culture of Cities, 1969; (with S. Thernstrom and contrib.) Nineteenth Century Cities, 1969; The Psychology of Society, 1977; (with C. Calhoun) Practicing Culture, 2007. **Address:** Department of Sociology, New York University, 295 Lafayette St., Rm. 4109, New York, NY 10012, U.S.A. **Online address:** richard.sennett@nyu.edu

SENOR, Dan. American (born United States), b. 1971. **Genres:** History. **Career:** Carlyle Group, investment professional, 2001-03; Rosemont Capital L.L.C., founding partner; Rosemont Solebury Capital Management, founding partner. Writer. **Publications:** (With S. Singer) Start-Up Nation: The Story of Israel's Economic Miracle, 2009. Contributor to periodicals. **Address:** New York, NY , U.S.A. **Online address:** dsenor@cfr.org

SENSEL, Joni. American (born United States), b. 1962. **Genres:** Novels. **Career:** University of Oregon, public relations writer, 1982-83; freelance communication and marketing consultant, 1983-; Weyerhauser, video production assistant, 1985-86, video producer, 1986-87, communication manager, 1987-93; Dream Factory Book, founder and publisher, 1999. Writer. **Publications:** Traditions through the Trees: Weyerhauser's First 100 Years, 1999; Bears Barge In, 2000; The Garbage Monster, 2001. YOUNG ADULT NOVELS: Reality Leak, 2007; The Humming of Numbers, 2008; The Farwalker's Quest, 2009. Contributor of articles to magazines. **Address:** Enumclaw, WA , U.S.A. **Online address:** joni@jonisensel.com

SENSIBAR, Judith L(evin). American (born United States), b. 1941?. **Genres:** Literary Criticism And History, Bibliography, Biography, Psychology, Cultural/Ethnic Topics, Social Sciences. **Career:** University of Chicago, lecturer, 1982; University of Illinois, visiting assistant professor, 1984; Arizona State University, Department of English, assistant professor and faculty affiliate in women's studies and humanities programs, 1985-88, associate professor, 1988-99, professor, 1999-2004, professor emeritus, 2004-; Chicago Institute for Psychoanalysis, visiting research fellow, 1991-92. Writer, biographer, literary critic and reviewer. **Publications:** The Origins of Faulkner's Art, 1984; (ed.) William Faulkner, Vision in Spring, 1984; (with N.L. Stegall) Faulkner's Poetry: A Bibliographical Guide to Texts and Criticism, 1988; Faulkner and Love: The Women Who Shaped His Art, 2009. Contributor to books and journals. **Address:** Yale University Press, 302 Temple St., New Haven, CT 06511, U.S.A. **Online address:** sensibar@asu.edu

SENTILLES, Sarah. American (born United States), b. 1973?. **Genres:** Women's Studies And Issues, Adult Non-fiction. **Career:** Journal of Feminist Studies in Religion, managing editor; California State University, faculty of critical thinking. **Publications:** Taught by America: A Story of Struggle and Hope in Compton, 2005; A Church of Her Own: What Happens when a Woman Takes the Pulpit, 2008; Breaking Up with God: A Love Story, 2011. **Address:** c/o Author Mail, Beacon Press, 25 Beacon St., Boston, MA 02108, U.S.A.

SEO, Audrey Yoshiko. American (born United States) **Genres:** Novels, History, Art/Art History. **Career:** University of Richmond, adjunct professor of art history; College of William and Mary, adjunct instructor in anthropology; Virginia Commonwealth University, assistant professor of Asian art. Writer and consultant. **Publications:** (With S. Addiss) How to Look at Japanese Art, 1996; (with S. Addiss) The Art of Twentieth-Century Zen: Paintings and Calligraphy by Japanese Masters, 1998; Zen No Sho: The Calligraphy of Fukushima Keido Roshi, 2003; Ensō: Zen Circles of Enlightenment, 2007; (with S. Addiss) The Sound of One Hand: Paintings and Calligraphy by Zen Master Hakuin, 2010. **Address:** College of William and Mary, P O Box 8795, Williamsburg, VA 23187-8795, U.S.A.

SEPINWALL, Alyssa Goldstein. American (born United States), b. 1970. **Genres:** History. **Career:** California State University, associate professor of history. Writer. **Publications:** The Abbé Grégoire and the French Revolution: The Making of Modern Universalism, 2005. Works appear in anthologies. Contributor to journals. **Address:** Department of History, California State University, San Marcos, CA 92096-0001, U.S.A. **Online address:** sepinwal@csusm.edu

SERAILE, William. American (born United States), b. 1941. **Genres:** History. **Career:** City University of New York, Herbert H. Lehman College, professor of African American history, 1971-2007, professor emeritus of African and African American studies, 2007-; Bank Street College, faculty, 1975-76; Schomburg Corp., second vice president, 1999-2006; Westchester Community College, lecturer; West Chester University, lecturer; Bronx Community College, lecturer. Writer. **Publications:** Voice of Dissent: Theophilus Gould Steward (1843-1924) and Black America, 1991; Fire in His Heart: Bishop Benjamin Tucker Tanner and the A.M.E. Church, 1998; New York Black Regiments during the Civil War, 2001; Bruce Grit: The Black Nationalist Writings of John Edward Bruce, 2003; Angels of Mercy: White Women and the History of New York's Colored Orphan Asylum, 2011. Contributor of articles to journals. **Address:** Department of Black Studies, Lehman College, City University of New York, 250 Bedford Park Blvd. W, Bronx, NY 10468, U.S.A. **Online address:** william.seraile@lehman.cuny.edu

SERAJI, Mahbod. American/Iranian (born Iran), b. 1956?. **Genres:** Novels. **Career:** Motorola Corp., engineer, 1990-2007. Writer. **Publications:** Rooftops of Tehran, 2009. **Address:** CA , U.S.A. **Online address:** mahbod@rooftopsoftehran.com

SERELS, M. Mitchell. American/Canadian (born Canada), b. 1948. **Genres:** Cultural/Ethnic Topics. **Career:** Yeshiva University, Safra Institute of Sephardic Studies, associate director, director, 1972-99; Magen David Sephardic Congregation, spiritual leader, 1983-; Petah Tikva Sephardic Congregation of Toronto, spiritual leader; Berkeley College, assistant professor of psychology and world civilization, School of Liberal Arts Humanities and Social Sciences, faculty. Writer. **Publications:** (Ed. with S. Gaon) Sephardim and the Holocaust, 1987; A History of the Jews of Tangier in the Nineteenth and Twentieth Centuries, 1991; Judísde Tánger en los siglos XIX y XX, 1994; (ed. with S. Gaon) Del Fuego: Sephardim and the Holocaust, 1995; Jews of Cape Verde: A Brief History, 1997; (ed. with I.J. Katz) Studies on the History of Portuguese Jews from their Expulsion in 1497 through their Dispersion, 2000; (ed.) Semana Sepharad: The Lectures: Studies on Sephardic Jewry, 2001; Birqat Teiman: Studies on the History of Yemenite Jews, 2002; Westchester Remembers: Anecdotal and Psychological Remembrances of September 11th, 2001 by the Citizens of Westchester County, 2006. **Address:** Magen David Sephardic Congregation, 1225 Weaver St., PO Box 129 H, Wykagyl, NY 10804, U.S.A. **Online address:** mitchser@aol.com

SERET, Roberta. American (born United States), b. 1945. **Genres:** Travel/Exploration, Art/Art History. **Career:** Ladycliff College, instructor in French, 1970-71; Briarcliff College, instructor in English, 1972-73; Bergen Community College, adjunct instructor in English, 1975-76; Marymount Manhattan College, adjunct instructor in English, 1976-78, Department of Continuing Education, affiliate, 1977-78, Department of Courses for Adults, affiliate, 1990; Hunter College of the City University of New York, adjunct instructor of English, 1976-79; Pace University, adjunct associate professor in English, 1979-83; American Welcome Services, founder and president, 1982-; NYC Chamber of Commerce, director of relocation, 1986-90; director of professional English at the United Nations, 2001-; International Cinema Education, president and founder, 2003-. Writer. **Publications:** Welcome to New York: How to Settle and Survive in New York, 1983, 5th ed., 2001; Voyage into Creativity: The Modern Kunstlerroman, 1992; World Affairs in Foreign Films: Getting the Global Picture, 2011; The Gift of Diamonds, forthcoming. Contributor to periodicals. **Address:** 180 E End Ave., New York, NY 10128-7763, U.S.A. **Online address:** rseret@aol.com

SERFOZO, Mary. American (born United States), b. 1925. **Genres:** Children's Fiction, Picture/Board Books, Animals/Pets. **Career:** Mademoiselle Magazine, assistant editor; California Advertising Agency, copywriter. **Publications:** Welcome, Roberto! Bienvenido, Roberto!, 1969; Who Said Red?, 1988, 1st ed., 1992; Who Wants One?, 1989, new ed., 1992; Rain Talk, 1990, new ed., 1993; Dirty Kurt, 1992; Benjamin Bigfoot, 1993; Joe Joe, 1993; There's a Square: A Book About Shapes, 1996; What's What? A Guessing

Game, 1996; A Head Is for Hats, 1999; The Big Bug Dug, 2001, 1st ed., 2006; Plumply, Dumply Pumpkin, 2001; Whooo's There?, 2007. **Address:** c/o Publicity Director, Margaret K. McElderry Books, 866 3rd Ave., New York, NY 10022, U.S.A.

SERLING, Carol. American (born United States), b. 1929. **Genres:** Adult Non-fiction. **Career:** Writer. **Publications:** (Intro. with E. Delavan) Grace in the Afternoon: A Cayuga Love Story, 1999; (with D. Brode) Rod Serling and the Twilight Zone, 2009. EDITOR: (with C.G. Waugh and M.H. Greenberg) Rod Serling's Night Gallery Reader, 1987; Journeys to the Twilight Zone, 1993; Return to the Twilight Zone, 1994; Adventures in the Twilight Zone, 1995; Twilight Zone Anthology, 2009; (and intro.) More Stories from the Twilight Zone, 2010. Contributor to periodicals. **Address:** 1940 Palisades Dr., Pacific Palisades, CA 90272, U.S.A.

SERRANO, Lucienne J. American/Moroccan (born Morocco), b. 1936. **Genres:** Novellas/Short Stories, Literary Criticism And History, Women's Studies And Issues, Poetry, Psychology. **Career:** City University of New York, Hunter College, instructor in French, 1968-73; York College, associate professor of French, 1974-, Department of Foreign Languages, professor of French. Writer. **Publications:** Jeux de Masques: Essai sur le Travesti Dérisoire dans la littérature, 1977. WITH E.H. BARUCH: Women Analyze Women: In France, England and the United States, 1988; She Speaks He Listens: Women on the French Analyst's Couch, 1995. **Address:** Department of Foreign Languages / ESL / Humanities, York College, City University of New York, AC-3D09, 94-20 Guy R. Brewer Blvd., Jamaica, NY 11451, U.S.A. **Online address:** lserrano@york.cuny.edu

SERRANO, Richard A. American (born United States), b. 1953. **Genres:** Documentaries/Reportage. **Career:** Kansas City Star/Times, reporter, 1972-87; Los Angeles Times, reporter, 1987-, Washington Bureau, correspondent, staff writer. **Publications:** One of Ours: Timothy McVeigh and the Oklahoma City Bombing, 1998; My Grandfather's Prison: A Story of Death and Deceit in 1940s Kansas City, 2009. **Address:** c/o Ronald Goldfarb, Goldfarb & Associates, 721 Gibbon St., Alexandria, DC 22314, U.S.A. **Online address:** richard.serrano@latimes.com

SERULNIKOV, Sergio. American (born United States), b. 1961. **Genres:** History. **Career:** Universidad de Buenos Aires, Department of History, assistant and faculty of arts, 1987-90, Department of History of Argentina and American Science Career Communication, assistant and faculty of social sciences, 1988-90, Department of Latin American History, Science Careers Policy, chief and faculty of social sciences, 1994-96, acting assistant professor and faculty of social sciences, 1996-97, researcher, 2005-; State University of New York, Department of History, teaching assistant, 1990-93, 1997-98; Harvard University, visiting assistant professor, 1998-99; University of Kentucky, Department of History, professor of American history, 1998-99; Boston College, Department of History, associate professor of history, professor of American history, 1999-2005, director of Latin American studies, 2004-05; Consejo Nacional de Investigaciones Científicas y Técnicas, research career scientist, 2005-; Universidad Nacional General Sarmiento-Instituto de Desarrollo Económico y Social, visiting professor of social sciences, 2006-. Writer. **Publications:** Su verdad y su justicia: Tomás Katari y la insurrección aymara de Chayanta, 1777-1780, 1994; Subverting Colonial Authority: Challenges to Spanish Rule in Eighteenth-Century Southern Andes, 2003; Conflictos sociales e insurrección en el mundo colonial andino: el norte de Potosí en el siglo XVIII, 2006; Revolución en los Andes: la era de Túpac Amaru, 2010. Contributor to periodicals. **Address:** Department of History, Boston College, 21 Campanella Way, Chestnut Hill, MA 02467-3859, U.S.A. **Online address:** sergio.serulnikov@bc.edu

SERVADIO, Gaia (Cecilia Gemmalina). (Gualtiero Malde' Myddelton Biddulph). British/Italian (born Italy), b. 1938. **Genres:** Novels, Criminology/True Crime, Travel/Exploration, Autobiography/Memoirs, Biography, Young Adult Fiction. **Career:** Il Mondo and L'Espresso, feature writer, 1963-64; British Broadcasting Corp., broadcaster and TV documentaries, 1964-67; La Stampa, feature writer, Corriere della Sera art correspondent, 1965-; Evening Standard, feature writer, 1967-68; Sunday Times, political writer, 1973-75; The Telegraph group, critic. **Publications:** Melinda (tanto gentile e tanto onesta), 1967; Don Juan-Salome (Don Giovanni-L'azione Consiste), 1968; Il Metodo, 1970; A Siberian Encounter, 1971; Angelo La Barbera: Profile of a Mafia Boss, 1974; Mafioso, 1976; Insider Outsider, 1978; To a Different World, 1979; Luchino Visconti, 1981; La donna nel Rinascimento, 1986; Il

Lamento di Arianna (novel), 1988; Una Infanzia Diversa (autobiography), 1988; La Vallata, 1990; La Storia di R, 1991; Incontri, 1993; The Real Traviata (biography of Giuseppina Strepponi), 1994; Motya (history), 1999; Mozia, 2003; Rossini (biography), 2003; Renaissance Woman (history), 2005; E i morti non sanno, 2005; Classic and Preclassic Syrian Wriings, 2007; Incoronata Pazza, 2010. **Address:** Anna Webber United Agents, 12 26 Lexingtn St., London, GL W1F 0LE, England. **Online address:** kdd39@dial.pipex.com

SERVER, Lee. American (born United States) **Genres:** Documentaries/Reportage, Bibliography, Biography, Autobiography/Memoirs. **Career:** Writer. **Publications:** Screenwriter: Words Become Pictures, 1987; Sharks, 1989; Danger Is My Business: An Illustrated History of the Fabulous Pulp Magazines, 1993; Over My Dead Body: The Sensational Age of the American Paperback: 1945-1955, 1994; Sam Fuller: Film Is a Battleground: A Critical Study, with Interviews, A Filmography, and a Bibliography, 1994; Golden Age of Ocean Liners, 1996; Tigers, 1997; (ed. with E. Gorman and M.H. Greenberg) The Book of Noir, 1998; Asian Pop Cinema: Bombay to Tokyo, 1999; Robert Mitchum: Baby I Don't Care, 2001; Encyclopedia of Pulp Fiction Writers, 2001; Ava Gardner: Love is Nothing, 2006. Contributor to periodicals. **Address:** c/o Roslyn Targ, Roslyn Targ Literary Agency Inc., 105 W 13th St. 15E, New York, NY 10011, U.S.A.

SERVICE, Pamela. (Pamela F. Service). American (born United States), b. 1945. **Genres:** Children's Fiction, Young Adult Fiction, Novels. **Career:** Indiana University, Art Museum, publicist, 1970-72; Monroe County Museum, curator, 1978-95; Clarke Historical Museum, director, 2000-, Clarke Historical Society, curator. Writer. **Publications:** FOR YOUNG ADULTS FICTION AS PAMELA F. SERVICE: Winter of Magic's Return, 1985; A Question of Destiny, 1986; Tomorrow's Magic, 1987; When the Night Wind Howls, 1987; The Reluctant God, 1988; Stinker from Space, 1988; Vision Quest, 1989; Under Alien Stars, 1990; Being of Two Minds, 1991; Weirdos of the Universe, Unite!, 1992; Stinker's Return, 1993; All's Faire, 1993; Phantom Victory, 1994; Storm at the Edge of Time, 1994; Yesterday's Magic, 2008; My Cousin, the Alien, 2008; Camp Alien, 2008; Earth's Magic, 2009; Alien Expedition, 2009; Alien Encounter, 2010; Alien Contact, 2010; Alien Envoy, 2011. WAY-TOO-REAL ALIENS SERIES: Escape from Planet Yastol, 2011; The Not-So-Perfect Planet, 2012. NONFICTION: The Ancient African Kingdom of Kush, 1998; Mesopotamia, 1999; Eureka and Humboldt County California, 2001; Around the World in . 300 BC, 2002; Around the World in . 1200, 2002. FOR CHILDREN: Wizard of Wind and Rock (picture book), 1990. Contributor to magazines. **Address:** Clark Historical Society, 430 Westfield Ave., Clark, NJ 07066-1732, U.S.A.

SERVICE, Pamela F. See **SERVICE, Pamela.**

SERVID, Carolyn. American/Indian (born India), b. 1953. **Genres:** Adult Non-fiction, Natural History, Autobiography/Memoirs, Essays, Cultural/Ethnic Topics. **Career:** Island Institute, co-founder and co-director, 1994-, The Island Institute Journal, editor; Sitka Symposium on Human Values and the Written Word, co-founder. **Publications:** Of Landscape and Longing: Finding a Home at the Water's Edge, 2000; (comp. with H. Lentfer) Arctic Refuge: A Circle of Testimony, 2001; (contrib.) Sitka: A Home in the Wild, 2009. EDITOR: From the Island's Edge: A Sitka Reader, 1995; (with D. Snow) The Book of the Tongass, 1999. **Address:** Island Institute, PO Box 2420, Sitka, AK 99835-2420, U.S.A.

SESHADRI, Vijay. American/Indian (born India), b. 1954. **Genres:** Poetry. **Career:** The New Yorker, editor, 1993-; New School for Social Research, adjunct professor, 1995-; Sarah Lawrence College, adjunct professor, 1995-, Graduate Program in Creative Non-fiction, director, Michele Tolela Myers Chair in Writing. **Publications:** POETRY: Wild Kingdom: Poems, 1996; The Long Meadow: Poems, 2004; The Disappearances, 2007. **Address:** Writing Program, Sarah Lawrence College, 1 Mead Way, Bronxville, NY 10708-5940, U.S.A. **Online address:** seshadri@slc.edu

SESSA, Valerie I. American (born United States), b. 1964. **Genres:** Administration/Management, Bibliography. **Career:** New York University, adjunct professor, 1990; Yeshiva University, adjunct professor, 1992; Marymount Manhattan College, adjunct professor, 1993; Center for Creative Leadership, research associate, 1993-95, director of research scientist, 1995-2000, New Frontiers, director, 1993-95, Executive Selection Research, director and co-director, 1993-95, research scientist, 1995-2001; Applied Research Corp., leadership consultant, 2001-02; Montclair State University, assistant profes-

sor, 2003-, associate professor of psychology. Writer. **Publications:** (With R.J. Campbell) Selection at the Top: An Annotated Bibliography, 1997; (co-author) Executive Selection: A Research Report on What Works and What Doesn't, 1998; (co-author) Geographically Dispersed Teams, 1999; (with J.J. Deal and J.J. Taylor) Choosing Executives: A Research Report on the Peak Selection Simulation, 1999; (with M. London) Selecting International Executives, 1999; (with J.J. Taylor) Executive Selection: Strategies for Success, 2000; (with M. London) Continuous Learning in Organizations: Individual, Group, and Organizational Perspectives, 2005; (ed. with M. London) Work Group Learning: Understanding, Improving & Assessing How Groups Learn in Organizations, 2007. Contributor of books to journals. **Address:** Department of Psychology, Montclair State University, 237 Dixon Hall, Montclair, NJ 07043, U.S.A. **Online address:** sessav@mail.montclair.edu

SESSIONS, William. American (born United States), b. 1938. **Genres:** Literary Criticism And History, Biography, Autobiography/Memoirs. **Career:** State University of West Georgia, assistant professor of English, 1959-60; Spring Hill College, assistant professor, 1960-62; St. John's University, assistant professor, 1962-66; Georgia State University, Department of English, associate professor, 1966-72, professor, 1972-93, Regent's professor of English, 1993-, now Regent's professor emeritus of English, Graduate Programs, director, 1969-75. Writer. **Publications:** Shakespeare's Romeo and Juliet, 1966; (with B.C. Bach and W. Walling) The Liberating Form: A Handbook-Anthology of English and American Poetry, 1972; Henry Howard, Earl of Surrey, 1986; (ed.) Francis Bacon's Legacy of Texts: The Art of Discovery Grows with Discovery, 1990; Francis Bacon Revisited, 1996; Henry Howard, the Poet Earl of Surrey: A Life, 1999. Contributor to books and journals. **Address:** Department of English, Georgia State University, 33 Gilmer St., PO Box 3970, Atlanta, GA 30303-3044, U.S.A. **Online address:** wsessions@gsu.edu

SESTI, Giuseppe Maria. Italian (born Italy), b. 1942. **Genres:** Mythology/Folklore, Astronomy. **Career:** The Wine Trio, staff. Writer and artist. **Publications:** The Phenomenon Book of Calendars, 1974, rev. ed., 1978; Le Dimore del Cielo, 1987; The Glorious Constellations: History and Mythology, 1991; Die Geheimnisse des Himmels, 1991. **Address:** The Wine Trio, Via del Gallo 28, Lucca, 55100, Italy. **Online address:** giuseppesesti@libero.it

SETH, Vikram. Indian (born India), b. 1952. **Genres:** Novels, Poetry, Travel/Exploration, Mythology/Folklore. **Career:** Stanford University Press, senior editor, 1985-86. **Publications:** Mappings (poems), 1980; From Heaven Lake: Travels Through Sinkiang and Tibet, 1983; The Humble Administrator's Garden (poems), 1985; The Golden Gate: A Novel in Verse, 1986; From Heaven Lake: Travels through Sinkiang and Tibet, 1987; All You Who Sleep Tonight (poetry), 1990; Beastly Tales from Here and There (animal fables), 1992; Three Chinese Poets (translations), 1992; A Suitable Boy (novel), 1993; Arion and the Dolphin (libretto), 1994; An Equal Music, 1999; Two Lives, 2005; A Suitable Girl, 2013. **Address:** The Orion Publishing Group Ltd., 5 Upper St Martin's Ln., Orion House, London, GL WC2H 9EA, England.

SETIAWAN, Erick. American/Indonesian (born Indonesia), b. 1975?. **Genres:** Novels. **Career:** Writer and software engineer. **Publications:** Of Bees and Mist (novel), 2009. **Address:** c/o Alex Glass, Trident Media Group, 41 Madison Ave., 36th Fl., New York, NY 10010, U.S.A. **Online address:** erick@ofbeesandmist.com

SETTERBERG, Fred. American (born United States), b. 1951. **Genres:** Essays, Writing/Journalism, Novels. **Career:** East Bay Center for the Performing Arts, executive director, 1980-83; Data Center, director, 1990-; Pacific News Service, associate editor, 1991-; East Bay Express, staff writer, 1993-; University of San Francisco, teacher of writing, 1993-; Chautauqua Writers Center, visiting writer. **Publications:** (With K. Schulman) Beyond Profit: The Complete Guide to Managing the Non-Profit Organization, 1985; (with B. Kibbe) Succeeding with Consultants: Self-Assessment for the Changing Nonprofit, 1992; The Roads Taken: Travels through America's Literary Landscapes (essays), 1993; (with L. Shavelson) Toxic Nation, 1993; (ed.) Travelers Tales America, 1999; (co-author) Grantmaking Basics: A Field Guide for Funders, 2005; (with L. Shavelson) Under the Dragon: California's New Culture, 2007; (with B. Somerville) Grassroots Philanthropy: Field Notes of a Maverick Grantmaker, 2008; Lunch Bucket Paradise: A True-Life Novel, 2011; Return of the Lost Souls, forthcoming. Contributor to periodicals. **Address:** 918 Vermont St., Oakland, CA 94610, U.S.A. **Online address:** fsetterberg@sbcglobal.net

SETTJE, David E. American (born United States), b. 1970?. **Genres:** History. **Career:** Concordia University Chicago, Department of history, associate professor and chair, 2002-, Department of political science, chair, 2002-. Writer. **Publications:** Lutherans and the Longest War: Adrift on a Sea of Doubt about the Cold and Vietnam Wars, 1964-1975, 2007; Faith and War: How Christians Debated the Cold and Vietnam Wars, 2011. **Address:** Concordia University Chicago, 7400 Augusta St., River Forest, IL 60305-1499, U.S.A. **Online address:** david.settje@cuchicago.edu

SETZER, (Cynthia) Lynn. American (born United States), b. 1955. **Genres:** Recreation, Adult Non-fiction, Travel/Exploration. **Career:** North Carolina State University, Kenan-Flagler Business School, lecturer, 1980-84; Global Software, manager of publications, 1984-94; State of North Carolina, manager of training, 1994-97; Global Software, manager. Writer. **Publications:** (With C. Filoreto) Working in T.V. News: The Insider's Guide, 1993; A Season on the Appalachian Trail: An American Odyssey, 1997, 2nd ed., 2001; Great Adventures in North Carolina, 1999, 2nd ed., 2001; 60 Hikes within 60 Miles, Raleigh, 2001; North Carolina Weekends, 2003. Contributor to magazines and newspapers. **Address:** Management and Corporate Communication, Kenan-Flagler Business School, University of North Carolina, CB 3490, McColl 4722, Chapel Hill, NC 27599-3490, U.S.A. **Online address:** hikester@ral.mindspring.com

SEVERANCE, Ben H. American (born United States), b. 1966?. **Genres:** History, Military/Defense/Arms Control. **Career:** Pellissippi State Technical Community College, instructor, 2000-02; University of Tennessee, adjunct history instructor, 2002-05, assistant editor; Auburn University, Department of History, assistant professor, 2005-, associate professor. Writer. **Publications:** Tennessee's Radical Army: The State Guard and Its Role in Reconstruction, 1867-1869, 2005. **Address:** Department of History, Auburn University, 356 Liberal Arts, PO Box 244023, Montgomery, AL 36124-4023, U.S.A. **Online address:** bseveran@aum.edu

SEVERANCE, John B(ridwell). American (born United States), b. 1935. **Genres:** Young Adult Fiction, Young Adult Non-fiction, Biography. **Career:** Harper and Row Publishers Inc., sales representative, 1958-61; Kent Place School, teacher and department head, 1987-91. Writer. **Publications:** FOR YOUNG ADULTS: Winston Churchill: Soldier, Statesman, Artist, 1996; Gandhi, Great Soul, 1997; Thomas Jefferson: Architect of Democracy, 1998; Einstein: Visionary Scientist, 1999; Skyscrapers: How America Grew Up, 2000; Braving the Fire, 2002. Contributor to periodicals. **Address:** 6 George St., Westerly, RI 02891, U.S.A.

SEVERSON, Kim. American (born United States), b. 1961. **Genres:** Food And Wine, Medicine/Health. **Career:** Anchorage Daily News, editor and reporter; San Francisco Chronicle, food writer; New York Times, staff writer, 2004-. **Publications:** (With G. Denkler) The New Alaska Cookbook: Recipes from the Last Frontier's Best Chefs, 2001, 2nd ed., 2009; (with C. Burke) The Trans Fat Solution: Cooking and Shopping to Eliminate the Deadliest Fat from Your Diet, 2003; Spoon Fed: How Eight Cooks Saved My Life, 2010. **Address:** Brooklyn, NY , U.S.A. **Online address:** seversonbooks@gmail.com

SEVERSON, Richard. Also writes as Richard J. Severson, Richard James Severson. American (born United States), b. 1955. **Genres:** Philosophy, Adult Non-fiction, Ethics. **Career:** Marylhurst University, electronic resources and reference librarian, 1995-. Writer. **Publications:** (As Richard James Severson) Time, Death, and Eternity: Reflecting on Augustine's Confessions in Light of Heidegger's Being and Time, 1995; The Confessions of Saint Augustine: An Annotated Bibliography of Modern Criticism, 1888-1995, 1996; (as Richard J. Severson) The Principles of Information Ethics, 1997. **Address:** Marylhurst University, 17600 Pacific Hwy, PO Box 261, Marylhurst, OR 97036-0261, U.S.A. **Online address:** rseverso@marylhurst.edu

SEVERSON, Richard J. See SEVERSON, Richard.

SEVERSON, Richard James. See SEVERSON, Richard.

SEWALL, Gilbert T. American (born United States) **Genres:** Education. **Career:** Phillips Academy, instructor in history, 1970-78; Newsweek Magazine, education editor, 1979-81; Columbia University, Teachers College, Institute of Politics and Philosophy of Education, research associate, 1981-82, 1986-87, co-director of educational excellence network, 1986-88; Boston University School of Education, senior research associate, 1986-87; Center for Education Studies, president, 1989-; American Textbook Council, director, 1989-; Huntington Library, reader, 1991-. Journalist. **Publications:** (With T.T. Lyons and A.C. Ganley) After Hiroshima: America Since 1945, 1979, 3rd ed. as The U.S.A. Since 1945: After Hiroshima, 1993; Necessary Lessons: Decline and Renewal in American Schools, 1983; (ed.) The Eighties: A Reader, 1997. Contributor to periodicals and books. **Address:** American Textbook Council, 1150 Park Ave., 12th Fl., New York, NY 10128-1244, U.S.A. **Online address:** sewall@columbia.edu

SEWARD, Desmond. British/French (born France), b. 1935. **Genres:** History, Biography, Military/Defense/Arms Control. **Career:** Writer and historian. **Publications:** The First Bourbon: Henry IV, King of France and Navarre, 1971; The Monks of War: The Military Religious Orders, 1972; Prince of the Renaissance: The Life of François I, 1973 in US as Prince of the Renaissance: The Golden Life of François I; The Bourbon Kings of France, 1976; Eleanor of Aquitaine: The Mother Queen, 1978 in US as Eleanor of Aquitaine, 1979; The Hundred Years War: The English in France, 1337-1453, 1978; Monks and Wine, 1979; Marie Antoinette, 1981; Richard III: England's Black Legend, 1983, rev. ed., 1997; (ed. and intro.) Naples: A Traveller's Companion, 1984; Napoleon's Family, 1986; Italy's Knights of St. George: The Constantinian Order, 1986; Henry V. as Warlord, 1987 in US as Henry V: The Scourge of God, 1988; Napoleon and Hitler: A Comparative Biography, 1988; (with S. Mountgarret) Byzantium, 1989; (ed. with P. Ziegler) Brooks's: A Social History, 1991; Metternich: The First European, 1991; The Dancing Sun: Journeys to the Miracle Shrines (travel), 1993; The War of the Roses: Through the Lives of Five Men and Women of the Fifteenth Century, 1995; Sussex (travel), 1995; Caravaggio: A Passionate Life, 1998; Brief History of the Hundred Years War: The English in France, 1337-1453, 2003; Eugénie: The Empress and Her Empire, 2004; Burning of the Vanities: Savonarola and the Borgia Pope, 2006; Wings Over the Desert, 2009; Jerusalem's Traitor, 2009; The Monks of War, 2009; Old Puglia: A Portrait of South Eastern Italy, 2009; The Last White Rose: the Spectre at the Tudor Court 1485-1547, 2010. Contributor to periodicals. **Address:** Andrew Lownie Literary Agency Ltd., 17 Sutherland St., London, GL SWIV 4JU, England.

SEWARD, Robert (Allen). Japanese/American (born United States), b. 1942. **Genres:** Communications/Media, Politics/Government, History, Travel/Exploration. **Career:** University of New Mexico, assistant professor, 1977-80; Wharton School, Analysis Center, associate director, 1980-82; Courant Institute, sponsored research administrator, 1982-87; Meiji Gakuin University, Faculty of International Studies, instructor, professor of international studies, 1987-. Writer. **Publications:** Radio Happy Isles: Media and Politics at Play in the Pacific, 1999. **Address:** Faculty of International Studies, Meiji Gakuin University, 1518 Kamikurata-cho Totsuka-ku, Yokohama, 244-8539, Japan. **Online address:** rseward@k.meijigakuin.ac.jp

SEWELL, Kitty. (Kitty Harri). Spanish/Swedish (born Sweden), b. 1951?. **Genres:** Novels, Biography. **Career:** British National Health Service, psychotherapist. Writer. **Publications:** (With R. Thompson) What Took You So Long? A Girl's Journey to Manhood: The Story of Raymond Thompson (biography), 1995; (ed.) My Cheating Heart: Contemporary Short Stories by Women from Wales, 2005; (as Kitty Harri) Hector's Talent for Miracles (fiction), 2007; Ice Trap, 2007; Bloodprint: A Novel of Psychological Suspense, 2009. **Address:** c/o Sheila Crowley, Curtis Brown Group Ltd., Haymarket House, 28-29, Haymarket, London, GL SW1Y 4SP, England.

SEWELL, Lisa. American (born United States), b. 1960. **Genres:** Poetry, Literary Criticism And History, Women's Studies And Issues. **Career:** Goldwater State Hospital for the Severely Disabled, instructor in creative writing, 1987-88; New York University, instructor in English, 1987-88; Texas Christian University, visiting lecturer in English, 1997-98; Villanova University, assistant professor, associate professor of English and creative writing, 1998-, Gender and Women's Studies Program, co-director. Writer. **Publications:** The Way Out: Poems, 1998; Name Withheld: Poems, 2006; (ed. with C. Rankine) American Poets in the 21st Century: The New Poetics, 2007; Long Corridor: Poems, 2008. Contributor to Periodicals. **Address:** Department of English, Villanova University, 456 Saint Augustine Ctr., Villanova, PA 19085, U.S.A. **Online address:** lisa.sewell@villanova.edu

SEWELL, Michael (John). British (born England), b. 1934. **Genres:** Mathematics/Statistics, Sciences. **Career:** University of Nottingham, assistant lecturer in mathematics, 1960-62, lecturer in mathematics, 1962-63; University of Bristol, research associate, 1963-66; University of Reading, reader in applied mathematics, 1966-67, professor, 1977-99, emeritus professor of applied mathematics, 1999-; University of Wisconsin, Mathematics Research Center, visiting professor, 1970-71; University of Surrey, Faculty of Engineering and Physical Sciences, associate tutor, 2010. Writer. **Publications:** (Ed. with H.G. Hopkins) Mechanics of Solids, 1982; Maximum and Minimum Principles: A Unified Approach with Applications, 1987; (ed.) Mathematics Masterclasses: Stretching the Imagination, 1997. **Address:** Department of Mathematics, University of Reading, Whiteknights, PO Box 220, Reading, BR RG6 6AX, England. **Online address:** m.j.sewell@reading.ac.uk

SEXTON, Linda Gray. American (born United States), b. 1953. **Genres:** Novels, Psychology, Women's Studies And Issues, Autobiography/Memoirs, Essays, Young Adult Fiction, Literary Criticism And History. **Career:** Writer. **Publications:** (Ed.) Anne Sexton: A Self-Portrait in Letters, 1977; (ed.) Words for Dr. Y.: Uncollected Poems with Three Stories, 1978; Between Two Worlds: Young Women in Crisis, 1979; Rituals, 1981; Mirror Images, 1985; Points of Light, 1988; Private Acts, 1991; Searching for Mercy Street: My Journey Back to My Mother, Anne Sexton, 1994; Anne Sexton: The Last Summer, 2000; Half in Love, 2010. Contributor to periodicals. **Address:** Little, Brown & Co., 237 Park Ave., New York, NY 10017, U.S.A.

SEYBOLD, Patricia B. American (born United States) **Genres:** Information Science/Computers, Business/Trade/Industry, Economics, Administration/Management. **Career:** Seybold Publications Inc., vice president, 1976-85; Patricia Seybold's Office Computing Group Inc., staff, 1985-92; Patricia Seybold Group Inc., founder and chief executive officer, 1992-, senior consultant and analyst. Writer. **Publications:** (Co-author) La Compo- Quel Avenir?: Séminaire Seybold, 1984; (with R.T. Marshak and M.D. Millikin) Integrated Desk-Top Environments: Symphony, Visi On, and DesQ, 1985; (with R.T. Marshak) Customers.com: How to Create a Profitable Business Strategy for the Internet and Beyond, 1998; (with R.T. Marshak and J.M. Lewis) The Customer Revolution: How to Thrive When Customers Are in Control, 2001; (with M. Lindstrom) Brandchild: Remarkable Insights Into the Minds of Today's Global Kids and their Relationships with Brands, 2003, rev. ed., 2004; Outside Innovation: How Your Customers will Co-design Your Company's Future, 2006. **Address:** Patricia Seybold Group, 47 Harvard St., Ste. B202, PO Box 290565, Boston, MA 02109-3504, U.S.A. **Online address:** pseybold@customers.com

SEYMOUR, Gerald. British (born England), b. 1941. **Genres:** Mystery/Crime/Suspense, Essays. **Career:** Independent Television News, reporter, 1963-78. **Publications:** Harry's Game, 1975; The Glory Boys, 1976; Kingfisher: A Novel, 1977; Red Fox, 1979 in US as The Harrison Affair, 1980; The Contract, 1981; Archangel, 1982; In Honour Bound, 1984; Field of Blood, 1985; A Song in the Morning, 1987; At Close Quarters in US as An Eye for an Eye, 1987; Home Run in US as The Running Target, 1989; Condition Black, 1990; Shadow on the Sun, 1990; The Journeyman Tailor, 1992, 2nd ed., 1993; The Fighting Man, 1993; The Heart of Danger, 1995; Killing Ground, 1997; The Waiting Time, 1998 in US as Dead Ground, 1999; A Line in the Sand: A Novel, 2000; Holding the Zero, 2000; The Untouchable, 2001; Traitor's Kiss, 2003; The Unknown Soldier, 2005; Rat Run, 2007; The Walking Dead, 2007; Timebomb, 2008; The Collabrator, 2009; The Dealer and the Dead, 2010; A Deniable Death, 2011; The Innocents, 2012. **Address:** PFD, Drury House, 34-43 Russell St., London, GL WC2B 5HA, England. **Online address:** webmaster@geraldseymour.co.uk

SEYMOUR, Tres. American (born United States), b. 1966. **Genres:** Novels, Children's Fiction, Social Sciences, Humor/Satire. **Career:** National Park Service, seasonal park ranger, 1987-. Writer. **Publications:** Life in the Desert (novel), 1992; Pole Dog, 1993; Hunting the White Cow, 1993; I Love My Buzzard, 1994; The Smash-Up Crash-Up Derby, 1995; Black Sky River, 1996; The Gulls of the Edmund Fitzgerald, 1996; Too Quiet for These Old Bones, 1997; The Revelation of Saint Bruce, 1998; We Played Marbles, 1998; Jake Johnson: The Story of a Mule, 1998; Our Neighbor Is a Strange, Strange Man, 1999; Auction!, 2005. **Address:** Mammoth Cave National Park, 1 Mammoth Cave Pkwy., Mammoth Cave, KY 42259, U.S.A.

SEYMOUR-JONES, Carole. British (born England), b. 1943. **Genres:** History, Biography, Theology/Religion. **Career:** Surrey University, history faculty. Writer. **Publications:** Beatrice Webb: A Life, 1992; Refugees, 1992; Homelessness, 1993; Journey of Faith the History of the World YWCA 1945-1994, 1994; Painted Shadow: A Life of Vivienne Eliot, First Wife of T.S. Eliot, and the Long-Suppressed Truth about Her Influence on his Genius,

2001; (ed. with L. Popescu) Writers under Siege: Voices of Freedom from Around the World, a PEN Anthology, 2007; (ed. with L. Popescu) Another Sky: Voices of Conscience from Around the World, 2007. **Address:** Constable Robinson Ltd., 3 The Lanchesters, 162 Fulham Palace Rd., London, GL W6 9ER, England.

SHAABAN, Bouthaina. Syrian (born Syrian Arab Republic), b. 1953. **Genres:** Literary Criticism And History, Cultural/Ethnic Topics, Area Studies. **Career:** University of Constantine, lecturer in English, 1982-84; University of Damascus, lecturer, 1984-89, professor of romantic poetry, 1985-2002, professor of world literature, 1987-2002, associate professor of English literature, 1988-93; Ministry of Foreign Affairs, advisor, 1988-2002, Foreign Media Department, director, 2002-03; Arab Writers Union, vice president, 2000-05; Cabinet Ministry of Expatriates, minister of expatriates, 2003-08. Writer. **Publications:** Both Right and Left Handed: Arab Women Talk about Their Lives, 1988, new ed., 2009; Poetry and Politics: Shelley and the Chartist Poets, 1993; (ed.) Al Sufūr Wa-al-ḥijāb, 1998; (ed.) Fatāḥ wa-al-shuyūkh, 1998; Mi'at ām min al-riwāyah al-nisā'īyah al-'Arabīyah (1899-1999), 1999; al-Mar'ah al-'Arabīyah fī al-qarn al-'ishrīn, 2000; Ma'ziq al-tadakhkhul al-Amīrkī wa-imkānāt al-fi'l al-'Arabī, 2006; Mar'ah ah fī al-siyāsah wa-al-mujtima', 2008; Voices Revealed: Arab Women Novelists, 1898-2000, 2009; The Prism and the Promise: Arab Women Novelists from Afifa Karam to Ghada Samman, forthcoming. Contributor of articles to periodicals. **Address:** Rawda Sq., PO Box 11103, Damascus, SAR, Syria. **Online address:** bouthaina@bouthainashaaban.com

SHABAZZ, Jamel. American (born United States), b. 1960?. **Genres:** Photography, Adult Non-fiction, Travel/Exploration. **Career:** New York City Department of Correction, staff. Freelance photographer and writer. **Publications:** Back in the Days, 2001; Last Sunday in June, 2003; A Time before Crack, 2005; Seconds of My Life, 2007. **Address:** PO Box 331, Canal Street Sta., New York, NY 10013, U.S.A.

SHABECOFF, Philip. American (born United States), b. 1934. **Genres:** Environmental Sciences/Ecology, History, Politics/Government. **Career:** New York Times, reporter, 1959-91, foreign correspondent in Europe and Asia, 1964-70, White House correspondent, chief environmental correspondent, 1977-99; Greenwire, founding publisher, 1991-95, executive producer; Environment & Energy Publishing L.L.C., staff, 2000-; Society of Environmental Journalists, founding member. **Publications:** A Fierce Green Fire: The American Environmental Movement, 1993, rev. ed., 2003; A New Name for Peace: International Environmentalism, Sustainable Development and Democracy, 1996; Earth Rising: American Environmentalism in the 21st Century, 2000; (with A. Shabecoff) Poisoned Profits: The Toxic Assault on Our Children, 2008; Places: A Personal Ecology, forthcoming. **Address:** 38 Garrison Rd., Brookline, MA 02445, U.S.A. **Online address:** shabeco@erols.com

SHACHNOW, Sid. American/Lithuanian (born Lithuania), b. 1934?. **Genres:** Military/Defense/Arms Control. **Career:** Writer. **Publications:** (With J. Robbins) Hope and Honor, 2004. Contributor to periodicals. **Address:** c/o Author Mail, Forge, 175 5th Ave., New York, NY 10010, U.S.A.

SHACKELFORD, Renae Nadine. American (born United States), b. 1958. **Genres:** Social Sciences, Young Adult Non-fiction, Urban Studies. **Career:** University of Michigan Library System, coordinator of student employment, 1982-84; University of Toledo, coordinator of student employment for the Upward Bound program, 1989, writing and editorial specialist, 1995, instructor, 1995-97; First Church of God Christian School, teacher, 1990-92; Purdue University, lecturer, 1997-99, continuing lecturer, 1999-; University of Virginia, visiting professor, 2004-05; Black American Student Experiences Program, founder and director, 2005-. Writer. **Publications:** WITH J.R. SAUNDERS: Urban Renewal and the End of Black Culture in Charlottesville, Virginia: An Oral History of Vinegar Hill, 1998; The Dorothy West Martha's Vineyard: Stories, Essays, and Reminiscences by Dorothy West Writing in the Vineyard Gazette, 2001. **Address:** Department of English, Purdue University, 307C, Heavilon Hall, 500 Oval Dr., West Lafayette, IN 47907-2038, U.S.A. **Online address:** rshackelford@purdue.edu

SHACKLETON, C. C. See **ALDISS, Brian (Wilson).**

SHADER, Rachel. See **SOFER, Barbara.**

SHAFER, Audrey. American (born United States) **Genres:** Novels, Poetry.

Career: University of Pennsylvania, resident in anesthesia, 1984-86; Veterans Affairs Palo Alto Health Care System, staff anesthesiologist, 1989-; Stanford University, School of Medicine, associate professor of anesthesia, 1997-, professor, Stanford Center for Biomedical Ethics, faculty, 2003-, Biomedical Ethics & Medical Humanities Scholarly Concentration, co-director, 2003-. Writer. **Publications:** Sleep Talker: Poems by a Doctor/Mother, 2001; The Mailbox, 2006. Contributor to books and journals. **Address:** Random House Inc., 1745 Broadway, New York, NY 10019, U.S.A. **Online address:** ashafer@stanford.edu

SHAFER, Byron E. American (born United States), b. 1947. **Genres:** International Relations/Current Affairs, Politics/Government, History. **Career:** Florida State University, associate professor of political science, 1984-85; Oxford University, Andrew W. Mellon professor of American government, 1985-2001, Politics Group, chairperson, 1993-97, Nuffield College, professional fellow, 1985-2001, acting warden, 2000-01; University of Wisconsin, Glenn B. and Cleone Orr Hawkins chair of political science, 2001-, Honors Program, board director, 2007-, La Follette School of Public Policy, faculty affiliate, 2008-; British Broadcasting Corp., BBC World Service, public commentator. Writer. **Publications:** Quiet Revolution: The Struggle for the Democratic Party and the Shaping of Post-Reform Politics, 1983; The Changing Structure of American Politics, 1986; Bifurcated Politics: Evolution and Reform in the National Party Convention, 1988; (with W.J.M. Claggett) The Two Majorities: The Issue Context of Modern American Politics, 1995; (co-author) Present Discontents: American Politics in the Very Late Twentieth Century, 1997; (co-author) Partisan Approaches to Postwar American Politics, 1998; The Two Majorities and the Puzzle of Modern American Politics, 2003; (with R. Johnston) The End of Southern Exceptionalism: Class, Race, and Partisan Change in the Postwar South, 2006; (with W.J.M. Claggett) American Public Mind, 2010. EDITOR: (with J.I. Lengle) Presidential Politics: Readings on Nominations and Elections, 1980, 2nd ed., 1983; Is America Different?: A New Look at American Exceptionalism, 1991; The End of Realignment?: Interpreting American Electoral Eras, 1991; Postwar Politics in the G-7: Orders and Eras in Comparative Perspective, 1996; (with A.J. Badger) Contesting Democracy: Substance and Structure in American Political History, 1775-2000, 2001; The State of American Politics, 2002. Contributor to books and periodicals. **Address:** Department of Political Science, University of Wisconsin, 322A North Hall, 1050 Bascom Mall, Madison, WI 53706-1316, U.S.A. **Online address:** bshafer@polisci.wisc.edu

SHAFER, D. Michael. American (born United States), b. 1953. **Genres:** History, Social Commentary, Politics/Government, Economics, Business/Trade/Industry. **Career:** U.S. Department of State, intern, 1976; Institute for Psychiatry and Foreign Affairs, executive director, 1976-77; Agency for International Development, Technical Assistance Bureau, consultant, 1977; Harvard University, teaching fellow, 1980-84; University of Cape Town, visiting professor, 1983; Rutgers University, assistant professor, 1984-90, associate professor of political science, 1990-97, professor of political science, 1997-2009, professor emeritus, 2009-, Rutgers Citizenship and Service Education Program, director, 1994-2004, Rutgers Center for Global Security and Democracy, director, 2004-08; University of Colombo, visiting professor, 1986; Korea University, visiting research fellow, 1986; New School for Social Research, adjunct professor, 1989-92; University of Natal-Pietermaritzberg, visiting professor, 1997; NJ Vietnam Veterans' Memorial Foundation, consultant, 2000-; Warm Heart Worldwide Inc., founder and director, 2008-, Warm Heart Foundation, founder, advisor, senior advisor, 2008-; Second Harvest Power Company (Thailand) Ltd., president, 2009-; Arts Network, co-founder; Cobalt Studios, co-founder. Writer. **Publications:** (Co-author) Back in the U.S.S.R., 1988; Deadly Paradigms: The Failure of U.S. Counterinsurgency Policy, 1988; (ed. and contrib.) The Legacy: The Vietnam War in the American Imagination, 1990; Counterinsurgency, 1993; Winners and Losers: How Sectors Shape the Developmental Prospects of States, 1994; The Political Economy of Sectors and Sectoral Change: Korea Then and Now, 1997. Contributor to journals. **Address:** Warm Heart Foundation, 290 T.Maewan, A.Phrao, Chiang Mai, 50190, Thailand. **Online address:** d.michael.shafer@gmail.com

SHAFER, Glenn (Ray). American (born United States), b. 1946. **Genres:** Mathematics/Statistics, Education. **Career:** Peace Corps, teacher, 1968-69; Princeton University, Department of Statistics, assistant professor, 1973-76; University of Kansas, Department of Mathematics, assistant professor, 1976-78, associate professor, 1978-83, professor, 1983-84, School of Business, professor, 1984-87, Ronald G. Harper distinguished professor, 1988-92; Journal of the American Statistical Association, associate editor, 1980-82; Rutgers University, Rutgers Business School, Department of Accounting and Information Systems, professor II, 1992-, chair, 1995-96, 1998-99, Rutgers Ph.D. in Management Program, director, 1997-2000, board of governors professor, 2004; Knowledge Engineering Review, associate editor, 1994-98; University of London, Royal Holloway College, Department of Computer Science, Computer Learning Research Centre, visiting professor, 1996-; Statistical Science, associate editor, 2008-. **Publications:** A Mathematical Theory of Evidence, 1976; (ed. with J. Pearl) Readings in Uncertain Reasoning, 1990; Probabilistic Expert Systems, 1996; The Art of Causal Conjecture, 1996; (with V. Vovk) Probability and Finance: It's Only a Game!, 2001; (with V. Vladimir and A. Gammerman) Algorithmic Learning in a Random World, 2005. **Address:** Department of Accounting and Information Systems, Rutgers Business School, Newark and New Brunswick, 1 Washington Pk., Newark, NJ 07102, U.S.A. **Online address:** gshafer@andromeda.rutgers.edu

SHAFER, Neil. American (born United States), b. 1933. **Genres:** Economics, Money/Finance, Music, Art/Art History, Literary Criticism And History. **Career:** Music teacher, 1959-62; Western Publishing Company Inc., numismatic editor, 1962-75, senior editor, 1976-; Racine Symphony Orchestra, assistant conductor, 1963-72; Kiwanis Youth Symphony, director and coordinator, 1966-79; Paper View, columnist, 1966; New England Journal of Numismatics, editor-in-chief, 1985-87; Paper Money News and Views, bank note reporter, columnist, 1987-; Christie's Auctions of the American Bank Note Co. Archives, consultant for cataloguing, 1990-91; Numismatic News, columnist, 1996-. **Publications:** United States Territorial Coinage for the Philippine Islands, 1961; A Guide Book of Philippine Paper Money, 1964; A Guide Book of Modern United States Currency, 1965, 8th ed., 1979; (comp. with H. Wallace) A Guide Book of Mexican Coins, 1822 to Date, 1969, 2nd ed., 1971; Philippine Emergency and Guerrilla Currency of World War II, 1974; Let's Collect Paper Money, 1976; (co-ed.) Standard Catalog of World Paper Money, 3 vols., 1982-2003; (R.A. Mitchell) Standard Catalog of Depression Scrip of the United States, 1984; Banknotes, Scrip and Paper Ephemera of Milwaukee, 1990; The Wonderful World of Paper Money, 1992; (ed.) College Currency, 1993; Collecting United States Postage and Fractional Currency, 1996. Contributor to journals. **Address:** PO Box 170138, Milwaukee, WI 53217, U.S.A. **Online address:** nelsshaf@aol.com

SHAFER, Yvonne. American (born United States), b. 1936. **Genres:** Literary Criticism And History, Theatre, Plays/Screenplays. **Career:** University of Georgia, faculty; University of Delaware, faculty; University of California, faculty; St. John's University, associate professor, professor of speech, communication sciences and theatre, now professor emeritus. Writer. **Publications:** Henrik Ibsen: Life, Work, and Criticism, 1985; (ed.) Approaches to Teaching Ibsen's A Doll House, 1985; (with M. Carlson) The Play's the Thing: An Introduction to Theatre, 1990; American Women Playwrights, 1900-1950, 1995; August Wilson: A Research and Production Sourcebook, 1998; (comp.) Performing O'Neill: Conversations with Actors and Directors, 2000. Contributor to periodicals. **Address:** MacMillan Publishers Inc., 175 5th Ave., New York, NY 10010-7703, U.S.A. **Online address:** shafery@stjohns.edu

SHAFFER, Donald R. (Donald Robert Shaffer). American (born United States), b. 1965?. **Genres:** History, Military/Defense/Arms Control. **Career:** University of Maryland, teaching assistant and lecturer in history, 1991-96; National Park Service, Chesapeake and Ohio Canal National Historical Park, lead historian, 1996-97; State University of New York, visiting assistant professor, 1998-99; University of Northern Colorado, lecturer in history, 2000-07; Upper Iowa University, Department of History, instructor, 2007-, assistant professor, 2007-10, Center for Distance Education, instructor, 2008-; American Public University System, instructor, 2010; University of Phoenix, facilitator, 2011-. Writer. **Publications:** (Contrib.) Southern Families at War, 2000; (contrib.) Union Soldiers and the Northern Home Front: Wartime Experiences, Post War Adjustments, 2002; After the Glory: The Struggles of Black Civil War Veterans, 2004; (ed. with E.A. Regosin) Voices of Emancipation: Understanding Slavery, the Civil War, and Reconstruction through the U.S. Pension Bureau Files, 2008. Contributor to periodicals. **Address:** Division of Liberal Arts, Upper Iowa University, 605 Washington St., PO Box 1857, Fayette, IA 52142, U.S.A. **Online address:** shafferd@uiu.edu

SHAFFER, Donald Robert. See SHAFFER, Donald R.

SHAFFER, Louise. American (born United States), b. 1942. **Genres:** Mystery/Crime/Suspense, Novels. **Career:** Home Sweet Home, operator. Writer. **Publications:** All My Suspects (mystery novel), 1994; Talked to Death, 1995;

The Three Miss Margarets: A Novel, 2003; The Ladies of Garrison Gardens: A Novel, 2005; Family Acts: A Novel, 2007; Serendipity, 2009; Looking for Love Story, 2010. **Address:** c/o Lisa Barnes, Random House Inc., 1745 Broadway, 10th Fl., New York, NY 10019, U.S.A. **Online address:** louise@louiseshaffer.com

SHAFFER, Paul. American/Canadian (born Canada), b. 1949. **Genres:** Autobiography/Memoirs. **Career:** Writer, musician and actor. **Publications:** (With D. Ritz) We'll Be Here for the Rest of Our Lives: A Swingin' Show-biz Saga (autobiography), 2009. **Address:** New York, NY , U.S.A. **Online address:** paulshaffer@envisionradio.com

SHAFFER, Peter (Levin). (Peter Antony). British (born England), b. 1926. **Genres:** Novels, Plays/Screenplays, Mystery/Crime/Suspense, inspirational/ Motivational Literature, Literary Criticism And History. **Career:** New York Public Library, staff, 1951-54, Boosey & Hawkes (music publishers), staff, 1954-55; Truth, literary critic, 1956-57; Time and Tide Magazine, music critic, 1961-62. Writer. **Publications:** (As Peter Antony) Woman in the Wardrobe, 1952; (with A. Shaffer) Withered Murder, 1955; (with A. Shaffer) How Doth the Little Crocodile?, 1957; The Private Ear and the Public Eye, 1964; Black Comedy, 1966; The White Liars; And Black Comedy, 1968; Equus, 1973; Equus and Shrivings, 1974; Shrivings, 1974; Ma, 1979; Three Plays, 1976; White Liars, 1976; Four Plays, 1981; Peter Shaffer's Amadeus, 1981; The Collected Plays of Peter Shaffer, 1982; Yonadab: A Play, 1988; (ed.) Elisabeth Frink Sculpture: Catalogue Raisonné, 1988; Yonadab: The Watcher, 1988; Realcacería del sol, 1989; Lettice & Lovage: A Comedy, 1990; Whom Do I Have the Honor of Addressing?: A Play, 1990; The Gift of the Gorgon: A Play, 1993; The Royal Hunt of the Sun, 1999. Contributor of articles to periodicals. **Address:** McNaughton-Lowe Representation Ltd., 200 Fulham Rd., London, GL SW10 9PN, England.

SHAFQUAT, Sofia. American/Pakistani (born Pakistan), b. 1959. **Genres:** Novels, Sports/Fitness, Medicine/Health, How-to Books, Self Help, Adult Non-fiction, Ghost Writer, Mystery/Crime/Suspense, Mystery/Crime/Suspense. **Career:** Freelance writer, 1980-85; graphics designer and illustrator, 1980-; Rodale Press, health and fitness editor, 1985-87. **Publications:** The Shadow Man (novel), 1993. Contributor of articles to periodicals. **Address:** PO Box 761, Cardiff, CA 92007, U.S.A.

SHAGAN, Ethan H. American (born United States), b. 1971. **Genres:** History. **Career:** Harvard University, Society of Fellows, junior fellow, 1999-2000; Northwestern University, assistant professor, 2000-04, associate professor, 2004-07, Wayne V. Jones research professor in history, 2006-07; University of California, associate professor, 2007-. Writer. **Publications:** Popular Politics and the English Reformation, 2003; (ed.) Catholics and the Protestant Nation: Religious Politics and Identity in Early Modern England, 2005; Rule of Moderation: Violence, Religion, and the Politics of Restraint in Early Modern England, 2011. Contributor of articles to books and journals. **Address:** Department of History, University of California, 3210 Dwinelle Hall, Berkeley, CA 94720-2550, U.S.A. **Online address:** shagan@berkeley.edu

SHAGAN, Steve. (Robert Barnett). American (born United States), b. 1927. **Genres:** Novels, Plays/Screenplays, Young Adult Fiction. **Career:** Writer. **Publications:** Save the Tiger, 1972; City of Angels, 1975; Voyage of the Damned, 1976; The Formula, 1979; The Circle, 1982; The Discovery, 1984; Vendetta, 1986; Pillars of Fire, 1989; Cast of Thousands, 1993. **Address:** c/o Ron Mardigian, William Morris Agency, 151 E1 Camino Dr., Beverly Hills, CA 90212, U.S.A.

SHAH, Jami J. American/Pakistani (born Pakistan), b. 1950. **Genres:** Business/Trade/Industry, Engineering. **Career:** PASMIC Steel Mills, project engineer, 1973-75; POL, product engineer, 1976-78, product manager for welding products, 1978-80; Ohio State University, lecturer in mechanical engineering, 1981-84; Arizona State University, Ira A. Fulton Schools of Engineering, Department of Mechanical and Aerospace Engineering, assistant professor, 1984-88, associate professor, 1989-93, professor of mechanical and aerospace engineering, 1994-, Mechanical Engineering Design Group, coordinator, 1990-91, Design Automation Laboratory, director, DEMAP, director; ASME Transactions, chief editor. **Publications:** (Ed. with M. Mäntylä and D.S. Nau) Advances in Feature Based Manufacturing, 1994; (with M. Mäntylä) Parametric and Feature-Based CAD/CAM: Concepts, Techniques, and Applications, 1995. Contributor to periodicals. **Address:** Department of Mechanical and Aerospace Engineering, Ira A. Fulton Schools of Engineering, Arizona State University, GWC 458, 501 E Tyler Mall, PO Box 876106, Tempe, AZ 85281, U.S.A. **Online address:** jami.shah@asu.edu

SHAH, Sayed Tahir. British (born England), b. 1966. **Genres:** Anthropology/Ethnology, Travel/Exploration. **Career:** Institute for Cultural Research, director; Institute for Study of Human Knowledge, director; Health Review Journal, contributing editor; The Institute for Health Sciences, advisor. **Publications:** The Baby Killer, 1974; (ed.) Middle East Bedside Book, 1992; (ed.) Cultural Research, 1993; Spectrum Guide to Jordan, 1994; (with M. Amin and D. Willetts) Journey through Namibia, 1994; Beyond the Devil's Teeth, 1995; Trail of Feathers, 2001; In Search of King Solomon's Mines: House of the Tiger King, 2002; Sorcerer's Apprentice, 1998, 1st ed., 2001; Trail of Feathers, 2001; House of The Tiger King, 2005; The Caliph's House: A Year in Casablanca, 2006; In Arabian Nights, 2007; Sorcerer's Apprentice: An Incredible Journey Into The World of India's Godmen, 2011. Contributor to journals. **Address:** 24 Woodseer St., Blvd. de Grande Ceinture, Ain Diab, London, GL E1 5HD, England. **Online address:** mangorains@aol.com

SHAH, Sonia. American (born United States), b. 1969?. **Genres:** History. **Career:** Nuclear Times, managing editor; Nation institute, writing fellow; Puffin Foundation, writing fellow. Freelance journalist. **Publications:** (Ed.) Between Fear and Hope: A Decade of Peace Activism, 1992; Dragon Ladies: Asian American Feminists Breathe Fire, 1997; Crude: The Story of Oil, 2004; The Body Hunters: Testing New Drugs on the World's Poorest Patients, 2006; The Fever: How Malaria Has Ruled Humankind for 500000 Years, 2010. **Address:** Farrar, Straus & Giroux, 18 W 18th St., New York, NY 10011, U.S.A. **Online address:** sonia@soniashah.com

SHAHAN, Sherry. American (born United States), b. 1949. **Genres:** Young Adult Fiction, Young Adult Non-fiction, Novels, Mystery/Crime/Suspense, Natural History, Music, Sports/Fitness, Romance/Historical, Romance/Historical. **Career:** Freelance travel journalist and children's book author. **Publications:** FICTION: One Sister Too Many, 1988; Wanted: A Date for Mom, 1988; Operation Dump the Boyfriend, 1988; The Baby-Sitting Crack-Up, 1989; There's Something in There, 1989; Fifth Grade Crush, 1993; Sixth-Grade Crush, 1993; Telephone Tag, 1996; Wait Until Dark: Seven Scary Sleepover Stories, 1996; Love Stories, 1996. NONFICTION: (contrib.) Barnacles Eat with Their Feet: Delicious Facts about the Tide Pool Food Chain, 1996; Dashing through the Snow: The Story of Alaska's Jr. Iditarod, 1997; Blowtorch@psycho.com, 1997; There's Something in There. OTHER: Frozen Stiff, 1998; Fountain of Wierd, 1998; The Little Butterfly, 1998; Eerie Indiana 6, 1998; Working Dogs, 1999; Feeding Time at the Zoo, 2000; Together for Kwanzaa, 2000; Jazzy Alphabet, 2002; Spicy Hot Colors=Colores Picantes, 2004; Willie Covan Loved to Dance, 2004; Cool Cats Counting, 2005; Death Mountain, 2005; That's Not How You Play Soccer, Daddy, 2007; Fiesta!: A Celebration of Latino Festivals, 2009; Purple Daze, 2011. Contributor of articles to periodicals. **Address:** Random House Publishing, 1540 Broadway, New York, NY 10036, U.S.A. **Online address:** kidbooks@thegrid.net

SHAHAR, Yuval. Israeli (born Israel), b. 1953?. **Genres:** Geography, History, Social Commentary. **Career:** Tel Aviv University, professor of Jewish history. Writer. **Publications:** (With Y. Tepper) Me'arot-mareshah u-ma'arkhot-ha- mistor: Mehkarim, 1988; Josephus Geographicus: The Classical Context of Geography in Josephus, 2004. **Address:** Department of Jewish History, Tel Aviv University, PO Box 39040, Ramat Aviv, 69978, Israel. **Online address:** syuval@gvat.org.il

SHAHEEN, Jack G. American (born United States), b. 1935. **Genres:** Film. **Career:** Southern Illinois University, now professor emeritus. Writer. **Publications:** NONFICTION: Nuclear War Films, 1978; The TV Arab, 1984; Arab and Muslim Stereotyping in American Popular Culture, 1997; Reel Bad Arabs: How Hollywood Vilifies a People, 2001; Guilty: Hollywood's Verdict on Arabs after 9/11, 2008. **Address:** U.S.A. **Online address:** jgshaheen1@juno.com

SHAHRIARI, Shahriar. American/Iranian (born Iran), b. 1956. **Genres:** Mathematics/Statistics. **Career:** University of Razi, instructor, 1979-80; Oberlin College, assistant professor of mathematics, 1985-86; California State University, assistant professor of mathematics, 1986-89; Pomona College, assistant professor, 1989-93, associate professor, 1993-2001, professor, 2001-08, William Polk Russell professor of mathematics, 2008-, associate dean of college, 2000-03, department of mathematics, chair, 2004-07; National Science Foundation, research assistant, University of Oxford, Mathematical

Institute, 1984; Mathematical Science Research Institute Program on Representations of Finite Groups, member, 1990; Institute for Studies in Theoretical Physics and Mathematics, visiting researcher, 1999, 2002, 2003, 2006; California Institute of Technology, visiting associate in mathematics, 1996-97, 2000; United Nations Mission to Sharif Institute of Technology, member, 1991-92; United Nations Mission to Institute for Studies in Theoretical Physics and Mathematics, member, 1995-96. Writer. **Publications:** Approximately Calculus, 2006. **Address:** Pomona College, 610 N College Ave., Claremont, CA 91711-6348, U.S.A. **Online address:** sshahriari@pomona.edu

SHAIN, Milton. South African (born South Africa), b. 1949. **Genres:** History, Social Sciences, Politics/Government. **Career:** University of Cape Town, assistant lecturer, 1983-85, lecturer, 1986-91, senior lecturer, 1991-94, Isaac and Jessie Kaplan Centre for Jewish Studies and Research, director, 1994-, associate professor of Jewish studies, 1995-. Writer. **Publications:** Jewry and Cape Society: The Origins and Activities of the Jewish Board of Deputies for the Cape Colony, 1983; The Roots of Antisemitism in South Africa, 1994; Antisemitism, 1998; (ed. with S.L. Gilman) Jewries at the Frontier: Accommodation, Identity, Conflict, 1999; (ed. with S.A. Cohen) Israel: Culture, Religion, and Society 1948-1998, 2000; (comp.) Looking Back: Jews in the Struggle for Democracy and Human Rights in South Africa, 2001; (ed. with R. Mendelsohn) Memories, Realities and Dreams: Aspects of the South African Jewish Experience, 2002; (comp. with J. Blumberg) First Twenty-Five Years: The Isaac & Jessie Kaplan Centre for Jewish Studies and Research, University of Cape Town, 2005; Helen Suzman: Fighter for Human Rights, 2005; (intro. and ed.) Opposing Voices: Liberalism and Opposition in South Africa Today, 2006; (with R. Mendelsohn) Jews in South Africa: An Illustrated History, 2008; (ed. with D. Cesarani and T. Kushner) Place and Displacement in Jewish History and Memory: Zakor V'makor, 2009. **Address:** Department of Jewish Studies, University of Cape Town, PO Box Rondebosch, Cape Town, 7700, South Africa. **Online address:** milton.shain@uct.ac.za

SHAIN, Yossi. Israeli (born Israel), b. 1956. **Genres:** Politics/Government, Social Sciences, Anthropology/Ethnology. **Career:** Wesleyan University, visiting assistant professor of political science, 1987-88; Yale University, visiting assistant professor of political science, 1988-89, Fulbright fellow, 1991-92; Tel-Aviv University, assistant professor of political science, 1989-93, associate professor, 1993-97, department head, 1996-99, Haver professor, 1997-2002, Romulo Betancourt professor of political science, Aba Eban Program of Diplomacy, head, MA Program in Political Leadership, co-chair, Hartog School of Government, head 2003-07; Middlebury College, visiting assistant professor, 1991-92; The Fletcher School of Law and Diplomacy, visiting associate professor, 1994; Oxford University, St. Antony's College, visiting senior fellow, 1995; Georgetown University, Department of Government, Aaron and Cecile Goldman visiting professor, professor of comparative government and diaspora politics, 1999-2002, Jewish Civilization Program, founding director; Western Galilee College, president, 2007. Writer. **Publications:** Frontier of Loyalty: Political Exiles in the Age of the Nation-State, 1989; (with J.J. Linz) Between States: Interim Governments and Democratic Transitions, 1995; Arab-Americans in the 1990s: What Next for the Diaspora?, 1996; Marketing the American Creed Abroad: Diasporas in the U.S. and Their Homelands, 1999; Frontier of Loyalty: Political Exiles in the Age of the Nation-State, 2005; Kinship & Diasporas in International Affairs, 2007; (ed. with E. Langenbacher) Power and the Past: Collective Memory and International Relations, 2010. EDITOR: Government in Exile in Contemporary World Politics, 1990; (with A. Kleiman) Democracy: The Challenges Ahead, 1997. Contributor to books, periodicals and journals. **Address:** Department of Government, Georgetown University, 681 Intercultural Ctr., PO Box 571034, Washington, DC 20057-1034, U.S.A. **Online address:** shain@post.tau.ac.il

SHAINBERG, Lawrence. American (born United States), b. 1936. **Genres:** Medicine/Health, Autobiography/Memoirs, Novels. **Career:** Freelance journalist and writer, 1963-. **Publications:** One on One, 1970; Brain Surgeon: An Intimate View of His World, 1979; Memories of Amnesia: A Novel, 1988; Ambivalent Zen: A Memoir, 1995; Crust: A Novel, 2008. Contributor of articles to periodicals. **Address:** c/o Jane Gelfman, Gelfman Schneider Literary Agents Inc., 250 W 57th St., Ste. 2122, New York, NY 10025, U.S.A.

SHAKAR, Alex. American (born United States), b. 1968. **Genres:** Novels, Novellas/Short Stories, Young Adult Fiction. **Career:** University of Illinois, Department of English, assistant professor, associate professor, Creative Writing Program, program director; University of Texas at Austin, Michener fellow. Writer. **Publications:** City in Love: The New York Metamorphoses

(stories), 1996; The Savage Girl (novel), 2001; Luminarium, 2011. **Address:** Department of English, College of Liberal Arts & Sciences, University of Illinois, 314 English, 608 S Wright St., Urbana, IL 61801-3630, U.S.A. **Online address:** ashakar@illinois.edu

SHAKERI, Khosrow. (Cosroe Chaquéri). French/Iranian (born Iran), b. 1938. **Genres:** History, Intellectual History, International Relations/Current Affairs, Politics/Government. **Career:** Mazdak Publications, general editor, 1969-78; University of Paris III, lecturer in modern Iranian history, 1977-80; Tehran University, assistant professor of economics, 1979-80; école des Hautes études en Sciences Sociales, lecturer, associate professor of history, 1982-85, research fellow, 1998-; University of California, visiting associate professor of history, 1987; Harvard University, Center for Middle Eastern Studies, research fellow, 1988-91, senior research fellow, 1992-94, 1996-; DePaul University, visiting associate professor of history, 1991-92; Columbia University, Center for Iranian Studies, assistant editor, 1994-96. **Publications:** (Ed. and trans.) Documentary History of the Worker's Social Democratic, and Communist Movement in Iran, 10 vols., 1975-91; Russo-Caucasian Origins of the Iranian Left, 2000; Az Islām-i inqilābī tā gūlāg: ash'ār-i inqilābī-i Zarrah, Lādbun, Hisābī va Lāhūtī, 2002; (co-author) Naqsh-i Arāminah dar sūsiyāl dimūkrāsī-i īrān: 1905-1911, 2003; Pīshīnah'hā-yi iqtiṣ ādī-ijtimāī-i junbish-i Mashrūṭīyat va inkishāf-i sūsiyāl dimūkrāsī dar ān ahd, 2005; Hasht nāmah bih Chirīk'hā-yi Fadāyī-i Khalq: naqd-i yak manish-i fikrī, 2007; Mīlād-i zakhm: Junbish-i Jangal va Jumhūrī-i Shūravī-i Sūsiyālīstī-i īrān, 2007; Taqī Arrānī dar āyinah-yi tārīkh, 2008. AS COSROE CHAQUéRI: (intro.) Social-démocratie en Iran, 1979; (ed.) Mouv[e]ment communiste en Iran, 1979; (ed.) Revolutionary Movement in Iran versus Great Britain and Soviet Russia, 1979; Premier Congrès des peuples de l'Orient: Bakou, 1920: documents inédits avec une introduction historique, 1982; Union soviétique et les tentatives de soviets en Iran, 1983; (ed.) Orient et la IIe Internationale: documents inédits du COMINTERN, 1984; Beginning Politics in the Reproductive Cycle of Children's Tales and Games in Iran: An [sic] Historical Inquiry, 1992, rev. ed., 1996; The Soviet Socialist Republic of Iran, 1920-1921: Birth of the Trauma, 1995; Armenians of Iran, 1998; Origins of Social Democracy in Modern Iran, 2001; Armíańe Irana i persislamskiǐ imperskiǐ kompleks Khospova Chakeri, 2002. Contributor to periodicals. **Address:** école des Hautes études en, Sciences Sociales, 54 Bd. Raspail, Bureau 827, Paris, 75006, France. **Online address:** shakeri@ehess.fr

SHAKESPEARE, Nicholas. British (born England), b. 1957. **Genres:** Biography, Novels, Adult Non-fiction, Young Adult Fiction. **Career:** British Broadcasting Corporation Television (BBC-TV), assistant producer, 1980-84; London Times, deputy arts editor, 1985-; London Daily Telegraph, literary editor, 1988-91; The Sunday Telegraph, literary editor, 1988-91; Telegraph, literary editor. **Publications:** BIOGRAPHIES: The Men Who Would Be King, 1984; Londoners, 1986; Bruce Chatwin, 1999. NOVELS: The Vision of Elena Silves, 1989; High Flyer, 1993; Dancer Upstairs, 1995; Snowleg, 2004; In Tasmania, 2004; The Secrets of the Sea, 2007; Inheritance, 2010; (ed. with E. Chatwin) Under the Sun: The Letters of Bruce Chatwin, 2010. OTHER: (co-author) Ox-Tales: Earth, 2009. **Address:** Aitken Alexander Associates Ltd., 18-21 Cavaye Pl., London, GL SW10 9PT, England.

SHAKIN, Ken. German/American (born United States), b. 1959. **Genres:** Romance/Historical, Gay And Lesbian Issues, History. **Career:** Writer and musician. **Publications:** Love Sucks: New York Stories of Love, Hate and Anonymous Sex, 1997; Real Men Ride Horses: Cowboys and Indians, Outlaws and In-laws, Mormons and Other Strange Bedfellows in the Pink Desert, 1999; The Cure for Sodomy, 2006; Grandma Gets Laid, 2008. **Address:** Berlin, Germany. **Online address:** kenshakin@gmail.com

SHAKOORI, Ali. Iranian (born Iran), b. 1962. **Genres:** Economics. **Career:** University of Tehran, Faculty of Social Sciences, associate professor, 2008, Department of Cooperative and Social Welfare, director. Writer. **Publications:** The State and Rural Development in Post-Revolutionary Iran, 2001; Agricultural Development Policies in Iran, 2006; Agricultural Development Policies in Iran, 2nd ed., 2010. Contributor to journals. **Address:** The Faculty of Social Sciences, University of Tehran, Near Ghisha Bridge, PO Box 14395/773, Tehran, 13577, Iran. **Online address:** shakoori@chamran.ut.ac.ir

SHALANT, Phyllis. American (born United States), b. 1949. **Genres:** Children's Fiction, Young Adult Non-fiction, Young Adult Fiction, Social Sciences, Novels. **Career:** Manhattanville College, professor of children's literature. Writer. **Publications:** NONFICTION: Look What We've Brought

You from Vietnam: Crafts, Games, Recipes, Stories, and Other Cultural Activities from New Americans, 1988, 2nd ed. as Look What We've Brought You from Vietnam: Crafts, Games, Recipes, Stories, and Other Cultural Activities from Vietnamese Americans, 1998; Look What We've Brought You from Mexico: Crafts, Games, Recipes, Stories, and Other Cultural Activities from Mexican-Americans, 1992; Look What We've Brought You from Korea: Crafts, Games, Recipes, Stories, and Other Cultural Activities from Korean Americans, 1995; Look What We've Brought You from India: Crafts, Games, Recipes, Stories, and Other Cultural Activities from Indian Americans, 1998; Look What We've Brought You from the Caribbean: Crafts, Games, Recipes, Stories and Other Cultural Activities, 1998. FICTION: The Rock Star, The Rooster & Me, The Reporter, 1990; The Transformation of Faith Futterman, 1990; Shalom, Geneva Peace, 1992; Beware of Kissing Lizard Lips, 1995; The Great Eye, 1996; When Pirates Came to Brooklyn, 2002; The Great Cape Rescue: Society of Super Secret Heroes, 2007. BARTLEBY SERIES: Bartleby of the Mighty Mississippi, 2000; Bartleby of the Big Bad Bayou, 2005. Contributor to books. **Address:** 17 Palisade Ave., White Plains, NY 10607, U.S.A. **Online address:** phyllis@phyllisshalant.com

SHALIT, Béatrice. French/American (born United States), b. 1945. **Genres:** Novels, Plays/Screenplays, Young Adult Fiction. **Career:** Educational Television, script writer and director, 1965-69; International Newsreel and News Film Association, assistant director, 1970-72; CDNP, producer, 1975-83. **Publications:** NOVELS: Roi de cœur, 1982; L'Année de Louise, 1984; Le Plus Jeune Frére, 1985; Comédie Américaine, 1987; Lisa, Lisa: Roman, 1990; L'Air du Brésil, 1994; Poudre D'ange, 1998; Famille Et Autres Supplices, 2000; Ne M'appelez Plus Varsovie: Roman, 2003; Merci D'êtreVenu: Roman, 2006; Danse Avec Ma Mère: Roman, 2009; Qui veut tuer Rosa Hoffmann?, 2011. **Address:** 3 Passage Rauch, Paris, 75011, France.

SHALLCRASS, John James. American/New Zealander (born New Zealand), b. 1922?. **Genres:** Education, Language/Linguistics, History. **Career:** Teacher, 1940-53; Wellington Teachers College, lecturer in education to senior lecturer in history and geography, 1953-63, vice-principal, 1963-67; broadcaster and commentator, 1957-; Price-Milburn & Company Ltd., Liberal Studies Briefs, editor, 1968-74; Victoria University, reader in education, 1968-. **Publications:** CONTRIBUTOR: The Right to Dissent, 1965; Women's Position in the World Today, 1968; Prospects in New Zealand Education, 1969; Wellington Prospect, 1970; New Horizons in Social Codes, 1971; Recreation in New Zealand, vol. II, 1972; A Guide to Education Research, 1975; New Directions in Secondary Education, 1976; Chance to Be Equal, 1978; Environmental Education Handbook, 1979; Schools in New Zealand Society, 1980; New Zealand 2000, 1981; Adventures in Curriculum, 1983; N.Z. (1984) Limited, 1984; English: An International Perspective, 1984; Prejudice and Pride, 1985. OTHERS: Educating New Zealanders: Essays in Education, 1967; Forward to Basics, 1978; (with P. Wilson) No Stone Unturned, 1981; Tales Out of School, 1981; He Tangata, Report on Non-formal Learning, 1987; (with J. Morris and H. Haines) Pornography, report on Ministerial Enquiry, 1989; (co-author) School Development, 1990; The New Zealand Oxford Junior Dictionary, 1992; The New Zealand Oxford Primary School Dictionary, 1994. EDITOR: (with J.L. Ewing) An Introduction to Maori Education, 1970; Secondary Schools in Change, 1974; (with J.L. Robson) The Spirit of an Age: New Zealand in the Seventies: Essays in Honour of W.B.Sutch, 1975; (with R. Stothart and R. Larkin) Recreation Reconsidered, 1981; Civil Liberties in a Changing World New Zealand: Papers Presented at a Seminar Held in Wellington on 8 September 1984, 1985. **Address:** 24 Newcombe Cres., Wellington, 0600, New Zealand.

SHALLECK, David. American (born United States) **Genres:** Food And Wine, Travel/Exploration, Autobiography/Memoirs, E-books. **Career:** Volochef Culinary Solutions (culinary production company), founder. Writer. **Publications:** Mediterranean Summer: A Season on France's Cote D'Azur and Italy's Costa Bella (memoir), 2007. **Address:** Volochef Culinary Solutions, 1125 Broadway, Ste. 203, San Francisco, CA 94109-2191, U.S.A. **Online address:** david@volochef.com

SHALLIT, Jeffrey (Outlaw). Canadian/American (born United States), b. 1957. **Genres:** Mathematics/Statistics, Information Science/Computers, Technology. **Career:** University of Chicago, Department of Computer Science, assistant professor of mathematics, 1983-88; Dartmouth College, Department of Mathematics and Computer Science, assistant professor of mathematics, 1988-90; University of Waterloo, Department of Computer Science, associate professor of computer science, 1990-2000, professor, 2000-. Writer. **Publica-**

tions: (With E. Bach) Algorithmic Number Theory, 1996; (with J.P. Allouche) Automatic Sequences: Theory, Applications, Generalizations, 2003; A Second Course in Formal Languages and Automata Theory, 2008. **Address:** School of Computer Science, University of Waterloo, Davis Ctr. 3134, Waterloo, ON N2L 3G1, Canada. **Online address:** shallit@cs.uwaterloo.ca

SHAMAS, Victor A. American/Cuban (born Cuba), b. 1959. **Genres:** Psychology, Music, Theology/Religion, Art/Art History. **Career:** University of Arizona, Department of Psychology, adjunct lecturer, 1994-, Center for Consciousness Studies, coordinator, 1998; Global Chant, co-founder and director, 1996; North American Consortium for Educational Restructuring, program evaluator, 1998-99; Center for Image Processing in Education, Visualizing Addiction Project, director, 2000-04. Writer. **Publications:** Visualizing Addiction, 2003; The Chanter's Guide: Sacred Chanting as a Shamanic Practice, 2007. Contributor to books and journals. **Address:** Department of Psychology, University of Arizona, Rm. 312, Psychology Bldg., 1503 E University Blvd., PO Box 210068, Tucson, AZ 85721, U.S.A. **Online address:** vas@email.arizona.edu

SHAMBAUGH, David L. American (born United States), b. 1953. **Genres:** Area Studies, Politics/Government. **Career:** University of London, London School of Oriental and African Studies, lecturer in Chinese politics, 1988-91, senior lecturer in Chinese politics, 1992-94, reader in Chinese politics, 1995-96; George Washington University, Elliott School of International Affairs, professor of political science and international affairs, 1996-, China Policy Program, director, 1998-. Writer. **Publications:** The Making of a Premier: Zhao Ziyang's Provincial Career, 1983; Beautiful Imperialist: China Perceives America, 1972-1990, 1991; China's Transition Into the Twenty-first Century: U.S. and PRC Perspectives, 1996; Modernizing China's Military: Progress, Problems and Prospects, 2003; (co-author) China-Europe Relations Perceptions, Policies and Prospects, 2007; China's Communist Party: Atrophy & Adaptation, 2008. EDITOR: Contemporary China Studies in the United States, 1993; (with T.W. Robinson) Chinese Foreign Policy, 1993; American Studies of Contemporary China, 1993; (with T.W. Robinson) Chinese Foreign Policy: Theory and Practice, 1994; Deng Xiaoping: Portrait of a Chinese Stateman, 1995; Greater China: The Next Superpower?, 1995; (with R.H. Yang) China's Military in Transition, 1997; Contemporary Taiwan, 1998; The China Reader: The Reform Era, 1999; (with J.R. Lilley) China's Military Faces the Future, 1999; Is China Unstable?, 2000; The Modern Chinese State, 2000; (with R. Myers and M. Oksenberg) Making China Policy: Lessons from the Bush and Clinton Administrations, 2001; Power Shift: China and Asia's New Dynamics, 2005; (with J.S. Elliot) Odyssey of China's Imperial Art Treasures, 2005; (co-ed.) China Watching: Perspectives from Europe, Japan and the United States, 2006; (ed. with M. Yahuda) International Relations of Asia, 2009; Charting China's Future, 2011. Works appear in anthologies. Contributor of articles to journals and newspapers. **Address:** Sigur Center for Asian Studies, George Washington University, 1957 E St. NW, Ste. 503, Washington, DC 20052, U.S.A. **Online address:** shambaug@gwu.edu

SHAMES, Germaine W. American (born United States) **Genres:** Novels, Business/Trade/Industry, Cultural/Ethnic Topics, Social Sciences. **Career:** Writer. **Publications:** (Ed. with W.G. Glover) World Class Service, 1989; Transcultural Odysseys: The Evolving Global Consciousness, 1997; Between Two Deserts: A Novel, 2002; Hotel Noir, forthcoming; The Echo Year, forthcoming, The Abstract Life, forthcoming. Works appear in anthologies. Contributor to periodicals. **Address:** c/o Kathleen Anderson, Anderson Grinberg Literary Management Inc., 266 W 23rd St., Ste. 3, New York, NY 10011, U.S.A. **Online address:** germainewrites@gmail.com

SHAMMAS, Anton. American/Israeli (born Israel), b. 1951?. **Genres:** Novels, Poetry. **Career:** Ha-Yir (weekly periodical), columnist and reporter; A'sharq (monthly literary journal), editor, 1970-75; University of Michigan, Center for Middle Eastern and North African Studies, Rockefeller Fellow, 1987-88, Institute for the Humanities, visiting fellow, 1988-89, Department of Near Eastern Studies and the Program in Comparative Literature, adjunct professor, 1989-98, professor of modern middle Eastern literature, 1997-, visiting literary translator, 1996. Freelance journalist, translator and television producer. **Publications:** Asīr yaqẓatī wa-nawmī, 1974; Krikha Kasha, 1974; Sifrut haArvit be-Yiśrael le-aḥar 1967, 1976; Sheṭaḥ hefḳer: shirim, 1979; The Biggest Liar in the World, 1982; ṣ ayd al-ghazālah: 12 qiṣ ṣ ah min al-adab al-ʾIbrī al-ḥadīth, 1984; ʿArabesḳot (novel), 1986; Arabesques,

1986. Contributor to periodicals. **Address:** Department of Near Eastern Studies, University of Michigan, 3163 Thayer Academic Bldg., Ann Arbor, MI 48104-1608, U.S.A. **Online address:** antons@umich.edu

SHAMSIE, Kamila. British/Pakistani (born Pakistan), b. 1973?. **Genres:** Novels, Young Adult Non-fiction. **Career:** Hamilton College, creative writing teacher. Writer. **Publications:** In the City by the Sea, 1998; Salt and Saffron, 2000; Kartography, 2002; Broken Verses, 2005; Offence: The Muslim Case, 2009; Burnt Shadows, 2009. **Address:** c/o Victoria Hobbs, AM Heath & Co., Ltd., 6 Warwick Ct., London, GL WC1R 5DJ, England.

SHANAHAN, Daniel (A.). American (born United States), b. 1947. **Genres:** Philosophy, Psychology, Humanities. **Career:** California State University, instructor, 1971-73, lecturer, 1978; Stanford University, instructor, 1974-78; Filozofski Fakultet of Zadar, senior Fulbright lecturer, 1979-80; Monterey Institute of International Studies, associate professor, 1980-92, Center for North American Studies, director, 1980-83, head of English programs, 1982-89, chair of faculty assembly, 1986-87; Ain Shams University, academic specialist, 1985; Univerzita Karlova, senior Fulbright lecturer, 1987-88; Ecole des Hautes Etudes Commerciales, Department of English, associate professor of English, 1989-2001, chair, 1990-97; Charles University, professor of communication. Writer. **Publications:** (Ed.) The Colonial Mind, 1989; Toward A Genealogy of Individualism, 1992; Language, Feeling and The Brain: The Evocative Vector, 2007; Waiting for Something That Never Arrived: Meditations on a Progressive America in Honor of Tony Judt, 2011; Sparky's Folks: A Tribute to the Life and Work of Charles Schulz, 2012. Works appear in anthologies. Contributor to periodicals and journals. **Address:** Charles University, U krize 8, Praha 5, 158 00, Czech Republic. **Online address:** danshanahan@volny.cz

SHANAHAN, Michael Edward. (Mike Shanahan). American (born United States), b. 1952. **Genres:** Sports/Fitness, Self Help. **Career:** Professional football coach. Writer. **Publications:** (With A. Schefter as Mike Shanahan) Think Like a Champion, 1999. Contributor to periodicals. **Address:** Executive Offices & Training Facility, Denver Broncos Football Club, 13655 Broncos Pkwy., Englewood, CO 80112, U.S.A.

SHANAHAN, Mike. *See* **SHANAHAN, Michael Edward.**

SHANDLER, Jeffrey. American (born United States) **Genres:** Social Commentary, Local History/Rural Topics, Adult Non-fiction, Autobiography/Memoirs, Translations. **Career:** University of Pennsylvania, School for Communication, fellow, Center for Judaic Studies, fellow; State University of New Jersey, Rutgers University, visiting fellow, 2000-01, associate professor of Jewish studies, 2001-, professor of Jewish studies and acting chair, German Department, professor, 2003-. Writer and curator. **Publications:** (Trans.) Mani-Leib, Yingl Tsingl Khvat, 1986; While America Watches: Televising the Holocaust, 1999; (contrib.) Lives Remembered, 2002; (trans.) Y. Glatshteyn, Emil and Karl, 2006; Adventures in Yiddishland: Postvernacular Language & Culture, 2006; Jews, God, and Videotape: Religion and Media in America, 2009; Keepers of Accounts: The Practice of Inventory in Modern Jewish Life, 2010. EDITOR: The Life and Work of S.M. Dubnov: Diaspora Nationalism and Jewish History, 1991; (with B.S. Wenger) Encounters with the Holy Land: Place, Past and Future in American Jewish Culture, 1997; (with D. Abramowicz) Profiles of a Lost World: Memoirs of East European Jewish Life before World War II, 1999; (with H.R. Diner and B.S. Wenger) Remembering the Lower East Side: American Jewish Reflections, 2000; Awakening Lives: Autobiographies of Jewish Youth in Poland before the Holocaust, 2002; (with J. Hoberman) Entertaining America: Jews, Movies, and Broadcasting, 2003. **Address:** Department of Jewish Studies, Rutgers University, 102 Miller Hall, 14 College Ave., New Brunswick, NJ 08901, U.S.A. **Online address:** shandler@rci.rutgers.edu

SHANDLING, Garry. American (born United States), b. 1949. **Genres:** Plays/Screenplays, Humor/Satire, Film. **Career:** Actor, writer and comedian. **Publications:** (With D. Rensin) Confessions of a Late Night Talk Show Host: The Autobiography of Larry Sanders, 1998. **Address:** c/o Author Mail, Simon & Schuster Inc., 1230 Ave. of the Americas, New York, NY 10020-1513, U.S.A.

SHANE, Scott. American (born United States), b. 1954. **Genres:** History, Politics/Government. **Career:** Washington Star, clerk and reporter, 1979-80; Greensboro News and Record, reporter, 1980-83; Baltimore Sun, reporter, 1983-2004, Moscow correspondent, 1988-91, project reporter, 1992-2004; Johns Hopkins University, teacher, 1991; New York Times, national security reporter, 2004-. **Publications:** Dismantling Utopia: How Information Ended the Soviet Union, 1994. **Address:** 705 Kingston Rd., Baltimore, MD 21212, U.S.A. **Online address:** shane@nytimes.com

SHANGÉ, Ntozake. American (born United States), b. 1948. **Genres:** Novels, Plays/Screenplays, Poetry, Novellas/Short Stories, Humanities. **Career:** University of California Extension, faculty in women's studies, 1972-75; California State College, faculty in women's studies, 1973-75; Sonoma Mills College, faculty in women's studies, 1975; City University of New York, City College, faculty in women's studies, 1975, creative writing instructor; Douglass College, faculty in women's studies, 1978; University of Houston, associate professor of drama, 1983-2001; University of Florida, African American Studies Program, professor, 2000-, Center for Women's Studies and Gender Research, professor, 2000-; DePaul University, visiting professor; Brown University, visiting artist; New Jersey State Council on the Arts, artist-in-residence; Yale University, lecturer; Howard University, lecturer; Detroit Institute of Arts, lecturer; New York University, lecturer. Writer. **Publications:** For Colored Girls Who Have Considered Suicide: When the Rainbow Is Enuf (play), 1975; Melissa and Smith, 1976; Sassafrass: A Novella, 1976, rev. ed. as Sassafrass, Cypress, and Indigo, 1982; A Photograph: Lovers in Motion: A Drama, 1977; Natural Disasters and other Festive Occasions, 1977; A Photograph: A Study of Cruelty, 1977, rev. ed. as A Photograph: Lovers in Motion, 1981; Nappy Edges (poetry), 1978; From Okra to Greens: A Different Kinda Love Story; A Play with Music and Dance, 1978, rev. ed. as Mouths, 1981; Black and White Two-Dimensional Planes, 1978; Spell No.7: A Geechee Quick Magic Trance Manual, 1979 as Spell No. 7: A Theatre Piece in Two Acts, 1981; (adapter) Mother Courage and Her Children, 1980; Some Men, 1981; Three Pieces, 1981; A Daughter's Geography (poetry), 1983; From Okra to Greens: Poems, 1984; See No Evil: Prefaces, Essays and Accounts, 1974-1983, 1984 as See No Evil: Prefaces, Essays and Accounts, 1976-1983, 1984; Betsey Brown (novel), 1985; (foreword) The Black Book, 1986; Ridin' the Moon in Texas (poetry), 1987; (contrib.) Selected from Contemporary American Plays: An Anthology, Literacy Volunteers of New York City, 1990; Love Space Demands: A Continuing Saga, 1991; Plays, One, 1992; I Live in Music: Poem, 1994; Liliane: Resurrection of the Daughter, 1994; (intro.) Plays by Women, Book Two: An International Anthology, 1994; Whitewash, 1997; If I Can Cook, You Know God Can, 1998; (ed.) The Beacon Best of 1999: Creative Writing by Women and Men of All Colors, 1999; Muhammad Ali, The Man Who could Float like a Butterfly and Sting Like a Bee, 2002; Daddy Says, 2003; Ellington Was Not a Street, 2004; Sweet Breath of Life: A Poetic Narrative of the African-American Family, 2004; We Troubled the Waters: Poems, 2009; Coretta Scott, 2009; (with I. Bayeza) Some Sing, Some Cry: A Novel, 2010; Lost in Language & Sound: Or, How I Found My Way to the Arts: Essays, 2011; Freedom's A-Calling Me, 2012. Works appear in anthologies. Contributor to periodicals. **Address:** c/o Author Mail, St. Martin's Press, 175 5th Ave., New York, NY 10010-7703, U.S.A. **Online address:** nshange@ufl.edu

SHANK, Theodore. (Theodore Junior Shank). American (born United States), b. 1929. **Genres:** Plays/Screenplays, Theatre, Literary Criticism And History. **Career:** University of California-Davis, Department of Dramatic Art, professor, 1956-89, department chair, 1956-69, College of Letters and Science, faculty chair, professor, 1990-, distinguished professor, distinguished professor emeritus of theatre, Theatre Forum, founding editor, 1992-, department founding chair, Graduate Playwriting Program, head; Drama Review, contributing editor, 1976-86; University of California-San Diego, Snake Theater, director, 1979-80, Graduate Directing Program, head; Magic Theatre, director. **Publications:** The Bowery Theatre 1826-1836, 1956; (ed.) 500 Plays: Outlines and Production Notes, 1963; The Art of Dramatic Art, 1969; Theatre in Real Time, 1980; American Alternative Theatre, 1982; California Performance, 1989; (ed.) Contemporary British Theatre, 1994; Beyond the Boundaries: American Alternative Theatre, 2002. Contributor to books and journals. **Address:** Department of Theatre, University of California, Galbraith Hall 307, 9500 Gilman Dr., La Jolla, CA 92093-0344, U.S.A. **Online address:** tshank@ucsd.edu

SHANK, Theodore Junior. *See* **SHANK, Theodore.**

SHANKAR, S. American/Indian (born India), b. 1962. **Genres:** Poetry, Novels, Social Sciences. **Career:** Purdue University, teaching assistant, 1987-89; University of Texas, assistant instructor, 1989-93; Rutgers University, assistant professor, 1993-2002; University of Hawaii, Department of English, assistant professor of English, 2002-, professor, Center for South Asian Studies, director. Writer. **Publications:** I As Man (poems), 1987; A Map of Where I Live (novel), 1997; Textual Traffic: Colonialism, Modernity, and the Economy of the Text, 2001; (trans.) K. Swaminathan, Water!, 2001; (ed. with L. Mendoza) Crossing into America: The New Literature of Immigration, 2003; No End to the Journey: A Novel, 2005. Contributor to periodicals. **Address:** Department of English, University of Hawaii, 720 Kuykendall Hall, 1733 Donaghho Rd., Honolulu, HI 96822-2315, U.S.A. **Online address:** subraman@hawaii.edu

SHANKER, S. G. *See* **SHANKER, Stuart G.**

SHANKER, Stuart G. Also writes as S. G. Shanker, S. G. Shanker. Canadian (born Canada) **Genres:** Cultural/Ethnic Topics, Language/Linguistics, History, Philosophy, Mathematics/Statistics. **Career:** York University, Atkinson College, associate professor, 1986-89, professor of philosophy, 1989-, professor of psychology, 1996-2002, distinguished research professor of philosophy and psychology, 2002, Milton & Ethel Harris Research Initiative, director, 2003-, Graduate Faculty of Education, professor, 2009; Interdisciplinary Council of Developmental and Learning Disorders, chair, 2000, board director, 2008-; Council of Human Development, director, 2002; Council of Early Child Development, president, 2006; Cuba-Mexico-Canada Research Initiative, director, 2007. Writer and psychologist. **Publications:** (Ed.) Ludwig Wittgenstein: Critical Assessments, 1986, (ed. with D. Kilfoyle) 2nd ed., 2002; (ed. with J.V. Canfield) Wittgenstein's Intentions, 1993; (ed.) Philosophy of Science, Logic, and Mathematics in the Twentieth Century, 1996; (with S. Savage-Rumbaugh and T.J. Taylor) Apes, Language, and the Human Mind, 1998; Wittgenstein's Remarks on the Foundations of AI, 1998; (ed. with D. Bakhurst) Jerome Bruner: Language, Culture, Self, 2001; (with S. Greenspan) Toward a Psychology of Global Interdependency: A Framework for International Collaboration, 2002; (with S.I. Greenspan) The First Idea: How Symbols, Language, and Intelligence Evolved from our Early Primate Ancestors to Modern Humans, 2004; (with P. Reygadas) Rizoma de la racionalidad, 2007; (with A. Fogel and B.J. King) Human Development in the Twenty-First Century: Visionary Ideas from Systems scientists, 2008. AS S.G. SHANKER: (ed.) Philosophy in Britain Today, 1986; Wittgenstein and the Turning-Point in the Philosophy of Mathematics, 1987; (ed. with G.H.R. Parkinson) Routledge History of Philosophy, 10 vols., 1994; (with V.A. Shanker) A Wittgenstein Bibliography, 1986; (ed.) Gödel's Theorem in Focus, 1998. Contributor to books. **Address:** Milton & Ethel Harris Research Initiative, York University, 5030 TEL Bldg., 4700 Keele St., Toronto, ON M3J 1P3, Canada. **Online address:** shanker@yorku.ca

SHANLEY, Mary Kay. American (born United States), b. 1943. **Genres:** Autobiography/Memoirs, Essays, Sex, inspirational/Motivational Literature, Biography, Humor/Satire. **Career:** Des Moines Register, reporter, 1965-69; Iowa State University, School of Journalism, instructor, 1983-87; West Des Moines Board of Education, president, 1985-; writer, 1991-; Drake University, School of Journalism and Mass Communication, faculty, 1992; University of Iowa, Summer Writing Festival, instructor, 1995-. **Publications:** She Taught Me to Eat Artichokes: The Discovery of the Heart of Friendship, 1993; Little Lessons for Teachers, 1994; The Memory Box: Gathering the Keepsakes of the Heart, 1996; (ed.) When I Think About My Father, 1996; (with M. Adams) Rhythm of the Seasons: A Journey Beyond Loss, 1997; (with J. Johnston) For Parents Only: Tips for Surviving the Journey from Homeroom to Dorm Room, 2000; Our State Fair: Iowa's Blue Ribbon Story, 2000; (with J. Johnston) Best Answers to the 201 Most Frequently Asked Questions About Getting into College, 2005; (with J. Johnston) Survival Secrets of College Students, 2007; (with J. Johnston) Survival Secrets of Colleges Students, 2012. Contributor to magazines. **Address:** Summer Writing Festival, University of Iowa, C215 Seashore Hall, Iowa City, IA 52242, U.S.A. **Online address:** mks@marykayshanley.com

SHANLEY, Mary L(yndon). American (born United States), b. 1944. **Genres:** Intellectual History, Law, Politics/Government, Women's Studies And Issues, Social Sciences, Human Relations/Parenting. **Career:** Regis College, assistant professor of political science, 1972-73; Vassar College, assistant professor, 1972-83, associate professor, 1982-88, acting director of program of women's studies, 1982-83, department head, 1987-90, professor of political science, 1988-, Margaret Stiles Halleck professor, 1991-, Margaret Stiles Halleck chair, Learning, Teaching and Research Center, director; Princeton University, University Center for Human Values, De Camp visiting fellow, 1991-92. Writer and speaker. **Publications:** Women's Rights, Feminism and Politics in the United States, 1987; Feminism, Marriage and the Law in Victorian England, 1850-1895, 1989; (ed. with C. Pateman) Feminist Interpretations and Political Theory, 1991; (ed. with U. Narayan) Reconstructing Political Theory: Feminist Perspectives, 1997; Making Babies, Making Families: What Matters Most in an Age of Reproductive Technologies, Surrogacy, Adoption and Same-Sex and Unwed Parents, 2001; Just Marriage, 2004; (ed. with D.I. O'Neill and I.M. Young) Illusion of Consent: Engaging with Carole Pateman, 2008. Contributor of articles to books and journals. **Address:** Department of Political Science, Vassar College, Rockefeller Hall 106, 124 Raymond Ave., PO Box 455, Poughkeepsie, NY 12604-0009, U.S.A. **Online address:** shanley@vassar.edu

SHANNON, Doris. (E. X. Giroux). Canadian/American (born United States), b. 1924. **Genres:** Novels, Mystery/Crime/Suspense, Young Adult Fiction, Horror. **Career:** Royal Bank of Canada, bank teller, 1942-49; writer, 1969-. **Publications:** The Whispering Runes, 1972; Twenty-two Hallowfield, 1974; The Seekers, 1975; Hawthorn Hill, 1976; Lodestar Legacy, 1976; Devil's Servant, 1978; Cain's Daughters, 1978; Beyond the Shining Mountains, 1979; The Punishment, 1980; Little Girls Lost, 1981; Family Money, 1984. MYSTERY NOVELS AS E.X. GIROUX: A Death for Adonis, 1984; Death for a Darling, 1985; A Death for a Dancer, 1985; A Death for a Doctor, 1986; A Death for a Dilettanter, 1987; A Death for a Dietitian, 1988; A Death for a Dreamer, 1989; A Death for a Double, 1990; A Death for a Dancing Doll, 1991; A Death for a Dodo, 1993; The Dying Room, 1993. **Address:** St. Martin's Press, 175 5th Ave., New York, NY 10010, U.S.A.

SHANNON, Elizabeth (McNelly). American (born United States), b. 1937. **Genres:** Women's Studies And Issues, Plays/Screenplays. **Career:** Two-W Program, community director, 1975-77; Harvard University Extension Program, teacher of expository writing, 1983-84; Boston University, International Visitors Program, director. Writer. **Publications:** American Ambassador's Residence-Dublin, 1979; Up in the Park: The Diary of the Wife of the American Ambassador to Ireland 1977-1981, 1983; I Am of Ireland: Women of the North Speak Out, 1989, rev. ed., 1997. Contributor of articles to periodicals. **Address:** Boston University, 1 Sherborn St., 7th Fl., Boston, MA 02215, U.S.A. **Online address:** eshannon@bu.edu

SHANNON, Harry. American (born United States), b. 1948. **Genres:** Novels, Mystery/Crime/Suspense, Horror. **Career:** ATV Music Group, executive director; Carolco Pictures Inc., vice president of music, 1988-93. Writer. **Publications:** Bad Seed, 2001; Night of the Beast, 2002; Night of the Werewolf, 2003; Night of the Daemon, 2005; Memorial Day, 2004; Eye of the Burning Man, 2005; Pressure of Darkness: A Thriller, 2006; Dead and Gone, 2007; Daemon, 2008; One of the Wicked, 2008; A Host of Shadows, 2010; (co-author) Die, Lover, Die!, 2011; Running Cold, 2011. Works appear in anthologies. Contributor to magazines. **Address:** c/o Author Mail, Five Star Publishing, 295 Kennedy Memorial Dr., Waterville, ME 04901, U.S.A. **Online address:** ghoulishguy@aol.com

SHANNON, Ray. *See* **HAYWOOD, Gar Anthony.**

SHANNON, Timothy J. American (born United States), b. 1964. **Genres:** Politics/Government, History, Anthropology/Ethnology. **Career:** Gettysburg College, professor. Writer and historian. **Publications:** Indians and Colonists at the Crossroads of Empire: The Albany Congress of 1754, 2000; (ed. with V.B. Brown) Going to the Source: The Bedford Reader in American History, 2004; Atlantic Lives: A Comparative Approach to Early America, 2004; Iroquois Diplomacy on the Early American Frontier, 2008. Contributor of articles to periodicals. **Address:** Gettysburg College, Weidensall Hall, N Washington St., PO Box 0401, Gettysburg, PA 17325-1400, U.S.A. **Online address:** tshannon@gettysburg.edu

SHAPCOTT, Thomas W(illiam). Australian (born Australia), b. 1935. **Genres:** Novels, Novellas/Short Stories, Plays/Screenplays, Poetry, Songs/Lyrics And Libretti, Art/Art History, Literary Criticism And History. **Career:** H.S. Shapcott, public accountant and clerk, 1951-60; Shapcott & Shapcott, accountant, partner, 1961-78; Literature Board of Australia Council, deputy chair, 1973-76, director, 1983-90; Ipswich, sole trader, 1974-78; full-time writer, 1975-; Copyright Agency Ltd., director, 1991-99, chair, 1997-99; University of Adelaide, professor of creative writing, 1997-2005, chair, professor emeritus, 2005-. **Publications:** POETRY: Time on Fire: Poems, 1961; Twelve Bagetelles, 1962; The Mankind Thing, 1964; Sonnets 1960/1963,

1964; A Taste of Salt Water: Poems, 1967; Inwards to the Sun: Poems, 1969; Fingers at Air: Experimental Poems, 1969; The Seven Deadly Sins: Poem for the Opera, 1970; Begin with Walking, 1972; Interim Report, 1972; Shabbytown Calendar: Poems, 1975; Seventh Avenue Poems, 1976; Selected Poems, 1978; Turning Full Circle: Prose Poems, 1978; Make the Old Man Sing, 1980; Those Who Are Compelled, 1980; Stump and Grape and Bopple-nut, 1981; Welcome!: Poems, 1983; Shapcott: Poems, 1989; Travel Dice, 1987; Selected Poems 1956-1988, 1989; The City of Home, 1995; The Sun's Waste is our Energy, 1998; Cities in Exile, 1998; Chekhov's Mongoose, 2000; Beginnings & Endings, 2003. EDITOR: (with R. Hall) New Impulses in Australian Poetry, 1968; Australian Poetry Now, 1970; Poets on Record, 1970-74; Contemporary American and Australian Poetry, 1976; Consolidation: The Second Paperback Poets Anthology, 1982; Contemporary Australian Poetry, 1989; Pamphlet Poets, 1991; The Moment Made Marvellous: A Celebration of UQP Poetry, 1998; (and trans. with I. Casule) An Island on Land: Contemporary Macedonian Poetry, 1999; A Circle around My Grandmother, 2010. NOVELS: Flood Children, 1981; The Birthday Gift: A Novel, 1982; White Stag of Exile, 1984; Holiday of the Ikon, 1985; Hotel Belleview, 1986; The Search for Galina, 1989; (with S. Spears) Mr. Edmund, 1990; (with A.R. Sijkpson) His Master's Ghost, 1990; Mona's Gift, 1993; Theatre of Darkness: Lillian Nordica as Opera, 1998; Spirit Wrestlers, 2004. OTHERS: Focus on Charles Blackman (art monograph), 1967; Limestone and Lemon Wine (stories), 1988, 2nd ed., 1990; The Literature Board: A Brief History, 1989; Art of Charles Blackman (art monograph), 1989; Biting the Bullet: A Literary Memoir, 1990; In the Beginning: Pamphlet Poets 6, 1990; What You Own (stories), 1991; Twins in the Family, 2001; (intro.) Tense Little Lives: Uncollected Prose of Ray Mathew, 2007; Gatherers and Hunters, 2010. **Address:** Discipline of English and Creative Writing, School of Humanities, University of Adelaide, Rm. 722, Napier Bldg. Level 7, Adelaide, SA 5005, Australia.

SHAPIN, Steven. American (born United States), b. 1943. **Genres:** History, Sociology. **Career:** Keele Univeristy, visiting research fellow, 1972; Edinburgh University, Science Studies Unit, lecturer in science studies, 1973-88, reader in Science Studies, 1988-89; University of Pennsylvania, Department of History and Sociology, visiting fellow, 1979-80; University of California, professor of sociology, 1989-2003, adjunct professor of history, 1994-98; Harvard University, professor of history of science 2004-, Franklin L. Ford professor of the history of science, 2004-. Writer, historian and sociologist. **Publications:** (With S. Schaffer) Leviathan and the Air-Pump: Hobbes, Boyle, and the Experimental Life, 1985; A Social History of Truth: Civility and Science in Seventeenth-Century England, 1994; The Scientific Revolution, 1996; The Scientific Life: A Moral History of a Late Modern Vocation. 2008; Never Pure: Historical Studies of Science as if it Was Produced by People With Bodies, Situated in Time, Space, Culture and Society and Struggling for Credibility and Authority, 2010. EDITOR: (with B. Barnes) Natural Order: Historical Studies of Scientific Cultures, 1979; (with C. Lawrence) Science Incarnate: Historical Embodiments of Natural Knowledge, 1998. **Address:** Department of the History of Science, Harvard University, 371 Science Ctr., 1 Oxford St., Cambridge, MA 02138, U.S.A. **Online address:** shapin@fas.harvard.edu

SHAPIRO, Barbara J(une). American (born United States), b. 1934. **Genres:** History, Biography. **Career:** Occidental College, assistant professor of history, 1965-66; Pitzer College, assistant professor, 1966-68, associate professor of history, 1968-70; University of California-Irvine, lecturer in social science, 1969-70; University of California-Berkeley, lecturer in history, 1970-71, professor of rhetoric, 1977-94, Graduate School, professor, 1994-, now professor emeritus; Wheaton College, professor of history and dean of faculty, 1971-73; University of California-San Diego, associate professor of history, 1973-76. Writer. **Publications:** John Wilkins, 1614-1672: An Intellectual Biography, 1969; (with R.G. Frank, Jr.) English Scientific Virtuosi in the 16th and 17th Centuries, 1979; History and Natural History in Seventeenth-Century England, 1981; Probability and Certainty in Seventeenth-Century England: A Study of the Relationships between Natural Science, Religion, History, Law, and Literature, 1983; Beyond Reasonable Doubt and Probable Cause: Historical Perspectives on the Anglo-American Law of Evidence, 1991; A Culture of Fact: England, 1550-1720, 2000. Contributor to journals. **Address:** Department of Rhetoric, University of California, 7408 Dwinelle Hall, Ste. 2670, Berkeley, CA 94720-2670, U.S.A. **Online address:** bshapiro@berkeley.edu

SHAPIRO, Barry M. American (born United States), b. 1944. **Genres:** His-

tory, Law. **Career:** Loop Jr. College, instructor of social science, 1968-69; Pembroke State University, instructor of political science, 1974-76; University of California, 1986-88; Allegheny College, Department of History, assistant professor, 1988-95, associate professor, 1995-2003, professor, 2003-. Writer. **Publications:** Revolutionary Justice in Paris, 1789-1790, 1993; Traumatic Politics: the Deputies and the King in the Early French Revolution, 2009. Contributor to periodicals. **Address:** Department of History, Allegheny College, 206 Arter Hall, 520 N Main St., PO Box 154, Meadville, PA 16335, U.S.A. **Online address:** bshapiro@allegheny.edu

SHAPIRO, Bonnie L. Canadian/American (born United States) **Genres:** Education, Psychology, Sciences. **Career:** Teacher and science specialist, 1972-77; University of Alberta, sessional lecturer and faculty consultant, 1977-86; Cornell University, visiting fellow, 1984; University of Surrey, visiting fellow, 1985; Alberta Elementary Science Network, initiator, editor, and coordinator, 1986-; University of Calgary, assistant professor, 1986-89, associate professor, 1989-95, Killam resident fellow, 1991, 1996, graduate coordinator for curriculum and instruction, 1993, associate dean for faculty research, 1994-99, professor of education, 1995-. Writer. **Publications:** What Children Bring to Light: A Constructivist Perspective on Children's Learning in Science, 1994. Contributor to books and journals. **Address:** Faculty of Education, University of Calgary, Rm. 926, 2500 University Dr. NW, Calgary, AB T2N 1N4, Canada. **Online address:** bshapiro@ucalgary.ca

SHAPIRO, Dan(iel). (Daniel E. Shapiro). American (born United States), b. 1966?. **Genres:** Medicine/Health, Psychology. **Career:** University of Arizona, associate professor of clinical psychiatry, 1995-2008, curricular thread director of humanism and behavioral medicine, 2005-08, director of program in medical humanities, 2005-08; Fertile Hope, board director, 2002-03; Sunstone Cancer Healing Center, board director, 2002-04; Cure Magazine, board director, 2006-; Penn State College of Medicine, Department of Humanities, chair and professor, 2008-, Arnold P. Gold Foundation professor of medical humanism. Writer. **Publications:** The Social Impact of Oil in Scotland: A Contribution to the Sociology of Oil, 1980; (ed. with M. Tauber and R. Traunmuller) The Design of Computer Supported Cooperative Work and Groupware Systems, 1996; Mom's Marijuana: Insights About Living, 2000 as Mom's Marijuana: Life, Love, and Beating the Odds, 2001; Delivering Doctor Amelia: The Story of a Gifted Young Obstetrician's Mistake and the Psychologist Who Helped Her, 2003. Contributor to periodicals. **Address:** Department of Humanities, Penn State College of Medicine, H 134 Milton Hershey Medical Ctr., 500 University Dr., Hershey, PA 17033, U.S.A. **Online address:** dshapiro@hmc.psu.edu

SHAPIRO, Daniel E. *See* **SHAPIRO, Dan(iel).**

SHAPIRO, Dani (J.). American (born United States), b. 1962. **Genres:** Novels, Autobiography/Memoirs. **Career:** Columbia University, Creative Writing Center, adjunct assistant professor; Wesleyan University, visiting writer; New School, M.F.A. program instructor; Travel & Leisure, contributing editor. **Publications:** NOVELS: Playing with Fire, 1990; Fugitive Blue, 1993; Picturing the Wreck, 1996; Family History, 2003; Black & White, 2007. OTHER: Slow Motion: A True Story (memoir), 1998; (ed.) Best New American Voices 2010, 2009; Devotion: A Memoir, 2010. Contributor to books and periodicals. **Address:** c/o Jennifer Rudolph Walsh, William Morris Endeavor L.L.C., 1325 Ave. of the Americas, New York, NY 10019, U.S.A. **Online address:** djs17@columbia.edu

SHAPIRO, David (Joel). American (born United States), b. 1947. **Genres:** Poetry, Art/Art History, Translations. **Career:** William Paterson University, art historian; professional violinist, 1963-; Art News, art historian, 1970; New Yorker, editorial associate, 1970-; Columbia University, instructor, 1972-73, assistant professor of English, 1973-81; Brooklyn College, visiting professor, 1979; Bard College, faculty; Princeton University, visiting lecturer, 1982-83; Cooper Union University, adjunct faculty, professor; Patterson College, faculty. Writer. **Publications:** January: A Book of Poems, 1965; Poems from Deal, 1969; A Man Holding an Acoustic Panel, 1971; The Page-Turner, 1973; Lateness (verse), 1977; (co-trans.) The New Art of Color: The Writings of Robert and Sonia Delaunay, 1978; John Ashbery: An Introduction to His Poetry, 1979; Jim Dine: Painting What One Is, 1981; To an Idea (verse), 1983; Jasper Johns: Drawings 1954-1984, 1984; House, Blown Apart (verse), 1988; Mondrian: Flowers, 1991; (with J. Stein) Alfred Leslie, 1991; (trans. with P. Auster and S. Romer) Selected Poems, 1992; After a Lost Original (verse), 1994; (with E. Longari and J. Gilbert-Rolfe) Michael Goldberg, 1997; Drawings of Richard Upton: Ireland and Italy, 1997; (with M. Govrin and J. Derrida) Body of Prayer, 2001; A Burning Interior (verse), 2002; (with T. Gere) After, 2005; New and Selected Poems, 1965-2006, 2007. EDITOR: (with K. Koch) Learn Something, America, 1968; Inventory, 1997; (with R. Padgett) An Anthology of New York Poets, 1970; (with B. Beckley) Uncontrollable Beauty, 1998. Contributor to periodicals. **Address:** 3001 Henry Hudson Pkwy., Linden House 3B, Bronx, NY 10463-4717, U.S.A. **Online address:** dajoshap@aol.com

SHAPIRO, Edward S. American (born United States), b. 1938. **Genres:** Adult Non-fiction, History. **Career:** St. John's University, assistant professor of history, 1965-69; Seton Hall University, professor of history, 1969-2000, professor emeritus, 2000-. Writer. **Publications:** Clio From the Right: Essays of a Conservative Historian, 1983; A Time for Healing: American Jewry since World War II, 1992; Letters of Sidney Hook: Democracy, Communism, and the Cold War, 1995; We Are Many: Reflections on American Jewish History and Identity, 2004; Crown Heights: Blacks, Jews, and the 1991 Brooklyn Riot, 2006; (ed.) Yiddish in America: Essays on Yiddish Culture in the Golden Land, 2008. Contributor to periodicals. **Address:** Department of History, Seton Hall University, Fahy Hall, South Orange, NJ 07079, U.S.A. **Online address:** shapired@shu.edu

SHAPIRO, Eileen C. American (born United States), b. 1949?. **Genres:** Business/Trade/Industry, Economics, inspirational/Motivational Literature. **Career:** McKinsey and Company Inc., strategy consultant; Hillcrest Group Inc., president and co-founder; Myomo Inc., board director; Tangerine Wellness Inc., board director. Writer. **Publications:** (Ed. with L.M. Lowenstein) Becoming a Physician: Development of Values and Attitudes in Medicine, 1979; How Corporate Truths Become Competitive Traps: How to Keep the Things that Everyone Knows Are True from Becoming Roadblocks to Success, 1991; Fad Surfing in the Boardroom: Reclaiming the Courage to Manage in the Age of Instant Answers, 1995; Fad Surfing in the Boardroom: Managing in the Age of Instant Answers, 1996; The Seven Deadly Sins of Business: Freeing the Corporate Mind from Doom-loop Thinking, 1998; (with H.H. Stevenson) Make Your Own Luck: 12 Practical Steps to Taking Smarter Risks in Business, 2005. **Address:** Hillcrest Group Inc., 20 University Rd., Cambridge, MA 02138-5756, U.S.A. **Online address:** eshapiro@hillcrestinc.com

SHAPIRO, Fred R(ichard). American (born United States), b. 1954. **Genres:** Law, Librarianship. **Career:** Raysor, Barbour & Iversen (law firm), associate, 1980-81; Catholic University of America, special assistant for circulation services, 1981-82; New York Law School, lawyer-librarian and adjunct assistant professor, 1982-84, head of reference services and adjunct associate professor, 1984-87; Yale Law School, lecturer in legal research, 1987-, assistant librarian for public services, 1987-93, associate librarian for public services, 1993-, Lillian Goldman Law Library, Department of Reference & Instruction, associate librarian for collections & access. Writer. **Publications:** (Comp.) The Most-Cited Law Review Articles, 1987; LEXIS: The Complete User's Guide, 1989; The Most-Cited Articles from the Yale Law Journal, 1991; (comp.) The Oxford Dictionary of American Legal Quotations, 1993; (ed. with J. Garry) Trial and Error: An Oxford Anthology of Legal Stories, 1998; (ed.) Stumpers!: Answers to Hundreds of Questions that Stumped the Experts, 1998; (comp.) Collected Papers on Legal Citation Analysis, 2001; (ed.) Yale Book of Quotations, 2006; (comp. with C.C. Doyle and W. Mieder) Dictionary of Modern Proverbs, 2012. **Address:** Lillian Goldman Law Library, Yale University, SLB314, 127 Wall St., PO Box 208215, New Haven, CT 06511, U.S.A. **Online address:** fred.shapiro@yale.edu

SHAPIRO, Harold T(afler). American/Canadian (born Canada), b. 1935. **Genres:** Economics, Business/Trade/Industry. **Career:** University of Michigan, assistant professor, 1964-67, associate professor, 1967-70, professor of economics, 1970-76, chairman of department, 1974-77, Research Seminar in Quantitative Economics, co-director, 1967-81, director of Graduate Program, 1967-73, Institute of Labor and Industrial Relations, research scientist, 1976-87, Institute of Public Policy Studies, research scientist, 1976-87, professor of economics and public policy and senior fellow, 1977-87, vice-president for academic affairs, 1977-79, president and chairman of board of regents, 1980-87; Unisys Corp., board director, 1981-89; Industrial Technology Institute, board director, 1982-89; Kellogg Co., board director, 1982-89; Dow Chemical Co., board director, 1985-2006; Association of American Universities, vice chair, 1986-87, chair, 1987-88; National Bureau of Economic Research Inc., board director, 1986-99; Princeton University, president, 1988-2001, Woodrow Wilson School of Public and International Affairs, Department

of Economics, professor, 1988-, professor of economics and public affairs and president emeritus, 2001-; The Edison Partnership, co-chair, 1998-2001; DeVry Inc., board director, 2001-, chairman, 2008-; HCA Inc., board director, 2001-06; The Hastings Center, board director, 2001-09; Institute for Advanced Study, board director, 2009-. Writer. **Publications:** (With G.A. Fulton) A Regional Econometric Forecasting System: Major Economic Areas of Michigan, 1985; Tradition and Change: Perspectives on Education and Public Policy, 1987; (ed. with M.J. Field) Employment and Health Benefits: A Connection at Risk, 1993; (ed. with W.G. Bowen) Universities and Their Leadership, 1998; Larger Sense of Purpose: Higher Education and Society, 2005; (ed. with J.F. Childress and E.M. Meslin) Belmont Revisited: Ethical Principles for Research with Human Subjects, 2005. **Address:** Woodrow Wilson School of Public, and International Affairs, Princeton University, 359 Wallace Hall, Princeton, NJ 08544-0015, U.S.A. **Online address:** hts@princeton.edu

SHAPIRO, Harvey. American (born United States), b. 1924. **Genres:** Poetry, History, Young Adult Fiction, Literary Criticism And History, Language/Linguistics, Humanities. **Career:** Cornell University, instructor in English, 1949-50, 1951-52; Bard College, creative writing fellow, 1950-51; Commentary Magazine, staff, 1953-54, assistant editor, 1955-56; New Yorker Magazine, staff member, 1954-55, fiction editor, 1956-57; New York Times Magazine, editor, 1957-64, assistant editor, 1964-75, deputy editor, 1983-93, consulting editor, 1993-2002; New York Times Book Review, editor, 1975-83. **Publications:** The Eye, 1953; The Book and Other Poems, 1955; Mountain, Fire, Thornbush, 1961; Battle Report, 1966; This World, 1971; Lauds, 1975; Lauds & Nightsounds, 1978; The Light Holds: Poems, 1984; (with P. Tumay) Murder in Soho, 1987; National Cold Storage Company, 1988; A Day's Portion, 1994; Selected Poems, 1997; How Charlie Shavers Died and Other Poems, 2001; (ed.) Poets of World War II, 2003; The Sights along the Harbor: New and Collected Poems, 2006. **Address:** 43 Pierrepont St., Brooklyn, NY 11201, U.S.A.

SHAPIRO, Herbert. American (born United States), b. 1929. **Genres:** History, Race Relations, Autobiography/Memoirs, Humanities. **Career:** Morehouse College, Atlanta University Center, assistant professor of history, 1962-66; University of Cincinnati, assistant professor, 1966-71, associate professor of history, 1971-2001, professor, 2001-, now professor emeritus. Writer. **Publications:** (Ed. with E. Winter) World of Lincoln Steffens, 1962; (ed. and intro.) The Muckrakers and American Society, 1968; White Violence and Black Response: From Reconstruction to Montgomery, 1988; (ed. with P.S. Foner) American Communism and Black Americans: A Documentary History, 1930-1934, 1991; (ed. with D.L. Sterling) I Belong to the Working Class: The Unfinished Autobiography of Rose Pastor Stokes, 1992; (ed. with P.S. Foner) Northern Labor and Antislavery: A Documentary History, 1994; (ed.) African American History and Radical Historiography: Essays in Honor of Herbert Aptheker, 1998. **Address:** Department of History, University of Cincinnati, 360 McMicken Hall, PO Box 210373, Cincinnati, OH 45221-0373, U.S.A. **Online address:** herbert.shapiro@uc.edu

SHAPIRO, H. Svi. American (born United States), b. 1948. **Genres:** Social Commentary, Education, Politics/Government. **Career:** University of North Carolina, school of education, 1980-, Department of Educational Leadership and Cultural Foundations, professor, 1991-, chair and director of graduate programs, 1991-97, director of the Ph.D. program in curriculum and teaching, 1997-2004, interim chair, 2003; Tikkun Magazine, contributor. Writer. **Publications:** (Ed. with D.E. Purpel) Schools and Meaning: Essays on the Moral Nature of Schooling, 1985; Between Capitalism and Democracy: Educational Policy and the Crisis of the Welfare State, 1990; (ed. with D.E. Purpel) Critical Social Issues in American Education: Toward the 21st Century, 1993, 3rd ed. as Critical Social Issues in American Education: Democracy and Meaning in a Globalizing World, 2005; (with D.E. Purpel) Beyond Liberation and Excellence: Reconstructing the Public Discourse on Education, 1995; (ed.) Strangers in the Land: Pedagogy, Modernity and Jewish Identity, 1999; (ed. with S. Shapiro) Body Movements: Pedagogy, Politics and Social Change, 2002; Losing Heart: The Moral and Spiritual Miseducation of America's Children, 2006; Educating Youth for a World beyond Violence: A Pedagogy for Peace, 2010. Contributor to books and (Ed. with D.E. Purpel) Schools and Meaning: Essays on the Moral Nature of Schooling, 1985; Between Capitalism and Democracy: Educational Policy and the Crisis of the Welfare State, 1990; (ed. with D.E. Purpel) Critical Social Issues in American Education: Toward the 21st Century, 1993, 3rd ed. as Critical Social Issues in American Education: Democracy and Meaning in a Globalizing World, 2005; (with D.E. Purpel) Beyond Liberation and Excellence: Reconstructing the Public

Discourse on Education, 1995; (ed.) Strangers in the Land: Pedagogy, Modernity and Jewish Identity, 1999; (ed. with S. Shapiro) Body Movements: Pedagogy, Politics and Social Change, 2002; Losing Heart: The Moral and Spiritual Miseducation of America's Children, 2006; Educating Youth for a World beyond Violence: A Pedagogy for Peace, 2010. Contributor to books and journals. **Address:** Dept. of Edu. Leadership & Cultural Foundations, University of North Carolina, 364 School of Education Bldg., PO Box 26170, Greensboro, NC 27402-6170, U.S.A. **Online address:** svishapiro@nc.rr.com

SHAPIRO, Ian. American/South African (born South Africa), b. 1956. **Genres:** Politics/Government, History, Law, Essays. **Career:** Yale University, Institution for Social and Policy Studies, assistant professor, 1984-88, associate professor, 1988-92, professor, 1992-, William R. Kenan Jr. Professor of Political Science, 2000-05, Sterling Professor of Political Science, 2005-, Yale Law School, adjunct professor, 2004, 2008, Program in Ethics, Politics, and Economics, director, 1992-98, 2000-01, chair of department, 1999-2004, Whitney and Betty MacMillan Center for International and Area Studies, Henry R. Luce Director, 2004-; University of Cape Town, visiting professor; Nuffield College, visiting professor. Writer. **Publications:** The Evolution of Rights in Liberal Theory, 1986; (ed. with G. Reeher) Power, Inequality, and Democratic Politics: Essays in Honor of Robert A. Dahl, 1988; Political Criticism, 1990; (ed. with J.W. Chapman) Democratic Community, 1993; (ed. with D.Morris and intro.) The Political Writings, 1993; (with D.P. Green) Pathologies of Rational Choice Theory: A Critique of Applications in Political Science, 1994; (ed.) The Rule of Law, 1994; (ed. and intro.) Abortion: The Supreme Court Decisions, 1995, 2nd ed. as Abortion: The Supreme Court Decisions, 1965-2000, 2001, 3rd ed. as Abortion: The Supreme Court Decisions, 1965-2007, 2007; (ed. with J.W. DeCew) Theory and Practice, 1995; (ed. with R. Hardin) Political Order, 1996; Democracy's Place, 1996; (ed. with W. Kymlicka) Ethnicity and Group Rights, 1997; (ed. with R. Adams) Integrity and Conscience, 1998; (ed. with C. Hacker-Cordón) Democracy's Edges, 1999; Democratic Justice, 1999; (ed. with L. Brilmayer) Global Justice, 1999; (ed. with C. Hacker-Cordón) Democracy's Value, 1999; (ed. with S. Macedo) Designing Democratic Institutions, 2000; The Moral Foundations of Politics, 2003; (ed. with R. Dahl and J.A. Cheibub) The Democracy Sourcebook, 2003; The State of Democratic Theory, 2003; (ed. with R. Grant and J. Dunn and contrib.) Two Treatises of Government and A Letter Concerning Toleration, 2003; (ed. with R.M. Smith and T.E. Masoud) Problems and Methods in the Study of Politics, 2004; The Flight from Reality in the Human Sciences, 2005; (with M.J. Graetz) Death by a Thousand Cuts: The Fight over Taxing Inherited Wealth, 2005; (ed. with S. Skowronek and D. Galvin) Rethinking Political Institutions: The Art of the State, 2006; (ed. with S. Bedi) Political Contingency: Studying the Unexpected, the Accidental, and the Unforeseen, 2007; Containment: Rebuilding a Strategy against Global Terror, 2007; (ed. with S. Benhabib and D. Petranovic) Identities, Affiliations, and Allegiances, 2007; (ed. with S.N. Kalyvas and T. Masoud) Order, Conflict, and Violence, 2008; (ed. with P.A. Swenson and D. Donno) Divide and Deal: The Politics of Distribution in Democracies, 2008. **Address:** MacMillan Center for Intl and Area Studies, Yale University, 34 Hillhouse Ave., PO Box 208206, New Haven, CT 06520-8206, U.S.A. **Online address:** ian.shapiro@yale.edu

SHAPIRO, Jerrold Lee. American (born United States), b. 1943. **Genres:** Psychology, Sciences, Medicine/Health, Adult Non-fiction. **Career:** St. Bonaventure University, assistant professor, 1969-70; University of Hawaii, assistant professor, professor, 1970-83; Chapman College, visiting associate professor, 1974; licensed clinical psychologist private practice, 1974; University of California-Santa Cruz, visiting professor and counselor, 1978-79; University of California-Los Angeles, visiting professor, 1978-80; California Graduate School of Family Psychology, professor, 1979-87; Santa Clara University, associate professor, 1982-, professor; Ohana Family Therapy Institute, managing partner, 1983-; California School of Professional Psychology, adjunct professor, 1983, 1988-89; University of California-Irvine, visiting professor, 1986; Family Business Solutions, managing partner and chief consultant, 1986-; Pacific Graduate School of Psychology, affiliate clinical faculty and adjunct professor, 1988-95; Wright Institute, adjunct professor, 1992-95; Institute for Transpersonal Psychology, 1992-96; Psyjourn Inc., president, 1994-. Writer. **Publications:** Methods of Group Psychotherapy and Encounter, 1978; (with H.I. Ayabe) Classic Readings in Educational Psychology, 1986; (with B.A. Edmiston and E. Wallace) Handbook of Ethical and Legal Guidelines for MFCC's and Psychologists, 1986; When Men Are Pregnant: Fears and Concerns of Expectant Fathers, 1987; (with A.W. Scheflin) Trance on Trial, 1989; The Measure of a Man: Becoming the Father You Wish Your Father Had Been, 1993; (ed. with M.J. Diamond and M. Greenberg) Becom-

ing a Father: Social, Emotional and Therapeutic Perspectives, 1993; (with S. Bernadett-Shapiro and L. Peltz) Brief Group Treatment, 1997. Contributor to books and periodicals. **Address:** Department of Counseling Psychology, Santa Clara University, Rm. 140 H, 500 El Camino Real, Santa Clara, CA 95053, U.S.A. **Online address:** jshapiro@scu.edu

SHAPIRO, Judith. American (born United States), b. 1953. **Genres:** Intellectual History, Politics/Government, Social Commentary, Adult Non-fiction. **Career:** U.S. Department of State, Chinese interpreter, 1981-; National Endowment for Democracy, senior program officer for Asia, 1992-94; American University, School of International Service, Global Environmental Politics MA Programs, director, Dual Degree in Natural Resources and Sustainable Development, director; New School for Social Research, faculty; University of Pennsylvania, faculty; Villanova University, faculty; University of Aveiro, faculty. Writer. **Publications:** (Co-author) Zui xi Mei yu chang yong shou ce=A Handbook of current Americanisms, 1981; (with J.H. Lennox) Lifechanges: How Women Can Make Courageous Choices, 1990; (ed. with V. Tismaneanu) Debates on the Future of Communism, 1991; (with B. Granville) Russian Inflation: A Statistical Pandora's Box, 1994; Mao's War Against Nature: Politics and the Environment in Revolutionary China, 2001. NONFICTION WITH L. HENG: Ge ming zhi zi, 1983; Son of the Revolution, 1983; Intellectual Freedom in China After Mao with a Focus on 1983, 1984; Intellectual Freedom in China: An Update, 1985; Cold Winds, Warm Winds: Intellectual Life in China Today, 1986; After the Nightmare: A Survivor of the Cultural Revolution Reports on China Today, 1986; After the Nightmare: Inside China Today, 1987. **Address:** Global Environmental Politics MA Programs, School of International Service, American University, Rm. 308, 4400 Massachusetts Ave. NW, Washington, DC 20016-8071, U.S.A. **Online address:** shapiro@american.edu

SHAPIRO, Karen Jo. American (born United States), b. 1964?. **Genres:** Young Adult Non-fiction, Children's Fiction. **Career:** Center for Creative Leadership, adjunct faculty. Psychologist and writer. **Publications:** Because I Could Not Stop My Bike and Other Poems, 2003; I Must Go Down to the Beach Again and Other Poems, 2007. **Address:** Charlesbridge Publishing, 85 Main St., Watertown, MA 02472-4411, U.S.A. **Online address:** kjshapiro@earthlink.net

SHAPIRO, NancyKay. American (born United States) **Genres:** Novels. **Career:** Sudler & Hennessey, copywriter, 1986-88, freelance copywriter, 2006; Lally McFarland & Pantello, copywriter, 1989-90; Kallir, Philips, Ross Inc., copywriter, 1990-92; S.J. Weinstein Associates, copywriter, 1992-93; Robert A. Becker, copy supervisor, 1993-95; Harrison, Star, Wiener, and Beitler, copy supervisor, 1995-2000; Harrison and Star, copy supervisor, 1995-2001; Infranco Moore Group, freelance copywriter, 2001; Draft FCB Healthcare, freelance copywriter, 2001-; Saatchi & Saatchi Healthcare, freelance copywriter, 2001-02; Accel, freelance copywriter, 2001-02; Surge, freelance copywriter, 2001-03; EURO RSCG Life Chelsea, freelance copywriter, 2001-03; FCB Healthcare, freelance copywriter, 2001-07; Grey Healthcare Group, freelance copywriter, 2001-; Draftfcb, freelance copy creative, 2001-08; Juice Pharma, freelance copywriter, 2004-07, freelance copywriter of advertising, 2007-, Juice Pharma Worldwide, freelance copywriter, 2010-; Centron, freelance copywriter, 2007; Brand Pharm, freelance copywriter, 2007; Wishbone, freelance copywriter, 2007; Area 23, freelance copywriter, 2008; Flashpoint Medica, freelance copywriter, 2009; AgencyRX, freelance copywriter, 2009-; Cline Davis & Mann, freelance copywriter, 2009-; GSW NY, freelance copywriter, 2010; Health4Brands, freelance copywriter, 2010-. **Publications:** What Love Means to You People, 2006. **Address:** c/o Author Mail, St. Martin's Press, 175 5th Ave., New York, NY 10010-7703, U.S.A. **Online address:** nk@nancykayshapiro.com

SHAPIRO, Rami M. American (born United States), b. 1951. **Genres:** Theology/Religion, inspirational/Motivational Literature. **Career:** Wright-Patterson Air Force Base, rabbi, 1979-81; Temple Beth Or, founding rabbi, 1981-; One River Foundation, director; Middle Tennessee State University, adjunct professor of religious studies; What Would a Mensch Do?, project, director; Sh'ma Center for Jewish Meditation, director. Writer. **Publications:** (Trans. and ed.) Wisdom of the Jewish Sages: A Modern Reading of Pirke Avot, 1995; Minyan: Ten Principles for Living a Life of Integrity, 1997; The Way of Solomon: Finding Joy and Contentment in the Wisdom of Ecclesiastes, 2000; (trans. and intro.) Proverbs: The Wisdom of Solomon, 2001; (trans.) The Hebrew Prophets: Selections Annotated and Explained, 2004; (trans.) Hasidic Tales: Annotated and Explained, 2004; Open Secrets: The

Letters of Reb Yerachmiel Ben Yisrael, 2004; (with M. Smith) Let Us Break Bread Together: A Passover Haggadah for Christians, 2005; The Divine Feminine in Biblical Wisdom Literature: Selections Annotated and Explained: Translation and Annotation, 2005; The Sacred Art of Lovingkindness: Preparing to Practice, 2006; (trans.) Ethics of the Sages: Pirke Avot-Annotated and Explained, 2006; Recovery-The Sacred Art, 2009; Angelic Way, 2009; (trans.) Ecclesiastes, 2010; (trans.) Tanya, the Masterpiece of Hasidic Wisdom, 2010; Guide to God, 2011. Contributor to books. **Address:** Temple Beth Or, 11715 SW 87th Ave., Miami, FL 33176-4305, U.S.A. **Online address:** rabbirami@gmail.com

SHAPIRO, Robert J. (Robert Jacob Shapiro). American (born United States), b. 1948. **Genres:** Business/Trade/Industry, Law. **Career:** U.S. News & World Report, associate editor, 1986-88; Progressive Policy Institute, co-founder, vice president, 1989-97; private consultant, 1991-97; Progressive Foundation, co-founder and director of economic studies, 1993-97; U.S. Government, under secretary of commerce, 1997-2001; Sonecon LLC, managing director and founding partner, 2001-; Slate.com, economic columnist. **Publications:** (co-author) Globaphobia: Confronting Fears about Open Trade, 1998; (with J.F. Canterbury, Jr.) Texas Construction Law Manual, 2005; Futurecast: How Superpowers, Populations, and Globalization Will Change the Way You Live and Work, 2008. Contributor to journals and periodicals. **Address:** Sonecon L.L.C., 633 Pennsylvania Ave. NW, Ste. 400, Washington, DC 20004-2605, U.S.A. **Online address:** rshapiro@sonecon.com

SHAPIRO, Robert Jacob. See **SHAPIRO, Robert J.**

SHAPIRO, Robert Y. American (born United States), b. 1953. **Genres:** Politics/Government, International Relations/Current Affairs, Social Commentary, Adult Non-fiction. **Career:** Columbia University, Department of Political Science, assistant professor, 1982-87, associate professor of political science, 1987-95, chair, School of International and Public Affairs, faculty, 1991-, professor of political science, 1995-, director of undergraduate studies, Institute for Social and Economic Research and Policy, acting director, 2008-09; University of Chicago, research associate, 1982-87, National Opinion Research Center, director; Roper Center for Public Opinion Research, director; American Association for Public Opinion Research, councilor-at-large. Writer. **Publications:** (With B.I. Page) The Rational Public: Fifty Years of Trends in Americans' Policy Preferences, 1992; (ed. with M.X.D. Carpini and L. Huddy) Research in Micropolitics, vol. IV: New Directions in Political Psychology, 1993; (ed.) Understanding Presidential Elections: Trends and New Developments, 1996; (with L.R. Jacobs) Myths and Misunderstandings About Public Opinion Toward Social Security: Knowledge, Support and Reformism, 1999; (with L.R. Jacobs) Politicians Don't Pander: Political Manipulations and the Loss of Democratic Responsiveness, 2000; (ed. with B.L. Nacos and P. Isernia) Decisionmaking in a Glass House: Mass Media, Public Opinion and American and European Foreign Policy in the Twenty-first Century, 2000; (ed. with M.J. Kumar and L.R. Jacobs) Presidential Power: Forging in the Presidency for the Twenty-first Century, 2000; (ed. with G. González and S. Minushkin) Mexican Public Opinion and Foreign Policy, 2004; (ed.) The Meaning of American Democracy, 2005; (with B.L. Nacos and Y. Bloch-Elkon) Selling Fear: Counterterrorism, The Media and Public Opinion, 2011; (ed. with L.R. Jacobs) The Oxford Handbook of American Public Opinion and the Media, 2011. Works appear in anthologies. Contributor of articles to journals. **Address:** Department of Political Science, Columbia University, 730 International Affairs Bldg., 420 W 118th St., PO Box 3320, New York, NY 10027, U.S.A. **Online address:** rys3@columbia.edu

SHAPIRO, Rochelle Jewel. American (born United States), b. 1947. **Genres:** Novels. **Career:** Writer. **Publications:** Miriam the Medium, 2004. Contributor to periodicals. **Address:** c/o Author Mail, Simon & Schuster Inc., 1230 Ave. of the Americas, PO Box 524, New York, NY 10020, U.S.A. **Online address:** rochelle@miriamthemedium.com

SHAPIRO, Sidney. Chinese/American (born United States), b. 1915. **Genres:** History, Biography, Law, International Relations/Current Affairs, Autobiography/Memoirs, Translations, Social Sciences. **Career:** Shapiro & Shapiro, law partner, 1939-41; H.D. Rodger, law partner, 1947-48; Foreign Languages Press, literary translator, 1953-80. Author. **Publications:** An American in China: Thirty Years in the People's Republic, 1979; (trans.) S. Nai'an, L. Guanzhong, Outlaws of the Marsh, 1980; Experiment in Sichuan: A Report on Economic Reform, 1981; (trans.) D. Pengcheng, Defend Yanan, 1983; (ed., comp. and trans.) Jews in Old China: Studies by Chinese Scholars,

1984; (trans.) Bene-Yiśra el be-Sin ha-atiḳah: Asupat Ma'Amarim Siniyim, 1987; (trans. with W. Mingjie) Selected Works of Ba Jin, 1988, 2nd ed., 2005; The Law and the Lore of Chinese Criminal Justice, 1990; Ma Haide: The Saga of American Doctor George Hatem in China (biography), 1993; (trans.) A Sampler of Chinese Literature from the Ming Dynasty to Mao Zedong, 1996; My China: The Metamorphosis of a Country anda Man (autobiography), 1996, 2nd ed., 1999; I Chose China: The Metamorphosis of a Country and a Man, 2000; (trans.) M. Dun, Lin jia pu zi: Chuncan, 2001; (co-trans.) Zhongguo xian dai ming jia duan pian xiao shuo xuan, 2002; (trans.) Shui hu Zhuan, 2003; Zhongguo gu dai Youtai ren, 2008. **Address:** 53 Nanguanfang, Beijing, 100009, China.

SHAPIRO, Susan. American (born United States), b. 1961?. **Genres:** Human Relations/Parenting, Young Adult Fiction. **Career:** New York University, lecturer; New School, lecturer. Journalist. **Publications:** The Male-to-Female Dictionary: The Handy Guide to the Babble of the Sexes, 1996; Internal Medicine, 1997; (ed. with E. Maxwell) Food for the Soul: Selections from the Holy Apostles Soup Kitchen Writers' Workshop, 2004; Five Men Who Broke My Heart: A Memoir, 2004; Lighting Up: How I Stopped Smoking, Drinking, and Everything Else I Loved in Life Except Sex, 2005; Only as Good as Your Word: Writing Lessons from My Favorite Literary Gurus, 2007; Secrets of a Fix-Up Fanatic: How to Meet & Marry Your Match, 2007; Speed Shrinking, 2009; Overexposed, 2010. Contributor to periodicals. **Address:** c/o Ryan Fischer-Harbage, Fischer-Harbage Agency, 115 W 29th St., 3rd Fl., New York, NY 10001-5080, U.S.A. **Online address:** profsue123@aol.com

SHAPIRO, Tricia. See **ANDRYSZEWSKI, Tricia.**

SHARKANSKY, Ira. Israeli/American (born United States), b. 1938. **Genres:** Economics, Politics/Government. **Career:** Ball State University, assistant professor of political science, 1964-65; Florida State University, assistant professor, 1965-66; University of Georgia, assistant professor, 1966-68; University of North Carolina, visiting professor, 1967; University of Wisconsin, associate professor, 1968-71; professor of political science, 1971-75; University of Nairobi, research associate, 1972; Brigham Young University, visiting professor, 1987-88; University of Utah, visiting professor, 1993-94; Hebrew University of Jerusalem, professor of political science, 1975-95, professor emeritus, 1995-. Writer. **Publications:** Spending in the American States, 1968; Politics of Taxing and Spending, 1969; Regionalism in American Politics, 1969; The Routines of Politics, 1970; Public Administration: Policy-Making in Government Agencies, 1970, 4th ed., 1978; Policy Analysis in Political Sciences, 1970; Public Administration; Policy-Making in Government Agencies, 1970, 4th ed., 1978; (ed. with R.I. Hofferbert) State and Urban Politics: Readings in Comparative Public Policy, 1971; (with R.L. Lineberry) Urban Politics and Public Policy, 1971, 3rd ed., 1978; The Maligned States: Policy Accomplishments, Problems and Opportunities, 1972, 2nd ed., 1978; (with D.V. Meter) Policy and Politics in American Governments, 1975; The United States: A Study of a Developing Country, 1975; (with G.C. Edwards) The Policy Predicament: Making and Implementing Public Policy, 1978; Wither the State?: Politics and Public Enterprise in Three Countries, 1979; Public Administration: Agencies, Policies and Politics, 1982; United States Revisited: A Study of a Still Developing Country, 1982; (with D.J. Elazar) Alternative Federal Solutions to the Problem of the Administered Territories, 1984; What Makes Israel Tick?: How Domestic Policy-Makers Cope with Constraints, 1985; The Political Economy of Israel, 1987; Ancient and Modern Israel: An Exploration of Political Parallels, 1991; Israel and Its Bible: A Political Analysis, 1996; Governing Jerusalem: Again on the World's Agenda, 1996; Rituals of Conflict: Religion, Politics and Public Policy in Israel, 1996; Policy Making in Israel: Routines for Simple Problems and Coping with the Complex, 1997; Ambiguity, Coping and Governance: Israeli Experiences in Politics, Religion and Policy Making, 1999; The Politics of Religion and the Religion of Politics: Looking at Israel, 2000; Politics and Policymaking: In Search of Simplicity, 2002; Coping with Terror: An Israeli Perspective, 2003; Governing Israel: Chosen People, Promised Land & Prophetic Tradition, 2005; (with G. Auerbach) Politics and planning in the Holy City, 2007. Contributor to journals. **Address:** Department of Political Science, Hebrew University of Jerusalem, Jerusalem, 91905, Israel. **Online address:** msira@mscc.huji.ac.il

SHARLET, Jeff. American (born United States), b. 1972?. **Genres:** Theology/Religion, History, Politics/Government, Social Sciences. **Career:** Killing the Buddha, founder and editor, 2000-; Harper's Magazine, contributing editor; Rolling Stone Magazine, contributing editor; The Revealer, editor; Religion Dispatches, books columnist; Pakn Treger, editor-in-chief; Chronicle of Higher Education, senior writer; New York University, faculty; Dartmouth College, Department of English, Mellon assistant professor. **Publications:** (With P. Manseau) Killing the Buddha: A Heretic's Bible, 2004; The Family: The Secret Fundamentalism at the Heart of American Power, 2008; (co-ed.) Believer, Beware: First Person Dispatches from the Margins of Faith, 2009; C Street: The Fundamentalist Threat to American Democracy, 2010; Sweet Heaven when I Die: Faith, Faithlessness and The Country in Between, 2011; The Hammer Song, 2012. **Address:** Department of English, Dartmouth College, 15 Sanborn House, Hanover, NH 03755, U.S.A. **Online address:** jeffsharlet@dartmouth.edu

SHARMA, Arvind. Canadian/Indian (born India), b. 1940. **Genres:** Theology/Religion. **Career:** Gujarat Industrial Development Corp., Indian Administrative Service, managing director, district development officer, 1962-68; Northeastern University, instructor in economics and statistics, 1972-76, instructor in Buddhism, Hinduism, mysticism and the great Western traditions, 1974-75; University of Queensland, lecturer in religious studies, 1976-80; Journal of South Asian Literature, associate editor, 1977-; Australian Association for the Study of Religions, vice president, 1978-79; University of Sydney, lecturer, 1980-86, senior lecturer in religious studies, 1986-87; McGill University, visiting associate professor, 1983-84, associate professor, 1987-89, professor of religious studies, 1989-, Birks professor of comparative religion, 1994-; Temple University, visiting assistant professor, 1982-83; Concordia University, visiting lecturer, 1989; R. M. Bucke Memorial Society for the Study of Religious Experience, president, 1990-91; University of California, lecturer, 1990; John F. Kennedy School of Government, fellow, 1995-96, lecturer, 1996; G.B. Pant Institute of Social Science Research, visiting lecturer, 1996. Writer. **Publications:** Visistadvaita Vedanta: A Study, 1978; Thresholds in Hindu-Buddhist Studies, 1979; The Hindu Scriptural Value System and the Economic Development of India, 1980; Textual Studies in Hinduism, 1980; (with H.W. French) Religious Ferment in Modern India, 1981; The Purusarthas: A Study in Hindu Axiology, Asian Studies Center, 1982; The Gitarthasangraha of Abhinavagupta, 1982; Studies in Alberuni's India, 1982; Spokes of the Wheel: Studies in Buddha's Dhamma, 1985; The Hindu Gita: Its Ancient and Classical Interpretations, 1986; (comp.) New Essays in the Bhagavad-Gita, 1987; (with K.K. Young, A. Ray and A. Hejib) Sati: Historical and Phenomenological Essays, 1988; Ramakrishna and Vivekananda: New Perspectives, 1989; A Hindu Perspective on the Philosophy of Religion, 1990; The Experiential Dimension of Advaita Vedanta, 1993; (with S.J. Palmer) The Rajneesh Papers: Studies in a New Religious Movement, 1993; The Philosophy of Religion and Advaita Vedanta, 1995; The Philosophy of Religion: A Buddhist Perspective, 1995; Hinduism for Our Times, 1996; Classical Hindu Thought: An Introduction, 2001; Her Voice, Her Faith: Women Speak on World Religions, 2002; Hinduism and Its Sense of History, 2003; The Study of Hinduism, 2003; Sleep as a State of Consciousness in Advaita Vedánta, 2004; Hinduism and Human Rights: A Conceptual Approach, 2004; Reservation and Affirmative Action: Models of Social Integration in India and the United States, 2005; A New Curve in the Ganges, 2005; Religious Studies and Comparative Methodology: The Case for Reciprocal Illumination, 2005; New Focus on Hindu Studies, 2005; Modern Hindu Thought, 2005; Goddesses and Women in the Indic Religious Tradition, 2005; Dharma, the Categorial Imperative, 2005; The World as Dream, 2006; Sea-shell as Silver: A Metaphorical Excursion into Advaita Vedánta, 2006; Ramana Maharshi: The Sage of Arunachala, 2006; A Primal Perspective on the Philosophy of Religion, 2006; A Guide to Hindu Spirituality, 2006; Are Human Rights Western? A Contribution to the Dialogue of Civilizations, 2006; The Philosophy of Religion: A Sikh Perspective, 2007; Fundamentalism and Women in World Religions, 2007; Christianity and Human Rights: Influences and Issues, 2007; (with R. Panikkar) Human Rights as a Western Concept, 2007; Islam for Hindus, 2009; World's Religions: a Contemporary Reader, 2010; One Religion Too Many: the Religiously Comparative Reflections of a Comparatively Religious Hindu, 2010; Hinduism as a Missionary Religion, 2010; Hindu Narratives on Human Rights, 2010; Christianity for Hindus, 2010. EDITOR: (co-ed.) Vignettes of Vrindavan, 1987; Women in World Religions, 1987; Neo-Hindu Views of Christianity, 1988; Essays on the Mahabharata, 1991; Fragments of Infinity: Essays in Religion and Philosophy, 1991; (with Young) The Annual Review of Women in World Religions, vol. I, 1991, vol. II, 1992, vol. III, 1993; Perspectives on History and Culture: Essays in Honour of D.P. Singhal (1925-1986), 1992; Our Religions, 1993; God, Truth and Reality: Essays in Honour of John Hick, 1993; Today's Woman in World Religions, 1994; Religion and Women, 1994; The Little Clay Cart: An English Translation of the Mrcchakatika of Sudraka as Adapted for the Stage, 1994; Feminism and

World Religions, 1998; Women Saints in World Religions, 2000; Hinduism and Secularism: After Ayodhya, Palgrave, 2001; Religion in a Secular City, 2001; Methodology in Religious Studies: The Interface with Women's Studies, 2002; Part of the Problem, Part of the Solution: Religion Today and Tomorrow, 2008; (with R. Sharma) Hermeneutics and Hindu Thought: Toward a Fusion of Horizons, 2008; Why I am a Believer: Personal Reflections on Nine World Religions, 2009; World's Religions After September 11, 2009; Problematizing Religious Freedom, 2011; Contributor of articles to books and periodicals. **Address:** Faculty of Religious Studies, McGill University, 3520 University St., Birks Bldg., Montreal, QC H3A 2A7, Canada. **Online address:** arvind.sharma@mcgill.ca

SHARMA, Nandita. American (born United States), b. 1964?. **Genres:** Economics, Politics/Government. **Career:** Simon Fraser University, research assistant, 1991, 1992, 1994-95; Capilano College, Department of Women's Studies, instructor, 1999-2001; Direct Action Against Refugee Exploitation, principal investigator, 2000; University of British Columbia, Department of Anthropology and Sociology, post-doctoral research fellow, 2000-02; International Council for Canadian Studies, researcher, 2001-03; University of British Columbia, assistant professor, 2003-04; York University, assistant professor, 2004-06; York University, Atkinson School of Social Sciences, assistant professor, 2004-06; Center for Refugee Studies, affiliate faculty, 2005-; University of Hawaii, Department of Sociology, assistant professor, 2006-08, associate professor, 2011-; Open the Borders! (activist group), co-founder. Writer. **Publications:** (Ed.) The National Action Committee on the Status of Women's Voters' Guide: A Women's Agenda for Social Justice, 1997; Home Economics: Nationalism and the Making of Migrant Workers in Canada, 2006. Contributor to periodicals. **Address:** Department of Sociology, University of Hawaii, Rm. 247, Saunders Hall, 2424 Maile Way, Honolulu, HI 96822-2287, U.S.A. **Online address:** nsharma@hawaii.edu

SHARMA, Poonam. American (born United States), b. 1977. **Genres:** Business/Trade/Industry, Economics, Young Adult Fiction, Young Adult Non-fiction. **Career:** Writer and real estate developer. **Publications:** The Harvard Entrepreneurs Club Guide to Starting Your Own Business, 1999; Chasing Success: Lessons We Can Learn from the Lives of Harvards Entrepreneurs, 2004; Girl Most Likely To, 2007; All Eyes on Her, 2008. **Address:** Red Dress Ink, PO Box 5190, Buffalo, NY 14240-5190, U.S.A.

SHARMAN, Cheryl Harris. American (born United States), b. 1972?. **Genres:** Young Adult Non-fiction. **Career:** Writer and researcher. **Publications:** (With R.L. Sharman) Nightshift NYC, 2008. Contributor of articles to periodicals and journals. **Address:** U.S.A. **Online address:** chs@cherylharrissharman.com

SHARMAN, Russell Leigh. American (born United States), b. 1972. **Genres:** Young Adult Non-fiction, History, Politics/Government. **Career:** Fordham University, adjunct assistant professor, 1999-2001; State University of New York, Purchase College, adjunct assistant professor, 1999-2001; City University of New York, adjunct assistant professor, 1999-2001; Brooklyn College, assistant professor, 2002-07, associate professor, 2007-. Writer. **Publications:** The Tenants of East Harlem, 2006; (with C.H. Sharman) Nightshift NYC, 2008. Contributor of articles to books and journals. **Address:** Department of Anthropology, Brooklyn College, 2900 Bedford Ave., Brooklyn, NY 11210, U.S.A. **Online address:** rsharman@brooklyn.cuny.edu

SHARMAT, Marjorie Weinman. (Wendy Andrews). American (born United States), b. 1928. **Genres:** Novels, Novellas/Short Stories, Mystery/Crime/Suspense, Children's Fiction, Picture/Board Books, Humor/Satire, Young Adult Fiction, Romance/Historical, Romance/Historical. **Career:** Writer, 1967-. **Publications:** Rex, 1967; Goodnight, Andrew Goodnight, Craig, 1969; Gladys Told Me to Meet Her Here, 1970; Hot Thirsty Day, 1971; 51 Sycamore Lane, 1971; Getting Something on Maggie Marmelstein, 1971; A Visit with Rosalind, 1971; Sophie and Gussie, 1973; Morris Brookside, A Dog, 1973; Morris Brookside Is Missing, 1974; I Want Mama, 1974; I'm Not Oscar's Friend Anymore, 1975; Walter the Wolf, 1975; Maggie Marmelstein for President, 1975; Burton and Dudley, 1975; The Lancelot Closes at Five, 1976; The Trip and Other Sophie and Gussie Stories, 1976; Mooch the Messy, 1976; Edgemont, 1977; I'm Terrific, 1977; I Don't Care, 1977; (co-author) Just for Fun, 1977; A Big Fat Enormous Lie, 1978; Thornton the Worrier, 1978; Mitchell Is Moving, 1978; Mooch the Messy Meets Prudence the Neat, 1978; Scarlet Monster Lives Here, 1979; Mr. Jameson and Mr. Phillips, 1979; Uncle Boris and Maude, 1979; The 329th Friend, 1979; (with M. Sharmat) I

Am Not a Pest, 1979; Octavia Told Me a Secret, 1979; Say Hello, Vanessa, 1979; Griselda's New Year, 1979; The Trolls of Twelfth Street, 1979; Little Devil Gets Sick, 1980; What Are We Going to Do about Andrew?, 1980; Sometimes Mama and Papa Fight, 1980; Taking Care of Melvin, 1980; Gila Monsters Meet You at the Airport, 1980; Grumley the Grouch, 1980; (with M. Sharmat) The Day I Was Born, 1980; Twitchell the Wishful, 1981; Chasing after Annie, 1981; Rollo and Juliet, Forever! 1981; The Sign, 1981; Lucretia the Unbearable, 1981; The Best Valentine in the World!, 1982; Two Ghosts on a Bench, 1982; Mysteriously Yours, Maggie Marmelstein, 1982; Frizzy the Fearful, 1983; I Saw Him First, 1983; How to Meet a Gorgeous Guy, 1983; Rich Mitch, 1983; The Story of Bently Beaver, 1984; (co-author) Sixteen, 1984; Bartholomew the Bossy, 1984; How to Meet a Gorgeous Girl, 1984; Sasha the Silly, 1984; He Noticed I'm Alive and Other Hopeful Signs, 1984; My Mother Never Listens to Me, 1984; Two Guys Noticed Me and Other Miracles, 1985; Attila the Angry, 1985; How to Have a Gorgeous Wedding, 1985; Get Rich Mitch!, 1985; The Son of the Slime Who Ate Cleveland, 1985; One Terrific Thanksgiving, 1985; Helga High-Up, 1986; Hooray for Mother's Day!, 1986; Who's Afraid of Ernestine?, 1986; Fighting over Me, 1986; Marjorie Sharmat's Sorority Sisters, 8 vols., 1986-87; Hooray for Father's Day!, 1987; (co-author) Visions, 1987; Go to Sleep, Nicholas Joe, 1987; (with M. Sharmat) Surprises, 1989; (with M. Sharmat) Treasures, 1989; (with M. Sharmat) Kingdoms, 1989; (with M. Sharmat) Olivia Sharp, Agent for Secrets, 4 vols., 1989-91; (with A. Sharmat) The Kids on the Bus, 6 vols., 1990-91; I'm Santa Claus and I'm Famous, 1990; I'm the Best!, 1991; (co-author) Funny You Should Ask, 1992; The Great Genghis Khan Look-Alike Contest, 1993; Genghis Khan: A Dog Star is Born, 1994; Genghis Khan: Doggone Hollywood, 1995; The Perfects, 1995; Tiffany Dino Works Out, 1995; Richie and the Fritzes, 1997; Dirty Tricks, 2000; Hollywood Hound, 2000. AS WENDY ANDREWS: Vacation Fever!, 1984; Supergirl, 1984; Are We There Yet?, 1985. NATE SERIES: Nate the Great, 1972, new ed., 2010; Nate the Great Goes Undercover, 1974, new ed., 2010; Nate the Great and the Lost List, 1975, new ed., 2010; Nate the Great and the Phony Clue, 1977, new ed., 2010; Nate the Great and the Sticky Case, 1978, new ed., 2006; Nate the Great and the Missing Key, 1981, new ed., 2007; Nate the Great and the Snowy Trail, 1982; Nate the Great And The Fishy Prize, 1985; Nate the Great Stalks Stupidweed, 1986, new ed., 2005; Nate the Great and the Boring Beach Bag, 1987, new ed., 2005; Nate the Great and the Halloween Hunt, 1989; Nate the Great Goes Down in the Dumps, 1989; (with C. Sharmat) Nate the Great and the Musical Note, 1990; Nate the Great and the Stolen Base, 1992, new ed., 2006; (with R. Weinman) Nate the Great and the Pillowcase, 1993; Nate the Great and the Mushy Valentine, 1994; (with C. Sharmat) Nate the Great and the Tardy Tortoise, 1995, new ed., 2005; (with C. Sharmat) Nate the Great and the Crunchy Christmas, 1996; Nate the Great Saves the King of Sweden, 1997; Nate the Great and Me: The Case of the Fleeing Fang, 1998; Nate the Great and the Monster Mess, 1999; (with M. Sharmat) Nate the Great, San Francisco Detective, 2000; (with M. Sharmat) Nate the Great and the Big Sniff, 2001; (with M. Sharmat) Nate the Great on the Owl Express, 2003; (with M. Sharmat) Nate the Great Talks Turkey, 2006; (with M. Sharmat) Nate the Great and the Hungry Book Club, 2009. OLIVIA SHARP, AGENT FOR SECRETS SERIES WITH M. SHARMAT: The Pizza Monster, 1989, 2nd ed., 2005; The Princess of the Fillmore Street School, 1989; The Sly Spy, 1990; The Green Toenails Gang, 1991, 2nd ed., 2005. THE KIDS ON THE BUS SERIES WITH A. SHARMAT: School Bus Cat, 1990; The Cooking Class, 1991; The Haunted Bus, 1991; Bully on the Bus, 1991; The Secret Notebook, 1991; The Field Day Mix-up, 1991. SORORITY SISTERS SERIES: For Members Only, 1986; Snobs, Beware, 1986; I Think I'm Falling in Love, 1986; Nobody Knows How Scared I Am, 1987; Here Comes Mr. Right, 1987; Getting Closer, 1987; I'm Going to Get Your Boyfriend, 1987. Works appear in anthologies. Contributor to magazines and newspapers. **Address:** Harold Ober Associates Inc., 425 Madison Ave., New York, NY 10017-1110, U.S.A.

SHAROT, Stephen. Israeli/British (born England), b. 1943. **Genres:** Sociology, Film. **Career:** University of Leicester, Department of Sociology, lecturer, 1970-74; Hebrew University of Jerusalem, Department of Sociology, lecturer, 1974-76, senior lecturer, 1976-79; The University of North Carolina, Department of Sociology, visiting associate professor, 1979-80; Ben-Gurion University of the Negev, Department of Behavioral Sciences, senior lecturer, 1980-84, associate professor, 1985-90, professor, 1990-2010, chair, 2000-03, professor emeritus, 2010-; State University of New York, Department of Sociology, visiting associate professor, 1984-85. Writer. **Publications:** Modern Judaism: A Sociology, 1976; Messianism, Mysticism and Magic: A Sociological Analysis of Jewish Religious Movements, 1982; (with E. Ben-Rafael) Ethnic-

ity, Religion and Class in Israeli Society, 1991; A Comparative Sociology of World Religions: Virtuosi, Priests and Popular Religion, 2001; Comparative Perspectives on Judaisms and Jewish Identities, 2011. **Address:** Department of Sociology & Anthropology, Ben-Gurion University of the Negev, PO Box 653, Beer Sheva, 84105, Israel. **Online address:** sharot@netvision.net.il

SHARP, Anne Wallace. American (born United States), b. 1947. **Genres:** Children's Non-fiction, Biography, Education. **Career:** Nurse, 1979-96; freelance journalist and author, 1994-. **Publications:** FOR CHILDREN: Daring Pirate Women, 2002; The Inuit, 2002; The Blackfeet, 2002; Australia, 2003; Pacific Islands, 2003; The Gypsies, 2003; Caribbean, 2003; The Amazon, 2004; Women of Ancient Egypt, 2005; Palestinians, 2005; Dream Deferred: The Jim Crow Era, 2005; Separate But Equal: The Desegregation of America's Schools, 2006; Condoleezza Rice, 2008; Nancy Lopez: Golf Hall of Famer, 2008; LeBron James, 2008; Coretta Scott King, 2009; Right to Die, 2009; Malcolm X and Black Pride, 2010; Ice Hockey, 2011; (and ed.) Sports Violence, 2011. OTHER: (with S.H. Terbay) Gifts: Two Hospice Professionals Reveal Messages from Those Passing On (inspirational), 1997. **Address:** 1867 N Longview St., Beavercreek, OH 45432, U.S.A. **Online address:** annebudd@aol.com

SHARP, Deborah. American (born United States), b. 1954. **Genres:** Novels. **Career:** News-Press, reporter, 1982; USA Today, reporter; Gannett News Service, staff. **Publications:** MACE BAUER MYSTERY NOVELS: Mama Does Time, 2008; Mama Rides Shotgun, 2009; Mama Gets Hitched, 2010. **Address:** c/o Whitney Lee, Fielding Agency L.L.C., 269 S Beverly Dr., Ste. 341, Beverly Hills, CA 90212, U.S.A.

SHARP, Luke. See **ALKIVIADES, Alkis.**

SHARPE, Graham. British (born England), b. 1950?. **Genres:** Sports/Fitness, History, Humor/Satire. **Career:** The William Hill Press, media relations director. Writer. **Publications:** Rare Stakes, 1986; Sporting Life Book of Amazing Bets, 1988; Turf Accounts, 1990; The World's Best Gambling Jokes, 1992; William Hill's Horse Racing Quiz Books, 1992; William Hill's Racing Data, 1993; William Hill's Book of Racing Quotations, 1994; William Hill's Book of Bizarre Bets, 1994; The Essential Gambler, 1995; Odds, Sods and Racing Certs: Horse Laughs, Winning One-Liners & Off-Beat Tales of the Turf, 1996; Gambling on Goals: A Century of Football Betting, 1997; 14 Million to One, 1998; Bizarre Book of Football, 2000; The Magnificent Seven, 2001; The Final Whistle, 2001; Free the Manchester United One, 2003; The Man Who was Screaming Lord Sutch, 2005; Gambling's Strangest Moments: Extraordinary but True Tales of Foolish Flutters and Preposterous Punts, 2005; The Magnificent Seven: Seven Winners in a Day: How Frankie Dettori Achieved the Impossible, 2006; What Are the Odds?: The Odds on Everything Book, 2006; Poker's Strangest Hands, 2007; (ed.) Essential Poker, 2007; 500 Strangest Racing Stories, 2007; A Gentleman's Guide to Calculating Winning Bets, 2007; 1001 Great Gambling Tips, 2008. **Address:** William Hill Organization Ltd., Greenside House, 50 Station Rd., Wood Green, London, GL N22 7TP, England. **Online address:** gsharpe@williamhill.co.uk

SHARPE, Isabel. See **SILL, Isabel Shehadi.**

SHARPE, Kevin. British (born England), b. 1949. **Genres:** Literary Criticism And History, History, Art/Art History, Humanities. **Career:** Oxford University, Oriel College, research fellow, 1974-78, Christ Church, lecturer, 1976-78; University of Southampton, lecturer, 1978-88, senior lecturer, 1988-89, reader, professor of early modern history, 1989-94, professor of history and director of research, 1994-2001; University of Warwick, professor of Renaissance studies, 2001-; BBC World Service, presenter and adviser for TV programs; Huntington Library, Fletcher Jones research professor, 2001-02; California Institute of Technology, Mellon professor, 2001-02; Queen Mary University of London, Leverhulme research professor, professor of renaissance studies and director, 2005; Princeton university, visiting professor; Stanford university, visiting professor; The California Institute of Technology, visiting professor; The Australian National University, visiting professor; The Max Planck Institute, visiting professor. Writer. **Publications:** Sir Robert Cotton, 1586-1631: History and Politics in Early Modern England, 1979; Criticism and Compliment: The Politics of Literature in the England of Charles I, 1987; Politics and Ideas in Early Stuart England: Essays and Studies, 1989; The Personal Rule of Charles I, 1992; Remapping Early Modern England: The Politics of Reading in Early Modern England, 2000; Reading Revolutions: The Politics of Reading in Early Modern England, 2000; Selling the Tudor Monarchy: Authority and Image in Sixteenth-century England, 2009; Image Wars: Promoting Kings and Commonwealths in England, 1603-1660, 2010. EDITOR: Faction and Parliament: Essays on Early Stuart History, 1978; (with S.N. Zwicker) The Politics of Discourse: The Literature and History of Seventeenth-Century England, 1987; (with P. Lake) Culture and Politics in Early Stuart England, 1993; (with S.N. Zwicker) Refiguring Revolutions: Aesthetics and Politics from the English Revolution to the Romantic Revolution, 1998; (with S. Zwicker) Reading, Society, and Politics in Early Modern England, 2003; (with S. Zwicker) Writing Lives: Biography and Textuality, Identity and Representation in Early Modern England, 2008. **Address:** Department of English, Queen Mary University of London, Mile End Rd., London, GL E1 4NS, England. **Online address:** k.m.sharpe@qmul.ac.uk

SHARPE, Myron E(manuel). American (born United States), b. 1928. **Genres:** Economics, Business/Trade/Industry, Sociology. **Career:** Modern Factors Corp., president, 1957; M.E. Sharpe Inc. (publisher), president, 1959-; Social Policy, co-founder and publisher, 1970-72; M.E. Sharpe Ltd. (arts and antiques), president, 1981-83; Economic Policy Center, co-founder and chair, 1982-; Pro Arte Chamber Singers of Connecticut, chairman, 1982-83; Waveny Chamber Music Society, vice president, 1982-87, president, 1987-98. Writer. **Publications:** (Ed.) Problems of Economics, 1958-60; (ed.) Soviet Review, 1960-67; (ed.) The Liberman Discussion: A New Phase in Soviet Economic Thought, 1966; (ed.) Reform of Soviet Economic Management, 1966; (ed.) Planning, Profit and Incentives in the USSR, 1966; John Kenneth Galbraith and the Lower Economics, 1973, 2nd ed., 1974; (intro.) The Challenge of Economics: Readings from Challenge Magazine, 1977; Thou Shalt Not Kill Unless Otherwise Instructed: Poems and Stories, 2005. Contributor to periodicals. **Address:** M. E. Sharpe Inc., 80 Business Park Dr., Armonk, NY 10504, U.S.A.

SHARPE, Tony. British/American (born United States), b. 1952?. **Genres:** Biography, Literary Criticism And History, Autobiography/Memoirs. **Career:** Lancaster University, County College, Department of English and Creative Writing, senior lecturer, head. Writer. **Publications:** T.S. Eliot: A Literary Life, 1991; Vladimir Nabokov, 1991; Wallace Stevens: A Literary Life, 2000; W.H. Auden, 2007. Contributor to books and periodicals. **Address:** Department of English and Creative Writing, County College, Lancaster University, B97 County, Lancaster, ES LA1 4YD, England. **Online address:** a.sharpe@lancaster.ac.uk

SHARPE, William Chapman. American (born United States), b. 1951. **Genres:** Literary Criticism And History, Urban Studies. **Career:** Edinburgh Tutorial College, lecturer, 1978-79; Columbia University, postdoctoral fellow in humanities, 1981-83; University of Nice, Fulbright lecturer, 1983-84; Columbia University, Barnard College, faculty, 1983-, assistant professor, 1984-92, associate professor of English, 1992-97, professor of English and American studies, 1997-. Writer. **Publications:** Unreal Cities: Urban Figuration in Wordsworth, Baudelaire, Whitman, Eliot, and Williams, 1990. EDITOR AND AUTHOR OF INTRODUCTION: (with L. Wallock) Visions of the Modern City: Essays in History, Art, and Literature, 1983; (with C. Baswell) The Passing of Arthur: New Essays in Arthurian Tradition, 1988. (contrib. with A. Nemerov) Frederic Remington: The Color of Night, 2003; New York Nocturne: The City After Dark in Art, Literature, and Photography, 2008. **Address:** Department of English, Barnard College, Columbia University, 408A Barnard Hall, 3009 Broadway, New York, NY 10027, U.S.A. **Online address:** wsharpe@barnard.edu

SHARPE, William F(orsyth). American (born United States), b. 1934. **Genres:** Business/Trade/Industry, Economics, Marketing. **Career:** Rand Corp., economist, 1956-61; University of Washington, Department of economics, assistant professor, 1961-63, associate professor, 1963-67, professor, 1967-68; The Journal of Financial and Quantitative Analysis, associate editor, 1966-72; University of California, professor, 1968-70; Management Science, associate editor, 1970-72; The Bell Journal of Economics and Management Science, associate editor, 1970-73; Stanford University, professor, 1970-73, Department of Finance, Timken professor, 1973-89, Timken professor emeritus, 1989-92, professor, 1992-95, STANCO 25 professor, 1995-99, STANCO 25 professor emeritus, 1999-; National Bureau of Economic Research, senior research associate, 1976-77, research associate, 1982-86; American Finance Association, director, 1977-78, vice president, 1979, president, 1980; Western Finance Association, director, 1978-80; Stanford-International Program inInvestment Management, co-director, 1983-85; Sharpe-Russell Research Inc., president, 1986-88; London Graduate School of Business of Manage-

ment Program, co-director, 1986; Academy of Financial Services, board director, 1986-87; William F. Sharpe Associates, president, 1986-92, chairman, 1990-92; Sharpe-Tint Inc., chairman, 1988-90; Stanford Management Co., director, 1993-2001; C-ATS Software, director, 1994-97; Financial Engines Inc., Chairman, 1996-2003, director, 1996-2009; Hong Kong Council on Innovation and Technology, special advisor, 1999-2002; C.M. Capital Corp., director, 1999-; The Mingly Corp., advisor; Stanford Center on Longevity, faculty affiliate, 2008. **Publications:** Mutual Fund Performance; Measurement and Prediction, 1965; (with A.A. Barbour and D.M. Fisk) The NATO Force Planning Cost Model, 1966; Business Finance, 1966; (with N.L. Jacob) Basic: An Introduction to Computer Programming Using the Basic Language, 1967, 3rd ed., 1979; The Economics of Computers, 1969; Portfolio Theory and Capital Markets, 1970; Introduction to Managerial Economics, 1973; Is Financial Analysis Useless?, 1975; (with G.J. Alexander and J.V. Bailey) Investments, 1978, 6th ed., 1999; (ed. with C.M. Cootner) Financial Economics: Essays in Honor of Paul Cootner, 1982; Asset Allocation Tools, 1987; (with G.J. Alexander and J.V. Bailey) Fundamentals of Investments, 1989, 3rd ed., 2001; (co-author) Quantifying the Market Risk Premium Phenomenon for Investment Decision Making, 1990; The Founders of Modern Finance: Their Prize-Winning Concepts and 1990 Nobel Lectures, 1991; Investors And Markets: Portfolio Choices, Asset Prices and Investment Advice, 2007. **Address:** Graduate School of Business, Stanford University, Stanford, CA 94305-5015, U.S.A. **Online address:** wtsharpe@stanford.edu

SHARRATT, Nick. British (born England), b. 1962. **Genres:** Children's Fiction, Illustrations, Children's Non-fiction. **Career:** Children's book illustrator and author. **Publications:** FOR CHILDREN SELF ILLUSTRATED: Monday Run-Day, 1992; The Green Queen, 1992; Look What I Found!, 1992; I Look Like This, 1992; Don't Put Your Finger in the Jelly, Nelly!, 1993; Mrs. Pirate, 1994; Snazzy Aunties, 1994; My Mum and Dad Make Me Laugh in US as My Mom and Dad Make Mc Laugh, 1994; Caveman Dave, 1994; The Pointy-Hatted Princesses, 1994; I Went to the Zoopermarket, 1995; Rocket Countdown, 1995; A Cheese and Tomato Spider, 1996; The Animal Orchestra, 1997; (with S. Tucker) My Day, 1997; (with S. Tucker) My Games, 1997; Come and Play!, 1997; Ketchup on Your Cornflakes?: A Wacky Mix-and Match Book, 1997; What Do I Look Like?, 1998; (with S. Tucker) The Time It Took Tom, 1998; The Best Pop-Up Magic Book Ever!, 1998; Dinosaurs' Day Out, 1998. (with S. Tucker) My Days Out, 1999; Croc with a Clock, 1999; Bear with a Pear, 1999; A Giraffe in a Scarf, 1999; Kangaroo in a Canoc, Campbell, 1999; Turning Points, Hodder, 1999; (with S. Tucker) My Friends, Oxford University, 1999; (with S. Tucker) My Colours, 2000; Buzz Buzz, Bumble Kitty, 2000; Split Ends, 2000; Mouse Moves House, 2000; (with S. Tucker) Cinderella, 2001; (reteller with S. Tucker) Three Little Pigs, 2001; (reteller with S. Tucker) Jack and the Beanstalk, 2002; (reteller with S. Tucker) Little Red Riding Hood, 2002; Once upon a Time, 2002; Shark in the Park, 2002; (with S. Heap) Red Rockets and Rainbow Jelly, 2003; (with G. Andreae) Pants, 2003; Pirate Pete, Walker, 2003 in US as Ahoy, Pirate Pete, 2003; (with S. Tucker) The Three Billy Goats Gruff, 2004; (reteller with S. Tucker) Goldilocks, 2004; (with H. Robinson) Mixed up Fairy Tales, 2005; Muddlewitch on the Farm, 2006; (with K. Gray) You Do!, 2006; (with K. Gray) 006 and a Half, 2007; Foggy, Foggy Forest, 2008. OTHERS: (with N. Sharratt) Eat your Peas, 2006; What's in the Witch's Kitchen?, 2011. Illustrator of books by others. **Address:** David Higham Associates, 5-8 Lower John St., Golden Sq., London, GL W1F 9HA, England.

SHASHA, Dennis (E.). American (born United States), b. 1955. **Genres:** Information Science/Computers, Mathematics/Statistics, Biography, Biology, Physics. **Career:** IBM Data Systems Division, hardware and microcode design of arithmetic, interrupt and processor-to-channel communication for the IBM 3090 central processor, 1977-80; New York University, assistant professor, 1984-90, associate professor of computer science, 1990-95, professor of computer science, 1995-; Courant Institute of Mathematical Sciences, assistant professor of computer science, 1984-90, associate professor of computer science, 1990-95, professor of computer science, 1995-; Bell Laboratories and Unix System Laboratories, Bell Communication Research, Union Bank of Switzerland American Telephone and Telegraph (AT&T), 1987-95; Ellis Island Restoration Commission, technical consultant (pro bono work) for the design of the immigrant database management system, 1987-91; Wall Street Investment Banks, Internet Gaming and Biotech, database tuning and design consulting, 1991-; Marble Associates Inc., staff, 1993-; Lucent Bell Laboratories and Bell Communication Research, database research collaboration, 1995-2000. Writer. **Publications:** The Puzzling Adventures of Dr. Ecco, 1988; Codes, Puzzles, and Conspiracy, 1992; Database Tuning: A Principled

Approach, 1992; (ed. with C. Beeri and A. Ohori) Database Programming Languages (DBPL-4): Proceedings of the Fourth International Workshop on Database Programming Languages, 1994; (with C. Lazere) Out of Their Minds: The Lives and Discoveries of 15 Great Computer Scientists, 1995; (ed. with J.T.L. Wang and B.A. Shapiro) Pattern Discovery in Bio molecular Data: Tools, Techniques and Applications, 1999; Dr. Ecco's Cyberpuzzles: Thirty-Six Puzzles for Hackers and Other Mathematical Detectives, 2002; (with M. Shron) Red Blues: Voices from the Last Wave of Russian Immigrants, 2002; (with P. Bonnet) Database Tuning: Principles, Experiments, and Troublshooting Techniques, 2003; (with Y. Zhu) High Performance Discovery in Time Series: Techniques and Case Studies, 2004; Dr. Ecco, Mathematical Detective, 2004; Puzzling Adventures: Tales of Strategy, Logic and Mathematical Skill, 2005; The Puzzler's Elusion: A Tale of Fraud, Pursuit, and the Art of Logic, 2006; Puzzles for Programmers and Pros, 2007; (with T. Morad and R. Shasha, eds.) Iraq's Last Jews: Stories of Daily Life, Upheaval and Escape from Modern Babylon, 2008; (with M. Wilson) Statistics is Easy!, 2009; (with C. Lazere) Natural Computing: DNA, Quantum Bits and The Future of Smart Machines, 2010. **Address:** Courant Institute of Mathematical Sciences, New York University, 251 Mercer St., New York, NY 10012, U.S.A. **Online address:** shasha@cs.nyu.edu

SHATTUCK, George C. American (born United States), b. 1927. **Genres:** Novels, Law, Literary Criticism And History. **Career:** Bond, Schoeneck & King (law firm), partner, 1954-94, retired. Writer. **Publications:** The Oneida Land Claims: A Legal History, 1991; Business Succession Planning, 1992; Estate Planning for the Small Business Owner, 1993; Letters to Room Five, 2001. **Address:** c/o B. K. Nelson, B. K. Nelson Literary Agency, 84 Woodland Rd., Pleasantville, NY 10570, U.S.A.

SHATZKY, Joel. American (born United States), b. 1943. **Genres:** Literary Criticism And History, Novels, Children's Fiction, Young Adult Fiction, Autobiography/Memoirs, Theology/Religion. **Career:** State University of New York College, professor of English, 1968-2005, professor emeritus, 2005-; Kingsborough Community College, adjunct instructor in English and writing, 2006-. Writer. **Publications:** (With D. Shatzky) Facing Multiple Sclerosis: Our Longest Journey (memoir), 1999; Iago's Tale, 2002; Well of Evil, 2004; Option Three, 2005; (with J. Napoli) Eternal Duet: The Story of Robert and Clara Schumann, 2005; Intelligent Design: A Fable, 2007; WAM, 2008. EDITOR: (with R. Ives and D. Rauch) Theresienstadt: Hitler's Gift to the Jews, 1991; (with M. Taub) Contemporary Jewish-American Novelists: A Bio-Critical Sourcebook, 1997; (with M. Taub) Contemporary Jewish-American Dramatists and Poets: A Bio-Critical Source Book, 1999; (with A. Wyman) Protective Custody Prisoner 34042, 2005. **Address:** Department of English, State University of New York College, 113-B Old Main, 4 Graham Ave., PO Box 2000, Cortland, NY 13045-2424, U.S.A. **Online address:** shatzkyj@cortland.edu

SHAUGHNESSY, Brenda. American/Japanese (born Japan), b. 1970. **Genres:** Poetry. **Career:** Lewis Center for the Arts, lecturer in creative writing; New School University, writing teacher. **Publications:** Interior with Sudden Joy, 1999; Human Dark with Sugar, 2008. **Address:** Princeton University, Lewis Center for the Arts, 185 Nassau St., Princeton, NJ 08541, U.S.A. **Online address:** bshaughn@princeton.edu

SHAUGHNESSY, Mary Alice. American (born United States), b. 1951. **Genres:** Biography, Music. **Career:** People, reporter, 1984-. **Publications:** Les Paul: An American Original (biography) 1993. **Address:** 41 Lowell Terr., Bloomfield, NJ 07003-2925, U.S.A.

SHAUL, David Leedom. American (born United States), b. 1952. **Genres:** Adult Non-fiction, Language/Linguistics, History, Literary Criticism And History. **Career:** Dave Shaul Productions, principal; Arizona State Library, Archives and Public Records, librarian and archivist; Institute of Museum and Library Services, librarian and archivist. Writer. **Publications:** (Comp. with R. Albert) A Concise Hopi and English Lexicon, 1985; Topics in Nevome Syntax, 1986; (with N.L. Furbee) Language and Culture, 1998; Hopi Traditional Literature, 2002; Celtic Lullabies, 2003; Celtic Christmas: Sing a Celtic Noël, 2003; The Celtic Year, 2003; (contrib.) Ópatas: In Search of a Sonoran People, 2010; Grammar of Literary Hopi, forthcoming; A Linguistic Prehistory of the American Southwest, forthcoming; Language, Music, and Dance in the Pimeria Alta, 1698-1798, forthcoming. **Address:** Dave Shaul Productions, PO Box 15576, Cheyenne, WY 82003, U.S.A. **Online address:** wyomingharp@yahoo.com

SHAVELSON, Lonny. American (born United States), b. 1952. **Genres:** Adult Non-fiction, Environmental Sciences/Ecology, Photography, Essays, Social Sciences, Philosophy. **Career:** University of Southern California, Annenberg, School of Communication, Health Journalism Fellow, 2005; California College of the Arts, faculty; Fotovision, faculty. Photojournalist and physician. **Publications:** Personal Ad Portraits, 1984; I'm Not Crazy, I Just Lost My Glasses, 1986; (with F. Setterberg) Toxic Nation: The Fight to Save Our Communities from Chemical Contamination, 1993; A Chosen Death: The Dying Confront Assisted Suicide, 1995; Hooked: Five Addicts Challenge Our Misguided Drug Rehab System, 2001; (with F. Setterberg) Under the Dragon: California's New Culture, 2007. Contributor of articles to newspapers and periodicals. **Address:** Felicia Eth Literary Representation, 555 Bryant St., Ste. 350, Palo Alto, CA 94301-1700, U.S.A. **Online address:** lonny@photowords.com

SHAVER, Phillip (Robert). American (born United States), b. 1944. **Genres:** Human Relations/Parenting, Psychology, Social Sciences, History. **Career:** Columbia University, assistant professor of psychology, 1971-75; New York University, associate professor of psychology, 1975-80, coordinator of doctoral program in personality and social psychology, 1978-80; Societal Data Corp., president 1977-82; University of Denver, associate professor, 1980-84, professor of psychology, 1984-87, Department of Experimental and Social Areas, head, 1987-88; State University of New York, professor of psychology, 1988-92, Doctoral Program in Social and Organizational Psychology, head, 1988-92; University of California, Department of Psychology, professor, 1992-, chair, 1993-96, 2001-06, head of personality/social area, 1998-2001, 2008-, distinguished professor of psychology, 2004-; International Association for Relationship Research, vice president, 2006-07, president, 2007-08. Consultant and writer. **Publications:** (Contrib.) Measures of Political Attitudes, 1968; (with J.P. Robinson) Measures of Social Psychological Attitudes, 1973; (with C. Rubenstein) In Search of Intimacy, 1982. EDITOR: Review of Personality and Social Psychology, (with L. Wheeler) vol. IV, 1983, vol. V: Emotions, Relationships and Health, 1984, vol. VI: Self, Situations, and Social Behavior, 1985, (with C. Hendrick) vol. VII: Sex and Gender, 1987; (with J.P. Robinson and L.S. Wrightsman) Measures of Personality and Social Psychological Attitudes, vol. I, 1991; (with J. Cassidy) Handbook of Attachment: Theory, Research and Clinical Applications, 1999, 2nd ed., 2008; (with M. Mikulincer) Attachment in Adulthood: Structure, Dynamics and Change, 2007; (with M. Mikulincer) Prosocial Motives, Emotions and Behavior: The Better Angels of Our Nature, 2010; (with M. Mikulincer) Human Aggression and Violence, 2011; (with M. Mikulincer) The Social Psychology of Morality, 2012. **Address:** Department of Psychology, University of California, 103 Young Hall, 1 Shields Ave., Davis, CA 95616-8686, U.S.A. **Online address:** prshaver@ucdavis.edu

SHAVIT, David. American (born United States), b. 1936. **Genres:** Librarianship, Social Sciences, History, Travel/Exploration, Business/Trade/Industry, Education. **Career:** New York Public Library, periodicals librarian, 1963-65; University of Massachusetts, acquisitions librarian, 1966-69; University of Denver, assistant director of library, 1970-72; Shekel Public Library, director, 1973-75; Libraries Department, director, 1976-80; Northern Illinois University, assistant professor, 1981-87, associate professor, 1988-94, professor of library science, 1995-2002, professor emeritus, 2003-. Writer. **Publications:** Federal Aid and State Library Agencies: Federal Policy Implementation, 1985; The United States in the Middle East: A Historical Dictionary, 1986; The Politics of Public Librarianship, 1986; The United States in Africa: A Historical Dictionary, 1989; The United States in Asia: A Historical Dictionary, 1990; (contrib.) Bücher und Bibliotheken in Ghettos und Lagern, 1933-1945, 1991; The United States in Latin America: A Historical Dictionary, 1992; The United States Relations with Russia and the Soviet Union: A Historical Dictionary, 1993; Hunger for the Printed Word: Books and Libraries in the Jewish Ghettoes of Nazi-Occupied Europe, 1997; Bali and the Tourist Industry: A History, 1906-1942, 2003; Amateurism Abroad: FDR's Political Ambassadors, forthcoming. Contributor to periodicals. **Address:** Northern Illinois University, 1425 W. Lincoln Hwy., DeKalb, IL 60115-2828, U.S.A. **Online address:** dshavit@niu.edu

SHAW, Ali. British (born England), b. 1982?. **Genres:** Novels. **Career:** Writer. **Publications:** The Girl with Glass Feet (novel), 2010. **Address:** Oxford, OX , England. **Online address:** ali@alishaw.co.uk

SHAW, Alison. British (born England), b. 1957. **Genres:** Race Relations, Sex, Social Sciences, Race Relations, Medicine/Health. **Career:** Asian Language Development Project, director, 1984-87; Brunel University, Department of Human Sciences, faculty, 1988-97, lecturer in social anthropology, 1997-2000; University of London, lecturer of social anthropology, 1991-92; University of Oxford, lecturer, 1993-97, senior research fellow, 2004-; Oxford Brukes University, lecturer, 1997; The Ethox Centre, Department of Public Health and Primary Care, senior research fellow in social anthropology; Oxford Centre for Islamic Studies, senior research associate. Writer. **Publications:** A Pakistani Community in Britain, 1988; Get by in Hindi and Urdu, 1989; Urdu and Hindi Part 1, 1991; Kinship and Continuity: Pakistani Families in Britain, 2000; (ed. with S. Ardener) Changing Sex and Bending Gender, 2005; Negotiating Risk: British Pakistani Experiences of Genetics, 2009. **Address:** Oxford Centre for Islamic Studies, George St., Oxford, OX OX1 2AR, England. **Online address:** alison.shaw@dphpc.ox.ac.uk

SHAW, Andrew. *See* **BLOCK, Lawrence.**

SHAW, Carolyn V. (Penelope). American (born United States), b. 1934. **Genres:** Children's Fiction, Poetry, Animals/Pets, Young Adult Fiction, Literary Criticism And History. **Career:** Youth choirs, director. Writer and educator. **Publications:** The Adventures of Pudgie Duck, 1995; (as Penelope) Portrait of Valor, forthcoming. **Address:** 7215 Root Rd., Spring, TX 77389, U.S.A.

SHAW, Christine. British (born England), b. 1952. **Genres:** History, Biography, Business/Trade/Industry, Economics. **Career:** European University Institute, chercheur, 1976-77; University of London, London School of Economics and Political Science, deputy editor, 1980-85, Westfield College, tutor, 1983-89, Institute of Historical Research, Seminar on Italian History, co-chairperson, 1988-, Business History Unit, research officer, 1989-91; University of Warwick, European Humanities Research Center, visiting fellow, 1991, senior research fellow, 1991-. **Publications:** (Comp. and ed.) A-Z of U.K. Marketing Information Sources, 1984; Julius II: The Warrior Pope, 1993; (ed. with S.Fletcher) The World of Savonarola: Italian Elites and Perceptions of Crisis: Papers from the Conference Held at the University of Warwick, 29-31 May 1998, to Mark the Fifth Centenary of the Death of Fra Girolamo Savonarola, 2000; The Politics of Exile in Renaissance Italy, 2000; L'ascesa al potere di Pandolfo Patnicci is Magnifico, signore di Siena (14871500), 2001; (ed.) Italy and The European Powers: The Impact of War, 1500-1530, 2006; Popular Government and Oligarchy in Renaissance Italy, 2006; The Political Role of the Orsini Family from Sixtus IV to Clement VII: Barons and Factions in the Papal States, 2007; (with C. Crabtree) Quilting, Patchwork & Applique. A World Guide, 2007; (ed.) Debrett's Peerage & Baronetage 2008, 2008. CONTRIBUTOR: (deputy ed.) Dictionary of Business Biography, vol. II-IV, 1983-86; Florence and Italy: Renaissance Studies in Honour of Nicolai Rubinstein, 1988; Business History: Concepts and Measurement, 1989; Business in the Age of War and Aggression, 1990; Management in the Age of the Corporate Economy, 1850-1990, 1995; French Descent into Renaissance Italy, 1494-5: Antecedents and Effects, 1995. **Address:** Centre for the Study of the Renaissance Humanities, University of Warwick, Rm. H448b, Bldg., Coventry, WM CV4 7AL, England.

SHAW, Daron R. American (born United States), b. 1966. **Genres:** Communications/Media, Politics/Government, Social Sciences. **Career:** University of Texas, professor of government. Survey research analyst and writer. **Publications:** (ed. with R. Hart) Communication in U.S. Elections: New Agendas, 2001; The Race to 270: The Electoral College and the Campaign Strategies of 2000 and 2004, 2006; (with K.M. Kaufmann and J.R. Petrocik) Unconventional Wisdom: Facts and Myths about American Voters, 2008. Contributor of articles to journals. **Address:** Department of Government, University of Texas at Austin, A1800, 1 University Sta., Austin, TX 78712-0119, U.S.A. **Online address:** dshaw@austin.utexas.edu

SHAW, Dash. American (born United States), b. 1983. **Genres:** Novels, Graphic Novels. **Career:** Comic writer and artist. **Publications:** Goddess Head (graphic novel), 2006; The Mother's Mouth, 2006; The Bottomless Belly Button, 2008; The Unclothed Man in the Thirty-Fifth Century A.D., 2009; BodyWorld, 2010. Work appears in anthology. **Address:** Brooklyn, NY , U.S.A. **Online address:** dash@dashshaw.com

SHAW, David W. American (born United States), b. 1961. **Genres:** Adult Non-fiction, Writing/Journalism, Military/Defense/Arms Control, Biography. **Career:** Star-Ledger, columnist and feature writer; Offshore, columnist and feature writer; Sail Magazine, staff; Cruising World Magazine, staff; Lakeland Boating Magazine, staff. **Publications:** Cheapskate's Guide to Weddings and Honeymoons, 1996; Inland Passage: On Boats and Boating in the Northeast, 1998; Daring the Sea: The True Story of the First Two Men to Row across the Atlantic Ocean, 1998; Flying Cloud: The True Story of America's Most Famous Clipper Ship and the Woman Who Guided Her, 2000; The Sea Shall Embrace Them: The Tragic Story of the Steamship Arctic, 2002; America's Victory: The Heroic Story of a Team of Ordinary Americans, and How They Won the Greatest Yacht Race Ever, 2002; Sea Wolf of the Confederacy: The Daring Civil War Raids of Naval Lt. Charles W. Read, 2004. Contributor to periodicals. **Address:** HarperCollins/William Morrow, 10 E 53rd St., New York, NY 10022-5244, U.S.A.

SHAW, Deborah Anne. British (born England), b. 1965. **Genres:** Film, Social Sciences. **Career:** University of Portsmouth, senior lecturer in film studies, 1990-2004. Writer. **Publications:** Contemporary Cinema of Latin America: Ten Key Films, 2003; (ed.) Contemporary Latin American Cinema: Breaking into the Global Market, 2007; (ed. with R. Doughty) Film: The Essential Study Guide, 2009. **Address:** c/o Author Mail, Continuum Publishing Group, 15 E 26th St., Ste. 17, New York, NY 10010-1505, U.S.A. **Online address:** deborahanneshaw@hotmail.com

SHAW, Fiona. British (born England) **Genres:** Autobiography/Memoirs, Young Adult Fiction. **Career:** Writer. **Publications:** Out of Me: The Story of a Postnatal Breakdown, 1997 in US as Composing Myself: A Journey through Postpartum Depression, 1998; The Sweetest Thing, 2004; The Picture She Took, 2006; Tell it to the Bees, 2009. Contributor to periodicals. **Address:** Viking Publicity, 80 Strand, London, GL WC2R 0RL, England.

SHAW, James E. British (born England), b. 1972. **Genres:** History, Law, Criminology/True Crime. **Career:** University of Sheffield, Department of History, lecturer, 2005-, senior lecturer in history. Writer. **Publications:** The Justice of Venice: Authorities and Liberties in the Urban Economy, 1550-1700, 2006. Contributor to books and periodicals. **Address:** Department of History, University of Sheffield, Jessop W, 1 Upper Hanover St., Sheffield, SY S3 7RA, England. **Online address:** j.e.shaw@sheffield.ac.uk

SHAW, Joseph M(inard). American (born United States), b. 1925. **Genres:** History, Theology/Religion, Translations. **Career:** St. Olaf College, instructor, 1957-59, assistant professor, 1959-62, associate professor, 1962-68, professor of religion, 1968-91, chairperson of department, 1985-88, professor emeritus of Religion, 1991-. Writer. **Publications:** Pulpit under the Sky: A Life of Hans Nielsen Hauge, 1955; (trans.) Carl F. Wisloeff, The Gift of Communion, 1964; If God Be for Us: A Study in the Meaning of Justification, 1966; Our New Testament Heritage, vol. I, 1968, vol. II, 1969; History of St. Olaf College 1874-1974, 1974; (trans.) A. Aarflot, Hans Nielsen Hauge: His Life and Message, 1979; (ed. with R.W. Franklin, H. Kaasa and C.W. Buzicky) Readings in Christian Humanism, 1982; The Pilgrim People of God Fortress, 1990; (with R.W. Franklin) The Case for Christian Humanism, Eerdmans, 1991; Dear Old Hill: The Story of Manitou Heights, the Campus of St. Olaf College, 1992; (ed.) The Carl and Martha Shaw Family: Reminiscences by Their Children, 1994; The St. Olaf Choir: A Narrative, 1997; Bernt Julius Muus: Founder of St. Olaf College, 1999; Th. N. Mohn: First President of St. Olaf College, 2006. **Address:** Department of Religion, St. Olaf College, Boe Memorial Chapel, 1520 St. Olaf Ave., Northfield, MN 55057-1098, U.S.A.

SHAW, Lisa. British (born England), b. 1966?. **Genres:** Film, Music, Area Studies. **Career:** University of Leeds, senior lecturer in Portuguese; University of California, visiting lecturer, 1999; University of Liverpool, reader in Portuguese and Brazilian studies, 2005. Writer. **Publications:** The Social History of the Brazilian Samba, 1999; (with S. Dennison) Popular Cinema in Brazil, 1930-2001, 2004; (ed. with S. Dennison) Latin American Cinema: Essays on Modernity, Gender and National Identity, 2005; (with S. Dennison) Pop Culture Latin America!: Media, Arts and Lifestyle, 2005; (with S. Dennison) Brazilian National Cinema, 2007. Contributor to journals and books. **Address:** School of Cultures, Languages and Area Studies, University of Liverpool, Cypress Bldg., Chatham St., Liverpool, L69 7ZR, England. **Online address:** lisa.shaw@liverpool.ac.uk

SHAW, Margret. British (born England), b. 1940. **Genres:** Novels, Young Adult Fiction, Children's Fiction. **Career:** Manchester Education Authority, careers officer, 1965-67; Lancashire Education Authority, district careers officer, 1967-71; Manchester Polytechnic, senior lecturer in vocational counselling, 1971-74; Department of Employment, careers service inspector,

1974-78; Open University, tutor and counselor, 1978-88; Local Government Management Board, moderator and consultant, 1980-86; educational consultant, 1986-. Writer. **Publications:** A Wider Tomorrow (young adult novel), 1989; Thirty Six Hours, 1993; The Chacer, 1994; Walking the Maze, 1998. **Address:** 17 Pagefield Cres., Clitheroe, LC BB7 1LH, England.

SHAW, Mark. American (born United States), b. 1945. **Genres:** Law. **Career:** Aspen Daily News, co-founded; ABC News, legal analyst, 1992-; London Channel Four, legal analyst, 1992-; ESPN, legal analyst, 1992-; Disney Channel program, host; Entertainment Tonight, correspondent; USA Today, columnist. Lawyer and writer. **Publications:** Down for the Count: The Shocking Truth behind the Mike Tyson Rape Trial, 1993; (with P. Dye) Bury Me in a Pot Bunker: A Personal Golf Odyssey, 1995; (with R. Hoover) Forever Flying: Fifty Years of High-Flying Adventures, From Barnstorming in Prop Planes to Dogfighting Germans to Testing Supersonic Jets: An Autobiography, 1996; (with D. Larsen) Perfect Yankee: The Incredible Story of the Greatest Miracle in Baseball History, 1996; Nicklaus, 1997; Diamonds in the Rough: Championship Golf on the Senior PGA Tour, 1998; Larry Legend, 1998; Miscarriage of Justice: The Jonathan Pollard Story, 2001; (with A. Dye) From Birdies to Bunkers: Discover How Golf Can Bring Love, Humor, and Success into Your Life, 2004; Melvin Belli: King of the Courtroom: Lawyer, Legend, Legal Revolutionary, 2007; Road to a Miracle, 2011. **Address:** 4154 N Covered Bridge Rd., Nashville, TN 47448, U.S.A. **Online address:** mshawin@yahoo.com

SHAW, Martin. British (born England), b. 1947. **Genres:** Sociology, International Relations/Current Affairs. **Career:** London School of Economics, part-time tutor in sociology, 1968-70; University of Durham, lecturer in sociology, 1970-72; University of Hull, lecturer, senior lecturer, 1972-92, Centre for Defence and Disarmament, director, 1989-92, Department of Sociology and Social Anthropology, head, 1992-95, reader, 1992-95, professor in sociology, 1992-95; University of Sussex, Department of International Relations, research professor, 1995-. Writer. **Publications:** Marxism and Social Science, 1975; Dialectics of War, 1988; Post-Military Society: Militarism, Demilitarization and War at the End of the Twentieth Century, 1991; Global Society and International Relations, 1994; Civil Society and Media in Global Crises, 1996; Theory of the Global State: Globaility as Unfinished Revolution, 2000; War and Genocide: Organized Killing in Modern Society, 2003; New Western Way of War: Risk-Transfer War and Its Crisis in Iraq, 2005; What is Genocide?, 2007. EDITOR: War, State and Society, 1984; Marxist Sociology Revisited, 1985; The Sociology of War and Peace, 1987; (with M. Banks) State and Society in International Relations, 1991; Politics and Globalisation: Knowledge, Ethics and Agency, 1999; (with W.D. Jong and N. Stammers) Global Activism, Global Media, 2005. **Address:** School of Social Sciences, University of Sussex, Arts E504, Brighton, BN1 9QN, England. **Online address:** m.shaw@sussex.ac.uk

SHAW, Miranda Eberle. American (born United States), b. 1954. **Genres:** Theology/Religion, Women's Studies And Issues, Mythology/Folklore, Social Sciences. **Career:** University of Richmond, assistant professor of religion, associate professor of religion. Writer. **Publications:** Passionate Enlightenment: Women in Tantric Buddhism, 1994; Buddhist Goddesses of India, 2006. Contributor of articles to journals. **Address:** Department of Religion, University of Richmond, 102G Weinstein Hall, 124 N Court, 28 Westhampton Way, Richmond, VA 23173-0001, U.S.A. **Online address:** mshaw@richmond.edu

SHAW, Patrick W. American (born United States), b. 1938. **Genres:** Literary Criticism And History, Young Adult Fiction. **Career:** University of Missouri, instructor in English, 1966-67; Louisiana State University, instructor in English, 1968-72; Texas Tech University, professor of English, 1972-2002, emeritus professor, 2002-. Writer. **Publications:** (Ed.) Literature: A College Anthology, 1977; Willa Cather and the Art of Conflict: Re-Visioning Her Creative Imagination, 1992; The Modern American Novel of Violence, 1999. Contributor to periodicals. **Address:** Department of English, Texas Tech University, PO Box 43091, Lubbock, TX 79409-3091, U.S.A. **Online address:** ditps@ttacs.ttu.edu

SHAW, Robert B. American (born United States), b. 1947. **Genres:** Poetry, Literary Criticism And History. **Career:** Harvard University, Briggs-Copeland lecturer in English, 1974-76; Yale University, assistant professor, 1976-80, associate professor of English, 1980-83; Mount Holyoke College, associate professor, 1983-91, professor of English, 1991-2010, Emily Dick-

inson professor of English, 2010-. Writer. **Publications:** POEMS: Curious Questions, 1970; In Witness, 1972; Comforting the Wilderness, 1977; The Wonder of Seeing Double, 1988; The Post Office Murals Restored, 1994; Below the Surface, 1999; Solving for X, 2002; Aromatics, 2011. CRITICISM: The Call of God: The Theme of Vocation in the Poetry of Donne and Herbert (monograph), 1981; Blank Verse: A Guide to Its History and Use, 2007. EDITOR: American Poetry Since 1960: Some Critical Perspectives, 1973; Henry Vaughan: Selected Poems, 1976. Contributor to periodicals. **Address:** Department of English, Mount Holyoke College, South Hadley, MA 01075, U.S.A. **Online address:** rshaw@mtholyoke.edu

SHAW, Ron W. Canadian (born Canada), b. 1951. **Genres:** Novellas/Short Stories, Novels. **Career:** Northern Times Publishing, journalist, 1969-71; Signal Star Publishing, journalist, 1971-74, 1976-77; Canadian Hunger Foundation, project administrator, 1974-75; CARE Intl., project administrator, 1977-85; Gibson-Shaw Visual Productions, creative director, 1981-82; Salzburg Seminar in American Studies Development, Communication, and Social Change, fellow, 1982; USAID Cameroon, development communications specialist, 1985-88; Medical Care Development Intl., administrative officer, 1988-89; Agricultural Cooperative Development Intl., monetization specialist, 1989-91; Marine Overseas Services, monetization and food assistance specialist, 1991-, food security advisor. Writer. **Publications:** Black Light: Ten Stories and a Novella, 1993. Contributor to periodicals. **Address:** 2336 Drummond Concession-7, R.R., Ste. 6, Perth, ON K7H 3C8, Canada. **Online address:** scdhrcda@perth.igs.net

SHAW, Russell B(urnham). American (born United States), b. 1935. **Genres:** Novels, Philosophy, Theology/Religion, Business/Trade/Industry. **Career:** Catholic Standard, reporter, 1956-57; National Catholic Welfare Conference News Service, staff writer, 1957-66; National Catholic Educational Association, director of publications and information, 1966-69; National Catholic Office for Information, director, 1969-73; U.S. Catholic Conference, associate secretary for communication, 1973-74, secretary for public affairs, 1975-87; Knights of Columbus, director of public information, 1987-97; Pontifical University, adjunct professor of communications, 1996-, Pontifical Council for Social Communications, consultor; Our Sunday Visitor, editor, 1997; The Pope Speaks, editor, 1998-2005; Catholic Distance University, vice-chairman. **Publications:** The Dark Disciple, 1961; Abortion on Trial, 1968; (with C.A. Koob) S.O.S. for Catholic Schools, 1970; (with G.G. Grisez) Beyond the New Morality, 1974, 3rd ed., 1988; Church and State, 1979; Choosing Well, 1982; Why We Need Confession, 1986, 2nd ed., 2000; Renewal, 1986; Signs of the Times, 1986; Does Suffering Make Sense, 1987, 2nd ed., 2000; (with G.G. Grisez) Fulfillment in Christ, 1991; To Hunt, to Shoot, to Entertain, 1993; Understanding Your Rights, 1994; Papal Primacy in the Third Millennium, 2000; Ministry or Apostolate, 2002; (with G.G. Grisez) Personal Vocation: God Calls Everyone by Name, 2003; Catholic Laity in the Mission of the Church, 2005; Nothing To Hide: Secrecy, Communication and Communion in the Catholic Church, 2008; Writing the Way: The Story of a Spiritual Classic, 2010. EDITOR: (with M.P. Sheridan) Catholic Education Today and Tomorrow, 1968; (with R.J. Hurley) Trends and Issues in Catholic Education, 1969; (with P. Riley) Anti-Catholicism in the Media, 1993; Encyclopedia of Catholic Doctrine, 1997. **Address:** 2928 44th Pl. NW, Washington, DC 20016, U.S.A. **Online address:** rshaw10290@aol.com

SHAW, Susan. American (born United States), b. 1951. **Genres:** Novels. **Career:** Writer and music educator. **Publications:** Black-eyed Suzie, 2002; The Boy from the Basement, 2004; Safe, 2007; One of the Survivors, 2009; Tunnel Vision, 2011. Contributor to periodicals. **Address:** c/o Author Mail, Dutton Books, 375 Hudson St., New York, NY 10014, U.S.A.

SHAW, Thurstan. (Peter Woods). British (born England), b. 1914. **Genres:** Archaeology/Antiquities, Autobiography/Memoirs. **Career:** Achimota College, Museum of Anthropology, curator, 1937-45; Cambridge Institute of Education, tutor, 1951-63; University of Ibadan, research professor of archaeology and head of department, 1963-74, now professor emeritus; West African Archaeological Newsletter, editor, 1964-70; West African Journal of Archaeology, 1971-75; Cambridge University, lecturer in archaeology, 1975-, retired; Magdalene College, director of studies in archaeology and anthropology, 1976-79. **Publications:** Excavation at Dawu, 1961; Archaeology and Nigeria, 1964; (ed. and co-author) Nigerian Prehistory and Archaeology, 1969; (ed.) Lectures on Nigerian Prehistory and Archaeology, 1969; (with J. Vanderburg) A Bibliography of Nigerian Archaeology, 1969; Igbo-Ukwu: An Account of Archaeological Discoveries in Eastern Nigeria, vol. II, 1970; Africa and the Origins of Man, 1973; Why, Darkest Africa?: Archaeological Light on an Old Problem, 1975; (ed.) Discovering Nigeria's Past, 1975; Unearthing Igbo-Ukwu: Archaeological Discoveries in Eastern Nigeria, 1977; Nigeria: Its Archaeology and Early History, 1978; Filling Gaps in Afric Maps: Fifty Years of Archaeology in Africa, 1984; (with S.G.H. Daniels) Excavations at Iwo Eleru, Ondo State, Nigeria, 1987; (with K.D. Aiyedun) Prehistoric Settlement and Subsistence in the Kaduna Valley, Nigeria, 1989; (contrib.) Cultural Resource Management, 1990; (co-ed.) The Archaeology of Africa: Food, Metals and Towns, 1993; (contrib.) Imprints of West Africa's Past, 1993; (as Peter Woods) Diary of a Grief, 1998; (co-ed.) Africa: The Challenge of Archaeology, 1998; (with P. Ucko and K. MacDonald) A Tribute to the Life and Work of Professor Bassey Wai Andah, 1999. **Address:** Department of Archaeology, University of Cambridge, The Old Schools, Trinity Ln., Cambridge, CB CB2 1TN, England.

SHAW, Tony. British (born England), b. 1965. **Genres:** Art/Art History. **Career:** University of Hertfordshire, professor of contemporary history. Writer. **Publications:** Eden, Suez, and the Mass Media: Propaganda and Persuasion during the Suez Crisis, 1996; British Cinema and the Cold War: The State, Propaganda and Consensus, 2001; Hollywood's Cold War, 2007; (with D.J. Youngblood) Cinematic Cold War: The American and Soviet Struggle for Hearts and Minds, 2010. Contributor to books and periodicals. **Address:** England. **Online address:** a.t.shaw@herts.ac.uk

SHAW, William. British (born England), b. 1959. **Genres:** Novels, Novellas/Short Stories, Social Sciences, Music. **Career:** ZigZag Magazine, assistant editor. Freelance journalist, 1983-. **Publications:** (With R. Lowe) Travellers, 1993; Happy Clappy: Spying in Guru Land, 1994; Westside: Young Men and Hip Hop in L.A., 2000; Superhero For Hire, 2004. **Address:** Fraser & Dunlop Peters, The Chambers, Chelsea Harbour, Lots Rd., London, GL SW10 0XF, England. **Online address:** wshaw@cix.co.uk

SHAWHAN, Dorothy Sample. American (born United States), b. 1942. **Genres:** Novels, Politics/Government. **Career:** Louisiana State University, instructor in English, 1966-69; Indiana University Publications, editor, 1970-74; Agency for Instructional Television, writer/editor, 1975-81; Delta State University, professor of English, 1981-2006, professor emerita, 2006-, chair of Division of Languages and Literature, 1992-2006; Habitat for Humanity, secretary, 1987-98. **Publications:** Lizzie (novel), 1995; (with M.H. Swain) Lucy Somerville Howorth: New Deal Lawyer, Politician and Feminist from the South, 2006. Contributor of articles and short stories to periodicals. **Address:** Delta State University, 250 Kethley Hall, 1003 W Sunflower Rd., Cleveland, MS 38733, U.S.A. **Online address:** dshawhan@deltastate.edu

SHAWL, Nisi. American (born United States), b. 1955?. **Genres:** Novellas/Short Stories. **Career:** Clarion West Writers Workshop, director. Writer. **Publications:** (With C. Ward) Writing the Other, 2005; Filter House: Short Fiction, 2008. Contributor to periodicals. **Address:** Seattle, WA, U.S.A. **Online address:** nisis@aol.com

SHAWVER, Lois. American (born United States), b. 1939. **Genres:** History, Human Relations/Parenting, Intellectual History, Philosophy, Psychology, Gay And Lesbian Issues, Military/Defense/Arms Control. **Career:** Patton State Hospital, clinical psychology intern, 1971-72; University of California, lecturer in psychology, 1973-74; California State University, lecturer, 1973; California Medical Facility, prison psychologist, 1974-89; California State University, lecturer, 1974; California School of Professional Psychology, lecturer, 1990-94; Massey University, Department of Psychology, contributing faculty; PMTH News, editor. **Publications:** And the Flag Was Still There: Straight People, Gay People and Sexuality in the U.S. Military, 1995; Nostalgic Postmodernism: Postmodern Therapy, 2005. Contributor to books and journals. **Address:** 385 Bellevue Ave., Oakland, CA 94610, U.S.A. **Online address:** rathbone@california.com

SHAY, Jonathan. American (born United States), b. 1941?. **Genres:** Ethics, Adult Non-fiction, Psychology, Medicine/Health. **Career:** Tufts Medical School, Department of Psychiatry, clinical psychiatrist; United States Department of Veterans Affairs, psychiatrist; Boston Veterans' Administration Hospital, Department of Veteran Affairs Veterans' Improvement Program, psychiatrist; Department of Veteran Affairs Outpatient Clinic, staff psychiatrist; U.S. Army, Office of the Deputy Chief of Staff for Personnel, chairman of ethics, leadership and personnel policy, 2004-05. Writer. **Publications:** Achilles in Vietnam: Combat Trauma and the Undoing of Character, 1994; Odysseus in

America: Combat Trauma and the Trials of Homecoming, 2002. Contributor to periodicals. **Address:** Department of Veterans' Services, 239 Causeway St., Ste. 100, Boston, MA 02114, U.S.A. **Online address:** jshay@world.std.com

SHAY, Kathryn. American (born United States) **Genres:** Adult Non-fiction, Romance/Historical, Novellas/Short Stories, Young Adult Fiction. **Career:** Teacher, through 2004. Writer. **Publications:** BAYVIEW HEIGHTS SERIES: Cop of the Year, 1998; Because It's Christmas, 1998. Count on Me, 2001. AMERICA'S BRAVEST SERIES: Feel the Heat, 1999; The Man Who Loved Christmas, 1999; Code of Honor, 2000; The Fire Within, 2001. SERENITY HOUSE TRILOGY SERIES: Practice Makes Perfect, 2002; A Place to Belong, 2002; Against the Odds, 2003. OTHERS: The Father Factor, 1995; A Suitable Bodyquard, 1996; Michael's Family, 1997; Just One Night, 1997; Finally a Family, 2000; A Christmas Legacy, 2000; Caught Off Guard, 2002; Promises to Keep, 2002; Trust in Me, 2003; Opposites Attract, 2003; Lipstick Chronicles: Book One, 2003; (with E. Carmichael and V. Leiber) More Lipstick Chronicles, 2004; After the Fire, 2003; The Unknown Twin, 2004; On the Line, 2004; Time to Give, 2005; Someone to Believe In, 2005; Nothing More to Lose, 2005; Our Two Sons, 2005; Ties that Bind, 2006; Tell Me No Lies, 2006; Close to You, 2007; Wrong Man for Her, 2007; Taking the Heat, 2008; Be my Babies, 2008; Man She Couldn't Forget, 2009; Back to Luke, 2009; The Perfect Family, 2010. Contributor to books. Works appear in anthologies. **Address:** c/o Author Mail, Berkley Books, Penguin Putnam, 375 Hudson St., New York, NY 10014, U.S.A. **Online address:** kshayweb@rochester.rr.com

SHEA, Lisa. American (born United States), b. 1953. **Genres:** Novels, Young Adult Fiction. **Career:** Novelist and freelance journalist. **Publications:** Hula (novel), 1994; (adapter) Iron Man's Friends and Foes, 2010; (adapter) Meet the Black Widow, 2010. Contributor to periodicals. **Address:** W. W. Norton & Company Inc., 500 5th Ave., New York, NY 10110, U.S.A.

SHEA, Mark P. American (born United States), b. 1958. **Genres:** Theology/Religion. **Career:** University of Washington, secretary to the vice president, 1987-89, secretary, 1989-91; Fred Hutchinson Cancer Research Center, program assistant, 1992-98; writer, 1998-; Catholic Exchange, senior content editor. **Publications:** This Is My Body: An Evangelical Discovers the Real Presence, 1993; By What Authority?: An Evangelical Discovers Catholic Tradition, 1996; Making Senses Out of Scripture: Reading the Bible as the First Christians Did, 1999; So Why Do We do This?: Understanding the Why and How of the Mass: Leader's Guide, 2003; Light and the Lens: Understanding Scripture and Tradition, 2003; Mary, Mother of the Son, 2009. Contributor to books and periodicals. **Address:** 5610 239th Pl. SW, Mountlake Terrace, WA 98043, U.S.A. **Online address:** mshea@catholicexchange.com

SHEA, Pegi Deitz. American (born United States), b. 1960. **Genres:** Children's Fiction. **Career:** Institute of Children's Literature, writing instructor; Pegi Deitz Public Relations, president and freelance writer 1986-; journalist. **Publications:** Bungalow Fungalow, 1991; The Whispering Cloth: A Refugee's Story, 1995; New Moon, 1996; Ekaterina Gordeeva, 1999; The Impeachment Process, 2000; I See Me, 2000; (with C. Weill) Ten Mice for Tet, 2003; Tangled Threads, 2003; The Carpet Boy's Gift, 2003; Liberty Rising, 2005; Patience Wright: America's First Sculptor, and Revolutionary Spy, 2007; The Boy and the Spell, 2007; Noah Webster: Weaver of Words, 2008; Abe in Arms, 2010; (with I.V. Rynbach) Taxing Case of the Cows: A True Story about Suffrage, 2010. Contributor of articles. **Address:** 27 Fox Hill Dr., Rockville, CT 06066, U.S.A. **Online address:** pegideitzshea@aol.com

SHEA, Suzanne Strempek. American (born United States) **Genres:** Adult Non-fiction, Novels. **Career:** Author, 1994-; Springfield Newspapers, staff writer; Providence Journal-Bulletin, staff writer; Billy Riordan Memorial Clinic, fouder; University of Southern Maine, faculty; Bay Path College, writer-in-residence; Emerson College, faculty; University of South Florida, creative writing program, faculty. **Publications:** Selling the Lite of Heaven, 1994; Hoopi Shoopi Donna, 1996; Lily of the Valley, 1999; Around Again, 2001; Songs from a Lead-lined Room: Notes-High and Low-from My Journey through Breast Cancer and Radiation, 2002; Becoming Finola: A Novel, 2004; Shelf Life: Romance, Mystery, Drama, and Other Page-Turning Adventures from a Year in a Bookstore, 2004; Sundays in America: A Yearlong Road Trip in Search of Christian Faith, 2008. **Address:** PO Box 468, Thorndike, MA 01079, U.S.A. **Online address:** sess7@comcast.net

SHEA, William M. American (born United States), b. 1935. **Genres:** Theology/Religion. **Career:** Catholic University of America, assistant professor and associate professor, 1972-80; University of South Florida, associate professor, professor, 1980-91; Saint Louis University, chair of theological studies, 1991-97, professor, 1991-2003; College of the Holy Cross, Center for Religion, Ethics and Culture, director, 2003-; Woodrow Wilson Center at the Smithsonian, resident fellow, 1986-87; St. John's University, Ecumenical Institute, resident fellow, 1999. Writer. **Publications:** The Naturalists and the Supernatural: Studies in Horizon and an American Philosophy of Religion, 1984; (ed. with P.A. Huff) Knowledge and Belief in America: Enlightenment Traditions and Modern Religious Thought, 1995; (ed. with D.V. Slyke) Trying Times: Essays on Catholic Higher Education in the 20th Century, 1999; The Lion and the Lamb: Evangelicals and Catholics in America, 2004. Contributor to journals and periodicals. **Address:** College of the Holy Cross, 1 College St., Worcester, MA 01610, U.S.A. **Online address:** wshea@holycross.edu

SHEAFFER, Mike. American (born United States), b. 1950. **Genres:** Adult Non-fiction. **Career:** American Karate Black Belt Association, professional instructor and competitor, 1967-75; Hi-Line Inc., distribution assistant, 1975-76, sales representative, 1976-78, sales manager, 1978-79, purchasing manager, 1980-82, national sales manager, 1983-86, president, director and chief executive officer, 1987-; Present American Pregnancy Association, founder and chairman, 1995-; America's Crisis Pregnancy Helpline, founder and chairperson. Writer. **Publications:** (With A. Sheaffer and J. Shaw) The Ultimate Gift: A True Life Story, 1998. **Address:** Hi-Line Inc., 2121 Valley View Ln., Dallas, TX 75234-8912, U.S.A. **Online address:** mike@hi-line.com

SHEAHAN, John. American (born United States), b. 1923. **Genres:** Economics. **Career:** U.S. Economic Cooperation Administration, economic analyst, 1951-54; Williams College, professor of economics, 1954-94, 1966-94, William Brough professor of economics, William Brough professor emeritus, 1994-; Brookings Institution, national research professor, 1959-60; Harvard University, Development Advisory Service, economic adviser, 1963-65; El Colegio de Mexico, visiting professor, 1970-71; Universite de Grenoble, Fulbright research professor, 1974-75; University of California, Center for U.S.-Mexican Studies, visiting research fellow, 1991. Writer. **Publications:** Promotion and Control of Industry in Postwar France, 1963; The Wage-Price Guideposts, 1967; An Introduction to the French Economy, 1969; Aspects of Planning and Development in Colombia, 1977; Early Industrialisation and Violent Reaction: Argentina and Brazil, 1982; Alternative International Economic Strategies and Their Relevance for China, 1986; Patterns of Development in Latin America: Poverty, Repression and Economic Strategy, 1987; Conflict and Change in Mexican Economic Strategy, 1992; Searching for a Better Society: The Peruvian Economy from 1950, 1999; El Economia Peruana Desde 1950: Buscando un Sociedad Mejor, 2001. Contributor to books. **Address:** Department of Economics, Williams College, Schapiro Hall, 24 Hopkins Hall Dr., PO Box 751, Williamstown, MA 01267, U.S.A. **Online address:** jsheahan@williams.edu

SHEAR, Jeff. American (born United States), b. 1947. **Genres:** Economics, History. **Career:** Junior Scholastic, associate editor, 1978-81; freelance writer, 1981-88; Insight, staff writer, 1988-91; National Journal, staff correspondent, 1994-. **Publications:** The Keys to the Kingdom: The FS-X and the Selling of America's Future to Japan, 1994. Contributor to magazines and newspapers. **Address:** National Journal, 1501 M St. NW, Washington, DC 20005-1700, U.S.A.

SHEARD, Sarah. Canadian (born Canada), b. 1953. **Genres:** Novels, Novellas/Short Stories, Literary Criticism And History, Politics/Government. **Career:** Literary Press Group, Ontario representative, 1980-81; Toronto-area high schools, instructor in creative writing, 1980-88; Toronto Book Fair, executive, 1983-84; Canada Council National Book Festival, Ontario coordinator, 1986-92; Bolton Public Library, writer-in-residence, 1988; Dr. Marian Hilliard Secondary School, electronic writer-in-residence, 1989; York University, Glendon College, instructor in creative writing, 1991; Ryerson Polytechnical University, instructor in creative writing, 1991-2006; Humber College, Humber School for Writers, mentor, 1995-. **Publications:** FICTION: Almost Japanese: A Novel, 1985, 2nd ed., 2000; The Swing Era, 1993; Hypnotist, 1999. NONFICTION: (ed. with L. Scheier and E. Wachtel) Language in Her Eye: Views on Writing and Gender by Canadian Women Writing in English, 1990. OTHER: (with M. Dragu and S. Swan) Mothers Talk Back: Momz Radio, 1991. Contributor to periodicals. **Address:** Writers Union of Canada, 90 Richmond St. E, Ste. 200, Toronto, ON M5C 1P1, Canada. **Online address:** ssheard@interlog.com

SHEDD, Warner. American (born United States), b. 1934. **Genres:** Adult Non-fiction, Children's Non-fiction, Zoology, Animals/Pets, Sciences, Natural History. **Career:** Vermont Department of Forests and Parks, municipal forester, 1958-66; Vermont Extension Service, area resource specialist, 1966-69; National Wildlife Federation, regional executive, 1969-89; freelance writer, 1990-. **Publications:** The Kids' Wildlife Book: Exploring Animal Worlds through Indoor/ Outdoor Experiences, 1994; Owls Aren't Wise and Bats Aren't Blind: A Naturalist Debunks Our Favorite Fallacies About Wildlife, 2000. Contributor to magazines. **Address:** PO Box 125, East Calais, VT 05650, U.S.A. **Online address:** woad3040@earthlink.net

SHEEHAN, Aurelie. American/French (born France), b. 1963. **Genres:** Novellas/Short Stories, Women's Studies And Issues, Young Adult Fiction. **Career:** Radcliffe College, Mary Ingraham Bunting Institute, administrative assistant, 1984-86; Child (magazine), assistant editor, 1987-90; City University, City College, administrative assistant, 1987-92, instructor in literature and composition, 1989-92; Ucross Foundation, Artists Residency Program, coordinator, 1993-96, writer-in-residence; Sanskriti Kendra, writer-in-residence; The Tyrone Guthrie Centre, writer-in-residence; Child Magazine, assistant editor; Sheridan College, instructor in creative writing, 1995; Johns Hopkins University, lecturer in arts and sciences, 1997-98; University of Arizona, assistant professor, 2000-05, associate professor of English and director of creative writing program, 2005-. **Publications:** Jack Kerouac is Pregnant (stories), 1994, rev. ed., 2001. NOVEL: The Anxiety of Everyday Objects, 2004; History Lesson for Girls, 2006. Works appear in anthologies. Contributor to periodicals. **Address:** Department of English, University of Arizona, Rm. 462, 1423 E University Blvd., Modern Languages Bldg., PO Box 210067, Tucson, AZ 85721, U.S.A. **Online address:** aurelie@aureliesheehan.com

SHEEHAN, Jason. American (born United States), b. 1973?. **Genres:** Biography, Autobiography/Memoirs. **Career:** La Cocinita and Weekly Alibi, restaurant critic, 2001; Westword, restaurant critic, 2002-10; Seattle Weekly, restaurant critic, 2010-. Writer and chef. **Publications:** Cooking Dirty: A Story of Life, Sex, Love, and Death in the Kitchen, 2009. Works appear in anthologies. Contributor to periodicals. **Address:** Seattle, WA , U.S.A. **Online address:** jsheehan@seattleweekly.com

SHEEHAN, Julie. American (born United States), b. 1964. **Genres:** Poetry. **Career:** Youth Speaks, visiting artist, 2000; Adelphi University, adjunct instructor, 2000; Dowling College, adjunct instructor, 2001-; Ross Institute, visiting artist, 2002-; Suffolk Community College of the State University of New York, adjunct instructor, 2002-; Stony Brook University, assistant professor; W.W. Norton & Company Inc., poet, 2006-. **Publications:** Thaw, 2001; Orient Point, 2006; Bar Book: Poems and Otherwise, 2010. Contributor to periodicals. **Address:** W. W. Norton & Company Inc., 500 5th Ave., New York, NY 10110, U.S.A. **Online address:** julie@tecsoft.com

SHEEHAN, Michael J. American (born United States), b. 1939. **Genres:** Westerns/Adventure, Writing/Journalism, Poetry, Literary Criticism And History, Novels. **Career:** Olive-Harvey College, Department of English, associate professor of English, 1968-94, retired, 1994. Writer. **Publications:** In the Shadow of the Bear (novel), 1990; The Cry of the Jackal (novel), 1991; (with N. Sheehan) Workbook for Basic Writers, 1991; (with N. Sheehan) Handbook for Basic Writers, 1991; Words! A Vocabulary Power Workbook, 1996; The Word Parts Dictionary: Standard and Reverse Listings of Prefixes, Suffixes, Roots and Combining Forms, 2000, 2nd ed., 2008; Words to the Wise: A Lighthearted Look at the English Language, 2004; On the Lamb in a Doggy Dog World: At Play with the English Language, 2006; More Words to the Wise: A Lighthearted Look at the English Language, 2009. **Address:** 3736 S Bay Bluffs Dr., Cedar, MI 49621-8413, U.S.A. **Online address:** seniorcorner@aol.com

SHEEHAN, Neil. American (born United States), b. 1936. **Genres:** International Relations/Current Affairs, History. **Career:** United Press Intl., bureau chief, 1962-64; New York Times, reporter, 1964, news staff, 1964-72, correspondent, 1965-69, foreign correspondent in Indonesia, 1965, foreign correspondent in Vietnam, 1965-66, Pentagon correspondent, 1966-68, White House correspondent, 1968-69, special investigative reporter, 1969-72; freelance writer, 1972-. Pulitzer Prize and National Book Award winner. **Publications:** The Pentagon Papers As Published by the New York Times: The Secret History of the Vietnam War, 1971; The Arnheiter Affair, 1972; A Bright Shining Lie: John Paul Vann and America in Vietnam, 1988; After The War was Over: Hanoi and Saigon, 1992; Two Cities, 1994; A Fiery Peace in a

Cold War: Bernard Schriever and the Ultimate Weapon, 2009. **Address:** 4505 Klingle St. NW, Washington, DC 20016, U.S.A.

SHEEHAN, Sean. British (born England), b. 1951. **Genres:** History, Geography. **Career:** English teacher, 1975-91; freelance writer, 1992-. **Publications:** Dictionary of Irish Quotations, 1993; (with P. Murray and G. Skelly) Limelight, 1993; (ed.) The Sayings of James Joyce, 1995; (with P. Levy) Ancient World of Rome, 1999; Great African Kingdoms, 1999; Ancient Rome, 2000; After the Holocaust, 2001; Allied Victory, 2001; Death Camps, 2001; Germany and Japan Attack, 2001; Illustrated Encyclopedia of Ancient Greece, 2002; South Africa since Apartheid, 2002; Cold War, 2003; D-Day, June 6, 1944, 2003; Technology of World War II, 2003; Castles, 2004; Greenpeace, 2004; World War II: The Pacific, 2004; (with P. Levy) From Compact Discs to the Gulf War: The Mid 1980s to the Early 1990s, 2005; Holocaust, 2005; (with P. Levy) From the World Wide Web to September 11, 2006; From Beatlemania to Watergate, 2006; From Jessie Owens to Hiroshima, 2006; From the Wright Brothers to the Treaty of Versailles, 2006; Jack's World, 2007; Endangered Species, 2009; War in the Pacific, 2009; Angola, 2010; Malta, 2010; Ancient African Kingdoms, 2011; Auschwitz, 2011; Cameroon, 2011; Trinidad and Tobago, 2011; Why did the Holocaust Happen?, 2011; (with P. Levy) Ancient Rome, 2011. CULTURES OF THE WORLD SERIES: Austria, 1992; Zimbabwe, 1993; Jamaica, 1994; Pakistan, 1994; Romania, 1994; Turkey, 1994; Cuba, 1995; Cambodia, 1996; Lebanon, 1997; Guatemala, 1998; Angola, 1999; Cameroon, 2001; Malta, 2001; Trinidad & Tobago, 2001; Africa, 2003; Genocide, 2005. **Address:** Bantry, CK , Ireland. **Online address:** thailand1@eircom.net

SHEEHAN, Susan. American/Austrian (born Austria), b. 1937. **Genres:** Writing/Journalism, Social Sciences, Social Commentary. **Career:** Esquire-Coronet Magazines, editorial researcher, 1959-60; freelance writer, 1960-61; New Yorker Magazine, staff writer, 1961-; Architectural Digest, contributing editor, 1997-. **Publications:** Ten Vietnamese, 1967; A Welfare Mother, 1976; A Prison and a Prisoner, 1978; Is There No Place on Earth for Me?, 1982; Kate Quinton's Days, 1984; A Missing Plane, 1986; Life for Me Ain't Been No Crystal Stair, 1993; (with H. Means) The Banana Sculptor, the Purple Lady and the All-Night Swimmer: Hobbies, Collecting and Other Passionate Pursiuts, 2002. Contributor to magazines. **Address:** New Yorker, 4 Times Sq., New York, NY 10036, U.S.A.

SHEEHY, Gail. American (born United States), b. 1937. **Genres:** Psychology, Social Commentary, Biography, Human Relations/Parenting, Sex, Literary Criticism And History, Self Help. **Career:** Democrat and Chronicle, fashion editor, 1961-63; New York Herald Tribune, feature writer, 1963-66; New York (magazine), contributing editor, 1968-77; Vanity Fair, contributing political editor, 1984-. **Publications:** Lovesounds, 1970; Panthermania: The Clash of Black against Black in One American City, 1971; Speed Is of the Essence, 1971; Hustling: Prostitution in Our Wide Open Society, 1973; Passages: The Predictable Crises of Adult Life, 1976; Pathfinders, 1981; Spirit of Survival, 1986; (contrib.) Hiśardut: sipur hatsalatah shel yaldah Ḳambodit, 1987; Character: America's Search for Leadership, 1988; The Man Who Changed the World: The Lives of Mikhail S. Gorbachev, 1990; The Silent Passage: Menopause, 1992, rev. ed., 1998; New Passages: Mapping Your Life Across Time, 1995; Understanding Men's Passages: Discovering the New Map of Men's Lives, 1998; Hillary's Choice, 1999; Middletown, America: One Town's Passage from Trauma to Hope, 2003; Sex and the Seasoned Woman: Pursuing the Passionate Life, 2006; (intro.) Power Of Experience: Great Writers Over 50 On the Quest For A Lifetime Of Meaning, 2007; Passages in Caregiving: Turning Chaos Into Confidence, 2010. Contributor to magazines. **Address:** c/o Richard S. Pine, InkWell Management L.L.C., 521 5th Ave., 26th Fl., New York, NY 10175-0003, U.S.A.

SHEEHY, Helen. American (born United States), b. 1948. **Genres:** Biography, Essays, Plays/Screenplays, Theatre, Novels. **Career:** Hartford Stage Co., dramaturg, 1981-85; Southern Connecticut State University, adjunct professor of theatre, 1985-2007. Writer and consultant. **Publications:** All about Theatre, 1981; Margo: The Life and Theatre of Margo Jones, 1989; Eva Le Gallienne: A Biography, 1996; (with L. Stainton) On Writers and Writing, 2000; Eleonora Duse: A Biography, 2003; Eleonora Duse: La Donna, Le Passioni, La Leggenda, 2005; Willa, A Novel, forthcoming. Contributor to magazines and newspapers. **Address:** 200 Ridgewood, Hamden, CT 06517, U.S.A. **Online address:** helen@helensheehy.org

SHEELER, Jackie. American (born United States), b. 1957. **Genres:** Poetry, Autobiography/Memoirs. **Career:** Poetz, founder and publisher. Writer. **Publications:** The Memory Factory, 2002; (ed.) Off the Cuffs: Poetry By and About the Police, 2003; Earthquake Came to Harlem, 2010; Autobiography of a Street Junkie, forthcoming. Contributor to journals and newspapers. **Address:** PO Box 1401, New York, NY 10026, U.S.A. **Online address:** jsheeler@mindspring.com

SHEELER, Jim. American (born United States), b. 1969?. **Genres:** inspirational/Motivational Literature, Documentaries/Reportage, Sports/Fitness. **Career:** Boulder Daily Camera, journalist, 1991-96; Boulder Planet, senior staff writer, 1996-2000; Denver Post, freelance writer, 1999-2003; Rocky Mountain News, staff writer, 2004-; University of Colorado, Department of Journalism and Mass Communication, adjunct professor, 2007. **Publications:** Obit: Inspiring Stories of Ordinary People Who Led Extraordinary Lives, 2007; After Words: Obituaries of Ordinary People that Lead Extraordinary Lives, 2007; Final Salute: A Story of Unfinished Lives, 2008. Works appear in anthologies. **Address:** Journalism and Mass Communication, University of Colorado at Boulder, 203A Armory, 1511 University Ave., PO BOX 478, Boulder, CO 80309, U.S.A. **Online address:** james.sheeler@colorado.edu

SHEEN, Barbara. American (born United States), b. 1949. **Genres:** Children's Non-fiction, Young Adult Non-fiction, Biography, Food And Wine. **Career:** Educator, 1970-2003. Writer. **Publications:** We Learn English, 1975; Attention Deficit Disorder, 2001; Arthritis, 2001; Hepatitis, 2002; Asthma, 2002; Diabetes, 2003; Chemical Dependency, 2003; Teen Alcoholism, 2003; Cerebral Palsy, 2003; Acne, 2004; Headaches, 2004; Heart Disease, 2004; Food Poisoning, 2005; Birth Defects, 2005; Mad Cow Disease, 2005; Ovarian Cancer, 2005; Deafness, 2006; Toxic Shock Syndrome, 2006; Foods of Italy, 2006; Foods of Mexico, 2006; Foods of Greece, 2006; Foods of China, 2006; Foods of Thailand, 2006; Foods of Japan, 2006; Foods of the Philippines, 2006; Foods of Vietnam, 2006; Foods of Iran, 2006; Flu, 2006; Foods of Russia, 2006; Foods of Germany, 2007; Nuclear Weapons, 2007; Foods of India, 2007; Foods of Brazil, 2008; Foods of the Caribbean, 2008; Foods of Ethiopia, 2008; Foods of Spain, 2008; Adolescence, 2008; Eating Right, 2008; Keeping Fit, 2008; Tony Hawk, 2008; Girl's Guide to Feeling Great, 2008; Allergies, 2008; Lung Cancer, 2008; Prostate Cancer, 2008; Danica Patrick, 2009; Derek Jeter, 2009; Pope Benedict XVI, 2009; ADHD, 2009; MRSA, 2010; Steve Jobs, 2010; Michael Phelps, 2010; Janet Guthrie, 2010; Stephenie Meyer, 2010; Foods of Egypt, 2010; Foods of Kenya, 2010; Foods of Australia, 2010; Kanye West, 2010; Foods of Scandinavia, 2010; Foods of Korea, 2010; Foods of Peru, 2011; Foods of Cuba, 2011; Foods of Ireland, 2011; Foods of Chile, 2011; Foods of Afghanistan, 2011; Foods of Morocco, 2011; Foods of Israel, 2011; Foods of Pakistan, 2011; Foods of Iceland, 2011; Foods of England, 2011; Foods of Poland, 2012; Foods of Canada, 2012. **Address:** 905 Conway, Ste. 32, Las Cruces, NM 88005, U.S.A. **Online address:** sheenbusby@hotmail.com

SHEERMAN, Barry. British (born England), b. 1940. **Genres:** Politics/Government, Biography. **Career:** University of Wales, lecturer, 1966-79; British Parliament, member of Parliament, 1979-83; European Monetary Union, Cross-Party Advisory Group, chair; National Education Research Trust, chair; European Economic Reform, Cross-Party Advisory Group, chair. Writer. **Publications:** Education and Training: A Policy for Labour, 1986; Community and Commitment: A Tourism Policy for the Labour Party, 1987; Seven Steps to Justice, 1992; (with I. Kramnick) Harold Laski: A Life on the Left, 1993. **Address:** 6 Cross Church St., Huddersfield, WY HD1 2TP, England. **Online address:** sheermanb@parliament.uk

SHEFCHIK, Rick. American (born United States), b. 1952. **Genres:** Sports/Fitness, Mystery/Crime/Suspense. **Career:** Duluth News-Tribune, reporter, 1978-; St. Paul Pioneer Press, columnist, enterprise reporter, feature writer, sportswriter and media critic, 1980-2006; novelist, 2006-. **Publications:** SAM SKARDA MYSTERIES: Amen Corner, 2007; Green Monster, 2008; Frozen Tundra, 2010. **Address:** Poisoned Pen Press, 6962 E 1st Ave., Ste. 103, Scottsdale, AZ 85251, U.S.A. **Online address:** rshefchik@comcast.net

SHEFTEL, Victor O. Israeli/Russian (born Russia), b. 1936. **Genres:** Medicine/Health, Environmental Sciences/Ecology, Sciences, Reference. **Career:** Research Institute of General and Commune Hygiene, scientific fellow, 1961-68; All-Union Research Institute of Hygiene and Toxicology of Pesticides, Polymers and Plastics, senior researcher, scientific fellow and team leader, 1968-89; Ministry of Health, chief environmental toxicologist, 1990-. Writer. **Publications:** Toxic Properties of Polymers and Additives,

1990; Handbook of Toxic Properties of Monomers and Additives, 1995; Farewell to Russian (poems), 1996; Indirect Food Additives: Migration and Toxicology, 2000. Contributor to journals. **Address:** Ministry of Health, 20 King David St., PO Box 1176, Jerusalem, 91010, Israel. **Online address:** victor.sheftel@moh.health.gov.il

SHEFTER, Martin. American (born United States), b. 1943. **Genres:** Politics/Government, History. **Career:** Harvard University, Department of Government, assistant professor, 1969-73, associate professor and director of graduate studies, 1973-74; Cornell University, Department of Government, associate professor, 1975-77, 1978-85, professor, 1986-, placement director, 1980-84, University Library, faculty; University of Chicago, associate professor of political science, 1979-80; Yale University Press, associate editor, 1988-92; Princeton University Press, series co-editor, 1992-. **Publications:** Patronage and Its Opponents: A Theory and Some European Cases, 1977; Political Crisis, Fiscal Crisis: The Collapse and Revival of New York City, 1985; (with B. Ginsberg) Politics by Other Means: The Declining Importance of Elections in America, 1990, rev. ed. as Politics by Other Means: Politicians, Prosecutors, and the Press from Watergate to Whitewater, 1999, 3rd. ed., 2002; (ed.) Capital of the American Century: The National and International Influence of New York City, 1993; Political Parties and the State: The American Historical Experience, 1994; (ed. with I. Katznelson) Shaped by War and Trade: International Influences on American Political Development, 2002. **Address:** Department of Government, Cornell University, 211 White Hall, Ithaca, NY 14853-7901, U.S.A. **Online address:** mas34@cornell.edu

SHEHADEH, Lamia Rustrum. Lebanese (born Lebanon), b. 1940?. **Genres:** Women's Studies And Issues, Military/Defense/Arms Control. **Career:** American University of Beirut, Civilization Sequence Program, director, 1988-94, Berytus Journal, associate editor, 1988-2003, associate professor of cultural studies, 2004. Writer and researcher. **Publications:** AS LAMIA RUSTUM SHEHADEH: (ed.) Women and War in Lebanon, 1999; The Idea of Women in Fundamentalist Islam, 2003. Contributor to journals. **Address:** c/o Author Mail, University Press of Florida, 15 NW 15th St., Gainesville, FL 32611, U.S.A. **Online address:** lshehade@cyberia.net.lb

SHEHADI, Fadlou. (Fadlou A. Shehadi). American/Lebanese (born Lebanon), b. 1926. **Genres:** Philosophy. **Career:** Princeton University, assistant instructor in Arabic, 1950-51; Rockefeller humanities fellow, 1951-53; Rutgers University, assistant professor, 1957-63, associate professor, 1963-72, professor of philosophy, 1972-, now professor emeritus, department head, 1963-68, 1977-81, Philosophy and Contemporary Issues Program, director of the program, 1979-81, Junior Year in France Program, director of the program, 1984-85, 1991-92; American Philosophical Association, chair, 1980-83; Robert Miller Fund for Music, vice-chair, 1986-; Friends of Music, president, 1988-97; Joy in Singing, president of the board, 1992-; Princeton Symphony Orchestra, president of the board. Writer. **Publications:** Ghazali's Unique Unknowable God, 1964; Ghazali's Al-Maqsad alAsná, 1971; Metaphysics in Islamic Philosophy, 1982; (ed. with D.M. Rosenthal) Applied Ethics and Ethical Theory, 1988; Philosophies of Music in Medieval Islam, 1995. **Address:** Department of Philosophy, Rutgers University, College Ave. Campus, 1 Seminary Pl., New Brunswick, NJ 08901, U.S.A.

SHEHADI, Fadlou A. See **SHEHADI, Fadlou.**

SHEINDLIN, Judith. American (born United States), b. 1942. **Genres:** Adult Non-fiction, Self Help, Human Relations/Parenting, Reference. **Career:** New York's Family Court, prosecuting attorney, 1972-82, judge, 1982-86, supervising judge, 1986-96, retired, 1996; Fox Broadcasting Co., television judge, 1996-. Writer. **Publications:** (With J. Getlin) Don't Pee on My Leg and Tell Me It's Raining: America's Toughest Family Court Judge Speaks Out, 1996; Beauty Fades, Dumb is Forever: The Making of A Happy Woman, 1999; Keep It Simple, Stupid: You're Smarter Than You Look, 2000; Judge Judy Sheindlin's Win or Lose by How You Choose!, 2000; You're Smarter Than You Look: Uncomplicating Relationships in Complicated Times, 2001; Judge Judy Sheindlin's You Can't Judge a Book By Its Cover: Cool Rules for School, 2001. Contributor to periodicals. **Address:** PO Box 949, Los Angeles, CA 90078, U.S.A.

SHEININ, David (M. K.). Canadian (born Canada), b. 1960. **Genres:** Bibliography, History. **Career:** Wilfrid Laurier University, Department of History, adjunct professor; Trent University, Department of History, associate professor of history, professor of history, associate faculty of comparative develop-

ment studies, Frost Centre for Canadian Heritage and Development Studies, faculty; University of Idaho, Martin Institute for Peace Studies and Conflict Resolution, associate, 1995-; University Press of the South, history editor of Latin America studies, 2000-; Academia Nacional de la Historia de la República Argentina, académico correspondiente, 2005-; Tri-University, Doctoral Program in History, faculty. **Publications:** Prospects for United States-Argentine Economic Relations in the Early 1990s, 1989; The Organization of American States: An Annotated Bibliography, 1996; (ed. with L.B. Barr) The Jewish Diaspora in Latin America: New Studies on History and Literature, 1996; (ed. with C.A. Mayo) Es Igual Pero Distinto: Essays in the Histories of Canada and Argentina, 1997; Searching for Authority: Pan Americanism, Diplomacy and Politics in United States-Argentine Relations, 1910-1930, 1998; (ed.) Beyond the Ideal: Pan Americanism in Inter-American Affairs, 2000; (contrib.) Diversidad Cultural: Multiples miradas del tiempo presente, 2005; Argentina and the United States: An Alliance Contained, 2006. Contributor of articles to books and periodicals. **Address:** Department of History, Trent University, S101.9 Lady Eaton College S, 1600 W Bank Dr., Peterborough, ON K9J 7B8, Canada. **Online address:** dsheinin@trentu.ca

SHEINMEL, Courtney. American (born United States), b. 1977. **Genres:** Human Relations/Parenting. **Career:** Writopia Lab, teacher of fiction writing. Author and attorney. **Publications:** My So-called Family, 2008; Positively, 2009; Sincerely Sophie/Sincerely Katie, 2010. Contributor to periodicals. **Address:** New York, NY , U.S.A. **Online address:** courtney@courtneysheinmel.com

SHELBY, Anne. American (born United States), b. 1948. **Genres:** Children's Fiction, Poetry, Young Adult Fiction, Literary Criticism And History, Environmental Sciences/Ecology. **Career:** Barbourville Elementary School, artist-in-residence, 1994-95; Kentucky Governor's School for the Arts, Department of Creative Writing, faculty. Writer. **Publications:** FOR CHILDREN: We Keep a Store, 1990; Potluck, 1991; What to Do about Pollution, 1993; Homeplace, 1995; The Someday House, 1996; (contrib.) Waiting for Daylight: For Soprano and Orchestra (1997), 1997; Appalachian Studies, 2006; Adventures of Molly Whuppie and other Appalachian Folktales, 2007; (with C. Hazelaar) The Man Who Lived in a Hollow Tree, 2009. Contributor to journals. Works appear in anthologies. **Address:** 15705 N Hwy. 11, PO Box 43, Oneida, KY 40972, U.S.A. **Online address:** oneida4792@aol.com

SHELBY, Graham. British (born England), b. 1939?. **Genres:** Romance/ Historical, Novels, Young Adult Fiction, Biography. **Career:** Copywriter and book reviewer. **Publications:** The Knights of Dark Renown, 1969; The Kings of Vain Intent, 1970; The Oath and the Sword, 1972; The Villains of the Piece, 1972; The Devil is Loose, 1973; The Wolf at the Door, 1975; The Cannaways, 1978; The Cannaway Concern, 1980; The Edge of the Blade, 1986; Demand the World, 1990. **Address:** c/o Lisa Eveleigh, 26A Rochester Sq., London, GL NW1 9SA, England.

SHELBY, Tommie. American (born United States), b. 1967?. **Genres:** Social Sciences, Philosophy, Politics/Government. **Career:** Ohio State University, assistant professor of philosophy, 1998-2000; Harvard University, assistant professor, 2000-04, professor African and African American studies and philosophy, 2007-, John L. Loeb associate professor of social sciences, 2004-07. Writer. **Publications:** We Who Are Dark: The Philosophical Foundations of Black Solidarity, 2005; (ed. with D. Darby) Hip Hop and Philosophy: Rhyme 2 Reason, 2005. Contributor to periodicals. **Address:** Department of African and African American Studies, Harvard University, Barker Ctr., 12 Quincy St., Cambridge, MA 02138, U.S.A. **Online address:** tshelby@fas.harvard.edu

SHELDEN, Michael. American (born United States), b. 1951. **Genres:** Biography, Novels, Young Adult Fiction. **Career:** Indiana State University, assistant professor, 1979-84, associate professor, 1984-89, professor of English, 1989-; Indiana University, visiting professor, 1990; Daily Telegraph, writer, 1995-2007; Baltimore Sun, fiction critic, 1996-2006. Consultant. **Publications:** (Ed.) George Orwell: Ten Animal Farm Letters to His Agent, Leonard Moore, 1984; Friends of Promise: Cyril Connolly and the World of Horizon, 1989; Orwell: The Authorized Biography, 1991; Graham Greene: The Enemy Within, 1994; George Orwell, 2000; Mark Twain: Man in White: The Grand Adventure of His Final Years, 2010. Contributor to periodicals. **Address:** Department of English, Indiana State University, Root Hall, 400 N 7th St., Terre Haute, IN 47809, U.S.A. **Online address:** michael.shelden@indstate.edu

SHELDON, Ann. See **WAGNER, Sharon Blythe.**

SHELDON, Dyan. British/American (born United States) **Genres:** Novels, Young Adult Fiction. **Career:** Writer. **Publications:** A Witch Got on at Paddington Station, 1987; Alison and the Prince, 1988; I Forgot, 1988; Jack and Alice, 1990; The Whales' Song, 1991; Seymour Finds a Home, 1991; Harry and Chicken, 1992; Harry the Explorer, 1992; Lilah's Monster, 1992; My Brother is a Visitor from Another Planet, 1992; Sky Watching, 1992; Harry's Holiday, 1992; The Garden, 1993; A Night to Remember, 1993; Only Binky, 1993; Counting Cows, 1994; Under the Moon, 1994; Ride On, Sister Vincent, 1994; Love, Your Bear, Pete, 1994; A Bad Place for a Bus Stop, 1994; My Brother is a Superhero, 1994; Elena the Frog, 1997; Unicorn Dreams, 1997; Lizzie and Charley Go Shopping, 1999; Leon Loves Bugs, 2000; Undercover Angel, 2000; Undercover Angel Strikes Again, 2000; Clara and Buster Go Moondancing, 2001; Lizzie and Charley Go to the Movies, 2001; He's Not My Dog, 2001; Lizzie and Charley Go Away for the Weekend, 2002; The Last Angel, 2003; Vampire across the Way, 2004; What Mona Wants Mona Gets, 2005; Deep and Meaningful Diaries from Planet Janet, 2007; Drusilla and Her Brothers, 2009; One or Two Things I Learned About Love, 2012. FOR YOUNG ADULTS: Tall, Thin, and Blonde, 1993; You Can Never Go Home Anymore, 1993; Save the Last Dance for Me, 1993; The Boy of My Dreams, 1997; Confessions of a Teenage Drama Queen, 1999; And Baby Makes Two, 2000; My Perfect Life, 2002; Planet Janet, 2002; Sophie Pitt-Turnbull Discovers America, 2003; Planet Janet in Orbit, 2004; Perfect, 2005; Confessions of a Hollywood Star, 2005; I Conquer Britain, 2006; The Difficult Job of Keeping Time, 2008; My Worst Best Friend, 2010; The Crazy Things Girls Do For Love, 2010. FOR ADULTS: Victim of Love, 1982; The Dreams of an Average Man, 1985; My Life as a Whale, 1992; On the Road Reluctantly, 1995. **Address:** Candlewick Press, 99 Dover St., Somerville, MA 02144, U.S.A. **Online address:** dyan@dyansheldon.co.uk

SHELDON, Garrett Ward. American (born United States), b. 1954. **Genres:** Ethics, Intellectual History, Politics/Government, Theology/Religion, Social Sciences. **Career:** University of New Mexico, Honors Program, instructor, 1976-77; Rutgers University, Livingston College, teaching assistant, 1978-80; University of Virginia, College at Wise, Department of Behavioral and Social Sciences, assistant professor, 1983-88, associate professor, 1988-93, professor, 1993-chair, 1988-95, 2001-02, 2005-, John Morton Beaty professor, 1997-; Regent University, distinguished visiting lecturer, 2001-02, 2002-03. Writer. **Publications:** The History of Political Theory: Ancient Greece to Modern America, 1988; (ed.) Religion and Politics: Major Thinkers on the Relation of Church and State, 1990; The Political Philosophy of Thomas Jefferson, 1991; (ed.) Major Concepts in Politics and Political Theory, 1991; (with D. Morris) What Would Jesus Do?: A Contemporary Retelling of Charles M. Sheldon's Classic In his Steps, 1993; The Political Thought of John Taylor; What Would Jefferson Say?, 1998; Jefferson and Atatürk: Political Philosophies, 2000; (ed. with D.L. Dreisbach) Religion and Political Culture in Jefferson's Virginia, 2000; (ed.) The Encyclopedia of Political Thought, 2001; The Political Philosophy of James Madison, 2001; (with C.W. Hill, Jr.) Liberal Republicanism of John Taylor of Caroline, 2008; The Political Philosophy of John Wycliffe, forthcoming; Searching for the Secularism in America, forthcoming; American Religious Freedom, forthcoming. **Address:** Department of Social Sciences, University of Virginia's College at Wise, 241 Smiddy Hall, 1 College Ave., Wise, VA 24293, U.S.A. **Online address:** g_sheldon@uvawise.edu

SHELDON, Joseph K(enneth). American (born United States), b. 1943. **Genres:** Environmental Sciences/Ecology, Biology, Theology/Religion, Bibliography, Education. **Career:** Eastern College, professor of biology, 1971-92; Messiah College, professor of biology, 1992-2007, distinguished professor, 2002-07. Writer. **Publications:** Rediscovery of Creation: A Bibliographical Study of the Church's Response to the Environmental Crisis, 1992; (co-author) Redeeming Creation: A Biblical Basis of Environmental Ethics, 1993. Contributor to journals and magazines. **Address:** 36 S Pheasant Run Rd., Coupeville, WA 98239, U.S.A. **Online address:** jsheldon@messiah.edu

SHELDON, Mary. American (born United States), b. 1955?. **Genres:** Novels, Young Adult Fiction, Literary Criticism And History. **Career:** Writer. **Publications:** Perhaps I'll Dream of Darkness, 1981; Portrait of Rosemary, 1983; The Shadow Girl, 1987; Special Stories for Special Children: The Summer, 1988; Under the Influence, 1990; Day in the City, 1992; Day at the Farm, 1992; Day at the Aquarium, 1992; Day at the Zoo, 1992; Audrey Hepburn's Enchanted Tales, 1993; I Am America: Get Hooked on Reading, 1995; (with S. Sheldon) The Adventures of Drippy the Runaway Raindrop, 1996; The Santasaurus, 1996; Raising My Titanic: The Diary of a Single Mother, 1996;

D Resolution, 2000; The Blue Unicorn, 2000; Halfway Home, 2002; Reflection, 2003; Pandora Brown, 2004. Contributor to periodicals. **Address:** c/o Author Mail, Kensington Publishing Corp., 850 3rd Ave., New York, NY 10022, U.S.A.

SHELEMAY, Kay Kaufman. American (born United States), b. 1948. **Genres:** Music, Autobiography/Memoirs, Science Fiction/Fantasy. **Career:** Columbia University, assistant professor of music, 1977-83; New York University, Department of Music, visiting professor, 1981-82, assistant professor, 1982-85, associate professor, 1985-90, Hagop Kevorkian Center for Near Eastern Studies, faculty; Wesleyan University, professor of music, 1990-92; Harvard University, professor of music, 1992-, G. Gordon Watts professor of music and of African and African American studies, 1992-, Walter Channing Cabot fellow, 2001-02; Society for Ethnomusicology, president, 1997-99; Harvard Humanities Center, board director, 1999-; Library of Congress, American Folklife Center, board chair, 2003-05; Harvard Magazine, board director, 2005-09. Writer. **Publications:** Liturgical Music of the Falasha of Ethiopia, 1977; The Jews of Ethiopia: A People in Transition, 1986; Music, Ritual and Falasha History, 1986; A Song of Longing: An Ethiopian Journey, 1991; Let Jasmine Rain Down: Song and Remembrance among Syrian Jews, 1998; Soundscapes Classical: Case Studies from the Western Classical Repertory, 2001; Soundscapes: Exploring Music in a Changing World, 2001, 2nd ed., 2006. EDITOR: The Garland Library of Readings in Ethnomusicology, 7 vols., 1990; Ethnomusicological Theory and Method, 1990; Century of Ethnomusicological Thought, 1990; Cross-Cultural Musical Analysis, 1990; History, Definitions, and Scope of Ethnomusicology, 1990; Music as Culture, 1990; (with P. Jeffery) Ethiopian Christian Liturgical Chant: An Anthology, 3 vols., 1993-97; Studies in Jewish Musical Traditions: Insights from the Harvard Collection of Judaica Sound Recordings, 2001; (with S. Coakley) Pain and Its Transformations: The Interface of Biology and Culture, 2007. Works appear in anthologies. Contributor to periodicals. **Address:** Department of Music, Harvard University, Rm. 6 Music Bldg., N Yard, Cambridge, MA 02138, U.S.A. **Online address:** shelemay@fas.harvard.edu

SHELL, Robert C.H. South African (born South Africa), b. 1949. **Genres:** History, Mathematics/Statistics, Social Sciences, Film, Bibliography. **Career:** ICL British Computer Firm, trainee computer programmer, 1968-69; South African Cultural History Museum, acting assistant director, 1977-78; University of California, visiting lecturer in African history, 1986-87; University of Rochester, teacher of colonial American history, 1988-89; State University of New York College, Oswego, visiting professor of African history, 1988; Princeton University, assistant professor of African history, 1988-96, director of African studies, 1989-93, executive secretary, 1991-92; University of the Western Cape, Department of Statistics, associate professor, 2001-05, professor of historical demography, 2005-, extraordinary professor of historical demography, 2006-07. Writer. **Publications:** Meillon's People of Colour, 1978; Children of Bondage: A Social History of the Slave Society at the Cape of Good Hope, 1652-1838, 1994; Diaspora to Diorama -The Slave Lodge, 2nd ed., 2007; Changing Hands: A Cadsatral Calender of the Cape, 1580 to 1875, 2007; (comp. with S.R. Shell and M. Kamedien) Bibliographies of Bondage: Selected Bibliographies of South African Slavery and Abolition, 2008. Contributor to books and journals. **Address:** Department of Statistics, University of Western Cape, Rm. 3.23, New Science Bldg., Modderdam Rd., Cape Town, 7535, South Africa. **Online address:** rshell@uwc.ac.za

SHELL, Susan Meld. American (born United States), b. 1948. **Genres:** Novels, Politics/Government, Philosophy. **Career:** Harvard University, Leverett House, resident tutor, 1972-74; Radcliffe College, Bunting Institute, research fellow, 1982; Concordia University, Department of Political Science, assistant professor, 1975-77; McMaster University, Department of Philosophy, postdoctoral fellow, 1977-80; Boston College, Department of Political Science, assistant professor, 1980-83, associate professor, 1983-96, professor of political science, 1996-, department chair, 2003-; Brock University, Department of Politics, visiting associate professor, 1985. Writer. **Publications:** The Rights of Reason: A Study of Kant's Philosophy and Politics, 1980; The Embodiment of Reason: Kant on Spirit, Generation, and Community, 1996; Kant and the Limits of Autonomy, 2009; (ed. with R. Faulkner and T.E. Schneider) America at Risk: Threats to Liberal Self-government in an Age of Uncertainty, 2009. **Address:** Department of Political Science, Boston College, 231 McGuinn Hall, 140 Commonwealth Ave., Chestnut Hill, MA 02467-3807, U.S.A. **Online address:** susan.shell@bc.edu

SHELLENBERGER, Michael. American (born United States), b. 1971?.

Genres: Environmental Sciences/Ecology. **Career:** Breakthrough Institute, co-founder and president, 2002-; Apollo Alliance, co-founder, 2003; American Environics (environmental research and consulting firm), co-founder and managing partner. Writer, consultant and environmental activist. **Publications:** (Ed. with K. Danaher) Fighting for the Soul of Brazil, 1995; Break Through: From the Death of Environmentalism to the Politics of Possibility, 2007 as Break Through: Why We Can't Leave Saving the Planet to Environmentalists, 2009. Contributor to periodicals. **Address:** Breakthrough Institute, 436 14th St., Ste. 820, Oakland, CA 94612, U.S.A. **Online address:** michael@thebreakthrough.org

SHELLER, Mimi Beth. American (born United States), b. 1967. **Genres:** Social Sciences. **Career:** University of Michigan, Dubois-Mandela-Rodney Postdoctoral Fellow Center for African and Afro-American Studies, fellow, 1997-98; Swarthmore College, visiting associate professor; Lancaster University, visiting senior research fellow. Writer. **Publications:** Democracy after Slavery: Black Publics and Peasant Radicalism in Haiti and Jamaica, 2000; Consuming the Caribbean: From Arawaks to Zombies, 2003; (co-ed.) Uprootings/Regroundings: Questions of Home and Migration, 2003; (ed. with J. Urry) Tourism Mobilities: Places to Play, Places in Play, 2004; (ed. with J. Urry) Mobile Technologies of the City, 2006; Citizenship From Below: Erotic Agency and Caribbean Freedom, 2012. Contributor to journals. **Address:** Department of Sociology & Anthropology, Swarthmore College, 238 Kohlberg Hall, 500 College Ave., Swarthmore, PA 19081, U.S.A. **Online address:** mshelle1@swarthmore.edu

SHELLEY, Deborah. *See* **MAZOYER, Deborah.**

SHELTON, Allen C. American (born United States) **Genres:** Cultural/Ethnic Topics, Area Studies. **Career:** Buffalo State College, associate professor of sociology; Auburn University, lecturer, 1988. Writer. **Publications:** Dreamworlds of Alabama (memoir), 2007. **Address:** Department of Sociology, Buffalo State College, Classroom Bldg. B307, 1300 Elmwood Ave., Buffalo, NY 14222, U.S.A. **Online address:** sheltoac@buffalostate.edu

SHELTON, Beth Anne. American (born United States), b. 1957. **Genres:** Sociology. **Career:** Oberlin College, Department of Sociology-Anthropology, assistant professor, 1984-86; State University of New York, assistant professor, 1986-90, associate professor of sociology and director of graduate studies, 1990-94; University of Texas, College of Liberal Arts, Department of Sociology and Anthropology, associate professor, 1994-96, professor, 1996-, Women's Studies Program, director, 1997-2010, graduate advisor, 2002-05. Writer. **Publications:** (Co-author) Houston: Growth and Decline in a Sunbelt Boomtown, 1989; Women, Men, and Time: Gender Differences in Paid Work, Housework and Leisure, 1992; (with B. Agger) Fast Families, Virtual Children: A Critical Sociology of Families and Schooling, 2007. Works appear in anthologies. Contributor of articles to journals. **Address:** Department of Sociology & Anthropology, University of Texas Arlington, PO Box 19599, Arlington, TX 76019-0599, U.S.A. **Online address:** shelton@uta.edu

SHELTON, Connie. American (born United States), b. 1951. **Genres:** Novels, Mystery/Crime/Suspense, Young Adult Fiction. **Career:** Pitney Bowes, collections supervisor, 1971-72; The March Co., partner, 1974-90; Columbine Publishing Group, president, 1994. Writer. **Publications:** Deadly Gamble, 1995; Vacations Can Be Murder, 1996; Publish Your Own Novel, 1996; Partnerships Can Kill, 1997; Small Towns Can Be Murder, 1998; Memories Can Be Murder, 1999; Honeymoons Can Be Murder, 2001; Reunions Can Be Murder, 2002; Competition Can Be Murder: A Charlie Parker Mystery, 2004; Balloons Can Be Murder: A Charlie Parker Mystery, 2005; Obsessions Can Be Murder: A Charlie Parker Mystery, 2006; Sweet Masterpiece, 2010; Gossip Can Be Murder, 2010; Stardom can be Murder, 2011; Sweet's Sweets, 2011; Sweet Holidays, forthcoming. **Address:** Columbine Publishing Group Inc., PO Box 416, Angel Fire, NM 87710-0416, U.S.A.

SHELTON, Hal T(erry). American (born United States), b. 1935. **Genres:** History, Biography, Autobiography/Memoirs, Social Sciences, Humanities. **Career:** Rice University, associate professor, professor, 1969-72; North Harris County College, adjunct instructor in history, 1986-88; University of Houston, lecturer in history, 1989-91; San Jacinto College, instructor in history, 1991-; American Military University, adjunct professor, 1993-; San Jacinto College Central, professor. **Publications:** General Richard Montgomery and the American Revolution: From Redcoat to Rebel, 1994. EDITOR: (and contrib.) Encyclopedia of American Political Parties and Elections, 1990; Ameri-

can History Reader, vol. II, 1992; (and contrib.) The American Revolution: An Encyclopedia, 1993. **Address:** San Jacinto College Central, 8060 Spencer Hwy., Pasadena, TX 77505, U.S.A. **Online address:** hshelt@sjcd.cc.tx.us

SHELTON, Mark L(ogan). American (born United States), b. 1958. **Genres:** Adult Non-fiction, Literary Criticism And History, Writing/Journalism, Medicine/Health. **Career:** University of Pittsburgh, instructor in writing, 1982-88; Presbyterian-University Hospital, editor, 1984-85; Ohio Magazine, editor, 1988-91; Ohio University, adjunct instructor in writing, 1988-94; College of the Holy Cross, lecturer, 1994; University of Massachusetts Medical School, director of public affairs and publications and managing editor, associate vice chancellor for communications, 1995-. Writer. **Publications:** Working in a Very Small Place: The Making of a Neurosurgeon, 1989; The Next Great Thing: The Sun, the Stirling Engine and the Drive to Change the World, 1994. Contributor to magazines. **Address:** Office of Communications, University of Massachusetts Medical School, 55 Lake Ave. N, Worcester, MA 01655, U.S.A. **Online address:** mark.shelton@umassmed.edu

SHELTON, Richard. American (born United States), b. 1933. **Genres:** Adult Non-fiction, Poetry. **Career:** Lowell School, teacher, 1958-62; Ruth Stephan Poetry Center, director, 1964-65; University of Arizona, instructor, 1960-70, assistant professor, 1970-74, associate professor, 1974-79, creative writing program, director, 1979-81, professor of English, 1979-91, regent's professor emeritus, 1991-, Poetry Center, faculty fellow; Arizona Commission on the Arts, director of writers workshop, 1974-80; Association of Writers & Writing Programs, board director, 1983-, president; National Federation of State Poetry Societies, national honorary chancellor. Writer. **Publications:** Journal of Return, 1969; The Tattooed Desert, 1971; The Heroes of Our Time, 1972; Of All the Dirty Words, 1972; Among the Stones, 1973; Chosen Place: Poems, 1975; You Can't Have Everything, 1975; The Bus to Veracruz, 1978; Selected Poems: 1969-1981, 1982; A Kind of Glory, 1982; Hohokam, 1986; The Other Side of the Story, 1987; (nonfiction) Going Back to Bisbee, 1992; Crossing the Yard: Thirty Years as a Prison Volunteer, 2007; Last Person to Hear Your Voice, 2007. **Address:** Department of English, University of Arizona, Rm. 445, Modern Languages Bldg., 1423 E University Blvd., PO Box 210067, Tucson, AZ 85721, U.S.A. **Online address:** rshelton@email.arizona.edu

SHEM, Samuel. American (born United States), b. 1944. **Genres:** Novels, Plays/Screenplays, Education, Psychology, Self Help, Literary Criticism And History. **Career:** Harvard Medical School, clinical instructor in psychiatry, Division on Addictions, chair of clinical projects; Center for Gender Relations, co-director; Boston Shakespeare Co., writer-in-residence. **Publications:** The House of God: A Novel, 1978; The Shem Plays, 1981; Napoleon's Dinner and Room for One Woman, 1981; Fine: A Novel, 1985; Mount Misery, 1997; (with J. Surrey) We Have to Talk: Healing Dialogues between Women and Men, 1998; (with J. Surrey) Bill W. and Dr. Bob, 2000; Spirit of the Place, 2008. Contributor to periodicals. **Address:** c/o Robert Barnett, Williams & Connolly, 725 12th St. NW, Washington, DC 20005, U.S.A.

SHEMESH, Haim. Israeli/Russian (born Russia), b. 1954. **Genres:** Politics/Government, History, International Relations/Current Affairs, Third World, Social Sciences. **Career:** Tel-Aviv University, Russian and East European Research Center, researcher, 1979-89; writer, 1989-. **Publications:** Soviet-Iraqi Relations, 1968-1988: In the Shadow of the Iraq-Iran Conflict, 1992. **Address:** Rehov Esther Hamalcha 10, Petah Tikva, 49386, Israel.

SHEMIE, Bonnie (Jean Brenner). Canadian/American (born United States), b. 1949. **Genres:** Architecture, Children's Non-fiction, Homes/Gardens, Literary Criticism And History, Illustrations. **Career:** Freelance illustrator, 1976-85. Writer and architectural artist. **Publications:** SELF-ILLUSTRATED NONFICTION: Building Canada, 2001. NONFICTION: Houses of Snow, Skin, and Bones, 1989; Hus av sno, hudar och ben, 1989; Hus av Bark och Naver, 1990; Houses of Bark, 1990; Maisons d'ecorce, 1990; Maisons de Peaux et de Terre, 1991; Houses of Hide and Earth, 1991; Maisons de Neighes, de pierres et d'os, 1992; Houses of Wood, 1992; Mounds of Earth and Shell, 1993; Maisons de Bois, 1994; Houses of Adobe, 1994; Maisons d'adobe, 1994; Houses of Stone and Adobe: Native Dwellings: Southwest, 1995; Houses of China, 1996; Ainsi s'est construit le Canada, 2002. **Address:** 4474 de Maisonneuve W, Montreal, QC H3Z 1L7, Canada.

SHEN, Aisling Juanjuan. American/Chinese (born China), b. 1974. **Genres:** Autobiography/Memoirs. **Career:** Wellington Management Co. (investment management firm), research associate. Writer, educator and researcher. **Publications:** A Tiger's Heart: The Story of a Modern Chinese Woman (memoir), 2009. Contributor to periodicals. **Address:** Wellington Management Co., 75 State St., Boston, MA 02109, U.S.A. **Online address:** aisling@atigersheart.com

SHEN, Dajun. (Sang Ye). Chinese (born China), b. 1955?. **Genres:** Area Studies. **Career:** Hong Kong Press, writer; China Daily News, feature writer. **Publications:** (With Z. Xinxin) Chinese Lives: An Oral History of Contemporary China, 1987; (with N. Jose and S. Trevaskes) The Finish Line: A Long March Through China and Australia, 1994; Lung lai ti che i nien, trans. as The Year the Dragon Came, 1996; 1949, 1989, 1999, 1999; China Candid: The People on the People's Republic, 2006. Contributor to journals. **Address:** China Daily News, Ste. 15, Huixin Dongjie, Chaoyang District, Beijing, 100029, China.

SHEN, Fan (A.). American/Chinese (born China), b. 1955?. **Genres:** Autobiography/Memoirs, Translations, History, Social Sciences. **Career:** Three Gorge Commune, farm hand, 1968-72; 5702 Aircraft Factory, assembly man, 1972-74, electrician, 1974-77; Tianjin Institute of Light Industry, lecturer, 1982-85; Marquette University, instructor, 1988-90, teaching assistant, 1988-90; Rockland Community College, assistant professor, 1991-93; Rochester Community and Technical College, professor, 1994-. Writer and translator. **Publications:** TRANSLATOR: S. Ostrander and L. Schroeder, Superlearning, 1983; B.C.J. Levegoed, Phases, 1986; M. Ende, Momo, 1988. OTHER: Gang of One: Memoirs of a Red Guard, 2004. Contributor of articles to journals. Works appear in anthologies. **Address:** Department of English, Rochester Community and Technical College, 336 Memorial Hall, 851 30th Ave. SE, Rochester, MN 55904-4999, U.S.A. **Online address:** fan.shen@roch.edu

SHENGOLD, Leonard. American (born United States), b. 1925. **Genres:** Psychology, Medicine/Health, Young Adult Non-fiction, Social Sciences. **Career:** New York University Medical School, clinical professor of psychiatry, 1980-; New York University Psychoanalytic Institute, training analyst. Writer. **Publications:** Halo in the Sky: Observations on Anality and Defense, 1988; Soul Murder: The Effects of Childhood Abuse and Deprivation, 1989; Father, Don't You See I'm Burning: Reflections on Sex, Narcissism, Symbolism and Murder: From Everything to Nothing, 1991; That Boy Will Come to Nothing: Freud's Ego Ideal and Freud as Ego Ideal, 1993; Delusions of Everyday Life, 1995; Soul Murder Revisited: Thoughts about Therapy, Hate, Love and Memory, 1999; Is There Life without Mother?: Psychoanalysis, Biography, Creativity, 2000; Haunted by Parents, 2006. Contributor to journals. **Address:** School of Medicine, Psychiatry, New York University, Rm 230, Bellevue C&D Bldg., 462 1st Ave., 2nd Fl., New York, NY 10016, U.S.A. **Online address:** lsheng@worldnet.att.net

SHENHAV, Yehouda A. Israeli (born Israel), b. 1952. **Genres:** Adult Nonfiction. **Career:** Stanford University, Department of Sociology, lecturer, 1985, visiting assistant professor, 1988-90; Tel Aviv University, Department of Sociology and Anthropology, assistant professor, 1986-89, senior lecturer, 1989-93, associate professor, 1994-2006, department chair, 1995-98, academic director of the advanced learning, 2005-09, professor, 2006-; University of Wisconsin-Madison, School of Business, visiting associate professor, 1992-93; Van Leer Jerusalem Institute, Jerusalem, Israel, senior research fellow, 1999-2006, Forum on Israeli Culture and Society, co-director, 1999-2002, 2004-06; Columbia University, Department of Sociology, visiting associate professor, 2002-04; Journal of Management Studies, editor; Organization Studies, senior editor, 2003-; Jerusalem Vanleer Institute, head of advanced studies, 2006-09. **Publications:** (With Y. Haberfeld) Beyond a Smoking Gun Type Discrimination: A Firm Level Analysis of Rewards and Opportunities, 1987; Ide'ologyot Nihul Be-'idan Ha-ratsyonaliyut, 1991; Mekhonat Ha-irgun: ḥakirah Biḳortit Bi-yesodot Torat Ha-nihul, 1995; Ma'avak Holekh ye-ne'lam: Yitsug Sikhsukhe Ha-'avodah Be-khitve 'et Shel Tenuat Ha-nihul Ben Ha-shanim 1887-1932: Kolel Taktsir 'Ivri Ve- Angli, 1995; Manufacturing Rationality: The Engineering Foundations of the Managerial Revolution, 1999; (with H. Haver and P.M. Haley) Mizrahim Be-Yiśra'el: 'Iyun Biḳorti Mehudash, 2002; Merḥav, Adamah, Bayit, 2003; Ha-Yehudim-ha- 'Arvim: Le'umiyut, Dat Ve-etniyut, 2003; ḳolonyaliyut yeha-matsav Ha-postḳolonyali: Antologyah Shel Targum U-makor, 2004; (with Y. Yonah) Rav Tarbutiyut Mahi? 'al Ha-politikah Shel Ha-shonut Be- Yiśra'el, 2005; The Arab Jews: A Postcolonial Reading of Nationalism, Religion, and Ethnicity, 2006; (with Y. Yonah) Gizanut be-Yiśrael, 2008; (with K. Shmidṭ S. Tselniḳer and orkhim) Le-fanim mi-shurat ha-din: he-ḥarig u-matsav ha-ḥefrum, 2009; Be-malkodet ha-ḳay ha-yaroḳ: masah poliṭit Yehudit, 2010. **Address:** Depart-

ment of Sociology and Anthropology, Tel Aviv University, Ramat-Aviv, Tel Aviv, 69978, Israel. **Online address:** shenhav@post.tau.ac.il

SHENK, David. American (born United States), b. 1966. **Genres:** Information Science/Computers, Communications/Media. **Career:** Columbia University, Freedom Forum Media Studies Center, fellow, 1995-96; The Japan Society, fellow, 1998; TheAtlantic.com, correspondent; Hotwired, author; National Public Radio, producer. Educator and radio commentator. **Publications:** (With S. Silberman) Skeleton Key: A Dictionary for Deadheads, 1994; Data Smog: Surviving the Information Glut, 1997; End of Patience: Cautionary Notes on the Information Revolution, 1999; The Forgetting, Alzheimer's, Portrait of An Epidemic, 2001; Immortal Game: A History of Chess or How 32 Carved Pieces on a Board Illuminated Our Understanding of War, Art, Science and the Human Brain, 2006; The Genius in All of Us: Why Everything You've Been Told about Genetics, Talent and IQ is Wrong, 2010; The Genius in All of Us: New Insights into Genetics, Talent and IQ, 2011. Contributor to periodicals. Works appear in anthologies. **Address:** 216 St. Johns Pl., Apt. D, Brooklyn, NY 11217, U.S.A. **Online address:** homepage@davidshenk.com

SHENKMAN, Richard (Bennett). American (born United States), b. 1954. **Genres:** Communications/Media, History, Mythology/Folklore. **Career:** WTVQ, general assignment reporter, 1981; KOCO TV, overnight reporter, 1981-82; KUTV News, investigative reporter, 1982-89, Washington bureau chief, 1989-90; NBC Sunday Today Show, contributing reporter, 1991; KIRO TV News, managing editor, 1993-95; Learning Channel, producer, host, writer, 1996; American University, adjunct lecturer, 1997-98; TomPaine.com, managing editor and co-founder, 1998-2000; History News Network, founder and editor, 2001-; George Mason University, associate professor of history, 2002-. **Publications:** (With K. Reiger) One-Night Stands with American History: Odd, Amusing, and Little-Known Incidents, 1980, rev. ed., 2003; Legends, Lies and Cherished Myths of American History, 1988; I Love Paul Revere, Whether He Rode or Not, 1991; Legends, Lies and Cherished Myths of World History, 1993; Presidential Ambition: How the President Gained Power, Kept Power and Got Things Done, 1999; Just How Stupid Are We?: Facing the Truth About the American Voter, 2008. **Address:** History News Network, 119 S Main St., Ste. 220, Seattle, WA 98104, U.S.A. **Online address:** editor@historynewsnetwork.org

SHEPARD, Alicia C. American (born United States), b. 1953. **Genres:** Biography. **Career:** San Jose Mercury News, reporter, 1982-87; American Journalism Review, senior writer; American University, adjunct professor of journalism; University of Texas, Times Mirror visiting professor, 2005-06; National Public Radio, staff, 2007-. **Publications:** (With C. Trost) Running Toward Danger: Stories Behind the Breaking News of 9/11, 2002; Woodward and Bernstein: Life in the Shadow of Watergate, 2007. **Address:** Gail Ross Literacy Agency, 1666 Connecticut Ave. NW, Ste. 500, Washington, DC 20009, U.S.A. **Online address:** alicia@woodwardandbernstein.net

SHEPARD, Charles E. American (born United States), b. 1954. **Genres:** Documentaries/Reportage, Young Adult Non-fiction, History. **Career:** Charlotte Observer, reporter, 1977-91; Washington Post, reporter. **Publications:** Forgiven: The Rise and Fall of Jim Bakker and the PTL Ministry (nonfiction), 1989, 2nd ed., 1991. **Address:** 3223 Morrison St. NW, Washington, DC 20015-1636, U.S.A.

SHEPARD, Geoff Carroll. American (born United States), b. 1944?. **Genres:** Politics/Government, History. **Career:** White House Domestic Policy Council, associate director. Writer and attorney. **Publications:** The Secret Plot to Make Ted Kennedy President: Inside the Real Watergate Conspiracy, 2008. **Address:** The Richard Nixon Foundation, 18001 Yorba Linda Blvd., Yorba Linda, CA 92886, U.S.A. **Online address:** geoff@thesecretplot.com

SHEPARD, Jim. (Scott Eller). American (born United States), b. 1956. **Genres:** Novels, Novellas/Short Stories, Literary Criticism And History. **Career:** University of Michigan, lecturer in creative writing, 1980-83; Williams College, Department of English, assistant professor, 1983-90, associate professor, 1990-95, professor of English, 1995-, J. Leland Miller professor of American history, literature, and eloquence. Writer. **Publications:** Flights (novel), 1983; Paper Doll (novel), 1987; Lights out in the Reptile House (novel), 1990; Kiss of the Wolf (novel), 1994; (ed. with R. Hansen) You've Got To Read This: Contemporary American Writers Introduce Stories That Held Them in Awe, 1994; (ed. with A. Hempel) Unleashed, 1995; Batting against Castro (short stories), 1996; Nosferatu: A Novel, 1998; (ed.) Writers at the Movies: Twenty-Six Contemporary Authors Celebrate Twenty-Six Memorable Movies, 2000; Project X, 2004; Love and Hydrogen: New and Selected Stories, 2004; Like You'd Understand, Anyway, 2007; Master of Miniatures, 2010; You Think That's Bad, 2011. Contributor to periodicals. **Address:** Department of English, Williams College, Rm. 212 Hollander Hall, 114 N Academic Bldg., Williamstown, MA 01267, U.S.A. **Online address:** james.r.shepard@williams.edu

SHEPARD, Molly Dickinson. American (born United States) **Genres:** Business/Trade/Industry, Communications/Media, Adult Non-fiction. **Career:** The Leader's Edge (women's career development firm), founder and chief executive officer, 2000-; Diversified Search, vice president; Hay Career Consultants, regional vice president; Manchester Inc. (career development firm), chairman, president and co-founder; Institute for Paralegal Training, director of admissions; The United Way of Southeastern Pennsylvania, chairman emeritus; WHYY Inc., chairman emeritus; Pennsylvania Women's Forum, president emeritus; The Greater Philadelphia Chamber of Commerce, vice chairman. Writer. **Publications:** (With J.K. Stimmler) Stop Whining & Start Winning: 8 Surefire Ways for Women to Thrive in Business, 2005; (with J.K. Stimmler and P.J. Dean) Breaking into the Boys' Club: 8 Ways for Women to Get Ahead in Business, 2009. **Address:** c/o Author Mail, Penguin Group, Plume Publicity, 375 Hudson St., New York, NY 10014, U.S.A.

SHEPARD, Neil. American (born United States), b. 1951. **Genres:** Poetry. **Career:** Louisiana State University, instructor in English, 1980-82; Rider College, assistant professor of English, 1982-85; Johnson State College, professor of creative writing and literature, 1985-2009, chairman of department, 1987-91; Green Mountains Review, senior editor, poetry editor, 1987-; Vermont Studio Center, writing program director, 1989-97; International Studies University, visiting professor, 1991; Chautauqua Institution, visiting writer, 2001, 2006, 2009; Wilkes University, faculty in MFA creative writing program, 2006-. **Publications:** Scavenging the Country for a Heartbeat (poems), 1992; I'm Here Because I Lost My Way (poems), 1998; This Far from the Source: Poems, 2006; Travel-Untravel, 2011. Contributor of articles, reviews and poetry to periodicals. **Address:** Department of Writing and Literature, Johnson State College, Martinetti 2nd Fl., Johnson, VT 05656, U.S.A. **Online address:** neil.shepard@jsc.edu

SHEPARD, Sam. American (born United States), b. 1943. **Genres:** Novels, Plays/Screenplays, Novellas/Short Stories, Novels, Young Adult Non-fiction, inspirational/Motivational Literature. **Career:** Conley Arabian Horse Ranch, stable hand, 1958-60; Bishop's Company Repertory Players, actor, 1962-63; writer, 1964-; Holy Modal Rounders, rock musician, 1968-71; Magic Theatre, playwright-in-residence, 1974-84. **Publications:** Cowboys, 1964; The Rock Garden, 1964; 4-H Club, 1965; Up to Thursday, 1965; Dog, 1965; Chicago, 1965; Icarus's Mother, 1965; Fourteen Hundred Thousand, 1966; Red Cross, 1966; Five Plays: Chicago, Icarus's Mother, Red Cross, Fourteen Hundred Thousand, Melodrama Play, 1967; Cowboys No.2, 1967; Forensic and the Navigators, 1967; Turista: A Play in Two Acts, 1968; The Unseen Hand, 1969; Holy Ghostly, 1970; Zabriskie Point, 1970 as Red Desert, 1972; Shaved Splits, 1970; Operation Sidewinder, 1970; The Unseen Hand and Other Plays, 1971; Cowboy Mouth, 1971; Mad Dog Blues and Other Plays, 1971; Back Bog Beast Bait, 1971; Sam Shepard: Mad Dog Blues & Other Plays, 1972; The Unseen Hand and Other Plays, 1972; The Tooth of Crime, 1972, rev. ed., 2006; Hawk Moon (short stories), 1973; Blue Bitch, 1973; (co-author) Nightwalk, 1973; The Tooth of Crime and Geography of a Horse Dreamer, 1974; Little Ocean, 1974; Action and The Unseen Hand, 1975; Killer's Head, 1975; Curse of the Starving Class: A Play in Three Acts, 1976, rev. ed., 1997; Angel City and Other Plays, 1976; Angel City, Curse of the Starving Class and Other Plays, 1976; Rolling Thunder Logbook, 1977, rev. ed., 2004; Buried Child, Seduced, Suicide in B-flat, 1978; Savage/Love, 1979; Four Two-Act Plays, 1980; True West, 1981; Seven Plays, 1981; Chicago and Other Plays, 1981; Motel Chronicles, 1982; The Sad Lament of Pecos Bill on the Eve of Killing His Wife, 1983; Fool for Love and Other Plays, 1983; Superstitions, 1983; (with W. Wenders) Paris, Texas, 1984; A Lie of the Mind, 1985; (with J. Chaikin) The War in Heaven, 1987; Joseph Chaikin and Sam Shepard: Letters and Texts, 1972-1984, 1989; States of Shock, 1991; States of Shock, Far North, and Silent Tongue, 1994; Simpatico, 1995; Cruising Paradise, 1996; Buried Child: A Play, 1997, rev. ed., 2006; Eyes for Consuela, 1999; Dash and Lilly, 1999; Late Henry Moss: Eyes for Consuela: When the World was Green: Three Plays, 2002; Great Dream of Heaven: Stories, 2002; (with S. Fife) Best Revenge: How the Theatre Saved My Life and Has Been Killing Me Ever Since, 2004; God of Hell: A Play, 2005; (with W. Wenders) Don't

Come Knocking: Das Buch Zum Film, 2005; Kicking a Dead Horse: A Play, 2008; Day Out of Days: Stories, 2010; Fifteen One-act Plays, 2012. **Address:** International Creative Management Inc., 8942 Wilshire Blvd., Beverly Hills, CA 90211-1934, U.S.A. **Online address:** admin@sam-shepard.com

SHEPHARD, Roy Jesse. Canadian (born Canada), b. 1929. **Genres:** Medicine/Health, Sports/Fitness, Young Adult Non-fiction. **Career:** Institute of Aviation Medicine, flying officer and flight lieutenant, 1954-56; University of Cincinnati, Department of Preventive Medicine and Applied Physiology, Fulbright Exchange fellow and assistant professor, 1956-58; Chemical Defense Experimental Establishment, senior scientific officer, 1958-59, principal scientific officer, 1959-64; Fitness Canada/Active Living, Health and Welfare Canada, consultant, 1964-; University of Toronto, Graduate School, professor, 1964-98, Fitness Research Unit/Life Style Center, director, 1964-94, professor of physiology, 1968-80, Institute of Medical Sciences, professor, 1968-80, School of Physical and Health Education, director, 1979-91, Center Cardiovascular Research, professor, 1993-2000, professor emeritus, 1994-, Center for Health Promotion, consultant, 2001-02; Toronto Rehabilitation Center, consultant, 1968-2002; York University, Department of Physical Education, professor, 1969-70; Trois Rivières, Department des Sciences de la Santé, professor, 1970-78; Toronto Hospitals, Gage Research Institute, consultant, 1971-2002; Defence and Civil Institute of Environmental Medicine, consultant and visiting scientist, 1978-2000; Université de Paris, Faculty of Medicine, associate professor, 1985-86; Institute for Aerobics Research, consultant, 1993-2000; School of Physical and Health Education, consultant, 1993-97; University of New Brunswick, School of Physical and Health Education, consultant, 1997-2000; Universite de Québec àTrois Rivières, Department d'éducation physique, consultant, 1997-; Finnish National Academy, consultant, 2001-03. **Publications:** (Ed.) Proceedings, International Symposium on Physical Activity and Cardiovascular Health, 1967; Endurance Fitness, 1969, 2nd ed. 1977; (co-author) Fundamentals of Exercise Testing, 1971; (ed. with R.J. Stephard) Frontiers of Fitness, 1971; Alive Man! The Physiology of Physical Activity, 1972; Sport Medicine: Physiology, 1973; Men at Work: Applications of Ergonomics to Performance and Design, 1974; (ed. with S. Itoh) Circumpolar Health: Proceedings of the 3rd International Symposium, Yellowknife, N.W.T., 1976; The Fit Athlete, 1978, 2nd ed. 1987; (with H. Lavallee) Physical Fitness Assessment: Principles, Practice, and Application, 1978; Human Physiological Work Capacity, 1978; Physical Activity and Aging, 1978; Ischaemic Heart Disease and Physical Activity, 1981; Textbook of Exercise Physiology and Biochemistry, 1982; Physical Activity and Growth, 1982; Physiology and Biochemistry of Exercise, 1982; The Risks of Passive Smoking, 1982; Carbon Monoxide, the Silent Killer, 1983; Exercise Biochemistry, 1983; Biochemistry of Physical Activity, 1984; (with P. Welsh and J. Tong) Current Therapy in Sports Medicine, 1985; Fitness and Health in Industry, 1986; Economic Benefits of Enhanced Fitness, 1986; Fitness of a Nation, 1986; Fundamentals of Exercise Physiology, 1987; (ed. with J. Taunton) Foot and Ankle in Sports and Exercise, 1987; Fitness in Special Populations, 1990; Body Composition in Biological Anthropology, 1990; (with S. Thomas) Fit after Fifty, 1990; (ed. with J. Pařízková) Human Growth, Physical Fitness, and Nutrition, 1991; (with A. Rode) Observations on the Soviet/Canadian Transpolar Ski Trek, 1992; (ed. with H.S. Miller) Exercise and the Heart in Health and Disease, 1992, 2nd ed. 1999; (with P.O. Astrand) Endurance in Sport, 1992 2nd ed., 2000; (with C. Bouchard and T. Stephens) Physical Activity, Fitness, and Health Consensus Statement, 1993; (with C. Bouchard and T. Stephens) Physical Activity, Fitness, and Health: International Proceedings and Consensus Statement, 1994; Aerobic Fitness and Health, 1994; (with A. Rode) The Health Consequences of Modernization: Evidence From Circumpolar Peoples, 1996; Aging Physical Activity and Aging, 1997; Physical Activity, Training and the Immune Response, 1997; Gender, Physical Activity and Aging, 2002; Body Composition in Biological Anthropology, 2005; (with B.D. Kirkcaldy and R.G. Siefen) Making of a Good Doctor, 2009. **Address:** 41390 Dryden Rd., PO Box 521, Brackendale, BC V0N 1H0, Canada. **Online address:** royjshep@shaw.ca

SHEPHERD, George W. American/Chinese (born China), b. 1926. **Genres:** Politics/Government, Race Relations, Area Studies, Civil Liberties/Human Rights, International Relations/Current Affairs, Essays, Autobiography/Memoirs, Biography, Biography. **Career:** African farmers' marketing organization, technical assistant, 1952-53; American Committee on Africa, director, 1953-55; Brooklyn College (now Brooklyn College of the City University of New York), lecturer in political science, 1955-58; University of Minnesota, visiting professor, 1961; University of Denver, assistant professor and research associate, 1961-65, Graduate School of International Studies, associate professor, 1965-68, professor, 1968-92, Center of International Race Relations, director, 1968-74, emeritus professor, 1992-; Africa Today, editor, 1965-; United Church of Christ, chairman, 1967-72; Global Human Rights, co-editor, 1981; University of New Mexico, adjunct professor, 1998. Writer. **Publications:** They Wait in Darkness, 1955; Politics of African Nationalism, 1962; The Study of Race in American Foreign Policy and International Relations, 1969; Nonaligned Black Africa, 1970; (co-ed.) Race Among Nations: A Conceptual Approach, 1970; Racial Influences on U.S. Foreign Policy, 1970; Anti-Apartheid: Transnational Conflict and Western Policy in the Liberation of South Africa, 1977; The Trampled Grass: Tributary States and Self-Reliance in the Indian Ocean Zone of Peace, 1987; Economic Justice in Africa, 1994; (contrib.) Africa, Human Rights, and the Global System: The Political Economy of Human Rights in a Changing World, 1994; Popular Politics: Renewing Democracy for a Sustainable World, 1998; They are Us: Fifty Years of Human Rights Advocacy, 2002. EDITOR: (with V.P. Nanda and J.R. Scarritt) Global Human Rights: Public Policies, Comparative Measures, and NGO Strategies, 1981; (co-ed.) Human Rights and Third World Development, 1985; (with M.O. Anikpo) Emerging Human Rights: The African Political Economy Context, 1990; (with D. Penna) Racism and the Underclass: State Policy and Discrimination Against Minorities, 1991; Effective Sanctions on South Africa: The Cutting Edge of Economic Intervention, 1991; (ed. with V.P. Nanda) World Debt and the Human Condition: Structural Adjustments and the Right to Development, 1993; (with K.N.M. Sonko) Economic Justice in Africa: Adjustment and Sustainable Development, 1994. **Address:** Graduate School of International Studies, University of Denver, 2201 S Gaylord St., Denver, CO 80208, U.S.A.

SHEPHERD, Joel. Australian (born Australia), b. 1974?. **Genres:** Young Adult Fiction. **Career:** Writer. **Publications:** Sasha: A Trial of Blood and Steel, 2007; Haven, 2010. CASSANDRA KRESNOV SERIES: Crossover, 2006; Breakaway, 2007; Killswitch, 2007; Petrodor, 2008; Breakaway: A Cassandra Kresnov (novel), 2009; Tracato, 2009. **Address:** Hachette Australia, Level 17, 207 Kent St., Sydney, NW 2000, Australia. **Online address:** joel@joelshepherd.com

SHEPHERD, John Scott. American (born United States), b. 1964?. **Genres:** Novels, Literary Criticism And History, Young Adult Fiction. **Career:** Warp & Weft (production company), co-founder, 2001; Valentine Radford, advertising executive, corporate video producer. Screenwriter and novelist. **Publications:** Joe Somebody, 2001; Henry's List of Wrongs, 2002; Eulogy for Joseph Way, 2003; The Dead Fathers Guide to Sex and Marriage: A Novel, 2004. Contributor to periodicals. **Address:** Endeavor Agency, 9601 Wilshire Blvd., 3rd Fl., Beverly Hills, CA 90210-5219, U.S.A.

SHEPHERD, Margaret. American (born United States) **Genres:** Adult Non-fiction, Language/Linguistics, History. **Career:** Boston University School for the Arts, teacher, 1998; Boston Arts Academy, gothic calligraphy, teacher, 2001. Writer and calligrapher. **Publications:** Learning Calligraphy: A Book of Lettering, Design and History, 1977; Using Calligraphy: A Workbook of Alphabets, Projects and Techniques, 1979; Borders for Calligraphy: How to Design a Decorated Page, 1980, rev. ed., 1984; Capitals for Calligraphy: A Sourcebook of Decorative Letters, 1981; Calligraphy Made Easy: A Beginner's Workbook, 1981; Margaret Shepherd's Calligraphy Projects for Pleasure and Profit, 1983; Calligraphy Now: New Light on Traditional Letters, 1984; Calligraphy Alphabets Made Easy, 1986; Basics of the New Calligraphy, 1987; Basics of Left-Handed Calligraphy, 1988; Manual of Modern Calligraphy, 1988; Modern Calligraphy Made Easy: A New Script for Streamlined Lettering, 1988; Calligraphy for Celebrating Your Newborn, 1990; Learn Calligraphy: The Complete Book of Lettering and Design, 2001; The Art of the Handwritten Note: A Guide to Reclaiming Civilized Communications, 2002; (with S. Hogan) The Art of Civilized Conversation: A Guide to Expressing Yourself with Style and Grace, 2005; (with S. Hogan) Art of the Personal Letter: A Guide to Connecting Through the Written Word, 2008; The Visionbuilder's Manual: 9 Steps to Panoramic Success for Your Company, Career or Cause, 2010; Learn World Calligraphy: Discover African, Arabic, Chinese, Ethiopic, Greek, Hebrew, Indian, Japanese, Korean, Mongolian, Russian, Thai, Tibetan Calligraphy and Beyond, 2011. **Address:** c/o Colleen Mohyde, The Doe Coover Agency, PO Box 668, Winchester, MA 01890, U.S.A. **Online address:** shepherdscribe@yahoo.com

SHEPHERD, Robert. British (born England), b. 1949. **Genres:** History, Politics/Government, Biography, Documentaries/Reportage, Social Sciences, Philosophy. **Career:** Department of Employment, special adviser to the secretary of state, 1979-83; Investor's Chronicle, leader and features writer, 1983; Channel 4 Television, parliamentary lobby correspondent, 1983-87, producer, 1986-89; Investor's Chronicle, leader and features writer, 1983-87; Wide Vision Productions Ltd. (television production), managing director. **Publications:** Public Opinion and European Integration, 1975; A Class Divided: Appeasement and the Road to Munich, 1938, 1988; Ireland's Fate: The Boyne and After, 1990; The Power Brokers: The Tory Party and Its Leaders, 1991; Iain Macleod: A Biography, 1994; Enoch Powell: A Biography, 1996; That Terrible Place, forthcoming. Contributor to books. **Address:** c/o Gordon Wise, Curtis Brown Ltd., Haymarket House, 28/29 Haymarket, London, GL SW1Y 4SP, England. **Online address:** rgbshepherd@msn.com

SHEPHERD, Sherri Evonne. American (born United States), b. 1967. **Genres:** Autobiography/Memoirs. **Career:** American Broadcasting Corp., The View, co-host, 2007-. Writer, actress and comedian. **Publications:** (With L. Kilmartin) Permission Slips: Every Woman's Guide to Giving Herself a Break (autobiography), 2009. **Address:** Faith Walker Productions, 1001 Ave. of the Americas, Ste. 1200, New York, NY 10018, U.S.A.

SHEPPARD, Alice. American (born United States), b. 1945. **Genres:** History, Art/Art History, Social Sciences. **Career:** Vassar College, instructor, assistant professor of psychology, 1970-73; Educational Testing Service, visiting fellow, 1971, 1973; Kalamazoo College, assistant professor of psychology, 1973-76; California State University, lecturer in psychology, 1976-78; California School of Professional Psychology, faculty, 1977-79; Eastern Oregon State College, associate professor of psychology, 1979-87; Oregon State University, adjunct faculty, 1981-82; Bloomsburg University, assistant professor of psychology, 1987-90; Susquehanna University, lecturer, 1988; Pennsylvania College of Technology, adjunct faculty, 1990-91; State University of New York College at Fredonia, assistant professor of psychology, 1991-94; State University of New York College at Geneseo, visiting assistant professor, 1991; University of Maine, assistant professor of psychology, 1995-, professor of psychology. Writer. **Publications:** Cartooning for Suffrage, 1994. Contributor to books. **Address:** University of Maine, 206 S, 181 Main St., Presque Isle, ME 04769, U.S.A. **Online address:** alice.sheppard@umpi.edu

SHEPPARD, John L. (John Lawrence Sheppard). American (born United States), b. 1963. **Genres:** Young Adult Fiction, Novellas/Short Stories, Humor/Satire. **Career:** Writer and educator. **Publications:** AS JOHN LAWRENCE SHEPPARD: Midnight in Monaco, 2000; Bad Men Driving, 2001; Carl Versus the Men from Mars: Bombast, Drivel, Odds and Ends, 2002. OTHERS: Small Town Punk, 2002, 2nd ed., 2007; The Runner-Up, 2003; Tales of the Peacetime Army, 2007; Loner: Stories, 2010. **Address:** Ig Publishing, 392 Clinton Ave., Ste. 1S, Brooklyn, NY 11238-1187, U.S.A. **Online address:** johnsheppard@mac.com

SHEPPARD, John Lawrence. See SHEPPARD, John L.

SHEPPARD, Mary C. Canadian (born Canada) **Genres:** Young Adult Fiction, Novels. **Career:** Ryerson University, journalism faculty; Women's Television Network, staff; Maclean's Magazine, staff; Canadian Broadcasting Corp., executive producer. **Publications:** Seven for a Secret (young-adult novel), 2001; One for Sorrow, 2008; Three for a Wedding, 2009. **Address:** Canadian Broadcasting Corp., PO Box 500, Sta. A, Toronto, ON M5W 1E6, Canada. **Online address:** mcsheppard@gmail.com

SHEPPARD, Rob. American (born United States) **Genres:** Photography, How-to Books, Art/Art History. **Career:** Werner Publishing Corp., PCPhoto, editor and co-founder, Outdoor Photographer Magazine, editor, editor-at-large. **Publications:** Telephoto Lens Photography, 1997; Computer Photography Handbook, 1998; Basic Scanning Guide: For Photographers and Other Creative Types, 2001; Beginner's Guide to Digital Imaging for Photographers and Other Creative Types, 2002; Epson Complete Guide to Digital Printing, 2003, rev. ed., 2005; National Geographic Photography Field Guide-Digital: Secrets to Making Great Pictures, 2003; Canon EOS Digital Rebel, Canon EOS 300D Digital, 2004; PCPhoto Digital SLR handbook, 2005, rev. ed., 2008; Canon EOS 20D, 2005; Digital Photography 1, 2, 3: Taking and Printing Great Pictures, 2005, rev. ed., 2008; PCPhoto Digital SRL Handbook, 2005, rev. ed., 2008; PCPhoto Digital Zoom Camera Handbook, 2005; Adobe Camera Raw for Digital Photographers Only, 2005, 2nd ed., 2008; Outdoor Photographer: Landscape and Nature Photography with Photoshop CS2, 2006; The Magic of Digital Nature Photography, 2007; Digital Photography: Top 100 Simplified Tips & Tricks, 3rd ed., 2007; Adobe Lightroom for Digital

Photographers Only, 2007; Canon EOS 30D Digital, 2007; Adobe Photoshop Lightroom for Digital Photographers Only, 2008; Canon EOS 40D, 2008; Digital Photography Simplified, 2008; Kodak Guide to Digital Photography, 2008; New Epson Complete Guide to Digital Printing, 2008, 2nd ed., 2011; PCPhoto Digital Compact Camera Handbook, 2009; Canon EOS 50D, 2009; Photoshop Elements 7: Top 100 Simplified Tips and Tricks, 2009; Photoshop Elements 8: Top 100 Simplified Tips and Tricks, 2009; Magic Lantern Guides: Canon EOS 20D, 2009; How To Take Great Photos With The Canon D-SLR System, 2009; (with M. Guncheon) Digital Photographer's Complete Guide to HD Video, 2010; The Magic of Digital Landscape Photography, 2010; Digital Photographers Complete Guide to HD Video, 2011. Contributor to periodicals. **Address:** Werner Publishing Corp., 12121 Wilshire Blvd., 12th Fl., Los Angeles, CA 90025, U.S.A. **Online address:** robsheppard@earthlink.net

SHER, Barbara. American (born United States), b. 1935. **Genres:** Business/Trade/Industry, Psychology, Self Help. **Career:** Real Simple Magazine, life coach columnist; psychotherapist, 1968-; career counselor, 1968-; Writer. **Publications:** (With A. Gottlieb) Wishcraft: How to Get What You Really Want, 1979; Moving Right Along, 1985; (with A. Gottlieb) Teamworks! Building Support Groups That Guarantee Success, 1989; Extraordinary Play with Ordinary Things: Recycling Everyday Materials to Build Motor Sills, 1992; (with B. Smith) I Could Do Anything If I Only Knew What It Was: How to Discover What you Really Want and How to Get It, 1994; Live the Life You Love: In Ten Easy Step-by-Step Lessons, 1996; (intro.) Different Drummers, Same Song: 400 Inclusion Games that Promote Cognitive Skills, 1996; Working in Music, 1996; It's Only Too Late If You Don't Start Now: How to Create Your Second Life after Forty, 1998; Self-esteem Games: 300 Fun Activities that Make Children Feel Good about Themselves, 1998; Spirit Games: 300 Fun Activities that Bring Children Comfort and Joy, 2002; Smart Play: 101 Fun, Easy Games that Enhance Intelligence, 2004; Refuse to Choose!: A Revolutionary Program for Doing Everything that You Love, 2006; Attention Games: 101 Fun, Easy Games that Help Kids Learn to Focus, 2006; Early Intervention Games: Fun, Joyful Ways to Develop Social and Motor Skills in Children with Autism Spectrum or Sensory Processing Disorders, 2009. Contributor to periodicals. **Address:** c/o Kristine Dahl, International Creative Management, 40 W 57th St., New York, NY 10019, U.S.A. **Online address:** bsherny@earthlink.net

SHER, Gila. American/Israeli (born Israel) **Genres:** Philosophy, Essays. **Career:** Columbia University, Graduate School of Arts and Sciences, fellow, 1981-82, president's fellow, 1983-84, Barnard College, Department of Philosophy, visiting assistant professor, 1988-89; University of California, Department of Philosophy, assistant professor, 1989-93, associate professor, 1993-2000, professor, 2000-; Hebrew University of Jerusalem, Sidney M. Edelstein Center for the History and Philosophy of Science, senior research fellow, 2000. Writer. **Publications:** The Bounds of Logic: A Generalized Viewpoint, 1991; (ed. with R. Tieszen) Between Logic and Intuition: Essays in Honor of Charles Parsons, 2000. **Address:** Department of Philosophy, University of California, 8042 Humanities & Social Sciences Bldg., 9500 Gilman Dr., Ste. 0119, La Jolla, CA 92093-0119, U.S.A. **Online address:** gsher@ucsd.edu

SHER, Gilead. Israeli (born Israel), b. 1953. **Genres:** International Relations/Current Affairs. **Career:** Israel Broadcasting Authority, senior editor, correspondent and radio anchorman, 1977-88; Gilead Sher & Co., Law Offices, founder, 1989-2004; Government of Israel, head of negotiation team, 1999-2001; Office of the Prime Minister, chief of staff and policy coordinator, 2000-01; Aaronsohn, Sher, Aboulafia, Amoday & Co., Law Offices, senior founding partner, 2004-; Israel Shotokan Karate Association, president, 2006-. **Publications:** Be-merhak Negiah: Ha-masa- u-matan Le-shalom, 1999-2001: Edut, Yediot Aharonot: Sifre hemed, 2001 in US as Israeli-Palestinian Peace Negotiations, 1999-2001: Within Reach, 2006; (contrib.) Neyar emdah medini, 2002. Contributor to periodicals. **Address:** Gilead Sher & Company Law Offices, 1 Azrieli Ctr., Round Twr., 17th Fl., Tel Aviv, 67021, Israel. **Online address:** gileads@asaa-law.co.il

SHER, Ira G. American (born United States), b. 1970. **Genres:** Communications/Media, Novels, Young Adult Fiction, Romance/Historical. **Career:** Writer. **Publications:** Gentlemen of Space (novel), 2003; Singer, 2009. Contributor of short stories to periodicals. **Address:** c/o Author Mail, Simon & Schuster, 1230 Ave. of the Americas, New York, NY 10020, U.S.A.

SHER, Julian. Canadian (born Canada), b. 1953?. **Genres:** History. **Career:** New York Times, investigative journalist; Globe and Mail and Toronto Star, investigative journalist; Canadian Broadcasting Corp. (CBC-TV), The Fifth Estate, investigative producer, 1990-2000; Media magazine, columnist; JournalismNet, creator and webmaster; Organisation for Economic Cooperation and Development (OECD), consultant; United Nation's Children's Fund (UNICEF), consultant. Television writer, producer and director. **Publications:** White Hoods: Canada's Ku Klux Klan, 1983; Until You Are Dead: Steven Truscott's Long Ride into History, 2002; (with W. Marsden) The Road to Hell: How the Biker Gangs Are Conquering Canada, 2003; (with W. Marsden) Angels of Death: Inside the Biker Gangs Global Crime Empire, 2006; Caught in the Web: Inside the Police Hunt to Rescue Children from Online Predators in UK as One Child at a Time: The Global Fight to Rescue Children from Online Predators, 2007; Somebody's Daughter: The Hidden Story of America's Prostituted Children and the Battle to Save Them, 2011. Contributor to periodicals and journals. **Address:** Chicago Review Press, 814 N Franklin St., Chicago, IL 60610, U.S.A. **Online address:** julian@sher.com

SHER, Richard B. American (born United States), b. 1948. **Genres:** History. **Career:** New Jersey Institute of Technology, Department of History, lecturer, 1979-85, assistant professor, 1985-86, associate professor, 1986-92, professor of history, 1992-2000, department chair, 1999-2008, 2011-, distinguished professor of history, 2000-, College of Science and Liberal Arts, director of honors program and associate dean, 1985-91; New York University, visiting professor, 1982; Rutgers University, graduate faculty, 1991-. Writer and historian. **Publications:** Church and University in the Scottish Enlightenment: The Moderate Literati of Edinburgh, 1985; (ed. with J.R. Smitten) Scotland and America in the Age of the Enlightenment, 1990; (ed. with J. Dwyer) Sociability and Society in Eighteenth-Century Scotland, 1993; (ed. with A. Hook) The Glasgow Enlightenment, 1995; The Enlightenment and the Book: Scottish Authors and Their Publishers in Eighteenth-Century Britain, Ireland, and America, 2006. Contributor to books and journals. **Address:** Federated Department of History, New Jersey Institute of Technology, University Hts., Newark, NJ 07102, U.S.A. **Online address:** sher@njit.edu

SHERBANIUK, Richard. Canadian (born Canada) **Genres:** Novels, Mystery/Crime/Suspense. **Career:** Writer, historian and consultant. **Publications:** The Fifth Horseman: A Novel of Biological Disaster, 2001. **Address:** c/o Author Mail, Forge Books, 175 5th Ave., New York, NY 10010-7703, U.S.A.

SHERIDAN, Lionel Astor. Welsh/British (born England), b. 1927. **Genres:** Law. **Career:** Queen's University of Belfast, lecturer in law, 1949-56, professor of comparative law, 1963-71; University of Malaya, professor of law, 1956-63; University of Wales, University College, professor of law, 1971-88, professor emeritus, 1988-. Writer. **Publications:** Fraud in Equity, 1957; (with T.B. Teik) Elementary Law: An Introduction for the Malayan Citizen, 1957; (with V.T.H. Delany) The Cy-Près Doctrine, 1959; The Federation of Malaya Constitution, 1961, (with H.E. Groves) 3rd ed. as The Constitution of Malaysia, 1967, 5th ed., 2004; (ed. and contrib.) Malaya and Singapore, the Borneo Territories: The Development of Their Laws and Constitutions, 1961; Constitutional Protection: Expropriation and Restrictions on Property Rights, 1963; Legal Education in the Seventies: An Inaugural Lecture Delivered Before the Queen's University of Belfast on 1 February 1967, 1967; (with G.W. Keeton) Equity, 1969, 2nd ed., 1976; Charitable Causes, Political Causes and Involvement: An Inaugural Lecture Given on 8 November 1972 at University College, Cardiff, 1970; (ed. and contrib.) Survey of the Land Law of Northern Ireland, 1971; (with G.W. Keeton) The Modern Law of Charities, 1971, 3rd ed., 1983; (with G.W. Keeton) A Case-book on Equity and Trusts, 2nd ed., 1974; Rights in Security, 1974; (with G.W. Keeton) The Law of Trusts, 1974; (with G.W. Keeton) The Comparative Law of Trusts in the Commonwealth and the Republic of Ireland, 1976; (with G.W. Keeton) Digest of the English Law of Trusts, 1979; (with G.W. Keeton) Rights Protected By Injunction, 1984. IRISH SUPPLEMENTS: Real Property, 3rd ed., 1956; An Introduction to Equity, 5th ed., 1961; (ed.) Law of Trusts, 10th ed., 1974; Law of Trusts, 11th ed., forthcoming. Contributor to books. **Address:** University College, University of Wales, Cardiff, SG CF1 1XL, Wales.

SHERIDAN, Thomas. Australian/British (born England), b. 1938. **Genres:** Industrial Relations, History, Organized Labor, Politics/Government, Social Sciences. **Career:** University of Adelaide, reader, 1968-, lecturer, 1968-72, Department of Economics, senior lecturer, 1973-, associate professor, visiting fellow. Writer. **Publications:** Mindful Militants: The Amalgamated Engineering Union in Australia 1920-1972, 1975; Division of Labour: Industrial Relations in the Chifley Years 1945-49, 1989; Australia's Own Cold War: The Waterfront Under Menzies, 2006. Contributor to journals. **Address:** Department of Economics, University of Adelaide, Rm. 13, 10 Pulteney St., 4th Fl., Adelaide, SA 5005, Australia. **Online address:** tom.sheridan@adelaide.edu.au

SHERIFF, Carol. American (born United States), b. 1966?. **Genres:** History, Military/Defense/Arms Control, Humanities. **Career:** College of William and Mary, Department of History, associate professor, professor. Writer. **Publications:** The Artificial River: The Erie Canal and the Paradox of Progress, 1817-1862, 1996; (with S.R. Nelson) A People at War: Civilians and Soldiers in America's Civil War, 1854-1877, 2007; A People and A Nation, 2008. Contributor to periodicals. **Address:** Department of History, College of William and Mary, Blair 314, PO Box 8795, Williamsburg, VA 23187-8795, U.S.A. **Online address:** cxsher@wm.edu

SHERLOCK, Patti. American (born United States) **Genres:** Young Adult Fiction, Adult Non-fiction, Animals/Pets, Self Help, Theology/Religion, Biography. **Career:** Eastern Idaho Technical College, creative writing instructor; Jackson Hole Writer's Conference, faculty. Writer. **Publications:** Alone on the Mountain: Sheepherding in the American West, 1979; Four of a Kind, 1991; Some Fine Dog, 1992; American West: Twenty New Stories, 2001; Taking Back Our Lives: Reflections for Survivors of Child Abuse, 2003; Letters from Wolfie, 2004; A Dog for All Seasons, 2010. **Address:** Jackson Hole Writers Conference, PO Box 1974, Jackson, WY 83001, U.S.A. **Online address:** pattisherlock@gmail.com

SHERMAN, Arnold. Greek/Israeli/American (born United States), b. 1932. **Genres:** Poetry, Air/Space Topics, Military/Defense/Arms Control, Humor/Satire, History, Politics/Government, Novels. **Career:** Aviation Week, news editor, 1957-63; Israel Aircraft Industries, public relations director, 1963-65; El Al-Israel Airlines, vice-president of public relations, 1965-82; Technion-Israel Institute of Technology, executive vice-president, 1983-. **Publications:** A Thought in the Night (poetry), 1950; Impaled on a Cactus Bush (humor), 1970; In the Bunkers of Sinai (military), 1971; To the Skies: The El Al Story, 1972; Lightning in the Skies (aviation), 1973; When God Judged and Men Died (military), 1973; The El Al Story, 1973; Impaled on a Rhino's Horn (humor), 1974; The Druse, 1975; Pomeranz Connection, 1976; In Search of Rahamim (autobiography), 1977; In Search for Rachamim, 1970; Blue Sky, Red Sea, 1977; The Ship (novel), 1978; Challenging the Skies (aviation), 1979; Israel on $10 a Day, 1980; Wings of Icarus (novel), 1980; Splintered Cedar (Lebanon), 1981; Levanon, ha-erez she-nigda, 1982; Israel High Technology, 1984; Tel Aviv-Jaffa, 1986; Ke-esh be-atsmotav: Aryeh Ben-Eliezer'ḥayav, 1986; Perfidy in the Balkans: The Rape of Yugoslavia, 1993; The Centaurs of Pelion, 1994; On the Threshold of Chaos, 1995; Cyprus: The Tormented Island, 1999. **Address:** 86 Neriedon, Paleo Faliron, 17561, Greece.

SHERMAN, Charlotte Watson. American (born United States), b. 1958. **Genres:** Novels, Novellas/Short Stories, Young Adult Fiction, Romance/Historical. **Career:** Garvey School, instructional assistant, 1987-88; Child Welfare Services, social worker, 1989-91; Group Health Cooperative, mental health specialist, 1991-92. Writer. **Publications:** Killing Color (fiction), 1992; A Kiss at Sunrise, 1993; (ed.) Sisterfire: Black Womanist Fiction and Poetry, 1994; Eli and the Swamp Man, 1996. NOVELS: One Dark Body: A Novel, 1993; Touch: A Novel, 1995; The Flight of the Pearl, forthcoming. Contributor to periodicals. Works appear in anthologies. **Address:** Beth Vesel, Sanford Greenberger Associates, 55 5th Ave., New York, NY 10003, U.S.A. **Online address:** readermail@charlottewatsonsherman.com

SHERMAN, Janette D. (Janette D. Sherman-Nevinger). American (born United States), b. 1930?. **Genres:** Medicine/Health. **Career:** U.S. Atomic Energy Commission, researcher; University of California, researcher; Michigan State University, researcher; U.S. Environmental Protection Agency, advisor; National Cancer Institute, advisor; Wayne State University, Medical School, clinical assistant professor, adjunct professor; Western Michigan University, Environmental Institute, adjunct professor of sociology; Radiation and Public Health Project, research associate and lecturer. Writer and toxicologist. **Publications:** Chemical Exposure and Disease: Diagnostic and Investigative Techniques, 1988; Life's Delicate Balance: Causes and Prevention of Breast Cancer, 2000; (ed. as Janette D. Sherman-Nevinger) Chernobyl: Consequences of the Catastrophe for People and the Environment, 2009. Contributor to journals. **Address:** Western Michigan University, 1903 W Michigan Ave., Kalamazoo, MI 49008-5211, U.S.A. **Online address:** toxdoc.js@verizon.net

SHERMAN, Jason. Canadian (born Canada), b. 1962. **Genres:** Plays/

Screenplays, Theatre, Poetry, Young Adult Fiction. **Career:** What (literary magazine), founding editor, 1985, editor, 1985-90; Tarragon Theater, playwright-in-residence, 1992-99; Soulpepper Theater, playwright-in-residence, 2002-03. **Publications:** The League of Nathans, 1992; Three in the Back, Two in the Head, 1995; The Retreat, 1996; Reading Hebron, 1997; None is Too Many, 1997; Patience, 2000; It's All True, 2000; An Acre of Time: Inspired by the Book of the Same Name by Phil Jenkins, 2001; Six Plays, 2001; Remnants: A Fable, 2003; (with J. Thompson and D. Young) The Wrecking Ball, 2004; Adapt Or Die: Plays New and Used, 2006; Afghanada, 2006. EDITOR: Canadian Brash: New Voices in Fiction, Drama and Poetry (fiction, drama and poetry), 1990; Solo (drama), 1994; Modern Jewish Plays, 2006. **Address:** c/o Jeff Alpern, The Alpern Group, 15645 Royal Oak Rd., Encino, CA 91436, U.S.A. **Online address:** shermlit@rogers.com

SHERMAN, Joe. American (born United States), b. 1945. **Genres:** Business/Trade/Industry, Politics/Government, Novellas/Short Stories, Social Sciences. **Career:** Johnson State College, adjunct professor, 1990-91; Black Fall Press, founder. Writer. **Publications:** The House at Shelburne Farms: The Story of One of America's Great Country Estates, 1986, rev. ed., 1992; A Thousand Voices: The Story of Nashville's Union Station, 1987; Nashville's Union Station, 1987; Fast Lane on a Dirt Road: Vermont Transformed, 1945-1990, 1991; In the Rings of Saturn, 1994; Charging Ahead, 1998; Gasp!: The Swift and Terrible Beauty of Air, 2004; (with M. Tesarova) Young Vermonters: Not an Endangered Species, 2010. **Address:** Black Falls Press, 2307 Broadway, PO Box 102, Montgomery, VT 05470, U.S.A. **Online address:** joesherman11@gmail.com

SHERMAN, John W. American (born United States), b. 1960. **Genres:** History, Social Sciences. **Career:** Wright State University, associate professor of history, 1994-, professor of history, History Graduate Program, director, 2000-07, chair, 2008-09. Writer. **Publications:** The Mexican Right: The End of Revolutionary Reform, 1929-1940, 1997; Latin America in Crisis, 2000; A Communist Front at Mid-Century: The American Committee for Protection of Foreign Born, 1933-1959, 2001. **Address:** Department of History, Wright State University, 366 Millett Hall, 3640 Colonel Glenn Hwy., Dayton, OH 45435-0001, U.S.A. **Online address:** john.sherman@wright.edu

SHERMAN, Nancy. American (born United States), b. 1951. **Genres:** History, Military/Defense/Arms Control, Essays. **Career:** Yale University, assistant professor, 1982-88, associate professor, 1988-89; Georgetown University, associate professor of philosophy, 1989-94, professor of philosophy, 1994-, university professor of philosophy, 2001-, Kennedy Institute of Ethics, faculty affiliate, 1994-, fellow, Law Center, adjunct professor of law, 2004-; U.S. Naval Academy, distinguished chair in ethics, 1997-99; University of Maryland, visiting professor; Johns Hopkins University, visiting professor; Walter Reed Army Hospital, lecturer; National Defense University, lecturer; Uniformed Services University, lecturer. Writer and consultant. **Publications:** The Fabric of Character: Aristotle's Theory of Virtue, 1989; Making a Necessity of Virtue: Aristotle and Kant on Virtue, 1997; (ed.) Aristotle's Ethics: Critical Essays, 1999; Stoic Warriors: The Ancient Philosophy behind the Military Mind, 2005; The Untold War: Inside the Hearts, Minds, and Souls of Our Soldiers, 2010. Contributor to books and periodicals. **Address:** Department of Philosophy, Georgetown University, 224 New North NW, Washington, DC 20057, U.S.A. **Online address:** shermann@georgetown.edu

SHERMAN, Richard B. American (born United States), b. 1929. **Genres:** History, Race Relations, Autobiography/Memoirs. **Career:** Pennsylvania State University, instructor in history, 1957-60; College of William and Mary, assistant professor, 1960-65, associate professor, 1965-70, professor of history, 1970-, William E. Pullen professor of history, 1994, now William E. Pullen professor emeritus of history; University of Stockholm, Fulbright professor, 1966-67. Writer. **Publications:** (Ed.) The Negro and the City, 1970; The Republican Party and Black America: From McKinley to Hoover, 1896-1933, 1973; The Case of Odell Waller and Virginia Justice, 1940-1942, 1992; (co-author) The College of William and Mary: A History, 1993; Learning from the Past: Memoirs of a Would-Be Historian, 1997. **Address:** Department of History, College of William and Mary, James Blair Hall 330, James Blair Dr., PO Box 8795, Williamsburg, VA 23185, U.S.A.

SHERMAN, Robert. American (born United States), b. 1928. **Genres:** Psychology, Biography, Music. **Career:** Farmer, 1951-54; schoolteacher, 1954-57; school counselor, 1957-60; Rutgers University, visiting professor, 1959, 1960; Yeshiva University, assistant professor of counseling, 1960-62; City

University of New York, Queens College, assistant professor, professor, 1962-92, coordinator of graduate programs in community mental health counseling, 1971-78, professor emeritus, 1993-; Newark State College, visiting professor, 1963; Fairleigh Dickinson University, visiting professor, 1962-64; University of Miami, visiting professor, 1967; Adelphi University, visiting professor, 1978; Alfred Adler Institutes of New York, visiting professor, 1982-; Bowie State College, visiting professor, 1983; National Academy For Certified Family Therapists, board director. Writer. **Publications:** (Co-author) Appraising the Guidance-Personnel Function in Secondary Schools and Colleges, 1959; (with N. Fredman) Handbook of Structured Techniques in Marriage and Family Therapy, 1986; (with D. Dinkmeyer) Systems of Family Therapy: An Adlerian Integration, 1987; (with N. Fredman) Handbook of Measurements for Marriage and Family Therapy, 1987; (with P. Oresky and Y.B. Rountree) Solving Problems in Couples and Family Therapy, 1991; (with A. Shumsky and Y.B. Rountree) Enlarging the Therapeutic Circle, 1994. Work appears in anthologies. Contributor to periodicals. **Address:** 12 Berkshire Dr., Monroe Township, NJ 08831-4718, U.S.A. **Online address:** sherman42@juno.com

SHERMAN, Spencer D. American (born United States), b. 1962?. **Genres:** Business/Trade/Industry, Economics, Money/Finance. **Career:** Abacus Wealth Partners L.L.C., co-founder, chief executive officer and financial planner. Writer. **Publications:** The Cure for Money Madness: Break Your Bad Money Habits, Live without Financial Stress-and Make More Money!, 2009. **Address:** Abacus Wealth Partners L.L.C., 17383 Sunset Blvd., Ste. A360, Pacific Palisades, CA 90272-4181, U.S.A. **Online address:** befree@curemoneymadness.com

SHERMAN, Steve (Barry). American (born United States), b. 1938. **Genres:** Travel/Exploration, Novels, Theology/Religion, Natural History, Food And Wine. **Career:** Glendale, high school teacher, 1961-63; Ruby, elementary school teacher, 1963-64; University of Alaska, research librarian, 1967-69; Anchorage Daily News, reporter, 1971; freelance writer, 1971-. **Publications:** ABC's of Library Promotion, 1971, 3rd ed., 1992; Bike Hiking, 1974; The Wood Stove & Fireplace Book, 1976; Home Heating With Coal: Energy for the Eighties, 1980; The Haägen-Dazs Book of Ice Cream, 1982; Cheese Sweets and Savories: Pies, Cheesecakes, Quiches, Appetizers, 1982; Basic Yankee, 1984; Wreaths for All Seasons, 1986; Christmas Wreaths: Text and Photographs, 1987; The Maple Sugar Murders, 1987; The White Mountain Murders, 1989; Tempered Iron, 1989; (with H.K. Nearing) A Scott Nearing Reader: The Good Life in Bad Times, 1989; Country Roads of New Hampshire, 1993, 3rd ed. as Country Roads of New Hampshire: Drives, Day Trips and Weekend Excursions, 1999; Country Roads of Connecticut and Rhode Island, 1994, 2nd ed. as Country Roads of Connecticut and Rhode Island: Day Trips and Weekend Excursions, 2000; Primary Crime: New England Cozy, 2000; Highboy, 2001; Revitalizing Theological Epistemology, 2008. WITH J. OLDER: Appalachian Odyssey: Walking the Trail from Georgia to Maine, 1977; Soup and Bread: 100 Recipes for Bowl & Board, 1978; The New Hampshire Dining Guide: A Compendium of Dining Places of Note and Flavorful Recipes Therefrom, 1979; (ed.) The Picture Perfect Encyclopedia of Cooking, 1985; Menus à Trois: The Soup, Bread, and Salad Menu Cookbook, 1987, 2nd ed., 1989; Grand Monadnock: Exploring the Most Popular Mountain in America, 1990; The Ultimate Soup Book: 250 Soups for Appetizers, Entrees, and Desserts, 1991; Nature Walks in Southern New Hampshire, 1994; Natural Wonders of New Mexico: A Guide to Parks, Preserves and Wild Places, 1997; Nature Walks in the New Hampshire Lakes Region, 1997; Nature Walks Along the Seacoast: Massachusetts, New Hampshire, Maine, 2003. **Address:** Wipf and Stock Publishers, 199 W 8th Ave., Ste. 3, Eugene, OR 97401-2960, U.S.A.

SHERMAN-NEVINGER, Janette D. *See* **SHERMAN, Janette D.**

SHERMER, Michael. American (born United States), b. 1954. **Genres:** Education, Sciences, Sports/Fitness, Psychology, Medicine/Health, Politics/Government. **Career:** Glendale College, instructor of psychology, 1980-86, assistant professor of psychology, 1986-91; Occidental College, Cultural Studies Program, adjunct professor of history of science, 1989-99; California State University, adjunct professor, 1991-93; California Institute of Technology, Skeptics Distinguished Lecture Series, host, 1991-; Skeptics Society, executive director, 1991-; Skeptic Magazine, founding publisher and editor-in-chief, 1991-; KPCC, science correspondent, 1998-; Fox Family, consulting producer and host, 1999-2000; Scientific American, contributing editor and monthly columnist, 2001-; Claremont Graduate University, adjunct professor of economics, 2007-. **Publications:** Sport Cycling: A Guide to Training,

Racing and Endurance, 1985; Cycling: Endurance and Speed, 1987; Teach Your Child Science, 1989; (with G. Yates) Meeting the Challenge of Arthritis, 1990; (with A. Benjamin) Teach Your Child Math, 1991; (with A. Benjamin) Mathemagics: How to Look like a Genius without Really Trying, 1993; Race Across America, 1993; Denying History: Who Says the Holocaust Never Happened and Why Do They Say It?, 1996; (ed. with B. Maidhof-Christig and L. Traynor) Argumente und Kritik: Skeptisches Jahrbuch. Rassiismus, die Leugnung des Holocaust, AIDS ohne HIV und andere fragwuerdige Behauptungen, 1997; Why People Believe Weird Things: Pseudoscience, Superstition and Other Confusions of Our Time, 1997, rev. ed., 2002; (co-ed.) Endzeittaumel: Propheten, Prognosen, Propaganda, 1998; O Ye of Little Faith: The Search for God in the Age of Science, 1999; How We Believe: The Search for God in the Age of Science, 2000; In Darwin's Shadow: The Life and Science of Alfred Russel Wallace, 2002; How We Believe: Science, Skepticism, and the Search for God, 2003; Science of Good and Evil: Why People Cheat, Gossip, Care, Share, and Follow the Golden Rule, 2004; Science Friction: Where the Known Meets the Unknown, 2005; Why Darwin Matters: The Case Against Intelligent Design, 2006; The Secrets of Mental Math: The Mathemagician's Guide to Lightning Calculation and Amazing Math Tricks, 2006; Soul of Science, 2006; (with A. Benjamin) Think Like a Math Genius, 2006; Mind of the Market: Compassionate Apes, Competitive Humans, and Other Tales from Evolutionary Economics, 2007; Believing Brain: From Ghosts and Gods to Politics and Conspiracies How We Construct Beliefs and Reinforce them As Truths, 2011. Contributor to periodicals. **Address:** c/o Tara Kennedy, Times Books, 115 W 18th St., New York, CA 10011, U.S.A. **Online address:** mshermer@skeptic.com

SHERR, Lynn B(eth). American (born United States), b. 1942. **Genres:** Documentaries/Reportage, Humanities, Biography, Adult Non-fiction. **Career:** Television news correspondent; Conde Nast Publications, writer and editor, 1963-65; Associated Press, writer and reporter, 1965-72; WCBS-TV News, correspondent, 1972-74; Public Broadcasting System, anchor and correspondent, 1975-77; ABC News, general assignment correspondent, 1977-, national correspondent, 1982-, 20/20, correspondent 1986-; WNET, staff. **Publications:** (With J. Kazickas) The Liberated Woman's Appointment Calendar, 1971, 1982; (with J. Kazickas) The American Woman's Gazetteer, 1976, rev. ed. as Susan B. Anthony Slept Here: A Guide to American Women's Landmarks, 1994; Failure is Impossible: Susan B. Anthony in Her Own Words, 1995; Tall Blondes: A Book About Giraffes, 1997; America the Beautiful: The Stirring True Story Behind Our Nations's Favorite Song, 2001; Outside the Box: A Memoir, 2006; (ed. with K. Darnton and K.F. Jennings) Peter Jennings: A Reporter's Life, 2007. Contributor to periodicals. **Address:** 20/20, 147 Columbus Ave., New York, NY 10023, U.S.A.

SHERRADEN, Michael (Wayne). American (born United States), b. 1948. **Genres:** Social Work. **Career:** Sight Point Camp, director, 1972-73, 1976; Piney Creek Ranch, director, 1972-74; University of Michigan, research associate, instructor and faculty adviser, 1975-79; Washington University, George Warren Brown School of Social Work, assistant professor, 1979-85, associate professor, 1985-92, Benjamin E. Youngdahl professor of social development, 1992-, Center for Social Development, founding director, 1994-; University of Arkansas, visiting professor, 1980; University of Mexico, visiting professor, 1987; National Autonomous University of Mexico, visiting professor, 1987-88; Hebrew University of Jerusalem, visiting professor, 1988; National University of Singapore, visiting professor, 1992-93, Fulbright research fellow, 1992-93; Hong Kong Polytechnic University, visiting chaired professor, 2008-11. Writer. **Publications:** Assets and the Poor: A New American Welfare Policy, 1991; (with M.S. Sherraden and C.K. Sanders) Kitchen Capitalism: Microenterprise in Low-Income Households, 2004; (with M. Schreiner) Can the Poor Save?: Saving & Asset Building in Individual Development Accounts, 2007. EDITOR: (with D.J. Eberly) National Service: Social, Economic and Military Impacts, 1982; (with D. Eberly) The Moral Equivalent of War? A Study of Non-Military Service in Nine Nations, 1990; (with J. Midgley) Alternatives to Social Security: An International Inquiry, 1997; (with N. Morrow-Howell and J. Hinterlong) Productive Aging: Concepts and Controversies, 2001; Inclusion in the American Dream: Assets, Poverty and Public Policy, 2005; (with A.M. McBride) Civic Service Worldwide: Impacts and Inquiry, 2007; (with S.M. McKernan) Asset Building and Low-Income Families, 2008; (with S.G. McKernan) Asset Building and Low-income Families, 2008. Contributor of articles to journals. **Address:** George Warren Brown School of Social Work, Washington University, 1 Brookings Dr., St. Louis, MO 63130, U.S.A. **Online address:** sherrad@wustl.edu

SHERRARD-JOHNSON, Cherene. American (born United States), b. 1973?. **Genres:** Adult Non-fiction. **Career:** Cornell University, teaching assistant, 1996-97; Spelman College, Writing Center, instructor, 1999-2000; University of Wisconsin, Anna Julia Cooper postdoctoral fellow, 2000-01, Department of English, assistant professor, 2001-06, associate professor, 2007-. Writer. **Publications:** Portraits of the New Negro Woman: Visual and Literary Culture in the Harlem Renaissance, 2007; (ed. and intro.) Comedy, American Style, 2010; Dorothy West: A Biography of Class and Color, 2012. Contributor to journals. **Address:** English Department, University of Wisconsin-Madison, 7187 Helen C. White Hall, 600 N Park St., Madison, WI 53706, U.S.A. **Online address:** csherrard@wisc.edu

SHERRER, Quin(ton M.). American (born United States), b. 1933. **Genres:** inspirational/Motivational Literature, Human Relations/Parenting. **Career:** Titusville Star Advocate, feature writer and columnist; Christian magazines and local newspapers, freelance journalist, 1979-. **Publications:** How to Pray for Your Children, 1986, rev. ed. (with R. Garlock), 1998; (with L. Watson) A Christian Woman's Guide to Hospitality, 1993; (with L. Watson) A House of Many Blessings, 1993; Miracles Happen When You Pray: True Stories of the Remarkable Power of Prayer, 1997; Listen, God Is Speaking to You: True Stories of His Love and Guidance, 1999; Good Night, Lord: Inspiration for the End of the Day, 2000; Prayers from a Grandma's Heart: Asking God's Blessing and Protection for Your Grandchildren, 2001; Grandma's Prayers, 2002; The Warm and Welcome Home: Sharing God's Love through Hospitality, 2002; A Mom's Guide to Spiritual Power: Finding God's Help for Parenting and Becoming a Spirit-Led Mom, 2003; Becoming a Spirit-Led Mom, 2004; A Mother's Guide to Praying for your Children, 2010. WITH R. GARLOCK: How to Forgive Your Children, 1989; How to Pray for Family and Friends, 1990; A Woman's Guide to Spiritual Warfare: A Woman's Guide for Battle, 1991; The Spiritual Warrior's Prayer Guide, 1992, 2nd ed., 2010; A Woman's Guide to Breaking Bondages, 1994; A Woman's Guide to Spirit-Filled Living, 1996; Prayers Women Pray: Intimate Moments with God, 1998; A Woman's Guide to Getting through Tough Times, 1998; The Making of a Spiritual Warrior: A Woman's Guide to Daily Victory, 1998; Praying Prodigals Home: How to Wait for the Promise, 2000; Prayer Partnerships: The Power of Agreement, 2001; God Be with Us: A Daily Guide to Praying for Our Nation, 2001; Grandma, I Need Your Prayers: Blessing Your Grandchildren through the Power of Prayer, 2002; The Beginner's Guide to Receiving the Holy Spirit, 2002; Lord, I Need Your Healing Power, 2006; Lord, I Need to Pray With Power, 2006; Lord, Help Me Break this Habit: You can be Free from Doing the Things You Hate, 2009. Contributor to magazines and newspapers. **Address:** Ann Spangler and Associates, 1420 Pontiac Rd. SE, Grand Rapids, MI 49506, U.S.A.

SHERRETT, James. Canadian (born Canada), b. 1975. **Genres:** Young Adult Non-fiction, Novels. **Career:** Jesse James Press, publisher and co-founder. Writer. **Publications:** Up in Ontario, 2003. **Address:** c/o Author Mail, Turnstone Press, 206-100 Arthur St., Winnipeg, MB R3B 1H3, Canada. **Online address:** james@upinontario.com

SHERRILL, Kenneth S. American (born United States), b. 1942. **Genres:** Politics/Government, Gay And Lesbian Issues, Social Sciences. **Career:** Oberlin College, instructor in government, 1965-67; Hunter College of the City University, Department of Political Science, professor, 1967-, now professor emeritus. Writer. **Publications:** (With D.J. Vogler) Power, Policy and Participation: An Introduction to American Government, 1977, 2nd ed., 1982; (ed. with M. Wolinsky) Gays and the Military: Joseph Steffan Versus the United States, 1993; Sources of Gay Power and Powerlessness in American Politics, forthcoming. **Address:** Department of Political Science, Hunter College of the City University, 695 Park Ave., New York, NY 10065, U.S.A. **Online address:** kenneth.sherrill@hunter.cuny.edu

SHERRILL, Steven. American (born United States), b. 1961. **Genres:** Novels. **Career:** Penn State University Altoona, assistant professor, 2000-06, associate professor of English, creative writing and integrative arts, 2006-; University of Iowa, Iowa Summer Writing Festival, summer writing instructor, 2001-06. Writer. **Publications:** NOVELS: The Minotaur Takes a Cigarette Break, 2000; Visits from the Drowned Girl, 2004; The Locktender's House, 2007. Contributor of books to periodicals. Works appear in anthologies. **Address:** Penn State Altoona, 3000 Ivyside Pk., Altoona, PA 16601, U.S.A. **Online address:** kss15@psu.edu

SHERRY, Dulcie Sylvia. See SHERRY, Sylvia.

SHERRY, Norman. British (born England), b. 1935. **Genres:** Literary Criticism And History, Biography. **Career:** University of Singapore, lecturer in English, 1960-66; University of Liverpool, lecturer, 1966-68, senior lecturer in English, 1968-70; University of Lancaster, professor of English, 1970-83; Trinity University, professor of English, 1983-, Mitchell Distinguished Professor of Literature, 1983-, now retired. Writer. **Publications:** Conrad's Eastern World, 1966; Jane Austen, 1966; Charlotte and Emily Brontë, 1969; Jane Austen, 1969; Conrad's Western World, 1971; Conrad and His World, 1972; Conrad, 1988; The Life of Graham Greene, vol. I: 1904-1939, 1989, vol. II: 1939-1955, 1994, vol. III, forthcoming; The Mystery That Was Graham Greene: An Inaugural Lecture, 1992; Books of the Century: A Hundred Years of Authors, Ideas and Literature, 1998. EDITOR: (with J. Conrad) An Outpost of Progress and Heart of Darkness, 1973; Conrad: The Critical Heritage, 1973; (intro.) Nostromo: A Tale of the Seaboard, 1974; (intro.) A Secret Tale, A Simple Tale, 1974; Lord Jim, 1974; The Nigger of the Narcissus, Typhoon, Falk and Other Stories, 1975; Joseph Conrad: A Commemorative: Papers from the 1974 International Conference on Conrad, 1976; (with C.B. Coy) Youth A Narrative, Heart of Darkness, The End of Tether, 1990. **Address:** Departmentt of English, Trinity University, 1 Trinity Pl., San Antonio, TX 78212-7200, U.S.A. **Online address:** nsherry@trinity.edu

SHERRY, Patrick. British (born England), b. 1938. **Genres:** Theology/Religion, Race Relations, Literary Criticism And History. **Career:** Lancaster University, lecturer, 1974-89, Department of Religious Studies, senior lecturer, 1989-93, reader, 1993-99, professor, 1999-, now professor emeritus. Writer. **Publications:** Religion, Truth and Language-Games, 1977; Spirit, Saints and Immortality, 1984; Spirit and Beauty: An Introduction to Theological Aesthetics, 1992, 2nd ed., 2002; Images of Redemption: Art, Literature, and Salvation, 2003. EDITOR: (with N. Smart, J. Clayton and S. Katz) Nineteenth-Century Religious Thought in the West, 3 vols., 1985; Philosophers on Religion: A Historical Reader, 1987. **Address:** Department Politics, Philosophy and Religion, Lancaster University, University House, Bailrigg, Lancaster, LC LA1 4YW, England. **Online address:** p.sherry@lancaster.ac.uk

SHERRY, Suzanna. American (born United States), b. 1954. **Genres:** Law, Education, Reference. **Career:** U.S. Court of Appeals, Fifth Circuit, law clerk, 1979-80; Miller, associate, 1980-82; Cassidy, associate, 1980-82; Larroca & Lewin, associate, 1980-82; University of Minnesota-Twin Cities, associate professor, 1982-88, professor, 1988-2000, Julius E. Davis professor of law, 1991-92, Earl R. Larson professor of civil rights and civil liberties law, 1992-2000; Vanderbilt University, Cal Turner professor of law and leadership, 2000-06, Herman O. Loewenstein professor of law, 2006-. Writer. **Publications:** (With D.A. Farber) A History of the American Constitution, 1990, 2nd ed., 2005; (with D.A. Farber) Beyond All Reason: The Radical Assault on Truth in American Law, 1997; (with M.H. Redish) Federal Courts: Cases, Comments, and Questions, 4th ed., 1998, 6th ed., 2007; (with D.A. Farber) Desperately Seeking Certainty: The Misguided Quest for Constitutional Foundations, 2002; (with T.D. Rowe and J. Tidmarsh) Civil Procedure, 2004, 2nd ed., 2008; (with J. Tidmarsh) Civil Procedure: Essentials, 2007; (with D.A. Farber) Judgment Calls: Principle and Politics in Constitutional Law, 2008; (with T.E. George) What Every Law Student Really Needs to Know: An Introduction to the Study of Law, 2009. Contributor to journals. **Address:** Law School, Vanderbilt University, Rm. 238, 131 21st Ave. S, Nashville, TN 37203-1181, U.S.A. **Online address:** suzanna.sherry@law.vanderbilt.edu

SHERRY, Sylvia. (Dulcie Sylvia Sherry). British (born England), b. 1932. **Genres:** Novels, Children's Fiction. **Career:** Primary school teacher, 1949-51; Church High School, teacher, 1951-53; Kenton Lodge College of Education, lecturer, 1953-61; College of Education, teacher and lecturer, 1955-64; editor, 1960-64; writer, 1964-. **Publications:** Street of the Small Night Market, 1966; Secret of the Jade Pavilion, 1967; Frog in a Coconut Shell, 1968; The Liverpool Cats, 1969; New Windmills: A Pair of Jesus Boots, 1969; The Loss of the Night Wind, 1970; Haven-Screamers, 1970; Snake in the Old Hut, 1972; Dark River, Dark Mountain, 1975; Mat, The Little Monkey, 1977; Girl in a Blue Shawl (for adults), 1978; South of Red River (for adults), 1981; A Pair of Desert-Wellies (for children), 1985; Pair of Desert Wellies, 1986; Rocky and the Ratman, 1988; Elephants Have Right of Way, 1996. **Address:** Jonathan Clowes Ltd., 10 Iron Bridge House, Bridge Approach, London, GL NW1 8BD, England.

SHERWIN, Michael S. Swiss (born Switzerland), b. 1963. **Genres:** Philosophy, Theology/Religion, Translations. **Career:** University of Fribourg, associate professor of theology; Dominican School of Philosophy and Theology, faculty. Writer. **Publications:** (trans.) Servais Pinckaers, Morality: The Catholic View, 2003; By Knowledge and By Love: Charity and Knowledge in the Moral Theology of St. Thomas Aquinas, 2005; (intro. and trans.) R. Pouivet, After Wittgenstein, St. Thomas, 2006. Contributor to periodicals. **Address:** Albert-Ludwigs-Universität, Fahnenbergplatz, Freiburg, 79085, Switzerland. **Online address:** michael.sherwin@unifr.ch

SHERWOOD, Ben. (Max Barclay). American (born United States), b. 1964. **Genres:** Novels, Biography, Self Help. **Career:** ABC News Prime Time Live, investigative producer and associate producer, 1989-93; NBC Nightly News with Tom Brokaw, senior broadcast producer, senior producer and broadcast producer, 1997-2001; ABC's Good Morning America, executive producer, 2004-06; The Survivors Club.org, founder, 2009, executive director. Writer. **Publications:** (As Max Barclay) Red Mercury: A Novel, 1996; The Man Who Ate the 747, 2000; The Death and Life of Charlie St. Cloud, 2004; Survivors Club: The Secrets and Science that Could Save Your Life, 2009; The Death and Life of Charlie St. Cloud, 2010. Contributor to periodicals. **Address:** Bantam Books, 1540 Broadway, New York, NY 10036, U.S.A. **Online address:** ben@bensherwood.com

SHERWOOD, Dolly. American (born United States) **Genres:** Art/Art History, Biography, Autobiography/Memoirs, Women's Studies And Issues. **Career:** West Virginia Heritage Truck, writer and developer; West Virginia Department of Culture and History, consultant and media specialist; University of Charleston, Carleton Varney School of Design, adjunct instructor, 1983-85; West Virginia College of Graduate Studies, adjunct instructor, 1986. **Publications:** Harriet Hosmer American Sculptor, 1830-1908, 1991. Contributor periodicals. **Address:** c/o George F. Scheer, 918 Kings Mill Rd., Chapel Hill, NC 27517-4923, U.S.A.

SHERWOOD, Frances. American (born United States), b. 1940. **Genres:** Novellas/Short Stories, Novels, Young Adult Fiction. **Career:** Indiana University, creative writing and journalism instructor, 1986-94, professor of English, 1994-, emeritus. Writer, novelist, and educator. **Publications:** Everything You've Heard Is True (short stories), 1989; Vindication (novel), 1993; Green (novel), 1995; The Book of Splendor (novel), 2002; Night of Sorrows, 2006. FORIEGN EDITION: Il Viscolo D'oro; Zidovka Rachel; Mary Larevendication; Poetess and Petticoats. Contributor to books and periodicals. Works appear in anthologies. **Address:** Department of English, Indiana University, Wiekamp Hall 3127, 1700 Mishawaka Ave., PO Box 7111, South Bend, IN 46634-7111, U.S.A. **Online address:** fsherwood@iusb.edu

SHERWOOD, Valerie. *See* **HINES, Jeanne.**

SHESOL, Jeff. American (born United States), b. 1969. **Genres:** Politics/Government, History. **Career:** United States Government, speechwriter, 1998-2001, senior presidential speechwriter, 1999-, deputy chief of presidential speechwriting; Princeton University, Anschutz Distinguished Fellow in American Studies, 2002; West Wing Writers, founding partner. Writer. **Publications:** Thatch: Featuring Politically Correct Person (comic collection), 1991; Mutual Contempt: Lyndon Johnson, Robert Kennedy, and the Feud That Defined a Decade, 1997; Supreme Power: Franklin Roosevelt vs. the Supreme Court, 2010. Contributor to periodicals and journals. **Address:** c/o Raphael Sagalyn, Sagalyn Literary Agency, 4922 Fairmont Ave., Ste. 200, Bethesda, MD 20814, U.S.A.

SHETTERLY, Aran. American (born United States), b. 1970. **Genres:** Adult Non-fiction, History. **Career:** Inside Mexico Magazine, co-founder. Writer. **Publications:** The Americano: Fighting with Castro for Cuba's Freedom, 2007. **Address:** 11010 NW 30th St., Ste. 104, Miami, FL 33172-5032, U.S.A.

SHEVELOW, Kathryn. American (born United States), b. 1951. **Genres:** Literary Criticism And History, Gay And Lesbian Issues, History, Popular Culture, Theatre, Women's Studies And Issues, Biography, Adult Non-fiction, Animals/Pets. **Career:** University of California, professor of British literature and culture, professor of English literature; University of Maine, faculty. Writer. **Publications:** Women and Print Culture: The Construction of Femininity in the Early Periodical, 1989; Charlotte: Being a True Account of an Actress's Flamboyant Adventures in Eighteenth-Century London's Wild and Wicked Theatrical World, 2005; For the Love of Animals: The Rise of the Animal Protection Movement, 2008. **Address:** Department of Literature, University of California, 9500 Gilman Dr., La Jolla, CA 92093-0410, U.S.A. **Online address:** kshevelow@ucsd.edu

SHEVITZ, Amy Hill. American (born United States), b. 1953?. **Genres:** History. **Career:** California State University, lecturer. Writer. **Publications:** Jewish Communities on the Ohio River: A History, 2007. **Address:** Center for Jewish History, 15 W 16th St., New York, NY 10011, U.S.A. **Online address:** amy@shevitz.net

SHEWARD, Tamara. American (born United States) **Genres:** Autobiography/Memoirs, Travel/Exploration. **Career:** The Travel Rag, co-editor. **Publications:** Bad Karma: Confessions of a Reckless Traveller in South-East Asia (memoir), 2005. Contributor to periodicals. **Address:** Academy Chicago Publishers, Chicago Distribution Ctr., 11030 South Langley Ave., Chicago, IL 60628, U.S.A.

SHIACH, Morag. British (born England), b. 1958. **Genres:** Cultural/Ethnic Topics, History, Politics/Government, Novels. **Career:** University of London, Queen Mary College, staff, 1987, professor of cultural history, head of the School of English and Drama, vice principal of teaching and learning and executive dean. Writer. **Publications:** NONFICTION: Discourse on Popular Culture: Class, Gender, and History in Cultural Analysis, 1730 to the Present, 1989; Hélène Cixous: A Politics of Writing, 1991; (ed.) Feminism and Cultural Studies, 1999; Modernism, Labour and Selfhood in British Literature and Culture, 1890-1930, 2004; (ed.) The Cambridge Companion to the Modernist Novel, 2007; (ed. and intro.) Room of One's Own, 2008. **Address:** Department of English, Queen Mary College, University of London, Mile End Rd., London, GL E1 4NS, England. **Online address:** m.e.shiach@qmul.ac.uk

SHIELDS, Jody. American (born United States), b. 1952?. **Genres:** Fashion/Costume, Novellas/Short Stories, Novels, Young Adult Non-fiction, Literary Criticism And History. **Career:** New York Times Magazine, design editor; Vogue, editor; House and Garden, editor; Details, editor. Artist. **Publications:** All That Glitters: The Glory of Costume Jewelry, 1987; Hats: A Stylish History and Collector's Guide, 1991; The Fig Eater (novel), 2000; Crimson Portrait (novel), 2006. Contributor to periodicals. **Address:** c/o Author Mail, Little, Brown and Company Inc., 1271 Ave. of the Americas, New York, NY 10020-1300, U.S.A.

SHIELDS, John M(ackie). Canadian (born Canada), b. 1954. **Genres:** Economics, Politics/Government. **Career:** University of Windsor, Canadian National Election Study, research officer, 1981; University of British Columbia, labor archival researcher, 1982; University of Saskatchewan, lecturer in politics, 1985-87; Ryerson University, professor of politics, 1988-, research professor, 1994, Graduate Programme in Communication and Culture, faculty, Political Economy of Communication and Culture, professor; Joint Center of Excellence for Research on Immigration and Settlement, associate director, 2002-05. Writer. **Publications:** (With S. McBride) Dismantling a Nation: Canada and the New World Order, 1993, 2nd ed., 1997; (with B.M. Evans) Shrinking the State: Globalization and Public Administration Reform, 1998. EDITOR: (with S. McBride and L. Haiven) Regulating Labour: The State, Neo-Conservatism, and Industrial Relations, 1991; (with M. Burke and C. Mooers) Restructuring and Resistance: Canadian Public Policy in an Age of Global Capitalism, 2000. Contributor to journals. **Address:** Department of Politics, Ryerson University, 350 Victoria St., Toronto, ON M5B 2K3, Canada. **Online address:** jshields@ryerson.ca

SHIELDS, Jon A. American (born United States), b. 1975. **Genres:** Humanities. **Career:** Claremont McKenna College, assistant professor of government; University of Colorado, assistant professor; Cornell University, visiting assistant professor. Writer. **Publications:** (With P.S. Nivola) Managing Green Mandates: Local Rigors of U.S. Environmental Regulation, 2001; The Democratic Virtues of the Christian Right, 2009. Contributor to periodicals. **Address:** U.S.A. **Online address:** jon.shields@cmc.edu

SHIGEKUNI, Julie. American (born United States) **Genres:** Novellas/Short Stories, Novels. **Career:** University of New Mexico, director of creative writing program, assistant professor of creative writing, 1998-, professor in English department, development director of Asian American studies program; Mills College, writer-in-residence; Hunter College, faculty; Institute of American Indian Arts, faculty; Sarah Lawrence College, faculty. Novelist. **Publications:** A Bridge Between Us, 1995; Invisible Gardens, 2003; Unending Nora, 2008. Works appear in anthologies. Contributor to periodicals. **Address:** Department of English Language and Literature, University of New Mexico, MSC03-2170, Humanities 374, Albuquerque, NM 87131-0001, U.S.A. **Online address:** jshig@unm.edu

SHIH, Chih-yu. Chinese/Taiwanese (born Taiwan), b. 1958. **Genres:** Area Studies, International Relations/Current Affairs, Psychology, Cultural/Ethnic Topics. **Career:** Winona State University, assistant professor of political science, 1987-88; Ramapo College of New Jersey, assistant professor of East Asian studies, 1988-90; National Taiwan University, associate professor of mainland Chinese affairs, 1990-96, professor, 1996-, national chair professor, 2001-04, university chair professor, 2007-10. Writer. **Publications:** The Spirit of Chinese Foreign Policy: A Psychocultural View, 1990; (with M. Cottam) Contending Dramas: A Cognitive Approach to International Organizations, 1992; China's Just World: The Morality of Chinese Foreign Policy, 1993; (with J. Adelman) Symbolic War: The Chinese Use of Force, 1840-1980, 1993; State and Society in Chinese Political Economy: Cultural Dynamics of Socialist Reform, 1995; Collective Democracy: Political and Legal Reform in China, 1999; Reform, Identity and Chinese Foreign Policy, 2000; Negotiating Ethnicity in China: Citizenship as a Response to the State, 2002; Navigating Sovereignty: World Politics Lost in China, 2003; Democracy (Made in Taiwan): The Success State as a Political Theory, 2007; Autonomy, Ethnicity and Poverty in Southwestern China: The State Turned Upside Down, 2007. **Address:** Department of Political Science, College of Social Science, National Taiwan University, 21 Hsu Chow Rd., Taipei, 10055, Taiwan. **Online address:** cyshih@ntu.edu.tw

SHIINA, Makoto. (Makoto cho Shiina). Japanese (born Japan), b. 1944?. **Genres:** Autobiography/Memoirs, Novels, Science Fiction/Fantasy, Young Adult Fiction. **Career:** Hon No Zasshi, editor-in-chief, publisher; Stores Report, editor-in-chief. **Publications:** Jon Mansaku no tōbō, 1982; Jōgai rantō wa kore kara da, 1982; Ima kono hito ga suki da!, 1983; Kaze ni korogaru eiga mo atta: sūpā essei, 1983; Gaku monogatari, 1985; Roshia Ni Okeru Nitarinofu no Benza ni Tsuite, 1987; Katsuji no sākasu, 1987; Ado bādo, 1990; Ginza no karasu, 1991; My Boy: A Father's Memories, 1993; Seishun, 1994. NOVELS IN JAPANESE: Aishu No Machi Ni Kiri Ga Furunoda; Shinbashi Karasumoriguchi Seishun Hen; Inu No Keifu. SCIENCE FICTION IN JAPANESE: Ad Bird, 1993; Chika Seikatsusha, 1993; Suiiki; Buso Shimada Soko. **Address:** Japan Foreign-Rights Center, 27-18-804, Naka Ochiai 2-chome, Shinjuku-ku, Tokyo, 161, Japan.

SHIINA, Makoto cho. *See* SHIINA, Makoto.

SHILLER, Robert J. American (born United States), b. 1946. **Genres:** Economics, Technology. **Career:** Yale University, Cowles Foundation, Stanley B. Resor professor of economics, Arthur M. Okun professor of economics, School of Management, professor, International Center for Finance, fellow; Case Shiller Weiss Inc., co-founder; Macro Securities Research L.L.C., co-founder; American Economic Association, vice-president, 2005; Eastern Economic Association, president, 2006-07; MacroMarkets L.L.C., co-founder and chief economist. Writer. **Publications:** Market Volatility, 1989; The Report of the Twentieth Century Fund Task Force on Market Speculation and Corporate Governance, 1992; Macro Markets: Creating Institutions for Managing Society's Largest Economic Risks, 1993; Irrational Exuberance, 2000, 2nd ed., 2005; The New Financial Order: Risk in the 21st Century, 2003; (with A.S. Blinder) The Quiet Revolution, 2004; Subprime Solution: How Today's Global Financial Crisis Happened and What to do About it, 2008; Animal Spirits: How Human Psychology Drives the Economy and Why it Matters for Global Capitalism, 2009; (with R.S. Kroszner) Reforming U.S. Financial Markets: Reflections before and beyond Dodd-Frank, 2011; Finance and the Good Society, 2012. Contributor to periodicals. **Address:** Cowles Foundation, Yale University, Rm. 23A, 30 Hillhouse Ave., PO Box 208281, New Haven, CT 06520-8281, U.S.A. **Online address:** robert.shiller@yale.edu

SHILLING, Michael. American (born United States), b. 1970. **Genres:** Novels. **Career:** University of Michigan, lecturer. Writer. **Publications:** Rock Bottom: A Novel, 2009. Contributor of to periodicals. **Address:** U.S.A. **Online address:** rockbottom09@bloodorphans.com

SHILLINGLAW, Gordon. American (born United States), b. 1925. **Genres:** Business/Trade/Industry. **Career:** Hamilton College, assistant professor of economics, 1951-52; Joel Dean Associates, consulting associate, 1952-55; Eliot-Pearson School, business manager and assistant treasurer,

1955-60; Massachusetts Institute of Technology, School of Industrial Management, assistant professor, 1955-61; Columbia University, Graduate School of Business, associate professor, 1961-66, professor of accounting, 1966-90, professor emeritus of accounting, 1991-; International Institute for Management Development, visiting professor, 1964-65, 1967-69. Writer. **Publications:** (With M.J. Gordon) La Comptabilité, 1960; Cost Accounting: Analysis and Control, 1961, 5th ed. as Managerial Cost Accounting, 1982; (with M.J. Gordon) Accounting: A Management Approach, 3rd ed., 1964, (with K.T. McGahran) 9th ed., 1993; (with J.C. Burton) Materials Management and the Profit Center Concept, 1964; Financial Accounting: Concepts and Applications, 1989. **Address:** Columbia Business School, Columbia University, 101 Uris, 3022 Broadway, New York, NY 10027, U.S.A. **Online address:** gs15@columbia.edu

SHILLINGSBURG, Miriam (Carolyn) Jones. American (born United States), b. 1943. **Genres:** History, Literary Criticism And History, Biography. **Career:** Mississippi State University, professor of English, 1970-88, associate vice-president of academic affairs, 1988-; Lamar University, professor of English, College of Arts and Sciences, dean, 1996-2000; Indiana University, professor of English, 2000-, College of Liberal Arts and Sciences, dean, 2000-04. Writer. **Publications:** At Home Abroad: Mark Twain in Australasia, 1988. EDITOR: (with E.N. Harbert) A Chronicle of the Conquest of Granada, 1988; The Cub of the Panther, 1997. Contributor to journals. **Address:** Department of English, Indiana University South Bend, Greenlawn Hall 101, 1700 Mishawaka Ave., PO Box 7111, South Bend, IN 46634, U.S.A. **Online address:** mshillin@iusb.edu

SHILLINGSBURG, Peter L(eRoy). American/Colombian (born Colombia), b. 1943. **Genres:** Literary Criticism And History. **Career:** University of South Carolina, research assistant to James B. Meriwether, 1966-70; Mississippi State University, Mississippi State, professor of English, 1970-97, William L. Giles distinguished professor, 1997; Australian Defence Force Academy, visiting professor, 1984, 1989; Lamar University, dean, 1996, associate director and associate dean, 1997-99; University of North Texas, professor, 1999-2003; De Montfort University, professor of English, 2003-08, The Centre for Textual Scholarship, director, 2005-08; Loyola University, Martin J. Svaglic professor of textual studies, 2008-; Society for Textual Scholarship, board director. Writer. **Publications:** Scholarly Editing in the Computer Age, 1984, rev. ed., 1996; Pegasus in Harness: Victorian Publishing and W.M. Thackeray, 1992; Resisting Texts: Authority and Submission in Constructions of Meaning, 1997; William Makepeace Thackeray: A Literary Life, 2001; From Gutenberg to Google: Electronic Representations of Literary Texts, 2006. EDITOR: Vanity Fair: A Novel Without a Hero, 1989; (with E. Harden) Henry Esmond, 1989; The History of Pendennis, 1991; Flore et Zéphyr, The Yellowplush Correspondence, The Tremendous Adventures of Major Gahagan, 1991; Vanity Fair: Authoritative Text, Backgrounds and Contents, Criticism, 1994; The Newcomes: Memoirs of a Most Respectable Family, 1996; (ed. with R. Modiano and L.F. Searle) Voice, Text, Hypertext: Emerging Practices in Textual Studies, 2004. Works appear in anthologies. Contributor to literature journals. **Address:** Department of English, Loyola University, 1032 W Sheridan Rd., Chicago, IL 60660, U.S.A. **Online address:** pshillingsburg@luc.edu

SHILLUE, Edith. American/Irish (born Ireland), b. 1963. **Genres:** History, Earth Sciences. **Career:** Shanghai Institute of Education, instructor in English, 1990; University of Ho Chi Minh City, instructor in English, 1993; University of Massachusetts, faculty, 1996-2001, Pre-enrollment Program, director, Directions for Student Potential Program, director, Dorchester Women's Program, instructor; College of the Holy Cross, Center for Interdisciplinary Studies, teacher, 1998-99; Queen's University, instructor in literature, 2005-. Writer. **Publications:** Earth and Water: Encounters in Viet Nam, 1997; Peace Comes Dropping Slow: Conversations in Northern Ireland, 2003. Contributor of articles to journals and books. **Address:** University of Massachusetts Press, East Experiment Sta., 671 N Pleasant St., Amherst, MA 01003, U.S.A. **Online address:** eshillue@hotmail.com

SHILOAH, Amnon. Israeli (born Israel), b. 1928. **Genres:** Music. **Career:** Ecole des Hautes Etudes, attache de recherches, 1962-65; Israel National Radio, Folk Music Department, director, 1965-69; Jewish Music Research Center, director and producer of musical and literary programs, 1965-69; Hebrew University of Jerusalem, lecturer, 1965-69, senior lecturer, 1969-71, Department of Musicology, chairman, 1971-74, 1992-94, associate professor 1971-78, professor, 1979-97, professor emeritus, 1997-; Illinois University,

George A. Miller visiting professor, 1968, 1974; University of Louisville, professor of humanities, 1978-79; University of Paris VIII, professor of Hebrew culture; Rothberg School for Overseas Students, Languages, Literatures and Arts, head, 1985-89; Center for Research and Study of Sephardi and Oriental Jewish Heritage, director. Writer. **Publications:** Caracteristiques de l'art vocal arabe au Moyen-age, 1963; (Ed. with B. Bayer) Yuval: Studies of the Jewish Music Research Centre, 1971; La Perfection des Connaissances Musicales, 1972; The Musical Subjects in the Zohar, 1977; (with R. Tenne) Noś'e musik(PTE)ah ba-Zohar, 1977; (trans.) The epistle on music of the Ikhwān al-Safā, 1978; The Theory of Music in Arabic Writings, 1979; Hemshekhiyut u-temurah ba-masoret ha-musik(PTE) alit shel Yehude Sefarad, 1985; Anu Lakh Homat Magen, 1990; Ule-fa'ate mizraḥ ḳadimah, 1990; Jewish Musical Traditions, 1992; The Dimension of Music in Islamic and Jewish Culture, 1993; A Music in the World of Islam Socio-Cultural Study, 1995; The Performance of Jewish and Arab Music in Israel Today, 1997; Musiḳah ba-'olam ha-Islam, 1999; The Theory of Music in Arabic Writings, 2003; Music and its Virtues in Islamic and Judaic Writings, 2007. **Address:** Department of Musicology, Hebrew University of Jerusalem, Rm. 6725, Jerusalem, 93116, Israel. **Online address:** shiloah@mscc.huji.ac.il

SHIM, Eunmi. American/Korean (born Korea (South)), b. 1964?. **Genres:** Music, Art/Art History. **Career:** Worcester Polytechnic Institute, associate professor of music. Writer. **Publications:** Lennie Tristano: His Life in Music, 2007. **Address:** Department of Humanities and Arts, Worcester Polytechnic Institute, 211 Alden Memorial, 100 Institute Rd., Worcester, MA 01609-2280, U.S.A. **Online address:** eshim@wpi.edu

SHIM, Jae K. American/Korean (born Korea (South)), b. 1943. **Genres:** Administration/Management, Business/Trade/Industry, Economics, Information Science/Computers, Technology. **Career:** Sam Ho Textile Corp., budget and cost analyst, 1965-66; City University of New York, Queens College, associate professor of accounting and information systems, 1973-81, visiting professor of economics, 1979-81; California State University, professor of accountancy, 1981-2008, professor emeritus, 2008-. Writer and consultant. **Publications:** WITH J.G. SIEGEL: Variance Analysis for Cost Control and Profit Maximization, 1982; Financial Accounting, 1982, 2nd ed., 1999; Accounting for and Evaluation of Process Cost Systems, 1983; Managerial Accounting, 1983; Schaum's Outline of Theory and Problems of Financial Accounting, 1983, 2nd ed. as Schaum's Outline of Theory and Problems of Managerial Accounting, 1998; Schaum's Outline of Theory And Problems of Managerial Finance, 1986; A Guide to Investments, 1986; Investments: A Self-teaching Guide, 1986; Accountants' Microcomputer Handbook, 1986; (and A.J. Simon) The Vest Pocket MBA, 1986, 3rd ed., 2004; Dictionary of Accounting Terms, 1987, 5th ed., 2010; Handbook of Financial Analysis, Forecasting, and Modeling, 1988, 3rd ed., 2007; (and N.A. Dauber) The Vest Pocket CPA, 1989, 4th ed., 2008; The Personal Financial Planning and Investment Pocket Guide, 1989; Encyclopedia of Accounting and Finance, 1989; Accounting Handbook, 1990, 5th ed., 2010; The Managerial Accountant's Standard Desk Reference, 1990; Thinking Finance: Everything Managers Need To Know About Finance And Accounting, 1990; Keys to Starting a Small Business, 1991; Financial Management, 1991, 3rd ed., 2008; Schaum's Outline of Theory and Problems of Personal Finance, 1991; Study Keys to Finance, 1991; Schaum's Outline Of Theory And Problems of Financial Management, 1991, 3rd ed., 2007; The Corporate Controller's Handbook of Financial Management, 1991, (and N. Dauber) 2nd ed., 1997; Modern Cost Management and Analysis, 1992, 3rd ed., 2009; Dictionary of Personal Finance, 1992; Keys to Managing Cash Flows, 1992; The McGraw-Hill Pocket Guide to Business Finance: 201 Decision-Making Tools For Managers, 1992; Source: The Complete Guide to Investment Information: Where To Find It and How To Use It, 1992; The Vest Pocket CFO, 1992, 3rd ed., 2008; The Loan Broker Manual, 1992; The Financial Troubleshooter: Spotting And Solving Financial Problems In Your Company, 1993; Study Keys to Macroeconomics, 1993; 569 Solutions to Your Personal Finance Problems, 1993; Macroeconomics, 1993, 2nd ed., 2005; Complete Budgeting Workbook and Guide, 1993; (and J. Lansner) 101 Investment Decision Tools: Barometers, Instruments, And Keys, 1993; Introduction To Accounting II, 1993; (and J. Lansner) 100 & One Investment Decision Tools: Barometers, Instruments, and Keys (Where to Find Them and How They're Used), 1994; (co-author) The Prentice-Hall Handbook of Budgeting, 1994; Budgeting Basics and Beyond: A Complete Step-By-Step Guide For Nonfinancial Managers, 1994, 3rd ed., 2009; What Every Engineer Should Know About Accounting And Finance, 1995; The Complete Book of Business Math: Every Manager's Guide To Analyzing Facts And Figures For Smart Business Decisions, 1995; Handbook of Budget-

ing for Nonprofit Organizations, 1996; Dictionary of Real Estate, 1996; The Encyclopedic Dictionary of Accounting & Finance, 1996; The Vest Pocket Investor: Everything You Need To Know To Invest Successfully, 1996; Financial Management for Nonprofits: The Complete Guide To Maximizing Resources And Managing Assets, 1997; (and with S. Hartman) Quick Study for Business Finance, 1997; The Vest-pocket Guide To Information Technology, 1997, 2nd ed., 2005; Managerial Economics, 1998; Schaum's Quick Guide To Business Formulas: 201 Decision-Making Tools For Business, Finance, And Accounting Students, 1998; Operations Management, 1999; Entrepreneurship 101, 2000; Dictionary of International Investment Terms, 2001; Fast Track Financial Analysis And Forecasting, 2001; The Manager's Handbook of Client/Server Computing In Business And Finance, 2003; Schaum's Outline of Financial Management, 3rd ed., 2007; (with A.I. Shim) Vest-pocket MBA, 2011; (with N.A. Dauber) Complete CPA Reference, 2012; (with A.I. Shim) CFO Fundamentals: Your Quick Guide to Internal Controls, Financial Reporting, IFRS, Web 2.0, Cloud Computing, and More, 4th ed., 2012. OTHERS: (with L. Geller) Readings in Cost and Managerial Accounting, 1980; Dictionary of Business Terms, 1987; (with C.J. Liew) Strategic Business Forecasting: The Complete Guide To Forecasting Real-World Company Performance, 1994, rev. ed., 2000; Budgeting Basics and Beyond, 1994; Information Systems Management Handbook, 1999; Accounting and Finance for the Nonfinancial Executive: An Integrated Resource Management Guide For The 21st Century, 2000; Information Systems And Technology for The Noninformation Systems Executive: An Integrated Resource Management Guide for The 21st Century, 2000; The International Handbook of Computer Security, 2000; (with J. Lansner) 101 Investment Tools For Buying Low And Selling High, 2001; (with M. Constas) Investment Sourcebook: The Complete Guide To Finding And Understanding Investment Information, 2001; (with M. Constas) Encyclopedic Dictionary of International Finance And Banking, 2001; Handbook of Financial Planning: An Expert's Guide For Advisors And Their Clients, 2004; The Financial Troubleshooter: Spotting and Solving Financial Problems in Your Company, 2005; Management Accountant's Standard Desk Reference, 2008; Art of Mathematics in Business: Analyzing Facts and Figures for Smart Business Decisions, 2009; Manager's Guide to Information Systems & Technology, 2010; Project Management: A Financial Perspective, 2010; Complete Guide to Investing, 2011; Internal Control and Fraud Detection, 2011; Managing and Improving Your Cash Flow, 2011. Contributor of articles to periodicals. **Address:** California State University, 1250 Bellflower Blvd., Long Beach, CA 90840-8504, U.S.A. **Online address:** jaeshim@csulb.edu

SHIMKO, Bonnie. American (born United States), b. 1941. **Genres:** Novels, Young Adult Fiction. **Career:** Peru Central School, second-grade teacher, 1963-94, now retired. Writer. **Publications:** NOVELS: Letters in the Attic, 2002; Kat's Promise, 2006; The Private Thoughts of Amelia E. Rye, 2010. **Address:** Wendy Schmalz Agency, PO Box 831, Hudson, NY 12534-0831, U.S.A. **Online address:** bonnie.shimko@verizon.net

SHIMPOCK, Kathy E(lizabeth). American (born United States), b. 1952. **Genres:** Business/Trade/Industry, Law. **Career:** Stanford University, assistant librarian, 1979-82; University of Bridgeport, law librarian and assistant professor of law, 1982-83; Law Library Administrative Services, director, 1983-85, owner and director, 1987-95; Arizona State University, executive assistant, 1985-87; Jennings, Strouss & Salmon, director of library services, 1988-89; O'Connor, Cavanagh, Anderson, Westover, Killingsworth & Beshears, director of research services, 1989-95; Muchmore & Wallwork, counsel, 1995-; Juris Research, president, 1995-; Bryan Cave L.L.P., research and legal information manager, 2000-11. Writer and speaker. **Publications:** (With M.A. Voges) The Bankruptcy Reform Act of 1978: Analysis, Legislative History and Selected Bibliography, 1981; (with M. Alcorn) Arizona Legal Research Guide, 1992; Business Research Handbook: Methods and Sources for Lawyers and Business Professionals, 1996. Contributor to books and periodicals. **Address:** 7650 S McClintock Dr., Ste. 103-136, f, Tempe, AZ 85284, U.S.A. **Online address:** kshimpock@jurisresearch.com

SHIN, Leo K. Canadian (born Canada), b. 1967. **Genres:** Cultural/Ethnic Topics, Sociology, History. **Career:** The Standard, education and political reporter, 1989-90; Columbia University, lecturer and fellow, 1995-96; Simon Fraser University, instructor, 1996-99, assistant professor, 1999-2001; University of British Columbia, assistant professor, 2001-08, associate professor of history and asian studies, 2008-. Writer. **Publications:** The Making of the Chinese State: Ethnicity and Expansion on the Ming Borderlands, 2006. Contributor of articles to books. **Address:** Department of History, University of British Columbia, 1297-1873 East Mall, Vancouver, BC V6T 1Z1, Canada. **Online address:** leo.shin@ubc.ca

SHINAGEL, Michael. American/Austrian (born Austria), b. 1934. **Genres:** Literary Criticism And History, Education, Adult Non-fiction. **Career:** Harvard University, Harvard Extension School, teacher, 1959, dean of continuing education and director of university extension, 1975-, teacher, 1976, tutor in English, senior lecturer in English, 1983-, Graduate and Career Plans, associate director, Peace Corps, liaison officer, director of the summer school, chair of dramatics, Harvard Graduate Society, board director, Continuing Higher Education Review, editor; Cornell University, assistant professor of English, 1964-67; Union College, associate professor, 1967-72, chair of department, 1967-75, professor of English, 1972-75; Council of Masters, chair; Harvard Review, publisher; Educational Exchange, president; Indian Computer Academy, chairman; Old South Meeting House, director; Harvard Coop, vice chair; Educational Exchange of Greater Boston, president; Old South Meeting House, board director. **Publications:** Daniel Defoe and Middle-Class Gentility, 1968; (ed.) Concordance to the Poems of Jonathan Swift, 1972; (ed.) Robinson Crusoe, by Daniel Defoe, 1975, rev. ed., 1993; (ed. with W.J. Bate and J. Engell) Harvard Scholars in English, 1890-1990, 1991; The Gates Unbarred: A History of University Extension at Harvard, 1910-2009, 2009. **Address:** Division of Continuing Education, Harvard University, Rm. 723, 51 Brattle St., Cambridge, MA 02138, U.S.A. **Online address:** michael_shinagel@harvard.edu

SHINE, Frances L(ouise). American (born United States), b. 1927. **Genres:** Novels, Writing/Journalism, Young Adult Fiction. **Career:** Boston Public Library, secretary, 1948-50; Cornell University, secretary, 1951-52; Hardy, Hall, Iddings & Grimes, secretary, 1952-53; teacher, 1953-56; Framingham Public Schools, teacher, 1956-. Writer. **Publications:** The Life-Adjustment of Harry Blake, 1968; Johnny Noon, 1973; Conjuror's Journal: Excerpts from the Journal of Joshua Medley, Conjuror, Juggler, Ventriloquist, and Sometime Balloonist: A Novel, 1978. **Address:** Curtis Brown Ltd., 10 Astor Pl., New York, NY 10003, U.S.A.

SHINE, Richard. (Rick Shine). Australian (born Australia), b. 1950. **Genres:** Biology, Zoology. **Career:** University of Utah, postdoctoral fellow, 1975-78; University of Sydney, postdoctoral fellow, 1978-80, lecturer, 1980-84, senior lecturer, 1985-87, reader in biology, 1988-92, professor of evolutionary biology, 1993-2005, professor in biology, 2011-; Carnegie Museum of Natural History, research associate, 1988; Australian Museum, research associate, 1988; Flinders University of South Australia, honorary research associate, 1991; Australian Research Council, professorial fellow, 2002-05, 2006-; University chair, 2004-. Writer. **Publications:** (Ed. with G.C. Grigg and H. Ehmann and contrib.) Biology of Australian Frogs and Reptiles, 1985; Diets and Abundances of Anuatic and Semi-Aquatic Reptiles in the Alligator Rivers Region, 1986; Australian Snakes: A Natural History, 1991, rev. ed. as Das Grosse Buch der Australischen Schlangen Eine Naturgeschichte, 1996; Snakes of the United States and Canada, 2003. Works appear in anthologies. Contributor of articles to scientific journals. **Address:** School of Biological Sciences, University of Sydney, Rm. 209, A08-Heydon-Laurence Bldg.,, Sydney, NW 2006, Australia. **Online address:** rick.shine@sydney.edu.au

SHINE, Rick. *See* SHINE, Richard.

SHINER, David. American/Israeli (born Israel), b. 1951. **Genres:** Sports/Fitness. **Career:** Shimer College, professor of humanities and the history of ideas, 1976-, faculty, 1977-. Writer. **Publications:** Baseball's Greatest Players: The Saga Continues, 2001. Contributor of articles to periodicals. **Address:** Shimer College, 3424 S State St., Chicago, IL 60616-3893, U.S.A. **Online address:** cunegonde@pcbb.net

SHINICHI, Kano. *See* JACKSON, G. Mark.

SHINN, Sharon. American (born United States), b. 1957. **Genres:** Science Fiction/Fantasy, Young Adult Fiction. **Career:** Professional Photographer, associate editor, 1979-83; Decor, managing editor, 1983-2001; BizEd, co-editor, 2001-. **Publications:** FANTASY/SCIENCE FICTION NOVELS: The Shape-Changer's Wife, 1995; Archangel, 1996; Jovah's Angel, 1997; The Alleluia Files, 1998; Wrapt in Crystal, 1999; Heart of Gold, 2000; Summers at Castle Auburn, 2001; Jenna Starborn, 2002; Angelica, 2003; Angel-Seeker, 2004; The Safe-Keeper's Secret, 2004; (co-author) To Weave a Web of Magic; 2004; Mystic and Rider, 2005; Truth-Teller's Tale, 2005; Dream-Maker's

Magic, 2006; Dark Moon Defender, 2006; Thirteenth House, 2006; (co-author) The Queen in Winter, 2006; Reader and Raelynx, 2007; General Winston's Daughter, 2007; (co-author) Elemental Magic, 2007; Fortune and Fate, 2008; Quatrain, 2009; Gateway, 2009; Troubled Waters, 2010; (co-author) Angels of Darkness, October 2011. **Address:** c/o Ethan Ellenberg, Ethan Ellenberg Literary Agency, 548 Broadway, Ste. 5E, New York, NY 10012-3916, U.S.A. **Online address:** sharon@sharonshinn.net

SHINN, Thelma J. American (born United States), b. 1942. **Genres:** Literary Criticism And History, Plays/Screenplays. **Career:** Connecticut State Department of Welfare, caseworker, 1965-66; New York City Social Services, caseworker, 1968; Bronx Aftercare, psychiatric social worker, 1968-70; College of Our Lady of the Elms, instructor in English, 1971-73; Westfield State College, assistant professor of English, Writing Laboratory, head, 1973-75; Urban Education English Program, head, 1973-75; Arizona State University, assistant professor, 1975-82, associate professor, 1982-85, professor of English, 1985-2004, professor emeritus of English, 2004-, founding director of women's studies, 1977-80. Writer. **Publications:** Radiant Daughters: Fictional American Women, 1986; Worlds within Women: Myth and Mythmaking in Fantastic Literature by Women, 1986; Women Shapeshifters: Transforming the Contemporary Novel, 1996. Contributor to books and journals. **Address:** Department of English, Arizona State University, PO Box 870302, Tempe, AZ 85287-0302, U.S.A. **Online address:** tjrichard@asu.edu

SHIPLER, David K(arr). American (born United States), b. 1942. **Genres:** International Relations/Current Affairs, Race Relations, Writing/Journalism. **Career:** New York Times, news clerk, 1966-68, reporter, 1968-73, foreign correspondent-Saigon, 1973-75, Moscow Bureau, foreign correspondent, 1975-79, chief, 1977-79, Israel Bureau, chief, 1979-84, Washington Bureau, state department diplomatic correspondent, 1985-88; Metropolitan Staff, reporter, 1968-73; Carnegie Endowment for International Peace, senior associate, 1988-90; Princeton University, Ferris professor of journalism and public affairs, 1990-91; freelance writer, 1991-; Dartmouth College, trustee, 1993-2003, visiting professor of government, 2003; American University, faculty. **Publications:** Russia: Broken Idols, Solemn Dreams, 1983, rev. ed., 1989; Arab and Jew: Wounded Spirits in a Promised Land, 1986, rev. ed., 2002; A Country of Strangers: Blacks and Whites in America, 1997; The Working Poor: Invisible in America, 2004; Rights of the People: How Our Search for Safety Invades our Liberties, 2011. **Address:** c/o Author Mail, Knopf Publishing, 1745 Broadway, New York, NY 10019, U.S.A.

SHIPMAN, Henry Longfellow. American (born United States), b. 1948. **Genres:** Astronomy. **Career:** California Institute of Technology, teaching assistant, 1969-71; Yale University, J.W. Gibbs Instructor, 1971-73; University of Missouri, assistant professor, 1973-74; University of Delaware, assistant professor, 1974-77, associate professor, 1977-81, professor of physics, 1981-, Annie Jump Cannon professor of astronomy; American Astronomical Society, Harlow Shapley visiting lecturer, 1976-; Center for Advanced Study, fellow, 1985-86; Writer. **Publications:** Black Holes, Quasars, and the Universe, 1976, 2nd ed., 1980; The Restless Universe: An Introduction to Astronomy, 1978; Space 2000: Meeting the Challenge of a New Era, 1987; Humans in Space: 21st Century Frontiers, 1989; Science, Technology and Society, 1993; The Way the World Works, 1995; (ed. with E.M. Sion and S. Vennes) White Dwarfs: Cosmological and Galactic Probes, 2005. Contributor to periodicals. **Address:** Department of Physics & Astronomy, University of Delaware, 00224, 104 The Green, Sharp Laboratory 124, Newark, DE 19716-2593, U.S.A. **Online address:** harrys@udel.edu

SHIPMAN, John Marlin. American (born United States), b. 1946. **Genres:** Writing/Journalism, Documentaries/Reportage, Adult Non-fiction. **Career:** Arkansas State University, professor of journalism, 1981-2007, retired, 2007. Journalist. **Publications:** The Penalty Is Death: U.S. Newspaper Coverage of Womens Executions, 2002. Contributor to periodicals. **Address:** 2607 Greenbriar, Jonesboro, AR 72401-5939, U.S.A.

SHIPMAN, Pat. American (born United States), b. 1949. **Genres:** Anthropology/Ethnology, Biography, History, Animals/Pets, Archaeology/Antiquities. **Career:** Jersey City State College, visiting lecturer in anthropology, 1974; Fordham University, EXCEL Program, adjunct instructor, 1975; American Institutes for Research, editor and research associate, 1976-78; Johns Hopkins University, research associate, 1978-81, assistant professor, 1981-86, associate professor of cell biology and anatomy, 1986-95, assistant dean of academic affairs, School of Medicine, 1985-90; full-time writer, 1990-;

Penn State University, adjunct professor of anthropology, 1995-. **Publications:** Life History of a Fossil: An Introduction to Taphonomy and Paleoecology, 1981; Reconstructing the Paleoecology and Taphonomic History of Ramapithecus Wickeri at Fort Ternan, Kenya, 1982; (with A. Walker and D. Bichell) The Human Skeleton, 1985; (with E. Trinkaus) The Neanderthals: Changing the Image of Mankind, 1993; The Evolution of Racism: Human Differences and the Use and Abuse of Science, 1994; (with A. Walker) The Wisdom of the Bones: In Search of Human Origins, 1996; Taking Wing: Archaeopteryx and the Evolution of Bird Flight, 1998; The Man Who Found the Missing Link, 2001; To the Heart of the Nile: Lady Florence Baker and the Exploration of Central Africa, 2004; The Stolen Woman: Florence Baker's Extraordinary Life from the Harem to the Heart of Africa, 2004; (with Alan Walker) Ape in the Tree: An Intellectual and Natural History of Proconsul, 2005; Femme Fatale: Love, Lies, and the Unknown Life of Mata Hari, 2007; The Animal Connection: A New Perspective on What Makes Us Human, 2011. Contributor to journals. **Address:** Department of Anthropology, Penn State University, 315 Carpenter Bldg., University Park, PA 16802, U.S.A. **Online address:** pat.shipman9@gmail.com

SHIPNUCK, Alan. American (born United States), b. 1973?. **Genres:** Sports/Fitness. **Career:** Sports Illustrated Magazine, writer, 1994-, senior writer. Sports journalist. **Publications:** Bud, Sweat, and Tees: A Walk on the Wild Side of the PGA Tour, 2001; The Battle for Augusta National: Hootie, Martha, and the Masters of the Universe, 2004; (with C. Kim) Swinging from My Heels: Confessions of an LPGA Star, 2010; (with M. Bamberger) The Swinger: A Novel, 2011. Contributor to periodicals. **Address:** Sports Illustrated Magazine, P O Box 30602, Tampa, FL 33630-0602, U.S.A.

SHIPP, Steve. American (born United States), b. 1937. **Genres:** History, Politics/Government, Sciences, Education. **Career:** Professional musician, 1953-; news reporter, 1965-; freelance writer, 1975-. **Publications:** Hong Kong, China: A Political History of the British Crown Colony's Transfer to Chinese Rule, 1995; American Art Colonies 1850-1930: A Historical Guide to America's Original Art Colonies and their Artists, 1996; Macau, China: A Political History of the Portuguese Colony's Transition to Chinese Rule, 1997; Rainforest Organizations: A Worldwide Directory of Private and Governmental Entities, 1997; Latin American and Caribbean Artists of the Modern Era: A Biographical Dictionary of More Than 12, 700 Persons, 2003; North Korea in Quotation: A Worldwide Dictionary, 1948-2004, 2005. **Address:** McFarland, 960 NC Hwy 88 W, PO Box 611, Jefferson, NC 28640, U.S.A. **Online address:** ekim@goodnet.com

SHIPPER, Apichai W. American (born United States), b. 1968. **Genres:** Politics/Government. **Career:** University of Tokyo, visiting researcher, 1992-94, 1998-99; United Nations University, visiting researcher, 1998-99; Hitotsubashi University, visiting researcher, 1998-99, 2005-06; Harvard University, visiting researcher, 2000-01; University of Southern California, assistant professor, 2002-; Japan Institute of Labour Policy and Training, visiting researcher, 2004, 2005-06, 2009; Stockholm University, visiting researcher, 2007, 2008; Swedish Institute of International Affairs, visiting researcher, 2008; Kyoto University, visiting researcher, 2008-09. Writer. **Publications:** Fighting for Foreigners: Immigration and Its Impact on Japanese Democracy, 2008. **Address:** University of Southern California, 318 Von KleinSmid Ctr., Los Angeles, CA 90089-0044, U.S.A. **Online address:** shipper@usc.edu

SHIRE, Michael J. British (born England) **Genres:** Theology/Religion. **Career:** Leo Baeck College, Centre for Jewish Education, vice president, Rabbinic Programme and Community of Learners Project, director, Department of Jewish Education, vice-principal and director; Centre for the Spirituality of Childhood and Adolescence, distinguished advisor. Writer. **Publications:** (Ed.) The Illuminated Haggadah: Featuring Medieval Illuminations from the Haggadah Collection of the British Library, 1998; (ed.) Lchaim! Prayers and Blessings for the Home, 2000; (ed.) The Jewish Prophet: Visionary Words from Moses and Miriam to Henrietta Szold and A.J. Heschel, 2002; Mazal tov! The Rituals and Customs of a Jewish Wedding, 2002. **Address:** Sternberg Ctr. for Judaism, Leo Baeck College Centre for Jewish Education, 80 E End Rd., London, GL N3 2SY, England. **Online address:** michael.shire@lbc-cje.ac.uk

SHIRK, David A. American (born United States), b. 1971?. **Genres:** Politics/Government, Law. **Career:** University of California, UCSD Center for U.S. Mexican Studies, pre-doctoral fellow, 1998-99, 2001-03, post-doctoral fellow, 2002-04; University of San Diego, Department of Political Science, assistant professor, Trans-Border Institute, director, associate professor of political science, faculty, 2003-, Joan B. Kroch School of Peace Studies, director, 2003-; California State University, faculty; Instituto Autónomo de México, faculty; Soka University of America, faculty; Woodrow Wilson fellow, 2009-10. Writer. **Publications:** (Contrib.) Subnational Politics and Democratization in Mexico, 1999; (contrib.) Party Politics and the Struggle for Democracy in Mexico: National and State-Level Analyses of the Partido Acci On Nacional, 2001; Mexico's New Politics: The PAN and Democratic Change, 2005; (ed. with C. Bardan and C.R. Alejandra) Análisis técnico de la propuesta de reforma al sistema de justicia mexicano, 2005; (ed. with W.A. Cornelius) Reforming the Administration of Justice in Mexico, 2007; (ed. with C.R. Alejandra) Evaluating Accountability and Transparency in Mexico: National, Local, and Comparative Perspectives, 2007; Contemporary Mexican Politics, 2009; (ed. with R.A. Donnelly) Police and Public Security in Mexico, 2009; Shared Responsibility: U.S.-Mexico Policy Options for Combatting Organized Crime, 2010. Contributor to periodicals. **Address:** Trans-Border Institute, University of San Diego, Rm. KIPJ 257, 5998 Alcalá Pk., San Diego, CA 92110, U.S.A. **Online address:** dshirk@sandiego.edu

SHIRKY, Clay. American (born United States), b. 1964?. **Genres:** Information Science/Computers. **Career:** New York University, Interactive Telecommunications Program, adjunct professor; Hard Place Theater, theater director & designer; Site Specific, chief technology officer; Hunter College, professor of new media. Consultant, educator and writer. **Publications:** The Internet by E-mail, 1994; Voices from the Net, 1995; Here Comes Everybody: The Power of Organizing without Organizations, 2008. Contributor to periodicals. **Address:** Brooklyn, NY , U.S.A. **Online address:** clay@shirky.com

SHIRLEY, Dennis. American (born United States), b. 1955. **Genres:** Education. **Career:** Ecole d'Humanite, teacher, 1980-83; Rice University, assistant professor, associate professor, 1988-97, department chair, 1992-94, professor of education, 1997-98; Alexander von Humboldt Foundation, chancellor's fellow, 1990-91; Rice University, Will Rice College, college master, 1992-97; Harvard University, research associate, 1997-98; Boston College, Lynch School of Education, Department of Teacher Education, Special Education, and Curriculum and Instruction, professor, 1998-, associate dean, 1998-2001, Massachusetts Coalition for Teacher Quality and Student Achievement, 1999-2005, chair, 2001-04, The Mindful Teacher, principal investigator, 2004-, The Teachers Union Reform Network, principal investigator, 2010-. Writer. **Publications:** The Politics of Progressive Education: The Odenwaldschule in Nazi Germany, 1992; Community Organizing for Urban School Reform, 1997; Valley Interfaith and School Reform, 2002; (with A. Hargreaves) The Long and Short of Educational Change, 2009; (with E. MacDonald) The Mindful Teacher, 2009; (with A. Hargreaves) The Fourth Way: The Inspiring Future for Educational Change, 2009; The Fourth Way in Action, forthcoming. **Address:** Lynch School of Education, Boston College, 221 Campion Hall, 140 Commonwealth Ave., Chestnut Hill, MA 02467-3807, U.S.A. **Online address:** shirleyd@bc.edu

SHIRLEY, Frances A. American (born United States), b. 1931. **Genres:** Literary Criticism And History, Theatre, inspirational/Motivational Literature, Photography, Archaeology/Antiquities. **Career:** Johns Hopkins University, McCoy College, instructor in English, 1955-56; Bryn Mawr College, 1956-59; Wheaton College, instructor, 1960-63, assistant professor, 1963-67, associate professor, 1967-73, professor of English, 1973-96, A. Howard Meneely research professor, 1980-81, Department of English, chairman, 1972-81, associate provost, 1984-88, professor emerita of English, 1996-; Land Preservation Society of Norton, founder, 1970-, co-president, 2008-09. Writer. **Publications:** Shakespeare's Use of Off-Stage Sound, 1963; Swearing and Perjury in Shakespeare's Plays, 1979. EDITOR: Devil's Law-Case, 1972; King John and Henry VIII: Critical Essays, 1988; Troilus and Cressida, 2005. **Address:** Department of English, Wheaton College, 26 E Main St., Norton, MA 02766-2322, U.S.A. **Online address:** fshirley@wheatonma.edu

SHIRLEY, Shirley. American (born United States), b. 1934. **Genres:** Local History/Rural Topics, Travel/Exploration, Business/Trade/Industry, History. **Career:** Iowa Valley Community College, instructor in nursing, 1991-2000; Iowa Artists, state president, 2003-. Writer. **Publications:** Restoring the Tallgrass Prairie: An Illustrated Manual for Iowa and the Upper Midwest, 1994; Evolution of the Prairie Border: Aggression and Succession, forthcoming. **Address:** 803 9th Ave., Eldora, IA 50627, U.S.A. **Online address:** shirshir52@juno.com

SHIVERS, Jay Sanford. American (born United States), b. 1930. **Genres:** Gerontology/Senior Issues, Public/Social Administration, Recreation, Administration/Management. **Career:** Hillside Psychiatric Hospital, recreational leader, 1952-53; Goldwater Memorial Hospital, director of recreational rehabilitation, 1953; University of Wisconsin, instructor in education, 1955-57; U.S. Veterans Administration Hospital, recreational supervisor, 1957-58; Mississippi Southern College, professor of recreational service education and chair of department, 1958-62; University of Connecticut, assistant professor, 1962-66, associate professor, 1967-69, professor of recreational service education, 1970-2003, now professor emeritus, 2003-. Writer. **Publications:** (With G. Hjelte) Public Administration of Park and Recreational Services, 1963; Leadership in Recreational Service, 1963; Principles and Practices of Recreational Service, 1967; Camping: Administration, Counseling, Programming, 1971; (with G. Hjelte) Planning Recreational Places, 1971; (with G. Hjelte) Public Administration of Recreational Services, 1972, 2nd ed., 1978; (with C.R. Calder) Recreational Crafts: Programming and Instructional Techniques, 1974; (with H.F. Fait) Therapeutic and Adapted Recreational Service, 1975; Essentials of Recreational Services, 1978; Leisure: Emergence and Expansion, 1979; Recreational Leadership: Group Dynamics and Interpersonal Behaviour, 1980, 2nd ed., 1986; Urban Recreational Problems, 1980; (with H.F. Fait) Recreational Service for the Aging, 1980; Leisure and Recreation Concepts: A Critical Analysis, 1981; (with C.A. Bucher and R.D. Bucher) Recreation for Today's Society, 2nd ed., 1984; (with H.F. Fait) Special Recreational Services Therapeutic and Adapted, 1985; Recreational Safety, 1986; Introduction to Recreational Service Administration, 1987; Camping: Organization and Operation, 1989; Introduction to Recreational Service, 1993; (with L.J. DeLisle) The Story of Leisure: Context, Concepts, and Current Controversy, 1997; Leadership and Groups in Recreational Service, 2001; Recreational Services for Older Adults, 2002; Programming Recreational Services, 2011; (ed. with J. Halper) Strategic Recreation Management, 2012. **Address:** University of Connecticut, U-110, 115 N Eagleville Rd., Storrs, CT 06269-9011, U.S.A.

SHLAES, Amity. American (born United States) **Genres:** Adult Non-fiction. **Career:** Council on Foreign Relations, senior fellow; National Public Radio, contributor; American Institute in Contemporary German Studies, trustee; American Academy in Berlin, J.P. Morgan fellow of economics and finance; Wall Street Journal (European edition), editorial features editor, 1986-90; Wall Street Journal, deputy editorial features editor, 1990-92, editorial features editor, 1992-94; Financial Times, columnist, 2000-09; Bloomberg, syndicated columnist, 2000-09; Marketplace Radio, commentator, 2005-. **Publications:** NONFICTION: Germany: The Empire Within, 1991; The Greedy Hand: How Taxes Drive Americans Crazy and What to Do about It, 1999; (contrib.) Turning Intellect into Influence: The Manhattan Institute at 25, 2004; The Forgotten Man: A New History of the Great Depression, 2007. Contributor to periodicals. **Address:** Council on Foreign Relations, 58 E 68th St., New York, NY 10065, U.S.A. **Online address:** ashlaes@cfr.org

SHLAIM, Avi. British/Israeli/Iraqi (born Iraq), b. 1945. **Genres:** International Relations/Current Affairs, History, Writing/Journalism, Military/Defense/Arms Control, Politics/Government. **Career:** Cambridge University, reader, 1966-69; University of Reading, lecturer, 1970-87, reader in politics, 1986-87; Hebrew University of Jerusalem, Leonard Davis Institute of International Relations, visiting fellow, 1975, Ford Fellow in department of international relations, 1981-82; Woodrow Wilson International Center for Scholars, fellow, 1980-81; University of Oxford, fellow of St. Antony's College and Alastair Buchan reader in international relations, 1987-96, professor of politics and international relations, 1987-, British academy research reader, 1995-97, research professor, 2003-06; Graduate Studies in International Relations, director, 1993-95, 1998-2001; University of Paris, visiting professor, 2009. Writer and consultant. **Publications:** (Ed. with G.N. Yannopoulos) EEC and the Mediterranean Countries, 1976; (with P. Jones and K. Sainsbury) British Foreign Secretaries since 1945, 1977; (ed. with G.N. Yannopoulos) EEC and Eastern Europe, 1978; The United States and the Berlin Blockade, 1948-49: A Study in Crisis Decision Making, 1983; Collusion Across the Jordan: King Abdullah, the Zionist Movement and the Partition of Palestine, 1988; Politics of Partition: King Abdullah, the Zionists and Palestine, 1921-1951, 1990; War and Peace in the Middle East: A Critique of American Policy, 1994, rev. ed. as War and Peace in the Middle East: A Concise History, 1995; (ed. with Y. Sayigh) The Cold War and the Middle East, 1997; (ed. with Y. Sayigh) The Cold War and the Middle East, 1997; The Politics of Partition: King Abdullah, the Zionists and Palestine, 1921-1951, 1998; The Iron Wall: Israel and the Arab World, 2000; (ed. with E.L. Rogan) The War of Palestine: Rewriting

the History of 1948, 2001, 2nd ed., 2007; (ed. with E.L. Rogan) The War for Palestine: Rewriting the History of 1948, 2001; Lion of Jordan: The Life of King Hussein in War and Peace, 2008; Israel and Palestine: Reappraisals, Revisions, Refutations, 2009. Contributor to periodicals. **Address:** St. Antony's College, University of Oxford, 62 Woodstock Rd., Oxford, OX OX2 6JF, England. **Online address:** avi.shlaim@sant.ox.ac.uk

SHLECHTER, Theodore M. American (born United States), b. 1952. **Genres:** Psychology, Technology, Education, Engineering. **Career:** U.S. Army Research Institute for the Behavioral and Social Sciences, research psychologist, 1984-; University of Louisville, adjunct instructor, 1990-. Writer. **Publications:** (Co-author) Educational Psychology: A Manual for Independent Study, 1979; (ed. with M.P. Toglia) New Directions in Cognitive Science, 1985; (ed.) Problems and Promises of Computer-Based Training, 1991. Contributor to books and periodicals. **Address:** U.S. Army Research Institute for the Behavioral, and Social Sciences, 2423 Bldg., 121 Morande St., Fort Knox, KY 40121-4141, U.S.A. **Online address:** drteds@earthlink.net

SHMANSKE, Stephen. American (born United States), b. 1954. **Genres:** Business/Trade/Industry, Economics, Transportation. **Career:** University of California, Department of Economics, teaching associate, 1977-79; United States Department of Justice, Antitrust Division, economist, 1978; California State University, Department of Economics, instructor, lecturer, assistant professor, associate professor, professor of economics, 1979-2010, College of Business and Economics, The Smith Center for Private Enterprise Studies, director, 2007-10; Law Offices of Stevens and Stevens, consultant, 1979-2010; National Center for State Courts, consultant, 1980; Anglia Polytechnic University, visiting professor, 1994. Writer. **Publications:** Public Goods, Mixed Goods, and Monopolistic Competition, 1991. Golfonomics, 2004, 2005. Contributor to journals. **Address:** Department of Economics, California State University, East Bay, Hayward, CA 94542, U.S.A. **Online address:** stephen.shmanske@csueastbay.edu

SHNEIDMAN, N(oah) N(orman). Canadian (born Canada), b. 1924. **Genres:** Literary Criticism And History, Politics/Government, Education. **Career:** University of Toronto, associate professor, 1975-79, professor of Slavic languages and literatures, 1979-90, associate chair of department, 1984-86, professor emeritus, 1990-, Centre for Russian and East European Studies, acting director, 1990; McMaster University, distinguished visiting professor, 1981. Writer. **Publications:** Literature and Ideology in Soviet Education, 1973; The Soviet Road to Olympus: The Theory and Practice of Soviet Physical Culture, 1978; Soviet Literature in the 1970s: Artistic Diversity and Ideological Conformity, 1979; Dostoevsky and Suicide, 1984; Soviet Literature in the 1980s: Decade of Transition, 1989; Russian Literature 1988-1994: The End of an Era, 1995; Jerusalem of Lithuania: The Rise and Fall of Jewish Vilnius, 1998; The Three Tragic Heroes of the Vilnius Ghetto: Witenberg, Sheinbaum, Gens, 2002; Russian Literature 1995-2002: On the Threshold of the New Millennium, 2004; Double Vision: The Jew in Post-Soviet Russian Literature, 2007. **Address:** Department of Slavic Languages & Literatures, University of Toronto, Toronto, ON M5S 1A1, Canada. **Online address:** nn.shneidman@utoronto.ca

SHNEOUR, Elie Alexis. American/French (born France), b. 1925. **Genres:** Biology, Chemistry, History, Medicine/Health, Military/Defense/Arms Control, Politics/Government, Psychology. **Career:** University of Utah, professor of biology, 1965-69; City of Hope Medical Center, researcher in neurosciences, 1969-71; Calbiochem Inc., director of research, 1971-74; Biosystems Associates Ltd., president, 1975-, chief executive offier. Consultant and writer. **Publications:** (With S. Moffat) Life Beyond the Earth, 1965; The Search for Extraterrestrial Life, 1966; The Malnourished Mind, 1974. Contributor to journals and newspapers. **Address:** Biosystems Associates Ltd., PO Box 1414, La Jolla, CA 92038, U.S.A.

SHOCKLEY, Ann Allen. American (born United States), b. 1927. **Genres:** Novels, Novellas/Short Stories, Librarianship, Romance/Historical, Young Adult Fiction, Young Adult Non-fiction. **Career:** Delaware State College, assistant librarian, 1959-60; University of Maryland, assistant librarian, associate librarian and curator of the Negro Collection, 1960-69; Fisk University, associate librarian, 1970, librarian for public services, 1975, university archivist, associate professor of library science, 1980-98, now retired; American Library Association, Black Caucus Newsletter, editor, 1972-74. Writer. **Publications:** (With S.P. Chandler) Living Black American Authors: A Biographical Directory, 1973; Loving Her (novel), 1974; (comp. and ed.

with E.J. Josey) A Handbook of Black Librarianship, 1977; The Black and White of It (short stories), 1980; Say Jesus and Come to Me (novel), 1982; (ed.) Afro-American Women Writers, 1746-1933: An Anthology and Critical Guide, 1988; Celebrating Hotchclaw: A Novel, 2005. Contributor of articles to magazines, newspapers and journals. **Address:** 5975 Post Rd., Nashville, TN 37205, U.S.A.

SHOEMAKER, Robert B(rink). American (born United States), b. 1956. **Genres:** History, E-books, Law. **Career:** Stanford University, lecturer in modern European history, 1984-86; Institute of European Studies, part-time lecturer in history, 1986-90; Richmond College, visiting lecturer, 1986; Stanford University, visiting lecturer, 1988; Lansdowne College, visiting lecturer, 1989-90; Lawrence University, part-time lecturer in history, 1990; University of Sheffield, lecturer, 1991-98, senior lecturer in history, 1998, professor of eighteenth-century British history, 2003, head of the department, 2004-08, director of research and innovation, Centre for Criminological Research, deputy director. Writer. **Publications:** Prosecution and Punishment: Petty Crime and the Law in London and Rural Middlesex, c.1660-1725, 1991; (co-ed.) Stilling the Grumbling Hive: The Response to Social and Economic Problems in England, 1689-1750, 1992; Gender in English Society, 1650-1850: The Emergence of Separate Spheres?, 1998; (ed. with M. Vincent) Gender and History in Western Europe, 1998; Proceedings of the Old Bailey, London 1674 to 1913, 2003; London Mob: Violence and Disorder in Eighteenth-Century England, 2004; (with T. Hitchcock) Tales from the Hanging Court, 2006. **Address:** Department of History, University of Sheffield, 1.08 Jessop W, Sheffield, SY S10 2TN, England. **Online address:** r.shoemaker@sheffield.ac.uk

SHOEMAKER, Sarah. See **WOLF, Sarah (Elizabeth).**

SHOESMITH, Kathleen A. British (born England), b. 1938. **Genres:** Romance/Historical, Children's Non-fiction, Novellas/Short Stories, Mystery/Crime/Suspense, Children's Fiction, Young Adult Fiction. **Career:** West Riding County Council, teacher, 1958-94; Lees County Primary School, teacher, 1973-. Writer. **Publications:** HISTORICAL ROMANCES: Jack O'Lantern, 1969; Cloud over Calderwood, 1969; The Tides of Tremannion, 1970; Mallory's Luck, 1971; Return of the Royalist, 1971; The Highwayman's Daughter, 1972; The Reluctant Puritan, 1972; Belltower, 1973; The Black Domino, 1975; Elusive Legacy, 1976; The Miser's Ward, 1977; Smuggler's Haunt, 1978; Guardian at the Gate, 1979; Brackenthorpe, 1980; Autumn Escapade, 1981; Rustic Vineyard, 1982; A Minor Bequest, 1984; Taste and Flavor, 1984. JUVENILE SERIES: Three Poems for Children, 1965; Playtime Stories, 1966; Judy Stories, 1968; Easy to Read, 1968; How Do They Grow?, 1969; Do You Know About?, 1970; Use Your Senses, 1973. **Address:** 351 Fell Ln., Keighley, WY BD22 6DB, England.

SHOGAN, Colleen J. American (born United States), b. 1975. **Genres:** Politics/Government, International Relations/Current Affairs, History, Women's Studies And Issues. **Career:** George Mason University, assistant professor of government and politics, 2000-; University of Virginia, Presidential Oral History Project, interviewer, 2003-; Center for the Study of the Presidency, faculty mentor, 2003-; Georgetown University, adjunct professor, Congressional Research Service, assistant director. Writer. **Publications:** (Contrib.) George Washington: Leadership and Legacy, 2001; (contrib.) Women and Congress: Running, Winning, and Ruling, 2002; (contrib.) Abraham Lincoln's American Dream: Critical Appreciations and Engagements, 2005; The Moral Rhetoric of American Presidents, 2006. Contributor to periodicals. **Address:** Department of Public and International Affairs, George Mason University, MSN 3F4, 4400 University Dr., Fairfax, VA 22030-4422, U.S.A. **Online address:** cshogan@gmu.edu

SHOGAN, Robert. American (born United States), b. 1930. **Genres:** History, Politics/Government, Documentaries/Reportage. **Career:** Detroit Free Press, reporter, 1956-59; Miami News, telegraph editor, 1959-61; Wall Street Journal, assistant editor, 1961-65; Peace Corps, evaluation officer, 1965-66; Newsweek Magazine, correspondent, 1966-73; Los Angeles Times, national political correspondent, 1973-98; Johns Hopkins University, adjunct professor, 1998-2010; University of Pennsylvania, Annenberg School of Communication, professional-in-residence, 1993; journalist. **Publications:** (With T. Craig) The Detroit Race Riot: A Study in Violence, 1964; A Question of Judgment: The Fortas Case and the Struggle of the Supreme Court, 1972; Promises to Keep: Carter's First Hundred Days, 1977; None of the Above: Why Presidents Fail-And What Can Be Done about It, 1982; The Riddle of Power: Presidential Leadership from Truman to Bush, 1991; Hard Bargain: How F.D.R.

Twisted Churchill's Arm, Evaded the Law, and Changed the Role of the American Presidency, 1995; The Fate of the Union: America's Rocky Road to Political Stalemate, 1998; The Double Edged Sword: How Character Makes and Ruins Presidents from Washington to Clinton, 1998; Bad News: Where the Press Goes Wrong in the Making of the President, 2001; War without End: Cultural Conflict and the Struggle for America's Political Future, 2002; The Battle of Blair Mountain: The Story of America's Largest Labor Uprising, 2004; Backlash: The Killing of the New Deal, 2006; No Sense of Decency: The Army-McCarthy Hearings, 2009; Prelude to Catastrophe: FDR'S Jews and the Menace of Nazism, 2010. **Address:** 3513 Raymond St., Chevy Chase, MD 20815, U.S.A. **Online address:** robertshogan@hotmail.com

SHOHAT, Ella Habiba. American/Israeli (born Israel), b. 1959. **Genres:** Politics/Government, Film, Communications/Media. **Career:** City University of New York, College of Staten Island, Department of Media Culture, professor, 1988-2001, Graduate Center, professor of film studies, 1992-2001; New York University, professor of cultural studies and women's studies, 2002-; Cornell University, School of Theory and Criticism, faculty. Writer, curator and activist. **Publications:** Israeli Cinema: East/West and the Politics of Representation, 1989, new ed., 2010; (with R. Stam) Unthinking Eurocentrism: Multiculturalism and the Media, 1994; Ha-Mahpekhah ha-Mizrahit: shalosh masot 'al ha-Tsiyonut veha-Mizrahim, 1999; Zikhronot asurim: likrat mahshavah rav-tarbutit: asupat-ma'amarim, 2001; Ha-Kolno'a ha-Yisre'eli: Mizrah/Ma'arav veha-politikah shel ha-yitsug, 2005; Taboo Memories, Diasporic Voices, 2006; (with R. Stam) Flagging Patriotism: Crises of Narcissism and Anti-Americanism, 2007. EDITOR: (with A. McClintock and A. Mufti) Dangerous Liaisons: Gender, Nation, and Postcolonial Perspectives, 1997; Talking Visions: Multicultural Feminism in Transnational Age, 1998; (and intro. with R. Stam) Multiculturalism, Postcoloniality, and Transnational Media, 2003. **Address:** Tisch School of the Arts, New York University, Rm. 603, 665 Broadway, 6th Fl., New York, NY 10003, U.S.A. **Online address:** ella.shohat@nyu.edu

SHOMER, Enid. American (born United States), b. 1944. **Genres:** Novellas/Short Stories, Poetry, Young Adult Fiction. **Career:** University of Miami, lecturer in English, 1974-80; Antioch Writer's Workshop, writer-in-residence, 1988-91; Ohio State University, Thurber House, writer-in-residence, 1994; Florida State University, visiting writer, 1997; University of Arkansas, visiting writer, 1999-2001, University of Arkansas Press, poetry series editor. **Publications:** POETRY: Startle Effect, 1983; Florida Postcards, 1987; Stalking the Florida Panther, 1987; This Close to the Earth, 1992; Black Drum, 1997; Stars at Noon: Poems from the Life of Jacqueline Cochran, 2001. OTHER: Imaginary Men (short stories), 1993; Tourist Season: Stories, 2007; The Twelve Rooms of the Nile, 2012. Works appeared in anthologies. Contributor of articles to periodicals. **Address:** c/o Diane Bartoli, Artists Literary Group, 27 W 20th St., 10th Fl., New York, NY 10011, U.S.A. **Online address:** eshomer1@tampabay.rr.com

SHONE, Anna. French/British (born England), b. 1947. **Genres:** Mystery/Crime/Suspense, Novels, Literary Criticism And History. **Career:** Department of Employment, clerical officer, 1970-72; Chamber of Commerce, teacher, 1985-92. Writer. **Publications:** MYSTERY NOVELS: Come Away Death, 1994 in US as Mr. Donaghue Investigates, 1995; Secrets in Stones, 1995. Contributor to magazines. **Address:** Teresa Chris Literary Agency, 43 Musard Rd., London, GL W6 8NR, England.

SHONE, Richard (N.). British (born England), b. 1949. **Genres:** Art/Art History. **Career:** The Burlington Magazine, associate editor, 1979-2003, editor, 2003-. **Publications:** Bloomsbury Portraits: Vanessa Bell, Duncan Grant, and Their Circle, 1976, rev. ed., 1993; The Century of Change: British Painting since 1900, 1977; (comp.) Vincent van Gogh, 1977; Toulouse-Lautrec, 1977; Manet, 1978; Augustus John, 1979; The Post-Impressionists, 1979; Sisley, 1979, rev. ed., 1999; (with J. Collins) Duncan Grant, Designer: An Exhibition, 1980; Walter Sickert, 1988; Rodrigo Moynihan, 1988; (ed. with W. Baron) Sickert, Paintings, 1992; (co-author) Sensation, 1997; About Face, 1998; (with I.G. Lumsden) Sargent to Freud: Modern British Paintings and Drawings in the Beaverbrook Collection, 1998; The Art of Bloomsbury: Roger Fry, Vanessa Bell, and Duncan Grant, 1999; Damien Hirst, 2001; Janice H. Levin Collection of French Art, 2002; (J. Stonard) The Books that Shaped Art History, 2012. Contributor to journals. **Address:** The Burlington Magazine, 14-16 Duke's Rd., London, GL WC1H 9SZ, England. **Online address:** shone@burlington.org.uk

SHONE, Ronald. Scottish/British (born England), b. 1946. **Genres:** Business/Trade/Industry, Economics, Mathematics/Statistics, Self Help, Money/Finance, Adult Non-fiction. **Career:** University of Sheffield, lecturer in economics, 1971-73, Esmee Fairbairn research fellow, 1974-76; University of Stirling, lecturer, 1976-82, senior lecturer in economics, 1982-; University of Wales, London School of Economics and Political Science, lecturer; University of York, lecturer; University of Edinburgh, lecturer; Haile Selassie I University, lecturer; University College, lecturer. Writer. **Publications:** The Pure Theory of International Trade, 1972; Microeconomics: A Modern Treatment, 1975; (with F. Neal) Economic Model Building, 1976; Applications in Intermediate Microeconomics, 1981; Autohypnosis: A Step-by-Step Guide to Self-hypnosis, 1983; Issues in Macroeconomics, 1984; Creative Visualization, 1984; Advanced Autohypnosis, 1985; (contrib.) Economic Perspectives on Key Issues, 1985; (contrib.) The Social Science Encyclopedia, 1985; Open Economy Macroeconomics, 1989; (with D.N. King) Microeconomics: An Introduction to Theory and Applications, 1987; Creative Visualization: How to use Imagery and Imagination for Self-improvement, 1988; Open Economy Macroeconomics, 1989; First Steps to Freedom, 1991; Economic Dynamics: Phase Diagrams and Their Economic Application, 1997, 2nd ed., 2002; Creative Visualization: Using Imagery and Imagination for Self-Transformation, 1998; An Introduction to Economic Dynamics, 2001. Contributor of articles to journals. **Address:** Department of Economics, University of Stirling, Stirling, FK9 4LA, Scotland. **Online address:** ronald@shoners3.freeserve.co.uk

SHONTZ, Franklin C(urtis). American (born United States), b. 1926. **Genres:** Psychology. **Career:** Western Reserve University, lecturer in psychology, 1953-60; Highland View Hospital, chief psychologist, 1954-60; Cuyahoga County Hospital, chief psychologist, 1954-60; Case Western Reserve University, School of Medicine, Department of Psychiatry, associate in psychology, 1954-59, Department of Psychology, clinical instructor in psychology, 1954-59; Fenn College, lecturer, 1958; Rehabilitation Psychology, consulting editor, 1962-69; University of Kansas, Department of Psychology, assistant professor, 1960-62, director of research and training in somatopsychology/rehabilitation, 1960-76, associate professor, 1962-66, acting co-chairperson, 1965-66, professor, 1966-92, director of undergraduate Education, 1970-73, Clinical Psychology Program, director, 1976-82, associate Chairperson, 1977-82, professor emeritus, 1992-; Institute for Community Studies, consultant, 1967-70; State of Wisconsin, Division of Vocational Rehabilitation, consultant, 1967-70; University of Wisconsin, honorary fellow in psychology, 1969-70, Christian Psychological Services Overland Park, clinical supervisor, 1988-; High Plains Comprehensive Community Mental Health Center, consultant, 1973; Greater Kansas City Mental Health Foundation, consultant, 1974-92; American Psychological Association, Division of Rehabilitation Psychology, president, 1975-76; University of Missouri Medical School, faculty, 1977-78; Center for Psychosocial Studies, consultant, 1981-88; American Occupational Therapy Association, research consultant, 1981-87; Mental Health Management Corp., Rehabilitation Agency Design, special consultant, 1982; American Journal of Psychiatry, statistical consultant, 1987-91; Resource Development Institute, director of evaluation, 1992-2000; Veterans Administration Center, consultant. Writer. **Publications:** Research Methods in Personality, 1965; Perceptual and Cognitive Aspects of Body Experience, 1969; (with W. Epstein) Psychology in Progress, 1971; Psychological Aspects of Physical Illness and Disability, 1975; (with J.V. Spotts) The Life Styles of Nine American Cocaine Users: Trips to the Land of Cockaigne, 1976; (with J.V. Spotts) Cocaine Users: A Representative Case Approach, 1980; Fundamentals of Research in the Behavioral Sciences: Principles and Practice, 1986. Contributor to journals. **Address:** Department of Psychology, University of Kansas, Rm. 426, 1415 Jayhawk Blvd., Lawrence, KS 66045-7556, U.S.A.

SHOOKMAN, Ellis. American (born United States), b. 1957. **Genres:** Literary Criticism And History, Biography, History, Poetry, Young Adult Fiction. **Career:** Dartmouth College, assistant professor, associate professor of German, 1987-. Writer. **Publications:** Noble Lies, Slant Truths, Necessary Angels: Aspects of Fictionality in the Novels of Christoph Martin Wieland, 1997; Thomas Mann's Death in Venice: A Novella and Its Critics, 2003; Thomas Mann's Death in Venice: A Reference Guide, 2004. EDITOR: (trans.) Eighteenth-Century German Prose, 1992; The Faces of Physiognomy: Interdisciplinary Approaches to Johann Caspar Lavater, 1993. Contributor to books and journals. **Address:** Department of German Studies, Dartmouth College, 332 Dartmouth Hall, Hanover, NH 03755-3511, U.S.A. **Online address:** ellis.shookman@dartmouth.edu

SHORE, Zachary. American (born United States), b. 1968?. **Genres:** Psychology, History. **Career:** U.S. Department of State, policy planning staff; Oxford Analytica, consultant; Naval Postgraduate School, professor. Writer and policy advisor. **Publications:** What Hitler Knew: The Battle for Information in Nazi Foreign Policy, 2003; Breeding Bin Ladens: America, Islam, and the Future of Europe, 2006; Blunder: Why Smart People Make Bad Decisions, 2008. Contributor of articles to periodicals and journals. **Address:** Berkeley, CA , U.S.A. **Online address:** z@zacharshore.org

SHORROCK, Tim. American (born United States), b. 1951?. **Genres:** Law, Politics/Government, International Relations/Current Affairs. **Career:** Freelance journalist. **Publications:** Spies for Hire: The Secret World of Intelligence Outsourcing, 2008. Contributor to periodicals and journals. **Address:** Simon & Schuster Inc., 1230 Ave. of the Americas, New York, NY 10020, U.S.A. **Online address:** timshorrock@gmail.com

SHORS, John. American (born United States), b. 1969. **Genres:** Novels. **Career:** English teacher, 1991-94; Des Moines Business Record, reporter; GroundFloor Media, co-founder and vice president, 2001-06. Novelist. **Publications:** Beneath a Marble Sky: A Novel of the Taj Mahal, 2004; Beside a Burning Sea, 2008; Dragon House, 2009; The Wishing Trees, 2010; Cross Currents, 2011. **Address:** New American Library, 375 Hudson St., New York, NY 10014-3657, U.S.A. **Online address:** shors@aol.com

SHORT, Brendan. American (born United States), b. 1969. **Genres:** Novels, Children's Fiction. **Career:** St. Albans School, writer-in-residence fellow, 2000-01. **Publications:** Dream City (novel), 2008. Contributor to periodicals. **Address:** InkWell Management, 521 5th Ave., 26th Fl., New York, NY 10175, U.S.A. **Online address:** brenshort@hotmail.com

SHORT, Brian (Michael). British (born England), b. 1944. **Genres:** Geography, History, Local History/Rural Topics, Sociology. **Career:** University of Sussex, lecturer in geography, 1974-, senior lecturer, 1992-, School of Cultural and Community Studies, dean, 1995-2000, professor of historical geography, 2000-09, geography department head, 2001-04, associate tutor; emeritus professor of historical geography, 2009-; Kellogg College, visiting fellow. Writer. **Publications:** The Geography of England and Wales in 1910, 1989; (with P. Brandon) The Southeast from A.D. 1000, 1990; Rural Housing Needs in Southeast England, 1991; (ed.) The English Rural Community, 1992; Land and Society in Edwardian Britain, 1997; (ed.) The Ashdown Forest Dispute 1876-1882, 1997; (with K. Leslie) An Historical Atlas of Sussex, 1999; (with C. Watkins, W. Foot and P. Kinsman) The National Farm Survey 1941-1943, 2000; (ed. with D. Gilbert and D. Matless) Geographies of British Modernity, 2003; England's Landscape: The South East, 2006; The Front Line of Freedom: British Farming in the Second World War, 2007. **Address:** Department of Geography, University of Sussex, Arts C C205, Brighton, ES BN1 9SJ, England. **Online address:** b.m.short@sussex.ac.uk

SHORT, Kathy G(nagey). American (born United States), b. 1952. **Genres:** Children's Fiction, Education, Picture/Board Books, International Relations/Current Affairs. **Career:** Teacher, 1975-80; Goshen College, assistant professor, 1980-83, associate professor of education, 1984-89; Indiana University, secretary/treasurer and graduate assistant, 1983-84, research assistant, 1984-85; Ohio State University, postdoctoral research fellow, 1985-86; University of Arizona, assistant professor, 1989-93, associate professor, 1993-99, professor of language, reading and culture, 1999-, Undergraduate Courses in Reading, associate professor, 1986-89; Center for the Expansion of Language and Thinking, board director, 1989-95; Rutgers University, lecturer; Columbia University, lecturer, 1996; University of Puerto Rico, lecturer, 1999; Language Arts, editor, 2000-06. **Publications:** (With J. Harste and C. Burke) Creating Classrooms for Authors, 1988, 2nd ed. as Creating Classrooms for Authors and Inquirers, 1996; (with C. Burke) Creating Curriculum, 1991; (with J. Harste) Creating Classrooms for Authors and Inquiries, 1996; (co-author) Learning Together through Inquiry, 1996; Literature as a Way of Knowing, 1997; (co-author) Teacher Study Groups, 1998; (with C. Lynch-Brown and C.M. Tomlinson) Essentials of Children's Literature, 7th ed., 2011. EDITOR: (with K.M. Pierce) Talking about Books, 1991; (co-ed.) Teachers as Researchers, 1993; Research & Professional Resources in Children's Literature, 1995; (with D. Fox) Stories Matter: The Complexity of Cultural Authenticity in Children's Literature, 2003. Contributor to books. **Address:** Department of Language, Reading and Culture, College of Education, University of Arizona, Tucson, AZ 85721, U.S.A. **Online address:** shortk@u.arizona.edu

SHORT, Philip. French/British (born England), b. 1945. **Genres:** Politics/ Government, Biography, Documentaries/Reportage, History, Autobiography/ Memoirs, Romance/Historical, Adult Non-fiction. **Career:** Freelance journalist, 1967-97; British Broadcasting Corp., foreign correspondent, 1967-97, Washington correspondent; University of Iowa, journalism professor, 1998. **Publications:** Banda, 1974; The Dragon And The Bear: Inside China and Russia Today, 1982; Dragon And The Bear: China and Russia in the Eighties, 1982; Mao: A Life, 2000; Pol Pot: Anatomy of A Nightmare, 2004; Pol Pot: The History of a Nightmare, 2005. Contributor to periodicals. **Address:** David Higham Associates Ltd., 5-8 Lower John St., Golden Sq., London, GL W1F 9HA, England. **Online address:** philip.short@free.fr

SHORT, Robert Stuart. British (born England), b. 1938. **Genres:** Art/Art History, Literary Criticism And History. **Career:** Tulse Hill School, teacher, 1959-60; Ecole Colbert, teacher of English, 1961-62; Hull University, assistant lecturer, 1965-67; University of East Anglia, School of Language, Linguistics and Translation Studies, senior lecturer, 1967-2001, reader, 2001-, senior fellow. Writer. **Publications:** (With R. Cardinal) Surrealism: Permanent Revelation, 1970; Paul Klee, 1979; (with P. Webb) Hans Bellmer, 1985; Dada and Surrealism, 1994; The Age of Gold: Surrealist Cinema, 2003. Contributor to journals. **Address:** School of Language, Linguistics and, Translation Studies, University of East Anglia, Colley Ln., Norwich, NF NR4 7UL, England. **Online address:** robert.short@uea.ac.uk

SHORTO, Russell. Dutch/American (born United States), b. 1959. **Genres:** History, Young Adult Non-fiction, Language/Linguistics. **Career:** John Adams Institute, director, 2008-. Writer. **Publications:** Thomas Jefferson and the American Ideal, 1987; Tecumseh and the Dream of an American Indian Nation, 1989; Geronimo and the Struggle for Apache Freedom, 1989; Cinderella: Cinderella's Stepsister, 1990; Abraham Lincoln and the End of Slavery, 1991; Abraham Lincoln: To Preserve the Union, 1991; David Farragut and the Great Naval Blockade, 1991; Jane Fonda: Political Activism, 1991; Careers for People Who Like to Perform: Interviews, 1992; Careers for the Curious: Interviews, 1992; How to Fly the Space Shuttle, 1992; Careers for Animal Lovers, 1992; Careers for Foreign Language Experts: Interviews, 1992; Careers for Hands-on Types: Interviews, 1992; Careers for People Who Like People: Interviews, 1992; Gospel Truth: The New Image of Jesus Emerging from Science and History and Why It Matters, 1997; Saints and Madmen: Psychiatry Opens Its Doors to Religion, 1999; (ed. with D. Rubel) The Civil War Chronicle: The Only Day-by-Day Portrait of America's Tragic Conflict as Told by Soldiers, Journalists, Politicians, Farmers, Nurses, Slaves and Other Eyewitnesses, 2000; The Island at the Center of the World: The Epic Story of Dutch Manhattan and the Forgotten Colony That Shaped America, 2004; Descartes' Bones: A Skeletal History of the Conflict between Faith and Reason, 2008. Contributor to periodicals and magazine. **Address:** John Adams Institute, West-Indisch Huis, 97 Herenmarkt, Amsterdam, 1013 EC, Netherlands. **Online address:** rs@russellshorto.com

SHORTT, Tim(othy Donald). Canadian (born Canada), b. 1961. **Genres:** Young Adult Fiction, Picture/Board Books, Children's Fiction, Illustrations. **Career:** Plastiglide Ltd., quality control inspector, 1986; Sentinel Investment, messenger, 1987. Illustrator and Writer. **Publications:** SELF-ILLUSTRATED: The Babe Ruth Ballet School, 1996. **Address:** 733 Talfourd St., Sarnia, ON N7T 1S1, Canada.

SHOSTAK, Seth. American (born United States), b. 1943. **Genres:** Sciences, Biology. **Career:** Search for Extraterrestrial Intelligence (SETI) Institute, senior astronomer; University of Groningen, astronomer; DIGIMA (a computer animation company), founder and operator; Project Phoenix, observer; International Academy of Astronautics SETI Permanent Study Group, chair; Explorer, science editor. Broadcaster, researcher and astronomer. **Publications:** (Ed.) Third Decennial US-USSR Conference on SETI, 1993; (ed.) Progress in the Search for Extraterrestrial Life: 1993 Bioastronomy Symposium, Santa Cruz, California, 16-20 August 1993, 1993; Sharing the Universe: Perspectives on Extraterrestrial Life, 1998; (with J. Bennett and B. Jakosky) Life in the Universe, 2003, 2nd ed., 2007, 3rd ed., 2012; (with A. Barnett) Cosmic Company: The Search for Life in the Universe, 2003; Confessions of an Alien Hunter: A Scientist's Search for Extraterrestrial Intelligence, 2009. Contributor to magazines and periodicals. **Address:** Search for Extraterrestrial Intelligence Institute, 189 Bernardo Ave., Ste. 100, Mountain View, CA 94043, U.S.A. **Online address:** sshostak@seti.org

SHOUP, Barbara. American (born United States), b. 1947. **Genres:** Novels,

Education, Documentaries/Reportage, Essays, Literary Criticism And History, Young Adult Fiction. **Career:** Indiana University, associate instructor in creative writing, 1979; Indianapolis Museum of Art, school programs coordinator, 1980; Broad Ripple High School, Center for the Humanities and the Performing Arts, writer-in-residence, 1982-2001; Prelude Academy, Indianapolis Children's Museum and Penrod Society, coordinator, 1985-97; Other Voices, associate editor, 1992-2007; OV Books, associate editor, 2007-; Indiana University/Purdue University, associate faculty, 2004-; Writers' Center of Indiana, program director 2006-08, executive director 2009-. **Publications:** NOVELS: Night Watch, 1982; Wish You Were Here, 1994, 2008; Stranded in Harmony, 1997; Faithful Women, 2001, Vermeer's Daughter, 2003, Everything You Want, 2008. OTHER: Living and Learning for Credit, 1978; (with J.G. Schine and D. Harrington) New Roles for Early Adolescents in Schools and Communities, 1981; (with F. Stevens-Jacobi) Learning Unlimited: A Model for Options Education, 1981; (with M.L. Denman) Novel Ideas: Contemporary Authors Share the Creative Process, 2001. Contributor to periodicals. **Address:** 6012 N Broadway, Indianapolis, IN 46220, U.S.A. **Online address:** barbshoup@aol.com

SHOUP, Donald. (Donald Curran Shoup). American (born United States), b. 1938. **Genres:** Public/Social Administration, Politics/Government. **Career:** University of California, Luskin School of Public Affairs, Institute of Government and Public Affairs, research economist, 1968-70, Department Of Urban Planning, associate professor of urban planning, 1974-80, professor, 1980- , chair, 1998-2002, Institute of Transportation Studies, director, 1996-2001; University of Michigan, assistant professor of economics and public policy, 1970-74; University of Hawaii, visiting assistant professor, 1972; American Institute of Certified Planners, fellow, 2004-; Access, editor, 2009-; University of Buffalo, Clarkson chair in urban planning, 2010. **Publications:** AS DONALD C. SHOUP: (with R.P. Mack) Advance Land Acquisition by Local Governments: Benefit-Cost Analysis as an Aid to Policy, 1968; (with A. Rosett) Fiscal Exploitation of Central Cities by Overlapping Governments: A Case Study of Law Enforcement Finance in Los Angeles County, 1969; (with S.L. Mehay) Program Budgeting for Urban Police Services, 1971; The High Cost of Free Parking, 2005; Parking Cash Out, 2005. **Address:** Department of Urban Planning, Luskin School of Public Affairs, University of California, 3250 Public Affairs Bldg., PO Box 951656, Los Angeles, CA 90095-1656, U.S.A. **Online address:** shoup@ucla.edu

SHOUP, Donald Curran. See **SHOUP, Donald.**

SHOVEN, John B. American (born United States), b. 1947. **Genres:** Economics, Money/Finance. **Career:** Stanford University, Department of Economics, assistant professor, 1973-79, professor, 1979-, Charles R. Schwab professor of economics, chair, 1986-89, Center for Economic Policy Research, director, 1988-93, dean of humanities and sciences, 1993-98, Stanford Institute for Economic Policy Research, Wallace R. Hawley director, 1999- , Hoover Institution, senior fellow, Center for Public and Private Finance, co-director; Finance Program, director; General Research Program, director; Tax and Budget Policy Program, co-director; National Bureau of Economic Research, research associate and director of West Coast office. Writer. **Publications:** (With C.L. Ballard, D. Fullerton and J. Whalley) A General Equilibrium Model for Tax Policy Evaluation, 1985; (with J. Whalley) Applying General Equilibrium, 1992; (with S.J. Schieber) The Real Deal: The History and Future of Social Security, 1999; (with H.J. Aaron) Should the United States Privatize Social Security?, 1999; (with S. Nataraj) Has the Unified Budget Undermined the Federal Government Trust Funds?, 2004; New Age Thinking: Alternative Ways of Measuring Age, Their Relationship to Labor Force Participation, Government Policies and GDP, 2007; (with G.P. Shultz, M. Gunn and G.S. Goda) Putting Our House in Order: A Guide to Social Security and Health Care Reform, 2008. WITH G.S. GODA AND S.N. SLAVOV: Removing the Disincentives in Social Security for Long Careers, 2007; Social Security and the Timing of Divorce, 2007; A Tax on Work for the Elderly: Medicare as a Secondary Payer, 2007. EDITOR (with Z. Bodie) Financial Aspects of the United States Pension System, 1983; (with H.E. Scarf) Applied General Equilibrium Analysis, 1984; (with Z. Bodie and D.A. Wise) Issues in Pension Economics, 1987; Government Policy towards Industry in the United States and Japan, 1988; (with Z. Bodie and D.A. Wise) Pensions in the U.S. Economy, 1988; (with J. Waldfogel) Debt, Taxes, and Corporate Restructuring, 1990; (with B.D. Bernheim) National Saving and Economic Performance, 1991; (with J. Whalley) Canada-U.S. Tax Comparisons, 1992; (with S.J. Schieber) Public Policy toward Pensions, 1997; Administrative Aspects of Investment-based Social Security Reform, 2000; (with W.G. Gale and M.J. Warshawsky) Private Pensions and Public Policies, 2004; (with W.G. Gale and M.J. Warshawsky and contrib.) The Evolving Pension System: Trends, Effects, and Proposals for Reform, 2005; Demography and the Economy, 2011. **Address:** Department of Economics, Stanford University, Rm. 132, 579 Serra Mall, 366 Galvez St., Stanford, CA 94305-6015, U.S.A. **Online address:** shoven@stanford.edu

SHOWALTER, Elaine. American (born United States), b. 1941. **Genres:** Gay And Lesbian Issues, Literary Criticism And History, Women's Studies And Issues, Humanities. **Career:** University of California, instructor, 1967-78; Rutgers University, Douglass College, assistant professor, 1970-74, associate professor, 1974-83, professor of English, 1983, faculty research fellow, 1972-73; University of Delaware, visiting professor of English and women's studies, 1976-77; Princeton University, Department of English, professor of English, 1984-, Avalon Foundation professor of the humanities, chair, now professor emeritus of English, professor of the humanities emeritus; Dartmouth College, visiting professor, 1986; Oxford University, Clarendon Lecturer, 1989. Writer. **Publications:** A Literature of Their Own: British Women Novelists from Brontë to Lessing, 1977, rev. ed., 1999; The Female Malady: Women, Madness and English Culture, 1830-1980, 1985; Sexual Anarchy: Gender and Culture at the Fin de Siècle, 1990; Sister's Choice: Tradition and Change in American Women's Writing, 1991; Modern American Women Writers, 1991; (co-author) Hysteria beyond Freud, 1993; Sister's Choice: Tradition and Change in American Women's Writing, 1991; Hystories: Hysterical Epidemics and Modern Media, 1997; Inventing Herself, 2000; Teaching Literature, 2003; Faculty Towers: The Academic Novel and its Discontents, 2005; Jury of her Peers: American Women Writers from Anne Bradstreet to Annie Proulx, 2009. EDITOR: Women's Liberation and Literature, 1971; Female Studies IV, 1971; (intro.) These Modern Women: Autobiographical Essays from the Twenties, 1978; New Feminist Criticism: Essays on Women, Literature and Theory, 1985; (intro.) Alternative Alcott, 1988; (intro.) Little Women, 1989; Speaking of Gender, 1989; (intro.) These Modern Women: Autobiographical Essays from the Twenties, 1989; (intro.) Daughters of Decadence: Women Writers of the Fin-de-Siècle, 1993; (intro.) Where are you Going, Where have you Been?, 1994; (intro.) Ethan Frome, 1996; (with G. Greer) The Cambridge Guide to Women's Writing in English, 1999; (intro.) Daddy Long Legs; and, Dear Enemy, 2004; (intro.) Vintage Book of American Women Writers, 2011. **Address:** Department of English, Princeton University, 22 McCosh Hall, Princeton, NJ 08544-1099, U.S.A. **Online address:** elaines@princeton.edu

SHOWALTER, Gena. American (born United States), b. 1975?. **Genres:** Romance/Historical, Young Adult Fiction, Literary Criticism And History. **Career:** Writer. **Publications:** IMPERIA: The Stone Prince, 2004; The Pleasure Slave, 2005. ALIEN HUNTRESS SERIES: Awaken Me Darkly, 2005; Enslave Me Sweetly, 2006; (contrib.) Mysteria, 2006; Savor Me Slowly, 2008; Seduce the Darkness, 2009. ATLANTIS: Heart of the Dragon, 2005; Jewel of Atlantis, 2006; The Nymph King, 2007; The Vampire's Bride, 2009; The Amazon's Curse, 2009. Lords of the Underworld: The Darkest Fire, 2008; The Darkest Night, 2008; The Darkest Kiss, 2008; The Darkest Pleasure, 2008; (contrib.) Mysteria Lane, 2008; The Darkest Prison, 2009; The Darkest Whisper, 2009; The Darkest Angel in Heart of the Darkness, 2010; The Darkest Passion, 2010; The Darkest Lie, 2010; (with M. Shayne and S. Krinard) Heart of Darkness, 2010; The Darkest Secret, 2011; The Darkest Surrender, 2011; Twisted, 2011; Mysteria Nights, 2011; Lord of the Vampires, 2011. TALES OF AN EXTRAORDINARY GIRL: Playing with Fire, 2006; Twice as Hot, 2010. YOUNG ADULT: Oh My Goth!, 2006; Red Handed, 2007; Blacklisted, 2007; Intertwined, 2009. CONTEMPORARY ROMANCE: Animal Instincts, 2006; Catch a Mate, 2007. **Address:** HQN Books, Harlequin Enterprises Ltd., 225 Duncan Mill Rd., Don Mills, ON M3B 3K9, Canada. **Online address:** managergenashowalter@yahoo.com

SHRADER, Charles R. (Charles Reginald Shrader). American (born United States), b. 1943. **Genres:** History, Military/Defense/Arms Control, Politics/Government. **Career:** U.S. War College, George C. Marshall Professor of Military Studies, 1983-84; independent historian and consultant, 1987-; Society for Military History, executive director, 1992-2000; National Coalition of Independent Scholars, president, 2000-02. Writer. **Publications:** (Ed.) Selected Readings in Military History: The Evolution of U.S. Army Logistics, 1978; (ed.) Proceedings of the 1982 International Military History Symposium: The Impact of Unsuccessful Military Campaigns on Military Institutions, 1860-1980, Carlisle Barracks, Pennsylvania, 1-4 August 1982, 1984; Amicicide: The Problem of Friendly Fire in Modern War, 1985; (ed. as Charles Reginald

Shrader) Reference Guide to United States Military History, 1991; U.S. Military Logistics, 1607-1991: A Research Guide, 1992; Communist Logistics in the Korean War, 1995; (ed.) United States Army Logistics, 1775-1992: An Anthology, 1997; The First Helicopter War: Logistics and Mobility in Algeria, 1954-1962, 1999; The Withered Vine: Logistics and the Communist Insurgency in Greece, 1945-1949, 1999; Muslim-Croat Civil War in Central Bosnia: A Military History, 1992-1994, 2003; History of Operations Research in the United States Army, 2006; (with C.R. Newell) Of Duty Well and Faithfully Done: A History of the Regular Army in the Civil War, 2011; (with T.J. Crackel) A Guide to the Papers of the Commanding Generals and Chiefs of Staff, United States Army, 1775-1987, forthcoming. **Address:** Texas A&M University Press, 4354 TAMU, John H. Lindsey Bldg., Lewis St., College Station, TX 77843-4354, U.S.A. **Online address:** heriger@aol.com

SHRADER, Charles Reginald. See SHRADER, Charles R.

SHRAER-PETROV, David. American/Russian (born Russia), b. 1936. **Genres:** Novels, Novellas/Short Stories, Theology/Religion, Young Adult Fiction. **Career:** Doctor and scientist, 1959-; Writer. **Publications:** Kholsty, 1967; Poèziia i nauka, 1974; Druzia i teni: roman suchastiem avtora, 1988; Druzia i teni: roman s uchastiem avtora, 1988; Pesnia o golubom slone: liubovnaia lirika, 1990; Gerberg i Nelli: roman vdvukh knigakh, 1992; Villa Borgeze: stikhotvoreniia, 1992; Moskvazlatoglavaia, 1993; Propashchaia dusha: stikhotvoreniia i poemy, 1987-1996, 1997; Frantsuzskii kottedzh: roman, 1999; Piterskii dozh: stikhotvoreniia i poema, 1995-1998, 1999; Zamok y Tystemaa, 2001; Barabanysud by, 2002; Jonah and Sarah: Jewish Stories of Russia and America, 2003; Forma liubvi, 2003; Etei strannye russkie evrei, 2004; Stikhotvoreniia ipoemy, 2004; (with M.D. Shrayer) Genrikh Sapgir: Klassik avangarda, 2004; Gerbert i Nelli: roman, 2006; Autumn in Yalta: A Novel and Three Stories, 2006; Vodka s pirozhnymi: roman s pisateliâ, 2007; Okhota na ryzhego d' iiàvola: Roman s mikrobiologami, 2010. Contributor of articles to periodicals. **Address:** 110 Overhill Rd., Providence, RI 02906, U.S.A. **Online address:** dshrayer@cox.net

SHREIBER, Maeera Yaffa. American (born United States), b. 1956. **Genres:** Poetry, Theology/Religion. **Career:** Brandeis University, instructor, 1980-86; Reed College, visiting assistant professor, 1987-92; University of Southern California, visiting assistant professor, 1994-99; University of Utah, faculty, 1999-. Writer and literary critic. **Publications:** (Ed. with Y. Prins) Dwelling in Possibility: Women Poets and Critics on Poetry, 1997; (ed. with K. Tuma) Mina Loy: Poet and Woman, 1998; Singing in a Strange Land: A Jewish American Poetics, 2007. Contributor to books, periodicals and journals. **Address:** Salt Lake City, UT, U.S.A. **Online address:** m.shreiber@english.utah.edu

SHRESTHA, Nanda R. American/Nepalese (born Nepal), b. 1949. **Genres:** Geography, History, Business/Trade/Industry, Economics, Social Sciences. **Career:** Georgia State University, lecturer, 1982-85; University of Wisconsin, associate professor of geography, 1985-94; Florida A&M University, professor of resource and cultural management. Writer. **Publications:** Socioeconomic Theory of Migration: A Political Economy Perspective, 1983; (with B.N. Kayastha) Midterm Evaluation of the Community Based Integrated Rural Development Project Implemented by Save the Children Federation of U.S.A, 1985; Landlessness and Migration in Nepal, 1990, 2nd ed. as The Political Economy of Land, Landlessness and Migration in Nepal, 2001; In the Name of Development, 1997; Nepal and Bangladesh: A Global Studies Handbook, 2002; (with K. Bhattarai) Historical Dictionary of Nepal, 2003; (with K. Gray and W. Smith) Culture Analysis and Global Business: A Multidimensional Perspective, forthcoming. Contributor to books. **Address:** School of Business and Industry, Florida A M University, Rm. 105, 500 Gamble St., 1 SBI Plz., Tallahassee, FL 32307-5200, U.S.A. **Online address:** nanda.shrestha@famu.edu

SHREVE, Anita. American (born United States), b. 1946. **Genres:** Novels, How-to Books, Psychology, Women's Studies And Issues, Young Adult Non-fiction. **Career:** Freelance writer, 1986-; Viva Magazine, deputy editor; U.S. Magazine, editor; Newsweek, special issue writer; high school English teacher; Amherst College, instructor in creative writing. **Publications:** NON-FICTION WITH L. BALTER: Dr. Balter's Child Sense: Understanding and Handling the Common Problems of Infancy and Early Childhood, 1985; Dr. Balter's Baby Sense, 1985; Who's in Control?: Dr. Balter's Guide to Discipline without Combat, 1988. NONFICTION: (with P.Lone) Working Woman: A Guide to Fitness + Health, 1986; Remaking Motherhood: How Working

Mothers Are Shaping Our Children's Future, 1987; Women Together, Women Alone: The Legacy of the Consciousness-Raising Movement, 1989. NOVELS: Eden Close: A Novel, 1989; Strange Fits of Passion, 1991; Where or When: A Novel, 1993; Resistance: A Novel, 1995; The Weight of Water, 1997; The Pilot's Wife: A Novel, 1998; Fortune's Rocks: A Novel, 2000; The Last Time They Met, 2001; Sea Glass, 2002; All He Ever Wanted, 2003; Light on Snow, 2004; Wedding in December, 2005; Body Surfing, 2007; Testimony, 2008; Change in Altitude, 2009; Rescue: A Novel, 2010. Contributor to periodicals and magazines. **Address:** c/o Michelle Aielli, Little, Brown & Co., 237 Park Ave., New York, NY 10017, U.S.A. **Online address:** askanita@hbgusa.com

SHREVE, Susan R(ichards). American (born United States), b. 1939. **Genres:** Novels, Children's Fiction, Essays, Young Adult Non-fiction, Writing/Journalism, Young Adult Fiction. **Career:** School teacher, 1962-72; Community Learning Center, co-founder, 1972-75; George Mason University, associate professor, 1976-80, professor of English literature, 1980-, MFA Creative Writing Program, founder, 1980-; George Washington University, Jenny McKean Moore chair in creative writing, 1977-78; Columbia University, visiting professor, 1983-87; Princeton University, visiting professor, 1991-94. Writer. **Publications:** A Fortunate Madness, 1974; The Nightmares of Geranium Street, 1977; A Woman Like That, 1977; Loveletters: A Novel, 1978; Children of Power, 1979; Family Secrets: Five Very Important Stories, 1979; The Masquerade, 1980; Miracle Play, 1981; The Bad Dreams of a Good Girl, 1982; The Revolution of Mary Leary, 1982; Dreaming of Heroes, 1984; The Flunking of Joshua T. Bates, 1984; How I Saved the World on Purpose, 1985; Queen of Hearts, 1986; Lily and the Runaway Baby, 1987; Lucy Forever and Miss Rosetree, Shrinks, 1987; A Country of Strangers, 1989; The Gift of the Girl Who Couldn't Hear, 1991; Wait for Me, 1992; Daughters of the New World, 1992; Amy Dunn Quits School, 1993; Joshua T. Bates Takes Charge, 1993; The Train Home, 1993; Lucy Forever, Miss Rosetree, and the Stolen Baby, 1994; A Will of Their Own, 1994; The Wimp, 1995; The Formerly Great Alexander Family, 1995; Zoe and Colombo, 1995; Goalie, 1996; The Visiting Physician, 1996; Warts, 1996; Jonah the Whale, 1997; Joshua T. Bates in Trouble Again, 1997; Ghost Cats, 1998; Goodbye, Amanda the Good, 2000; Plum and Jaggers (novel), 2000; (co-author) It's Fine to Be Nine, 2000; Blister, 2001; Trout and Me, 2002; Under the Watsons' Porch, 2004; Kiss Me Tomorrow, 2006; (co-author) Tripping Over the Lunch Lady, 2006; A Student of Living Things, 2006; Warm Springs: Traces of A Childhood At FDR's Polio Haven, 2007; Left at Wichita, 2009; The Lovely Shoes, 2011; Failing with Children, forthcoming; What Are You Going to Do with a Boy Like Me, forthcoming. EDITOR: (with M. Golden) Skin Deep: Black Women and White Women Write About Race, 1995; (with P. Shreve) Outside the Law: Narratives on Justice in America, 1997; (with P. Shreve) How We Want to Live: Narratives on Progress, 1998; (with P. Shreve) Tales Out of School: Contemporary Writers on Their Student Years, 2000; Dream Me Home Safely: Writers on Growing up in America, 2003. Contributor to periodicals. **Address:** Department of English, George Mason University, Rm. 3E4, 4400 University Dr., Fairfax, VA 22030, U.S.A. **Online address:** sshreve@gmu.edu

SHRIMSLEY, Bernard. British (born England), b. 1931. **Genres:** Novels, Social Sciences, Literary Criticism And History. **Career:** Sunday Express, deputy editor, 1958-61; Daily Mirror, editor, 1961-64, assistant editor, 1964-68; Daily Post, editor, 1968-69; The Sun, deputy editor, 1969-72, editor, 1972-75; News of the World, editor, 1975-80, director, 1980-82; Daily Express, assistant editor, 1983-86, associate editor, 1986-96; Press Gazette, leader writer, 1991-2002; British Newspaper, editor and writer. **Publications:** The Candidates, 1968; Lion Rampant, 1984; The Silly Season: A Novel, 2003. **Address:** 11 Chiswick Wharf, Chiswick, London, GL W4 2SR, England. **Online address:** bernardshrimsley@btopenworld.com

SHRIVER, Jean Adair. American (born United States), b. 1932. **Genres:** Novels. **Career:** Palos Verdes Friends of the Library, president, 1965, 1980; Writer and librarian. **Publications:** Mayflower Man, 1991. **Address:** c/o William Reiss, John Hawkins & Associates Inc., 71 W 23rd St., Ste. 1600, New York, NY 10010-4185, U.S.A.

SHRIVER, Lionel. British/American (born United States), b. 1957. **Genres:** Novels, Young Adult Fiction. **Career:** BBC Radio, political commentator. Novelist and journalist. **Publications:** NOVELS: The Female of the Species, 1987; Checker and the Derailleurs, 1988; The Bleeding Heart in UK as Ordinary Decent Criminals, 1990; Game Control, 1994; A Perfectly Good Family,

1996; Double Fault, 1997; We Need to Talk About Kevin, 2003; The Post-Birthday World, 2007; So Much for That: A Novel, 2010; The New Republic, 2012. Contributor to journals. **Address:** c/o Kathleen Anderson, Scovil, Chichak, Galen Literary Agency Inc., 381 Park Ave. S, Ste. 1020, New York, NY 10016, U.S.A.

SHROPSHIRE, Kenneth (L.). American (born United States), b. 1955. **Genres:** Sports/Fitness, Law, Social Sciences. **Career:** Manatt, Phelps, Rothenberg and Tunney, associate, 1980-82; Southwestern University, adjunct professor, 1981-86; Los Angeles Olympic Organizing Committee, assistant vice-president and sports manager, 1982-85; University of Pennsylvania, Wharton School, assistant professor, 1986-91, associate professor of legal studies and real estate, 1991-, Afro-American Studies Program, acting director, 1997-98, David W. Hauck professor, 2001-, professor of legal studies and business ethics, Legal Studies Department, chairperson, 2000-05, Wharton Sports Business Initiative, director, 2004-; University of San Diego, visiting professor, 1990; Sports Lawyers Association, president, 2005-07; Florida Coastal School of Law, trustee; Womens Sports Foundation, trustee. Commentator, consultant and writer. **Publications:** Agents of Opportunity: Sports Agents and Corruption in Collegiate Sports, 1990; Careers in Sports Law, 1990; The Sports Franchise Game: Cities in Pursuit of Sports Franchises, Events, Stadiums and Arenas, 1995; In Black and White: Race and Sports in America, 1996; (with T. Davies) Business of Sports Agents, 2003, 2nd ed., 2008; Being Sugar Ray: The Life of Sugar Ray Robinson, America's Greatest Boxer and First Celebrity Athlete, 2007; Negotiate like the Pros, 2009. EDITOR: (with T. Davis and A. Mathewson) Sports and the Law: A Modern Anthology, 1999; (with T. Boyd) Basketball Jones, 2000; (with S.R. Rosner) Business of Sports, 2004, 2nd ed., 2010. Contributor to books and periodicals. **Address:** Wharton School, University of Pennsylvania, 660 Jon M Huntsman Hall, 3730 Walnut St., Philadelphia, PA 19104-6340, U.S.A. **Online address:** shrop@wharton.upenn.edu

SHROUT, Richard Neil. (R. N. Shrout). American (born United States), b. 1931. **Genres:** Adult Non-fiction, Medicine/Health, Psychology. **Career:** Youth For Christ Intl., representative, 1954-62; Dade County Juvenile and Domestic Relations Court, correctional officer and juvenile probation officer with Spanish-speaking delinquents, 1962-65; Intl. Institute for Hypnosis Studies, clinical hypnotherapist and consultant to health professionals and agencies, 1966-81, president. Writer, 1984-. **Publications:** Principles and Techniques of Hypnotism, 1971; Hypnology: Hypnotherapy and Hypnoanalysis, 3 vols., 1981; Survey of Hypnology, 3 vols., 1982; Abnormal Psychology, 1982; Diencephalic Physiology and Psychosomatic Disorders, 1982; Ericksonian Hypnotherapy: A Critique, 1982; Medical Terminology Simplified, 1982; Psycholinguistics and the Collective Unconscious, 1982; Psychodynamics, 1982; Socio-Medical Hypnosis, 1982; Symptomatology and Psychopathology, 1982. NONFICTION: (as R.N. Shrout) Modern Scientific Hypnosis: From Ancient Mystery to Contemporary Science, 1985; (as R.N. Shrout) Self-improvement through Self-hypnosis: A Complete Programme to Help You Shape Your Own Destiny, 1987; Resource Directory for the Disabled: Mobility Impaired, Vision Impaired, and Hearing Impaired, 1991. Contributor to periodicals and magazines. **Address:** Richard Curtis Associates Inc., 171 E 74th St., 2nd Fl., New York, NY 10021-3221, U.S.A.

SHROUT, R. N. See SHROUT, Richard Neil.

SHRUM, Robert. American (born United States), b. 1943?. **Genres:** Young Adult Non-fiction, Autobiography/Memoirs. **Career:** Senator Edward M. Kennedy, press secretary, 1980-84; Doak, Shrum & Associates (consulting firm), partner, 1985-2004; New York University, Robert F. Wagner Graduate School of Public Service, senior fellow; Yale University, teacher; Boston College, teacher; Kennedy Institute, fellow; The Los Angeles Times, columnist. Writer and consultant. **Publications:** No Excuses: Concessions of a Serial Campaigner (nonfiction), 2007. Contributor to periodicals. **Address:** Robert F. Wagner Graduate School of Public Service, New York University, 295 Lafayette St., New York, NY 10012-9604, U.S.A. **Online address:** robert.shrum@nyu.edu

SHTEINER, E. S. See STEINER, Evgeny.

SHTEINER, Evgenii. See STEINER, Evgeny.

SHTEYNGART, Gary. American/Russian (born Russia), b. 1972?. **Genres:** Novels, Humor/Satire. **Career:** Hunter College, faculty; Columbia University, faculty; Princeton University, faculty. Writer. **Publications:** The Russian Debutante's Handbook, 2002; Absurdistan, 2006. Super Sad True Love Story, 2010. **Address:** c/o Author Mail, Riverhead Books, Penguin Putnam Inc., 375 Hudson St., New York, NY 10014, U.S.A.

SHUBIN, Neil. American (born United States), b. 1960. **Genres:** History. **Career:** University of Chicago, Department of Anatomy, professor, chair, associate dean & provost of the Field Museum. Educator, paleontologist and writer. **Publications:** Your Inner Fish: A Journey into the 3.5-billion-year History of the Human Body, 2008. **Address:** Department of Organismal Biology & Anatomy, University of Chicago, 1027 E 57th St., Chicago, IL 60637, U.S.A. **Online address:** nshubin@uchicago.edu

SHUBIN, Seymour. American (born United States), b. 1921. **Genres:** Novels, Medicine/Health, Psychiatry, Documentaries/Reportage. **Career:** Triangle Publications, editor, 1943-48; Official Detective Stories Magazine, managing editor, 1944-47, reporter; writer, 1948-; J.B. Lippincott Publishing Co., editor, 1966-69. **Publications:** Anyone's My Name: A Novel, 1953; Stranger to Myself, 1954; Manta, 1958; Wellville, U.S.: A Novel, 1961; The Captain, 1982; Holy Secrets, 1984; Voices, 1985; Never Quite Dead, 1989; Remember Me Always, 1994; Fury's Children, 1997; Man from Enterprise: The Story of John B. Amos, Founder of AFLAC, 1998; My Face among Strangers, 1999; The Good and the Dead, 2000; A Matter of Fear, 2002; The Man From Yesterday, 2005; Witness to Myself, 2006; The Hunch, 2009. **Address:** 309 Paoli Pointe Dr., Paoli, PA 19301, U.S.A. **Online address:** sishu@aol.com

SHUGART, Herman H(enry). American (born United States), b. 1944. **Genres:** Environmental Sciences/Ecology. **Career:** Oak Ridge National Laboratory, scientist, 1971-84; University of Tennessee, associate professor, 1971-80, professor, 1980-84; University of Virginia, W.W. Corcoran professor of environmental sciences, 1984-, Department of Biology, professor, Global Environmental Change Program, director, Center for Regional Environmental Studies, director; Australian National University, visiting fellow, 1978-79, 1993-94. Writer. **Publications:** A Theory of Forest Dynamics: The Ecological Implications of Forest Succession Models, 1984; Terrestrial Ecosystems in Changing Environments, 1998; Theory of Forest Dynamics: The Ecological Implications of Forest Succession Models, 2003; How the Earthquake Bird got Its Name and Other Tales of an Unbalanced Nature, 2004; (with F.I. Woodward) Global Change and the Terrestrial Biosphere: Achievements and Challenges, 2011. EDITOR: Time Series and Ecological Processes, 1978; (with R.V. O'Neill) Systems Ecology, 1979; (with D.C. West and D.B. Botkin) Forest Succession: Concepts and Application, 1981; (with R. Leemans and G.B. Bonan) A Systems Analysis of the Global Boreal Forest, 1992; (with A.M. Solomon) Vegetation Dynamics and Global Change, 1993; (with T.M. Smith and F.C. Woodward) Plant Functional Types: Their Relevance to Ecosystem Properties and Global Change, 1997. **Address:** Department of Environmental Sciences, University of Virginia, 376 Clark Hall, Charlottesville, VA 22903, U.S.A. **Online address:** hhs@virginia.edu

SHUGHART, William F. American (born United States), b. 1947. **Genres:** Economics, Politics/Government, Money/Finance. **Career:** Center for Naval Analyses, systems analyst, 1973-74; University of Arizona, visiting lecturer in economics, 1978-79; Federal Trade Commission, Bureau of Economics, economist, 1979-82, special assistant, 1982-83; Clemson University, assistant professor, 1983-84, associate professor of economics, 1984-85; George Mason University, associate professor of economics, Center for the Study of Public Choice, research associate, 1985-88; University of Mississippi, Department of Economics and Finance, P.M.B. Self, William King Self and Henry C. Self Free Enterprise Chair and professor, 1988-98, Robert M. Hearin Chair, 1998-2006, Frederick A.P. Barnard Distinguished Professor of Economics, 1998-. Writer. **Publications:** The Organization of Industry, 1990, 2nd ed., 1997; Antitrust Policy and Interest-Group Politics, 1990; (with W.F. Chappell and R.L. Cottle) Modern Managerial Economics: Economic Theory for Business Decisions, 1994; (with J.F. Couch) The Political Economy of the New Deal, 1998. EDITOR: (with F.S. McChesney) The Causes and Consequences of Antitrust: The Public-Choice Perspective, 1995; Taxing Choice: The Predatory Politics of Fiscal Discrimination, 1997; (with L. Razzolini) The Elgar Companion to Public Choice, 2001; (with C.K. Rowley and R.D. Tollison) The Economics of Budget Deficits, 2 vols., 2002; (with R.D. Tollison) Policy Challenges and Political Responses: Public Choice Perspectives on the Post9/11 World, 2005. **Address:** Department of Economics, University of Mississippi, 229 N Hall, PO Box 1848, University, MS 38677-1848, U.S.A. **Online address:** wfs2@aggienetwork.com

SHUKEN, Julia. American (born United States), b. 1948. **Genres:** Adult Non-fiction, History, Romance/Historical. **Career:** Yorba Linda Star, editor; Biomedical and Aerospace Industries, technical editor. **Publications:** Day of the East Wind, 1993; In the House of My Pilgrimage, 1995. **Address:** 18 Filare, Irvine, CA 92620-2578, U.S.A.

SHUKMAN, Harold. British (born England), b. 1931. **Genres:** History, Translations. **Career:** Marconi Telecommunications, executive, 1956-57; St. Antony's College, fellow, 1961-98, lecturer in modern Russian history, 1969-, emeritus fellow, 1998-; Longman's History of Russia, general editor; British Broadcasting Corp., consultant. **Publications:** Lenin and the Russian Revolution, 1967; (with G. Katkov) Lenin's Path to Power, 1971; (with F.W. Deakin and H.T. Willetts) A History of World Communism, 1975; Rasputin, 1997; The Russian Revolution, 1998; Stalin, 1999; (with G. Elliott) Secret Classrooms, 2002; War or Revolution: Russian Jews and Conscription in Britain 1917, 2006, 8 vols., 2010; (with F. Patrikeeff) Railways and the Russo-Japanese War, 2007. TRANSLATOR: (with M. Hayward) E. Shvarts: The Dragon, 1965; (with M. Glenny) I. Babel: Marya, 1965; (with M. Hayward) V. Kataev: The Holy Well, 1967; A. Rybakov, Heavy Sand, 1981; R. Medvedev, All Stalin's Men, 1983; R. Medvedev, China and the Superpowers, 1986; A. Rybakov, Children of the Arbat, 1988; A. Gromyko, Memories, 1989. EDITOR: The Blackwell Encyclopedia of the Russian Revolution, 1988; Stalin's Generals, 1993; Agents for Change, 2000; (and intro.) Stalin and the Soviet-Finnish War, 1939-1940, 2002; Redefining Stalinism, 2003. TRANSLATOR and EDITOR: D. Volkogonov, Stalin: Triumph and Tragedy, 1991; D. Volkogonov, Lenin: Life and Legacy, 1994; D. Volkogonov, Trotsky: Eternal Revolutionary, 1995; D. Volkogonov, The Rise and Fall of the Soviet Empire, 1998. **Address:** St. Antony College, 62 Woodstock Rd., Oxford, OX OX2 6JF, England. **Online address:** harold.shukman@sant.ox.ac.uk

SHULEVITZ, Judith Anne. American (born United States), b. 1963. **Genres:** Young Adult Non-fiction. **Career:** Lingua Franca, co-editor, 1991-94; New York, deputy editor, 1994-95; Slate (online journal), editor, 1996-, cultural editor and columnist. **Publications:** (Ed. with J. Kantor and C. Krohn) The Slate Diaries, 2000; The Sabbath World: Glimpses of a Different Order of Time (nonfiction), 2010. Contributor to periodicals. **Address:** c/o Tina Bennett, Janklow and Nesbit Associates, 445 Park Ave., New York, NY 10022-2606, U.S.A. **Online address:** judith@judithshulevitz.com

SHULL, Steven A. American (born United States), b. 1943. **Genres:** Politics/Government, Young Adult Fiction, Economics, History. **Career:** High school social science teacher, 1965-67; Millikin University, instructor in political science, 1968-70; Ohio State Senate, legislative intern, 1970-71, budget analyst, administrative assistant, 1973-74; University of New Orleans, assistant professor, professor of political science, 1974-89, university research professor, 1989, now research professor emeritus; Chinese University of Hong Kong, Fulbright professor, 1985; University of Innsbruck, Fulbright professor, 2001, now professor emeritus; Ohio State University, Political Science Department, visiting professor, 2006-07. Writer. **Publications:** Interrelated Concepts in Policy Research, 1977; Presidential Policy-Making: An Analysis, 1979; Domestic Policy Formation: Presidential-Congressional Partnership?, 1983; The President and Civil Rights Policy: Leadership and Change, 1989; (with L.T. LeLoup) Congress and the President: The Policy Connection, 1993; A Kinder, Gentler Racism? The Reagan-Bush Civil Rights Legacy, 1993, rev. ed. as American Civil Rights Policy from Truman to Clinton: The Role of Presidential Leadership, 1999; Presidential-Congressional Relations: Policy and Time Approaches, 1997; (foreword) Presidents as Candidates, 1997; American Civil Rights Policy from Truman to Clinton: The Role of Presidential Leadership, 1999; (with T.C. Shaw) Explaining Congressional-Presidential Relations: A Multiple Perspectives Approach, 1999; (with L.T. LeLoup) The President and Congress: Collaboration and Combat in National Policymaking, 1999, 2nd ed., 2003; Policy by Other Means: Alternative Adoption by Presidents, 2006. EDITOR: (with L.T. LeLoup and contrib.) The Presidency: Studies in Public Policy, 1979; (with G.C. Edwards and N.C. Thomas and contrib.) American Presidency and Public Policy-Making, 1985; (with J.E. Cohen and contrib.) Economics and Politics of Industrial Policy: The United States and Western Europe, 1986; The Two Presidencies: A Quarter Century Assessment, 1991; Presidential Policymaking: An End-of-Century Assessment, 1999. Contributor to books and journals. **Address:** Department of Political Science, University of New Orleans, New Orleans, LA 70148, U.S.A. **Online address:** sshull@uno.edu

SHULMAN, Mark R(ussell). American (born United States), b. 1963.

Genres: Law, Military/Defense/Arms Control. **Career:** University of California at Berkeley, Department of History, graduate student instructor, 1986-89; U.S. Naval War College, research associate, 1989-; Yale University, International Security Program Colloquium, head, 1990-93, Olin Fellow, 1990-91, lecturer in history, 1991-94; Columbia University, School of International and Public Affairs, adjunct assistant professor, 1993, 1998, School of Law, lecturer in law, 2000-04; Georgetown University, fellow in foreign affairs, 1994-; National Strategy Information Center, Bradley Fellow, 1994-95, lecturer in law, 2000-04; Air War College, associate professor of military and diplomatic history, 1995-96; Debevoise & Plimpton, associate in the corporate department, 1999-2003; EastWest Institute, senior fellow and director of worldwide security initiative, 2003-04; Pace University, adjunct professor of law, 2004-, Graduate Programs/International Affairs, assistant dean, 2004-; Columbia Journal of Transnational Law, editor-in-chief. **Publications:** Navalism and the Emergence of American Sea Power, 1995; Proliferation Security Initiative as a New Paradigm for Peace and Security, 2006. EDITOR: (with M. Howard and G.J. Andreopoulos) The Laws of War: Constraints on Warfare in the Western World, 1994; (and intro.) An Admiral's Yarn: The Autobiography of Harris Laning, 1995; Admiral's Yarn, 1999; (with J.R. Silkenat) Imperial Presidency and the Consequences of 9/11: Lawyers React to the Global War on Terrorism, 2007. Contributor of articles to books and journals. **Address:** Pace University School of Law, Pace Law School, 78 N Broadway, White Plains, NY 10603, U.S.A. **Online address:** mshulman@law.pace.edu

SHULMAN, Myra Ann. American (born United States), b. 1941. **Genres:** Art/Art History, Communications/Media, Business/Trade/Industry, Economics. **Career:** American University, language specialist, 1976-2003; Georgetown University, faculty, 1998, adjunct instructor, adjunct professor, 2003-, English for Heritage Language Speakers Program, academic coordinator and instructor, 2007-; U.S. Department of State, English language specialist, 2005. Writer. **Publications:** Selected Readings in Business, 1991; (comp.) Journeys through Literature, 1995; Cultures in Contrast, 1998; Journeys through American Literature, 2000, 2nd ed., 2009; Thinking Critically: World Issues for Reading, Writing and Research, 2004; In Focus: Strategies for Academic Writers, 2005; In Focus: Strategies for Business Writers, 2006. **Address:** Center for Language Education and Development, Georgetown University, Rm. 3607, O St NW, Washington, DC 20007, U.S.A. **Online address:** shulmanm@georgetown.edu

SHULMAN, Seth. American (born United States), b. 1960. **Genres:** Adult Non-fiction, Sciences, Information Science/Computers, History, Technology, Adult Non-fiction. **Career:** Nature (journal), Boston correspondent, 1988-91; Technology Review, contributing writer, 1993-2004; contributing writer, 2001-03; Massachusetts Institute of Technology, Dibner Institute in the History of Science and Technology, Dibner science writer fellow, 2004-05, Amherst College, Copeland fellow, 2009-10. **Publications:** Biohazard, 1991; The Threat at Home: Confronting the Toxic Legacy of the U.S. Military, 1992; Owning the Future: Staking Claims on the Knowledge Frontier, 1999; Trouble on the Endless Frontier: Science Invention and the Erosion of the Technological Commons, 2002; Unlocking the Sky: Glenn Hammond Curtiss and the Race to Invent the Airplane, 2002; Undermining Science: Suppression and Distortion in the Bush Administration, 2006; Telephone Gambit: Chasing Alexander Graham Bell's Secret, 2008. **Address:** Brockman Inc., 123 E 54th St., Ste. 8-D, New York, NY 10022, U.S.A.

SHULTZ, George P(ratt). American (born United States), b. 1920. **Genres:** Business/Trade/Industry, Economics, Industrial Relations, Autobiography/Memoirs. **Career:** Massachusetts Institute of Technology, instructor, 1948-49, faculty, 1949-57, assistant professor, 1949-55, associate professor of industrial relations, 1955-57; President's Council of Economic Advisers, senior staff economist, 1955-56; University of Chicago, professor of industrial relations, 1957-68, Graduate School of Business, dean, 1962-68; Office of U.S. Secretary of Labor, consultant, 1959-60; Advisory Commission on Labor-Management Policy, consultant to president, 1961-62; National Opinion Research Center, board director, 1962-69; U.S. Employment Service, U.S. Department of Labor Task Force, chairman, 1965-68; Center for Advanced Study in the Behavioral Sciences, fellow, 1968-69; Industrial Relations Research Association, president, 1968; U.S. secretary of labor, 1969-70; Office of Management and Budget, director, 1970-72; Secretary of the Treasury, assistant to the president, Cost of Living Council, chairman, 1972-74; Stanford University, professor of management and public policy, 1974, Graduate School of Business, professor of international economics, 1989-; Jack Steele Parker professor of international economics, Hoover Institution,

senior fellow in economics, Thomas W. and Susan B. Ford distinguished fellow, 1989-, Energy Policy Task Force, chair; President's Economic Advisory Board, chairman, 1981-82; Bechtel Corp., executive vice president, 1974-75, president, 1975-77, vice chairman, 1977-81, president, 1981-82, director and senior counselor, 1989-; General Motors Corp., director, 1981-82, 1989-91; U.S. secretary of state, 1982-89; Boeing Corp., director, 1989-92; Tandem Computers Inc., director, 1989-92; Fremont Group, board director; American Economic Association, distinguished fellow; Tulane University, Sperry & Hutchinson lecturer; Stanford Institute for Economic Policy Research, senior fellow and director. Writer. **Publications:** Pressures on Wage Decisions, 1951; (with C. Myers) The Dynamics of a Labor Market; a Study of the Impact of Employment Changes on Labor Mobility, Job Satisfactions, and Company and Union Policies, 1951; (with J.R. Coleman) Labor Problems: Cases and Readings, 1953; (with G.B. Baldwin) Automation, a New Dimension to Old Problems, 1955; (with T. Whisler) Management Organization and the Computer, 1960; (with A. Weber) Strategies for the Displaced Worker, 1966; (with R. Aliber) Guidelines, Informal Controls and the Marketplace, 1966; (with A. Rees) Workers and Wages in the Urban Labor Market, 1970; Leaders and Followers in an Age of Ambiguity, 1975; (with K.W. Dam) Economic Policy Beyond the Headlines, 1977; Risk, Uncertainty and Foreign Economic Policy, 1981; Turmoil and Triumph: My Years as Secretary of State, 1993; Economics in Action: Ideas, Institutions, Policies, 1995; Putting Our House in Order: A Guide to Social Security and Health Care Reform, 2008; Implications of the Reykjavik Summit on Its Twentieth Anniversary: Conference Report, 2008; (ed. with K.E. Scott and J.B. Taylor) Ending Government Bailouts as We Know Them, 2009. Contributor to periodicals. **Address:** Hoover Institution, 434 Galvez Mall, Stanford, CA 94305-6010, U.S.A. **Online address:** schendel@hoover.stanford.edu

SHULTZ, Richard H. American (born United States), b. 1947. **Genres:** Cultural/Ethnic Topics. **Career:** Tufts University, Fletcher School, professor of international politics, 1983-, director of international security studies program, 1988-; Armed Groups Project, National Strategic Information Center, director; Columbia University, senior guest lecturer, 1991, 1992; U.S. Military Academy, Olin distinguished professor of National Security Studies, 1994-95; U.S. Marine Corps, Brigadier General H.L. Oppenheimer Chair of War fighting Strategy, 1997-98; George C. Marshall European Center for Security Studies, senior lecturer, 1998; Africa Center for Strategic Studies, senior fellow, 2000. Writer. **Publications:** Responding to the Terrorist Threat: Security and Crisis Management, 1980; (with R. Godson) Dezinformatsia: Active Measures in Soviet Strategy, 1984; The Soviet Union and Revolutionary Warfare: Principles, Practices and Regional Comparisons, 1988; In the Aftermath of War: U.S. Support for Reconstruction and Nation-building in Panama following Just Cause, 1993; The Secret War against Hanoi: Kennedy's and Johnson's Use of Spies, Saboteurs and Covert Warriors in North Vietnam, 1999; (with D. Farah and I.V. Lochard) Armed Groups: A Tier-one Security Priority, 2004; (with A.J. Dew) Insurgents, Terrorists and Militias: The Warriors of Contemporary Combat, 2006. EDITOR: (with R.A. Hunt) Lessons from an Unconventional War: Reassessing U.S. Strategies for Future Conflicts, 1982; (with F.R. Barnett and B.H. Tovar) Special Operations in U.S. Strategy, 1984; (with J. Salmon and J.P. O'Leary) Power, Principles & Interests: A Reader in World Politics, 1985; (co-author) Guerrilla Warfare and Counterinsurgency: U.S.-Soviet Policy in the Third World, 1989; (with R.L. Pfaltzgraff) U.S. Defense Policy in an Era of Constrained Resources, 1990; (with R.L. Pfaltzgraff) The Future of Air Power in the Aftermath of the Gulf War, 1992; (with R. Godson and T. Greenwood) Security Studies for the 1990s, 1993; (with R.L. Pfaltzgraff) Naval Forward Presence and the National Military Strategy, 1993; (with R.L. Pfaltzgraff) Ethnic Conflict and Regional Instability: Implications for U.S. Policy and Army Roles and Missions, 1994; (with R.L. Pfaltzgraff and W.B. Stock) Special Operations Forces: Roles and Missions in the Aftermath of the Cold War, 1995; (with R.L. Pfaltzgraff) War in the Information Age: New Challenges for U.S. Security Policy, 1997; (with R. Godson and G.H. Quester) Security Studies for the 21st Century, 1997; (with R.L. Pfaltzgraff) The Role of Naval Forces in 21st Century Operations, 2000. **Address:** The Fletcher School, Tufts University, 160 Packard Ave., Medford, MA 02155, U.S.A. **Online address:** richard.shultz@tufts.edu

SHULTZ, Suzanne M. (Suzanne Marie Shultz). American (born United States), b. 1947. **Genres:** Librarianship, Medicine/Health, Bibliography, Sports/Fitness. **Career:** Polyclinic Medical Center, medical librarian, 1969-96, co-founder of archives, 1989, archivist and historian, 1990-96, medical editor, 1991-96; Pennsylvania Medical Assistant, assistant editor, 1978-80, editor, 1987-88; Medical Reference Services Quarterly, interim book review editor, 1984-86; York Health System, director of library services, 1996-

. **Publications:** (Comp. with M.S. Wood) Three Mile Island: A Selectively Annotated Bibliography, 1988; Body Snatching: The Robbing of Graves for the Education of Physicians in Early Nineteenth Century America, 1992; A History of Polyclinic Medical Center, 1909-1986, 1994. Contributor to journals. **Address:** Wellspan Health, York Hospital, 1001 S George St., York, PA 17405-7198, U.S.A. **Online address:** sshultz@wellspan.org

SHULTZ, Suzanne Marie. *See* **SHULTZ, Suzanne M.**

SHUMAKER, David M. American (born United States), b. 1970. **Genres:** Medicine/Health. **Career:** Massachusetts General Hospital Department of Psychiatry, Children and the Law Program, instructor; Suffolk University, adjunct professor; Harvard University Medical School, lecturer. Writer. **Publications:** (with R.V. Heckel) Children Who Murder: A Psychological Perspective, 2001; (with R.V. Heckel) Kids of Character: A Guide to Promoting Moral Development, 2007. Contributor to journals. **Address:** Suffolk University, 8 Ashburton Pl., Boston, MA 02108, U.S.A. **Online address:** dshumake@suffolk.edu

SHUMAKER, Peggy. American (born United States), b. 1952. **Genres:** Poetry, Adult Non-fiction, Women's Studies And Issues. **Career:** University of Arizona, graduate assistant instructor, 1976-79; Arizona Commission on the Arts, writer-in-residence, 1979-85; Epoch Universal Publications, managing editor, 1980-81; Arizona State University, faculty associate in creative writing, 1983-85; University of Alaska, visiting assistant professor in creative writing, 1985-86; Old Dominion University, director of creative writing, 1987-88; University of Alaska, co-director of creative writing, 1988-99, Department of English, head, 1991-93, associate professor, 1991-93, professor, 1993-99, professor emeritus 1999-; Pacific Lutheran University, Rainier Writing Workshop, professor, 2003-; Bucknell University, Stadler Center for Poetry, poet-in-residence; Boreal Books, founding editor. **Publications:** POETRY: Esperanza's Hair, 1985; The Circle of Totems, 1988; Braided River (chapbook), 1993; Wings Moist from the Other World, 1994; Underground Rivers, 2001; Blaze, 2005; Greatest Hits (chapbook), 2006. ADULT NON-FICTION: Just Breathe Normally, 2007. **Address:** Deptartment of English, University of Alaska Fairbanks, PO Box 755720, Fairbanks, AR 99775-5720, U.S.A. **Online address:** peggyzoe@gmail.com

SHUMAN, George D. American (born United States), b. 1952?. **Genres:** Novels, Adult Non-fiction, Young Adult Non-fiction, Mystery/Crime/Suspense. **Career:** Metropolitan Police Force, undercover narcotics detective; Metropolitan Police Academy, operations commander; Internal Affairs Division, Public Integrity Branch, lieutenant commander, Special Assignments Branch, sergeant; Shuman and Associates, president. **Publications:** NOVELS: 18 Seconds, 2006; Last breath: A Sherry Moore Novel, 2007; Lost Girls: A Sherry Moore Novel, 2008; Second Sight: A Novel of Psychic Suspense, 2009. **Address:** c/o Simon Schuster, 1230 Ave. of the Americas, New York, NY 10020, U.S.A. **Online address:** author@georgedshuman.com

SHUMAN, Joel James. American (born United States) **Genres:** Theology/Religion. **Career:** Duke University Divinity School, instructor in theological ethics; King's College, Department of Theology, associate professor, professor, chair. Writer. **Publications:** The Body of Compassion: Ethics, Medicine and the Church, 1999; (with K.G. Meador) Heal Thyself: Spirituality, Medicine and the Distortion of Christianity, 2003; (with B. Volck) Reclaiming the Body: Christians and the Faithful Use of Modern Medicine, 2006; To Live is to Worship: Bioethics and the Body of Christ, 2007; (ed. with L.R. Owens) Wendell Berry and Religion: Heaven's Earthly Life, 2009. **Address:** Department of Theology, Kings College, 133 N River St., Wilkes Barre, PA 18711, U.S.A. **Online address:** jjshuman@kings.edu

SHUMAN, Malcolm K. (M. S. Karl). American (born United States), b. 1941?. **Genres:** Novels, Mystery/Crime/Suspense, Young Adult Fiction. **Career:** North Texas State University (now University of North Texas), lecturer, 1974-75; Texas A&I University (now Texas A&M University-Kingsville), faculty, 1975-76; Louisiana State University, faculty, 1977-92; Surveys Unlimited Research Associates Inc. (SURA), co-founder and co-operator, 1986-. Writer and archaeologist. **Publications:** ALAN GRAHAM MYSTERY NOVELS: Burial Grounds, 1998; The Meriwether Murder, 1998; Assassin's Blood, 1999; Past Dying, 2000; The Last Mayan, 2001. NOVELS: (as M.S. Karl) Mayab, 1981; (as M.S. Karl) The Mobius Man, 1982; The Levee: A Novel of Baton Rouge, 2008. MICA DUNN MYSTERY NOVELS: AS M.K. SHUMAN: The Maya Stone Murders, 1989; The Caesar Clue, 1990; Deep

Kill, 1991; The Last Man to Die, 1992. MICA DUNN MYSTERY NOVELS: AS M.S. KARL: Killer's Ink, Dodd, 1988; Death Notice, 1990; Deerslayer, 1991. Contributor to periodicals. **Address:** Surveys Unlimited Research Associates Inc., PO Box 14414, Baton Rouge, LA 70898-4414, U.S.A.

SHUMAN, Samuel I. American (born United States), b. 1925. **Genres:** Law, Philosophy, Politics/Government, Administration/Management. **Career:** Temple University, assistant instructor in philosophy, 1949-50; University of Pennsylvania, assistant instructor in philosophy, 1949-51; Wayne State University, assistant professor, 1954-55, associate professor, 1955-57, professor of law, 1957-80; C.N. Davidson & Co., partner, 1957-71; International Faculty of Comparative Law, lecturer, 1964; Michigan Department of Mental Health, Lafayette Clinic, professor of forensic psychiatry, 1967-; Art Tax Information Center, president, 1980-; Legislative Research Center, research assistant. Writer. **Publications:** Legal Positivism: Its Scope and Limitations, 1963; (trans. with N.D. West) Austrian Penal Code, 1966; (ed.) The Future of Federalism, 1968; (ed. with G.L. Dorsey) Validation of New Forms of Social Organization, 1968; (comp.) Law and Disorder, 1971; (ed. with N.D. West) Introduction to American Law: Cases and Materials, 1971; Psychosurgery and the Medical Control of Violence: Autonomy and Deviance, 1977. **Address:** Art Tax Information Center, 1 West Loop S, Ste. 703, Houston, TX 77027, U.S.A. **Online address:** sishuman@ev1.net

SHUMSKY, Zena. *See* **COLLIER, Zena.**

SHUSTERMAN, Neal (Douglas). American (born United States), b. 1962. **Genres:** Science Fiction/Fantasy, Children's Fiction, Young Adult Fiction, Plays/Screenplays, Novels, Plays/Screenplays. **Career:** Irvin Arthur Associates, assistant. Playwright and novelist. **Publications:** FOR YOUNG PEOPLE: Just for Boys Presents Guy Talk, 1987; The Shadow Club, 1988; It's O.K. to Say No to Cigarettes and Alcohol!: A Parent/Child Manual for the Protection of Children, 1988; Dissidents, 1989; (with C. Currie) Neon Angel: The Cherie Currie Story, 1989; Speeding Bullet, 1990; What Daddy Did, 1990; Kid Heroes, 1990; The Eyes of Kid Midas, 1992; Neal Shusterman's Darkness Creeping: Tales to Trouble Your Sleep, 1993, vol. II, 1995; Piggyback Ninja, 1994; Scorpion Shards, 1995; Mind Quakes, 1996; Mind Storms, 1996; The Dark Side of Nowhere, 1997; MindTwisters, 1997; Mind Benders, 1999; Thief of Souls, 1999; Downsiders, 1999; Shattered Sky, 2002; The Shadow Club Rising, 2002; Full Tilt, 2003; The Schwa Was Here, 2004; Dread Locks, 2005; Red Rider's Hood, 2005; Bruiser, 2005; Everlost, 2006; Duckling Ugly, 2006; Unwind, 2007; Antsy Does Time, 2008; Everwild, 2009; Everfound, 2011; Antsy Floats, 2012. **Address:** Lido Deck Productions, PO Box 80093, Rancho Santa Margarita, CA 92688-0093, U.S.A. **Online address:** nstoryman@aol.com

SHUSTERMAN, Richard (M.). American (born United States), b. 1949. **Genres:** Music, Philosophy, Essays, Art/Art History, Cultural/Ethnic Topics, Sports/Fitness. **Career:** Ben-Gurion University of the Negev, lecturer, 1980-82, senior lecturer in English and philosophy, 1983-87; Bezalel Academy of Art, lecturer, 1980-81; Hebrew University of Jerusalem, lecturer, 1981-83; Oxford University, St. John's College, visiting fellow, 1984-85; Temple University, Department of Philosophy, visiting associate professor, 1985-87, associate professor, 1987-92, professor of philosophy, 1992-2004, chair of philosophy, 1998-2004, Institute for Aesthetics and Cultural Studies, director, 1991-2004, Institute for the Study of Literature, Literacy, and Culture, fellow, 1997-99; école des Hautes études en Sciences Sociales, director of studies, 1990, 1992; Collège International de Philosophie, correspondent, 1992-95, 2001-, director, 1995-2001; New School for Social Research, Department of Liberal Studies, visiting professor, 1993-2004; Freie Universität, Fulbright professor in philosophy and American studies, 1995-96; Princeton University, Department of Comparative Literature, Eberhard L. Faber Class of 1915 memorial lecturer, 1996-97; Hiroshima University, visiting professor, 2002-03; Florida Atlantic University, Dorothy F. Schmidt College of Arts and Letters, Dorothy F. Schmidt eminent scholar chair in the humanities and professor of philosophy, 2004-, Center for Body, Mind, and Culture, director; Journal of Comparative Literature and Aesthetics, international editor, 2009-. **Publications:** The Object of Literary Criticism, 1984; T.S. Eliot and the Philosophy of Criticism, 1988; L'art a l'etat vif, 1991; Pragmatist Aesthetics: Living Beauty, Rethinking Art, 1992, 2nd ed., 2000; Sous l'interpretation, 1994; Kunst Leben, 1994; Practicing Philosophy: Pragmatism and the Philosophical Life, 1997; Performing Live: Aesthetic Alternatives for the Ends of Art, 2000; Surface and Depth: Dialectics of Criticism and Culture, 2002; Body Consciousness: A Philosophy of Mindfulness and Somaesthetics, 2008. EDITOR: (with

D. Heyd, Y. Mathias and S. Scolnicov) Sources for the Study of Philosophy in High School, vol. V: Aesthetics (in Hebrew), 1986; Analytic Aesthetics, 1989; (with D.R. Hiley and J.F. Bohman) The Interpretive Turn: Philosophy, Science, Culture, 1991; (with F. Gaillard and J. Poulain) Modernité en questions, 1998; (with M. Krausz) Interpretation, Relativism, and the Metaphysics of Culture: Themes in the Philosophy of Joseph Margolis, 1999; Bourdieu: A Critical Reader, 1999; Range of Pragmatism and the Limits of Philosophy, 2004; (with A. Tomlin) Aesthetic Experience, 2008. Contributor of articles to journals. **Address:** Dorothy F. Schmidt College of Arts and Letters, Florida Atlantic University, 777 Glades Rd., Boca Raton, FL 33431-0991, U.S.A. **Online address:** shuster1@fau.edu

SHUTE, Jenefer. American/British (born England), b. 1956. **Genres:** Novels, Psychology, Young Adult Non-fiction. **Career:** University of Cape Town, junior lecturer in English, 1977-78; Smith College, assistant professor of English, 1983-85, writer-in-residence; Tufts University, instructor in writing, 1985-86; Emerson College, Department of Writing, Literature and Publishing, assistant professor, associate professor, 1986-94; City University of New York, Hunter College, professor of English, 1995-; University of Paris, visiting professor. **Publications:** NOVELS: Life-Size, 1992; Sex Crimes, 1996; Free Fall, 2002, User ID, 2005. Contributor to periodicals. **Address:** Department of English, Hunter College, City University of New York, Rm. 1212, West Bldg., 695 Park Ave., New York, NY 10065, U.S.A. **Online address:** jpshute@earthlink.net

SHUTER, Jane Margaret. Also writes as Margaret Hudson. British/Zambian (born Zambia), b. 1955. **Genres:** History, Young Adult Non-fiction, Children's Fiction, Theology/Religion, Cultural/Ethnic Topics. **Career:** Teacher, 1977-83; Hamlyn Publishing Group, educational advisor. Editor and writer. **Publications:** (With P. Taylor) Invaders and Settlers, 1992; (with J. Maguire) Tudor and Stuart Times, 1992; Victorian Britain, 1992; Tudor Times, 1995; The Tudor Court, 1995; Shakespeare and the Theatre, 1995; The Poor in Tudor England, 1995; Life in a Tudor Town, 1995; Victorian Children, 1995; Tudor Children, 1996; (as Margaret Hudson) Teacher, 1996; (as Margaret Hudson) Shopkeeper, 1996; Russia and the U.S.S.R., 1996; Exploration Overseas, 1996; Country Life, 1996; Medieval Times, 1996; Clothes and Costume, 1997; Victorian Family Life, 1997; Tudor Family Life, 1997; Tudors and Stuarts, 1998; Egypt, 1999; Ancient Egypt, 1999; Anne Frank, 2000; Ancient Greece, 2001; Britian since 1930, 2001; Ancient Chinese Art, 2001, rev. ed., 2006; The Egyptians, 2003; Ancient China, 2006; Mesopotamia, 2006; How the Ancient Egyptians Lived, 2011. HISTORY EYEWITNESS, FIRST SERIES (EDITOR): Edmund Ludlow and the English Civil War, 1994; (and intro.) Helen Williams and the French Revolution, 1994; (and intro.) Sarah Royce and the American West, 1994; (intro.) Christabel Bielenberg and Nazi Germany, 1994. HISTORY EYEWITNESS, SECOND SERIES (EDITOR): (intro.) Exquemlin and the Pirates of the Caribbean, 1993; (and intro.) Charles Ball and American Slavery, 1993; (and intro.) Francis Parkman and the Plains Indians, 1993. HISTORY OPENS WINDOWS SERIES: The Ancient Egyptians, 1997, rev. ed., 2007; The Ancient Greeks, 1997, rev. ed., 2007; The Ancient Chinese, 1998, rev. ed., 2007; The Ancient Romans, 1998, rev. ed., 2007; The Middle Ages, 2000, rev. ed., 2007; The Renaissance, 2000, rev. ed., 2007; The Sumerians, 2002, rev. ed., 2009; The Aztecs, 2002; The Incas, 2002; The Maya, 2002; Ancient West African Kingdoms, 2003, rev. ed., 2009; The Indus Valley, 2003, rev. ed., 2009; The Vikings, 2003, rev. ed., 2009. LIVING THROUGH HISTORY SERIES (with N. Kelly and R. Rees): Medieval Realms, 1997; The Making of the United Kingdom, 1998; Britain, 1750-1900, 1998; The Twentieth Century World, 1998; Black Peoples of the Americas, 1998. LIVES AND TIMES SERIES: (as Margaret Hudson) Pocahontas, 1997; (as Margaret Hudson) The Wright Brothers, 1999; Alexander Graham Bell, 2000; Thomas Edison, 2000; Henry Ford, 2001. ANCIENT EGYPT SERIES: Builders and Craftsmen, 1998; Discoveries and Inventions, 1998; Farming and Food, 1998; Pharaohs and Priests, 1998. ANCIENT GREECE SERIES: Builders, Traders, and Craftsmen, 1998 in US as Builders, Craftsmen, and Traders, 1999; Cities and Citizens, 1999; Farmers and Fighters, 1999; Discoveries, Inventions, and Ideas, 1999. A CENTURY OF CHANGE SERIES: Transport, 1999; Health and Medicine, 1999; Space and Technology, 1999; Communications, 1999. VISITING THE PAST SERIES: Carisbrooke Castle, 1999; The Acropolis, 1999; Hadrian's Wall, 1999; Auschwitz, 1999; Mesa Verde, 2000; Shakespeare's Birthplace, 2002. HOLOCAUST SERIES: Prelude to the Holocaust, 2002; Resistance to the Nazis, 2002; Life and Death in the Camps, 2002; The Camp System, 2002; Life and Death in Hitler's Europe, 2003; Aftermath of the Holocaust, 2003; Survivors of the Holocaust, 2003. TRAVEL THROUGH TIME SERIES: Cycle Power: Two-Wheeled Travel Past and Present, 2004; Flying High: Air Travel Past and Present, 2004; Making Waves: Water Travel Past and Present, 2004; On the Road: Road Travel Past and Present, 2004; Riding the Rails: Rail Travel Past and Present, 2004; War Machines: Military Vehicles Past and Present, 2004. PICTURE THE PASTSERIES: Shops, 1997; Work, 1997; School, 1997; Transport, 1997; Leisure, 1997; Toys, 1997; Life along the Nile River, 2005; Life in a Roman Fort, 2005; Life in a Roman Town, 2005; Life in a Roman Villa, 2005; Life in an Egyptian Town, 2005; Life in a Greek Trading Port, 2005; Life in an Egyptian Workers' Village, 2005; Life in Ancient Athens, 2005; Life on a Viking Ship, 2005; Life in a Greek Temple, 2005; Life in a Medieval Castle, 2005; Life in a Viking Town, 2005. **Address:** 30 Portland Rd., Oxford, OX OX2 7EY, England.

SHUTTLE, Penelope (Diane). British (born England), b. 1947. **Genres:** Novels, Plays/Screenplays, Poetry, Young Adult Non-fiction, Young Adult Fiction. **Career:** Arvon Foundation, tutor. Writer. **Publications:** NOVELS: An Excusable Vengeance, 1967; All the Usual Hours of Sleeping, 1969; Jesusa, 1972; Wailing Monkey Embracing a Tree, 1973; (with P. Redgrove) The Terrors of Dr. Treviles, 1974; (with P. Redgrove) The Glass Cottage: A Nautical Romance, 1976; Rainsplitter in the Zodiac Garden, 1977; The Mirror of the Giant, 1980; The Orchard Upstairs, 1980; The Child-Stealer, 1983; Redgrove's Wife, 2006. POETRY: Moon Meal, 1973; The Dream, 1975; Webs of Fire, 1975; Period, 1976; Four American Sketches, 1976; The Lion from Rio, 1986; Adventures with My Horse, 1988; Taxing the Rain, 1992; Building a City for Jamie, 1996; Selected Poems, 1980-96, 1998; A Leaf out of His Book, 1999; Sandgrain and Hourglass, 2010. OTHERS: Nostalgia Neurosis, 1968; (with P. Redgrove) The Hermaphrodite Album, 1973; Midwinter Mandala, 1973; Photographs of Persephone, 1974; Autumn Piano and Other Poems, 1974; The Songbook of the Snow and Other Poems, 1974; (with P. Redgrove) The Wise Wound: Menstruation and Everywoman (non-fiction) in US as The Wise Wound: Eve's Curse and Everywoman, 1978, rev. ed., 1986, 2nd ed., 1999; Prognostica, 1980; The Wise Wound: Myths, Realities and Meanings of Menstruation, rev. ed., 1988; (with P. Redgrove) Alchemy for Women (non-fiction), 1995; A Shared Solitude: A Memoir, forthcoming. **Address:** David Higham Assocs, 5-8 Lower John St., Golden Sq., London, GL W1R 4HA, England.

SHVETS, Yuri B. American/Ukranian (born Ukraine), b. 1953. **Genres:** Autobiography/Memoirs, Young Adult Non-fiction. **Career:** KGB Intelligence Service, American Department, officer, 1980-84; TASS News Agency, correspondent, 1984-87; freelance journalist, 1990-. **Publications:** Washington Station: My Life as a KGB Spy in America, 1995. **Address:** c/o Brockman Inc., 5 E 59th St., New York, NY 10022-1027, U.S.A.

SHVIDKOVSKII, D. O. *See* **SHVIDKOVSKY, Dimitri.**

SHVIDKOVSKY, Dimitri. (D. O. Shvidkovskii). Russian (born Russia), b. 1959. **Genres:** Architecture. **Career:** Academy of Art of the Russian Federation, Institute of Theory and History of Fine Arts, fellow, 1986-, Department of the History and Theory of Art, chairman, 1991-; Moscow Architectural Institute, professor of architectural history and chair, 1991-, 1982 alumnus and long-term professor, rector, 2007-. Writer. **Publications:** (Co-ed.) Zakazchik v istorii russkoî arkhitektury, 1994; The Empress and the Architect: Architecture and Gardens at the Court of Catherine the Great, 1996; (contrib.) St. Petersburg, 1996; (contrib.) Zurab TSéreteli=Zurab Ceret'el=Zurab Tsereteli, 1996; (with E. Shorban) Moskovskie osobniaki, 1997; The Moscow Mansions, 1997; (ed. with J.M.P. de Montclos) Moscou: Patrimoine architectural, 1997; (as D.O. Shvidkovskii) Khudozhestvennye Modeli Mirozdaniiá, 1997; (as D.O. Shvidkovskii) Na Poroge Tret'ego Tysíacheletií á: Problemy Khudozhestvennoî Kul'tury: Materialy Nauchnoî Konferentsii, 1997; (as D.O. Shvidkovskii with V.P. Tolstoi and V.V. Tolstoi) Khudozhestvennaiá Kul'tura XX Veka: Razvitie Plasticheskikh Iskusstv, 2002; Russian Architecture and the West, 2007; (as D.O. Shvidkovskii) Charl'z Kameron I Arkhitektura Imperatorskikh Rezidentsií, 2008; (co-author; as D.O. Shvidkovskii) Nauka, obrazovanie i e'ksperimental'noe proektirovanie, 2010; Charlz Kameron pri dvore Ekateriny II, 2010. **Address:** Department of the History of Architecture, Moscow Architectural Institute, Rozhdestvenka Str. 11, Moscow, 107031, Russia. **Online address:** shvid@rah.ru

SIBLEY, Katherine A. S. (Katherine A. S. Siegel). American (born United States), b. 1961. **Genres:** International Relations/Current Affairs, History. **Career:** University of California, lecturer, 1991; St. Joseph's University, assistant professor, 1991-97, associate professor of history, 1998-, professor and chair. Writer. **Publications:** The Cold War, 1998; Red Spies in America: Stolen Secrets and the Dawn of the Cold War, 2004; First Lady Florence Harding: Behind the Tragedy and Controversy, 2009. AS KATHERINE A.S. SIEGEL: Loans and Legitimacy: The Evolution of Soviet-American Relations, 1919-1933, 1996. Contributor of articles to journals. **Address:** Department of History, St. Joseph's University, B/L 112M, 5600 City Ave., Philadelphia, PA 19131-1308, U.S.A. **Online address:** sibley@sju.edu

SIBSON, Caroline. *See* **DRACUP, Angela.**

SIBUM, Norm. Canadian/German (born Germany), b. 1947. **Genres:** Poetry. **Career:** Poet. **Publications:** POETRY: Among Other Howls in the Storm, 1982; Cafe Poems, 1988; Narratives and Continuations, 1990; In Laban's Field, 1993; The November Propertius, 1998; Girls and Handsome Dogs, 2002; Intimations of a Realm in Jeopardy, 2004; The Pangborn Defence, 2008; Smoke and Lilacs, 2009; William Hoffer and the Theology of Snooker, 2011. **Address:** 6077 Sherbrooke St. W, Ste. 202, Montreal, QC H4A 1Y2, Canada. **Online address:** sibum@videotron.ca

SICHEL, Kim Deborah. American (born United States), b. 1955. **Genres:** History, Photography. **Career:** National Museum of American Art, fellow, 1977; Zabriskie Gallery, director of photography department, 1977-80; Yale University, Art Gallery, teaching fellow, 1981-83, National Museum Act, fellow, 1982-83, Art Gallery, printroom assistant, 1982-85, lecturer, 1985-86; Smith College, visiting assistant professor, 1986-87; Boston University, Department of History of Art and Architecture, assistant professor, 1987-2000, director, 1987-, associate professor, 2000-, chair, 2002-05, Museum Studies, director, 1990-92, 1998-99, Art Gallery, director, 1992-98, junior fellow, 1996-97, 1989-90, senior fellow, 2005-06, American and New England Studies Program, director, 2009-. Writer. **Publications:** Brancusi: Photographer, 1980; Turn-of-the-Century Photographs by Robert Demachy, 1983; Brassai: Paris le jour, Paris la nuit, 1988; Mapping the West: Nineteenth-Century American Landscape Photographs from the Boston Public Library, 1992; Elbert Weinberg, 1928-1991: A Retrospective Exhibition, 1993; (co-author) Black Boston: Documentary Photography and the African American Experience, 1994; (with M.D. McInnes) Philip Guston, 1975-1980: Private and Public Battles, 1994; (with M.D. McInnes) Philip Guston, 1975-1980: Private and Public Battles, 1995; From Icon to Irony: German and American Industrial Photography, 1995; Germaine Krull, 1897-1985: An International Photographic Eye, 1999; (ed.) Street Portraits, 1946-1976: The Photographs of Jules Aarons, 2002; To Fly: Contemporary Aerial Photography, 2007; Aerial Vision: Aerial Photography and Landscape Photography, forthcoming. Contributor to books and journals. **Address:** Department of History of Art and Architecture, Boston University, Rm. 202E, 725 Commonwealth Ave., Boston, MA 02215, U.S.A. **Online address:** ksichel@bu.edu

SICHEL, Werner. American/German (born Germany), b. 1934. **Genres:** Economics, Business/Trade/Industry, Sciences, Technology, Reference, Engineering. **Career:** Roosevelt University, assistant professor, 1959-60; Lake Forest College, instructor, 1959-62; Western Michigan University, Department of Economics, instructor, 1960-64, assistant professor, 1964-66, associate professor, 1966-72, professor of economics, 1972-, chairman, 1985-, now professor emeritus; University of Belgrade, Fulbright senior lecturer, 1968-69. Writer. **Publications:** Industrial Organization and Public Policy: Selected Readings, 1967; (with P. Eckstein) Basic Economic Concepts, 1974, 2nd ed., 1977; (with M. Bronfenbrenner and W. Gardner) Microeconomics, 1983, 3rd ed., 1990; (with M. Bronfenbrenner and W. Gardner) Macroeconomics, 1984, 3rd ed., 1989; (with M. Bronfenbrenner and W. Gardner) Economics, 1984, 3rd ed., 1990; (comp. with B. Sichel) Economics Journals and Serials: An Analytical Guide, 1986; (with D.L. Alexander) Promoting Competition in Michigan Telecommunication Markets Through Innovative Legislation, 1998. EDITOR: Antitrust Policy and Economic Welfare, 1970; (with T.G. Gies) Public Utility Regulation, 1975; The Economic Effects of Multinational Corporations, 1975; Salvaging Public Utility Regulation, 1976; Economic Advice and Executive Policy: Recommendations from Past Members of the Council of Economic Advisers, 1978; Public Utility Rate Making in an Energy Conscious Environment, 1979; (with T.G. Gies) Applications of Economic Principles in Public Utility Industries, 1981; (with T.G. Gies) Deregulation: Appraisal Before the Fact, 1982; The State of Economic Science: Views of Six Nobel Laureates, 1989; (with D.L. Alexander) Networks, Infrastructure, and the New Task for Regulation, 1996. Contributor of articles to

journals. **Address:** Department of Economics, Western Michigan University, 5307 Friedmann Hall, 1903 W Michigan Ave., Kalamazoo, MI 49008, U.S.A. **Online address:** werner.sichel@wmich.edu

SICHER, Efraim. Israeli (born Israel), b. 1954. **Genres:** Literary Criticism And History, Novels. **Career:** Ben-Gurion University of the Negev, professor. Writer. **Publications:** Beyond Marginality: Anglo- Jewish Literature after the Holocaust, 1985; Style and Structure in the Prose of Isaak Babel, 1986; Jews in Russian Literature after the October Revolution: Writers and Artists between Hope and Apostasy, 1995; (ed.) Breaking Crystal: Writing and Memory after Auschwitz, 1998; Rereading the City, Rereading Dickens: Representation, the Novel, and Urban Realism, 2003; (ed.) Holocaust Novelists, 2004; The Holocaust Novel, 2005. **Address:** Department of Foreign Literatures & Linguistics, Ben-Gurion University of the Negev, PO Box 653, Beer Sheva, 84105, Israel. **Online address:** sicher@bgu.ac.il

SICHERMAN, Carol. (Carol Marks Sicherman). American (born United States), b. 1937. **Genres:** Education, Literary Criticism And History, Bibliography. **Career:** Cornell University, instructor, 1963-65, assistant professor of English, 1965-69; City University of New York, Herbert H. Lehman College, assistant professor, 1969-74, associate professor, 1975-90, professor of English and graduate coordinator, 1991-99, professor emerita, 1999-; Harvard University Press, writer consultant; Bucknell University, writer consultant; Cornell University Press, writer consultant; National Endowment for the Humanities, writer consultant. **Publications:** Ngugi Wa Thiong'o: A Bibliography of Primary and Secondary Sources, 1989; Ngugi Wa Thiong'o, the Making of a Rebel: A Source Book in Kenyan Literature and Resistance, 1990; Becoming an African University: Makerere, 1922-2000, 2004. **Address:** Department of English, Herbert H. Lehman College, City University of New York, 302 Carman Hall, 250 Bedford Park Blvd. W, Bronx, NY 10468-1589, U.S.A. **Online address:** sicherc@msn.com

SICHERMAN, Carol Marks. *See* **SICHERMAN, Carol.**

SICHROVSKY, Peter. Austrian (born Austria), b. 1947. **Genres:** Sociology, Plays/Screenplays. **Career:** Teacher, 1973-74; Freelance writer and journalist, 1980-86; Männer-Vogue Newspaper, editor-in-chief, 1986-, co-founder, 1988; Der Spiegel Newspaper, co-founder, 1988; Der Standard Newspaper, co-founder, 1988; Freedom Party of Austria, secretary-general, 2000-03, parliamentary member. **Publications:** Wir wissen nicht was morgen wird, wir wissen wohl was gestern war, 1986, (ed.) Schuldig geboren, 1987; Seelentrainig, 1989; Kinder Abrahams, 1990; Mein Freund David, 1990; (with P. Scheer) Liebe, Hass und Gleichgültigkeit: die moderne Beziehung in der Sackgasse, 1991; Unheilbar Deutsch, 1993; Die Kobra-Falle, 1994; Das Bild des Roten Drachen, 1995; (with I. Bubis) Damit Bin ich Noch längst Nicht Fertig: Die Autobiographie, 1996; Verklemmt: Jüdische Liebesgeschichten, 1998. Contributor of articles to periodicals. **Address:** European Office of the Socialist Party, Schenkenstrasse 8/5, Vienna, 1017, Austria. **Online address:** peter.sichrovsky@fpoe.at

SICK, Gary G(ordon). American (born United States), b. 1935. **Genres:** International Relations/Current Affairs, History. **Career:** Persian Gulf Sheikhdoms and Indian Ocean area, Office of the Assistant Secretary of Defense for International Security Affairs, country director, 1973-76; National Security Council, staff, 1976-81; Columbia University, Middle East Institute, research associate, 1981-82, School of International and Public Affairs, adjunct professor, 1982-, Gulf/2000 Project, executive director, 1993-; Ford Foundation, deputy director for international affairs, 1982-87. Writer. **Publications:** All Fall Down: America's Tragic Encounter with Iran, 1985; October Surprise: America's Hostages in Iran and the Election of Ronald Reagan, 1991. CO-EDITOR: The Persian Gulf at the Millennium: Essays in Politics, Economy, Security and Religion, 1997; Security in the Persian Gulf: Origins, Obstacles and the Search for Consensus, 2002; Iran, Iraq and the Legacies of War, 2004. Contributor to journals. Works appear in anthologies. **Address:** School of International and Public Affairs, Columbia University, International Affairs Bldg., 420 W 118th St., 11th Fl., New York, NY 10027, U.S.A. **Online address:** ggs2@columbia.edu

SICKELS, Noelle. American (born United States), b. 1945. **Genres:** Novels, Plays/Screenplays, Novellas/Short Stories. **Career:** North Caroline High School, teacher of life skills, 1971-72; Caroline County Migrant School, teacher of life skills, 1971-72; Philadelphia Child Guidance Clinic, psychoeducation specialist, 1974-77; Behavioral Health Services, coordinator of medicine education program, 1977-79; Neighborhood Nursery School, teacher, 1984-93, teacher-director, 1995-; Sequoyah School, assistant to the director, 1993-95. Writer. **Publications:** (Ed.) Time Was (reminiscences collection), 1992; Walking West (novel), 1995; The Shopkeeper's Wife, 1998; The Medium, 2007; Relics, forthcoming. Contributor of articles to periodicals. Works appear in anthologies. **Address:** c/o Jeffery McGraw, The August Agency, 4200 60th Ct., Vero Beach, FL 32967, U.S.A. **Online address:** noellesickels@mac.com

SICKER, Martin. American (born United States), b. 1931. **Genres:** Politics/Government, International Relations/Current Affairs, Reference. **Career:** U.S. Government, senior executive, associate commissioner for program development on aging, 1957-82; American Association of Retired Persons, Work Force Programs Department, director, 1990-97. Writer. **Publications:** The Making of a Pariah State, 1987; The Judaic State, 1988; The Strategy of Soviet Imperialism, 1988; The Bear and the Lion, 1988; Between Hashemites and Zionists: The Struggle for Palestine, 1908-1988, 1989; Israel's Quest for Security, 1989; The Genesis of the State, 1991; Judaism, Nationalism, and the Land of Israel, 1992; What Judaism Says about Politics: The Political Theology of the Torah, 1994; Reshaping Palestine: From Muhammad Ali to the British Mandate, 1831-1922, 1999; Pangs of the Messiah: The Troubled Birth of the Jewish State, 2000; The Pre-Islamic Middle East, 2000; The Islamic World in Ascendancy: From the Arab Conquests to the Siege of Vienna, 2000; The Islamic World in Decline, 2001; Between Rome and Jerusalem: 300 years of Roman-Judaean Relations, 2001; The Middle East in the Twentieth Century: From the Treaty of Karlowitz to the Disintegration of the Ottoman Empire, 2001; Political Culture of Judaism, 2001; Between Man and God: Issues in Judaic Thought, 2001; Geopolitics of Security in the Americas: Hemispheric Denial from Monroe to Clinton, 2002; Reading Genesis Politically: An Introduction to Mosaic Political Philosophy, 2002; Political Economy of Work in the 21st Century: Implications for an Aging American Workforce, 2002; Rise and Fall of the Ancient Israelite States, 2003; Orthocratic State, 2003; Passover Seder Companion and Analytic Introduction to the Haggadah, 2004; Trials of Abraham: The Making of a National Patriarch, 2004; Aspects of Jewish Metarational Thought, 2005; Kohlet: The Reflections of a Judean Prince: A New Translation and Commentary, 2006; Introduction to Judaic Thought and Rabbinic Literature, 2007; Ten Commandments: Background, Meaning and Implications: From a Judaic Perspective, 2008; Convocation at Sinai: A Study in Biblical Interpretation, 2008. **Address:** 6483 E Baker Pl., Denver, CO 80222, U.S.A. **Online address:** msicker@pcisys.net

SIDAHMED, Abdel Salam. British (born England), b. 1956. **Genres:** Politics/Government. **Career:** Sudanow, senior reporter and sub-editor for current affairs, 1985-; Cambridge University, researcher and lecturer in modern Middle Eastern history, 1991-95; Amnesty Intl., human rights researcher, 1995-, Middle East program, director, 1995-2005; Sudan Studies Centre, consultant; University of Windsor, Middle East Studies, staff, Department of Political Science, assistant professor, associate professor, 2005-. Writer. **Publications:** (Ed. with A. Ehteshami) Islamic Fundamentalism, 1996; Politics and Islam in Contemporary Sudan, 1996; (with A. Sidahmed) Sudan, 2005; (with W.C. Soderlund and E.D Briggs) The Responsibility to Protect in Darfur: The Role of Mass Media, 2010. **Address:** Department of Political Science, University of Windsor, 1149 Chrysler Hall N, 401 Sunset Ave., Windsor, ON N9B 3P4, Canada. **Online address:** sidahmed@uwindsor.ca

SIDAK, J. Gregory. American (born United States), b. 1955. **Genres:** Business/Trade/Industry, Technology, Communications/Media, Economics. **Career:** U.S. Court of Appeals for the Seventh Circuit, law clerk, 1981-82; O'Melveny and Myers, associate, 1982-84; The Boston Consulting Group Inc., management consultant, 1984-86; Council of Economic Advisers, Executive Office of the President, senior counsel and economist, 1986-87; Federal Communications Commission, deputy general counsel, 1987-89; Covington and Burling, associate, 1989-92; American Enterprise Institute for Public Policy Research, director, 1992-95, F.K. Weyerhaeuser fellow in law and economics, 1995-2002, emeritus, 2002-05; Yale University, Yale School of Management, senior lecturer, 1993-99; Criterion Economics, founder, president and chief executive officer, 1999, chairman, 2008-; Journal of Competition Law and Economics, founding editor, 2004-; Georgetown University, visiting professor of law, 2005-07; Tilburg University, Ronald Coase professor of law and economics, 2009-. **Publications:** (Ed.) Governing the Postal Service, 1994; (with W.J. Baumol) Toward Competition in Local Telephony, 1994; (with W.J. Baumol) Transmission Pricing and Stranded Costs in the Electric Power Industry, 1995; (with D.F. Spulber) Protecting Competition from the Postal Monopoly, 1996; Foreign Investment in American Telecommunications, 1997; (with D.F. Spulber) Deregulatory Takings and the Regulatory Contract: The Competitive Transformation of Network Industries in the United States, 1997; (ed.) Is the Telecommunications Act of 1996 Broken? If So, How Can we Fix It?, 1999; (with C. Engel and G. Knieps) Competition and Regulation in Telecommunications: Examining Germany and America, 2001; (co-author) Broadband in Europe: How Brussels Can Wire the Information Society, 2005. Contributor to books and periodicals. **Address:** Criterion Economics L.L.C., 1614 20th St. NW, Washington, DC 20009, U.S.A. **Online address:** jgsidak@criterioneconomics.com

SIDDALI, Silvana R. American (born United States) **Genres:** History, Social Sciences, Military/Defense/Arms Control. **Career:** Saint Louis University, Department of History, assistant professor, associate professor. Writer. **Publications:** From Property to Person: Slavery and the Confiscation Acts, 1861-1862, 2005; (ed.) Missouri's War: The Civil War in Documents, 2008. Contributor to periodicals. **Address:** Department of History, Saint Louis University, 3800 Lindell Blvd., 221 N Grand Blvd., Saint Louis, MO 63108, U.S.A. **Online address:** siddalis@slu.edu

SIDDIQA, Ayesha. (Ayesha Siddiqa-Agha). Pakistani (born Pakistan), b. 1966. **Genres:** Military/Defense/Arms Control, Economics, History, Politics/Government. **Career:** Pakistan Navy, civil servant, director of naval research, deputy director in audit defence services, 1988-2001; Sustainable Development Policy Institute, visiting fellow; Sandia National Laboratories, Cooperative Monitoring Center, research fellow. Writer. **Publications:** (As Ayesha Siddiqa-Agha) Pakistan's Arms Procurement and Military Build-Up, 1979-99: In Search of a Policy, 2001; (as Ayesha Siddiqa-Agha with U. Sen) Governance in Plural Societies and Security: An Overview, 2001; Confrontation to Conciliation: India-Pakistan Relations, 2004; Development of Pakistan's Foreign Policy: Case Study of the Gulf Crisis, 1990, 2004; (with F.R. Frankel) Security Perspectives from Pakistan; Indo-US Relations, Changing Perceptions, 2006; Military Inc.: Inside Pakistan's Military Economy, 2007; Military Autonomy and the Prospects of Democratic Consolidation in Pakistan, 2008. Contributor to periodicals. **Address:** Rm. No. 7, 9th Ave., Islamabad, 44000, Pakistan. **Online address:** info@ayeshasiddiqa.com

SIDDIQA-AGHA, Ayesha. See **SIDDIQA, Ayesha.**

SIDDONS, Anne Rivers. (Sybil Anne Rivers Siddons). American (born United States), b. 1936. **Genres:** Novels, Essays, Young Adult Non-fiction, Children's Non-fiction, Young Adult Fiction. **Career:** Retail Credit Co., advertiser, 1959; Citizens & Southern National Bank, advertiser, 1961-63; Atlanta, senior editor, 1964-67; Burke-Dowling Adams, advertiser, 1967-69; Burton Campbell Advertising, advertiser, 1969-74. Full-time writer, 1974-. **Publications:** NONFICTION: John Chancellor Makes Me Cry, 1975; Go Straight on Peachtree, 1977. NOVELS: Heartbreak Hotel, 1976; The House Next Door, 1978; Fox's Earth, 1981; Homeplace: A Novel, 1987, rev. ed., 1988; Peachtree Road: A Novel, 1988, rev. ed., 1994; King's Oak: A Novel, 1990, rev. ed., 1991; Outer Banks: A Novel, 1991; Colony: A Novel, 1992, rev. ed., 1993; Hill Towns: A Novel, 1993; Downtown: A Novel, 1994; Fault Lines: A Novel, 1995, rev. ed., 2007; Up Island: A Novel, 1997; Low Country: A Novel, 1998; Nora, Nora: A Novel, 2000; Islands, 2004; (with E. Goudge and J. Gould) Trilogy of Romances, 2004; Sweetwater Creek: A Novel, 2005; Off Season, 2008; Burnt Mountain: A Novel, 2010. **Address:** c/o Jennifer Rudolph Walsh, William Morris Agency L.L.C., 1325 Ave. of the Americas, New York, NY 10019-6026, U.S.A.

SIDDONS, Sybil Anne Rivers. See **SIDDONS, Anne Rivers.**

SIDES, W(ade) Hampton. American (born United States), b. 1962. **Genres:** Documentaries/Reportage, History, Biography. **Career:** Washingtonian, staff writer, 1986-88; City Paper, associate editor, 1988-89; freelance writer, 1989-; Stanford University, Edwards Media fellow. **Publications:** Stomping Grounds: A Pilgrim's Progress through Eight American Subcultures, 1992; (ed.) Why Moths Hate Thomas Edison and Other Urgent Inquiries into the Odd Nature of Nature: The Best of Outside Magazine's The Wild File, 2001; Ghost Soldiers: The Forgotten Epic Story of World War II's Most Dramatic Mission, 2001; Ghost Soldiers: The Epic Account of World War II's Greatest Rescue Mission, 2002; Americana: Dispatches from the New Frontier, 2004; Blood and Thunder: An Epic of the American West, 2006; Hellhound on His Trail: The Stalking of Martin Luther King, Jr., and the International Hunt for His Assassin, 2010. Contributor to periodicals. **Address:** c/o Joy Harris, Lantz-Harris Literary Agency, 156 5th Ave., Ste. 617, New York, NY 10010, U.S.A.

SIDKY, H. American (born United States), b. 1956. **Genres:** Anthropology/ Ethnology, Psychology, Social Sciences, Agriculture/Forestry. **Career:** Miami University, assistant professor of anthropology, 1994-2000, associate professor of anthropology, 2000-08, professor of sociology, 2008-, Black World Studies Program, affiliate. Writer. **Publications:** Hunza: An Ethnographic Outline, 1995; Irrigation and State Formation in Hunza: The Anthropology of a Hydraulic Kingdom, 1996; Witchcraft, Lycanthropy, Drugs and Disease: An Anthropological Study of the European Witch-Hunts, 1997; The Greek Kingdom of Bactria: From Alexander to Eucratides the Great, 2000; (with J. Subedi) Bitan, Oracles and Healers in the Karakorams, 2000; (co-author) Halfway to the Mountain: The Jirels of Eastern Nepal, 2002; An Ethnographic Description, 2002; A Critique of Postmodern Anthropology: In Defense of Disciplinary Origins and Traditions, 2003; Perspectives on Culture: A Critical Introduction to Theory in Cultural Anthropology, 2004; Haunted by the Archaic Shaman: Himalayan Jhakris and the Discourse on Shamanism, 2008; Phombos and Jhankris: Spirit Masters and Healers, forthcoming. Contributor to journals. **Address:** Department of Sociology, Gerontology and, Anthropology, Miami University, 375 Upham Hall, 501 E High St., Oxford, OH 45056, U.S.A. **Online address:** sidkyh@muohio.edu

SIDLOW, Edward I. American (born United States), b. 1952. **Genres:** Politics/Government. **Career:** Arizona State University, faculty; Miami University, assistant professor, 1979-85; Northwestern University, assistant professor, associate professor, 1985-89; Loyola University, assistant dean, 1989-92, director of academic affairs, 1992-95; Eastern Michigan University, Honors College, public administration, Department of Political Science, professor, 2000-, department head, 1995-2000. Writer and political scientist. **Publications:** (With B. Henschen) America at Odds: An Introduction to American Government, 1998, rev. ed. as America at Odds, the Essentials: An Introduction to American Government, 1999, 6th ed., 2008; Challenging the Incumbent: An Underdogs Undertaking, 2004; Freshman Orientation: Home Style and House Style, 2006; (with B. Henschen) Govt, 2010. **Address:** Department of Political Science, Eastern Michigan University, 601C Pray-Harrold, Ypsilanti, MI 48197, U.S.A. **Online address:** ed.sidlow@emich.edu

SIDNEY, Neilma. Also writes as Neilma Myer, Neilma Gantner. Australian/ American (born United States), b. 1922. **Genres:** Novellas/Short Stories, Travel/Exploration, Young Adult Fiction. **Career:** Australian Executive International Social Service, staff, 1955-91; International Social Service, international executive, 1965-69; Myer Foundation, executive; Sidney Myer Fund, executive; Four Winds Cultural Festival, founder. Writer. **Publications:** Saturday Afternoon (short stories), 1959; Beyond the Bay, 1966; The Eye of the Needle (short stories), 1970; The Return, 1976; Journey to Mourilyan (travel), 1986; Sunday Evening (short stories), 1988; The Sweet Cool South Wind, 1993. **Address:** PO Box 497, South Yarra, VI 3141, Australia.

SIDOR, Steven. American (born United States), b. 1968?. **Genres:** Mystery/ Crime/Suspense, Novels, Horror. **Career:** Writer. **Publications:** NOVELS: Skin River, 2004; Bone Factory, 2005; The Mirror's Edge, 2008; Pitch Dark, 2011. Contributor to books. **Address:** Rees Literary Agency, 14 Beacon St., Ste. 710, Boston, MA 02108-3735, U.S.A. **Online address:** ssidor@msn.com

SIEBOLD, Cathy. American (born United States), b. 1951. **Genres:** Medicine/Health, Social Work, Social Sciences, Sociology. **Career:** Todd Nursing Home Inc., admissions and case aide, 1972-75; Fifth Avenue Center for Counseling, supervisor, 1984-88; National Institute for Psychotherapy, staff, 1984-88; Fordham University, adjunct professor, 1986-88, chair of advanced training program in clinical social work, 1993-; Pennsylvania State University, assistant professor of social welfare, 1988-90; University of Southern Maine, assistant professor of social work, 1990-. Writer. **Publications:** The Hospice Movement: Easing Death's Pains, 1992. Works appear in anthologies. Contributor of articles to journals. **Address:** School of Social Work, University of Southern Maine, Masterton Hall, 3rd Fl., 96 Falmouth St., PO Box 9300, Portland, ME 04104-9300, U.S.A. **Online address:** csiebolddsw@verizon.net

SIEBOLD, Jan. American (born United States), b. 1953. **Genres:** Children's Fiction, Novels, Librarianship, Writing/Journalism. **Career:** East Aurora Schools, library media specialist, 1977-2009; writer, 1985-. **Publications:** NOVELS: Rope Burn, 1998; Doing Time Online, 2002; My Nights at the

Improv, 2005. OTHERS: Writing and Publishing: The Librarian's Handbook, 2010; Librarians as Community Partners, 2010. **Address:** Albert Whitman & Co., 250 S Northwest Hwy., Ste. 320, Park Ridge, IL 60068, U.S.A. **Online address:** jansiebold@roadrunner.com

SIEGAL, Nina. Dutch/American (born United States), b. 1969. **Genres:** Novels. **Career:** Amsterdam Weekly, associate editor; Time Out Amsterdam, founding editor, editor-in-chief, 2008-. Journalist. **Publications:** A Little Trouble with the Facts: A Novel, 2008. Contributor to periodicals. **Address:** Time Out Amsterdam, West-Indisch Pakhuis, s-Gravenhekje 1a, Amsterdam, 1011TG, Netherlands. **Online address:** nina@ninasiegal.com

SIEGEL, Bernard S(hepard). American (born United States), b. 1932. **Genres:** Children's Fiction, Medicine/Health, Psychology, Self Help. **Career:** Surgical Associates, practitioner of pediatric and general surgery, 1961-89; Exceptional Cancer Patients, founder and director. Lecturer and writer. **Publications:** Love, Medicine & Miracles: Lessons Learned about Self-Healing from a Surgeon's Experience with Exceptional Patients, 1986, rev. ed., 1990; Peace, Love & Healing: Bodymind Communication and the Path to Self-Healing: An Exploration, 1989; How to Live Between Office Visits: A Guide to Life, Love and Health, 1993; Prescriptions for Living: Inspirational Lessons for a Joyful, Loving Life, 1999; (intro.) Ancient Secret of the Fountain of Youth, 1999; (with Y. August) Help Me to Heal: A Practical Guidebook for Patients, Visitors and Caregivers, 2003; 365 Prescriptions for the Soul: Daily Messages of Inspiration, Hope and Love, 2003; Smudge Bunny, 2004; 101 Exercises for the Soul: A Divine Workout Plan for Body, Mind and Spirit, 2005; Love, Magic & Mudpies: Raising Your Kids to Feel Loved, Be Kind and Make a Difference, 2006; (intro.) The Language of Miracles: A Celebrated Psychic Teaches You to Talk to Animals, 2006; Buddy's Candle, 2008; Faith, Hope and Healing, 2009; A Book of Miracles: Inspiring True Stories of Healing, Gratitude and Love, 2011. Contributor of articles to newspapers and magazines. **Address:** 61 Ox Bow Ln., Woodbridge, CT 06525-1525, U.S.A.

SIEGEL, Daniel J. American (born United States), b. 1957. **Genres:** Psychiatry, Medicine/Health, Sciences. **Career:** University of California, Infant and Pre-School Evaluation Service, medical director, 1990-99, School of Medicine, associate clinical professor, 1997-2009, clinical professor of psychiatry, 2009-, Mindful Awareness Research Center, co-director and founding member, 2005-; Children's Mental Health Alliance, director of interdisciplinary studies, 1998-2003; Center for Human Development and Mindsight Institute, executive director, 1999-; Lifespan Learning Institute, medical director, 2004-; Garrison Institute, Leadership Council on Awareness and Concentration in Education, staff, 2006-. Writer and psychiatrist. **Publications:** (Ed. with S. Richeimer) The Handbook of Psychiatry, 1990; The Developing Mind: Toward a Neurobiology of Interpersonal Experience, 1999 as The Developing Mind: How Relationships and the Brain Interact to Shape Who We Are, 2001; (with M. Hartzell) Parenting from the Inside Out: How a Deeper Self-Understanding Can Help You Raise Children Who Thrive, 2003; (ed. with M.F. Solomon) Healing Trauma: Attachment, Mind, Body and Brain, 2003; The Mindful Brain: Reflection and Attunement in the Cultivation of Well-Being, 2007; Mindsight: The New Science of Personal Transformation, 2009; (co-ed.) The Healing Power of Emotion: Affective Neuroscience, Development and Clinical Practice, 2009; The Mindful Therapist: A Clinician's Guide to Mindsight and Neural Integration, 2010. Contributor to books and periodicals. **Address:** Mindsight Institute, 11980 San Vicente Blvd., Ste. 809, Los Angeles, CA 90049, U.S.A. **Online address:** info@drdansiegel.com

SIEGEL, Daniel M. American (born United States), b. 1939. **Genres:** Sciences, Adult Non-fiction, Essays. **Career:** San Francisco State College (now University), assistant professor of physical science, 1965-66; University of Wisconsin, assistant professor, 1970-, associate professor, through 1990, professor of history of science and integrated liberal studies, 1990-, Department of the History of Science, head, 1981-84, 1990-91, Integrated Liberal Studies Program, head, 1991-93, now professor emeritus. Writer. **Publications:** Innovation in Maxwell's Electromagnetic Theory: Molecular Vortices, Displacement Current, and Light, 1991; (ed. with A.J. Kox) No Truth Except in the Details: Essays in Honor of Martin J. Klein, 1995. Contributor of articles to journals. **Address:** Department of History of Science, University of Wisconsin, 7143 Social Science Bldg., 1180 Observatory Dr., Madison, WI 53706-1393, U.S.A.

SIEGEL, James. American (born United States), b. 1954?. **Genres:** Novels, Mystery/Crime/Suspense, Young Adult Fiction. **Career:** BBDO (advertising agency), senior creative director and vice president. Writer. **Publications:** Epitaph, 2001; Derailed, 2003; Detour, 2005; Deceit, 2006; Detour/Derailed, 2007; (co-author) Adventure Pack: Five Gripping Novels, 2008. **Address:** c/o Author Mail, Warner Books Inc., 1271 Ave. of the Americas, New York, NY 10020, U.S.A.

SIEGEL, Jennifer. American (born United States) **Genres:** History, Politics/Government, Social Sciences. **Career:** Ohio State University, assistant professor, associate professor of history; University of Pennsylvania, lecturer; Boston University, assistant professor; Yale University, lecturer; Bennington College, assistant professor; Yale University, International Security Studies, postdoctoral fellow; Olin Foundation postdoctoral fellow; Mellon Foundation, dissertation fellow. Writer and historian. **Publications:** Endgame: Britain, Russia, and the Final Struggle for Central Asia, 2002; (ed. with P. Jackson) Intelligence and Statecraft: The Use and Limits of Intelligence in International Society, 2005. **Address:** Department of History, Ohio State University, 342 Dulles Hall, 230 W 17th Ave., Columbus, OH 43210, U.S.A. **Online address:** siegel.83@osu.edu

SIEGEL, Jonah. American (born United States), b. 1963. **Genres:** Art/Art History, Cultural/Ethnic Topics. **Career:** Rutgers University, professor of English. Writer. **Publications:** Desire and Excess: The Nineteenth-Century Culture of Art, 2000; Haunted Museum: Longing, Travel and the Art-Romance Tradition, 2005; (ed.) The Emergence of the Modern Museum: An Anthology of Nineteenth-Century Sources, 2008. Contributor to periodicals. **Address:** Department of English, Rutgers University, College Ave., New Brunswick, NJ 08901, U.S.A. **Online address:** jonah.siegel@rutgers.edu

SIEGEL, Katherine A. S. *See* **SIBLEY, Katherine A. S.**

SIEGEL, Mona L. American (born United States) **Genres:** Social Sciences, Politics/Government, Philosophy. **Career:** California State University, Department of History, assistant professor, 2003-08, associate professor, 2008-, director of graduate studies, 2007-. Writer. **Publications:** The Moral Disarmament of France: Education, Pacifism and Patriotism, 1914-1940, 2004. Contributor to journals. **Address:** California State University, 6000 J St., Sacramento, CA 95819-6056, U.S.A. **Online address:** msiegel@csus.edu

SIEGEL, Robert Anthony. American (born United States) **Genres:** Novels. **Career:** University of North Carolina, assistant professor of creative writing, associate professor, MFA coordinator. Writer. **Publications:** NOVELS: All the Money in the World, 1997; All Will Be Revealed, 2007. Contributor to periodicals. **Address:** c/o Geri Thoma, Markson Thoma Literary Agency, 44 Greenwich Ave., New York, NY 10011-8347, U.S.A. **Online address:** robert@robertanthonysiegel.com

SIEGELBAUM, Lewis H. American (born United States), b. 1949. **Genres:** History, Politics/Government. **Career:** La Trobe University, Department of History, lecturer, 1976-80, senior lecturer, 1980-83; Michigan State University, Department of History, assistant professor, 1983-85, associate professor, 1985-88, professor, 1988-, chair of department, 1994-2004, associate chairperson and graduate director, 1995-98; University of Michigan, Department of History, visiting associate professor, 1986; University of California at Los Angeles, Department of History, visiting professor, 1998; école des hautes études en sciences sociales, research professor, 2005; Netherlands Institute for Advanced Study in the Humanities and Social Sciences, fellow, 2007-08; Université de Toulouse, visiting professor, 2007. Writer. **Publications:** The Politics of Industrial Mobilization in Russia, 1914-1917: A Study of the War-Industries Committees, 1983; Stakhanovism and the Politics of Productivity in the USSR, 1935-1941, 1988; (with T.H. Friedgut) Soviet Miners' Strike, July 1989: Perestroika from Below, 1990; The Soviet State and Society between Revolutions, 1918-1929, 1992; (ed.) Borders of Socialism: Private Spheres of Soviet Russia, 2006; Cars for Comrades: The Life of the Soviet Automobile, 2008; The Faustian Bargain of the Soviet Automobile, 2008. CO-EDITOR: (with W.O. McCagg) Disabled in the Soviet Union: Past and Present, Theory and Practice, 1989; (with W.G. Rosenberg) Social Dimensions of Soviet Industrialization, 1993; (with R.G. Suny) Making Workers Soviet: Power, Class and Identity, 1994; (with D.J. Walkowitz) Workers of the Donbass Speak: Survival and Identity in the New Ukraine, 1989-1992, 1995; (with A. Sokolov) Stalinism as a Way of Life: A Narrative in Documents, 2000, rev. ed., 2004. **Address:** Department of History, Michigan State University, 304 Morrill Hall, East Lansing, MI 48824, U.S.A. **Online address:** siegelba@msu.edu

SIEGELSON, Kim L. American (born United States), b. 1962?. **Genres:** Children's Non-fiction, History. **Career:** Author. **Publications:** FOR YOUNG READERS: The Terrible, Wonderful Tellin' at Hog Hammock, 1996; In the Time of the Drums, 1999; Escape South, 2000; Honey Bea, 2003; Dancing the Ring Shout!, 2003; Trembling Earth, 2004. **Address:** c/o Publicity Department, Philomel Books, 375 Hudson St., New York, NY 10014, U.S.A. **Online address:** ksiegelson@earthlink.net

SIEGFRIED, Tom. American (born United States), b. 1950. **Genres:** Physics. **Career:** Fort Worth Press, business and science writer, 1974-75; Texas Christian University, journalism faculty, 1979-83; Dallas Morning News, science editor, 1985-2004; Why Files, columnist; University of Wisconsin, science journalist-in-residence, 1992; Council for the Advancement of Science Writing, editor-in-chief, secretary, board director, 1999-; freelance science writer, 2004-; Science News, editor in chief, 2008-. **Publications:** The Bit and the Pendulum: From Quantum Computing to M Theory-The New Physics of Information, 2000; Strange Matters: Undiscovered Ideas at the Frontiers of Space and Time, 2002; A Beautiful Math: John Nash, Game Theory, and the Modern Quest for a Code of Nature, 2006. Contributor to periodicals. **Address:** Council for the Advancement of Science Writing, PO Box 910, Hedgesville, WV 25427, U.S.A. **Online address:** tsiegfried@nasw.org

SIEGMUND, Stefanie. American (born United States) **Genres:** History. **Career:** University of Florida, Department of History, assistant professor, Samuel Melton legislative professor in Jewish studies; University of Michigan, Department of History and Frankel Center for Judaic Studies, associate professor, 2005-, professor, International Institute, assistant professor; The Jewish Theological Seminary, associate professor of Jewish history. Writer. **Publications:** The Medici State and the Ghetto of Florence: The Construction of an Early Modern Jewish Community, 2006. **Address:** The Jewish Theological Seminary, 3080 Broadway, New York, NY 10027-4650, U.S.A. **Online address:** stsiegmund@jtsa.edu

SIEMENS, Alfred H. Canadian (born Canada), b. 1932. **Genres:** Geography, History, Adult Non-fiction, Earth Sciences, Agriculture/Forestry. **Career:** University of British Columbia, acting head of department, professor of geography, 1962-98, professor emeritus, 1998-; Xalapa Institute of Ecology, visiting investigator, 1998-. Writer. **Publications:** (Ed.) The Lower Fraser Valley: Evolution of a Cultural Landscape, 1968; The Americas: A Comparative Introduction to Geography, 1977; Special Issue: The Rio Hondo Project, an Investigation of the Maya of Northern Belize, 1977; Tierra Configurada, 1989; Between the Summit and the Sea: Central Veracruz in the Nineteenth Century, 1990; A Favored Place: San Juan River Wetlands, Central Veracruz, A.D. 500 to the Present, 1998; (co-author) Tabasco Prehispánico, 2001. Contributor to periodicals. **Address:** Department of Geography, University of British Columbia, 1984 W Mall, Vancouver, BC V6T 1Z2, Canada. **Online address:** asiemens@interchange.ubc.ca

SIGGINS, Lorna. Irish/Scottish (born Scotland), b. 1958. **Genres:** Biography, Adult Non-fiction, inspirational/Motivational Literature. **Career:** Irish Times, senior reporter and marine correspondent, 1988-97, western and marine correspondent, 1997-. Journalist. **Publications:** Everest Calling: Ascent of the Dark Side: The Mallory-Irvine Ridge, 1994; The Woman Who Took Power in the Park: Mary Robinson, President of Ireland, 1990-97, 1997; Mayday! Mayday!: Heroic Air-Sea Rescues in Irish Waters, 2004; Once Upon a Time in the West: The Corrib Gas Controversary, 2010. **Address:** c/o Jonathan Williams, 2 The Mews, 10 Sandycove Ave. W, Sandycove, DU 2, Ireland. **Online address:** lsiggins@irishtimes.com

SIGGINS, Maggie. Canadian (born Canada), b. 1942. **Genres:** Documentaries/Reportage, Biography, Autobiography/Memoirs, History. **Career:** Toronto Telegram, reporter; University of Regina, instructor of journalism, Max Bell chair in journalism, 1983-84; CBC Radio, reporter; New China News Agency, staff; 4 Square Entertainment Ltd., vice-president; Beijing Broadcast Institute, instructor. Author, journalist, broadcaster and filmmaker. **Publications:** A Guide to Eastern Ski Resorts, 1969; Bassett: John Bassett's Forty Years in Politics, Publishing, Business and Sports, 1979; Brian and the Boys: The Story of a Gang Rape, 1984; A Canadian Tragedy: JoAnn and Colin Thatcher, a Story of Love and Hate, 1985; Revenge of the Land: A Century of Greed, Tragedy and Murder on a Saskatchewan Farm, 1991; Louis Riel: A Life of Revolution, 1994; In Her Own Time: A Class Reunion Inspires a Cultural History of Women, 2000; Bitter Embrace: White Society's Assault on the Woodland Cree, 2005; Marie-Anne: The Extraordinary Life of Louis

Riel's Grandmother, 2008; Pelican Narrows in 1924, forthcoming. Contributor to periodicals. **Address:** 4 Square Entertainment Ltd., 39 Borden St., Toronto, ON M5S 2M8, Canada. **Online address:** msiggins@4square.ca

SIJIE, Dai. French/Chinese (born China), b. 1954. **Genres:** Plays/Screenplays, Psychiatry. **Career:** Film director and writer. **Publications:** Balzac et la petite tailleuse chinoise, 2000; Le Complexe de Di, 2003; Par une nuit où la lune ne s'est pas levée, 2007; Trois vies chinoises, 2011. Contributor to periodicals. **Address:** c/o Author Mail, Knopf Publishing, 299 Park Ave., New York, NY 10171-0002, U.S.A.

SIKÉLIANÒS, Eleni. American (born United States) **Genres:** Poetry. **Career:** Teachers & Writers Collaborative, poet-in-residence; Bard College, Clemente Program, teacher; University of Denver, Department of English, associate professor, director of creative writing; Princeton University, Seeger fellow. **Publications:** To Speak While Dreaming, 1993; The Book of Tendons, 1997; Earliest Worlds, vol. I: Blue Guide, vol. II: Of Sun, Of History, Of Seeing, 2001. CHAPBOOKS: Gold Trout, 1994; Poetics of the X, 1995; Poetics of the Exclamation Point: A Book of Ease, 1995; Color, 1998; The Lover's Numbers, 1998; From Blue Guide, 1999; The Book of Jon, 2004; The California Poem, 2004; Body Clock: Poems, 2008; The Blue Coat Narrative. Contributor to periodicals. **Address:** Department of English, University of Denver, 487D Sturm Hall, 2000 E Asbury Ave., Denver, CO 80208, U.S.A. **Online address:** esikelia@du.edu

SIKES, Gini. American (born United States), b. 1957. **Genres:** Novels. **Career:** Metropolis, senior editor and staff writer, 1983-86; Mademoiselle, entertainment editor and senior writer, 1986-88; freelance writer, 1988-; Columbia University, adjunct writing professor; Voice of America Radio, freelance correspondent, 2005-. **Publications:** 8 Ball Chicks: A Year in the Violent World of Girl Gangsters, 1997. Contributor to magazines and newspapers. **Address:** c/o Laurie Fox, Linda Chester and Associates, 2342 Shattuck Ave., Ste. 506, Berkeley, CA 94704-1517, U.S.A. **Online address:** eightballchicks@earthlink.net

SIKES, Melvin P. (Melvin Patterson Sikes). American (born United States), b. 1917. **Genres:** Race Relations, Social Sciences, Law, Cultural/Ethnic Topics. **Career:** Veterans Counseling Service, director, 1945-47; Wilberforce University, College of Liberal Arts and Sciences, dean, 1950-52; Bishop College, administrative dean, 1952-55; Veterans Administration Hospital, trainee in clinical and counseling psychology, 1959, clinical and counseling psychologist, 1960-68; Baylor University of Medicine, clinical assistant professor of psychiatry, 1961-68; United States Department of Justice, community relations specialist, 1968-69; University of Texas, professor of educational psychology, 1969-83, professor emeritus of educational psychology, 1983-, program director of research and development for teacher education, 1978-81; Wiley College, visiting professor; National Drug Education Center, faculty. Writer. **Publications:** The Administration of Injustice, 1975; (with J.R. Feagin) Living with Racism: The Black Middle-Class Experience, 1994. Contributor to books and journals. **Address:** University of Texas, 1616 Guadalupe St., Austin, TX 78701-1204, U.S.A. **Online address:** msikes@austin.rr.com

SIKES, Melvin Patterson. See **SIKES, Melvin P.**

SIKKINK, Kathryn. American (born United States), b. 1955. **Genres:** Business/Trade/Industry, Economics, Civil Liberties/Human Rights. **Career:** Washington Office on Latin America, staff associate, 1979-81; Columbia University, teaching assistant, 1983-84; Yale University, Center for International and Area Studies, visiting fellow, 1986-88; University of Minnesota, Department of Political Science, assistant professor, 1988-94, associate professor, 1994-98, professor, 1998-2001, Arleen Carlson professor of political science, 2001-07, distinguished McKnight university professor, 2005-09, regents professor of political science, 2006-, McKnight presidential chair in political science, 2008-, Law School, affiliate faculty, 2001-. Writer. **Publications:** Ideas and Institutions: Developmentalism in Brazil and Argentina, 1991; (with M.E. Keck) Activists beyond Borders: Advocacy Networks in International Politics, 1998; (ed. with T. Risse and S.C. Ropp) The Power of Human Rights: International Norms and Domestic Change, 1999; (ed. with S. Khagram and J.V. Riker) Restructuring World Politics: Transnational Social Movements, Networks, and Norms, 2002; Mixed Signals: U.S. Human Rights Policy and Latin America, 2004; Justice Cascade: How Human Rights Prosecutions are Changing World Politics, 2011. CONTRIBUTOR: Ideas and Foreign Policy, 1993; The International Dimensions of Democratization: Europe and the Americas, 1996; International Development and the Social Sciences: Essays in the History and Politics of Knowledge, 1997; Global Prescriptions: The Production, Exportation and Importation of a New Legal Orthodoxy, 2002; The Judicialization of Politics in Latin America, 2005. Contributor to periodicals and journals. **Address:** Department of Political Science, University of Minnesota, 1414 Social Sciences Bldg., 267 19th Ave. S, Minneapolis, MN 55455, U.S.A. **Online address:** sikkink@umn.edu

SIKORSKI, Radek (Tomasz). Polish (born Poland), b. 1963. **Genres:** Adult Non-fiction, History. **Career:** National Review, journalist and correspondent, 1986-89; Spectator, journalist and correspondent, 1986-89; National Review, roving correspondent, 1989-; Warsaw Sunday Telegraph, newspaper correspondent, 1990-91; Poland News Corporation Inc., reporter, 1990-92; deputy defense minister for Poland, 1992; Foreign Affairs of Poland, deputy minister, 1998-2001; Polish Solidarity Party, secretary of foreign affairs, 1999-2002; American Enterprise Institute, resident fellow, 2002-05; New Atlantic Initiative, resident fellow and executive director, 2002-05; National Defense of Poland, minister, 2005-07. **Publications:** NONFICTION: Moscow's Afghan War: Soviet Motives and Western Interests, 1990; Dust of the Saints: A Journey to Heart in Time of War in US as Dust of the Saints: A Journey through War-Torn Afghanistan, 1990; Full Circle: A Homecoming to Free Poland, 1997 in UK as The Polish House: An Intimate History of Poland, 1998; Strefa Zdekomunizowana: Wywiad Rzeka Z Radkiem Sikorskim, 2007. Contributor to periodicals. **Address:** National Review, 150 E 35th St., New York, NY 10016, U.S.A.

SILBER, John (Robert). American (born United States), b. 1926. **Genres:** Education, Law, Philosophy, Humanities. **Career:** Yale University, instructor in philosophy, 1952-55; University of Texas, assistant professor, 1955-62, professor of philosophy, 1962-70, chairman, 1962-67, College of Arts and Sciences, dean, 1967-70; University of Bonn, visiting professor, 1960; Kant-Studien, associate editor, 1968; Boston University, College of Arts and Sciences, president, 1971-96, chancellor, 1996-2003, university professor, professor of philosophy and international relations, president emeritus, 2003-, School of Law, professor; Massachusetts Board of Education, head, 1996-99. Writer. **Publications:** The Ethical Significance of Kant's Religion, 1960; (ed.) Religion within the Limits of Reason Alone, 1960; Being and Doing: A Study of Status Responsibility and Voluntary Responsibility, 1967; Soul Politics and Political Morality, 1968; The Thicket of Law and the Marsh of Conscience, 1974; Democracy: Its Counterfeits and Its Promises, 1976; The Past, Present and Future of American Higher Education, 1978; Education at the Antipodes: Problems of the American University, 1989; Straight Shooting: What's Wrong with America and How to Fix It (education), 1989; Higher Education in America: Its Problems and its Promise, 1989; 1st Amerika zu retten?, 1992; From Thebes to Auschwitz: Moral Responsibility in Sophocles and Wiesel, 1998; Procedure or Dogma: The Core of Liberalism, 1999; Architecture of the Absurd: How Genius Disfigured a Practical Art, 2007; Kant's Ethics: The Good, Freedom and the Will, 2012. **Address:** Office of President Emeritus, Boston University, 73 Bay State Rd., Boston, MA 02215-1812, U.S.A.

SILBER, Lee T. American (born United States), b. 1965. **Genres:** Business/Trade/Industry, Self Help. **Career:** Lee Silber Designs Hawaii, founder and owner, 1986-87; Waves 7 Wheels Surfcenters, founder and owner, 1987-92; Tales from the Tropics Publishing Co., founder and publisher, 1992-2004; SkillPath Seminars, lead trainer, 1995-2000; Creative Lee Speaking, founder, principal and lecturer, 1998-; Environmental Lee Speaking, founder and principal, 2002-; Deep Impact Corporate Training, founder and lead trainer. Writer. **Publications:** Successful San Diegans: The Stories behind San Diego's Most Successful People both Past and Present, 1993; Time Management for the Creative Person, 1998; Aim First! Get Focused and Fired Up to Follow Through on Your Goals, 1999; Career Management for the Creative Person: Right-Brain Techniques to Run Your Professional Life and Build Your Business, 1999; Self-Promotion for the Creative Person: Get the Word Out about Who You Are and What You Do, 2001; Money Management for the Creative Person: Right Brain Strategies to Build Your Bank Account and Find the Financial Freedom to Create, 2002; Summer Stories, 2002; Organizing from the Right Side of the Brain: A Creative Approach to Getting Organized, 2004; (contrib.) Chicken Soup For The Beach Lover's Soul, 2007; (with A. Chapman) Rock To Riches, 2008; (with A. Chapman and L. Krall) The Wild Idea Club, 2009; (with M. Metz) Bored Games: Entertain Your Kids With Things From Your Pocket and Purse, 2009; Creative Careers, 2010; Ripple Effect,

2011; No Brown M&Ms, 2011; Show and Tell Organizing, 2011. **Address:** Creative Lee Speaking, 822 Redondo Ct., San Diego, CA 92109, U.S.A. **Online address:** leesilber@earthlink.net

SILBER, Nina. American (born United States), b. 1959. **Genres:** History, Sex, Social Sciences, Military/Defense/Arms Control. **Career:** University of California, Project on American Culture, research assistant, 1984-85; University of Delaware, Department of History, visiting assistant professor, 1989-90; Boston University, Department of History, assistant professor, 1990-96, associate professor, 1996-2007, professor, 2007-, director of graduate studies, 2000-02, 2008-09, director of undergraduate studies, 2005-07, director of women's studies, 1994-96, 1998-99; Charles University, Fulbright Program, senior lecturer, 1999-2000; Organization of American Historians, distinguished lecturer, 2001-06. Writer. **Publications:** (Ed. with C. Clinton) Divided Houses: Gender and the Civil War, 1992; The Romance of Reunion: Northerners and the South, 1865-1900, 1993; (ed. with M.B. Sievens) Yankee Correspondence: Civil War Letters between New England Soldiers and the Home Front, 1996; Landmarks of the Civil War, 2003; Daughters of the Union: Northern Women fight the Civil War, 2005; (ed. with C. Clinton) Battle Scars: Gender and Sexuality in the American Civil War, 2006; Gender and the Sectional Conflict, 2008; America Transformed: Blue, Gray, and Black: Essays on the Civil War Era, 2009; The Civil War in American Life, 1929-1941, forthcoming. Contributor to periodicals. **Address:** Department of History, Boston University, Rm. 408, 226 Bay State Rd., Boston, MA 02215-1403, U.S.A. **Online address:** nsilber@bu.edu

SILBER, Sherman J(ay). American (born United States), b. 1941. **Genres:** Medicine/Health. **Career:** Stanford University, surgical intern, 1966-67; U.S. Public Health Service in Alaska, gynecology assistant, 1967-69; University of Michigan, researcher in nephrology, 1969-70; University of Michigan, researcher in urology, 1970-73; University of Melbourne, Department of Surgery, assistant surgeon, 1973-74; Veterans Administration Hospital, chief of urology, 1974-76; University of California Medical Center, assistant professor of urology, Division of Urology, vice-chairman; University of California Medical Center, assistant professor of urology, Division of Urology, vice-chairman, 1974-76; St. Luke's Hospital, consulting urologist, urologist and reproductive microsurgeon; The Infertility Center of Saint Louis, staff, director, IVF Program, director; Dutch-speaking Brussels Free University, consultant in IVF; Tel Hashomer Hospital, consultant in male infertility; New Hope Infertility Center, associate director; Kato Ladies Clinic, consultant; Massachusetts Institute of Technology, Whitehead Institute, consultant; ABC News, consultant; NPR St. Louis, consultant; KMOX Radio, consultant; FOX News, consultant; British Broadcasting Corp., consultant; Wall Street Journal, consultant; St. Louis Zoo, consultant; Tulsa Zoo, consultant; National Zoo, consultant. Writer. **Publications:** Transurethral Resection, 1977; (ed.) Microsurgery, 1979; How to Get Pregnant, 1980; The Male: From Infancy to Old Age, 1981; Reproductive Infertility Microsurgery in the Male and Female, 1984; How to Get Pregnant, 1980; How Not to Get Pregnant: Your Guide to Simple, Reliable Contraception, 1987; How to Get Pregnant with the New Technology, 1991, rev. ed., 1998. **Address:** The Infertility Center of St. Louis, St. Luke's Hospital, 224 S Woods Mill Rd., Ste. 730, St. Louis, MO 63017, U.S.A.

SILBERMAN, Jerome. See **WILDER, Gene.**

SILBERMAN, Marc (D.). American (born United States), b. 1948. **Genres:** Literary Criticism And History, Film, Theatre, Novels. **Career:** Indiana University, visiting assistant professor of German, 1975-76; University of Texas, assistant professor of German, 1976-86, associate professor of German, 1986-88; University of Wisconsin, associate professor of German, 1988-93, professor of German, 1993-, Department of Theater and Drama, affiliate professor, Vilas fellow, 1995-97, department chair, 1999-2003, 2009-10, Center for German and European Studies, director, 2008-10. Writer. **Publications:** Literature of the Working World: A Study of the Industrial Novel in East Germany, 1976; Heiner Müller, 1980; (ed.) Zum Roman in der DDR, 1980; German Cinema: Texts in Context, 1995; (ed. with J. Hermand) Contentious Memories: Looking Back at the GDR, 1998; (ed. with J. Hermand) Rethinking Peter Weiss, 2000; (ed. with P. Cooke) Screening War: Perspectives on German Suffering, 2010; (ed.) German Wall: Fallout in Europe, 2011. Contributor to journals. Works appear in anthologies. **Address:** Department of German, University of Wisconsin, 818 Van Hise Hall, 1220 Linden Dr., Madison, WI 53706-1557, U.S.A. **Online address:** mdsilber@wisc.edu

SILBEY, David. (David J. Silbey). American (born United States), b. 1968. **Genres:** History, Military/Defense/Arms Control. **Career:** Alvernia College, associate professor of history; North Carolina State University, faculty; Duke University, faculty; Bowdoin College, senior fellow; Cornell University, senior lecturer, Cornell in Washington Program, associate director. Writer and historian. **Publications:** The British Working Class and Enthusiasm for War, 1914-1916, 2005; (as David J. Silbey) A War of Frontier and Empire: The Philippine-American War, 1899-1902, 2007; (as David J. Silbey) The Boxer Rebellion and the Great Game in China, 2012. Contributor to books and periodicals. **Address:** Cornell University, B20 Day Hall, Ithaca, NY 14853-2801, U.S.A. **Online address:** ds90@cornell.edu

SILBEY, David J. See **SILBEY, David.**

SILBIGER, Alexander. American/Dutch (born Netherlands), b. 1935. **Genres:** Music. **Career:** University of Chicago, teaching assistant, 1956-57; University of Miami, research instructor in physics, 1957-58; Columbia University, research assistant, 1959-60; Cambridge Acoustical Associates, staff engineer, 1960-62, senior scientist, 1962-68; Longy School of Music, instructor, 1962-72; Northeastern University, lecturer, 1965; Brandeis University, Department of Music, teaching assistant, 1970, lecturer, 1972-74; University of Wisconsin, School of Music, instructor, 1974-76, assistant professor, 1976-80, associate professor, 1980-85, professor, 1985, chair of music history and ethnomusicology area, 1976-77, 1981-82, 1983-84; Duke University, visiting associate professor, 1984-85, professor of music, 1985-2002, director of graduate studies, 1986-88, 1995-96, 1999-2000, chair of department, 1988-93, professor emeritus, 2002-. Writer. **Publications:** Italian Manuscript Sources of Seventeenth-Century Keyboard Music, 1980; Mathias Weckmann: Sacred Concertos, 1984. EDITOR: John Reid, Sonata for Recorder (or Flute) and Keyboard, 1968; Four Sacred Concertos, 1984; Frescobaldi Studies, 1987; Seventeenth-Century Keyboard Music, 28 vols., 1987-89; Four Enharmonic Madrigals: For Four Voices, 1990; Keyboard Music before 1700, 1995, 2nd ed., 2004; Fiori Musicali, 2010. Contributor of articles to journals. **Address:** Department of Music, Duke University, Rm. 059 Mary Duke Biddle Bldg., PO Box 90665, Durham, NC 27708-0665, U.S.A. **Online address:** alexander.silbiger@duke.edu

SILCOTT, Loma G. Davies. American (born United States), b. 1934?. **Genres:** Food And Wine, Gerontology/Senior Issues, How-to Books, Theology/Religion, Travel/Exploration, Writing/Journalism, Young Adult Nonfiction, Reference, Reference. **Career:** High school, teacher and counselor, 1970-87; State Association of Kansas Watersheds, staff writer, 1988-94; Cook's Corner, columnist, 1988-96; Wamego Smoke Signal, writer, 1988-96; Topeka Capital Journal, correspondent, 1990-94; Oglala-Lakota Indian College, English writing associate professor, 1995-. Freelance writer. **Publications:** The Nuts and Bolts Writer's Manual, 1991; 201 Happy Hints, 1991; Cook's Corner Recipe Collection, 1991; Senior Sense: 42 Ways to Improve Your Life, 1995. Contributor to magazines. **Address:** 1786 N Neel St., Rapid City, SD 57703, U.S.A. **Online address:** lomasilcott@cs.com

SILER, Jenny. (Alex Carr). American (born United States), b. 1971?. **Genres:** Novels, Mystery/Crime/Suspense, Young Adult Fiction. **Career:** Tutor and writer. **Publications:** Easy Money, 1998; Iced, 2000; Shot: A Novel, 2002; Flashback, 2004; (as Alex Carr) An Accidental American, 2007; (as Alex Carr) Prince of Bagram Prison: a Novel, 2008; (with M.J. Connnor) The Art of the Heist: Confessions of a Master Art Thief, Rock 'n' Roller and Prodigal Son, 2009. **Address:** c/o Dan Conaway, Writer's House, 21 W 26th St., New York, NY 10010, U.S.A. **Online address:** jenny@jennysiler.com

SILESKY, Barry. American (born United States), b. 1949. **Genres:** Novellas/Short Stories, Poetry, Biography, Art/Art History. **Career:** School of the Art Institute, adjunct associate professor, adjunct professor, 1984-, visiting professor, 1984-; Urban Gateways, poet, 1984-98; Another Chicago Magazine, editor. **Publications:** Twin Cities Family Fun Guide, 1981; In the Ruins (prose poetry), 1983; Ferlinghetti: The Artist in His Time, 1990; The New Tenants (poetry), 1991; One Thing That Can Save Us (prose poetry), 1994; Greatest Hits (poetry), 2002; John Gardner: Literary Outlaw (biography), 2004; This Disease (poems), 2006. **Address:** c/o Nat Sobel, Sobel Weber Associates Inc., 146 E 19th St., New York, NY 10003-2404, U.S.A. **Online address:** bsiles@artic.edu

SILIOTTI, Alberto. Italian (born Italy), b. 1950?. **Genres:** Archaeology/Antiquities. **Career:** Egypt Exploration Society, correspondent. Journalist, photographer and documentarian. **Publications:** Viaggiatori veneti alla scoperta dell'Egitto: itinerari di storia e arte, 1985; Magia in Egitto ai tempi dei faraoni: atti, convegno internazionale di studi, Milano, 29-31 ottobre 1985, 1987; (with A. Roccati) La Magia in Egitto ai tempi dei faraoni, 1987; Nefertari e la valle delle regine, 1993; Egypt: Splendors of an Ancient Civilization, 1996; (ed. with M. Forte) Virtual Archaeology: Re-Creating Ancient Worlds, 1997; Discovery of Ancient Egypt, 1998; Egypt Lost and Found: Explorers and Travelers on the Nile, 1999; Valley of the Kings and the Theban Tombs, 2000; Egypt: Temples, Men and Gods, 2000; (ed.) The Dwellings of Eternity, 2000; (ed.) Belzoni's Travels: Narrative of the Operations and Recent Discoveries in Egypt and Nubia, 2000; Valley of the Kings and the Theban Tombs, 2000; Abu Simbel and the Nubian Temples, 2000; Alexandria and the North Coast, 2002; Islamic Cairo, 2002; Aswan, 2002; Luxor, Karnak and the Theban Temples, 2002; Pyramids, 2002; Sinai, 2002; Fayoum and Wadi El-Rayan, 2003; (ed.) Hidden Treasures of Antiquity, 2006. **Address:** Harry N. Abrams Inc., 115 W 18th St., 6th Fl., New York, NY 10011, U.S.A.

SILJAK, Ana. Canadian (born Canada), b. 1967. **Genres:** History. **Career:** Northwestern University, faculty; University of Chicago, faculty; Queen's University, assistant professor of history. Writer and historian. **Publications:** (Ed.) The Balkans, 2001; (ed. with P. Ther) Redrawing Nations: Ethnic Cleansing in East-Central Europe, 1944-1948, 2001; Angel of Vengeance: The Girl Assassin, the Governor of St. Petersburg, and Russia's Revolutionary World, 2008. Contributor to books and journals. **Address:** Department of History, Queen's University, Rm. 212, Watson Hall, 49 Bader Ln., Kingston, ON K7L 3N6, Canada. **Online address:** siljaka@queensu.ca

SILJANDER, Mark D. American (born United States), b. 1951. **Genres:** Autobiography/Memoirs. **Career:** United States Congress, member of house of representatives, 1981-87; United Nations General Assembly, alternate representative, 1987-88; Global Strategics Inc. (a consulting firm), president. Writer, politician, business executive, commentator and ambassador. **Publications:** (With J.D. Mann) A Deadly Misunderstanding: A Congressman's Quest to Bridge the Muslim-Christian Divide (memoir), 2008. **Address:** Reston, VA , U.S.A. **Online address:** info@adeadlymisunderstanding.com

SILK, Gerald. American (born United States), b. 1947. **Genres:** Art/Art History, History, Cultural/Ethnic Topics, Photography. **Career:** University of Virginia, graduate teaching assistant, 1970-74, Department of Art History, instructor, 1974; Columbia University, lecturer, 1975, assistant professor of art history, 1975-83; University of Pennsylvania, assistant professor of art history, 1983-87; Center for Advanced Study in the Visual Arts, senior fellow, 1987-88; Temple University, Tyler School of Art, Department of Art History, associate professor, 1992-94, professor of modern and contemporary art, 2000-, chair, 2004-. Writer. **Publications:** (Contrib.) The Great Drawings of All Time: The Twentieth Century, 1979; Museums Discovered: The Wadsworth Atheneum, 1982; (contrib.) The Automobile in American Culture, 1982; (co-author) The Automobile and Culture, 1984; Investigations/Robert Colescott: The Artist and His Model, 1984; (with P. Colombo) Aeropittura Futurista: Images of Flight in Italian Art from 1913 to 1942, 1989; Reva Urban: Shaping Things to Come, 1991; Ralph Goings: A Retrospective View of Watercolors, 1972- 1994, 1994; Susan Fenton: Hand Painted Photographs, 2002. Contributor to books. **Address:** Department of Art History, Tyler School of Art, Temple University, 2001 N 13th St., Ste. 211, Philadelphia, PA 19122, U.S.A. **Online address:** gerald.silk@temple.edu

SILK, Joseph (Ivor). British (born England), b. 1942. **Genres:** Astronomy, Sciences. **Career:** Cambridge University, research fellow, 1968-69; Princeton University, research associate, 1969-70; University of California, assistant professor, associate professor, 1970-78, professor of astronomy, 1978-; Miller Foundation of Basic Research, Miller professor, 1980-81; University of Oxford, Department of Physics, Savilian professor of astronomy and head, New College, fellow. Writer. **Publications:** The Big Bang, 1980, 3rd ed., 2001; (with I. Appenzeller and J. Lequeux) Star Formation, 1980; (with J.D. Barrow) The Left Hand of Creation, 1983; Cosmic Enigmas, 1994; (ed. with N. Vittorio) Galaxy Formation, 1994; A Short History of the Universe, 1994; On the Shores of the Unknown: A Short History of the Universe, 2005; The Infinite Cosmos: Questions from the Frontiers of Cosmology, 2006; Horizons of Cosmology: Exploring Worlds Seen and Unseen, 2009; (ed. with V. Antonuccio-Delogu) AGN Feedback in Galaxy Formation: Proceedings of the Workshop Held in Vulcano, Italy, May 18-22, 2008, 2011. **Address:** Department of Physics, University of Oxford, Rm. 715, Denys Wilkinson Bldg., Keble Rd., Oxford, OX OX1 3RH, England. **Online address:** silk@astro.ox.ac.uk

SILL, Isabel Shehadi. Also writes as Isabel Sharpe. American (born United States), b. 1962?. **Genres:** Novels. **Career:** Writer. **Publications:** AS ISABEL SHARPE: ROMANCE NOVELS: The Wild Side, 2001; Hot on His Heels, 2002; A Taste of Fantasy, 2003; Take Me Twice, 2004; Before I Melt Away, 2004; Thrill Me, 2005; All I Want, 2005; What Have I Done for Me Lately?, 2006; Women on the Edge of a Nervous Breakthrough, 2007; Indulge Me, 2008; My Wildest Ride, 2008; As Good as It Got, 2008; No Holding Back, 2009; (with S. Sala and L. Cardillo) A Mother's Heart, 2009; Surprise Me--, 2010; Knit in Comfort, 2010; While She was Sleeping..., 2010; Hot to the Touch, 2011. AS ISABEL SHARPE: OMNIBUS NOVELS: (with C. Linz) The Cowboy Finds a Bride; The Way We Weren't, 2000; (with C. Linz) The Lawman Gets Lucky/Beauty and the Bet, 2000; (with C. Alexander) Tryst of Fate/Counterfeit Cowboy, 2000; (with J. Diamond) Excuse Me?, Whose Baby?, 2001; One Fine Prey/Two Catch a Fox, 2002. AS ISABEL SHARPE: ANTHOLOGIES: Windfall, 2003; (with J. Sullivan and J. Kistler) Always a Bridesmaid, 2004; (with J. Denison and J. LaBrecque) Secret Santa: A Naughty but Nice Christmas Collection, 2006 as Secret Santa: He'd Better Watch Out!/The Nights before Christmas/Mistletoe Madness, 2006. **Address:** Harlequin Books, 225 Duncan Mill Rd., 6th Fl., Don Mills, ON M3B 3K9, Canada. **Online address:** isabel@isabelsharpe.com

SILL, John. American (born United States), b. 1947. **Genres:** Humor/Satire, Illustrations, Natural History, Environmental Sciences/Ecology. **Career:** Freelance artist and illustrator, 1971-; Viking Penguin, bird calendar artist, 1978-; freelance writer, 1987-; South Carolina Wildlife Magazine, illustrator, 1991-; Institute for Field Ornithology, Field Sketching and Bird Illustration Workshop, instructor. **Publications:** SELF-ILLUSTRATED: (with B.L. Sill and C.P. Sill) A Field Guide to Little-Known and Seldom-Seen Birds of North America, 1988; (with B.L. Sill and C.P. Sill) Another Field Guide to Little-Known and Seldom-Seen Birds of North America, 1990. OTHERS: (with B.L. Sill and C.P. Sill) Beyond Birdwatching: More than There Is to Know about Birding: Ornipsychology, A Primer for Novices and Beginners Alike, 1993. Illustrator of books by others. **Address:** c/o Author Mail, Peachtree Publishers Ltd., 1700 Chattahoochee Ave., Atlanta, GA 30318-2112, U.S.A.

SILLIMAN, Matthew R. American (born United States), b. 1956. **Genres:** Novels. **Career:** Earlham College, visiting assistant professor of philosophy, 1985; North Adams State College, assistant professor of philosophy, 1986-93; Massachusetts College of Liberal Arts, faculty, 1986-, associate professor, 1993-2000, professor of philosophy, 2000-. Academician and writer. **Publications:** Sentience and Sensibility: A Conversation About Moral Philosophy, 2006. Contributor to periodicals. **Address:** Department of Philosophy, Massachusetts College of Liberal Arts, Rm. 6, 100 Porter St., 375 Church St., North Adams, MA 01247, U.S.A. **Online address:** m.silliman@mcla.edu

SILLS, Judith. American (born United States), b. 1948?. **Genres:** Human Relations/Parenting, How-to Books, Psychology, Self Help. **Career:** Clinical psychologist; Family Circle, contributing editor; O, The Oprah Magazine, staff. **Publications:** How to Stop Looking for Someone Perfect and Find Someone to Love, 1984; A Fine Romance: The Psychology of Successful Courtship, 1987; Excess Baggage: Getting out of Your Own Way, 1993; Biting the Apple: Women Getting Wise about Love, 1996 as Loving Men More, Needing Men Less, 1997; Comfort Trap, or, What if You're Riding a Dead Horse?, 2004; Getting Naked Again: Dating, Romance, Sex and Love When You've Been Divorced, Widowed, Dumped, or Distracted, 2009. Contributor to magazines. **Address:** c/o Joni Evans, William Morris Agency, 1325 Ave. of the Americas, New York, NY 10019-6047, U.S.A.

SILLS, Leslie (Elka). American (born United States), b. 1948. **Genres:** Art/Art History, Children's Non-fiction, Photography, Biography. **Career:** Artist and sculptor, 1970-; Children's Creative Clay Studio School, founder, director and teacher, 1975-; writer, 1986-. **Publications:** Inspirations: Stories about Women Artists, 1989; Visions: Stories about Women Artists, 1993; In Real Life: Six Women Photographers, 2000; From Rags to Riches: A History of Girl's Clothing in America, 2005. Contributor to books. **Address:** 38 St Paul St., Apt. 3, Brookline, MA 02446-6502, U.S.A. **Online address:** lesills38@gmail.com

SILMAN, Roberta. American (born United States), b. 1934. **Genres:** Novels, Novellas/Short Stories, Children's Fiction, Young Adult Fiction. **Career:**

Saturday Review Magazine, secretary and science editor, 1957-61; writer, 1961-. **Publications:** Somebody Else's Child, 1976; Blood Relations, 1977; Boundaries: A Novel, 1979; The Dream Dredger: A Novel, 1986; Beginning the World Again, 1990; Astronomers, 2002. FORTHCOMING: A Country of Their Own; Souls in Motion; Secrets and Shadows. Contributor to periodicals. **Address:** c/o Lois Wallace, Wallace & Sheil Agency Inc., 177 E 70th St., New York, NY 10021, U.S.A. **Online address:** rsilman@verizon.net

SILVA, Daniel (Joseph). American (born United States), b. 1960. **Genres:** Novels, Documentaries/Reportage, Literary Criticism And History, Young Adult Fiction. **Career:** Newspaper and television journalist; United Press International (UPI), foreign news editor, 1985-86; Cable News Network (CNN), executive producer of political news, 1988. **Publications:** NOVELS: The Unlikely Spy, 1996; The Mark of the Assassin, 1998; The Marching Season, 1999; Kill Artist: A Novel, 2000; The English Assassin, 2002; The Confessor, 2003; A Death in Vienna, 2004; Prince of Fire, 2005; The Messenger, 2006; The Secret Servant, 2007; Criado Secreto, 2007; Moscow Rules, 2008; Artista Da Morte, 2008; Defector, 2009; Rembrandt Affair, 2010; Portrait of a Spy, 2011. **Address:** Cable News Network, 247 CNN Ctr., Atlanta, GA 30303, U.S.A. **Online address:** daniel@danielsilvabooks.com

SILVA, Noenoe. (Noenoe K. Silva). American (born United States), b. 1954. **Genres:** History, Politics/Government, Humanities. **Career:** University of Hawaii, faculty, 2001-, associate professor; Bishop Museum, research affiliate, 2007-. Writer. **Publications:** Aloha Betrayed: Native Hawaiian Resistance to American Colonialism, 2004. Contributor to periodicals. **Address:** Department of Political Science, University of Hawaii, 2424 Maile Way, Saunders Hall, Rm. 640, Honolulu, HI 96822-2223, U.S.A. **Online address:** noenoe@hawaii.edu

SILVA, Noenoe K. *See* **SILVA, Noenoe.**

SILVA-CORVALÁN, Carmen. American (born United States) **Genres:** Language/Linguistics. **Career:** Universidad de Chile, assistant professor, 1970-73, associate professor of English, 1973-78, associate professor of linguistics, 1978-79; University of Southern California, Department of Spanish and Portuguese, assistant professor of Spanish, 1979-84, associate professor of Spanish, 1984-92, professor of Spanish, 1992-, department chair, 1999-2002, Department of Linguistics, associate professor of linguistics, 1978-79, professor of linguistics, 1995-. Writer. **Publications:** (Ed. with O. Jaeggli) Studies in Romance Linguistics, 1986; Sociolingüística: Teoría y análisis, 1989; (ed. with H.U. Cárdenas) Bilingüismo y adquisición del español, 1992; Language Contact and Change: Spanish in Los Angeles, 1994; (ed.) Spanish in Four Continents: Studies in Language Contact and Bilingualism, 1995; Sociolingüística y pragmática del español, 2001. **Address:** Department of Spanish and Portuguese, University of Southern California, THH 156G, 3501 Trousdale Pkwy., Los Angeles, CA 90089-0358, U.S.A. **Online address:** csilva@usc.edu

SILVER, Anna Krugovoy. American (born United States) **Genres:** Literary Criticism And History. **Career:** Mercer University, Department of English, assistant professor of English and interdisciplinary studies, 2000-, associate professor of English and interdisciplinary studies, director of women's and gender studies. Writer. **Publications:** Victorian Literature and the Anorexic Body, 2002. **Address:** Department of English, Mercer University, 210 Groover, 1400 Coleman Ave., Macon, GA 31207-0001, U.S.A. **Online address:** silver_ak@mercer.edu

SILVER, Brenda R. American (born United States), b. 1942. **Genres:** Literary Criticism And History, Young Adult Non-fiction, History. **Career:** Dartmouth College, associate professor of English, Mary Brinsmead Wheelock professor. Writer. **Publications:** Virginia Woolf's Reading Notebooks, 1983; (ed. with L.A. Higgins) Rape and Representation, 1991; Virginia Woolf Icon, 1999. Contributor of articles to periodicals. Works appear in anthologies. **Address:** Department of English, Dartmouth College, 206 Sanborn House, Ste. 207, Hanover, NH 03755, U.S.A. **Online address:** brenda.silver@dartmouth.edu

SILVER, Carole G(reta). American (born United States), b. 1937. **Genres:** Literary Criticism And History, Language/Linguistics, Social Sciences. **Career:** Vassar College, instructor in English, 1966; City University of New York, Hunter College, instructor in English, 1967-68; Yeshiva University, Stern College for Women, assistant professor, 1968-74, associate professor,

1974-82, professor of English, 1982-, Humanities Division, chairperson, 1983-. Writer. **Publications:** (Ed.) Studies in the Late Romances of William Morris, 1976; The Romance of William Morris, 1982; (co-ed.) The Golden Chain: Essays on William Morris and Pre-Raphaelitism, 1982; (with J.S. Neaman) Kind Words: A Thesaurus of Euphemisms, 1983, rev. ed., 1990; (ed. with F.S. Boos) Socialism and the Literary Artistry of William Morris, 1990; (ed. with K.A. Lochnan and E.E. Schoenherr) The Earthly Paradise: Arts and Crafts by William Morris and His Circle from Canadian Collections, 1993; Strange and Secret Peoples: Fairies and Victorian Consciousness, 1999; Sarah Heckford: A Lady Trader in the Transvaal, 2008. Contributor to journals. **Address:** Stern College for Women, Yeshiva University, 245 Lexington Ave., New York, NY 10016, U.S.A. **Online address:** csilver@ymail.yu.edu

SILVER, Harold. British (born England), b. 1928. **Genres:** Education, History, Sociology, Bibliography, Translations. **Career:** Hull College of Commerce, lecturer, 1956-58; Huddersfield College of Technology, lecturer, 1958-60; University of London, Chelsea College, senior lecturer, 1961-71, reader, 1972-73, professor of education, 1974-78; Bulmershe College of Higher Education, principal, 1978-86; University of Plymouth, visiting professor of higher education, 1992-, professor; Open University, visiting research professor, 1993-; Access-Ability Communications Technology, staff; Cued Speech Association, staff. Writer. **Publications:** (Trans.) V.I. Chuikov: The Beginning of the Road in US as The Battle for Stalingrad, 1963; The Concept of Popular Education, 1965; (with J. Ryder) Modern English Society: History and Structure, 1850-1970, 1970, 3rd ed., 1985; (with S.J. Teague) The History of British Universities 1800-1969, 1970; (with J. Lawson) A Social History of Education in England, 1973; (with P. Silver) The Education of the Poor: The History of a National School 1824-1974, 1974; English Education and the Radicals 1780-1850, 1975; Nothing but the Present, or Nothing but the Past?, 1977; Education and the Social Condition, 1980; Education as History: Interpreting Nineteenth-and Twentieth-Century Education, 1983; (with J. Brennan) A Liberal Vocationalism, 1988; A Higher Education: The Council for National Academic Awards and British Higher Education, 1964-89, 1990; Education, Change and the Policy Process, 1990; (with P. Silver) An Educational War on Poverty: American and British Policy-Making, 1960-1980, 1991; Student Feedback, 1992; External Examiners: Changing Roles?, 1993; Good Schools, Effective Schools: Judgements and their Histories, 1994; The External Examiner System: Possible Futures, 1995; (with P. Silver) Students: Changing Roles, Changing Lives, 1997; Researching Education, 1999; (with A. Hannan) Innovating in Higher Education: Teaching, Learning and Institutional Culture, 2000; Higher Education and Opinion Making in Twentieth-Century England, 2003; Tradition and Higher Education, 2007. EDITOR: (and intro.) Robert Owen on Education, 1969; Equal Opportunity in Education: A Reader in Social Class and Educational Opportunity, 1973; (with S.J. Teague) Chelsea College, a History, 1977; Poverty, Power and Authority in Education, 1981. **Address:** Cued Speech Association UK, 9 Jawbone Hill, Dartmouth, DN TQ6 9RW, England. **Online address:** harold.silver@plymouth.ac.uk

SILVER, Lee M(errill). American (born United States), b. 1952. **Genres:** Medicine/Health, Sciences, Biology. **Career:** Harvard University, Dunster House, tutor, 1975-77; National Endowment for the Humanities, fellow, 1978-79; Cornell University Graduate School of Medical Sciences, Sloan-Kettering Division, assistant professor of biology, 1979-80, Sloan-Kettering Institute for Cancer Research, postdoctoral fellow, 1977-80, associate, 1979-80; Cold Spring Harbor Laboratory, senior staff investigator, 1980-84, director, 1981-84; Yeshiva University, Albert Einstein College of Medicine, visiting assistant professor of genetics, 1980; State University of New York, assistant professor of genetics and adjunct assistant professor of microbiology, 1982-84; Princeton University, Department of Molecular Biology, assistant professor, 1984-87, associate professor, 1987-92, professor of molecular biology and public affairs, 1992-, Mathey College, faculty fellow, 1986-96, Department of Ecology and Evolutionary Biology, faculty associate, 1990-99, Forbes College, faculty fellow, 1998-, Woodrow Wilson School of Public and International Affairs, professor, 1999-; Institut Pasteur, visiting scientist, 1989-90; Université de Nice, Faculté de Médecine, visiting scientist, 1996-97. Writer. **Publications:** (Ed. with G.R. Martin and S. Strickland) Teratocarcinoma Stem Cells, 1983; Mouse Genetics: Concepts and Applications, 1995; Remaking Eden: Cloning and Beyond in a Brave New World, 1997, rev. ed. as Remaking Eden: How Genetic Engineering and Cloning will Transform the American Family, 1998; (co-author) Genetics: From Genes to Genomes with Genetics, 1999, 3rd ed. 2007; Challenging Nature: The Clash of Science and Spirituality at the New Frontiers of Life, 2006. **Address:** c/o Theresa Park, Sanford J. Greenburger Associates, 55 5th Ave., 15th Fl., New York, NJ 10003, U.S.A. **Online address:** lsilver@princeton.edu

SILVER, Marisa. American (born United States), b. 1960. **Genres:** Novellas/Short Stories, Novels, Young Adult Fiction. **Career:** Director and writer. **Publications:** Babe in Paradise (fiction), 2001; No Direction Home, 2005; The God of War, 2008; Alone With You: Stories, 2010. Contributor to periodicals. **Address:** Dunow, Carlson & Lerner Literary Agency Inc., 27 W 20th St., Ste. 1107, New York, NY 10011, U.S.A. **Online address:** marisa@marisasilver.com

SILVER, Norman. British/South African (born South Africa), b. 1946. **Genres:** Children's Fiction, Young Adult Fiction, Poetry, Young Adult Non-fiction, Children's Non-fiction, Education, Reference. **Career:** Information Technology Centre, teacher of computer programming, 1984-87; full-time writer, 1987-; Aldeburgh Poetry Festival, writer-in-residence, 1995. **Publications:** YOUNG ADULTS FICTION: An Eye for Colour, 1991; No Tigers in Africa, 1992; Python Dance, 1992; A Monkey's Wedding, 2000. POETRY: Words on a Faded T-Shirt, 1991; The Comic Shop, 1992; The Walkmen Have Landed, 1994; Choose Your Superhero, 1998. FOR CHILDREN: Cloud Nine, 1995; The Blue Horse, 1996; Temper Temper, 1999. **Address:** c/o Laura Cecil, 17 Alwyne Villas, London, GL N1 2HG, England. **Online address:** norman@storybook.demon.co.uk

SILVER, Peter Rhoads. American (born United States) **Genres:** Intellectual History. **Career:** Princeton University, assistant professor of history. Writer. **Publications:** Our Savage Neighbors: How Indian War Transformed Early America, 2007. **Address:** Department of History, Princeton University, 129 Dickinson Hall, Princeton, NJ 08544-1017, U.S.A. **Online address:** psilver@princeton.edu

SILVERBERG, Robert. Also writes as Lee Sebastian, David Osborne, Calvin M. Knox, Ivar Jorgenson, Robert Randall. American (born United States), b. 1935. **Genres:** Novellas/Short Stories, Science Fiction/Fantasy, Children's Fiction, Young Adult Fiction, Children's Non-fiction, History, Sciences, Biography, Biography. **Career:** Writer, 1955-. **Publications:** SCIENCE FICTION: Revolt on Alpha C (juvenile), 1955; Starmen's Quest, 1956; The Thirteenth Immortal, 1957; The Dawning Light, 1957; Master of Life and Death, 1957; The Shrouded Planet, 1957; Invaders from Earth, 1958; Aliens from Space, 1958; Invisible Barriers, 1958; Stepsons of Terra, 1958; Lest We Forget Thee, Earth, 1958; (as Ivar Jorgenson) Starhaven, 1958; The Planet Killers, 1959; The Plot Against Earth, 1959; Lost Race of Mars (juvenile), 1960; Collision Course, 1961; The Seed of Earth, 1962; Recalled to Life, 1962; Next Stop the Stars (short stories), 1962; The Silent Invaders, 1963; One of Our Asteroids Is Missing, 1963; Time of the Great Freeze, 1963; Regan's Planet, 1964; Godling, Go Home! (short stories), 1964; The Mask of Akhnaten, 1965; Conquerors from the Darkness (juvenile), 1965; To Worlds Beyond: Stories of Science Fiction, 1965; Needle in a Timestack (short stories), 1966; The Gate of Worlds (juvenile), 1967; To Open the Sky, 1967; Thorns, 1967; Those Who Watch, 1967; The Time-Hoppers, 1967; Planet of Death, 1967; Hawksbill Station, 1968 in UK as The Anvil of Time, 1969; The Masks of Time, 1968 in UK as Vornan-19, 1970; The Calibrated Alligator and Other Science Fiction Stories, 1969; Dimension Thirteen (short stories), 1969; Up the Line, 1969; Nightwings, 1969; Across a Billion Years (juvenile), 1969; The Man in the Maze (juvenile), 1969; Three Survived (juvenile), 1969; To Live Again, 1969; World's Fair, 1992 (juvenile), 1970; Downward to the Earth, 1970; Tower of Glass, 1970; Parsecs and Parables: Ten Science Fiction Stories, 1970; The Cube Root of Uncertainty (short stories), 1970; Moonferns and Starsongs (short stories), 1971; The World Inside, 1971; A Time of Changes, 1971; Son of Man, 1971, rev. ed., 2003; The Reality Trip and Other Implausibilities (short stories), 1972; The Book of Skulls, 1972, rev. ed., 2006; Dying Inside, 1972; The Second Trip, 1972; Valley Beyond Time (short stories), 1973; Unfamiliar Territory (short stories), 1973; Earth's Other Shadow: Nine Science Fiction Stories, 1973; Born with the Dead: Three Novellas about the Spirit of Man, 1974; Sundance and Other Science Fiction Stories, 1974; Sunrise on Mercury and Other Science Fiction Stories, 1975; The Feast of St. Dionysus: Five Science Fiction Stories, 1975; The Stochastic Man, 1975; Shadrach in the Furnace, 1976; The Shores of Tomorrow (short stories), 1976; The Best of Robert Silverberg, vol. I, 1976, vol. II, 1978; Capricorn Games (short stories), 1976; The Songs of Summer (short stories), 1979; Lord Valentine's Castle, 1980; A Robert Silverberg Omnibus, 1981; The Desert of Stolen Dreams, 1981; Majipoor Chronicles, 1982; (ed. with C.G. Waugh and

M.H. Greenberg) The Science Fictional Dinosaur, 1982; World of a Thousand Colors (short stories), 1982; Valentine Pontifex, 1983; Lord of Darkness, 1983; The Conglomeroid Cocktail Party, 1984; Gilgamesh the King, 1984; Tom O'Bedlam, 1985; Sailing to Byzantium, 1985; Star of Gypsies, 1986, rev. ed., 2005; Beyond the Safe Zone: Collected Short Fiction of Robert Silverberg, 1986; Project Pendulum, 1987; (intro.) At Winter's End, 1988, rev. ed., 2005; To the Land of the Living, 1989; (with K. Haber) The Mutant Season, 1989; Lion Time in Timbuctoo, 1990; The New Springtime, 1990; Letters from Atlantis, 1990; In Another Country: Vintage Season, 1990; (with I. Asimov) Nightfall, 1990; Time Gate II, 1990; The Face of the Waters, 1991; (with I. Asimov) Child of Time, 1991; (with I. Asimov) The Ugly Little Boy, 1992; The Collected Stories of Robert Silverberg, vol. I: Secret Sharers, 1992; (with I. Asimov) The Positronic Man, 1993; Kingdoms of the Wall, 1993; Hot Sky at Midnight, 1994; The Mountains of Majipoor, 1995; Starborne, 1996; Sorcerers of Majipoor, 1997; Reflections and Refractions: Thoughts on Science-Fiction, Science, and Other Matters, 1997; The Alien Years, 1998; Lord Prestimion, 2000; Shadowon the Stars, 2000; Cronos, 2001; King of Dreams, 2001; Longest Way Home, 2002; In Another Country, and Other Short Novels, 2002; Roma Eterna, 2003; (intro.) The Queen of Springtime, 2005. NONFICTION: First American into Space, 1961; Lost Cities and Vanished Civilizations, 1962; The Fabulous Rockefellers: A Compelling, Personalized Account of One of America's First Families, 1963; Empires in the Dust: Ancient Civilizations Brought to Light, 1963; Akhnaten: The Rebel Pharaoh, 1964; Man before Adam: The Story of Man in Search of His Origins, 1964; (ed.) Great Adventures in Archaeology, 1964; Scientists and Scoundrels: A Book of Hoaxes, 1965, rev. ed., 2007; The Great Wall of China, 1965, rev. ed. as The Long Rampart: The Story of the Great Wall of China, 1966; Frontiers of Archaeology, 1966; The Long Rampart, 1966; Bridges, 1966; The Auk, The Dodo, and the Oryx: Vanished and Vanishing Creatures, 1967; Men Against Time: Salvage Archaeology in the United States, 1967; Light for the World: Edison and the Power Industry, 1967; Mound Builders of Ancient America: The Archaeology of a Myth, 1968; The Challenge of Climate: Man and His Environment, 1969; The World of Space, 1969; If I Forget Thee, O Jerusalem: American Jews and the State of Israel, 1970; The Pueblo Revolt, 1970; Before the Sphinx: Early Egypt, 1971; Clocks for the Ages: How Scientists Date the Past, 1971; To the Western Shore: Growth of the United States, 1776-1853, 1971; The Longest Voyage: Circumnavigators in the Ageof Discovery, 1972; The Realm of Prester John, 1972; Drug Themes in Science Fiction, 1974; The Stochastic Man, 1975; Lord Valentine's Castle, 1980; Lord of Darkness, 1983; The New Springtime, 1990; To the Land of the Living, 1990; The Face of the Waters, 1991; Thebes of the Hundred Gates, 1991; Kingdoms of the Wall, 1992; The Positronic Man, 1992; The Ugly Little Boy, 1992; Hot Sky at Midnight, 1994; The Mountains of Majipoor, 1995; Starborne, 1996; The Alien Years, 1997; Sorcerers of Majipoor, 1997; Lord Prestimion, 1999; King of Dreams, 2000; The Longest Way Home, 2001; At Winter's End, 2005; Book of Skulls, 2006; Shadrach in the Furnace, 2008; Time of Changes, 2009; Dying Inside, 2009. JUVENILE NONFICTION: Treasures beneath the Sea, 1960; 15 Battles That Changed the World, 1963; Home of the Red Man: Indian North America before Columbus, 1963; Sunken History: The Story of Underwater Archaeology, 1963; The Great Doctors, 1964; The Man Who Found Nineveh: The Story of Austen Henry Layard, 1964; Men Who Mastered the Atom, 1965; Niels Bohr: The Man Who Mapped the Atom, 1965; The Old Ones: Indians of the American Southwest, 1965; Socrates, 1965; The World of Coral, 1965; Forgotten by Time: A Book of Living Fossils, 1966; To the Rock of Darius: The Story of Henry Rawlinson, 1966; The Adventures of Nat Palmer: Antarctic Explorer and Clipper Ship Pioneer, 1967; The Dawn of Medicine, 1967; The Morning of Mankind: Prehistoric Man in Europe, 1967; The World of the Rain Forest, 1967; Four Men Who Changed the Universe, 1968; Ghost Towns of the American West, 1968; Stormy Voyager: The Story of Charles Wilkes, 1968; The World of the Ocean Depths, 1968; Bruce of the Blue Nile, 1969; Vanishing Giants: The Story of the Sequoias, 1969; Wonders of Ancient Chinese Science, 1969; Mammoths, Mastodons, and Man, 1970; The Seven Wonders of the Ancient World, 1970; (with A.C. Clarke) Into Space: A Young Person's Guide to Space, 1971; John Muir: Prophet among the Glaciers, 1972; The World within the Ocean Wave, 1972; The World within the Tide Pool, 1972; Scientists and Scoundrels: A Book of Hoaxes, 2005. EDITOR: SCIENCE FICTION: Earthmen and Strangers: Nine Stories of Science Fiction, 1966; Voyagers in Time: Twelve Stories of Science Fiction, 1967; Men and Machines: Ten Stories of Science Fiction, 1968; Dark Stars, 1969; Tomorrow's Worlds: Ten Stories of Science Fiction, 1969; The Ends of Time: Eight Stories of Science Fiction, 1970; Great Short Novels of Science Fiction, 1970; The Mirror of Infinity: A Critics' Anthology of Science Fiction, 1970; The Science

Fiction Hall of Fame, vol. I, 1970, vol. II, 1972; Worlds of Maybe: Seven Stories of Science Fiction, 1970; Four Futures, 1971; Mind to Mind: Nine Stories of Science Fiction, 1971; The Science Fiction Bestiary: Nine Stories of Science Fiction, 1971; To the Stars: Eight Stories of Science Fiction, 1971; Beyond Control: Seven Stories of Science Fiction, 1972; Invaders from Space: Ten Stories of Science Fiction, 1972; Chains of the Sea: Three Original Novellas of Science Fiction, 1973; Deep Space: Eight Stories of Science Fiction, 1973; Other Dimensions: Ten Stories of Science Fiction, 1973; Three Trips in Time and Space, 1973; Infinite Jests: The Lighter Side of Science Fiction, 1974; Mutants: Eleven Stories of Science Fiction, 1974; Threads of Time: Three Original Novellas of Science Fiction, 1974; Windows into Tomorrow: Nine Stories of Science Fiction, 1974; (with R. Elwood) Epoch, 1975; Explorers of Space: Eight Stories of Science Fiction, 1975; The New Atlantis and Other Novellas of Science Fiction, 1975; Strange Gifts: Eight Stories of Science Fiction, 1975; The Aliens: Seven Stories of Science Fiction, 1976; The Crystal Ship: Three Original Novellas of Science Fiction, 1976; Earth Is the Strangest Planet: Ten Stories of Science Fiction, 1977; Galactic Dreamers: Science Fiction as Visionary Literature, 1977; Alpha, 9 vols., 1977-78; The Infinite Web: Eight Stories of Science Fiction, 1977; Tri-ax: Three Original Novellas, 1977; Trips in Time: Nine Stories of Science Fiction, 1977; Lost Worlds, Unknown Horizons: Nine Stories of Science Fiction, 1978; The Androids Are Coming: Seven Stories of Science Fiction, 1979; (with M.H. Greenberg and J.D. Olander) Car Sinister, 1979; (with M.H. Greenberg and J.D. Olander) Dawn of Time: Prehistory through Science Fiction, 1979; The Edge of Space: Three Original Novellas of Science Fiction, 1979; (with M.H. Greenberg) The Arbor House Treasury of Great Science Fiction Short Novels, 1980; (with M.H. Greenberg) The Arbor House Treasury of Modern Science Fiction, 1980; The Best of Randall Garrett, 1982; The Nebula Awards, 1983; (with M.H. Greenberg) The Arbor House Treasury of Science Fiction Masterpieces, 1983; (with M.H. Greenberg) The Fantasy Hall of Fame, 1983; (with M.H. Greenberg) The Time Travelers: A Science Fiction Quartet, 1985; (with M.H. Greenberg and C.G. Waugh) Neanderthals, 1987; Robert Silverberg's Worlds of Wonder, 1987; (with M.H. Greenberg) The Mammoth Book of Fantasy All-Time Greats, 1988; Worlds Imagined: Fifteen Short Stories, 1989; (with K. Haber) Universe 1, 1990; (with K. Haber) Universe 2, 1992; Virtual Unrealities: The Short Fiction of Alfred Bester, 1997; Legends: Short Novels by the Masters of Modern Fantasy, 1997; A Century of Fantasy, 1980-1989, 1997; A Century of Science Fiction, 1950-1959, 1997; Far Horizons: All New Tales from the Greatest Worlds of Science Fiction, 1999; Legends II: New Short Novels by the Masters of Modern Fantasy, 2004. EDITOR: NEW DIMENSIONS SERIES: The Best of New Dimensions, 1979; New Dimensions, vol. I-X, (with M. Randall) vol. XI-XII, 1980-81. AS WALKER CHAPMAN: The Loneliest Continent: The Story of Antarctic Discovery, 1965; Kublai Khan: Lord of Xanadu (juvenile), 1966; (ed.) Antarctic Conquest: The Great Explorers in Their Own Words, 1966; The Golden Dream: Seekers of El Dorado, 1967, rev. ed. as The Search for El Dorado, 1967. AS IVAR JORGENSEN: Starhaven, 1958; Whom the Gods Would Slay, 1968; The Deadly Sky, 1971. AS CALVIN M. KNOX: Lest We Forget Thee, Earth, 1958; The Plot against Earth, 1959; One of Our Asteroids Is Missing, 1964. AS DAVID OSBORNE: InvIsible Barriers, 1958; Aliens from Space, 1958. AS ROBERT RANDALL: The Shrouded Planet, 1957; The Dawning Light, 1959. AS LEE SEBASTIAN: Rivers (juvenile), 1966; The South Pole (juvenile), 1968. AS DON ELLIOTT: Flesh Peddlers, 1960; Passion Trap, 1960; Backstage Sinner, 1961; Lust Goddess, 1961; Sin Cruise, 1961; Kept Man, 1962; Shame House, 1962; Sin Hellion, 1963; Sin Servant, 1963; Beatnik Wanton, 1964; Flesh Bride, 1964; Flesh Prize, 1964; Flesh Taker, 1964; Sin Warped, 1964; Switch Trap, 1964; Nudie Packet, 1965; The Young Wanton, 1965; Depravity Town, 1973; Jungle Street, 1973; Summertime Affair, 1973. AS WALTER DRUMMOND: Philosopher of Evil, 1962; How to Spend Money, 1963. AS FRANKLIN HAMILTON: 1066, 1963; The Crusades, 1965; Challenge for a Throne: The Wars of the Roses, 1967. AS PAUL HOLLANDER: The Labors of Hercules, 1965; Sam Houston, 1968. AS LLOYD ROBINSON: The Hopefuls: Ten Presidential Candidates, 1966; The Stolen Election: Hayes versus Tilden, 1968. CHAPBOOKS: Absolutely Inflexible, 1998; Hunters in the Forest, 2001; Seventh Shrine, 2004. OTHERS: (intro.) The Disappearance, 1951; (as Alexander Blade) 3117 Half-Credit Uncirculated, 1958; (as Roy Cook) Leaders of Labor, 1966; (ed. with M.H. Greenberg) The Horror Hall of Fame, 1991; Classic Science Fiction, 2010; The Palace At Midnight, 2010; (co-author) Enter A Future: Fantastic Tales from Asimov's Science Fiction, 2010; The Last Song of Orpheus, 2010; Dangerous Dimensions, 2011; Multiples, 2011; Something Wild is Loose: The Collected Stories of Robert Silverberg, 2011; (co-author) Science Fiction Gems, 2011; The Chalice of Death, 2011; Hunt the Space-Witch!: Seven Adventures in Time and Space, 2011; We Are For The Dark, 2012; Blood on the Mink, 2012; Hot Times in Magma City, 2013; Tales of Majipoor, 2013; The Millennium Express, 2014. **Address:** Orb Books, 175 5th Ave., New York, NY 10010, U.S.A. **Online address:** ragberg@attglobal.net

SILVERBLATT, Art. American (born United States), b. 1949. **Genres:** Communications/Media, Reference, Adult Non-fiction. **Career:** Webster University, director of media programs, 1981-96, associate professor, 1985-95, Department of Media Communications, head, 1985-96, Department of Communications and Journalism, professor, 1995-, head, 1996-97. Writer. **Publications:** Media Literacy: Keys to Interpreting Media Messages, with Instructor's Manual, 1995, 3rd ed., 2008; (with E.M.E. Eliceiri) Dictionary of Media Literacy, 1997; (with J. Ferry and B. Finan) Approaches to Media Literacy: A Handbook, 1999, 2nd ed., 2009; (with N. Zlobin) International Communications: A Media Literacy Approach, 2004; Approaches to Genre Studies: A Media Literacy Approach, 2007; Genre Studies in Mass Media: A Handbook, 2007. Contributor to books and periodicals. **Address:** Department of Communication and Journalism, Webster University, 470 E Lockwood, 815 Olive St., Ste. 20, St. Louis, MO 63119-3194, U.S.A. **Online address:** silveram@webster.edu

SILVERBURG, Sanford R. American (born United States), b. 1940. **Genres:** Politics/Government, International Relations/Current Affairs, Bibliography, Social Sciences. **Career:** American University, Special Operations Research Office, Counterinsurgency Information Analysis Center, information systems analyst, 1965-67; American Institute of Research, Center for Research in Social Systems, Cultural Information Analysis Center, research associate, 1967-69; Catawba College, Department of Political Science, assistant professor, 1970-75, associate professor, 1975-79, head, 1975-2006, professor, 1979-95, 1997-2006, Jefferson-Pilot professor, 1995-97, Summer Sessions and Programs, director, 1982-85, director of summer sessions, 1985-2000, Department of History and Politics, professor, 2006-; University of North Carolina at Charlotte, lecturer, 1974-75; Columbia Pacific University, faculty mentor, 1988-; Educational Testing Service, consultant, 1999-2006, 2008; Troy University, Instructor, 2008-. Writer. **Publications:** Palestinian Arab-Israeli Conflict, 1982; (with B. Reich) United States Foreign Policy and the Middle East/North Africa: A Bibliography of Twentieth-Century Research, 1990; Middle East Bibliography, 1992; (with B. Reich) U.S. Foreign Relations with the Middle East and North Africa, 1994; (with B. Reich) Asian States' Relations with the Middle East: A Bibliography, 1950-1993, 1994; Index to Law School Theses and Dissertations, 1995; (ed.) Palestine and International Law: Essays on Politics and Economics, 2002; (ed.) International Law: Contemporary Issues and Future Developments, 2011. **Address:** Department of History and Politics, Catawba College, 2300 W Innes St., Salisbury, NC 28144-2488, U.S.A. **Online address:** ssilver@catawba.edu

SILVERMAN, Jerry. American (born United States), b. 1931. **Genres:** Novellas/Short Stories, Civil Liberties/Human Rights, Cultural/Ethnic Topics, History, How-to Books, Music, Mythology/Folklore, Translations, Translations. **Career:** State University of New York, faculty, 1981; Saw Mill Music Corp., president; Sing Out Magazine, editor; Hastings-on-Hudson, owner. Musicologist, folksinger and guitarist. **Publications:** Folksinger's Guitar Guide, vol. I, 1962, vol. II, 1966; Art of the Folk Blues Guitar, 1964; Beginning the Folk Guitar, 1964; (trans.) Russian Songs, 1966; Flat Picker's Guitar Guide, 1966; Sixty-Two Outrageous Songs, 1966; A Folksinger's Guide to Note Reading and Music Theory, 1966; The Chord Player's Encyclopedia, 1967; How to Play the Guitar, 1968; Graded Guitar, 10 vols., 1970; That Good Old Razza Ma Tazz, 1970; Folksongs for Schools and Camps, 1971; The Liberated Woman's Songbook, 1971; How to Play Better Guitar, 1972; Beginning the Five-String Banjo, 1974; Jerry Silverman Folk Guitar Method Book, 1974; Jerry Silverman Folk Harmonica, 1974; Jerry Silverman Blues Harmonica, 1974; The Folk Song Encyclopedia, 2 vols., 1975; How to Play Country Fiddle, 1975; Favorite Folk Songs, 1976; Children's Songs, 1976; Blues, 1976; Love Songs, 1976; Bluegrass, 1976; Folksongs for Flute, 1977; Folk Guitar-Folk Songs, 1977; How Can I Keep from Singing, 1977; Folksongs for Voice and Classical Guitar, 1977; The Back Packer's Song Book, 1977; Favorite Christmas Songs and Carols, 1977; Ragtime Solos and Duets, 1978; No More Booze, 1978; Look, Listen and Learn Guitar, 1979; Guitar Folk Styles, 1979; The Young Guitarist, 1980; Sing and Play Blues, 1980; Sing and Play Ragtime, 1980; Easy Folk Fiddle, 2 vols., 1980; Play Guitar in 15 Lessons, 1982; Bass Runs and Arpeggios for Guitar, 1982; How to Play Blues Guitar, 1982; How to Play Ragtime Guitar, 1982; How to Play Bluegrass Guitar, 1982; How to Sing Higher and Lower, 1982; Scales into

Chords, 1982; The Dirty Song Book, 1982; Pop Guitar Hits Fingerstyle, 1983; Country and Western Guitar Hits-Fingerstyle, 1983; The Yiddish Song Book, 1983; Recorder Music for Children, 1990; Campfire Songbook, 1990; Ragtime Songbook, 1990; Kidsongs, 1990; Kidfiddle, 1990; Songs of England, 1991, Songs of Scotland, 1991; Complete Folk Guitar, 1991; Songs of the Western Frontier, 1991; The American History Songbook, 1991; Train Songs, 1991; Songs of Fun and Foolishness, 1991; The Animal Songbook, 1991; Good Times, Hard Times and Ragtimes, 1991; The Holiday Songbook, 1991; Songs of the Great Outdoors, 1991; A Treasury of Christmas Carols, 1991; Traditional Black Music: Songs of Protest and Civil Rights (15 vols.), 1992; Children's Songs, 1992; African Roots, 1993; Slave Songs, 1993; Blues, 1993; Good-Time Songs; Gospel Songs; Outlaws and Outcasts; Spirituals; Wartime Songs; West Indian and Calypso; Work Songs; Earth and Nature Song, 1992; Children Sing around the World, 1992; Immigrant Song Book, 1992; Songs of the Sea, Rivers, Lakes and Canals, 1992; Songs of the American People, 1993; (comp.) Ballads and Songs of the Civil War, 1993; Songs That Made History around the World, 1993; Songs of the British Isles, 1993; Blues Classics, 1993; You Can Teach Yourself Folk-Singing Guitar, 1993; British and American Victorian Vocal Varieties, 1994; American Love Songs and Ballads, 1994; America Sings, 1994; Work Songs, 1994-95; Songs and Stories the Revolutionary War, 1994; Mel Bay Presents Songs of Latin America, 1994; Songs of Mexico, 1994; Mexican Songs for Guitar, 1994; Songs of France, 1994; Songs of Latin America, 1994; (comp.) Songs of the British Isles for Guitar, 1995; Songs and Stories from Colonial America, 1995; Just Listen to this Song I'm Singing, 1996; Songs of Latin America for Guitar, 1996; Songs of the Jewish People, 1996; Australian Songs, 1996; Songs of Spain for Guitar, 1996; Backpacker's Harmonica Songbook, 1996; Russian and Hungarian Gypsy Songs, 1997; Russian and Hungarian Gypsy Songs for Guitar, 1997; Ballads and Songs of World War I, 1997; The Complete Chorales of J.S. Bach, 1997; Of Thee I Sing: America's Most Patriotic Songs, 2002; Songs and Stories of the Civil War, 2002; The Baseball Songbook, 2007. **Address:** 160 High St., Hastings on Hudson, NY 10706, U.S.A. **Online address:** sawmillmus@aol.com

SILVERMAN, Joseph H. American (born United States), b. 1955. **Genres:** Mathematics/Statistics, Sciences. **Career:** Massachusetts Institute of Technology, Moore Instructor, 1982-85, postdoctoral fellow, 1983-86; Boston University, associate professor of mathematics, 1986-88; Brown University, associate professor, 1988-91, professor of mathematics, 1991-, chairman, 2001-04, 2008; University of Paris VII, visiting professor, 1992, 1995; NTRU Crypto Systems Inc., vice-president, 1998-. Writer. **Publications:** The Arithmetic of Elliptic Curves, 1986, 2nd ed., 2009; (ed. with G. Cornell) Arithmetic Geometry, 1986, rev. ed., 1998; (with J. Tate) Rational Points on Elliptic Curves, 1992; Advanced Topics in the Arithmetic of Elliptic Curves, 1994; (ed. with G. Cornell and G. Stevens) Modular Forms and Fermat's Last Theorem, 1997; (contrib.) Diophantus and Diophantine Equations, 1997; A Friendly Introduction to Number Theory, 1997, 4th ed., 2013; (with M. Hindry) Diophantine Geometry: An Introduction, 2000; A Friendly Introduction to the Number Theory, 2006; Arithmetic of Dynamical Systems, 2007; (co-ed.) Introduction to Mathematical Cryptography, 2008; (contrib.) Introduction to the Theory of Numbers, 2008. Contributor of articles to journals. **Address:** Department of Mathematics, Brown University, 202 Kassar House, PO Box 1917, Providence, RI 02912, U.S.A. **Online address:** joseph_silverman@brown.edu

SILVERMAN, Mark P. American (born United States), b. 1945?. **Genres:** Physics, Sciences. **Career:** Hitachi Advanced Research Laboratory, chief researcher; University of Canterbury, Erskine Professor of Physics; Trinity College, Department of physics, faculty, 1982-, Jarvis professor of physics, professor, department head; Ecole Supérieure de Physique et Chimie, Frédéric Joliot Chair of Physics and National Science Foundation, senior scientist and consultant. **Publications:** And Yet It Moves: Strange Systems and Subtle Questions in Physics, 1993; More Than One Mystery: Explorations in Quantum Interference, 1995; Waves and Grains: Reflections on Light and Learning, 1998; Probing the Atom: Interactions of Coupled States, Fast Beams and Loose Electrons, 2000; A Universe of Atoms, an Atom in the Universe, 2002; Quantum Superposition: Counterintuitive Consequences of Coherence, Entanglement and Interference, 2008; A Certain Uncertainty: Nature's Random Ways, forthcoming. Contributor of articles to journals. **Address:** Department of Physics, Trinity College, McCook 216, 300 Summit St., Hartford, CT 06106, U.S.A. **Online address:** mark.silverman@trincoll.edu

SILVERMAN, Robin L(andew). American (born United States), b. 1954. **Genres:** Documentaries/Reportage, Young Adult Non-fiction, Children's Non-fiction, Young Adult Fiction, Children's Fiction, Self Help, Education, inspirational/Motivational Literature, Travel/Exploration, Cultural/Ethnic Topics. **Career:** Freelance writer, 1975-; Silverman's Inc., marketing director, 1978-; Y Family Center, president, 1987-88. **Publications:** A Bosnian Family, 1997; Where Do We Turn? What Should We Do?: Processes to Help Educators and Their Students Recover from a Natural Disaster, 1999; The Ten Gifts, 2000; North Dakota, 2003; Something Wonderful is About to Happen: True Stories of People Who Found Happiness in Unexpected Places, 2003; Reaching Your Goals, 2004. Contributor to magazines and newspapers. **Address:** PO Box 398062, Edina, MN 55439-8062, U.S.A. **Online address:** robin@robinsilverman.com

SILVERMAN, Stephen M. (Stephen Meredith Silverman). American (born United States), b. 1951. **Genres:** Film, Documentaries/Reportage, Social Sciences, Photography, Art/Art History. **Career:** Coast, editor-in-chief, 1975-77; New York Post, chief cultural correspondent, 1977-88; City University of New York, Hunter College, film teacher, 1978-80; Marymount Manhattan College, film teacher, 1978-80; Columbia University, Graduate School of Journalism, cultural arts writing and reporting teacher, 1995-, Teachers College, professor, Department of Biobehavioral Sciences, chair; People Magazine, news editor, 1996-; Time Inc., news editor, 1996-; PEOPLE.com, news editor. **Publications:** Public Spectacles, 1981; The Fox That Got Away: The Last Days of the Zanuck Dynasty at Twentieth Century-Fox, 1988; David Lean, 1989, rev. ed., 1991; Where There's a Will...: Who Inherited What and Why, 1991; The Last Wills and Testaments of the Rich and Renowned, 1991; Dancing on the Ceiling: Stanley Donen and His Movies, 1996; (with intro.) The Last Remaining Seats: Movie Palaces of Tinsel Town, 1997; Funny Ladies: The Women Who Make Us Laugh, 1999; Movie Mutts: Hollywood Goes to the Dogs, 2001; Envy, Anger and Sweet Revenge: Hey, It Works in Hollywood!, 2002; (contrib.) Divas!: The Fabulous Photography of Kenn Duncan, 2008. **Address:** Teachers College, Columbia University, 1056 Thndk, 525 W 120th St., New York, NY 10027, U.S.A. **Online address:** ss928@columbia.edu

SILVERMAN, Stephen Meredith. See SILVERMAN, Stephen M.

SILVERMAN, Willa Z. American (born United States), b. 1959?. **Genres:** Biography. **Career:** Pennsylvania State University, assistant professor of French, associate professor of French and Jewish studies, professor of French and Jewish studies; Association for French Cultural Studies, president. Writer. **Publications:** The Notorious Life of Gyp: Right-Wing Anarchist in Fin-de-Siècle France (biography), 1995; (trans.) Gyp, la derni Fre des Mirabeau, 1998; (co-author) Confrontations. Politics and Aesthetics in Nineteenth-Century France, 2001; The New Bibliopolis: French Book Collectors and the Culture of Print, 1880-1914, 2008. **Address:** Department of French and Francophone Studies, The Pennsylvania State University, 237 Burrowes Bldg., University Park, PA 16802, U.S.A. **Online address:** wzs1@psu.edu

SILVERSTEIN, Amy. American (born United States), b. 1963. **Genres:** Novels, Biography. **Career:** Writer and lawyer. **Publications:** Sick Girl, 2007. Contributor to periodicals. **Address:** c/o Deb Seager, Grove/Atlantic Inc., 841 Broadway, 4th Fl., New York, NY 10003, U.S.A. **Online address:** amy_silverstein@mail.vresp.com

SILVERSTEIN, Clara. American (born United States), b. 1960?. **Genres:** Autobiography/Memoirs, Food And Wine, Race Relations. **Career:** Boston Herald, editor and food correspondent; go2 Media (mobile media co.), food correspondent; Chautauqua Writers' Center, program director, 2000-; Grub Street Inc., non-fiction instructor. **Publications:** White Girl: A Story of School Desegregation (memoir), 2004; (contrib.) Oxford Encyclopedia of American Food and Drink, 2004; (with M. Druker) The New England Soup Factory Cookbook, 2007; The Boston Chef's Table, 2008; A White House Garden Cookbook, 2010. Contributor of articles to periodicals and journals. **Address:** Red Rock Press, 331 W 57th St., Ste. 175, New York, NY 10019, U.S.A. **Online address:** clara@clarasilverstein.com

SILVERSTEIN, Herma. American (born United States), b. 1945. **Genres:** Children's Non-fiction, Children's Fiction, Young Adult Fiction, Education, History. **Career:** Tibetan Terriers, breeder; instructor of writing for children; writer, 1978-. **Publications:** (With C. Arnold) Anti-Semitism: A Modern Perspective, 1985; Mary Lou Retton and the New Gymnasts, 1985; (with C. Arnold) Hoaxes That Made Headlines, 1986; Scream Machines: Roller Coasters Past, Present and Future, 1986; Mad, Mad Monday (fiction), 1988; Spies among Us: The Truth about Modern Espionage, 1988; David Ben-Gurion,

1988; Teenage and Pregnant: What You Can Do, 1988; Teen Guide to Single Parenting, 1989; Alcoholism, 1990; Teenage Depression, 1990; The Alamo, 1992; Date Abuse, 1994; (with T.J. Donnahoo) Baseball Hall of Fame, 1994; (with T.J. Donnahoo) Basketball Hall of Fame, 1994; (with T.J. Donnahoo) Pro Football Hall of Fame, 1994; Yearbooks in Science: 1990 and Beyond, 1995; Threads of Evidence: Using Forensic Science to Solve Crimes, 1996; Kids Who Kill, 1997. Contributor to periodicals. **Address:** Andrea Brown Literary Agency, 1076 Eagle Dr., Salinas, CA 93905, U.S.A.

SILVERSTEIN, Jake Phillip. American (born United States), b. 1975. **Genres:** Young Adult Fiction. **Career:** Big Bend Sentinel, reporter, 1999-2000; Texas Monthly, senior editor, 2006-08, editor, 2008-. **Publications:** Nothing Happened and Then It Did: A Chronicle in Fact and Fiction, 2010. Works appear in anthologies. **Address:** Austin, TX , U.S.A. **Online address:** jakesilverstein@gmail.com

SILVERSTEIN, Ken. American (born United States), b. 1958?. **Genres:** Politics/Government, History. **Career:** Associated Press, Brazil correspondent, 1989-93; Los Angeles Times, reporter; Harper's Magazine, editor. Journalist. **Publications:** (With E. Sader) Without Fear of Being Happy: Lula, the Workers Party and Brazil, 1991; (with A. Cockburn) Washington Babylon, 1996; Washington on $10 Million a Day: How Lobbyists Plunder the Nation, 1998; Private Warriors, 2000; The Radioactive Boy Scout: The True Story of a Boy and His Backyard Nuclear Reactor, 2004; Turkmeniscam: How Washington Lobbyists Fought to Flack for a Stalinist Dictatorship, 2008. Contributor to magazines. **Address:** U.S.A. **Online address:** ken@harpers.org

SILVERSTONE, Scott A. American (born United States), b. 1963. **Genres:** Politics/Government, Social Sciences. **Career:** University of Pennsylvania, instructor, 1996-99, assistant professor of international relations and assistant director of Christopher Browne Center for International Politics, 1999-2000; Williams College, visiting assistant professor of international relations, 2000-01; U.S. Military Academy, associate professor of international relations, 2001-, West Point Model United Nations, faculty adviser, 2002-; U.S. Naval War College, analyst, 1997, 1998; Bard College, adjunct professor of international relations, 2007-. Writer. **Publications:** Divided Union: The Politics of War in the Early American Republic, 2004; Preventive War and American Democracy, 2007. CONTRIBUTOR: Understanding International Relations: The Value of Alternative Lenses, 2004; Defence Politics: International and Comparative Perspectives, 2008; American National Security, 2008. Contributor to periodicals. **Address:** Department of Social Sciences, United States Military Academy, 600 Thayer Rd., West Point, NY 10996, U.S.A. **Online address:** js6300@usma.edu

SILVERTON, Nancy. American (born United States), b. 1954. **Genres:** Food And Wine, How-to Books. **Career:** Campanile (restaurant), owner and pastry chef, 1989-; La Brea Bakery, owner and head baker, 1989-; Michael's Restaurant, assistant pastry chef; Wolfgang Puck's Spago Restaurant, head pastry chef. Writer. **Publications:** (With H. Yorkshire) Desserts, 1986; (with M. Peel and E. Waycott) Mark Peel and Nancy Silverton at Home: Two Chefs Cook for Family and Friends, 1994; (with L. Ochoa) Breads from the La Brea Bakery, 1996; (with M. Peel) The Food of Campanile, 1997; (with T. Gelber) Nancy Silverton's Pastries from the La Brea Bakery, 2000; (with T. Gelber) Nancy Silverton's Sandwiches Book: The Best Sandwiches Ever from Thursday Nights at Campanile, 2002; (with C. Carreño) Twist of the Wrist: Quick Flavorful Meals with Ingredients from Jars, Cans, Bags and Boxes, 2007; (with M. Molina and C. Carreño) The Mozza Cookbook: Recipes from Los Angeles's Favorite Italian Restaurant and Pizzeria, 2011. **Address:** Janis A. Donnaud & Associates Inc., 525 Broadway, Ste. 201, New York, NY 10012, U.S.A.

SILVESTER, Peter (John). British (born England), b. 1934. **Genres:** Music, Social Commentary, History, Art/Art History, Young Adult Fiction. **Career:** Teacher, 1956-68; Inner London Education Authority, senior lecturer, 1968-71. Writer. **Publications:** A Left Hand Like God: A History of Boogie-Woogie Piano, 1989, rev. ed. as Story of Boogie-Woogie: A Left Hand Like God, 2009. **Address:** Quartet Books, 27 Goodge St., London, GL W1T 2LD, England. **Online address:** ken@wardston.freeserve.co.uk

SILVEY, Diane F. Canadian (born Canada), b. 1946?. **Genres:** Children's Fiction, Children's Non-fiction, Novels, Cultural/Ethnic Topics. **Career:** Greater Victoria School District, First Nations Education Division, teacher. Writer. **Publications:** Little Bear's Vision Quest, 1995; Brittney Diana Read-

ing Series, 1995; Whale Girl, 1996; Spirit Quest, 1997; Tidepools and Book Report, 1997; Brittney Diana First Nations Cultural Series, 1997; (with D. Mumford) From Time Immemorial: The First People of the Pacific Northwest Coast (teacher's guide), 1999; Raven's Flight, 2001. **Address:** c/o Author Mail, Raincoast Books, 9050 Shaughnessy St., Vancouver, BC V6P 6E5, Canada.

SIM, Dorrith M. Scottish/German (born Germany), b. 1931. **Genres:** Children's Fiction, Autobiography/Memoirs, Romance/Historical. **Career:** Secretary and freelance writer. **Publications:** In My Pocket, 1997. Works appear in anthologies. Contributor of articles to magazines. **Address:** c/o Marilyn Malin, Marilyn Malin Consultancy, 5/33 Ferncroft Ave., London, GL NW3 7PG, England. **Online address:** dorrithmsim@aol.com

SIMA, Carol Ann. American (born United States), b. 1956?. **Genres:** Science Fiction/Fantasy, Novels. **Career:** New York School System, grade school language arts teacher. Writer. **Publications:** Jane's Bad Hare Day: A Novel, 1995; The Mermaid that Came between Them, 2001. Contributor to periodicals. **Address:** c/o Author Mail, Coffee House Press, 79 13th Ave. NE, Ste. 110, Minneapolis, MN 55413, U.S.A.

SIMETI, Mary Taylor. Italian/American (born United States), b. 1941. **Genres:** Food And Wine, Biography, Travel/Exploration, Writing/Journalism, Autobiography/Memoirs. **Career:** Writer. **Publications:** Sariddu, 1975; On Persephone's Island: A Sicilian Journal, 1986; Pomp and Sustenance: Twenty-Five Centuries of Sicilian Food, 1989; (with M. Grammatico) Bitter Almonds: Recollections and Recipes from a Sicilian Girlhood, 1994; Travels with a Medieval Queen, 2001. Contributor to books and periodicals. **Address:** Robert Cornfield Literary Agency, 145 W 79th St., New York, NY 10024-6407, U.S.A.

SIMIC, Charles. American (born United States), b. 1938. **Genres:** Poetry, Translations. **Career:** Aperture Magazine, editorial assistant, 1966-69; State University of California, visiting assistant professor of English, 1970-73; University of New Hampshire, professor of English, 1973-, now professor emeritus of English; Boston University, visiting professor, 1975; Columbia University, visiting professor, 1979; Chicago Sun Times, staff. **Publications:** What the Grass Says, 1967; Somewhere Among Us a Stone is Taking Notes, 1969; Dismantling the Silence, 1971; White, 1972; Return to a Place Lit by a Glass of Milk, 1974; (co-ed.) Another Republic, 1976; Biography and a Lament, 1976; Charon's Cosmology, 1977; (trans.) Key to Dreams According to Djordje, 1978; Brooms: Selected Poems, 1978; School for Dark Thoughts, 1978; Classic Ballroom Dances, 1980; Shaving at Night, 1982; Austerities, 1982; Weather Forecast for Utopia and Vicinity: Poems 1967-1982, 1983; Selected Poems 1963-1983, 1985, rev. ed., 1990; The Uncertain Certainty, 1985; Unending Blues, 1986; The World Doesn't End, 1989; Nine Poems, 1989; The World Doesn't End, 1989; The Book of Gods and Devils, 1990; Wonderful Words, Silent Truth, 1990; Dime-Store Alchemy: The Art of Joseph Cornell, 1992; Hotel Insomnia, 1992; A Wedding in Hell: Poems, 1994; The Unemployed Fortune-Teller: Essays and Memoirs, 1994; Frightening Toys, 1995; Walking the Black Cat, 1996; Orphan Factory: Essays and Memoirs, 1997; Jackstraws: Poems, 1999; A Fly in the Soup: Memoirs, 2000; Selected Early Poems, 2000; (ed.) Feast, 2000; (contrib.) On Great Bay, 2001; Night Picnic, 2001; (ed. And foreword) Mermaids Explained, 2001; The Voice at 3: 00 A.M.: Selected Late and New Poems, 2003; Metaphysician in the Dark, 2003; (contrib.) Private View, 2004; (ed. with D. Paterson) New British Poetry, 2004; Aunt Lettuce, I Want to Peek Under Your Skirt, 2005; My Noiseless Entourage: Poems, 2005; Memory Piano, 2006; Sixty Poems, 2007; (ed.) Thomas Campion, 2007; That Little Something: Poems, 2008; Monster Loves his Labyrinth: Notebooks, 2008; (co-author) Seven American Poets in Conversation, 2008; Renegade: Writings on Poetry and a Few Other Things, 2009; Master of Disguises, 2010. TRANSLATOR: I.V. Lalic, Fire Gardens, 1970; V. Popa, The Little Box: Poems, 1970; Four Modern Yugoslav Poets: Ivan V. Lalic, Branko Miljkovic, Milorad Pavic, Ljubomir Simovic, 1970; (and ed. With M. Strand) Another Republic: Seventeen European and South American Writers, 1976; V. Popa, Homage to the Lame Wolf: Selected Poems, 1979; (with P. Kastmiler) Slavko Mihalic, Atlantis, 1983; I.V. Lalic, Roll Call of Mirrors, 1987; A. Ristovic, Some Other Wine or Light, 1989; S. Janevski, Bandit Wind, 1991; N. Tadic, Night Mail: Selected Poems, 1992; Horse Has Six Legs: Contemporary Serbian Poetry, 1992; A. Ristovic, Devil's Lunch, 1999; R. Lazic, A Wake for the Living, 2003; G. Grass, The Gunter Grass Reader, 2004; (and intro.) N. Tadić, Dark Things, 2009; (and intro.) M. Djordjević, Oranges and Snow, 2010; (ed. And intro.) The Horse has Six

Legs: An Anthology of Serbian Poetry, 2010. **Address:** Department of English, University of New Hampshire, 229 Hamilton Smith Hall, 95 Main St., Durham, NH 03824, U.S.A. **Online address:** csimic@cisunix.unh.edu

SIMIC, Goran. Canadian (born Canada), b. 1952. **Genres:** Poetry, Plays/Screenplays, Novellas/Short Stories, Songs/Lyrics And Libretti, Translations. **Career:** University of Toronto, senior resident; University of Guelph, writer-in-exile, 2006, writer-in-residence; Luna Publications, founder, 2006-; University of Alberta, faculty, 2010. **Publications:** Sorrow of Sarajevo, 1996; Sprinting from the Graveyard, 1997; Peace and War: Poems, 1999; Immigrant Blues, 2003; From Sarajevo, with Sorrow, Poems, 2005; Yesterday's People, Stories, 2005; Looking for Tito, 2010; Sunrise in the Eyes of the Snowman, 2011. FORTHCOMING: When You Die as a Cat. IN BOSNIA-HERZEGOVINA: A Period next to a Circle; or, A Journey, 1976; Vertigo, 1977; Mandragora, 1982; Young Playwrights of Bosnia-Herzegovina, 1986; A Step into the Dark, 1987; Cut: Younger Literature of Bosnia-Herzegovina, 1987; Korak u mrak, 1987; Fantasy Book, 1989; Sarajevo Sorrow, 1995; Tree Plays for Puppets, 1998; Zapisi O Bivsim Ljudima: Price, 2005; My Happy Days in the Madhouse, 2010; Somebody Told Me that Tito has Died, 2011. **Address:** 200 72nd Ave., Apt. 207, St. Petersburg, FL 33702-5938, U.S.A. **Online address:** goransimic8@aim.com

SIMIEN, Evelyn M. American (born United States), b. 1974. **Genres:** Politics/Government, Social Sciences. **Career:** University of Connecticut, associate professor; Texas A&M University, lecturer; Minnesota State University, lecturer; American University, lecturer; Louisiana State University, lecturer; Loyola University of New Orleans, lecturer; University of Mississippi, lecturer. Writer. **Publications:** Black Feminist Voices in Politics, 2006. Contributor to periodicals and journals. **Address:** Department of Political Science, University of Connecticut, U-1024, 341 Mansfield Rd., Storrs, CT 06269-1024, U.S.A. **Online address:** evelyn.simien@uconn.edu

SIMKINS, Ronald A. American (born United States), b. 1960. **Genres:** Theology/Religion, Women's Studies And Issues, History. **Career:** Creighton University, professor of theology and classical and Near Eastern studies, Kripke Center for the Study of Religion and Society, director. Writer. **Publications:** Yahweh's Activity in History and Nature in the Book of Joel, 1991; Creator & Creation: Nature in the Worldview of Ancient Israel, 1994; Women and Judaism, 2003; (with G.S. Risch) Religion and the Family, 2005. EDITOR: (with L.J. Greenspoon) A Land Flowing with Milk and Honey: Visions of Israel from Biblical to Modern Times, 2001; (with L.J. Greenspoon) Millennialism from the Hebrew Bible to the Present, 2002; (with L.J. Greenspoon) Spiritual Dimensions of Judaism, 2003; (with L.J. Greenspoon and B. Horowitz) The Jews of Eastern Europe, 2005; (with L.J. Greenspoon and G. Shapiro) Food and Judaism, 2005; (with L.J. Greenspoon) American Judaism in Popular Culture, 2006. **Address:** Creighton University, 2500 California Pl., Omaha, NE 68178, U.S.A. **Online address:** rsmkns@creighton.edu

SIMMER-BROWN, Judith. American (born United States), b. 1946. **Genres:** Cultural/Ethnic Topics, Theology/Religion. **Career:** Fordham University, Bensalem College, adjunct teacher, 1969-71; Western Washington University, lecturer in general studies and history, 1971-75; Fairhaven College, adjunct lecturer, 1973-75; Whatcom Community College, Religious Studies Program, chair, 1974-77; Naropa University, religious studies faculty, 1978-, department chair, 1979-97, 1999-2001, Semester-Abroad Program, director, 1988; Vajradhatu Seminary, faculty, 1982, Rocky Mountain Dharma Center, director, 1985, 1986, lead acharya (senior dharma teacher), 2000, 2002, 2004; Ngedon School of Higher Learning, core faculty, 1982-, co-director, 1987-95, director, 1995-; Regis College, adjunct faculty of religion, 1983-84; University of Pittsburgh, visiting professor, 1985; University of Colorado, adjunct faculty, 1987-88; Prudential Relocation Services, consultant and trainer, 1989-90; Tucker Intl., consultant and trainer, 1994-2000; National Prison Hospice Association, board director, 1994-96; Shambhala Intl., board director, 1995-2000, teacher. Writer. **Publications:** (Co-author) Buddhists Comment on the Rule of St. Benedict, 2001; Dakini's Warm Breath: The Feminine Principle in Tibetan Buddhism, 2001; (ed. with F. Grace) Meditation and the Classroom: Contemplative Pedagogy for Religious Studies, 2011. Contributor to books and periodicals. **Address:** Naropa University, 2130 Arapahoe Ave., Boulder, CO 80302, U.S.A. **Online address:** jsb@naropa.edu

SIMMIE, James (Martin). British (born England), b. 1941. **Genres:** Economics, Regional/Urban Planning, Sociology, Urban Studies, Bibliography. **Career:** Oxford Polytechnic, lecturer, 1965-67, senior lecturer in sociology, 1967-70; University of California, lecturer, 1970; University of London, University College, faculty, 1970-97, reader in planning and sociology, 1970-; Sociology, Politics, and Cities, editor, 1976-; Reading University, faculty, 1998; Oxford Brookes University, Department of Planning, professor of innovation studies, research associate, 2000-. Writer. **Publications:** The Sociology of Internal Migration, 1972; Sociology of Town Planning: A Bibliography, 1972; Citizens in Conflict, 1974; Bibliography on the Political Sociology of Urban Development, 1978; The Power, Property, and Corporation: The Political Sociology of Planning, 1981; (with S. French) Corporatism, Participation, and Planning: The Case of Contemporary London, 1989; Changing City: Population, Employment, and Land Use Change Since the 1943 County of London Plan, 2002. EDITOR: Sociology, Politics, and Cities, 1976; (with R. King) The State in Action: Public Policy and Politics, 1990; (with J. Dekleca) Yugoslavia in Turmoil: After Self-Management?, 1991; Planning London, 1994; Innovation, Networks, and Learning Regions?, 1997; (with J. Cohen and D. Hart) Recherche et développement régional: travaux franco-britanniques, 1997; Innovative Cities, 2001. **Address:** Department of Planning, Oxford Brookes University, Gypsy Ln., Headington Campus, Oxford, OX OX3 0BP, England. **Online address:** jsimmie@brookes.ac.uk

SIMMIE, Lois (Ann). Canadian (born Canada), b. 1932. **Genres:** Children's Fiction, Novellas/Short Stories, Novels, Psychology, Poetry, Young Adult Non-fiction. **Career:** Saskatoon Public Library, writer-in-residence, 1987-88; University of Saskatchewan, Saskatoon Summer School of the Arts, Extension Department, fiction instructor. **Publications:** ADULT FICTION: Ghost House (short stories), 1976; They Shouldn't Make You Promise That (novel), 1981; Pictures (short stories), 1984; Betty Lee Bonner Lives There (short stories) 1993. FOR CHILDREN: Auntie's Knitting a Baby (poems), 1984; An Armadillo Is Not a Pillow (poems), 1986; What Holds Up the Moon?, 1987; Who Greased the Shoelaces? (poems), 1989; Oliver's Chickens, 1992; Mister Got to Go: The Cat that Wouldn't Leave, 1995 in US as No Cats Allowed, 1996. OTHER: The Secret Lives of Sgt. John Wilson: A True Story of Love and Murder (nonfiction), 1995; What I'm Trying to Say is Goodbye, 2003. Contributor to periodicals. **Address:** 1501 Cairns Ave., Saskatoon, SK S7H 2H5, Canada.

SIMMONDS, Posy. British (born England), b. 1945. **Genres:** Cartoons, Graphic Novels, Picture/Board Books, Young Adult Fiction, Illustrations. **Career:** The Sun, cartoonist, 1969-; writer and illustrator of books for children and adults, 1969-; London Times, contributor of daily cartoons, 1969-72; The Guardian, illustrator, 1972; Manchester Guardian Newspaper, contributor of weekly cartoons, 1977-87, 1988-90; Spectator Magazine, contributor of cartoons, 1988-90; Cartoon Trust, lecturer; University of Sussex, lecturer, 2000; Central Saint Martin's College of Art and Design, instructor in graphic arts. **Publications:** FOR ADULTS SELF-ILLUSTRATED CARTOON COLLECTIONS: The Posy Simmonds Bear Book, 1969; More Bear, 1975; Mrs. Weber's Diary, 1979; Pick of Posy, 1982; Very Posy, 1985; Pure Posy, 1987; Mustn't Grumble, 1993; Literary Life, 2003; Tamara Drewe, 2007. SELF-ILLUSTRATED GRAPHIC NOVELS: True Love, 1985; Gemma Bovery, 1999. FOR CHILDREN SELF-ILLUSTRATED PICTURE BOOKS: Fred, 1987; Lulu and the Flying Babies, 1988; The Chocolate Wedding, 1991; Bouncing Buffalo, 1994; F-Freezing ABC, 1996; Lavender, the Bravest Rabbit in the World, 2000; Baker Cat, 2005. Contributor to books. **Address:** Peters Fraser and Dunlop, Drury House, 34-43 Russell St., London, GL WC2B 5HA, England.

SIMMONS, Beth A. American (born United States), b. 1958?. **Genres:** Civil Liberties/Human Rights. **Career:** Duke University, assistant professor, 1991-96; University of California, associate professor, 1996-2002; Harvard University, Clarence Dillon professor of international affairs and director of weatherhead center for international affairs, 2002-; United States Institute of Peace, senior fellow, 1996-97; Center for the Advanced Study of the Behavioral Sciences, fellow, 2002-03; New York University, Straus Institute for the Advanced Study of Law and Justice, fellow, 2009-10. Writer. **Publications:** Who Adjusts? Domestic Sources of Foreign Economic Policy during the Interwar Years, 1994; Territorial Disputes and Their Resolution: The Case of Ecuador and Peru, 1999; Mobilizing for Human Rights: International Law in Domestic Politics, 2009. EDITOR: (with L.L. Martin) International Institutions: An International Organization Reader, 2001; (with W. Carlsnaes and T. Risse) Handbook of International Relations, 2002; (with R.H. Steinberg) International Law and International Relations, 2006; International Law, 2008;

(with F. Dobbin and G. Garrett) The Global Diffusion of Markets and Democracy, 2008. Contributor to periodicals. **Address:** Harvard University, 1737 Cambridge St., Ste. N212, Cambridge, MA 02138, U.S.A. **Online address:** bsimmons@wcfia.harvard.edu

SIMMONS, Cal. American (born United States), b. 1951?. **Genres:** Money/Finance, Business/Trade/Industry. **Career:** Angel Investor Clubs, co-founder and co-manager; Cal Simmons Travel, founder, president; ASAP Ventures, founder, managing partner; The Five Star Alliance, founder, chairman; Blue Cotton Tech Services L.L.C., co-founder, chairman; The Informed Traveler, founder, publisher; Adcision, founder; Washington Dinner Club, founder, manager; EMedia Club, founder, manager. **Publications:** (With J. May) Every Business Needs an Angel: Getting the Money You Need to Make Your Business Grow, 2001. Contributor to periodicals. **Address:** 1 Wales Alley, Ste. 201, Alexandria, VA 22314, U.S.A. **Online address:** cal@calsimmons.com

SIMMONS, Charles A(lexander). American (born United States), b. 1933. **Genres:** Writing/Journalism, History. **Career:** University of Central Oklahoma, assistant professor of journalism, associate professor, 1981-, professor of journalism, professor emeritus; Beach Beacon, reporter; Savannah Tribune, reporter; Savannah Herald, reporter. Photographer. **Publications:** The African American Press: A History of News Coverage during National Crises, with Special Reference to Four Newspapers, 1827-1965, 1998. Contributor of articles to magazines. **Address:** Department of Mass Communication, University of Central Oklahoma, 207J Communications Bldg., 100 N University Dr., Edmond, OK 73034-5209, U.S.A. **Online address:** csimmons@uco.edu

SIMMONS, Curt. American (born United States), b. 1968?. **Genres:** Information Science/Computers, Business/Trade/Industry. **Career:** Writer. **Publications:** MCSE Study Tips for Dummies, 1998; MCSE Windows 98 Ace It!, 1999; MCSE Exchange Server 5.5 for Dummies, 1999; Microsoft Proxy Server 2.0 MCSE Study System, 1999; Windows 2000 Hardware and Disk Management, 2000; Configuring Windows 2000 Server, 2000; Creating Active Directory Infrastructures, 2000; Active Directory Bible, 2000; MCSE Windows 2000 Server for Dummies, 2000; Master Active Directory Visually, 2000; MCSE: Designing a Windows 2000 Directory Services Infrastructure, 2000; Microsoft ISA Configuration and Administration, 2001; How to Do Everything with Windows ME, 2001; How to Do Everything with Your BlackBerry, 2001, 2nd ed., 2004; How to Do Everything with Windows XP, 2001, 3rd ed., 2005; Wireless Internet Access for Dummies, 2001; MCSE Internet Security and Acceleration Server 2000 Study Guide; Exam 70-227, 2001; Microsoft Windows XP Networking Inside Out, 2002; How Howard Crenshaw Stopped the Flood, 2002; MCSE Windows XP Professional Study Guide (Exam 70-270), 2002; Windows XP Headaches: How to Fix Common (and Not So Common) Problems in a Hurry, 2002, 2nd ed., 2005; Windows XP Secrets, 2002; (with A. Rofail) The Microsoft.NET Platform and Technologies, 2002; MCSA: All-in-One Desk Reference for Dummies, 2003; Microsoft Office 2003: The Complete Reference, 2003; A-plus Technicians On-the-Job Guide to Networking, 2003; A-plus; Technicians On-the-Job Guide to Windows XP, 2003; Microsoft Office FrontPage 2001 Bible, 2003; How to Do Everything with Photoshop Album, 2003; iPhoto 2 for Dummies, 2003; Mac OS X Headaches: How to Fix Common (and Not So Common) Problems in a Hurry, 2003; Windows XP for Power Users: Power Pack, 2004; Absolute Beginner's Guide to Keynote for Mac OS X, 2004; How to Do Everything with Windows XP Digital Media, 2004; PC Magazine Windows XP Speed Solutions, 2005; How to Do Everything with Windows Vista, 2007; CNET Do-It-Yourself Windows Vista Projects: 24 Cool Things You Didn't Know You Could Do!, 2007; MCTS Windows Vista Client Configuration Study Guide (exam 70-620), 2007. **Address:** c/o Author Mail, Wiley Publishing Inc., 111 River St., 5th Fl., Hoboken, NJ 07030, U.S.A. **Online address:** curt.simmons@hotmail.com

SIMMONS, Cynthia Francene. American (born United States), b. 1949. **Genres:** Novels, Adult Non-fiction, Language/Linguistics, Literary Criticism And History, Autobiography/Memoirs. **Career:** University of New Hampshire, lecturer of department of German and Russian, 1973-74; University of Wisconsin, department of Slavic languages and literatures, assistant professor, 1980-87, associate professor, 1987-90; Massachusetts Institute of Technology, visiting associate professor, foreign languages and literatures, literature, 1990-94; Boston College, Department of Slavic and Eastern Languages, associate professor, 1994-, chair, 2002-05, professor of Slavic studies, 2003-, undergraduate program director, 2006-. Writer. **Publications:** (Ed. with A.W. Mackie and T.K. McAuley) For Henry Kucera: Studies in Slavic Philology

and Computational Linguistics, 1992; Their Fathers Voice: Vassily Aksyonov, Venedikt Erofeev, Eduard Limonov and Sasha Sokolov, 1993; Writing the Siege of Leningrad: Womens, Diaries Memoirs and Documentary Prose, 2002. Contributor to periodicals. **Address:** Department of Slavic and Eastern Languages, Boston College, 210 Lyons Hall, Chestnut Hill, MA 02467-3804, U.S.A. **Online address:** simmonsc@bc.edu

SIMMONS, D(avid) R(oy). New Zealander (born New Zealand), b. 1930. **Genres:** Anthropology/Ethnology, Art/Art History, History, Theology/Religion. **Career:** Otago Museum, assistant keeper, 1962-64, keeper in anthropology, 1965-68; Auckland Institute and Museum, ethnologist, 1968-85, assistant director, 1978-85. Writer. **Publications:** Little Papanui and Otago Prehistory, 1967; The Lake Hauroko Burial and the Evolution of Maori Clothing, 1968; The Great New Zealand Myth, 1976; A Catalogue of Maori Artefacts in the Museums of Canada and the United States America, 1982; Whakairo: Maori Tribal Art, 1985; Ta Moko: The Art of Maori Tattooing, 1986, rev. ed., 1997; Iconography of New Zealand Maori Religion, 1986; Maori Auckland, 1987; (with K. Te Riria) Maori Tattoo, 1989; Ko Huiarau, 1991; An Index of Maori Items Held in Overseas Museums, 1996; (with G.S. Park) An Index of Chatham Islands Material in Overseas Museums, 1997; The Maori Meeting House, 1997; (with K. Te Riria) Moko Rangatira, 1999; The Carved Pare, 2001; Nga Taurere: An Anthology of Ancient Maori Poetry, 2003; Meeting-Houses of Ngati Porou o Te Tai Rawhiti: An Illustrated Guide, 2006. EDITOR: Habits and Customs of the New Zealanders 1838-42, 1972; Maori History and Place Names of Hawkes Bay, 1973; The Māori History and Place Names of Hawke's Bay, 2004. Contributor to books. **Address:** 12 Minto Rd., Remuera, 1050, New Zealand.

SIMMONS, Diane E. American (born United States), b. 1948. **Genres:** Novels, Literary Criticism And History, History. **Career:** Daily News-Miner, features editor, 1973-76; Seattle Post-Intelligencer, writer and editor, 1978-80; The City University of New York, adjunct lecturer, 1984-87, Borough of Manhattan Community College, assistant professor of English, 1988-, associate professor of English, professor of English; Fiction (magazine), associate editor, 1985-88; Hunter College, adjunct lecturer, 1987-93; Upsala College, assistant professor of English, 1993-94; New Jersey Institute of Technology, lecturer, 1994-98. **Publications:** NOVELS: Let the Bastards Freeze in the Dark, 1980; Dreams like Thunder, 1992; Narcissism of Empire, 2007; Little America, 2011. UNITED STATES AUTHOR SERIES: Jamaica Kincaid, 1994; Maxine Hong Kingston, 1999. **Address:** Department of English, Borough of Manhattan Community College, City University of New York, 199 Chambers St., Rm. N-719, New York, NY 10007-1044, U.S.A. **Online address:** dsimmons@bmcc.cuny.edu

SIMMONS, Earl. American (born United States), b. 1970. **Genres:** Biography, Music, Art/Art History. **Career:** Columbia Records, label artist, 1992; Ruff Ryders/Def Jam Records, label artist, 1997-2005, actor, 1998-; Bloodline Films, founder, 2003-; Sony, label artist, 2005-. Writer. **Publications:** (With S.D. Fontaine) E.A.R.L.: Ever Always Real Life: The Autobiography of DMX, 2002. Contributor to periodicals. **Address:** Bloodline Records, c/o Def Jam Records, 160 Varick St., Fl. 12, New York, NY 10003, U.S.A.

SIMMONS, James C(oleman). American (born United States), b. 1939. **Genres:** Literary Criticism And History, Travel/Exploration, Biography, Essays, Young Adult Non-fiction. **Career:** Boston University, assistant professor of British and American literature, 1966-73; San Diego State University, instructor in British and American literature, 1976-80. Freelance writer. **Publications:** The Novelist as Historian: Essays on the Victorian Historical Novel, 1973; (with M. Rudisill) Truman Capote: The Story of His Bizarre and Exotic Boyhood by an Aunt Who Helped Raise Him (biography), 1983; (with K. Druck) The Secrets Men Keep (nonfiction), 1985; Passionate Pilgrims: English Travelers to the World of the Desert Arabs, 1987; (comp.) Americans: The View from Abroad, 1990; The Big Book of Adventure Travel, 1990, 4th ed., 2001; Castaway in Paradise: The Incredible Adventures of True-Life Robinson Crusoes, 1993; (with D.E. Clippinger) David E. Clippinger Story: A Family Chronicle, 2000; Star-Spangled Eden: 19th Century America through the Eyes of Dickens, Wilde, Frances Trollope, Frank Harris, and Other British Travelers, 2000; (with M. Rudisill) The Southern Haunting of Truman Capote, 2000; Gypsy in My Soul: The Life and History of James C. Simmons, 2004; (with R.H. Baker) Against All Odds: The Robert H. Baker Story, 2005; (with M. Gibbons) Hooray for Hollywood: Marian Gibbons and the Founding of Hollywood Heritage, 2006. Contributor to periodicals. **Address:** Sheridan House Inc., 145 Palisade St., Dobbs Ferry, NY 10522, U.S.A.

SIMMONS, Jane. British (born England) **Genres:** Children's Fiction, Science Fiction/Fantasy, Psychology, Young Adult Fiction, Illustrations, Animals/Pets. **Career:** Writer and illustrator. **Publications:** Daisy and the Egg, 1998; Come Along Daisy!, 1998; Ebb and Flo and the New Friend, 1999; Daisy's Favorite Things, 1999; Go to Sleep Daisy, 1999; Daisy's Day Out, 2000; Daisy Says Coo!, 2000; Ebb and Flo and the Greed Gulls, 2000; Ebb and Flo and the Baby Seal, 2000; Daisy and the Beastie, 2000; Daisy: The Little Duck with Big Feet!, 2001; Where the Fairies Fly, 2001; Daisy's Hide-and-Seek: A Lift-the-Flap Book, 2001; Little Fern's First Winter, 2001; Daisy Says Here We Go Round the Mulberry Bush, 2002; Daisy Says If You're Happy and You Know It, 2002; Quack Daisy Quack!, 2002; The Dreamtime Fairies, 2002; Bouncy Bouncy Daisy, 2003; Splish Splash Daisy, 2003; Goodnight Daisy Goodnight Pip, 2003; Together, 2007; Beryl: A Pig's Tale, 2010; Ship's Cat Doris, 2011. **Address:** c/o Author Mail, Little Brown and Company Children's Publishing, 1271 Ave. of the Americas, New York, NY 10020, U.S.A. **Online address:** jane@janesimmons.com

SIMMONS, Marc (Steven). American (born United States), b. 1937. **Genres:** History. **Career:** University of New Mexico, visiting assistant professor of history, 1965-66, 1967-68; St. John's College, director, 1968. Writer. **Publications:** (Ed. and intro.) Indian And Mission Affairs In New Mexico, 1773, 1965; (ed. and intro.) Border Comanches: Seven Spanish Colonial Documents, 1785-1819, 1967; Spanish Government in New Mexico, 1968, 2nd ed., 1990; Two Southwesterners: Charles Lummis and Amado Chaves, 1968; Yesterday in Santa Fe: Episodes In A Turbulent History, 1969, rev. ed., 1989; The Little Lion of the Southwest: A Life of Manuel Antonio Chaves, 1973; Witchcraft in the Southwest: Spanish And Indian Supernaturalism On The Rio Grande, 1974; Turquoise and Six-Guns: The Story of Cerrillos, New Mexico, 1974, 3rd ed., 1990; New Mexico: A Bicentennial History, 1977; New Mexico: An Interpretive History, 1977; People of the Sun: Some Out-Of-Fashion Southwesterners, 1979; Southwestern Colonial Ironwork: The Spanish Blacksmithing Tradition From Texas To California, 1980; Albuquerque: A Narrative History, 1982; Ranchers, Ramblers and Renegades: True Tales Of Territorial New Mexico, 1984; Following the Santa Fe Trail: A Guide For Modern Travelers, 1984, (with H. Jackson) 3rd ed., 2001; Taos to Tome, 1986; Along the Santa Fe Trail, 1986; On the Santa Fe Trail, 1986; The Battle At Valley's Ranch: First Account Of The Gettysburg Of The West, 1862, 1987; Murder on the Santa Fe Trail: An International Incident, 1843, 1987; Spanish Government in New Mexico, 1990; When Six-Guns Ruled: Outlaw Tales Of The Southwest, 1990; Coronado's Land: Essays On Daily Life In Colonial New Mexico, 1991; The Last Conquistador: Juan de Oñate and The Settling Of The Far Southwest, 1991; Santiago: Saint of Two Worlds, 1991; Treasure Trails of the Southwest, 1994; The Old Trail to Santa Fe, 1996; Rio Grande Series, 1996; The Mexican War Correspondence Of Richard Smith Elliott, 1997; Massacre on the Lordsburg Road: A Tragedy of the Apache Wars, 1997; The Santa Fe Trail Association: A History of Its First Decade, 1986-1996, 1997; Spanish Pathways: Readings In The History Of Hispanic New Mexico, 2001; Millie Cooper's Ride: A True Story From History, 2002; Kit Carson And His Three Wives: A Family History, 2003; José's Buffalo Hunt: A Story From History, 2003; Hispanic Albuquerque, 1706-1846, 2003; Friday, The Arapaho Boy: A Story From History, 2004; Teddy's Cattle Drive: A Story From History, 2005; New Mexico Mavericks: Stories From A Fabled Past, 2005; Billy Blackfeet In The Rockies: A Story From History, 2006; Stalking Billy The Kid: Brief Sketches of a Short Life, 2006; (foreword) Villages & Villagers: Stories From New Mexico Villages, 2007; Charles F. Lummis: Author and Adventurer: A Gathering, 2008; (ed. with F.V. Scholes and J. Antonio) Juan Domínguez de Mendoza: soldier and frontiersman of the Spanish Southwest, 1627-1693, 2012. Contributor to periodicals. **Address:** University of New Mexico Press, 1720 Lomas Blvd. NE, Albuquerque, NM 87131, U.S.A.

SIMMONS, Sylvie. British (born England) **Genres:** Novels, Young Adult Non-fiction, Photography. **Career:** Mojo Magazine, contributing editor. **Publications:** NONFICTION: Motley Crue: Lewd, Crude and Rude, 1994; (intro.) Kiss, 1997; Neil Young: Reflections in Broken Glass, 2001; Serge Gainsbourg: A Fistful of Gitanes: Requiem for a Twister, 2002. OTHER: Too Weird for Ziggy, 2004. Contributor to periodicals. **Address:** Mojo Magazine, Mappin House, 4 Winsley St., London, GL W1W 8HF, England.

SIMMONS, Thomas. American (born United States), b. 1956. **Genres:** Adult Non-fiction, Literary Criticism And History, Education. **Career:** Stanford University, Freshman Writing Program, acting instructor in English, 1979-81, instructor, 1987-88; University of California, graduate student instructor, 1985-88; Massachusetts Institute of Technology, Program in Writing and Humanistic Studies, assistant professor of writing, 1988-92, associate professor in writing and humanistic studies, 1992-; University of Iowa, assistant professor, 1992-94, associate professor of English and nonfiction writing, 1994-, Nonfiction Writing Program, co-director, 1993-94; Iowa City Press Citizen, columnist, 1999-2000. **Publications:** The Unseen Shore: Memories of a Christian Science Childhood (nonfiction), 1991; A Season in the Air: One Man's Adventures in Flying (nonfiction), 1993; Erotic Reckonings: Mastery and Apprenticeship in the Work of Poets and Lovers (literary criticism and biography), 1994; Ghost Man: Reflections on Evolution, Love, and Loss, 2001; The Burning Child: Essays on Mental Health and Illness, 2005; Imperial Affliction: Eighteenth-century British Poets and Their Twentieth-century Lives, 2010. Contributor to periodicals. **Address:** Department of English, University of Iowa, Rm. 451 EPB, 308 English-Philosophy Bldg., Iowa City, IA 52242-1492, U.S.A. **Online address:** tom-simmons@uiowa.edu

SIMMONS, Valerie. *See* **GILLIES, Valerie.**

SIMMS, Brendan. British/Irish (born Ireland), b. 1967. **Genres:** History. **Career:** Christ Church, research fellow, 1992-93; University of Cambridge, Centre of International Studies, director of studies in history, 1993-99, 2003-, admissions tutor, 1997-2002, lecturer in international relations, 1998-2004, professor of international history, 2004-, Newton-Sheehy teaching fellow. Historian and author. **Publications:** The Impact of Napoleon: Prussian High Politics, Foreign Policy, and the Crisis of the Executive, 1797-1806, 1997; The Struggle for Mastery in Germany, 1779-1850, 1998; Unfinest Hour: How Britain Helped to Destroy Bosnia, 2002; (ed. with H. Scott) Cultures of Power in Europe During the Long Eighteenth Century, 2007; (ed. with T. Riotte) Hanoverian Dimension in British History, 1714-1837, 2007; Three Victories and a Defeat: The Rise and Fall of the First British Empire, 1714-1783, 2007; (ed. with W. Mulligan) Primacy of Foreign Policy in British History, 1660-2000: How Strategic Concerns Shaped Modern Britain, 2010; (ed. with K. Urbach) Die Rückkehr der grossen Männer, 2010; (ed.) Humanitarian Intervention: A History, 2011. Contributor to periodicals. **Address:** Center of International Studies, University of Cambridge, POLIS, 32 Trumpington St., Fitzwilliam House, Cambridge, CB CB2 1QY, England. **Online address:** bps11@cam.ac.uk

SIMOEN, Jan. Belgian (born Belgium), b. 1953. **Genres:** Young Adult Fiction. **Career:** House Theatre, artistic director. Photographer and writer. **Publications:** En Met Anna?, 1999; I'm Alice, forthcoming. **Address:** 75 bus Fontcinstraat 44, Louvain, 3000, Belgium. **Online address:** jsimoen@skynet.be

SIMON, Alvah. American (born United States), b. 1950?. **Genres:** Geography, Autobiography/Memoirs. **Career:** Midland College Foundation, lecturer. Producer, journalist and writer. **Publications:** North to the Night: A Year in the Arctic Ice, 1999. Contributor to magazines. **Address:** c/o Author Mail, International Marine Publishing, PO Box 220, Camden, ME 04843, U.S.A.

SIMON, Daniel (Martin). American/British (born England), b. 1957. **Genres:** Translations, Biography, Writing/Journalism, Essays, Literary Criticism And History. **Career:** Four Walls Eight Windows (book publishers), co-founder and co-publisher, 1986-. Writer. **Publications:** (Ed.) Best of Abbie Hoffman, 1989; (trans.) P. Bonafoux, Van Gogh: Self-Portraits (nonfiction), 1989; (with J. Hoffman) Run Run Run: The Lives of Abbie Hoffman (biography), 1994; (ed.) Nonconformity: Writing on Writing (essays), 1996; (ed.) A Man Without a Country, 2005; (ed. with B. Horvath) Entrapment and Other Writings, 2009. Contributor to periodicals. **Address:** Four Walls Eight Windows, 39 W 14th St., Ste. 503, New York, NY 10011, U.S.A.

SIMON, Diane. American (born United States) **Genres:** Business/Trade/Industry, Fash Ion/Costume, Politics/Government. **Career:** Freelance writer. **Publications:** Hair: Public, Political, Extremely Personal, 2000. Contributor to periodicals. **Address:** c/o Author Mail, St. Martin's Griffin, 175 5th Ave., New York, NY 10010, U.S.A.

SIMON, Francesca. British/American (born United States), b. 1955. **Genres:** Children's Fiction, Novels, Novellas/Short Stories, Adult Non-fiction, Children's Non-fiction, Picture/Board Books. **Career:** Freelance journalist, 1980-93; Sunday Times, writer; Guardian, writer; Mail on Sunday, writer; Telegraph, writer; Vogue, writer. **Publications:** FOR CHILDREN: But What Does the Hippopotamus Say?, 1994; Horrid Henry, 1994; Higgledy Piggledy: The Hen Who Loved to Dance, 1995; The Topsy Turvies, 1995; Cafe at the Edge of the Moon, 1996; Spider School, 1996; Papa Forgot, 1996; When the

Moon Comes Out, 1996; The Topsy-Turvies, 1996; Whoops a Daisy!, 1996; What's That Noise?, 1996; Horrid Henry and the Secret Club, 1996; Horrid Henry and the Tooth Fairy, 1997; Fussy Frieda, 1997; Moo Baa Baa Quack: Seven Farmyard Stories, 1998; Camels Don't Ski, 1998; Horrid Henry's Nits, 1998; Horrid Henry Strikes it Rich, 1998; Horrid Henry Gets Rich Quick, 1998; Where Are You?, 1998; Rosie's Swing, 1998; Don't Wake the Baby, 1998; Calling All Toddlers, 1999; Helping Hercules: And Other Stories, 1999; Horrid Henry's Haunted House, 1999; Hugo and the Bully Frogs, 1999; Horrid Henry and the Mummy's Curse, 2000; Toddler Times, 2000; Horrid Henry's Head Lice, 2000; Miaow Miaow Bow Wow, 2000; Three Cheers for Ostrich!, 2001; Horrid Henry Tricks The Tooth Fairy, 2001; Horrid Henry's Revenge, 2001; Horrid Henry's Stink Bomb, 2002; Horrid Henry and the Bogey Babysitter, 2002; Little Yellow Dog Says Look at Me, 2003; Little Yellow Dog Gets a Shock, 2003; Horrid Henry's Big Bad Book, 2004; Horrid Henry Joke Book, 2004; Horrid Henry Meets the Queen, 2004; Little Yellow Dog Bites the Builder, 2004; Adventures of Harry, 2004; Horrid Henry's Bedtime, 2005; Horrid Henry's Wicked Ways, 2005; Horrid Henry's Evil Enemies, 2006; Horrid Henry and the Football Fiend, 2006; Horrid Henry's Christmas Cracker, 2006; Horrid Henry Rules the World, 2007; Horrid Henry and the Abominable Snowman, 2007; Horrid Henry's House of Horrors, 2008; Horrid Henry's Annual 2009, 2008; Little Yellow Dog Meets His Match, 2008; Horrid Henry Robs the Bank, 2008; Horrid Henry's Underpants, 2009; Horrid Henry and the Soccer Fiend, 2009; Horrid Henry Wakes the Dead, 2009; Horrid Henry's Double Dare, 2009; Horrid Henry and the Mega-Mean Time Machine, 2009; Horrid Henry and the Scary Sitter, 2009; Horrid Henry's Holiday, 2009; Horrid Henry's Stinky School, 2009; Horrid Henry and Moody Margaret, 2009; Horrid Henry's Annual 2010, 2009; Moody Margaret Strikes Back, 2009; Horrid Henry's Christmas, 2009; Horrid Henry's Football Kit, 2010; Horrid Henry Rocks, 2010; Horrid Henry Annual 2011, 2010; Christmas Chaos with Horrid Henry: How to Survive, 2010; Horrid Henry's Dreadful Deeds, 2010; Horrid Henry Shows Who's Boss, 2010; Horrid Henry's Sleepover, 2010; Horrid Henry's Horrid Holidays, 2010; Horrid Henry's Hilariously Horrid Joke Book, 2010; Bodies, 2011; Do You Speak English, Moon?, 2011; Horrid Henry Reads a Book, 2011; Horrid Henry Tricks and Treats, 2011; Dinosaurs, 2011; Horrid Henry's Birthday Party, 2011; Horrid Henry's Car Journey, 2011; Horrid Henry's Christmas Play, 2011; A Greedy Gulp of Horrid Henry, 2011; Horrid Henry's Thank You Letter, 2011; Moody Margaret's School, 2011; Horrid Henry's Purple Hand Joke Book, 2011; Horrid Henry and the Zombie Vampire, 2011; Horrid Henry Annual 2012, 2011; Horrid Henry's A-Z of Everything Horrid, 2011; Horrid Henry's Rainy Day, 2012; Horrid Henry's Fab Facts, 2012; Horrid Henry's Author Visit, 2012; Horrid Henry's Christmas Presents, 2012; Horrid Henry's Sports Day, 2012. NOVELS: Big Class, Little Class, 1996; The Parent Swap Shop, 2011; The Sleeping Army, 2011. **Address:** Orion Children's Books, Orion House, 5 Upper St Martin's Ln., London, GL WC2H 9EA, England.

SIMON, Fritz B(ernhard). German (born Germany), b. 1948. **Genres:** Psychology, Psychiatry, Sociology, Economics. **Career:** University of Heidelberg, Department for Basic Research and Psychoanalytic Family Therapy, head physician, 1982-89, medical faculty, 1987; Carl-Auer-Systeme Verlag GmbH (publishing company), founder and managing partner, 1989, chief executive officer; Heidelberg Institute for Systemic Research, director, 1990-99; European Family Therapy Association, vice president, 1994-2001; German-Chinese Academy for Psychotherapy, co-founder, 1995, vice president, 1995-2005; Family Dynamics, editor, 1996-2001; University of Witten-Herdecke, Institute for Family Business, Faculty of Economics, founding professor and chair of leadership and organization, 1999-2004, adjunct professor, 2004-; Management Centre Witten GmbH, co-founder, 2000; Simon, Weber and Friends Organisation Consulting GmbH, systemic co-founder and managing partner, 2001; Helmet-Stierlin Institute, co-founder, 2002. **Publications:** Der Prozess der Individuation: über den Zusammenhang von Vernunft und Gefühlen, 1984; (with H. Stierlin) Die Sprache der Familientherapie: ein Vokabular: überblick, Kritik und Integration systemtherapeutischer Begriffe, Konzepte und Methoden, 1984; (with H. Stierlin and L.C. Wynne) The Language of Family Therapy: A Systemic Vocabulary and Sourcebook, 1985; (ed. with H. Stierlin and G. Schmidt) Familiar Realities: The Heidelberg Conference, 1987; (ed. with G. Weber) Strange Encounters with Carl Auer, 1991; Tödliche Konflikte: zur Selbstorganisation privater und öffentlicher Kriege, 2001, 2nd ed., 2004; (with K. König) Zwischen Couch und Einwegspiegel: Systemisches für Psychoanalytiker-Psychoanalytisches für Systemiker; ein Gespräch, 2001; (ed. with D. Baecker and P. Krieg) Terror im System: der 11. September 2001 und die Folgen, 2002; (ed.) Die Familie des Familienunternehmens: ein System zwischen Gefühl und Geschäft, 2002; Gemeinsam

sind wir blöd, 2004, 2nd ed., 2006; (with G. Weber) Vom Navigieren beim Driften, 2004, 2nd ed., 2006; (with G. Weber and G. Schmidt) Aufstellungsarbeit revisited, 2005; (with T. Groth and R. Wimmer) Mehr-Generationen-Familienunternehmen, 2005; Einführung in Systemtheorie und Konstruktivismus, 2006, 3rd ed., 2008; Einführung in die systemische Organisationstheorie, 2007; (with C. Rech-Simon) Survival-Tipps für Adoptiveltern, 2008; Einführung in die systemische Wirtschaftstheorie, 2009; (ed.) Vor dem Spiel ist nach dem Spiel, 2009. **Address:** University of Witten-Herdecke, Ifred-Herrhausen-Strabe 50, Witten, 58448, Germany. **Online address:** fbsimon@t-online.de

SIMON, Harvey B(ruce). American (born United States), b. 1942. **Genres:** Sports/Fitness, Medicine/Health, Administration/Management. **Career:** U.S. Public Health Service, wartime affiliate, 1969-71; Georgetown University, clinical instructor of medicine, 1971-72; Harvard Medical School, instructor, 1973-74, assistant professor, 1974-, associate professor of medicine, Harvard Men's Health Watch, founding editor, editor-in-chief; Massachusetts General Hospital, affiliate staff, 1973-. **Publications:** (With S.R. Levisohn) Tennis Medic: Conditioning, Sports Medicine, and Total Fitness for Every Player, 1984; (with S.R. Levisohn) The Athlete Within: A Personal Guide to Total Fitness, 1987; Staying Well: Your Complete Guide to Disease Prevention, 1992; Conquering Heart Disease: New Ways to Live Well without Drugs or Surgery, 1994; The Harvard Medical School Guide to Men's Health, 2002; No Sweat Exercise Plan: Lose Weight, Get Healthy, and Live Longer, 2006. Contributor to periodicals. **Address:** Harvard Medical School, 25 Shattuck St., Boston, MA 02115-6092, U.S.A.

SIMON, James F. American (born United States), b. 1938. **Genres:** Law. **Career:** Ford Foundation, fellow, 1964-65; Time, editor and correspondent, 1969-74; University of California, lecturer, 1973; Yale University, visiting lecturer, 1974-75; New York Law School, assistant professor, 1975-77, associate professor, 1977-78, professor of law, 1978-93, dean pro tempore, 1983-84, dean, 1983-92, Martin professor of law, 1993, dean emeritus; University of Pennsylvania, lecturer, 1981; Franklin and Marshall College, lecturer, 1982, 1986; University of Latvia, lecturer, 1990. Writer. **Publications:** In His Own Image: The Supreme Court in Richard Nixon's America, 1973; The Judge, 1976; Independent Journey: The Life of William O. Douglas, 1980; The Antagonists: Hugo Black, Felix Frankfurter and Civil Liberties in Modern America, 1989; The Center Holds: The Power Struggle Inside the Rehnquist Court, 1995; What Kind of Nation: Thomas Jefferson, John Marshall and the Epic Struggle to Create a United States, 2002; Lincoln and Chief Justice Taney: Slavery, Secession and the President's War Powers, 2006; FDR and Chief Justice Hughes: the President, the Supreme Court, and the Epic Battle Over the New Deal, 2012; The Modern Supreme Court and Civil Liberties, forthcoming. Contributor to periodicals. **Address:** New York Law School, 57 Worth St., New York, NY 10013, U.S.A. **Online address:** jsimon@nyls.edu

SIMON, Lizzie. American (born United States), b. 1975. **Genres:** Travel/Exploration. **Career:** Columbia University, Arts Department, WKCR 89.9 FM, head; Flea Theatre, creative producer. Freelance writer. **Publications:** Detour: My Bipolar Road Trip in 4-D, 2002. **Address:** Atria Books Publicity, Simon & Schuster, 1230 Ave. of the Americas, New York, NY 10020, U.S.A. **Online address:** lizzie@lizziesimon.com

SIMON, Michele. American (born United States) **Genres:** Food And Wine, Business/Trade/Industry, Economics. **Career:** Lieff, Cabraser, Heimann, & Bernstein, attorney, 1994-96; nutrition advocate, 1996-; public health lawyer and consultant, 1998-; John F. Kennedy University, School of Law, adjunct professor of law, 1999; Center for Informed Food Choices (CIFC), founder and director, 2002-07; University of California-San Francisco, Hastings College of the Law, assistant professor of health policy, 2005-06, adjunct assistant professor, 2005-06; University of California-Berkeley, School of Public Health, instructor, 2005, 2007-08; Marin Institute, research and policy director, 2007-11; Eat Drink Politics, president, 2011-; Yale University, Rudd Center for Food Policy and Obesity, consultant; Prevention Institute, consultant; Public Health Institute, consultant. Writer. **Publications:** Appetite for Profit: How the Food Industry Undermines Our Health and How to Fight Back, 2006. Contributor to periodicals. **Address:** Center for Informed Food Choices, PO Box 16053, Oakland, CA 94610, U.S.A. **Online address:** michele@informedeating.org

SIMON, Neil. American (born United States), b. 1927. **Genres:** Plays/Screenplays, Autobiography/Memoirs, Young Adult Fiction, Literary Criticism And History. **Career:** Television script writer, 1951-60; playwright and screenwriter, 1961-. **Publications:** PLAYS: (with W. Friedberg) Adventures of Marco Polo: A Musical Fantasy, 1959; Come Blow Your Horn: A Comedy in Three Acts, 1961; Little Me, 1962, rev. ed., 1982; Barefoot in the Park, 1963; The Odd Couple, 1965; Sweet Charity, 1966; The Star-Spangled Girl, 1967; Plaza Suite, 1968; Promises, Promises, 1969; Last of the Red Hot Lovers, 1969; The Gingerbread Lady, 1970; The Prisoner of Second Avenue, 1971; The Sunshine Boys, 1972; The Good Doctor, 1974; God's Favorite, 1974; California Suite, 1976; Chapter Two, 1979; They're Playing our Song, 1979; I Ought to be in Pictures, 1980; Fools, 1981; Brighton Beach Memoirs, 1983; Biloxi Blues, 1985; Broadway Bound, 1986; Rumors, 1988; Lost in Yonkers, 1991; Jake's Women, 1993; The Goodbye Girl, 1993; Laughter on the 23rd Floor, 1993; London Suite, 1995; Rewrites, 1996; Rumours, 1997, rev. ed., 2007; The Dinner Party, 1999; The Odd Couple I and II, 2000; 45 Seconds from Broadway, 2001; Oscar and Felix: A New Look at the Odd Couple, 2002; Rose's Dilemma, 2004. OTHERS: (with W. Friedberg) Heidi, 1959; The Comedy of Neil Simon, 1971; The Collected Plays of Neil Simon, vol. II, vol. III, 1991, vol. IV, 1998; A Memoir, 1996; (contrib.) Hold Fast Your Dreams, 1996; The Play Goes On, 1999; (with R. Karshner) Neil Simon Scenes: Scenes from the Works of America's Foremost Playwright, 2000. **Address:** Gary N. Da Silva, 111 N Sepulveda Blvd., Ste. 250, Manhattan Beach, CA 90266-6850, U.S.A.

SIMON, Rachel. American (born United States), b. 1959?. **Genres:** Novels, Novellas/Short Stories, Autobiography/Memoirs. **Career:** Barnes & Noble, event coordinator; Bryn Mawr College, lecturer in creative writing, 1995-; Pennsylvania State University, faculty; full-time writer, 2007-. **Publications:** Little Nightmares, Little Dreams, 1990; The Magic Touch, 1994; The Writer's Survival Guide, 1997; Riding the Bus with My Sister: A True Life Journey, 2002; Building A Home With My Husband, 2009; The House On Teacher's Lane, 2010; Story of Beautiful Girl, 2011. **Address:** Grand Central Publishing, 237 Park Ave., New York, NY 10017, U.S.A. **Online address:** rachelsimon2008@gmail.com

SIMON, Rita J(ames). American (born United States), b. 1931. **Genres:** Law, Sociology, Women's Studies And Issues. **Career:** University of Chicago, Law School, research associate, 1958-61, assistant professor of sociology, 1959-61; Columbia University, School of Social Work, research associate, 1961-63; Yale University, Graduate School of Nursing, Annie W. Goodrich visiting professor, 1962-63; University of Illinois, associate professor, 1963-68, professor of sociology, 1968-, College of Law, research professor of communications and professor, 1971-74, professor of law and communications research, 1980-, Department of Sociology, head, 1968-70, Law and Society Program, director, 1975-80, Center for Advanced Study, fellow, 1980-81; Hebrew University of Jerusalem, visiting lecturer, 1967-68, visiting professor, 1970-71, 1974-75; American Sociological Review, editor, 1977-80; Justice Quarterly, editor, 1983-86; American University, School of Justice, dean, 1983-87, School of Public Affairs, university professor, 1989-, College of Law, university professor, 1989-; Gender Issues, editor, 1998; The Shula Ankary Foundation, founder, 2000-; Women's Freedom Network, president. **Publications:** The Jury and the Defense of Insanity, 1967; (with J. O' Connell) Payment for Pain and Suffering, 1972; American Public Opinion: 1937-1970, 1974; Women and Crime, 1975; (with H. Altstein) Transracial Adoption, 1977 as Transracial Adoption, A Follow-up, 1981; Continuity and Change, 1978; The American Jury, 1980; Public Opinion and the Immigrant, 1985; New Lives, 1985; (with D. Aaronson) The Defense of Insanity, 1987; (with J. Landis) The Crimes Women Commit: The Punishments They Receive, 1990, (with H. Ahn-Redding) 3rd ed., 2005; (with G. Danziger) Women's Movements in America, 1991; (with H. Altstein) Adoption, Race and Identity, 1992; (with S. Alexander) The Ambivalent Welcome, 1993; Rabbis, Lawyers, Immigrants, and Thieves, 1993; (with H. Altstein and M. Melli) The Case for Transracial Adoption, 1994; (with J. Fyfe) Editors as Gatekeepers, 1994; In the Golden Land, 1997; (with R. Erickson) Social Science Data and Supreme Court Decisions, 1998; Abortion, 1998; (with J. Scherer) Euthanasia and the Right to Die, 1998; (with L. van der Does) Renaissance Women of Science, 1999; (with R. Roorda) In Their Own Voices: Transracial Adoptees Tell Their Stories, 2000; (with H. Altstein) Adoption across Borders: Serving the Children in Transracial and Intercountry Adoptions, 2000; A Life Against the Grain: The Autobiography of An Unconventional Economist, 2002; A Comparative Analysis of Capital Punishment: Statutes, Policies, Frequencies, and Public Attitudes the World Over, 2002; (with R. Procida) Global Perspectives On Social Issues: Pornography, 2003; (with H. Altstein) Global Perspectives on Social Issues: Marriage and Divorce, 2003; Immigration the World Over: Statutes, Policies, and Practices, 2003; (with L. Banks) Global Perspec-

tives on Social Issues: Education, 2003; (with P. Zalkind) Global Perspectives On Social Issues: Juvenile Justice Systems, 2004; (with C.G. Roman and M. Ahn-Redding) Illicit Drug Policies, Trafficking, and Use the World Over, 2005; (with S. Hepburn) Women's Roles and Statuses the World Over, 2006; (with with H. Ahn-Redding) The Insanity Defense, the World Over, 2006; (with R.M. Roorda) In Their Parents' Voices: Reflections On Raising Transracial Adoptees, 2007; (with S. Hernandez) Native American Transracial Adoptees Tell Their Stories, 2008; (with A. Brooks) Rights and Responsibilities of Citizenship the World Over, 2009; (with M.A. Abdel-Moneim) Public Opinion in the United States: Studies of Race, Religion, Gender, and Issues that Matter, 2009; (with C.A. de Waal) Prisons the World Over, 2009; (with R.M. Roorda) In their Siblings' Voices: White Non-adopted Siblings Talk about their Experiences Being Raised with Black and Biracial Brothers and Sisters, 2009; (with A.M. Brooks) Gay and Lesbian Communities the World Over, 2009; (with V. Gueorguieva) Voting and Elections the World Over, 2009; (with M.A. Abdel-Moneim) Handbook of Military Conscription and Composition the World Over, 2011. EDITOR: As We Saw the Thirties, 1967; Readings in the Sociology of Law, 1968; The Jury System, 1975; Research in Law and Sociology, 1978; (with F. Adler) The Criminology of Deviant Women, 1979; (with C.B. Brettell) International Migration, 1986; Neither Victim nor Enemy, 1995; From Data to Public Policy, 1996; Women in the Military, 1999; Immigrant Women, 2000; A Look Backward and Forward at Professional Women and Their Families, 2000; A Comparative Perspective On Major Social Problems, 2001; Sporting Equality: Title IX Thirty Years Later, 2005; (ed. with H. Ahn-Redding) Intercountry Adoptees Tell Their Stories, 2007. Contributor to newspapers, magazines and journals. **Address:** School of Public Affairs, American University, 246 Ward Circle Bldg., 4400 Massachusetts Ave. NW, Washington, DC 20016-8001, U.S.A. **Online address:** rsimon@american.edu

SIMON, Robert. See MUSTO, Barry.

SIMON, Roger (Mitchell). American (born United States), b. 1948. **Genres:** Mystery/Crime/Suspense, Civil Liberties/Human Rights, Communications/Media, Ethics, Law, Politics/Government, Social Commentary, Writing/Journalism, Essays, Humor/Satire, Adult Non-fiction. **Career:** City News Bureau, reporter, 1970; Waukegan News-Sun, columnist, 1970-72; Chicago Sun-Times, investigative reporter and columnist, 1972-84; Baltimore Sun, staff columnist, 1984-95; WMAR-TV, commentator, 1986; Chicago Tribune, White House correspondent, 1998-; U.S. News & World Report, chief political correspondent, 1999-, political editor; Bloomberg News, chief political correspondent, 2006-; Politico.com, chief political columnist; Yale university, fellow; Stanford University, fellow; Commercial-News, staff. **Publications:** Simon Says: The Best of Roger Simon, 1985; Road Show: In America, Anyone Can Become President, It's One of the Risks We Take, 1990; Show Time: The American Political Circus and the Race for the White House, 1998; High Horses on a Low Road, 2001; Divided We Stand: How Al Gore Beat George Bush and Lost the Presidency, 2001. Contributor of articles to periodicals and magazines. **Address:** Creators Syndicate, 5777 W Century Blvd., Ste. 700, Los Angeles, CA 90045, U.S.A. **Online address:** rogersimon@bloomberg.net

SIMON, Scott. American (born United States), b. 1952. **Genres:** Sports/Fitness, Novels, Politics/Government. **Career:** National Public Radio, host, commentator and chief of Chicago bureau, 1977-, Weekend Edition Program, host and co-creator, 1985-; National Broadcast Corp., television co-anchor, 1994; Broadcast journalist. **Publications:** Home and Away: Memoir of a Fan, 2000; Jackie Robinson and the Integration of Baseball, 2002; Pretty Birds: A Novel, 2005; (foreword) A Russian Diary, 2007; Windy City: A Novel of Politics, 2008; Baby, We Were Meant for Each Other: In Praise of Adoption, 2010. Contributor to books. **Address:** National Public Radio, 635 Massachusetts Ave. NW, Washington, DC 20001-3740, U.S.A. **Online address:** scottsimonbooks@gmail.com

SIMON, Seymour. American (born United States), b. 1931. **Genres:** Children's Non-fiction, Children's Fiction, E-books, Picture/Board Books, Sciences, Natural History, Animals/Pets, Photography, Photography. **Career:** New York Public Schools, teacher, 1955-79; author, 1968-; Seymour Science L.L.C., digital application writer and publisher. **Publications:** Animals in Field and Laboratory: Science Projects in Animal Behaviour, 1968; The Look-It-Up Book of the Earth, 1968; Motion, 1969; Soap Bubbles, 1969; Discovering What Earthworms Do, 1969; Discovering What Frogs Do, 1969; Exploring with a Microscope, 1969; Wet and Dry, 1969; Weather and Climate,

1969; Discovering What Goldfish Do, 1970; Handful of Soil, 1970; Light and Dark, 1970; Science in a Vacant Lot, 1970; Chemistry in the Kitchen, 1971; Discovering What Gerbils Do, 1971; Finding Out with Your Senses, 1971; The Paper Airplane Book, 1971; Science at Work: Easy Models You Can Make, 1971; Science at Work: Projects in Space Science, 1971; Hot and Cold, 1972; Science at Work: Projects in Oceanography, 1972; Science Projects in Ecology, 1972; Science Projects in Pollution, 1972; A Building on Your Street, 1973; Discovering What Crickets Do, 1973; From Shore to Ocean Floor: How Life Survives in the Sea, 1973; Projects with Plants, 1973; The Rock-Hound's Book, 1973; A Tree on Your Street, 1973; About Your Heart, 1974; Birds on Your Street, 1974; Life in the Dark: How Animals Survive at Night, 1974; Water on Your Street, 1974; Pets in a Jar: Collecting and Caring for Small Wild Animals, 1975; Projects with Air, 1975; Discovering What Garter Snakes Do, 1975; Ghosts, 1976; Life on Ice: How Animals Survive In The Arctic, 1976; Everything Moves, 1976; The Optical Illusion Book, 1976, rev. ed. as Now You See It, Now You Don't: The Amazing World of Optical Illusions, 1998; Tropical Saltwater Aquarium Book: How to Set Them up and Keep Them Going, 1976; Life and Death in Nature, 1976; Animals in Your Neighborhood, 1976; Discovering What Puppies Do, 1977; Beneath Your Feet, 1977; Space Monsters: From Movies, TV, and Books, 1977; What Do You Want to Know about Guppies?, 1977; Look to the Night Sky, 1977; Exploring Fields and Lots: Easy Science Project, 1978; Killer Whales, 1978; About Your Lungs, 1978; Animal Fact/Animal Fable, 1979; Danger from Below: Earthquakes, Past, Present, and Future, 1979; The Secret Clocks: Time Senses of Living Things, 1979; Meet the Giant Snakes, 1979; Creatures from Lost Worlds, 1979; The Long View into Space, 1979; Deadly Ants, 1979; About the Foods You Eat, 1979; Meet Baby Animals, 1980; Animals Nobody Loves, 1980; Einstein Anderson, Science Sleuth, 1980; Einstein Anderson Shocks His Friends, 1980; Goony Birds, Bush Babies, and Devil Rays, 1980; Strange Mysteries from Around the World, 1980; Mirror Magic, 1980; Silly Animal Jokes and Riddles, 1980; Poisonous Snakes, 1981; About Your Brain, 1981; Strange Creatures, 1981; Body Sense/Body Nonsense, 1981; Einstein Anderson Makes Up For Lost Time, 1981; Einstein Anderson Tells A Comet's Tale, 1981; Mad Scientists, Weird Doctors, & Time Travelers in Movies, TV, & Books, 1981; Einstein Anderson Goes To Bat, 1982; Einstein Anderson Lights Up The Sky, 1982; The Smallest Dinosaurs, 1982; How to Be a Space Scientist in Your Own Home, 1982; The Long Journey from Space, 1982; Einstein Anderson Sees Through The Invisible Man, 1983; Hidden Worlds: Pictures: The Invisible, 1983; Little Giants, 1983; Chip Rogers, Computer Whiz, 1984; Computer Sense, Computer Nonsense, 1984; The Dinosaur Is The Biggest Animal That Ever Lived, and Other Wrong Ideas You Thought Were True, 1984; Earth: Our Planet in Space, 1984; The Moon, 1984; 101 Questions and Answers About Dangerous Animals, 1985; The BASIC Book, 1985; Bits and Bytes: A Computer Dictionary For Beginners, 1985; How to Talk to Your Computer, 1985; Meet the Computer, 1985; Saturn, 1985; Shadow Magic, 1985; Your First Home Computer: Buying It, Using It, and Keeping It Working, 1985; The Largest Dinosaurs, 1986; Stars, 1986, rev. ed., 2006; The Sun, 1986; Turtle Talk: A Beginner's Book of LOGO, 1986; Mars, 1987; Uranus, 1987; Icebergs and Glaciers, 1987; Galaxies, 1988; Volcanoes, 1988; How to Be an Ocean Scientist in Your Own Home, 1988; Jupiter, 1988; Storms, 1989; Whales, 1989, rev. ed., 2006; Oceans, 1990, rev. ed., 2006; Deserts, 1990; The New Question and Answer Book About Dinosaurs, 1990; Space Words: A Dictionary, 1991; Neptune, 1991; Big Cats, 1991; Earthquakes, 1991, rev. ed., 2006; Mercury, 1992; Our Solar System, 1992, rev. ed., 2007; Snakes, 1992; Venus, 1992; Professor I.Q. Explores the Brain, 1993; Wolves, 1993; Autumn across America, 1993; Weather, 1993, rev. ed., 2006; Winter across America, 1994; Science Dictionary, 1994; Comets, Meteors, and Asteroids, 1994; Mountains, 1994; Earth Words: A Dictionary of the Environment, 1995; (ed.) Star Walk, 1995; Sharks, 1995, rev. ed., 2006; The Heart: Our Circulatory System, 1996, rev. ed., 2006; Journeys through the Air: Life on the Move, 1996; The Heart, 1996; Wildfires, 1996; Spring Across America, 1996; The Brain: Our Nervous System, 1997, rev. ed., 2006; Lightning, 1997, rev. ed., 2006; The Machine and Other Cases, 1997; Gigantic Ants and Other Cases, 1997; Halloween Horror and Other Cases, 1997; Howling Dog and Other Cases, 1997; On-line Spaceman and Other Cases, 1997; Ride The Wind: Airborne Journeys: Animals and Plants, 1997; The Time Machine and Other Cases, rev. ed., 1997; Wild Babies, 1997; Invisible Man and Other Cases, rev. ed., 1998; Bones: Our Skeletal System, 1998; Destination Jupiter, 1998; They Swim the Seas: The Mystery: Animal Migration, 1998; Wings of Darkness and Other Cases, 1998; Mysterious Lights and Other Cases, 1998; The Universe, 1998, rev. ed., 2006; Muscles: Our Muscular System, 1998; Crocodiles and Alligators, 1999; Tornadoes, 1999; Destination Mars, 2000; From Paper Airplanes To Outer Space, 2000; Gorillas, 2000; Out of Sight,

2000; Seymour Simon's Book of Trucks, 2000; They Walk the Earth: The Extraordinary Travels: Animals On Land, 2000; Animals Nobody Loves, 2001; (with N. Fauteux) Let's Try It Out In The Air: Hands-On Early Learning Science Activities, 2001; (with N. Fauteux) Let's Try It Out In The Water: Hands-On Early Learning Science Activities, 2001; Amazing Aircraft, 2002; Baby Animals, 2002; Danger! Earquakes, 2002; Danger! Volcanoes, 2002; Destination, Space, 2002; Fighting Fires, 2002; Giant Machines, 2002; (with N. Fauteux) Let's Try It Out On The Playground, 2002; Planets Around The Sun, 2002; Seymour Simon's Book: Trains, 2002; Destination Space, 2002; Super Storms, 2002; Wild Bears, 2002; Cool Cars, 2003; Eyes and Ears, 2003; Hurricanes, 2003, rev. ed., 2007; Incredible Sharks, 2003; (with N. Fauteux) Let's Try It Out In The Kitchen, 2003; (with N. Fauteux) Let's Try It Out With Towers and Bridges: Hands-On Early-Learning Science Activities, 2003; Pyramids and Mummies, 2003; Space Travelers, 2003; Spiders, 2003; Cats, 2004; Dogs, 2004; Amazing Bats, 2005; Big Bugs, 2005; Bridges, 2005; Guts: Our Digestive System, 2005; Skyscrapers, 2005; Wild Weather, 2005; Aeronaves Asombrosos, 2006; Creatures of the Dark, 2006; Creepy Creatures, 2006; Emergency Vehicles, 2006; Giant Snakes, 2006; Horses, 2006; Knights and Castles, 2006; Planets, 2006; Tiburones Fabulosos, 2006; Lungs: Your Respiratory System, 2007; Murciélagos Asombrosos, 2007; Penguins, 2007; The Human Body, 2008; under the Sea, 2008; Dolphins, 2009; Tropical Rainforests, 2010; Global Warming, 2010; (with N. Fauteux) Let's Try It Out With Cold Hands and Warm Feet, 2010; Butterflies, 2011; Strange Mysteries: From Around the World, 2012; Body Sense, Body Nonsense, 2012; Seymour Simon's Extreme Earth Records, 2012. **Address:** PO Box 420, Craryville, Copake Lake, NY 12521, U.S.A. **Online address:** simon@seymoursimon.com

SIMON, Sheldon Weiss. American (born United States), b. 1937. **Genres:** Politics/Government, Third World, Social Sciences. **Career:** University of Minnesota, Center for International Relations, assistant director, 1961-62; U.S. Government, foreign affairs analyst, 1963-66; George Washington University, lecturer, 1965-66; University of Kentucky, Department of political science, assistant professor, 1966-69, associate professor, 1969-74, professor, 1974-75; Institute of Sino-Soviet Studies, research associate, 1967-; Patterson School of Diplomacy, acting director, 1970-71; University of Hawaii, department of political science, visiting assistant professor, 1968-; University of British Columbia, Institute of International Relations, visiting research associate, 1972-73, department of political science, visiting professor, 1979-80; Arizona State University, department of political science, chairman, 1975-79, professor of political science department, 1975-79, Center for Asian Studies, director, 1980-88; Carleton University, Paterson School of International Affairs, visiting professor, 1976-; The Orkand Corp., consultant, 1985-88; Research Analysis Corp., consultant; Bendix Research Corp., consultant; Orkand Corp., consultant. Writer. **Publications:** Assessing Pekings Perception of Southeast Asia: A Research Approach, 1967; Threat Perception and Prospects for Southeast Asian Regional Cohesion: Some Considerations, 1967; The Broken Triangle: Peking, Djakarta and the PKI, 1969; A Systems Approach to Security in the Indian Ocean Arc, 1970; War and Politics in Cambodia: A Communications Analysis, 1974; Asian Neutralism and U.S. Policy, 1975; (ed.) The Military and Security in the Third World: Domestic and International Impacts, 1978; The ASEAN States and Regional Security, 1982; The Future of Asian-Pacific Security Collaboration, 1988; (ed.) East Asian Security in the Post-Cold War Era, 1993; (with R.J. Ellings) Southeast Asian Security in the New Millennium, 1996; The Many Faces of Asian Security, 2001; (ed. with L.E. Cady) Religion and Conflict in South and Southeast Asia: Disrupting Violence, 2006; ASEAN and Its Security Offspring: Facing New Challenges, 2007; (ed. with E. Gohn) China, the United States, and Southeast Asia: Contending Perspectives on Politics, Security and Economics, 2008. Contributor to journals. **Address:** Department of Political Science, Arizona State University, Lattie Coor Hall 6716, PO Box 3902, Tempe, AZ 85287-3902, U.S.A. **Online address:** shells@asu.edu

SIMON, Uriel. Israeli (born Israel), b. 1929. **Genres:** Theology/Religion. **Career:** Bar-Ilan University, lecturer, 1962-73, associate professor, 1973-82, professor of Bible, 1982-97, head of department, 1964-75, Institute for the History of Jewish Bible Research, director, 1974-92, professor emeritus, 1997-; Jewish Theological Seminary, visiting associate professor, 1970-71; Tel-Aviv University, visiting senior lecturer, 1972-73; Hebrew University of Jerusalem, Institute for Advanced Studies, fellow, 1982-83, 1988-89; Yale University, visiting professor, 1991-92, 1996-97; Harvard University, visiting professor, 1994-95. Writer. **Publications:** Four Approaches to the Book of Psalms: From Saadya Gaon to Abraham Ibn-Ezra, 1982; The Book of Jonah, 1992; Jona: ein jüdischer Kommentar, 1994; Reading Prophetic Narratives,

1997; (with J. Cohen) Abraham Ibn Ezra's Yesod Mora Ve-Sod Torah (title means: 'The Foundation of Piety and the Secret of Torah'), 2002, 2nd ed., 2007; Joseph and His Brothers: A Story of Change, 2002. ENGLISH TITLES OF BOOKS PUBLISHED IN HEBREW: Abraham Ibn Ezra's Two Commentaries on the Minor Prophets: An Annotated Critical ed., Volume I: Hosea, Joel, Amos, 1989; Seek Peace and Pursue It: Topical Issues in the Light of the Bible, the Bible in the Light of Topical Issues, 2002. EDITOR: The Bible and Us, 1979; Studies in Bible and Exegesis, vol. I, 1980, vol. II, 1986. Contributor to periodicals. **Address:** Bar-Ilan University, Ramat Gan, 52900, Israel.

SIMONDS, Merilyn. (Merilyn Mohr). Canadian (born Canada), b. 1949. **Genres:** Children's Fiction, Novellas/Short Stories, Crafts, Adult Non-fiction, Homes/Gardens. **Career:** Freelance magazine writer, 1979-; Kingston School of Writing, instructor in creative nonfiction, 1988-90; Loyalist College of Applied Arts and Technology, instructor in freelance writing, 1995-96; Kwantlen University, adjunct professor, 2009-11; Kingston Writers Fest, artistic director, 2009-12; University of British Columbia, MFA in Creative Writing, Optional Residency Program, adjunct professor, 2011-12. **Publications:** NON-FICTION: The Art of Soapmaking, 1979; (with T. Moores) Canoecraft, 1983; Sunwings, 1985; Home Playgrounds, 1987; A Chronicle of Our House, 1988; (with M. Weisbord) The Valour and the Horror: The Untold Story of Canadians in the Second World War, 1991; (with T. Forsyth) The Harrowsmith Salad Garden, 1992; The Games Treasury, 1993; The Convict Lover: A True Story, 1996; The New Games Treasury, 1997. FOR CHILDREN: Fit to Drink (nonfiction), 1995. FOR ADULTS: The Lion in the Room Next Door (short stories), 2000. FICTION: The Holding, 2004. OTHERS: (with W. Grady) Breakfast at the Exit Cafe: Travels in America, 2010. MEMOIR: A New Leaf, 2011. **Address:** Anne McDermid Agency, 64 Bloem Ave., Toronto, ON M6E 1S1, Canada. **Online address:** info@merilynsimonds.com

SIMONELLI, Jeanne M(arie). American (born United States), b. 1947. **Genres:** Novellas/Short Stories, Poetry, Anthropology/Ethnology, Adult Non-fiction, Sociology. **Career:** State University of New York College-Oneonta, chair, 1990-92, 1998-99, professor of anthropology, 1995; Wake Forest University, Department of Anthropology, professor of anthropology, 1999-, chair, 1999-2007, acting chair, 2009. Writer. **Publications:** (Contrib.) Training Manual in Medical Anthropology, 1985; Two Boys, A Girl, and Enough!: Reproductive and Economic Decisionmaking on the Mexican Periphery, 1986; (contrib.) Too Wet to Plow: The Family Farm in Transition, 1990; (contrib.) The Politics of Birth, 1990; (contrib.) Bridges to Humanity: Anthropological Friendships in the Field, 1995; Crossing Between Worlds: The Navajos of Canyon de Chelly, 1997, (with L. McClanahan) 2nd ed., 2008; (with D. Earle) Uprising of Hope: Sharing the Zapatista Journey to Alternative Development, 2005. Contributor of articles to books and journals. **Address:** Department of Anthropology, Wake Forest University, Anthropology Museum Bldg, Anthropology Lab Bldg, 296 Torrance Dr., PO Box 7807, Winston-Salem, NC 27106-3634, U.S.A. **Online address:** simonejm@wfu.edu

SIMONETTA, Joseph R. American (born United States), b. 1943. **Genres:** inspirational/Motivational Literature, Theology/Religion, Young Adult Fiction, Humanities, Self Help. **Career:** World Business Academy, editor, senior editor. Public speaker. **Publications:** The Heroes Are Us: A Call to Rescue Our World, 1985; Russell, Alexandra, and John: A Story of Personal and Planetary Change, 1990; The Book of Pithies, 2 vols., 1995; The Simple Truth: A New Understanding of Sacredness, 2000; Seven Words That Can Change the World: A New Understanding of Sacredness, 2001; The Skeptic's Book of Religious Quotes & Anecdotes, 2006; Religion, An Obstacle to Human Progress, 2006; The Book of Observations, Life on Earth, 2006; Siete Palabras Que Pueden Cambiar El Mundo En Español, 2009; Sete Palavras Que Podem Mudar O Mundo Em Português, 2009; Will Humanity Survive?, 2010. **Address:** 1589 Shadow Ridge Cir., Sarasota, FL 34240-9462, U.S.A. **Online address:** jrsimonetta@comcast.net

SIMONETTA, Marcello. American/Italian (born Italy), b. 1968?. **Genres:** History, Mystery/Crime/Suspense. **Career:** Yale University, faculty; Wesleyan University, faculty. Writer. **Publications:** Rinascimento segreto: il mondo del segretario da Petrarca a Machiavelli, 2004; The Montefeltro Conspiracy: A Renaissance Mystery Decoded, 2008. EDITOR: Dei pericoli della lingua Italiana, 1995; (and intro.) Non faccio niente senza gioia: Leonardo Sciascia e la cultura francese, 1996; (with M. Meserve) Commentaries, vol. I, 2003, vol. II, 2007; Federico Da Montefeltro and His Library, 2007. **Address:** Curtis

Brown Group Ltd., Haymarket House, 28-29 Haymarket, London, GL SW1Y 4SP, England. **Online address:** marcello.simonetta@gmail.com

SIMONS, Daniel J. American (born United States), b. 1969?. **Genres:** Psychology. **Career:** Harvard University, assistant professor of psychology, 1997-2001, John L. Loeb associate professor of the social sciences, 2001-02; University of Illinois, associate professor, 2002-06, professor of psychology, 2006-; Viscog Productions Inc., founder, 2003. Writer and psychologist. **Publications:** (With C.F. Chabris) The Invisible Gorilla: And Other Ways Our Intuitions Deceive Us, 2010. Contributor to periodicals. **Address:** Department of Psychology, Beckman Institute for Advanced Science, and Technology, University of Illinois, Rm. 807, 603 E Daniel St., Champaign, IL 61820, U.S.A. **Online address:** dsimons@illinois.edu

SIMONS, Les. See **PTACEK, Kathryn.**

SIMONS, Paullina. American/Russian (born Russia), b. 1963?. **Genres:** Novels, Young Adult Fiction. **Career:** Writer. **Publications:** Tully, 1994; Red Leaves, 1996; Eleven Hours, 1998; The Bronze Horseman: A Novel, 2001; Lily, 2004; The Girl in Times Square, 2004; Tatiana and Alexander, 2005; The Summer Garden, 2005; Tatiana's Table, 2007; Road To Paradise, 2007; A Song in the Daylight, 2008; I Love My Baby Because..., 2013. **Address:** c/o Author Mail, HarperCollins, 10 E 53 St., New York, NY 10020, U.S.A. **Online address:** paullinasimons@aol.com

SIMONS, Rae. See **SANNA, Ellyn.**

SIMONS, Rita Dandridge. See **DANDRIDGE, Rita B(ernice).**

SIMONS, Thomas W(inston). American (born United States), b. 1938. **Genres:** History, International Relations/Current Affairs. **Career:** U.S. Foreign Service, career civil servant, 1963-98; American Embassy-Warsaw, political officer, 1968-71; Department of State, Bureau of Political-Military Affairs and Policy Planning, staff, 1972-75; American Embassy-Moscow, External Reporting Unit, chief, 1975-77; American Embassy-Bucharest, deputy chief of mission, 1977-79; American Embassy-London, political counselor, 1979-81; Office of Soviet Union Affairs, Bureau of European and Canadian Affairs, director, 1981-85; State for European and Canadian Affairs, deputy assistant secretary, 1986-89; Brown University, professor, 1989-90; ambassador-Poland, 1990-93; coordinator of U.S. assistance to the new states of the former Soviet Union, 1993-95; ambassador-Pakistan, 1996-98; Stanford University, professor, 1998-2002; Cornell University, provost's visiting professor, 2005-07; Harvard University, Department of Government, lecturer, 2007-10. Writer. **Publications:** The End of the Cold War?, 1990; Eastern Europe in the Postwar World, 1991, 2nd ed., 1993; Islam in a Globalizing World, 2003; Eurasia's New Frontiers: Young States, Old Societies, Open Futures, 2008. **Address:** Davis Center for Russian and Eurasian Studies, Harvard University, 1730 Cambridge St., 3rd Fl., Cambridge, MA 02138, U.S.A. **Online address:** tsimons@fas.harvard.edu

SIMONSON, Helen. American/British (born England), b. 1963. **Genres:** Novels. **Career:** Writer. **Publications:** Major Pettigrew's Last Stand (novel), 2010. Contributor to periodicals. **Address:** c/o Julie Barer, Barer Literary L.L.C., 270 Lafayette St., Ste. 1504, New York, NY 10012, U.S.A. **Online address:** helen@majorpettigrew.com

SIMONTACCHI, Carol. American (born United States), b. 1947. **Genres:** Medicine/Health, Self Help, Sports/Fitness, Politics/Government. **Career:** Health Haus Inc., chief executive officer, 1985-98; Island Nutrition Center, owner and proprietor. **Publications:** Your Fat is Not Your Fault: How to Overcome Your Body's Resistance to Permanent Weight Loss, 1997, rev. ed., 2007; All About Chitosan, All about Flax Seeds and Flax Seed Oil, and All About Evening Primrose Oil, 1999; The Crazy Makers: How the Fast Food Industry is Destroying Our Brains and Harming Our Children, 2000; Heart Health For Women, 2000; WINGS: Weight Success for a Lifetime, 2000; A Woman's Guide to a Healthy Heart, 2004; Weight Success for a Lifetime, 2005; A New Holistic You, 2005; Natural Alternatives to Vioxx, Celebrex and Other Anti-Inflammatory Prescription Drugs, 2005; The Crazy Makers: How the Food Industry Is Destroying Our Brains and Harming Our Children, 2007. **Address:** Island Nutrition Center, 1633C Periwinkle Way, Sanibel, FL 33957-4404, U.S.A. **Online address:** csimontacchi@cs.com

SIMOSKO, Vladimir. Canadian/American (born United States), b. 1943.

Genres: Music, Biography, Autobiography/Memoirs. **Career:** AeroChem Research Laboratories, librarian, 1967-69; Rutgers University, Institute of Jazz Studies, curator, 1968-70; Princeton University, Forrestal Campus, librarian, 1969-74; University of Manitoba, science librarian, 1974-81, music librarian, 1981-. Writer and musician. **Publications:** (With B. Tepperman) Eric Dolphy: A Musical Biography and Discography, 1974, rev. ed., 1996; Serge Chaloff: A Musical Biography and Discography, 1998; Artie Shaw: A Musical Biography and Discography, 2000; Jazz as an Evolving Art Form, forthcoming. Contributor of articles to periodicals. **Address:** Eckhardt-Gramatté Music Library, University of Manitoba, Faculty of Music Bldg., Rm. 223, 65 Dafoe Rd., Winnipeg, MB R3T 2N2, Canada. **Online address:** vladimir_simosko@umanitoba.ca

SIMPSON, Adrienne. American/New Zealander (born New Zealand), b. 1943. **Genres:** Social Commentary, Popular Culture, Music, Biography. **Career:** Victoria University of Wellington, John David Stout research fellow, 1993. Writer. **Publications:** (Ed.) Opera in New Zealand: Aspects of History and Performance, 1990; Southern Voices: International Opera Singers of New Zealand, 1992; The Greatest Ornaments of Their Profession: The New Zealand Tours by the Simonsen Opera Companies, 1876-1889, 1993; (ed.) Classic Kiwi Sport: Cricket, 1996; Opera's Farthest Frontier: A History of Professional Opera in New Zealand, 1996; (with G. Newson) Alex Lindsay: The Man and His Orchestra, 1998; Capital Opera: Wellington's Opera Company, 1982-1999, 2000; Alice May: Gilbert and Sullivan's First Prima Donna, 2003; Hallelujahs and History: Auckland Choral, 1855-2005, 2005; Women at the Wicket-a Social History of Women's Cricket in New Zealand, forthcoming. **Address:** c/o Author Mail, Routledge, 270 Madison Ave., New York, NY 10016, U.S.A. **Online address:** a.simpson@clear.net.nz

SIMPSON, Anne. Canadian (born Canada), b. 1956?. **Genres:** Poetry. **Career:** St. Francis Xavier University, Writing Centre, coordinator and director, Department of English, professor; University of New Brunswick, writer-in-residence, 2002-03; Dalhousie University, Medical Humanities Program, artist-in-residence; Saskatoon Public Library, writer-in-residence, 2009-10; Banff Centre, faculty. **Publications:** Light Falls through You (poetry), 2000; Canterbury Beach, 2001; Loop (poetry), 2003; Orange from Portugal: Christmas Stories from the Maritimes and Newfoundland, 2003; Quick, 2007; Marram Grass, 2009. Works appear in anthologies. **Address:** Department of English, St. Francis Xavier University, PO Box 5000, Antigonish, NS B2G 2W5, Canada. **Online address:** asimpson@stfx.ca

SIMPSON, Brooks D. American (born United States), b. 1957?. **Genres:** History, Biography. **Career:** Arizona State University, ASU Foundation professor of history. Writer. **Publications:** Let Us Have Peace: Ulysses S. Grant and the Politics of War and Reconstruction, 1861-1868, 1991; America's Civil War, 1996; The Political Education of Henry Adams, 1996; The Reconstruction Presidents, 1998; (with M. Grimsley) Gettysburg: A Battlefield Guide, 1999; Ulysses S. Grant: Triumph Over Adversity, 1822-1865, 2000; The Civil War in the East: Struggle, Stalemate, and Victory, 2011; (with A. Castel) Victors in Blue, 2011. EDITOR: (with L.P. Graf and J. Muldowny) Advice after Appomattox: Letters to Andrew Johnson, 1865-1866, 1987; (with D.W. Blight) Union and Emancipation: Essays on Politics and Race in the Civil War Era, 1997; Think Anew, Act Anew: Abraham Lincoln on Slavery, Freedom and Union, 1998; (with J.V. Berlin) Sherman's Civil War: Selected Correspondence of William T. Sherman, 1860-1865, 1999; (with M. Grimsley) The Collapse of the Confederacy, 2001; (with S.W. Sears and A. Sheehan-Dean) The Civil War: The First Year Told By Those Who Lived It, 2011. **Address:** School of Historical, Philosophical and Religious, Arizona State University, Coor Hall, PO Box 874302, Tempe, AZ 85287-4302, U.S.A. **Online address:** brooks.simpson@asu.edu

SIMPSON, Dick. American (born United States), b. 1940. **Genres:** Politics/Government. **Career:** University of Illinois, instructor, 1967-68, assistant professor, 1968-72, associate professor, 1972-96, professor of political science, 1996-, department head, 2006-; City of Chicago, 44th Ward, alderman, 1971-79; Metro-Chicago Clergy and Laity Concerned, executive director, 1987-89. Writer. **Publications:** Who Rules? Introduction to the Study of Politics, 1970; (co-author) The Politics of Cultural Subnationalism, 1972; Winning Elections: A Handbook in Participatory Politics, 1972, 4th ed., 1996; (with G. Beam) Strategies for Change, 1976; Neighborhood Government in Chicago's 44th Ward, 1979; (co-author) Illinois: Political Processes and Government Performance, 1980; (co-author) Volunteerism in the Eighties, 1982; (with G. Beam) Political Action, 1984; The Politics of Compassion and Transformation, 1989; Rogues, Rebels, and Rubber Stamps: The Politics of the Chicago City Council, 1863 to the Present, 2001; Inside Urban Politics: Voices from America's Cities and Suburbs, 2003; (with J. Nowlan and B. O'Shaughnessy) Struggle for Power in Cities and States, 2010. EDITOR: (with R.L. Randall) Science Administration, Education, and Career Mobility, 1966; Chicago's Future, in a Time of Change, 1976, 5th ed., 1993; (with C. Williams) Blueprint of Chicago Government, 1983; (with C. Stockwell) Justice Ministries: Fighting Against Hunger, Homelessness and Joblessness, 1984; (with C. Stockwell) Justice Ministries: The Struggle for Peace, Justice and Sanctuary, 1985; Chicago's Future: In a Time of Change, 1988; Blueprint of Chicago Government: 1989; The Crazy Quilt of Government, 1994; (with D. Judd) The City, Revisited, 2011; (with C. Mixon) Twenty-First Century Chicago. **Address:** Department of Political Science, University of Illinois, 1007 W Harrison St., BSB 1126C, PO Box 276, Chicago, IL 60607-7137, U.S.A. **Online address:** simpson@uic.edu

SIMPSON, Dorothy. British/Welsh (born Wales), b. 1933. **Genres:** Mystery/Crime/Suspense, Novels, Literary Criticism And History, Young Adult Fiction, Horror. **Career:** Dartford Grammar School for Girls, teacher of English and French, 1955-59; Erith Grammar School, teacher of English and French, 1959-61; Senacre School, teacher of English, 1961-62; marriage guidance counselor, 1969-82; writer, 1975-. **Publications:** Harbingers of Fear (suspense novel), 1977. INSPECTOR THANET SERIES: The Night She Died, 1981; Six Feet Under, 1982; Puppet for a Corpse, 1983; Close Her Eyes, 1984; Last Seen Alive, 1985; Dead on Arrival, 1986; Element of Doubt, 1987; Suspicious Death, 1988; Dead by Morning, 1989; Doomed to Die, 1991; Wake the Dead, 1992; No Laughing Matter, 1993; A Day for Dying, 1995; (co-author) A Dead Giveaway, 1995; Once Too Often, 1998; Dead and Gone, 1999. Contributor to magazines. **Address:** c/o Peter Robinson, Curtis Brown Group Ltd., Haymarket House, 28-29 Haymarket, London, GL SW1Y 4SP, England.

SIMPSON, Elizabeth. American (born United States), b. 1947. **Genres:** Archaeology/Antiquities. **Career:** The University of Pennsylvania Museum of Archaeology and Anthropology, research associate, director; Gordion Furniture Project, director; University Museum, project director, 1983-; Metropolitan Museum of Art, Department of Ancient Near Eastern Art, assistant curator, 1986-89; Sarah Lawrence College, visiting professor, 1990-92; Duke University, visiting professor, 1992-93; Bard College, Bard Graduate Center for Studies in the Decorative Arts, associate professor, 1993-2006, assistant dean, 1993-95, professor, 2006-; Archaeological Institute of America, traveling lecturer; Writer. **Publications:** Gordion Wooden Furniture: The Study, Conservation and Reconstruction of the Wooden Furniture from Gordion, 1981-1990, 1992, rev. ed., 1999; (ed.) Spoils of War: World War II and Its Aftermath: The Loss, Reappearance, and Recovery of Cultural Property, 1997; The Gordion Wooden Objects, vol. I: The Furniture from Tumulus MM, 2008, vol. II, 2010. Contributor to journals. **Address:** Bard Graduate Center for, Studies in the Decorative Arts, Bard College, 18 W 86th St., New York, NY 10024, U.S.A. **Online address:** simpson@bgc.bard.edu

SIMPSON, Jacqueline (Mary). British (born England), b. 1930. **Genres:** History, Language/Linguistics, Mythology/Folklore, Translations. **Career:** Writer and researcher of medieval Icelandic literature and folklore, 1955-79; Folklore Society, editor, 1979-93, president, 1993-96, secretary, 1996-2002; University of Chichester, Sussex Centre for Folklore, Fairy Tales and Fantasy, visiting professor of folklore, 2010-. Writer. **Publications:** (Comp. with G.N. Garmonsway) The Penguin Dictionary of English, 1965, 3rd ed. as The Penguin English Dictionary, 1979; Everyday Life in the Viking Age, 1967; A Dictionary of Historical Slang, 1972; (comp.) Icelandic Folktales and Legends, 1972; (contrib.) Routledge Dictionary of Historical Slang, 1973; The Folklore of Sussex, 1973; The Folklore of the Welsh Border, 1976; The Viking World, 1980; British Dragons, 1980; European Mythology, 1987; (with S. Roud) A Dictionary of English Folklore, 2000; (with J. Westwood) The Lore of the Land: A Guide to England's Legends, From Spring-Heeled Jack to the Witches of Warboys, 2005; (with T. Pratchett) The Folklore of Discworld, 2008; Country Lore and Legends, 2009; Green Men and White Swans: The Folklore of British Pub Names, 2010. TRANSLATOR: Heimskringla: The Olaf Sagas, 2 vols., 1964; (and intro.) The Northmen Talk: A Choice of Tales from Iceland, 1965; (with G.N. Garmonsway) Beowulf and Its Analogues, 1968; Legends of Icelandic Magicians, 1975; (and ed.) Scandinavian Folktales, 1988. Contributor to journals. **Address:** 9 Christchurch Rd., Worthing, WS BN11 1JH, England.

SIMPSON, James. American/Australian (born Australia), b. 1954. **Genres:**

History. **Career:** University of Melbourne, tutor, 1977-78; Westfield College, lecturer in English literature, 1981-89; Girton College, lecturer and fellow, 1989-99, professor of Medieval and Renaissance English and professorial fellow, 1999-2003, life fellow, 2003; Harvard University, professor, 2004-06, Donald P. and Katherine B. Loker professor of English, 2006-, college professor, 2008-, chair of English department, 2010-. Writer. **Publications:** (Ed. with G. Kratzmann) Medieval English Religious and Ethical Literature: Essays in Honour of G.H. Russell, 1986; A Handlist of Manuscripts Containing Middle English Prose in Parisian Libraries, 1989; Piers Plowman: An Introduction, 1990, 2nd rev. ed., 2007; Sciences and the Self in Medieval Poetry: Alan of Lille's Anticlaudianus and John Gower's Confessio Amantis, 1995; (ed. with J. Dimmick and N. Zeeman) Images, Idolatry, and Iconoclasm in Late Medieval England: Textuality and the Visual Image, 2002; The Oxford English Literary History, vol. II: Reform and Cultural Revolution, 1350-1547, 2002; (ed. with A. David) Norton Anthology of English Literature, 2006; (ed. with L. Scanlon) John Lydgate: Poetry, Culture, and Lancastrian England, 2006; Burning to Read: English Fundamentalism and Its Reformation Opponents, 2007; (ed. with D. Donoghue and N. Watson) The Morton W. Bloomfield Lectures, 1989- 2005, 2010; The Routledge Handbook of Applied Linguistics, 2010. Contributor to books. **Address:** U.S.A. **Online address:** jsimpson@fas.harvard.edu

SIMPSON, Jeffrey (Carl). Canadian/American (born United States), b. 1949. **Genres:** History, Politics/Government. **Career:** Globe and Mail Inc., reporter, 1974-79, Ottawa bureau chief, 1979-81, European correspondent, 1981-83, London correspondent, 1981-84, national affairs columnist, 1984-; Stanford University, John S. Knight fellow, 1983, 1993-94; Order of Canada, officer, 2000-; Queen's University, Skelton-Clark fellow, Institute of Policy Studies, adjunct professor; University of Ottawa, Law School, adjunct professor, Graduate School of Public and International Affairs, senior fellow; University of British Columbia, John V. Clyne fellow. **Publications:** Discipline of Power: The Conservative Interlude and the Liberal Restoration, 1980; (co-author) The Canadian Guide to Britain, 1985; Spoils of Power: The Politics of Patronage, 1988; (with G. Martin) Canada's Heritage in Scotland, 1989; Faultlines: Struggling for a Canadian Vision, 1993; The Anxious Years, 1996; Star-Spangled Canadians: Canadians Living the American Dream, 2000; The Friendly Dictatorship: Reflections on Canadian Democracy, 2001; (with M. Jaccard and N. Rivers) Hot Air: Meeting Canada's Climate Change Challenge, 2007. Contributor to periodicals. **Address:** Globe and Mail Inc., 444 Front St. W, Toronto, ON M5V 2S9, Canada. **Online address:** jsimpson@globeandmail.com

SIMPSON, John (Cody Fidler). British (born England), b. 1944. **Genres:** Documentaries/Reportage, Military/Defense/Arms Control. **Career:** British Broadcasting Corp., radio news sub-editor, producer and reporter, 1966-72, foreign correspondent, 1972-78, BBC Television News, diplomatic correspondent, 1978-80, Nine O'Clock News, political editor and presenter, 1980-82, diplomatic editor, 1982-88, foreign affairs editor, 1988, reporter, 1989-, world affairs editor; Spectator, contributing editor; Granta Magazine, editor. **Publications:** (Co-ed.) The Best of Granta, 1966; Moscow Requiem (novel), 1981; A Fine and Private Place (novel), 1983; (with J. Bennett) The Disappeared and the Mothers of the Plaza: The Story of the 11,000 Argentinians Who Vanished in UK as The Disappeared: Voices from a Secret War, 1985; Inside Iran: Life under Khomeini's Regime, 1988; Despatches from the Barricades: An Eye-Witness Account of the Revolutions That Shook the World, 1989-90, 1990; From the House of War: John Simpson in the Gulf, 1991; In the Forests of the Night: Encounters in Peru with Terrorism, Drug-Running and Military Oppression, 1993; Lifting the Veil: Life in Revolutionary Iran, 1995; (ed.) The Oxford Book of Exile, 1995; Strange Places, Questionable People, 1998; A Mad World My Masters, 2000; News from No Man's Land, 2002; Simpson's World, 2003; The Wars against Saddam: Taking the Hard Road to Baghdad, 2003; Days from a Different World: A Memoir of Childhood, 2005; Not Quite World's End: A Traveller's Tales, 2007; Twenty Tales From The War Zone, 2007; Unreliable Sources, 2010. **Address:** Kruger Cowne Ltd., Chelsea Wharf, 15 Lots Rd., Ste. 18G, London, GL SW10 0QJ, England. **Online address:** gina@johnsimpson.tv

SIMPSON, John Warfield. American (born United States) **Genres:** Adult Non-fiction, Environmental Sciences/Ecology, Politics/Government. **Career:** Nitschke Godwin Bohm Inc., assistant landscape architect, 1974-75; John Brown Associates Inc., associate landscape architect, 1976; Tennessee Valley Authority, consulting landscape architect, 1977-84; Harvard University, Graduate School of Design, Landscape Architecture Section, teaching assis-

tant, 1977, occasional critic and lecturer, 1978; Ohio State University, Department of Landscape Architecture, assistant professor, 1978-80, 1983-89, associate professor of landscape architecture, 1989-2001, director of graduate studies, 1990-91, professor, 2001-, Environmental Sciences Program, graduate faculty, 1991-, associate professor of natural resources, 1998-; Oak Ridge National Laboratory, consulting landscape architect, 1979-80; Ohio Department of Natural Resources, consulting landscape architect, 1979-80; Duke University, Center for Resource and Environmental Policy Research, research fellow, 1980-81; United States Agency for International Development, principal instructor, 1981; HOH Associates Inc., associate, 1982; Council of Educators in Landscape Architecture, regional director, 1992-94; Heriot-Watt University, visiting research fellow, 2001. Writer. **Publications:** Visions of Paradise: Glimpses of Our Landscape's Legacy, 1999; Yearning for the Land: A Search for the Importance of Place, 2002; Dam!: Water, Power, Politics, and Preservation in Hetch Hetchy and Yosemite National Park, 2005. Contributor to journals. **Address:** Austin E. Knowlton School of Architecture, Ohio State University, 233 Knowlton Hall, 275 W Woodruff Ave., Columbus, OH 43210-1138, U.S.A. **Online address:** simpson.10@osu.edu

SIMPSON, Marc. American (born United States) **Genres:** Art/Art History, History, Architecture. **Career:** Writer. **Publications:** Winslow Homer: Paintings of the Civil War, 1988; (with S. Mills and J. Saville) The American Canvas: Paintings from the Collection of the Fine Arts Museums of San Francisco, 1989; (with S. Mills and P. Hills) Eastman Johnson: The Cranberry Harvest, Island of Nantucket, 1990; (ed. with D. Bolger, J. Wilmerding and T.T. Mickel) William M. Harnett, 1992; (with A. Henderson and S. Mills) Expressions of Place: The Art of William Stanley Haseltine, 1992; Rockefeller Collection of American Art at the Fine Arts Museum of San Francisco, 1994; (with R. Ormond and H.B. Weinberg) Uncanny Spectacle: The Public Career of the Young John Singer Sargent, 1997; (ed.) Like Breath on Glass: Whistler, Inness, and the Art of Painting Softly, 2008. **Address:** Yale University Press, 302 Temple St., PO Box 209040, New Haven, CT 06511-8909, U.S.A.

SIMPSON, Michael Andrew. South African (born South Africa), b. 1944. **Genres:** Plays/Screenplays, Poetry, Education, Law, Medicine/Health, Meteorology/Atmospheric Sciences, Psychiatry, Psychology, Documentaries/Reportage, Essays, Humor/Satire, Bibliography. **Career:** Guy's Hospital, psychiatrist, 1970-73; McMaster University, assistant professor of psychiatry, 1973-76; University of London, Royal Free Hospital School of Medicine, senior lecturer in psychiatry and medicine and senior research fellow, 1976-79; Temple University, Family Practice and Community Health, professor of psychiatry, 1979; University of Natal, professor of medical education and deputy dean, 1984-87; Clinic Holdings, director of program development, 1987-90; Dalhousie University, visiting professor, 1991; National Centre for Psychosocial and Traumatic Stress, director; Pulse and Intermedica, editor. **Publications:** Medical Education: A Critical Approach, 1972; Continuing Education in the Health Sciences, 1978; The Facts of Death: A Complete Guide for Being Prepared, 1979; Dying, Death and Grief: A Critical Annotated Bibliography, 1979; (co-ed.) Primary Care and Medical Education, 1979; Psycholinguistics in Clinical Practice: Languages of Illness and Healing, 1980; MCQ Ttutor: Psychiatry, 1983; Self-Tutor Guide to Psychiatry, 1983; Death and Ideology: Political Thanatology and the 'Femme Fatale' Syndrome, 1985; Dying, Death and Grief: A Critical Bibliography, 1987; Schizophrenia: Exploring the Spectrum of Psychosis, 1993; Beyond Trauma, 1995; Death and Trauma, 1995; Reforming Health Care: The Philosophy and Practice of International Health Reform, 1995; Multiple Personality Disorder: Controversies and Cultural Issues, 1995. Contributor to books and international journals. **Address:** Intermedica, PO Box 51, Pretoria, 0001, South Africa.

SIMPSON, Myrtle Lillias. Scottish/British (born England), b. 1931. **Genres:** Children's Fiction, Travel/Exploration, Writing/Journalism, Autobiography/Memoirs, Biography. **Career:** Writer. **Publications:** Home is a Tent, 1964; White Horizons, 1967; Due North, 1970; Simpson the Obstetrician, 1972; Greenland Summer: Based on True Expedition, 1973; Armadillo Stew, 1975; Vikings, Scots and Scraelings, 1977; Skisters: The Story of Scottish Skiing, 1982. FAR AND NEAR READERS SERIES: Journey to Amazon, 1960; Black Fellows and Buffaloes, 1960; Lapland Journey, 1960; Spitsbergen Adventure, 1960; Three in the Andes, 1960. Contributor to periodicals. **Address:** Towers Winant Ltd., Clerkenwell House, 45-47 Clerkenwell Green, London, GL EC1R 0HT, England.

SIMPSON, Penny Claire. British (born England), b. 1962. **Genres:** Novels, Novellas/Short Stories. **Career:** Welsh International Opera, head of media.

Writer and journalist. **Publications:** Dogdays (short stories), 2003; The Banquet of Esther Rosenbaum (novel), 2008; The Deer Wedding (novel), 2010. **Address:** Alcemi, c/o Y Lolfa, Wales, SY24 5AP, United Kingdom. **Online address:** penny.simpson@ukonline.co.uk

SIMPSON, Peter. See **SIMPSON, Peter L. Phillips.**

SIMPSON, Peter L. Phillips. (Peter Simpson). American/British (born England), b. 1951. **Genres:** Philosophy. **Career:** National University of Ireland, University College, professor of philosophy, 1982-84; Catholic University of America, professor of philosophy, 1984-88; Manchester Polytechnic, staff; City University of New York, College of Staten Island, professor of philosophy, 1988-, Department of Politics, Economics, and Philosophy, deputy head, Graduate Center, professor of philosophy and classics, Center for Hellenic Studies, junior fellow, 1991-92; Earhart Foundation, fellow, 1994-95. Writer. **Publications:** Goodness and Nature: A Defense of Ethical Naturalism, 1987; (trans. and intro.) Politics of Aristotle, 1997; (trans.) A Philosophical Commentary on the Politics of Aristotle, 1998; Vices, Virtues, and Consequences: Essays in Moral and Political Philosophy, 2001; On Karol Wojyla, 2001. **Address:** Department of Philosophy, College of Staten Island, City University of New York, Rm. 232, Bldg. 2N, Staten Island, NY 10314, U.S.A. **Online address:** psimpson@gc.cuny.edu

SIMS, Anastatia. American (born United States), b. 1953. **Genres:** History. **Career:** Indiana University South Bend, adjunct lecturer, 1981; North Carolina State University, Raleigh, visiting instructor, 1982-84; Virginia Polytechnic Institute and State University, visiting instructor, 1984-85, visiting assistant professor, 1986-87; Georgia Southern University, assistant professor, 1987-93, associate professor of history, 1993-, professor; Vanderbilt University, visiting assistant professor, 1989; Duke University, Center for Research on Women, Rockefeller humanist-in-residence, 1990-91. Writer. **Publications:** The Power of Femininity in the New South: Women and Politics in North Carolina, 1880-1930, 1997; (co-ed.) Negotiating the Boundaries of Southern Womanhood: Dealing with the Powers That Be, 2000; (ed.) Reading Southern History: Essays on Interpreters and Interpretations, 2001. Contributor to books and periodicals. **Address:** Department of History, Georgia Southern University, 1143 Forest Bldg., PO Box 8054, Statesboro, GA 30460-8054, U.S.A. **Online address:** asims@georgiasouthern.edu

SIMS, Elizabeth. American (born United States), b. 1957?. **Genres:** Novels. **Career:** Writer's Digest Magazine, contributing editor, 2009-. **Publications:** Holy Hell, 2002; Damn Straight, 2003; Lucky Stiff, 2004; Easy Street, 2005; The Actress, 2008; The Extra, 2009; On Location, 2010; NON FICTION: (with N. Thomas) The Port Angeles Symphony Orchestra, 2007; (contrib.) Crafting Novels & Short Stories; (contrib.) The Complete Handbook of Novel Writing. Contributor to books and periodicals. **Address:** St. Martin's Minotaur, 175 5th Ave. 18th Fl., New York, NY 10010, U.S.A. **Online address:** esims@elizabethsims.com

SIMS, Henry P. American (born United States), b. 1939. **Genres:** Business/Trade/Industry, Industrial Relations, Institutions/Organizations, Administration/Management, Economics, Mathematics/Statistics. **Career:** Hong Kong Baptist University, visiting professor, 1995, Fulbright fellow; Pennsylvania State University, Human Resources Management Program, founding academic director; Ford Motor Co., project engineer, design engineer, skilled trades supervisor in steel division and corporate staff management consultant; Indiana University-Bloomington, faculty; University of California-Irvine, faculty, 1975; Stanford University, faculty; George Mason University, faculty; University of Maryland, Robert H. Smith School of Business, director of PhD program, professor of management and organization; U.S. Steel Corp., management trainee; Armco Steel Corp., management trainee. Writer. **Publications:** (With D.A. Gioia) The Thinking Organization: Dynamics of Organizational Social Cognition, 1986; (with C.C. Manz) Super Leadership: Leading Others to Lead Themselves, 1989; (with P. Lorenzi) The New Leadership Paradigm: Social Learning and Cognition in Organizations, 1992; (with C.C. Manz) Business without Bosses: How Self-Managing Teams Are Building High-Performance Companies, 1993; (with C.C. Manz) Company of Heroes: Unleashing the Power of Self-Leadership, 1996; (with C.C. Manz and G.L. Stewart) Team Work and Group Dynamics, 1999; (with C.C. Manz) The New Super Leadership: Leading Others to Lead Themselves, 2001. Contributor to periodicals. **Address:** Robert H. Smith School of Business, University of Maryland, 4510 Van Munching Hall, College Park, MD 20742, U.S.A. **Online address:** hsims@rhsmith.umd.edu

SIMS, Michael. American (born United States), b. 1958. **Genres:** Essays, Novels, Mystery/Crime/Suspense, Astronomy, Sciences, Young Adult Nonfiction, Mythology/Folklore, Natural History, Natural History, Zoology, Animals/Pets, Literary Criticism And History, Biography. **Career:** Anthologist and freelance journalist. **Publications:** Darwin's Orchestra: An Almanac of Nature in History and the Arts, 1997; Adam's Navel: A Natural and Cultural History of the Human Form, 2003; (ed. and intro.) Annotated Archy and Mehitabel, 2006; Apollo's Fire: A Day on Earth in Nature and Imagination, 2007; (ed. and intro.) Arsène Lupin, Gentleman-Thief, 2007; In the Womb: Animals, 2009; (ed. and intro.) The Penguin Book of Gaslight Crime: Con Artists, Burglars, Rogues and Scoundrels from the Time of Sherlock Holmes, 2009; (ed. and intro.) Dracula's Guest: A Connoisseur's Collection of Victorian Vampire Stories, 2010; (ed. and intro.) The Penguin Book of Victorian Women in Crime: Forgotten Cops and Private Eyes from the Time of Sherlock Holmes, 2011; (ed. and intro.) The Dead Witness: A Connoisseur's Collection of Victorian Detective Stories, 2011; The True Story of Charlotte's Web: E.B. White's Eccentric Life in Nature and the Birth of an American Classic, 2011. **Address:** c/o Author Mail, Walker & Co., 175 5th Ave., New York, NY 10010, U.S.A. **Online address:** letters@michaelsimsbooks.com

SIMS, Norman (Howard). American (born United States), b. 1948. **Genres:** Writing/Journalism, Documentaries/Reportage, Essays, Travel/Exploration. **Career:** United Press Intl., reporter and editor, 1971-72; Telefood, associate editor, 1972; University of Illinois News, editor, 1974-75; University of Illinois, instructor, 1975-77, lecturer in communications, 1975-77; University of Wisconsin, assistant professor of mass communications, 1978-79; University of Massachusetts, department chair and professor of journalism, 1979-; Massachusetts Public Radio News and Information Service, humanist adviser, 1982-83; University of Colorado, visiting professor, 1984; Humanities Institute, fellow. **Publications:** The Deerfield River Guidebook, 1993; True Stories: A Century of Literary Journalism, 2007. EDITOR: (and intro.) The Literary Journalists: The New Art of Personal Reportage, 1984; (ed.) Literary Journalism in the Twentieth Century, 1990; (ed. and intro. with M. Kramer) Literary Journalism: A New Collection of the Best American Nonfiction, 1995; Literary Journalism in the Twentieth Century, 2008. Contributor of articles to journals. **Address:** University of Massachusetts, 108C Bartlett Hall, 40 Campus Ctr. Way, Amherst, MA 01003-9244, U.S.A. **Online address:** sims@journ.umass.edu

SIMS, Patsy. American (born United States), b. 1938. **Genres:** Writing/Journalism, Education. **Career:** New Orleans States-Item, reporter, 1962-63, assistant women's editor, 1963-67, acting women's editor, 1967-69, women's editor, 1969-71, special assignments writer, 1972-73; San Francisco Chronicle, acting women's editor, 1971, feature writer and assistant women's editor, 1971-72; Philadelphia Inquirer, feature writer, 1973-74; American University, lecturer, 1986; University of Maryland, lecturer, 1986; University of California, visiting writer, 1987; Austin Peay State University, writer-in-residence, 1988; Pacific Lutheran University, writer-in-residence, 1989; University of Pittsburgh, associate professor of creative non-fiction and associate director, 1989-2002; Goucher College, MFA in Creative Nonfiction Program, director, 2001-. **Publications:** The Klan, 1978, rev. ed., 1996; New Orleans: The Passing Parade, 1980; Cleveland Benjamin's Dead!: A Struggle for Dignity in Louisiana's Cane Country, 1981; (co-author) The Klan: A Legacy of Hate, 1982; Can Somebody Shout Amen!: Inside the Tents and Tabernacles of American Revivalists, 1988, rev. ed., 1996; (ed.) Literary Nonfiction, 2002. **Address:** Welch Center for Graduate and Professional Studies, Goucher College, 1021 Dulaney Valley Rd., Baltimore, MD 21204-2794, U.S.A. **Online address:** psims@goucher.edu

SIMS, William. See **SAMS, Ferrol.**

SINCLAIR, Alison. Canadian/British (born England), b. 1959?. **Genres:** Novels, Science Fiction/Fantasy. **Career:** Writer. **Publications:** NOVELS: Legacies, 1995; Blueheart, 1996; Cavalcade, 1998; (with L. Williams) Throne Price, 2002. DARKBORN FANTASY TRILOGY: Darkborn, 2009; Lightborn, 2010; Shadowborn, 2011. Contributor to books and periodicals. **Address:** Victoria, BC , Canada. **Online address:** alixsin@gmail.com

SINCLAIR, Andrew (Annandale). British (born England), b. 1935. **Genres:** Novels, Plays/Screenplays, History, Translations, Children's Fiction, Art/Art History. **Career:** University of Cambridge, Churchill College, founding fellow and director of historical studies, 1961-63; University College, lecturer in American history, 1965-67; Lorrimer Publishing Ltd., managing director,

1967-91; Timon Films, film director and screenwriter, 1969-95. **Publications:** The Breaking of Bumbo, 1959; My Friend Judas, 1959; The Project, 1960; Prohibition: The Era of Excess, 1962; The Hallelujah Bum in US as The Paradise Bum, 1963; The Raker, 1964; The Available Man: The Life behind the Masks of Warren Gamaliel Harding, 1965; The Better Half, 1965; Adventures in the Skin Trade, 1967; A Concise History of the United States, 1967, new ed., 2010; Gog: A Novel, 1967; Viva Che!: The Strange Death and Life of Che Guevara, 1968; The Last of the Best, 1969; Che Guevara, 1970; Guevara, 1970; Magog: A Novel, 1972; Dylan Thomas: Poet of His People, 1975; Dylan Thomas No Man More Magical, 1975; The Surrey Cat, 1976; Patriot for Hire, 1977; The Savage: A History of Misunderstanding, 1977; Jack: A Biography of Jack London, 1977; John Ford, 1979; (ed.) The Facts in the Case of E.A. Poe, 1979; Corsair: The Life of J. Pierpont Morgan, 1981; (ed.) Call of the Wild, White Fang, and Other Stories, 1981; Better Half: The Emancipation of the American Woman, 1981; The Other Victoria: The Princess Royal and the Great Game of Europe, 1981 in US (with L. Farago) as Royal Web, 1982; Sir Walter Raleigh and the Age of Discovery, 1984; Beau Bumbo, 1985; The Red and the Blue, 1986; Prohibition, the Era of Excess, 1986; Spiegel, the Man behind the Pictures, 1987; King Ludd: A Novel, 1988; War Like a Wasp, 1989; The War Decade, 1989; The Need to Give, 1990; The Far Corners of the Earth, 1991; The Naked Savage, 1991; The Strength of the Hills, 1992; The Sword and the Grail, 1992; Francis Bacon: His Life and Violent Times, 1993; In Love and Anger, 1993; Arts and Cultures: The History of the 50 Years of the Arts Council of Great Britain, 1995; Jerusalem: The Endless Crusade, 1995; Discovery of the Grail, 1998; Death by Fame: A Life of Elisabeth, Empress of Austria, 1999; Dylan the Bard: A Life of Dylan Thomas, 1999; The Secret Scroll, 2002; Blood and Kin, 2002; An Anatomy of Terror: A History of Terrorism, 2003; Rosslyn, 2006; Grail: The Quest for a Legend, 2007; Man and Horse: Four Thousand Years of the Mounted Warrior, 2008; The Rebel Masons, 2008. TRANSLATOR: Selections from the Greek Anthology, 1967; (with C.P. Hansen) Bolivian Diary: Ernesto Che Guevara, 1968; (with M. Alexandre) C. Spaak, La Grande Illusion, 1968. OTHERS: (intro.) The Iliad, 1969; Inkydoo, the Wild Boy (children's story), 1976 as Carina and the Wild Boy, 1977; (ed.) The Call of the Wild, White Fang, and Other Stories, 1981; (ed. and intro.) The Sea Wolf and Other Stories, 1989; (comp.) The War Decade: An Anthology of the 1940s, 1989; (ed.) Greece: A Literary Companion, 1994. Contributor to periodicals. **Address:** Birlinn Ltd., West Newington House, 10 Newington Rd., Edinburgh, EH9 1QS, Scotland.

SINCLAIR, Barbara Louise. American (born United States), b. 1940. **Genres:** Politics/Government. **Career:** University of California, assistant professor, associate professor, professor, 1970-96; University of California, American Political Science Association, fellow, 1978-79, Marvin Hoffenberg professor of American politics, 1996-, professor emeritus; University of California, president's chair, 1990-92, 1993-96. Academic, political scientist and writer. **Publications:** (As Barbara Sinclair Deckard) The Women's Movement, Political, Socioeconomic and Psychological Issues, 1975, 3rd ed., 1983; Congressional Realignment, 1925-1978, 1982; Majority Leadership in the U.S. House, 1983; The Transformation of the U.S. Senate, 1989; Legislators, Leaders and Lawmaking: The U.S. House of Representatives in the Postreform Era, 1995; Unorthodox Lawmaking: New Legislative Processes in the U.S. Congress, 1997, 3rd ed., 2007; Party Wars: Polarization and the Politics of National Policy Making, 2006. **Address:** Political Science Department, University of California, 4289 Bunche Hall, Los Angeles, CA 90095-1472, U.S.A. **Online address:** sinclair@polisci.ucla.edu

SINCLAIR, Billy Wayne. American (born United States), b. 1945. **Genres:** Biography, Autobiography/Memoirs, Criminology/True Crime, Politics/Government. **Career:** Angolite-Angola Prison Magazine, journalist, 1977-86; John T. Floyd Law Firm, senior paralegal. **Publications:** (With J. Sinclair) A Life in the Balance: The Billy Wayne Sinclair Story, 2000; (with J. Sinclair) Capital Punishment: An Indictment by a Death-row Survivor, 2009. **Address:** John T. Floyd Law Firm, The Kirby Mansion, 2000 Smith St., Houston, TX 77002, U.S.A. **Online address:** billy@johntfloyd.com

SINCLAIR, Brett J(ason). American (born United States), b. 1942. **Genres:** Economics, Money/Finance, Information Science/Computers, Law, Medicine/Health. **Career:** Sinclair On-Line Services, technical consultant, 1981-; International Business Machines (IBM), developer; Merrill Lynch, developer; Chase Manhattan Bank, developer; American Telephone and Telegraph (AT&T), developer; International Telephone and Telegraph (IT&T), developer, 1983-; United Nations, developer of communications, 1988. Writer. **Publications:** Cut Your Real Estate Taxes Down to Size: How to Win the Battle

against Spiraling Property Taxes, 1992; Alternative Health Care Resources: A Directory and Guide, 1992. Contributor to periodicals. **Address:** 68 Spencer Rd., Basking Ridge, NJ 07920, U.S.A.

SINCLAIR, Carla. American (born United States), b. 1964. **Genres:** Documentaries/Reportage, Children's Fiction, Medicine/Health. **Career:** BOING BOING magazine, editor-in-chief, co-founder, 1988-. **Publications:** (Ed. with M. Frauenfelder and G. Branwyn) The Happy Mutant Handbook, 1995; Net Chick: A Smart-Girl Guide to the Wired World, 1996; Signal to Noise, 1997; (intro.) From Girls to Grrlz: A History of Women's Comics from Teens to Zines, 1999; Braid Crazy: Simple Steps for Daring Dos, 2003. Contributor to periodicals. **Address:** c/o Dan Mandel, Sanford J. Greenburger Associates Inc., 55 5th Ave., New York, CA 10003, U.S.A. **Online address:** carla@well.com

SINCLAIR, Elizabeth. See **SMITH, Marguerite.**

SINCLAIR, Iain. British/Welsh (born Wales), b. 1943. **Genres:** Novels, Poetry, Documentaries/Reportage, Essays, Young Adult Fiction. **Career:** Albion Village Press, founder. Writer. **Publications:** (With C. Bamford) An Explanation, 1963; (with C. Bamford) Chords, 1964; Back Garden Poems, 1970; Kodak Mantra Diaries, October 1966 to June 1971, 1971; Muscat's Wuerm, 1972; The Birth Rug, 1973; Lud Heat: A Book of the Dead Hamlets, 1975; Brown Clouds: In the Tin Zone Pendeen, Cornwall, April-May 1977, 1977; The Penances, 1977; Fluxions, 1983; Autistic Poses, 1985; White Chappell: Scarlet Tracings, 1987; Flesh Eggs and Scalp Metal: Selected Poems, 1970-1987, 1989; Jack Elam's Other Eye, 1991; The Shamanism of Intent: Some Flights of Redemption, 1991; Downriver, 1991; The Vessels of Wrath: A Narrative in Twelve Tales, 1993; Radon Daughters: A Voyage, Between Art and Terror, from the Mound of Whitechapel to the Limestone Pavements of the Burren, 1994; Suicide Bridge, 1995; (ed.) Conductors of Chaos, 1996; Lights Out for the Territory: 9 Excursions in the Secret History of London, 1997; Slow Chocolate Autopsy: Incidents From the Notorious Career of Norton, Prisoner of London, 1997; The Ebbing of the Kraft, 1997; (with R. Lichtenstein) Rodinsky's Room, 1999; (with M. Atkins) Liquid City, 1999; Crash: David Cronenberg's Post-mortemon J.G. Ballard's 'Trajectory of Fate', 1999; Old Elgin, 2000; Landor's Tower, or, The Imaginary Conversations, 2001; White Chappell, 2002; London Orbital: A Walk around the M25, 2002; Verbals: Iain Sinclair in Conversation with Kevin Jackson, 2003; Dining on Stones, or, The Middle Ground, 2004; Edge of the Orison, 2005; Buried at Sea, 2006; (ed.) London: City of Disappearances, 2007; The Firewall: Selected Poems 1979-2006, 2006; (with R. Ryan) Gritty Brits: New London Architecture, 2007; Hackney Novel: Black Teeth, 2007; Hackney, That Rose-Red Empire: A Confidential Report, 2009; Postcards from the 7th Floor, 2010; Ghost Milk: Calling Time on the Grand Project, 2011. Contributor to periodicals. **Address:** Zeno Literary Agency, Primrose Hill Business Ctr., 110 Gloucester Ave.,, London, GL NW1 8HX, England.

SINCLAIR, Olga (Ellen). Also writes as Olga Daniels, Ellen Clare. British (born England), b. 1923. **Genres:** Novels, Children's Fiction, Children's Non-fiction, History, Adult Non-fiction, Young Adult Fiction. **Career:** Writer. **Publications:** Gypsies, 1967; Man at the Manor, 1967; Man of the River, 1968; Hearts by the Tower, 1968; Night of the Black Tower, 1968; Dancing in Britain, 1970; Bitter Sweet Summer, 1970; Children's Games, 1972; Wild Dream, 1973; Tenant of Binningham Hall, 1975; Toys and Toymaking, 1975; My Dear Fugitive, 1976; Where the Cigale Sings, 1976; Never Fall in Love, 1977; Master of Melthorpe, 1979; Gypsy Julie, 1979; Gypsy Girl, 1981; Orchids from the Orient, 1986; When Wherries Sailed By, 1987; Gretna Green, 1989; Potter Heigham: The Heart of Broadland, 1989; Come Sail with Me, 1990; Where the Cigale Sings, 1997; An Heir for Ashingby, 2004; The Countess and the Miner, 2005. AS ELLEN CLARE: Ripening Vine, 1981. AS OLGA DANIELS: Lord of Leet Castle, 1984; The Gretna Bride, 1985; The Bride from Faraway, 1987; The Untamed Bride, 1988; The Arrogant Cavalier, 1991; A Royal Engagement, 2000. **Address:** Sycamore, 10 Norwich Rd., Lingwood, NF NR13 4BH, England. **Online address:** olga@albatross.co.uk

SINDEN, Donald (Alfred). British (born England), b. 1923. **Genres:** Theatre, Autobiography/Memoirs, Theology/Religion, Photography. **Career:** Royal Shakespeare Co., associate artist, 1967-; Federation of Playgoers Societies, president, 1968-; Theatre Museum Advisory Council, chair, 1973-80; Royal General Theatrical Fund, president, 1982-. Writer. **Publications:** A Touch of the Memoirs, 1982; Laughter in the Second Act, 1985; (ed.) Everyman Book of Theatrical Anecdotes, 1987; The English Country Church, 1988;

(ed.) The Last Word: A Sparkling Collection of Put-downs, Epitahs, Final Utterances, Touching Tributes and Damning Dismissals, 1994. Contributor to periodicals. **Address:** c/o Richard Scott Simon, 32 College Cross, London, GL N1 1PR, England.

SINDERMANN, Carl J(ames). American (born United States), b. 1922?. **Genres:** Biology, Environmental Sciences/Ecology, Marine Sciences/Oceanography, Business/Trade/Industry, Engineering, Earth Sciences. **Career:** National Marine Fisheries Service, Oxford Laboratory, senior scientist, scientific editor, 1981-84; University of Miami, Rosenstiel School of Marine and Atmospheric Sciences, adjunct professor; University of Rhode Island, adjunct professor; University of Guelph, adjunct professor; Cornell University, adjunct professor; Georgetown University, adjunct professor. Writer. **Publications:** Blood Properties of Prespawning and Postspawning Anadromous Alewives (Alosa pseudoharengus), 1961; Serological Studies of Atlantic Redfish, 1961; (with G.L. Hoffman) Common Parasites of Fishes, 1962; Principal Diseases of Marine Fish and Shellfish, 1970, 2nd ed., 1990; (ed.) Disease Diagnosis and Control in North American Marine Aquaculture, 1977, 2nd ed., 1988; (ed. with P.N. Kaul) Drugs and Food from the Sea: Myth or Reality?, 1978; (ed. with R.L. Swanson) Oxygen Depletion and Associated Benthic Mortalities in New York Bight, 1976, 1980; Winning the Games Scientists Play, 1982, rev. ed. as Winning The Games Scientists Play: Strategies for Enhancing Your Career in Science, 2001; (ed.) Proceedings of the Ninth and Tenth U.S.-Japan Meetings on Aquaculture, 1984; Joy of Science: Excellence and Its Rewards, 1985; (ed.) Proceedings of the Eleventh U.S.-Japan Meeting on Aquaculture: Salmon Enhancement: Tokyo, Japan, October 19-20, 1982, 1985; (ed. with M. Bilio and H. Rosenthal) Realism in Aquaculture: Achievements, Constraints, Perspectives: Review Papers, World Conference on Aquaculture: Venice, Italy, 21-25 September 1981, 1986; Survival Strategies for New Scientists, 1987; (with C.M. Yentsch) The Woman Scientist: Meeting the Challenges for a Successful Career, 1992; (ed. with B. Steinmetz and W. Hershberger) Introductions and Transfers of Aquatic Species: Selected Papers from a Symposium Held in Halifax, Nova Scotia, 12-13 June 1990, 1992; Quantitative Effects of Pollution on Marine and Anadromous Fish Populations, 1994; Ocean Pollution: Effects on Living Resources and Humans, 1996; (with T.K. Sawyer) The Scientist as Consultant: Building New Career Opportunities, 1997; Coastal Pollution: Effects on Living Resources and Humans, 2006. Works appear in anthologies. **Address:** 7660 Tred Avon Cir., Easton, MD 21601, U.S.A.

SINE, Tom. American (born United States), b. 1936. **Genres:** History. **Career:** Mustard Seed Associates, co-founder; Fuller Theological Seminary, adjunct faculty; University of Washington, faculty; Seattle Pacific University, faculty. Writer and historian. **Publications:** The Mustard Seed Conspiracy: You Can Make a Difference in Tomorrow's Troubled World, 1981; Taking Discipleship Seriously: A Radical Biblical Approach, 1985; Why Settle for More and Miss the Best? Linking Your Life to the Purposes of God, 1987; Wild Hope, 1991; Live It Up! How to Create a Life You Can Love, 1993; Cease Fire: Searching for Sanity in America's Culture Wars, 1995; Mustard Seed vs. McWorld: Reinventing Life and Faith for the Future, 1999; (with C. Sine) Living on Purpose: Finding God's Best for Your Life, 2002; The New Conspirators: Creating the Future One Mustard Seed at a Time, 2008. **Address:** Mustard Seed Associates, PO Box 45867, Seattle, WA 98145, U.S.A.

SINGER, A. L. *See* LERANGIS, Peter.

SINGER, Alan. American (born United States), b. 1948. **Genres:** Novels, Literary Criticism And History, Young Adult Fiction. **Career:** Temple University, professor of English, 1980-, Graduate Creative Writing Program, Graduate Studies, director, 1980-, graduate chair. Writer. **Publications:** FICTION: The Ox-Breadth, 1978; Dirtmouth, 1984; The Charnel Imp, 1984; Memory Wax, 1996; Aesthetic Reason: Artworks and the Deliberative Ethos, 2003; Self-Deceiving Sense: Notice and Knowledge in the Work of Art, 2010. LITERARY CRITICISM: A Metaphorics of Fiction, 1983; The Subject as Action, 1993. EDITOR: (with A. Dunn) Literary Aesthetics: A Reader, 2000. **Address:** Department of English, Temple University, Rm. 1020, Anderson Hall, 10th Fl., 1114 W Berks St., Philadelphia, PA 19122-6090, U.S.A. **Online address:** alan.singer2@verizon.net

SINGER, Barry. American (born United States), b. 1957. **Genres:** Plays/Screenplays, Songs/Lyrics And Libretti, Music, Photography, Theatre, Writing/Journalism, Biography, Humor/Satire, Humor/Satire. **Career:** Chartwell Booksellers, founder and proprietor, 1983-. Writer. **Publications:** (With S. Weil) Steppin' Out: A Guide to Live Music in Manhattan, 1980; Black and Blue: The Life and Lyrics of Andy Razaf, 1992; Three Times We Parted: Three Poems for Chorus SATB, 1993; Ever After: The Last Years of Musical Theater and Beyond, 2004; (with L. Gordon) Alive at the Village Vanguard: My Life in and Out of Jazz Time, 2006; Churchill Style: The Art of Being Winston Churchill, 2012. Contributor to periodicals. **Address:** Chartwell Booksellers, Park Ave. Plz., 55 E 52nd St., New York, NY 10055, U.S.A.

SINGER, Bayla. American (born United States), b. 1940?. **Genres:** Air/Space Topics, Transportation, History, Adult Non-fiction. **Career:** Smithsonian Institution, consultant. Writer. **Publications:** Like Sex with Gods: An Unorthodox History of Flying, 2003. Contributor to magazines and journals. **Address:** c/o Author Mail, John Texas A & M University Press, John H. Lindsey Bldg., Lewis St., 4354 TAMU, College Station, TX 77843-4354, U.S.A.

SINGER, Benjamin D. Canadian/American (born United States), b. 1931. **Genres:** Communications/Media, Social Commentary, Sociology, Advertising/Public Relations, Social Sciences. **Career:** Grosse Pointe Press, editor, 1952; Palmer-Pann Corp., advertising manager, 1953-55; Singer-Kings Wood Advertising Co., president, 1957-61; University of Western Ontario, associate professor, 1966-72, professor of sociology, 1972, now professor emeritus of sociology. Writer. **Publications:** (With R.W. Osborn and J.A. Geschwender) Black Rioters: A Study of Social Factors and Communication in the Detroit Riot, 1970; (ed.) Communications in Canadian Society, 1972, 2nd ed., 1975; (with L. Green) Social Functions of Radio in a Community Emergency, 1972; Feedback and Society: A Study of the Uses of Mass Channels for Coping, 1973; (contrib.) Learning for Tomorrow, 1974; Racial Factors in Psychiatric Intervention, 1977; Social Functions of the Telephone, 1981; Advertising and Society, 1994. Contributor to journals. **Address:** University of Western Ontario, Rm. 5306, Social Science Ctr., London, ON N6A 5C2, Canada. **Online address:** singer@uwo.ca

SINGER, Jerome L(eonard). American (born United States), b. 1924. **Genres:** Psychology, Medicine/Health. **Career:** Veterans Administration, Mental Hygiene Clinic, staff, 1946-50; Franklin D. Roosevelt Veterans Administration Hospital, chief of research section, 1950-55, acting chief of psychotherapy section, 1951-52; William Alanson White Institute of Psychiatry, Psychoanalysis and Psychology, psychotherapist, 1954-59; Tappan Zee Mental Health Center Inc., psychotherapist, 1954-55; Northshore Neuro-Psychiatric Center, research consultant, 1956-62; Astor Home for Childern, research consultant, 1956-66; Columbia University, Teachers College, Institute of Psychological Research, lecturer in clinical psychology and research associate, 1957-63; Adelphi University, visiting professor, 1962; City University of New York, professor of psychology, 1963-72, Center for Research in Cognition and Affect, program director, 1969-72; Atherton-Aldine Press, editor, 1968-72; Yale University, professor of psychology, 1972-, director of clinical psychology training program, 1972-91, Family Television Research and Consultation Center, co-director, 1976-, director of graduate studies in psychology, 1988-93, now professor emeritus. Writer. **Publications:** Daydreaming, 1966; (co-author) The Child's World of Make-Believe, 1973; Imagery and Daydream Methods in Psychotherapy and Behavior Modification, 1974; The Inner World of Daydreaming, 1975; Daydreaming and Fantasy, 1976; (with D.G. Singer) Partners in Play: A Step-By-Step Guide to Imaginative Play in Children, 1977; (with E. Switzer) Mind Play: The Creative Uses of Fantasy, 1980; (with D.G. Singer) Television, Imagination and Aggression, 1981; (with D.M. Zuckerman and D.G. Singer) Getting the Most out of TV, 1981; (with D.M. Zuckerman and D.G. Singer) Teaching Television: How to use TV to Your Child's Advantage, 1981; The Human Personality, 1984; (with D.G. Singer) Make Believe: Games and Activities to Foster Imaginative Play in Young Children, 1985; The House of Make-Believe, 1990; The Parent's Guide: Use TV to Your Child's Advantage, 1990; (with D.G. Singer) Creating Critical Viewers, 1992; (with D.G. Singer) Make-Believe, 2001; (with D.G. Singer) Imagination and Play in the Electronic Age, 2005; Imagery in Psychotherapy, 2006. EDITOR: The Control of Aggression and Violence, 1971; (with K.S. Pope) The Stream of Consciousness, 1978; (with K.S. Pope) The Power of Human Imagination: New Methods in Psychotherapy, 1978; (co-ed.) Stream of Consciousness: Scientific Investigations into the Flow of Human Experience, 1978; Repression and Dissociation: Implications for Personality Theory, Psychopathology and Health, 1990; (with H. Morowitz) Mind, Brain and Complex Adaptive Systems, 1994; (with D.G. Singer) Handbook of Children and the Media, 2001, 2nd ed., 2011; (co-ed.) Creativity: From Potential to Realization, 2004. **Address:** Department of Psychology, Yale University, PO Box 208205, New Haven, CT 06520-8205, U.S.A.

SINGER, Judy Reene. American (born United States) **Genres:** Novels. **Career:** Author. **Publications:** Horseplay (novel), 2004; Still Life with Elephant (novel), 2007; An Inconvenient Elephant, 2010. **Address:** PO Box 25, Chester, NY 10918, U.S.A. **Online address:** judyreene@hotmail.com

SINGER, Marcus George. American (born United States), b. 1926. **Genres:** Philosophy, Sociology, History, Young Adult Non-fiction, Reference. **Career:** Cornell University, instructor in philosophy, 1951-52; University of Wisconsin, Department of Philosophy, instructor, 1952-55, assistant professor, 1955-59, associate professor, 1959-63, professor, 1963-92, chairman, 1963-68, professor emeritus, 1992-; American Philosophical Association, president, 1985-86. Writer. **Publications:** Generalization in Ethics, 1961, 2nd ed., 1971; The Ideal of a Rational Morality: Philosophical Compositions, 2002. EDITOR: (with R. Ammerman) Introductory Readings in Philosophy, 1962, 2nd ed., 1974; (with W.H. Hay) Reason and the Common Good: Selected Essays of Arthur E. Murphy, 1963; (with R. Ammerman) Belief, Knowledge, and Truth, 1970; Morals and Values, 1977; American Philosophy, 1985; (with R. Martin) Legislative Intent and Other Essays on Law, Politics, and Morality, 1993; Reason, Reality, and Speculative Philosophy, 1996; (and intro.) Essays on Ethics and Method, 2000. **Address:** Department of Philosophy, University of Wisconsin, White Hall, Helen C, 600 N Park St., Madison, WI 53706, U.S.A. **Online address:** mgsinger@facstaff.wisc.edu

SINGER, Marilyn. American (born United States), b. 1948. **Genres:** Young Adult Fiction, Children's Fiction, Poetry, Adult Non-fiction, Children's Non-fiction. **Career:** Daniel S. Mead Literary Agency, editor, 1967; Where (magazine), assistant editor, 1969; NYC Public High Schools, teacher of English, 1969-74; Writer, 1974-. **Publications:** YOUNG ADULT FICTION: No Applause, Please, 1977; The First Few Friends, 1981; The Course of True Love Never Did Run Smooth, 1983; Horsemaster, 1985; Ghost Host, 1987; Several Kinds of Silence, 1988; Storm Rising, 1989; Deal with a Ghost, 1997. PICTURE BOOKS: The Dog Who Insisted He Wasn't, 1976; The Pickle Plan, 1978; Will You Take Me to Town on Strawberry Day?, 1981; Archer Armadillo's Secret Room, 1985; Minnie's Yom Kippur Birthday, 1989; The Golden Heart of Winter, 1991; Chester, the Out-of-Work Dog, 1992; The Painted Fan, 1994; The Maiden on the Moor, 1995; In the Palace of the Ocean King, 1995; Good Day, Good Night, 1998; Solomon Sneezes, 1999; The One and Only Me, 2000; Didi and Daddy on the Promenade, 2001; Fred's Bed, 2001; Boo Hoo Boo-Boo, 2002; Quiet Night, 2002; Block Party Today!, 2004; Let's Build a Clubhouse, 2006; City Lullaby, 2007; I'm Your Bus, 2009; I'm Getting a Checkup, 2009; Tallulah's Tutu, 2011; What Is Your Dog Doing?, 2011. CHILDREN'S FICTION: It Can't Hurt Forever, 1978; Tarantulas on the Brain, 1982; Lizzie Silver of Sherwood Forest, 1986; The Lightey Club, 1987; Mitzi Meyer, Fearless Warrior Queen, 1987; Charmed, 1990; 20 Ways to Lose Your Best Friend, 1990; California Demon, 1992; Big Wheel, 1993; Josie to the Rescue, 1999; The Circus Lunicus, 2000. SAM AND DAVE MYSTERY SERIES: Leroy Is Missing, 1984; The Case of the Sabotaged School Play, 1984; A Clue in Code, 1985; The Case of the Cackling Car, 1985; The Case of the Fixed Election, 1989; The Hoax on You, 1989. SAMANTHA SPAYED MYSTERY SERIES: The Fido Frame-Up, 1983; A Nose for Trouble, 1985; Where There's a Will, There's a Wag, 1986. NONFICTION: Exotic Birds, 1990; A Wasp Is Not a Bee, 1995; Bottoms Up!, 1997; Prairie Dogs Kiss and Lobsters Wave, 1998; A Dog's Gotta Do What a Dog's Gotta Do, 2000; A Pair of Wings, 2001; Tough Beginnings: How Baby Animals Survive, 2001, What Stinks?, 2006; Cats to the Rescue, 2006; Venom, 2007; Eggs, 2008. POETRY: Turtle in July, 1989; Nine O'Clock Lullaby; 1991; In My Tent, 1992; It's Hard to Read a Map with a Beagle on Your Lap, 1993; Sky Words, 1994; Family Reunion, 1994; The Morgans Dream, 1995; Please Don't Squeeze Your Boa, Noah!, 1995; All We Needed to Say, 1996; On the Same Day in March, 2000; Monster Museum, 2001; Footprints on the Roof, 2002; The Company of Crows, 2002; Fireflies at Midnight, 2003; How to Cross a Pond, 2003; Creature Carnival, 2004; Central Heating, 2005; Monday on the Mississippi, 2005; First Food Fight This Fall and Other School Poems, 2008. Shoe Bop!, 2008; Mirror, Mirror, 2010; Twosomes: Love Poems from the Animal Kingdom, 2011; A Full Moon Is Rising, 2011. ADULT NONFICTION: The Fanatic's Ecstatic, Aromatic Guide to Onions, Garlic, Shallots and Leeks, 1981. FORTHCOMING: Caterpillars; A Stick Is an Excellent Thing; Every Day's a Dog's Day; The Boy Who Cried Alien; Tallulah's Solo; Tallulah's Toe Shoes; The Superheroes Employment Agency. EDITOR: (and intro.) A History of Avant-Garde Cinema, 1976; (and contrib.) New American Filmmakers, 1976; Stay True, 1998 (and contrib.) I Believe in Water, 2000; (and

contrib.) Face Relations, 2004; (and contrib.) Make Me Over: Eleven Stories about Transforming Ourselves, 2005. Contributor to books and magazines. **Address:** 42 Berkeley Pl., Brooklyn, NY 11217, U.S.A. **Online address:** marilyn@marilynsinger.net

SINGER, Mark. American (born United States), b. 1950. **Genres:** Documentaries/Reportage, Biography, Autobiography/Memoirs, Criminology/True Crime, History, Travel/Exploration, Essays, Business/Trade/Industry, Social Sciences. **Career:** New Yorker magazine, staff writer, 1974-. **Publications:** Funny Money, 1985; Mr. Personality: Profiles and Talk Pieces, 1989; Citizen K: The Deeply Weird American Journey of Brett Kimberlin, 1996; Somewhere in America: Under the Radar with Chicken Warriors, Left-Wing Patriots, Angry Nudists and Others, 2004; Character Studies: Encounters with the Curiously Obsessed, 2005; (with A.C. Greenberg) The Rise and Fall of Bear Stearns, 2010. Contributor to periodicals. **Address:** The New Yorker, 4 Times Sq., New York, NY 10036, U.S.A.

SINGER, Max. Israeli/American (born United States), b. 1931. **Genres:** Economics, Money/Finance. **Career:** Hudson Institute Inc., co-founder, 1961, president, 1965-73, 1978-82, adjunct senior fellow, senior fellow, trustee, now trustee emeritus; World Institute, managing director, 1974-76; Institute for Jewish Policy Planning and Research, director, 1977-78; Potomac Organization Inc., president, 1983-; American Law Institute, lawyer; U.S. Atomic Energy Commission, lawyer; Bar Ilan University, Begin-Sadat Center for Strategic Studies (BESA), senior fellow, senior research associate; Institute for Zionist Strategies, research director. Writer. **Publications:** Policy Concerning Drug Abuse in New York State: Final Report, 1970; Passage to a Human World: The Dynamics of Creating Global Wealth, 1987; (with A. Wildavsky) The Real World Order: Zones of Peace, Zones of Turmoil, 1993, rev. ed., 1996; History of the Future: The Shape of the World to Come is Visible Today, 2011. Contributor to periodicals. **Address:** Hudson Institute Inc., 1015 15th St. NW, 6th Fl., Washington, DC 20005-2605, U.S.A. **Online address:** maxsinger@bogriver.net

SINGER, Maxine. (Maxine Frank Singer). American (born United States), b. 1931. **Genres:** Biology, Sciences, Business/Trade/Industry. **Career:** U.S. Public Health Service, National Institute for Arthritis, Metabolism and Digestive Diseases, National Institutes of Health, research fellow, 1956-58, research chemist, 1958-72, Nucleic Acid Enzymology Division of Cancer Biology and Diagnosis, chief, 1974-80, Division of Cancer Biology and Diagnosis's Laboratory of Biochemistry, chief, 1980-88, scientist emeritus 1988-; Weizman Institute of Science, Department of Genetics, visiting scientist, 1971-72, Scientific Advisory Council, Board of Governors, member, 1978-; University of California, instructor, 1981; Carnegie Institution, president, 1988-2002, president emeritus; First Light, founder, 1989; CASE, founder, 1993; American Academy of Arts and Sciences, fellow. Writer. **Publications:** (With P. Berg) Genes and Genomes: A Changing Perspective, 1991; (with Berg) Dealing with Genes: The Language of Heredity, 1992; (ed. with P. Berg) Exploring Genetic Mechanisms, 1997; (with R.M. Hazen) Why Aren't Black Holes Black?: The Unanswered Questions at the Frontiers of Space, 1997; (with P. Berg) George Beadle, and Uncommon Farmer: The Emergence of Genetics in the 20th Century, 2003. Contributor to scientific journals and periodicals. **Address:** Carnegie Institution, 1530 P St. NW, Washington, DC 20005-1910, U.S.A.

SINGER, Maxine Frank. See **SINGER, Maxine.**

SINGER, Peter. American/Australian (born Australia), b. 1946. **Genres:** Animals/Pets, Philosophy, Ethics, Sciences. **Career:** Oxford University, University College, Radcliffe Lecturer, 1971-73; New York University, visiting assistant professor of philosophy, 1973-74; La Trobe University, senior lecturer in philosophy, 1975-76; Monash University, professor of philosophy, 1977-99, chair, 1977-78, 1980-81, associate dean, 1982, director, 1987-91, deputy director, 1992-97, co-director, 1992-95, Centre for Human Bioethics, part-time faculty, 1983-87, 1997-99, full-time faculty, 1987-97; Princeton University, Ira W. DeCamp professor of bioethics, 1999-2004, part-time faculty, 2005-; University of Melbourne, Centre for Applied Philosophy and Public Ethics, Laureate professor, 2005-. Writer. **Publications:** Democracy and Disobedience, 1973; Animal Liberation: A New Ethics for Our Treatment of Animals, 1975, 2nd ed., 1990; Practical Ethics, 1979, 3rd ed., 2011; (with J. Mason) Animal Factories, 1980, rev. ed., 1990; Marx, 1980, rev. ed. as Marx: A Very Short Introduction, 2000; The Expanding Circle: Ethics and Sociobiology, 1981; Hegel, 1983, rev. ed. as Hegel: A Very Short Introduction, 2001;

(with D. Wells) The Reproduction Revolution: New Ways of Making Babies, 1984, 2nd ed. as Making Babies: The New Science and Ethics of Conception, 1985; (with H. Kuhse) Should the Baby Live?: The Problem of Handicapped Infants, 1985; (with L. Gruen) Animal Liberation: A Graphic Guide, 1987; (co-author) Save the Animals, 1991; How Are We to Live?: Ethics in An Age of Self-interest, 1993; (with H. Kuhse) Individuals, Humans and Persons: Questions of Life and Death, 1994; Rethinking Life & Death: The Collapse of Our Traditional Ethics, 1995; (with B. Brown) The Greens, 1996; Henry: One Man's Way, 1997; Ethics into Action: Henry Spira and The Animal Rights Movement, 1998; A Darwinian Left: Politics, Evolution, and Cooperation, 2000; Writings on an Ethical Life, 2000; One World: The Ethics of Globalization, 2002, 2nd ed., 2004; Pushing Time Away: My Grandfather and the Tragedy of Jewish Vienna, 2003; (with T. Gregg) How Ethical is Australia?: An Examination of Australia's Record as a Global Citizen, 2004; President of Good & Evil: Questioning the Ethics of George W. Bush, 2004; President of Good & Evil: The Ethics of George W. Bush, 2004; Comment Vivre Avec Les Animaux, 2004; (with T. Gregg) How Ethical is Australia? An Examination of Australia's Record as a Global Citizen, 2004; (with J. Mason) The Way We Eat: Why Our Food Choices Matter/The Ethics of What We Eat, 2006; The Life You Can Save: Acting Now to End World Poverty, 2009. EDITOR: (with T. Regan) Animal Rights and Human Obligations, 1976, 2nd ed., 1989; (with W.A.W. Walters) Test-Tube Babies: A Guide to Moral Questions, Present Techniques, and Future Possibilities, 1982; In Defence of Animals, 1985; Applied Ethics, 1986; (co-ed.) Embryo Experimentation, 1990; A Companion to Ethics, 1991; Ethics, 1994; (with P. Cavalieri) Great Ape Project: Equality Beyond Humanity, 1994; (with H. Kuhse) Companion to Bioethics, 1998, 2nd ed., 2009; (with H. Kuhse) Bioethics: An Anthology, 1999, 2nd ed., 2006; (with R. Singer) Moral of the Story: An Anthology of Ethics Through Literature, 2005; In Defense of Animals: The Second Wave, 2005; (with L.Gruen and L. Grabel) Stem Cell Research: The Ethical Issues, 2007; (co-ed.) Editors' Choice, 2007; (with A. Leist) J. M. Coetzee and Ethics: Philosophical Perspectives on Literature, 2010. OTHER: (foreword) The Future of Animal Farming: Renewing the Ancient Contract, 2008. **Address:** University Center for Human Values, Princeton University, Rm. 203, 5 Ivy Ln., Princeton, NJ 08544-1013, U.S.A. **Online address:** psinger@princeton.edu

SINGER, P. W. American (born United States) **Genres:** History, Technology, History, Military/Defense/Arms Control, Social Sciences. **Career:** Duke University, instructor, 1994-96; International Peace Academy, special assistant, 1996-97; Office of the Secretary of Defense, Balkans Task Force, action officer, 1998-99; JFK School of Government, International Security Program, Belfer Center for Science and International Affairs, post doctoral fellow, 1999-2001; Brookings Institution, Foreign Policy Studies Program, national security fellow and project coordinator, 2001-03, Project on U.S. Policy towards the Islamic World, senior fellow and director, 2003-06, 21st Century Defense Initiative, senior fellow and director, 2006-. Writer. **Publications:** Corporate Warriors: The Rise of the Privatized Military Industry, 2003; Children at War, 2005; Wired For War: The Robotics Revolution And Conflict In The Twenty-first Century, 2009. Contributor of journals and periodicals. **Address:** Brookings Institution, 1775 Massachusetts Ave. NW, Washington, DC 20036-2188, U.S.A. **Online address:** author@pwsinger.com

SINGH, Amritjit. American/Indian (born India), b. 1945. **Genres:** Literary Criticism And History, Race Relations, Biography, Cultural/Ethnic Topics, Young Adult Fiction. **Career:** University of Delhi, lecturer, 1965-68; City University of New York, Herbert H. Lehman College, lecturer/assistant professor, 1970-71, 1973-74; New York University, instructor, 1971-72; American Studies Research Centre, research associate, 1974-77; University of Hyderabad, associate professor of English, 1977-78; University of Rajasthan, professor of English, 1978-83; Yale University, ACLS visiting fellow, 1983-84; Hofstra University, associate professor of English, 1984-86; Rhode Island College, professor of English, 1986-2006; Rhode Island College, Mary Tucker Thorp distinguished professor of arts and sciences, 1991-92; Du Bois Institute, Harvard University, NEH visiting fellow, 1991-92; University of Calgary, visiting Killam fellow, 1995; JFK Institute, Freie University, visiting Fulbright professor, 2002; Ohio University, professor, Langston Hughes professor of English, 2006-. Writer and Fulbright senior specialist. **Publications:** The Novels of the Harlem Renaissance: Twelve Black Writers, 1923-1933, 1976, 1994; (with R. Verma and I.M. Joshi) Indian Literature in English 1827-1979: A Guide to Information Sources, 1981. EDITOR: (co-ed.) Afro-American Poetry and Drama, 1760-1975 (annotated bibliography), 1979; (co-ed.) India: An Anthology of Contemporary Writing, 1983; (with W.S. Shiver and S. Brodwin) The Harlem Renaissance: Revaluations, 1989; (with

K.A. Paniker) The Magic Circle of Henry James: Essays in Honor of Darshan Singh Maini, 1989; George Houston Bass: A Memorial Volume, 1991; Wallace Thurman, Infants of the Spring, 1992; (with J.T. Skerrett Jr. and R.E. Hogan) Memory, Narrative and Identity: New Essays in Ethnic Literatures, 1994; (co-ed.) American Studies Today, 1995; (with M. Graham) Conversations with Ralph Ellison, 1995; (with B. Dick) Conversations with Ishmael Reed, 1995; Richard Wright, The Color Curtain, 1995; Richard Wright, Black Power, 1995; (with J.T. Skerrett, Jr. and R.E. Hogan) Memory and Cultural Politics: New Approaches to American Ethnic Literatures, 1996; (co-ed.) New Perspectives on Indian Literature in English, 1996; (with P. Schmidt) Postcolonial Theory and the United States: Race, Ethnicity and Literature, 2000; (with D.M. Scott III) The Collected Writings of Wallace Thurman: A Harlem Renaissance Reader, 2003; (with B.G. Johnson) Interviews with Edward W. Said, 2004: (co-ed.) Pedagogy, Canon and Context: Toward a Redefinition of Ethnic American Literary Studies, MELUS Special Number, 2004. **Address:** Department of English, Ohio University, Ellis 332, 360 Ellis Hall, 1 Park Pl., Athens, OH 45701-2979, U.S.A. **Online address:** singha@ohio.edu

SINGH, Chetan. Indian (born India), b. 1955. **Genres:** Environmental Sciences/Ecology, History, Local History/Rural Topics, Area Studies. **Career:** Jawaharlal Nehru University, Centre for Historical Studies, junior research fellow, 1978-80, senior research fellow, 1980-83; Panjab University, lecturer in history, 1985-87; Himachal Pradesh University, assistant professor, 1987-98, associate professor of history, 1998-2002, professor, 2002-, Studies in Humanities and Social Sciences, editor, 1995-99. Writer. **Publications:** Region and Empire: Panjab in the Seventeenth Century, 1991; Natural Premises: Ecology and Peasant Life in the Western Himalaya, 1800-1950, 1998; (ed.) Social Transformation in North-Western India During the 20th Century, 2010; (ed.) Recognizing Diversity: Society and Culture in the Himalaya, 2011. **Address:** Department of History, Himachal Pradesh University, Summer Hill, Shimla, HP 171005, India. **Online address:** thakurchetan@sify.com

SINGH, D(asharath). Indian (born India), b. 1937. **Genres:** Mathematics/Statistics, Sciences. **Career:** University of Bihar, lecturer in mathematics, 1961-71; University of Basrah, foreign expert, 1972-80; Princeton University, visiting fellow, 1981; University of Bihar, reader in mathematics, 1981-85; Indian Institute of Technology, professor of mathematics, 1986-97. Writer. **Publications:** (With F.R. Drake) Intermediate Set Theory, 1996. **Address:** c/o Machaha Niwas, G.D. College Rd., Professor's Colony, Mirganj, Begusarai, BH 851101, India.

SINGH, Nikhil Pal. American (born United States) **Genres:** Theology/Religion. **Career:** University of Washington, associate professor & Walker Family professor of history. Writer and educator. **Publications:** Black Is a Country: Race and the Unfinished Struggle for Democracy, 2004. Contributor to journals. **Address:** Department of History, University of Washington, 315 Smith Hall, PO Box 353560, Seattle, WA 98195-3560, U.S.A. **Online address:** nsingh@u.washington.edu

SINGH, Simon. British (born England), b. 1964. **Genres:** Mathematics/Statistics. **Career:** British Broadcasting Co., Department of Science and Features, producer and director, 1990-96; freelance author, 1997-. **Publications:** Fermats Enigma: The Epic Quest to Solve the World's Greatest Mathematical Problem, 1997, rev. ed. as Fermat's Last Theorem: The Story of a Riddle That Confounded the Worlds Greatest Minds for 358 Years, 1998; The Code Book: The Evolution of Secrecy from Mary, Queen of Scots, to Quantum Cryptography, 1999 as The Code Book: The Evolution of Secrecy from Ancient Egypt to Quantum Cryptography, 1999 as The Code Book: The Secret History of Codes and Code-Breaking, 2000; The Science of Secrecy: The Secret History of Codes and Codebreaking, 2000; The Code Book: How to Make It, Break It, Hack It, Crack It, 2002; Big Bang: The Origin of the Universe, 2004; (with E. Ernst) Trick or Treatment? Alternative Medicine, 2008. Contributor to journals and newspapers. **Address:** Morley House, 36 Acreman St., Sherborne, DS DT9 3NX, England. **Online address:** simon@simonsingh.net

SINGLETON, Elyse. See **SINGLETON, Janet Elyse.**

SINGLETON, Janet Elyse. (Elyse Singleton). American (born United States) **Genres:** Novels, Young Adult Fiction. **Career:** USA Today, freelance journalist; The Miami Herald, freelance journalist; Chicago Tribune, freelance journalist. **Publications:** (As Elyse Singleton) This Side of the Sky: A Novel, 2002. Contributor to periodicals. **Address:** c/o Sally Wofford-Girand,

Brickhouse Literary Agents, 80 5th Ave., Ste. 1101-03, New York, NY 10011-8002, U.S.A. **Online address:** thissideofthesky@aol.com

SINGLETON, Linda Joy. Also writes as L. J. Singleton. American (born United States), b. 1957. **Genres:** Novels. **Career:** Writer. **Publications:** Almost Twins, 1991; Opposites Attract, 1991; Barnyard Battle, 1992; Almost Perfect, 1992; Love to Spare, 1993; Spring Break!, 1994; Deep in My Heart, 1994; The Saturday Night Bash, 1994; Twin Again, 1995; Dreamboat, 1995; Escape from Ghostland, 1995; Stand up and Cheer, 1996; Teacher Trouble, 1996; Babysitter Beware, 1996; Crazy for Cartwheels, 1996; Spirit Song, 1996; Spring to Stardom, 1997; Gimme a C-A-M-P!, 1997; Boys Are Bad News, 1997; Regeneration: The Impostor, 2000; The Search, 2000; The Truth, 2000; The Impostor, 2000; The Killer, 2001; Double Vision, 2003; Don't Die Dragonfly, 2004; Oh No! UFO!, 2004; Sea Switch, 2005; Last Dance, 2005; Shamrocked!, 2005; Sword Play, 2006; Witch's Ball, 2006; Fatal Charm, 2007; Dead Girl Walking, 2008; Dead Girl Dancing, 2009; Dead Girl in Love, 2009; Magician's Muse, 2010; Buried, 2012. **Address:** PO Box 1357, Galt, CA 95632, U.S.A. **Online address:** ljscheer@inreach.com

SINGLETON, L. J. *See* **SINGLETON, Linda Joy.**

SINGTON, David. British (born England) **Genres:** Documentaries/Reportage, Earth Sciences, Adult Non-fiction. **Career:** Dox Productions Ltd., principal, 1999-, director and executive producer. Journalist. **Publications:** (With S. Lamb) Earth Story: The Shaping of Our World, 1998; (with S. Lamb) Earth Story: The Forces that Have Shaped Our Planet, 1998. **Address:** c/o Author Mail, Princeton University Press, 41 William St., Princeton, NJ 08540, U.S.A. **Online address:** david.sington@tvdox.com

SINGTON, Philip. (Patrick Lynch). British (born England), b. 1962. **Genres:** Mystery/Crime/Suspense, Children's Fiction, Young Adult Fiction, Novels. **Career:** Euromoney Publications, financial journalist and editor, 1986-95. **Publications:** AS PATRICK LYNCH: The Annunciation, 1993; The Immaculate Conception, 1994; Carriers, 1995; Omega, 1997; The Policy, 1998; Figure of Eight, 2000. AS PHILIP SINGTON: Zoia's Gold: A Novel, 2006; The Einstein Girl, 2009; The Valley of Unknowing, 2012. Contributor to periodicals. **Address:** c/o Peter Straus, Rogers, Coleridge & White Ltd., 20 Powis Mews, London, GL W11 1JN, England. **Online address:** philip.sington@philipsington.com

SINHA, Indra. British/Indian (born India), b. 1950. **Genres:** Novels, Novellas/Short Stories, Translations. **Career:** The Creative Business, advertising copywriter, 1976-79; Ogilvy & Mather, advertising copywriter, 1980-83; Collett, Dickenson, Pearce & Partners, advertising copywriter, 1984-95; Amnesty Intl., copywriter. **Publications:** The Cybergypsies: A True Tale of Lust, War, and Betrayal on the Electronic Frontier, 1999; Tantra: The Cult of Ecstasy, 2000; Death of Mr. Love, 2004; Animal's People, 2008. TRANSLATOR: The Love Teachings of Kama Sutra: With Extracts from Koka shastra, Ananga Ranga, and Other Famous Indian Works on Love, 1980; (and ed.) The Great Book of Tantra: Translations and Images from the Classic Indian Texts with Commentary, 1993. **Address:** The Wylie Agency Ltd., 17 Bedford Sq., London, GL WC1B 3JA, England.

SINISALO, Johanna. Finnish (born Finland), b. 1958. **Genres:** Novels, Novellas/Short Stories, Science Fiction/Fantasy. **Career:** Writer. **Publications:** Kotikatu, 1995; Elämän suola, 1996; Samaa sukua eri maata, 1998; Ennen Päivänlaskua ei voi, 2000; Troll: A Love Story, 2004; Käenpesä, 2004; (ed.) The Dedalus Book of Finnish Fantasy, 2005; Lasisilmä, 2006; Linnunlaivot, 2008; Birdbrain, 2010. Contributor to books. **Address:** c/o Author Mail, Grove Atlantic Inc., 841 Broadway, New York, NY 10003, U.S.A.

SINISTER, Bucky. American (born United States), b. 1969. **Genres:** Poetry. **Career:** Writer. **Publications:** Get Up: A 12-Step Guide to Recovery for Misfits, Freaks, & Weirdos, 2008; Still Standing: Addicts Talk About Living Sober, 2011. POETRY: Twelve Bowls of Glass, 1990; Asphalt Rivers, 1991; King of the Roadkills, 1995; Tragedy and Bourbon, 2001; Whiskey & Robots, 2004; All Blacked Out & Nowhere to Go, 2007. **Address:** 65 Parker St., Ste. 7, Newburyport, MA 01950, U.S.A. **Online address:** buckyofoakland@yahoo.com

SINIVER, Asaf. British (born England), b. 1976. **Genres:** Politics/Government, Social Sciences. **Career:** International Coalition for Israel's MIAs and POWs, project manager, 1996-97; National Bank of Israel, personal banker, 2001; Language Services to Business, tutor of Hebrew, 2002; University of Birmingham, lecturer in international security and director of undergraduate studies. Author and translator. **Publications:** Nixon, Kissinger, and U.S. Foreign Policy Making: The Machinery of Crisis, 2008; (ed.) International Terrorism Post-9/11: Comparative Dynamics and Responses, 2010. Contributor to books and journals. **Address:** Nottingham, NT , England. **Online address:** a.siniver@bham.ac.uk

SINN, Hans Werner. German (born Germany), b. 1948. **Genres:** Economics, Business/Trade/Industry, Politics/Government. **Career:** University of Münster, Institute of Public Economics, lecturer, 1972-74; University of Mannheim, Department of Economics and Statistics, lecturer, 1974-83, associate professor, 1983; University of Western Ontario, professor of economics, 1978-79, 1984-85; University of Vienna, honorary professor, 1980; University of Munich, professor of economics and public finance, 1984-, chairman of economics faculty, 1991-93, IFO Center for Economic Studies, director, 1991-, chief executive officer, 1999-, IFO Institute for Economic Research, president, 1999-; CESifo Inc., chief executive officer, 1999-; National Bureau of Economic Research, research associate, 1989-; Verein für Socialpolitik, chairman, 1997-2000; International Institute of Public Finance, president, 2006-09, honorary president, 2009-. Writer. **Publications:** ökonomische Entscheidungen bei Ungewissheit, 1980; Economic Decisions Under Uncertainty, 1983; Vacant Land and the Role of Government Intervention, 1985; Kapitalein kommensbesteuerung: eine Analyse derintertemporalen, internationalen und intersektoralen Allokationswirkungen, 1985; Capital Income Taxation and Resource Allocation, 1987; (with J.M.G. Schulenburg) Theorie der Wirtschaftspolitik: Festschrift zum fünfundsiebzigsten Geburtstag von Hans Möller, 1990; (co-author) Influence of Tax Differentials on International Competitiveness: Proceedings of the Munich Symposium on International Taxation: Papers, 1990; (with G. Sinn) Kaltstart: volkswirtschaftliche Aspekte der deutschen Vereinigung, 1991; (ed. with E. Baltensperger) Exchange-Rate Regimes and Currency Unions: Proceedings of a Conference Held by the Confederation of European Economic Associations at Frankfurt, Germany, 1990, 1992; (with G. Sinn) Jumpstart: The Economic Unification of Germany, 1992; (co-author) Making Sense of Subsidiarity: How Much Centralization for Europe?, 1993; Staat im Bankwesen: zur Rolle der Landesbanken in Deutschland, 1997; (with E. Nowotny) Fiskalföderalismus in Europa, 1997; The German State Banks: Global Players in the International Finance Markets, 1999; (with M. Thum) Gesetzliche Rentenversicherung: Prognosen im Vergleich, 1999; (co-ed.) EU-Erweiterung und Arbeitskräftemigration: Wege zu einer schrittweisen Annäherung derArbeitsmärkte, 2001; Fusion E.ON-Ruhrgas: die volkswirtschaftlichen Aspekte, 2002; Ist Deutschland noch zu retten?, 2003; (ed. with S. Cnossen) Public Finance and Public Policy in the New Century, 2003; New Systems Competition, 2003; Sick Man of Europe: A Desk Socialist's Diagnosis and Therapy: Der kranke Mann Europas: Diagnose und Therapieeines Kathedersozialisten, 2003; Migration, Social Standards and Replacement Incomes: How to Protect Low-Income Workers in the Industrialized Countries Against the Forces of Globalization and Market Integration, 2004; (ed. with M. Widgrén and M. Köthenbürger) European Monetary Integration, 2004; Dilemmader Globalisierung, 2004; Basar-ökonomie: Deutschland, Exportweltmeister oder Schlusslicht?, 2005; (ed. with J. Whalley and M. Köthenbürger) Privatization Experiences in the European Union, 2006; (co-author) Redesigning the Welfare State: Germany's Current Agenda for an Activating Social Assistance, 2006; Can Germany be Saved?: The Malaise of the World's First Welfare State, 2007; (ed. with G. Cette and M. Fouquin) Divergences in Productivity Between Europe and the United States: Measuring and Explaining Productivity Gaps Between Developed Countries, 2007; (ed. with A. Chopra) Sustainable Public Finance in Aging Societies: Documentation of the Symposium Long-Term Fiscal Sustainability in Germany=Nachhaltigkeit öffentlicher Finanzen in einer alternden Gesellschaft, 2007; (ed.) Projektionen zur langfristigen Tragfähigkeit der öffentlichen Finanzen, 2008; (ed.) Steuerausfälle im Bereich der Mehrwertsteuer: Gründe, Ausmass und Abhilfemöglichkeiten, 2008; Kasino-Kapitalismus: wie es zur Finanzkrise kam, und was jetzt zu tun ist, 2009; Casino Capitalism: How the Financial Crisis Came about and What Needs to be Done Now, 2010; (ed. with E. Phelps) Perspectives on the Performance of the Continental Economies, 2011; Green Paradox, 2012. Contributor to periodicals and journals. **Address:** Ifo Institute for Economic Research, Poschingerstr. 5, Munich, 81679, Germany. **Online address:** sinn@info.de

SINNETT, Mark C. Canadian/British (born England), b. 1963. **Genres:** Poetry, Novels, Mystery/Crime/Suspense. **Career:** Writer. **Publications:** The Landing, 1997; Bull, 1998; Some Late Adventure of the Feelings: Poems,

2000; The Border Guards, 2004; Carnivore: A Novel, 2009. **Address:** c/o Author Mail, HarperCollins Canada, 1995 Markham Rd., Scarborough, ON M1B 5M8, Canada. **Online address:** marksinnett@yahoo.com

SINNETTE, Elinor Des Verney. American (born United States), b. 1925. **Genres:** Biography, History, Bibliography, Humanities. **Career:** New York Public Library, librarian, 1947-55; New York City Board of Education, district school librarian, 1960-65; University of Ibadan, Institute of African Studies, founding librarian, 1965-66, lecturer in librarianship, 1966-69; Ahmadu Bello University, senior lecturer in librarianship, 1969-70; UNESCO, Library Assistants Training Program, director, 1976-77; Howard University, Moorland-Spingarn Research Center, Oral History Department, head, 1980-88, chief librarian, 1988-91. Writer. **Publications:** Arthur Alfonso Schomburg, Black Bibliophile and Collector: A Biography, 1989; (ed. with W.P. Coates and T.C. Battle) Black Bibliophiles and Collectors: Preservers of Black History, 1990. **Address:** 1016 S Wayne St., Ste. 409, Arlington, VA 22204-4435, U.S.A.

SINNOTT-ARMSTRONG, Walter. American (born United States), b. 1955. **Genres:** Theology/Religion, Essays. **Career:** Dartmouth College, professor of philosophy, Hardy professor of legal studies; Duke University, Kenan Institute for Ethics, Chauncey Stillman professor in practical ethics; MacArthur Law and Neuroscience Project, co-director; University of Oxford, Centre for Neuroethics, co-investigator; Johns Hopkins University, visiting professor; Princeton University, visiting professor. Writer. **Publications:** Moral Dilemmas, 1988; (with R.J. Fogelin) Understanding Arguments: An Introduction to Informal Logic, 4th ed., 1991, 8th ed., 2010; (with W.L. Craig) God? A Debate Between a Christian and an Atheist, 2004; Moral Skepticisms, 2006; Moral Psychology, 3 vols., 2008; Morality without God?, 2009. EDITOR: (with S.J. Brison) Contemporary Perspectives on Constitutional Interpretation, 1993; (with N.A. Raffman) Modality, Morality, and Belief: Essays in Honor of Ruth Barcan Marcus, 1995; Moral Knowledge? New Readings in Moral Epistemology, 1996; (with F. Schauer) The Philosophy of Law: Classic and Contemporary Readings with Commentary, 1996; (with R. Audi) Rationality, Rules, and Ideals: Critical Essays on Bernard Gert's Moral Theory, 2002; Pyrrhonian Skepticism, 2004; Conscious Will and Responsibility: A Tribute to Benjamin Libet, 2010. **Address:** Kenan Institute for Ethics, Duke University, 102 W Duke Bldg., PO Box 90432, Durham, NC 27708, U.S.A. **Online address:** ws66@duke.edu

SINYARD, Neil. British (born England), b. 1945. **Genres:** Film, Literary Criticism And History, Art/Art History, Adult Non-fiction, Biography, Autobiography/Memoirs. **Career:** University of Hull, professor in film studies, 1989-. Writer and film critic. **Publications:** (With A. Turner) Journey down Sunset Boulevard: The Films of Billy Wilder, 1979; Classic Movies, 1985; Directors: All-Time Greats, 1985; (ed.) All-Time Box-Office Hits, 1985; The Films of Richard Lester, 1985; Filming Literature: The Art of Screen Adaptation, 1986; The Films of Alfred Hitchcock, 1986; (with A. Goldau and H. Prinzler) Zinnemann, 1986; The Films of Steven Spielberg, 1987; The Films of Woody Allen, 1987; The Films of Mel Brooks, 1988; The Best of Disney, 1988; Marilyn, 1989; Silent Movies, 1990; The Films of Nicolas Roeg, 1991; Classic Movie Comedians, 1992; Mel Gibson, 1992; Children in the Movies, 1992; Clint Eastwood, 1995; Jack Clayton, 2000; Graham Greene: A Literary Life, 2003; (ed. with I. MacKillop) British Cinema of the 1950s: A Celebration, 2003; Fred Zinnemann: Films of Character and Conscience, 2003; Richard Lester, 2010. **Address:** Department of Film Studies, University of Hull, Larkin Bldg., Hull, HB HU6 7RX, England. **Online address:** n.r.sinyard@hull.ac.uk

SINYKIN, Sheri Cooper. *See* **SINYKIN, Sheril C.**

SINYKIN, Sheril C. (Sheri Cooper Sinykin). American (born United States), b. 1950. **Genres:** Children's Fiction. **Career:** Rockford Newspapers, reporter, 1972; Madison General Hospital, public relations coordinator, 1972-75; Greater Madison Convention and Visitors Bureau, assistant executive director, 1975-78. Writer. **Publications:** AS SHERI COOPER SINYKIN: Shrimpboat and Gym Bags, 1990; Come out, Come out, Wherever You Are!, 1990; Apart at the Seams, 1991; Next Thing to Strangers, 1991; The Buddy Trap, 1991; Slate Blues, 1993; Sirens, 1993; The Shorty Society, 1994. MAGIC ATTIC CLUB SERIES: The Secret of the Attic, 1995; Heather at the Barre, 1995; Heather, Belle of the Ball, 1995; Heather Takes the Reins, 1996; Viva Heather, 1996; Alison Walks the Wire, 1996; Heather Goes to Hollywood, 1997; Trapped beyond the Magic Attic, 1997; A Matter of Time, 1998; Giving

Up the Ghost, 2007; Zayde Comes to Live, 2012. Contributor to books and periodicals. **Address:** 9622 E Sundune Dr., Sun Lakes, AZ 85248, U.S.A. **Online address:** scsinykin@gmail.com

SIPHERD, Ray. American (born United States), b. 1935. **Genres:** Novels, Novellas/Short Stories, Children's Fiction, Mystery/Crime/Suspense, Literary Criticism And History, Young Adult Fiction. **Career:** CBS-TV, story editor, 1957-61; WNET-TV, writer and producer, 1962-65; freelance writer, 1965-68; Reader's Digest Books, editor, 1968-96; Children's Television Workshop, writer, 1968-85. **Publications:** The Courtship of Peggy McCoy (novel), 1990; The Christmas Store (stories), 1993; Dance of the Scarecrows (mystery novel), 1996; The Audubon Quartet, 1998; The Devil's Hawk, 2002. JUVENILE FICTION: The White Kite, 1972; Ernie and Bert's Telephone Call, 1978; The Count's Poem, 1978; Down on the Farm with Grover, 1980; Sherlock Hemlock and the Creatures from Outer Space, 1981; Big Bird's Animal Alphabet, 1987; When is My Birthday?, 1988. Contributor to periodicals. **Address:** c/o Author Mail, St. Martin's Press, 175 5th Ave., New York, NY 10010, U.S.A.

SIPIERA, Paul P. American (born United States), b. 1948. **Genres:** Air/Space Topics, Astronomy, Children's Non-fiction, Earth Sciences, Biography, Autobiography/Memoirs. **Career:** William Rainey Harper College, adjunct professor, 1974, professor of geology and astronomy, 1976-, now professor emeritus; Planetary Studies Foundation, president; Harrison H. Schmitt Meteorite Research Group, director. Writer. **Publications:** FOR CHILDREN: (with C.B. Moore) Identification of Meteorites, 1975; (with R.L. Leary) Inventory of Meteorites in the Collection of the Illinois State Museum, 1977; I Can Be an Astronomer, 1986; I Can Be a Geologist, 1986; I Can Be an Oceanographer, 1987; Gerald Ford: Thirty-Eighth President of the United States, 1989; I Can Be a Geographer, 1990; Roald Amundsen and Robert Scott, 1990; Globes, 1991; I Can Be a Physicist, 1991; I Can Be a Biologist, 1992; I Can Be a Chemist, 1992; Meteorites, 1994; (with D.M. Sipiera) Constellations, 1997; The Solar System, 1997; Comets and Meteor Showers, 1997; Stars, 1997; Galaxies, 1997; Black Holes, 1997; (with D.M. Sipiera) Project Mercury, 1997; (with D.M. Sipiera) Project Gemini, 1997; (with D.M. Sipiera) Project Apollo, 1997; (with D.M. Sipiera) Hubble Space Telescope, 1997; (with D.M. Sipiera) Space Stations, 1997; (with D.M. Sipiera) Seasons, 1998; (with D.M. Sipiera) Floods, 1998; (with D.M. Sipiera) Thunderstorms, 1998; (with D.M. Sipiera) Wildfires, 1998; Earthquakes, 1998; Volcanoes, 1998; Ernest Shackleton: A Life of Antarctic Exploration, 2002. Contributor to periodicals. **Address:** Harper College, 1200 W Algonquin Rd., Palatine, IL 60067, U.S.A. **Online address:** psipiera@harpercollege.edu

SIPLE, Molly. American (born United States), b. 1942. **Genres:** Food And Wine, Medicine/Health, Information Science/Computers, Art/Art History. **Career:** Writer and artist. **Publications:** (With J. Naar) Living in One Room, 1976; (with I. Sax) Foodstyle: The Art of Presenting Food Beautifully, 1982; (with L.G. DeAngelis) Recipes for Change: Gourmet Wholefood Cooking for Health and Vitality at Menopause, 1996; (with L.G. DeAngelis) SOS for PMS: Whole-Food Solutions for Premenstrual Syndrome, 1999; Healing Foods for Dummies, 1999; (with D. Gordon) Menopause the Natural Way, 2001; Low-Cholesterol Cookbook for Dummies, 2004; Eating for Recovery: The Essential Nutrition Plan to Reverse the Physical Damage of Alcoholism, 2008; (with J. Stern) California Light: A Century of Landscapes: Paintings of the California Art Club, 2011. **Address:** 2178 Moreno Dr., Los Angeles, CA 90039, U.S.A. **Online address:** msiple@earthlink.net

SIRACUSA, Catherine (Jane). American (born United States), b. 1947. **Genres:** Children's Fiction, Art/Art History, Cartoons, Illustrations, Animals/Pets, Literary Criticism And History. **Career:** Harper's Bazaar, editorial assistant, 1968-69; freelance illustrator, 1969-87; Montclair State University, visiting specialist (editorial illustration), 1983-84; author and illustrator of children's books, 1986-; Miami University, children's book illustration craft, instructor, 2000, 2003-04. **Publications:** SELF-ILLUSTRATED: No Mail for Mitchell, 1990; The Giant Zucchini, 1993; The Parrot Problem, 1994; The Banana Split from Outer Space, 1995; The Peanut-Butter Gang, 1996. OTHER: Bingo, The Best Dog in the World, 1991. Illustrator of books by others. **Address:** Joanna Lewis Cole Literary Agency, 404 Riverside Dr., New York, NY 10025, U.S.A. **Online address:** siracusalevitt@hotmail.com

SIRC, Ljubo. British/Scottish/Slovenian (born Slovenia), b. 1920. **Genres:** Economics, History, Politics/Government, Autobiography/Memoirs, Business/Trade/Industry, Money/Finance. **Career:** Government of Slovenia, Daily News Section of Press Office, editor and translator, 1945; Yugoslav News Agency, editor and translator, 1945; freelance translator, 1954-55; British Broadcasting Corp., Monitoring Service, Serbo-Croat and Russian monitor, 1957-58; University of Dacca, visiting lecturer in economics, 1960-61; Institute of Economic Affairs, researcher, 1961-62; University of St. Andrews, lecturer in economics, 1962-65; University of Glasgow, lecturer, 1965-68, senior lecturer in economics, 1968-83; Centre for Research into Communist Economies (now Centre for Research into Post-Communist Economies), founding president, 1983-, director, 2006-. **Publications:** Kommunistische Agrarpolitik und Asien, Unter Besonderer: Unter Besonderer Berücksichtigung Jugoslwiens Und Pakistans, 1963; (with M. Miller, T.M. Piotrowicz and H. Smith) Communist Economy under Change, 1963; Nesmisel in Smisel, 1968; Economic Devolution in Eastern Europe, 1969; Outline of International Trade: Commodity Flows and Division of Production Between Countries, 1973; Outline of International Finance: Exchange Rates and Payments Between Countries, 1974; (co-author) Can Workers Manage?, 1977; The Yugoslav Economy Under Self-management, 1979; Between Hitler and Tito: Nazi Occupation and Communist Oppression, 1989; What Must Gorbachev Do?, 1989; Med Hitlerjem in Titom, 1992; Why Communist Economies Failed, 1994; True Fight for Freedom, 1995; Political Morality in Yugoslavia, 1996; In Search of Entrepreneurs, 1996; Da Li Je Kritika samoupravljanja Još Uvek Aktuelna?, 1997; Encouraging Entrepreneurship in Eastern Europe: A CRCE Conference in Bled, Slovenia, October 2005, No 22, 2006. Contributor of articles to journals and newspapers. **Address:** Centre for Research into Communist Economies, 57 Tufton St., London, GL SW1P 3QL, England.

SIRE, H. J. A. British/Spanish (born Spain), b. 1949. **Genres:** History, Biography, Autobiography/Memoirs, Philosophy, Art/Art History. **Career:** Aston University, representative, 1988-93. Educator and writer. **Publications:** Gentlemen Philosophers (history), 1988; The Knights of Malta (history), 1994; Father Martin D'Arcy (biography), 1997. **Address:** Travellers Club, 106 Pall Mall, London, GL SW1Y 5EP, England.

SIRIAS, Silvio. Panamanian/American (born United States), b. 1954. **Genres:** Novels. **Career:** Florida State University, faculty. Writer. **Publications:** (Ed. with B. Dick) Conversations with Rudolfo Anaya, 1998; (ed. and intro.) Tropical Town and Other Poems, 1999; Julia Alvarez: A Critical Companion, 2001; Bernardo and the Virgin (novel), 2005; Meet Me under the Ceiba (novel), 2009. **Address:** Panama. **Online address:** silvio@silviosirias.com

SIRIMARCO, Elizabeth. Also writes as E. S. Budd, Hal Rogers. American (born United States), b. 1966. **Genres:** Children's Fiction, Children's Nonfiction, Sciences, Natural History, Transportation. **Career:** Writer and editor, 1989-. **Publications:** Canada, 1990; Motherhood, 1991; Illiteracy, 1991; Health, 1991; War and the Environment, 1993; Tennis, 1994; AIDS, 1994; Eating Disorders, 1994; Yanomamis, 2000; Gypsies, 2000; At the Orchard, 2000; At the Construction Site, 2000; At the Barber, 2000; At the Bank, 2000; Tiger Woods, 2001; Steven Spielberg, 2002; Thomas Jefferson: Our Third President, 2002; American Voices from the Cold War, 2005; American Voices from the Civil Rights Movement, 2005; American Voices from Slavery, 2005; The Time of Slavery, 2007. CHILDREN'S NONFICTION AS E.S. BUDD: Fire Engines, 1999; Street Cleaners, 2001; Humvees, 2002; Military Helicopters, 2002; Military Trucks, 2002; Tanks, 2002; BMX Bicycles, 2004; Dune Buggies, 2004; ATVs, 2004; Off-Road Motorcycles, 2004; Personal Watercraft, 2004; Snowmobiles, 2004; Street Sweepers, 2008. CHILDREN'S NONFICTION AS HAL ROGERS: Generals, 1992; Skiing, 1994; Graders, 1999; Cranes, 1999; Earth Movers, 1999; Fire Engines, 1999; Rescue Helicopters, 2000; Cherry Pickers, 2000; Ambulances, 2000; Tow Trucks, 2000; Combines, 2001; Cars, 2001; Buses, 2001; Airplanes, 2001; Milking Machines, 2001; Plows, 2001; Snowplows, 2001; Tractors, 2001; Trains, 2001. **Address:** c/o Author Mail, Chelsea House Publishers, 1974 Sproul Rd., Ste. 400, Broomall, PA 19008, U.S.A. **Online address:** esbudd28@netscape.net

SIROTA, David. (David J. Sirota). American (born United States), b. 1975. **Genres:** Money/Finance, Politics/Government, Social Sciences, History. **Career:** University of Denver, instructor; Progressive Legislative Action Network (PLAN), co-chair; In These Times, senior editor. **Publications:** Hostile Takeover: How Big Money & Corruption Conquered Our Government-and How We Take It Back, 2006; The Uprising: An Unauthorized Tour of the Populist Revolt Scaring Wall Street and Washington, 2008; Back to Our Future: How The 1980s Explain The World We Live In Now Our Culture, Our Politics, Our Everything, 2011. **Address:** Creators Syndicate Inc., 5777 W Century Blvd., Ste. 700, Los Angeles, CA 90045-5652, U.S.A. **Online address:** ds@davidsirota.com

SIROTA, David J. *See* **SIROTA, David.**

SIROWITZ, Hal. American (born United States), b. 1949. **Genres:** Essays, Poetry, Humor/Satire, Literary Criticism And History. **Career:** New York Public School System, special education teacher. Poet, performance artist and teacher. **Publications:** Mother Said: Poems, 1996; My Therapist Said: Poems, 1998; Before, During, and After: Poems, 2003; Father Said: Poems, 2004. Works appear in anthologies. **Address:** The Joy Harris Literary Agency Inc., 156 5th Ave., Ste. 617, New York, NY 10010-7787, U.S.A. **Online address:** halsirowitz@yahoo.com

SIRR, Peter. Irish (born Ireland), b. 1960?. **Genres:** Poetry, Humanities. **Career:** Irish Writers' Centre, director, 1991-2002; Poetry Ireland Review, editor, 2003-07. Poet and translator. **Publications:** Marginal Zones, 1984; Talk, Talk, 1987; Ways of Falling, 1991; The Ledger of Fruitful Exchange, 1995; Bring Everything, 2000; Nonetheless, 2004; Selected Poems, 1982-2004, 2004; The Thing Is, 2009. Contributor to journals and books. **Address:** The Gallery Press, Loughcrew, Oldcastle, ME 1, Ireland. **Online address:** petersirr@mac.com

SIRVAITIS (CHERNYAEV), Karen (Ann). American (born United States), b. 1961. **Genres:** Travel/Exploration, History. **Career:** Skyway News, reporter and photographer, 1984-86; Lerner Publications Co., editor, 1986-; freelance translator. **Publications:** Virginia, 1991, 2nd ed., 2002; Utah, 1991; Tennessee, 1991; Nevada, 1992; Florida, 1994; Michigan, 1994; South Dakota, 1995; Nevada State History, 2007; Barack Obama: A Leader in a Time of Change, 2010; Seven Wonders of Green Building Technology, 2010; Guyana in Pictures, 2010; The Asian Pacific American Experience, 2011; Danica Patrick, 2011; The European American Experience, 2011. **Address:** Lerner Publishing Group, 1251 Washington Ave. N, Minneapolis, MN 55401, U.S.A.

SISK, David W. American (born United States), b. 1963. **Genres:** Science Fiction/Fantasy, Literary Criticism And History, Language/Linguistics, Social Commentary, Humor/Satire. **Career:** University of North Carolina, microcomputer lab manager, 1987-92, graduate English instructor, 1988-92, Office of Information Technology, microcomputer technical trainer, 1992-94; Knox College, user services specialist, 1994-96, instructor, 1995; Macalester College, assistant director for academic computing, 1996-98, Information Technology Services Office, associate director and team leader for desktop services, 1998-2008, associate director for administration, 2008-. Writer. **Publications:** Transformations of Language in Modern Dystopias, 1997. **Address:** Information Technology Services, Macalester College, Rm. 307-A, Humanities Bldg., 1600 Grand Ave., Saint Paul, MN 55105-1899, U.S.A. **Online address:** dwsisk@gmail.com

SISSON, Rosemary Anne. British (born England), b. 1923. **Genres:** Novels, Children's Fiction, Plays/Screenplays, Biography, Social Sciences. **Career:** University of Wisconsin, instructor in English, 1949-50; University of London, University College, assistant lecture in American literature, 1950-54; University of Birmingham, assistant lecturer in English, 1954-55; Stratford-upon-Avon Herald, Stratford-upon-Avon, drama critic, 1955-57. Writer. **Publications:** The Adventures of Ambrose, 1951; The Impractical Chimney Sweep, 1956; Mr. Nobody, 1956; The Queen and the Welshman (play), 1958; The Treasures of Our Time: Embroidered Kneelers in Chelsea Old Church, 1958; Fear Came to Supper (play), 1959; The Splendid Outcasts (play), 1959; The Young Shakespeare, 1959; The Isle of Dogs, 1959; The Young Jane Austen, 1962; The Young Shaftesbury, 1964; Bitter Sanctuary (play), 1964; The Man in the Case (play), 1965; The Exciseman, 1972; Catherine of Aragon: Six Wives of Henry VIII (television play), 1972; The Killer of Horseman's Flats, 1973; The Stratford Story, 1974; (with R. Morley) A Ghost on Tiptoe (play), 1975; Will in Love, 1975; Escape from the Dark, 1976; Will in Love, 1977; The Dark Horse (play), 1979; The Queen and the Welshman, 1979; (with A. Nixon) The Manions of America, 1981; Mole's Cousin, 1984; Bury Love Deep, 1985; Beneath the Visiting Moon, 1986; The Bretts, 1987; Rosemary for Remembrance, 1995; Footstep on the Stair, 1999; First Love, Last Love, 2002; We'll Meet Again, 2003. **Address:** Andrew Mann Ltd., 1 Old Compton St., London, GL W1D 5JA, England.

SITA, Lisa. American (born United States), b. 1962. **Genres:** Children's Non-fiction, Natural History, Cultural/Ethnic Topics, Biology, Theology/Religion, Biography. **Career:** Museum of the American Indian/Heye Foundation, assistant educator, 1987-88; American Museum of Natural History, senior museum educator in anthropology, 1988-; New York Historical Society, educational program coordinator. Writer. **Publications:** FOR CHILDREN: The Rattle and the Drum: Native American Rituals and Celebrations, 1994. EXPLORING SCIENCE SERIES: Rocks, Gems, and Minerals, 1995; Human Biology and Evolution, 1995. OUR HUMAN FAMILY SERIES: Worlds of Belief: Religion and Spirituality, 1995; Search for Beauty: Art and Music, 1996. OTHERS: Woodland Peoples of the Northeast, 1996; Peoples of the Great Plains, 1996; Cliff Dwellers and Pueblo Peoples, 1996; Coming of Age, 1999; Indians of the Southwest: Traditions, History, Legends, and Life, 2000; Indians of the Great Plains: Traditions, History, Legends, and Life, 2000; Indians of the Northeast: Traditions, History, Legends, and Life, 2000; (with L.J. Krizner) Peter Stuyvesant: New Amsterdam and the Origins of New York, 2001; (with L.J. Krizner) Nathan Hale: Patriot and Martyr of the American Revolution, 2002; Pocahontas: The Powhatan Culture and the Jamestown Colony, 2005. Contributor to periodicals. **Address:** Department of Education, American Museum of Natural History, Central Park W, 79th St., New York, NY 10024-5192, U.S.A.

SITES, Kevin. American (born United States) **Genres:** Military/Defense/Arms Control, Biography, History. **Career:** California Polytechnic State University, broadcast lecturer in journalism, 2000-01; National Broadcasting Company Inc., freelance solo journalist, 2004, NBC News, producer; Microsoft/NBC in Asia, freelance solo journalist, 2004; Cable News Network, correspondent; Kevin Sites in the Hot Zone, war news correspondent, 2005-; People of the Web, Yahoo! News, correspondent, 2007-; American Broadcasting Companies Inc., producer. **Publications:** In the Hot Zone: One Man, One Year, Twenty Wars, 2007. Contributor of articles to periodicals. **Address:** CA , U.S.A. **Online address:** ksinhz@hotmail.com

SITKOFF, Harvard. American (born United States) **Genres:** Social Sciences. **Career:** University of New Hampshire, professor of history, now professor emeritus. Writer and educator. **Publications:** A New Deal for Blacks: The Emergence of Civil Rights as a National Issue: The Depression Decade, 1978; The Struggle for Black Equality, 1954-1980, 1981, 25th ed. as The Struggle for Black Equality, 2008; A History of Our Time: Readings on Postwar America, 1983, 7th ed., 2008; Fifty Years Later: The New Deal Evaluated, 1985; Postwar America: A Student Companion, 2000; Perspectives on Modern America: Making Sense of the Twentieth Century, 2001; King: Pilgrimage to the Mountaintop, 2008; Toward Freedom Land: The Long Struggle For Racial Equality in America, 2010. **Address:** University of New Hampshire, Horton Social Science Ctr., 20 Academic Way, Durham, NH 03824, U.S.A. **Online address:** his@cisunix.unh.edu

SITTENFELD, Curtis. American (born United States), b. 1975. **Genres:** Novels, Natural History. **Career:** St. Albans School, writer-in-residence, 2002-03, teacher of English, 2003-. **Publications:** NOVELS: Prep, 2005; The Man of My Dreams, 2006; American Wife, 2008. Contributor to periodicals. **Address:** c/o Jennifer Hershey, Random House Inc., 1745 Broadway, New York, NY 10019, U.S.A.

SITTER, John E(dward). American (born United States), b. 1944. **Genres:** Literary Criticism And History. **Career:** University of Massachusetts, assistant professor, 1969-75, associate professor of English, 1975-80; Emory University, professor of English, 1980-85, chairman of department, 1982-85, 1994-97, Dobbs professor, 1985-93, Charles Howard Candler professor, 1987-2004, now professor emeritus; University of Kent, visiting lecturer; University of Notre Dame, English professor, Mary Lee Duda professor of literature, chair of department. Writer. The Poetry of Pope's Dunciad, 1971; Literary Loneliness in Mid-Eighteenth-Century England, 1982; (ed.) Eighteenth-Century British Poets, 2 vols., 1990-91; Arguments of Augustan Wit, 1991; (ed.) The Cambridge Companion to Eighteenth-Century Poetry, 2001; Cambridge Introduction to Eighteenth-Century Poetry, 2011. Contributor to journals. **Publications:** The Poetry of Pope's "Dunciad," 1971; Literary Loneliness in Mid-Eighteenth-Century England, 1982; (ed.) Eighteenth-Century British Poets, 2 vols., 1990-91; Arguments of Augustan Wit, 1991; (ed.) The Cambridge Companion to Eighteenth-Century Poetry, 2001. Contributor to journals. **Address:** Department of English, University of Notre Dame, 181 Decio Faculty Hall, 356 O'Shaughnessy, Notre Dame, IN 46556, U.S.A. **Online address:** john.sitter.1@nd.edu

SITTSER, Gerald L. American (born United States), b. 1950. **Genres:** Theology/Religion, Sociology, Social Sciences. **Career:** Reformed church in Paramount, associate pastor, 1975-79; Northwestern College, chaplain, 1979-85; Whitworth University, associate professor, professor of religion, 1989-, Certification in Ministry program, director, Master of Arts in Theology Program, chair. Writer. **Publications:** The Adventure: Putting Energy into Your Walk with God, 1985; Loving Across Our Differences, 1994; A Grace Disguised: How the Soul Grows through Loss, 1996; A Cautious Patriotism: The American Churches and the Second World War, 1997; The Will of God as a Way of Life, 2002, rev. ed. as The Will of God as a Way of Life: How to Make Every Decision with Peace and Confidence, 2004; Discovering God's Will: How to Make Every Decision with Peace and Confidence, 2002; When God Doesn't Answer Your Prayer, 2003, 2nd ed., 2007; Water from a Deep Well: Christian Spirituality from Early Martyrs to Modern Missionaries, 2007; Love One Another: Becoming the Church Jesus Longs For, 2008; When Your Rope Breaks, 2009. **Address:** Whitworth University, 117 Westminster Hall, 300 W Hawthorne Rd., Spokane, WA 99251, U.S.A. **Online address:** gsittser@whitworth.edu

SIVERLING, Michael. See **SIVERLING, Mike.**

SIVERLING, Mike. (Michael Siverling). American (born United States) **Genres:** Mystery/Crime/Suspense, Young Adult Fiction. **Career:** Office of the District Attorney, supervising criminal investigator; Midnight Investigations Agency, supervising criminal investigator. Writer. **Publications:** The Sterling Inheritance, 2004; The Sorcerer's Circle, 2006. **Address:** c/o Author Mail, St. Martins Press, 175 5th Ave., New York, NY 10010, U.S.A. **Online address:** catfelon1@msn.com

SIVERSON, Randolph M. American (born United States), b. 1940. **Genres:** Politics/Government, Adult Non-fiction, Social Sciences, Military/Defense/Arms Control. **Career:** Stanford University, Department of Political Science, teaching assistant, 1964-66, lecturer, 1967; University of California, Riverside, acting assistant professor, 1967-69, assistant professor, 1969-70; University of California, Davis, assistant professor, 1970-75, associate professor, 1975-81, professor, 1981-2007, distinguished professor, 2007-09, distinguished professor emeritus and research professor emeritus, 2009, acting university librarian, 2010-11; International Interactions, editor, 1986-91, co-editor, 1992-99. **Publications:** (Ed. with O.R. Holsti and A.L. George) Change in the International System, 1980; (with H. Starr) The Diffusion of War: A Study of Opportunity and Willingness, 1991; (ed.) Strategic Politicians, Institutions and Foreign Policy, 1998; The Logic of Political Survival, 2003. Contributor to periodicals. **Address:** Department of Political Science, University of California-Davis, 578 Kerr Hall, 1 Shields Ave., Davis, CA 95616, U.S.A. **Online address:** rmsiverson@ucdavis.edu

SIZEMORE, Christine Wick. American (born United States), b. 1945. **Genres:** Literary Criticism And History, Women's Studies And Issues, Young Adult Fiction. **Career:** Georgia State University, instructor, 1971-72, assistant professor of English, 1972-78; Emory University, visiting professor, 1976; Spelman College, Department of English, assistant professor, 1978-84, associate professor, 1984-92, professor, 1992-. Writer. **Publications:** A Female Vision of the City: London in the Novels of Five British Women, 1989; Negotiating Identities in Women's Lives: English Postcolonial and Contemporary British Novels, 2002. Contributor to journals. **Address:** Department of English, Spelman College, 309 Cosby Academic Ctr., 305 Spelman Ln. SW, Atlanta, GA 30314, U.S.A. **Online address:** csizemor@spelman.edu

SIZER, Mona D. See **JAMES, Deana.**

SJOSTRAND, Sven-Erik. Swedish (born Sweden), b. 1945. **Genres:** Economics, Administration/Management, Business/Trade/Industry. **Career:** Stockholm School of Economics, professor, 1978-, Matts Carlgren Chair in Management, 1995-, Economic Research Institute, chairman, 1995-2001. Writer. **Publications:** Företagsorganisation: En Taxonomisk Ansats. Med en typisering av 38 svenska byggnadsföretag, 1973; Organisationspraktik, 1977; Inlärningsorganisation: Fallet Kista, 1977; Organizational Myths, 1979; (ed.)

Företagsledning: Bortom Etablerad Teori, 1992; (ed.) Institutional Change: Theory and Empirical Findings, 1993; (ed. with J. Groenewegen and C. pitelis) On Economic Institutions, 1995; The Two Faces of Management: The Janus Factor, 1997; Invisible Management, 2001; (ed. with P.G. de Monthoux and C. Gustafsson) Aesthetic Leadership: Managing Fields of Flow in Art and Business, 2007; (with M. Kallifatides and S. Nachemson-Ekwall) Corporate Governance in Modern Financial Capitalism: Old Mutual's Hostile Takeover of Skandia, 2010. **Address:** Stockholm School of Economics, Saltmatargatan 13-17, 6th Fl., PO Box 6501, Stockholm, S-11383, Sweden. **Online address:** sven-erik.sjostrand@hhs.se

SKAL, David J. American (born United States), b. 1952. **Genres:** Horror, Novels, Young Adult Non-fiction. **Career:** Hartford Stage Co., publicity director; American Conservatory Theatre, staff writer; David J. Skal Associates Inc., president and creative director, 1982-92. Consultant. **Publications:** Scavengers, 1980; When We Were Good, 1981; (ed.) Graphic Communications for the Performing Arts, 1981; Antibodies, 1988; Hollywood Gothic: The Tangled Web of Dracula from Novel to Stage to Screen, 1990, rev. ed., 2004; The Monster Show: A Cultural History of Horror, 1993, rev. ed., 2001; (ed.) Dracula: The Ultimate, Illustrated Edition of the World-Famous Vampire Play, 1993; (with E. Savada) Dark Carnival: The Secret World of Tod Browning-Hollywood's Master of the Macabre, 1995; V is for Vampire: The A to Z Guide to Everything Undead, 1996; (with E. Savada) Carnaval de Las Tinieblas: El Mundo Secreto de Tod Browning, Maestro de lo Macabro en el Cine de Hollywood, 1996; (ed. with N. Auerbach) Dracula: Authoritative Text, Contexts, Reviews and Reactions, Dramatic and Film Variations, Criticism, 1997; Screams of Reason: Mad Science and Modern Culture, 1998; (ed.) Vampires: Encounters with the Undead, 2001; Death Makes a Holiday: A Cultural History of Halloween, 2002; (with J. Rains) Claude Rains: An Actor's Voice, 2008; Romancing the Vampire, 2009; Citizen Clone: The Morphing of America, forthcoming. **Address:** c/o Author Mail, Faber and Faber Inc., 19 Union Sq. W, New York, NY 10003-3304, U.S.A.

SKANDERA-TROMBLEY, Laura Elise. *See* **TROMBLEY, Laura Skandera.**

SKARIA, Ajay. American/Indian (born India) **Genres:** History, Social Sciences. **Career:** University of Virginia, assistant professor of history, 1995-98; University of Minnesota, assistant professor of history, 1999-, McKnight Land-Grant professor, 2000-02, associate professor, Institute for Advanced Study, interdisciplinary doctoral fellow, 2011-. Writer. **Publications:** Hybrid Histories: Forests, Frontiers, and Wildness in Western India, 1999; (ed. with S. Mayaram and M.S.S. Pandian) Muslims, Dalits, and the Fabrications of History, 2005. **Address:** Department of History, University of Minnesota, 924 Heller Hall, 271 19th Ave. S, Minneapolis, MN 55455-0425, U.S.A. **Online address:** skari002@umn.edu

SKARSAUNE, Oskar. Norwegian (born Norway), b. 1946?. **Genres:** Theology/Religion, Cultural/Ethnic Topics. **Career:** Norwegian Lutheran School of Theology, assistant professor, 1980-90, professor of church history, 1990-; Norwegian Lutheran School of Theology, assistant professor, 1980-90, professor of patristic studies and early church history, 1990-; Caspari Center, curriculum writer, 1983. Writer. **Publications:** (With T. Bjerkholt and J. Gossner) Skjulte Gud, 1971; The Proof from Prophecy: A Study in Justin Martyr's Proof-Text Tradition; Text-Type, Provenance, Theological Profile, 1987; Daskriften ble åpnet: Den første kristne tolkning av det gamletestamente, 1987; Incarnation, myth or Fact?, 1991; Kristendommens Jødiske rødder, 1996; Jewish Influences in the Early Church, 1997; Jewish Roots of the New Testament, 1997; Troens ord: De tre oldkirkeligebekjennelsene, 1997; In the Shadow of the Temple: Jewish Influences on Early Christianity, 2002; Den ukjente Jesus: Nye kilder til hvem Jesusvirkelig var?: Da Vinci-koden, Gralsfortellingene, 2005; (ed. with R. Hvalvik) Jewish Believers in Jesus: The Early Centuries, 2007. Contributor to journals. **Address:** PO Box 84, Rygge, N-1581, Norway. **Online address:** oskar.skarsaune@mf.no

SKEET, Ian. British (born England), b. 1928. **Genres:** Area Studies, International Relations/Current Affairs, History, Travel/Exploration. **Career:** Royal Dutch Shell, staff, 1953-, Qatar, general manager, 1958-, Petroleum Development Oman, management liaison representative, 1966-, manager of shell relations, 1973-85. Consultant and writer. **Publications:** Muscat and Oman: End of an Era, 1974; Oman before 1970: End of an Era, 1985; OPEC: Twenty-Five Years of Prices and Politics, 1988; (ed.) Paul Frankel: Common Carrier of Common Sense, 1989; Oman: Politics and Development, 1992. **Address:** 27 Christchurch Rd., Winchester, SO23 9SU, England.

SKELTON, William B(arott). American (born United States), b. 1939. **Genres:** History, Military/Defense/Arms Control, Humanities. **Career:** University of Wisconsin, professor of history, 1969-2002, professor emeritus, 2002-. Writer. **Publications:** An American Profession of Arms: The Army Officer Corps, 1784-1861, 1992. **Address:** Department of History, University of Wisconsin, 477 Collins Classroom Ctr., 1801 4th Ave., Stevens Point, WI 54481-3897, U.S.A. **Online address:** wskelton@uwsp.edu

SKEMER, Don C. (Don Cornel Skemer). American (born United States), b. 1948. **Genres:** History, Bibliography. **Career:** New Jersey Historical Society, keeper of manuscripts, 1974-79, director of publishing, 1979-86, associate executive director, 1986; New Jersey History, managing editor, 1983-86; State University of New York, head of special collections and archives, adjunct lecturer, 1986-91; Princeton University Libraries, curator of manuscripts, 1991-. **Publications:** American History in Belgium and Luxembourg: A Bibliography, 1975; (comp. with R.C. Morris) Guide to the Manuscript Collections of the New Jersey Historical Society, 1979; Binding Words: Textual Amulets in the Middle Ages, 2006. Contributor to periodicals. **Address:** Department of Rare Books and Special Collections, Princeton University Library, 1 Washington Rd., Princeton, NJ 08544-2002, U.S.A. **Online address:** dcskemer@princeton.edu

SKEMER, Don Cornel. *See* **SKEMER, Don C.**

SKERPAN-WHEELER, Elizabeth (Penley). American (born United States), b. 1955. **Genres:** Literary Criticism And History, Politics/Government, Biography, History. **Career:** Madison Area Technical College, substitute instructor, 1983; Southwest Texas State University, assistant professor of English, 1983-90, associate professor of English, 1990-97, professor of English, 1997-. Writer. **Publications:** The Rhetoric of Politics in the English Revolution, 1642-1660, 1992; Life Writings, 2 vols., 2000. Contributor of articles to periodicals. Works appear in anthologies. **Address:** Department of English, Texas State University, Flowers Hall 331, 601 University Dr., San Marcos, TX 78666, U.S.A. **Online address:** es10@txstate.edu

SKIBA, Katherine M. American (born United States) **Genres:** Young Adult Non-fiction, Military/Defense/Arms Control, Biography, Autobiography/Memoirs, History. **Career:** Milwaukee Journal Sentinel, reporter, 1982-, Washington correspondent, 2000-; Marquette University, staff; Chicago Tribune, reporter. Photographer. **Publications:** Sister in the Band of Brothers: Embedded with the 101st Airborne in Iraq, 2005. Contributor to periodicals. **Online address:** kskiba@tribune.com

SKIDMORE, David (G.). American (born United States), b. 1958. **Genres:** Economics, Politics/Government. **Career:** Hamilton College, instructor, 1986-88; University of Notre Dame, instructor, 1988-89; Drake University, assistant professor, 1989-94, associate professor of political science, 1994-2001, divisional representative to arts and sciences council, 1990-92, faculty senate, 1993-94, International Relations Program, director, 1997, Elsworth and Sylvia Woods Fund, director, 1997-2001, Drake Curriculum and First Year Seminar Programs, director, 1998-2002, acting chair in political science, 1998-99, College of Arts and Sciences, acting assistant dean, 1998, associate dean for curriculum development, 1999-2001 Department of Politics and International Relations, professor, 2001-, Center for Global Citizenship, founding director, 2000-; Rollins College, visiting associate professor, 1996; Johns Hopkins-Nanjing University, Center for Chinese and American Studies, visiting associate professor, 1996-97. Writer. **Publications:** (With T.D. Lairson) International Political Economy: The Struggle for Power and Wealth, 1993, 3rd ed., 2003; Reversing Course: Carter's Foreign Policy, Domestic Politics, and the Failure of Reform, 1996. EDITOR and CONTRIBUTOR: (with V. Hudson) The Limits of State Autonomy: Societal Groups and Foreign Policy Formulation, 1993; Contested Social Orders and International Politics, 1997; Paradoxes of Power: U.S. Foreign Policy in a Changing World, 2007; The Unilateralist Temptation in American Foreign Policy, 2011. Contributor of articles to periodicals. **Address:** Department of Political Science, Drake University, 213 Meredith Hall, 2507 University Ave., Des Moines, IA 50311, U.S.A. **Online address:** david.skidmore@drake.edu

SKIDMORE, Max J(oseph). American (born United States), b. 1933. **Genres:** Adult Non-fiction, Politics/Government, Travel/Exploration. **Ca-**

reer: Missouri Public Schools, teacher, 1954-55; City of Climax Springs, superintendent of schools, 1956-57; Department of Health, Education and Welfare, Social Security Administration, management analyst, 1959-62; Office of Commissioner of Social Security, administrative assistant, 1962-64; U.S. Office of Education, program review officer, 1964-65; University of Alabama, associate professor and director of American studies, 1965-68; Southwest Missouri State University, Department of Political Science, professor and head, 1968-82; American Studies Research Center, director and distinguished Fulbright lecturer, 1978-79; Eastern New Mexico University, dean of arts and sciences, 1982-84; University of Missouri, College of Arts and Sciences, dean, 1985-92, Department of Political Science, professor of political science, 1985-92, Curators' professor of political science, 1999-, Thomas Jefferson fellow, Thomas Jefferson professor, 2007-. Writer. **Publications:** Medicare and the American Rhetoric of Reconciliation, 1970; (with M.C. Tripp) American Government: A Brief Introduction, 1974, 6th ed., 1993; American Political Thought, 1978; (with J.F. Barnes and M. Carter) The World of Politics: A Concise Introduction, 1980, 2nd ed., 1984; Ideologies: Politics in Action, 1989, 2nd ed., 1993; The Future of Hong Kong, 1996; Hong Kong and China, 1997; Legacy to the World: A Study of America's Political Ideas, 1998; Social Security and Its Enemies: The Case for America's Most Efficient Insurance Program, 1999; After the White House: Former Presidents as Private Citizens, 2004; Presidential Performance: A Comprehensive Review, 2004; Moose Crossing: Portland to Portland on the Theodore Roosevelt International Highway, 2007; Securing America's Future: A Bold Plan to Preserve and Expand Social Security, 2008. EDITOR: Word Politics: Essays on Language and Politics, 1972; (with A. Singh and I. Sequeira) American Studies Today, 1995; (with A. Cline) Politics and Language, 2007. Contributor of articles to periodicals. **Address:** Department of Political Science, University of Missouri, 303D Manheim Hall, 5120 Rockhill Rd., Kansas City, MO 64110, U.S.A. **Online address:** skidmorem@umkc.edu

SKILLINGSTEAD, Jack. American (born United States), b. 1955. **Genres:** Novels, Graphic Novels. **Career:** Author, 2000-; Boeing Corp, staff. **Publications:** Empty Mansions (graphic novel), 2008; Are You There and Other Stories, 2009; Harbinger (novel), 2009. Works appear in anthologies. Contributor to magazines and periodicals. **Address:** Seattle, WA , U.S.A. **Online address:** jskillingstead@yahoo.com

SKILLMAN, Don. American (born United States), b. 1932. **Genres:** Travel/Exploration. **Career:** Freelance feature writer and photographer, 1953-55; Natural History Museum, director, 1992-97. **Publications:** (With L. Skillman) Pedaling across America, 1988; (with L. Skillman) Twenty-Five Hikes along the Pacific Crest Trail, 1994; Moving to the Country, 1996; Adventure Kayaking: Trips in Glacier Bay, 1998; Adventure Kayaking: Inland Waters of the Western United States, 1999. **Address:** PO Box 1120, Ashland, OR 97520, U.S.A. **Online address:** lark541@charter.net

SKINNER, Ainslie. See **GOSLING, Paula.**

SKINNER, Anthony David. Israeli/American (born United States), b. 1962?. **Genres:** Biography, Translations, Autobiography/Memoirs, Theology/Religion. **Career:** Al-Quds University, writer-in-residence, faculty. Author, historian and researcher. **Publications:** Gershom Scholem: A Life in Letters, 1914-1982, 2002; The Patron: A Life of Salman Schocken, 1877-1959, 2003; (ed. and trans.) Lamentations of Youth: The Diaries of Gershom Scholem, 1913-1919, 2007; (with S. Nusseibeh) Once Upon a Country: A Palestinian Life, 2007; The Sky's the Limit, 2008; Mr. Viral, forthcoming. **Address:** Al-Quds University, Abdel Hamaid Shoman St., Beit Hanina, Jerusalem, 02138, Israel. **Online address:** antonydavidd@gmail.com

SKINNER, Gloria Dale. Also writes as Amelia Grey, Charla Cameron. American (born United States), b. 1951. **Genres:** Romance/Historical, Young Adult Fiction. **Career:** Writer. **Publications:** Passion's Choice, 1990; Georgia Fever, 1992; Tender Trust, 1993; Starlight, 1994; Midnight Fire, 1994; Bewitching, 1995; Ransom, 1996; Juliana, 1997; Cassandra, 1998; Hellion, 1998. AS CHARLA CAMERON: Diamond Days, 1991; Sultry Nights, 1992; Glory Nights, 1993. AS AMELIA GREY: Never a Bride, 2001; A Dash of Scandal, 2002; A Little Mischief, 2003; A Hint of Seduction, 2004; Taste of Temptation, 2005; Duke to Die For, 2009; A Marquis to Marry, 2009. **Address:** 2211 Thomas Dr., Panama City Beach, FL 32408, U.S.A. **Online address:** gloriadaleskinner@worldnet.att.net

SKINNER, June O. See **O'GRADY, Rohan.**

SKINNER, Knute (Rumsey). American/Irish (born Ireland), b. 1929. **Genres:** Poetry. **Career:** University of Iowa, faculty, 1960-61; Oklahoma College for Women, faculty, 1961-62; Western Washington University, assistant professor, 1962-63, lecturer, 1964-71, associate professor, 1971-73, professor of English, 1973-97; Signpost Press, Bellingham, editor and publisher, 1977-95. **Publications:** Stranger with a Watch, 1965; A Close Sky over Killaspuglonane, 1968; In Dinosaur Country, 1969; The Sorcerers: A Laotian Tale, 1972; Hearing of the Hard Times, 1981; The Flame Room, 1982; Selected Poems, 1985; Learning to Spell Zucchini: Poems, 1988; The Bears and Other Poems, 1991; (ed.) Roughly Speaking, 1991; What Trudy Knows and Other Poems, 1994; The Cold Irish Earth: New and Selected Poems of Ireland, 1965-1995, 1996; An Afternoon Quiet and Other Poems, 1998; Greatest Hits 1964-2000, 2001; Stretches, 2002; The Other Shoe, 2004; Fifty Years: Poems, 1957-2007, 2007; Help Me to a Getaway (a memoir), 2010. **Address:** Killaspuglonane, Lahinch, CL , Ireland. **Online address:** knuteskinner@eircom.net

SKINNER, Margaret. American (born United States), b. 1942. **Genres:** Novels, Horror. **Career:** University of Memphis, Department of English, instructor, 1988, 1992, 1993, assistant professor of creative writing, 1993-, Creative Writing Program, faculty; Sweet Briar College, writer-in-residence, 1996. **Publications:** Old Jim Canaan, 1990; Molly Flanagan and the Holy Ghost, 1995; (ed. with B.L. Parker and T. Lewis) Thrips Biology and Management, 1995; The Road to Finisterre, forthcoming. Contributor to periodicals. **Address:** Creative Writing Program, Department of English, University of Memphis, 471A Patterson Hall, Memphis, TN 38152, U.S.A.

SKINNER, Michael. American (born United States), b. 1953. **Genres:** Military/Defense/Arms Control, Novels, History, Literary Criticism And History. **Career:** St. Petersburg Times, writer and editor, 1979-81; Washington Star, writer and editor, 1981; Cable News Network, writer and producer, 1982-85, writer and editor, 1992-. **Publications:** U.S.A.F.E.: A Primer of Modern Air Combat in Europe, 1983, rev. ed., 1988; Red Flag: Air Combat for the Eighties, 1984, rev. ed., 1993; USN: Naval Operations in the Eighties, 1986; USAREUR: United States Army in Europe, 1989; First Air: A Novel of Air Combat in the Persian Gulf, 1991; Boomtown (novel), 1994. **Address:** c/o Al Zuckerman, Writers House Inc., 21 W 26th St., New York, NY 10010-1003, U.S.A. **Online address:** michael.skinner@turner.com

SKINNER, Quentin (Robert Duthie). British (born England), b. 1940. **Genres:** History, Intellectual History, Travel/Exploration. **Career:** Cambridge University, Christ's College, fellow, 1962-, lecturer in history, 1967-78, professor of political science, 1978-96, Regius professor of modern history, 1996-, pro-vice-chancellor, 1999-; University of London, Barber Beaumont professor of the humanities, 2008-, distinguished visiting professor, 2007-08. Writer. **Publications:** CO-EDITOR AND CONTRIBUTOR: Philosophy, Politics and Society, 1972; Philosophy in History, 1984; The Return of Grand Theory in the Human Sciences, 1985; The Cambridge History of Renaissance Philosophy, 1988; Machiavelli and Republicanism, 1990; Political Discourse in Early-Modern Britain, 1993; Republicanism: A Shared European Heritage, 2 vols., 2002. OTHERS: The Foundations of Modern Political Thought, vol. I, The Renaissance, 1978, vol. II, The Age of Reformation, 1978; Machiavelli, 1981; Meaning and Context, 1988; (co-author) Great Political Thinkers, 1992; Reason and Rhetoric in the Philosophy of Hobbes, 1996; Liberty before Liberalism, 1998; Visions of Politics, vol. I: Regarding Method, 2002, vol. II: Renaissance Virtues, 2002, vol. III: Hobbes and Civil Science, 2002; Hobbes and Republican Liberty, 2008; Families and States in Western Europe, 2011. CO-EDITOR: Machiavelli, The Prince, 1988; Milton and Republicanism, 1995; Machiavelli: A Very Short Introduction, 2000; (with B. Strath) States and Citizens: History, Theory, Prospects, 2003; A Dialogue Between a Philosopher and a Student, of the Common Laws of England, 2005; Sovereignty in Fragments: The Past, Present and Future of a Contested Concept, 2010. **Address:** Faculty of History, University of Cambridge, West Rd., Cambridge, CB3 9EF, England. **Online address:** qrds2@cam.ac.uk

SKINNER, Stephen. British/Singaporean (born Singapore), b. 1948?. **Genres:** Adult Non-fiction, Biography, Theology/Religion. **Career:** Feng Shui for Modern Living (magazine), publisher, 1998-. Writer, lecturer and consultant. **Publications:** (With N. Drury) The Search for Abraxas, 1972; Aleister Crowleys Astrology, 1974; (with F. King) Techniques of High Magic: A Manual of Self-Initiation, 1975; The Living Earth Manual of Feng-shui: Chinese Geomancy, 1976, rev. ed. as Feng Shui: The Living Earth Manual, 2006; In Pursuit of Gold: Alchemy in Theory and Practice, 1976; (ed. and intro.) Aleister Crowleys Tao the King: Liber CLVII, 1976; Terrestrial Astrology: Divination by Geomancy, 1980; The Oracle of Geomancy: Divination by Earth, 1986; Techniques of High Magic: A Guide to Self-Empowerment, 1991; Nostradamus: Prophecies of the Worlds Greatest Seer: Prophecies Fulfilled and Predictions for the Millennium and Beyond, 1994; Millennium Prophecies: Predictions for the Year 2000 and Beyond, 1994; The Magical Diaries of Aleister Crowley: Tunisia 1923, 1996; Feng Shui: The Traditional Oriental Way to Enhance Your Life, 1997; Feng Shui, 1998; Feng Shui for Modern Living, 2000; KISS Guide to Feng Shui, 2001; Feng Shui Before and After: Practical Room-by-Room Makeovers for Your House, 2001; Flying Star Feng Shui, 2003; Feng Shui Style: The Asian Art of Gracious Living, 2003; The Practical Angel Magic of John Dees Enochian Tables, 2004; Tibetan Feng Shui Oracle Pack, 2005; (ed. and intro.) The Fourth Book of Occult Philosophy, 2005; (with D. Rankine) The Keys to the Gateway of Magic: Summoning the Solomonic Archangels and Demon Princes, 2005; Sacred Geometry: Deciphering the Code, 2006; The Water Dragon, vol. I, 2006; Complete Magician's Tables: The Most Complete Set of Magic, Kabbalistic, Angelic, Astrologic, Alchemic, Demonic, Geomantic, Grimoire, Gematria, I Ching, Tarot, Planetary, Pagan Pantheon, Plant, Perfume, Emblem and Character Correspondences in More Than 777 Tables, 2nd ed., 2006; The Original Eight Mansions Formula, 2007; The Key San He Feng Shui Formulas, 2007; (ed. with D. Rankine) The Goetia of Dr Rudd, 2007; Mountain Dragon Formulas, 2008; Guide to the Feng Shui Compass, 2008; The Veritable Key of Solomon, 2008; (intro.) Byzantine Magic: Michael Psellus on the Operation of Daæmons, 2009; Geomancy in Theory & Practice, 2009; (with D. Rankine) The Grimoire of St. Cyprian- Clavis Inferni, 2009. **Address:** Tuttle Publishing, 153 Milk St., Boston, MA 02109, U.S.A. **Online address:** perscon@gmail.com

SKINNER-LINNENBERG, **Virginia (M.).** American (born United States), b. 1951. **Genres:** Young Adult Fiction, Education, Writing/Journalism, Communications/Media, Travel/Exploration. **Career:** Bowling Green State University, teaching fellow, 1989-92; North Central Michigan College, professor of English, dean of liberal arts and department chair, 1992-98; Nazareth College, professor of English, director of writing programs, 1998-2010, interim department chair, 2010-11, Rosemary White chair; Society for Technical Communication, education manager, 1999-2006; Brescia College, instructor; Dousman Index, editor. **Publications:** Dramatizing Writing: Reincorporating Delivery in the Classroom, 1997. Contributor to books. **Address:** Department of English, Nazareth College, 4245 East Ave., Rochester, NY 14618-3703, U.S.A. **Online address:** vskinne5@naz.edu

SKIPP, **John.** Also writes as Maxwell Hart, John Mason Skipp. American (born United States), b. 1957?. **Genres:** Novels, Sex, Horror, Young Adult Non-fiction. **Career:** Musician and writer, 1980-; Ravenous Shadows Inc., editorial director, 2011. **Publications:** (With C. Spector) Fright Night, 1985; The Light at the End, 1986; (with C. Spector) The Cleanup, 1987; (with C. Spector) The Scream, 1988; Class of 1999, 1988; Nightmare on Elm Street 5: The Dream Child, 1989; Dead Lines, 1989; (ed. with C. Spector) Book of the Dead, 1989; The Bridge, 1991; (ed. with C. Spector) Still Dead: Book of the Dead II, 1992; Animals, 1993; The Emerald Burrito of Oz, 2000; Stupography, 2004; Misty Beethoven: The Musical, 2004; Conscience, 2004; The Long Last Call, 2006; Opposite Sex, 2008; (with C. Goodfellow) Jake's Wake, 2008; (with C. Goodfellow) Spore, 2010. Contributor to magazines. **Address:** c/o Joel Gotler, IPGLM, 9200 Sunset Blvd., Ste. 900, Los Angeles, CA 90069, U.S.A. **Online address:** info@johnskipp.com

SKIPP, **John Mason.** See **SKIPP, John.**

SKIPP, **Victor (Henry Thomas).** British (born England), b. 1925. **Genres:** Business/Trade/Industry, Economics, History, Philosophy, Theology/Religion, Education. **Career:** Sheldon Heath Comprehensive School, head of history, 1955-59; Bordesley College of Education, Department of Environmental Studies, principal lecturer in history and head, 1964-78. Writer. **Publications:** Discovering Sheldon: A Brief History of a Birmingham Parish from Anglo-Saxon to Modern Times, 1960; (with R.P. Hastings) Discovering Bickenhill, 1963; An Eighteenth Century Farm Labourer's Family, 1963; Out of the Ancient World, 1967; (with H.P.R. Finberg) Local History: Objective and Pursuit, 1967; Honest to Man: A Religious Alternative to Christianity, 1967; Medieval Yardley: The Origin and Growth of a West Midland Community, 1970; The Origins of Solihull, 1977, 2nd ed., 1984; Crisis and Development: An Ecological Case Study of the Forest of Arden, 1570-1674, 1978; The Centre of England: Warwickshire, Worcestershire, Staffordshire, East Shrop-

shire, North Gloucestershire, Eyre Methuen, 1979, rev. ed., 1980; A History of Greater Birmingham: Down to 1830, 1980, 2nd ed., 1997; The Making of Victorian Birmingham, 1983; Industrial Revolution Then and Now: Or Understanding Globalization-The Birmingham Experience, 2002. Contributor to journals and periodicals. **Address:** The Old Rectory, Greyhound Ln., Hopton, NF 1P22 2NU, England.

SKLAR, **Kathryn Kish.** American (born United States), b. 1939. **Genres:** History, Women's Studies And Issues, Politics/Government. **Career:** University of Michigan, Department of History, faculty, 1969-74; Harvard University, Radcliffe Institute, faculty, 1973-74; University of California, associate professor, 1974-81, professor of history, 1981-88; Binghamton University, distinguished Bartle professor of history, 1988-, Center for the Historical Study of Women and Gender, co-director, Center for the Teaching of American History, co-director; Oxford University, Harmsworth professor of U.S. history, 2005-06. Writer. **Publications:** Catharine Beecher: A Study in American Domesticity 1973; (ed.) Notes of Sixty Years: The Autobiography of Florence Kelley, 1859-1926, 1985; (ed. with T. Dublin) Women and Power in American History: A Reader, 2 vols., 1991, 3rd ed., 2009; (ed. with M. Bulmer and K. Bales) The Social Survey Movement in Historical Perspective, 1992; Florence Kelley and the Nation's Work: The Rise of Women's Political Culture, 1830-1900, 1995; (ed. with L.K. Kerber and A. Kessler-Harris) U.S. History as Women's History: New Feminist Essays, 1995; (ed. with A. Sch'ler and S. Strasser) Social Justice Feminists in the United States and Germany: A Dialogue in Documents, 1885-1933, 1998; Women's Rights Emerges within the Anti-Slavery Movement, 1830-1870: A Brief History with Documents, 2000; (ed. with J.B. Stewart) Women's Rights and Transatlantic Antislavery in the Era of Emancipation, 2007; (ed. with B.W. Palmer) The Selected Letters of Florence Kelley, 1869-1931, 2009; (ed. with C. Shemo and B. Reeves-Ellington) Competing Kingdoms: Women, Mission, Nation and the American Protestant Empire, 1812-1960, 2010. Contributor to periodicals. **Address:** Department of History, Binghamton University, LT 607, PO Box 6000, Binghamton, NY 13902-6000, U.S.A. **Online address:** kksklar@binghamton.edu

SKLOOT, **Floyd.** American (born United States), b. 1947. **Genres:** Novels, Poetry, Essays, Adult Non-fiction, Young Adult Fiction, Novellas/Short Stories. **Career:** Novelist. **Publications:** Kaleidoscope: Poems, 1986; Wild Light: Poems, 1989; Pilgrim's Harbor, 1992; Summer Blue: A Novel, 1994; Music Appreciation, 1994; Poppies: Poems, 1994; Lawrence B. Salander: Small Landscapes, 1995; Jedd Novatt, Sculpture, 1996; The Night-Side: Chronic Fatigue Syndrome and the Illness Experience, as The Night-Side: Years in the Kingdom of the Sick, 1996; The Open Door: A Novel, 1997; The Evening Light: Poems, 2001; The Fiddler's Trance, 2001; In the Shadow of Memory, 2003; (with L. Wieseltier) Lawrence Salander: Paintings, 2004; Approximately Paradise, 2005; World of Light, 2005; End of Dreams: Poems, 2006; Patient 002 (novel), 2007; Selected Poems, 2008; The Snow's Music: Poems, 2008; Wink of the Zenith: The Shaping of a Writer's Life, 2008; Cream of Kohlrabi (short stories), 2011; Close Reading: Poems, 2012. Contributor of articles to periodicals. **Address:** 0836 SW Curry St., Ste. 602, Portland, OR 97239, U.S.A. **Online address:** floyd@floydskloot.com

SKLOOT, **Rebecca.** American (born United States), b. 1972. **Genres:** Young Adult Non-fiction. **Career:** Radiolab, correspondent; WNYC, correspondent; Nova ScienceNOW, correspondent; Public Broadcasting System, correspondent; Popular Science, associate editor, 2002-03, contributing editor, 2003-; New York University, adjunct assistant professor of science, health, and environmental reporting, 2006-07; University of Memphis, assistant professor of English, 2007-10; Henrietta Lacks Foundation, founder and president. **Publications:** The Immortal Life of Henrietta Lacks (nonfiction), 2010. Contributor to books and periodicals. **Address:** c/o Simon Lipskar, Writers House, 21 W 26th St., New York, NY 10010, U.S.A. **Online address:** rebecca@rebeccaskloot.com

SKOCPOL, **Theda (Ruth).** American (born United States), b. 1947. **Genres:** History, Politics/Government, Social Sciences, Sociology. **Career:** Harvard University, assistant professor, 1975-78, associate professor, 1978-81, professor of sociology, 1986-95, professor of government and sociology, 1995-97, Victor S. Thomas professor of government and of sociology, 1998-, Center for American Political Studies, director, 2000-06, dean of the Graduate School of Arts and Sciences, 2005-07; University of Chicago, professor, 1981-84, Center for Study of Industrial Societies, director, 1982-85, professor of sociology and political science, 1984-86; Radcliffe Institute for Advanced Study, senior advisor, 2006-. Writer. **Publications:** States and Social Revolutions: A

Comparative Analysis of France, Russia and China, 1979; (with L. Paramio and W. Roy) Sociología histórica, 1988; (with J. Goldstone) Sociología y historia de larevolución, 1988; Protecting Soldiers and Mothers: The Political Origins of Social Policy in the United States, 1992; Social Revolutions in the Modern World, 1994; Time is Never Ripe: The Repeated Defeat of Universal Health Insurance in the 20th Century United States, 1995; (with K. Finegold) State and Party in America's New Deal, 1995; Social Policy in the United States: Future Possibilities in Historical Perspective, 1995; Boomerang: Clinton's Health Security Effort and the Turn against Government in U.S. Politics, 1996, rev. ed. as Boomerang: Health Care Reform and the Turn against Government, 1997; The Missing Middle: Working Families and the Future of American Social Policy, 2000; Diminished Democracy: From Membership to Management in American Civic Life, 2003; (with A. Liazos and M. Ganz) What a Mighty Power We Can Be: African American Fraternal Groups and the Struggle for Racial Equality, 2006; Voice and Inequality: The Transformation of American Civic Democracy, 2006; (with L.R. Jacobs) Health Care Reform and American Politics: What Everyone Needs to Know, 2010; (with V. Williamson) Tea Party and the Remaking of Republican Conservatism, 2012; Obama and America's Political Future, 2012. EDITOR: (with M. Burawoy) Marxist Inquiries: Studies of Labor, Class and States, 1982; Vision and Method in Historical Sociology, 1984; (with P.B. Evans and D. Rueschemeyer) Bringing the State Back In, 1985; (with M. Weir and A.S. Orloff) The Politics of Social Policy in the United States, 1988; (with J.L. Campbell) American Society and Politics: Institutional, Historical and Theoretical Perspectives, 1995; (with D. Rueschemeyer) States, Social Knowledge and the Origins of Modern Social Policies, 1996; (with S.B. Greenberg) The New Majority: Toward a Popular Progressive Politics, 1997; (with G. Ross, T. Smith and J.E. Vichniac) Democracy, Revolutions and History, 1998; (with M.P. Fiorina) Civic Engagement in American Democracy, 1999; (with L.R. Jacobs) Inequality and American Democracy: What We Know and What We Need to Learn, 2005; (with P. Pierson) The Transformation of American Politics: Activist Government And The Rise of Conservatism, 2007; (with L.R. Jacobs) Reaching for a New Deal: Ambitious Governance, Economic Meltdown and Polarized Politics in Obama's First Two Years, 2011. Contributor to periodicals. **Address:** Department of Government, Harvard University, Rm. K416, CGIS Knafel Bldg., 1737 Cambridge St., Cambridge, MA 02138, U.S.A. **Online address:** skocpol@fas.harvard.edu

SKOLNIKOFF, Eugene B. American (born United States), b. 1928. **Genres:** Environmental Sciences/Ecology, International Relations/Current Affairs, Politics/Government, Sciences. **Career:** Massachusetts Institute of Technology, research assistant, 1948-50, administrative staff, 1952-55, Department of Political Science, professor, 1965-, head, 1970-74, Center for International Studies, director, 1972-87, now professor emeritus of political science; Institute for Defense Analyses, systems analyst, 1957-58; Executive Office of the President, Office of Science and Technology Policy, staff, 1958-63, senior consultant, 1977-81; Harvard University, Center for European Studies, research associate, 1973-. Writer. **Publications:** Science, Technology and American Foreign Policy, 1967; (with D.A. Kay) World Eco-Crisis, 1972; The International Imperatives of Technology, 1972; (with S. Friedlander, G. Holton and L. Marx) Visions of Apocalypse, 1985; The Elusive Transformation: Science, Technology, and the Evolution of International Politics, 1993; (with D.G. Victor and K. Raustiala) The Implementation and Effectiveness of International Environmental Commitments, 1998. **Address:** Department of Political Science, Massachusetts Institute of Technology, E53-366, 77 Massachusetts Ave., Cambridge, MA 02139, U.S.A. **Online address:** ebskol@mit.edu

SKORUPSKI, John. Scottish (born Scotland), b. 1946. **Genres:** Philosophy, Young Adult Non-fiction, Humanities. **Career:** Obafemi Awolowo University, visiting lecturer, 1971-72; Katholieke Universiteit Leuven, visiting professor, 1974; University of Wales, research fellow, 1974-76; University of Glasgow, educator, 1976-84; University of Sheffield, professor of philosophy, 1984-90, chair, 1984-; University of St. Andrews, chair and professor of moral philosophy, 1990-, Stirling Graduate Programme, director. Writer. **Publications:** Symbol and Theory: A Philosophical Study of Theories of Religion in Social Anthropology, 1976; John Stuart Mill, 1989; English-Language Philosophy, 1750-1945, 1993; (ed. with D. Knowles) Virtue and Taste: Essays on Politics, Ethics and Aesthetics: In Memory of Flint Schier, 1993; Ethical Explorations, 1999; (ed.) Cambridge Companion to Mill, 1998; Why Read Mill Today, 2006; (ed.) Routledge Companion to Ethics, 2010;

The Domain of Reasons, 2010; Ethics and the Social Good, forthcoming. **Address:** Department of Moral Philosophy, University of St. Andrews, Edgecliffe, The Scores, St. Andrews, FF KY16 9AR, Scotland. **Online address:** jms2@st-andrews.ac.uk

SKOUG, Kenneth N. American (born United States), b. 1931. **Genres:** International Relations/Current Affairs, History. **Career:** U.S. Department of State, foreign service officer, 1957-90, minister counselor, 1980-90, charge d'affaires in Caracas, 1989-90, Office of German affairs, deputy director, 1969-73, foreign service inspector, 1974-76; writer and public speaker on foreign policy issues, 1990-. **Publications:** Cuba as a Model and a Challenge, 1984; A Spotlight on Cuba, 1986; The U.S.-Cuba Migration Agreememnt, 1988; The United States and Cuba under Reagan and Shultz: A Foreign Service Officer Reports, 1996; Czechoslovakia's Lost Fight for Freedom, 1967-1969: An American Embassy Perspective, 1999; An Interview with Kenneth N. Skoug, 2000. Contributor to periodicals. **Address:** 8320 Fort Hunt Rd., Alexandria, VA 22308-1812, U.S.A.

SKOVER, David M. American (born United States), b. 1951. **Genres:** Communications/Media, Law, Biography. **Career:** U.S. Court of Appeals for the Second Circuit, law clerk, 1978-79; Levi Strauss and Co., trademark and patent attorney, 1979-82; University of Puget Sound, School of Law, assistant professor, 1982-85, associate professor, 1985-90, professor, 1990-94; Indiana University, School of Law, visiting professor, 1988-89; Seattle University, professor of law, 1994-, Fredric C. Tausend professor of law; National Endowment for the Humanities, consultant; Washington Commission for the Humanities, consultant; Advisory Commission on Inter-Governmental Relations, consultant. Writer. **Publications:** (With P. Schlag) Tactics of Legal Reasoning, 1986; (with R.K.L. Collins) The Death of Discourse, 1996, 2nd ed., 2005; (with R.K.L. Collins) The Trials of Lenny Bruce: The Fall and Rise of an American Icon, 2002; (with R. Collins) On Dissent, 2012; (with R. Collins) Mania: The Madcap Story of the Lives That Launched a Generation, forthcoming; (with R. Collins) The Judge, forthcoming. Contributor of articles to books and journals. **Address:** School of Law, Seattle University, SLLH-422, 901 12th Ave., Seattle, WA 98122-4338, U.S.A. **Online address:** davidskover@qwest.net

SKOWRONEK, Stephen. American (born United States), b. 1951. **Genres:** Politics/Government, Social Sciences. **Career:** Cornell University, instructor in American government, 1977; University of California, assistant professor, 1978-82, associate professor of American government, 1982-85; Yale University, professor of American government and American studies, 1986-90, director of undergraduate studies in political science, 1989-94, Pelitiah Peul professor of political and social sciences, 1998-, director of graduate studies in political science, 2003-; Woodrow Wilson International Center for Scholars, fellow, 1985-86; University of Notre Dame, Exxon Education Foundation lecturer, 1986; Reed College, Ducey lecturer, 1990; Yale University Press, founder and managing editor of journal studies in American political development; Ecole des Hautes Etudes, chair in American civilization. Writer. **Publications:** Building a New American State: The Expansion of National Administrative Capacities, 1877-1920, 1982; The Politics Presidents Make: Leadership from John Adams to George Bush, 1993, The Politics Presidents Make: Leadership from John Adams to Bill Clinton, 1997; (with K. Orren) The Search for American Political Development, 2004; (ed.) Rethinking Political Institutions: The Art of the State, 2006; (with M. Glassman) Formative Acts: American Politics In The Making, 2007; Presidential Leadership In Political Time: Reprise and Reappraisal, 2008, 2nd ed., 2011. CONTRIBUTOR: The Presidency and the Political System, 1984, 4th ed., 1994; Studies in American Political Development: An Annual, vol. I, 1986; The Dynamics of American Politics, 1993. Contributor of articles to books and journals. **Address:** Department of Political Science, Yale University, Rm. 330, 115 Prospect St., Rosenkranz Hall, New Haven, CT 06520-8301, U.S.A. **Online address:** stephen.skowronek@yale.edu

SKRENTNY, John D. (John David Skrentny). American (born United States) **Genres:** Politics/Government, History, Social Sciences. **Career:** Harvard University, teaching fellow, 1991-94; University of Pennsylvania, assistant professor of sociology, 1994-98, Janice and Julian Bers assistant professor of the social sciences, 1998; Princeton University, Center for Human Values, Laurance S. Rockefeller visiting fellow, 1997-98; University of California, Department of Sociology, assistant professor, 1999-2000, associate professor, 2000-02, professor of sociology, 2002-, vice chair, 2002-03, Center for Comparative Immigration Studies, research associate, 2000-, director,

2009-; Yonsei University, visiting professor, 2001. Writer. **Publications:** The Ironies of Affirmative Action: Politics, Culture, and Justice in America, 1996; (ed.) Color Lines: Affirmative Action, Immigration, and Civil Rights Options for America, 2001; The Minority Rights Revolution, 2002. CONTRIBUTOR: Seeking the Center: Politics and Policymaking at the New Century, 2001; Controlling Immigration: A Global Perspective, 2004; Rightward Bound: Making America Conservative in the 1970s, 2008. Contributor to periodicals and journals. **Address:** Department of Sociology, University of California, 490 Social Science Bldg., 9500 Gilman Dr., Ste. 0533, La Jolla, CA 92093-0533, U.S.A. **Online address:** jskrentny@ucsd.edu

SKRENTNY, John David. *See* SKRENTNY, John D.

SKRESLET, Paula Youngman. American (born United States) **Genres:** Adult Non-fiction, Bibliography, Literary Criticism And History, Reference, History. **Career:** Union Theological Seminary and Presbyterian School of Christian Education, reference and archives librarian, William Smith Morton Library, acquisitions and reference librarian. Writer. **Publications:** NON-FICTION: Northern Africa: A Guide to Reference and Information Sources, 2000; (with R. Skreslet) The Literature of Islam: A Guide to the Primary Sources in English Translation, 2006. **Address:** William Smith Morton Library, Union Theological Seminary and, Presbyterian School of Christian Education, 3401 Brook Rd., Richmond, VA 23227, U.S.A. **Online address:** pskreslet@union-psce.edu

SKRZYNECKI, Peter. Australian/German (born Germany), b. 1945. **Genres:** Novels, Novellas/Short Stories, Poetry, Autobiography/Memoirs. **Career:** Teacher, 1967-87; Milperra College of Advanced Education, lecturer in English, 1987-; University of Western Sydney, School of Humanities, adjunct associate professor, senior lecturer. Writer. **Publications:** POETRY: There, Behind the Lids, 1970; Head-waters, 1972; Immigrant Chronicle, 1975; The Aviary: Poems 1975-1977, 1978; The Polish Immigrant, 1982; Night Swim, 1989; Easter Sunday, 1993; Time's Revenge, 1999. NOVELS: The Beloved Mountain, 1988; The Cry of the Goldfinch, 1996. STORIES: The Wild Dogs, 1987; Rock 'n' Roll Heroes, 1992. OTHER: The Sparrow Garden (memoir), 2004; Old/new World: New & Selected Poems, 2007. EDITOR: Joseph's Coat: An Anthology of Multicultural Writing, 1985; Influence: Australian Voices, 1997. **Address:** c/o Barbara Mobbs, PO Box 126, Edgecliff, NW 2027, Australia. **Online address:** p.skrzynecki@uws.edu.au

SKULTETY, Nancy Laney. American (born United States), b. 1960. **Genres:** How-to Books. **Career:** Brody's Department Store, sales clerk, 1981-83; Homer-Center School District, reading specialist, 1993-. Writer. **Publications:** From Here to There, 2005; 101 Words Your Child Will Read by the End of Grade 1, 2006; 101 Words Your Child Will Spell by the End of Grade 1, 2007. **Address:** Barrons Educational Series Inc., 250 Wireless Blvd., Hauppauge, NY 11788-3924, U.S.A. **Online address:** nancy@nancyskultety.com

ŠKVORECKÝ, Josef. *See* Obituaries.

SKYE, Christina. (Roberta Helmer). American (born United States) **Genres:** Romance/Historical, Novels, Young Adult Non-fiction, Crafts, Novellas/Short Stories. **Career:** Writer. **Publications:** REGENCY ERA SERIES: Defiant Captive, 1990; The Black Rose, 1991; East of Forever, 1993. DELAMERE SERIES: Come the Night, 1994; Come the Dawn, 1995. DRAYCOTT ABBEY SERIES: Hour of the Rose, 1994; Bridge of Dreams, 1995; Bride of the Mist, 1996; Key to Forever, 1997; Season of Wishes, 1997; Enchantment, 1998; Christmas Knight, 1998; The Perfect Gift, 1999; Bound by Dreams, 2009. NAVY SEALS SERIES: Going Overboard, 2001; My Spy, 2002; Hot Pursuit, 2003. CODE NAME SERIES: Nanny, 2004; Princess, 2004; Baby, 2005; Blondie, 2006; Bikini, 2007. NOVELS: The Ruby, 1992; 2000 Kisses, 1999; (with E. Harbison) A Walk Down the Aisle, 1999; To Catch A Thief, 2008; A Home by the Sea, 2011. OTHERS: (with R. Brandewyne, S. Drake and K. Michaels) Bewitching Love Stories, 1992; (co-author) More Than Words, vol. VI, 2010. AS ROBERTA HELMER: The Poems of the Hanshan Collection, 1977; China's Crafts: The Story of How They're Made and What They Mean, 1980; China's Puppets, 1984; Shopping in China: Arts, Crafts, and The Unusual, 1986. **Address:** c/o Author Mail, Dell Publishing Co., 1745 Broadway, New York, NY 10019, U.S.A. **Online address:** christinaskye@christinaskye.com

SKYLER, Heather. American (born United States) **Genres:** Adult Non-fiction, Novels. **Career:** Beloit College, instructor in fiction writing, Beloit Fiction Journal, managing editor, 2000-04, editor-in-chief, 2004-06; W.W. Norton & Company Inc., publisher, 2004; freelance journalist and fiction writer, 2004; In Business Magazine, business journalist, 2006-07, features editor/business journalist, 2007-08, editorial director/business journalist, 2008-09; freelance writer, 2009-. **Publications:** The Perfect Age, 2004; Found Elsewhere, forthcoming. **Address:** W.W. Norton & Company Inc., 500 5th Ave., New York, NY 10110-0002, U.S.A.

SLADE, Arthur G(regory). Canadian (born Canada), b. 1967. **Genres:** Young Adult Fiction, Novels, Biography, Mystery/Crime/Suspense. **Career:** Advertising copywriter, 1990-95; writer, 1995-. **Publications:** YOUNG ADULT NOVELS: Draugr, 1997; Hallowed Knight, 1997; The Haunting of Drang Island, 1998; The Loki Wolf, 2000; John Diefenbaker: An Appointment With Destiny, 2000; Dust, 2001; Return of the Grudstone Ghosts, 2002; Tribes, 2002; Ghost Hotel, 2004; Monsterology: The Fabulous Lives of the Creepy, the Revolting, and the Undead, 2005; Megiddo's Shadow, 2006; Invasion of the IQ Snatchers, 2007; Villainology: Fabulous Lives of the Big, the Bad, and the Wicked, 2007; Jolted: Newton Starker's Rules for Survival, 2008; The Hunchback Assignments, 2009; The Dark Deeps, 2010; Empire of Ruins, 2011; Delilah Red, forthcoming; Calvin 13, forthcoming; Gallows Club, forthcoming. **Address:** 404 10th St. E, Saskatoon, SK S7N 0C9, Canada. **Online address:** art@arthurslade.com

SLADE, Bernard. American/Canadian (born Canada), b. 1930. **Genres:** Plays/Screenplays, Autobiography/Memoirs, Literary Criticism And History. **Career:** Actor, 1948-57; Garden Centre Theatre, co-founder, 1954; Columbia Pictures, television writer, 1957-74; Canadian Broadcasting Corp., scriptwriter, 1958-64. **Publications:** Same Time, Next Year, 1975; Tribute, 1978; Fling!, 1979; Romantic Comedy, 1980; Special Occasions, 1982; Fatal Attraction, 1986; An Act of the Imagination, 1988; Sweet William, 1988; Return Engagements, 1989; Every Time I See You (musical) 1991; You Say Tomatoes, 1994; I Remember You, 1994; Same Time, Another Year, 1995; Moving, 2007. **Address:** 650 Park Ave., New York, NY 10021, U.S.A. **Online address:** bernslade@aol.com

SLADE, Leonard A. American (born United States), b. 1942. **Genres:** Poetry, Essays, Language/Linguistics, Literary Criticism And History. **Career:** Kentucky State University, instructor, 1965-70, Department of English, associate professor, 1972-73, chair, 1972-78, professor, 1973-78, Department of Literature and Languages, chair, 1978-83, Division of Humanities and Fine Arts, chair, 1981-83, Division of Literature, Languages and Philosophy, chairman, 1982-85, College of Arts and Sciences, dean, 1985-88; Bennington College, writer-in-residence, 1983, 1986; State University of New York, University of Albany, Department of Africana Studies, professor, 1988-, chair, 1988-93, Department of English, adjunct professor, Doctor of Arts in Humanistic Studies Program, director, Master of Arts in Liberal Studies Program, director. **Publications:** Critical Essays on Language and Literature, 1973; (with K.J. Lawless) A Selected Working Bibliography of Twenty-Four American Authors, 1974; (ed.) A Collection of Short Stories, 1974; Another Black Voice: A Different Drummer, 1988; The Beauty of Blackness, 1989; I Fly Like a Bird: The Poetry of Leonard A. Slade, Jr., 1992; The Whipping Song: Poems, 1993; (ed.) Black Essays, 1995; Vintage: New and Selected Poems, 1995; Fire Burning, 1995; Pure Light, 1996; Neglecting the Flowers: Book of Poems, 1997; Symbolism in Herman Melville's Moby Dick: From the Satanic to The Divine, 1998; Lilacs in Spring, 1998; Elisabeth and Other Poems, 1999; For the Love of Freedom: Poems, 2000; Jazz After Dinner: Selected Poems, 2006; Sweet Solitude: New and Selected Poems, 2010; George Moses Horton: A Bio-Critical Study, forthcoming. Contributor to periodicals. **Address:** Department of Africana Studies, State University of New York, 1400 Washington Ave., Albany, NY 12222, U.S.A. **Online address:** lslade@albany.edu

SLADER, John M. Welsh/British (born England), b. 1924. **Genres:** History, Local History/Rural Topics, Novels, Marine Sciences/Oceanography, Military/Defense/Arms Control. **Career:** Evans and Reid Company Ltd., navigating officer of merchant shipping, 1940-48; Vantona Textiles Ltd., import/export manager, 1949-70; Vantona International Ltd., export director, 1971-76; Compton Webb Ltd., export director, 1977-81. Writer. **Publications:** Dicky Slader: The Exmoor Pedlar Poet, 1963; Days of Renown: The Story of Mining on Exmoor and the Border Parishes, 1965; Down along the Exe: The Story of the Devonshire Exe from Source to Estuary, 1966; The Churches of Devon, 1968; The Red Duster at War: A History of the Merchant Navy During the Second World War, 1988; The Fourth Service: Merchantmen at War, 1939-1945, 1994; British Merchant Ship Losses in World War II: Lifeline of the World, 1997; The Maritime Poets of the Second World War, forthcoming; Son of the Manse, forthcoming. Contributor to magazines. **Address:** 5 Station Rd., Govilon, Abergavenny, NP7 9RG, Wales.

SLAN, Joanna. *See* **SLAN, Joanna Campbell.**

SLAN, Joanna Campbell. Also writes as Joanna Slan, Joanna Campbell-Slan. American (born United States), b. 1953?. **Genres:** Mystery/Crime/Suspense. **Career:** Herald & Review, Advertising Department, staff; Forensic University, Sisters in Crime Inc., co-founder. Writer and public speaker. **Publications:** (as Joanna Slan) Using Stories and Humor: Grab Your Audience!, 1998; Scrapbook Storytelling: Save Family Stories and Memories with Photos, Journaling and Your Own Creativity, 1999; Storytelling with Rubber Stamps, 2001; One-Minute Journaling, 2001; Quick & Easy Pages, 2001; (as Joanna Campbell-Slan) Bless This Mess: Motivation for Moms, 2001; (as Joanna Campbell-Slan) I'm Too Blessed to Be Depressed, 2001; Adventures in Journaling: Paper Adventures, 2002; The Best of British Scrapbooking and Cardmaking, 2004. KIKI LOWENSTEIN SCRAP-N-CRAFT MYSTERY SERIES: Paper, Scissors, Death, 2008; Cut, Crop & Die, 2009. Contributor to books and periodicals. **Address:** Near St., St. Louis, MO 63103, U.S.A. **Online address:** joannaslan@aol.com

SLATER, Jim. British (born England), b. 1929. **Genres:** Children's Fiction, Autobiography/Memoirs. **Career:** Park Royal Vehicles Ltd., secretary and chief accountant; AEC Ltd., director, commercial manager; Leyland Motor Corp., deputy sales director, 1963-64; Children's Book Centre, owner; Slater Walker Securities Ltd., founder, managing director, 1964-72, chair, 1964-75; Salar Properties Ltd., chair, 1983-; Agrifirma Services Ltd., deputy chairman; BioProjects International PLC, co-founder, 2002, executive chairman; ViaLogy Corp., board director; Galahad Gold PLC, co-founder, 2003, deputy chairman and finance director; Agrifirma Brazil, co-founder, 2008, investment director; Dohm Group, staff, general manager. Writer. **Publications:** NONFICTION: Return to Go: My Autobiography, 1977; The Zulu Principle: Making Extraordinary Profits from Ordinary Shares, 1992; Investment Made Easy, 1994; Pep up Your Wealth, 1994; Beyond the Zulu Principle, 1996. JUVENILE FICTION: Goldenrod, 1978, new ed., 1981; Goldenrod and the Kidnappers, 1979; The Boy Who Saved Earth, 1979; Grasshopper and the Unwise Owl, 1979; Grasshopper and the Pickle Factory, 1980; The Boy Who Found Atlantis, 1980; Grasshopper and the Poisoned River, 1982. ROGER ROBOT SERIES: Roger the Robot at the Circus; Roger the Robot at the Safari Park; Roger the Robot at the Seaside; Roger the Robot Goes Fishing; AMAZING MONSTER SERIES: The Great Gulper, 1979; Bignose, 1979; The Tricky Troggle, 1979; Dimmo, 1979; Webfoot, 1979; Greeneye, 1979; The Winkybird, 1979; Wormball, 1979; Snuggly, 1980; Kleenum, 1980; Swiggo, 1980; Big Snowy, 1980. **Address:** BioProjects International PLC, 39 Cornhill, London, GL EC3V 3RR, England.

SLATER, Judith (Carol). American (born United States), b. 1951. **Genres:** Novellas/Short Stories. **Career:** University of Nebraska, professor of English, 1987-, reader. Writer. **Publications:** The Baby Can Sing and Other Stories, 1999. **Address:** Department of English, University of Nebraska, 202 Andrews Hall, Lincoln, NE 68588-0333, U.S.A. **Online address:** jslater1@unl.edu

SLATER, Michael. British (born England), b. 1936?. **Genres:** Young Adult Fiction, Biography, Literary Criticism And History. **Career:** University of London, Birkbeck College, Department of victorian literature, professor, now professor emeritus; Ohio State University, distinguished visiting professor; University of Debrecen, visiting lecturer; University of Kyoto, visiting lecturer; Hendrix College, Murphy lecturer in English, 1982, 1983 and 1984; Dickens Society of America, president. Writer. **Publications:** Dickens and Women, 1983; An Intelligent Person's Guide to Dickens, 1999; Douglas Jerrold: 1803-1857, 2002; Charles Dickens, 2007. EDITOR: Dickens 1970: Centenary Essays, 1970; (and intro. and notes) The Christmas Books, 1971; (and intro.) The Catalogue of the Suzannet Charles Dickens Collection, 1975; Dickens on America and the Americans, 1978; (and intro. and notes) Nicholas Nickleby, 1978; Big House, 1978; (intro.) The Life and Adventures of Nicholas Nickleby: Reproduced in Facsimile from the Original Monthly Parts of 1838-39, 1982; (and intro.) Thomas Love Peacock, Headlong Hall; and Gryll Grange, 1987; (with N. Bentley and N. Burgis) The Dickens Index, 1988; A Guide to Risc Microprocessors, 1992; Sketches by Boz and Other Early

Papers 1833-39, 1994; The Amusements of the People and Other Papers: Reports, Essays, and Reviews, 1834-51, 1996; Gone Astray and Other Papers from Household Words, 1851-59, 1998; (with J. Drew) The Uncommercial Traveller and Other Papers, 1859-70, 2000; (and intro.) A Christmas Carol and Other Christmas Writings, 2003. **Address:** Department of English, Birkbeck College, University of London, Malet St., Bloomsbury, GL WC1E 7HX, England. **Online address:** m.slater@eng.bbk.ac.uk

SLATER, Nigel. British (born England), b. 1958. **Genres:** Autobiography/Memoirs, Food And Wine, Essays. **Career:** Marie Claire, food editor, 1988-93; The Observer, food columnist, 1993-; BBC One, food host; BBC Two, food host. Author and broadcaster. **Publications:** Tiger, 1986; The 30-Minute Cook: The Best of the Worlds Best Cooking, 1996; Real Fast Food: 350 Recipes Ready-to-Eat in 30 Minutes, 1996; Real Cooking, 1997; Real Fast Desserts, 1997; Nigel Slater's Real Food, 1998; Appetite: So What Do You Want to Eat Today?, 2000; Thirst, 2002; Toast: The Story of a Boys Hunger (biography), 2003; Nigel Slater: The Kitchen Diaries, 2005; The Kitchen Diaries: A Year in the Kitchen with Nigel Slater, 2006; Eating for England, 2008; Tender, vol. I: A Cook and His Vegetable Patch, 2009, vol. II: A Cook's Guide to the Fruit Garden, 2010. Contributor to magazine. **Address:** c/o Araminta Whitley, Lucas Alexander Whitley Ltd., 14 Vernon St., London, GL W14 0RJ, England. **Online address:** nigel.slater@observer.co.uk

SLATER, Thomas J. American (born United States), b. 1955. **Genres:** Film, Biography, Bibliography, Reference. **Career:** Northwest Missouri State University, lecturer in English, 1985-86; University of Missouri, lecturer in English, 1986-87; Missouri Western State College, lecturer in English, 1986-87; Illinois State University, assistant professor of English, 1987-90; Indiana University of Pennsylvania, assistant professor of English, 1990-, professor. Writer. **Publications:** Milos Forman: A Bio-Bibliography, 1987; (ed. and contrib.) A Handbook of Soviet and East European Film and Filmmakers, 1991; (ed. with G. Bachman) American Silent Film: Discovering Marginalized Voices, 2002; Womens Studies: An Interdisciplinary Journal October, 2008; The Vision and the Struggle: June Mathis's Work on Ben-Hur, 1922-24, 2008; (co-ed. and intro.) June Mathis's The Legion of Death (1918): Melodrama and the Realities of Women in WWI, 2008. **Address:** Department of English, Indiana University of Pennsylvania, 345 Sutton Hall, 421 N Walk, Indiana, PA 15705-1094, U.S.A. **Online address:** thomas.slater@iup.edu

SLATTA, Richard W(ayne). American (born United States), b. 1947. **Genres:** Westerns/Adventure, History, Popular Culture, Education, Reference, Social Sciences. **Career:** University of Colorado, visiting instructor in history, 1979-80; North Carolina State University, assistant professor, 1980-85, associate professor, 1985-90, professor of history, 1990-. Writer. **Publications:** Gauchos and the Vanishing Frontier, 1983; (ed.) Bandidos: The Varieties of Latin American Banditry, 1987; Cowboys of the Americas, 1990; The Cowboy Encyclopedia, 1994; Comparing Cowboys and Frontiers, 1997; (foreword) The Cowboy: An Unconventional History of Civilization on the Old-Time Cattle Range, 1997; The Mythical West: An Encyclopedia of Legend, Lore and Popular Culture, 2001; Simón Bolívar's Quest for Glory, 2003; Cowboy: The Illustrated History, 2006; National Cowboy Symposium & Celebration, 2010. Contributor to periodicals. **Address:** Department of History, North Carolina State University, 277 Withers Hall, 313 Chapanoke Rd., Ste. 100, PO Box 8108, Raleigh, NC 27603, U.S.A. **Online address:** slatta@ncsu.edu

SLATTERY, Brian Francis. American (born United States) **Genres:** Novels, Young Adult Fiction. **Career:** Interact Nova, teacher of English, 1997-98; Harry Frank Guggenheim Foundation, assistant program officer, 1998-2001; Columbia University, School of International and Public Affairs, Journal of International Affairs, senior editor, 2002-03; Bernard F. and Alva B. Gimbel Foundation, program officer, 2003-04; freelance writer and editor, 2003-; Health Literacy Project, consultant; New Haven Review, editor. **Publications:** Spaceman Blues: A Love Song (novel), 2007; Liberation: Being the Adventures of the Slick Six after the Collapse of the United States of America (novel), 2008; Lost Everything, 2012. Contributor to periodicals. **Address:** c/o Cameron McClure, Donald Maass Literary Agency, 121 W 27th St., Ste. 801, New York, NY 10001, U.S.A. **Online address:** bfs@bfslattery.com

SLATTERY, Dennis Patrick. American (born United States), b. 1944?. **Genres:** Novels, Literary Criticism And History, Psychology. **Career:** Palmyra Elementary School, instructor, 1968-70; Lorain Catholic High School, instructor in English and psychology, 1970-72; Mountain View College, instructor of English and composition, 1976-80; University of Dallas, instructor of English, 1976-78, assistant professor of English, 1978-79; Texas Christian University, instructor, 1980-81; Southern Methodist University, instructor, 1981-87; The Dallas Institute of Humanities and Culture, faculty, 1983-86, visiting lecturer, seminar leader, 1999-2005; Incarnate Word College's Summer Study Abroad Program in Italy, director, 1989-95; University of South Alabama, faculty, 1992-93; Pacifica Graduate Institute, visiting lecturer, 1993-95, interdisciplinary coordinator, 1995-98, core faculty, 1998-. Writer. **Publications:** The Idiot: Dostoevsky's Fantastic Prince: A Phenomenological Approach, 1983; The Wounded Body: Remembering the Markings of Flesh, 2000; (ed. with L. Corbett) Depth Psychology: Meditations in the Field, 2001; Casting the Shadows: Selected Poetry, 2002; Psychology at the Threshold, 2002; Grace in the Desert: Awakening to the Gifts of Monastic Life, 2004; Just below the Water Line: Selected Poems, 2004; (with C.W. Asher) Simon's Crossing, 2010. Contributor of articles to professional journals. **Address:** Pacifica Graduate Institute, 249 Lambert Rd., Carpinteria, CA 93013-3019, U.S.A. **Online address:** dslattery@pacifica.edu

SLAUGHTER, Anne-Marie. American (born United States), b. 1958. **Genres:** Law, History. **Career:** Harvard University, assistant to professor Abram Chayes, 1984-88, assistant to professor Hal S. Scott, 1986-87, The Center for International Affairs, Ford fellow in European society and Western security, 1985-86, Harvard Law School, fellow in international law, 1988-89, J. Sinclair Armstrong professor of Intl., foreign and comparative law, 1994-2002, professor, 2001-02, John F. Kennedy School of Government, director of graduate and international legal studies, 1997-2002, Harvard Colloquium on International Affairs, founder and director, 1999-2002, Hauser Center, faculty fellow; University of Chicago Law School, assistant professor of law and international relations, 1989-93, professor of law and international relations, 1993-94; University of Richmond, T.C. Williams School of Law, Allen Chair professor, 1994; American Society of International Law, vice president, 2000-02, president, 2002-04, editor, 2004; Princeton University, Woodrow Wilson School of Public and International Affairs, dean, 2002-09, Bert G. Kerstetter '66 University professor of politics and international affairs, 2004-, Princeton Project on National Security, co-director, 2004-06; Shanghai Institute for International Studies, visiting fellow, 2007-08; Worcester College, honorary fellow; U.S. Department of State, Policy Planning for the United States, director, 2009-11; Board, Bridge Fund, vice-president; Business for Diplomatic Action, senior advisor; New America Foundation, board director. **Publications:** (Ed. with A.S. Sweet and J.H.H. Weiler) The European Court and National Courts Doctrine and Jurisprudence: Legal Change in Its Social Context, 1998; International Law and International Relations Theory: Millennial Lectures, 2000; (co-ed.) Legalization and World Politics, 2001; A New World Order, 2004; (ed. with S.R. Ratner) Methods of international law, 2004; (with G.J. Ikenberry) Forging a World of Liberty under Law, 2006; The Idea that is America: Keeping Faith with Our Values in a Dangerous World, 2007. **Address:** Woodrow Wilson School of Public, and International Affairs, Princeton University, 440 Robertson Hall, Princeton, NJ 08544-1013, U.S.A. **Online address:** slaughtr@princeton.edu

SLAUGHTER, Karin. American (born United States), b. 1971. **Genres:** Mystery/Crime/Suspense, Novels. **Career:** Writer. **Publications:** GRANT COUNTY MYSTERY SERIES: Blindsighted, 2001; Kisscut, 2002; A Faint Cold Fear: A Novel, 2003; (ed.) Like a Charm: A Novel in Voices, 2004; Indelible, 2004; Faithless, 2005; Triptych, 2006; Skin Privilege in US as Beyond Reach, 2007; Fractured, 2008; Martin Misunderstood, 2008; Undone in UK as Genesis, 2009; Broken, 2010; Fallen, 2011; The Unremarkable Heart, 2011; Criminal, 2012. Contributor to periodicals. **Address:** c/o Author Mail, William Morrow Publishing, 1350 Ave. of the Americas, New York, NY 10019, U.S.A.

SLAVICEK, Louise Chipley. American (born United States), b. 1956. **Genres:** Children's Non-fiction, Biography. **Career:** Writer. **Publications:** Life among the Puritans, 2001; Confucianism, 2001; The Women of the American Revolution, 2002; Israel, 2002, 2nd ed., 2009; Juan Ponce de Leon, 2003; Mao Zedong, 2004; Abraham Lincoln, 2004; Jimmy Carter, 2004; Annie Montague Alexander: Naturalist and Fossil Hunter, 2004; The Great Wall of China, 2004; Alexander the Great, 2005; Bloody Mary, 2005; Carlos Santana, 2006; Harriet Tubman and the Underground Railroad, 2006; Run-DMC, 2007; Daniel Inouye, 2007; Mother Teresa: Caring for the World's Poor, 2007; The San Francisco Earthquake and Fire of 1906, 2008; The Black Death, 2008; King David, 2008; Women and the Civil War, 2009; New York City's Central Park, 2009; The Prohibition Era: Temperance in the United States, 2009; Chinese Cultural Revolution, 2010; I.M. Pei, 2010; The Treaty of Versailles, 2010; Jane Addams, 2011; Paul Robeson, 2011; Anne Hutchinson, 2011; The Boer War, 2011; The Establishment of the State of Israel, 2011; The Salem Witchcraft Trials, 2011; The Protestant Reformation, 2012. Contributor of articles to journals and periodicals. **Address:** 2195 Gnarled Pine Dr., Dublin, OH 43016, U.S.A.

SLAVIN, Barbara. American (born United States), b. 1951?. **Genres:** Politics/Government, History. **Career:** USA Today, senior diplomatic reporter, 1996-; United Press Intl., reporter & editor; New York Times, reporter, editor & foreign news writer; Los Angeles Times, staff; Newsday, staff; Business Week, staff. **Publications:** Bitter Friends, Bosom Enemies: Iran, the U.S. and the Twisted Path to Confrontation, 2007. Contributor to periodicals. **Online address:** bslavin@usip.org

SLAVIN, Bill. Canadian (born Canada), b. 1959. **Genres:** Animals/Pets, Illustrations, Literary Criticism And History. **Career:** Tele-Direct, layout artist, 1978-81; General Store Publishing House, art director, 1982-87; freelance illustrator, 1988-. Writer. **Publications:** SELF-ILLUSTRATED: The Stone Lion, 1996; (with J. Slavin) Transformed: How Everyday Things Are Made, 2005. **Address:** Red Deer Press, 195 Allstate Pkwy, Markham, ON L3R 4T8, Canada. **Online address:** bslavin@nexicom.net

SLAVIN, Helen. British (born England), b. 1966?. **Genres:** Novels, Literary Criticism And History, Young Adult Fiction. **Career:** Writer. **Publications:** The Extra Large Medium (novel), 2007; The Stopping Place, 2008; Cross My Heart, 2009. Contributor to periodicals. **Address:** PFD, Drury House, 34-43 Russell St., London, GL WC2B 5HA, England.

SLAVIN, Robert E(dward). British/American (born United States), b. 1950. **Genres:** Education. **Career:** Aloha Children's Center, teacher, 1972-73; Johns Hopkins University, Center for Social Organization of Schools, associate research scientist, 1975-78, research scientist, 1978-85, Center for Research on Effective Schooling for Disadvantaged Students, director of elementary program, 1985-90, principal research scientist and co-director, 1989-94, Center for Research and Reform in Education, director; University of York, Institute for Effective Education, director, 1994-, professor; Success for All Foundation, chairman and director, 1997-. Writer. **Publications:** Using Student Team Learning, 1978, 3rd ed., 1986; (co-author) Teams-Games-Tournament: The Team Learning Approach, 1980; Cooperative Learning in Student Teams: What Research Says to the Teacher, 1982, rev. ed., 1987; Student Team Learning: An Overview and Practical Guide, 1983, rev. ed., 1988; Research Methods in Education: A Practical Guide, 1984, 2nd ed., 1992; Educational Psychology: Theory into Practice, 1986, 10th ed., 2012; Cooperative Learning: Theory, Research, and Practice, 1990, 2nd ed., 1995; Education for All, 1996; (co-author) Every Child, Every School: Success for All, 1996; (with O.S. Fashola) Show Me the Evidence!: Proven and Promising Programs for America's Schools, 1998; (with N.A. Madden) One Million Children: Success for All, 2001, 2nd ed. as 2 Million Children: Success for All, 2009; (with D. Morris) Every Child Reading, 2003; Educational Research in an Age of Accountability, 2007. EDITOR: (with S. Sharan, S. Kagan and C. Webb) Learning to Cooperate, Cooperating to Learn, 1985; School and Classroom Organization, 1989; (with N.L. Karweit and N.A. Madden) Effective Programs for Students at Risk, 1989; (with N.L. Karweit, B.A. Wasik and N.A. Madden) Preventing Early School Failure: Research, Policy, and Practice, 1994; (with N.A. Madden) One Million Children: Success for All, 2000; (with N.A. Madden) Success for All: Research and Reform in Elementary Education, 2001; (with M. Calderon) Effective Programs for Latino Students, 2001; (with G.D. Bornman and S.C. Stringfield) Title I, Compensatory Education at the Crossroads, 2001. **Address:** Institute for Effective Education, University of York, Berrick Saul Bldg., Heslington, York, NY YO10 5DD, England. **Online address:** rslavin@jhu.edu

SLAWSON, Douglas J. American (born United States), b. 1947. **Genres:** Theology/Religion. **Career:** National University, vice president for student services. Writer. **Publications:** (with S. Poole) Church and Slave in Perry County, Missouri, 1818-1865, 1986; The Foundation and First Decade of the National Catholic Welfare Council, 1992; The Department of Education Battle, 1918-1932: Public Schools, Catholic Schools and the Social Order, 2005; Ambition and Arrogance: Cardinal William O'Connell of Boston and the American Catholic Church, 2007. **Address:** San Diego, CA, U.S.A. **Online address:** dslawson@nu.edu

SLAYTON, Robert A(llen). American (born United States), b. 1951. **Genres:** Urban Studies, Politics/Government, Biography, Military/Defense/Arms Control, History, Women's Studies And Issues. **Career:** Chicago Urban League, research specialist, 1984-88; Humanities Council, consultant, 1986-87; Chapman University, Department of History, assistant professor, 1988-94, associate professor, 1994-2002, professor, 2002-, Henry Salvatori professorship in American values and traditions; Writer. **Publications:** Back of the Yards: The Making of a Local Democracy, 1986; (with C. Hoch) New Homeless and Old: Community and the Skid Row Hotel, 1989; Empire Statesman: The Rise and Redemption of Al Smith, 2001; Westchester County: Headquarters to the World, 2002; Arms of Destruction: Ranking the World's Best Land Weapons of World War II, 2004; New York State: Prime Mover, 2004; Master of the Air: William Tunner and the Success of Military Airlift, 2010. **Address:** Department of History, 114 Roosevelt Hall, 1 University Dr., Chapman University, Orange, CA 92866, U.S.A. **Online address:** slayton@chapman.edu

SLEE, Debora A. American (born United States), b. 1949. **Genres:** Language/Linguistics, Law, Medicine/Health, Reference, Social Sciences, Sports/Fitness. **Career:** Schmidt & Slee, attorney, 1979-84; American Institute for Paralegal Studies, instructor, 1982-84; Mid-America Research Institute, senior staff attorney, 1984-85; Tringa Press, managing editor, 1985-2007; Health NorthEast Inc., director of quality management, 1987-90; The Tringa Group (a consulting firm), partner, 1990-. Attorney and designer. **Publications:** (Contrib.) The Law of Hospital and Health Care Administration, 1988; (with V.N. Slee) Health Care Terms, 2nd ed., 1991; (with V.N. Slee) Health Care Reform Terms: An Eplanatory Glossary of Words, Phrases and Acronyms Used in Today's U.S. Health Care Reform Movement, 1993, 3rd ed. as Health Care Terms: Healthy Communities Edition, 1996, (with V.N. Slee and H.J. Schmidt) 4th ed. as Slee's Health Care Terms, 2001, 5th ed. as Slee's Health Care Terms, 2008; (with V.N. Slee and H.J. Schmidt) The Endangered Medical Record: Ensuring Its Integrity in the Age of Informatics, 2000. **Address:** The Tringa Group, 2074 Highland Pkwy., Saint Paul, MN 55116, U.S.A. **Online address:** dslee@tringa.com

SLEE, Vergil N(elson). American (born United States), b. 1917. **Genres:** Law, Medicine/Health, Language/Linguistics. **Career:** Barry County Health Department (now Barry County Health Center), director, 1947-48, 1949-56; University of Michigan, lecturer, 1947-78; Southwestern Michigan Hospital Council, Professional Activity Study (PAS), founding director, 1953-55; Commission on Professional and Hospital Activities, founding director, 1956-71, president, 1971-80, president emeritus, 1980-; Estes Park Institute, director, 1981-; Tringa Group, chief executive officer, 1982-, managing director; Transylvania Community Hospital, trustee, 1990-; Helena Health Institute, director, 1991-93; Health Commons Institute, chairperson of the board, 1993-; Council on Clinical Classifications, president. Writer. **Publications:** Slee's Health Care Terms, 1991, (with D.A. Slee and H.J. Schmidt) 5th ed., 2008; (with D.A. Slee) Health Care Reform Terms: An Explanatory Glossary of Words, Phrases and Acronyms Used in Today's U.S. Health Care Reform Movement, 1993, 2nd ed., 1994; (with D.A. Slee and H.J. Schmidt) The Endangered Medical Record: Ensuring Its Integrity in the Age of Informatics, 2000. Contributor to periodicals. **Address:** The Tringa Group, 2074 Highland Pkwy., Saint Paul, MN 55116, U.S.A. **Online address:** vslee@juno.com

SLEGMAN, Ann. American (born United States), b. 1954. **Genres:** Novels, Young Adult Non-fiction. **Career:** Abarta Publications, columnist, 1999-; Writers Place, vice president. Writer. **Publications:** Return to Sender: A Novel, 1995; Conversation, 2004. Contributor to periodicals. **Address:** The Writers Place, 3607 Pennsylvania, Kansas City, MO 64111-2820, U.S.A. **Online address:** slegdog@aol.com

SLEIGH, Charlotte. British (born England), b. 1973?. **Genres:** History, Animals/Pets, Sciences, Philosophy. **Career:** University of Kent, Rutherford College, School of History, senior lecturer in history of science, 2000-; University of California, visiting assistant professor. Writer. **Publications:** Ant, 2003; Six Legs Better: A Cultural History of Myrmecology, 2007; Literature and Science, 2011. **Address:** School of History, Rutherford College, University of Kent, Canterbury, KT CT2 7NX, England. **Online address:** c.l.sleigh@kent.ac.uk

SLEIGH, Tom. American (born United States), b. 1953?. **Genres:** Poetry, Literary Criticism And History, Young Adult Fiction. **Career:** Dartmouth College, professor of English and creative writing, 1986-; University of Iowa, faculty; University of California, faculty; Johns Hopkins University, faculty; New York University, Creative Writing Program, visiting professor in poetry; Hunters College, senior poet and program director, Program in Creative Writing, faculty. Writer. **Publications:** POETRY: After One, 1983; Waking, 1990; The Chain, 1996; The Dreamhouse, 1999; Far Side of the Earth, 2003; Interview With a Ghost, 2006; Space Walk, 2007. OTHER: (trans.) Herakles / Euripides, 2001. **Address:** Department of English, Hunter College, City University of New York, 695 Park Ave., New York, NY 10065-5024, U.S.A. **Online address:** thomas.r.sleigh@dartmouth.edu

SLEMON, Gordon Richard. Canadian (born Canada), b. 1924. **Genres:** Engineering, Technology. **Career:** Nova Scotia Technical College, assistant professor of electrical engineering, 1953-55; University of Toronto, associate professor, 1955-63, professor of electrical engineering, 1964-90, Department of Electrical and Computer Engineering, chair, 1966-76, dean of faculty of applied science and engineering, 1979-86, professor emeritus, 1990-; Microelectronics Development Center, chairman, 1982-87; Inverpower Controls Ltd., director, 1982-99. Writer. **Publications:** (With J.M. Ham) Scientific Basis of Electrical Engineering, 1961; Magnetoelectric Devices: Transducers, Transformers, and Machines, 1966; (with A. Straughen) Electric Machines, 1980; (with S.B. Dewan and A. Straughen) Power Semiconductor Drives, 1984; Electric Machines and Drives, 1992. **Address:** Faculty of Applied Science and Engineering, University of Toronto, SF 1021A, 35 St. George St., Toronto, ON M5S 1A4, Canada. **Online address:** g.slemon@utoronto.ca

SLEMROD, Joel (B.). American (born United States), b. 1951. **Genres:** Money/Finance, Economics, Law, Economics. **Career:** Harvard University, teaching fellow, 1975-77, research assistant, 1977-79; U.S. Department of Treasury, Office of Tax Analysis, intern, 1976, consultant; University of Minnesota, assistant professor of economics, 1979-85, associate professor of economics, 1985-87; Council of Economic Advisers, senior staff economist, 1984-85; University of Michigan Business School, Business Economics and Public Policy, associate professor, 1987-89, professor, 1989-, Office of Tax Policy Research, director, 1987-; University of Michigan, Department of Economics, associate professor, 1987-89, professor of economics, 1989-, chair, Paul W. McCracken collegiate professor of business economics and public policy; University of Michigan Law School, adjunct professor of law, 2003-04; Columbia Law School, visiting professor, 2007; Canadian Department of Finance, consultant; South African Ministry of Finance, consultant; World Bank, consultant; OECD, consultant. Writer. **Publications:** (With M. Feldstein and S. Yitzhaki) The Effects of Taxation on the Selling of Corporate Stock and the Realization of Capital Gains, 1978; (with A. Shah) Tax Sensitivity of Foreign Direct Investment: An Empirical Assessment, 1990; (with J. Bakija) Taxing Ourselves: A Citizen's Guide to the Great Debate over Tax Reform, 1996, 4th ed., 2008; (with J. Bakija) Do the Rich Flee from High State Taxes?, 2004; (with K.J. Crocker) Corporate Tax Evasion with Agency Costs, 2004; (with D.S. Hamermesh) The Economics of Workaholism, 2005; (with W. Kopczuk) Denial of Death and Economic Behavior, 2005; Tax Law Changes, Income Shifting and Measured Wage Inequality, 2006; Tax Competition and Parasitic Tax Havens, 2006; (with A.J. Auerbach and J.R. Hines, Jr.) Taxing Corporate Income in the 21st Century, 2007; (with M.D. Shapiro) Did the 2008 Tax Rebates Stimulate Spending?, 2009; (with J.M. Sallee) Car Notches, 2010; (with C.R. Sahm and M.D. Shapiro) Check in the Mail or More in the Paycheck, 2010. EDITOR: Do Taxes Matter? TheImpact of the Tax Reform Act of 1986, 1990; (with A. Razin) Taxation in the Global Economy, 1990; Why People Pay Taxes: Tax Compliance and Enforcement, 1992; (ed. with A. Giovannini and R.G. Hubbard) Studies in International Taxation, 1993; Tax Progressivity and Income Inequality, 1994; The Taxation of Multinational Corporations, 1996; Tax Policy in the Real World, 1999; Does Atlas Shrug?: The Economic Consequences of Taxing the Rich, 2000; (with W.G. Gale and J.R. Hines, Jr.) Rethinking Estate and Gift Taxation, 2001; (with H.J. Aaron) The Crisis in Tax Administration, 2004; (ed. with R.M. Bird and J.M. Poterba) Fiscal Reform in Colombia: Problems and Prospects, 2005; (with E.J. McCaffery) Behavorial Public Finance, 2006; (with E.J. McCaffery) Behavioral Public Finance, 2006. Contributor to periodicals. **Address:** Stephen M. Ross School of Business, University of Michigan, Rm. R5396, 701 Tappan St., Ann Arbor, MI 48109-1234, U.S.A. **Online address:** jslemrod@umich.edu

SLEPIAN, Jan(ice B.). American (born United States), b. 1921. **Genres:** Children's Fiction, Young Adult Fiction, Education, Novels. **Career:** Massachusetts General Hospital, language therapist, 1947-49; private speech therapist, 1952-58; Red Seal Clinic, speech therapist, 1953-55; Matheny School for Cerebral Palsy, speech therapist, 1955-57; Writer, 1962-. **Publications:** LISTEN-HEAR SERIES (with A. Seidler): Alfie and the Dream Machine, 1964; The Cock Who Couldn't Crow, 1964; Lester and the Sea Monster, 1964; Magic Arthur and the Giant, 1964; Mister Sipple and the Naughty Princess, 1964; The Roaring Dragon of Redrose, 1964; Mr. Sipple and the Naughty Princess, 1964. JUNIOR LISTEN-HEAR SERIES (with A. Seidler): Bendemolena, 1967; Ding-Dong, Bing-Bong, 1967; An Ear Is to Hear, 1967; The Hungry Thing, 1967; The Silly Listening Book, 1967; The Cat Who Wore a Pot on Her Head, 1981. FOR CHILDREN (with A. Seidler): The Best Invention of All, 1967; The Hungry Thing Returns, 1990; The Hungry Thing Goes to a Restaurant, 1992; Lost Moose, 1995; Emily Just in Time, 1998; Astonishment, 2009. NOVELS FOR YOUNG ADULTS: The Alfred Summer, 1980; Lester's Turn, 1981; The Night of the Bozos, 1983; Getting On with It, 1985; Something beyond Paradise, 1987; The Broccoli Tapes, 1988; Risk n' Roses, 1990; Back to Before, 1993; Pinocchio's Sister, 1995; The Mindreader, 1997. OTHERS: Building Foundations for Better Speech and Reading (teachers' training series), 1974. **Address:** c/o Sheldon Fogelman, 10 E 40th St., New York, NY 10016, U.S.A. **Online address:** dslepian@comcast.net

SLEPYAN, Kenneth D. American (born United States) **Genres:** History, Military/Defense/Arms Control. **Career:** Transylvania University, professor of history. Writer and historian. **Publications:** Stalin's Guerrillas: Soviet Partisans in World War II, 2006. **Address:** Transylvania University, 300 N Broadway, Haupt Humanities 109B, Lexington, KY 40508-1797, U.S.A. **Online address:** kslepyan@mail.transy.edu

SLESINGER, Warren. American (born United States), b. 1933. **Genres:** Poetry, Literary Criticism And History. **Career:** Macmillan Co., sales staff, 1961-64; Holt, Rinehart and Winston, manager, 1961-68; Olivet College, part-time instructor, 1963-67; D.C. Heath and Co., editor, 1969; College of Wooster, assistant professor of English, 1969-75; University of Pennsylvania Press, editor and market manager, 1976-81; University of Chicago Press, east coast representative, 1981-86; University of South Carolina Press, senior editor, 1986-97; Oregon State University Press, senior editor, 1997-2000; University of South Carolina-Beaufort, adjunct professor, 2000-. **Publications:** Field with Figurations, 1970; Heartland II, 1975; With Some Justification, 1985; (ed.) The Whole Story: Editors on Fiction, 1994; (ed.) Spreading the Word: Editors on Poetry, 1996, (with S. Corey) rev. ed., 2001; Warren Slesinger: Greatest Hits, 2002; A Word For It, 2008. **Address:** University of South Carolina, 801 Carteret St., Beaufort, SC 29902, U.S.A. **Online address:** slcsin@islc.net

SLETHAUG, Gordon E. Canadian/American (born United States), b. 1940. **Genres:** Humanities, Literary Criticism And History. **Career:** University of Waterloo, assistant professor, 1968-74, associate professor, 1974-93, Department of English, chair, 1985-94, professor of English, 1993-95, associate dean of arts, graduate studies and research, 1994-95; University of Hong Kong, Program in American Studies, chairman, 1995-, honorary professor, Visiting Lingnan Professor; Sun Yat-sen University, visiting Lingnan professor; University of Southern Denmark, research assistant, professor. Writer. **Publications:** (With S. Fogel) Understanding John Barth, 1990; The Play of the Double in Postmodern American Fiction, 1993; Beautiful Chaos: Chaos Theory and Metachaotics in Recent American Fiction, 2000; (ed. with J. Ryan) International Education and the Chinese Learner, 2010. Contributor of articles to periodicals and books. **Address:** School of Modern Languages and Cultures, University of Hong Kong, Rm. 706, K.K. Leung Bldg., Pokfulam Rd., Hong Kong, Hong Kong. **Online address:** slethaug@hkucc.hku.hk

SLIDE, Anthony (Clifford). (Anna Kate Sterling). American/British (born England), b. 1944. **Genres:** Communications/Media, Film, Gay And Lesbian Issues, Theatre, Biography, Autobiography/Memoirs, Essays, Reference, Reference. **Career:** Silent Picture, founder and editor, 1968-74; International Film Guide, assistant editor, 1968-74; American Film Institute, Louis B. Mayer Research Associate, 1971-72; associate archivist, 1972-75; Academy of Motion Picture Arts and Sciences, resident film historian, 1975-80; Producers Library Service, co-owner, 1986-90; Classic Images, book review editor, 1989-2001. Freelance writer, researcher, archivist and consultant. **Publications:** Early American Cinema, 1970, rev. ed., 1994; (contrib.) Griffith and the Rise of Hollywood, 1971; The Griffith Actresses, 1973; (with E. Wagenknecht) The Films of D.W. Griffith, 1975; The Idols of Silence, 1976; The Big V: A History of the Vitagraph Company, 1976, rev. ed., 1987; Early Women Directors, 1977, rev. ed., 1984; Aspects of American Film History Prior to 1920, 1978; Films on Film History, 1979; The Kindergarten of the Movies: A

History of the Fine Arts Company, 1980; (with E. Wagenknecht) Fifty Great American Silent Films 1912-1920: A Pictorial Survey, 1980; The Vaudevillians: A Dictionary of Vaudeville Performers, 1981; Great Radio Personalities in Historic Photographs, 1982; A Collector's Guide to Movie Memorabilia with Prices, 1983; Fifty Classic British Films 1932-1982, 1985; A Collector's Guide to TV Memorabilia, 1986; The American Film Industry, 1986; Great Pretenders, 1986; Fifty French Films, 1912-1982, 1987; (comp.) The Picture Dancing on a Screen: Poetry of the Cinema: An Anthology, 1988; (with P.K. Hanson and S.L. Hanson) Sourcebook for the Performing Arts: A Directory of Collections, Resources, Scholars, and Critics in Theatre, Film, and Television, 1988; The Cinema and Ireland, 1988; The International Film Industry: A Historical Dictionary, 1989; Silent Portraits: Stars of the Silent Screen in Historic Photographs, 1989; The Television Industry, 1991; Nitrate Won't Wait: A History of Film Preservation in the United States, 1992; Before Video: A History of the Non-Theatrical Film, 1992; The Slide Area: Film Book Reviews, 1898-1991, 1992; Gay and Lesbian Themes and Characters in Mystery Novels: A Critical Guide to Over 500 works in English, 1993; The Encyclopedia of Vaudeville, 1994; The Hollywood Novel, 1995; Some Joe You Don't Know, 1996; The Silent Feminists, 1996; Lois Weber: The Director Who Lost Her Way in History, 1996; Before, in, and after Hollywood, 1997; The New Historical Dictionary of the American Film Industry, 1998; Eccentrics of Comedy, 1998; Banned in the USA: British Films in the U.S. and Their Censorship, 1933-1960, 1998; Actors on Red Alert: Career Interviews With Five Actors and Actresses Affected By the Blacklist, 1999; Silent Players, 2002; Biographical and Autobiographical Study of 100 Silent Film Actors and Actresses, 2002; Lost Gay Novels: A Reference Guide to Fifty Works From the First Half of the Twentieth Century, 2003; American Racist: The Life and Films of Thomas Dixon, 2004; Silent Topics: Essays on Undocumented Areas of Silent Film, 2005; New York City Vaudeville, 2006; (with J.B. Powell and L.G. Berthelsen) Now Playing: Hand-Painted Poster Art From the 1910s Through the 1950s, 2007; Incorrect Entertainment, 2007; Frank Lloyd: Master of Screen Melodrama, 2009; Inside the Hollywood Fan Magazine: A History of Star Makers, Fabricators, and Gossip Mongers, 2010; Hollywood Unknowns, 2012; The Encyclopedia of Vaudeville, 2012. EDITOR: Selected Film Criticism, 5 vols., 1982; Selected Film Criticism: Foreign Films 1930-1950, 1984, Selected Film Criticism: 1951-1960, 1985; International Film, Radio and Television Journals, 1985; The Best of Rob Wagner's Script, 1985; Selected Theatre Criticism, 3 vols., 1985; Filmfront, 1986; The Memoirs of Alice Guy Blaché, 1986; Selected Radio and Television Criticism 1987; Selected Vaudeville Criticism, 1988; Highlights and Shadows: The Memoirs of a Hollywood Cameraman, 1989; They Also Wrote for the Fan Magazines: Film Articles by Literary Giants from E.E. Cummings to Eleanor Roosevelt, 1920-1939, 1992; (comp.) Robert Goldstein and the Spirit of '76, 1993; The Ultimate Directory of the Silent Screen Performers: A Necrology of Births and Deaths and Essays on 50 Lost Players, De Toth on De Toth, 1997; (comp.) Ravished Armenia and the Story of Aurora Mardiganian, 1997; Marihuana, Motherhood & Madness, 1998; (and intro.) On Actors and Acting, 1998; Paramount in Paris, 1998; Encyclopedia of British Film, 2003; D. W. Griffith, 2012. EDITOR AS ANNA KATE STERLING: Celebrity Articles from the Screen Guild Magazine, 1987; (and comp.) The Best of Shadowland, 1987. COMPILED AS ANNA KATE STERLING: Cinematographers on the Art and Craft of Cinematography, 1987. **Address:** 4118 Rhodes Ave., Studio City, CA 91604, U.S.A.

SLINGER, Joey. Canadian (born Canada), b. 1943. **Genres:** Humor/Satire. **Career:** Guelph Mercury, reporter; The Canadian Press, city editor; Victoria Times, bureau chief; Globe and Mail, bureau chief, 1970-; Toronto Star, humour columnist, 1979-, now retired; Toronto Sun, gossip columnist. **Publications:** No Axe Too Small to Grind: The Best of Joey Slinger, 1985; If It's a Jungle Out There, Why Do I Have to Mow the Lawn?, 1992; Down & Dirty Birding: From the Sublime to the Ridiculous-Here's All the Outrageous But True Stuff You Ever Wanted to Know about North American Birds, 1996; Punch Line, 2005. Contributor to periodicals. **Address:** Simon & Schuster, 1230 Ave. of the Americas, New York, NY 10020, U.S.A.

SLIVE, Seymour. American (born United States), b. 1920. **Genres:** Art/Art History. **Career:** Oberlin College, faculty, 1950-51; Pomona College, assistant professor of art and chair of department, 1952-54; Harvard University, assistant professor, 1954-57, associate professor, 1957-61, professor of fine arts, 1961-, Gleason professor of fine arts, 1973-, chair of department, 1968-71, Fogg Art Museum, director, 1975-; University of Leningrad, exchange professor, 1961; Yale University, Ryerson lecturer, 1962; Oxford University,

Slade professor of fine art, 1972-73. Writer. **Publications:** Rembrandt and His Critics, 1630-1730, 1953; Dutch Painting, 1953; Masterpieces of Dutch Painting, 1954; (contrib.) Great Landscapes, 1955; (contrib.) Bible Paintings, 1956; (intro.) Drawings of Rembrandt, with a Selection of Drawings by His Pupils and Followers, vol. II, 1965; (J. Rosenberg and E.H. ter Kuile) Dutch Art and Architecture 1600-1800, 1966, rev. ed., 1972; (intro. and ed.) Frans Hals, vol. III, 1970-74; Jacob van Ruisdael, 1981; Jacob van Ruisdael, 1628/29-1682: Tentoonstelling: Mauritshuis, Den Haag, 1982; Frans Hals, 1989; Dutch Painting 1600-1800, 1995; (contrib.) Shop Talk, 1995; Jacob van Ruisdael: A Complete Catalogue of His Paintings, Drawings and Etchings, 2001; Jacob van Ruisdael: Master of Landscape, 2005; Rembrandt Drawings, 2009; Jacob van Ruisdael: Windmills and Water Mills, 2011. **Address:** Fogg Art Museum, Harvard University, 32 Quincy St., Cambridge, MA 02138, U.S.A.

SLOAN, Cliff. American (born United States), b. 1958?. **Genres:** History. **Career:** Washingtonpost.Newsweek Interactive, general counsel, 2000-08, vice president, business development, 2002-05; Slate magazine, publisher, 2005-08; Skadden, Arps, Slate, Meagher & Flom IP, partner, 2008-; Georgetown University Law Center, adjunct professor; George Washington University Law School, adjunct professor; American University's Washington College of Law, adjunct professor. Writer. **Publications:** (With D. McKean) The Great Decision: Jefferson, Adams, Marshall and the Battle for the Supreme Court, 2009. **Address:** Skadden, Arps, Slate, Meagher & Flom IP, 1440 New York Ave. NW, Washington, DC 20005, U.S.A. **Online address:** cliff.sloan@skadden.com

SLOAN, Don. American (born United States), b. 1928. **Genres:** Medicine/ Health, Politics/Government, Sex, History. **Career:** Albert Einstein Medical Center, rotating intern, 1963-64; Temple University, Health Sciences Center, resident in obstetrics and gynecology, 1964-67; National Board of Medical Examiners, diplomate, 1964; New York Medical College, associate professor of clinical gynecology, 1967-, Department of Obstetrics and Gynecology, director of psychosomatic Service; American Board of Obstetrics and Gynecology, diplomate, 1970; American Society of Psychoprophylaxis in Obstetrics, national board director, 1969, vice-president, 1970-77; Society for Sex Therapy and Research, president, 1974-76; Cuban Ministry of Public Health, exchange professor, biannually, 1977-; Metropolitan Hospital, exchange professor, 1977-; Masters and Johnson Institute, fellow, 1979; New York Gynecologic Society, president, 1981; Milbank Memorial Fund, consulting staff, 1989; Political Affairs, assistant editor; American College of Obstetrics and Gynecology, fellow. **Publications:** The Dual Therapy Approach to the Treatment of Sexual Dysfunction, 1983; (with P. Hartz) Abortion: A Doctor's Perspective, a Woman's Dilemma, 1992; Anything Goes: A Complete Guide to Sexual Diversity, 1997; (with P. Hartz) Choice: A Doctor's Experience with the Abortion Dilemma, 2nd ed., 2002; (with R. Feman) Practicing Medicine Without A License: The Corporate Takeover Of Healthcare In America, 2006. Works appear in anthologies. Contributor to medical and sex therapy journals. **Address:** Betsy Nolan Agency, 50 W 29th St., Ste. 9W, New York, NY 10001, U.S.A. **Online address:** donsloan@whereitis.com

SLOAN, Jane. American (born United States), b. 1946. **Genres:** Film, Bibliography. **Career:** Pacific Film Archive, librarian, 1977-79; San Francisco State University, instructor in film, 1978-79; University of Southern California, government documents librarian, 1980-83, cinema and television librarian, 1985-89; Los Angeles Times, Editorial Library, librarian, 1984-85; Rutgers University, Douglass Library, women's studies librarian, 1990-98, media and cinema studies librarian. Writer. **Publications:** Robert Bresson: A Guide to References and Resources, 1983; Alfred Hitchcock: A Guide to References and Resources, 1993; Alfred Hitchcock: A Filmography and Bibliography, 1995; Reel Women: An International Directory of Contemporary Feature Films About Women, 2007; (ed. with M.Z. Stange and C.K. Oyster) Encyclopedia of Women in Today's World, 2011. **Address:** Kilmer Library, Rutgers University, Rm. 409A, Livingston Campus, New Brunswick, NJ 08903, U.S.A. **Online address:** jsloan@rci.rutgers.edu

SLOAN, John. British/Scottish (born Scotland), b. 1948. **Genres:** Literary Criticism And History, Poetry. **Career:** Oxford University, Balliol College, lecturer in English, 1985-96; Harris Manchester College, fellow, tutor, lecturer in English, 1996-. Writer. **Publications:** George Gissing: The Cultural Challenge, 1989; John Davidson: First of the Moderns, 1995; (ed.) Selected Poems and Prose of John Davidson, 1995; Oscar Wilde, 2003, (ed. and intro.)

The Complete Short Stories, 2010. **Address:** Harris Manchester College, Oxford University, Mansfield Rd., City Ctr., Oxford, OX OX1 3TD, England. **Online address:** john.sloan@hmc.ox.ac.uk

SLOAN, Mark. American (born United States), b. 1953?. **Genres:** Medicine/Health. **Career:** Permanente Medical Group, pediatrician, 1982-90; Permanente Medical Group, pediatrician, 1990-, chief of pediatrics, 1997-2002. University of California, Department of Community and Family Medicine, assistant clinical professor. Writer, mentor and physician. **Publications:** Birth Day: A Pediatrician Explores the Science, the History and the Wonder of Childbirth, 2009. Contributor to periodicals. **Online address:** mark@marksloanmd.com

SLOAN, Susan R. American (born United States) **Genres:** Novels, Young Adult Non-fiction, Romance/Historical. **Career:** Attorney and novelist. **Publications:** Guilt by Association, 1995; An Isolated Incident, 1998; Act of God, 2002; Behind Closed Doors, 2004. **Address:** c/o Author Mail, Warner Books, 1271 Ave. of the Americas, New York, NY 10020-1300, U.S.A. **Online address:** feedback@sloanbooks.com

SLOAN, Tod (Stratton). American (born United States), b. 1952. **Genres:** Psychology. **Career:** University of Tulsa, assistant professor, associate professor, professor of psychology, 1982-2001, chair of department, 1999-2001, Center for Community Research and Development, founder, 1988; Psychologists for Social Responsibility, national co-coordinator, 2001-04; Lewis & Clark College, Graduate School of Education and Counseling, department chair and professor of counseling psychology, 2004-. Writer. **Publications:** Deciding: Self-Deception in Life Choices, 1987; Damaged Life: The Crisis of the Modern Psyche, 1996; Life Choices: Understanding Dilemmas and Decisions, 1996. EDITOR: Ráfaga: The Life Story of a Nicaraguan Miskito Comandante, 1992; Critical Psychology: Voices for Change, 2000; (with S.C. Carr) Poverty and Psychology: From Global Perspective to Local Practice, 2003. **Address:** Graduate School of Education and Counseling, Lewis & Clark College, Rm. 335, Rogers Hall, 0615 SW Palatine Hill Rd., Portland, OR 97219, U.S.A. **Online address:** sloan@lclark.edu

SLOANE, Peter J(ames). Welsh/British (born England), b. 1942. **Genres:** Economics, Industrial Relations, E-books, Social Commentary, Adult Non-fiction. **Career:** University of Aberdeen, assistant lecturer, 1966-67, lecturer in political economy, 1967-69, Department of Economics, Jaffrey professor of political economy and head, 1984-96, Department of Political Economy, Jaffrey professor of political economy, vice-principal and dean of the faculty of social sciences and law, 1996-2002, now professor emeritus; University of Nottingham, lecturer in industrial economics, 1969-75; Department of Employment Unit for Manpower Studies, economic adviser, 1973-74; University of Paisley, professor of economics and management, 1975-84; McMaster University, visiting professor, 1978; Swansea University, School of Business and Economics, Welsh Economic Labour Market Evaluation and Research Center, director, 2002-08, professor emeritus, 2008-; University of Melbourne, visiting professor, 2007-10; Flinders University, National Institute of Labour Studies, adjunct professor, 2010-. Writer. **Publications:** Changing Patterns of Working Hours, 1975; (with B. Chiplin) Sex Discrimination in the Labour Market, 1976; Sport in the Market?: The Economic Causes and Consequences of the Packer Revolution, 1980; (ed.) Women and Low Pay, 1980; The Earnings Gap Between Men and Women in Britain: The Current State of Research Knowledge, 1981; (with H.C. Jain) Equal Employment Issues: Race and Sex Discrimination in the United States, Canada, and Britain, 1981; (with B. Chiplin) Tackling Discrimination at the Workplace: An Analysis of Sex Discrimination in Britain, 1982; (co-author) Labour Economics, 1985; (ed. with R. Asplund and I. Theodossiou) Low Pay and Earnings Mobility in Europe, 1998; (co-author) Employment Equity and Affirmative Action: An International Comparison, 2003; (co-author) The Economics of Sport: An International Perspective, 2004. Contributor to journals. **Address:** Department of Economics, WELMERC, School of Business and Economics, Swansea University, Richard Price Bldg., Singleton Pk., Swansea, WG SA2 8PP, Wales. **Online address:** p.j.sloane@swan.ac.uk

SLOAT, Teri. American (born United States), b. 1948. **Genres:** Illustrations, Children's Fiction, Young Adult Fiction, Poetry, Animals/Pets, Humor/Satire. **Career:** Elementary school teacher in rural villages, 1970-75; developer and illustrator of bilingual materials used in classrooms, 1975-81; freelance textbook developer and illustrator, Alaska, 1981-83; teacher of sixth grade and art, 1984-87; freelance writer and illustrator-Sebastopol, 1988-. Writer. **Publications:** FOR CHILDREN: From Letter to Letter, 1989; From One to One Hundred, 1991; The Thing That Bothered Farmer Brown, 1995; (with R. Sloat) Rib-ticklers: A Book of Punny Animals, 1995; Little Red Hen's Christmas, 1996; Really, Really Bad Monster Jokes, 1998; There Was An Old Lady Who Swallowed a Trout, 1998; Farmer Brown Goes Round and Round, 1999; Patty's Pumpkin Patch, 1999; Farmer Brown Shears His Sheep: A Yarn About Wool, 2000; Hark! The Aardvark Angels Sing: A Story of Christmas Mail, 2001; Pieces of Christmas, 2002; (with B. Huffmon) Berry Magic, 2004; This Is the House That Was Tidy & Neat, 2005; There Was an Old Man Who Painted the Sky, 2009. SELF-ILLUSTRATED: (reteller) Eye of the Needle, 1990; (reteller) Hungry Giant of the Tundra, 1993; (reteller) Sody Sallyratus, 1997; Hungry Giant of the Tundra, 2001; I'm a Duck!, 2006. Illustrator of books by J.R. Howard, B. Winslow. **Address:** c/o Kendra Marcus, 67 Meadow View Dr., Orinda, CA 94563-3246, U.S.A. **Online address:** teri@terisloat.com

SLOMAN, Albert Edward. British (born England), b. 1921. **Genres:** Education, Literary Criticism And History, Young Adult Fiction. **Career:** University of California, lecturer in Spanish, 1946-47; University of Dublin, Trinity College, reader in Spanish, 1947-53; University of Liverpool, professor of Spanish, 1953-62; University of Essex, vice-chancellor, 1962-87. Writer. **Publications:** The Sources of Calderón's El Príncipe Constante: With a Critical Edition of Its Immediate Source, La Fortuna Adversa Del infante Don Fernando De Portugal, 1950; The Dramatic Craftsmanship of Calderon, 1960; (ed. and intro.) La Vida es Sueño, 1961; A University in the Making, 1964; British Universities and Their Students, 1970. **Address:** 19 Inglis Rd., Colchester, EX CO3 3HU, England.

SLOMP, Hans. Dutch (born Netherlands), b. 1945. **Genres:** Politics/Government, Industrial Relations. **Career:** Radboud University, assistant professor political science, 1970-, Institute for Management Research, faculty; Cornell University, New York State School of Industrial and Labor Relations, lecturer, 1994; Universidad Autonoma de Bucaramanga, lecturer, 1996; Pontificia Universidad Catolica del Peru, lecturer, 1998. Writer. **Publications:** (With T. Mierlo) Arbeidsverhoudingen in Belgie, 1984; Labor Relations in Europe: A History of Issues and Developments, 1990; Between Bargaining and Politics: An Introduction to European Labor Relations, 1996; European Politics into the Twenty-First Century: Integration and Division, 2000; Europe, A Political Profile: An American Companion to European Politics, 2011. **Address:** Institute for Management Research, Radboud University, PO Box 9108, Nijmegen, 6500 HK, Netherlands. **Online address:** h.slomp@fm.ru.nl

SLOSBERG, Mike. American (born United States), b. 1934. **Genres:** Novels, Advertising/Public Relations, Humor/Satire, Poetry. **Career:** Young & Rubicam (advertising agency), copy writer, 1960-63, copy supervisor, 1963-66, vice-president and creative supervisor, 1966-69, vice-president and creative director, 1969-71, senior vice-president and associate creative director, 1971-84; Digitas, co-founder and chief executive officer, 1986-2002, retired, 2002; Fairfield University, part-time instructor; Mike Slosberg Inc., owner, 2003-. **Publications:** SELF-ILLUSTRATED: Klan-Destined, 1965; The August Strangers (novel), 1977; Hitler Error: A Novel, 2006; Pimp My Walker: The Official Book of Old Age Haiku, 2007. **Address:** c/o Eugene Wenick, Ernst, Cane, Berner & Gitlin, 7 W 51st St., New York, NY 10019-6910, U.S.A. **Online address:** mslosberg@digitas.com

SLOTE, Alfred. (A. H. Garnet). American (born United States), b. 1926. **Genres:** Novels, Novellas/Short Stories, Mystery/Crime/Suspense, Children's Fiction, Plays/Screenplays, Young Adult Fiction, Politics/Government, Young Adult Non-fiction, Young Adult Non-fiction, Social Commentary. **Career:** Williams College, instructor in English, 1953-56; University of Michigan, lecturer, Television Center, producer and writer, 1956-68, associate director, 1968-73, executive producer, 1973-82; University of California, lecturer. **Publications:** CHILDREN'S FICTION: The Princess Who Wouldn't Talk, 1964; The Moon in Fact and Fancy (non-fiction), 1967, rev. ed., 1971; Air in Fact and Fancy, 1968; Stranger on the Ball Club, 1970; Jake, 1971; The Biggest Victory, 1972; My Father, the Coach, 1972; Hang Tough, Paul Mather, 1973; Tony and Me, 1974; Matt Gargan's Boy, 1975; My Robot Buddy, 1975; The Hotshot, 1977; My Trip to Alpha I, 1978; Love and Tennis, 1979; The Devil Rides with Me and Other Fantastic Stories, 1980; C.O.L.A.R.: A Tale of Outer Space, 1981; Clone Catcher, 1982; Rabbit Ears, 1982; Omega Station, 1983; The Trouble on Janus, 1985; Moving In, 1988; A Friend Like That, 1988; Make-Believe Ball Player, 1989; The Trading Game, 1990; Finding Buck McHenry, 1991. ADULT FICTION: Denham Proper, 1953; Lazarus in

Vienna, 1956; Strangers and Comrades, 1964; (with W.W. Hunter) Preparation for Retirement (short stories), 1968; Termination: The Closing at Baker Plant (non-fiction), 1969. AS A.H. GARNET WITH G. GARRISON: The Santa Claus Killer, 1981; Maze, 1982. **Address:** HarperCollins Publishers, 10 E 53rd St., New York, NY 10022-5244, U.S.A.

SLOTTEN, Ross A. American (born United States), b. 1954. **Genres:** Biography, Biology. **Career:** Physician in private practice, 1984-; Northwestern University School of Medicine, faculty; St. Joseph Hospital, associate attending physician, 1984-, Acquired Immune Deficiency Syndrome (AIDS) Unit, co-founder, Human Immune Deficiency Virus (HIV) and Aging Study, adviser, Ad Hoc AIDS Task Force, member; Bonaventure House (homeless shelter for AIDS patients), board director; Howard Brown Memorial Clinic, board director, 1987; Horizon Hospice, adviser. Writer. **Publications:** The Heretic in Darwin's Court: The Life of Alfred Russel Wallace, 2004. Contributor to periodicals. **Address:** Klein Slotten & French Medical Associates, 711 W North Ave., Ste. 209, Chicago, IL 60610, U.S.A. **Online address:** rslotten@aol.com

SLOUKA, Mark. American (born United States) **Genres:** Information Science/Computers, Novels, Novellas/Short Stories, Psychology, Adult Nonfiction. **Career:** Columbia University, associate professor; University of Chicago, professor of English, Creative Writing Program, chair; University of California, lecturer in literature and culture. Writer. **Publications:** War of the Worlds: Cyberspace and the Hi-Tech Assault on Reality, 1995; Lost Lake, 1998; God's Fool, 2002; Visible World, 2007; Essays from the Nick of Time: Reflections and Refutations, 2010. Contributor to periodicals. **Address:** Department of English, The University of Chicago, 415A Rosenwald, 1115 E 58th St., Chicago, IL 60637-1511, U.S.A. **Online address:** mslouka@uchicago.edu

SLOVENKO, Ralph. American (born United States), b. 1926. **Genres:** Criminology/True Crime, Law, Psychiatry, Psychology. **Career:** Louisiana Supreme Court, law clerk, 1953; Tulane University of Louisiana, professor of law, 1954-64, School of Medicine, associate in psychiatry, 1963-65; U.S. District Court, commissioner, 1960; Senior assistant district attorney, 1964-65; Menninger Foundation, professor of law, 1965-67; University of Kansas, professor of law, 1965-67; Wayne State University, professor of law and psychiatry, 1969-; American Academy of Psychoanalysis, scientific associate; American Series in Behavioral Science and Law, editor; Tulane Law Review, editor-in-chief. **Publications:** Symposium on LMRDA: The Labor-Management Reporting and Disclosure Act of 1959, 1961; (ed.) Civil Code of Louisiana and Ancillaries: Revision of 1870 with Amendments to July 1, 1961, 1961; (ed.) Symposium, 1961; (ed.) Symposium on Labor Relations Law, 1961; (ed.) Louisiana Civil Code, Ancillaries and Code of Civil Procedure, 1961; (ed.) Cases and Materials on Louisiana Security Rights: The Law of Debtor's and Creditor's Rights, 1962; Louisiana Security Rights, 4 vols., 1962; (ed.) Mineral and Tidelands Law, 1963; (ed.) Oil and Gas Operations: Legal Considerations in the Tidelands and on Land, 1963; Sexual Behavior and the Law, 1965; (ed.) Crime, Law and Corrections, 1966; (with G.L. Usdin) Psychotherapy, Confidentiality and Privileged Communications, 1966; (ed. with J. Knight) Motivations in Play, Games and Sports, 1967; Handbook of Criminal Procedure and Forms, 1967; Creditor's and Debtor's Rights in Louisiana Civil Law, 1968; Psychiatry and Law, 1973; Tragicomedy in Court Opinions, 1973; Psychiatry and Criminal Culpability, 1995; Psychotherapy and Confidentiality: Testimonial Privileged Communication, Breach of Confidentiality and Reporting Duties, 1998; Psychiatry in Law/Law in Psychiatry, 2002, 2nd ed., 2009; (foreword) Contemporary Issues in Family Law and Mental Health, 2008. **Address:** Wayne State University Law School, Rm. 3363, 471 W Palmer St., Detroit, MI 48202-3986, U.S.A. **Online address:** ad4847@wayne.edu

SLOVIC, Scott H. American (born United States), b. 1960. **Genres:** Writing/Journalism, Literary Criticism And History. **Career:** Southwest Texas State University, faculty, 1991-95; University of Nevada, professor, 1995-, Center for Environmental Arts and Humanities, director, 1995-2002. Writer. **Publications:** Seeking Awareness in American Nature Writing: Henry Thoreau, Annie Dillard, Edward Abbey, Wendell Berry, Barry Lopez, 1992; (ed. with T.F. Dixon) Being in the World: An Environmental Reader for Writers, 1993; (comp. with L. Anderson and J.P. O'Grady) Literature and the Environment: A Reader on Nature and Culture, 1999; (ed.) Getting Over the Color Green: Contemporary Environmental Literature of the Southwest, 2001; (ed. with M.P. Branch) The ISLE Reader: Ecocriticism, 1993-2003, 2003; (ed. with G.

Hart) Literature and the Environment, 2004; (ed. with T. Satterfield) What's Nature Worth? Narrative Expressions of Environmental Values, 2004; (ed. with R. Moore) Wild Nevada: Testimonies on Behalf of the Desert, 2005; Going Away to Think: Engagement, Retreat, and Ecocritical Responsibility, 2008. **Address:** University of Nevada, 1664 N Virginia St., Reno, NV 89557-0208, U.S.A. **Online address:** slovic@unr.edu

SLUGLETT, Peter. American/British (born England), b. 1943. **Genres:** History, Translations. **Career:** Riyadh University (now King Saud University), lecturer in English, 1966-67; Algiers University, lecturer in English, 1973; Royal Commission on Historical Manuscripts, research assistant, 1974; University of Durham, lecturer in modern Middle Eastern history, 1974-93; British Journal of Middle Eastern Studies, review editor, 1990-94; Harvard University, visiting professor and Gibb memorial fellow at the Center for Middle Eastern Studies, 1991-92; University of California, visiting professor, 1992; University of Utah, associate professor of history, 1994-97, professor of history, 1997-, Middle East Center, director, 1994-2000. Historian and translator. **Publications:** Britain in Iraq, 1914- 1932, 1976; (comp.) Theses on Islam, the Middle East and North-West Africa, 1880-1978: Accepted by Universities in the United Kingdom and Ireland, 1983; (with M. Farouk-Sluglett) Iraq since 1958: From Revolution to Dictatorship, 1987, rev. ed., 2001; (trans.) A. Maalouf, Leo Africanus, 1989. EDITOR: (and trans. with M. Farouk-Sluglett) B. Tibi, Arab Nationalism: A Critical Enquiry, 1981, 2nd ed., 1990; (and contrib. with K. Brown, M. Jolé and S. Zubaida) Middle Eastern Cities in Comparative Perspective/Points de Vue sur les Villes du Maghreb et du Machrek, 1986; (co-ed.) Etat, Ville et Mouvements Sociaux au Maghreb et au Moyen Orient/Arab and Muslim Cities; the State, Urban Crisis and Social Movements, 1989; (with M. Farouk-Sluglett) Tuttle Guide to the Middle East, 1992; (and contrib. with M. Farouk-Sluglett) The Times Guide to the Middle East: The Arab World and Its Neighbours, 1993; (and contrib. with N. Meouchy) The British and French Mandates in Comparative Perspectives, 2004; (and contrib. with G.D. Khoury, N. Méouchy and H. Laurens) états et Sociétés de l'Orient Arabe en Quête d'Avenir (1945-2005): vol. I: Fondements et Sources I, 2006, vol. II: Dynamiques et enjeux, 2007; The Urban Social History of the Middle East, 1750-1950, 2008; (with S. Weber) Syria and Bilad al-Sham under Ottoman Rule, 2010; (with M.H. Yavuz) War and Diplomacy, 2011. Contributor to books and periodicals. **Address:** Middle East Center, University of Utah, Rm. 250, Carolyn Tanner Irish Humanities Bldg., 215 S Central Campus Dr., Salt Lake City, UT 84112-9199, U.S.A. **Online address:** sluglett@aol.com

SLUHOVSKY, Moshe. Israeli (born Israel), b. 1958. **Genres:** Cultural/Ethnic Topics. **Career:** Hebrew University of Jerusalem, professor of history; Brown University, visiting associate professor of history. Writer and educator. **Publications:** Patroness of Paris: Rituals of Devotion in Early Modern France, 1998; (with Y. Kaplan) Sifriyot ye-osfe Sefarim, 2006; Believe Not Every Spirit: Possession, Mysticism and Discernment in Early Modern Catholicism, 2007. **Online address:** msl@mscc.huji.ac.il

SMAIL, Daniel Lord. American (born United States), b. 1961. **Genres:** Law, History. **Career:** Fordham University, assistant professor of history, 1995-2001, associate professor of history, 2001-04, professor of history, 2004-05, Center for Medieval Studies, co-director, 2001-02; Harvard University, professor of history, 2006-. Writer and historian. **Publications:** Imaginary Cartographies: Possession and Identity in Late Medieval Marseille, 2000; (ed. and intro. with T. Fenster) Fama: The Politics of Talk and Reputation in Medieval Europe, 2003; The Consumption of Justice: Emotions, Publicity, and Legal Culture in Marseille, 1264-1423, 2003; On Deep History and the Brain, 2008. Contributor to books and journals. **Address:** Harvard University, Robinson Hall, 35 Quincy St., Cambridge, MA 02138, U.S.A. **Online address:** smail@fas.harvard.edu

SMALL, Bertrice. American (born United States), b. 1937. **Genres:** Romance/Historical, Young Adult Fiction. **Career:** Young and Rubicam Advertising, secretary, 1959-60; Weed Radio and TV Representatives, sales assistant, 1960-61; Edward J. Petrie and Co., sales assistant, 1961-63; freelance writer, 1969-; The Fat Cat Gift Shop, owner, 1976-81. **Publications:** The Kadin, 1978; Love Wild and Fair, 1978; Adora, 1980; Skye O'Malley, 1980; Unconquered, 1982; Beloved, 1983; All the Sweet Tomorrows, 1984; This Heart of Mine, 1985; A Love for All Time, 1986; Enchantress Mine, 1987; Blaze Wyndham, 1988; Lost Love Found, 1989; The Spitfire, 1990; A Moment in Time, 1991; Wild Jasmine, 1992; To Love Again, 1993; Love, Remember Me, 1994; The Love Slave, 1995; Hellion, 1996; Darling Jasmine,

1997; Betrayed, 1998; Deceived, 1998; The Innocent, 1999; Bedazzled, 1999; Besieged, 2000; (co-author) Fascinated, 2000; A Memory of Love, 2000; Intrigued, 2001; The Dutchess, 2001; Just beyond Tomorrow, 2002; (co-author) Delighted, 2002; Rosamund, 2002; Vixens, 2003; Until You, 2003; I Love Rogues, 2003; The Dragon Lord's Daughters, 2004; Private Pleasures, 2004; Philippa, 2004; Lara, 2005; The Last Heiress, 2005; Distant Tomorrow, 2006; Dangerous Love, 2006; Forbidden Pleasures, 2006; Border Lord's Bride, 2007; Skye O'Malley, 2007; Sudden Pleasures, 2007; The Twilight Lord, 2007; Dangerous Pleasures, 2008; Sorceress of Belmair, 2008; Captive Heart, 2008; The Shadow Queen, 2009; Crown of Destiny, 2010; The Border Vixen, 2010; Passionate Pleasures, 2010; Guilty Pleasures, 2011; Bond of Passion, 2011. Contributor to periodicals. **Address:** PO Box 765, Southold, NY 11971-0765, U.S.A. **Online address:** bertricesmall@hotmail.com

SMALL, Hugh. American (born United States), b. 1943?. **Genres:** Novels, Military/Defense/Arms Control, Autobiography/Memoirs, History. **Career:** Writer, consultant and historian. **Publications:** Florence Nightingale: Avenging Angel, 1999; The Crimean War: Queen Victoria's War with the Russian Tsars, 2007. Contributor to periodicals. **Address:** c/o Author Mail, St. Martin's Press Inc., 175 5th Ave., New York, NY 10010-7703, U.S.A. **Online address:** hugh@hugh-small.co.uk

SMALLEY, Stephen S(tewart). British (born England), b. 1931. **Genres:** Theology/Religion, Essays, How-to Books. **Career:** Ordained minister of Church of England, 1958; St. Paul's Church of England, assistant curate, 1958-60; Cambridge University, Peterhouse, dean and chaplain, 1960-63, preacher, 1963-64; University of Ibadan, lecturer, 1963-67, senior lecturer in religious studies, 1967-69; Victoria University of Manchester, lecturer, 1970-77, senior lecturer in new testament studies, 1977; Coventry Cathedral, canon resident and precentor, 1977-86; Chester Cathedral, dean, 1987-2001, dean emeritus, 2001-. Writer. **Publications:** Building for Worship: Biblical Principles in Church Design, 1967; Heaven and Hell: A Study of Last Things, 1968; The Spirit's Power: The Teaching of the Bible about the Holy Spirit, 1972; John, Evangelist and Interpreter, 1978, 2nd ed., 1998; 1, 2, 3 John, 1984; Thunder and Love: John's Revelation and John's Community, 1994; Revelation to John: A Commentary on the Greek Text of the Apocalypse, 2005. CONTRIBUTOR: (and ed.) Work, 1968; Encounter with Books: A Guide to Christian Reading, 1970; (and ed. with B. Lindars) Christ and Spirit in the New Testament: Essays in Honor of Professor C.F.D. Moule, 1973; Jesus under Menschensohn: Fuer A Voegtle, 1975; New Testament Interpretation, 1977; Pauline Studies in Honor of Professor F.F. Bruce, 1980. Contributor to journals. **Address:** Chester Cathedral, 12 Abbey Sq., Chester, CH CH1 2HU, England. **Online address:** stephen@fsworld.co.uk

SMARANDACHE, Florentin. American/Romanian (born Romania), b. 1954. **Genres:** Novels, Novellas/Short Stories, Children's Fiction, Plays/Screenplays, Poetry, Art/Art History, Education, Mathematics/Statistics, Philosophy, Theatre, Autobiography/Memoirs, Translations, Politics/Government, Physics, Language/Linguistics, Engineering. **Career:** University of Craiova, analyst and programmer, 1979-81; College of Balcesti, teacher of mathematics, 1981-82; Sidi El Hassan Lyoussi College, teacher of mathematics, 1982-84; N. Balcescu College, teacher of mathematics, 1983-85; Honeywell Inc., software engineer, 1990-95; Pima Community College, adjunct professor of mathematics, 1995-97; University of New Mexico, assistant professor of mathematics, professor of mathematics, 1997-; Chandler Gilbert Community College, adjunct professor, 1997. Writer. **Publications:** Formulas for the Spirit, 1981; Collection of Poetical Exercises, 1982; Feelings Made in Laboratory, 1982; The Sense of the Nonsense, 1983; Ante-rooms and Anti-poems or Bizarreries, 1984; Integer Algorithms to Solve Linear Equations and Systems, 1984; NonPoems, 1990; Only Problems, Not Solutions!, 1991; Dark Snow, 1992; Circles of Light, 1992; (trans.) Keys of the Earth, 1992; The PARADOXISM: A New Literary Movement, 1992; Without Me, How Is the Poetry Going?, 1993; NonNovel, 1993; Silence's Bell (poetry), 1993; Escaped, 1994; Trickster's Famous Deeds (children's plays), 1994; I Exist against Myself, 1995; Emigrant towards Infinity (poems); Collected Papers I-III, 1996-2000, 2nd ed., 2007; Word Tunnels (poetry), 1997; Scrieri defecte, 1997; (trans.) Afinitati, 1998; Professor in Africa, 1999; Intreaba-ma sa te-ntreb, 1999; Cum am descoperit America, 2000; Destin, 2000; Cantece de mahala, 2000; In Seven Languages, 2000; Dedications, 2000; A Unifying Field in Logics (essay), 2000; Second International Anthology on Paradoxism, 2000; Outer-Art, the Worst Possible Art in the World, vol. I, 2000, vol. II, 2002, vol. III, 2006; Third International Anthology on Paradoxism, 2002; Ultrapolemici cu LiTeRe mari şi MICI, 2002; Fourth International Anthology on Paradoxism, 2004; Frate cu Meridianele si Paralelele, vol. I, 2004, vol. II, 2005, vol. III, 2006; (with H. Tilton) Begin the Adventure, 2004, 3rd ed., 2010; (with F. Liu) Neutrosophic Dialogues, 2004; A Trilogy in pAradOXisM/Avant-Garde Political Dramas, 2004; (with G. Niculescu) Creionari facute cu pixul, 2004; India Magica (note de calatorie), 2005; Parallel Universes (experimental digital art), 2006; Mama vitrega Rusia (note de calatorie), 2006; (with W.B.V. Kandasamy) Neutrosophic Rings, 2006; Fifth International Anthology on Paradoxism, 2006; Unfolding the Labyrinth: Open Problems in Physics, Mathematics, Astrophysics and Other Areas of Science, 2006; Defective Writing: Short Paradoxist Prose, 2006; (with G. Niculescu) Perorari Paradoxiste, 2007; Exotica si cutremuratoarea Indonezie, 2007; Unification of Art Theories, 2007; (with S. Osman) Neutrosophy in Arabic Philosophy, 2007; (with W.V.B. Kandasamy) Special Fuzzy Matrices for Social Scientists, 2007; (ed.) I Drive Like You Do! (American pArAdOxIsT Folklore), 2007; Neogeometrism: Composed, Found, Changed, Modified, Alternated or Computer-programmed Art Works in a Geometrized World, 2007; Quantum Cyberart: The World of Micro-infinity, 2007; Maximus in minimis (aphlorisms), 2008; (with W.B.V. Kandasamy) Super Linear Algebra, 2008; 601 Paradoxist Distiches, 2008; Zhong dao bian zheng fa yu wei dao zhu yi zi ran zhe xue, 2008; Aflorisme, 2008; Frate cu meridianele si paralelele, vol. IV, 2008; Totul este posibil, chiar si imposibilul, 2008; (with W.B.V. Kandasamy) Super Fuzzy Matrices and Super Fuzzy Models for Social Scientists, 2008; (with W.B.V. Kandasamy and K. Ilanthenral) Set Linear Algebra and Set Fuzzy Linear Algebra, 2008; (with W.B.V. Kandasamy) Special Classes of Set Codes and Their Applications, 2008; Experimental Paradoxist Linguistics (Florentin's Lexicon), 2008; Global Totalitarianism and the Working Animals, 2008; (with V. Christianto) The Art of Wag/Awaken the Dog Inside, 2008; (with W.B.V. Kandasamy) New Classes of Codes for Cryptologists and Computer Scientists, 2008; Life Strategies, vol. I-III, 2008; (with W.B.V. Kandasamy) N-linear Algebra of Type I and Its Applications, 2008; (with W.B.V. Kandasamy) Methods in Industrial Biotechnology for Chemical Engineers, 2008; (with G. Niculescu) Amprente Paradoxiste, 2009; (ed. and comp. with F. Yuhua and V. Christianto) Cultural advantages in China, 2009; (with W.B.V. Kandasamy) Superbimatrices and their Generalizations, 2009; Multispace & Multistructure: Neutrosophic Transdisciplinarity, 2010; (ed.) Helluo librorum, 2010; Proposed Problems of Mathematics, 2010; (with W.B.V. Kandasamy and K. Ilanthenral) New Classes of Neutrosophic Linear Algebras, 2010; Dragă Domnule Rotaru: Antiscrisori, 2011. **Address:** University of New Mexico, 200 College Rd., Gallup, NM 87301, U.S.A. **Online address:** smarand@unm.edu

SMART, Alexa. See STUCKART, Diane A. S.

SMART, Bradford D. American (born United States), b. 1944. **Genres:** Business/Trade/Industry, Marketing. **Career:** Smart & Associates, president. Psychologist, consultant and writer. **Publications:** Selection Interviewing: A Management Psychologist's Recommended Approach, 1983; The Smart Interviewer, 1989; Topgrading: How Leading Companies Win by Hiring, Coaching, and Keeping the Best People, 1999, rev. ed., 2005; (with K.S. Mursau) Resourcefulness Parenting: How to Raise Happy, Successful Kids, 2003; (with G. Alexander) Topgrading for Sales: World-Class Methods to Interview, Hire, and Coach Top Sales Representatives, 2008. Contributor to periodicals. **Address:** 37202 N Black Velvet Ln., Wadsworth, IL 60083, U.S.A.

SMART, Ian Isidore. American (born United States), b. 1944. **Genres:** Literary Criticism And History, Novels, Cultural/Ethnic Topics. **Career:** National Autonomous University, faculty, 1970; St. James Secondary School, teacher of French and Spanish, 1970-71; University of California, instructor, 1975-76; University of Arkansas, assistant professor, 1976-77; Howard University, assistant professor, 1977-81, associate professor, 1981-84, professor of Spanish, 1984-. Writer. **Publications:** LITERARY CRITICISM: Central American Writers of West Indian Origin: A New Hispanic Literature, 1984; Nicolás Guillén: Popular Poet of the Caribbean, 1990; Amazing Connections: Kemet to Hispanophone Africana Literature, 1996. NOVELS: Sanni Mannitae: A Tall Tale for Our Times, 1994; Affirmative Action and West Indian Intellectual Tradition, 2004; Dude, Where's My HBCU?, 2005, 2nd ed., 2009; Willie Lynch to the World Trade Center: An African American Response to Nine-One-One, 2008, 3rd ed., 2011; From Pharaoh Narmer to President Obama: Keeping Audacious Hope Alive, 2009; (with K.A. Bedeau) Decoding Carnival: Creole Bacchanak, Pan-African Festival, 2010. EDITOR: (with K.S.K. Nehusi) Ah Come Back Home: Perspectives on the Trinidad and Tobago Carnival, 2000. TRANSLATOR: C.G. Wilson, Short Stories by Cubena, 1987; N.E. Bass, Pastrana's Last River (novel), 1992. Contributor to periodicals. **Address:** Department of Modern Languages and Literatures, Howard University, Rm. 350, Locke Hall, 2441 6th St. NW, Washington, DC 20059, U.S.A. **Online address:** ismart@fac.howard.edu

SMART, John Jamieson Carswell. Australian (born Australia), b. 1920. **Genres:** Philosophy, History. **Career:** Corpus Christi College, junior research fellow, 1948-50; University of Adelaide, Hughes professor of philosophy, 1950-72, emeritus professor, 1972-, Gavin David Young lecturer, 1987; La Trobe University, reader in philosophy, 1972-76; Australian National University, Institute of Advanced Studies, professor of philosophy, 1976-85, emeritus professor, 1986-; Stanford University, Center for Advanced Study in the Behavioral Sciences, fellow, 1979; Monash University, honorary research fellow. Writer. **Publications:** An Outline of a System of Utilitarian Ethics, 1961; Philosophy and Scientific Realism, 1963; (ed. and intro.) Problems of Space and Time, 1964; Between Science and Philosophy: An Introduction to the Philosophy of Science, 1968; (with B. Williams) Utilitarianism: For and Against, 1973; Ethics, Persuasion and Truth, 1984; Metaphysics and Morality, 1987; Our Place in the Universe: A Metaphysical Discussion, 1989; (with J.J. Haldane) Atheism and Theism, 1996, 2nd ed., 2002. **Address:** School of Philosophy and Bioethics, Monash University, Bldg. 11, 10/1-131 Wellington Rd., Clayton, VI 3168, Australia. **Online address:** john.smart@arts.monash.edu.au

SMART, S(tephen) Bruce. American (born United States), b. 1923. **Genres:** Business/Trade/Industry, Local History/Rural Topics, Economics, Sports/Fitness. **Career:** Permutit Co., sales engineer, 1947-51; Continental Group, staff, 1953-60, Central Metal Division, vice-president and general manager, 1961-64, vice-president for marketing and corporate planning, 1965-68, executive vice-president for forest products, 1969-73, vice-chairperson in charge of U.S. Operations, 1973-75, president and chief operating officer, 1975-80, chairman and chief executive officer, 1981-85; U.S. Department of Commerce, under secretary of commerce for international trade, 1985-88; World Resources Institute, senior fellow, 1989-; Chase Manhattan Corp., director; Chase Manhattan Bank, director; Celanese Corp., director; GTE Corp., director; Rexnord Inc., director; CCL Industries of Canada, director; Life Insurance Co., director; Chevron Corp., director. Writer. **Publications:** Beyond Compliance: A New Industry View of the Environment, 1992; Indian Summer: A Memoir, 1999; A Community of the Horse: Partnerships, 2003. Contributor to periodicals. **Address:** World Resources Institute, 1709 New York Ave. NW, Washington, DC 20006, U.S.A.

SMARTT, J(oseph). British (born England), b. 1931. **Genres:** Agriculture/Forestry, Biology, Botany, Sciences. **Career:** Colonial Research Service, scientific officer, 1954-, senior scientific officer, through 1962; North Carolina State University, research assistant; Cambridge University, School of Agriculture, postdoctoral fellow, 1965-67; University of Southampton, Botany Department, lecturer, 1967-73, senior lecturer, 1973-90, Department of Biological Sciences, reader, 1990-, senior visiting research fellow. Writer. **Publications:** Tropical Pulses, 1976; Grain Legumes: Evolution and Genetic Resources, 1990; (with N.W. Simmonds) Principles of Crop Improvement, 2nd ed., 1999; Goldfish Varieties and Genetics: A Handbook for Breeders, 2001. EDITOR: The Groundnut Crop; (with N.W. Simmonds) Evolution of Crop Plants, 2nd ed., 1995. **Address:** Department of Biology, School of Biological Sciences, University of Southampton, Biomedical Sciences Bldg., Bassett Cres. E, Southampton, HM SO9 3TU, England.

SMEDLEY, Audrey. American (born United States), b. 1930?. **Genres:** Social Sciences, Anthropology/Ethnology, Race Relations. **Career:** Wayne State University, assistant professor of anthropology, 1964-69; Oakland University, associate professor of anthropology, 1969-71; Radcliffe Institute, fellow, 1971-73; Tufts University, visiting associate professor, 1972-73; State University of New York, associate professor 1973-95, professor of anthropology, 1995-; Virginia Commonwealth University, professor of anthropology, 1995-2002, professor emeritus, 2002-; University of Michigan, faculty; Charles H. Wright Museum of Afro-American History, co-founder; Museum of Afro-American History, co-founder; National Endowment for the Humanities, proposal writer; National Science Foundation, proposal writer; Smithsonian Institution, consultant. Writer. **Publications:** Race in North America: Origin and Evolution of a World View, 1993, 4th ed., 2011; Women Creating Patrilyny: Gender and Environment in West Africa, 2004. Contributor to books. **Address:** School of World Studies, Virginia Commonwealth University, 312 Shafer St., PO Box 842040, Richmond, VA 23284, U.S.A. **Online address:** asmedley@saturn.vcu.edu

SMELIANSKY, Anatoly. Russian (born Russia) **Genres:** Plays/Screenplays, Theatre. **Career:** Moscow Art Theatre, literary director, 1980-, associate artistic director, 1996; Moscow Art Theatre School for Academic Studies, dean, 1986-, head, 2000-; Harvard University, Institute for Advanced Theatre Training, associate director; Yale University, lecturer; Carnegie Mellon University, lecturer; Columbia University, lecturer; Princeton University, lecturer; Georgetown University, lecturer; Sorbonne University, lecturer; Oxford University, lecturer; Cambridge University, lecturer. Writer. **Publications:** Nashi sobesedniki, 1981; Mikhail Bulgakov v Khudozhestvennom teatre, 1986; Oleg Efremov, 1987; (ed.) Klassika i sovremennost, 1987; Teatr-vremi, 1987; (ed.) Russkoe rezhisserskoe iskusstvo, 1898-1907, 1989; (ed.) O teatre i o sebe, 1997; Moskovskii khudozhestvennyi teatr, 1998; Rezhisserskii teatr, 1999; The Russian Theatre after Stalin, 1999; Predlagaemye obstoi a te'stva, 1999; Our Collocutors: Russian Classics on Stage; Mezhdometiia vremeni, 2002; Semeinyi al'bom, 2003. Contributor to periodicals. **Address:** A.R.T./ MXAT Institute, Loeb Drama Center, 64 Brattle St., Cambridge, MA 02138, U.S.A.

SMELLIE, Jim. (J. S. Smyllie). British (born England), b. 1955. **Genres:** Novels, Young Adult Fiction. **Career:** Sherman-Cardiff University Theater, house manager, 1980-83; British Paediatric Association, assistant secretary, 1984-89; East London Homeless Health Team, coordinator, 1989-92; East London and the City Health Authority, senior commissioning manager, 1993-. Writer. **Publications:** AS J.S. SMYLLIE: The Fifth Sun, 1990. Contributor to periodicals. **Address:** East London Homeless Health Team, 42 Carnegie House, 20 Osborn St., London, GL E1 6TD, England.

SMELSER, Neil Joseph. American (born United States), b. 1930. **Genres:** Sociology, Economics, Psychology, History. **Career:** University of California, Department of Sociology, assistant professor, 1958-60, associate professor, 1960-62, professor, 1962-72, university professor of sociology, 1972-94, professor emeritus, 1994-, vice chair, 1965, chair, 1974-76, 1991-92, assistant chancellor for educational development, 1966-68, Institute of International Studies, associate director, 1969-70, 1972-73, 1981-89, Center for Studies in Higher Education, acting director, 1987-89, director; Center for Advanced Study in the Behavioral Sciences, director, 1994-2001. Writer. **Publications:** (With T. Parsons) Economy and Society: A Study in the Integration of Economic and Social Theory, 1956, rev. ed., 1998; Social Change in the Industrial Revolution: An Application of Theory to the Lancashire Cotton Industry, 1770-1840, 1959; Theory of Collective Behavior, 1962; The Sociology of Economic Life, 1963, 2nd ed., 1976; Essays in Sociological Explanation, 1968; Sociological Theory: A Contemporary View, 1971; (contrib.) The American University, 1974; (contrib.) Economics and Sociology: Towards an Integration, 1976; (with S. Warner) Sociological Theory: Historical and Formal, 1976; Comparative Methods in the Social Sciences, 1976; (with R. Content) The Changing Academic Market, 1980; Social Paralysis and Social Change: British Working-Class Education in the Nineteenth Century, 1991; Effective Committee Service, 1993; Social Change in the Industrial Revolution: An Application of Theory to the British Cotton Industry, 1994; Sociology, 1995; Problematics of Sociology: The Georg Simmel Lectures, 1995, 1997; The Social Edges of Psychoanalysis, 1998; Faces of terrorism: Social and Psychological Dimensions, 2007; The Odyssey Experience, 2009; Reflections on the University of California: From the Free Speech Movement to the Global University, 2010. EDITOR: (with S.M. Lipset) Sociology: The Progress of a Decade: A Collection of Articles, 1961; (with W.T. Smelser) Personality and Social Systems, 1963, 2nd ed., 1970; Readings on Economic Sociology, 1965; (with S.M. Lipset) Social Structure and Mobility in Economic Development, 1966; Sociology: An Introduction, 1967, 2nd ed., 1973; (and intro.) On Society and Social Change, 1973; (with G. Almond) Public Higher Education in California, 1974; (with E.H. Erikson) Themes of Work and Love in Adulthood, 1980; (with H. Makler and A. Martinelli) New International Economy, 1982; The Handbook of Sociology, 1988; (with A. Martinelli) Economy and Society: Overviews in Economic Sociology, 1990; (with R. Münch) Theory of Culture, 1992; (with H. Haferkamp) Social Change and Modernity, 1992; (with R. Swedberg) The Handbook of Economic Sociology, 1994; (with J.C. Alexander) Diversity and its Discontents: Cultural Conflict and Common Ground in Contemporary American Society, 1999; (with P.B. Baltes) International Encyclopedia of the Social and Behavioral Sciences, 2001; (W.J. Wilson and F. Mitchell) America Becoming: Racial Trends and Their Consequences, 2001; (with F. Mitchell) Discouraging Terrorism: Some Implications Of 9/11: Panel on Understanding Terrorists In Order To Deter Terrorism, 2002; (with F. Mitchell) Terrorism: Perspectives From The Behavioral And Social Sciences: Panel On Behavioral, Social, And Institutional Issues, Committee On Science And Technology For Countering Terrorism, 2002; (with R. Swedberg) Handbook of Economic Sociology, 2005; (with S.M. Lipset) Social Structure and Mobility in Economic Development, 2005. Contributor to books. **Address:** Department of Sociology, University of California, 410 Barrows Hall, Berkeley, CA 94720-1980, U.S.A. **Online address:** nsmelser@berkeley.edu

SMERK, George M. American (born United States), b. 1933. **Genres:** Transportation, Urban Studies, History. **Career:** Illinois Central Railroad, traffic analyst, 1958-60; Indiana University, teaching associate, 1960-63, associate professor, 1966-69, Kelley School of Business, professor of transportation, 1969-, Institute for Urban Transportation, director, 1969-, director of transportation, 1992-; University of Maryland, assistant professor of transportation, 1963-66; Transportation Research Board, Newsline Newsletter, writer, 1976-99; Bus Ride Magazine, columnist, 1982-; Railfan and Railroad Magazine, columnist, 1982-; Transit Connections, associate editor, 1993-95; Railroads Past and Present, editor, 1997-. **Publications:** The Northeast Corridor Region: Main Line Rail Passenger Service in the Southern Section, 1947-1963, 1964; Urban Transportation: The Federal Role, 1965; (co-author) Mass Transit Management: A Handbook for Small Cities, 1971, 3rd ed., 1988; Mass Transit Technical Study for Bloomington, Indiana, 1971; (co-author) City of Bloomington, Indiana: Mass Transit Technical Study, 1973; Urban Mass Transportation: A Dozen Years of Federal Policy, 1974; Handbook for Management Performance Audits, 1979; The Federal Role in Urban Mass Transportation, 1991. EDITOR: Transportation Horizons: A Selection of Articles on the Subject of Transportation From Business Horizons, 1966, 2nd ed., 1970; Readings in Urban Transportation, 1968; Essays on Transportation Problems of the 1970s, 1969; (with W.D. Middleton and R.L. Diehl) Encyclopedia of North American Railroads, 2007; From Telegrapher to Titan: The Life of William C. Van Horne, 2010. **Address:** Kelley School of Business, Indiana University, Bryan Hall, 107 S Indiana Ave., Bloomington, IN 47405-7000, U.S.A.

SMIGEL, Robert. American (born United States), b. 1960. **Genres:** Science Fiction/Fantasy, Novels, Humor/Satire, Literary Criticism And History. **Career:** Writer and animator. **Publications:** (Co-author) If They Mated, 1995; (with A. McKay) X-Presidents, 2000. Contributor to periodicals. **Address:** NBC, 30 Rockefeller Plz., Galen Hall Rd., New York, NY 10112, U.S.A.

SMILES, Sam. British (born England) **Genres:** Art/Art History, History, Architecture. **Career:** Plymouth University, Exeter School of Art and Design, principal lecturer in art history, research coordinator for history of art, Faculty of Arts, director of studies duties. Writer. **Publications:** The Image of Antiquity: Ancient Britain and the Romantic Imagination, 1994; (with M. Pidgley) The Perfection of England: Artist Visitors to Devon c.1750-1870, 1995; (ed. with J. Gould, D. Jeremiah and D. Fitch) Going Modern and Being British: Art, Architecture and Design in Devon, 1910-1960, 1998; J.M.W. Turner, 2000; Eye Witness: Artists and Visual Documentation in Britain 1770-1830, 2000; (ed. with S. Moser) Envisioning the Past: Archaeology and the Image, 2005; Light into Colour: Turner in the South West, 2006; The Turner Book, 2007; J.M.W. Turner: The Making of a Modern Artist, 2007; (ed.) Sir Joshua Reynolds: The Acquisition of Genius, 2009; (ed. with S. Shaw-Miller) Samuel Palmer Revisited, 2010; (ed.) Into the Light, 2011. **Address:** School of Humanities, Plymouth University, Rm. 105, 6 Portland Villas, Drake Circus, Plymouth, DN PL4 8AA, England. **Online address:** s.smiles@plymouth.ac.uk

SMILEY, Bob. American (born United States), b. 1977. **Genres:** Children's Fiction. **Career:** Columbia Broadcasting System Inc. (CBS) television, staff writer, 1999-2005; ESPN.com, golf columnist, 2007-. **Publications:** (With J. Florea) Growing Up Super Average: The Adventures of Average Boy, 2007; Follow the Roar: Tailing Tiger for All 604 Holes of His Most Spectacular Season, 2008. **Address:** Los Angeles, CA , U.S.A. **Online address:** forerightbob@gmail.com

SMILEY, Gene. (William Gene Smiley). American (born United States), b. 1940. **Genres:** Economics, Business/Trade/Industry. **Career:** Bradley University, visiting assistant professor of economics, 1972-73; Marquette University, assistant professor, 1973-79, associate professor, 1979-94, chair of department, 1982-85, 1988-91, professor of economics, 1994-, now professor emeritus. Writer. **Publications:** The American Economy in the Twentieth Century, 1994; Rethinking the Great Depression: A New View of Its Causes and Consequences, 2002. Contributor to books, journals and periodicals. **Address:**

Department of Economics, Marquette University, PO Box 1881, Milwaukee, WI 53201-1881, U.S.A. **Online address:** william.smiley@marquette.edu

SMILEY, Jane (Graves). American (born United States), b. 1949. **Genres:** Novels, Crafts, Young Adult Fiction, Adult Non-fiction, Novellas/Short Stories. **Career:** Iowa State University, instructor in English, 1981-90, distinguished professor of English, 1992-96; University of Iowa, visiting assistant professor, 1981, 1987. Writer. **Publications:** Barn Blind: A Novel, 1980; At Paradise Gate: A Novel, 1981; Duplicate Keys, 1984; Age of Grief: A Novella and Stories, 1987; Greenlanders, 1988; Catskill Crafts: Artisans of the Catskill Mountains, 1988; Ordinary Love & Good Will: Two Novellas, 1989; Life of the Body: A Story, 1990; A Thousand Acres, 1991; (intro.) Of Human Bondage, 1991; (co-author) The True Subject: Writers on Life and Craft, 1993; Moo, 1995; (intro.) Nancy's Mysterious Letter, 1996; All-true Travels and Adventures of Lidie Newton: A Novel, 1998; (intro.) Return of the Native, 1999; (ed. with R. Rosenblatt and B. Mukherjee) Consumption Culture and the Pursuit of Happiness, 1999; (contrib.) The Barbie Chronicles: A Living Doll Turns Forty, 1999; Horse Heaven, 2000; (intro.) Uncle Tom's Cabin, 2001; Charles Dickens, 2002; (afterword) Millon the Floss, 2002; Good Faith, 2003; (intro. with W.H. Gass) Horses: Photographs, 2003; (co-author) Deborah Butterfield, 2003; (ed.) Writers on Writing, vol. II: More Collected Essays from The New York Times, 2003; Year at the Races: Reflections on Horses, Humans, Love, Money and Luck, 2004; Thirteen Ways of Looking at the Novel, 2005; (with A. Wilson) Anglo-Saxon Attitudes, 2005; (ed. with J. Kulka and N. Danford) Best New American Voices 2006, 2005; Ten Days in the Hills, 2007; Georges and the Jewels, 2009; (intro.) School for Love, 2009; Private Life: A Novel, 2010; The Man Who Invented the Computer: The Biography of John Atanasoff, Digital Pioneer, 2010; A Good Horse, 2010; True Blue, 2011; Pie in the Sky, 2012. **Address:** c/o Knopf Publicity, Random House Inc., 1745 Broadway, New York, NY 10019, U.S.A. **Online address:** jane.smiley@sbcglobal.net

SMILEY, William Gene. *See* **SMILEY, Gene.**

SMIRAGLIA, Richard P(aul). American (born United States), b. 1952. **Genres:** Information Science/Computers, Music. **Career:** University of Illinois, assistant music catalog librarian and assistant professor of library administration, 1974-78, music catalog librarian and associate professor of library administration, 1978-86, Graduate School of Library and Information Science, visiting instructor, 1985-86; Columbia University, School of Library Service, assistant professor of library service, 1987-93; Long Island University, Palmer School of Library and Information Science, faculty, 1993-97, professor of library and information science, 1997-2009, professor emeritus, 2009-; University of Wisconsin, School of Information Studies, visiting professor of information studies, 2009-; Royal Netherlands Academy of the Arts and Sciences, e-Humanities Group, associate researcher, 2011-. Writer. **Publications:** Shelflisting Music: Guidelines for Use with the Library of Congress Classification, M, 1981, 2nd ed., 2008; Cataloging Music: A Manual for Use with AACR2, 1983, 2nd ed., 1986; Music Cataloging: The Bibliographic Control of Printed and Recorded Music in Libraries, 1989; (with T. Pavlovsky) Describing Music Materials, 3rd ed., 1996; The Nature of a Work: Implications for the Organization of Knowledge, 2001; Bibliographic Control of Music: A Retrospective Bibliography, 1882-2000, 2005; Bibliographic Control of Music, 1897-2000, 2006. EDITOR: (with S.S. Intner) Policy and Practice in Bibliographic Control of Nonbook Media, 1987; (and foreword) Music Subject Headings, 1988; Describing Archival Materials: The Use of the MARC AMC Format, 1990; Origins, Content, and Future of AACR2 Revised, 1992; Works as Entities for Information Retrieval, 2002; Metadata: A Cataloger's Primer, 2005. **Address:** School of Information Studies, University of Wisconsin, Bolton Hall, 3210 N Maryland Ave., 5th Fl., Milwaukee, WI 53211, U.S.A. **Online address:** smiragli@uwm.edu

SMIRNOFF, Marc. American (born United States), b. 1963. **Genres:** Art/Art History, Writing/Journalism. **Career:** Oxford American, founder and editor, 1992-. **Publications:** (Co-author) Best of the Oxford American: Ten Years from the Southern Magazine of Good Writing, 2002; (ed.) The Oxford American Book of Great Music Writing, 2008. **Address:** The Oxford American, 201 Donaghey Ave., Conway, AR 72035, U.S.A. **Online address:** smirnoff@oxfordamericanmag.com

SMITH, Adam I.P. British (born England), b. 1973. **Genres:** Reference. **Career:** University College London, senior lecturer in American history; Cambridge University, junior research fellow; Harvard University, visiting fellow;

Queen Mary College, lecturer in American history. Writer. **Publications:** (Ed. with S. Grant) The North and the Nation in the Era of the Civil War, 2003; The Republican Party: An Illustrated History of the GOP, 2003; No Party Now: Politics in the Civil War North, 2006; The American Civil War, 2007. Contributor to books and journals. **Address:** Department of History, University College London, Gower St. 409, 25 Gordon Sq., London, GL WC1E 6BT, England. **Online address:** a.i.p.smith@ucl.ac.uk

SMITH, Ali. British/Scottish (born Scotland), b. 1962. **Genres:** Literary Criticism And History, Novellas/Short Stories, Plays/Screenplays, Novels, Mythology/Folklore. **Career:** University of Strathclyde, lecturer in Scottish, English, and American literature, 1990-92. Writer, 1992-. **Publications:** (Ed.) Poems, Plays, and Prose of J.M. Synge, 1992; Free Love, 1995; Like (novel), 1997; Other Stories and Other Stories, 1999; Trace of Arc, 1999; (co-ed.) The Virago Book of 20th Century Fiction, 2000; Shorts 3: The Macallan/Scotland on Sunday Short Story Collection, 2000; (ed. with K. Boddy and S. Wood) Brilliant Careers: The Virago Book of Twentieth-Century Fiction, 2000; Hotel World, 2001; Whole Story and Other Stories, 2003; (ed. with T. Litt) New Writing 13, 2005; (with L. de Bernières, M. Rosoff and J. Winterson) The Brighton Book, 2005; Accidental, 2005; Writ, 2006; The Reader, 2006; Girl Meets Boy: The Myth of Iphis, 2007; The Book Lover, 2008; First Person and Other Stories, 2008; (co-author) Ox-tales: Fire, 2009; (foreword) A State of Change, 2009. Contributor to periodicals. **Address:** Wylie Agency Ltd., 17 Bedford Sq., London, GL WC1B 3JA, England.

SMITH, Andrew Anselmo. American (born United States), b. 1959?. **Genres:** Children's Fiction, Young Adult Non-fiction. **Career:** Writer and educator. **Publications:** Ghost Medicine, 2008; In the Path of Falling Objects, 2009; Marbury Lens, 2010; Stick, 2011. **Address:** Feiwel and Friends, 175 5th Ave., New York, NY 10010, U.S.A. **Online address:** andrew@ghostmedicine.com

SMITH, Angela Thompson. American/British (born England), b. 1946. **Genres:** Psychology, Young Adult Fiction, Sciences. **Career:** Manchester University, Medical School, research nurse, 1978-81; Robert Wood Johnston Medical School, researcher, 1985-88; Princeton University, researcher, 1988-92; The Bigelow Foundation, research coordinator, 1992-94; Gaining the Edge Inc., chief operations officer, 1998-2000; International Remote Viewing Association, founding member, 1999-; Inner Vision Research Institute, executive director; Nevada Remote Viewing Group, founder, 2002-, director, 2002-05; Boulder City Senior Center, executive director, 2003-05; University of Medicine and Dentistry of New Jersey, research analyst; Princeton University, Engineering Anomalies Research Laboratory, research analyst; Mindwise Consulting, head. Writer and researcher. **Publications:** Remote Perceptions: Out-of-body Experiences, Remote Viewings, and Other Normal Abilities, 1998; Diary of an Abduction: A Scientist Probes the Enigma of Her Alien Contact, 2001; Shire, 2006; River of Passion, 2007; Simple Living: An Eclectic Gathering of Practical, Common Sense Knowledge to Live Longer, Feel Better and Live Simply, forthcoming. **Address:** Nevada Remote Viewing Group, 509 5th St., Boulder City, NV 89005, U.S.A. **Online address:** catalyst13@cox.net

SMITH, Annick. American/French (born France), b. 1936. **Genres:** Environmental Sciences/Ecology, Natural History, Poetry, Photography, Autobiography/Memoirs. **Career:** Writer, 1974-. Producer and director. **Publications:** (Ed. with W. Kittredge) The Last Best Place: A Montana Anthology, 1988; (intro.) Fireweed, 1994; Homestead, 1995; Big Bluestem: Journey into the Tall Grass, 1996; (contrib.) Writing Down the River, 1998; (contrib.) Monte Dolack: The Works, 2000; In This We Are Native: Memoirs and Journeys (memoir), 2001; (ed. with S. O'Connor) The Wide Open: Prose, Poetry, and Photographs of the Prairie, 2008; The River Guide, forthcoming. Works appear in anthologies. Contributor to periodicals. **Address:** c/o Amanda Urban, International Creative Management, 730 5th Ave., New York, NY 10019, U.S.A. **Online address:** annick@blackfoot.net

SMITH, Anthony. British (born England), b. 1926. **Genres:** Environmental Sciences/Ecology, Sciences, Travel/Exploration. **Career:** Guardian, reporter, 1953, 1956-57; Drum, general manager, 1954-55; Daily Telegraph, science correspondent, 1957-63. Journalist, broadcaster, science writer and explorer. **Publications:** Blind White Fish in Persia, 1953; Sea Never Dry, 1958; High Street Africa, 1961; Jambo: African Balloon Safari in UK as Throw Out Two Hands, 1966; The Body, 1968, 2nd ed., 1970; Corps et ses secrets. Traduit de l'anglais par Claude Pagani, 1969; The Seasons: Life and Its Rhythms in UK as The Seasons: Rhythms of Life, Cycles of Change, 1970; The Dangerous

Sort: The Story of a Balloon, 1970; Mato Grosso: Last Virgin Land: An Account of the Mato Grosso, Based on the Royal Society and Royal Geographical Society Expedition to Central Brazil, 1967-9, 1971; Beside the Seaside, 1972; (with J. Southam) Good Beach Guide, 1973; Human Pedigree: Inheritance and the Genetics of Mankind, 1975; Animals on View: An Illustrated Guide to Britain's Safari Parks, Zoos, Aquariums, and Bird Gardens, 1977; Wilderness, 1978; A Persian Quarter Century, 1979; A Sideways Look, 1983; The Mind, 1984; Smith & Son: An Expedition into Africa, 1984; Which Animal Are You?, 1988; The Great Rift, 1988; Explorers of the Amazon, 1990; Swaps, 1992; (with M. Wagner) Ballooning, 1998; Weather: The Truth About the Health of Our Planet, 2000; Machine Gun: The Story of the Men and the Weapon that Changed the Face of War, 2003; Lost Lady of the Amazon: The Story of Isabela God in Her Epic Journey, 2003. **Address:** Curtis Brown Ltd., Haymarket House, 28-29 Haymarket, London, GL SW1Y 4SP, England.

SMITH, Arthur L. *See* **ASANTE, Molefi K.**

SMITH, Arthur L. American (born United States), b. 1927. **Genres:** History, International Relations/Current Affairs. **Career:** Occidental College, instructor in European history, 1955-56; California State University, assistant professor, 1957-62, associate professor, 1962-65, professor of history, 1965-92, professor emeritus, 1992-, resident director of international programs, 1972-73. Writer. **Publications:** The Deutschtum of Nazi Germany and the United States, 1965; Churchill's German Army: Wartime Strategy And Cold War Politics, 1943-1947, 1977; (with H. Jacobsen) World War II: Policy and Strategy: Selected Documents With Commentary, 1979; Die Hexe von Buchenwald, 1983; Heimkehr aus dem Zweiten Weltkrieg, 1985; Hitler's Gold: The Story Of The Nazi War Loot, 1989; Die Vermisste Million, 1992; The War for the German Mind, 1996; Kidnap City: Cold War Berlin, 2002; (with H. Jacobsen) The Nazi Party and the German Foreign Office, 2007. Contributor of articles to journals. **Address:** Department of History, California State University, C4066 King Hall, 5151 State University Dr., Los Angeles, CA 90032-8223, U.S.A. **Online address:** arthursmith@cox.net

SMITH, Barbara Herrnstein. American (born United States), b. 1932. **Genres:** Literary Criticism And History, Humanities, Language/Linguistics, Intellectual History, Philosophy. **Career:** Sanz School of Languages, instructor in English, 1956-57; Brandeis University, Department of English and American Literature, graduate assistant, 1959-60, teaching and research assistant, 1960-61, instructor in English, 1961-62; University of Pennsylvania, visiting lecturer, 1973-74, professor of English and communications, 1974-87; Duke University, Braxton Craven professor of comparative literature and English, 1987-2011, Braxton Craven professor emeritus of comparative literature and English, 2011-, Center for Interdisciplinary Studies in Science and Cultural Theory, director, 1991-2011; University of Toronto, Northrop Frye chair in literary theory, 1990; Brown University, distinguished professor of English, 2003-11. Writer. **Publications:** Discussions of Shakespeare's Sonnets, 1964; Poetic Closure: A Study of How Poems End, 1968; (ed. and intro.) Sonnets, 1969; (ed.) Shakespeare's Sonnets, 1969; (contrib.) New Directions in Literary History, 1974; On the Margins of Discourse: The Relation of Literature to Language, 1978; Contingencies of Value: Alternative Perspectives for Critical Theory, 1988; (ed. with D.J. Gless) The Politics of Liberal Education, 1992; (ed. with A. Plotnitsky) Mathematics, Science and Postclassical Theory, 1996; Belief and Resistance: Dynamics of Contemporary Intellectual Controversy, 1997; Scandalous Knowledge: Science, Truth and the Human, 2006; Natural Reflections: Human Cognition at the Nexus of Science and Religion, 2009. **Address:** Duke University, PO Box 90015, Durham, NC 27708, U.S.A. **Online address:** bhsmith@duke.edu

SMITH, Bernard (William). Australian (born Australia), b. 1916. **Genres:** Art/Art History, Autobiography/Memoirs, Biography, History. **Career:** New South Wales Department of Education, teacher, 1935-44; National Art Gallery of New South Wales, education officer, 1944-48, 1951-52; University of Melbourne, lecturer, 1955, senior lecturer, 1956-63, reader, 1964-66, Department of Art History, professorial fellow; The Age, art critic; University of Sydney, Power Institute of Fine Arts, professor of contemporary art, 1967-77, director; Australian Academy of the Humanities, president, 1977, 1980. Writer. **Publications:** Place, Taste and Tradition: A Study of Australian Art since 1788, 1945, rev. ed., 1979; Education through Art in Australia, 1958; European Vision and the South Pacific, 1960, rev. ed., 1980; Australian Painting, 1962, 4th ed., 2001; (with K. Smith) The Architectural Character of Glebe, Sydney, 1973; (ed.) Concerning Contemporary Art, 1975; (ed.) Documents on Art and Taste in Australia, 1975; Antipodean Manifesto: Essays in Art and History, 1976; Art as Information: Reflections on the Art from Captain Cook's Voyages, 1979; The Spectre of Truganini (Boyer Lectures), 1980; Culture and History: Essays Presented to Jack Lindsay, 1984; The Boy Adeodatus, 1984; European Vision and the South Pacific, 1985; (with R. Joppien) Art of Captain Cook's Voyages, 1985; The Death of the Artist as Hero, 1988; (with B. Smith) Terra Australis: The Furthest Shore, 1988; (with A. Wheeler) The Art of the First Fleet, 1988; The Critic as Advocate, 1989; Imagining the Pacific, 1992; Noel Counihan, 1993; Modernism's History, 1998; (ed.) Tales from Sydney Cove, 2000; A Pavane for Another Time, 2002; Formalesque: A Guide to Modern Art and its History, 2007. **Address:** Australian Academy of the Humanities, 168 Nicholson St., Fitzroy, VI 3065, Australia.

SMITH, Bobbi. Also writes as Julie Marshall. American (born United States), b. 1949. **Genres:** Romance/Historical, Novels, Young Adult Fiction. **Career:** Famous-Barr, sales person, 1966-70, assistant buyer, 1971-72, department manager, 1972-73; writer, 1982-. **Publications:** ROMANCE NOVELS: Rapture's Rage, 1982; Forbidden Fires, 1983; Wanton Splendor, 1984; Raptures Tempest, 1985; Arizona Temptress, 1986; Island Fire, 1986; Desert Heart, 1987; Captive Pride, 1987; Texas Splendor, 1988; Pirate's Promise, 1988; Arizona Caress, 1989; Sweet Silken Bondage, 1990; Bayou Bride, 1991; Kiss Me Forever, 1991; Capture My Heart, 1992; Beneath Passion's Skies, 1993; Dream Warrior, 1993; (co-author) Timeless Love, 1993; Heaven, 1994; (with J. Hohl, B. Hutchinson and E. Rogers) Love beyond Time, 1994; (co-author) A Christmas Embrace, 1994; Passion, 1995; (with P. Hagan, B. Hutchinson and L. Madl) Cupid's Kiss, 1996; Lady Deception, 1996; The Lady's Hand, 1996; Renegade's Lady, 1997; The Lady and the Texan, 1997; (contrib.) Celebrations, 1998; Outlaw's Lady, 1998; Half-Breed's Lady, 1998; Weston's Lady, 1999; (with E. Barbieri, C. O'Banyon and E. Rogers) Something Borrowed, Something Blue, 2000; Cinnamon and Roses, 2000; Half-Breed, 2001; Eden, 2001; Lone Warrior, 2002; Forever Autumn, 2003; Hunter's Moon, 2003; Brazen, 2004; Halfbreed Warrior, 2005; Defiant, 2006; Hired Gun, 2006; Lawless, Texas, 2007; Wanted!: The Half-Breed, 2008; Runaway, 2009; The Gunfighter, 2009; Wanted: The Texan, 2009; The Viking, 2010; A Cowboy for Christmas, 2010; Relentless, 2010. BRIDES OF DURANGO SERIES: Elise, 1999; Tessa, 2000; Jenny, 2000. AS JULIE MARSHALL: Haven, 2005; Miracles, 2006. **Address:** Dorchester Publishing, PO Box 6640, Wayne, PA 19087, U.S.A.

SMITH, Bradley A. American (born United States), b. 1958. **Genres:** Politics/Government, Law, Money/Finance. **Career:** Small Business Association of Michigan, legislative analyst, 1979-80, legislative and political director, 1980, general manager, 1980-81; U.S. Department of State, U.S. vice-consult and foreign service officer, 1981-83; IBA Health and Life Assurance Co., assistant vice president, 1983-85; VHA Health Ventures, senior consultant, 1986-87; Capital University, Law School, visiting assistant professor of law, 1993-94, assistant professor, 1994-96, associate professor, 1996-99, professor of law, 1999-2009, Josiah H. Blackmore II/Shirley M. Nault designated professor of law; U.S. Federal Election Commission, commissioner, 2000-05; George Mason University, School of Law, adjunct professor, 2002-04. Writer. **Publications:** Unfree Speech: The Folly of Campaign Finance Reform, 2001; (with M. Dimino, Jr. and M. Solimine) Voting Rights and Election Law, 2010. Contributor to periodicals and journals. **Address:** Law School, Capital University, 303 E Broad St., Columbus, OH 43215-3200, U.S.A. **Online address:** bsmith@law.capital.edu

SMITH, Bradley F. American (born United States), b. 1931. **Genres:** Education, History, Biography. **Career:** Cabrillo College, instructor, 1960-66, 1969-; Miles College, instructor, 1967-69; Western Washington University, Huxley College of Environmental Studies, professor, 1975-90, dean, 1994-; U.S. Environmental Protection Agency, director, special assistant, acting associate administrator, senior executive, 1992; Air Force Institute of Technology, adjunct faculty. Writer. **Publications:** Adolf Hitler: His Family, Childhood and Youth, 1967; Heinrich Himmler: A Nazi in the Making, 1971, 1974; (ed. with A.F. Peterson) Himmler Geheimreden, 1974; Reaching Judgement at Nuremberg, 1977; (with E. Agarossi) Operation Sunrise, 1979; The Road to Nuremberg, 1981; The American Road to Nuremberg: The Documentary Record, 1981; The Shadow Warriors, 1984; The War's Long Shadow, 1986; The Ultra-Magic Deals and the Most Secret Special Relationship, 1993; Sharing Secrets with Stalin, How the Allies Traded Intelligence, 1941-45, 1996; (with E.D. Egner) Environmental Science, 2010. **Address:** Huxley College of Environmental Studies, Western Washington University, 516 High St., Bellingham, WA 98225-9079, U.S.A. **Online address:** bfs@admsec.wwu.edu

SMITH, Brenda. American (born United States), b. 1946. **Genres:** History, Politics/Government, Law. **Career:** Middle school instructor, 1968-69; Reynoldsburg, middle and high school instructor, 1970-71; Ohio Statehouse, political speech writer, 1972-74; Josephinum College, public relations writer, 1976-78; Merrill Publishing, editor, 1979-91, Social Studies Department, interim manager, 1990; editor of elementary and secondary social studies texts, 1991-. **Publications:** The Collapse of the Soviet Union, 1994; Egypt: Land of the Pharoahs, 1995; (ed. with S. Brown) Research, Teaching and Learning in Higher Education, 1995; Egypt of the Pharoahs, 1996; Wake Up, Charlie Dragon!, 1997; (with R.T. Sataloff) Choral Pedagogy, 1999; Breaking Through, 2001; Bridging The Gap College Reading, 2003; Lawyers Gone Wild, 2005; 500 Tips on Assessment, 2007; A Football Goalpost Killed My Son, 2008. EDITOR: Human Heritage: A World History, 1985; World History: The Human Experience, 1992; (with G. Williams) The Best Kept Secrets for Winning Scholarships, 2003. **Address:** c/o Publicity Director, Lucent Books Inc., PO Box 289011, San Diego, CA 92198-9011, U.S.A.

SMITH, Brian. Irish (born Ireland), b. 1949. **Genres:** Animals/Pets, Cultural/Ethnic Topics, History, Sports/Fitness, Mythology/Folklore, Genealogy/Heraldry, Theology/Religion. **Career:** Irish Horse Board, education officer, 1977-83; Ericsson Systems Expertise Ltd., publishing manager, 1987-. Writer. **Publications:** The Horse in Ireland, 1992; (with I. Mostafa) The Militarisation of Public Administration in Bangladesh, 1996; A Guide to Tracing Your Mayo Ancestors, 1997, 2nd ed., 2010; The Christmas Rose, 1997; (with J.G. Ryan) A Guide to Tracing Your Dublin Ancestors, 1998; (with D. Duke) Prayer Quest: Breaking through to Your God-Given Dreams and Destiny, 2004; (ed. with T. Williams) Operating Department Practice A-Z, 2004; (with S. Harris and J. Harris) Not Even a Hint: A Study Guide for Women, 2004; 3Ds Max 2009 Architectural Visualization: Intermediate to Advanced, 2007. **Address:** Ericsson Systems Expertise Ltd., Adelphi Ctr., Upper Georges St., Dun Laoghaire, DU 2, Ireland. **Online address:** bcsmith@eircom.net

SMITH, Bruce L. R. American (born United States), b. 1936. **Genres:** Politics/Government, Education, Young Adult Non-fiction. **Career:** Columbia University, professor of political science, 1966-79; U.S. Department of State, staff, 1980-81; Brookings Institution, Center for Public Policy Education, senior staff, 1981-99; George Mason University, visiting professor. Writer. **Publications:** The governance of Berlin, 1959; Concept of Scientific Choice, 1965; The Rand Corporation: Case Study of a Non-Profit Advisory Corporation, 1966; (with W.S. Sayre) Government, Technology, and Social Problems, 1969; (with J.J. Karlesky) The State of Academic Science, vol. I: The Role of the Universities in the Nation's Research and Development Effort, vol. II: Background Papers, Transaction Publishers, 1977; (with M.G. Fromm) The Facilitating Environment: Clinical Applications of Winnicot's Theories, 1989; American Science Policy since World War II, 1990; The Advisers: Scientists in the Policy Process, 1992; (with J.D. Mayer and A.L. Fitschler) Closed Minds: Politics and Ideology in American Universities, 2008. EDITOR: (with D.C. Hague) The Dilemma of Accountability in Modern Government: Independence versus Control, 1971; (eith N. Hollander) The Administration of Medicare, 1973; The Politics of School Decentralization, 1973; New Political Economy, 1975; (with J.D. Carroll) Improving the Accountability and Performance of Government, 1982; The Higher Civil Service in Europe and Canada: Lessons for the United States, 1984; The State of Graduate Education, 1985; The Next Steps in Central America, 1991; (with G. Danilenko) Law and Democracy in the New Russia, 1993; (with C.E. Barfield) Technology, R&D and the Economy, 1996; (with A. Harwood) Sequencing?: Financial Strategies for Developing Countries, 1997; Future of Biomedical Research, 1997. **Address:** School of Public Policy, George Mason Univeristy, 3401 N Fairfax Dr., Arlington, VA 22201, U.S.A. **Online address:** brucelrsmith@aol.com

SMITH, Bruce R. American (born United States), b. 1946. **Genres:** Literary Criticism And History, Theatre, Art/Art History, Cultural/Ethnic Topics, Gay And Lesbian Issues. **Career:** Georgetown University, assistant professor, 1972-78, associate professor, 1978-87, professor of English, 1987-2003, director of graduate program in English, 1987-91, director of undergraduate studies in English, 1992-95; Shakespeare Association of America, president, 1994-95; Middlebury College, Bread Loaf School of English, faculty, 1994-98, 2000-10; University of Southern California, professor of English, 2003-04, College distinguished professor of English, 2004-08, Dean's professor of English, 2008-, director of graduate program in English, 2005-06, Department of English, chair, 2006-08. Writer. **Publications:** Ancient Scripts and Modern Experience on the English Stage, 1500-1700, 1988; Homosexual Desire in Shakespeare's England: A Cultural Poetics, 1991; Roasting the Swan of Avon: Shakespeare's Redoubtable Enemies and Dubious Friends, 1994; The Acoustic World of Early Modern England: Attending to the O-Factor, 1999; Shakespeare and Masculinity, 2000; (ed.) Twelfth Night, or, What You Will: Text and Contexts, 2001; The Key of Green: Passion and Perception in Renaissance Culture, 2008; Phenomenal Shakespeare, 2010. Works appear in anthologies. Contributor to literature journals. **Address:** Department of English, University of Southern California, THH 404G, 3551 Trousdale Pkwy., Los Angeles, CA 90089-4012, U.S.A. **Online address:** brucesmi@usc.edu

SMITH, Carolyn Jeanne. American (born United States), b. 1946. **Genres:** Music, Biography, Bibliography. **Career:** Kansas State University, instructor, 1979-83, assistant professor, 1983-86, associate professor, 1986-93, professor of library studies, 1994; humanities reference librarian, 1983-86, humanities collection librarian, 1983-94, music librarian, 1986-94; Texas A&M University, Evans Library, music collection and development librarian, 1994-, senior lecturer in library science and in philosophy and humanities, cataloging and performance studies librarian and associate professor. Writer. **Publications:** William Walton: A Bio-Bibliography, 1988; Peter Maxwell Davies: A Bio-Bibliography, 1995; Kenneth Leighton: A Bio-Bibliography, 2004. **Address:** Sterling C. Evans Library Annex, Texas A & M University, Rm. 316L, 5000 TAMU, College Station, TX 77843-5000, U.S.A. **Online address:** c-smith50@library.tamu.edu

SMITH, Charles R. American (born United States), b. 1969?. **Genres:** Novels, Novellas/Short Stories, Picture/Board Books, Young Adult Non-fiction. **Career:** Photographer and writer. **Publications:** Dance with Me, 2004; Let's Play Basketball!, 2004; Let's Play Baseball!, 2006; Twelve Rounds to Glory: The Story of Muhammad Ali, 2007; Chameleon (young- adult novel), 2008; The Mighty Twelve: Superheroes of Greek Myth, 2008. OTHERS: Rim Shots: Basketball Pix, Rolls, and Rhythms, 1999; Brown Sugar Babies, 2000; Tall Tales, 2000; Short Takes: Fast-Break Basketball Poetry, 2001; Loki and Alex: The Adventures of a Dog and His Best Friend, 2001; Perfect Harmony: A Musical Journey with the Boys Choir of Harlem, 2002; I Am America, 2003; Hoop Queens (poems), 2003; Hoop Kings (poems), 2004; Diamond Life: Baseball Sights, Sounds, and Swings, 2004; Winning Words: Sports Stories and Photographs, 2008. **Address:** Poughkeepsie, NY , U.S.A. **Online address:** charles@charlesrsmithjr.com

SMITH, Charles Robert Saumarez. (Charles Saumarez Smith). British (born England), b. 1954. **Genres:** Architecture, Antiques/Furnishings, Art/Art History. **Career:** University of Essex, visiting lecturer, 1979-81; Christ's College, Christie's research fellow, 1979-82, honorary fellow; Victoria and Albert Museum, assistant keeper, 1982-90, head of research, 1990-94; Yale Center for British Art, visiting fellow, 1983; Soane Monuments Trust, trustee, 1988-; National Portrait Gallery, secretary, 1994-2002; National Gallery, director, 2002-07; Royal Academy of Arts, secretary and chief executive, 2007-; University of the Arts London, governor. Writer. **Publications:** AS CHARLES SAUMAREZ SMITH: The Building of Castle Howard, 1990; (comp. and ed. with M.H. Wilson) Introducing the Victoria and Albert Museum, 1991; Eighteenth-Century Decoration: Design and the Domestic Interior in England, 1993; (contrib. with A. Shulman) Mario Testino Portraits, 2002; The National Gallery: A Short History, 2009. **Address:** Royal Academy of Arts, Burlington House, Piccadilly, London, GL W1J 0BD, England.

SMITH, Charles Saumarez. See **SMITH, Charles Robert Saumarez.**

SMITH, Christopher. (Christopher John Smith). Scottish/British (born England), b. 1965. **Genres:** History, Archaeology/Antiquities, Autobiography/Memoirs, Economics, Literary Criticism And History. **Career:** University of St. Andrews, School of Classics, professor of ancient history, St. Leonard's College, provost, 1992-; British School at Rome, director, 2009-14. Writer and historian. **Publications:** (As Christopher John Smith) Early Rome and Latium: Economy and Society c. 1000 to 500 BC, 1996; (contrib.) Approaches to the Study of Ritual, 1996; (contrib.) The Development of the Polis in Archaic Greece, 1997; (ed. with H. Parkins) Trade, Traders, and the Ancient City, 1998; (ed. with J. Serrati) Sicily from Aeneas to Augustus: New Approaches in Archaeology and History, 2000; (ed. with E. Bispham) Religion in Archaic and Republican Rome and Italy: Evidence and Experience, 2000; (contrib.) The City of Rome, 2000; (contrib.) Mediterranean Urbanization 800-600, 2005; (as C.J. Smith) The Roman Clan: The Gens from Ancient Ideology to Modern Anthropology, 2006; (contrib.) Ancient Tyranny, 2006; (ed. with A. Powell) Lost Memoirs of Augustus and the Development of Roman Autobiography, 2009. Contributor to periodicals. **Address:** University of Saint Andrews, School of Classics, Swallowgate, St. Andrews, FF KY16 9AL, Scotland. **Online address:** cjs6@st-andrews.ac.uk

SMITH, Christopher John. *See* **SMITH, Christopher.**

SMITH, C(hristopher) U. M. British (born England), b. 1930. **Genres:** Biology, History, Philosophy, Sciences, Medicine/Health. **Career:** University of Aston, assistant lecturer, lecturer, 1959-73, senior lecturer in biological science, 1973, senior tutor, sub-dean, 1987-90, dean of faculty of science, 1990-91, dean of the faculty of life and health science, 1991-94, honorary visiting fellow; British Association for the Advancement of Science, Archaeology and Anthropology Sectioin, honorary secretary, 1984-92, Birmingham Branch, chair, 2002-University of Birmingham, honorary research fellow; Royal Society of Medicine, fellow; Royal Society of Arts, fellow; International Society for the History of the Neurosciences, founding memeber, president, 1998-99; Institute of Biology, fellow, West Midlands Branch, chair, 1999-2003. Writer. **Publications:** The Architecture of the Body, 1964; Molecular Biology: A Structural Approach, 1968; The Brain: Towards an Understanding, 1970; The Problem of Life: An Essay on the Origins of Biological Thought, 1976; Elements of Molecular Neurobiology, 1989, 3rd ed., 2002; Biology of Sensory Systems, 2000, 2nd ed., 2008; (ed. with R. Arnott and S. Finger) Trepanation: History-Discovery Theory, 2003; (ed. with R. Arnott) The Genius of Erasmus Darwin, 2005; (ed. with H. Whitaker and S. Finger) Brain, Mind and Medicine: Essays in Eighteenth Century Neuroscience, 2007; (with S. Finger, E. Frixione, W. Clower) Animal Spirits: A Physiological Odyssey, 2010. Contributor to journals. **Address:** Department of Vision Sciences, Aston University, Aston Triangle, Birmingham, B4 7ET, England. **Online address:** c.u.m.smith@aston.ac.uk

SMITH, Clive Stafford. British (born England), b. 1959. **Genres:** Biography, Law. **Career:** Louisiana Crisis Assistance Center, founder, 1993-; Reprieve, founder, lawyer, 1999-, UK Branch, legal director; Guantánamo Bay, attorney for prisoners, 2004-; Southern Center for Human Rights, lawyer; Gulf Region Advocacy Center, founding member, 2002. Writer. **Publications:** (Contrib.) Welcome To Hell, 2nd ed., 2004; Bad Men: Guantanamo Bay and the Secret Prisons, 2007; The Eight O'Clock Ferry to the Windward Side, 2007. **Address:** Reprieve, PO Box 52742, London, GL EC4P 4WS, England. **Online address:** clive@reprieve.org.uk

SMITH, Craig. Swiss/American (born United States), b. 1950?. **Genres:** Novels. **Career:** Arkansas State University, professor; University of Northern Colorado, professor. Writer. **Publications:** Silent She Sleeps in UK as The Whisper of Leaves, 1997; The Painted Messiah, 2007; The Blood Lance, 2008; Cold Rain, 2009; Every Dark Place, 2011. Contributor to periodicals. **Address:** c/o Author Mail, Southern Illinois University Press, PO Box 3697, Carbondale, IL 62902-3697, U.S.A.

SMITH, Cynthia Leitich. American (born United States), b. 1967. **Genres:** Children's Fiction, Humor/Satire. **Career:** Department of Health and Human Services, law clerk, 1994-95; Vermont College, M.F.A. Program in Writing for Children and Young Adults, faculty, 2005-. Writer. **Publications:** Jingle Dancer, 2000; Rain Is Not My Indian Name, 2001; Indian Shoes, 2002; (with G.L. Smith) Santa Knows, 2006; Tantalize, 2007; Eternal, 2009; Holler Loudly, 2010; Blessed, 2011; Tantalize: Kieren's Story, 2011. Contributor to periodicals. **Address:** c/o. Ginger Knowlton, Curtis Brown Ltd., Ten Astor Pl., New York, NY 10003, U.S.A. **Online address:** cynthia@cynthialeitichsmith.com

SMITH, Dale L. American (born United States), b. 1953. **Genres:** Politics/Government, Business/Trade/Industry, Economics, Military/Defense/Arms Control. **Career:** GLOBUS Research Group, Science Center Berlin, research fellow, 1982-88; Florida State University, Department of Political Science, assistant professor, 1988-94, associate professor, 1994-2009, professor, 2009-, director of graduate studies, 1995-99, International Affairs Program, interim director, 1996-97, chair of department, 1999-, William A. Kerr Intercultural Education and Dialogue Initiative, faculty affiliate, 2010-. Writer. **Publications:** (Co-author) The Challenge of Japan: Before World War II and After, 1992; (ed. with J.L. Ray) The 1992 Project and the Future of Integration in Europe, 1993. Contributor to journals. **Address:** Department of Political Science, Florida State University, 531 Bellamy Bldg., Tallahassee, FL 32306-2230, U.S.A. **Online address:** dale.smith@fsu.edu

SMITH, Daniel Jordan. American (born United States), b. 1961. **Genres:** History, Young Adult Non-fiction, Cultural/Ethnic Topics. **Career:** Brown University, Population Studies and Training Center, Mellon Postdoctoral Research Fellow, 1999-2001, assistant professor, 2001-04, associate professor, 2007-, Stanley J. Bernstein assistant professor for the social sciences and international relations, 2004-07, Population Studies and Training Center, associate director, 2006-09, anthropology undergraduate advisor. Writer. **Publications:** A Culture of Corruption: Everyday Deception and Popular Discontent in Nigeria, 2007. Contributor to books and periodicals. **Address:** Population Studies and Training Center, Brown University, Cabinet 306, 68 Waterman St., PO Box 1836, Providence, RI 02912, U.S.A. **Online address:** daniel_j_smith@brown.edu

SMITH, Dave. American (born United States), b. 1942. **Genres:** Novels, Novellas/Short Stories, Poetry, Literary Criticism And History. **Career:** Poquoson High School, teacher of English and French, football coach, 1965-67; Christopher Newport College, part-time instructor, 1970-72, Thomas Nelson Community College, instructor, 1970-72; College of William and Mary, instructor, 1971; Western Michigan University, instructor, 1973-74; Cottey College, assistant professor, 1974-75; University of Utah, assistant professor, 1976-79, associate professor of English, 1979-81, director of the creative writing program, 1976-81; State University of New York, visiting professor of English, 1980-81; University of Florida, associate professor of English and director of creative writing, 1981-82; Bennington College, faculty, 1981-87; Virginia Commonwealth University, professor of English, 1982-90; Louisiana State University, Boyd professor of English, The Southern Review, editor, 1990-2002; University of Cincinnatti, Elliston professor of poetry, 1996; Johns Hopkins University, The Writing Seminars, Elliott Coleman professor of poetry, 2002-, chairman, 2005-. **Publications:** Bull Island, 1970; Mean Rufus Throw Down, 1973; The Fisherman's Whore, 1974; Drunks, 1975; Cumberland Station, 1976; In Dark, Sudden with Light, 1977; Goshawk, Antelope, 1979; Blue Spruce, 1981; Apparitions, 1981; Homage to Edgar Allan Poe, 1981; Onliness (novel), 1981; Dream Flights, 1981; Photograph of a Confederate Soldier Standing on Rocks in the James River at Richmond, Virginia, 1983; Gray Soldiers, 1983; In the House of the Judge, 1983; Southern Delights (short stories), 1984; Local Assays: On Contemporary American Poetry, 1985; The Roundhouse Voices (poems), 1985; The Roadhouse Voices, 1985; Cuba Night (poems), 1990; Night Pleasures (poems), 1992; Fate's Kite: Poems, 1991-1995 (poems), 1995; Tremble, 1996; Floating on Solitude: Three Volumes of Poetry, 1996; The Wick of Memory: New and Selected Poems, 1974-2000, (poems), 2000; Little Boats, Unsalvageable, 2005; Hunting Men: Reflections on a Life in American Poetry, 2006; (with R. Demott) Afield: American Writers on Bird Dogs, 2010; Hawks on Wires: Poems, 2005-2010, 2011. EDITOR: New Virginia Review, 1980; The Pure Clear Word: Essays on the Poetry of James Wright, 1982; (with D. Bottoms) The Morrow Anthology of Younger American Poets, 1985; (and intro.) The Essential Poe, 1991. **Address:** The Writing Seminars, Johns Hopkins University, 3400 N Charles St., Baltimore, MD 21218, U.S.A. **Online address:** davesmith@jhu.edu

SMITH, David A(lden). American (born United States), b. 1956. **Genres:** Third World, Social Sciences, History. **Career:** University of South Carolina, visiting assistant professor of sociology, 1983-84; East-West Center, population fellow, 1984; University of California, assistant professor to associate professor of sociology and urban planning, 1984-98, acting chairperson of department, 1993, 1996, School of Social Sciences, professor of sociology, 1999-; Center for Far Eastern Studies, fellow, 1988; Social Problems (academic journal), editor. **Publications:** (Ed. with J. Borocz and contrib.) A New World Order? Global Transformations in the Late Twentieth Century, 1995; Third World Cities in Global Perspective: The Political Economy of Uneven Urbanization, 1996; (ed. with D.J. Solinger and S.C. Topik) States and Sovereignty in the Global Economy, 1999; (ed. with J. Lardner) Inequality Matters: The Growing Economic Divide in America and Its Poisonous Consequences, 2005; State, Sewing and Global Sourcing: Garment Production in Vietnam's Economic Transition, 2008. Contributor of articles to books and journals. **Address:** Department of Sociology, University of California, 160 Aldrich Hall, 5291 Social Sciences Plz. B, PO Box 5100, Irvine, CA 92697-5100, U.S.A. **Online address:** dasmith@uci.edu

SMITH, David Alexander. American (born United States), b. 1953. **Genres:** Novels, Urban Studies. **Career:** Boston Financial, senior vice president, 1975-89; Recapitalization Advisors, founder and president, 1989-2007; CAS Financial Advisory Services, founder and chief executive officer, 2007-; Affordable Housing Institute, founder. **Publications:** Subsidized Housing as a Tax Shelter, 1982. NOVELS: Marathon, 1982; Rendezvous, 1988; Homecoming, 1990; In the Cube: A Novel of Future Boston, 1993; (ed.) Future Boston: The History of a City, 1990-2100, 1994. Works appear in anthologies. Contributor to journals. **Address:** Affordable Housing Institute, 38 Chauncy St., Ste. 600, Boston, MA 02111-2301, U.S.A. **Online address:** dsmith@affordablehousinginstitute.org

SMITH, David E(lvin). American (born United States), b. 1939. **Genres:** Medicine/Health, Photography. **Career:** Haight Ashbury Free Clinic, founder, 1967-, medical director and president; Merritt Perralta Chemical Dependence Recovery Hospital, research director, 1967-; Journal of Psychoactive Drugs, founder and publisher, 1967-, executive editor; University of California Medical Center, assistant clinical professor, associate clinical professor, 1967-, adjunct professor; MPI Treatment Services at Summit Medical Center, research director, 1984-; University of Nevada Medical School, visiting associate clinical professor; State of California, Department of Alcohol and Drug Programs, technical assistance, 1998-2000, medical director, 2005-06, Department of Health Alcohol and Drug Program, Substance Abuse Prevention and Treatment, staff, 1998-2005, Substance Abuse Policy Research, California Collaborative Center, medical director, staff, 2000-03; Betty Ford Center, advisor; Newport Academy in Southern California, Adolescent Addiction Medicine, chair; Center Point Drug Rehabilitation Center, medical director; Prometa Center, executive medical director. **Publications:** Drug Abuse Papers, 1969; (ed.) The New Social Drug: Cultural, Medical and Legal Perspectives on Marijuana, 1970; (with J. Luce) Love Needs Care: A History of San Francisco's Haight-Ashbury Free Medical Clinic and its Pioneer Role in Treating Drug-Abuse Problems, 1971; The Free Clinic: Community Approaches to Health Care and Drug Abuse, 1972; (ed. with G.R. Gay) It's So Good, Don't Even Try it Once: Heroin in Perspective, 1972; (ed. with D.R. Wesson) Uppers and Downers, 1973; (with H.J. Cornacchia and D.J. Bentel) Drugs in the Classroom: A Conceptual Model for School Programs, 1973, 2nd ed., 1978; (with D.R. Wesson) Barbiturates, Their Use, Misuse and Abuse, 1977; (co-ed.) A Multicultural View of Drug Abuse: Proceedings of the National Drug Abuse Conference, 1977, 1978; (co-ed.) Amphetamine Use, Misuse and Abuse: Proceedings of the National Amphetamine Conference, 1978, 1979; (co-ed.) PCP, Problems and Prevention, 1982; (co-ed.) Substance Abuse in the Workplace, 1984; (ed. with D.R. Wesson) Treating the Cocaine Abuser, 1985; (ed. with D.R. Wesson) The Benzodiazepines: Current Standards for Medical Practice, 1985; (with R.B. Seymour) Drugfree: A Unique, Positive Approach to Staying Off Alcohol and Other Drugs, 1987; (with R.B. Seymour) Guide to Psychoactive Drugs: An Up-To-The-Minute Reference to Mind-Altering Substances, 1987; (with R.B. Seymour) Physician's Guide to Psychoactive Drugs, 1987; (ed. with D.R. Wesson) Treating Cocaine Dependency, 1988; Treating Opiate Dependency, 1989; (contrib. with R.B. Seymour) A New Connection: A Problem-Solving Approach to Chemical Dependency, 1992; (with D.R. Wesson and S.C. Steffens) Crack and Ice: Treating Smokable Stimulant Abuse, 1992; Clinicians Guide to Substance Abuse, 2001. **Address:** Haight Ashbury Free Clinics, 558 Clayton St., PO Box 29917, San Francisco, CA 94117-2999, U.S.A. **Online address:** drsmith@drdave.org

SMITH, David L(awrence). British (born England), b. 1963. **Genres:** History, Politics/Government. **Career:** Cambridge University, Selwyn College, fellow, 1988-, tutor for admissions, 1992-2003, director of studies in history, 1992-, affiliated lecturer in history, 1995-, praelector, 1996-2006, tutor for graduate students, 2004-; University of Chicago, visiting assistant professor, 1991; Kyungpook National University, visiting professor, 2004. Writer. **Publications:** Oliver Cromwell: Politics and Religion in the English Revolution, 1640-1658, 1991; Louis XIV, 1992; Constitutional Royalism and the Search for Settlement, 1640-1649, 1994; A History of the Modern British Isles, 1603-1707: The Double Crown, 1998; The Stuart Parliaments, 1603-1689, 1999; (with G. Seel) The Early Stuart Kings, 1603-1642, 2001; (with G. Seel) Crown and Parliaments, 1558-1689, 2001; (with P. Little) Parliaments and Politics During the Cromwellian Protectorate, 1654-1659, 2007. EDITOR: (with R. Strier and D. Bevington) The Theatrical City: Culture, Theatre, and Politics in London, 1576-1649, 1995; Cromwell and the Interregnum, 2003; (with J. McElligott) Royalists and Royalism During the English Civil Wars, 2007; (with J. McElligott) Royalists and Royalism During the Interregnum, 2010; (with M.J. Braddick) The Experience of Revolution in Stuart Britain and Ireland: Essays for John Morrill, 2011. Contributor to journals. **Address:** Selwyn College, Cambridge University, Cambridge, CB CB3 9DQ, England. **Online address:** dls10@cam.ac.uk

SMITH, David Livingstone. American (born United States), b. 1953?. **Genres:** Philosophy, Psychology, Intellectual History, Race Relations. **Career:** Antioch University, Center for British Studies, lecturer in psychology; Regent's College London, interim dean and director of graduate programs; University of New England, associate professor of philosophy; New England Institute for Cognitive Science and Evolutionary Psychology, founding director; University of London, visiting professor; Middlesex University, visiting professor; Surrey University, visiting professor; Ithaca College, visiting professor. Writer. **Publications:** Hidden Conversations: An Introduction to Communicative Psychoanalysis, 1991; Freuds Philosophy of the Unconscious, 1999; Approaching Psychoanalysis, 1999; Psychoanalysis in Focus, 2003; Why We Lie: The Evolutionary Roots of Deception and the Unconscious Mind, 2004; The Most Dangerous Animal: Human Nature and the Origins of War, 2007; Less Than Human: Why We Demean, Enslave, and Exterminate Others, 2011. **Address:** Department of Philosophy, University of New England, 11 Hills Beach Rd., Biddeford, ME 04005, U.S.A. **Online address:** dsmith@une.edu

SMITH, Deborah. Also writes as Jackie Leigh. American (born United States), b. 1955. **Genres:** Novels, Novellas/Short Stories. **Career:** Neighbor Newspapers, reporter and editor, 1980-83; American Health Consultants, medical writer, 1983-86; author, 1986-; Belle Books, founding partner, publisher and editor, 2000-, editorial director. **Publications:** AS JACKIE LEIGH: Proud Surrender, 1986; Cupid's Verdict, 1987; No Holds Barred, 1987; A Sweet Talkin' Man, 1987; Young At Heart, 1987; Angel On My Shoulder, 1987. NOVELS: Jed's Sweet Revenge, 1988; Hold on Tight, 1988; Caught by Surprise, 1988; Hot Touch, 1989; Legends, 1990; Silver Fox and the Red-Hot Dove, 1990; Sara's Surprise, 1990; Honey and Smoke, 1990; Stranger in Camelot, 1991; Heart of the Dragon, 1991; Follow the Sun, 1991; The Beloved Woman, 1991; Miracle, 1991; Blue Willow, 1993; Silk and Stone, 1994; A Place to Call Home, 1997; When Venus Fell, 1998; On Bear Mountain: A Novel, 2001; (co-author) Reunion at Mossy Creek: A Collective Novel, 2002; The Stone Flower Garden: A Novel, 2002; Alice at Heart, 2002; Sweet Hush: A Novel, 2003; Summer at Mossy Creek, 2003; Diary of a Radical Mermaid' 2004; Charming Grace: A Novel, 2004; Crossroads Café, 2006; At Home in Mossy Creek: A Collective Novel Featuring the Voices of, 2007; A Gentle Rain, 2007; (co-author) On Grandma's Porch, 2007; (co-author) Mossy Creek: A Collective Novel, 2007. CHEROKEE TRILOGY SERIES: Kat's Tale, 1989; Tempting the Wolf, 1989; Sundance and the Princess, 1989. **Address:** BelleBooks, PO Box 300921, Memphis, TN 38130, U.S.A. **Online address:** deb@deborah-smith.com

SMITH, Delia. British (born England), b. 1941. **Genres:** Food And Wine. **Career:** Daily Mirror Magazine, cookery writer, 1969; Evening Standard, columnist, 1972-85; Radio Times, columnist, through 1986; Sainsbury's, consultant, 1991-; Sainsbury's The Magazine, consultant editor of food pages and founder, 1993-; television showhost, through 2003. **Publications:** How to Cheat at Cooking, 1971; Country Fare, 1973; Recipes from Country Inns and Restaurants, 1973; Family Fare, parts 1, 2 and 3, 1973-75; The Evening Standard Cook Book, 1974; Country Recipes from Look East, 1975; More Country Recipes from Look East, 1976; Frugal Food, 1976; Delia Smith's Book of Cakes, 1977; Recipes from Look East, 1977; Food for Our Times, 1978; Cookery Course, 3 vols., 1978-81; Delia Smith's The Complete Cookery Course, 1982; A Feast for Lent: Readings and Prayer, 1983; A Feast for Advent, 1983; One Is Fun, 1985; (ed.) Food Aid Cookery Book, 1986; A Journey into God, 1988; Complete Illustrated Cookery Course, 1989; Delia Smith's Christmas, 1992; Delia Smith's Summer Collection, 1993; Delia Smith's Winter Collection, 1995; Delia Smith's Frugal Food: Tempting Recipes for Careful Cooks, 1997; Delia's How to Cook: Book One, 1998, Book Two, 1999, Book Three, 2001; Delia's Hot to Cook, 2001; Delia's Vegetarian Collection, 2002; The Delia Collection: Soup, 2003; Delia Collection: Fish, 2003; Delia Collection; Chocolate, 2003; Delia Collection: Chicken, 2003; Delia's Kitchen Garden: A Beginners' Guide to Growing and Cooking Fruit and Vegetables, 2004; The Smart Cook Collection: Italian, 2005; Soup, 2005; Chicken, 2005; Fish, 2006; The Delia Collection-Puddings, 2006; Delia's Kitchen Garden, 2007; Delia's Happy Christmas, 2009. **Address:** Deborah Owen Ltd., 78 Narrow St., Limehouse, London, GL E14 8BP, England.

SMITH, Denis. Canadian (born Canada), b. 1932. **Genres:** History, Politics/Government, Biography. **Career:** University of Toronto, lecturer in political science, 1956-58; York University, assistant professor of political science, 1960-63; Canadian Forum, editor, 1962-64; Trent University, associate professor to professor of political science, 1963-82, vice-president of the university, 1964-67; Journal of Canadian Studies, editor, 1966-75; Canadian Forum, editor, 1975-79; University of Western Ontario, professor of political science, 1982-96, dean of social science, 1982-88, professor emeritus, 1996-. Writer. **Publications:** Bleeding Hearts Bleeding Country: Canada and Quebec Crisis, 1971; Gentle Patriot: A Political Biography of Walter Gordon, 1973; Diplomacy of Fear: Canada and the Cold War, 1988; Rogue Tory: The Life and Legend of John G. Diefenbaker, 1995; The Prisoners of Cabrera: Napoleon's Forgotten Soldiers, 1809-1814, 2001; Ignatieff's World: A Liberal Leader for the 21th century?, 2006; Ignatieff's World Updated: Iggy Goes to Ottawa, 2009. **Address:** 119 Dunbarton Ct., Ottawa, ON K1K 4L5, Canada. **Online address:** smith_3@sympatico.ca

SMITH, Derek D. (Derek Delbert Smith). American (born United States), b. 1978. **Genres:** Novels. **Career:** Latham & Watkins, associate; University of Oxford, lecturer in international relations. Writer. **Publications:** Deterring America: Rogue States and the Proliferation of Weapons of Mass Destruction, 2006. **Address:** Washington, DC 20001, U.S.A. **Online address:** derek@derekdsmith.com

SMITH, Derek Delbert. *See* **SMITH, Derek D.**

SMITH, Diane. American (born United States), b. 1949. **Genres:** Novels, Young Adult Fiction, Westerns/Adventure. **Career:** Writer. **Publications:** Letters from Yellowstone, 1999; Pictures from an Expedition, 2002. **Address:** c/o Author Mail, Penguin Putnam, 345 Hudson St., New York, NY 10014, U.S.A.

SMITH, D. J. *See* **SMITH, D. James.**

SMITH, D. James. (D. J. Smith). American (born United States), b. 1955. **Genres:** Novels, Young Adult Fiction, Poetry, Animals/Pets, History, Humor/Satire. **Career:** Writer and educator. **Publications:** (As D.J. Smith) Prayers for the Dead Ventriloquist, 1995; Fast Company, 1999; My Brother's Passion (novel), 2004; Boys of San Joaquin, 2005; Dog Days for the Boys of San Joaquin, 2006; Probably the World's Best Story About a Dog and the Girl Who Loved Me, 2006; It Was September When We Ran Away the First Time, 2008. Contributor to periodicals. **Address:** c/o Barbara Markowitz, Barbara Markowitz Literary Agency, PO Box 41709, Los Angeles, CA 90041, U.S.A.

SMITH, Douglas K. American (born United States), b. 1949?. **Genres:** Administration/Management, Business/Trade/Industry, Philosophy, Psychology. **Career:** Columbia School of Journalism, Punch Sulzberger Leadership Program, executive-director; Web River Media, chief executive officer and co-founder. Writer, lawyer, educator and consultant. **Publications:** (With R.J. Cohen and M.E. Swerdlik) Psychological Testing and Assessment: An Introduction to Tests and Measurement, 1988; (with R.C. Alexander) Fumbling the Future: How Xerox Invented, then Ignored, the First Personal Computer, 1988; (with J.R. Katzenbach) The Wisdom of Teams: Creating the High-Performance Organization, 1993, rev. ed., 2003; Taking Charge of Change: 10 Principles for Managing People and Performance, 1996; Make Success Measurable!: A Mindbook-workbook for Setting Goals and Taking Action, 1999; (co-author) Sources of the African Past Case Studies of Five Nineteenth-Century African Societies, 1999; (with J.R. Katzenbach) Discipline of Teams: A Mindbook-Workbook for Delivering Small Group Performance, 2001; On Value and Values: Thinking Differently About We in an Age of Me, 2004; (with J.R. Katzenbach) The Discipline of Teams, 2008. Contributor to periodicals. **Address:** Graduate School of Journalism, Columbia University, Rm. 702A, 2950 Broadway, New York, NY 10027, U.S.A. **Online address:** dougsmith@douglasksmith.com

SMITH, Duane Allan. American (born United States), b. 1937. **Genres:** History, Social Sciences. **Career:** Fort Lewis College, assistant professor, 1964-67, associate professor, 1967-72, professor of history, 1972-. Writer. **Publications:** Rocky Mountain Mining Camps: The Urban Frontier, 1967; (with Ubbelohde and Benson) A Colorado History, 1972, 8th ed., 2001; Horace Tabor: His Life and the Legend, 1973; Silver Saga: The Story of Caribou, Colorado, 1974, rev. ed., 2003; Colorado Mining, 1977; (with Weber) Fortunes Are for the Few: Letters of Forty-Niner, 1977; Rocky Mountain Boom Town: A History of Durango, 1980; Secure the Shadow: Lachlan McLean, Colorado Mining Photographer, 1980; (with Vandenbusche) A Land Alone: Colorado's Western Slope, 1981; (with Ubbelohde and Benson) A Colorado Reader, 1982; Song of the Hammer and Drill, 1982; When Coal Was King: A History of Crested Butte, Colorado 1880-1952, 1984; (with Lamm) Pioneers and Politicans: Ten Colorado Governors in Profile, 1984; (with Metcalf and

Noel) Colorado: Heritage of the Highest State, 1984; Mining America: The Industry and the Environment 1800-1980, 1987; Mesa Verde National Park, 1988; The Birth of Colorado, 1989; Sacred Trust: The Birth and Development of Fort Lewis College, 1991; (with Ellis) Colorado: A History in Photographs, 1991; Prisoner of the Emperor: An American POW in World War II, 1992; Rocky Mountain West: Colorado, Wyoming, and Montana 1859-1915, 1992; (with Noel) Colorado: The Highest State, 1995; Durango Diary, 1996; A Tale of Two Towns: A Mining and a Farming Community in the 1890s, 1997; They Came to Play: A Photographic History of Colorado Baseball, 1997; Colorado: Our Colorful State, 1999; The Legendary Line: Durango to Silverton, 1999; The Substance and the Shadow: Capturing the Spirit of Southwestern Colorado: A Pictorial History, 1880s-1920s, 2000; (with Brown) No One Ailing Except a Physician, 2001; Staking a Claim in History: The Evolution of the Homestake Mining Company, 2001; Henry M. Teller, 2002; The Ballad of Baby Doe, 2002; A Visit with the Tomboy Bride, 2003; Night Journey to Vicksburg, 2003; Quick History of Silverton, 2003; Colorado: A History in Photographs, 2005; The Rise of the Silver Queen: Georgetown, Colorado, 1859-1896, 2005; Sacred Trust: The Birth and Development of Fort Lewis College, 2005; Crested Butte: From Coal Camp to Ski Town, 2005; San Juan Bonanza: Western Colorado's Mining legacy, 2006; A Time for Peace: Fort Lewis, Colorado, 1878-1891, 2006; Rocky Mountain Heartland: Colorado, Montana, and Wyoming in the Twentieth Century, 2008; Mountain Idylls and Other Poems, 2008; (with R.D. Lamm) Pioneers and Politicians: Colorado Governors in Profile, 2008; Trail of Gold and Silver: Mining in Colorado, 1859-2009, 2009; San Juan Legacy: Life in the Mining Camps, 2009; Mesa Verde National Park, 2009; Sisters in Sin: The Nellie Spencer Story, 2011; The Eighth Illinois Cavalry and Henry Teller, forthcoming. **Address:** Department of History, Fort Lewis College, 1000 Rim Dr., Durango, CO 81301, U.S.A.

SMITH, Dustin Beall. American (born United States), b. 1940?. **Genres:** Autobiography/Memoirs. **Career:** University of Scranton, visiting writer; Columbia University, Artist-as-Teacher Program, faculty; Gettysburg College, Peer Learning Program, creative writing teacher and coordinator; Adams County Arts Council, Imagination Station, faculty of creative writing, adjunct assistant professor of English. **Publications:** Key Grip: A Memoir of Endless Consequences, 2008. Contributor to periodicals. **Address:** Department of English, Gettysburg College, Rm. 409, Breidenbaugh Hall, N Washington St., PO Box 0397, Gettysburg, PA 17325, U.S.A. **Online address:** dsmith@gettysburg.edu

SMITH, Elizabeth. *See* **HAY, Elizabeth (Jean).**

SMITH, Elizabeth A(ngele) T(aft). American (born United States), b. 1958. **Genres:** Architecture, Art/Art History, Essays, History. **Career:** Sylvia Leonard Wolf Inc., fine arts specialist and associate, 1977-82; Museum of Contemporary Art-Los Angeles, assistant curator, 1983-86, associate curator, 1987-90, curator, 1990-99, Museum of Contemporary Art, Chicago, James W. Alsdorf chief curator, 1999-2009, deputy director for programs; University of Southern California, School of Fine Arts, adjunct professor, 1992-99; Art Gallery of Ontario (AGO), executive director of curatorial affairs, 2010-. Writer. **Publications:** Blueprints for Modern Living: History and Legacy of the Case Study Houses, 1989; Rebecca Horn: Diving through Buster's Bedroom, 1990; Eloquent Abstraction (essay), 1991; (intro.) Rita and Taft Schreiber Collection, 1991; Erik Levine: Essay, 1993; Urban Revisions: Current Projects for the Public Realm, 1994; Uta Barth, 1995; Paradise Cage: Kiki Smith and Coop Himmelblau, 1996; (with A. Cruz and A. Jones) Cindy Sherman: Retrospective, 1997; (co-ed.) Fin de siglo: cien añ de arquitectura, 1998; (co-ed.) At the End of the Century: One Hundred Years of Architecture, 1998; Techno Architecture, 2000; (contrib.) Architecture of R.M. Schindler, 2001; (contrib.) Katharina Fritsch, 2001; (contrib.) Matta in America: Paintings and Drawings of the 1940s, 2001; Case Study Houses, 2002; Donald Moffett: What Barbara Jordan Wore, 2002; Life Death Love Hate Pleasure Pain, 2002; (ed. and contrib.) Lee Bontecou: A Retrospective, 2003; Between the Museum and the City: Garofalo Architects, 2004; Case Study Houses: 1945-1966: The Californian Impetus, 2006. Contributor to periodicals. **Address:** Art Gallery of Ontario, 317 Dundas St. W, Toronto, ON M5T 1G4, Canada.

SMITH, Emily Wing. American (born United States), b. 1980?. **Genres:** Novels. **Career:** Writer. **Publications:** The Way He Lived (novel), 2008. Contributor to periodicals. **Address:** c/o Michael Bourret, Dystel & Goderich Literary Management, 1 Union Sq. W, Ste. 904, New York, NY 10003, U.S.A. **Online address:** emilywingsmith@gmail.com

SMITH, Emma. British (born England), b. 1923. **Genres:** Novels, Children's Fiction, Biography, Autobiography/Memoirs. **Career:** Freelance writer. **Publications:** Maidens' Trip, 1948, rev. ed., 1964; The Far Cry, 1949, 2nd ed., 1950; Emily: The Story of a Traveller in US as Emily: The Travelling Guinea Pig, 1959; Out of Hand, 1964; Emily's Voyage, 1966; No Way of Telling, 1972; The Opportunity of a Lifetime, 1978, 2nd ed., 1980; Village Children: A Soviet Experience, 1982; The Great Western Beach: A Memoir of a Cornish Childhood Between the Wars, 2008. **Address:** Curtis Brown Group Ltd., Haymarket House, 28/29 Haymarketm, 4th Fl., London, GL SW1Y 4SP, England.

SMITH, Erin A(nn). American (born United States), b. 1970. **Genres:** Women's Studies And Issues, Theology/Religion, Literary Criticism And History, Social Sciences. **Career:** Duke University, University Writing Program and English Department, instructor, 1993-94, instructor in English, 1994-95, University Writing Program, veteran assistant, 1994-95, Women's Studies Program, teaching assistant, 1994-95, Simone de Beauvoir instructor in literature, 1996-97, Duke University Women's Studies Program, staff assistant, 1996-97; Center for Teaching and Learning, fellow, 1995-96, Partnership for Literacy, adult literacy tutor, 1995-96; University of Texas, assistant professor, 1997-2003, associate professor of American studies and literature, 2003-, associate director of gender studies program, 2007; National Humanities Center, fellow, 2002-03. Writer. **Publications:** Hard-Boiled: Working Class Readers and Pulp Magazines, 2000; Souls and Commodities: Liberal Religion and Print Culture in Twentieth-Century America, forthcoming; What Would Jesus Read?, forthcoming. Contributor of articles to books and periodicals. **Address:** School of Interdisciplinary Studies, University of Texas, 2304, Hoblitzelle Hall, 800 W Campbell Rd., Richardson, TX 75080-3021, U.S.A. **Online address:** erins@utdallas.edu

SMITH, Faye McDonald. American (born United States), b. 1950. **Genres:** Novels, Plays/Screenplays, Writing/Journalism, Education, Literary Criticism And History. **Career:** Journalist and screenwriter. **Publications:** Flight of the Blackbird: A Novel, 1996; Seeking Solutions: A Three-Part Conference Series on Community-Building Strategies, Resident Mobilization and Governance, 1997; Promising Practices, A Vision for Early Childhood Education: Convened December 10-11, 1998, 1999. Contributor to periodicals. **Address:** PO Box 42402, Atlanta, GA 30311-0402, U.S.A.

SMITH, Felipe. Japanese/Jamaican/Argentine (born Argentina), b. 1978. **Genres:** Graphic Novels. **Career:** Manga artist and writer. **Publications:** MBQ, vol. I, 2005, vol. II, 2006, vol. III, 2007. Works appear in anthologies. **Address:** Japan. **Online address:** contact@felipesmith.com

SMITH, Frederick E(screet). (David Farrell). British (born England), b. 1922. **Genres:** Novels, Novellas/Short Stories, Plays/Screenplays, Mystery/Crime/Suspense, Young Adult Fiction. **Career:** Writer. **Publications:** 633 SQUADRON SERIES: 633 Squadron, 1956; Operation Rhine Maiden, 1975; Operation Crucible, 1977; Operation Valkyrie, 1978; Operation Crisis, 1993; Operation Thor, 1994; Operation Cobra, 1995; Operation Defiant, 1995; Operation Titan, 1996; Operation Safeguard, 2007. PERSUADERS SERIES: The Persuaders, 1971; Persuaders... Again, 1976; Persuaders at Large, 1976. NOVELS: Of Masks and Minds, 1954; Laws be Their Enemy, 1955; Lydia Trendennis, 1957; The Sin and the Sinners, 1958; The Grotto of Tiberius, 1961; The Devil Behind Me, 1962; The Storm Knight, 1966; A Killing for the Hawks, 1966; The Wider Sea of Love, 1969; Waterloo, 1970; The Tormented, 1974; Saffron's War, 1975; Saffron's Army, 1976; The War God, 1980; Turning Points in History, 1982; The Dark Cliffs, 1983; The Obsession, 1984; Rage of the Innocent, 1986; Meeting of Stars, 1987; Clash of Stars, 1987; The Devil Behind Me, 1994; Saffron's Trials, 1996; Years of the Fury, 1997; In Presence of My Foes, 1997; The Mysterious Affair, 2010. NONFICTION: Write a Successful Novel, 1991. AS DAVID FARRELL: Temptation Isle, 1962; The Other Cousin, 1962; Two Loves, 1963; Valley of Conflict, 1967; Strange Enemy, 1967; Mullion Rock, 1968. **Address:** c/o Moe Sherrard-Smith, Garthend House, Millington, York, NY YO42 1TX, England. **Online address:** frederickesmith@hathawayroad.fsnet.co.uk

SMITH, F. Todd. American (born United States), b. 1957. **Genres:** Anthropology/Ethnology. **Career:** University of South Dakota, Department of History, teaching assistant, 1981-82; Tulane University, Department of History, teaching assistant, 1985-87; Xavier University of Louisiana, instructor in history, 1987-88, assistant professor of history, 1991-96; Louisiana State University, Museum of Geoscience, historian, 1988-89; Austin Community College, instructor in history, 1990-91; U.S. Military Academy, History fellow, 1992; University of West Florida, assistant professor of history, 1996-; University of North Texas, assistant professor, 1996-2000, associate professor, 2000-07, professor, 2007-. Writer. **Publications:** The Caddo Indians: Tribes at the Convergence of Empires, 1542-1854, 1995; The Wichita and Caddo Indians: Relations With the United States, 1846-1901, 1996; Wichita Indians: Traders of Texas and the Southern Plains, 1540-1845, 2000; From Dominance to Disappearance: The Indians of Texas and the near Southwest, 1786-1859, 2005; (with H.S. Burton) Colonial Natchitoches: A Creole Community on the Louisiana-Texas Frontier, 2008; Colonial Louisiana and the Gulf Coast Frontier, 1500-1821, forthcoming. Contributor of articles to books and journals. **Address:** Department of History, University of North Texas, 254 Wooten Hall, 1155 Union Cir., PO Box 310650, Denton, TX 76203, U.S.A. **Online address:** ftsmith@unt.edu

SMITH, Gary Scott. American (born United States), b. 1950?. **Genres:** History, Art/Art History. **Career:** Grove City College, professor of history, 1978-, department chair. Writer. **Publications:** The Seeds of Secularization: Calvinism, Culture and Pluralism in America, 1870-1915, 1985; (ed. with W.A. Hoffecker) Building a Christian World View, 1986; (ed.) God and Politics: Four Views on the Reformation of Civil Government: Theonomy, Principled Pluralism, Christian America, National Confessionalism, 1989; The Search for Social Salvation: Social Christianity and America, 1880-1925, 2000; Faith and the Presidency: From George Washington to George W. Bush, 2006; Heaven in the American Imagination, 2011. **Address:** Department of History, Grove City College, Rm. HAL 300J, 100 Campus Dr., PO Box 3039, Grove City, PA 16127, U.S.A. **Online address:** gssmith@gcc.edu

SMITH, Gavin D. Scottish/British (born England), b. 1960. **Genres:** Poetry, Writing/Journalism, Biography, History. **Career:** Wordsworth Trust, retail manager, 1983-; Whisky-Pages.com, contributing editor; The Serpent Press, co-founder. **Publications:** Whisky: A Book of Words, 1993; The Year of the Prince, 1995; Flambard New Poets 2, 1995; Gavin D. Smith's Lake District, 1997; A to Z of Whisky, 1997; (comp. with D. Ross) Scots-English, English-Scots Dictionary, 1998; (with J. McDougall) Wort, Worms and Washbacks: Memoirs from the Stillhouse, 1999; Whisky Wit & Wisdom: A Verbal Distillation, 2000; Secret Still: Scotland's Clandestine Whisky Makers, 2002; The Scottish Smuggler, 2004; The Whisky Men, 2005; Whisky: A Brief History, 2007; Discovering Scotland's Distilleries, 2010; The Lake Poets, 2010; Malt Whisky Companion, 6th ed., 2010; Ardbeg: A Peaty Provenance and Goodness Nose, forthcoming. Works appear in anthologies. Contributor of articles to periodicals. **Address:** Whisky-Pages.com, Glasgow, G12, Scotland. **Online address:** gavin@whisky-pages.com

SMITH, Geof. American (born United States), b. 1969. **Genres:** Novellas/Short Stories, Young Adult Fiction, Mystery/Crime/Suspense. **Career:** McGraw-Hill Book Co., School Division, textbook editor, 1991-. **Publications:** Above 95th Street and Other Basketball Stories, 1997; (co-author) Million Dollar Bucket: And Other Stories About Your Favorite Sports, 2000; Return of the Monster Tracker's Guide: Monsterzine 1, 2001; City Tales, 2002; (with K. Oshima) Ultrafiltration-based Extraction for Biological Agents in Early Warning Systems, 2006; (contrib.) Mr. Fancy Pants!, 2009; Midnight Hockey League, forthcoming. Contributor to anthologies. **Address:** School Division, McGraw-Hill Book Co., 1221 Ave. of the Americas, New York, NY 10021, U.S.A.

SMITH, George P(atrick). American (born United States), b. 1939. **Genres:** Economics, Ethics, Law, Medicine/Health. **Career:** Indiana University Law School, Krannert teaching fellow, 1953-54, 1964-65; University of Michigan, instructor in law, 1965-66; State University of New York, assistant professor of law and assistant dean, 1967-69; George Washington University, visiting assistant professor, 1968; University of Arkansas, associate professor of law, 1969-71; Georgetown University, adjunct professor of law, 1971-75, Johns Hopkins Program on Law and Public Health, visiting fellow, 2001-02; United States Environmental Protection Agency, Special Counsel, 1971-74; Catholic University of America, lecturer, 1973-75, professor of law, 1977-, school of nursing, occasional lecturer, 1981-86, Rosemary Donley lecturer, 1986; Columbia University Law School, university fellow, 1974-75; University of Pittsburgh, associate professor of law, 1975-77; University of Connecticut, visiting professor, 1977; Uniformed Services University of the Health Sciences, lecturer, 1979-86; University of New South Wales, distinguished university, visiting lecturer, 1982, Fulbright visiting professor of law, 1984, medical jurisprudence, Julius Stone Memorial lecturer, 1987, visiting professor of law, 1987, 1990 and 2001; University of Notre Dame, Thomas J. White lecturer, 1986; Cleveland State University, Medical Institute for Law Faculty, Cleveland Clinic Center for Creative Thinking in Medicine, associate, 1991; University of Otago, visiting professor of legal research, 1994; University of Sydney, visiting professor of law, 2003; Macquarie University, distinguished visiting professor of law, 2005; Saint Edmund's College, visiting fellow, 2008; University of Michigan School of Public Health Ann Arbor, University Center for Law, Ethics and Health, instructor, 1965-66, visiting fellow, 2007; University of Saint Andrews, visiting fellow, 2006-07. Writer. **Publications:** Financing Growth of the Electric Utilities, 1976; The Legacy of Peter Zenger (monograph), 1977; Restricting the Concept of Free Seas, 1980; Genetics, Ethics, and the Law, 1981; A Bibliography with Subject Index of Legal Theses and Dissertations at the Squire and Bodleian Libraries (monograph), 1981; Ethical, Legal and Social Challenges to a Brave New World, 2 vols., 1982; Medical-Legal Aspects of Cryonics, 1983; The New Biology, 1989; Final Choices, 1989; Bioethics and the Law, 1993; Legal and Healthcare Ethics for the Elderly, 1996; Challenging Family Values in The New Society, 1996; Lard Use, Economic Jurisprudence, and Nuisance Law (monograph), 1996; Ethical Imperatives in Law and Medicine (monograph), 1996; Family Values and the New Society: Dilemmas of the 21st Century, 1998; Human Rights and Biomedicine, 2000; The Christian Religion and Biotechnology: A Search for Principled Decision-Making, 2005; Distributive Justice and the New Medicine, 2008. **Address:** Columbus School of Law, Catholic University of America, 3600 John McCormack Rd. NE, Washington, DC 20064, U.S.A. **Online address:** smithg@law.edu

SMITH, Glenn D. American (born United States), b. 1970?. **Genres:** Photography. **Career:** Mississippi State University, assistant professor of communication. Writer and historian. **Publications:** Something on My Own: Gertrude Berg and American Broadcasting, 1929-1956, 2007. Contributor to periodicals. **Address:** U.S.A. **Online address:** gsmith@comm.msstate.edu

SMITH, Glenn Robert. American (born United States), b. 1952. **Genres:** Plays/Screenplays, Art/Art History, Biography, Photography. **Career:** Magician, 1970-76; antiques dealer, 1977-79; builder of estates, 1980-91. writer, 1991-. **Publications:** (With R. Kenner) Discovering Ellis Ruley, 1993. **Address:** PO Box 1031, Cardiff by the Sea, CA 92007-7031, U.S.A. **Online address:** diniart@aol.com

SMITH, Gordon. American (born United States), b. 1951?. **Genres:** Mystery/Crime/Suspense. **Career:** Tower Advertising, art director, 1980-85; Tremain Smith (graphic design firm), partner, 1985-89; California Lawyer, art director, 1989-95; freelance graphic designer, 1999-; School Wise Press, design director, 2005-07; Antioch College Fire Department, chief; Legal Magazine, director. Writer. **Publications:** The Forest in the Hallway, 2006. Contributor to periodicals. **Address:** Clarion Books, 215 Park Ave. S, New York, NY 10003, U.S.A. **Online address:** info@beatriz.co.uk

SMITH, Gordon Roland. British (born England), b. 1931. **Genres:** Children's Non-fiction, Crafts, Theology/Religion, Young Adult Fiction, Art/Art History, Communications/Media, Adult Non-fiction. **Career:** Cannock School, teacher, 1951-55, 1958-64, 1966-68, Art and Junior Department, head, 1968-83; Marley Group, graphic designer, 1955-57; Outlook, editor, 1992-; freelance design consultant. **Publications:** First Models in Cardboard, 1963, 1969; Creative Crayon Craft, 1964; My Side of the Grave, 1970; Making a Model Village, 1970; The Zebra Book of Papercraft, 1972; Make It from Paper, 1974; Paper for Play, 1975; Thinks, 1979; The Educational Uses of Paper Fasteners, 1981; I Suppose I Shall Survive, 1981; 100 Plus Calligraphy Projects: Creative Ideas for Putting Basic Calligraphy to Practical Use, 1989; The Strange Case of the Swedish Reporter, 1996. Contributor to magazines. **Address:** Melilot, Well Hill Ln., Chelsfield, Orpington, KT BR6 7QJ, England.

SMITH, Greg Leitich. American (born United States) **Genres:** Children's Fiction, Novels, Picture/Board Books, Young Adult Fiction. **Career:** Writer. **Publications:** NOVELS: Ninjas, Piranhas, and Galileo, 2003; Tofu and T. Rex, 2005; Chronal Engine, 2012. PICTURE BOOK: (with C.L. Smith) Santa Knows, 2006. **Address:** PO Box 3255, Austin, TX 78764-3255, U.S.A. **Online address:** greg@gregleitichsmith.com

SMITH, Gregory Blake. American (born United States), b. 1951. **Genres:** Novels, Mystery/Crime/Suspense, Young Adult Fiction. **Career:** Carleton College, associate professor of American literature and creative writing, 1987-, professor of English. Writer. **Publications:** The Devil in the Dooryard, 1986; The Divine Comedy of John Venner, 1992; The Madonna of Las Vegas: A Novel, 2005; The Law of Miracles: Short Fiction, 2011. **Address:** Department of English, Carleton College, 1 N College St., Northfield, MN 55057, U.S.A.

SMITH, Gregory White. American (born United States), b. 1951. **Genres:** Documentaries/Reportage, Autobiography/Memoirs. **Career:** Morrison & Foerster, staff; Woodward/White Inc., president, 1981-; Best Lawyers, editor and co-founder; 1983-; Best Doctors Inc., chairman, 1994-2000. Writer and lawyer. **Publications:** WITH S.W. NAIFEH: Moving Up in Style: The Successful Man's Guide to Impeccable Taste, 1980; Gene Davis, 1982; What Every Client Needs to Know about Using a Lawyer, 1982; The Bargain Hunter's Guide to Art Collecting, 1982; (with M. Morgenstern) How to Make Love to a Woman, 1986; The Best Lawyers in America, 1983; Why Can't Men Open Up?: Overcoming Men's Fear of Intimacy, 1984; (with P. Donahue) The Human Animal, 1985; The Mormon Murders: A True Story of Greed, Forgery, Deceit and Death, 1988; Jackson Pollock: An American Saga, 1989; The Best Lawyers in America: Directory of Expert Witnesses, 1990; The Best Doctors in America, 1992, rev. ed., 1994; Final Justice: The True Story of the Richest Man Ever Tried for Murder, 1993; Stranger in the Family: A True Story of Murder, Madness and Unconditional Love, 1995; The Best Doctors in America: Southeast Region, 1995; Midwest Region, 1995; Pacific Region, 1996; Central Region, 1996; Northeast Region, 1996; On a Street Called Easy, in a Cottage Called Joye, 1996; Making Miracles Happen, 1997; The Best Dentists in America, 2003; Vincent van Gogh: The Life, 2011. Contributor to periodicals. **Address:** Woodward/White Inc., 129 1st Ave. SW, Aiken, SC 29801, U.S.A.

SMITH, Gwen. American (born United States), b. 1970. **Genres:** Theology/Religion. **Career:** Girlfriends in God (conference and devotional ministry), co-founder and worship leader; Brentwood and Benson Publishing Group, staff songwriter; Audio 31, founder. **Publications:** Broken into Beautiful: How God Restores the Wounded Heart, 2008. **Address:** Audio 31 Music, PO Box 1311, Huntersville, NC 28070, U.S.A. **Online address:** audio31@aol.com

SMITH, Hedrick (Laurence). American (born United States), b. 1933. **Genres:** International Relations/Current Affairs. **Career:** Journalist, 1959-; United Press Intl., reporter, 1959-62; New York Times, foreign affairs reporter, 1962-63, Saigon correspondent, 1963-64, Cairo correspondent, 1964-66, chief diplomatic correspondent, 1966-71, Moscow bureau chief, 1971-74; deputy national editor, 1975-76, Washington bureau chief, 1976-79, chief Washington correspondent, 1979-85, Washington correspondent, 1987-88; Harvard University, Nieman fellow, 1969-70; American Enterprise Institute, visiting journalist, 1985-86; Hedrick Smith Productions, documentary producer and correspondent, 1988-2010. **Publications:** (With N. Sheehan, E.W. Kentworthy and F. Butterfield) The Pentagon Papers, 1971; The Russians, 1976; (with A. Clymer, R. Bart and L. Silk) Reagan: The Man, the President, 1980; (co-author) Beyond Reagan: The Politics of Upheaval, 1986; The Power Game: How Washington Works, 1988; The New Russians, 1990; (ed.) Media and the Gulf War, 1992; Rethinking America: A New Game Plan from the American Innovators: Schools, Business, People, Work, 1995. **Address:** Hedrick Smith Productions, 4630 Montgomery Ave., Ste. 400, Bethesda, MD 20814, U.S.A. **Online address:** hsmithprod@aol.com

SMITH, Helmut Walser. American/German (born Germany), b. 1962. **Genres:** History. **Career:** Vanderbilt University, associate professor of history, director of graduate studies, department of history, co-director, 1992-, Martha Rivers Ingram professor of history, Martha Rivers Ingram chair of history, director of the Max Kade Center for European and German Studies, professor of European studies. Writer. **Publications:** German Nationalism and Religious Conflict: Culture, Ideology, Politics, 1870-1914, 1995; The Butcher's Tale: Murder and Anti-Semitism in a German Town, 2002; The Continuities of German History: Nation, Religion, and Race across the Long Nineteenth Century, 2008. EDITOR: Protestants, Catholics and Jews in Germany, 1800-1914, 2001; (co-ed.) The Holocaust and Other Genocides: History, Representation, Ethics, 2002; (with C. Hoffmann and W. Bergmann) Exclusionary Violence: Antisemitic Riots in Modern German History, 2002. Contributor to journals and books. **Address:** Department of History, Vanderbilt University, 243 Buttrick Hall, 2301 Vanderbilt Pl., PO Box 351802, Nashville, TN 37235-1802, U.S.A. **Online address:** helmut.w.smith@vanderbilt.edu

SMITH, H. Jeff. (H. Russell Smith). American (born United States), b. 1957. **Genres:** Information Science/Computers, Administration/Management. **Career:** U.S. Environmental Protection Agency, statistical analyst and programmer, 1977-79; North Carolina State University, Computer Science Department, teaching assistant and aide, 1978-79; Fulcrum Computer Group Inc., systems analyst, 1981-82; IBM Corp., manager of software development, 1982-87; Harvard Business School, research associate, 1987-89; Georgetown University, School of Business, assistant professor of business, 1991-96, associate professor, 1996-98; Wake Forest University, Babcock Graduate School of Management, associate professor of management, 1998-2003, IT concentration coordinator, 2003-06, professor of management, 2005-06, Sisel fellow in information technology; Miami University, Farmer School of Business, Department of Decision Sciences and Management Information Systems, professor and chair, 2006-. Writer. **Publications:** Managing Privacy: Information Technology and Corporate America, 1994. Contributor to books. **Address:** Department of Decision Sciences &, Management Information Systems, Farmer School of Business, Miami University, 3095 A, 800 E High St., Oxford, OH 45056, U.S.A. **Online address:** smithhj@muohio.edu

SMITH, Hobart Muir. American (born United States), b. 1912. **Genres:** Biology, Zoology, Bibliography, Animals/Pets, Environmental Sciences/Ecology. **Career:** University of Rochester, instructor of biology, 1941-45; University of Kansas, associate professor, 1945-46; Texas A&M University, associate professor of wildlife management, 1946-47; University of Illinois, assistant professor, 1947-51, associate professor, 1951-57, professor of zoology, 1957-68, Museum of Natural History, curator of herpetology, 1947-68; University of Colorado, professor of biology, 1968-83, professor emeritus, 1983-, chairman, 1971-74. Writer. **Publications:** The Mexican and Central American Lizards of the Genus Sceloporus, 1939; (with B.C. Brown) A New Subspecies of Sceloporus Jarrovii from Mexico, 1941; Notes on Mexican Snakes of the Genus Geophis, 1941; Further Notes on Mexican Snakes of the Genus Salvadora, 1941; The White Sands Earless Lizard, 1943; (with K.P. Schmidt) Notes on Coral Snakes from Mexico, 1943; Mexican Herpetological Miscellany, 1943; Mexican Subspecies of the Snake Coniophanes Fissidens, 1943, Notes on the Snake Genus Trimorphodon, 1943; Snakes of the Hoogstraal Expeditions to Northern Mexico, 1944; (with E.H.Taylor) An Annotated Checklist and Key to the Snakes of Mexico, 1945; Handbook of Lizards: Lizards of the United States and of Canada, 1946; (with E.H. Taylor) An Annotated Checklist and Key to the Amphibia of Mexico, 1948; Handbook of Amphibians and Reptiles of Kansas, 1950, (with E.H. Taylor) An Annotated Checklist and Key to the Reptiles of Mexico Exclusive of the Snakes, 1950; (with H.S. Zim) Reptiles and Amphibians: A Guide to Familiar American Species, 1953, rev. ed., 2001; Snakes as Pets 1953, 4th ed., 1977; Lectures in Comparative Anatomy, 1954; (with J.L. Bronson) Pet Turtles, 1954; Pet Turtles, 1955; Evolution of Chordate Structure: An Introduction to Comparative Anatomy, 1957, 1960; Laboratory Studies of Chordate Structure, 1957, 7th ed., 1973; A Golden Stamp Book: Snakes, Turtles and Lizards, 1958; (with F.G. Boys) Poisonous Amphibians and Reptiles: Recognition and Bite Treatment, 1959; Glossary of Terms for Comparative Anatomy, 1961; (with D.A. Langebartel and K.L. Williams.) Herpetological Type-Specimens in the University of Illinois Museum of Natural History, 1964; (with T.P. Maslin and R.L. Brown) Summary of the Distribution of the Herpetofauna of Colorado, 1965; (with E.H. Taylor) Herpetology of Mexico, 1966; Turtles in Colour, 1967; Early Foundations of Mexican Herpetology: An Annotated and Indexed Bibliography of the Herpetological Publications of Alfredo Duges 1826-1910, 1969; (with J.C. Oldham and S.A. Miller) A Laboratory Perspectus of Snake Anatomy, 1970; (with R.B. Smith) Synopsis of the Herpetofauna of Mexico, 7 vols., 1971-93; (with R.B. Smith) Analysis of the Literature on the Mexicanaxolotl, 1971; (with R.B. Smith) Analysis of the Literature Exclusive of the Mexican Axolotl, 1973; (with J.C. Oldham) Laboratory Anatomy of the Iguana, 1974; (with R.B. Smith) Source Analysis and Index for Mexican Reptiles, 1976; (with R.B. Smith) Source Analysis and Index for Mexican Amphibians, 1976; Guide to Mexican Amphibaenians and Crocodilians: Bibliographic Addendum II Amphibians of North America, 1979; (with E.D.Brodie) Reptiles of North America: A Guide to Field Identification, 1982; (with E.L. Marca) Eleutherodactylus Colostichos: A New Frog Species from the Páramo de Los Conejos, in the Venezuelan Andes (Anura, Leptodactylidae), 1982; (with H.S. Zim) Reptiles and Amphibians: 212 Species in Full Color, rev. ed., 1987; (with G. Pérez-Higareda) Ofidiofauna de Veracruz: An álisis taxonómico y zoogeográfiico, 1991; (with R.B. Smith) Synopsis of the Herpetofauna of Mexico, vol. VII: Bibliographic Addendum IV and Index, Bibliographic Addenda II-IV, 1979-1991, 1993; (with D. Chiszar) Species-Group Taxa of the False Coral Snake Genus Pliocercus, 1996. Contributor to books and journals. **Address:** Department of Ecology & Evolutionary Biology, University of Colorado, 334 UCB, PO Box 334, Boulder, CO 80309-0334, U.S.A. **Online address:** hsmith@colorado.edu

SMITH, H. Russell. See **SMITH, H. Jeff.**

SMITH, Hugh. Australian (born Australia), b. 1943. **Genres:** Bibliography, Military/Defense/Arms Control. **Career:** Australian Defence Force Academy, Department of Politics, teacher; Armed Forces & Society, Inter University Seminar, fellow. Writer. **Publications:** (with S. Broome) A Bibliography of Armed Forces and Society in Australia, 1979; On Clausewitz: A Study of Military and Political Ideas, 2005. EDITOR: Officer Education: Problems and Prospects; Papers Presented to a Conference of the Australian Study Group on Armed Forces and Society, R.M.C., Duntroon, 30-31 May 1980, 1980; Rewarding the Defence Force: Proceedings of a Conference Held on 3 July 1987, 1987; The Military Profession in Australia: Proceedings of a Conference Held on 1 July 1988 by the Australian Defence Studies Centre and the Australian Study Group on Armed Forces and Society, 1988; Australia and Peacekeeping, 1990; (with A. Bergin) Naval Power in the Pacific: Toward the Year 2000, 1993; Peacekeeping: Challenges for the Future, 1993; The Force of Law: International Law and the Land Commander, 1994; International Peacekeeping: Building on the Cambodian Experience, 1994; The Strategists, 2001. **Address:** Defence Studies Forum, School of Humanities & Social Sciences, Canberra, 2600, Australia. **Online address:** h.smith@adfa.edu.au

SMITH, James K. A. American/Canadian (born Canada), b. 1970?. **Genres:** Philosophy, Theology/Religion. **Career:** Villanova University, lecturer in philosophy, 1995-99; University of the Sciences in Philadelphia, Department of Humanities, adjunct assistant professor of biomedical writing, 1998-2002; Loyola Marymount University, assistant professor of philosophy, 1999-2002; Vanguard University, Graduate Program in Religion, adjunct professor of theology and ethics, 2001; Calvin College, associate professor of philosophy, 2002-, professor, Department of Congregational and Ministry Studies, adjunct professor, Seminars in Christian Scholarship, director, 2003-06, Center for Social Research, fellow, 2006-08, Calvin Institute of Christian Worship, research fellow; Pneuma Journal, associate editor, 2004-; Calvin Theological Seminary, adjunct professor of philosophical theology, 2005-; Fuller Theological Seminary, visiting associate professor of Christian philosophy, 2006; Society of Christian Philosophers, executive director, 2009-; Regent College, visiting professor. **Publications:** The Fall of Interpretation: Philosophical Foundations for a Creational Hermeneutic, 2000; Speech and Theology: Language and the Logic of Incarnation, 2002; (with K.J. Clark and R. Lints) 101 Key Terms in Philosophy and Their Importance for Theology, 2004; Introducing Radical Orthodoxy: Mapping a Post-secular Theology, 2004; Jacques Derrida: Live Theory, 2005; Who's Afraid of Postmodernism?: Taking Derrida, Lyotard, and Foucault to Church, 2006; Desiring the Kingdom: Worship, Worldview, and Cultural Formation, 2009; Devil Reads Derrida: And Other Essays on the University, the Church, Politics, and the Arts, 2009; Letters to a Young Calvinist: An Invitation to the Reformed Tradition, 2010; Thinking in Tongues: Pentecostal Contributions to Christian Philosophy, 2010. EDITOR: (with H.I. Venema) The Hermeneutics of Charity: Interpretation, Selfhood, and Postmodern Faith, 2004; (with J.H. Olthuis) Radical Orthodoxy and the Reformed Tradition: Creation, Covenant, and Participation, 2005; (with K.J. Vanhoozer and B.E. Benson) Hermeneutics at the Crossroads, 2006; After Modernity?: Secularity, Globalization, and the Re-enchantment of the World, 2008; (with A. Yong) Science and the Spirit: A Pentecostal Engagement with the Sciences, 2010; (with D.I. Smith) Teaching and Christian Practices: Reshaping Faith and Learning, 2011. Contributor to periodicals. **Address:** Department of Philosophy, Calvin College, 342H Hiemenga Hall, 1845 Knollcrest Cir. SE, Grand Rapids, MI 49546, U.S.A. **Online address:** jkasmith@calvin.edu

SMITH, James L(eslie Clarke). British (born England), b. 1936. **Genres:** Theatre. **Career:** Yale University, Henry Fellow, 1962-63; University of British Columbia, lecturer in English, 1963-64; University of Southampton, Department of English, lecturer, 1965-80, senior lecturer, 1980-93. Writer. **Publications:** (Contrib.) Christopher Marlowe, 1968; Melodrama, 1973. EDITOR: The Great McGonagall: Poetical Pearls from the Pen of William McGonagall, 1968; The Last Poetic Gems Selected from the Works of William McGonagall, Poet and Tragedian, 1968; Sir John Vanbrugh's The Provoked Wife, 1974. (intro.) Victorian Melodramas: Seven English, French, and

American Melodrams, 1976; William Wycherley's The Plain Dealer, 1979, rev. ed., 1991; Dion Boucicault's London Assurance, 1984. **Address:** Sansomes Farmhouse, Whiteparish, WT SP5 2SS, England.

SMITH, James M. American (born United States), b. 1966?. **Genres:** Architecture. **Career:** Boston College, adjunct faculty, 1996-99, associate professor of English and Irish studies, 2000-; Pennsylvania State University, assistant professor, 1999-2000. Writer. **Publications:** Ireland's Magdalen Laundries and the Nation's Architecture of Containment, 2007. Contributor to periodicals. **Address:** Boston College, Connolly House, 300 Hammond St., Chestnut Hill, MA 02467, U.S.A. **Online address:** smithbt@bc.edu

SMITH, Janna M(alamud). American (born United States), b. 1952. **Genres:** Adult Non-fiction, Autobiography/Memoirs, Biography, Young Adult Fiction, Literary Criticism And History. **Career:** Harvard University, Cambridge Hospital, The Cambridge Health Alliance, Department of Psychiatry, faculty, 1979-. Writer. **Publications:** (Contrib.) The Psychotherapist's Guide to Pharmacotherapy, 1989; (contrib.) Women and Group Psychotherapy, 1996; Private Matters: In Defense of the Personal Life (nonfiction), 1997, rev. ed., 2003; A Potent Spell: Mother Love and the Power of Fear, 2003; My Father is a Book: A Memoir of Bernard Malamud, 2006. Contributor to books, journals and newspapers. **Address:** The Cambridge Health Alliance, 1493 Cambridge St., Cambridge, MA 02139, U.S.A. **Online address:** jms@jannamalamudsmith.com

SMITH, Jason Scott. American (born United States), b. 1970. **Genres:** Politics/Government, History. **Career:** Harvard University, Harvard-Newcomen postdoctoral fellow in business history, 2001-02, Graduate School of Business Administration lecturer, 2002-04; Cornell University, Mellon postdoctoral fellow in American Studies, visiting assistant professor, 2004-06; University of New Mexico, assistant professor of history, 2006-. Academic, historian and writer. **Publications:** Building New Deal Liberalism: The Political Economy of Public Works, 1933-1956, 2006. Contributor to periodicals and journals. **Address:** Department of History, University of New Mexico, MSC06 3760, Albuquerque, NM 87131-1181, U.S.A. **Online address:** jssmith@unm.edu

SMITH, Jean Edward. American (born United States), b. 1932. **Genres:** Civil Liberties/Human Rights, History, Politics/Government, Biography. **Career:** Dartmouth College, assistant professor of government, 1963-65; Princeton University, Center for International Studies, research associate, 1967-68; Columbia University, adjunct professor, 1998-99; University of Toronto, professor of political science, now professor emeritus; Marshall University, associate professor, John Marshall professor of political science; Ashland University, professor of history and government; Freie Universitat, visiting professor; Georgetown University, visiting professor; University of Virginia, Woodrow Wilson Department of Government and Foreign Affairs, visiting professor; University of California, visiting professor. Writer. **Publications:** The Defense of Berlin, 1963; Der Weg ins Delimma, 1965; Germany beyond the Wall, People, Politics ... and Prosperity, 1969; (with H.M. Levine) Civil Liberties and Civil Rights Debated, 1988; Lucius D. Clay: An American Life, 1990; George Bush's War, 1992; John Marshall: Definer of a Nation, 1996; Grant, 2001; Eisenhower, 2012. EDITOR: The Papers of General Lucius D. Clay: Germany, 1945-1949, 1974; The Constitution and American Foreign Policy, 1989; (with H.M. Levine) The Conduct of American Foreign Policy, 1990; Face of Justice: Portraits of John Marshall, 2001; Grant, 2001; FDR, 2007. **Address:** Department of Political Science, Marshall University, 1 John Marshall Dr., Huntington, WV 25755-2014, U.S.A.

SMITH, Jeanne Rosier. American (born United States), b. 1966?. **Genres:** Novels, Social Sciences, Literary Criticism And History, Young Adult Fiction. **Career:** Seton Hall University, instructor of American literature, professor; Fountain Street Studios, visiting artist; Jeanne Smith Fine Art, instructor and owner, 2007-. Writer. **Publications:** Writing Tricksters: Mythic Gambols in American Ethnic Fiction, 1997. Contributor to periodicals. **Address:** Fine Art America, 2103 Brentwood St., 2120 Berkeley Way, High Point, NC 27263, U.S.A.

SMITH, Jessie. See **KUNHARDT, Edith.**

SMITH, Joan Gerarda. (Jennie Gallant). Canadian (born Canada), b. 1932. **Genres:** Mystery/Crime/Suspense, Romance/Historical, Children's Fiction, Young Adult Fiction, Novels, Horror. **Career:** High school teacher, 1965-67; St. Lawrence College, instructor in English, 1970-73; novelist, 1977-; Smith-

Gallant Productions, president, 1981-. **Publications:** ROMANCE NOVELS: Folk Doll of Sion, 1973; Dittany Bush, 1975; Affair of the Heart, 1976; Escapade, 1977; Aunt Sophies Diamond, 1977; Dame Durden's Daughter, 1978; Harry McShane: No Mean Fighter, 1978; Imprudent Lady, 1978; Sweet and Twenty, 1979; Talk of the Town, 1979; Lace for Milady, 1980; Endure My Heart, 1980; Rose Trelawney, 1980; Perdita, 1981; Valerie, 1981; Blue Diamond, 1981; Lovers' Vows, 1981; Delsie, 1982; Gift of Umtal, 1982; The Reluctant Bride, 1982; Reprise, 1982; Love's Way, 1982; Wiles of a Stranger, 1982; Caprice, 1983; Prelude to Love, 1983; Lady Madeline's Folly, 1983; Love Bade Me Welcome, 1983; From Now on, 1983; Chance of a Lifetime, 1984; Next Year's Blonde, 1984; Trouble in Paradise, 1984; Future Perfect, 1984; Midnight Masquerade, 1984; Best of Enemies, 1985; Tender Takeover, 1985; The Yielding Art, 1985; Royal Revels, 1985; Devious Duchess, 1985; True Lady, 1985; Bath Belles, 1986; The Infamous Madame X, 1986; Where There's a Will, 1986; Strange Capers, 1986; A Country Wooing, 1987; Love's Harbinger, 1987; Letters to a Lady, 1987; Country Flirt, 1987; Dear Corrie, 1987; Larcenous Lady, 1987; Memoirs of a Hoyden, 1988; By Hook or by Crook, 1988; Silken Secrets, 1988; Drury Lane Darling, 1988; After the Storm, 1988; The Hermit's Daughter, 1988; Thrill of the Chase, 1989; Maybe Next Time, 1989; The Royal Scamp, 1989; It Takes Two, 1989; Lover's Quarrels, 1989; Madcap Miss, 1989; Sealed With a Kiss, 1990; The Merry Month of May, 1990; Cousin Cecilia, 1990; Her Nest Egg, 1990; Winter Wedding, 1990; Romantic Rebel, 1990; Her Lucky Break, 1991; Waltzing Widow, 1991; The Notorious Lord Havergal, 1991; Bath Scandal, 1991; Jennie Kissed Me, 1991; For Richer, for Poorer, 1992; Barefoot Baroness, 1992; Dangerous Dalliance, 1992; Francesca, 1992; Getting to Know You, 1992; Wife Errant, 1992; The Spanish Lady, 1992; Headed for Trouble, 1993; Gather Ye Rosebuds, 1993; Can't Buy Me Love, 1993; John Loves Sally, 1993; The Savage Lord Griffin, 1993; The Great Christmas Ball, 1993; Poor Little Rich Girl, 1993; Behold, a Mystery!, 1994; Old Lover's Ghost, 1994; Regency Masquerade, 1994; Never Let Me Go, 1994; The Kissing Bough, 1994; Damsel in Distress, 1994; No Place for a Lady, 1994; An Autumn Perspective, 1995; A Kiss in the Dark, 1995; The Virgin and the Unicorn, 1995; Kissing Cousins, 1995; Tea and Scandal, 1996; A Christmas Gambol, 1996; Daughters of the Law, 1996; An Infamous Proposal, 1996; A Tall Dark Stranger, 1996; Petticoat Rebellion, 1997; Blossom Time, 1997; A Highwayman Came Riding, 1998; Little Coquette, 1998; Is He a Devil, 1999; Oh Miranda!, 2001; Aurora, 2007; Friends and Lovers, 2009. BERKELY BRIGADE SERIES: Murder Will Speak, 1996; Murder and Misdeeds, 1997; Murder While I Smile, 1997; Murder Comes to Mind, 1998. ROMANTIC SUSPENSE NOVELS: The Polka Dot Nude, 1989; Capriccio, 1989; A Brush With Death, 1990; Follow That Blonde, 1990. OTHERS: La Comtesse, 1978; Destiny's Dream, 1988; Emerald Hazard, 1988; Silver Water, Golden Sand, 1989; A Whisper on the Wind, 1990; (with L. Lynn, P. Veryan and B. Metzger) Autumn Loves, 1993. AS JENNIE GALLANT: Lady Hathaway's House Party, 1980; Minuet, 1980; The Moonless Night, 1980; The Black Diamond, 1981; Olivia, 1981; Friends & Lovers, 1982; Thick as Thieves, 1993; (with L. Lynn and B. Metzger) A Regency Christmas, 1994. **Address:** Robert Hale Ltd., Clerkenwell House, 45-47 Clerkenwell Green, London, GL EC1R 0HT, England. **Online address:** joansmith@aztec-net.com

SMITH, (John) Geddeth. American (born United States), b. 1934. **Genres:** Theatre, Biography, Film. **Career:** Actor, 1958-; writer, 1967-; Actors and Directors Lab, faculty, 1984-85. **Publications:** BIOGRAPHY: The Brief Career of Eliza Poe, 1988; Thomas Abthorpe Cooper: America's Premier Tragedian, 1996; Walter Hampden: Dean of the American Theatre, 2008. **Address:** 900 W End Ave., New York, NY 10025, U.S.A. **Online address:** geddethsmith@yahoo.com

SMITH, John M. American (born United States), b. 1942. **Genres:** Medicine/Health, Documentaries/Reportage, Sociology. **Career:** University of Colorado, rotating intern in obstetrics and gynecology, 1969, resident in obstetrics and gynecology, 1969-72, Colorado Springs Center for Entrepreneurship, founder; Peak Health Plan Ltd., medical director, 1979-83; Colorado Springs Medical Center, director of ambulatory surgery unit, 1980-84; Peak Health Care Inc., founder and executive vice president, 1982-86; Colorado Springs Symphony Orchestra, board director, 1984-86, vice president, 1986-88, president, 1988-90; The Prelude (music store), owner, 1986-; Navajo Hogan Restaurant, owner, 1987-; CSSO Foundation, board president, 1991-; Alten Ozone Corp., director, 1992-. Writer. **Publications:** Women and Doctors: A Physician's Explosive Account of Women's Medical Treatment-and Mistreatment-in America Today and What You Can Do About It, 1992. Ad-

dress: c/o Elizabeth Wales, Levant & Wales Inc., 108 Hayes St., Seattle, WA 98109, U.S.A. **Online address:** summitven@aol.com

SMITH, Jonathan. British (born England), b. 1942. **Genres:** Novels, Plays/Screenplays. **Career:** Tonbridge School, head of humanities; Christ Church, schoolteacher fellow, 1982; Writer. **Publications:** (Ed.) William Shakespeare, King Lear, 1970; (with C. Cowdrey) Good Enough?, 1986. NOVELS: Wilfred and Eileen, 1976; The English Lover, 1977; In Flight, 1980; Come Back, 1983; Summer in February, 1995; The Learning Game, 2000; Night Windows, 2004. Contributor to periodicals. **Address:** Tonbridge School, High St., Tonbridge, KT TN9 1JP, England.

SMITH, Judie. See **SMITH, Judie R.**

SMITH, Judie R. (Judie Smith). American (born United States), b. 1936. **Genres:** Medicine/Health, Human Relations/Parenting, Self Help. **Career:** Richland Junior College, instructor, 1975-81; Suicide Crisis Center, program director, 1981-87; Dallas Independent School District, crisis specialist, 1987-. Writer. **Publications:** Coping with Suicide: A Resource Book for Teenagers and Young Adults, 1986; Suicide Prevention: A Crisis Intervention Curriculum for Teenagers and Young Adults, 1988; Drugs and Suicide, 1992; School Crisis Management Manual: Guidelines for Administrators, 1997, 2nd ed., 2001; (co-author) Curriculum Standards on Suicide; Postvention Guidelines. Contributor to books. **Address:** 5319 W University, Dallas, TX 75209, U.S.A.

SMITH, Judith E. American (born United States), b. 1948. **Genres:** History, Film, Cultural/Ethnic Topics, Popular Culture, Race Relations. **Career:** University of Rhode Island, visiting instructor, 1975, visiting assistant professor, 1978-79; Boston College, assistant professor, 1981-86, associate professor, 1986-93, director of American studies program, 1986-87, 1991-93; Harvard University, visiting professor, 1989, Charles Warren Center in American History, fellow in film and history, 2002-03; Stanford University, visiting professor, 1990; University of Massachusetts, associate professor, 1993-2004, professor of American studies, 2004-, director of graduate program in American studies. Writer and historian. **Publications:** (With J.D. Blum) Nothing Left to Lose: Studies of Street People, 1972; Family Connections: A History of Italian and Jewish Immigrant Lives in Providence, Rhode Island, 1900-1940, 1985; (with H.P. Chudacoff) The Evolution of American Urban Society, 3rd ed., 1988, 7th ed., 2010; Visions of Belonging: Family Stories, Popular Culture and Postwar Democracy, 1940-1960, 2004; (ed. with L.P. Rudnick and R.L. Rubin) American Identities: An Introductory Textbook, 2006. **Address:** Department of American Studies, University of Massachusetts, 100 Morrissey Blvd., Boston, MA 02125-3393, U.S.A. **Online address:** judith.smith@umb.edu

SMITH, Julian C(leveland). American (born United States), b. 1919. **Genres:** Engineering, History. **Career:** E.I. duPont de Nemours, chemical engineer, 1942-46; Cornell University, assistant professor, 1946-49, associate professor, 1949-53, professor of chemical engineering, 1953-86, professor emeritus, 1986-, director of continuing engineering education, 1965-71, School of Chemical Engineering, associate director, 1973-75, director, 1975-83; University of Edinburgh, visiting professor, 1971-72; United Nations Educational, Scientific, and Cultural Organization (UNESCO), consultant, 1975; consultant on nuclear waste disposal. Writer. **Publications:** (With W.L. McCabe) Unit Operations of Chemical Engineering, 1956, 7th ed., 2005; The School of Chemical Engineering at Cornell: A History of the First Fifty Years, 1988; Breaking Ninety: A History of the Country Club of Ithaca, 1900-1989, 1990. Contributor to scientific journals. **Address:** School of Chemical and Biomolecular Engineering, Cornell University, 120 Olin Hall, Ithaca, NY 14853-5201, U.S.A. **Online address:** jcs29@cornell.edu

SMITH, J. Walker. American (born United States), b. 1955. **Genres:** inspirational/Motivational Literature, Marketing. **Career:** Yankelovich Inc., senior vice president and managing partner, 1991-95, Yankelovich Monitor, managing partner and head, 1995-99, president, 1999-; Premiere Global Services, director, 2001-; University of Notre Dame, School of Marketing Research, lecturer; Dow Brands Inc., director of research; Cyber Dialogue, director; Ptek Holdings, director; American Marketing Association Foundation, director; University of North Carolina, School of Journalism and Mass Communications, board advisor. Writer, marketing consultant and researcher. **Publications:** (With A. Clurman) Rocking the Ages: The Yankelovich Report on Generational Marketing, 1997; (with R.K. Johnston) Life Is Not Work, Work Is Not Life: Simple Reminders for Finding Balance in a 24/7 World, 2001;

(with A. Clurman and C. Wood) Coming to Concurrence: Addressable Attitudes and the New Model for Marketing Productivity, 2004; (with A. Clurman) Generation Ageless: How Baby Boomers Are Changing the Way We Live Today-and They're Just Getting Started, 2007. Contributor to magazines and periodicals. **Address:** Yankelovich Inc., 400 Meadowmont Village Cir., Ste. 431, Chapel Hill, NC 27517, U.S.A.

SMITH, Kevin. American (born United States), b. 1970. **Genres:** Plays/Screenplays, Film. **Career:** Writer. **Publications:** (With J. Pierson) Spike, Mike, Slackers and Dykes: A Guided Tour Across a Decade of American Independent Cinema, 1997; Jay & Silent Bob: Chasing Dogma, 1999; Clerks: The Comic Books, 2000; Quiver: Green Arrow, 2002; (contrib.) Spike Mike eReloaded: A Guided Tour Across a Decade of American Independent Cinema, 2003; Green Arrow: Sounds of Violence, 2003; Silent Bob Speaks: The Collected Writings of Kevin Smith, 2005; My Boring-Ass Life: The Uncomfortably Candid Diary Of, 2009; Shootin' the shit with Kevin Smith, 2009; Batman, 2009; (intro.) Gallery 1988's Crazy 4 Cult: Cult Movie Art, 2011; Tough Sht: Life Advice from a Fat, Lazy Slob Who Did Good, 2012. **Address:** Creative Artists Agency Inc., 9830 Wilshire Blvd., Beverly Hills, CA 90212-1825, U.S.A.

SMITH, Kirsten. American (born United States), b. 1970. **Genres:** Novels. **Career:** CineTel Films, director of development; MacDowell Colony, writer-in-residence. Poet and novelist. **Publications:** The Geography of Girlhood (young-adult novel), 2006. Contributor to magazines. **Address:** Los Angeles, CA, U.S.A. **Online address:** kiwi@kiwilovesyou.com

SMITH, Lane. American (born United States), b. 1959. **Genres:** Children's Fiction, Illustrations, Sciences, Animals/Pets. **Career:** Freelance illustrator, 1983-. Writer. **Publications:** SELF-ILLUSTRATED: Flying Jake, 1988; The Big Pets, 1991; Glasses: Who Needs 'Em?, 1991; (with J. Scieszka) Squids Will Be Squids: Fresh Morals, Beastly Fables, 1998; Pinocchio, the Boy or: Incognito in Collodi, 2002; The Happy Hocky Family Moves to the Country!, 2003; John, Paul, George & Ben, 2006. OTHERS: (with J. Scieszka) Stinky Cheese Man and Other Fairly Stupid Tales, 1992; The Happy Hocky Family!, 1993; (with J. Scieszka) Math Curse, 1995; (with K. Kirkpatrick) Disney's James & the Giant Peach, 1996; (contrib.) Hooray for Diffendoofer Day!, 1998; (with J. Scieszka) Science Verse, 2004; (with J. Scieszka) Seen Art?, 2005; (with J. Scieszka) Cowboy and Octopus, 2007; Madam President, 2008; Big Elephant in the Room, 2009; It's a Book, 2010; It's a Little Book, 2011; Grandpa Green, 2011. Illustrator of books by others. **Address:** c/o Steven Malk, Writers House, 21 W 26th St., New York, NY 10010, U.S.A. **Online address:** lanesmithbooks@gmail.com

SMITH, Lee Harold. American (born United States), b. 1962. **Genres:** Politics/Government. **Career:** Ecco Press, staff; Atheneum, staff; GQ Magazine, staff; Grand Street, staff; Hudson Review, staff; Talk Magazine, staff; Voice Literary Supplement, editor-in-chief, 1995-96; Weekly Standard, Middle East correspondent. **Publications:** The Strong Horse: Power, Politics and the Clash of Arab Civilizations, 2010. Contributor to periodicals. **Address:** c/o Chris Calhoun, Sterling Lord Literistic Inc., 65 Bleecker St., New York, NY 10012, U.S.A.

SMITH, Lora Roberts. (Leigh Roberts). American (born United States), b. 1949. **Genres:** Novels, Mystery/Crime/Suspense, Romance/Historical, Young Adult Fiction, Horror. **Career:** Writer. **Publications:** Revolting Development, 1988. ROMANCE NOVELS AS LEIGH ROBERTS: Moonlight Splendor, 1983; Love Circuits, 1984; Siren Song, 1985; Birds of a Feather, 1986; Head Over Heels, 1987; The Wishing Pool, 1988; A Piece of Cake, 1990; Built to Last, 1992. The Problem of the Contentious Jewel, forthcoming. AS LORA ROBERTS: Murder in a Nice Neighborhood, 1994; Murder in the Marketplace, 1995; Murder Mile-High, 1996; Murder Bone by Bone, 1997; Murder Crops Up, 1998; Murder Follows Money, 2000; Another Fine Mess: A Bridget Montrose Mystery, 2002; The Affair of the Incognito Tenant: A Mystery with Sherlock Holmes, 2004. Contributor to periodicals. **Address:** PO Box 957, Palo Alto, CA 94302, U.S.A. **Online address:** myslora@pacbell.net

SMITH, Lori. American (born United States), b. 1971. **Genres:** Autobiography/Memoirs, Theology/Religion. **Career:** Freelance writer. **Publications:** The Single Truth: Challenging the Misconceptions of Singleness with God's Consuming Truth, 2002; A Walk with Jane Austen: A Journey into Adventure, Love and Faith, 2007. Contributor to periodicals. **Address:** Destiny Image, PO Box 310, Shippensburg, PA 17257, U.S.A. **Online address:** austenquotes@gmail.com

SMITH, Marguerite. (Elizabeth Sinclair). American (born United States), b. 1940. **Genres:** Romance/Historical, Science Fiction/Fantasy. **Career:** Rondout Valley Publishing, supervisor, 1980-88; Flagler County School District, creative writing teacher, 1989-97. Writer. **Publications:** ROMANCE NOVELS AS ELIZABETH SINCLAIR: Jenny's Castle, 1994; Eight Men and a Lady, 1997; Gabriel's Angel, 1998; The Overnight Groom, 1999; The Pregnancy Clause, 2000; For Your Love, 2000; Honey's Heroes. OTHER: The Dreaded Synopsis: A Writing and Plotting Guide (non-fiction), 1999; A Question of Love, 2002; Miracle in the Mist, 2005; Baptism in Fire, 2006; Eye of the Dream, 2006; Touched By Fire, 2007; Into the Mist, 2008; Angel Unaware, 2008; Garden of the Moon, 2009; Burning Secrets, 2009. Contributor to magazines and newspapers. **Address:** c/o Pattie Steele-Perkins, Steele-Perkins Literary Agency, 26 Island Ln., Canandaigua, NY 14424, U.S.A. **Online address:** esinclair1@aol.com

SMITH, Marisa. American (born United States), b. 1956. **Genres:** Theatre, Women's Studies And Issues, Plays/Screenplays, Reference. **Career:** Smith and Kraus Inc., president and publisher, 1990-. Writer. **Publications:** Women Playwrights, vol. I: The Best Plays of 1992, 1993, vol. II: The Best Plays of 1993, 1994, vol. III: The Best Plays of 1994, 1995; EST Marathon 1994, 1995; Book Group: A Comedy in Two Acts, 2005. EDITOR: (with A. Schewel) The Actor's Book of Movie Monologues, 1986; (with K. Graham) Monologues from Literature: A Sourcebook for Actors, 1990; (with J. Beard) Contemporary Movie Monologues: A Sourcebook for Actors, 1991; (with J. Beard) Contemporary Movie Monologues 1960-1989: For Audition and Study, 1991; Humana Festival '93: The Complete Plays, 1994; Humana Festival '94: The Complete Plays, 1995; Showtime's Act One Festival of One-Act Plays, 1994, 1995; Act One '95: The Complete Plays, 1996; The Seattle Children's Theatre: Seven Plays for Young Actors, 1996; Women Playwrights, vol. IV: The Best Plays of 1996, 1997, vol. V: The Best Plays of 1999, 2001; The One-Act Plays 1996, 1997. **Address:** 1 Main St., PO Box 127, Lyme, NH 03768, U.S.A.

SMITH, Mark Haskell. American (born United States), b. 1957?. **Genres:** Adult Non-fiction, Novels, Sex, Travel/Exploration, Humor/Satire, Botany, Food And Wine, Popular Culture, Essays, Plays/Screenplays. **Career:** University of California, Palm Desert Graduate Center, MFA in Creative Writing and Writing for the Performing Arts Program, adjunct assistant professor. Writer. **Publications:** NOVELS: Moist, 2002; Delicious, 2005; Salty, 2007; Baked, 2010. NON-FICTION: Heart of Dankness: Underground Botanists, Outlaw Farmers and the Race for the Cannabis Cup, 2012. **Address:** Mary Evans Literary Agency, 242 E 5th St., New York, NY 10003-8501, U.S.A. **Online address:** mhs@markhaskellsmith.com

SMITH, Mark M. British (born England), b. 1968. **Genres:** History, Natural History, Social Sciences, Humanities. **Career:** University of Birmingham, lecturer in economic and social history, 1994-96; University of South Carolina, assistant professor, 1996-99, associate professor, 1999-2001, professor of history, 2001-, Carolina distinguished professor of history, 2004-. Writer. **Publications:** Mastered by the Clock: Time, Slavery and Freedom in the American South, 1997; Debating Slavery: Economy and Society in the Antebellum American South, 1998; Listening to Nineteenth-Century America, 2001; How Race is Made: Slavery, Segregation and the Senses, 2006; Sensory History, 2007; Sensing the Past: Seeing, Hearing, Smelling, Tasting and Touching in History, 2008; Camille, 1969: Histories of a Hurricane, 2011. EDITOR: The Old South, 2001; Hearing History: A Reader, 2004; Stono: Documenting and Interpreting a Southern Slave Revolt, 2005; Writing the American Past: U.S. History to 1877, 2009; (with R.L. Paquette) Oxford Handbook of Slavery in the Americas, 2010. Contributor of articles to journals. **Address:** Department of History, University of South Carolina, 211 Gambrell Hall, Columbia, SC 29208, U.S.A. **Online address:** smithmm@gwm.sc.edu

SMITH, Martha Nell. American (born United States), b. 1953. **Genres:** Literary Criticism And History, Gay And Lesbian Issues, Women's Studies And Issues, Technology, Biography. **Career:** Rutgers University, assistant director of writing program, 1985-86; University of Maryland, Department of English, assistant professor, 1986-92, associate professor, 1992-98, associate director of graduate English, 1990-94, professor of English, 1998-, advance professor, Maryland Institute for Technology in the Humanities, founding director,

1999-2005. Writer. **Publications:** Rowing in Eden: Rereading Emily Dickinson, 1992; (with S. Juhasz and C. Miller) Comic Power in Emily Dickinson, 1993; (ed. with E.L. Hart) Open Me Carefully: Emily Dickinson's Intimate Letters to Susan Huntington Dickinson, 1998; (ed. with M. Loeffelholz) A Companion to Emily Dickinson, 2008; (with L. Vetter and E.L. Hart) Emily Dickinson's Correspondences: A Born-Digital Inquiry, 2008; Emily Dickinson, A User's Guide, 2010; (with B. Armand) Life Before Last: Reminiscences of a Country Girl, forthcoming; Eroto Biographies, forthcoming; The Life of Susan Dickinson, forthcoming. Contributor of articles to books and journals. **Address:** Department of English, University of Maryland, 3238 Tawes Hall, College Park, MD 20742, U.S.A. **Online address:** mnsmith@umd.edu

SMITH, Martin. *See* **SMITH, Martin Cruz.**

SMITH, Martin Cruz. Also writes as Simon Quinn, Nick Carter, Martin Smith, Jake Logan. American (born United States), b. 1942. **Genres:** Novels, Mystery/Crime/Suspense, Young Adult Fiction. **Career:** Philadelphia Daily News, reporter, 1965; Magazine Management, writer, editor, 1966-69; Associated Press, correspondent. **Publications:** NOVELS AS MARTIN SMITH: The Indians Won, 1970; Gypsy in Amber, 1971; Canto for a Gypsy, 1972. NOVELS AS SIMON QUINN: His Eminence, Death, 1974; Nuplex Red, 1974; The Devil in Kansas, 1974; The Last Time I Saw Hell, 1974; The Midas Coffin, 1975; Last Rites for the Vulture, 1975; The Human Factor, 1975; The Adventures of the Wilderness Family, 1976. NOVELS AS JAKE LOGAN: North to Dakota, 1976; Ride for Revenge, 1977; Slocum Bursts Out, 1990; Slocum, No. 150: Trail of Death, 1991; Slocum, No. 154: Slocum's Standoff, 1991; Slocum, No. 155: Death Council, 1991; Slocum, No. 156: Timber King, 1992; Slocum, No. 157: Railroad Baron, 1992; Slocum, No. 158: River Chase, 1992; Slocum, No. 159: Tombstone Gold, 1992; Slocum, No. 163: Slocum and the Bush wackers, 1992; Slocum, No. 165: San Angelo Shootout, 1992; Slocum, No. 166: Blood Fever, 1992; Revenge at Devil's Tower, 1993; Ambush at Apache Rocks, 1993; Slocum, No. 167: Hell town Trail, 1993; Slocum, No. 168: Sheriff Slocum, 1993; Slocum, No. 169: Virginia City Showdown, 1993; Slocum, No. 170: Slocum and the Forty Thieves, 1993; Slocum, No. 171: Powder River Massacre, 1993; Slocum, No. 173: Slocum and the Tin Star Swindle, 1993; Slocum, No. 174: Slocum and the Nightriders, 1993; Slocum, No. 176: Slocumat Outlaw's Haven, 1993; Pikes Peak Shoot-Out, 1994; Slocum and the Cow Town Kill, 1994; Slocum and the Gold Slaves, 1994; Slocum and the Invaders, 1994; Slocum and the Mountain of Gold, 1994; Slocum and the Phantom Gold, 1994; Slocum, No. 179: Slocum and the Buffalo Soldiers, 1994; Ghost Town, 1994; Blood Trail, 1994. NOVELS: The Analog Bullet, 1972; Nightwing, 1977; Gorky Park, 1981; Park im Gorkogo, 1985; Stallion Gate, 1986; Polar Star, 1989; Red Square, 1992; Rose, 1996; Havana Bay: A Novel, 1999; (ed.) Death By Espionage: Intriguing Stories of Betrayal and Deception, 1999; December 6: A Novel, 2002; Wolves Eat Dogs, 2004; Stalin's Ghost, 2007; The Golden Mile, 2009. OTHERS: (with S. Shagan and B. Shrake) Nightwing, 1979; (ed.) Death By Espionage: Intriguing Stories of Betrayal and Deception, 1999; Three Stations: An Arkady Renko Novel, 2010. AS NICK CARTER: Inca Death Squad, 1972; The Devil's Dozen, 1972. **Address:** c/o Knox Burger, Harold Ober Associates Inc., 425 Madison Ave., Fl. 10, New York, NY 10017, U.S.A. **Online address:** mcsmith@literati.net

SMITH, Marya. American (born United States), b. 1945. **Genres:** Children's Fiction, Plays/Screenplays, Advertising/Public Relations, Essays. **Career:** Seventeen magazine, editorial assistant, 1967-68; University of Chicago Press, copywriter, 1968-70; Drucilla Handy Co., publicity writer, 1970-72; freelance writer, 1972-74, 1978-; Cornell University, Department of Communications, lecturer in magazine writing, 1976-77; Oak Park Public Library, reading tutor. **Publications:** Across the Creek, 1989; Winter-Broken, 1990. Contributor to newspapers and magazines. **Address:** c/o Perry Browne, Pema Browne Ltd., Pine Rd., HCR 104-B, Neversink, NY 12765, U.S.A. **Online address:** marya@creekwinter.com

SMITH, Michael. British (born England), b. 1952. **Genres:** Novels, Biography. **Career:** British Broadcasting Corporation Monitoring Service, journalist; Financial Times and Sunday Times, journalist; Daily Telegraph, defense correspondent covering intelligence and espionage matters. **Publications:** Odd Man Out: The Story of the Singapore Traitor, 1993; New Cloak, Old Dagger: How Britain's Spies Came in from the Cold, 1996; Station X: The Code breakers of Bletchley Park, 1998; Foley: The Spy Who Saved 10000 Jews, 1999; The Emperor's Codes: The Breaking of Japan's Secret Ciphers, 2000; (ed. with R. Erskine) Action This Day, 2001; Killer Elite: The Inside

Story of America's Most Secret Special Operations Team, 2007; SIX: A History of Britain's Secret Intelligence Service, 2010. **Address:** c/o Robert Kirby, Drury House, 34-43 Russell St., London, GL WC2B 5HA, England. **Online address:** mick@michaelsmithwriter.com

SMITH, Mitchell. (Roy LeBeau). American (born United States), b. 1935. **Genres:** Novels, Young Adult Fiction, Science Fiction/Fantasy, Westerns/Adventure. **Career:** Writer. **Publications:** NOVELS: Daydreams, 1987; Stone City, 1990; Due North, 1992; Karma, 1994; Sacrifice, 1997; Reprisal, 1999. OTHERS: Snowfall, 2002; Kingdom River, 2003; Moonrise, 2004; (as Roy LeBeau) 12 Westerns. **Address:** c/o Anne Sibbald, JandN Associates, 445 Park Ave., New York, NY 10022, U.S.A.

SMITH, M. J. American (born United States), b. 1955. **Genres:** Food And Wine, Medicine/Health, Self Help, How-to Books, Adult Non-fiction, Education. **Career:** Writer and dietitian. **Publications:** All-American Low-Fat Meals in Minutes: Recipes and Menus for Special Occasions or Every Day, 1990; 60 Days of Low-Fat, Low-Cost Meals in Minutes: Over 150 Delicious, Healthy Recipes and Menus that Fit Your Budget, 1992; 366 Low-Fat, Brand-Name Recipes in Minutes!: More than One Year of Healthy Cooking Using Your Family's Favorite Brand-Name Foods, 1994; Miracle Foods Cookbook: Easy, Low-Cost Recipes and Menus with Antioxidant-Rich Vegetables and Fruits that Help You Lose Weight, Fight Disease, and Slow the Aging Process, 1995; Diabetic Low-Fat and No-Fat Meals in Minutes: More than 250 Delicious, Easy, and Healthy Recipes and Menus for People with Diabetes, Their Families, and Their Friends, 1996; Daily Bread: A Day Book of Recipes and Reflections for Healthy Eating, 1997; All-American Low-Fat and No-Fat Meals in Minutes: 300 Delicious Recipes and Menus for Special Occasions or Every Day-in Thirty Minutes or Less, 2nd ed., 1997; Seafood Meals in Minutes!, 1998; Cream of the Crop, 1998; (ed. with K. Freiberg) Farm Journal's Cream of the Crop Cookbook: 300 Classic Dishes Picked from Farm Journal's Famous Test Kitchens, plus! Fat-Skimming Options with Each Recipe, 1998; Low-Fat Bed and Breakfast Cookbook: 300 Tried-and-True Recipes from North American B & Bs, 1998; Mother's Cry: A Novel, 2004; A Better You, 2005; Kevin Murphy Takes on the Father of Lies, 2005; (with F. Smith) The Smart Student's Guide to Healthy Living: How to Survive Stress, Late Nights, and the College Cafeteria, 2006. **Address:** Smart Student's Guide, 207 Lorenz Ln., Guttenberg, IA 52052, U.S.A. **Online address:** mj@lowfatkitchen.com

SMITH, Morris. American (born United States), b. 1928. **Genres:** Novellas/Short Stories, Young Adult Fiction, Novels, Literary Criticism And History. **Career:** School teacher, social worker and writer. **Publications:** Spencer Road: A Short Story Sequence, 1997; Zambian Text: Stories from Ngambe Mission, 2005; Better Than Jail: A Novel, 2009. **Address:** 2947 Loch Laurel Rd., Valdosta, GA 31601, U.S.A.

SMITH, Neil. Canadian (born Canada), b. 1964?. **Genres:** Novels. **Career:** Writer. **Publications:** Bang Crunch, 2008. **Address:** Montreal, QC , Canada. **Online address:** eepie@sympatico.ca

SMITH, Neil. Scottish (born Scotland), b. 1954. **Genres:** Geography, Politics/Government. **Career:** Columbia University, assistant professor, 1982-86, director, 2000-08; Rutgers University, assistant professor, 1986-88, associate professor, 1988-90, professor of geography, 1990-2000, department chair, 1991-94, Princeton University, adjunct assistant professor, 1988; University of Queensland, visiting research professor, 1988; University of Utrecht, visiting professor, 1990; City University New York, Center for Place Culture and Politics Graduate Center, director, 2000, distinguished professor of anthropology and geography; University Toronto, visiting research professor, 2002, Visiting Distinguished Johnson-Connaught Professor in American Studies, 2002; University of Oslo, visiting professor, 2002; University of Pennsylvani, visiting professor, 2003; Queens University, visiting professor, 2005. Writer. **Publications:** Geography Social Welfare and Underdevelopment, 1977; Uneven Development: Nature, Capital and the Production of Space, 1984, 3rd ed., 2008; Gentrification of the City, 1986; (ed. with A. Godlewska) Geography and Empire, 1994; The New Urban Frontier: Gentrification and the Revanchist City, 1996; Globalización, 2000; American Empire: Roosevelts Geographer and the Prelude to Globalization, 2003; The Endgame of Globalization, 2005; (ed.) The Politics of Public Space, 2006. **Address:** Department of Anthropology and Geography, Graduate Center and Hunter College, City University of New York, 365 5th Ave., New York, NY 10016, U.S.A. **Online address:** nsmith@gc.cuny.edu

SMITH, Neil(son) V(oyne). British (born England), b. 1939. **Genres:** Language/Linguistics. **Career:** University of London, School of Oriental and African Studies, lecturer in West African languages, 1964-72, lecturer in linguistics, 1970-72, University College, reader, 1972-81, professor of linguistics, 1981-2006, Department of Phonetics and Linguistics, head, 1983-90, now professor emeritus. Writer. **Publications:** An Outline Grammar of Nupe, 1967; The Acquisition of Phonology, 1973; (with D. Wilson) Modern Linguistics: The Results of Chomsky's Revolution, 1979; (ed.) Mutual Knowledge, 1982; Speculative Linguistics, 1983; The Twitter Machine: Reflections on Language, 1989; (with I. Tsimpli) The Mind of a Savant: Language Learning and Modularity, 1995; Chomsky: Ideas and Ideals, 1999, rev. ed., 2004; Language, Bananas, and Bonobos: Linguistic Problems, Puzzles, and Polemics, 2002; Language, Frogs and Savants: More Linguistic Problems, Puzzles and Polemics, 2005; Acquiring Phonology: A Cross-generational Case-study, 2010; (with I. Tsimpli, G. Morgan and B. Woll) The Signs of a Savant: Language Against the Odds; 2011. **Address:** Research Department of Linguistics, University College London, Chandler House, 2 Wakefield St., London, GL WC1N 1PF, England. **Online address:** smithnv@gmail.com

SMITH, Nicholas D. American (born United States), b. 1949. **Genres:** Classics, Philosophy, Literary Criticism And History, Theology/Religion. **Career:** University of Wisconsin-Parkside, lecturer, 1975-76, assistant professor of philosophy, 1976-77; Virginia Polytechnic Institute and State University, assistant professor, professor of philosophy, 1977-94; University of Santa Clara, visiting associate professor, 1982-83; Michigan State University, professor, 1994-99; Lewis & Clark College, James F. Miller professor of humanities, 1999-; Hong Kong University, Department of Philosophy, outside evaluator, 2009-. Writer. **Publications:** (Comp. with F.D. Miller) Thought Probes: Philosophy Through Science Fiction, 1981, 2nd ed., 1989; (ed.) Philosophers Look at Science Fiction, 1982; (ed. with M. Barr) Women and Utopia: Critical Interpretations, 1983; (ed.) Utopian Studies, vol. I (with G. Beauchamp and K. Roemer), 1987, (with M. Cummings) vol. II, 1989, (with L. Leibacher-Ouvrard) vol. III-IV, 1991; (with T.C. Brickhouse) Socrates on Trial, 1989; (ed. with J. Klagge) Methods of Interpreting Plato and His Dialogues, 1992; (with T.C. Brickhouse) Plato's Socrates, 1994; (co-ed.) Knowledge, Teaching and Wisdom, 1996; (with T.C. Brickhouse) The Philosophy of Socrates, 2000; (ed. with P.B. Woodruff) Reason and Religion in Socratic Philosophy, 2000; (ed. with P. Woodruff) Reason and Religion in Socratic Philosophy, 2000; (ed. and trans. with T.C. Brickhouse) The Trial and Execution of Socrates: Sources and Controversies, 2002; (with T.C. Brickhouse) Routledge Philosophy Guidebook to Plato and the Trial of Socrates, 2004; (ed. with P. Destrée) Socrates' Divine Sign: Religion, Practice, and Value in Socratic Philosophy, 2005; (ed. with F. Ilhoff and A.J. Vaidya) Ancient Philosophy: Essential Readings With Commentary, 2008; (with M. McPherran) Socrates, 2008; (ed. with J. Bussanich) A Companion to Socrates, 2008; (with T.C. Brickhouse) Socratic Moral Psychology, 2010. **Address:** Department of Philosophy, Lewis & Clark College, 0615 SW Palatine Hill Rd., Portland, OR 97219-7899, U.S.A. **Online address:** ndsmith@lclark.edu

SMITH, Nigel. American (born United States), b. 1958. **Genres:** Poetry, Social Sciences, Language/Linguistics. **Career:** Princeton University, professor of English and Senior Behrman Fellow; Oxford University, reader in English; Keble College, tutor in English and fellow. Writer. **Publications:** Perfection Proclaimed: Language and Literature in English Radical Religion, 1640-1660, 1989; Literature and Revolution in England, 1640-1660, 1994; Is Milton Better Than Shakespeare?, 2008. EDITOR: A Collection of Ranter Writings from the 17th Century, 1983; Literature and Censorship, 1993; (and intro.) George Fox, The Journal, 1998; (with T. Morton) Radicalism in British Literary Culture, 1650-1830: From Revolution to Revolution, 2002; The Poems of Andrew Marvell, 2003, rev. ed., 2006. **Address:** Center for the Study of Religion, Princeton University, 5 Ivy Ln., Princeton, NJ 08540, U.S.A. **Online address:** nsmith@princeton.edu

SMITH, Noel W. Also writes as N. W. Smith, Noel Wilson Smith. American (born United States), b. 1933. **Genres:** Psychology. **Career:** State University of New York College, assistant professor, 1963-66, associate professor, 1966-71, professor of psychology, 1971-. Writer. **Publications:** (With J.R. Kantor) The Science of Psychology: An Interbehavioral Survey, 1975; (ed. with P.T. Mountjoy and D.H. Ruben) Reassessment in Psychology: The Interbehavioral Alternative, 1983; Greek and Interbehavioral Psychology: Selected and Revised Papers of Noel W. Smith, 1990, rev. ed., 1993; An Analysis of Ice Age

Art: Its Psychology and Belief System, 1992; Current Systems in Psychology: History, Theory, Research and Applications, 2001. **Address:** 3027 Willow Green, Sarasota, FL 34235, U.S.A. **Online address:** nwilsmith@yahoo.com

SMITH, Noel Wilson. *See* **SMITH, Noel W.**

SMITH, N. W. *See* **SMITH, Noel W.**

SMITH, Pamela (A.). American (born United States), b. 1947. **Genres:** inspirational/Motivational Literature, Romance/Historical, Theology/Religion. **Career:** Roman Catholic nun of the Sisters of Saints Cyril and Methodius; Saints Cyril and Methodius Seminary, associate dean and director of lay ministry programs, 1996-; Duquesne University, faculty; University of Scranton, faculty; Marywood College, faculty; Villanova University, faculty; Lehigh University, faculty; Writer. **Publications:** Waymakers, 1982; Woman Story: Biblical Models for Our Time, 1992; Life after Easter, 1993; Woman Gifts: Biblical Models for Forming a Church, 1994; Days of Dust and Ashes: Hope-Filled Lenten Reflections, 1997; What Are They Saying about Environmental Ethics?, 1997; Days of Light and Darkness: Prayerful Reflections for Advent, 1999; Aquinas and Today's Environmental Ethics, forthcoming. Contributor to periodicals. **Address:** Saints Cyril & Methodius Seminary, 3535 Indian Trl., Orchard Lake, MI 48324, U.S.A.

SMITH, Patricia. American (born United States), b. 1955. **Genres:** Poetry, Music, History, Children's Fiction, Popular Culture, Race Relations, Women's Studies And Issues, Mystery/Crime/Suspense, Mystery/Crime/Suspense. **Career:** Chicago Daily News, music and entertainment reviewer; Chicago Sun-Times, entertainment writer, 1978-90; Boston Globe, entertainment critic, regular columnist and reporter, 1990-98; Georgia Institute of Technology, Bruce McEver chair in writing; Cave Canem (a writers center), faculty; City University of New York, professor, 2009-. **Publications:** Life According to Motown, 1991; Big Towns, Big Talk, 1992; Close to Death, 1993; Africans in America: America's Journey through Slavery, 1998; Janna and the Kings, 2003; Teahouse of the Almighty, 2006; Blood Dazzler, 2008. Works appear in anthologies. Contributor to periodicals. **Address:** c/o Alison Granucci, Blue Flower Arts, 373 Mabbettsville Rd., PO Box 1361, Millbrook, NY 12545, U.S.A. **Online address:** patricia@wordwoman.ws

SMITH, Paul. American/British (born England), b. 1954. **Genres:** Cultural/Ethnic Topics, Business/Trade/Industry. **Career:** Carnegie Mellon University, School of Computer Science, The Robotics Institute, professor of cultural studies and senior mechanical engineer. Writer. **Publications:** Pound Revised, 1983; (ed. with A. Jardine) Men in Feminism, 1987; Discerning the Subject, 1988; (ed. with L. Frank) Madonnarama: Essays on Sex and Popular Culture, 1993; Clint Eastwood: A Cultural Production, 1993; (ed. and trans.) J. Schefer, Enigmatic Body: Essays on the Arts, 1995; (ed.) Boys: Masculinities in Contemporary Culture, 1996; Millenial Dreams: Contemporary Culture and Capital in the North, 1997; Primitive America: The Ideology of Capitalist Democracy, 2007; (ed.) Renewal of Cultural Studies, 2011. **Address:** School of Computer Science, Carnegie Mellon University, 37 National Robotics Engineering Ctr., 10 40th St., Pittsburgh, PA 15201, U.S.A. **Online address:** pksmith@rec.ri.cmu.edu

SMITH, Paul. British (born England), b. 1937?. **Genres:** History, Biography. **Career:** University of Southampton, professor of history. Writer. **Publications:** Disraelian Conservatism and Social Reform, 1967; (ed. and intro.) Lord Salisbury on Politics; A Selection from his Articles in the Quarterly Review, 1860-1883, 1972; (ed.) The Historian and film, 1976; (ed. with K. Koufa and A. Suppan) Ethnic Groups in International Relations, 1991; Disraeli: A Brief Life, 1996; (ed.) Government and the Armed Forces in Britain, 1856-1990, 1996; (ed. with C. Richmond) The Self-Fashioning of Disraeli, 1818-1851, 1998; (ed.) Bagehot: The English Constitution, 2001. Contributor to periodicals. **Address:** Department of History, School of Humanities, University of Southampton, Southampton, S017 1BJ, England.

SMITH, Paul Julian. British/American (born United States), b. 1956. **Genres:** Cultural/Ethnic Topics, History, Language/Linguistics, Literary Criticism And History, Reference. **Career:** Cambridge University, Trinity Hall, research fellow, 1983-84, Department of Spanish and Portuguese, professor, 1991-2010, head, 1991-; University of London, Queen Mary College, lecturer, 1984-88, reader in Spanish, 1988-91; Journal of Spanish Cultural Studies, founding editor; City University of New York, Hispanic and Luso-Brazilian Literatures and Languages, Graduate Center, distinguished profes-

sor, 2010-. Visiting professor and writer. **Publications:** Quevedo on Parnassus: Allusive Context and Literary Theory in the Love-Lyric, 1987; Writing in the Margin: Spanish Literature of the Golden Age, 1988; The Body Hispanic: Gender and Sexuality in Spanish and Spanish American Literature, 1989; A Critical Guide to Quevedo's Buscon, 1991; Representing the Other: Race, Text and Gender in Spanish and Spanish American Narrative, 1992; Laws of Desire: Questions of Homosexuality in Spanish Writing and Film, 1960-1990, 1992; (ed. with C. Davis) Art and Literature in Spain, 1600-1800: Studies in Honour of Nigel Glendinning, 1993; Desire Unlimited, 1994; (ed. with Emilie L. Bergmann) Entiendes?: Queer Readings, Hispanic Writings, 1995; García Lorca/Almodóva, 1995; The Vision Machines, 1996; The Theatre of Garcia Lorca: Text, Performance, Psychoanalysis, 1998; The Moderns: Time, Space and Subjectivity in Contemporary Spanish Culture, 2000; Contemporary Spanish Culture: TV, Fashion, Art and Film, 2003; Amores Perros: Modern Classic, 2003; Television in Spain: From Franco to Almodóvar, 2006; Spanish Visual Culture: Cinema, Television, Internet, 2006. Contributor to journals. **Address:** Hispanic and Luso BrazilianLiteratures, Graduate Center, City University of New York, 365 5th Ave., New York, NY 10016, U.S.A. **Online address:** pjs1001@cam.ac.uk

SMITH, Peter Charles Horstead. British (born England), b. 1940. **Genres:** Novels, History, Military/Defense/Arms Control, Engineering, Technology. **Career:** General Post Office, overseas telegraph officer, 1965-70; W&J MacKay Ltd., manager of printing sales office, 1970-72; Photo Precision Ltd., editor, 1972-74; Cape Sun, editor and journalist, 1974-75; British Telecomms, tutor and instructor in communication skills, 1976-91; fulltime author, 1991-; RSPB, publications coordinator, 2000-. **Publications:** Destroyer Leader: The Story of HMS Faulknor, 1968, 3rd ed., 2004; Task Force 57, 1969; Pedestal, 1970, 6th ed., 2007; Hard Lying, 1971; Stuka at War, 1971; (with E.R. Walker) War in the Aegean: The Campaign for the Eastern Mediterranean in World War II, 1972; Royal Navy Ships Badges, 1973; Royal Air Force Squadron Badges, 1973; Per Mare Per Terram, 1974; (with E. Walker) Battles of the Malta Striking Forces, 1974; The Story of the Torpedo Bomber, 1975; Arctic Victory, 1975; Midway, 1976; Fighting Flotilla, 1976, 2nd ed., 2010; The Great Ships Pass, 1977; Hit First, Hit Hard, 1979; Action Imminent, 1980; Impact!, 1981; (with J.R. Dominy) Cruisers in Action, 1981; Dive Bomber! An Illustrated History, 1982; Rendezvous Skerki Bank, 1982; Hold the Narrow Sea: Naval Warfare in the English Channel, 1939-45, 1984; H.M.S. Wild Swan, 1985; Into the Assault: Famous Dive Bomber Aces of the Second World War, 1985; Vengeance! Vultee Vengeance Dive Bomber, 1986; Jungle Dive: Bombers at War, 1987; Victorias Victories: Seven Classic Battles of the British Army, 1987; Pedestal: Malta Convoy of August 1942, 1987; Massacre at Tobruk: The Story of Operation Agreement, 1987; (with D. Oakley) The Royal Marines, 1988; Dive Bombers in Action, 1988; Battleship Royal Sovereign, 1988; Stuka Squadron: St. G 77, 1990; T-6: The Texan, Harvard and Wirraway, 1995; Eagles War: The War Diary of an Aircraft Carrier, 1996; Behind the Black Curtain, 1996; Stuka Spearhead: The Lightning War from Poland to Dunkirk, 1939-1940, 1998; Douglas SBD Dauntless, 1998; Stukas over the Mediterranean, 1940-1945, 1999; Stukas over the Steppe: The Blitzkrieg in the East, 1941-1945, 1999; Curtiss SB2C Helldiver, 1999; Straight Down! The A-36 in Combat, 2000; Junkers Ju 87 Stuka, 2000; Lockheed C-130 Hercules, 2001; North American Harvard, Texan, and Wirraway, 2001; Fairchild-Republic A-10A Thunderbolt II, 2001; Sea Eagles: The Luftwaffes Maritime Operations, 2001; Into the Minefields: British Destroyer Minelaying 1916-1960, 2005; Skua!: The Royal Navys Dive-bomber, 2006; Fist from the Sky, 2006; Midway: Dauntless Victory: Fresh Perspectives on Americas Seminal Naval Victory of World War II, 2007; The Story of the Torpedo Bomber: Rare Photographs from Wartime Archives, 2007; History of Dive-bombing, 2007; Naval Warfare in the English Channel, 1939-1945, 2007; Dive Bomber!: Aircraft, Technology, and Tactics in World War II, 2008; Great Ships: British Battleships in World War II, 2008; Massacre at Tobruk: The British Assault on Rommel, 1942, 2008; The Battle-cruiser HMS Renown, 1916-1948, 2008. EDITOR: Destroyer Action, 1974; The Haunted Sea, 1975; Undesirable Properties, 1977; The Phantom Coach, 1979; Haunted Shores, 1980; Uninvited Guests: Thirteen Unwelcome Visitors, 1984. **Address:** Foxden, 12 Brooklands Rd., Riseley, Bedford, BD MK44 1EE, England. **Online address:** petercsmith@supanet.com

SMITH, Peter J. (P. J. Smith). Canadian/New Zealander (born New Zealand), b. 1931. **Genres:** Geography, Regional/Urban Planning. **Career:** City Planning Department, research planner, 1956-59; University of Alberta, assistant professor, 1959-64, associate professor, 1964-69, chairman of department, 1967-75, professor of geography, 1969-94, associate dean of science, 1975-

77, emeritus professor, 1994-; Canada Council, fellow, 1970-71; Social Sciences and Humanities Research Council of Canada, fellow, 1977-78, 1984-85; Canadian Geographer, editor, 1978-84. Writer. **Publications:** Population and Production: An Introduction to Some Problems in Economic Geography, 1967, rev. ed., 1971; The Edmonton-Calgary Corridor, 1978; Edinburgh Redivivus: Urban Renewal in a Victorian City and Its Implications for the Planning Idea, forthcoming. EDITOR: Studies in Canadian Geography: The Prairie Provinces, 1972; Edmonton: The Emerging Metropolitan Pattern, 1978; (with B.M. Barr) Environment and Economy: Essays on the Human Geography of Alberta, 1984; (with E.L. Jackson) A World of Real Places, 1990. **Address:** Department of Earth & Atmospheric Sciences, University of Alberta, Tory 2-5, 1-26 Earth Sciences Bldg., Edmonton, AB T6G 2E3, Canada. **Online address:** peterjsmith@shaw.ca

SMITH, Peter Moore. American/Panamanian (born Panama), b. 1965?. **Genres:** Novels, Criminology/True Crime. **Career:** Publicis, executive creative director and executive vice president. Writer. **Publications:** NOVELS: Raveling, 2000; Strange Bliss, 2002; Die vergessene Zeit, 2002; Los Angeles, 2005. Contributor to journals. **Address:** c/o Author Mail, Little, Brown and Company Inc., 1271 Ave. of the Americas, New York, NY 10020-1300, U.S.A.

SMITH, P. J. See **SMITH, Peter J.**

SMITH, Ralph Lee. American (born United States), b. 1927. **Genres:** Music, Art/Art History. **Career:** National Better Business Bureau, editor, 1954-58; freelance writer and consultant, 1959-71; Sloan Commission on Cable Communications, senior staff assistant, 1970-71; Howard University, associate professor, 1972-76; MITRE Corp., writer and researcher, 1972; Berner & Smith Associates, partner, 1977-79; Appalachian State University, faculty; Western Carolina University, faculty; Shenandoah University, faculty; Davis College, faculty; Elkins College, faculty; Technology & Economics Inc., director, 1979-. **Publications:** The Wired Nation, 1970; (ed. with N. Jesuale) CTIC Cablebooks, 1982; The Story of the Dulcimer, 1986; American Dulcimer Traditions, 1997, 2nd ed., 2010; Songs and Tunes of the Wilderness Road, 1999; Folk Songs of Old Kentucky, 2003; Greenwich Village: The Happy Folksinging Days, 1950s and 1960s, 2008; Folk Songs of Old Virginia, 2009. **Address:** Technology & Economics Inc., 204 G St. NE, Washington, DC 20002, U.S.A. **Online address:** ralphlecsmith@comcast.net

SMITH, Richard L. American (born United States), b. 1950. **Genres:** Medicine/Health, Gay And Lesbian Issues. **Career:** Spokane Resource Advocates, research assistant, 1972; Pacific Institute for Community Organizations, community organizer, 1973-75; St. Leo's Church, associate pastor, 1981-83; St. Aloysius Parish, pastor, 1983-87; Quality Rehabilitation Services, vocational rehabilitation counselor, 1991-94; AIDS Resource and Information Services, trainer of volunteers, 1992-95; San Jose State University, lecturer in comparative religious studies, 1994-95; Pacific School of Religion, adjunct professor, 1995; Santa Clara University, adjunct faculty, 1996; Chabot College, lecturer; University of California-Berkeley, lecturer. Writer. **Publications:** AIDS, Gays and the American Catholic Church, 1994. Contributor to periodicals. **Address:** 842 Teresita Blvd., San Francisco, CA 94127-2323, U.S.A.

SMITH, Rick. Canadian (born Canada), b. 1968?. **Genres:** Sciences. **Career:** International Fund for Animal Welfare, executive director, 1997-2002, acting director; Environmental Defence Canada, executive director, 2003-. Writer. **Publications:** (With S. Dopp) Slow Death by Rubber Duck: The Secret Danger of Everyday Things in Canada as Slow Death by Rubber Duck: How the Toxic Chemistry of Everyday Life Affects Our Health, 2009. **Address:** Environmental Defence, 317 Adelaide St. W, Ste. 705, Toronto, ON M5V 1P9, Canada.

SMITH, R. J. American (born United States), b. 1959?. **Genres:** History, Social Sciences. **Career:** Los Angeles magazine, senior editor; Details, senior contributing editor; historian. **Publications:** The Great Black Way: L.A. in the 1940s and the Lost African-American Renaissance, 2006; The Life and Music of James Brown, 2012. Contributor to periodicals. **Address:** Los Angeles Magazine, 5900 Wilshire Blvd., 10th Fl., Los Angeles, CA 90036, U.S.A.

SMITH, Robert Ellis. American (born United States), b. 1940. **Genres:** Civil Liberties/Human Rights, Law, Humanities, Literary Criticism And History, Information Science/Computers. **Career:** Detroit Free Press, reporter, 1962-63, 1966; The Southern Courier, editor, 1965-66; Newsday, reporter, 1967-70; U.S. Department of Health, Education and Welfare, Office for Civil Rights, staff, 1970-73, assistant director, 1973-74; Privacy Journal, publisher, 1974-; Americans Abroad, editor and publisher, 1977-78. **Publications:** Compilation of State and Federal Laws on Privacy, 1976; (with K.D. Snyder) Compilation of State and Federal Privacy Laws, 1976, 8th ed., 1997; Privacy: How to Protect What's Left of It, 1979; Workrights, 1983; (co-author) The Big Brother Book of Lists, 1984; The Law of Privacy Explained, 1993; Law of Privacy in a Nutshell, 1993; Our Vanishing Privacy and What You Can do to Protect Yours, 1993; Ben Franklin's Web Site: Privacy and Curiosity from Plymouth Rock to the Internet, 2000; A National ID Card: A License to Live, 2001; Block Island Trivia, 2003; (ed.) Naked in Nature: Great Skinny Dipping Moments in Art and Literature, 2006. Contributor of articles to periodicals. **Address:** Privacy Journal, PO Box 28577, Providence, RI 02908-0577, U.S.A. **Online address:** ellis84@rcn.com

SMITH, Roger T. American (born United States), b. 1953. **Genres:** Sciences, Bibliography, Biography, Astronomy, Reference. **Career:** Nevada Magazine, associate editor, 1981-82; Associated Press, legislative correspondent, 1986; Fairleigh Dickinson University, assistant professor of English, 1987-89; writer, 1989-; Willamette University, adjunct instructor, 1989-94; Linfield College, adjunct instructor, 1989-94; Concordia College, adjunct instructor, 1989-94. **Publications:** (With P. Allen and A. Bearne) Energy Matter and Form: Toward a Science of Consciousness, 1977; (contrib.) Magill's Survey of Science, 1990; Popular Physics and Astronomy: An Annotated Bibliography, 1996; (ed.) The Solar System, 1998; (ed. with R. Olson) The Biographical Encyclopedia of Scientists, 1998; Biographies of Scientists: An Annotated Bibliography, 1998; (ed.) Inventions and Inventors, 2002. **Address:** 2644 NE 24th Ave., Portland, OR 97212, U.S.A. **Online address:** irtnogebw@msn.com

SMITH, Rollin. American (born United States), b. 1942. **Genres:** Music, Biography, Sciences. **Career:** Church of Our Lady of Angels, organist and director of music, 1970-92; Saint Catherine of Alexandria Church, organist and director of music, 1992-; Brooklyn Museum, artist-in-residence; The Organ Historical Society, tracker staff and tracker editor, director of publications. Educator and writer. **Publications:** Toward an Authentic Interpretation of the Organ Works of César Franck, 1983, 2nd ed., 2002; Saint-Saëns and the Organ, 1992; Organist's Book of Days, 1994; Playing the Organ Works of César Franck, 1997; The Aeolian Pipe Organ and Its Music, 1998; Louis Vierne: Organist of Notre-Dame, 1999; Stokowski and the Organ, 2004. Contributor to journals. **Address:** 313 Fulton St., Westbury, NY 11590-2127, U.S.A. **Online address:** tracker@organsociety.org

SMITH, Rosamond. See **OATES, Joyce Carol.**

SMITH, Rupert. Also writes as Rupert James, James Lear. British (born England), b. 1960. **Genres:** Novels, Young Adult Fiction. **Career:** Radio Times Magazine, staff. Writer. **Publications:** (With J. County) Man Enough to Be a Woman (autobiography), 1995; Physique: The Life of John S. Barrington (biography), 1997; I Must Confess (novel), 1998; On the Edge (novel), 2000; Fly on the Wall (novel), 2002; (with G. Morecambe) Life's Not Hollywood, It's Cricklewood (biography), 2003; Service Wash (novel), 2006; (with M. Barrymore) Awight Now! (biography), 2006. TELEVISION TIE-INS: The Forsyte Saga Companion, 2002; Cold Feet: The Complete Companion, 2003; A Year at Kew, 2004; East Enders: 20 Years in Albert Square, 2005; Strictly Come Dancing, 2005; The Museum, 2007. ADULT GAY FICTION-UNDER PSEUDONYM JAMES LEAR: The Low Road, 2001; The Palace of Varieties, 2003; The Back Passage, 2006; Hot Valley, 2007; Secret Tunnel, 2008; Sticky End, 2010; Man's World, 2011. (As Rupert James) Silk, 2009; Stepsisters, 2010. Contributor to periodicals. **Address:** London, England. **Online address:** rupert.smith@virgin.net

SMITH, Ryan K. American (born United States) **Genres:** Archaeology/Antiquities, Popular Culture, Theology/Religion, History. **Career:** Virginia Commonwealth University, Department of History, collateral assistant professor and assistant, 2004-07, assistant professor of history, 2007-09, associate professor, 2009-. Writer and historian. **Publications:** Gothic Arches, Latin Crosses: Anti-Catholicism and American Church Designs in the Nineteenth Century, 2006. Contributor to periodicals. **Address:** Department of History, Virginia Commonwealth University, Rm. 106, 813 S Cathedral Pl., PO Box 842001, Richmond, VA 23284-2001, U.S.A. **Online address:** rksmith3@vcu.edu

SMITH, Sam. American (born United States), b. 1948. **Genres:** Sports/Fitness, Biography, Politics/Government. **Career:** Arthur Young and Co., staff auditor, 1970-72; News-Sentinel, investigative reporter, 1973-75; State News Service, congressional reporter, 1975-79; U.S. Senate, press secretary for Senator Lowell Weicker, 1979; Chicago Tribune, sportswriter/columnist, 1979-, now retired; Professional Basketball Writers Association, president; Sporting News magazine, NBA writer; Bulls.com, NBA writer. **Publications:** The Jordan Rules: The Inside Story of a Turbulent Season with Michael Jordan and the Chicago Bulls, 1992; Second Coming: The Strange Odyssey of Michael Jordan-From Courtside to Home Plate and Back Again, 1995. Contributor to periodicals. **Address:** c/o Shari Lesser Wenk, Burns Sports, 320 N Michigan Ave., Chicago, IL 60611, U.S.A. **Online address:** sasmith@tribune.com

SMITH, Sandra Lee. (Sandy Wardman). American (born United States), b. 1945. **Genres:** Romance/Historical, Self Help, Children's Fiction, Novels. **Career:** McKinleyville School District, teacher, 1967-70; Ft. Bragg Elementary School District, teacher, 1970-73; Phoenix Elementary School District, teacher, 1975-2000; Arizona State University, consultant, 1984-90; California State Universities, consultant, 1987-88. Writer. **Publications:** FICTION: Love's Miracles, 1989; Dream Song, 1989; A Flower for Angela, 1999. NONFICTION: Coping with Decision Making, 1989; Coping with Cross-Cultural and Interracial Relationships, 1990; Value of Self Control, 1991; Coping through Self-Control, 1991; Marijuana, 1991, rev. ed., 1999; Heroin, 1991, rev. ed., 2000; Discovering Personal Resources, 1992; Setting Goals, 1992; Discovering Your Own Space, 1992; Great Grooming for Girls, 1993; Coping with Changing Schools, 1993; Peyote and Magic Mushrooms, 1995; The Price of Victory, 2011. AS SANDY WARDMAN: Jesus Saves!: Take-Home Mini-Books, 2007; God's Spirit Within Me, 2008; (with C. Frankel) God's Spirit Calls Me, 2010; Hector Wants to Play, Percival, The Naughty Prairie Dog. Contributor of articles to periodicals. **Address:** 5433 S Mill Ave., Tempe, AZ 85283, U.S.A. **Online address:** sandyward@yahoo.com

SMITH, Sarah (W. R.). American (born United States), b. 1947. **Genres:** Mystery/Crime/Suspense, Science Fiction/Fantasy, Film, Information Science/Computers, Literary Criticism And History, Bibliography, Translations, Young Adult Fiction, Young Adult Fiction, Paranormal, Humanities, E-books. **Career:** Northeastern University, assistant professor of English, 1975-76; Tufts University, assistant professor of English, 1976-82; G.K. Hall, field editor, 1977-83; LISP Machine, director of documentation, 1982-86; Bachman Information Systems, director of documentation, 1986-88; ITP Systems Inc., manager of training and documentation, 1988-90; writer and consultant, 1990-2004; Effective Educational Technologies, staff, 2004-07; Pearson L.L.C., staff, 2007-. **Publications:** NOVELS: King of Space (science fiction), 1991; The Vanished Child (mystery), 1992; (co-author) Future Boston, 1994; The Knowledge of Water (mystery), 1996; The Dolls, 1996; A Citizen of the Country (mystery), 2000; Chasing Shakespeare, 2003; Other Side of Dark, 2010. OTHERS: (trans.) Colette, Colette at the Movies, 1980; Samuel Richardson: A Critical Bibliography, 1984; A New Shakespearean Poem, 2011. Contributor to periodicals. **Address:** c/o Christopher Schelling, Selectric Artists, 56 Planetarium Sta., New York, NY 10024, U.S.A. **Online address:** sarahwriter@gmail.com

SMITH, Scott. (Scott Bechtel Smith). American (born United States), b. 1965. **Genres:** Adult Non-fiction, Novels, Horror. **Career:** Writer. **Publications:** A Simple Plan: A Novel, 1993; The Ruins: A Novel, 2006. Contributor to periodicals. **Address:** c/o Gail Hochman, Robert A. Freedman Dramatic Agency Inc., 1501 Broadway, Ste. 2310, New York, NY 10036-5600, U.S.A.

SMITH, Scott Bechtel. *See* **SMITH, Scott.**

SMITH, Sheldon. American/Trinidadian (born Trinidad and Tobago), b. 1940. **Genres:** Social Sciences, History, Natural History, Anthropology/Ethnology, Environmental Sciences/Ecology. **Career:** Umqua Community College, instructor, 1968-69; University of Wisconsin-La Crosse, Department of Sociology and Archaeology, instructor, professor of anthropology and archaeology, 1969-2005, emeritus professor of anthropology and archaeology, 2005-, Institute of Latin American Studies, director; University of Wisconsin-Milwaukee, Center for Latin American and Caribbean Studies, regional associate. Writer. **Publications:** Anthropology: A Human Systems Ecology Approach, vol. I: Prehistoric World, vol. II: Culture and Community, 1986; (ed. with E. Reeves) Human Systems Ecology, 1989; World in Disorder: An Interdisciplinary Approach to Global Issues, 1993; World in Disorder, 1994-1995: An Anthropological and Interdisciplinary Approach to Global Issues,

1995; (with P.D. Young) Cultural Anthropology: Understanding a World in Transition, 1998; Latin America in Transition: The Influence of Culture on Ecology, Power, and Diversity, 2003. Contributor to books and periodicals. **Address:** Department of Sociology & Archaeology, University of Wisconsin, 1725 State St., La Crosse, WI 54601-3742, U.S.A. **Online address:** smith.shel@uwlax.edu

SMITH, Sherri L. American (born United States), b. 1971. **Genres:** Novels. **Career:** Disney TV Animation, development assistant, 1996-97, development associate, 1997-99; Los Angeles Construction Co., staff; Bongo Comics, office manager. Writer. **Publications:** Lucy the Giant, 2002; Sparrow, 2006; Hot, Sour, Salty, Sweet, 2008; Flygirl, 2009. Contributor to periodicals. **Address:** Delacorte Press, Dell Publishing Group Inc., 1540 Broadway Ave., New York, NY 10036, U.S.A. **Online address:** letters@sherrilsmith.com

SMITH, Sherry L. American (born United States), b. 1951. **Genres:** History. **Career:** University of Colorado, Department of History, visiting lecturer in history, 1981-82, 1984-85; University of Wyoming, Department of History, visiting assistant professor of history and field historian, 1982-84; University of Texas, visiting assistant professor, 1985-87, assistant professor of history, 1988-92, associate professor, 1992-99, faculty senate, 1993-95, Centennial Museum, faculty associate, 1989-90; Southern Methodist University, Department of History, associate professor, 1999-2000, professor, 2000-08, university distinguished professor, 2008-, William P. Clements Center for Southwest Studies, acting director, 2000-01, William P. Clements Center for Southwest Studies, associate director, 2001-, director of graduate studies, 2004-. Writer. **Publications:** Sagebrush Soldier: Private William Earl Smith's View of the Sioux War of 1876, 1989; The View from Officers' Row: Army Perceptions of Western Indians, 1990; Reimagining Indians: Native Americans Through Anglo Eyes, 1880-1940, 2000; (ed.) Future of the Southern Plains, 2003; (contrib.) Lanterns on the Prairie, 2009; (ed. with B. Frehner) Indians & Energy: Exploitation and Opportunity in the American Southwest, 2010; Hippies, Indians and the Fight for Red Power, 2012. Contributor of articles to journals. **Address:** William P. Clements Center for Southwest Studies, Southern Methodist University, Rm. 356, 3225 University Ave., PO Box 750176, Dallas, TX 75275-0176, U.S.A. **Online address:** sherrys@mail.smu.edu

SMITH, Sherwood. Also writes as Robyn Tallis, Nicholas Adams. American (born United States), b. 1951. **Genres:** Science Fiction/Fantasy, Young Adult Fiction, Novels, Novellas/Short Stories. **Career:** Teacher, now retired. Writer. **Publications:** YOUNG ADULT FANTASY: Wren to the Rescue, 1990; Wren's Quest, 1993; Wren's War, 1995; Crown Duel, 1997; Court Duel, 1998; A Stranger to Command, 2008. SCIENCE FICTION FOR ADULTS WITH D. TROWBRIDGE: The Phoenix in Flight, 1993; Ruler of Naught, 1993; A Prison Unsought, 1994; The Rifter's Covenant, 1995; The Thrones of Kronos, 1996. SCIENCE FICTION FOR ADULTS WITH A. NORTON: Derelict for Trade, 1997; A Mind for Trade, 1998; Echoes in Time, 1999; Atlantis Endgame, 2002. SCIENCE FICTION FOR ADULTS: Journey to Otherwhere, 2000. YOUNG ADULT SCIENCE FICTION AS ROBYN TALLIS: Fire in the Sky, 1989; The Giants of Elenna, 1989; Rebel from Alphorion, 1989; Visions from the Sea, 1989. YOUNG ADULT AS JESSE MAGUIRE: The Beginning, 1989; Crossing Over, 1990; Getting It Right, 1991; Breaking the Rules, 1992. YOUNG ADULT AS NICHOLAS ADAMS: School Play, 1991. INDA SERIES: Inda, 2005; The Fox, 2007; The King's Shield, 2008; Treason's Shore, 2009. OTHERS: The Borrowers, 1997; Augur's Teacher, 2001; Paradise Drift, 2005; The Emerald Wand of Oz, 2005; Trouble Under Oz, 2006; Senrid, 2007; Over the Sea, 2007; Mearsies Heili Bounces Back, 2008; A Posse of Princesses, 2008; The Trouble with Kings, 2008; Once a Princess, 2009; (contrib.) Lace and Blade. 2, 2009; Twice a Prince, 2009; Coronets and Steel, 2010; Blood Spirits, 2011; Poor World, 2011; Barefoot Pirate, 2011; Fleeing Peace, 2011; Hunt Across Worlds, 2011; Banner of the Damned, 2012. Contributor to periodicals. **Address:** c/o Valerie Smith, 1746 Rte. 44-55, Modena, NY 12548, U.S.A. **Online address:** sherwood-smith@worldnet.att.net

SMITH, Stephanie A. (Stephanie Ann Smith). American (born United States), b. 1959. **Genres:** Novels, Adult Non-fiction, Literary Criticism And History, Science Fiction/Fantasy, Education. **Career:** Western Imprints, assistant editor, 1982-85; Representations, editorial assistant, 1987-89; University of California, English department teaching assistant, 1987-89, women's studies teaching associate, 1989; University of Florida, assistant professor, 1990-95, associate professor, 1995-2007, professor, 2007-; Michigan University Press, assistant editor, 1997-. **Publications:** Conceived by Liberty: Maternal Figures and Nineteenth-Century American Literature, 1994; Household Words: Bloomers, Sucker, Bombshell, Scab, Nigger, Cyber, 2006. SCIENCE FICTION NOVELS: Snow-Eyes, 1985; The Boy Who Was Thrown Away, 1987; Other Nature, 1995; Baby Rocket, forthcoming. **Address:** Department of English, University of Florida, 4348 Turlington Hall, PO Box 117300, Gainesville, FL 32611, U.S.A. **Online address:** ssmith@english.ufl.edu

SMITH, **Stephanie Ann.** *See* **SMITH**, **Stephanie A.**

SMITH, **Steven.** American (born United States), b. 1964. **Genres:** How-to Books, inspirational/Motivational Literature, Administration/Management, Business/Trade/Industry. **Career:** Franklin Covey, staff, through 2001; MarcumSmith LC (business consulting firm), co-founder and founding partner, 2001-. Writer. **Publications:** (With D. Marcum and M. Khalsa) Business Think: Rules for Getting It Right-Now, and No Matter What!, 2002; (with D. Marcum) Egonomics: What Makes Ego Our Greatest Asset (or Most Expensive Liability), 2007. **Address:** MarcumSmith LC, 10939 N Alpine Hwy., PO Box 127, Highland, UT 84003, U.S.A. **Online address:** info@marcumsmith.com

SMITH, **Steven G(arry).** American (born United States), b. 1953. **Genres:** Theology/Religion, Philosophy. **Career:** North Carolina Wesleyan College, assistant professor of philosophy and religion, 1980-85; Millsaps College, Department of Philosophy and Religious studies, assistant professor, 1985-89, associate professor, 1989-95, professor, 1995-, director of honors program, 1987-90, chair, 1992-2005, 1996-2005, 2008-, director of heritage program (first-year humanities course) 1996-98, 2005-07, acting chair, 2003-04, Golding chair in philosophy, 2010-; American Association of University Professors, president, 1996-97; Nash-Edgecombe Research and Dialectic Society, founder and director. Writer. **Publications:** The Argument to the Other: Reason beyond Reason in the Thought of Karl Barth and Emmanuel Levinas, 1983; The Concept of the Spiritual: An Essay in First Philosophy, 1988; Gender Thinking, 1992; Worth Doing, 2004; Appeal and Attitude: Prospects for Ultimate Meaning, 2005. Works appear in anthologies. Contributor of articles to journals. **Address:** Department of Philosophy, Millsaps College, 1701 N State St., PO Box 150390, Jackson, MS 39210, U.S.A. **Online address:** smithsg@millsaps.edu

SMITH, **Steven Trent.** American (born United States), b. 1947?. **Genres:** Military/Defense/Arms Control, Transportation, History. **Career:** Videosmith Inc., founder, 1977-; Quarterly, editor, 1986-96. Freelance television photojournalist. **Publications:** The Rescue: A True Story of Courage and Survival in World War II, 2001; Wolf Pack: The American Submarine Strategy that Helped Defeat Japan, 2003. **Address:** Videosmith Inc., 200 Spring Garden St., Ste. C, Philadelphia, PA 19123-2944, U.S.A. **Online address:** stscam@bellatlantic.net

SMITH, **Susan Arnout.** (Susan Arnout). American (born United States) **Genres:** Cultural/Ethnic Topics. **Career:** Writer and host. **Publications:** (As Susan Arnout) The Frozen Lady, 1983; The Timer Game, 2008; Out at Night, 2009. **Address:** PO Box 60061, San Diego, CA 92166, U.S.A. **Online address:** saswriter1s@aol.com

SMITH, **Tara Bray.** American (born United States), b. 1970?. **Genres:** Young Adult Fiction, Biography, Autobiography/Memoirs. **Career:** Writer. **Publications:** West of Then: A Mother a Daughter and a Journey Past Paradise, 2004; Betwixt, 2007. Contributor to periodicals. **Address:** Simon & Schuster Inc., 1230 Ave. of the Americas, 12th Fl., New York, NY 10020, U.S.A. **Online address:** tara@tarabraysmith.com

SMITH, **Timothy B.** American (born United States), b. 1967?. **Genres:** Psychology, Social Sciences. **Career:** Drexel University, adjunct assistant professor; University of South Dakota, assistant professor; Brigham Young University, McKay School of Education, professor of counseling psychology, 1999-, Department of Counseling Psychology and Special Education, chair. Writer. **Publications:** Practicing Multiculturalism: Affirming Diversity in Counseling and Psychology, 2004. **Address:** David O. McKay School of Education, Brigham Young University, 301 McKay Bldg., Provo, UT 84602, U.S.A.

SMITH, **Timothy B.** American (born United States), b. 1974?. **Genres:** History. **Career:** University of Tennessee at Martin, professor; National Park Service, staff. Author and historian. **Publications:** Champion Hill: Decisive Battle for Vicksburg, 2004; This Great Battlefield of Shiloh: History, Memory, and the Establishment of a Civil War National Military Park, 2004; The Untold Story of Shiloh: The Battle and the Battlefield, 2006; (co-ed.) Shiloh and the Western Campaign of 1862, 2007; The Golden Age of Battlefield Preservation: The Decade of the 1890s and the Establishment of America's First Five Military Parks, 2008; A Chickamauga Memorial: The Establishment of America's First Civil War National Military Park, 2009; Mississippi in the Civil War: The Home Front, 2010. Contributor of articles to journals. **Address:** Department of History and Philosophy, University of Tennessee at Martin, 322 Humanities Bldg., Martin, TN 38238, U.S.A. **Online address:** tims@utm.edu

SMITH, **Tim(othy R.).** American (born United States), b. 1945?. **Genres:** Children's Fiction, Animals/Pets. **Career:** Writer, entrepreneur and speaker. **Publications:** (With M. Herrick) Buck Wilder's Small Fry Fishing Guide: A Complete Introduction to the World of Fishing for Small Fry of All Ages, 1995; (with M. Herrick) Buck Wilder's Small Twig Hiking and Camping Guide: A Complete Introduction to the World of Hiking and Camping for Small Twigs of All Ages, 1997; Buck Wilder's Little Skipper Boating Guide: A Complete Introduction to the World of Boating for Little Skippers of All Ages, 2001; (with M. Herrick) Buck Wilder's Animal Wisdom, 2006; Buck Wilder's Who Stole the Animal Poop?, 2006; Buck Wilder's The Work Bees Go On Strike, 2006; Buck Wilder's The Ants Dig to China, 2007; Buck Wilder's The Owls Don't Give a Hoot, 2007; Buck Wilder's The Salmon Stop Running, 2008; Buck Wilder's The Squirrels Go Nuts, 2010. **Address:** Mackinac Island Press Inc., 216 E Front St., Ste. 205, Traverse City, MI 49684, U.S.A. **Online address:** buckwilder@charter.net

SMITH, **Tommie C.** American (born United States), b. 1944. **Genres:** Autobiography/Memoirs, Sports/Fitness. **Career:** Oberlin College, assistant professor of physical education, athletic director, sports coach; Santa Monica College, educator and track-and-field coach, now retired. Writer. **Publications:** (With D. Steele) Silent Gesture: The Autobiography of Tommie Smith, 2007. **Address:** DELO 2K Enterprises, PO Box 870010, Stone Mountain, GA 30087, U.S.A.

SMITH, **Vivian (Brian).** Australian (born Australia), b. 1933. **Genres:** Poetry, Children's Non-fiction, Literary Criticism And History, Biography, Bibliography. **Career:** University of Tasmania, lecturer in French, 1955-67; University of Sydney, lecturer, 1967-74, senior lecturer, 1974-82, reader in English, 1982-96, honorary associate, now retired; Quadrant, literary editor, 1975-90. Writer. **Publications:** The Other Meaning: Poems, 1956; (with G. Casey) The Writing of Novels and Short Stories, 1964; James McAuley, 1965, 2nd ed., 1970; An Island South, 1967; Les Vigaé en Australie, 1967; Vance Palmer, 1971; The Poetry of Robert Lowell, 1974; Vance and Nettie Palmer, 1975; Familiar Places: Poems, 1978; Tide Country, 1982; Tasmania and Australian Poetry, 1984; Selected Poems, 1985; New Selected Poems, 1995; Late News (poems), 2001; (with B. Hubber) Patrick White: A Bibliography, 2004. EDITOR: Letters of Vance and Nettie Palmer, 1915-1963, 1977; Young St. Poets Anthology, 1981; (with P. Coleman and L. Shrubb) Quadrant: Twenty-Five Years, 1982; (with M. Scott) Effects of Light: The Poetry of Tasmania, 1985; Australian Poetry, 1986: The Finest of Recent Australian Poetry, 1986; Australian Poetry 1988: The Finest of Recent Australian Poetry, 1988; Nettie Palmer: Her Private Journal Fourteen Years, Poems, 1988; (with R. Gray) Sydney's Poems: 1842-1992, 1992; (with N. Rowe) Windchimes: Asia in Australian Poetry, 2006. **Address:** 19 McLeod St., Mosman, NW 2088, Australia. **Online address:** smith@sydney.dialix.com.au

SMITH, **Wanda VanHoy.** American (born United States), b. 1926. **Genres:** Children's Fiction, Young Adult Fiction, Cartoons, Novellas/Short Stories, Art/Art History. **Career:** Associated Press, teletype attendant, 1944; California State Office of Vital Statistics, computer operator, 1946; Redondo Beach Sailing Academy, sailing coordinator, 1968-75; Capital Yachts (advertising agency), copywriter, 1970-88; Society of Children's Book Writers, program chair, 1986; Southwest Manuscripters, president. **Publications:** Ash Brooks, Super Ranger (children), 1984; Love Knots (young adult), 1987; Let's Talk to Lynn Frost, Fashion Designer; Let's Talk to Cody Collins, Farrier. FORTHCOMING: Mainstreet Chronicles; Thanks for the Dance; Pocketful of Poems. Works appear in anthologies. **Address:** 144 Monterey Blvd., Hermosa Beach, CA 90254, U.S.A. **Online address:** wandavanhoy@yahoo.com

SMITH, Wesley J. American (born United States), b. 1949. **Genres:** Documentaries/Reportage, Adult Non-fiction, Law, Animals/Pets, Politics/Government, Science Fiction/Fantasy. **Career:** Attorney, 1975-; Discovery Institute, Human Rights and Bioethics, senior fellow; Center for Bioethics and Culture, consultant; International Task Force on Euthanasia and Assisted Suicide, consultant; Writer, lawyer and educator. **Publications:** NONFICTION: The Lawyer Book: A Nuts and Bolts Guide to Client Survival, 1986; The Doctor Book: A Nuts and Bolts Guide to Patient Power, 1987 as Getting the Best from Your Doctor: A Nuts and Bolts Guide to Consumer Health, 1994; The Senior Citizens' Handbook: A Nuts and Bolts Approach to More Comfortable Living, 1989; (with R. Nader) Winning the Insurance Game: The Complete Consumer's Guide to Saving Money, 1990, rev. ed., 1993; (with N. Wexler) Mama Can't Remember Anymore, 1991; (with R. Nader) Collision Course: The Truth about Airline Safety, 1994; (with R. Nader) No Contest: Corporate Lawyers and the Perversion of Justice in America, 1996; Forced Exit: The Slippery Slope from Assisted Suicide to Legalized Murder, 1997, rev. ed., 2003; Culture of Death: The Assault on Medical Ethics in America, 2000; Fighting for Public Justice: Cases and Trial Lawyers That Made a Difference, 2001; (with E.M. Chevlen) Power Over Pain: How to Get the Pain Control You Need, 2002; A Consumer's Guide to a Brave New World, 2004; Forced Exit: Euthanasia, Assisted Suicide, and the New Duty to Die, 2006; Rat is a Pig is a Dog is a Boy, 2010. **Address:** Discovery Institute, 208 Columbia St., Seattle, WA 98104-1508, U.S.A. **Online address:** wjs@wesleyjsmith.com

SMITH, Wilbur (Addison). British/Zambian (born Zambia), b. 1933. **Genres:** Novels, Animals/Pets, Natural History, Romance/Historical, Young Adult Fiction, Mystery/Crime/Suspense. **Career:** Goodyear Tire & Rubber Co., staff, 1954-58; H.J. Smith & Son Ltd., staff, 1958-63; full-time writer, 1964-. **Publications:** When the Lion Feeds: A Novel, 1964; The Train from Katanga: A Novel in UK as The Dark of the Sun, 1965; The Roar of Thunder, 1966; The Sound Of Thunder, 1966; Shout at the Devil, 1968; Gold Mine, 1970; The Diamond Hunters, 1971; The Sunbird, 1972; Eagle in the Sky, 1974; The Eye of the Tiger, 1975; Cry Wolf, 1976; A Sparrow Falls, 1977 Hungry as the Sea, 1978; Wild Justice, 1978; A Falcon Flies, 1979, rev. ed. as Flight of the Falcon, 1982; Men of Men, 1981; The Delta Decision, 1981; Selected Works, 1983; The Angels Weep, 1983; The Leopard Hunts in Darkness, 1984; The Burning Shore, 1985; Power of the Sword, 1986; Rage, 1987; The Courtneys, 1988; A Time to Die, 1989; Golden Fox, 1990; Elephant Song, 1991; River God, 1993; Seventh Scroll, 1995; Birds of Prey, 1997; Monsoon, 1999; Warlock: A Novel of Ancient Egypt, 2001; The Blue Horizon, 2003; Triumph of the Sun, 2005; The Quest, 2007; Assegai, 2009; Those in Peril, 2011. **Address:** Charles Pick Consultancy Ltd., 21 Dagmar Terr., London, GL N1 2BN, England. **Online address:** wilbur.smith@stmartins.com

SMITH, Wilda M(axine). American (born United States), b. 1924. **Genres:** History, Biography, Military/Defense/Arms Control, Autobiography/Memoirs. **Career:** Teacher, 1943-45, 1946-49, 1953-57; Fort Hays State University, assistant professor, 1960-63, associate professor, 1963-66, professor of history, 1966-86, department chair, 1981-86. Writer. **Publications:** (With E.A. Bogart) The Wars of Peggy Hull: The Life and Times of a War Correspondent, 1991. Contributor to journals. **Address:** 2924 Walnut St., Hays, KS 67601-1721, U.S.A.

SMITH, William Jay. American/French (born France), b. 1918. **Genres:** Poetry, Literary Criticism And History, Autobiography/Memoirs, Humor/Satire, Translations, Children's Fiction, Adult Non-fiction, Social Sciences, Social Sciences. **Career:** Washington University, assistant in French, 1939-41; Columbia University, instructor in English and French, 1946-47, visiting professor of writing, acting chair of writing division, chair of writing division, 1973-75, Translation Center, board chairman; Williams College, lecturer in English, 1951, poet-in-residence, 1959-67, lecturer in English, 1956-64, 1966-67; Arena Stage, writer-in-residence, 1964-65; Hollins University, writer-in-residence, 1965-66, professor of English, 1970-80, professor emeritus, 1980-; Library of Congress, consultant in poetry, 1968-70, honorary consultant, 1970-76; Salzburg Seminar in American Studies, lecturer, 1975; Moscow State University, Fulbright lecturer, 1981; Cathedral of St. John the Divine, poet-in-residence, 1985-88. **Publications:** POETRY: Poems, 1947; Celebration at Dark: Poems, 1950; Type Writer Birds, 1954; Laughing Time, 1955, rev. ed. as Laughing Time: Collected Nonsense, 1990; The Bead Curtain: Calligrams, 1957; Poems 1947-1957, 1957; Boy Blue's Book of Beasts, 1957; Puptents and Pebbles: A Nonsense ABC, 1959; Typewriter Town, 1960; What Did I See?, 1962; My Little Book of Big and Little, 3 vols., 1963; (with R. Wilbur) Prince Souvanna Phouma: An Exchange between Richard Wilbur

and William Jay Smith, 1963; Ho for a Hat!, 1964; The Tin Can and Other Poems, 1966; If I Had a Boat, 1966; Mr. Smith and Other Nonsense, 1968; Around My Room and Other Poems, 1969; Grandmother Ostrich and Other Poems, 1969; (with V. Haviland) Children and Poetry (bibliography), 1969; New and Selected Poems, 1970; A Rose for Katherine Anne Porter, 1970; Louise Bogan: A Woman's Words, 1972; At Delphi: For Allen Tate on His 75th Birthday, 1974; Venice in the Fog, 1975; (with R. Wilbur) Verses on the Times, 1978; Journey to the Dead Sea, 1979; The Tall Poets, 1979; The Traveler's Tree: New and Selected Poems, 1980; Laughing Time: Nonsense Poems, 1980; The Tin Can, 1988; Journey to the Interior, 1988; Plain Talk, 1988; Collected Poems: 1939-1989, 1990; Birds and Beasts, 1990; Big and Little, 1992; The Cyclist, 1995; The World below the Window: Poems, 1937-1997, 1998; The Cherokee Lottery: A Sequence of Poems, 2000; The Girl in Glass: Love Poems, 2002; Hey Diddle, A Riddle, 2002; Words by the Water, 2008. OTHERS: Spectra Hoax, 1961, 2nd ed., 2000; The Straw Market, 1965; (with L. Bogan) The Golden Journey: Poems for Young People, 1965; The Streaks of the Tulip: Selected Criticism, 1972; Modern Hungarian Poetry, 1977; Children and Poetry: A Selective, Annotated Bibliography, 1979; Army Brat: A Memoir, 1980; Green, 1980; (comp.) A Green Place: Modern Poems (for children), 1982; (comp. with C. Ra) The Sun is Up: A Child's Year of Poems, 1996; Here Is My Heart (poems), 1999; (comp.) Up the Hill and Down: Poems for the Very Young, 2003; Dancing in the Garden: A Bittersweet Love Affair with France, 2008; My friend Tom, 2012. TRANSLATOR: R. Romano, Scirocco, 1951; V. Larbaud, Poems of a Multimillionaire, 1955; (and ed.) Selected Writings of Jules Laforgue, 1956; Two Plays by Charles Bertin: Christopher Columbus and Don Juan, 1970; E. Beskow, The Children of the Forest, 1970; L. Hellsing, The Pirate Book, 1972; (with M. Hayward) K. Chukovsky, The Telephone, 1977; (and intro. with L. Sjöberg) A. Lundkvist, Agadir, 1979; J. Laforgue, Moral Tales, 1985; (with L. Sjoberg) H. Martinson, Wild Bouquet: Nature Poems 1985; (with E. Morgan and others) S. Weores, Eternal Moment, 1989; (with S.H. Smith) T. U Tam'Si, The Madman and the Medusa, 1989; F.G. Lorca, Songs of Childhood 1993; C. Bartin, Christopher Columbus, 1994; J. Laforgue, Berlin, the City and the Court, 1996; (and ed. with L. Sjoberg) The Forest of Childhood, Poems from Sweden, 1996. EDITOR: Herrick, 1962; Poems from France, 1967; Poems from Italy, 1972; Light Verse and Satires, 1978; (and intro. with E. Brasil) Brazilian Poetry 1950-1980, 1983; (with J.S. Holmes) Dutch Interior: Post-war Poetry of the Netherlands and Flanders, 1984; Collected Translations, 1985; (with F.D. Reeve) An Arrow in the Wall: Selected Poetry and Prose, 1987; (and intro.) Life Sentence: Selected Poems, 1989; (with C. Ra) Behind the King's Kitchen, 1992; (and intro.) What You Have Almost Forgotten: Selected Poems, 1999. Contributor of articles to periodicals and magazines. **Address:** Hollins University, PO Box 9707, Roanoke, VA 24020-1707, U.S.A.

SMITH, Zadie. American/Italian/British (born England), b. 1975. **Genres:** Novels. **Career:** Columbia University, School of the Arts, faculty; Harper Magazine, reviewer; New York University, Creative Writing Program, professor, 2010-; Royal Society of Literature, fellow. Novelist. **Publications:** NOVELS: White Teeth, 2000; The Autograph Man, 2002; On Beauty, 2005. OTHERS: Zadie Smith Introduces The Burned Children of America, 2003; (ed.) The Book of Other People, 2007; Changing My Mind, 2010. **Address:** Creative Writing Program, New York University, Lillian Vernon Creative Writers House, 58 W 10th St., New York, NY 10011, U.S.A.

SMITH, Zak. American (born United States), b. 1976. **Genres:** Art/Art History, Photography. **Career:** Writer and artist. **Publications:** (With S. Momin) Zak Smith: Pictures of Girls, 2005; Pictures Showing What Happens on Each Page of Thomas Pynchon's Novel Gravity's Rainbow 2009; We Did Porn: Memoir and Drawings, 2009. **Address:** Tin House Books, 2617 NW Thurman St., Portland, OR 97210, U.S.A. **Online address:** zakzsmith@hotmail.com

SMITH AND DOE See **Debin, David.**

SMITH-ANKROM, M. E. (Martha McFarland). American (born United States), b. 1942. **Genres:** Children's Fiction, Children's Non-fiction, Language/Linguistics. **Career:** Growing Place, preschool teacher, 1976-84; Dade County Public Schools, junior high school history teacher, 1984-85; elementary school teacher, 1985-90; Viewpoint Press Inc., co-founder and president, 1998-. Writer. **Publications:** FOR CHILDREN AS MARTHA McFARLAND: The Super, Stupendous, and Tremendously Terrific Show-and-Tell Day, 1998; Nora's Terrible Picture Day, 2000. **Address:** Viewpoint Press Inc., 707 Walker Ave., Greensboro, NC 27403-2525, U.S.A. **Online address:** vpressbks@att.net

SMITH-AYALA, Emilie. Canadian/Argentine (born Argentina), b. 1964. **Genres:** Children's Fiction, Documentaries/Reportage, Social Sciences, History. **Career:** Writer. **Publications:** The Granddaughters of Ixmucané: Guatemalan Women Speak, 1991; Marisol and the Yellow Messenger (children's picture book), 1994; Clouds on the Mountain (children's picture book), 1996. **Address:** 2292 Parker St., Vancouver, BC V5L 2L9, Canada.

SMITHER, Elizabeth. New Zealander (born New Zealand), b. 1941. **Genres:** Novels, Children's Fiction, Young Adult Fiction, Poetry, Literary Criticism And History, Young Adult Non-fiction. **Career:** New Plymouth Public Library, library assistant, 1959-62, cataloguer, 1962-63, children's librarian, 1963-79, relieving librarian, 1979-. Writer. **Publications:** Here Come the Clouds: Poems, 1975; You're Very Seductive, William Carlos Williams, 1978; The Sarah Train, 1978; The Legend of Marcello Mastroianni's Wife, 1981; Casanova's Ankle, 1981; Tug Brothers, 1983; Shakespeare Virgins, 1984; Professor Musgrove's Canary, 1986; Gorilla, 1986; Animaux, 1988; A Pattern of Marching, 1989; A Cortège of Daughters, 1993; The Tudor Style: Poems, New and Selected, 1993; Lola, 2010; The Sea Question, 2010. NOVELS: First Blood, 1983; Brother-love, Sister-love, 1986; The Sea between Us, 2003; Different Kinds of Pleasure, 2006. STORIES: Nights at the Embassy: Stories, 1990; Mr. Fish and Other Stories, 1994; The Journal Box, 1996; The Mathematics of Jane Austen and Other Stories, 1997; The Lark Quartet, 1999; Listening to the Everly Brothers and Other Stories, 2002; Red Shoes, 2003; A Question of Gravity, 2004; Horse Playing the Accordion, 2007; The Year of Adverbs, 2007; The Girl Who Proposed, 2008; The Commonplace Book: A Writer's Journey Through Quotations, 2011. EDITOR: (with D. Hill) The Seventies Connection, 1980; (with C.K. Stead and K. Smithyman) The New Gramophone Room: Poetry and Fiction, 1985; (with D. Hill) Taranaki, 1987. Contributor to magazines. **Address:** 19-A Mount View Pl., New Plymouth, 4310, New Zealand.

SMITH-HUNTER, Andrea E. American (born United States), b. 1969. **Genres:** Business/Trade/Industry, Economics. **Career:** Exxon Corp., financial analyst, 1990-91, marketing analyst, 1991-93; Siena College, visiting assistant professor, 1999-2000, associate professor of marketing management, 2000-, professor of management, professor of sociology, Hickey chair; Eastern Academy of Management, representative, 2004-07; White House Council for Women and Girls, director; New Covenant Charter School, director. Writer. **Publications:** Diversity and Entrepreneurship: Analyzing Successful Women Entrepreneurs, 2003; Women Entrepreneurs Across Racial Lines: Issues of Human Capital, Financial Capital and Network Structures, 2006; Women Entrepreneurs in the Global Marketplace, 2009. Contributor of articles to periodicals. **Address:** Department of Marketing and Management, Siena College, 213 Colbeth Hall, 515 Loudon Rd., Loudonville, NY 12211, U.S.A. **Online address:** ahunter@siena.edu

SMITH-REX, Susan J. American (born United States), b. 1950. **Genres:** Children's Non-fiction, Education. **Career:** Winthrop University, professor of education, 1979-85, professor emeritus of education, 2002-, Winthrop's Project for At Risk Initiatives, director, 1985-90, Winthrop's Involvement in Nurturing and Graduating Students (WINGS) Program, director, 1990-; Phone Friend (talk line for York County children), director, 1984-; York County Parent Educators in the Work Force Program, director, 1990-. Writer. **Publications:** (Ed.) Teaching Reading in South Carolina Secondary Schools, 1978; Art, Fine Motor, and Cognitive Ideas for Special Education, 1985; (with K. Frank) Getting a Grip on ADD: A Kids Guide to Understanding and Coping with Attention Disorders, 1994; (with Frank) Getting a Life of Your Own: A Kid's Guide to Understanding and Coping with Family Alcoholism, 1995; (with Frank) Getting over the Blues: A Kids Guide to Understanding and Coping with Unpleasant Feelings and Depression, 1996; (with K. Frank) ADHD: 102 Practical Strategies for Reducing the Deficit, 1996; (with K. Frank) Getting with It: A Kids Guide to Forming Good Relationships and Fitting In, 1997; (with B.H. Boatwright and T.A. Mathis) Getting Equipped To Stop Bullying: A Kids Survival Kit for Understanding and Coping with Violence in the Schools, 1998; (with S. Castillo and T.A. Mathis) Getting Face to Face with Your Fears: A Kids Guide to Understanding and Coping with Fears and Phobias, 2000; (with T.A. Mathis and S.C. Castillo) Getting Your Second Wind: Living a Smoke-Free Life: A Kid's Guide to Saying No to Smoking, 2000; (with T.A. Mathis) Getting Ahead: Strategies to Motivate and Assist Students with Classroom Learning, 2001; (with T.A. Mathis) Getting Your Life on Track: A Female Teen's Guide to Saying No to Sex, 2002; (with J.H. Rex) 101 Creative Strategies for Reaching Unmotivated Student Learners: A Practical Resource of Approaches and Activities for Helping Unmotivated, Discour-

aged and/or Disruptive Students (grades 2-8), 2005; (with J.H. Rex) Pursuit of Happiness: Practical Strategies to Help Young People Increase Their Level of Happiness, 2006. Contributor to journals and newspapers. **Address:** College of Education, Winthrop University, 114 Tillman Hall, 701 Oakland Ave., Rock Hill, SC 29733-7001, U.S.A. **Online address:** smithsj@winthrop.edu

SMOAK, Gregory E. American (born United States), b. 1962. **Genres:** History, Theology/Religion. **Career:** Colorado State University, associate professor of history. Writer. **Publications:** Ghost Dances and Identity: Prophetic Religion and American Indian Ethnogenesis in the Nineteenth Century, 2006. Contributor to books and periodicals. **Address:** Department of History, Colorado State University, 8356 Clark, Fort Collins, CO 80523, U.S.A. **Online address:** gsmoak@loma.colostate.edu

SMOCK, Raymond W. American (born United States), b. 1941. **Genres:** Essays. **Career:** U.S. House of Representatives, Office of the Bicentennial, historian, 1983-85; Association for Documentary Editing, co-founder; Robert C. Byrd Center for Legislative Studies, director; WGBH, senior historical consultant for A Biography of America, 2000; National Constitution Center, historical consultant; Shepherd University, adjunct history faculty. Writer. **Publications:** (With P. Daniel) A Talent for Detail: The Photographs of Miss Frances Benjamin Johnston, 1889- 1910, 1974; (with D.A. Burton and J.B. Rhoads) A Guide to Manuscripts in the Presidential Libraries, 1985; (with L. Boggs and the U.S. House of Representatives) Final Report of the Commission on the Bicentenary of the U.S. House of Representatives, 1990: Including a Summary of the Activities and Programs of the Office for the Bicentennial of the House of Representatives, 1983-1989, 1990; (with R.H. Davidson and S.W. Hammond) Masters of the House: Congressional Leadership over Two Centuries, 1998; Booker T. Washington: Black Leadership in the Age of Jim Crow, 2009. EDITOR: (with L.R. Harlan) The Booker T. Washington Papers, vol. I-XIV, 1972-89, Booker T. Washington in Perspective: Essays of Louis R. Harlan, 1988; Landmark Documents on the U.S. Congress, 1999. **Address:** Shepherd University, PO Box 5000, Shepherdstown, WV 25443-5000, U.S.A. **Online address:** rsmock@shepherd.edu

SMOLENS, John (Harrison). American (born United States), b. 1949. **Genres:** Novels, Novellas/Short Stories. **Career:** Michigan State University, Department of American Thought and Language, assistant professor, 1985-; Western Michigan University, M.F.A. Program, adjunct assistant professor, 1993-96; Northern Michigan University, professor and director of creative writing program, 1996-; University of New Mexico, Department of English, visiting writer, 1995. **Publications:** NOVELS: Winter by Degrees, 1988; Angel's Head, 1994; Cold, 2001; The Invisible World, 2002; Fire Point, 2004; The Anarchist, 2009; The Schoolmaster's Daughter, 2011. COLLECTION: My One and Only Bomb Shelter, 2000. Works appear in anthologies. Contributor of articles to periodicals, magazines and newspapers. **Address:** Department of English, Northen Michiigan University, 237 Gries Hall, 1401 Presque Isle Ave., Marquette, MI 49855-5301, U.S.A. **Online address:** jsmolens@nmu.edu

SMOLEY, Richard. American (born United States), b. 1956?. **Genres:** Cultural/Ethnic Topics, Theology/Religion, Intellectual History, Philosophy, Paranormal, Mythology/Folklore, Humanities, Popular Culture, Self Help, Adult Non-fiction, Theology/Religion. **Career:** Gnosis Magazine, co-editor, 1985-99; Quest Books, editor, 2005-; Quest: Journal of the Theosophical Society in America, editor, 2008; Holyoke Community College, faculty. **Publications:** (With J. Kinney) Hidden Wisdom: A Guide to the Western Inner Traditions, 1999, rev. ed., 2006; Inner Christianity: A Guide to the Esoteric Tradition, 2002; The Essential Nostradamus: Literal Translation, Historical Commentary and Biography, 2006, rev. ed., 2010; Forbidden Faith: The Secret History of Gnosticism, 2006; Conscious Love: Insights from Mystical Christianity, 2008; (contrib.) A Disclosure of Secrets of Heaven Contained in Sacred Scripture or the Word of the Lord: Here First Those in Genesis, Together with Amazing Things Seen in the World of Spirits and In the Heaven of Angels, 2008; The Dice Game of Shiva: How Consciousness Creates the Universe, 2009; (intro.) Christian Gnosis, 2011. Contributor to periodicals. **Address:** The Theosophical Society in America, PO Box 270, Wheaton, IL 60187, U.S.A.

SMOOT, George Fitzgerald. American (born United States), b. 1945. **Genres:** Sciences. **Career:** University of California, research physicist and professor of physics, 1971-; Paris Diderot University, professor of physics, 2010-. Writer, astrophysicist and cosmologist. **Publications:** (With K. Davidson) Wrinkles in Time, 1993 as Wrinkles in Time: Witness to the Birth of the Universe, 2007. **Address:** Lawrence Berkeley National Laboratory, 50-5005 Bldg., 1 Cyclotron Rd., Berkeley, CA 94720, U.S.A. **Online address:** gfsmoot@lbl.gov

SMYLLIE, J. S. *See* **SMELLIE, Jim.**

SMYTH, Denis. Canadian (born Canada), b. 1948?. **Genres:** International Relations/Current Affairs, History. **Career:** University of Toronto, Department of History, professor, 1985-, International Relations Program, professor, 1985-. Writer and historian. **Publications:** (With P. Preston) Spain, the EEC, and NATO, 1984; Diplomacy and Strategy of Survival: British Policy and Franco's Spain, 1940-41, 1986; (with P. Preston and M. Partridge) British Documents on Foreign Affairs-Reports and Papers from the Foreign Office Confidential Print, 2000; Deathly Deception: The Real Story of Operation Mincemeat, 2010. Contributor to books and periodicals. **Address:** Department of History, University of Toronto, Rm. 2074, Sidney Smith Hall, 100 St George St., Toronto, ON M5S 3G3, Canada.

SMYTH, Iain. British (born England), b. 1959. **Genres:** Children's Fiction. **Career:** Papersmyths Ltd., designer. Writer. **Publications:** The Mystery of the Russian Ruby, 1994; Pirate Plunder's Treasure Hunt, 1996; Dig, Dig, Dig It, 1997; Zoom, Zoom, Fire Engine!, 1997; (with F. Cony) Old McDonald Had a Farm, 1999. SELF-ILLUSTRATED: (with J. Crawford) The Eye of the Pharaoh, 1995; Dug the Digger, 1997; Ruby the Fire Engine, 1997; The Quest for the Aztec Gold, 1997; Professor Screwloose, 1998; (with M. Ratnett and J. Goulding) Monster Train, 2000; Angel Fish: A Pull and Lift Book, 2002. **Address:** Papersmyths Ltd., 11 Southfield Rd., Bristol, BS6 6AX, England. **Online address:** iain@papersmyths.com

SMYTH, William J. Irish (born Ireland), b. 1949. **Genres:** History, Intellectual History. **Career:** University of Toronto, assistant professor, 1975-78; St. Patrick's College, professor of geography, 1978-94, vice president, 1986-94, master, 1994-97; National University of Ireland, president, 1997-, now president emeritus; University of College Cork, professor of geography, now professor emeritus. Writer. **Publications:** (With C.J. Houston) The Sash Canada Wore: A Historical Geography of the Orange Order in Canada, 1980; (ed. with K. Whelan) Common Ground: Essays on the Historical Geography of Ireland, 1988; (with C.J. Houston) Irish Emigration and Canadian Settlement, 1990; (intro.) Census of Ireland, Circa 1659: With Essential Materials from the Poll Money Ordinances 1660-1661, 2002; Map-making, Landscapes and Memory: A Geography of Colonial and Early Modern Ireland, c.1530-1750, 2006. Contributor of articles to journals. **Address:** Department of Geography, College of Arts, Celtic Studies & Social Sciences, University College Cork, Geography Bldg., Maynooth, CK 1, Ireland. **Online address:** w.smyth@ucc.ie

SNADON, Patrick A. American (born United States), b. 1952. **Genres:** Architecture. **Career:** University of Cincinnati, College of Design, Architecture, Art, and Planning, associate professor. Writer. **Publications:** (With M.W. Fazio) The Domestic Architecture of Benjamin Henry Latrobe, 2006. **Address:** U.S.A. **Online address:** patrick.snadon@uc.edu

SNADOWSKY, Daria. American (born United States), b. 1979?. **Genres:** Novels, Sex. **Career:** Lawyer. Writer. **Publications:** Anatomy of a Boyfriend: A Novel, 2007. Contributor to periodicals. **Address:** Las Vegas, NV, U.S.A. **Online address:** daria@daria-snadowsky.com

SNAY, Mitchell. American (born United States), b. 1954. **Genres:** Theology/Religion, Race Relations, History. **Career:** Harvard University, lecturer in history and literature, 1983-86; Denison University, Department of History, associate professor, 1986-, professor of history, chair, 2001-03, William T. Utter/Clyde E. Williams, Jr. professor, 2008-; Ohio State University, adjunct professor of history. Writer. **Publications:** Gospel of Disunion: Religion and Separatism in the Antebellum South, 1993; (ed. with J.R. McKivigan) Religion and the Antebellum Debate over Slavery, 1998; Fenians, Freedmen, and Southern Whites: Race and Nationality in the Era of Reconstruction, 2007. Contributor to periodicals. **Address:** Department of History, Denison University, Granville, OH 43023, U.S.A. **Online address:** snay@denison.edu

SNELL, Daniel C. American (born United States), b. 1947. **Genres:** History, Anthropology/Ethnology, Language/Linguistics, Theology/Religion, Classics. **Career:** University of Washington, instructor in near Eastern languages and literature, 1975-76; City University of New York, Graduate Center, An-

drew W. Mellon postdoctoral fellow, 1976-77; Connecticut College, assistant professor of religious studies, 1977-78; Yale University, visiting part-time lecturer in Near Eastern languages, 1978-79; Barnard College, assistant professor of religious studies, 1978-80; Gustavus Adolphus College, assistant professor of religion, 1981-82; University of Aleppo, visiting professor and professor, 1982-83; The National Museum, Fulbright researcher, 1982-83; University of Oklahoma, assistant professor, 1987-92, associate professor, 1992-, professor of history, 1992-, L.J. Semrod presidential professor of history, 2001-, associates distinguished lecturer, 1986-87, faculty senate, 1987-89, Humanities Center, director, 1995-2001; National Humanities Center, fellow, 1989-90. Writer. **Publications:** A Workbook of Cuneiform Signs, 1979; The E. A. Hoffman Collection and Other American Collections, 1979; Ledgers and Prices: Early Mesopotamian Merchant Accounts, 1982; (with R. Caplice) Introduction to Akkadian, 3rd ed., 1988; (and ed. and intro. with C.H. Lager) Economic Texts from Sumer, 1991; Twice-Told Proverbs and the Composition of the Book of Proverbs, 1993; Life in the Ancient Near East, 3100-332 B.C.E., 1997; Flight and Freedom in the Ancient Near East, 2001; (with G. Rubio, S. Garfinkle and G. Beckman) Current Issues and the Study of the Ancient Near East, 2007; Religions of the Ancient Near East, 2011. EDITOR: (with M.E. Cohen and D.B. Weisberg) The Tablet and the Scroll: Near Eastern Studies in Honor of William W. Hallo, 1993; Companion to the Ancient Near East, 2005. Contributor of articles to journals. **Address:** Department of History, University of Oklahoma, Rm. 420, 455 W Lindsey St., Norman, OK 73019-0535, U.S.A. **Online address:** dcsnell@ou.edu

SNELL, K. D. M. British (born England), b. 1955. **Genres:** Theology/Religion, Geography, History. **Career:** University of Leicester, School of Historical Studies, reader, personal chair, professor of rural and cultural history. Writer. **Publications:** Annals of the Labouring Poor: Social Change and Agrarian England, 1660-1900, 1985; (ed. and intro.) The Whistler at the Plough, 1989; Church and Chapel in the North Midlands: Religious Observance in the Nineteenth Century, 1991; (ed. and intro.) Letters from Ireland during the Famine of 1847, 1994; (ed.) The Regional Novel in Britain and Ireland, 1800-1990, 1998; (with P.S. Ell) Rival Jerusalems: The Geography of Victorian Religion, 2000; The Bibliography of Regional Fiction in Britain and Ireland, 1800-2000, 2002; (ed. with P. Lane and N. Raven) Women, Work, and Wages in England, 1600-1850, 2004; Parish and Belonging: Community, Identity, and Welfare in England and Wales, 1700-1950, 2006. Contributor of articles to periodicals. **Address:** School of Historical Studies, University of Leicester, Rm. 20, Marc Fitch House, 16 Salisbury Rd., Leicester, LE LE1 7QR, England. **Online address:** kdm@le.ac.uk

SNELL, Michael. American (born United States), b. 1945. **Genres:** Business/Trade/Industry, Economics, Education. **Career:** Wadsworth Publishing Co., editor, 1967-77; Addison-Wesley Publishing Co., executive editor, 1978-79; Michael Snell Literary Agency, owner, president and editorial director, 1979-. **Publications:** (With S.J. Bennett) Executive Chess, 1987; (with E.C. Murphy) The Genius of Sitting Bull: Thirteen Heroic Strategies for Today's Business Leaders, 1993; (with C. Hickman) The Strategy Game, 1993; (with T. Connor and R. Smith) The Oz Principle, 1993; (with M. Silva) Crisis Management, 1993; (with E.C. Murphy) Forging The Heroic Organization: A Daring Blueprint for Revitalizing American Business, 1994; (with C. Hickman) The Organization Game, 1994; (with C. Hickman) The Productivity Game, 1995; (with C. Hickman) The Fourth Dimension, 1995; (with J. Cotter) The Twenty Percent Solution, 1995; Leadership IQ, 1996; (with M. Murphy) Dogperfect, 1997; (with M. Milani) From Book Idea to Bestseller: What You Absolutely, Positively Must Know to Make Your Book a Success, 1997; Cost-Benefit Analysis for Engineers and Planners, 1997; (with P. Gilberd) The Twelfth Commandment of Wildly Successful Women, 1998; Salisbury Gunsmiths: A History of Guns, Gunsmiths, Cutlers, Fishing Tackle Makers and Other Sporting and More Belligerent Pursuits in Sarum, 1999; (with E. Murphy) The New Murphy's Law, 1999; (with M. Milani) Preparing for the Loss of Your Pet, 1999; (with D. Swiss) The Male Mind at Work, 2000; (with C. McCoy) Why Didn't I Think of That, 2002; (with S. Edwards) Fit and Fat, 2003. **Address:** Michael Snell Literary Agency, 32 Castle Rd., PO Box 1206, Truro, MA 02666, U.S.A.

SNELL, Patricia. American (born United States), b. 1978. **Genres:** Theology/Religion. **Career:** University of Notre Dame, Center for the Study of Religion and Society, assistant director; Northern Indiana Congregation Study, principal investigator; Science of Generosity project, co-investigator; National Study of Youth and Religion, interviewer. Writer and sociologist. **Publications:** (With C. Smith and M.O. Emerson) Passing the Plate: Why

American Christians Don't Give Away More Money, 2008; (with C. Smith) Souls in Transition: The Religious and Spiritual Lives of Emerging Adults, 2009. **Address:** Notre Dame, IN , U.S.A. **Online address:** psnell@nd.edu

SNELLGROVE, David L(lewellyn). British (born England), b. 1920. **Genres:** Cultural/Ethnic Topics, Theology/Religion. **Career:** University of London, lecturer, 1950-60, reader, 1960-74, professor of Tibetan studies, 1974-82, professor emeritus, 1982-; British Academy, fellow; Institute of Tibetan Studies, founding director, 1966-82. Consultant and writer. **Publications:** Buddhist Himalaya, 1957; The Hevajra Tantra, vol. II, 1959; Himalayan Pilgrimage, 1961 as Himalayan Pilgrimage: A Study of Tibetan Religion by a Traveller through Western Nepal, 1989; (with H.E. Richardson) A Cultural History of Tibet, 1968; The Chester Beatty Library: A Catalogue of the Tibetan Collection, 1969; (with T. Skorupski) The Cultural Heritage of Ladakh, vol. I: Central Ladakh, 1979, vol. II: Zangskar and the Cave Temples of Ladakh, 1980; Indo-Tibetan Buddhism: Indian Buddhists and Their Tibetan Successors, 1987; (trans. and ed. with E. Conze, I.B. Horner and A. Waley) Buddhist Texts through the Ages, 1990; Asian Commitment: Studies of Travels in the Indian Sub-Continent and South East Asia, 2000; Khmer Civilization and Angker, 2001; Angkor, Before and After: A Cultural History of the Khmers, 2004; Religion as History, Religion as Myth, 2006. EDITOR: (trans.) Four Lamas of Dolpo, 1967; (trans.) The Nine Ways of Bon, 1967; (and contrib.) The Image of the Buddha, 1978, 1979. Contributor to encyclopedias and periodicals. **Address:** University of London, Senate House, Malet St., London, GL WC1E 7HU, England.

SNELLGROVE, Laurence Ernest. British (born England), b. 1928. **Genres:** Novellas/Short Stories, History, Language/Linguistics, Military/Defense/Arms Control, Women's Studies And Issues, Children's Fiction. **Career:** Rose Hill School, assistant master, 1950-53; Cheshunt County Secondary School, assistant master, 1953-55; Yaxley School, assistant master, 1955-57; Caterham Valley County Secondary School, History Department, head, 1957-66; De Stafford Comprehensive School, History Department, head, 1966-73; writer, 1973-. **Publications:** From Kitty Hawk to Outer Space: The Story of the Aeroplane, 1960; From Steamcarts to Minicars: A History of Motor Cars, 1961; From Coracles to Cunarders, 1962; From Rocket to Railcar: An Outline of Rail Development since 1804, 1963; Suffragettes and Votes for Women, 1964, 2nd ed., 1984; Franco and the Spanish Civil War, 1965; Modern World since 1870, 1968, rev. ed. as The Modern World since 1900, 1973; (with R.J. Cootes) The Ancient World, 1970, 2nd ed., 1991; Early Modern Age, 1972, 2nd ed., 1989; World War II, 1974; Hitler, 1974; (with J.R.C. Yglesias) Mainstream English, 6 vols., 1974-75; Picture the Past, 5 vols., 1978-82; Wide Range Histories, 4 vols., 1978-79; (with D. Thornton) History around You, 4 vols., 1982-83; Modern World, 1984; Britain since 1700, 1985; Storyline Histories, 4 vols., 1985; Modern World History, 1989; Making of the United Kingdom, 1992; (with M. Haisman) Dear Merv, Dear Bill, 1992; (with R.J. Cootes) Expansion, Trade and Industry, 1993; (with R.J. Cootes) The Era of the Second World War, 1994. Contributor to periodicals. **Address:** Kitty Hawk, 23 Harvest Hill, East Grinstead, ES RH19 4BU, England.

SNELLING, Dennis (Wayne). American (born United States), b. 1958. **Genres:** Sports/Fitness, Young Adult Fiction, History, Biography. **Career:** Stanislaus County, accountant, 1981-87; Modesto City Schools, director of business, 1987-; Salida Area Public Facilities Financing Agency, controller; Schools Infrastructure Financing Agency, controller. Writer. **Publications:** SPORTS HISTORIES: A Glimpse of Fame: Brilliant but Fleeting Major League Careers, 1993; The Pacific Coast League: A Statistical History, 1903-1957, 1995; The History of High School Football in Modesto, 1999. **Address:** Modesto City Schools, 426 Locust St., Modesto, CA 95351, U.S.A.

SNELLING, Lauraine. American (born United States), b. 1942. **Genres:** Novels, Adult Non-fiction, Young Adult Fiction. **Career:** Writer and educator. **Publications:** NOVELS: Song of Laughter, 1986; Dakota: Four Inspirational Love Stories on the Northern Plains, 1996; Race for the Roses, 1999; Hawaiian Sunrise, 1999; The Healing Quilt, 2002; The Gift: A Horse, a Boy and a Miracle of Love, 2002; The Way of Women, 2004; Amethyst, 2005; Once Upon a Christmas, 2005; Saturday Morning: A Novel, 2005; Brushstroke Legacy: A Novel, 2006; Breaking Free: A Novel, 2007; What about Cimmaron?, 2008; One Perfect Day, 2008; (with J. Hart) Yuletide treasure, 2008; On Hummingbird Wings, 2011; Valley of Dreams, 2011; Reunion, 2012. DAUGHTERS OF BLESSING SERIES: A Promise for Ellie, 2006; Sophie's Dilemma, 2007; A Touch of Grace, 2008; Rebecca's Reward, 2008. RED RIVER OF THE NORTH SERIES: An Untamed Land, 1996; A New

Day Rising, 1996; A Land to Call Home, 1997; The Reapers' Song, 1998; Blessing in Disguise, 1999; Tender Mercies, 1999. RETURN TO RED RIVER SERIES: A Dream to Follow, 2001; Believing the Dream, 2002; More than a Dream, 2003. A SECRET REFUGE SERIES: Daughter of Twin Oaks, 2000; Sisters of the Confederacy, 2000; The Long Way Home, 2001. DAKOTAH TREASURES SERIES: Ruby, 2003; Pearl, 2004; Opal, 2005. GOLDEN FILLY SERIES: The Race, 1990; Eagle's Wings, 1991; Go for the Glory, 1991; Kentucky Dreamer, 1991; Call for Courage, 1992; Out of the Mist, 1993; Shadow Over San Mateo, 1993; Close Call, 1994; Second Wind, 1994; The Winner's Circle, 1994. HIGH HURDLES SERIES: DJ's Challenge, 1995; Olympic Dreams, 1995; Setting the Pace, 1996; Out of the Blue, 1996; Storm Clouds, 1997; Close Quarters, 1997; Moving Up, 1998; Letting Go, 1999; Raising the Bar, 1999; Class Act, 2000. HOME TO BLESSING: A Measure of Mercy, 2009; No Distance Too Far, 2010; Heart for Home, 2011. NON-FICTION: Start Your Own Business: After 50, 60, or 70, 1990; 100 Good Things That Happen as You Grow Older, 1992; A Hand to Hold: Helping Someone Through Grief, 2004. OTHERS: Whispers in the Wind, 2012. **Address:** c/o Author Mail, Bethany House Publishers, 11400 Hampshire Ave. S, Minneapolis, MN 55483, U.S.A. **Online address:** tlsnelling@yahoo.com

SNICKET, Lemony. (Daniel Handler). American (born United States), b. 1970. **Genres:** Novels, Children's Fiction, Young Adult Fiction. **Career:** Writer. **Publications:** FOR CHILDREN: The Bad Beginning, 1999; The Reptile Room, 1999; The Wide Window, 1999; The Miserable Mill, 1999; The Austere Academy, 2000; The Ersatz Elevator, 2001; The Vile Village, 2001; The Hostile Hospital, 2001; Lemony Snicket: The Unauthorized Autobiography, 2002; A Box of Unfortunate Events: The Situation Worsens, 2002; The Carnivorous Carnival, 2002; A Box of Unfortunate Events: The Dilemma Deepens, 2003; The Slippery Slope, 2003; The Grim Grotto, 2004; The Penultimate Peril, 2005; A Box of Unfortunate Events: The Loathsome Library, 2005; The End, 2006; The Complete Wreck, 2006; The Beatrice Letters, 2006. ADULT FICTION AS DANIEL HANDLER: The Basic Eight, 1999; Watch Your Mouth, 2000; (intro.) Nonsense Novel, 2005; Adverbs, 2006; Why We Broke Up, 2012. OTHER: Lemony Snicket: The Unauthorized Autobiography, 2002; Series of Unfortunate Events Calendar 2004: Thirteen Alarming Months!, 2003; The Blank Book, 2004; Behind the Scenes with Count Olaf, 2004; Series of Unfortunate Events Calendar 2005: Thirteen Alarming Months!, 2004; The Notorious Notations (blank journal), 2006; The Puzzling Puzzles: Bothersome Games Which Will Bother Some People (activity book), 2007; Horseradish: Bitter Truths You Can't Avoid, 2007; The Latke Who Wouldn't Stop Screaming: A Christmas Story, 2007; Baby in the Manger, 2007; The Composer Is Dead, 2008; Lump of Coal, 2008; 13 Words, 2010. **Address:** c/o Author Mail, HarperCollins Children's Books, 10 E 53rd St., New York, NY 10022, U.S.A. **Online address:** lsnicket@harpercollins.com

SNIDER, J. H. American (born United States), b. 1958. **Genres:** Business/Trade/Industry, Technology, Social Sciences. **Career:** University of Vermont, instructor, 1993-; Northwestern University, Department of Political Science, university fellow, 1994-; Office of U.S. Senator Ron Wyder, congressional fellow in information policy, 1999-2000; New America Foundation, Markle fellow and senior research fellow, 2001-07, research director; Harvard Kennedy School, residential fellow, 2008; Harvard Business School, senior research assistant; Harvard University, Edmond J. Safra Center for Ethics, network fellow, 2011-12; Vermont Secretary of State, Task Force, chair; iSolon.org, president. Writer and consultant. **Publications:** (With T. Ziporyn) Future Shop: How New Technologies Will Change the Way We Shop and What We Buy, 1992; Explanation of the Citizen's Guide to the Airwaves, 2003; Speak Softly and Carry A Big Stick: How Local TV Broadcasters Exert Political Power, 2005. **Address:** iSolon.org, 945 Old County Rd., Severna Park, MD 21146-4830, U.S.A. **Online address:** snider@isolon.org

SNIEGOSKI, Thomas E. (Tom Sniegoski). American (born United States) **Genres:** Novels. **Career:** Novelist. **Publications:** (with C. Golden and Stephen R. Bissette) Buffy the Vampire Slayer: The Monster Guide (nonfiction), 2000; NOVELS: Angel: Soul Trade, 2001; (with C. Golden) Force Majeure, 2002; (with C. Golden) Monster Island, 2003; Hellboy: The God Machine, 2006; A Kiss before the Apocalypse, 2008; Dancing on the Head of a Pin, 2009; Mean Streets (novella), 2009; Lobster Johnson: The Satan Factory, 2009; THE FALLEN NOVEL SERIES: The Fallen, 2003; Leviathan, 2003; Aerie, 2003; Reckoning, 2004; OUTCAST NOVEL SERIES: (with C. Golden) The Un-Magician, 2004; (with C. Golden) Dragon Secrets, 2004; (with C. Golden) Ghostfire, 2005; (with C. Golden) Wurm War, 2005; MENAGERIE NOVEL SERIES: (with C. Golden) The Nimble Man, 2004; (with C.

Golden) Tears of the Furies, 2005; (with C. Golden) Stones Unturned, 2006; (with C. Golden) Crashing Paradise, SLEEPER CONSPIRACY NOVEL SERIES: Sleeper Code, 2006; Sleeper Agenda, 2006; BILLY HOOTEN NOVEL SERIES: Billy Hooten, Owlboy, 2007; The Girl with the Destructo Touch, 2007; Tremble at the Terror of Zis-Boom-Bah, 2008; The Flock of Fury, 2008; BRIMSTONE NETWORK NOVEL SERIES: The Brimstone Network, 2008; The Shroud of A'ranka, 2008; Specter Rising, 2009. **Address:** Stoughton, MA , U.S.A. **Online address:** tsniegoski@comcast.net

SNIEGOSKI, Tom. *See* **SNIEGOSKI, Thomas E.**

SNODGRASS, Anthony McElrea. British (born England), b. 1934. **Genres:** Archaeology/Antiquities. **Career:** University of Edinburgh, lecturer, 1961-69, reader, 1969-75, professor of classical archaeology, 1975-76; Cambridge University, Laurence professor of classical archaeology, 1976-2001, Laurence professor emeritus of classical archaeology, 2001-, Clare College, fellow; British Academy, vice president, 1990-92. Writer. **Publications:** Early Greek Armour and Weapons, 1964; Arms and Armour of the Greeks, 1967; The Dark Age of Greece, 1971; Archaeology and the Rise of the Greek State, 1977; Archaic Greece, 1980; (contrib.) Sources for Ancient History, 1983; An Archaeology of Greece, 1987; Homer and the Artists, 1998; (ed. with G.R. Tsetskhladze and A.J.N.W. Prag) Periplous, 2000; (ed. with G.R. Tsetskhladze) Greek Settlements in the Eastern Mediterranean and the Black Sea, 2002; Archaeology and the Emergence of Greece, 2006; (with J. Bintliff and P. Howard) Testing the Hinterland, 2007. Contributor to journals. **Address:** Clare College, Cambridge University, Trinity Ln., Cambridge, CB CB2 1TL, England. **Online address:** ams1002@hermes.cam.ac.uk

SNODGRASS, Mary Ellen. American (born United States), b. 1944. **Genres:** Children's Non-fiction, Literary Criticism And History, Young Adult Non-fiction, Reference. **Career:** Hickory High School, teacher of English and Latin, 1966-85, city language arts chair, 1968-70, English Department, chair, 1968-75; North Carolina State Textbook Commission, evaluator, 1972; freelance writer, 1985-; North Carolina Humanities Commission, lecturer, 2006-; Lenoir Rhyne University, professor of Latin and young adult literature, 2008-; Perma-Bound, consultant; Friends of the Hickory Library, founding member and president; Salem Books, reviewer. Writer. **Publications:** 55 Lessons in Latin I and II, 1986; Library Skills, 1988; Poetry Skills, 1988; Greek Classics Notes, 1988; Roman Classics Notes, 1988; Wise Words, The Gifted Child Today, 1989; (with P. Gammond) Bluffer's Guide to Bluffing, 1989; Bluff Your Way in the Deep South, 1990; The English Book, 1990; Cliffs Notes in the Classroom, 1990; Reading the Newspaper, 1990; Writing Letters, 1990; Characters from Young Adult Literature, 1991; Environmental Awareness, vol. I: Acid Rain, vol. II: Air Pollution, vol. III: Land Pollution, vol. IV: Solid Waste, vol. V: Toxic Waste, vol. VI: Water Pollution, 1991; Silver: A Study Guide, 1991; Late Achievers, 1992; Crossing Barriers, 1993; Auctori Latini, 1993; Japan vs. U.S.A., 1993; (with L. Patterson) Indian Terms of the Americans, 1994; Voyages in Classical Mythology, 1994; Encyclopedia of Utopian Literature, 1995; An Illustrated Dictionary of Little-Known Words from Literary Classics, 1996; Encyclopedia of Satirical Literature, 1997; Encyclopedia of Frontier Literature, 1997; Signs of the Zodiac, 1997; Encyclopedia of Southern Literature, 1997; (with C. Miller) Contemporary Storytellers, 1998; (with G. Carey) Multicultural Dictionary of Literary Terms, 1998; Encyclopedia of Fable, 1998; Historical Encyclopedia of Nursing, 1999; Modern American Poets, 1999; The Light in the Forest: Notes, 1999; Religious Sites in America, 2000; Encyclopedia of World Scripture, 2001; Literary Treks: Characters on the Move, 2003; Coins and Currency: An Historical Encyclopedia, 2003; World Epidemics: A Cultural Chronology of Disease from Prehistory to the Era of SARS, 2003; Amy Tan: A Literary Companion, 2004; August Wilson: A Literary Companion, 2004; Barbara Kingsolver: A Literary Companion, 2004; Encyclopedia of Kitchen History, 2004; Facts on File Encyclopedia of Gothic Literature, 2005; World Shores and Beaches: A Descriptive and Historical Guide to 50 Coastal Treasures, 2005; (trans.) W. Shakespeare, Hamlet, 2006; (trans.) W. Shakespeare, Macbeth, 2006; (trans.) W. Shakespeare, Romeo and Juliet, 2006; Encyclopedia of Feminist Literature, 2006; Walter Dean Myers: A Literary Companion, 2006; Kaye Gibbons: A Literary Companion, 2007; Underground Railroad: An Encyclopedia of People, Places, and Operations, 2008; Beating the Odds: A Teen Guide to 75 Superstars Who Overcame Adversity, 2008; Jamaica Kincaid: A Literary Companion, 2008; (trans.) W. Shakespeare, Othello, 2008; (trans.) W. Shakespeare, Midsummer Night's Dream, 2008; (trans.) Taming of the Shrew, 2008; (trans.) Twelfth Night, 2008; Civil Disobedience: An Encyclopedic History of Dissidence in the United States, 2009; Reading Nora Roberts, 2010; Encyclopedia of the

Literature of Empire, 2010; Peter Carey: A Literary Companion, 2010; Civil War Era and Reconstruction: An Encyclopedia of Social, Political, Cultural and Economic History, 2011; Leslie Marmon Silko: A Literary Companion, 2011. EDITOR: The Great American English Handbook, 1987; Contests for Students: All You Need to Know to Enter and Win 600 Contests, 1990; Black History Month Resource Book, 1993; Literary Maps, 1995; Celebrating Women's History, 1996. Contributor to periodicals. **Address:** Lenoir Rhyne University, 625 7th Ave. NE, Hickory, NC 28601-3984, U.S.A. **Online address:** aphra@charter.net

SNOW, Carol. American (born United States), b. 1965?. **Genres:** Novels. **Career:** Author. **Publications:** YOUNG-ADULT NOVELS: Switch, 2008; Snap, 2009. ADULT NOVELS: Been There, Done That, 2006; Getting Warmer, 2007; Here Today, Gone to Maui, 2009; Just Like Me, Only Better, 2010. Contributor to magazine. **Address:** c/o Stephanie Kip Rostan, Levine Greenberg Literary Agency, 307 7th Ave., New York, NY 10001, U.S.A. **Online address:** carolsnow@roadrunner.com

SNOW, Donald. American (born United States), b. 1951. **Genres:** Environmental Sciences/Ecology, Ethics, Economics, Literary Criticism And History. **Career:** Northern Lights Institute, executive director, 1984; Northern Lights magazine, editor, 1985-; University of Montana, visiting instructor, 1990, Environmental Writing Institute, director, 1998; Aspen Institute, seminar moderator; Whitman College, senior lecturer of environmental humanities and general studies. **Publications:** EDITOR: Inside the Environmental Movement: Meeting the Leadership Challenge, 1992; Voices From the Environmental Movement: Perspectives for a New Era, 1992; (with D. Clow) Northern Lights: A Selection of New Writing from the American West, 1994; (with J.A. Balden) The Next West: Public Lands, Community, and Economy in the American West, 1994; (with C. Servid) Book of the Tongass, 1999; Do Economists Know About Lupines?, 1999; (with P. Brick and S.V. DeWetering) Across the Great Divide: Explorations in Collaborative Conservation and the American West, 2001. **Address:** Whitman College, 345 Boyer Ave., Walla Walla, WA 99362, U.S.A. **Online address:** snowdr@whitman.edu

SNOW, Keith Ronald. British (born England), b. 1943. **Genres:** Biology, Children's Non-fiction, Medicine/Health, Zoology, Animals/Pets. **Career:** South West Essex Technical College, lecturer in biology, 1967-68; Waltham Forest Technical College, lecturer in biology, 1968-70; University of East London, lecturer in zoology, 1970-77, senior lecturer in biology, 1977-94, Department of Environmental Sciences, head and professor, now professor emeritus. Writer. **Publications:** The Arachnids: An Introduction, 1970; Insects and Disease, 1974; Flies, 1978; A Garden of Birds, 1981, vol. II, 1984; Birds in Your Garden, 1984; British Mosquitoes (Culicidae), 1987; Mosquitoes, 1990; Mosquito Control in Britain, 1995; (co-author) A Revised Bibliography of the Mosquitoes of the British Isles, 1997; (co-author) A Provisional Atlas of the Mosquitoes of Britain, 1998. WITH F.E. WILLIAMS: I Am a Fox, 1978; I Am a Squirrel, 1978; I Am a Badger, 1979; I Am a Hedgehog, 1979; I Am a Frog, 1981; I Am a Rabbit, 1981. Contributor to books, periodicals and magazines. **Address:** Department of Environmental Sciences, University of East London, Romford Rd., London, GL E15 4LZ, England. **Online address:** k.r.snow@uel.ac.uk

SNOW, Kimberley. American (born United States), b. 1939. **Genres:** Cultural/Ethnic Topics, Popular Culture. **Career:** University of California, visiting lecturer, 1980-2001; Kentucky Horse Center, executive chef; Vairotsana Foundation, administrator. Writer. **Publications:** Word Play, Word Power: A Woman's Personal Growth Workbook, 1989; Writing Yourself Home: A Woman's Guided Journey of Self-Discovery, 1992; Keys to the Open Gate: A Woman's Spirituality Sourcebook, 1994; In Buddha's Kitchen: Cooking, Being Cooked, and Other Adventures in a Meditation Center, 2003; Jeannie and Leo, forthcoming. **Address:** 1111 Bath St., Santa Barbara, CA 93101, U.S.A. **Online address:** ksnow@snowlight.com

SNOW, Philip (Albert). British (born England), b. 1915. **Genres:** Novellas/Short Stories, Administration/Management, Anthropology/Ethnology, Archaeology/Antiquities, History, Sports/Fitness, Travel/Exploration, Autobiography/Memoirs, Bibliography, Biography. **Career:** Government of Fiji and Western Pacific, provincial commissioner, magistrate and assistant colonial secretary, 1938-52, liaison officer, 1942-44; Fiji Cricket Team, captain, 1948; Figi Museum, trustee, 1950-52; Rugby School, bursar, 1952-76; Oxford and Cambridge Universities, examiner on Pacific subjects, 1955-; Great Britain and Commonwealth Public Schools Bursars Association, chairman, 1962-65;

Order of the British Empire, officer, 1985; Lord Snow, executor and literary executor. Writer. **Publications:** Civil Defence Services, 1942; Cricket in the Fiji Islands, 1949; Rock Carvings in Fiji, 1950; The Nature of Fiji and Tonga, 1956; Bula, 1959; (with D.M. Sherwood and F.J. Walesby) Visit of Three Bursars to Schools and Universities, 1964; (with J.S. Woodhouse) Visit of Her Majesty the Queen and H.R.H. Prince Philip to Rugby School on the Occasion of the Quatercentenary, 1967; Bibliography of Fiji, Tonga and Rotuma, vol. I, 1969; (with S. Waine) The People from the Horizon, 1979; Stranger and Brother: A Portrait of C.P. Snow, 1982; (with R. Lovegrove) River Birds: Bird Life from Mountain Stream to Estuary, 1984; The Star Raft: China's Encounter with Africa, 1988; The Rarest Printed Work on the Pacific: A Bibliographer's Proposition, 1988; The Years of Hope, 1997; A Time of Renewal: Clusters of Characters, C.P. Snow, and Coups, 1998; Fall of Hong Kong: Britain, China, and the Japanese Occupation, 2003. EDITOR: (with G.K. Roth) Fijian Customs, 1944; Best Stories of the South Seas, 1967. Contributor to books and journals. **Address:** 46 Bennett Ct., Station Rd., Letchworth, HF SG6 3WA, England.

SNOW, Robert L. American (born United States), b. 1949. **Genres:** Documentaries/Reportage, Criminology/True Crime, History. **Career:** Indianapolis Police Department, Homicide Branch, detective, field training coordinator, 1978-80, director of planning, 1980-86, chief executive officer, 1986; law enforcement officer and administrator, retired. Writer. **Publications:** Protecting Your Life, Home, and Property: A Cop Shows You How, 1995; Swat Teams: Explosive Face-offs with America's Deadliest Criminals, 1996; Family Abuse: Tough Solutions to Stop the Violence, 1997; Stopping a Stalker: A Cop's Guide to Making the System Work for You, 1998; Looking for Carroll Beckwith: The True Story of a Detective's Search for His Past Life, 1999; Complete Guide to Personal and Home Safety: What You Need to Know, 2002; Terrorists Among Us: The Militia Threat, 2002; Deadly Cults: The Crimes of True Believers, 2003; Murder 101: Homicide and Its Investigation, 2005; Sex Crimes Investigation: Catching and Prosecuting the Perpetrators, 2006; Technology and Law Enforcement: From Gumshoe to Gamma Rays, 2007; Child Abduction: Prevention, Investigation, and Recovery, 2008; Policewomen Who Made History: Breaking through the Ranks, 2010; Finding Runaways and Missing Adults: When No One Else is Looking, 2012. Contributor of articles to magazines. **Address:** c/o Author Mail, Kluwer Academic Publishers Group, PO Box 358, Accord Sta., Hingham, MA 02018-0358, U.S.A.

SNOWDON, David A. American (born United States), b. 1952. **Genres:** Gerontology/Senior Issues, Medicine/Health. **Career:** University of Minnesota, School of Public Health, Division of Epidemiology, resident fellow, 1977-; University of Kentucky, Sanders-Brown Center on Aging, professor of neurology, 1986-, director of nun study. Writer. **Publications:** Aging with Grace: What the Nun Study Teaches Us About Leading Longer, Healthier and More Meaningful Lives, 2001. **Address:** Sanders-Brown Center on Aging, University of Kentucky, 101 Sanders-Brown Bldg., 900 S Limestone St., Lexington, KY 40536-0230, U.S.A. **Online address:** dsnowdon@nunstudy.mi8.com

SNOWMAN, Daniel. British (born England), b. 1938. **Genres:** Environmental Sciences/Ecology, History, Music, Politics/Government. **Career:** University of Sussex, lecturer in politics and American studies, 1963-67; British Broadcasting Corp., chief producer, 1967-95; University of London, Institute of Historical Research, senior research fellow. Writer. **Publications:** USA: The Twenties to Vietnam, 1968 as America since 1920, 1969, rev. ed., 1978; Eleanor Roosevelt, 1969; Kissing Cousins, 1977 in US as Britain and America, 1977; (ed. and intro.) If I Had Been, 1979; The Amadeus Quartet: The Men and the Music, 1981; The World of Plácido Domingo, 1985; (with J. Darras) Beyond the Tunnel of History, 1990; Pole Positions: The Polar Regions and the Future of the Planet, 1993; Frozen Future: The Arctic, the Antarctic, and the Survival of the Planet, 1993; Plácido Domingo's Tales from the Opera, 1994; (ed. with A. Briggs) Fins de Siecle: How Centuries End, 1400-2000, 1996; The Hitler é?migrés: The Cultural Impact on Britain of Refugees from Nazism, 2002; (ed.) Past Masters: The Best of History Today, 2001; Historians, 2006; The Gilded Stage: A Social History of Opera, 2009. **Address:** Dinah Wiener Ltd., 12 Cornwall Grove, London, GL W4 2LB, England. **Online address:** daniel@danielsnowman.org.uk

SNYDER, Brad M. American (born United States), b. 1972. **Genres:** Sports/Fitness. **Career:** Baltimore Sun, staff writer, 1994-96; Williams and Connally L.L.P., associate, 2001-04; Writer, 2004-08; University of Wisconsin Law School, assistant professor, 2008-. **Publications:** (With D.Parent)

Police-Corrections Partnerships, 1999; Beyond the Shadow of the Senators: The Untold Story of the Homestead Grays and the Integration of Baseball, 2003; Well-Paid Slave: Curt Flood's Fight for Free Agency in Professional Sports, 2006; (with Q. Lee) The Strategos Guide to Value Stream & Process Mapping, 2006. Contributor of stories to periodicals. **Address:** University of Wisconsin Law School, Rm. 9101, 975 Bascom Mall, Madison, WI 53706, U.S.A. **Online address:** bsnyder2@wisc.edu

SNYDER, Cecil. (Cecil K. Snyder). American (born United States), b. 1927. **Genres:** Novels. **Career:** Santa Ana College, instructor in English, 1961-62; University of California-Riverside, lecturer in English, 1962-69; University of California-Los Angeles, lecturer, 1964-66; California State Polytechnic University, lecturer in English, 1968-71. Writer. **Publications:** Big with Vengeance, 1969. **Address:** Harold Matson Company Inc., 276 5th Ave., New York, NY 10001-4509, U.S.A.

SNYDER, Cecil K. *See* **SNYDER, Cecil.**

SNYDER, Francis Gregory. British/American (born United States), b. 1942. **Genres:** Law, Politics/Government, Business/Trade/Industry, Economics, Agriculture/Forestry, Social Sciences. **Career:** Yale Law School, fellow, 1970-71; York University, Osgoode Hall Law School, Division of Social Science, assistant professor, 1971-74, associate professor, 1974-78; Journal of Legal Pluralism, European law journal editor, founding editor, 1975-; Warwick University, School of Law, senior lecturer, 1979-82, reader, 1982-87; Review of African Political Economy, editor, 1983-; University of London (University College), reader in European law, 1987-89, professor of European law, 1989-92; Modern Law Review, European law editor, 1988-; College of Europe, visiting professor of law, 1989-; European University Institute, part-time professor of European economic law, 1989-92, professor of European law, 1992-2000, head of the law department, 1993, Academy of European Law, co-director, 1997-2000; Academy of International Trade Law, founder and director, 1999-; Institute for Advanced Study, fellow, 2000-01; The Hague Academy of International Law, Centre for Studies and Research, director, 2003; London School of Economics, Department of Law, centennial professor of law, visiting professor of law; Université d'Aix-Marseille, associate professor; Université Paul Cézanne Aix-Marseille III, Jean Monnet chair, university professor and professor of law; Peking University, School of Transnational Law, C.V. Starr professor of law, Centre for Research on Transnational Law, co-director. **Publications:** One-party Government in Mali: Transition Toward Control, 1965; (with M.A. Savane) Law and Population in Senegal: A Survey of Legislation, 1977; Capitalism and Legal Change: An African Transformation, 1981; Law of the Common Agricultural Policy, 1985; New Directions in European Community Law, 1990; The Common Agricultural Policy of the European Economic Community, 1990; Introduction to European Union Law (in Chinese), 1996; International Trade and Customs Law of the European Union, 1998; Comment Protéger les intérêts du citoyen dans l'Union Européene d'aujourd'hui?: premiére rencontre internationale des jeuneschercheurs (RIJC)/Protecting the Interests of The Citizen in Today's European Union: First International Workshop of Young Scholars (WISH), 2003; (intro.) La sécurité Alimentaire dans l'Union Européenne, 2003; (intro.) Designing the European Union, 2007; (intro.) Evolution of the European Courts, 2009; European Union and China, 1949-2008: Basic Documents and Commentary, 2009; EU, The WTO and China: Legal Pluralism and International Trade Regulation, 2010. EDITOR: Law in Rural Africa, 1973; (with Y. Ghai and R. Luckham) The Political Economy of Law: A Third World Reader, 1987; (with D. Hay) Labour, Law and Crime: An Historical Perspective, 1987; (with P. Slinn) International Law of Development: Comparative Perspectives, 1987; (with D. Hay) Policing and Prosecution in Britain, 1750-1850, 1989; European Community Law, 2 vols., 1993; Constitutional Dimensions of European Economic Integration European, 1996; The Europeanisation of Law: The Legal Effects of European Integration, 2000; Regional and Global Regulation of International Trade, 2002; (with A. Mahiou) La sécurité alimentaire/publié sous la direction de Ahmed Mahiou, FrancisSnyder/Food Security and Food Safety, 2006. Contributor of articles to journals. **Address:** Department of Law, London School of Economics, Houghton St., London, GL WC2A 2AE, England. **Online address:** f.g.snyder@lse.ac.uk

SNYDER, Gary (Sherman). American (born United States), b. 1930. **Genres:** Poetry, Environmental Sciences/Ecology, Philosophy, Essays, Photography. **Career:** University of California, lecturer in English, 1964-65, professor of English, 1986-, professor emeritus of English. Writer. **Publications:** Riprap, 1959; Myths and Texts, 1960; Riprap and Cold Mountain Poems,

1965; Six Sections from Mountains and Rivers without End, 1965; A Range of Poems, 1966; Three Worlds, Three Realms, Six Roads, 1966; The Back Country, 1967; The Blue Sky, 1969; Four Changes, 1969; Sours of the Hills, 1969; Earth House Hold, 1969; Regarding Wave, 1970; The Fudo Trilogy, 1973; Turtle Island, 1974; The Old Ways: Six Essays, 1977; He Who Hunted Birds in His Father's Village: The Dimensions of a Haida Myth, 1978; The Real Work: Interviews & Talks, 1964-1979, 1980; True Night, 1980; Axe Handles, 1983; Passage through India, 1984; Good Wild Sacred, 1984; Left out in the Rain: New Poems, 1947-1985, 1986; The Practice of the Wild (essays), 1990; No Nature (poems), 1992; North Pacific Lands & Waters: A Further Six Sections, 1993; A Place in Space: Ethics, Aesthetics, and Watersheds: New and Selected Prose (essays), 1995; Mountains and Rivers without End, 1996; The Gary Snyder Reader, 1999; Look Out: A Selection of Writings, 2002; Danger on Peaks, 2004; Back on the Fire: Essays, 2007; (foreword) Pharmako Poeia: Plant Powers, Poisons, and Herbcraft, 2009; (with T. Killion) Tamalpais Walking, 2009. **Address:** Department of English, University of California, Voorhies Hall, 1 Shields Ave., Davis, CA 95616-8581, U.S.A. **Online address:** gssnyder@ucdavis.edu

SNYDER, Graydon F. American (born United States), b. 1930. **Genres:** Theology/Religion, Essays, History, Earth Sciences, Medicine/Health. **Career:** Bethany Theological Seminary, professor of biblical studies, 1959-86, dean, 1975-86; Chicago Theological Seminary, professor of New Testament, 1986-98, academic dean, 1987-99, now retired. Writer. **Publications:** (Ed. with W. Klassen) Current Issues in New Testament Interpretation, 1962; In His Hands, 1965; (ed.) The Shepherd of Hermas, 1967; (with R. Ruether) Power and Violence, 1971; (with D. Eugene) Using Biblical Simulations, 1973; Ante Pacem: Archaeological Evidence of Church Life Before Constanine, 1985, rev. ed., 2003; Tough Choices: Health Care Decisions and the Faith Community, 1988; (with K.M. Shaffer) Texts in Transit II, 1991; First Corinthians: A Faith Community Commentary, 1992; Health and Medicine in the Anabaptist Tradition: Care in Community, 1995; Religion and Health in the Anabaptist Tradition, 1995; (co-ed.) Putting Body and Soul Together, 1997; Inculturation of the Jesus Tradition: The Impact of Jesus on Jewish and Roman Cultures, 1999; Irish Jesus, Roman Jesus: The Formation of Early Irish Christianity, 2002; Fundamentalism: An Essay, 2003; (with D.M. McFarlane) People are Holy: The History and Theology of Free Church Worship, 2005; (co-ed.) Bound On Earth: A Festschrift for Edmon Lewin Rowell Jr., 2006. **Address:** 1407 E 60th St., Chicago, IL 60615-5314, U.S.A. **Online address:** graydonsny@aol.com

SNYDER, Gregory J. American (born United States), b. 1968?. **Genres:** Criminology/True Crime. **Career:** Baruch College of the City University of New York, Department of Sociology and Anthropology, assistant professor, 2007-. Writer and sociologist. **Publications:** Graffiti Lives: Beyond the Tag in New York's Urban Underground, 2009; The Grind: Professional Street Skateboarding in an Age of Spatial Constraint, 2012. **Address:** Department of Sociology and Anthropology, Baruch College, City University of New York, Vertical Campus 4-251, 17 Lexington Ave., New York, NY 10010, U.S.A. **Online address:** gregory.snyder@baruch.cuny.edu

SNYDER, James D. Also writes as James Donald Snyder. American (born United States), b. 1937. **Genres:** Adult Non-fiction, History, Novels, Theology/Religion. **Career:** Clissold Publishing Co., editor, 1960-63; Snyder Associates Inc., president, 1964-85; Enterprise Communications Inc., associate, 1985-. **Publications:** All Gods Children: How the First Christians Challenged the Roman World and Shaped the Next 2000 Years: An Historical Novel, 1999; The Faith and the Power: The Inspiring Story of the First Christians & How They Survived the Madness of Rome: A First Century History, 2002; Life and Death on the Loxahatchee: The Story of Trapper Nelson, 2002; Five Thousand Years on the Loxahatchee: A Pictorial History of Jupiter-Tequesta Florida, 2003; Black Gold and Silver Sands: A Pictorial History of Agriculture in Palm Beach County, 2004; A Light in the Wilderness: The Story of Jupiter Inlet Lighthouse & the Southeast Florida Frontier, 2006. **Address:** c/o Author Mail, Pharos Books, 8657 SE Merritt Way, Jupiter, FL 33458-1007, U.S.A. **Online address:** jsnyder@adelphia.net

SNYDER, James Donald. *See* SNYDER, James D.

SNYDER, Jane McIntosh. American (born United States), b. 1943. **Genres:** Classics, History, Women's Studies And Issues, Social Sciences, Adult Non-fiction. **Career:** Ohio State University, assistant professor, 1968-72, associate professor, 1973-86, professor, 1986-95, College of Humanities, associate

dean, 1986-88, Department of Classics, head, 1988-92, professor emeritus, 1995-. Writer. **Publications:** Puns and Poetry in Lucretius' De Rerum Natura, 1980; (with M. Maas) Stringed Instruments of Ancient Greece, 1989; The Woman and the Lyre: Women Writers in Classical Greece and Rome, 1989; Sappho, 1995; Lesbian Desire in the Lyrics of Sappho, 1997; Cleaning Up the Park: Learning to Count by Fives, 2003. Contributor of articles to books and journals. **Address:** Department of Greek and Latin, Ohio State University, 414 University Hall, 230 N Oval Mall, Columbus, OH 43210-1319, U.S.A. **Online address:** snyder.6@osu.edu

SNYDER, Laurel. American (born United States), b. 1974?. **Genres:** Adult Non-fiction, Poetry. **Career:** Writer and educator. **Publications:** Daphne and Jim: A Choose-Your-Own- Adventure Biography in Verse (for adults), 2005; (ed.) Half/Life: Jew-ish Tales from Interfaith Homes, 2006; The Myth of the Simple Machines (poetry; for adults), 2007; Inside the Slidy Diner, 2008; Up and Down the Scratchy Mountains; or, The Search for a Proper Princess, 2008; Any Which Wall, 2009; Baxter, the Pig Who Wanted to Be Kosher, 2010; (intro.) E. Nesbit, Five Children and It, 2010; Penny Dreadful, 2010; Nosh, Schlep, Schluff, 2011. Contributor to periodicals. **Address:** Decaturc, GA, U.S.A. **Online address:** laurelsnyder@hotmail.com

SNYDER, Lucy A. American (born United States), b. 1971?. **Genres:** Poetry, Novels, Novellas/Short Stories. **Career:** Seton Hill University, mentor, 2010-. Writer. **Publications:** Installing Linux on a Dead Badger (short stories), 2007; Chimeric Machines (poetry), 2009; Spellbent (novel), 2009; Sparks and Shadows (short stories and poetry), 2010; Shotgun Sorceress (novel), 2010. **Address:** Worthington, OH, U.S.A. **Online address:** lusnyde@gmail.com

SNYDER, Midori. American (born United States), b. 1954. **Genres:** Science Fiction/Fantasy, Children's Non-fiction, Animals/Pets, Young Adult Fiction. **Career:** Freelance writer, 1985-. **Publications:** FANTASY NOVELS: Soulstring, 1987; The Flight of Michael McBride, 1994; Hatchling, 1995; The Innamorati, 1998; Hannah's Garden, 2002. ORAN TRILOGY SERIES: New Moon, 1989; Sadar's Keep, 1990; Beldane's Fire, 1993; (with J. Yolen) Except the Queen, 2010. Works appear in anthologies. **Address:** c/o Howard Morhaim, Howard Morhaim Agency, 11 John St., Ste. 407, New York, NY 10038, U.S.A. **Online address:** msnylabyrinth@yahoo.com

SNYDER, Timothy. American (born United States), b. 1969. **Genres:** Biography, History. **Career:** Yale University, Department of History, assistant professor, 2001-04, associate professor, 2004-06, professor of history, 2006-, Bird White Housum professor of history, director of graduate studies, 2006-08; Harvard Academy for International and Area Studies, executive secretary. Writer and historian. **Publications:** Nationalism, Marxism and Modern Central Europe: A Biography of Kazimierz Kelles-Krauz, 1872-1905, 1997; (ed. with P. Andreas) The Wall around the West: State Borders and Immigration Controls in North America and Europe, 2000; The Reconstruction of Nations: Poland, Ukraine, Lithuania, Belarus, 1569-1999, 2003; Sketches from a Secret War: A Polish Artist's Mission to Liberate Soviet Ukraine, 2005; The Red Prince: The Secret Lives of a Habsburg Archduke, 2008; Bloodlands: Europe Between Hitler and Stalin, 2010; (with J. Judt) Thinking the Twentieth Century, 2012. Contributor to books, periodicals and journals. **Address:** Department of History, Yale University, WLH 107, 320 York St., PO Box 208324, New Haven, CT 06520-8324, U.S.A. **Online address:** timothy.snyder@yale.edu

SNYDER, Zilpha Keatley. American (born United States), b. 1927. **Genres:** Novels, Children's Fiction, Young Adult Fiction, Poetry, Picture/Board Books, Novellas/Short Stories. **Career:** Teacher, 1948-62; University of California, master, teacher and demonstrator for education classes, 1959-61. Writer. **Publications:** NOVELS: Season of Ponies, 1964; The Velvet Room, 1965; Black and Blue Magic, 1966; The Egypt Game, 1967; Eyes in the Fishbowl, 1968; Today Is Saturday (verse), 1969; The Changeling, 1970; The Witches of Worm, 1972; The Princess and the Giants, 1973; The Truth about Stone Hollow, 1974 in UK as The Ghosts of Stone Hollow, 1978; Heirs of Darkness (for adults), 1978; A Fabulous Creature, 1981; Come On, Patsy, 1982; The Birds of Summer, 1983; The Changing Maze, 1985; The Three Men, 1986; And Condors Danced, 1987; Squeak Saves the Day and Other Tooley Tales, 1988; Libby on Wednesday, 1990; Song of the Gargoyle, 1990; Fool's Gold, 1993; Cat Running, 1994; The Trespassers, 1995; The Gypsy Game, 1997; Gib Rides Home, 1998; The Gypsy Game Teacher's Guide, 1998; The Runaways, 1999; Gib and the Gray Ghost, 2000; Spyhole Secrets, 2001; The Ghosts of Rathburn Park, 2002; The Unseen, 2004; The Magic Nation Thing, 2005; The Treasures of Weatherby, 2007; The Bronze Pen, 2008; William S.

and the Great Escape, 2009; William's Midsummer Dreams, 2011. STAN-LEY FAMILY SERIES: The Headless Cupid, 1971; The Famous Stanley Kidnapping Case, 1979; Blair's Nightmare, 1984; Janie's Private Eyes, 1989. GREEN SKY SERIES: Below the Root, 1975; And All Between, 1976; Until the Celebration, 1977. CASTLE COURT KIDS SERIES: The Diamond War, 1995; The Box and the Bone, 1995; Ghost Invasion, 1995; Secret Weapons, 1995. OTHER: Alexis Danger, 2001. **Address:** 52 Miller Ave., Mill Valley, CA 94941-1920, U.S.A. **Online address:** zilpha@zksnyder.com

SOBEL, Dava. American (born United States), b. 1947. **Genres:** Medicine/Health, Documentaries/Reportage, Sciences, Translations, Astronomy, History, Biography, Sports/Fitness, Sports/Fitness. **Career:** IBM, technical writer; Cornell University News Bureau, science writer; New York Times, science reporter, 1979-82; East Hampton Independent, astronomy columnist, 1994-; Discovery Channel Online, astronomy columnist, 1996-. **Publications:** (With F.D. Drake) Is Anyone Out There?: The Scientific Search for Extraterrestrial Intelligence, 1992; Longitude: The True Story of a Lone Genius Who Solved the Greatest Scientific Problem of His Time, 1995; (with W.J.H. Andrewes) Illustrated Longitude, 1998; Galileo's Daughter: A Historical Memoir of Science, Faith and Love, 1999; (trans.) M.C. Galilei, Letters to Father: Suor Maria Celeste to Galileo, 1623-1633, 2001; (ed.) The Best American Science Writing 2004, 2004; The Planets, 2005; Longitude: A Play, 2006. WITH A.C. KLEIN: Backache Relief: The Ultimate Second Opinion from Back-Pain Sufferers Nationwide Who Share Their Successful Healing Experiences, 1985; Arthritis: What Works, 1989; Arthritis: What Exercises Work, 1993, rev. ed. as Arthritis: What Exercises Works: Breakthrough Relief for the Rest of Your Life, Even After Drugs and Surgery Have Failed, 1995; Backache: What Exercises Work, 1994. Contributor to periodicals. **Address:** c/o Michael V. Carlisle, InkWell Management, 521 5th Ave., 26th Fl., New York, NY 10175, U.S.A. **Online address:** web_submit@davasobel.com

SOBEL, David T. American (born United States), b. 1949. **Genres:** Adult Non-fiction, Education, Education. **Career:** The Harrisville School, co-founder, director and teacher, 1972-75; Antioch New England Graduate School, Department of Education and Environmental Studies, core faculty, 1977-86, Education Department, chairperson, 1983-97, Center for Place-based Education, director, 1997-, Teacher Certification Programs, director, 1997-, Community-based School Environmental Education, director of project; Harrisville Children's Center, founder; Yankee Lands: A Land Use Curriculum Project, curriculum coordinator, 1980-83; Know Nukes Institute, project director, 1982-87. Writer. **Publications:** Children's Special Places: Exploring the Role of Forts, Dens, and Bush Houses in Middle Childhood, 1993; Beyond Ecophobia: Reclaiming the Heart in Nature Education, 1996; Mapmaking with Children: Sense-of-Place Education for the Elementary Years, 1998; Standing Strong in My Rightful Place, 2003; Place-Based Education: Connecting Classrooms & Communities, With Index, 2004; (co-author) Living a Healthy Life with Chronic Conditions: Self-Management of Heart Disease, Fatigue, Arthritis, Worry, Diabetes, Frustration, Asthma, Pain, Emphysema, and Others, 2006; Teaching with Nature: Inspiration for Educators, 2007; Childhood and Nature: Design Principles for Educators, 2008; (with G.A. Smith) Place- and Community-based Education in Schools, 2010; Wild Play: Parenting Adventures In The Great Outdoors, 2011. **Address:** Antioch New England Graduate School, 40 Avon St., Keene, NH 03431-3516, U.S.A. **Online address:** dsobel@antiochne.edu

SOBEL, Ileene Smith. American (born United States), b. 1953?. **Genres:** Children's Fiction, Biography, Theology/Religion. **Career:** Random House, vice president and senior editor, 2003-. **Publications:** Moses and the Angels (children's book), 1999. **Address:** Random House, 1745 Broadway, New York, NY 10019, U.S.A. **Online address:** ismith@randomhouse.com

SOBEL, Russell S(teven). American (born United States), b. 1968. **Genres:** Economics. **Career:** West Virginia University, College of Business and Economics, Bureau of Business and Economic Research, faculty research associate, 1995-, visiting assistant professor, 1994-95, Department of Economics, assistant professor of economics, 1995-, James Clark Coffman distinguished chair and professor, 2005-, Entrepreneurship Center, founding director, 2002-06, senior research advisor, 2006-; Public Policy Foundation of West Virginia, Center for Economic Growth, senior economist and director. Writer. **Publications:** (With R.G. Holcombe) Growth and Variability in State Tax Revenue: An Anatomy of State Fiscal Crises, 1997; (with J.D. Gwartney and R.L. Stroup) Microeconomics: Private and Public Choice, 9th ed., 2000; (with J.D. Gwartney and R.L. Stroup) Macroeconomics: Private and Public Choice,

9th ed., 2000; (with J.D. Gwartney and R.L. Stroup) Economics: Private and Public Choice, 9th ed., 2000; (ed. with J.C. Hall and M.E. Ryan) Unleashing Capitalism: Why Prosperity Stops at the West Virginia Border and How to Fix It, 2007. Contributor of articles to journals. **Address:** Department of Economics, West Virginia University, 1601 University Ave., PO Box 6025, Morgantown, WV 26506-6025, U.S.A. **Online address:** russell.sobel@mail.wvu.edu

SOBER, Elliott (Reuben). American (born United States), b. 1948. **Genres:** Philosophy, Natural History, Sciences. **Career:** University of Wisconsin, Department of Philosophy, assistant professor, 1974-80, associate professor of philosophy, 1980-84, professor, 1984-, Hans Reichenbach professor, 1989-, William F. Vilas research professor, 1993-, chair, 1993-97; Harvard University, fellow in population genetics, 1980-81; University of Otago, Department of Philosophy, William Evans visiting fellow, 1990; International Union for History and Philosophy of Science, secretary, 1991-99; American Philosophical Association, president, 1998-99; London School of Economics and Political Science, Centennial professor, 1999-2002, visiting professor, 2003-08; University of Vienna, Institute Vienna Circle, International Summer School, co-director, 2001; Stanford University, Department of Philosophy, professor, 2003-04; Philosophy of Science Association, president, 2003-05. Writer. **Publications:** Simplicity, 1975; The Nature of Selection: Evolutionary Theory in Philosophical Focus, 1984; (ed.) Conceptual Issues in Evolutionary Biology, 1984, 3rd ed., 2006; Reconstructing the Past: Parsimony Evolution and Inference, 1988; Core Questions in Philosophy, 1991, 5th ed., 2009; Reconstructing Marxism, 1991; Philosophy of Biology, 1993, 2nd ed., 2000; From a Biological Point of View, 1994; (with D.S. Wilson) Unto Others: the Evolution and Psychology of Unselfish Behavior, 1998; (ed. with S.H. Orzack) Adaptationism and Optimality, 2001; Evidence and Evolution: The Logic Behind the Science, 2008; Did Darwin Write the Origin Backwards?: Philosophical Essays on Darwin's Theory, 2010. Contributor to books and professional journals. **Address:** Department of Philosophy, University of Wisconsin, 5185 Helen C. White Hall, Madison, WI 53706, U.S.A. **Online address:** ersober@wisc.edu

SOBOL, Donald J. American (born United States), b. 1924. **Genres:** Novellas/Short Stories, Children's Fiction, Children's Non-fiction, Novels, Mystery/Crime/Suspense, Young Adult Non-fiction. **Career:** New York Sun, reporter, 1946-47; Long Island Daily Press, reporter, 1947-52; New York Daily News, reporter, 1949-51; freelance writer, 1954-; R.H. Macy, columnist, 1959-68. **Publications:** FOR YOUNG ADULTS: The Double Quest, 1957; The Lost Dispatch: A Story of Antictam, 1958; The First Book of Medieval Man, 1959 in UK as The First Book of Medieval Britain, 1960; Two Flags Flying, 1960; A Civil War Sampler, 1961; The Wright Brothers at Kitty Hawk, 1961; The First Book of the Barbarian Invaders, A.D. 375-511, 1962; (with R. Sobel) Stocks and Bonds, 1963; Lock, Stock, and Barrel, 1965; Secret Agents Four, 1967; Two Minute Mysteries, 1967; Mastermind!, 1968; Greta the Strong, 1970; Milton, the Model A, 1970; More Two-Minute Mysteries, 1971; The Amazons of Greek Mythology, 1972; Great Sea Stories, 1975; Still More Two-Minute Mysteries, 1975; Strange but True, 1975; True Sea Adventures, 1975; Disasters, 1979; Angie's First Case, 1981; The Amazing Power of Asher Fine: A Fine Mystery, 1986; My Name Is Amelia, 1994; Two-minute Mysteries Collection, 2004. ENCYCLOPEDIA BROWN: BOY DETECTIVE SERIES: Encyclopedia Brown: Boy Detective, 1963; Encyclopedia Brown and the Case of the Secret Pitch, 1965; Encyclopedia Brown Finds the Clues, 1966; Encyclopedia Brown Gets His Man, 1967; Encyclopedia Brown Solves Them All, 1968; Encyclopedia Brown Keeps the Peace, 1969; Encyclopedia Brown Saves the Day, 1970; Encyclopedia Brown Tracks Them Down, 1971; Encyclopedia Brown Shows the Way, 1972; Encyclopedia Brown Takes the Case, 1973; Encyclopedia Brown Lends a Hand, 1974; Encyclopedia Brown and the Case of the Dead Eagles, 1975; Encyclopedia Brown and the Eleven: Case of the Exploding Plumbing and Other Mysteries, 1976; Encyclopedia Brown and the Case of the Midnight Visitor, 1977; Encyclopedia Brown's Record Book of Weird and Wonderful Facts, 1979; Encyclopedia Brown Carries On, 1980; Encyclopedia Brown's Second Record Book of Weird and Wonderful Facts, 1981; Encyclopedia Brown's Third Record Book of Weird and Wonderful Facts, 1981; Encyclopedia Brown Sets the Pace, 1982; Encyclopedia Brown's Book of Wacky Crimes, 1982; Encyclopedia Brown, 1983; (with G. Andrews) Encyclopedia Brown Takes the Cake!: A Cook and Case Book, 1983; Encyclopedia Brown Book of Wacky Spies, 1984; Encyclopedia Brown's Book of Wacky Sports, 1984; Encyclopedia Brown and the Case of the Mysterious Handprints, 1985; Encyclopedia Brown Book of Wacky Animals, 1985; (with C. Elliot) Encyclopedia Brown's Book of Comic Strips, 1985; Encyclopedia Brown Book of the Wacky Outdoors, 1987; Encyclopedia Brown Book of Wacky Cars, 1987; Encyclopedia Brown and the Case of the Treasure Hunt, 1988; Encyclopedia Brown and the Case of the Disgusting Sneakers, 1990; The Best of Encyclopedia Brown, 1990; (with R. Sobol) Encyclopedia Brown's Book of Strange but True Crimes, 1991; Encyclopedia Brown and the Case of the Two Spies, 1994; Encyclopedia Brown and the Case of Pablo's Nose, 1996; Encyclopedia Brown and the Case of the Sleeping Dog, 1998; Encyclopedia Brown and the Case of the Slippery Salamander, 1999; Encyclopedia Brown and the Case of the Jumping Frogs, 2003; Encyclopedia Brown Cracks the Case, 2007; Encyclopedia Brown, Super Sleuth, 2009; Encyclopedia Brown and the Case of the Secret UFOs, 2010; Encyclopedia Brown and the Case of the Carnival Crime, 2011; Encyclopedia Brown and the Case of the Soccer Scheme, 2012. EDITOR: An American Revolutionary War Reader, 1964; (and comp.) The Strongest Man in the World: Stories, 1967; Best Animal Stories of Science Fiction and Fantasy, 1979. Contributor of articles to magazines. **Address:** McIntosh & Otis Inc., 353 Lexington Ave., New York, NY 10016-0941, U.S.A.

SOBOL, Joshua. (Yehoshua Sobol). Israeli (born Israel), b. 1939?. **Genres:** Plays/Screenplays, Novels. **Career:** Theater Co., founder, 1977; Tel Aviv University, Seminar Hakibutsim and Beit Tzvi Drama Schools, teacher of aesthetics and workshop director; Haifa Municipal Theater, artistic director, 1984-88; Atlantic Center for the Arts, artist-in-residence, 1989; Al Hamishmar (socialist newspaper), journalist. Dramatist. **Publications:** Lel ha-'eśrim, 1977, trans. as The Night of the twentieth, 1978; Ha-Lailah ha-aḥaron shel Oṭo Vaininger, 1982; El alma de un judío: la última noche de Otto Weininger: drama en dos actos, 1984; Geṭo, 1984, trans. as Ghetto: Schauspiel in drei Akten, 1984; Ha-Paleṣ tinait, 1985; Sindrom Yerushalayim, 1987; Adam, 1989; Ba-martef, 1990; Solo, 1991; Almah: maḥazeh, 1999; Silence (novel), 2000; Shetiḳah: roman, 2000; 'Ed reiyah: be-hashraat parashat Frants Yegershṭeṭer, 2004; Whiskey's Fine (novel), 2004; Viṣḳi zeh be-seder: sipur, 2005; Gibor ma'amad ha-po'alim, 2006; Here and Now: Amir Peretz and the Israeli Situation (non-fiction), 2006; She ato ha-aḥaronah shel ḳol: monodramah, 2008; Ani lo Draifus: monodramah, 2008; Devash: (ha-lailah ha-shelishi), 2008; ḳolot ba-lailah: Libera me, 2009. **Address:** Or-Am Publishing House, PO Box 22096, Tel Aviv, 61220, Israel.

SOBOL, Yehoshua. See **SOBOL, Joshua.**

SOBOTT-MOGWE, Gaele. South African/Australian (born Australia), b. 1956. **Genres:** Novels, Children's Fiction, Young Adult Fiction. **Career:** University of Botswana, English Department, lecturer. Writer. **Publications:** FICTION FOR CHILDREN: The Magic Pool, 1991; Thara and the Cassipoohkaman, 1992; Speckled Eggs, 1993; Weird Wambo, 1994; Tumelo and the Blue Birds, 1995; Mare's Aunt, 1995; Tickles, 1997. FICTION FOR ADULTS: Colour Me Blue, 1995. Works appears in anthologies. Contributor to periodicals and journals. **Address:** c/o Heinemann, Halley Ct., Jordan Hill, Oxford, OX OX2 8EJ, England. **Online address:** sobottmogwe@msn.com

SODEN, Dale E.(Edward). American (born United States), b. 1951. **Genres:** Biography, History. **Career:** Oklahoma Baptist University, assistant professor of history, 1980-85; Whitworth College, associate professor, professor of history and vice president for planning, 1985-, executive assistant to president; Pacific Lutheran Theological Seminary, board director; Young Men's Christian Association, board director. Writer. **Publications:** A Venture of Mind and Spirit: An Illustrated History of Whitworth University, 1990, rev. ed., 2010; The Reverend Mark Matthews: An Activist in the Progressive Era, 2001; (ed.) Historic Photos of Washington State, 2008. **Address:** Whitworth College, Weyerhaeuser Hall 210 J, 300 W Hawthorne Rd., Spokane, WA 99251, U.S.A. **Online address:** dsoden@whitworth.edu

SODEN, Garrett. American (born United States), b. 1952. **Genres:** Administration/Management, Business/Trade/Industry, History. **Career:** Occidental College, graphic designer and writer; Kenwood USA, communications executive; GetPlugged.com, marketing manager, editorial director; Waves Inc., marketing manager, director of pro-audio marketing and communications, 2004-06; Clear Moon Music, co-founder, 2006-; SD Ray Associates, marketing director. **Publications:** (With J. Book) The One Minute Maniac, 1987; I Went to College for This?: True Stuff about Life in the Business World-And How to Make Your Way through It, 1994; Looking Good on Paper: How to Create Eye-Catching Reports, Proposals, Memos, and Other Business Documents, 1995; Hook, Spin, Buzz: How to Command, Attention, Change Minds and Influence People, 1996; Falling: How Our Greatest Fear Became Our Greatest Thrill: A History, 2003; Defying Gravity: Land Divers, Roller Coast-

ers, Gravity Bums, and the Human Obsession with Falling, 2005. **Address:** Dystel & Goderich Literary Management, 1 Union Sq. W, Ste. 904, New York, NY 10003-3313, U.S.A. **Online address:** garrett@garrettsoden.com

SOEHNLEIN, Karl M. American (born United States) **Genres:** Novels, Gay And Lesbian Issues, Sex, Young Adult Fiction. **Career:** Release Print (film magazine), associate editor; San Fransisco State University, teacher; University of San Fransisco, creative writing teacher; Seton Hall University, adjunct professor of communication, M.A.S.C.L program director; freelance writer, film producer and magazine publisher. **Publications:** The World of Normal Boys (novel), 2000; You Can Say You Knew Me When, 2005; Robin and Ruby, 2010. Contributor to periodicals. **Address:** c/o Craig Bentley, Kensington Publishing Corp., 119 W 40th St., New York, NY 10018, U.S.A. **Online address:** karl@kmsoehnlein.com

SOERENS, Matthew. American (born United States), b. 1983. **Genres:** Politics/Government. **Career:** World Relief DuPage, immigration and citizenship counselor. Writer and advocate. **Publications:** (With J. Hwang) Welcoming the Stranger: Justice, Compassion, & Truth in the Immigration Debate, 2009. Contributor to periodicals. **Address:** World Relief DuPage, 1825 College Ave., Ste. 230, Wheaton, IL 60187, U.S.A.

SOFER, Barbara. (Rachel Shader). American/Israeli (born Israel), b. 1949. **Genres:** Novels, Children's Fiction, Travel/Exploration, Children's Nonfiction, Young Adult Fiction. **Career:** English teacher, 1971-76; Kibbutz Experimental School, English teacher, 1977-; Hadassah Medical Center, public relations and communications director, 1999-; Inside Magazine, contributing editor; Ohr Torah Stone Newsbriefs, editor; Jerusalem Post Newspaper, columnist; Hadassah Magazine, contributing editor. **Publications:** The Holiday Adventures of Achbar (juvenile fiction), 1983; Kids Love Israel, Israel Loves Kids: A Travel Guide for Families, 1988, rev. ed., 1996; Shalom Haver, Goodbye Friend (memorial album), 1996; The Thirteenth Hour (novel), 1996; Ilan Ramon, Israel's Space Hero, 2004; Keeping Israel Safe: The Israel Defense Forces, 2008; The Human Spirit, 2010, At Home with God, forthcoming. Contributor to books, magazines and newspapers. **Address:** 5 Hahish Dr., Jerusalem, 93223, Israel. **Online address:** bsofer@netvision.net.il

SOFFER, Joshua. American (born United States), b. 1959. **Genres:** Philosophy, Psychology, Humanities, History. **Career:** Writer. **Publications:** Sense and Affect, 2003. Contributor to periodicals. **Address:** 5701 N Sheridan Rd., Ste. 29R, Chicago, IL 60660-4720, U.S.A. **Online address:** joshsoffer@uron.cc

SOFFER, Olga. American (born United States), b. 1942?. **Genres:** History, Local History/Rural Topics, Area Studies, Adult Non-fiction, Women's Studies And Issues, Social Sciences. **Career:** City University of New York, Hunter College, adjunct instructor of anthropology, 1978-80, Lehman College, adjunct instructor of anthropology, 1979-80; University of Wisconsin, instructor of anthropology, 1980-85; University of Illinois, Department of Anthropology, assistant professor, 1985-88, associate professor, 1988-92, professor, 1992-, Russian and East European Center, acting director, 1992-93, Department of Slavic Languages and Literature, head, 1993-98, now professor emeritus; Illinois State Museum, adjunct research associate, 1990-; Centre de Recherches Archeologiques, visiting professor, 1992; University of California, Cotsen Institute of Archaeology, research associate. Writer. **Publications:** The Upper Paleolithic of the Central Russian Plain, 1985; (ed.) The Pleistocene Old World: Regional Perspectives, 1987; (ed. with with C. Gamble) The World at 18000 BP, 1990; Archaeological Dictionary of Stone Tools, 1991; (ed. with N.D. Praslov) From Kostenki to Clovis: Upper Paleolithic Paleo-Indian Adaptations, 1993; (ed. with S.A. Vasil'ev and J. Kozlowski) Perceived Landscapes and Built Environments: The Cultural Geography of Late Paleolithic Eurasia, 2003; (with J.M. Adovasio and J. Page) The Invisible Sex: Uncovering the True Roles of Women in Prehistory, 2007. **Address:** Department of Anthropology, University of Illinois, 109 Davenport Hall, MC-148, 607 S Matthew Ave., PO Box 148, Urbana, IL 61801, U.S.A. **Online address:** o-soffer@illinois.edu

SOFTLY, Barbara (Charmian). British (born England), b. 1924. **Genres:** Novellas/Short Stories, Children's Fiction, Children's Non-fiction, History, Animals/Pets. **Career:** Manor House, teacher of history, 1944-57. Writer. **Publications:** Plain Jane, 1961; Place Mill, 1962; A Stone in a Pool, 1964; Ponder and William, 1966; Magic People, 1966; Ponder and William on Holiday, 1968; More Magic People, 1969; Hippo, Potta and Muss, 1969; Magic

People Around the World, 1970; A Lemon-yellow Elephant Called Trunk, 1971; Geranium, 1972; Ponder and William at Home, 1972; Ponder and William at the Weekend, 1974; Queens of England, 1976; The Story of the Village of Sidbury, Devon, England 1800-1900; Tapping on the Garden Gate, 1995; Further Tappings at Sidbury Gates, 1998; Within the Bounds, Sidbury Parish Past and Present, 1998; Sidbury's Church of a Thousand Years, 2000. Contributor of articles to magazines. **Address:** Bundels, Ridgway Ln., Sidbury, DN EX10 0SF, England.

SOHN, Amy. American (born United States), b. 1973?. **Genres:** Novels, Young Adult Non-fiction, Sex. **Career:** New York magazine, contributing editor; Writer. **Publications:** Run Catch Kiss, 1998; Sex and the City: Kiss and Tell, 2002; My Old Man, 2004; Prospect Park West: A Novel, 2009. Contributor to magazines. **Address:** c/o Author Mail, Simon & Schuster, 1230 Ave. of the Americas, New York, NY 10020, U.S.A.

SOK-KYONG, Kang. Korean (born Korea (South)), b. 1951. **Genres:** Novels, Literary Criticism And History. **Career:** Writer, painter and essayist. **Publications:** Sullyeja ŭi norae: Kang Sŏk-kyŏng ŭi sosŏl, 1981; Pam kwa yoram, 1983; Pam kwa yoram, 1983; Il hanŭn yesulgadŭl: Kang Sŏk-kyŏng ŭi in gan t amgu, 1986; Pomnal esŏ pomnal ro, 1986; Sup sok ŭi pang, 1986; (with Y. Kwi-ja and Y. Chong-mo) Sŏ gyang kkot, 1987; Kŭ dae ŭ i hanŭ l e tal i toeŏ ttŭ rira, 1988; Sojunghan tangsin ŭi sam ŭl wihayŏ, 1989; Kakkaun koltchagi, 1989; (K. Chi-wŏn and O. Chŏng-hŭi) Words of Farewell: Stories by Korean Women Writers, 1989; Sam ŭl sarang hanŭn yŏsŏngdŭl ŭl wihayŏ, 1990; Indo kihaeng, 1990; Uridŭl ŭi p yŏnghwajuŭi, 1991; Kakkun koltchagi (novel), 1997; Valley Nearby, 1997; Sŏul: Ch angjak kwa Pip yŏngsa, 2001; Nae maŭm c namŭn chŏl: Han guk munhwagye rŭl taep yŏ hanŭn 52-myŏng ŭi sachal inyŏngi, 2007; Sŏul-si: Purŭn Sasangsa, 2008; Work appears in anthologies. Contributor of short stories to periodicals. **Address:** Publicity Department, Heinemann, 361 Hanover St., Portsmouth, NH 03801, U.S.A.

SOKOL, B. J. British (born England), b. 1942. **Genres:** Psychology, Literary Criticism And History. **Career:** Goldsmith's University of London, emeritus professor of English. Writer. **Publications:** (Ed.) The Undiscover'd Country: New Essays on Psychoanalysis and Shakespeare, 1993; Art and Illusion in the Winter's Tale, 1994; (Ed. with H. Klein and P. Davidhazi) Shakespeare and Hungary: Special Theme Section: The Law and Shakespeare, 1996. (with M. Sokol) Shakespeare's Legal Language: A Dictionary, 2000. (with M. Sokol) Shakespeare, Law, and Marriage, 2003; A Brave New World of Knowledge: Shakespeare's "The Tempest" and Early Modern Epistemology, 2003; Shakespeare and Tolerance, 2008. Contributor to periodicals. **Address:** England. **Online address:** j.sokol@gold.ac.uk

SOKOL, Julia. American (born United States) **Genres:** Novels, Social Sciences, Self Help, Psychology, Women's Studies And Issues, Adult Non-fiction. **Career:** Writer. **Publications:** (With S. Carter) Men Who Can't Love: When a Man's Fear Makes Him Run from Commitment (and What a Smart Woman Can Do about It), 1987; (with S. Carter) What Really Happens in Bed: A Demystification of Sex, 1989; (with S. Carter) Lives without Balance: When Youre Giving Everything Youve Got and Still Not Getting What You Hoped For, 1992; (with S. Carter) He's Scared Shes Scared: Understanding the Hidden Fears That Sabotage Your Relationships, 1993; (with S. Carter) Men Like Women Who Like Themselves: (and Other Secrets That the Smartest Women Know about Partnership), 1996; (with S. Carter) Getting to Commitment: Overcoming the Eight Greatest Obstacles to Lasting Connection (and Finding the Courage to Love), 1998; (with S. Carter) Help! I'm in Love with a Narcissist, 2005. **Address:** c/o Author Mail, M. Evans & Company Publishing, 216 E 49th St., New York, NY 10017, U.S.A.

SOKOLOFF, Naomi B. American (born United States), b. 1953. **Genres:** Literary Criticism And History. **Career:** Princeton University, English Composition, assistant in instruction, 1976, assistant in instruction Spanish, 1976-80; University of Arizona, Department of Oriental Studies, visiting assistant professor, 1980-81, assistant professor, 1981-84; University of Maryland, course consultant, 1984; Jewish Theological Seminary of America, faculty fellow, 1984-85; Jewish Education Council, consultant, 1986-87; University of Washington, assistant professor, 1985-92, associate professor, 1992-99, Near Eastern Languages and Civilization, chair, 1993-97, adjunct associate professor, 1993-, professor, 1999-, Samuel and Althea Stroum endowed chair in Jewish studies, 2003-; Jackson School of International Studies, Jewish Studies Program, chair, 1997-2000. Writer. **Publications:** (Ed. with A.L. Lerner and A. Norich) Gender and Text in Modern Hebrew and Yiddish Literature, Jewish Theological Seminary of America, 1992; Imagining the Child in Modern Jewish Fiction, 1992; (ed. with E. Goodenough and M.A. Heberle) Infant Tongues: The Voice of the Child in Literature, 1994; (ed. and intro.) Israel and America: Cross-Cultural Encounters and the Literary Imagination, 1998; (ed. with with S. Rahn) The Jewish Presence in Children's Literature, 2003; (co-ed.) Traditions and Transitions in Israel Studies, vol. VI, 2003; (ed. with S.A. Glenn) Boundaries of Jewish Identity, 2010. Contributor to periodicals. **Address:** Department of Near East Lang & Civilization, University of Washington, 229A Denny Hall, PO Box 353120, Seattle, WA 98195, U.S.A. **Online address:** naosok@u.washington.edu

SOLARES, Ignacio. Mexican (born Mexico), b. 1945. **Genres:** Novels, Novellas/Short Stories, Young Adult Fiction, History. **Career:** Plural, editor, 1969-71; Excélsior (daily), writer and editor of cultural section diorama de la cultura, 1971-76; Universidad Nacional Autónoma de México, professor of literature, Theater and Dance Department, head. **Publications:** FICTION: El hombre habitado, 1975; Puerta del cielo, 1976; Anónimo, 1979; El árbol del deseo, 1980; La fórmula de la inmortalidad, 1982; Serafín (novel), 1985; Casas de encantimiento, 1987; Madero, el otro (historical novel), 1989; El gran elector (historical novel), 1993; Nen, la inútil, trans. as The Idle Dreamer, 1995; Muérete y sabrás: Cuentos (short stories), 1995; Columbus (novel), 1996; Los mártires; Serafín; El árbol de deseo (selected stories), 1997; Lost in the City: Tree of Desire and Serafín, 1998. OTHER: El problema es otro, 1978; Delirium tremens (essay), 1979; Problema es otro; y, Desenlace, 1983; De cuerpo entero, 1990; La noche de ángeles, 1991; (ed.) Gustavo A. Madero: epistolario (letters), 1991; El jefe máximo, 1991; Teatro histórico, 1996; El sitio, 1998; Great Mexican Electoral Game: A Novel, 1999; Madero's judgement=Madero, el otro: a novel, 1999; Cartas a una joven psicóloga, 2000; Espía del aire, 2001; Imagen de Julio Cortázar, 2002; (with H. Bonilla and J.R. Enriquez) Tríptico de Guerra, 2003; Golden Coin: Freud or Jung?, 2004; Invasión, 2005; La instrucción y otros cuentos, 2007; There is no Such Place, 2008; Ficciones de la Revolución Mexicana, 2009. Contributor to periodicals. **Address:** Department de Teatro y Danza, Universidad Nacional Autonoma de Mexico, Ciudad Universitaria, Mexico, DF 04510, Mexico. **Online address:** ignaciosolares@servidor.unam.mx

SOLBRIG, Dorothy J. American (born United States), b. 1945. **Genres:** Biology, Sciences, Adult Non-fiction, Earth Sciences. **Career:** Harvard University, librarian, 1971-. Writer. **Publications:** (With O.T. Solbrig) Introduction to Population Biology and Evolution, 1979; (with O.T. Solbrig) So Shall You Reap: Farming and Crops in Human Affairs, 1994. **Address:** Biological Laboratories Library, Harvard University, Massachusetts Hall, 16 Divinity Ave., Cambridge, MA 02138, U.S.A.

SOLBRIG, Otto Thomas. American/Argentine (born Argentina), b. 1930. **Genres:** Environmental Sciences/Ecology, Biology, Botany, Natural History, Philosophy, Sciences. **Career:** Harvard University, curator of botany, 1959-66, professor of biology, 1969-84, Bussey Professor of Biology, 1984-, now Bussey professor emeritus of biology, Bussey Institute, supervisor, 1978-84, Gray Herbarium, director, 1978-84; University of Michigan, associate professor, 1966-68, professor of botany, 1968-69. Writer. **Publications:** Evolution and Systematics, 1966; Principles and Methods of Plant Biosystematics, 1970; (ed. with W.J.T. Gadella) Biosystematic Literature, 1970; (ed. with G.H. Orians) Convergent Evolution in Warm Deserts, 1977; (with D.J. Solbrig) Introduction to Population Biology and Evolution, 1979; (co-ed.) Topics in Plant Population Biology, 1979; (ed.) Demography and Evolution in Plant Populations, 1980; (trans.) G. Sarmiento, The Ecology of Neotropical Savanas, 1984; (ed.) From Genes to Ecosystems: A Research Agenda for Biodiversity, 1991; (with G. Nicolis) Perspectives on Bioilogical Complexity, 1991; (ed. with H. van Emdem and P.G.W.J. van Oordt) Biodiversity and Global Change, 1992; (ed. with M.D. Young) The World's Savannas, 1993; (with D.J. Solbrig) So Shall You Reap, 1994; (ed. with E. Medina and J.F. Silva) Biodiversity and Savanna Ecosystem Processes: A Global Perspective, 1996; Towards a Sustainable Pampa Agriculture: Past Performance and Prospective Analysis, 1997; (comp. with J. Morello) Argentina granero del mundo, hasta cuando?, 1997; (with L. Vainesman) Hacia Una Agricultura Productiva y Sostenible en la Pampa, 1998; (with E. Viglizzo) Sustainable Farming in the Argentine Pampas: History, Society, Economy, and Ecology, 2000; (ed. with R. Paarlberg and F. di Castri) Globalization and the Rural Environment, 2001. Contributor of articles to journals. **Address:** Department of Organismic and Evolutionary, Biology, Harvard University, 421 Herbaria, 26 Oxford St., Cambridge, MA 02138, U.S.A. **Online address:** solbrig@fas.harvard.edu

SOLEY, Lawrence C(harles). American (born United States), b. 1949. **Genres:** Communications/Media. **Career:** University of Alabama, assistant professor, 1980-81; Pennsylvania State University, State College, assistant professor, 1981-82; University of Georgia, assistant professor, 1982-83; City University of New York, Bernard M. Baruch College, associate professor, 1983-86; freelance writer, 1986-87; University of Minnesota, associate professor to professor, 1987-92; Marquette University, Department of Journalism, professor of communication, 1992-. **Publications:** NONFICTION: (with J. Nichols) Clandestine Radio Broadcasting, 1987; Radio Warfare (history), 1989; The News Shapers (media criticism), 1992; Leasing the Ivory Tower, 1995; Free Radio (media criticism), 1999; Censorship Inc.: The Corporate Threat to Free Speech in the United States, 2001; Advertising Censorship (media criticism), 2002; (with A.L. Smith) Projective Techniques for Social Science and Business Research, 2008. Contributor to journals. **Address:** College of Communication, Marquette University, Johnston Hall 520, Milwaukee, WI 53233, U.S.A. **Online address:** lawrence.soley@marquette.edu

SOLHEIM, James. American (born United States) **Genres:** Food And Wine, Adult Non-fiction, Children's Fiction. **Career:** Writer. **Publications:** It's Disgusting and We Ate It!: True Food Facts from Around the World and Throughout History, 1998; Santa's Secrets Revealed: All Your Questions Answered about Santa's Super Sleigh, His Flying Reindeer, and Other Wonders, 2004; Born Yesterday: The Diary of a Young Journalist, 2010. **Address:** 3707 S 97th St., Omaha, NE 68124-3740, U.S.A. **Online address:** jim@jamessolheim.com

SOLINGER, Rickie. American (born United States), b. 1947. **Genres:** Documentaries/Reportage, Politics/Government, Education, History, Women's Studies And Issues, Social Sciences. **Career:** Writer and historian. **Publications:** Wake up Little Susie: Single Pregnancy and Race Before Roe v. Wade, 1992, 2nd ed., 2000; The Abortionist: A Woman Against the Law, 1994; (ed.) Abortion Wars: A Half Century of Struggle, 1950-2000, 1998; Beggars and Choosers: How the Politics of Choice Shapes Adoption, Abortion and Welfare in the United States, 2001; (ed. with G. Mink) Welfare: A Documentary History of U.S. Policy and Politics, 2003; Pregnancy and Power: A Short History of Reproductive Politics in America, 2005; (ed. with M. Fox and K. Irani) Telling Stories to Change the World, 2008; (co-ed.) Interrupted Life, 2010. Contributor to books and periodicals. **Address:** University of California Press, 2120 Berkeley Way, Berkeley, CA 94704-1012, U.S.A. **Online address:** rsolinger@mochamail.com

SOLMSSEN, Arthur R(obert) G(eorge). American (born United States), b. 1928. **Genres:** Novels, Young Adult Fiction, History, Literary Criticism And History. **Career:** Saul Ewing Remick and Saul L.L.P., lawyer, 1953-, Public Finance Department, founding member, Dechert L.L.P., partner and chair of the private client group. Writer. **Publications:** Rittenhouse Square, 1968; Alexander's Feast, 1971; The Comfort Letter, 1975; A Princess in Berlin, 1980; Takeover Time, 1986; The Wife of Shore, 2000; Comfort Letter, 2002. **Address:** Dechert L.L.P., Cira Ctr., 2929 Arch St., Philadelphia, PA 19104-2808, U.S.A. **Online address:** arthur.solmssen@dechert.com

SOLOMITA, Stephen. (David Cray). American (born United States), b. 1943. **Genres:** Novels, Mystery/Crime/Suspense. **Career:** Writer. **Publications:** MYSTERY NOVELS: A Twist of the Knife, 1988; Force of Nature, 1989; Law According to Moodrow, 1989; Forced Entry, 1990; Bad to the Bone, 1991; A Piece of the Action, 1992; A Good Day to Die, 1993; Last Chance for Glory, 1994; Damaged Goods, 1996; Trick Me Twice, 1998; The Poster Boy, 1998; No Control, 1999; (as David Cray) Keeplock, 1995; (as David Cray) Bad Lawyer, 2001; (as David Cray) Little Girl Blue, 2002; (as David Cray) What You Wish For, 2002; (as David Cray) Partner, 2004; (as David Cray) Dead is Forever, 2005; Monkey in the Middle, 2008; Cracker Bling, 2008; Mercy Killing, 2010; Angel Face, 2011. Contributor to periodicals. **Address:** c/o Author Mail, Carroll & Graf Publishers, 161 William St., 16th Fl., New York, NY 10038, U.S.A.

SOLOMON, Andrew. (Andrew Wallace Solomon). American (born United States), b. 1963. **Genres:** Art/Art History, Novels, Gay And Lesbian Issues, Dance/Ballet, Politics/Government, Psychiatry, Psychology. **Career:** The New York Times, contributing writer, 1993-2001; Weill-Cornell Medical College, lecturer in psychiatry; Berkeley College, fellow. **Publications:** The Irony Tower: Soviet Artists in a Time of Glasnost, 1991; Art in Embassies, U.S. Department of State, 1993; A Stone Boat, 1994; (contrib.) New Russian Art: Paintings from the Christian Keesee Collection, 1994; The Noonday Demon:

An Atlas of Depression, 2001; A Dozen Kinds of Love: Bringing Up Challenging Children, 2010. Contributor to periodicals. **Address:** Wylie, Aitken & Stone, 250 W 57th St., Ste. 2106, New York, NY 10107, U.S.A.

SOLOMON, Andrew Wallace. See SOLOMON, Andrew.

SOLOMON, Barry D. American (born United States), b. 1955. **Genres:** Geography. **Career:** University of California-Irvine, Cooperative Recycling Center, commissioner and co-founder, 1976-77; Indiana University, Department of Geography, associate instructor and research assistant, 1979-82; West Virginia University, Regional Research Institute, visiting assistant professor of geography and energy economics and research associate, 1982-84; Federal Energy Regulatory Commission, Office of Electric Power Regulation, industry economist, 1984-86; U.S. Department of Energy, Office of Energy Markets and End Use, Energy Information Administration, economist, 1986-89; U.S. Environmental Protection Agency, Climate Change Division, international energy economist, 1989-91, Office of Atmospheric Programs, Acid Rain Division, senior economist, 1991-95; Michigan Technological University, associate, Department of Social Sciences, associate professor of geography and environmental policy, 1995-2003, professor of geography and environmental policy, 2003-, Graduate Program, Environmental Policy, director; National Audubon Society, vice president, 2001-; University of California-Santa Barbara, Donald Bren School of Environmental Science and Management, visiting associate professor, 2002-03. Writer. **Publications:** (Ed. with F.J. Calzonetti) Geographical Dimensions of Energy, 1985; (with A. Blowers and D. Lowry) The International Politics of Nuclear Waste, 1991; (ed.) Readings in American Socioeconomic Institutions, 2000, 3rd ed., 2006; (ed. with V.A. Luzadis and contrib.) Renewable Energy from Forest Resources in the United States, 2009. Work appears in anthologies. Contributor of articles to journals. **Address:** Department of Social Sciences, Michigan Technological University, 224 Academic Offices, 1400 Townsend Dr., Houghton, MI 49931-1295, U.S.A. **Online address:** bdsolomo@mtu.edu

SOLOMON, Evan. Canadian (born Canada), b. 1968?. **Genres:** Novels, Adult Non-fiction, Social Sciences, Business/Trade/Industry. **Career:** South China Morning Post, reporter; Shift, co-founder and editor-in-chief, 1992-99; Canadian Broadcasting Corp., showhost, FutureWorld, host, 1994-97; The Globe and Mail, columnist. Writer. **Publications:** Crossing the Distance (novel), 1999; (ed. with A. Heintzman) Fueling the Future: How the Battle Over Energy is Changing Everything, 2003; (ed. with A. Heintzman) Feeding the Future: From Fat to Famine, How to Solve the World's Food Crises, 2003. Contributor to periodicals. **Address:** Canadian Broadcasting Corp., PO Box 500, Sta. A, Toronto, ON M5W 1E6, Canada. **Online address:** futureworld@toronto.cbc.ca

SOLOMON, Marion F. American (born United States), b. 1935. **Genres:** Psychiatry. **Career:** Psychologist, 1964-; Las Palmas School for Girls, intake officer, 1965-66; City of Hope and Streissand Center for Jewish Cultural Arts, associate; Lifespan Learning Institute, director; University of California, USC Social Work Students, field work instructor, 1968-70, psychological consultant, 1969-75, Social Work Students, field work instructor, 1970-73, Neuropsychiatric Institute, Department of Legal Psychiatry, adjunct clinical professor, 1972-75, Department of Humanities, Sciences and Social Sciences, program consultant/coordinator of psychological, 1974-, parent education consultant, 1978-84, director of clinical training, 1978-, coordinator of mental health training programs, 1981-95, senior extension instructor, 2000-; Park Century School, Parent-Child Issues, psychological consultant, 1969-75; Beverly Hills Unified School District, family therapist, consultant, 1978-84; American Behavioral Studies Institute, professor, 1995-2001. Writer. **Publications:** (Ed. with J.S. Grotstein and J.A. Lang) The Borderline Patient: Emerging Concepts in Diagnosis, Etiology, Psychodynamics and Treatment, 1987; Narcissism and Intimacy: Love and Marriage in an Age of Confusion, 1989; Lean on Me: The Power of Positive Dependency in Relationships, 1994; (ed. with J.P. Siegel) Countertransference in Couples Therapy, 1997; Short Term Therapy for Long Term Change, 2001; (ed. with D.J. Siegel) Healing Trauma: Attachment, Mind, Body and Brain, 2003; (ed. with D. Fosha and D.J. Siegel) The Healing Power of Emotion: Affective Neuroscience, Development and Clinical Practice, 2009; (with S. Tatkin) Love and War in Intimate Relationships: Connection, Disconnection and Mutual Regulation in Couple Therapy, 2011. **Address:** 1023 Westholme Ave., Los Angeles, CA 90024, U.S.A.

SOLOMON, Nina. American (born United States), b. 1961. **Genres:** Young

Adult Fiction, Novels. **Career:** Wilkes University, faculty of creative writing. Writer. **Publications:** Single Wife: A Novel, 2003. **Address:** c/o Author Mail, Algonquin Books, PO Box 2225, Chapel Hill, NC 27515-2225, U.S.A.

SOLOMON, Richard H(arvey). American (born United States), b. 1937. **Genres:** International Relations/Current Affairs, Politics/Government, Military/Defense/Arms Control, History, Social Sciences. **Career:** University of Michigan, assistant professor, 1966-70, associate professor, 1970-75, professor of political science, 1976; National Security Council, senior staff, 1971-76, Department of State, director of policy planning; Rand Corp., Department of Political Science, head, 1976-86; U.S. Department of State, Policy Planning Staff, director, 1986-89; U.S. States for East Asian and Pacific Affairs, assistant secretary, 1989-92; United States Institute of Peace, president, 1993-. Writer. **Publications:** Mao's Revolution and the Chinese Political Culture, 1971, rev. ed., 1998; A Revolution Is Not a Dinner Party: A Feast of Images of the Maoist Transformation of China, 1975; China Policy and America's Public Debate: Ten Arguments in Search of Normalized U.S.-PRC Relations, 1977; (with J.D. Pollack) Sino-Soviet Conflict and American Security Concerns, 1979; (ed.) Asian Security in the 1980's: Problems and Policies for a Time of Transition, 1979, 2nd ed., 1980; China Factor in America's Foreign Relations: Perceptions and Policy Choices, 1981; Choices for Coalition-Building: The Soviet Presence in Asia and American Policy Alternatives, 1981; The China Factor: Sino-American Relations and the Global Scene, 1981; Chinese Political Negotiating Behavior: A Briefing Analysis, 1985; (ed. with M. Kosaka) The Soviet Far East Military Build-up: Nuclear Dilemmas and Asian Security, 1986; Chinese Political Negotiating Behavior, 1967-1984, 1995; Chinese Political Negotiating Behavior: Pursuing Interests Through Old Friends, 1995; Exiting Indochina: U.S. Leadership of the Cambodia Settlement and Normalization of Relations with Vietnam, 2000; In Memoriam of John Wallach: A Sower of Seeds of Peace, 2002; Teaching Peace or War?, 2003; Managing the Great Asian Transformation: Challenges and Opportunities in U.S.-China Relations, 2004; (ed. with N. Quinney) American Negotiating Behavior: Wheeler-dealers, Legal Eagles, Bullies and Preachers, 2009. **Address:** United States Institute of Peace, 2301 Constitution Ave. NW, Washington, DC 20037, U.S.A. **Online address:** usip_requests@usip.org

SOLOMON, Steven. American (born United States), b. 1953. **Genres:** Business/Trade/Industry, Economics. **Career:** Marketplace, commentator; National Public Radio, commentator. Journalist. **Publications:** Small Business USA: The Role of Small Companies in Sparking America's Economic Transformation, 1986; The Confidence Game: How Unelected Central Bankers Are Governing the Changed Global Economy, 1995; Water: The Epic Struggle for Wealth, Power, and Civilization, 2010. Contributor to periodicals. **Address:** Washington, DC , U.S.A. **Online address:** snsolwater@gmail.com

SOLOMONSON, Katherine M. American (born United States) **Genres:** Architecture, Engineering, History. **Career:** Stanford University, professor; University of Minnesota, Department of Architecture, associate professor of architecture, Departments of American Studies, faculty, Department of Art History, faculty, Department of Cultural Studies and Comparative Literature, faculty. Writer. **Publications:** The Chicago Tribune Tower Competition: Skyscraper Design and Cultural Change in the 1920s, 2001. **Address:** Department of Architecture, University of Minnesota, Rm. 145F Arch 0811, 111 Rapson Hall, 89 Church St., Minneapolis, MN 55455, U.S.A. **Online address:** solom003@umn.edu

SOLOTAROFF, Ivan. American (born United States), b. 1956. **Genres:** Documentaries/Reportage, Essays, Adult Non-fiction, Social Sciences. **Career:** Journalist, 1988-; Esquire, senior editor; Village Voice, senior writer; ESPN: The Magazine, senior writer; Philadelphia Magazine, senior writer. **Publications:** No Success like Failure: The American Love of Self-Destruction, Self-Aggrandizement and Breaking Even, 1994; The Last Face You'll Ever See: The Private Life of the American Death Penalty, 2001. **Address:** c/o Author Mail, HarperCollins Publishers Inc., 10 E 53rd St., New York, NY 10022, U.S.A.

SOLOVE, Daniel J. American (born United States), b. 1972?. **Genres:** Information Science/Computers, Technology, Law, Social Sciences. **Career:** U.S. District Court for the District of Columbia, Honorable Stanley Sporkin, law clerk, 1997-98; Arnold and Porter, associate, 1998-99; U.S. Court of Appeals for the Ninth Circuit, Honorable Pamela Ann Rymer, law clerk, 1999-2000; Seton Hall Law School, associate professor of law, 2000-04; George Washington University Law School, associate professor, 2004-08, profes-

sor of law, 2008-10, John Marshall Harlan research professor of law, 2010-; American Association of Law Schools, Defamation and Privacy Section, chair, 2006-07; TeachPrivacy L.L.C., principal and founder, 2010-; Hogan Lovells L.L.P., senior policy advisor, 2011-. Writer. **Publications:** (With M. Rotenberg) Information Privacy Law, 2003, (with P.M. Schwartz) 3rd ed., 2009; The Digital Person: Technology and Privacy in the Information Age, 2004; (with M. Rotenberg and P.M. Schwartz) Privacy, Information and Technology, 2006, (with P.M. Schwartz) 2nd ed., 2009; The Future of Reputation: Gossip, Rumor and Privacy on the Internet, 2007; Understanding Privacy, 2008; (with P.M. Schwartz) Information Privacy: Statutes and Regulations, vol. I, 2008, vol. II, 2009; (with P.M. Schwartz) Privacy and the Media, 2008; (with P.M. Schwartz) Privacy Law Fundamentals, 2011; Nothing to Hide: The False Tradeoff Between Privacy and Security, 2011. Contributor of articles to journals and periodicals. **Address:** George Washington University Law School, 2000 H St. NW, Washington, DC 20052, U.S.A. **Online address:** dsolove@law.gwu.edu

SOLSONA, S. See **SCHWARTZ, Stephen (Alfred).**

SOLTER, Aletha. American (born United States), b. 1945. **Genres:** Human Relations/Parenting, Psychology. **Career:** Aware Parenting Institute, founder and director, 1990-. Writer, psychologist, speaker and consultant. **Publications:** The Aware Baby: A New Approach to Parenting, 1984, rev. ed., 2001; Helping Young Children Flourish, 1989; Tears and Tantrums: What to Do When Babies and Children Cry, 1998; Raising Drug-free Kids: 100 Tips for Parents, 2006. **Address:** Aware Parenting Institute, PO Box 206, Goleta, CA 93116, U.S.A. **Online address:** solter@awareparenting.com

SOLTIS, Jonas F. American (born United States), b. 1931. **Genres:** Education, Ethics, Philosophy. **Career:** University of Connecticut, instructor in history and philosophy, 1958-60; Wesleyan University, instructor in education, 1962-64; Columbia University, Teachers College, assistant professor, 1964-68, associate professor, 1968-71, professor, 1971-79, Division of Instruction, director, 1971-75, Division of Philosophy and the Social Sciences, director, 1977-79, William Heard Kilpatrick professor of philosophy and education, 1979-92, William Heard Kilpatrick professor emeritus of philosophy and education, 1992-; Addison-Wesley Publishing Co., consultant, 1965-68; Teachers College Record, editor; Teachers College Press, consultant, 1992-. **Publications:** Seeing, Knowing and Believing, a Study of the Language of Visual Perception, 1966; An Introduction to the Analysis of Educational Concepts, 1968, 2nd ed., 1985; (with B.R. Joyce) Performance-Based Teacher Education Design Alternatives: The Concept of Unity, 1974; (with K. Strike) The Ethics of Teaching, 1985, 5th ed., 2009; (with D.C. Phillips) Perspectives on Learning, 1985, 5th ed., 2009; (with W. Feinberg) School and Society, 1985, 5th ed., 2009; (with D. Walker) Curriculum and Aims, 1986, 5th ed., 2009; (with G. Fenstermacher) Approaches to Teaching, 1986, 5th ed., 2009; (with K. Strike and E.J. Haller) The Ethics of School Administration, 1988, 3rd ed., 2005; (with B. Zubay) Creating the Ethical School: A Book of Case Studies, 2005. EDITOR: (with B. Chazan) Moral Education, 1973; Philosophy of Education since Mid-Century, 1981; Philosophy and Education: Eightieth Yearbook of the National Society for the Study of Education, 1981; Reforming Teacher Education: The Impact of the Holmes Group Report, 1987; (with B. Zoobay) Creating the Ethical School, 2004. **Address:** Teachers College, Columbia University, 525 W 120th St., New York, NY 10027, U.S.A.

SOLUM, John. American (born United States), b. 1935. **Genres:** Music. **Career:** Concert flutist, 1957-; Vassar College, lecturer, 1969-71, 1977-; Indiana University, visiting professor, 1973; Oberlin College, visiting professor, 1976. Writer and lawyer. **Publications:** The Early Flute, 1992. EDITOR: Massenet and Delibes: Three Original Pieces for the Concours de Flute of the Paris Conservatory, 1978; Popp: Bagatelle, 1980; Popp: Thirty Easy Studies for Flute, 1981; Andersen: Five Songs without Words, 1982; Boccherini: Sextet for Flute, 2 Violins, Viola and 2 Cellos, Opus 15, no. 16, 1990; de la Barre: Two Suites for Two Flutes from Eleventh Book of Suites (1724), 1990; Foote: At Dusk, 1991; The NFA 20th-Anniversary Anthology of American Flute Music, 1993; The American Flute: New Works for Flute Solo, 1996; D. Scarlatti: Sonata in E Minor, K. 81, 1997. Contributor of articles to journals. **Address:** 10 Bobwhite Dr., Westport, CT 06880, U.S.A. **Online address:** jhsolum@optonline.net

SOLURI, John. American (born United States), b. 1967. **Genres:** Agriculture/Forestry, Environmental Sciences/Ecology, Sciences, History. **Career:** Society for Latin American and Caribbean Environmental History, founding member; Hispanic American Historical Review, associate editor; Carnegie Mellon University, associate professor of history, 1999-. **Publications:** Banana Cultures: Agriculture, Consumption, and Environmental Change in Honduras and the United States, 2005. Contributor to books and periodicals. **Address:** Department of History, Carnegie Mellon University, 240 Baker Hall, Pittsburgh, PA 15213, U.S.A. **Online address:** jsoluri@andrew.cmu.edu

SOLVANG, Elna K. American (born United States) **Genres:** Women's Studies And Issues, Theology/Religion, Gay And Lesbian Issues. **Career:** Lutheran Church, Division for Mission in North America, Women in Church and Society, assistant and director, 1979-87; Evangelical Lutheran Church, Commission for Women, assistant executive director and director of education and training, 1988-93; Concordia College, instructor, 1998-2000, assistant professor of religion, 2000-. Writer. **Publications:** A Woman's Place Is in the House: Royal Women of Judah and Their Involvement in the House of David, 2003. Contributor to periodicals. **Address:** Concordia College, 901 8th St. S, Moorhead, MN 56562, U.S.A. **Online address:** solvang@cord.edu

SOMEL, Selcuk Akscin. Turkish (born Turkey), b. 1961. **Genres:** History. **Career:** Bogazici University, research assistant, 1985-88; University of Freiburg, instructor, 1988-91; University of Bilkent, assistant professor, 1993-2002, acting department chair, 1993-99, Institute of Economic and Social Sciences, co-director, 1997-2002; Sabanci University, assistant professor, 2002-. Writer. **Publications:** Das Grundschulwesen in den Provinzen des Osmanischen Reiches Während der Herrschaftsperiode Abdulhamid II (1876-1908), 1995; The Modernization of Public Education in the Ottoman Empire, 1839-1908, 2001; Historical Dictionary of the Ottoman Empire, 2003; (ed. with A. Singer and C.K. Neumann) Untold Histories of the Middle East: Recovering Voices From the 19th and 20th Centuries, 2011; 1885 Tarihli Istanbul Istatistikleri, forthcoming; (with M. Kalpakli) Ali Fuad Türkgeldinin Maruf Simalar, forthcoming. **Address:** Faculty of Arts and Social Sciences, Sabanci University, Tuzla, 34956, Turkey. **Online address:** somel@sabanciuniv.edu

SOMERS, Jane. See **LESSING, Doris (May).**

SOMERS, Jeff. American (born United States), b. 1971?. **Genres:** Novels, Adult Non-fiction, Young Adult Fiction, Science Fiction/Fantasy. **Career:** Inner Swine, publisher, 1995-. Writer. **Publications:** (Co-author) Sliders: Blood and Splendor (comic book), 1996; Lifers (novel), 2001; The Freaks Are Winning: The Inner Swine Collection, 2002; The Electric Church, 2007; The Digital Plague, 2008; The Eternal Prison, 2009; The Terminal State, 2010; The Final Evolution, 2011. Contributor to periodicals. **Address:** The Inner Swine, PO Box 3024, Hoboken, NJ 07030, U.S.A. **Online address:** mreditor@innerswine.com

SOMERSET, Anne. British (born England), b. 1955. **Genres:** Biography, History, Mystery/Crime/Suspense. **Career:** Writer, 1980-. **Publications:** The Life and Times of William IV, 1980; Ladies-in-Waiting: From the Tudors to the Present Day, 1984; Elizabeth I, 1991; Unnatural Murder: Poison At the Court of James I, 1997; The Affair of the Poisons: Murder, Infanticide and Satanism At the Court of Louis XIV, 2003. **Address:** Ed Victor Ltd., 6 Bayley St., London, GL WC1B 3HE, England.

SOMERVILL, Barbara A(nn). American (born United States), b. 1948. **Genres:** Children's Non-fiction, Young Adult Non-fiction. **Career:** Karastan/Bigelow, public relations manager, 1986-88; PYA/Monarch, editor of trade publication, 1988-94; Somervill Inc., president, 1994-. Writer. **Publications:** The Best Guide to Success, 1999; Historical Case Studies: The Great Migration, 2000; (with L. Parker) Survival Guide for Computer Literacy, 2000; Pacemaker United States History:, 2001; Ida M. Tarbell: Pioneer Investigative Reporter, 2002; Franklin Pierce, 2002; Votes for Women!: The Story of Carrie Chapman Catt, 2003; Enchantment of the World: Iceland, 2003; Andrew Jackson, 2003; Backstage at a Newscast, 2003; Scott O'Grady: Behind Enemy Lines, 2003; Wolverines, 2003; Warren G. Harding, 2003; Australia, 2004; James K. Polk, 2004; Mary McLeod Bethune: African-American Educator, 2004; Animal Survivors of the Arctic, 2004; Animal Survivors of the Wetlands, 2004; Great Empires of the Past: The Incas, 2004; Brown The Board of Education, 2004; Amistad: Fighting for Freedom, 2004; Wetlands, 2004; Grasslands, 2004; Tundra, 2004; Forests, 2004; Deserts, 2004; Rivers, Streams, Lakes and Ponds, 2004; Oceans, Seas and Reefs, 2004; The Gold Rush, 2005; Empire of the Inca, 2005, rev. ed., 2009; Catherine de Medici: The Power Behind the French Throne, 2005; Amistad Mutiny: Fighting for Freedom, 2005; Nicolaus Copernicus: Father of Modern Astronomy, 2005;

Machu Picchu: City in the Clouds, 2005; William Penn: Founder of Pennsylvania, 2006; Martin Luther: Father of the Reformation, 2006; Eleanor Roosevelt: First Lady of the World, 2006; Abigail Adams: Courageous Patriot and First Lady, 2006; Women of the Confederacy, 2007; What's the Big Idea?: Forming Hypotheses, 2007; What Do You Want to Prove?: Planning Investigations, 2007; What Did You Find Out?: Reporting Conclusions, 2007; What are the Facts?: Collecting Information, 2007; Sorting It Out: Evaluating Data, 2007; Indira Gandhi: Political Leader in India, 2007; Golden Lion Tamarin, 2007; First Response: By Air, 2007; Does this Make Sense?: Constructing Explanations, 2007; Clara Barton: Founder of the American Red Cross, 2007; Gray Wolf, 2008; Gray Squirrel, 2008; Fleas: Feasting on Blood, 2008; Electrical Circuits and Currents, 2008; Colorado, 2008; Cane Toad, 2008; Asian Carp, 2008; American Bison, 2008; Africanized Honey Bee, 2008; Samurai, Shoguns and Soldiers: The Rise of the Japanese Military, 2008; Pierre-Auguste Renoir, 2008; Mountain Gorilla, 2008; Mosquitoes: Hungry for Blood, 2008; Life and Times of James Madison, 2008; Lice: Head Hunters, 2008; Leeches: Waiting in the Water, 2008; Human Body, 2008; How Life Changes, 2008; Vampire Bats: Hunting for Blood, 2008; Ticks: Digging for Blood, 2008; Teens in Egypt, 2008; Plant Reproduction, 2009; Plains and Plateaus, 2009; Oral Reports, 2009; Grizzly Bear, 2009; Florida Panther, 2009; Fire Ant, 2009; Elizabeth Blackwell: America's First Female Doctor, 2009; Brown Treesnake, 2009; Written Reports, 2009; Wildlife Photographer, 2009; Wild Boar, 2009; Veterinarian, 2009; Team Projects, 2009; Studying and Tests, 2009; Sea Lamprey, 2009; Glaciers, 2010; Marine Biologist, 2010; Graphing Natural Disasters, 2010; Food Scientist, 2010; Empires of Ancient Mesopotamia, 2010; Graphing Health and Disease, 2010; Dental Hygienist, 2010; Empire of the Aztecs, 2010; Speed and Acceleration, 2011; Commercial Fisher, 2011; Animal Cells and Life Processes, 2011; Cells and Disease, 2011; Distance, Area and Volume, 2011; Green General Contractor, 2011; It's Cool to Learn About Countries: Japan, 2011; It's Cool to Learn About Countries: Mexico, 2011; Mass and Weight, 2011. THE TIMELINE LIBRARY SERIES: The History of the Telephone, 2005; History of the Clock, 2005; History of the Airplane, 2005; History of Space Travel, 2005; History of the Post Office, 2006; History of the Motion Picture, 2006; History of the Library, 2006; History of the Computer, 2006; History of the Calendar, 2006; History of Money, 2006. THE MOUNTAINS SERIES: The Magnificent Himalayas, 2004; The Timeworn Urals, 2005; The Land of the Andes, 2005; The Rugged Rockies, 2005; The Awesome Alps, 2005. SIGNATURE LIVES SERIES: Michelangelo, 2005; Francisco Pizarro, 2005; John Hancock: Signer for Independence, 2005. SEA TO SHINING SEA SERIES: Florida, 2001; Alaska, 2002; Maryland, 2003; Pennsylvania, 2003; West Virginia, 2003; Mississippi, 2003; Illinois, 2008. AMERICA THE BEAUTIFUL SERIES: New York, 2008; Alabama, 2008; Texas, 2009; South Carolina, 2009; Arizona, 2009; Tennessee, 2010; Small Indian Mongoose, 2010; Python, 2010; Plant Cells and Life Processes, 2010; Monitor Lizard, 2010. SPIRIT OF AMERICA SERIES: Massachusetts Colony, 2004; New York Colony, 2004; The Rhode Island Colony, 2004. ENCHANTMENT OF THE WORLD SERIES: Japan, 2011. COOL CAREERS SERIES: Musician, 2011; Actor, 2011. OTHERS: Producing Grain, 2011; Producing Fish, 2011; West, 2011; The Story Behind Coal, 2011; The Story Behind Glass, 2011; The Story Behind Paper, 2011; The Story Behind Rubber, 2011; The Story Behind Maps, 2011. **Address:** c/o Author Mail, Editorial Directions, 1000 W Washington Blvd., Ste. 203, Chicago, IL 60607, U.S.A. **Online address:** somervill@aol.com

SOMMER, Jason. American (born United States) **Genres:** Poetry, Young Adult Fiction. **Career:** St. Louis University, faculty; Webster University, faculty; University College, faculty; Fontbonne College, professor of English and poet-in-residence, 1985-. Writer. **Publications:** (Trans.) G. Rosenstock, Portrait of the Artist as an Abominable Snowman: Selected Poems, 1989; Lifting the Stone, 1991; Other People's Troubles, 1997; Man who Sleeps in My Office, 2004; (trans. and intro. with H. Zhang) W. Xiaobo, Wang in Love and Bondage: Three Novellas, 2007. Contributor to periodicals. **Address:** Fontbonne College, 6800 Wydown Blvd., St. Louis, MO 63105, U.S.A.

SOMMERS, Christina Hoff. American (born United States), b. 1950?. **Genres:** Philosophy, Ethics, Sciences, Women's Studies And Issues. **Career:** University of Massachusetts, instructor, 1978-80; Clark University, assistant professor, 1980-86, associate professor of philosophy, 1986-99; University of Pittsburgh, visiting lecturer, 1987-88; American Enterprise Institute for Public Policy Research, W.H. Brady fellow, 1997-; Independent Womens Forum, chairman, 2000-; Center for the American Experiment, advisor, 2001-. Writer. **Publications:** (Comp.) Vice and Virtue in Everyday Life: Introductory Readings in Ethics, 1985, 8th ed. 2010; (comp.) Right and Wrong: Basic Readings in Ethics, 1986; Who Stole Feminism?: How Women Have Betrayed Women, 1994; The War Against Boys: How Misguided Feminism is Harming our Young Men, 2000; (with S. Satel) One Nation Under Therapy: How the Helping Culture is Eroding Self-Reliance, 2005; (ed.) Science on Women in Science, 2009. Contributor to journals and periodicals. **Address:** American Enterprise Institute for, Public Policy Research (AEI), 1150 17th St. NW, Washington, DC 20036-4603, U.S.A. **Online address:** csommers@aei.org

SOMMERS, Susan Mitchell. American (born United States), b. 1961. **Genres:** History, Politics/Government, Humanities. **Career:** Saint Vincent College, Department of History, associate professor and chair, professor. Writer. **Publications:** Parliamentary Politics of a County and Its Town: General Elections in Suffolk and Ipswich in the Eighteenth Century, 2002. Contributor to periodicals and journals. **Address:** Department of History, Saint Vincent College, Rm. 322, Placid Hall, 300 Fraser Purchase Rd., Latrobe, PA 15650-2690, U.S.A. **Online address:** susan.sommers@email.stvincent.edu

SOMMERVILLE, C(harles) John. American (born United States), b. 1938. **Genres:** History, Theology/Religion. **Career:** Stanford University, instructor in Western civilization, 1968-71; University of Florida, Department of History, professor of English history, 1971-2005, now professor emeritus. Writer. **Publications:** Popular Religion in Restoration England, 1977; The Rise and Fall of Childhood, 1982, rev. ed., 1990; The Discovery of Childhood in Puritan England, 1992; The Secularization of Early Modern England: From Religious Culture to Religious Faith, 1992; The News Revolution in England: Cultural Dynamics of Daily Information, 1996; How the News Makes Us Dumb, 1999; The Decline of the Secular University, 2006; Religion in the National Agenda: What We Mean by Religious, Spiritual, Secular, 2009; Religious Ideas for Secular Universities, 2009. Contributor to books, periodicals and journals. Works appear in anthologies. **Address:** Department of History, University of Florida, 025 Keene-Flint Hall, PO Box 117320, Gainesville, FL 32611, U.S.A. **Online address:** cjsommerv@gmail.com

SONENBERG, Maya. American (born United States), b. 1960. **Genres:** Novels, Novellas/Short Stories, Autobiography/Memoirs, Young Adult Fiction, Literary Criticism And History. **Career:** Sonoma State University, lecturer, 1986; Chabot College, instructor in English, 1989-90; Oregon State University, assistant professor of English, 1990-93; University of Washington, Department of English, assistant professor, 1993-2000, associate professor, 2000-, Creative Writing Program, director, 2001-. Writer. **Publications:** Cartographies, 1989; Noctambus, 2000; Voices From the Blue Hotel, 2007; Learning to Paint, forthcoming. Contributor of articles to magazines. **Address:** Department of English, University of Washington, PO Box 354330, Seattle, WA 98195-4330, U.S.A. **Online address:** mayas@u.washington.edu

SONG, Yuwu. American/Chinese (born China), b. 1958. **Genres:** How-to Books, Information Science/Computers, History. **Career:** Arizona State University, Hayden Library, web developer, assistant librarian and instructor, 1999-. Writer. **Publications:** Building Better Web Sites: A How-to-Do-It Manual for Librarians, 2003; (ed.) Encyclopedia of Chinese American Relations, 2006; Chinese Stamps, 2006; Chinese Filmography, 2006; A Historical Dictionary of Sino-American Relations, 2006. Contributor to periodicals. **Address:** University Libraries, Arizona State University, PO Box 871006, Tempe, AZ 85287, U.S.A. **Online address:** yuwu.song@asu.edu

SONN, Richard D. American (born United States), b. 1949. **Genres:** History. **Career:** University of California, acting instructor in history, 1980-81; St. Olaf College, visiting assistant professor, assistant professor of history, 1981-83, Paracollege, tutor; Gustavus Adolphus College, visiting assistant professor, assistant professor of history, 1983-87; University of Arkansas, assistant professor, 1987-92, associate professor of history, 1999-2010, professor, 2010-. Writer. **Publications:** Anarchism and Cultural Politics in Fin-de-Siècle France, 1989; Anarchism, 1992; Sex, Violence, and the Avant-Garde: Anarchism in Interwar France, 2010. Works appear in anthologies. Contributor to periodicals. **Address:** Department of History, University of Arkansas, MAIN 409, 416 Old Main, Fayetteville, AR 72701, U.S.A. **Online address:** rsonn@uark.edu

SONNENBERG, Susanna Sophia. American/British (born England), b. 1965. **Genres:** Autobiography/Memoirs. **Career:** Writer. **Publications:** (contrib.) About What Was Lost: Twenty Writers on Miscarriage, Healing and Hope, 2006; Her Last Death (memoir), 2008. Contributor to periodicals. **Address:** c/o Molly Friedrich, Friedrich Agency, 136 E 57th St., New York, NY 10022, U.S.A.

SONNENFELD, Jeffrey. American (born United States), b. 1954. **Genres:** Business/Trade/Industry, Economics. **Career:** Heir & Gentry Shop, retailer, 1968-72; Harvard Radio Broadcasting, president, 1974-76; Scott Paper, IBM, management intern, 1976-78; Harvard College, tutor, 1976-80; Harvard University, research assistant, 1977-80, assistant professor, 1980-84, associate professor of Harvard Business School, 1984-89; Emory University, professor, 1989-97, director of the Center of Leadership and Career Studies, 1989-97; Yale Chief Executive Leadership Institute, founder and president, 1989-; American Association of Retired Persons, director, 1992; Yale University, Lester Crown Professor in the Practice of Management, 2001-, School of Management, senior associate dean of executive programs, 2001-. Writer. **Publications:** Corporate Views of the Public Interest: Perceptions of the Forest Products Industry, 1981; Career Management: An Introduction to Self-Assessment, Career Development and Career Systems, 1984; Managing Career Systems: Channeling the Flow of Executive Careers, 1984; The Hero's Farewell: What Happens When CEOs Retire, 1988; (ed.) Concepts of Leadership, 1995; (ed. with R. Gandossy) Leadership and Governance from the Inside Out, 2004; (with A. Ward) Firing Back: How Great Leaders Rebound after Career Disasters, 2007. Contributor to books and periodicals. **Address:** Yale School of Management, 135 Prospect St., PO Box 208200, New Haven, CT 06520-8200, U.S.A. **Online address:** jeffrey.sonnenfeld@yale.edu

SONNEVI, Göran. Swedish (born Sweden), b. 1939. **Genres:** Poetry, Young Adult Fiction. **Career:** Writer. **Publications:** Outfört: dikter, 1961; Abstrakta dikter, 1963; Ingrepp-modeller, 1965; Och nu!, 1967; Göran Sonnevi: On the War. A Bilingual Pamphlet of Poems from the Swedish, 1968; Det gäller oss: dikter 1959-1968, 1969; Et maintenant!: Göran Sonnevi; traduit du suédois et présentépar François-Noël Simoneau, 1970; Del måste gå: dikter, 1970; Det oavslutade språket: dikter, 1972; Dikter 1959-1973, 1974; Det omöjliga: dikter, 1975; Språk; Verktyg; Eld: dikter, 1979; Små klanger; en röst: dikter, 1981; Göran Sonnevi: Poetry in Translation, 1982; Dikter utan ordning, 1983; Oavslutade dikter, 1987; Trädet: dikter, 1991; Framför ordens väggar: dikter iöversättning 1959-1992, 1992; Mozarts tredje hjärna: dikter, 1996; Klangernas bok: dikter, 1998; Dikter, 2000; Oceanen: dikter, 2005. **Address:** Trålargränd 49, Järfälla, 17555, Sweden.

SOODALTER, Ron. American (born United States) **Genres:** Social Sciences, History. **Career:** History Colorado, curator. Writer and educator. **Publications:** Hanging Captain Gordon: The Life and Trial of an American Slave Trader, 2006; (with K. Bales) The Slave Next Door: Human Trafficking and Slavery in America Today, 2009; Annex Cuba! A History of the United States' Nation-Long Obsession with Its Caribbean Neighbor, 2010. Contributor to periodicals. **Address:** Abraham Lincoln Institute, 94 Cumberland Ct., Frederick, MD 21702, U.S.A. **Online address:** ron@ronsoodalter.com

SOOS, Troy. American (born United States), b. 1957. **Genres:** Mystery/Crime/Suspense, Sports/Fitness, Children's Fiction, Young Adult Fiction. **Career:** Research physicist, 1984-95; Lake Howell High School, Department of Physics, teacher, 1999-; Massachusetts Institute of Technology, Laboratory for Nuclear Science, research physicist; Los Alamos National Laboratory, research physicist; Thermal Physics Research Laboratory, director. Writer. **Publications:** Murder at Fenway Park, 1994; Murder at Ebbets Field, 1995; Murder at Wrigley Field, 1996; Hunting a Detroit Tiger, 1997, rev. ed., 2006; Before the Curse: The Glory Days of New England Baseball, 1858-1918, 1997, rev. ed., 2006; The Cincinnati Red Stalkings, 1998; Hanging Curve, 1999; Island of Tears, 2001; The Gilded Cage, 2002; Burning Bridges, 2004; Streets of Fire, 2008. Works appear in anthologies. **Address:** Lake Howell High School, 4200 Dike Rd., Winter Park, FL 32792, U.S.A. **Online address:** troysoos@aol.com

SOOTHILL, Keith (Leonard). British (born England), b. 1941?. **Genres:** Criminology/True Crime, Medicine/Health, Sociology, Social Sciences. **Career:** Queen Elizabeth College, research assistant, 1965-66; Apex Charitable Trust, research officer, 1966-69; University of London, Institute of Psychiatry, researcher, 1970-72; Lancaster University, applied social science lecturer, 1972-78, senior lecturer, 1978-90, professor of social research, through 1990, Centre for Applied Statistics, faculty, now professor emeritus. Writer. **Publications:** (With P. Pope) Medical Remands in Magistrates' Courts, 1974; The Prisoner's Release: A Study of the Employment of Ex-prisoners, 1974; (with

T.C.N. Gibbens and P.J. Pope) Medical Remands in the Criminal Court, 1977; Contemporary British Society, 1988, 3rd ed., 2000; (with S. Walby) Sex Crime in the News, 1991; New Technology and Practical Police Work, 1992; Medicine and Nursing: Professions in a Changing Health Service, 1994; Homicide in Britain, 1999; (with C. Taylor and M. Peelo) Making Sense of Criminology, 2002; (with B. Francis and C. Fitzpatrick) Understanding Criminal Careers, 2009. EDITOR: Themes and Perspectives in Nursing, 1992, 2nd ed., 1996; Interprofessional Relations in Health Care, 1995; (with R. Hugman and M. Peelo) Concepts of Care: Developments in Health and Social Welfare, 1997; (with L. Mackay and K. Melia) Classic Texts in Health Care, 1998; Criminal Conversations: An Anthology of the Work of Tony Parker, 1999; (with M. Peelo) Questioning Crime and Criminology, 2005; (with M. Dolan and P. Rogers) Handbook of Forensic Mental Health, 2008. **Address:** Department of Applied Social Science, Lancaster University, B63, Bowland North, Lancaster, ES LA1 4YT, England. **Online address:** k.soothill@lancaster.ac.uk

SOPER, Kate. British (born England), b. 1943?. **Genres:** Philosophy, Environmental Sciences/Ecology, Cultural/Ethnic Topics, Humanities, Women's Studies And Issues, Business/Trade/Industry. **Career:** University of Sussex, faculty; London Metropolitan University, professor in philosophy, 1987-, Department of Humanities, Arts and Languages, professor, Institute for the Study of European Transformations, professor, now professor emeritus; University of Brighton, Department of Humanities, visiting professor. Writer and translator. **Publications:** (Trans.) S. Timpanaro, The Freudian Slip, 1976; (trans.) P. Chiodi, Sartre and Marxism, 1976; On Human Needs: Open and Closed Theories in a Marxist Perspective, 1981; Humanism and Anti-Humanism, 1986; Troubled Pleasures: Writings on Politics, Gender, and Hedonism, 1990; What Is Nature?: Culture, Politics, and the Non-Human, 1995; (trans. with M. Ryle) C. Ginzburg, Wooden Eyes: Nine Reflections on Distance, 2001; (with M. Ryle) To Relish the Sublime?: Culture and Self-Realisation in Postmodern Times, 2002; (ed. with F. Trentmann) Citizenship and Consumption, 2008; (ed. with M. Ryle and L. Thomas) The Politics and Pleasures of Consuming Differently, 2009. **Address:** Institute for the Study of European, Transformations, London Metropolitan University, Tower Bldg., 166-220 Holloway Rd., London, GL N7 8DB, England. **Online address:** k.soper@londonmet.ac.uk

SOPER, Tony. British (born England), b. 1929. **Genres:** Writing/Journalism, Natural History. **Career:** British Broadcasting Corp., Radio, features producer, Natural History Unit, co-founder. Freelance writer. **Publications:** The Bird Table Book, 1966; (with C. Gill and F. Booker) The Wreck of the Torrey Canyon, 1967; (with J. Sparks) Penguins, 1967; (with J. Sparks) Owls: Their Natural and Unnatural History, 1970, rev. ed., 1989; The Shell Book of Beachcombing, 1972; Wildlife Begins at Home, 1975; Everyday Birds, 1976; Beside the Sea, 1978; Birdwatch, 1982; Discovering Birds, 1983; The National Trust Guide to the Coast, 1984; Go Birding, 1988; Birds in Your Garden, 1989; Oceans of Birds, 1989; The Shell Book of the Shore, 1991; Antarctica: a Guide to the Wildlife, 1994, 5th ed., 2008; The Arctic: A Guide to Coastal Wildlife, 2001, 3rd ed., 2012; Wildlife of the North Atlantic, 2008. **Address:** The Venture, Slapton, Kingsbridge, DN TQ7 2PN, England. **Online address:** tonysoper@btinternet.com

SOREL, Julia. See **DREXLER, Rosalyn.**

SOREL, Nancy Caldwell. American (born United States), b. 1934. **Genres:** Biography, Humor/Satire, Art/Art History, Autobiography/Memoirs, Graphic Novels, Cartoons, Medicine/Health, Biography, Biography. **Career:** First Encounters, Atlantic Magazine, columnist; Massachusetts Institute of Technology, news writer, 1958-60; Columbia Encyclopedia, staff editor, 1962-63; New School for Social Research, English teacher, 1963-65; Brooklyn Friends School, English teacher, 1965-66. Writer. **Publications:** Word People, 1970; (co-ed.) An Historic Biographical Profile of the Town of Kent, Putnam County, New York, 1976; Ever since Eve: Personal Reflections on Childbirth, 1984; (with E. Sorel) First Encounters: A Book of Memorable Meetings, 1994; Reporting World War II vol. I: American Journalism 1938-1944, 1995; The Women Who Wrote the War, 1999. Contributor of articles. **Address:** 156 Franklin St., New York, NY 10013, U.S.A.

SØRENSEN, Georg. Danish (born Denmark), b. 1948. **Genres:** International Relations/Current Affairs. **Career:** Aarhus University, assistant lecturer, 1978-79, senior lecturer of international politics, 1989-95, professor of international politics and economics, 1995-, head of department, 2001-04; Aalborg University, lecturer, 1979-81, research fellow in international studies, 1981-83, senior lecturer, 1984-89; Danish Institute of International Studies,

chairman, 2003-10. Writer. **Publications:** (With J.J. Simonsen) Chile 1970-73: et eksempel på østeuropæisk udviklingsstrategi?, 1976; International politik og marxisme, 1980, 6th ed., 1988; Transnationale selskaber og udviklingsprocessen i perifere samfund: med en case-studie af Brasilien, 1983; Transnational Corporations in Peripheral Societies: Contributions Towards Self-Centered Development?, 1983; Udviklingsteori og den Tredje verden, 1988; Democracy, Dictatorship, and Development: Economic Development in Selected Regimes of the Third World, 1990; Democracy and Democratization: Processes and Prospects in a Changing World, 1993, 3rd ed., 2008; (with H. Holm) Whose World Order?: Uneven Globalization and the End of the Cold War, 1995; (with R. Jackson) An Introduction to International Relations, 1999, 4th ed., 2010; Changes in Statehood: The Transformation of International Relations, 2001; The Transformation of the State: Beyond the Myth of Retreat, 2004; A Liberal World Order in Crisis: Choosing Between Imposition and Restraint, 2011. EDITOR: (with O.J. Sorensen) State Enterprise: Development or Business as Usual?, 1982; Political Conditionality: Problems and Promises, 1993; (with A. Kohli and C. Moon) States, Markets, and Just Growth: Development in the Twenty-First Century, 2003; (with T.B. Knudsen and J.D. Pedersen) Danmark og de fremmede, 2009. Contributor to journals. **Address:** Department of Political Science, Aarhus University, Rm. 224, Bldg. 1331, Bartholins Allé 7, Aarhus, DK-8000, Denmark. **Online address:** georgs@ps.au.dk

SORENSEN, Roy A. American (born United States), b. 1957. **Genres:** Philosophy, Social Sciences. **Career:** LaRoche College, adjunct faculty, 1983; Illinois State University, assistant professor of philosophy, 1984; University of Delaware, assistant professor of philosophy, 1984-87; New York University, assistant professor, 1987-90, associate professor of philosophy, 1990-95, chairman of department, 1991-94, professor, 1995-99; Dartmouth College, professor, 1999-2008; Washington University, professor, 2008-. Writer. **Publications:** Blindspots, 1988; Thought Experiments, 1992; Pseudo-Problems: How Analytic Philosophy Gets Done, 1993; Vagueness and Contradiction, 2001; A Brief History of the Paradox: Philosophy and the Labyrinths of the Mind, 2003; Seeing Dark Things: The Philosophy of Shadows, 2008. Works appear in anthologies. Contributor of articles to journals. **Address:** Department of Philosophy, Washington University, Rm. 102 Wilson Hall, One Brookings Dr., PO Box 1073, St. Louis, MO 63130, U.S.A. **Online address:** sorensen@wustl.edu

SORENSON, John L. American (born United States), b. 1924. **Genres:** Anthropology/Ethnology, Social Sciences, Young Adult Non-fiction. **Career:** Brigham Young University, faculty, 1953-55, 1958-64, 1971-86, professor of anthropology, through 1986, professor emeritus of anthropology, 1986-; General Research Corp., head of social sciences, 1964-69; Bonneville Research Corp., president, 1969-71. Writer. **Publications:** Nephite Culture, 1977; (with W. Bray and J.R. Moriarty) Metallurgy in ancient Mexico, 1982; An Ancient American Setting for the Book of Mormon, 1985, rev. ed., 1996; (with M.H. Raish) Pre-Columbian Contact with the Americas Across the Oceans: An Annotated Bibliography, 2 vols., 1990, 2nd ed., 1996; (ed. with M.J. Thorne) Rediscovering the Book of Mormon, 1991; Mormon Culture: Four Decades of Essays on Mormon Society and Personality, 1997; Images of Ancient America: Visualizing Book of Mormon Life, 1998; Mormon's Map, 2000; (with C.L. Johannessen) World Trade and Biological Exchanges Before 1492, 2009. Contributor of articles to periodicals. **Address:** 3401 N Canyon Rd., Provo, UT 84604, U.S.A. **Online address:** johnsorenson@byu.edu

SORENSON, Margo. (Marcie Kremer). American (born United States), b. 1946?. **Genres:** Children's Fiction, Children's Non-fiction, Young Adult Non-fiction, Sports/Fitness, Young Adult Fiction, Humor/Satire, Adult Non-fiction, Picture/Board Books, Picture/Board Books. **Career:** Teacher, 1967-85. Writer. **Publications:** (As Marcie Kremer) Aloha, Love (young adult romance novel), 1995; Danger Canyon, 1996; The Hidden Dagger, 1996; Soccer Blaster, 1996; Kimo and the Secret Waves, 1996; Nothing Is for Free, 1996; The Gotcha Plot, 1996; Firewatch, 1996; Time Trap, 1996; Who Stole the Bases?, 1996; Don't Bug Me, 1996; Tsunami!, 1997; Hurricane, 1997; Fight in the Fields: The Story of Cesar Chavez, 1998; Leap into the Unknown: The Story of Albert Einstein, 1998; Danger Marches to the Palace: The Story of Queen Lili'uokalani, 1998; Death of Lies: The Story of Socrates, 1998; Fight in the Fields: Cesar Chavez, 1998; Shatter with Words: The Story of Langston Hughes, 1998; Clubhouse Threat, 2001; Funny Man, 2002; Soccer Battle, 2002; Tori and the Sleigh of Midnight Blue, 2002; Secret Heroes,

2003; Funny Man Gets Rolling, 2004; Armando's Backpack, 2004; Ambrose and the Princess, 2005; Ambrose and the Cathedral Dream, 2006; Aloha for Carol Ann, 2011. **Address:** 55802 Brae Burn, La Quinta, CA 92253, U.S.A. **Online address:** ms@margosorenson.com

SORKIN, Adam J. American (born United States), b. 1943. **Genres:** Literary Criticism And History, Translations. **Career:** University of Illinois, instructor in English, 1965-66; University of North Carolina, instructor in English, 1970-71; Stockton State College, instructor in literature, 1971-73; Bluefield State College, assistant professor of English, 1974-78; Penn State Brandywine, assistant professor, 1978-85, associate professor, 1985-94, professor, 1994-2000, distinguished professor of English, 2000-; University of Bucharest, Fulbright lecturer, 1980-81, Department of English, Masters Program for the Translation of the Contemporary Literary Text, visiting professor, 2008. Writer. **Publications:** City of Dreams and Whispers: An Anthology of Contemporary Poets of Lasi, 1998. EDITOR: (with K.W. Treptow and trans.) An Anthology of Romanian Women Poets, 1994; (with L. Bleoca) Transylvanian Voices: An Anthology of Contemporary Poets From Cluj-Napoca, 1994, 2nd ed., 1997; (and co-trans.) Day after Night: Twenty Romanian Poets for the Twenty-First Century, 1999; (and trans. with B. Stefanescu) Speaking the Silence: Prose Poets of Contemporary Romania, 2001; (and trans. with R. Andriescu) Club 8: Poems, 2001; (with C. Cirstea and S. Cotter and trans. with C. Cirstea) Singular Destinies: Contemporary Poets of Bessarabia, 2003. TRANSLATOR: (with I.G. Pana and contrib.) Selected Poems of Anghel Dumbraveanu in Romanian and English: Love and Winter, 1992; (with L. Ursu) Fires on Water/Focuri pe apa: Seven Poets from Sibiu/7 poeti din Sibiu, 1992; (with L. Ursu and T. Gallagher) L. Ursu, The Sky behind the Forest (poetry), 1997; (co-trans.) D. Crasnaru, Sea-Level Zero, 1999; (with V. Mihaiu and L. Bleoca) V. Mihaiu, Recensamant de epifanii/Census of Epiphanies, 1999; M. Cartarescu, Bebop Baby, 1999; (with M. Carneci) M. Carneci, Poeme/Poems, 1999; (with I. Ieronim) I. Ieronim, The Triumph of the Water Witch, 2000; (with A. Carac) I. Flora, Medeea si masinile ei derazboi/Medea and Her War Machines, 2002; (with S. Stanescu) S. Stanescu, Diary of a Clone: Five Poems Written in English, 2003; (with I. Ieronim) I. Ieronim, 41 Poems, 2003; (with L. Vianu) M. Sorescu, The Bridge, 2004; (with R. Cesereanu) R. Cesereanu, Lunacies, 2004; (with D. Crasnaru) D. Crasnaru, The Grand Prize And Other Stories, 2004; (co-trans.) M. Sorescu, The Past Perfect of Flight, 2004; (with L. Vianu) M. Sorescu, The Bridge, 2004; Bridge, 2004; (with I. Ieronim) I. Ieronim, Scara rulanta, 2005; (co-trans.) M. Ursachi, The March To The Stars, 2006; (co-trans.) M. Marin, Paper Children, 2006; (with M. Carneci) M. Carneci, Chaosmos 2006; Born In Utopia: An Anthology of Modern And Contemporary Romanian Poetry, 2006; (with R. Andriescu) R. Andriescu, The Catalan Within, 2007; (with A. Carac) M. Carneci, A Bucharest of Smells, 2007; (co-trans.) R. Cesereanu, Crusader-Woman, 2008; (co-trans.) Elena Stefoi, Somewhere in a Different Realm, 2008; (with D. Hurezanu) M. Marin, The Factory of the Past, 2008; (co-trans.) Visteriile cetatii: 18 poeti din Sibiu/Treasury of the City: 18 Poets of Sibiu, 2008; (with R. Andriescu, B. Stefanescu and M. Ivanescu) Memory Glyphs: Prose Poems from Romania, 2009; (with L. Vianu) M. Ivanescu, Lines Poems Poetry, 2009; (co-trans.) C. Firan, Rock and Dew, 2010. Works appear in anthologies. Contributor to journals. **Address:** Department of English, Penn State Brandywine, 25 Yearsley Mill Rd., Media, PA 19063, U.S.A. **Online address:** ajs2@psu.edu

SOROUSH, Abdolkarim. Iranian (born Iran), b. 1945?. **Genres:** Essays, Humanities. **Career:** Laboratory for Food Products, director; Teacher Training College, Islamic culture group, director; Institute for Cultural Studies, researcher; Tehran Academy of Philosophy, professor of ethics; Imam Sadeq Mosque, lecturer; Tehran University, instructor; Harvard University, visiting professor; Kiyan, co-founder; Princeton University, teacher, 2002-03. Writer. **Publications:** Naqdī va Darā Madī bar Tazā dd-i diyā Liktīkī, 1978; Dā Nish va Arzish, 1980; Ilm va ī mā n: Bi-zamī mah-i jahā n dar Asòr-i mawud, 1980; Yā Dnāmah-i Ustā d Shahī d Murtazá Mutòahharī, 1981; Taḥrī rī -i Naw az Naqdī va Darā Madī bar Tazād-i Diyā Liktī kī, 1982; Rawshanfikrī va dī Ndārī, 1988; Tafarruj-i ş un': Guftārhā-yi darmaqūlāt-i akhlāq va sòanat va ilm-i insānī, 1988; Tamsīl dar shir-i Mawlā Nā VaguftgūyīpīrāmuMCNn-i hunar, 1988; Qabz va Basṭ-itiūrīk-i Sharīat, 1991; Awş āf-i Pārsāyān, 1992; ḥikmat va Maīshat, 1994. Qiş ş ah-i Arbāb-imarifat, 1994; Qabzva Basṭ-i Tiūrīk-i sharīat: Naẓariyah-i takā mul-i marifat-i dīnī, 1995; Darshāyī dar falsafah-i ilm al-ijtimā: Ravish-i tafsī rdar ulū m-i ijtimāī, 1995; Hòadī s-i bandagi vadilburdagī, 1996; Farbahtar az īdiūlūzhī, 1997; Madārā va mudīriyat, 1997; ş irāṭhā-yimustaqīm, 1998; Siyāsat-nāmah, 1999; Basṭ-i tajrubah-inabavī, 1999; Reason, Freedom, and Democracy in Islam: Essential Writings

of Abdolkarim Soroush, 2000; Qimār-i āshiqānah: Shamsva Mawlānā, 2000; Guftimān-i Rawshangar: darbārah-iandīshah hā-yi Bunyādīn, 2000; Akhlāq-ikhudāyān, 2001; Az Sharīatī, 2006; Adab-i Qudrat, Adab-i Adālat, 2007; Expansion of Prophetic Experience: Essays on Historicity, Contingency and Plurality in Religion, 2009. **Address:** c/o Author Mail, Oxford University Press, 198 Madison Ave., New York, NY 10016, U.S.A. **Online address:** info@drsoroush.com

SORRENSON, Maurice Peter Keith. New Zealander (born New Zealand), b. 1932?. **Genres:** History, Race Relations, Biography. **Career:** Makerere University, East African Institute of Social Research, research fellow, 1963-64; University of Auckland, lecturer, 1964-65, senior lecturer, 1965-66, associate professor, 1966-67, professor of history, 1968-95, head of the department of history, 1974-76, 1978-80, 1984-87, professor emeritus, 1995-. Writer. **Publications:** Land Reform in the Kikuyu Country, 1967; Maori and European since 1870: A Study in Adaptation and Adjustment, 1967; New Zealand and the Rhodesia Crisis: The Lessons of History, 1968; The Origins of European Settlement in Kenya, 1968; Europe and Southern Africa, 1972; Integration or Identity: Cultural Integration in New Zealand since 1911, 1977; Separate and Unequal: Cultural Integration in South Africa 1919-1961, 1977; Maori Origins and Migrations, 1979; (ed.) Na To Hoa Aroha: From Your Dear Friend: The Correspondence between Sir Apirana Ngata and Sir Peter Buck, 1925-50, 3 vols., 1986-88; Manifest Duty: The Polynesian Society over a 100 Years, 1992; Waitangi: New Zealand's Enduring Struggle, 1998. **Address:** Department of History, University of Auckland, 5 and 7 Wynyard St., Auckland, 1010, New Zealand. **Online address:** r.sorrenson@auckland.ac.nz

SORROW, Barbara Head. American (born United States), b. 1945. **Genres:** Education, Librarianship, How-to Books, Social Sciences. **Career:** Teacher, 1969, 1976, 1977-79, 1984-; Red Bank High School, librarian, 1984-; Chattanooga State Community College, part-time librarian, 1985. Writer. **Publications:** (With L. Sparks) Teachers and Librarians Working Together: To Make Students Lifelong Library Users, 1991; (with B.S. Lumpkin) CD-ROM for Librarians and Educators: A Resource Guide to over 300 Instructional Programs, 1993, 2nd ed., 1996; Multimedia Activities for Students: A Teachers' and Librarians' Handbook, 1997. **Address:** 4 S Bluff Rd., Chattanooga, TN 37419, U.S.A.

SOSNOWSKI, David (J.). American (born United States), b. 1959. **Genres:** Novels. **Career:** University of Michigan, tutor in English, 1980-85; instructor in composition, 1986-88; University of Alaska-Fairbanks, instructor, 1983-85; Madonna College, instructor, 1985; Wayne State University, instructor, 1985-88; University of Detroit, instructor in composition, 1985-86; U.S. Environmental Protection Agency, budget and program analyst for Office of Mobile Sources, Office of Air and Radiation, 1988-90, National Vehicle and Fuels and Emission Laboratory, environmental protection specialist, 1990-. Writer. **Publications:** Rapture, 1996; Vamped: A Novel, 2004. Contributor of articles to periodicals. **Address:** U.S. Environmental Protection Agency, 2565 Plymouth Rd., Ann Arbor, MI 48105, U.S.A. **Online address:** sosnowskid@aol.com

SOTO, Gary. American (born United States), b. 1952. **Genres:** Poetry, Essays, Picture/Board Books, Novels, Novellas/Short Stories, Biography, Adult Non-fiction, Plays/Screenplays, Criminology/True Crime. **Career:** University of California-Berkeley, assistant professor, 1979-85, associate professor of English and ethnic studies, 1985-91, part-time senior lecturer in English department, 1991-93; University of Cincinnati, Elliston poet, 1988; University of California-Riverside, distinguished professor of creative writing; Wayne State University, Martin Luther King/Cesar Chavez/Rosa Parks visiting professor of English, 1990; full-time writer, 1992-. **Publications:** (With M. Peich) Heaven, 1970; The Level at Which the Sky Begins, 1976; The Elements of San Joaquin, 1977; The Tale of Sunlight, 1978; Father is a Pillow Tied to a Broom, 1980; (with E. Trejo) Comoarbustos de Niebla, 1980; Where Sparrows Work Hard, 1981; Living up the Street, 1985; Black Hair, 1985; Small Faces, 1986; The Cat's Meow (picturebook), 1987, 2nd ed., 1995; (ed.) California Childhood, 1988; Lesser Evils, 1988; Who Will Know Us?, 1990; Baseball in April, 1990, 2nd ed., 1991; A Fire in My Hands, 1990; A Summer Life, 1990; Home Course in Religion, 1991; Taking Sides, 1991; Too Many Tamales (picture book), 1992; (ed.) Pieces of the Heart: New Chicano Fiction, 1993; Pacific Crossing, 1993; Crazy Weekend, 1994; Neighborhood Odes, 1992; Jesse, 1994, rev. ed., 2006; New and Selected Poems, 1995; Chato's Kitchen, 1995; Boys at Work, 1995; Canto Familiar, 1995; Junior College,

1997; Buried Onions, 1997, 2nd ed., 1999; Novio Boy (play), 1997; Big Bushy Mustache, 1998; Petty Crimes, 1998; Béisbol en Abril y Otras Historias, 1998; A Natural Man, 1999; Nerd-landia (play and opera libretto), 1999; Nickel and Dime, 2000; Poetry Lover, 2001; Effects of Knut Hamsun on a Fresno Boy, 2000; Chato and the Party Animals, 2000; Jessie De La Cruz: A Profile of a United Farm Worker, 2000; If the Shoe Fits, 2002; Fearless Fernie, 2002; Shadow of the Plum: Poems, 2002; Cesar Chavez: A Hero for Everyone, 2003; The After Life, 2003; Amnesia in a Republican County: A Novel, 2003; One Kind of Faith, 2003; Chato Goes Cruisin', 2005; Marisol, 2005; Worlds Apart: Traveling with Fernie and Me, 2005; Help Wanted: Stories, 2005; My Little Car/Micarrito, 2006; Accidental Love, 2006; Novio Boy: A Play, 2006; Mercy on These Teenage Chimps, 2007; A Simple Plan, 2007; Facts of Life: Stories, 2008; Chato's Day of Dead, 2008; Skirt, 2008; Partly Cloudy: Poems of Love and Longing, 2009; Human Nature: Poem, 2010; Hey 13!, 2011; Lucky Luis, 2012. **Address:** Soto & Friends Booksellers, 43 The Crescent, Berkeley, CA 94708, U.S.A.

SOTO, Hernando de. Spanish (born Spain), b. 1941. **Genres:** History, Politics/Government. **Career:** General Agreement on Tariffs and Trade, economist; Universal Engineering Corp., managing director; Swiss Bank Corporation Consultant Group, principal; Peru's Central Reserve Bank, governor; Instituto Libertad y Democracia, president. **Publications:** (With E. Ghersi and M. Ghibellini) El otro sendero: la revolución informal, 1986; Estimación de la magnitud de la actividad económica informal en el peru, 1989; Compendio técnico y estadístico de el otro sendero, 1989; Caminando el otro sendero, 1990; (ed. with S. Schmidheiny) Las nuevas reglas del juego: hacia un desarrollo sostenible en américa latina, 1991; (with F.M. Pandolfi) Hacia la consolidación de la democracia, 1996; The Mystery of Capital: Why Capitalism Triumphs in the West and Fails Everywhere Else, 2000; (with P. Masías) El Mito Del Capital, 2001. (foreword) A Possible Way Out: Formalizing Housing Informality in Egyptian Cities, 2004. Contributor to periodicals. **Address:** Instituto Libertad y Democracia, Las Begonias 441, Oficina 901, San Isidro, Lima, 27, Peru.

SOTO, Lourdes Díaz. American (born United States), b. 1945?. **Genres:** Education, Language/Linguistics, Cultural/Ethnic Topics, Social Sciences. **Career:** Kindergarten teacher, 1970-74; school head teacher, 1974-78; junior and senior high school teacher of chemistry and health, 1978-80; elementary school teacher of mathematics, science and language arts, 1980-82; Florida Atlantic University, assistant professor of education, 1986-87; Pennsylvania State University, assistant professor of education, 1987-91, director of comprehensive bilingual early childhood project, professor of education, 1995-2006, coordinator of bilingual and multicultural education; Lehigh University, associate professor of education, 1991-95, coordinator of bilingual education program; Columbia University, Teachers College, visiting professor, 2001-02; University of Texas-Austin, professor of Education, 2006-, director/coordinator bilingual and bicultural education, 2006-; Dalton State College, Goizueta endowed chair and professor of early childhood education. Writer. **Publications:** Language, Culture and Power: Bilingual Families and the Struggle for Quality Education, 1997; (ed. and contrib.) The Politics of Early Childhood Education, 2000; (ed.) Making a Difference in the Lives of Bilingual/Bicultural Children, 2001; (ed. with B.B. Swadener) Power and Voice in Research with Children, 2005; The Praeger Handbook of Latino Education In the U.S., 2007; (ed. with H. Kharem) Teaching Bilingual/Bicultural Children: Teachers Talk about Language and Learning, 2010; (ed. with G.S. Cannella) Childhoods: A Handbook, 2010. Contributor to books and journals. **Address:** Dalton State College, 650 College Dr., Dalton, GA 30720, U.S.A. **Online address:** lsoto@daltonstate.edu

SOUEIF, Ahdaf. British (born England), b. 1950?. **Genres:** Novels, Novellas/Short Stories, Civil Liberties/Human Rights, Cultural/Ethnic Topics, Politics/Government, Documentaries/Reportage, Translations, Social Sciences, Social Sciences. **Career:** University of Cairo, lecturer; University of King Seoud, lecturer; Riyadh University, lecturer; Castle Publishing, editing counselor; Engaged Events, founder and chairman; Royal Society of Literature, fellow. Writer. **Publications:** Aisha (short stories), 1983; In the Eye of the Sun, 1992; Sandpiper, 1996; The Map of Love, 1999; (trans.) Mourid al-Barghouti, I Saw Ramallah, 2000; Mezzaterra: Fragments from the Common Ground, 2004; I Think of You: Stories, 2007; (foreword) Education Under Occupation, 2005. **Address:** Bloomsbury Publishing, 38 Soho Sq., London, GL W1D 3HB, England.

SOULE, Maris Anne. American (born United States), b. 1939. **Genres:** Novels, Romance/Historical, Young Adult Fiction, Mystery/Crime/Suspense. **Career:** Rio Americano High School, teacher, 1963-67; La Cumbre Junior High School, teacher, 1968-70; Augusta High School, teacher, 1970-72; Kellogg Community College, instructor, 1990; Galesburg-Augusta High School, teacher. Writer. **Publications:** FICTION: First Impressions, 1983; Lost and Found, 1985; Sounds Like Love, 1986; A Winning Combination, 1987; The Best of Everything, 1988; The Law of Nature, 1988; Storybook Hero, 1989; Jared's Lady, 1991; Missy's Proposition, 1992; Lyon's Pride, 1993; Con Man, 1993; No Strings Attached, 1993; No Promises Made, 1994; Stop the Wedding!, 1994; Dark Temptation, 1995; Thrill of the Chase, 1995; Substitute Mom, 1996; Destiny Strikes Twice, 1996; Destiny Unknown, 1997; Heiress Seeking Perfect Husband, 1997; Shelter from the Storm, 1997; Chase the Dream, 1999; The Bachelor, the Beauty and the Blizzard, 1999; The Crows, 2007; As the Crow Flies, 2011. OTHER: No Room for Love, 1984. **Address:** Five Star Publications Inc., PO Box 6698, Chandler, AZ 85246, U.S.A. **Online address:** soulem@aol.com

SOULSBY, E. J. L. (Ernest Jackson Lawson Soulsby). British (born England), b. 1926. **Genres:** Animals/Pets, Medicine/Health, Biology, Zoology. **Career:** Veterinary officer, 1949-52; Clinical Parasitology, University of Bristol, lecturer, 1952-54; Cambridge University, Wolfson College, lecturer, 1954-63, fellow, 1978-, professor of animal pathology, 1978-93, honorary and emeritus fellow, now professor emeritus; World Association for the Advancement of Veterinary, president, 1963-67; University of Pennsylvania, professor of parasitology, 1964-78, Department of Veterinary Biology, chairman, now retired; Helminthological Society of Washington, president, 1970-71; Royal College of Veterinary Surgeons, president, 1984-85; Royal Society of Medicine, president, 1998-2000; Royal Institute of Public Health, president, 2003-; Windward Islands Research and Education Foundation, president, 2007-. Writer. **Publications:** (Ed.) The Evaluation of Anthelmintics, 1964; Textbook of Veterinary Clinical Parasitology, 1965; (ed.) Biology of Parasites, 1966; Reaction of the Host to Parasitism, 1968; Helminths, Arthropods and Protozoa of Domesticated Animals, 6th ed. 1968, 7th ed. 1982; (ed.) Immunity to Animal Parasites, 1972; (ed.) Parasitic Zoonoses, 1974; (ed.) Pathophysiology of Parasitic Infections, 1976; Epidemiology and Control of Nematodiasis in Cattle, 1981; (ed.) Immune Responses in Parasitic Infections: Immunology, Immunopathology and Immunoprophylaxis, 1987; (ed. with D.I.H. Simpson and S.R. Palmer) Zoonoses: Biology, Clinical Practice and Public Health Control, 1998; (ed. with R. Wilbur) Antimicrobial Resistance, 2001; (ed.) Pain: Its Nature and Management In Man and Animals, 2001. **Address:** Wolfson College, University of Cambridge, Cambridge, CB CB3 9BB, England.

SOULSBY, Ernest Jackson Lawson. *See* **SOULSBY, E. J. L.**

SOUPER, Patrick C(harles). British (born England), b. 1928. **Genres:** Education, Reference. **Career:** Royal Opera House Orchestra, musician, 1942-52; ordained Anglican minister, 1957; Anglican Cathedral, chaplain, 1957-62; University of London, Central Colleges, chaplain, 1963-65; St. Paul's School (private boys' secondary school), senior chaplain, 1965-70; University of Southampton, lecturer in education, 1970-; South Hampshire Industrial Mission, chairman, 1981-. Writer. **Publications:** About to Teach: An Introduction to Method in Teaching, 1976; (with W.K. Kay) The School Assembly Debate 1942-1982, 1982; (with W.K. Kay) The School Assembly in Hampshire, 1982; (with W.K. Kay) Worship in the Independent Day School, 1983; (ed. and contrib.) The Spiritual Dimension of Education, 1985. **Address:** Department of Education, University of Southampton, University Rd., Southampton, HM SO17 1BJ, England.

SOUSSLOFF, Catherine M. American (born United States), b. 1951. **Genres:** Art/Art History, Theology/Religion. **Career:** Virginia Polytechnic Institute and State University, assistant professor of art history, 1983-86; University of North Carolina, visiting lecturer in art history, 1986-87; University of California, assistant professor, 1987-91, associate professor, 1991-97, professor of art history and visual culture, 1997-, presidential chair, 2006-09, Visual and Performance Studies Faculty Research Group, director; KUSP-Radio, film reviewer, 1995-. Writer. **Publications:** The Absolute Artist: The Historiography of a Concept, 1997; (ed.) Jewish Identity in Art History: Ethnicity and Discourse, 1999; Subject in Art: Portraiture and the Birth of the Modern, 2006. Contributor to periodicals. **Address:** Porter College, University of California, 1156 High St., 203 Cowell College, Santa Cruz, CA 95064, U.S.A. **Online address:** cmsoussl@cats.ucsc.edu

SOUSTER, Raymond. Also writes as John Holmes, Raymond Holmes. Canadian (born Canada), b. 1921. **Genres:** Novels, Poetry, History, Sports/Fitness, Bibliography, Travel/Exploration, Young Adult Fiction. **Career:** Canadian Imperial Bank of Commerce, accountant, 1939-85, retired, 1985; Direction Journal, founder, 1941-46; Contact Magazine, founder, 1952-54; Contact Press, founder, 1952-67; Combustion Journal, founder, 1957-60; League of Canadian Poets, co-founder, 1966, president, 1967-72. **Publications:** Unit of Five: Louis Dudek, 1944; When We Are Young, 1946; Go to Sleep World, 1947; (as Raymond Holmes) The Winter of Time, 1949; City Hall Street, 1951; (with L. Dudek and I. Layton) Cerberus: Poems, 1952; Selected Poems, 1956; A Local Pride, 1962; Place of Meeting, 1962; Ten Elephants on Yonge Street, 1965; As Is, 1967; The Colour of the Times, 1967; Lost and Found, 1968; So Far So Good, 1969; The Years, 1971; Selected Poems, 1972; (as John Holmes) On Target: A Novel, 1972; (with R. Woollatt) Sights and Sounds, 1973; Change Up, 1974; (with R. Woollatt) These Loved, These Hated Lands, 1975; Double-Header, 1975; Rain-Check, 1975; Extra Innings, 1977; Vapour and Blue: The Poetry of W.W. Campbell, 1978; Hanging In: New Poems, 1979; Collected Poems, 10 vols., 1940-93; (with D. Alcorn) From Hell to Breakfast (memoir), 1980; (with R. Woollatt) Poems of a Snow-Eyed Country, 1980; Going the Distance: New Poems 1979-82, 1983; (with B. Brooks) Queen City, Toronto in Poems and Pictures, 1984; Jubilee of Death, 1984; (with J. Deahl) Into this Dark Earth, 1985; Flight of the Roller-Coaster: Poems for Younger Readers, 1985; It Takes All Kinds: New Poems, 1986; The Eyes of Love, 1987; Asking for More, 1988; Running Out the Clock, 1991; Riding the Long Black Horse, 1993; Old Bank Notes, 1993; No Sad Songs Wanted Here, 1995; Close to Home, 1996; An Acadian Easter: The Collected Poems of Francis Sherman, 1999; No Choice but to Trust: The Winning Poems of the 1999 Sandburg-Livesay Anthology Contest, 2000; Of Time & Toronto, 2000; Making the Damn Thing Work: The First 4 Years of the League of Canadian Poets, 1968-1972, 2001; Take Me Out to the Ballgame (poetry), 2002; Twenty-Three New Poems, 2003. EDITOR: (and intro.) New Wave Canada, 1966; Contact 1952-1954: Being an Index to the Contents of Contact, a Little Magazine, 1966; (with R. Woollatt) Generation Now, 1970; (with D. Lochhead) Made in Canada, 1970; (with D. Lochhead) 100 Poems of Nineteenth Century Canada, 1974; (with D. Lochhead) Comfort of the Fields: The Best Known Poems of Archibald Lampman, 1979; (with D. Lockhead) Powassan's Drum: Selected Poems of Duncan Campbell Scott, 1985; (with D. Lochhead) Windflower: The Selected Poems of Bliss Carman, 1985. **Address:** 39 Baby Point Rd., Toronto, ON M6S 2G2, Canada.

SOUTAR, Carolyn. British (born England) **Genres:** Biography, Autobiography/Memoirs. **Career:** English National Opera, Stage manager. Writer. **Publications:** Noureiev Intime, 2004; The Real Nureyev: An Intimate Memoir of Ballet's Greatest Hero, 2004; Staging Events, a Practical Guide, 2005; Dave Allen: The Biography, 2005. Contributor to periodicals. **Address:** c/o Author Mail, Redhammer Management Ltd., 186 Bickenhalls Mansions, Bickenhall St., London, GL W1U 6BX, England.

SOUTH, Mary. American (born United States) **Genres:** Adult Non-fiction, Autobiography/Memoirs. **Career:** Rodale, deputy editor women's health books; Riverhead Books, founding editor, senior editor, associate publisher; Little, Brown Book Group, editor; Ballantine, associate editor; Houghton Mifflin, editor; Yachting magazine, senior editor. **Publications:** (Contrib.) The Limestone Valley, 1976; The Cure for Anything Is Salt Water: How I Threw My Life Overboard and Found Happiness at Sea (memoir), 2007. **Address:** Yachting Magazine, PO Box 420235, Palm Coast, FL 32142-0235, U.S.A. **Online address:** bossanova12@qgmail.com

SOUTH, Sheri Cobb. American (born United States), b. 1959. **Genres:** Romance/Historical, Mystery/Crime/Suspense, Young Adult Fiction. **Career:** J.C. Penney and Company Inc., sales clerk, 1978. Writer. **Publications:** Wrong-Way Romance, 1991; That Certain Feeling, 1991; The Cinderella Game, 1992; Blame It on Love, 1995; Don't Bet on Love, 1996; Miss Darby's Duenna, 1999; Weaver Takes A Wife, 1999; Brighton Honeymoon, 2000; Restless Hearts, 2001; French Leave, 2001; The Cobra and the Lily, 2002; In Milady's Chamber, 2006; Of Paupers and Peers, 2006; Dead Bore: Another John Pickett Mystery, 2008; The Chance of a Lifetime, 2008. **Address:** Andrea Brown Literary Agency Inc., 1076 Eagle Dr., Salinas, CA 93905-4466, U.S.A. **Online address:** cobbsouth@aol.com

SOUTHER, J. Mark. American (born United States), b. 1971?. **Genres:** History. **Career:** Cleveland State University, History Internships program co-ordinator, Center for Public History and Digital Humanities co-director, faculty member, 2003-; U.S. Department of Education, academic director. Writer. **Publications:** (ed.) Reconstructing Louisiana, 2001; New Orleans on Parade: Tourism and the Transformation of the Crescent City, 2006. **Address:** Department of History, Cleveland State University, 2121 Euclid Ave., RT 1904, Cleveland, OH 44115, U.S.A. **Online address:** m.souther@csuohio.edu

SOUTHEY, Roz. British (born England), b. 1952. **Genres:** Novels, Music, History. **Career:** Newcastle University, teaching assistant. Writer. **Publications:** NOVELS: Broken Harmony, 2007; Chords and Discords, 2008; Secret Lament, 2009; Sword and Song, 2010. OTHERS: Music-Making in North-East England during the Eighteenth Century, 2006; (with S. Quigley and D. King) Radgepacket, vol. II: Tales from the Inner Cities, 2009. **Address:** School of Arts and Cultures, Newcastle University, Newcastle upon Tyne, TW NE1 7RU, England. **Online address:** rosemary.southey@ncl.ac.uk

SOUTHWICK, Leslie H. American (born United States), b. 1950. **Genres:** Politics/Government, Biography. **Career:** Texas Supreme Court of Criminal Appeals, briefing attorney, law clerk for Judge John F. Onion, 1975-76; Fifth Circuit U.S. Court of Appeals, law clerk for Judge Charles Clark, 1976-77; Brunini Law Firm, associate, 1977-83, partner, 1983-89; Mississippi College School of Law, adjunct professor, 1985-89, 1998-2006; U.S. Department of Justice, deputy assistant, 1989-93; Mississippi Court of Appeals, judge, 1995-2006; 155th Brigade Combat Team, Iraq, deputy and staff judge advocate, 2004-06; United States Court of Appeals for the Fifth Circuit, federal judge, 2007-; Mississippi College School of Law, visiting professor of law, 2007-. Attorney and writer. **Publications:** Presidential Also-Rans and Running Mates, 1788-1980, 1984, (comp.) 2nd ed. as Presidential Also-Rans and Running Mates, 1788 Through 1996, 1998. Contributor of articles to journals. **Address:** 501 E Court St., Ste. 3.750, Jackson, MS 39201, U.S.A. **Online address:** jsouthwick@mssc.state.ms.us

SOWELL, David (Lee). American (born United States), b. 1952. **Genres:** History, Adult Non-fiction, Business/Trade/Industry, Economics. **Career:** Fort Hays State University, assistant professor of history, 1986-87; Allegheny College, assistant professor of history, 1987-88; University of South Carolina at Columbia, visiting assistant professor of history, 1988-89; Juniata College, assistant professor, 1989-92, associate professor, 1992-2001, chair of history department, 1993-2004, 2001-, director of international programs, 1996-99, professor of history, 2001-. Writer. **Publications:** (Comp.) Santander y la opinion Anglo americana: Vision de viajeros y periodicos, 1821-1840, 1991; The Early Colombian Labor Movement: Artisans and Politics in Bogota, 1832-1919, 1992; Contact, Conquest, and Consequences: Originally Presented as a Lecture Series in Commemoration of the Quincentennial of 1492, 1993; The Tale of Healer Miguel Perdomo Neira: Medicine, Ideologies and Power in the Nineteenth-Century Andes, 2001. Works appear in anthologies. Contributor of articles to journals. **Address:** Department of History, Juniata College, 311 Founders Hall, 1700 Moore St., Huntingdon, PA 16652-2196, U.S.A. **Online address:** sowell@juniata.edu

SOWELL, Mike. American (born United States), b. 1948. **Genres:** Sports/Fitness, Biography. **Career:** Tulsa Tribune, sports editor, 1977-92; writer, 1992-; Oklahoma State University, faculty, 1999-, School of Journalism and Broadcasting, associate professor. **Publications:** The Pitch That Killed, 1989; July 2, 1903: The Mysterious Death of Hall-of-Famer Big Ed Delahanty, 1992; One Pitch Away: The Players' Stories of the 1986 League Championships and World Series, 1995. **Address:** 206-B Paul Miller Bldg., Stillwater, OK 74078, U.S.A. **Online address:** mike.sowell@okstate.edu

SOYINKA, Wole. American/Nigerian (born Nigeria), b. 1934. **Genres:** Novels, Plays/Screenplays, Poetry, Literary Criticism And History, Essays, Translations, Young Adult Fiction. **Career:** Royal Court Theatre, play reader and dramaturgist, 1958-59; University of Ibadan, research fellow in drama, 1960-61, Department of Theatre Arts, chairman, 1967-71, School of Drama, director, 1969-72; Black Orpheus, co-editor, 1961-64; University of Ife, lecturer in English, 1962-64, research professor of drama, 1972-75, professor of comparative literature, 1975-85; University of Lagos, senior lecturer in English, 1964-67, now professor emeritus; Transition, editor, 1974-76; University of Sheffield, visiting professor, 1974; University of Ghana, visiting professor, 1975; Yale University, visiting professor, 1979-80; Cornell University, visiting professor, 1986, Goldwin Smith professor of African studies and theatre arts, 1988-91; University of Nevada, Department of English, Elias Ghanem professor of creative writing; Emory University, Robert W. Woodruff professor of the arts; Obafemi Awolowo University, now professor emeritus. **Pub-**

lications: Camwood on the Leaves, 1960; A Dance of the Forest, 1963; The Lion and the Jewel, 1963; Three Plays, 1963; Five Plays, 1964; Before the Blackout, 1965; The Interpreters (novel), 1965; The Road, 1965; Idanre, and Other Poems, 1967; Kongi's Harvest, 1967; (trans.) D.O. Fagunwa, Forest of a Thousand Daemons: A Hunter's Saga, 1968; Poems From Prison, 1969; Madmen and Specialists, 1971; The Jero Plays, 1972; A Shuttle in the Crypt (poems), 1972; The Man Died: Prison Notes of Wole Soyinka, 1972; The Bacchae of Euripides: A Communion Rite, 1973; (ed. and intro.) Anthology of Black Verse, 1973 in UK as Poems of Black Africa, 1975; Collected Plays, 2 vols., 1973-74; Season of Anomy (novel), 1973; Death and the King's Horseman, 1975; Myth, Literature, and the African World, 1976; Ogun Abibiman (verse), 1976; (adapter) Opera Wonyosi, 1981; Aké: The Years of Childhood (autobiography), 1981; A Play of Giants, 1984; Six Plays, 1984; Requiem for a Futurologist, 1985; Climate of Art, 1986; Childe Internationale, 1987; Mandela's Earth and Other Poems, 1988; Art, Dialogue and Outrage: Essays on Literature and Culture, 1988; La Récolte de Kongi, 1988; Ìsarà: A Voyage around Essay, 1989; The Search: With Fountain Notes and Exercises, 1989; The Credo of Being and Nothingness: First in the Series of Olufosoye Annual Lectures on Religions, Delivered at the University of Ibadan, on 25 January, 1991, 1991; La Ronde Dans La Forêt, 1991; From Zia, with Love: And, A Scourge of Hyacinths (plays), 1992; (foreword) Nigeria, 1993; Blackman and the Veil (lectures), 1993; Ikuú Olókun-Esin, 1994; Ibadan: The Penkelemes Years (memoir), 1994; The Beatification of Area Boy: A Lagosian Kaleidoscope, 1995; Collected Plays 2, 1996; Open Sore of a Continent: A Personal Narrative of the Nigerian Crisis, 1996; Early Poems, 1998; La Muerte Y El Jinete Del Rey: Threno Nigeriano, 1998; (co-author) Scourge Of Hyacinths: An Opera in Twelve Scenes: Libretto, 1999; Burden of Memory, the Muse of Forgiveness, 1999; Salutation to the Gut, 2002; Samark and and Other Markets I Have Known, 2002; King Baabu, 2002; The Deceptive Silence of Stolen Voices, 2003; (contrib.) WS: A Life in Full, 2004; Climate of Fear: The Quest for Dignity in a Dehumanized World, 2005; Interventions, 2005; The Invention; And The Detainee, 2005; (contrib.) Strategie Di Sviluppo E Aiuto Internazionale: Le Proposte Africane, 2006; You Must Set Forth at Dawn: A Memoir, 2006; New Imperialisms, 2010. Contributor to periodicals. **Address:** Random House Inc., 1745 Broadway, New York, NY 10019, U.S.A.

SPACK, Ruth. American (born United States), b. 1947. **Genres:** Humanities, Language/Linguistics, Literary Criticism And History, Education. **Career:** Teacher, 1970-71; Prince George's County, Adult Education Department, teacher, 1973-79; Boston University, Department of English, lecturer, 1978-88; Tufts University, Department of English, lecturer and director of ESOL composition, 1980-98, director of composition program, 1988-98; Bentley University, associate professor of English, 1998-2006, English for Speakers of Other Languages, director, 1999-, director of communication across the curriculum, 2006-08, professor of English and media studies, 2006-. Writer. **Publications:** Guidelines: A Cross-Cultural Reading/Writing Text, 1990, 3rd ed., 2007; The International Story: An Anthology with Guidelines for Reading and Writing about Fiction, 1994; English as a Second Language, 1994, 3rd ed., 2000; (ed. with V. Zamel) Negotiating Academic Literacies: Teaching and Learning across Languages and Cultures, 1998; America's Second Tongue: American Indian Education and the Ownership of English 1860-1900, 2002; (ed. with V. Zamel) Enriching ESOL Pedagogy: Readings and Activities for Engagement, Reflection, and Inquiry, 2002; (ed. with V. Zamel) Crossing the Curriculum: Multilingual Learners in College Classrooms, 2004; Teaching Writing for ESL Students, 4th ed., 2005; (ed. with V. Zamel) Language Lessons: Stories for Teaching and Learning English, 2008. **Address:** Department of English, Bentley University, Morison Hall 233, 175 Forest St., Waltham, MA 02452-4705, U.S.A. **Online address:** rspack@bentley.edu

SPACKS, Barry. American (born United States), b. 1931. **Genres:** Novels, Poetry, History, Literary Criticism And History. **Career:** University of Florida, assistant professor, 1957-59; Massachusetts Institute of Technology, professor of literature, 1960-81; University of Kentucky, faculty, 1978-79; University of California, Berkeley, Department of English, visiting professor, 1980-, distinguished professor in humanities and fine arts, 1991; University of California, Santa Barbara, visiting professor. Writer. **Publications:** POETRY: Twenty Poems, 1967; The Company of Children: Poems, 1968; Something Human: Poems, 1972; Teaching the Penguins to Fly, 1975; Imagining a Unicorn, 1978; Spacks Street: New and Selected Poems, 1982; Brief Sparrow, 1988; Regarding Women, 2004; The Hope of the Air: Poems, 2004; Food for the Journey: Poems, 2008. NOVELS: The Sophomore, 1968; Orphans: A

Novel, 1972. Contributor to periodicals. **Address:** College of Creative Studies, University of California, Santa Barbara, CA 93106, U.S.A. **Online address:** barry.spacks@verizon.net

SPACKS, Patricia Meyer. American (born United States), b. 1929. **Genres:** Literary Criticism And History. **Career:** Indiana University, instructor in English, 1954-56; University of Florida, instructor in Humanities, 1958-59; Wellesley College, instructor, 1959-61, assistant professor, 1961-65, associate professor, 1965-68, department chair, 1968-71, professor of English, 1968-79; Yale University, professor of English, 1979-89, department chairman, 1985-88; University of Virginia, Edgar F. Shannon professor of English, 1989-, Department of English, chairman, 1991-97. Writer. **Publications:** The Insistence of Horror, 1962; John Gay, 1965; Poetry of Vision, 1967; The Varied God, 1969; An Argument of Images, 1971; Female Imagination, 1975; Imagining a Self, 1976; The Adolescent Idea, 1981; (with W.B. Carnochan) A Distant Prospect, 1982; (contrib.) Women and Society in the Eighteenth Century, 1983; Gossip, 1985; Desire and Truth, 1990; Boredom, 1995; Privacy: Concealing the Eighteenth-Century Self, 2003; Novel Beginnings: Experiments in Eighteenth-Century English Fiction, 2006; Reading Eighteenth-Century Poetry, 2009; On Rereading, 2011. EDITOR: 18th Century Poetry, 1964; Late Augustan Prose, 1971; Late Augustan Poetry, 1973; The Contemporary Women Novelists, 1977; Persuasion, 1995; Advocacy in the Classroom: Problems and Possibilities, 1996; Selections from The Female Spectator, 1999; Pride and Prejudice, 2010. **Address:** Department of English, University of Virginia, 219 Bryan Hall, PO Box 400121, Charlottesville, VA 22903, U.S.A. **Online address:** pms2b@virginia.edu

SPAETH, Anthony. Korean/American (born United States), b. 1955. **Genres:** Novels, Writing/Journalism, Literary Criticism And History. **Career:** Asahi Evening News, desk editor and film critic, 1977-78; Forbes, reporter, researcher and staff writer, 1978-80; Asian Wall Street Journal, regional industry correspondent, Manila bureau chief, South Asia bureau chief, 1980-91; writer, 1991-94; Time Magazine, executive editor for Asia, 1993-2006; Bloomberg News, editor, head of Asian political news, 2006-08, Asian Government Team, leader; POWER Magazine, Hong Kong, founding editor, 2008-09; Joong Ang Daily, Seoul, chief editor, 2010-. **Publications:** The Hong Kong Foreign Correspondents Club, 1990; May and June, 1992; The Thousand-Headed Snake, 1993. **Address:** JoongAng Daily, 7 Soonhwa-dong, Jung-gu, Seoul, 100-759, Korea (South). **Online address:** anthonyspaeth@mac.com

SPAHR, Juliana. American (born United States), b. 1966. **Genres:** Poetry, Literary Criticism And History. **Career:** Siena College, visiting assistant professor of English, 1996-97; University of Hawaii, assistant professor of English, 1997-2002, associate professor of English, 2003; Mills College, associate professor of English, 2003-11, professor of English, 2011-, Aurelia Henry Reinhardt chair. Writer. **Publications:** POETRY: Nuclear, 1992; Testimony, 1995; Choosing Rooms, 1995; Response, 1996; Spiderwasp or Literary Criticism, 1998; Live, 2000; Fuck You, Aloha, I Love You, 2001; (ed. with C. Rankine) American Women Poets in the 21st Century, 2002; This Connection of Everyone with Lungs: Poems, 2005; Transformation, 2007. OTHERS: (ed. with P. Gizzi) Writing from the New Coast: Technique, 1993; (co-ed.) A Poetics of Criticism, 1993; Everybody's Autonomy: Connective Reading and Collective Identity, 2001; (ed. with J. Retallack) Poetry & Pedagogy: The Challenge of the Contemporary, 2005; Well then there Now, 2011. **Address:** Department of English, Mills College, 316 Mills Hall, 5000 MacArthur Blvd., Oakland, CA 94613, U.S.A. **Online address:** jspahr@mills.edu

SPALDING, Andrea. Canadian/British (born England), b. 1944. **Genres:** Children's Fiction, Young Adult Fiction, Travel/Exploration, Biography, Picture/Board Books, Language/Linguistics, Novels, Mystery/Crime/Suspense, Adult Non-fiction. **Career:** Writer, 1979-. Actress, educator, musician and consultant. **Publications:** CHILDREN'S BOOKS: The Most Beautiful Kite in the World (picture book), 1988, rev. ed., 2003; (comp. and reteller) A World of Stories (folktale collection), 1989, rev. ed., 1999; A Special Gift, 1995; Finders Keepers (young adult novel), 1995; Sarah May and the New Red Dress, 1998; Island of My Own, 1998; Phoebe and the Gypsy, 1999; Me and Mr. Mah (picture book), 1999; (with D. Spalding) The Lost Sketch (adventure), 1999; The Keeper and the Crows, 2000; (with D. Spalding) The Silver Boulder, 2000; It's Raining, It's Pouring, 2001; The Disappearing Dinosaur (adventure), 2002; Solomon's Tree, 2002; The White Horse Talisman, 2002; Dance of the Stones, 2003; Heart of the Hill, 2005; Behind the Sorcerer's Cloak, 2006; (with A. Scow) Secret of the Dance, 2006; Dance Baby Dance,

2009; (with P. Milelli) Seal Song, 2011. FOR ADULTS: (with P. Holmes) Never a Dull Moment, 1984; (with D. Spalding) The Whistlers, Jasper National Park, 1986; (with G. Montgomery) The Pender Palate: Tastes and Flavours from Our Favorite Island, 1992; (with D. Spalding) The Flavours of Victoria, 1994; (with D. Spalding, G. Montgomery and L. Pitt) Southern Gulf Islands of British Columbia (Altitude Superguide), 1995; (with D. Spalding and L. Pitt) B.C. Ferries and the Canadian West Coast, 1996. Contributor of articles to periodicals and newspapers. **Address:** 1105 Ogden Rd., R.R. 1, Pender Island, BC V0N 2M1, Canada. **Online address:** andrea@andreaspalding.com

SPALDING, Frances. British (born England), b. 1950. **Genres:** Art/Art History, Biography, Architecture. **Career:** Sheffield City Polytechnic, lecturer in art history, 1978-88; freelance writer, 1989-; Newcastle University, School of Arts and Cultures, professor of art history, 2000-; Royal College of Art, honorary fellow. **Publications:** Magnificent Dreams: Burne-Jones and the Late Victorians, 1978; Whistler, 1979; Roger Fry: Art and Life, 1980; Vanessa Bell, 1983; British Art Since 1900, 1986; Stevie Smith: A Critical Biography, 1988; 20th Century Painters and Sculptors, 1990; Dance Till the Stars Come Down: A Life of John Minton, 1991; (ed. and intro.) Paper Darts: Selected Letters of Virginia Woolf, 1991; Duncan Grant: A Biography, 1997; The Tate: A History, 1998; Gwen Raverat: Friends, Family and Affection, 2001; (with D.F. Jenkins) John Piper in the Thirties: Abstraction On The Beach, 2003; John Minton: Dance till the Stars Come Down, 2005; The Bloomsbury group in the National Portrait Gallery Insights Series, 2005; John Piper, Myfanwy Piper Lives in Art, 2009. Contributor to periodicals. **Address:** c/o Gill Coleridge, Rogers, Coleridge & White Ltd., 20 Powis Mews, London, GL W11 1JN, England. **Online address:** frances.spalding@ncl.ac.uk

SPALL, James C. American (born United States) **Genres:** Physics, Sciences. **Career:** U.S. Department of Transportation, staff, 1979-82; National Highway Traffic and Safety Administration, staff, 1979-82; General Motors Research Laboratory, staff, 1979-82; Johns Hopkins University, Applied Physics Laboratory, senior professional staff, 1983-91, principal professional staff, 1991-, Strategic Education Program, instructor, 1996-, Whiting School of Engineering, instructor, 1997-, part-time faculty, 1999-, research professor of applied mathematics and statistics, 2004-, Dunning professor, 2004-05, Applied and Computational Mathematics Program, chair and adviser, 1999-; Applied Technology Institute Inc., instructor, 2004-. Writer. **Publications:** (Ed.) Bayesian Analysis of Time Series and Dynamic Models, 1988; Introduction to Stochastic Search and Optimization: Estimation, Simulation, and Control, 2003. Contributor to books and journals. **Address:** Applied Physics Laboratory, Johns Hopkins University, 11100 Johns Hopkins Rd., Laurel, MD 20723-6005, U.S.A. **Online address:** james.spall@jhuapl.edu

SPANGER, Hans-Joachim. German (born Germany), b. 1953. **Genres:** International Relations/Current Affairs, Politics/Government, Young Adult Non-fiction. **Career:** Peace Research Institute Frankfurt (PRIF), research fellow, 1980-, deputy director, 1997-2006, Cross-sectional Tasks Research Group, head, 2004-; International Institute for Strategic Studies, research associate, 1987-88. Writer. **Publications:** SED und der Sozialdemokratismus: Ideologische Abgrenzung in der DDR, 1982; (with L. Brock) Beiden deutschen Staaten in der Dritten Welt: Die Entwicklungspolitik der DDR, eine Herausforderung für die Bundesrepublik Deutschland, 1987; (with V. Handl) Wie weiter bei der Vertrauensbildung?: Zu den Wiener VSBM-Verhandlungen und darüber hinaus, 1989; The GDR in East-West Relarions, 1992; Auf dem Weg zum europäischen Wirtschaftsraum?: Der Systemwandel im Osten als Herausforderung für den Westen, 1992; (ed. with V. Baranovsky) In From the Cold: German, Russian and the Future of Europe, 1992; (with P. Vale) Security, Development, and Cooperation in Southern Africa: The Midgard Conference Report, 1993; Marginalisiert?: Russland und die politische Ökonomie der Transformationsperiode, 1994; (ed. with P. Vale) Bridges to the Future: Prospects for Peace and Seccurity in Southern Africa, 1995; (with A. Kokeev) Brücken, Achsen-und neue Gräben: Die deutsch-russischen Beziehungen im multilateralen Spannungsfeld, 1995; (ed.) Russland und der Westen: von der strategischen Partnerschaft zur Strategie der Partnerschaft, 1998; (ed. with P.W. Schulze) Zukunft Russlands: Staat und Gesellschaft nach der Transformationskrise, 2000; Vor einer Renaissance des asiatischen Modells'?: Die Krisen in Asien und ihre strukturpolitischen Folgen, 2000; Wiederkehr des Staates: Staatszerfall als wissenschaftliches und entwicklungspolitisches Problem, 2001; Demarcation versus Cooperation: Peculiarities of Western Democracy Promotion in Russia, 2002; (with J. Wolff) Armutsreduzierung durch Demokratisierung?: PRSP, Chancen und Widersprüche einer neuen entwicklungspolitischen Strategie, 2003; (with J. Wolff) Poverty Reduc-

tion through Democratisation?: PRSP Challlenges of a New Devolopment Assistant Strategy, 2003; Modernisierung contra Demokratisierung: Putins russischer Weg, 2004; Paradoxe Kontinuitäten: die deutsche Russlandpolitik und die koalitionären Farbenlehren, 2005; Zwischen Ground Zcro und Square One: George W. Bush und die Folgen der Simulation amerikanischer Russlandpolitik, 2007; (ed. with S. Weiss and W. van Meurs) Diplomacy, Development and Defense: A Paradigm for Policy Coherence: A Comparative Analysis of International Strategies, 2009. Contributor to books. **Address:** Peace Research Institute Frankfurt, Baseler Str. 27-31, Frankfurt, D-60329, Germany. **Online address:** spanger@hsfk.de

SPANGLER, Catherine. American (born United States) **Genres:** Novels, Young Adult Fiction, Romance/Historical. **Career:** Novelist. **Publications:** THE SHIELDER SERIES: Shielder, 1999; Shadower, 2000; Shamara, 2001; Shadow Crossing, 2003; Shadow Fires, 2004. THE SENTINEL SERIES: Touched by Darkness, 2007; Touched by fire, 2007; Touched by Light, 2009. **Address:** c/o Roberta M. Brown, Brown Literary Agency, 410 7th NW, Naples, FL 34120, U.S.A. **Online address:** romance@catherinespangler.com

SPANGLER, David. American (born United States), b. 1945. **Genres:** Theology/Religion, Autobiography/Memoirs. **Career:** Lorian Association, co-founder, 1973-; University of Wisconsin, teacher, 1978-84. Writer. **Publications:** The Christ Experience and the New Age (booklet), 1967; The New Age Vision, 1974; (with R.O. Crombie and D. Maclean) Man, Nature and the New Age, 1974; Manifestation (booklet), 1975; Attunement (booklet), 1975; (R. McVicar) Festivals in the New Age, 1975; Synergy (booklet), 1975; The Laws of Manifestation, 1975, new ed., 2009; Revelation: The Birth of a New Age, 1976; Vision of Findhorn: Anthology, 1976; The Little Church, 1976; Relationship & Identity, 1977; Towards a Planetary Vision, 1977; Reflections on the Christ, 1977; Conversations with John, 1980; Explorations: Emerging Aspects of the New Culture, 1980; Emergence: The Rebirth of the Sacred (autobiography), 1984; Channeling in the New Age, 1988; (with W.I. Thompson) Reimagination of the World: A Critique of the New Age, Science and Popular Culture, 1991; Everyday Miracles: The Inner Art of Manifestation, 1996; The Call, 1996; A Pilgrim in Aquarius, 1996; Parent as Mystic, Mystic as Parent, 1998; (with S. Koke) Hidden Millennium: The Doomsday Fallacy, 1998; Blessing: The Art and the Practice, 2001; Story Tree, 2003; The Incarnational Card Deck, 2008; Apprenticed to Spirit, 2011. Contributor to periodicals. **Address:** c/o Author Mail, Riverhead Books/Penguin Putnam, 375 Hudson St., New York, NY 10014, U.S.A.

SPANGLER, Jewel L. Canadian (born Canada), b. 1961. **Genres:** Theology/Religion. **Career:** University of Calgary, Department of History, assistant professor of history, associate professor. Writer. **Publications:** (Co-ed.) The Papers of James Madison, Presidential Series, vol. IV, 1999, vol. V, 2004; Virginians Reborn: Anglican Monopoly, Evangelical Dissent, and the Rise of the Baptists in the Late Eighteenth Century, 2008. Contributor to journals. **Address:** University of Calgary, 2500 University Dr. NW, Calgary, AB T2N 1N4, Canada. **Online address:** spangler@ucalgary.ca

SPANIER, Sandra Whipple. American (born United States), b. 1951. **Genres:** Literary Criticism And History, Novels. **Career:** State College, English teacher, 1973-81; State University of New York at Stony Brook, lecturer in engineering and applied sciences, 1982-86; Oregon State University, assistant professor, 1986-89, associate professor of English, 1989-92, Center for the Humanities, fellow, 1991-92; University of Nebraska, associate professor of English, 1992-95; National Endowment for the Humanities, fellow, 1993-94; Pennsylvania State University, associate professor, 1995-2003, professor of English, 2003-. Writer. **Publications:** Kay Boyle: Artist and Activist, 1986. EDITOR: (and intro.) Life Being the Best and Other Stories, 1988; (and afterword) Love Goes to Press: A Comedy in Three Acts, 1995, 2nd ed., 2009; (intro.) American Fiction, American Myth: Essays, 2000; (and intro.) Process: A Novel, 2001. Contributor to periodicals. **Address:** Department of English, Pennsylvania State University, 17 Burrowes Bldg., University Park, PA 16802, U.S.A. **Online address:** sxs74@psu.edu

SPANOGLE, Joshua. American (born United States), b. 1970?. **Genres:** Novels, Mystery/Crime/Suspense, Medicine/Health. **Career:** University of Pennsylvania, Center for Bioethics, researcher. Writer. **Publications:** Isolation Ward, 2006; Flawless, 2007. **Address:** c/o Author Mail, Delacorte Press, 1745 Broadway, New York, NY 10019-4368, U.S.A. **Online address:** spanogle@stanford.edu

SPAR, Debora L. American (born United States), b. 1963?. **Genres:** Economics, Business/Trade/Industry, International Relations/Current Affairs, Human Relations/Parenting, Politics/Government, Women's Studies And Issues. **Career:** Barnard College, president, 2008-; Harvard Business School, Spangler Family professor of business administration. Writer. **Publications:** (With R. Vernon) Beyond Globalism: Remaking American Foreign Economic Policy, 1989; (with R. Vernon and G. Tobin) Iron Triangles and Revolving Doors: Cases in U.S. Foreign Economic Policymaking, 1991; The Cooperative Edge: The Internal Politics of International Cartels, 1994; Cyberrules: Problems and Prospects for On-line Commerce, 1996; Attracting High Technology Investment: Intel's Costa Rican Plant, 1998; Ruling the Waves: Cycles of Discovery, Chaos and Wealth from the Compass to the Internet, 2001; The Baby Business: How Money, Science and Politics Drive the Commerce of Conception, 2006. **Address:** Barnard College, 3009 Broadway, New York, NY 10027, U.S.A. **Online address:** dspar@barnard.edu

SPARKE, Penny. British (born England), b. 1948. **Genres:** Art/Art History, Design, Photography. **Career:** Brighton Polytechnic, principal lecturer in the history of design, 1975-; Royal College of Art, senior lecturer, 1981-99, School of Humanities, head, 1994-99, senior fellow; Kingston University, Faculty of Art, Design and Architecture, dean of design faculty, 1999-, professor and pro vice-chancellor of arts. Writer. **Publications:** Ettore Sottsass Jnr, 1982; Consultant Design: The History and Practice of the Designer in Industry, 1983; Design and Culture, 1986; Introduction to Design and Culture in the Twentieth Century, 1986; Furniture, 1986; (co-author) Design Source Book, 1986; Design in Context, 1987; Electrical Appliances: Twentieth-Century Design, 1987; Modern Japanese Design, 1987; Design in Italy: 1870 to the Present, 1988; As Long as It's Pink: The Sexual Politics of Taste, 1995; A Century of Design, 1998; Design Lexikon Grossbritannien, 2000; Design Directory Great Britain, 2001; Introduction to Design and Culture: 1900 to the Present, 2nd ed., 2004; Elsie De Wolfe: The Birth of Modern Interior Decoration, 2005; (with R.C. Miller and C. McDermott) European Design Since 1985: Shaping the New Century, 2009; (with P. Antonelli) Japanese Design, 2009. EDITOR: Design by Choice, 1981; Did Britain Make It?: British Design in Context, 1946-86, 1986; The Cutting Edge, 1992; The Plastics Age: From Bakelite to Beanbags and Beyond, 1993; A Century of Design, 1999; A Century of Car Design, 2002; (with B. Martin) Women's Places: Architecture and Design 1860-1960, 2003; (with S. McKellar) Interior Design and Identity, 2004; (with T. Keeble and B. Martin) Modern Period Room: The Construction of the Exhibited Interior 1870 to 1950, 2006; (co-ed.) Designing the Modern Interior: From the Victorians to Today, 2009. **Address:** Faculty of Art, Design & Architecture, University of Kingston, River House, 53-57 High St., Kingston upon Thames, SR KT1 1LQ, England. **Online address:** p.sparke@kingston.ac.uk

SPARKES, Ali. (Alison Sparkes)., b. 1966?. **Genres:** Novels, Children's Fiction. **Career:** BBC Radio Solent, presenter & producer; London's West End theatre district, staff. Novelist. **Publications:** NOVELS: Frozen in Time, 2010. SHAPESHIFTER SERIES-YOUNG ADULT NOVELS: Finding the Fox, 2006; Running the Risk, 2007; Going to Ground, 2007; Dowsing the Dead, 2007; Stirring the Storm, 2008. MONSTER MAKERS SERIES-JUVENILE FICTION: Electrotaur and Slashermite, 2008; Introducing Stinkermite, 2008; Bashertaur, 2008. **Online address:** info@alisparkes.com

SPARKES, Alison. See **SPARKES, Ali.**

SPARKS, John. American (born United States), b. 1961. **Genres:** Biography, Autobiography/Memoirs. **Career:** St. Joseph Hospital, lab technician; Baptist Church, ordained minister. Writer. **Publications:** The Roots of Appalachian Christianity: The Life and Legacy of Elder Shubal Stearns, 2001; Raccoon John Smith: Frontier Kentucky's Most Famous Preacher, 2005; The Last Dance of Gus Finley: A Tale of Eastern Kentucky Justice, 2009; Kentucky's Most Hated Man, 2009. **Address:** Hager Hill, KY , U.S.A. **Online address:** jgsprks@bellsouth.net

SPARKS, Kenton L. (Kenton Lane Sparks). American (born United States), b. 1963. **Genres:** Cultural/Ethnic Topics. **Career:** North Carolina Wesleyan College, instructor of religion, 1992-94; University of North Carolina, teaching fellow, 1993-95; Providence Baptist Church, special assistant, 1993-2000; Eastern University, professor of biblical studies, 2000-, Office of the Provost, special assistant. Writer. **Publications:** Ethnicity and Identity in Ancient Israel: Prolegomena to the Study of Ethnic Sentiments and Their Expression in the Hebrew Bible, 1998; The Pentateuch: An Annotated Bibliography, 2002; Ancient Texts for the Study of the Hebrew Bible: A Guide to the Background Literature, 2005; God's Word in Human Words: An Evangelical Appropriation of Critical Biblical Scholarship, 2008; Sacred Word, Broken Word, 2011. **Address:** Department of Biblical Studies, Eastern University, 1300 Eagle Rd., St. Davids, PA 19087-3696, U.S.A. **Online address:** ksparks@eastern.edu

SPARKS, Kenton Lane. See **SPARKS, Kenton L.**

SPARKS, Nicholas. American (born United States), b. 1965. **Genres:** Novels. **Career:** Writer and novelist, 1993-. **Publications:** NOVELS: (with B. Mills) Wokini: A Lakota Journey to Happiness and Self-Understanding, 1990; The Notebook, 1996; Message in a Bottle, 1998; A Walk to Remember, 1999; The Rescue, 2000; A Bend in the Road, 2001; Nights in Rodanthe, 2002; The Guardian, 2003; The Wedding, 2003; Three Weeks with My Brother, 2004; At First Sight, 2005; True Believer, 2005; (with B. Mills) Lessons of a Lakota: A Young Man's Journey to Happiness and Self-Understanding, 2005; Dear John, 2006; The Choice, 2007; Lucky One, 2008; Last Song, 2009; Safe Haven, 2010; Best of Me, 2011. **Address:** The Park Literary Group L.L.C., 270 Lafayette St., Ste. 1504, New York, NY 10012, U.S.A.

SPARKS, Randy J. American (born United States), b. 1957. **Genres:** History, Adult Non-fiction. **Career:** Mississippi State University, teaching assistant, 1980-82, instructor, 1987-88; University of Georgia, instructor, 1988-89; College of Charleston, assistant professor, 1989-95, associate professor, 1995-2000, Woodrow Wilson Summer Teachers' Institutes in History for High School Teachers, coordinator, 1991-95, Program in the Carolina Lowcountry and the Atlantic World, co-director and co-associate director, 1994-2000; Tulane University, associate professor, 2000-05, professor, 2005-, Deep South Regional Humanities Center, director, 2003-05, Department of History, chair, 2007-10. Writer. **Publications:** The Papers of Hilde Bruch: A Manuscript Collection in the Harris County Medical Archive, 1985; On Jordan's Stormy Banks: Evangelicalism in Mississippi, 1773-1876, 1994; (ed. with J.P. Greene and R.B. Shute) Money, Trade and Power: The Evolution of Colonial South Carolina's Plantation Society, 2001; Religion in Mississippi, 2001; (ed. with B.V. Ruymbeke) Memory and Identity: The Huguenots in France and the Atlantic Diaspora, 2003; The Two Princes of Calabar: An Eighteenth-Century Atlantic Odyssey, 2004; (ed. with R.B. Shute) Paths to Freedom: Manumission in the Atlantic World, 2009. **Address:** Department of History, Tulane University, Rm. 118, Hebert Hall, 6823 St. Charles Ave., New Orleans, LA 70118, U.S.A. **Online address:** rsparks1@tulane.edu

SPARROW, Jeff. Australian (born Australia), b. 1969?. **Genres:** History, Novellas/Short Stories. **Career:** Victoria University, Department of Communication, Culture and Languages, research fellow; Small Press Underground Networking Community, director; Crikey, contributor; New Matilda, contributor; ABC The Drum Unleashed, contributor; Overland, writer and editor. **Publications:** (With J. Sparrow) Radical Melbourne: A Secret History, 2001; (with J. Sparrow) Radical Melbourne 2: The Enemy Within, 2004; Communism: A Love Story, 2007; Killing: Misadventures In Violence, 2009. Contributor of articles to journals and magazines. **Address:** Victoria University, PO Box 14428, Melbourne, VI 8001, Australia. **Online address:** overland@vu.edu.au

SPARROW, Rebecca. Australian (born Australia), b. 1972?. **Genres:** Novels. **Career:** Trips Magazine, travel writer, editor, 1997. **Publications:** The Girl Most Likely: A Novel, 2003; The Year Nick McGowan Came to Stay, 2006; (with N. Earls) Joel and Cat Set the Story Straight (young adult), 2007. Contributor to periodicals. **Address:** Brisbane, QL , Australia. **Online address:** bec@rebeccasparrow.com

SPARROWDANCER, Mary. American (born United States) **Genres:** Songs/Lyrics And Libretti, Self Help. **Career:** Wild-Animal Rehabilitation Facility, founder and president, 1978-96. Writer. **Publications:** The Love Song of the Universe, 2001. Contributor to periodicals. **Address:** 529 E Jennings St., PO Box 535, Tallahassee, FL 32302, U.S.A. **Online address:** mary@sparrowdancer.com

SPARSHOTT, F. E. See **SPARSHOTT, Francis (Edward).**

SPARSHOTT, Francis (Edward). Also writes as Cromwell Kent, F. E. Sparshott. Canadian/British (born England), b. 1926. **Genres:** Poetry, Philosophy, Dance/Ballet. **Career:** University of Toronto, Victoria College, lecturer in philosophy, 1950-55, assistant professor, 1955-62, associate professor, 1962-64, professor of philosophy, 1964-91, chair of department, 1965-70, university professor, 1982-91, now professor emeritus, 1991-; Northwestern University, visiting associate professor, 1958-59; University of Illinois, visiting professor, 1966; Canadian Philosophical Association, president, 1975-76; League of Canadian Poets, 1977-79; American Society for Aesthetics, president, 1981-82. Writer. **Publications:** An Enquiry into Goodness and Related Concepts, 1958; The Structure of Aesthetics, 1963; The Concept of Criticism, 1967; A Book by Cromwell Kent (humour), 1970; Looking for Philosophy, 1972; The Theory of the Arts, 1982; Off the Ground: First Steps to a Philosophical Consideration of the Dance, 1988; Taking Life Seriously: A Study of the Argument of the Nicomachean Ethics, 1994; A Measured Pace: Toward a Philosophical Understanding of the Arts of Dance, 1995; The Future of Aesthetics, 1998; Scoring in Injury Time, 2006. POETRY: A Divided Voice, 1965; A Cardboard Garage, 1969; The Naming of the Beasts, 1979; The Rainy Hills, 1979; The Cave of Trophonius, 1983; The Hanging Gardens of Etobicoke, 1983; Storms and Screens, 1985; Sculling to Byzantium, 1989; Views from the Zucchino Gazebo, 1994; Home from the Air: Residual Verses, 1997; The City Dwellers and Other Verses, 2000. Contributor to periodicals. **Address:** 50 Crescentwood Rd., Scarborough, ON M1N 1E4, Canada.

SPASH, Clive L(aurence). British (born England), b. 1962. **Genres:** Economics, Environmental Sciences/Ecology. **Career:** University of British Columbia, Forest Economic Policy Association, research assistant, 1985-87; University of Wyoming, teaching assistant, 1987-88, 1988-90, research associate, 1988-90; University of Stirling, lecturer in environmental economics, 1990-96, Environmental Economics Research Group, assistant director, 1992-96; Lincoln University, visiting lecturer, 1993-94; University of Cambridge, Department of Land Economy, university lecturer in environmental economics and policy, Cambridge Research for the Environment, director, 1996-2001; University of Aberdeen, Department of Agriculture and Forestry, research chair, 2001-02, Department of Land Economy, research chair, 2002-03, Department of Geography and Environment, research chair, 2003-06; Macaulay Land Use Research Institute, Socio-Economic Research Programme, head, 2001-06; Commonwealth Scientific Industrial Research Organisation, Chief Executive Officers, science leader, 2006-09; Norwegian University of Life Sciences, Department of International Environment and Development Studies, professor, 2010-; WU Vienna University of Economics and Business, Department of Socio-Economics, chair of public policy and governance, 2010-. Writer. **Publications:** (With N. Hanley) Cost-Benefit Analysis and the Environment, 1993; (ed. with M. O'Connor) Valuation and the Environment: Theory, Method, and Practice, 1999; (ed. with D. Requier-Desjardins and J. van der Straaten) Environmental Policy and Societal Aims, 1999; (with J. O'Neill) Conceptions of Value in Environmental Decision-making, 2000; Concerted Action on Environmental Valuation in Europe (EVE): An Introduction, 2000; (with C. Carter) Environmental Valuation in Europe: Findings from the Concerted Action, 2001; (with S. McNally) Managing Pollution: Economic Valuation and Environmental Toxicology, 2001; Greenhouse Economics: Value and Ethics, 2002; (ed. with M. Getzner and S. Stagl) Alternatives for Environmental Valuation, 2005; (ed.) Ecological Economics: Critical Concepts in the Environment, 2009; (ed. with R.P.F. Holt and S. Press) Post Keynesian and Ecological Economics: Confronting Environmental Issues, 2009. Contributor to books and periodicals. **Address:** Sustainable Ecosystems Division, CSIRO, PO Box 284, Canberra, AC 2601, Australia. **Online address:** clive.spash@csiro.au

SPATZ, Gregory. American (born United States), b. 1964?. **Genres:** Novels, Novellas/Short Stories. **Career:** Eastern Washington University, Inland Northwest Center for Writers, MFA Program, director; University of Iowa, teacher of fiction; University of Memphis, teacher of fiction. Writer. **Publications:** FICTION: No One but Us: A Novel, 1995; Wonderful Tricks: Stories, 2002; Fiddler's Dream: A Novel, 2006; Inukshuk: A Novel, 2012. **Address:** 2020 S Post St., Spokane, WA 99203, U.S.A. **Online address:** gspatz1@earthlink.net

SPATZ, Kenneth Christopher. American (born United States), b. 1940. **Genres:** Mathematics/Statistics, Psychology, Social Sciences. **Career:** University of the South, instructor in psychology, 1966-69; University of Arkansas, associate professor of psychology, 1971-73; Hendrix College, professor of psychology and chair, 1973-2003, professor emeritus of psychology, 2003-. Writer. **Publications:** A Laboratory Manual for Experimental Psychology, 1970; (with J.O. Johnston) Basic Statistics: Tales of Distributions, 1976, 10th ed., 2010; (with E.P. Kardas) Research Methods in Psychology: Ideas, Techniques and Reports, 2008. **Address:** Department of Psychology, DW Reyn-

olds Center for Life Sciences, Hendrix College, 1600 Washington Ave., Ste. 108, Conway, AR 72032, U.S.A. **Online address:** spatz@hendrix.edu

SPAUGH, Jean Christopher. American (born United States) **Genres:** Novels, Food And Wine, Young Adult Fiction. **Career:** Ashley Hall, teacher, 1968; College of Charleston, faculty; Salem Academy, faculty; Columbia College, faculty; John F. Blair Publisher, reader, editor. **Publications:** (With D. O'Brien) Georgia's Historic Restaurants and Their Recipes, 1987, rev. ed., 1996; Something Blue (novel), 1997. **Address:** John F. Blair Publisher, 1406 Plaza Dr., Winston-Salem, NC 27103, U.S.A.

SPEAKES, Larry (Melvin). American (born United States), b. 1939. **Genres:** Politics/Government, Adult Non-fiction, History. **Career:** Oxford Eagle, news editor, 1961-62; Bolivar Commercial, news editor, 1962-63, managing editor, 1965-66; Bolivar County Civil Defense, deputy director, 1963-65; Progress Publishers, general manager and editor, 1966-68; U.S. Senate, press secretary to Senator James Eastland of Mississippi, 1968-74; Executive Office of the President, staff assistant, press assistant, 1974; White House, assistant press secretary, 1974-76; U.S. President, assistant press secretary, 1976-77; Gerald Ford, press secretary, 1977; Hill & Knowlton, vice president, 1977-81; White House, chief spokesman, 1981-87; Merrill Lynch & Company Inc., senior vice president of communications, 1987-88; Northern Telecom Ltd., senior vice president of communications, 1991-93; U.S. Postal Service, corporate relations and legislative affairs vice president, 1994, head of advertising. Writer. **Publications:** (With R. Pack) Speaking Out: The Reagan Presidency from Inside the White House (nonfiction), 1988. **Address:** 4800 Thiban Terr., Annandale, VA 22003, U.S.A.

SPEAR, Hilda D. Scottish/British (born England), b. 1926. **Genres:** Literary Criticism And History, Biography. **Career:** University of Leicester, tutor in English, 1954-56, lecturer in English and education, 1965-68; Purdue University, lecturer in English, 1956-57; University of Dundee, lecturer, 1969-87, senior adviser of studies, 1979-83, senior lecturer in English, 1987-93, retired, 1993, honorary research fellow, 1993-; International Biographical Association, fellow. Writer. **Publications:** Remembering, We Forget, 1979; Hardy's The Mayor of Casterbridge, 1980; Lawrence's The Rainbow, 1980; Conrad: Youth and Typhoon, 1980; William Golding: The Inheritors, 1983; Emily Brontë Wuthering Heights, 1985; William Golding: The Spire, 1986; E.M. Forster: A Passage to India, 1986; (ed. with A.M. Aly) Forster in Egypt: A Graeco-Alexandrian Encounter, 1987; (with A.M. Aly) The Uncollected Egyptian Essays of E.M. Forster, 1988; John Fowles: The French Lieutenant's Woman, 1990; (with O. Yamada and D.S. Robb) The Contribution to Literature of Orcadian Writer George Mackay Brown: An Introduction and a Bibliography, 1991; Iris Murdoch, 1995, 2nd ed., 2007. EDITOR: The English Poems of Charles Stuart Calverley, 1974; The Poems and Selected Letters of C.H. Sorley, 1978; (with A.M. Aly) Forster in Egypt: A Graeco-Alexandrian Encounter: E. M. Forster's First Interview, 1987; The Uncollected Egyptian Essays of E.M. Forster, 1988; (with B. Pandrich) Sword and Pen: Poems of 1915 from Dundee and Tayside, 1989; George Mackay Brown: A Survey of His Work and a Full Bibliography, 2000. Contributor to periodicals. **Address:** Department of English, University of Dundee, Nethergate, Dundee, DD1 4HN, Scotland.

SPEARS, Sally. American (born United States), b. 1938. **Genres:** Biography, Military/Defense/Arms Control. **Career:** Attorney, 1981-. Writer. **Publications:** Call Sign Revlon: The Life and Death of Navy Fighter Pilot Kara Hultgreen, 1998. **Address:** 8151 Broadway, Ste. 106, San Antonio, TX 78209-1938, U.S.A. **Online address:** sespears@swbell.net

SPEAR-SWERLING, Louise. American (born United States), b. 1954. **Genres:** Education, Psychology, Sciences, Sports/Fitness. **Career:** Jefferson Middle School, teacher, 1976-77; Toffolon School, learning disabilities resource teacher, 1977-78; Yale University, Institute on Teaching Thinking, teacher, 1987; Southern Connecticut State University, Department of Special Education and Reading, professor; LD OnLine, contributor. Writer. **Publications:** (Contrib.) Handbook of Cognitive, Social, and Neuropsychological Aspects of Learning Disabilities, 1987; (contrib.) Cognitive Science and Clinical Disorders, 1992; (with R.J. Sternberg) Off Track: When Poor Readers Become Learning Disabled, 1996; (with R.J. Sternberg) Teaching for Thinking, 1996; (contrib.) Self-Awareness: Its Nature and Development, 1997; (ed. with R.J. Sternberg) Perspectives on Learning Disabilities: Biological, Cognitive, Contextual, 1999. Contributor to books and journals. **Address:** Department of Special Education & Reading, Southern Connecticut State University, 501 Crescent St., New Haven, CT 06515-1330, U.S.A. **Online address:** spearswerll1@southernct.edu

SPECK, Bruce W. American (born United States), b. 1948. **Genres:** Writing/Journalism, Bibliography, Language/Linguistics, Education. **Career:** University of Nebraska, instructor in English, 1980-84; Norden Laboratories, science writer, 1984-86; Kamterter Inc., associate and office manager, 1986-87; Indiana University, assistant professor and linguistics, 1987-90; University of Memphis, assistant professor, 1990-93, associate professor of English, 1993, Center for Academic Excellence, acting director; Lincoln School of Commerce and American Field Service, teacher; University of North Carolina, associate vice chancellor for academic affairs and professor of English, 2000-01, College of Arts and Sciences, interim dean, 1999-2000, dean, 2000-01; Austin Peay State University, vice president for academic affairs, 2001-05, provost, 2005-08, professor of English; Missouri Southern State University, president, 2008-. Writer. **Publications:** Editing: An Annotated Bibliography, 1991; (comp.) Publication Peer Review: An Annotated Bibliography, 1993; Managing Editing: An Annotated Bibliography, 1994; Managing the Publishing Process: An Annotated Bibliography, 1995; Grading Student Writing: An Annotated Bibliography, 1998; Grading Students' Classroom Writing: Issues and Strategies, 1999; (with T.R. Johnson, C.P. Dice and L.B. Heaton) Collaborative Writing: An Annotated Bibliography, 1999; (with R.S. Anderson) Using Technology in K-8 Literacy Classrooms, 2001; Without Rage Against the Dark: Selected Poems by Bruce W. Speck, 2001; Facilitating Students' Collaborative Writing, 2002; (with D.A. Hinnen and K. Hinnen) Teaching Revising and Editing: An Annotated Bibliography, 2003; (ed. with S.L. Hoppe) Service-Learning: History, Theory, and Issues, 2004; (contrib.) Teaching Online, 2005; (with R.S. Anderson and M.M. Grant) Technology To Teach Literacy: A Resource for K-8 Teachers, 2005; (with J. Rocheleau) Rights and Wrongs in the College Classroom: Ethical Issues in Postsecondary Teaching, 2007; (with S.L. Hoppe) Maxine Smith's Unwilling Pupils: Lessons Learned in Memphis's Civil Rights Classroom, 2007; (ed. with S.L. Hoppe) Searching for Spirituality in Higher Education, 2007; (with R.S. Anderson and M.M. Grant) Technology to Teach Literacy: A Resource for K-8 Teachers, 2008. Works appear in anthologies. Contributor of articles to journals and magazines. **Address:** Missouri Southern State University, 3950 E Newman Rd., Joplin, MO 64801-1595, U.S.A.

SPECK, Katie. American (born United States) **Genres:** Novels. **Career:** Writer. **Publications:** Maybelle in the Soup, 2007; Maybelle Goes to Tea, 2008. **Address:** Kansas City, MO , U.S.A. **Online address:** kspeck@katiespeck.com

SPECK, Nancy. American (born United States), b. 1959. **Genres:** Children's Fiction, Westerns/Adventure, Sports/Fitness, Literary Criticism And History. **Career:** Social worker in foster care, 1981-85; recruiter of foster parents, 1984-85; medical social worker at a nursing home, 1985-87; writer and public speaker, 1994-. **Publications:** FOR YOUNG PEOPLE. FAIRFIELD FRIENDS DEVOTIONAL ADVENTURE SERIES: The Lightning Escape and Other Stories, 1997; Firecracker Power and Other Stories, 1997; Blaze on Rocky Ridge and Other Stories, 1997; Cave Hill Treasure and Other Stories, 1998. OTHER: The Secret of the Hidden Room, 1999; Freedom Trail Mystery: Going to Boston, 2001. Work appears in anthologies. Contributor to magazines. **Address:** 337 Juniper St., Carlisle, PA 17013, U.S.A. **Online address:** brispeck@aol.com

SPECTOR, Jack Jerome. American (born United States), b. 1925. **Genres:** Art/Art History, Psychology, History. **Career:** Teacher of art, 1956-59; Rutgers University, instructor, 1962-64, assistant professor, 1964-67, associate professor, 1967-72, Department of Art History, chairman, graduate program in art history, director, 1969-71, professor, 1972-88, distinguished professor of art history, 1988-, professor emeritus of art history; American Imago journal, editor. **Publications:** The Murals of Eugene Delacroix at Saint-Sulpice, 1967; The Aesthetics of Freud: A Study in Psychoanalysis and Art, 1973; Delacroix: The Death of Sardanapalus, 1974; (intro.) Surrealism and American art, 1931-1947, 1976; Surrealist Art and Writing, 1919-1939: The Gold of Time, 1997. **Address:** Department of Art History, Rutgers University, Voorhees Hall, 71 Hamilton St., New Brunswick, NJ 08901, U.S.A.

SPECTOR, Robert. American (born United States), b. 1947. **Genres:** History. **Career:** Speaker, educator and writer. **Publications:** The Legend of Eddie Bauer, 1994; (with P.D. McCarthy) The Nordstrom Way: The Inside Story of America's #1 Customer Service Company, 1995, 2nd ed., 2000; Shared Values: A History of Kimberly-Clark, 1997; (with B. Grant) The Ale Master: How I Pioneered America's Craft Brewing Industry, Opened the First Brewpub, Bucked Trends, and Enjoyed Every Minute of It, 1998; Seattle Fur Exchange: 100 Years, 1998; Amazon.com: Get Big Fast, 2000; Lessons from the Nordstrom Way: How Companies Are Emulating the #1 Customer Service Company, 2001; Anytime, Anywhere: How the Best Bricks-and-Clicks Businesses Deliver Seamless Service to Their Customers, 2002; Category Killers: The Retail Revolution and Its Impact on Consumer Culture, 2005; (with P.D. McCarthy) The Nordstrom Way to Customer Service Excellence: A Handbook for Implementing Great Service in Your Organization, 2005; Generations: Kemper Freeman, Jr., and the Freeman Family, 2006; The Mom & Pop Store: How the Unsung Heroes of the American Economy Are Surviving and Thriving, 2009. Contributor to periodicals. **Address:** Seattle, WA , U.S.A. **Online address:** robert@robertspector.com

SPECTOR, Sheila A. American (born United States), b. 1946?. **Genres:** Bibliography, Psychology, History, Essays. **Career:** Writer. **Publications:** Jewish Mysticism: An Annotated Bibliography on the Kabbalah in English, 1984; Wonders Divine: The Development of Blake's Kabbalistic Myth, 2001; Glorious Incomprehensible: The Development of Blake's Kabbalistic Language, 2001; (ed.) British Romanticism and the Jews: History, Culture, Literature, 2002; (ed.) The Jews and British Romanticism: Politics, Religion, Culture, 2005; Byron and the Jews, 2010; (ed.) Romanticism/Judaica: A Convergence of Cultures, 2011. **Address:** Palgrave Macmillan, 175 5th Ave., New York, NY 10010-7703, U.S.A. **Online address:** sheilaspector@aol.com

SPECTOR, Stephen. American (born United States), b. 1946. **Genres:** Humanities. **Career:** State University of New York at Stony Brook, assistant professor, 1973-80, associate professor, 1980-90, professor of English, 1990-, chair. Writer. **Publications:** The Genesis of the N-Town Cycle, 1988; Operation Solomon: The Daring Rescue of the Ethiopian Jews, 2004; Evangelicals and Israel: The Story of American Christian Zionism, 2009. EDITOR: Essays in Paper Analysis, 1986; (with R.R. Edwards) The Olde Daunce: Love, Friendship, Sex, and Marriage in the Medieval World, 1990; The N-Town Play: Cotton MS Vespasian D.8, 1992; I Will Bless Those Who Bless You, forthcoming. Contributor to periodicals. **Address:** Department of English, State University of New York at Stony Brook, Humanities Bldg., Stony Brook, NY 11794-5350, U.S.A. **Online address:** sspector@notes.cc.sunysb.edu

SPEDALE, Darren R. American (born United States) **Genres:** Adult Nonfiction, Gay And Lesbian Issues. **Career:** White & Case L.L.P., corporate attorney. Writer. **Publications:** (With W.N. Eskridge, Jr.) Gay Marriage: For Better or for Worse? What We've Learned from the Evidence, 2006. **Address:** Writers' Representatives L.L.C., 116 W 14th St., 11th Fl., New York, NY 10011-7305, U.S.A.

SPEEL, Erika. British (born England), b. 1932?. **Genres:** Art/Art History, Crafts, Humanities. **Career:** Researcher, cataloger, lecturer and writer on enamel work, 1977-; Guild of Enamellers, enamel historian and publicity officer, chairman. **Publications:** Popular Enamelling, 1984; Dictionary of Enamelling, 1998. (contrib.) Maleremails des 16. und 17. Jahrhunderts aus Limoges, 2002; Painted Enamels: Fifteenth Century To The Early Twentieth Century, 2008; Painted Enamels: An Illustrated Survey 1500-1920, 2008. Contributor to books and periodicals. **Address:** 60 Deane Croft Rd., Eastcote, Pinner, Middlesex, GL HA5 1SP, England. **Online address:** erikaspeel@yahoo.co.uk

SPEER, Laurel. American (born United States), b. 1940. **Genres:** Poetry, Novellas/Short Stories, Essays, Plays/Screenplays, Young Adult Fiction, Adult Non-fiction. **Career:** Poet and essayist. **Publications:** POETRY: The Sitting Duck, 1978; A Bit of Wit, 1979; Lovers and Others, 1980; Don't Dress Your Cat in an Apron, 1981; The Hobbesian Apple, 1982; T. Roosevelt Tracks the Last Buffalo (prose poems), 1982; Hokum: Visions of a Gringa, 1982; I'm Hiding from the Cat, 1983; One Lunch, 1984; Weird Sister I, 1984; Vincent et al., 1985; The Scandal of Her Bath, 1986; Second Thoughts over Bourget, 1987; Very Frightened Men, 1988; Cold Egg, 1989; Sin, 1990; Grant Drank, 1991; Slavery, 1992; The Destruction of Lions, 1993; Rebecca at the Port Authority, 1995; Blue Salmon in the Mines, 1997; Under a Scorpion Sun, 1998; Cookies, 1999. OTHERS: The Hundred Percent Black Steinway Grand (stories), 1979; The Self-Mutilation of an Aged Apple Woman (plays), 1980; The

Book That Couldn't Be Saved (essay), 1995; Blood & Puppets (short prose), 1996; Sacks (short prose), 1997; Our LBJ (short prose), 2000. **Address:** PO Box 12220, Tucson, AZ 85732, U.S.A.

SPEHR, Paul C(hristopher). American (born United States), b. 1931. **Genres:** Film. **Career:** Library of Congress, Motion Picture Broadcasting and Recorded Sound Division, assistant chief, 1958-93, now retired; George Washington University, instructor in American studies, 1994; film historian and archival consultant, 1994-. Writer. **Publications:** The Civil War in Motion Pictures, 1961; The Movies Begin: Making Movies in New Jersey, 1887-1920, 1977; (with G. Lundquist) American Film Personnel and Company Credits, 1908-1920, 1996; Man Who Made Movie: W.K.L. Dickson, 2008. Contributor to periodicals. **Address:** 17 Valley View Trl., Fairfield, PA 17320, U.S.A. **Online address:** spehr@supernet.com

SPELLMAN, Frank R. American (born United States), b. 1944. **Genres:** Environmental Sciences/Ecology, Social Sciences. **Career:** HRSD, safety manager, 1989-; Old Dominion University, adjunct assistant professor, 2007-, assistant professor of environmental health. Freelace writer. **Publications:** (With J.E. Drinan) Stream Ecology & Self-Purification: An Introduction for Wastewater and Water Specialist, 1996, 2nd ed., 2001; Safe Work Practices for Wastewater Treatment Plants, 1996, 2nd ed., 2001; Microbiology for Water/Wastewater Operators, 1997, rev. ed., 2000; Wastewater Biosolids to Compost, 1997; Dewatering Biosolids, 1997; Incinerating Biosolids, 1997; Guide To Compliance For Process Safety Management/Risk Management Planning (PSM/RMP), 1997; The Science of Water: Concepts and Applications, 1998, 2nd ed., 2008; Safe Work Practices for the Environmental Laboratory, 1998; Surviving an OSHA Audit: A Management Guide, 1999; Hazard Communication Made Easy: A Practical Guide to OSHA Compliance, 1999; (with N.E. Whiting) Safety Engineering: Principles and Practices, 1999, 2nd ed., 2005; (with N.E. Whiting) Water Pollution Control Technology: Concepts and Applications, 1999; (with N.E. Whiting) Environmental Science and Technology: Concepts and Applications, 1999, 2nd ed., 2006; Choosing Disinfection Alternatives for Water/Wastewater Treatment, 1999; Confined Space Entry: A Guide to Compliance, 1999; The Science of Air: Concepts & Applications, 1999, 2nd ed., 2009; Machine Guarding Handbook: A Practical Guide To Osha Compliance And Injury Prevention, 1999; The Science of Environmental Pollution, 1999, 2nd ed., 2010; Spellman's Standard Handbook for Wastewater Operators, 1999, 2nd ed., 2011; (with J.E. Drinan) The Drinking Water Handbook, 2000, 2nd ed., 2012; The Handbook for Waterworks Operator Certification: Intermediate Level vol. II, 2001; (with J. Drinan) Electronics, 2001; (with J.E. Drinan) Electricity, 2001; (with J. Drinan) Water Hydraulics, 2001; (with J.E. Drinan) Pumping, 2001; (with J.E. Drinan and N.E. Whiting) Transportation of Hazardous Materials: A Practical Guide to Compliance, 2001; Advanced Level, 2001; The Handbook for Waterworks Operator Certification, 2001; Pumping, 2001; (with J. Drinan) Piping and Valves, 2001; Transportation of Hazardous Materials Post-9/11, 2007; (with N.E. Whiting) Environmental Management of Concentrated Animal Feeding Operations (CAFOs), 2007; Water Infrastructure Protection and Homeland Security, 2007; (with R.M. Bieber) Occupational Safety and Health Simplified for the Food Manufacturing Industry, 2008; (with R.M. Bieber) Chemical Infrastructure Protection and Homeland Security, 2009; (with N.E. Whiting) Handbook of Safety Engineering Principles and Applications, 2010; (with R.M. Bieber) Energy Infrastructure Protection and Homeland Security, 2010; (with R.M. Bieber) Encyclopedia of Environmental Health and Science, 2010. OTHERS: (with J.E. Drinan) Blueprint Reading, 2002; Handbook of Water and Wastewater Treatment Plant Operations, 2003, 2nd ed., 2009; (ed. with J.E. Drinan) Stormwater Discharge Management: A Practical Guide to Compliance, 2003; Mathematics Manual for Water and Wastewater Treatment Plant Operators, 2004; (with N.E. Whiting) Environmental Engineer's Mathematics Handbook, 2005; Chemistry for Non-Chemists: Principles and Applications for Environmental Practitioners, 2006; Industrial Hygiene Simplified: A Guide to Anticipation, Recognition, Evaluation and Control of Workplace Hazards, 2006; Biology for Non- Biologists, 2007; Ecology for Non-Ecologists, 2008; Food Supply Protection and Homeland Security, 2008; Geology for Nongeologists, 2009; Physics for Non-Physicists, 2009; Occupational Safety and Health Simplified for the Chemical Industry, 2009; Geography for Non-Geographers, 2010; (with J. Price-Bayer) In Defense of Science: Why Scientific Literacy Matters, 2011; (with M.L. Stoudt) Nuclear Infrastructure Protection and Homeland Security, 2011; The Science of Renewable Energy,

2011; Physical Hazard Control, 2011; Forest-based Biomass Energy, 2012; Handbook of Nature, 2012. **Address:** College Of Health Sciences, School of Community And Environmental Health, Old Dominion University, 3134 Health Science Bldg., 5115 Hampton Blvd., Norfolk, VA 23529, U.S.A. **Online address:** fspellman@odu.edu

SPELLMAN, W. M. American (born United States), b. 1956. **Genres:** Theology/Religion, Politics/Government, Social Sciences. **Career:** University of North Carolina, assistant professor of history, 1988-, professor of history, Council of Public Liberal Arts Colleges, executive director. Writer. **Publications:** John Locke and the Problem of Depravity, 1988; The Latitudinarians and the Church of England, 1660-1700, 1993; John Locke, 1997; European Political Thought 1600-1700, 1998; (ed. with C.O. Ho and S.D. Sawin) Medieval and Renaissance World, 1998; (with C. Levin) Extraordinary Women of the Medieval and Renaissance World, 2000; Monarchies, 1000-2000, 2001; The Global Community: Migration and the Making of the Modern World, 2002; (with A.D. Frankforter) The West: Culture and Ideas, 2003, 2nd ed., 2009; A Concise History of the World Since 1945: States and Peoples, 2006; Uncertain Identity: International Migration Since 1945, 2008; A Short History of Western Political Thought, 2011; Death: A Short Global History, forthcoming. **Address:** Department of History, University of North Carolina, 118B Carmichael Hall, PO Box 16101, Asheville, NC 28804-8505, U.S.A. **Online address:** spellman@unca.edu

SPELMAN, Cornelia Maude. American (born United States), b. 1946. **Genres:** Children's Fiction, Children's Non-fiction, Autobiography/Memoirs, Animals/Pets, Humor/Satire, Social Commentary, Literary Criticism And History. **Career:** Roosevelt University, teacher; Loyola University, teacher. Writer. **Publications:** Talking about Child Sexual Abuse (pamphlet), 1987; After Charlotte's Mom Died, 1996; Your Body Belongs to You, 1997; Mama and Daddy Bear's Divorce, 1998; When I Feel Angry, 2000; When I Feel Scared, 2002; When I Feel Sad, 2002; When I Care about Others, 2002; When I Feel Good about Myself, 2003; When I Feel Jealous, 2003; When I Miss You, 2004; Dogs: Beensie Book, 2009; Missing, 2010; My Mother's Heart, forthcoming. **Address:** c/o Author Mail, Albert Whitman and Co., 6340 Oakton St., Morton Grove, IL 60053-2723, U.S.A. **Online address:** cornelia@corneliaspelman.com

SPELVIN, George. See **DOUGLAS, Kirk.**

SPENCE, Bill. See **SPENCE, William John Duncan.**

SPENCE, Jonathan D(ermot). American/British (born England), b. 1936. **Genres:** History, Biography. **Career:** Yale University, assistant professor of history, 1966-68, associate professor of history, 1968-71, professor, 1971-, George Burton Adams professor of history, chair, Sterling professor of history emeritus; Queens University, Wiles lecturer, 1985; Princeton University, Gauss lecturer, 1987; Peking University, visiting professor, 1987; American Historical Association, president; Council on East Asian Studies, chair. Writer. **Publications:** Tsáo Yin and the Káng-hsi Emperor; Bondservant and Master, 1966; Chūgoku o Kaeta Seiyòjin Komon, 1620-1960 in UK as The China Helpers: Western Advisers to China, 1620-1960, 1969; Emperor of China: Self-Portrait of Káng-His, 1974; (contrib. with C. Worswick) Imperial China: Photographs 1850-1912, 1978; The Death of Woman Wang, 1978; (ed. with J.E. Wills, Jr.) From Ming to Ch'ing: Conquest, Region, and Continuity in Seventeenth-Century China, 1979; (with P. Cohen and S. Levine) The Historical Precedents for Our New Regulations with China, 1980; The Gate of Heavenly Peace: The Chinese and Their Revolution, 1895-1980, 1981; The Memory Palace of Matteo Ricci, 1984; The Question of Hu (biography), 1988; (ed. with P. Cheng and M. Lestz) The Search for Modern China: A Documentary Collection, 1990, 2nd ed. 1999; Chinese Roundabout: Essays in History and Culture, 1992; God's Chinese Son: The Taping Heavenly Kingdom of Hong Xiuquan, 1996; (with A. Chin) The Chinese Century: The Photographic History of the Last Hundred Years, 1996; Wen Hua Lei Tong Yu Wen Hua Li Yong, 1997; The Chan's Great Continent: China in Western Minds, 1998; The Taiping Vision of a Christian China, 1836-1864, 1998; (contrib.) A Century in Crisis: Modernity and Tradition in the Art of Twentieth-Century China, 1998; Mao Zedong, 1999; Treason by the Book, 2001; Return to Dragon Mountain: Memories of a Late Ming Man, 2007; The Chinese and Their Revolution, 1895-1980, 2007; Chinas Weg in Die Moderne, 2008. Contributor to books. **Address:** Department of History, Yale University, 320 York St., PO Box 208324, New Haven, CT 06520-8324, U.S.A. **Online address:** jonathan.spence@yale.edu

SPENCE, William John Duncan. Also writes as Bill Spence, Kirk Ford, Jim Bowden, Hannah Cooper, Jessica Blair. British (born England), b. 1923. **Genres:** Novels, Novellas/Short Stories, Romance/Historical, Westerns/Adventure, History. **Career:** School teacher, 1940-42; Ampleforth College, store manager, 1946-77; Writer, 1977-. **Publications:** AS DUNCAN SPENCE: Dark Hell, 1959. AS BILL SPENCE: (with J. Spence) Romantic Ryedale, 1977; Harpooned: The Story of Whaling, 1980; Bomber's Moon, 1981; (with J. Spence) The Medieval Monasteries of Yorkshire, 1981; (with J. Spence) Handy Facts: North Yorkshire, 1984; Secret Squadron, 1986; (with J. Spence) Stories from Yorkshire Monasteries, 1993. AS JIM BOWDEN: The Return of the Sheriff, 1960; Waymans Ford, 1960; Two Gun Justice, 1961; Roaring Valley, 1962; Revenge in Red Springs, 1962; Black Water Canyon, 1963; Arizona Gold, 1963; Trail of Revenge, 1964; Brazos Feud, 1965; Guns along the Brazos, 1967; Gun Loose, 1969; Valley of Revenge, 1971; Trail to Texas, 1973; Thunder in Montana, 1973; Showdown in Salt Fork, 1975; Hired Gun, 1976; Incident at Bison Creek, 1977; Cap, 1978; Dollars of Death, 1979; Renegade Riders, 1980; Gunfight at Elm Creek, 1980; Shadow of Eagle Rock, 1982; Pecos Trail, 1983; Incident at Elm Creek, 1984; Hangman's Trail, 1986; Return of the Gunmen, 1988; Robbery at Glenrock, 1992; A Man Called Abe, 1993. AS FLOYD ROGERS: The Man from Cheyenne Wells, 1964; Revenge Rider, 1964; The Stage Riders, 1967; Montana Justice, 1973; Hangman's Gulch, 1974; Incident at Elk River, 1979. AS KIRK FORD: Trail to Sedalia, 1967; Feud Riders, 1974. AS HANNAH COOPER: Time Will Not Wait, 1983. AS JESSICA BLAIR: The Red Shawl, 1993; A Distant Harbour, 1993; Storm Bay, 1995; The Restless Spirit, 1996; The Other Side of the River, 1997; The Seaweed Gatherers, 1998; Portrait of Charlotte, 1999; The Locket, 2000; The Long Way Home, 2001; The Restless Heart, 2001; Time and Tide, 2002; Echoes of the Past, 2003; Secrets of the Sea, 2004; Yesterday's Dreams, 2005; Reach For Tomorrow, 2006; Dangerous Shores, 2007; Wings of Sorrow, 2008; Stay With Me, 2009; Sealed Secrets, 2010; Secrets of a Whitby Girl, 2011; The Road Below Me, 2012. **Address:** Ampleforth College, York, YO62 4ER, England. **Online address:** me@jessicablair.co.uk

SPENCER, Brent. American (born United States), b. 1952. **Genres:** Novels, Novellas/Short Stories, Plays/Screenplays, Autobiography/Memoirs, Poetry. **Career:** Stanford University, Stegner fellow, 1987-88, Jones lecturer in creative writing, 1988-91; Creighton University, director of creative writing, 1992-96, 2009-, assistant professor of creative writing, 1992-97, associate professor, 1997-2005, professor, 2005-, chair of the department 2005-08; Creighton University Press, editor, 1994-2005, coordinator of film studies, 2006-; Pennsylvania State University, faculty; University of Iowa, grad student and faculty. Writer. **Publications:** The Lost Son (novel), 1995; Are We Not Men? (short fiction), 1996; Rattlesnake Daddy, 2011. Contributor to periodicals. Works appears in anthologies. **Address:** Department of English, Creighton University, Creighton Hall 141B, Omaha, NE 68178, U.S.A. **Online address:** spencer@creighton.edu

SPENCER, Charles. British (born England), b. 1920. **Genres:** Art/Art History, Theatre, History. **Career:** Anglo-Jewish Association, director, 1956-66; Grosvenor Gallery, consultant, 1966-71; Art and Artists, consultant, 1968-71; Editions Alecto, editor, 1971-. Writer. **Publications:** Erté, 1970; Alecto Monographs, 1973; Leon Bakst, 1973; Kenneth Armitage, 1973; Ciussi 64-74, 1974; (with P. Dyer) The World of Serge Diaghilev, 1974, rev. ed., 1979; Cecil Beaton: Stage and Film Designs, 1975, rev. ed., 1994; André Volten, 1976; (with V.D. Lipman) The Immigrant Generations: Jewish Artists in Britain, 1900-1945: Essays, 1983; Left, Two, Three: A Novel of the Great Depression, 1987; Leon Bakst and the Ballets Russes, 1995. EDITOR: Decade of Printmaking, 1973; (and contrib.) The Aesthetic Movement, 1869-1890: Catalogue of an Exhibition at the Camden Arts Centre, London, 15 August-7 October 1973, 1973; (with C. Bernard) The World of Flo Ziegfeld, 1974. Contributor to journals and books. **Address:** 24 A Ashworth Rd., London, GL W9 1JY, England.

SPENCER, Colin. British (born England), b. 1933. **Genres:** Novels, Food And Wine, Gay And Lesbian Issues, Young Adult Non-fiction, Children's Non-fiction, Young Adult Fiction. **Career:** Writers Guild of Great Britain, co-chairman, 1982, chairman, 1988-90, vice-president, 1990-99; Guild of Food Writers, president, 1994-99; University of Reading, professor of international politics and strategic studies. Writer. **Publications:** NOVELS: An

Absurd Affair, 1961; Asylum, 1966; Poppy, Mandragora, and the New Sex: A Novel, 1966; Panic, 1971; How the Greeks Kidnapped Mrs. Nixon, 1974. GENERATION SERIES: Anarchists in Love, 1963 in US as The Anarchy of Love, 1967; The Tyranny of Love, 1967; Lovers in War, 1969; The Victims of Love, 1978. NONFICTION: Summer at Camber-39, 1973; Gourmet Cooking for Vegetarians, 1978; Good and Healthy, 1983; Cordon Vert: 52 Vegetarian Gourmet Dinner Party Menus, 1985; Mediterranean Vegetarian Cooking, 1986; (with T. Sanders) The Vegetarian's Healthy Diet Book, 1986; The New Vegetarian: Cooking with Style the Vegetarian Way, 1986; (with T. Sanders) The Vegetarian Kitchen: A Natural Program for Health & Nutrition, 1986; Colin Spencer's Fish Cookbook, 1986; One Course Feasts, 1986; Feast for Health: A Gourmet Guide to Good Food, 1987; Al Fresco: A Feast for Outdoor Entertaining, 1987; The Romantic Vegetarian, 1988; The Adventurous Vegetarian, 1989; Which of Us Two?: The Story of a Love Affair, 1991; Vegetable Pleasures, 1992; The Heretic's Feast: A History of Vegetarianism, 1993, rev. ed. as Vegetarianism: A History, 2002; (with C. Clifton) The Faber Book of Food, 1994; Homosexuality in History, 1995; The Vegetable Book, 1995; Green Gastronomy, 1996; The Gay Kama Sutra, 1997; British Food: An Extraordinary Thousand Years of History, 2002; From Microliths to Microwaves, 2011. Contributor to periodicals. **Address:** c/o Richard Scott Simon, Anthony Sheil Associates, 43 Doughty St., London, GL WC1N 2LF, England. **Online address:** spencerhist@aol.com

SPENCER, Duncan. American (born United States), b. 1940. **Genres:** Autobiography/Memoirs, Documentaries/Reportage, Travel/Exploration, Biography, Social Sciences. **Career:** Washington Star, reporter, 1965-81; National Endowment for the Humanities, consultant and speech writer, 1970; Fathers magazine, vice-president and managing editor, 1986-90; Roll Call (the newspaper of Capitol Hill), columnist; The Hill (Congressional weekly), columnist. **Publications:** Love Gone Wrong: The Jean Harris/Scarsdale Murder Case, 1981; (with W. Groom) Conversations with the Enemy: The Story of PFC Robert Garwood, 1983; Facing the Wall: Americans at the Vietnam Veterans Memorial, 1986; (with T.M. Booth) Paratrooper, 1994. Contributor of articles to periodicals. **Address:** 643 E Capitol St. SE, Washington, DC 20003, U.S.A. **Online address:** dcspencer9@aol.com

SPENCER, Elizabeth. American (born United States), b. 1921. **Genres:** Novels, Novellas/Short Stories, Autobiography/Memoirs, Plays/Screenplays, Young Adult Non-fiction, History, Literary Criticism And History, Adult Non-fiction, Essays. **Career:** Northwest Junior College, instructor of English, 1943-44; Ward-Belmont School, instructor of English, 1944-45; Nashville Tennessean, reporter, 1945-46; University of Mississippi, instructor in English and creative writing, 1948-51, 1952-53; Bryn Mawr College, writer-in-residence, 1962; University of North Carolina, writer-in-residence, 1969; Hollins College, writer-in-residence, 1972; Concordia University, writer-in-residence, adjunct professor, 1976-86; University of North Carolina, Chapel Hill, visiting professor of creative writing, 1986-92. **Publications:** NOVELS: Fire in the Morning, 1948; This Crooked Way, 1952; The Voice at the Back Door, 1956; The Light in the Piazza, 1960; Knights and Dragons, 1965; No Place for an Angel, 1967; The Snare, 1972; The Salt Line, 1984; The Night Travellers, 1991. SHORT STORY COLLECTIONS: Ship Island and Other Stories, 1968; The Stories of Elizabeth Spencer, 1981; Marilee, 1981; Jack of Diamonds and Other Stories, 1988; On the Gulf, 1991; The Light in the Piazza and Other Italian Tales, 1996; The Southern Woman: New and Selected Fiction, 2001. NON-FICTION: Landscapes of the Heart, 1998. Works appear in anthologies. Contributor to periodicals. **Address:** 402 Longleaf Dr., Chapel Hill, NC 27517-3042, U.S.A.

SPENCER, Irene. American (born United States), b. 1937. **Genres:** Autobiography/Memoirs, History. **Career:** Writer, memoirist and public speaker. **Publications:** Shattered Dreams: My Life as a Polygamist's Wife (memoir), 2007; Cult Insanity: A Memoir of Polygamy, Prophets, and Blood Atonement, 2009. **Address:** Center St., 237 Park Ave., New York, NY 10017-3140, U.S.A. **Online address:** irene@irenespencerbooks.com

SPENCER, John Francis Theodore. See SPENCER, John (Walter).

SPENCER, John (Walter). (John Francis Theodore Spencer). British (born England), b. 1922. **Genres:** Poetry, Language/Linguistics, Literary Criticism And History. **Career:** University of Lund, university lecturer in English, 1949-52; University of Edinburgh, faculty, 1952-56, lecturer in phonetics, 1955-56; University of Allahabad, associate professor of phonetics, 1956-58;

University of Lahore, reader in phonetics, 1958-59; University of Ibadan, Department of Phonetics, head, 1959-62; University of Leeds, faculty, 1962-82, senior lecturer in modern English; West African Language Monograph Series, editor, 1963-74; Journal of West African Languages, editor, 1964-71; Hong Kong University, professor of English, 1982-84; University of Bayreuth, professor of English language, 1984-91; University of Warwick, honorary professor of English linguistics, 1990-2000. **Publications:** (With Bhandari and Ram) An English Pronouncing Vocabulary, 1959; (with L.F. Brosnahan) Language and Society, 1962; Workers for Humanity, 1962; (with N.E. Enkvist and M. Gregory) Linguistics and Style, 1964. EDITOR: Language in Africa, 1963; (with M. Wollmann) Modern Poems for the Commonwealth, 1966; The English Language in West Africa, 1971. Contributor of articles. **Address:** Hawthorn Cottage, Blockley, GC GL56 9HF, England.

SPENCER, Jon Michael. American (born United States) **Genres:** Music, Race Relations, Theology/Religion, Art/Art History, Social Sciences, Sociology. **Career:** Duke University, Divinity School, faculty; Bowling Green State University, Department of Popular Culture, associate professor; University of North Carolina, Department of Popular Culture, professor of religious studies, African American religious music; University of Richmond, Tyler and Alice Haynes professor of American Studies and professor of music, now retired. Writer. **Publications:** As the Black School Sings: Black Music Collections at Black Universities and Colleges with a Union List of Book Holdings, 1987; (comp.) Sacred Symphony: The Chanted Sermon of the Black Preacher, 1987; Protest & Praise: Sacred Music of Black Religion, 1990; Theological Music: Introduction to Theomusicology, 1991; Black Hymnody: A Hymnological History of the African-American Church, 1992; Blues and Evil, 1993; The Rhythms of Black Folk: Race, Religion, and Pan-Africanism, 1995; Sing a New Song: Liberating Black Hymnody, 1995; Researching Black Music, 1996; Self-Made & Blues-Rich, 1996; The New Negroes and Their Music: The Success of the Harlem Renaissance, 1997; The New Colored People: The Mixed-Race Movement in America, 1997, rev. ed., 2000; In Search of Elvis: Music, Race, Art, Religion, 1997; Tribes of Benjamin, 1999. Contributor to books and periodicals. **Address:** Africa World Press Inc., 541 W Ingham Ave., Ste. B, PO Box 1892, Trenton, NJ 08638-5001, U.S.A.

SPENCER, Mark. American (born United States), b. 1956. **Genres:** Novellas/Short Stories, Novels, History. **Career:** Southwest Missouri State University, assistant professor of English, 1983-87; Cameron University, assistant professor of English, 1987-92, associate professor, 1992-99, professor and chair, 1999; University of Arkansas, professor of English, 2005-, School of Arts and Humanities, dean, 2005-. Writer. **Publications:** Spying on Lovers (short stories), 1988; Wedlock, 1989; Love and Reruns in Adams County: A Novel, 1994; The Weary Motel (novel), 2000; Images of America: Monticello (history), 2011; A Haunted Love Story (nonfiction novel), 2011; The Masked Demon (novel), 2012. **Address:** School of Arts and Humanities, University of Arkansas, PO Box 3460, Monticello, AR 71656, U.S.A. **Online address:** spencer@uamont.edu

SPENCER, Paul. British (born England), b. 1932. **Genres:** Anthropology/Ethnology, Area Studies, Dance/Ballet, Demography, Gerontology/Senior Issues, Sociology. **Career:** Tavistock Institute, Institute for Operational Research, researcher, 1962-71, representative, 1967-68; University of London, School of Oriental and African Studies, lecturer, 1971-82, senior lecturer, 1982-88, reader, 1988-93, professor of African anthropology, 1988-97, professor emeritus, 1997-, International African Institute, honorary director, 1996-. Writer. **Publications:** The Samburu: A Study of Gerontocracy in a Nomadic Tribe, 1965; General Practice and Models of the Referral Process, 1971; Nomads in Alliance: Symbiosis and Growth among the Rendille and Samburu of Kenya, 1973; The Maasai of Matapato: A Study of Rituals of Rebellion, 1988; The Pastoral Continuum: The Marginalization of Tradition in East Africa, 1998; Time, Space and the Unknown: Maasai Configurations of Power and Providence, 2003. EDITOR: Society and the Dance: The Social Anthropology of Process and Performance, 1985; Anthropology and the Riddle of the Sphinx: Paradoxes of Change in Life Course, 1990. **Address:** School of Oriental and African Studies, University of London, Thornhaugh St., Russell Sq., London, GL WC1H 0XG, England. **Online address:** paul.spencer100@googlemail.com

SPENCER, Robert H. American (born United States), b. 1950. **Genres:** Business/Trade/Industry, Administration/Management, Environmental Sciences/Ecology. **Career:** U.S. Department of Defense, systems design, programmer and analyst, 1970-84; Condominium Realty Corp., real estate broker

and developer, 1975-80; U.S. Navy, software analyst and design, 1980-84; University of West Florida, associate professor, Department of Accounting and Information Technology, adjunct professor, 1983-97; Saltmarsh, Cleaveland and Gund (public accountants), principal and consultant, 1984-95; author, 1985-; Novell Corp., staff, 1992; Monsanto Employees Credit Union, executive vice president, 1995-96; Twenty Seconds in the Future, writer and educator, 1996-; Microsoft Corp., consultant, 1997; K2 Enterprises, associate. **Publications:** Client/Server Accounting: Reengineering Financial Systems, 1997; (with A.E. Davis) The Year 2000 Problem and the Legal Profession: Managing the Risks, 1998; (with A.E. Davis and M. Gordon) Risk Management: A CPA's Toolkit for a Changing Environment, 2001; (with R.P. Johnson) Technology Best Practices, 2002; (with R.P. Johnson) Accounting Software Solutions, 2003. Contributor of articles to periodicals. **Address:** 1522 Knob Hill Rd., Elizabethtown, KY 42701, U.S.A. **Online address:** bob@bobspencer.com

SPENCER, Scott. American (born United States), b. 1945. **Genres:** Novels, Literary Criticism And History, Young Adult Fiction. **Career:** Writer. **Publications:** Last Night at the Brain Thieves Ball, 1973; Preservation Hall, 1976; Endless Love, 1979; Waking the Dead, 1986; Magic Room, 1987; Secret Anniversaries, 1990; Men in Black, 1995; The Rich Man's Table, 1998; A Ship Made of Paper, 2003; Willing, 2008; ZBrush Character Creation: Advanced Digital Sculpting, 2008; Man in the Woods, 2010. Contributor of stories and articles to periodicals. **Address:** Janklow & Nesbit Associates, 445 Park Ave., 13th Fl., New York, NY 10022, U.S.A.

SPENCER, Stuart S. American (born United States), b. 1957. **Genres:** Theatre, How-to Books, Plays/Screenplays. **Career:** Sarah Lawrence College, faculty, 1991-. Writer. **Publications:** (With M. McDuffee) Arrayed for the Bridal, Trifocal, 1998; Plays by Stuart Spencer, 2000; The Playwright's Guidebook, 2002. **Address:** Rosenstone/Adams L.L.C., 448 W 44 St., New York, NY 10036, U.S.A. **Online address:** stuartspencer@nyc.rr.com

SPENCER, Wen. (Wendy Kosak). American (born United States), b. 1963?. **Genres:** Politics/Government. **Career:** Medical researcher and writer. **Publications:** Alien Taste, 2001; Tainted Trail, 2002; Bitter Waters, 2003; Tinker, 2003; Dog Warrior, 2004; A Brother's Price, 2005; Wolf Who Rules, 2006; Endless Blue, 2007. Works appear in anthologies. **Address:** Outside Boston, MA, U.S.A. **Online address:** wen_spencer@livejournal.com

SPENCER, William Browning. American (born United States), b. 1946. **Genres:** Novels, Science Fiction/Fantasy, Psychology, Young Adult Fiction. **Career:** Freelance graphic artist and writer. **Publications:** Maybe I'll Call Anna (novel), 1990; The Return of Count Electric and Other Stories, 1993; Résumé with Monsters, 1995; Zod Wallop, 1995; Irrational Fears, 1998; Resume with Monsters, 2000; The Ocean and All Its Devices, 2005. **Address:** c/o Jonathan Matson, Harold Matson Company Inc., 276 5th Ave., New York, NY 10001-4509, U.S.A. **Online address:** zodwallop1@netzero.net

SPENDER, Matthew. Italian/British (born England), b. 1945?. **Genres:** Art/Art History, Travel/Exploration. **Career:** Writer and artist. **Publications:** (With P. Rylands) Arshile Gorky: Works on Paper, 1992; Within Tuscany: Reflections on a Time and Place, 1993; (co-author) Arshile Gorky and the Genesis of Abstraction: Drawings from the Early 1930s, 1994; From a High Place: A Life of Arshile Gorky, 1999; (with G. Cordoni) La Grazia Indifesa: Ventotto Sculture Di Matthew Spender, 2000; (ed.) Arshile Gorky: Goats on the Roof: A Life in Letters and Documents, 2009. **Address:** Alfred A. Knopf Inc., Random House, 299 Park Ave., New York, NY 10171-0002, U.S.A.

SPENS, Christiana. Australian (born Australia), b. 1987?. **Genres:** Novels, Literary Criticism And History. **Career:** Writer. **Publications:** The Wrecking Ball: A Novel, 2008; The Socialite Manifesto, 2009. Works appear in anthologies. Contributor of articles to journals and periodicals. **Address:** c/o Caroline Hardman, The Marsh Agency Ltd., 50 Albemarle St., London, GL W1S 4BD, England.

SPENSER, Jay P. American (born United States), b. 1952. **Genres:** Air/Space Topics, History. **Career:** Smithsonian Institution, National Air and Space Museum, assistant curator, 1975-86; freelance writer, 1986-87, 1989-; Museum of Flight, staff, 1987-89; Boeing, technical writer, 1990-. Historian. **Publications:** Aeronca C-2: The Story of the Flying Bathtub, 1978; Bellanca C.F.: The Emergence of the Cabin Monoplane in the United States, 1982; Moskito, 1983; Focke-Wulf FW 190, Workhorse of the Luftwaffe, 1987; Vertical Challenge: The Hiller Aircraft Story, 1992; Whirlybirds: A History of the U.S. Helicopter Pioneers, 1998; (with J. Sutter) 747: Creating the World's First Jumbo Jet and Other Adventures from a Life in Aviation, 2006; The Airplane: How Ideas Gave Us Wings, 2008. **Address:** Seattle, WA , U.S.A. **Online address:** jay@jayspenser.com

SPERBER, Jonathan. American (born United States), b. 1952. **Genres:** History. **Career:** Leo Baeck Institute, archivist, 1979-82; Northwestern University, visiting assistant professor, 1982-84; University of Missouri, assistant professor, 1984-87, associate professor, 1987-92, professor of history, 1992-2003, curators' professor of history, 2003-, department chair, 2005; German Academic Exchange Service, Graduate student fellow, 1976-78, summer research fellow, 1986, 1999; John Simon Guggenheim Memorial Foundation, visiting research fellow & fellow, 1988-89. Writer. **Publications:** Popular Catholicism in Nineteenth-Century Germany, 1984; Rhineland Radicals: The Democratic Movement and the Revolution of 1848-1849, 1991; The European Revolutions, 1848-1851, 1994, 2nd ed., 2005; The Kaiser's Voters: Electors and Elections in Imperial Germany, 1997; Revolutionary Europe, 1780-1850, 2000; (ed. with D. Dowe, H.G. Haupt and D. Langewiesche) Europe in 1848, Revolution and Reform, 2002; (ed.) Germany, 1800-1870, 2004; Property and Civil Society in South-Western Germany, 1820-1914, 2005; Europe, 1850-1914: Progress, Participation and Apprehension, 2009. Contributor to periodicals. **Address:** Department of History, University of Missouri, 101 Read Hall, Columbia, MO 65211-7500, U.S.A. **Online address:** sperberj@missouri.edu

SPERLING, Daniel. American (born United States), b. 1951. **Genres:** Transportation. **Career:** Peace Corps, city planner, 1973-75; Environmental Protection Agency, environmental scientist, 1976-77; University of California, assistant professor, 1982-87, associate professor, 1987-91, professor, 1991-, Energy Efficiency Center, associated director, 2006-, Energy Initiative, co-director, 2006-07. Writer. **Publications:** (With A. Kanafani) National Transportation Planning, 1982; New Transportation Fuels: A Strategic Approach to Technological Change, 1988; (ed.) Alternative Transportation Fuels: An Environmental and Energy Solution, 1989; (with M.A. Delucchi, P.M. Davis and A.F. Burke) Future Drive: Electric Vehicles and Sustainable Transportation, 1995; (ed. with S.A. Shaheen) Transportation and Energy: Strategies for a Sustainable Transportation System, 1995; (ed. with J.S. Cannon) The Hydrogen Energy Transition: Moving toward the Post Petroleum Age in Transportation, 2004; (with J.E. Hughes and C.R. Knittel) Evidence of a Shift in the Short-run Price Elasticity of Gasoline Demand, 2006; (ed. with J.S. Cannon) Driving Climate Change: Cutting Carbon from Transportation, 2007; (with D. Gordon) Two Billion Cars: Driving toward Sustainability, 2009. **Address:** Institute of Transportation Studies, University of California, 2028 Academic Surge, 1 Shields Ave., Davis, CA 95616, U.S.A. **Online address:** dsperling@ucdavis.edu

SPERLING, L(es) H. American (born United States), b. 1932. **Genres:** Chemistry, Sciences, Young Adult Fiction. **Career:** Buckeye Cellulose Corp., research chemist, 1958-65; Princeton University, fellow, 1965-67; Lehigh University, senior staff, associate professor of chemical engineering, professor of chemical engineering, 1967-2002, professor emeritus, 2002-, Center for Polymer Science and Engineering, Education Committee, co-chairman. Writer. **Publications:** (Ed.) Recent Advances in Polymer Blends, Grafts and Blocks, 1974; Polymer Blends and Composites, 1976; Interpenetrating Polymer Networks, 1981; (ed. with C.E. Carraher) Polymer Applications of Renewable Resource Materials, 1983; Introduction to Physical Polymer Science, 1986, 4th ed., 2006; (ed. with D.R. Paul) Multicomponent Polymer Materials, 1986; (ed.) Sound and Vibration Damping with Polymers, 1990; Fruit Wine: A Home Winemaker's Guide to Making Wine from Fruits, 1993; (ed. with D.L. Lohse and T.P. Russell) Interfacial Aspects of Multicomponent Polymer Materials, 1997; (ed. with S.C. Kim) IPNs Around the World: Science and Engineering, 1997; Polymeric Multicomponent Materials: An Introduction, 1997; Adventurous Home Wine Maker, 2007. **Address:** Lehigh University, 5 E Packer Ave., Bethlehem, PA 18015, U.S.A. **Online address:** lhs0@lehigh.edu

SPICER, Michael. British (born England), b. 1943. **Genres:** Mystery/Crime/Suspense, Young Adult Fiction. **Career:** Economic Models Ltd., managing director, 1969-74; British Parliament, minister for trade and consumer affairs, 1979-81, parliamentary under-secretary of state for transport 1984-87, minister for aviation, 1984-87, minister for coal and electricity, 1987-90, minister for housing, 1990; Conservative Parliamentary Party, vice-chair 1981-83, deputy chair 1983-84, chairman, 2001-10, chairman finance and audit committee, 2007-10. Writer. **Publications:** Final Act, 1980; Prime Minister Spy, 1983; Cotswold Manners, 1987; The Cotswold Murders (mystery novel), 1990; Cotswold Mistress, 1992; Cotswold Moles, 1993; A Treaty Too Far, 1993; Challenge of the East-Rebirth of the West, 1996. **Address:** House of Commons, London, GL SW1A 0AA, England.

SPICER, Ron. *See* **KELLY, Ronald.**

SPICHER KASDORF, Julia. *See* **KASDORF, Julia.**

SPIEGEL, David. American (born United States), b. 1945. **Genres:** Medicine/Health, Psychology, Psychiatry. **Career:** Harvard College, resident tutor and premedical advisor, 1972-74; Stanford University, School of Medicine, clinical instructor in psychiatry, 1974-75, Department of Psychiatry and Behavioral Sciences, acting assistant professor of psychiatry and behavioral sciences, 1975-76, assistant professor of psychiatry and behavioral sciences, 1976-82, associate professor of psychiatry and behavioral sciences, 1982-91, professor of psychiatry and behavioral sciences, 1991-2002, associate chair, 1997-, associate chair of psychiatry and behavioral sciences, 2000-, Jack, Lulu and Sam Willson professor, 2002-, Medical Center, Psychiatric Inpatient Therapeutic Community, Psychiatry Clinic, director, 1980-89, associate director, 1981-83, Stanford University Clinic, medical director, 1986-87, Faculty Medical Psychotherapy Clinic, director, 1989-96, Stanford Center for Integrative Medicine, medical director, 1997-; San Mateo County Mental Health Program, staff psychiatrist, 1974-75; Palo Alto Veterans Administration Medical Center, Brief Treatment Inpatient Unit, chief, 1975-76, Social Psychiatry/Community Services, director, 1976-80; University of California, associate research psychiatrist, 1986-91; U.S. Department of Veterans Affairs Medical Center, physician and consultant, 1994-. Writer. **Publications:** (With H. Spiegel) Trance and Treatment: Clinical Uses of Hypnosis, 1978, 2nd ed., 2004; Living Beyond Limits: New Hope and Help for Facing Life-Threatening Illness, 1993; (with C. Classen) Group Therapy for Cancer Patients: A Research-Based Handbook of Psychosocial Care, 2000; (co-author) Everyone's Guide to Cancer Survivorship: A Road Map for Better Health, 2007. EDITOR AND CONTRIBUTOR: Dissociative Disorders: A Clinical Review, 1993; Dissociation: Culture, Mind and Body, 1994; Efficacy and Cost-Effectiveness of Psychotherapy, 1999; (with R.J. Moore) Cancer, Culture and Communication, 2004; (with J. Lake) Complementary and Alternative Treatments in Mental Health Care, 2007; (with E. Vermetten and M.J. Dorahy) Traumatic Dissociation: Neurobiology and Treatment, 2007. Contributor to books and journals. **Address:** Department of Psychiatry and Behavioral Sciences, School of Medicine, Stanford University, 401 Quarry Rd., Stanford, CA 94305-5718, U.S.A. **Online address:** dspiegel@stanford.edu

SPIEGELMAN, Annie. American (born United States) **Genres:** Film, Homes/Gardens, Adult Non-fiction, Agriculture/Forestry, Biography. **Career:** Writer and film director. **Publications:** Annie's Garden Journal: Reflections on Roses, Weeds, Men, and Life, 1996; Dear Jack-I'll Be with You When the Sky Is Full of Colors, 2001; Growing Seasons: Half-baked Garden Tips, Cheap Advice on Marriage, and Questionable Theories on Motherhood, 2003; Talking Dirt: The Dirt Diva's Down-to-Earth Guide to Organic Gardening, 2010; The Dirt Diva's Almanac, forthcoming. **Address:** Fredrica S. Friedman & Company Inc., 136 E 57th St., 14th Fl., New York, NY 10022-2940, U.S.A. **Online address:** annie@dirtdiva.com

SPIEGELMAN, Ian. American (born United States), b. 1974. **Genres:** Young Adult Non-fiction, Novels. **Career:** Queens Courier, staff; New York Magazine, staff writer; New York Post, reporter; Details Magazine, contributing editor. Journalist. **Publications:** Everyone's Burning: A Novel, 2003; Welcome to Yesterday: A Novel, 2006; (with A. Raymond) How to Rig an Election: Confessions of a Republican Operative, 2008. **Address:** c/o Joseph Regal, Regal Literary Inc., The Capitol Bldg., 236 W 26th St., Ste. 801, New York, NY 10001, U.S.A. **Online address:** ian@ianspiegelman.com

SPIEGELMAN, Peter. American (born United States) **Genres:** Novels. **Career:** Writer. **Publications:** Black Maps, 2003; Death's Little Helpers, 2005; Red Cat, 2007; (ed.) Wall Street Noir, 2007; Thick as Thieves, 2011. **Address:** c/o Author Mail, Knopf Publishing, 1745 Broadway, New York, NY 10019, U.S.A. **Online address:** peter@peterspiegelman.com

SPIEGELMAN, Willard. American (born United States), b. 1944. **Genres:** Literary Criticism And History. **Career:** Southern Methodist University,

Hughes professor of English, 1971-; Southwest Review, editor-in-chief, 1984-. **Publications:** Wordsworth's Heroes, 1985; The Didactic Muse: Scenes of Instruction in Contemporary American Poetry, 1989; Majestic Indolence: English Romantic Poetry and the Work of Art, 1995; (ed.) Love, Amy: The Selected Letters of Amy Clampitt, 2005; How Poets See the World: The Art of Description in Contemporary Poetry, 2005. (ed. with J. Hedley and N. Halpern) In the Frame: Women's Ekphrastic Poetry from Marianne Moore to Susan Wheeler, 2009; Seven Pleasures: Essays on Ordinary Happiness, 2009; Imaginative Transcripts: Selected Literary Essays, 2009. Contributor to periodicals. **Address:** Department of English, Southern Methodist University, PO Box 750435, Dallas, TX 75275-0435, U.S.A. **Online address:** wspiegel@smu.edu

SPIELBERG, Peter. American/Austrian (born Austria), b. 1929. **Genres:** Novels, Literary Criticism And History, Young Adult Fiction. **Career:** University of Buffalo (now State University of New York at Buffalo), instructor in English, 1958-61; City University of New York, Brooklyn College, assistant professor, 1961, professor of English and American literature and creative writing, now professor emeritus. Writer. **Publications:** (Comp. and intro.) James Joyce's Manuscripts & Letters at the University of Buffalo, 1962; (with S. Galin) Reference Books: How to Select and Use Them, 1969; Bedrock: A Work of Fiction Composed of Fifteen Scenes from My Life, 1973; Twiddledum Twaddledum, 1974; (ed. with J. Baumbach) Statements 2: New Fiction, 1977; The Hermetic Whore, 1977; Crash-Landing: A Novel, 1985; Hearsay, 1992; Noctambulists and Other Fictions, 2001; The New Abolitionists: (Neo) Slave Narratives and Contemporary Prison Writings, 2005. CONTRIBUTOR: Joyce's Portrait: Criticisms and Critiques, 1962; Modern Occasions, 1966; Statements 1: New Fiction, 1975. Contributor to periodicals. **Address:** Department of English, Brooklyn College, City University of New York, Rm. 208, Boylan Hall, 2900 Bedford Ave., Brooklyn, NY 11210-2850, U.S.A.

SPIER, Peter (Edward). American/Dutch (born Netherlands), b. 1927. **Genres:** Children's Fiction, Illustrations. **Career:** Elsevier's Weekblad, junior editor, 1949-51; Elsevier Publishing, junior editor, 1951-52; Author and illustrator, 1952-. **Publications:** SELF-ILLUSTRATED: Hurrah, We're Outward Bound!, 1968; Of Dikes and Windmills, 1970; Gobble, Growl, Grunt, 1971; Crash! Bang! Boom!, 1972; Fast-Slow, High-Low: A Book of Opposites, 1972; The Star-Spangled Banner, 1973; Tin Lizzie, 1975; Noah's Ark, 1977; Bored--Nothing to Do!, 1978; Oh, Were They Ever Happy!, 1978; The Legend of New Amsterdam, 1979; People, 1980; The Pet Store, 1981; My School, 1981; The Fire House, 1981; The Food Market, 1981; The Toy Shop, 1981; Bill's Service Station, 1981; Rain, 1982; Peter Spier's Christmas!, 1983; Peter Spier's Little Bible Storybooks, 1983; Peter Spier's Little Cats, 1984; Peter Spier's Little Dogs, 1984; Peter Spier's Little Ducks, 1984; Peter Spier's Little Rabbits, 1984; (and reteller) The Book of Jonah, 1985; Dreams, 1986; Peter Spier's Advent Calendar: Silent Night, Holy Night, 1987; We the People: The Story of the U.S. Constitution, 1987; Peter Spier's Little Animal Books, 1987; Trucks That Dig and Dump, Random House, 1988; Here Come the Fire Trucks, Random House, 1988; Big Trucks, Little Trucks, Random House, 1988; Fast Cars, Slow Cars, Random House, 1988; Pop-Up Peter Spier's Birthday Cake, 1990; Peter Spier's Circus, 1991; Father, May I Come?, 1992; Doubleday, 1993. Contributor to periodicals. **Address:** Warden Cliff Rd., PO Box 210, Shoreham, NY 11786, U.S.A.

SPIERENBURG, Pieter (Cornelis). Dutch (born Netherlands), b. 1948. **Genres:** History, Criminology/True Crime. **Career:** Teacher, 1973-74; University of Amsterdam, faculty, 1978; International Association for the History of Crime and Criminal Justice, secretary, 1978-; Posthumus Institute, program on Group Cultures, research director, 1993-2005; Erasmus University, staff, 1977-, professor of historical criminology and law faculty, 2005-, faculty of history and Art, senior lecturer. Writer. **Publications:** The Spectacle of Suffering: Executions and the Evolution of Repression, from a Preindustrial Metropolis to the European Experience, 1984; Verbroken betovering: mentaliteitsgeschiedenis van preïndustrieel Europa, 1988; The Broken Spell, 1988; The Prison Experience: Disciplinary Institutions and Their Inmates in Early Modern Europe, 1991; Zwarte schapen: Losbollen, Dronkaards en Levensgenieters in a Achttiende-Eeuwse Beterhuizen, 1995; Written in Blood: Fatal Attraction in Enlightenment Amsterdam, 2004; History of Murder: Personal Violence in Europe from the Middle Ages to the Present, 2008. EDITOR: The Emergence of Carceral Institutions: Prisons, Galleys, and Lunatic Asylums, 1550-1900, 1984; (with C.Fijnaut) Scherp toezicht, 1990; (with A. Schuurman) Private Domain, Public Inquiry: Families and Life-Styles in the Netherlands and Europe, 1550 to the Present, 1996; Men and Violence: Gender,

Honor and Rituals in Modern Europe and America, 1998; (with S. Body-Gendrot) Violence in Europe: Historical and Contemporary Perspectives, 2008; (with L. Mucchielli) Histoire de l'homicide en Europe, 2009. **Address:** Department of History, Erasmus University, PO Box 1738, Rotterdam, 3000, Netherlands. **Online address:** spierenburg@fhk.eur.nl

SPIERLING, Karen E. American (born United States), b. 1970. **Genres:** History, Humanities. **Career:** University of Wisconsin, teaching assistant, 1996, 2001; University of Louisville, Department of History, assistant professor, 2001-07, associate professor, 2007-. Writer. **Publications:** Infant Baptism in Reformation Geneva: The Shaping of a Community, 1536-1564, 2005; (with M.J. Halvorson) Defining Community in Early Modern Europe, 2008. Contributor to journals. **Address:** Department of History, University of Louisville, 103B Gottschalk Hall, Louisville, KY 40292, U.S.A. **Online address:** spierling@louisville.edu

SPIERS, Edward M(ichael). British (born England), b. 1947. **Genres:** History, Military/Defense/Arms Control, Biography. **Career:** ICI Fibres, market research executive, 1970-71; City of London Polytechnic, lecturer, 1974-75; Edinburgh District Council, councilor, 1974; University of Leeds, defense lecturer, 1975-85, lecturer, 1985-87, reader, 1987-93, Leverhulme research fellow, 1991-92, professor of strategic studies, 1993-, School of History, chairman, 1994-97, Faculty of Arts, dean of research, 1999-2002, pro-dean of research, 2006-; University of Alberta, visiting lecturer, 1987; British Army, chief examiner, 1992-2002; South Africa's National Research Foundation, external reviewer, 2007; Asian Human Rights Commission, staff, 2009. Writer. **Publications:** Haldane: An Army Reformer, 1980; The Army and Society 1815-1914, 1980; Radical General: Sir George de Lacy Evans, 1787-1870, 1983; Chemical Warfare, 1986; Chemical Weaponry, 1989; The Late Victorian Army, 1868-1902, 1992; Chemical and Biological Weapons: A Study of Proliferation, 1994; (ed.) Sudan: The Reconquest Reappraised, 1998; Weapons of Mass Destruction: Prospects for Proliferation, 2000; The Victorian Soldier in Africa, 2004; Scottish Soldier and Empire, 1854-1902, 2006; Letters from Ladysmith, 2010; A History of Chemical and Biological Weapons, 2010; The Learning Curve in the South African War: Soldiers Perspectives in Historia, forthcoming; The Highland Soldier: Imperial Impact and Image, forthcoming. **Address:** School of History, University of Leeds, Michael Sadler Bldg., Leeds, WY LS2 9JT, England. **Online address:** e.m.spiers@leeds.ac.uk

SPIKES, Daniel. French/American (born United States), b. 1953. **Genres:** Third World, Politics/Government, Military/Defense/Arms Control, History. **Career:** Teacher in special education; Moulin de l'Auro, accountant and chief financial officer. Writer. **Publications:** Angola and the Politics of Intervention: From Local Bush War to Chronic Crisis in Southern Africa, 1993. **Address:** Chemin de la Muscadelle, Isle sur Sorgue, 84800, France.

SPILLANE, Mickey. *See* COLLINS, Max Allan.

SPINDLER, George Dearborn. American (born United States), b. 1920. **Genres:** Anthropology/Ethnology, Education, Psychology, Social Sciences, Cultural/Ethnic Topics, Young Adult Non-fiction. **Career:** Stanford University, School of Education, assistant professor, 1952-55, associate professor, 1955-60, professor, 1960-78, emeritus professor of anthropology and education, 1978-; Center for Advanced Study in the Behavioral Sciences, fellow, 1956-57; Harvard University, Burton lecturer, 1957; Holt, Rinehart and Winston, series editor, 1960-, consulting editor, 1965; San Francisco State College (now San Francisco State University), Edith P. Merritt Lecturer, 1969. Writer. **Publications:** Menomini Acculturation, 1955; Sociocultural and Psychological Processes in Menomini Acculturation, 1955; Transmission of American Culture, 1959; (with A. Beals and L. Spindler) Culture in Process, 1967, 2nd ed., 1973; (with L. Spindler) Dreamers without Power: The Menomini Indians, 1971; Burgbach: Urbanization and Identity in a German Village, 1973; (with L. Spindler, H. Trueba and M.D. Williams) The American Cultural Dialogue and its Transmission, 1990; (with M.M. Suarez-Orozco and L. Spindler) The Making of Psychological Anthropology II, 1994; (with L. Spindler) Fifty Years of Anthropology and Education 1950-2000: A Spindler Anthology, 2000. EDITOR: Education and Anthropology, 1955; (and contrib.) Education and Culture, 1963; (and contrib.) Being an Anthropologist, 1970; (and contrib.) Education and Cultural Process: Toward an Anthropology of Education, 1974, 3rd ed., 1997; (with L. Spindler) Native North American

Cultures: Four Cases, 1977; (with L. Spindler) Cultures around the World, 1977; (with L. Spindler) Urban Anthropology in the United States: Four Cases: Chicano Prisoners, Black Families in Chicago, Portland Longshoremen, Fun City, 1978; The Making of Psychological Anthropology, 1978; Doing the Ethnography of Schooling: Educational Anthropology in Action, 1982; Education and Cultural Process: Anthropological Approaches, 1987, 3rd ed., 1997; (with L. Spindler) Interpretive Ethnography of Education at Home and Abroad, 1987; (with H.T. Trueba and L. Spindler) What do Anthropologists have to Say about Dropouts?, 1989; (with L. Spindler) Pathways to Cultural Awareness, 1994; (with L. Hammond) Innovations in Educational Ethnography: Theory, Methods and Results, 2006; (with J.E. Stockard) Globalization and Change in Fifteen Cultures: Born in One World, Living in Another, 2007. **Address:** Department of Anthropological Sciences, Stanford University, Rm. 361D, Main Quad, Bldg. 360, 450 Serra Mall, PO Box 3096, Stanford, CA 94305-2117, U.S.A. **Online address:** geospinner@aol.com

SPINELLI, Jerry. American (born United States), b. 1941. **Genres:** Young Adult Fiction, Young Adult Non-fiction, Children's Fiction, Picture/Board Books, Novels. **Career:** Chilton Co. (magazine publishers), editor, 1966-89. **Publications:** Space Station Seventh Grade, 1982; Who Put That Hair in My Toothbrush?, 1984; Night of the Whale, 1985; Jason and Marceline, 1986; Dump Days, 1988; The Bathwater Gang, 1990; Maniac Magee, 1990; Fourth Grade Rats, 1991; Report to the Principal's Office, 1991; There's a Girl in My Hammerlock, 1991; School Daze: Report to the Principal's Office, 1991; The Bathwater Gang Gets down to Business, 1992; Do the Funky Pickle, 1992; Who Ran My Underwear up the Flagpole?, 1992; Picklemania, 1993; Tooter Pepperday, 1995; Crash, 1996; In My Own Words, 1997; The Library Card, 1997; Wringer, 1997; Blue Ribbon Blues, 1998; Knots in My Yo-Yo String, 1998; (co-author) It's Fine to Be Nine, 2000; Stargirl, 2000; Loser, 2002; The Mighty Crashman, 2002; Milkweed, 2003; My Daddy and Me, 2003; Eggs, 2007; Love, Stargirl, 2007; Smiles to Go, 2008; (with E. Spinelli) Today I Will: A Year of Quotes, Notes, and Promises to Myself, 2009; I Can be Anything!, 2010. Contributor to books. Works appear in anthologies. **Address:** 319 Shaker Ln., West Chester, PA 19380, U.S.A. **Online address:** jerry@jerryspinelli.com

SPINK, Ian. See Obituaries.

SPINNER, Jackie. American (born United States) **Genres:** Novels, Writing/Journalism. **Career:** Washington Post, military affairs correspondent, staff writer, 1995-2009; Angel Says: Read, founder and executive director; The American University of Iraq, AUI-S Voice, director of media relations; Sultan Qaboos University, faculty, 2010-11, Al Mir'ah, founder; Columbia College Chicago, Department of Journalism, assistant professor. **Publications:** (With J. Spinner) Tell Them I Didn't Cry: A Young Journalist's Story of Joy, Loss, and Survival in Iraq, 2006. **Address:** c/o Jeff Kleinman, Folio Literary Management L.L.C., 505 8th Ave., Ste. 603, New York, NY 10018-4629, U.S.A. **Online address:** jspinner@colum.edu

SPINOSA, Tony. See **COLEMAN, Reed Farrel.**

SPITZ, Bob Stephen. (Robert Stephen Spitz). American (born United States) **Genres:** Sports/Fitness, Recreation, Food And Wine, Biography, Essays. **Career:** The New School, teacher of rock music. Writer and screenwriter. **Publications:** NONFICTION: (as Robert Stephen Spitz) Barefoot in Babylon: The Creation of the Woodstock Music Festival, 1969, 1979, rev. ed. as Bob Spitz, 1989; The Making of Superstars: Artists and Executives of the Rock Music Business, 1978; Dylan: A Biography, 1989; Shoot Out the Lights: The Amazing, Improbable, Exhilarating Saga of the 1969-70 New York Knicks, 1995; The Beatles: The Biography, 2005; Yeah! Yeah! Yeah!: The Beatles, Beatlemania, and the Music that Changed the World, 2007; The Saucier's Apprentice: One Long Strange Trip through the Great Cooking Schools of Europe, 2008. Contributor of articles to periodicals. **Address:** c/o Author Mail, Little Brown and Co., 1271 Ave. of the Americas, New York, NY 10020, U.S.A. **Online address:** thebeatles@bobspitz.com

SPITZ, Robert Stephen. See **SPITZ, Bob Stephen.**

SPIVACK, Charlotte. American (born United States), b. 1926. **Genres:** Literary Criticism And History, Theatre, Biography, Young Adult Fiction. **Career:** University of Missouri, instructor in English, 1952-54; College of

William and Mary, assistant professor of English, 1954-56; Fisk University, assistant professor, associate professor, 1956-64; University of Massachusetts, visiting lecturer, 1964-66, associate professor, 1967-71, professor of English, 1971-. Writer. **Publications:** (With W. Bracy) Early English Drama from the Middle Ages to the Early Seventeenth Century, 1966; George Chapman, 1967; The Comedy of Evil on Shakespeare's Stage, 1978; Ursula K. Le Guin, 1984; Merlin's Daughters: Contemporary Women Writers of Fantasy, 1987; (ed.) Merlin versus Faust: Contending Archetypes in Western Culture, 1992; Merlin: A Thousand Heroes with One Face, 1994; (with R.L. Staples) The Company of Camelot: Arthurian Characters in Romance and Fantasy, 1994; (ed. with C. Herold) Archetypal Readings of Medieval Literature, 2002. **Address:** Department of English, University of Massachusetts, 170 Bartlett Hall, PO Box 30515, Amherst, MA 01003, U.S.A.

SPIVACK, Kathleen (Romola Drucker). American (born United States), b. 1938. **Genres:** Novels, Poetry, Adult Non-fiction, Education, Novellas/Short Stories, Literary Criticism And History. **Career:** Advanced Writing Workshop, director, 1978-; University of Paris VII-VIII, visiting professor, 1991-; University of Francoise Rabelais, faculty; University of Versailles, faculty; Ecole Superieure (Polytechnique), faculty. Writer. **Publications:** Flying Inland, 1973; The Jane Poems, 1974; Swimmer in the Spreading Dawn, 1981; The Beds We Lie In: Selected and New Poems, 1986, The Honeymoon, 1986; The Breakup Variations, 2002; Moments of Past Happiness, 2007; A History of Yearning, 2010; Robert Lowell, A Personal Memoir, 2011; Unspeakable Things, forthcoming. POEMS: Penelope; Playing Ping Pong with Elizabeth Bishop; a Sestina; The Frost Farm in Derry, New Hampshire; Works appear in anthologies. Contributor to magazines. **Address:** 53 Spruce St., Watertown, MA 02472, U.S.A. **Online address:** kspivack@earthlink.net

SPIVAK, Dawnine. American (born United States) **Genres:** Children's Fiction, Biography. **Career:** Hobart and William Smith Colleges, faculty; Sterling College, faculty. Writer. **Publications:** Grass Sandals: The Travels of Basho, 1997; Winter into Spring; Inanna (theater piece); Merlin of the Wildwood; The Open World; Wild and Secret Wings, forthcoming. **Address:** Carter Rd., Lowell, VT 05847, U.S.A.

SPIVAK, Gayatri Chakravorty. American/Indian (born India), b. 1942. **Genres:** Young Adult Non-fiction, Essays, Translations. **Career:** Emory University, Longstreet professor of English; University of Pittsburgh, Andrew W. Mellon Professor of English, through 1991; Columbia University, Avalon Foundation professor in the humanities, 1991-2007, university professor, 2007-, Institute for Comparative Literature and Society, founding member. Writer. **Publications:** NONFICTION: Myself Must I Remake: The Life and Poetry of W.B. Yeats, 1974; In Other Worlds: Essays in Cultural Politics, 1987; (ed. with R. Guha) Selected Subaltern Studies, 1988; The Post-Colonial Critic: Interviews, Strategies, Dialogues, 1990; (contrib.) Inscription, 1990; Outside in the Teaching Machine, 1993; A Critique of Postcolonial Reason: Toward a History of the Vanishing Present, 1999; Death of a Discipline, 2003; Other Asias, 2008; Aesthetic Education in the Era of Globalization, 2011. TRANSLATOR: J. Derrida, Of Grammatology, 1976; (and intro.) M. Devi, Imaginary Maps, 1995; (and intro.) M. Devi, Breast Stories, 1997; M. Devi, Old Women, 1999; N. Mazumdar, Song for Kali: A Cycle of Images and Songs, 2000; (and intro.) M. Devi, Chotti Munda and His Arrow, 2002. Works appear in anthologies. Contributor to journals. **Address:** Department of English, Columbia University, 401A Interchurch Bldg., 602 Philosophy Hall, 1150 Amsterdam Ave., PO Box 4927, New York, NY 10027, U.S.A. **Online address:** gcs4@columbia.edu

SPOLLEN, Anne. American (born United States), b. 1958. **Genres:** Novels, Young Adult Non-fiction, Children's Fiction. **Career:** Writer and educator. **Publications:** The Shape of Water (young adult novel), 2008; Light beneath Ferns, 2010. Works appear in anthologies. Contributor to magazines and periodicals. **Address:** Flux, 2143 Wooddale Dr., Woodbury, MN 55125-2989, U.S.A. **Online address:** aspollen@comcast.net

SPOLTER, Pari (Dokht). American (born United States), b. 1930. **Genres:** Sciences, Astronomy, Physics. **Career:** Temple University, postdoctoral fellow, 1961-62, research fellow and instructor, 1962-65; U.S. Public Health Service Hospital, research biochemist, 1966-68; Orb Publishing Co., founder and publisher, 1988-. Writer. **Publications:** Gravitational Force of the Sun, 1993. **Address:** Orb Publishing Co., 11862 Balboa Blvd., Ste. 182, Granada Hills, CA 91344-2753, U.S.A. **Online address:** orbpublishing@msn.com

SPOONER, Mary Helen. American (born United States), b. 1951. **Genres:** History, Adult Non-fiction, Local History/Rural Topics, Humanities. **Career:** St. Louis Post Dispatch, stringer and contributor, 1976; Guatemala News, staff reporter and editor, 1977; American Broadcast Corp., staff reporter and Venezuela correspondent, 1977-79, Interpress, freelance reporter and editor, 1979, Financial Times, Chile correspondent, 1980-89; Time, staff reporter and Venezuela correspondent, 1977-79; Washington Star, staff reporter and Venezuela correspondent, 1977-79; Radio News, reporter, 1991-94. **Publications:** Soldiers in a Narrow Land: The Pinochet Regime in Chile, 1994; General's Slow Retreat: Chile after Pinochet, 2011. Contributor to journals and periodicals. **Address:** c/o Deborah Schneider, Gelfman Schneider Literary Agents Inc., 250 W 57th St., Ste. 2515, New York, NY 10107-0001, U.S.A. **Online address:** spoostep@aol.com

SPOONER, Michael. American (born United States), b. 1954. **Genres:** Poetry, Young Adult Fiction, Mythology/Folklore, Education. **Career:** ERIC Clearinghouse for Reading and Communication, assistant director and project manager, 1986-88; National Council of Teachers of English, senior editor, 1988-93; Utah State University, University Press, director, 1993-. Writer. **Publications:** A Moon in Your Lunch Box (poetry), 1993; Old Meshikee and the Little Crabs: An Ojibwe Story, 1996; Daniel's Walk: A Novel, 2001; Last Child, 2005. Entrapment: A Comedy in Chat, 2009. Contributor to books and journals. **Address:** University Press, Utah State University, 3078 Old Main Hill, Logan, UT 84322-3078, U.S.A. **Online address:** michael.spooner@usu.edu

SPRACKLAND, Jean. British (born England), b. 1962?. **Genres:** Poetry. **Career:** Bedfordshire County Council, writer-in-residence, 1998; Manchester Metropolitan University, associate lecturer, senior lecturer in creative writing, 2009-, education director of the poetry archive; Arvon Foundation, tutor; educator and writer. **Publications:** Tattoos for Mothers Day, 1997; Hard Water, 2003; (with M. Coe) Our Thoughts are Bees: Working with Writers and Schools, 2005; Ellipsis, vol. I, 2005; Tilt, 2007. **Address:** Department of English, Manchester Metropolitan University, Rm. 116, Geoffrey Manton Bldg., Manchester, M15 6LL, England. **Online address:** jean@sprackland.demon.co.uk

SPRACKLING, Michael Thomas. (M. T. Sprackling). British (born England), b. 1934?. **Genres:** Physics, Sciences, Chemistry. **Career:** King Edward VI School, assistant master, 1958-60; Queen Elizabeth College, assistant lecturer, 1960-62, lecturer, 1962-83, senior lecturer in physics, 1983-85; King's College, senior lecturer in physics, 1985-95. Writer. **Publications:** AS M.T. SPRACKLING: The Mechanical Properties of Matter, 1970; Plastic Deformation of Simple Ionic Crystals, 1976; Liquids and Solids, 1985; Thermal Physics, 1991; Heat and Thermodynamics, 1993. **Address:** 35 Princes Gardens, London, GL W3 0LX, England. **Online address:** michael@sprackling0.freeserve.co.uk

SPRACKLING, M. T. See **SPRACKLING, Michael Thomas.**

SPRAGGON, Julie. American (born United States), b. 1962. **Genres:** History. **Career:** University of London, Institute of Historical Research, deputy editor. Academic and historian. **Publications:** Puritan Iconoclasm during the English Civil War, 2003. **Address:** Institute of Historical Research, University of London, Senate House, London, GL WC1E 7HU, England. **Online address:** julie.spraggon@sas.ac.uk

SPRATFORD, Becky Siegel. American (born United States) **Genres:** How-to Books, Librarianship. **Career:** Berwyn Public Library, reference librarian, readers advisory librarian, 2000-; Dominican University, instructor, Graduate School of Library and Information Science, adjunct faculty, 2004-. Writer. **Publications:** (With T.H. Clausen) The Horror Readers' Advisory: The Librarian's Guide to Vampires, Killer Tomatoes, and Haunted Houses, 2004, 2nd ed. as The Readers' Advisory Guide to Horror, 2012. **Address:** Berwyn Public Library, 2701 S Harlem Ave., Berwyn, IL 60402-2140, U.S.A. **Online address:** becky@berwynlibrary.net

SPREIREGEN, Paul (David). American (born United States), b. 1931. **Genres:** Architecture, Urban Studies, History, Essays, Business/Trade/Industry. **Career:** Adams Howard & Greeley, Boston Government Center, urban designer, 1958-59; Downtown Progress, urban designer, 1960-62; Ball State University, Emons distinguished professor of architecture, 1973-74. Writer,

consultant and architect. **Publications:** SELF-ILLUSTRATED: Urban Design: The Architecture of Towns and Cities, 1965. OTHERS: (ed. and intro.) The Modern Metropolis: Its Origins, Form, Characteristics, and Planning: Selected Essays of Hans Blumenfeld, 1967; (ed. and intro.) On the Art of Designing Cities: Selected Essays of Elbert Peets, 1968; (with H. von Hertzen) Building a New Town: Finland's New Garden City, Tapiola, 1971, rev. ed., 1973; (ed.) Metropolis and Beyond: Selected Essays, 1979; Design Competitions, 1979; The Architecture of William Morgan, 1987; Pre-Design 2, 1991; Pre-Design 1, 1997; Pre-Design, 2005. Contributor to magazines and journals. **Address:** 2215 Observatory Pl. NW, Washington, DC 20007-1813, U.S.A. **Online address:** paulspreiregen@verizon.net

SPRENGLE, Artie. See **LERANGIS, Peter.**

SPRETNAK, Charlene. (Charlene Marie Spretnak). American (born United States), b. 1946. **Genres:** Art/Art History, Environmental Sciences/Ecology, Humanities, Intellectual History, Mythology/Folklore, Social Commentary, Theology/Religion, Women's Studies And Issues, Women's Studies And Issues. **Career:** University of California, lecturer and director of writing program, 1978-86; Holy Names College, instructor, 1985-86; California Institute of Integral Studies, professor of philosophy and religion, 1992-, visiting professor of philosophy and religion, 1993-; Green Institute, senior fellow, 2005-; Green Party of the United States, co-founder. Writer. **Publications:** Lost Goddesses of Early Greece: A Collection of Pre-Hellenic Myths, 1978, rev. ed., 1992; (ed.) The Politics of Women's Spirituality: Essays on the Rise of Spiritual Power within the Feminist Movement, 1982, rev. ed. as The Politics of Women's Spirituality: Essays by Founding Mothers of the Movement, 1994; (with F. Capra) Green Politics: The Global Promise, 1984; The Spiritual Dimension of Green Politics, 1986; States of Grace: The Recovery of Meaning in the Postmodern Age, 1991; The Resurgence of the Real: Body, Nature, and Place in a Hypermodern World, 1997; Missing Mary: The Queen of Heaven and Her Re-emergence in the Modern Church, 2004; Relational Reality, 2011. Contributor to periodicals. **Address:** PO Box 133, Ojai, CA 93024, U.S.A.

SPRETNAK, Charlene Marie. See **SPRETNAK, Charlene.**

SPRIGGS, James F. American (born United States), b. 1966. **Genres:** Law, Politics/Government. **Career:** University of California, assistant professor, 1994-2000, associate professor, 2000-06, professor of political science, 2006-, School of Law, professor, 2006-; Washington University, Department of political science, professor of political science and law, Center for Empirical Research in Law, fellow, 2006-, Sidney W. Souers professor of government, 2009-12, department chair, 2011-. Writer. **Publications:** (With F. Maltzman and P.J. Wahlbeck) Crafting Law on the Supreme Court: The Collegial Game, 2000; (with T.G. Hansford) The Politics of Precedent on the U.S. Supreme Court, 2006. Contributor to periodicals. **Address:** Departmentt of Political Science, Washington University, 1 Brookings Dr., PO Box 1063, St. Louis, MO 63130-4899, U.S.A. **Online address:** jspriggs@artsci.wustl.edu

SPRING, Eileen. American/Canadian (born Canada), b. 1923. **Genres:** History, Law, Social Sciences. **Career:** University of Toronto Press, staff, 1945-48; Johns Hopkins University, Press, staff, 1952-59, School of Continuing Studies, lecturer in British history, 1974-82. Freelance historian and writer. **Publications:** (Ed. with D. Spring) Ecology and Religion in History, 1974; Law, Land & Family: Aristocratic Inheritance in England, 1300-1800, 1993. **Address:** 5605 Wexford Rd., Baltimore, MD 21209-4432, U.S.A.

SPRINGER, Claudia. American (born United States), b. 1956. **Genres:** Novels. **Career:** Rhode Island College, professor of English and film studies, 1986-; Framingham State University, Department of English, assistant professor of English, 2009-. Writer. **Publications:** Electronic Eros: Bodies and Desire in the Postindustrial Age, 1996; James Dean Transfigured: The Many Faces of Rebel Iconography, 2007. **Address:** Department of English, Framingham State University, 100 State St., PO Box 9101, Framingham, MA 01702-2499, U.S.A. **Online address:** claudia_springer@emerson.edu

SPRINGER, Margaret. Canadian/British (born England), b. 1941. **Genres:** Children's Fiction. **Career:** McGill School of Library Science, librarian, 1964-66; Saint Paul's United College, librarian, 1966-74, 1977-80; freelance writer, 1982-; Institute of Children's Literature, faculty, 1988-; Boyds Mills Press, consulting editor, 1989-; Conestoga College, Continuing Education

Department, faculty, 1993-95. **Publications:** A Royal Ball, 1992; Move Over, Einstein!, 1997; Dr. Beastly's Lab, 1998; Finding Annie, 2005. Contributor to periodicals. **Address:** Boyds Mills Press, 815 Church St., Honesdale, PA 18431, U.S.A. **Online address:** mgtspr@sympatico.ca

SPRINGFIELD, David. *See* **LEWIS, J(ohn) R(oyston).**

SPRINKLE, Annie (M.). American (born United States), b. 1954. **Genres:** Film, Sex, Biography, Social Sciences. **Career:** The New School of Erotic Touch, faculty. Writer and educator. **Publications:** Love Vibration, 1994; (co-author) Metamorphosex: Personal and Society Tranformation Through Creative Sexual Experiments, 1996; Annie Sprinkle, Post-Porn Modernist: My Twenty-five Years as a Multi-media Whore, 1998; Hardcore from the Heart: The Pleasures, Profits, and Politics of Sex Performance, 2001; Dr. Sprinkle's Spectacular Sex: Make Over Your Love Life With One of the World's Great Sex Experts, 2005. Contributor to periodicals. **Address:** c/o Author Mail, Cleis Press, 2246 6th St., Berkeley, CA 94710-2219, U.S.A. **Online address:** drsprinkle@anniesprinkle.org

SPRINKLE, Patricia Houck. American (born United States), b. 1943. **Genres:** Novels, Mystery/Crime/Suspense, How-to Books, Human Relations/Parenting, Self Help, Theology/Religion, Women's Studies And Issues, Songs/Lyrics And Libretti, Songs/Lyrics And Libretti. **Career:** Freelance writer, 1977-; Presbyterian Hunger Program, Education, Public Policy and Lifestyle Integrity Department, interim associate, 1987-89. **Publications:** MYSTERY NOVELS: Murder at Markham, 1988; Murder in the Charleston Manner, 1990; Murder on Peachtree Street: A Sheila Travis Mystery, 1991; Somebody's Dead in Snellville, 1992; Death of a Dunwoody Matron, 1993; A Mystery Bred in Buckhead, 1994; Deadly Secrets on the St. Johns, 1995; When Did We Lose Harriet?, 1997; But Why Shoot the Magistrate?, 1998; Carley's Song, 2001; Who Invited the Dead Man?: A Thoroughly Southern Mystery, 2002; Who Left That Body in the Room?: A Thoroughly Southern Mystery, 2002; Who Left That Body in the Rain?: A Thoroughly Southern Mystery, 2002; Who Let That Killer in the House?: A Thoroughly Southern Mystery, 2003; When Will the Dead Lady Sing?: A Thoroughly Southern Mystery, 2004; Who Killed the Queen of Clubs?: A Thoroughly Southern Mystery, 2005; Did You Declare the Corpse?: A Thoroughly Southern Mystery, 2006; Guess Who's Coming to Die?: A Thoroughly Southern Mystery, 2007; What Are You Wearing to Die?, 2008; Deadly Secrets on The St. Johns, 2008. FAMILY TREE SERIES: Death on the Family Tree, 2007; Sins of the Fathers, 2007; Daughter of Deceit, 2008. OTHER: The Church and Young Women: A Case of Mutual Neglect, 1968; The Birthday Book: First Fifty Years, 1972; (comp. and ed.) Hunger: Understanding the Crisis through Games, Dramas & Songs, 1980; In God's Image: Meditations for the New Mother, 1988; Stress and the Christian Superwoman, 1991; Women Who Do Too Much: Stress and the Myth of the Superwoman, 1992, rev. ed. as Women Who Do Too Much: How to Stop Doing it All and Start Enjoying Your Life, 2002; House Warmings: For those Who Make a House a Home, 1992; Do I have To?: What to Do about Children Who Do Too Little around the House, 1993, 3rd ed., 2007; A Gift from God, 1995; Children Who Do Too Little: Why Your Kids need to Work Around the House (and How to Get Them to Do It), 1996; Women Home Alone: Learning to Thrive: Help for Women, Single Moms, Widows and Wives who are Frequently Alone, 1996; The Remember Box, 2000; The Grandmother's Bible, 2008; Hold up the Sky, 2010; Friday's Daughter, 2011. **Address:** Zondervan, 5300 Patterson Ave. SE, Grand Rapids, MI 49530, U.S.A. **Online address:** patriciasprinkle@hotmail.com

SPROAT, Robert. British/Scottish (born Scotland), b. 1944. **Genres:** Novels, Novellas/Short Stories, Romance/Historical, Young Adult Fiction. **Career:** British Telecom, manager, 1965-90; freelance writer and computer programmer, 1990-. **Publications:** Stunning the Punters (stories), 1986; Chinese Whispers (novel), 1988. Work appears in anthologies. Contributor of short stories to periodicals. **Address:** Peters, Fraser & Dunlop, Drury House, 34-43 Russell St., London, GL WC2B 5HA, England.

SPROTT, Duncan. British (born England), b. 1952. **Genres:** Novels. **Career:** Writer. **Publications:** NOVELS: The Clopton Hercules, 1991 in US as The Rise of Mr. Warde, 1992; Our Lady of the Potatoes, 1995; The House of the Eagle in US as The Ptolemies, 2004; Daughter of the Crocodile, 2006. OTHER: 1784, 1984; Sprottichronicon (genealogy), 2000. **Address:** Rogers Coleridge & White Ltd., 20 Powis Mews, London, GL W11 1JN, England. **Online address:** duncansprott@mac.com

SPRUILL, Steven. Also writes as Steven Harriman. American (born United States), b. 1946. **Genres:** Mystery/Crime/Suspense, Novels, Novellas/Short Stories. **Career:** Hazleton Laboratories Inc., biological technician, 1969-73; Veterans Administration Hospital, psychology intern, 1978-79; Mount Vernon Community Mental Health Center, staff, 1979-80; full-time writer, 1981-. **Publications:** MEDICAL THRILLERS: Keepers of the Gate, 1977; The Psychopath Plague, 1978; Hellstone, 1980; The Janus Equation, 1980; The Imperator Plot, 1983; The Genesis Shield, 1985; Paradox Planet: A Kane and Pendrake Novel, 1988; Painkiller: A Novel of Medical Terror, 1990; Rulers of Darkness, 1995; (with F.P. Wilson) Nightkill, 1997. OTHER NOVELS: Before I Wake, 1992; My Soul to Take, 1994; Daughter of Darkness, 1997; Lords of Light, 1999; Octave, 2000; Sleeper, 2003; (as Steven Harriman) Absorbing SpongeBob: Ten Ways to Squeeze More Happiness Out of Life, 2005. Contributor to periodicals. **Address:** c/o Al Zuckerman, 21 W 26th St., New York, NY 10010, U.S.A.

SPRUYT, Hendrik. Dutch (born Netherlands), b. 1956. **Genres:** Adult Nonfiction, Public/Social Administration. **Career:** Columbia University, Institute of War and Peace Studies, assistant professor, 1991-99; Arizona State University, instructor, 1999-2003; Northwestern University, Department of Political Science, Norman Dwight Harris professor of international relations and chair, 2003-, Buffett Center for International and Comparative Studies, director. Political scientist and writer. **Publications:** The Sovereign State and Its Competitors: An Analysis of Systems Change, 1994; Ending Empire: Contested Sovereignty and Territorial Partition, 2005; Global Horizons: An Introduction to International Relations, 2009; (with A. Cooley) Contracting States: Sovereign Transfers in International Relations, 2009. Contributor to books, periodicals and journals. **Address:** Department of Political Science, Weinberg College of Arts & Sciences, Northwestern University, Scott Hall, 601 University Pl., Evanston, IL 60208, U.S.A. **Online address:** h-spruyt@northwestern.edu

SPUFFORD, Francis. British (born England), b. 1964. **Genres:** Adult Nonfiction, Novels, Autobiography/Memoirs. **Career:** Chatto & Windus Ltd., chief publishers reader, 1987-90; full-time writer, 1990-2004; University College London, writer-in-residence, 2004-05; Anglia Ruskin University, royal literary fund fellow, 2005-07; University of London, Goldsmiths College, Department of English and Comparative Literature, senior lecturer in creative writing, 2007-. **Publications:** I May Be Some Time: Ice and the English Imagination, 1997; The Child that Books Built: A Life in Reading, 2002; Backroom Boys: The Secret Return of the British Boffin, 2003; Red Plenty, 2010. EDITOR: The Chatto Book of Cabbages and Kings: Lists in Literature, 1989; The Chatto Book of the Devil: With an Introduction by Himself, 1992; (with J. Uglow) Cultural Babbage: Technology, Time and Invention, 1996; (with E. Kolbert) The Ends of the Earth: An Anthology of the Finest Writing on the Arctic and the Antarctic, 2007. Contributor to books and journals. **Address:** Department of English and Comparative Literature, University of London, Rm. 312, Warmington Twr., New Cross, GL SE14 6NW, England. **Online address:** f.spufford@gold.ac.uk

SPUNGIN, Charlotte I(sabelle). American (born United States), b. 1929. **Genres:** Education, Gay And Lesbian Issues, Psychology, Business/Trade/Industry. **Career:** South Broward High School, teacher of psychology; American government, and economics, social science department, head, 1961-90; Broward Community College, instructor in psychology and sociology; Florida Performance Measurement System, teacher trainer. Writer. **Publications:** (With N. Tallent) Psychology: Understanding Ourselves and Others, 2nd ed., 1977; (with H.F. Besner) Gay and Lesbian Students: Understanding Their Needs, 1995; (with H.F. Besner) Training for Professionals Who Work with Gays and Lesbians in Educational and Workplace Settings, 1998. Contributor to periodicals. **Address:** PO Box 8833, Fort Lauderdale, FL 33310, U.S.A. **Online address:** spunbar@attbi.com

SPURLING, Hilary. British (born England), b. 1940. **Genres:** Art/Art History, Literary Criticism And History, Biography, Adult Non-fiction, History, Novellas/Short Stories. **Career:** Spectator, arts editor and theatre critic, 1964-70; literary editor, 1967-69; The Daily Telegraph, biographer and reviewer; freelance writer, 1970-. **Publications:** Ivy when Young: The Early Life of I. Compton-Burnett, 1884-1919, 1974, rev. ed., 1983 in US as Ivy, The Life of I. Compton-Burnett, 1984; (ed.) The Drawings of Mervyn Peake, 1974; Handbook to Anthony Powell's Music of Time, 1977; Invitation to the Dance: A Guide To Anthony Powell's Dance To The Music Of Time, 1977; Secrets of a Woman's Heart: The Later Life of Ivy Compton Burnett, 1984; Elinor Fettiplace's Receipt Book: Elizabethan Country House Cooking, 1986; Paul

Scott: Novelist And Historian, Or, The End Of The Party And The Beginning Of The Washing Up, 1990; Paul Scott: A Life Of The Author Of The Raj Quartet, 1991; Paper Spirits: Collage Portraits by Vladimir Sulgagin, 1992; The Unknown Matisse: A Life of Henri Matisse, The Early Years, 1869-1908, 1998; Grande Thérèse, or, The Greatest Swindle of The Century, 1999 in US La Grande Thérèse: The Greatest Scandal of the Century, 2000; Henri Matisse, Man of the North, 2000; The Girl from the Fiction Department: A Portrait of Sonia Orwell, 2002; Matisse, His Art And His Textiles: The Fabric Of Dreams, 2004; Matisse the Master: A Life of Henri Matisse, the Conquest of Colour, 1909-1954, 2005; (intro.) The Raj Quartet, 2007; (contrib.) Ann Stokes: Artists' Potter, 2009; Pearl Buck in China: Journey to the Good Earth, 2010; Burying The Bones: Pearl Buck in China, 2010. **Address:** c/o Lizzy Kremer, David Higham Associates Ltd., 5-8 Lower John St., Golden Sq., London, GL W1F 9HA, England.

SPURLING, John. (Henry Tube). British/Kenyan (born Kenya), b. 1936. **Genres:** Novels, Plays/Screenplays, Art/Art History, Literary Criticism And History, Language/Linguistics. **Career:** British Government, Southern Cameroons, UN plebiscite officer, 1960-61; BBC Radio, announcer, 1963-66; freelance writer, 1966-; University of East Anglia, Henfield writing fellow, 1973; New Statesman, art critic, 1976-88. **Publications:** MacRune's Guevara (play), 1969; In the Heart of the British Museum (play), 1972; (with J. Fletcher) Beckett: A Study of His Plays, 1972, 3rd ed. as Beckett the Playwright, 1985; Shades of Heathcliff and Death of Captain Doughty (plays), 1975; (ed.) Hill Station: An Unfinished Novel, and an Indian Diary, 1981; (and intro.) The British Empire, vol. I: A Play, 1982; Graham Greene, 1983; The Ragged End (novel), 1989; (contrib. with J. Bryant) Trojan War: Sculptures by Anthony Caro, 1994; After Zenda: A Novel, 1995; A Book of Liszts, 2011; Arcadian Nights, forthcoming. **Address:** MLR Ltd., Douglas House, 16-18 Douglas St., London, GL SW1P 4PB, England.

SPYCKET, Jerome. French (born France), b. 1928. **Genres:** Literary Criticism And History, Music, Biography, Photography. **Career:** Singer, 1959-73. Writer. **Publications:** Clara Haskil: Illustrated Album, 1984; Nadia Boulanger, 1987. IN FRENCH: Les scandales de l'assurance automobile, 1972; Clara Haskil, 1975; Laceinture qui tue, 1975; Un diable de musicien: Hughes Cuénod, 1979; Et apres-Antione Golea, 1981; Je suis un violoniste raté, 1981; Scarbo: Le roman de Samson Francois, 1985; Kathleen Ferrier, 1990; L'Etatmeurtrier: les impostures de la sécurité routière, 1994; Viebréve dc Kathleen Ferrier, 2003; A la recherche de Lili Boulanger: essai biographique, 2004. **Address:** 79 rue d'Amsterdam, Paris, 75008, France.

SQUIRES, Richard D(onald). American (born United States), b. 1957. **Genres:** Biography. **Career:** General Code Publishers Corp., editor, 1981-88; Rochester Institute of Technology, reference librarian, 1991-95; Monroe Community College, collection development librarian, 1995-. **Publications:** Stern Fathers 'neath the Mould: The Lovecraft Family in Rochester, 1995. **Address:** Monroe Community College, Brighton Campus, Bldg. 3, Rm. 106B, 1000 E Henrietta Rd., Rochester, NY 14623, U.S.A. **Online address:** rsquires@monroecc.edu

SRAGOW, Michael. American (born United States), b. 1952. **Genres:** Biography, Young Adult Fiction. **Career:** Baltimore Sun, film critic. Writer. **Publications:** (Intro.) Sheerly Avni, Cinema by the Bay, 2006; Victor Fleming: An American Movie Master, 2008. EDITOR: Produced and Abandoned: The Best Films You've Never Seen, 1990; James Agee: Film Writing and Selected Journalism, 2005; James Agee: Let Us Now Praise Famous Men, A Death in the Family, Shorter Fiction, 2005. Contributor to periodicals. **Address:** Baltimore, MD , U.S.A. **Online address:** michael.sragow@baltsun.com

SRIGLEY, Susan. Canadian (born Canada), b. 1967?. **Genres:** Art/Art History. **Career:** Nipissing University, associate professor of religions and cultures & chair of the department of philosophy and religions and cultures. Writer, theologian, scholar, critic and educator. **Publications:** Flannery O'Connor's Sacramental Art, 2004. **Address:** Department of Philosophy, Religions & Cultures, Nipissing University, 100 College Dr., PO Box 5002, North Bay, ON P1B 8L7, Canada. **Online address:** susans@nipissingu.ca

SRIVASTAVA, Vinayak N. Indian (born India), b. 1961. **Genres:** Politics/Government, Economics. **Career:** Indian Council For Social Sciences Research Institute, Centre for Policy Research, visiting lecturer, 1995-97; Institute For Social Sciences, senior research officer, 1998-99; Maulana Abul Kalam Azad Institute For Asian Studies, honorary fellow, 1998-2001; Nehru

Memorial Museum and Library, Centre for Contemporary Studies, fellow, 2001-. Writer. **Publications:** The Separation of the Party and the State: Political Leadership in Soviet and Post-Soviet Phases, 1998; Rethinking Panchayatiraj: Politics And Economics Of Democracy And Governance With Special Reference To Uttar Pradesh, forthcoming. **Address:** Centre for Contemporary Studies, Nehru Memorial Museum & Library, Teen Murti Bhawan, New Delhi, DH 110011, India. **Online address:** vns1@rediffmail.com

SRIVER, Tom. *See* **PYENSON, Lewis (Robert).**

STAAR, Richard F. American/Polish (born Poland), b. 1923. **Genres:** International Relations/Current Affairs, Politics/Government, Autobiography/Memoirs, Biography. **Career:** U.S. Government, research specialist, 1949-54; Harding College, professor of political science, 1954-57; Voice of America Radio, speaker, 1957-; Arkansas State College (now University), professor, 1957-58; University of Maryland, lecturer in government, 1958-59; Emory University, professor of political science, 1959-67, chairman of department, 1966-67; U.S. Naval War College, Fleet Admiral Nimitz professor of social and political philosophy, 1963-64; National War College, professor of foreign affairs, 1967-69, visiting professor; Stanford University, Hoover Institution, associate director, senior fellow, 1969-; Mutual and Balanced Force Reductions, U.S. Ambassador, 1981-83, chief of mission; U.S. Arms Control and Disarmament Agency, consultant, 1983-87; Sandia National Laboratories, consultant, 1991-92; Boston University, visiting research professor, 1997-99; Duquesne University, visiting professor of political science, 1999-2000; San Jose State University, distinguished visiting professor of political science, 2003-; U.S. Department of Defense, consultant; Harvard University, Davis Center for Russian Studies, associate. Writer. **Publications:** Poland 1944-1962, 1962; Yearbook on International Communist Affairs, 1966; Communist Regimes in Eastern Europe, 1967, 5th ed., 1988; USSR Foreign Policies after Detente, 1985, 2nd ed., 1987; (with W.T. Lee) Soviet Military Policy since World War II, 1986; Soviet Deception at MBFR: A Case Study, 1986; Foreign Policies of the Soviet Union, 1991; The New Russian Armed Forces: Preparing for War or Peace?, 1992; Transition to Democracy in Poland, 1993, 2nd ed., 1998; The New Military in Russia, 1996; Born under a Lucky Star: Reminiscences, 2002. EDITOR: (and intro.) Aspects of Modern Communism, 1968; Arms Control: Myth Versus Reality, 1984; Public Diplomacy: USA versus USSR, 1986; The Future Information Revolution in the USSR, 1988; United States-East European Relations in the 1990s, 1989; East-Central Europe and the USSR, 1991; Transition to Democracy in Poland, 1993, 2nd ed., 1998. **Address:** Hoover Institution, Stanford University, 434 Galvez Mall, Stanford, CA 94305-6010, U.S.A.

STAATS, Marilyn Dorn. American (born United States), b. 1939. **Genres:** Novels, Novellas/Short Stories, Children's Fiction, Education. **Career:** Atlanta Buckhead, feature writer, 1977; Purple Cow, editor/publisher, 1977-83; Goodlife, Atlanta, senior editor, 1983-85; freelance writer, 1985-; Veranda, copy editor and writer, 1991-, now retired. **Publications:** (With E. Bloodworth) A Parent's Guide to Atlanta Area Private Schools, 1971; Primer for Pebble Pups, 1971; Looking for Atlanta: A Novel, 1992; Goodnight, Lady Joan (novel), 1993. Contributor of articles to periodicals. **Address:** Miriam Altshuler, Russell & Volkening Inc., 50 W 29th St., Ste. 7E, New York, NY 10001, U.S.A.

STABENOW, Dana. American (born United States), b. 1952. **Genres:** Mystery/Crime/Suspense, Science Fiction/Fantasy. **Career:** Cook Inlet Aviation, staff; Whitney-Fidalgo Seafoods, egg grader, bookkeeper and expediter; Alyeska Pipeline, staff; British Petroleum, staff. Writer. **Publications:** NOVELS: STAR SVENSDOTTER SERIES: Second Star, 1991; A Handful of Stars, 1991; Red Planet Run, 1995. KATE SHUGAK SERIES: A Cold Day for Murder, 1992; Dead in the Water, 1993; A Fatal Thaw, 1993; A Cold-Blooded Business, 1994; Play with Fire, 1995; Blood Will Tell, 1996; Breakup, 1997; Killing Grounds, 1998; Hunter's Moon, 1999; Midnight Come Again, 2000; The Singing of the Dead, 2001; A Fine and Bitter Snow, 2002; A Grave Denied, 2003; A Taint in the Blood, 2004; A Complement to Rage, 2007; Whisper to the Blood, 2009; A Night Too Dark, 2010; Though Not Dead, 2011. LIAM CAMPBELL/WYANET CHOUINARD SERIES: Fire and Ice, 1998; So Sure of Death, 1999; Nothing Gold Can Stay, 2000; Better to Rest, 2002; Out for Blood, forthcoming. OTHERS: Blindfold Game, 2006; Deeper Sleep, 2007; Prepared for Rage, 2008; Restless in the Grave, 2012; Silk and Song, forthcoming. EDITOR: Mysterious North: Tales of Suspense from Alaska, 2002; Powers of Detection: Stories of Mystery & Fantasy, 2004; Unusual Suspects: Stories of Mystery & Fantasy, 2008. Contributor to periodicals. **Ad-**

dress: c/o Richard Henshaw Group, 22 W 23rd St., 5th Fl., New York, NY 10010, U.S.A. **Online address:** dana@stabenow.com

STABILE, Don. American (born United States), b. 1944. **Genres:** Intellectual History, History. **Career:** Standard and Poor's Corp., statistician, 1968-70; National Association of Accountants, associate editor, 1972-74; Drury College, assistant professor of economics, 1978-80; St. Mary's College assistant professor, 1980-85, associate professor, 1985-89, professor of economics, 1989-, head of department, 1994-2002, Yeager endowed chair, 2000-04, associate provost, 2002-05, professor of the college, 2005-, Center for Economic Education, director, 1982-95; Cremona Conferences on Institutional Economics, co-organizer, 1985, 1987. Writer. **Publications:** Prophets of Order: The Rise of the New Class, Technocracy, and Socialism in America, 1984; (with J.A. Cantor) The Public Debt of the United States: An Historical Perspective, 1775-1988, 1991; Activist Unionism: The Institutional Economics of Solomon Barkin, 1993; Work and Welfare: The Social Costs of Labor in the History of Economic Thought, 1996; The Origins of American Public Finance, 1998; Community Associations, 2000; Forerunners of Modern Financial Economics, 2005; Economics, Comepetition and Academia, 2007; The Living Wage, 2008. Contributor to journals. **Address:** St. Mary's College of Maryland, 18952 East Fisher Rd., St. Marys City, MD 20686, U.S.A. **Online address:** drstabile@smcm.edu

STABLEFORD, Brian M(ichael). Also writes as Francis Amery, Brian Craig. British (born England), b. 1948. **Genres:** Science Fiction/Fantasy, Young Adult Fiction, Literary Criticism And History, Translations, Novels, Young Adult Non-fiction, Essays. **Career:** Writer, 1965-; University of Reading, lecturer in sociology, 1976, 1977-88, instructor of creative writing, 1988-95; University of the West of England, School of Cultural and Media Studies, part-time lecturer, 1995-96; King Alfred's College, part-time lecturer in creative writing. **Publications:** Cradle of the Sun, 1969; The Blind Worm, 1970; The Days of Glory, 1971; In the Kingdom of the Beasts, 1971; Day of Wrath, 1971; To Challenge Chaos, 1972; The Halcyon Drift, 1972; Rhapsody in Black, 1973; Promised Land, 1974; The Paradise Game, 1974; The Fenris Device, 1974; Swan Song, 1975; Scientific Imagination in Literature, 1975; Man in a Cage, 1975; The Face of Heaven, 1976; The Florians, 1976; The Mind Riders, 1976; Mysteries of Modern Science, 1977; Critical Threshold, 1977; The Realms of Tartarus, 1977; Wildeblood's Empire, 1977; The City of the Sun, 1978; The Last Days of the Edge of the World (juvenile), 1978; Balance of Power, 1979; The Walking Shadow, 1979; The Paradox of The Sets, 1979; A Clash of Symbols: The Triumph of James Blish, 1979; Optiman, 1980 in UK as War Games, 1981; Masters of Science Fiction, 1981; The Castaways of Tanagar, 1981; Journey to the Center, 1982, rev. ed., 1989; The Gates of Eden, 1983; (contrib.) Science in Science Fiction, 1983; Future Man: Brave New World or Genetic Nightmare?, 1984; (with D. Langford) The Third Millennium: A History of the World, A.D. 2000-3000, 1985; Scientific Romance in Britain, 1985; The Cosmic Perspective, 1985; The Sociology of Science Fiction, 1987; The Empire of Fear, 1988; The Way to Write Science Fiction, 1989; Invaders from the Centre, 1990; The Centre Cannot Hold, 1990; The Werewolves of London, 1990; Sexual Chemistry: Sardonic Tales of the Genetic Revolution, 1991; The Angel of Pain, 1991; Slumming in Voodooland, 1991; Young Blood, 1992; The Innsmouth Heritage, 1992; The Carnival of Destruction, 1994; Firefly: A Novel of The Far Future, 1994; Algebraic Fantasies And Realistic Romances: More Masters of Science Fiction, 1995; Serpent's Blood, 1995; Opening Minds: Essays On Fantastic Literature, 1995; Outside The Human Aquarium: Masters of Science Fiction, 1995; Salamander's Fire, 1996; The Hunger And Ecstasy of Vampires, 1996; Chimera's Cradle, 1997; Space, Time, and Infinity: Essays On Fantastic Literature, 1998; Inherit the Earth, 1998; Yesterday's Bestsellers: A Journey Through Literary History, 1998; Slaves of The Death Spiders: Essays On Fantastic Literature, 1998; Writing Fantasy & Science Fiction, And Getting Published, 1998; Glorious Perversity: The Decline and Fall of Literary Decadence, 1998; Architects of Emortality, 1999; The Dictionary of Science Fiction Places, 1999; The Fountains of Youth, 2000; Year Zero, 2000; The Cassandra Complex, 2001; Eleventh Hour, 2001; Dark Ararat, 2002; (trans. and intro.) Lumen, 2002; The Omega Expedition, 2002; Year Zero, 2003; Complications: And Other Stories, 2003; Asgard's Conquerors, 2004; Asgard's Secret, 2004; Designer Genes: Tales of The Biotech Revolution, 2004; Salome and Other Decadent Fantasies, 2004; Historical Dictionary of Science Fiction Literature, 2004; Curse of the Coral Bride, 2004; The A to Z of Science Fiction Literature, 2005; Historical Dictionary of Fantasy Literature, 2005; Asgard's Heart, 2005; Sheena and Other Gothic Tales, 2005; Kiss the Goat, 2005; Streaking, 2005; The Wayward Muse, 2005; Science Fact

and Science Fiction: An Encyclopedia, 2006; The Stones of Camelot, 2006; The Cure for Love: And Other Tales of the Biotech Revolution, 2007; The Haunted Bookshop: And Other Apparitions, 2007; The Tree of Life, 2007; Heterocosms, 2007; The New Faust at the Tragicomique, 2007; An Oasis of Horror: Decadent Tales and Contes Cruels, 2008; The Gardens of Tantalus: And Other Delusions, 2008; The Shadow of Frankenstein, 2008; The Dragon Man: A Novel of the Future, 2009; The World Beyond, 2009; Alien Abduction: The Wiltshire Revelations, 2009; Prelude to Eternity: A Romance of the First Time Machine, 2009; The Innsmouth Heritage And Other Sequels, 2009; Changelings and Other Metamorphic Tales, 2009; The Return of the Djinn, 2009; The Best of Both Worlds, 2009; Sherlock Holmes and the Vampires of Eternity, 2009; Jaunting on the Scoriac Tempests: And Other Essays on Fantastic Literature, 2009; The Devil's Party: A Brief History of Satanic Abuse, 2009; Gothic Grotesques: Essays on Fantastic Literature, 2009; The Moment of Truth, 2009; The A to Z of Fantasy Literature, 2009; Against the New Gods: And Other Essays on Writers of Imaginative Fiction, 2009; Narrative Strategies in Science Fiction: And Other Essays on Imaginative Fiction, 2009; Creators of Science Fiction, 2009; News of the Black Feast: And Other Random Reviews, 2009; The Great Chain of Being: And Other Tales of the Biotech Revolution, 2009; Frankenstein and the Vampire Countess, 2009; Frankenstein in London, 2010; The Decadent World-View, 2010; Exotic Encounters: Selected Reviews, 2010; Luscinia: A Romance of Nightingales and Roses, 2010. EDITOR: (and comp.) The Dedalus Book of Decadence (Moral Ruins), 1990; Tales of the Wandering Jew: A Collection of Contemporary and Classic, 1991; The Dedalus Book of British Fantasy, 1991; The Dedalus Book of Femmes Fatales, 1992; The Second Dedalus Book of Decadence (Black Feast), 1992; (and intro.) Deluge, 2003. TRANSLATOR: P. Feral, Vampire City, 1999; P. Feral, Knightshade, 2001. AS BRIAN CRAIG: Zaragoz, 1990; Plague Daemon, 1990; Storm Warriors, 1991; Ghost Dancers, 1991; Pawns of Chaos, 1996; The Wine of Dreams, 2000; The Unquiet Dead, 2003. TRANSLATOR AS FRANCIS AMERY: The Angels of Perversity, 1992; (intro. and foreword) Monsieur de Phocas, 1994. Works appear in anthologies. Contributor of articles to magazines. **Address:** 113 St. Peter's Rd., Reading, BR RG6 1PG, England. **Online address:** bstableford@cix.compulink.co.uk

STACEY, Cherylyn. (R. F. Darion). Canadian (born Canada), b. 1945. **Genres:** Mystery/Crime/Suspense, Young Adult Fiction, Plays/Screenplays, Criminology/True Crime. **Career:** University of Alberta, teacher, 1968-70; Red Deer College, teacher, 1971-72; Edmonton Catholic Schools, researcher and writer on children's literature, 1984-95. Writer. **Publications:** I'll Tell You Tuesday if I Last That Long, 1989; How Do You Spell Abducted?, 1996; Gone to Maui, 1996. AS R.F. DARION: Tip of the Halo, 2001; Beyond Spite, 2002; The Tao of Laurenson, 2005. **Address:** 3104 1190 Hooke Rd., Edmonton, AB T5A 4A4, Canada. **Online address:** cherylynstacey@yahoo.ca

STACEY, Judith. American (born United States), b. 1943. **Genres:** Sociology, Women's Studies And Issues, Novellas/Short Stories. **Career:** City University of New York, Richmond College, instructor in education, 1971-73; University of California, assistant professor, 1978-84, associate professor 1984-89, professor of sociology, women's studies and ethnography, 1990-97; University of Southern California, Streisand Professor of Contemporary Gender Studies and professor of sociology, 1997-2008; New York University, Department of Sociology, professor, Department of Social and Cultural Analysis, professor, director of undergraduate studies, Institute for Public Knowledge, senior fellow; Council on Contemporary Families, co-founder. Writer. **Publications:** (Ed. with S. Bereaud and J. Daniels) And Jill Came Tumbling After: Sexism in American Education, 1974; Patriarchy and Socialist Revolution in China, 1983; Brave New Families: Stories of Domestic Upheaval in Late Twentieth Century America, 1990; In the Name of the Family: Rethinking Family Values in the Postmodern Age, 1996; Unhitched: Love, Marriage, and Family Values from West Hollywood to Western China, 2011. Contributor to journals. **Address:** Institute for Public Knowledge, New York University, 20 Cooper Sq., 5th Fl., New York, NY 10003, U.S.A. **Online address:** judith.stacey@nyu.edu

STACEY, Kathryn. See FENTON, Kate.

STACEY, Susannah. See STAYNES, Jill.

STACEY, Susannah. See STOREY, Margaret.

STACEY, Tom. (Kendal J. Peel). British (born England), b. 1930. **Genres:** Novels, Novellas/Short Stories, Plays/Screenplays, Literary Criticism And

History, Travel/Exploration, Writing/Journalism, Social Sciences. **Career:** Lilliput Magazine, staff writer, 1951-52; Picture Post, staff writer, 1952-54; Daily Express, African correspondent, 1954, 1956-60, American columnist, 1957, diplomatic and roving correspondent, 1957-60; Montreal Star, correspondent, 1955-56; Sunday Times, roving correspondent, chief foreign correspondent, 1960-65; Christopher Wren School, governor, 1960-68; Evening Standard, columnist, 1965-67; Correspondents World Wide, managing director, 1967-71, editor-in-chief, 1967-73; Stacey Intl. (formerly Tom Stacey Ltd.), owner, managing director, 1969-, chairman, 1974-; Wandsworth School, governor, 1971-79; St. David's and St. Katharine's School, governor, 1992-. Writer. **Publications:** The Hostile Sun: A Malayan Journey, 1953; Summons to Ruwenzori, 1965; Immigration and Enoch Powell, 1970; Peoples of the World, 1972; Thomas Brassey, the Greatest Railway Builder in the World, 2005. NOVELS: The Brothers M, 1960; The Living and the Dying, 1976; The Pandemonium, 1980; (as Kendal J. Peel) The Twelfth Night of Ramadan, 1983; The Worm in the Rose, 1985; Deadline, 1988; Decline, 1991; Tribe: The Hidden History of the Mountains of the Moon: An Autobiographical Study, 2003; The First Dog to be Somebody's Best Friend, 2007, The Man Who Knew Everything, 2008, Absolutiion, forthcoming; Blackness and Darkness, forthcoming. EDITOR: (with A.G. Nicolson and C. Hayman) Today's World: A Map Notebook of World Affairs, 1968; (with C. Hayman) Correspondents World Wide, 1968; (with R.S. Oswald) Here Come the Tories, 1970. STORIES/NOVELLAS: Bodies and Souls, 1989; The Same Old Story, 1999; The Tether of the Flesh, 2001; Golden Rain, 2003; Grief, 2003; Mary's Visit, forthcoming. Contributor to books. **Address:** c/o Max, Stacey International Publisher, 128 Kensington Church St., London, GL W8 4BH, England. **Online address:** tom@stacey.international.co.uk

STACHEL, John Jay. American (born United States), b. 1928. **Genres:** Intellectual History, Philosophy, Physics, Politics/Government, Sciences, Essays. **Career:** Lehigh University, instructor in physics, 1959-61; University of Pittsburgh, instructor in physics, 1961-62, research associate, 1962-64; Institute for Theoretical Physics, visiting research associate, 1962; Boston University, Department of physics, assistant professor, 1964-69, associate professor, 1969-72, professor, 1972-97, professor emeritus, 1997-, Center for Einstein Studies, director, 1985-; University of London, King's College, visiting professor, 1970-71; Einstein Papers, editor, 1977-89; Princeton University, Department of Physics, visiting senior research fellow, 1977-84; University of Paris, visiting professor, 1990-91; Max Planck Institute for History of Science, visiting professor, 1994-; University of California, research associate, 1994; California Institute of Technology, visiting professor, 1998. **Publications:** Einstein from B to Z, 2002; (co-author) Revisiting the Foundations of Relativistic Physics, 2003; Going Critical: Selected Essays, vol. I, The Challenge of Practice, 2004. EDITOR: (with R.S. Cohen and M.W. Wartofsky) For Dirk Struik, 1974; (with R.S. Cohen) Selected Papers of Léon Rosenfeld, 1979; (with J. Earman and C. Glymour) Foundations of Space-Time Theories, 1977; The Collected Papers of Albert Einstein, vol. I: The Early Years, 1879-1902 (texts in German with English commentary), 1987, vol. II: The Swiss Years, Writing 1900-1909, 1989; (with D. Howard) Einstein and the History of General Relativity, 1989; (with A. Ashtekar) Conceptual Problems of Quantum Gravity, 1991; (with K. Gavroglu and M.W. Wartofsky) Physics, Philosophy, and the Scientific Community, 1994; (with K. Gavroglu and M.W. Wartofsky) Science, Politics, and Social Practice, 1995; (with K. Gavroglu and M.W. Wartofsky) Science, Mind, and Art, 1995; (with R.S. Cohen and M. Horne) Experimental Metaphysics, 1997; (with R.S. Cohen and M. Horne) Potentiality, Entanglement, and Passion-at-a-Distance, 1997; (with R.S. Cohen and M. Horne) Quantum Mechanical Studies for Abner Shimony, 1997; (and intro.) Einstein's Miraculous Year, 1998; (with D. Howard) Einstein: The Formative Years, 1879-1909, 2000. **Address:** Department of Philosophy, Boston University, Rm.STH, 745 Commonwealth Ave., Boston, MA 02215-1401, U.S.A. **Online address:** stachel@bu.edu

STACHNIAK, Eva. (Eva Maria Stachniak). Canadian/Polish (born Poland), b. 1952. **Genres:** Novels. **Career:** University of Wroclaw, Department of English, faculty; Radio Canada Intl., staff, 1984-86; Sheridan College, School of Business, teacher, 1988-2007. Writer. **Publications:** Necessary Lies, 2000; Garden of Venus, 2005; The Winter Palace: A Novel of Catherine the Great, 2011. **Address:** Random House, 1745 Broadway, 3rd Fl., New York, NY 10019, U.S.A. **Online address:** eva.stachniak@sheridanc.on.ca

STACHNIAK, Eva Maria. See STACHNIAK, Eva.

STACK, Andy. See RULE, Ann.

STACK, George. (George J. Stack). American (born United States), b. 1931. **Genres:** Humanities, Literary Criticism And History, Philosophy, Young Adult Non-fiction, Politics/Government. **Career:** Long Island University, instructor, 1963-64, assistant professor, 1964-67; State University of New York, The College at Brockport, assistant professor, 1967-68, associate professor, 1968-70, professor, 1970-95, professor emeritus of philosophy, 1995-. Writer. **Publications:** Berkeley's Analysis of Perception, 1970; On Kierkegaard: Philosophical Fragments, 1976; Kierkegaard's Existential Ethics, 1977; Sartre's Philosophy of Social Existence, 1977; Lange and Nietzsche, 1983; Nietzsche and Emerson: An Elective Affinity, 1992; Nietzsche: Man, Knowledge, Will to Power, 1994; Nietzsche's Anthropic Circle: Man, Science and Myth, 2005. **Address:** The College at Brockport, State University of New York, 350 New Campus Dr., Brockport, NY 14420-2914, U.S.A. **Online address:** gjstack@yahoo.com

STACK, George J. See STACK, George.

STACK, Megan K. American (born United States), b. 1977?. **Genres:** History, Education. **Career:** Los Angeles Times, Houston bureau chief, 2001-03, Jerusalem bureau chief, 2003, Cairo bureau chief, 2003-07, Moscow bureau chief, 2007-; El Paso Times, staff; Associated Press, staff. **Publications:** Every Man in This Village Is a Liar: An Education in War, 2010. **Online address:** megan.stack@latimes.com

STACKPOLE, Michael A(ustin). American (born United States), b. 1957. **Genres:** Novels, Science Fiction/Fantasy, Ghost Writer. **Career:** Flying Buffalo Inc., game designer, 1979-87; writer, 1987-; FASA Corp., writer, 1987-; Coleco Industries, consultant. **Publications:** NOVELS: Natural Selection, 1992; Assumption of Risk, 1993; Once a Hero, 1994; Mutant Chronicles: Dementia, 1994. WARRIOR SERIES: Warrior: En Garde, 1988; Warrior: Riposte, 1988; Warrior: Coupe, 1989. BLOOD OF KERENSKY SERIES: Lethal Heritage, 1990; Blood Legacy, 1990; Lost Destiny, 1991. DARK CONSPIRACY SERIES: A Gathering Evil, 1991; Evil Ascending, 1991; Evil Triumphant, 1992. STAR WARS X-WING SERIES: Rogue Squadron, 1996; Wedge's Gamble, 1996; The Krytos Trap, 1996; The Bacta War, 1997; Battleground: Tatooine, 1998; The Phantom Affair, 1998; The Warrior Princess, 1998; (co-author) Blood and Honor, 1999; In the Empire's Service, 1999; Isard's Revenge, 1999; Requiem for a Rogue, 1999; Masquerade, 2000; Mandatory Retirement, 2001. GAMES: Citybook I, 1983; Stormhaven, 1984; Wasteland, 1988; Neuromancer, 1989; Wolf and Raven, 1998; (foreword) Core Rulebook, 2000. BATTLETECH SERIES: Bred for War, 1995; Malicious Intent, 1996; The Twilight of the Clans II: Grave Covenant, 1997; Prince of Havoc, 1998; Warrior: Coupe, 1998. REALMS OF CHAOS SERIES: A Hero Born, 1997; (with W.F. Wu) An Enemy Reborn, 1998. STAR WARS: THE NEW JEDI ORDER SERIES: Onslaught: Dark Tide I, 2000; Dark Tide II: Ruin, 2000; At the Queen's Command SC, 2010. DRAGONCROWN WAR CYCLE SERIES: Fortress Draconis, 2001; When Dragons Rage, 2002; The Grand Crusade, 2003. MECHWARRIOR: DARK AGE SERIES: Ghost War, 2002; Masters of War, 2007. AGE OF DISCOVERY SERIES: A Secret Atlas, 2005; Cartomancy, 2006; The New World, 2007. OTHERS: City of Terrors, 1978; Sewers of Oblivion, 1980; (ed. with L. Danforth) Mages Blood and Old Bones, 1992; Talion Revenant (fantasy), 1997; Star Wars: X-Wing Rogue Squadron, 1998; Eyes of Silver, 1998; I, Jedi, 1998; (with T. Zahn) Star Wars-Mara Jade: By the Emperor's Hand, 1999; Star Wars: Union, 2000; The Dark Glory War, 2000; Perchance to Dream and Other Stories, 2005; (contrib.) Timeshares, 2010; Of Limited Loyalty, 2011; Ungrateful Rabble, 2012. Works appear in anthologies. Contributor to magazines. **Address:** c/o Author Mail, Ricia Mainhardt Agency, 612 Argyle Rd., Ste. L5, Brooklyn, NY 11230-1682, U.S.A.

STACKS, Don W. American (born United States), b. 1949. **Genres:** Communications/Media, Language/Linguistics. **Career:** University of South Alabama, associate professor, 1978-84; University of Georgia, associate professor, 1984; University of Alabama, associate professor, 1985-90, adjunct professor, 1990; University of Miami, School of Communication, associate professor, 1990-93, professor, 1993-, acting program director, 1994, associate director, 1995-96, Program in Advertising and Public Relations, director, 1996-2005, Public Relations Program, coordinator, 1998-, director, 2005-09, associate dean for research, 2009-. Writer. **Publications:** (With M.L. Hickson III) NVC, Nonverbal Communication: Studies and Applications, 1985, (with N. Moore and M.L. Hickson III) 5th ed., 2010; (with J.E. Hocking) Communication Research, 1990, (with J.E. Hocking and S.T. McDermott) 3rd ed., 2003; (with M.L. Hickson III and S.R. Hill, Jr.) Introduction to Communication Theory, 1991; (ed. with M.L. Hickson) Effective Communication for Academic Chairs, 1992; (with J.E. Hocking) Essentials of Communication Research, 1992; (ed. with M.B. Salwen) An Integrated Approach to Communication Theory and Research, 1996, 2nd ed., 2009; (with M.L. Hickson III and M. Padgett-Greely) Organizational Communication in the Personal Context: From Interview to Retirement, 1998; Primer of Public Relations Research, 2002, 2nd ed., 2011; (with D. Michaelson) A Practitioner's Guide to Public Relations Research, Measurement and Evaluation, 2010. **Address:** School of Communication, University of Miami, 3007 Frances L. Wolfson Bldg., 5100 Brunson Dr., Coral Gables, FL 33146, U.S.A. **Online address:** don.stacks@miami.edu

STADDON, John (E. R.). American/British (born England), b. 1937. **Genres:** Psychology, Biology, Philosophy. **Career:** Massachusetts Institute of Technology, Electronic Systems Laboratory, researcher in experimental psychology, 1962-63; University of Toronto, assistant professor of psychology, 1964-67; Duke University, assistant professor, professor of psychology and neuroscience, 1979-, professor of zoology, 1983-, professor of biology and neurobiology, 1988-, James B. Duke professor of psychology and brain sciences, 1983-, head of department, 1985-87; University of York, honorary visiting professor. Writer. **Publications:** (Ed. with W.K. Honig) Handbook of Operant Behavior, 1977; (ed.) Limits to Action: The Allocation of Individual Behavior, 1980; Adaptive Behavior and Learning, 1983; (with R.H. Ettinger) Learning: An Introduction to the Principles of Adaptive Behavior, 1989; (ed. with M.L. Commons and S. Grossberg and contrib.) Neural Networks of Conditioning and Action, 1991; (ed. with C.D.L. Wynne) Models of Action: Mechanisms for Adaptive Behavior, 1998; The New Behaviorism: Mind, Mechanism and Society, 2001; Adaptive Dynamics: The Theoretical Analysis of Behavior, 2001; New Behaviorism: Mind, Mechanism and Society, 2001; (contrib.) Reflections on Adaptive Behavior: Essays in Honor of J.E.R. Staddon, 2008. Contributor to journals, magazines and books. **Address:** Department of Psychology, Duke University, 304 W Campus Union Bldg., 125 Science Dr., PO Box 90338, Durham, NC 27708-0086, U.S.A. **Online address:** jers@duke.edu

STADE, George. American (born United States), b. 1933. **Genres:** Cultural/Ethnic Topics, Literary Criticism And History, Psychiatry. **Career:** Rutgers University, instructor, 1961-62; Columbia University, assistant professor, 1965-68, associate professor, 1968-71, professor of English and comparative literature, 1971-, now professor emeritus; Barnes and Noble Classics, senior consulting director. Writer. **Publications:** (Ed. with F.W. Dupee) Selected Letters of E. E. Cummings, 1968; Robert Graves, 1969; (ed.) Six Modern British Novelists, 1974; (ed.) Six Contemporary British Novelists, 1976; (ed.) Columbia Essays on Modern Writers, 1976; Confessions of a Lady-Killer, 1979; (ed.) European Writer, 1983; (ed.) British Writers: Supplement II: Kingsley Amis to J.R.R. Tolkien, 1992; (ed.) British Writers: Supplement III: James M. Barrie to Mary Wollstonecraft, 1996; (ed. with C. Howard) British Writers: Supplement IV, 1997; (ed.) British Writers Supplement V, Ayckbourn to G. Swift, 1999; Sex and Violence: A Love Story, 2005; Love Is War, 2006; Literature, Moderns, Monsters, Popsters and Us, 2007; Equipment for Living: Moderns, Monsters, Popsters and Us, 2007; (ed.) Encyclopedia of British Writers, 1800 to the Present, 2009. Contributor of articles to periodicals. **Address:** Department of English, Columbia University, 604 Philosophy Hall, New York, NY 10027, U.S.A. **Online address:** ggs3@columbia.edu

STAFFORD, Barbara Maria. American/Austrian (born Austria), b. 1941. **Genres:** Art/Art History. **Career:** National College of Education, assistant professor, 1969-70, 1971-72; Loyola University, assistant professor, 1972-73; University of Delaware, assistant professor, associate professor of art history, 1973-81; University of Chicago, professor, 1981-2010, chair, William B. Ogden distinguished service professor of art history, 1995-2010, William B. Ogden distinguished service professor emeritus, 2007-10; American Society for Eighteenth-Century Studies, president, 1995; University of Southern California, Templeton Research Fellow, 2007-08; Georgia Institute of Technology, Distinguished University Visiting Professor, 2010-. Writer. **Publications:** Symbol and Myth: Humbert de Superville's Essay on Absolute Signs in Art, 1979; Voyage into Substance: Art, Science, Nature and the Illustrated Travel Account, 1760-1840, 1984; Body Criticism: Imaging the Unseen in Enlightenment Art and Medicine, 1991; Artful Science: Enlightenment Entertainment and the Eclipse of Visual Education, 1994; Good Looking, 1995; Visual Analogy: Consciousness as the Art of Connecting, 1999; Devices of Wonder: From the World in a Box to Images on a Screen, 2001; Echo Objects: The Cognitive Work of Images, 2007; A Field Guide to a New Metafield:

Bridging the Humanities-Neurosciences Divide, 2008. Contributor to periodicals. **Address:** Department of Art History, 166 Cochrane-Woods Art Ctr., University of Chicago, 5540 S Greenwood Ave., Chicago, IL 60637, U.S.A. **Online address:** bms6@uchicago.edu

STAFFORD, Edward Peary. American (born United States), b. 1918. **Genres:** History, Military/Defense/Arms Control, Natural History. **Career:** Speech writer, 1969-80; University of Nevada, English teacher; Miami-Dade Junior College, English teacher. **Publications:** The Big E: The Story of the USS Enterprise, 1962; The Far and the Deep, 1967; Sun, Earth and Man, 1982; Little Ship, Big War: The Saga of DE343, 1984; Subchaser, 1988. **Address:** 101 La Costa St., Apt. B-1, Melbourne Beach, FL 32951-3480, U.S.A. **Online address:** patronops@webtv.net

STAFFORD, Fiona (Jane). British (born England), b. 1960. **Genres:** Intellectual History, Literary Criticism And History, Mythology/Folklore. **Career:** University of Evansville, British Campus, lecturer in English, 1985-87; Oxford University, British academy postdoctoral fellow in English literature, 1987-99. Nene College, English lecturer, 1990-91; Oxford University, English lecturer, 1991-92; Oxford University, Somerville College, tutor in English literature, CUF lecturer, university reader in English, 1992, fellow, professor of English language and literature. Writer. **Publications:** The Sublime Savage: James Macpherson and the Poems of Ossian, 1988; The Last of the Race: The Growth of a Myth from Milton to Darwin, 1994; Starting Lines in Scottish, Irish and English Poetry: From Burns to Heaney, 2000; (intro. and contrib.) Pride and Prejudice, 2004; Reading Romantic Poetry, 2012. EDITOR: (and intro.) Emma, 1996; Lodore, 1996; (contrib.) From Gaelic to Romantic: Ossianic Translations, 1998; Jane Austen's Emma: A Casebook, 2007; Local Attachments: The Province of Poetry, 2010; (with D. Sergeant) Burns and other Poets, 2012. **Address:** Department of English Language & Literature, Somerville College, University of Oxford, St Cross Bldg., Manor Rd., Oxford, OX OX1 3UL, England. **Online address:** fiona.stafford@some.ox.ac.uk

STAFFORD, William. British/American (born United States), b. 1945. **Genres:** Social Sciences, History. **Career:** University of Huddersfield, professor of history, 1972-, School of Music and Humanities, director of research, now professor emeritus. Writer, historian and biographer. **Publications:** Socialism, Radicalism and Nostalgia: Social Criticism in Britain, 1775-1830, 1987; The Mozart Myths: A Critical Reassessment, 1991; Mozart's Death: A Corrective Survey of the Legends, 1991; John Stuart Mill, 1998; English Feminists and Their Opponents in the 1790s: Unsex'd and Proper Females, 2002; Kansas Poems of William Stafford, 2nd ed., 2010. Contributor to books and journals. **Address:** School of Music, Humanities & Media, University of Huddersfield, West Bldg., Huddersfield, WY HD1 3DH, England. **Online address:** w.stafford@hud.ac.uk

STAFFORD-DEITSCH, Jeremy. British/American (born United States), b. 1958. **Genres:** Natural History, Social Sciences, Archaeology/Antiquities. **Career:** Writer and photographer. **Publications:** Shark: A Photographer's Story, 1987; (contrib.) Reef: A Safari through the Coral World, 1991; Mangroves: The Forgotten Habitat, 1995; The Monuments of Ancient Egypt, 2001; Kingdoms of Ruin: The Art and Architectural Splendours of Ancient Turkey, 2010; Red Sea Sharks and Mangrove: The Forgotten Habitat, forthcoming. **Address:** c/o Carol Smith, Carol Smith Literary Agency, 22 Adam & Eve Mews, Kensington High St., London, GL W8 6UJ, England.

STAGGENBORG, Suzanne. American/Canadian (born Canada), b. 1955. **Genres:** Sociology. **Career:** Washington University, Department of Sociology, teaching assistant, 1978-79; Northwestern University, Center for Urban Affairs and Policy Research, research fellow, 1981-84, instructor, 1982-83; Northwestern Memorial Hospital, Medical School, faculty associate and project director for alcohol and crime study, 1985-86; Indiana University, assistant professor, 1986-92, associate professor of sociology, 1992-93; McGill University, Department of Sociology, associate professor, 1993-99, professor, 1999-2008, acting chair, 2003-04, chair, 2005-08; American Sociological Association, Section on Collective Behavior and Social Movements, chair, 1999-2000; University of Pittsburgh, professor of sociology, 2008-; Cambridge University Press, co-editor, 2008-12. Writer. **Publications:** The Pro-Choice Movement: Organization and Activism in the Abortion Conflict, 1991; Gender, Family and Social Movements, 1998; (ed. with B. Klaudermans) Methods of Social Movement Research, 2002; Social Movements,

2008. Contributor to books. **Address:** Department of Sociology, University of Pittsburgh, 2409 Wesley W Posvar Hall, 230 Bouquet St., Pittsburgh, PA 15260, U.S.A. **Online address:** suzstagg@pitt.edu

STAHL, Saul. American/Belgian (born Belgium), b. 1942. **Genres:** Mathematics/Statistics, Sciences. **Career:** International Business Machines (IBM) Corp., systems programmer, 1969-73; Wright State University, assistant professor of mathematics, 1975-77; University of Kansas, professor of mathematics, 1977-. Writer. **Publications:** The Poincaré Half-Plane: A Gateway to Modern Geometry, 1993, 2nd ed., 2008; Introductory Modern Algebra: A Historical Approach, 1997; A Gentle Introduction to Game Theory, 1999; Real Analysis: A Historical Approach, 1999, 2nd ed., 2011; Geometry from Euclid to Knots, 2003; Introduction to Topology and Geometry, 2005; (with P.E. Johnson) Understanding Modern Mathematics, 2007. Contributor to journals. **Address:** Department of Mathematics, University of Kansas, 603 Snow Hall, Lawrence, KS 66045, U.S.A. **Online address:** stahl@math.ku.edu

STAINBACK, Berry. American (born United States), b. 1935. **Genres:** Sports/Fitness, Biography, Documentaries/Reportage, Adult Non-fiction, Autobiography/Memoirs. **Career:** Metro-Goldwyn-Mayer (MGM) Pictures, publicity writer, 1960; Sport Magazine, assistant managing editor, 1961-64, managing editor, 1965-67, executive editor, 1975-76, editor, 1977-79; Life Magazine, Articles Department, associate editor, 1967-72; New Times Magazine, managing editor, 1972; True Magazine, editor, 1973; CBS Publications, editor of sports annuals, 1980-82; School of Visual Arts, faculty advisor to student newspaper, 1982-83; Winter Olympic Games, assistant managing editor, 1983-84, 1986; Sports Inc. (magazine), managing editor, 1987. **Publications:** NONFICTION: (with S. Gelman) Basketball Stars of 1966, 1965; Basketball Stars of 1969, 1968; Pro Football Forecast for 1969, 1969; Pro Basketball Forecast for 1969-70, 1969; How the Pros Play Football, 1970; Pro Football Heroes of Today, 1973; (with J. Pepitone) Joe, You Coulda Made Us Proud, 1975; A Very Different Love Story: Burt and Linda Pugach's Intimate Account of Their Triumph Over Tragedy, 1976; (with E. Weaver) It's What You Learn After You Know It All That Counts, 1982, rev. ed. as It's What You Learn After You Know It All That Counts: Updated to Include the 1982 Season, 1983; (with K. Stabler) Snake, 1986; (with A. Goldstein) Overcoming Agoraphobia: Conquering Fear of the Outside World, 1987; (with F. Robinson) Extra Innings, 1988; (with P. Ragonese) The Soul of a Cop, 1991. **Address:** c/o Mel Berger, William Morris Agency L.L.C., 1325 Ave. of the Americas, New York, NY 10019-6026, U.S.A.

STAINTON, Leslie. American (born United States), b. 1955. **Genres:** Literary Criticism And History, History, Theatre, Essays. **Career:** University of Michigan, Museum of Art, editor, 1990-96, School of Public Health, editor and writer, 1998-; Borders Books, editor, 1996-98. **Publications:** (With H. Sheehy) On Writers and Writing: A Desk Diary, 1992; Lorca: A Dream of Life, 1999. **Address:** Carol Mann Agency, 55 5th Ave., New York, NY 10003, U.S.A. **Online address:** stainton@umich.edu

STAINTON, Robert J. (H.). Canadian (born Canada), b. 1964. **Genres:** Philosophy, Language/Linguistics. **Career:** York University, research coordinator, 1988-91; Salem State College, lecturer in philosophy, 1991; Carleton University, assistant professor of philosophy, 1993-97, associate professor of philosophy and linguistics, 1997-2001, clerk, 1997-2000, Theoretical Linguistics Organized Research Unit, director, 1996-97, research chair in cognitive science, 2001-04, Doctoral Program in Cognitive Science, director, 2001-03, Department of Philosophy and Institute of Cognitive Science, adjunct research professor, 2004-09; University of Ottawa, Department of Philosophy and Faculty of Graduate and Postdoctoral Studies, adjunct professor, 2001-04; University of Western Ontario, visiting adjunct research professor, 2003-04, associate professor, 2004-06, Mind and Language Graduate Field, director, 2005-07, professor of philosophy, 2006-11, acting associate dean, 2007-08, associate dean, 2008-10; Simon Fraser University, Department of Philosophy, James S. McDonnell distinguished visiting professor of neurophilosophy, 2010-11. Writer. **Publications:** Philosophical Perspectives on Language, 1996; (with A. Brook) Knowledge and Mind: A Philosophical Introduction, 2000; Words and Thoughts: Subsentences, Ellipsis, and the Philosophy of Language, 2006. EDITOR: (with K. Murasugi) Philosophy and Linguistics, 1999; Perspectives in the Philosophy of Language: A Concise Anthology, 2000; (with M. Ezcurdia and C. Viger) New Essays in the Philosophy of Language and Mind, 2004; (with R. Elugardo) Ellipsis and Nonsentential Speech, 2005; Contemporary Debates in Cognitive Science, 2006; (with C. Viger) Compositionality, Context and Semantic Values, 2009; (with

S. Brennan) Philosophy and Death, 2010. **Address:** Department of Philosophy, University of Western Ontario, Rm. 3126, Stevenson Hall, 1151 Richmond St., London, ON N6A 5B8, Canada. **Online address:** rstainto@uwo.ca

STALEY, Allen (Percival Green). American (born United States), b. 1935. **Genres:** History, Art/Art History, Photography. **Career:** Frick Collection, lecturer, 1962-65; Philadelphia Museum of Art, assistant curator, 1965-69; Columbia University, assistant professor of art history, 1969-71, associate professor of art history, 1971-76, professor of art history, 1976-2007, professor emeritus of art history, 2007-. Writer. **Publications:** (With F.J. Cummings) Romantic Art in Britain: Paintings and Drawings, 1760-1860, 1968; The Pre-Raphaelite Landscape, 1973, 2nd ed., 2001; (contrib.) Whistler Lithographs: An Illustrated Catalogue Raisonné, 1975; (with H.V. Erffa) The Paintings of Benjamin West, 1986; (contrib.) Impossible Picturesqueness: Edward Lear's Indian Watercolours, 1873-1875, 1989; Benjamin West, American Painter at the English Court: June 4-August 20, 1989, 1989; (intro.) Unfaded Pageant: Edwin Austin Abbey's Shakespearean Subjects, 1994; (co-author) Post-pre-Raphaelite Print: Etching, Illustration, Reproductive Engraving, and Photography in England in and around the 1860s, 1995; (with C. Newall) Pre-Raphelite Vision, 2004; New Painting of the 1860s, 2011. Works appear in anthologies. Contributor to periodicals. **Address:** Department of Art History and Archaeology, Columbia University, 826 Schermerhorn Hall, 1190 Amsterdam Ave., PO Box 5517, New York, NY 10027, U.S.A. **Online address:** as60@columbia.edu

STALEY, Lynn. (Lynn Staley Johnson). American (born United States), b. 1947. **Genres:** Literary Criticism And History, Poetry, Young Adult Fiction. **Career:** Colgate University, instructor, 1974-75, assistant professor of history 1975-81, associate professor, 1981-86, professor of English, 1986-95, Harrington and Shirley Drake professor of the humanities and medieval and renaissance studies, 1995-, MARS, director. Writer. **Publications:** (As L.S. Johnson) The Voice of the Gawain-Poet, 1984; (as L.S. Johnson) The Shepheardes Calendar: An Introduction, 1990; Margery Kempe's Dissenting Fictions, 1994; (ed.) The Book of Margery Kempe, 1996; (with D. Aers) The Powers of the Holy: Religion, Politics and Gender in Late Medieval English Culture, 1996; (ed. and trans.) The Book of Margery Kempe: A New Translation, Contexts, Criticism, 2001; Languages of Power in the Age of Richard II, 2005. Contributor of articles to books and journals. **Address:** Department of English, Colgate University, 306 Lawrence Hall, 13 Oak Dr., Hamilton, NY 13346, U.S.A. **Online address:** lstaley@colgate.edu

STALLARD, Michael L. (Michael Lee Stallard). American (born United States), b. 1959. **Genres:** inspirational/Motivational Literature, Adult Non-fiction, Business/Trade/Industry. **Career:** Van Kampen Investments, senior vice-president, director of business and product development, 1993-98; Morgan Stanley, principal and chief marketing officer, 1998-2001; Charles Schwab/U.S. Trust, managing director and chief marketing officer, 2001-02; E Pluribus Partners, co-founder and president, 2002-; Citigroup Private Bank, managing director, head of U.S. marketing, 2006-07. Writer. **Publications:** (With C. Dewing-Hommes and J. Pankau) Fired Up or Burned Out: How to Reignite Your Team's Passion, Creativity, and Productivity, 2007. Contributor to periodicals. **Address:** c/o Lee Hough, Alive Communications, 7680 Goddard St., Ste. 200, Colorado Springs, CO 80920, U.S.A. **Online address:** mstallard@epluribuspartners.com

STALLARD, Michael Lee. See STALLARD, Michael L.

STALLMAN, Richard Matthew. American (born United States), b. 1953. **Genres:** Technology. **Career:** Massachusetts Institute of Technology, software developer, 1971-84; GNU Project, founder, 1984-; Free Software Foundation, founder and president, 1985-. Writer. **Publications:** GNU Emacs Manual, 1986; No Sir, No Monopoly!: Free Software: A Perspective, 2002; (contrib.) Free Software, Free Society, 2002; (with T. Vadén) Koodi Vapaaksi: Hakkerietiikan vaativuus, 2002. **Address:** Free Software Foundation, 51 Franklin St., Ste. 500, Boston, MA 02110-1335, U.S.A. **Online address:** rms@gnu.org

STALLWORTHY, Jon (Howie). British (born England), b. 1935. **Genres:** Poetry, Literary Criticism And History, Biography, Translations. **Career:** Oxford University Press, editor, 1959-71; British Academy, Chatterton lecturer, 1970; Oxford University, visiting fellow, 1971-72; Clarendon Press, editor, 1972-77; Cornell University, John Wendell Anderson professor of English literature, 1977-86; Wolfson College, acting president, fellow, 1986-, reader in

English literature, 1986-92, professor of English literature, 1992-2000, literary critic; University of Oxford, now professor emeritus of English. **Publications:** Between the Lines: Yeats's Poetry in the Making, 1963; Vision and Revision in Yeats's Last Poems, 1969; Wilfred Owen, 1974; Louis MacNeice, 1995; Singing School: The Making of a Poet, 1998; Anthem for Doomed Youth: 12 Soldier Poets of the First World War, 2002. POETRY: The Earthly Paradise: The Newdigate Prize Poem, 1958; The Astronomy of Love, 1961; Out of Bounds, 1963; The Almond Tree, 1967; A Day in the City, 1967; Root and Branch, 1969; Positives, 1969; A Dinner of Herbs, 1970; Hand in Hand, 1974; Poets of the First World War, 1974; The Apple Barrel: Selected Poems 1956-1963, 1974; A Familiar Tree, 1978; The Anzac Sonata (poems), 1986; The Guest from the Future, 1989; Rounding the Horn (poems), 1998; Body Language, 2004. TRANSLATOR: (with J. Peterkiewicz) Five Centuries of Polish Poetry, rev. ed., 1970; (with P. France) A. Blok, The Twelve and Other Poems, 1970, as Alexander Blok, Selected Poems, 1974; (with P. France) B. Pasternak, Selected Poems, 1982. EDITOR/CO-EDITOR: Yeats: Last Poems: A Casebook, 1968; (with S. Heaney and A. Brownjohn) New Poems 1971; The Penguin Book of Love Poetry in US as A Book of Love Poetry, 1973; W. Owen, The Complete Poems and Fragments, vol. II, 1983; The Oxford Book of War Poetry, 1984; (and intro.) The Poems of Wilfred Owen, 1985; (and intro.) First Lines: Poems Written in Youth from Herbert to Heaney, 1988; Henry Reed: Collected Poems, 1991; The Norton Anthology of English Literature, 7th ed., 2000; The Norton Anthology of Poetry, 5th ed., 2005. **Address:** Faculty of English Language & Literature, Oxford University, St Cross Bldg., Manor Rd., Oxford, OX OX1 3UL, England.

ST. AMANT, Mark. American (born United States), b. 1967. **Genres:** Sports/Fitness, Biography. **Career:** Arnold Worldwide, creative director; Sports Rag online, creator, 2002-. Writer. **Publications:** Committed: Confession of a Fantasy Football Junkie, 2004; Just Kick It: Tales of an Underdog, Over-age, Out-of-place, Semi-pro Football Player, 2006. Contributor to periodicals. **Address:** Creative Book Services, 66 Grand St., New York, NY 10013-2263, U.S.A. **Online address:** mark@markstamant.com

STAMBLER, Irwin. American (born United States), b. 1924. **Genres:** Air/Space Topics, Children's Non-fiction, History, Music, Recreation, Sports/Fitness, Travel/Exploration. **Career:** R.H. Macy Bureau of Standards, mechanical engineer, 1946; Chase Aircraft, senior engineer, 1950-53; Republic Aviation, structures engineer, 1953-54; Space/Aeronautics, associate editor, 1954-66; Industrial Research, western editor, 1966-; Airline Management and Marketing, correspondent, 1967-69; Technology Forecasts and Technology Surveys Newsletter, co-publisher and editorial director, 1969-; Tape Cartridge/Cassette Industry, editor, 1970-69; Alternative Energy Newsletter, publisher and editor, 1980-. Writer. **Publications:** Find a Career in Aviation, 1960; Space Ship: Story of the X-15, 1961; The Battle for Inner Space: Undersea Warfare and Weapons, 1962; (with G. Ashmead) Find a Career in Engineering, 1962; Wonders of Underwater Exploration, 1962; Breath of Life: Story of Our Atmosphere, 1963; Build the Unknown, 1963; (with G. Ashmead) Project Mariner, 1964; Build the Unknown: How Scientists Create the Materials of Tomorrow for the Designs of Today, 1964; Project Gemini, 1964; Encyclopedia of Popular Music, 1965; Supersonic Transport, 1965; Orbiting Space Stations, 1965; Orbiting Stations, 1965; Automobiles of the Future, 1966; Great Moments in Auto Racing, 1967; Guide to Model Car Racing, 1967; Worlds of Sound, 1967; Weather Instruments, 1968; Ocean Liners of the Air, 1969; (with G. Landon) Encyclopedia of Folk, Country and Western Music, 1969, 2nd ed., 1983; World of Microelectronics, 1969; Project Viking, 1970; Guitar Years: Popular Music from Country and Western to Hard Rock, 1970; (with G. Landon) Golden Guitars: The Story of Country Music, 1971; Great Moments in Stock Car Racing, 1971; Unusual Automobiles of Today and Tomorrow, 1972; Shorelines of America, 1972; Automobile Engines of Today and Tomorrow, 1972; Revolution in Light, 1972; The Supercars and the Men Who Drive Them, 1974; Speed Kings, 1974; Women in Sports, 1975; Encyclopedia of Pop, Rock and Soul, 1975, rev. ed., 1990; The Supercars and the Men Who Race Them, 1975; Bill Walton, Super Center, 1976; Catfish Hunter, 1976; Here Come the Funny Cars, 1976; Minibikes and Small Cycles, 1977; New Automobiles of the Future, 1978; Top Fuelers, 1978; Racing the Sprint Cars, 1979; Dream Machines: Vans and Pickups, 1980; Off-Roading: Racing and Riding, 1984; (with G. Landon) Country Music: The Encyclopedia, 1997; (with L. Stambler) Encyclopedia of Folk and Blues, 2000; (with L. Stambler) Folk and Blues: The Encyclopedia, 2001. Contributor to journals. **Address:** c/o Willard Wilks, Technology Forecasts & Technology Surveys, 205 S Beverly Dr., Ste. 208, Beverly Hills, CA 90212, U.S.A. **Online address:** nodnyl@aol.com

STAMETS, Paul. American (born United States), b. 1955. **Genres:** Agriculture/Forestry, Homes/Gardens, Sciences. **Career:** Fungi Perfecti, founder; Rainforest Mushroom Genome and Mycodiversity Preservation Project, co-director and founder; University of Arizona Medical School, Program for Integrative Medicine, consultant. Writer and mycologist. **Publications:** (With J.S. Chilton) The Mushroom Cultivator: A Practical Guide to Growing Mushrooms at Home, 1983; Growing Gourmet and Medicinal Mushrooms, 1993, 3rd ed., 2000; Psilocybin Mushrooms of the World: An Identification Guide, 1996; (with C.D.W. Yao) Mycomedicinals: An Informational Booklet on Medicinal Mushrooms, 1998; Mycelium Running: How Mushrooms Can Help Save the World, 2005. **Address:** Fungi Perfecti L.L.C., PO Box 7634, Olympia, WA 98507, U.S.A. **Online address:** info@fungi.com

STAMFORD KRAUSE, Shari. American (born United States), b. 1961. **Genres:** Air/Space Topics, Technology, Engineering. **Career:** Martin Marietta Aerospace Co., engineer, 1984-85; Embry-Riddle Aeronautical University, instructor, 1990-96; Writer, 1996-; Federal Aviation Administration, licensed single-engine land pilot, 1980-. **Publications:** Avoiding Mid-Air Collisions, 1995; Aircraft Safety: Accident Investigations, Analyses, and Applications, 1996, 2nd ed., 2003. Contributor to periodicals. **Address:** The McGraw-Hill Co., P.O. Box 182604, Columbus, OH 43272, U.S.A. **Online address:** sskrause@aol.com

STAMM, Peter. Swiss (born Switzerland), b. 1963. **Genres:** Novels, Theatre, Novellas/Short Stories, Children's Fiction. **Career:** Freelance writer, 1990-. **Publications:** Ich und die Anderen, 1991; Die Nacht der Gewohnheiten, 1993; In Vitro, 1994; Alles ueber die Maenner, 1995; Der Letzte Autofahrer, 1995; Bildnis eines Knaben mit Peitsche, 1996; Gotthard-die Steinerne Seele derSchweiz, 1997; Ableben, 1997; Warum wir Vor der Stadt Wohnen, 1999; Nachtkampf oder die Kunst des Tee-Wegs, 1999; Blitzeis: Erzaehlungen, 1999; Agnes: A Roman, 1998; Passion, 2000; Ungefaehre Landschaft, 2001; Was Wir Koennen, 2002; (ed.) Diensttage, 2003; Der Kuss des Kohaku: Stuecke, 2004; Unformed Landscape, 2004; An einem Tag wie diesem: Roman, 2006; In Strange Gardens and Other Stories, 2006; On a Day Like This: A Novel, 2007; Wir Fliegen: Erzaehlunge, 2008; Sieben Jahre, 2009; Seeruecken: Erzaehlungen, 2011. Contributor to periodicals. Works appear in anthologies. **Address:** c/o Author Mail, Liepman AG, Englischviertelstrasse 59, Zurich, 8032, Switzerland. **Online address:** post@peterstamm.ch

STAMMERS, John. British (born England), b. 1954?. **Genres:** Poetry, Literary Criticism And History. **Career:** King's College, associate; Birkbeck College, faculty; University of London, faculty; City Lit, teacher in creative writing; University of Cambridge, Judith E. Wilson fellow, 2002-03. Writer and poet. **Publications:** POETRY: Panoramic Lounge Bar, 2001; Buffalo Bills, 2004; Stolen Love Behaviour, 2005; Interior Night, 2010. Contributor to magazines and periodicals. **Address:** c/o Author Mail, Pan Macmillan, 20 New Wharf Rd., London, GL N1 9RR, England.

STAMP, Terence (Henry). British (born England), b. 1939. **Genres:** Autobiography/Memoirs, Novels, Westerns/Adventure, Food And Wine. **Career:** Actor in films, 1962-. Writer. **Publications:** Stamp Album, 1987; Coming Attractions, 1988; Double Feature, 1989; The Night, 1993; (with E. Buxton) The Stamp Collection Cookbook, 1995. **Address:** Markham & Froggatt Ltd., 4 Windmill St., London, GL W1P 1HF, England.

STAMPF, Günter. German/Austrian (born Austria), b. 1968. **Genres:** Young Adult Non-fiction. **Career:** Niederösterreichische Nachrichten, columnist and editor, 1985-87; Rennbahn Express (youth magazine), chief music editor, 1988-91; Basta Magazine, writer, 1991; Bunte Illustrierte Magazine, Lifestyle Department, editor, 1992-93; Bild (newspaper), senior journalist, 1993-94; Bunte Magazine, deputy editor-in-chief, 1995-96; Orf, editor-in-chief, 1996-97; Prassl & Stampf Medienprodukktion, managing director, 1998-2001; Stampfwerk (media production company), founder and chief executive officer, 2001-. **Publications:** Interview with a Cannibal: The Secret Life of the Monster of Rotenburg, 2008. **Address:** Stampfwerk, Spielbudenplatz 24/25, Entertainmentcenter, Hamburg, 20359, Germany. **Online address:** g.stampf@stampfwerk.de

STANCYKOWNA *See* **Szymborska, Wislawa.**

STANDAGE, Virginia. *See* **RANDALL, Rona.**

STANDEN, John Derek. (John J. Standen). British (born England), b.

1937?. **Genres:** History, Literary Criticism And History. **Career:** Kingsdale School, assistant master, 1960-64; Kingston Polytechnic (now Kingston University), lecturer, 1964-67, senior lecturer, 1967-74, principal lecturer in history, 1974-89; Young Historian Newsletter, editor, 1990-96. **Publications:** The Victorian Age, 1967; The End of an Era, 1968; The Edwardians, 1968; After the Deluge: English Society Between the Wars, 1969; The Great Exhibition of 1851, 1973. **Address:** 30 New Compton St., Flat 1, London, GL WC2H 8DN, England.

STANDEN, John J. *See* **STANDEN, John Derek.**

STANDIFORD, Natalie. Also writes as Emily James. American (born United States), b. 1961. **Genres:** Science Fiction/Fantasy, Children's Fiction, Young Adult Fiction, Children's Non-fiction. **Career:** Writer. **Publications:** The Best Little Monkeys in the World, 1987; Dollhouse Mouse (picture book), 1989; The Bravest Dog Ever: The True Story of Balto, 1989; The Headless Horseman, 1992; Brave Maddie Egg, 1995; Astronauts Are Sleeping (picture book), 1996. SPACE DOG SERIES: Space Dog and Roy, 1990; Space Dogand the Pet Show, 1990; Space Dog in Trouble, 1991; Space Dog the Hero, 1991; The Stone Giant, 2001. THE DATING GAME SERIES: The Dating Game, 2004; Breaking Up is Really, Really Hard to Do, 2005; Can True Love Survive High School?, 2005; Ex-Rating, 2006; Speed Dating, 2006; Parallel Parking, 2006. THE ELLE WOODS SERIES: Blonde at Heart, 2006; Beach Blonde, 2006; Vote Blonde, 2006; Blonde Love, 2007; How to Say Goodbye in Robot, 2009; Confessions of the Sullivan Sisters, 2010. **Address:** c/o Sarah Burnes, The Gernert Co., 136 E 57th St., New York, NY 10022, U.S.A. **Online address:** natstand@aol.com

STANFORD, Craig (Britton). American (born United States), b. 1956?. **Genres:** Anthropology/Ethnology, Environmental Sciences/Ecology, Politics/Government. **Career:** University of Southern California, Departments of Anthropology and Biology, professor, 1992-, Jane Goodall Research Center, co-director; Los Angeles County Museum of Natural History, research associate in vertebrate biology; University of Michigan, lecturer. Writer. **Publications:** The Capped Langur in Bangladesh: Behavioral Ecology and Reproductive Tactics, 1991; Chimpanzee and Red Colobus: The Ecology of Predator and Prey, 1998; The Hunting Apes: Meat Eating and the Origins of Human Behavior, 1999; Significant Others: The Ape-Human Continuum and the Quest for Human Stature, 2001; Meat-Eating and Human Evolution, 2001; Upright: The Evolutionary Key to Becoming Human, 2003; (with J.S. Allen, S.C. Anton) Biological Anthropology: The Natural History of Humankind, 2006; Apes of the Impenetrable Forest: The Behavioral Ecology of Sympatric Chimpanzees and Gorillas, 2008; (with M. Bearzi) Beautiful Minds: The Parallel Lives of Great Apes and Dolphins, 2008; (with J.S. Allena and S.C. Antón) Exploring Biological Anthropology: The Essentials, 2008, 2nd ed., 2010; (with J.S. Allen and S.C. Antón) Biological Anthropology: The Natural History of Humankind, 2010; Last Tortoise: A Tale of Extinction In Our Lifetime, 2010. **Address:** Department of Anthropology, University of Southern California, Rm. 349, Hancock B54, 3518 Trousdale Pkwy., Von KleinSmid Ctr., Los Angeles, CA 90089-0032, U.S.A. **Online address:** stanford@usc.edu

STANGROOM, Jeremy. British (born England) **Genres:** Philosophy, Sciences, Humor/Satire. **Career:** The Philosophers' Magazine, co-founder, 1997, owner, co-editor, new media editor; Butterflies and Wheels Website, co-founder. Website designer and computer programmer. **Publications:** (Ed. with J. Baggini) New British Philosophy, 2002; (ed. with J. Baggini) What Philosophers Think, 2003; (ed. with J. Baggini) Great Thinkers A-Z, 2004; (with Ophelia Benson) The Dictionary of Fashionable Nonsense: A Guide for Edgy People, 2004; (ed.) What Scientists Think, 2005; The Great Philosophers, 2005; (with O. Benson) Why Truth Matters, 2006; (ed. with J. Baggini) What More Philosophers Think, 2007; (with J. Baggini) Do You Think What You Think You Think?: The Ultimate Philosophical Handbook, 2007; Little Book of Big Ideas: Philosophy, 2007; Identity Crisis: Against Multiculturalism, 2008; (with O. Benson) Does God Hate Women?, 2009; Einstein's Riddle: Riddles, Paradoxes and Conundrums to Stretch Your Mind, 2009. **Address:** Butterflies & Wheels, 98 Mulgrave Rd., Sutton, SR SM2 6LZ, England. **Online address:** jerry@jeremystangroom.com

STANISH, Charles. American (born United States), b. 1956?. **Genres:** Environmental Sciences/Ecology, History, Social Sciences. **Career:** University of Illinois, Department of Anthropology, postdoctoral research fellow and visiting assistant professor, 1986-87, adjunct associate professor, 1988-97; Field Museum of Natural History, Department of Anthropology, assistant curator, 1988-92, associate curator, 1992, vice-chair, 1993-95, chair, 1995-97; University of Chicago, Department of Anthropology, research associate, 1990-97; University of California, Department of Anthropology, associate professor, 1997-2000, professor, 2001-, The Cotsen Institute of Archaeology, director, 2001-; Los Angeles County Museum of Natural History, Department of Anthropology, research associate, 2001-. Writer. **Publications:** (Ed. with D.S. Rice and P.R. Scarr) Ecology, Settlement, and History in the Osmore Drainage, Peru, 1989; Ancient Andean Political Economy, 1992; (with B.S. Bauer) Ritual and Pilgrimage in the Ancient Andes: The Islands of the Sun and the Moon, 2001; Ancient Titicaca: The Evolution of Complex Society in Southern Peruand Northern Bolivia, 2003; (ed. with B.S. Bauer) Archaeological Research on the Islands of the Sun and Moon, Lake Titicaca, Bolivia: Final Results of the Proyecto Takai Kjarka, 2004; (ed. with A.B. Cohen and M.S. Aldenderfer) Advances in Titicaca Basin Archaeology-1, 2005; (ed. with J. Marcus) Agricultural Strategies, 2006; Lake Titicaca: Legend, Myth and Science, 2011. Contributor to periodicals. **Address:** Cotsen Institute of Archaeology, University of California Los Angeles, A210D Fowler Bldg., 308 Charles E Young Dr. N, PO Box 951510, Los Angeles, CA 90095-1553, U.S.A. **Online address:** stanish@anthro.ucla.edu

STANLEY, Autumn. (Autumn Joy Stanley). American (born United States), b. 1933. **Genres:** Mystery/Crime/Suspense, Children's Fiction, Archaeology/Antiquities, History, Technology, Women's Studies And Issues, Biography, Autobiography/Memoirs, Autobiography/Memoirs. **Career:** Stanford University Press, editor of scholarly books, 1969-74; Wadsworth Publishing Co., senior developmental editor of science textbooks, 1974-80; researcher, 1980-; Montalvo Center for the Arts, resident artist, 1983; Pacific Lutheran College, instructor; Canada College, instructor. **Publications:** Sparrowgrass: The Asparagus Cookbook, 1977; Mainder the Buttercup, 1977; The Enchanted Quill, 1978; Mothers and Daughters of Invention: Notes for a Revised History of Technology, 1993; Raising More Hell and Fewer Dahlias: The Public Life of Charlotte Smith, 1840-1917, 2009. Work appears in anthologies. Contributor of articles to magazines. **Address:** 241 Bonita Rd., Los Trancos Woods, Portola Valley, CA 94028, U.S.A.

STANLEY, Autumn Joy. *See* **STANLEY, Autumn.**

STANLEY, Diane. American (born United States), b. 1943. **Genres:** Children's Fiction, Children's Non-fiction, Illustrations. **Career:** Freelance medical illustrator, 1970-74; Dell Publishing, graphic designer, 1977; Putnam's Publishers, art director of children's books, 1977-79; Author and illustrator, 1979-. **Publications:** SELF-ILLUSTRATOR: The Conversation Club, 1983; Birdsong Lullaby, 1985; (with P. Vennema) Shaka, King of the Zulus, 1988; Good Queen Bess: The Story of Queen Elizabeth I of England, 1990; Bard of Avon: The Story of William Shakespeare, 1992; (with P. Vennema) Charles Dickens: The Man Who Had Great Expectations, 1993; (with P. Vennema) Cleopatra, 1994; Giant and the Beanstalk, 2004. OTHERS: Farmer in the Dell, 1978; Fiddle-i-fee: A Traditional American Chant, 1979; A Country Tale, 1985; The Good Luck Pencil, 1986; Peter the Great, 1986; Captain Whiz-Bang, 1987; Fortune, 1990; Siegfried, 1991; Moe the Dog in Tropical Paradise, 1992; The Gentleman and the Kitchen Maid, 1994; The True Adventure of Daniel Hall, 1995; Woe is Moe, 1995; Elena, 1996; Leonardo da Vinci, 1996; Saving Sweetness, 1996; Rumpelstiltskin's Daughter, 1997; Joan of Arc, 1998; A Time Apart, 1999; Raising Sweetness, 1999; Roughing it on the Oregon Trail, 1999; Michelangelo, 2000; Joining the Boston Tea Party, 2001; The Mysterious Matter of I.M. Fine, 2001; Saladin: Noble Prince of Islam, 2002; Goldie and the Three Bears, 2003; Thanksgiving on Plymouth Plantation, 2004; Bella at Midnight: The Thimble, the Ring and the Slippers of Glass, 2006; The Trouble With Wishes, 2007; The Mysterious Case of the Allbright Academy, 2008; Mozart, the Wonder Child: A Puppet Play in Three Acts, 2009; Saving Sky, 2010; Silver Bowl, 2011. **Address:** c/o Author Mail, HarperCollins Publishers, 10 E 53rd St., 7th Fl., New York, NY 10022, U.S.A. **Online address:** dianley@aol.com

STANLEY, J. B. (Jennifer B. Stanley). American (born United States), b. 1970?. **Genres:** Mystery/Crime/Suspense. **Career:** Leland Little Auctions, sales associate. Educator and writer. **Publications:** COLLECTIBLE MYSTERY SERIES: A Killer Collection, 2006; A Fatal Appraisal, 2006; A Deadly Dealer, 2007. SUPPER CLUB MYSTERY SERIES: Carbs & Cadavers, 2006; Fit to Die, 2007; Chili con Corpses, 2008; Stiffs and Swine, 2008. **Address:** Richmond, VA , U.S.A. **Online address:** jbstanleyauthor@comcast.net

STANLEY, Jennifer B. *See* **STANLEY, J. B.**

STANLEY, Jerry. American (born United States), b. 1941. **Genres:** Biography, Young Adult Non-fiction, Children's Fiction, History. **Career:** California State University, assistant professor, 1973-77, associate professor, 1977-81, professor of history, 1981-98. Freelance writer. **Publications:** Children of the Dust Bowl: The True Story of the School at Weedpatch Camp, 1992; I Am an American: A True Story of Japanese Internment, 1994; Big Annie of Calumet: A True Story of the Industrial Revolution, 1996; Digger: The Tragic Fate of the California Indian from the Missions to the Gold Rush, 1997; Frontier Merchants: Lionel and Barron Jacobs and the Jewish Pioneers Who Settled the West, 1998; Hurry Freedom!: African Americans in Gold Rush California, 2000; Cowboys & Longhorns, 2003. **Address:** 3504 Robinwood, Bakersfield, CA 93309, U.S.A. **Online address:** jdstanle@pacbell.net

STANLEY, Kelli. American (born United States), b. 1964. **Genres:** Mystery/Crime/Suspense. **Career:** Funny Papers (a comic book store), co-owner, 1989-97; San Francisco State University, publications director, 2007-. Writer. **Publications:** Nox Dormienda: A Long Night for Sleeping: An Arcturus Mystery, 2008; City of Dragons, 2010; Curse-Maker, 2011; City of Secrets, 2011. **Address:** c/o Kimberley Cameron, Reece Halsey North Literary Agency, 98 Main St., Ste. 704, Tiburon, CA 94920, U.S.A. **Online address:** kelli@kellistanley.com

STANLEY, Oliver. British (born England), b. 1925. **Genres:** Law, Money/Finance. **Career:** Weymouth, H.M. inspector of taxes, 1952-65; Middle Temple, part-time barrister, 1963; Gray Dawes Company Ltd., director, 1966-71; Comprehensive Financial Services L.L.C., founder, 1971; Rathbone Bros P.L.C., chairman, 1971-96; Profile Books Ltd., chairman, 1996-2005, director, 2004-. Writer. **Publications:** A Guide to Taxation, 1967; Tax and Insurance, 1969; (co-author) Simon's Taxes, 1970; Taxology: The Perpetual Battle of Wits Between the Inland Revenue and the Taxpayer, 1972; (ed.) The Creation and Protection of Capital, 1974; Taxation of Farmers and Landowners, 1981, rev. ed., 2003; (with G. Clarke) Offshore Tax Planning, 1989; Hotel Victoire, 2007; 1941, 2008; Happy Families, forthcoming. **Address:** 159 New Bond St., London, GL W1Y 9PA, England. **Online address:** oliverstanley@compuserve.com

STANLEY, Patricia H. (Patricia Hass Stanley). American (born United States) **Genres:** Literary Criticism And History, Essays, Translations, History. **Career:** Indiana University, instructor in German, 1970-72; University of Virginia, instructor, 1972-75, assistant professor of German, 1976-77; Florida State University, assistant professor, 1977-82, associate professor of German, 1982-94, professor, 1994-2005; Columbia University, College of Physicians and Surgeons, faculty; Dickstein Cancer Center, staff. Writer. **Publications:** Wolfgang Hildesheimer's Tynset, 1978; The Realm of Possibilities: Wolfgang Hildesheimer's Non-traditional, Nonfictional Prose, 1988; Wolfgang Hildesheimer and His Critics, 1993; (trans. and intro.) The Writer in Her Writing, Selected Stories of Adelheid Duvanel, 2002; (trans.) I. Kaiser, Rosa and The Wolves, 2008; (trans.) V. Jehele, Come, Let's Dream, 2008. Contributor of articles to periodicals. **Address:** Rowman & Littlefield Publishing Group, University Press of America, 4501 Forbes Blvd., Ste. 200, Lanham, MD 20706, U.S.A. **Online address:** phstanley@embarqmail.com

STANLEY, Patricia Hass. See **STANLEY, Patricia H.**

STANLEY, Peter W(illiam). American (born United States), b. 1940. **Genres:** History, Military/Defense/Arms Control, Travel/Exploration, Social Sciences. **Career:** University of Illinois, assistant professor of history, 1970-72; Harvard University, assistant professor, 1972-78, lecturer in history, 1978-79; Foreign Service Institute, lecturer, 1977-89; Carleton College, dean, 1979-84; Ford Foundation, program officer in charge of education and culture, 1984-87, director of education and culture program, 1987-91; Pomona College, president, 1991-2003; Johns Hopkins University, Center for Research on Effective Schooling for Disadvantaged Students, member of national advisory board, 1989-; National Association of Latino Elected and Appointed Officials Educational Fund, director, 1992-; Isaacson, vice president. Writer. **Publications:** A Nation in the Making: The Philippines and the United States, 1899-1921, 1974; (with J.C. Tomson, Jr. and J.C. Perry) Sentimental Imperialists: The American Experience in East Asia, 1981; (ed. and intro.) Reappraising an Empire: New Perspectives on Philippine-American History, 1984. Contributor to books and periodicals. **Address:** 345 N College Ave., Claremont, CA 91711-4408, U.S.A.

STANLEY, Susie Cunningham. American (born United States), b. 1948.

Genres: Theology/Religion, Women's Studies And Issues, Race Relations, Autobiography/Memoirs. **Career:** Church of God, ordained ecumenical minister; Western Evangelical Seminary, professor, 1983-95; Wesleyan/Holiness Women Clergy Intl., founder and executive director, 1991-2006; Messiah College, professor of historical theology, retired, 2011. Writer. **Publications:** (Co-author) Women, Authority and the Bible, 1986; Called to Ministry,1989. NONFICTION: Feminist Pillar of Fire: The Life of Alma White, 1993; (comp.) Wesleyan/Holiness Women Clergy: A Preliminary Bibliography, 1994; (comp.) Honoring God's Call: A Celebration of Holiness Women Preachers, 1994; Holy Boldness: Women Preachers Autobiographies and the Sanctified Self, 2002; (co-ed.) Faith and Gender Equity, 2007. **Address:** 130 Sholly Dr., Mechanicsburg, PA 17055, U.S.A. **Online address:** sstanley@messiah.edu

STANNARD, Martin (J.). British (born England), b. 1947. **Genres:** Literary Criticism And History, Biography. **Career:** University of Edinburgh, Leverhulme research fellow in English literature, 1976-79; University of Leicester, lecturer in English literature, 1979-93, reader in English, 1993-95, professor of modern English literature, 1995-. Writer. **Publications:** Evelyn Waugh: The Early Years, 1903-1939, 1986; Evelyn Waugh: The Later Years, 1939-1966, 1992; Muriel Spark: The Biography, 2009. EDITOR: Evelyn Waugh: The Critical Heritage, 1984; The Good Soldier by Ford Madox Ford, 1995, 2nd ed., 2011. Contributor to periodicals. **Address:** Department of English, University of Leicester, Leicester, LE LE1 7RH, England. **Online address:** maj@le.ac.uk

STANNARD, Richard M. American (born United States), b. 1925. **Genres:** Military/Defense/Arms Control, History. **Career:** Peninsula Newspapers Inc., journalist, 1951-64; Examiner & Chronicle, correspondent, 1951-64; Office of Economic Opportunity, inspector and writer, 1966-82; Princeton University, fellow, 1975-76. **Publications:** Infantry Combat: An Oral History of a World War II American Infantry Battalion, 1993. **Address:** 2424 Hobart Ave. SW, Apt. C, Seattle, WA 98116, U.S.A.

STANSBERRY, Domenic (Joseph). American (born United States), b. 1952. **Genres:** Plays/Screenplays, Novels, Literary Criticism And History, Mystery/Crime/Suspense. **Career:** Daily Hampshire Gazette, feature writer, 1981-83; Northampton Veterans Administration, writing teacher, 1982-83; University of New Orleans, instructor of composition and creative writing, 1984-87; Lynx House Press, consulting editor, 1984-85; Tulane University, visiting lecturer, 1985-86; Eastern Washington University, Publications Department, editor and writer of public relations and marketing material, 1987-; California State University, writing instructor, 1990-92; Stansberry Communications, dialogue writer and media consultant, 1992-; Vermont College, visiting writer; Black River Publishing, co-founder and co-editor; Willow Springs, contributing editor. **Publications:** The Spoiler: A Novel, 1987; Exit Paradise: Stories, 1992; Labyrinths: The Art of Interactive Writing & Design: Content Development for New Media, 1998; Last Days of Il Duce, 1998; Manifesto for the Dead, 2000; Confession, 2004; Chasing the Dragon, 2004; The Big Boom, 2006; The Ancient Rain, 2008; Naked Moon, 2010. **Address:** PO Box 657, Corte Madera, CA 94976-0657, U.S.A. **Online address:** domenic.stansberry@pacbell.net

STANSFIELD, Gareth R.V. British (born England), b. 1973. **Genres:** Politics/Government, History. **Career:** University of Durham, Centre for Middle Eastern and Islamic Studies, research associate, 1997-2001; University of Exeter, Leverhulme Trust special research fellow in political development, 2002-04, lecturer in Middle East politics, 2004-05, reader in Middle East politics, 2005-06, Institute of Arab and Islamic Studies, professor of Middle East politics, 2006-, Centre for Ethno-Political Studies, director; Royal Institute for International Affairs (Chatham House), Middle East and North Africa Program, associate fellow; United Nations Assistance Mission for Iraq, senior political advisor, 2008-. Writer. **Publications:** Iraqi Kurdistan: An Analysis and Assessment of the Development and Operation of the Political System, 2001; The 1995-96 Yemen-Eritrea Conflict over the Islands of Hanish and Jabal Zuqar: A Geopolitical Analysis, 2001; Iraqi Kurdistan: Political Development and Emergent Democracy, 2003; (with L. Anderson) The Future of Iraq: Dictatorship, Democracy, or Division?, 2004; The Iraq War and Democratic Politics, 2005; Iraq: People, History, Politics, 2007; (ed. with R. Visser) An Iraq of Its Regions: Cornerstones of a Federal Democracy?, 2008; (with L. Anderson) Crisis in Kirkuk: The Ethnopolitics of Conflict and Compromise, 2009; (ed. with R. Lowe) The Kurdish Policy Imperative, 2010; (ed.

with N. Caspersen) Unrecognized States in the International System, 2011. Contributor of articles to journals. **Address:** England. **Online address:** g.r.v.stansfield@exeter.ac.uk

STANSKY, Peter (David Lyman). American (born United States), b. 1932. **Genres:** History, Literary Criticism And History, Biography, Military/Defense/Arms Control, Politics/Government. **Career:** Harvard University, instructor, 1961-64, assistant professor of history, 1964-68; Stanford University, associate professor, 1968-74, professor, 1974-75, Frances and Charles Field professor of history, 1975-2005, department chair, 1975-78, 1979-82, 1989-90, professor emeritus, 2005-, Center for the Advanced Study of the Behavioral Sciences, fellow, 1988-89, Stanford Humanities Center, director, 2000-01, honorary fellow, 2002-, fellow, 2003-04; Cambridge University Press, editor, 1970-74; Oxford University, All Souls College, visiting fellow, 1979, St. Catherine's College, Christensen Fellow, 1983. Writer. **Publications:** Ambitions and Strategies: The Struggle for the Leadership of the Liberal Party in the 1890s, 1964; (with W. Abrahams) Journey to the Frontier: Two Roads to the Spanish Civil War, 1966; (with W. Abrahams) The Unknown Orwell, 1972; England since 1867: Continuity and Change, 1973; Gladstone, A Progress Politics, 1979; (with W. Abrahams) Orwell: The Transformation, 1980; William Morris, 1983; William Morris, C.R. Ashbee and the Arts and Crafts, 1984; Redesigning the World: William Morris, the 1880s and the Arts and Crafts, 1985; (with W. Abrahams) London's Burning: Life, Death and Art in the Second World War, 1994; On or about December 1910: Early Bloomsbury and Its Intimate World, 1996; Another Book That Never Was: William Morris, Charles Gere, The House of the Wolfings, 1998; From William Morris to Sergeant Pepper: Studies in the Radical Domestic, 1999; Sassoon: The Worlds of Philip and Sybil, 2003; The First Day of The Blitz: September 7, 1940, 2007; (with W. Abrahams) Julian Bell: From Bloomsbury to the Spanish Civil War, 2012. EDITOR: The Left and War: The British Labour Party and World War I, 1969; John Morley: 19th Century Essays, 1970; Churchill: A Profile, 1973; The Victorian Revolution: Government and Society in Victoria's Britain, 1973; On Nineteen Eighty-Four, 1983. **Address:** Department of History, Stanford University, Rm. 314, Bldg. 200, Stanford, CA 94305-2024, U.S.A. **Online address:** stansky@stanford.edu

ST. ANTOINE, Sara L. American (born United States), b. 1966. **Genres:** Children's Fiction, Children's Non-fiction, Mystery/Crime/Suspense. **Career:** Environmental Law Institute, associate editor, 1988-89; National Wildlife Federation, School Programs Division, project editor, 1989-91; Conservation Intl., research associate, 1991-92; World Wildlife Fund, education consultant, 1993-; Echoing Green Foundation, public service fellow, 1993-95; American Association for the Advancement of Science, writer for children's science radio drama, 1995-; Children & Nature Network, senior writer. **Publications:** Dress Code Mess, 1992; The Green Musketeers and the Fabulous Frogs, 1994; The Green Musketeers and the Incredible Energy Escapade, 1994; (contrib.) The Biophilia Hypothesis, 1993. EDITOR: Stories from Where We Live, 2000; Stories from Where We Live, The Great North American Prairie, 2001; Stories from Where We Live, The California Coast, 2001; Stories from Where We Live, The Gulf Coast, 2002; Stories from Where We Live, The Great Lakes, 2003; The South Atlantic Coast and Piedmont: Stories from Where We Live, 2006. **Address:** Children & Nature Network, 7 Avenida Vista Grande B-7, Ste. 502, Santa Fe, NM 87508, U.S.A. **Online address:** sstantoine@aol.com

STANTON, Doug. American (born United States) **Genres:** Documentaries/Reportage, History. **Career:** Esquire, contributing editor; Outside, contributing editor; Men's Journal, contributing editor; Sports Afield, contributing editor. **Publications:** In Harm's Way: The Sinking of the USS Indianapolis and the Extraordinary Story of Its Survivors, 2001; Horse Soldiers: The Extraordinary Story of a Band of U.S. Soldiers Who Rode to Victory in Afghanistan, 2009. **Address:** c/o Author Mail, Henry Holt, 115 W 18th St., New York, NY 10011-4113, U.S.A.

STANTON, Joseph. American (born United States), b. 1949. **Genres:** Biography, Poetry, Literary Criticism And History. **Career:** University of Hawaii, associate professor. Writer. **Publications:** British & European Literatures, 1983; (ed. with D.H.Y. Lum and E. Enoki) The Quietest Singing, 2000; The Important Books: Children's Picture Books as Art and Literature, 2005; Stan Musial: A Biography, 2007. POETRY: (with M. Ooka, W.T. Lum and J.Y. Toyama) What the Kite Thinks: A Linked Poem, 1994; Imaginary Museum: Poems on Art, 1999; Cardinal Points: Poems on St. Louis Cardinals Baseball, 2002; A Field Guide to the Wildlife of Suburban O'ahu, 2006. Contributor

of articles to periodicals. **Address:** Department of Art and Art History, University of Hawaii, 2535 McCarthy Mall, Honolulu, HI 96822-2318, U.S.A. **Online address:** jstanton@hawaii.edu

STANTON, Richard C. Australian (born Australia), b. 1951. **Genres:** Adult Non-fiction, Public/Social Administration, Social Sciences, Young Adult Fiction. **Career:** Australian British Chamber of Commerce, director, 1989-95; Public Relations Institute of Australia, Industry Liaison, chair, 1997-99, director, 2004-07; Australian Institute of Professional Communicators, director, 1998-99, president, 1999-2001, fellow; Temple University, School of Communication and Theater, visiting professor, 2009; University of North Carolina, Department of Communication Studies, visiting adjunct professor; University of Sydney, Faculty of Arts, associate dean; Sookmyung University, Department of Advertising and Public Relations, visiting fellow; Rydges Business Journal, journalist and editor; International Communication Association, Political Communication Report, editor; Academy of Journalism and Social Sciences, visiting fellow. Publisher, political consultant and public relations executive. **Publications:** (With R. Phillipps) Public Relations Precepts and Practices, 1998; When Your Partner Dies: Stories of Women Who Have Lost Their Husbands, 1999; Innovation Management: Strategic Positioning in a Global and Local World, 2001; Media Relations, 2006; All News is Local: The Failure of the Media to Reflect World Events in a Globalized Age, 2007; Spinning Towards Earth: Public Relations and Death in Postmodernity, 2009. Contributor to periodicals. **Address:** Department of Media and Communications, University of Sydney, Rm. 208, Footbridge Theatre Terr., Sydney, NW 2006, Australia. **Online address:** richard.stanton@sydney.edu.au

STANTON, Shelby L(ee). American (born United States), b. 1948. **Genres:** Military/Defense/Arms Control, History. **Career:** Teacher, 1976-77; attorney, 1977-; writer, 1981-; Centers for Disease Control and Prevention, consultant; Smithsonian Institution, consultant; U.S. Army, infantry officer, paratrooper platoon leader. **Publications:** Vietnam Order of Battle, 1981; Order of Battle, U.S. Army, World War II, 1984; The Rise and Fall of an American Army: U.S. Ground Forces in Vietnam, 1965-1973, 1985, rev. ed., 1999; The Green Berets at War: U.S. Army Special Forces in Southeast Asia, 1956-1975, 1985; Anatomy of a Division: The 1st Cav in Vietnam, 1987; U.S. Army Special Forces A-Team Vietnam Combat Manual, 1988; America's Tenth Legion: X Corps in Korea, 1950, 1989; U.S. Army Uniforms of the Vietnam War, 1989; Soldiers: A Portrait of the United States Army, 1990; Special Forces at War: An Illustrated History, Southeast Asia, 1957-1975, 1990; U.S. Army Uniforms of World War II, 1991, U.S. Army Uniforms of the Korean War, 1992; Rangers at War: Combat Recon in Vietnam, 1992; U.S. Army Uniforms of the Cold War, 1948-1973, 1994; World War II Order of Battle, U.S. Army, 2006; Special Forces at War: An Illustrated History, Southeast Asia 1957-1975, 2008. **Address:** c/o Al Zuckerman, Writers House, 21 W 26th St., New York, MD 10010-1003, U.S.A.

STAPLES, Robert Eugene. American (born United States), b. 1942. **Genres:** Human Relations/Parenting, Humanities, Race Relations, Sociology, Social Sciences, Women's Studies And Issues. **Career:** St. Paul Urban League, director of research, 1966; Bethune-Cookman College, associate professor of sociology, 1967-68; California State University, assistant professor, 1968-69; Fisk University, assistant professor of sociology and visiting professor, 1969-70; University of California, faculty, 1970-71, associate professor, 1973-84, professor of sociology, 1984, now professor emeritus; University of Maryland, adjunct professor, 1970-72; Howard University, associate professor of sociology, 1970-73. Writer. **Publications:** The Lower-Income Negro Family in Saint Paul, 1967; The Black Family: Essays and Studies, 1971, (comp.) 6th ed., 1999; The Black Woman in America: Sex, Marriage and the Family, 1973; Introduction to Black Sociology, 1976; The World of Black Singles: Changing Patterns of Male/Female Relations, 1981; Singles in Australian Society, 1982; Black Masculinity: The Black Male's Role in American Society, 1982; (with L.B. Johnson) Black Families at the Crossroads: Challenges and Prospects, 1993, rev. ed., 2004; Exploring Black Sexuality, 2006. **Address:** Department of Sociology, University of California, LHts-455, 3333 California St., PO Box 0612, San Francisco, CA 94143-0612, U.S.A. **Online address:** robert.staples@ucsf.edu

STAPLES, Suzanne Fisher. American (born United States), b. 1945. **Genres:** Novels, Young Adult Fiction, Human Relations/Parenting, Novellas/Short Stories. **Career:** Business International Corp., Asian marketing director, 1974-76; United Press Intl., news editor and correspondent, 1976-83, South Asia Bureau, chief; Washington Post, part-time editor for foreign desk,

1983-85; U.S. Agency for International Development, consultant, 1986-87; freelance writer, 1988-. **Publications:** Shabanu: Daughter of the Wind, 1989; Haveli, 1993; Dangerous Skies, 1996; Storm, 1998; Shiva's Fire, 2000; The Green Dog: A Mostly True Story, 2003; Under the Persimmon Tree, 2005; Under the Same Stars, 2007; The House of Djinn, 2008. Contributor to periodicals. **Address:** Farrar, Straus and Giroux, 19 Union Sq. W, New York, NY 10003-3304, U.S.A.

STAPLETON, **Richard M.** American (born United States), b. 1942. **Genres:** Environmental Sciences/Ecology, Sciences, Medicine/Health. **Career:** Hartford Times, general assignment reporter, 1962-63; WNOS-Radio, radio reporter, 1963-64; Southern Broadcasting Company Inc., WGHP-TV, reporter, 1965; WTOP-Radio, reporter, 1966-67; Avco Broadcasting Co., WWDC-Radio, news and editorial director, 1968-71, national reporter, 1968-69; WCAU-Radio, managing editor, 1971-74; Metromedia Broadcasting Inc., WNEW-Radio, news director, 1974; National Broadcasting Co., WNBC-Radio, director of news, 1975, WNWS-Radio, director of news, 1975; freelance writer, 1976-80; American Broadcasting Co., ABC Network Radio, writer and editor, 1980-81, ABC Network Radio, senior editor, 1983-87; Columbia Broadcasting System, CBS News, producer, 1987-91, acting executive producer, 1989; American Broadcasting Co., ABC Television News, Capital Cities, writer, 1992-93; U.S. Environmental Protection Agency, External Services Division, Public Affairs Branch, chief, 1993-; Columbia University, adjunct faculty, 1985-87; City University of New York, Brooklyn College, adjunct faculty, 1989. **Publications:** Lead is a Silent Hazard, 1994; (ed.) Pollution A to Z, 2 vols., 2004. Contributor to books and periodicals. **Address:** Carol Mann Agency, 55 5th Ave., New York, NY 10003, U.S.A.

STAPLETON, **Timothy J.** Canadian (born Canada), b. 1967?. **Genres:** History, Military/Defense/Arms Control, Biography, Autobiography/Memoirs. **Career:** University of Botswana, research associate; University of Zimbabwe, research associate; Rhodes University, faculty; University of Fort Hare, faculty; Trent University, Department of History, assistant professor, professor and chair. Writer and historian. **Publications:** Maqoma: Xhosa Resistance to Colonial Advance, 1798-1873, 1994; (ed. with C. Youe) Agency and Action in Colonial Africa: Essays for John E. Flint, 2001; Faku: Rulership and Colonialism in the Mpondo Kingdom, c. 1760-1867, 2001; No Insignificant Part: The Rhodesia Native Regiment and the East Africa Campaign of the First World War, 2006; A Military History of South Africa: From the Dutch-Khoi Wars to the End of Apartheid, 2010; African Police and Soldiers in Colonial Zimbabwe 1923-80, 2011. **Address:** Department of History, Traill College, Trent University, Crawford House 201, 1600 W Bank Dr., Peterborough, ON K9J 7B8, Canada. **Online address:** tstapleton@trentu.ca

STARER, **Daniel.** American (born United States), b. 1954. **Genres:** How-to Books, Self Help, Novels, Education, Reference, Human Relations/Parenting. **Career:** Research for Writers, president and founder, 1980-. Writer. **Publications:** (With J. Boswell) Five Rings, Six Crises, Seven Dwarfs and 38 Ways to Win an Argument: Numerical Lists You Never Knew or Once Knew and Probably Forgot, 1990; Who to Call: The Parents Sourcebook, 1992; Who Knows What: The Essential Business Resource Book, 1992; Hot Topics: Everything You Ever Wanted to Know About the Fifty Major Controversies Everyone Pretends to Know All About, 1995. **Address:** Research for Writers, 59 W 85th St., New York, NY 10024, U.S.A. **Online address:** dstarer@researchforwriters.com

STARITA, **Joe.** American (born United States), b. 1948. **Genres:** Adult Non-fiction. **Career:** Miami Herald, Naples Bureau, reporter, 1979-80, Fort Lauderdale-Broward Bureau, city hall reporter, 1980-81, city desk reporter, 1981-83, New York bureau chief, 1983-87; freelance writer, 1991-97; Lincoln Star Journal, city editor, 1997-2000; University of Nebraska, College of Journalism & Mass Communications, associate professor of news-editorial professor, Pike professor of journalism, 2000-. **Publications:** The Dull Knifes of Pine Ridge: A Lakota Odyssey (nonfiction), 1995; A Day in the Life, The Fans of Memorial Stadium, 1996; I Am A Man: Chief Standing Bear's Journey for Justice (nonfiction), 2009. Contributor to newspapers. **Address:** College of Journalism and Mass Communications, University of Nebraska, 239 Andersen Hall, Lincoln, NE 68588-0443, U.S.A. **Online address:** jstarita2@unl.edu

STARK, **Evan.** American (born United States), b. 1942. **Genres:** Young Adult Non-fiction, Human Relations/Parenting, Medicine/Health, Women's Studies And Issues, Law, Public/Social Administration, Sociology, Race Relations, Social Sciences, Criminology/True Crime. **Career:** City College of New York, lecturer in sociology, 1967; Citizens Community Centers, administrator, 1968-70; Quinnipiac College, assistant professor of sociology, 1971-75; Yale University, Institution for Social and Policy studies, assistant, 1975-77, research associate, senior research scientist, 1978-84; Rutgers University, School of Public Affairs and Administration, Department of Urban Health Administration, professor, 1976-, chair, 1994-, director of public health, 1998-; University of Essex, Department of Sociology, Fulbright research professor, 1980-81; Shoreline Mental Health Center, co-leader, 1984-95; Domestic Violence Training Project Inc., co-director, 1986-99; State University of New York, School of Social Welfare, visiting professor, 1991-92; University of Bristol, School of Policy Studies, international fellow, 2006. Writer. **Publications:** Wife Abuse in the Medical Setting: An Introduction for Health Personnel, 1981; Everything You Need to Know about Sexual Abuse, 1988; Everything You Need to Know about Family Violence, 1989, rev. ed., 1991; Everything You Need to Know about Boys, 1992; Everything You Need to Know about Street Gangs, 1995; (with A. Flitcraft) Women at Risk: Domestic Violence and Women's Health, 1996; (ed. with R.C. Rosen) Everything You Need to Know about Aids, 1998; (ed.) Everything You Need to Know about Alcohol, 1999; Coercive Control: The Entrapment of Women in Personal Life, 2007; (ed. with E. Buzawa) Violence against Women in Families and Relationships, 4 vols., 2009; (with E.S. Buzawa and C.G. Buzawa) Responding to Domestic Violence: The Integration of Criminal Justice and Human Services, 4th ed., 2011. **Address:** 11 Forest Trl., Woodbridge, CT 06525, U.S.A. **Online address:** eds203@juno.com

STARK, **John.** *See* **STOKOE**, **E(dward) G(eorge).**

STARK, **Marisa Kantor.** American (born United States), b. 1973. **Genres:** Poetry, Plays/Screenplays, Novels. **Career:** Asbury Park Press, staff writer, 1992-94; Princeton Arts Council, coordinator and teacher of writing seminars, 1995; New Yorker, writing assistant, 1995-96; Bruriah High School, teacher of English, speech and communication, 1996-97. Freelance writer, 1997-. **Publications:** Bring Us the Old People, 1998; Another Different Life, 2001. Contributor of articles to magazines and newspapers. **Address:** c/o Diana Finch, Ellen Levine Literary Agency Inc., 15 E 26th St., Ste. 1801, New York, NY 10010-1505, U.S.A. **Online address:** marisa.stark@gte.net

STARK, **Rodney.** American (born United States), b. 1934. **Genres:** Theology/Religion, Social Sciences, Politics/Government, Criminology/True Crime, Economics, Sociology. **Career:** Denver Post, reporter, 1955-56; Oakland Tribune, reporter, 1959-61; University of California, Survey Research Center, research assistant, 1961-70, Center for the Study of Law and Society, research sociologist, 1968-71; University of Washington, professor of sociology and of comparative religion, 1971-2003; Micro Case Corp., co-founder and director, 1987-99; Baylor University, university professor of the social sciences, 2004-, distinguished professor of social sciences, Institute for Studies of Religion, co-director; Interdisciplinary Journal of Research on Religion, founding editor; Institute for Jewish and Community Research, senior research fellow; Peking University, honorary professor of sociology. **Publications:** NONFICTION: (with C.Y. Glock) Religion and Society in Tension, 1965; (with C.Y. Glock) Christian Beliefs and Anti-Semitism, 1966; (with C.Y. Glock) Patterns of Religious Commitment, 1968; (co-author) Wayward Shepherds: Prejudice and the Protestant Clergy, 1971; Police Riots: Collective Violence and Law Enforcement, 1972; (co-author) Society Today, 1973; (co-author) Social Problems, 1975; (with C.Y. Glock) The Northern California Church Member Study, 1978; Sociology, 1985, 10th ed., 2007; (ed.) Religious Movements: Genesis, Exodus and Numbers, 1985; (with W.S. Bainbridge) The Future of Religion: Secularization, Revival and Cult Formation, 1985; Crime and Deviance in North America, 1986; (with W.S. Bainbridge) A Theory of Religion, 1987; Criminology: An Introduction through Micro Case, 1989; (with R. Finke) The Churching of America, 1776-1990: Winners and Losers in Our Religious Economy, 1992, 2nd ed., 2005; Doing Sociology: An Introduction through Micro Case, 1992, 4th ed., 2002; The Rise of Christianity: A Sociologist Reconsiders History, 1996 as The Rise of Christianity: How the Obscure, Marginal Jesus Movement Became the Dominant Religious Force in the Western World in A Few Centuries, 1997; (with W.S. Bainbridge) Religion, Deviance and Social Control, 1996; Contemporary Social Research Methods, 1996, 3rd ed., 2002; Acts of Faith: Explaining the Human Side of Religion, 2000; One True God: Historical Consequences of Monotheism, 2001; For the Glory of God: How Monotheism Led to Reformations, Science, Witch-hunts and the End of Slavery, 2003; Dio eternato: indagine sulla rivincita delle religioni in occidente, 2003; Exploring the Religious Life, 2004; The Rise of a New World Faith: Rodney Stark on Mormonism, 2005; The Rise of Mormonism, 2005; The Victory of Reason: How Christianity, Freedom and Capitalism Led to Western Success, 2005; Cities of God: Christianizing the Urban Empire, 2006; Discovering God: The Origins of the Great Religions and the Evolution of Belief, 2007; (co-author) What Americans Really Believe: New Findings from the Baylor Surveys of Religion, 2008; God's Battalions: A History of the Crusades as the First Western War on Muslim Terror and Aggression, 2009; Triumph of Christianity: How the Jesus Movement Became the World's Largest Religion, 2011. **Address:** Department of Sociology, Baylor University, 1 Bear Pl., Ste. 97326, Waco, TX 76798-7326, U.S.A. **Online address:** rs@rodneystark.com

STARKEY, David. American (born United States), b. 1962?. **Genres:** Poetry, Plays/Screenplays, Humanities. **Career:** Francis Marion University, instructor, 1990-94, assistant professor of English, 1994-95; South Carolina Governor's School for the Arts, instructor, 1991, Rural Outreach Program, instructor, 1991-95; North Central College, assistant professor of English, 1995-99, associate professor, 1999-2001; University of Oulu, Fulbright professor of English, 1999; Antioch University, MFA Program, director pedagogy track and faculty, 2001-05; Santa Barbara City College, English professor. Writer. **Publications:** POETRY: Koan Americana, 1992; A Year with Gayle, and Others (chapbook), 1993; Adventures of the Minor Poet (chapbook), 1994; Starkey's Book of States, 1995; Open Mike Night at the Cabaret Voltaire, 1996; Fear of Everything (chapbook), 2000; David Starkey's Greatest Hits (chapbook), 2002; Ways of Being Dead: New and Selected Poems, 2006; It Must be Like the World, 2011. HUMANITIES: (with W. Bishop) Keywords in Creative Writing, 2006; Creative Writing: Four Genres in Brief, 2008; Few Things You Should Know About the Weasel, 2010. EDITOR: (with R. Guzman) Smokestacks and Skyscrapers: An Anthology of Chicago Writing, 1998; Teaching Writing Creatively, 1998; (with W. Bishop) In Praise of Pedagogy, 2000; Genre by Example: Writing What We Teach, 2001; (with P.J. Willis) In a Fine Frenzy: Poets Respond to Shakespeare, 2005; Living Blue in the Red States, 2007. OTHER: Poetry Writing: Theme and Variations, 2000. Works appear in anthologies. Contributor of articles to magazines. **Address:** Department of English, Santa Barbara City College, HT-12/05, 721 Cliff Dr., Santa Barbara, CA 93109, U.S.A. **Online address:** starkey_d@hotmail.com

STARMER, Aaron. American (born United States), b. 1976?. **Genres:** Novels. **Career:** Longitude Books (online publisher), website editor, 1999-2007; Micato Safaris, operations director, 2007-09, America Share (nonprofit), school sponsorship program coordinator, 2009; freelance author, 2009-. **Publications:** (With C. Wells and T. Starmer) The Best in Tent Camping-New York State: A Guide for Car Campers Who Hate RV's, Concrete Slabs, and Loud Portable Stereos, 2007; Dweeb: Burgers, Beasts, and Brainwashed Bullies, 2009; The Only Ones (young-adult novel), 2011. Contributor to books. **Address:** Hoboken, NJ , U.S.A. **Online address:** drajwells@gmail.com

STARNES, Richard D. American (born United States), b. 1970. **Genres:** Cultural/Ethnic Topics, History. **Career:** Western Carolina University, Department of History, Sossomon associate professor and chair, Western North Carolina Oral History Project, founder and director. Writer and historian. **Publications:** (Ed.) Southern Journeys: Tourism, History and Culture in the Modern South, 2003; Creating the Land of the Sky: Tourism and Society in Western North Carolina, 2005; (ed. with G.E. Harvey and G. Feldman) History and Hope in the Heart of Dixie: Scholarship, Activism and Wayne Flynt in the Modern South, 2006. Contributor to periodicals and journals. **Address:** Department of History, Western Carolina University, 226 McKee Bldg., Cullowhee, NC 28723, U.S.A. **Online address:** starnes@email.wcu.edu

STARR, Jason. American (born United States), b. 1966. **Genres:** Novels, Mystery/Crime/Suspense, Young Adult Fiction, Plays/Screenplays. **Career:** Richmond Review, editor; St. Martin's Press, staff. Telemarketer. **Publications:** Cold Caller, 1998; Nothing Personal, 1998; Fake I.D., 2000; Hard Feelings, 2002; Tough Luck, 2003; Twisted City, 2004; (ed. with M. Estep) Bloodlines: A Hhorse Racing Anthology, 2006; Lights Out, 2006; (with K. Bruen) Bust, 2006; (with K. Bruen) Slide, 2007; The Follower, 2007; (with K. Bruen) Max, 2008; Panic Attack, 2009; The Chill, 2010; The Pack, 2011. Contributor to periodicals. Works appear in anthologies. **Address:** c/o Brian DeFiore, DeFiore & Co., 47 E 19th St., 3rd Fl., New York, NY 10003, U.S.A. **Online address:** jason@jasonstarr.com

STARR, Larry. American (born United States), b. 1946. **Genres:** Music. **Career:** University of Washington, faculty, 1977-, professor of music. Writer. **Publications:** A Union of Diversities: Style in the Music of Charles Ives,

1992; The Dickinson Songs of Aaron Copland, 2002; (with C. Waterman) American Popular Music: From Minstrelsy to MTV, 2003, 2nd ed. as American Popular Music: From Minstrelsy to MP3, 2007, 3rd ed., 2010; (with C. Waterman) American Popular Music: The Rock Years, 2006; George Gershwin, 2011; (with J. Schloss and C. Waterman) Rock: Music, Culture, and Business, 2012. Contributor to journals. **Address:** School of Music, University of Washington, PO Box 353450, Seattle, WA 98195-3450, U.S.A. **Online address:** lstarr@u.washington.edu

STARR, Patricia. See **STARR, Patti.**

STARR, Patti. (Patricia Starr). Canadian (born Canada), b. 1943. **Genres:** Novels, Adult Non-fiction, Romance/Historical. **Career:** Ontario Place Corp., chairperson and chief executive officer, 1987-89; Reid & Lyons, co-owner and co-manager; Blue Book of Canadian Business, associate editor. Public speaker. **Publications:** Tempting Fate: A Cautionary Tale of Power and Politics (nonfiction), 1993; Deadly Justice (novel), 1995; Final Justice, 2002; (as Patricia Starr) Angel on My Handlebars, 2009. Contributor to periodicals. **Address:** 45 Riderwood Dr., Willowdale, ON M3L 2E7, Canada. **Online address:** info@patriciastarr.com

STARZL, Thomas E(arl). American (born United States), b. 1926. **Genres:** Medicine/Health, Young Adult Fiction, Autobiography/Memoirs. **Career:** Northwestern University, instructor, 1958-59, associate in surgery, 1959-61, assistant professor of surgery, 1961-62; University of Colorado, associate professor, 1962-64, professor of surgery, 1964-80, chair of surgery, 1972-80; University of the Witwatersrand, Jane and Michael Miller visiting professor, 1966; Royal College of Physicians, special lecturer, 1969; Fondazione Giovanni Lorenzini, lecturer, 1985; University of Pittsburgh, professor of surgery and distinguished service professor of health sciences, 1986, Transplantation Institute, director, 1990-91; University of Madrid, honorary professor, 1989, now retired. Writer. **Publications:** Experience in Renal Transplantation, 1964; Experience in Hepatic Transplantation, 1969; (with C-G Groth and L. Makowka) Liver Transplantation, 1988; (with A.J. Demetris) Liver Transplantation: A 31-Year Perspective, 1990; The Puzzle People: Memoirs of a Transplant Surgeon, 1992, rev. ed., 2003; (ed. with R. Shapiro and R. Simmons) Atlas of Organ Transplantation, 1992. Contributor to journals. **Address:** Falk Clinic, 3601 5th Ave., Pittsburgh, PA 15213, U.S.A.

STASHOWER, Daniel (Meyer). American (born United States), b. 1960. **Genres:** Novels, Mystery/Crime/Suspense, Biography, Literary Criticism And History. **Career:** Professional magician, 1974-79; Liggett Stashower Advertising Inc., advertising copywriter, 1979-84; Time-Life Books, staff writer, 1984-86; freelance writer, 1986-. **Publications:** The Adventure of the Ectoplasmic Man (novel), 1985; Elephants in the Distance (novel), 1989; Magic Box, 1995; Hocus Pocus, 1997; Teller of Tales: The Life of Arthur Conan Doyle (biography), 1999; The Dime Museum Murders (novel), 1999; (ed. with M.H. Greenberg and J. Lellenberg) Ghosts in Baker Street, 1999; The Floating Lady Murder: A Harry Houdini Mystery, 2000; (ed. with M. Greenberg and J.L. Lellenberg) Murder in Baker Street: New Tales of Sherlock Holmes, 2001; The Boy Genius and the Mogul: The Untold Story of Television, 2002; The Houdini Specter, 2002; (ed. with M.H. Greenberg and J. Lellenberg) Murder, My Dear Watson: New Tales of Sherlock Holmes, 2002, The Beautiful Cigar Girl: Mary Rogers, Edgar Allan Poe and the Invention of Murder, 2006; (ed. with M.H. Greenberg and J. Lellenberg) Ghosts in Baker Street, 2006; (ed. with J. Lellenberg and C. Foley) Arthur Conan Doyle: A Life in Letters, 2007; (ed. with M.H. Greenberg and J.L. Lellenberg) Sherlock Holmes in America, 2009. **Address:** c/o Donald Maass, Donald Maass Literary Agency, 121 W 27th St., Ste. 801, New York, NY 10001, U.S.A. **Online address:** daniel@stashower.com

STASSINOPOULOS, Arianna. See **HUFFINGTON, Arianna.**

STATEN, Vince. American (born United States), b. 1947?. **Genres:** Biography, Food And Wine, Sports/Fitness. **Career:** Kingsport Times-News, metro columnist. Writer. **Publications:** The Real Elvis: Good Old Boy, 1978; Golly Wally: The Story of Leave It to Beaver, 1984; (with G. Johnson) Real Barbecue: The Only Barbecue Book You'll Ever Need: A Guide to the Best Joints, the Best Sauces, the Best Cookers-And Much More, 1988; Unauthorized America: A Travel Guide to the Places the Chamber of Commerce Won't Tell You About, 1990; Jack Daniel's Old Time Barbecue Cookbook, 1991; Ol' Diz: A Biography of Dizzy Dean, 1992; Can You Trust a Tomato in January?: Everything You Wanted to Know (and a Few Things You Didn't) about

Food in the Grocery Store, 1993; Did Monkeys Invent the Monkey Wrench?: Hardware Stores and Hardware Stories, 1996; Do Pharmacists Sell Farms?: A Trip Inside the Corner Drugstore, 1998; Do Bald Men Get Half-price Haircuts?: In Search of America's Great Barbershops, 2001; Kentucky Curiosities: Quirky Characters, Roadside Oddities & Other Offbeat Stuff, 2003; Why Is the Foul Pole Fair? or, Answers to the Baseball Questions Your Dad Hoped You'd Never Ask, 2003; (G. Johnson) Real Barbecue: The Classic Barbecue Guide to the Best Joints across the USA, with Recipes, Porklore, and More!, 2007. **Address:** c/o Author Mail, Simon & Schuster Inc., 1230 Ave. of the Americas, 11th Fl., New York, NY 10020-1513, U.S.A.

STATHAM, E. Robert. American (born United States), b. 1963. **Genres:** Civil Liberties/Human Rights, Law, Philosophy, Politics/Government, Social Sciences, History, Young Adult Non-fiction. **Career:** American River College, faculty, 1990; College of St. Francis, instructor in political science, 1991-93; University of Nevada, instructor in political science, 1992-93; South Georgia College, assistant professor of political science, 1993-94; University of Guam, assistant professor, associate professor of political science, 1994-, professor, Micronesian Area Research Center, research affiliate, Division of Social and Behavioral Sciences, chair, 1999-, Political Science Library, founder, 1997; Guam Cable Television, political science analyst, 1995-97; Pacific Daily News, political science analyst, 1995-2000. Writer. **Publications:** Between Inquiry and Advocacy: A Critique of the Pragmatic Foundations of Academic Public Policy, 1995; The Constitution of Public Philosophy: Toward a Synthesis of Freedom and Responsibility in Postmodern America, 1998; (ed.) Public Philosophy and Political Science: Crisis and Reflection, 2002; Colonial Constitutionalism: The Tyranny of United States' Offshore Territorial Policy and Relations, 2002. CONTRIBUTOR: Problems and Prospects for Nuclear Waste Disposal Policy, 1993; Emerging from Empire? Decolonisation in the Pacific, 1997; Foreign in a Domestic Sense: Puerto Rico, American Expansion and the Constitution, 2001. Contributor to periodicals and books. **Address:** Division of Social and Behavioral Sciences, College of Liberal Arts, University of Guam, HSS Bldg., 2nd Fl., Ste. 220C, Mangilao, 96923, Guam. **Online address:** estatham@uog9.uog.edu

STATHIS, Pete. American (born United States) **Genres:** Novels, Cartoons, Science Fiction/Fantasy. **Career:** Writer and cartoonist. **Publications:** Evenfall, vol. I: Lay Me Down, 2004, vol. II: Soul to Keep, 2007, vol. III: Before I Wake, forthcoming. **Address:** Philadelphia, PA , U.S.A. **Online address:** pstathis@earthlink.net

STATLANDER, Jane (B.). Israeli/American (born United States), b. 1943. **Genres:** Cultural/Ethnic Topics, Novels, Young Adult Fiction. **Career:** Negev Academic College of Engineering, lecturer in English, 1997-; Miami Dade County College, faculty, literature professor; Miami University, faculty; Thomas Edison State College, faculty. Journalist. **Publications:** A Family Affair, 1996; Cultural Dialectic: Cynthia Ozick and Ludwig Lewisohn, 2002; Story of a Newark Girl, 2006. **Address:** Department of English, Negev Academic College of Engineering, Bazel St., Beer Sheva, 84100, Israel. **Online address:** drbjanes@yahoo.com

STAUB, Wendy Corsi. Also writes as Wendy Markham, Wendy Morgan. American (born United States), b. 1964. **Genres:** Romance/Historical, Horror, Young Adult Fiction. **Career:** Macmillan, textbook marketing division administrator, 1986; Backer Spielvogel Bates (advertising), account coordinator, 1988-90; Silhouette Books, editor, 1990-92; freelance writer, 1993-; Long Ridge Writer's Institute, writing instructor, 1993-95; Cupid Literary Services, owner. **Publications:** JUVENILE AND YOUNG-ADULT NOVELS: Summer Lightning, 1993; Halloween Party, 1994; Witch Hunt, 1995; Help Me, 1995; Mitzi Malloy and the Anything-but-Heavenly-Summer, 1995; Brittany Butterfield and the Back-to-School Blues, 1995; But-Heavenly Summer, 1995; Henry Hopkins and the Horrible Halloween Happening, 1995; College Life 101/Cameron: The Sorority, 1997; College Life 101/Zara: The Roommate, 1997; College Life 101/Kim: The Party, 1997; College Life 101/Bridget: The Fling, 1997; College Life 101/Allison: The Townie, 1997; College Life 101/Christmas Break: The Reunion, 1998; Lily Dale: Connecting, 2008; Lily Dale: Believing, 2008; Lily Dale: Discovering, 2009. NOVELS: Getting It Together, 1994; Getting Attached, 1994; Getting Hitched, 1995; (as Wendy Morgan) Obsession, 1996; Dearly Beloved, 1996, rev. ed., 2003; (with E.I. Koch) Murder on Broadway, 1996; (with Fabio) Dangerous, 1996; (with Fabio) Wild, 1997; (with E.I. Koch) Murder on 34th Street, 1997; (with Fabio) Mysterious, 1998; (with E.I. Koch) The Senator Must Die, 1998; Fade to Black, 1998; Party of Five: A Family Album, 1998; All the Way Home, 1999;

(as Wendy Morgan) Loving Max, 1999; The Long Way Home, 1999; Gossip, 2000; Voodoo Moon: An Original Novel, 2000; More than This, 2000; The Last to Know, 2001; This Boy Is Mine, 2001. OTHERS: Real Life: Help Me, 1995; (as Wendy Morgan) Ask Me Again, 2000; In the Blink of an Eye, 2002; (as Wendy Morgan) Slightly Single, 2002; She Loves Me Not, 2003; (as Wendy Markham) The Nine Month Plan, 2003; Thoroughly Modern Princess, 2003; Possession: The Other Side of Darkness, 2003; Kiss Her Goodbye, 2004; (as Wendy Markham) Once Upon a Blind Date, 2004; (as Wendy Markham) Slightly Settled, 2004; Lullaby and Goodnight, 2005; (as Wendy Markham) Mike, Mike and Me, 2005; (as Wendy Markham) Hello, It's Me, 2005; (as Wendy Markham) Bride Needs Groom, 2005; The Final Victim, 2006; If Only In My Dreams, 2006; (as Wendy Markham) The Best Gift, 2006; (as Wendy Markham) Slightly Engaged, 2006; Lily Dale: Awakening, 2007; (with L. Jackson and B. Barton) Most Likely To Die, 2007; Love, Suburban Style, 2007; Don't Scream, 2007; (as Wendy Markham) Slightly Married, 2007; (as Wendy Markham) That's Amore, 2008; Dying Breath, 2008; Slightly Suburban, 2008; Dying Breath, 2008; Dead Before Dark, 2009; Live to Tell, 2010; Scared to Death, 2011; Hell to Pay, 2011; Sleepwalker, 2012; Shadowkiller, 2013. Contributor to periodicals. **Address:** c/o Laura Blake Peterson, Curtis Brown Ltd., 10 Astor Pl., New York, NY 10003, U.S.A. **Online address:** corsistaub@aol.com

STAUBER, John (Clyde). American (born United States), b. 1953. **Genres:** Documentaries/Reportage, History, Military/Defense/Arms Control, Ethics, Business/Trade/Industry, Economics. **Career:** Consultant, 1974-93; Center for Media and Democracy, founder, 1993-, executive director, 1993-2009; PR Watch, contributing editor. **Publications:** (With S. Rampton) Toxic Sludge Is Good for You: Lies, Damn Lies and the Public Relations Industry, 1995; (with S. Rampton) Mad Cow, U.S.A.: Could the Nightmare Happen Here?, 1997; (with S. Rampton) Trust Us, We're Experts! How Industry Manipulates Science and Gambles With Your Future, 2001; (with S. Rampton) Weapons of Mass Deception: The Uses of Propaganda in Bush's War on Iraq, 2003; (with S. Rampton) Banana Republicans: How the Right Wing Is Turning America into a One-party State, 2004; (with S. Rampton) The Best War Ever: Lies, Damned Lies and The Mess in Iraq, 2006. **Address:** Center for Media and Democracy, 520 University Ave., Ste. 260, Madison, WI 53703, U.S.A. **Online address:** john.stauber@gmail.com

STAUBUS, Martin. American (born United States), b. 1952. **Genres:** Business/Trade/Industry, Economics, Humanities. **Career:** University of California, Rady School of Management, Beyster Institute, senior principal, associate director, director of employee ownership consulting, consultant. Writer. **Publications:** (With R. Bernstein and D. Binns) Transitioning Ownership in the Private Company, 2nd ed., 2004; (with C. Rosen and J. Case) Equity: Why Employee Ownership is Good for Business, 2005; (with D. Binns and R. Bernstein) The Entrepreneur's Guide to Equity Compensation, 4th ed., 2006. **Address:** Beyster Institute, Rady School of Management, University of California, 1241 Cave St., La Jolla, CA 92037, U.S.A. **Online address:** mstaubus@ucsd.edu

ST. AUBYN, Giles (Rowan). British (born England), b. 1925. **Genres:** Philosophy, Biography, History, Autobiography/Memoirs, Civil Liberties/Human Rights. **Career:** Eton College, staff, 1947-85, house master, 1959-76, History Department, head, 1961-71. Writer. **Publications:** Macaulay, 1952; (with W.A. Barker and R.L. Ollard) A General History of England, 1952; A Victorian Eminence, 1958; The Art of Argument, 1962; The Royal George, 1963; A World to Win, 1968; Infamous Victorians, 1971; (ed.) William of Gloucester: Pioneer Prince, 1977; Edward VII, Prince and King, 1979; The Year of Three Kings: 1483, 1983; Queen Victoria: A Portrait, 1991; Souls in Torment: Victorian Faith in Crisis, 2011. **Address:** Saumarez Park Manor, Apt. 2, Route de Saumarez, Catel, Guernsey, Channel Islands, GY5 7TH, England.

STAUNTON, Ted. Canadian (born Canada), b. 1956. **Genres:** Picture/Board Books, Children's Fiction, Young Adult Fiction. **Career:** City of Etobicoke, Parks and Recreation Department, community programmer, 1974-80; University of Toronto, St. Michael's College Library, library technician, 1983-84; Ministry of Consumer and Commercial Relations, education officer, 1984-85; full-time writer and speaker, 1985-; George Brown College, teacher of writing; Haliburton School of the Arts, teacher of writing. **Publications:** PICTURE BOOKS: Puddleman, 1983, new. ed., 1999; Taking Care of Crumley, 1984; Simon's Surprise, 1986; Miss Fishley Afloat, 1990; Anna Takes Charge, 1993. JUNIOR FICTION: Morgan Makes Magic, 1997; Hope Springs a Leak,

1998; Morgan and the Money, 1998; Morgan's Secret, 2000; Great Play, Morgan!, 2001; Morgan's Birthday, 2002; Stinky, 2002; Trouble with Girls, 2002; Morgan's Pet Plot, 2003; Morgan makes a Splash, 2004; Sounding Off, 2004; Morgan Makes a Deal, 2005; The Dreadful Truth: Confederation, 2005; The Northwest Passage, 2005; The Dreadful Truth: Building a Railway, 2005; Canadian Crime, 2006; Super move, Morgan, 2006; Campfire Morgan, 2007; Pucker Up, Morgan!, 2008; Gold Rush, 2008; Daredevil Morgan, 2009; Acting Up, 2010; Morgan and the Dune Racer, 2011; Power Chord, 2011. CHILDREN'S FICTION: Maggie and Me, 1986; Greenapple Street Blues, 1987; Mushmouth and the Marvel, 1988; Great Minds Think Alike, 1989; Taking the Long Way Home, 1992; Forgive Us Our Travises, 2000; Monkey Mountain Monster, 2000; Two False Move, 2000; Music By Morgan, 2010. **Address:** 202 Yeovil St., Port Hope, ON L1A 1W9, Canada. **Online address:** tedstaunton@sympatico.ca

STAUROWSKY, Ellen J. American (born United States), b. 1955. **Genres:** Sports/Fitness. **Career:** Oberlin College, assistant professor of physical education, head field hockey coach and women's lacrosse coach, assistant professor of physical education, 1979-83; Colby Sawyer College, dean of student staff and consultant to athletic department, 1983-84; Daniel Webster College, assistant professor, director of athletics and men's soccer coach, 1984-86; Rutgers University, Livingston College, director of physical education, recreation and intramurals, 1986-87; William Smith College, director of physical education, recreation and athletics, 1987-92; Ithaca College, assistant professor, 1992-96, associate professor, 1996-2002, coordinator, 1996-2011, professor, 2002-11, Sport Media Program, coordinator, 1992-2006, Graduate Program in Exercise & Sport Sciences, associate professor, 1996-99, Graduate Program in Sport Management, professor, 2005-11, Graduate Program, chair, 2006-11; Drexel University, Goodwin College of Professional Studies, professor, 2011-. Writer. **Publications:** (With A.L. Sack) College Athletes for Hire: The Evolution and Legacy of the NCAA's Amateur Myth, 1998. Contributor of articles to books, journals and newspapers. **Address:** School of Technology and Professional Studies, Goodwin College of Professional Studies, Drexel University, 1 Drexel Plz., Ste. 53, 3141 Chestnut St., Philadelphia, PA 19104, U.S.A. **Online address:** ejs95@drexel.edu

STAVE, Bruce M. American (born United States), b. 1937. **Genres:** History, Politics/Government, Urban Studies. **Career:** Samuel Lubell Associates, political pollster, 1958-64; University of Bridgeport, instructor, 1965-66, assistant professor of history, 1966-70; University of Connecticut, Department of History, assistant professor, associate professor, professor of history, 1970-2002, chairman, 1985-94, Board of Trustees distinguished professor, 2000, distinguished professor emeritus, 2002-, director of oral history project, 1979-81, Center for Oral History, director, 1981-2006, Oral History Office, director, 2006-; University of Hartford, Henry Jack Gray/NEH Distinguished Visiting Humanist, 2003. Writer. **Publications:** The New Deal and the Last Hurrah: Pittsburgh Machine Politics, 1970; The Making of Urban History: Historiography through Oral History, 1977; (with M. Palmer) Mills and Meadows: A Pictorial History of Northeast Connecticut, 1991; (with J.F. Sutherland and A. Salerno) From the Old Country: An Oral History of European Migration to America, 1994, rev. ed., 1999; (with M. Palmer and L. Frank) Witnesses to Nuremberg: An Oral History of American Participants at the War Crimes Trials, 1998; Red Brick in the Land of Steady Habits: Creating the University of Connecticut, 1881-2006, 2006. EDITOR: (and intro.) Urban Bosses, Machines and Progressive Reformers, 1971, 2nd ed., 1984; (with L. Ashby) The Discontented Society: Interpretations of Twentieth-Century American Protest, 1972; Socialism and the Cities, 1975; Modern Industrial Cities: History, Policy and Survival, 1981; (with J.F. Sutherland) Talking about Connecticut: Oral History in the Nutmeg State, 1985. Contributor to periodicals. **Address:** Oral History Office, University of Connecticut, 405 Babbidge Rd., U-1132, Storrs, CT 06269-1132, U.S.A. **Online address:** bruce.stave@uconn.edu

STAVE, Shirley A. American (born United States), b. 1952. **Genres:** Paranormal, Mythology/Folklore, Literary Criticism And History, Sociology. **Career:** Gustavus Adolphus College, visiting instructor in English, 1980-82; West Virginia University, visiting instructor in English, 1984-86; Oxford College of Emory University, assistant professor of English, 1986-93; University of Wisconsin-Waukesha, assistant professor, 1993-97, associate professor of English, 1997-98; Northwestern State University of Louisiana, associate professor of English, 1998-. Writer. **Publications:** (With A. Scarboro and N. Campbell) Living Witchcraft: A Contemporary American Coven, 1994; The Decline of the Goddess: Nature, Culture and Women in Thomas Hardy's Fiction, 1995; (ed.) Gloria Naylor: Strategy and Technique, Magic and Myth,

2001; (ed.) Toni Morrison and the Bible: Contested Intertextualities, 2006. Contributor to periodicals. **Address:** Louisiana Scholars' College, Northwestern State University of Louisiana, 119 Morrison Hall, 715 University Pkwy., Natchitoches, LA 71497, U.S.A. **Online address:** stavesh@nsula.edu

STAVEACRE, Tony. British/Irish (born Ireland), b. 1942. **Genres:** Plays/Screenplays. **Career:** British Broadcasting Corp. (BBC), television producer, 1972-92. writer, 1992-. **Publications:** (With S. Colin) Al Bowlly, 1978; The Songwriters, 1980; Slapstick! The Illustrated Story of Knockabout Comedy, 1988; Wodehouse behind the Scenes, 1990. **Address:** Tony Staveacre Productions, Channel View, Rhodyate, Blagdon, Bristol, AV BS40 7TP, England. **Online address:** newstaving@btinternet.com

STAVITSKY, Gail. American (born United States), b. 1954. **Genres:** Art/Art History, Cultural/Ethnic Topics. **Career:** Carnegie Museum of Art, assistant curator of fine arts, 1981-83; Museum of Modern Art, instructor, 1986-; Montclair Art Museum, curator of collections and exhibitions, 1994-98, Curatorial Department, chief curator, 1998-. Writer. **Publications:** From Vienna to Pittsburgh: The Art of Henry Koerner, 1983; Gertrude Stein: The American Connection, 1990; Life and Art of Esphyr Slobodkina, 1992; (co-author) Precisionism in America: Reordering Reality, 1915-1941, 1994; (contrib.) Paris 1900: The American School at the Universal Exposition, 1999; Waxing Poetic, 1999; (co-author) Will Barnet: A Timeless World, 2000; Reflecting Culture: The Evolution of American Comic Book Super Heroes, 2007; (ed. with K. Rothkopf) Cézanne and American Modernism, 2009. Contributor to books. **Address:** Montclair Art Museum, 3 S Mountain Ave., Montclair, NJ 07042, U.S.A. **Online address:** gstavitsky@montclairartmuseum.org

STAVRAKIS, Peter J(acob). American (born United States), b. 1955. **Genres:** Politics/Government, History, Social Sciences, Economics. **Career:** Rio Hondo Project, assistant director, 1973-74; Marquette University, lecturer in political science, 1985-86; University of Wisconsin-Madison, instructor, 1985-86; University of Vermont, assistant professor, 1986-92, associate professor of political science, 1992-2005, Russian and East European Area Studies Program, head, 1994; University of Copenhagen, lecturer, 1987, 1991; Harvard University, Russian Research Center, fellow, 1989, 1991; Middlebury College, lecturer, 1992; Georgetown University, lecturer, 1992; Woodrow Wilson International Center for Scholars, Kennan Institute for Advanced Russian Studies, deputy director, 1994-97; National Defense University, professor, 2001-; George Washington University, Institute for European, Russian, and Eurasian Studies, research associate, 2001, adjunct professor of political science. Writer. **Publications:** Moscow and Greek Communism, 1944-1949, 1989; (contrib.) The U.S.S.R. and the World Economy: Challenges for the Global Integration of Soviet Markets under Perestroika, 1992; (contrib.) Greece at the Crossroads, 1944-1950: Essays on the Greek Civil War and Its Legacy, 1995; (contrib.) States and Regimes in Transition: Russia and East Europe after Communism, 1996; (ed. with J. De Bardeleben, L. Black and contrib.) Beyond the Monolith: The Emergence of Regionalism in Post-Soviet Russia, 1997; Shadow Politics: The Russian State in the 21st Century, 1997; Dark Visions: Contemporary Feudalism Confronts the Global World Order, forthcoming. Contributor to journals and magazines. **Address:** Industrial College of the Armed Forces, National Defense University, 408 4th Ave., Fort McNair, DC 20319, U.S.A. **Online address:** stavrakisp@ndu.edu

STAYNES, Jill. Also writes as Susannah Stacey, Elizabeth Eyre. British (born England) **Genres:** Mystery/Crime/Suspense, Romance/Historical, Literary Criticism And History, Young Adult Fiction, Children's Fiction. **Career:** Writer. **Publications:** AS SUSANNAH STACEY WITH MARGARET STOREY: Goodbye, Nanny Gray, 1987; A Knife at the Opera, 1988; Body of Opinion, 1990; Grave Responsibility, 1990; The Late Lady, 1992; Bone Idle, 1993; Dead Serious, 1995; Hunter's Quarry, 1998. AS ELIZABETH EYRE WITH MARGARET STOREY: Death of the Duchess, 1991; Curtains for the Cardinal, 1992; Poison for the Prince, 1993; Bravo for the Bride, 1994; Axe for an Abbot, 1995; Dirge for the Doge, 1996. OTHERS: Out of That World, 1979. Contributor to periodicals. **Address:** A.M. Heath & Company Ltd., 6 Warwick Ct., London, GL WC1R 5DJ, England.

ST. CLAIR, William. British (born England), b. 1937. **Genres:** Administration/Management, History, Literary Criticism And History, Biography. **Career:** Royal Society of Literature, fellow, 1973-; All Souls College, visiting fellow, 1981-82, fellow, 1992-96; Huntington Library, fellow, 1985; Joint International President, Byron Society, 1988; British Academy, fellow, 1992-; Trinity College, visiting fellow, 1997-98, visiting fellow commoner, 1998-

99, fellow, 1999-2006; British Treasury, secretary; University of London, Institute of English Studies, senior research fellow, 2005-; Cambridge and Harvard, Centre for history and economics, senior research fellow, 2008-; Open Book Publishers, chairman, 2008-. Writer. **Publications:** Lord Elgin and the Marbles, 1967; That Greece Might still Be Free: The Philhellenes in the War of Independence, 1972; (ed.) Trelawny's Adventures of a Younger Son, 1974; Trelawny: The Incurable Romancer, 1977; Policy Evaluation: A Guide for Managers, 1988; The Godwins and the Shelleys: The Biography of a Family, 1989; Executive Agencies: A Guide to Setting Targets and Judging Performance, 1992; (ed. with I. Maasen) Conduct Literature for Women, 1500 to 1640, 2000; (ed. with I. Maasen) Conduct Literature for Women, 1640 to 1710, 2002; (ed. with P. France) Mapping Lives: The Uses of Biography, 2002; The Reading Nation in the Romantic Period, 2004; The Grand Slave Emporium: Cape Coast Castle and the British Slave Trade, 2006; Door of No Return: The History of Cape Coast Castle and the Atlantic Slave Trade, 2007. **Address:** Institute of English Studies, School of Advanced Study, University of London, Rm. 239, Senate House, Malet St., London, WC1E 7HU, England. **Online address:** ws214@cam.ac.uk

ST. CLAIRE, Erin. *See* **BROWN, Sandra.**

STEAD, C(hristian) K(arlson). New Zealander (born New Zealand), b. 1932. **Genres:** Novels, Poetry, Literary Criticism And History, Novellas/Short Stories, Autobiography/Memoirs, Biography, Essays. **Career:** University of New England, lecturer in English, 1956-57; University of Auckland, lecturer, 1960-61, senior lecturer, 1962-64, associate professor, 1964-67, professor of English, 1967-86, professor emeritus, 1986-; NZ Literary Fund, chairman, 1972-75; full-time writer, 1986-; New Zealand PEN, national vice-president, 1988-89; NZ Authors' Fund, chairman, 1989-91; University of Oxford, St. John's College, visiting fellow, 1996-97. **Publications:** POETRY: New Poetic, 1964; Whether the Will is Free: Poems 1954-62, 1964; Crossing the Bar, 1972; Quesada: Poems 1972-74, 1975; Walking Westward, 1979; Geographies, 1982; Poems of a Decade, 1983; Paris, 1984; Between, 1988; Voices, 1990; Straw into Gold: Poems New and Selected, 1997; The Right Thing, 2000, Dog, 2002; The Red Tram, 2004; Black River, 2007; Collected Poems, 1951-2006, 2008. LITERARY CRITICISM: The New Poetic: Yeats to Eliot, 1967; Pound, Yeats, Eliot, and the Modernist Movement, 1985. EDITOR: New Zealand Short Stories: Second Series, 1966; Shakespeare: Measure for Measure, 1971; Letters and Journals of Katherine Mansfield: A Selection, 1977; Collected Stories, 1981; The Faber Book of Contemporary South Pacific Stories, 1994; Katherine Mansfield Letters and Journals: A Selection, 2004. NOVELS: Smith's Dream, 1971; All Visitors Ashore, 1984; The Death of the Body, 1986; Sister Hollywood, 1989; The End of the Century at the End of the World, 1992; The Singing Whakapapa, 1994; Villa Vittoria, 1997; Talking about O'Dwyer, 2000; The Secret History of Modernism, 2001; Mansfield: A Novel, 2004; My Name was Judas, 2006. SHORT STORIES: Five for the Symbol, 1981; The Blind Blonde with Candles in Her Hair: Stories, 1998. ESSAYS: In the Glass Case: Essays on New Zealand Literature, 1981; Answering to the Language: Essays on Modern Writers, 1989; The Writer at Work: Essays, 2000; Kin of Place: Essays on 20 New Zealand Writers, 2002. OTHER: Book Self: The Reader as Writer and the Writer as Critic, 2008; South-West of Eden: A Memoir 1932-1956, 2010. **Address:** 37 Tohunga Cres., Parnell, Auckland, 1, New Zealand.

STEANS, Jill A. (Jill A. Krause). British (born England), b. 1961. **Genres:** International Relations/Current Affairs. **Career:** Nottingham Trent University, faculty, 1990-95; University of Keele, lecturer in international relations, 1995-2000; University of Birmingham, Department of Political Science and International Studies, senior lecturer, 2000-; Open University, part-time tutor and consultant; International Feminist Journal, associate editor. **Publications:** (Ed. as Jill A. Krause with N. Renwick) Identities in International Relations, 1996; Gender and International Relations: An Introduction, 1997, 2nd ed. as Gender and International Relations: Issues, Debates and Future Directions, 2006; (with L. Pettiford) International Relations: Perspectives and Themes, 2001; An Introduction to International Relations, 2001, (with L. Pettiford, T. Diez and I. El-Anis) 3rd ed., 2010; The Politics of Women's Human Rights, 2009; (co-author) Global Political Economy: Current Debates and Controversies, forthcoming. Contributor to periodicals. **Address:** Department of Political Science, and International Studies, University of Birmingham, Muirhead Twr., Edgbaston, WM B15 2TT, England. **Online address:** j.a.steans@bham.ac.uk

STEARNS, Maureen. American (born United States) **Genres:** Novels. Ca-

reer: Educator and writer. **Publications:** Conscious Courage: Turning Everyday Challenges into Opportunities, 2004; Multiply and Divide with Sticks and Steps: Teach This Easy Method in Just 5 Minutes, 2010. **Address:** Enrichment Books, PO Box 3362, Seminole, FL 33775-3362, U.S.A. **Online address:** info@enrichmentbooks.com

STEAVENSON, Wendell. French/American (born United States), b. 1970?. **Genres:** Adult Non-fiction, Biography, Autobiography/Memoirs. **Career:** Time Magazine, correspondent. Journalist. **Publications:** Stories I Stole from Georgia, 2002; The Weight of a Mustard Seed: An Iraqi General's Moral Journey during the Time of Saddam, 2009; (contrib.) Le printemps géorgien, 2009. Contributor to periodicals. **Address:** c/o Author Mail, Grove/Atlantic Inc., 841 Broadway, New York, NY 10003-4793, U.S.A.

STEBBINS, Robert A. Canadian/American (born United States), b. 1938. **Genres:** Recreation, Sociology, Social Sciences. **Career:** Presbyterian College, associate professor of sociology, 1964-65; Memorial University of Newfoundland, assistant professor of sociology, 1965-68, Department of Sociology and Anthropology, associate professor and head, 1968-71, professor, 1971-73; The University of Texas at Arlington, professor, 1973-76; University of Calgary, Department of Sociology, professor and head, 1976-82, professor of sociology, 1982-99, faculty professor, 2000-06, professor emeritus of sociology, 2006-; Calgary Institute for the Humanities, fellow, 1987-88; World Leisure and Recreation Association International Centre of Excellence (WICE), faculty, 1992-2004; Leisure Sciences, associate editor, 1997-; Deviant Behavior, associate editor, 1999-; Leisure/Loisir, associate editor, 2003-05; World Leisure Journal, editor, 2004-; University of Bedfordshire, visiting professor, 2005-09; University of Luton, visiting professor, 2005-09; University of New Brunswick, graduate studies, honorary research associate, 2009-. **Publications:** Commitment to Deviance: The Nonprofessional Criminal in the Community, 1971; The Disorderly Classroom: Its Physical and Temporal Conditions, 1974; Teachers and Meaning: Definitions of Classroom Situations, 1975; Amateurs: On the Margin Between Work and Leisure, 1979; Fieldwork Experience: Qualitative Approaches to Social Research, 1980; The Sociology of Deviance, 1982; The Magician: Career, Culture and Social Psychology in a Variety Art, 1984, 3rd ed., 1993; Sociology: The Study of Society, 1987, 2nd ed., 1990; Canadian Football: The View from the Helmet, 1987; Deviance: Tolerable Differences, 1988; The Laugh Makers: Stand-Up Comedy as Art, Business, and Life-Style, 1990; The Laugh Makers: Stand-Up Comedy as Art, Business, and Life- Style, 1990; Experiencing Fieldwork: An Inside View of Qualitative Research, 1991; Amateurs, Professionals, and Serious Leisure, 1992; Predicaments: Moral Difficulty in Everyday Life, 1993; The Franco-Calgarians: French Language, Leisure, and Linguistic Life-Style in an Anglophone City, 1994; The Connoisseur's New Orleans, 1995; Tolerable Differences: Living with Deviance, 1996; The Barbershop Singer: Inside the Social World of a Musical Hobby, 1996; The French Enigma: Survival and Development in Canada's Francophone Societies, 2000; Exploratory Research in the Social Sciences, 2001; New Directions in the Theory and Research of Serious Leisure, 2001; The Organizational Basis of Leisure Participation, 2002; Volunteering as Leisure/Leisure as Volunteering: An International Assessment, 2004; Between Work & Leisure: The Common Ground of Two Separate Worlds, 2004; Challenging Mountain Nature: Risk, Motive and Lifestyle in Three Hobbyist Sports, 2005; (with D.H. Smith and M.A. Dover) A Dictionary of Nonprofit Terms and Concepts, 2006; Serious Leisure: A Perspective for Our Time, 2007; Personal Decisions in the Public Square: Beyond Problem Solving into a Positive Sociology, 2009; Leisure and Consumption: Common Ground, Separate Worlds, 2009; (with M.B. Durieux) Social Entrepreneurship for Dummies, 2010; (with L. Davidson) Serious Leisure and Nature: Sustainable Consumption in the Outdoors, 2011; Idea of Leisure, 2011. Contributor of articles to journals. **Address:** Department of Sociology, Faculty of Arts, University of Calgary, 2500 University Dr. NW, Calgary, AB T2N 1N4, Canada. **Online address:** stebbins@ucalgary.ca

STEBENNE, David. (David Lawler Stebenne). American (born United States), b. 1960. **Genres:** Biography, History. **Career:** Yale University, lecturer in history, 1991-93; Ohio State University, College of Arts and College of Humanities, Department of History, assistant professor of history, 1993-97, associate professor of history, 1997-, Moritz College of Law, adjunct professor of law, 2004-10, associate professor of law, 2010-. Writer. **Publications:** Arthur J. Goldberg: New Deal Liberal, 1996; Modern Republican: Arthur Larson and the Eisenhower Years, 2006; (with J.R. Mitchell) New City upon a Hill: A History of Columbia, Maryland, 2007. Contributor of articles to periodicals. **Address:** Department of History, Ohio State University, 240 Dulles Hall, 230 W 17th Ave., Columbus, OH 43210-1367, U.S.A. **Online address:** stebenne.1@osu.edu

STEBENNE, David Lawler. *See* **STEBENNE, David.**

STECKEL, Richard. American (born United States), b. 1944. **Genres:** Social Work, Adult Non-fiction, Business/Trade/Industry. **Career:** Denver Children's Museum, executive director, 1976-84; AddVenture Network Inc., founder and president, 1984-; Consultative Group on International Research and Future Harvest, advisor; Sustainable Cities Trust, associate; E Source Corp., director. Writer. **Publications:** (With R. Simons and P. Lengsfelder) Filthy Rich and Other Nonprofit Fantasies: Changing the Way Nonprofits Do Business in the 90s, 1989, (with R. Simons, J. Lehman and P. Lengsfelder) rev. ed. as Filthy Rich: How to Turn Your Nonprofit Fantasies into Cold, Hard Cash, 2000; (with R. Simons) Doing Best by Doing Good: How to Use Public Purpose Partnerships to Boost Corporate Profits and Benefit Your Community, 1992, (co-author) rev. ed. as Making Money While Making a Difference: How to Profit with a Nonprofit Partner, 1999; (with J. Lehman) In Search of America's Best Nonprofits, 1997; (with M. Steckel) The Milestones Project: Celebrating Childhood around the World, 2004; (with E. Ford and C. Hilliard) Cold Cash for Warm Hearts: 101 Best Social Marketing Initiatives, 2004; (with M. Steckel) Happy Birthday! A Milestones Project Chewable, 2007; (with M. Steckel) Milestones Project: My Teeth, 2008; (with M. Steckel) Go Baby!, 2008. **Address:** AddVenture Network Inc., 5443 S Prince St., Littleton, CO 80120-1123, U.S.A.

STECKER, Ann Page. American (born United States), b. 1942?. **Genres:** Local History/Rural Topics, History, Business/Trade/Industry. **Career:** Colby-Sawyer College, faculty, 1980-, Department of Humanities, professor, David H. Winton endowed chair, Wesson Honors Program, coordinator. Historian and writer. **Publications:** WITH NANCY COFFEY HEFFERNAN: New Hampshire: Crosscurrents in Its Development, 1986, 3rd ed., 2004; Sisters of Fortune: Being the True Story of How Three Motherless Sisters Saved Their Home in New England and Raised Their Younger Brother While Their Father Went Fortune Hunting in the California Gold Rush, 1993. OTHER: Our Voices, Our Town: A History of New London, New Hampshire, 1950-2000, 2000. **Address:** Department of Humanities, Colby-Sawyer College, 541 Main St., New London, NH 03257, U.S.A. **Online address:** astecker@colby-sawyer.edu

STEEDMAN, Carolyn (Kay). British (born England), b. 1947. **Genres:** History, Business/Trade/Industry, Cultural/Ethnic Topics. **Career:** University of Warwick, Department of History, faculty, 1984-, professor. Writer. **Publications:** The Tidy House: Little Girls Writing, 1982; Policing the Victorian Community: The Formation of English Provincial Police Forces, 1856-80, 1984; (ed. with C. Urwin and V. Walkerdine) Language, Gender, and Childhood, 1985; Landscape for a Good Woman: A Story of Two Lives, 1986; The Radical Soldier's Tale: John Pearman, 1819-1908, 1988; Childhood, Culture, and Class in Britain: Margaret McMillan, 1860-1931, 1990; Past Tenses: Essays on Writing, Autobiography, and History, 1992; Strange Dislocations: Childhood and the Idea of Human Interiority, 1780-1930, 1995; Dust: The Archive and Cultural History, 2002; Master and Servant. Love and Labour in the English Industrial Age, 2007; Labours Lost: Domestic Service and the Making of Modern England, 2009. **Address:** Department of History, University of Warwick, Rm. 326, Humanities Bldg., University Rd., Coventry, WM CV4 7AL, England. **Online address:** c.k.steedman@warwick.ac.uk

STEEGE, Paul. American (born United States), b. 1970. **Genres:** History. **Career:** Villanova University, associate professor. Writer. **Publications:** Black Market, Cold War: Everyday Life in Berlin, 1946-1949, 2007. Works appear in anthologies. Contributor to periodicals and journals. **Address:** Department of History, Villanova University, 800 Lancaster Ave., Villanova, PA 19085-1699, U.S.A. **Online address:** paul.steege@villanova.edu

STEEL, Danielle. American (born United States), b. 1947. **Genres:** Romance/Historical, Children's Fiction, Young Adult Fiction, Picture/Board Books, Young Adult Non-fiction, Children's Non-fiction, Novels, Biography, Biography. **Career:** Supergirls Ltd., vice president of public relations, 1968-71; Grey Advertising, copywriter, 1973-74; Nick Traina Foundation, founder; Yo! Angel!, founder. Writer and educator. **Publications:** Going Home, 1973; Passion's Promise, 1976; The Promise, 1978; Now and Forever, 1978; Season of Passion, 1978; Summer's End, 1979; Golden Moments, 1979; The Ring, 1980; Loving, 1980; To Love Again, 1980; Remembrance, 1981; Palomino, 1981; Love: Poems, 1981; A Perfect Stranger, 1981; Crossings, 1982; Once in a Lifetime, 1982; Changes, 1983; Thurston House, 1983; Full Circle, 1984; (co-author) Having a Baby, 1984; Secrets, 1985; Family Album, 1985; Amando, 1985; Wanderlust, 1986; Fine Things, 1987; Kaleidoscope, 1987; Zoya, 1988; Star, 1989; Daddy, 1989; Martha's Best Friend, 1989; Martha's New Daddy, 1989; Martha's New School, 1989; Max and the Baby-Sitter, 1989; Max's Daddy Goes to the Hospital, 1989; Max's New Baby, 1989; Message from Nam, 1990; Max and Grandma and Grampa Winky, 1990; Martha's New Puppy, 1990; Max Runs Away, 1990; Heartbeat, 1991; No Greater Love, 1991; Martha and Hilary and the Stranger, 1991; Freddie's Trip, 1992; Freddie's First Night Away, 1992; Freddie's Accident, 1992; Freddie and the Doctor, 1992; Mixed Blessings, 1992; Jewels, 1992; Vanished, 1993; The Gift, 1994; Accident, 1994; Wings, 1994; Five Days in Paris: A Novel, 1995; Lightning, 1995; Malice, 1996; Silent Honor, 1996; The Ranch, 1997; Special Delivery, 1997; The Ghost, 1997; The Long Road Home, 1998; The Klone and I: A High-Tech Love Story, 1998; Mirror Image, 1998; His Bright Light: The Story of Nick Traina, 1998; Bittersweet, 1999; Granny Dan, 1999; Irresistible Forces, 1999; The House on Hope Street, 2000; The Wedding, 2000; Journey, 2000; Leap of Faith, 2001; Lone Eagle, 2001; The Kiss, 2001; The Cottage, 2002; Answered Prayers, 2002; Sunset in St. Tropez, 2002; Dating Game, 2003; Johnny Angel, 2003; Safe Harbour, 2003; Echoes, 2004; Miracle, 2004; Ransom, 2004; Second Chance, 2004; Impossible, 2005; Toxic Bachelors, 2005; Coming Out, 2006; H.R.H, 2006; The House, 2006; First Sight, 2006; Amazing Grace, 2007; Bungalow 2, 2007; Sisters, 2007; Honor Thyself, 2008; Rogue, 2008; Good Woman, 2008; One Day at a Time, 2009; Matters of the Heart, 2009; Southern Lights: A Novel, 2009; Happiest Hippo in the World, 2009; Big Girl, 2010; Family Ties, 2010; Legacy, 2010; 44 Charles Street, 2011; Happy Birthday: A Novel, 2011; Hotel Vendome: A Novel, 2011; Gift of Hope, 2012; Betrayal, 2012; Sins of the Mother, 2012; Friends Forever, 2012. Contributor of articles to periodicals. **Address:** Delacorte Press, 1745 Broadway, 9th Fl., New York, NY 10019-4368, U.S.A.

STEEL, David (Martin Scott). British/Scottish (born Scotland), b. 1938. **Genres:** Politics/Government, Autobiography/Memoirs, History. **Career:** Scottish Liberal Party, assistant secretary, 1962-64; Liberal Democrat, member of parliament (U.K.), 1965-97; Liberal Party, leader, 1976-88; Liberal Intl., vice president, 1978-, president 1994-96; Social and Liberal Democrats, co-founder, 1988; Scottish Parliament, presiding officer, 1999-2003. Writer. **Publications:** Boost for the Borders, 1964; Out of Control, 1968; No Entry: The Background and Implications of the Commonwealth Immigrants Act, 1969; The Liberal Way Forward, 1975; A New Political Agenda, 1976; Militant for the Reasonable Man, 1977; New Majority for a New Parliament, 1978; High Ground of Politics, 1979; A House Divided, 1980; (with J. Steel) David Steel's Border Country, 1985; Scotland's Border Country, 1985; Partners in One Nation, 1985; Decade of Realignment: The Leadership Speeches of David Steel (1976-1986), 1986; (with D. Owen) The Time Has Come, 1987; (with J. Steel) Mary Stuart's Scotland, 1987; Against Goliath (autobiography), 1989; (with L. Parsons) Admiralty and Commercial Court: Forms and Precedents, 2nd ed., 1993; Achievements of the Scottish Parliament, 2003. **Address:** The House of Lords, London, GL SW1A 0PW, England.

STEEL, D(avid) R(obert). Scottish/British (born England), b. 1948?. **Genres:** Administration/Management, Politics/Government, Medicine/Health, Public/Social Administration, Social Sciences. **Career:** University of Exeter, lecturer in politics, 1972-84; National Association of Health Authorities, assistant director, 1984-86; Scottish Health Board Chairmen's and General Managers' Group, secretary, 1986-90; National Health Service in Scotland, director of corporate affairs, 1990-95, head of health gain, 1995-, chief executive officer. Writer. **Publications:** (With R.G.S. Brown) The Administrative Process in Britain, 2nd ed., 1979; (ed. with D. Heald) Privatizing Public Enterprises, 1984. **Address:** National Health Service, Elliott House, 8-10 Hillside Cres., Edinburgh, EH 7 5EA, Scotland.

STEEL, Gayla R(uth). American (born United States), b. 1933. **Genres:** Literary Criticism And History, Social Sciences, Women's Studies And Issues. **Career:** Northern Illinois University, instructor, 1979-87, lecturer, 1991; Whitson Publishing Co., assistant editor, 1980-84. **Publications:** Sexual Tyranny in Wessex: Hardy's Witches and Demons of Folklore, 1993. Works appear in anthologies. Contributor to periodicals. **Address:** 825 N Bennett St., Geneva, IL 60134-1467, U.S.A.

STEEL, Nigel. British (born England), b. 1962. **Genres:** History, Military/Defense/Arms Control, Travel/Exploration. **Career:** Imperial War Museum, Department of Documents, research assistant, archivist, 1988-99, Research and Information Department, head, 1999-2006, Lord Ashcroft Gallery, principal historian, 2008-10, First World War Centenary Programme, principal historian, 2010-; Australian War Memorial, visiting senior historian, 2006-08. Writer. **Publications:** The Gallipoli Battlefields: Then and Now, 1990; (with P. Hart) Defeat at Gallipoli, 1994, rev. ed., 1997; Tumult in the Clouds: The British Experience of the War in the Air, 1914-1918, 1997; Gallipoli, 1999; (with P. Hart) Passchendaele: The Sacrificial Ground, 2000; (with P. Hart) Jutland, 1916: Death in the Grey Wastes, 2003. Contributor to periodicals. **Address:** First World War Centenary Programme, Imperial War Museum, Lambeth Rd., London, GL SE1 6HZ, England. **Online address:** nsteel@iwm.org.uk

STEEL, Ronald. American (born United States), b. 1931. **Genres:** History, Politics/Government, Biography. **Career:** U.S. Foreign Service, vice consultant, 1957-58; New Republic, contributing editor; Scholastic Magazines, editor, 1959-62; Jonathan Edwards College, visiting fellow, 1970-73; University of Southern California, professor of international relations, 1986-, now professor emeritus of international relations. Writer. **Publications:** Federal Aid to Education, 1961; U.S. Foreign Trade Policy, 1962; Italy, 1963; The End of Alliance: America and the Future of Europe, 1964; (with G.H.T. Kimble) Tropical Africa Today, 1966; Pax Americana, 1967, rev. ed., 1977; North Africa, 1967; New Light on Juvenile Delinquency, 1967; (trans.) The American Challenge, 1968; Imperialists and Other Heroes: A Chronicle of the American Empire, 1971; Walter Lippmann and the American Century, 1980; (contrib.) The Jewish Experience at Harvard and Radcliffe: An Introduction to an Exhibition Presented by the Harvard Semitic Museum on the Occasion of Harvard's 350th Anniversary, September, 1986, 1986; Temptations of a Superpower, 1995; In Love with Night: The American Romance with Robert Kennedy, 2000. **Address:** School of International Relations, University of Southern California, 304 Von Kleinsmid Ctr., Los Angeles, CA 90089-0043, U.S.A. **Online address:** steel@usc.edu

STEELE, Cynthia. American (born United States), b. 1951. **Genres:** Literary Criticism And History, Poetry, Novels, Translations, Novellas/Short Stories. **Career:** Ohio State University, assistant professor of Spanish, 1980-85; Columbia University, assistant professor of Spanish, 1985-86; University of Washington, Department of Comparative Literature, assistant professor, 1986-90, associate professor, 1990-96, professor and chair, 1996-, Center for Human Rights, faculty. Writer. **Publications:** Narrativa Indigenista en Los Estados Unidos y México, 1985; (with G. Rojo) Ritos de Iniciación: Tres Novelas cortas de Hispanoamérica, 1988; Politics, Gender and the Mexican Novel, 1968-1988: Beyond the Pyramid, 1992; (trans.) I. Arredondo, Underground River and Other Stories, 1996; (trans. with D. Lauer) J.E. Pacheco, City of Memory and Other Poems, 1997. **Address:** Department of Comparative Literature, University of Washington, B537 Padelford, PO Box 354338, Seattle, WA 98195-4338, U.S.A. **Online address:** cynthias@u.washington.edu

STEELE, Mary. Australian (born Australia), b. 1930. **Genres:** Novellas/Short Stories, Autobiography/Memoirs, Children's Fiction, Biography. **Career:** Office of the Federal Attorney General, research officer, 1953-54; Melbourne University, tutor, 1955-57; Australian Scientific Liaison Office, research officer, 1958-59; Monash University, lecturer in English, 1961-62; research assistant and book reviewer, 1965-80. Writer. **Publications:** (With G. Weed) Collected Field Reports on the Phonology of Konkomba, 1966. SELF-ILLUSTRATED: Arkwright, 1985; Mallyroots' Pub at Misery Ponds, 1988; Citizen Arkwright, 1990; Featherbys, 1993; A Bit of a Hitch, 1996; Tenterhooks (for children), 1997; Beside the Lake: A Ballarat Childhood, 2000. Works appear in anthologies. Contributor to periodicals. **Address:** Hyland House Publishing, 50 Pin Oak Cres., PO Box 122, Flemington, VI 3031, Australia.

STEELE, Peter. Canadian/British (born England), b. 1935. **Genres:** Biography, Medicine/Health, Travel/Exploration, Sports/Fitness. **Career:** St. George's Hospital, intern, 1960-61; United Mission Hospital, physician and surgeon, 1961-62; West Suffolk Hospital, resident in obstetrics and gynecology and in anesthetics, 1963-64; Grenfell Association, acting medical officer in charge of flying doctor service, 1964-65; Cambridge University, demonstrator in anatomy, 1967; Bristol Eye Hospital, resident in ophthalmology, 1967-70, clinical assistant, 1973-74; Frenchay Hospital, resident in plastic surgery, 1970-71, resident in general surgery, 1971-72; Bristol University

Health Service, general practice of medicine, 1973-74. Writer. **Publications:** Two and Two Halves to Bhutan, 1970; Doctor on Everest, 1972; Medical Care for Mountain Climbers, 1976; Far from Help, 1990; Atlin's Gold, 1995; Eric Shipton: Everest and Beyond, 1998; Medical Handbook for Walkers and Climbers, 1999; Backcountry Medical Guide, 2nd ed., 1999; The Man Who Mapped the Arctic: The Intrepid Life of George Back, Franklin's Lieutenant, 2003. Contributor to periodicals. **Address:** 138 Dalton Trl., Whitehorse, YT Y1A 3G1, Canada. **Online address:** peter.steele@yt.sympatico.ca

STEELE, Philip. (Nikki Bundey). Welsh/British (born England), b. 1948. **Genres:** Children's Fiction, Children's Non-fiction, Picture/Board Books, Young Adult Non-fiction, Young Adult Fiction, History. **Career:** ULP/EUP (Hodder Group), educational promotions assistant, 1971-73; Hamlyn Children's Books, assistant editor, 1973-76; Macdonald Educational, editor, 1977-79, senior editor, 1979-80; freelance writer and editor, 1981-. **Publications:** FOR CHILDREN: Joseph and His Coat of Many Colours, 1985; Joseph and His Brothers, 1985; Last of the Monsters, 1987; Fairy Post Box, 1987; Goblins of Griddlestone Gap, 1987; The Witches Who Came to Stay, 1987; The Ghost Train, 1987; Grandma Goosegog, 1987; The Wizard and the Weasel, 1987; The King Who Loved Yellow, 1987; Rainbow's End, 1987; The Giving Book, 1987. POCKET FACTS SERIES: Reptiles, 1990; Wild Animals, 1991; Deserts, 1991; Cars and Trucks, 1991; Boats, 1991; Planes, 1991; Trains, 1991; Boats, 1991; Astronomy, 1991; Space Travel, 1991; Mountains, 1991. EXTINCT AND ENDANGERED SERIES: Reptiles, 1991; Birds, 1991; Amphibians, 1991; Insects, 1991; Underwater Life, 1991. KILLERS! SERIES: Fish, 1991; Insects, 1991; Mammals, 1991; Prehistoric Animals, 1991. WEATHER WATCH SERIES: Frost: Causes and Effects, 1991; Heatwave: Causes and Effects, 1991; Storms: Causes and Effects, 1991; Wind: Causes and Effects, 1991; Rain: Causes and Effects, 1991; Snow: Causes and Effects, 1991. THROUGH THE AGESSERIES: City, 1993; Eagle, 1993; Road, 1993; Farm, 1993; House, 1993; River, 1993; Factory, 1994. PAST AND PRESENT SERIES: Censorship, 1992; Kidnapping, 1992; Terrorism, 1992; Riots, 1993; Smuggling, 1993; Thermopylae, 1993. DISCOVERING CHILDREN'S NONFICTION SERIES: Discovering Germany, 1993; Discovering Great Britain, 1993. GEOGRAPHY DETECTIVES CHILDREN'S NONFICTION: Grasslands, 1996; Islands, 1996; Tundra, 1996. STEP INTO CHILDREN'S NONFICTION SERIES: Step into Ancient Rome, 1997 as Find out about Ancient Rome, 2000; Step into Ancient Egypt, 1997 as Find out about Ancient Egypt, 2000; Step into the Viking World, 1998; Step into the Chinese Empire, 1999; Step into the Inca World, 2000. NONFICTION FOR CHILDREN: (with B.R. Lewis and L. Williams) 1000 Great Events, 1973; (with K. Lye) Pictorial Atlas, 1983; Counting and Numbers: Blue Book, 1983; Reading and Writing: Blue Book, 1983; Festivals Around the World, 1983; Red Book, 1984; Children's Picture Atlas, 1985; Do You Know How Animals Live, 1985; Do You Know About Life in the Sea, 1986; Land Transport around the World, 1986; Money, 1986; Tactics of Terror, 1986; Whatever the Weather, 1988; First Book of Questions and Answers, 1989; China, 1990; Food and Diet, 1991; The People Atlas, 1991; Sharks and Other Creatures of the Deep, 1991; Children's Illustrated Atlas of the World, 1992; Little Bighorn, 1992; Europe in World War Two, 1993; Incas and Machu Picchu, 1993; Thor Heyerdahl and Kon-Tiki Voyage, 1993; Thermopylai, 1994; The Romans and Pompeii, 1994; The Egyptians and Valley of the Kings, 1994; Between Two World Wars, 1994; I Wonder Why Castles Had Moats and Other Questions About Long Ago, 1994; The Samurai Warriors, 1994; The Blue Whale, 1994; The Giant Panda, 1994; In Ancient Rome, 1994; Farming Village, 1994; Flags, 1994; Countries Fly Flags, 1995; Great Discoveries, 1995; I Wonder Why Pyramids Were Built? And Other Questions About Ancient Egypt, 1995; Castles, 1995; Black Holes and Other Space Phenomena, 1995; Vampire Bats and Other Creatures of the Night, 1996; Eyes of the Skull, 1996; The Aztec News, 1997; In Ancient Greece, 1997; In Victorian Times, 1997; Ancient Rome, 1997; Rocking and Rolling, 1997; Best-Ever Book of Pirates, 1997; Freedom of Speech, 1997; Kingfisher Young People's Atlas of the World, 1997; Beaumaris, Story of the Town, 1997; Snow and Ice, 1998; Censorship, 1998; Children's Atlas, 1998; Knights, 1998; An Explorer, 1998; Crime and Punishment, 1999; Time Capsule of 20th Century, 1999; Volcanoes, 1999; Ultimate Atlas of Almost Everything, 1999; Ultimate Atlas of the World, 1999; A Tidal Pool, 1999; Toys and Games, 1999; (with A. Powell) The Greek News, 2000; Pirates, 2000; Going to School, 2000; My Best Book of Mummies, 2000; Animal Matters, 2000; Encyclopedia of British History, 2001; Jesse Owens: An Unauthorised Biography, 2001; Citizenship, 2001; Children's Atlas of the World, 2001. EDITOR: The Birds from Africa, 1980; Flight into Danger, 1980; Cars, 1980; Airport, 1980; Red Racing Car, 1980. AS NIKKI BUNDEY: (co-author) Encyclopaedia of Lands and

Peoples, 1995; Best-Ever Book of Castles, 1995; Anglesey: Ynys Môn, 1996; In the Park, 1998; On a Bike, 1998; In the Water, 1998; In the Snow, 1998; In the Gym, 1999; On the Field, 1999; Rain and the Earth, 2000; Rain and People, 2000; Drought and People, 2001; Ice and the Earth, 2001; Snow and the Earth, 2001; Storms and People, 2001; Snow and People, 2001; Wind and People, 2001; Wind and the Earth, 2001; Ice and People, 2001; Drought and the Earth, 2001; Storms and the Earth, 2001. OTHERS: America's Natural Beauty (adult travelog), 1986; About Life in the Sea, 1986; Journey Through China, 1991; Reader's Digest Children's World Atlas, 1991; Extinct Birds, and Those in Danger of Extinction, 1991; Extinct Land Mammals and those in Danger of Extinction, 1991; Extinct Reptiles, and those in Danger of Extinction, 1991; Extinct Underwater Creatures and those in Danger of Extinction, 1991; Collage, 1993; First Atlas, 1993; Over 50 Years Ago in Europe: During World War II, 1993; Banderas, 1994; Food & Feasts between the Two World Wars, 1994; Food & Feasts in Ancient Rome, 1994; I Wonder Why Countries Fly Flags, and Other Questions About People and Places, 1995; World of Festivals, 1996; Clothes & Crafts in Roman Times, 1997; The Best Book of Mummies, 1998; Wannabe an Explorer, 1998; Clothes & Crafts in Ancient Greece, 1998; Clothes & Crafts in Victorian Times, 1998; Sharks and Other Monsters of the Deep, 1998; (co-author) Peoples of the Americas, 10 vols., 1999; Human Race, 2000; (co-author) Peoples of the Africa, 10 vols., 2000; Human Race, 2000; Medieval World, 2000; People in Place and Time, 2000; Scholastic Atlas of the World, 2001; History of the British Isles, 2001; Atlas of People & Places, 2002; Long Ago, 2002; Ho Chi Minh, 2003; Rosa Parks and her Protest for Civil Rights, 2003; City Through Time, 2004; World of Pirates, 2004; I Wonder Why Castles had Moats and Other Questions About Long Ago, 2004; (contrib.) Scholastic Pocket United States Atlas, 2004; Moscow, 2004; Pocket World Atlas, 2004; Sydney, 2004; Galileo: The Genius Who Faced the Inquisition, 2005; History of Fashion and Costume, vol. II: The Medieval World, 2005; Nineteenth Century, 2005; World of Castles, 2005; Population Growth, 2005; Marie Curie: The Woman Who Changed the Course of Science, 2006; Middle East, 2006; Inside Volcanoes, 2007; Isaac Newton: The Scientist Who Changed Everything, 2007; Wonders of the World, 2007; History of Science, 2007; Pirates: With Jake Rattlebones, 2007; I Wonder Why Venetians Walk on Water: And Other Questions about People and Places, 2007; Eyewitness Mesopotamia, 2007; Ancient Iraq, 2007; Knight's City, 2008; Navigators: Knights & Castles, 2008; The Chinese Empire, 2009; Roman Empire, 2009; Mariner's Tale, 2009; Saving Water and Energy, 2010; Hail! Tudors, 2010; Documenting Slavery and Civil Rights, 2010; Documenting World War I, 2010; Activists, 2011; Hail! Ancient Romans, 2011. **Address:** Ty Cerrig, Llangoed, Beaumaris, Ynys Mon, LL58 8SA, Wales. **Online address:** phil_steele@btinternet.com

STEELE, Timothy (Reid). American (born United States), b. 1948. **Genres:** Poetry, Literary Criticism And History, Adult Non-fiction. **Career:** California State University, lecturer, 1973-74, professor of English, 1987-; Stanford University, Jones lecturer in poetry, 1975-77; University of California-Los Angeles, lecturer in English, 1977-83; University of California-Santa Barbara, lecturer in English, 1986; West Chester University, faculty. Poet. **Publications:** Uncertainties and Rest, 1979; The Prudent Heart, 1983; Nine Poems, 1984; On Harmony, 1984; Short Subjects, 1985; Sapphics Against Anger and Other Poems, 1986; Beatitudes, 1988; Missing Measures: Modern Poetry and the Revolt against Meter, 1990; The Color Wheel, 1994; Sapphics and Uncertainties: Poems 1970-1986, 1995; (ed. and intro.) The Poems of J.V. Cunningham, 1997; All the Fun's in How You Say a Thing: An Explanation of Meter and Versification, 1999; Toward the Winter Solstice, 2006. Contributor to books. **Address:** Department of English, California State University, 5151 State University Dr., Los Angeles, CA 90032, U.S.A. **Online address:** timothyrsteele@sbcglobal.net

STEELE-PERKINS, Christopher Horace. British/Myanmar (born Myanmar), b. 1947. **Genres:** Photography. **Career:** Freelance photographer; Polytechnic of Central London, lecturer in photography, 1976-77. Writer. **Publications:** Teds, 1979; In Our Time, 1989; The Pleasure Principle, 1990; St. Thomas's Hospital, 1992; Fuji: Images of Contemporary Japan, 2002. **Address:** Magnum Photos, 63 Gee St., London, GL EC1V 3RS, England. **Online address:** chrissteeleperkins@hotmail.com

STEENSLAND, Brian. American (born United States), b. 1967. **Genres:** Politics/Government, Social Sciences. **Career:** Indiana University, Department of Religious Studies, associate professor of sociology and adjunct professor, 2002-. Writer. **Publications:** The Failed Welfare Revolution: America's Struggle over Guaranteed Income Policy, 2008. Contributor to books and

periodicals. **Address:** Department of Religious Studies, College of Arts and Sciences, Indiana University, Sycamore Hall 230, Bloomington, IN 47405-7005, U.S.A. **Online address:** bsteens@indiana.edu

STEFANIAK, Mary Helen. American (born United States), b. 1951. **Genres:** Novels, Novellas/Short Stories, Essays. **Career:** Teacher of English, French and journalism, 1973-82; Stratton Business College, instructor in literature and composition, 1980-81; Marquette University, upward bound instructor, 1981; freelance editor and copy editor, 1984-87; Iowa Review, assistant editor, 1984-86, fiction editor, 1986-87; Eastern Iowa Community College, instructor in English, 1990-92; University of Iowa, fiction faculty, 1991-2007; Iowa Time, codirector, 1991-92; Iowa Humanities Board, promotions and publications specialist, 1992-95; Iowa City Community School District Music Carnival, co-chair, 1995-96; Kirkwood Community College, instructor in writing, 1995-96, English faculty, 1996-97; University of Nebraska, writer-in-residence, 1997; Iowa Source, columnist, 1997-2003; Creighton University, visiting assistant professor, 1998-99, associate professor, 2004-, director of creative writing, 1999-2007; Iowa Public Radio, commentator; Pacific University, faculty; University of Nebraska, faculty. **Publications:** Self Storage and Other Stories, 1997; The Turk and My Mother (novel), 2004; Cailiffs of Baghdad, Georgia: A Novel, 2010. Works appear in anthologies. Contributor of essays and stories to magazines. **Address:** Department of English, Creighton University, 2500 California Plz., Omaha, NE 68178, U.S.A. **Online address:** mhs@creighton.edu

STEGER, Manfred B. Australian (born Australia), b. 1961. **Genres:** Translations. **Career:** First Austrian Bank, investment and loan officer, 1980-86; Kapiolani Community College, lecturer in religious studies, 1990; Rutgers University, lecturer in political science and philosophy, 1992-95; Whitman College, assistant professor of politics, 1995-96; Illinois State University, assistant professor, 1996-99, associate professor, 1999-2003, professor of politics and government, 2003-05; University of Hawaii at Manoa, visiting professor of sociology, 1999-2004, Globalization Research Center, director of publications, 2001-02, Globalization Research Center, senior research fellow, 2002-, Department of Political Science, visiting professor of political science and affiliated graduate faculty, 2005-; U.S. Embassy in Minsk, Academic consultant on globalization, 2002; Royal Melbourne Institute of Technology, professor of global studies, 2005-, School of International and Community Studies, head, 2005-06, Globalism Research Centre, academic director, 2005-07, director, 2007-09, China-Australia Forum, executive director, 2006-, Global Cities Institute, Globalization and Culture Program, research leader, 2006-; U.S. State Department, Academic consultant on globalization; United Nations Global Compact Cities Program, associate director, 2007-. Consultant and writer. **Publications:** (With P. Besserman) Crazy Clouds: Zen Radicals, Rebels, and Reformers, 1991, 2nd ed. as Zen Radicals, Rebels, and Reformers, 2011; (ed., trans. and intro.) Selected Writings of Eduard Bernstein, 1900-1921, 1996; The Quest for Evolutionary Socialism: Eduard Bernstein and Social Democracy, 1997; (ed. with T. Carver) Engels after Marx, 1999; (ed. with N.S. Lind) Violence and Its Alternatives: An Interdisciplinary Reader, 1999; Gandhi's Dilemma: Nonviolent Principles and Nationalist Power, 2000; (with P. Besserman) Grassroots Zen, 2001; Globalism: The New Market Ideology, 2002, 2nd ed. as Globalism: Market Ideology Meets Terrorism, 2005, 3rd ed. as Globalisms: The Great Ideological Struggle of the Twenty-first Century, 2009; (ed. with S.L. McLean and D.A. Schultz) Social Capital: Critical Perspectives on Community and Bowling Alone, 2002; Judging Nonviolence: The Dispute between Realists and Idealists, 2003; Globalization: A Very Short Introduction, 2003, 2nd ed., 2009; (ed.) Rethinking Globalism, 2004; The Rise of the Global Imaginary: Political Ideologies from the French Revolution to the Global War on Terror, 2008; (ed.) Globalization: The Greatest Hits, a Global Studies Reader, 2010; (with R.K. Roy) Neoliberalism: A Very Short Introduction, 2010; (ed. with P. James) Ideologies of Globalization, 2010. Contributor to books. **Address:** Royal Melbourne Institute of Technology, PO Box 2476, Melbourne, VI 3001, Australia. **Online address:** manfred.steger@rmit.edu.au

STEGGLE, Matthew. British (born England), b. 1970. **Genres:** Theatre, Literary Criticism And History, Humanities, Reference. **Career:** Oxford University, Trinity College, lecturer in English, 1997-99; Sheffield Hallam University, lecturer, 1999-2005, senior lecturer, 2005-07, reader in English, 2007-. Writer. **Publications:** Wars of the Theatres: The Poetics of Personation in the Age of Jonson, 1998; Richard Brome: Place and Politics on the Caroline Stage, 2004; (with L. Hopkins) Renaissance Literature and Culture, 2006; Laughing and Weeping in Early Modern Theatres, 2007. **Address:** Department of English, Sheffield Hallam University, City Campus, 38-40 Howard St., Sheffield, SY S1 1WB, England. **Online address:** m.steggle@shu.ac.uk

STEIDLE, Brian. American (born United States), b. 1976?. **Genres:** History. **Career:** Joint Military Commission, team leader, senior operations officer, 2004; African Union, U.S. State Department, military observer, 2004; African Union Cease Fire Commission, military observer and US representative, 2004-05; Steidle Consulting, president, 2005-; Seldon Technologies Inc., business development manager, 2010-. Writer and consultant. **Publications:** (With G.S. Wallace) The Devil Came on Horseback: Bearing Witness to the Genocide in Darfur, 2007. **Address:** PublicAffairs Books, 1094 Flex Dr., Jackson, TN 38301, U.S.A. **Online address:** brian@globalgrassroots.org

STEIDLE WALLACE, Gretchen. American (born United States) **Genres:** History. **Career:** PMD International Inc., international project finance associate, 1996-99; Youth Venture, director, 2003; Global Grassroots, founder and president, 2004; Allwin Initiative for Corporate Citizenship, co-founder; Ashoka: Innovators for the Public, director. Writer. **Publications:** (With B. Steidle) The Devil Came on Horseback: Bearing Witness to the Genocide in Darfur, 2007. **Address:** Global Grassroots, 45 Lyme Rd., Ste. 206, Hanover, NH 03755, U.S.A. **Online address:** info@globalgrassroots.org

STEIKER, Valerie. American (born United States), b. 1969?. **Genres:** Autobiography/Memoirs, History, Biography. **Career:** ArtForum Magazine, editor; Vogue magazine, senior editor. **Publications:** The Leopard Hat: A Daughters Story, 2002; (ed. with C. Knutsen) Brooklyn was Mine, 2008. **Address:** c/o Author Mail, Pantheon, 1745 Broadway, New York, NY 10019, U.S.A.

STEIL, Benn. American (born United States), b. 1963. **Genres:** Money/Finance, Business/Trade/Industry, Economics. **Career:** Royal Institute of International Affairs, International Economics Programme, director, 1992-98; Virt-X Securities Exchange, nonexecutive director, 2000-02; Efficient Frontiers L.L.C., co-founder; Council on Foreign Relations, senior fellow and director of international economics; British-American Project, fellow; International Finance Journal, editor. Economist and consultant. **Publications:** Illusions of Liberalization: Securities Regulation in Japan and the EC, 1995; The European Equity Markets, 1996; (with E.P. Davis) Institutional Investors, 2001; Building a Transatlantic Securities Market, A Council Report, 2002; (with R.E. Litan) Financial Statecraft: The Role of Financial Markets in American Foreign Policy, 2006; (with M. Hinds) Money, Markets, and Sovereignty, 2009. EDITOR: International Financial Market Regulation, 1994; (with S.J. Evenett and A. Lehmann) Antitrust Goes Global: What Future for Transatlantic Cooperation?, 2000; (with D.G. Victor) Technological Innovation and Economic Performance, 2002. Contributor to periodicals. **Address:** U.S.A. **Online address:** mholden@cfr.org

STEIN, Ben. *See* STEIN, Benjamin J.

STEIN, Benjamin J. (Ben Stein). American (born United States), b. 1944. **Genres:** Novels, Money/Finance, Social Commentary, Business/Trade/Industry, Economics. **Career:** Federal Trade Commission, trial lawyer, 1970-73; speech writer for president Richard M. Nixon, 1973-74; University of California, instructor, 1973; speech writer for president Gerald Ford, 1974; Wall Street Journal, editorial page staff, 1976-76; creative consultant and scriptwriter for norman lear, 1976-77; Los Angeles Herald Examiner, columnist; Los Angeles Magazine, columnist; American University, adjunct faculty; Pepperdine University, adjunct faculty; The Wall Street, columnist and editorial writer; The Los Angeles Herald Examiner, syndicated columnist; King Features Syndicate, syndicated columnist; writer, 1977-. **Publications:** Fernwood U.S.A: An Illustrated Guide from the Folks Who Brought You Mary Hartman, Mary Hartman, 1977; (with H. Stein) On the Brink: A Novel, 1977; The Croesus Conspiracy, 1978; Dreemz, 1978; (as Ben Stein) The View from Sunset Boulevard: America as Brought to You by the People Who Make Television, 1979; (as Ben Stein with H. Stein) Moneypower: How to Make Inflation Make You Rich, 1979; Bunkhouse Logic: How to Bet on Yourself and Win, 1981; Ludes: A Ballad of the Drug and the Dreamer, 1982; The Manhattan Gambit, 1983; Financial Passages, 1985; Her Only Sin: A Novel of Hollywood, 1985; Hollywood Days, Hollywood Nights: The Diary of a Mad Screenwriter, 1988; Will You Still Love Me Tomorrow?, 1991; A License to Steal: The Untold Story of Michael Milken and the Conspiracy to Bilk the Nation, 1992; Tommy and Me: The Making of a Dad, 1998; How to Ruin Your Life, 2002; (with P. DeMuth) Yes, You Can Time the Market!, 2003; How to Ruin Your Love Life, 2003; How to Ruin Your Financial Life, 2004; (with P.

DeMuth) Can America Survive?: The Rage of the Left, the Truth, and What To Do About It, 2004; The Gift of Peace: Guideposts on the Road to Serenity, 2005; Yes, You Can be a Successful Income Investor!: Reaching for Yield inToday's Market, 2005; Yes, You Can Still Retire Comfortably!: The Baby-Boom Retirement Crisis and How to Beat It, 2005; How to Ruin Your Life: An Anthology Including How to Ruin Your Life, How to Ruin Your Love Life, How to Ruin Your Financial Life, 2006; How Successful People Win: Using Bunkhouse Logic to Get What You Want in Life, 2006; 26 Steps to Succeed in Hollywood or Any Other Business, 2006; (with P. DeMuth) Yes, You Can Get a Financial Life!: Your Lifetime Guide to Financial Planning, 2007; Real Stars: In Today's America, Who Are the True Heroes?, 2007; (with P. DeMuth) How to Ruin the United States of America, 2008; (with P. DeMuth) Yes, You can Supercharge Your Portfolio!: Six Steps for Investing Success in the 21st Century, 2008; Eyes of Faith: How to Not Go Crazy: Things to Bear in Mind to Get through Even the Worst Days, 2009; (with P. DeMuth) Little book of bulletproof investing: Do's And Don'ts to Protect Your Financial Life, 2010; Little Book of Alternative Investments: Reaping Rewards By Daring to Be Different, 2011; What Would Ben Stein Do?: Applying the Insights of a Modern-day Pundit to Tackle the Challenges of Business and Life, 2011. **Address:** c/o Lois Wallace, Wallace & Sheil Agency Inc., 177 E 70th St., New York, NY 10021, U.S.A. **Online address:** benstein99@aol.com

STEIN, Dan. *See* STEIN, Dan J(oseph).

STEIN, Dan J(oseph). (Dan Stein). South African (born South Africa), b. 1962. **Genres:** Psychiatry, Medicine/Health. **Career:** Columbia-Presbyterian Hospital, resident in psychiatry, 1987-91; Columbia University, New York State Psychiatric Institute, resident in psychiatry, 1987-91, fellow in psychiatric research, 1991-93; City University of New York, Mount Sinai School of Medicine, assistant professor of clinical psychiatry, 1993-94, visiting professor of psychiatry; University of Stellenbosch, director of psychiatry research, 1994-, Medical Research Council Research Unit on Anxiety Disorders, director, 1998-; University of Florida, research associate professor of psychiatry, 1999-; University of Cape Town, Department of Psychiatry and Mental Health, professor, founding editor, chair, Brain and Behaviour Initiative, director. **Publications:** (Co-author) Mental Health Resource Guide for South Africa, 1996; (with N. Fineberg and D. Marazitti) Obsessive Compulsive Disorder: A Practical Guide, 2000; (with N.J. Keuthen and G.A. Christenson) Help for Hair Pullers, 2001; Cognitive-Affective Neuroscience of Depression and Anxiety Disorders, 2003; (with N.A. Fineberg) Obsessive-Compulsive Disorder, 2007; Philosophy of Psychopharmacology: Smart Pills, Happy Pills, and Pepp Pills, 2008. EDITOR: (with J.E. Young) Cognitive Science and Clinical Disorders, 1992; (with E. Hollander) Impulsivity and Aggression, 1995; (with M. Stone) Essential Papers on Obsessive-Compulsive Disorders, 1997; Cognitive Science and the Unconscious, 1997; (with E. Hollander) Obsessive-Compulsive Disorders: Diagnosis, Etiology, Treatment, 1997; (with J. Ludik) Neural Networks and Psychopathology, 1998; (with E. Hollander and G.A. Christenson) Trichotillomania, 1999; (with J. Fawcett and K.O. Jobson) Textbook of Treatment Algorithms in Psychopharmacology, 1999; (with E. Hollander) The American Psychiatric Publishing Textbook of Anxiety Disorders, 2002, 2nd ed. (with E. Hollander and B.O. Rothbaum) as Textbook of Anxiety Disorders, 2010; (with B. Bandelow) Social Anxiety Disorder, 2004; Clinical Manual of Anxiety Disorders, 2004; (with D.J. Kupfer and A.F. Schatzberg) The American Psychiatric Publishing Textbook of Mood Disorders, 2005; (with B. Lerer and S. Stahl) Evidence-based Psychopharmacology, 2005; (with E. Hollander) Clinical Manual of Impulse-control Disorders, 2006; (with M. Friedman and C. Blanco) Post-Traumatic Stress Disorder, 2011. Contributor to journals. **Address:** Department of Psychiatry & Mental Health, University of Capetown, Rm. 75, J-2 Block, Groote Schuur Hospital, Observatory 7925, Anzio Rd., Capetown, 7505, South Africa. **Online address:** dan.stein@curie.uct.ac.za

STEIN, Edith Sarah. *See* SARAH, Edith.

STEIN, Edward D. American (born United States), b. 1965. **Genres:** Law, Philosophy, Adult Non-fiction, Social Sciences. **Career:** Williams College, visiting assistant professor of philosophy, 1991-92; New York University, assistant professor of philosophy, 1992-95, Law School, adjunct professor, 1994, 2008-; Mount Holyoke College, visiting assistant professor of philosophy, 1995-96; Yale University, visiting assistant professor of philosophy, 1996-97; Benjamin N. Cardozo School of Law, associate professor of law, 2000-05, professor of law, 2005-, Program in Family Law, Policy and Bioethics, director, 2003-, vice dean, 2009-. Writer. **Publications:** (Ed.) Forms of

Desire: Sexual Orientation and the Social Constructionist Controversy, 1990; Without Good Reason: The Rationality Debate in Philosophy and Cognitive Science, 1996; The Mismeasure of Desire: The Science, Theory and Ethics of Sexual Orientation, 1997; The Story of Goodridge v. Department of Public Health: Bumpy Road to Marriage for Same-Sex Couples, in Family Law Stories, 2006; Miscegenation, forthcoming; Spousal Secrets, in Secrets of Law, forthcoming. **Address:** Benjamin N. Cardozo School of Law, 55 5th Ave., New York, NY 10003, U.S.A. **Online address:** ed@edstein.com

STEIN, Eugene. American (born United States), b. 1960. **Genres:** Novels, Young Adult Fiction, Literary Criticism And History. **Career:** Pfizer Inc., marketing research analyst, 1985-86, staff writer, 1986-87; ABC Entertainment, supervisor, manager and director, 1987-90; freelance television writer, 1990-93; ABC Productions, vice president of comedy, 1993-95; CBS, director of drama development and vice president of nontraditional programs, 1995-96, vice president and senior vice president, 1996-2000. Writer. **Publications:** Straitjacket and Tie (novel), 1994; Touch & Go (short stories), 1997. Contributor to periodicals. **Address:** c/o Molly Friedrich, Aaron M. Priest Literary Agency, 708 3rd Ave., 23rd Fl., New York, NY 10017-4103, U.S.A.

STEIN, Kevin. American (born United States), b. 1954. **Genres:** Poetry, Literary Criticism And History. **Career:** Ball State University, instructor, 1978-79; Indiana University, associate instructor, 1980-84; Bradley University, assistant professor, 1984-88, associate professor, 1988-94, professor of English, 1994-2000, Caterpillar professor of English, 2000-, Bradley's Vital Creative Writing Program, director; Illinois Poet Laureate, 2003-. Writer. **Publications:** POETRY: A Field of Wings, 1986; The Figure Our Bodies Make, 1988; A Circus of Want, 1992; Bruised Paradise, 1996; Chance Ransom, 2000; American Ghost Roses, 2005; Sufficiency of the Actual, 2009. OTHER: James Wright: The Poetry of a Grown Man (literary criticism), 1988; The Brothers Majere, 1989; Private Poets, Worldly Acts: Public and Private History in Contemporary American Poetry (essays), 1996; (ed. with G.E. Murray) Illinois Voices: An Anthology of Twentieth-Century Poetry, 2001; Bread & Steel: An Anthology of Illinois Poets, 2007; Poetry's Afterlife: Verse in the Digital Age, 2010. Contributor of essays to periodicals. **Address:** Department of English, Bradley University, 364 Bradley Hall, 1501 W Bradley Ave., Peoria, IL 61625, U.S.A. **Online address:** kstein@bradley.edu

STEIN, Leslie. (Leslie A. Stein). Australian/American (born United States), b. 1945. **Genres:** Adult Non-fiction, Novels, Architecture, Law. **Career:** Sydney Metropolitan Strategy, chief counsel; Western Australian Town Planning Appeal Tribunal, chief judge and chairman; Pace Law School, adjunct professor; Monash University, adjunct professor of law, professor of law; barrister, 1996-. Writer. **Publications:** Urban Legal Problems, 1974; The Relevance of Legal Density Controls in Town Planning to the Human Use of Space, 1976; (ed.) Locus Standi, 1979; The Journey of Adam Kadmon: A Novel, 2000; Principles of Planning Law, 2008. **Address:** Pace Law School, 78 North Broadway, White Plains, NY 10603, U.S.A. **Online address:** lstein@ca.com.au

STEIN, Leslie A. See **STEIN, Leslie.**

STEIN, Mary Kay. American (born United States), b. 1953. **Genres:** Education, Reference. **Career:** Pennsylvania State University, assistant, 1976-80; University of Pittsburgh, School of Education, teaching assistant, 1980-81, teaching fellow, 1981-83, Learning Research and Development Center (LRDC), graduate research assistant, 1983-86, postdoctoral fellow, 1986-89, research associate, 1989-98, research scientist, 1998-2005, senior scientist, 2005-, associate director for education research and practice, 2008-, School of Education, Department of Administrative and Policy Studies, associate professor, 1999-2005, professor, 2005-, Learning Policy Center, founding director, 2006-, Learning Sciences and Policy Program, chair, 2007-. Writer. **Publications:** (Co-author) Implementing Standards-Based Mathematics Instruction: A Casebook for Professional Development, 2000, 2nd ed., 2009; (co-author) Improving Instruction in Algebra, 2005; (co-author) Improving Instruction in Geometry and Measurement, 2005; (co-author) Improving Instruction in Rational Numbers and Proportionality, 2005; (with L. Hubbard and H. Mehan) Reform as Learning: School Reform, Organizational Culture and Community Politics in San Diego, 2006; (ed. with C.E. Coburn) Research and Practice in Education, 2010; (ed. with L. Kucan) Instructional Explanations in the Disciplines, 2010; (with M.S. Smith) Five Practices For Orchestrating Productive Mathematics Discussions, 2011. Contributor to journals, books and periodicals. **Address:** School of Education, University of Pitts-

burgh, Posvar Hall, 828 LRDC Bldg., 5th Fl., 3939 O'Hara St., Pittsburgh, PA 15260, U.S.A. **Online address:** mkstein@pitt.edu

STEIN, Michael B. Canadian (born Canada), b. 1940. **Genres:** Politics/Government. **Career:** Carleton University, assistant professor of political science, 1965-68; McGill University, associate professor of political science, 1968-77; Hebrew University, associate professor, 1973-74; McMaster University, professor of political science, 1977-2007, chairman, 1980-83, professor emeritus, 2007-; University of Toronto, visiting professor of political science, 2007-10. Writer. **Publications:** (With R.J. Jackson) Issues in Comparative Politics: A Text with Readings, 1971; The Dynamics of Right-Wing Protest: A Political Analysis of Social Credit in Quebec, 1973; Canadian Constitutional Renewal, 1968-1981: A Case Study in Integrative Bargaining, 1989; Constitutional Reform in Canada, 1968-81: A Case Study in Integrative Bargaining, 1990; (ed. with D. Easton and J.G. Gunnell) Regime and Discipline: Democracy and the Development of Political Science, 1995. **Address:** Department of Political Science, University of Toronto, 100 St. George St., Toronto, ON M5S 3G3, Canada. **Online address:** michael.stein@utoronto.ca

STEIN, Michael D. American (born United States), b. 1960. **Genres:** Young Adult Fiction, Medicine/Health, Novels. **Career:** Rhode Island Project AIDS, board director, 1988-93; University Medicine Foundation, board director, 1991-2000; Brown University, Program in Medicine, assistant professor, 1991-96, associate professor, 1996-2003, associate professor of medicine and community health, 2002-03, professor of medicine and community health, 2003-; Rhode Island Hospital Medical Foundation, board director, 1991-99; Lifespan Outcomes Assessment Project, director, 1995-2008; Lifespan Employee Health Services, medical director, 1996-2008; Stanley Street Treatment & Resources, board director, 2000-. Writer. **Publications:** (With J.K. Davis) Therapies for Adolescents, 1982; The Lonely Patient: How We Experience Illness (nonfiction), 2007. NOVELS: Probabilities, 1995; The White Life, 1999; The Lynching Tree, 2000; This Room is Yours, 2004; In the Age of Love, 2007. **Address:** Division of Biology and Medicine, Brown University, PO Box G-A, Providence, RI 02912, U.S.A. **Online address:** michael_stein@brown.edu

STEIN, Peter (Gonville). British (born England), b. 1926. **Genres:** History, Law, Essays. **Career:** Supreme Court, solicitor, 1951; University of Nottingham, assistant lecturer in law, 1952-53; University of Aberdeen, lecturer in jurisprudence, 1953-56, professor of jurisprudence, 1956-68, Faculty of Law, dean, 1961-64; Cambridge University, Queens' College, fellow, 1968-74, Regius professor of civil law, 1968-93, Regius Professor of Civil Law Emeritus, 1993, vice president, 1974-81, acting president, 1976, 1980-81; University of Virginia, visiting professor, 1965-66, 1978-79; University of Colorado, visiting professor, 1966; University of Witwatersrand, visiting professor, 1970; University of Louisiana, visiting professor, 1974, 1977, 1983, 1985; University of Chicago, visiting professor, 1985, 1988, 1990, 1992, 1995; Tulane university, visiting professor, 1992, 1996, 1998; University of Salerno, visiting professor, 1994; Lateran university, visiting professor, 1997. Writer. **Publications:** Fault in the Formation of Contract in Roman Law and Scots Law, 1958; Regulae Iuris: From Juristic Rules to Legal Maxims, 1966; Lösung derlinearen gewöhnlichen Differential Gleichungen und simultaner Systememit Hilfe der Stabstatik, 1969; Roman Law and English Jurisprudence, 1969; (with J. Shand) Legal Values in Western Society, 1974; Legal Evolution: The Story of an Idea, 1980; Legal Institutions: The Development of Dispute Settlement, 1984; The Character and Influence of the Roman Civil Law: Historical Essays, 1988; (with F. de Zulueta) The Teaching of Roman Law in England around 1200, 1990; (with C.W. Brooks and R.H. Hemholz) Notaries Public in England since the Reformation, 1991; Romisches Recht und Europa, 1996; Roman Law in European History, 1999. EDITOR/CO-EDITOR: W.W. Buckland's Textbook of Roman Law, 3rd ed., 1963; (with R.L. Meck and D.D. Raphael) Adam Smith's Lectures on Jurisprudence, 1978; (with A.D.E. Lewis) Studies in Justinian's Institutes: In Memory of J. A. C. Thomas, 1983; Droit romain et lEurope: Essai dinterprètation historique, 2003. **Address:** 36, Wimpole Rd., Great Eversden, Cambridge, CB CB3 7HR, England. **Online address:** gonville@waitrose.com

STEIN, Rebecca L. American (born United States), b. 1969. **Genres:** History, Travel/Exploration, Anthropology/Ethnology, Social Sciences. **Career:** Stanford University, lecturer, 1999-2000; University of California, lecturer, 2000-01; Amherst College, visiting professor in law and jurisprudence, 2001-02; University of Minnesota, assistant professor, 2002-03; Duke University, assistant professor of cultural anthropology and women's studies, 2003-, associate professor of cultural anthropology and women's studies, director of undergraduate studies. Writer. **Publications:** (Ed. with T. Swedenburg) Palestine, Israel and the Politics of Popular Culture, 2005; (ed. with J. Beinin) The Struggle for Sovereignty: Palestine and Israel, 1993-2005, 2006; Itineraries in Conflict: Israelis, Palestinians and the Political Lives of Tourism, 2008. Contributor to journals and periodicals. **Address:** Cultural Anthropology & Womens Studies Dept., Duke University, 212 Friedl Bldg., PO Box 90091, Durham, NC 27708, U.S.A. **Online address:** rlstein@duke.edu

STEIN, Sherman K. American (born United States), b. 1926. **Genres:** Mathematics/Statistics, Education. **Career:** University of California, Department of Mathematics, professor of mathematics, 1953-93, professor emeritus, 1993-. Writer. **Publications:** Mathematics: The Man-made Universe, 1963, 2nd ed., 1969; Calculus in the First Three Dimensions, 1967; Calculus for the Natural and Social Sciences, 1968; Calculus and Analytic Geometry, 1968, (with A. Barcellos) 5th ed., 1992; (with C.D. Crabill) Elementary Algebra: A Guided Inquiry, 1972; (with G.D. Chakerian and C.D. Crabill) Geometry: A Guided Inquiry, 1972; (with A. Barcellos) An Introduction to Differential Equations to Accompany Stein/Barcellos, Calculus and Analytic Geometry, Fifth Edition, 1994; (with S. Szabo) Algebra and Tiling, 1994; Strength in Numbers, 1996; Archimedes: What Did He Do Besides Cry Eureka?, 1999; How the Other Half Thinks, 2001; Survival Guide for Outsiders: How to Protect Yourself from Politicians, 2010. Contributor to periodicals. **Address:** Department of Mathematics, University of California, Mathematical Sciences Bldg., 1 Shields Ave., Davis, CA 95616-8633, U.S.A. **Online address:** stein@math.ucdavis.edu

STEIN, Wendy. American (born United States), b. 1951. **Genres:** Young Adult Non-fiction, Mystery/Crime/Suspense. **Career:** Syracuse Herald-Journal, reporter, 1974-75; New Readers Press, managing editor of periodicals department and senior editor; freelance writer and editor, 1983-. **Publications:** GREAT MYSTERIES SERIES: Filling Out Forms, 1986; Atlantis: Opposing Viewpoints, 1989; Shamans: Opposing Viewpoints, 1991; Dinosaurs: Opposing Viewpoints, 1994; Witches: Opposing Viewpoints, 1995. OTHER: Taking the Wheel, 1979; Making a Budget, 1980; Communication Skills That Work (workbook), 1991; (with J. Haley) The Truth about Abuse, 2005, 2nd ed., 2010; Ready, Set, Study! (workbook). **Address:** 1909 Collins Rd., LaFayette, NY 13084, U.S.A.

STEINBERG, Blema S. Canadian (born Canada), b. 1934. **Genres:** Politics/Government, Psychology, Women's Studies And Issues, Biography. **Career:** McGill University, lecturer, 1961-64, assistant professor, 1964-67, associate professor, 1967-96, professor of political science, 1996-2004, professor emeritus, 2004-, director of graduate studies, 1980-83. Writer. **Publications:** (Ed. with A. Legault, J. Stein and J. Sigler) L'Analyse des Conflits Internationaux: Quatre Etudes de Cas, 1979; (ed. with P. Marantz) Superpower Involvement in the Middle East: Dynamics of Foreign Policy, 1985; Shame and Humiliation: Presidential Decision Making on Vietnam, 1996; Women in Power: The Personalities and Leadership Styles of Indira Gandhi, Golda Meir, and Margaret Thatcher, 2008. Contributor of articles to books, journals and newspapers. **Address:** Department of Political Science, McGill University, Rm. 414, Leacock Bldg., 855 Sherbrooke St. W, Montreal, QC H3A 2T7, Canada. **Online address:** bstein@mcgill.ca

STEINBERG, Bruce Robb. See **ROBB, B. R.**

STEINBERG, Clarence B. American (born United States), b. 1929. **Genres:** Agriculture/Forestry, History. **Career:** Delaware Valley College, assistant professor of English, 1960-68; University of Maryland, assistant professor of language and literature, 1968-75, professor of English literature; Board of Veterans Appeals, management analyst, 1980-86; U.S. Department of Agriculture, public affairs specialist, 1986, now retired. Writer. **Publications:** (With A.D. Lavender) Jewish Farmers of the Catskills: A Century of Survival, 1995. Contributor to periodicals. **Address:** University of Florida Press, 15 NW 15th St., Gainesville, FL 32603, U.S.A. **Online address:** csteinberg@usda.gov

STEINBERG, David. Canadian (born Canada), b. 1942. **Genres:** Young Adult Fiction, Humor/Satire. **Career:** Executive producer of television programs and writer. **Publications:** The Book of David, 2007. Contributor to periodicals. **Address:** Simon & Schuster, 1230 Ave. of the Americas, New York, NY 10020, U.S.A. **Online address:** info@davidsteinberg.tv

STEINBERG, Erwin R. American (born United States), b. 1920. **Genres:** Language/Linguistics, Administration/Management, Literary Criticism And History, History. **Career:** Carnegie-Mellon University, instructor, 1946-49, assistant professor, 1949-55, associate professor, 1955-61, professor of English, 1961-75, professor of English, interdisciplinary studies, and rhetoric, 1975-2006, now retired, Thomas S. Baker professor of English and interdisciplinary studies, 1980-93, department head, 1956-60, Margaret Morrison Carnegie College, dean, 1960-73, College of Humanities and Social Sciences, dean, 1965-75, Carnegie-Mellon Education Center, chairman of board, 1968-75, Carnegie-Mellon Communications Design Center, director, 1979-81, vice provost for education, 1991-96; U.S. Office of Education, coordinator, 1963-64. Writer. **Publications:** (With W.M. Schutte) Communication in Business and Industry, 1960; (with W.M. Schutte) Communication Problems in Business and Industry, 1961; Needed Research in the Teaching of English; Proceedings of a Project English Research Conference, May 5-7, 1962, 1963; (co-author) Curriculum Development and Evaluation in English and Social Studies: A Report on Research Development Conference for Personnel of USOE Curriculum Study Centers in English and Social Studies, 1965; (with A.M. Markman) English, then and Now, 1970; The Stream of Consciousness and Beyond in Ulysses, 1973. EDITOR: (with W.M. Schutte) Personal Integrity, 1961; The Rule of Force, 1962; Insight: The Experience of Literature, 14 vols., 1968-74; (with A. Markman) English Then and Now: Readings and Exercises, 1970; (with L. Josephs) English Education Today, 1970; Insight: Literature of Imagination; Discovery and Growth, 1972; The Stream of Consciousness Technique in the Modern Novel, 1979; (with L.W. Gregg) Cognitive Processes in Writing, 1980; La Technica del Fluir de la Consciencia en la Novela Moderna, 1982; (with A.M. Markman) Exercises in the History of English, 1983; Plain Language: Principles and Practice, 1991; (with K. McCormick) Approaches to Teaching Joyce's Ulysses, 1993; (with A. Midani) Ulysses on Montmartre: An Earlier Ulysses in Another Nighttown: A French Shadow Play (1910), Its Translation, and an Essay on Its Relation to Joyce's Ulysses, 2002. **Address:** Department of English, Carnegie Mellon University, 5000 Forbes Ave., Pittsburgh, PA 15213, U.S.A. **Online address:** es2t@andrew.cmu.edu

STEINBERG, Jonathan. American (born United States), b. 1934. **Genres:** History, Translations, Biography. **Career:** Cambridge University, university lecturer in history, 1966-93, Trinity Hall, fellow, vice-master, director of studies in history, 1966-, emeritus fellow, reader in modern history, 1993-99; Harvard University, visiting lecturer, 1968-69; University of Pennsylvania, Walter H. Annenberg professor of modern European history, 2000-. Writer. **Publications:** Yesterday's Deterrent: Tripitz and the Birth of the German Battle Fleet, 1965; Why Switzerland?, 1976, 2nd ed., 1996; All or Nothing: The Axis and the Holocaust, 1941-43, 1990; Deutsche, Italiener und Juden: deritalienische Widerstand gegen den Holocaust, 1992; Fountain Pens: The Collector's Guide to Selecting, Buying, and Enjoying New and Vintage Fountain Pens, 1994; Midas Investing: How You Can Make at Least 20% in the Stock Market This Year and Every Year, 1996; Tutto o niente L'Asseand ali Ebrei nei territori occupati, 1997; Die Deutsche Bank und ihre Goldtransaktionen wahrend des Zweiten Weltkrieges, trans. as The Deutsche Bank and Its Gold Transactions during the Second World War, 1999; Bismarck: A Life, 2011. TRANSLATOR: M. Boveri, Treason in the Twentieth Century, 1961; F. Heer, Intellectual History of Europe, 1966; P. Arlacchi, Mafia, Peasants and Great Estates: Society in Traditional Calabria, 1983; L. Karina and M. Kant, Hitler, Dancers: German Modern Dance and the Third Reich, 2002. **Address:** Department of History, University of Pennsylvania, 206E College Hall, Philadelphia, PA 19104-6379, U.S.A. **Online address:** steinbej@history.upenn.edu

STEINBERG, Laurence. (Laurence D. Steinberg). American (born United States), b. 1952. **Genres:** Psychology, Human Relations/Parenting, Education, Reference. **Career:** Cornell University, lecturer, 1976-77; University of California, assistant professor of social ecology, 1977-82, associate director for undergraduate studies, 1981-82, Public Policy Research Organization, faculty associate, 1979-83, associate professor of social ecology, 1982-83; University of Wisconsin, professor, 1983-89; University of Wisconsin, School of Education, National Center on Effective Secondary Schools, faculty associate, 1985-89; Temple University, professor, 1988-, division of developmental psychology, director, 1991-94; department of psychology, director of graduate studies, 1994-99, 2001-07, John D. and Catherine T. MacArthur Foundation Research Network on Adolescent Development and Juvenile Justice, director, 1997-2008, Laura H. Carnell professor of psychology, 1998-, distinguished university professor, 1999-; Society for Research on Adolescence, president. Writer. **Publications:** (Comp.) The Life Cycle: Readings in Human Development, 1981; Adolescence, 1985, 9th ed., 2010; (with E.

Greenberger) When Teenagers Work: The Psychological and Social Costs of Adolescent Employment, 1986; (with A. Levine) You and Your Adolescent: A Parent's Guide for Ages 10 to 20, 1990, rev. ed., 1997; (with R.B. Meyer and J. Belsky) Infancy, Childhood & Adolescence: Development in Context, 1991; (with W. Steinberg) Crossing Paths: How Your Child's Adolescence Triggers Your Own Crisis, 1994; (with R. Meyer) Childhood, 1995; (with S.M. Dornbusch and B.B. Brown) Beyond the Classroom: Why School Reform Has Failed and What Parents Need To Do, 1996; (ed. with V.C. McLyod) Studying Minority Adolescents: Conceptual, Methodological and Theoretical Issues, 1998; Ten Basic Principles of Good Parenting, 2004; (ed. with R.M. Lerner) Handbook of Adolescent Psychology, 2004, 3rd ed., 2009; Rethinking Juvenile Justice, 2008; Life-Span Development, 2010; (with M.H. Bornstein and D.L. Vandell) Development: Infancy Through Adolescence, 2010; You and Your Adolescent: The Essential Guide for Ages 10-25, 2011. Contributor to books. **Address:** Department of Psychology, Temple University, Weiss Hall 1701, N 13th St., Philadelphia, PA 19122-6085, U.S.A. **Online address:** lds@temple.edu

STEINBERG, Laurence D. *See* **STEINBERG, Laurence.**

STEINBERG, Mark D(avid). American (born United States), b. 1953. **Genres:** History, Literary Criticism And History, Urban Studies. **Career:** University of Oregon, visiting instructor in Russian history, 1987; Harvard University, assistant professor of Russian history, 1987-89; Yale University, assistant professor, 1989-94, Morse junior faculty fellow in humanities, 1991-92, associate professor of Russian history, 1994-96; National Geographic Television, consultant, 1996-97; University of Illinois, assistant professor, 1996-98, associate professor of history, 1998-2003, Helen Corley Petit professor, 1998-99, professor of history, 2003-, Russian and East European Center, director, 1998-2004; Slavic Review, editor, 2006-. **Publications:** Moral Communities: The Culture of Class Relations in the Russian Printing Industry, 1867-1907, 1992; (ed. with S. Frank and contrib.) Cultures in Flux: Lower Class Values, Practices, and Resistance in Late Imperial Russia, 1994; (with V. Khrustalev) The Fall of the Romanovs: Political Dreams and Personal Struggles in a Time of Revolution, 1995; Voices of Revolution, 1917, 2001; Proletarian Imagination: Self, Modernity, and the Sacred in Russia, 1910-1925, 2002; (with N.V. Riasanovsky) A History of Russia, 8th ed., 2010; (ed. with H.J. Coleman) Sacred Stories: Religion and Spirituality in Modern Russia, 2007; (with C. Wanner) Religion, Morality, and Community in Post-Soviet Societies, 2008; (ed. with V. Sobol) Interpreting Emotion in Russia and Eastern Europe, 2011; Petersburg Fin de Siecle, 2011. Contributor to books. **Address:** Department of History, University of Illinois, 309 Gregory Hall, 810 S Wright St., Urbana, IL 61801, U.S.A. **Online address:** steinb@illinois.edu

STEINBERG, Neil. American (born United States), b. 1960. **Genres:** Humor/Satire, Novels, Adult Non-fiction. **Career:** Chicago Sun-Times, feature writer and reporter, 1987-95, columnist, 1995-. **Publications:** If at All Possible, Involve a Cow: The Book of College Pranks, 1992; Complete and Utter Failure: A Celebration of Also-rans, Runners-up, Never-weres, and Total Flops, 1994; Alphabet of Modern Annoyances, 1996; Don't Give up the Ship: Finding My Father While Lost at Sea, 2002; Hatless Jack: The President, The Fedora, and The History of an American Style, 2004; Drunkard: A Hard-drinking Life, 2008; You Were Never in Chicago, 2012. Contributor to periodicals. **Address:** Chicago Sun-Times, 350 N Orleans St., 10th Fl., Chicago, IL 60654, U.S.A. **Online address:** nsteinberg@suntimes.com

STEINBERG, Susan. American (born United States) **Genres:** Novellas/Short Stories. **Career:** University of San Francisco, Department of English, associate professor, department co-chair. Writer. **Publications:** The End of Free Love (short stories), 2003; Hydroplane (short stories), 2006. Contributor to periodicals and journals. **Address:** University of San Francisco, 2130 Fulton St., San Francisco, CA 94117, U.S.A. **Online address:** ssteinberg@usfca.edu

STEINBERG, Warren. American (born United States), b. 1944. **Genres:** Psychology, Medicine/Health, Adult Non-fiction, Social Sciences. **Career:** College of New Rochelle, faculty, 1975; Ulster County Community College, faculty, 1976; Delaware County Community College, faculty, 1976; C.G. Jung Training Institute of New York, director, 1988-93, faculty. Writer. **Publications:** Circle of Care: Clinical Issues in Jungian Therapy, 1990; Masculinity: Identity, Conflict and Transformation, 1993. Contributor to journals. **Address:** 275 Central Pk. W, Ste. 1A, New York, NY 10024-3035, U.S.A.

STEINBERG, Wendy. American (born United States), b. 1952. **Genres:** Human Relations/Parenting, Psychology, Social Sciences. **Career:** Institute of Contemporary Art (ICA), public relations director. Writer. **Publications:** (With L. Steinberg) Crossing Paths: How Your Child's Adolescence Triggers Your Own Crisis, 1994. **Address:** Institute of Contemporary Art, 118 S 36th St., Philadelphia, PA 19104-3289, U.S.A.

STEINBROOK, Gordon L. American (born United States), b. 1942. **Genres:** Autobiography/Memoirs, Military/Defense/Arms Control, History, Biography. **Career:** Columbus High School, history instructor, 1969-. Writer. **Publications:** Allies & Mates: An American Soldier with the Australians and New Zealanders in Vietnam, 1966-67, 1995. **Address:** Columbus High School, 2200 26th St., Columbus, NE 68601-2614, U.S.A.

STEINER, Evgeny. Also writes as Antony Iwajin, E. S. Shteĭner, Evgenii Shteĭner. British/American/Russian (born Russia), b. 1955. **Genres:** Novellas/Short Stories, Art/Art History, Language/Linguistics, Literary Criticism And History, Biography. **Career:** Pushkin State Museum of Fine Arts, assistant archivist, 1975-80; Iskusstvo Publishing House, editor, 1981-83, senior editor, 1983-90; Moscow State University, Faculty of Philosophy, adjunct lecturer, 1988-89; Hebrew University of Jerusalem, Department of East Asian Studies, lecturer, 1991-93; Tel-Aviv University, Department of Art History, lecturer, 1991-94; Russian State University for Humanities, visiting professor, 1994; Meiji Gakuin University, visiting researcher, 1996-97; New York University, adjunct faculty member in history of art, 1998-; Yeshiva University Museum, archivist, 1999-2000; State University of New York at Oswego, Art Department, visiting professor, 2002-05; University of Manchester, Leverhulme visiting professor, 2006-07; University of London, School of Oriental and African Studies, Japan Research Centre, professorial research associate; Russian Institute for Cultural Research, principal research fellow, 2006-. **Publications:** (As E.S. Shteĭner) Ikkiu Sodzíiun: Tvorcheskaia Lichnost' v Kontekste Srednevekovoĭ Kul'tury, 1987; Stories for Little Comrades, 1999; Gonsuke from Shinjuku, 1999; English-Japanese Children's Dictionary, 2000; Japanese-English and English/Japanese Dictionary and Phrasebook, 2000; Letters from the Space, 2000, rev. ed., 2005; (as Evgenii Shteĭner) Avangard i postroenie novogo cheloveka: iskusstvo sovetskoi detskoi knigi 1920 godov, 2002; Avant-Garde and Construction of the New Man, 2002; Russian-English-Japanese Phrasebook, 2003; Zen Life: Ikkyu and Others, 2005; Reflections of the Japanologist, 2005. Contributor to periodicals and books. **Address:** School of Oriental and African Studies, University of London, Thornhaugh St., Russell Sq., London, GL WC1H 0XG, England. **Online address:** evgeny.steiner@manchester.ac.uk

STEINER, George. British/French (born France), b. 1929. **Genres:** Novels, Literary Criticism And History, Language/Linguistics, Essays. **Career:** The Economist, editorial staff, 1952-56; Princeton University, Institute for Advanced Study, fellow, 1956-58, Gauss lecturer, 1959-60, visiting professor; Cambridge University, Churchill College, fellow, 1961-69, extraordinary fellow, 1969-, Leslie Stephen lecturer, 1985; University of California, visiting professor, 1973-74; University of Geneva, professor of English and comparative literature, 1974-94, emeritus professor of comparative literature, 1994-; University of London, Maurice lecturer, 1984; University of Glasgow, W.P. Ker lecturer, 1986, Gifford lecturer, 1990; College of France, visiting professor, 1992; Oxford University, St. Anne's College, First Lord Weidenfeld professor of comparative literature and fellow, 1994-95, Balliol College, honorary fellow, 1995; Harvard University, visiting professor, Norton professor of poetry, 2001-02; Yale University, visiting professor, Stanford University, visiting professor. **Publications:** Tolstoy or Dostoevsky, 1958, 2nd ed., 1996; The Death of Tragedy, 1961; (ed. with R. Fagles) Homer: A Collection of Critical Essays, 1962; Anno Domini: Three Stories, 1964; (ed. and intro.) Penguin Book of Modern Verse Translation, 1966; Language and Silence: Essays 1958-1966, 1967; (ed. and intro.) Poem into Poem: World Poetry in Modern Verse Translation, 1970; Extraterritorial, 1971; In Bluebeard's Castle: Some Notes Towards The Redefinition of Culture, 1971; The Sporting Scene: White Knights of Reykjavik, 1973 in US as Fields of Force: Fischer and Spassky at Reykjavik, 1974; Nostalgia for the Absolute, 1974; After Babel: Aspects of Language and Translation, 1975, 2nd ed., 1992; Why English?, 1975; Heidegger, 1978; The Uncommon Reader, 1978; On Difficulty and Other Essays, 1978; Martin Heidegger, 1978; Antigones, 1979; The Portage to San Cristóbal of A.H., 1981; George Steiner: A Reader, 1984; Real Presences, 1986; (with R. Jahanbegloo) Entretiens, 1992; Proofs and Three Parables, 1993; Dialogues: Sur le Mythe d'Antigone, sur le Sacrifice d'Abraham, 1994; What Is Comparative Literature?, 1995; (intro.) Trial, 1995; The Deeps of the Sea and Other Fiction, 1996; (ed. and intro.) Homer in English, 1996; No Passion Spent: Essays 1978-1995, 1996; Errata: An Examined Life, 1998; Language and Silence: Essays on Language, Literature, and the Inhuman, 1998; (with A. Spire) Barbarie de l ignorance: Juste l'ombre d'un certain ennui, 1998; (with A. Spire) Ce qui me hante, 1999; Grammars of Creation: Originating in the Gifford Lectures for 1990, 2001; Lessons of the Masters, 2003; (contrib.) The Legacy of Homer, 2005; The Idea of Europe, 2005; My Unwritten Books, 2008; (ed. and intro.) George Steiner at the New Yorker, 2009; Avec George Steiner: Les Chemins de la Culture, 2010; Poetry of Thought, 2011. Contributor of articles to periodicals. **Address:** Churchill College, Storey's Way, Churchill, Cambridge, CB CB3 0DS, England.

STEINER, George A. American (born United States), b. 1912. **Genres:** Administration/Management, Business/Trade/Industry, Public/Social Administration, Economics, Ethics, Politics/Government, History. **Career:** Indiana University, instructor, 1937-39, assistant professor of finance, 1939-42, Bureau of Business Research, associate director, 1937-39; University of Illinois, professor of economics, 1947-56; Lockheed Aircraft Corp., chief economist, 1953-55; University of California, Graduate School of Management, professor of management theory, 1956-, Division of Research, director, 1956-71, Center for Research and Dialogue on Business in Society, director, 1971-80, now professor emeritus, Harry and Elsa Kunin Chair in Business and Society; Cleveland State University, Nance Distinguished Lecturer, 1981; U.S. Federal Government, Defense Production Administration, director of policy, Office of Defense Mobilization, director of policy. Writer. **Publications:** Tax System and Industrial Development, 1938; Business Turnover of Indiana Retail Trades, 1939; Indiana State Disbursements, 1939; Economic Problems Of National Defense, 1941; Economic Problems of War, 1942; (with N. David) Wartime Industrial Statistics, 1949; Government's Role in Economic Life, 1953; National Defense and Southern California, 1961-70, 1961; (ed. with R. Fagles) Homer: A Collection of Critical Essays, 1962; Problems in Implementing Program Budgeting, 1965; (with W.M. Cannon) Multinational Corporate Planning, 1966; Industrial Project Management, 1968; Strategic Factors in Business Success, 1969; Top Management Planning, 1969; (with J.F. Steiner) Business, Government, and Society: A Managerial Perspective, 1971, 13th ed., 2012; Contemporary Challenges in the Business-Society Relationship, 1972; (comp.) Issues in Business and Society, 1972, 2nd ed., 1977; Redefinition of Capitalism and Its Impact on Management Theory and Practice, 1973; Selected Major Issues In Business' Role in Modern Society, 1973; The Changing Business Role In Modern Society, 1974; Nostalgia for the Absolute, 1974; (with J.J. Corson) Measuring Business's Social Performance: The Corporate Social Audit, 1974; Changing Business-Society Interrelationships, 1975; Casebook in Business and Society, 1975, 2nd ed., 1980; Management Policy and Strategy: Text, Readings and Cases, 1977, 3rd ed., 1986; (ed.) Business and Its Environment, 1977; The Uncommon Reader, 1978; (ed.) Business and Its Changing Environment, 1978; Strategic Planning: What Every Manager Must Know, 1979; Casebook for Business, Government and Society, 2nd ed., 1980; New CEO, 1983; (co-author) Barbarie de l ignorance: Juste I ombre d un certainennui, 1998; Errata: An Examined Life, 1998; (co-author) Ce qui me hante, 1999. **Address:** Graduate School of Management, University of California, 110 Westwood Plz., PO Box 951481, Los Angeles, CA 90095-1481, U.S.A. **Online address:** george.steiner@anderson.ucla.edu

STEINER, Michael C. American (born United States), b. 1947. **Genres:** Urban Studies, History. **Career:** Carleton College, instructor, 1971-72; University of Minnesota, instructor, 1973-74; California State University, professor of American studies, 1975-, graduate Program adviser. Writer. **Publications:** (With C. Mondale) Region and Regionalism in the United States, 1988; (ed. with W. Franklin) Mapping American Culture, 1992; (ed. with D. Wrobel) Many Wests: Place, Culture & Regional Identity, 1997; (co-ed.) Changing Borders: Legal and Economic Aspects of European Englargement, 1998; (co-ed.) Innovation, Networks and Localities, 1999. Contributor to journals. **Address:** Department of American Studies, California State University, UH-410, 800 N State College Blvd., Fullerton, CA 92831, U.S.A. **Online address:** msteiner@fullerton.edu

STEINHARDT, Bernice. American (born United States) **Genres:** Novels. **Career:** Esther Project and Art and Remembrance, founder. Writer. **Publications:** (with mother, Esther Nisenthal Krinitz) Memories of Survival, 2005. **Address:** Art & Remembrance, 5505 Connecticut Ave. NW, Ste. 131, Washington, DC 20015-2601, U.S.A.

STEINHARDT, Nancy Shatzman. American (born United States), b. 1954.

Genres: Architecture, Area Studies, Art/Art History, Translations, Social Sciences. **Career:** Bryn Mawr College, lecturer, 1981-83; University of Delaware, faculty; University of Pennsylvania, lecturer, 1982-, associate professor of Oriental studies, Department of East Asian Languages and Civilizations, professor of East Asian art and architecture, Museum of Archaeology and Anthropology, curator of Chinese art; Kunsthistorische Institute, visiting professor, 1996. Writer. **Publications:** (Trans. with M.N. Parent) Early Buddhist Architecture in Japan, 1980; (co-author) Chinese Traditional Architecture, 1984; Chinese Imperial City Planning, 1990; Liao Architecture, 1997; (ed.) A History of Chinese Architecture, 2002; (ed. with V.H. Mair and P.R. Goldin) Hawai'i Reader in Traditional Chinese Culture, 2005. (ed. with J.W. Cody and T. Atkin) Chinese Architecture and The Beaux-Arts, 2011. Contributor to journals. **Address:** Department of Asian and Middle Eastern Studies, University of Pennsylvania, 853 Williams Hall, 255 S 36th St., Philadelphia, PA 19104-6305, U.S.A. **Online address:** nssteinh@sas.upenn.edu

STEINHOFF, Judith B. American (born United States), b. 1953. **Genres:** Art/Art History, Politics/Government. **Career:** Trinity College, visiting lecturer, 1987-88; Rice University, visiting assistant professor, 1988-93; National Gallery of Art, Department of Italian Painting, research assistant, 1995; University of Houston, assistant professor, 1996-2005, associate professor, 2005-, area coordinator. Writer. **Publications:** Sienese Painting after the Black Death: Artistic Pluralism, Politics, and the New Art Market, 2007; (with T.B. Smith) Art As Politics In Late Medieval and Renaissance Siena, 2012. Contributor of articles to journals. **Address:** School of Art, University of Houston, Rm. 104F, Fine Arts Bldg., 4800 Calhoun Rd., Houston, TX 77204-4019, U.S.A. **Online address:** jsteinhoff@uh.edu

STEINKE, Darcey. American (born United States), b. 1964?. **Genres:** Novels, Young Adult Fiction. **Career:** University of Mississippi, writing instructor, Renee and John Grisham Southern writer-in-residence, Ole Miss, Department of English, professor. **Publications:** Up through the Water, 1989; Suicide Blonde, 1992; (ed. with R. Moody) Joyful Noise: The New Testament Revisited, 1997; Jesus Saves, 1997; Milk, 2005; Easter Everywhere: A Memoir, 2007. Contributor to periodicals. **Address:** University of Mississippi, PO Box 1848, University, MS 38677, U.S.A.

STEINLAUF, Michael C. American (born United States), b. 1947. **Genres:** History, Theology/Religion, Reference, Regional/Urban Planning. **Career:** University of Michigan, visiting assistant professor of history, 1988; Carleton University, lecturer, 1988; Hebrew University of Jerusalem, lecturer, 1988; Harvard University, lecturer, 1989; Brandeis University, assistant professor of east European Jewish history and culture, 1989-90; U.S. Holocaust Memorial Museum, project director for Poland, 1990; Gratz College, Department of History, assistant professor, 1991-93, associate professor, 1998-; University of California, lecturer, 1992; McGill University, lecturer, 1993; Franklin and Marshall College, visiting assistant professor of Judaic studies, 1994-96; YIVO Institute for Jewish Research, senior research fellow, 1996-98; Reconstructionist Rabbinical College, adjunct instructor. Writer. **Publications:** (Contrib.) From Shtetl to Socialism: Studies from Polin, 1993; (contrib.) The World Reacts to the Holocaust, 1996; (contrib.) Between Two World Wars: On the Cultural Life of the Jews in Poland in Its Three Languages, 1997; Bondage to the Dead: Poland and the Memory of the Holocaust, 1997; Ida Kaminska (1899-1980): Grande Dame of the Yiddish Theater, 2001; Polin: Studies in Polish Jewry, 2003; (ed.) Emergence of Modern Jewish Politics: Bundism and Zionism in Eastern Europe, 2003; (ed.) Worlds of S. An-sky, 2006; (ed.) Jewish Theatre: A Global View, 2009. Contributor of articles to periodicals. **Address:** Department of History, Gratz College, 7605 Old York Rd., Melrose Park, PA 19027, U.S.A. **Online address:** msteinlauf@earthlink.net

STEINMAN, David. American (born United States), b. 1958. **Genres:** Novels, Adult Non-fiction, Medicine/Health, Environmental Sciences/Ecology. **Career:** Freedom Press, founder, publisher and editor, 1997-; Green Patriot Radio, host, 2008-. Journalist, consumer health advocate. **Publications:** Diet for a Poisoned Planet: How to Choose Safe Foods for You and Your Family, 1990; Seafood Safety, 1991; (ed. and comp.) Life Extenders and Memory Boosters!, 1993; (with S.S. Epstein) The Safe Shopper's Bible: A Consumer's Guide to Nontoxic Household Products, Cosmetics and Food, 1995; (with R.M. Wisner) Living Healthy in a Toxic World: Simple Steps to Protect You and Your Family from Everyday Chemicals, Poisons and Pollution, 1996; (with S.S. Epstein and S. Levert) Breast Cancer Prevention Program, 1997; (with L.S. Coles) Nature's Ultimate Anti-Cancer Pill: The IP6 with Inositol Question & Answer Book: How to Use Nature's Ultimate Anti-Cancer

Pill for the Prevention and Treatment of all Forms of Cancer, 1999; (with M. Loes) Non-drug European Secret to Healing Sports Injuries Naturally, 1999; (with G. Ross) Cure Indigestion, Heartburn, Cholesterol, Triglyceride and Liver Problems with Artichoke Extract, 1999; (with M. Loes) Aspirin Alternative: The Natural Way to Overcome Chronic Pain, Reduce Inflammation and Enhance the Healing Response, 2001; Safe Trip to Eden: 10 Steps to Save Planet Earth from the Global Warming Meltdown, 2007; (intro.) 50 Simple Steps to Save the Earth from Global Warming, 2008. **Address:** Freedom Press Inc., 1801 Chart Trl., Topanga, CA 90290, U.S.A. **Online address:** info@freedompressonline.com

STEINMAN, Louise. American (born United States), b. 1951. **Genres:** Literary Criticism And History, Plays/Screenplays, Adult Non-fiction, Theatre, Writing/Journalism, Dance/Ballet, Photography. **Career:** Freelance critic, 1975-; SO&SO&SO&SO Inc., theater critic, co-founder and artistic co-director, 1976-86; Willamette Week, performance editor, 1982; Los Angeles Public Library, ALOUD, curator, 1983-, cultural programs director, 1993-; Pro Arts, executive director, 1985-86; San Francisco State University, Center for Experimental and Interdisciplinary Arts, lecturer, 1985-87; City of Los Angeles Cultural Affairs Department, performance curator, 1986-91; Centrum Foundation, writer-in-residence, 1992; Los Angeles Institute for Humanities, Sundance Institute Arts Writing Program, co-director and senior creative advisor, 1995-2000; University of California, lecturer; Mills College, lecturer. **Publications:** The Knowing Body: Elements of Contemporary Performance and Dance, 1986; The Knowing Body: The Artist as Storyteller in Contemporary Performance, 1995; The Souvenir: A Daughter Discovers Her Father's War, 2001; The Crooked Mirror: A Conversation with Poland, forthcoming. Contributor to journals. **Address:** Los Angeles Public Library, 630 W 5th St., Los Angeles, CA 90071, U.S.A. **Online address:** louisesteinman@members.authorsguild.net

STEINMAN, Michael. American (born United States), b. 1952. **Career:** Hofstra University, assistant professor of English, 1977-82; Nassau Community College, associate professor of English, professor, 1982-. Writer. **Publications:** Yeats's Heroic Figures: Wilde, Parnell, Swift, Casement, 1983; Frank O'Connor at Work, 1990; (ed.) A Frank O'Connor Reader, 1994; (ed.) Happiness of Getting it Down Right: Letters of Frank O'Connor and William Maxwell, 1945-1966, 1996; (ed.) Element of Lavishness: Letters of Sylvia Townsend Warner and William Maxwell, 1938-1978, 2001; (ed. and afterword) Music at Long Verney: Twenty Stories, 2001. Contributor to magazines. **Address:** Department of English, Nassau Community College, 230 Bradley Hall, 1 Education Dr., Garden City, NY 11530-6793, U.S.A. **Online address:** michael.steinman@ncc.edu

STEINMAN, Ron. American (born United States), b. 1934. **Genres:** Documentaries/Reportage, History. **Career:** Today Show, producer, senior producer, 1975-92; NBC News, bureau chief, 1966, news writer, through 1992; Sunday Today, producer; ABC News, producer, writer on documentaries for arts and entertainment, 1993-; Douglas/Steinman Productions, partner; The Digital Journalist, executive editor and columnist; The Digital Filmmaker, executive editor and columnist. **Publications:** The Soldiers' Story: Vietnam in Their Own Words, 2000; Women in Vietnam: The Oral History, 2000; Inside Television's First War: A Saigon Journal, 2002; Death in Saigon, a Novel, 2007. **Address:** Douglas/Steinman Productions, 1841 Broadway, Ste. 1103, New York, NY 10023, U.S.A. **Online address:** ron@douglas-steinman.com

STEINMANN, Andrew E. American (born United States), b. 1954. **Genres:** Biography, Theology/Religion. **Career:** Lutheran church, associate pastor, 1981-86; Concordia College, visiting instructor, 1986-88, instructor, 1988-90, assistant professor of language and religious studies, 1990-91; St. Paul Lutheran School, chair of board of education, 1990-91; Gods Word to the Nations Bible Society, editor and translation coordinator, 1991-94; Lutheran Home, staff pastor, 1995-2000; Ashland University, adjunct professor, 1996-2000; Ashland Theological Seminary, adjunct professor, 1998; Concordia University, associate professor, 2000-06, Masters of Arts in Religion program, coordinator, 2003, professor of theology and Hebrew, 2006-; Walther Lutheran High School, chair of board of directors, 2005. **Publications:** (Ed. and trans.) Gods Word, 1995; Are My Prayers Falling on Deaf Ears? A Biblical Scholar Takes a Personal Look at Prayer, 1997; The Oracles of God: The Old Testament Canon, 1999; Fundamental Biblical Aramaic (bound with Fundamental Biblical Hebrew by A.H. Bartelt), 2004; Is God Listening? Making Prayer a Part of Your Life, 2004; Intermediate Biblical Hebrew, 2004; (ed.

and contrib.) Called to Be Gods People: An Introduction to the Old Testament, 2006; (with A.H. Bartelt) Workbook and Supplementary Exercises for Fundamental Biblical Hebrew and Fundamental Biblical Aramaic, 2006; Intermediate Hebrew Grammar, 2007; Daniel, 2008; Proverbs, 2009; Ezra and Nehemiah, 2010; From Abraham to Paul, 2011. **Address:** Concordia University, 7400 August St., River Forest, IL 60305-1499, U.S.A. **Online address:** andrew.steinmann@cuchicago.edu

STEINMETZ, Christian. German (born Germany), b. 1960. **Genres:** History, Language/Linguistics. **Career:** Otto Group, staff member. Writer. **Publications:** Deutscher Bund und Europäische Friedensordnung: die Krise der Wiener Ordnung 1848-1850, 2002. **Address:** Beiden Rauhen Bergen 80, Grosshansdorf, 22927, Germany. **Online address:** cauthades@aol.com

STEINMETZ, Devora. American (born United States), b. 1959?. **Genres:** Law. **Career:** Mechon Hadar, Yeshivat Hadar, senior faculty; Drisha Institute for Jewish Education and Jewish Theological Seminary, teacher of rabbinic literature; Beit Rabban, founder; Mandel Foundation, educational leadership consultant. Writer. **Publications:** From Father to Son: Kinship, Conflict, and Continuity in Genesis, 1991; Punishment and Freedom: The Rabbinic Construction of Criminal Law, 2008. Contributor to periodicals. **Address:** Mechon Hadar, 190 Amsterdam Ave., New York, NY 10023, U.S.A. **Online address:** steinmetz@mechonhadar.org

STEINMETZ, Lawrence Leo. American (born United States), b. 1938. **Genres:** Administration/Management, Business/Trade/Industry, Human Relations/Parenting, Marketing, Economics, Money/Finance. **Career:** The Kroger Co., management training staff, 1959-61; Henry Ford Community College, lecturer, 1961-63; University of Colorado, Graduate School of Business, assistant professor, 1964-66, associate professor, 1966-69, professor of management, 1969-77, Management and Organization Division, head, 1971-74; High Yield Management Inc., president, 1968-, vice president, 1968-69. Writer. **Publications:** Grass-roots Approach to Industrial Peace: Planning And Promoting Area Development Through The Labor-Management Community Council, 1966; (with R. Johnson and A.D. Allen) Labor Law, 1967; (with J.B. Kline and D.P. Stegall) Managing the Small Business, 1968, 3rd ed., 1982; Managing the Marginal and Unsatisfactory Performer, 1969, 2nd ed., 1985; Interviewing Skills for Supervisory Personnel, 1971; (with H.R. Todd, Jr.) First-Line Management: Approaching Supervision Effectively, 1975, 4th ed., 1986; The Art and Skill of Delegation, 1976; Human Relations, People and Work, 1979; Nice Guys Finish Last: Management Myths And Reality, 1983; (with H.R. Todd, Jr.) Supervision: First Line Management, 5th ed., 1992; (with W.T. Brooks) How To Sell At Margins Higher Than Your Competitors: Winning Every Sale At Full Price, Rate Or Fee, 2006. **Address:** High Yield Management Inc., 5340 Waterstone Dr., Boulder, CO 80301-6503, U.S.A.

STEINS, Richard. American (born United States), b. 1942. **Genres:** History, Biography, Military/Defense/Arms Control, Politics/Government, Young Adult Fiction, Autobiography/Memoirs. **Career:** Columbia University Press, editor, 1970-78; Harcourt Brace Jovanovich, School Division, editor, 1978-80; St. Martin's Press, director of development, 1981-93. **Publications:** Berlin, 1991; Morality, 1992; The Mideast after the Gulf War, 1992; The Nation Divides: The Civil War, 1820-1880, 1993; A Nation is Born: Rebellion and Independence in America, 1700-1820, 1993; Postwar Years: The Cold War and the Atomic Age, 1950-1959, 1993; Leontyne Price: Opera Superstar, 1993; The Death Penalty: Is it Justice?, 1993; The Allies against the Axis: World War II, 1940-1950, 1993; Our National Capital, 1994; Our Elections, 1994; Alcohol Abuse: Is This Danger on the Rise?, 1995; Censorship: How Does it Conflict with Freedom?, 1995; Transportation Milestones and Breakthroughs, 1995; The Complete History of Our Presidents, 1997; Hungary: Crossroads of Europe, 1997; Shiloh, 1997; Colonial America, 2000; Exploration and Settlement, 2000; Colin Powell: A Biography, 2003; Arthur Ashe: A Biography, 2005. Contributor to periodicals. **Address:** 425 Riverside Dr., New York, NY 10025-7775, U.S.A.

STEKETEE, Gail. American (born United States), b. 1949. **Genres:** Medicine/Health. **Career:** Boston University, professor, School of Social Work, dean. Writer. **Publications:** (With K. White) When Once Is Not Enough: Help for Obsessive-Compulsives, 1990; Treatment of Obsessive Compulsive Disorder, 1993; (ed. with T.A. Pigott and T. Schemmel) Obsessive Compulsive Disorder: The Latest Assessment and Treatment Strategies, 1999, 3rd ed., 2006; Overcoming Obsessive-Compulsive Disorder: A Behavioral and

Cognitive Protocol for the Treatment of OCD: Client Manual, 1999; (with S. Wilhelm) Cognitive Therapy for Obsessive-Compulsive Disorder: A Guide for Professionals, 2006. WITH R.O. FROST: (co-ed.) Cognitive Approaches to Obsessions and Compulsions: Theory, Assessment, and Treatment, 2002; Buried in Treasures: Help for Compulsive Acquiring, Saving, and Hoarding, 2007; Compulsive Hoarding and Acquiring: Client Workbook, 2007; Compulsive Hoarding and Acquiring: Therapist Guide, 2007; Stuff: Compulsive Hoarding and the Meaning of Things, 2010. Contributor to books and periodicals. **Address:** School of Social Work, Boston University, 264 Bay State Rd., Boston, MA 02215, U.S.A. **Online address:** steketee@bu.edu

STELL, Elizabeth P(arker). American/British (born England), b. 1958. **Genres:** Homes/Gardens, Horticulture, Sciences, Music. **Career:** Stellar Productions, writer and editor, 1982-; Storey Communications, horticultural consultant and editor, 1995-. **Publications:** Landscaping with Perennials, 1995; Secrets to Great Soil: A Grower's Guide to Composting, Mulching, and Creating Healthy, Fertile Soil for Your Garden and Lawn, 1998; Easy Guide to Perennials, 2002; The Civil War Ballroom Band Book, 2005. CO-AUTHOR: All the Onions, 1999; Fertilizers for Free, 1999; Improving Your Soil, 1999. Contributor to magazines. **Address:** Stellar Productions, 33 Stormview Rd., Lanesboro, MA 01237-9769, U.S.A. **Online address:** liz@bfv.com

STELLA, Santiago Villasmil. See **VILLASMIL, Omar (Santiago).**

STEN, Christopher (W.). American (born United States), b. 1944. **Genres:** Literary Criticism And History, Administration/Management, Education, Writing/Journalism. **Career:** George Washington University, instructor, 1970, assistant professor, 1971-78, associate professor, 1978-88, professor of English, 1988-, head of department, 1987-91, 1994-98, director of graduate studies in English, 1985-87, Writing in the Disciplines Program, director, 2003-; University of Wuerzburg, senior Fulbright lecturer in American literature, 1975-76. Writer. **Publications:** (Ed.) Savage Eye: Melville and the Visual Arts, 1991; The Weaver-God, He Weaves: Melville and the Poetics of the Novel, 1996; Sounding the Whale: Moby-Dick as Epic Novel, 1996; (ed. with J. Barnum and W. Kelley) Whole Oceans Away: Melville and the Pacific, 2007; (ed.) Literary Capital: A Washington Reader, 2011. Works appear in anthologies. Contributor of articles to journals. **Address:** Department of English, George Washington University, Rm. 673, Rome Hall, 801 22nd St. NW, Washington, DC 20052, U.S.A. **Online address:** csten@gwu.edu

STENGEL, Joyce A. American (born United States), b. 1938. **Genres:** Children's Fiction, Novels, Picture/Board Books, Humor/Satire. **Career:** Hartford Hospital, nurse, 1959-62; Central Connecticut State University, Writing Center, coordinator, 1982-89; University of Hartford, faculty. Writer. **Publications:** NOVELS: The Caribbean Jewels Mystery, 1996; Letting Go, 1997; Sara Takes Charge, 1998; Kittiwake Bay, 1999; Katie O', 2000; Mystery at Kittiwake Bay, 2001; Mystery of the Island Jewels, 2002. PICTURE BOOK: St. Patrick and the Three Brave Mice, 2009. Contributor of articles to periodicals. Works appear in anthologies. **Address:** c/o Author Mail, Simon & Schuster Inc., 1230 Ave. of the Americas, New York, NY 10020-1513, U.S.A. **Online address:** jastengel@me.com

STENGER, Victor J. American (born United States), b. 1935. **Genres:** Adult Non-fiction, Sciences. **Career:** Hughes Aircraft Co., technical staff, 1956-59; University of California, graduate teaching assistant, 1959-60, graduate research assistant, 1960-63; University of Hawaii, assistant professor, 1963-68, associate professor, 1968-73, acting principal investigator, 1968-69, professor of physics and astronomy, 1973-2000, deputy director, 1979-91, DUMAND Project, co-principal investigator, 1992-95, professor emeritus of physics and astronomy, 2000-; University of Heidelberg, visiting professor, 1969-70; Oxford University, visiting professor, 1977-78, 1993; Instituto Nazionale Fisica Nucleare, visiting professor, 1987; University of Colorado, adjunct professor of philosophy, 2000-. Writer. **Publications:** Not by Design: The Origin of the Universe, 1988; Physics and Psychics: The Search for a World beyond the Senses, 1990; The Unconscious Quantum: Metaphysics in Modern Physics and Cosmology, 1995; Timeless Reality: Symmetry, Simplicity and Multiple Universes, 2000; Has Science Found God? The Latest Results in the Search for Purpose in the Universe, 2003; The Comprehensible Cosmos: Where Do the Laws of Physics Come From?, 2006; God: The Failed Hypothesis. How Science Shows That God Does Not Exist, 2007; Quantum Gods: Creation, Chaos, and the Search for Cosmic Consciousness, 2009; The New Atheism: Taking a Stand for Science and Reason, 2009; The Fallacy of Fine-Tuning.

Why the Universe Is Not Designed for Us, 2011. **Address:** c/o Author Mail, Prometheus Books, 59 John Glenn Dr., Amherst, NY 14228-2197, U.S.A. **Online address:** vic.stenger@comcast.net

STENING, Bruce W. Australian (born Australia), b. 1949?. **Genres:** Administration/Management, Industrial Relations, Business/Trade/Industry. **Career:** Australian National University, Australia Asia Management Centre, professor and executive director; University of New South Wales-Asia, faculty. Writer. **Publications:** (With J.E. Everett and A.R. Krishnan) South-East Asian Managers: Mutual Perceptions of Japanese and Local Counterparts, 1984; (co-author) Japanese Organization Behaviour and Management: An Annotated Bibliography, 1984; (with C.R. Milton and L. Entrekin) Organizational Behaviour in Australia, 1984; (ed. with G. Redding) Cross-Cultural Management, 2003; (with F. Jiang) The Chinese Business Environment: An Annotated Bibliography, 2006; (with M.Y. Zhang) China 2.0, 2010. Contributor to periodicals. **Address:** ANU College of Business and Economics, Australian National University, Copland Bldg. 26C, Canberra, AC 0200, Australia.

STENNETT, Rob. American (born United States), b. 1977. **Genres:** Humor/Satire. **Career:** New Life Church, creative director, 1998-. Novelist. **Publications:** The Almost True Story of Ryan Fisher, 2008; The End Is Now, 2009. **Address:** U.S.A. **Online address:** robstennett3@yahoo.com

STENTIFORD, Barry M. American (born United States), b. 1964. **Genres:** Military/Defense/Arms Control. **Career:** Grambling State University, assistant professor of history, 1997-, associate professor; School of Advanced Military Studies, associate professor of History; U.S. Army's Command and General Staff College, Distance Education, adjunct faculty; American Public University, faculty. Writer. **Publications:** The American Home Guard: The State Militia in the Twentieth Century, 2002; (ed. with N.L.M. Brown) Jim Crow Encyclopedia, 2008; Tuskegee Airmen, 2012. **Address:** American Public University System, 111 W Congress St., Charles Town, WV 25414, U.S.A. **Online address:** bstent2746@aol.com

STENZEL, Anabel. American (born United States), b. 1972?. **Genres:** Novels, Biography, Autobiography/Memoirs, Human Relations/Parenting. **Career:** Lucile Packard Children's Hospital, genetic counselor. Writer. **Publications:** (With I.S. Byrnes) The Power of Two: A Twin Triumph over Cystic Fibrosis, 2007. **Address:** Redwood City, CA , U.S.A. **Online address:** ana@stenzeltwins.com

STENZEL BYRNES, Isabel. American (born United States), b. 1972?. **Genres:** Novels. **Career:** Lucile Packard Children's Hospital, health educator & social worker; Genentech's Heroes of Hope Living with Cystic Fibrosis Program, chair. Writer. **Publications:** (with A. Stenzel) The Power of Two: A Twin Triumph over Cystic Fibrosis, 2007. **Address:** Redwood City, CA , U.S.A. **Online address:** isa@stenzeltwins.com

STEPAKOFF, Jeffrey. American (born United States), b. 1964?. **Genres:** Novels, Children's Non-fiction. **Career:** Kennesaw State University, professor of film and television writing. Writer. **Publications:** Billion-Dollar Kiss: The Kiss That Saved Dawson's Creek and Other Adventures in TV Writing, 2007; Fireworks Over Toccoa, 2010; Orchard, 2011. Contributor to books and periodicals. **Address:** Daniel Greenberg, Levine Greenberg Literary Agency Inc., 307 7th Ave., Ste. 2407, New York, NY 10001, U.S.A. **Online address:** jstepakoff@billiondollarkiss.com

STEPANCHEV, Stephen. American (born Yugoslavia), b. 1915. **Genres:** Poetry, Literary Criticism And History, Local History/Rural Topics. **Career:** Purdue University, instructor in English, 1938-41; New York University, instructor in English, 1946-48; City University of New York, Queens College, professor of English, 1949-85, professor emeritus of English, 1985-; English Graduate Association of New York University, president. Writer. **Publications:** Three Priests in April, 1956; American Poetry since 1945: A Critical Survey, 1965; Spring in the Harbor, 1967; A Man Running in the Rain, 1969; The Mad Bomber, 1972; Mining the Darkness, 1975; Medusa and Others, 1975; The Dove in the Acacia, 1977; What I Own, 1978; Descent: A Selection of Eight Poems, 1988; (ed.) The People's College on the Hill: Fifty Years at Queens College, 1937-1987 (local history), 1990; Seven Horizons, 1997; Beyond the Gate: New and Selected Poems, 2005. **Address:** Queens College, The City University of New York, 65-30 Kissena Blvd., Flushing, NY 11367, U.S.A.

STEPANIANTS, Marietta. (M. T. Stepaniants). Russian (born Russia), b. 1935. **Genres:** Philosophy, Theology/Religion, History, Social Work, Social Sciences, Cultural/Ethnic Topics. **Career:** Russian Academy of Sciences, Institute of Philosophy, fellow, researcher, 1959-80, director of Center for the Study of Oriental Philosophies, 1980-; Diplomatic Academy of the U.S.S.R., professor, 1980-94; State University of Humanities, chair of Oriental philosophical and political thought, 1996-. Writer. **Publications:** AS M. T. STEPANIANTS: Pakistan: Philosophy and Sociology, 1971; The Philosophical Aspects of Sufism, 1989; Islamic Philosophy and Social Thought (XIX-XX Centuries), 1989; Sufi Wisdom, 1994; Gandhi and the World Today: A Russian Perspective, 1998; Introduction to Eastern Thought, 2002. EDITOR: Philosophy and Religion in the East XX Century, 1985; Rationalistic Tradition and Modernity, 1988, 3 vol., 2000; Muslim Philosophy in Soviet Studies, 1988; God- Man-Society in Traditional Cultures of the East, 1993; Feminism: East-West-Russia, 1993; History of Indian Philosophy: A Russian Viewpoint, 1993; (with R. Bontekoe) Justice and Democracy: Cross-cultural Perspectives, 1997; Universals of the Eastern Cultures, 2001; (with P. Hershock and R.T. Ames) Technology and Cultural Values: On the Edge of the Third Millennium, 2003; (with J. Johnson and B. Forest) Religion and Identity in Modern Russia: The Revival of Orthodoxy and Islam, 2005; Comparative Ethics in a Global Age, 2007; Knowledge and Belief in the Dialogue of Cultures, 2009. **Address:** Institute of Philosophy, Russian Academy of Sciences, 14 Volkhonka St., 420, Moscow, 199991, Russia. **Online address:** mstepani@iph.ras.ru

STEPANIANTS, M. T. See **STEPANIANTS, Marietta.**

STEPHEN, Jaci. British (born England), b. 1958?. **Genres:** Novels, Young Adult Fiction. **Career:** Educator and freelance writer, 1990-. **Publications:** Definitions of a Horse (novel), 1990. Contributor to periodicals. **Address:** c/o Hutchinson/Random House, 20 Vauxhall Bridge Rd., London, GL SW1V 2SA, England.

STEPHEN, Martin. British (born England), b. 1949. **Genres:** Romance/Historical, Literary Criticism And History, Military/Defense/Arms Control, History, Poetry. **Career:** Haileybury College, house master, 1976-83; Sedbergh School, second master, 1983-86; Perse School, headmaster, 1986-94; Manchester Grammar School, high master, 1994-2004; St. Paul's School, high master, 2004-11. Writer. **Publications:** An Introductory Guide to English Literature, 1984; Studying Shakespeare, 1984; British Warship Designs since 1906, 1985; Sea Battles in Close Up, 1986, 2nd ed., 1996; English Literature, 1986, 3rd ed. as English Literature: A Student Guide, 1999; (ed. and intro.) Never Such Innocence: A New Anthology of Great War Verse, 1988; Never Such Innocence: A New Anthology of Great War Verse, 1988, 3rd ed., 1993; The Fighting Admirals: British Admirals of the Second World War, 1991; The Best of Saki, 1993, 2nd ed., 1998; The Price of Pity: Poetry, History and Myth in the Great War, 1996; The Desperate Remedy: Henry Gresham and the Gunpowder Plot, 2002; The Conscience of the King: Henry Gresham and the Shakespeare Conspiracy, 2003; The Galleon's Grave: Hendry Gresham and The Spanish Armada, 2005; The Rebel Heart: Hendry Gresham and The Earl of Essex, 2006. Contributor to periodicals. **Address:** Little, Brown Book Group, 100 Victoria Embankment, London, GL EC4Y 0DY, England. **Online address:** g.m.stephen@mgs.org

STEPHENS, Andy. British (born England), b. 1956. **Genres:** Librarianship, History, Bibliography. **Career:** British Library, affiliate, 1977-, head of chief executive's office, 1992, secretary and head of international engagement. Writer. **Publications:** The History of the British National Bibliography: 1950-1973, 1994. Contributor to journals. **Address:** British Library, St. Pancras, 96 Euston Rd., London, GL NW1 2DB, England. **Online address:** andy.stephens@bl.uk

STEPHENS, Blythe. See **WAGNER, Sharon Blythe.**

STEPHENS, Casey. See **WAGNER, Sharon Blythe.**

STEPHENS, Evelyne Huber. See **HUBER, Evelyne.**

STEPHENS, F(rank) Douglas. Australian (born Australia), b. 1913. **Genres:** Medicine/Health. **Career:** Royal Melbourne and Children's Hospitals, medical officer, 1937-39; Hospital for Sick Children, Nuffield research fellow, 1947-50; University of Melbourne, clinical surgical teacher, 1950-75; Royal Women's Hospital, consultant, 1953-75; Royal Children's Hospital Research Foundation, Surgical Research Unit, director, 1957-75, honorary senior research fellow, 1986-; Northwestern University, professor, 1975-84, professor emeritus of surgery and urology, 1984-; Children's Memorial Hospital, Surgical Education and Research, director, 1982-86. Writer. **Publications:** Congenital Malformations of Rectum, Anus and Genito-urinary Tracts, 1963; (with E.D. Smith) Anorectal Malformations in Children, 1971; Congenital Malformations of the Urinary Tract, 1983; (with E.D. Smith and N.W. Paul) Anorectal Malformations in Children: Update 1988, 1988; (with E.D. Smith and J.M. Hutson) Congenital Anomalies of the Urinary and Genital Tracts, 1996, 2nd ed. as Congenital Anomalies of the Kidney, Urinary and Genital Tracts, 2002. **Address:** Feinberg School of Medicine, Department of Surgery, Northwestern University, 300 E Superior, Tarry Bldg., Rm. 16-703, Chicago, IL 60611, U.S.A. **Online address:** hutsonj@cryptic.rch.unimelb.edu.au

STEPHENS, J. B. See **BRASWELL, Elizabeth.**

STEPHENS, John D(avid). American (born United States), b. 1947. **Genres:** Politics/Government, Area Studies. **Career:** Kenyon College, visiting assistant professor of political science, 1976-77; Brown University, visiting assistant professor, 1977-78, assistant professor, 1979-86, associate professor of political science, 1985-86; Northwestern University, associate professor, 1985-89, professor of political science, 1989-92; American Journal of Sociology, consulting editor, 1988-90; University of North Carolina, Gerhard E. Lenski, Jr., distinguished professor of political science and sociology, 1992-, Center for European Studies, director; Swedish Collegium for Advanced Study in the Social Sciences, fellow, 1995; American Sociological Association, chair, 1996-99; Harvard University, national fellow, 1998-; Radcliffe Institute for Advanced Study, fellow, 2009-10; Collegio Carlo Alberto, visiting fellow, 2010; John Simon Guggenheim Memorial Foundation, fellow, 2010. Writer. **Publications:** The Transition from Capitalism to Socialism, 1979; (with E.H. Stephens) Democratic Socialism in Jamaica: The Political Movement and Social Transformation in Dependent Capitalism, 1986; (with E.H. Stephens and D. Rueschemeyer) Capitalist Development and Democracy, 1992; (with E. Huber) The Political Economy of Pension Reform: Latin America in Comparative Perspective, 2000; (with E. Huber) Development and Crisis of the Welfare State: Parties and Policies in Global Markets, 2001. Contributor to books, political science and sociology journals. **Address:** Department of Political Science, University of North Carolina, 361 Hamilton Hall, CB 3265, Chapel Hill, NC 27599-3449, U.S.A. **Online address:** jdsteph@unc.edu

STEPHENS, Meic. Welsh (born Wales), b. 1938. **Genres:** Poetry, Language/Linguistics, Literary Criticism And History. **Career:** Ebbw Vale Grammar School, French master, 1962-66; Triskel Press, director, 1962-67; Poetry Wales magazine, editor, 1965-73; Western Mail, journalist, 1966-67; Welsh Arts Council, assistant literature director, 1967-75, literature director, 1975-90; University of Wales Press, staff, 1969-74; Brigham Young University, visiting professor, 1991-92; University of Glamorgan, lecturer, 1994-2000, professor of Welsh writing in English, 2001-03, professor emeritus, 2003-. **Publications:** Triad, 1962; Exiles All, 1973; Linguistic Minorities in Western Europe, 1976; Celfyddydau yng Nghymru, 1979; A Bibliography of Literature in 20th-Century Wales, 1994; Ponies, Twynyrodyn and Other Poems, 1997; Cydymaith i Lenyddiaeth Cymru, 1997; A Militant Muse: Selected Literary Journalism of Harri Webb, 1998; Wales in Quotation, 1999; Welsh Names for Your Children: The Complete Guide, 2000, new ed., 2003; The Literary Pilgrim in Wales, 2000; A Semester in Zion: A Journal with Memoirs, 2003. EDITOR: (with J.S. Williams) The Lilting House, 1969; (with R.B. Jones) Writers of Wales Series, 1970; Artists in Wales vol. I-III, 1971-77; The Welsh Language Today, 1973; A Reader's Guide to Wales, 1973; (with P. Finch) Green Horse, 1978; The Arts in Wales 1950-75, 1979; (and intro.) The Curate of Clyro: Extracts from the Diary of Francis Kilvert, 1983; The Oxford Companion to the Literature of Wales, 1986; A Book of Wales, 1987; A Cardiff Anthology, 1987; A Dictionary of Literary Quotations, 1989; The Bright Field, 1991; Changing Wales, 1991-97; (and comp.) A Most Peculiar People: Quotations about Wales and the Welsh, 1992; The Oxford Illustrated Literary Guide to Great Britain and Ireland, 1992; Rhonndda Anthology, 1993; A Rhondda Anthology, 1994; The Collected Poems of Harri Webb, 1995; (and comp.) The Collected Poems of Glyn Jones, 1996; (and comp.) No Half-way House: Selected Political Journalism of Harri Webb, 1997; A Little Book of Welsh Quotations, 1997; (and comp.) The Collected Stories of Rhys Davies III, 1998; A Little Book of Welsh Sayings, 1998; Looking Up Englands Arsehole, 2000; The Corgi Series, 2000; Rhys Davies, 2001; Decoding the Hare: Rhys Davies, 2001; (with D. Smith) A University and Its Community,

2003; Poetry, 1900-2000, 2007; Necrologies: A Book of Welsh Obituaries, 2008; (with T. Hadley) Eagle in the Maze: An Anthology of Stories from the Rhys Davies Short Story Competition 2008, 2008; Yeah Dai Dando, 2008. TRANSLATOR: The White Stone, 1987; For the Sake of Wales: The Memoirs of Gwyn for Evans, 1996; The Basques: Their Struggle for Independence, 1996; (trans.) Monica, 1997; (and ed.) Illuminations: An Anthology of Welsh Short Prose, 1998; A White Afternoon and Other Stories, 1998; Shadow of the Sickle, 1998; Return to Lleifior, 1999; The Plum Tree, 2004. **Address:** 10 Heol Don, Whitchurch, Cardiff, SG CF14 2AU, Wales. **Online address:** hwmcomanco@hotmail.co.uk

STEPHENS, Randall J. American (born United States), b. 1973. **Genres:** History. **Career:** University of Florida, adjunct professor, 2003-04; Eastern Nazarene College, associate professor of history, 2004-, department chair; Indiana University-Purdue University, young scholars in American religion fellow, 2007-09. Writer and historian. **Publications:** The Fire Spreads: Holiness and Pentecostalism in the American South, 2008; (ed.) Recent Themes in American Religious History: Historians in Conversation, 2009. Contributor to magazines. **Address:** James R. Cameron Center for History, Law, and, Government, Eastern Nazarene College, 23 E Elm Ave., Quincy, MA 02170, U.S.A. **Online address:** randall.stephens@enc.edu

STEPHENS, Thomas M. American (born United States), b. 1931. **Genres:** Education, Social Sciences, Psychology. **Career:** Teacher and psychologist, 1955-58; Montgomery County Schools, psychologist, 1958-60; Ohio Department of Education, educational specialist, 1960-62, administrator of programs for gifted and slow learning children, 1962-64, Title I-E.S.E.A. state coordinator, 1965-66; United States Office of Education, consultant, 1966-; University of Pittsburgh, associate professor of education, 1966-70; National Evaluation of Project Follow Through, co-director, 1967-68; Ohio State University, Department of Exceptional Children, associate professor, chair, 1970-92, professor emeritus, 1992-; School Study Council of Ohio, executive director emeritus; Rutgers, The State University of New Jersey, professor, 1981-, School of Arts and Science, associate professor, 1998-2000. Writer. **Publications:** (Ed. with W.B. Barbe) Educating Tomorrow's Leaders, 1961; Ohios Academically Gifted, 1960-61, 1961; (ed. with W.B. Barbe) Attention to the Gifted Child a Decade Later, 1962; A Look at Ohios Gifted-Status Study, 1962; Some Problems in the Definition and Identification of Gifted High School Students, 1962; (with A.R. Gibson) Ohio's Academically Gifted, 1961-62, 1962; (contrib. and ed. with A.R. Gibson) Pathways to Progress, 1963; (ed. with A.R. Gibson) Pathways to Progress, 1963; (ed. with A.R. Gibson) Accelaration and the Gifted, 1963; (with S.J. Bonham) Psychological Evaluation and Screening Procedures of Slow Learning Children, 1963; (ed. with S.J. Bonham) Mental Health Planning in Education, 1964; (with H.N. Menapace and C.E. Grover) Orthopedically Handicapped Children in Ohio Public Schools, 1964; (with H. McPherson) Developing a Work Experience Program for Slow Learning Youth, 1964; (contrib.) Progress and Promise in Reading Instruction, 1966; (co-ed.) Three Views of Human Behavior, 1967; (contrib.) Teaching Migrant Children, 1969; (with M. Kurfurst) The National Evalution of Project Follow Through, 1967-68, 1969; Directive Teaching of Children with Learning and Behavioral Handicaps, 1970, 2nd ed., 1976; Using Behavioral Approaches with Delinquent Youth and Implications for Vocational Assessment: A Selected Review, 1970; Implementing Behavior Approaches in Elementary and Secondary Schools, 1975; Teaching Skills to Children with Learning and Behavioral Disorders, 1977, 2nd ed., 1983; (with A.C. Hartman and V.H. Lucas) Teaching Children Basic Skills: A Curriculum Handbook, 1978, 2nd ed., 1983; (ed. with A.C. Hartman) Inservice Training: The Future of Professional Education, 1978; Social Skills in the Classroom, 1978, rev. ed., 1992; (with A.E. Blackhurst and L.A. Magliocca) Teaching Mainstreamed Students, 1982, 2nd ed., 1988; Dictionary of Latin American Racial and Ethnic Terminology, 1989, 2nd ed., 1999; Social Behavior Assessment Inventory, 1992; Game of Mirrors: The Changing Face of Ethno-Racial Constructs and Language in the Americas, 2003. Contributor to journals. **Address:** School Study Council of Ohio, 936 Eastwind Dr., Ste. 100, Westerville, OH 43081, U.S.A. **Online address:** etstephens@copper.net

STEPHENS, Walter. American (born United States), b. 1949?. **Genres:** Novels, Art/Art History, History. **Career:** Cornell University, lecturer in Italian literature, 1978-79; University of Washington, assistant professor of romance languages and literature, 1981-83; Dartmouth College, assistant professor, 1983-88, associate professor, 1988-93, Paul D. Paganucci professor of Italian, 1993-98, professor of French, Italian and comparative literature, 1998-2003; Johns Hopkins University, Charles Singleton Center, Charles S. Singleton professor of Italian studies, Medieval and Renaissance Italian Literature, vice chair of romance languages and literature, 1999-, director of Villa Spelman, 2001-. Writer. **Publications:** Giants in Those Days: Folklore, Ancient History and Nationalism, 1989; (ed. with K. Brownlee) Discourses of Authority in Medieval and Renaissance Literature, 1989; Demon Lovers: Witchcraft, Sex and the Crisis of Belief, 2002; (ed. with J.L. Hairston) The Body in Early Modern Italy, 2010; (ed.) Studia Humanitatis: A Tribute to Salvatore Camporeale, forthcoming. Contributor to books and periodicals. **Address:** Charles Singleton Center, Johns Hopkins University, 408 Gilman Hall, 3400 N Charles St., Baltimore, MD 21218, U.S.A. **Online address:** walter.stephens@jhu.edu

STEPHENS, William Peter. British (born England), b. 1934. **Genres:** History, Intellectual History, Theology/Religion, Translations, Transportation, Biography, Autobiography/Memoirs, Sciences, Sports/Fitness. **Career:** Hartley Victoria College, assistant tutor in New Testament, 1958-61, Ranmoor chair of church history, 1971-73; University of Nottingham, Methodist chaplain, 1961-65; Shirley Methodist Church, minister, 1967-71; Shirley Group of Churches, chair, 1969-70; Croydon Anti-Apartheid Group, chair, 1970-72; World Development Movement, chair, 1972-73; Wesley College, Randles chair of historical and systematic theology, 1973-80; Bristol City Councilor, 1976-83; Duke University, James A. Gray lecturer, 1976; Queen's College, research fellow, 1980-81, lecturer in church history, 1981-86; University of Aberdeen, King's College, Department of Church History, professor of church history, 1986-99, dean of faculty of divinity, 1987-89, provost of faculty of divinity, 1989-90; Mint Methodist Church, minister, 2000-02; University of Exeter, chaplain, 2000-02, visiting professor, 2001-04, honorary fellow, 2004-; Liskeard and Looe Circuit, superintendent minister, 2002-03; Methodist Church, chairman and general superintendent, 2003-04; Mid-Sussex Circuit, minister, 2004-. Writer. **Publications:** (Trans.) Luther's Works vol. IV1; Church and Ministry, 1966; The Holy Spirit in the Theology of Martin Bucer, 1970; Faith and Love (sermons), 1971; Christians Conferring, 1978; (with J. Todd) Our Churches, 1978; Methodism in Europe, 1981; The Theology of Huldrych Zwingli, 1986; Zwingli: An Introduction to His Thought, 1992; (ed.) The Bible, the Reformation and the Church, 1995; Zwingli: Einfuehrung in Sein Denken, 1997; Zwingli le theologien, 1999; American Yachting, 2010; The Theology of Heinrich Bullinger, forthcoming. Contributor to books. **Address:** 42 Hart Close, Uckfield, ES TN22 2DA, England.

STEPHENS WARD-THOMAS, Evelyn Bridget Patricia. *See* **ANTHONY, Evelyn.**

STEPP, Laura Sessions. American (born United States), b. 1951. **Genres:** Medicine/Health, Human Relations/Parenting, Women's Studies And Issues, Sex. **Career:** Television reporter, 1971-72; Palm Beach Times, government reporter, 1974; Evening Bulletin, investigative reporter, 1975-78; Charlotte Observer, newsroom projects editor, 1979-81; Washington Post, editor, 1982-86, religion editor, 1987-92, style section writer, 1992-. **Publications:** Our Last Best Shot: Guiding Our Children through Early Adolescence, 2000; Unhooked: How Young Women Pursue Sex, Delay Love and Lose at Both, 2007. Contributor to books. **Address:** Washington Post Co., 1150 15th St. NW, Washington, DC 20071-0002, U.S.A. **Online address:** lstepp@aol.com

STERK, Andrea. American (born United States) **Genres:** Theology/Religion, Humanities. **Career:** Princeton University, lecturer, 1993-94; Trenton State College (now College of New Jersey), adjunct assistant professor, 1993-94; Calvin College, assistant professor of history, 1994-95; University of Notre Dame, adjunct assistant professor, 1995-2001; Lilly Seminar on Religion and Higher Education, administrator, 1996-2000; University of Florida, Department of History, assistant professor, 2002-06, associate professor, 2006-, affiliate faculty in religion, 2005-, affiliate faculty in early modern studies. Writer. **Publications:** (With H. Louthan) John Comenius: The Labyrinth of the World and the Paradise of the Heart, 1998; (ed.) Religion, Scholarship and Higher Education: Perspectives, Models and Future Prospects: Essays from the Lilly Seminar on Religion and Higher Education, 2001; (ed. with J.W. Coakley) Readings in World Christian History, 2004; Renouncing the World yet Leading the Church: The Monk-Bishop in Late Antiquity, 2004. **Address:** Department of History, University of Florida, 225 Keene-Flint Hall, PO Box 117320, Gainesville, FL 32611-7320, U.S.A. **Online address:** sterk@ufl.edu

STERKEN, Christiaan (L.). Belgian (born Belgium), b. 1946. **Genres:** Astronomy, History, Physics, Earth Sciences, Sciences. **Career:** University of Ghent, assistant professor, 1969-70, 1974-75; European Southern Observatory, staff astronomer, 1971-73; University of Brussels, research fellow, 1975-76, 1978-82; University of Heidelberg, research fellow, 1977; Vrije University, Belgian Fund for Scientific Research, research director, 1983-; International Astrological Union, Division IX Optical & Infrared Techniques, president, 2003-06. Writer. **Publications:** (With G. Evon) Pulsating B Stars, 1981; (with C. Jaschek) Coordination of Observational Projects in Astronomy, 1988; Quelques Nouvelles Contributions a l'etude Observationnelle des Etoiles, 1988; (ed. with J. Percy and J. Mattei) Variable Star Research: An International Perspective, 1992; (with J. Manfroid) Astronomical Photometry, a Guide, 1992; (with M. Jerzykiewicz) Beta Cephei Stars from a Photometric Point of View, 1993; (with M. de Groot) The Impact of Long-Term Monitoring on Variable Star Research, 1994; (ed. with C. Jaschec) Typical Light Curves of Variable Stars: A Pictorial Atlas, 1996; (with K. Staubermann) K.F. Zoellner and the Historical Dimension of Astronomical Photometry, 2000; (with M. de Groot) Pcygni 400 Years of Progress, 2001; First Corot-Mons-Most Ground-Based Workshop, 2001; (ed. with D.W. Kurtz) Observational Aspects of B and A Stars, 2002; (with J. Hearnshaw) Homage to Miklos Konkoly Thege; Interplay of Periodic, Cyclic, and Stochastic Variability in Selected Areas of the H-R Diagram, 2003; Stars with Extended Atmospheres, 2003; (ed. with H.W. Duerbeck) Astronomical Heritages: Astronomical Archives and the Historic Transits of Venus, 2005; (ed.) Future of Photometric, Spectrophotometric and Polarimetric Standardization, 2007; (ed. with H.U. Kaufl) Deep Impact as a World Observatory Event: Synergies in Space, Time, and Wavelength, 2009. **Address:** Astronomy Group, Vrije University Brussel, Pleinlaan 2, Brussel, 1050, Belgium. **Online address:** csterken@vub.ac.be

STERLE, Francine. (Francine M. Sterle). American (born United States), b. 1952. **Genres:** Poetry. **Career:** Lake Superior Writers, mentor. Educator and writer. **Publications:** POETRY: The White Bridge, 1999; Every Bird Is One Bird, 2001; Nude in Winter, 2006. Works appears in anthology. **Address:** c/o Author Mail, Tupelo Press, PO Box 539, Dorset, VT 05251, U.S.A. **Online address:** fmsterle@northlc.com

STERLE, Francine M. See STERLE, Francine.

STERLING, Anna Kate. See SLIDE, Anthony (Clifford).

STERLING, Bruce. American (born United States), b. 1954. **Genres:** Science Fiction/Fantasy, Novels. **Career:** European Graduate School, professor of internet studies and science fiction. Writer. **Publications:** Involution Occan, 1977; The Artificial Kid, 1980; Schismatrix, 1985; (ed.) Mirrorshades, 1986; Islands in the Net, 1988; Crystal Express, 1989; (with W. Gibson) The Difference Engine, 1990; The Hacker Crackdown (nonfiction), 1992; Global Head, 1992; Heavy Weather, 1994; Holy Fire, 1996; Distraction, 1998; A Good Old-Fashioned Future, 1999; Zeitgeist, 2000; Tomorrow Now: Envisioning the Next Fifty Years, 2002; Zenith Angle, 2004; (intro.) The Mysterious Island, 2004; Shaping Things, 2005; Visionary in Residence: Stories, 2006; (intro.) Art of Alex Gross: Paintings and Other Works, 2007; Ascendancies: The Best of Bruce Sterling, 2007; Phantasmagoria: Specters of Absence, 2007; Caryatids, 2009; (with R. Rucker) Good Night, Moon, 2011; Gothic High-Tech, 2011. **Address:** European Graduate School, 151 1st Ave., Ste. 14, New York, NY 10003, U.S.A. **Online address:** bruces@well.com

STERLING, Jessica. See RAE, Hugh C(rawford).

STERLING, Keir B(rooks). American (born United States), b. 1934. **Genres:** History, Natural History, Biography, Sciences, Environmental Sciences/Ecology. **Career:** Columbia University, School of General Studies, assistant, 1959-65, research associate, 1980; Pace University, adjunct professor, 1966-83, research professor, 1980; Brooklyn College of the City University of New York, general counselor, 1967-68; Marymount College, adjunct instructor in history, assistant academic dean and chair of American studies program, 1968-71; Rockland Community College, State University of New York, assistant dean, 1971-74; State Colleges of New Jersey, full-time consultant, 1974-75; University of Wisconsin-Madison, visiting professor of history of science, 1983; U.S. Army Ordnance Branch, historian, 1983-98, Harford Community College, adjunct professor, 1987-94; U.S. Army Combined Arms Support Command, civilian command historian, 1998-. Writer. **Publications:** Last of the Naturalists: The Career of C. Hart Merriam, 1974, rev. ed., 1977; Serving the Line With Excellence: The Development of the U.S. Army Ordnance Corps as Expressed Through the Lives of Its Chiefs of Ordnance, 1812-1987, with a Short Sketch of the History of Army Ordnance, 1775-1987, 1987, rev. ed., 1992; Addere Flammam: Commanders of the United States

Army Ordnance Center and School, 1918-1993, 1993; (co-author) 125th Anniversary History of the American Ornithologists Union, 1883-2008, forthcoming; U.S. Army Ordnance: The First Century, 1812-1912, forthcoming. EDITOR: (and intro.) Essays in South American Ornithogeography, 1978; An International History of Mammalogy, vol. I, 1987; Biographical Dictionary of American and Canadian Naturalists and Environmentalists, 1997. Contributor to books and periodicals. **Address:** U.S. Army Combined Arms Support Command, 3901 Adams Ave., Ste. 120, Fort Lee, VA 23801-1807, U.S.A. **Online address:** sterlink@lee.army.mil

STERLING, Susan Fisher. American (born United States), b. 1955. **Genres:** Art/Art History. **Career:** Corcoran Gallery of Art, curatorial assistant, 1979; National Museum of Women in the Arts, associate curator, 1988-90, curator of modern and contemporary art, 1990-, director, 2008-; River Market Regional Exhibition, juror, 1993; Kansas City Artists Coalition, juror, 1993; Inter-American Development Bank, member of art acquisition board, 1994; Very Special Arts, member of national advisory board, 1994. Writer. **Publications:** (With H. Posner) Forefront: Cheryl Laemmle, 1989; Forefront: Hollis Sigler, 1993; (with A. Kirsh) Carrie Mae Weems, 1993; Women Artists: The National Museum of Women in the Arts, 1995; (with B.M. Sichel and F. Pedroso) Virgin Territory, 2001; Role Models: Feminine Identity in Contemporary American Photography, 2008. **Address:** National Museum of Women in the Arts, 1250 New York Ave. NW, Washington, DC 20005-3970, U.S.A.

STERN, Daniel N. Swiss/American (born United States), b. 1934. **Genres:** Human Relations/Parenting, Psychology. **Career:** Columbia University, Psychoanalytic Center, psychoanalysis lecturer, 1977-; Cornell University, Medical School-New York Hospital, adjunct professor of psychiatry, 1977-; University of Geneva, honorary professor of psychology, 1985-, now professor emeritus; Massachusetts School of Professional Psychology, instructor. Writer. **Publications:** The First Relationship: Mother and Infant, 1977; The Interpersonal World of the Infant: A View from Psychoanalysis and Developmental Psychology, 1985; Diary of a Baby, 1990; Rappresentazioni e narrazioni, 1991; (ed. with M. Ammaniti) Psychoanalysis and Development: Representations and Narratives, 1994; The Motherhood Constellation: A Unified View of Parent-Infant Psychotherapy, 1995; (with N. Bruschweiler-Stern) The Birth of a Mother: How the Motherhood Experience Changes You Forever, 1998; The First Relationship: Infant and Mother, 2002; The Present Moment in Psychotherapy and Everyday Life, 2004; Forms of Vitality: Exploring Dynamic Experience in Psychology, the Arts, Psychotherapy, and Development, 2010. **Address:** Universite de Geneve, 4141 M, 40 Blvd. du Pont d'Arve, Uni Mail, Geneve, 1211, Switzerland. **Online address:** daniel.stern@unige.ch

STERN, David. American (born United States), b. 1949. **Genres:** Theology/Religion, Literary Criticism And History. **Career:** University of Pennsylvania, assistant professor, 1980-90, associate professor, 1990-95, professor, 1995-, Ruth Meltzer professor, 2002-09, Moritz and Josephine Berg professor, 2009-. Writer. **Publications:** Rabbinic Fantasies, 1990; Parables in Midrash, 1991; Ha-Mashal ba-Midrash: siporet u-farshanut be-sifrut Ḥazal, 1995; Midrash and Theory: Ancient Jewish Exegesis And Contemporary Literary Studies, 1997; (ed.) Anthology in Jewish Literature, 2004; Chosen: Philadelphia's Great Hebraica, 2007; (ed. with N.B. Dohrmann) Jewish Biblical Interpretation and Cultural Exchange: Comparative Exegesis in Context, 2008; The Washington Haggadah, 2011. **Address:** Department of Near Eastern Language and Civilizati, University of Pennsylvania, 847 Williams Hall, Philadelphia, PA 19104-6305, U.S.A. **Online address:** dstern@sas.upenn.edu

STERN, Ellen Norman. American/German (born Germany), b. 1927. **Genres:** Children's Non-fiction, Young Adult Fiction, Biography, Romance/Historical, Biography, Autobiography/Memoirs, History. **Career:** WAVE-TV, production assistant, 1950-55; National Broadcasting Corp., production assistant, 1955-57; Children's Aid Society, Foster Home Department, secretary to director, 1957-59. Writer. **Publications:** Embattled Justice: The Story of Louis Dembitz Brandeis, 1971; Dreamer in the Desert: A Portrait of Nelson Glueck, 1980; Elie Wiesel: Witness for Life, 1982; Elie Wiesel: A Voice for Humanity, 1996; The French Physician's Boy, 2001. Contributor of stories and articals to journals. **Address:** 135 Anbury Ln., Willow Grove, PA 19090, U.S.A.

STERN, Fritz. American (born United States), b. 1926. **Genres:** History, Politics/Government, Essays. **Career:** Columbia University, instructor, 1949-51, assistant professor, 1953-57, associate professor, 1957-63, professor of history, 1963-67, Seth Low professor of history, 1967-92, provost, 1980-83, university professor, 1992-96, university professor emeritus, 1997-; Cornell University, acting assistant professor of history, 1951-53; Yale University, visiting professor, 1964-65; U.S. Department of State, consultant, 1966-67; University of Konstanz, visiting professor, 1967; International Archive for the Social History of German Literature, editorial consultant, 1974-; University of Paris, Elie Halevy professor, 1979; U.S. Embassy, senior adviser, 1993-94; Free University of Berlin, visiting professor. Writer. **Publications:** The Politics of Cultural Despair, A Study in the Rise of the Germanic Ideology, 1961; Bethman Hollweg und der Krieg: die Grenzen der Verantwortung, 1968; The Failure of Illiberalism: Essays on the Political Culture of Modern Germany, 1972, rev. ed., 1992; Um Eine Neue Deutsche Vergangenheit, 1972; Ernst Reuter: Festvortr Anlässl D Hrsg D 4 ULetzten Bd D Reden U Schriften Von Ernst Reuter Am 27 April 1976, 1976; Gold and Iron: Bismarck, Bleichröder and the Building of the German Empire, 1977; Germany 1933: Fifty Years Later, 1984; Dreams and Delusions: The Drama of German History, 1987; Verspielte Grösse: Essays ZurDeutschen Geschichte, 1996; Einstein's German World, 1999; Das Feine Schweigen; Historisch Essays, 1999; Leo Baeck Institute Tenth Annual Dinner: Fritz Stern Awarded the Leo Baeck Medal by German Foreign Minister Joschka Fischer, 2004; Five Germanys I Have Known, 2006. EDITOR: The Varieties of History, From Voltaire to the Present, 1956, 2nd ed., 1970; Geschichte und Geschichtschreibung, 1963; (with L. Krieger) The Responsibility of Power: Historical Essays in Honor of Hajo Holborn, 1967; (with H. Jonas) Reflexionen finsterer Zeit: Zwei Vorträge, 1984. Contributor to books and periodicals. **Address:** Department of History, Columbia University, 413 Fayerweather Hall, 1180 Amsterdam Ave., MC 2527, New York, NY 10027, U.S.A. **Online address:** fs20@columbia.edu

STERN, Gerald. American (born United States), b. 1925. **Genres:** Poetry, Social Sciences, Theology/Religion. **Career:** Lake Grove School, English teacher and principal, 1951-53; Victoria Drive Secondary School, English teacher, 1953-54; Raritan Valley Community College, faculty; Temple University, instructor, 1957-63; Indiana University, associate professor of English, 1963-67; Somerset County College, professor, 1968-82; Pennsylvania Arts Council, consultant in poetry, 1973-; Columbia University, visiting professor, 1980; University of Iowa, professor of English, 1982-, Writers Workshop, teacher of poetry writing; University of Alabama, chair of creative writing, 1984; New England College, Masters of Fine Arts Program, co-founder and faculty; Academy of American Poets, chancellor, 2006; Pennsylvania Council on the Arts, consultant; University of Pittsburgh, faculty; Associated Writing Programs, board director; Drew University, distinguished poet-in-residence, 2009-. Writer. **Publications:** Pineys, 1971; The Naming of Beasts and Other Poems, 1973; Rejoicings, 1973; Lucky Life, 1977; The Red Coal, 1981; Paradise Poems, 1984; Lovesick, 1987; Leaving Another Kingdom: Selected Poems, 1990; Two Long Poems, 1990; Bread without Sugar, 1992; Odd Mercy, 1995; This Time: New and Selected, 1998; Last Blue, 2000; American Sonnets, 2002; What I Can't Bear Losing: Notes from a Life, 2003; Not God after All, 2004; Everything is Burning, 2005; Preacher: A Poem, 2007; Save the Last Dance: Poems, 2008; Early Collected Poems: 1965-1992, 2010. Contributor to periodicals. **Address:** Drew University, 36 Madison Ave., Madison, NJ 07940, U.S.A.

STERN, Jessica Eve. American (born United States), b. 1958. **Genres:** Theology/Religion. **Career:** National Security Council, director, 1994-95; Hoover Institution, national fellow, 1995-96; Council on Foreign Relations, next- generation fellow, 1998-99; Harvard University, Center for Science and International Affairs, senior fellow, 1999; Hoover Institute Task Force on National Security and Law, staff, 2009-; Harvard Law School, lecturer; Somali Youth at Children's Hospital, founder of a project. Writer. **Publications:** The Ultimate Terrorists, 1999; Terror in the Name of God: Why Religious Militants Kill, 2003; Denial: A Memoir of Terror, 2010. Contributor to periodicals. **Address:** Cambridge, MA , U.S.A. **Online address:** info@jessicasternbooks.com

STERN, Judith M. American (born United States), b. 1951. **Genres:** Children's Non-fiction, Education, Psychology. **Career:** Charles E. Smith Jewish Day School, coordinator of special education services, 1983-; consultant, 1985-. Writer. **Publications:** (With P. Quinn) Putting on the Brakes: Young People's Guide to Understanding Attention Deficit Hyperactivity Disorder (ADHD), 1991, (with P.O. Quinn) 3rd ed. as Putting on the Brakes: Understanding and Taking Control of your ADD or ADHD, 2012; (with U. Ben-Ami) Many Ways to Learn: Young People's Guide to Learning Disabilities,

1996; (ed. with P. Quinn) The Best of Brakes: An Activity Book For Kids with ADD, 2000; (with U. Ben-Ami) Many Ways to Learn: A Kid's Guide to LD, 2010, 2nd ed., 2011; (with S.F. Rief) The Dyslexia Checklist, 2010. **Address:** Charles E. Smith Jewish Day School, 1901 E Jefferson St., Rockville, MD 20852-4029, U.S.A. **Online address:** jstern@cesjds.org

STERN, Kenneth S. (Kenneth Saul Stern). American (born United States), b. 1953. **Genres:** History, Race Relations, Theology/Religion, Politics/Government, Military/Defense/Arms Control. **Career:** Attorney at Law, 1979-89; Multnomah Defenders Inc., board of director, 1983-88; International Association of Jewish Lawyers and Jurists, board director, 1983-88; Oregon Law Firm, managing partner. 1989; American Jewish Committee, anti-semitism specialist, 1989-.Writer. **Publications:** Dr. Jeffries and the Anti-Semitic Branch of the Afrocentrism Movement, 1991; Holocaust Denial, 1993; Demjanjuk: An Analysis of the Sixth Circuit Court of Appeals Decision in Demjanjuk v. Petrovsky, 1993; Loud Hawk: The United States Versus the American Indian Movement, 1994; A Force upon the Plain: The American Militia Movement and the Politics of Hate, 1996, rev. ed., 1997; Antisemitism Today: How it is the Same, How it is Different, and How to Fight it, 2006. BOOKLETS: Bigotry on Campus: A Planned Response, 1989; Anti-Zionism: The Sophisticated Anti-Semitism, 1990; Skinheads: Who They are & What To Do When They Come to Town, 1990; Patrick Buchanan: A Backgrounder, 1990; Hate on Talk Radio, 1991; David Duke: A Nazi in Politics, 1991; Crown Heights: A Case Study in Anti-Semitism and Community Relations, 1991; Politics and Bigotry, 1992; Farrakhan and the Jews in the 1990s, 1992, rev. ed., 1994; Militias, a Growing Danger: An American Jewish Committee Background Report, 1995; Hate and the Internet, 1999; Why Campus Anti-Israel Activity Flunks Bigotry 101, 2002; Anti-Semitism Matters, 2004. Contributor to articles and periodicals. **Address:** American Jewish Committee, 165 E 56th St., New York, NY 10022-2746, U.S.A. **Online address:** sternk@ajc.org

STERN, Kenneth Saul. See **STERN, Kenneth S.**

STERN, Paul C(linton). American (born United States), b. 1944. **Genres:** Environmental Sciences/Ecology, International Relations/Current Affairs, Psychology, Social Sciences. **Career:** Clark University, Psychological Services Center, staff, 1965-68, 1969-70; Elmira College, instructor, 1971-75, assistant professor of psychology, 1975-78, Counseling Center, staff, 1976-78, director, 1978; Yale University, Institution for social and policy studies, postdoctoral fellow, 1978-79, research associate, 1979-80; National Research Council (National Academy of Sciences), Commission on Behavioral and Social Sciences and Education, senior staff officer, 1980-89, principal staff officer, 1989-, Committee on the Human Dimensions of Global Climate Change, director; George Mason University, research professor of sociology, 1993-; Social and Environmental Research Institute, president, 1996-; Elmira Correctional Facility, consultant; Consumer Energy Council of America, consultant; U.S. Department of Energy, consultant. Writer. **Publications:** Evaluating Social Science Research, 1979, (with L. Kalof) 2nd ed., 1996; (with J. Black and J. Elworth) Home Energy Conservation, 1981; (with G.T. Gardner) Environmental Problems and Human Behavior, 1996, 2nd ed., 2002; Human Interactions with the Carbon Cycle, 2002. EDITOR: (with E. Aronson) Energy Use, 1984; Improving Energy Demand Analysis, 1984; Energy Efficiency in Buildings, 1984; (co-ed.) Perspectives on Deterrence, 1989; (co-ed.) Behavior, Society, and Nuclear War, vol. I, 1989, vol. II, 1991, vol. III: Behavior, Society, and International Conflict, 1993; (with O.R. Young and D. Druckman) Global Environmental Change, 1992; (with J.L. Comaroff) Perspectives on Nationalism and War, 1995; (with H.V. Fineberg) Understanding Risk, 1996; (co-ed.) Environmentally Significant Consumption, 1997; (co-ed.) People and Pixels, 1998; (with W.E. Easterling) Making Climate Forecasts Matter, 1999; (with L.L. Carstensen) The Aging Mind, 2000; (with D. Druckman) International Conflict Resolution after the Cold War, 2000; (co-ed.) The Drama of the Commons, 2002; (with T. Dietz) New Tools for Environmental Protection, 2002; (with G. Brewer) Decision Making for the Environment: Social and Behavioral Science Priorities, 2005; (with B. Entwisle) Population, Land Use, Environment: Research Directions, 2005; Strategy for Assessing Science, 2007; (with H.M. Ingram) Research and Networks for Decision Support in the NOAA Sectoral Applications Research Program, 2008; (with T. Dietz) Public Participation in Environmental Assessment and Decision Making, 2008; (with R.E. Kasperson) Facilitating Climate Change Responses: A Report of Two Workshops on Knowledge from the Social and Behavioral Science, 2010. Contributor of articles to periodicals. **Address:** Social and

Environmental Research Institute, 278 Main St., Ste. 404, Greenfield, MA 01301-3230, U.S.A. **Online address:** pstern@nas.edu

STERN, Richard G(ustave). American (born United States), b. 1928. **Genres:** Novels, Novellas/Short Stories, Essays. **Career:** Jules Ferry College, lecturer, 1949-50; University of Heidelberg, assistant professor, 1950-51; Connecticut College, instructor, 1951-52; University of Chicago, assistant professor, 1956-61, associate professor, 1962-64, professor of English, 1965-, Helen A. Regenstein professor of English, 1990-2002, now Helen A. Regenstein emeritus professor of English; University of Venice, visiting lecturer, 1962-63; University of California, visiting lecturer, 1964, 1968; State University of New York, visiting lecturer, 1966; Harvard University, visiting professor, 1969; University of Nice, visiting lecturer, 1970; University of Urbino, visiting lecturer, 1977. Writer. **Publications:** Golk, 1960; Europe; or, Up and Down with Schreiber and Baggish in UK as Europe: or, Up and Down with Baggish and Schreiber, 1961; In Any Case, 1963 as The Chaleur Network, 1981; Teeth, Dying, and Other Matters, and The Gamesman's Island: A Play, 1964; Stitch, 1965; (ed.) Honey and Wax: Pleasures and Powers of Narrative: An Anthology, 1966; A Short Novel, an Urban Idyll, Five Stories and Two Trade Notes, 1970; The Books in Fred Hampton's Apartment (essays), 1973; Other Men's Daughters, 1973; Natural Shocks, 1978; Packages, 1980; The Invention of the Real, 1982; A Father's Words, 1986; The Position of the Body, 1987; Noble Rot: Stories 1949-1988, 1989; Shares and Other Fictions, 1992; One Person and Another: On Writers and Writing, 1993; A Sistermony, 1995; Pacific Tremors, 2001; What Is What Was, 2002; Almonds to Zhoof: Collected Stories, 2005; Still On Call, 2010. Contributor to periodicals. **Address:** University of Chicago, 5801 S Ellis Ave., Chicago, IL 60637, U.S.A. **Online address:** rstern@uchicago.edu

STERN, Robert A. M. American (born United States), b. 1939. **Genres:** Architecture, Art/Art History, History. **Career:** Architectural League of New York, program director, 1965-66; Richard Meier, designer, 1966; Housing and Development Administration, assistant to assistant administrator and urban designer, 1966-70; Robert Stern and John Hagmann, Architects, partner, 1969-76; Columbia University, lecturer, 1970-73, assistant professor, 1973-77, associate professor, 1977-82, professor of architecture, 1982-, Temple Hoyne Buell Center for American Architecture, director, 1984-88, director historic preservation, 1990-; Yale University, visiting lecturer, 1972, 1973; Rhode Island School of Design, visiting critic, 1976; University of Pennsylvania, visiting critic, 1977; Robert A.M. Stern Architects, principal partner, 1977-; North Carolina State University, visiting critic, 1978. Writer. **Publications:** New Directions in American Architecture, 1969, 1977; George Howe: Towards a Modern American Architecture, 1975; (with D. Nevins) The Architect's Eye, 1979; (co-author) East Hampton's Heritage, 1982; Raymond Hood, 1982; (co-author) New York 1900, 1983; Pride of Place, 1986; Buildings and Projects, 1981-1985, 1986; (co-author) New York 1930, 1987; (foreword) Images of Fin-de-siecle Architecture and Interior Decoration, 1988; Modern Classicism, 1988; The House That Bob Built, 1991; (with T. Mellins and D. Fishman) New York 1960, 1995; (with T. Mellins and D. Fishman) New York 1880: Architecture and Urbanism in the Guilded Age, 1999; (intro.) David M. Schwarz/Architectural Services, 2002; New York 2000: Architecture and Urbanism between the Bicentennial and the Millennium, 2006; Architecture on the Edge of Postmodernism, 2009; (foreword) Ike Kligerman Barkley: Houses, 2010; (epilogue) Further Lane, 2011. **Address:** Robert A.M. Stern Architects LLP, 460 W 34th St., New York, NY 10001, U.S.A.

STERN, Sheldon M. American (born United States), b. 1939. **Genres:** History. **Career:** Federal City College, assistant professor of history, 1968-70; University of Massachusetts, assistant professor of history, 1970-77; John F. Kennedy Library, historian, 1977-99; JFK Library, American History Project for High School Students, founder and director, 1993-99; self-employed historian and educational consultant, 2000-. Writer. **Publications:** What Elementary Teachers Need to Know: College Course Outlines for Teacher Preparation, Core Knowledge Foundation, 2002; Effective State Standards for U.S. History: A 2003 Report Card, Fordham Institute, 2003; Averting the Final Failure: John F. Kennedy and the Secret Cuban Missile Crisis Meetings, 2003; The Week the World Stood Still: Inside the Secret Cuban Missile Crisis, 2005; The State of State U.S. History Standards, Fordham Institute, 2011; Arbiters of Apocalypse-JFK Versus his Advisers: The Real Story of How the Cuban Missile Crisis was Settled Peacefully, 2012. **Address:** c/o Author Mail, Stanford University Press, 1450 Page Mill Rd., Palo Alto, CA 94304-1124, U.S.A. **Online address:** shjjstern@comcast.net

STERN, Sol. American/Israeli (born Israel), b. 1935?. **Genres:** Business/Trade/Industry, Education, Social Sciences. **Career:** Ramparts (magazine), editor and writer, 1966-72; freelance writer and editor, 1972-84; Office of the City Council President, press secretary, senior policy advisor, director of issues, 1985-94; New York State Commission on Juvenile Justice Reform, executive director, 1994-95; Manhattan Institute, senior fellow; City journal, contributing editor. **Publications:** Breaking Free: Public School Lessons and the Imperative of School Choice, 2003. Contributor to periodicals. **Address:** c/o Author Mail, Encounter Books, 116 New Montgomery St., San Francisco, CA 94105, U.S.A.

STERN, Steve. American (born United States), b. 1947. **Genres:** Novels, Novellas/Short Stories, Children's Fiction. **Career:** Center for Southern Folklore, Ethnic Heritage Program, director, 1983; Memphis College of Art, visiting lecturer, 1985-86; University of Wisconsin, visiting lecturer, 1987; Skidmore College, visiting lecturer, 1988, 1990-91, professor of English, 1993; West Side YMCA, writer-in-residence, 1988. **Publications:** STORIES: Isaac and the Undertaker's Daughter, 1983; Lazar Malkin Enters Heaven, 1986; A Plague of Dreamers, 1994; The Wedding Jester, 1999. NOVELS: The Moon and Ruben Shein, 1984; Harry Kaplan's Adventures Underground, 1991; The Angel of Forgetfulness, 2005; The Frozen Rabbi, 2010. OTHERS: Mickey and the Golem: A Child's Hanukkah in the South (for children), 1986; Hershel & the Beast (for children), 1987; North of God, 2008. **Address:** Skidmore College, 815 N Broadway, Saratoga Springs, NY 12866-1729, U.S.A. **Online address:** sstern@skidmore.edu

STERN, Steve J. American (born United States), b. 1951?. **Genres:** History, Cultural/Ethnic Topics, Politics/Government, Anthropology/Ethnology. **Career:** Universidad Nacional de San Cristóbal de Huamanga, visiting professor of historical-social sciences, 1977; University of Wisconsin, Department of History, assistant professor, 1979-83, associate professor, 1983-88, professor of history, 1988-2006, director of graduate studies, 1997-99, chair, 2003-06, Alberto Flores Galindo professor, 2006-, Hilldale professor of history, 2011-, Latin American and Iberian Studies Program, director, 1992-95, vice provost for faculty and staff, 2008-; Stanford University, Center for Advanced Study in the Behavioral Sciences, fellow, 1990-91. Writer. **Publications:** Peru's Indian Peoples and the Challenge of Spanish Conquest: Huamanga to 1640, 1982, 2nd ed., 1993; (ed.) Resistance, Rebellion, and Consciousness in the Andcan Peasant World, 18th to 20th Centuries, 1987; (co-author and intro.) Confronting Historical Paradigms: Peasants, Labor and the Capitalist World System in Africa and Latin America, 1993; The Secret History of Gender: Women, Men, and Power in Late Colonial Mexico, 1995; (ed.) Shining and Other Paths: War and Society in Peru, 1980-1995, 1998; Remembering Pinochet's Chile: On the Eve of London, 1998, 2004; Battling for Hearts and Minds: Memory Struggles in Pinochet's Chile, 1973-1988, 2006; Recordando el Chile de Pinochet, 2009; Reckoning with Pinochet: The Memory Question in Democratic Chile, 1989-2006, 2010. CONTRIBUTOR: The Inca and Aztec States, 1400-1800: Anthropology and History, 1982; The Peru Reader: History, Culture, Politics, 1995; Reclaiming the Political in Latin American History: Essays from the North, 2001. Contributor to periodicals and journals. **Address:** Department of History, University of Wisconsin, 5105 Mosse Humanities Bldg., 455 N Park St., Madison, WI 53706-1483, U.S.A. **Online address:** sjstern@wisc.edu

STERN, Stuart. See **RAE, Hugh C(rawford).**

STERN, Vivien. British (born England), b. 1941. **Genres:** Public/Social Administration, Adult Non-fiction. **Career:** National Council for the Care and Resettlement of Offenders, director, 1977-96; University Of Oxford, Nuffield College, visiting fellow, 1984-91; Penal Reform Intl., honorary secretary general, 1989-2006; King's College, International Centre for Prison Studies, senior research fellow, 1997-; London School of Economics, honorary fellow. Writer. **Publications:** (Ed. with S. Gardiner) A Second Chance: Further Education in Multi-racial Areas, 1976; A Home from Home?: Some Policy Considerations on Black Children in Residential Care, 1977; (with C. Carmichael) The Multi-racial Community: A Guide for Local Councillors, 1977; Caring for Under-Fives in a Multi-racial Society, 1978; Failures in Penal Society, 1987; Imprisoned by Our Prisons: A Programme of Reform, 1989; Deprived of Their Liberty, 1990; Creativity in Captivity, 1992; Bricks of Shame: Britain's Prisons, 1993; A Sin against the Future: Imprisonment in the World, 1998; Alternatives to Prison in Developing Countries, 1999; Sentenced to Die?: The Problem of TB in Prisons in Eastern Europe and Central Asia, 1999; Creating Criminals: Prisons and People in a Market Society, 2006;

(foreword) Making Good: Prisons, Punishment and Beyond, 2008. **Address:** International Centre for Prison Studies, King's College, The Merchant Ctr., 1 New Street Sq., 1st Fl., London, GL EC4A 3BF, England. **Online address:** vivien.stern@bushinternet.com

STERNBERG, Robert J(effrey). American (born United States), b. 1949. **Genres:** Psychology, Adult Non-fiction, Education, Reference. **Career:** The Psychological Corp., research assistant, 1968-69; Yale University, Office of Institutional Research, research assistant, 1970-71, Department of Psychology, assistant professor, 1975-80, associate professor, 1980-83, professor, 1983-86, director of graduate studies, 1983-88, IBM professor of psychology and education, 1986-2005, professor of management, 2005, Center for the Psychology of Abilities, Competencies, and Expertise (PACE Center), director, 2000-05; Tufts University, Center for the Enhancement of Learning and Teaching (CELT), director, 2005-08, Center for the Psychology of Abilities, Competencies, and Expertise (PACE Center), director, 2005-10, School of Arts and Sciences, dean, 2005-10, Department of Psychology, professor, 2006-10, Department of Education, professor, 2006-10; University of Heidelberg, Department of Psychology, provost, professor of psychology, honorary professor, 2007-; Oklahoma State University, provost and senior vice president, 2010-, professor of psychology, 2010-. Writer. **Publications:** Barron's How to Prepare for the Miller Analogies Test, 1974, 8th ed., 2001; Intelligence, Information Processing, and Analogical Reasoning: The Componential Analysis of Human Abilities, 1977; Writing the Psychology Paper, 1977; Beyond IQ: A Triarchic Theory of Human Intelligence, 1985; Intelligence Applied: Understanding and Increasing Your Intellectual Skills, 1986; Psychologist's Companion: A Guide to Scientific Writing for Students and Researchers, 1988, (with K. Sternberg) 5th ed. as The Psychologist's Companion: A Guide to Writing Scientific Papers for Students and Researchers, 2010; The Triangle of Love: Intimacy, Passion, Commitment, 1988; The Triarchic Mind: A New Theory of Human Intelligence, 1988; Metaphors of Mind: Conceptions of the Nature of Intelligence, 1990; (with C. Whitney) Love the Way You Want It: Using Your Head in Matters of the Heart, 1991; (with T.I. Lubart) Defying the Crowd: Cultivating Creativity in a Culture of Conformity, 1995; In Search of the Human Mind, 1995, 3rd ed., 2001; Successful Intelligence: How Practical and Creative Intelligence Determine Success in Life, 1996; (with L. Spear-Swerling) Off Track: When Poor Readers Become Learning Disabled, 1996; Cognitive Psychology, 1996, 5th ed., 2009; (with W.M. Williams) How to Develop Student Creativity, 1996; (with L. Spear-Swerling) Teaching for Thinking, 1996; Pathways to Psychology, 1997, 4th ed., 2004; Introduction to Psychology, 1997; Cupid's Arrow: The Course of Love through Time, 1998; Love is a Story: A New Theory of Relationships, 1998; (with E.L. Grigorenko) Our Labeled Children: What Every Parent and Teacher Needs to Know About Learning Disabilities, 1999; (co-author) Practical Intelligence in Everyday Life, 2000; (with A.V. Azzara and A. Freer) Cracking the A.P. Psychology, 2000; (with E.L. Grigorenko) Teaching for Successful Intelligence: To Increase Student Learning and Achievement, 2000, 2nd ed., 2007; (with E.L. Grigorenko) Dynamic Testing: The Nature and Measurement of Learning Potential, 2000; (with T. Ben-Zeev) Complex Cognition: The Psychology of Human Thought, 2001; (with J.C. Kaufman and J.E. Pretz) The Creativity Conundrum: A Propulsion Model of Kinds of Creative Contributions, 2002; (with E.L. Grigorenko) Dynamic Testing: The Nature and Measurement of Learning Potential, 2002; (with W.M. Williams) Educational Psychology, 2002, 2nd ed., 2010; Wisdom, Intelligence and Creativity Synthesized, 2003; (with A.T. Cianciolo) Intelligence: A Brief History, 2004; Psychology 101 1/2: The Unspoken Rules for Success in Academia, 2004; Psychology, 2004; (with D.D. Preiss) Intelligence and Technology: The Impact of Tools on the Nature and Development of Human Abilities, 2005; (with L. Zhang) Nature of Intellectual Styles, 2006; (with J.C. Kaufman and E.L. Grigorenko) Applied Intelligence, 2008; (with K. Sternberg) Nature of Hate, 2008; (with L. Jarvin and E.L. Grigorenko) Teaching for Wisdom, Intelligence, Creativity, and Success, 2009; (foreword) Impact of 9/11 on Psychology and Education: The Day that Changed Everything?, 2009; (with W.M. Williams) Educational Psychology, 2010; College Admissions for the 21st Century, 2010; (with L. Jarvin and E.L. Grigorenko) Explorations in Giftedness, 2011. EDITOR: (with D.K. Detterman) Human Intelligence: Perspectives on its Theory and Measurement, 1979; Handbook of Human Intelligence, 1982; (and contrib.) Advances in the Psychology of Human Intelligence, 5 vols., 1982-89; (with D.K. Detterman) How and How Much Can Intelligence be Increased, 1982; (and contrib.) Mechanisms of Cognitive Development, 1984; Human Abilities: An Information-Processing Approach, 1985; (with R.F. Dillon) Cognition and Instruction, 1986; (with J.E. Davidson) Conceptions of Giftedness,

1986, 2nd ed., 2005; (with R.K. Wagner) Practical Intelligence: Nature and Origins of Competence in the Everyday World, 1986; (with D.K. Detterman) What is Intelligence?: Contemporary Viewpoints on its Nature and Definition, 1986; (with J.B. Baron) Teaching Thinking Skills: Theory and Practice, 1987; (and contrib.) Nature of Creativity: Contemporary Psychological Perspectives, 1988; (with E.E. Smith) The Psychology of Human Thought, 1988; (with M.L. Barnes) The Psychology of Love, 1988; (with P.L. Ackerman and R. Glaser) Learning and Individual Differences: Advances in Theory and Research, 1989; (with J. Kolligian, Jr.) Competence Considered, 1990; Wisdom: Its Nature, Origins, and Development, 1990; (with L. Okagaki) Directors of Development: Influences on the Development of Children's Thinking, 1991; (with P.A. Frensch) Complex Problem Solving: Principles and Mechanisms, 1991; (with C.A. Berg) Intellectual Development, 1992; (with D.K. Detterman) Transfer on Trail: Intelligence, Cognition, and Instruction, 1993; (with A.E. Beall and A.H. Eagly) The Psychology of Gender, 1993, 2nd ed., 2004; Encyclopedia of Human Intelligence, 1994; (with R.K. Wagner) Mind in Context: Interactionist Perspectives on Human Intelligence, 1994; (with P. Ruzgis) Personality and Intelligence, 1994; Thinking and Problem Solving, 1994; (with J.E. Davidson) The Nature of Insight, 1995; (with E.L. Grigorenko) Intelligence, Heredity, and Environment, 1996; (with T. Ben-Zeev) The Nature of Mathematical Thinking, 1996; Teaching Introductory Psychology: Survival Tips from the Experts, 1997; (with M. Hojjat) Satisfaction in Close Relationships, 1997; (with E.L. Grigorenko and P. Ruzgis) Psychology of Russia: Past, Present, Future, 1997; Career Paths in Psychology: Where Your Degree Can Take You, 1997, 2nd ed., 2007; Thinking Styles, 1997; (with W.M. Williams) Intelligence, Instruction, and Assessment: Theory into Practice, 1998; (with M. Ferrari) Self-Awareness: Its Nature and Development, 1998; Handbook of Creativity, 1999; (with P.A. Frensch) Nature of Cognition, 1999; (with L. Spear-Swerling) Perspectives on Learning Disabilities: Biological, Cognitive, Contextual, 1999; (with R.K. Wagner) Readings in Cognitive Psychology, 1999; (with J.A. Horvath) Tacit Knowledge in Professional Practice: Researcher and Practitioner Perspectives, 1999; Guide to Publishing in Psychology Journals, 2000; Handbook of Intelligence, 2000; (with L. Zhnag) Perspectives on Thinking, Learning and Cognitive Styles, 2001; (with B. Torff) Understanding and Teaching the Intuitive Mind: Student and Teacher Learning, 2001; (with E.L. Grigorenko) Family Environment and Intellectual Functioning: A Life-span Perspective, 2001; (with J.C. Kaufman) The Evolution of Intelligence, 2001; (with E.L. Grigorenko) Environmental Effects on Cognitive Abilities, 2001; (with E.L. Grigorenko) The General Factor of Intelligence: How General Is It?, 2002; Why Smart People Can Be So Stupid, 2002; International Handbook of Intelligence, 2003; (with J. Lautrey and T.I. Lubart) Models of Intelligence: International Perspectives, 2003; Psychologists Defying the Crowd: Stories of Those Who Battled the Establishment and Won, 2003; (with E.L. Grigorenko) The Psychology of Abilities, Competencies, and Expertise, 2003; (with J.E. Davidson) The Psychology of Problem Solving, 2003; The Anatomy of Impact: What Makes the Great Works of Psychology Great, 2003; (with D.Y. Dai) Motivation, Emotion, and Cognition: Integrative Perspectives on Intellectual Functioning and Development, 2004; (with E.L. Grigorenko and J.L. Singer) Creativity: From Potential to Realization, 2004; (with E.L. Grigorenko) Culture and Competence: Contexts of Life Success, 2004; Definitions and Conceptions of Giftedness, 2004; (with J. Antonakis and A.T. Cianciolo) Nature of Leadership, 2004; (with J.P.Leighton) Nature of Reasoning, 2004; (with T.M. Newman) Students With Both Gifts and Learning Disabilities: Identification, Assessment, and Outcomes, 2004; Unity in Psychology: Possibility or Pipe dream?, 2005; Psychology of Hate, 2005; (with J. Jordan) Handbook of Wisdom: Psychological Perspectives, 2005; (with J.E. Pretz) Cognition and Intelligence: Identifying the Mechanisms of the Mind, 2005; (with M.A. Constas) Translating Theory and Research into Educational Practice: Developments in Content Domains, Large Scale Reform, and Intellectual Capacity, 2006; Reviewing Scientific Works in Psychology, 2006; (with C.D. Goodheart and A.E. Kazdin) Evidence-based Psychotherapy: Where Practice and Research Meet, 2006; (with J.C. Kaufman) International Handbook of Creativity, 2006; (with K. Weis) The New Psychology of Love, 2006; (with R.F. Subotnik) Optimizing Student Success in School with the Other Three Rs: Reasoning, Resilience and Responsibility, 2006; (with L. Barbanel) Psychological Interventions in Times of Crisis, 2006; (with H.J. Roediger, III and D.F. Halpern) Critical Thinking in Psychology, 2007; (with J.C. Kaufman and E.L. Grigorenko) Essential Sternberg: Essays on Intelligence, Psychology, and Education, 2009; (with L. Zhang) Perspectives on the Nature of Intellectual Styles, 2009; (with D.D. Preiss) Innovations in Educational Psychology: Perspectives on Learning, Teaching, and Human Development, 2010; (with J.C. Kaufman) Cambridge Handbook of Creativity, 2010. Contributor of articles to journals. **Address:**

Office of Academic Affairs, Oklahoma State University, 101 Whitehurst Hall, Stillwater, OK 74078-1010, U.S.A. **Online address:** robert.sternberg@okstate.edu

STERNE, Richard Clark. American (born United States), b. 1927. **Genres:** Literary Criticism And History, Politics/Government. **Career:** North Carolina State College of Agriculture and Engineering (now North Carolina State University), instructor in social studies, 1948-49; Simmons College, instructor, professor of English, 1952-, now professor emeritus; Northeastern University, lecturer, 1957, 1962; University of Lille, lecturer, 1958-59; University of Rennes, lecturer, 1958-59; University of Bordeaux, lecturer, 1958-59; University of Toulouse, lecturer, 1958-59; University of Lisbon, lecturer, 1962-63; Harvard University, extension lecturer, 1963-64; Newton PAX, president. Writer. **Publications:** Political, Social and Literary Criticism in the New York Nation, 1865-1881: A Study in Change of Mood, 1987; Dark Mirror: The Sense of Injustice in Modern European and American Literature, 1994. Contributor of articles and reviews to academic journals and popular magazines. **Address:** Department of English, Simmons College, 300 The Fenway, Boston, MA 02115, U.S.A.

STERNGOLD, James (S.). American (born United States), b. 1954. **Genres:** Business/Trade/Industry. **Career:** Associated Press, Hong Kong correspondent, 1981-84; New York Times, wall street reporter, 1984-89, correspondent, 1989-95, business and culture correspondent, 1995-2002; San Francisco Chronicle, bureau chief, national correspondent. Writer. **Publications:** Burning Down the House: How Greed, Deceit and Bitter Revenge Destroyed E. F. Hutton, 1990. Contributor to periodicals. **Address:** San Francisco Chronicle, 901 Mission St., San Francisco, CA 94103, U.S.A. **Online address:** jsterngold@sfchronicle.com

STERNLICHT, Sanford. American (born United States), b. 1931. **Genres:** Poetry, History, Literary Criticism And History, Biography, Plays/Screenplays, Young Adult Fiction. **Career:** Colgate University, instructor in remedial reading, 1953-55; State University of New York-Oswego, instructor of English, 1959-60, assistant professor, 1960-62, associate professor, 1962, professor of English, 1962-72, professor of theatre, 1972-86, chair of department, 1973-85, professor emeritus of theatre, 1986-; University of York, Leverhulme Fellow and visiting professor of English, 1965-66; Syracuse University, adjunct professor of English, 1982-86, professor of English, 1986-2010, professor emeritus, 2010-; University of Pés, visiting professor of English, 2004. Writer. **Publications:** Gull's Way (poems), 1961; Uriah Phillips Levy: The Blue Star Commodore (biography), 1961; Love in Pompeii (poems), 1967; Jean Rhys, 1997; A Reader's Guide to Modern Irish Drama, 1998; A Reader's Guide to Modern American Drama, 2002; New Plays from the Abbey Theatre 1999-2001, 2003; A Student Companion to Elie Wiesel, 2003; A Reader's Guide to Modern British Drama, 2004; Masterpieces of Modern British and Irish Drama, 2005; Masterpieces of Jewish American Literature, 2007; Modern Irish Drama: W.B. Yeats to Marina Carr, 2010. LITERARY CRITICISM: John Webster's Imagery and the Webster Canon, 1972; John Masefield, 1978; C.S. Forester, 1981; John Galsworthy, 1987; R.F. Delderfield, 1988; Stevie Smith, 1990; Stephen Spender, 1992; Siegfried Sassoon, 1993; All Things Herriot: James Herriot and His Peaceable Kingdom, 1995; C.S. Forester and the Hornblower Saga, 1999; Chaim Potok: A Critical Companion, 2001; The Tenement Saga: The Lower East Side and Early Jewish American Writers, 2004. HISTORY: (with E.M. Jamison) The Black Devil of the Bayous: The Life and Times of the United States Steam-Sloop Hartford, 1858-1957, 1970; McKinley's Bulldog: The Battleship Oregon, 1978; (with E.M. Jameson) U.S.F. Constellation: Yankee Racehorse, 1981. EDITOR: Selected Short Stories of Padraic Colum, 1985; Padraic Colum, 1985; Selected Plays of Padraic Colum, 1986; Selected Poems of Padraic Colum, 1988; (intro.) In Search of Stevie Smith, 1991; (and intro. with C. Fitz-Simon) New Plays from the Abbey Theatre, 1996; New Plays from the Abbey Theatre, 1996-1998, 2001. Contributor to books and periodicals. **Address:** Department of English, Syracuse University, 306 Tolley, 401 Hall of Languages, Syracuse, NY 13244-1170, U.S.A. **Online address:** svsternl@syr.edu

STERNS, Kate. Canadian (born Canada), b. 1961. **Genres:** Novels. **Career:** Concordia University, Department of English, associate professor. Writer. **Publications:** Thinking about Magritte, 1992; Down There by the Train, 2001. **Address:** Department of English, Concordia University, 1455 de Maisonneuve Blvd. W, Montreal, QC H3G 1M8, Canada. **Online address:** sternsk@sympatico.ca

STERRITT, Laurence Lux. (Laurence Lux-Sterritt). French (born France) **Genres:** Theology/Religion, Women's Studies And Issues, Military/Defense/Arms Control, History. **Career:** Universite de Provence, Aix-en-Provence, faculty, Département des Etudes du Monde Anglophone, lecturer. Writer and historian. **Publications:** AS LAURENCE LUX-STERRITT: Redefining Female Religious Life: French Ursulines and English Ladies in Seventeenth-Century Catholicism, 2005; (ed. with G. Teulié) War Sermons, 2009; (ed. with C.M. Mangion) Gender, Catholicism and Spirituality: Women and the Roman Catholic Church in Britain and Europe, 1200-1900, 2011. Contributor to periodicals. **Address:** Lab d'études et de Recherche sur le Monde Angl, Université de Provence, Centre d'Aix, 29, Ave. Robert Schuman, Cedex, 13621, France. **Online address:** sterritt@up.univ-aix.fr

STERTZ, Bradley A. American (born United States), b. 1960. **Genres:** Adult Non-fiction, History, Business/Trade/Industry. **Career:** Times, reporter, 1983-87; Wall Street Journal, reporter, 1987-93; Detroit News, journalist, assistant managing editor, Washington bureau chief, 1993-; Daily Press, news editor. **Publications:** (With B. Vlasic) Taken for a Ride: How Daimler-Benz Drove Off with Chrysler (nonfiction), 2000. **Address:** William Morrow/HarperCollins Publishers, 10 E 53rd St., New York, NY 10022, U.S.A. **Online address:** bstertz@dailypress.com

STETSON, Brad. American (born United States), b. 1963. **Genres:** Politics/Government, History, Social Sciences, Music, Humanities. **Career:** David Institute, director, 1993-; California State University, lecturer, 1995-; State Long Beach, Department of Religious Studies and Communication Studies, faculty; Chapman University, Department of Religious Studies and Communication Studies, faculty. Writer. **Publications:** (With J.G. Conti) Challenging the Civil Rights Establishment: Profiles of a New Black Vanguard, 1993; Pluralism and Particularity in Religious Belief, 1994; Human Dignity and Contemporary Liberalism, 1998; Tender Fingerprints: A True Story of Loss and Resolution, 1999; (with J.L. Peterson) From Rage To Responsibility: Black Conservative Jesse Lee Peterson and America Today, 2000; Living Victims, Stolen Lives: Parents of Murdered Children Speak to America, 2003; (with J.G. Conti) Truth About Tolerance: Pluralism, Diversity, and the Culture Wars, 2005. EDITOR: The Silent Subject: Reflections on the Unborn in American Culture, 1996; (with S. Faryna and J.G. Conti) Black and Right: The Bold New Voice of Black Conservatives in America, 1997; (with J.L. Friedmann) Jewish Sacred Music and Jewish Identity: Continuity and Fragmentation, 2008. Contributor of articles and magazines. **Address:** PO Box 1248, Tustin, CA 92781, U.S.A. **Online address:** bradleystetson@hotmail.com

STEUERLE, C. Eugene. American (born United States), b. 1946. **Genres:** Economics, Public/Social Administration. **Career:** U.S. Treasury, staff, 1974-83, Project for Fundamental Tax Reform, economic staff coordinator, 1984-86, deputy assistant secretary, 1987-89; Urban Institute, Richard B. Fisher chair, senior fellow, 1989-, institute fellow; Brookings Institution, federal executive fellow, 1983-84; American Enterprise Institute for Public Policy Research, fellow, director of finance and taxation, 1986-87; National Tax Association, president, 2001-02; National Economists Club Educational Foundation, president. Writer, consultant and columnist. **Publications:** Taxes, Loans and Inflation: How the Nation's Wealth Becomes Misallocated, 1985; Who Should Pay for Collecting Taxes?: Financing the IRS, 1986; The Tax Decade: How Taxes Came to Dominate the Public Agenda, 1992; Economic Effects of Health Reform, 1994; (with J.M. Bakija) Retooling Social Security for the Twenty-First Century: Right and Wrong Approaches to Reform, 1994; (ed. with M. Kawai) The New World Fiscal Order: Implications for Industrialized Nations, 1996; (with L.Y. Aron and P.J. Loprest) Serving Children with Disabilities: A Systematic Look At the Programs, 1996; (with E.M. Gramlich, H. Heclo and D.S. Nightingale) The Government We Deserve: Responsive Democracy and Changing Expectations, 1998; (ed. with E. Boris) Nonprofits and Philanthropy: Collaboration and Conflict, 1999; (ed. with E.T. Boris) Nonprofits and Government: Collaboration & Conflict, 1999, 2nd ed., 2006; (ed. with G. Peterson, R.D. Reischauer and V.D. Ooms) Vouchers and the Provision of Public Services, 2000; (ed. with M.M. Favreault and F.J. Sammartino) Social Security and the Family: Addressing Unmet Needs in An Underfunded System, 2002; Contemporary U.S. Tax Policy, 2004, 2nd ed., 2008; (ed. with H.J. Aaron and L.E. Burman) Taxing Capital Income, 2007; (ed. with J.J. Cordes) Nonprofits and Business, 2009. Contributor to journals and magazines. **Address:** The Urban Institute Press, 2100 M St. NW, Washington, DC 20037, U.S.A.

STEVENS, Bryna. American (born United States), b. 1924. **Genres:** Poetry,

Songs/Lyrics And Libretti, Adult Non-fiction, Children's Non-fiction, History, Music, Photography, Women's Studies And Issues, Young Adult Non-fiction, Biography, Essays, Humor/Satire, Novels, Military/Defense/Arms Control. **Career:** Private piano teacher, 1942-62, 1965-; freelance writer, 1954-. **Publications:** (Ed.) Borrowed Feathers and Other Fables, 1977; How to Succeed in Popular Music, 1987; Handel and the Famous Sword Swallower of Halle, 1990; Frank Thompson, Her Civil War Story, 1992. FOR CHILDREN: The Harbor Book (juvenile), 1977; Borrowed Feathers and Other Fables, 1978; Ben Franklin's Glass Armonica, 1983; Deborah Sampson Goes to War, 1984; Witches: Opposing Viewpoints, 1987; The Golden Mountain. Contributor to newspapers and magazines. **Address:** Simon and Schuster, 1230 Ave. of the Americas, New York, NY 10020, U.S.A. **Online address:** riteon@jps.net

STEVENS, David. Israeli (born Israel), b. 1940?. **Genres:** Novels, Film, Young Adult Fiction. **Career:** Writer. **Publications:** (With A. Haley) Alex Haley's Queen: The Story of an American Family, 1993; (with A. Haley) Mama Flora's Family, 1998; The Waters of Babylon: A Novel of Lawrence after Arabia, 2000. **Address:** c/o Author Mail, Simon Schuster, 1230 Ave. of the Americas, New York, NY 10020, U.S.A.

STEVENS, Diane. American (born United States), b. 1939. **Genres:** Children's Fiction, Novels, Mystery/Crime/Suspense. **Career:** Writer and educator. **Publications:** Labyrinth, 1976; Elves Chasm: A Novel, 1980; Liza's Blue Moon, 1995; Liza's Star Wish, 1997. **Address:** PO Box 422, Cambria, CA 93428-0422, U.S.A. **Online address:** fruitheart@aol.com

STEVENS, Dick. (Richard Stevens). American (born United States), b. 1928. **Genres:** Literary Criticism And History, Photography. **Career:** Notre Dame Magazine, photographer; University of Notre Dame, professor of photography. Writer. **Publications:** (With T. Musial) Reading and Writing about and Discussing the Great Books, 1970; Making Kallitypes, 1993. **Address:** 2905 Rockwood Cove, Sarasota, FL 34234, U.S.A. **Online address:** rstev24559@aol.com

STEVENS, Garry. Australian (born Australia) **Genres:** Architecture, Sociology, History, Social Commentary, Sciences. **Career:** Architectural sociologist; University of Sydney, research associate; Key Centre for Architectural Sociology, founder. Writer. **Publications:** CADD Made Easy: A Comprehensive Guide for Architects and Designers, 1987; The Reasoning Architect: Mathematics and Science in Design, 1990; The Favored Circle: The Social Foundations of Architectural Distinction, 1998. Contributor to periodicals. **Address:** 16 Piper St., Annandale, NW 2038, Australia.

STEVENS, Greg. See **COOK, Glen (Charles).**

STEVENS, Karl. American (born United States), b. 1978. **Genres:** Graphic Novels, Novellas/Short Stories. **Career:** Writer, illustrator and artist. **Publications:** SELF-ILLUSTRATED: Guilty (graphic novel), 2005; Whatever (graphic short stories), 2008. **Address:** Alternative Comics, 644 NE 9th Ave., Gainesville, FL 32601-4440, U.S.A. **Online address:** karlstevensart@gmail.com

STEVENS, Kathy. American (born United States), b. 1949. **Genres:** Human Relations/Parenting, How-to Books, Adult Non-fiction, Education, Social Sciences. **Career:** Gurian Institute, training director, executive director; Rocky Mountain Learning Enterprises, co-owner and operator. Writer, entrepreneur, trainer and educator. **Publications:** (With M. Gurian) The Minds of Boys: Saving Our Sons from Falling behind in School and Life, 2005; (with M. Gurian and K. King) Strategies for Teaching Boys and Girls, Elementary Level: A Workbook for Educators, 2008; (with M. Gurian and K. King) Strategies for Teaching Boys and Girls, Secondary Level: A Workbook for Educators, 2008; (with M. Gurian and P. Daniels) Successful Single-sex Classrooms: A Practical Guide to Teaching Boys and Girls Separately, 2009. Contributor to periodicals. **Address:** Rocky Mountain Learning Enterprises, 1301 S 8th St., Ste. 102C, PO Box 60160, Colorado Springs, CO 80905-7306, U.S.A. **Online address:** kathy@gurianinstitute.com

STEVENS, Lawrence L. (Lawrence Steven London). American (born United States), b. 1950. **Genres:** How-to Books, Money/Finance. **Career:** Attorney, 1975-; Baltimore County Adult Education Program, lecturer. Writer. **Publications:** Landlording as a Second Income: The Survival Handbook, 1994. **Address:** 2404 Diana Rd., Baltimore, MD 21209-1526, U.S.A.

STEVENS, Lee. See **LEIGH, Stephen.**

STEVENS, Marcus. American (born United States), b. 1959?. **Genres:** Novels, Young Adult Fiction. **Career:** Writer and director. **Publications:** The Curve of the World: A Novel, 2002; Useful Girl: A Novel, 2004. **Address:** Algonquin Books, 708 Broadway, New York, NY 10003, U.S.A.

STEVENS, M. L. Tina (L.). American (born United States) **Genres:** Ethics, Philosophy. **Career:** University of California, research assistant, 1978-80; National Center for State Courts, consultant, 1980; California State University, U.S. history, lecturer, 1997-99; Ben Manilla Productions, script writer, 1997-99; San Francisco State University, U.S. History, lecturer, 1999-. Writer. **Publications:** Bioethics in America: Origins and Cultural Politics, 2000. Contributor to books and periodicals. **Address:** Department of History, San Francisco State University, SCI 227, 1600 Holloway Ave., San Francisco, CA 94132-1722, U.S.A. **Online address:** mstevens@sfsu.edu

STEVENS, Peter (Stanley). Canadian/British (born England), b. 1927. **Genres:** Poetry, Literary Criticism And History, Bibliography. **Career:** Hillfield College, Department of English, chairman, 1957-64; McMaster University, lecturer, 1961-64; University of Saskatchewan, assistant professor of English, 1964-69; University of Windsor, associate professor, professor of English, 1969-94, professor emeritus, 1996-; Ontario Review, contributing editor; Sesame Press, founding director. Writer. **Publications:** Plain Geometry, 1968; Nothing but Spoons, 1969; The McGill Movement: A.J.M. Smith, F.R. Scott, and Leo Kennedy, 1969; A Few Myths, 1970; Breadcrusts and Glass, 1972; Family Feelings & Other Poems, 1974; Momentary Stay, 1974; And the Dying Sky Like Blood: A Bethune College for Several Voices, 1974; The Bogman Pavese Tactics, 1977; Modern English-Canadian Poetry: A Guide to Information Sources, 1978; Coming Back, 1981; Revenge of the Mistresses, 1981; Miriam Waddington and Her Works, 1984; Out of the Willow Trees, 1986; Swimming in the Afternoon: New and Selected Poems, 1992; Dorothy Livesay: Patterns in a Poetic Life, 1992; Rip Rap: Yorkshire Ripper Poems for Several Voices, 1995; (with D.M. Yach) Community Policing in Action: A Practitioner's Guide, 1995; Thinking into the Dark, 1997; Attending to this World, 1998; States of Mind, 2001; Bread from Stones, 2002. EDITOR: (with J.L. Granatstein) Forum: Canadian Life and Letters 1920-1970: Selections from The Canadian Forum, 1972; The First Day of Spring: The Prose of R. Knister, 1977; (and comp.) The New England Collection of Martial Music: Being a Compendium of Martial Tunes Published in the United States Before 1840, 1995. **Address:** Department of English, University of Windsor, 401 Sunset Ave., Windsor, ON N9B 1K6, Canada. **Online address:** prichmond5@cogico.ca

STEVENS, Richard. See **STEVENS, Dick.**

STEVENS, Robert E(llis). American (born United States), b. 1942. **Genres:** Marketing. **Career:** Angelo Manufacturing Co., sales representative, 1963-65; Stevens Cafeteria, assistant manager, 1965-66; University of Arkansas, instructor in marketing, 1966-68; University of Southern Mississippi, assistant professor, 1968-72, associate professor of marketing, 1972-76; Oral Roberts University, associate professor, 1976-80, professor of marketing, 1980-86; Ruddick Research Intl., senior consultant, 1982-83; Tulsa Marketing Research Group, partner, 1983-86; Northeast Louisiana University, professor of marketing, 1986-, adjunct professor of marketing; Professional Marketing Systems, incorporator, 1988-; South West Dental Care Inc., owner; Southeastern Oklahoma State University, John Massey School of Business, John Massey professor of business; Journal of Professional Services Marketing, editor. **Publications:** (With S.K. Keiser and L.J. Loudenback) Contemporary Marketing: A Study Guide, 1977; Strategic Marketing Plan Master Guide, 1982; (with P.K. Sherwood) How to Prepare a Feasibility Study, 1982; (co-author) Marketing Research Handbook: A Decision Oriented Approach, 1983; (with P.K. Sherwood) Marketing Opportunity Analysis, 1986; (with PK. Sherwood) Market Opportunity Analysis, 1987; (with D.L. Loudon) Legal Services Marketing: A Planning Guide, 1989; (with Loudon and W.E. Warren) Marketing Planning Guide, 1991, 3rd ed., 2006; (with Loudon) Marketing for Churches and Ministries, 1992; Market Analysis: Assessing Your Business Opportunities, 1993; Strategic Planning for Churches and Ministries, 1993; Church and Ministry Strategic Planning, 1994; The Marketing Research Guide, 1997, 2nd ed., 2006; Strategic Planning for Not-for-Profit Organizations, 1997; Strategic Planning for Private Higher Education, 1997; (co-author) Marketing Research: Text and Cases, 2002, 2nd ed., 2007; (co-author) Marketing Management: Text and Cases, 2004; (co-author) Concise

Encyclopedia of Church and Religious Organization Marketing, 2006; (with K.E. Clow) Concise Encyclopedia of Professional Services Marketing, 2009; (with L.S. Silver and K.E. Clow) Concise Encyclopedia of Insurance Terms, 2010. Works appear in anthologies. Contributor to marketing and business journals and newspapers. **Address:** Department of Marketing, Northeast Louisiana University, 700 University Ave., Monroe, LA 71209, U.S.A. **Online address:** mmstevens@alpha.nlu.edu

STEVENS, Susan. American (born United States), b. 1961?. **Genres:** Novels, Young Adult Fiction, Theology/Religion. **Career:** Writer and methodist pastor. **Publications:** (With M. Horsfall) Double Honor, 2002. **Address:** c/o Author Mail, WaterBrook Press, 12265 Oracle Blvd. Ste. 200, Colorado Springs, CO 80921, U.S.A.

STEVENS, Suzanne H. American (born United States), b. 1938. **Genres:** Education, Self Help, Psychology. **Career:** Salem College, Center for Special Education, supervisor of interns and learning disabilities therapist, 1975-78; learning enhancement consultant and workshop leader, 1978-; Winston-Salem/Forsyth County Schools, learning disabilities teacher, 1976-78; Learning Development Network, founder, 1987, executive director, 1987-94. Writer. **Publications:** The Learning-Disabled Child: Ways That Parents Can Help, 1980; Classroom Success for the Learning Disabled, 1984; Enabling Disorganized Students to Succeed, 1987; Shifters: How to Help Students Concentrate, 1987; Helping the LD Student with Homework, 1987; How to Rescue At-Risk Students, 1990; Getting the Horse to Drink, 1994; The LD Child and the ADHD Child: Ways Parents and Professionals Can Help, 1996; Classroom Success for the LD and ADHD Child, 1997. Contributor of articles to periodicals. **Address:** 1001 S Marshall St., Ste. 37, Winston-Salem, NC 27101-5851, U.S.A. **Online address:** shstevens@multas.net

STEVENSON, David. British (born England), b. 1954?. **Genres:** Economics, History, Humanities. **Career:** London School of Economics and Political Science, Department of International History, lecturer, 1982, professor of international history, 1998-. Writer. **Publications:** French War Aims against Germany, 1914-1919, 1982; (ed. with K. Bourne and D.C. Watt) British Documents on Foreign Affairs: Reports and Papers from the Foreign Office Confidential Print, vol. I: From the Mid-nineteenth Century to the First World War, 1987, vol. II: From the First to the Second World War, 1989; The First World War and International Politics, 1988; Armaments and the Coming of War: Europe, 1904-1914, 1996; The Outbreak of the First World War: 1914 in Perspective, 1997; 1914-1918: The History of the First World War, 2004; Cataclysm: The First World War as Political Tragedy, 2004; (ed. with H. Afflerbach) Improbable War?: The Outbreak of World War I and European Political Culture Before 1914, 2007; With our Backs to the Wall, 2011; The Organization of Victory: The Sources of Allied Success in World War One, forthcoming. Contributor to books. **Address:** Department of International History, London School of Economics and Political Science, Rm. EAS. E604, Houghton St., London, GL WC2A 2AE, England. **Online address:** d.stevenson@lse.ac.uk

STEVENSON, David. Scottish (born Scotland), b. 1942. **Genres:** History, Politics/Government, Biography. **Career:** University of Aberdeen, Department of History, lecturer, 1970-78, senior lecturer in history, 1978-84, reader in Scottish history, Center for Scottish Studies, director, 1984-; University of St. Andrews, School of History, Department of Scottish History, professor, 1991-94, professor emeritus, 1994-. Writer. **Publications:** The Scottish Revolution, 1637-44: The Triumph of the Covenanters, 1973; Battle of Mauchline Moor 1648, 1973; Revolution and Counter-Revolution in Scotland 1644-51, 1977; Alasdair MacColla and the Highland Problem in the Seventeenth Century, 1980; Scottish Covenanters and Irish Confederates, 1981; (ed.) The Government of Scotland under the Covenanters 1637-1651, 1982; (ed.) From Lairds to Louns: Country and Burgh Life in Aberdeen, 1600-1800, 1986; (with W.B. Stevenson) Scottish Texts and Calendars: An Analytical Guide to Serial Publications, 1987; The Origins of Freemasonry, 1988; The First Freemasons: The Early Scottish Lodges and Their Members, 1988; (ed. with J.S. Smith) Aberdeen in the Nineteenth Century, 1988; (ed. with J.S. Smith) Fermfolk & Fisherfolk: Rural Life in Northern Scotland in the Eighteenth and Nineteenth Centuries, 1989; The Covenanters, 1989; King's College, Aberdeen, 1560-1641: From Protestant Reformation to Covenanting Revolution, 1990; (ed. and intro.) The Diary of a Canny Man: 1818-28: Adam Mackie, Farmer, Merchant, and Innkeeper in Fyvie, 1991; Highland Warrior: Alasdair MacColla and the Civil Wars, 1994; King or Covenant?: Voices from Civil War, 1996; Scotland's Last Royal Wedding, 1997; Union, Revolution and Re-

ligion in 17th-Century Scotland, 1997; The Beggar's Benison: Sex Clubs of the Scottish Enlightenment, 2001; The Hunt for Rob Roy: The Man and the Myths, 2006; (ed.) Letters of Sir Robert Moray to the Earl of Kincardine, 1657-73, 2007. **Address:** School of History, Department of Scottish History, University of St. Andrews, St Katharine's Lodge, The Scores, St. Andrews, FF KY16 9AR, Scotland. **Online address:** david.stevenson@btinternet.com

STEVENSON, Doug. American (born United States), b. 1950. **Genres:** Speech/Rhetoric. **Career:** Professional actor, 1972-85; Story Theater Intl., founder and president. Writer. **Publications:** Never Be Boring Again: Make Your Business Presentations Capture Attention, Inspire Action and Produce Results, 2003 as Story Theater Method, 2008. **Address:** Story Theater International, 2504 Shalimar Dr., Colorado Springs, CO 80915, U.S.A. **Online address:** doug@dougstevenson.com

STEVENSON, Garth. Canadian (born Canada), b. 1943. **Genres:** Politics/Government, History, Social Sciences, Social Commentary. **Career:** Carleton University, assistant professor, associate professor of political science, 1968-78; University of Alberta, associate professor, professor of political science, 1978-87; Brock University, professor of political science, 1987-. Writer. **Publications:** Mineral Resources and Australian Federalism, 1976; The Control of Foreign Direct Investment in a Federation: Canada & Australian Experience, 1976; (ed. with N. Hillmer) A Foremost Nation: Canadian Foreign Policy and a Changing World, 1978; Unfulfilled Union, 1979, 4th ed., 2004; (ed. with L. Pratt) Western Separatism: The Myths, Realities and Dangers, 1981; Rail Transport and Australian Federalism, 1987; The Politics of Canada's Airlines: From Diefenbaker to Mulroney, 1987; (ed. with D. Latouche and D. Duchacek) Perforated Sovereignties and International Relations: Trans-Sovereign Contacts and Subnational Governments, 1988; Ex Uno Plures: Federal-Provincial Relations in Canada, 1867-1896, 1993; Community Besieged: The Anglophone Minority and the Politics of Quebec, 1999; Parallel Paths: The Development of Nationalism in Ireland and Quebec, 2006. **Address:** Department of Political Science, Brock University, PL336, Saint Catharines, ON L2S 3A1, Canada. **Online address:** gstevenson@brocku.ca

STEVENSON, James. American (born United States), b. 1929?. **Genres:** Novels, Children's Fiction, Novellas/Short Stories, Cartoons, Poetry, Autobiography/Memoirs, Young Adult Fiction, Cartoons, Illustrations. **Career:** Life, reporter, 1954-56; New Yorker, cartoonist, cover artist and writer, 1956-63; Writer and illustrator, 1962-. **Publications:** CHILDREN'S FICTION: The Bear Who Had No Place to Go, 1972; Here Comes Herb's Hurricane!, 1973; Could be Worse!, 1977; Wilfred the Rat, 1977; The Sea View Hotel, 1978; Winston, Newton, Elton and ed., 1978; The Worst Person in the World, 1978; Fast Friends: Two Stories, 1979; Monty, 1979; Clams Can't Sing, 1980; Howard, 1980; That Terrible Halloween Night, 1980; The Night after Christmas, 1981; The Wish Card Ran Out!, 1981; Oliver, Clarence, and Violet, 1982; We Can't Sleep, 1982; Barbara's Birthday, 1983; Grandpa's Great City Tour: An Alphabet Book, 1983; The Great Big Especially Beautiful Easter Egg, 1983; What's under My Bed!, 1983; Worse Than Willy!, 1984; Yuck!, 1984; Are We Almost There?, 1985; Emma, 1985; That Dreadful Day, 1985; Fried Feathers for Thanksgiving, 1986; No Friends, 1986; There's Nothing to Do!, 1986; When I Was Nine, 1986; Higher on the Door, 1987; Happy Valentine's Day, Emma!, 1987; No Need for Monty, 1987; Will You Please Feed Our Cat?, 1987; The Supreme Souvenir Factory, 1988; We Hate Rain!, 1988; The Worst Person in the World at Crab Beach, 1988; Oh No, It's Waylon's Birthday!, 1989; Grandpa's too Good Garden, 1989; Unhappy New Year, Emma!, 1989; July, 1990; Which One Is Whitney?, 1990; Mr. Hacker, 1990; National Worm Day, 1990; Quick! Turn the Page!, 1990; Emma at the Beach, 1990; The Stowaway, 1990; That's Exactly the Way It Wasn't, 1991; BRRR, 1991; The Worst Person's Christmas, 1991; Don't You Know There's a War On?, 1992; Rolling Rose, 1992; And Then What?, 1993; The Flying Acorns, 1993; The Pattaconk Brook, 1993; Fun No Fun, 1994; The Mud Flat Olympics, 1994; The Sea View Hotel, 1994; Worse than the Worst, 1994; A Village Full of Valentines, 1995; All Aboard, 1995; The Bones in The Cliff, 1995; I Meant to Tell You, 1995; The Royal Nap, 1995; Sweet Corn: Poems, 1995; The Worst Goes South, 1995; I Had a Lot of Wishes, 1995; Daddy, Could I Have an Elephant?, 1996; The Oldest Elf, 1996; What You Do Is Easy, What I Do Is Hard, 1996; Yard Sale, 1996; Heat Wave at Mud Flat, 1997; The Mud Flat Mystery, 1997; The Unprotected Witness, 1997; Mud Flat April Fool, 1998; Popcorn: Poems, 1998; Sam the Zamboni Man, 1998; Candy Corn: Poems, 1999; Don't Make Me Laugh, 1999; Mud Flat Spring, 1999; Christmas at Mud Flat, 2000; The Most Amazing Dinosaur, 2000; The Castaway, 2001; Corn Chowder, 2003; Runaway Horse!: A Novel, 2003; Flying Feet: A

Mud Flat Story, 2004; No Laughing, No Smiling, No Giggling, 2004. FOR ADULTS: Do Yourself a Favor, Kid (novel), 1962; The Summer Houses (novel), 1963; Sorry, Lady-This Beach Is Private! (cartoons), 1963; Sometimes, But Not Always (novel), 1967; Annual Report, 1969; Miss Florence and the Artists of Old Lyme, 1971; Something Marvelous Is about to Happen, 1971; Cool Jack and the Beanstalk (comic strip novel), 1976; Let's Boogie! (cartoons), 1978; Uptown Local, Downtown Express, 1983. SELF ILLUSTRATED: Walker, The Witch, and the Striped Flying Saucer, 1969; (with E. Stevenson) Help! Yelled Maxwell, 1978; Cornflakes: Poems, 2000; Just Around the Corner: Poems, 2001; Corn-fed: Poems, 2002; Lost and Found New York: Oddballs, Heroes, Heart breakers, Scoundrels, Thugs, Mayors and Mysteries, 2007. **Address:** Darhansoff and Verrill Literary, 236 W 26th St., Ste. 802, New York, NY 10001-6736, U.S.A.

STEVENSON, Jonathan. Irish/American (born United States), b. 1956. **Genres:** Documentaries/Reportage, Military/Defense/Arms Control. **Career:** Le Boeuf, Lamb, Greene & MacRae, attorney, 1981-85, 1988-92; Corcoran, Mallin & Aresco, P.C., attorney, 1985-88; freelance author, 1992-; International Institute for Strategic Studies, senior fellow, 1999-2005; IISS US, director of studies, 2004-05; U.S. Naval War College, Center for Naval Warfare Studies, Strategic Research Department, associate professor, professor, 2005-, National Security Affairs, associate professor. Writer. **Publications:** Losing Mogadishu: Testing U.S. Policy in Somalia, 1995; We Wrecked the Place: Contemplating an End to the Northern Irish Troubles, 1996; Preventing Conflict: The Role of the Bretton Woods Institutions, 2000; Hard Men Humble: Vietnam Veterans Who Wouldn't Come Home, 2002; Counter-terrorism: Containment and Beyond, 2004; Thinking Beyond The Unthinkable: Harnessing Down From The Cold War To The War On Terror, 2008. Contributor to periodicals. **Address:** Center for Naval Warfare Studies, U.S. Naval War College, 686 Cushing Rd., Newport, RI 02841, U.S.A.

STEVENSON, Louise L. American (born United States), b. 1948. **Genres:** Intellectual History, Education, Women's Studies And Issues. **Career:** University of New Hampshire, visiting lecturer in history, 1981-82; Franklin and Marshall College, assistant professor, 1982-89, associate professor of history and American studies, 1989-96, professor of history and American studies, 1996-, chair of department of history, 1991-94, chair women's studies program, 1995-2001. Writer. **Publications:** Scholarly Means to Evangelical Ends: The New Haven Scholars and the Transformation of Higher Learning in America, 1830-1890, 1986; Miss Porter's School: A History in Documents, 1847-1948, 1987; (ed. with A.K. Baxter) Women's History, 1987, 4th ed., 1998; The Victorian Homefront: American Thought and Culture, 1860-1880, 1991; Victorian Homefront: American Thought and Culture, 1860-1880: With a New Preface, 2001. Contributor to periodicals. **Address:** Department of American Studies, Franklin and Marshall College, Stager Hall, PO Box 3003, Sta. 301, Lancaster, PA 17604-3003, U.S.A. **Online address:** louise.stevenson@fandm.edu

STEVENSON, Matthew. Swiss/American (born United States), b. 1954?. **Genres:** Travel/Exploration, Sports/Fitness. **Career:** Harper's Magazine, associate editor, contributing editor. **Publications:** Letters of Transit: Essays on Travel, History, Politics and Family Life Abroad, 2001; Mentioned in Dispatches: The Travel Essays of An Expatriate American, 2005; April Across America, 2006; Remembering the Twentieth Century Limited, 2009; (ed. with M. Martin) Rules of the Game: The Best Sports Writing from Harper's Magazine, 2010. Contributor to periodicals. **Address:** c/o Author Mail, Odysseus Books, 4 White Brook Rd., PO Box 89, Gilsum, NH 03448, U.S.A. **Online address:** matthewstevenson@freesurf.ch

STEVENSON, Robert G. American (born United States), b. 1945. **Genres:** Psychology, Education, Human Relations/Parenting. **Career:** River Dell High School, teacher of social studies and psychology and athletic coach, 1970-; grief counselor, 1975-; Columbia University, Seminar on Death, chairperson, 1984-94; New Jersey Special Olympics, coordinator of field events, 1988-; Goals and Assists Hockey Club, president, 1994-95. Writer. **Publications:** EDITOR: Grief and Healing, 1979; Children and Death: Perspectives from Birth through Adolescence, 1987; What Will We Do? Preparing the School Community to Cope with Crises, 1994, 2nd ed., 2002; Death Education in Schools (K-12): Curing Death Ignorance, 1995; (with E.P. Stevenson) Teaching Students About Death: A Comprehensive Resource for Educators and Parents, 1996; (with G.R. Cox and R.A. Bendiksen) Complicated Grieving and Bereavement: Understanding and Treating People Experiencing Loss, 2002; (with G.R. Cox and R.A. Bendiksen) Making Sense Of Death: Spiri-

tual, Pastoral and Personal Aspects of Death, Dying and Bereavement, 2003; (with G.R. Cox) Perspectives on Violence and Violent Death, 2008. Contributor to books and journals. **Address:** River Dell Regional Schools, Pyle St., Oradell, NJ 07649, U.S.A.

STEVENSON, Robin H. Canadian/British (born England), b. 1968. **Genres:** Young Adult Fiction, Novels. **Career:** University of Victoria, sessional instructor in social work and fine arts, 2001-. Writer. **Publications:** YOUNG ADULT NOVELS: Out of Order, 2007; Big Guy, 2008; Dead in the Water, 2008; A Thousand Shades of Blue, 2008; Inferno, 2009; In the Woods, 2009; Liars and Fools, 2010. OTHERS: Impossible Things, 2008; Ben's Robot (novel for children), 2009. Works appear in anthologies. **Address:** Victoria, BC , Canada. **Online address:** robin@robinstevenson.com

STEVENSON, Seth. American (born United States), b. 1974. **Genres:** Travel/Exploration. **Career:** Writer and journalist. **Publications:** Grounded: A Down to Earth Journey around the World, 2010. Contributor to periodicals. **Address:** Washington, DC , U.S.A. **Online address:** seth@sethstevenson.com

STEVENSON, Sucie. American (born United States), b. 1956?. **Genres:** Children's Fiction, Illustrations, Picture/Board Books, Literary Criticism And History. **Career:** Illustrator and author of children's books. **Publications:** SELF-ILLUSTRATED FOR CHILDREN: Do I Have to Take Violet?, 1987; I Forgot, 1988; Christmas Eve, 1988; Jessica The Blue Streak, 1989; (reteller) The Princess and the Pea, 1992; (reteller) The Twelve Dancing Princesses, 1995; (reteller) The Emperor's New Clothes, 1997. Illustrator of books by others. **Address:** c/o Liza Pulitzer-Voges, Kirchoff-Wohlberg Inc., 897 Boston Post Rd., Madison, CT 06443, U.S.A. **Online address:** artist@suciestevenson.com

STEVENSON, Talitha. British (born England), b. 1977?. **Genres:** Novels, Literary Criticism And History. **Career:** Writer. **Publications:** An Empty Room, 2004; Exposure, 2005. Disappear, 2010. Contributor to periodicals. **Address:** Carroll and Graf Publishers, 245 W 17th St., 11th Fl., New York, NY 10011-5300, U.S.A.

STEVENSON (LUCAS), Anne. American/British (born England), b. 1933. **Genres:** Poetry, Literary Criticism And History, Biography, Young Adult Fiction, Essays. **Career:** Lillesden School, school teacher, 1955-56; A&C Black Publishers Ltd., advertising manager, 1956-57; Westminster School, school teacher, 1959-60; Cambridge School of Weston, school teacher, 1962-65; University of Glasgow, tutor of extra-mural studies, 1970-73; Open University, counselor, 1972-73; University of Dundee, fellow in writing, 1973-75; Lady Margaret Hall, fellow, 1975-77; Bulmershe College, writer-in-residence, 1977-78; The Poetry Bookshop, co-founder, 1979-81; Newcastle University, Northern Arts Literary Fellow, 1981-82; University of Durham, Northern Arts Literary Fellow, 1981-82; University of Edinburgh, fellow, 1987, writer-in-residence, 1987-89. **Publications:** POETRY: Living in America, 1965; Reversals, 1969; Correspondences: A Family History in Letters, 1974; Travelling Behind Glass: Selected Poems, 1963-1973, 1974; Enough of Green, 1977; Cliff Walk: A Poem, 1977; A Morden Tower Reading 3, 1977; Sonnets for Five Seasons, 1979; Green Mountain, Black Mountain, 1982; Minute by Glass Minute, 1982; New Poems, 1982; Making Poetry, 1983; A Legacy, 1983; Black Grate Poems, 1984; The Fiction-Makers, 1985; Winter Time, 1986; (ed.) Selected Poems, 1986; (ed. with A. Clampitt and C. Raine) 1985 Anthology: The Observer and Ronald Duncan Foundation International Poetry Competition on Behalf of the Arvon Foundation, 1987; Selected Poems, 1956-1986, 1987; The Other House: New Poems, 1990; Four and a Half Dancing Men, New Poems, 1993; (ed. with D. Abse) The Gregory Anthology, 1991-1993, 1994; The Collected Poems of Anne Stevenson, 1955-1995, 1996; Once Upon a Time This Morning, 1997; Granny Scarecrow, 2000; Report from the Border: New and Rescued Poems, 2003; Way You Say the World: A Celebration for Anne Stevenson, 2003; Poems, 1955-2005, 2004; Stone Milk, 2007; Selected Poems, 2008; Astonishment, 2012. PROSE BOOKS: Elizabeth Bishop, 1966; Bitter Fame: A Life of Sylvia Plath, 1989; Between the Iceberg and the Ship: Selected Essays, 1998; Five Looks at Elizabeth Bishop, 1998. Works appear in anthologies. Contributor to periodicals. **Address:** c/o Neil Astley, Bloodaxe Books, Highgreen, Tarset, NM NE48 1RP, England. **Online address:** annestevenson38@gmail.com

STEWARD, H. Leighton. American (born United States), b. 1934. **Genres:** Medicine/Health, Food And Wine, Children's Fiction. **Career:** Shell Oil Co., staff, 1962-77, chief of exploration operations, 1977-79; Burlington Northern Inc., vice president of energy and minerals, 1979-81; Kilroy Company of Texas, executive vice president and chief operations officer, 1981-82; Louisiana Land and Exploration Co., senior vice president, 1982-84, president and chief operating officer, 1984-88, chairman and chief executive officer, 1989-97; Burlington Resources, vice chairman, 1997-2000; EOG Resources Inc., director, 2004-; American Petroleum Institute, honorary director; Southern Methodist University, Institute for Study of Earth and Man, chairman; Sugar Busters L.L.C., partner. Writer. **Publications:** WITH M.C. BETHEA, S.S. ANDREWS AND L.A. BALART: Sugar Busters! Cut Sugar to Trim Fat, 1998, rev. ed. as The New Sugar Busters! Cut Sugar to Trim Fat, 2003; Sugar Busters! Shopper's Guide, 1998; Sugar Busters!: Quick & Easy Cookbook, 1999; Sugar Busters! For Kids, 2001; El Nuevo Sugar Busters!, 2003; Fire, Ice, and Paradise, 2008. **Address:** PO Box 56180, Metairie, LA 70055, U.S.A.

STEWART, Christopher S. American (born United States) **Genres:** Novellas/Short Stories. **Career:** Writer. **Publications:** Hunting the Tiger: The Fast Life and Violent Death of the Balkans Most Dangerous Man, 2008. Contributor of articles to periodicals. **Address:** New York, NY , U.S.A. **Online address:** christophersstewart@gmail.com

STEWART, David O. American (born United States) **Genres:** Business/Trade/Industry, Economics. **Career:** Ropes & Gray LLP, partner, 1989-, counsel; Washington Independent Review of Books, president. Educator and writer. **Publications:** (Ed.) Representing Small Businesses, 1986; The Summer of 1787: The Men Who Invented the Constitution, 2007; Impeached: The Trial of President Andrew Johnson and the Fight for Lincoln's Legacy, 2009; American Emperor, 2011. **Address:** Ropes & Gray L.L.P., 1 Metro Ctr., 700 12th St. NW, Ste. 900, Washington, DC 20005-3948, U.S.A. **Online address:** david@davidostewart.com

STEWART, David W. (David Wood Stewart). American (born United States), b. 1929. **Genres:** Education. **Career:** Electrical Information Publications, editor, 1960-66; University of Wisconsin System, assistant to the chancellor of the Extension, 1967-72, senior academic planner, 1972-80; Coalition of Adult Education Organizations, president, 1988-89; American Council on Education, Center for Adult Learning and Educational Credentials, director of program development, 1985-. Consultant and writer. **Publications:** Adult Learning in America: Edvard Lindeman and His Agenda for Lifelong Education, 1987; (with H.A. Spike) Diploma Mills: Degrees of Fraud, 1988; Immigration and Education: The Crises and the Opportunities, 1993; (with E. Sullivan and H.A. Spille) External Degrees in the Information Age: Legitimate Choices, 1997. Contributor to professional journals. **Address:** American Council on Education, 1 Dupont Cir., Ste. 250, Washington, DC 20036, U.S.A.

STEWART, David Wood. *See* **STEWART, David W.**

STEWART, Elizabeth A. American (born United States), b. 1954. **Genres:** Adult Non-fiction, Mystery/Crime/Suspense, History. **Career:** Office of the State Attorney, Court Administrators Office, staff, 1981-83; McKinley and Blenk P. A., associate; U.S. Access Board, deputy general counsel, 1986-2006, staff, 2006-09. Writer and lawyer. **Publications:** (With B. Hendon) An Enormous Crime: The Definitive Account of American POWs Abandoned in Southeast Asia, 2007. Contributor to periodicals. **Address:** McKinley & Blenk P.A., 190 E Davidson St., Bartow, FL 33830-3932, U.S.A.

STEWART, Gail B. American (born United States), b. 1949. **Genres:** Children's Non-fiction, Young Adult Non-fiction, Children's Fiction. **Career:** English teacher, 1971-82; University of Minnesota, teaching assistant, 1977-79. Writer. **Publications:** China, 1988; Stunt People, 1988; Smoke Jumpers and Forest Firefighters, 1988; Coal Miners, 1988; Offshore Oil Rig Workers, 1988; The Facts about Teen Suicide, 1988; Motorcycle Racing, 1988; 1900s, 1989; 1910s, 1989; 1920s, 1989; 1930s, 1989; Peer Pressure, 1989; Chicago, 1989; Death, 1989; Child Abuse, 1989; Adoption, 1989; In Space, 1989; New York, 1989; In the Deserts, 1989; On the Water, 1989; In the Future, 1989; In the Mountains, 1989; In the Polar Regions, 1989; Houston, 1989; Los Angeles, 1989; Discrimination, 1989; Lumbermen, 1990; South Africa, 1990; The Soviet Union, 1990; Acid Rain, 1990; Rivermen, 1990; Scouts, 1990; Panama, 1990; Northern Ireland, 1990; Poland, 1990; Trappers and Traders, 1990; Drought, 1990; Texans, 1990; Drug Trafficking, 1990; Germany, 1990; Lebanon, 1990; Colombia, 1991; El Salvador, 1991; The Philippines, 1991; Cuba, 1991; Romania, 1991; The Revolutionary War, 1991; Antarctica, 1991; Ethiopia, 1991; Iraq, 1991; World War I, 1991; (with J. Duden) 1980s, 1991;

Microscope: Bringing the Unseen World into Focus, 1992; Benjamin Franklin, 1992; What Happened to Judge Crater?, 1992; Where Lies Butch Cassidy?, 1992; Why Buy Quantrill's Bones?, 1992; Liberia, 1992; India, 1992; Egypt, 1992; The Baltic States, 1992; The New Deal, 1993; Alexander the Great, 1994; Hitler's Reich, 1994; Cowboys in the Old West, 1995; The Quarter Horse, 1995; The Appaloosa Horse, 1995; The Thoroughbred Horse: Born to Run, 1995; Horseback Riding, 1995; Life in the Eskimo Village, 1995; Life in the Warsaw Ghetto, 1995; The Arabian Horse, 1995; Life during the French Revolution, 1995; Mustangs and Wild Horses, 1996; The Shetland Pony, 1996; The Palomino Horse, 1996; The Pinto Horse, 1996; The Elderly, 1996; People with AIDS, 1996; The Homeless, 1996; Teen Mothers, 1996; Teens in Prison, 1997; Battered Women, 1997; Gangs, 1997; Illegal Immigrants, 1997; Teen Runaways, 1997; Gay and Lesbian Youth, 1997; The Death Penalty, 1998; Drugs and Sport, 1998; Life during the Spanish Inquisition, 1998; Militias, 1998; Mothers on Welfare, 1998; Teens and Depression, 1998; Teen Fathers, 1998; Diabetes, 1999; F. Scott Fitzgerald, 1999; Homeless Teens, 1999; 1970s, 1999; Teen Dropouts, 1999; Teen Addicts, 2000; Teen Alcoholics, 2000; Weapons of War, 2000; Teen Parenting, 2000; Teens and Divorce, 2000; Teens with Eating Disorders, 2001; Teens with Disabilities, 2001; Suez Canal, 2001; Soccer, 2001; Phobias, 2001; Gambling, 2001; Tuberculosis, 2002; Terrorism, 2002; Teens with Cancer, 2002; Teens and Violence, 2002; Guns and Violence, 2002; Divorce, 2002; Drugs, 2002; America under Attack: September 11, 2001, 2002; Drugs, 2002; Smoking, 2003; Sleep Disorders, 2003; Racism, 2003; People with Mental Illness, 2003; Lyme Disease, 2003; Life of a Soldier in Washington's Army, 2003; Life in Elizabethan London, 2003; Great Women Comedians, 2003; Written Communications, 2004; War at Home, 2004; Teens in Mexico, 2004; SARS, 2004; Saddam Hussein, 2004; Medicine, 2004; Defending the Borders: the Role of Border and Immigration Control, 2004; American Revolution, 2004; Police Brutality, 2005; Life Under the Taliban, 2005; Human Rights in the Middle East, 2005; Fetal Alcohol Syndrome, 2005; Enlightenment, 2005; Catastrophe in Southern Asia: The Tsunami of 2004, 2005; Renaissance, 2006; London Transit System Bombings, 2006; Forensics, 2006; Fighting for Freedom: Blacks in the American Military, 2006; French Revolution, 2006; Bombings, 2006; Arson, 2006; UFOs, 2007; Ripped from the Headlines: Smoking, 2007; Illegal Immigration, 2007; Identity Theft, 2007; Forgery, 2007; Fat in America, 2007; Population, 2008; Larry Page and Sergey Brin: The Google Guys, 2008; John McCain, 2008; Ghosts, 2008; Crime Scene Photographer, 2008; (with P.H. Phillips) Portrait of Passion, 2008; Stephanie Kwolek, 2009; Maya Angelou, 2009; Drowning in a Bottle: Teens and Alcohol Abuse, 2009; Criss Angel, 2009; Bulimia, 2009; Anorexia, 2009; Bermuda Triangle, 2009; Area 51, 2009; Underwater Forensics, 2010; K-9 Police Units, 2010; Hauntings, 2010; Do Vampires Exist?, 2010; Cold Cases, 2010; Cesar Millan, 2010; Water Monsters, 2011; Missing Persons, 2011; Trolls, 2011; Urban Legends, 2011. **Address:** Lucent Books, 15822 Bernardo Centre Dr., PO Box 289001, San Diego, CA 92127-2320, U.S.A. **Online address:** gail@twohand.org

STEWART, Gary. American (born United States), b. 1944. **Genres:** Music, Novels, History. **Career:** Michigan Ladder Co., production manager, 1978-83; freelance writer, 1983-; Smith, Ellison, Stewart, & Miller, partner and researcher, 1985-87. **Publications:** Tenth Virgin, 1983; The Zarahemla Vision, 1988; Breakout: Profiles in African Rhythm, 1992; Downwinder Dance, 1992; Rumba on the River: A History of the Popular Music of the Two Congos, 2000; (with T.J. Demy) In the Name of God, 2002; (with J. Amman) Black Man's Grave: Letters from Sierra Leone, 2007. Contributor of articles to periodicals. **Address:** 605 K St. NE, Washington, DC 20002, U.S.A.

STEWART, Harry E. American (born United States), b. 1931. **Genres:** History, Theatre. **Career:** University of Richmond, instructor, assistant professor, 1958-61; Kent State University, assistant professor, associate professor, 1961-69; Tulsa University, professor and head of department of languages, 1969-71; Clemson University, professor of French, 1971-96, professor emeritus, 1996-, Department of Languages, head, 1971-84. Writer. **Publications:** (With R.R. McGregor) Jean Genet: A Biography of Deceit, 1910-1951, 1989; (with R.R. McGregor) Jean Genet: From Fascism to Nihilism, 1993. Contributor to periodicals. **Address:** Department of Languages, Clemson University, 717 Strode Twr., PO Box 340535, Clemson, SC 29634-0535, U.S.A.

STEWART, Ian (Nicholas). British (born England), b. 1945. **Genres:** Mathematics/Statistics, Graphic Novels, Translations. **Career:** Warwick University, lecturer, 1969-84, reader, 1984-90, professor of mathematics, 1990-, now professor emeritus of mathematics; University of Tuebingen, Humboldt Foundation fellow, 1974; Auckland University, visiting fellow, 1976; University of Connecticut, associate professor, 1977-78; University of Illinois, professor, 1978; University of Houston, professor, 1983-84. Writer. **Publications:** (With J. Jaworski) Nut-Crackers, 1971; Galois Theory, 1973, 3rd ed., 2004; (with R.K. Amayo) Infinite-Dimensional Lie Algebras, 1974; Concepts of Modern Mathematics, 1975; (with J. Jaworski) Get Knotted!, 1976; (with D. Tall) The Foundations of Mathematics, 1977; (with T. Poston) Catastrophe Theory and Its Applications, 1978; (with D. Tall) Algebraic Number Theory, 1979; (co-author) Aspects of Abstract Algebra, 1980; (with J. Jaworski) Seven Years of MANIFOLD: 1968-1980, 1981; (with D. Tall) Complex Analysis, 1983; The Problems of Mathematics, 1987; (with M. Golubitsky and D. Schaeffer) Singularities and Groups in Bifurcation Theory, vol. II, 1988; Does God Play Dice?, 1989; Game, Set, and Math, 1989; (with M. Golubitsky) Fearful Symmetry, 1992; Another Fine Math You've Got Me Into..., 1992; (with J. Cohen) The Collapse of Chaos, 1994; Nature's Numbers 1995; From Here to Infinity, 1996; (with J. Cohen) Figments of Reality, 1997; The Magical Maze, 1997; Life's Other Secret, 1998; (with T. Pratchett and J. Cohen) The Science of Discworld, 1999, vol. II: The Globe, 2002; (with J. Cohen) Wheelers, 2000; Flatterland, 2001; The Annotated Flatland, 2001; What Shape is a Snowflake?, 2001; (with J. Cohen) Evolving the Alien, 2002; (with M. Golubitsky) The Symmetry Perspective, 2002; (with D. Tall) Algebraic Number Theory and Fermat's Last Theorem, 2002; (with J. Cohen) Heaven, 2004; Math Hysteria: Fun and Games with Mathematics, 2004; (co-author) The Colours of Infinity: The Beauty, and Power of Fractals, 2004; (with J. Cohen and T. Pratchett) The Science of Discworld III: Darwin's Watch, 2005; The Mayor of Uglyville's Dilemma, 2005; Letters to a Young Mathematician, 2006; How to Cut a Cake and Other Mathematical Conundrums, 2006; Why Truth is Beauty, 2007; Game, Set and Math: Enigmas and Conundrums, 2007; Taming the Infinite: The Story of Mathematics from the First Numbers to Chaos Theory, 2008; Professor Stewart's Cabinet of Mathematical Curiosities, 2009; Professor Stewart's Hoard of Mathematical Treasures, 2009; The Story of Mathematics, 2008; Cows in the Maze And Other Mathematical Explorations, 2010; Mathematics of Life, 2011. COMIBOOKS SELF-ILLUSTRATED: Oh Catastrophe!, 1982; Les Fractals, 1982; Ah, les beaux groupes!, 1983. TRANSLATOR: J. Petit, Flight of Fancy, 1982; J. Petit, Informagic, 1982; J. Petit, Euclid Rules OK?, 1982; J. Petit, The Black Hole, 1985; J. Petit, Everything Is Relative, 1985; J. Petit, Run, Robot, Run, 1985; J. Petit, Big Bang, 1986; J. Petit, The Silence Barrier, 1986; K.H. Becker and M. Doerfler, Dynamical Systems and Fractals, 1989. **Address:** Mathematics Institute, University of Warwick, Rm. B211, Zeeman Bidg., Coventry, WM CV4 7AL, England. **Online address:** i.n.stewart@warwick.ac.uk

STEWART, Jack (F.). Canadian/Scottish (born Scotland), b. 1935. **Genres:** Literary Criticism And History, Poetry, Art/Art History. **Career:** University of Southern California, instructor of English, 1963-67; University of British Columbia, Department of English, assistant professor, 1967-71, associate professor, 1971-, professor, professor emeritus, 2000-. Writer. **Publications:** The Incandescent Word: The Poetic Vision of Michael Bullock, 1990; (ed. with P. Loeffler) Selected Works, 1936-1996, 1998; The Vital Art of D.H. Lawrence: Vision and Expression, 1999; Color, Space, and Creativity: Art and Ontology in Five British Writers, 2008. Contributor of articles to periodicals. **Address:** Department of English, University of British Columbia, 397-1873 East Mall, Buchanan Twr., Vancouver, BC V6T 1Z1, Canada. **Online address:** jackst@mail.ubc.ca

STEWART, Jeffrey C. American (born United States), b. 1950. **Genres:** Art/Art History, History. **Career:** George Mason University, associate professor of history, 1985-, professor of history and art history; National Humanities Center, fellow, 1990-91; Smithsonian Institution, Anacostia Museum, director of research; University of Rome, Fulbright professor of American intellectual history; University of California, Department of Black Studies, professor and chair. Writer. **Publications:** (Ed.) The Critical Temper of Alain Locke: A Selection of His Essays on Art and Culture, 1983; Winold Reiss: An Illustrated Checklist of His Portraits, 1990; (intro.) Narrative of Sojourner Truth, a Bondswoman of Olden Time: With a History of Her Labors and Correspondence Drawn from Her Book of Life, 1991; (ed. and intro.) Race Contacts and Inter-Racial Relations: Lectures on the Theory and Practice of Race, 1992; 1001 Things Everyone Should Know About African American History, 1996; (ed., intro. and contrib.) Paul Robeson: Artist and Citizen, 1998; Enter the New Negro: A Biography of Alain Locke, forthcoming. Contributor to periodicals. **Address:** Department of History, George Mason University, 4400 University Dr., Robinson Hall B 373B, Fairfax, VA 22030, U.S.A. **Online address:** jstewart@blackstudies.ucsb.edu

STEWART, Kathleen. Australian (born Australia), b. 1958?. **Genres:** Poetry, Novels, Autobiography/Memoirs, Biography. **Career:** Upsidedown House, singer-songwriter. Writer. **Publications:** Victim Train, 1992; Louis: A Normal Novel, 1993; Snow, 1994; Spilt Milk, 1995; Nightflowers, 1996; The White Star, 1997; The Red Room, 1999; The Black Butterfly, 2001; Waiting Room; The After Life: A Memoir, 2008; Men of Bad Character, 2010. **Address:** c/o Author Mail, Allen and Unwin, PO Box 8500, St. Leonards, NW 1590, Australia.

STEWART, Kaye. See HOWE, Muriel.

STEWART, Kenneth. (Kenneth L. Stewart). American (born United States), b. 1949. **Genres:** Sociology, Social Commentary, Politics/Government, Race Relations, History. **Career:** Angelo State University, assistant professor, 1975-80, associate professor, 1980-93, professor of sociology and university studies, 1993-, department head, 1984-93, Community Development Initiatives, co-director, 2007-, director. Writer. **Publications:** (As Kenneth L. Stewart with A.D. Léon) Tejanos and the Numbers Game: A Socio-Historical Interpretation from the Federal Censuses, 1850-1900, 1989; (as Kenneth L. Stewart with A.D. Léon) Not Room Enough: Mexicans, Anglos, and Socio-Economic Change in Texas, 1850-1900, 1993; Race and Ethnic Relations in America: AnIntroduction Using MicroCase, 1997; (ed.) The Angelo State University Symposium on American Values, 1998; (ed. with D.S. Eitzen) Solutions to Social Problems from the Bottom Up: Successful Social Movements, 2007. Contributor to books and journals. **Address:** Angelo State University, A104B, 2601 West Ave. N, ASU Sta., PO Box 10907, San Angelo, TX 76909-2601, U.S.A. **Online address:** kenneth.stewart@angelo.edu

STEWART, Kenneth L. See STEWART, Kenneth.

STEWART, Leah. American (born United States), b. 1973. **Genres:** Novels. **Career:** DoubleTake Magazine, associate editor, 1999; Vanderbilt University, assistant visiting professor, 2001-02, visiting professor; Murray State University, instructor, Nancy and Rayburn Watkins endowed visiting professor of creative writing, 2007-08; University of the South, Tennessee Williams fellow, visiting writer; Sewanee Young Writers' Conference, instructor; Sewanee Writers' Conference, staff, magazine editor, copy editor; University of Cincinnati, Creative Writing Program, faculty. **Publications:** Body of a Girl, 2000. The Myth of You and Me, 2005; Husband and Wife, 2010. Contributor of short stories to periodicals. **Address:** Gail Hochman, Brandt & Hochman Literary Agency, 1501 Broadway, Ste. 2310, New York, NY 10036, U.S.A. **Online address:** leahandmatt@mindspring.com

STEWART, Lucretia. British/Singaporean (born Singapore), b. 1952?. **Genres:** Novels, Travel/Exploration, Education, Reference. **Career:** Granta, commissioning editor, 1998-90, contributing editor. **Publications:** Tiger Balm: Travels in Laos, Vietnam and Cambodia, 1992; The Weather Prophet: A Caribbean Journey, 1995; Making Love: A Romance (novel), 1999; (ed.) Erogenous Zones: An Anthology of Sex Abroad, 2000; (ed. and intro.) Travelling Hopefully: A Golden Age of Travel Writing, 2006. **Address:** Random House, 20 Vauxhall Bridge Rd., London, GL SW1V 2SA, England. **Online address:** lucretia@dircon.co.uk

STEWART, Mart A. American/Canadian (born Canada), b. 1947. **Genres:** Cultural/Ethnic Topics, Geography, History. **Career:** Western Washington University, associate professor of history, professor of history, 1992-, Huxley College of Environmental Studies, affiliate professor; National Humanities Center, MacArthur ecological humanities fellow, 2002-03; Collective Memory Research Group, research consultant. Writer. **Publications:** What Nature Suffers to Groe: Life, Labor, and Landscape on the Georgia Coast, 1680-1920, 1996, 2nd ed., 2002. Contributor to periodicals. **Address:** Department of History, Western Washington University, Bond Hall 320, 516 High St., Bellingham, WA 98225-9061, U.S.A. **Online address:** mart.stewart@wwu.edu

STEWART, Martha. American (born United States), b. 1941. **Genres:** Homes/Gardens, How-to Books, Food And Wine. **Career:** Monness, Williams and Sidel (brokerage firm), stockbroker, 1965-73; House Beautiful, food and entertainment editor and columnist; K-mart Corp., lifestyle consultant, 1987-; Family Circle Magazine, contributing editor; Martha Stewart Living, editor-in-chief, 1990-. **Publications:** LIFESTYLE BOOKS: (with E. Hawes) Entertaining, 1982; Martha Stewart's Quick Cook, 1983; Hors D'oeuvres: The Creation and Presentation of Fabulous Finger Foods, 1984; Pies and Tarts, 1985; (with Hawes) Weddings, 1987; The Wedding Planner,

1988; Martha Stewart's Quick Cook Menus: Fifty-Two Meals You Can Make in under an Hour, 1988; Christmas: Entertaining, Decorating and Giving, 1989; Martha Stewart's Gardening, Month by Month, 1991; Martha Stewart's New Old House: Restoration, Renovation, Decoration, 1992; Martha Stewart's Quick Cook: Two Hundred Easy and Elegant Recipes, 1992; Holidays: Recipes, Gifts and Decorations, Thanksgiving and Christmas, 1993; Martha Stewart's Menus for Entertaining, 1994; Special Occasions: The Best of Martha Stewart Living, 1995; Handmade Christmas: The Best of Martha Stewart Living, 1995; The Martha Stewart Cookbook: Collected Recipes for Everyday, 1995; What to Have for Dinner: The Best of Martha Stewart Living, 1995; How to Decorate: The Best of Martha Stewart Living, 1996; Great American Wreaths: The Best of Martha Stewart Living, 1996; Martha Stewart's Healthy Quick Cook: Four Seasons of Great Menus to Make Every Day, 1997; Great Parties: Recipes, Menus and Ideas for Perfect Gatherings: The Best of Martha Stewart Living, 1997; Desserts: Our Favorite Recipes for Every Season and Every Occasion: The Best of Martha Stewart Living, 1998; Decorating Details: Projects and Ideas for a More Comfortable, More Beautiful Home: The Best of Martha Stewart Living, 1998; Favorite Comfort Food: A Satisfying Collection of Home Cooking Classics, 1999; Christmas with Martha Stewart Living, 2000; Halloween: The Best of Martha Stewart Living, 2001; Martha Stewart's Baking Handbook, 2005; Martha Rules: 10 Essentials for Achieving Success as You Start, Build or Manage A Business, 2005; World According to Martha, 2006; Martha Stewart's Homekeeping Handbook: The Essential Guide to Caring for Eveything in Your Home, 2006; (with W. Kromer) Martha Stewart's Wedding Cakes, 2007; (with S. Carey) Martha Stewart's Cooking School: Lessons and Recipes for the Home Cook, 2008; Martha Stewart's Dinner at Home: 52 Quick Meals to Cook for Family & Friends, 2009; Martha Stewart's Cupcakes: 175 Inspired Ideas for Everyone's Favorite Treat, 2009; (foreword) Ask the Dog Keeper, 2009; Holiday Sweets, 2009; Martha Stewart's Encyclopedia of Sewing and Fabric Crafts: Basic Techniques for Sewing, Applique, Embroidery, Quilting, Ddyeing and Printing, Plus 150 Inspired Projects From A to Z, 2010; (foreword) Man for all Species: the Remarkable Adventures of an Animal Lover and Expert Pet Keeper, 2010; Martha Stewart's New Pies and Tarts, 2011; Martha Stewart's American Food, 2012. **Address:** c/o Susan Magrino, Susan Magrino Agency, 641 Lexington Ave., 28th Fl., New York, NY 10022, U.S.A. **Online address:** mstewart@marthastewart.com

STEWART, Mary (Florence Elinor). British (born England), b. 1916. **Genres:** Romance/Historical, Children's Fiction, Poetry, Mystery/Crime/Suspense, inspirational/Motivational Literature, Theology/Religion, Young Adult Fiction, Novels, Novels. **Career:** University of Durham, lecturer, 1941-45, part-time lecturer, 1948-55; writer, 1954-. **Publications:** Madam, Will You Talk?, 1955; Wildfire at Midnight, 1956; Thunder on the Right, 1957; Nine Coaches Waiting, 1958; My Brother Michael, 1959; The Ivy Tree, 1961; The Moon-Spinners, 1962; Three Novels of Suspense, 1963; This Rough Magic, 1964, 2nd ed., 1992; Airs above the Ground, 1965; The Gabriel Hounds, 1967; The Wind off the Small Isles, 1968; Spell of Mary Stewart: Three Complete Novels, 1968; Mary Stewart Omnibus, 1969; The Crystal Cave, 1970; The Little Broomstick (for children), 1971; The Hollow Hills, 1973; Ludo and the Star Horse (for children), 1974; Touch Not the Cat, 1976; Triple Jeopardy, 1978; Selected Works, 1978; The Last Enchantment, 1979; A Walk in Wolf Wood: A Tale of Fantasy and Magic, 1980; Mary Stewart's Merlin Trilogy, 1980; The Wicked Day, 1983; Mary Stewart: Four Complete Novels, 1983; Thornyhold, 1988; Frost on the Window: Poems, 1990; The Stormy Petrel, 1991, 2nd ed., 1992; The Prince and the Pilgrim, 1995, 2nd ed., 1996; Rose Cottage, 1997, rev. ed., 1998; Blustery Weather Storms: A Suffering Church, 2008; Being On the Edge, 2008; Jesus' Life and Mission, 2008; A Man Named Zacchaeus: Jesus Miracle Stops and Parables, 2008. **Address:** c/o Author Mail, William Morrow & Co., 105 Madison Ave., New York, NY 10016, U.S.A.

STEWART, Matthew. American (born United States), b. 1963?. **Genres:** Popular Culture, Business/Trade/Industry, Economics, Philosophy, History. **Career:** Mitchell Madison Group L.L.C., founding partner. Writer, consultant and philosopher. **Publications:** The Truth About Everything: An Irreverent History of Philosophy, with Illustrations, 1997; Monturiol's Dream: The Extraordinary Story of the Submarine Inventor Who Wanted to Save the World, 2003; The Courtier and the Heretic: Leibniz, Spinoza, and the Fate of God in the Modern World, 2006; The Management Myth: Why the Experts Keep Getting it Wrong, 2009. **Address:** c/o Author Mail, Random House Inc., 1745 Broadway, New York, NY 10019, U.S.A.

STEWART, Michael. British/Irish (born Ireland), b. 1946?. **Genres:** Novels, Young Adult Fiction, Mystery/Crime/Suspense. **Career:** P.A. Management Consultants Ltd., management consultant, 1971-73; Northern Ireland Finance Corp., senior executive, 1974-77. Writer. **Publications:** Belladonna, 1982; Monkey Shines, 1983; A Far Cry, 1984; Blindsight, 1987; Prodigy, 1988; Grace, 1989; Birthright, 1990; Compulsion, 1994. **Address:** Wytham Abbey, Wytham, Oxford, OX OX2 8QE, England.

STEWART, Michael (James). British (born England), b. 1933. **Genres:** Economics. **Career:** Oxford Institute of Statistics, assistant research officer, 1955-56; Cornell University, visiting research fellow, 1956-57; National Institute of Economic and Social Research, assistant editor of economic review, 1962-64; Cabinet Office, economic adviser, 1964-67, senior economic advisor, 1967; Kenya Treasury, economic advisor, 1967-69; University College, reader in political economy, 1969-94, emeritus, 1994-; Foreign and Commonwealth Secretary, special economic advisor, 1977-78. Writer. **Publications:** Keynes and After, 1967; Labour and the Economy: A Socialist Strategy, 1972; The Jekyll and Hyde Years: Politics and Economic Policy since 1964, 1977; Politics and Economic Policy in the U.K. since 1964: The Jekyll and Hyde Years, 1978; The Age of Interdependence: Economic Policy in a Shrinking World, 1983; Controlling the Economic Future: Policy Dilemmas in a Shrinking World, 1983; (with P. Jay) Apocalypse 2000: Economic Breakdown and the Suicide of Democracy 1989-2000, 1987; Keynes in the 1990s: A Return to Economic Sanity, 1993. **Address:** University College London, Gower St., London, GL WC1E 6BT, England. **Online address:** m.stewart@ucl.ac.uk

STEWART, Patricia. See GUSSIN, Patricia.

STEWART, Ron(nie). American (born United States), b. 1956. **Genres:** Sociology, Social Sciences, Human Relations/Parenting. **Career:** Alabama State University, instructor in sociology, 1984-86; Mobile County Urban League, research assistant, 1985; University of the District of Columbia, Unsheltered Homeless Research Project, field coordinator, 1988; State University of New York College, associate professor of sociology, 1990-, professor, Prevention Resource Center, consultant, 1991-92. Writer. **Publications:** African-American Husbands: A Study of Black Family Life, 1991. Works appear in anthologies. Contributor to periodicals. **Address:** Department of Sociology, State University of New York College, B 313, Classroom Bldg., 1300 Elmwood Ave., Buffalo, NY 14222, U.S.A. **Online address:** stewarr@buffalostate.edu

STEWART, Rosemary. British (born England), b. 1945. **Genres:** Administration/Management, Economics. **Career:** Acton Society Trust, director, 1956-61; London School of Economics, fellow in management studies, 1964-66; University of Oxford, Green Templeton College, Oxford Center for management studies, fellow in organizational behavior, 1966-92, honorary fellow, 2000-05, emeritus fellow in organizational behavior, 2005-. Writer. **Publications:** (Co-author) Management Succession, 1956; (with R. Lewis) The Boss: The Life and Times of the British Businessman, 1958; (with R. Lewis) The Managers: A New Examination of the English, German and American Executive, 1961; Mergers, 1963; The Reality of Management, 1963, 3rd ed., 1997; (with J. Sleeman) Continuously Under Review: A Study of the Management of Out-Patient Departments, 1967; Managers and Their Jobs: A Study of the Similarities and Differences in the Ways Managers Spend Their Time, 1967, rev. ed., 1987; The Reality of Organizations: A Guide For Managers, 1970, 3rd ed., 1993; How Computers Affect Management, 1971; The Reality of Organizations: A Guide for Managers and Students, 1972; Contrasts in Management: A Study of Different Types of Managers' Jobs, Their Demands and Choices, 1976; Management Education and Managerial Work, 1977; (co-author) The District Administrator in the National Health Service, 1980; (ed. with J. Machin and C. Hales) Toward Managerial Effectiveness: Applied Research Perspectives on the Mangerial Task, 1981; Choices for the Manager, 1982; Leading in the NHS: A Practical Guide, 1989, rev. ed., 1996; Managing Today and Tomorrow, 1991; (with J. Barsoux) The Diversity of Management, 1994; (co-author) Managing in Britain and Germany, 1994; (ed.) Management of Health Care, 1998; (ed.) Managerial Work, 1998; Evidence-based Management: A Practical Guide for Health Professionals, 2002. **Address:** Green Templeton College, University of Oxford, 43 Woodstock Rd., Oxford, OX OX2 6HG, England. **Online address:** rosemary.stewart@templeton.ox.ac.uk

STEWART, Sarah. American/Mexican (born Mexico), b. 1939?. **Genres:** Children's Fiction, Education, Travel/Exploration, Librarianship. **Career:** Western Michigan University, artist-in-residence, 2000, Department of History, faculty. Writer. **Publications:** The Money Tree, 1991; The Library, 1995;

The Gardener, 1997; The Journey, 2001; The Friend, 2004; Quiet Place, 2012. **Address:** 17A Piedras Chinas, San Miguel de Allenda Gto., 37700, Mexico.

STEWART, Susan. American (born United States), b. 1952. **Genres:** Poetry, Literary Criticism And History, Art/Art History, Translations. **Career:** Temple University, Department of English, assistant professor, 1978-81, associate professor, 1981-85, professor of English, 1986-97, MA Program in Creative Writing, director, 1984-85; University of Pennsylvania, Regan professor in English, 1997-2004; Princeton University, Department of English, Annan professor of English, 2004-, placement officer, 2007-09, Avalon Foundation University professor in the humanities, Society of Fellows in the Liberal Arts, director, 2010-; Academy of American Poets, chancellor, 2005-. Poet and critic. **Publications:** POETRY: Yellow Stars and Ice, 1981; The Hive, 1987; The Forest, 1995; The Elements, 2002; Columbarium, 2003; Red Rover, 2008; Poet's Freedom: A Notebook on Making, 2011. LITERARY AND ART CRITICISM: Nonsense: Aspects of Intertextuality in Folklore and Literature, 1979; On Longing: Narratives of the Miniature, the Gigantic, the Souvenir, the Collection, 1984; Crimes of Writing: Problems in the Containment of Representation, 1991; Poetry and the Fate of the Senses, 2002; The Open Studio: Essay on Art and Aesthetics, 2005; (contrib.) William Kentridge Prints, 2006; (with A. Vidler and W.J.T. Mitchell) Antony Gormley: Blind Light, 2007. TRANSLATION: (and ed. with B. Antomarini) Scipione: poesie e prose, 2001; (with W. Smith) Euripides, Andromache, 2001; (with R.P. Harrison) Contemporary Italian Poetry/TriQuarterly 127, 2007; Love Lessons: Selected Poems of Alda Merini, 2009. Contributor to journals. **Address:** Department of English, Princeton University, 44A McCosh Hall, Princeton, NJ 08544-1016, U.S.A. **Online address:** stewart1@princeton.edu

STEWART, Thomas A(lan). American (born United States), b. 1948. **Genres:** Money/Finance, Economics, Administration/Management, Organized Labor. **Career:** Grossman Publishers, editor, 1970-73; Farrar, Straus, and Giroux, editor, 1973-76; Harcourt Brace Jovanovich, senior editor, 1976-79; Atheneum Publishers, vice president and editor-in-chief, 1979-83, senior vice president and director, 1983-85, president and publisher, 1985-89; Fortune Magazine, editor and columnist, 1989-; Business 2.0, editorial director; Harvard Business Review, editor and managing director, 2002-08; Booz & Company Inc., chief marketing and knowledge officer, 2008-. **Publications:** Intellectual Capital: The New Wealth of Organizations, 1997; The Wealth of Knowledge: Intellectual Capital and the Twenty-first Century Organization, 2001. **Address:** Bantam Doubleday, Dell Publishing Group Inc., 1745 Broadway, New York, NY 10019-4039, U.S.A. **Online address:** thosstew@aol.com

STEYN, Mark. American/Canadian (born Canada), b. 1959. **Genres:** Music, Essays. **Career:** British Broadcasting Corp., host. Writer. **Publications:** (With E. Behr) The Story of Miss Saigon, 1991; Broadway Babies Say Goodnight: Musicals Then and Now, 1999; Stephen Sondheim, 2000; The Face of the Tiger and Other Tales from the New War, 2002; From Head to Toe: An Anatomical Anthology, 2004; America Alone: Our Countrys Future as a Lone Warrior, 2005; America Alone: The End of The World As We Know It, 2006; After America, 2011. **Address:** PO Box 30, Woodsville, NH 03785, U.S.A. **Online address:** steyn@marksteyn.com

ST. GEORGE, Andrew. American (born United States), b. 1962. **Genres:** Travel/Exploration, Biography, Reference, Adult Non-fiction. **Career:** Edelman PR, staff, 1985-86; Columbia University, professor of literature and film, 1986-90; Oxford University, staff, 1987-93; Landmark Film Corp., consultant; Oxford Writing Ltd., director; McLuham-McLuhan First Media Group, consultant; Wenham-St George Media Group, director. Writer. **Publications:** The Sosnow Travel Essays, 1988; JOH: Jocelyn Hambro of Hambros Bank, 1992; Browning and Conversation, 1993; The Descent of Manners, 1993; A History of Norton Rose, 1995. **Address:** Chatto & Windus, The Hogarth Press, 30 Bedford Sq., London, GL WC1B 3SG, England.

ST. GEORGE, Judith. American (born United States), b. 1931. **Genres:** Children's Fiction, Children's Non-fiction, Adult Non-fiction, Mystery/Crime/Suspense. **Career:** Suburban Frontiers, president, 1968-71; writer, 1970-; teacher, 1979-81; Brooklyn Bridge Centennial Commission, commissioner, 1981-83; York Correctional Institution, instructor in creative writing. **Publications:** FICTION: Turncoat Winter, Rebel Spring, 1969; The Shad Are Running, 1972; The Girl with Spunk, 1975; By George, Bloomers!, 1977, rev. ed., 1989; The Chinese Puzzle of Shag Island, 1976; The Shadow of the Shaman, 1977; The Halo Wind, 1978; The Halloween Pumpkin Smasher, 1978; Mystery at St. Martin's, 1979; Haunted, 1980; Call Me Margo, 1981;

The Mysterious Girl in the Garden, 1981; Do You See What I See?, 1982; In the Shadow of the Bear, 1983; What's Happening to My Junior Year?, 1986; Who's Scared? Not Me!, 1987. NONFICTION: The Amazing Voyage of the New Orleans, 1980, rev. ed., 1989; The Brooklyn Bridge: They Said It Couldn't Be Built, 1982; The Mount Rushmore Story, 1985; Panama Canal: Gateway to the World, 1989; The White House: Cornerstone of a Nation, 1990; Mason and Dixon's Line of Fire, 1991; Dear Dr. Bell-Your Friend, Helen Keller, 1992; Crazy Horse, 1994; To See with the Heart: The Life of Sitting Bull, 1996; Sacagawea, 1997; Betsy Ross: Patriot of Philadelphia, 1997; In the Line of Fire: Presidents Lives at Stake, 1999; So You Want to Be President?, 2000, rev. ed., 2004; John & Abigail Adams: An American Love Story, 2001; So You Want to Be an Inventor?, 2002; You're on Your Way, Teddy Roosevelt!, 2004; So You Want to Be an Explorer?, 2005; Take the Lead, George Washington!, 2005; The Journey of the One and Only Declaration of Independence, 2005; Stand Tall, Abe Lincoln, 2007; The Ghost, the White House and Me, 2007; Make Your Mark, Franklin Roosevelt, 2007; Mystery Isle, 2007; Stand Tall, Abe Lincoln, 2008; Duel: The Parallel Lives of Alexander Hamilton and Aaron Burr, 2009; Zarafa: The Giraffe Who Walked to the King, 2009. OTHERS: Tales of the Gold Monkey, 1983; (adapter) Grand Constructions, 1983; (adapter) Great Painters, 1984; A View to a Kill, 1985. **Address:** Philomel Books, 345 Hudson St., New York, NY 10014, U.S.A.

STIBBE, Mark W. G. British (born England), b. 1960. **Genres:** Theology/Religion, Literary Criticism And History. **Career:** Church of England, clerk in holy orders, 1986-; Sheffield University, honorary lecturer in biblical studies, 1989-93; St. Mark's Church, vicar; The Father's House Trust, founder, 2008-; St. Andrew's, vicar, through 2009. Writer. **Publications:** John as Storyteller: Narrative Criticism and the Fourth Gospel, 1992; John: A New Commentary, 1993; (ed. and intro.) The Gospel of John as Literature, 1993; John's Gospel, 1994; A Kingdom of Priests: Deeper into God in Prayer, 1993; Explaining Baptism in the Holy Spirit, 1995; O Brave New Church, 1996; Times of Refreshing, 1996; Know Your Spiritual Gifts, 1997. Contributor to journals and magazines. **Address:** Father's House Trust, Arnold House, 15 Clarendon Rd., Watford, HF WD17 1JR, England.

STIDWORTHY, David Earl. American (born United States), b. 1947. **Genres:** Film, Horror, Education. **Career:** Writer. **Publications:** (As D. Earl Worth) Sleaze Creatures: An Illustrated Guide to Obscure Hollywood Horror Movies, 1956-1959, 1995; High on the Hogs: A Biker Filmography, 2003. **Address:** c/o Author Mail, McFarland & Company Inc., PO Box 611, Jefferson, NC 28640-0611, U.S.A.

STIEBING, William H(enry). American (born United States), b. 1940. **Genres:** Archaeology/Antiquities, History. **Career:** University of New Orleans, instructor, 1967-70, assistant professor, 1970-73, associate professor, 1973-85, professor of ancient history and archaeology, 1985-2001, Seraphia D. Leyda teaching professor of ancient history and archaeology, 2001-05, professor emeritus, 2005-. Writer. **Publications:** Ancient Astronauts, Cosmic Collisions, and Other Popular Theories about Man's Past, 1984; Out of the Desert? Archaeology and the Exodus/Conquest Narratives, 1989; Uncovering the Past: A History of Archaeology, 1993; Ancient Near Eastern History and Culture, 2003, 2nd ed., 2009. Contributor to periodicals. **Address:** Department of History, University of New Orleans, Rm. 135, Liberal Arts Bldg., 2000 Lakeshore Dr., New Orleans, LA 70148, U.S.A. **Online address:** wstiebing@msn.com

STIEFVATER, Maggie. American (born United States), b. 1981. **Genres:** Novels. **Career:** Writer and educator. **Publications:** Lament: The Faerie Queen's Deception, 2008; Ballad: A Gathering of Faerie, 2009; Shiver, 2009; Linger, 2010. **Address:** VA , U.S.A. **Online address:** stiefvaterreadermail@gmail.com

STIERLIN, Helm. American/German (born Germany), b. 1926. **Genres:** Philosophy, Psychiatry, Human Relations/Parenting. **Career:** Washington School of Psychiatry, faculty, 1957-62, 1971-; Sanatorium Bellevue, senior supervising analyst, 1963-64; National Institute of Mental Health, Family Studies Section, Adult Psychiatry Branch, visiting scientist, 1965, Family Studies Section, head of psychotherapy unit, 1966-71, acting chief, 1969-74; Johns Hopkins University, assistant professor of psychiatry, 1969-74; University of Maryland, associate professor of psychiatry, 1972-74; Washington Psychoanalytic Institute, faculty, 1972-; University of Heidelberg Medical

School, professor and chief psychoanalyst, 1974-92, now professor emeritus; Family Therapy Institute, founder, 1974-. Writer. **Publications:** Der gewalttaetige Patient, 1956; Conflict and Reconciliation, 1969; Das Tun der Einen ist das Tun des Anderen, 1971; Separating Parents and Adolescents, 1974, rev. ed. 1981; Adolf Hitler: Familienperspektiven, 1975; Von der Psychoanalyse zur Familien therapie: Theorie, Klinik, 1975; Hitler: A Family Perspective, 1977; Psychoanalysis and Family Therapy, 1977; (co-author) Das erste Familiengesprach Theorie, Praxis, Beispiele 1977; Delegation und Familie, 1978; (co-author) The First Interview with the Family, 1980; Eltern und Kinder: das Drama von Trennung und Versohnung im Jugendalter, 1980; (with M. Wirsching) Krankheit und Familie, 1982; Die Christen in der Weltfamilie, 1982; Psychotherapie und Sozialtherapie der Schizophrenie, 1984; (with F. Simon) Die Sprache der Familientherapie: EinVokabular: Uberblick, Kritik und Integration Systemtherapeutischer Begriffe, Konzepte und Methoden, 1984; (with F. Simon and L.C. Wynne) The Language of Family Therapy: A Systemic Vocabulary and Sourcebook, 1985; Familiaere Wirklichkeiten, 1987; Ob sich das Herz zum Herzen findet, 1987; (with G. Weber) Unlocking the Family Door: A Systemic Approach to the Understanding and Treatment of Anorexia Nervosa, 1989; Individuation und Familie-Studien zur Theorie und therapeutischen Praxis, 1989; Ich und dieanderen-Psychotherapie in einer sich wandelnden Gesellschaft, 1994; Psychosomatische Krankheiten in der Familie. Texte zur Familiendynamik, 1995; Haltsuche in Haltlosigkeit, 1997; (with R. Grossarth-Maticek) Krebsrisiken-Uberlebenschancen, 1998; Christsein hundert Jahre nach Nietzsche: Systemisch-Therapeutische Perspektiven, 2001; Die Demokratisierung der Psychotherapie, 2003. EDITOR: (with L.C. Wynne and M. Wirsching) Psychosocial Intervention in Schizophrenia, 1983; (with F.B. Simon and G. Schmidt) Familiar Realities: The Heidelberg Conference, 1987. Contributor of articles to journals. **Address:** University of Heidelberg, 1 Kirchheimer Mühle, Sandhausen, 69207, Germany. **Online address:** helmstierlin@t-online.de

STILES, T. J. American (born United States) **Genres:** Biography, History, Literary Criticism And History. **Career:** Writer, biographer, historian and critic. **Publications:** (Comp.) The Citizen's Handbook: Essential Documents and Speeches from American History, 1993; (ed.) Civil War Commanders, 1995; (ed.) Warriors and Pioneers, 1996; (ed.) Robber Barons and Radicals, 1997; (ed.) The Colonizers, 1998; (ed.) Founding Fathers, 1999; Jesse James: Last Rebel of the Civil War, 2002; The First Tycoon: The Epic Life of Cornelius Vanderbilt, 2009. Contributor to newspapers and magazines. **Address:** c/o Jill Grinberg, Jill Grinberg Literary Management, 16 Court St., Ste. 3306, Brooklyn, NY 11241, U.S.A. **Online address:** tjstiles@tjstiles.net

STILL, William N. American (born United States), b. 1932. **Genres:** History. **Career:** Mississippi University for Women, instructor, 1959-, assistant professor of history; East Carolina University, associate professor, 1968-74, professor of history, 1974-94, Maritime history and Underwater archaeology, director, 1982-94; University of Hawaii, adjunct researcher, 1995-. Writer. **Publications:** Confederate Shipbuilding, 1969; Iron Afloat: The Story of the Confederate Armorclads, 1971; North Carolina's Revolutionary War Navy, 1976; American Sea Power in the Old World: The United States Navy in European and Near Eastern Waters 1865-1917, 1980; Ironclad Captains: The Commanding Officers of the USS Monitor, 1988; Monitor Builders, 1988; (co-author) Raiders & Blockaders: The American Civil War Afloat, 1998; (ed.) The Confederate Navy, the Ships, Men and Organization, 1861-65, 1999; Crisis at Sea: The United States Navy in European Waters in World War I, 2007. **Address:** 2005B Quail Ridge Rd., Greenville, NC 27858, U.S.A. **Online address:** still@hawaii.edu

STILLERMAN, Marci. American (born United States) **Genres:** Children's Non-fiction, Autobiography/Memoirs. **Career:** Marshall Field's, assistant. Writer. **Publications:** Nine Spoons: A Chanukah Story, 1998; Swimming Lessons, 2007; Something Terrible Happened on Kenmore, 2009; The First Thirteen Years of a Catawamptious Life, forthcoming. Contributor to periodicals. **Address:** 15 Lake Shore Dr., Rancho Mirage, CA 92270-4054, U.S.A. **Online address:** marciess@aol.com

STILLINGER, Jack. American (born United States), b. 1931?. **Genres:** Literary Criticism And History, Poetry, Bibliography, Essays. **Career:** Harvard University, teaching fellow, 1955-58; University of Illinois, assistant professor, 1958-61, associate professor, 1961-64, professor of English, 1964-, Center for Advanced Study, professor of English, 1970-, now professor emeritus. Writer. **Publications:** The Hoodwinking of Madeline and Other Essays on

Keats's Poems, 1971; The Texts of Keats's Poems, 1974; Multiple Authorship and the Myth of Solitary Genius, 1991; Coleridge and Textual Instability: The Multiple Versions of the Major Poems, 1994; Reading The Eve of St. Agnes: The Multiples of Complex Literary Transaction, 1999; Romantic Complexity: Keats, Coleridge, and Wordsworth, 2006; Nina and the Balloon: Poems, 2008. EDITOR: The Early Draft of John Stuart Mill's Autobiography, 1961; Anthony Munday's Zelauto, 1963; Wordsworth: Selected Poems and Prefaces, 1965; The Letters of Charles Armitage Brown, 1966; Twentieth Century Interpretations of Keats's Odes: A Collection of Critical Essays, 1968; J.S. Mill: Autobiography and Other Writings, 1969; The Poems of John Keats, 1978; (with J.M. Robson) J.S. Mill: Autobiography and Literary Essays, 1981; John Keats: Complete Poems, 1982; John Keats: Poetry Manuscripts at Harvard, 1990. **Address:** Department of English, University of Illinois, 608 S Wright St., Urbana, IL 61801, U.S.A. **Online address:** jstill@illinois.edu

STILLMAN, David A. American (born United States) **Genres:** Human Relations/Parenting, Adult Non-fiction. **Career:** DAS Creative, founding director, 1995-; BridgeWorks L.L.C., co-founder and partner, 1998-; Michigan State University, Mass Media in Britain Program, fellow. Writer and consultant. **Publications:** (With L.C. Lancaster) When Generations Collide: Who They Are, Why They Clash, How to Solve the Generational Puzzle at Work, 2002; (with L.C. Lancaster) M-factor: How The Millennial Generation is Rocking the Workplace, 2010. **Address:** c/o Author Mail, HarperCollins Publishers, 10 E 53rd St., New York, MN 10022, U.S.A. **Online address:** info@generations.com

STILLMAN, (John) Whit(ney). American (born United States), b. 1952. **Genres:** Plays/Screenplays, Novels, Literary Criticism And History. **Career:** Doubleday, editorial assistant and first reader, 1974-78; Access News Summary, editorial assistant and first reader, 1979-81; Riley Illustration, owner and operator, 1984-91. Director. **Publications:** Barcelona and Metropolitan: Tales of Two Cities, 1994; The Last Days of Disco, 2000. Contributor to periodicals. **Address:** William Morris Agency Inc., 151 El Camino Dr., Beverly Hills, CA 90212-2704, U.S.A.

STILLMAN, Norman A(rthur). American (born United States), b. 1945. **Genres:** History, Language/Linguistics, Cultural/Ethnic Topics, Theology/Religion. **Career:** University of Chicago, Momigliano lecturer; University of London, School of Oriental and African Studies, Sherman lecturer; New York University, assistant professor of Near Eastern language and literature, 1970-73; State University of New York, associate professor, 1973-85, professor of history and Arabic, 1985-95; Haifa University, visiting associate professor, 1979-80; University of Oklahoma, professor, 1995-, Schusterman/Josey professor of Judaic history, Schusterman-Josey chair of Judaic history, Judaic Studies Program, director; AJS Review, editor, 1989-99; Hebrew University, Lady Davis Fellow, 1994-95; Tel-Aviv University, Moshe Dayan Center for Middle Eastern and African Studies, visiting fellow; National Endowment for the Humanities, consultant; National Geographic, consultant; Social Science Research Council, consultant. **Publications:** (Comp.) The Jews of Arab Lands: A History and Source Book, 1979; The Language and Culture of the Jews of Sefrou (monograph), 1988; (trans. with Y.K. Stillman) S. Romanelli, Travail in an Arab Land, 1989; The Jews of Arab Lands in Modern Times, 1991; Sephardi Religious Responses to Modernity, 1995; (intro.) Studies in Islamic History and Institutions, 2010. EDITOR: (with I. Ben-Ami and S. Morag) Studies in Judaism and Islam, 1981; (with Y.K. Stillman) From Iberia to Diaspora, 1999; Arab Dress: A Short History, 2000, 2nd ed., 2003; (co-ed.) Encyclopedia of Jews in the Islamic World, 2010. Contributor to periodicals. **Address:** Department of History, University of Oklahoma, Rm. 403A, 455 W Lindsey St., Norman, OK 73019-2004, U.S.A. **Online address:** nstillman@ou.edu

STILLSON, Alan. American (born United States), b. 1945. **Genres:** Trivia/Facts, Theatre. **Career:** Mathematics teacher, 1967-74; Commercial Real Estate Finance Co., owner, 1978-95; Beneficial Capital, marketing coordinator, 1981-83; Calcomp Financial, marketing coordinator, 1983-95; Best Buy, marketing coordinator, 1995-2001. Writer. **Publications:** The Mensa Genius A-B-C Quiz Book, 1998; (co-author) Match Wits with Mensa: The Complete Quiz Book, 1998; One-Minute Brainteasers, 2001; (with K.C. Richards and B.R. Santos) Classic Brain Teasers, 2002; Middle School Word Puzzles, 2002; What's Your CQ?, 2003; Ninety-Second Brainteasers, 2003; Two-Minute Brainteasers, 2005; (with F. Longo) Sudokugrams, 2008; I Remember Lou, 2010; Brain Warmer Uppers, 2011; Thank You, Minerva, 2011. **Address:** 5515 Keokuk Ave., Woodland Hills, CA 91367, U.S.A. **Online address:** astillson@sbcglobal.net

STILTNER, Brian. American (born United States), b. 1966. **Genres:** History. **Career:** Sacred Heart University, associate professor of religious studies, 1998-; Hersher Institute for Applied Ethics, director, 1998-2003; Center for Catholic Thought, Ethics and Culture, director, 2003-06, department of philosophy and religious studies, chair, 2006-. **Publications:** Religion and the Common Good: Catholic Contributions to Building Community in a Liberal Society, 1999; (with D.L. Clough) Faith and Force: A Christian Debate about War, 2007. **Address:** Sacred Heart University, Rm. 200, Administrative Bldg., 5151 Park Ave., Fairfield, CT 06825, U.S.A. **Online address:** stiltner@sacredheart.edu

STIMMLER, Jane K. American (born United States) **Genres:** Novels, Marketing, Business/Trade/Industry. **Career:** Grant Thornton (accounting and consulting firm), director of marketing programs; Hansen Group, senior vice president and director of marketing and public relations; The Marketing Edge, consulting and communications principal, president, co-founder and chief executive officer, 1990-; ElderNet of Lower Merion and Narberth, board director; Wharton Small Business Development Center, marketing teacher; Small Business Board, chair; Philadelphia Finance Association, president. Writer. **Publications:** (With M.D. Shepard) Stop Whining & Start Winning: 8 Surefire Ways for Women to Thrive in Business, 2005; (with M.D. Shepard and P.J. Dean) Breaking into the Boys' Club: 8 Ways for Women to Get Ahead in Business, 2009. Contributor to periodicals. **Address:** The Marketing Edge, 24 N Bryn Mawr Ave., Ste. 280, Bryn Mawr, PA 19010, U.S.A. **Online address:** jks@mktgedge.com

STIMPSON, Jeff. American (born United States) **Genres:** Autobiography/Memoirs, Biography. **Career:** Ithaca Journal, journalist; Patuxent Publications, journalist. Writer. **Publications:** Alex: The Fathering of a Preemie (memoir), 2004; Alex the Boy: Episodes From a Family's Life With Autism, 2008. Contributor to periodicals. **Address:** c/o Author Mail, Academy Chicago Publishers, 363 W Erie St., 7E, Chicago, IL 60610, U.S.A. **Online address:** jeff@jeffslife.net

STIMSON, Tess. British/American (born United States), b. 1966. **Genres:** Novels, Young Adult Non-fiction. **Career:** British Broadcasting Corp., staff; Cable News Network, staff; University of South Florida, professor of creative writing; Daily Mail Newspaper, columnist. Writer. **Publications:** (With Jackie and S. Mann) Yours till the End (nonfiction), 1992; NOVELS: Hard News, 1993; Soft Focus, 1995; Pole Position, 1996; The Infidelity Chain, 2008; The Adultery Club, 2008; One Good Affair, 2009; The Cradle Snatcher, 2009; Who Loves You Best: A Novel, 2010; Beat the Bitch, 2010; What's Yours is Mine: A Novel About Sisters Who Share Just a Little too much, 2011; The Wife Who Ran Away, 2012; Someone Else's Child, forthcoming. **Address:** c/o Carole Blake, Blake Friedmann, 122 Arlington Rd., London, GL NW1 7HP, England. **Online address:** tess@tessstimson.com

STINCHECUM, Amanda Mayer. American (born United States), b. 1941. **Genres:** Art/Art History, Cultural/Ethnic Topics, Children's Fiction, History, Travel/Exploration, Translations, Children's Non-fiction, Business/Trade/Industry, Business/Trade/Industry. **Career:** Harper's Bazaar, editorial assistant, 1964-65; Women's Wear Daily, fashion reporter, 1965-69; Metropolitan Museum of Art, research fellow, 1981-82; Tokyo National Institute for Research on Cultural Properties, research fellow, 1983-84; Textile Museum, consulting specialist, 1985; Tokyo National Institute for Research on Cultural Properties, research fellow, 1987-88; Hosei University, Institute of Okinawan Studies, research fellow, 1988-; Okinawa Prefectural Government, Department of Education, special liaison, 1990; University of Illinois, adjunct assistant professor, 1991-92; Art Institute of Chicago, lecturer; Fashion Institute of Technology, lecturer; American Museum of Natural History, consultant; Calvin Klein Inc., Japanese translator; Los Angeles County Museum of Art, Japanese translator; Columbia University Translation Service, Japanese translator. **Publications:** Kosode: 16th-19th Century Textiles from the Nomura Collection, 1984; (contrib.) Mingei: Japanese Folk Art, 1995; Robert Mose Mingei: Japanese Folk Art: From the Montgomery Collection, 1995. TRANSLATIONS: Girl from the Snow Country, 1986; Grandpa's Town, 1991; Everyone Poops, 1993; Holes in Your Nose, 1994; The Gas We Pass, 1994; Contemplating Your Bellybutton, 1995; Animal Faces, 1996; All About Scabs, 1998; Breasts, 1999.

Contributor to periodicals. **Address:** 39 Remsen St., Ste. 3A, Brooklyn, NY 11201, U.S.A. **Online address:** amandams@earthlink.net

STINE, Catherine. American (born United States) **Genres:** Children's Non-fiction, Adult Non-fiction, Novellas/Short Stories, Children's Fiction, History. **Career:** New School University, writing instructor in continuing education division; Elementary-and secondary-school writing workshops, teacher. Writer. **Publications:** Building Your Babys Brain: A Parents Guide to the First Five Year, 1999; The Joy of Weight Loss, 1999; Refugees, 2005; From Chapter Book to Teen Fiction, 2006; Girl's Best Friend, 2010. SELF ILLUSTRATED: Fireseed One, 2011. FORTHCOMING: Girl with Goat; The Smoky Beats of My Tri-Colored Heart. Contributor to periodicals. **Address:** Transatlantic Literary Agency Inc., 72 Glengowan Rd., Toronto, ON M4N 1G4, Canada. **Online address:** info@catherinestine.com

STINE, Scott A(aron). American (born United States), b. 1968. **Genres:** Adult Non-fiction, Film, Popular Culture, Reference, Novels, Novellas/Short Stories, Horror, Science Fiction/Fantasy, Science Fiction/Fantasy. **Career:** Stigmata Press, publisher, 1992-2002; Studio Scordatura, contributor, 2009-11. Writer. **Publications:** The Gorehound's Guide to Splatter Films of the 1960s and 1970s, 2001; (with M. von Sacher-Masoch) The Trashfiend's Guide to Collecting Videotapes, 2003; The Gorehound's Guide to Splatter Films of the 1980s, 2003; Trashfiend: Disposable Horror Fare of the 1960s and 1970s, 2006. Contributor to periodicals. Works appear in anthologies. **Address:** PO Box 5273, Everett, WA 98206-5273, U.S.A. **Online address:** hiddennoise@fidalgo.net

STINGEL, Janine. Canadian (born Canada), b. 1966. **Genres:** Sociology, Theology/Religion, History, Adult Non-fiction. **Career:** University of Ottawa, sessional lecturer in history, 1996-99; Carleton University, sessional lecturer in history, 1996-99; McGill University, sessional lecturer in history, 1996-99; Joan Holmes and Associates, aboriginal land claims researcher, 1999-2000; National Archives of Canada, Indian and Northern Affairs in Government Records Branch, archivist of records, 2000-01. Writer. **Publications:** Social Discredit: Anti-Semitism, Social Credit and the Jewish Response, 2000. Contributor of articles to periodicals. **Address:** 40 Chemin de la Mésange, Val-des-Monts, QC J8N 6B7, Canada.

STINNETT, Robert B. American (born United States) **Genres:** Politics/Government, Military/Defense/Arms Control, History. **Career:** Oakland Tribune, staff, sports photographer, 1982, journalist, retired, 1986; The Independent Institute, research fellow; British Broadcasting Corp., consultant; NHK Television, consultant. Photojournalist. **Publications:** George Bush: His World War II Years, 1991; Day of Deceit: The Truth about FDR and Pearl Harbor, 2000. **Address:** c/o Author Mail, Simon & Schuster Inc., 1230 Ave. of the Americas, 10th Fl., New York, NY 10020-1513, U.S.A.

STINSON, Jim. American (born United States), b. 1937. **Genres:** Novels, Communications/Media, Education, Reference. **Career:** Videomaker Magazine, columnist and contributing editor; Harvard University, faculty; University of California-Los Angeles, College of Design, Media History and Criticism, Art Center, teacher of film production; La Canada High School, teacher of video production. **Publications:** Double Exposure, 1985; Low Angles: A Stoney Winston Mystery, 1986; TruckShot: A Stoney Winston Mystery, 1989; TV Safe: A Stoney Winston Mystery, 1991; Video Communication and Production, 2002, 3rd ed., 2011; Video: Digital Communication & Production, 2nd ed., 2008, 3rd ed., 2012; Tassy Morgan's Bluff, 2011; San Andreas Fault, forthcoming. **Address:** 252 Annandale Rd., Pasadena, CA 91105, U.S.A.

STIRT, Joseph A. American (born United States), b. 1948. **Genres:** Medicine/Health, Plays/Screenplays. **Career:** University of California, Medical School, assistant professor of anesthesiology, 1980-83; University of California Hospital, medical director, 1980-83, Outpatient Surgical Unit, director, 1980-83; University of Virginia Medical School, assistant professor of anesthesiology, 1983-88, associate professor of anesthesiology and neurosurgery, 1988-95, associate professor of neurological surgery, 1990-95; University of Southern California School of Medicine, clinical associate professor of anesthesiology, 1996-2001; Richmond Community Hospital, staff anesthesiologist, 2002-; Central District of Virginia, medical examiner, 2009-. Writer. **Publications:** (With R.J. Sperry and D.J. Stone) Manual of Neuroanesthesia, 1989; Baby, 1992. **Address:** 2809 Magnolia Dr., Charlottesville, VA 22901, U.S.A. **Online address:** info@anesthesiologyexpert.com

STIVALE, Charles J. American (born United States), b. 1949. **Genres:** Literary Criticism And History, Language/Linguistics, Cultural/Ethnic Topics, Philosophy, Translations. **Career:** Western Michigan University, instructor, 1980-81; Council on International Educational Exchange, Cooperative Study Center, resident director, 1981-82; Franklin and Marshall College, assistant professor of French, 1982-86; Tulane University, assistant professor of French, 1986-90; Wayne State University, Department of Classical and Modern Languages, Literatures, and Cultures, associate professor of French, 1990-96, professor, 1996-2005, chairman, 1996-2002, distinguished professor of French, 2005-, Department of Art and Art History, interim chair, 2002-03. Writer. **Publications:** Oeuvre de Sentiment, Oeuvre de Combat: La Trilogie de Jules Valles, 1988; La Temporalité Romanesque Chez Stendhal: L'échafaudage de la Bâtisse, 1989; (trans. with M. Lester) G. Deleuze, The Logic of Sense, 1990; The Art of Rupture: Narrative Desire and Duplicity in the Tales of Guy de Maupassant, 1994; (trans.) L'Abecedaire de Gilles Deleuze, 1995; The Two-Fold Thought of Deleuze and Guattari: Intersections and Animations, 1998; Disenchanting Les Bons Temps: Identity and Authenticity in Cajun Music and Dance, 2003; (ed.) Modern French Literary Studies in the Classroom: Pedagogical Strategies, 2004; (ed.) Gilles Deleuze: Key Concepts, 2005; Gilles Deleuze's ABCs: The Folds of Friendship, 2008; (ed. and trans. with G. Mecchia) F. Berardi, Félix Guattari: Thought, Friendship and Visionary Cartography, 2008; (ed. with E.W. Holland and D.W. Smith) Gilles Deleuze: Image and Text, 2009. Contributor to periodicals. **Address:** Department of Classical and Modern Languages,, Literatures, and Cultures, Wayne State University, 361 Manoogian Hall, 906 W Warren St., Detroit, MI 48202, U.S.A. **Online address:** ad4928@wayne.edu

STIVENDER, Ed. (Edi Lee Jalan). American (born United States), b. 1946. **Genres:** Theology/Religion, Biography. **Career:** Writer. **Publications:** Raised Catholic (Can You Tell?), 1992; Still Catholic after All These Fears, 1995. **Address:** 26616 Willowmere Dr., Ste. E-35, Millsboro, DE 19966, U.S.A. **Online address:** storyclan@aol.com

ST. JAMES, Lyn. American (born United States), b. 1947. **Genres:** How-to Books, Sports/Fitness, Travel/Exploration, Autobiography/Memoirs. **Career:** U.S. Steel Corp., secretary, 1967-69; Mike Roth Sales Corp., secretary, 1969-70; Dynasales, co-owner and vice president, 1970-79; professional race car driver, 1979-2001, retired, 2001; Autodyne, president, 1974-91; Ford Motor Co., race car driver and spokesperson, 1981-96; Lyn St. James Enterprises, owner, 1979-; Women in the Winner's Circle Foundation, founder, 1994-. Writer, motivational speaker and sports commentator. **Publications:** Lyn St. James's Car Owner's Manual for Women, 1984; Ride of Your Life: A Race Car Driver's Journey (memoir), 2002; Oh By the Way... A Letter From My Mother, 2005; (ed.) Only this Morning, You're All Grown Up: An Inspiring Message from a Mother to Her Daughter, 2006. Contributor to periodicals. **Address:** Lyn St. James Enterprises, PO Box 10357, Phoenix, AZ 85064, U.S.A. **Online address:** lsjweb@aol.com

ST. JAMES, Sierra. *See* **RALLISON, Janette.**

STJERNØ, Steinar. Norwegian (born Norway), b. 1945. **Genres:** History, Sociology. **Career:** Norwegian State College of Local Government Administration and Social Work, lecturer, 1971-78, research team leader, 1978-80, department head, 1981-84, associate professor and research team leader, 1983-88, professor, 1987, dean of faculties, 1988-92, associate professor, 1992-94, professor, 2002-; Norwegian Research Council, National Research Programme on Immigration, Migration and Ethnic Minorities, leader, 1991-95; Oslo University College, rector, 1994-2000, professor, 2002-; Evaluation of Research on Norwegian Social Welfare Agencies, project leader, 1996-97; National Research Program on Welfare, Family and Adolescence, leader, 1999-2004. Writer, political scientist and researcher. **Publications:** Solidarity in Europe: The History of an Idea, 2005; (with K. Halvorsen) Work, Oil, and Welfare: The Welfare State in Norway, 2008; (contrib.) Culture and Welfare State: Values and Social Policy in Comparative Perspective, 2008. IN NORWEGIAN: (ed.) Velferd eller Nød?: Helse-og sosialpolitikk i 80-åra, 1982; Den moderne fattigdommen: Om økonomisk knapphet og ydmykelse i 1980-åra, 1985; (with A. Marie and L.I. Terum) Et bedre sosialkontor!: Organisasjonsutvikling for klienter og ansatte, 1988; Mellom kirke og kapital: Tysk velferdspolitikk, med sideblikk til britisk, svensk og norsk, 1995. **Address:** Oslo University College, Pb 4 St. Olavs plass, Oslo, 0130, Norway. **Online address:** steinar.stjerno@sam.hio.no

ST. JOHN, Bob J. American (born United States), b. 1937. **Genres:** Sports/Fitness, Biography, Essays, Novels, Picture/Board Books, Young Adult Fiction, History, Autobiography/Memoirs, Autobiography/Memoirs. **Career:** Dallas Morning News, sports columnist and writer, 1960-77, general columnist, 1977-2000; El Centro College, creative writing instructor, lecturer on creative writing. **Publications:** We Love You Cowboys, 1972; (with S. Blair and R. Staubach) Staubach: First Down, Lifetime to Go (biography), 1974; The Dallas Cowboys (picturebook), 1974; On Down the Road: The World of the Rodeo Cowboy, 1977; The Man Inside... Landry (biography), 1979; Sketches in His Own Key (collected columns), 1981; Tex! The Man Who Built the Dallas Cowboys (biography), 1988; While the Music Lasts (collected columns), 1988; The Landry Legend: Grace Under Pressure (biography), 1989; South Padre: The Island and Its People, 1991; Heart of a Lion: The Wild and Woolly Life of Bobby Layne (biography), 1991; Landry: The Legend and the Legacy, 2000; Texas Sports Writers: The Wild and Wacky Years, 2001; Postscripts in a Rearview Mirror, 2003; Never Just a Game: Tex Schramm, 2006. NOVEL: The End of Autumn, 1985. Contributor to periodicals. **Address:** 800 Sherbrook Dr., Richardson, TX 75080-3014, U.S.A.

ST. JOHN, David. American (born United States), b. 1949. **Genres:** Poetry, Essays. **Career:** The University of Iowa, Iowa Writers' Workshop, teaching and writing fellow, 1973-74; Oberlin College, assistant professor of English, 1975-77; Johns Hopkins University, assistant professor, 1977-81, associate professor of writing seminars, 1981-87; University of Southern California, Department of English, professor, 1987-, director of creative writing, 1994-2001, director of Ph.D. program in literature and creative writing, 2003-06; The Antioch Review, editor, 1996-; Washington University, Hurst professor in creative writing, 2005; Bucknell University, West Branch, contributing editor, 2005-; PEN, Emerging Voices Program, Mentor, 2007; University of Cincinnati, Elliston chair, 2007. **Publications:** POETRY: (contrib.) Wright a Profile, 1979; Hush, 1976; The Shore, 1980; The Man in the Yellow Gloves: A Poem, 1984; No Heaven, 1985; Terraces of Rain, 1991; Study for the World's Body: New and Selected Poems, 1994; Watchfire, 1994; The Red Leaves of Night, 1999; In the Pines: Lost Poems, 1972-1997, 1998; Prism, 2002; The Face: A Novella in Verse, 2004; (ed.) Pushcart, 2006; Auroras, 2012. OTHER: Where the Angels Come toward Us: Selected Essays, Reviews and Interviews, 1995; (afterword) Selected Levis, 2000; (ed. with C. Swensen) American Hybrid: A Norton Anthology of New Poetry, 2009. Contributor of articles to periodicals. **Address:** Department of English, University of Southern California, Rm. THH 431, University Pk., Los Angeles, CA 90089, U.S.A. **Online address:** dstjohn@usc.edu

ST. JOHN, Ronald Bruce. American (born United States), b. 1943. **Genres:** International Relations/Current Affairs. **Career:** Writer, 1969-; Caterpillar Inc., marketing manager, 1973-2001; Bradley University, affiliate professor, 1982-2006. **Publications:** Qaddafi's World Design: Libyan Foreign Policy, 1969-1987, 1987; The Foreign Policy of Peru, 1992; The Land Boundaries of Indochina: Cambodia, Laos and Vietnam, 1998; La Politica Exterior del Peru, 1999; The Ecuador-Peru Boundary Dispute, 1999; Libya and the United States: Two Centuries of Strife, 2002; Historical Dictionary of Libya, 4th ed., 2006; Revolution, Reform and Regionalism in Southeast Asia: Cambodia, Laos and Vietnam, 2006; Libya: From Colony to Independence, 2008; Toledo's Peru: Vision and Reality, 2010; Libya: Continuity and Change, 2011; Libya: From Colony to Revolution, 2011. Contributor to periodicals. **Address:** 10121 Elena Dr. NE, Albuquerque, NM 87122, U.S.A. **Online address:** rbstjohn@comcast.net

ST. JOHN, Warren. American (born United States) **Genres:** Sports/Fitness, Social Sciences, Biography. **Career:** New York Times, journalist. **Publications:** Rammer Jammer Yellow Hammer: A Journey into the Heart of Fan Mania, 2004; Outcasts United: A Refugee Team, An American Town, 2009. **Address:** New York Times, 229 W 43rd St., New York, NY 10036, U.S.A. **Online address:** stjohn@nytimes.com

STOCK, Gregory. American (born United States) **Genres:** Essays, Biology, Sciences, History, Philosophy. **Career:** University of California, School of Public Health, Program on Science, Technology and Society, director, senior fellow; Bioagenda Institute, associate director; biophysicist; ethicist; speaker. Writer. **Publications:** The Book of Questions, 1987; The Kids' Book of Questions, 1988; Love & Sex: The Book of Questions, 1989; The Book of Questions: Business, Politics, and Ethics, 1991; Metaman: The Merging of Humans and Machines into a Global Superorganism, 1993; (ed. with J. Campbell) Engineering the Human Germline: An Exploration of the Science and Ethics of Altering the Genes We Pass to Our Children, 2000; Redesigning

Humans: Our Inevitable Genetic Future, 2002; Redesigning Humans: Choosing Our Genes, 2003. Contributor to journals and periodicals. **Address:** University of California, 760 Westwood Blvd., PO Box 951567, Los Angeles, CA 90095, U.S.A. **Online address:** gstock@ess.ucla.edu

STOCKBRIDGE, Sara Jane. British (born England), b. 1966?. **Genres:** Novels. **Career:** Writer and model. **Publications:** Grace Hammer: A Novel of the Victorian Underworld, 2009 as Hammer: A Novel of the Victorian Underworld, 2009 as The Fortunes of Grace Hammer: A Novel of the Victorian Underworld, 2010. Contributor to periodicals. **Address:** Free Word, 60 Farringdon Rd., London, GL EC1R 3GA, England.

STOCKEL, H. Henrietta. American (born United States), b. 1938. **Genres:** Anthropology/Ethnology, Women's Studies And Issues, History, Education, Cultural/Ethnic Topics, Biography. **Career:** University of New Mexico, School of Medicine Library, special projects bibliographer; Cochise College, associate faculty and researcher; Albuquerque Indian Center, co-founder and executive director. Writer. **Publications:** (With B. Perrone and V. Krueger) Medicine Women, Curanderas, and Women Doctors, 1989; Women of the Apache Nation: Voices of Truth, 1991; Survival of the Spirit: Chiricahua Apaches in Captivity, 1993; The Lightning Stick: Arrows, Wounds, and Indian Legends, 1995; (with R.S. Ove) Geronimo's Kids, 1997; (ed.) LaDonna Harris: A Comanche Life, 2000; Chiricahua Apache Women and Children: Safekeepers of the Heritage, 2000; On the Bloody Road to Jesus: Christianity and the Chiricahua Apaches, 2004; Shame & Endurance: The Untold Story of the Chiricahua Apache Prisoners of War, 2004; (with W. Billingslea) Lost Cultures: The Aztecs, 2007; Salvation through Slavery: Chiricahua Apaches and Priests on the Spanish Colonial Frontier, 2008; (with M.D. Kelley) Drumbeats from Mescalero: Conversations with Apache Elders, Warriors, and Horseholders, 2011. Contributor of articles to periodicals. **Address:** PO Box 698, Hereford, AZ 85615-0698, U.S.A. **Online address:** stockelh@theriver.com

STOCKENBERG, Antoinette. Also writes as Antoinette Hardy, Antoinette Hale. American (born United States), b. 1943?. **Genres:** Novels, Romance/Historical, Horror. **Career:** Writer. **Publications:** (As Antoinette Hale) Trouble in Paradise, 1984; Fit Be Loved, 1984; (as Antoinette Hardy) Fit to Be Loved, 1984; (as Antoinette Hale) Island of Desire, 1985; The Challenge and the Glory, 1987; Emily's Ghost, 1992; Beloved, 1993; Embers, 1995; Time after Time, 1995; Beyond Midnight, 1996; Dream a Little Dream, 1998; A Charmed Place, 1998; Keepsake, 1999; Safe Harbor, 2000; Tidewater, 2001; Sand Castles, 2002; A Month at the Shore, 2003. **Address:** PO Box 735, Newport, RI 02840-0007, U.S.A. **Online address:** antoinet@cox.net

STOCKLER, Bruce. American (born United States), b. 1960?. **Genres:** Humor/Satire, Biography, Autobiography/Memoirs, Medicine/Health. **Career:** Media-relations consultant, humorist and writer. **Publications:** I Sleep at Red Lights: A True Story of Life after Triplets, 2003. Contributor to periodicals. **Address:** c/o Author Mail, St. Martin's Press, 175 5th Ave., New York, NY 10010, U.S.A.

STOCKLEY, Grif. American (born United States), b. 1944. **Genres:** Mystery/Crime/Suspense, History, Social Sciences, Young Adult Non-fiction. **Career:** Center for Arkansas Legal Services, attorney, 1972-; University of Arkansas, adjunct professor, 1987-92, visiting professor of law; Disability Rights Center, staff, 2002; American Civil Liberties Union, staff; Butler Center for Arkansas Studies, Dee Brown Fellow, 2006-; Disability Rights Center, attorney; American Civil Liberties Union, attorney. Writer. **Publications:** Expert Testimony, 1991; Probable Cause: A Novel, 1992; Religious Conviction, 1994; Illegal Motion: A Gideon Page Mystery, 1995; Blind Judgment: A Gideon Page Novel, 1997; Blood in Their Eyes: The Elaine Race Massacres of 1919, 2001; Salted with Fire, 2001; Daisy Bates: Civil Rights Crusader from Arkansas, 2005; Race Relations in the Natural State, 2007; Ruled by Race: Black/White Relations in Arkansas from Slavery to the Present, 2009. Contributor to periodicals. **Address:** Butler Center for Arkansas Studies, 401 President Clinton Ave., Little Rock, AR 72201, U.S.A. **Online address:** grif@aristotle.net

STOCKWIN, J. A. A. British (born England), b. 1935. **Genres:** Area Studies, Politics/Government, Biography, Translations. **Career:** Australian National University, lecturer, 1964-66, senior lecturer, 1966-72, reader in political science, 1972-81; Australian Department of Foreign Affairs, academic-in-residence, 1975-76; University of Oxford, Nissan Institute of Japanese Studies,

director, 1982-2003, Nissan Professor of Modern Japanese Studies, 1982-2003, St. Antony's College, emeritus fellow, 2003-. Writer. **Publications:** The Japanese Socialist Party and Neutralism: A Study of a Political Party and its Foreign Policy, 1968; (ed.) Japan and Australia in the Seventies, 1972; Japan: Divided Politics in a Growth Economy, 1975, 3rd ed. as Governing Japan: Divided Politics in a Growth Economy, 1999, 4th ed. as Governing Japan: Divided Politics in a Resurgent Economy, 2008; (co-author) Dynamic and Immobilist Politics in Japan, 1988; (trans.) Junji Banno, The Establishment of the Japanese Constitutional System, 1992; The Story of Tim, 1993; Dictionary of the Modern Politics of Japan, 2003; Collected Writings of J.A.A. Stockwin, vol. I, 2004; Thirty-Odd Feet below Belgium: An Affair of Letters in the Great War, 1915-1916, 2005, 2nd ed. 2009; Japanese Foriegn Policy and Understanding Japanese Politics, 2012. Contributor to journals. **Address:** Nissan Institute of Japanese Studies, Oxford University, 27 Winchester Rd., Oxford, OX OX2 6NA, England. **Online address:** arthur.stockwin@nissan.ox.ac.uk

STODDARD, Robert H. American (born United States), b. 1928. **Genres:** Geography, Theology/Religion, Education, Sciences. **Career:** Woodstock School, teacher, 1952-58; Nebraska Wesleyan University, instructor, assistant professor, 1961-67; University of Nebraska, assistant professor, professor, 1967-2002, professor emeritus, 2002-; Tribhuvan University, visiting professor, 1975-76; University of Colombo, visiting professor, 1986-. Writer. **Publications:** Planning College Geography Facilities: Guidelines for Space and Equipment, 1973; Field Techniques and Research Methods in Geography, 1982; (with D.J. Wishart and B.W. Blouet) Human Geography: People, Places, and Cultures, 1986, 2nd ed., 1989; (ed. with A. Morinis) Sacred Places, Sacred Spaces: The Geography of Pilgrimages, 1997. Contributor to books and periodicals. **Address:** Department of Geography, University of Nebraska, 618 Hardin Hall, 3310 Holdrege St., Lincoln, NE 68583-6996, U.S.A. **Online address:** rstoddard1@unl.edu

STODDART, Brian. Malaysian/New Zealander (born New Zealand), b. 1946. **Genres:** Sports/Fitness. **Career:** University of Western Australia, senior tutor in history, 1975-76; Curtin University, lecturer in social science, 1977-80; University of Canberra, lecturer, senior lecturer in sports studies, 1981-90, dean of communication, 1991-95; ADORNA-RMIT, academic director, 1995-; University of New England. pro vice-chancellor; La Trobe University, interim vice-chancellor, 2005-06, professor, 2006, now professor emeritus. Writer. **Publications:** (With R. Sissons) Cricket and Empire, 1984; Saturday Afternoon Fever: Sport in the Australian Culture, 1986; (with C. Tatz) The Royal Sydney Golf Club: The First Hundred Years, 1993; (ed. with W. Vamplew) Sport in Australia, 1994; (ed. with H. Beckles) Liberation Cricket, 1995; (co-ed.) The Oxford Companion to Australian Cricket, 1996; (ed. with K.A.P. Sandiford) The Imperial Game: Cricket, Culture, and Society, 1998; (ed.) Sport in the Australian Culture Revisited: Saturday Afternoon Fever II, 2006; (ed. with W. Vamplew) Sport in Australia: A Social History, 2008. **Address:** La Trobe University, Melbourne, VI 3086, Australia. **Online address:** bstoddar@metz.une.edu.au

STODGHILL, Ron. American (born United States) **Genres:** Mystery/Crime/Suspense, Autobiography/Memoirs. **Career:** Business Week Magazine, correspondent, 1989-97, staff editor, 1993-97; Time Magazine, Midwest bureau chief, senior writer, 1997-2002; Savoy Magazine/Vanguarde Media, editor-in-chief, 2002-03; Fortune Small Business, senior editor, 2004-06; New York Times, staff writer, 2006-08; The Charlotte Observer, columnist, 2010-, Magazine Division, editorial director. **Publications:** (With K. Mfume) No Free Ride: From the Mean Streets to the Mainstream, 1996; Redbone: Money, Malice, and Murder in Atlanta, 2007. Works appear in anthologies. **Address:** The Charlotte Observer, 600 S Tryon St., Charlotte, NC 28202, U.S.A. **Online address:** ronstodghill@aol.com

STOEHR, Shelley. American (born United States), b. 1969. **Genres:** Novels, Young Adult Fiction. **Career:** Writer. **Publications:** Crosses, 1991, rev. ed., 2003; Weird on the Outside, 1995; Wannabe, 1997; Tomorrow Wendy: A Love Story, 1998, rev. ed., 2003; Lost and Found (anthology), 2000; Girl Broken, 2005; Let Her Cry, 2007; Somebody's Daughter, 2011. Birth Mother, forthcoming. Contributor to books and periodicals. **Address:** Delacorte Press Publicity, 1745 Broadway, New York, NY 10019, U.S.A. **Online address:** christiancarthy@sbcglobal.net

STOFF, David M. American (born United States), b. 1945?. **Genres:** Medicine/Health, Sciences. **Career:** City University of New York, Hunter College, adjunct assistant professor of psychology, 1970-72; National Institute of Mental Health, postdoctoral fellow, 1972-73, Perpetrators of Violence Research Program, Division of Epidemiology and Services Research, chief, research fellow, 1992-94, Training and Health Disparities Programs, assistant director, Division of Clinical and Treatment Research, Clinical Neuroscience Research Program, chief, 1994-97, Division of Mental Disorders, Behavioral Research, and AIDS, Developmental Disorders Research Program, chief, 1997-2000, HIV Neuropsychiatry Research Program, chief, 1997-; St. Elizabeth's Hospital, Laboratory of Clinical Psychopharmacology, staff fellow, 1973-81, Laboratory of Behavioral Pharmacology, unit chief, 1978-81; University of Maryland, adjunct assistant professor, 1977-78, adjunct professor, 1997-; University of Chicago, Illinois State Psychiatric Institute, assistant professor of psychiatry, 1981-82; Eastern Pennsylvania Psychiatric Institute, Medical College of Pennsylvania, Department of Psychiatry, assistant professor, 1982-85, associate professor of psychiatry and director of behavioral pharmacology, 1985-92; Villanova University, adjunct assistant professor, 1987-88; LaSalle University, adjunct assistant professor, 1991-92; Montgomery Community College, adjunct assistant professor, 1996-97. **Publications:** (Co-author) Mental Health Care for People Living with or Affected by HIV/AIDS: A Practical Guide, 1999. EDITOR: (with R.B. Cairns and contrib.) Aggression and Violence: Neurobiological, Biosocial, and Genetic Perspectives, 1996; (with J. Breiling and J.D. Maser) Handbook of Antisocial Behavior, 1997; (with J.J. Mann) Neurobiology of Suicide: From the Bench to the Clinic, 1997; (with E.J. Susman) Developmental Psychobiology of Aggression, 2005. Contributor to books and journals. **Address:** Division of Mental Disorders, National Institute of Mental Health, Rm. 6210, MSC 9619, 6001 Executive Blvd., Bethesda, MD 20892-9619, U.S.A. **Online address:** dstoff@nih.gov

STOKER, Dacre. American/Canadian (born Canada), b. 1958. **Genres:** Novels. **Career:** Aiken Land Conservancy, executive director. Writer. **Publications:** (With I. Holt) Dracula: The Un-Dead, 2009. **Address:** Aiken, SC , U.S.A. **Online address:** dacre@draculatheun-dead.com

STOKER, Gerry. British (born England), b. 1955?. **Genres:** Young Adult Non-fiction. **Career:** Leicester Polytechnic, faculty; University of Southampton School of Social Sciences, faculty; Local Governance Programme research project, program director, 1992-97; Manchester University, professor, 2000-; New Local Government Network, founding chair, trustee. Writer. **Publications:** NONFICTION: The Politics of Local Government, 1988, 2nd ed., 1991; (ed. with J. Stewart and contrib.) The Future of Local Government, 1989; (with T. Brindley and Y. Rydin) Remaking Planning: The Politics of Urban Change in the Thatcher Years, 1989, 2nd ed., 1996; (ed. with R. Batley and contrib.) Local Government in Europe: Trends and Development, 1991; (with S. Young) Cities in the 1990s, 1993; (with S. Leach, D. Wilson and C. Game) Local Government in the United Kingdom, 1994; (ed. with J. Stewart) Local Government in the 1990s, 1995; (ed. with D. Marsh) Theory and Methods in Political Science, 1995, 2nd ed., 2002; (ed. with D. Lorrain and contrib.) La Privatisation Des Services Urbains En Europe, 1995, trans. as The Privatisation of Urban Services in Europe, 1997; (ed. with D. Judge and H. Wolman and contrib.) Theories of Urban Politics, 1995; (ed. with D. King) Rethinking Local Democracy, 1996; More Than the Flower Show: Elected Mayors and Democracy, 1997; (ed.) The New Management of British Local Governance, 1999; Social Capital and Urban Governance: A Contextualized Approach, 1999; Proportional Representation and Local Government: Lessons from Europe, 2000; The New Politics of British Local Governance, 2000; (with W. Miller and M. Dickson) Models of Local Governance: Public Opinion and Political Theory in Britain, 2000; A New Account? Choices in Local Government Finance, 2001; (with Perri, D. Leat and K. Setzler) Holistic Governance, 2002; (with R. Aldridge) Advancing a New Public Service Ethos, 2002; Money Talks: Creating a Dialogue between Taxpayers and Local Government, 2002; Council Tax Consultation: Guidelines for Local Authorities, 2002; Transforming Local Governance: From Thatcherism to New Labour, 2004; (ed. with D. Wilson and contrib.) British Local Government into the 21st Century, 2004; Why Politics Matters: Making Democracy Work, 2006; (ed. with T. Brannan and P. John and contrib.) Re-Energizing Citizenship: Strategies for Civil Renewal, 2007; (ed. with J. Pierre and B. G. Peters) Debating Institutionalism, 2008; (with V. Chhotray) Governance Theory and Practice: A Cross-Disciplinary Approach, 2008. Contributor to books. **Address:** University of Southampton, University Rd., Southampton, SO17 1BJ, England. **Online address:** g.stoker@soton.ac.uk

STOKER, R. Bryan. American (born United States), b. 1962. **Genres:** Money/Finance, Business/Trade/Industry, Economics. **Career:** U.S. Department of Defense, principal engineer, 1984-; Lifestyle Publishing, founder and president, 1993-. Writer. **Publications:** Financial Freedom: A Wealth Manual for the Middle Class, 1994; Growth and Income: How to Build a Mutual Fund Money Machine, 1999; Money Secrets, 2003; The Car Book, 2003; Money Secrets Personal Wealth Program, 2004. **Address:** Lifestyle Publishing, 6685 Slacks Rd., Eldersburg, MD 21784-6245, U.S.A. **Online address:** rbstoker@netzero.net

STOKES, Donald W. American (born United States), b. 1947. **Genres:** Sciences, Biology, Environmental Sciences/Ecology. **Career:** Writer. **Publications:** Guide to Nature in Winter: Northeast and North Central North America, 1976; Guide to the Behavior of Common Birds, 1979; The Natural History of Wild Shrubs and Vines, 1981; A Guide to Observing Insect Lives, 1983; A Guide to Enjoying Wildflowers, 1985; The Hummingbird Book, 1986; The Bird Feeder Book, 1987. WITH LILLIAN STOKES: A Guide to Bird Behavior, vol. I, 1978, vol. II, 1983, vol. III, 1989; A Guide to Enjoying Wildflowers, 1985; A Guide to Animal Tracking and Behavior, 1986; The Bird Feeder Book: An Easy Guide to Attracting, Identifying and Understanding Your Feeder Birds, 1987; The Hummingbird Book, 1989; (ed.) Guide to Amphibians and Reptiles, 1990; The Complete Birdhouse Book, 1990; Bluebird Book: The Complete Guide to Attracting Bluebirds, 1991; The Butterfly Book: An Easy Guide to Butterfly Gardening, Identification and Behavior, 1991; Wildflower Book: East of the Rockies, 1992; Wildflower Book: From the Rockies West, 1993; Stokes Beginner's Guide to Birds, 1996; Stokes Field Guide to Birds, Eastern Region, 1996; Western Region, 1996; (with J.L. Brown) Stokes Purple Martin Book: The Complete Guide to Attracting and Housing Purple Martins, 1997; Stokes Bird Gardening Book: The Complete Guide to Creating a Bird-Friendly Habitat in Your Backyard, 1998; Stokes Oriole Book: The Complete Guide to Attracting, Identifying and Enjoying Oriole, 2000; Stokes Beginner's Guide to Butterflies, 2001; Stokes Beginner's Guide to Shorebirds, 2001; (with K. Williams and R. Mies) Stokes Beginner's Guide to Bats, 2002; Stokes Beginner's Guide to Bird Feeding, 2002; Stokes Beginner's Guide to Hummingbirds, 2002; (with B. Nikula and J. Sones) Stokes Beginner's Guide to Dragonflies and Damselflies, 2002; Stokes Backyard Bird Book: The Complete Guide to Attracting, Identifying and Understanding the Birds in Your Backyard: A Treasury of The Best from Donald and Lillian Stokes, 2003; Stokes Field Guide to Warbler, 2004; The Stokes Field Guide to the Birds of North America, 2010. Contributor to periodicals. **Address:** c/o Author Mail, Little, Brown & Co., 1271 Ave. of the Americas, New York, NY 10020, U.S.A.

STOKES, Gale. American (born United States), b. 1933. **Genres:** History, Politics/Government. **Career:** Rice University, instructor, 1968, chair of department, 1980-82, 1997-2000, Mary Gibbs Jones professor of history, 1997-2005, Mary Gibbs Jones professor emeritus of history, 2005-, dean of humanities, 2000-03; George Washington University, Institute for Sino Soviet Studies, fellow, 1991; American Association for the Advancement of Slavic Studies, president, 2003. Writer. **Publications:** Legitimacy through Liberalism: Vladimir Jovanovic and the Transformation of Serbian Politics, 1975; (ed.) Nationalism in the Balkans: An Annotated Bibliography, 1984; (co-ed. with B. Kiraly) War, Insurrection, and the Eastern Crisis, 1875-78, 1985; Politics as Development: The Emergence of Political Parties in Nineteenth-Century Serbia, 1990; From Stalinism to Pluralism: A Documentary History of Eastern Europe since 1945, 1991, 2nd ed., 1995; The Walls Came Tumbling Down: The Collapse of Communism in Eastern Europe, 1993, 2nd ed., 2012; Three Eras of Political Change in Eastern Europe, 1997; The West Transformed: A History of Western Civilization, 2000; Yugoslavia: Oblique Insights and Observations, 2008. Contributor to journals. **Address:** Rice University, 6100 Main St., PO Box 1892, Houston, TX 77251, U.S.A. **Online address:** gstokes@rice.edu

STOKES, Susan C. American (born United States), b. 1959?. **Genres:** Politics/Government, History. **Career:** University of Washington, assistant professor, 1988-91; University of Chicago, assistant professor, 1991-96, associate professor, 1996-2000, professor, 2000-05, director of the Chicago Center on Democracy, 1995-2005; Yale University, John S. Saden Professor of Political Science and director of the Yale Program on Democracy, 2005-. Writer. **Publications:** Cultures in Conflict: Social Movements and the State in Peru, 1995; (ed. with A. Przeworski and B. Manin) Democracy, Accountability and Representation, 1999; (ed.) Public Support for Market Reforms in New Democracies, 2001; Mandates and Democracy: Neoliberalism by Surprise in Latin America, 2001; Democracia Local: clientelismo, capital social e innovacion politica en la Argentina, 2005; (with M.R. Cleary) Democracy and the Culture of Skepticism: Political Trust in Argentina and Mexico, 2006 (ed. with C. Boix) The Oxford Handbook of Comparative Politics, 2007. Contributor to periodicals. **Address:** Department of Political Science, Yale University, 124 Prospect St., PO Box 208301, New Haven, CT 06520-8301, U.S.A. **Online address:** susan.stokes@yale.edu

STOKOE, E(dward) G(eorge). Also writes as John Stark, Charles Clos, Paul Daner, Ross Dexter, Brian Peters. British (born England), b. 1919?. **Genres:** Westerns/Adventure, Young Adult Fiction, Children's Fiction, Novels, Literary Criticism And History. **Career:** North Eastern Electricity Board, employee, 1936-84, welfare officer, 1960-84. Writer. **Publications:** Cade, 1954; (as Paul Daner) End of the Trail, 1954; (as Ross Dexter) Carson's Killer, 1955; (as Brian Peters) Starbuck, 1957; Once a Marine, 1957; (as Charles Clos) Call It Experience, 1959; (as John Stark) Marine Commando, 1959; Last of the Napiers, 1960; Death at Sundown, 1961; Once an Outlaw, 1961; Once a Marshal, 1961; Showdown at Mesa, 1963; Lower the Ramps: Experiences with the 43rd Royal Marine Commando in Yugoslavia, 1974; Greed is the Spur, 1988; The Judas Trail, 1988; A Nest of Rattlers, 1990. **Address:** 474 Station Rd. N, Wallsend, TW NE28 8NF, England.

STOKOE, James. Canadian (born Canada), b. 1985. **Genres:** Literary Criticism And History, Humor/Satire, Food And Wine. **Career:** Comic book writer and artist. **Publications:** Wonton Soup: Space Trucker Opera, 2007. Contributor to magazines. **Address:** U.S.A. **Online address:** spikes@redcarp.com

STOLL, Steven. American (born United States), b. 1966. **Genres:** History, Economics. **Career:** Yale University, lecturer, 1994-96, assistant professor, 1996-2002, associate professor, 2002-08; Fordham University, associate professor of history, 2008-; Rural America Institute for the Humanities and Rural America Arts Partnership, consultant. Writer. **Publications:** The Fruits of Natural Advantage: Making the Industrial Countryside in California, 1998; Larding the Lean Earth: Soil and Society in Nineteenth-Century America, 2002; U.S. Environmentalism since 1945: A Brief History with Documents, 2006; The Great Delusion: A Mad Inventor, Death in the Tropics and the Utopian Origins of Economic Growth, 2008. Contributor to books and periodicals. **Address:** Garamond Agency Inc., 12 Horton St., Newburyport, MA 01950, U.S.A. **Online address:** stoll@fordham.edu

STOLLER, Debbie. American (born United States) **Genres:** Art/Art History, How-to Books. **Career:** Bust (magazine), co-owner, co-founder and editor-in-chief, 1993. **Publications:** The Bust Guide to the New Girl Order, 1999; Stitch n Bitch: The Knitters Handbook, 2003; Happy Hooker: Stitch n Bitch Crochet, 2006; Son of Stitch n Bitch: 45 Projects to Knit & Crochet for Men, 2007; Stitch n Bitch Superstar Knitting: Go Beyond the Basics, 2010; Bust DIY Guide to Life, 2011. **Address:** c/o Author Mail, Workman Publishing, 708 Broadway, New York, NY 10003, U.S.A. **Online address:** stitchnbitch@bust.com

STOLLMAN, Arveh Lev. American/Canadian (born Canada), b. 1954?. **Genres:** Novels, Literary Criticism And History, Young Adult Fiction. **Career:** Mount Sinai Medical Center, neuroradiologist. Writer. **Publications:** The Far Euphrates, 1997; The Illuminated Soul, 2002; The Dialogues of Time and Entropy, 2003. **Address:** The Susan Golomb Literary Agency, 875 Ave. of the Americas, Ste. 2302, New York, NY 10001, U.S.A.

STOLTENBERG, John (Vincent). American (born United States), b. 1944. **Genres:** Human Relations/Parenting, Women's Studies And Issues, Essays, Sex, Politics/Government. **Career:** The Open Theatre, administrative director and writer-in-residence, 1971-74; Essence, managing editor, 1980-85; Working Woman, consulting and project development editor, 1985-87; Lear's, managing editor, 1988-91; New School of Social Research, instructor, 1991; On the Issues Magazine, special projects advisor, 1993-94, executive editor and editorial director, 1994-96; Golf Digest Woman, managing editor, 1999; Men Can Stop Rape Inc., creative director, 2000-10; AARP The Magazine, managing editor, 2003-; DC Rape Crisis Center, communications consultant, 2010-. **Publications:** Refusing to Be a Man: Essays on Sex and Justice, 1989, rev. ed., 2000; The End of Manhood: A Book for Men of Conscience, 1993, 2nd ed. as End of Manhood: Parables on Sex and Selfhood, 1999; What Makes Pornography Sexy?, 1994. Works appear in anthologies. Contributor to periodicals. **Address:** Elaine Markson Literary Agency Inc., 44 Greenwich Ave., New York, NY 10011-8347, U.S.A.

STOLTZFUS, Ben. American (born United States), b. 1927. **Genres:** Novels, Literary Criticism And History, Translations. **Career:** Smith College, instructor in French, 1958-60; University of California, assistant professor, 1960-65, associate professor, 1965-66, professor, 1967-97, professor emeritus of French, comparative literature, and creative writing, 1997-, Division of Humanities, vice chair, 1962, Humanities Interdisciplinary Program, chair, 1973-76, Education Abroad Program, chair, 1976-78. Writer. **Publications:** Alain Robbe-Grillet and the New French Novel, 1964; Georges Chenneviere et l'unanimisme, 1964; The Eye of the Needle, 1967; Gide's Eagles, 1969; Black Lazarus, 1972; Gide and Hemingway: Rebels against God, 1978; Alain Robbe-Grillet: The Body of the Text, 1985; Postmodern Poetics: Nouveau Roman and Innovative Fiction, 1987; Alain Robbe-Grillet: Life, Work, and Criticism, 1987; Red, White, and Blue, 1989; (trans. and contrib.) A. Robbe-Grillet and R. Magritte, Belle Captive, 1995; Lacan and Literature: Purloined Pretexts, 1996; Valley of Roses, 2003; (trans. and contrib.) The Target: Alain Robbe-Grillet, Jasper Johns, 2006; Hemingway and French Writers, 2010. Contributor to journals and magazines. **Address:** University of California, 2401 Humanities & Social Sciences Bldg., 900 University Ave., Riverside, CA 92521, U.S.A. **Online address:** benstoltzfus@tstonramp.com

STOLZ, Joëlle. Austrian/French (born France), b. 1952?. **Genres:** Novels, Politics/Government, Children's Fiction. **Career:** Radio France Internationale, journalist; Le Monde, Vienna correspondent. **Publications:** Ombres de Ghadamès, 2004. Contributor to books and periodicals. **Address:** c/o Author Mail, Delacorte Press, 1745 Broadway, New York, NY 10019, U.S.A.

STOLZ, Karen. See Obituaries.

STOMFAY-STITZ, Aline M. American (born United States) **Genres:** Education, Young Adult Non-fiction, Social Sciences. **Career:** College of Saint Scholastica, assistant professor of education, 1984-85; St. Leo College, assistant professor of education, 1985-87; Nicholls State University, assistant professor of education, 1989-91; Christopher Newport University, associate professor of education, 1991-. Writer. **Publications:** Peace Education in America, 1828-1990: A Sourcebook for Education and Research, 1993; Nurturing a Non-Violent Child, forthcoming. Works appear in anthologies. Contributor to journals. **Address:** The Scarecrow Press Inc., 4501 Forbes Blvd., Ste. 200, Lanham, MD 20706, U.S.A.

STONE, Alan A. American (born United States), b. 1929. **Genres:** Law, Psychiatry, Film. **Career:** Harvard University, associate professor of medical school, 1954-66, instructor, 1961-65, assistant professor, 1966-69, associate professor, 1969-72, lecturer on law, 1969-, Faculties of Law and Medicine, professor of law and psychiatry, 1972-, Touroff-Glueck professor of law and psychiatry, 1982-; pediatric intern, 1955-56; McLean Hospital, resident in psychiatry, 1956-58, Resident Education, director, 1962-63, associate psychiatrist, 1966-69. Writer. **Publications:** (With G.C. Onque) Longitudinal Studies of Child Personality, 1959; (ed. with S.S. Stone) The Abnormal Personality Through Literature, 1966; (with C.D. Stromberg) Mental Health and Law: A System in Transition, 1975; Law, Psychiatry, and Morality: Essays and Analysis, 1984; Movies and the Moral Adventure of Life, 2007. **Address:** Law School, Harvard University, Hauser 400, 1563 Massachusetts Ave., Cambridge, MA 02138-2903, U.S.A. **Online address:** stone@law.harvard.edu

STONE, Cynthia L. American (born United States), b. 1962. **Genres:** Theology/Religion, History, Literary Criticism And History. **Career:** College of the Holy Cross, associate professor and director of the Latin American and Latino Studies Program. Writer. **Publications:** In Place of Gods and Kings: Authorship and Identity in the Relación de Michoacán, 2004. Contributor to books and periodicals. **Address:** College of the Holy Cross, 1 College St., Worcester, MA 01610-2395, U.S.A. **Online address:** cstone@holycross.edu

STONE, David. See STROUD, Carsten.

STONE, David Lee. (David Grimstone). American/British (born England), b. 1978. **Genres:** Novels. **Career:** Blockbuster Video, clerk, assistant manager, 1999-2001. Novelist. **Publications:** The Ratastrophe Catastrophe, 2003; The Yowler Foul-Up, 2004; The Shadewell Shenanigans, 2005; The Dwellings Debacle, 2006; The Vanquish Vendetta, 2006; The Coldstone Conflict, 2007; The Adventures of Davey Swag, 2008. Contributor to periodicals. **Address:** Hodder Children's Books, 338 Euston Rd., London, GL NW1 3BH, England.

STONE, David R. (David Russell Stone). American (born United States), b. 1968. **Genres:** History, Military/Defense/Arms Control, Humanities. **Career:** Yale University, International Security Studies, post-doctoral fellow, 1997-98; Hamilton College, visiting assistant professor of history, 1998-99; Kansas State University, assistant professor of history, 1999-2002, associate professor of history, 2002-07, professor of history, 2007-08, Pickett professor of military history, 2008-; Center for Advanced Study in the Behavioral Sciences, fellow, 2005-06. Writer. **Publications:** Hammer and Rifle: The Militarization of the Soviet Union, 1926-1933, 2000; A Military History of Russia: From Ivan the Terrible to the War in Chechnya, 2006; (ed.) The Soviet Union at War, 1941-1945, 2010. **Address:** Department of History, Kansas State University, 208 Eisenhower Hall, Manhattan, KS 66506-1002, U.S.A. **Online address:** stone@ksu.edu

STONE, David Russell. See **STONE, David R.**

STONE, Dawna. American (born United States), b. 1969?. **Genres:** Business/Trade/Industry, Economics, Self Help. **Career:** Morgan Stanley and Co., financial analyst, 1991-93; Deloitte Consulting Group, LLP, strategy consultant and manager, 1995-99; PR Nutrition, president and general manager, 1999-2000; Active Sports Network, senior vice president, 2000-01; Marine-Max Inc., chief marketing officer, 2001-03; Her Sports, president, publisher and founder, 2003-; Martha Stewart Living Omnimedia, staff, 2005, vice president of business development, through 2006. Writer and financial consultant. **Publications:** (With M. Dieter) Winning Nice: How to Succeed in Business and Life without Waging War, 2007. Contributor to periodicals. **Address:** Her Sports Corporate Headquarters, 1499 Beach Dr., SE, Ste. B, Saint Petersburg, FL 33701-5623, U.S.A.

STONE, Del. American (born United States), b. 1955. **Genres:** Horror. **Career:** Northwest Florida Daily News, associate editor, deputy managing editor, online editor; Wasted Lands project, writing partner. **Publications:** Roadkill, 1993; December, 1994; Dead Heat, 1996. Contributor of stories to magazine. Works appear in anthologies. **Address:** Northwest Florida Daily News, 200 Racetrack Rd., PO Box 2949, Fort Walton Beach, FL 32547, U.S.A. **Online address:** dels@nwfdailynews.com

STONE, Eric. American (born United States), b. 1952?. **Genres:** Novels, Mystery/Crime/Suspense, Archaeology/Antiquities, Sex, Sports/Fitness, Travel/Exploration, Biography, Novellas/Short Stories, Criminology/True Crime. **Career:** Editor, publisher and photographer. **Publications:** In a Heartbeat, 1996; Wrong Side of the Wall: The Life of Blackie Schwamb, the Greatest Prison Baseball Player of All Time, 2004; The Living Room of the Dead, 2005; Grave Imports, 2007; Flight of the Hornbill, 2008; Shanghaied, 2009. **Address:** c/o Vicky Bijur, Vicky Bijur Literary Agency, 333 W End Ave., Ste. 5B, New York, NY 10023, U.S.A. **Online address:** eric@ericstone.com

STONE, Gerald (Charles). British (born England), b. 1932. **Genres:** History, Language/Linguistics. **Career:** University of Nottingham, lecturer, 1966-71; Cambridge University, assistant director of research, 1971-72; Oxford University, university lecturer, 1972-99, Hertford College, fellow and tutor, 1972-99, emeritus fellow, 1999-. Writer. **Publications:** The Smallest Slavonic Nation: The Sorbs of Lusatia, 1972; (with B. Comrie) The Russian Language since the Revolution, 1978; An Introduction to Polish, 1980, 2nd ed., 1992; (with B. Comrie and M. Polinsky) The Russian Language in the Twentieth Century, 1995; (comp.) Kerluse, 1995; Upper Sorbian-English Dictionary, 2002; Der erste Beitrag zur sorbischen Sprachgeographie, 2003; The Goda Manuscript 1701, 2009. EDITOR: (with D. Worth) The Formation of the Slavonic Literary Languages, 1985; (with intro.) A Dictionarie of the Vulgar Russe Tongue Attributed to Mark Ridley, 1996. **Address:** 6 Lathbury Rd., Oxford, OX OX2 7AU, England. **Online address:** gerald.stone@hertford.ox.ac.uk

STONE, Glenn D(avis). American (born United States), b. 1954. **Genres:** Anthropology/Ethnology, Agriculture/Forestry. **Career:** School of American Research, Weatherhead fellow, 1987-88; Columbia University, assistant professor of anthropology, 1988-93, associate professor of anthropology, 1993-95, professor of anthropology, 1988-95; Washington University, associate professor of anthropology and environmental studies, 1995-2004, professor of anthropology and environmental studies, 2004-; University College London, research fellow, 2001-02. Writer. **Publications:** Settlement Ecology: The Spatial and Social Organization of Kofyar Agriculture, 1996. Contributor to journals. **Address:** Department of Anthropology, Washington University, 332 McMillan Hall, 1 Brookings Dr., PO Box 1114, St. Louis, MO 63130-4899, U.S.A. **Online address:** stone@wustl.edu

STONE, Harry. American (born United States), b. 1926. **Genres:** Literary Criticism And History, Novels, How-to Books, Essays, History. **Career:** Northwestern University, assistant professor of English, 1955-60; California State University, assistant professor, 1960-63, associate professor, 1963-66, professor of English, 1966-, now emeritus; Victorian Studies, reader; Dickens Quarterly, reader; University of California Press, reader; Wayne State University Press, reader; University of Georgia Press, reader. Consultant and writer. **Publications:** Dickens the Craftsman, 1970; Dickens Centennial Essays, 1971; Dickens and the Invisible World: Fairy Tales, Fantasy and Novel-Making, 1979; The Night Side of Dickens: Cannibalism, Passion, Necessity, 1994. EDITOR AND INTRODUCTION: Uncollected Writings from Household Words, 1850-1859, 2 vols., 1968 in UK as The Uncollected Writings of Charles Dickens: Household Words (1850-1859), 1969; Night Walks, 1982; Travelling Abroad, 1982; A Flight, 1982; George Silverman's Explanation, 1984; Dickens' Working Notes for His Novels, 1987; The Bride's Chamber, 1996. Contributor to books. **Address:** 641 Lorna Ln., Los Angeles, CA 90049, U.S.A.

STONE, James S(tuart). (Jim Stone). Canadian (born Canada), b. 1919. **Genres:** Literary Criticism And History, Women's Studies And Issues, Biography, Social Sciences, Civil Liberties/Human Rights. **Career:** Canada Roof Products, clerk, 1937-41; University of British Columbia, lecturer in English, 1949-50; Elphinstone High School, English teacher, 1951-52; Royal Canadian Air Force, Officer's School, supervisor and lecturer in effective writing course, 1952-54, Telecommunications Section, officer-in-charge, 1954-56, No. 1 Communications Unit, officer commanding, 1956-58; Waterloo University College, department of English, lecturer in English, 1958-60; University of Waterloo, lecturer, 1960-61, assistant professor, 1961-67, associate professor, 1967-86, adjunct professor of English, 1986, now professor emeritus. Writer. **Publications:** George Meredith's Politics: As Seen in His Life, Friendships and Works, 1986; Emily Faithfull, Victorian Champion of Women's Rights, 1994; (as Jim Stone) My Dad, the Rum Runner, 2002. Contributor to books and periodicals. **Address:** 263 Hemlock St., Waterloo, ON N2L 3R4, Canada. **Online address:** stone.james@sympatico.ca

STONE, Jim. See **STONE, James S(tuart).**

STONE, Judith F. American (born United States), b. 1946. **Genres:** History, Politics/Government, Law, Biography. **Career:** State University of New York, lecturer in history, 1976, The Journal of the Fernand Braudel Center, managing editor of review, 1976-77, Empire State College, Long Island Regional Learning Center, mentor and tutor, 1977-80, Center for Labor Studies, adjunct instructor, 1979-80, assistant professor, 1981-84; Central Michigan University, assistant professor of history, 1980-81; Reed College, visiting assistant professor, 1984-86; Burnham-Macmillan, research fellow, 1987-88, 1992, interim department chair, 2000-01; Western Michigan University, assistant professor, 1986-89, associate professor, 1989-96, director of undergraduate studies in history, 1995, 2003, professor of history, 1996-2003, Mary U. Meader professor of modern European history, 1997-2000, professor emeritus, 2003-. Writer. **Publications:** The Search for Social Peace: Reform Legislation in France, 1890-1914, 1985; Sons of the Revolution: Radical Democrats in France, 1862-1914, 1996. Contributor to books. Contributor of articles to journals. **Address:** Department of History, Western Michigan University, 4301 Friedmann Hall, 1903 W Michigan Ave., Kalamazoo, MI 49008-5334, U.S.A. **Online address:** judith.stone@wmich.edu

STONE, Katherine. American (born United States), b. 1949?. **Genres:** Romance/Historical, Mystery/Crime/Suspense, Novels. **Career:** Writer. **Publications:** Roommates, 1987; Twins, 1989; Bel Air, 1990; All That Glitters, 1990; Love Songs, 1991; Rainbows, 1992; Promises, 1993; Illusions, 1994; Happy Endings, 1994; Pearl Moon, 1995; Imagine Love, 1996; The Carleton Club, 1997; Bed of Roses, 1998; Sisters and Secrets, 1998; Home At Last, 1999; A Midnight Clear, 1999; Thief of Hearts, 1999; Island of Dreams, 2000; Star Light, Star Bright, 2002; The Other Twin, 2003; Another Man's Son, 2004; The Cinderella Hour, 2006; Caroline's Journal, 2006. Contributor to periodicals. **Address:** Time Inc., Time & Life Bldg., 1271 Ave. of the Americas, New York, NY 10020-1393, U.S.A.

STONE, Laurie. American (born United States), b. 1946. **Genres:** Novels,

Documentaries/Reportage. **Career:** Village Voice, writer, 1974-; Viva, contributing editor and columnist, 1978; National Public Radio, program Fresh Air, critic, 1987-90; City University of New York, Hunter College, instructor, 1969-75, Queens College, instructor, 1969-75; Ohio State University, creative writing, faculty; Pratt Institute, writer-in-residence; Antioch University, MFA in Creative Writing Program, faculty; Sarah Lawrence college, Department of Graduate Theater, faculty; Fordham University, faculty; Fairleigh Dickinson University, MFA in creative writing, faculty. **Publications:** Starting with Serge (novel), 1990; Laughing in the Dark: A Decade of Subversive Comedy, 1997; Close to the Bone: Memoirs of Hurt, Rage, and Desire, 1997. Contributor of articles to periodicals. **Address:** 808 W End Ave., Apt. 511, New York, NY 10025, U.S.A. **Online address:** lstone@echonyc.com

STONE, Linda. American (born United States), b. 1947. **Genres:** Anthropology/Ethnology, Social Sciences, Cultural/Ethnic Topics, Sciences. **Career:** University of California, International Population and Urban Research Institute, research anthropologist, 1977; Tribhuvan University, Research Center for Nepal and Asian Studies, reader in anthropology, 1978-80; Washington State University, Department of Anthropology, assistant professor, 1981-89, associate professor, 1989-99, professor, 1999-, now professor emeritus; University of Naples, visiting professor, 1989-90; University of South Carolina, visiting professor, 1996-97; Eastern Michigan University, visiting professor, 1996-97. Writer. **Publications:** (With J.G. Campbell, L. Bennett and R. Shrestha) The Use and Misuse of Social Science Research in Nepal, 1979; Illness Beliefs and Feeding the Dead in Hindu Nepal: An Ethnographic Analysis, 1988; Kinship and Gender: An Introduction, 1997, 4th ed., 2010; (with N.P. McKee) Gender and Culture in America, 1999, 2nd ed., 2002; (ed.) New Directions in Anthropological Kinship, 2001; (ed. with N.P. McKee) Readings in Gender and Culture in America, 2002; (ed. with R. Parkin) Kinship and Family: An Anthropological Reader, 2004; (with P.F. Lurquin) A Genetic and Cultural Odyssey: The Life and Work of L. Luca Cavalli-Sforza, 2005; (with P.F. Lurquin) Evolution and Religious Creation Myths: How Scientists Respond, 2007; (with P.F. Lurquin) Genes, Culture, and Human Evolution: A Synthesis, 2007. Contributor to journals. **Address:** Department of Anthropology, Washington State University, PO Box 644910, Pullman, WA 99164-4910, U.S.A. **Online address:** lstone@wsu.edu

STONE, Margaret N. See **DRESSER, Norine.**

STONE, Merlin (David). British (born England), b. 1948?. **Genres:** Economics, Information Science/Computers, Marketing. **Career:** University of Manchester, Institute of Science and Technology, Department of Management Sciences, lecturer, 1972-75; Iscar Ltd., product manager and market analyst, 1977-78; Jerusalem Institute of Management, course co-ordinator, 1978-79; Rank Xerox, business planning manager, 1980-83; Henley Management College, lecturer in marketing, 1983-86; Taba Midas Ltd., managing director, 1985-90; Kingston University, Faculty of Human Sciences, dean, 1991-93; APEX Centre, director, 1989-93, School of Economics and Politics, senior lecturer, 1975-77, School of Management Education, senior lecturer, 1979-80; QCI Ltd., partner, 1993-, director; Swallow Information Systems and Consultancy Ltd., director, 1995-; Customer Foresight Ltd., director, 1995-; Surrey University of Surrey, European Management School, senior research fellow, 1995; International Business Machines, business research leader; University of the West England, Bristol Business School, IBM professor of relationship marketing. Writer. **Publications:** (With M. Lipton and R. Pryce) An Enlarged European Community and the Less Developed Countries, 1973; Product Planning, 1976; Marketing and Economics, 1980; (with H. MacArthur) How to Market Computers and Office Systems, 1984; (with A. Wild) Field Service Management, 1985; (with R. Shaw) Database Marketing, 1988; (with P. Mounsey) Managing Direct Marketing, 1990; (with A. Thomson and C. Wheeler) Telemanage Your Customers, 1990; Leisure Service Marketing, 1990; (with L. Young) Competitive Customer Care, 1992; (with H. MacArthur) How to Market Computers and I.T., 1994; (with D. Davies and A. Bond) Direct Hit, 1995; (with N. Woodcock) Relationship Marketing, 1995; (with B. Foss) CRM in Financial Services: A Practical Guide to Making Customer Relationship Management Work, 2002; (with N. Woodcocks and B. Foss) The Customer Management Scorecard: Managing CRM for Profit, 2003; (with M. Cerasale) Business Solutions on Demand: Transform the Business to Deliver Real Customer Value, 2004; (ed. with A. Bond and B. Foss) Consumer Insight: How to use Data and Market Research to get Closer to your Customer, 2004. **Address:** Department of Marketing, Bristol Business School, University of the West England, Coldharbour Ln., Bristol, BS16 1QY, England.

STONE, Nick. British (born England), b. 1966. **Genres:** Novels, Mystery/Crime/Suspense, Young Adult Fiction. **Career:** Financial Times, staff. Author. **Publications:** Death Waves, 1987; Killer Cruise, 1988; Mr. Clarinet (novel), 2007; King of Swords: A Novel, 2008; Voodoo Eyes, 2011. **Address:** Harper Group, 120 E 56th St., New York, NY 10022, U.S.A. **Online address:** nick@nickstone.co.uk

STONE, Robert (Anthony). American (born United States), b. 1937. **Genres:** Novels, Plays/Screenplays, Young Adult Non-fiction, Children's Fiction, Novellas/Short Stories. **Career:** New York Daily News, caption writer, 1958-60; National Mirror, writer, 1965-67; freelance writer, 1967-71; Princeton University, writer-in-residence, 1971-72, faculty, 1985, 1986; Amherst College, associate professor of English, 1972-75, writer-in-residence, 1977-78; Stanford University, faculty, 1979; University of Hawaii, faculty, 1979-80; Harvard University, faculty, 1981; University of California-Irvine, faculty, 1982; New York University, faculty, 1983-84; University of California-San Diego, faculty, 1985; Johns Hopkins University, faculty, 1993; Yale University, faculty, 1994-2003; Texas State University, Department of English, endowed chair, 2010-11. **Publications:** A Hall of Mirrors, 1967; Dog Soldiers: A Novel, 1974; A Flag for Sunrise: A Novel, 1981; (contrib.) Images of War, 1986; Children of Light, 1986; (intro.) Deeds of War, 1989; (co-author) Paths of Resistance: The Art and Craft of the Political Novel, 1989; Outerbridge Reach, 1992; TESTKEY SBIE Outerbridge Reach, 1993; Day Hikes in Aspen, Colorado, 1996; Bear and His Daughter (collection), 1997; Damascus Gate, 1998; Bay of Souls, 2003; Prime Green: Remembering the Sixties, 2007; (intro.) Dispatches, 2009; Fun with Problems: Stories, 2010. Contributor of articles to periodicals. **Address:** c/o Neal Olson, Donadio & Olson Inc., 121 W 27th St., Ste. 704, New York, NY 10001-6207, U.S.A.

STONE, Rodney. (Matthew Hunter). British (born England), b. 1932. **Genres:** Mystery/Crime/Suspense, Young Adult Fiction. **Career:** His Majesty's Government, Office of Arts and Libraries, deputy head; Ministry of Agriculture, Treasury Department, staff, Education Department, staff. Writer. **Publications:** Cries in the Night, 1991; The Dark Side of the Hill, 1992. AS MATTHEW HUNTER: Cambridgeshire Disaster, 1967; Schiller, 1989; Comrades, 1990; The Kremlin Armoury, 1990; The Gibraltar Factor, 1991. **Address:** 75 Maze Hill, Greenwich, London, GL SE10 8XQ, England.

STONE, Ruth. See Obituaries.

STONE, R. W. American (born United States) **Genres:** Young Adult Non-fiction, Literary Criticism And History. **Career:** Veterinary Trauma Center, veterinarian. Writer. **Publications:** Trail Hand: A Western Story, 2006; A Very Shiny Nose, 2010. Contributor to periodicals. **Address:** Veterinary Trauma Center, 244 W Orange St., Groveland, FL 34736, U.S.A. **Online address:** vettcenter0001@aol.com

STONE, Sarah. American (born United States), b. 1961. **Genres:** Novels, Literary Criticism And History, Writing/Journalism, Novellas/Short Stories, Art/Art History, Theatre. **Career:** California Institute of Integral Studies, MFA in Writing and Consciousness, core faculty; Warren Wilson College, MFA Program for Writers, faculty; University of Michigan, MFA in Fiction, faculty. Writer. **Publications:** The True Sources of the Nile, 2002; (with R. Nyren) Deepening Fiction: A Practical Guide for Intermediate and Advanced Writers, 2005; (with R. Nyren) The Longman Guide to Intermediate and Advanced Fiction Writing, 2007. **Address:** MFA in Writing and Consciousness, California Institute of Integral Studies, 1453 Mission St., San Francisco, CA 94103-2557, U.S.A. **Online address:** sstone@ciis.edu

STONE, Thomas H. See **GILMAN, George G.**

STONE, Zachary. See **FOLLETT, Ken(neth Martin).**

STONECASH, Jeffrey M. American (born United States), b. 1946. **Genres:** Politics/Government. **Career:** Lord Fairfax Community College, instructor in economics, 1970-71; University of Illinois Champaign, Institute of Government and Public Affairs, research associate, 1974-76; Case Western Reserve University, Department of Urban Studies, assistant professor of urban studies and political science, 1976-77; Syracuse University, assistant professor, 1977-81, associate professor, 1981-82, director of graduate studies, 1980-82, 1993-96, professor, 1992, director of undergraduate studies, 1996-98, Maxwell professor of political science, 2006-; New York State Assembly Internship Program, professor-in-residence. Writer. **Publications:** (With P.F.

Nardulli) Politics, Professionalism and Urban Services, 1981; (ed. with J.K. White and P.W. Colby) Governing New York State, 3rd ed., 1994, (ed. with R.P. Pecorella) 5th ed., 2006; American State and Local Politics, 1995; Class and Party in American Politics, 2000; (with M.P. McGuire) The Emergence of State Government: Parties and New Jersey Politics, 1950-2000, 2003; (with M.D. Brewer and M.D. Mariani) Diverging Parties: Social Change, Realignment and Party Polarization, 2003; Political Polling: Strategic Information in Campaigns, 2003; Political Parties Matter: Realignment and the Return of Partisan Voting, 2006; (with M.D. Brewer) Split: Class and Cultural Divides in American Politics, 2007; Reassessing the Incumbency Effect, 2008; (with M.D. Brewer) Dynamics of American Political Parties, 2009; (ed.) New Directions in American Political Parties, 2010; (with H.L. Reiter) Counter Realignment: Political Change in the Northeastern United States, 2010. Contributor to books. **Address:** Department of Political Science, Maxwell School of Syracuse University, 405B Maxwell Hall, Syracuse, NY 13244, U.S.A. **Online address:** jstone@syr.edu

STONEHOUSE, Bernard. British (born England), b. 1926. **Genres:** Natural History, Travel/Exploration, Zoology, Biology, Environmental Sciences/Ecology. **Career:** University of Canterbury, senior lecturer, 1960-64, reader in zoology, 1964-69; University of British Columbia, Commonwealth research fellow in zoology, 1969-70; Yale University, visiting associate professor of biology, 1969; teacher and freelance writer, 1970-72; University of Bradford, senior lecturer in ecology and chair of Postgraduate School of Environmental Science, 1972-83; University of Cambridge, Scott Polar Research Institute, Polar Record, editor, 1983-92, senior associate, emeritus fellow and emeritus associate. Writer and consultant. **Publications:** Het Bevroren Continent: The Frozen Continent: A History of Antarctic Exploration, 1958; Wideawake Island: The Story of B.O.U Centenary Expedition to Ascension Island, 1960; Whales, 1963; Gulls and Terns, 1964; Penguins, 1968; Birds of the New Zealand Shore, 1968; Animals of the Arctic: The Ecology of the Far North, 1971; Animals of the Arctic: The Ecology of the Far South, 1972; Young Animals: Invertebrates, Fish and Amphibia, Reptiles, Birds, Mammals and Man, 1973; Young Animals: The Search for Independent Life, 1973; Mountain Life, 1975; Penguins, 1975; Frontiers of Life: Animals of Mountains and Poles, 1976; Kangaroos, 1977; A Closer Look at Plant Life, 1978; A Closer Look at Whales and Dolphins, 1978; The Living World of the Sea, 1979; A Closer Look at Reptiles, 1979; (with M. Borner) Orang-Utan, 1979; Penguins, 1979; Bears, 1980; Saving the Animals, 1981; Charles Darwin and Evolution, 1981; Venomous Snakes, 1981; Parrots, 1981; Buffaloes, 1981; Britain from the Air, 1982; Life in the Sea, 1984; Pocket Guide to the World, 1985; Sea Mammals of the World, 1985; Facts on File Pocket Guide to the World, 1985; Philips Pocket Guide to the World, 1985; Living at the Poles, 1987; Polar Ecology, 1989; North Pole-South Pole, 1990; (with R. Burton and R. Cavendish) Journeys of the Great Explorers, 1992; Snow, Ice and Cold, 1992; Bears: A Visual Introduction to Bears, 1998; Whales: A Visual Introduction to Whales, Dolphins, and Porpoises, 1998; Camouflage, 1999; Predators, 1999; Sharks: A Visual Introduction to Sharks, Skates, and Rays, 1999; Visual Introduction to Wild Cats, 1999; Against the Odds, 2000; The Last Continent: A Guide to Antarctica, 2000; Defenders, 2000; Fighters, 2000; Growing Up: Strange Beginnings, 2000; Partners, 2000; Show-offs, 2000; Visual Introduction to Monkeys and Apes, 2000; Visual Introduction to Penguins, 2000; Alone, 2000; Growing Up: Protected, 2001; Growing Up: Alone, 2001; Poles, 2001; (with E. Bertram) Truth About Animal Senses, 2002; (with E. Bertram) Truth About Animal Intelligence, 2002; (with E. Bertram) Truth About Animal Builders, 2003; (with E. Bertram) Truth About Animal Communication, 2003; (with E. Bertram) How Animals Live: The Amazing World of Animals in the Wild, 2004; Antarctica from South America, 2006; (with J. Snyder) Polar Tourism: An Environmental Perspective, 2010. EDITOR: The Way Your Body Works, 1974; The Biology of Penguins, 1974; (with D. Gilmore) Biology of Marsupials, 1977; (with C. Perrins) Evolutionary Ecology, 1977; Animal Marking: Recognition Marking of Animals in Research, 1978; (co-ed.) Atlas of Earth Resources, 1979; Philips Illustrated Atlas of the World, 1980; Biological Husbandry, 1981; Prentice-Hall Illustrated Atlas of the World, 1982; Aerofilms Book of Britain from the Air, 1982; Arctic Ocean: The Hydrographic Environment and the Fate of Pollutants, 1982; Arctic Air Pollution, 1986; (ed. with C.M. Harris) Antarctica and Global Climatic Change, 1991; Encyclopedia of Antarctica and the Southern Oceans, 2002; (with J. Snyder) Prospects for Polar Tourism, 2007; Polar Tourism, 2010. Contributor to magazines. **Address:** Scott Polar Research Institute, University of Cambridge, Lensfield Rd., Cambridge, CB CB2 1ER, England. **Online address:** bs111@cus.cam.ac.uk

STONEMAN, Richard (John). British (born England), b. 1951. **Genres:**

Literary Criticism And History, Travel/Exploration, Theology/Religion. **Career:** Croom Helm Ltd., humanities editor, 1977-88; Routledge & Kegan Paul, classics and philosophy editor, 1988-. **Publications:** (Comp.) Daphne Into Laurel: English Translations of Classical Poetry From Chaucer to the Present, 1982; (contrib.) Aischylus und Pindar, 1982; A Literary Companion to Travel in Greece, 1984; Land of Lost Gods: The Search for Classical Greece, 1987; Fvs to Freya Strak, 1987; (comp. with R. Wallace) Roman Italy, 1989; (comp. with R. Wallace) Ancient Greece and the Aegean, 1989; (comp.) The Roman Empire in the Flavian Period, 1989; (comp. with R. Wallace) The Empire of Alexander, The Great, 1991; (contrib.) The Greek Alexander Romance, 1991; Greek Mythology: An Encyclopedia of Myth and Legend, 1991; (comp. with R. Wallace) The Roman Empire in the Flavian Period, 1991; (contrib. and intro.) The Education of Cyrus, 1992; Palmyra and Its Empire: Zenobia's Revolt against Rome, 1992; (ed.) The Odyssey, 1992; (ed.) Satires, 1992; A Travellers History of Turkey, 1993; (ed. with J.R. Morgan) Greek Fiction: The Greek Novel in Context, 1994; Alexander the Great, 1997, 2nd ed., 2004; (ed.) Pindar: The Odes & Selected Fragments, 1997; A Luminous Land: Artists Discover Greece, 1998; Travellers History of Athens, 2004; Il Romanzo di Alessandro, 2007; Making the Gods Speak: The Ancient Oracles, 2011. Contributor of articles to periodicals. **Address:** c/o Routledge, 11 New Fetter Ln., London, GL EC4 P4EE, England. **Online address:** richard.stoneman@tandf.co.uk

STONER, K. Lynn. American (born United States), b. 1946. **Genres:** Cultural/Ethnic Topics, History, Women's Studies And Issues, Bibliography, Social Sciences. **Career:** Arizona State University, assistant professor, 1985-91, associate professor of history, 1991-, Center for Latin American Studies, director, 1993-, 2004-05. Writer. **Publications:** (With C.L. Lombardi and J.V. Lombardi) Latin American History, A Teaching Atlas, 1983; (ed.) Latinas of the Americas: A Source Book, 1989; From the House to the Streets: The Cuban Woman's Movement for Legal Reform, 1898-1940, 1991; (ed. and comp. with L. Hipólito and S. Pérez) Cuban and Cuban-American Women: An Annotated Bibliography, 2000; De La Casa A La Calle: El Movimiento Cubano De La Mujer En Favor De La Reforma Legal (1898-1940), 2003. Contributor to periodicals. **Address:** Department of History, Arizona State University, 975 S Myrtle Ave., PO Box 4302, Tempe, AZ 85287-4302, U.S.A. **Online address:** lynn.stoner@asu.edu

STONER, Tom. American (born United States), b. 1948. **Genres:** Novels, Literary Criticism And History. **Career:** Writer. **Publications:** The Comfort of Our Kind (novel), 2008. Contributor to periodicals. **Address:** St. Martin's Press, 175 5th Ave., New York, NY 10010, U.S.A.

STONICH, Sarah. American (born United States), b. 1958. **Genres:** Plays/Screenplays, Novels, E-books, Humor/Satire, Writing/Journalism. **Career:** Writer. **Publications:** NOVELS: These Granite Islands, 2001; Ice Chorus, 2005, Shelter, 2011. FORTHCOMING: Vacationland; Fishing with Ray-Anne. **Address:** c/o Erica Spellman Silverman, Trident Media Group, 41 Madison Ave., 36th Fl., New York, NY 10010, U.S.A. **Online address:** sarah@sarahstonich.com

STOPFORD, John M(orton). British (born England), b. 1939. **Genres:** Administration/Management, International Relations/Current Affairs. **Career:** Baker Perkins Ltd., skilled fitter, 1957-58; Shell Chemicals (U.K.), engineer, 1962-64, non-executive director, 1973-77; Guyana Stockfeeds Ltd., acting managing director, 1965; Manchester Business School, senior lecturer in business administration, 1968-70; Harvard University, Business School, visiting assistant professor of business administration, 1971-72; London Business School, professor of international business, 1972-, academic dean, 1979-84, now emeritus professor of international business; Bracken Kelner and Associates, director, 1974-79; Webtec Industrial Technology Ltd., director, 1975-90; Centre on Business Responsibility, chair, 1976-77; United Nations Centre on Transnational Corporations, senior staff, 1977-78; London and International Publishers Ltd., director, 1983-89; British Army, Land Warfare Centre, non-executive director, 1999-2003; Goodenough College, trustee, 2004-10. Writer. **Publications:** (With L. Wells, Jr.) Managing the Multinational Enterprise: Organization of the Firm and Ownership of the Subsidiaries, 1972; (with D. Channon and D. Norburn) British Business Policy, 1976; (ed.) Transnational Corporations in World Development: A Re-Examination, 1978; (ed. with B. Garratt) Breaking Down Barriers: Practice and Priorities for International Management Education, 1980; (ed. with D. Channon and J. Constable) Cases in Strategic Management, 1980; Growth and Organizational Change in the Multinational Firm, 1980; (with J. Dunning and K. Haberich)

The World Directory of Multinational Enterprises, 1980, 2nd ed., 1982; (with J. Dunning) Multinationals: Company Performance and Global Trends, 1983; (with L. Turner) Britain and the Multinationals, 1985; (with S. Strange and J.S. Henley) Rival States, Rival Firms: Competition for World Market Shares, 1991; (with C. Baden-Fuller) Rejuvenating the Mature Business, 1992, 2nd ed., 1994; Offensive and Defensive Responses by European Multinationals to a World of Trade Blocs, 1992; (ed.) The Directory of Multinationals, 4th ed., 1992; (co-author) Annotated Bibliography of Organizational Learning, 1999; FDI Determinants and TNC Strategies: The Case of Brazil, 2000; (co-author) The Future of the Multinational Company, 2004. **Address:** 6 Chalcot Sq., London, GL NW1 8YB, England. **Online address:** jstopford@london.edu

STOPPARD, Miriam. British (born England), b. 1937. **Genres:** Medicine/Health, Psychology. **Career:** University of Bristol, Department of Chemical Pathology, resident fellow, 1963-65, registrar in dermatology, 1965-66, senior registrar in dermatology, 1966-68; Syntext Pharmaceuticals Ltd., associate medical director, 1968-71, deputy medical director, 1971-74, medical director, 1974-76, deputy managing director, 1976-77, managing director, 1977-81; LifeTime Ltd., executive chairman; Royal College of Physicians, fellow. Writer. **Publications:** Miriam Stoppard's Book of Baby Care, 1977; (co-author) My Medical School, 1978; Miriam Stoppard's Book of Health Care, 1979; (ed.) Good Looks Book, 1980; (ed.) The Face and Body Book, 1980; Everywoman's Lifeguide, 1982; Talking Sex: A Book about Growing Up, 1982; Being a Well Woman, 1982; Your Baby, 1982; Fifty Plus Lifeguide, 1982; Your Growing Child, 1983; Baby Care Book, 1983; Day by Day Baby Care, 1983; Best Years of your Life, 1984; Pregnancy and Childbirth, 1985; Baby and Child Medical Handbook, 1986; Every Girl's Life Guide, 1987; Dr. Miriam Stoppard's Pregnancy and Birth Book, 1987; Feeding Your Family, 1987; My First Food Book, 1987; Health and Beauty Book, 1988; Everywoman's Medical Handbook, 1989; The First Weeks of Life, 1989; Your Family's Diet, 1990; The Boot's Guides to Pregnancy and Babycare, 1990; Tach Your Child, 1991, rev. ed., 2001; Test Your Child: How to Discover and Enhance Your Child's True Potential, 1991; Know Your Child: How to Discover and Enhance Your Child's Potential, 1991; Magic of Sex, 1991; Lose Seven Pounds in Seven Days, 1991; First Food Made Fun, 1993; Conception, Pregnancy and Birth, 1993, rev. ed., 2008; Menopause, 1994; (ed.) Woman's Body, 1994; Complete Baby and Child Care, 1995, rev. ed., 2008; The Breast Book, 1996; Breast Care, 1997; Sex Ed, 1997; Questions Children Ask and How to Answer Them, 1997; Your New Baby, 1998; Well Woman, 1998; Birth, 1998; Breast Health, 1998; Child Health, 1998; First Foods, 1998; Healthy Pregnancy, 1998; Healthy Sex, 1998; Natural Menopause, 1998; The New Parent, 1998; Prenatal Care, 1998; You and Your Toddler, 1999; HRT: Hormone Replacement Therapy, 1999; Healthy Weight Loss, 1999; Dr. Miriam Stoppard's New Pregnancy and Birth Book, 2000, rev. ed., 2009; Baby's Learn and Play Pack, 2000; Women's Health Handbook, 2001; Test Your Child: How to Discover and Enhance Your Childs True Potential, 2001; Baby First Aid, 2003; Dr. Miriam Stoppard's Family Health Guide, 2003; Defying Age: How to Think, Act & Stay Young, 2004; Baby's First Skills, 2005, rev. ed., 2009; Shapes, 2006; On the Move, 2006; First Time Parents: What Every New Parent Needs to Know, 2006, rev. ed., 2009; Colors, 2006; Busy Day, 2006; New Babycare, 2007, rev. ed., 2009; Teach Your Child: How to Discover and Enhance Your Child's True Potential, 2001; Let's Play Baby Talking, 2007; Let's Play Baby Senses, 2007; Let's Play Baby Games, 2007; Happy Baby, 2007; Your Pregnancy Planner, 2008; Bonding before Birth: Prenatal Nurturing for Your Baby, 2008; Bonding with Your Bump, 2008; You and Your Toddler: A Practical Guide to Life with Your Toddler from 18 Months to Five Years, 2011; Your Healthy Pregnancy: A Practical Guide to Enjoying Your Pregnancy, 2011. **Address:** The Media Village, Miriam Stoppard Lifetime Ltd., 131-151 Great Titchfield St., London, GL W1W 5BB, England.

STOPPARD, Tom. British/Czech (born Czech Republic), b. 1937. **Genres:** Novels, Novellas/Short Stories, Plays/Screenplays, Translations, Biography, Art/Art History. **Career:** Western Daily Press, reporter and critic, 1958-60; Bristol Evening World, reporter, 1958-60; freelance reporter, 1960-63; Scene, drama critic, 1962-63. **Publications:** (Co-author) Introduction 2 (short stories), 1964; Lord Malquist and Mr. Moon (novel), 1966; Tango, 1966; A Separate Peace, 1966; Rosencrantz and Guildenstern Are Dead, 1967; Enter a Free Man, 1968; The Real Inspector Hound, 1968; Albert's Bridge, 1968; After Magritte, 1971; Jumpers, 1972; Artist Descending a Staircase, and Where are They Now?, 1973; Travesties, 1974; Dirty Linen and New-Found-Land, 1976; The Fifteen Minute Hamlet, 1976; Albert's Bridge and Other Plays, 1977; Every Good Boy Deserves Favour, 1977; Night and Day, 1978; Dogg's

Hamlet, 1980; Real Thing, 1982; The Dog It Was That Died and Other Plays, 1983; Squaring the Circle, 1985; Rough Crossing, 1985; Dalliance, 1986; Hapgood, 1988; Boundary: A Play, 1991; In the Native State, 1991; Stoppard: The Plays for Radio 1964-1983, 1991; Arcadia (play), 1993; A Stylistics of Drama, 1993; The Television Plays, 1965-1984, 1993; Tom Stoppard in Conversation, 1994; Conversations with Stoppard, 1995, rev. ed., 2003; Indian Ink, 1995; (and intro.) Plays Two, 1996; Arkádie, 1997; Invention of Love, 1997; (with M. Norman) Shakespeare in Love, 1998; Plays Five, 1999; Doing It, 2001; (trans.) A. Chekhov, The Seagull, 2001; The Coast of Utopia, 2002; Voyage, 2003; Shipwreck, 2003; Salvage, 2003; Pirandello's Henry IV, 2004; (trans.) G. Sibleyras, Heroes, 2005; (intro.) Bach at Leipzig: A Play, 2005; Rock n Roll, 2006, rev. ed., 2007; (trans.) A. Chekhov, Ivanov, 2008; (trans.) A. Chekhov, Cherry Orchard, 2009. Contributor to periodicals. **Address:** Peters Fraser & Dunlop Group Ltd., Drury House, 34-43 Russell St., London, GL WC2B 5HA, England.

STOPS, Sue. British (born England), b. 1936. **Genres:** Children's Fiction, Young Adult Fiction, History, Picture/Board Books. **Career:** Primary and Secondary Schools, teacher, 1960-95. Writer. **Publications:** (With M.V. Jones) Maurice, 1988; Dulcie Dando, 1990; Dulcie Dando, Soccer Star, 1992; Dulcie Dando Football Player, 1992; Dulcie Dando Disco Dancer, 1993; Dulcie Dando-Soccer Super Star Pkgt, 1994; Sally Moves South, 1994; Mystery in the Peaks, 1994; (with H. Reid) On the Waterfront: The Hotwells Story, 2002; Hotwells and Clifton, 2005. **Address:** 9 Freeland Pl., Hotwells, Bristol, GL BS8 4NP, England. **Online address:** suestops@aol.com

STORCH, Margaret. American/British (born England), b. 1941. **Genres:** Education, Literary Criticism And History, Social Sciences. **Career:** Newcastle Polytechnic, assistant professor of English, 1964-67; St. Joseph's Teachers College, assistant professor of English, 1967-70; Polytechnic of the South Bank, assistant professor of English, 1971-73; Tufts University, assistant professor of English, 1973-77; Open University, assistant professor, 1974-75; University of Massachusetts, assistant professor of English, 1978-81; Bentley College, assistant professor of English, 1981-90, New England Heritage Center, acting director, 1989-90; Massachusetts State Department of Education, consultant, 1991-; Framingham State College, director of college publications. Writer. **Publications:** Sons and Adversaries: Women in William Blake and D.H. Lawrence, 1990; (ed.) Directions in Urban Education for the Nineties: Report of the Boston, 1992. Contributor of articles to journals. Works appear in anthologies. **Address:** Framingham State University, 100 State St., PO Box 9101, Framingham, MA 01701-9101, U.S.A. **Online address:** mstorch@frc.mass.edu

STORER, James Donald. Scottish/British (born England), b. 1928. **Genres:** Air/Space Topics, Engineering, Technology, Transportation. **Career:** British Aircraft Corp., staff, 1948-66; Royal Scottish Museum, Department of Technology, assistant keeper, 1966-78, keeper, 1978-85; National Museums of Scotland, Department of Science, Technology and Working Life, keeper, 1985-88; museum consultant, 1988-; British Aviation Preservation Council, chairman. Writer. **Publications:** Steel and Engineering, 1959; Behind the Scenes in an Aircraft Factory, 1965; It's Made Like This: Cars, 1967; The World We Are Making: Aviation, 1968; A Simple History of the Steam Engine, 1969; How to Run an Airport, 1971; How We Find Out about Flight, 1973; World of Flight, 1974; Flying Feats, 1977; Book of the Air, 1979; Great Inventions, 1980; (co-author) Encyclopaedia of Transport, 1983; (co-author) East Fortune: Museum of Flight and History of the Airfield, 1983; (co-author) The Hamlyn Colour Encyclopedia of Transport, 1983; (co-author) The Silver Burdett Encyclopedia of Transport, 1984; Ship Models in the Royal Scottish Museum, Edinburgh: A Catalogue of Models Representing the History of Shipping from 1500 BC to the Present Day, 1986; The Conservation of Industrial Collections, 1989; (co-author) Industry and Transport in Scottish Museums, 1997; (co-author) Liverpool on Wheels, 1998. **Address:** Royal Museum of Scotland, Chambers St., Edinburgh, EH1 1JF, Scotland.

STOREY, David (Malcolm). British (born England), b. 1933. **Genres:** Novels, Plays/Screenplays, Literary Criticism And History, Young Adult Fiction, Novellas/Short Stories. **Career:** Royal Court Theatre, associate artistic director, 1972-74; University College London, fellow, 1974-. Novelist. **Publications:** NOVELS: This Sporting Life, 1960; Flight into Camden, 1960; Radcliffe, 1963; The Contractor, 1970; Pasmore, 1972; The Changing Room, 1972; A Temporary Life, 1973; Edward, 1973; The Farm, 1973; Life Class, 1975; Saville, 1976; A Prodigal Child, 1982; Present Times, 1984; The March on Russia: A Play, 1989; (and intro.) Plays, One, 1992; Storey's Lives: Poems,

1951-1991, 1992; The Phoenix, 1993; A Serious Man, 1998; A Star in the West, 1999; As It Happened, 2002; Thin-Ice Skater, 2004. OTHERS: Stories to Remember, 1956; (contrib.) Writers on Themselves, 1964; Restoration of Arnold Middleton, 1967; In Celebration, 1969; Home, 1970; Cromwell, 1973; Early Days, 1980; Stages, 1992; Plays, Three, 1998. Contributor to books and periodicals. **Address:** Jonathan Cape Ltd., 20 Vauxhall Bridge Rd., London, GL SW1V 2SA, England.

STOREY, Dee. American (born United States), b. 1950. **Genres:** Literary Criticism And History, Bibliography, Young Adult Fiction, Education. **Career:** Teacher, 1973; Michigan State University, instructor, 1975-78; University of Nebraska, assistant professor, 1978-85; Marycrest College, assistant professor of education, 1986-87; Saginaw Valley State University, associate professor of children's literature, language arts and reading, 1987-, coordinator of elementary education curriculum, 1989-. Writer. **Publications:** Twins in Children's and Adolescent Literature: An Annotated Bibliography, 1993. Contributor of articles to journals. **Address:** College of Education, Saginaw Valley State University, 238 Wickes Hall, Education Bldg-N Wing 291, 7400 Bay Rd., University Center, MI 48710-0001, U.S.A. **Online address:** storey@svsu.edu

STOREY, Edward. Welsh/British (born England), b. 1930. **Genres:** Poetry, Songs/Lyrics And Libretti, Travel/Exploration, Autobiography/Memoirs, Biography, Literary Criticism And History. **Career:** Peterborough City Education Authority, arts organizer, 1959-64; Peterborough College of Adult Education, registrar and tutor, 1964-69; freelance writer, 1969-. **Publications:** North Bank Night, 1969; Portrait of the Fen Country, 1971, 3rd ed., 1982; A Man in Winter, 1972; Four Seasons in Three Countries: A Year's Journey Through England, Scotland and Wales, 1974; The Solitary Landscape, 1975; Call It a Summer Country, 1978; The Dark Music, 1979; Old Scarlett: A Cantata for Treble and Baritone Soloists, Semichorus, Chorus & Organ (libretto), 1982; A Right to Song: The Life of John Clare, 1982; A Slant of Light, 1983; Spirit of the Fens: A View of Fenland Life, Past and Present, 1985; Fen, Fire and Flood, 1986; Summer Journeys through theFens, 1988; Fen Boy First, 1993; The Winter Fens, 1994; Last Train to Ely, 1995; Fen Country Christmas, 1995; In Fen Country Heaven, 1996; A Changein the Climate, 1998; Letters from the Fens, 1998; New and Selected Poems, 2000. **Address:** Kites Drift, Discoed nr Presteigne, PW LD8 2NW, Wales.

STOREY, Gail Donohue. American (born United States), b. 1947. **Genres:** Novels, Poetry, Literary Criticism And History. **Career:** Maclean-Hunter Publishing Corp., Inland Printer/American Lithographer, assistant editor, 1969; Idea Communications, assistant film producer, 1970; Peer Enterprises, publishing production coordinator, 1971; Newberry Library, Office of the Director, assistant, Atlas of Early American History, research secretary and bibliographic assistant, 1971-72; Champaign Public Library and Information Center, adult services librarian, 1974-77; Public Library of Annapolis and Anne Arundel County, project director of service to homebound and individuals confined in institutions, 1977-80; University of Houston, teacher of basic writing, 1980-81, teacher of freshman composition, 1981, administrative director of creative writing program, 1982-86, teacher, 1984-86; St. John's College, visiting faculty, 1983; Houston Community College, literacy tutor, 1990-91. Writer. **Publications:** AS GAIL DONOHUE: First Poems of Gail Donohue, 1974. NOVELS: The Lord's Motel, 1992; God's Country Club, 1996. Contributor to periodicals. **Address:** Ellen Levine Literary Agency Inc., 15 E 26th St., Ste. 1801, New York, NY 10010-1505, U.S.A.

STOREY, Margaret. Also writes as Susannah Stacey, Elizabeth Eyre. British (born England), b. 1924?. **Genres:** Mystery/Crime/Suspense, Children's Fiction, History, Romance/Historical, Young Adult Fiction. **Career:** Miss Ironside's School, English teacher, 1959-69. Writer. **Publications:** Kate and the Family Tree, 1965 in US as The Family Tree, 1973; The Smallest Doll, 1966; The Smallest Bridesmaid, 1966; Timothy and Two Witches, 1966; The Stone Sorcerer, 1967; Pauline, 1967; The Dragon's Sister and Timothy Travels, 1967; A Quarrel of Witches, 1970; The Mollyday Holiday, 1971; The Sleeping Witch, 1971; Wrong Gear, 1973; Keep Running, 1974 in US as Ask Me No Questions, 1975; A War of Wizards, 1976; The Double Wizard, 1979. AS SUSANNAH STACEY: Goodbye, Nanny Gray, 1987; Hunter's Quarry, 1998. WITH J. STAYNES: A Knife at the Opera, 1988; Body of Opinion, 1988; Grave Responsibility, 1990; The Late Lady, 1992; Bone Idle, 1993; Dead Serious, 1995; Quarry, 1998. AS ELIZABETH EYRE: Death of the Duchess, 1991; Curtains for the Cardinal, 1992; Poison for the Prince, 1993;

Bravo for the Bride, 1994; Axe for an Abbot, 1995; Dirge for a Doge, 1996. **Address:** A. M. Heath & Company Ltd., 6 Warwick Ct., Holborn, London, GL WC1R 5DJ, England.

STOREY, Margaret M. American (born United States), b. 1969. **Genres:** History. **Career:** Emory University, teaching associate, 1996; De Paul University, instructor, 1998-99, assistant professor, 1999-2004, associate professor, 2004-; Emory University, Graduate School of Arts and Sciences fellow, 1992-96; Emory University, Mellon fellow in Southern Studies, 1996-97; Newberry Library summer fellow for undergraduate seminar instructors, 2000; Pierpont Morgan Library, Gilder Lehrman Institute of American History, American Civilization fellow, 2002. **Publications:** Loyalty and Loss: Alabama's Unionists in the Civil War and Reconstruction, 2004. Contributor to periodicals and journals. **Address:** Department of History, DePaul University, 2320 N Kenmore Ave., Chicago, IL 60614, U.S.A. **Online address:** mstorey@depaul.edu

STOREY, Mark. British/American (born United States), b. 1944. **Genres:** Literary Criticism And History, Bibliography, Young Adult Fiction, Humanities. **Career:** University of Birmingham, instructor in English literature, professor emeritus, 2000-. Writer. **Publications:** Clare: The Critical Heritage, 1973; The Poetry of John Clare: A Critical Introduction, 1974; Poetry and Humour from Cowper to Clough, 1979; (ed.) The Letters of John Clare, 1985; Byron and the Eye of Appetite, 1986; (ed.) The Private Papers of Henry Ryecroft, 1987; (ed.) John Clare: Selected Letters, 1988; Poetry and Ireland since 1800: A Source Book, 1988; Robert Southey: A Life, 1997; The Problem of Poetry in the Romantic Period, 2000; (ed.) Selected Poetry of Ebenezer Elliott, 2008; Ebenezer Elliott, The Corn Law Rhymer, forthcoming. Contributor to periodicals. **Address:** University of Birmingham, Edgbaston, Birmingham, WM B15 2TT, England. **Online address:** m.g.storey@bham.ac.uk

STOREY, R(obin) L(indsay). British (born England), b. 1927. **Genres:** History. **Career:** Public Record Office, assistant keeper, 1953-62; Nottingham University, lecturer, 1962-64, senior lecturer, 1964-66, reader in history, 1966-73, professor of English history, 1973-83, dean of faculty of arts, 1979-82, professor of medieval history, 1983-90, professor emeritus, 1990-; Canterbury and York Society, honorary general editor, 1994-2004. **Publications:** Thomas Langley and the Bishopric of Durham, 1961; The End of the House of Lancaster, 1966, new. ed., 1986; The Reign of Henry VII, 1968; Chronology of the Expanding World, 1492 to 1762, 1994. EDITOR: Register of Thomas Langley, Bishop of Durham 1406-1437, vol. VI, 1956-70; (and contrib.) The Study of Medieval Records, 1971; Chronology of the Medieval World 800-1491, 1973; Register of John Kirkby, Bishop of Carlisle 1332-52, vol. I, 1993, vol. II, 1995; Register of Gilbert Welton, Bishop of Carlisle 1353-62, 1999; Register of Thomas Appleby, Bishop of Carlisle 1363-1395, 2006. **Address:** School of History, University of Nottingham, University Pk., Nottingham, NT NG7 2RD, England.

STORK, Francisco X. American (born United States), b. 1953?. **Genres:** Literary Criticism And History. **Career:** MassHousing (housing bank), attorney. Writer. **Publications:** The Way of the Jaguar, 2000; Behind the Eyes, 2006; Marcelo in the Real World, 2009; Irises, Last Summer of the Death Warriors, forthcoming. **Address:** MassHousing, 1 Beacon St., Boston, MA 02108, U.S.A. **Online address:** fstork@masshousing.com

STORLIE, Erik Fraser. American (born United States), b. 1940. **Genres:** Autobiography/Memoirs, Biography. **Career:** Minneapolis Community College, instructor, 1965-, faculty, through 2000; University of Minnesota, Center for Spirituality & Healing, faculty. Writer. **Publications:** Nothing on My Mind: Berkeley, LSD, Two Zen Masters, and a Life on the Dharma Trail, 1996. Contributor to magazines. **Address:** Center for Spirituality & Healing, University of Minnesota, MMC 505, 420 Delaware St. SE, Minneapolis, MN 55455-0341, U.S.A. **Online address:** estorlie@visi.com

STORM, Dirk. See NEALON, Kevin.

STORM, Elizabeth. See SANDSTROM, Eve K.

STORTZ, Martha E. (Martha Ellen Stortz). American (born United States), b. 1952. **Genres:** Theology/Religion. **Career:** Graduate Theological Union, Pacific Lutheran Theological Seminary, professor of historical theology and ethics & core doctoral faculty member, 1981-. Writer, historian, theologian, scholar, lecturer and educator. **Publications:** Pastorpower, 1993; A World According to God: Practices for Putting Faith at the Center of Your Life, 2004; Blessed to Follow: The Beatitudes as a Compass for Discipleship, 2008. Contributor to books and periodicals. **Address:** Department of Historical Theology & Ethics, Graduate Theological Union, Pacific Lutheran Theological Seminary, 2400 Ridge Rd., Berkeley, CA 94709, U.S.A. **Online address:** mstortz@plts.edu

STORTZ, Martha Ellen. *See* **STORTZ, Martha E.**

STORY, Jonathan. French/British/Welsh (born Wales), b. 1940. **Genres:** Politics/Government, Economics, Adult Non-fiction. **Career:** Agence Europe, staff, 1969-70; EC Commission Office, staff, 1970-72; Hudson Institute, lecturer, 1972-74; INSEAD, assistant professor, 1974-77, associate professor, 1977-87, professor, 1987-2006, emeritus professor of international political economy, 2006-, Shell fellow in economic transformation, 1997-2006, Shell emeritus fellow in economic transformation, 2006-; Rensselaer Polytechnic Institute, Lally School of Management and Technology, Marusi professor of global business, Marusi chair of global business and political economy; Story Productions, chairman. Writer. **Publications:** (Co-author) L'Envol de La France, 1972; (ed. with P.F. della Torre and E. Mortimer) Eurocommunism: Myth or Reality?, 1979; (with G. de Carmoy) Western Europe in World Affairs: Continuity, Change, and Challenge, 1986; The New Europe: Politics, Government, and Economy Since 1945, 1993; (ed. with R. Gillespie and F. Rodrigo) Democratic Spain: Reshaping External Relations in a Changing World, 1995; (ed. with R. Gillespie and F. Rodrigo) Relaciones exteriores de la España democrá, 1995; (with I. Walter) Political Economy of Financial Integration in Europe: The Battle of the Systems, 1997; Frontiers of Fortune: Predicting Capital Prospects and Casualties in the Markets of the Future, 1999; China: The Race to Market: What China's Transformation Means for Business, Markets and the New World Order, 2003; China Uncovered: What You Need to Know to Do Business in China, 2010. **Address:** INSEAD, Boulevard de Constance, Fontainebleau, 77305, France. **Online address:** jonathan.story@insead.edu

STOSKOPF, Neal C. Canadian (born Canada), b. 1934. **Genres:** Agriculture/Forestry, Earth Sciences, Sciences, Technology. **Career:** Michigan State University, lecturer; University of Guelph, professor, 1958-95, retired, 1995. Writer. **Publications:** Understanding Crop Production, 1981; Cereal Grain Crops, 1985; (with D.T. Tomes and B.R. Christie) Plant Breeding: Theory and Practice, 1993; Crop Production Systems, forthcoming. **Address:** 12 Evergreen Dr., Guelph, ON N1G 2M6, Canada. **Online address:** nstoskop@uoguelph.ca

STOTT, Annette. American (born United States) **Genres:** Art/Art History, History. **Career:** University of Maine, assistant professor, 1986-87; Winthrop University, assistant professor, 1987-91; Harvard University, Mellon faculty fellow in the humanities, 1989-90; University of Denver, School of Art and Art History, assistant professor, 1991-93, associate professor of art history and women's studies, 1994-, professor, director, 1999-. Writer. **Publications:** Holland Mania: The Unknown Dutch Period in American Art and Culture, 1998; (ed. with J.D. Goodfriend and B. Schmidt) Going Dutch: The Dutch Presence in America, 1609-2009, 2008; Pioneer Cemeteries: Sculpture Gardens of the Old West, 2008. Contributor to periodicals. **Address:** School of Art & Art History, University of Denver, Rm. 132, Shwayder Art Bldg., 2121 E Asbury Ave., Denver, CO 80208, U.S.A. **Online address:** astott@du.edu

STOTTER, Mike. Also writes as Jim A. Nelson. British (born England), b. 1957. **Genres:** Novellas/Short Stories, Mystery/Crime/Suspense, Westerns/Adventure, Children's Non-fiction, Novels. **Career:** BBC, clerk, 1974-78; Westerner Magazine, editor, 1978-80, co-creator and consultant, 1981-82; Centre-File Ltd., clerk, 1980-82; Alpine Drinks, supervisor, 1982-84; Morgan Grenfell, Laurie Property Consultants, bank messenger, 1986-93; Shots (crime and mystery magazine), editor, 1997-, editor-in-chief; Deutsche Bank, administrator, 1987-99, 2006-; Aberdeen Asset Management, legal administrator; Mystery Scene Magazine, contributor and reviewer; Mystery Review Magazine, contributor and reviewer; Crime Writers Association, dagger liaison officer. **Publications:** NOVELS: McKinney's Revenge, 1990; Tombstone Showdown, 1991; McKinney's Law, 1993; Tucson Justice, 1994; (as Jim A. Nelson) Death in the Canyon, 1997; World of North American Indians, 2009. CHILDREN'S NONFICTION: I Wonder Why Encyclopedia, 1996; The Best Ever Book of the Wild West, 1997; Conquests and Discoveries through the Ages, 2001; Everyday Life in the Ancient World, 2001; The Encyclopedia of the Ancient Americans, 2001; Politics, Society and Leadership through the

Ages, 2001; Pirates and Pioneers, 2001; Find Out about Native Americans, 2002; How Ancient Americans Lived, 2006. Contributor to magazines. Works appear in anthologies. **Address:** 189 Snakes Ln. E, Woodford Green, EX IG8 7JH, England. **Online address:** mike_stotter@yahoo.co.uk

STOURTON, Ivo. British (born England), b. 1982?. **Genres:** Novels, Literary Criticism And History. **Career:** Writer. **Publications:** The Night Climbers: A Novel, 2007. Contributor to periodicals. **Address:** The Ampersand Agency, Ryman's Cottages, Little Tew, Chipping Norton, Oxfordshire, OX OX7 4JJ, England.

STOUT, Chris E. American (born United States), b. 1959. **Genres:** Medicine/Health, Social Sciences, Technology, International Relations/Current Affairs, Sciences. **Career:** Forest Hospital, chief of psychology and director of research, 1985-; Chicago Medical School, associate professor of clinical psychology, 1990-; Forest Health Systems Inc., senior vice-president of clinical applications, policy and development; Alliance Research Group, director; Stout Ventures, principal; University of Illinois, College of Medicine, Department of Psychiatry, clinical full professor, Illinois School, associate professor of clinical psychology, 1990-, International Center on Responses to Catastrophes, faculty; Northwestern University, Feinberg Medical School, Department of Psychiatry and Behavioral Science Mental Health Services and Policy Program, faculty; Rush University, Department of Health Systems Management, visiting professor; United Nations, NGO Special Representative; Illinois Psychological Association, president; School of Public Health Leadership Institute, fellow. Writer. **Publications:** From the Other Side of the Couch: Candid Conversations of Psychotherapists About the Profession, 1993; The Complete Guide to Managed Behavioral Healthcare, 1996; Psychological Assessment in Managed Care, 1997; (with A.E. Jongsma, Jr.) Continuum of Care Treatment Planner, 1998; Technology Solutions Sourcebook, 1998; Continuum of Care Clinical Documentation Sourcebook: A Comprehensive Collection of Inpatient, Outpatient and Partial Hospitalization Forms, Handouts, and Records, 1999; Building Your Best Practice, 2003; The College Counseling Treatment Planner, 2003; (with S.G. Fairley) Getting Started in Personal and Executive Coaching: How To Create A Thriving Coaching Practice, 2004; (with C. Helkowski and A.E. Jongsma, Jr.) College Student Counseling Treatment Planner, 2004; (with L.C. Grand) Getting Started in Private Practice, 2005; The Evidence Based Practice: Methods, Models and Tools for Mental Health Professionals, 2005. EDITOR: (with J.L. Levitt and D.H. Ruben) Handbook for Assessing and Treating Addictive Disorders, 1992; (with M.B. Squire and D.H. Ruben) Current Advances in Inpatient Psychiatric Care, 1993; (with L.F. Koziol and D.H. Ruben) Handbook of Childhood Impulse Disorders and ADHD, 1993; (with D.H. Ruben) Transitions, 1993; (with L.F. Koziol) The Neuropsychology of Mental Disorders, 1994; The Integration of Psychological Principles in Policy Development, 1996; The Psychology of Terrorism, vol. I: A Public Understanding, 2002, vol. II: Clinical Aspects and Responses, 2002, vol. III: Theoretical Understandings and Perspectives, 2002, vol. IV: Programs and Practices in Response and Prevention, 2002; Psychology of Terrorism: Coping with the Continuing Threat, 2004; (with H.J. Langholtz) The Psychology of Diplomacy, 2004; (with R.A. Hayes) Evidence-based Practice, 2005; (with M. Fitzduff) The Psychology of Resolving Global Conflicts: From War to Peace, 2006; (with P.R. Kimmel) Collateral Damage: The Psychological Consequences of America's War on Terrorism, 2006; The New Humanitarians: Inspiration, Innovations, and Blueprints for Visionaries, 2009. Contributor to journals. **Address:** College of Medicine, University of Illinois, 808 S Wood St., Chicago, IL 60612-7301, U.S.A. **Online address:** cstout@ix.netcom.com

STOUT, Harry S. American (born United States), b. 1947. **Genres:** Theology/Religion, History, Local History/Rural Topics, Novels, Intellectual History. **Career:** University of Connecticut, assistant professor, 1974-78, associate professor, 1979-85; American National Biography, associate editor, 1980-85, 1992-99; Cobblestone Magazine, consulting editor, 1985-89; Yale University, professor of American religious history, 1986-90, John B. Madden master, 1990-2000, Jonathan Edwards professor of American christianity, 1991-, Pew Program in Religion in American History, associate director, 1993-, Center for Religion and American Life, co-director. **Publications:** Remigration and Revival: Two Case Studies in the Social and Intellectual History of New England, 1630-1745, 1974; The New England Soul: Preaching and Religious Culture in Colonial New England, 1986; (with D.H. DeFord) An Enemy Among Them (novel), 1987; The Divine Dramatist: George Whitefield and the Rise of Modern Evangelicalism, 1991; (with C. Brekus) A New England Congregation: First Church, New Haven, 1638-1988, 1994; (with R. Balmer and G.

Wacker) Stories of Faith, Stories of America: Religion in United States History, 2003; Upon the Altar of the Nation: A Moral History of the American Civil War, 2006. EDITOR: (with N.O. Hatch) Jonathan Edwards and the American Experience, 1988; (co-ed.) Dictionary of Christianity in America, 1990; (with B. Oberg) Benjamin Franklin, Jonathan Edwards, and the Representation of American Culture, 1993; (with J.E. Smith and K.P. Minkema) A Jonathan Edwards Reader, 1995; (with D.G. Hart) New Directions in American Religious History, 1997; (with J. Butler) Reading in American Religious History: 1997; (with R.M. Miller and C.R.Wilson) Religion and the American Civil War, 1998; (with J. Butler) Women and American Religion, 1999; (with J. Butler) Protestants in America, 2000; (ed. with N.O. Hatch and K.P. Farley) Sermons and Discourses, 1739-1742, 2003. **Address:** Department of Religious Studies, Yale University, 451 College, Rm. 401, PO Box 208287, New Haven, CT 06520-8287, U.S.A. **Online address:** harry.stout@yale.edu

STOUT, Janis P. American (born United States), b. 1939. **Genres:** Novels, Novellas/Short Stories, Literary Criticism And History. **Career:** Rice University, director of graduate programs and English lecturer, 1977-87; Texas A&M University, College of Liberal Arts, associate dean, 1987-94, associate professor, 1987-89, professor of English, 1989-, dean of faculties and associate provost, 1998-2002, now professor emeritus; Auburn University, College of Liberal Arts, acting associate dean, 1992-93. Writer. **Publications:** Sodoms in Eden: The City in American Fiction before 1860, 1976; A Family Likeness, 1982; The Journey Narrative in American Literature: Patterns and Departures, 1983; Eighteen Holes, 1984; Strategies of Reticence: Silence and Meaning in the Works of Jane Austen, Willa Cather, Katherine Anne Porter and Joan Didion, 1990; Home Truth, 1992; Katherine Anne Porter: A Sense of the Times, 1995; Through the Window, Out the Door: Women's Narratives of Departure, 1998; Willa Cather: The Writer and Her World, 2000; (ed.) A Calendar of the Letters of Willa Cather, 2002; (ed.) Willa Cather and Material Culture, 2004; Coming Out of War: Poetry, Culture, and the World Wars, 2005; Willa Cather and Material Culture: Real-World Writing, Writing the Real World, 2005; Picturing a Different West: Vision, Illustration, and the Tradition of Austin and Cather, 2007; This Last House: A Retirement Memoir, 2010. Author of scholarly articles, essays, and short stories. **Address:** Department of English, Texas A & M University, Blocker 227, PO Box 4227, College Station, TX 77843-4227, U.S.A.

STOUT, Jay A. American (born United States), b. 1959. **Genres:** Biography, Military/Defense/Arms Control, Young Adult Non-fiction, Autobiography/Memoirs. **Career:** The United States Marine Corps (USMC), staff, lieutenant colonel, now retired; Delta Air Lines, pilot; Kuwait Air Force, instructor. Writer. **Publications:** NONFICTION: Hornets Over Kuwait (memoir), 1997; (with H. McWhorter III) The First Hellcat Ace (memoir), 2000; Fortress Ploesti: The Campaign to Destroy Hitler's Oil, 2003; To Be a U.S. Naval Aviator, 2005; Hammer from Above: Marine Air Combat over Iraq, 2005; Slaughter at Goliad: The Mexican Massacre of 400 Texas Volunteers, 2008; Men Who Killed the Luftwaffe: The U.S. Army Air Forces Against Germany in World War II, 2010. Contributor of articles to periodicals. **Address:** c/o Author Mail, Presidio Publicity, 1745 Broadway, New York, NY 10019, U.S.A. **Online address:** jayastout@usa.net

STOUT, Joseph A. (Joseph A(llen) Stout). American (born United States), b. 1939. **Genres:** History, Third World, Humor/Satire. **Career:** Missouri Southern College, assistant professor of history, 1971-72; Oklahoma State University, director of Will Rogers Project, 1972-74; Department of History, assistant professor, 1972-74, associate professor, 1974-83, professor, 1983-99, Regents professor, 1999-2005, Regents professor emeritus, 2005-. Writer. **Publications:** The Liberators: The Filibustering Expeditions into Mexico, 1848, and the Last Gasp of Manifest Destiny, 1973; Apache Lightning: The Last Great Battles of the Ojo Calientes, 1974; (with O.B. Faulk) A Short History of the American West, 1974; Letters of a Self-made Diplomat to His President, 1977; Cattle Country: A History of the Oklahoma Cattleman's Association, 1981; The Professionalization of Veterinary Medicine in Oklahoma, 1991; (with A.N. Hanson) A History of the Oklahoma State University College of Arts and Sciences, 1992; Border Conflict: Villistas, Carrancistas, and the Punitive Expedition, 1915-1920, 1999; Schemers and Dreamers: Filibustering in Mexico, 1848-1921, 2002; Spies, Politics, and Power, 2012. EDITOR: (with O.B. Faulk) The Mexican War: Changing Interpretations, 1973; Ether and Me or Just Relax, 1973; There's Not a Bathing Suit in Russia and Other Bare Facts, 1974; The Cowboy Philosopher on the Peace Conference, 1974; Frontier Adventurers: American Exploration In Oklahoma, 1976. **Address:** Department of History, Oklahoma State University, LSW 508, Stillwater, OK 74078-3054, U.S.A. **Online address:** jas1624@okstate.edu

STOUT, Joseph A(llen). *See* **STOUT, Joseph A.**

STOUT, Martha. American (born United States), b. 1953. **Genres:** Psychology, Medicine/Health, Social Sciences. **Career:** Harvard Medical School, clinical faculty; The New School for Social Research, faculty; Massachusetts School of Professional Psychology, faculty; Wellesley College, faculty; Massachusetts General Hospital, clinical psychologist. Writer. **Publications:** The Myth of Sanity: Divided Consciousness and the Promise of Awareness, 2001; The Sociopath Next Door: The Ruthless Versus the Rest of Us, 2005; The Paranoia Switch: How Terror Rewires Our Brains and Reshapes Our Behavior and How We Can Reclaim Our Courage, 2007. **Address:** c/o Author Mail, Broadway Books, 1745 Broadway, New York, NY 10019, U.S.A. **Online address:** dr_martha_stout@worldnet.att.net

STOUT, Maureen. Canadian (born Canada) **Genres:** Social Sciences, Education, Reference. **Career:** California State University, assistant professor of education, 1994-2000; Simon Fraser University, professor, Imaginative Education Research Group, post-doctoral fellow; University of British Columbia, professor; University of Victoria, professor. Writer and realtor. **Publications:** The Feel-Good Curriculum: The Dumbing Down of America's Kids in the Name of Self-Esteem, 2000; (ed. with K. Egan and K. Takaya) Teaching and Learning Outside The Box: Inspiring Imagination Across The Curriculum, 2007. Contributor to books. **Address:** Sutton Group - West Coast Realty, 1508 W Broadway, Ste. 301, Vancouver, BC V6J 1W8, Canada. **Online address:** maureenstout@telus.net

STOUT, Nancy. American (born United States), b. 1942. **Genres:** Photography, Architecture, Travel/Exploration, Sports/Fitness. **Career:** State of Ohio, regional preservation officer, 1976-80; Ohio Historic Preservation Office, research and survey contractor, 1980-82; Clarion Music Society Inc., executive director. Fordham University, academic librarian, 2004-. Writer. **Publications:** Great American Thoroughbred Racetracks, 1991; Havana/La Habana, 1994; Habanos, The Book of the Havana Cigar, 1997; Homestretch, 2000; The West Side YMCA: A Social and Architectural Retrospective, 2001. Contributor to periodicals. **Address:** 419 E 64th St., Ste. 3D, New York, NY 10065-7562, U.S.A. **Online address:** newyorkstout@yahoo.com

STOVALL, Tyler. American (born United States), b. 1954. **Genres:** History, Social Sciences, Politics/Government. **Career:** University of California, professor of history, 1988-, Ford Foundation and National Endowment for the Humanities, fellow. **Publications:** The Rise of the Paris Red Belt, 1990; Paris Noir: African Americans in the City of Light, 1996; France Since the Second World War, 2001; (ed. with G.V.D. Abbeele) French Civilization and Its Discontents: Nationalism, Colonialism, Race, 2003; (ed. with S. Peabody) Color of Liberty: Histories of Race in France, 2003; Paris and the Spirit of 1919: Consumer Struggles, Transnationalism and Revolution, 2012; (ed. with T.D. Keaton and T.D. Sharpley-Whiting) Black France/France Noire: The History and Politics of Blackness, 2012. **Address:** Department of History, University of California, 2213 Dwinelle Hall, Berkeley, CA 94720-2550, U.S.A. **Online address:** tstovall@socrates.berkeley.edu

STOVER, Matthew Woodring. American (born United States), b. 1962?. **Genres:** Science Fiction/Fantasy, Novellas/Short Stories, Novels. **Career:** Novelist and producer. **Publications:** Iron Dawn, 1997; Jericho Moon, 1998; The Real Flash Gordon, 2001; (with R.E. Vardeman) God of War, 2010; Caine's Law, 2012. THE ACTS OF CAINE: Heroes Die, 1998; Blade of Tyshalle, 2001; Caine Black Knife, 2008; Act of Faith Trilogy, forthcoming; Dead Man's Heart, forthcoming. STAR WARS: Traitor, 2002; Shatterpoint, 2003; Revenge of the Sith, 2005; Star Wars on Trial: Science Fiction and Fantasy Writers Debate the Most Popular Science Fiction Films of all Time, 2006; The Prequel Trilogy, 2007; Luke Skywalker and the Shadows of Mindor, 2008. **Address:** c/o Author Mail, Del Rey Books, 201 E 50th St., New York, NY 10022, U.S.A.

STOW, Kenneth R. Israeli/American (born United States) **Genres:** Theology/Religion, History. **Career:** University of Haifa, emeritus professor of Jewish history. Historian and writer. **Publications:** Catholic Thought and Papal Jewry Policy, 1555-1593, 1977; Taxation, Community and State: The Jews and the Fiscal Foundations of the Early Modern Papal State, 1982; The "1007 Anonymous" and Papal Sovereignty: Jewish, Perceptions of the Papacy and Papal Policy in the High Middle Ages, 1984; (ed.) The Church and the Jews in the XIIIth Century, 2 vols., 1989; Alienated Minority: The Jews of Medieval Latin Europe, 1992; The Jews: A Mediterranean Culture, 1994; The Jews in Rome, 2 vols., 1995; Theater of Acculturation: The Roman Ghetto in the Sixteenth Century, 2001; Jewish Dogs: An Image and Its Interpreters: Continuity in the Catholic-Jewish Encounter, 2006; Popes, Church and Jews in the Middle Ages: Confrontation and Responses, 2007; Jewish Life in Early Modern Rome: Challenge, Conversion and Private Life, 2007. Contributor to periodicals and journals. **Address:** Department of Jewish History, University of Haifa, Mount Carmel, Haifa, 31905, Israel. **Online address:** kstow@research.haifa.ac.il

STOWE, Steven M. American (born United States), b. 1946?. **Genres:** Medicine/Health, Biography, Autobiography/Memoirs, History. **Career:** Indiana University, Department of History, professor. Writer and historian. **Publications:** Intimacy and Power in the Old South: Ritual in the Lives of the Planters, 1987; (ed.) A Southern Practice: The Diary and Autobiography of Charles A. Hentz, M.D., 2000; Doctoring the South: Southern Physicians and Everyday Medicine in the Mid-Nineteenth Century, 2004. **Address:** Department of History, Indiana University, Rm. 824, Ballantine Hall, 1020 E Kirkwood Ave., Bloomington, IN 47405-7103, U.S.A. **Online address:** sstowe@indiana.edu

STOWE, William W. American (born United States), b. 1946. **Genres:** Literary Criticism And History, Poetry, Essays, Travel/Exploration. **Career:** Coleytown Junior High School, English teacher, 1968-73; Princeton University, visiting instructor, 1976-77; Yale University, visiting instructor, 1977; Wesleyan University, assistant professor to associate professor, 1978-90, professor of English, 1990-, Department of English, chair, 1992-96, 2001-, Benjamin L. Waite professor of English, 1998-, professor of environmental studies. Writer. **Publications:** Balzac, James and the Realistic Novel, 1983; (ed. with G.W. Most) The Poetics of Murder: Detective Fiction and Literary Theory, 1983; Going Abroad: European Travel in Nineteenth-Century American Culture, 1994. Contributor to periodicals. **Address:** Department of English, Wesleyan University, 294 High St., Middletown, CT 06459, U.S.A. **Online address:** wstowe@wesleyan.edu

STOYLE, Mark. British (born England) **Genres:** Social Sciences, History. **Career:** University of Southampton, professor of history. Writer and historian. **Publications:** Loyalty and Locality: Popular Allegiance in Devon during the English Civil War, 1994; From Deliverance to Destruction: Rebellion and Civil War in an English City, 1996; West Britons: Cornish Identities and the Early Modern British State, 2002; Circled with Stone: Exeter's City Walls, 1485-1660, 2003; Soldiers and Strangers: An Ethnic History of the English Civil War, 2005. Contributor to books and periodicals. **Address:** University of Southampton, Faculty of Humanities, Department of History, 65 Bldg., University Rd., Avenue Campus, Southampton, HM SO17 1BF, England. **Online address:** mjs@soton.ac.uk

STRACHAN, Ian. Also writes as Nikki Fisher, Maria Palmer, Ben Taylor, Robin Campbell. British (born England), b. 1938. **Genres:** Novels, Picture/Board Books, Literary Criticism And History. **Career:** British Broadcasting Corp., television producer and radio presenter, 1990. Writer. **Publications:** Moses Beech, 1981; The Soutar Retrospective, 1982, rev. ed. as Pebble on the Beach, 1991; Journey of a Thousand Miles, 1985; Bang! Bang! You're Dead!, 1988; Picking Up the Threads, 1989; The Flawed Glass, 1989; (with A. Dalton) Heartache: A Book of Love Stories, 1989; Wayne Loves Custard?, 1990; The Ferryman's Son, 1990; The Second Step, 1991; (as Ben Taylor) Star for a Month, 1991; (co-author) Haunting Christmas Tales, 1991; (as Ben Taylor) Falling Star, 1991; (as Ben Taylor) Summer Special, 1991; Throwaways, 1992; The Upside Down World of Ginger Nutt, 1992; The Boy in the Bubble, 1993; (as Robin Campbell) The Final Act, 1994; Kidnap!, 1994; Hidden Depths, 1995; House of Danger, 1995; The Stray Cat's Tale, 1995; (as Maria Palmer) Gemini: Sliced Apart, 1995; (as Nikki Fisher) Lucky Break, 1995; (as Nikki Fisher) Undercurrents, 1995; Which Way Is Home?, 1996; The Joke Shop, 1997; The Iliad, 1997; Dan's Den, 1997; (co-author) Best of Friends, 1997; Wastelanders, 1997; Underwater World, 1998; Circus Twins in Dynamite Summer, 1998; Monster School, 1999. Contributor to books. Works appear in anthologies. **Address:** Caroline Sheldon Literary Agency Ltd., 71 Hillgate Pl., London, GL W8 7SS, England.

STRACHMAN, Daniel A. American (born United States), b. 1971. **Genres:** Money/Finance, Business/Trade/Industry, Biography, Economics. **Career:** Answers & Co., managing director, 2001-; New York University, School of Continuing Education, adjunct professor; Institutional Investor, columnist. **Publications:** Getting Started in Hedge Funds, 2000, 3rd ed. as Getting Started in Hedge Funds: From Launching a Hedge Fund to New Regulation, the Use of Leverage, and Top Manager Profiles, 2010; Essential Stock Picking Strategies: What Works on Wall Street, 2002; Julian Robertson: A Tiger in the Land of Bulls and Bears, 2004; Fundamentals of Hedge Fund Management: How to Successfully Launch and Operate a Hedge Fund, 2007; Long and Short of Hedge Funds: A Complete Guide to Hedge Fund Evaluation and Investing, 2008; (with R.S. Bookbinder) Fund of Funds Investing: A Roadmap to Portfolio Diversification, 2010. Contributor to magazines. **Address:** Answers & Co., 1120 Ave. of the Americas, 4th Fl., New York, NY 10036-6700, U.S.A. **Online address:** strach@mindspring.com

STRADLING, R. A. (Robert Stradling). British/Welsh (born Wales), b. 1942. **Genres:** History, Music. **Career:** University of Wales, reader in history, 1970-, professor of history, now professor emeritus. Writer. **Publications:** Europe and the Decline of Spain, 1981; Philip IV and the Government of Spain, 1988; Armada of Flanders, 1992; (with M. Hughes) The English Musical: Renaissance 1860-1940, 1993; The Spanish Monarchy and Irish Mercenaries, 1994; (with M. Vincent) Cultural Atlas of Spain and Portugal, 1994; Spain's Struggle for Europe, 1598-1668, 1994; Cardiff and the Spanish Civil War, 1996; (ed. with S. Newton and D. Bates) Conflict and Coexistence: Nationalism and Democracy in Modern Europe: Essays in Honor of Harry Hearder, 1997; (ed.) Brother Against Brother: Experiences of a Volunteer in the Spanish Civil War, 1998; The Irish and the Spanish Civil War-Crusades in Conflict, 1999; (with M. Hughes) The English Musical Renaissance, 1840-1940, 2nd ed. 2001; History and Legend: Writing the International Brigades, 2003; Wales and the Spanish Civil War: The Dragon's Dearest Cause, 2004; Your Children Will Be Next: Bombing and Propaganda in the Spanish Civil War, 1936-1939, 2008. **Address:** 1 Rectory Rd., Penarth, Penarth, CF64 3AN, Wales. **Online address:** dr.robert@lineone.net

STRADLING, Robert. See **STRADLING, R. A.**

STRAHINICH, Helen C. American (born United States), b. 1949. **Genres:** Young Adult Fiction, Education, Young Adult Non-fiction, Writing/Journalism, History. **Career:** Jamaica Plain High School, Boston, special needs teacher, 1974-76; Belmont High School, learning disabilities specialist, 1976-77; Boston Center for Adult Education, teacher, 1977; The Reading Institute, supervisor and reading specialist, 1977-79; Holt, Rinehart and Winston, textbook editor, 1979-80; freelance writer, 1980-. **Publications:** Think about Guns in America, 1992; The Holocaust: Understanding and Remembering, 1996; Surprising World of Plants, 2002; Saving the Zog, 2003; Tales from Gull Island, 2003; (comp. and adapter) Sounds of Our Heritage series, 1979-80. Contributor to newspapers. **Address:** 32 Southbourne Rd., Jamaica Plain, MA 02130, U.S.A.

STRAIGHT, Susan. American (born United States), b. 1960. **Genres:** Novels, Novellas/Short Stories, Mystery/Crime/Suspense. **Career:** Inland Empire Job Corps, teacher of gang members, dropouts and refugees, 1984-85; Lao Family Community, teacher of recent refugees, 1985-86; Riverside City College, teacher of English, 1986-89; University of California, lecturer, 1988-92, professor of creative writing, 1993-; California Youth Authority (prison for young offenders), leader of a writing workshop. Writer. **Publications:** NOVELS: Aquaboogie: A Novel in Stories, 1991; I Been in Sorrow's Kitchen and Licked out All the Pots, 1993; Blacker Than a Thousand Midnights, 1994; Bear E. Bear, 1995; The Gettin Place, 1996; Highwire Moon, 2001; Million Nightingales, 2006; Friskative Dog, 2007; Take One Candle Light a Room, 2010. Contributor to books and periodicals. **Address:** Department of Creative Writing, University of California, 4109 INTS Bldg., 900 University Ave., Riverside, CA 92521, U.S.A. **Online address:** susan.straight@ucr.edu

STRAIN, Christopher B. American (born United States), b. 1970?. **Genres:** History. **Career:** Florida Atlantic University, Harriet L. Wilkes Honors College, associate professor, assistant professor; Honors College Judicial Review Board, faculty advisor; Black Student Union, faculty advisor; Triple-H, faculty advisor; University of California, Department of history, instructor; University of Georgia, Department of history, instructor, graduate assistant; Institute of Reading Development, instructor; Harvard University, W.E.B. Du Bois Institute, visiting fellow, 2006 Writer. **Publications:** Pure Fire: Self-Defense as Activism in the Civil Rights Era, 2005; Burning Faith: Church Arson in the American South, 2008; Reload: Rethinking Violence in American Life,

2010. Contributor to periodicals. **Address:** Harriet L. Wilkes Honors College, Florida Atlantic University, 5353 Parkside Dr., Jupiter, FL 33458, U.S.A. **Online address:** cstrain@fau.edu

STRANE, Susan. American (born United States), b. 1944. **Genres:** Biography, Autobiography/Memoirs, History, Women's Studies And Issues, Race Relations. **Career:** Macmillan Publishing Company Inc., editorial art editor, 1972-74; freelance writer. **Publications:** A Whole-Souled Woman: Prudence Crandall and the Education of Black Women, 1990. **Address:** c/o Nancy Trichter, 5 W 86th St., New York, NY 10024-3603, U.S.A.

STRANGE, Julie-Marie. British (born England), b. 1973. **Genres:** Social Sciences, Cultural/Ethnic Topics. **Career:** University of Manchester, faculty, 2003-; University of London, Birkbeck College, lecturer; United Africa Co., research assistant. Writer. **Publications:** Death, Grief and Poverty in Britain, 1870-1914, 2005; (ed. with F. Carnevali) Twentieth-Century Britain: Economic, Cultural and Social Change, 2nd ed., 2007. Contributor to journals. **Address:** School of Arts, Histories & Cultures, University of Manchester, Oxford Rd., Manchester, M13 9PL, England. **Online address:** Julie-marie.strange@manchester.ac.uk

STRANGE, Lily. American (born United States), b. 1965. **Genres:** Novels. **Career:** Writer. **Publications:** Eternal Death: Lost Beneath The Surface, 2007; Eternal Death I: Lost Beneath the Surface, 2009. **Address:** Outskirts Press Inc., 10940 S Parker Rd., Ste. 515, Parker, CO 80134, U.S.A. **Online address:** lily@lilystrange.com

STRASSER, Todd. (Morton Rhue). American (born United States), b. 1950. **Genres:** Novels, Children's Fiction, Young Adult Fiction, Plays/Screenplays, Young Adult Non-fiction, Essays. **Career:** Beloit College, staff in public relations, 1973-74; Times Herald Record, reporter, 1974-76; freelance writer, 1975-; Compton Advertising, copywriter, 1976-77; Esquire, researcher, 1977-78; Toggle Inc. (fortune cookie co.), owner, 1978-89. **Publications:** YOUNG ADULT FICTION: Angel Dust Blues: A Novel, 1979; Friends till the End: A Novel, 1981; (as Morton Rhue) The Wave, 1981; Rock 'n' Roll Nights: A Novel, 1982; Workin' for Peanuts, 1983; Turn It Up!: A Novel, 1984; A Very Touchy Subject, 1985; Ferris Bueller's Day Off, 1986; Wildlife, 1987; The Accident, 1988; Cookie, 1989; Beyond the Reef, 1989; Moving Target, 1989; Home Alone, 1990; (as Morton Rhue) Devil in Vienna, 1991; Honey, I Blew Up the Kid: A Novel, 1992; Home Alone II, 1992; The Diving Bell, 1992; Disney's The Villains Collection, 1993; Lifeguards Serves, 1993; Free Willy: A Novelization, 1993; Hocus Pocus: A Novel, 1993; The Three Musketeers: A Novel, 1993; Rookie of The Year, 1993; Walt Disney's Peter Pan, 1994; (with R. Duke) Disney's It's Magic!: Stories From the Films, 1994; Street Fighter, 1994; Tall Tale: The Unbelievable Adventures Of Pecos Bill, 1994; Walt Disney's Lady and the Tramp, 1994; How I Changed My Life, 1995; Man of the House: A Novel, 1995; Hey Dad, Get a Life, 1996; Girl Gives Birth to Own Prom Date, 1996; The Villains Collection: Stories From The Films, 1996; Kidnap Kids, 1998; How I Spent My Last Night on Earth, 1998; Kids' Book Of Gross Facts & Feats, 1998; Close Call, 1999; Give a Boy a Gun, 2000; Con-fidence, 2002; Thief of Dreams, 2003; Can't Get There from Here, 2004; Battle Drift, 2006; Is That A Dead Dog In Your Locker?, 2006; Wild, 2006; Boot Camp, 2007; Cheap Shot, 2007; Count Your Blessings, 2007; For Money and Love, 2007; Is That A Sick Cat In Your Backpack?, 2007; Is That A Glow-In-The-Dark Bunny in Your Halloween Sack?, 2007; Is That an Angry Penguin in Your Gym Bag?, 2008. HELP! I'M TRAPPED SERIES: Help! I'm Trapped in My Teacher's Body, 1993; Help! I'm Trapped in the First Day of School, 1994; Help! I'm Trapped in Obedience School, 1995; Help! I'm Trapped in Santa's Body, 1997; Help! I'm Trapped in My Sister's Body, 1997; Help! I'm Trapped in My Gym Teacher's Body, 1997; Help! I'm Trapped in the President's Body, 1997; Help! I'm Trapped in Obedience School Again, 1997; Help! I'm Trapped in the First Day of Summer Camp, 1998; Help! I'm Trapped in the Principal's Body, 1998; Help! I'm Trapped in an Alien's Body, 1998; Help! I'm Trapped in a Movie Star's Body, 1999; Help! I'm Trapped in My Lunch Lady's Body, 1999; Help! I'm Trapped in the Camp Counselor's Body, 1999; Help! I'm Trapped in a Professional Wrestler's Body, 2000; Help! I'm Trapped in a Vampire's Body, 2000; Help! I'm Trapped in a Supermodel's Body, 2001; Help! I'm Trapped in Summer Camp, 2006. WORDSWORTH SERIES: Wordsworth And The Cold Cut Catastrophe, 1995; Wordsworth and the Kibble Kidnapping, 1995; Wordsworth and the Roast Beef Romance, 1995; Wordsworth and the Mail-Order Meatloaf Mess, 1995; Wordsworth and the Tasty Treat Trick, 1995; The Lip-Smacking Licorice Love Affair, 1996. CAMP RUN-A-MUCK SERIES: Greasy Grimy

Gopher Guts, 1997; Mutilated Monkey Meat, 1997; Chopped-Up Birdy's Feet, 1997. AGAINST THE ODDS SERIES: Shark Bite, 1998; Grizzly Attack, 1998; Buzzard's Feast, 1999; Gator Prey, 1999. HERE COMES HEAVENLY SERIES: Here Comes Heavenly, 1999; Dance Magic, 1999; Pastabilitics, 2000; Spell Danger, 2000. DON'T GET CAUGHT SERIES: Driving the School Bus, 2000; In the Girl's Locker Room, 2001; In the Teacher's Lounge, 2001; Wearing the Lunch Lady's Hairnet, 2001. IMPACT ZONE SERIES: Take Off, 2004; Cut Back, 2004; Close Out, 2004. DRIFT X SERIES: Battle Drift, 2006; Sidewayz Glory, 2006; Slide or Die, 2006. MOB PRINCESS SERIES: Count Your Blessings, 2007; For Money and Love, 2007; Stolen Kisses, Secrets, and Lies, 2007. TARDY BOYS SERIES: Is That a Dead Dog in Your Locker?, 2006; Is That a Sick Cat in Your Backpack?, 2007. OTHERS: The Complete Computer Popularity Program, 1984; The Mall from Outer Space, 1987; The Family Man, 1988; Super Mario Brothers: A Novel, 1993; Summer's End, 1993; Summer's Promise, 1993; Free Willy 2: The Adventure Home, 1995; Playing for Love, 1995; The Boys in the Band, 1996; (with D. Reynolds) Kids' Book of Insults, 1996; Nighttime, 2007; Too Scared To Sleep, 2007; How I Created My Perfect Prom Date, 2008; How I Spent My Last Night on Earth, 2008; If I Grow Up, 2009; Wish You were Dead, 2009; Is that an Unlucky Leprechaun in your Lunch?, 2009; Too Dark To See, 2009; Too Afraid to Scream, 2009; Is That A Glow-in-the-Dark Bunny In Your Pillowcase?, 2009; Blood on My Hands, 2010; Famous, 2011; Kill You Last, 2011. Contributor to periodicals. **Address:** PO Box 859, Larchmont, NY 10538-2041, U.S.A. **Online address:** todd@toddstrasser.com

STRATHERN, Paul. British (born England), b. 1940. **Genres:** Novels, Philosophy, Sciences, Travel/Exploration, Biography, Art/Art History, Adult Non-fiction, Autobiography/Memoirs, Autobiography/Memoirs. **Career:** Kingston University, lecturer. Writer. **Publications:** NOVELS: Pass by the Sea, 1968; A Season in Abyssinia, 1972; One Man's War, 1973; Vaslav: An Impersonation of Nijinsky, 1974; The Adventures of Spiro, 1979; Exploration by Land, 2002; Napoleon in Egypt, 2008. TRAVEL GUIDES: The Silk and Spice Routes, 1993; Greece and the Greek Islands: Trip Planner & Guide, 1994; Turkey, 1995; Florida, 1996; Australia, 1997. THE BIG IDEAS SCIENCE SERIES: Crick, Watson and DNA, 1997; Einstein and Relativity, 1997; Newton and Gravity, 1997; Pythagoras and His Theorem, 1997; Archimedes and the Fulcrum, 1998; Bohr and Quantum Theory, 1998; Curie and Radium, 1998; Darwin and Evolution, 1998; Galileo and the Solar System, 1998; Hawking and Black Holes, 1998; Oppenheimer and the Bomb, 1998; Turing and the Computer, 1998; Mendeleyev's Dream: The Quest for the Elements, 2000; Dr. Strangelove's Game: A Brief History of Economic Genius, 2001; The Medici: Godfathers of the Renaissance, 2003; A Brief History of Medicine: From Hippocrates to Gene Therapy, 2005. PHILOSOPHERS IN 90 MINUTES SERIES: Aristotle in 90 Minutes, 1996; Descartes, 1996; Kant in 90 Minutes, 1996; Nietzsche in 90 Minutes, 1996; Plato in 90 Minutes, 1996; Wittgenstein in 90 Minutes, 1996; Hegel in 90 Minutes, 1997; Kierkegaard in 90 Minutes, 1997; Socrates in 90 Minutes, 1997; St. Augustine in 90 Minutes, 1997; Machiavelli in 90 Minutes, 1998; Sartre in 90 Minutes, 1998; Spinoza in 90 Minutes, 1998; Thomas Aquinas in 90 Minutes, 1998; Confucius in 90 Minutes, 1999; Hume in 90 Minutes, 1999; Locke in 90 Minutes, 1999; Schopenhauer in 90 Minutes, 1999; Berkeley in 90 Minutes, 2000; Derrida in 90 Minutes, 2000; Foucault in 90 Minutes, 2000; Leibniz in 90 Minutes, 2000; Marx in 90 Minutes, 2001; Bertrand Russell in 90 Minutes, 2001; Dewey in 90 Minutes, 2002; Heidegger in 90 Minutes, 2002; J.S. Mill in 90 Minutes, 2002; Rousseau in 90 Minutes, 2002; James Joyce in 90 Minutes, 2005; Tolstoy in 90 Minutes, 2006. WRITERS IN 90 MINUTES SERIES: García Márquez in 90 Minutes, 2004; Dostoevsky in 90 Minutes, 2004; Kafka in 90 Minutes, 2004; Virginia Woolf in 90 Minutes, 2005; Nabokov in 90 Minutes, 2005; Hemingway in 90 Minutes, 2005; D.H. Lawrence in 90 Minutes, 2005; Beckett in 90 Minutes, 2005; Poe in 90 Minutes, 2006; Borges in 90 Minutes, 2006. OTHERS: The Artist, the Philosopher, and the Warrior: The Intersecting Lives of da Vinci, Machiavelli, and Borgia and the World They Shaped, 2009; The Artist, the Philosopher, and the Warrior: Leonardo, Machiavelli, and Borgia: A Fateful Collusion, 2009. Contributor to newspapers and journals. **Address:** c/o Julian Alexander, Lucas Alexander Whitley Ltd., 14 Vernon St., London, GL W14 ORJ, England.

STRATTON, Allan. Canadian (born Canada), b. 1951?. **Genres:** Film, Novels, Plays/Screenplays, inspirational/Motivational Literature. **Career:** Etobicoke School of the Arts, head of drama department. Writer. **Publications:** 72 under the O: A Farce, 1977; Nurse Jane Goes to Hawaii, 1981; Rexy!, 1981; Joggers, 1983. OTHERS: Friends of a Feather, 1984; Papers, 1985; Bing!, 1987; Words in Play: Three Comedies by Allan Stratton, 1988; Bag Babies: A

Comedy of (Bad) Manners, 1990; Canada Split: A Flush of Tories & Rexy!: Two Plays, 1991; Grave Robber's Apprentice, 2012. NOVELS: The Phoenix Lottery, 2000; Leslie's Journal, 2000; Chanda's Secrets, 2004; Chanda's Wars: A Novel, 2008; Borderline, 2010; The Resurrection of Mary Mabel McTavish, forthcoming. **Address:** c/o Denise Bukowski, The Bukowski Agency, 14 Prince Arthur Ave., Ste. 202, Toronto, ON M5R 1A9, Canada. **Online address:** allanstratton@excite.com

STRATTON, Thomas. *See* DEWEESE, Gene.

STRAUB, Peter (Francis). American (born United States), b. 1943. **Genres:** Novels, Novellas/Short Stories, Poetry, Young Adult Non-fiction, Graphic Novels, Literary Criticism And History. **Career:** University School of Milwaukee, English teacher, 1966-69; writer, 1969-. **Publications:** TALISMAN SERIES WITH S. KING: The Talisman, 1984; Black House, 2001. CRIMINAL RECORDS SERIES: Pork Pie Hat, 1999. NOVELS: Marriages, 1973; Julia, 1975 as Full Circle, 1977; If You could See Me Now, 1976; Ghost Story, 1979; Shadowland, 1980; Generals' Wife, 1982; Floating Dragon, 1982; Leeson Park and Belsize Square: Poems 1970-1975, 1983; Under Venus, 1984; Koko, 1988; Mystery, 1990; Mrs. God, 1990; The Throat, 1993; Blue Rose, 1995; The Hellfire Club, 1995; Misterr X, 1999; Lost Boy Lost Girl, 2003; In the Night Room, 2004; (ed.) H.P. Lovecraft: Tales, 2005; The Skylark, 2009; Dark Matter: A Novel, 2010; The Juniper Tree: And Other Blue Rose Stories, 2010; The Ballad of Ballard and Sandrine, 2011. OMNIBUS: Wild Animals, 1984. COLLECTIONS: Ishmael, Poems, 1972; Open Air, Poems, 1972; Houses without Doors, 1990; Ghosts, 1995; Magic Terror, 1997; 5 Stories, 2008. NON-FICTION: (with P. Conroy, J. Grisham and S. King) The Wavedancer Benefit, 2002; Sides, 2006. AUTHOR OF INTRODUCTION: In a Lonely Place, 1983; The Island of Dr. Moreau, 1996; Are You Loathsome Tonight? A Collection of Short Stories, 1998; Peter and Ptr, 1999; Secret Windows: Essays and Fiction on the Craft of Writing, 2000; Hopes to Die, 2001; Dracula, 2001; The Darkest Part of the Woods, 2002; The Stepford Wives, 2002. AFTERWORD: Tales of Pain and Wonder, 2000; Dystopia: Collected Stories, 2000. GRAPHIC NOVELS: Ashputtle, 2006; (with S. King) The Talisman: The Road of Trials, vol. I, 2010; (with M. Easton) The Green Woman, 2010. OTHERS: (ed.) Peter Straub's Ghosts, 1995; Magic Terror: Seven Tales, 2000; (ed.) Poe's Children, 2008; (ed.) American Fantastic Tales: Terror and the Uncanny from the 1940s to Now, 2009; (ed.) American Fantastic Tales: Terror and the Uncanny from Poe to the Pulps, 2009; A Special Place: The Heart of a Dark Matter, 2010. Contributor to periodicals. **Address:** 53 W 85th St., New York, NY 10024-4132, U.S.A.

STRAUS, Jillian. American (born United States), b. 1973?. **Genres:** Young Adult Fiction. **Career:** ABC News, television producer; Woodhull Institute for Ethical Leadership, fellow; Straus Strategic Communications, founder; writer, 2006-. **Publications:** Unhooked Generation: The Truth about Why We're Still Single, 2006. **Address:** c/o Author Mail, Hyperion Books, 114 5th Ave., New York, NY 10011, U.S.A. **Online address:** jillian@unhookedgeneration.com

STRAUS, Murray A. American (born United States), b. 1926. **Genres:** Criminology/True Crime, Psychology, Sociology, Human Relations/Parenting. **Career:** University of Ceylon, lecturer in sociology, 1949-52; University of Wisconsin, Department of Economics and Sociology, instructor, 1949, assistant professor of sociology, 1957-59; Washington State University, assistant professor of sociology, 1954-57; Cornell University, associate professor, 1959-61; University of Minnesota, College of Liberal Arts, professor of sociology, 1961-68, School of Home Economics, Division of Family Social Science, chairman, 1961-64; National Council on Family Relations, director, 1963-70, president, 1972-73; University of Bombay, visiting professor, 1964-65; Groves Conference on the Family, director, 1968-70, chairman, 1968; University of New Hampshire, professor of sociology, 1968-, Family Violence Research Program, director, 1970-, Family Research Laboratory, founder and co-director, 1979-, State and Regional Indicators Archives, director, 1979-88; Teaching Sociology, founding editor, 1973-76; University of York, visiting professor, 1974; University of Massachusetts, visiting professor, 1975; Eastern Sociological Society, vice-president, 1976-78; Columbia University, visiting professor, 1982; U.S. National Institute of Mental Health and National Science Foundation, consultant. Writer. **Publications:** (With J.I. Nelson) Sociological Analysis: An Empirical Approach through Replication, 1968; Family Analysis: Readings and Replications, 1969; Family Measurement Techniques, 1969, (with B. Brown) rev. ed., 1978; (co-ed.) Fam-

ily Problem Solving, 1971; (co-ed.) Violence in the Family, 1974; (with G. Hotaling) The Social Causes of Husband-Wife Violence, 1980; (co-author) Behind Closed Doors: Violence in the American Family, 1980; (co-author) The Dark Side of Families: Current Family Violence Research, 1983; (with A. Lincoln) Crime and the Family, 1985; (with A.S. Linsky) Social Stress in the United States: Links to Regional Patterns of Crime and Illness, 1986; (with R. Gelles) Intimate Violence, 1988; (with L. Baron) The Four Theories of Rape in the United States, 1989; (with R. Gelles) Physical Violence in American Families, 1990; Beating the Devil Out of Them: Corporal Punishment in American Families and the Effects on Children, 1994, 2nd ed., 2001; (ed. with S.M. Stith) Understanding Partner Violence, 1995; (with A.S. Linsky and R. Bachman) Stress, Culture, and Aggression, 1995; (ed. with J. Touliatos and B.F. Perlmutter) Handbook of Family Measurement Techniques, 2001; (ed. with M. Donnelly) Corporal Punishment of Children in Theoretical Perspective, 2005; Violence against Dating Partners in World Perspective: The International Dating Violence Study, forthcoming; The Primordial Violence: Corporal Punishment By Parents, Cognitive Development, And Crime, forthcoming. Contributor to periodicals. **Address:** Family Research Laboratory, University of New Hampshire, 126 Horton Social Science Ctr., Durham, NH 03824, U.S.A. **Online address:** murray.straus@unh.edu

STRAUSBAUGH, John. American (born United States), b. 1951?. **Genres:** History, Cultural/Ethnic Topics, Politics/Government, Popular Culture. **Career:** New York Press, editor, 1990-2002. **Publications:** Flying Fish, 1986; (ed. with D. Blaise) The Drug User: Documents 1840-1960, 1991; Alone with the President, 1993; E: Reflections on the Birth of the Elvis Faith, 1996; Rock 'til You Drop: The Decline from Rebellion to Nostalgia, 2001; Black Like You: Blackface, Whiteface, Insult and Imitation in American Popular Culture, 2006; Sissy Nation: How America Became a Nation of Wimps and Stoopits, 2007. **Address:** Author Mail, Verso Books, 180 Varick St., 10th Fl., New York, NY 10014, U.S.A. **Online address:** press@johnstrausbaugh.com

STRAUSS, David Levi. American (born United States), b. 1953?. **Genres:** Art/Art History. **Career:** Bard College, Avery Graduate School of the Arts, Center for Curatorial Studies, faculty; School of Visual Arts, MFA Art Criticism and Writing Department, chair; Art Center College of Design, faculty; Columbia University, faculty; Naropa Institute, faculty; New York University, faculty; San Francisco Art Institute, faculty; Tyler School of Art, faculty; Yale University, faculty; critic; art curator. Writer. **Publications:** The Things You See when You Don't Have a Grenade!, 1995; Miguel Rio Branco (essay), 1998; Between Dog & Wolf: Essays on Art & Politics, 1999; Jorge Zeno: Semilla Abierta=Open Seed (exhibit catalog), 2000; Miguel Rio Branco: entre os olhos, o deserto, 2001; Between the Eyes: Essays on Photography and Politics, 2003; From Head to Hand: Art and the Manual, 2010; The Fighting is a Dance, Too: Leon Golub and Nancy Spero, 2000; Odile & Odette, forthcoming; Artists and Photography, forthcoming; Beuys in Ireland: 7000 Oaks on the Hill of Uisneach, forthcoming; Nine Latin American Photographers, forthcoming. Contributor to books. **Address:** c/o Author Mail, Aperture's Book Ctr., 20 E 23rd St., New York, NY 10010, U.S.A. **Online address:** dstrauss@bard.edu

STRAUSS, Gwen. French/Haitian (born France), b. 1963. **Genres:** Poetry, Children's Fiction. **Career:** Park School, creative writing teacher, 1986-87; Frank Books, editorial assistant, 1992. Writer. **Publications:** Trail of Stones (poems), 1990; The Night Shimmy (children's book), 1992; Ruth and the Green Book, 2010. Contributor to periodicals. **Address:** c/o Publicity Director, Alfred Knopf, 201 E 50th St., New York, NY 10022, U.S.A.

STRAUSS, Jennifer (Wallace). Australian (born Australia), b. 1933. **Genres:** Poetry, Literary Criticism And History, History, Reference, Adult Non-fiction. **Career:** University of Melbourne, lecturer, 1961-63; Monash University, lecturer, 1964-71, senior lecturer, 1971-91, associate professor, 1991-98, senior research fellow, 1998-, honorary senior research fellow; University of Toronto, Centre for Medieval Studies, visiting professor, 1982. Writer. **Publications:** Children and Other Strangers: Poems, 1975; (co-ed.) Middle English Verse: An Anthology, 1976, rev. ed., 1985; Winter Driving: Poems, 1981; Labour Ward, 1988; Stop Laughing! I'm Being Serious: Three Studies in Seriousness and Wit in Contemporary Australian Poetry, 1990; Boundary Conditions: The Poetry of Gwen Harwood, 1992, new ed., 1996; (ed.) The Oxford Book of Australian Love Poems, 1993; Judith Wright, 1995; Tierra del Fuego: New and Selected Poems, 1997; (ed. with B. Bennett) The Oxford Literary History of Australia, 1998; (ed.) Family Ties: Australian Poems of the Family, 1998; (ed.) The Collected Verse of Mary Gilmore, 2004. **Address:** Monash University, 10/1-131 Wellington Rd., Clayton, VI 3800, Australia. **Online address:** jstrauss@bigpond.com

STRAUSS, Susan (Elizabeth). American (born United States), b. 1954. **Genres:** Children's Fiction, Animals/Pets, Biology, Children's Non-fiction, Education, Environmental Sciences/Ecology, Language/Linguistics, Mythology/Folklore, Natural History, Sciences. **Career:** Professional storyteller, 1979-; San Diego State University, visiting professor, 1989; Colorado State University, affiliate faculty, 1990-; University of Idaho, affiliate faculty; Oregon State University, faculty. Writer. **Publications:** Oh that Coyote!: Native American Coyote Stories for Reading Aloud, 1983; Coyote Stories for Children, 1991; Wolf Stories: Myths and True Life Tales from around the World, 1993; The Passionate Fact: Storytelling in Science and History Interpretation, 1996; When Woman Became the Sea: A Costa Rican Creation Myth, 1998; (ed. with S. Sawyer) Polshek Partnership Architects: Joseph L. Fleischer, Timothy P. Hartung, Duncan R. Hazard, Richard M. Olcott, James S. Polshek, Susan T. Rodriguez, Todd H. Schliemann, 2005. **Address:** PO Box 1141, Bend, OR 97709, U.S.A. **Online address:** susan@straussstoryteller.com

STRAVINSKAS, Peter M. J. American (born United States), b. 1950. **Genres:** Theology/Religion, inspirational/Motivational Literature, Cultural/Ethnic Topics. **Career:** Catholic Educational Institutions, teacher and administrator; Catholic Answer, founding editor; Newman House Press, Scranton Diocesan Oratory of St. Philip Neri, founder and provost; Seton Hall University, adjunct professor of education; Holy Apostles Seminary, adjunct professor of education and classics; Drew University, Casperson Graduate School, adjunct professor of humanities; Priestly Society of the Venerable John Henry Cardinal Newman, founder. **Publications:** (With R.A. McBain) The Church after the Council: A Primer for Adults, 1975; Catholic Education: A New Dawn?, 1977; The Catholic Response, 1985, rev. ed., 2001; Essentials of Religious Life Today, 1987; The Catholic Church and the Bible, 1987, 2nd ed., 1996; (with H. Dieterich) Understanding the Sacraments: A Guide for Prayer and Study, 1989; The Bible and the Mass: Understanding the Scriptural Basis of the Liturgy, 1989, rev. ed., 2000; The Catholic Answer Book (annual), 1990; (with L. Klenicki) A Catholic Jewish Encounter, 1994; A Tour of the Catholic Catechism, 1996; La Sicologia y Metodos de Proselitismo, 1998; Mary and the Fundamentalist Challenge, 1998; Priestly Celibacy: Its Scriptural, Historical, Spiritual and Psychological Roots, 2001; Advent Meditations: Helps to Wait in Joyful Hope, 2001; Salvation Outside the Church?, 2002; Lenten Meditations, 2003; Constitutional Rights and Religious Prejudice, 2nd ed., 2009; What Mary Means to Christians, 2012. EDITOR: Our Sunday Visitor's Catholic Dictionary, 1993, rev. ed., 2002; Our Sunday Visitor's Catholic Encyclopedia, rev. ed., 1998; The Catholic Answer Book of Mary, 2000; Lauds and Vespers, 2001. Contributor to periodicals. **Address:** Newman House, 601 Buhler Ct., Pine Beach, NJ 08741, U.S.A. **Online address:** fstravinskas@hotmail.com

STRAW, Deborah. American (born United States), b. 1948. **Genres:** Animals/Pets. **Career:** Community College of Vermont, English instructor, 1989-; Trinity College, writing instructor; Champlain College, teacher; Saint Michael's College, teacher; Johnson State College, teacher of writing and literature. Writer. **Publications:** Natural Wonders of the Florida Keys: Exploring Wild and Scenic Places, 1999; Why Is Cancer Killing Our Pets? How You Can Protect and Treat Your Animal Companion, 2000; Healthy Pet Manual: A Guide to the Prevention and Treatment of Cancer, 2005. Contributor to periodicals. **Address:** 31 Pine Pl., Burlington, VT 05401, U.S.A. **Online address:** ligature@together.net

STRAWN, Martha A. American (born United States), b. 1945. **Genres:** Art/Art History. **Career:** Florida State University, instructor in art, 1969-70; Northeast Louisiana University, assistant professor of art, 1970-71; University of North Carolina, professor of art and women studies, 1971-2004, professor emeritus, 2005-; Light Factory Arts Organization, founder, 1973, board director, 1973-75; Charlotte Dance Guild, board director, 1973-76; University of Florida, courtesy professor, 1985; Center for American Places, trustee, 1993-2001; Davidson Lands Conservancy, founder and board director, 2000-, vice president, president, 2001-. Writer. **Publications:** Alligators: Prehistoric Presence in the American Landscape, 1997; Across the Threshold of India, 2004; (contrib.) Religion: From Place to Placelessness, 2009. **Address:** Department of Art, University of North Carolina, 9201 University City Blvd., Charlotte, NC 28223-0001, U.S.A. **Online address:** mstrawn@earthlink.net

STRAY, Christopher. Welsh/British (born England), b. 1943. **Genres:** Classics, History, Politics/Government. **Career:** Colloquium on Textbooks, Schools and Society, founder, 1988, convenor, 1988-; University of Wales, University College of Swansea, honorary research fellow in classics, 1989-; University of London, Institute of Classical Studies, senior research fellow. Writer. **Publications:** The Living Word: W. H. D. Rouse and the Crisis of Classics in Edwardian England, 1992; Grinders and Grammers: A Victorian Controversy, 1996; Classics Transformed: Schools, Universities and Society in England 1830-1960, 1998; (intro.) The Clarendon Report: English Public Schools in the Nineteenth Century, 2004; Classics in Britain 1800-2000, forthcoming. EDITOR: Winchester Notions: The English Dialect of Winchester College, 1998; Classics in 19th and 20th Century Cambridge: Curriculum, Culture and Community, 1999; (with J. Smith) Teaching and Learning in Nineteenth-Century Cambridge, 2002; (with J. Smith) Cambridge in the 1830s: The Letters of Alexander Chisholm Gooden, 1831-1841, 2003; Promoting and Defending: Reflections on the History of the Hellenic Society (1879) and the Classical Association (1903), 2003; The Classical Association: The First Century, 1903-2003, 2003; Travellers to Greece, 2006; Gilbert Murray Reassessed: Hellenism, Theatre and International Politics, 2007; (and contrib.) Classical Books, 2007; Oxford Classics, 2007; Remaking the Classics, 2007; Gilbert Murray Reassessed, 2007; (with L. Hardwick) A Companion to Classical Receptions, 2008; (with J.P. Hallett) British Classics Outside England: The Academy and Beyond, 2009; (with D. Butterfield and contrib.) A.E. Housman, 2009; Classical Dictionaries, 2010. **Address:** Department of Classics and Ancient History, University of Wales Swansea, Singleton Pk., Swansea, WG SA2 8PP, Wales. **Online address:** c.a.stray@swansea.ac.uk

STREB, Matthew J(ustin). American (born United States), b. 1974. **Genres:** Politics/Government, Law. **Career:** Indiana University, The United States Congress, instructor, 1998, Elections 2000, instructor, 2000; Loyola Marymount University, visiting assistant professor, 2000-02, assistant professor, 2002-05; Northern Illinois University, Department of Political Science, assistant professor, 2005-08, associate professor, 2008-, chair, 2012-, director of undergraduate studies, 2006-, president, 2010-. Writer. **Publications:** The New Electoral Politics of Race, 2002; (comp. with C. Barbour) Clued in to Politics: A Critical Thinking Reader in American Government, 2004, 3rd ed., 2010; (ed. with M.A. Genovese) Polls and Politics: The Dilemmas of Democracy, 2004; (co-ed.) Election Law and Electoral Politics, 2004; (ed.) Law and Election Politics: The Rules of the Game, 2005; (with C. Barbour, G.C. Wright and M.R. Wolf) Keeping the Republic: Power and Citizenship in American Politics, the Essentials, 3rd ed., 2006; (ed. with E. Gerstmann) Academic Freedom at the Dawn of a New Century: How Terrorism, Governments, and Culture Wars Impact Free Speech, 2006; (ed.) Running for Judge: The Rising Political, Financial and Legal Stakes of Judicial Elections, 2007; Rethinking American Electoral Democracy, 2008, 2nd ed., 2011; (with B.F. Schaffner and G.C. Wright) Politics without Parties, forthcoming. Contributor to periodicals. **Address:** Department of Political Science, Northern Illinois University, 1425 W Lincoln Hwy., DeKalb, IL 60115-2828, U.S.A. **Online address:** mstreb@niu.edu

STRECKERT, Hal. American (born United States), b. 1955. **Genres:** Travel/Exploration, Westerns/Adventure. **Career:** General Atomics, senior principal scientist, 1982-. Writer. **Publications:** Kilimanjaro Adventure: One Family's Quest to Reach the Top of the African Continent, 1998. **Address:** General Atomics, 3550 General Atomics Ct., PO Box 85608, San Diego, CA 92121-1122, U.S.A. **Online address:** h.streckert@gat.com

STREET, Brian Jeffrey. Canadian (born Canada), b. 1955. **Genres:** Documentaries/Reportage, Plays/Screenplays, Adult Non-fiction, History, Military/Defense/Arms Control, Biography. **Career:** Ross Briggs Ltd., film editor, 1974-75; director of documentary films, 1975-79; Crawley Films Ltd., staff writer, 1979-80; freelance writer, 1980-; Royal Canadian Mounted Police, writer/producer communications advisor, 1991-96. **Publications:** The Parachute Ward: A Canadian Surgeon's Wartime Adventures in Yugoslavia, 1987; (with B. Nolan) Champagne Navy: Canada's Small Boat Raiders of the Second World War, 1991; (with M. Berger) Invasions without Tears: The Story of Canada's Top-Scoring Spitfire Wing in Europe During the Second World War, 1994. Contributor to periodicals. **Address:** c/o Carol Bonnett, MGA Agency Inc., 10 Saint Mary St., Ste. 510, Toronto, ON M4Y 1P9, Canada.

STREETEN, Paul Patrick. American/Austrian (born Austria), b. 1917. **Genres:** Economics, Public/Social Administration, Social Commentary, Adult

Non-fiction, Business/Trade/Industry. **Career:** Stanford University, visiting professor, 1956; University of Buenos Aires, visiting professor, 1963; Ministry of Overseas Development, deputy director-general of economic planning staff, 1964-66; University of Sussex, Institute of Development Studies, professor of economics, acting director and fellow, 1966-68, director; Institute of Commonwealth Studies, director, 1968-78; Economic Development Institute of the World Bank, visiting professor, 1972; World Development Journal, founding editor, 1972; World Bank, senior adviser, 1976-80, 1984-85; Boston University, professor of economics, 1980-93, Center for Asian Development, director, 1980-94, World Development Institute, director, 1984-89, professor emeritus, 1993-; European University Institute, Jean Monet professor, 1991; University of Oxford, Queen Elizabeth House, warden. Writer and consultant. **Publications:** Value in Social Theory, 1958; Economic Integration: Aspects and Problems, 1962, 2nd ed., 1964; Obstacles to Development, 1967; (ed. with M. Lipton) The Crisis of Indian Planning, 1968; (ed.) Unfashionable Economics: Essays in Honor of Lord Balogh, 1970; (with H. Sutch) Capital for Africa: The British Contribution, 1971; (ed. with H. Corbet) Commonwealth Policy in a Global Context, 1971; (with D. Elson) Diversification and Development: The Case of Coffee, 1971; The Frontiers of Development Studies, 1972; Aid to Africa, 1972; Trade Strategies for Development, 1973; The Limits of Development Research, 1975; (with S. Lall) Foreign Investment, Transnationals, and Developing Countries, 1977; Development Perspectives, 1981; First Things First: Meeting Basic Human Needs In The Developing Countries, 1981; (ed. with R. Jolly) Recent Issues in World Development, 1981; What Price Food?: Agricultural Price Policies In Developing Countries, 1987; Beyond Structural Adjustment, 1988; (ed.) Beyond Adjustment: The Asian Experience, 1988; Mobilizing Human Potential, 1989; Paul Streeten in South Africa: Reflections on a Journey, 1992; (with L. Emmerij and C. Fortin) International Governance, 1992; The Role of Direct Private Foreign Investment in Developing Countries, 1993; Strategies for Human Development, 1994; (co-author) The United Nations and the Bretton Woods Institutions: New Challenges for the 21st Century, 1994; Thinking about Development, 1995; Globalisation: Threat or Opportunity, 2001; Technological Nightmares: Frederick S. Pardee Distinguished Lecture, October 2003, 2006. **Address:** Department of Economics, Boston University, 270 Bay State Rd., Boston, MA 02215, U.S.A. **Online address:** ppstreeten@taconic.net

STREETER, Patrick. British (born England), b. 1946?. **Genres:** Biography, Young Adult Fiction, Autobiography/Memoirs. **Career:** Accountant, political activist and writer. **Publications:** The Heath Mount Register, 1992; Streeter of Bond Street, 1993; For Whom the Bell Tolls, 1996; Mad for Zion: A Biography of Colonel J.H. Patterson, 2004. **Address:** Matching Press, Waterman's End Cottage, 1 Watermans End, Matching Green, Harlow, EX CM17 0RQ, England.

STREEVER, Bill. American (born United States), b. 1961?. **Genres:** Economics. **Career:** University of Newcastle, Kooragang Wetland Rehabilitation Project, research program developer; Waterways Experiment Station, researcher; Alaskan North Slope Oil Fields, applied research program director. Writer. **Publications:** Bringing Back the Wetlands, 1999; (ed. as W. Streever) An International Perspective on Wetland Rehabilitation, 1999; Saving Louisiana? The Battle for Coastal Wetlands, 2001; (with R.E. Turner) Approaches to Coastal Wetlands Restoration: Northern Gulf of Mexico, 2002; Green Seduction: Money, Business, and the Environment, 2007; Cold: Adventures in the World's Frozen Places, 2009. **Address:** Anchorage, AR , U.S.A. **Online address:** bill_streever@hotmail.com

STREITWIESER, Andrew. American (born United States), b. 1927. **Genres:** Chemistry, Sciences. **Career:** Massachusetts Institute of Technology, postdoctoral fellow, 1951-52; University of California, instructor, 1952-54, assistant professor, 1954-59, associate professor, 1959-63, professor of chemistry, 1963-93, professor emeritus, 1993-, Graduate School, professor, 1995-99; National Science Foundation, science faculty fellow, 1959-60; Wiley Interscience, Progress in Physical Organic Chemistry, editor, 1963-74; American Chemical Society, fellow, 2009. **Publications:** Molecular Orbital Theory for Organic Chemists, 1961; Solvolytic Displacement Reactions, 1962; Progress in Physical Organic Chemistry, 1963; (with J.I. Brauman) Supplemental Tables of Molecular Orbital Calculations, 1965; (with C.A. Coulson) Dictionary of Electron Calculations, 1965; (with P.H. Owens) Orbital and Electron Density Diagrams: An Application of Computer Graphics, 1973; (with C.H. Heathcock) Organic Chemistry: An Introductory Text, 1976, 4th ed. (with C.H. Heathcock and E.M. Kosower), 1992; A LifeTime of Syn-

ergy with Theory and Experiment, 1996. **Address:** Department of Chemistry, University of California, 325B Lewis Hall, Berkeley, CA 94720-1460, U.S.A. **Online address:** astreit@berkeley.edu

STRELKOFF, Tatiana. Italian/American (born United States), b. 1957. **Genres:** Novels, Children's Fiction, Young Adult Fiction, Plays/Screenplays, Adult Non-fiction, Translations, Gay And Lesbian Issues. **Career:** Translator, 1981-; writer, 1987-; International Fund for Agricultural Development, writer and proofreader. **Publications:** Allison, 1998. THE CHANGER SERIES: The Changer, 1993; Jeremy and the Crow Nation, 1996; Kelly, 1997. **Address:** c/o Author Mail, O'Brien Press Ltd., 12 Terenure Rd. E, Dublin, 6, Ireland.

STRETTON, Charles. *See* **DYER, Charles (Raymond).**

STRETTON, Hugh. Australian (born Australia), b. 1924?. **Genres:** Economics, Politics/Government, Urban Studies, Architecture, Business/Trade/Industry. **Career:** University of Adelaide, professor, 1954-68, reader, 1969-89, emeritus professor of history, 1989-, visiting research fellow; Smith College, visiting lecturer, 1960-61; Australian National University, visiting lecturer, 1966; Centre for Environmental Studies, visiting researcher, 1973; York University, visiting lecturer, 1981. Writer. **Publications:** The Political Sciences: General Principles of Selection in Social Science and History, 1969; Ideas for Australian Cities, 1971, 3rd ed., 1989; Housing and Government, 1974; Capitalism, Socialism and the Environment, 1976; Urban Planning in Rich and Poor Countries, 1978; Political Essays, 1987; Markets, Morals, and Public Policy, 1989; (with L. Orchard) Public Goods, Public Enterprise, Public Choice, 1994; (ed.) Compassionate Town Planning, 1994; Economics: A New Introduction, 1999; Australia Fair, 2005. **Address:** School of Economics, The University of Adelaide, Levels 3 & 4, 10 Pulteney St., Adelaide, SA 5005, Australia. **Online address:** hugh.stretton@adelaide.edu.au

STRICK, Wesley. American (born United States), b. 1954. **Genres:** Novels. **Career:** Screenwriter, 1989-; Sundance Institute, Screenwriters Laboratory, creative advisor, 1995-. **Publications:** Out There in the Dark, 2006; Whirlybird, 2011. Contributor to periodicals. **Address:** c/o Ken Stovitz, Creative Artists Agency, 9830 Wilshire Blvd., Beverly Hills, CA 90212-1825, U.S.A. **Online address:** stricken@ibm.net

STRICKLAND, Craig (A.). American (born United States), b. 1956. **Genres:** Novellas/Short Stories, Horror, Children's Fiction, Young Adult Fiction, Science Fiction/Fantasy. **Career:** U.S. Postal Service, postal carrier, 1989-. Writer. **Publications:** Scary Stories from 1313 Wicked Way, 1996; Scary Stories for Sleep-Overs No. 8, 1997; Spirit Horse, forthcoming; Curiosity and the Silver, forthcoming; Seven Clocks, forthcoming. Contributor of articles to magazines. **Address:** 2933 Bonanza, San Clemente, CA 92673, U.S.A. **Online address:** strickland_4@cox.net

STRICKLAND, Michael R. American (born United States), b. 1965. **Genres:** Poetry, Children's Non-fiction, History, Biography. **Career:** Kean College of New Jersey, admissions representative and instructor, 1987-88; Glassboro State College (now Rowan University), instructor in composition, 1988-89; Worall Publications, reporter, 1989-90; New Jersey Star Ledger, reporter, 1990; LifeQuest (health company), staff writer, 1991-92; Strickland Group L.L.C., partner, 1992-; Jersey City State College (now New Jersey City University), instructor in English, 1992-96, assistant professor, 1997-2001; Institute for Arts and Humanities Education, Robeson Fellow, 1993-94; Literacy Place (reading program), poetry consultant, 1994-96; Boyds Mills Press, manuscript internal reviewer, 1995-; Washington State University College of Education, teaching/research fellow, 1997; Aquinas Academy, computer instructor, 2001-02; School District 91 and 93, teacher, 2002-; Utah State University, adjunct professor, 2003; Eastern Idaho Technical College, instructor in English, 2003-. **Publications:** African-American Poets, 1996; Haircuts at Sleepy Sam's, 1998; A-to-Z of African-American History, 2001; Black Snake and the Eggs: A Tale Told in Liberia, 2001; (with L. Bahlinger) The Club, 2002; (with L. Bahlinger) Shell's Gold, 2002. EDITOR: Poems That Sing to You, 1993; (with D.S. Strickland) Families: Poems Celebrating the African-American Experience, 1994; My Own Song: And Other Poems to Groove To, 1997; (with S.D. Hatch) African-American Writers: A Dictionary, 2000. **Address:** 510 E 17th St., PO Box 422, Idaho Falls, ID 83404, U.S.A. **Online address:** strick@michaelrstrickland.com

STRICKLAND, (William) Brad(ley). American (born United States), b. 1947. **Genres:** Science Fiction/Fantasy, Young Adult Fiction, Mystery/

Crime/Suspense. **Career:** Truett-McConnell Junior College, Department of Humanities, chair, 1976-85; Lakeview Academy, Department of Secondary English, head, 1985-87; Gainesville College, professor of English, 1987-. Writer. **Publications:** To Stand beneath the Sun (science fiction), 1986; Moon Dreams (fantasy), 1988; Shadowshow (horror), 1988; Nul's Quest (fantasy), 1989; Children of the Knife (thriller), 1990; Wizard's Mole (novel), 1990; Dragon's Plunder (fantasy), 1992; Ark Liberty (science fiction), 1992; The Star Ghost (science fiction), 1994. YOUNG ADULT FANTASY: The Ghost in the Mirror, 1993; The Vengeance of the Witch-Finder, 1994; (comp.) The Drum, the Doll, and the Zombie, 1995; The Hand of the Necromancer, 1996; The Bell, the Book and the Spellbinder, 1997; The Specter from the Magician's Museum, 1998; When Mack Came Back, 2000; John Bellairs's Lewis Barnavelt in The Beast Under the Wizard's Bridge, 2000; (with T.E. Fuller) Disoriented Express, 2000; (with A. Capeci and C. Jablonski) The Wishbone Halloween Adventure, 2000; No-Rules Weekend, 2001; Survive!, 2001; The Tower at the End of the World, 2001; Pirate Hunter: Mutiny!, 2002; Heart of Steele, 2003; John Bellairs's Lewis Barnavelt in The Whistle, the Grave, and the Ghost, 2003; (with T.E. Fuller) Pirate Hunter: The Guns of Tortuga, 2003; Pirate Hunter: Heat of Steele, 2003; Mars: Year One, 2004; Marooned!, 2004; (with J. Michlig) Kong: King of Skull Island, 2004; (with T.E. Fuller) Missing!, 2004; Mars Year One: Marsquake!, 2005; (with J. DeVito) Merian C. Cooper's King Kong, 2005; The Roanoke Adventure, 2005; The House Where Nobody Lived, 2006; Grimoire: Curse of the Midions, 2006; Storm, 2006; Race for the Gold, 2007; The Flying Tomato: The Shaun White Story, 2007; Grimoire: Tracked by Terror, 2007; The Sign of the Sinister Sorcerer, 2008; Flight of the Outcast, 2010. **Address:** Department of English, Gainesville State College, 3820 Mundy Mill Rd., PO Box 1358, Gainesville, GA 30503, U.S.A. **Online address:** bstrickland@gsc.edu

STRIEBER, Anne. American (born United States) **Genres:** Novels, Literary Criticism And History. **Career:** Unknowncountry.com, editor-in-chief. **Publications:** (Ed. with W. Strieber) The Communion Letters, 1997; An Invisible Woman, 2004; Little Town Lies, 2005. Contributor to periodicals. **Address:** c/o Author Mail, St. Martin's Press, Publicity Dept., 175 5th Ave., New York, NY 10010-7703, U.S.A.

STRIEDER, Leon F. American (born United States), b. 1950. **Genres:** Theology/Religion, History, Institutions/Organizations. **Career:** Diocese of Austin, priest, 1976-82; Diocesan Liturgical Commission, chair, 1977-, director of campus ministries, 1998; Texas A&M University, director of campus ministry, 1982-90; St. Mary's Seminary, formation director, 1990-2002; University of St. Thomas, School of Theology, adjunct professor of liturgy and sacraments, 1991-2002, associate professor of liturgy and sacraments, 2002-. Writer. **Publications:** The Promise of Obedience: A Ritual History, 2001. **Address:** University of St. Thomas, 3800 Montrose, Houston, TX 77006-4626, U.S.A. **Online address:** strieder@stthom.edu

STRIEGEL, Jana. American (born United States), b. 1955. **Genres:** Children's Fiction, Sports/Fitness, Dance/Ballet, Medicine/Health. **Career:** New Mexico Ballet Co., dancer; Ballet del Monte Sol, dancer; Six Flags Over Mid-America, dancer; American Southwest Ballet Co., dancer; Jana's Academy of Music and Dance, owner and artistic director, 1982-90; writer, 1990-. Dance instructor and choreographer. **Publications:** Homeroom Exercise, 2002. Contributor to periodicals. **Address:** c/o Author Mail, Holiday House Inc., 425 Madison Ave., New York, NY 10017-1110, U.S.A. **Online address:** jana@janastriegel.com

STRIER, Karen B. American (born United States), b. 1959. **Genres:** Animals/Pets, Biology, Natural History. **Career:** Fulbright fellow, 1983-84; Harvard University, instructor in anthropology and sophomore tutor in biological anthropology, 1985, lecturer in anthropology, 1986-87; Beloit College, assistant professor of anthropology, 1987-89, adjunct professor, 1989-92; University of Wisconsin-Madison, Department of Anthropology, assistant professor, 1989-92, associate professor, 1992-95, affiliate associate professor of zoology, 1992-95, chair, 1994-96, professor of anthropology and affiliate professor of zoology, 1995-2006, Hilldale professor of anthropology, 2006-11, Irven DeVore professor of anthropology, 2009-, Vilas professor, 2011-; American Journal of Physical Anthropology, associate editor, 2000-05; Pontifica Universidade Catolica, affiliate professor, 2003-; Primates, A Journal of Primatology, associate editor, 2006-11; Current Zoology, editor, 2008-10. **Publications:** Faces in the Forest: The Endangered Muriqui Monkeys of Brazil, 1992; (with J.P. Hailman) Planning, Proposing and Presenting Science Effectively: A Guide for Graduate Students and Researchers in the Behavioral Sciences

and Biology, 1997, 2nd ed., 2006; Primate Behavioral Ecology, 2000, 4th ed., 2011. Contributor to scientific journals. **Address:** Department of Anthropology, University of Wisconsin, 1180 Observatory Dr., 5403 Social Science Bldg., Madison, WI 53706, U.S.A. **Online address:** kbstrier@wisc.edu

STRINGER, Christopher. Also writes as Christopher B. Stringer. British (born England), b. 1947. **Genres:** Sciences, Biology, Natural History, Earth Sciences. **Career:** Natural History Museum-London, senior research fellow, senior scientific officer, principal scientific officer, 1973-, head of anthropology, 1989-90, Human Origins Programme, head, 1990-93, 1999-2005, research leader in human origins, 2005-, Human Origins Group, anthropologist and principal researcher, Palaeontology Research Division, Department of Palaeontology, merit researcher, Ancient Human Occupation of Britain project, director; Journal of Human Evolution, associate editor, 1984-2003; Centre for Ecology and Evolution London, Darwin Lecturer, 2003; University College, Centre for Ecology and Evolution, research associate. Writer. **Publications:** EDITOR: (as C.B. Stringer) Aspects of Human Evolution, 1981; (with P. Mellars) The Human Revolution: Behavioural and Biological Perspectives on the Origins of Modern Humans, 1989; (with J.J. Hublin and A.M. Tiller) Aux origines d'Homo sapiens, 1991; (with M.J. Aitken and P.A. Mellars) The Origin of Modern Humans and the Impact of Chronometric Dating: A Discussion, 1993. OTHERS: (with E. Trinkaus) The Emergence of Modern Humans, 1989; (with P. Andrews) Human Evolution: Behavioural and Biological Perspectives on the Origins of Modern Humans, 1989; (with C. Gamble) In Search of Neanderthals: Solving the Puzzle of Human Origins, 1993; Paleoclimate and Evolution with Emphasis on Human Origins, 1995; (with R. McKie) African Exodus: The Origins of Modern Humanity, 1997; (with P. Andrews and A. Currant) Westbury Cave The Natural History Museum Excavations 1976-1984, 1999; (with P. Andrews) Complete World of Human Evolution, 2005; Homo Britannicus: The Incredible Story of Human Life in Britain, 2006; The Origin of our Species, 2011; Lone Survivors, 2012. **Address:** Palaeontology Research Division, Department of Palaeontology, Natural History Museum, Cromwell Rd., London, GL SW7 5BD, England.

STRINGER, Christopher B. See **STRINGER, Christopher.**

STRINGER, C. Vivian. American (born United States), b. 1948. **Genres:** Sports/Fitness, Biography, Autobiography/Memoirs, Sports/Fitness. **Career:** Cheyney State University, women's basketball coach, 1971-83; University of Iowa, women's basketball coach, 1983-95; Rutgers University, women's basketball coach, 1995-, head coach; U.S. Olympic, Women's Basketball Team, assistant coach, 2004. Writer. **Publications:** (With L. Tucker) Standing Tall: A Memoir of Tragedy and Triumph, 2008. Contributor to periodicals. **Address:** Louis Brown Athletic Center, 83 Rockefeller Rd., Piscataway, NJ 08854, U.S.A.

STRINGER, Vickie M. American (born United States), b. 1971. **Genres:** Novels, Young Adult Non-fiction, Business/Trade/Industry. **Career:** Triple Crown Publications, founder, owner, president, chief executive officer and publisher; Valen Foundation, founder. Writer. **Publications:** (With M. McPherson) How to Succeed in the Publishing Game, 2005. NOVELS: Let That Be the Reason, 2001; Imagine This, 2004; Dirty Red, 2006; Still Dirty, 2008; The Reason Why, 2009; Dirtier Than Ever, 2010. Contributor to periodicals. **Address:** Triple Crown Publications, 2184 Citygate Dr., Columbus, OH 43219, U.S.A.

STROBY, Wallace. American (born United States) **Genres:** Novels, Mystery/Crime/Suspense. **Career:** Star-Ledger, editor. **Publications:** HARRY RANE MYSTERY SERIES: The Barbed-Wire Kiss, 2003; The Heartbreak Lounge, 2005. NOVELS: Gone 'Til November, 2010; Cold Shot to the Heart, 2011; Kings of Midnight, 2012. **Address:** Minotaur Books, 175 5th Ave., New York, NY 10010-7703, U.S.A. **Online address:** wallace@wallacestroby.com

STROCK, Ian Randal. American (born United States), b. 1966. **Genres:** Novellas/Short Stories, Science Fiction/Fantasy, Air/Space Topics, Sciences, Writing/Journalism. **Career:** Freelance writer, 1985-; Daily Free Press, editorial page editor, 1986-87; Asimov's Science Fiction Magazine, associate editor, 1989-95; Analog Science Fiction and Fact Magazine, associate editor, 1989-95; Mphasis, editor and publisher, 1990-91; Lunar Resources Co., vice president of publications, 1995-; Artemis Magazine, editor, 1995-; LRC Publications Inc., president and publisher, 1996-; Artemis Society Intl., director of publications and board director. **Publications:** (Co-ed.) Writing Science Fiction and Fantasy, 1991; The Presidential Book of Lists: From Most to Least,

Elected to Rejected, Worst to Cursed-Fascinating Facts About Our Chief Executives, 2008. Contributor to periodicals. **Address:** LRC Publications Inc., 1380 E 17th St., Ste. 202, Brooklyn, NY 11230-6011, U.S.A.

STROH, Linda K. American (born United States), b. 1948. **Genres:** Business/Trade/Industry, Economics, Engineering. **Career:** Northwestern University, research professor, 1988-89; Loyola University, Graduate School of Business, professor, 1989-. Writer. **Publications:** (With G.B. Northcraft and M.A. Neale) Organizational Behavior: A Management Challenge, 3rd ed., 2002; (co-author) International Assignments: An Integration of Strategy, Research, and Practice, 2006; (with H.H. Johnson) The Basic Principles of Effective Consulting, 2006; Trust Rules: How to Tell the Good Guys from the Bad Guys in Work and Life, 2007. **Address:** Graduate School of Business, Loyola University Chicago, 456 Maguire Hall, 820 N Michigan Ave., 1032 W Sheridan Rd., Chicago, IL 60660, U.S.A. **Online address:** lstroh@luc.edu

STROM, Robert. American (born United States), b. 1935. **Genres:** Education, Psychology. **Career:** Teacher, 1958-60, 1961-62; University of Connecticut, assistant professor of education, 1962-63; National Education Association, School Dropouts Project, assistant director, 1963-64; The Ohio State University, associate professor of psychology and education, 1964-67, professor of psychology and education, 1967-69; University of Ankara, lecturer, 1967; Arizona State University, Department of Elementary Education, chairman, 1969-73, professor of curriculum and instruction, 1973-85, professor of lifespan developmental psychology, 1985-2010, Office of Parent Development Intl., director, 1985-; Canberra College of Advanced Education, lecturer, 1975, professor of educational leadership and innovation, 2010-. Writer. **Publications:** Tragic Migration; School Dropouts, 1964; Teaching in the Slum School, 1965; Inner-City Classroom: Teacher Behaviors, 1966; Psychology for the Classroom, 1969; The Urban Teacher, 1971; Growing Together: Parent and Child Development, 1978; (with H.W. Bernard) Educational Psychology, 1982; (with H.W. Bernard and S.K. Strom) Human Development and Learning, 1987; (with S.K. Strom) Becoming a Better Grandparent: Viewpoints on Strengthening the Family, 1991; (with S.K. Strom) Becoming a Better Grandparent: A Guidebook for Strengthening the Family, 1991; (with S.K. Strom) Grandparent Education: A Guide for Leaders, 1991; (with S.K. Strom) Achieving Grandparent Potential: Viewpoints on Building Intergenerational Relationships, 1992; Achieving Grandparent Potential: A Guidebook for Building Intergenerational Relationships, 1992; Grandparent Strengths and Needs Inventory, 1993; Parent as a Teacher Inventory, 1995; Parent Success Indicator, 1998; Interpersonal Intelligence Inventory, 2001; (with P.S. Strom) Adolescents in the Internet Age, 2009; (with P.S. Strom) Parenting Young Children: Exploring the Internet, Television, Play and Reading, 2009; Adult Learning and Relationships, 2011. EDITOR: (with P. Torrance) Mental Health and Achievement, 1965; Teacher and the Learning Process, 1971; Elementary Education Today: Its Impact on Children, 1971; Values and Human Development, 1973; (with P. Torrance) Education for Affective Achievement, 1973; Teaching and Its Preconditions, 1974; Parent and Child in Fiction, 1977; Growing Through Play, 1981. **Address:** Mary Lou Fulton College of Education, Arizona State University, EDB 446E, PO Box 1811, Tempe, AZ 85287-0211, U.S.A. **Online address:** bob.strom@asu.edu

STROM, Yale. American (born United States), b. 1957. **Genres:** Cultural/Ethnic Topics. **Career:** Ethnographer, photographer, musician, composer, filmmaker and writer. **Publications:** The Last Jews of Eastern Europe, 1986; A Tree Still Stands: Jewish Youth in Eastern Europe Today, 1990; Expulsion of the Jews: Five Hundred Years of Exodus, 1992; The Hasidim of Brooklyn: A Photo Essay, 1993; Uncertain Roads: Searching for the Gypsies, 1993; Quilted Landscapes: Voices of Immigrant Youth in America, 1996; The Book of Klezmer: The History, the Music, the Folklore, 2002; Wandering Feast: A Journey through the Jewish Culture of Eastern Europe, 2005; World Music Play-Along: Klezmer, 2005; The Absolutely Complete Klezmer Songbook, 2006; The Wedding that Saved a Town, 2008; Dave Tarras: The King of Klezmer, 2010. **Address:** 3834 Goldfinch St., San Diego, CA 92103, U.S.A. **Online address:** yitztyco@aol.com

STROMBERG, Peter G. American (born United States), b. 1952. **Genres:** Anthropology/Ethnology, Language/Linguistics, Social Sciences, Psychology, Sociology, Communications/Media, Theology/Religion. **Career:** University of Arizona, visiting assistant professor of anthropology, 1985-87; University of Tulsa, assistant professor, 1987-93, associate professor of anthropology, 1993-2008; professor of anthropology, 2008-. Writer. **Publications:** Symbols of Community: The Cultural System of a Swedish Church, 1986; Language and Self-Transformation: A Study of the Christian Conversion Narrative, 1993; Caught in Play: How Entertainment Works on You, 2009. **Address:** Department of Anthropology, University of Tulsa, Harwell Hall, Fl. 2, Tulsa, OK 74104, U.S.A. **Online address:** peter-stromberg@utulsa.edu

STRONACH, Bruce. American (born United States), b. 1950. **Genres:** International Relations/Current Affairs, Politics/Government, Social Sciences, History. **Career:** Keio University, International Center and Center for Communications Research, visiting researcher, 1976-78, lecturer, 1980-85; International Education Center, School of International Studies, chair, 1980-85; Merrimack College, assistant professor, 1985-90, associate professor and associate dean, 1990-94; International University of Japan, Graduate School of International Relations, associate professor of Japanese studies, 1990-94, professor and dean, 1994-97; University of Virginia, Darden Graduate School of Business Administration, visiting professor, 1997-98; Becker College, provost and chief operating officer, 1998-2003, acting president, 2003-04; Yokohama City University, acting president, 2003-04, president, 2005-08; Temple University, dean, 2008-. Writer. **Publications:** Japan and America: Opposites That Attract, 1988; (ed. with R.G. Powers and H. Kato) The Handbook of Japanese Popular Culture, 1989; Popular Culture in Japan and America, 1991; (with C.H. Martin) Politics East and West: A Comparison of Japanese and British Political Culture, 1992; Beyond the Rising Sun: Nationalism in Contemporary Japan, 1995. **Address:** Temple University, Garden Level, Sullivan Hall, 1330 W Polett Walk, Philadelphia, PA 19122, U.S.A. **Online address:** bruce.stronach@temple.edu

STRONG, Albertine. American (born United States) **Genres:** Novels, History. **Career:** Writer. **Publications:** Deluge, 1997. Contributor to periodicals. **Address:** c/o Random House, 1745 Broadway, New York, NY 10019-4368, U.S.A.

STRONG, Carson. American (born United States), b. 1946. **Genres:** Medicine/Health, Sports/Fitness. **Career:** University of Tennessee, College of Medicine, Department of Human Values and Ethics, professor of human values and ethics. Writer. **Publications:** (With T.F. Ackerman) A Casebook of Medical Ethics, 1989; Ethics in Reproductive and Perinatal Medicine: A New Framework, 1997. Contributor to periodicals. **Address:** Department of Human Values and Ethics, College of Medicine, University of Tennessee, 956 Court Ave., PO Box 11, Memphis, TN 38103-2814, U.S.A. **Online address:** cstrong@utmem.edu

STRONG, Douglas M. American (born United States), b. 1956. **Genres:** Theology/Religion, Social Sciences. **Career:** Aldersgate United Methodist Church, associate pastor, 1981-89; Wesley Theological Seminary, professor, 1989-2007, Summer School, director, 2001-07, associate dean for church relations, 2005-07; Lutheran Theological Seminary, visiting professor, 1990-94; St. Mary's Seminary and University, The Ecumenical Institute, visiting professor, 1994-2004; Catholic University of America, visiting professor, 1995; Oakdale Emory United Methodist Church, teacher and group leader, 1996-2007; Wesleyan Theological Society, president, 1997-99; Indiana Wesleyan University, visiting professor, 1998; Russia United Methodist Theological Seminary, visiting professor, 1999, 2000, 2003; Chautauqua Institution, United Methodist House, chaplain, 1999, 2005; International Reform Federation, vice president, 2002-; Methodist History, editorial board, 2004-; Seattle Pacific University, School of Theology, dean and professor, 2007-; Queen Anne United Methodist Church, resident theologian, 2007-. **Publications:** (Ed. with J.P. Wogaman) Readings in Christian Ethics: A Historical Sourcebook, 1996; They Walked in the Spirit: Personal Faith and Social Action in America, 1997; Perfectionist Politics: Abolitionism and the Religious Tensions of American Democracy, 1999; (co-author) Reclaiming the Wesleyan Tradition: John Wesley's Sermons for Today, 2007. **Address:** School of Theology, Seattle Pacific University, 109 Alexander Hall, 3307 3rd Ave. W, Ste. 102, Seattle, WA 98119-1950, U.S.A. **Online address:** dstrong@spu.edu

STRONG, John S. American (born United States), b. 1956. **Genres:** Air/Space Topics, Technology, Sciences. **Career:** College of William and Mary, assistant professor, 1985-91, associate professor of business, 1991-95, professor of business, 1996-, CSX professor of business administration economics and finance; Harvard University, assistant professor, 1989-90; National Science Foundation, graduate fellow. Writer and consultant. **Publications:** (With J.R. Meyer and C.V. Oster) Deregulation and the New Airline Entrepreneurs, 1984; (with J.R. Meyer and C.V. Oster) Airline Deregulation and the Future of Intercity Travel, 1987; (with K. Dominguez and R. Weiner)

Oil and Money, Energy and Environmental Policy Center, 1989; (with C.V. Oster, Jr. and C.K. Zorn) Why Airplanes Crash, 1992; (with G. Smith, J.R. Meyer and C.G. Harral) Moving to Market: Restructuring Transport in the Former Soviet Union, 1996; (with C.V. Oster, Jr.) Managing the Skies: Public Policy, Organization and Financing of Air Traffic Management, 2007. **Address:** Graduate School of Business, College of William & Mary, 3003 Miller Hall, PO Box 8795, Williamsburg, VA 23187, U.S.A. **Online address:** John.Strong@mason.wm.edu

STRONG, Marilee. American (born United States), b. 1957. **Genres:** Criminology/True Crime, Young Adult Non-fiction. **Career:** Journalist. **Publications:** A Bright Red Scream: Self-Mutilation and the Language of Pain, 1998; (with M. Powelson) Erased: Missing Women, Murdered Wives, 2008. **Address:** Jossey-Bass, 1 Montgomery St., Ste. 1200, San Francisco, CA 94104-4594, U.S.A. **Online address:** marileestrong@gmail.com

STRONG, Roy (Colin). British (born England), b. 1935. **Genres:** Art/Art History, History, Homes/Gardens, Photography. **Career:** National Portrait Gallery, assistant keeper, 1959-67, director, 1967-73, keeper and secretary; Victoria & Albert Museum, director, 1973-87; The Garden History Society, president, 2000-06; The Friends of Croome Park, president, 2008-. Writer, art historian and broadcaster. **Publications:** Portraits of Queen Elizabeth I, 1963; The House of Tudor, 1967; Holbein and Henry VIII, 1967; Tudor and Jacobean Portraits, 1969; The English Icon, 1969; Van Dyck, Charles I on Horseback, 1972; The Destruction of the Country House, 1875-1975, 1974; Splendour at Court, 1973; Nicholas Hilliard, 1975; The Cult of Elizabeth, 1977; Recreating the Past: British History and the Victorian Painter, 1978; When Did You Last See Your Father? The Victorian Painter and British History, 1978; The Renaissance Garden in England, 1979; Britannia Triumphant: Inigo Jones, Rubens, and Whitehall Palace, 1980; The English Renaissance Miniature, 1983; Art and Power: Renaissance Festivals, 1450-1650, 1984; Strong Points, 1985; Henry, Prince of Wales and England's Lost Renaissance, 1986; Creating Small Gardens, 1986; Gloriana: Portraits of Queen Elizabeth Portraits of Queen Elizabeth I, 1963; The House of Tudor, 1967; Holbein and Henry VIII, 1967; Tudor and Jacobean Portraits, 1969; The English Icon, 1969; Van Dyck, Charles I on Horseback, 1972; The Destruction of the Country House, 1875-1975, 1974; Splendour at Court, 1973; Nicholas Hilliard, 1975; The Cult of Elizabeth, 1977; Recreating the Past: British History and the Victorian Painter, 1978; When Did You Last See Your Father? The Victorian Painter and British History, 1978; The Renaissance Garden in England, 1979; Britannia Triumphant: Inigo Jones, Rubens, and Whitehall Palace, 1980; The English Renaissance Miniature, 1983; Art andI, 1987; The Small Garden Designer's Handbook, 1987; Cecil Beaton: The Royal Portraits, 1988; Creating Small Formal Gardens, 1989; Lost Treasures of Britain, 1990; A Celebration of Gardens, 1991; The Garden Trellis, 1991; Small Period Gardens, 1992; Royal Gardens, 1992; William Larkin, 1994; A Country Life, 1994; Successful Small Gardens, 1994; The Tudor and Stuart Monarchy (collected papers), 3 vols., 1995-1997; The Story of Britain, 1996; Country Life, 1897-1997: The English Arcadia, 1996; The Roy Strong Diaries, 1967-1987, 1997; The English Arcadia, 1996; On Happiness, 1997; The Spirit of Britain, 1999; Garden Party, 2000; The Artist and the Garden, 2000; Ornament in the Small Garden, 2002; Feast: A History of Grand Eating, 2002; The Laskett: The Story of a Garden, 2003; Country Life: At Home in the English Countryside, 2003; Passions Past and Present, 2005; Coronation: A History of Kingship and the British Monarchy, 2005; A Little History of the English Country Church, 2007. CO-AUTHOR: (with J.A. Van Dorsten) Leicester's Triumph, 1964; (with J.T. Oman) Elizabeth R. Evocation, 1971; (with J.T. Oman) Mary Queen of Scots, 1972; (with S. Orgel) Inigo Jones: The Theatre of the Stuart Court, 1973; (with C. Ford) An Early Victorian Album, 1974; The English Miniature, 1981; Designing for the Dancer, 1981; (with J.T. Oman) The English Year, 1982; The New Pelican Guide to English Literature, 1982; (with J. Murrell) Artists of the Tudor Court Catalogue, 1983; Glyndebourne: A Celebration, 1984; For Veronica Wedgwood These, 1986; Sir Philip Sidney's Achievements, 1990; England and the Continental Renaissance, 1990; (with T. Pepper) Beaton Portraits, 2004; (with J. Evelyn) The Diary of John Evelyn, 2006. **Address:** The Laskett, Much Birch, HF HR2 8HZ, England.

STRONG, Terence. British (born England), b. 1946. **Genres:** Romance/Historical, Novels, Young Adult Fiction. **Career:** News Trade Weekly, assistant editor, editor, 1964-67; New English Library, publicity director, 1967-70; TM Associates, owner, 1970-77; Welbeck/Golin/Harris, senior account executive and publications editor, 1977-81. **Publications:** Whisper Who Dares, 1982; The Fifth Hostage, 1983; Conflict of Lions, 1985; Dragon Plague, 1987; That

Last Mountain, 1989; Sons of Heaven, 1990; This Angry Land, 1992; Stalking Horse, 1993; The Tick Tock Man, 1994; White Viper, 1996; Rogue Element, 1997; Deadwater Deep, 1998; Cold Monday, 2004; Wheels of Fire, 2005; President Down, 2007; Some Unholy War, 2010. **Address:** c/o Anthony Goff, David Higham Associates Ltd., 5-8 Lower John St., Golden Sq., London, GL W1F 9HA, England.

STRONGE, James H. American (born United States), b. 1950. **Genres:** Education, Sciences, Mathematics/Statistics. **Career:** Fairfield Board of Education, middle-school social studies teacher, 1974-76, guidance/counselor, 1976-77, special education coordinator, 1977-78, director of student services, 1978-83; Bradley University, assistant professor, 1983-87, associate professor of educational administration, 1987-89, Institute for Gifted and Talented Youth, director, 1986-88, Center for Research and Service, director, 1986-89; College of William and Mary, associate professor of educational administration, 1989-95, professor of education, 1995-, Heritage Professor of Educational Policy, Planning and Leadership Area, 1996-. Writer. **Publications:** Evaluation of Ancillary School Staff Training Manual, 1988; (with V.M. Helm) Evaluating Professional Support Personnel in Education, 1991; (ed. and contrib.) Educating Homeless Children and Adolescents: Evaluating Policy and Practice, 1992; (contrib.) Program Leadership for Serving Students with Disabilities, 1993; (with P.D. Tucker) Evaluation Handbook for Professional Support Staff, 1995; (ed. and contrib.) Evaluating Teaching: A Guide to Current Thinking and Best Practice, 1997, 2nd ed., 2006; (contrib.) A School Administrator's Guide to School Counseling, 1998; (ed. with P. Popp) The Education and Youth: A Compendium of Research and Information, 1999; (contrib.) Educating Everybody's Children: Diverse Teaching Strategies for Diverse Learners, 2000; (with P.D. Tucker) Teacher Evaluation and Student Achievement, 2000; (ed. with E. Reed-Victor) Educating Homeless Students: Promising Practices, 2000; (contrib.) Children on the Streets of the Americas: Globalization, Homelessness and Education in the United States, Brazil and Cuba, 2000; (with P.D. Tucker and C.R. Gareis) Handbook on Teacher Portfolios for Evaluation and Professional Development, 2002; Qualities of Effective Teachers, 2002, 2nd ed., 2007; (with P.D. Tucker) Handbook on Teacher Evaluation: Assessing and Improving Performance, 2003; (with M.F. DiPaola) Superintendent Evaluation Handbook, 2003; (with P.D. Tucker and J.L. Hindman) Handbook for Qualities of Effective Teachers, 2004; (with P.D. Tucker) Linking Teacher Evaluation and Student Learning, 2005; (with C.A. Little and C.R. Gareis) Teacher Pay & Teacher Quality: Attracting, Developing and Retaining the Best Teachers, 2006; (with J.L. Hindman) The Teacher Quality Index: A Protocol for Teacher Selection, 2006; (with H.B. Richard and N. Catano) Qualities of Effective Principals, 2008; (with L.W. Grant) Student Achievement Goal Setting: Using Data to Improve Teaching and Learning, 2009; (with L.W. Grant and J.L. Hindman) Planning, Instruction and Assessment: Effective Teaching Practices, 2010; (with L.W. Grant and J.L. Hindman) Supportive Learning Environment: Effective Teaching Practices, 2010; Evaluating what Good Teachers do: Eight Research-Based Standards for Assessing Teacher Excellence, 2010; Effective Teachers- Student Achievement: What the Research Says, 2010; Human Resources Administration in Education: The Importance of People, forthcoming. Contributor to journals. **Address:** School of Education, College of William and Mary, 301 Monticello Ave., PO Box 8795, Williamsburg, VA 23187-8795, U.S.A. **Online address:** jhstro@wm.edu

STRONGIN, Laurie. American (born United States) **Genres:** Autobiography/Memoirs. **Career:** Hope for Henry Foundation, founder and executive director. Writer and lawyer. **Publications:** Saving Henry: A Mother's Journey, 2010. Contributor to magazines. **Address:** Washington, DC , U.S.A. **Online address:** laurie@hopeforhenry.org

STROOT, Michel. American/Belgian (born Belgium), b. 1938. **Genres:** Food And Wine, How-to Books. **Career:** The Golden Door Spa, executive chef, master chef, 1974-. Writer. **Publications:** (With D. Szekely) Golden Door Cookbook: The Greening of American Cuisine, 1982; The Golden Door Cookbook: 200 Recipes from the World's Most Luxurious Spa, 1997; The Golden Door Cooks Light & Easy: Delicious Recipes from America's Premier Spa, 2003. **Address:** Golden Door Spa, PO Box 463077, Escondido, CA 92046-3077, U.S.A.

STROSS, Charles. Scottish/British (born England), b. 1964. **Genres:** Science Fiction/Fantasy. **Career:** Datacash, senior programmer, through 1999; Fma Ltd. (Web site consultants), senior programmer. Computer Shopper, writer, 1994-2004; PerlCGI Scripts, staff. Writer. **Publications:** The Web Architect's Handbook, 1996; Toast and Other Rusted Futures, 2002; Festival of Fools, 2003; Singularity Sky, 2003; Atrocity Archives, 2004; Family Trade, 2004; Iron Sunrise, 2004; Hidden Family, 2005; Accelerando, 2005; Clan Corporate, 2006; Jennifer Morgue, 2006; Glasshouse, 2006; Halting State, 2007; Missile Gap, 2007; Merchants' War, 2007; Saturn's Children, 2008; Revolution Business, 2009; Wireless, 2009; Down on the Farm, 2010; Fuller Memorandum, 2010; The Trade of Queens, 2010; Rule 34, 2011. **Address:** c/o Author Mail, Ace Books, 375 Hudson St., New York, NY 10014, U.S.A. **Online address:** charles@fma.com

STROSS, Randall E. American (born United States) **Genres:** Biography, Autobiography/Memoirs, Business/Trade/Industry, Economics, History, Adult Non-fiction. **Career:** San Jose State University, Organization and Management, professor; New York Times, digital domain columnist. Writer. **Publications:** NONFICTION: The Stubborn Earth: American Agriculturalists on Chinese Soil, 1898-1937, 1986; (ed.) Technology and Society in Twentieth Century America: An Anthology, 1989; Bulls in the China Shop: And Other Sino-American Business Encounters, 1990; Steve Jobs and the NeXT Big Thing, 1993; The Microsoft Way: The Real Story of How the Company Outsmarts Its Competition, 1996; EBoys: The First Inside Account of Venture Capitalists at Work, 2000; The Wizard of Menlo Park: How Thomas Alva Edison Invented the Modern World, 2007; Planet Google: One Company's Audacious Plan to Organize Everything We Know, 2008; Startups in Silicon Valley, forthcoming. **Address:** San Jose State University, BT Bldg., Fl. 06, Rm. 658, 1 Washington Sq., San Jose, CA 95192-0065, U.S.A. **Online address:** randall.stross@sjsu.edu

STROSSEN, Nadine. American (born United States), b. 1950. **Genres:** Law, Civil Liberties/Human Rights, Sex. **Career:** Harvard Law Review, editor, 1975; Minnesota Supreme Court, judicial clerk, 1975-76; Lindquist and Vennum, associate, 1976-78; Sullivan and Cromwell, associate, 1978-84; New York University, School of Law, associate professor of clinical law and supervising attorney, 1984-88; American Civil Liberties Union, general counsel, 1986-91, president, 1991-2008; New York Law School, professor of law, 1988-; Columbia University Graduate School of Business, adjunct professor, 1990; Yale University, Calhoun College, adjunct fellow, 1997-. Writer. **Publications:** (With H.L. Gates, Jr., A. Griffin and D. Lively) Speaking of Race, Speaking of Sex: Hate Speech, Civil Rights and Civil Liberties, 1995; Defending Pornography: Free Speech, Sex, and the Fight for Women's Rights, 1995; (foreword) The Government vs. Erotica: The Siege of Adam and Eve, 2001. Contributor to books and periodicals. **Address:** New York Law School, E914, 57 Worth St., 185 West Broadway, New York, NY 10013-2960, U.S.A. **Online address:** nstrossen@nyls.edu

STROTHER, Ruth. (Berman). American (born United States), b. 1958. **Genres:** Animals/Pets, Children's Non-fiction, Young Adult Non-fiction, Zoology, Sciences, Natural History, Biography, Biology, How-to Books. **Career:** Lerner Publications, children's book editor, senior editor, 1987-95; Bowtie Press, editor-in-chief, 1995-2000. Freelance writer and editor. **Publications:** American Bison, 1992, rev. ed. 2009; El Bisonte Americano, 1994; Sharks, 1995, rev. ed. 2009; Peacocks, 1996; Ants, 1996; Squeaking Bats, 1998, rev. ed. 2010; Fishing Bears, 1998; Buzzing Rattlesnakes, 1998; Spinning Spiders, 1998; Climbing Tree Frogs, 1998; Watchful Wolves, 1998; (ed.) Guys and Dogs, 1999; My Pet Dog, 2001; Bill Gates, 2007; W is for Woof: A Dog Alphabet, 2008; Girls' Box, 2008; Margaret Mead, 2009; B Is for Blue Planet: An Earth Science Alphabet, 2011; The Dog Friendly Home: DIY Projects for Dog Lovers, 2011. **Address:** 11517 Tulane Ave., Riverside, CA 92507-6650, U.S.A. **Online address:** rstrother@earthlink.net

STROUD, Bettye. American (born United States), b. 1939. **Genres:** Children's Fiction, Children's Non-fiction, Picture/Board Books, Cultural/Ethnic Topics, Social Commentary, Human Relations/Parenting. **Career:** Winder Middle Grade Schools, media specialist, 1960-72; Barnett Shoals School, media specialist, 1972-92; University of Georgia, lecturer of writing for children. Writer. **Publications:** Down Home at Miss Dessa's, 1996; Dance Y'All, 2001; A Personal Tour of Tuskegee Institute, 2001; The Leaving, 2001; (ed.) The World's Wide Open, 2003; Patchwork Path: A Quilt Map to Freedom, 2005; (with V. Schomp) The Reconstruction Era, 2007; (with C.A. Ramsey) Belle, the Last Mule at Gee's Bend, 2011. Contributor to magazines. **Address:** c/o Lynda Tinari, Marshall Cavendish Corp., 99 White Plains Rd., PO Box 2001, Tarrytown, NY 10591, U.S.A. **Online address:** bjstroud@bellsouth.net

STROUD, Carsten. (David Stone). Canadian (born Canada), b. 1946. **Genres:** Mystery/Crime/Suspense, Plays/Screenplays, Adult Non-fiction, Novels. **Career:** Mair, Stroud and Associates Inc., partner; Absaroke Communications Inc., co-owner. Journalist. **Publications:** NON-FICTION: The Blue Wall: Street Cops in Canada, 1983; Close Pursuit: A Week in the Life of an NYPD Homicide Cop, 1987; Contempt of Court, 1993; Iron Bravo: Hearts, Minds and Sergeants in the U.S. Army, 1995; Deadly Force: In the Streets with the U.S. Marshals, 1996. NOVELS: Sniper's Moon, 1990; Lizardskin, 1992; Black Water Transit, 2001; Cuba Strait, 2003; Cobraville, 2004. AS DAVID STONE: The Echelon Vendetta, 2007; The Orpheus Deception, 2008; The Venetian Judgment, 2009; The Skorpion Directive, 2010. **Address:** Karpfinger Agency, 357 W 20th St., New York, NY 10011, U.S.A. **Online address:** carsten@carstenstroudbooks.com

STROUD, Joanne. See BILBY, Joanne Stroud.

STROUD, Joanne H. See BILBY, Joanne Stroud.

STROUD, Jonathan. British (born England), b. 1970. **Genres:** Children's Fiction, Young Adult Fiction. **Career:** Freelance writer, 1993-; Walker Books Ltd., editor, 1994-98; Kingfisher Books, editor, 1998-2001. **Publications:** Justin Credible's Word Play World, 1994; The Lost Treasure of Captain Blood: How the Infamous Spammes Escaped the Jaws of Death and Won a Vast and Glorious Fortune, 1996; The Viking Saga of Harri Bristlebeard: A Heroic Puzzle Adventure, 1997; Buried Fire, 1999; Word Puzzles, 1999; Ancient Rome: A Guide to the Glory of Imperial Rome, 2000; The Leap, 2001; The Last Siege, 2003; The Amulet of Samarkand, 2003; Buried Fire, 2004; The Golem's Eye, 2004; Ptolemy's Gate, 2006; Heroes of the Valley, 2009; The Ghost of Shadow Vale, 2009; Ring of Solomon: A Bartimaeus Novel, 2010; (adapted with A. Donkin) Amulet of Samarkand: A Bartimaeus Graphic Novel, 2010. **Address:** c/o Laura Cecil, Laura Cecil Literary Agency, 17 Alwyne Villas, London, GL N1 2HG, England.

STROUD, Patricia Tyson. American (born United States), b. 1932. **Genres:** Environmental Sciences/Ecology, Natural History, Zoology, Biography, History, Autobiography/Memoirs. **Career:** Wildlife Expo, editor, 1979-83; Academy of Natural Sciences, Frontiers Publication, editor, 1980-82. **Publications:** Thomas Say: New World Naturalist, 1992; The Emperor of Nature: Charles-Lucien Bonaparte and His World, 2000; The Man Who Had Been King: The American Exile of Napoleon's Brother Joseph, 2005; (with R.M. Peck) A Glorious Enterprise, 2012. **Address:** 613 Maplewood Rd., Wayne, PA 19087-4720, U.S.A.

STROUHAL, Eugen. Czech (born Czech Republic), b. 1931. **Genres:** Anthropology/Ethnology, Archaeology/Antiquities, Geography, History, Medicine/Health. **Career:** Charles University, Institute of Biology, assistant in medical faculty, 1957-60, Czechoslovak Institute of Egyptology, science staff, 1961-68, Institute for the History of Medicine, professor and director, 1990-2004; National Museum, Naprstek Museum, curator and science staff, 1969-92. Writer. **Publications:** Stareogyptské Mumie, 1971; Do Srdce Maretánské Sahary, 1974; Egyptian Mummies in Czechoslovak Collections, 1979; Setkání S Aljaškou, 1981; (with J. Jungwirth) Anthropologische Untersuchung der C-Gruppenund Pan-Gräber-Skelette aus Sayala, ägyptisch-Nubien, 1984; Wadi Qitna and Kalabsha-South: Late Roman-Early Byzantine Tumuli Cemeteries in Egyptian Nubia, vol. I: Archaeology, 1984; Zivot Starých Egypt'anů, 1989, 2nd ed., 1994; Sedmkrát do Núbie, 1989; Begegnungen mit Alaska, 1990; Vivre au Temps des Pharaons, 1992; Secondary Cemetery in the Mastaba of Ptahshepses at Abusir, 1993; Zaklady paleopatologie, 2004; Trpeli i davni lide nádory?, 2008; The Memphite Tomb of Horemheb, Commander-in-Chief of Tutankhamun IV, Human Skeletal Remains, 2008; Lekarstvi starych Egyptanu I. Chirurgie a pece o zenu a dite, 2010. **Address:** First Faculty of Medicine, Institute for History of Medicine and Foreign Lang, Charles University, U nemocnice 4, Prague, 121 08, Czech Republic. **Online address:** eugen.strouhal@lf1.cuni.cz

STROUP, George W. American (born United States), b. 1944. **Genres:** Theology/Religion. **Career:** University of the South, assistant professor of religion, 1973-74; ordained minister of word and sacrament, 1973; Princeton Theology Seminary, assistant professor, 1974-80; Austin Presbyterian Theological Seminary, associate professor of theology, 1980-86; Columbia Theological Seminary, J.B. Green professor of theology, 1986-; Writer. **Publications:** The Promise of Narrative Theology: Recovering the Gospel in the

Church, 1981; Jesus Christ for Today, 1982; Reformed Reader: A Sourcebook in Christian Theology, 1993; (ed. with W. Brueggemann) Many Voices, One God: Being Faithful in a Pluralistic World: In Honor of Shirley Guthrie, 1998; Before God, 2004; Calvin, 2009; Why Jesus Matters, 2011. Contributor to books and periodicals. **Address:** Columbia Theological Seminary, 701 Columbia Dr., PO Box 520, Decatur, GA 30031-0520, U.S.A. **Online address:** stroupg@ctsnet.edu

STRUBE, Cordelia. Canadian (born Canada), b. 1960. **Genres:** Novels, Young Adult Fiction. **Career:** Ryerson University, instructor. Actress and writer. **Publications:** NOVELS: Alex & Zee, 1994; Milton's Elements, 1995; Teaching Pigs to Sing, 1996; Dr. Kalbfleisch And The Chicken Restaurant, 1997; The Barking Dog, 2000; Blind Night: A Novel, 2004; Planet Reese, 2007; Lemon, 2009. **Address:** Anne McDermid & Associates Ltd., 64 Bloem Ave., Toronto, ON M6E 1S1, Canada.

STRUYK, Raymond J(ay). American (born United States), b. 1944. **Genres:** Demography, Economics. **Career:** Rutgers University, assistant professor, 1968-69; National Bureau of Economic Research, Urban Studies Group, research associate, 1968-72; Rice University, visiting assistant professor of economics, 1971-72; Urban Institute, Housing Studies Group, research associate, 1972-77, International Activities Center, director, senior fellow, 1980-2006; U.S. Department of Housing and Urban Development, Office of Policy Development and Research, deputy assistant secretary for research, 1977-79; University of Chicago, National Opinion Research Center, Department of International Projects, senior fellow, 2007-. Writer. **Publications:** (With F.J. James) A Comparative Study of Manufacturing Employment Location in the Boston and Phoenix Metropolitan Areas, 1974; (with F.J. James) Intrametropolitan Industrial Location, 1975; (with F. de Leeuw) The Web of Urban Housing, 1975; A Simulation Model of Urban Housing Markets in Developing Countries, 1976; (with L. Ozanne) Housing from the Existing Stock, 1976; (with S.A. Marshall) Urban Home Ownership, 1976; Should Government Encourage Home Ownership?, 1977; (with J. Follain) Home Ownership Effects of Alternate Mortgage Instruments, 1977; (with S.A. Marshall and L.J. Ortiz) Housing Policies for the Urban Poor, 1978; A New System for Public Housing, 1980; (with B.J. Soldo) Improving the Elderly's Housing, 1980; (with D.W. Rasmussen) A Housing Strategy for the City of Detroit, 1981; (with J.P. Zais and T. Thibodeau) Housing Assistance for Older Americans, 1982; (with R. Kolodny and R.D. Baron) The Insider's Guide to Managing Public Housing, vol. I: Diagnosing Management Problems, vol. II: Analysis Guides, 1983; (with N. Mayer and J.A. Tuccillo) Federal Housing Policy at President Reagan's Midterm, 1983; (with M.A. Turner) Urban Housing in the 1980s, 1984; (with M.A. Turner) Finance and Housing Quality in Two Developing Countries: Korea and the Philippines, 1986; Aging at Home, 1987; Future U.S. Housing Policy, 1988; (with R.J. Struyk and S.J. Newman) Housing for the Elderly in 2010: Projections and Policy Options, 1989; (with M. Hoffman and H. Katsura) The Market for Shelter in Indonesian Cities, 1990; (with J. Telgarsky) Toward a Market-Oriented Housing Sector in Eastern Europe Developments in Bulgaria, Czechoslovakia, Hungary, Romania and Yugoslavia, 1990; (with J. Hegedus and I. Toscis) Integrating State Rental Housing with the Private Market, 1991; (with R.M. Ravicz) Housing finance in LDCs: India's National Housing Bank as a Model?, 1992; Making Aid Work, 1997; Reconstructive Critics: Think Tanks In Post-Soviet Bloc Democracies, 1999; Managing Think Tanks: Practical Guidance for Maturing Organizations, 2006; (co-author) Policy Analysis for Effective Development: Strengthening Transition Economies, 2006; Efektivnye resheniia v ekonomike perekhodnogo perioda: analiticheskie instrumenty razrabotki i realizatsii sotsialno-ėkonomicheskoĭ politiki, 2007; Guide to Preparing a Housing Finance Strategy, 2009. EDITOR: (with M. Bendick) Housing Vouchers for the Poor, 1981; (with K. Stahl) The U.S. and West German Housing Markets, 1985; Homeownership and Housing Financial Policy in the Former Soviet Bloc, 2000. **Address:** National Opinion Research Center, University of Chicago, 4350 East-West Hwy., Bethesda, MD 20814, U.S.A. **Online address:** struyk3@yahoo.com

STRYK, Lucien. American/Polish (born Poland), b. 1924. **Genres:** Poetry, Philosophy, Translations, Theology/Religion. **Career:** Freelance writer, 1952-54; Northern Illinois University, Department of English, assistant professor, professor, 1958-91, professor emeritus, 1991-, now distinguished research professor emeritus; Niigata University, visiting lecturer, 1956-58; Yamaguchi University, visiting lecturer, 1962-63. Writer. **Publications:** Taproot: A Selection of Poems, 1953; The Trespasser: Poems, 1956; Notes for a Guidebook, 1965; The Pit and Other Poems, 1969; Awakening, 1973; (trans.

with T. Ikemoto) Zen Poems of China & Japan, 1973 as The Crane's Bill: Zen Poems of China and Japan, 1981; (trans. with T. Ikemoto) Twelve Death Poems of the Chinese Zen Masters, 1973; Three Zen Poems, after Shinkichi Takahashi, 1976; Selected Poems, 1976; The Duckpond, 1978; Encounter with Zen, 1981; Cherries, 1983; Collected Poems 1953-1983, 1984; (trans.) B. Matsuo, Traveler, My Name, Haiku of Bashō, 1984; (trans. and intro.) B. Matsuo, On Love and Barley: Haiku of Basho, 1985; Bells of Lombardy, 1986; Of Pen and Ink and Paper Scraps, 1989; The Dumpling Field: Haiku of Issa, 1991; (ed. and intro.) The Gift of Great Poetry, 1992; Zen, Poetry, the Art of Lucien Stryk, 1993; Cage of Fireflies: Modern Japanese Haiku, 1993; Zen Poems, 1995; The Awakened Self: Encounters with Zen, 1995; Where We Are: Selected Poems and Zen Translations, 1997; And Still Birds Sing, 1998. EDITOR: (trans. with T. Ikemoto) Zen: Poems, Prayers, Sermons, Anecdotes, Interviews, 1965, 2nd ed., 1981; Heartland: Poets of the Midwest, 1967; (intro.) World of the Buddha: A Reader, 1968 as World of Buddha: An Introduction to Buddhist Literature, 1982; (trans. with T. Ikemoto) After Images: Zen Poems of Shinkichi Takahashi, 1970; HeartlandII: Poets of the Midwest, 1975; (and trans.) The Penguin Book of Zen Poetry, 1977; Prairie Voices: A Collection of Illinois Poets, 1980; (trans. with T. Ikemoto) Triumph of the Sparrow: Zen Poems of Shinkichi Takahashi, 1986; (ed. and trans. with T. Ikemoto) Zen Poetry: Let the Spring Breeze Enter, 1995; (with K. Bailey) The Acorn Book of Contemporary Haiku, 2000. **Address:** Department of English, Northern Illinois University, 101 Williston Hall, 1425 W Lincoln Hwy., DeKalb, IL 60115-2828, U.S.A.

STRYKER, Daniel. See **MORRIS, Chris(topher Crosby).**

STUART, Alexander. American/British (born England), b. 1955. **Genres:** Novels, Children's Fiction, Plays/Screenplays, Film, Travel/Exploration, Autobiography/Memoirs, Biography. **Career:** Films and Filming Magazine, film critic, 1972-80; University of Miami, professor of film, 1994-. Screenwriter. **Publications:** Glory B (novel), 1983; Joe, Jo-Jo, and the Monkey Masks (children's fiction) 1988; The War Zone (novel), 1989; (with J.B. Stuart) Henry and the Sea (children's fiction), 1989; (with A. Totterdell) 5-1/2x3: The Short Life and Death of Joe Buffalo Stuart (biography), 1990; Tribes (novel), 1992; Life on Mars: Gangsters, Runaways, Exiles, Drag Queens and Other Aliens in Florida (travel/autobiography), 1996; Chinatown Nights, 1999. **Address:** c/o Charles Walker, Peter Fraser and Dunlop, Drury House, 34-43 Russell St., London, GL WC2B 5HA, England. **Online address:** singleword@alexanderstuart.com

STUART, Anne. Also writes as Anne Kristine Stuart. American (born United States), b. 1948. **Genres:** Romance/Historical, Novels. **Career:** Writer and public speaker. **Publications:** Barretts Hill, 1974; Cameron's Landing, 1977; Demonwood, 1979; The Demon Count, 1980; The Demon Count's Daughter, 1980; Lord Satan's Bride, 1981; The Spinster and the Rake, 1982; Chain of Love, 1983; Hearts Ease, 1983; The Museum Piece, 1984; Catspaw, 1984; Tangled Lies, 1984; Crazy like a Fox, 1984; Against the Wind, 1985; The Houseparty, 1985; Banish Misfortune, 1985; Housebound, 1985; Rocky Road, 1985; Bewitching Hour, 1986; Hand in Glove, 1987; Escape out of Darkness, 1987; Darkness before the Dawn, 1987; At the Edge of the Sun, 1987; Blue Sage, 1987; Cry for the Moon, 1988; Catspaw II, 1988; Partners in Crime, 1988; Seen and Not Heard, 1988; Glass Houses, 1989; Angels Wings, 1990; Special Gifts, 1990; Rancho Diablo, 1990; Night of the Phantom, 1991; Lazarus Rising, 1991; Chasing Trouble, 1991; My Valentine, 1992; Rafe's Revenge, 1992; Now You See Him, 1992; Heat Lightning, 1992; Highland Fling, 1993; Falling Angel, 1993; A Rose at Midnight, 1993; (contrib.) Avon Books Presents, 1993; Shadow Dance, 1993; One More Valentine, 1993; Cinderman, 1994; To Love a Dark Lord, 1994; Strangers in the Night, 1995; Nightfall, 1995; Moonrise, 1996; Lovers Dark and Dangerous, 1996; Break the Night, 1996; Winters Edge, 1996; Prince of Swords, 1996; The Soldier and the Baby, 1996; Summer Love, 1997; Lord of Danger, 1997; Ritual Sins, 1997; A Dark and Stormy Night, 1997; Sisters and Secrets, 1998; Prince of Magic, 1998; Now or Never, 1999; Shadow Lover, 1999; Shadows at Sunset, 1999; Valentine Affairs, 1999; The Right Man, 1999; Lady Fortune, 2000; Looking for Trouble, 2000; Wild Thing, 2000; Kissing Frosty Santa in a Stetson, 2000; The Widow, 2001; Still Lake, 2002; (with G. Wilson) Night and Day, 2002; Into the Fire, 2003; The Road to Hidden Harbor, 2003; (with M. Shayne and J. Arnold) Burning Bright, 2004; Hidden Honor, 2004; (with B. Hutchinson) Undercover Summer, 2004; (with C. Adair and M. Jensen) Date with a Devil, 2004; Black Ice, 2005; Cold as Ice, 2006; the Devil's Waltz, 2006; (with J. Crusie and E. Dreyer) Unfortunate Miss Fortunes, 2007; Ice Blue, 2007; Fire and Ice, 2008; Ice Storm, 2008; (with T. Leonard and M.

Lennox) Christmas Getaway, 2008; Dogs and Goddesses, 2009; Silver Falls, 2009; Ruthless, 2010; Reckless, 2011; Breathless, 2011; Shameless, 2011. Works appear in anthologies. Contributor to books. **Address:** Harlequin. com, PO Box 5190, Buffalo, NY 14240-5190, U.S.A. **Online address:** anne@anne-stuart.com

STUART, Anne Kristine. *See* **STUART, Anne.**

STUART, Dabney. American (born United States), b. 1937. **Genres:** Novellas/Short Stories, Poetry, Literary Criticism And History. **Career:** College of William and Mary, instructor in English, 1961-65; Washington and Lee University, instructor, 1965-66, assistant professor, 1966-69, associate professor, 1969-74, professor of English, 1974-91, S. Blount Masson Professor of English, 1991-2002, professor emeritus, 2002-; University of Virginia, poet-in-residence, 1981, 1982-83; Shenandoah, poetry editor, 1966-76, editor-in-chief, 1988-95. Writer. **Publications:** The Diving Bell: Poems, 1966; A Particular Place: Poems, 1969; (co-author) Corgi Modern Poets in Focus 3, 1971; Other Hand: Poems, 1974; Friends of Yours, Friends of Mine: Poems, 1975; Round and Round: A Triptych, 1977; Nabokov: The Dimensions of Parody, 1978; Rockbridge Poems, 1981; Common Ground: Poems, 1982; Don't Look Back: Poems, 1987; Narcissus Dreaming: Poems, 1990; Sweet Lucy Wine: Stories, 1992; Light Years: New and Selected Poems, 1994; Second Sight: Poems for Paintings by Carroll Cloar, 1996; Long Gone: Poems, 1996; The Way to Cobbs Creek: Stories, 1997; Strains of the Old Man, 1999; Settlers: Poems, 1999; No Visible Means of Support: Stories, 2001; Man Who Loves Cézanne: Poems, 2003; Family Preserve: Poems, 2005. **Address:** 30 Edmondson Ave., Lexington, VA 24450, U.S.A.

STUART, Mark. British (born England), b. 1970?. **Genres:** Politics/Government, Biography. **Career:** University of Nottingham, School of Politics and International Relations, Centre for British Politics, research fellow. Writer and biographer. **Publications:** Douglas Hurd: The Public Servant: An Authorised Biography, 1998; John Smith: A Life, 2005. Contributor to periodicals. **Address:** Centre for British Politics, School of Politics and International Relations, University of Nottingham, Law and Social Sciences Bldg., University Pk., Nottingham, NT NG7 2RD, England. **Online address:** mark.stuart@nottingham.ac.uk

STUART, Sally E(lizabeth). American (born United States), b. 1940. **Genres:** Education, Writing/Journalism, How-to Books, Reference, Young Adult Fiction, Novels. **Career:** Writer and speaker. **Publications:** Teaching and Reaching: A How-To and Idea Book for Sunday School Teachers, 1981; The All-Occasion Game Book: A How-To-Book for Parties and Holidays, 1981; Teaching and Reaching Kindergarten Resources, 1984; Teaching and Reaching Primary Resources, 1984; Teaching and Reaching Junior Resources, 1984; The All-Occasion Craft and Gift Book, 1984; Sally Stuart's Inspirational Writers Topical Market Guide, 1985; Inspirational Writers Market Guide, 1987; (with W. Young) Copyright Not Copycat: A Writers Guide to Copyright, 1987; The Way It Was in Bible Times (juvenile), 1988; 100 Plus Party Games: Fun & Easy Ideas for Parties, 1988; 100 Plus Holiday Crafts and Gifts: Fun & Easy Ideas for Parties, 1990; Christian Writers' Market Guide, 1990-91, 1990; Spirit's Gold (western novel), 1990; 1991-92 Christian Writers' Market Guide, 1991; 1992-93 Christian Writers' Market Guide, 1992; 1993-94 Christian Writers' Market Guide, 1993; 1994-95 Christian Writers' Market Guide, 1994; Christian Writers' Market Guide, 1995-1996, 1995; Christian Writers' Market Guide, 1996, 1996; Christian Writers' Market Guides, 1997, 1997; Sally Stuart's Guide to Getting Published, 1999; (foreword) Sowing Seeds, 2010; The Writer's Bloc, 2012. Contributor to books and periodicals. **Address:** 11080 SW Allen Blvd., Beaverton, OR 97005, U.S.A. **Online address:** stuartcwmg@aol.com

STUART, Sarah Payne. American (born United States), b. 1952. **Genres:** Novels, Autobiography/Memoirs, Documentaries/Reportage, Essays, Plays/Screenplays, Biography, Romance/Historical. **Career:** Writer. **Publications:** Men in Trouble (novel), 1988; The Year Roger Wasn't Well (novel), 1994; My First Cousin Once Removed: Money, Madness and the Family of Robert Lowell, 1998. **Address:** Darhansoff & Verrill Literary Agents, 236 W 26th St., Ste. 802, New York, NY 10001, U.S.A.

STUBBS, Jean. British (born England), b. 1926. **Genres:** Mystery/Crime/Suspense, Romance/Historical, Novels, Adult Non-fiction, Young Adult Non-fiction, Young Adult Fiction. **Career:** Writers' Summer Schools and Seminars, lecturer, 1968; London Metropolitan University, Department of Humanities, Arts, Languages and Education, professor of Caribbean studies, Caribbean Studies Centre, director; International Journal of Cuban Studies, co-editor, 2008-; University of London, School of Advanced Study, Institute for the Study of the Americas, professor of Caribbean history. **Publications:** NOVELS: The Rose-Grower, 1962; The Travellers, 1963; Hanrahan's Colony, 1964; The Straw Crown, 1966; My Grand Enemy, 1967; The Case of Kitty Oglivie: A Novel, 1970; Eleanora Duse in UK as The Passing Star, 1970; An Unknown Welshman: A Historical Novel, 1972; Dear Laura, 1973; The Painted Face: An Edwardian Mystery, 1974; The Golden Crucible, 1976; By Our Beginnings, 1979; An Imperfect Joy in UK as The Ironmaster, 1981; Love is of the Valley, 1981; A Lasting Spring, 1987; Like We Used to Be, 1989; Summer Secrets, 1990 in US as Light in Summer, 1991; Kelly Park, 1992; Family Games, 1994; Charades, 1994; The Witching Time, 1998; I'm a Stranger Here Myself, 2005. NON-FICTION: One Hundred Years Around the Lizard, 1985; Tobacco on the Periphery: A Case Study in Cuban Labour History, 1860-1958, 1985; Great Houses of Cornwall, 1987; Cuba: The Test of Time, 1989; (co-ed.) Cuba in Transition: Crisis and Transformation, 1992; (ed. with P.P. Sarduy) Afro-Cuba: An Anthology of Cuban Writing on Race, Politics and Culture, 1993; (comp. with L. Haines and M.F. Haines) Cuba, 1996; (ed. with P.P. Sarduy) Afro-Cuban Voices: On Race and Identity in Contemporary Cuba, 2000. SERIES: Kits' Hill, 1978; The Vivan Inheritance, 1982; The Northern Correspondent 1831-1851, 1984. OTHER: The Vivian Inheritance, 1982. **Address:** Institute for the Study of the Americas, School of Advanced Study, University of London, Senate House, Malet St., London, GL WC1E 7HU, England. **Online address:** j.stubbs@londonmet.ac.uk

STUBBS, Peter Charles. British (born England), b. 1937. **Genres:** Economics, Education, Technology, Law, Politics/Government, Business/Trade/Industry, History. **Career:** The Economist Magazine, staff writer, 1960-62; University of Melbourne, Institute of Applied Economic Research, research fellow, 1963-68; University of Manchester, lecturer, 1969-72, senior lecturer, 1972-80, reader, 1980-90, dean of faculty, 1985-87, professor of economics, 1990-97, professor emeritus, 1997-. Writer. **Publications:** Innovation and Research, 1968; The Australian Motor Industry, 1972; (with N. Lee) The History of Dorman Smith, 1972; (with W.J. Tyson and M.Q. Dalvi) Transport Economics, 1980, rev. ed., 1984; Technology and Australia's Future, 1980; Australia and the Maritime Industries, 1983; (with J. Froud, R. Boden, and A. Ogus) Controlling the Regulators, 1998. Contributor to academic journals. **Address:** Department of Economics, University of Manchester, Manchester, M13 9PL, England. **Online address:** peter.stubbs@man.ac.uk

STUBBS, Richard W. Canadian (born Canada), b. 1946. **Genres:** Economics, Social Sciences. **Career:** McMaster University, Department of Political Science, professor, chair. Writer and educator. **Publications:** Counter-insurgency and the Economic Factor: The Impact of the Korean War Prices Boom on the Malayan Emergency, 1974; Facing the 1990s, 1989; Hearts and Minds in Guerrilla Warfare: The Malayan Emergency, 1948-1960, 1989, 2nd ed., 2004; (ed. with G.R.D. Underhill) Political Economy and the Changing Global Order, 1994, 3rd ed., 2006; (with A. Acharya) New Challenges for ASEAN: Emerging Policy Issues, 1995; (ed. with P.B. Rich) The Counter-insurgent State: Guerrilla Warfare and State Building in the Twentieth Century, 1997; (ed. with A. Acharya and B.M. Frolic) Democracy, Human Rights and Civil Society in Southeast Asia, 2001; Rethinking Asia's Economic Miracle: The Political Economy of War, Prosperity and Crisis, 2005. Contributor of articles to books and journals. **Address:** Department of Political Science, McMaster University, Hamilton, ON L8S 4M4, Canada. **Online address:** stubbs@mcmaster.ca

STUCKART, Diane A. S. (Alexa Smart). American (born United States) **Genres:** Novels. **Career:** Writer. **Publications:** AS ALEXA SMART: Masquerade, 1994; Shadows of the Heart, 1995; A Touch of Paradise, 1996; Roses at Midnight, 1997; (as Anna Gerard) Desert Hearts, Zebra, 1999; The Queen's Gambit: A Leonardo Da Vinci Mystery, 2008; Portrait of a Lady, 2009. **Address:** 1805 Walnut St., Philadelphia, PA 19103, U.S.A. **Online address:** diane@dianestuckart.com

STUCKEY, Peter J(ames). Australian (born Australia), b. 1963. **Genres:** Information Science/Computers, Sciences. **Career:** International Business Machines Co., T.J. Watson Research Center, research fellow, 1988-89; University of Melbourne, Machine Intelligence Project, research fellow, 1990, lecturer, 1991-93, senior research fellow, 1993, senior lecturer, 1994-98, reader and associate professor of computer science, 1999-, professor, 2003-; NICTA Victoria Laboratory, program leader. Writer. **Publications:** (Ed.

with R. Ramakrishnan) Constraints and Databases, 1998; (with K. Marriott) Programming with Constraints: An Introduction, 1998; (ed.) Logic Programming: 18th International Conference, ICLP, 2002, 2002; (ed. with Y. Kameyama) Functional and Logic Programming: 7th International Symposium, FLOPS 2004, Nara, Japan, April 7-9, 2004; (ed.) Principles and Practice of Constraint Programming: 14th International Conference, CP 2008, Sydney, Australia, September 14-18, 2008: Proceedings, 2008; (ed.) Proceedings of the Fourteenth International Conference on Principles and Practice of Constraint Programming, 2008; In Proceedings of 17th International Symposium on Graph Drawing, 2010. Contributor to journals. **Address:** Department of Computer Science, University of Melbourne, Rm. 5.27, 111 Barry St., Carlton, VI 3053, Australia. **Online address:** peter.stuckey@nicta.com.au

STUDDERT-KENNEDY, (William) Gerald. British/Indian (born India), b. 1933. **Genres:** Politics/Government, Social Sciences, Theology/Religion. **Career:** British Broadcasting Corp., producer, 1957-62; University of York, lecturer, 1966-70; University of Birmingham, senior lecturer in political science, 1970-92, reader in politics, 1992-98, School of Social Sciences, honorary professor, 1998-. Writer. **Publications:** (With G.C. Moodie) Opinions, Publics and Pressure Groups: An Essay on Vox Populi and Representative Government, 1970; Evidence and Explanation in Social Science: An Interdisciplinary Approach, 1975; Dog-collar Democracy: The Industrial Christian Fellowship, 1919-1929, 1982; British Christians, Indian Nationalists, and the Raj, 1991, rev. ed., 1999; Providence and the Raj: Imperial Mission and Missionary Imperialism, 1998. Contributor to journals. **Address:** University of Birmingham, Edgbaston, Birmingham, WM B15 2TT, England.

STUEVER, Hank. American (born United States), b. 1968. **Genres:** Adult Non-fiction. **Career:** Albuquerque Tribune, reporter; Austin American-Statesman, reporter; Washington Post, staff writer, 1999, TV critic, 2009. **Publications:** Off-Ramp: Adventures and Heartache in the American Elsewhere, 2004; Tinsel: A Search for America's Christmas Present, 2009. Works appear in anthologies. **Address:** The Washington Post, 1150, 15th St. NW, Washington, DC 20071, U.S.A. **Online address:** hank@hankstuever.com

STUHR(-ROMMEREIM), Rebecca (Ann). American (born United States), b. 1958. **Genres:** Bibliography, Biography, Literary Criticism And History. **Career:** University of Kansas Libraries, reference librarian and German bibliographer, 1984-88; Grinnell College Libraries, Burling Library, acting archivist and acting head of circulation sabbatical replacement, 1989-90, preservation officer, 1989-, collection development and preservation librarian, 1992-, associate professor; public service and outreach. Writer and musician. **Publications:** Autobiographies by Americans of Color, 1980-1994: An Annotated Bibliography, 1997; (with D. Iwabuchi) Autobiographies by Americans of Color, 1995-2000: An Annotated Bibliography, 2003; Reading Khaled Hosseini, 2009. Contributor to periodicals. **Address:** Burling Library, Grinnell College, 1127 Park St., Grinnell, IA 50112-1640, U.S.A. **Online address:** stuhrr@grinnell.edu

STUKAS, David. American (born United States) **Genres:** Mystery/Crime/Suspense, Novels, Gay And Lesbian Issues, Horror. **Career:** Writer. **Publications:** Someone Killed His Boyfriend, 2001; Going Down for the Count, 2002; Wearing Black to the White Party, 2003; Biceps of Death, 2004. **Address:** Kensington Publishing Corp., 119 W 40th St., New York, NY 10018, U.S.A. **Online address:** davidstukas@yahoo.com

STULBERG, Adam N. American (born United States), b. 1963. **Genres:** Politics/Government, Economics, Humanities. **Career:** RAND Corp., political consultant, 1987-99; Monterey Institute of International Studies, Center for Nonproliferation Studies, senior research associate, 1997-98; Carnegie Corp., consultant, 2000-; U.S. Secretary of Defense, staff, 2000-; Georgia Institute of Technology, assistant professor, 1998-2006, associate professor, 2006-, Center for International Strategy, Technology and Policy, co-director, 2007-, GT Suburu professor of excellence, 2010-. Writer. **Publications:** Setting the Agenda in the Caspian Basin: The Political Economy of Russia's Energy Leverage, 2003; (ed. with J.C. Moltz and V.A. Orlov) Preventing Nuclear Meltdown: Managing Decentralization of Russia's Nuclear Complex, 2004; (with M.D. Salomone and A.G. Long) Managing Defense Transformation: Agency, Culture and Service Change, 2007; Well-Oiled Diplomacy: Strategic Manipulation and Russia's Energy Statecraft in Eurasia, 2007. Contributor to periodicals. **Address:** Ctr for Intl Strategy, Technology and Policy,

Sam Nunn School of International Affairs, Georgia Institute of Technology, Rm. 314, 781 Marietta St. NW, Atlanta, GA 30332, U.S.A. **Online address:** adam.stulberg@inta.gatech.edu

STUPPLES, Peter (Cecil). New Zealander/British (born England), b. 1936. **Genres:** Biography, Art/Art History. **Career:** University of York, faculty, 1967-72; University of Otago, associate professor of art history, 1973, head of the department of art history, 1990-98; Dunedin Public Art Gallery Society, vice president, 1988-; Otago Polytechnic, Art History and Theory, senior lecturer. Writer. **Publications:** Vpered!, 1971; Gottfried Lindauer, 1985; (with B. Gordon) Charles Heaphy, 1987; John Clark Hoyte, 1987; Pavel Kuznetsov: His Life and Art, 1989. Contributor to periodicals. **Address:** Department of Art History & Theory, Otago Polytechnic, The Geoff Mason Administration Ctr., 4th St., PO Box 1910, Dunedin, 9054, New Zealand. **Online address:** peter.stupples@stonebow.otago.ac.nz

STUPPY, Wolfgang. British/German (born Germany), b. 1966. **Genres:** Botany. **Career:** National Herbarium of the Netherlands, Leiden University branch, researcher, 1997-99; Royal Botanic Gardens, threatened plants officer, 1999-2002, Seed Conservation Department, seed morphologist, 2002-, seed anatomist, 2004-; botanist. Writer. **Publications:** (With R. Kesseler) Seeds: Time Capsules of Life, 2006; (with R. Kesseler) Fruit: Edible, Inedible, Incredible, 2008; (with R. Kesseler and M. Harley) The Bizarre and Incredible World of Plants, 2009. **Address:** The Royal Botanic Gardens, Kew, Richmond, SR TW9 3AB, England. **Online address:** w.stuppy@rbgkew.org.uk

STURGEON, Janet C. Canadian (born Canada) **Genres:** Politics/Government. **Career:** Simon Fraser University, professor of social geography and human ecology, 2004-. Educator and writer. **Publications:** Border Landscapes: The Politics of Akha Land Use in China and Thailand, 2005. Contributor of articles to journals. **Address:** Simon Fraser University, Burnaby Campus, 8888 University Dr., Burnaby, BC V5A 1S6, Canada. **Online address:** sturgeon@sfu.ca

STURGES, Robert S(tuart). American (born United States), b. 1953. **Genres:** Gay And Lesbian Issues, Literary Criticism And History. **Career:** French teacher, 1978-79; Massachusetts Institute of Technology, assistant professor of literature, 1980-81; Wesleyan University, assistant professor of English, 1981-88; University of New Orleans, assistant professor, 1988-91, associate professor, 1991-95, professor of English, 1995-2002, university research professor of English, 2002-; Arizona State University, professor of English, director of graduate studies. Writer. **Publications:** Medieval Interpretation: Models of Reading in Literary Narrative, 1100-1500, 1991; Chaucer's Pardoner and Gender Theory: Bodies of Discourse, 2000; Dialogue and Deviance: Male-Male Desire in the Dialogue Genre, 2005; Law and Sovereignty in the Middle Ages and the Renaissance, 2011. **Address:** Department of English, Arizona State University, G. Homer Durham Language & Literature Bldg., Rm. LL 204, PO Box 0302, Tempe, AZ 85287-0302, U.S.A. **Online address:** robert.sturges@asu.edu

STURGIS, Ingrid. American (born United States) **Genres:** Human Relations/Parenting, Psychology, Women's Studies And Issues. **Career:** Journalist. New York City Board of Education, teacher, 1978-80; Chocolate Singles, staff writer, 1982-87; WBAI-FM radio, reporter, 1985-86; New York Pulse, business editor, 1985-87; Bank Systems and Equipment, associate editor, 1987-88; Times-Herald Record, business reporter, 1988-89; Emerge, contributing editor, 1989-95; Poughkeepsie Journal, features editor, 1990-92; Courier-News, special sections editor, 1992-94; Philadelphia Inquirer, copy editor, 1994-97; BET Weekend, managing editor, 1997-2000; Savoy, managing editor, 2000-01; Essence.com, editor, 2001-, editor-in-chief; Black Voices, senior program manager; Howard University, assistant professor of new media. **Publications:** The Nubian Wedding Book: Words and Rituals to Celebrate and Plan an African-American Wedding, 1997; (ed.) Aunties: Thirty-five Writers Celebrate Their Other Mother, 2004. Contributor to periodicals. **Address:** Department of Journalism, Howard University, W5-233F, 525 Bryant St. NW, Washington, DC 20059, U.S.A. **Online address:** isturgis@howard.edu

STURM, Circe. American (born United States), b. 1967. **Genres:** Young Adult Non-fiction. **Career:** University of Oklahoma, adjunct assistant professor & professor, 1992-; University of California, faculty, 1993-96. Writer. **Publications:** Blood Politics: Race, Culture, and Identity in the Cherokee Nation of Oklahoma (nonfiction), 2002. Contributor to books. **Address:** Department of Anthropology, University of Oklahoma, Dale Hall Twr. 521, 455 W Lindsey, Norman, OK 73019, U.S.A. **Online address:** circe@ou.edu

STURM, Douglas E. American (born United States), b. 1929. **Genres:** Ethics, Philosophy, Politics/Government, Theology/Religion. **Career:** Bucknell University, assistant professor, 1959-64, associate professor, 1964-70, professor of religion and political science, 1970-95, presidential professor, 1974-80, Institute for the Study of Human Values, director, 1966-67, Department of Religion, chairperson, 1969-74, 1989-90, professor emeritus, 1995-; Southern Methodist University, Perkins School of Theology, visiting professor, 1963; St. John's College, Graduate Institute in Liberal Education, visiting tutor, 1972; Andover-Newton Theological School, visiting professor, 1972-73; University of Chicago, visiting professor, 1976-77, lecturer, 1983-84; University of Tennessee, visiting research professor, 1991-92. Writer. **Publications:** Community and Alienation: Essays on Process Thought and Public Life, 1988; Solidarity and Suffering: Toward a Politics of Relationality, 1998; Belonging Together: Faith and Politics in a Relational World, 2003. Works appear in anthologies. Contributor of articles to periodicals. **Address:** Department of Religion and Political Science, Bucknell University, Coleman Hall, Lewisburg, PA 17837, U.S.A. **Online address:** sturm@bucknell.edu

STURMA, Michael Thomas. American (born United States), b. 1950. **Genres:** Novels. **Career:** Australian Capital Territory, tutor, 1980; University of New England, lecturer, 1981-91; Murdoch University, Department of History, senior lecturer, 1991-, professor. Writer. **Publications:** Vice in a Vicious Society: Crime and Convicts in Mid-Nineteenth-Century New South Wales, 1983; Australian Rock 'n' Roll: The First Wave, 1991; South Sea Maidens: Western Fantasy and Sexual Politics in the South Pacific, 2002; Death at a Distance: The Loss of the Legendary USS Harder, 2006; The USS Flier: Death and Survival on a World War II Submarine, 2008; Surface and Destroy, 2011. **Address:** School of Social Sciences & Humanities, Division of Arts, Murdoch University, 90 S St., Murdoch, WA 6150, Australia. **Online address:** m.sturma@murdoch.edu.au

STURMAN, Jennifer. American (born United States) **Genres:** Mystery/Crime/Suspense, Novels, Literary Criticism And History. **Career:** Goldman, Sachs and Co., investment banking staff, 1991-93; McKinsey and Co., management consulting executive, 1995-2000; Time Warner Books, corporate strategy executive, 2002-. Writer. **Publications:** The Pact, 2004; The Jinx, 2005; The Key, 2006; The Hunt, 2007; And then Everything Unraveled, 2009; And then I Found Out the Truth, 2010. Contributor to periodicals. **Address:** c/o Author Mail, Red Dress Ink, Harlequin Enterprises Ltd., 225 Duncan Mill Rd., Don Mills, ON M3B 3K9, Canada. **Online address:** jen@jennifersturman.com

STURMER, Michael. German (born Germany), b. 1938?. **Genres:** Antiques/Furnishings, Economics, International Relations/Current Affairs, Military/Defense/Arms Control, Philosophy, Politics/Government. **Career:** University of Sussex, lecturer in European history, 1970-71; University of Erlangen-Nuernberg, professor of medieval and modern history, 1973-; Harvard University, research fellow, 1976-77; University of Toronto, visiting professor, 1983-84; University of Paris, associate professor, 1984-85; Johns Hopkins School for Advanced International Studies, visiting professor, 1985-; Die Welt, chief correspondent, 1998-; Stiftung Wissenschaft und Politik, director. Writer. **Publications:** Das Ruhelose Reich: Deutschland, 1866-1918, 1983, 4th ed., 1994; Scherbendes Gluecks: Klassizismus und Revolution, 1987; Die Grenzen der Macht: Begegnung der Deutschen mit der Geschichte, 1992; Striking the Balance: Sal. Oppenheim Jr. et Cie, a Family and a Bank, 1994; Die Reichsgruendung, 4th ed., 1997; (ed. with R. Blackwill) Allies Divided: Transatlantic Policies for the Greater Middle East, 1997; The German Century, 1998; Welt ohne Weltordnung, Wer wird die Erde erben, 2007. **Address:** c/o Die Welt, 65 Axel Springer St., Berlin, 10888, Germany. **Online address:** michael.stuermer@welt.de

STURTEVANT, Katherine. American (born United States), b. 1950. **Genres:** Children's Fiction, Women's Studies And Issues, History, Novels, Travel/Exploration, Young Adult Fiction. **Career:** Author. **Publications:** A Mistress Moderately Fair, 1988; Our Sisters' London: Feminist Walking Tours, 1990: Nineteen Feminist Walks, 1991; At the Sign of the Star, 2000; True and Faithful Narrative, 2006; Brothers Story, 2009. **Address:** c/o Author Mail, Farrar, Straus & Giroux, 19 Union Sq. W, New York, NY 10003, U.S.A. **Online address:** author@katherinesturtevant.com

STUTCHBURY, Bridget Joan. Canadian (born Canada), b. 1962?. **Genres:** Natural History, Biology, Animals/Pets. **Career:** Smithsonian Institution, postdoctoral fellow and research associate; York University, faculty of science and engineering, Department of Biology, associate professor, professor and Canada research chair in ecology and conservation biology. Writer. **Publications:** (With E.S. Morton) Behavioral Ecology of Tropical Birds, 2001; Silence of the Songbirds: How We Are Losing the World's Songbirds and What We Can Do to Save Them, 2007; Private Lives of Birds, 2010; The Bird Detective, 2010. **Address:** Department of Biology, York University, 203F Lumbers Bldg., 4700 Keele St., Toronto, ON M3J 1P3, Canada. **Online address:** bstutch@yorku.ca

STUTSON, Caroline. American (born United States), b. 1940. **Genres:** Children's Fiction, Children's Non-fiction. **Career:** Bemis Public Library, children's librarian, 1961-65; Highlands Ranch Library, staff. Writer. **Publications:** FOR CHILDREN: By the Light of the Halloween Moon, 1993; On the River ABC, 1993; Mountain Meadow 1 2 3, 1995; Prairie Primer A to Z, 1996; Cowpokes, 1999; Star Comes Home: A True Story, 1999; Night Train, 2002; Mama Loves You, 2005; Pirate Pup, 2005; By the Light of the Halloween Moon, 2009; Cats' Night Out, 2010. Contributor of poetry to magazines. **Address:** c/o Nancy Gallt, 273 Charlton Ave., South Orange, NJ 07079, U.S.A. **Online address:** astutson@aol.com

STÜTZLE, Walther. German (born Germany), b. 1941. **Genres:** International Relations/Current Affairs, Politics/Government. **Career:** Theodor Heuss Akademie, Gummersbach, lecturer, 1967-68; International Institute for Strategic Studies, research associate, 1968; German Society for Foreign Affairs, researcher, 1969; German Ministry for Defense, founding member of planning staff, 1969-71, Independent Armed Forces Structure Commission, secretary, 1971-72, private secretary to the minister of defense, 1973-76, head of planning staff, 1976-82; Stuttgarter Zeitung, international security and defense correspondent, 1983; Stockholm International Peace Research Institute, director, 1986-91; Der Tagesspiegel, editor-in-chief, 1992-98; deputy secretary of defense, 1998-2002; German Institute for International and Security Affairs, senior distinguished fellow, 2004-; Potsdam University, visiting professor, 2004-, honorary professor. **Publications:** Kennedy und Adenauer in der Berlin Krise, 1961-1962, 1973; Politik and Kraefteverhaeltnis, 1983; (with A. Buchan and C.B.C. Gasteyger) Europe's Future, Europe's Choices (bilingual in English and German), 1967; (ed.) SIPRI Yearbook World Armament and Disarmament, 1986-91; (ed. with B. Jasani and R. Cowen) The ABM Treaty: To Defend or Not to Defend? 1987; (co-author) Die Architektur europaeischer Sicherheit: Probleme, Kriterien, Perspektiven, 1989; (ed. with A. Rotfeld) Germany and Europe in Transition, 1991; (with W. Wiedenfeld) Abschied vonder alten Ordnung: Europas neue Sicherheit, 1993. (ed.) From Alliance to Coalitions: The Future of Transatlantic Relations, 2005. Contributor to periodicals. **Address:** Faculty of Economics and Social Science, University of Potsdam, 89 August-Bebel-Strabe, Potsdam, 14482, Germany. **Online address:** wkastuetzle@web.de

STUTZMAN, Linford L. American (born United States), b. 1950. **Genres:** Theology/Religion. **Career:** Mennonite Missionary, staff, 1978-90; Eastern Mennonite University, Department of Bible and Religion, assistant professor of culture and mission, 1990-, associate professor of culture and mission, 1991; Coffman Center, director. Writer. **Publications:** With Jesus in the World: Mission in Modern, Affluent Societies, 1992; (ed. with D.W. Shenk) Practicing Truth: Confident Witness in Our Pluralistic World, 1999; (ed. with J.R. Krabill and D.W. Shenk) Anabaptists Meeting Muslims: A calling for Presence in the Way of Christ, 2005; Sailing Acts: Following an Ancient Journey, 2006. **Address:** Department of Bible and Religion, Eastern Mennonite University, 1200 Park Rd., Harrisonburg, VA 22802-2462, U.S.A. **Online address:** stutzmal@emu.edu

STYCHIN, Carl F. British/Canadian (born Canada), b. 1964. **Genres:** Gay And Lesbian Issues, Law, Sex, Social Sciences. **Career:** Supreme Court of Canada, Chief Justice Brian Dickson, law clerk, 1989-90; University of Keele, lecturer, 1992-96, senior lecturer in law, 1996-98; McGill University, visiting professor, 1996; University of Reading, School of Law, professor of law and social theory, 1998-, head, dean of the faculty of economic and social sciences 2003-05, pro vice-chancellor, 2005-08; Université Paris X-Nanterre, visiting professor of law; Griffith University, adjunct professor of law, 2009-. Writer. **Publications:** Law's Desire: Sexuality and the Limits of Justice, 1995; A Nation by Rights: National Cultures, Sexual Identity Politics and the Discourse of Rights, 1998; Legal Methods and System, 1999, 3rd ed. (with L. Mulcahy), 2007; Governing Sexuality: The Changing Politics of Citizenship and Law Reform, 2003; (ed. with V.E. Munro) Sexuality and the Law: Feminist Engagements, 2007. EDITOR WITH D. HERMAN: Legal Inversions: Lesbians, Gay Men and the Politics of Law, 1995; Sexuality in the Legal Arena, 2000; Law and Sexuality: The Global Arena, 2001. Contributor to books and journals. **Address:** School of Law, University of Reading, Foxhill House, Whiteknights Rd., Reading, BR RG6 7BA, England. **Online address:** c.f.stychin@reading.ac.uk

STYLES, John. British (born England), b. 1949. **Genres:** Art/Art History. **Career:** AHRC Centre for the Study of the Domestic Interior, associate director, 2001-04; University of Hertfordshire, research professor in history, 2004-; Bradford University, lecturer in history; Bath University, lecturer in history; Bristol University, lecturer in history; Victoria and Albert Museum, head of graduate studies, British Galleries, honorary research fellow and historical advisor; Royal College of Art, honorary fellow; Huntington Library, Pasold Research Fund research reader in the history of fashion and clothing and Fletcher Jones distinguished chair in humanities. Writer. **Publications:** (With M. Snodin) Design & the Decorative Arts: Britain, 1500-1900, 2001; (with M. Snodin) Design & the Decorative Arts: Georgian Britain, 1714-1837, 2004; (with M. Snodin) Design & the Decorative Arts: Tudor and Stuart Britain 1500-1714, 2004; (with M. Snodin) Design & the Decorative Arts: Victorian Britain 1837-1901, 2004; (ed. with A. Vickery) Gender, Taste, and Material Culture in Britain and North America, 1700-1830, 2006; The Dress of the People: Everyday Fashion in Eighteenth-Century England, 2007. **Address:** School of Humanities, University of Hertfordshire, Hatfield, HF AL10 9AB, England. **Online address:** j.a.styles@herts.ac.uk

STYNES, Barbara White. American (born United States) **Genres:** Children's Non-fiction, Illustrations, Children's Fiction. **Career:** Red Cedar Review, assistant editor; City of Lansing, Parks Department, art instructor; Michigan State University, Communication Technology Laboratory, CD-ROM illustrator. **Publications:** Walking with Mama, 1997; A Snowshoe Story, forthcoming; The Legend of Paintbox: The Story of a Turtle, forthcoming. **Address:** c/o Author Mail, Dawn Publications, 12402 Bitney Springs Rd., Nevada City, CA 95959-9016, U.S.A. **Online address:** bwhitestynes@usa.net

STYRON, Alexandra. American (born United States), b. 1966. **Genres:** Novels, Young Adult Fiction. **Career:** Hunter College, MFA Program, teacher. Writer and actress. **Publications:** All the Finest Girls: A Novel, 2001; Im Licht der Karibik, 2001; Reading My Father, 2011. **Address:** c/o Esther Newberg, International Creative Management, 730 5th Ave., New York, NY 10019, U.S.A. **Online address:** astyron@me.com

SUAREZ, Daniel. American (born United States), b. 1964. **Genres:** Novels. **Career:** Computer systems consultant and writer. **Publications:** Daemon (novel), 2009. **Address:** CA , U.S.A. **Online address:** dasuarez@thedaemon.com

SUAREZ, Ray. American (born United States), b. 1957. **Genres:** Sociology. **Career:** CNN, correspondent; ABC Radio Network, producer; CBS Radio, reporter; WMAQ-TV, reporter, through 1993; Public Radio Intl., host; National Public Radio, host, 1993-99; The NewsHour, senior correspondent, 1999-; Si Magazine, contributing editor; National Public Radio (NPR), corecipient, 1993-94. Writer. **Publications:** The Old Neighborhood: What We Lost in the Great Suburban Migration 1966-1999, 1999; (foreword.) Local Heroes Changing America: Indivisible, 2000; The Holy Vote: The Politics of Faith in America, 2006. Contributor of articles to periodicals. **Address:** The NewsHour, 3620 S 27th St., Arlington, VA 22206, U.S.A. **Online address:** totn@npr.org

SUBOTNIK, Rena F. American (born United States), b. 1948. **Genres:** Education, Psychology, Sciences, Reference. **Career:** Gifted Education specialist, 1977-84; West Virginia University, assistant in special education, 1984-86; City University of New York, Hunter College, assistant professor, 1986-91, professor in educational foundations, 1986-91, professor, 1991-2001; Western Washington University, visiting professor, 1986-88; Greenpeace Intl., curriculum evaluator, 1989-91; Simon Fraser University, visiting professor, 1995; National Alliance for Excellence Academic Merit Scholarships, judge, 1998-; American Psychological Association, Center for Psychology in the Schools and Education, director, 2002-, Center for Gifted Education Policy, director. Writer. **Publications:** (Co-author) Genius Revisited: High IQ Children Grown Up, 1993; (ed. with K.D. Arnold) Beyond Terman:

Contemporary Longitudinal Studies of Giftedness and Talent, 1994; (ed. with K.D. Arnold and K.D. Noble) Remarkable Women: Perspectives on Female Talent Development, 1996; (co-ed.) The International Handbook of Research on the Development of Giftedness and Talent, 2nd ed., 2000; (ed. with H.J. Walberg) Scientific Basis of Educational Productivity, 2005; (ed. with R.J. Sternberg) Optimizing Student Success in School with the Other Three Rs: Reasoning, Resilience and Responsibility, 2006; (ed. with F.D. Horowitz and D.J. Matthews) Development of Giftedness and Talent across the Life Span, 2009; (ed. with B. Thompson) Methodologies for Conducting Research on Giftedness, 2010. Contributor of articles to periodicals, books and journals. **Address:** Center for Gifted Education Policy, American Psychological Association, 750 1st St. NE, Washington, DC 20002-4242, U.S.A. **Online address:** rsubotnik@apa.org

SUBRAHMANYAM, Sanjay. American/Indian (born India), b. 1961?. **Genres:** History, Area Studies. **Career:** Delhi School of Economics, research associate, 1983, reader, 1989; University of Delhi, professor of economic history, 1993-95; École des Hautes Etudes en Sciences Sociales, director of studies and research professor, 1995-2002; University of Oxford, professor of Indian history and culture, 2002-04; St. Cross College, fellow, 2003-; University of California, professor, Navin and Pratima Doshi chair in pre-modern Indian history, 2004-, UCLA's Center for India and South Asia, founding director, 2005-; University of Minnesota, staff; University of Michigan, staff; Federal University of Minas Gerais, staff; New University of Lisbon, staff. Historian and author. **Publications:** Improvising Empire: Portuguese Trade and Settlement in the Bay of Bengal, 1500-1700, 1990; The Political Economy of Commerce: Southern India, 1500-1650, 1990; (with V.N. Rao and D. Shulman) Symbols of Substance, Court and State in Nāyaka Period Tamilnadu, 1992; The Portuguese Empire in Asia, 1500-1700: A Political and Economic History, 1993, 2nd ed., 2012; The Career and Legend of Vasco da Gama, 1997; Penumbral Visions: Making Polities in Early Modern South India, 2001; (with V.N. Rao and D. Shulman) Textures of Time: Writing History in South India, 1600-1800, 2001; Explorations in Connected History, 2005; Mughals and Franks, 2005; From the Tagus to the Ganges, 2005; (with M. Alam) Indo-Persian Travels in the Age of Discoveries, 1400-1800, 2007; Three Ways to be Alien: Travails and Encounters in the Early Modern World, 2011; (with M. Alam) Writing the Mughal World, 2012. EDITOR: Money and the Market in India, 100-1700, 1994; (with B. Stein) Institutions and Economic Change in South Asia, 1996; Merchant Networks in the Early Modern World, 1996; (with K. Basu) Unravelling the Nation: Sectarian Conflict and India's Secular Identity, 1996; (with A. Muzaffar) The Mughal State, 1526-1750, 1998; Sinners and Saints: The Successors of Vasco da Gama, 1998; (with C. Markovits and J. Pouchepadass) Society and Circulation: Mobile People and Itinerant Cultures in South Asia, 1750-1950, 2003; Land, Politics, and Trade in South Asia, 2004; (with K. McPherson) From Biography to History: Essays in the History of Portuguese Asia (1500-1800), 2006; (with D. Armitage) The Age of Revolutions in Global Context, c. 1760-1840, 2009. Contributor to periodicals. **Address:** Department of History, University of California, 9347 Bunche Hall, PO Box 951473, Los Angeles, CA 90095-1473, U.S.A. **Online address:** subrahma@history.ucla.edu

SUCH, David G. American (born United States), b. 1954. **Genres:** Music. **Career:** Freelance soloist, recording artist, composer and producer, 1978-; Theatre of the Ear, KPKF radio, music director and composer, 1981-82; AVAZ International Music and Dance Troupe, music director, 1986-87; University of California, visiting assistant professor of folklore and mythology and of music, 1986-87, visiting assistant professor of ethnomusicology and systematic musicology, 1987-89; California State University, lecturer in music, 1987-88, lecturer in anthropology, 1989-91; California Polytechnic University, lecturer in music, 1989; recording artist, 1991-; New College of California, administrative director, 1991-92; performer, 1991-94; Hope University, music director, 1995-; Mount San Antonio College, lecturer in anthropology, 1996-; California Institute for Men, producer for the educational concert series, 1996; Spokane Community College, professor of music, 1998-, music instructor. Writer. **Publications:** Avant-Garde Jazz Musicians: Performing Out There, 1993. Contributor to books, articles and reviews to periodicals. **Address:** Department of Social Sciences & Humanities, Spokane Community College, Old Main Bldg., 1810 N Greene St., PO Box 2011, Spokane, WA 99217-5399, U.S.A. **Online address:** dsuch@scc.spokane.edu

SUDA, Zdenek Ludvik. American/Slovak (born Slovakia), b. 1920. **Genres:** Economics, History, Politics/Government, Sociology, Social Sciences. **Career:** International Secretariate of the European Movement, assistant head of department, 1951-54, supervisor of education program, 1954-68; University of Pittsburgh, associate professor of sociology, 1968-, professor emeritus of sociology, 1968-. Writer. **Publications:** La division internationale socialiste du travail, 1967; The Czechoslovak Socialist Republic, 1969; Zealots and Rebels, 1980; (ed. with M.O. Attir and B. Holzner) Directions of Change, 1981; The Globalization of Labor Markets, 1994; (ed. with J. Musil) The Meaning of Liberalism: East and West, 2000. Contributor to periodicals. **Address:** Department of Sociology, University of Pittsburgh, 2400 Wesley W Posvar Hall, 230 Bouquet St., Pittsburgh, PA 15260, U.S.A. **Online address:** zlsuda_1999@yahoo.com

SUDJIC, Deyan. American/British (born England), b. 1952. **Genres:** Homes/Gardens, Architecture, History. **Career:** Blueprint magazine, founding editor, 1983-96; Academy of Applied Arts in Vienna, visiting professor, 1993; Yokohama Design Center, advisor; Sunday Times and Guardian, architecture and design critic; Kingston University, dean of the faculty of art, architecture and design; Royal College of Art, visiting professor; U.K. City of Architecture, director of Glasgow, 1999; Domus, editor, 2000-04; Venice Architecture Biennale, director, 2002; Design Museum of London, director, 2006-. **Publications:** Cult Objects: The Complete Guide to Having It All, 1985; (ed.) House Style Book, 1985; The Lighting Book: A Complete Guide to Lighting Your Home, 1985; (with S. Bayley and P. Garner) Twentieth-Century Style & Design, 1986; Norman Foster, Richard Rogers, James Stirling: New Directions in British Architecture, 1986; English Extremists: The Architecture of Campbell Zogolovitch Wilkinson Gough, 1988; (with F.Shimizu) The British Architecture & Interior, 1989; (ed.) From Matt Black to Memphis and Back Again: An Anthology from Blueprint Magazine, 1989; Ron Arad: Restless Furniture, 1989; Cult Heroes: How to Be Famous for More than Fifteen Minutes, 1990; Rei Kawakubo and Commes des Garcons, 1990; The 100 Mile City, 1992; Banque De Luxembourg: Architectes, Arquitectonica, 1994; The Architecture of Richard Rogers, 1995; The Architecture Pack: A Unique, Three-Dimensional Tour of Architecture Over the Centuries: What Architects Do, How They Do It and the Great Buildings They Have Given Us Around the World, 1997; Erick Van Egeraat: Six Ideas About Architecture, 1997; (intro.) Cool Medium Hot: Erick Van Egeraat Architect: Exhibition January-February, 1997, 1997; Aedes East Galerie Und Architekturforum, 1997; (with T. Beyerle) Home: The Twentieth-Century House, 1999; John Pawson: Works, 2000, rev. ed., 2005; (with H. Jones) Architecture and Democracy, 2001; (with N. Foster and S.D. Grey) Norman Foster and the British Museum, 2001; Edifice Complex: How the Rich and Powerful Shape the World, 2005; Future Systems 2006, 2006; The Endless City, 2008; Language of Things, 2008; Norman Foster: A Life in Architecture, 2010; (ed. with R. Burdett) Living in the Endless City: The Urban Age Project by the London School of Economics and Deutsche Bank's Alfred Herrhausen Society, 2011. **Address:** Alfred A. Knopf, 201 E 50th St., New York, NY 10022, U.S.A.

SUEN, Anastasia. American (born United States) **Genres:** Children's Nonfiction, Children's Fiction, Poetry, Adult Non-fiction, How-to Books, Ghost Writer, Picture/Board Books. **Career:** Southern Methodist University, writing teacher; University of North Texas, children's literature teacher. Writer. **Publications:** Man on the Moon, 1997; Window Music, 1998; Baby Born, 1998; Delivery, 1999; Recien Nacido, 2000; One Hundred Day, 2000; El día 100, 2000; Here Comes the Bus, 2000; Ya viene el autobús, 2000; Toddler Two, 2000; Funny Clowns, 2000; The Statue of Liberty, 2000; Guitars, 2000; Making Mount Rushmore, 2000; Hamster Chase, 2000; Willie's Birthday, 2000; Air Show, 2001; The Clubhouse, 2001; Loose Tooth, 2001; Splash!, 2001; The Letter, 2001; Make a Turkey, 2002; Hacer un pavo, 2002; Fruit Salad, 2002; Dos años, 2002; ASPCA: The American Society for the Prevention of Cruelty to Animals, 2002; Doctors without Borders, 2002; Habitat for Humanity, 2002; The Peace Corps, 2002; The Red Cross, 2002; UNICEF: United Nations Children's Fund, 2002; The Story of Baseball, 2002; The Story of Basketball, 2002; The Story of Figure Skating, 2002; The Story of Football, 2002; The Story of Hockey, 2002; The Story of Soccer, 2002; Picture Writing: A New Approach to Writing for Kids and Teens, 2002; Block Party, 2003; Fiesta de barrio, 2003; Raise the Roof!, 2003; La historia del béisbol, 2003; La historia del fútbol, 2003; La historia del baloncesto, 2003; La historia del hockey, 2003; La historia del patinaje artistico, 2003; La historia del fútbol americano, 2003; Hábitat para la Humanidad, 2003; La Cruz Roja, 2003; ASPCA: Sociedad Protectora de Animales, 2003; UNICEF: Fondo de las Naciones Unidas para la Infancia, 2003; Médicos sin Fronteras, 2003; El Cuerpo de Paz, 2003; Splish, Splash!, 2004; Ice Cream Money, 2004; Dinero para comprar un helado, 2004; Fractals: The Art of Math, 2004; Remarkable Robots, 2004; Subway, 2004; Finding a Way: Six Historic U.S. Routes, 2005; Mysterious Magnets, 2005; Pencil Talk and Other School Poems, 2005; Los lápices hablan y otras poemas poemas de la escuela, 2005; Red Light, Green Light, 2005; Wetlands, 2005; A Lion Grows Up, 2006; A Rhinoceros Grows Up, 2006; A Tiger Grows Up, 2006; A Elephant Grows Up, 2006; A Hippopotamus Grows Up, 2006; A Baboon Grows Up, 2006; BMX Bully, 2007; Face-Off, 2007; Free Throw, 2007; Go-Kart Rush, 2007; Mr. Strike Out, 2007; Skate Park Challenge, 2007; Wired, 2007; Tyrannosaurus Rex, 2007; Trappers & Mountain Men, 2007; Cutting in Line isn't Fair!, 2008; Show Some Respect, 2008; Raising the Flag, 2008; Scissors, Paper, and Sharing, 2008; Times Tables Cheat, 2008; Helping Sophia, 2008; What Do You See At the Pond?, 2008; Qué ves en la charca?, 2008; U.S. Supreme Court, 2009; Uncle Sam, 2009; Game Over: Dealing with Bullies, 2009; Don't Forget!: A Responsibility Story, 2009; Trust Me: A Loyalty Story, 2009; Good Team: A Cooperation Story, 2009; Vote for Isaiah!: A Citizenship Story, 2009; Girls Can, Too!: A Tolerance Story, 2009; Toco Toucan: Bright Enough to Disappear, 2010; Pirate Map: A Robot and Rico Story, 2010; Dino Hunt: A Robot and Rico Story, 2010; Snow Games: A Robot and Rico Story, 2010; Test Drive: A Robot and Rico Story, 2010; Prize Inside: A Robot and Rico Story, 2010; Scary Night: A Robot and Rico Story, 2010; Skate Trick: A Robot and Rico Story, 2010; Big Catch: A Robot and Rico Story, 2010; Read and Write Sports: Readers Theatre and Writing Activities for Grades 3-8, 2011; Road Work Ahead, 2011; Tick Tock, Taylor, 2011; The Zombie Project, 2011; Can You Eat a Rainbow?, 2011; Puedes comer el arco iris?, 2011; Golden Dragon Parade, 2011; El desfile del dragón dorado, 2011; Girl's Guide to Volleyball, 2012; Save the Best for Last, Abby, 2012; Just So, Brianna, 2012; Fly, Emma, Fly, 2012; Gran pesca: un cuento sobre Robot y Rico, 2012; Un noche de terror: un cuento sobre Robot y Rico, 2012; Premio adentro: un cuento sobre Robot y Rico, 2012; Trucos en la patineta: un cuento sobre Robot y Rico, 2012. **Address:** c/o Author Mail, Lee & Low Books, 95 Madison Ave., Ste. 1205, New York, NY 10016, U.S.A. **Online address:** asuen@asuen.com

SUGIMOTO, Yoshio. Australian/Japanese (born Japan), b. 1939. **Genres:** Sociology, Cultural/Ethnic Topics, Politics/Government. **Career:** Mainichi Newspapers, staff writer, 1964-67; La Trobe University, lecturer, 1973-75, senior lecturer, 1976-82, department chairman, 1979-81, reader, 1983-87, dean of social sciences, 1988-91, professor of sociology, 1988, professor emeritus; Monash University Japanese Studies Centre, foundation director, 1981-82, president, 1985-; Australian Academy of the Humanities, fellow, 1988-; Cambridge University Press, Contemporary Japanese Society Series, series editor, 1996-; Trans Pacific Press, founder. **Publications:** Marxism and New Left Ideology, 1977; (with R. Mouer) Japanese Society: Stereotypes and Realities, 1982; (with R.M. Cho) Nihonjin wa Nihon-teki ka: Tokushuron o koe Tagenteki Bunseki e, 1982; Process of Unity in Caribbean Society: Ideologies and Literature, 1983; Chō kanri rettō Nippon: Watakushitachi wa Hontō ni jiyū na no ka, 1983; Primer inventario del invasor, 1984; Literatura y crisis en Centroamérica: ponencias, 1986; (ed. with G. McCormack) Democracy in Contemporary Japan, 1986; (with R. Maoa) Kojin Kanjin Nihonjin: Japanorogī o Koete, 1987; Shinkashinai Nihonjin e: Sono Kokusai kankaku wa Jigazō no Han'ei de aru, 1988; (with S. Yoshiro) Dentō shūkyō to shakai seijiteki tōgō, 1988; (ed. with G. McCormack) Japanese Trajectory: Modernization and Beyond, 1988; Registradas en la historia: diez años del quehacer feminista en Nicaragua, 1990; Nihonjin o Yameru hōhō, 1990; (with R. Mouer) Images of Japanese Society: A Study in the Social Construction of Reality, 1990; Dentō Shūkyō to Chishiki, 1991; ōsutoraria 6000-nichi, 1991; House/Garden/Nation: Space Gender and Ethnicity in Post-colonial Latin-American Literatures by Women, 1994; (ed. with J. Arnason) Japanese Encounters with Postmodernity, 1995; Women Guerrillas and Love: Understanding War in Central America, 1996; An Introduction to Japanese Society, 1997, 3rd ed., 2010; The Latin American Subaltern Studies Reader, 2001; Convergencia de tiempos: estudios subalternos/contextos Latinoamericanos estado cultura subalternidad, 2001; Cánones literarios masculinos y relecturas transculturales: los trans-femenino/masculine/queer, 2002; Fukuin to Bunmeika no Jinrui Gakuteki kenkyū, 2002; Transatlantic Topographies: Islands Highlands Jungles, 2004; Liberalism at its Limits: Crime and Terror in the Latin American Cultural Text, 2009; (ed.) The Cambridge Companion to Modern Japanese Culture, 2009. Contributor to periodicals. **Address:** Department of Humanities & Social Science, School of Social Sciences, La Trobe University, Rm. 454, Martin Bldg., Melbourne, VI 3083, Australia. **Online address:** y.sugimoto@latrobe.edu.au

SUINN, Richard M. American (born United States), b. 1933. **Genres:** Psychology, Sports/Fitness. **Career:** Veterans Administration Hospitals, intern in psychology, 1955-58; Stanford University, Department of Psychology, clinical psychology teaching assistant, 1957-58, counselor, 1958-59, School of Medicine, research associate, 1965-66, research consultant, 1967; Whitman College, Department of Psychology, assistant professor, 1959-64, acting head, 1962; Central Washington State College, visiting professor, 1961-64; University of Washington, visiting professor, 1963; University of Hawaii, associate professor of psychology and coordinator, 1966-68; Colorado State University, Department of Psychology, associate professor, 1968-69, professor, 1969-99, associate head, 1969-72, acting head, 1972, head, 1973-93, now professor emeritus and emeritus department head; University of Vera Cruz, visiting professor, 1971; Chinese University of Hong Kong, external examiner, 1998-2003; University of Hong Kong, external examiner, 2002-; University Waikato, dissertation examiner, 2004; University of Pune, dissertation examiner. Writer. **Publications:** (Contrib.) Theories Personality: Primary Sources and Research, 1965; (with W.L. Dauterman) The Stanford Ohwaki-Kohs Tactile Block Design Intelligence Test for the Blind, 1966; (with S. Oskamp) The Predictive Validity of Projective Measures: A Fifteen Year Evaluation Review of Research, 1969, 2nd ed., 1975; The Fundamentals of Behavior Pathology, 1970, 2nd ed., 1975; (ed. with R.G. Weigel) The Innovative Psychological Therapies: Critical and Creative Contributions, 1975; (ed. with R.G. Weigel) The Innovative Medical-Psychiatric Therapies, 1976; (ed. with R.D. Clayton) Psychology in Sports: Methods and Applications, 1980; Fundamentals of Abnormal Psychology, 1984; Seven Steps to Peak Performance: The Mental Training Manual for Athletes, 1986; Anxiety Management Training: A Behavior Therapy, 1990; (ed. with J.R. Whitfield) Cancer: Abstracts of the Psychological and Behavioral Literature, 1990-1999, 1999; (ed. with G.R. VandenBos) Cancer Patients and Their Families: Readings on Disease Course, Coping and Psychological Interventions, 1999. Contributor to journals. **Address:** Department of Psychology, Colorado State University, C7 Andrew Clark Bldg., Fort Collins, CO 80523-1876, U.S.A. **Online address:** suinn@lamar.colostate.edu

SUKLA, Ananta Charana. Indian (born India), b. 1942. **Genres:** Art/Art History. **Career:** College teacher, 1965-82; Vishvanatha Kaviraja Institute of Comparative Literature and Aesthetics, director, founding secretary, 1977; Sambalpur University, professor of English, comparative aesthetics and literature, 1982-2002; University of Siena, visiting professor and honorary associate of Loro group of studies in comparative aesthetics; Uppsala University, visiting professor; University of Helsinki, visiting professor; National University of Wales, visiting professor; University College, visiting professor; University of Liverpool, visiting professor; Cambridge University, visiting professor; Journal of Comparative Literature and Aesthetics, founder editor; University of Uppsala, Institute of Aesthetics, visiting professor. Writer. **Publications:** Model Expansions, 1965; The Concept of Imitation in Greek and Indian Aesthetics, 1977; Representation in Contemporary Criticism, 1989; Deconstruction in Contemporary Criticism, 1989; (ed.) Art and Representation: Contributions to Contemporary Aesthetics, 2001; (ed.) Art and Experience, 2003; (ed. with S. Davies) Art and Essence, 2003; (with M. Mitias) Art and Expression, 2003; Visvanatha Kaviraja (monograph), forthcoming. Contributor to periodicals. **Address:** A/42, Sector 7, Markat Nagar, Cuttack, OR 753014, India. **Online address:** anantasukla@hotmail.com

SULEIMAN, Susan Rubin. American/Hungarian (born Hungary), b. 1939. **Genres:** Art/Art History, Cultural/Ethnic Topics, Intellectual History, Literary Criticism And History, Women's Studies And Issues, Autobiography/Memoirs, Translations, Philosophy, Essays. **Career:** Columbia University, instructor, 1966-68, assistant professor of French, 1969-76, director of study program at Reid Hall, 1973; Occidental College, assistant professor, associate professor of French, 1976-81, director of study in France, 1978-79, 1981, Interdisciplinary Colloquium on Women and Society, coordinator, 1979-80; Harvard University, associate professor of romance languages and literatures, 1981-83, John L. Loeb associate professor of humanities, 1983-84, Department of Romance Languages and Literatures, professor, 1984-, chair, 1997-2000, 2003-04, head of French section and director of graduate studies in French, 2001-05, C. Douglas Dillon professor of the civilization of France and professor of comparative literature, 1997-, acting chair, The Minda de Gunzburg Center for European Studies, literary and cultural critic and theorist. Writer. **Publications:** EDITOR: (and intro.) Pour une nouvelle culture, 1971; (with I. Crosman) The Reader in the Text: Essays on Audience and Interpretation, 1980; The Female Body in Western Culture: Contemporary Perspectives, 1986; Social Control and the Arts, 1990; Exile and Creativity: Signposts, Travelers, Outsiders, Backward Glances, 1998; (with E. Forgács) Contemporary Jewish Writing in Hungary: An Anthology, 2003; (ed. with C. McDonald) French Global: A New Approach to Literary History, 2010; (with J. Lothe and J. Phelan) After Testimony, 2012. TRANSLATOR: G. Apollinaire, Apollinaire on Art: Essays and Reviews, 1902-1918, 1972; S. Friedlander, History and Psychoanalysis, 1978. OTHERS: Authoritarian Fictions: The Ideological Novel as a Literary Genre, 1983; Subversive Intent: Gender, Politics and the Avant-Garde, 1990; Risking Who One Is: Encounters with Contemporary Art and Literature, 1994; Budapest Diary: In Search of the Motherbook, 1996; Crises of Memory and the Second World War, 2006. **Address:** The Minda de Gunzburg Center for European Studies, Harvard University, 27 Kirkland St., Cambridge, MA 02138, U.S.A. **Online address:** suleiman@fas.harvard.edu

SULKIN, Tracy. American (born United States), b. 1975. **Genres:** Politics/Government. **Career:** University of Washington, graduate fellow, 1997-99 and 2001-02; National Science Foundation graduate research fellow, 1998-2001; University of Illinois at Urbana-Champaign, assistant professor, 2002-; Center for the Study of Democratic Governance, research fellow, 2006-07. **Publications:** Issue Politics in Congress, 2005. Contributor to periodicals and journals. **Address:** Department of Political Science, University of Illinois, Urbana- Champaign, 361 Lincoln Hall, 702 S Wright St., Urbana, IL 61801, U.S.A. **Online address:** tsulkin@uiuc.edu

SULLIVAN, Amy. American (born United States), b. 1973. **Genres:** Politics/Government, Social Sciences. **Career:** Washington Monthly, editor; Pew Forum on Religion and Public Life, editorial director; Time, national correspondent. **Publications:** (Contrib.) The Best American Political Writing 2006, 2006; The Party Faithful: How and Why Democrats are Closing the God Gap, 2008. Contributor to periodicals. **Address:** U.S.A. **Online address:** thepartyfaithful@gmail.com

SULLIVAN, Brad. American (born United States), b. 1961. **Genres:** Intellectual History, Education, Literary Criticism And History, Sciences, Philosophy. **Career:** Freelance writer, 1984-87; University of Richmond, adjunct faculty, 1987, 1988; freelance copy editor, 1992-96; Ball State University, instructor, 1994-96; Florida Gulf Coast University, instructor, 1996-97, assistant professor, 1997-2001; University of North Carolina, visiting assistant professor of English, 2002-03; Western New England College, associate professor of English, 2003-, professor; Polling Institute, director, 2005-06. **Publications:** Wordsworth and the Composition of Knowledge: Refiguring Relationships among Minds, Worlds and Words, 2000; Artful Knowing: British Romantic Poetry, Cognitive Science and the Practice of Learning, forthcoming. Contributor to journals. **Address:** Department of English, Western New England College, Emerson 111B, 1215 Wilbraham Rd., PO Box E-5322, Springfield, MA 01119, U.S.A. **Online address:** dsulliva@wnec.edu

SULLIVAN, C(harles) W(illiam). American (born United States), b. 1944. **Genres:** Literary Criticism And History, Science Fiction/Fantasy, Mythology/Folklore. **Career:** State University of New York, instructor in English, 1968-71; University of Oregon, instructor, 1976-77; East Carolina University, Thomas Harriot College of Arts and Sciences, Department of English, assistant professor, professor of English, 1977-, distinguished professor of arts and sciences, 2003-, university distinguished research professor of English, now professor emeritus; Hollins University, faculty of children's literature. Writer. **Publications:** (Ed.) As Tomorrow Becomes Today, 1974; Welsh Celtic Myth in Modern Fantasy, 1989; (co-ed.) Herbal Magical Medicine, 1992; (ed.) Science Fiction for Young Readers, 1993; (ed.) The Mabinogi: A Book of Essays, 1996; (ed.) Dark Fantastic: Selected Essays from the Ninth International Conference on the Fantastic in the Arts, 1997; (ed.) Young Adult Science Fiction, 1999; (co-ed.) Worldviews and The American West: The Life of the Place Itself, 2000; (ed. and intro.) Fenian Diary: Denis B. Cashman on Board the Hougoumont, 2001; Heinlein's Juvenile Novels: A Cultural Dictionary, 2011. Contributor to journals and periodicals. **Address:** Department of English, Thomas Harriot College of Arts and Sciences, East Carolina University, 2116 Bate Bldg., Greenville, NC 27858-4353, U.S.A. **Online address:** sullivanc@ecu.edu

SULLIVAN, Claudia. (Claudia N. Sullivan). American (born United States), b. 1950. **Genres:** Theatre, Food And Wine, Photography. **Career:** Schreiner College, professor of theatre and communication, 1977; Notre Dame Church, liturgical movement director, pastoral council, director of lectors and liturgical dance. Writer. **Publications:** (As Claudia N. Sullivan) The Actor Moves, 1990; (comp. and ed.) Summer Come, Summer Go (memoir), 1991; (as Claudia N. Sullivan) The Actor Alone: Exercises for Work in Progress, 1993; M-m-m that Good Mystic Food (cookbook), 1993; And In Return, 2000; Heartfelt, 2001. **Address:** Department of Theatre and Communication, Schreiner College, Hanszen Fine Arts, Ste. 2, 2100 Memorial Blvd., Kerrville, TX 78028, U.S.A. **Online address:** csulliva@schreiner.edu

SULLIVAN, Claudia N. *See* **SULLIVAN, Claudia.**

SULLIVAN, David M. American (born United States), b. 1942. **Genres:** History, Military/Defense/Arms Control, Biography, Autobiography/Memoirs. **Career:** Company of Military Historians, Military Collector and Historian (journal), administrator, editor; International Naval Research Organization, president; Warship (journal), executive production editor; Journal of the Company of Military Historians, editor; United States Marine Corps, staff; August A. Busch Inc., employee. **Publications:** The United States Marine Corps in the Civil War: The First Year, 1997; The United States Marine Corps in the Civil War: The Second Year, 1997; The United States Marine Corps in the Civil War: The Third Year, 1998; The United States Marine Corps in the Civil War: The Final Year, 2003; (with R.W. Donnnelly) Biographical Sketches of the Commissioned Officers of the Confederate States Marine Corps, 3rd ed., 2001. **Address:** Warship International, PO Box 48, Holden, MA 01520-0048, U.S.A. **Online address:** dsulli7875@aol.com

SULLIVAN, Dolores P. American (born United States), b. 1925. **Genres:** History, Biography. **Career:** Teacher of journalism, American history and English, 1945-53; Boardman High School, teacher of journalism and English, 1969-92; Duane-Jones Advertising Agency, staff; Winston Publishing Co., staff. Writer. **Publications:** History of the Youngstown Vindicator, 1974; William Holmes McGuffey: Schoolmaster to the Nation, 1994. Contributor to journals. **Address:** 204 Forest Park Dr., Youngstown, OH 44512-1449, U.S.A. **Online address:** dps425@cs.com

SULLIVAN, (Donovan) Michael. British/Canadian (born Canada), b. 1916. **Genres:** Art/Art History, History, Biography. **Career:** West China Union University, lecturer and assistant museum curator, 1942-45; Ginling College, Chengtu, English professor, 1945-46; University of Malaya, curator of art museum and lecturer in history of art, 1954-60; University of London, lecturer in Asian art, 1960-66; University of Michigan, visiting professor of fine art, 1964; Stanford University, Department of Oriental Art, professor of oriental art, 1966-75, head, 1966-84, Christensen professor of oriental art, 1975-85, now professor emeritus; Oxford University, Slade professor of fine art, 1973-74, St. Catherine's College, fellow, 1979-87, fellow emeritus, 1987-; Cambridge University, Slade professor of fine art, 1983-84. Writer. **Publications:** Chinese Art in the Twentieth Century, 1959; An Introduction to Chinese Art, 1961; The Birth of Landscape Painting in China, 1962; Chinese Ceramics, Bronzes and Jades in the Collection of Alan and Lady Barlow, 1963; Chinese and Japanese Art, 1965; A Short History of Chinese Art, 1967; The Cave Temples of Maichishan, 1969; Chinese Art: Recent Discoveries, 1973; The Arts of China, 1973, 5th ed., 2008; The Meeting of Eastern and Western Art, 1973, rev. ed., 1989; The Three Perfections, 1974, rev. ed., 1999; Chinese Landscape Painting in the Sui and T'ang Dynasties, 1979; Symbols of Eternity: The Art of Landscape Painting in China, 1979; Chinese Landscaping: Sui and T'ang Dynasties, 1980; Zhongguo yi shu shi, 1985; Studies in the Art of China and South-East Asia, 1991; (contrib.) Wu Guanzhong, 1992; Art and Artists of Twentieth Centruy China, 1996; (contrib.) Dong xi fang mei shu di jiao liu, 1998; (contrib.) Zhu Dequn, 2004; (contrib.) Zhu Ming tai ji diao su, 2006; Modern Chinese Artists: A Biographical Dictionary, 2006; Night Entertainments of Han Xizai: A Scroll by Gu Hongzhong, 2008. **Address:** St. Catherine College, Manor Rd., Oxford, OX OX1 3UJ, England.

SULLIVAN, Faith. American (born United States), b. 1933. **Genres:** Novels, Young Adult Fiction. **Career:** Legal secretary, employment counselor, 1957-61; North High School, instructor in history, 1962-65; writer, 1965-; Southwest State University, visiting instructor; The Loft Literary Center, instructor. **Publications:** Repent, Lanny Merkel, 1981; Watchdog, 1982; Mrs. Demming and the Mythical Beast, 1985; The Cape Ann, 1988; The Empress of One, 1996; What a Woman Must Do, 2000; Gardenias, 2005. **Address:** 4258 Russell Ave. N, Minneapolis, MN 55412-1550, U.S.A. **Online address:** faith@faithsullivan.com

SULLIVAN, Garrett A. American (born United States) **Genres:** History, Literary Criticism And History, Theatre. **Career:** Charlotte Country Day School, teacher of English, 1983-89; University of Massachusetts, Writing Program, teaching assistant, 1989-91; Brown University, teaching assistant of English, 1992-95; Pennsylvania State University, Department of English, assistant professor, 1995-2001, associate professor, 2001-06, professor, 2006-, Graduate Studies, director; Shakespeare Studies, associate editor, 2004-08, co-editor, 2008-; Georgetown University, visiting associate professor of English, 2006-07. **Publications:** The Drama of Landscape: Land, Property and Social Relations on the Early Modern Stage, 1998; Memory and Forgetting in English Renaissance Drama: Shakespeare, Marlowe, Webster, 2005; (ed. with P. Cheney and A. Hadfield) Early Modern English Drama: A Critical Companion, 2006; (ed. with M. Floyd-Wilson) Environment and Embodiment in Early Modern England, 2007; (ed. with E. Smith) Cambridge Companion to English Renaissance Traged, 2010; (ed. with A. Stewart) Encyclopedia of English Renaissance Literature, 2012. **Address:** Department of English, Pennsylvania State University, 136 Burrowes Bldg., 417 Old Main, University Park, PA 16802-1505, U.S.A. **Online address:** gas11@psu.edu

SULLIVAN, George E(dward). American (born United States), b. 1927. **Genres:** Children's Non-fiction, Photography, Sciences, Sports/Fitness, Young Adult Non-fiction, Biography, Autobiography/Memoirs, Politics/Government, Politics/Government. **Career:** Popular Library, public relations director, 1952-55; American Machine and Foundry Co., publicity manager, 1955-62; freelance writer, 1962-; Fordham University, Fordham College, adjunct professor of nonfiction writing, 1969-72, 1979-81. Writer. **Publications:** NONFICTION: (with F. Clause) How to Win at Bowling, 1961; (with F. Clause and P. McBride) Junior Guide to Bowling, 1963; The Story of Cassius Clay, 1964; Harness Racing, 1964; (with I. Crane) The Young Sportsman's Guide to Pocket Billiards, 1964; The Story of the Peace Corps, 1964, rev. ed., 1965; Boats: A Guidebook to Boating Procedures, Maintenance and Fun!, 1965; (with L. Lassiter) Billiards for Everyone, 1965; Camping Guidebook: Outdoor Living, from Luxury to Roughing It, 1965; The Complete Guide to Softball, 1965; (with L. Scott) Fell's Teen-Age Guide to Skin and Scuba Diving, 1965, rev. ed., 1975; How Do They Make It?, 1965; Better Boxing for Boys, 1966; Camping: Skills, Places, Pleasures, 1966; The Champions' Guide to Golf, 1966; How Do They Grow It?, 1966; The Personal Story of Lynda and Luci Johnson, 1966; Philip Vampatella, Fighter Pilot: The Complete Life Story of a College Dropout Who Became One of the First Aircraft Carrier Pilots to Fly over Vietnam, 1966; (with F.E. Larsen) Skiing for Boys and Girls, 1966; (with H. Kramp) Swimming for Boys and Girls, 1966; Tennis, 1966; Wilt Chamberlain, 1966, rev. ed., 1971; (with W. Ellis) All-Weather Golf, 1967; Better Swimming and Diving for Boys and Girls, 1967, rev. ed., 1982; Better Track and Field Events for Boys, 1967, rev. ed. as Better Track for Boys, 1985; The Complete Book of Family Skiing, 1967; The Modern Guide to Skin and Scuba Diving, 1967; Pro Football's Unforgettable Games, 1967; Touchdown! The Picture History of the American Football League, 1967; The Boom in Going Bust: The Threat of a National Scandal in Consumer Bankruptcy, 1968; The Complete Book of Family Bowling, 1968; Face-Off: A Guide to Modern Ice Hockey, 1968; Guide to Badminton, 1968; The New World of Construction Engineering, 1968; Pass to Win: Pro Football Greats, 1968; Pro Football's All-Time Greats: The Immortals in Pro Football's Hall of Fame, 1968; Seven Wonders of the World, 1968; (with G.L. Seewagen) Tennis, 1968; Better Horseback Riding for Boys and Girls, 1969; The Complete Book of Skin and Scuba Diving, 1969; Hockey Heroes: The Game's Greatest Players, 1969; (with E. Morrall) In the Pocket: My Life As a Quarterback, 1969; More How Do They Make It?, 1969; The New World of Communications, 1969; Plants to Grow Indoors, 1969; They Flew Alone, 1969; (with J. Fanning) Work When You Want to Work: The Complete Guide for the Temporary Worker-From the President of Uniforce, 1969, rev. ed., 1985; Bart Starr, the Cool Quarterback, 1970; Better Archery for Boys and Girls, Dodd, 1970; The Dollar Squeeze and How to Beat It, 1970; Knute Rockne: Notre Dame's Football Great, 1970; This Is Pro Football, 1970, rev. ed., 1975; Trees, 1970; (with E. Morrall) Comeback Quarterback: The Earl Morrall Story, 1971; The Complete Book of Autograph Collecting, 1971; The Gamemakers: Pro Football's Great Quarterbacks-From Baugh to Namath, 1971; Jim Thorpe, All-Around Athlete, 1971; How Do They Run It?, 1971; (with E.J. Zegarowicz) Inflation-Proof Your Future, 1971; Pro Football Plays in Pictures, 1971; Rise of the Robots, Dodd, 1971; (with G. Kirby) Soccer, 1971; (with H. Kramp) Swimming, 1971; Tom Seaver of the Mets, 1971; Understanding Architecture, 1971; The Backpacker's Handbook, 1972; Better Table Tennis for Boys and Girls, 1972; By Chance a Winner: The History of Lotteries, 1972; Football, 1972; The Great Running Backs, 1972; How Do

They Build It?, 1972; Pitchers and Pitching, 1972; Pro Football's Great Upsets, 1972; Pro Football's Passing Game, 1972; Understanding Photography, 1972; Do-It-Yourself Moving, 1973; How Does It Get There?, 1973; Pro Football's Kicking Game, 1973; Sports for Your Child, 1973; Willie Mays, 1973; Baseball's Art of Hitting, 1974; Better Bicycling for Boys and Girls, 1974, rev. ed., 1984; Linebacker!, 1974; Queens of the Court, 1974; Roger Staubach: A Special Kind of Quarterback, 1974; Better Softball for Boys and Girls, 1974; Hank Aaron, 1975; How Do They Find It?, 1975; Larry Csonka, Power and Pride, 1975; The Modern Treasure Finder's Manual, 1975; Paddle: The Beginner's Guide to Platform Tennis, 1975; Pro Football A to Z: A Fully Illustrated Guide to America's Favorite Sport, 1975; Winning Plays in Pro Football, 1975; Additives in Your Food, 1976; Better Ice Skating for Boys and Girls, 1976; Bobby Bonds, Rising Superstar, 1976; The Catcher, Baseball's Man in Charge, 1976; How Do They Package It?, 1976; On the Run, Franco Harris, 1976; Pro Football and the Running Back, 1976; This Is Pro Hockey, 1976; Understanding Hydroponics: Growing Plants without Soil, 1976; Winning Basketball, 1976; Bert Jones: Born to Play Football, 1977; Better Gymnastics for Girls, 1977; Dave Cowens: A Biography, 1977; Home Run!, 1977; Making Money in Autographs, Coward, 1977; The Picture Story of Catfish Hunter, 1977; The Picture Story of Nadia Comaneci, 1977; The Picture Story of Reggie Jackson, 1977; This Is Pro Basketball, 1977; Better Basketball for Girls, 1977; Amazing Sports Facts, 1978; Better Soccer for Boys and Girls, 1978; Sports Superstitions, Coward, 1978; Supertanker! The Story of the World's Biggest Ships, 1978; Wind Power for Your Home: The First Complete Guide That Tells How to Make the Wind's Energy Work for You, 1978; Wood-Burning Stoves, 1978; Better Volleyball for Girls, 1979; The Complete Beginner's Guide to Pool and Other Billiard Games, 1979; The Complete Sports Dictionary, 1979, rev. ed., 1993; Modern Olympic Superstars, 1979; This Is Pro Soccer, 1979; The All-Sports Puzzle and Quiz Book, 1980; Better Basketball for Boys, 1980; Better Football for Boys, 1980; Better Roller Skating for Boys and Girls, 1980; Charms and Spells, Witches, and Demons, 1980; Cross-Country Skiing: A Complete Beginner's Book, 1980; Discover Archaeology: An Introduction to the Tools and Techniques of Archaeological Fieldwork, 1980; (with G. Player) Gary Player's Golf Book For Young People, 1980; Marathon-The Longest Race, 1980; Run, Run Fast!, 1980; The Supercarriers, 1980; Track and Field: Secrets of the Champions, 1980; Better Baseball for Boys, rev. ed., 1981; Better Field Hockey for Girls, 1981; Better Track for Girls, 1981; The Gold Hunter's Handbook, 1981; Sadat: The Man Who Changed Mid-East History, 1981; Superstars of Women's Track, 1981; The Art of Base-Stealing, 1981; Better Field Events for Girls, 1982; Famous Firsts, 1982; Great Impostors, 1982; Inside Nuclear Submarines, 1982; Picture Story of George Brett, 1982; Quarterback, 1982; Better Cross-Country Running for Boys and Girls, 1983; The Complete Book of Baseball Collectibles, 1983; The Complete Car Book, 1983; Computer Puzzles and Quizzes, 1983; Great Sports Hoaxes, 1983; Return of the Battleship, 1983; Screen Play: The Story of Video Games, 1983; Strange but True Stories of World War II, 1983, rev. ed., 1991; (with T. Sullivan) Stunt People, 1983; Video Games, Puzzles and Quizzes, 1983; Baseball's Wacky Players, 1984; Better Weight Training for Boys, 1984; Better BMX Riding and Racing for Boys and Girls, 1984; Computer Kids, 1984; Mr. President: A Book of U.S. Presidents, 1984, rev. ed., 2005; Pope John Paul II: The People's Pope, 1984; Famous Air Force Bombers, 1985; Famous Air Force Fighters, 1985; Mary Lou Retton: A Biography, 1985; Ronald Reagan, 1985, rev. ed., 1991; Baseball Backstage, 1986; Better Wrestling for Boys, 1986; Famous Navy Attack Planes, 1986; Famous Navy Fighter Planes, 1986; Pitcher, 1986; The Thunderbirds, 1986; All about Football, 1987; Better Tennis for Boys and Girls, 1987; Facts and Fun about the Presidents, 1987, rev. ed., 1993; Famous U.S. Spy Planes, 1987; Great Racing Cars, 1987; Treasure Hunt: The Sixteen-Year Search for the Lost Treasure Ship Atocha, 1987; Work Smart, Not Hard, 1988; All about Baseball, 1988; Center, 1988; Famous Blimps and Airships, 1988; Great Escapes of World War II, 1988; Great Lives: Sports, 1988; Mikhail Gorbachev, 1988, rev. ed., 1990; Big League Spring Training, 1989; Cars, 1989; George Bush, 1989; Here Come the Monster Trucks, 1989; How the White House Really Works, 1989; Any Number Can Play, 1990, as Any Number Can Play: The Numbers Athletes Wear, 2000; Baseball Kids, 1990; The Day We Walked on the Moon, 1990; Football Kids, 1990; All about Basketball, 1990; Campaigns and Elections, 1991; Modern Fighter Planes, 1991; Choosing the Candidates, 1991; The Day They Bombed Pearl Harbor, 1991; Sluggers!: Twenty-seven of Baseball's Greatest, 1991; Disaster!: The Destruction of Our Planet, 1992; Modern Bombers and Attack Planes, 1992; Racing Indy Cars, 1992; Unsolved Famous Real-Life Mysteries, 1992; How an Airport Really Works, 1993; Blading for Beginners: A Compete Guide to In-Line Skating, 1993; Modern Combat Helicopters, 1993; The Official Price Guide to American Stoneware,

1993; They Shot the President: Ten True Stories, 1993; The Day Women Got the Vote: A Photo History of the Women's Rights Movement, 1994; Mathew Brady: His Life and Photographs, 1994; Slave Ship: The Story of the Henrietta Marie, 1994; Great Impostors, 1994; Unsolved II: More Famous Real-Life Mysteries, 1994; Elite Warriors: The Special Forces of the United States and Its Allies, 1995; Presidents at Play, 1995; Glovemen: Twenty-seven of Baseball's Greatest, 1996; Women War Spies, 1996; Alamo!, 1996; Black Artists in Photography, 1840-1940, 1996; (with J. Powers) The Yankees: An Illustrated History, 1997; Not Guilty: Six Times when Justice Failed, 1997; Snowboarding: A Complete Guide for Beginners, 1997; The Yankees Fan's Little Book of Wisdom: 101 Truths Learned the Hard Way, 1998; Trapped, 1998; All about Hockey, 1998?; Burnin' Rubber: Behind the Scenes in Stock Car Racing, 1998; Portraits of War: Civil War Photographers and Their Work, 1998; Quarterbacks!: Eighteen of Football's Greatest, 1998; 100 Years in Photographs, 1999; Lewis and Clark, 1999; Paul Revere, 1999; To the Bottom of the Sea: The Exploration of Exotic Life, the Titanic and Other Secrets of the Oceans, 1999; Picturing Lincoln: Famous Photographs That Popularized the President, 2000; Helen Keller, 2000; Abraham Lincoln, 2000; Don't Step on the Foul Line: Sports Superstitions, 2000; All about Soccer, 2001; The Civil War at Sea, 2001; Power Football: The Greatest Running Backs, 2001; Davy Crockett, 2001; Harriet Tubman, 2001; Pocahontas, 2001; Thomas Edison, 2001; The Wright Brothers, 2002; Baseball's Boneheads, Bad Boys and Just Plain Crazy Guys, 2003; In the Wake of Battle: The Civil War Images of Mathew Brady, 2004; Built to Last: Building America's Amazing Bridges, Dams, Tunnels and Skyscrapers, 2005; Journalists at Risk: Reporting America's Wars, 2006; Berenice Abbott, Photographer: An Independent Vision, 2006; Helen Keller: Her Life in Pictures, 2007; Knockout!: A Photobiography of Boxer Joe Louis, 2008; Geronimo: Apache Renegade, 2010. EDITOR: The Champion's Guide to Bowling, 1964; The Modern Guide to Pocket Billiards, 1964; Bowling Secrets of the Pros, 1968; Baseball Rules Illustrated, 1981; Football Rules Illustrated, 1981; Soccer Rules Illustrated, 1981; Tennis Rules Illustrated, 1981; Racquetball Rules and Techniques Illustrated, 1982. **Address:** c/o Eleanor Wood, Spectrum Literary Agency, 320 Central Pk. W, Ste. 1-D, New York, NY 10025, U.S.A. **Online address:** george@georgesullivanauthor.com

SULLIVAN, John Jeremiah. American (born United States), b. 1974?. **Genres:** Sports/Fitness, Animals/Pets, Homes/Gardens, Essays. **Career:** Sewanee Review, editorial assistant; Oxford American, editor; Oxford University Press, Department of History, staff; Harper's Magazine, senior editor, contributing editor; Gentleman's Quarterly, writer-at-large; The Paris Review, southern editor; New York Times Magazine, contributing writer. **Publications:** Blood Horses: Notes of a Sportswriter's Son, 2004; Pulphead: Essays, 2011; The Key of the Fields, forthcoming. Contributor to magazines. **Address:** Harpers Magazine, 666 Broadway, 11th Fl., New York, NY 10012, U.S.A.

SULLIVAN, Michael Joseph. American (born United States), b. 1941. **Genres:** International Relations/Current Affairs, Politics/Government, History, Travel/Exploration. **Career:** Drexel University, professor of political science, 1970-; WUHY-FM Radio, The Press and Foreign Policy, moderator, 1973; Abington Township Zoning Hearing Board, chair, 1980; United Nations Secretary General Special Representative for World Summit for Social Development, consultant, 1992. Writer. **Publications:** Measuring Global Values: The Ranking of One-Hundred-Sixty-Two Countries, 1991; Comparing State Polities: A Framework for Analyzing One-Hundred Governments, 1996; American Adventurism Abroad: 30 Invasions, Interventions, and Regime Changes Since World War II, 2004, rev. ed., 2008. Contributor of articles and reviews to scholarly journals. **Address:** Department of Political Science, Drexel University, 3021 MacAlister Hall, Philadelphia, PA 19104, U.S.A. **Online address:** sullivmj@drexel.edu

SULLIVAN, M(ichael) J(ustin). Also writes as Tōshoin no Seihō, Seiho. American (born United States), b. 1940. **Genres:** Novels, Mystery/Crime/Suspense, Philosophy, History, Sports/Fitness, Young Adult Fiction. **Career:** Eckerd College, teacher; Takamatsu Dai-ichi Koto Gakko, English teacher, 1979-80. Writer. **Publications:** (As Seiho) Seiho's Kanji Workbook, 1991; Japanese Calligraphy: Practice, Learning, and Art, 1993; Japanese Calligraphy: A First-Year Curriculum, 1993; (with A. Kalla) Velvet (mystery novel), 1993; Mark Messier: Star Center, 1997; Sports Great Shaquille O'Neal, 1998; (as Toshoin no Seiho) Sword and Psyche: Hachigenri and Other Writings on the Martial Arts, 2001; Waza: A Trans-Pacific Novel, 2002; Necessary Heartbreak: A Novel of Faith and Forgiveness, 2010. **Address:** 295 Catamount Ridge, Bailey, CO 80421, U.S.A.

SULLIVAN, Patricia. American (born United States), b. 1950. **Genres:** Civil Liberties/Human Rights, Politics/Government, History. **Career:** University of South Carolina, associate professor. Writer. **Publications:** Days of Hope: Race and Democracy in the New Deal Era, 1996; Lift Every Voice: The NAACP and the Making of the Civil Rights Movement, 2009. EDITOR: (with A.L. Robinson) New Directions in Civil Rights Studies, 1991; (with W.E. Martin, Jr.) Civil Rights in the United States, 2 vols., 2000; Freedom Writer: Virginia Foster Durr, Letters from the Civil Rights Years, 2003. **Address:** Department of African American Studies, University of South Carolina, 202 Flinn Hall, Columbia, SC 29208, U.S.A.

SULLIVAN, Paul. American (born United States), b. 1939. **Genres:** Novels, Young Adult Fiction, Art/Art History. **Career:** Novelist. **Publications:** (Co-author) Calligraphy: From Beginner to Expert (Usborne Kid Kits), 1993; Legend of the North, 1995; Keewatin, 1996; The Unforgiving Land, 1996; The Spirit Walker, 1997; Maata's Journal: A Novel, 2003; Burning of Prayers, 2010; Breaker at Dawn, 2010; Torn from the Sun, 2010. Illustrator of books by others. **Address:** Royal Fireworks Publishing Company Inc., 1 Ave., PO Box 388, Unionville, NY 10988, U.S.A.

SULLIVAN, Randall. American (born United States), b. 1951. **Genres:** Novellas/Short Stories, Travel/Exploration, Autobiography/Memoirs, Documentaries/Reportage, Essays, Social Sciences. **Career:** New York Daily News, reporter, 1978-79; Los Angeles Herald Examiner, columnist, 1979-83; Rolling Stone Magazine, contributing editor, 1983-91, 1999-; Men's Journal, contributing editor, 1997-; freelance writer, 1991-. **Publications:** The Price of Experience: Power, Money, Image, and Murder in Los Angeles, 1996; Labyrinth, 2002; The Miracle Detective, 2004. Contributor of articles to books. **Address:** Rolling Stone Magazine, 1290 Ave. of the Americas, New York, NY 10104-0298, U.S.A. **Online address:** randysul@aol.com

SULLIVAN, Sherry E. American (born United States), b. 1961?. **Genres:** Psychology, Women's Studies And Issues, Business/Trade/Industry, Economics. **Career:** Memphis State University, assistant professor, associate professor, 1988-93; Bowling Green State University, Small Business Institute, associate professor, 1993-, director. Writer. **Publications:** (With L.A. Mainiero) The Opt-Out Revolt: Why People Are Leaving Companies to Create Kaleidoscope Careers, 2006; (ed. with Y. Baruch and H.N. Schepmyer) Winning Reviews: A Guide for Evaluating Scholarly Writing, 2006; (ed. with S.G. Baugh) Maintaining Focus, Energy and Options Over the Career, 2009. Contributor to periodicals. **Address:** Department of Management, College of Business Administration, Bowling Green State University, 3008A Business Administration, Bowling Green, OH 43403, U.S.A. **Online address:** ssulliv@bgsu.edu

SULLIVAN, Silky. See MAKOWSKI, Silky.

SULLIVAN, Steve (Joseph). American (born United States), b. 1954?. **Genres:** Women's Studies And Issues, Young Adult Non-fiction, Biography. **Career:** Glamour Girls: Then and Now Magazine, founder, editor, writer and publisher. Journalist. **Publications:** Pop Memories: The History of American Popular Music, 1890-1954, 1986; Va Va Voom!: Bombshells, Pin-ups, Sexpots and Glamour Girls, 1995; Bombshells: Glamour Girls of a Lifetime, 1998; Glamour Girls: The Illustrated Encyclopedia, 1999. Contributor to books. **Address:** Glamour Girls: Then and Now Magazine, PO Box 34501, Washington, DC 20043, U.S.A. **Online address:** stevesul@aol.com

SULLIVAN, Winnifred Fallers. American (born United States), b. 1950. **Genres:** Theology/Religion. **Career:** State University of New York, Buffalo School of Law, associate professor of law, professor of law, Law and Religion Program, director; National Humanities Center, Lilly foundation fellow, 2007-08. Writer. **Publications:** Paying the Words Extra: Religious Discourse in the Supreme Court of the United States, 1994; The Impossibility of Religious Freedom, 2005; Prison Religion: Faith-based Reform and the Constitution, 2009; (ed. with R.A. Yelle and M. Taussig-Rubbo) After Secular Law, 2011. **Address:** State University of New York, University at Buffalo Law School, 715 O'Brian Hall, North Campus, Buffalo, NY 14260-1100, U.S.A. **Online address:** wfs2@buffalo.edu

SULLIVAN-BLUM, Louise A(gnes). See BLUM, Louise A(gnes).

SULLIVAN HARPER, Donna Akiba. American (born United States), b. 1954. **Genres:** Literary Criticism And History, Young Adult Fiction. **Career:** Oberlin College, African Heritage House, dormitory director, 1975-77, lecturer in black studies program (now department), 1976-77; Emory University, graduate teaching assistant in English, 1979, programming assistant, 1982-83; Oglethorpe University, part-time instructor of English, 1980-81; Georgia Institute of Technology, part-time instructor of English, 1985-87; Spelman College, Department of English, instructor, 1987-88, assistant professor, 1988-94, associate professor, 1994-2000, interim chair, 1995-96, professor of English, 2000-, Fuller E. Callaway professor, chair, dean of undergraduate studies; Hillside Presbyterian Church, Evangelism Ministry, chairperson, 1989-90; Dana Foundation, Preparing Minorities for Academic Careers Program, project director, 1991-94; UNCF-Mellon Undergraduate Program, campus coordinator, 1998-. Writer. **Publications:** Not So Simple: The Simple Stories by Langston Hughes (literary criticism), 1995. EDITOR: The Return of Simple (short fiction), 1994; Short Stories (short fiction), 1996; (and intro.) The Early Simple Stories, 2002; (and intro.) The Later Simple Stories, 2002. Contributor to books and periodicals. **Address:** Spelman College, 350 Spelman Ln. SW, PO Box 745, Atlanta, GA 30314, U.S.A. **Online address:** dharper@spelman.edu

SULLUM, Jacob. American (born United States), b. 1965. **Genres:** Medicine/Health, Self Help. **Career:** Times Leader, reporter, 1987-88; News and Courier/Evening Post, reporter, 1988-89; Reason magazine, assistant editor, 1989-, associate editor, managing editor, 1989-94, senior editor, 1995-; National Review, articles editor, 1994-95; Reason.com, senior editor. **Publications:** For Your Own Good: The Anti-Smoking Crusade and the Tyranny of Public Health, 1998; Saying Yes: In Defense of Drug Use, 2003. Contributor to magazines and newspapers. **Address:** Glen Hartley and Lynn Chu, Writers' Representatives, 116 W 14th St., 11th Fl., New York, NY 10011-7305, U.S.A. **Online address:** jsullum@reason.com

SULMASY, Daniel P. American (born United States), b. 1956. **Genres:** Medicine/Health, Philosophy, Theology/Religion. **Career:** New York Medical College, professor of medicine, 1998-, Bioethics Institute director, 1998-; University of Chicago, Department of Medicine, Kilbride-Clinton professor of medicine and ethics, 2009-, MacLean Center for Clinical Medical Ethics, associate director, 2009-, Divinity School, Kilbride-Clinton professor of medicine and ethics, 2009-; Georgetown University, faculty; Theoretical Medicine and Bioethics, editor-in-chief. **Publications:** The Healer's Calling: A Spirituality for Physicians and Other Health Care Professionals, 1997; (ed. with J. Sugarman) Methods in Medical Ethics, 2001, 2nd ed., 2010; The Rebirth of the Clinic: An Introduction to Spirituality in Health Care, 2006; A Balm for Gilead: Meditations on Spirituality and the Healing Arts, 2006. **Address:** Department of Medicine, University of Chicago, 5841 S Maryland Ave., PO Box 6098, Chicago, IL 60637, U.S.A. **Online address:** dsulmasy@uchicago.edu

SULSTON, John (Edward). British (born England), b. 1942. **Genres:** Biology, Sciences, Philosophy, Engineering. **Career:** Salk Institute, staff; Medical Research Council Laboratory of Molecular Biology, staff scientist, 1969-92; Wellcome Trust Sanger Institute, director, 1992-2000, research scientist, 2000-. Writer. **Publications:** (With G. Ferry) The Common Thread: A Story of Science, Politics, Ethics, and the Human Genome, 2002. Contributor of articles to scientific journals. **Address:** 39 Mingle Ln., Stapleford, Cambridge, CB2 5BG, England.

SULTAN, Alan. American (born United States), b. 1948. **Genres:** Mathematics/Statistics, Education, Sciences, Information Science/Computers. **Career:** Mellon Fellow, 1973; City University of New York, Queens College, assistant professor, 1975-80, associate professor, 1981-96, professor of mathematics, 1996-; Howard Hughes fellow, 1992. Writer. **Publications:** Linear Programming: An Introduction with Applications, 1993; (with A.F. Artzt) Mathematics that Every Secondary School Math Teacher Needs to Know, 2010. **Address:** Department of Mathematics, Queens College, City University of New York, Rm. 505, Kiely, 65-30 Kissena Blvd., Flushing, NY 11367-1575, U.S.A. **Online address:** asultan956@aol.com

SULTAN, Stanley. American (born United States), b. 1928. **Genres:** Novels, Novellas/Short Stories, History, Literary Criticism And History, Recreation, Young Adult Fiction. **Career:** National Lexicographic Board Ltd., assistant editor, 1951-55; Smith College, instructor in English, 1955-59; Clark University, Department of English, assistant professor, 1959-62, associate professor, 1962-68, professor of English, 1968-, now professor emeritus; National Defense Education Institute in English, director, 1965; University of Trier, lecturer, 1980. **Publications:** The Argument of Ulysses, 1965; (ed.) The Playboy of the Western World, 1971; Yeats at His Last, 1975; Ulysses, The Waste Land, and Modernism: A Jubilee Study, 1977; Rabbi: A Tale of the Waning Year, 1977; (co-author) Galley Bliss, 1980; Eliot, Joyce, and Company, 1987; Joyce's Metamorphosis, 2001; Interpreting Modernist Writers: Macro History, Personal History, and Manuscript History, 2008. Works appear in anthologies. **Address:** Department of English, Clark University, 950 Main St., Worcester, MA 01610-1477, U.S.A. **Online address:** ssultan@clarku.edu

SULTANA, Donald Edward. Scottish/Maltese (born Malta), b. 1924. **Genres:** Literary Criticism And History, Biography. **Career:** Royal University of Malta, lecturer in English literature, 1951-64; University of Edinburgh, lecturer, 1965-72, senior lecturer, 1973-78, reader in English literature, 1979-81, honorary fellow, 1982-99. Writer. **Publications:** Samuel Taylor Coleridge in Malta and Italy 1804-1806, 1969; Benjamin Disraeli in Spain, Malta, and Albania 1830-32, 1976; The Siege of Malta Rediscovered: An Account of Sir Walter Scott's Mediterranean Journey and His Last Novel, 1977; (ed.) New Approaches to Coleridge: Biographical and Critical Essays, 1981; The Journey of Sir Walter Scott to Malta, 1987; The Journey of William Frere to Malta in 1832, 1988; From Abbotsford to Paris and Back: Sir Walter Scott's Journey of 1815, 1993. **Address:** Department of Rhetoric & English Literature, University of Edinburgh, George Sq., David Hume Twr., Edinburgh, 8, Scotland.

SUM, Ngai-Ling. British/Hong Kong (born Hong Kong), b. 1952. **Genres:** International Relations/Current Affairs, Politics/Government, Sociology, Cultural/Ethnic Topics, Economics. **Career:** City Polytechnic of Hong Kong, part-time lecturer, 1988-92; University of Sheffield, Political Economy Research Centre, Alec Horsley research fellow, 1994-97; University of Manchester, Manchester International Centre for Labour Studies, Simon research fellow, 1998-2000; Lancaster University, Department of Politics, Philosophy and Religion, lecturer in politics, 2001-05, senior lecturer 2005-. Writer. **Publications:** (With E.V. Roberts and P. Bradshaw) Historical Dictionary of Hong Kong and Macau, 1992; (ed. with M. Perkmann) Globalization, Regionalization, and Cross-Border Regions, 2002; (with B. Jessop) Beyond the Regulation Approach, 2006; (with B. Jessop) Towards a Cultural Political Economy, 2011. **Address:** Department of Politics, Philosophy and Religion, Lancaster University, Rm. B73, County South, Lancaster, LC LA1 4YL, England. **Online address:** n.sum@lancaster.ac.uk

SUMARSAM. American/Indonesian (born Indonesia), b. 1944. **Genres:** Cultural/Ethnic Topics, History, Social Sciences, Young Adult Non-fiction. **Career:** Kasatriyan Junior High School, Gamelan instructor, 1965-69; Indonesian National Academy of Music, assistant lecturer, 1967-71; Indonesian National Conservatory of Music, teacher, 1966-71; Expo '70, staff, 1970; Indonesian Embassy, instructor in Gamelan, 1971-72; Wesleyan University, visiting artist and instructor, 1972-76, director of Wesleyan Gamelan Ensemble, 1972-90, artist-in-residence and lecturer, 1976-90, adjunct associate professor, 1990-92, adjunct professor of music, 1992-; Brown University, visiting instructor of Javanese music, 1980; Cornell University, consultant on exhibition of Javanese puppet at the Herbert F. Johnson Museum, 1980-88, co-director of gamelan ensemble, 1983-84, director, 1984; Williams College, visiting instructor of Javanese music, 1991; Smith College, visiting instructor of Javanese music, 1995-97. **Publications:** Inner Melody in Javanese Gamelan, 1976; Kendhangan Gaya Solo: Kendag Kalih and Setunggal Dengan Selintas Pengetahuan Gamelan, 1976; (trans.) Menakjingga Lena, 1981; Introduction to Javanese Gamelan (monograph), 1988; Gamelan: Cultural Interaction and Musical Development in Central Java, 1995; Hayatan gamelan: kedalaman lagu, teori, dan perspektif, 2002; Gamelan: interaksi budaya dan perkembangan musikal di Jawa, 2003; Opportunity and Interaction: The Gamelan from Java to Wesleyan, 2004. Contributor of articles to periodicals and books. **Address:** Department of Music, Wesleyan University, 70 Wyllys Ave., Wesleyan Sta., Middletown, CT 06459, U.S.A. **Online address:** sumarsam@wesleyan.edu

SUMMER, Lauralee. American (born United States), b. 1976?. **Genres:** Autobiography/Memoirs. **Career:** Boston Public Schools, high school teacher; Charlestown High School, teacher of English and writing. Writer. **Publications:** Learning Joy from Dogs Without Collars: A Memoir, 2003. **Address:**

c/o Author Mail, Simon & Schuster Inc., 1230 Ave. of the Americas, New York, NY 10020, U.S.A. **Online address:** lauraleesummer@gmail.com

SUMMERHAWK, Barbara. American (born United States), b. 1946. **Genres:** Literary Criticism And History, Gay And Lesbian Issues. **Career:** Daito Bunka University, professor of American studies, 1987-. Writer. **Publications:** Invitation to a New Yarn, 1989; Mariko's Choice, 1993; (co-trans. and co-ed.) Queer Japan: Personal Stories of Japanese Lesbians, Gays, Transsexuals and Bisexuals, 1998; (with L.V. Gagehabib) Circles of Power: Shifting Dynamics in a Lesbian-Centered Community, 2000; (ed. with K. Hughes) Sparkling Rain: And Other Fiction from Japan of Women Who Love Women, 2009. **Address:** Daito Bunka University, 1-9-1 Takashimadaira, Itabashi-ku, Tokyo, 175, Japan. **Online address:** barbara@ic.daito.ac.jp

SUMMERHILL, Thomas. American (born United States), b. 1962. **Genres:** History, Technology, Engineering. **Career:** University of California, Regents Fellow, 1987-88; dissertation research fellow, 1990-91; Smithsonian National Museum of American History, graduate fellow, 1991; Babson College, visiting lecturer, 1993; Boston College, visiting lecturer, 1993-94; University of Massachusetts, visiting lecturer, 1994; University of California, visiting lecturer, 1994-95; Drake University, assistant professor of history, 1995-97; Yale University, Institute for Social and Policy Studies, Program in Agrarian Studies, postdoctoral fellow, 1996-97; Michigan State University, assistant professor of history, 1997-2004, associate professor of history, 2004-, associate dean for academic and student affairs, Michigan State University Museum, adjunct curator, 2000-, Michigan Agricultural Heritage Project, investigator, head. Writer, academic and historian. **Publications:** (Ed. with J.C. Scott) Transatlantic Rebels: Agrarian Radicalism in Comparative Context, 2004; Harvest of Dissent: Agrarianism in Nineteenth-Century New York, 2005; Fighting the Union: Anti-War Politics in the Civil War North, forthcoming. Contributor to journals and periodicals. **Address:** Department of History, Michigan State University, 202 Berkey Hall, East Lansing, MI 48824, U.S.A. **Online address:** summerhi@msu.edu

SUMMERLIN, Vernon. American (born United States), b. 1943. **Genres:** Travel/Exploration, Food And Wine. **Career:** Gallivant Travel Magazine, editor and publisher; WDCN-TV, Tennessee Outdoorsmen, field host; Tennessee Angler Radio, producer and host of daily four-minute radio broadcast; Gallivant: Whimsical Travel, co-founder, 2003; Southeastern Outdoor Press Association, president; Tennessee Outdoor Writers Association, president. **Publications:** Two Dozen Fishin' Holes: A Guide to Middle Tennessee, 1992; (with C. Summerlin) Traveling the Trace, 1995; (with C. Summerlin) Traveling the Southern Highlands, 1997; (with C. Summerlin) Traveling Tennessee, 1998; (with C. Summerlin) Highroad Guide to the Tennessee Mountains, 1999; The Compleat Tennessee Angler: Everything you Need to Know about Fishing in the Volunteer State, 1999; (with C. Summerlin) Traveling Florida, 2002; (with J. Holt) Tennessee Outdoorsmen Cookbook, 2002; Great Outdoorsman Cookbook, 2003. Contributor of articles to magazines. **Address:** 5550 Boy Scout Rd., Franklin, TN 37064, U.S.A. **Online address:** vsummerlin@mindspring.com

SUMMERS, Anthony (Bruce). Irish/British (born England), b. 1942. **Genres:** History, Documentaries/Reportage, Young Adult Non-fiction. **Career:** Granada-TV, World in Action Program, researcher, 1963; Swiss Broadcasting Corp., newsreader and writer, 1964-65; British Broadcasting Corp., journalist, BBC TV News, scriptwriter, 1965; BBC TV Current Affairs Program, producer, 1965-73. **Publications:** (With T. Mangold) The File on the Tsar, 1976, rev. ed., 2002; Conspiracy, 1980; Goddess: The Secret Lives of Marilyn Monroe, 1985; (with S. Dorril) Honeytrap: The Secret Worlds of Stephen Ward, 1987; Official and Confidential: The Secret Life of J. Edgar Hoover, 1993; The Kennedy Conspiracy, 1998; Not in Your Lifetime, 1998; (with R. Swan) The Arrogance of Power: The Secret World of Richard Nixon, 2000; (with R. Swan) Sinatra: The Life, 2005. **Address:** c/o Jonathan Lloyd, Curtis Brown Literary Agency, Haymarket House, 48/49 Haymarket, London, GL SW1Y 4SP, England. **Online address:** johndoe@homestead.com

SUMMERS, Judith (Anne). British (born England), b. 1953?. **Genres:** Novels, History, Writing/Journalism, Biography, Adult Non-fiction. **Career:** Full-time writer, 1985-; freelance london tourist guide, 1976-85; lecturer, 1976-85; British Broadcasting Corp., assistant film editor, 1978-81. **Publications:** Dear Sister, 1985; I, Gloria Gold, 1988; Soho: A History of London's Most Colourful Neighbourhood, 1989; Crime and Ravishment, 1996; Frogs and Lovers, 1997; The Empress of Pleasure: The Life and Adventures of Teresa

Cornelys, Queen of Masquerades and Casanova's Lover, 2003; Casanova's Women: The Great Seducer and the Women He Loved, 2006; My Life With George: What I Learned About Joy from One Neurotic (and Very Expensive) Dog, 2007; Who Gets Fluffy?, 2008; The Badness of King George, 2010. **Address:** c/o Clare Alexander, Gillon Aitken Associates Ltd., 18-21 Cavaye Pl., London, GL SW10 9PT, England. **Online address:** judithsammers@aol.com

SUMMERS, Mark Wahlgren. American (born United States), b. 1951. **Genres:** History. **Career:** University of Kentucky, Thomas D. Clark professor of history. Writer. **Publications:** Railroads, Reconstruction and the Gospel of Prosperity: Aid under the Radical Republicans, 1865-1877, 1984; The Plundering Generation: Corruption and the Crisis of the Union, 1849- 1861, 1987; The Era of Good Stealings, 1993; The Press Gang: Newspapers and Politics, 1865-1878, 1994; The Gilded Age or The Hazard of New Functions, 1997; Rum, Romanism and Rebellion: The Making of a President, 1884, 2000; Party Games: Getting, Keeping and Using Power in Gilded Age Politics, 2004; Dangerous Stir: Fear, Paranoia and the Making of Reconstruction, 2009. **Address:** Department of History, University of Kentucky, 1715 Patterson Office Twr., Lexington, KY 40506-0027, U.S.A. **Online address:** msumm2@pop.uky.edu

SUMMERS, Rowena. See SAUNDERS, Jean (Innes).

SUMMERSCALE, Kate. British (born England), b. 1965?. **Genres:** Biography, Adult Non-fiction, History, Social Sciences. **Career:** The Independent, staff writer; Daily Telegraph, obituaries writer, obituaries editor, 1995-96, features writer, 1996-2005, literary editor. **Publications:** The Queen of Whale Cay: The Eccentric Story of Joe Carstairs, Fastest Woman on Water (biography), 1997; The Suspicions of Mr. Whicher: A Shocking Murder and the Undoing of a Great Victorian Detective, 2008; Suspicions of Mr. Whicher, or, The Murder at Road Hill House, 2009. **Address:** Viking Press, 375 Hudson St., New York, NY 10014-3657, U.S.A.

SUMNER, David E. American (born United States), b. 1946. **Genres:** History, Education. **Career:** Episcopal Diocese of Southern Ohio, editor of interchange and director of communications, 1981-86; University of Tennessee, School of Journalism, graduate teaching associate, 1986-88; Knoxville News-Sentinel, feature writer, 1988-90; Knoxville Journal, part-time columnist, 1988-90; Christian Writers Newsletter, editor and publisher, 1988-89; Ball State University, assistant professor, 1990, associate professor, 1995, professor of journalism, 2000-, head magazine program, 1990-, Ball Bearings Magazine, coordinator; Association for Education in Journalism and Mass Communication, webmaster, 2000-; Indiana Collegiate Press Association, executive director, 2004-06. **Publications:** The Episcopal Church's History, 1945-1985, 1987; Graduate Programs in Journalism and Mass Communication, 1996; (with H.G. Miller) Feature and Magazine Writing: Action, Angle and Anecdotes, 2005, 2nd ed., 2009; (S. Rhoades) Magazines: A Complete Guide to the Industry, 2006; Magazine Century: American Magazines Since 1900, 2010. **Address:** Department of Journalism, Ball State University, Rm. 300, 391 Art and Journalism Bldg., 2000 W University Ave., Muncie, IN 47306, U.S.A. **Online address:** dsumner@bsu.edu

SUMNER, (Edith) Aurea. British (born England), b. 1913. **Genres:** Novels, Children's Non-fiction, Children's Fiction, Romance/Historical. **Career:** Scotholme Central Girls School, music mistress, 1934-38; Hill Secondary Modern School, divinity mistress, 1948-53. Writer. **Publications:** Listen and Do, 1958; More Listen and Do, 1959; The Hand, 1982; A Man May Not, 1992. **Address:** Galatea, 535 Main Rd., Dovercourt Bay, Harwich, EX CO12 4NH, England.

SUMNER, George R. Canadian/American (born United States), b. 1955?. **Genres:** Theology/Religion, Essays, History, Humanities. **Career:** Anglican Theological College, missionary teacher; Wycliffe College, principal, Helliwell Professor of World Mission; St. Paul's Anglican Church, honorary assistant. Pastor and writer. **Publications:** (Ed. with E. Radner) Reclaiming Faith: Essays on Orthodoxy in the Episcopal Church and the Baltimore Declaration, 1993; (ed. with E. Radner) The Rule of Faith: Scripture, Canon and Creed in a Critical Age, 1998; The First and the Last: The Claim of Jesus Christ and the Claims of Other Religious Traditions, 2004; (with J.P. Greenman) Unwearied Praises: Exploring Christian Faith through Classic Hymns, 2004; Unwearied Praises, 2005; Being Salt: A Theology of an Ordered Church, 2007; (ed. with C.S. Hamilton and P.M.B. Robinson) In Spirit and in Truth: The Challenge of

Discernment for Canadian Anglicans Today, 2009. **Address:** Department of Theology, Wycliffe College, 5 Hoskin Ave., Toronto, ON M5S 1H7, Canada. **Online address:** george.sumner@utoronto.ca

SUMNER, Mark (C.). (Kenyon Morr). American (born United States) **Genres:** Novels, Young Adult Fiction. **Career:** Author. **Publications:** AS KENYON MORR: Kingdom of Sorrow, 1995; See No Weevil, 1996. THREE BOOKS OF BLOOD SERIES: The Principal, 1994; The Substitute, 1994; The Coach, 1994; Three Books of Blood, 1994. NEWS FROM THE EDGE SERIES: The Monster of Minnesota, 1997; Insanity, Illinois, 1998; The Vampires of Vermont, 1999; Evolution of Everything, 2010. EXTREME ZONE SERIES: Night Terrors, 1997; Dark Lies, 1997; Unseen Powers, 1997; Deadly Secrets, 1997; Common Enemy, 1997; Inhuman Fury, 1997; Lost Soul, 1997; Dead End, 1998. OTHERS: A Handful of Hatchlings (short stories), 1993; Rent-to-Own (short stories), 1994; The Dark, 1994; Deadly Stranger, 1993; (contrib.) Magic-The Gathering: The Prodigal Sorcerer, 1995; (contrib.) The Cursed Land, 1996; Devil's Tower, 1996; Devil's Engine, 1997; Unfinished Tales, forthcoming. **Address:** PO Box 515286, St. Louis, MO 63151, U.S.A. **Online address:** range@inlink.com

SUMPTION, Jonathan. British (born England), b. 1948. **Genres:** History, Theology/Religion, Military/Defense/Arms Control, Social Sciences. **Career:** Oxford University, Magdalen College, fellow of history, 1971- 75; barrister, 1975-; High Court, chancery division judge, deputy judge; Royal Academy of Music, governor; Jersey and Guernsey Court of Appeal, judge. Writer. **Publications:** Pilgrimage: An Image of Medieval Religion, 1975; The Albigensian Crusade, 1978; (with K. Joseph) Equality, 1979; The Hundred Years War I: Trial by Battle, 1991; The Hundred Years War II: Trial by Fire, 1999; Age of Pilgrimage: The Medieval Journey to God, 2003; The Hundred Years War III, 2009. Contributor to periodicals. **Address:** 7-8 Essex St., Crooms Hill, London, GL WC2R 3LD, England. **Online address:** jonathan.sumption@brickcourt.co.uk

SUN, Chyng Feng. American/Taiwanese (born Taiwan), b. 1959. **Genres:** Children's Fiction, Young Adult Fiction. **Career:** Min-sheng Daily Newspaper, Journalist, 1980-88, reporter, 1984-89; Family, Friends and Community, associate director; Linking Publishing Co., part-time editor, 1984-89; New York University, clinical associate professor, professor, 2003-. **Publications:** UNTRANSLATED WORKS: Bao-Bao in America, 1986; The Magic Jar, 1988; The Diary of an E.T., 1988; Leaves-Birds, 1988; Cooking Something Up: How to Teach Children Creative Writing, 1988; Little Red, 1989; The Magic Egg, 1995. FOR CHILDREN: Two Together, 1991; Square Beak, 1993; On a White Pebble Hill, 1994; Mama Bear, 1994; Cat and Cat-face, 1996. OTHER: Fantasies Matter: Pornography, Sexuality and Relationships, forthcoming. Contributor to children's magazines. **Address:** Paul McGhee Division, School of Continuing and Professional Studies, New York University, 7 E 12th St., Ste. 923, New York, NY 10003, U.S.A. **Online address:** chyng.sun@nyu.edu

SUN, Yifeng. Chinese (born China), b. 1957?. **Genres:** Translations, Literary Criticism And History, Cultural/Ethnic Topics. **Career:** Lingnan University, associate professor of translation, professor of translation studies, Chinese Language Education and Assessment Centre, head; Southwest University, affiliate professor. Writer. **Publications:** (Trans.) Contemporary Chinese Women Writers VI: Four Novellas by Zhang Xin, 1998; (trans.) King of the Wizards: Selected Works by Lin Xi, 1998; (contrib.) The Construction of Translation Theory and Cultural Perspectives, 2000; Fragments and Dramatic Moments: Zhang Tianyi and the Narrative Discourse of Upheaval in Modern China, 2002; Translation Terminology, 2004; Perspective, Interpretation and Culture: Theory of Literary Translation, 2004, 2nd ed., 2006; Cultural Exile and Homeward Journey: R.L. Stevenson and American Fiction, 2005; (ed. with N. Wang) Translation, Globalisation and Localisation, 2008. FORTHCOMING: Perspective, Interpretation and Utterance: Theory of Literary Translation; Norms and Translation: Toury's Translation Theory; Studies: Dialogue in the New Century; Barriers to Translation: Transcending Ideologies in China. Contributor to books and journals. **Address:** Department of Translation, Lingnan University, 8 Castle Peak Rd., Tuen Mun, Hong Kong, 999077, Hong Kong. **Online address:** sunyf@ln.edu.hk

SUNDAHL, Daniel James. American (born United States), b. 1947. **Genres:** Novels, Poetry, Literary Criticism And History, Humanities. **Career:** College of the Ozarks, assistant professor, 1979-83; Hillsdale College, Russell Amos Kirk professor of English and American studies and director of American studies program, 1983-. Writer. **Publications:** Loss of Habitat, 1993; Hiroshima Maidens: Imaginary Translations From the Japanese, 1994; (contrib.) The Permanent Things: Hillsdale College, 1900-1994, 1998; The Small Logics, 2000. **Address:** Department of English, Hillsdale College, 33 E College St., Hillsdale, MI 49242, U.S.A. **Online address:** dsundahl@hillsdale.edu

SUNDEEN, Mark. American (born United States), b. 1970?. **Genres:** Novels, Autobiography/Memoirs, Technology, Young Adult Non-fiction. **Career:** Great God Pan (magazine), cofounder and managing editor, 1996; Outward Bound instructor; El Camino College, writing tutor. **Publications:** Car Camping: The Book of Desert Adventures, 2000; The Making of Toro: Bullfights, Broken Hearts and One Author's Quest for the Acclaim He Deserves, 2003; (with S. Hansen) North by Northwestern: A Seafaring Family on Deadly Alaskan Waters, 2010. **Address:** c/o Author Mail, Simon Andamp Schuster, 1230 Ave. of the Americas, New York, NY 10020, U.S.A.

SUNDELL, Joanne. American (born United States), b. 1946?. **Genres:** Civil Liberties/Human Rights, Novels, Romance/Historical. **Career:** Writer. **Publications:** HISTORICAL ROMANCE NOVELS: Matchmaker, Matchmaker, 2006; A . My Name's Amelia, 2007; The Parlor House Daughter, 2008; Meggie's Remains, 2009; Hearts Persuaded, 2010; Hearts Divided, 2010. **Address:** Tabernash, CO , U.S.A. **Online address:** author@joannesundell.com

SUNDELSON, David. American (born United States), b. 1946. **Genres:** Literary Criticism And History, Psychology, Young Adult Fiction. **Career:** State University of New York College, assistant professor of English, 1979-80; California Institute of Technology, instructor, 1980-82; State Public Defender's Office, deputy state public defender, 1990-91; appellate attorney, 1991-; Claremont Graduate School, adjunct professor of English, 1994-96. Writer. **Publications:** Shakespeare's Restorations of the Father, 1983; (with C. Bollas) The New Informants: The Betrayal of Confidentiality in Psychoanalysis and Psychotherapy, 1995; Defending Your Practice, 1996. **Address:** 1678 Shattuck Ave., Ste. 330, Berkeley, CA 94709-1631, U.S.A.

SUNDIATA, Ibrahim K. (I. K. Sundiata). American (born United States), b. 1944. **Genres:** History, Social Sciences. **Career:** Rutgers University, assistant professor, 1971-72; Northwestern University, assistant professor, 1972-78; University of Illinois, associate professor, 1978-91; Brandeis University, professor of African and Afro-American studies, 1991-98, 2003-, professor of history, 2003-; Howard University, Department of History, professor and chair, 1998-2002; Harvard University, W.E.B. Du Bois Insitute, resident research fellow, 2002-03, non-resident fellow, 2008. Writer. **Publications:** (As I.K. Sundiata) Black Scandal, America and the Liberian Labor Crisis, 1929-1936, 1980; Equatorial Guinea: Colonialism, State Terror, and the Search for Stability, 1990; From Slaving to Neoslavery: The Bight of Biafra and Fernando Po in the Era of Abolition, 1827-1930, 1996; Brothers and Strangers, Black Zion, Black Slavery, 1914-1940, 2003. **Address:** Department of African and Afro-American Studies, Brandeis University, 415 South St., Mandel Ctr., Ste. 218, Waltham, MA 02453, U.S.A. **Online address:** sundiata@brandeis.edu

SUNDIATA, I. K. See **SUNDIATA, Ibrahim K.**

SUNDQUIST, James (Lloyd). American (born United States), b. 1915. **Genres:** Politics/Government. **Career:** Tribune, reporter, 1935-39; U.S. Bureau of the Budget, administrative analyst, 1941-47, 1949-51; U.S. Office of Defense Mobilization, reports and statistics officer, 1951-53; Democratic National Committee, assistant to chair, 1953-54; assistant secretary to the governor of New York, 1955-56; U.S. Senate, administrative assistant to senator clark, 1957-62; U.S. Department of Agriculture, deputy undersecretary, 1963-65; Smith College, adjunct professor; Brookings Institution, senior fellow, 1965-, senior fellow emeritus. Writer. **Publications:** (Comp.) The British Defense Program and Local Government, 1940; British Cities at War, 1941; Politics and Policy: The Eisenhower, Kennedy and Johnson Years, 1968; (with C.S. Schelling) On Fighting Poverty: Perspectives from Experience, 1969; (with D.W. Davis) Making Federalism Work, 1969; Dynamics of the Party System, 1973, rev. ed., 1983; Where Shall They Live, 1970; Whither the American Party System: Highlights of Dynamics of the Party System, 1973, rev. ed., 1983; Dispersing Population, 1975; The Decline and Resurgence of Congress, 1981; Dynamics of the Party System: Alignment and Realignment of Political Parties in the United States, 1983; Constitutional Reform and Effective Government, 1986, rev. ed., 1992; (ed.) Beyond Grid-

lock?, 1993; (ed.) Back to Gridlock?: Governance in the Clinton Years, 1995. **Address:** Brookings Institution, 1775 Massachusetts Ave. NW, Washington, DC 20036, U.S.A.

SUNDQUIST, Josh. American (born United States), b. 1984. **Genres:** Biography, Autobiography/Memoirs. **Career:** LessThanFour.org, founder. Author and motivational speaker. **Publications:** A Leg Up, 2009; Just Don't Fall: How I Grew Up, Conquered Illness, and Made It Down the Mountain, 2010. Contributor to Magazines. **Address:** Sundquist Company L.L.C., 3132 N 10th St., Ste. 101, Arlington, VA 22201, U.S.A. **Online address:** josh@joshsundquist.com

SUNDSTRAND, David. American (born United States) **Genres:** Novels, Young Adult Fiction, Mystery/Crime/Suspense. **Career:** Writer and educator. **Publications:** DESERT SKY MYSTERY SERIES: Shadow of the Raven (novel), 2007; Shadows of Death, 2009. **Address:** Minotaur Books, 175 5th Ave., New York, NY 10010-7703, U.S.A. **Online address:** sundstrand@pyramid.net

SUNEE, Kim. American/Korean (born Korea (South)), b. 1970?. **Genres:** Autobiography/Memoirs, Biography. **Career:** Cottage Living Magazine, founding food editor; Southern Living Magazine, food editor. **Publications:** Trail of Crumbs: Hunger, Love and the Search for Home (memoir), 2008. **Address:** Birmingham, AL , U.S.A. **Online address:** info@kimsunee.com

SUNLEY, Christina. American (born United States) **Genres:** Young Adult Fiction. **Career:** Writer. **Publications:** The Tricking of Freya, 2009. Contributor to journals. **Address:** San Francisco, CA , U.S.A. **Online address:** info@christinasunley.com

SUNSHINE, Linda. American (born United States), b. 1948. **Genres:** Humor/Satire, Essays, Novels, Art/Art History, Poetry. **Career:** Crown Publishers, Harmony Books, executive editor, 1970-78; Simon and Schuster, Fireside Books, editor-in-chief, 1978-80; Stewart, Tabori and Chang, editorial director, 1993-. Writer. **Publications:** Constant Stranger, 1982; Plain Jane Works Out, 1983; The Plain Jane 1984 Calendar: A Year of Twinkies and Diet Soda, 1983; Plain Jane's Thrill of Very Fattening Foods Cookbook, 1985; The Memoirs of Bambi Goldbloom, Or, Growing Up in New Jersey (novel), 1987; (with J.W. Wright) The Best Hospitals in America, 1987, 2nd ed., 1995; Women Who Date Too Much (and Those Who Should Be So Lucky): A Guide for Singles in Search of Significant Others (humor), 1988; (with Wright) The 100 Best Treatment Centers for Alcoholism and Drug Abuse, 1988; Mom Loves Me Best and Other Lies You Told Your Sister (humor), 1990; One-Hundred-One Uses for Silly Putty (humor), 1990; How NOT to Turn Into Your Mother (humor), 1991; Lovers (nonfiction), 1992; (contrib.) A Day in the Life of Hollywood: As Seen by 75 of the World's Leading Photographers on One Day, May 20, 1992, 1992; Dating Iron John and Other Pleasures: A Woman's Survival Guide for the '90s (humor), 1993; (with W. Allen) The Illustrated Woody Allen Reader, 1993; It Could Happen to You (novelization), 1994; A Teacher Affects Eternity, 1995; (with M. Tiegreen) A Passion for Shoes, 1995; Bogus (novelization), 1996; (with M. Tiegreen) The Family Dog: Celebrating Our Favorite Relative, 2003; All Things Alice: The Wit, Wisdom and Wonderland of Lewis Carroll, 2004; Women Who Date Too Much and Those Who Should be so Lucky: Happy Dating, Great Sex, Healthy Relationships and Other Delusions, 2005; She's Just that into You!: The No-Excuses Truth about Women's Obsessions with Men, 2005; How Not to Turn into Your Mother: For the Woman Who Loves Her Mother but Never Follows Mom's Advice, 2006; (with D. Rich) Through Maria's Eyes, 2010. EDITOR: Victoria's Book of Days, 1989; The HBO Guide to Videocassettes, 1989; Victoria's On Being a Mother, 1990; Portrait of Great Britain and Northern Ireland, 1990; By Any Other Name: A Celebration of Roses, 1990; In the Company of Cats, 1991; It's a Boy!, 1992; It's a Girl!, 1992; A Vow of Love, 1992; To Grandmother, With Love, 1992; Victoria's No Friend Like a Sister, 1993; Victoria's A Love Is Born: A Keepsake Journal for Mothers, 1993; The Illustrated Woody Allen Reader, 1993; Newborn Joy, 1993; N. Shange, I Live in Music (poems), 1994; In the Heart of a Friend, 1994; L. Cohen, Dance Me to the End of Love (poems), 1995; May I Feel Said He (poems), 1995; Victoria: Father of My Heart, 1996; Words of Comfort, 1996; Women of Flowers: A Tribute to Victorian Women Illustrators, 1996; Our Grandmothers: Loving Portraits by 74 Granddaughters, 1998; Shape of My Heart: Poem, 1998; (with J. Kornbluth) Now you Know: Reactions After Seeing Saving Private Ryan, 1999; Cabaret: The Illustrated Book and Lyrics, 1999; Phenomenal Woman, 2000; Stuart Little: The Art, the Artists and the Story Behind the Amazing Movie, 2000; Waiting for My Baby: A Celebration of Pregnancy, 2001; (with A. Felix) Pearl Harbor: The Movie and the Moment, 2001; Still I Rise, 2001; E.T., the Extra-Terrestrial from Concept to Classic: The Illustrated Story of the Film and the Filmmakers, 2002; Catch Me If You Can: A Steven Spielberg Film, 2002; All Things Oz: Words by L. Frank Baum, 2003; (with M. Tiegreen) The Family Dinner: A Celebration of Love, Laughter and Leftovers, 2003; Cold Mountain: The Journey From Book to Film, 2003; Van Helsing: The Making of the Legend, 2004; Ray: A Tribute to the Movie, the Music and the Man, 2004. Contributor to books and magazines. **Address:** Stewart Tabori & Chang, 115 W 18th St., New York, NY 10011, U.S.A.

SUPPLE, Barry E(manuel). British (born England), b. 1930. **Genres:** Business/Trade/Industry, Economics, Transportation, History. **Career:** Harvard University, Graduate School of Business Administration, assistant professor of business history, 1955-60; McGill University, associate professor of economic history, 1960-62; University of Sussex, lecturer, reader, professor of economic and social history, 1962-78, School of Social Sciences, dean, 1965-68, pro-vice-chancellor, 1968-72, 1978; Economic History Review, co-editor, 1973-82; Nuffield College, Oxford University, professorial fellow, reader in recent social and economic history, 1978-81; University of Cambridge, Christ's College, professorial fellow, 1981-83, honorary fellow, 1984, now professor emeritus of economic history; Cambridge University, professor of economic history, 1981-93; Saint Catharine's College, master, 1984-93, honorary fellow, 1993; Worcester College, honorary fellow, 1986; Yale University, Trumbull College, associate fellow, 1986; British Academy, president, 1987; Economic History Society, president, 1992-95; Leverhulme Trust, director, 1993-2001; foreign secretary, 1995-99. **Publications:** The Entrepreneur, 1957; Commercial Crisis and Change in England 1600-42, 1959; (ed.) The Experience of Economic Growth, 1963; Boston Capitalists and Western Railroads, 1967; The Royal Exchange Assurance: A History of British Insurance 1720-1970, 1970; (ed.) Essays in Business History, 1977; History of British Coal Industry, 1987; (ed. with M.O. Furner) The State and Economic Knowledge: The American and British Experience, 1990; (ed.) The Rise of Big Business, 1992. **Address:** 3 Scotts Gardens, Whittlesford, Cambridge, CB CB2 4N4, England.

SURAGNE, Pierre. See **PÉLOT, Pierre.**

SUROWIECKI, James (Michael). American (born United States), b. 1967. **Genres:** Adult Non-fiction, Business/Trade/Industry, Economics. **Career:** Rogue Magazine, editor-in-chief, 1995-96; Motley Fool, staff writer, 1996-98; Slate, finance columnist, 1997-2000; New York Magazine, business columnist, 1998-99; Talk, contributing editor, 1999-2000; Fortune, contributing editor, 1999-2000; New Yorker, staff writer, 2000-. **Publications:** (Ed.) Best Business Crime Writing of the Year, 2002; The Wisdom of Crowds: Why the Many Are Smarter than the Few and How Collective Wisdom Shapes Business, Economies, Societies, and Nations, 2004. Contributor to periodicals. **Address:** New Yorker, 4 Times Sq., New York, NY 10036-6518, U.S.A. **Online address:** jamessuro@aol.com

SURRIDGE, Lisa. Canadian (born Canada), b. 1963?. **Genres:** Young Adult Non-fiction, Novels. **Career:** University of Victoria, Department of English, faculty, 1992-, University of Victoria Speaker's Bureau, graduate advisor. Writer and educator. **Publications:** (ed. with R. Nemesvari) Aurora Floyd (novel), 1988; Bleak Houses: Marital Violence in Victorian Fiction (nonfiction), 2005. Contributor to periodicals. **Address:** Department of English, University of Victoria, PO Box 1700, Victoria, BC V8W 2Y2, Canada. **Online address:** lsurridg@uvic.ca

SUSI, Geraldine Lee. American (born United States), b. 1942. **Genres:** Children's Fiction, Young Adult Fiction, Illustrations, History. **Career:** Reading teacher, now retired. Writer. **Publications:** For My People: The Story of Jennie Dean, 2003. HISTORICAL NOVELS: Looking for Pa: A Civil War Journey from Catlett to Manassas, 1861, 1995, 2nd ed., 2000. SELF-ILLUSTRATED: Looking Back: A Boy's Civil War Memories, 2001; My Father, My Companion: Life at the Hollow, Chief Justice John Marshall's Boyhood Home in Virginia, 2001. Contributor to periodicals. **Address:** 7939 Kettle Creek Dr., Catlett, VA 20119, U.S.A. **Online address:** rsusi@mnsinc.com

SUSKIND, Ron(ald Steven). American (born United States), b. 1959. **Genres:** Autobiography/Memoirs. **Career:** New York Times, news assistant and interim reporter, 1983-85; St. Petersburg Times, reporter, 1985-86; Boston Business Magazine, senior editor, 1987-88, editor, 1988-90; Harvard

University, instructor in advanced journalism, 1987-93; Big Ideas, consultant, 1988-90; WBUR, radio commentator, 1989-93; Wall Street Journal, staff reporter, 1990-93, Washington senior national affairs writer, 1993-2000. **Publications:** A Hope in the Unseen: An American Odyssey From the Inner City to the Ivy League, 1998; The Price of Loyalty: George W. Bush, The White House, and the Education of Paul O'Neill, 2004; One Percent Doctrine: Deep Inside America's Pursuit of Its Enemies Since 9/11, 2006; Way of the World: A Story of Truth and Hope in an Age of Extremism, 2008; Confidence Men: Wall Street, Washington, and the Education of a President, 2011. **Address:** The Harry Walker Agency Inc., 355 Lexington Ave., 21st Fl., New York, NY 10017, U.S.A. **Online address:** info@ronsuskind.com

SUSMAN, Gerald I. American (born United States), b. 1941. **Genres:** Industrial Relations, Administration/Management, Business/Trade/Industry. **Career:** Pennsylvania State University, professor of organizational behavior, 1976-88, Robert and Judith Klein professor of management, 1988-, Department of Management and Organization, chair, 1991-99, emeritus Klein professor of management, Center for the Management of Technological and Organizational Change, director, Sustainability Council, director, Quality and Manufacturing Management Program, co-director, 2000-05; Smeal College of Business, associate dean for research, 2005-09; National Academy of Sciences, study director, 1983-87; Harvard University, Harvard Business School, visiting professor business administration, 1992-93. Writer. **Publications:** Autonomy at Work: A Aociotechnical Analysis of Participative Management, 1976; Labor-Management Committees in State and Local Government, 1980; Integrating Design and Manufacturing for Competitive Advantage, 1992; (ed. with S. O'Keefe) The Defense Industry in the Post-Cold War Era: Corporate Strategies and Public Policy Perspectives, 1998; Small and Medium-Sized Enterprises and the Global Economy, 2007. **Address:** Department of Management & Organization, Pennsylvania State University, 351 Business Bldg., University Park, PA 16802-1014, U.S.A. **Online address:** gis1@psu.edu

SUSSEX, Lucy (Jane). Australian/New Zealander (born New Zealand), b. 1957. **Genres:** Novels, Novellas/Short Stories, Mystery/Crime/Suspense, Horror, Science Fiction/Fantasy, Children's Fiction, Young Adult Fiction. **Career:** Librarian, 1982-87; University of Melbourne, research assistant, senior research fellow in English, 1987-; Victorian College of the Arts, teacher of creative writing and course coordinator, 1989-; Hodder Headline, consultant editor for children's fiction, 1996-98; Clarion West Writers' Workshop, writer-in-residence, 1998; Mavis, dramaturge and storyline advisor, 1998; Deakin University, tutor in professional writing, 1999. **Publications:** NOVELS: The Peace Garden, 1989; Deersnake, 1994; The Scarlet Rider, 1996; Black Ice, 1997; The Penguin Friend, 1997; (with K. Greenwood and S. Jay) Alien Invasions, 2000; The Revognase: Quentaris Chronicles Series, 2003. OTHERS: The Fortunes of Mary Fortune, 1989; My Lady Tongue & Other Tales, 1990; (intro.) Force and Fraud, 1993; (ed.) The Lottery, 1994; (ed.) The Pattern Maker, 1994; Shadow Alley: Nine Crime Stories, 1995; (ed. with J.R. Buckrich) She's Fantastical, 1995; (comp. with K. Dyer and S. Martin) Canadian Women's History Bibliography: Catalogue, 1997; (comp. with E. Gibson) Mary Helena Fortune: A Bibliography, 1997; (ed.) Altered Voices, 1999; (ed.) Australian Women's Speculative Fiction, Magical Realism and Fantasy, 2002; A Tour Guide in Utopia, 2005; Absolute Uncertainty, 2006; Women Writers and Detectives in Nineteenth-Century Crime Fiction: The Mothers of the Mystery Genre, 2010; Matilda Told Such Dreadful Lies: The Essential Lucy Sussex, 2011. **Address:** Margaret Connolly & Associates, PO Box 945, Wahroonga, NW 2076, Australia. **Online address:** lsussex@netspace.net.au

SUSSKIND, Leonard. American (born United States), b. 1940?. **Genres:** Earth Sciences, Geography, Sciences, Philosophy. **Career:** Cornell University, national science foundation postdoctoral fellow, 1965-66; Yeshiva University, Belfer Graduate School of Science, assistant professor, 1966-68, associate professor, 1968-70, professor of physics, 1970-79; University of Tel Aviv, professor of physics, 1971-72; Harvard University, Loeb lecturer, 1976; Stanford University, professor of physics, 1979-, Felix Bloch professor of physics, 2000-, Stanford Institute for Theoretical Physics, director, 2009-. Writer. **Publications:** (With J. Lindesay) An Introduction to Black Holes, Information and the String Theory Revolution: The Holographic Universe, 2005; The Cosmic Landscape: String Theory and the Illusion of Intelligent Design, 2005; The Black Hole War: My Battle with Stephen Hawking to Make the World Safe for Quantum Mechanics, 2008. Contributor to periodicals. **Address:** Department of Physics, Stanford University, Rm. 332, Varian Physics Bldg., 382 Via Pueblo Mall, Stanford, CA 94305-4060, U.S.A. **Online address:** susskind@stanford.edu

SUSSMAN, Peter Y. American (born United States), b. 1941. **Genres:** Writing/Journalism, Biography, Autobiography/Memoirs, Civil Liberties/Human Rights, Communications/Media, Ethics, Politics/Government, Social Commentary, Social Commentary. **Career:** San Francisco Chronicle, copy editor, 1964-67, assistant news editor, 1967-81; Sunday Magazine, This World, editor, 1981-83, Sunday Punch, editor, 1983-93; freelance writer, 1993-. **Publications:** (With D.M. Martin) Committing Journalism: The Prison Writings of Red Hog, 1993; Reaching for the Dream: Profiles in Affirmative Action, 1998; (ed.) Decca: The Letters of Jessica Mitford, 2006. Contributor to magazines and newspapers. **Address:** 2636 Woolsey St., Berkeley, CA 94705-2537, U.S.A. **Online address:** peter@psussman.com

SUTCLIFFE, Jane. American (born United States), b. 1957. **Genres:** Children's Non-fiction, Biography, Adult Non-fiction. **Career:** Writer. **Publications:** Babe Didrikson Zaharias: All-Around Athlete, 2000; Jesse Owens, 2000; Paul Revere, 2002; Helen Keller, 2002; Amelia Earhart, 2003; Chief Joseph of the Nez Perce, 2003; Milton Hershey, 2004; John F. Kennedy, 2005; Juan Ponce de León, 2005; George S. Patton Jr., 2005; The Attack on Pearl Harbor, 2006; Abigail Adams, 2006; John Adams, 2006; John Deere, 2007; Marian Anderson, 2008; Ronald Reagan, 2008; Walt Disney, 2009; Sacagawea, 2009; Barack Obama, 2010; Leonardo's Monster, 2010. Contributor of articles to periodicals. **Address:** 128 Eaton Rd., Tolland, CT 06084, U.S.A. **Online address:** jane@janesutcliffe.com

SUTCLIFFE, Katherine. American (born United States), b. 1952. **Genres:** Romance/Historical, Novels, Young Adult Fiction. **Career:** Freelance writer, 1982-. **Publications:** Desire and Surrender, 1985; Windstorm, 1987; A Heart Possessed, 1988; Renegade Love, 1988; (co-author) Christmas Romance: Love Stories, 1990; A Fire in the Heart, 1990; Shadow Play, 1991; Dream Fever, 1991; Love's Illusion, 1991; My Only Love, 1994; Once a Hero, 1995; Miracle, 1996; Devotion, 1997; (co-author) Tis the Season, 1997; Jezebel, 1997; (co-author) Moonglow, 1998; (co-author) Secret Valentines, 1998; Hope and Glory, 1998; Whitehorse, 1999; Notorious, 2000; Darkling I Listen, 2001; Fever, 2001; Bad Moon Rising, 2003; Lover Beware, 2003; Obsession, 2004; Black Bayou, 2005. Contributor to books. **Address:** c/o Evan M. Fogelman, Fogelman Literary Agency, 7515 Greenville Ave., Ste. 712, Dallas, TX 75231, U.S.A. **Online address:** katherine@katherinesutcliffe.net

SUTCLIFFE, William. Scottish/British (born England), b. 1971. **Genres:** Novels, Literary Criticism And History, Young Adult Fiction. **Career:** Writer. **Publications:** New Boy, 1996; Are You Experienced?, 1999; The Love Hexagon, 2000; Bad Influence, 2004; Whatever Makes You Happy: A Novel, 2008. Contributor to periodicals. **Address:** c/o Hamish Hamilton, 80 Strand, London, GL WC2R 0RL, England.

SUTHERLAND, Elizabeth. *See* MARSHALL, Elizabeth Margaret.

SUTHERLAND, J. A. *See* SUTHERLAND, John.

SUTHERLAND, John. Also writes as J. A. Sutherland. British (born England), b. 1938. **Genres:** History, Language/Linguistics. **Career:** University of Edinburgh, lecturer, 1964-72; University College of London, lecturer, 1972-76, reader, 1976-84, Lord Northcliffe professor of modern English literature, now emeritus; California Institute of Technology, faculty, 1984-92, visiting professor. Writer. **Publications:** (With M. Greenfield) The History of Henry Esmond, 1970; (ed.) Phineas Finn: The Irish Member, 1972; Thackeray at Work (criticism), 1974; Victorian Novelists and Publishers (criitcism), 1976; Fiction and the Fiction Industry, 1978; The Book of Snobs, 1978; Bestsellers: Popular Fiction of the 1970s, 1981; (ed. and intro.) The Way We Live Now, 1982; (ed. and intro.) Vanity Fair: A Novel without a Hero, 1983; Offensive Literature, 1983; (ed. and intro.) He Knew He Was Right, 1985; Is He Popenjoy?, 1986; The Longman Companion to Victorian Fiction, 1988, 2nd ed., 2009; John Barleycorn: Alcoholic Memoirs, 1989; Mrs. Humphrey Ward: Eminent Victorian Pre-eminent Edwardian, 1990; Ralph the Heir, 1990; An Old Mans Love, 1991; An Eye for an Eye, 1992; He Knew He Was Right, 1994; Early Short Stories, 1994; Rachel Ray, 1995; Later Short Stories, 1995; Victorian Fiction: Writers Publishers Readers, 1995; The Life of Walter Scott: A Critical Biography, 1995; Barchester Towers, 1996; The Woman in White, 1996; (ed.) The Oxford Book of English Love Stories, 1996; Is Heathcliff a Murderer?: Great Puzzles in Nineteenth-Century Literature, 1996; Can Jane Eyre Be Happy?: More Puzzles in Classic Fiction, 1997; Where Was Rebecca Shot?: Curiosities Puzzles and Conundrums in Modern Fiction, 1998; (ed. and intro.) The Moonstone, 1999; The History of Pendennis: His Fortunes

and Misfortunes His Friends and His Greatest Enemy, 1999; Who Betrays Elizabeth Bennet?: Further Puzzles in Classic Fiction, 1999; Henry V War Criminal?: And Other Shakespeare Puzzles, 2000; The Literary Detective: 100 Puzzles in Classic Fiction, 2000; (ed. and intro.) The Sea-Wolf, 2000; Literary Lives, 2001; Reading the Decades: Fifty Years of the Nations Bestselling Books, 2002; (intro.) The Shooting Party, 2004; Stephen Spender: The Authorized Biography, 2005; (with D. Le Faye) So You Think You Know Jane Austen?: A Literary Quizbook, 2005; So you Think You Know Thomas Hardy?, 2005; How to Read a Novel: A User's Guide, 2006; Boy who Loved Books: A Memoir, 2007; Bestsellers: A Very Short Introduction, 2007; (ed. and intro.) Woman in White, 2008; (ed. and intro.) Moonstone, 2008; Curiosities of literature, 2008; Magic Moments: Life-changing Encounters with Books, Films, Music, 2008; Longman Companion to Victorian Fiction, 2009; (ed. and intro.) Eminent Victorians, 2009; (ed. and intro.) John Barleycorn: 'Alcoholic Memoirs', 2009; 50 Literature Ideas You Really Need to know, 2010; How Literature Works: 50 Key Concepts, 2011; (ed.) Oxford Companion to Popular Fiction, forthcoming. **Address:** Department of English Language & Literature, University College London, Gower St., London, GL WC1E 6BT, England. **Online address:** j.sutherland@ukcl.ac.uk

SUTHERLAND, Luke. British (born England), b. 1971?. **Genres:** Music, Young Adult Fiction, Romance/Historical, Gay And Lesbian Issues. **Career:** Band Long Fin Killie, founding member, vocalist. Musician and writer. **Publications:** Jelly Roll, 1998; Sweetmeat, 2002; Venus as a Boy, 2004. **Address:** David Godwin Associates, 55 Monmouth St., London, GL WC2H 9DG, England.

SUTHERLAND, Margaret. New Zealander/Australian (born Australia), b. 1941. **Genres:** Novels, Novellas/Short Stories, Education, Children's Fiction. **Career:** Music teacher; writer, 1968-; Auckland University, literary fellow, 1981. **Publications:** The Fledgling, 1974; Hello I'm Karen (for children), 1976; The Love Contract, 1976; Getting Through, 1977; (contrib.) A little Pandamonium, 1979; Dark Places, Deep Regions, 1980; The Fringe of Heaven, 1984; The City Far from Home, 1991; Is That Love?, 1999; Thanksgiving is for Giving Thanks, 2000; Valentines are for Saying I Love You, 2007; Developing the Gifted and Talented Young Learner, 2008. **Address:** 10 Council St., Speers Point, NW 2284, Australia. **Online address:** chapsuth@idl.com.au

SUTPHEN, Mona. American (born United States) **Genres:** History. **Career:** Stonebridge International LLC., managing director; U.S. presidential candidate, advisor; Illinois Senator Barack Obama on foreign policy, advisor; U.S. National Security Advisor Samuel R. Berger, White House special assistant; U.S. Ambassador to the United Nations Bill Richardson, advisor; Ron Brown Scholarship Program, advisory board; Global Rights, director; Women's Foreign Policy Group; International Human Rights Law Group, director; Council on African American Affairs, director. Writer. **Publications:** (with N. Hachigian) The Next American Century: How the U.S. Can Thrive as Other Powers Rise, 2008. **Address:** Stonebridge Intl., 875 3rd Ave., 25th Fl., New York, NY 10017, U.S.A. **Online address:** msutphen@stonebridge-international.com

SUTTER, Robert G. American/Italian (born Italy), b. 1943. **Genres:** History. **Career:** Georgetown University, visiting professor of Asian studies, 2001-; Library of Congress, Congressional Research Service, Foreign Affairs and National Defense Division, senior specialist & director; George Washington University, faculty; Johns Hopkins University, faculty; University of Virginia, faculty. Writer. **Publications:** China-Watch: Toward Sino-American Reconciliation, 1978; Chinese Foreign Policy after the Cultural Revolution, 1966-1977, 1978; Playing the China Card: Implications for United States-Soviet-Chinese Relations: Report, 1979; Recognizing the People's Republic of China: The Experience of Japan, Australia, France and West Germany, 1979; Executive-Legislative Consultations on China Policy, 1978-79, 1980; The China Quandary: Domestic Determinants of U.S. China Policy, 1972-1982, 1983; Chinese Foreign Policy: Developments after Mao, 1986; Taiwan: Entering the 21st Century, 1988; (ed. with H. Sungjoo) Korea-U.S. Relations in a Changing World, 1990; The Cambodian Crisis and U.S. Policy Dilemmas, 1991; East Asia and the Pacific: Challenges for U.S. Policy, 1992; (ed. with W.R. Johnson) Taiwan in World Affairs, 1994; China and the United States, 1996; (with S.E. Choi) Shaping China's Future in World Affairs: The Role of the United States, 1996; U.S. Policy toward China: An Introduction to the Role of Interest Groups, 1998; Chinese Policy Priorities and Their Implications for the United States, 2000; The United States and East Asia: Dynamics and Implications, 2003; China's Rise in Asia: Promises and Perils, 2005; China's Rise: Implications for U.S. Leadership in Asia, 2006; Historical Dictionary of United States-China Relations, 2006; Chinese Foreign Relations: Power and Policy since the Cold War, 2008; The United States in Asia, 2008. **Address:** Georgetown University, Intercultural Center, Rm. 512, 37th St., NW, Washington, DC 20057, U.S.A. **Online address:** sutterr@georgetown.edu

SUTTON, Allan. American (born United States), b. 1952?. **Genres:** Travel/Exploration, Adult Non-fiction, Art/Art History. **Career:** American Bibliographical Center-Clio Books, project editor. Freelance writer. **Publications:** (Comp.) A Guide to Pseudonyms on American Records, 1892-1942, 1993; Directory of American Disc Record Brands and Manufacturers, 1891-1943, 1994; Potomac Trails: D.C., Virginia, Maryland and West Virginia, 1997; American Record Labels and Companies (1891-1943), 2000; (comp.) Pseudonyms on American records, 1892-1942: A Guide to False Names and Label Errors, 2001, 2nd ed., 2005; (comp.) Cakewalks, Rags and Novelties: The International Ragtime Discography (1894-1930), 2002; Columbia Record Recording and Release Dates (1896-1934), 2004; (comp.) Edison Blue Amberol Records: A Discography (1912-1929), 2005; (with B.W. Thomas) Plaza-ARC discography, 2006; American Stage Performers Discography: Actors, Vaudevillians and Musical Comedy Stars, 2007; Recording the 'Twenties: The Evolution of the American Recording Industry, 1920-29, 2008; Edison Blue Amberol Cylinders: U.S., Special and Foreign Issues (1912-1929), 2009; Phonograph in Every Home: The Evolution of the American Recording Industry, 1900-19, 2010. Contributor to periodicals. **Address:** 501 S Cherry St., Ste. 350, Denver, CO 80246, U.S.A. **Online address:** asutton02@sprynet.com

SUTTON, C(live) (Julian). British (born England), b. 1937?. **Genres:** Economics, Business/Trade/Industry. **Career:** Esso Petroleum Co., staff, 1960-62; Polytechnic of Central London, lecturer, 1962-66; University of Bristol, lecturer, 1966-69; University of Stirling, senior lecturer, 1969-78; Sheffield Hallam University, assistant principal, 1978-93. Writer. **Publications:** (With R.W. Shaw) Industry and Competition, 1976; Economics and Corporate Strategy, 1980; Strategic Concepts, 1998. **Address:** Cambridge University Press, 32 Ave. of the Americas, New York, NY 10013-2473, U.S.A.

SUTTON, Dana F. (Dana Ferrin Sutton). American (born United States), b. 1942. **Genres:** Classics, Humanities, Language/Linguistics, Theatre, Translations, Poetry. **Career:** The University of Minnesota, Department of Humanities and classics, instructor, 1967-68; The University of Wisconsin, department of classics, teaching assistant, 1968-69; The City University of New York, Herbert Lehman College, Department of Classical and Oriental Languages, lecturer, 1969-72; The University of Illinois, assistant professor, 1975-79; University of California at Irvine, School of Humanities, assistant professor, 1979-81, associate professor, 1981-88, professor, 1988-2005, professor emeritus, 2005-; Southern California Classics Resource Sharing Consortium, senior administrative officer, 1990-92. Writer. **Publications:** Date of Euripides' Cyclops, 1974; Sophocles' Inachus, 1979; Greek Satyr Play, 1980; Self and Society in Aristophanes, 1980; Concordance to the Greek Satyr Play, 1980; A Concordance to the Anonymous Constitution ofAthens, 1981; Dramaturgy of the Octavia, 1983; The Lost Sophocles, 1984; Seneca on the Stage, 1986; Papyrological Studies in Dionysiac Literature, 1987; Two Lost Plays of Euripides, 1987; Dithyrambographi Graeci, 1989; Ancient Comedy: The War of the Generations, 1993; (trans. and ed.) T. Legge, Solymitana clades: The Destruction of Jerusalem, 1993; (trans. and ed.) T. Legge, Richardus Tertius, 1993; (trans. and ed.) T. Legge, Complete Plays, 1993; (trans. and ed.) William Gager: The Complete Works, 1994; The Catharsis of Comedy, 1994; Oxford Poetry by Richard Eedes and George Peele, 1995; (ed.) The Complete Works of Thomas Watson, 1556-1592, 1997; (ed.) The Complete Latin Poetry of Walter Savage Landor, 1999. Contributor to journals. **Address:** Department of Classics, University of California, 120 Humanities Office Bldg. 2, Irvine, CA 92697-2000, U.S.A. **Online address:** danasutton@mac.com

SUTTON, Dana Ferrin. See **SUTTON, Dana F.**

SUTTON, David John. British (born England), b. 1944. **Genres:** Poetry, Young Adult Fiction. **Career:** International Computers Ltd., computer programmer, 1966-98. Writer. **Publications:** Out on a Limb, 1969; Absences and Celebrations, 1982; Finders Keepers (poems), 1986; Flints, 1986; Settlements, 1991; The Planet Happiness, 1996; A Holding Action, 2000; Selected Poems, 2005. **Address:** 46 W Chiltern, Woodcote, Reading, BR RG8 0SG, England.

SUTTON, Garrett. American (born United States), b. 1953. **Genres:** Business/Trade/Industry, Economics. **Career:** Sutton Law Center, founder. Writ-

er, attorney and publisher. **Publications:** Own Your Own Corporation: Why the Rich Own Their Own Companies and Everyone Else Works for Them, 2001; (ed.) How Your Company can Raise Money to Grow and Go Public, 2001; How to Use Limited Liability Companies and Limited Partnerships, 2001; (with D. de Roos) Success DNA Guide to Real Estate Investment and Management, 2003; (with D. Kennedy) Real Estate Loopholes: Secrets of Successful Real Estate Investing, 2003; How to Buy & Sell a Business: How You Can Win in the Business Quadrant, 2003; The ABC's of Getting Out of Debt: Turn Bad Debt into Good Debt and Bad Credit into Good Credit, 2004; Bullet Proof Your Corporation, Limited Liability Company and Limited Partnership: Protecting the Corporate Veil, 2005; ABC's of Writing Winning Business Plans: How to Prepare a Business Plan that Others Will Want to Read and Invest in, 2005; Buy-sell Agreements: Creating a Will for Your Business or Real Estate Investment, 2005; (with S.L. Lechter) Rich Dad's Real Estate Advantages: Tax and Legal Secrets of Successful Real Estate Investors, 2006. **Address:** Sutton Law Center, 348 Mill St., Reno, NV 89501, U.S.A. **Online address:** gsutton@sutlaw.com

SUTTON, Jane. American (born United States), b. 1950. **Genres:** Picture/Board Books, Children's Fiction, Young Adult Fiction. **Career:** Harlem Valley State Hospital, mental health worker, 1972-74; Mid-Hudson Leisure, staff writer, 1974-75; Instrumentation Laboratory Inc., advertising writer, 1975-80; Lexington Public Schools, special education tutor, 1994-99; Fisher College, Academic Center for Enrichment, writing tutor, 1999-; private writing tutor, 2006-; Lexington Community Education, instructor, 2010-. **Publications:** What Should a Hippo Wear?, 1979; Me and the Weirdos, 1981; Confessions of an Orange Octopus, 1983; Not Even Mrs. Mazursky, 1984; Definitely Not Sexy, 1988; The Trouble with Cauliflower, 2006; Don't Call Me Sidney, 2010. Works appear in anthologies. **Address:** Dial Books for Young Readers, Publicity Department, 345 Hudson St., New York, NY 10014, U.S.A. **Online address:** jane@jane-sutton.com

SUTTON, Matthew Avery. American (born United States), b. 1975. **Genres:** History, Theology/Religion, Politics/Government. **Career:** Oakland University, Department of History, assistant professor of history; Washington State University, Department of History, associate professor of history. Writer. **Publications:** Aimee Semple McPherson and the Resurrection of Christian America, 2007; American Evangelicals and the Politics of Apocalypse, forthcoming; Jerry Falwell and the Rise of the Religious Right, forthcoming. Contributor to journals and periodicals. **Address:** Department of History, Washington State University, 352 Wilson-Short Hall, PO Box 644030, Pullman, WA 99164-4030, U.S.A. **Online address:** sutton@wsu.edu

SUTTON, Peter C. American (born United States), b. 1949. **Genres:** Art/Art History, History. **Career:** Philadelphia Museum of Art, associate curator of paintings, 1979-85; Museum of Fine Arts, Baker curator of European paintings, 1985-94; Christie's, senior director, 1994-96; Wadsworth Atheneum, director, 1996-2000; Bruce Museum of Arts and Science, executive director and chief executive officer, 2001-. Writer. **Publications:** (With O. Naumann) Dutch Religious Art of the Seventeenth Century, 1975; Pieter de Hooch, 1980; Jan Steen, 1983; Masters of Seventeenth-Century Dutch Genre Painting: Philadelphia Museum of Arts, March 18 to May 13, 1984, Gemäldegalerie, Staatliche Museen Preussischer kulturbesitz, Berlin (West), June 8 to August 12, 1984, 1984; A Guide to Dutch Art in America, 1986; (ed. with T.E. Stebbins, Jr.) Masterpiece Paintings from the Museum of Fine Arts, Boston, 1986; Masters of 17th-century Dutch Landscape Painting, 1987; Northern European Paintings in the Philadelphia Museum of Art: From the Sixteenth through the Nineteenth Century, 1990; (with P.H. Janssen) The Hoogsteder Exhibition of Dutch Landscapes, 1991; Dutch & Flemish Seventeenth-Century Paintings: The Harold Samuel Collection, 1992; (co-author) Prized Possessions: European Paintings from Private Collections of Friends of the Museum of Fine Arts, Boston, 1992; (co-author) The Age of Rubens, 1993; The William Appleton Coolidge Collection, 1995; Pieter de Hooch, 1629-1684, 1998; (with G. Jansen) Michael Sweerts: 1618-1664, 2002; (with L. Vergara and A.J. Adams) Love Letters: Dutch Genre Paintings in the Age of Vermeer, 2003; (with A.K. Wheelock Jr.) Rembrandt's Late Religious Portraits, 2005; Jan van der Heyden (1637-1712), 2006; Reclaimed: Paintings from the collection of Jacques Goudstikker, 2008; (with W.W. Robinson) Drawings by Rembrandt, His Students and Circle from the Maida and George Abrams Collection, 2012. **Address:** Bruce Museum of Arts and Science, 1 Museum Dr., Greenwich, CT 06830, U.S.A. **Online address:** pcsutton@brucemuseum.org

SUTTON, R. Anderson. American (born United States), b. 1949. **Genres:**

Music, inspirational/Motivational Literature. **Career:** University of Hawaii, lecturer in music, 1975-76; University of Wisconsin, assistant professor, 1982-88, associate professor, 1988-93, professor of music, 1993-, Center for Southeast Asian Studies, director, 1991-94, 1999-2001, 2006-09, Madison's Research Circle, co-director, professor of ethnomusicology. Writer. **Publications:** Traditions of Gamelan Music in Java: Musical Pluralism and Regional Identity, 1991; Variation in Central Javanese Gamelan Music: Dynamics of a Steady State, 1993; Calling Back the Spirit: Music, Dance, and Cultural Politics in Lowland South Sulawesi, 2002. Works appear in journals and anthologies. **Address:** School of Music, University of Wisconsin, 5541 Mosse Humanities Bldg., 455 N Park St., Madison, WI 53706, U.S.A. **Online address:** rasutton@wisc.edu

SUTTON, Robert I. American (born United States) **Genres:** Administration/Management, Business/Trade/Industry, Economics, Reference. **Career:** Stanford University, Stanford Engineering School, assistant professor, professor of management science and engineering, 1983-92, Stanford Center for Organizations Research, associate director, 1988-91, professor of organizational behavior, 1989-, associate professor, 1989-92, professor of management science and engineering, 1992-, Center for Work, Technology and Organization, co-director, 1996-, Stanford Technology Ventures Program, co-founder, research director, 1997-99, Stanford Design Institute, founding team, 2003-, Customer-Focused Innovation Executive Program, co-director, Stanford Business School, professor of organizational behavior; Center for Advanced Study in Behavioral Sciences, fellow, 1986-87, 1994-95, 2002-03; Haas Business School, professor of organizational behavior, 1997-98; IDEO Product Development, fellow; Reactivity, fellow; Administrative Science Quarterly, editor; Research in Organizational Behavior, co-editor, editor. **Publications:** (Ed. with K.S. Cameron and D.A. Whetten) Readings in Organizational Decline, 1988; (with J. Pfeffer) The Knowing-Doing Gap: How Smart Firms Turn Knowledge into Action, 2000; Weird Ideas That Work: 11 1/2 Practices for Promoting, Managing and Sustaining Innovation, 2002; (with J. Pfeffer) Hard Facts, Dangerous Half-truths and Total Nonsense: Profiting from Evidence-based Management, 2006; The No Asshole Rule: Building a Civilized Workplace and Surviving One that Isn't, 2007; Good Boss, Bad Boss: How to Be the Best-and Learn From the Worst, 2010. Contributor to books. **Address:** Department of Management Science & Engineering, Graduate School of Business, Stanford University, 209 Huang Engineering Ctr., PO Box 4026, Stanford, CA 94305-4024, U.S.A. **Online address:** bobsut@stanford.edu

SUTTON, Roger. American (born United States), b. 1956. **Genres:** Gay And Lesbian Issues, Librarianship, Technology, Reference, Adult Non-fiction. **Career:** Zion-Benton Public Library District, young adult services librarian, 1981-83; Chicago Public Library, librarian, 1983-87, manager; Columbia University, Children's Literature Institute, director and teacher of children's literature classes, 1987-91; Bulletin of the Center for Children's Books, senior editor, 1988-92, executive editor, 1992-94, editor-in-chief, 1994-96; Rosary College, lecturer, 1991; Horn Book Inc., The Horn Book Magazine, editor-in-chief, 1996-, The Horn Book Guide, editor-in-chief, 1996-; Simmons College, teacher; University of Chicago, teacher; University of Illinois, faculty. Consultant. **Publications:** (And ed. with B. Hearne and Z. Sutherland) The Best in Children's Books: The University of Chicago Guide to Children's Literature, 1985-1990, 1991; (ed. with B. Hearne) Evaluating Children's Books: A Critical Look: Aesthetic, Social, and Political Aspects of Analyzing and Using Children's Books, 1993; Hearing Us Out: Voices from the Gay and Lesbian Community, 1994; (ed.) The Newbery and Caldecott Medal Books, 1986-2000: A Comprehensive Guide to the Winners, 2001; (ed.) Secure Communications: Applications and Management, 2002; (with M.V. Parravano) A Family of Readers: The Book Lover's Guide to Children's and Young Adult Literature, 2010. Contributor of articles to periodicals. **Address:** Horn Book Inc., 56 Roland St., Ste. 200, Boston, MA 02129, U.S.A. **Online address:** rsutton@hbook.com

SUZUKI, Akihito. Japanese (born Japan), b. 1963. **Genres:** Medicine/Health, Psychology, History, Anthropology/Ethnology, Psychiatry. **Career:** Keio University, School of Economics, professor of history, 2004-. Writer. **Publications:** Madness at Home: The Psychiatrist, the Patient, and the Family in England, 1820-1860, 2006; (with C. Aldous) Reforming Public Health in Occupied Japan, 1945-52: Alien Prescriptions?, 2012. **Address:** Keio University, 4-1-1 Hiyoshi, Kohoku-ku, Yokohama-shi, 223-8521, Japan. **Online address:** asuzuki@hc.keio.ac.jp

SUZUKI, Kōji. Japanese (born Japan), b. 1957. **Genres:** Novels, Horror,

Translations. **Career:** Writer. **Publications:** RING SERIES: Ring, 1991; Rasen, 1995; Loop, 1998; Birthday, 1999. OTHERS: Enso-kun kisha ni noru, 1986; Rauken, 1990; (co-author) Hikon, hōkai, shōshika: doko e yuku Nihon nokazoku, 2006; Dark Water, 2006; Death and the Flower, 2007; Namida; Kamigami no Promenãde, 2008; Drop, 2009; Edge, 2012; Fusei no Tanjo, Kazoku no Kizuna; Papa-ism. **Address:** c/o Author Mail, Vertical Inc., 451 Park Ave. S, 7th Fl., New York, NY 10016, U.S.A.

SVALLFORS, Stefan. Swedish (born Sweden), b. 1961. **Genres:** Economics, Sociology. **Career:** Umeå Universitet, Department of Sociology, research assistant, 1984-89, lecturer, 1989-99, 1992-99, research fellow, 1992-96, acting professor, 1996-97, professor of sociology, 2000-; Institute for Futures Studies, affiliate researcher, 2011-. Writer. **Publications:** Vem älskar välfärdsstaten? Attityder, organiserade intressen och svensk välfärdspolitik, 1989; (ed.) In the Eye of the Beholder: Opinions on Welfare and Justice in Comparative Perspective, 1995; Välfärdsstatens moraliska ekonomi: Välfärdsopinionen i 90-talets Sverige, 1996; (ed. with P. Taylor-Gooby) The End of the Welfare State?: Responses to State Retrenchment, 1999; Mellan risk och tilltro, 1999; (ed. with T.P. Boje) The New Millennium: Essays on the Current State of Sociology, 2000; Sidospår: essäer om klass & politik, 2000; Klassamhällets kollektiva medvetande: Klass och attityder i jämförande perspektiv, 2004; (ed.) Analyzing Inequality: Life Chances and Social Mobility in Comparative Perspective, 2005; The Moral Economy of Class: Class and Attitudes in Comparative Perspective, 2006; (ed.) The Political Sociology of the Welfare State: Institutions, Social Cleavages, and Orientations, 2007. Contributor to periodicals. **Address:** Department of Sociology, Umeå Universitet, Beteendevetarhuset, Vindarnas torg 1, Umeå, SE-901 87, Sweden. **Online address:** stefan.svallfors@soc.umu.se

SVARTVIK, Jan. Swedish (born Sweden), b. 1931. **Genres:** Language/Linguistics, Education, Humanities, Reference. **Career:** University of London, University College, research assistant, 1961-64, lecturer in English, 1964-65; Gothenburg University, lecturer in English, 1965-66, docent, 1966-70; University of Lund, professor of English, 1970-95, professor emeritus, 1995-. Writer. **Publications:** On Voice in the English Verb, 1966; (with R. Quirk) Investigating Linguistic Acceptability, 1966; The Evans Statements: A Case for Forensic Linguistics, 1968; (with H.T. Carvell) Computational Experiments in Grammatical Classification, 1969; (with R. Quirk, S. Greenbaum and G. Leech) A Grammar of Contemporary English, 1971; (co-author) A Typology of Grammatical Errors, 1973; (with G. Leech) A Communicative Grammar of English, 1975, 2nd ed., 1994; (with O. Sager) Engelsk Universitetsgrammatik, 1978; (co-author) Survey of Spoken English: Report on Research, 1975-81, 1982; (with R. Svartvik) Handbok i Engelska, 2000; (with G. Leech) English: One Tongue, Many Voices, 2006. EDITOR: Errata: Papers in Error Analysis, 1973; (with R. Quirk) A Corpus of English Conversation, 1980; (with K. Aijmer) English Corpus Linguistics: Studies in Honour of Jan Svartvik, 1991; Directions In Corpus Linguistics: Proceedings of Nobel Symposium 82, Stockholm, 4-8 August 1991, 1992; Words: Proceedings of an International Symposium, Lund, 25-26 August 1995, 1996. **Address:** Department of English, University of Lund, Paradisgatan 2, PO Box 117, Lund, SE-221 00, Sweden.

SVARTVIK, Jesper. Swedish (born Sweden), b. 1965. **Genres:** Theology/Religion. **Career:** Ordained lutheran minister, 1991; International Council for Christians and Jews, chair, 1994-98; Lund University, Swedish Research Council, fellow, New Testament Exegesis, docent, 2002-, assistant professor pro tempore in New Testament studies, associate professor, 2002-, Department for Introductory Religious Studies, head, 2003-, Department of Religion, director, 2003-05, Research Council, professor, 2006-, Krister Stendahl professor of theology, 2009. Writer. **Publications:** Mark and Mission: Mark 7: 1-23 in Its Narrative and Historical Contexts, 2000; Skriftens ansikten: Konsten att lasa mellan raderna i Bibeln, 2001; (with B. Frid) Thomasevangeliet: Med Jesusorden fran Oxyrhynchus, 2002, 2nd ed., 2004; (co-author) Jossel Rakovers samtal med Gud, 2003; Ordet: bli skickliga vaxlare!, 2004. Contributor of articles and reviews to periodicals. **Address:** Center for Theology & Religious Studies, Lund University, Hämtställe 36, Allhelgona Kyrkogata 8, Lund, SE-223 62, Sweden. **Online address:** jesper.svartvik@teol.lu.se

SVENDSEN, Linda. Canadian/American (born United States), b. 1954. **Genres:** Novels, Plays/Screenplays, Young Adult Fiction, Children's Fiction. **Career:** Stanford University, Stegner fellow, 1980-81; Radcliffe College, Bunting Institute, fellow, 1981-82; Writers Community, writer-in-residence, 1982-85; Tri-Star Pictures, freelance story analyst, 1984; University of British

Columbia, professor of creative writing program, 1989-2009; Howe Sound Films, producer, 1998-. **Publications:** (Ed.) Words We Call Home: Celebrating Creative Writing at UBC, 1990; Marine Life, 1992. **Address:** University of British Columbia, Buchanan E470, 1866 Main Mall, Vancouver, BC V6T 1Z1, Canada. **Online address:** linda.svendsen@ubc.ca

SVENSON, Bo. American/Swedish (born Sweden), b. 1941. **Genres:** Plays/Screenplays, Novels. **Career:** Northwestern Mutual Life Insurance Co., staff, 1965-70; Motion Picture Group of America, chairman and chief executive officer, 1984-95; MagicQuest Entertainment, president. Writer, actor, ice hockey player and director. **Publications:** A Love Story; For Love and Country. **Address:** Agency for the Performing Arts, 405 S Beverly Dr., Beverly Hills, CA 90212, U.S.A. **Online address:** business@bosvenson.com

SVENVOLD, Mark. American (born United States), b. 1958?. **Genres:** Adult Non-fiction, Poetry, Biography. **Career:** Fordham University, poet-in-residence; Seton Hall University, Department of English, assistant professor. **Publications:** Soul Data: Poems, 1998; Elmer McCurdy: The Misadventures in Life and Afterlife of an American Outlaw, 2002; Big Weather: Chasing Tornadoes in the Heart of America, 2005; Empire Burlesque, 2007. Contributor to periodicals. **Address:** Department of English, Seton Hall University, Rm. 361, Fahy Hall, 400 S Orange Ave., South Orange, NJ 07079, U.S.A. **Online address:** smark.svenvold@shu.edu

SVOBODA, Terese. American (born United States), b. 1950. **Genres:** Novels, Poetry, Writing/Journalism, Autobiography/Memoirs, Essays, Translations, Novellas/Short Stories, Film, Film. **Career:** McGill University, rare manuscript curator, 1969; Voices and Visions, co-producer, 1980-82; University of Hawaii, distinguished visiting professor, 1992; Museum of Modern Art, Between Word and Image, curator, 1992; New School, instructor, 1993; Sarah Lawrence College, professor, 1993; Williams College, associate professor; College of William and Mary, visiting professor; Davidson College, McGee professor. Writer. **Publications:** POETRY: All Aberration, 1985; Laughing Africa, 1990; Mere Mortals, 1995; Treason, 2002; Weapons Grade, 2009. OTHERS: (trans.) Cleaned the Crocodile's Teeth, 1985; Cannibal (fiction), 1995; A Drink Called Paradise(fiction), 1999; Trailer Girl (fiction), 2001; Tin God (fiction), 2006; Black Glasses Like Clark Kent (memoir), 2008; Pirate Talk or Mermalade (fiction), 2010; Bohemian Girl (fiction), 2011. Contributor to periodicals. **Address:** 56 Ludlow, New York, NY 10002, U.S.A. **Online address:** svoboda@el.net

SWAAB, Neil. American (born United States), b. 1978. **Genres:** Graphic Novels, Illustrations. **Career:** Rehabilitating Mr. Wiggles (comic strip), creator, 1999-; Time Out New York, ad designer, 2000-01; HarperCollins Publishers, senior designer, 2001-06, art director; Parsons The New School For Design, instructor in illustration, 2004-, adjunct professor. Writer. **Publications:** SELF-ILLUSTRATOR: Rehabilitating Mr. Wiggles, vol. I, 2003, vol. II, 2005. Contributor of articles to periodicals. **Address:** Nantier Beall Minoustchine Publishing Inc., 40 Exchange Pl., Ste. 1308, New York, NY 10005-2742, U.S.A. **Online address:** mail@neilswaab.com

SWADE, Doron. American/British/South African (born South Africa), b. 1946. **Genres:** Adult Non-fiction, Technology. **Career:** London Science Museum, senior curator, assistant director and head of collections; University of Portsmouth, visiting professor; Computer History Museum, director; University of London, Computer Science, honorary research fellow; Computer Conservation Society, co-founder, 1989; British Computer Society, fellow, Chartered Engineer; Royal Holloway University, honorary research fellow. Writer. **Publications:** Charles Babbage and His Calculating Engines, 1991; (with J. Palfreman) The Dream Machine: Exploring the Computer Age, 1991; The Cogwheel Brain: Charles Babbage and the Quest to Build the First Computer, 2000 in US as The Difference Engine: Charles Babbage and the Quest to Build the First Computer, 2001. **Address:** Computer History Museum, 1401 N Shoreline Blvd., South Kensington, Mountain View, CA 94043, U.S.A. **Online address:** doron.swade@blueyonder.co.uk

SWAFFORD, Jan Johnson. American (born United States), b. 1946. **Genres:** Biography, Music, Autobiography/Memoirs, Reference, Literary Criticism And History. **Career:** Boston University School for the Arts, assistant professor, 1977-78; Hampshire College, visiting assistant professor, 1979-81; Amherst College, visiting assistant professor, 1980-81; Tufts University Arts, lecturer in English; freelance composer and writer, 1981-. **Publications:**

The Vintage Guide to Classical Music, 1992; The New Guide to Classical Music, 1993; Charles Ives: A Life with Music (biography), 1996; Johannes Brahms: A Biography, 1997; They Who Hunger: For Piano and Strings, 2007. **Address:** Department of English, Tufts University, Rm. 312, 210 E Hall, Medford, MA 02155, U.S.A. **Online address:** jswaffor@tufts.edu

SWAIN, Carol. British (born England), b. 1962. **Genres:** Novels, Graphic Novels, Humor/Satire. **Career:** Comic writer and artist, 1989-. **Publications:** Way Out Strips (collected comic strips), 1992; Invasion of the Mind Sappers (graphic novel), 1996; Foodboy (graphic novel), 2004; (with B. Paley) Giraffes in My Hair: A Rock n Roll Life, 2009. **Address:** 109 Southend Close, Hampstead, London, GL NW3 2RE, England. **Online address:** bpaley@compuserve.com

SWAIN, Gwenyth. American (born United States), b. 1961. **Genres:** Children's Fiction, Children's Non-fiction, History, Cartoons. **Career:** Fine Print (magazine), circulation manager, 1987-88; Hungry Mind bookstore, clerk, 1989-90; Carolrhoda Books, senior editor, 1990-2000. **Publications:** Indiana, 1992, 2nd ed., 2002; Pennsylvania, 1994; Bookworks: Making Books by Hand, 1995; The Road to Seneca Falls: A Story about Elizabeth Cady Stanton, 1996; Smiling, 1999; Carrying, 1999; Celebrating, 1999; Eating, 1999; Civil Rights Pioneer: A Story about Mary Church Terrell, 1999; President of the Underground Railroad: A Story about Levi Coffin, 2001; Johnny Appleseed, 2001; Bedtime!, 2002; Get Dressed!, 2002; Tidy Up!, 2002; Tigers, 2002; Wash Up!, 2002; I Wonder as I Wander, 2003; Chig and the Second Spread, 2003; Freedom Seeker: A Story about William Penn, 2003; Dred and Harriet Scott: A Family's Struggle for Freedom, 2004; Little Crow=Taoyateduta: Leader of the Dakota, 2004; Declaring Freedom: A Look at the Declaration of Independence, the Bill of Rights, and the Constitution, 2004; Theodore Roosevelt, 2005; Sojourner Truth, 2005; Wanda Gág: Storybook Artist, 2005; Hunger for Learning: A Story about Booker T. Washington, 2006; Riding to Washington, 2008; World War I: An Interactive History Adventure, 2012; Documents of Freedom: A Look at the Declaration of Independence, The Bill of Rights, and the U.S. Constitution, 2012. Contributor to periodicals. **Address:** 957 Palace Ave., St. Paul, MN 55102, U.S.A. **Online address:** gswain@gwenythswain.com

SWAIN, Joseph P(eter). American (born United States), b. 1955. **Genres:** Songs/Lyrics And Libretti, Music. **Career:** Music teacher, 1980-84; Colgate University, assistant professor, 1984-89, associate professor of music, 1989-, chairman of department, 1991-94, 2004-07; St. Mary's Church, music director, 1988-90; Tapestry, All-Centuries Singers, music director, 1992-; St. Malarchy's Church, staff, 2000-. Writer. **Publications:** Sound Judgment: Basic Ideas about Music, 1987; The Broadway Musical: A Critical and Musical Survey, 1990, 2nd ed., 2002; Musical Languages, 1997; Harmonic Rhythm: Analysis and Interpretation, 2002; Historical Dictionary of Sacred Music, 2006; Sacred Treasure: Understanding Catholic Liturgical Music, 2012. Contributor to journals. **Address:** Department of Music, Colgate University, 105 Charles Dana Arts Ctr., 13 Oak Dr., Hamilton, NY 13346-1398, U.S.A. **Online address:** jswain@mail.colgate.edu

SWAN, Annalyn. American (born United States) **Genres:** Biography. **Career:** Time Magazine, staff writer; Newsweek, music critic and senior arts editor; ASAP Media, co-founder; U.S. News & World Report, staff; Fortune Magazine, staff. **Publications:** (With M. Stevens) De Kooning: An American Master, 2004; (ed. with P.W. Bernstein) All the Money in the World: How the Forbes 400 Make and Spend Their Fortunes, 2007; (ed. with P.W. Bernstein) Access to Life, 2009; One World, Two Artists, 2011. Contributor to periodicals. **Address:** c/o Author Mail, Alfred A. Knopf Inc., 1745 Broadway, New York, NY 10019, U.S.A.

SWAN, Claudia. American (born United States), b. 1963. **Genres:** Botany, Art/Art History, Politics/Government, Economics. **Career:** Rembrandt Research Project, assistant, 1986; Columbia University, instructor, 1995-96; Pennsylvania State University, assistant professor of Northern European renaissance and baroque art, 1996-98; Northwestern University, Department of Art History, assistant professor, 1998-2003, associate professor of art history, 2003-, chair, 2007-10, Program in the Study of Imagination, founding director, 2001-04. Writer. **Publications:** The Clutius Botanical Watercolors: Plants and Flowers of the Renaissance, 1998; (ed. with L. Schiebinger) Colonial Botany: Science, Commerce, and Politics in the Early Modern World, 2005; Art, Science, and Witchcraft in Early Modern Holland: Jacques De Gheyn

II (1565-1629), 2005. Works appear in anthologies. Contributor of articles to journals. **Address:** Department of Art History, Northwestern University, 3-132 Crowe, Kresge Hall, 1880 Campus Dr., Evanston, IL 60208-2208, U.S.A. **Online address:** c-swan@northwestern.edu

SWAN, Robert. British (born England), b. 1956. **Genres:** Young Adult Nonfiction, Natural History. **Career:** Leeds Metropolitan University, visiting professor, 1992; Robert Swan Foundation, founder, 1993; One Step Beyond South Pole Challenge Expedition, planner and fundraiser, 1994-96; Countryside Management Association, vice president, 1995; 2041, founder and president. Writer, polar explorer and environmental activist. **Publications:** NONFICTION: (With R. Mear and L. Fulcher) A Walk to the Pole: To the Heart of Antarctica in the Footsteps of Scott in UK as In the Footsteps of Scott, 1987; (with R. Mear and R. Ward) Destination, Antarctica, 1988; (with G. Reavill) Antarctica 2041: My Quest to Save the Earth's Last Wilderness, 2009. **Address:** Robert Swan Foundation, Cottage Camphill, Bedale, NY DL8 2LS, England. **Online address:** rswan@2041.com

SWAN, Sharon. American (born United States) **Genres:** Romance/Historical, Novels. **Career:** Writer. **Publications:** ROMANCE NOVELS: Cowboys and Cradles, 2002; Home-grown Husband, 2002; Husbands, Husbands...Everywhere!, 2002; Four-Karat Fiancee, 2003; Her Necessary Husband, 2003; Husband in Harmony, 2004; Husband by Necessity, forthcoming. **Address:** c/o Pamela Hopkins, Hopkins Literary Associates, 2117 Buffalo Rd., Ste. 327, Rochester, NY 14624, U.S.A.

SWANN, E. L. See **LASKY, Kathryn.**

SWANSON, David. American (born United States), b. 1935. **Genres:** How-to Books, Business/Trade/Industry, Writing/Journalism. **Career:** Manpower Inc., director of corporate personnel, 1965-71; Jim Weller and Partners (advertising agency), vice-president and account supervisor, 1971-73; Waukesha County Technical College, Career Center, director, 1973-82; Advertising Ltd., owner and president, 1973-82; Career Seminars, owner and president, 1982-. Writer. **Publications:** The Resume Solution: How to Write (and Use) a Resume That Gets Results, 1991, rev. ed., 1995. **Address:** Career Seminars & Workshops, 7235 W Wells St., Wauwatosa, WI 53213-3607, U.S.A. **Online address:** dswanson@wi-rr.com

SWANSON, Doug J. American (born United States), b. 1953?. **Genres:** Mystery/Crime/Suspense, Novels, Young Adult Fiction. **Career:** The Dallas Morning News, staff writer, 1982-, bureau chief, 1986-91, investigative journalist; Stanford University, John S. Knight fellow in journalism, 1998-99. **Publications:** JACK FLIPPO MYSTERY NOVELS: Big Town, 1994; Dream Boat, 1995; 96 Tears, 1996; Umbrella Man, 1999; House of Corrections, 2000. Contributor to periodicals. **Address:** c/o Author Mail, HarperCollins Publishers, 10 E 53rd St.,, New York, NY 10022-5299, U.S.A. **Online address:** dswanson@dallasnews.com

SWANSON, Eric. American (born United States) **Genres:** Novels, Theology/Religion. **Career:** Writer. **Publications:** The Greenhouse Effect, 1990; The Boy in the Lake, 1999; (co-author) Karmapa the Sacred Prophecy, 1999; Police Field Guide, 2000; What the Lotus Said: A Journey to Tibet and Back, 2002; (with M. Piazzesi) Futures Prices as Risk-Adjusted Forecasts of Monetary Policy, 2004; (with Y.M. Rinpoche) The Joy of Living: Unlocking the Secret and Science of Happiness, 2007; (with Y.M. Rinpoche) Joyful Wisdom: Embracing Change and Finding Freedom, 2009; Ideal Face, 2009; Ideal Facelift, 2009; Ideal Breast, 2009; Ideal Body, 2009. Contributor to periodicals. **Address:** c/o Author Mail, St. Martins Press, 175 5th Ave., New York, NY 10010, U.S.A.

SWANSON, Gerald J. American (born United States), b. 1940?. **Genres:** Economics, Politics/Government, Education. **Career:** University of Illinois, instructor in economics, 1964-68, Liberal Arts College, assistant dean, 1968-70; University of Arizona, assistant professor of economics, 1970, professor, Thomas R. Brown chair in economic education, Thomas R. Brown chair in economics education emeritus. Writer. **Publications:** The Hyperinflation Survival Guide-Strategies for American Businesses, 1990; (with H.E. Figgie, Jr.) Bankruptcy 1995: The Coming Collapse of America and How to Stop It, 1992; America the Broke: How the Reckless Spending of the White House and Congress is Bankrupting Our Country and Destroying Our Children's Future, 2004. Contributor to journals. **Address:** Eller College of Management, University of Arizona, Rm. 401U, McClelland Hall, 1130 E Helen St., PO Box 210108, Tucson, AZ 85721-0108, U.S.A. **Online address:** swansong@eller.arizona.edu

SWANSON, Heather (Crichton). British/Hong Kong (born Hong Kong), b. 1949. **Genres:** History, Architecture. **Career:** Middle Temple and British Broadcasting Corp., librarian, 1971-76; University of Birmingham, Institute for Advanced Research in the Humanities, fellow, 1987-; Open University, tutor and counselor, 1989-, associate lecturer. Writer. **Publications:** Building Craftsmen in Late Medieval York, 1983; Medieval Artisans: An Urban Class in Late Medieval England, 1989; Medieval British Towns, 1999. Contributor to periodicals. **Address:** Centre for Reformation and Early Modern Studies, University of Birmingham, Edgbaston, Edgbaston, WM B15 2TT, England. **Online address:** swanpeople@blueyonder.co.uk

SWANSON, James L. American (born United States) **Genres:** History, Novels, Mystery/Crime/Suspense, Young Adult Fiction. **Career:** Cato Institute, senior fellow in constitutional studies; U.S. International Trade Commission, assistant; Department of Justice, Office of Legal Counsel, special assistant. Attorney, historian and author. **Publications:** (With K. Essex) Bettie Page: The Life of a Pin-up Legend, 1995; The Stuff That Dreams Are Made Of, 1999; (with D.R. Weinberg) Lincoln's Assassins: Their Trial and Execution: An Illustrated History, 2001; Manhunt: The Twelve-Day Chase for Lincoln's Killer, 2006; Chasing Lincoln's Killer, 2009; Bloody Crimes: The Chase for Jefferson Davis and the Death Pageant for Lincoln's Corpse, 2010; Bloody Times, 2011. Contributor to periodicals. **Address:** c/o Author Mail, HarperCollins Publishing Inc., 10 E 53rd St., New York, NY 10022-5244, U.S.A.

SWANSON, Judith A(nn). American (born United States), b. 1957. **Genres:** Humanities, Philosophy, Politics/Government. **Career:** University of Chicago, writing tutor, 1982-83, teaching assistant, 1983-84; Ethics, editorial assistant, 1982-83; State's Attorney's Office, Division of Juvenile Justice, Repeat Offender Unit, systems analyst, 1984-85; Yale University, lecturer in political philosophy, 1985-86, visiting fellow, 1987; University of Georgia, assistant professor, 1986-88; Boston University, Department of Philosophy, assistant professor of political philosophy, 1988-95, associate professor, 1996-, associated faculty, 1997-; California Institute of Technology, Division of Social Sciences, visiting associate, 1991. **Publications:** The Public and the Private in Aristotle's Political Philosophy, 1992; (with D.C. Corbin) Aristotle's Politics: A Reader's Guide, 2009. Contributor to journals. **Address:** Department of Political Science, Boston University, Rm. PLS 311C, 232 Bay State Rd., Boston, MA 02215-1403, U.S.A. **Online address:** jswanson@bu.edu

SWANSON, June. American (born United States), b. 1931. **Genres:** Children's Non-fiction, History, Business/Trade/Industry. **Career:** Teacher, 1952-54; freelance writer, 1954-. **Publications:** NONFICTION: The Spice of America, 1983; I Pledge Allegiance, 1990, 2nd ed., 2002; David Bushnell and His Turtle: The Story of America's First Submarine, 1991. OTHER: That's for Shore: Riddles from the Beach, 1991; Summit Up: Riddles about Mountains, 1994; Out to Dry: Riddles about Deserts, 1994; Punny Places: Jokes to Make You Mappy, 2004. Contributor to magazines and periodicals. **Address:** 1010 Park Ln., Eagle, ID 83616, U.S.A.

SWANSON, Logan. See **MATHESON, Richard (Burton).**

SWARD, Robert S. (Robert Stuart Sward). American (born United States), b. 1933. **Genres:** Poetry, Autobiography/Memoirs, History, Writing/Journalism, Novels, Gerontology/Senior Issues, Human Relations/Parenting, Humanities, Local History/Rural Topics, Paranormal, Philosophy, Biography, Humor/Satire, Plays/Screenplays, Literary Criticism And History, Theology/Religion, Humor/Satire, Sex. **Career:** Connecticut College, instructor in English, 1958-59; University of Victoria, writer-in-residence, 1969-73; Soft Press, founding editor, 1970-77; Hancock House Publishers, editor, 1976-79; The Toronto Star, reviewer and feature writer, 1980-85; The Globe & Mail, reviewer and feature writer, 1980-85; York University, associate fellow, 1984-; University of California, visiting writer, 1986-; Monterey Peninsula College, visiting writer, 1986-; Cultural Council of Santa Cruz County, visiting writer-in-the-schools, 1986-; Uncle Dog Audio, founder and director, 2002-. **Publications:** Advertisements: Poems, 1958; Uncle Dog and Other Poems, 1962; Kissing the Dancer, 1964; Thousand-Year-Old Fiancee, 1965; In Mexico and Other Poems, 1966; Horgbortom Stringbottom, I Am Yours, You Are History, 1970; Quorum/Noah, 1970; Letter to a Straw Hat, 1974; The Jurassic Shales (novel), 1975; Honey Bear on Lasqueti Island, B.C., 1978; Six Poems, 1980;

Twelve Poems, 1982; Half-a-Life's History: Poems New and Selected, 1983; Movies: Left to Right, 1983; The Toronto Islands: An Illustrated History, 1983; (with R. Priest and R. Zend) The Three Roberts, 1984; Four Incarnations: New and Selected Poems, 1957-1991, 1991; Autobiography in Contemporary Authors Autobiography Series, vol. XIII, 1991, rev. ed., 2003; (with C. Atkinson, T. Shaw and D. Swanger) Family, 1994; A Much-Married Man, A Novel, 1996; Rosicrucian in the Basement & Other Poems, 2001; Heavenly Sex and Other Poems, 2002; The Collected Poems, 1957-2004, 2004; God is in the Cracks, A Narrative in Voices, 2006; New & Selected Poems, 1957-2011. EDITOR: Vancouver Island Poems, 1973; Cheers for Muktananda, 1974; Emily Carr, the Untold Story, 1979. Contributor to periodicals. **Address:** 435 Meder St., PO Box 7062, Santa Cruz, CA 95061, U.S.A. **Online address:** robert@robertsward.com

SWARD, Robert Stuart. See **SWARD, Robert S.**

SWARTZ, Jon David. American (born United States), b. 1934. **Genres:** Novellas/Short Stories, Psychology, Science Fiction/Fantasy, Adult Nonfiction, Literary Criticism And History, Popular Culture, Mythology/Folklore, Mystery/Crime/Suspense, Biography, Art/Art History. **Career:** University of Texas, faculty, 1962-78, Department of psychology, assistant professor, 1969-72, associate professor, 1974-78, chairman, 1974-78, Hogg Foundation, research scientist, 1972-74, chairman of department of anthropology and sociology, 1975-78; National University of Mexico, visiting lecturer, 1962; Current Anthropology, editorial associate, 1971-77; Southwestern University, visiting professor, 1978-82, director of testing and guidance, 1978, 1981, professor of education and psychology, 1978-90, associate dean for libraries and learning resources, 1981-90, series editor, 1985-90; Journal of Personality Assessment, consulting editor, 1981-91; Journal of Biological Psychology, book review editor, 1982-80; Revista Interamericana de Psicologia, book review editor, 1983-90; CCCMHMRS, chief of psychological services, 1990-2000. **Publications:** (With W.H. Holtzman) Inkblot Perception and Personality, 1961; (with C.C. Cleland) Mental Retardation, 1969; (with Cleland) Administrative Issues in Institutions for the Mentally Retarded, 1972; Multihandicapped Mentally Retarded, 1973; Holtzman Inkblot Technique Annotated Bibliography, 1973; (with R. Diaz-Guerrero and W.H. Holtzman) Personality Development in Two Cultures, 1975; (with Cleland and L.W. Talkington) The Profoundly Mentally Retarded: Second Annual Conference Proceedings, 1976; (with R.K. Eyman and Cleland) Research with the Profoundly Retarded, 1978; (with Cleland) Exceptionalities through the Lifespan: An Introduction, 1982; (with Holtzman and R.C. Reinehr) Holtzman Inkblot Technique, 1956-1982: An Annotated Bibliography, 1983; The Osborne Collection of Melville Materials at Southwestern University, 1985; Jessie Daniel Ames: An Exhibition at Southwestern University, 1986; Supplement to Holtzman Annotated Bibliography, 1988; (with Reinehr) Handbook of Old-Time Radio, 1993; (with Reinehr and Holtzman) Holtzman Inkblot Technique Research Guide, 1999; (with J.D. Swartz) Historical Dictionary of Old-Time Radio, 2008; A to Z of Old-Time Radio, 2010; Pseudonyms of Science Fiction, Fantasy, and Horror Authors, 2010. Contributor to periodicals. **Address:** 12115 Missel Thrush Ct., Austin, TX 78750-2101, U.S.A. **Online address:** jon_swartz@hotmail.com

SWARTZ, Mark. American (born United States), b. 1968. **Genres:** Novels, Art/Art History. **Career:** Gale Research Co., editor, 1990-93; University of Chicago Press, staff, 1994-96; American Hospital Association, editor, 1996-97; Museum of Modern Art, writer/editor, 1999-2006; Robin Hood Foundation, communications manager, 2006-10. **Publications:** Artists: From Michelangelo to Maya Lin, 1995; Instant Karma, 2002; H2O: A Novel, 2006. **Address:** New York, NY, U.S.A. **Online address:** swartzmark@yahoo.com

SWASY, Alecia. American (born United States), b. 1963. **Genres:** Documentaries/Reportage, Business/Trade/Industry. **Career:** The Lexington Herald-Leader, staff; Wall Street Journal, staff writer, 1988-, bureau reporter; St. Petersburg Times, assistant managing editor and business editor, 1996-; Dow Jones Newswires, assistant managing editor; Virginian Pilot, deputy managing editor; The News Journal, managing editor. **Publications:** Soap Opera: The Inside Story of Procter and Gamble, 1993; Changing Focus: Kodak and the Battle to Save a Great American Company, 1997. Contributor to journals and periodicals. **Address:** c/o Kris Dahl, International Creative Management, 40 W 57th St., New York, NY 10019, U.S.A.

SWATUK, Larry A(nthony). Canadian (born Canada), b. 1957?. **Genres:** Area Studies, Philosophy. **Career:** University of Windsor, lecturer, 1991-93;

York University, Centre for International Studies, research fellow, 1993-95; African Centre for Development and Strategic Studies, senior research fellow, 1995-96; University of Botswana, lecturer, 1996-2002, associate professor, 2003-07, Harry Oppenheimer Okavango Research Centre, research professor of natural resources governance, 1996-2007; Dalhousie University, adjunct professor, 2007-, Centre for Foreign Policy Studies, visiting research fellow, 2007-08; University of Waterloo, associate professor, 2008-, International Development program, director; University of Western Cape, co-principal investigator. Writer. **Publications:** (With D.R. Black and J.B. Mugyenyi) Foreign Policy in Small States: Botswana, Lesotho, Swaziland and Southern Africa, 1988; Between Choice in a Hard Place: Contending Theories of International Relations, 1991; Re-Making the State: Assessing South Africa's Developmental Agenda, 1998; (with P. Vale) Swimming Upstream: Water and Discourses of Security, 2000. EDITOR and CONTRIBUTOR: (with T.M. Shaw) Prospects for Peace and Development in Southern Africa in the 1990s: Canadian and Comparative Perspectives, 1991; (with T.M. Shaw) The South at the End of the Twentieth Century, 1994; (with D.R. Black) Bridging the Rift: The New South Africa in Africa, 1997; (with P. Vale and B. Oden) Theory, Change and Southern Africa's Future, 2001; Transboundary Water Governance in Southern Africa: Examining Underexplored Dimensions, 2009. **Address:** International Development Program, University of Waterloo, Rm. 224, Environment 1, 200 University Ave. W, Waterloo, ON N2L 3G1, Canada. **Online address:** lswatuk@uwaterloo.ca

SWEARER, Donald K(eeney). American (born United States), b. 1934. **Genres:** Theology/Religion. **Career:** Bangkok Christian College, instructor of English, 1957-60; Edward W. Hazen Foundation, administrative assistant, 1961-63; Oberlin College, instructor and assistant professor, 1965-70; University of Pennsylvania, acting associate professor, 1970-72; Swarthmore College, associate professor, 1970-75, professor of religion, 1975-87, acting chairperson, 1973-74, 1979-80, 1992-93, 1999-2000, chairman of religion department, 1986-91, Eugene M. Lang research professor, 1987-92, Charles and Harriet Cox McDowell professor, 1992-2004, professor emeritus religion; American Broadcasting Co., consultant, 1972; British Broadcasting Co., consultant, 1977; Journal of Asian Studies, assistant editor, 1978-80; University of Pennsylvania, adjunct professor of religious studies, 1979-93; Temple University, adjunct professor of religion, 1992-; University of Hawaii, Numata visiting professor of Buddhist studies, 1993; Harvard Divinity School, Hershey visiting professor of Buddhist studies, 2000-01; Payap University, visiting professor, 2002-04, Center for the Study of World Religions, director and distinguished visiting professor of Buddhist studies, 2004-. Writer. **Publications:** Buddhism in Transition, 1970; (ed.) Secrets of the Lotus: Studies in Buddhist Mediation, 1971; Southeast Asia, 1973; Theology of Dialogue, 1973; Wat Haripuñjaya: A Study of the The Royal Temple of the Buddha's Relic, Lamphun, Thailand, 1976; Buddhism, 1977; Dialogue: The Key to Understanding Other Religions, 1977; Buddhism and Society in South East Asia, 1981; (co-author) Focus on Buddhism: Audio-Visual Resources for Teaching Religion, 1981; Phutthathāt Phikkhu, nakpatirupPhutthasātsanā nai Muang Thai, 1983; The Dhammic Socialism of Buddhadasa Bhikkhu, 1986; (with P. Henry) For the Sake of the World: The Spirit of Buddhist and Christian Monasticism, 1989; The Buddhist World of Southeast Asia, 1995, 2nd ed., 2010; Mountains, Myth and History, 2003; Becoming the Buddha, 2004; (with S. Premchit and P. Dokbuakaew) Sacred Mountains Of Northern Thailand and Their Legends, 2004. EDITOR: Toward the Truth, 1971; (and intro.) Me-and-Mine: Selected Essays of Bhikkhu Buddhadāsa, 1989; (with R. Sizemore) Ethics, Wealth and Salvation, A Study in Buddhist Social Ethics, 1990; The State of Buddhist Studies in the World, 1972-1997, 2000; (with D. Little) Religion and Nationalism in Iraq: A Comparative Perspective, 2006; (with S.L. McGarry) Ecology and the Environment: Perspectives from the Humanities, 2008; (with J.M. Molina and S.L. McGarry) Rethinking the Human, 2010; (with S.L. McGarry) Ecologies of Human Flourishing, 2011. Contributor to journals. **Address:** Hardvard divinity School, Swarthmore College, 45 Francis Ave., Cambridge, MA 02138, U.S.A. **Online address:** dsweare1@swarthmore.edu

SWEDBERG, Richard. American/Swedish (born Sweden), b. 1948. **Genres:** Sociology, Politics/Government, Economics. **Career:** University of Uppsala, researcher in sociology, 1981-85, assistant, 1983-86; University of Stockholm, associate professor of sociology, 1984-96, professor of sociology, 1996-2001; Theory and Society, senior editor, 1999-; Center for Advanced Study in the Behavioral Sciences, fellow, 2001-02; Maison de Science de l'

Homme, fellow, 2001; Cornell University, Center for the Study of Economy and Society, associate director, 2002-, Department of Sociology, professor of sociology, 2002-, director of graduate studies, 2004-08; Sociological Theory, associate editor, 2008-; Copenhagen University, Department of Sociology, adjunct professor, 2009-13, Copenhagen Business School, International Center for Business and Politics, visiting professor, 2009-. **Publications:** Sociology as Disenchantment: The Evolution of the Work of Georges Gurvitch, 1982; (with D.S. Krusé) El Salvador Bibliography and Research Guide, 1982; (intro.) Confidential IMF and World Bank Reports on El Salvador and Nicaragua, 1982; Honduran Trade Union Movement, 1920-1982, 1983; Honduras Bibliography and Research Guide, 1984; Une histoire de la sociologieéconomique, trans. as Economic Sociology: Past and Present, 1987; Economics and Sociology: Redefining their Boundaries: Conversations with Economists and Sociologists, 1990; Economics and Society, 1990; Economics and Sociology of Capitalism, 1991; Joseph A. Schumpeter: His Life and Work, 1991; Schumpeter: A Biography, 1991; (ed. with M. Granovether) Sociology of Economic Life, 1992; (ed.) Explorations in Economic Sociology, 1993; (ed. with N.J. Smelser) Handbook of Economic Sociology, 1994, 2nd ed., 2005; (ed.) Economic Sociology, 1996; Max Weber and the Idea of Economic Sociology, 1998; (ed. with P. Hedstrom) Social Mechanisms: An Analytical Approach to Social Theory, 1998; (ed. with E. Udddhammar) Sociological Endeavor, 1998; (ed. and intro.) Stridsskrifter och Samhällsekonomiska Analyser, 1998; (ed.) Essays in Economic Sociology, 1999; (ed.) Entrepreneurship: The Social Science View, 2000; (ed. with U. Hedtke) Briefe/Letters, 2000; (ed. with M. Granovetter) The Sociology of Economic Life, 2001, 3rd ed., 2011; Principles of Economic Sociology, 2003; Max Weber Dictionary: Key Words and Central Concepts, 2005; Interest, 2005; (ed.) New Developments in Economic Sociology, 2005; Handbook of Economic Sociology, 2005; (ed. with V. Nee) Economic Sociology of Capitalism, 2005; (ed. with V. Nee) On Capitalism, 2007; (ed. with T. Pinch) Living in a Material World: Economic Sociology Meets Science and Technology Studies, 2009; (ed.) Protestant Ethic and the Spirit of Capitalism: The Talcott Parsons Translation Interpretations, 2009; Tocqueville's Political Economy, 2009. **Address:** Department of Sociology, Cornell University, 328 Uris Hall, Ithaca, NY 14853-7601, U.S.A. **Online address:** rs328@cornell.edu

SWEENEY, Aoibheann. American (born United States), b. 1969. **Genres:** Novels, Young Adult Fiction. **Career:** City University of New York, Center for the Humanities, executive director; University of Virginia, MFA Program, Henry Hoyns Fellow. Writer. **Publications:** Among Other Things, I've Taken Up Smoking, 2007. Contributor to periodicals. **Address:** Center for the Humanities, City University of New York, The Graduate Ctr., Rm. 5103, 365 5th Ave., New York, NY 10016-4309, U.S.A. **Online address:** asweeney@gc.cuny.edu

SWEENEY, Eamonn. Irish (born Ireland), b. 1968. **Genres:** Novels, Autobiography/Memoirs. **Career:** Dublin magazine, staff journalist; Roscommon Champion, journalist, 1987-88; Echo Newspapers, journalist, 1988-92; Rte Radio, researcher, 1995-96; full time writer, 1996-. **Publications:** There's Only One Red Army (memoir), 1997; Waiting for the Healer (novel), 1998; The Photograph (novel), 2000. Munster Hurling Legends, 2002; The Road to Croker: A GAA Fanatic on the Championship Trail, 2004; O'Brien Pocket History of Gaelic Sports, 2005; Down Down Deeper and Down: Ireland in the 70s and 80s, 2010. Contributor to periodicals. **Address:** Patricia Kavanagh, Peters, Fraser & Dunlop, 503/4 The Chambers, Chelsea Harbour, London, GL SW10 0XF, England. **Online address:** thephotograph@hotmail.com

SWEENEY, Emma. American (born United States), b. 1956?. **Genres:** Horticulture, Romance/Historical, Photography. **Career:** Harold Ober Associates Inc., literary agent and director. Writer. **Publications:** (With J. O'Connor) The Complete Idiot's Guide to Gardening, 1996, 2nd ed., 1999; Annuals: A Growing Guide for Easy, Colorful Gardens, 1998; Perennials: A Growing Guide for Easy, Colorful Gardens, 1998; (with W. Lemmers) Tulipa: A Photographer's Botanical, 1999; As Always, Jack: A Wartime Love Story, 2002. **Address:** Harold Ober Associates Inc., 425 Madison Ave., Ste. 1001, New York, NY 10017-1183, U.S.A.

SWEENEY, Fionnghuala. British (born England), b. 1968. **Genres:** Biography. **Career:** University of Liverpool, lecturer. Writer. **Publications:** Frederick Douglass and the Atlantic World, 2007; (with D. Dolowitz and S. Buckler) Researching Online, 2008. **Address:** England. **Online address:** fsweeney@liv.ac.uk

SWEENEY, Marvin A. American (born United States), b. 1953. **Genres:** Literary Criticism And History, Theology/Religion. **Career:** University of Jerusalem, Yad Hanadiv/Barecha Foundation, visiting fellow; University of Miami, assistant professor, associate professor of religious studies, 1983-94; Claremont School of Theology, professor of Hebrew Bible, 1994-; Claremont Graduate University, professor of religion, 1994-; Academy for Jewish Religion, professor of Bible, 2000-; Ancient Biblical Manuscript Center for Preservation and Research, CEO; Hebrew University of Jerusalem, faculty; W.F. Albright Institute for Archaeological Research, faculty; Lilly Theological Research Fund, staff; Hebrew Union College-Jewish Institute of Religion, faculty. Writer. **Publications:** Isaiah 1-4 and the Post- exilic Understanding of the Isaianic Tradition, 1988; (ed. with R.F. Melugin) New Visions of Isaiah, 2006; Isaiah 1-39, 1996; (ed. with D.W. Cotter, J.T. Walsh and Chris Franke) The Twelve Prophets, vol. I: Hosea, Joel, Amos, Obadiah, Jonah, vol. II: Micah, Nahum, Habakkuk, Zephaniah, Malachi, 2000; (ed. with J.D. Nogalski) Reading and Hearing the Book of the Twelve, 2000; King Josiah of Judah: The Lost Messiah of Israel, 2001; (ed. with E.B. Zvi) The Changing Face of Form Criticism for the Twenty-first Century, 2003; Zephaniah: A Commentary, edited by Paul D. Hanson, 2003; The Prophetic Literature, 2005; Form and Intertextuality in Prophetic and Apocalyptic Literature, 2005; I & II Kings: A Commentary, 2007; Reading the Hebrew Bible after the Shoah: Engaging Holocaust Theology, 2008. Contributor of articles to periodicals. **Address:** Claremont School of Theology, 1325 N College Ave., Claremont, CA 91711, U.S.A. **Online address:** marvin.sweeney@cgu.edu

SWEENEY, Matthew. British/Irish (born Ireland), b. 1952. **Genres:** Children's Fiction, Poetry, Education, Young Adult Fiction. **Career:** Farnham College, writer-in-residence, 1984-85; West Surrey College of Art and Design, external adviser in creative writing, 1986-89; Poetry Society, publicist and events assistant, 1988-90; Hereford & Worcester, poet-in-residence, 1991; South Bank Center, writer-in-residence, 1994-95. **Publications:** Without Shores, 1978; A Dream of Maps, 1981; A Round House, 1983; The Lame Waltzer, 1985; Blue Shoes, 1989; (ed.) One for Jimmy: An Anthology from the Hereford and Worcester Poetry Project, 1992; Cacti, 1992; The Blue Taps, 1994; (ed. with J. Shapcott) Emergency Kit: Poems For Strange Times, 1996; (ed. with K. Smith) Beyond Bedlam: Poems Written out of Mental Distress, 1997; The Bridal Suite, 1997; (with J.H. Williams) Write Poetry and Get it Published, 1997; (with J. Shapcott and H. Dunmore) Penguin Modern Poets 12, 1997; Smell of Fish, 2000; (ed.) The New Faber Book of Children's Verse, 2001; Where Fishermen Can't Swim, 2001; Selected Poems, 2002; (ed.) Irish Poems, 2005; Selected Poems of Walter de la Mare, 2006; Stories, 2006; Night Post: A New Selection, 2010. FOR CHILDREN: The Chinese Dressing-Gown, 1987; The Snow Vulture, 1992; The Flying Spring Onion, 1992; Fatso in the Red Suit, 1995; Up on the Roof, 2001; The Man with the Fox, 2002; Sanctuary, 2004; Black Moon, 2007. **Address:** Jonathan Cape Ltd., Random House UK Ltd., 20 Vauxhall Bridge Rd., London, GL SW1V 2SA, England. **Online address:** matthewsweeney@writersartists.net

SWEENEY, Terrance (Allen). American (born United States), b. 1945. **Genres:** Theology/Religion, Plays/Screenplays, Novels, Young Adult Nonfiction. **Career:** Ordained Catholic priest, 1973; Paulist Productions, writer and creative consultant, 1974-75, producer, 1975-77, producer and director of development, 1980-83, senior vice president; Jesuit Media Associates, president, 1983-84; Michael Media, president, 1985-. Actor. **Publications:** Streets of Anger, Streets of Hope: Youth Gangs in East Los Angeles (nonfiction), 1980; God and (nonfiction), 1985; A Church Divided: The Vatican versus American Catholics (nonfiction), 1992; (with P.S. Sweeney) What God Hath Joined: The Real Life Love Story That Shook the Catholic Church (nonfiction), 1993. **Address:** Michael Media Inc., 3935 Benedict Canyon Dr., Sherman Oaks, CA 91423, U.S.A.

SWEET, O. Robin. American (born United States), b. 1952. **Genres:** Self Help, Food And Wine. **Career:** Nanny Connection, founder, president, 1983-87; SweetBloom Productions, partner; The Well Fed Baby Inc., president and co-founder, Spectrum College Transition Program, executive director; Country School Inc., president and co-owner; writer, 1985-. **Publications:** The Original Nanny Cookbook, 1985; The Nanny Connection Coloring Calendar, 1985; (with M.E. Siegel) The Nanny Connection, 1987; (with P. Bryan) Working Woman's Lamaze Handbook: The Essential Guide to Pregnancy, Lamaze, and Childbirth, 1992; (with T.A. Bloom) The Well-Fed Baby, 1994; (with P. Bryan) Adopt International: Everything You Need to Know to Adopt a Child from Abroad, 1996. **Address:** Spectrum College Transition Program, 7655 E Gelding Dr., Ste. A-3, Scottsdale, AZ 85260, U.S.A.

SWEET, William. Canadian (born Canada), b. 1955?. **Genres:** Philosophy, Theology/Religion, Ethics. **Career:** Canadian Philosophical Association, president; Canadian Jacques Maritain Association, president; University of Ottawa, lecturer, 1979-80, 1983-85, 1987-88; University of Saskatchewan, Saint Thomas More College, lecturer, 1980-83; Carleton University, lecturer, 1989-90; St. Francis Xavier University, assistant professor, 1990-95, associate professor, 1995-2000, professor of philosophy, 1990-, Centre for Philosophy, Theology and Cultural Traditions, director; Catholic University, Hoover chair of economic and social ethics, 1996; Dominican College of Philosophy, research professor, 1999-, adjunct professor in the graduate programmes; Saint Paul University, research professor, 2004-, adjunct professor in the graduate programmes; Saint Thomas University, professor of philosophy and professor of religious studies, 2007-, vice president, 2007-08; University of New Brunswick, adjunct professor in the graduate programmes; World Union of Catholic Philosophical Societies, president; Istituto Internazionale Jacques Maritain, president; John Paul II Catholic University, visiting professor; Soochow University, visiting professor; University of Pune, visiting professor. Writer. **Publications:** Venice of America: The American Dream Come True, 1976; Idealism and Rights, 1997; Science, Religion, and Non-Science, 2003; Religious Belief: The Contemporary Debate, 2003; (with H. Hart) Responses to the Enlightenment: Foundations, Faith, and Community, 2009. EDITOR: God and Argument, 1999; The Collected Works of Bernard Bosanquet, 20 vols., 1999; The Bases of Ethics, 2001; (with G.F. Gaus) The Philosophical Theory of the State and Related Essays by Bernard Bosanquet, 2001; Natural Law: Reflections on Theory and Practice by Jacques Maritain, 2001; Idealism, Metaphysics, and Community, 2001; Philosophy, Culture, and Pluralism, 2002; Bernard Bosanquet: Essays in Philosophy and Social Policy, 1883-1922, 3 vols., 2003; Philosophical Theory and the Universal Declaration of Human Rights, 2003; (with E.E. Harris) The Philosophical Remains of Arthur Ritchie Lord, vol. I: Foundational Problems in Philosophy: Politics, Ethics, Aesthetics, and Religion, vol. II: The History of Philosophy from Descartes to Hegel; vol. III: The Principles of Politics, 2006; The Philosophy of History, 2004; Approaches to Metaphysics, 2004; Politics, Ethics, and the Challenges to Democracy in the New Independent States, 2005; Freedom of Religions, 2006; Philosophy of Religion (Proceedings of XXI World Congress of Philosophy), 2006; Kicking the Carbon Habit: Global Warming and the Case for Renewable and Nuclear Energy, 2006; Bernard Bosanquet and the Legacy of British Idealism, 2007; Religion and the Challenges of Science, 2007; Dialogue of Cultural Traditions, 2008; (ed. with P. Van Duc) Rethinking the Role of Philosophy in the Global Age, 2009; (ed.) Biographical Encyclopedia of British Idealism, 2010. Contributor of articles to journals. **Address:** Department of Philosophy, St. Francis Xavier University, PO Box 5000, Antigonish, NS B2G 2W5, Canada. **Online address:** wsweet@stfx.ca

SWENSON, Kristin M. American (born United States) **Genres:** Social Sciences. **Career:** Virginia Commonwealth University, School of World Studies, assistant professor of religious studies. Writer, theologian and educator. **Publications:** Living through Pain: Psalms and the Search for Wholeness, 2005. **Address:** Virginia Commonwealth University, Rm. 203, 312 N Shafer St., Richmond, VA 23220, U.S.A. **Online address:** kswenson@vcu.edu

SWETMAN, Glenn R(obert). American (born United States), b. 1936. **Genres:** Poetry, Novellas/Short Stories, History, Young Adult Fiction. **Career:** Arkansas State University, instructor in English, 1958-59; McNeese State University, instructor in English, 1959-61; Mississippi State Times, book reviewer and literary consultant, 1961-64; University College of Tulane University, instructor, 1961-64; University of Southern Mississippi, assistant professor, 1964-66; Louisiana Technical University, associate professor, 1966-67; Nicholls State University, professor of English, 1967-, now professor emeritus; State University, Department of English, head, 1968-71, professor of English, 1971-91; William Carey College, writer-in-residence and professor of literature, 1971-91, associate professor emeritus; Nicholls Paon Press, consulting editor, 1974-. **Publications:** (With C. Whittington and W. Sullivan) Poems from the McNeese Review, 1961; (with W. Read and J.R. Swetman) The Pagan Christmas, 1962; Tunel de Amor, 1973; Deka No. 1: Poems, 1973; Shards, 1979; Deka No. 2, 1979; Concerning Carpenters and Childhood Saints & Other Poems, 1980; Son of Igor, 1980; Poems of the Fantastic, 1992; (with G.L. Swetman) Biloxi: A Bankers Daybook: An Outline of the History of Biloxi, Mississippi, the Swetman Family and the Peoples Bank, 1994. **Address:** William Carey College on the Coast, 1856 Beach Dr., Gulfport, MS 39507, U.S.A.

SWETT, Pamela E. Canadian (born Canada), b. 1970. **Genres:** Intellectual History, History, Politics/Government, Humanities. **Career:** McMaster University, assistant professor of history, associate professor and chair. Writer and historian. **Publications:** Neighbors and Enemies: The Culture of Radicalism in Berlin, 1929-1933, 2004; (ed. with J.R. Zatlin and S.J. Wiesen) Selling Modernity: Advertising in Twentieth-Century Germany, 2007; (ed. with C. Ross and F. d'Almeida) Pleasure and Power in Nazi Germany, 2011. **Address:** Department of History, McMaster University, 619 Chester New Hall, 1280 Main St. W, Hamilton, ON L8S 4L9, Canada. **Online address:** swettp@mcmaster.ca

SWETZ, Frank J. American (born United States), b. 1937. **Genres:** Sciences, History, Mathematics/Statistics, Writing/Journalism, Education. **Career:** Daystrom Electric Co., mechanical Designer, 1957-58; Ford Instrument Co., test engineer, 1958-60; Marist College, instructor, 1963-64; U.S. Peace Corps, teacher trainer, 1964-67; Columbia University, Teachers College, instructor, 1967-69; Pennsylvania State University, School of Science, Engineering and Technology, instructor in mathematics and education, 1969-72, assistant professor, 1972-75, associate professor, 1975-80; professor, 1980-, now professor emeritus; Technical University of Malaysia, consultant; U.S. Office of Education, consultant; Addison-Wesley Publishing Co., consultant; Convergence, co-founding editor. **Publications:** Mathematics Education in China: Its Growth and Development, 1974; (with T.I. Kao) Was Pythagoras Chinese?: An Examination of Right Triangle Theory in Ancient China, 1977; (ed.) Socialist Mathematics Education, 1978; The Mathematics Laboratory in the Elementary School: What? Why? and How?, 1981; Capitalism and Arithmetic: The New Math of the 15th Century, 1987; (ed. with J.S. Hartzler) Mathematical Modeling in the Secondary School Curriculum: A Resource Guide of Classroom Exercises, 1991; The Sea Island Mathematical Manual, 1992; (ed.) From Five Fingers to Infinity: A Journey through the History of Mathematics, 1994; (co-ed.) Learn from the Masters!, 1995; The Legacy of the Luoshu, 2002; Mathematical Expeditions: Exploring Word Problems Across the Ages, 2012. Contributor of articles to journals. **Address:** Department of Computer Science and, Mathematical Sciences, Pennsylvania State University, W-256 Olmsted Bldg., 777 Harrisburg Pke., Middletown, PA 17057, U.S.A. **Online address:** fjs2@psu.edu

SWICK, Marly. American (born United States), b. 1949. **Genres:** Language/Linguistics, Novellas/Short Stories, Young Adult Fiction, Novels. **Career:** University of Missouri, Department of English, professor, 1987-; University of Nebraska, associate professor of fiction writing, 1987-. Writer. **Publications:** A Hole in the Language, 1990; Monogamy: Stories, 1992; The Summer Before the Summer of Love: Stories, 1995; Paper Wings, 1996; Evening News: A Novel, 1999. Contributor of articles to periodicals. **Address:** Department of English, University of Missouri, 222 Tate, 365 McReynolds Hall, Columbia, MO 65211-1500, U.S.A. **Online address:** swickm@missouri.edu

SWICK, Thomas. American (born United States), b. 1952. **Genres:** Travel/Exploration, Biography, History. **Career:** Trenton Times, feature writer, 1977-79; English Language College, teacher of English, 1980-82; Providence Journal, editorial writer, 1987-89; Sun-Sentinel, travel editor, 1989-; American College of Physicians, feature writer. **Publications:** Unquiet Days: At Home in Poland, 1991; A Way to See the World: From Texas to Transylvania with a Maverick Traveler, 2003. Works appear in antologies. **Address:** Sun-Sentinel, 200 E Las Olas Blvd., Fort Lauderdale, FL 33301-2293, U.S.A. **Online address:** swickt@bellsouth.net

SWIDEY, Neil. American (born United States) **Genres:** Adult Non-fiction, Biography. **Career:** Boston Globe Magazine, staff writer; Times Herald-Record, assistant managing editor; Boston Globe Magazine, editor and staff writer, Sunday Magazine, metro editor. **Publications:** The Assist: Hoops, Hope, and the Game of Their Lives, 2008; Last Lion: The Fall and Rise of Ted Kennedy, 2009. Works appear in anthologies. **Address:** c/o Sarah Chalfant, The Wylie Agency, 250 W 57th St., Ste. 2114, New York, NY 10107, U.S.A. **Online address:** neil@theassist.net

SWIDLER, Ann. American (born United States), b. 1944. **Genres:** Education, Sociology, Psychology, Philosophy, Theology/Religion. **Career:** Harvard University, Department of Sociology, assistant professor, 1975-79; Stanford University, Department of Sociology, assistant professor, 1979-87; University of California, Department of Sociology, associate professor, 1987-96, professor, 1996-. Writer. **Publications:** Organization Without Authority: Dilemmas of Social Control in Free Schools, 1979; (co-author) Habits of the

Heart: Individualism and Commitment in American Life, 1985; (co-author) The Good Society, 1991; (co-author) Inequality by Design: Cracking the Bell Curve Myth, 1996; Talk of Love: How Culture Matters, 2001; (co-ed.) Meaning and Modernity, 2001. Contributor to periodicals. **Address:** Department of Sociology, University of California, 404b Barrows Hall, Berkeley, CA 94720-1980, U.S.A. **Online address:** swidler@berkeley.edu

SWIERENGA, Robert P. American/Dutch (born Netherlands), b. 1935. **Genres:** History, Local History/Rural Topics, Social Sciences, Theology/Religion, Genealogy/Heraldry, Geography, Translations. **Career:** Pella Christian High School, instructor in social studies, 1958-61; Calvin College, visiting lecturer, 1961, assistant professor of history, 1965-68; Kent State University, associate professor of history, 1968-72, professor of history, 1972-96, professor emeritus, 1996-; Hope College, A.C. Van Raalte Institute, research professor of history, 1996-. Writer. **Publications:** Pioneers and Profits: Land Speculation on the Iowa Frontier, 1968; Dutch Emigration Records, 1847-1877: A Computer Alphabetical Listing of Heads of Household and Independent Persons, 1974; Acres for Cents: Delinquent Tax Auctions in Frontier Iowa, 1976; (with Y. Schreuder) Catholic Emigration from the Southern Provinces of The Netherlands in the Nineteenth Century, 1982; (comp.) Dutch Immigrants in U.S. Ship Passenger Manifests, 1820-1880: An Alphabetical Listing by Household Heads and Independent Persons, 1983; (comp.) Dutch Emigrants to the United States, South Africa, South America, and Southeast Asia, 1835-1880: An Alphabetical Listing by Household Heads and Independent Persons, 1983; (comp.) Dutch Households in U.S. Population Censuses, 1850, 1860, 1870: An Alphabetical Listing by Family Heads, 1987; The Forerunners: Dutch Jewry in the North American Diaspora, 1994; (with E. Bruins) Family Quarrels in the Dutch Reformed Churches in the Nineteenth Century, 1999; Faith and Family: Dutch Immigration and Settlement in the United States, 1820-1920, 2000; Dutch Chicago: A History of the Hollanders in the Windy City, 2002; Elim: A Chicago Christian School and Life-Training Center for the Disabled, 2005. EDITOR: Quantification in American History: Theory and Research, 1970; Beyond the Civil War Synthesis: Political Essays of the Civil War Era, 1975; (with J.W.S. Nordholt) Bilateral Bicentennial: A History of Dutch-American Relations 1782-1982, 1982; History and Ecology: Studies of the Grassland, 1984; (J. van Hinte) Netherlanders in America: A Study of Emigration and Settlement in the Nineteenth and Twentieth Centuries in the United States of America, 1985; The Dutch in America: Immigration, Settlement, and Cultural Change, 1985; (with P. Vandermeer) Belief and Behavior: Essays in the New Religious History, 1991; For Food and Faith: Dutch Immigration to Western Michigan, 1846-1960, 2000; (J. Stellingwerff) Iowa Letters: Dutch Immigrants on the American Frontier, 2004; (with D. Sinnema and H. Krabbedam) The Dutch in Urban America, 2004; (with P. Fessler and H.R. Krygsma) Dutch Immigrants on the Plains, 2006; (with W. van Appledorn) Old Wing Mission: Cultural Interchange as Chronicled by George and Arvilla Smith in Their Work With Chief Wakazoo's Ottawa Band on the West Michigan Frontier, 2008; (with J.E. Nyenhuis and N. Kennedy) Dutch-American Arts and Letters in Historical Perspective, 2008; (with J.E. Nyenhuis and L.M. Berka) Aunt Tena, Called to Serve: Journals and Letters of Tena A. Huizenga, Missionary Nurse to Nigeria, 2009; (with J.E. Nyenhuis and S.M. Sinke) Across Borders: Dutch Immigration to North America and Australia, 2010. Contributor to journals. **Address:** A.C. Van Raalte Institute, Hope College, 9 E 10 St., PO Box 9000, Holland, MI 49422-9000, U.S.A. **Online address:** swierenga@hope.edu

SWIFT, Donald C. American (born United States), b. 1937. **Genres:** History. **Career:** Edinboro University, Department of History & Anthropology, professor of history, 1968-99, professor emeritus, 1999-, Friends of the Baron-Forness Library, board director, board secretary and treasurer. Writer. **Publications:** Politics and Society in America, 1607-1865, 1976; Religion and the American Experience: A Social and Cultural History, 1765-1997, 1998. **Address:** Department of History & Anthropology, Edinboro University, 235 Scotland Rd., Hendricks Hall 146, Edinboro, PA 16444, U.S.A. **Online address:** swiftdon@edinboro.edu

SWIFT, Graham. (Graham Colin Swift). British (born England), b. 1949. **Genres:** Novels, Novellas/Short Stories, Mystery/Crime/Suspense, Biography, Literary Criticism And History, Autobiography/Memoirs. **Career:** Teacher, 1974-83. Writer. **Publications:** The Sweet Shop Owner, 1980; Shuttlecock, 1981; Learning to Swim and Other Stories, 1982; Waterland, 1983; (ed. and intro. with D. Profumo) The Magic Wheel: An Anthology of Fishing in Literature, 1985; Out of This World, 1988; Ever After, 1992; Last Orders, 1996; The Light of Day, 2003; Tomorrow, 2007; (co-author) Poolside, 2007;

Chemistry, 2008; Making an Elephant: Writing from Within, 2009; Wish You Were Here, 2011. **Address:** A.P. Watt Ltd., 20 John St., London, GL WC1N 2DR, England.

SWIFT, Graham Colin. See **SWIFT**, Graham.

SWIFT, Jamie. Canadian (born Canada), b. 1951?. **Genres:** Local History/ Rural Topics, Business/Trade/Industry, Economics. **Career:** Whig Standard, reporter. Journalist. **Publications:** The Big Nickel: Inco at Home and Abroad, 1977; Cut and Run: The Assault on Canada's Forests, 1983; (with M. Czerny) Getting Started on Social Analysis in Canada, 1984; Odd Man Out: The Life and Times of Eric Kierans, 1988; (ed. with B. Tomlinson) Conflicts of Interest: Canada and the Third World, 1991; Wheel of Fortune: Work and Life in the Age of Falling Expectations, 1995; Civil Society in Question, 1999; Walking the Union Walk: Stories from CEP's First Ten Years, 2003; (with K. Stewart) Hydro: The Deline and Fall of Ontario's Electric Empire, 2004; (with B. Balmer and M. Dineen) Persistent Poverty: Voices from the Margins, 2010. **Address:** c/o Author Mail, Between the Lines, 720 Bathurst St., Ste. 404, Toronto, ON M5S 2R4, Canada.

SWIFT, Rachel. See **MASTERS**, Alexander.

SWIFT, Sue. American (born United States), b. 1955?. **Genres:** Romance/ Historical, Humor/Satire, Literary Criticism And History. **Career:** Trial attorney, 1981-2001. Writer. **Publications:** Hopelessly Compromised, 2000; His Baby, Her Heart, 2001; The Ranger & the Rescue, 2002; In the Sheikh's Arms, 2003; Engaged to the Sheik, 2005; Triangle, 2006; Walk Like a Man, 2006; Spy Game, 2008; Puckheads, 2009; Fashion Victim, 2011. **Address:** PO Box 241, Citrus Heights, CA 95611-0241, U.S.A. **Online address:** suzswift@yahoo.com

SWIFT, Will. American (born United States), b. 1947. **Genres:** History, Biography. **Career:** Clinical psychologist, 1978. Writer. **Publications:** The Roosevelts and the Royals: Franklin and Eleanor, the King and Queen of England, and the Friendship That Changed History, 2004; The Kennedys amidst the Gathering Storm: A Thousand Days in London, 1938-1940, 2008. Contributor to periodicals. **Address:** John Wiley & Sons Inc., 111 River St., Hoboken, NY 07030, U.S.A. **Online address:** drwswift@gmail.com

SWILLER, Josh. American (born United States) **Genres:** Humanities, Biography, Autobiography/Memoirs, Speech/Rhetoric. **Career:** Peace Corps, officer, 1994-96; Gallaudet University, visiting professor. Writer. **Publications:** The Unheard: A Memoir of Deafness and Africa, 2007. Contributor to periodicals. **Address:** New York City, NY , U.S.A. **Online address:** joshswiller@gmail.com

SWINBURNE, Richard (Granville). British (born England), b. 1934. **Genres:** Philosophy, Theology/Religion. **Career:** St. John's College, Fereday Fellow, 1958-61; University of Leeds, Leverhulme research fellow in the history and philosophy of science, 1961-63; University of Hull, lecturer in philosophy, 1963-69, senior lecturer, 1969-72; University of Maryland, visiting associate professor of philosophy, 1969-70; University of Keele, professor of philosophy, 1972-85; Oxford University, Wilde lecturer in natural and comparative religion, 1975-78, Nolloth professor of the philosophy of the Christian religion, 1985-2002, emeritus Nolloth professor of the philosophy of the Christian religion, 2002-; University of Aberdeen, Gifford lecturer, 1983-84; University of Liverpool, Forwood lecturer in the history and philosophy of religion, 1977; Exeter College, Marrett Memorial lecturer, 1980; University of London, special lecturer, 1981; University of Aberdeen, Gifford lecturer, 1982-84; University College, theology lecturer, 1983; Syracuse University, visiting professor of philosophy, 1987; University of Birmingham, Edward Cadbury lecturer, 1987; St Louis University, Wade Memorial lecturer, 1990; Penn State University., Dotterer Lecturer, 1992; Marquette University, Aquinas lecturer, 1997; University of Minnesota, Paul Holmer lecturer, 2006; Stetson University, Lawson lecturer, 2008; Oriel College, emeritus fellow. Writer. **Publications:** Space and Time, 1968, 2nd ed., 1981; The Concept of Miracle, 1970; An Introduction to Confirmation Theory, 1973; (ed.) The Justification of Induction, 1974; The Coherence of Theism, 1977, rev. ed., 1993; The Existence of God, 1979, 2nd ed., 2004; Faith and Reason, 1981, 2nd ed., 2005; (ed.) Space, Time and Causality, 1983; (with S. Shoemaker) Personal Identity, 1984; The Evolution of the Soul, 1986, rev. ed., 1997; Responsibility and Atonement, 1989; (ed.) Miracles, 1989; Revelation: From Metaphor to Analogy, 1992, 2nd ed., 2007; The Christian God, 1994; Is

There a God?, 1996, 2nd ed., 2010; Simplicity as Evidence of Truth, 1997; Providence and the Problem of Evil, 1998; Epistemic Justification, 2001; (ed.) Bayes's Theorem, 2002; The Resurrection of God Incarnate, 2003; Was Jesus God?, 2008. Contributor to journals. **Address:** Oriel College, University of Oxford, Oriel Sq., Oxford, OX OX1 4EW, England. **Online address:** richard.swinburne@oriel.ox.ac.uk

SWINDELLS, Robert (Edward). British (born England), b. 1939. **Genres:** Novellas/Short Stories, Children's Fiction, Picture/Board Books, Young Adult Non-fiction, Novels, History, Translations. **Career:** Telegraph and Argus, copyholder, 1954-57, advertising clerk, 1960-67; Hepworth & Grandage, engineer, 1967-69; Undercliffe First, teacher, 1972-77; Southmere First, part-time teacher, 1977-80; writer, 1980-. **Publications:** When Darkness Comes, 1973; A Candle in the Night, 1974; Voyage to Valhalla, 1976; The Very Special Baby, 1977; The Ice Palace, 1977; Dragons Live Forever, 1978; The Weather Clerck, 1979; The Moonpath and Other Stories, 1979 in US as The Moonpath and Other Tales of the Bizarre, 1983; Norah's Ark, 1979; Norah's Shark, 1979; You're a Sly One, 1979; Ghost Ship to Ganymede, 1980; Norah and the Whale, 1981; Norah to the Rescue, 1981; World Eater, 1981; The Wheaton Book of Science Fiction Stories, 1982; Night School, 1983; Brother in the Land, 1985; The Thousand Eyes of Night, 1985; The Ghost Messengers, 1986; Staying Up, 1986; Mavis Davis, 1988; The Postbox Mystery, 1988; A Serpent's Tooth, 1989; Night School, 1989; Room 13, 1989; Daz 4 Zoe, 1990; Follow a Shadow, 1990; Tim Kipper, 1990; Dracula's Castle, 1991; Hydra, 1991; Rolf and Rosie, 1992; You Can't Say I'm Crazy, 1992; Fallout, 1992; The Go-Ahead Gang, 1992; Inside the Worm, 1993; Sam and Sue and Lavatory Lou, 1993; The Secret of Weeping Wood, 1993; The Siege of Firmly Prim, 1993; We Didn't Mean to, Honest!, 1993; Stone Cold, 1994; Timesnatch, 1994; Kidnap at Denton Farm, 1994; The Muckitups, 1995; The Ghosts of Givenham Keep, 1995; Unbeliever, 1995; Jacqueline Hyde, 1996; Last Bus, 1996; Hurricane Summer, 1997; Nightmare Stairs, 1997; Peril in the Mist, 1997; Smash!, 1997; Abomination, 1998; The Strange Tale of Ragger Bill, 1998; Dosh, 1999; Roger's War, 1999; The Orchard Book of Vikings, 1999; The Orchard Book of Egyptian Gods and Pharaohs, 2000; The Orchard Book of Stories from Ancient Egypt, 2000; Invisible!, 2000; Doodlebug Alley, 2000; A Wish for Wings, 2001; Wrecked, 2001; Egyptian Gods and Pharaohs, 2001; Blitzed, 2002; No Angels, 2003; Ruby Tanya, 2004; Roger's War, 2004; Branded, 2005; Snapshot, 2005; Snakebite, 2006; In the Nick of Time, 2007; Burnout, 2007; The Shade of Hettie Daynes, 2008; The Tunnel, 2008; Knife-Edge, 2008; Shrapnel, 2009; A Midsummer Night's Dream, 2009; The First Hunter, 2009; Just a Bit of Fun, 2009; Henry V, 2010; Dan's War, 2010; Blackout, 2011; A Skull in Shadows Lane, 2012. TRANSLATOR: ALFIE SERIES BY G. BERGSTROM: Alfie and His Secret Friend, 1979; Who'll Save Alfie Atkins?, 1979; Alfie and the Monster, 1979; You're a Sly One, Alfie Atkins, 1979; Is That a Monster, Alfie Atkins?, 1989. Contributor to books. **Address:** 4 Spring Row, Denholme Rd., Oxenhope, Keighley, WY BD22 9NR, England.

SWINFEN, Ann. Scottish/American (born United States) **Genres:** Novels, Literary Criticism And History, Young Adult Non-fiction, History. **Career:** Writer. **Publications:** NON-FICTION: In Defence of Fantasy: A Study of the Genre in English and American Literature since 1945, 1984. NOVELS: The Anniversary, 1996; The Travellers, 1997; A Running Tide, 1998; Mere Incidents Of War, 1999; The Testament of Mariam, 2009. **Address:** c/o Judith Murray, Greene & Heaton Ltd., 37 Goldhawk Rd., London, GL W12 8QQ, England. **Online address:** ann.swinfen@onet.co.uk

SWINTON, Elizabeth de Sabato. American (born United States), b. 1937. **Genres:** Art/Art History, Biography, History. **Career:** Tufts University, assistant professor, 1977-84; Worcester Art Museum, research curator for Asiatic art, 1978-81, consulting curator, 1981-84, curator of Asian art, 1985-2001, director of curatorial affairs, 1995-2001; Harvard University, Edwin O. Reischauer Institute of Japanese Studies, research associate, 1980-, lecturer, 1981-. Writer. **Publications:** The Graphic Art of Onchi Koshiro (1891-1955): Innovation and Tradition, 1985; The Women of the Pleasure Quarter: Painting and Prints of the Floating World, 1995; Terrific Tokyo: A Panorama in Prints, 1999. Contributor to periodicals. **Address:** 121 Suffolk Rd., Chestnut Hill, MA 02467, U.S.A.

SWITZER, Jacqueline Vaughn. See VAUGHN, Jacqueline.

SWITZER, Janet. American (born United States), b. 1963. **Genres:** Business/Trade/Industry, Theology/Religion, Self Help. **Career:** Leading Experts Magazine, founder and editor. Writer. **Publications:** (With J. Canfield) The Success Principles: How to Get from Where You Are to Where You Want to Be, 2005; Instant Income: Strategies That Bring in the Cash for Small Businesses, Innovative Employees and Occasional Entrepreneurs, 2007. **Address:** Success Resources Intl., 107 N Reino Rd., Ste. 415, Newbury Park, CA 91320, U.S.A. **Online address:** clientservices@janetswitzer.com

SWITZER, Les. American (born United States), b. 1935. **Genres:** Communications/Media, History, Politics/Government, Theology/Religion. **Career:** Journalist, 1964-72; California State University, assistant professor of journalism and broadcasting and department head, 1972-73; Rhodes University, lecturer, 1972-76, senior lecturer, 1977-79, professor of journalism and media studies, 1980-83, department head, 1979-82; University of Houston, adjunct professor, professor of communication, 1983-2004, professor of African-American studies, 1983-86, Telecommunications Research Institute, associate director, 1985-86, professor of history, 1987-90, Center for Critical Cultural Studies, co-founder and co-director, 1990-96, head of journalism area, 1993-98, professor emeritus of communication. **Publications:** Politics and Communication in the Ciskei, 1979; (with D. Switzer) The Black Press in South Africa and Lesotho, 1836-1976, 1979; Media and Dependency in South Africa, 1985; Media Studies and the Critique of Development, 1987; Power and Resistance in an African Society: The Ciskei Xhosa and the Making of South Africa, 1993; South Africa's Alternative Press, 1880-1960, 1997; (with M. Adhikari) South Africa's Resistance Press, 2000; God in the Corridors of Power: Christian Conservatives, the Media and Politics in America, 2009. Works appear in anthologies. Contributor to journals and newspapers. **Address:** School of Communication, University of Houston, Rm. 101, Communications Bldg, Houston, TX 77204-3002, U.S.A. **Online address:** lswitzer@uh.edu

SWOPE, Sam. American (born United States) **Genres:** Children's Fiction, Children's Non-fiction, Education, inspirational/Motivational Literature, Literary Criticism And History, Writing/Journalism, Autobiography/Memoirs, Documentaries/Reportage, Essays, Humor/Satire, Picture/Board Books, Novels, Young Adult Non-fiction. **Career:** New York Public Library, Cullman Center Institute, dean. Writer. **Publications:** The Araboolies of Liberty Street, 1989; (ed. with D.L. Goddard) Saving Wildlife: A Century of Conservation, 1995; (with K. Arnold) Katya's Book of Mushrooms, 1997; The Krazees, 1997; Gotta Go! Gotta Go!, 2000; Jack and the Seven Deadly Giants, 2004; I Am a Pencil: A Teacher, His Kids, and Their World of Stories, 2004; Jack and the Seven Deadly Giants, 2004. Contributor to periodicals. **Address:** c/o Author Mail, Farrar Straus & Giroux Inc., 19 Union Sq. W, New York, NY 10003, U.S.A. **Online address:** readermail@samswope.org

SWORD, Wiley. American (born United States), b. 1937. **Genres:** History, Military/Defense/Arms Control, Literary Criticism And History. **Career:** Techni-Cast Inc., Automotive and Industrial supplies, manufacturer's agent, 1960-, president, 1960-2000, now retired. Writer. **Publications:** Shiloh: Bloody April, 1974, rev. ed., 2001; President Washington's Indian War, 1985; Firepower from Abroad, 1986; Sharpshooter: Hiram Berdan, His Famous Sharpshooters, and Their Sharps Rifles, 1988; Embrace an Angry Wind, 1991; Confederacy's Last Hurrah: Spring Hill, Franklin and Nashville, 1993; Mountains Touched with Fire, 1995; Southern Invincibility, 1999; The Historic Henry Rifle, 2002; Courage Under Fire: Profiles in Bravery from the Battlefields of the Civil War, 2007. **Address:** 5640 Kolly Rd., Bloomfield Hills, MI 48301, U.S.A. **Online address:** wileysword@msn.com

SYAL, Meera. Indian (born India), b. 1961. **Genres:** Novels, Plays/Screenplays, Literary Criticism And History, Young Adult Fiction. **Career:** Novelist, journalist and screenwriter. **Publications:** NOVELS: Anita and Me, 1996; Life Isn't all Ha Ha Hee Hee, 2000; Sari, Jeans und Chilischoten, 2003. Contributor to periodicals. **Address:** c/o New Press, 450 West 41st St., New York, NY 10036, U.S.A.

SYDOR, Colleen. Canadian (born Canada), b. 1960?. **Genres:** Children's Fiction, Social Commentary, Human Relations/Parenting. **Career:** Writer and floral designer. **Publications:** Ooo-cha!, 1999; Smarty Pants, 1999; Fashion Fandango, 2000; Maxwell's Metamorphosis, 2000; Camilla Chameleon, 2005; Raising a Little Stink, 2006; My Mother Is a French Fry and Further Proof of My Fuzzed-up Life, 2008; Timmerman Was Here, 2009. **Address:** Tundra Books, 75 Sherbourne St. 5th Fl., Toronto, ON M5A 2P9, Canada. **Online address:** sydor123@mts.net

SYKES, Charles J. American (born United States), b. 1954?. **Genres:** Education. **Career:** Milwaukee Magazine, editor; Milwaukee Journal, reporter; Hoover Institution, research fellow. **Publications:** ProfScam: Professors and the Demise of Higher Education, 1988; The Hollow Men: Politics and Corruption in Higher Education, 1990; (ed. with B. Miner) The National Review College Guide: America's 50 Top Liberal Arts School, 1991, rev. ed., 1993; A Nation of Victims: The Decay of the American Character, 1992; (ed. with B. Miner) National Review College Guide: America's Top Liberal Arts Schools, 1993; Dumbing Down Our Kids: Why America's Children Feel Good about Themselves But Can't Read, Write or Add, 1995, 2nd ed., 1996; The End of Privacy, 1999; 50 Rules Kids Won't Learn in School: Real World Antidotes to Feel-Good Education, 2007; Nation of Moochers: America's Addiction to Getting Something for Nothing, 2012. Contributor to periodicals. **Address:** c/o St. Martin's Press, 175 5th Ave., New York, NY 10010, U.S.A. **Online address:** colleen.schwartz@stmartins.com

SYKES, Plum. (Victoria Sykes). British (born England), b. 1969. **Genres:** Novels. **Career:** British Vogue, fashion writer, 1993-97; American Vogue, contributing editor, 1997-. **Publications:** Bergdorf Blondes, 2004; The Debutante Divorcee: A Novel, 2006. **Address:** Janklow & Nesbit, 445 Park Ave., New York, NY 10022, U.S.A.

SYKES, Victoria. See **SYKES, Plum.**

SYKTUS, Jozef. (Jozef I. Syktus). Australian/Polish (born Poland), b. 1959. **Genres:** Meteorology/Atmospheric Sciences. **Career:** University of Adelaide, research associate, 1980-92; Commonwealth Scientific and Industrial Research Organisation (CSIRO), Division of Atmospheric Research, research scientist, 1992-94; Queensland Department of Natural Resources, chief scientist. Writer. **Publications:** (With L.A. Frakes and J.E. Francis) Climate Modes of the Phanerozoic: The History of the Earth's Climate Over the Past 600 Million Years, 1992; Palaeoclimate and Climate Modeling, forthcoming. **Address:** Department of Natural Resources, QCCA Bldg., 80 Meiers Rd., Indooroopilly, QL 4068, Australia. **Online address:** jozef.syktus@dar.csiro.au

SYKTUS, Jozef I. See **SYKTUS, Jozef.**

SYLVAN, Dianne. American (born United States), b. 1977?. **Genres:** Novels, Psychology. **Career:** Blessedways Temple, co-founder and president. Writer. **Publications:** NEW AGE BOOKS: The Circle Within: Creating a Wiccan Spiritual Tradition, 2003; The Body Sacred, 2005; Queen of Shadows, 2010, Shadowflame, 2011; Shadow's Fall, 2012. Contributor to magazines. **Address:** c/o Author Mail, Llewellyn Worldwide Ltd., 2143 Wooddale Dr., Woodbury, MN 55125-2989, U.S.A. **Online address:** circlewithin@yahoo.com

SYLVESTER, Janet. (Terry Sylvester). American (born United States), b. 1950. **Genres:** Poetry, Young Adult Fiction. **Career:** University of South Carolina, staff; Harvard University, professor of expository and creative writing. University of Tampa, visiting writer, visiting assistant pofessor of English; University in Cambridge, faculty. Writer. **Publications:** That Mulberry Wine, 1985; A Visitor at the Gate (poetry chapbook), 1996; The Mark of Flesh (poems), 1997. Contributor to Periodicals. **Address:** Department of English, University of Tampa, PH 502 Bldg., 401 W Kennedy Blvd., PO Box R, Tampa, FL 33606, U.S.A. **Online address:** jsylvester@earthlink.net

SYLVESTER, Terry. See **SYLVESTER, Janet.**

SYMMONS, Sarah. British (born England) **Genres:** Art/Art History, Photography. **Career:** Cambridge University, lecturer; London University, lecturer; University of Georgia, lecturer; Savannah College of Art and Design, lecturer; University of Santiago de Compostela, lecturer; University of Essex, faculty. Writer. **Publications:** Goya, 1977; Daumier, 1979, 2nd ed., 2004; Flaxman and Europe: The Outline Illustrations and Their Influence, 1984; Goya: In Pursuit of Patronage, 1988; Art and Ideas, 1998; (ed. and intro.) Goya: A Life in Letters, 2004. AS NATALYA LOWNDES: Chekago, 1988; Angel in the Sun, 1989; Snow Red, 1992. Contributor to periodicals. **Address:** University of Essex, Wivenhoe Pk., Colchester, C04 3SQ, England.

SYMONDS, Deborah A(nn). American (born United States), b. 1951. **Genres:** History. **Career:** University of Iowa, Rockefeller Foundation Fellow, 1988; Drake University, associate professor of history, 1989-, profes-

sor of history. Writer. **Publications:** Weep Not for Me: Women, Ballads, and Infanticide in Early Modern Scotland, 1997; Notorious Murders, Black Lanterns and Moveable Goods: Transformation of Edinburgh's Underworld in the Early Nineteenth Century, 2006. Contributor of articles to books. **Address:** Department of History, Drake University, 220 Meredith Hall, 2507 University Ave., Des Moines, IA 50311-4505, U.S.A. **Online address:** deborah.symonds@drake.edu

SYMONS, Leslie John. Welsh/British (born England), b. 1926. **Genres:** Geography, Travel/Exploration. **Career:** Queen's University, lecturer in geography, 1953-63; University of Canterbury, senior lecturer in geography, 1963-70; University of Manchester, Simon senior research fellow, 1967-68; University of Wales, University College of Swansea, senior lecturer, 1970-73, reader, 1973-80, professor of geography, 1980-91, professor emeritus, 1991-, honorary research fellow. Writer. **Publications:** Agricultural Geography, 1967, rev. ed., 1979; (with L. Hanna) Northern Ireland: A Geographical Introduction, 1967; Russian Agriculture: A Geographical Survey, 1972; (co-author) The Soviet Union: A Systematic Geography, 1983, 2nd ed., 1990; To Ride the Mountain Winds, 2011. EDITOR: Land Use in Northern Ireland, 1964; (with C. White) Russian Transport: An Historical and Geographical Survey, 1975; (with J. Ambler and D.J.B. Shaw) Soviet and East European Transport Problems, 1985; (with J.F. Tismer and J. Ambler) Transport and Economic Development: Soviet Union and Eastern Europe, 1987. **Address:** Department of Geography, University College of Swansea, University of Wales, Singleton Pk., Swansea, WG SA2 8PP, Wales.

SYMYNKYWICZ, Jeffrey. See **SYMYNKYWICZ, Jeffrey B(ruce).**

SYMYNKYWICZ, Jeffrey B(ruce). (Jeffrey Symynkywicz). American (born United States), b. 1954. **Genres:** International Relations/Current Affairs, History, Biography, Young Adult Non-fiction, Theology/Religion. **Career:** First Universalist Society, minister, 1982-85; First Universalist Church, minister, 1985-93; First Parish Universalist Church, minister and chair, 1993-. Writer. **Publications:** Germany, United Again, 1995; Vaclav Havel and the Velvet Revolution, 1995; 1989: The Year the World Changed, 1995; The Soviet Collapse, 1996; Civil War in Yugoslavia, 1997; The Soviet Turmoil, 1997; Gospel According to Bruce Springsteen: Rock and Redemption, from Asbury Park to Magic, 2008. **Address:** First Parish Universalist Church, 790 Washington St., PO Box 284, Stoughton, MA 02072, U.S.A. **Online address:** revjeff@peoplepc.com

SYNAN, (Harold) Vinson. American (born United States), b. 1934. **Genres:** History, Social Commentary, Theology/Religion. **Career:** Pentecostal Holiness Church, pastor, 1956-74, officially commissioned historian, 1973-85, general secretary, 1973-77, acting president, 1980, director of evangelism; teacher, 1960-62; Emmanuel College, instructor, 1962-75, Division of Social and Behavioral Sciences, chairperson, 1967-75; Southwestern College, teacher, 1973-77; Oral Roberts University, professor of pentecostal and charismatic history, 1990-94, Holy Spirit Research Center, director, 1990-94; Regent University, School of Divinity, professor of church history, dean, 1994-2006, dean emeritus, 2006-. Writer. **Publications:** Emmanuel College: The First Fifty Years, 1969; Holiness-Pentecostal Movement in the United States, 1971, 2nd ed. as The Holiness-Pentecostal Tradition: Charismatic Movements in the Twentieth Century, 1997; The Old Time Power, 1973; Charismatic Bridges, 1974; In the Latter Days: The Outpouring of the Holy Spirit in the Twentieth Century, 1984, rev. ed., 2001; The Twentieth-Century Pentecostal Explosion, 1987; The Spirit Said Grow, 1992; Under His Banner, 1992; Holiness-Pentecostal Tradition, 1997; Oldtime Power: A Centennial History of the International Pentecostal Holiness Church, 1998; Century of the Holy Spirit, 2001; The Synans of Virginia, 2003; Voices of Pentecost, 2003; A Seminary to Change the World, 2007; An Eyewitness Remembers the Century of the Holy Spirit, 2010. EDITOR: Aspects of Pentecostal-Charismatic Origins, 1975; Azusa Street, 1976; Spirit-empowered Christianity in the Twenty-first Century, 2011. **Address:** School of Divinity, Regent University, 247 Robertson Hall, 1000 Regent University Dr., Virginia Beach, VA 23464, U.S.A. **Online address:** vinssyn@regent.edu

SYNGE, Ursula. British (born England), b. 1930. **Genres:** Children's Fiction, Mythology/Folklore, Science Fiction/Fantasy. **Career:** Writer. **Publications:** Weland: Smith of the Gods, 1972; The People and the Promise, 1974; Audun and the Bear, 1975; Kalevala: Heroic Tales from Finland, 1977; Margaret McElderry, 1978; Land of Heroes: A Retelling of the Kalevala, 1978; The Giant at the Ford: And Other Legends of the Saints, 1980; (adaptor and trans.) M. Anno, Anno's Medieval world, 1980; Swan's Wing, 1981. Contributor to periodicals. **Address:** 10 Highbury Villas, St. Michael's Hill, Bristol, GL BS2 8DB, England.

SZABÓ, Istvan. Hungarian (born Hungary), b. 1938. **Genres:** Plays/Screenplays, Young Adult Non-fiction, Education, Reference. **Career:** Hungarian Film Studios, staff, 1961-; Hungarian Film School, professor, 1970-, Objektiv Studio, staff, 1978-, department head, 1980-92; Deutsche Film Fernsehakademie, docent, 1982-84. Writer and film director. **Publications:** Hohere Technische Mechanik: Nach Vorlesungen, 1972; Hutte, Taschenbucher Der Technik: Mathematik, 1974; A Magyar Mezogazdasag Tortenete a XIV. Szazadtol Az 1530-as evekig, 1975; Einfuhrung in Die Technische Mechanik: Nach Vorlesungen, 1975; Agrarforradalom a Viharsarokban, 1976; Jobbagyok, Parasztok: Ertekezesek a Magyar Parasztsag Tortenetebol, 1976; Irodalom Esztorszagban, 1976; Szolnok: Utikalauz, 1977; Iskola a Magasban, 1977; Hajnalok Hajnala, 1978; Hazulrol Odaig, 1979; Geschichte Der Mechanischen Prinzipien Und Ihrer Wichtigsten Anwendungen, 1979; Jaszbereny, 1979; Hazulrol Odaig, 1979; (with P. Dobai) Mephisto, 1980; Szabo Istvan, 1898-1969, 1982; Legtechnikai Berendezesek Akusztikai Tervezese, 1984; (with Dobai) Redl Ezredes (title means: 'Colonel Redl'), 1985; Alphornsinfonie, 1985; A Forradalom Szemtanui, 1987; Sweet Emma, Dear Bobe: Sketches, Nudes, 1993; Bevezetes a Szocialpszichologiaba, 1995; Kisvarosi Kremtortenetek, 1995; Fejezetek Az Eszt Kultura Tortenetebol, 1995; Offenbach's Secret, 1996; Steadying the Boat, 1996; Sunshine, 1999; A Novenytan es Novenyelettan Tortenete Keszthelyen, 1999; (ed.) Hammered Dulcimer Treasury of Tunes, 2000; Taking Sides, 2001; Gazdasagi Folyamatok, 2000-2004, 2004. **Address:** I.S.L. Film, Rona utca 174, Budapest, 1145, Hungary.

SZAKOLCZAI, árpád. Irish/Hungarian (born Hungary), b. 1958. **Genres:** Politics/Government, Sociology, Theology/Religion. **Career:** Hungarian Academy of Sciences, Institute of Sociology, research associate, 1981-90; Polytechnic of Central London, Centre for Democracy, British council research fellow, 1989-90; European University Institute, lecturer, 1990-98; University College Cork, Department of Sociology, professor, 1998-, head. Writer. **Publications:** (With H. ágnes) Senkiföldjén: A politikai instruktorok tevékenységéröl az állampártban, 1989; Fejlödés megkérdöjelezése: a gazdasági fejlödés modern mitosza és valós alapjai, 1990; (with A. Horváth) The Dissolution of Communist Power: The Case of Hungary, 1992; Max Weber and Michel Foucault: Parallel Life-Works, 1998; (ed. with D. Della Porta and M. Greco) Identità, riconoscimento, scambio: saggi in onore di Alessandro Pizzorno, 2000; Reflexive Historical Sociology, 2000; Genesis of Modernity, 2003; Sociology, Religion, and Grace 2006; (ed. with A. Horvath) Gli interpreti degl interpreti: l'Ione di Platone oggi, 2008. **Address:** Department of Sociology, University College Cork, Safari, O'Donovan's Rd., Cork, CK 1, Ireland. **Online address:** a.szakolczai@ucc.ie

SZALAVITZ, Maia. American (born United States) **Genres:** Psychiatry, Psychology. **Career:** Public Broadcasting Service, associate producer; Charlie Rose talk show, segment producer for series; Statistical Assessment Service, senior fellow. Writer. **Publications:** (With J. Volpicelli) Recovery Options: The Complete Guide, 2000; (with B.D.D. Perry) The Boy Who Was Raised as a Dog and Other Stories from a Child Psychiatrist's Notebook: What Traumatized Children Can Teach Us about Loss, Love, and Healing, 2006; Help at Any Cost: How the Troubled-Teen Industry Cons Parents and Hurts Kids, 2006; Lost Boy, 2009; (with B.D. Perry) Born for Love: Why Empathy is Eessential and Endangered, 2010. **Address:** Statistical Assessment Service, 2100 L St., Ste. 300, Washington, DC 20037, U.S.A. **Online address:** maiasz@gmail.com

SZALAY, Miklós. Swiss/Hungarian (born Hungary), b. 1940. **Genres:** Anthropology/Ethnology, Art/Art History, History, Sociology, Social Sciences. **Career:** Küenstlerhaus Wien, archivist, 1968-70; University of Zurich, Department of African Art at Völkerkundemuseum, director, 1975-, professor of anthropology, 1992-. Writer. **Publications:** Biológia a mérnöki gyakorlatban, 1967; (with N. László) Síkvidéki tározók tervézese és üzeme, 1977; Ethnologie und Geschichte: zur Grundlegung einer ethnologischen Geschichtsschreibung: mit Beispielen aus der Geschichte der Khoi-San in Südafrika, 1983; The San and the Colonization of the Cape, 1770-1879: Conflict, Incorporation, Acculturation, 1995; Schön Hässlich: Gegensätze; afrikanische Kunst aus der Sammlung des Völkerkundemuseums der Universität Zürich, 2001. EDITOR: Der Sinn des Schöenen: ästhetik, Soziologie und Geschichte der afrikanischen Kunst, 1990; African Art from the Han Coray Collection,

1916-1928, 1998; The Moon as Shoe: Drawings of the San, 2002. **Address:** Völkerkundemuseum, University of Zurich, Pelikanstrasse 40, Zurich, 8001, Switzerland.

SZANTON, Andrew (Emlen). American (born United States), b. 1963. **Genres:** Autobiography/Memoirs, Psychology, Ghost Writer. **Career:** Smithsonian Institution, oral historian in video history, 1986-88. Freelance writer, 1988-; Harvard University Extension School, faculty. **Publications:** (With C. Evers) Have No Fear: The Charles Evers Story, 1997; (ed.) Forensic Ethics and the Expert Witness, 2007. **Address:** 162 Powderhouse Blvd., Somerville, MA 02144, U.S.A. **Online address:** aszanton@rcn.com

SZASZ, Andrew. American (born United States), b. 1947. **Genres:** Environmental Sciences/Ecology. **Career:** University of California, professor and chair of sociology. Writer. **Publications:** EcoPopulism: Toxic Waste and the Movement for Environmental Justice, 1994; (ed. with W.L. Goldfrank and D. Goodman) Ecology and the World-System, 1999; Shopping Our Way to Safety: How We Changed from Protecting the Environment to Protecting Ourselves, 2007. Contributor to journals. **Address:** U.S.A. **Online address:** szasz@ucsc.edu

SZASZ, Thomas Stephen. American/Hungarian (born Hungary), b. 1920. **Genres:** Ethics, Law, Medicine/Health, Philosophy, Politics/Government, Psychiatry, Psychology. **Career:** Boston City Hospital, intern, 1944-45; Cincinnati General Hospital, assistant resident, 1945-46, clinician, 1946; University of Chicago Clinics, assistant resident in psychiatry, 1946-48; Chicago Institute for Psychoanalysis, research assistant, 1949-50, staff, 1951-56; State University of New York, Upstate Medical Center, professor of psychiatry, 1956-90, professor emeritus, 1990-; Postgraduate Center for Mental Health, fellow, 1962; Cornell University Law School, Civil Liberties Carey lecturer, 1968; Citizens Commission on Human Rights, co-founder, 1969; Ithaca University, C.P. Snow lecturer, 1970; New York University School of Law, Root Tilden lecturer, 1971; International Commission for Human Rights, honorary president, 1974; University of Essex, Noel Buxton lectureship, 1975; University of Cincinnati College of Law, Robert S. Marx lectureship, 1976; Hartwick College, Hardy chair lectureship, 1976; University of Queensland Medical School, E.S. Meyer memorial lecturer, 1977; University of New Mexico, visiting professor, 1981. Writer. **Publications:** Pain and Pleasure: Study of Bodily Feelings, 1957, 2nd ed. 1988; The Myth of Mental Illness: Foundations of a Theory of Personal Conduct, 1961, rev. ed., 1974; Law, Liberty, and Psychiatry: An Inquiry into the Social Uses of Mental Health Practices, 1963; Psychiatric Justice, 1965; The Ethics of Psychoanalysis: The Theory and Method of Autonomous Psychotherapy, 1965; Ideology and Insanity: Essays on the Psychiatric Dehumanization of Man, 1970; The Manufacture of Madness, A Comparative Study of the Inquisition and the Mental Health Movement, 1970; (ed. and intro.) The Age of Madness: The History of Involuntary Mental Hospitalization, 1973; The Second Sin, 1973; Ceremonial Chemistry: The Ritual Persecution of Drugs, Addicts and Pushers, 1974, rev. ed. 2003; Heresies, 1976; Schizophrenia: The Sacred Symbol of Psychiatry, 1976; Karl Kraus and the Soul-Doctors: A Pioneer Critic and His Criticism of Psychiatry and Psychoanalysis, 1976; Psychiatric Slavery, 1977; Paresis and Plunder: The Models of Madness in Psychiatry and Anti-Psychiatry, 1977; The Theology of Medicine: The Political-Philosophical Foundations of Medical Ethics, 1977; The Myth of Psychotherapy: Mental Healing as Religion, Rhetoric, and Repression, 1978; Sex by Prescription: The Startling Truth about Today's Sex Therapy, 1980; The Therapeutic State: Psychiatry in the Mirror of Current Events, 1984; Insanity: The Idea and Its Consequences, 1987; Anti-Freud: Karl Kraus's Criticism of Psychoanalysis and Psychiatry, 1990; The Untamed Tongue: A Dissenting Dictionary, 1990; Friedman & Szasz On Liberty and Drugs: Essays on the Free Market and Prohibition, 1992; Our Right to Drugs: The Case for A Free Market, 1992; A Lexicon of Lunacy: Metaphoric Malady, Moral Responsibility and Psychiatry, 1993; Cruel Compassion: Psychiatric Control of Society's Unwanted, 1994; The Meaning of Mind: Language, Morality and Neuroscience, 1996; The Manufacture Of Madness: A Comparative Study Of The Inquisition And The Mental Health Movement, 1997; (and intro.) Fatal Freedom: The Ethics and Politics of Suicide, 1999; (and intro.) Pharmacracy: Medicine and Politics in America, 2001; Liberation by Oppression, 2002; Faith in Freedom: Libertarian Principles and Psychiatric Practices, 2004; Words to the Wise: A Medical-Philosophical Dictionary, 2004; My Madness Saved Me: The Madness and Marriage of Virginia Woolf, 2006; The Medicalization of Everyday Life: Selected Essays, 2007; Coercion As Cure: A Critical History of Psychiatry, 2007; Psychiatry: The Science of Lies, 2008; Antipsychiatry: Quackery Squared, 2009; Suicide Prohibition: The Shame of

Medicine, 2011. **Address:** Upstate Medical Center, State University of New York, 750 E Adams St., Syracuse, NY 13210-2375, U.S.A. **Online address:** tszasz@aol.com

SZE, Arthur C. American (born United States), b. 1950. **Genres:** Poetry, Literary Criticism And History, History, Social Sciences. **Career:** Institute of American Indian Arts, instructor in English, 1984-89, director of creative writing program, 1989-96, professor of creative writing program, 1986-2006, professor emeritus, 2006-; Tooth of Time Books, director, 1985-88; Naropa Institute, artist-in-residence, 1989, 1995, 1998, 2004; Brown University, faculty, 1991; Bard College, faculty, 1991; Mary Baldwin College, Elizabeth Kirkpatrick Doenges visiting artist, 2004-05; Washington University, visiting Fannie Hurst professor of creative literature, 2005. Writer. **Publications:** The Willow Wind, 1972, rev. ed. as The Willow Wind: Poems and Translations from the Chinese, 1981; Two Ravens, 1976, rev. ed. as Two Ravens: Poems and Translations from the Chinese, 1984; Dazzled (poems), 1982; River River (poems), 1987; Archipelago (poems), 1995; The Redshifting Web: Poems 1970-1998, 1998; The Silk Dragon: Translations from the Chinese, 2001; Quipu, 2005; The Ginkgo Light, 2009; (ed.) Chinese Writers on Writing, 2010. Works appear in anthologies. Contributor of poems to magazines. **Address:** PO Box 457, Santa Fe, NM 87504, U.S.A. **Online address:** asze@cybermesa.com

SZEKELY, Istvan P(al). Hungarian (born Hungary), b. 1959. **Genres:** Economics, Translations. **Career:** Budapest University of Economics, lecturer, 1983-85, Department of Econometrics and Mathematical Economics, associate professor, 1983-, senior lecturer, 1987-89; University of Bonn, research fellow, 1985-87; United Nations Secretariat, economic affairs officer, 1991-; Centre for Economic Policy Research, research associate, 1991-; European Commission, Office of the Chief Economist, consultant, 1995, 1996, 1998, Directorate-General for Economic and Financial Affairs, Economic Studies and Research, research director, 2007-; European Bank for Reconstruction and Development, Office of the Chief Economist, consultant, 1995; National Bank of Hungary, Department of Economics and Research, general manager and advisor to the governor, 1996-99; International Monetary Fund, European I Department, mission chief, 1999-2007; Corvinus University of Budapest, honorary associate professor, honorary professor, now professor emeritus. Writer. **Publications:** (With K. Gábor and M. László) Gyakorlati ökonometria, 1990, (with G. Kórösi and L. Mátyás) trans. as Practical Econometrics, 1992; Development Strategy and Management of the Market Economy, 1997; (with I. ábel and P.L. Siklos) Money and Finance in the Transition to a Market Economy, 1998. EDITOR: (with D.M.G. Newbery) Hungary: An Economy in Transition, 1993; (with J.P. Bonin) The Development and Reform of Financial Systems in Central and Eastern Europe, 1994; (with M.A. Landesmann) Industrial Restructuring and Trade Reorientation in Eastern Europe, 1995; (with K. Mizsei) Bad Enterprise Debts in Central and Eastern Europe, forthcoming. Contributor to books and journals. **Address:** Directorate General for Economic, and Financial Affairs, European Commission, Ste. R 4, Brussels, B-1049, Belgium. **Online address:** iszekely@imf.org

SZEKERES, Cyndy. American (born United States), b. 1933. **Genres:** Illustrations, Children's Fiction, Animals/Pets, Young Adult Fiction, Theology/Religion, Literary Criticism And History. **Career:** Illustrator and writer. **Publications:** FOR CHILDREN SELF-ILLUSTRATED: Long Ago, 1977; Cyndy Szekeres ABC, 1983; Puppy Too Small, 1984; Scaredy Cat!, 1984; Thumpity Thump Gets Dressed, 1984; Baby Bear's Surprise, 1984; Cyndy Szekeres' Counting Book 1 to 10, 1984; Suppertime for Frieda Fuzzypaws, 1985; Hide-and-Seek Duck, 1985; Nothing-to-Do Puppy, 1985; Good Night, Sammy, 1986; Puppy Lost, 1986; Sammy's Special Day, 1986; Little Bear Counts His Favorite Things, 1986; Melanie Mouse's Moving Day, 1986; Cyndy Szekeres' Good Night, Sweet Mouse, 1988; Cyndy Szekeres' Favorite Two-Minute Stories, 1989; Things Bunny Sees, 1990; What Bunny Loves, 1990; Cyndy Szekeres' Nice Animals, 1990; Cyndy Szekeres' Hugs, 1990; Cindy Szekeres' Little Puppy Learns to Share, 1991; Cyndy Szekeres' Ladybug, Ladybug, Where Are You?, 1991; Cyndy Szekeres' Fluffy Duckling, 1992; Cyndy Szekeres' Teeny Mouse Counts Herself, 1992; Cyndy Szekeres' Colors, 1992; Cyndy Szekeres' Kisses, 1993; Cyndy Szekeres' Little Puppy Cleans His Room, 1993; Cyndy Szekeres' Baby Animals, 1994; Cyndy Szekeres' I Am a Puppy, 1994; Cyndy Szejeres' Christmas Mouse, 1995; Cyndy Szekeres' Giggles, 1996; Yes, Virginia, There Is a Santa Claus, 1997; Cyndy Szekeres' I Love My Busy Book, 1997; The Mouse that Jack Built, 1997; The Deep Blue Sky Twinkles with Stars, 1998; I Can Count 100 Bunnies: And So Can You!, 1998; Cyndy Szekeres' Learn to Count, Funny Bunnies, 2000;

Toby!, 2000; Toby's Alphabet Walk, 2000; Toby's Rainbow Clothes, 2000; Toby's New Brother, 2000; Toby Counts His Marbles, 2000; Toby's Flying Lesson, 2000; Toby's Holiday Hugs and Kisses, 2000; Wilbur Bunny's Funny Friends A to Z, 2000; Do You Love Me?, 2001; I Can Do It, 2001; Toby's Good Night, 2001; Toby's Please and Thank You, 2001; Toby's Dinosaur Halloween, 2001; Santa Toby's Busy Christmas, 2001. TINY PAW LIBRARY SERIES SELF-ILLUSTRATED: A Busy Day, 1989; The New Baby, 1989; Moving Day, 1989; A Fine Mouse Band, 1989; A Mouse Mess, 1990. OTHERS: (ed.) Cyndy Szekeres' Favorite Mother Goose Rhymes, 1992; A Very Merry Mouse Country Christmas, 1998. Illustrator of books for children by others. **Address:** PO Box 280, Putney, VT 05346-0280, U.S.A.

SZENBERG, Michael. American/Polish (born Poland), b. 1934. **Genres:** Economics. **Career:** Long Island University, professor of economics and finance, 1965-83; Lecture Bureau of Economics, founder and director, 1972-80; The American Economist, editor-in-chief, 1974-; U.S. Department of Labor, Bureau of International Labor Affairs, consultant and director of research project, 1974-77; Abrasco Technological Services Inc., president and principal, 1979-2002; Pace University, Department of Finance and Graduate Economics, Lubin Graduate School of Business, Center for Applied Research, director, 1993-2007, distinguished professor of economics, 1998-, chairman, 2000-; Manufacturers Hanover Trust Co., consultant, 1984-87; American Economics Association, co-ordinator and chair, 1984-; Economics Journals affiliated with the American Economics Association, coordinator and chair, 1984-; Cambridge University Press, Cambridge Dictionary of American Biography, consultant, 1991-92, Cambridge University Encyclopedia, Economics Categories, editor, 1992-94. **Publications:** Economics of the Israeli Diamond Industry, 1973; (co-author) The Welfare Effects of Trade Restrictions, 1977; (co-author) Paul A. Samuelson in Five Parts, 2005; (with L. Ramrattan) Distressed US Industries in the Era of Globalization, 2007; (with L. Ramrattan) Franco Modigliani: A Mind That Never Rests, 2008. EDITOR: Essays in Economics: The John Commons Memorial Lectures, 1986; Eminent Economists, 1992; Craft and Passion: Economists at Work, 1998: New Frontiers in Economics, 2004; (with L. Ramrattan) Reflections of Eminent Economists, 2004; (with L. Ramrattan and A.A. Gotteman) Samuelsonian Economics and the 21st Century, 2006. **Address:** Department of Finance/Economics, Lubin School of Business, Pace University, Rm. W-425, 1 Pace Plz., New York, NY 10038, U.S.A. **Online address:** mszenberg@pace.edu

SZIRTES, George. British/Hungarian (born Hungary), b. 1948. **Genres:** Poetry, Translations, Essays, Art/Art History. **Career:** Cheshunt School, teacher of art, 1973-74; Hitchin School, teacher of art, 1974-75; Hitchin Girls School, head of art, 1975-81; Starwheel Press, proprietor, 1978-88; St. Christopher School, director of art, 1982-89; writer and translator, 1987-; Norfolk Institute of Art and Design, senior lecturer in poetry, 1991-; Norwich University College of the Arts, School of Art and Design, visiting lecturer, 1989-91, senior lecturer in poetry, 1992-2006, coordinator of creative writing, 1994-; Norwich Puppet Theatre, board chair, 1997-2000, board director, 1996-97, through 2002; University of East Anglia, reader in creative writing, 2006-. **Publications:** Poems, 1972; The Iron Clouds, 1975; Visitors, 1976; An Illustrated Alphabet, 1977; (with N. Powell and P. Scupham) A Mandeville Troika, 1977; At the Sink, 1978; Silver Age, 1978; The Slant Door, 1979; Sermon on a Ship, 1980; Homage to Cheval, 1980; November and May, 1981; The Kissing Place, 1982; Short Wave, 1983; The Photographer in Winter, 1986; Metro, 1988; (intro.) The Least Thing, 1989; Bridge Passages, 1991; Blind Field, 1994; Selected Poems, 1976-1996, 1996; The Red All Over Riddle Book (poems for children), 1997; Portrait of My Father in an English Landscape, 1998; (intro.) I Am God's Goldfish, 1999; (intro.) There is a Land, 2000; (intro.) Camp Notebook, 2000; The Budapest File, 2000; An English Apocalypse, 2001; (intro.) Between Words and Silence, 2001; (intro.) John the Valiant, 2004; Reel, 2004; József Attila 43 vers, 2005; New and Collected Poems, 2008; The Burning of the Books and Other Poems, 2009; Niki, 2009; (intro.) The Song of Solomon. EDITOR: Blood of the Walsungs: Selected Poems of Otto Orban, 1993; Collected Poems of Freda Downie, 1995; (with G. Gömöri) Colonnade of Teeth: Modern Hungarian Poetry, 1996; (and ed.) The Lost Rider, 1998; (with P. Lively) New Writing 10, 2001; (with M. Vajda and intro.) An Island of Sound, 2004; (and intro.) New Order, 2010. TRANSLATOR: The Tragedy of Man, by I. Madach, 1989; D. Kosztolanyi, Anna Edes, 1992; O. Orban, The Blood of the Walsungs, 1992; Z. Rakovszky, New Life, 1994; G. Krudy, The Adventures of Sindbad, 1998; L. Krasznahorkai, The Melancholy of Resistance, 1999; A.N. Nagy, The Night of Akhenaton, 2004; S. Márai, Casanova in Bolanzo, 2004; L. Krasznahorkai, War and War, 2006; S. Márai, Rebels, 2007; F. Karinthy, Metropole, 2008; S. Márai, Esther's Inheritance, 2008; L. Krasznahorkai, Satantango, 2009; S. Márai, The Intended, 2009; S. Márai, Portraits of a Marriage, 2010. MONOGRAPH: Exercise of Power, The Art of Ana Maria Pacheco, 2001. ESSAYS: Fortinbras at the Fishhouses, 2010. Works appear in anthologies. **Address:** Bloodaxe Books Ltd., Highgreen, Tarset, NM NE48 1RP, England. **Online address:** georgeszirtes@gmail.com

SZOSTAK, Rick. Canadian (born Canada), b. 1959. **Genres:** Economics, History, Humanities, Social Sciences, Technology. **Career:** University of Alberta, Department of Economics, visiting assistant professor, 1985-86, assistant professor, 1986-92, associate professor, 1992-97, professor of economic history and development, 1997-, Faculty of Arts, associate dean, 2002-05; University of New South Wales, visiting fellow, 1991-92; European University Institute, visiting fellow, 2006-07. Writer. **Publications:** The Role of Transportation in the Industrial Revolution, 1991; (with G. Cross) Technology and American Society: A History, 1995, 2nd ed. 2005; Technological Innovation and the Great Depression, 1995; Econ-Art: Divorcing Art from Science in Modern Economics, 1999; (with R. Szostak) Tales of Narcissus, 2000; A Schema for Unifying Human Science: Interdisciplinary Perspectives on Culture, 2003; Classifying Science: Phenomena, Data, Theory, Method, Practice, 2004; Unifying Ethics 2005; The Causes of Economic Growth: Interdisciplinary Perspectives 2009; (ed. with A.F. Repko and W.H. Newell) Case Studies in Interdisciplinary Research, 2012. Contributor to journals. **Address:** Department of Economics, University of Alberta, Rm. 9-18, Tory Bldg., Rm. 8-14, HM Tory Bldg., Edmonton, AB T6G 2H4, Canada. **Online address:** rick.szostak@ualberta.ca

SZPIRO, George G. Swiss/Austrian (born Austria), b. 1950. **Genres:** Mathematics/Statistics. **Career:** University of Pennsylvania, Wharton School, assistant professor, 1984-86; Hebrew University, lecturer, 1986-92; Neue Zürcher Zeitung (Swiss newspaper), Israel political correspondent and mathematics columnist, 1987-; University of Zurich, faculty. Writer and mathematician. **Publications:** Kepler's Conjecture: How Some of the Greatest Minds in History Helped Solve One of the Oldest Math Problems in the World, 2003; Secret Life of Numbers: 50 Easy Pieces on How Mathematicians Work and Think, 2006; Poincarés Prize: The Hundred-year Quest to Solve One of Math's Greatest Puzzles, 2007; Mathematical Cocktail: 50 Further Stories About How Mathematicians Work and Think, 2010; Numbers Rule: The Vexing Mathematics of Democracy, from Plato to the Present, 2010; Pricing the Future: Finance, Physics, and the 300-year Journey to the Black-Scholes Equation, 2011. **Address:** New England Publishing Associates Inc., PO Box 66066, Lawrenceville, NJ 08648-6066, U.S.A. **Online address:** egroeg@georgeszpiro.com

SZTOMPKA, Piotr. Polish (born Poland), b. 1944. **Genres:** Sociology, Social Sciences, Sciences, Social Commentary, Biography. **Career:** University of California, Berkeley, Fulbright fellow, 1972-73; Harvard University, Fulbright fellow, 1972-73; Jagiellonian University, head of theoretical sociology section, 1975-, Institute of Sociology, director, 1978-87, professor of sociology, 1980-, university professor, 1987-, chair; Columbia University, visiting professor, 1975-79; Universidad Nacional Autonoma de Mexico, visiting professor, 1984; University of California, Los Angeles, visiting professor, 1987, 1988-92; St. Catherines College, visiting professor, 1988-96; Johns Hopkins University, School of Advanced International Studies, special visiting research professor, 1981-82, 1991; University of Michigan, fellow, 1984-85; Oxford University, St. Catherine's College, fellow, 1988; Swedish Collegium for Advanced Studies in the Social Sciences, fellow, 1990, 1992; Wissenschaftekolleg, Berlin, fellow, 1998; Center for Analysis of Social Change, chair; Tischner's European University, professor. Writer. **Publications:** Teoria I Wyjaśnienie: Z Metodologicznych Problemów Socjologii, 1973; System and Function: Toward a Theory of Society, 1974; Sociological Dilemmas: Toward a Dialectic Paradigm, 1979; Robert K. Merton: An Intellectual Profile, 1986; Society in Action: The Theory of Social Becoming, 1991; The Sociology of Social Change, 1994; Trust: A Sociological Theory, 1999; Trauma Wielkiej Zmiany: Spoleczne Koszty Transformacji, 2000; (with A.K. Kozmiński) Rozmowa O Wielkiej Przemianie, 2004; Stawanie się Spoleczeństwa: Szkice Ofiarowane Piotrowi Sztompce z Okazji 40-lecia Pracy Naukowej, 2006. EDITOR: Masters of Polish Sociology, 1984; New Technological Challenge and Socialist Societies, 1987; (with J.C. Alexander and contrib.) Rethinking Progress: Movements, Forces and Ideas at the End of the 20th Century, 1990; (with B. Nedelman) Sociology in Europe: In Search of Identity, 1993; Agency and Structure: Reorienting Social Theory, 1994; (and intro.) On Social Structure and Science, 1996; Imponderabilia Wielkiej Zmiany: Mentalność, Wartości i

Wiezi Spoleczne Czasów Transformacji, 1999; (with A. Koj) Images of the World: Science, Humanities, Art, 2001. Contributor to books and journals. **Address:** Institute of Sociology, Jagiellonian University, Grodzka 52, Krakow, 31-044, Poland. **Online address:** ussztomp@cyf-kr.edu.pl

SZYBIST, Mary. American (born United States), b. 1970?. **Genres:** Poetry. **Career:** Kenyon College, visiting assistant professor of English, 2003-04; Lewis & Clark College, Department of English, associate professor, 2004-; Warren Wilson College, MFA Program, faculty, 2011; University of Tennessee, Governor's School for the Humanities, faculty; West High School, staff; University of Virginia, Young Writers' Workshop, faculty; University of Iowa, Writers' Workshop, teaching-writing fellow. Poet. **Publications:** POETRY: Granted, 2003; Incarnadine, 2013. Contributor of articles to books. **Address:** Department of English, Lewis & Clark College, Rm. 405, Miller Ctr., 0615 SW Palatine Hill Rd., Portland, OR 97219-7879, U.S.A. **Online address:** szybist@lclark.edu

SZYMAŃSKI, Leszek. Polish (born Poland), b. 1933. **Genres:** Novels, History, Politics/Government, Biography, Young Adult Fiction. **Career:** Wspotczesnosc, chief editor, 1956. **Publications:** Escape to the Tropics, 1960; Naneczona, 1965; On the Wallaby Track, 1967; Living with the Weird Mob, 1973; (contrib.) Warsaw Aflame: The 1939-1945 Years, 1973; Kazimierz Pulaski in America: A Monograph, 1777-1779, 1979; Putaski Bohetar Niozmany, 1980; Candle for Poland: 469 Days of Solidarity, 1982; Candle for Poland-Solidarity, 1988; Casimir Pulaski: A Hero of the American Revolution, 1994; Jose Rizal: L'uomo Universale, 2009. **Address:** c/o Publicity Director, Hippocrene Books Inc., 171 Madison Ave., New York, NY 10016, U.S.A.

SZYMANSKI, Lois. American (born United States), b. 1957. **Genres:** Children's Fiction, Natural History, Animals/Pets, Young Adult Fiction, Ghost Writer. **Career:** Carroll County Times, correspondent, 1989-95; freelance writer, 1990-; Lancaster Farming (newspaper), correspondent, 1994-; The Carroll Sun, correspondent, 1995-; Carroll Community College, instructor in continuing adult education. **Publications:** Patches, 1993; A New Kind of Magic, 1994; Little Icicle, 1995; A Pony Promise, 1996; A Perfect Pony, 1996; Pony Legend, 1997; Silver Lining, 1997; Sea Feather, 1998; On the Track, 1999; Hugs and Kisses, 2000; (with S. Sykes) Whisper of War, 2003; Out of the Sea: Today's Chincoteague Pony, 2007; Pony to the Rescue, 2007; Pony to Remember, 2007; Pony Named Patches, 2008; Grandfather's Secret, 2010; True Story of Sea Feather, 2010. GETTYSBURG GHOST SERIES: (with S. Sykes): The Ghost Comes Out, 2001; Ghost on Board, 2001; Night Mare, 2001; Soldier in the Cellar, 2002; Ghost Hunter, 2003. **Address:** 3377 Littlestown Pke., Westminster, MD 21158, U.S.A.

SZYMBORSKA, Wislawa. (Stancykowna). Polish (born Poland), b. 1923. **Genres:** Poetry. **Career:** Zycie Literackie, poetry editor and columnist, 1953-81. Poet and critic. **Publications:** Dlatego zyjemy, 1952; Pytania zadawane sobie, 1954; Wolanie do Yeti, 1957; Sol, 1962; Cienie wybrane, 1964, new ed., 2004; Sto pociech, 1967; Poezje wybrane, 1967; Poezje 1970; Wybor poezje, 1970; Wszelki wypadek, 1972; Lektury nadobowiązkowe, 1973; Wybor wierszy, 1973; Tarsjusz i inne wiersze, 1976; Wielka liczba, 1977; Vokabeln, 1979; Sounds, Feelings, Thoughts: Seventy Poems, 1981; Poezje wybrane (II), 1983; Ludzie na moscie, 1986; Poezje=Poems (bilingual edition), 1989; People on a Bridge: Poems, 1990; Wieczór autorski: wiersze, 1993; Koniec i początek, 1993; View with a Grain of Sand: Selected Poems, 1995; Widok z ziarnkiem piasku: 102 wiersze, 1996; Zycie na poczekaniu: lekcja literatury z Jerzym Kwiatkowskim i Marianem Stala, 1996; Koniec i poczatek, 1996; Hundert Gedichte, Hundert Freuden, 1997; Nothing Twice: Selected Poems, 1997; O śmierci bez przesady=de la mort sans exagérer, 1997; Poems: New and Collected 1957-1997, 1998; Nulla è in regalo, 1998; Nic darowane, 1999; Poczta literacka, czyli, Jak zostać (lub nie zostać) pisarzem, 2000; (contrib.) Godzina dla Adama: wspomnienia, wiersze, przeklady, 2000; Nowe lektury nadobowiazkowe: 1997-2002, 2002; Chwila, 2002; Nonrequired Reading: Prose Pieces, 2002; Wiersze, 2003; Rymowanki dla duzych dzieci: z wyklejankami autorki, 2003; Fin y principio, 2004; Monologue of a Dog: New Poems, 2005; Dwukropek, 2005; Zmysl udzialu: wybór wierszy, 2006; Here: New Poems, 2010. Works appear in anthologies. Contributor to periodicals. **Address:** Ul. Krolewska 82/89, Cracow, 30-079, Poland.

SZYMCZAK, Leonard K. American (born United States), b. 1947. **Genres:** Novels, Plays/Screenplays, Young Adult Fiction. **Career:** Psychotherapy Services Inc., psychotherapist, 1988-90; Metropolitan Family Services, senior social worker, 1991-2001; Northwestern University, Family Institute, senior affiliate therapist, 1996-2008; Northwestern University, senior affiliate therapist; Marriage Guidance Council of New South Wales, director of family therapy program; Royal North Shore Hospital, Department of Child and Family Psychiatry, senior social worker; Wollongong Marriage and Family Centre, director. Writer. **Publications:** (Ed. with A. Jones) Ethnic Differences in Marriage and Family Living in Australia: Personal Viewpoints, 1980; Cuckoo Forevermore (novel), 1996; The Roadmap Home: Your GPS to Inner Peace, 2009; Kookaburra's Last Laugh, 2010; Kookaburra Hereafter, forthcoming. Contributor to journals. **Address:** 4010 Barranca Pkwy., Ste. 252, Irvine, CA 92604, U.S.A. **Online address:** szymczak@aol.com

T

TAAFFE, Sonya. American (born United States) **Genres:** Novellas/Short Stories, Poetry, Young Adult Fiction, Literary Criticism And History. **Career:** Not One of Us, contributing editor. **Publications:** Dybbuk in Love, 2005; Singing Innocence and Experience (short fiction), 2005; FICTION: Postcards from the Province of Hyphens (short fiction and poems), 2005. Contributor to periodicals. **Address:** Not One of Us, 12 Curtis Rd., Natick, MA 01760-3206, U.S.A.

TABACK, Simms. American (born United States), b. 1932. **Genres:** Children's Fiction, Illustrations, Novels. **Career:** School of Visual Arts, instructor in illustration and design, 1967-82; Syracuse University, faculty; CBS Records, graphic designer, art director; New York Times, designer, art director; William Douglas McAdams, advertising art director; The Illustrators Guild, founding president. Illustrator and writer. **Publications:** SELF-ILLUSTRATED: Too Much Noise, 1967; There's Motion Everywhere, 1970; Joseph Had a Little Overcoat, 1977; Jason's Bus Ride, 1987; Book of Cards for Kids, 1992; There Was an Old Lady Who Swallowed a Fly, 1997; This is the House that Jack Built, 2001; Simms Taback's Great Big Book of Spacey, Snakey, Buggy Riddles, 2008. WITH H. ZIEFERT: Where Is My Dinner?, 1984; Where Is My House?, 1984; Where Is My Friend?, 1984; On Our Way to the Barn, 1985; On Our Way to the Forest, 1985; On Our Way to the Water, 1985; On Our Way to the Zoo, 1985; Zoo Parade!, 1990; Noisy Barn!, 1990; Where Is My Baby?, 1994; Who Said Moo?, 1996; Beach Party!, 2005. OTHERS: Two Little Witches: A Halloween Counting Story, 1996; There was an Old Lady Who Swallowed a Fly, 1997; Joseph Had a Little Overcoat, 1999; This is the House that Jack Built, 2002; Kibitzers and Fools: Tales My Zayda (grandfather) Told Me, 2005; Peek-a-Boo Who?: A Peek and Flap Book, 2006; I Miss You Every Day, 2007; Can You Smile?, 2007; Do You Have a Tail?, 2007; Simms Taback's Safari Animals, 2008; Simms Taback 1-2-3, 2009; Simms Taback Animals, 2009; Simms Taback Colors, 2009; Simms Taback's City Animals, 2009; 4, 5, 6, 2010; Mommies and Babies, 2010; Zoom, 2010; Simms Taback's Farm Animals, 2011. **Address:** c/o Author Mail, Penguin Group USA, 345 Hudson St., New York, NY 10014, U.S.A.

TABBI, Joseph. American (born United States), b. 1960. **Genres:** Adult Nonfiction. **Career:** Universität Hamburg, Fulbright professor, 1993-94; Kansas State University, assistant professor of English, 1991-95; University of Illinois, assistant professor, 1996-2002, associate professor, 2002-, professor of English; Electronic Book Review, editor; Electronic Literature Organization, director. **Publications:** Postmodern Sublime: Technology and American Writing from Mailer to Cyberpunk, 1995; (ed. with M. Wutz) Reading Matters: Narrative in the New Media Ecology, 1997; Cognitive Fictions, 2002; (ed. and intro.) The Rush for Second Place: Essays and Occasional Writings, 2002; (ed. with R. Shavers and intro.) Paper Empire: William Gaddis and The World System, 2007. Contributor to journals. **Address:** Department of English, University of Illinois, University Hall, 601 S Morgan St., Ste. 1912, PO Box 162, Chicago, IL 60607-7100, U.S.A. **Online address:** jtabbi@uic.edu

TABER, Stephen Welton. American/Canadian (born Canada), b. 1956. **Genres:** Environmental Sciences/Ecology, Natural History, Biology. **Career:** St. Edward's University, faculty, 1986-; Saginaw Valley State University, Department of Biology, assistant professor, associate professor of biology. Writer. **Publications:** The World of the Harvester Ants, 1998; Fire Ants, 2000;

(with S.B. Fleenor) Life in the Lost Pines, 2002; (with S.B. Fleenor) Insects of the Texas Lost Pines, 2003; (with S.B. Fleenor) Invertebrates of Central Texas Wetlands, 2005; (with S.B. Fleenor) Plants of Central Texas Wetlands, 2009; Plants of the Texas Lost Pines, forthcoming; Life in the Ottine Swamps, forthcoming. **Address:** Department of Biology, Saginaw Valley State University, 260 Science W, 7400 Bay Rd., University Center, MI 48710, U.S.A. **Online address:** swtaber@svsu.edu

TABIOS, Eileen. (Eileen R. Tabios). American (born United States), b. 1960?. **Genres:** Biography, Autobiography/Memoirs, Novels, Poetry. **Career:** Asian Pacific American Journal, editor; Meritage Press, founder. Writer, banker and stock market analyst. **Publications:** After the Egyptians Determined the Shape of the World As a Circle, 1996; Black Lightning: Poetry in Progress, 1998; Beyond Life Sentences, 1998; (ed.) The Anchored Angel: Selected Writings of José Garcia Villa, 1999; Ecstatic Mutations: Experiments in the Poetry Laboratory, 2000; (ed. with N. Carbó) Babaylan: An Anthology of Filipina and Filipina American Writers, 2000; My Romance, 2001; Reproductions of the Empty Flagpole (poems), 2002; (ed. with M.E. Galang) Screaming Monkeys: Critiques of Asian American Images, 2003; Ménage a Trois with the 21st Century, 2004; Behind the Blue Canvas: Stories, 2004; Post Bling Bling, 2005; I Take Thee, English, for My Beloved, 2005; The Secret Lives of Punctuations, vol. I, 2006; Dredging for Atlantis, 2006; The Light That Left His Body Entered Thine Eyes, 2007; The Light Sang as it Left Your Eyes: Our Autobiography: Poetry, 2007; The Blind Chatelaine's Keys: Her Biography Through Your Poetics, 2008; Footnotes to Algebra: Uncollected Poems 1995-2009, 2009; Nota bene eiswein, 2009; The Thorn Rosary: Selected Prose Poems & New (1998-2010), 2010. Contributor to journals. **Address:** 256 North Fork Crystal Springs Rd., Saint Helena, CA 94574, U.S.A.

TABIOS, Eileen R. *See* **TABIOS, Eileen.**

TAEUBER, Cynthia M. American (born United States), b. 1947. **Genres:** Demography, History. **Career:** National Academy of Sciences, research analyst, 1971-72; Oak Ridge Associated Universities, staff, 1972-73, Southern Regional Demographic Group, executive secretary, 1973-74; U.S. Bureau of the Census, social science analyst, 1974-76, survey statistician, 1976-83, Age and Sex Statistics Branch, Population Division, chief, 1983-94, congressional associate, 1994-95, customer liaison office, senior program advisor and director, 1994-96, American Community Survey, program policy adviser, 1997-99; Census Bureau, staff, 1999-2004; University of Baltimore, researcher, 2005-. Writer. **Publications:** (With B.L. Damon and D.G. Fowles) Guide to 1980 Census Data on the Elderly, 1986; (with V. Valdisera) Women in the American Economy, 1986; (with B.B. Torrey and K. Kinsella) An Aging World, 1987; (with G. Spencer and A.A. Goldstein) America's Centenarians: Data From the 1980 Census, 1987; (ed. and comp.) Statistical Handbook on Women in America, 1991, 2nd ed., 1996; Sixty-Five Plus in America, 1993; (with N. Carroll) A Profile of Older Workers in Idaho, 2004. Contributor of books to journals. **Address:** University of Baltimore, 1420 N Charles St., Baltimore, MD 21201, U.S.A. **Online address:** ctaeuber@ubalt.edu

TAFFEL, Ron Walter. American (born United States), b. 1946. **Genres:** Human Relations/Parenting, Psychology. **Career:** Downstate Medical Center, Child and Adolescent Treatment Division, director of treatment, 1974-79;

private therapist, 1979-; Institute for Contemporary Psychotherapy, director, 1982-95, Family and Couples Treatment Services, founder; National Parenting Network Inc., founder, 1995; Parents Magazine, contributing editor. Consultant. **Publications:** (With M. Blau) Parenting by Heart: How to Connect with Your Kids in the Face of Too Much Advice, Too Many Pressures, and Never Enough Time, 1991, rev. ed. as Parenting by Heart: How to Stay Connected to Your Child in a Disconnected World, 2002; (with R. Israeloff) Why Parents Disagree: How Women and Men Parent Differently and How We Can Work Together, 1994, rev. ed. as When Parents Disagree and What You Can Do about It, 2003; (with M. Blau) Nurturing Good Children Now: 10 Basic Skills to Protect and Strengthen Your Child's Core Self, 1999; Getting through to Difficult Kids and Parents: Uncommon Sense for Child Professionals, 2001; (with M. Blau) The Second Family: How Adolescent Power Is Challenging the American Family, 2001; Breaking through to Teens: A New Psychotherapy for the New Adolescence, 2005; Childhood Unbound: Saving Our Kids' Best Selves: Confident Parenting in a World of Change, 2009. **Address:** Institute of Contemporary Psychotherapy, 1 W 91 St., New York, NY 10024-1404, U.S.A. **Online address:** ron@listentomeplease.com

TAFT, John (Thomas). American/Irish (born Ireland), b. 1950. **Genres:** Documentaries/Reportage, International Relations/Current Affairs, Politics/Government. **Career:** Taft Associates, TV Productions, president; Harper's, editor, 1987-89; producer and consultant. **Publications:** Mayday at Yale: A Case Study in Student Radicalism, 1976; American Power: The Rise and Decline of U.S. Globalism, 1918-1988, 1989. **Address:** Taft Associates, 2221 Ontario Rd. NW, Washington, DC 20009, U.S.A.

TAFURI, Nancy. American (born United States), b. 1946. **Genres:** Children's Fiction, Illustrations, Animals/Pets. **Career:** Simon and Schuster (publisher), assistant art director, 1967-69; One Plus One Studio (graphic design firm), co-founder, graphic designer and illustrator, 1971-82. Writer and illustrator of children's books, 1980-. **Publications:** SELF-ILLUSTRATED FOR CHILDREN: All Year Long, 1983, 2nd ed., 1984; Early Morning in the Barn, 1983, 2nd ed., 1986; Have You Seen My Duckling?, 1984; Rabbit's Morning, 1985; Who's Counting, 1986; In a Red House, 1987; Where We Sleep, 1987; My Friends, 1987; Do Not Disturb, 1987; Spots, Feathers and Curly Tails, 1988; Two New Sneakers, 1988; One Wet Jacket, 1988; Junglewalk, 1988; The Ball Bounced, 1989; Follow Me!, 1990; This Is the Farmer, 1994; The Barn Party, 1995; The Brass Ring, 1996; What the Sun Sees, What the Moon Sees, 1997; I Love You, Little One, 1998; Counting to Christmas, 1998; Snowy Flowy Blowy: A Twelve Months Rhyme, 1999; Will You Be My Friend? A Bunny and Bird Story, 2000; Silly Little Goose!, 2001; Where Did Bunny Go?: A Bunny and Bird Story, 2001; Mama's Little Bears, 2002; The Donkey's Christmas Song, 2002; You Are Special, Little One, 2003; Goodnight, My Duckling, 2005; Five Little Chicks, 2006; The Busy Little Squirrel, 2007; Whose Chick are You?, 2007; Blue Goose, 2008; The Big Storm-A Very Soggy Counting Book, 2009; All Kinds of Kisses, 2011. Illustrator of books by others. **Address:** 44 Tophet Rd., PO Box 168, Roxbury, CT 06783, U.S.A. **Online address:** nancytafuri@gmail.com

TAGER-FLUSBERG, Helen. British/American (born United States), b. 1951. **Genres:** Psychology, Communications/Media. **Career:** University of Massachusetts, professor of psychology, 1978-; Eunice Kennedy Shriver Center, senior scientist, 1997-; Boston University, Boston University School of Medicine, professor of anatomy and neurobiology, professor, professor of psychology, Developmental Science Program, director and principal investigator. Writer. **Publications:** (Ed. with S. Baron-Cohen and D.J. Cohen) Understanding Other Minds: Perspectives from Autism, 1993, 2nd ed., 2000; (ed.) Constraints on Language Acquisition: Studies of Atypical Children, 1994; (ed.) Neurodevelopmental Disorders, 1999; Autism and William's Syndrome, 2002. **Address:** Department of Psychology, Boston University, Rm. 117 64 Cummington St., Boston, MA 02215, U.S.A. **Online address:** htagerf@bu.edu

TAGG, Christine Elizabeth. British (born England), b. 1962. **Genres:** Children's Fiction, Music. **Career:** Ridings Shopping Centre, secretary, 1985-97. Writer. **Publications:** Who Will You Meet on Scary Street?, 2001; Silly Stories, 2001; Monster Stories, 2001; Metal Mutz!, 2001; Buzz Off, I'm Busy, 2002; When I'm Big, 2002; Home Sweet Home, 2002; Little Owl in the Snow, 2002; Cinderlily: A Floral Fairy Tale in Three Acts, 2003. **Address:** Casatina, 32 The Spinney, Sandal, Wakefield, WY WF2 6JN, England. **Online address:** casatina32@hotmail.com

TAGGARD, Mindy Nancarrow. *See* **NANCARROW, Mindy.**

TAGLIAFERRO, Linda. American (born United States) **Genres:** Sciences. **Career:** School of Visual Arts, teacher. Illustrator and writer. **Publications:** Genetic Engineering: Progress or Peril?, 1997; Destination New York, 1998; The Complete Idiot's Guide to Decoding Your Genes, 1999; Bruce Lee, 2000; Galápagos Islands: Nature's Delicate Balance at Risk, 2001; Polar Bears, 2002; Thomas Edison: Inventor of the Age of Electricity, 2003; Spiders and Their Webs, 2004; Robins and Their Chicks, 2004; Rabbits and Their Burrows, 2004; Puerto Rico in Pictures, 2004; Ants and Their Nests, 2004; Dogs and Their Puppies, 2004; Birds and Their Nests, 2004; Bees and Their Hives, 2004; Bears and Their Dens, 2004; Bears and Their Cubs, 2004; Baboons and Their Infants, 2004; Palace of Versailles: France's Royal Jewel, 2005; Service Dogs, 2005; Taj Mahal: India's Majestic Tomb, 2005; Therapy Dogs, 2005; Explore the Tropical Rain Forest, 2007; Explore the Tundra, 2007; How Many Fish in the Sea?: A Book about Oceans, 2007; Explore the Deciduous Forest, 2007; How Does a Volcano Become an Island?, 2010; How Does a Plant Become Oil?, 2010; How Does an Earthquake Become a Tsunami?, 2010; Genetic Engineering: Modern Progress or Future Peril?, 2010; Who Lands Planes on a Ship?: Working on an Aircraft Carrier, 2011; Who Walks in Space?: Working in Space, 2011; World's Smartest Machines, 2011. PLANT LIFE CYCLES SERIES: Sunflowers, 2007; Apple Trees, 2007; Oak Trees, 2007; Pine Trees, 2007; Carrots, 2007; Bean, 2007. **Address:** Capstone Press, 151 Good Counsel Dr., PO Box 669, Mankato, MN 56002, U.S.A. **Online address:** nyclindat@gmail.com

TAGLIAVINI, Gabriela. American/Argentine (born Argentina), b. 1968. **Genres:** Novels, Plays/Screenplays, Young Adult Fiction, Translations. **Career:** CNN, entertainment writer. Director. **Publications:** Los colores de la memoria (novel), 1999, trans. as The Colors of Memory, 2001; La mujer que todo hombre quiere, 2001. **Address:** c/o Michael Lewis, Diverse Talent Group, 1875 Century Pk. E, Los Angeles, CA 90067-2501, U.S.A. **Online address:** gaboo_t@yahoo.com

TAGUIEFF, Pierre André. French (born France), b. 1946. **Genres:** Novels, Philosophy, History. **Career:** Centre National de la Recherche Scientifique, research director; Institut d' Etudes Politiques de Paris, professor. Writer. **Publications:** La force du préjugé: essai sur le racisme et ses doubles, 1988; (with G. Delannoi) Théories du nationalisme, 1991; Face au racisme, 1991; Les protocoles des sages de sion, 1992; Sur la nouvelle droit: jalons dune analyse critique, 1994; Les fins de lantiracisme: essai, 1995; La république menacée: entretiens ave Philippe petit, 1996; Leracisme: Un exposé pour comprendre un essai pour réfléchir, 1997; (with M. Tribalat) Face au front national: Arguments pour unecontre-offensive, 1998; La coleur et la sang: doctrines racistes lafrançaise, 1998; (co-author) Léantisémitisme de plume 1940-1944, 1999; Leffacement de lavenir, 2000; Résister au bougisme: démocratie forte contre mondialisation techno-marchande, 2001; Duprogress: biographie dune utopie moderne, 2001; (with G. Delannoi) Nationalismes en perspective, 2001; Lillusion populiste: de larchaque aumédiatique, 2002; La nouvelle judéophobie, 2002; Le sens duprogress: une approche historique et philosophique, 2004; Le retour dupopulisme: Un dé fi pour les démocraties europeénes, 2004; Precheurs de haine: Traversée de la judéophobie planétaire, 2004; La foire aux illuminés: Esotérisme, théorie du complot, extrémisme, 2005; Les contre-réactionnaires: Le progressisme entreillusion et imposture, 2007; Bioéthique ou le juste milieu, 2007; Julien Freund: au coeur du politique, 2008; Judéophobie des Modernes, 2008; Le Racisme, 2010; La Nouvelle Propagande Antijuive, 2010; Israël et la question juive, 2011. **Address:** Centre National de la Recherche Scientifique, 98 rue de l'Universite, Paris, 75794, France. **Online address:** pierreandre.taguieff@sciences-po.fr

TAHERI, Amir. Iranian (born Iran), b. 1942. **Genres:** Theology/Religion, History, Politics/Government, Theology/Religion, Social Sciences. **Career:** Kayhan Daily, editor-in-chief, 1972-79; Sunday Times, writer, 1980-84; Jeune Afrique, editor-in-chief, 1985-87; Mideast Horizon, director, 1987; Die Welt, editorial writer, 1989, 1995; Politique Internationale, editor, 1999-. **Publications:** The Spirit of Allah: Khomeini and the Islamic Revolution, 1985; Holy Terror: Inside the World of Islamic Terrorism, 1987; Nest of Spies: America's Journey to Disaster in Iran, 1988; The Cauldron: The Middle East Behind the Headlines, 1988; Crescent in a Red Sky: The Future of Islam in the Soviet Union, 1989; The Unknown Life of the Shah, 1991; Irak: le dessous des cartes, 2002; Persian Night: Iran under the Khomeinist Revolution, 2009; The

Kingdom of Allah: The Struggle for Saudi Arabia, 2010. **Address:** c/o Toby Eady, 5 Glendhow Grounds, London, GL 5W5 OBL, England. **Online address:** ataheri@hhsaudi.com

TAICHERT, Pari Noskin. American (born United States), b. 1958?. **Genres:** Novels, Young Adult Fiction, History. **Career:** Murderati.com, founder. Writer and educator. **Publications:** FICTION: The Clovis Incident, 2004; The Belen Hitch: A Sasha Solomon Mystery, 2005; Socorro Blast: A Sasha Solomon Mystery, 2008. Contributor to periodicals. **Address:** University of New Mexico Press, 1 University of New Mexico, PO Box 05-3185, Albuquerque, NM 87131-0001, U.S.A. **Online address:** pari@parinoskintaichert.com

TAINTER, Frank H(ugh). American (born United States), b. 1941. **Genres:** Agriculture/Forestry, Bibliography, Young Adult Fiction. **Career:** University of Minnesota, instructor in forest pathology, 1966-70; University of Arkansas, assistant professor, 1970-74, associate professor, 1974-79, professor of forestry, 1979; Clemson University, Department of Forest Resources, professor, 1979-, now professor emeritus. Writer. **Publications:** Microscopic identification of commercial Chilean woods. La identificación microscópia de las maderas comerciales chilenas, 1968; Diseases of Arkansas Forests, 1979; (with G.M. Weste and P.A. Mistretta) Annotated Bibliography of Littleleaf and Tree Decline Diseases Caused by Phytophthora Cinnamomi Rands, 1987; How the Biltmore Forest School Came to Be, 1992; Deforestation in Southwestern Colombia, 1995; (with F.A. Baker) Principles of Forest Pathology, 1996. **Address:** Department of Forest Resources, Clemson University, Lehotsky Hall, Clemson, SC 29634-1003, U.S.A. **Online address:** ftntr@clemson.edu

TAKAHASHI, Rumiko. Japanese (born Japan), b. 1957. **Genres:** Novels, Children's Fiction, Graphic Novels. **Career:** Manga (comics), writer and artist. **Publications:** Mermaid Forest, 1994; Ranma 1/2, 32 vols., 1995-2005; Mermaids Scar, 1996; Rumic World Trilogy, 1996; Rumic Theater, 1996; One-Pound Gospel, 1996; One-Pound Gospel: Hungry for Victory, 1997; Maison Ikkoku, 14 vols., 1997-2000; Mermaids Gaze, 1997; Return of Lum, 8 vols., 1997; Lum Urusei Yatsura: Perfect Collection, 1997; Inu-Yasha: A Feudal Fairy Tale, 23 vols., 1998-2005; One-Pound Gospel: Knuckle Sandwich, 1998; Rumic Theater: One of Double, 1998. **Address:** c/o Author Mail, VIZ L.L.C., 655 Bryant St., PO Box 77010, San Francisco, CA 94107, U.S.A.

TAKÁS, Tibor. Hungarian (born Hungary), b. 1954. **Genres:** Horror, Film. **Career:** Director of films. Writer. **Publications:** Deathline, 1997. **Address:** Agency for the Performing Arts, 9200 W Sunset Blvd., Ste. 900, Los Angeles, CA 90069-3604, U.S.A.

TAKASHIMA, Misako. (Misako Rocks). American/Japanese (born Japan) **Genres:** Novels, Graphic Novels, Mystery/Crime/Suspense. **Career:** Writer. **Publications:** GRAPHIC NOVELS AS MISAKO ROCKS: Biker Girl, 2006; Rock and Roll Love, 2007; Detective Jermain, vol. I, 2008. Contributor to periodicals. **Address:** Henry Holt and Company Inc., 175 5th Ave., Newyork, NY 10010, U.S.A. **Online address:** misako@misakorocks.com

TAKAYAMA, Sandi. American (born United States), b. 1962. **Genres:** Children's Fiction, Literary Criticism And History. **Career:** Librarian, 1991-. Educator and writer. **Publications:** The Musubi Man: Hawaii's Gingerbread Man, 1996; Sumorella: A Hawaii Cinderella Story, 1997; The Prince and the Li Hing Mui: Hawaii's Princess and the Pea, 1998; Musubi Man's New Friend, 2002; The Musubi Baby, 2007. **Address:** c/o Bess Press, 3565 Harding Ave., Honolulu, HI 96816, U.S.A.

TAKENAKA, Heizo. Japanese (born Japan), b. 1951. **Genres:** Economics, Politics/Government. **Career:** Ministry of Finance, senior economist, 1982; Osaka University, associate professor, 1987-88; Harvard University, visiting associate professor, 1988-89; Institute for International Economics, visiting fellow, 1989-90; Keio University, visiting associate professor, 1989, associate professor, 1990-96, professor, 2007-, Global Security Research Institute, director; NLI Research Institute, research associate. Writer. **Publications:** The Contemporary Japanese Economy and Economic Policy, 1991. IN JAPANESE: The Economics of Business Investment, 1984; Kenkyū kaihatsu to setsubi tōshi no keizaigaku: keizai katsuryoku o sasaeru mekanizumu, 1984; An Economic Analysis of External Imbalance, 1987; Taigai fukinkō no makuro bunseki: chochiku tōshi baransu to seisaku kyōchō, 1987; (with I. Naoko) Nichi-Bei keizai ronsō: iiwake no jidai wa owatta=Japan-U.S. Economic Controversy, 1988; Nichi-Bei masatsu no keizaigaku, 1991; Nihon keizai no kokusaika to kigyō tōshi, 1993; Nihon kenkokuron: shinseiki e no keizaigaku,

1993; Wealth of People, 1994; Minfuron, 1994; Nihon keizai wa ikinokoreru ka: shintensuru APEC, NAFTA, EU, 1995. **Address:** 5322 Endo, Fujisawa, Kanagawa, 252-8520, Japan.

TAL, Alon. Israeli/American (born United States), b. 1960?. **Genres:** Environmental Sciences/Ecology. **Career:** Office of Attorney General, assistant, 1985-86; Camp Tel Yehudah-Bet, director, 1987; Harvard University, Harvard School of Public Health, research associate, 1987-89, adjunct lecturer, 1989-97; Yael Solel Law Offices, staff, 1990; Ben-Gurion University, adjunct lecturer in environmental law and policy, 1990-94, Mitrani Department of Desert Ecology, senior lecturer, associate professor, 2005-09; Adam Teva V'din (Israel Union for Environmental Defense), founder, 1991, chairman, 1996-98; Tel Aviv University, faculty, 1991-2005; Arava Institute, founder and director of research, 1996-2005; University of Otago, faculty, 1998, visiting professor, 2003-04; Hebrew University, adjunct lecturer, 2000-03. Writer. **Publications:** (With A. Edelman and N. Ben-Aharon) Sevivah u-mediniyut: Kovets mehkarim, 2002; Pollution in a Promised Land: An Environmental History of Israel, 2002; Zihum avir mi-kele rekhev: Neyar 'emdah, 2002; (ed.) Speaking of Earth: Environmental Speeches That Moved the World, 2006; (ed. with A.A. Rabbo) Water Wisdom: Preparing the Groundwork for Cooperative and Sustainable Water Management in the Middle East, 2010. **Address:** Mitrani Department of Desert Ecology, Jacob Blaustein Institutes for Desert Research, Ben-Gurion University of the Negev, Sede Boqer Campus, Midreshet Ben-Gurio, 84990, Israel. **Online address:** alontal@bgu.ac.il

TALALAY, Kathryn M(arguerite). American (born United States), b. 1949. **Genres:** Songs/Lyrics And Libretti, Biography, Race Relations. **Career:** Indiana University School of Music, head reference librarian and research librarian, 1975-90; American Academy of Arts and Letters, assistant archivist and researcher, 1990-96; W.W. Norton and Co., senior developmental editor, 1996-. **Publications:** (Trans.) A Literal Translation of Joseph Haydn's Cantata, 1977; The Deserter (comic opera), 1980; Scores by Women Composers, 1988; (co-author) Notable Black American Women, 1992; Composition in Black and White: The Life of Philippa Schuyler, 1995; (co-author) Encyclopedia of African-American Culture and History, 1996; (co-author) The International Dictionary of Black Composers, 1999. Contributor to professional journals. **Address:** W.W. Norton & Company Inc., 500 5th Ave., New York, NY 10110, U.S.A. **Online address:** ktalalay@wwnorton.com

TALBOT, Emile J. American (born United States), b. 1941. **Genres:** Literary Criticism And History, Poetry, Intellectual History. **Career:** University of Illinois, instructor, 1967-68, assistant professor, 1968-73, associate professor, 1973-86, professor of French, 1986-2003, Center for Advanced Study, fellow, 1973-, coordinator of undergraduate studies, 1974-75, director of graduate studies, 1977-87, 1997-98, department head, 1988-94, now professor emeritus; National Endowment for the Humanities, fellow, 1973-74; The French Review, review editor, 1979-82; Québec Studies, editor, 2004-08. **Publications:** La Critique Stendhalienne de Balzac a Zola: Textes, 1979; Stendhal and Romantic Esthetics, 1985; Stendhal Revisited, 1993; Reading Nelligan, 2002. **Address:** Department of French, University of Illinois, Rm. 106, 1205 1/2 Nevada St, Urbana, IL 61801, U.S.A. **Online address:** ejtalbot@uiuc.edu

TALEB, Nassim Nicholas. British/American (born United States), b. 1960?. **Genres:** Social Sciences, Young Adult Fiction. **Career:** Union Bank of Switzerland, managing director and head currency derivatives trader; CIBC-Wood Gundy, managing director and worldwide head of financial option arbitrage; Chicago Mercantile Exchange, option market maker; Credit Agricole, trader; Empirica Capital L.L.C., founder, 1998; Courant Institute of Mathematical Sciences, fellow and adjunct professor of mathematics, 1999-2007; University of Massachusetts, Isenberg School of Management, dean's professor in the sciences of uncertainty, 2005-07; Wharton School Financial Institutions Center, fellow, professor; London Business School, visiting professor, 2007-09, professor of marketing and co-director of decision science laboratory, 2007-; New York University, Polytechnic Institute, distinguished professor of risk engineering, 2007-. Writer. **Publications:** Dynamic Hedging: Managing Vanilla and Exotic Options, 1997; Fooled by Randomness: The Hidden Role of Chance in the Markets and in Life, 2001, rev. ed., 2005; The Black Swan: The Impact of the Highly Improbable, 2007, 2nd ed., 2010; The Bed of Procrustes: Philosophical and Practical Aphorisms, 2010; Antifragility, 2012. Contributor to periodicals. **Address:** London Business School, Regents Pk., London, GL NW1 4SA, England. **Online address:** gamma@fooledbyrandomness.com

TALESE, Gay. American (born United States), b. 1932. **Genres:** Novels,

Autobiography/Memoirs, Essays, Literary Criticism And History, Travel/Exploration, Photography, History. **Career:** New York Times, reporter, 1956-65; writer, 1965-; University of Southern California, Master of Professional Writing Program, visiting writer. **Publications:** New York: A Serendipiter's Journey, 1961; The Bridge: The Building of the Verrazano-Narrows Bridge, 1964; The Over-Reachers, 1965; The Kingdom and the Power, 1969; Fame and Obscurity, 1970; Honor Thy Father, 1971; Thy Neighbor's Wife, 1980; (ed. with R. Atwan) The Best American Essays, 1987; Unto the Sons, 1992; (with B. Lounsberry) Writing Creative Nonfiction: The Literature of Reality, 1995; Origins of a Nonfiction Writer, 1996; The Gay Talese Reader: Portraits and Encounters, 2003; A Writer's Life, 2006; (intro.) New York: 365 Days, 2006; The Silent Season of a Hero, 2010. Contributors of articles to magazines. **Address:** Knopf Publicity Department, 1745 Broadway, 21st Fl., New York, NY 10019-4368, U.S.A.

TALIAFERRO, Charles. American (born United States), b. 1952. **Genres:** Theology/Religion, Philosophy, Essays. **Career:** University of Rhode Island, teaching fellow and assistant, 1975-77; Brown University, teaching fellow and assistant, 1979-84; University of Massachusetts, instructor, 1982-84; University of Notre Dame, instructor, 1984-85; St. Olaf College, Department of Philosophy, faculty, 1985-, acting chair of department, 1996, professor, 1998-; Princeton University, visiting fellow, 1998-99; University of Oxford, fellow, 2005. Writer. **Publications:** NONFICTION: Consciousness and the Mind of God, 1994; (ed. with P.L. Quinn) A Companion to Philosophy of Religion, 1997, (ed. with P.L. Quinn and P. Draper) 2nd ed., 2010; Contemporary Philosophy of Religion, 1997; Praying with C.S. Lewis, 1998; (ed. with P.J. Griffiths) Philosophy of Religion: An Anthology, 2003; (ed. and intro. with A.J. Teply) Cambridge Platonist Spirituality, 2004; Evidence and Faith: Philosophy and Religion since the Seventeenth Century, 2005; Love, Love, Love and Other Essays: Light Reflections on Love, Life, and Death, 2006; (with W.L. Craig) Is God Real?, 2007; (with S. Goetz) Naturalism, 2008; Dialogues about God, 2008; (ed. with C.V. Meister) The Cambridge Companion to Christian Philosophical Theology, 2010. OTHERS: (J. Evans) Image in Mind, 2010; (ed. with E.J. Marty) A Dictionary of Philosophy of Religion, 2010; (with E. Marty) A Dictionary in Philosophy of Religion, 2010; (ed. with V.S. Harrison and S. Goetz) The Routledge Companion to Theism, 2011; The Golden Cord, 2011; Aesthetics, 2011; (with S. Goetz) A Brief History of the Soul, 2011; (ed. with C. Meister) Investigating Philosophy of Religion, forthcoming; (ed. with J. Evans) Turning Images in Philosophy, Science, and Religion, forthcoming; (ed. with C. Meister) The History of Evil, vol. I: Evil in Antiquity, vol. II: Evil in the Middle Ages, vol. III: Evil in the Early Modern Age, vol. IV: Evil in the 18th and 19th Centuries, vol. V: Evil in the Early 20th Century, vol. VI: Evil from the Mid-20th Century to Today, forthcoming; (ed. with C. Meister) Provocateurs, forthcoming. Contributor of articles to books and journals. **Address:** Department of Philosophy, St. Olaf College, 506 Holland Hall, 1520 St. Olaf Ave., Northfield, MN 55057, U.S.A. **Online address:** taliafer@stolaf.edu

TALLEY, Colin L. American (born United States), b. 1963?. **Genres:** History. **Career:** University of California, lecturer, 1997; Vanderbilt University, assistant professor, 1999; San Diego State University, adjunct professor, 2000-03, lecturer, 2002-03; Emory University, consulting research historian, 2001-03, assistant research professor, 2006-. Writer. **Publications:** A History of Multiple Sclerosis, 2008. Contributor of articles to books and periodicals. **Address:** Rollins School of Public Health, Emory University, 1518 Clifton Rd. NE, Atlanta, GA 30322, U.S.A. **Online address:** cltalle@sph.emory.edu

TALLICHET, Suzanne E. American (born United States), b. 1956?. **Genres:** Young Adult Non-fiction, Social Sciences, Women's Studies And Issues. **Career:** Pennsylvania State University, instructor; Morehead State University, assistant professor, 1993-, associate professor, professor of sociology. Writer. **Publications:** Daughters of the Mountain: Women Coal Miners in Central Appalachia, 2006. Contributor to books and journals. **Address:** Department of Sociology, Social Work & Criminology, Morehead State University, 313 Rader Hall, Morehead, KY 40351-1689, U.S.A. **Online address:** s.tallic@moreheadstate.edu

TALLIS, Frank. American (born United States) **Genres:** Law, Mystery/Crime/Suspense, Novels, Young Adult Non-fiction, Self Help. **Career:** Clinical psychologist, neuroscientist; Florence Nightingale Hospital (formerly Charter Nightingale Hospital), clinical psychologist. Writer. **Publications:** LIEBERMANN PAPERS: Mortal Mischief, 2005; Vienna Blood: A Novel, 2006. NOVELS: Killing Time, 1999; Sensing Others, 2001; Fatal Lies, 2008.

NONFICTION: How to Stop Worrying, 1990; Understanding Obsessions and Compulsions: A Self-Help Manual, 1992; (with S. Jones) Coping with Schizophrenia, 1994; Obsessive Compulsive Disorder: A Cognitive and Neuropsychological Perspective, 1995; Cognition and Cognitive Neuropsychology, 1995; Changing Minds: The History of Psychotherapy as an Answer to Human Suffering, 1998; Hidden Minds: A History of the Unconscious, 2002; Love Sick: Love As a Mental Illness, 2004. OTHERS: (ed. with G.C.L. Davey) Worrying: Perspectives on Theory, Assessment and Treatment, 1994; (with S. Hodgson and G.C.L. Davey) Worried Sick: The Relationship between Worrying and Psychological and Physical Health Status, 1997; Death in Vienna, 2005; Darkness Rising, 2009; Deadly Communion, 2010; Vienna Secrets: A Max Liebermann Mystery, 2010; Death And The Maiden, 2011. **Address:** Florence Nightingale Hospital, 11-19 Lisson Grove, London, GL NW1 6SH, England. **Online address:** author@franktallis.com

TALLIS, Robyn. See MACDONALD, James D.

TALLIS, Robyn. See SMITH, Sherwood.

TALLIS, Robyn. See ZAMBRENO, Mary Frances.

TALLIS, Robyn. See DOYLE, Debra.

TALLMAN, Shirley. (Erin Ross). American (born United States) **Genres:** Mystery/Crime/Suspense, Plays/Screenplays. **Career:** KNTV, traffic manager, script writer, director. **Publications:** SARAH WOOLSON MURDER MYSTERIES SERIES: Please Stand By-Your Mother's Missing, 1980; (as Erin Ross) Second Harvest, 1982; Flower of the Orient, 1983; (as Erin Ross) Time for Tomorrow, 1983; (as Erin Ross) Fragrant Harbor, 1984; Tide's End, 1984; Odds Against, 1984; Child of My Heart, 1984; (as Erin Ross) Roses for Remembering, 1985; (as Erin Ross) Willing Spirit, 1986; (as Erin Ross) Carnival Madness, 1987; The Babysitter's Seduction, 1996; Murder on Nob Hill, 2004; The Russian Hill Affair, 2005; The Russian Hill Murders, 2005; The Cliff House Strangler, 2007; Scandal on Rincon Hill: A Sarah Woolson Mystery, 2010. **Address:** Incline Village, NV 89451, U.S.A. **Online address:** shirleytallman@comcast.net

TAMAR, Erika. American/Austrian (born Austria), b. 1934. **Genres:** Children's Fiction, Young Adult Fiction, Picture/Board Books, Sports/Fitness. **Career:** Freelance writer, 1982-; Leo Burnett Company Inc., production assistant and casting director; Play Troupe of Port Washington (community theater), actress and director. **Publications:** YOUNG ADULT NOVELS: Blues for Silk Garcia, 1983; Good-bye, Glamour Girl, 1984; It Happened at Cecilia's, 1989; High Cheekbones, 1990; Out of Control, 1991; The Truth about Kim O'Hara, 1992; Fair Game, 1993; The Things I Did Last Summer, 1994. MID-GRADE NOVELS: Soccer Mania!, 1993; The Junkyard Dog, 1995; Alphabet City Ballet, 1996; The Midnight Train Home, 2000; Venus and the Comets, 2003; The Girls of Lighthouse Lane, vol. V, 2004; Katherine's Story: A Cape Light Novel, 2004; Rose's Story: A Cape Light Novel, 2004; Lizabeth's Story: A Cape Light Novel, 2004; Amanda's Story: A Cape Light Novel, 2004. PICTURE BOOKS: The Garden of Happiness, 1996; Donnatalee: A Mermaid Adventure, 1998. Contributor of articles to magazines. **Address:** 399 E 72nd St., New York, NY 10021, U.S.A.

TAMBLYN, Amber. American (born United States), b. 1983. **Genres:** Poetry, Literary Criticism And History, Humor/Satire. **Career:** Actress and poet. **Publications:** Free Stallion (poems), 2005; Bang Ditto, 2009. **Address:** The Bartel's Co., PO Box 57593, Sherman Oaks, CA 91403, U.S.A. **Online address:** amber@amtam.com

TAMBURRI, Anthony Julian. American (born United States), b. 1949. **Genres:** Cultural/Ethnic Topics, Language/Linguistics, Literary Criticism And History, Essays. **Career:** Smith College, instructor of Italian, 1981-83; Middlebury College, visiting assistant professor of Italian, 1984-86; Auburn University, assistant professor of Italian, 1986-87; Purdue University, assistant professor, 1987-89, associate professor, 1990-94, Section of Classics and Italian, chair, 1999-2000, professor of Italian and comparative literature, 1995-2000; Florida Atlantic University, Department of Languages and Linguistics, Research, Graduate and Interdisciplinary Programs, associate dean for research, graduate and interdisciplinary studies, 2003-06, professor of Italian and comparative literature, director of program; Queens College, John D. Calandra Italian American Institute, dean, 2006-. Writer. **Publications:** Of Saltimbanchi and Incendiari: Aldo Palazzeschi and Avant-Gardism in Italy,

1990; To Hyphenate or Not to Hyphenate: The Italian/American Writer: An Other American?, 1991; Per una lettura retrospettiva: Prosegiovanili di Aldo Palazzeschi, 1994; A Reconsideration of Aldo Palazzeschi's Poetry, 1905-1974: Revisiting the Saltimbanco, 1998; A Semiotic of Ethnicity: In Recognition of the Italian/American Writer, 1998; A Semiotic of Re-reading: Italo Calvino's 'Snow Job', 1998; Italian/American Briefs, 2000; Italian/American Short Films and Music Videos: A Semiotic Reading, 2002; Semiotics of Re-Reading: Guido Gozzano, Aldo Palazzeschi and Italo Calvino, 2003; Una semiotioca dellari-lettura: Guido Gozzano, Aldo Palazzeschi, Italo Calvino, 2003; (with F. Gardaphé and P. Giordano) Introducing Italian Americana: Generalities on Literature and Film: A Bilingual Forum, 2006; Narrare Altrove: Diversesegnalature letterarie, 2007; Semiotica dell'etnicità: Nuove Segnalature per la Scrittura Italiano/Americana, 2010. EDITOR: (co-ed.) Italiana 1988, 1990; (with B. Lawton) Romance Languages Annual 1990, 1990; (with P.S. Isolani) Italian Americans Celebrate Life: The Arts and Popular Culture, 1990; (with P.A. Giordano and F.L. Gardaphé) From the Margin: Writings in Italian Americana, 1991, rev. ed., 2000; (with C. Ganelin) Romance Languages Annual 1991, 1991; (with M.J. Bona) Through the Looking Glass: Italian and Italian/American Images in the Media: Selected Essays from the 27th Annual Conference of the American Italian Historical Association, 1996; (with P.A. Giordano) Beyond the Margin: Readings in Italian Americana, 1998; (co-ed.) Shades of Black and White: Conflict and Collaboration between Two Communities: Selected Essays from the 30th Annual Conference of the American Italian Historical Society, 1999; (with P.A. Giordano) Italian Americans: A Retrospective on the Twentieth Century, 2001; (with P.A. Giordano) Esilio, migrazione, e sogno Americano, 2002; (with A.C. Hostert) Screening Ethnicity: Cinematographic Representations of Italian Americans in the United States, 2002; (with C. Headley) Same-sex Unions: A Symposium, 2004; (co-ed.) Italian Cultural Studies, 2001: Selected Essays, 2004; (co-ed.) Italian Cultural Studies, 2002: Selected Essays, 2005; (with M.J. Bona and D. Esposito) Italian Americans and the Arts & Culture, 2005; Global Diaspsoristics and the United States: Exile, Migration, Race, Ethnicity: Selected Papers, 2005; (with G. Parati) The Cultures of Italian Migration, 2011. Contributor to journals. **Address:** John D. Calandra Italian American Institute, Queens College, The City University of New York, 65-30 Kissena Blvd., Flushing, NY 33431, U.S.A. **Online address:** tamburri@fau.edu

TAMURA, Linda. American/Japanese (born Japan), b. 1949. **Genres:** Cultural/Ethnic Topics, Education, History. **Career:** McMinnville Schools, elementary school teacher, 1971-75; Oregon State University, graduate teaching assistant, 1975-77; Pacific University, professor of education, 1977-94, Education Department, chair, 1977-92, director of teacher education, 1992-94; Willamette University, professor of education, 1994-. Writer. **Publications:** In This Great Land of Freedom: Japanese Pioneers of Oregon: Curriculum Guide, 1993; The Hood River Issei: An Oral History of Japanese Settlers in Oregon's Hood River Valley, 1993; (ed. with K.D. Hamlin and R. Fromherz) Turning Points in Teaching: Narrative Reflection on Professional Practice, 2001. Contributor to periodicals and books. **Address:** School of Education, Willamette University, GSE Rm. 18, Executive Bldg., 900 State St., Salem, OR 97301, U.S.A. **Online address:** ltamura@willamette.edu

TAN, Amy. American (born United States), b. 1952. **Genres:** Novels, Children's Fiction, Young Adult Non-fiction, Essays. **Career:** Consultant to programs for disabled children, 1976-81; Emergency Room Reports (now Emergency Medicine Reports), reporter, managing editor, associate publisher 1981-83; freelance technical writer, 1983-87. **Publications:** NOVELS: The Joy Luck Club, 1989; The Kitchen God's Wife, 1991; The Hundred Secret Senses, 1995; The Bonesetter's Daughter, 2001; The Opposite of Fate, 2003; Saving Fish from Drowning, 2005. OTHER: The Moon Lady (children's book), 1992; Sagwa: The Chinese Siamese Cat, 1994; (contrib.) Mid-Life Confidential: The Rock Bottom Remainders Tour America With Three Cords and an Attitude, 1994; (contrib.) Mother, 1966; (ed.) The Best American Short Stories 1999, 1999. **Address:** c/o Sandra Dijkstra, Sandra Dijkstra Literary Agency, 1155 Camino Del Mar, PO Box 515, Del Mar, CA 92014, U.S.A.

TAN, Kok-Chor. American/Singaporean (born Singapore), b. 1964. **Genres:** Philosophy, Politics/Government. **Career:** University of Pennsylvania, assistant professor of philosophy, 2002-, associate professor of philosophy, graduate chair. Writer. **Publications:** Toleration, Diversity and Global Justice, 2000; Justice without Borders: Cosmopolitanism, Nationalism and Patriotism, 2004; Institutions, Luck, and Justice, forthcoming. **Address:** Department of Philosophy, University of Pennsylvania, 464 Cohen Hall, 249 S 36th St., Philadelphia, PA 19104, U.S.A. **Online address:** kctan@sas.upenn.edu

TAN, Sor-hoon. Singaporean (born Singapore), b. 1965. **Genres:** Politics/Government, Law, History. **Career:** National University of Singapore, faculty member, 2000-, Department of Philosophy, associate professor and head, 2007-. Writer. **Publications:** Confucian Democracy: A Deweyan Reconstruction, 2003. EDITOR: (and contrib. with K. Chong and C.L. Ten) The Moral Circle and the Self: Chinese and Western Approaches, 2003; (and contrib. with A.K.L. Chan) Filial Piety in Chinese Thought and History, 2004; (and contrib.) Challenging Citizenship: Group Membership and Cultural Identity in a Global Age, 2005; (with J. Whalen-Bridge and contrib.) Democracy as Culture: Dewey Pragmatism in a Globalising World, 2008. Contributor of articles to books and journals. **Address:** Department of Philosophy, Faculty of Arts and Social Sciences, National University of Singapore, 3 Arts Link, Singapore, 117570, Singapore. **Online address:** phitansh@nus.edu.sg

TANAKA, Stefan. American (born United States), b. 1952. **Genres:** History. **Career:** University of California, associate professor of history. **Publications:** Japan's Orient: Rendering Pasts into History, 1993; New Times in Modern Japan, 2004. **Address:** Department of History, University of California, 9500 Gilman Dr., La Jolla, CA 92093-0104, U.S.A. **Online address:** stanaka@ucsd.edu

TANAKA, Yukiko. American/Japanese (born Japan), b. 1940. **Genres:** Literary Criticism And History, Women's Studies And Issues, Translations, Social Sciences. **Career:** Freelance writer, translator and educator. **Publications:** EDITOR: (with E. Hanson) This Kind of Woman: Ten Stories by Japanese Women Writers, 1960-1976, 1982; To Live and To Write: Selections by Japanese Women Writers, 1913-1938, 1987; Unmapped Territories: New Women's Fiction from Japan, 1991. OTHERS: Contemporary Portraits of Japanese Women, 1995; Women Writers of Meiji and Taishō Japan: Their Lives, Works, and Critical Reception, 1868-1926, 2000; (trans.) S. Kishida, Nihon ga Amerika wo yurusu hi (title means: 'A Place for Apology: War, Guilt, and US-Japan Relations'), 2004. **Address:** 324 NE 88th St., Seattle, WA 98115-2933, U.S.A. **Online address:** foxytanaka@yahoo.com

TANCER, Bill. American (born United States), b. 1966. **Genres:** Information Science/Computers, Marketing. **Career:** Gartner Group, Internet Sector, senior technology marketplace consultant; Hitwise, general manager of global research, 2004-; LookSmart, team leader; Zaplet, team leader, strategy director; NBC Internet, team leader; Pacific Bell Internet Services, team leader; NBIC, strategy director; SEMPO, board director; Time Magazine, columnist; Wall Street Journal, columnist.. Marketing executive. **Publications:** Click: What Millions of People Are Doing Online and Why It Matters, 2008. **Address:** Hitwise, 300 Park Ave. S, 9th Fl., New York, NY 10010, U.S.A.

TANEN, Sloane A. American (born United States), b. 1970. **Genres:** Humor/Satire, Children's Fiction, Animals/Pets. **Career:** Writer. **Publications:** Bitter with Baggage Seeks Same: The Life and Times of Some Chickens (humor), 2003; Where Is Coco Going?, 2004; Going for the Bronze: Still Bitter, More Baggage, 2005; Coco all Year Round, 2006; Coco Counts, 2007; C is for Coco, 2007; Hatched!: The Big Push From Pregnancy to Motherhood, 2007; Appetite for Detention, 2008. Contributor to periodicals. **Address:** VHPS Distribution Ctr., 16365 James Madison Hwy., Gordonsville, VA 22942-8501, U.S.A. **Online address:** tanens@aol.com

TANG, Victor. American (born United States), b. 1942. **Genres:** Information Science/Computers, Technology, Mathematics/Statistics, Engineering, Business/Trade/Industry. **Career:** RCA Corp., systems programmer, 1965-67; Pennsylvania State University, research assistant in mathematics and computer science, 1967-69; International Business Machines (IBM) Corp., Palo Alto Systems Center, systems engineer, manager of strategy and business development, IBM Communications Group, manager of strategy development, 1969-85, director of strategy and technology development, 1986-89, director of market analysis, 1990-91, Santa Teresa Laboratory, director of strategy, planning, and quality, 1992-, vice president; St. Mary's Graduate School of Business, adjunct assistant professor of strategy; Center for Innovation in Product Development, researcher; United Nations Development Programme, lecturer on market planning and strategy; Massachusetts Institute of Technology, Department of Mechanical Engineering, faculty. Writer. **Publications:** (Co-author) The Silverlake Project: Transformation at IBM, 1992; Innovations in Software Engineering Methodologies, 1993; (with C. Kaplan and R.

Clark) Secrets of Software Quality: 40 Innovations From IBM, 1995; (with R. Bauer) Competitive Dominance: Beyond Strategic Advantage and Total Quality Management, 1995. Contributor to books and journals. **Address:** Santa Teresa Laboratory, International Business Machines Corp., 555 Bailey Ave., San Jose, CA 95141, U.S.A. **Online address:** victang@mit.edu

TANNER, Jo A. American (born United States) **Genres:** Plays/Screenplays, Theatre, Humor/Satire, Photography, Literary Criticism And History. **Career:** City College of the City University of New York, adjunct lecturer in African American literature and world humanities, 1987-88; Queens College of the City University of New York, assistant professor, associate professor of drama, theatre and dance, head of black theatre program, 1988-2003; Double Image Theatre, instructor, 1990; Mosaic Jewels, writer/performer; Dusky Divas Productions, founder/executive director. Writer. **Publications:** Dusky Maidens: The Odyssey of the Early Black Dramatic Actress, 1992; Black Patti's Troubadours, 1998; Fighting All the Way: The Anita Bush Story, 1999; Drama Mama: The Life of Anita Bush, 1999. Contributor of articles and reviews to periodicals. **Address:** Department of Drama, Theatre, and Dance, Queens College of the City University of New York, Flushing, NY 11367-1597, U.S.A.

TANNER, John S. American (born United States), b. 1950. **Genres:** Literary Criticism And History, Business/Trade/Industry. **Career:** Florida State University, assistant professor of English, 1980-82; Brigham Young University, Department of English, assistant professor, 1982-86, associate professor, 1987-92, professor of English, 1992-, chair of the department, 1998-2003, associate academic vice president, 1992-98, academic vice president, 2004-. Writer. **Publications:** Anxiety in Eden: A Kierkegaardian Reading of Paradise Lost, 1992. **Address:** Office of the Academic Vice President, Brigham Young University, A-387 ASB, Provo, UT 84602, U.S.A. **Online address:** john_tanner@byu.edu

TANNER, Karen Holliday (Olson). American (born United States), b. 1940. **Genres:** History, Biography. **Career:** Restaurant manager and owner, 1981-86; accountant, 1986-. Writer. **Publications:** Doc Holliday: A Family Portrait, 1998. WITH J.D. TANNER, JR.: Last of the Old-Time Outlaws: The George West Musgrave Story, 2002; Climax Jim: The Tumultuous Tale of Arizona's Rustling Cowboy, 2005; New Mexico Territorial Penitentiary (1884-1912) Directory of Inmates, 2006; Bronco Bill Gang, 2011. Contributor to magazines. **Address:** c/o Jon Tuska, Golden West Literary Agency, 2327 SE Salmon St., Portland, OR 97214, U.S.A. **Online address:** khtanner@aol.com

TANNER, Kathryn. American (born United States), b. 1957. **Genres:** Theology/Religion. **Career:** Yale University, teaching fellow, 1980-83, Department of Religious Studies, acting instructor, 1984-85, assistant professor, 1985-91, associate professor, 1991-94, Yale Divinity School, Pitt Lecturer, 2003, professor of systematic theology, 2010-; University of Chicago, Divinity School, Sharpe Lecturer, 1992, associate professor of theology, 1994-2000, professor of theology, 2000-04, Dorothy Grant Maclear Professor of Theology, 2006-10; Journal of Religion, Theology and Philosophy of Religion Division, general editor, 1993-97; Methodist School of Theology, Williams Lecturer, 1997-98; Journal of Religion, co-editor, 1998-2003; University of Aberdeen, Scottish Journal of Theology Lecturer, 1999; Harvard Divinity School, Horace De Y. Lentz Memorial Lecturer, 2002; Austin Theological Seminary, Thomas White Currie Lecturer, 2003; Vanderbilt Divinity School, Cole Lecturer, 2003; Katholieke Universiteit Leuven, Walgrave Lecturer, 2003; Brown University, Brooke Anderson Lecturer, 2005; Trinity Theological College, Rollie Busch Lecturer, 2005; University of Nottingham, Firth Lecturer, 2005; Davidson College, Otts-Maloney Lecturer, 2006; Princeton Theological Seminary, Warfield Lecturer, 2007; Eureka College, Humbert Lecturer on Religion and Society, 2009; Memphis Theological Seminary, Lowrie-Johns Lecturer, 2009; Seminary of the Southwest, Harvey Lecturer, 2010; Union Theological Seminary, Sprunt Lecturer, 2011. Theologian. **Publications:** God and Creation in Christian Theology: Tyranny or Empowerment, 1988; The Politics of God: Christian Theologies and Social Justice, 1992; Theories of Culture: A New Agenda for Theology, 1997; (ed. with D. Brown and S.G. Davaney) Converging on Culture: Theologians in Dialogue with Cultural Analysis and Criticism, 2001; Jesus, Humanity and the Trinity: A Brief Systematic Theology, 2001; (ed.) Spirit in the Cities: Searching for Soul in the Urban Landscape, 2004; Economy of Grace, 2005; (ed. with J. Webster and I. Torrance) The Oxford Handbook of Systematic Theology, 2007; Christ the Key, 2010. **Address:** Yale Divinity School, Yale University, 409 Prospect St., New Haven, CT 06511, U.S.A. **Online address:** kathryn.tanner@yale.edu

TANNER, Marcus. British (born England), b. 1961. **Genres:** Documentaries/Reportage, Biography, History. **Career:** The Independent, Balkan correspondent, 1988-94, deputy foreign editor, 1995-2000; The Institute for War and Peace Reporting, editor and trainer, teacher of journalism in the Balkans, 2004; Balkan Investigative Reporting Network, Balkan Insight, editor and trainer, 2005-. Journalist. **Publications:** Ticket to Latvia: A Journey from Berlin to the Baltic, 1989; Croatia: A Nation Forged in War, 1997, 3rd ed., 2010; Ireland's Holy Wars: The Struggle for A Nation's Soul, 1500-2000, 2001; Last of the Celts, 2004; The Raven King: Matthias Corvinus and the Fate of His Lost Library, 2008; (ed.) Ivan Mestrovic: The Making of a Master, 2008. **Address:** Yale University Press, 302 Temple St., PO Box 209040, New Haven, CT 06511, U.S.A. **Online address:** marcusgt@gmail.com

TANNER, Michael (K.). British (born England), b. 1935?. **Genres:** Music, Philosophy, Humanities. **Career:** Cambridge University, Corpus Christi College, instructor in philosophy, life fellow. Writer. **Publications:** Nietzsche, 1994; A Critical History of Opera, 1994; Wagner, 1996; (with R. Scruton, P. Singer and C. Janaway) German Philosophers: Kant, Hegel, Schopenhauer, Nietzsche, 1997; Schopenhauer: Metaphysics and Art, 1998. EDITOR: (intro.) W. Furtwaengler, Notebooks, 1924-1954, 1989; F.W. Nietzsche, The Birth of Tragedy out of the Spirit of Music, 1993. Contributor to periodicals. **Address:** Corpus Christi College, Cambridge University, Cambridge, CB2 1RH, England.

TANNER, Norman P. Italian/British (born England), b. 1943. **Genres:** History, Theology/Religion, Translations. **Career:** Ordained Roman Catholic priest, 1976; Farm Street Parish, assistant priest, 1977-78; University of Oxford, teacher of history, 1978-89, senior tutor, 1981-97, theology, 1989-97, research lecturer, 1997-; Pontifical Gregorian University, professor of church history, Faculty of the History and Cultural Patrimony of the Church, dean. Writer. **Publications:** The Church in Late Medieval Norwich, 1370-1532, 1984; The Councils of the Church: A Short History, 2001; Is the Church too Asian?: Reflections on the Ecumenical Councils, 2002; (co-author) History of Vatican II, vol. IV, 2002; Was the Church Too Democratic?: Councils, Collegiality and the Church's Future, 2003; Church and the World: Gaudium et Spes, Inter Mirifica, 2005; Church in the Later Middle Ages, 2008; Ages of Faith, 2009; The Church in Council: Conciliar Movements, Religious Practice and the Papacy from Nicea to Vatican II, 2011. EDITOR: Heresy Trials in the Diocese of Norwich, 1428-31, 1977; Decrees of the Ecumenical Councils, 2 vols., 1990; Kent Heresy Proceedings 1511-12, 1997; (and trans. with S. McSheffrey) Lollards of Coventry, 1486-1522, 2003. Contributor to books and periodicals. **Address:** Pontifical Gregorian University, 4 Piazza della Pilotta, Rome, 00187, Italy. **Online address:** tanner@unigre.it

TANNER, Stephen L. American (born United States), b. 1938. **Genres:** Literary Criticism And History, Biography, History. **Career:** University of Idaho, assistant professor, associate professor, 1969-78; Universidade Federal de Minas Gerais, senior Fulbright lecturer, 1974-76, 1983, 1989; Brigham Young University, associate professor, 1978-81, professor of English, 1981-2006; University of Coimbra, faculty, 1979. Writer. **Publications:** Ken Kesey, 1983; Paul Elmer More: Literary Criticism as the History of Ideas, 1987; Lionel Trilling, 1988; Ernest Haycox, 1996. **Address:** Department of English, Brigham Young University, Provo, UT 84602, U.S.A. **Online address:** sltanner@gmail.com

TANSELLE, G(eorge) Thomas. American (born United States), b. 1934. **Genres:** Literary Criticism And History, Bibliography, Art/Art History. **Career:** Chicago City Junior College, instructor in English, 1958-60; University of Wisconsin, instructor, 1960-61, assistant professor, 1961-63, associate professor, 1963-68, professor of English, 1968-78; Northwestern University Press, co-editor, 1968-; John Simon Guggenheim Memorial Foundation, vice president, 1978-, fellow, senior vice president, through 2006, now vice president emeritus; Literary Classics of the United States Inc., board director, 1979-; Columbia University, adjunct professor of English and comparative literature, 1980-, professor of bibliographic studies, School of Library Service, Summer Rare Book School, faculty, 1984-87; North America Inc., director, 1988-, chair, 1994-. **Publications:** Royall Tyler, 1967; (ed. with H. Hayford and H. Parker) Writings, 1968; Copyright Records and the Bibliographer, 1969; Guide to the Study of United States Imprints, 1971; A Checklist of Editions of Moby-Dick, 1851-1976, 1976; Selected Studies in Bibliography,

1979; The History of Books as a Field of Study, 1981; (ed. with H. Hayford and H. Parker) Israel Potter: His Fifty Years of Exile, 1982; Textual Criticism since Greg: A Chronicle, 1950-1985, 1987, rev. ed. as Textual Criticism since Greg: A Chronicle, 1950-2000, 2005; (ed. and intro.) Books as a Way of Life: Essays, 1988; A Rationale of Textual Criticism, 1989; Textual Criticism and Scholarly Editing, 1990; Introduction to Bibliography: Seminar Syllabus, 12th ed., 1990, 13th ed., 1992; Libraries, Museums, and Reading, 1991; A Description of Descriptive Bibliography, 1992; The Life and Work of Fredson Bowers, 1993; (ed. with D.L.V. Meulen) Samuel Johnson's Translation of Sallust, 1993; (co-ed.) Piazza Tales, 1996; Literature and Artifacts, 1998; (ed. with H. Hayford and H. Parker) Mardi and a Voyage Thither, 1998; (ed. with H. Hayford and H. Parker) Omoo: A Narrative of Adventures in the South Seas, 1999; (ed. with H. Hayford and H. Parker) White-jacket, or, The World in a Man-of-War, 2000; (ed. with P.F. Kardon and E.R. Schwager) The John Simon Guggenheim Memorial Foundation, 1925-2000: A Seventy-Fifth Anniversary Record, 2001; (ed. with H. Hayford and H. Parker) Moby-Dick, or, The Whale, 2001; (ed. with H. Hayford and H. Parker) The Confidence-man: His Masquerade, 2002; (ed. with H. Hayford and H. Parker) Typee: A Peep at Polynesian Life, 2003; (ed.) Art Deco Book in France, 2005; Bibliographical Analysis: A Historical Introduction, 2009; Book-jackets: Their History, Forms, and Use, 2011. Contributor to books and journals. **Address:** John Simon Guggenheim Memorial Foundation, 90 Park Ave., New York, NY 10016-1301, U.S.A.

TANZI, Rudolph E(mile). American (born United States), b. 1958. **Genres:** Medicine/Health. **Career:** Harvard University, Harvard Medical School, professor of neurobiology, 1990-, Joseph P. and Rose F. Kennedy professor of child neurology and mental retardation, Program in Neuroscience, affiliate faculty; Massachusetts General Hospital, Genetics and Aging Research Unit, director, 1990-, principal investigator; Neurogenetics Inc., scientific founder; Prana Biotechnology, scientific founder. Writer. **Publications:** (With A.B. Parson) Decoding Darkness: The Search for the Genetic Causes of Alzheimer's Disease, 2000. EDITOR: (with W. Wasco) Molecular Mechanisms of Dementia, 1997; (with S.G. Younkin and Y. Christen) Presenilins and Alzheimer's Disease, 1998; (with S.S. Sisodia) Alzheimer's Disease: Advances in Genetics, Molecular and Cellular Biology, 2007. **Address:** Genetics and Aging Research Unit, Massachusetts General Hospital, Rm. 2003, 114 Bldg., Charlestown Navy Yard, 114 16th St., Charlestown, MA 02129, U.S.A. **Online address:** tanzi@helix.mgh.harvard.edu

TANZMAN, Carol M. American (born United States) **Genres:** Novels, Young Adult Fiction. **Career:** Educator, consultant, administrator and writer. **Publications:** The Shadow Place (young adult novel), 2002; Dancergirl, 2011; Circle of Silence, forthcoming. **Address:** c/o Author Mail, Lerner Publishing Group, 1251 Washington Ave. N, Minneapolis, MN 55401-1607, U.S.A. **Online address:** carol@caroltanzman.com

TAPAHONSO, Luci. American (born United States), b. 1953. **Genres:** Poetry, Novellas/Short Stories, Songs/Lyrics And Libretti, Natural History, Children's Fiction. **Career:** University of New Mexico, assistant professor of English, 1987-89; University of Kansas, assistant professor, 1990-94, associate professor of English, 1994-99; University of Arizona, professor of of American Indian studies and English, 1999-. Writer. **Publications:** One More Shiprock Night: Poems, 1981; Seasonal Woman (poems), 1982; A Breeze Swept Through (poems), 1987; Sáanii Dahataał: The Women Are Singing: Poems and Stories, 1993; A Song for the Direction of North, 1994; Bah and Her Baby Brother, 1994; (ed.) Hayoolkaal: Dawn-An Anthology of Navajo Writers, 1995; (with E. Schick) Navajo ABC: A Diné Alphabet Book, 1995; Blue Horses Rush In: Poems and Stories, 1997; Songs of Shiprock Fair, 1999; Radiant Curve: Poems and Stories, 2008. Contributor to books. **Address:** American Indian Studies, University of Arizona, Harvill 226B, 218 Harvill Bldg., 1103 E 2nd St., PO Box 210076, Tucson, AZ 85721-0076, U.S.A. **Online address:** tapahons@email.arizona.edu

TAPIA, Richard A(lfred). American (born United States), b. 1939. **Genres:** Mathematics/Statistics, Education. **Career:** Todd Shipyards, mathematician, 1961-63; International Business Machines, part-time scientific programmer, 1963-66; University of California-Los Angeles, instructor, 1967-68; University of Wisconsin, assistant professor, 1968-70; Rice University, Department of Mathematical Sciences, assistant professor, 1970-72, associate professor, 1972-76, professor, 1976-, department chair, 1978-83, Office of Graduate Studies, associate director for minority affairs, 1989-, Noah Harding professor, 1991-2005, Center for Excellence and Equity in Education, director,

1995-, Alliances for Graduate Education and the Professoriate, cluster leader, 1999-, Maxfield and Oshman professor in engineering, 2005-, university professor, 2005-, Empowering Leadership Alliance, director, Office of Research and Graduate Studies, associate director; consultant, 1973-; Baylor College, Texas Institute of Rehabilitation and Research, adjunct professor, 1978-83, lecturer, 1986-88; Stanford University, lecturer, 1986-88, visiting associate professor; Center for Research on Parallel Computation (CRPC), director of education and outreach programs, 1989-2000-; University of Houston, College of Natural Sciences and Mathematics, adjunct professor, 2000-. Writer. **Publications:** (With J.R. Thompson) Nonparametric Probability Density Estimation, 1978; (with J.R. Thompson) Nonparametric Function Estimation, Modeling, and Simulation, 1978, rev. ed., 1990; (ed. with S. Gomez and J.P. Hennart) Advances in Numerical Partial Differential Equations and Optimization: Proceedings of the Fifth Mexico-United States Workshop, 1991; An Introduction to Mathematical Optimization Theory, forthcoming. **Address:** Department of Computational and Applied, Mathematics, Rice University, CAAM-MS 134, 6100 Main St., Houston, TX 77005-1892, U.S.A. **Online address:** rat@rice.edu

TAPLIN, Oliver. British (born England), b. 1943. **Genres:** Classics, Translations, Literary Criticism And History, Theatre. **Career:** Center for Hellenic Studies, junior fellow, 1970-71; University of Bristol, lecturer, 1972-73; Oxford University, Archive of Performances of Greek and Roman Drama, director, 1973-2008, Magdalen College, fellow and tutor, professor of classical languages and literature, professor emeritus, 2008-; Dartmouth College, visiting professor, 1981; University of California, visiting professor, 1987. Writer. **Publications:** The Stagecraft of Aeschylus: The Dramatic Use of Exits And Entrances in Greek Tragedy, 1977; Greek Tragedy in Action, 1978, 2nd ed., 2003; (with B. Rubens) An Odyssey Round Odysseus, 1989; Greek Fire, 1990; Homeric Soundings: The Shaping of the Iliad, 1992; Comic Angels: And Other Approaches to Greek Drama Through Vase Paintings, 1992; (ed.) Literature in the Greek World, 2001; (ed.) Literature in the Roman World, 2001; Pots & Plays: Interactions Between Tragedy And Greek Vase-Painting of the Fourth Century B.C, 2007; (co-ed.) The Pronomos Vase and its Context, 2010. Contributor to journals. **Address:** Magdalen College, Oxford University, High St., Oxford, OX OX1 4AU, England. **Online address:** oliver.taplin@magd.ox.ac.uk

TAPPAN, Mark B. American (born United States), b. 1957. **Genres:** Young Adult Non-fiction. **Career:** Colby College, professor and director. Writer. **Publications:** NONFICTION: (ed. with M.J. Packer) Narrative and Storytelling: Implications for Understanding Moral Development, 1991; (ed. with M.J. Packer) Cultural and Critical Perspectives on Human Development, 2001; (with L.M. Brown and S. Lamb) Packaging Boyhood: Saving Our Sons from Superheroes, Slackers, and Other Media Stereotypes, 2009. Contributor to books and journals. **Address:** Colby College, 4426 Mayflower Hill, Waterville, ME 04901-8844, U.S.A. **Online address:** mbtappan@colby.edu

TAPPER, Nancy. *See* **LINDISFARNE-Tapper, Nancy.**

TARABORRELLI, J. Randy. American (born United States), b. 1956. **Genres:** Biography, Music, Adult Non-fiction. **Career:** Biographer, 1984-; CBS News, televison reporter; Soul, editor and publisher. **Publications:** BIOGRAPHY: (with R. Wilson and D. Minger) Diana, 1985; Cher: A Biography, 1986; Laughing Till It Hurts: The Complete Life and Career of Carol Burnett, 1988; Call Her Miss Ross: The Unauthorized Biography of Diana Ross, 1989; Michael Jackson: The Magic and the Madness, 1991, rev. ed. as Michael Jackson-The Magic, the Madness, the Whole Story, 1958-2009, 2009; Roseanne Arnold, 1993; Sinatra: Behind the Legend, 1997; Jackie, Ethel, Joan: Women of Camelot, 2000; Madonna: An Intimate Biography, 2001; Once upon a Time: Behind the Fairy Tale of Princess Grace and Prince Rainier, 2003; Elizabeth, 2006. OTHERS: Motown: Hot Wax, City Cool and Solid Gold (non-fiction), 1986; Diana Ross, 2007; The Secret Life of Marilyn Monroe, 2009; After Camelot, 2012. **Address:** Bart Andrews and Associates, 7510 Sunset Blvd., Ste. 100, Los Angeles, CA 90046-3418, U.S.A.

TARANTINO, Quentin (Jerome). American (born United States), b. 1963. **Genres:** Plays/Screenplays, Novels, Animals/Pets. **Career:** Video Archives, clerk, 1985-90; Cinetel Productions, production assistant, 1990-92; A Band Apart Productions, co-founder, 1991-; screenwriter, filmmaker, director, producer and actor, 1992-; Rolling Thunder Distribution Co., co-founder, 1995-; A Band Apart Records, co-founder, 1997. **Publications:** Pulp Fiction: A Quentin Tarantino Screenplay, 1994; Jackie Brown: A Screenplay, 1997;

Quentin Tarantino: Interviews, 1998; (with C. Heard) Ten Thousand Bullets: The Cinematic Journey of John Woo, 1999; True Romance, 2000; Reservoir Dogs, 2000; Natural Born Killers, 2000; Quentin Tarantino: The Film Geek Files, 2000; Kill Bill, 2003; (contrib.) Grindhouse, 2007; Inglourious Basterds: A Screenplay, 2009. Contributor to periodicals. **Address:** A Band Apart Productions, 7966 Beverly Blvd., 2nd Fl., Los Angeles, CA 90048-4511, U.S.A.

TARAS, Raymond (C.). Canadian (born Canada), b. 1946. **Genres:** Politics/Government, Novels, International Relations/Current Affairs, Cultural/Ethnic Topics. **Career:** University of Essex, Department of Government, teaching assistant, 1969-71, Department of Sociology, research associate, 1970-72; Lanchester Polytechnic, lecturer in politics, 1972-76; freelance translator of historical and sociological monographs, 1978-81; Concordia University, research associate, 1981-82; University of Michigan, Center for Russian and East European Studies, visiting assistant professor of political science and research associate, 1982-83; University of Kentucky, visiting assistant professor of political science, 1983-84; University of Illinois, Russian and East European Center, research fellow, 1983; Ohio State University, Center for Slavic and East European Studies, fellow, 1984; Tulane University, assistant professor, 1984-88, associate professor of political science, 1988-96, professor of political science, 1996-, World Literature Program, director, 2008-08; University of Vermont, Department of Political Science, visiting professor, 1997; Hoover Institution on War, Revolution, and Peace, national fellow, 1990-91; Aalborg University, visiting professor, 1999; European University Institute, Robert Schuman Centre, visiting fellow. 2010. Writer. **Publications:** Ideology in a Socialist State: Poland, 1956-83, 1984; Poland: Socialist State, Rebellious Nation, 1986; (with D. Taddeo) Le debat linguistique au Quebec, 1987; (with R. Ebel and J. Cochrane) Political Culture and Foreign Policy in Latin America: Case Studies from the Circum-Caribbean, 1991; Polish Communists and the Polish Road to Socialism, 1993; Consolidating Democracy in Poland, 1995; (with R. Ganguly) Understanding Ethnic Conflict: The International Dimension, 1998, 4th ed., 2010; Liberal and Illiberal Nationalisms, 2002; (with M. Castle) Democracy in Poland, 2002; Europe Old and New: Transnationalism, Xenophobia, Belonging, 2009; Islamophobia and Europe's Values, 2011. EDITOR AND CONTRIBUTOR: Leadership Change in Communist States, 1989; The Road to Disillusion: From Critical Marxism to Post-Communism in Eastern Europe, 1992; Handbook of Political Science Research on the USSR and Eastern Europe: Trends from the 1950s to the 1990s, 1992; (with I. Bremmer) Nations and Politics in the Soviet Successor States, 1992; (with I. Bremmer) New States, New Politics: Building the Post-Soviet Nations, 1997; Postcommunist Presidents, 1997; National Identities and Ethnic Minorities in Eastern Europe, 1998. Works appear in anthologies. Contributor of articles to journals. **Address:** Department of Political Science, Tulane University, 306 Norman Mayer Bldg., 6823 St Charles Ave., New Orleans, LA 70118-5698, U.S.A. **Online address:** taras@tulane.edu

TARCOV, Nathan. American (born United States), b. 1948. **Genres:** Politics/Government. **Career:** Harvard University, Instructor, 1974-75, assistant professor, 1975-77; University of Chicago, Department of Political Science, assistant professor, 1978-81, associate professor, 1981-92, professor, 1992-, Political Theory Workshop, coordinator, The Leo Strauss Center, director; U.S.Naval War College, secretary, 1987-88. Writer. **Publications:** Locke's Education for Liberty, 1984; (trans. with H.C. Mansfield) N. Machiavelli, Discourses on Livy, 1996. EDITOR: (and intro. with R.W. Grant) Some Thoughts Concerning Education: And of the Conduct of the Understanding, 1996; (with C. Orwin) The Legacy of Rousseau, 1997. **Address:** Department of Political Science, University of Chicago, Foster 316, 5828 S University Ave., Chicago, IL 60637, U.S.A. **Online address:** n-tarcov@uchicago.edu

TARGETTI, Ferdinando. Italian (born Italy), b. 1945. **Genres:** Economics, Politics/Government, Essays. **Career:** Bocconi University, assistant, 1971-78, lecturer in problems of economic development and comparative economic systems, 1979-90; University of Trento, lecturer of economic policy, associate, 1974-96, professor, School of International Studies, director, 2001-05; University of Brescia, lecturer, 1982-84; New York University, visiting professor, 1984; University of Paris XIII, lecturer in theory of economic growth, 1991-93; Free University, Institute of Castellanza, lecturer, 1994-96. Writer. **Publications:** (With M. Baranzini and A. Chiancone) Nicholas Kaldor: teoria e politica economica di un capitalismo in mutamento, 1988; (ed. with A.P. Thirlwall) The Essential Kaldor, 1989; (ed. with A.P. Thirlwall) Further Essays on Economic Theory and Policy, 1989; Nicholas Kaldor: The Economics

and Politics of Capitalism as a Dynamic System, 1992; (ed.) Privatization in Europe: West and East Experiences, 1992. UNTRANSLATED WORKS: Valore e accumulazione, 1978; Lezioni di economia: L'inflazione, 1979; L'intervento dello Stato per lemaggiori scuole di pensiero economico, 1979; (ed.) Occupazione, moneta etassazione, 1987; (ed. with L. Marcolungo and M. Pugno) L'economiamondiale in trasformazione, 1988; (ed.) Economia e politica di uncapitalismo in mutamento, 1988; Le conseguenze economiche del governo Berlusconi, 2003; (with A. Fracasso) Le sfide della globalizzazione: Storia, politica e istituzioni, 2008. Works appear in anthologies. Contributor to journals. **Address:** Department of Economics, University of Trento, Via Inama 5, Trento, 38100, Italy. **Online address:** ferdinando.targetti@unitn.it

TARGOFF, Ramie. American (born United States), b. 1967?. **Genres:** Education, Literary Criticism And History. **Career:** Brandeis University, professor of English. Writer. **Publications:** Common Prayer: The Language of Public Devotion in Early Modern England, 2001; John Donne, Body and Soul, 2008. Contributor to periodicals. **Address:** Brandeis University, Rabb 238, 415 South St., Waltham, MA 02453, U.S.A. **Online address:** targoff@brandeis.edu

TARK, Ji-il. Korean (born Korea (South)), b. 1964. **Genres:** Race Relations, Theology/Religion. **Career:** Busan Presbyterian University, associate professor, professor, 2003-; Information Network on Christian Heresies, Modern Religion Monthly, editor. **Publications:** Family-Centered Belief & Practice in the Church of Jesus Christ of Latter-day Saints & the Unification Church, 2003. Contributor of periodicals to journals. **Address:** Busan Presbyterian University, 764 Gusan-Dong, Gimhae-Shi, Kyungnam, 1, Korea (South). **Online address:** tarkjiil@yahoo.com

TARLING, (Peter) Nicholas. New Zealander/British (born England), b. 1931. **Genres:** History, Business/Trade/Industry. **Career:** Royal Historical Society, assistant editor, 1956-57; University of Queensland, lecturer, 1957-61, senior lecturer in history, 1961-65; University of Auckland, associate professor, 1965-68, professor of history, 1968-97, deputy vice-chancellor, Faculty of Arts, dean, 1972-74, Southeast Asian Studies Centre, director and fellow, New Zealand Asia Institute, fellow; Royal Asiatic Society, fellow; Association of University Teachers of New Zealand, president, 1970-71, 1973-74; New Zealand Asian Studies Society, president, 1974-. **Publications:** Anglo-Dutch Rivalry in the Malay World, 1780-1824, 1962; Piracy and Politics in the Malay World, 1963; A Concise History of Southeast Asia, 1966; Southeast Asia, Past and Present, 1966; British Policy in the Malay Peninsula and Archipelago, 1824-1871, 1969; Britain, the Brookes and Brunei, 1971; Imperial Britain in Southeast Asia, 1975; (with O. Johnson) Cautions and Diversions: or, Dotty Lines and Road Remarks, 1975; Sulu and Sabah, 1978; The Burthen, The Risk, and the Glory, 1982; The Sun Never Sets, 1986; The Fourth Anglo-Burmese War, 1987; The Fall of Imperial Britain in South East Asia, 1993; (with R. Butterworth) A Shakeup Anyway: Government and the Universities in New Zealand in a Decade of Reform, 1994; Britain, Southeast Asia and the Onset of the Pacific War, 1996; Nations and States in Southeast Asia, 1998; Britain, Southeast Asia and the Cold War, 1998; Auckland: The Modern University, 1999; Professionals and Unionists, 2000; Historians and Southeast Asian History, 2000; Southeast Asia: A Modern History, 2001; (with M. Lamb) From Versailles to Pearl Harbor, 2001; A Sudden Rampage: The Japanese Occupation of Southeast Asia, 1941-1945, 2001; Imperialism in Southeast Asia, 2001; Nationalism in Southeast Asia, 2004; International Students in New Zealand, 2004; Britain, Southeast Asia, and the Impact of the Korean War, 2005; Imperialism in Asia, 2005; Regionalism in Southeast Asia, 2006; Wit, Eloquence and Commerce: A History of Auckland's Mercury Theatre, 2007; Britain and the West New Guinea Dispute, 1949-1962, 2008; Imparting Asia: Five Decades of Asian Studies at the University of Auckland, 2010; Eighty Years On: A Further Memoir, 2010. EDITOR: China and Its Place in the World, 1967; (with J. Ch'en) Studies in the Social History of China and Southeast Asia, 1970; Mrs. Pryer in Sabah, 1989; The Cambridge History of Southeast Asia, 1992; Singapore and the Singaporeans since 1819, 1992; The Journal of Henry Burney in the Capital of Burma, 1830-1832, 1995; On and Off: Opera in Auckland, 1970-2000, 2002; Corruption and Good Governance in Asia, 2005; Historians and Their Discipline: The Call of Southeast Asian History, 2007; (with E.T. Gomez) The State, Development, and Identity in Multi-Ethnic Societies: Ethnicity, Equity, and the Nation, 2008; History Boy, 2009; Southeast Asia and The Great Power, 2010. **Address:** New Zealand Asia Institute, University of Auckland Business School, Owen G Glenn Bldg., 12 Grafton Rd., Auckland, 1142, New Zealand. **Online address:** n.tarling@auckland.ac.nz

TARLOW, Sarah Alexandra. British (born England), b. 1967?. **Genres:** Archaeology/Antiquities. **Career:** University of Wales, lecturer in archaeology; University of Leicester, senior lecturer in archaeology, 2000-. Writer and archaeologist. **Publications:** Metaphors of Death in Orkney, 1560-1945 A.D., 1995; (ed. with S. West) The Familiar Past? Archaeologies of Later Historical Britain, 1998; Bereavement and Commemoration: An Archaeology of Mortality, 1999; (ed. with Y. Hamilakis and M. Pluciennik) Thinking through the Body: Archaeologies of Corporeality, 2002; The Archaeology of Improvement in Britain, 1750-1850, 2007; Ritual, Belief, and the Dead Body in Early Modern Britain and Ireland, 2010. Contributor to journals. **Address:** School of Archaeology and Ancient History, University of Leicester, University Rd., Leicester, LE LE1 7RH, England. **Online address:** sat12@le.ac.uk

TARLTON, John S. American (born United States), b. 1950?. **Genres:** Novels, Young Adult Fiction, Literary Criticism And History. **Career:** Writer. **Publications:** A Window Facing West, 1999; The Cost of Doing Business, 2001. Contributor to periodicals. **Address:** c/o Author Mail, Bridge Works Publishing, Bridge Ln., PO Box 1798, Bridgehampton, NY 11932, U.S.A.

TARN, Nathaniel. American/French (born France), b. 1928. **Genres:** Poetry, Translations, Literary Criticism And History, Anthropology/Ethnology. **Career:** University of London, School of Oriental and African Studies, lecturer of South East Asian anthropology, 1960-67; Jonathan Cape Ltd., Cape Goliard Press, founder and director, Cape Editions, editor, 1967-69; State University of New York, visiting professor, 1969-70; Princeton University, visiting professor, 1969-70; Rutgers University, professor, 1970-85, professor emeritus of comparative literature, 1984-; Wenner Gren Foundation for Anthropological Research, fellow, 1979-81; Commonwealth of Pennsylvania, poetry fellow, 1983; Rockefeller Foundation, fellow in Bellagio, 1988; University of Chicago, lecturer. Writer. **Publications:** Old Savage, Young City, 1964; (with R. Murphy and J. Silkin) Penguin Modern Poets 7, 1965; (trans.) P. Neruda, The Heights of Macchu Picchu, 1966; Richard Murphy, Jon Silkin, Nathaniel Tarn, 1966; Where Babylon Ends, 1968; (trans.) V. Segalen, Stelae, 1969; (ed. and co-trans.) Con Cuba: An Anthology of Cuban Poetry of the Last Sixty Years, 1969; The Beautiful Contradictions, 1969; October: A Sequence of Ten Poems Followed by Requiem Pro Duabus Filiis Israel, 1969; (trans.) Stelae, 1969; The Silence, 1970; (ed.) Selected Poems, 1970; Nathaniel Tarn Reading His Poems with Comment in the Recording Laboratory, 1971; Robin Skelton and Nathaniel Tarn Reading and Discussing Their Poems in the Coolidge Auditorium, 1971; A Nowhere for Vallejo: Choices, October, 1971; Lyrics for the Bride of God: Section: The Artemision, 1973; The Persephones, 1975; Lyrics for the Bride of God, 1975; Narrative of This Fall, 1975; The House of Leaves, 1976; The Microcosm, 1977; (with J. Rodney) From Alashka: The Ground of Our Great Admiration of Nature, 1977; Bird Scapes, with Seaside, 1978; (with J. Rodney) From Alaska: The Ground of Our Great Admiration of Nature, 1978; (with J. Rodney) The Forest: In Part, 1978; (with J. Rodney) Atitlan/Alashka: New and Selected, 1979; The Land Songs: Further Annotations from Baja California, 1981; Weekends in Mexico, 1982; The Desert Mothers, 1984; At the Western Gates, 1985; Palenque: Selected Poems, 1972-1984, 1986; Seeing America First, 1989; Mothers of Matagalpa, 1989; (trans.) Four Odes, One Song, 1990; Views from the Weaving Mountain: Selected Essays in Poetics and Anthropology, 1991; Flying the Body, 1992; Drafts For: The Army Has Announced That Body Bags Will From Now On Be Known As Human Remains Pouches, 1992; Multitude of One, 1994; I Think This May Be Eden, 1994; (with M. Prechtel) Scandals in the House of Birds: Shamans and Priests on Lake Atitlan, 1997; The Architextures, 2000; The St. Petersburg Poems, 2000; The Architextures: 1988-1994, 2000; Three Letters from the City: The St. Petersburg Poems, 1968-98, 2001; Selected Poems 1950-2000, 2002; Recollections of Being, 2004; Embattled Lyric: Essays and Conversations in Poetics and Anthropology, 2007; Avia: A Poem of International Air Combat, 1939-1945, 2008; Ins and Outs of the Forest Rivers, 2008. Works appear in anthologies. **Address:** PO Box 8187, Santa Fe, NM 87504, U.S.A. **Online address:** kandahar@worldnet.att.net

TARNAWSKY, Maxim. Canadian/American (born United States), b. 1955. **Genres:** Literary Criticism And History, Translations, Language/Linguistics. **Career:** Harvard University, Comparative Literature Department, faculty, 1986, summer school instructor, 1986-87; University of Toronto, Department of Slavic Languages and Literatures, assistant professor, 1987-92, associate professor, 1992-, undergraduate coordinator, 1995-99; Canadian Institute of Ukrainian Studies Press, director, 1992-2001; Ukrainian Literature, editor-in-chief, 2001-. **Publications:** Between Reason and Irrationality: The Prose of Valerijan Pidmohyl'nyj, 1994; (trans.) Weekdays and Sunday, 1999. **Address:** Department of Slavic Languages and Literatures, University of Toronto, Alumni Hall 403, 121 St. Joseph St., Toronto, ON M5S 1J4, Canada. **Online address:** tarn@chass.utoronto.ca

TARNOPOLSKY, Yuri. American/Ukranian (born Ukraine), b. 1936. **Genres:** Poetry, Adult Non-fiction, History, Biography, Autobiography/Memoirs. **Career:** Siberian Institute of Technology, professor of chemistry, 1964-77; SepTech Inc., senior scientist, 1988-91; Technic Inc., senior scientist, 1994-99; research scientist, 2001. Writer. **Publications:** La Clairiere dans la Pinede (poetry), 1985; Memoirs of 1984 (nonfiction), 1993. Contributor to journals. **Address:** 84 Pettaquamscutt Lake Rd., Saunderstown, RI 02874, U.S.A.

TARNOWSKI, Andrew. British/Saudi/Swiss (born Switzerland), b. 1940?. **Genres:** Novels, Biography, History. **Career:** Reuters News Agency, foreign correspondent, 1965-97; Gulf News, journalism coach, 1995-. **Publications:** The Last Mazurka: A Family's Tale of War, Passion and Loss, 2007. **Address:** c/o Marcella Edwards, PFD Group, Drury House, 34-43 Russell St., London, GL WC2B 5HA, England.

TARR, Hope. American (born United States) **Genres:** Romance/Historical, Young Adult Fiction. **Career:** Romance novelist. **Publications:** A Rogue's Pleasure, 2000; My Lord Jack, 2002; Tempting, 2002; Vanquished, 2006; It's a Wonderfully Sexy Life, 2006; The Haunting, 2007; Enslaved, 2007; Strokes of Midnight, 2007; Bound to Please, 2008; Untamed, 2008; Every Breath You Take, 2009; Twelve Nights, 2009; The Tutor, 2010; Tomorrow's Destiny, 2010. **Address:** Harlequin.com, PO Box 5190, Buffalo, NY 14240-5190, U.S.A. **Online address:** hope@hopetarr.com

TARR, Joel Arthur. American (born United States), b. 1934. **Genres:** Environmental Sciences/Ecology, History, Regional/Urban Planning, Politics/Government, Economics, Philosophy. **Career:** Northwestern University, instructor in history, 1959-61; Long Beach State College (now California State University), instructor, 1961-63, assistant professor of American history, 1963-65; University of California, visiting assistant professor of American history, 1966-67; Carnegie-Mellon University, assistant professor, 1967-70, associate professor, 1970-76, Program in Technology and Society, director, 1975-87, professor of history, technology, and urban affairs, 1976-78, Program in Applied History and Social Science, co-director, 1977-86, Engineering and Public Policy, professor of history and public policy, 1978-, School of Urban and Public Affairs, acting dean, 1986, College of Humanities and Social Science, academic associate dean, 1988-91, acting dean, 1991-92, Department of History, acting head, 1992-93, Richard S. Caliguiri University professor of history and policy, John Heinz III School of Public Policy and Management, faculty; Public Works Historical Society, president, 1982-83. Writer. **Publications:** A Study in Boss Politics: William Lorimer of Chicago, 1971; Transportation Innovation and Changing Spatial Patterns in Pittsburgh, 1850-1934: Essays in Public Works History, 1978; Infrastructure and Urban Growth in the Nineteenth Century, 1985; (with C.D. Jacobson) Ownership and Financing of Infrastructure: Historical Perspectives, 1995; The Search for the Ultimate Sink: Urban Pollution in Historical Perspective, 1996; Explorations in Environmental History: Essays, 1998; (with B.L. Jones and E.K. Muller) Born of Fire: The Valley of Work: Industrial Scenes of Southwestern Pennsylvania, 2006; (with C. McShane) Horse in the City: Living Machines in the Nineteenth Century, 2007. EDITOR: Living in Urban America, 1974; Patterns in City Growth, 1975; Retrospective Technology Assessment-1976, 1977; Pittsburgh-Sheffield, Sister Cities: Proceedings of the Pittsburgh-Sheffield Symposium on Industrial Cities, 1986; (with G. Dupuy) Technology and the Rise of the Networked City in Europe and America, 1988; Devastation and Renewal: An Environmental History of Pittsburgh and Its Region, 2004. **Address:** Department of History, Carnegie-Mellon University, 236C Baker Hall, 5000 Forbes Ave., Pittsburgh, PA 15213-3890, U.S.A. **Online address:** jt03@andrew.cmu.edu

TARROW, Sidney G. American (born United States), b. 1938. **Genres:** Politics/Government. **Career:** University of California, Falk Foundation fellow, 1961-62, N.D.E.A. Fellow, 1962-63; Yale University, instructor, 1965-66, assistant professor, 1966-69, associate professor, 1970-71; Cornell University, associate professor, 1971-75, professor, 1975-85, emeritus Maxwell M. Upson professor of government, 1986-, professor of sociology, 1999-; Hebrew University, visiting associate professor, 1973; Western Societies Program, founder and director, 1973-75; University of Rennes, visiting professor, 1978; Fulbright lecturer, 1978-79; Center for Advanced Study in the Behavioral Sciences, fellow, 1980-81, 1999; Conference Group on Italian Politics, vice-president, 1983-85, president, 1985-87; European University Institute, visiting fellow, 1985-86, visiting professor, 2005; University of Florence, visiting professor, 1990, 1999; Sydney University, visiting professor, 1994; Oxford University, Jemelo visiting fellow, 1994; The Institut d'Etudes Politiques, visiting professor, 1997; University of Pavia, visiting professor, 2000; Robert Schumann Center Advanced Study Institute, fellow, 2001; American Political Science Association, Comparative Politics Section, vice-president, 2003-04, president, 2005-07; Ford Foundation, Global Civil Society Program, program consultant, 2006; Central European University, visiting professor, 2007; Social Sciences in Madrid, Juan March Center for Advanced Study, visiting professor; Social Science Research Council, Pre Dissertation Research Program on Contentious Politics, co-director, 2010. Writer. **Publications:** Peasant Communism in Southern Italy, 1967; (with F.I. Greenstein) Political Orientations of Children; The Use of a Semi-Projective Technique in Three Nations, 1970; Partisanship and Political Exchange in French and Italian Local Politics: A Contribution to the Typology of Party Systems, 1974; Between Center and Periphery: Grassroots Politicians in Italy and France, 1977; Democracy and Disorder: Protest and Politics in Italy, 1965-1975, 1989; Struggle, Politics, and Reform: Collective Action, Social Movements, and Cycles of Protest, 1989; Power in Movement: Social Movements, Collective Action, and Politics, 1994; Power in Movement: Social Movements and Contentious Politics, 1998, 3rd ed., 2011; Contentious Politics in Western Europe and the United States, 2000; (with D. McAdam and C. Tilly) Dynamics of Contention, 2001; New Transnational Activism, 2005; (C. Tilly) Contentious Politics, 2007; Strangers At the Gates: Movements and States in Contentious Politics, 2012. EDITOR: (with D.L.M. Blackmer) Communism in Italy and France, 1975; (with P.J. Katzenstein and L. Graziano) Territorial Politics in Industrial Nations, 1978; (with P. Lange) Italy in Transition: Conflict and Consensus, 1980; (with P.J. Katzenstein and T. Lowi) Comparative Theory and Political Experience: Mario Einaudi and the Liberal Tradition, 1990; (with D.S. Meyer) The Social Movement Society: Contentious Politics for a New Century, 1998; (with D. Imig) Contentious Europeans: Protest and Politics in an Emerging Polity, 2001; (with D.D. Porta) Transnational Protest and Global Activism, 2005. **Address:** Department of Government, Cornell University, 202A White Hall, Ithaca, NY 14853-7901, U.S.A. **Online address:** sgt2@cornell.edu

TART, Charles T. American (born United States), b. 1937. **Genres:** Psychology, Medicine/Health, Psychiatry, Adult Non-fiction. **Career:** Round Table Foundation, research assistant, 1957; Duke University, research assistant for psychophysiology laboratory, 1958-60; University of North Carolina, teaching assistant, 1960-61, research assistant, 1961; Stanford University, lecturer in psychology, 1964-65; University of Virginia, School of Medicine, instructor in psychiatry, 1965-66; University of California, assistant professor, 1966-69, associate professor, 1969-74, professor of psychology, 1974-94, professor emeritus of psychology, 1994-; Institute of Noetic Sciences, senior research fellow, 1987-; Institute of Transpersonal Psychology, core faculty, professor of psychology, 1994-; California Institute of Integral Studies, visiting professor of east-west psychology, 1994-95; University of Nevada, distinguished visiting professor, Bigelow chair of consciousness studies, 1997-98; The Archives of Scientists' Transcendent Experiences, editor, 1999-. **Publications:** On Being Stoned: A Psychological Study of Marijuana Intoxication, 1971; States of Consciousness, 1975; Application of Learning Theory to ESP Performance, 1975; (co-author) States of Consciousness, 1975; Learning to Use Extrasensory Perception, 1976; PSI: Scientific Studies of the Psychic Realm, 1977; Waking Up: Overcoming the Obstacles to Human Potential, 1986; Open Mind, Discriminating Mind: Reflections on Human Possibilities, 1989; Living the Mindful Life, 1994; Mind Science: Meditation Training for Practical People, 2001; The End of Materialism: How Evidence of the Paranormal is Bringing Science and Spirit Together, 2009. EDITOR: Altered States of Consciousness, 1969, 3rd ed., 1990; Transpersonal Psychologies: Perspectives on the Mind from Seven Great Spiritual Traditions, 1975, 3rd ed., 1992; (with H.E. Puthoff and R. Targ) Mind at Large, 1979, rev. ed., 2002; Body, Mind, Spirit: Exploring the Parapsychology of Spirituality, 1997. Contributor to books. **Address:** Institute of Transpersonal Psychology, 1069 E Meadow Cir., Palo Alto, CA 94303, U.S.A. **Online address:** cttart@ucdavis.edu

TARTE, Bob. American (born United States), b. 1952. **Genres:** Autobiography/Memoirs, Biography, Animals/Pets. **Career:** The Beat Magazine, columnist. Writer. **Publications:** (Contrib.) Duplicity, 1991; Enslaved by Ducks: How One Man Went from Head of the Household to Bottom of the Pecking Order (memoir), 2003; Fowl Weather (memoir), 2007; Kitty Cornered: How

Frannie and Five Other Incorrigible Cats Seized Control of Our House and Made It Their Home, 2012; The Funnel of Happiness, forthcoming. Contributor to periodicals. **Address:** Algonquin Books, PO Box 2225, Chapel Hill, NC 27515-2225, U.S.A. **Online address:** theduckpen@att.net

TARUSKIN, Richard. American (born United States), b. 1945. **Genres:** Music, History, Essays. **Career:** Columbia University, assistant professor, 1975-81, associate professor, 1981-87; University of Pennsylvania, visiting professor, 1985; University of North Carolina, visiting professor, 1987; University of California, Department of Music, associate professor, 1986-89, professor of music, 1989-. Writer, critic and musician. **Publications:** Opera and Drama in Russia As Preached and Practiced in the 1860s, 1981; (ed.) T'Andernaken, 1981; (with P. Weiss) Music in the Western World: A History in Documents, 1984, 2nd ed., 2008; Stravinsky and the Russian Traditions: A Biography of the Works through Mavra, 2 vols., 1986; Musorgsky: Eight Essays and an Epilogue, 1993; Text and Act: Essays on Music and Performance, 1995; Defining Russia Musically: Historical and Hermeneutical Essays, 1997; The Oxford History of Western Music, 6 vols., 2005; Danger of Music and Other Anti-utopian Essays, 2009; Music from the Earliest Notations to the Sixteenth Century, 2009; On Russian Music, 2009; Music in the Early Twentieth Century, 2010; Music in the Seventeenth and Eighteenth Centuries, 2010; Music in the Nineteenth Century, 2010; Music in the Late Twentieth Century, 2010. **Address:** Department of Music, University of California, 216 Morrison Hall, PO Box 1200, Berkeley, CA 94720-1200, U.S.A. **Online address:** taruskin@berkeley.edu

TASHJIAN, Janet. American (born United States), b. 1956. **Genres:** Children's Fiction, Young Adult Fiction. **Career:** Consultant, 1978-93. Writer, 1993-. **Publications:** FICTION FOR CHILDREN: Tru Confessions, 1997; Marty Frye, Private Eye, 1998; Multiple Choice, 1999; The Gospel According to Larry, 2001; Fault Line, 2003; Vote for Larry, 2004; Larry and the Meaning of Life, 2008; My Life as a Book, 2010; My Life as a Stuntboy, 2011. OTHER: (contrib.) Felicity, 1999. Contributor of articles to journals. **Address:** isty Ottaviano Books, Henry Holt and Co, 175 5th Ave., New York, NY 10010, U.S.A.

TATALOVICH, Raymond. American (born United States), b. 1943. **Genres:** Politics/Government, Economics, Business/Trade/Industry, Philosophy, Humanities. **Career:** University of Illinois, visiting instructor in political science, 1971-72; University of Southern Mississippi, assistant professor of political science, 1972-74; Chicago State University, Department of Economics and Political Science, assistant professor, 1974-78, associate professor, 1978, chairperson, 1977-78; Loyola University of Chicago, associate professor, 1978-85, professor of political science, 1985-, Center for Urban Policy, director, 1980-88; Jackson Policy Academy, part-time teacher; Roxbury Publishing Co., consulting editor, 2001-07. **Publications:** An Introduction to American Government: Study Guide, 1976; (ed. with B.W. Daynes) Contemporary Readings in American Government, 1980; (with B.W. Daynes) The Politics of Abortion: A Study of Community Conflict in Public Policy-Making, 1981; (with R.M. Aduddell and E. Warren) Impact of Subsidized Housing on Property Values, 1983; (with B.W. Daynes) Presidential Power in the United States, 1984; (ed. with Daynes) Social Regulatory Policy: Moral Controversies in American Politics, 1988; (with J. Frendreis) The Modern Presidency and Economic Policy, 1994; Nativism Reborn: The Official English Language Movement and the American States, 1995; Abortion Controversy in Canada and the United States, 1996; The Politics of Abortion in the United States and Canada: A Comparative Study, 1996; (ed. with B.W. Daynes) Moral Controversies in American Politics: Cases in Social Regulatory Policy, 1998, 4th ed., 2011; (with B.W. Daynes and D. Soden) To Govern a Nation: Presedential Power and Politics, 1998; (with T.A. Smith) Cultures at War: Moral Conflicts in Western Democracies, 2003; (with T.S. Engeman) Presidency and Political Science, 2003; (with C.J. Dolan and J. Frendreis) Presidency and Economic Policy, 2008. Contributor of articles books to journals. **Address:** Department of Political Science, Loyola University of Chicago, Water Tower Campus - LT601, 820 N Michigan Ave., Chicago, IL 60611, U.S.A. **Online address:** rtatalo@luc.edu

TATCHELL, Jo. British/Indian (born India) **Genres:** Business/Trade/Industry. **Career:** Journalist. **Publications:** Nabeel's Song: A Family Story of Survival in Iraq, 2006 as The Poet of Baghdad: A True Story of Love and Defiance, 2008; A Diamond in the Desert: Behind the Scenes in the World's Richest City, 2009. Contributor to journals. **Address:** Sceptre, 338 Euston Rd., London, GL NW1 3BH, England. **Online address:** nabeelssong@hotmail.com

TATE, Eleanora E(laine). American (born United States), b. 1948. **Genres:** Children's Fiction, Young Adult Fiction, Civil Liberties/Human Rights, Writing/Journalism, Biography, Novels, Young Adult Non-fiction. **Career:** Iowa Bystander, news editor, 1966-68; Des Moines Register, staff writer, 1968-76; Des Moines Tribune, staff writer, 1968-76; Jackson Sun, staff writer, 1976-77; Kreative Koncepts Inc., writer and researcher, 1979-81; Positive Images Inc., president and co-owner, 1983-93; Tate and Associates, media consultant, 1993-99; Institute of Children's Literature, instructor; Hamline University, School of Graduate Studies, associate professor. **Publications:** Just an Overnight Guest, 1980; The Secret of Gumbo Grove, 1987; Thank You, Dr. Martin Luther King, Jr.!, 1990; Front Porch Stories: At the One-Room School, 1992; Retold African Myths, 1993; A Blessing in Disguise, 1995; Don't Split the Pole: Tales of Down-Home Folk Wisdom, 1997; African American Musicians, 2000; The Minstrel's Melody, 2001; To Be Free, 2004; Celeste's Harlem Renaissance, 2007. EDITOR: (with Z.E. Hamlett III and contrib.) Eclipsed (poetry), 1975; (and contrib.) Wanjiru: A Collection of Blackwomanworth, 1976. Contributor to books and periodicals. **Address:** Hamline University, 1536 Hewitt Ave., Saint Paul, MN 55104-1284, U.S.A. **Online address:** ablessing@members.authorsguild.net

TATE, Elodia. American (born United States), b. 1963. **Genres:** Humor/Satire. **Career:** Expert Financial Services, mortgage broker, 1984-88; Lamas Loan Group, loan officer, 1988-92; Adobe Mortgage, owner and mortgage broker, 1992-94; Writer, health coach and public speaker, 1995-. **Publications:** (With Y. King) Open My Eyes, Open My Soul: Celebrating Our Common Humanity, 2003; (contrib.) Chicken Soup For The African-American Soul, 2004; Infinite Paths to Wellness: Stories and Resources to Offer Hope, Health, and Humor, forthcoming. Contributor to books. **Address:** PO Box 578325, Modesto, CA 95357, U.S.A. **Online address:** info@elodiatate.com

TATE, Greg. American (born United States) **Genres:** Art/Art History, Social Sciences, Anthropology/Ethnology, Literary Criticism And History. **Career:** Village Voice, staff writer 1987-2003; Burnt Sugar, musical director; Black Rock Coalition, co-founder. **Publications:** Flyboy in the Buttermilk: Essays on Contemporary America, 1992; (contrib.) Brooklyn Kings: New York City's Black Bikers, 2000; (with J. Morgan and R. Storr) Ellen Gallagher, 2001; Midnight Lightning: Jimi Hendrix and the Black Experience, 2003; (ed.) Everything but the Burden: What White People Are Taking from Black Culture, 2003; (contrib.) Hard Truths, 2011. **Address:** c/o Alison Loerke, ALIA Agency, 12258 12th Ave. NW, Seattle, WA 98177, U.S.A.

TATE, James (Vincent). American (born United States), b. 1943. **Genres:** Novels, Poetry, Novellas/Short Stories. **Career:** Pym Randall Press, associate editor; Barn Dream Press, associate editor; University of Iowa, visiting lecturer, 1965-67; The Dickinson Review, poetry editor, 1967-; University of California, visiting lecturer, 1967-68; Columbia University, assistant professor, 1969-71; Emerson College, assistant professor, 1970-71; University of Massachusetts, faculty, 1971-, professor of English, distinguished university professor; Literary Magazines, Coordinating Council, consultant, 1971-74; The Best American Poetry, editor, 1997; Academy of American Poets, chancellor, 2001. **Publications:** Cages, 1966; The Destination, 1967; The Lost Pilot, 1967; The Torches, 1968, rev. ed. 1971; Notes of Woe: Poems, 1968; Mystics in Chicago, 1968; Camping in the Valley, 1968; Row with Your Hair, 1969; Is There Anything, 1969; Shepherds of the Mist, 1969; The Oblivion Ha-Ha, 1970, 2nd ed., 1984; Immortals, 1970; Amnesia People, 1970; Deaf Girl Playing, 1970; (with B. Knott) Are You Ready Mary Baker Eddy?: Poems, 1970; Wrong Songs, 1970; Hints to Pilgrims, 1971, rev. ed., 1982; Nobody Goes to Visit the Insane Anymore, 1971; Apology for Eating Geoffrey Movius's Hyacinth, 1972; Absences: New Poems, 1972; Hottentot Ossuary (stories), 1974; Viper Jazz, 1976; (with B. Holt) Lucky Darryl: A Novel, 1977; Riven Doggeries, 1979; The Land of Little Sticks, 1981; Constant Defender: Poems, 1983; Just Shades: Poems, 1985; Reckoner, 1986; Distance from Loved Ones, 1990; Selected Poems, 1991; Worshipful Company of Fletchers, 1994; Shroud of the Gnome: Poems, 1997; Route as Briefed, 1999; Memoir of the Hawk: Poems, 2001; Dreams of a Robot Dancing Bee: 44 Stories, 2002; Lost River, 2003; Return to the City of White Donkeys: Poems, 2004; Ghost Soldiers: Poems, 2008. **Address:** Department of English, University of Massachusetts, 466 Bartlett Hall, Amherst, MA 01003, U.S.A. **Online address:** tate@hfa.umass.edu

TATE, Michael L. American (born United States), b. 1947. **Genres:** History. **Career:** University of Nebraska, Ralph Wardle Diamond professor of history, 1998-2003, Charles and Mary Martin chair of Western history, 2003-, professor of history and Native American studies, Graduate Studies, chair. Writer. **Publications:** The Indians of Texas: An Annotated Research Bibliography, 1986; The Upstream People: An Annotated Research Bibliography of the Omaha Tribe, 1991; The Frontier Army in the Settlement of the West, 1999; (ed. and intro.) Crossing the Plains to Oregon in 1853, 2000; Indians and Emigrants: Encounters on the Overland Trails, 2006; The American Army in Transition, 1865-1898, 2007. **Address:** Department of History, University of Nebraska, 287 Arts & Sciences Hall, West Wing, 2nd Fl., 6001 Dodge St., Omaha, NE 68182, U.S.A. **Online address:** mtate@mail.unomaha.edu

TATHAM, David. American (born United States), b. 1932. **Genres:** Art/Art History. **Career:** Syracuse University, lecturer, 1962-71, associate professor, 1972-78, chair of department, 1973-77, 1980-86, professor of fine arts, 1978-2002, professor emeritus, 2002-. Writer. **Publications:** The Lure of the Striped Pig: The Illustration of Popular Music in America, 1820-1970, 1973; Robert Frost's White Mountains, 1974; (ed. and contrib.) Prints and Printmakers of New York State, 1986; Winslow Homer and the Illustrated Book, 1992; Fishing in the Northwoods: Winslow Homer, 1995; Winslow Homer in the Adirondacks, 1996; Winslow Homer and the Pictorial Press, 2003; (ed.) North American Prints, 1913-1947: An Examination at Century's End, 2006; (ed.) Winslow Homer in London, 2010. **Address:** Department of Art & Music Histories, Syracuse University, 308 Bowne Hall, Syracuse, NY 13244-1200, U.S.A. **Online address:** dftatham@syr.edu

TATTLIN, Isadora. American (born United States) **Genres:** Autobiography/Memoirs, Women's Studies And Issues. **Career:** Writer. **Publications:** Cuba Diaries: An American Housewife in Havana, 2002. Contributor to periodicals. **Address:** c/o Author Mail, Algonquin Books, 127 Kingston Dr., Ste. 105, PO Box 2225, Chapel Hill, NC 27514, U.S.A.

TATUM, Beverly Daniel. American (born United States), b. 1954. **Genres:** Environmental Sciences/Ecology, Education. **Career:** Counseling psychologist, 1979-83; University of California, center for black studies, fellow, 1980-81, lecturer of black studies, 1982-83; Westfield State College, assistant professor, 1983-86, associate professor of psychology, 1986-89; Equity Institute, director, 1985-90, chair, 1988-90; Mt. Holyoke College, Department of Psychology and Education, associate professor, 1989-96, professor, 1996-2002, chair, 1997-98, dean of college and vice president for student affairs, 1998-2002; Spelman College, president, 2002-; licensed clinical psychologist in private practice, 1988-98. Writer. **Publications:** Assimilation Blues: Black Families in a White Community, 1987; Outside the Circle? The Relational Implications for White Women Working against Racism, 1996; Why Are All the Black Kids Sitting Together in the Cafeteria? and Other Conversations about Race, 1997; Can We Talk about Race? and Other Conversations in an Era of School Resegregation, 2007. Contributor to books. **Address:** Office of the President, Spelman College, 350 Spelman Ln. SW., Atlanta, GA 30314-4399, U.S.A. **Online address:** btatum@spelman.edu

TAUBES, Gary. American (born United States), b. 1956. **Genres:** Sciences. **Career:** Science journalist. Writer. **Publications:** Nobel Dreams: Power, Deceit and the Ultimate Experiment, 1986; Bad Science: The Short Life and Weird Times of Cold Fusion, 1993; Good Calories, Bad Calories: Challenging the Conventional Wisdom on Diet, Weight Control and Disease, 2007. Contributor to periodicals. **Address:** New York, NY, U.S.A.

TAUBES, Timothy. American (born United States), b. 1955. **Genres:** Art/Art History, Philosophy, Adult Non-fiction. **Career:** Artists Choice Museum, director, 1983-86; Education Center, instructor in art history, 1987-94; American Scene Gallery, owner and director, 1989-94; AMS Inc., staff. Writer. **Publications:** Art and Philosophy, 1993. **Address:** 585 Barrack Hill Rd., Ridgefield, CT 06877, U.S.A.

TAUBMAN, Bruce. American (born United States), b. 1947. **Genres:** Medicine/Health, Sports/Fitness. **Career:** Children's Hospital of Philadelphia, resident in pediatrics, 1972-75; Cherry Hill Pediatric Group, physician, 1975-; University of Pennsylvania, assistant instructor, 1975-86, clinical assistant professor, 1986-91, clinical associate professor, 1992-. Writer. **Publications:** Curing Infant Colic: The 7-minute Program for Soothing the Fussy Baby, 1990; Your Child's Symptoms: A Parent's Guide to Understanding Pediatric Medicine, 1992; Why is My Baby Crying?: The 7-minute Program for Soothing the Fussy Baby, 1992, 3rd ed., 2000; (contrib.) Mothercare New

Guide to Pregnancy and Child Care: An Illustrated Guide to Caring for Your Child from Pregnancy through Age Five, 1994, rev. ed., 2000. Contributor to journals. **Address:** Cherry Hill Pediatric Group, 600 Marlton Pke. W, Cherry Hill, NJ 08003, U.S.A.

TAUBMAN, Philip. American (born United States), b. 1948?. **Genres:** Air/Space Topics, History, Military/Defense/Arms Control, Politics/Government. **Career:** Time Magazine, correspondent, Esquire, sports editor; Stanford Daily, editor-in-chief, 1969; New York Times, journalist and editor, 1979-, Moscow correspondent and bureau chief, 1985-88, deputy Washington bureau chief, 1989-92, deputy editorial page editor, 1993-94, assistant editorial page editor, 1994-2001; Stanford University, Center for International Security and Cooperation, consulting professor, 2008-. **Publications:** Secret Empire: Eisenhower, the CIA and the Hidden Story of America's Space Espionage, 2003; Shen mi di guo: Aisenhauowe'ier, zhong qing ju bei hou de Meiguo kong jian da zhan yi mi shi, 2004; The Partnership: Five Cold Warriors and their Quest to Ban the Bomb, 2012. **Address:** CISAC, Stanford University, E215, Encina Hall,, Stanford, CA 94305-6165, U.S.A. **Online address:** ptaubman@stanford.edu

TAUNTON, Eric. *See* **WESTCOTT-JONES, Kenneth.**

TA VĂN TÀI. American/Vietnamese (born Vietnam), b. 1938. **Genres:** History, Law, Politics/Government. **Career:** Saigon Law School and Institute of Administration, professor, 1965-75; Tang Thi Thanh Trai & Ta Van Tai, attorney-at-law and partner, 1968-75; Harvard Law School, adjunct lecturer on Vietnamese law, research associate and research fellow, 1975-; State Courts, attorney-at-law, 1986-, consultant; Federal Courts, attorney-at-law, 1987-; Ford Foundation, consultant; Bank of America, consultant. Writer. **Publications:** (With T.T.T. Trai and K. Kirkwood) Doing Business in Vietnam: Legal and Commercial Considerations, 1970, 2nd ed., 1974; Research Methods (in Vietnamese), 1972, 2nd ed., 1974; (ed. with Hooker) The Laws of Southeast Asia, 1986; (with N.N. Huy and T.V Liêm) The Lê Code: Law in Traditional Vietnam: A Comparative Sino-Vietnamese Legal Study with Historical-Juridical Analysis and Annotations, 1987; (ed. with B. McKnight) Law and the State in Traditional East Asia, 1987; (co-author) The Code of the Le Dynasty, 1987; The Vietnamese Tradition of Human Rights, 1989; (with J.A. Cohen and N.N Bich) Investment Law and Practice in Vietnam, 1989. **Address:** Harvard Law School, 145 Naples Rd., 1563 Massachusetts Ave., Cambridge, MA 02138, U.S.A. **Online address:** taivanta@yahoo.com

TAVERNE, Dick. British/Indonesian (born Indonesia), b. 1928. **Genres:** Politics/Government, Economics, Sciences. **Career:** Labour Member of Parliament, 1962-72, home office minister, 1966-68, financial secretary to the treasury, 1969-70; Institute for Fiscal Studies, founder and director, 1970, director-general, 1979-81; Axa Equity & Law Life Assurance, director, 1972-99; independent M.P. for Lincoln, 1973-74; BOC Intl., board director, 1975-; Public Policy Centre (U.K.), President PRIMA Europe, director, 1987-97; Research Defence Society, president, 2004; Sense About Science, founder; National Secular Society, honorary associate. Writer. **Publications:** Economic and Monetary Union in Europe (monograph), 1971; The Future of the Left: Lincoln and After, 1974; The Case for Biotechnology, 1990; The Pension Time Bomb in Europe, 1995; Majority Voting in Europe, 1996; (contrib.) Pension Reform in Europe: Enlightening the Debate on Good Governance, 2001; The March of Unreason: Science, Democracy, and the New Fundamentalism, 2005. Contributor to magazines and newspapers. **Address:** 60 Cambridge St., London, GL SW1V 4QQ, England.

TAVERNOR, Robert (William). British (born England), b. 1954. **Genres:** Architecture, Urban Studies, Translations, Mathematics/Statistics. **Career:** Polytechnic of Central London (now University of Westminster), part-time tutor in design, 1980-82; Cambridge University, part-time lecturer in design, 1982-86; University of Bath, lecturer in architecture, 1986-92, founding director of Centre for Advanced Studies in Architecture, 1991-92, professor and head of architecture, 1995-2005; University of Edinburgh, Forbes professor of architecture, 1992-95; University of California, visiting professor, 1998; London School of Economics, Cities Programme, director, professor, now professor emeritus of architecture and urban design . Writer. **Publications:** (Trans. with J. Rykwert and N. Leach and ed.) L.B. Alberti, On the Art of Building, in Ten Books, 1988; Palladio and Palladianism, 1991; (trans. with R. Schofield and ed.) A. Palladio: The Four Books on Architecture, 1997; On Alberti and the Art of Building, 1998; (ed. with G. Dodds) Body and Building: Essays on the Changing Relation of Body and Architecture, 2002;

Smoot's Ear: The Measure of Humanity, 2007. **Address:** London School of Economics and Political Science, University of London, Houghton St., London, GL WC2A 2AE, England. **Online address:** r.tavernor@lse.ac.uk

TAVIANI, Paolo. Italian (born Italy), b. 1931. **Genres:** Plays/Screenplays, Documentaries/Reportage, Translations, Young Adult Fiction. **Career:** Screenwriter and director. **Publications:** PUBLISHED SCREENPLAYS: San Michele aveva un gallo/Allonsafàn, 1974; Padre Padrone (title means: 'Father Master'), 1977; I sovrani di Ériu, 1983; (with T. Guerra) Good Morning Babylon, 1987; La Bottega Taviani: unviaggio nel cinema da San Miniato a Hollywood: comune di San Miniato, Amministrazione provinciale di Pisa, Regione Toscana, 1987; (with Guerra) Kaos, 1997; (with V. Taviani) Tu ridi: sceneggiatura originale e integraledell'omonimo film, 1999. OTHERS: (with V. Orsini) Un uomo dabruciare, trans. as A Man for the Killing, 1962; I fuorilegge del matrimonio, 1963; I sovversivi (title means: 'The Subversives'), 1967; Sotto il segno dello scorpione (title means: 'Under the Sign of the Scorpion'), 1969; Il prato, 1979 in US as The Meadow, 1979; (with T. Guerra and G.G. De Negri) La notte di San Lorenzo (title means: 'The Night of San Lorenzo'), 1982 in US as The Night of the Shooting Stars, 1983; (with Guerra) Il sole anche di notte in US as Night Sun, 1990; (with S. Petraglia) Fiorille, 1993. Contributor to periodicals. **Address:** Via dell'Ongaro 41, Rome, 06 5817231, Italy.

TAWA, Nicholas E. *See* Obituaries.

TAWIL, Ezra. American (born United States), b. 1967. **Genres:** History, Race Relations, Literary Criticism And History. **Career:** Columbia University, Department of English, associate professor. Writer. **Publications:** The Making of Racial Sentiment: Slavery and the Birth of the Frontier Romance, 2006; (intro.) The Deerslayer, 2011; Literary Exceptionalism and the Invention of the American Style, forthcoming. Contributor to books. **Address:** Departmentt of English, University of Rochester, 412 Morey Hall, PO Box 270451, Rochester, NY 14627-0451, U.S.A. **Online address:** eft2001@columbia.edu

TAYLER, Irene. American (born United States), b. 1934?. **Genres:** Literary Criticism And History, Women's Studies And Issues, Art/Art History. **Career:** Columbia University, lecturer, 1961-71; City College of the City University of New York, assistant professor, 1971-75, associate professor, 1975-76; Graduate Center of the City University of New York, faculty, 1973-76; Massachusetts Institute of Technology, associate professor, 1976-82, Thomas Meloy professor of rhetoric, 1979-83, professor literature, 1982-97, professor emeritus, 1997-. Writer. **Publications:** Blake's Illustrations to the Poems of Gray, 1971; Holy Ghosts: The Male Muses of Emily and Charlotte Bronte, 1990; (ed.) Between Worlds: The Paintings and Drawings of Samuel Bak from 1946 to 2001, 2002. Works appear in anthologies. **Address:** Department of Literature, Massachusetts Institute of Technology, 77 MAssachusetts Ave., Bldg. 14N, Cambridge, MA 02139, U.S.A.

TAYLER, Jeffrey. Russian/American (born United States), b. 1961. **Genres:** Crafts, Travel/Exploration. **Career:** American Security Co., co-manager; National Public Radio, commentator; Atlantic Monthly, Russia correspondent. **Publications:** Siberian Dawn: A Journey across the New Russia, 1999; Facing the Congo, 2000; Glory in a Camel's Eye: Trekking through the Moroccan Sahara, 2003; Angry Wind: Through Muslim Black Africa by Truck, Bus, Boat and Camel, 2005; River of No Reprieve: Descending Siberia's Waterway of Exile, Death and Destiny, 2006; The Lost Kingdoms of Africa: Through Muslim Africa by Truck, Bus, Boat and Camel, 2006; Murderers in Mausoleums: Riding the Back Roads of Empire between Moscow and Beijing, 2009. Contributor to periodicals. **Address:** Author Mail, Trade Division, Adult Editorial, Houghton Mifflin Co., 222 Berkeley St., Boston, MA 02116, U.S.A.

TAYLEUR, Karen. Australian (born Australia), b. 1961?. **Genres:** Novels, Novellas/Short Stories. **Career:** Author. **Publications:** Rubbish and Recycling, 2001; Forgetting to Remember, 2004; Bree, Centre, 2005; Mel, Goal Attack, 2006; Chasing Boys, 2007; Hostage, 2009; Halloween in Christmas Hills: The Legend of Stingy Jack, 2009; (ed.) Short and Scary (story collection), 2010. DAVID MORTIMORE BAXTER SERIES: Liar! The True Story of David Mortimore Baxter, 2003; Excuses: Survive and Succeed with David Mortimore Baxter, 2004; The Truth! David Mortimore Baxter Comes Clean, 2004; Manners! Staying out of Trouble with David Mortimore Baxter, 2005; Secrets! David Mortimore Baxter, 2005; Promises! Vote David Mortimore Baxter, 2005; Chicken! Be Brave with David Mortimore Baxter, 2008;

Haunted! The Scary Life of David Mortimore Baxter, 2008; Spies! David Mortimore Baxter Cracks the Case, 2008; Wild! Get Lost with David Mortimore Baxter, 2008; Exposed! In the Spotlight with David Mortimore Baxter, 2009; Famous! The Awesome Life of David Mortimore Baxter, 2009; Jealous! On the Sidelines with David Mortimore Baxter, 2009; Stranded! David Mortimore Baxter Gets Trapped, 2009. **Address:** Australia. **Online address:** kaygeetee@optusnet.com.au

TAYLOR, Allegra. British/Australian (born Australia), b. 1940. **Genres:** Medicine/Health, Psychology, Theology/Religion, Travel/Exploration, Women's Studies And Issues, Young Adult Non-fiction, Children's Fiction, Young Adult Fiction, Young Adult Fiction. **Career:** Orpheus Productions, partner, co-director; music teacher, 1975-85; freelance writer, 1980-. **Publications:** And For Children: Tal Niv's Kibbutz, 1987; A Kibbutz in Israel (juvenile), 1987; I Fly out with Bright Feathers: The Quest of a Novice Healer, 1987; Tal Niv's Kibbutz (juvenile), 1987; Acquainted with the Night: A Year on the Frontiers of Death, 1989; Prostitution: What's Love Got to Do with It?, 1991; Healing Hands, 1992; Older Than Time: A Grandmother's Search for Wisdom, 1993; Ladder to the Moon, 1999. **Address:** c/o Toby Eady, Toby Eady Associates, 9 Orme Ct., 3rd Fl., London, GL W2 4RL, England. **Online address:** brightfeathers@mac.com

TAYLOR, Andrew J. American/British (born England) **Genres:** Politics/Government, Young Adult Non-fiction. **Career:** WUNC, on-air political commentator; WRAL-5 television, on-air political commentator; WPTF-680 radio, on-air political commentator; University of Connecticut, adjunct instructor, 1991-95; North Carolina State University, Department Of Political Science, assistant professor, 1995-2001, associate professor, 2001-07, chair, 2006-, professor, 2007-, Distance Education Program (cable TV educational program), instructor. Writer. **Publications:** (Contrib.) Survey of Social Science: Government and Politics Series, 1995; Elephant's Edge: The Republicans as a Ruling Party, 2005. Contributor to journals and periodicals. **Address:** Department of Political Science, School of Public and International Affairs, North Carolina State University, 212 Caldwell Hall, PO Box 8102, Raleigh, NC 27695-8102, U.S.A. **Online address:** andrew_taylor@ncsu.edu

TAYLOR, Andrew (John Robert). Also writes as Andrew Saville, John Robert Taylor. British (born England), b. 1951. **Genres:** Mystery/Crime/Suspense, Romance/Historical, Children's Fiction. **Career:** Brent Public Libraries, library assistant, 1976-78, librarian, 1979-81.Writer. **Publications:** AS ANDREW TAYLOR: Caroline Minuscule, 1982; Waiting for the End of the World, 1984; Our Fathers' Lies, 1985; An Old School Tie, 1986; Freelance Death, 1987; The Second Midnight, 1987; Blacklist, 1988; Snapshot, 1989; Toyshop, 1990; Blood Relation, 1990; The Raven on the Water, 1991; The Sleeping Policeman, 1992; Negative Image, 1992; The Barred Window, 1993; Odd Man Out, 1993; The Invader, 1994; An Air That Kills, 1994; The Mortal Sickness, 1995; The Four Last Things, 1997; The Lover of the Grave, 1997; The Judgement of Strangers, 1998; The Suffocating Night, 1998; Where Roses Fade, 2000; The Office of the Dead, 2001; Death's Own Door, 2001; The American Boy, 2003; An Unpardonable Crime, 2004; Call the Dying, 2004; A Stain on the Silence, 2006; Naked to the Hangman, 2007; Bleeding Heart Square, 2009; The Anatomy of Ghosts, 2010. CHILDREN'S NOVELS AS JOHN ROBERT TAYLOR: Hairline Cracks, 1988; Snapshot, 1988; Double Exposure, 1989; The Private Nose, 1990. BERGERAC SERIES AS ANDREW SAVILLE: Bergerac, 1985; Bergerac Is Back!, 1985; Bergerac and the Fatal Weakness, 1988; Bergerac and the Jersey Rose, 1988; Bergerac and the Moving Fever, 1988; Bergerac and the Traitor's Child, 1989. **Address:** Sheil Land Associates, 52 Doughty St., London, GL WC1N 2LF, England. **Online address:** andrew@andrew-taylor.co.uk

TAYLOR, Andrew (McDonald). Australian (born Australia), b. 1940. **Genres:** Poetry, Songs/Lyrics And Libretti, Translations. **Career:** University of Melbourne, tutor, 1962-63, Lockie fellow in Australian literature, 1965-69; British Institute, English teacher, 1964-65; University of Adelaide, lecturer, 1971-74, senior lecturer in English, 1974-92, associate professor, 1992; Edith Cowan University, professor of English, 1992-2003, professor emeritus and honorary professor, 2003-. Writer. **Publications:** The Cat's Chin and Ears: A Bestiary, 1976; Bernie the Midnight Owl, 1984; (trans. with B. Josephi) Miracles of Disbelief, 1985; Reading Australian Poetry, 1987. POETRY: The Cool Change, 1971; Ice Fishing, 1973; The Invention of Fire, 1976; Parabolas: Prose Poems, 1976; The Crystal Absences, The Trout, 1978; Selected Poems, 1960-1980, 1982, rev. ed., 1988; Traveling, 1986; Travelling, 1986; Selected Poems 1960-1985, 1988; Folds in the Map, 1991; Sandstone, 1995;

Götterdämmerung Café, 2001; The Stone Threshold, 2001; Collected Poems, 2004; Rome, 2005; Regret about the Wolves, 2006; The Unhaunting, 2009. EDITOR: (intro.) Byron: Selected Poems, 1970; (with I. Reid) Number Two Friendly Street, 1978; (with J. Rodriguez) Poems Selected from The Australian's 20th Anniversary Poetry Competition, 1985; Unsettled Areas, 1986; (with R. McDougall) (Un)Common Ground, 1990; (with G. Phillips) Contrary Rhetoric, 2007; An Alphabetical Amulet, 2010. **Address:** School of Communication and Arts, Edith Cowan University, Rm. ML17.231, 270 Joondalup Dr., Perth, WA 6027, Australia. **Online address:** a.taylor@ecu.edu.au

TAYLOR, Andy. Spanish/British (born England), b. 1961. **Genres:** Biography, Autobiography/Memoirs, History. **Career:** Writer and musician. **Publications:** Wild Boy: My Life in Duran Duran, 2008. **Address:** Ibiza, Spain. **Online address:** grandcentralpublishing@hbgusa.com

TAYLOR, Anne Marie. American (born United States), b. 1964. **Genres:** Adult Non-fiction, Biography, Autobiography/Memoirs, History, Politics/Government. **Career:** Teacher, 1987; Université de Bordeaux III, reader, 1989-90; Université François Rabelais, reader, 1990-91; Mount Holyoke College, visiting assistant professor, 2001-; Greenfield Community College, adjunct instructor in French, 2002; University of Massachusetts, lecturer in French, 2002-. Writer. **Publications:** Young Charles Sumner and the Legacy of the American Enlightenment, 1811-1851, 2001. **Address:** Department of Languages, Literatures, & Cultures, University of Massachusetts, 300 Massachusetts Ave., Amherst, MA 01003-9290, U.S.A. **Online address:** ataylor@wellesley.edu

TAYLOR, Barbara Gold. British (born England), b. 1950. **Genres:** Philosophy. **Career:** University of London, Extra-Mural Department and Workers' Educational Association, staff, 1975-85; University of Saskatchewan, sessional lecturer, 1978; Hillcroft College, part-time lecturer in political theory, 1979-80; Bulmershe College of Higher Education, lecturer in history, 1980-85; University of East London, School of Humanities and Social Sciences, senior lecturer in history, 1993-2001, professor of modern history, 2001-; University of East London, Raphael Samuel History Centre, co-director; universities of Amsterdam, visiting professor; Indiana University, visiting professor. Writer. **Publications:** Eve and the New Jerusalem: Socialism and Feminism in the Nineteenth Century, 1983; Mary Wollstonecraft and the Feminist Imagination, 2003; (ed. with S. Knott) Women, Gender and Enlightenment, 2004; (with A. Phillips) On Kindness, Farrar, 2009. Contributor to periodicals. **Address:** School of Humanities and Social Sciences, University of East London, Docklands Campus, University Way, London, GL E16 2RD, England. **Online address:** b.taylor@uel.ac.uk

TAYLOR, Ben. See STRACHAN, Ian.

TAYLOR, Benjamin. American (born United States), b. 1952?. **Genres:** Novels. **Career:** Washington University, instructor; New School, Graduate Writing Program, faculty member; 92nd Street Y Poetry Center, instructor; Bennington College, seminar leader; Columbia University, adjunct associate professor. Writer. **Publications:** Into the Open: Reflections on Genius and Modernity, 1995; Tales Out of School: A Novel, 1995; The Book of Getting Even: A Novel, 2008. **Address:** School of the Arts, Columbia University, 415 Dodge Hall, 2960 Broadway, New York, NY 10027-6950, U.S.A.

TAYLOR, Beverly (White). American (born United States), b. 1947. **Genres:** Literary Criticism And History, Young Adult Fiction. **Career:** Memphis State University, instructor in English, 1970-72; Duke University, graduate teaching assistant, 1973-76; University of North Carolina, Department of English and Comparitive Literature, assistant professor of English, 1977-84, associate professor, 1984-92, professor, 1992-, chair, director of graduate studies. Writer. **Publications:** (With E. Brewer) The Return of King Arthur: British and American Arthurian Literature since 1800, 1983; (co-author) Arthurian Legend and Literature, vol. I, 1984; Francis Thompson, 1987; (ed. with R. Bain) The Cast of Consciousness, 1987; (ed. with R. Bain) The Cast of Consciorsness: Concepts of the Mind in British and American Romanticism, 1987; (ed. with A.H. Harrison) Gender and Discourse in Victorian Literature and Art, 1992; (ed. with M. Stone) Elizabeth Barrett Browning, 2009; Women of Victorian Camelot, forthcoming; Elizabeth Barrett Browning: The Poetics of Engagement, forthcoming; Elizabeth Barrett Browning's Early Writings, forthcoming. Contributor to journals. **Address:** Department of English and Comparitive Literature, University of North Carolina, Greenlaw Hall, CB 3520, Chapel Hill, NC 27599-3520, U.S.A. **Online address:** btaylor@email.unc.edu

TAYLOR, Billy. (William J. Taylor). American (born United States), b. 1960. **Genres:** Novels. **Career:** Writer. **Publications:** Based on the Movie: A Novel, 2008. **Address:** San Antonio, TX , U.S.A. **Online address:** bt@billytaylor.com

TAYLOR, Bob Pepperman. (Robert Pepperman Taylor). American (born United States), b. 1958. **Genres:** Politics/Government, Economics. **Career:** University of Vermont, visiting assistant professor, 1986-88, assistant professor, 1988-94, associate professor, 1994-2002, professor of political science, 2002-, College of Arts and Sciences, secretary, 1989-92, John Dewey Honors Program, associate director, 1998, John Dewey Honors Program, director, 1999-2003, Honors College, dean, 2003-. Consultant and writer. **Publications:** Our Limits Transgressed: Environmental Political Thought in America, 1992; America's Bachelor Uncle: Thoreau and the American Polity, 1996; (ed. with B.A. Minteer and contrib.) Democracy and the Claims of Nature: Critical Perspectives for a New Century, 2002; Citizenship and Democratic Doubt: The Legacy of Progressive Thought, 2004; Horace Mann's Troubling Legacy: The Education of Democratic Citizens, 2010. CONTRIBUTOR: Democracy and the Environment, 1996; Conservation Reconsidered, 2000; Friends and Citizens, 2000; The Moral Austerity of Environmental Decision Making, 2002. Contributor to periodicals. **Address:** Department of Political Science, University of Vermont, Rm. 100, Allen House, 94 University Pl., PO Box 54110, Burlington, VT 05405-4110, U.S.A. **Online address:** robert.taylor@uvm.edu

TAYLOR, Bron Raymond. American (born United States), b. 1955. **Genres:** Environmental Sciences/Ecology, Ethics, Civil Liberties/Human Rights, Philosophy, Popular Culture, Social Sciences, Theology/Religion, Economics, Economics. **Career:** California State Department of Parks and Recreation, ocean lifeguard, 1977-89; University of San Francisco, adjunct professor, 1986-89; California State University, lecturer in religious studies and philosophy, 1988-89; University of Wisconsin-Oshkosh, assistant professor of religion, social ethics and environmental ethics, 1989-93, Environmental Studies Program, director, 1993, associate professor of religion and social ethics, 1993-94, professor of religion and environmental studies, 1998; The University of Florida, Samuel S. Hill professor of Christian ethics, 2002-, professor of religion and nature, 2009-, School of Natural Resources and Environment, affiliate, 2002-. Writer. **Publications:** Affirmative Action at Work: Law, Politics, and Ethics, 1991; (ed.) Ecological Resistance Movements: The Global Emergence of Radical and Popular Environmentalism, 1995; (ed.) The Encyclopedia of Religion and Nature, 2005; Dark Green Religion: Nature Spirituality and the Planetary Future, 2010. Contributor to periodicals. **Address:** Department of Religion, University of Florida, 107 Anderson Hall, PO Box 117410, Gainesville, FL 32611-7410, U.S.A. **Online address:** bron@religion.ufl.edu

TAYLOR, Bruce. American (born United States), b. 1947. **Genres:** Novellas/Short Stories, Theology/Religion, Novels. **Career:** Harborview Medical Center, mental health therapist, 1974-2002, stress management specialist, 1974-; private practice of hypnotherapist, 1974-; Shakespeare and Co., writer-in-residence, 1986; Magic Realist Writers International Network, founder and director, 2001-. Writer. **Publications:** The Final Trick of Funny man and Other Stories, 1997; Mountains of the Night, 1998; Kafka's Uncle and Other Strange Tales, 2005; Edward: Dancing on the Edge of Infinity, 2005; The Bizarro Starter Kit, 2006; Kafka's Uncle: The Ghastly Prequel and Other Stories of Love and Pathos in the World's Most Powerful, 2007; Third-World Banana Republic and The Magic of Wild Places, 2007; (with J. Lake, R. Vuckevich and J.V. Pelt) Alembical, 2008. FORTHCOMING: (with B. Herbert) Stormworld; The Tails of Alley Manderous and Other Odd Tales; Kafka's Uncle: The Unfortunate Sequel and Other Insults to the Morally Perfect; Kafka's Uncle: The Ghastly Prequel and Other Tales of Love and Pathos From the World's Most Powerful, Third-World Banana Republic; (ed.) The Magic of Wild Places; (ed.) In the Majesty of the World; (ed.) Industrial Carpet Drag; (ed.) Fiction Writing for Fun, Profit and Possible Jail Time; The Tails of Alleymanderous and Other Odd Tales. **Address:** c/o Hans Joachim Alpers, Utoprop Literarisch Agent, Gross Flottbeker Strasse, Hamburg, 22607, Germany. **Online address:** bbtaylor@drizzle.com

TAYLOR, Bruce. (Bruce Edward Taylor). American (born United States), b. 1947. **Genres:** Poetry, Novellas/Short Stories. **Career:** Jinan University,

lecturer; University of Wisconsin, professor of English, 1972-2007, professor emeritus, 2007-; Upriver Press, editor and publisher, 1974-78; Red Weather Press, editor and publisher, 1974-78; Transactions: Journal of Wisconsin Academy of Arts and Sciences, poetry editor, 1988-92; Drexel University, FYE Program Development and Implementation, consultant, 2000. **Publications:** POETRY: Idle Trade: Early Poems, 1979; The Darling Poems, 1982; This Day, 1993; Why That Man Talks That Way, 1994; Pity the World: Poems Selected and New, 2005. EDITOR: (as Bruce Edward Taylor) Eating the Menu: A Contemporary American Poetry, 1970-1974, 1974; Upriver: Wisconsin Poetry and Prose, 1981; Wisconsin Poetry (anthology), 1991; (with P. See) Higher Learning: Reading and Writing about College, 2001, 3rd ed., 2012. Contributor to periodicals. **Address:** Department of English, University of Wisconsin, Rm. 405, Hibbard Hall, 105 Garfield Ave., Eau Claire, WI 54702-4004, U.S.A. **Online address:** taylorb@uwec.edu

TAYLOR, Bruce Edward. See **TAYLOR, Bruce.**

TAYLOR, Carl S. American (born United States), b. 1949. **Genres:** Human Relations/Parenting, Young Adult Non-fiction, Criminology/True Crime, Social Sciences. **Career:** Centrax Diversified Services Inc., manager, 1977-89; Michigan State University, Department of Sociology, assistant professor, 1984-90, professor, Institute for Children Youth and Families, director of community youth development programs, 1994-, professor of Family and Child Ecology, University Outreach and Engagement, senior fellow, Michigan Gang Research Project, principal investigator; Jackson Community College, Department of Criminal Justice and Public Safety, director, 1989-90; National Institute for Corrections, instructor, 1990-93; Grand Valley State University, professor of criminal justice, Youth Culture Studies Center, director, 1991-94, clinical professor, 1994-; Guggenheim Foundation, staff; C. S. Mott Foundation, staff; FBI Academy, staff; Children's Defense Fund, staff; National Institute of Justice, consultant. Writer. **Publications:** Rock Concerts: A Parents Guide, 1984; Private Security Training Manual, 1985; Urban Gangs and Public Schools, 1987; The Sociology and Distribution of Gangs, 1989; Dangerous Society, 1990; Girls, Gangs, Women and Drugs, 1993; (with G. Thiele) Jugendkulturen und gangs: eine Betrachtung zur Raumaneignung und Raumverdrängung, nachgewiesen an Entwicklungen in den neuen Bundesländern und den USA (Youth culture and gangs), 1998. Works appear in anthologies. Contributor to journals. **Address:** Institute for Children, Youth and Families, Michigan State University, 410B Berkey Hall, East Lansing, MI 48824, U.S.A. **Online address:** taylor36@msu.edu

TAYLOR, Claire. British (born England), b. 1965. **Genres:** History. **Career:** University of Nottingham, lecturer in history. Historian and writer. **Publications:** Heresy in Medieval France: Dualism in Aquitaine and the Agenais, 1000-1249, 2005. Contributor to books, journals and periodicals. **Address:** School of History, University of Nottingham, University Pk., Nottingham, NT NG7 2RD, England. **Online address:** claire.k.taylor@nottingham.ac.uk

TAYLOR, Daniel (William). American (born United States), b. 1948. **Genres:** Adult Non-fiction, Humanities, Theology/Religion, Autobiography/Memoirs, Essays, Travel/Exploration. **Career:** Northwestern College, English teacher, 1974-76; Westmont College, English teacher, 1976; Bethel University, professor of English, 1977-2010. Writer. **Publications:** (Ed. with L. Eitel) The Treasury of Christian Poetry, 1982; The Myth of Certainty: The Reflective Christian and the Risk of Commitment, 1986; Letters to My Children: A Father Passes on His Values, 1989; The Healing Power of Stories: Creating Yourself through the Stories of Your Life, 1996; (with R. Hoekstra) Before Their Time: Lessons in Living from Those Born Too Soon, 2000; Tell Me a Story: The Life-Shaping Power of Our Stories, 2001; Is God Intolerant?: A Christian Response to the Call for Tolerance, 2003; In Search of Sacred Places: Looking for Wisdom on Celtic Holy Islands, 2005; Creating a Spiritual Legacy: Telling the Stories of Your Life, 2011; The Expanded Bible, 2011. Contributor to books and periodicals. **Address:** 1605 Lake Johanna Blvd., St. Paul, MN 55112, U.S.A. **Online address:** dwtaylor321@gmail.com

TAYLOR, Dave. (David Taylor). Canadian (born Canada), b. 1948. **Genres:** Zoology, Natural History, Environmental Sciences/Ecology, Education, Young Adult Non-fiction, Illustrations, Sciences. **Career:** Peel Board of Education, teacher, 1972-; T.L. Kennedy Secondary School, head of business studies. Writer. **Publications:** SELF-ILLUSTRATED WITH PHOTOGRAPHS: (as David Taylor) Sharks (Nature's Children), 1987; Game Animals of North America, 1988; Ontario's Wildlife, 1988; (co-author) Cycles I & II, 1990; (co-author) Cycles I & II Teacher's Guide, 1990; (with Kettle) The

Fishing Book, 1990; Safari: Journey to the End, 1990; The Alligator and the Everglades, 1990; The Bison and the Great Plains, 1990; The Elephant and the Scrub Forest, 1990; The Lion and the Savannah, 1990; Endangered Forest Animals, 1992; Endangered Grassland Animals, 1992; Endangered Wetland Animals, 1992; Endangered Mountain Animals, 1992; Endangered Island Animals, 1993; Endangered Ocean Animals, 1993; Endangered Savannah Animals, 1993; Endangered Desert Animals, 1993; Algonquin Park, Excursions with a Photographer, 1994; Dave Taylor's Wildlife Reference Library, 1998; Dave Taylor's African Safari: Understanding the Serengeti-Mara Ecosystem, 1999, Florida Manatees, 2004; Black Bears: A Natural History, 2006; Deer World, 2008; Predators of North America, 2009. **Address:** Crabtree Publishing Company Ltd., 350 5th Ave., 59th Fl., PO Box 59051, New York, NY 10118, U.S.A. **Online address:** dtaylor@lifestories.com

TAYLOR, David. *See* **TAYLOR, Dave.**

TAYLOR, Debbie A. American (born United States), b. 1955. **Genres:** Children's Fiction, Picture/Board Books. **Career:** University of Michigan, career planning and placement counselor, 1992-97, graduate experience project, 1997-2000, graduate recruiter, 2000-01, Women in Science and Engineering, assistant director, director, 2002-. Writer. **Publications:** Sweet Music in Harlem, 2004. **Address:** WISE Engineering Office, Center for Engineering Diversity Office, University of Michigan, 153 Chrysler Ctr., 2121 Bonisteel Blvd., Ann Arbor, MI 48109-2092, U.S.A. **Online address:** dpoet@umich.edu

TAYLOR, Diana. American (born United States), b. 1950?. **Genres:** History, Literary Criticism And History. **Career:** New York University, Department of Performance Studies, professor of performance studies and Spanish, university professor, chair of department of performance studies, Hemispheric Institute of Performance and Politics, founding director, 1998-. Writer. **Publications:** Fernando Arrabal: El aquitecto y el emperador de asiria y Cementerio de automóviles, 1984; En busca de una imagen: el arquitecto y el emperador de arisia y Cementerio de automóviles, 1989; Theatre of Crisis: Drama and Politics in Latin America, 1991; (ed. with J. Villegas) Negotiating Performance: Gender, Sexuality, and Theatricality in Latin/o America, 1995; (ed. with A. Jetter and A. Orleck) The Politics of Motherhood: Activist Voices from Left to Right, 1997; Disappearing Acts: Spectacles of Gender and Nationalism in Argentina's Dirty War, 1997; Defiant Acts: Four Plays, 2002; (ed. with R. Costantino) Holy Terrors: Latin American Women Perform, 2003; The Archive and the Repertoire: Performing Cultural Memory in the Americas, 2003; (ed. with S.J. Townsend) Stages of Conflict: A Reader of Latin-American Theatre and Performance, 2004; (ed. with S.J. Townsend) Stages of Conflict: A Critical Anthology of Latin American Theatre and Performance, 2008. **Address:** Hemispheric Institute of Performance & Politics, New York University, 20 Cooper Sq., 5th Fl., New York, NY 10003, U.S.A. **Online address:** diana.taylor@nyu.edu

TAYLOR, Donathan. American (born United States), b. 1962. **Genres:** Travel/Exploration, History, Reference. **Career:** Hardin-Simmons University, Department of History, assistant professor, 1995-2000, associate professor, 2000-07, chairman, 2000-10, professor and Rupert N. Richardson distinguished chair of history, 2007-, Rupert N. Richardson professor of history. Writer. **Publications:** (With R.N. Richardson and B.W. Aston) Along the Texas Forts Trail, 1990. **Address:** Department of History, Cynthia Ann Parker College of Liberal Arts, Hardin-Simmons University, 2200 Hickory St., PO Box 16125, Abilene, TX 79698, U.S.A. **Online address:** dtaylor@hsutx.edu

TAYLOR, Drew Hayden. Canadian (born Canada), b. 1962. **Genres:** Plays/Screenplays. **Career:** University of Michigan, writer-in-residence; University of Western Ontario, writer-in-residence. Playwright. **Publications:** PLAYS: Toronto at Dreamers Rock, 1989; Education Is Our Right, 1990; Talking Pictures, 1990; The Bootlegger Blues, 1991; Someday, 1991; (ed.) Voices: Being Native in Canada, 1992; A Contemporary Gothic Indian Vampire Story, 1992; The Baby Blues, 1995; Girl Who Loved Her Horses, 1995; Only Drunks and Children Tell the Truth, 1996; Fearless Warriors, 1998; 400 Kilometres, 1999; Alternatives, 1999; Boy in the Treehouse, Girl Who Loved Her Horses, 2000; The Buz'gem Blues, 2002; In a World Created by a Drunken God, 2006; The Berlin Blues, 2007; The Night Wanderer: A Native Gothic Novel, 2007; Motorcycles & Sweetgrass (novel), 2010; Dead White Writer on the Floor, 2011. NONFICTION: Funny, You Don't Look like One: Observations of a Blue-Eyed Ojibway, 1998; Further Adventures of a Blue-Eyed Ojibway: Funny, You Don't Look like One II, 1999; Furious Observations of a Blue-Eyed Ojibway: Funny, You Don't Look like One III, 2002; Futile Observations of a Blue-Eyed Ojibway: Funny, You Don't Look like One IV, 2004; (ed.) Me Funny, 2006; Me Sexy, 2008; News: Postcards From the Four Directions, 2011. Contributor to books and newspapers. **Address:** Curve Lake, ON K0L 1R0, Canada. **Online address:** dhtaylor1@yahoo.com

TAYLOR, Elisabeth (D.). Also writes as Hester Pennie, Liz McNeill Taylor. British/Scottish (born Scotland), b. 1931. **Genres:** Romance/Historical, Antiques/Furnishings, How-to Books, Self Help, Novels. **Career:** Writer. **Publications:** (With T. Curtis) Twentieth Century Antiques, 1990. AS ELISABETH MCNEILL: The Shanghai Emerald, 1987; Lark Returning, 1988; A Woman of Gallantry, 1989; Mistress of Green Tree Mill, 1990; Perseverance Place (historical novel), 1991; A Bridge in Time, 1994; St. James' Fair, 1992; A Garden of Briars, 1993; Wild Heritage, 1995; Dusty Letters, 1997; Turn Back Time, 1998; Money Troubles, 1999; Debt Of Love, 2000; A Bombay Affair, 2000; The Send Off, 2001; The Golden Days, 2001; The Last Cocktail Party, 2002; Unforgettable, 2002; Hot News, 2003; Press Relations, 2003; The Lady of Cawnpore, 2004; The Storm, 2006; Flodden Field, 2007; The Turn of the Tide, 2007; Blood Royal, 2008; The Heartbreaker, 2009; East of Aden, 2011. AS HESTER PENNIE: Highland Lady, 1990. AS LIZ MCNEILL TAYLOR: Living with Loss, 1981; Bringing up Children on Your Own, 1982; The Writing Business, 1983; Living Alone, 1984; (with A. Curtis) Cash in on Collecting, 1986; (with T. Curtis) 20th Century Antiques, 1989. **Address:** Cairnhill, 40 Main St., Newstead, Melrose, TD6 9DX, England. **Online address:** liztal@aol.com

TAYLOR, Elizabeth Atwood. American (born United States), b. 1936. **Genres:** Mystery/Crime/Suspense, Novels, Young Adult Fiction, Novellas/Short Stories. **Career:** Writer, documentary film editor, social worker. **Publications:** MAGGIE ELLIOTT MYSTERIES: The Cable Car Murder, 1981, 2nd ed., 1982; Murder at Vassar, 1987; The Northwest Murders, 1992. **Address:** c/o Ruth Cohen, PO Box 7626, Menlo Park, CA 94025, U.S.A. **Online address:** etindia@techemail.com

TAYLOR, Frederick. British (born England), b. 1947?. **Genres:** Novels, Young Adult Non-fiction, Translations, History. **Career:** Writer and historian. **Publications:** NONFICTION: (trans. and ed.) J. Goebbels, The Goebbels Diaries, 1939-1941, 1982; The Kinder Garden, 1991; Operation Thunderclap, 2003; Dresden, Tuesday, February 13, 1945, 2004; The Berlin Wall: A World Divided, 1961-1989, 2006; Exorcising Hitler: The Occupation and Denazification of Germany, 2011. NOVELS: Walking Shadows, 1984; The Peacebrokers, 1992. **Address:** Bloomsbury Publishing Plc., 36 Soho Sq., London, GL W1D 3QY, England. **Online address:** fred@fredericktaylor.com

TAYLOR, Gary. American (born United States), b. 1953?. **Genres:** Literary Criticism And History, Race Relations, Sex, Sociology, Poetry, Humanities. **Career:** University of Oxford, professor, 1978-86; Brandeis University, professor, 1989; University of Alabama, professor, 1995-2005; Florida State University, George Matthew Edgar professor of English, 2005-; Catholic University of America, professor. Writer. **Publications:** Modernizing Shakespeare's Spelling, 1979; Three Studies in the Text of Henry, 1979; To Analyze Delight: A Hedonist Criticism of Shakespeare, 1985 in UK as Moment by Moment by Shakespeare, 1985; William Shakespeare, the Complete Works, 1986; (with S. Wells) William Shakespeare: A Textual Companion, 1987; Complete Oxford Shakespeare, 1987; Complete Works, 1988; Reinventing Shakespeare: A Cultural History, from the Restoration to the Present, 1989; (with J. Jowett) Shakespeare Reshaped, 1606-1623, 1993; Cultural Selection, 1996; Castration: An Abbreviated History of Western Manhood, 2000; The History of King Lear, 2000; Oeuvre's Complètes Comédies, 2000; Reconstructed Text of Pericles, Prince of Tyre, 2003; Buying Whiteness: Race, Sin, Slavery from the European Renaissance to African-American Literature, 2004; Buying Whiteness: Race, Culture and Identity from Columbus to Hip Hop, 2005; Thomas Middleton: The Collected Works, 2007. EDITOR: W. Shakespeare, Henry V, 1982, 3rd ed., 1994; (with M. Warren) The Division of the Kingdoms: Shakespeares Two Versions of King Lear, 1983; (with P.D. Beidler) Writing Race Across the Atlantic World: Medieval to Modern, 2005; (with J. Lavagnino) Thomas Middleton and Early Modern Textual Culture: A Companion to the Collected Works, 2007. Contributor to periodicals. **Address:** English Department, Florida State University, 420 Williams Bldg., Tallahassee, FL 32306-1580, U.S.A. **Online address:** gtaylor@fsu.edu

TAYLOR, Goldie. American (born United States), b. 1968. **Genres:** Novels. **Career:** Atlanta Journal Constitution, reporter; Fortune 500, external affairs executive and political consultant; Goldie Taylor Advertising and Public Relations, managing director and chief creative officer; NATIVE Brand Communications, chief creative officer. Writer and advertising executive. **Publications:** In My Father's House (novel), 2006; The January Girl (novel), 2006. **Address:** Goldie Taylor Brand Communications, 265 Ponce de Leon Ave., Ste. 3318, Atlanta, GA 30308, U.S.A.

TAYLOR, Greg. American (born United States), b. 1951?. **Genres:** Reference. **Career:** Writer. **Publications:** Killer Pizza, 2009. **Address:** c/o Scott Miller, Trident Media Group, 41 Madison Ave., Fl. 36, New York, NY 10010, U.S.A.

TAYLOR, Greg(ory Thomas). American/Canadian (born Canada), b. 1963?. **Genres:** Film, Art/Art History. **Career:** Hollins College, visiting assistant professor, 1992-93; State University of New York, Purchase College, assistant professor of film, 1993-2000, associate professor, 2000-10, professor of film, 2010-, Conservatory of Theatre Arts & Film, interim dean, 2007-10, Conservatory of Dance, interim dean, 2009-10, Conservatory of Theatre Arts, director, 2010-. Writer. **Publications:** Artists in the Audience: Cults, Camp, and American Film Criticism, 1999; Art/Movies: Film Criticism and the Ascent of an American Vanguard, forthcoming. Contributor to periodicals. **Address:** Conservatory of Theatre Arts, Purchase College, State University of New York, Rm. 1020, Dance Bldg., 735 Anderson Hill Rd., Purchase, NY 10577-1402, U.S.A. **Online address:** gregory.taylor@purchase.edu

TAYLOR, Helen. British (born England), b. 1947. **Genres:** Communications/Media, Women's Studies And Issues, Literary Criticism And History. **Career:** Louisiana State University, Department of English, research assistant, 1969-70, teaching assistant, 1970-71; William Collins Publishers, personal assistant, nonfiction editor, 1971; University of the West of England, lecturer, 1972-73, senior lecturer, 1973-90; University of Bristol, extramural tutor, 1972-; Bristol Polytechnic, lecturer, senior lecturer in literary studies, 1972-90; University of Warwick, Department of English and Comparative Literary Studies, senior lecturer in American literature, 1990-97, reader, 1997-98; University of Exeter, American Teaching and Research, lecturer, 1990-, staff development officer, 1994-96, deputy chair of department, 1996-98, professor of English, 1999-2008, School of English, head, 2000-05, director of postgraduate research, 1999-2000, university arts and culture development fellow, 2008-. **Publications:** (Co-author) Half the Sky: An Introduction to Women's Studies, 1979; (ed. and intro.) Portraits, 1979; Gender, Race, and Region in the Writings of Grace King, Ruth McEnery Stuart, and Kate Chopin, 1989; Scarlett's Women: Gone with the Wind and Its Female Fans, 1989; (ed. with R.H. King) Dixie Debates: Perspectives on Southern Cultures, 1996; Circling Dixie: Contemporary Southern Culture through a Transatlantic Lens, 2001; (ed.) Daphne du Maurier Companion, 2007. Contributor to books and journals. **Address:** School of Arts, Languages & Literatures, University of Exeter, Rm. 221, Queen's Bldg., The Queen's Dr., Exeter, DN EX4 4QH, England. **Online address:** helen.taylor@exeter.ac.uk

TAYLOR, Henry. American (born United States), b. 1942. **Genres:** Poetry, Literary Criticism And History, Translations, inspirational/Motivational Literature. **Career:** Roanoke College, instructor in English, 1966-68; University of Utah, assistant professor of English, 1968-71; University of Utah, Writers Conference, director, 1969-72; American University, associate professor, 1971-76, professor of literature, 1976-2003, professor emeritus, 2003-, MFA Program in Creative Writing, co-director, 1971-2003, American Studies Program, director, 1983-85; Hollins College, writer-in-residence, 1978; Wichita State University, distinguished poet-in-residence, 1994; Randolph-Macon Woman's College, poet-in-residence, 1997. Writer. **Publications:** The Horse Show at Midnight, 1966; Breakings, 1971; Poetry: Points of Departure, 1974; An Afternoon of Pocket Billiards, 1975; (ed.) The Water of Light: A Miscellany in Honor of Brewster Ghiselin, 1976; Desperado, 1979; (comp.) A Map of the Loudoun Valley in Virginia Showing Principal Roads, Towns, and Separately Taxed Parcels of Land: Spring 1980, 1980; (trans. with R.A. Brooks) Euripides, The Children of Herakles, 1981; The Flying Change, 1985; Compulsory Figures: Essays on Recent American Poets, 1992; Understanding Fiction: Poems, 1986-1996, 1996; (trans.) V. Levchev, Leaves from the Dry Tree, 1997; (trans.) Sophocles, Electra, 1998; (trans. with V. Levchev) V. Levchev, Black Book of the Endangered Species, 1999; Brief Candles: 101 Clerihews, 2000; Crooked Run: Poems, 2006; (foreword) Roses from the Desert of My Heart, 2007; (trans.) R. Pernoud, Templars, 2009; (trans.) M. Aillet, Old Mass and the New, 2010. Contributor to periodicals. Works appear in anthologies. **Address:** Department of Literature, American University, 4400 Massachusetts Ave. NW, Washington, DC 20016, U.S.A. **Online address:** htaylor@american.edu

TAYLOR, Jacqueline. American (born United States), b. 1951. **Genres:** Autobiography/Memoirs. **Career:** DePaul University, professor of communication, 1980-, chair, 1990-95, College of Liberal Arts and Sciences, associate dean of graduate studies, Women's Studies Program, director, College of Communication, dean, 2007-, associate vice president of academic affairs, DePaul Humanities Center, founding director; Kent State University, American Council on Education Fellow, 2005-06; National Communication Association, chair. Writer. **Publications:** Grace Paley: Illuminating the Dark Lives, 1990; (ed. with L.C. Miller and M.H. Carver) Voices Made Flesh: Performing Women's Autobiography, 2003; Waiting for the Call: From Preacher's Daughter to Lesbian Mom (memoir), 2007. Contributor to periodicals. **Address:** College of Communication, DePaul University, 14 E Jackson Blvd., Ste. 1802, Chicago, IL 60604-2259, U.S.A. **Online address:** jtaylor@depaul.edu

TAYLOR, Janelle (Diane Williams). American (born United States), b. 1944. **Genres:** Poetry, Romance/Historical, Science Fiction/Fantasy, Westerns/Adventure, Novels. **Career:** Nurse, 1969-72; Medical College of Georgia, research technologist, 1975-77. Writer. **Publications:** Savage Ecstasy, 1981; Defiant Ecstasy, 1982; Forbidden Ecstasy, 1982; Brazen Ecstasy, 1983; Love Me with Fury, 1983; Tender Ecstasy, 1983; First Love, Wild Love, 1984; Golden Torment, 1984; Valley of Fire, 1984; Savage Conquest, 1985; Stolen Ecstasy, 1985; Destiny's Temptress, 1986; Moondust and Madness, 1986; Sweet, Savage Heart, 1986; Bittersweet Ecstasy, 1987; Wild Is My Love, 1987; Fortune's Flames, 1988; Passions Wild and Free, 1988; Wild Sweet Promise, 1989; Kiss of the Night Wind, 1989; Whispered Kisses, 1990; Follow the Wind, 1990; Christmas Rendezvous, 1991; Forever Ecstasy, 1991; Promise Me Forever, 1991; Stardust and Shadows, 1992; Midnight Secrets, 1992; Taking Chances, 1993; Three Complete Novels, 1993, vol. II, 1994, vol. III, 1996; Chase the Wind, 1994; Starlight and Splendor, 1994; Destiny Mine, 1995; Anything for Love, 1995; Moonbeams and Magic, 1995; Defiant Hearts, 1996; Love with a Stranger, 1996; Wild Winds, 1997; By Candlelight, 1997; Summer Love, 1997; Lakota Winds, 1998; Lakota Dawn, 1998; Someday Soon, 1999; In too Deep, 2001; Can't Stop Loving You, 2001; Night Moves, 2002; Don't Go Home, 2003; Lakota Flower, 2003; Dying to Marry, 2004; Watching Amanda, 2005; Haunting Olivia, 2006; Shadowing Ivy, 2007; Cherokee Storm, 2010. Contributor to books. **Address:** Kensington Publishing Corp., 119 W 40th St., New York, NY 10018, U.S.A. **Online address:** jnataylor@aol.com

TAYLOR, Jean. *See* **TAYLOR, Jean Gelman.**

TAYLOR, Jean Gelman. (Jean Taylor). Australian (born Australia), b. 1944. **Genres:** History, Social Sciences. **Career:** University of New South Wales, associate professor of history and history discipline coordinator; Royal Institute of Southeast Asian and Caribbean Studies, visiting research fellow; Asia Research Group, coordinator. Historian and writer. **Publications:** The Social World of Batavia: European and Eurasian in Dutch Asia, 1983; (ed. and contrib.) Women Creating Indonesia: The First Fifty Years, 1997; Indonesia: Peoples and Histories, 2003; Social World of Batavia: Europeans and Eurasians in Colonial Indonesia, 2009. Contributor to journals. **Address:** School of History and Philosophy, University of New South Wales, Rm. 343, Morven Brown Bldg., Sydney, NW 2052, Australia. **Online address:** jeant@unsw.edu.au

TAYLOR, Jennifer (Evelyn). Australian (born Australia), b. 1935. **Genres:** Architecture, Art/Art History, Photography. **Career:** University of Sydney, tutor, 1970, lecturer, 1971-79, senior lecturer, 1980-82, associate professor of architecture, 1983-98; Queensland University of Technology, adjunct professor, 1998-; ICOMOS, founding member; DOCOMOMO, founding member. Writer and architect. **Publications:** An Australian Identity: Houses for Sydney 1953-63, 1972, 2nd ed., 1984; (with J. Andrews) John Andrews: Architecture a Performing Art, 1982; Australian Architects: Ken Woolley (monograph), 1985; Australian Architecture Since 1960, 1986, 2nd ed., 1989; (comp.) The Brock Family History, 1988; (comp.) World Architecture 1900-2000: A Critical Mosaic, vol. X (Oceania), 1999; (co-author) Tall Buildings: Australian Business Going Up, 1945-1970, 2001; The Architecture of Fumihiiko Maki: Space, City, Order and Making, 2003. **Address:** Oxford University Press, 253 Normanby Rd., PO Box 2784, South Melbourne, VI 3205, Australia. **Online address:** je.taylor@qut.edu.au

TAYLOR, Joan E(lizabeth). New Zealander/British (born England), b. 1958. **Genres:** Archaeology/Antiquities, History, Philosophy, Theology/Religion, Women's Studies And Issues, Humanities, Novels. **Career:** University of Waikato, fellow, 1992-93, lecturer, 1994-97, senior lecturer in history and religious studies, 1998-2000, Department of Philosophy and Religious Studies, research associate and adjunct senior lecturer, 2002-; Harvard University, visiting lecturer and research associate in women's studies in religion, 1996-97; University College London, Department of History and Jewish Studies, honorary research fellow, 2002-; King's College, Department of Theology and Religious Studies, lecturer. Writer. **Publications:** HISTORY AND RELIGION: Christians and the Holy Places: The Myth of Jewish-Christian Origins, 1993; (with S. Gibson) Beneath the Church of the Holy Sepulchre, Jerusalem, 1994; The Immerser: John the Baptist within Second Temple Judaism, 1997; Jewish Women Philosophers of First Century Alexandria, 2003; (ed.) The Onomasticon by Eusebius of Caesarea: Palestine in the Fourth Century AD, 2003; The Englishman, the Moor and the Holy City, 2005. FICTION: Conversations with Mr Prian, 2006. Contributor of articles to periodicals. **Address:** Departmentof Philosophy and Religious Studies, University of Waikato, PO Box 3105, Hamilton, 3240, New Zealand. **Online address:** jetaylor@waikato.ac.nz

TAYLOR, Joe. American (born United States), b. 1949. **Genres:** Novels, Novellas/Short Stories, Young Adult Fiction, Humanities. **Career:** Swallow's Tale Press, staff, 1982-; Peachtree Press, reader, 1986-; University of West Alabama, professor, 1990-; Livingston Press, director, 1993-. Writer. **Publications:** Oldcat and Ms. Puss: A Book of Days for You and Me, 1997; (ed. with T.N. Jones) Belles' Letters: Contemporary Fiction by Alabama Women, 1999; Some Heroes, Some Heroines, Some Others: Stories, 2002; World's Thinnest Fat Man: Stories, 2005; (ed. with D. Davis, G. Jones and T. Jones) Tartts: Incisive Fiction from Emerging Writers, 2005; (ed. with D. Davis, G. Jones and T. Jones) Tartts 2: Incisive Fiction From Emerging Writers, 2006; (ed. with T. Jones and T. Taylor) Tartts 4: Incisive Fiction from Emerging Writers, 2008; Masques for the Fields of Time, 2009; The Theoretics of Love, forthcoming; The First, Spinning Moment, forthcoming; Dappled Things, forthcoming. **Address:** University of West Alabama, 110 Wallace Hall, Sta. 22, Livingston, AL 35470, U.S.A. **Online address:** jwt@uwa.edu

TAYLOR, John A. American (born United States), b. 1942. **Genres:** History, Economics, Cultural/Ethnic Topics. **Career:** Southern Illinois University, faculty, 1970-, associate professor, 1976-96, professor of history, 1996-2009, professor emeritus, 2009-; Harvard University, visiting fellow, 1983-84; Waseda University, visiting professor, 2000; Saint Petersburg State University, visiting professor of history, 2008-. Writer. **Publications:** (Contrib.) The American Revolution: An Encyclopedia, 1993; British Monarchy, English Church Establishment and Civil Liberty, 1996; Popular Literature and the Construction of British National Identity, 1707-1850, 1997; (ed. and intro.) William Covel's A Just and Temperate Defence of the Five Books of Ecclesiastical Polity, 1998; Diana, Self-Interest and British National Identity, 2000; (contrib.) Dictionary of British Economists, 2004; British Empiricism and Early Political Economy: Gregory King's 1696 Estimates of National Wealth and Population, 2005; Prince William, the Internet and the Tabloids: Contemporary Celebrity and the Monarchy, 2010. Contributor to periodicals and journals. **Address:** College of Arts and Sciences, Southern Illinois University, Rm. 3225, Peck Hall, PO Box 1454, Edwardsville, IL 62026, U.S.A. **Online address:** john_taylor84@post.harvard.edu

TAYLOR, John (Gerald). British (born England), b. 1931. **Genres:** Information Science/Computers, Mathematics/Statistics, Physics, Psychology. **Career:** Institute for Advanced Study, staff, 1956-58, 1961-63; Cambridge University, Christ's College, fellow, 1958-60, assistant maths lecturer, 1959-60, Churchill College, senior research fellow, 1963-64; Rutgers University, professor of physics, 1964-66; Hertford College, Maths Institute, lecturer and fellow, 1966-67; University of London, Queen Mary College, reader in particles and fields, 1967-69, King's College, professor of mathematics, 1971-, Center for Neural Networks, director, 1990-, Neural Networks, European editor-in-chief, 1990-, now professor emeritus, International Neural Network Society, president; University of Southampton, professor of physics, 1969-71. **Publications:** Quantum Mechanics: An Introduction, 1969; The Shape of Minds to Come, 1970; The New Physics, 1972; Black Holes: The End of the Universe?, 1973, rev. ed., 1998; New Worlds in Pphysics, 1974; Superminds, 1975; Special Relativity, 1975; Science and the Supernatural, 1980; The Frontiers of Knowledge, 1982; Finite Superstrings, 1992; The Promise of Neural Networks, 1993; When the Clock Struck Zero, 1994; The Race for

Consciousness, 1999; Mind: A User's Manual, 2006. EDITOR: Supergravity '81, 1982; Supersymmetry and Supergravity '82, 1983; Tributes to Paul Dirac, 1987; New Developments in Neural Computing, 1989; Coupled Oscillating Newons, 1992; Neural Network Applications, 1992; (co-ed.) Neural Network Dynamics, 1992; Coupled Oscillating Neurons, 1992; Theory and Applications of Neural Networks, 1992; Mathematical Approaches to Neural Networks, 1993; Neural Networks and Their Applications, 1996; (with J. Shadbolt) Neural Networks and the Financial Markets: Predicting, Combining and Portfolio Optimization, 2002. **Address:** Department of Mathematics, King's College, Rm. 320, Strand Bldg., London, GL WC2R 2LS, England. **Online address:** john.g.taylor@kcl.ac.uk

TAYLOR, John H(ilton). British (born England), b. 1958. **Genres:** Archaeology/Antiquities, History, Social Sciences. **Career:** University of Birmingham, part-time lecturer in Egyptology, 1985-88; British Museum, Department of Ancient Egypt and Sudan, curator, 1988-, assistant keeper. Writer. **Publications:** Egyptian Coffins, 1989; Egypt and Nubia, 1991; (with N. Reeves) Howard Carter: Before Tutankhamun, 1993; Unwrapping a Mummy: The Life, Death and Embalming of Horemkenesi, 1996; (co-author) Ancient Faces: Mummy Portraits from Roman Egypt, 1996; Death and the Afterlife in Ancient Egypt, 2001; (ed. with N. Strudwick) The Theban Necropolis: Past, Present and Future, 2003; Mummy: The Inside Story, 2004; (ed. with R. Gundlach) Egyptian Royal Residences: London, June, 1st-5th 2004, 2009; (ed.) Journey Through the Afterlife: Ancient Egyptian Book of the Dead, 2010; Spells For Eternity: the Ancient Egyptian Book of the Dead, 2010; Egyptian Mummies, 2010. **Address:** Department of Ancient Egypt & Sudan, British Museum, Great Russell St., London, GL WC1B 3DG, England. **Online address:** jtaylor@thebritishmuseum.ac.uk

TAYLOR, John Robert. *See* **TAYLOR, Andrew (John Robert).**

TAYLOR, John Russell. British (born England), b. 1935. **Genres:** Communications/Media, Film, Theatre, Humanities, Biography, Autobiography/Memoirs. **Career:** University of London, Courtauld Institute of Art, researcher on art, 1956-58; Times Educational Supplement, sub-editor, 1959-60; Times, entertainment correspondent, 1959-63, film critic, 1963-73, art critic, 1978-; Times Literary Supplement, editorial assistant, 1961-63; Tufts University, lecturer in film, 1970-71; Films and Filming, editor, 1983-90; University of Southern California, Cinema Division, professor, 1972-78. **Publications:** Joseph L. Mankiewicz: An Index, 1960; Anger and After: A Guide to the New British Drama in US as The Angry Theatre, 1962; Anatomy of a Television Play, 1962; Cinema Eye, Cinema Ear: Some Key Film-Makers of the 60s, 1964; Penguin Dictionary of the Theatre, 1966; The Art Nouveau Book in Britain, 1966; Art in London: A Guide, 1966; The Rise and Fall of the Well-Made Play, 1967; The Art Nouveau Book in Britain, 1967; Look Back in Anger: A Casebook, 1968; The Art Dealers, 1969; Anger, and After: A Guide to the New British Drama, 1969; Harold Pinter, 1969; A Dictionary of the Theatre, 1970; (with A. Jackson) The Hollywood Musical, 1971; The Second Wave: British Dramatists for the Seventies, 1971; David Storey, 1974; Fifty Superstars, 1974; Peter Shaffer, 1975; Directors and Directions: Cinema for the Seventies, 1978; Hitch: The Life and Times of Alfred Hitchcock, 1978; Impressionism, 1981; Strangers in Paradise: The Hollywood Emigres 1933-1950, 1982; Ingrid Bergman, 1983; Alec Guinness: A Celebration, 1984; Vivien Leigh, 1984; Hollywood 1940s, 1985; (with J. Kobal) Portraits of the British Cinema, 1985; Orson Welles: A Celebration, 1986; Edward Wolfe, 1986; Great Movie Moments, 1987; Journeys, 1988; Impressionist Dreams: The Artists and the World They Painted, 1990; Bernard Meninsky, 1990; Liz Taylor, 1991; Ricardo Cinalli, 1992; Muriel Pemberton, 1993; Igor Mitoraj, 1994; Claude Monet: Impressions of France, 1995; Michael Parkes, 1996; Bill Jacklin, 1997; The Sun Is God: The Life and Work of Cyril Mann, 1999; Peter Coker, 2001; Geoffrey Dashwood, 2001; (with R. Humphreys) Peter Coker RA, 2002; Roboz: A Painter's Paradox, 2006; Ana Maria Pacheco, 2006; (with S. Tait) Philip Sutton, 2008; The Art of Jeremy Ramsey, 2008; Exactitude, 2009; (co-author) Kurt Jackson, 2010. EDITOR: Three Plays of John Arden, 1964; New English Dramatists 8, 1965; John Osborne: Look Back in Anger: A Casebook, 1968; The Playwrights Speak, 1969; The Pleasure Dome: Collected Film Criticism of Graham Greene, 1972; Masterworks of British Cinema, 1974. **Address:** The Times, 3 Thomas More Sq., London, GL E98 1XY, England.

TAYLOR, Jonathan. British (born England), b. 1973. **Genres:** Literary Criticism And History, Autobiography/Memoirs. **Career:** De Montfort University, senior lecturer in creative writing; Crystal Clear Creators, co-director and co-founder. Writer. **Publications:** Mastery and Slavery in Victorian Writing (literary criticism), 2003; (ed. with A. Dix) Figures of Heresy: Radical Theology in English and American Writing, 1800-2000 (literary criticism), 2006; Science and Omniscience in Nineteenth Century Literature (literary criticism), 2007; Take Me Home: Parkinson's, My Father, Myself (memoir), 2007; (ed. with M. Taylor) Fizzle & Sizzle: An Anthology of New Writing by Young Writers in Leicestershire (poetry and stories), 2008. Contributor of articles to newspapers and magazines. **Address:** Department of English and Creative Writing, Faculty of Humanities, De Montfort University, Clephan Bldg., Leicester, LE LE1 9BH, England. **Online address:** crystalclearjt@hotmail.co.uk

TAYLOR, Jon E. American (born United States), b. 1968. **Genres:** History. **Career:** University of Central Missouri, professor of history. Writer. **Publications:** A President, a Church, and Trails West: Competing Histories in Independence, Missouri, 2008. **Address:** University of Central Missouri, Rm. 136G, Wood Bldg., Warrensburg, MO 64093, U.S.A. **Online address:** jtaylor01@ucmo.edu

TAYLOR, Justin. New Zealander (born New Zealand), b. 1943. **Genres:** History, Theology/Religion. **Career:** Downing College, research fellow, 1970-73; Mount St. Marys Seminary, lecturer, 1974-88; Ecole Biblique, assistant professor, 1988-91, associate professor, 1991-96, professor, 1996-, vice-director. Writer. **Publications:** As it was Written: An Introduction to the Bible, 1987; Les Actes des deux Apotres, 3 vols., 1994-2000; (with E. Nodet) The Origins of Christianity: An Exploration, 1998; Where Did Christianity Come From?, 2001; Pythagoreans and Essenes: Structural Parallels, 2004. **Address:** Ecole Biblique, 6 Nablus Rd., PO Box 19053, Jerusalem, 91190, Israel. **Online address:** taylor@ebaf.edu

TAYLOR, Karen E. American (born United States), b. 1954?. **Genres:** Horror, Romance/Historical. **Career:** Writer, 1993-. **Publications:** VAMPIRE LEGACY SERIES: Blood Secrets, 1994; Bitter Blood, 1994; Blood Ties, 1995; Blood of My Blood, 2000; The Vampire Vivienne, 2001; Resurrection, 2002; Fangs and Angel Wings, 2003; Blood Red Dawn, 2004; Twelve Steps from Darkness, 2007; Hunger, 2011; Crave, 2011. **Address:** c/o Author Mail, Kensington Publishing Corp., 119 W 40th St., New York, NY 10018, U.S.A. **Online address:** ket@karenetaylor.com

TAYLOR, Katherine. American (born United States), b. 1973. **Genres:** Young Adult Fiction, Novels. **Career:** Writer. **Publications:** Rules for Saying Goodbye, 2007. **Address:** Curtis Brown Ltd., Haymarket House, 28-29 Haymarket, London, GL SW1Y 4SP, England.

TAYLOR, Kathy. American (born United States), b. 1950. **Genres:** Literary Criticism And History, History, Young Adult Fiction. **Career:** Scattergood High School, instructor in Spanish, 1974-78; University of Iowa, teaching assistant, 1979-82, 1984-87, adjunct instructor in Spanish, 1987; Earlham College, assistant professor, 1988-94, associate professor of Spanish, 1994-, professor of Spanish and Hispanic studies. Writer. **Publications:** The New Narrative of Mexico: Sub-versions of History in Mexican Fiction, 1994; Por el espejo retrovisor/Through the Rearview Mirror, 1999; Trees and Other Witnesses, forthcoming. Contributor of articles to periodicals. **Address:** Department of Languages & Literatures, Earlham College, 801 National Rd. W, Richmond, IN 47374-4095, U.S.A.

TAYLOR, Larissa J(uliet). American (born United States), b. 1952. **Genres:** History, Theology/Religion, Biography. **Career:** Brown University, teaching assistant in history, 1982-87; Massachusetts Institute of Technology, instructor in history, 1987; Wellesley College, assistant professor of history, 1988-93, 1991-93; Harvard University, lecturer in history, 1991-92, assistant professor, 1991-94; Assumption College, assistant professor of history, 1993-94; Colby College, professor of history, 1994-. Writer. **Publications:** Soldiers of Christ: Preaching in Late Medieval and Reformation France, 1992; Heresy and Orthodoxy in Sixteenth-Century Paris: Francois Le Picart and the Beginnings of the Catholic Reformation, 1999; (ed.) Preachers and People in the Reformations and Early Modern Period, 2001; (contrib.) Nahua Confraternities in Early Colonial Mexico: The 1552 Nahuatl Ordinances of Fray Alonso de Molina, OFM, 2002; (ed.) Great Events from History: The 17th Century, 1601-1700, 2005; (ed.) Great Lives from History: The 17th Century, 2005; (co-ed.) The Encyclopedia of Medieval Pilgrimage, 2009; The Virgin Warrior: The Life and Death of Joan of Arc, 2009; Giovanna d'Arco e la Guerra dei Cent' Anni, 2010. Contributor to periodicals. **Address:** Department of

History, Colby College, 5330 Mayflower Hill, Waterville, ME 04901-8853, U.S.A. **Online address:** ljtaylor@colby.edu

TAYLOR, Lester D. American (born United States), b. 1938. **Genres:** Economics, Communications/Media, Mathematics/Statistics, Technology, Essays. **Career:** Harvard University, instructor, 1963-64, assistant professor of economics, 1964-68; U.S. Council of Economic Advisers, staff economist, 1964-65; University of Michigan, associate professor of economics, 1969-74; National Bureau of Economic Research, research associate, 1972; University of Arizona, professor of economics, 1974, now professor emeritus. Writer. **Publications:** (With H.S. Houthakker) Consumer Demand in the United States, 1929-1970, 1966, 3rd ed., 2010; (with M.L. Ingbar) Hospital Costs in Massachusetts: An Econometric Study, 1968; (with S.J. Turnovsky and T.D. Wilson) Inflationary Process in North American Manufacturing, 1972; Processus Inflationnaire et le Secteur Manufacturier Nord Américain, 1973; Probability and Mathematical Statistics, 1974; Telecommunications Demand: A Survey and Critique, 1980; (ed. with L. Philips) Aggregation, Consumption and Trade: Essays in Honor of H.S. Houthakker, 1992; Telecommunications Demand in Theory and Practice, 1994; (ed. with D.G. Loomis) The Future of the Telecommunications Industry: Forecasting and Demand Analysis, 1999; Capital, Accumulation and Money: An Integration of Capital, Growth and Monetary Theory, 2000; (ed. with D.G. Loomis) Forecasting the Internet: Understanding the Explosive Growth of Data, 2002. Contributor to journals. **Address:** Department of Economics, Eller College of Management, University of Arizona, 432 McClelland Hall, 1130 E Helen St., PO Box 210108, Tucson, AZ 85721-0108, U.S.A. **Online address:** ltaylor@eller.arizona.edu

TAYLOR, Liza Pennywitt. American/British (born England), b. 1955. **Genres:** Novels, Novellas/Short Stories, Romance/Historical, Women's Studies And Issues, Mystery/Crime/Suspense. **Career:** Professional flutist and flute instructor, 1970-81; University California, Department of Immunology and Microbiology, research associate, 1983-90; writer, 1990-; Los Angeles Times, fiction reviewer, 1998-2008. **Publications:** The Drummer was the First to Die, 1992; The Inland Sea, forthcoming. Contributor to periodicals. **Address:** c/o Sandra Dijkstra, Sandra Dijkstra Literary Agency, 1155 Camino del Mar, Del Mar, CA 92014, U.S.A. **Online address:** lizaonavon@hotmail.com

TAYLOR, Liz McNeill. *See* **TAYLOR, Elisabeth (D.).**

TAYLOR, Margaret. Canadian (born Canada), b. 1950?. **Genres:** Adult Non-fiction, Science Fiction/Fantasy, Travel/Exploration. **Career:** School District 72, library technician and clerk, 1987-, school secretary. Writer. **Publications:** Three Against Time, 1997. **Address:** PO Box 64, Heriot Bay, BC V0P 1H0, Canada. **Online address:** marg.taylor@sd72.bc.ca

TAYLOR, Mark Kline. *See* **TAYLOR, Mark Lewis.**

TAYLOR, Mark Lewis. (Mark Kline Taylor). American (born United States), b. 1951. **Genres:** Theology/Religion, Politics/Government, Anthropology/Ethnology, Cultural/Ethnic Topics, History. **Career:** Agape: Neighborhood Crime Victims Assistance Program, co-founder and director, 1978-82; Princeton Theological Seminary, Department of Theology, assistant professor, 1982-88, associate professor, 1988-99, professor, 1999-, Maxwell M. Upson professor of theology and culture, 2003-. Writer. **Publications:** (Ed. with R.S. Chopp) Reconstructing Christian Theology, 1994; The Executed God: The Way of the Cross in Lockdown America, 2001; Religion, Politics, and the Christian Right: Post-9/11 Powers and American Empire, 2005; The Theological and the Political: On the Weight of the World, 2010. AS MARK KLINE TAYLOR: Beyond Explanation: Religious Dimensions in Cultural Anthropology, 1986; Paul Tillich: Theologian of the Boundaries, 1987; Remembering Esperanza: A Cultural-Political Theology for North American Praxis, 1990. **Address:** Department of Theology, Princeton Theological Seminary, 115 Hodge Hall, 64 Mercer St., PO Box 821, Princeton, NJ 08542-0803, U.S.A. **Online address:** mark.taylor@ptsem.edu

TAYLOR, Mary F. American (born United States) **Genres:** Food And Wine, How-to Books, Medicine/Health. **Career:** Author and counselor. **Publications:** New Vegetarian Classics: Soups, 1994; New Vegetarian Classics: Entrées, 1995; Lunch Crunch: Beating the Lunchbox Blues, 1997; (with L. Ginsburg) What Are You Hungry For?: Women, Food, and Spirituality, 2002. **Address:** c/o Jane Dystel, Dystel & Goderich Literary Management,

1 Union Sq. W, Ste. 904, New York, NY 10003, U.S.A. **Online address:** authors@whatareyouhungryfor.net

TAYLOR, Max. *See* **ERLBACH, Arlene.**

TAYLOR, Michael J. (M. J. Taylor). American (born United States), b. 1942. **Genres:** Politics/Government. **Career:** University of Essex, computer programmer, 1965-66, research fellow, 1966-68, lecturer, 1968-71, senior lecturer & reader, 1971-85; University of Washington, professor, 1985-, Program in Environmental Anthropology, adjunct faculty member, 1997-; Yale University, visiting research associate, 1967-68, visiting lecturer, 1970-71; Institute for Advanced Studies, guest professor, 1970, 1971; Board of the European Branch of the Public Choice Society, director, 1972-74; European University Institute, faculty, 1987; Australian National University, visiting fellow, 1988; Committee on the Political Economy of the Good Society, founding board member, 1989-. Political theorist, political economist and writer. **Publications:** (with D.W. Rae) The Analysis of Political Cleavages, 1970; (ed. with C.W. Lomas) The Rhetoric of the British Peace Movement, 1971; Anarchy and Cooperation, 1976; (ed. with N. Thrift) The Geography of Multinationals: Studies in the Spatial Development and Economic Consequences of Multinational Corporations, 1982; Community, Anarchy and Liberty, 1982; The Possibility of Cooperation, 1987; (ed.) Rationality and Revolution, 1988; Rationality and the Ideology of Disconnection, 2006. **Address:** Department of Political Science, University of Washington, PO Box 353530, Seattle, WA 98195-3530, U.S.A. **Online address:** mjtaylor@u.washington.edu

TAYLOR, Michael J(oseph). American (born United States), b. 1924. **Genres:** Theology/Religion, Self Help, History. **Career:** Gonzaga University, instructor in theology, 1956-59; Seattle University, assistant professor, 1961-66, associate professor, 1967-72; professor of theology, 1973-95, professor emeritus of theology and religious studies, 1995-. Writer. **Publications:** The Protestant Liturgical Renewal, 1963; (with R.P. Marshall) Liturgy and Christian Unity, 1965; (comp.) The Sacred and the Secular, 1968; A Companion to John: Readings in Johannine Theology, 1977; John: The Different Gospel, 1983; The Sacraments as Encasement, 1986; Korean Edition of The Sacraments as Encasement, 1991; Paul: His Letters, Message and Heritage, 1997; Purgatory, 1998; Theological Reflections on the Trinity, Christology, and Monotheism, 2001. EDITOR: Liturgical Renewal in the Christian Churches, 1967; The Mystery of Sin and Forgiveness, 1971; Sex: Thoughts for Contemporary Christians, 1972; The Mystery of Suffering and Death, 1973; A Companion to Paul: Topical Readings in Pauline Theology, 1975; Companion to John, 1977; Status of Endangered Australasian Wildlife, 1979; The Sacraments: Readings in Contemporary Sacramental Theology, 1981. **Address:** Department of Theology and Religious Studies, Seattle University, 901 12th Ave., Seattle, WA 98122, U.S.A.

TAYLOR, Michael Ray. American (born United States), b. 1959. **Genres:** Air/Space Topics, Biology, Earth Sciences, Natural History, Travel/Exploration, Autobiography/Memoirs, Documentaries/Reportage, Essays, Essays, Environmental Sciences/Ecology. **Career:** Dominican College, creative writing instructor, 1987-90; Henderson State University, assistant professor of journalism, 1991-96, associate professor, 1996-, Department of Communication and Theatre Arts, professor. Writer. **Publications:** (Ed.) Lechuguilla: Jewel of the Underground, 1990; Cave Passages: Roaming the Underground Wilderness, 1996; Dark Life: Martian Nanobacteria, Rock-Eating Cave Bugs, and Other Extreme Organisms of Inner Earth and Outer Space, 1999; Caves: Exploring Hidden Realms, 2000. Contributor to periodicals. **Address:** Department of Communication and Theatre Arts, Henderson State University, 1100 Henderson St., PO Box 7502, Arkadelphia, AR 71999-0001, U.S.A. **Online address:** taylorm@hsu.edu

TAYLOR, Mildred D. American (born United States), b. 1943. **Genres:** Children's Fiction, Novellas/Short Stories, Novels, History, Young Adult Fiction, Romance/Historical. **Career:** United States Peace Corps, recruiter, 1967-68; University of Colorado, study skills coordinator, 1969-71; proofreader and editor, 1971-73. **Publications:** Song of the Trees, 1975; Roll of Thunder, Hear My Cry, 1976; Let the Circle Be Unbroken, 1981; The Friendship, 1987; The Gold Cadillac, 1987; The Friendship and Other Stories, 1989; Mississippi Bridge, 1990; The Road to Memphis, 1990; The Well: David's Story, 1995; The Land, 2001; The Bliss, 2002. Contributor to periodicals. **Address:** Dial Books for Young Readers, 345 Hudson St., New York, NY 10014-4502, U.S.A.

TAYLOR, M. J. *See* **TAYLOR, Michael J.**

TAYLOR, Nick. American (born United States), b. 1945. **Genres:** Adult Non-fiction, Literary Criticism And History. **Career:** WQXI, reporter, through 1976; reporter, 1967-76; Writer, 1981-; Authors Guild, president, 2002-06. **Publications:** (With S. Linver) Speak and Get Results: The Complete Guide to Speeches and Presentations that Work in any Business Situation, 1983; Bass Wars: A Story of Fishing Fame and Fortune, 1988; Sins of the Father: The True Story of a Family Running from the Mob, 1989; Ordinary Miracles: Life in a Small Church, 1993; A Necessary End, 1994; (with Y. Svoray) In Hitler's Shadow, 1994; (with S.J. Winawer) Healing Lessons, 1998; (with J. Glenn) John Glenn: A Memoir, 1999; Laser: The Inventor, the Nobel Laureate and the Thirty-Year Patent War, 2000; American-Made: The Enduring Legacy of the WPA, When FDR Put the Nation to Work, 2008. **Address:** c/o Lynn Nesbit, Janklow & Nesbit Associates, 445 Park Ave., Fl. 13, New York, NY 10022, U.S.A. **Online address:** nicktaylornyc@mac.com

TAYLOR, Nick. American (born United States), b. 1976?. **Genres:** Novels, Politics/Government. **Career:** San Jose State University, assistant professor of English and comparative literature. Writer and computer programmer. **Publications:** (contrib.) Politically Inspired, 2003; The Disagreement: A Novel, 2008. Contributor to periodicals. **Address:** Department of English, San Jose State University, Faculty Offices 102, 1 Washington Sq., San Jose, CA 95192-0090, U.S.A. **Online address:** nicholas.taylor@sjsu.edu

TAYLOR, Patrick. Canadian/British/Irish (born Ireland), b. 1941?. **Genres:** Novels, Translations, Medicine/Health, Children's Fiction, Young Adult Fiction. **Career:** University of Calgary, faculty, 1971-87; Bourn Hall Clinic, staff, 1987-89; University of Manitoba, faculty, 1989-91; University of British Columbia, faculty, 1991-2001, professor of medicine, chairman of obstetrics and gynaecology, now professor emeritus; St. Paul's Hospital, head of obstetrics and gynecology, through 2001. **Publications:** Only Wounded: Ulster Stories, 1997; (with T.F. Baskett) The Complete Anthology of En Passant 1989-1999, 1999. NOVELS: Pray for Us Sinners, 2000; The Apprenticeship of Doctor Laverty, 2004; Now and in the Hour of Our Death, 2005; Irish Country Doctor, 2007; Irish Country Christmas: A Novel, 2008; An Irish Country Village, 2008; Irish Country Girl, 2010; Irish Country Courtship, 2011; Dublin Student Doctor, 2011. OTHERS: (co-author) Laparoscopy and Hysteroscopy in Gynecologic Practice, 1986; (trans.) J.E. Hamou, Hysteroscopy and Microhysteroscopy: Text and Atlas, 1991; (with J.A. Collins) Unexplained Infertility, 1992; (with A.G. Gordon) Practical Laparoscopy, 1993; (with A.G. Gordon) Practical Hysteroscopy, 1993; (with V. Gomel) Diagnostic and Operative Gynecologic Laparoscopy, 1995. **Address:** BC , Canada. **Online address:** editere@yahoo.com

TAYLOR, Paul F. American (born United States), b. 1927. **Genres:** Organized Labor, Children's Fiction. **Career:** Harlan County Board of Education, teacher, 1946-47; Bell County Board of Education, teacher, 1949-51; De Kalb County Board of Education, teacher, 1955-59; Georgia Military Academy, staff, 1959-63; Augusta College, associate professor, 1967-94; Westminster School, board director, 1972-79. Writer. **Publications:** Bloody Harlan: The United Mine Workers of America in Harlan County, Kentucky, 1931-1941, 1990; ABC-CLIO Companion to the American Labor Movement, 1993. **Address:** 925 Stonecase Ct., Lexington, KY 40509, U.S.A.

TAYLOR, Quintard. American (born United States), b. 1948. **Genres:** History, Humanities. **Career:** Washington State University, Black Studies Program, assistant professor, 1971-75; California Polytechnic State University, Department of History, professor, 1977-90; University of Lagos, Department of History, visiting Fulbright professor, 1987-88; University of Oregon, Folklore and Ethnic Studies Program, adjunct professor, 1990-94, acting director, 1992-93, Department of History, professor, 1990-99, Knight distinguished professor of liberal arts and sciences, 1998-99, department head, 1997-99; University of Utah, David E. Miller lecturer, 1997; University of Washington, Scott and Dorothy Bullitt professor of American history, 1999-, chair of American history. Writer. **Publications:** The Making of the Modern World: A Reader in Twentieth-Century Global History, 1990; The Forging of a Black Community: A History of Seattle's Central District, 1870 through the Civil Rights Era, 1994; In Search of the Racial Frontier: African Americans in the American West, 1528-1990, 1998; Ica I am Black Facts: The Story of a People Through Timelines, 1601-2008, 2009; (with S.E. Kelly) Dr. Sam, Soldier, Educator, Advocate, Friend: The Autobiography of Samuel Eugene Kelly, 2010. EDITOR: (with L.B. de Graaf and K. Mulroy) Seeking Eldorado:

African Americans in California, 2001; (with S.A. Moore) African American Women in the American West, 1600-2000, 2003; From Timbuktu to Katrina: Readings in African American History, 2008; (with E. Gamboa) Peoples of Color in the Pacific Northwest, 1788-1970, forthcoming; Urban Archipelago: African American Communities in the Twentieth Century American West, forthcoming; Erasmo Gamboa and Quintard Taylor, Eds. Peoples of Color in the Pacific Northwest, 1788-1970, forthcoming. Contributor to journals. **Address:** Department of History, University of Washington, Smith Hall Rm. 316-A, PO Box 353560, Seattle, WA 98195, U.S.A. **Online address:** qtaylor@u.washington.edu

TAYLOR, Ranald J. Australian (born Australia), b. 1962. **Genres:** Economics. **Career:** Murdoch University, professor. Writer and consultant. **Publications:** Technical Progress and Economic Growth: An Empirical Case Study of Malaysia, 2007. **Address:** Australia. **Online address:** ranald.taylor@murdoch.edu.au

TAYLOR, Robert. British (born England), b. 1941?. **Genres:** Politics/Government, International Relations/Current Affairs. **Career:** University of Auckland, lecturer, senior lecturer in Asian politics; University of Stirling, Centre for Japanese Studies, senior research fellow; University of Sheffield, School of East Asian Studies, reader in modern Chinese studies and director of Chinese studies, 1993-2007. Writer. **Publications:** Education and University Enrolment Policies in China, 1949-1971, 1973; China's Intellectual Dilemma: Politics and University Enrolment, 1949-1978, 1981; The Sino-Japanese Axis: A New Force in Asia?, 1985; China, Japan, and the European Community, 1990; Greater China and Japan: Prospects for an Economic Partnership in East Asia, 1996. Contributor to books and journals. **Address:** The School of East Asian Studies, The University of Sheffield, The Arts Twr., Fl. 5, Rm. 02, Western Bank, Sheffield, SY S10 2TN, England. **Online address:** r.i.d.taylor@shef.ac.uk

TAYLOR, Robert Allan. American (born United States), b. 1958. **Genres:** History, Military/Defense/Arms Control. **Career:** University of South Alabama, visiting instructor of history, 1990-91; Florida Atlantic University, adjunct instructor of history, 1992-96; University of St. Francis, adjunct instructor of history, 1992-98; Indian River Community College, adjunct instructor of history, 1992-99; Florida Institute of Technology, College of Psychology and Liberal Arts, Department of Humanities and Communication, adjunct professor, 1997-99, assistant professor, 1999-2001, associate professor of history, 2001-, professor and head, Creative Writing Institute, faculty; Indian River State College, faculty; University of Saint Francis, faculty; Florida State University, faculty. Writer. **Publications:** Archeological Investigations in the Van Buren Water Supply Project Area, West Central Arkansas, 1977; Rebel Storehouse: Florida in the Confederate Economy, 1995; World War II in Fort Pierce, 1999; (with L.N. Wynne) Florida in the Civil War, 2001; Rebel Storehouse: Florida's Contribution to the Confederacy, 2003; Florida: An Illustrated History, 2005. EDITOR: (with L.N. Wynne) This War So Horrible: The Civil War Diary of Hiram Smith Williams, 1993; A Pennsylvanian in Blue: The Civil War Diary of Thomas Beck Walton, 1995; (with A.K. Blomquist) This Cruel War: The Civil War Letters of Grant and Malinda Taylor, 1862-1865, 2000; Controversy at Port Canaveral: Cat Futch and the U.S.S. FINBACK, forthcoming. Contributor to journals and periodicals. **Address:** Department of Humanities and Communication, College of Psychology and Liberal Arts, Florida Institute of Technology, 604 Crawford Twr., 150 W University Blvd., Melbourne, FL 32901-6975, U.S.A. **Online address:** rotaylor@fit.edu

TAYLOR, Robert H(enry). British/American (born United States), b. 1943. **Genres:** Area Studies, History. **Career:** Cardozo High School, social studies teacher, 1965-67; Wilberforce University, instructor in political science, 1967-69; University of Sydney, lecturer in government, 1974-79; University of London School of Oriental and African Studies, lecturer, 1980-88, senior lecturer in politics, 1988-89, professor of politics, 1989-96, pro-director, 1991-96, Centre of South East Asian Studies, professorial research associate, 2002-05; University of Buckingham, vice chancellor and professor of international studies, 1997-2000; Institute of Southeast Asian Studies, visiting senior research fellow, 2003-05, associate senior fellow. Writer. **Publications:** Foreign and Domestic Consequences of the KMT Intervention in Burma, 1973; An Undeveloped State: The Study of Modern Burma's Politics, 1983; Marxism and Resistance in Burma, 1942-1954, 1984; The State in Burma, 1987; The State in Myanmar, 2009. EDITOR: (with M. Hobart) Context, Meaning, and Power in Southeast Asia, 1986; Asia and the Pacific, 1991; The Politics of

Elections in Southeast Asia, 1996; (co-ed.) Burma: Political Economy under Military Rule, 2001; The Idea of Freedom in Asia and Africa, 2002; (with K.Y. Hlaing and T.M.M. Than) Myanmar: Beyond Politics to Societal Imperatives, 2005; (comp.) Dr. Maung Maung: Gentleman, Scholar, Patriot, 2008. Contributor to books. **Address:** 13 Baron Close, Friern Village, London, GL N11 3PS, England. **Online address:** r_h_taylor@btopenworld.com

TAYLOR, Robert Larry. American (born United States), b. 1940. **Genres:** Novels, History, Military/Defense/Arms Control, Novellas/Short Stories. **Career:** National Home Study Council, editor, 1968-72; Music Educators National Conference, assistant editor, 1972-76; U.S. Department of Transportation, editor, 1976-80; U.S. Information Agency, deputy text editor, 1980-86; freelance writer, 1986-; Pierre Monteux Memorial Foundation, treasurer, 1994-97. **Publications:** The Innocent, 1997; All We Have is Now, 2002; Revelation and Other Stories (short stories), 2002; Whose Eye is on which Sparrow?, 2004; A Few Hints and Clews, 2007. **Address:** Morgan Bay Rd., Blue Hill, ME 04614, U.S.A. **Online address:** kailuum@oberlin.net

TAYLOR, Robert Pepperman. See **TAYLOR, Bob Pepperman.**

TAYLOR, Rogan. British (born England), b. 1945. **Genres:** Anthropology/Ethnology, History, Sports/Fitness, Autobiography/Memoirs. **Career:** Football Supporters Association, chairperson and campaigns coordinator, 1985-89; University of Leicester, Sir Norman Chester Centre for Football Research, research associate, 1989-94; University of Liverpool, Football Research Unit, director, 1995-, School of Management, senior lecturer; Share Liverpool, founder, 2008. Writer and presenter of television and radio programs. **Publications:** The Death and Resurrection Show: From Shaman to Superstar, 1985; Football and Its Fans: Supporters and Their Relations with the Game, 1885-1985, 1992; (with A. Ward) Three Sides of the Mersey: An Oral History of Everton, Liverpool, and Tranmere Rovers, 1993; (with A. Ward) Kicking and Screaming: An Oral History of Football in England, 1995; (ed. and comp. with A. Ward and T. Newburn) The Day of the Hillsborough Disaster: A Narrative Account, 1995; (with K. Jamrich) Magyar Gold: The Footballing Lives of Ference Puskas, 1997; Puskas on Puskas: The Life and Times of a Football Legend, 1997. Contributor to books. Contributor of articles to books, magazines and newspapers. **Address:** Football Industry Group, School of Management, University of Liverpool, Chatham St., Chatham Bldg., Ste. GE22, Liverpool, MS L69 7ZH, England. **Online address:** sam.johnstone@liverpool.ac.uk

TAYLOR, Ronald B. American (born United States), b. 1930. **Genres:** Organized Labor, Writing/Journalism, Novels, Young Adult Non-fiction, Social Sciences. **Career:** Fresno Bee, reporter, 1955-75; Los Angeles Times, reporter, 1977-. **Publications:** NONFICTION: Sweatshops in the Sun: Child Labor on the Farm, Beacon, 1973; Chavez and the Farm Workers, Beacon, 1975; The Kid Business, and How It Exploits the Children It Should Help, 1981; Preventing Violence Against Women and Children, 1997. OTHERS: Long Road Home (novel), 1988; Wild Card: A Novel, 2010. **Address:** Los Angeles Times, 202 W 1st St., Los Angeles, CA 90012, U.S.A.

TAYLOR, Sarah McFarland. American (born United States), b. 1968?. **Genres:** Theology/Religion, Environmental Sciences/Ecology, Sciences. **Career:** Northwestern University, Department of Religious Studies, assistant professor of religion, 2000, associate professor of religion, director of undergraduate studies; University of Chicago, Martin Marty Center Institute for the Advanced Study of Religion, senior research fellow, 2008-09. **Publications:** Green Sisters: A Spiritual Ecology, 2007; Eternally Green: American Religion and the Ecology of Death, forthcoming; Eco-Prophecy: Religious Responses to Global Climate Change, forthcoming. Contributor to periodicals. **Address:** Department of Religious Studies, Northwestern University, Crowe Hall, 1860 Campus Dr., Ste. 4-144, Evanston, IL 60208-2164, U.S.A. **Online address:** sarah@northwestern.edu

TAYLOR, Sarah Stewart. American (born United States), b. 1971?. **Genres:** Novels, Biography, Autobiography/Memoirs, Young Adult Fiction, Mystery/Crime/Suspense. **Career:** Journalist and writer. **Publications:** SWEENEY ST. GEORGE SERIES, MYSTERY NOVELS: O' Artful Death, 2003; Mansions of the Dead, 2004; Judgment of the Grave, 2005; Still as Death, 2006; Amelia Earhart: This Broad Ocean, 2010. Contributor to magazines and newspapers. **Address:** St. Martin's Press, 175 5th Ave., New York, NY 10010, U.S.A. **Online address:** sweeneystgeorge@aol.com

TAYLOR, Simona. See **CARRINGTON, Roslyn.**

TAYLOR, Stephen. British/South African (born South Africa), b. 1948. **Genres:** Biography, History, Military/Defense/Arms Control, Autobiography/Memoirs. **Career:** Times, foreign correspondent and sub-editor, 1978-. **Publications:** The Mighty Nimrod: A Life of Frederick Courteney Selous, African Hunter and Adventurer, 1851-1917 (biography), 1989; Shaka's Children: A History of the Zulu People, 1994; Livingstone's Tribe: A Journey from Zanzibar to the Cape (travel), 1999; Caliban's Shore: The Wreck of the Grosvenor and the Strange Fate of Her Survivors, 2004; Caliban Shore: The Fate of the Grosvenor Castaways, 2004; Storm and Conquest: The Battle for the Indian Ocean, 1809, 2007 in US as Storm and Conquest: The Clash of Empires in the Eastern Seas, 1809, 2008. **Address:** London Times, 1 Virginia St., London, GL E98 1TH, England. **Online address:** steve.taylor@the-times.co.uk

TAYLOR, Stuart. American (born United States), b. 1948. **Genres:** Social Sciences, Politics/Government. **Career:** Baltimore Evening Sun, reporter; Sun, reporter, 1971-74; Harvard Law School, Harvard Law Review, note editor; Brookings Institution, non-resident senior fellow in governance studies; American Lawyer Media, senior writer; The New York Times, Washington Bureau, staff, 1980, legal affairs staff, 1980-85, reporter, supreme court correspondent, 1985-88; Princeton University, lecturer, 1989-97; National Journal, columnist, 1998-2010, contributing editor, 1998; Newsweek, contributing editor, 1998-. **Publications:** (With K.C. Johnson) Until Proven Innocent: Political Correctness and the Shameful Injustices of the Duke Lacrosse Rape Case, 2007. Contributor to journals. **Address:** Brookings Institution, 1775 Massachusetts Ave. NW, Washington, DC 20036, U.S.A. **Online address:** stuarttaylorjr@gmail.com

TAYLOR, Sue. American (born United States), b. 1949. **Genres:** Art/Art History, History, Photography. **Career:** School of the Art Institute of Chicago, visiting lecturer, 1983-87, 1995-97; University of Illinois, School of Art and Design, adjunct assistant professor, 1985; University of Chicago, David and Alfred Smart Museum of Art, associate curator, 1986-91; Art in America, corresponding editor, 1986-; Alliance of Independent Colleges of Art, art historian-in-residence, 1986, 1988; Northwestern University, adjunct assistant professor, 1987-88; Milwaukee Art Museum, curator of prints and drawings, 1991-93; Portland State University, assistant professor of art history, 1997-2002, associate professor, 2002-08, professor, 2009-. Writer. **Publications:** (Ed. with H.A. Vanderstappen and R.A. Born) Ritual and Reverence: Chinese Art at the University of Chicago: Catalogue, 1989; Alice and Harris Weston collection of Post-War Art: Exhibition Catalogue, November 3, 1989-January 7, 1990, 1989; (ed. with R.A. Born) David and Alfred Smart Museum of Art: A Guide to the Collection, 1990; (ed.) Winslow Homer in Gloucester, 1990; (ed.) Refco Collection, 1990; (comp.) Breadth of Vision: The Ritz Collection, 1992; Hans Bellmer: The Anatomy of Anxiety, 2000; Grant Wood beyond Regionalism, forthcoming. **Address:** Department of Art, Portland State University, AB 310E, 2000 SW 5th Ave., PO Box 751, Portland, OR 97201-4936, U.S.A. **Online address:** taylorsc@pdx.edu

TAYLOR, Terence. American (born United States), b. 1954. **Genres:** Novels, Horror. **Career:** Writer and producer. **Publications:** VAMPIRE TESTAMENT NOVELS: Bite Marks, 2009; Blood Pressure, 2010. Works appear in anthologies. **Address:** New York, NY , U.S.A. **Online address:** terence@gocornerstore.com

TAYLOR, Terry. American (born United States), b. 1952?. **Genres:** Novels, Humor/Satire. **Career:** Lark Books, editor and project coordinator. **Publications:** Lets Eat!, 2000; (with J.E. Kilby and D. Morgenthal) The Book of Wizard Craft: In Which the Apprentice Finds Spells Potions Fantastic Tales and Fifty Enchanting Things to Make, 2001; Decorating Candles, 2001; (with J.E. Kilby) The Book of Wizard Parties: In Which the Wizard Shares the Secrets of Creating Enchanted Gatherings, 2002; Paper Crafting: 20 Projects to Fold, Cut, Mold, Weave & Pierce, 2003; (with J.E. Kilby) The Book of Wizard Magic: In Which the Apprentice Finds Marvelous Magic Tricks Mystifying Illusions and Astonishing Tales, 2003; Creative Candlescaping: Seventy Bright Ideas for Home and Garden, 2003; Paper Crafting: Twenty Projects to Fold Cut Mold Weave and Pierce, 2003; Altered Art: Techniques for Creating Altered Books Boxes Cards and More, 2004; The Artful Eggs: Six Dozen Extraordinary Ways to Decorate an Egg, 2004; (with J. O'Sullivan) The New Napkin Folding: Fresh Ideas for a Well-Dressed Table, 2004; (with J. O'Sullivan) Elegant Napkin Folding, 2004; (co-author) Encyclopedia of Projects for the Weekend Crafter, 2004; New Crochet: 40 Wonderful Wearables, 2005; Fabulous Crocheted Ponchos, 2005; (with D. Whyte) Chain Mail Jewelry: Contemporary Designs from Classic Techniques, 2006; Altered Object: Techniques, Projects, Inspiration, 2006; Artful Paper Dolls: New Ways to Play with a Traditional Form, 2006; Art of Jewelry Wood: Techniques, Projects, Inspiration, 2007; Jewelry with a Hook: Crocheted Fiber Necklaces, Bracelets & More, 2007; (with C. Cooper) Designer Needle Felting: Contemporary Styles, Easy Techniques, 2007; Button! Button!: 50 Cute & Crafty Projects, 2008; Eco Books: Inventive Projects from the Recycling Bin, 2009; Very Beaded Christmas: 46 Projects That Glitter, Twinkle & Shine, 2009; Stache: Frivolous Facts & Fancies About That Space Between the Nose and Lip, 2010; (ed.) Masters: Collage: Major Works by Leading Artists, 2010. **Address:** Lark Books, 67 Broadway, Asheville, NC 28801, U.S.A.

TAYLOR, T(homas) F(ish). British/Scottish (born Scotland), b. 1913. **Genres:** Theology/Religion, Biography. **Career:** Writer. **Publications:** A Profest Papist, S.P.C.K., 1958; Thematic Catalog of the Works of Jeremiah Clarke, 1977; J. Armitage Robinson: Eccentric, Scholar and Churchman, 1858-1933, 1991. **Address:** Digby House, 40 Avenue Rd., Wimborne, DS BH21 1BT, England.

TAYLOR, Walter Kingsley. American (born United States), b. 1939. **Genres:** Homes/Gardens, Zoology, Genealogy/Heraldry, Biography, Poetry, Natural History. **Career:** University of Central Florida, faculty, 1969-2004, professor emeritus of biology, 2004. Writer. **Publications:** The Lives, Families, and Descendants of Arnold, Philip, and Benjamin Taylor: From Pennsylvania and New Jersey to Kentucky, 1984; The Guide to Florida Wildflowers, 1992; Wild Shores: Exploring the Wilderness Areas of Eastern North Carolina, 1993; (with R.L. Wallace) Invertebrate Zoology: A Laboratory Manual, 1997; Florida Wildflowers in Their Natural Communities, 1998; (with D.B. Ward) Discovery of Tree-form Gopher Apple (Licania michauxii), with Implication of an Arboreous Ancestor, 1999; (with E.M. Norman) André in Michaux in Florida: An Eighteenth Century Botanical Journey, 2002; A Guide to Florida Grasses, 2009. **Address:** Department of Biology, College of Sciences, University of Central Florida, 4000 University Blvd., Orlando, FL 32816-2368, U.S.A. **Online address:** walter.taylor@ucf.edu

TAYLOR, Welford Dunaway. American (born United States), b. 1938. **Genres:** Art/Art History, History, Literary Criticism And History, Biography, Humor/Satire. **Career:** Randolph-Macon Academy, faculty, 1959; St. Christopher's School, faculty, 1960; Virginia Commonwealth University, instructor, 1961-63; University of Richmond, assistant professor, 1964-69, associate professor, 1969-73, professor of English, 1973-2004, Department of English, chairman, 1978-86, James A. Bostwick professor of English, James A. Bostwick chair of English 1991-2004, professor emeritus, 2004-. Writer. **Publications:** Amélie Rives (Princess Troubetzkoy), 1973; Sherwood Anderson, 1977; Robert Frost and J.J. Lankes: Riders on Pegasus, 1996; The Woodcut Art of J.J. Lankes, 1999. EDITOR: The Buck Fever Papers, 1971; (co-ed.) Virginia Authors Past and Present, 1972; (with intro.) Our American Cousin, 1990; (and intro.) The Newsprint Mask, 1991; (with C.E. Modlin) Southern Odyssey: Selected Writings by Sherwood Anderson, 1997; (with G.C. Longest) Regarding Ellen Glasgow, 2001; (and intro.) A Woodcut Manual, 2006; With One's Own Eyes: Sherwood Anderson's Realities, 2007; Sherwood Anderson Remembered, 2009. **Address:** English Department, University of Richmond, Ryland Hall 307, Richmond, VA 23173, U.S.A. **Online address:** wtaylor@richmond.edu

TAYLOR, William. New Zealander (born New Zealand), b. 1938. **Genres:** Young Adult Fiction, Children's Fiction, Novels, Adult Non-fiction, Literary Criticism And History. **Career:** Ohakune School, principal, 1979-85; Mayor of Borough of Ohakune, 1981-88; Palmerston North College of Education, writer-in-residence, 1992. **Publications:** NOVELS FOR CHILDREN AND YOUNG ADULTS: Pack Up, Pick Up and Off, 1981; My Summer of the Lions, 1986; Possum Perkins, 1987 in US as Paradise Lane, 1987; Shooting Through, 1987; Break a Leg!, 1987; Making Big Bucks, 1987; The Worst Soccer Team Ever, 1987; I Hate My Brother Maxwell Potter, 1989; The Kidnap of Jessie Parker, 1989; Agnes the Sheep, 1990; The Porter Brothers, 1990; Beth & Bruno, 1992 in UK as Secret Lives, 1993; Fast Times at Greenhill High, 1992; Knitwits, 1992; Supermum and Spike the Dog, 1992; The Southside War against Terrorists, 1993; Numbskulls, 1995; Annie & Co. and Marilyn Monroe, 1995; The Fatz Katz, 1995; Circles, 1996; Nick's Story, 1996; The Fatz Twins and the Haunted House, 1996; Hark the Herald Angel, 1997; The Fatz Twins and the Cuckoo in the Nest, 1997; Jerome, 1999; Harry Houdini: Wonderdog, 1999; The Blue Lawn, 1999; Crash! The Story of Poddy, 2000; (with T. Duder) Hot Mail, 2000; Scarface and the Angel, 2000; Spider, 2002; Pebble in a Pool, 2003; Albert, 2003; Gladys the Goat, 2005;

Albert the Cat, 2005; Land of Milk and Honey, 2005; Telling Tales: A Life in Writing, 2010. FOR ADULTS: Episode, 1970; The Mask of the Clown, 1971; The Plekhov Place, 1971; Pieces in a Jigsaw, 1972; The Persimmon Tree, 1973; The Chysalis, 1974; Burnt Carrots Don't Have Legs, 1976; At the Big Red Rooster, 1998. Contributor to periodicals. Works appear in anthologies. **Address:** Scholastic NZ Ltd., PO Box 94407, Botany, Manukau, 2163, New Zealand. **Online address:** wrt@xtra.co.nz

TAYLOR, William J. *See* **TAYLOR, Billy.**

TAYLOR, William R(obert). American (born United States), b. 1922. **Genres:** History. **Career:** Harvard University, assistant professor of history, 1956-61; University of Wisconsin, professor of history, 1961-68; Educational Development Corp., director, 1961-68; State University of New York, professor of history, 1968-94, professor emeritus, 1994-; New York University, New York Institute for Humanities, director, 1987-89, program director, 1989-94; Russell Sage Foundation, research fellow, 1990-91. Writer. **Publications:** Cavalier and Yankee: The Old South and American National Character, 1961; Auto Museum Directory USA, 1983; (ed.) Discovery of the Great West: La Salle, 1986; Auto Museum Directory USA Supplement with Canadian Museums, 1989; (ed.) Inventing Times Square: Commerce and Culture at the Crossroads, 1991; In Pursuit of Gotham: Culture and Commerce in New York, 1992; (contrib.) Painting the Town: Cityscapes of New York, 2000; American Confusion from Vietnam to Kosovo: Coping with Chaos in High Places, 2001. **Address:** Department of History, State University of New York, Social Science 145, 1400 Washington Ave., Albany, NY 12222, U.S.A.

TAYLOR-HALL, Mary Ann. American (born United States), b. 1937. **Genres:** Novels, Novellas/Short Stories. **Career:** Auburn University, faculty; University of Puerto Rico, faculty; University of Kentucky, faculty; Transylvania University, faculty. Writer. **Publications:** Come and Go, Molly Snow (novel), 1995; How She Knows What She Knows about Yo-Yos (short stories), 2000; (co-ed.) Missing Mountains: We Went to the Mountaintop but It Wasn't There, 2005; At the Breakers: A Novel, 2009. Works appear in anthologies. Contributor to periodicals. **Address:** c/o Geri Thomas, Elaine Markson Literary Agency Inc., 44 Greenwich Ave., New York, NY 10011, U.S.A.

TAZE, James E. American (born United States), b. 1938. **Genres:** Novels, Humor/Satire. **Career:** Automation Industries, manager of financial planning, 1972-77; Jet Propulsion Laboratory, resources administrator, 1977-85; Wilber Publishing Co., principal, 1998-. Writer. **Publications:** The System: Jay Learns to Handicap and Develops a Diversified System (novel), rev. ed., 1997. **Address:** Wilber Publishing Co., 1625 Howard Rd., Ste. 256, Madera, CA 93637-5128, U.S.A. **Online address:** jtaze@tampabay.rr.com

TEACHOUT, Terry. American (born United States), b. 1956. **Genres:** Autobiography/Memoirs, Social Commentary, Dance/Ballet, Literary Criticism And History, Music, Biography, Essays, Novels, Novels. **Career:** Jazz bassist, 1975-83; Star and Times, music critic, 1977-83; Harper's Magazine, assistant editor, 1985-86, senior editor, 1986-87; New York Daily News, editorial writer, 1987-93, classical music and dance critic, 1993-2000; Commentary, culture critic, 1995-; Time, contributor, 1998-; Washington Post, arts columnist, 1999-; The Wall Street Journal, drama critic; National Council on the Arts, National Endowment for the Arts, review panel, 2004-10; Vile Body, founder. **Publications:** City Limits: Memories of a Small-Town Boy, 1991; Skeptic: A Life of H.L. Mencken, 2002; All in the Dances: A Brief Life of George Balanchine, 2004; A Terry Teachout Reader, 2004; Pops: A Life of Louis Armstrong, 2009; Black Beauty: A Life of Duke Ellington, 2014. EDITOR: (intro.) Ghosts on the Roof: Selected Journalism of Whittaker Chambers, 1931-1959, 1989; Beyond the Boom: New Voices on American Life, Politics, and Culture, 1990; (intro.) A Second Mencken Chrestomathy, 1994. Contributor to books and periodicals. **Address:** Writers Representatives L.L.C., 116 W 14th St., 11th Fl., New York, NY 10011-7305, U.S.A. **Online address:** tteachout@artsjournal.com

TEAGUE, Frances. (Frances Nicol Teague). American/Canadian (born Canada), b. 1949. **Genres:** History, Theatre, Women's Studies And Issues, Humor/Satire, Essays. **Career:** University of Georgia, Josiah Meigs Professor of English, 1977-, Josiah Meigs distinguished teaching professor, Institute for Women's Studies, faculty. Writer. **Publications:** (With J.W. Velz as Frances N. Teague) An Index to the Letters of Joseph Crosby to Joseph Parker Norris in Folger Ms. Yc. 1372, 1978; The Curious History of Bartholomew Fair, 1985; (ed. with J.W. Velz) One Touch of Shakespeare: Letters of Joseph

Crosby to Joseph Parker Norris, 1875-1878, 1986; Shakespeare's Speaking Properties, 1991; (ed.) Acting Funny: Comic Theory and Practice in Shakespeare's Plays, 1994; Bathsua Makin: Woman of Learning, 1998; (ed. and intro.) Educational and Vocational Books: A Facsimile Library of Essential Works, 2000; Shakespeare and the American Popular Stage, 2006. **Address:** Department of English, University of Georgia, 263 Park Hall, Athens, GA 30602-6205, U.S.A. **Online address:** fteague@uga.edu

TEAGUE, Frances Nicol. *See* **TEAGUE, Frances.**

TEAGUE, Mark (Christopher). American (born United States), b. 1963. **Genres:** Children's Fiction, Illustrations, Picture/Board Books. **Career:** Barnes & Noble, staff; freelance illustrator and writer, 1989-. **Publications:** SELF-ILLUSTRATED FOR CHILDREN: The Trouble with the Johnsons, 1989; Moog-Moog, Space Barber, 1990; Frog Medicine, 1991; The Field beyond the Outfield, 1992; Pigsty, 1994; How I Spent My Summer Vacation, 1995; Secret Shortcut, 1996; Baby Tamer, 1997; Lost and Found, 1998; One Halloween Night, 1999; Dear Mrs. Larue: Letters from Obedience School, 2002; Detective LaRue: Letters from the Investigation, 2004; LaRue across America, 2011. OTHERS: (with J. Yolen) How Do Dinosaurs Count to Ten?, 2004; (with J. Yolen) How Do Dinosaurs Clean Their Rooms?, 2004; Funny Farm, 2009; Doom machine: a novel, 2009; (with C. Rylant) The Great Gracie Chase Stop that Dog, 2010; Firehouse!, 2010; (with J. Yolen) How Do Dinosaurs Love Their Dogs?, 2010; How Do Dinosaurs Laugh Out Loud?, 2010; (with J. Yolen) How Do Dinosaurs Love Their Cats?, 2010. **Address:** 87 Mansion St., Coxsackie, NY 12051-1216, U.S.A.

TEAHAN, Sheila. American (born United States), b. 1961. **Genres:** Literary Criticism And History, Young Adult Fiction, History. **Career:** Michigan State University, assistant professor, 1989-95, associate professor of English, 1995-. Writer. **Publications:** The Rhetorical Logic of Henry James, 1995. **Address:** Department of English, Michigan State University, 225A Morrill Hall, East Lansing, MI 48824, U.S.A. **Online address:** teahan@msu.edu

TEARLE, John L. British (born England), b. 1917. **Genres:** Biography, Genealogy/Heraldry, Writing/Journalism, Autobiography/Memoirs. **Career:** Kodak Ltd., research physicist, 1939-47, manufacturing manager, 1947-69, director, 1969-76, retired, 1976. Writer. **Publications:** Mrs. Piozzi's Tall Young Beau: William Augustus Conway, 1991; Tearle: A Bedfordshire Surname, 1996; (ed.) An American Journal, 1839-40, 2002. Contributor to magazines. **Address:** Frithsden Copse, Castle St., Berkhamsted, HF HP4 1RQ, England.

TE AWEKOTUKU, Ngahuia. New Zealander (born New Zealand), b. 1949. **Genres:** Novellas/Short Stories, Literary Criticism And History, Cultural/Ethnic Topics, Anthropology/Ethnology, Young Adult Fiction. **Career:** Waikato Museum of Art and History, curator, 1985-87; Auckland University, lecturer in art history, 1987-96; Victoria University of Wellington, professor of Māori studies, 1997-2004; University of Waikato at Tauranga, Centre for Māori and Pacific Development Research, professor, 2004-, Department of Psychology, professor. Writer. **Publications:** FICTION: Tahuri, 1993; Ruahine: Mythic Women, 2003. NONFICTION: Mana Wahine Maori: Selected Writings on Maori Women's Art, Culture, and Politics, 1991; He Tinkanga Whakaaro: Research Ethics in the Maori Community, 1991; (with L.W. Nikora, M. Rua and R. Karapu) Mau Moko: The World of Māori Tattoo, 2007. Works appear in anthologies. Contributor to books and periodicals. **Address:** School of Māori and Pacific Development, Research, University of Waikato, Rm. A1.04, PO Box 3105, Hamilton, 3240, New Zealand. **Online address:** ngahuia@waikato.ac.nz

TEBBIT, Norman. British/American (born United States), b. 1931. **Genres:** Plays/Screenplays, Autobiography/Memoirs, Documentaries/Reportage, Food And Wine. **Career:** British Overseas Airways (now British Airways), staff, 1953-70; House of Commons, Parliament for Epping, member, 1970-74, Parliament for Chingford, member, 1974-92; British Parliament, parliamentary under-secretary of state for trade, 1979-81, minister of state for industry, 1981, secretary of state for employment, 1981-83, secretary of state for trade and industry, 1983-85, Duchy of Lancaster, chancellor, 1985-87, chairman of conservative party, 1985-87; BBC-TV, co-presenter of the current affairs program Target, 1989-98, The Church's One Salvation, presenter, 1991; House of Lords, member of parliament, 1992-; Sun Newspaper, columnist, 1995-97; Sunday Newspaper, columnist, 1997-2001. **Publications:** Britain's Future: A Conservative Vision, 1985; Britain in the 1990s, 1986; Values of Freedom,

1986; New Consensus, 1988; Upwardly Mobile, 1988; Unfinished Business, 1991; Disappearing Britain, 2005; The Game Cookbook, 2009. Contributor to newspapers. **Address:** House of Lords, Westminster, London, GL SW1A 0PW, England.

TECHINÉ, André. French (born France), b. 1943. **Genres:** Plays/Screenplays, Young Adult Fiction. **Career:** Screenwriter and director. **Publications:** (With P. Bonitzer) Les Sœurs Brontè: Un filmdé André Techiné, 1979. Contributor to periodicals. **Address:** French Film Office, 424 Madison Ave., Ste. 8, New York, NY 10017-1106, U.S.A.

TEDROW, John C. F. (John Charles Fremont Tedrow). American (born United States), b. 1917. **Genres:** Earth Sciences. **Career:** U.S. Department of Agriculture, junior soil surveyor, 1941-42, 1946-47; Rutgers University, faculty, 1947-84, professor emeritus, 1984-. Writer and consultant. **Publications:** (Ed.) Antarctic Soils and Soil-Forming Processes, 1966; Soil Investigations in Inglefield Land, Greenland, 1970; (with R.C. Murray) Forensic Geology: Earth Sciences and Criminal Investigation, 1975; Soils of the Polar Landscapes, 1977; (with K.A. Linnell) Soil and Permafrost Surveys in the Arctic, 1981; Soils of New Jersey, 1986; (with R.C. Murray) Forensic Geology, 1992. **Address:** Department of Ecology, Rutgers University, 125 ENRS Bldg., Cook Campus, 14 College Farm Rd., New Brunswick, NJ 08901, U.S.A.

TEDROW, John Charles Fremont. See **TEDROW, John C. F.**

TEECE, David J(ohn). American/New Zealander (born New Zealand), b. 1948. **Genres:** Business/Trade/Industry, Economics, Environmental Sciences/Ecology, Money/Finance, Technology. **Career:** University of Canterbury, assistant lecturer in economics, 1971; Stanford University, assistant professor, 1975-78, associate professor of business economics, 1978-82; University of Pennsylvania, Department of Economics, visiting associate professor of economics, 1978-79; University of California, Walter A. Haas School of Business, professor of business administration, 1982-, Center for Research in Management, director, 1983-94, Mitsubishi Bank Chair in International Business and Finance, 1989-2007, Management of Technology Program, co-director, Institute of Management, Innovation and Organization, director, 1994-2008, Thomas W. Tusher chair in global business, 2007-, Center for Global Strategy and Governance, director, 2007-; University of Reading, Esmee Fairbairn senior research fellow, 1982; Law and Economics Consulting Group Inc., principal and chairman, board director, 1988-98; Atlas Funds, director, 1989-2007; Atlas Insurance Trust, trustee, 1997-2007; Industrial and Corporate Change, co-editor and co-founder, 1999-; IQUANTIC Inc., director, 2000-01; I-Cap partners, chairman, 2000-03; LECG L.L.C., chairman, 2000-03; Canterbury International Ltd., chairman, 2001-02; Russian Management Journal, co-editor and co-founder, 2003-; LECG Corp., chairman, 2003-07, vice-chairman, 2007-09; New Zealand Australia Private Equity Fund, vice-chairman, 2004-10; International Journal of Internet Technology and Secured Transactions, co-editor, 2007-; Palgrave Encyclopedia on Strategic Management, co-editor, 2007-; Puredepth Inc., director, 2009-; Berkeley Research Group L.L.C., chairman and chief executive officer. **Publications:** Vertical Integration and Vertical Divestiture in the U.S. Oil Industry, 1976; The Multinational Corporation and the Resource Cost of International Technology Transfer, 1976; (co-author) Technology Transfer, Productivity, and Economic Policy, 1982; (with J. Griffin) OPEC Behavior and World Oil Prices, 1982; Strategy, Technology, and Public Policy, 1998; Managing Intellectual Capital: Organizational, Strategic, and Policy Dimensions, 2000; Essays in Technology Management and Policy, 2003; Transfer and Licensing of Know-How and Intellectual Property: Understanding the Multinational Enterprise in the Modern World, 2008; Technological Know-how, Organizational Capabilities, and Strategic Management: Business Strategy and Enterprise Development in Competitive Environments, 2008; Dynamic Capabilities and Strategic Management: Organizing for Innovation and Growth, 2009. EDITOR: (and contrib.) R and D in Energy: Implications of Petroleum Industry Reorganization, 1977; The Competitive Challenge: Strategies for Industrial Innovation and Renewal, 1987; (with T.M. Jorde) Antitrust, Innovation, and Competitiveness, 1992; (with R.P. Rumelt and D.E. Schendel) Fundamental Issues in Strategy: A Research Agenda, 1994; Economic Performance and the Theory of the Firm, 1998; (with G. Dosi and J. Chytry) Technology, Organization, and Competitiveness: Perspectives on Industrial and Corporate Change, 1998; (G.R. Caroll) Firms, Markets, and Hierarchies: The Transaction Cost Economics Perspective, 1999; (with I. Nonaka) Managing Industrial Knowledge: Creation, Transfer and Utilization, 2001; (with G. Dosi and J. Chytry) Understanding Industrial and Corporate Change, 2005; (with M. Augier) Fundamentals of Business Strategy, 2008. **Address:** Inst. of Mgmt., Innovation & Organization, University of California, F402 Haas School of Business, Ste. 1930, Berkeley, CA 94720-1930, U.S.A. **Online address:** teece@haas.berkeley.edu

TEECE, Philip. Canadian (born Canada), b. 1940. **Genres:** Astronomy, Autobiography/Memoirs, Reference, Novellas/Short Stories. **Career:** Librarian, 1963-78; Greater Victoria Public Library, science specialist, reference and research librarian, 1978-98, retired, 1998. Writer. **Publications:** (With J. Newton) The Guide to Amateur Astronomy, 1988, 2nd ed., 1995; A Dream of Islands (memoir), 1988; Raincoast Macabre (short stories), 1991; A Shimmer on the Horizon (memoir), 1999. Contributor to magazines. **Address:** 1061 Fort St., Ste. 202, Victoria, BC V8V 5A1, Canada.

TEFERTILLER, Casey (Orie). American (born United States), b. 1952. **Genres:** Biography, Psychology. **Career:** San Francisco Examiner, baseball writer, 1981-95; freelance writer, 1995-. **Publications:** Wyatt Earp: The Life Behind the Legend, 1997; (with K. Kuehl and J. Kuehl) Mental Toughness: A Champion's State of Mind, 2005. Contributor to magazines. **Address:** c/o Gerard McCauley, Gerard McCauley Agency Inc., PO Box 844, Katonah, NY 10536, U.S.A.

TEHAN, Arline Boucher. American (born United States), b. 1930. **Genres:** Art/Art History, Theology/Religion, Biography, History, Autobiography/Memoirs. **Career:** Hartford Courant, feature writer and book reviewer; SALT, arts editor. **Publications:** Prince of Democracy: A Life of James Cardinal Gibbons, 1962; Henry Adams in Love: The Pursuit of Elizabeth Sherman Cameron, 1983. **Address:** 17 Westfield Rd., West Hartford, CT 06119-1534, U.S.A.

TEICHER, Craig Morgan. American (born United States), b. 1979. **Genres:** Poetry. **Career:** Publishers Weekly, senior web editor and poetry reviews editor; contributing editor, Pleiades; National Book Critics Circle, vice president; Columbia University, faculty; The New School, faculty; New York University, Creative Writing Program, faculty. **Publications:** Brenda is in the Room and Other Poems, 2007; Cradle Book: Stories & Fables, 2010. Contributor to periodicals. **Address:** BOA Editions Ltd., 250 N Goodman St., Ste.306, Rochester, NY 14607, U.S.A. **Online address:** craig@craigmorganteicher.com

TEICHMAN, Judith A. Canadian (born Canada), b. 1947. **Genres:** Area Studies, Politics/Government. **Career:** Ontario Institute for Studies in Education, research associate in educational administration, 1971-73; York University, teaching assistant in political science, 1976-77; Trent University, lecturer in comparative development studies and political studies, 1978-79; Ryerson Polytechnical Institute, instructor in politics, 1979-80; University of Waterloo, assistant professor, 1980-87, associate professor of political science, 1987; University of Toronto, assistant professor, 1987-89, associate professor, 1989-97, professor of political science, 1997-. Writer. **Publications:** Policymaking in Mexico: From Boom to Crisis, 1988; Privatization and Political Change in Mexico, 1995; The Politics of Freeing Markets in Latin America: Chile, Argentina and Mexico, 2001; Social Forces and States: Poverty and Distributional Outcomes in South Korea, Chile, and Mexico, 2012. Contributor of articles to books and periodicals. **Address:** Department of Political Science, University of Toronto, UTSC B-508, 100 George St., Toronto, ON M5S 1A1, Canada. **Online address:** judith.teichman@utoronto.ca

TEISER, Stephen F. American (born United States), b. 1947. **Genres:** Theology/Religion, History. **Career:** Princeton University, D.T. Suzuki professor in Buddhist studies, 2010-, Program in East Asian Studies, director, 2010-; École Pratique des Hautes Études, visiting professor in history and philosophy. Writer. **Publications:** The Ghost Festival in Medieval China, 1988; The Scripture on the Ten Kings and the Making of Purgatory in Medieval Chinese Buddhism, 1994; Reinventing the Wheel: Paintings of Rebirth in Medieval Buddhist Temples, 2006; (ed. with J.I. Stone) Readings of the Lotus Sutra, 2009. **Address:** Department of Religion, Princeton University, 1879 Hall, Princeton, NJ 08544, U.S.A. **Online address:** sfteiser@princeton.edu

TEITELBAUM, Matthew. Canadian (born Canada), b. 1956. **Genres:** Art/Art History, History. **Career:** London Regional Art Gallery, assistant curator, 1982-83, curator of contemporary art, 1983-85; Mendel Art Gallery, curator, 1986-89; University of Western Ontario, lecturer, 1983-85; Institute of Contemporary Art (Boston), curator, 1989-93, acting co-director, 1991; Lesley College, lecturer, 1990; Harvard University, John F. Kennedy School of Government, Institute of Politics Study Group on Art, Politics and Art, leader, 1991; York University, faculty; Association of Art Museum Directors, president; Art Gallery of Ontario, chief curator, 1993-98, director, 1998-, Michael and Sonja Koerner director, chief executive officer. Writer. **Publications:** Duncan de Kergommeaux, 1986; Wyn Geleynse: Filmwork and Apparatus, 1985; Ron Benner, Other Lives, 1988; The Mendel Art Gallery: Twenty-Five Years of Collecting, Mendel Art Gallery, 1989; Edward Poitras: Indian Territory, 1989; (with D. Ring) From Regionalism to Abstraction: Mashel Teitelbaum & Saskatchewan Art in the 1940s, 1991; (with O. Debroise and E. Sussman) El Corazón Sangrante/the Bleeding Heart, 1991; (and ed.) Paterson Ewen, 1996; (co-author) Frank Gehry in Toronto: Transforming the Art Gallery of Ontario Featuring Photographs by Edward Burtynsky, 2009. EDITOR: (and intro.) Montage and Modern Life, 1919-1942, 1992; (with J. Bradley) Art of Betty Goodwin, 1998; (with D. Reid) Greg Curnoe: Life and Stuff, 2001. Contributor to articles to journals. **Address:** Art Gallery of Ontario, 317 Dundas St. W, Toronto, ON M5T 1G4, Canada. **Online address:** director@ago.net

TEIWES, Helga. American/German (born Germany), b. 1930. **Genres:** Anthropology/Ethnology, Art/Art History, Social Sciences, Adult Non-fiction. **Career:** Hehmke-Winterer Studio, commercial, portrait and industrial photographer, 1950-57, teacher of photography, 1955-57; Bagel Printing Co., staff photographer, 1957-60; Brodatz Custom Lab, photographer, 1960-61; Cartier's, assistant to the photographer, staff photographer, 1961-62; CCF Color Lab, retoucher, 1962-64; archaeological field photographer, 1964-65; University of Arizona, Arizona State Museum, photographer, 1965-93. Writer. **Publications:** (Trans.) Mission San Xavier del Bac, 1973; Kachina Dolls: The Art of Hopi Carvers, 1991; Hopi Basket Weaving: Artistry in Natural Fibers, 1996. Contributor to books and periodicals. **Address:** 2611 N Teresa Ln., Tucson, AZ 85745-1007, U.S.A.

TEJA, Jesus F(rancisco) de la. American/Cuban (born Cuba), b. 1956. **Genres:** History, Local History/Rural Topics, Intellectual History. **Career:** Seton Hall University, Department of History, graduate assistant, 1979-81; University of Texas, graduate opportunity fellow, 1981-82, research assistant, 1982-84; Texas General Land Office, assistant archivist, 1985-89, archivist, 1989-90, director of archives and records, 1990-91; Austin Community College, adjunct instructor, 1988-90; Catholic Southwest: A Journal of History and Culture, managing editor, 1990-2005; Texas State University, Department of History, assistant professor, 1991-96, associate professor, 1996-2001, professor of history, 2001-11, chairman, 2005-11, university distinguished professor, 2011-; United States Department of the Interior, consultant, 1997-98; Texas State Historical Association, vice president, 2005-07, president, 2007-08. **Publications:** San Antonio de Béxar: A Community on New Spain's Northern Frontier, 1995; (with P.M. Marks and R. Tyler) Texas: Crossroads of North America, 2004; (with E.L. Ayers, R.D. Schulzinger and D.G. White) American Anthem, 2007. EDITOR: A Revolution Remembered: The Memoirs and Selected Correspondence of Juan N. Seguín, 1991; Preparing the Way: Preliminary Studies of the Texas Catholic Historical Society I, 1997; Wilderness Mission: Preliminary Studies of the Texas Catholic Historical Society II, 1999; New Foundations: Preliminary Studies of the Texas Catholic Historical Society III, 2000; (with T. Cashion) Human Tradition in Texas, 2001; (with R. Frank) Choice, Persuasion, and Coercion: Social Control on Spain's North American Frontiers, 2005; Tejano Leadership in Mexican and Revolutionary Texas, 2010. Contributor of articles to books and periodicals. **Address:** Department of History, Texas State University, 209 Taylor Murphy Hall, 601 University Dr., San Marcos, TX 78666, U.S.A. **Online address:** delateja@txstate.edu

TELLER, Astro. American/British (born England), b. 1970. **Genres:** Novels. **Career:** Phoenix Laser Technologies, algorithmic consultant and computer programmer, 1990; Stanford University, lecturer, 1991-92, Center for Integrated Systems, researcher in configuration management, 1991-93; Carnegie Group Inc. (CGI), senior engineer in machine learning, 1996; Sandbox Advanced Development, chief executive officer, 1998-99, co-founder, chairman; BodyMedia Inc., co-founder, 1999-, chief executive officer, 1999-2007, director, chairman and chief research and strategy officer, 2007-; Zivio Technologies, co-founder and chairman, 2003-10; Cerebellum Capital Inc., founding chief executive officer, 2008-10, co-founder and director, 2010-; Google Inc., director of new projects, 2010-. Write and scientist. **Publications:** Exegesis, 1997; Among These Savage Thoughts, 2008. Contributor to journals. **Address:** Cerebellum Capital Inc., 425 California St., Ste. 1250, San Francisco, CA 94104-2119, U.S.A. **Online address:** astro@bodymedia.com

TELLER, Neville. British/Israeli (born Israel), b. 1931. **Genres:** Mystery/Crime/Suspense, Plays/Screenplays, Classics, Novels, Politics/Government, Romance/Historical, Autobiography/Memoirs, Biography, Biography, Marketing. **Career:** Writer, 1956-; Butterworth Publishing Ltd., marketing manager, 1966-68; Granada Publishing, marketing director, 1968-69; The Times, marketing coordinator, 1969-70; Cancer Relief Macmillan Fund, director of operations, 1989-99. **Publications:** Bluff Your Way in Marketing, 1966, 2nd ed., 1969; One Man's Israel, 2008; One Year in the History of Israel and Palestine, 2011. EDITOR: Whodunit: Ten Tales of Crime and Detection, 1970; (with J.C. Saunders and D.H. Summers) Hospice: The Living Idea, 1981; British Architectural Design Awards, 1983; British Construction Profile, 1984. **Address:** 483 Green Lanes, London, GL N13 4BS, England. **Online address:** teller.neville@gmail.com

TELLERMANN, Esther. French (born France), b. 1947. **Genres:** Poetry. **Career:** Writer and educator. **Publications:** Premiére apparition avec épaisseur, 1986; Trois plans inhumains, 1989; Distance de fuite, 1993; Pangéia, 1996; Guerre extrême, 1999, trans. as Mental Ground, 2002; Encre plus rouge, 2003; Une odeur humaine, 2004; Terre exacte, 2007; Contre l'épisode, 2011. Contributor to periodicals. **Address:** c/o Author Mail, Flammarion, 26 rue Racine, Paris, 75278, France.

TELLKAMP, Uwe. German (born Germany), b. 1968. **Genres:** Literary Criticism And History, Young Adult Fiction. **Career:** Writer. **Publications:** Der Hecht, Die Träume Und Das Portugiesische Cafe, 2000; Der Eisvogel, 2005; Der Turm: Geschichte aus einem versunkenen Land, 2008; Reise Zur Blauen Stadt, 2009; Die Sandwirtschaft: Anmerkungen zu Schrift und Zeit; Leipziger Poetikvorlesung, 2009. **Address:** Freiburg, Germany. **Online address:** info@rowohlt.de

TELSER, Lester G(reenspan). American (born United States), b. 1931. **Genres:** Economics, Business/Trade/Industry. **Career:** University of Chicago, Cowles Commission for Research in Economics, research assistant, 1952-54, U.S. Department of Agriculture, cooperative agent, 1954-55, assistant professor, 1958-60, associate professor, 1960-63, professor of economics, 1965-97, now professor emeritus of economics; Iowa State University, assistant professor of economics, 1955-56; Journal of American Statistical Assignment, associate editor, 1966-69. Writer. **Publications:** Competition, Collusion and Game Theory, 1972; (with R.L. Graves) Functional Analysis in Mathematical Economics: Optimization Over Infinite Horizons, 1972; Economic Theory and the Core, 1978; A Theory of Efficient Cooperation and Competition, 1987; Theories of Competition, 1988; Joint Ventures of Labor and Capital, 1997; Classic Futures: Lessons from the Past for the Electronic Age, 2000; The Core Theory in Economics: Problems and Solutions, 2006. **Address:** Department of Economics, University of Chicago, 1126 E 59th St., Chicago, IL 60637, U.S.A. **Online address:** ltelser@midway.uchicago.edu

TEM, Melanie. American (born United States), b. 1949?. **Genres:** Novels, Novellas/Short Stories. **Career:** Writer. **Publications:** NOVELS: Prodigal, 1991; Blood Moon, 1992; Wilding, 1992; (with N. Holder) Making Love, 1993; Revenant, 1994; Desmodus, 1995; (with N. Holder) Witch-light, 1996; The Tides, 1996; Black River, 1997; (with S.R. Tem) Daughters, 2001; Slain in the Spirit, 2002; Deceiver, 2003; (with S.R. Tem) The Man on the Ceiling, 2008; Round the Earth, forthcoming; Roaming About, forthcoming. SHORT STORY COLLECTIONS: Daddy's Side, 1991; (with S.R. Tem) Beautiful Strangers, 1992; The Ice Downstream, 2001. **Address:** 2500 Irving St., Denver, CO 80211, U.S.A. **Online address:** melanie@m-s-tem.com

TEM, Steve Rasnic. American (born United States), b. 1950. **Genres:** Horror, Science Fiction/Fantasy, Young Adult Fiction. **Career:** Science fiction writer and editor. **Publications:** EDITOR: The Umbral Anthology of Science Fiction Poetry, 1982; (with C.L. Grant, T. Lee and A. Ryan) Night Visions No. 1, 1984; (with C.L. Grant, T. Lee and A. Ryan) Night Visions: In the Blood, 1987; High Fantastic: Colorado's Fantasy, Dark Fantasy and Science Fiction, 1995; City Fishing, 2000. FICTION: Excavation (novel), 1987; Fairytales (short stories), 1990; Absences, 1991; Celestial Inventory (short stories), 1991; Decoded Mirrors: 3 Tales after Lovecraft (short stories), 1992; (with M. Tem) Beautiful Strangers, 1992; City Fishing (short stories), 2000; The Far Side of the Lake (short stories), 2001; (with M. Tem) Daughters, 2002; The Book of Days (novel), 2002; The Hydrocephalic Ward, 2003. OTHERS: One View: Creating Characters in Fantasy and Horror Fiction,

1991; Prodigal, 1991; Blood Moon, 1992; Wilding, 1992; Revenant, 1994; Desmodus, 1995; In These Final Days of Sales, 2001; The Ice Downstream, 2001; Slain In The Spirit, 2002; The Deceiver, 2003; The World Recalled, 2004; (with M. Tem) Man on the Ceiling, 2008; Invisible, 2009; In Concert, 2010; Tales From the Crossroad, 2011; Among The Living, 2011; Deadfall Hotel, 2012. **Address:** 2500 Irving St., Denver, CO 80211, U.S.A. **Online address:** tems@m-s-tem.com

TEMES, Peter S. American (born United States), b. 1966. **Genres:** Young Adult Non-fiction, Theology/Religion. **Career:** Harvard University, Faculty of Arts and Sciences, faculty; University of Chicago, faculty; Goldman Sachs, Ernst & Young, researcher; Infonet Services, researcher; Prodigy Internet, researcher; BankOne, researcher; Antioch New England Graduate School, president; Great Books Foundation, head; I L O Institute, founder and president. Writer. **Publications:** NONFICTION: (ed.) Teaching Leadership: Essays in Theory and Practice, 1996; One School Now: Real Life at Lynn English High, 1998; (ed. with J. Coulson and J. Baldwin) Modern American Poetry, 2002; Against School Reform (And in Praise of Great Teaching), 2002; The Just War: An American Reflection on the Morality of War in Our Time, 2003; The Power of Purpose: Living Well by Doing Good, 2006; Future of the Jewish People in Five Photographs, 2012. **Address:** I L O Institute, 1275 Post Rd., Ste. A3, Fairfield, CT 06825, U.S.A. **Online address:** peter@ilo-institute.org

TEMIANKA, Dan(iel). American (born United States), b. 1948. **Genres:** Language/Linguistics, Reference. **Career:** Case Western Reserve University, resident, 1974-77; Healthcare Partners, director of quality management, medical director, quality manager, internist. Writer. **Publications:** (Ed. and intro.) The Jack Vance Lexicon: From Ahulph to Zipangote, 1992, as The Jack Vance Lexicon: The Coined Words of Jack Vance from Ahulph to Zipangote, 1995. Contributor to periodicals. **Address:** Health Care Partners, Los Angeles Urgent Care Center, 1025 W Olympic Blvd., Los Angeles, CA 90015, U.S.A. **Online address:** temianka@ix.netcom.com

TEMIN, Peter. American (born United States), b. 1937. **Genres:** Economics. **Career:** Massachusetts Institute of Technology, Woodrow Wilson Fellow, 1959-60, National Science Foundation cooperative fellow, 1960-61, teaching assistant, 1961-62, assistant professor of industrial history, 1965-67, associate professor of economic history, 1967-70, professor of economics, 1970-90, department head, 1990-93, Elisha Gray II professor of economics, 1993-2009, Gray professor emeritus of economics, 2009-; Harvard University, resident fellow, 1961-62, junior fellow, 1962-65, Charles Warren Center for Studies in American History, visiting fellow, 1976-77; National Bureau of Economic Research, research associate, 1982-; University of Cambridge, Pitt professor of American history and institutions, 1985-86; Economic History Association, president, 1995-96; Eastern Economic Association, president, 2001-02. Writer. **Publications:** Iron and Steel in Nineteenth-Century America: An Economic Inquiry, 1964; The Jacksonian Economy, 1969; Causal Factors in American Economic Growth in the Nineteenth Century, 1975; Did Monetary Forces Cause the Great Depression?, 1976; Economics, 1976; Taking Your Medicine: Drug Regulation in the United States, 1980; The Fall of the Bell System, 1987; Lessons from the Great Depression, 1989; (with G. Toniolo and C.H. Feinstein) European Economy Between the Wars, 1997; (N.R. Lamoreaux and D.M.G. Raff) Learning by Doing in Markets, Firms and Countries, 1999; (co-author) Research Bulletin Series on Jewish Law and Economics, 2002; (with F. Levy) Inequality and Institutions in 20th Century America, 2007; (with G. Toniolo and C.H. Feinstein) World Economy Between the World Wars, 2008; (with S. Finkelstein) Reasonable Rx: Solving the Drug Price Crisis, 2008; Great Recession and The Great Depression, 2010. EDITOR: New Economic History, 1972; Inside the Business Enterprise, 1991; (intro.) Industrialization in North America, 1994; (with E.S. Brezis) Elites, Minorities and Economic Growth, 1999; Engines of Enterprise: An Economic History of New England, 2000. **Address:** Department of Economics, Massachusetts Institute of Technology, Rm. 280A, Bldg. E52, 50 Memorial Dr., Cambridge, MA 02142-1347, U.S.A. **Online address:** ptemin@mit.edu

TEMPERLEY, David. American (born United States) **Genres:** Music, Photography. **Career:** Columbia University, Department of Music, instructor, teaching assistant, 1989-96, adjunct assistant professor, 1996-97, 1999-2000; Ohio State University, lecturer, 1998-99; Eastman School of Music, assistant professor of music theory, 2000-05, associate professor of music theory, 2005-; music composer. Writer. **Publications:** The Cognition of Basic Musical Structures, 2001; Music and Probability, 2007. Contributor to journals. **Address:** Eastman School of Music, 26 Gibbs St., Rochester, NY 14604, U.S.A. **Online address:** dtemperley@esm.rochester.edu

TEMPERLEY, Nicholas. American/British (born England), b. 1932. **Genres:** History, Music, Theology/Religion. **Career:** University of Illinois, postdoctoral fellow, 1959-61, associate professor, 1967-72, Center for Advanced Studies, associate, 1970-71, professor, 1972-96, professor emeritus of musicology, 1996-, Musicology Division, chairman, 1972-75, 1992-96; Cambridge University, assistant lecturer in music, 1961-66, Clare College, fellow and director of studies in music, 1961-66, Clare Hall, visiting fellow, 1970-71; Yale University, assistant professor of music, 1966-67; Midwest Victorian Studies Association, founding member, 1977-, vice president, 1982-84, president, 1984-86; Journal of the American Musicological Society, editor-in-chief, 1978-80; Oxford Studies in British Church Music, editor, 1986-. **Publications:** Jonathan Gray and Church Music in York, 1770-1840, 1977; The Music of the English Parish Church, 1979; (with C.G. Manns) Fuging Tunes in the Eighteenth Century, 1983; (with G. Abraham and H. Searle) New Grove Early Romantic Masters 1: Chopin, Schumann, Liszt, 1985; Chopin, 1985; Haydn: The Creation, 1991; The Hymn Tune Index, 1998; Bound for America: Three British Composers, 2003; Music of the English Parish Church, 2005; Studies in English Church Music, 1550-1900, 2009. EDITOR: Symphonie Fantastique, 1972; The Athlone History of Music in Britain, vol. V: The Romantic Age 1800-1914, 1981; (and intro.) Sonatas for Pianoforte Solo, 1984; (and intro.) Gradus ad Parnassum, 1984; (and intro.) Works for Pianoforte Solo, 1984; (wtih M. Greenbaum) One Symphony, 1984; (with M. Greenbaum) Overture in England, 1800-1840, 1984; (and intro.) Early Victorian Composers, 1830-1860: S.S. Wesley, Macfarren, Best, and Contemporaries, 1985; (and intro.) Samuel Wesley and Contemporaries: Works for Pianoforte Solo by Late Georgian Composers: Published from 1766 to 1830, 1985; (and intro.) Works for Pianoforte Solo by Continental Composers in London: From 1810 to 1850, 1985; (and intro.) Pieces for Pianoforte Solo, 1985; (and intro.) Studio per il piano forte, 1985; (and intro.) Complete Works for Pianoforte Solo, 1985; (and intro.) Works for Two Pianos Published between 1778 and 1860, 1986; (and intro.) Selection of Four-Hand Duets Published between 1777 and 1857, 1986; Three Quintets for Keyboard and Strings, 1987; Lost Chord: Essays on Victorian Music, 1989; Sonata for Flute and Piano, 1990; (and intro. With Y. Yang) Lectures on Musical Life, 2006; (with S. Drage) Eighteenth-Century Psalmody, 2007; (with S. Drage) Sing We Merrily, 2008; Christmas is Coming, 2009; (with S. Banfield) Music and the Wesleys, 2010. **Address:** The School of Music, University of Illinois, 2136 Music Bldg., 1114 W Nevada St., Urbana, IL 61801-3859, U.S.A. **Online address:** ntemp@illinois.edu

TEMPLE, Brian. American (born United States), b. 1955. **Genres:** History, Technology. **Career:** Macy's, shipping clerk, 1977-. Writer. **Publications:** The Origin of Knighthood, 1991; The Union Prison at Fort Delaware: A Perfect Hell on Earth, 2003. **Address:** c/o Author Mail, McFarland & Company Inc., 960 NC Hwy. 88 W, PO Box 611, Jefferson, NC 28640-8813, U.S.A. **Online address:** briant@voicenet.com

TEMPLE, Charles. American (born United States), b. 1947. **Genres:** Children's Fiction, Education. **Career:** Colegio San Patricio, teacher of English, 1967-68; Alston High School, teacher of English, 1969-70; Powhatan County Schools, director of special reading programs and adult education, 1970-75; University of Houston, assistant professor of education, 1978-81; Hobart and William Smith Colleges, faculty, 1982-, assistant professor of education 1982-86, associate professor of education, 1986-92, professor of education, 1992-, chair, 1983-85, 1988-90, 2002-05; Critical Thinking International Inc., director. Writer. **Publications:** FOR CHILDREN: On the Riverbank, 1992; Shanty Boat, 1994; Cadillac, 1994; Train, 1996. OTHERS: (with F. Temple, R. Nathan and K. Juntunen) Classroom Strategies That Work: An Elementary Teacher's Guide to Process Writing, 1988; (ed. with P. Collins) Stories and Readers: New Perspectives on Literature and Children, 1992; (with R. Nathan, C.F. Temple and N. Burris) The Beginnings of Writing, 1982, (with R. Nathan and C.F. Temkple) 4th ed. as The Beginnings of Writing: Observing and Nurturing Emergent Literacy, 2012; (with J. Gillet) Understanding Reading Problems: Assessment and Instruction, 1982, (with J. Gillet, A. Crawford and C.F. Temple) 8th ed., 2012; (with J. Gillet) Language Arts: Learning Processes and Teaching Practices, 1984, 3rd ed., 1994; (with J. Gillet) Language and Literacy: A Lively Approach, 1996; (with A. Naylor, J. Yokota and M. Martinez) Children's Books in Children's Hands: An Introduction to Their Literature, 1998, (with M. Martinez and J. Yokota) 4th ed., 2010; (co-author)

Intervening for Literacy: The Joy of Reading to young Children, 2005; (co-author) All Children Read, 2005, (with D. Ogle, A. Crawford and P. Freppon) 3rd ed., 2011; (with A. Crawford and J. Gillet) Developmental Literacy Inventory: Kindergarten through Grade Eight, 2008. Contributor to journals. **Address:** Departmentof Education, Hobart & William Smith Colleges, 202 Merritt Hall, Geneva, NY 14456, U.S.A. **Online address:** temple@hws.edu

TEMPLE, Norman J. Canadian/British (born England), b. 1947. **Genres:** Medicine/Health. **Career:** University of Surrey, postdoctoral scientist, 1978-80; School of Medicine, lecturer in biochemistry and nutrition, 1981-85; University of Alberta, postdoctoral fellow in nutrition, 1985-87; Alberta Environmental Centre, Division of Animal Sciences, scientist, 1988-90; Athabasca University, professor of nutrition, 1991-. Writer. **Publications:** (Ed. with D.P. Burkitt) Western Diseases: Their Dietary Prevention and Reversibility, 1994; (co-author) Health for the New Century: A Commonsense Nutritional Approach, 1996; (ed. with T.K. Basu and M.L. Garg) Antioxidants in Human Health and Disease, 1999; (ed. with T. Wilson) Nutritional Health: Strategies for Disease Prevention, 2001, 2nd ed., 2006; (ed. with T. Wilson) Beverages in Nutrition and Health, 2004; (ed. with A. Thompson) Excessive Medical Spending: Facing the Challenge, 2007; (ed. with N.P. Steyn) Community Nutrition Textbook for South Africa, 2008; (ed. with T. Wilson, G. Bray and M.B. Strubble) Nutritional Guide for Physicians, 2010. Contributor to journals. **Address:** Centre for Science, Athabasca University, 1 University Dr., Athabasca, AB T9S 3A3, Canada. **Online address:** normant@athabascau.ca

TEMPLE, Robert (Kyle Grenville). British/American (born United States), b. 1945. **Genres:** Plays/Screenplays, Intellectual History, Psychology, Mythology/Folklore, History, Translations, Mystery/Crime/Suspense, Sciences, Sciences. **Career:** Robert Temple Productions Ltd., director; Second Look Magazine, senior editor, 1978-80; New Horizons Research Foundation, senior research fellow in history of science, 1985-86; British Aerospace, consultant, 1991; Sunday Times, science writer; Guardian, science writer; Time-Life, science reporter; New Scientist, profile writer; Tsinghua University, visiting professor of the history and philosophy of science; American University, visiting professor. **Publications:** The Sirius Mystery, 1976, rev. ed. as The Sirius Mystery: New Scientific Evidence of Alien Contact 5,000 Years Ago, 1998; Goetter, Orakel, und Visionen, 1982; Strange Things: A Collection of Modern Scientific Curiosities, 1983; (intro.) The Dream of Scipio, 1983; Conversations with Eternity, 1984; China: Land of Discovery and Invention in US as The Genius of China: 3,000 Years of Science, Discovery, and Invention, 1986, rev. ed., 2007; Open to Suggestion: The Uses and Abuses of Hypnosis, 1989; He Who Saw Everything: A Verse Translation of the Epic of Gilgamesh, 1991; (trans. with O. Temple) Aesop, The Complete Fables, 1995; Vision of the Grail (verse libretto), 1995; (reteller) The Illustrated Golden Bough: A Study in Magic and Religion, 1996; (trans. and intro.) The Complete Fables of Aesop, 1998; The Crystal Sun, 2000; Netherworld, 2002; The Oracles of the Dead: Ancient Techniques for Predicting the Future, 2005; (with O. Temple) Sphinx Mystery: The Forgotten Origins of the Sanctuary of Anubis, 2009; Egyptian Dawn, 2010. Contributor to books and periodicals. **Address:** David Higham Associates Ltd., 5-8 Lower John St., Golden Sq., London, GL W1F 9HA, England.

TEMPLE, Wayne C(alhoun). American (born United States), b. 1924. **Genres:** Architecture, History, Biography. **Career:** University of Illinois, research assistant, 1949-53, teaching assistant, 1953-54; Illinois State Museum, curator, 1954-58; Lincoln Herald Quarterly, associate editor, 1958-74, editor-in-chief, 1974-; Lincoln Memorial University, ssociate professor of American history, 1958, John Wingate Weeks professor of history and director of department of lincolniana, 1958-64, chairman of department of history, 1959-62; Illinois State Archives, archivist, 1964-77, deputy director, 1977-, chief deputy director; Illinois State Militia, staff; Lincoln Land Community College, lecturer; U.S. Military Academy, lecturer; Midwest Conference on Masonic Education, president, 1984-85. Writer. **Publications:** (Ed.) Sketch of Tad Lincoln, 1958; Indian Villages of the Illinois Country: Historic Tribes, 1958, 4th ed., 1987; (with J.H. James) Mrs. Lincoln's Clothing, 1960; (ed.) Lincoln's Marriage Ceremony, 1960; Lincoln Rides the Circuit, 1960; Lincoln the Railsplitter, 1961; (ed.) Campaigning with Grant, 1961; (ed.) The Civil War Letters of Henry C. Bear, 1961; Lincoln as Seen by C.C. Brown, 1963; Lincoln and the Burners at New Salem, 1965; Lincoln and Bennett: The Story of a Store Account, 1967; Abraham Lincoln and Others at the St. Nicholas, 1968; Reminders of Lincoln in a Cornerstone, 1969; Alexander Williamson, Tutor to the Lincoln Boys, 1971; Indian Villages of the Illinois Country: Atlas, 1975; First Steps to Victory: Grant's March to Naples, 1977; Lincoln as a Lecturer on

Discoveries, Inventions and Improvements, 1982; Stephen A. Douglas: Freemason, 1982; By Square and Compasses: The Building of Lincoln's Home and Its Sage, 1984, rev. ed., 2002; Lincoln's Connections with the Illinois and Michigan, His Return from Congress in '48 and His Invention, 1986; Illinois' Fifth Capitol, 1988, 2nd ed. as Abraham Lincoln and Illinois' Fifth Capitol, 2006; Alfred Henry Piquenard: Architect of Illinois' Sixth Capitol, 1988; Dr. Anson G. Henry, Personal Physician to the Lincolns, 1988; Abraham Lincoln: From Skeptic to Prophet, 1995; Thomas and Abraham Lincoln as Farmers, 1996; Alexander Williamson: Friend of the Lincolns, 1997; By Square & Compass: Saga of the Lincoln Home, 2002; (comp. and ed.) Taste is in My Mouth a Little: Lincoln's Victuals and Potables, 2004; Lincoln's Travels on the River Queen during the Last Days of His Life, 2007; Mrs. Lincoln's Cookbook, forthcoming. **Address:** Illinois State Archives, Springfield, IL 62756, U.S.A.

TEMPLETON, Ty. Canadian (born Canada), b. 1962. **Genres:** Humor/Satire. **Career:** Writer; illustrator; comic book creator. **Publications:** How to Draw Superman, 1998; (and illus.) How to Draw Batman, 1998; (illus. with R. Boyd and J. Delaney) How to Draw Batman and the DC Comics Super Heroes, 2000; Batman: Gotham Adventures, 2000; Bigg Time: A Farcical Fable of Fleeting Time, 2002; (with D. Slott and S. Peterson) Batman Adventures, 2004; (contrib.) The Exterminators, Bug Brothers Forever, 2008. Contributor to periodicals. **Address:** c/o Author Mail, Vertigo, DC Comics, 1700 Broadway, New York, NY 10019, U.S.A.

TENBROOK, Gretchen W. American (born United States), b. 1972. **Genres:** Autobiography/Memoirs, inspirational/Motivational Literature, Medicine/Health, Psychology, Theology/Religion. **Career:** Dartmouth-Hitchcock Medical Center, clinical research coordinator, 1993-95; John's Hopkins Hospital, clinical pastoral education intern, 1997-99, adjunct chaplain; Sinai Hospital, clinical pastoral education intern, 1997-99; writer, 1999-. **Publications:** Broken Bodies, Healing Hearts: Reflections of a Hospital Chaplain, 2000. **Address:** 318 Warren St., Needham, MA 02492, U.S.A.

TENENBAUM, Shelly. American (born United States), b. 1955. **Genres:** Sociology. **Career:** Clark University, assistant professor, 1986-93, Department of Sociology, associate professor, 1993-, professor and chair, Department of Jewish Studies, associate professor, 1993-, adjunct professor, Strassler Family Center for Holocaust and Genocide Studies, coordinator of undergraduate activities. Writer. **Publications:** A Credit to Their Community: Jewish Loan Societies in the United States, 1880-1945, 1993. EDITOR: (with L. Davidman) Feminist Perspectives on Jewish Studies, 1994; (with J.R. Baskin) Gender and Jewish Studies: A Curriculum Guide, 1994. **Address:** Department of Sociology, Clark University, Jefferson 413, 950 Main St., Worcester, MA 01610-1400, U.S.A. **Online address:** stenenbaum@clarku.edu

TENNEN, Howard. American (born United States), b. 1948. **Genres:** Psychiatry, Medicine/Health. **Career:** State University of New York, assistant professor of psychology, 1975-78; University of Connecticut Health Center, assistant professor, professor of psychiatry, 1978-, board of trustees distinguished professor. Journal of Personality, associate editor, 1986-91, editor, 1991-. **Publications:** (With G. Affleck and J. Rowe) Infants in Crisis: How Parents Cope With Newborn Intensive Care and Its Aftermath, 1991. Contributor to periodicals. **Address:** Department of Community Medicine and Health Care, University of Connecticut Health Center, MC 6325, 263 Farmington Ave., Farmington, CT 06030-6325, U.S.A. **Online address:** tennen@nsol.uchc.edu

TENNER, Edward. American (born United States), b. 1944. **Genres:** Technology, History, Design, Humor/Satire, Business/Trade/Industry, Social Sciences. **Career:** Princeton University Press, acquisition editor, 1975-91; Princeton Council of the Humanities, visiting lecturer, 1990; independent writer, editor, speaker and consultant, 1991-; Smithsonian Institute, National Museum of American History, Jerome and Dorothy Lemelson Center for the Study of Invention and Innovation, senior research associate. Writer. **Publications:** Tech Speak, or How to Talk High Tech: An Advanced Post-Vernacular Discourse Modulation Protocol (humor), 1986; Why Things Bite Back: Technology and the Revenge of Unintended Consequences (history of technology), 1996; Inviting Disaster: Lessons from the Edge of Technology in Harvard Magazine, 2001; Our Own Devices: The Past and Future of Body Technology (history of technology), 2003; Our Own Devices: How

Technology Remakes Humanity, 2004. Contributor to periodicals. **Address:** 4316 Hunters Glen Dr., Plainsboro, NJ 08536-3911, U.S.A. **Online address:** tenner@alumni.princeton.edu

TENNYSON, Brian. (Brian Douglas Tennyson). Canadian (born Canada), b. 1939. **Genres:** Local History/Rural Topics, Biography. **Career:** University College of Cape Breton, Department of History and Fine Arts, professor, chairman, professor emeritus, 2003-; CBU Press, editor; Old Sydney Society, president; Atlantic Association of Historians, president; Federation of Nova Scotia Heritage, board director; Bridgewater Museum Commission, chairman. **Publications:** (Ed.) Essays in Cape Breton History, 1973; (ed. and comp.) Cape Breton: A Bibliography, 1978; (ed. with D. Macgillivray) Cape Breton Historical Essays, 1980; Canadian Relations with South Africa: A Diplomatic History, 1982; International Studies: An Annotated Bibliography, 1982, 3rd ed., 1989; Impressions of Cape Breton, 1986; (ed.) Canada and the Commonwealth Caribbean, 1988; (ed.) Canadian-Caribbean Relations, 1990; (with R. Schneider and S. Atwell) A Study of Cape Breton Exports, 1995; The Role of Microenterprise in Community Economic Development: An International Perspective, 1999; (with R. Sarty) Guardian of the Gulf: Sydney, Cape Breton and the Atlantic Wars, 2000; (comp.) Cape Bretoniana: an Annotated Bibliography, 2005; (with W.S. White) Historic Mahone Bay, 2006; Percy Willmot: Cape Bretoner at War, 2007. **Address:** Cape Breton University, 1250 Grand Lake Rd., PO Box 5300, Sydney, NS B1P 6L2, Canada. **Online address:** tennyson@uccb.ns.ca

TENNYSON, Brian Douglas. See **TENNYSON, Brian.**

TENPAS, Kathryn Dunn. American (born United States), b. 1963. **Genres:** Politics/Government, Social Commentary, Social Sciences. **Career:** Commission on Presidential Debates, production assistant, 1988; Leiden University, lecturer, 1992-93; University of South Florida, Department of Government and International Affairs, associate professor, 1993-99; University of Pennsylvania, associate director of the Washington semester program, 1999-2004, Washington semester program, director and adjunct associate professor of political science, 2006-; The Governance Institute, fellow, 2003-; The Brookings Institution, visiting fellow, 2004, non-resident senior fellow, 2004-; Washington University, The Weidenbaum Center on the Economy, Government and Public Policy, visiting fellow, 2004, Department of Political Science, senior lecturer, 2004-05, senior fellow, 2005. Writer. **Publications:** Presidents as Candidates: Inside the White House for the Presidential Campaign, 1997. CONTRIBUTOR: The Other Elites: Women, Politics, and Power in the Executive Branch, 1997; The 1996 Presidential Election in the South, 1997; New Perspectives on Old Age Policies, 1998; (with M. Dickinson) White House Staff Turnover, forthcoming. Contributor to books and journals. **Address:** University of Pennsylvania, 1608 Rhode Island Ave. NW, Washington, DC 20036, U.S.A. **Online address:** tenpas@sas.upenn.edu

TENT, Pam. American (born United States), b. 1949?. **Genres:** Autobiography/Memoirs, Biography. **Career:** Cockettes (theatrical troupe), co-founder and performer, 1970. Writer. **Publications:** Midnight at the Palace: My Life As a Fabulous Cockette (memoir), 2004. **Address:** c/o Author Mail, Alyson Books, 245 W 17th St., 12th Fl., New York, NY 10011-5373, U.S.A. **Online address:** pam@sweetpam.com

TEPPER, Ellen Jean. See **GLAZER, Ellen Sarasohn.**

TEPPER, Sheri S. Also writes as A. J. Orde, B. J. Oliphant, Sheri S. Eberhart, Shirley Stewart Douglas, E. E. Horlak. American (born United States), b. 1929. **Genres:** Mystery/Crime/Suspense, Science Fiction/Fantasy, Novels, Young Adult Fiction. **Career:** Rocky Mountain Planned Parenthood, executive director, 1962-86. Writer. **Publications:** TRUE GAME FANTASY NOVELS: King's Blood Four, 1983; Necromancer Nine, 1983; Wizard's Eleven, 1984; The Song of Mavin Manyshaped, 1985; The Flight of Mavin Manyshaped, 1985; The Search of Mavin Manyshaped, 1985; Jinian Footseer, 1985; Dervish Daughter, 1986; Jinian Star Eye, 1986. SCIENCE FICTION/FANTASY: The Revenants, 1984; Marianne, the Magus, and the Manticore, 1985; After Long Silence, 1987; Northshore: The Awakeners, vol. I, 1987; Southshore: The Awakeners, vol. II, 1987; Marianne, the Madame, and the Momentary Gods, 1988; The Gate to Women's Country, 1988; Grass, 1989; Marianne, the Matchbox, and the Malachite Mouse, 1989; Raising the Stones, 1990; Beauty, 1991; Sideshow, 1992; Plague of Angels, 1993; Shadow's End, 1994; True Game, 1996; Gibbons Decline and Fall, 1996; The Family Tree, 1997; Six Moon Dance, 1998; Singer from the Sea, 1999; The Fresco, 2000;

The Visitor, 2002; The Companions, 2003; The Visitor, 2003; The Margarets, 2007; The Waters Rising, 2010. AS B.J. OLIPHANT: Dead in the Scrub, 1990; The Unexpected Corpse, 1990; Deservedly Dead, 1992; Death and the Delinquent, 1993; Death Served up Cold, 1994; A Ceremonial Death, 1996; Here's to the Newly Deads, 1997. AS A.J. ORDE: A Little Neighborhood Murder: A Jason Lynx Novel, 1989; Death and the Dogwalker: A Jason Lynx Novel, 1990; Death for Old Times' Sake: A Jason Lynx Novel, 1992; Looking for the Aardvark, 1993 in UK as Dead on Sunday; A Long Time Dead, 1995; Death of Innocents, 1997. OTHERS: Blood Heritage, 1986; The Bones, 1987; (as E.E. Horlak) Still Life, 1989. **Address:** c/o Author Mail, HarperCollins Publishers, 10 E 53rd St., 11th Fl., New York, NY 10022, U.S.A.

TERAN, Boston. American (born United States) **Genres:** Novels. **Career:** Writer. **Publications:** God is a Bullet, 1999; Never Count out the Dead, 2001; The Prince of Deadly Weapons, 2002; Trois Femmes, 2006; Giv-the Story of a Dog and America, 2009; The Creed of violence, 2009; Gardens of Grief, 2010. **Address:** c/o Author Mail, St. Martins Minotaur Press, 175 5th Ave., New York, NY 10010, U.S.A. **Online address:** boston@bostonteran.com

TERASAWA, Mizuho. Japanese (born Japan), b. 1951. **Genres:** Adult Nonfiction, Literary Criticism And History. **Career:** Wako University, lecturer, 1981-85, associate professor of humanities, 1985-90; Waseda University, lecturer, 1990-91, associate professor, 1991-96, professor of American literature, 1996-; Macalester College, visiting professor, 1993-94. Writer. **Publications:** Minzoku gokan to shojomaku genso: Nihon kindai amerika nambu fokuna, 1992; (ed. with T. Kuribayashi) The Outsider Within: Ten Essays on Modern Japanese Women Writers, 2002; The Rape of the Nation and the Hymen Fantasy: Japan's Modernity, the American South and Faulkner, 2003. **Address:** Department of English, School of Education, Waseda University, 1-104 Totsukamachi, Shinjuku-ku, Tokyo, 169-8050, Japan. **Online address:** mizuho@waseda.jp

TERBORGH, John W. American (born United States), b. 1936. **Genres:** Environmental Sciences/Ecology, Natural History, Essays, Animals/Pets, Biology. **Career:** Tyco Laboratories Inc., scientist, 1963-65; University of Maryland, assistant professor of botany, 1965-70; Princeton University, associate professor of biology, 1971-78, professor of biology, 1978-88, Class of 1877 Professor of Biology, 1988-89; Duke University, Ruth F. DeVarney professor of environmental science, 1989-91, James B. Duke professor of environmental science, 1991-2006, Center for Tropical Conservation, research professor, director; Nicholas School of the Environment and Earth Sciences, research professor, 2006-; Pew conservation fellow, 1992-95; MacArthur fellow, 1992-97. Writer. **Publications:** Five New World Primates: A Study in Comparative Ecology, 1983; (with J.W. Fitzpatrick and L. Emmons) Annotated Checklist of Bird and Mammal Species of Cocha Cashu Biological Station, Manu National Park, Peru, 1984; Where Have All the Birds Gone?: Essays on the Biology and Conservation of Birds that Migrate to the American Tropics, 1989; Diversity and the Tropical Rain Forest, 1992; (ed. with M.E. Soulé) Continental Conservation: Scientific Foundations of Regional Reserve Networks, 1999; Requiem for Nature, 1999; (co-ed.) Making Parks Work: Strategies for Preserving Tropical Nature, 2002; (ed. with J.A. Estes) Trophic Cascades: Predators, Prey and the Changing Dynamics of Nature, 2010. Contributor to books and periodicals. **Address:** Center for Tropical Conservation, Duke University, Simon's Bldg., PO Box 90381, Durham, NC 27708, U.S.A. **Online address:** manu@duke.edu

TERPENING, Ron. Also writes as Ronnie H. Terpening, Sarah Rapalje-Bergen, Gerret Lambertzen. American (born United States), b. 1946. **Genres:** Novels, Literary Criticism And History. **Career:** University of California, teaching assistant, 1971-76, instructor, 1977-78; Loyola University, assistant professor, 1978-82, associate professor of Italian, 1982; University of Arizona, Department of French and Italian, visiting associate professor, 1982-84, associate professor, 1984-98, co-acting head, 1996, professor, 1998-2008, professor emeritus, 2008-, director of study abroad program, 1987. Writer. **Publications:** NONFICTION: (as Ronnie H. Terpening) Charon and the Crossing: Ancient, Medieval and Renaissance Transformations of a Myth (literary criticism), 1985; (as Ronnie H. Terpening) Lodovico Dolce: Renaissance Man of Letters (literary criticism), 1997; (as Gerret Lambertzen and Sarah Rapalje-Bergen) Beautiful Italy, Beloved Shores: An Illustrated Cultural History of Italy, vol. I: From Prehistoric Times to the Fall of the Roman Empire (cultural studies), 2001. NOVELS: In Light's Delay (young adult), 1988; Storm Track, 1989; The Turning (young adult), 2001; League of Shadows, 2005; Tropic of Fear, 2006; Nine Days in October, 2008. **Address:**

Department of French & Italian, University of Arizona, Modern Languages Bldg., Tucson, AZ 85721-0067, U.S.A. **Online address:** terp@u.arizona.edu

TERPENING, Ronnie H. *See* **TERPENING, Ron.**

TERPSTRA, John. Canadian/Dutch (born Netherlands), b. 1953. **Genres:** Poetry, Geography, History, Natural History, Autobiography/Memoirs, Theology/Religion. **Career:** Writer. **Publications:** Scrabbling for Repose, 1982; Forty Days and Forty Nights, 1987; Naked Trees, 1990; Captain Kintail, 1992; The Church Not Made with Hands: Poems, 1997; Devil's Punch Bowl, 1998; Falling into Place, 2002; Disarmament, 2003; The Boys: Or, Waiting for the Electrician's Daughter, 2005; Brendan Luck, 2005; Two or Three Guitars: Selected Poems, 2006; Skin Boat: Acts of Faith and Other Navigations, 2009. **Address:** 62 Locke St. N, Hamilton, ON L8R 3A5, Canada. **Online address:** j.terpstra@sympatico.ca

TERPSTRA, Vern. American (born United States), b. 1927. **Genres:** Business/Trade/Industry, Marketing, Social Sciences. **Career:** University of Pennsylvania, assistant professor, 1964-66; University of Michigan, Ross School of Business, professor of international business, 1966-92, professor emeritus of international business, 1992-; Holt Rinehart & Winston, consulting editor, 1971-; Academy of International Business, fellow. Writer. **Publications:** (With B. Liander and A.A. Sherbini) Marketing Development in the European Economic Community, 1964; (ed. with W. Alderson and S.J. Shapiro) Patents and Progress, 1965; (co-author) Comparative Analysis for International Marketing, 1967; American Marketing in the Common Market, 1967; University Education for International Business, 1969; International Marketing, 1972, 9th ed., 2006; (with K. David) The Cultural Environment of International Business, 1978, 3rd ed., 1991; International Dimensions of Marketing, 1982, 4th ed., 2000; (ed.) Global Environment of Business, 2006. **Address:** Stephen M Ross School of Business, University of Michigan, Rm. E1434, 701 Tappan St., Ann Arbor, MI 48109-1234, U.S.A. **Online address:** vterp@umich.edu

TERR, Lenore (C.). (Lenore Cagen Terr). American (born United States), b. 1936. **Genres:** Human Relations/Parenting, Psychiatry, Psychology. **Career:** University of California-San Francisco, Langley Porter Psychiatric Institute, clinical professor of psychiatry, 1972-; University of California-Davis, lecturer in law and psychiatry, 1978-; University of California-San Francisco, clinical professor; Case Western Reserve University, academic psychiatrist; Terr Medical Corp., adult and child psychiatrist; Harvard University, lecturer; Vanderbilt University, lecturer; University of Michigan, lecturer; Smithsonian Institution, lecturer. Writer. **Publications:** Too Scared to Cry (nonfiction), 1990; Unchained Memories (nonfiction), 1994; Beyond Love and Work (nonfiction): Why Adults Need to Play, 1999; Magical Moments of Change: How Psychotherapy Turns Kids Around, 2008. Contributor to journals. **Address:** Department of Psychiatry, University of California, 401 Parnassus Ave., San Francisco, CA 94143, U.S.A.

TERR, Lenore Cagen. *See* **TERR, Lenore (C.).**

TERRILL, Marshall. American (born United States), b. 1963. **Genres:** Biography, Sports/Fitness. **Career:** American Continental Corp., runner, 1984-89; Glendale Community College, instructor, 1994-; Mesa Community College, instructor, 1994-; East Valley Tribune, reporter, 1999-; Chandler Connection, staff, 1999-; Arizona State University, Public Affairs Division, information specialist and media relations officer. **Publications:** Steve McQueen: Portrait of an American Rebel, 1994; (with E. Byrnes) Edd Byrnes: Kookie No More, 1996; (with A. Pryor) Flight of the Hawk, 1996; (with K. Norton) Ken Norton: Going the Distance, 2000; (with B. Leigh) The King, McQueen, and the Love Machine: My Secret Hollywood Life with Elvis Presley, Steve McQueen, and James Aubrey, 2001; Earnie Shavers: Welcome to the Big Time, 2002; Sergeant Presley, 2002; David Thompson: Skywalker, 2003; (with W. Federman and J. Maravich) Maravich: The Dazzling Game and Miraculous Heart of Pistol Pete, 2006; (with S. West) Elvis: Still Taking Care of Business, 2007; (with W. Federman and J. Maravich) Pete Maravich: The Authorized Biography of Pistol Pete, 2008; (with M. Haber) Palm Springs á la carte: The Colorful World of the Caviar Crowd at Their Favorite Desert Hideaway, 2009; Steve McQueen: The Life and Legacy of a Hollywood Icon, 2010. **Address:** Arizona State University, 411 N Central Ave., Phoenix, AZ 85004, U.S.A. **Online address:** marshall.terrill@asu.edu

TERRIO, Susan J. American (born United States), b. 1950. **Genres:** History, Social Sciences. **Career:** Elizabethtown College, instructor in French, 1980-86; Georgetown University, visiting assistant professor of French, 1993-94, assistant professor of French civilization, adjunct assistant professor of anthropology, 1994-, associate professor of French, 2000-, associate professor of anthropology, professor of anthropology and French studies, chair of anthropology department, Edmund Walsh School of Foreign Service, chair, Culture and Politics Program, 2001-; Association for French Cultural Studies, vice president; Anthropological Quarterly, book review editor. **Publications:** Crafting the Culture and History of French Chocolate, 2000; Judging Mohammed: Juvenile Delinquency, Immigration and Exclusion at the Paris Palace of Justice, 2009. Contributor to journals. **Address:** Department of French, Georgetown University, 308-I Car Barn, 416 Intercultural Ctr., 3700 O St. NW, Washington, DC 20057-1047, U.S.A. **Online address:** terrios@georgetown.edu

TERRIS, Susan. (Susan Dubinsky Terris). American (born United States), b. 1937. **Genres:** Children's Fiction, Poetry. **Career:** Writer and educator. **Publications:** Children's NS Books: The Upstairs Witch and the Downstairs Witch, 1970; The Backwards Boots, 1971; On Fire, 1972; The Drowning Boy, 1972; Plague of Frogs, 1973; Pickle, 1973; Whirling Rainbows, 1974; Amanda, the Panda, and the Redhead, 1975; The Pencil Families, 1975; No Boys Allowed, 1976; The Chicken Pox Papers, 1976; Two P's in a Pod, 1977; Tucker and the Horse Thief, 1979; Stage Brat, 1980; No Scarlet Ribbons, 1981; Wings and Roots, 1982; Octopus Pie, 1983; Baby-Snatcher, 1984; The Latchkey Kids, 1986; Nell's Quilt, 1987; Author! Author!, 1990; Poetry: Killing in the Comfort Zone, 1994; Curved Space, 1998; Eye of the Holocaust, 1999; Angels of Bataan, 1999; Fire Is Favorable to the Dreamer, 2003; Natural Defenses, 2004; Poetic License, 2004; (ed. with C.B. Follet) Runes, A Review Of Poetry: Hearth, 2006; Contrariwise, 2008; Homelessness of Self, 2011. **Address:** 11 Jordan Ave., San Francisco, CA 94118, U.S.A. **Online address:** sdt11@aol.com

TERRIS, Susan Dubinsky. *See* **TERRIS, Susan.**

TERRY, Ken J. American (born United States), b. 1948. **Genres:** Medicine/Health. **Career:** Writer and public speaker. **Publications:** Rx for Health Care Reform, 2007. Contributor to periodicals and magazines. **Online address:** kenjterry@comcast.net

TERRY, Megan. American (born United States), b. 1932. **Genres:** Novellas/Short Stories, Plays/Screenplays, Songs/Lyrics And Libretti, Photography, Theatre, Humor/Satire. **Career:** Cornish School of Allied Arts, drama teacher and director of the cornish players, 1954-56; Open Theater, founding member and director of playwright's workshop, 1963-68; Yale University, writer-in-residence, 1966-67; New York Theater Strategy, founding member and vice president, 1971; Women's Theater Council, founding member, 1971; Omaha Magic Theater, playwright-in-residence and literary manager, 1974-; University of Nebraska at Omaha, adjunct professor of theater, through 1977; University of Louisville, Bingham professor of humanities, 1981; University of Minnesota, Hill professor of fine arts, 1983; Minneapolis Playwright's Center, national artist-in-residence, 1993. Director and consultant. **Publications:** Calm Down Mother, 1966; The People vs. Ranchman, 1967; Keep Tightly Closed in a Cool Dry Place, The Gloaming Oh My Darling: Four Plays, 1967; Viet Rock, Comings and Goings, Keep Tightly Closed in a Cool Dry Place, The Gloaming Oh My Darling; Four Plays, 1967; Ex-Miss Copper Queen On a Set Of Pills, 1968; Couplings and Groupings, 1972; Three One-Act Plays, 1972; Approaching Simone: A Play, 1973; Henna for Endurance, 1974; Fifteen Million Fifteen Year Olds, 1974; Hospital Play, 1974; Hothouse, 1974; Comings and Goings, 1974; Pro Game, The Pioneer: Two One-Act Plays, 1975; Willie-Walla-Bill's Dope Garden, 1977; Brazil Fado, 1977; Sleazing towards Athens, 1977; American King's English for Queens, 1978; (co-author) 100, 001 Horror Stories of the Plains, 1979; Attempted Rescue on Avenue B, 1979; Babes in the Big House, 1979; Advances, 1980; Objective Love, 1980; The Trees Blew Down, 1981; (with J. Metcalf) Mollie Bailey's Traveling Family Circus: Featuring Scenes from the Life of Mother Jones, 1983; Goona Goona, 1984; Two by Terry Plus One, 1984; (with J.A. Schmidman) Walking through Walls, 1987; Do You see What I'm Saying, 1991; (ed. with J.A. Schmidman and S. Kimberlain) Right Brain Vacation Photos: New Plays and Production Photographs, 1972-1992, 1992; Fireworks, 1996; College Money, 2003. **Address:** c/o Elisabeth Marton, 96 5th Ave., New York, NY 10011, U.S.A. **Online address:** frogheed@aol.com

TERRY, William. *See* **GILMAN, George G.**

TERTZAKIAN, Peter. Canadian (born Canada) **Genres:** Social Sciences, Economics, Business/Trade/Industry. **Career:** Chevron Corp., geophysicist, 1982; ARC Financial Corp., staff, 2002-, chief energy economist and managing director. Writer. **Publications:** A Thousand Barrels a Second: The Coming Oil Break Point and the Challenges Facing an Energy Dependent World, 2006; (with K. Hollihan) The End of Energy Obesity: Breaking Today's Energy Addiction for a Prosperous and Secure Tomorrow, 2009. Contributor to periodicals. **Address:** Julia Tanen, Mavens & Moguls, 46 Winterberry Dr., Franklin, MA 02038, U.S.A.

TERVALON, Jervey. American (born United States), b. 1958. **Genres:** Novels, Novellas/Short Stories. **Career:** Locke High School, teacher, 1986-90; University of California-Santa Barbara, College of Creative Studies, lecturer, 1992-95, 1997-98; freelance writer, 1994-; St. Mary's College, instructor, 1996; California State University, Department of English, lecturer, 1997-2002; University of California-Los Angeles, Program in African American Studies, lecturer, 2000-07; Occidental College, Remsen Bird artist-in-residence, 2002, lecturer, 2003-07; Pitzer College, writer-in-residence, 2003; University of Southern California, lecturer, 2004-10. **Publications:** Understand This (novel), 1994; Living For the City, 1998; Dead Above Ground, 2000; All the Trouble You Need, 2002; Lita: A Novel, 2003; (ed. with G. Phillips) The Cocaine Chronicles, 2005. Works appear in anthologies. Contributor of articles to periodicals. **Address:** 55 W Manor St., Altadena, CA 91001, U.S.A. **Online address:** jerveytervalon@yahoo.com

TESELLE, Eugene (Arthur). American (born United States), b. 1931. **Genres:** Theology/Religion, Politics/Government. **Career:** First Presbyterian Church, assistant minister, 1955-58; Yale University, Department of Religious Studies, instructor, 1962-65, assistant professor, 1966-69; Vanderbilt University, associate professor, 1969-74, professor of church history and theology, 1974-99, now professor emeritus, chair of the faculty senate, Oberlin Alumni/ae professor of church history and theology, now Oberlin Alumni/ae professor of church history and theology emeritus. Writer. **Publications:** Augustine the Theologian, 1970; Augustine's Strategy as an Apologist, 1974; Christ in Context: Divine Purpose and Human Possibility, 1975; Thomas Aquinas: Faith and Reason, 1988; Living in Two Cities: Augustinian Trajectories in Political Thought, 1998; (ed. with D. Patte) Engaging Augustine on Romans: Self, Context and Theology in Interpretation, 2002; Augustine: Abington Pillars of Theology, 2006. **Address:** Divinity School, Vanderbilt University, 411 21st Ave. S, Nashville, TN 37240-1121, U.S.A.

TESH, Jane. American (born United States), b. 1950. **Genres:** Mystery/Crime/Suspense, Novels. **Career:** Jones Elementary School, school librarian, 1975-2004. Writer. **Publications:** The Dewey Decimal System, or, I've Got Your Number, 1997; A Case of Imagination (mystery novel), 2006; Hard Bargain, 2007; A Little Learning, 2009; Stolen Hearts, 2011. **Address:** c/o Author Mail, Poisoned Pen Press, 6962 E 1st Ave., Ste. 103, Scottsdale, AZ 85251, U.S.A. **Online address:** teshwriter@hotmail.com

TESKE, Paul Eric. American (born United States), b. 1958. **Genres:** Politics/Government, Economics, Social Sciences. **Career:** NYC Partnership Inc., research associate, 1983; NYC Transit Authority, strategic planner and senior economist, 1984; State University of New York, assistant professor, 1988-93, associate professor, 1994-97, director of PhD program, 1996-2001, director of MA in public policy, 1997-2002; Columbia University Business School Institute for Tele-Information, affiliated research fellow, 1991-2003; Princeton University, Woodrow Wilson School, visiting professor of politics and public affairs, 1999; University of Colorado, Health Sciences Center, School of Public Affairs, professor, 2003-, dean, distinguished professor, GSPA Center for Education Policy Analysis, director, 2004-, GSPA Ph.D. program, director, 2004-, GSPA Center on Reinventing Public Education Denver, director, 2007-, GSPA Ph.D. Program Concentration in Homeland Security, director, 2007-. Writer. **Publications:** After Divestiture: The Political Economy of State Telecommunications Regulation, 1990; (ed. and contrib.) American Regulatory Federalism and Telecommunications Infrastructure, 1995; (with M. Mintrom and M. Schneider) Public Entrepreneurs: Agents for Change in American Government, 1995; (with S. Best and M. Mintrom) Deregulating Freight Transportation: Delivering the Goods, 1995; (with M. Schneider and M. Marschall) Choosing Schools: Consumer Choice and The Quality of American Schools, 2000; Regulation in the States, 2004; Implementing Teacher Pay for Performance: An Inside Story of Denver's Pro

Comp, 2007; Extraordinary Times, Extraordinary Powers? President George W. Bush's Influence over Bureaucracy and Policy, 2009. Contributor to books and periodicals. **Address:** School of Public Affairs, University of Colorado, CB 142, 1380 Lawrence St., Ste. 500,, PO Box 173364, Denver, CO 80217-3364, U.S.A. **Online address:** paul.teske@cudenver.edu

TESS AKAEKE. *See* **ONWUEME, Tess Osonye.**

TESSARO, Kathleen. British/American (born United States), b. 1965?. **Genres:** Novellas/Short Stories, Novels. **Career:** Writer. **Publications:** NOVELS: Elegance, 2003; Innocence, 2005; The Flirt, 2007; The Debutante, 2009; My Sin, 2012. Contributor to periodicals. **Address:** c/o Author Mail, HarperCollins Publishers, 10 E 53rd St., 7th Fl., New York, NY 10022, U.S.A.

TESTA, Judith (Anne). American (born United States), b. 1943. **Genres:** Art/Art History, Architecture, Travel/Exploration, Biography. **Career:** Northern Illinois University, art historian, art history teacher, professor of art, 1969-2000, now professor emeritus; Fra Noi Magazine, writer, 1992-. **Publications:** The Beatty Rosarium: A Manuscript with Miniatures by Simon Bening, 1986; Rome Is Love Spelled Backward: Enjoying Art and Architecture in the Eternal City, 1998; Sal Maglie: Baseball's Demon Barber, 2007. **Address:** School of Art, Northern Illinois University, Ab 216, 330 Gilbert Way, DeKalb, IL 60115, U.S.A. **Online address:** jtesta@niu.edu

TETER, Magda. American (born United States), b. 1970?. **Genres:** Theology/Religion, History. **Career:** Fordham University, adjunct instructor, 1998; Wesleyan University, Department of History, assistant professor, 2000-07, associate professor, 2007-11, professor, 2011-, associate professor of feminist, gender, and sexuality studies, 2008-, director of Jewish and Israel studies program, 2010-, Jeremy Zwelling associate professor of Jewish studies, 2010-11, Jeremy Zwelling professor of Jewish studies, 2011-; Harvard University, Center for Jewish Studies, Harry Starr fellow, 2002, Radcliffe Institute for Advanced Studies, Emeline Bigelow Conland fellow, 2007-08; University of Pennsylvania, Center for Advanced Judaic Studies, adjunct fellow, 2002-03; Early Modern Workshop Project (an online resource for scholars of Early Modern History and Jewish studies), director. Writer, historian and theologian. **Publications:** Jews and Heretics in Catholic Poland: A Beleaguered Church in the Post-Reformation Era, 2006; (ed. with A. Teller and A. Polonsky) Social and Cultural Boundaries in Pre-Modern Poland, 2010; Sinners on Trial: Jews and Sacrilege after the Reformation, 2011. Contributor to books and periodicals. **Address:** Department of History, Wesleyan University, PAC 313, Middletown, CT 06459-0002, U.S.A. **Online address:** mteter@wesleyan.edu

TEYBER, Edward C. American (born United States), b. 1950. **Genres:** Psychology, Self Help, Education, Psychiatry. **Career:** University of California, Laboratory for Family Studies, coordinator, 1978-79; California State University, professor of psychology, 1979-, director of community counseling center, 1979-; Option House, staff consultant, 1982-83; American Cable System, producer, moderator, 1986-87; University Foundation Board, executive secretary, 1989-93. Writer. **Publications:** Helping Your Children with Divorce, 1985; Interpersonal Process in Psychotherapy: A Guide for Clinical Training, 1988, 4th ed., 2000; Helping Children Cope with Divorce, 1992, 2nd ed., 2001; (ed. with F.H. McClure) Child and Adolescent Therapy: A Multicultural-Relational Approach, 1996; Interpersonal Process in Psychotherapy: A Relational Approach, 1997; (with F.H. McClure) Casebook in Child and Adolescent Treatment: Cultural and Familial Contexts, 2003; Interpersonal Process in Psychotherapy: An Integrative Model, 2006. Contributor to journals and magazines. **Address:** Department of Psychology, California State University, SB-505, San Bernardino, CA 92407, U.S.A. **Online address:** eteyber@csusb.edu

THACKER, Robert. American (born United States), b. 1951?. **Genres:** History, Literary Criticism And History, Essays. **Career:** St. Lawrence University, professor of Canadian studies and English, 1983, associate dean of academic advising, Molson research fellow, 2003, Charles A. Dana professor of Canadian studies. Writer. **Publications:** The Great Prairie Fact and Literary Imagination, 1989; English-Canadian Literature, 1996; (ed. with M.A. Peterman) Willa Cather's Canadian and Old World Connections, 1999; (ed.) The Rest of the Story: Critical Essays on Alice Munro, 1999; (ed. with C.L. Higham) One West, Two Myths: A Comparative Reader, 2004; Alice Munro: Writing Her Lives: A Biography, 2005; (ed. with C.L. Higham) One West, Two Myths II: Essays on Comparison, 2006; (ed. with J.J. Murphy and F. Palleau-Papin) Willa Cather: A Writer's Worlds, 2010. **Address:** St. Lawrence University, Canadian Studies Program, 688 Judson Street Rd., Canton, NY 13617, U.S.A. **Online address:** rthacker@stlawu.edu

THACKERAY, Frank W. American (born United States), b. 1943. **Genres:** History, Politics/Government, Social Sciences, Bibliography. **Career:** Anne Arundel Community College, visiting lecturer, 1976; Rutgers University, Camden Campus, visiting lecturer, 1977; Indiana University Southeast, assistant professor, 1977-82, associate professor, 1982-88, professor of history and Slavic studies, 1988-. Writer. **Publications:** Antecedents of Revolution: Alexander I and the Polish Congress Kingdom, 1815-1825, 1980; (ed.) The Greenwood Histories of the Modern Nations Series, 1997; (ed.) Events that Changed Germany, 2004; (ed.) Events that Changed Russia since 1855, 2007. EDITOR WITH J.E. FINDLING: Statesmen Who Changed the World: A Bio-Bibliographical Dictionary of Diplomacy, 1993; (co-ed.) Events That Changed the World, 1994; Events That Changed the World in the Twentieth Century, 1995; Events that Changed America in the Twentieth Century, 1996; Events that Changed the World in the Nineteenth Century, 1996; Events that Changed America in the Nineteenth Century, 1997; Events that Changed America in the Eighteenth Century, 1998; Events that Changed the World in the Eighteenth Century, 1998; Events that Changed the World in the Seventeenth Century, 1999; Events that Changed America through the Seventeenth Century, 2000; Events that Changed the World Through the Sixteenth Century, 2001; Events that Changed Great Britain Since 1689, 2002; Events that Changed Great Britain, from 1066 to 1714, 2003; What Happened?: An Encyclopedia of Events that Changed America Forever, 2011; Events That Formed The Modern World: From The European Renaissance Through The Sixteenth Century, 2012. Contributor to books and journals. **Address:** School of Social Sciences, Indiana University Southeast, CV 024, 4201 Grant Line Rd., New Albany, IN 47150-2158, U.S.A. **Online address:** fthacker@ius.edu

THADEN, Barbara Z. American (born United States), b. 1955. **Genres:** Autobiography/Memoirs, History, Humanities, Intellectual History, Social Sciences, Paranormal, Literary Criticism And History. **Career:** Bainbridge High School, English teacher, 1978-80; Florida State University, teaching and research assistant, 1980-81; Hillside High School, teacher, 1981-85; University of North Carolina, teaching assistant, 1985-94, lecturer in English, 1994-96; Triangle Research Collaborative, technical writer, 1990-91, 1994; Durham Technical Community College, instructor, 1991-92; Saint Augustine's College, assistant professor, 1997-2003, associate professor of English, 2003-; My Own Home Sweet Home, executive director, 2010-. Writer. **Publications:** (Ed. and contrib.) New Essays on the Maternal Voice in the Nineteenth Century, 1995; The Maternal Voice in Victorian Fiction: Rewriting the Patriarchal Family, 1997; A Student Companion to Charlotte and Emily Brontë, 2001. **Address:** Department of English, Saint Augustine's College, Boyer 304-C, 1315 Oakwood Ave., Raleigh, NC 27610-2298, U.S.A. **Online address:** bzthaden@st-aug.edu

THAGARD, Paul. Canadian (born Canada), b. 1950. **Genres:** Philosophy, Psychology. **Career:** University of Michigan, assistant professor, 1977-81, associate professor of philosophy, 1981-86, visiting associate research scientist in psychology, 1983-85; Princeton University, visiting research fellow and visiting associate professor of psychology, 1985-86, research psychologist, 1986-89, senior research cognitive scientist, 1989-92; University of Pennsylvania, adjunct professor, 1990-91; University of Waterloo, professor of philosophy and adjunct professor of psychology and computer science, 1992-, university research chair, Cognitive Science Program, director. Writer. **Publications:** (With J. Holland, K. Holyoak and R.E. Nisbett) Induction: Processes of Inference, Learning and Discovery, 1986; Computational Philosophy of Science, 1988; Conceptual Revolutions, 1992; (with K. Holyoak) Mental Leaps: Analogy in Creative Thought, 1995; Mind: Introduction to Cognitive Science, 1996, 2nd ed., 2005; (ed.) Mind Readings: Introductory Selections on Cognitive Science, 1998; (co-ed.) Model-based Reasoning in Scientific Discovery, 1999; How Scientists Explain Disease, 1999; Coherence in Thought and Action, 2000; Hot Thought: Mechanisms and Applications of Emotional Cognition, 2006; (ed.) Philosophy of Psychology and Cognitive Science, 2007; Brain and the Meaning of Life, 2010. Contributor of articles to journals and books. **Address:** Department of Philosophy, University of Waterloo, HH 368, Waterloo, ON N2L 3G1, Canada. **Online address:** pthagard@uwaterloo.ca

THALER, M. N. *See* **KERNER, Fred.**

THALER, Richard H. American (born United States), b. 1945. **Genres:** Economics, Money/Finance, Psychology. **Career:** University of Rochester, instructor, 1971-74, Rochester-Monroe County Criminal Justice Pilot City Program, associate, 1972-75, assistant professor, 1974-78; Center for Naval Analyses, Public Research Institute, research economist, 1975; Cornell University, assistant professor, 1978-80, associate professor, 1980-86, professor of economics, 1986-88, Henrietta Johnson Louis professor of economics, Center for Behavioral Economics and Decision Research, director, 1988-95; Center for the Study of American Political Economy, associate director, 1981-83; University of British Columbia, visiting associate professor, 1984-85; National Bureau of Economic Research, co-director of project on behavioral economics, 1992-; Massachusetts Institute of Technology, Sloan School of Management, visiting professor, 1994-95; University of Chicago, Robert P. Gwinn professor of behavioral science and economics and director of the Center for Decision Research, 1995-; Center for Advanced Study in the Behavioral Sciences, fellow, 1998; Fuller and Thaler Asset Management Inc., principal. Writer. **Publications:** Quasi Rational Economics, 1991; The Winner's Curse: Paradoxes and Anomalies of Economic Life, 1992; (ed.) Advances in Behavioral Finance, 1993; (with C.R. Sunstein) Nudge: Improving Decisions about Health, Wealth, and Happiness, 2008. Contributor to books and periodicals. **Address:** Chicago Booth School of Business, University of Chicago, 1101 E 58th St., Chicago, IL 60637, U.S.A. **Online address:** richard.thaler@chicagobooth.edu

THALMANN, William. American (born United States), b. 1947?. **Genres:** Poetry. **Career:** Yale University, assistant professor of classics, associate professor of classics, 1975-84; Hobart and William Smith Colleges, associate professor of classics, 1984-87; University of Southern California, professor of classics, 1987-2001, professor of classics and comparative literature, 2001-, Department of Comparative Literature, director of graduate studies, 2005-08. Writer. **Publications:** Dramatic Art in Aeschylus's Seven Against Thebes, 1978; Conventions of Form and Thought in Early Greek Epic Poetry, 1984; The Odyssey: An Epic of Return, 1992; The Swineherd and the Bow: Representations of Class in The Odyssey, 1998; The Norton Anthology of World Literature, 2006; The Production of Space in Apollonius of Rhodes' Argonautica, 2009; Apollonius of Rhodes and the Spaces of Hellenism, 2011. **Address:** Department of Classics & Comparative Literature, University of Southern California, THH 256P, KAP 462, 3620 S Vermont Ave., Los Angeles, CA 90089, U.S.A. **Online address:** thalmann@usc.edu

THANDEKA. (Sue Booker). American (born United States), b. 1946. **Genres:** Social Commentary, Philosophy, History. **Career:** Children's Television Workshop, production assistant for Sesame Street, 1968-69; KUON-TV, producer, director and writer for the series The Black Frontier, 1969-70; KCET-TV, staff producer and writer, 1970-73; California State University, associate professor of journalism, 1973; KNBC-TV, staff producer and writer, 1975-84; San Francisco State University, assistant professor of philosophy, 1987-91; Community Church of New York, affiliate minister, 1990-91; Williams College, assistant professor of religion, 1991-96; Massachusetts Institute of Technology, lecturer, 1994; Iliff School of Theology, lecturer, 1994; Vanderbilt University, lecturer, 1995; University of Wisconsin-Madison, lecturer, 1996; Columbia University, lecturer, 1997; Brandeis University, lecturer, 1998; Meadville Lombard Theological School, associate professor of theology and culture, 1998-2005, senior research professor, 2005-08; arvard Divinity School, faculty; Stanford University, Stanford Humanities Center, fellow; Lancaster Theological Seminary, faculty, 2012-. **Publications:** (Co-ed. as Sue Booker) Cry at Birth, 1971; The Embodied Self: Friedrich Schleiermacher's Solution to Kant's Problem of the Empirical Self, 1995; (contrib.) Horizons in Feminist Theology: Identity, Tradition and Norms, 1997; Learning to Be White: Money, Race and God in America, 1998; Research for Intersubjective Theology: An Introduction, forthcoming; Affect Theology: Returning Rational Theology to Its Senses, forthcoming. Contributor of articles to books, journals and newspapers. **Address:** Lancaster Theological Seminary, 555 W James St., Lancaster, PA 17603, U.S.A. **Online address:** thandeka@meadville.edu

THAPAR, Valmik. Indian (born India), b. 1952. **Genres:** Zoology, Animals/Pets, Natural History, Young Adult Non-fiction. **Career:** Nigaar Film Workshop, partner, 1973-. Naturalist and writer. **Publications:** NONFICTION: (with F.S. Rathore and T. Singh) With Tigers in the Wild: An Experience in an Indian Forest, 1983; Tiger: Portrait of a Predator, 1986; Tigers: The Secret

Life, 1989; The Tiger's Destiny, 1992; Land of the Tiger: A Natural History of the Indian Subcontinent, 1997; Tiger, 1999; The Tiger: Habitats, Life Cycles, Food Chains, Threats, 2000; Wild Tigers of Ranthambhore, 2000, 2nd ed., 2005; Bridge of God: 20 Days in Masai Mara, 2001; Cult of the Tiger, 2002; Tigers and Tigerwallahs, 2002; Tiger: The Ultimate Guide, 2005; The Last Tiger: Struggling for Survival, 2006; The Illustrated Tigers of India, 2007; Ranthambhore: 10 Days in the Tiger Fortress, 2008; Secret Life of Tigers, 2008; African Diary: 12 Days in Kenya's Magical Wilderness, 2009; The Tiger: Soul of India, 2010. EDITOR: Saving Wild Tigers, 1900-2000: The Essential Writings, 2001; Battling for Survival: India's Wilderness Over 2 Centuries, 2003. Contributor to periodicals. **Address:** 19, Kautilya Marg, Chanakyapuri, New Delhi, DH 110021, India. **Online address:** tiger@vsnl.com

THAROOR, Shashi. Indian/British (born England), b. 1956. **Genres:** Novels, Novellas/Short Stories, Politics/Government. **Career:** United Nations, High Commissioner for Refugees, assistant to the director of external affairs, 1978-79, public information officer, 1980-81, head of Singapore office, 1981-84, senior external affairs officer, 1985-87, executive assistant to the deputy high commissioner, 1987-89, United Nations Headquarters, special assistant to the under-secretary-general for peacekeeping operations, 1989-96, director of communications and special projects, 1996-2001, senior adviser and executive assistant to the secretary-general, 1996-98, under-secretary-general for communications and public information, 2001-07, Department of Public Information, head, 2001-02; Indian Parliament, minister of state for external affairs, 2009-10, member of Thiruvananthapuram constituency, 2009-; Afras Ventures, chairman. Writer. **Publications:** Reasons of State: Political Development and India's Foreign Policy under Indira Gandhi, 1966-1977, 1982; The Great Indian Novel, 1989; The Five-Dollar Smile: Fourteen Early Stories and a Farce in Two Acts, 1990; Show Business, 1991; Five-dollar Smile and Other Stories, 1993; India: From Midnight to the Millennium, 1997; Riot, 2001; Nehru: The Invention of India, 2003; (contrib.) Kerala, God's Own Country, 2003; Bookless in Baghdad: Reflections on Writing and Writers, 2005; Elephant, the Tiger, and the Cell Phone: Reflections on India, the Emerging 21st-Century Power, 2007; (with S. Khan) Shadows Across the Playing Field: 60 years of India-Pakistan Cricket, 2009. Contributor of articles to books and magazines. **Address:** Arcade Publishing, 307 W 36th St., 11th Fl., New York, NY 10018, U.S.A. **Online address:** office@tharoor.in

T HART, Marjolein C. Dutch (born Netherlands), b. 1955. **Genres:** History. **Career:** University of Groningen, research assistant, research fellow project social revolutions, 1981-85; University of Leiden, Political Science, research assistant, research fellow project Bureaucratisation, 1985-86; Free University of Amsterdam, assistant professor of history, 1988-89; Erasmus University, assistant professor of history, 1988-89; University of Amsterdam, senior lecturer in history, 1990-, Department of Economic and Social History, assistant professor, 1988-90, 1990-2002, associate professor, 2002-; Netherlands Institute for Advanced Studies, fellow, 1992-93; Columbia University, visiting professor Queen Wilhelmina chair. Writer. **Publications:** The Making of a Bourgeois State: War, Politics and Finance during the Dutch Revolt, 1993; (ed. with J. Jonker and J.L.V. Zanden) A Financial History of the Netherlands 1550-1990, 1997; (ed. with D. Bos) Humour and Social Protest, 2007; (Comp.) Van vlas naar glas, 2009. **Address:** Department of Economic and Social History, University of Amsterdam, Rm. 526, Spuistraat 134, 1012 VB Amsterdam, Amsterdam, 1012 VB, Netherlands. **Online address:** m.t.hart@hum.uva.nl

THARU, Susie. (Susie Jacob Tharu). Indian/Ugandan (born Uganda), b. 1943. **Genres:** History, Literary Criticism And History, Women's Studies And Issues. **Career:** Indian Institute of Technology-Delhi, associate lecturer in humanities and social sciences, 1968-70; Indian Institute of Technology-Kanpur, lecturer in humanities and social sciences, 1970-73; Central Institute of English and Foreign Languages, lecturer, 1973-82, reader in English literature, 1982-96, professor, 1996-. Writer. **Publications:** The Sense of Performance: Studies in the Post-Artaud Theatre, 1984; (co-author) Manaku Teliyani Mana Charitralu, 1986, trans. as We Were Making History: Women in the Telangana People's Struggle, 1988; (ed. with K. Lalita) Women Writing in India, vol. I: 600 B.C. to the Present, 1991, vol. II: The Twentieth Century, 1993; (ed.) Subject to Change: Teaching Literature in the Nineties, 1998; (co-ed.) French Feminism: An Indian Anthology, 2003; (ed. with A. Zachariah and R. Srivatsan) Towards a Critical Medical Practice: Reflections on the Dilemmas of Medical Culture Today, 2010; (with K. Satyanarayana)

No Alphabet In Sight, 2011. Contributor to periodicals. **Address:** Department of English Literature, Central Institute of English & Foreign Languages, 106 CIEFL Campus, Hyderabad, AP 500 007, India.

THARU, Susie Jacob. *See* **THARU, Susie.**

THATAMANIL, John J. American (born United States), b. 1966. **Genres:** Theology/Religion. **Career:** Boston University, researcher, 1995-98; Millsaps College, assistant professor of religious studies, 1998-2003; Vanderbilt University, assistant professor of theology, 2003-. Writer. **Publications:** (Ed. with J.M. Athyal) Mission in the Marketplace: Metropolitan Chrysostom on the Identity and Mission of the Mar Thoma Church, 2002; The Immanent Divine: God, Creation, and the Human Predicament, 2006; No One Comes to the Father but by Me: The Gospel of John and the Challenge of Religious Diversity, 2012. Contributor to books and periodicals. **Address:** Vanderbilt Divinity School, 411 21st Ave. S, Nashville, TN 37240, U.S.A. **Online address:** john.j.thatamanil@vanderbilt.edu

THATCHER, Margaret (Hilda). British (born England), b. 1925. **Genres:** Politics/Government, Speech/Rhetoric, Autobiography/Memoirs. **Career:** House of Commons-Finchley, parliamentary representative, 1959-79, 1991-; Ministry of Pensions and National Insurance, joint parliamentary secretary, 1961-64; secretary of state for education and science, 1970-74; Conservative Party, leader, 1975; prime minister and first lord of the treasury, 1979-90; University of Buckingham, chancellor, 1992-. Writer. **Publications:** What's Wrong with Politics?, 1968; Let Our Children Grow Tall: Selected Speeches, 1975-1977, 1977; Europe as I See It: Discorso Pronunciato a Roma, il 24 giugno 1977, nella sede del Banco di Roma, Sotto gli auspicidel Centro italiano di studi per la Conciliazione internazionale, 1977; (with G. Howe and K. Joseph) Right Angle: Three Studies in Conservatism, 1978; Sinews of Foreign policy: An Address, 1978; In Defence of Freedom: Speeches on Britain's Relations with the World, 1976-1986, 1987; The Revival of Britain: Speeches on Home and European Affairs, 1975-1988, 1989; (contrib.) Talking with David Frost. Margaret Thatcher, 1991; The Downing Street Years, 1979-1990 (memoir), 1993; The Path to Power, 1995; The Collected Speeches of Margaret Thatcher, 1997; As I Said to Denis: The Margaret Thatcher Book of Quotations, 1998; Messages from Croatia, 1998; Margaret Thatcher: Complete Public Statements 1945-1990, 1999; Statecraft: Strategies for a Changing World, 2002; (foreword) Afghanistan: Agony of a Nation, 2005. Contributor to periodicals. **Address:** House of Lords, 20 Dean's Yard, London, GL SW1P 3PA, England.

THAYER, Bradley A. American (born United States) **Genres:** Social Sciences, History, Politics/Government. **Career:** Dartmouth College, faculty; University of Minnesota, faculty; Harvard University's Kennedy School of Government, Belfer Center for Science and International Affairs, fellow; Missouri State University, Department of Defense and Strategic Studies, associate professor of political science; Writer. **Publications:** (With R.A. Falkenrath and R.D. Newman) America's Achilles' Heel: Nuclear, Biological and Chemical Terrorism and Covert Attack, 1998; Pax Americana and The Middle East: U.S. Grand Strategic Interests in The Region After September 11, 2003; Darwin and International Relations: On the Evolutionary Origins of War and Ethnic Conflict, 2004; (ed.) American National Security Policy: Essays in Honor of William R. Van Cleave, 2007; (with C. Layne) American Empire: A Debate, 2007; (with N.V. Ibryamova) Debates in international relations, 2010. **Address:** Department of Defense and Strategic Studies, Missouri State University, 9302 Lee Hwy., Ste. 760, Fairfax, VA 22031, U.S.A. **Online address:** dss1@missouristate.edu

THAYER, Helen. American (born United States), b. 1937. **Genres:** Travel/Exploration, Autobiography/Memoirs. **Career:** Writer, explorer and photographer. **Publications:** TRAVEL MEMOIRS: Polar Dream, 1993 as Polar Dream: The First Solo Expedition by a Woman and Her Dog to the Magnetic North Pole, 2002; Three among the Wolves: A Couple and Their Dog Live a Year with Wolves in the Wild, 2004; Walking the Gobi: A 1600-Mile Trek across a Desert of Hope and Despair, 2007. **Address:** Snohomish, WA , U.S.A. **Online address:** helen@helenthayer.com

THAYER, Terri. American (born United States) **Genres:** Mystery/Crime/Suspense. **Career:** Writer and educator. **Publications:** Wild Goose Chase: A Quilting Mystery, 2008; Old Maid's Puzzle: A Quilting Mystery, 2008; Stamped Out: A Stamping Sisters Mystery, 2008; Ocean Waves, 2009; Inked Up, 2009; False Impressions, 2010; Monkey Wrench: A Quilting Mystery,

2012. **Address:** Berkley Publishing Group, 375 Hudson St., New York, NY 10014, U.S.A. **Online address:** terri@territhayer.com

THEISMANN, Joe. American (born United States), b. 1949. **Genres:** Sports/Fitness. **Career:** Toronto Argonauts, Canadian Football League, football player, 1971-74; Washington Redskins, football player, 1974-86; CBS National Football League broadcasts, analyst, 1987-88; ESPN National Football League broadcasts, commentator, 1988-2005; J.R.T. Associates, president and chief executive officer; Offense-Defense Football Camp, teacher. Writer. **Publications:** Quarterbacking, 1973, 2nd ed., 1983; (with D. Kindred) Theismann (autobiography), 1987; (foreword) G. Janklowicz and A.M. Brown, Bodies in Motion: Finding Joy in Fitness, 1992; (with B. Tarcy) The Complete Idiot's Guide to Understanding Football Like a Pro, 1997, 2nd ed., 2001. Contributor to periodicals. **Address:** J.R.T. Associates, 5661 Columbia Pke., Ste. 100B, Falls Church, VA 22041-2868, U.S.A.

THEISS, Janet M. American (born United States), b. 1964. **Genres:** History, Politics/Government. **Career:** University of Utah, Department of History, assistant professor of history, 1997-2004, associate professor of history, 2004-, Asian Studies Program, interim director, 2005-06, director, 2006-09, The Asia Center, director, 2007-; Late Imperial China, co-editor, 2006-; Johns Hopkins University, The Society for Qing Studies, co-director, 2007-. Historian. **Publications:** Disgraceful Matters: The Politics of Chastity in Eighteenth-Century China, 2004. Contributor to periodicals and journals. **Address:** Department of History, University of Utah, Rm. 255, Carolyn Tanner Irish Humanities Bldg., 215 S Central Campus Dr., Salt Lake City, CT 84112, U.S.A. **Online address:** janet.theiss@m.cc.utah.edu

THEISZ, R. D. American (born Yugoslavia), b. 1941. **Genres:** Literary Criticism And History, Anthropology/Ethnology, Biography. **Career:** Long Island University, instructor, 1965-67; Fordham University, assistant professor, 1967-72; Sinte Gleska College, professor, 1972-77; Black Hills State University, professor of English, Department of Humanities, chair of humanities, 1977-, professor, now professor emeritus of English and American Indian studies. Writer. **Publications:** Das dokumentartheater und seine zeit, 1973; (ed.) Buckskin Tokens: Contemporary Oral Narratives of the Lakota, 1975; (with B.B. Bear, Sr.) Songs and Dances of the Lakota, 1976; Perspectives on Teaching American Indian Literature, 1977; (with S.Y. Bear) Standing in the Light: A Lakota Way of Seeing (biography), 1994; Sending their Voices: Essays on Lakota Musicology, 1996. **Address:** Department of Humanities, Black Hills State University, MH 326, 1200 University St., Ste. 9666, Spearfish, SD 57799-9666, U.S.A. **Online address:** ronnietheisz@bhsu.edu

THE MEDIEVAL MURDERERS See **Sansom, C. J.**

THEOBALD, William F. American (born United States), b. 1934. **Genres:** Travel/Exploration, Recreation, Business/Trade/Industry. **Career:** Village of Garden City, assistant superintendent of recreation, 1960-63; Village and School District of West Hempstead, director of community recreation, 1963-67; City University of New York, Brooklyn College, Department of Health, physical education, and recreation, chairperson, 1967-74, assistant, 1971-73; University of Waterloo, Department of Recreation and Leisure Studies, head, 1974-77; Purdue University, Department of Health, Kinesiology and Leisure Studies (now Department of Health and Kinesiology), divisional chairperson, 1977-, professor of recreation and tourism, now professor emeritus, Interdisciplinary Graduate Program in Travel and Tourism, director, through 1988; New York University, visiting professor, 1982; George Washington University, visiting professor, 1984; University of Surrey, visiting professor, 1985. Writer. **Publications:** (Ed.) Catalogue of Ontario Research in Leisure and Recreation, 1975; The Female in Public Recreation: A Study of Participation and Administrative Attitudes, 1976; The Evaluation of Recreation and Park Programs, 1979; (contrib.) New Space for Women, 1980; (contrib.) Tourism and the Next Decade, 1981; The Evaluation of Human Service Programs, 1985; (ed.) Global Tourism: The Next Decade, 1994, 3rd ed., 2004; (co-ed. and contrib.) Reducing the Barriers to International Tourism, 1995; (contrib.) Issues in Tourism: Case Studies in Planning, Development and Marketing, 1997; (contrib.) Quan Qiu Lü You Xin Lun, 2001. Contributor to journals. **Address:** Department of Health and Kinesiology, Purdue University, 800 W Stadium Ave., West Lafayette, IN 47907, U.S.A. **Online address:** theobald@purdue.edu

THEODORE, Mary. See **HEGEMAN, Mary Theodore.**

THEODORE, Wayne. American (born United States), b. 1958?. **Genres:** Biography, Self Help, Psychology, Autobiography/Memoirs. **Career:** Business owner and writer. **Publications:** (With L.A. Horvitz) Wayne: An Abused Child's Story of Courage, Survival and Hope, 2003. **Address:** c/o Author Mail, Harbor Press, PO Box 1656, Gig Harbor, WA 98335, U.S.A.

THEORELL, (Per Gunnar) Toeres. Swedish (born Sweden), b. 1942. **Genres:** Medicine/Health, Psychology. **Career:** Karolinska Institute, ward physician, 1967-73, assistant professor, 1973-78; University of Texas, visiting researcher, 1973-74; Huddinge Hospital, assistant chief physician in department of social medicine, 1978-80; National Institute for Psychosocial Factors and Health, professor, 1981-95; Johns Hopkins University, School of Public Health, senior research associate, 1989-; Karolinska Institute, director, professor, 1995-2006, professor emeritus of psychosocial environmental medicine, 2006-; Institute for Psycho-social Medicine, stress researcher. **Publications:** (With U. de Faire) Life Stress and Coronary Heart Disease, 1984; (with R. Karasek) Healthy Work, 1990. EDITOR: Socialmedicin och psykosocial medicin, 1988; Everyday Biological Stress Mechanisms, 2001; (with K. Konarski) Swedish Anthology of Psychosomatic Therapies. Contributor to books and journals. **Address:** Department of Public Health Sciences, Karolinska Institute, Solna Road 1, Solna, Alfred Nobels Alle 8, Stockholm, S-171 77, Sweden. **Online address:** tores.theorell@ki.se

THEORIN, Johan. Swedish (born Sweden), b. 1963. **Genres:** Novels. **Career:** Journalist. **Publications:** Echoes from the Dead, 2008; The Darkest Room, 2009. **Address:** Bonnier Group Agency, PO Box 3159, Stockholm, SE-103 63, Sweden.

THE ROCK. American (born United States), b. 1972. **Genres:** Sports/Fitness, Biography, Young Adult Non-fiction. **Career:** Wrestler and writer. **Publications:** (With J. Layden) The Rock Says: The Most Electrifying Man in Sports Entertainment, 2000. **Address:** World Wrestling Federation Inc., 1241 E Main St., Stamford, CT 06902-3520, U.S.A.

THEROUX, Joseph (Peter). American (born United States), b. 1953. **Genres:** Novels, Young Adult Fiction. **Career:** Tuasivi High School, school librarian, 1976; Teachers Training College, instructor in English, 1977; Avele College, English teacher, 1978; Leone High School, American Samoa, English teacher, 1978-80, Division of Instructional Development, secondary English specialist, 1980-85, Department of Education Newsletter, staff writer, 1983-85; Mountain View School, English teacher, 1985-86; Hilo High School, English teacher, 1986-90, vice-principal, 1990-91, 1993-2001; Keaukaha Elementary School, principal, 2001-. **Publications:** Black Coconuts, Brown Magic, 1983. Contributor to books. **Address:** Keaukaha Elementary School, 240 Desha Ave., Hilo, HI 96720-4815, U.S.A. **Online address:** joseph_theroux@lotus.k12.hi.us

THEROUX, Louis Sebastian. American/Singaporean (born Singapore), b. 1970. **Genres:** History, Travel/Exploration. **Career:** Metro Silicon Valley, journalist; Spy magazine, writer. Television host and producer. **Publications:** The Call of the Weird: Travels in American Subcultures, 2007. **Address:** Capel & Land Ltd., 29 Wardour St., London, GL W1D 6PS, England.

THEROUX, Paul. American (born United States), b. 1941. **Genres:** Novels, Children's Fiction, Literary Criticism And History, Travel/Exploration, Children's Non-fiction, Young Adult Non-fiction, Young Adult Fiction, Plays/Screenplays, Adult Non-fiction. **Career:** Soche Hill College, lecturer in English, 1963-65; Makerere University, lecturer in English, 1965-68; University of Singapore, lecturer in English, 1968-71; writer, 1971-; University of Virginia, visiting lecturer, 1972-73. **Publications:** Education By Radio: An Experiment in Rural Group Listening for Adults in Uganda, 1966; Waldo, 1967; Fong and the Indians, 1968; Girls at Play, 1969; Murder in Mount Holly, 1969; Jungle Lovers, 1971; Sinning with Annie and Other Stories, 1972; V.S. Naipaul: An Introduction to His Works, 1972; Saint Jack, 1973; The Black House, 1974; The Great Railway Bazaar: By Train Through Asia, 1975; The Family Arsenal, 1976; The Consul's File, 1977; Picture Palace, 1978; A Christmas Card, 1978; The Old Patagonian Express: By Train through the Americas, 1979; London Snow: A Christmas Story, 1979; World's End: and Other Stories, 1980; The Mosquito Coast, 1981; The London Embassy, 1983; The Kingdom by the Sea: A Journey around Great Britain, 1983; Sailing through China, 1983 in UK as Down the Yangtze, 1995; Doctor Slaughter, 1984; Half Moon Street: Two Short Novels, 1984; (with S. McCurry) The Imperial Way: By Rail from Peshawar to Chittagong, 1985; Sunrise with

Seamonsters: Travels and Discoveries 1964-1984, 1985; (with B. Chatwin) Patagonia Revisited, 1985; O-Zone, 1986; The Shortest Day of the Year: A Christmas Fantasy, 1986; The White Man's Burden: A Play in Two Acts, 1987; Riding the Iron Rooster: By Train through China, 1988; My Secret History, 1989; Dr. DeMarr, 1990; To the Ends of the Earth: The Selected Travels of Paul Theroux, 1990; Travelling the World: The Illustrated Travels of Paul Theroux, 1990; Chicago Loop, 1990; The Happy Isles of Oceania: Paddling the Pacific, 1992; Millroy the Magician, 1994; The Pillars of Hercules: A Grand Tour of the Mediterranean, 1995; My Other Life, 1996; On the Edge of the Great Rift: Three Novels of Africa, 1996; Kowloon Tong, 1997; The Collected Stories, 1997; Sir Vidia's Shadow: A Friendship Across Five Continents, 1998, rev. ed., 2000; The Collected Short Novels, 1998; Fresh Air Fiend: Travel Writings, 1985-2000, 2000; Hotel Honolulu, 2001; Nurse Wolf and Dr. Sacks, 2001; Dark Star Safari: Overland from Cairo to Cape Town, 2003; The Stranger at the Palazzo d'Oro: And Other Stories, 2004; Vineyard Days, Vineyard Nights: The Romance Of Martha's Vineyard, 2004; Blinding Light, 2005; The Elephanta Suite, 2007; Ghost Train to the Eastern Star, 2008; A Dead Hand: A Crime in Calcutta, 2009; The Tao of Travel, 2011; The Lower River, 2012. **Address:** c/o Author Mail, Houghton Mifflin Harcourt Publishing Co., Trade Division, Adult Editorial, 8th Fl., 222 Berkeley St., Boston, MA 02116-3764, U.S.A. **Online address:** erinn@paultheroux.com

THEROUX, Peter. American (born United States), b. 1956. **Genres:** Novels, Translations, Travel/Exploration. **Career:** Long Beach Project Read, volunteer tutor, 1986-92, part-time staff, 1987-91; Wall Street Journal, staff reporter. Journalist. **Publications:** (Trans.) A. Munif, Cities of Salt: A Novel, 1987; The Strange Disappearance of Imam Moussa Sadr, 1987; Sandstorms: Days and Nights in Arabia, 1990; (trans.) A. Munif, The Trench, 1991; (trans.) A. Munif, Variations on Night and Day, 1993; Translating LA: A Tour of the Rainbow City, 1994; (trans. and intro.) A. Qasim, Rites of Assent: Two Egyptian Short Novels, 1995; (trans.) N. Mahfouz, Children of the Alley, 1996; (trans.) A. Mamdouh, Mothballs, 1996; (trans.) I. Ali, Dongola: A Novel of Dubia, 1998; (trans.) A. Mamdouh, Naphtalene: A Novel of Baghdad, 2005; (trans.) E. Habiby, Saraya, The Ogre's Daughter: A Palestinian Fairy Tale, 2006; (trans.) E. Khoury, Yalo, 2008. Contributor to periodicals. **Address:** Wylie Aitken & Stone Inc., 250 W 57th St., Ste. 2114, New York, NY 10107-2199, U.S.A.

THESEN, Sharon. Canadian (born Canada), b. 1946. **Genres:** Poetry, Biography, Literary Criticism And History. **Career:** Capilano College, English instructor; Capilano Review, poetry editor, 1978-89; University of British Columbia, faculty of creative and critical studies, Department of Creative Studies, associate professor of creative writing, 2005-, professor. **Publications:** Artemis Hates Romance, 1980; Holding the Pose, 1983; Confabulations: Poems for Malcolm Lowry, 1984; The Beginning of the Long Dash, 1987; The Pangs of Sunday, 1990; Aurora, 1995; News & Smoke: Selected Poems, 1999; A Pair of Scissors, 2000; Weeping Willow, 2005; The Good Bacteria, 2006. EDITOR: Selected Poems: The Vision Tree, 1982; The New Long Poem Anthology, 1991, 2nd ed., 2001; (with R. Maud) Charles Olson and Frances Boldereff: A Modern Correspondence, 1999. **Address:** Faculty of Creative and Critical Studies, University of British Columbia Okanagan, ARTS 131, 3333 University Way, Kelowna, BC V1V 1V7, Canada. **Online address:** sharon.thesen@ubc.ca

THEVOZ, Michel. Swiss (born Switzerland), b. 1936. **Genres:** Art/Art History, Psychiatry. **Career:** Musee des beaux-arts, curator, 1965-75; Collection de l'Art Brut, curator, 1975-2001; University of Lausanne, professor, 1982-2001, Faculty of Arts, honorary professor. Writer. **Publications:** Louis Soutter, 1970; Art Brut, 1974; The Painted Body, 1984. IN FRENCH: Louis Soutter: ou, L'ecriture du desir, 1974; Le langage de la rupture, 1978; (contrib. and intro.) écrits Bruts, 1979; L'Academisme et ses fantasmes, 1980; Dubuffet, 1986; Jean Lecoultre, 1989; Détournement d'écriture, 1989; Le Theatre du crime: Essai sur la peinture de David, 1989; Art Brut, psychose et mediumnite, 1990; (with P. Restany) Sosno, 1992; Manifeste pour une mort douce, 1992; Requiem pour la folie, 1995; Le Miroir infidele, 1996; L'Esthétique du suicide, 2003; Le syndrome vaudois, 2003; Tout va bien, 2004; L'heure d'hiver, 2008. **Address:** Faculty of Arts, University of Lausanne, Rm. 2049, Anthropole, Lausanne, CH-1015, Switzerland. **Online address:** michel.thevoz@bluefin.ch

THIBODEAU, Serge Patrice. Canadian (born Canada), b. 1959. **Genres:** Poetry. **Career:** Radio Canada, staff, 1990-92; Editions Perce-Neige, editorial director. Poet. **Publications:** Septième chute: poèsie, 1982-1989, 1990;

Passage des glaces, 1992; Appel des mots: lecture de Saint-Denys-Garneau: essai, 1993; Nous, l'étranger, 1995; Quatuor de l'errance; suivi de La traversée du désert: poeésie, 1995; Nocturnes, 1997; Dans la cité; suivi de Paci'fica: poeésie, 1997; Disgrâce de l'humanité: essai sur la torture, 1999; Roseau: poèmes, 1997-2000, 2000; Seuils, 2002; Que repose, 2004; Let Rest, 2005; Lieux cachés: récits de voyage, 2005; Sept dernières paroles de Judas, 2008; One, 2009; (ed.) Anthologie de la poésie acadienne, 2009; Journal de John Winslow à Grand Pré, 2010. **Address:** c/o Editions de l, Division of Le Groupe Ville Marie Litterature, 1010 rue de la Gauchetiere Est., Montreal, QC H2L 2N5, Canada.

THIEL, Diane. American (born United States), b. 1967. **Genres:** Poetry, Translations, Essays, Humanities, Mythology/Folklore, Adult Non-fiction, Environmental Sciences/Ecology, Language/Linguistics, Language/Linguistics. **Career:** Brown University, teaching fellow, 1988-90; University of Miami, lecturer, 1990-99, visiting poet and assistant professor, 2000-01; Florida International University, intermittent lecturer, 1992-99; University of New Mexico, assistant professor, 2002-05, associate professor, 2005-10, professor, 2010-. Writer. **Publications:** Cleft in the Wall, 1999; Echolocations, 2000; Writing Your Rhythm: Using Nature, Culture, Form and Myth, 2001; Resistance Fantasies, 2004; The White Horse: A Colombian Journey, 2004; Crossroads: Creative Writing Exercises in Four Genres, 2005; Open Roads: Exercises in Writing Poetry, 2005; Winding Roads: Exercises in Writing Creative Nonfiction, 2008; American Fugue, 2008. Contributor to periodicals. **Address:** Department of English, University of New Mexico, MSC03-2170, Humanities 333, Albuquerque, NM 87131-0001, U.S.A. **Online address:** diane@dianethiel.net

THIELE, Leslie Paul. American/Canadian (born Canada), b. 1959. **Genres:** Philosophy, Politics/Government. **Career:** Swarthmore College, assistant professor of political science, 1989-91; University of Florida, assistant professor, 1991-95, associate professor, 1995-98, College of Natural Resources and the Environment, faculty, 1997-, Department of Political Science, head, 1997-2002, professor of political science, 1998-, graduate placement director, 2003-04, Minor in Sustainability Studies, faculty advisor, 2008-; Social Science Research Council and MacArthur Foundation, fellow, 1994-96. Writer. **Publications:** Friedrich Nietzsche and the Politics of the Soul: A Study of Heroic Individualism, 1990; Timely Meditations: Martin Heidegger and Postmodern Politics, 1995; Thinking Politics: Perspectives in Ancient, Modern, and Postmodern Political Theory, 1997, 2nd ed., 2003; Environmentalism for a New Millennium: The Challenge of Co-evolution, 1999; Heart of Judgment: Practical Wisdom, Neuroscience, and Narrative, 2006; Indra's Net and the Midas Touch: Living Sustainably in a Connected World, 2011. Contributor to periodicals. **Address:** Department of Political Science, University of Florida, 234 Anderson Hall, PO Box 117325, Gainesville, FL 32611-7325, U.S.A. **Online address:** thiele@polisci.ufl.edu

THIEMANN, Ronald F. American (born United States), b. 1946. **Genres:** Theology/Religion, Politics/Government, Literary Criticism And History, Ethics. **Career:** Yale University, acting instructor in religious studies, 1975-76; Haverford College, faculty, 1978-82, associate professor, 1982-85, professor of religion, 1985-86, department head and chair, 1978-84, acting provost, 1985, acting president, 1986; Trinity Lutheran Seminary, Fendt lecturer, 1984; Harvard University, Divinity School, John Lord O'Brian professor of divinity and dean, 1986-98, professor of theology, religion and society, 1998-2005, Lutheran Academy of Scholars, director, 1999-, Harvard Seminars on Business Across Religious Traditions, director, 2006-, John F. Kennedy School of Government, Hauser Center for Non-Profit Organizations, faculty fellow, 1999-, Center for Public Leadership, faculty affiliate, 2002-, Benjamin Bussey Professor of Theology, 2006-, Faculty of Arts and Sciences, Weatherhead Center for International Affairs, faculty associate, 2006-; University of Virginia, distinguished visiting theologian, 1988; Valparaiso University, O.P. Kretzmann lecturer, 1988; University of California, St. Augustine lecturer, 1993; Lutheran Southern Seminary, Yost lecturer, 1995; Yale Divinity School, St. John lecturer; Lutheran Theological Seminary, Holman lecturer, 2006; Kalamazoo College, William Weber lecturer in government and society. Writer. **Publications:** Revelation and Theology: The Gospel as Narrated Promise, 1985; Toward an American Public Theology: The Church in a Pluralistic Culture, 1991; (ed.) The Legacy of H. Richard Niebuhr, 1991; Religion in Public Life: A Dilemma for Democracy, 1996; (ed. with W.C. Placher) Why are We Here?: Everyday Questions and the Christian Life, 1998; (ed. with M.A. Noll) Where Shall My Wond'ring Soul Begin? The Landscape of Evangelical Piety and Thought, 2000; (ed. with M.J. Bane and B. Coffin) Who Will Provide:

The Changing Role of Welfare in American Society, 2000. Contributor of articles to books and journals. **Address:** Divinity School, Harvard University, Divinity 302, 45 Francis Ave., Cambridge, MA 02138, U.S.A. **Online address:** ronald_thiemann@harvard.edu

THIER, Marian J. American (born United States) **Genres:** How-to Books, Business/Trade/Industry. **Career:** WVIA-TV, on-air host, producer, writer, 1964-72; Keystone College, dean of academic support services, 1972-84; Communication Link, consultant, 1984-87; Expanding Thought Inc., founder, president and consultant, 1984-; Sixth Grade Center School, teacher. **Publications:** Coaching C.L.U.E.S., 2003. **Address:** Expanding Thought Inc., 3180 Westwood Ct., Boulder, CO 80304-2967, U.S.A. **Online address:** mjthier@xtho.com

THIER, Marlene. American (born United States) **Genres:** Education, Language/Linguistics, Sciences, Reference. **Career:** Elementary school teacher, 1955-57; public schools learning specialist, 1969-84; Simon Fraser University, visiting lecturer, 1972; California State University, extension instructor, 1974, lecturer and student teacher supervisor, 1993-2000, adjunct professor; reading specialist, 1986-87; classroom teacher, 1987-93; science mentor, 1988-89; University of California, Lawrence Hall of Science, staff associate, 1993-96, teacher, education coordinator and program developer, 1996-2002; Pittsburg-Antioch Teacher Credentialing Headstart Program, director, 1994-95; writer, 2002-. **Publications:** (With B. Daviss) The New Science Literacy: Using Language Skills to Help Students Learn Science, 2002; Media Literacy: Transforming Curriculum and Teaching, The 104th Yearbook of the National Society for the Study of Education, 2005; Merging Media and Science: Learning to Weigh Sources, Not Just Evidence, The 104th Yearbook of the National Society for the Study of Education, 2005; English Through Science: A Guide for Teaching Science (K-8) to English Language Learners, 2005; Media and Science: Developing Skepticism and Critical Thinking, 2008. **Address:** 142 Hodges Dr., Moraga, CA 94556, U.S.A. **Online address:** mthier@berkeley.edu

THIERAUF, Robert James. American (born United States), b. 1933. **Genres:** Administration/Management, Business/Trade/Industry, Information Science/Computers, Economics. **Career:** Coopers and Lybrand, staff, 1958-63; PriceWaterhouseCooper, staff auditor and consultant; Xavier University, Department of Management and Information Systems, chairman, 1968-80, D.J.O'Conor endowed chair of business administration, 1973-, now professor emeritus of information systems. Writer. **Publications:** Decision Making through Operation Research, 1970, 2nd ed., 1975; Data Processing for Business and Management, 1973; Systems Analysis and Design of Real-Time Management Information Systems, 1975; Management Principles and Practices: A Contingency and Questionnaire Approach, 1977; An Introductory Approach to Operations Research, 1978; Distributed Processing Systems, 1978; Management Auditing: A Questionnaire Approach, 1980; An Introduction to Data Processing for Business, 1980; Systems Analysis and Design: A Case Study Approach, 1980, 2nd ed., 1986; Effective Information Systems Management, 1982; Decision Support Systems for Effective Planning and Control, 1982; A Manager's Complete Guide to Effective Information Systems, 1983; Effective Management and Information Systems, 1984, rev. ed., 1987; Management Science: A Model Formulation Approach with Computer Applications, 1985; A Problem-Finding Approach to Effective Corporate Planning, 1987; User-Oriented Decision Support Systems, 1988; Effective Information Centers, 1988; New Directions in MIS Management, 1988; Group Decision Support Systems for Effective Decision Making, 1989; Expert Systems in Finance and Accounting, 1990; Electronic Data Interchange in Finance and Accounting, 1990; Executive Information Systems: A Guide for Senior Management and MIS Professionals, 1991; Image Processing Systems in Business: A Guide for MIS Professionals and End Users, 1992; Creative Computer Software for Strategic Thinking and Decision Making, 1993; Effective Management and Evaluation of Information Technology, 1994; Virtual Reality Systems for Business, 1995; On-Line Analytical Processing Systems for Business, 1997; Knowledge Management Systems for Business, 1999; Effective Business Intelligence Systems, 2001; (with J.J. Hoctor) Smart Business Systems for the Optimized Organization, 2003; (with J.J. Hoctor) Optimal Knowledge Management: Wisdom Management Systems Concepts and Applications, 2006. **Address:** Department of Management and Information Systems, Xavier University, 3800 Victory Pkwy., Cincinnati, OH 45207, U.S.A.

THIERING, Barbara (Elizabeth). Australian (born Australia), b. 1930. **Genres:** Theology/Religion. **Career:** Teacher, 1953-61; University of Sydney, lecturer in Old Testament studies, Hebrew and feminist theology, lecturer, 1967-93, faculty of board of studies in divinity, 1973-91, lecturer in continuing education, School of Divinity, student advisor, 1980-91, now retired. Writer. **Publications:** Created Second?: Aspects of Women's Liberation in Australia, 1973; (ed.) Deliver Us from Eve: Essays on Australian Women and Religion, 1977; Redating the Teacher of Righteousness, 1979; The Gospels and Qumran: A New Hypothesis, 1981; The Qumran Origins of the Christian Church, 1983; Jesus & the Riddle of the Dead Sea Scrolls, 1992 in UK as Jesus the Man: A New Interpretation from the Dead Sea Scrolls, 1992; Jesus of the Apocalypse: The Life of Jesus after the Crucifixion, 1995; The Book That Jesus Wrote, 1998; Jesus the Man: Decoding the Real Story of Jesus and Mary Magdalene, 2006. Contributor of books to journal. **Address:** 16 Wyong Rd., Mosman, NW 2088, Australia. **Online address:** thiering@ozemail.com.au

THIESSEN, Elmer John. Canadian (born Canada), b. 1942. **Genres:** Philosophy, Education, Theology/Religion. **Career:** Medicine Hat College, teacher of philosophy, 1971-2005; University of Lethbridge, lecturer, 1977; Tyndale University College and Seminary, research professor of education, 2008-11. Writer. **Publications:** (With H. Coward) Humanities in Alberta Post-Secondary Technical-Vocational Education, 1985; Teaching for Commitment: Liberal Education Indoctrination and Christian Nurture, 1993; In Defence of Religious Schools and Colleges, 2001; The Ethics of Evangelism: A Philosophical Defense of Proselytizing and Persuasion, 2011. **Address:** 305 Bushview Cres., Waterloo, ON N2V 2A6, Canada. **Online address:** ejthiessen@sympatico.ca

THIRLWELL, Adam. American/British (born England), b. 1978. **Genres:** Art/Art History. **Career:** Areté Magazine, editor-in-chief, assistant editor; Oxford University, All Soul's College, fellow, Quondam fellow. **Publications:** Politics, 2003; Miss Herbert, 2007; The Delighted States: A Book of Novels, Romances & Their Unknown Translators, Containing Ten Languages, Set on Four Continents & Accompanied by Maps, Portraits, Squiggles, Illustrations & a Variety of Helpful Indexes, 2008; Escape: A Novel in Five Parts, 2009; Escape: A Novel, 2010. **Address:** Rogers, Coleridge & White Ltd., 20 Powis Mews, London, GL W11 1JN, England. **Online address:** adam.thirlwell@all-souls.ox.ac.uk

THIRSK, (Irene) Joan. British (born England), b. 1922. **Genres:** Agriculture/Forestry, Environmental Sciences/Ecology, History, Horticulture, Local History/Rural Topics, Women's Studies And Issues. **Career:** University of London, London School of Economics and Political Science, assistant lecturer in sociology, 1951-52; University of Leicester, senior research fellow in Agrarian history, 1952-65; Agricultural History Review, editor, 1963-72; University of Oxford, St. Hilda's College, reader in economic history, 1965-83, Ford lecturer in English history, 1975, honorary fellow, 1983-, Kellogg College, reader emeritus in economic history; Cambridge University Press, deputy general editor, 1966-74, general editor, 1974-2000; History of Lincolnshire, general editor, 1970-76; British Agricultural History Society, president, 1983-86, 1995-98; British Association for Local History, president, 1986-92; Past and Present Society, vice president, 2003-. **Publications:** (Intro.) Fenland Farming in the Sixteenth Century, 1953; English Peasant Farming: The Agrarian History of Lincolnshire from Tudor to Recent Times, 1957; Tudor Enclosures, 1959; Sources of Information on Population, 1500-1760, and Unexplored Sources in Local Records, 1965; The Restoration, 1976; Economic Policy and Projects: The Development of a Consumer Society in Early Modern England, 1978; The Rural Economy of England, 1984; Agricultural Regions and Agrarian History in England, 1500-1750, 1987; Alternative Agriculture: A History from the Black Death to the Present Day, 1997; Food in Early Modern England: Phases, Fads, Fashions 1500-1760, 2007. EDITOR: (with J. Imray) Suffolk Farming in the Nineteenth Century, 1958; Land, Church, and People: Essays Presented to H.P.R. Finberg, 1970; History of Lincolnshire, 1970; (with J.P. Cooper) Seventeenth-Century Economic Documents, 1972; (with J. Goody and E.P. Thompson) Family and Inheritance: Rural Society in Western Europe, 1200-1800, 1976; Chapters from the Agrarian History of England and Wales, 1500-1750, 1990; Alternative Agriculture: A History from the Black Death to the Present Day, 1997; The English Rural Landscape, 2000; Hadlow: Life, Land, and People in a Wealden Parish, 1460-1600, 2007. Contributor to periodicals. **Address:** Kellogg College, University of Oxford, 62 Banbury Rd., Oxford, OX OX2 6PN, England.

THIS, Herve. French (born France), b. 1955. **Genres:** Food And Wine, Sciences, Chemistry, Philosophy. **Career:** Belin Co., editor, 1980-81; Pour la Science, editor, 1980-84, vice editor-in-chief, 1984-97, editor-in-chief,

1997-2000; Molecular Gastronomy Newsletter, editor-in-chief, 1994; Institut National de la Recherche Agronomique, physical chemist, 2000-; Foundation Science and Culture Alimentaire of the French Academy of Sciences, scientific director, 2006-. **Publications:** Les Secrets de la Casserole, 1993; La Casserole des enfants, 1997; Révélations Gastronomiques, 1999; Ateliers experimentaux du gout, 2001; Traité élémentaire de cuisine, 2002; Casserole eprouvette, 2002; Molecular Gastronomy: Exploring the Science of Flavor, 2006; La cuisine c'est de l'amour, de l'art, de la technique, 2006; (with P. Gagnaire) Cooking: The Quintessential Art, 2008; Sagesse du chimiste, 2009; Building a Meal: From Molecular Gastronomy to Culinary Constructivism, 2009; Cours de Gastronomie Moléculaire. No 1, Science, Technologie, Technique Culinaires: Quelles Relations?, 2009; Science of the Oven, 2009. **Address:** Institut National Agronomique Paris-Grignon, 16 rue Claude Bernard, Paris, 75005, France. **Online address:** herve.this@paris.inra.fr

THISELTON, Anthony C(harles). British (born England), b. 1937. **Genres:** Theology/Religion, Philosophy, Essays. **Career:** University of Bristol, recognized teacher, 1965-70; University of Sheffield, lecturer, 1970-79, senior lecturer in biblical studies, 1979-86; University of Nottingham, St. John's College, principal, 1986-88, professor of Christian theology, head of department of theology, 1992-2001, professor emeritus in residence, 2001-; University of Durham, St. John's College, principal, 1988-92, Cranmer Hall, honorary fellow; Church of England, ordained minister. Writer. **Publications:** Language, Liturgy, and Meaning, 1975; The Two Horizons: New Testament Hermeneutics and Philosophical Description with Special Reference to Heidegger, Bultmann, Gadamer, and Wittgenstein, 1980; (with R. Lundin and C. Walhout) The Responsibility of Hermeneutics, 1985; New Horizons in Hermeneutics, 1992; Interpreting God and the Postmodern Self: On Meaning, Manipulation and Promise, 1995; (with R. Lundin and C. Walhout) Promise of Hermeneutics, 1999; The First Epistle to the Corinthians: A Commentary on the Greek Text, 2000; A Concise Encyclopedia of the Philosophy of Religion, 2005; (ed. with C.G. Bartholomew and J.B. Green) Reading Luke: Interpretation, Reflection, Formation, 2005; First Corinthians: A Shorter Exegetical and Pastoral Commentary, 2006; Thiselton on Hermeneutics: The Collected Works and New Essays of Anthony Thiselton, 2006; The Hermeneutics of Doctrine, 2007; Hermeneutics: An Introduction, 2009; Living Paul: An Introduction to the Apostle's Life and Thought, 2009; 1 and 2 Thessalonians: Through the Centuries, 2011; Life After Death: A New Approach to the Last Things, 2011. Contributor to journals. **Address:** Department of Theology and Religious Studies, University of Nottingham, University Pk., Nottingham, NT NG7 2RD, England. **Online address:** anthony.thiselton@nottingham.ac.uk

THOBANI, Sunera. Canadian (born Canada), b. 1957?. **Genres:** Race Relations, Women's Studies And Issues. **Career:** Simon Fraser University, Ruth Wynn Woodward endowed professor in women's studies, 1996-2000; University of British Columbia, professor of women's studies, 2000-. Writer. **Publications:** (Ed. with T. Hellwig) Asian Women: Interconnections, 2006; Exalted Subjects: Studies in the Making of Race and Nation in Canada, 2007; (ed. with S.H. Razack and M.S. Smith) States of Race: Critical Race Feminism for the 21st Century, 2010. Contributor of articles to journals and periodicals. **Address:** Women's and Gender Studies Program, University of British Columbia, 1896 E Mall, Vancouver, BC V6T 1Z1, Canada.

THOENE, Bodie. American (born United States), b. 1951?. **Genres:** Young Adult Fiction, Novels. **Career:** Writer; researcher; U.S. News and World Report, journalist; American West, journalist; Saturday Evening Post, journalist; John Wayne's Batjac Productions, writer and researcher; ABC Circle Films, writer and researcher. **Publications:** CHRISTIAN FICTION: The Gates of Zion, 1986; A Daughter of Zion, 1987; The Return to Zion, 1987; The Key to Zion, 1988; A Light in Zion, 1988; Vienna Prelude, 1989; Munich Signature, 1990. FICTION: RESEARCHED BY BROCK THOENE: Prague Counterpoint, 1989; Jerusalem Interlude, 1990; Danzig Passage, 1991; Warsaw Requiem, 1991; In My Father's House, 1992; Say to This Mountain, 1993. FICTION (UNLESS OTHER WISE NOTED): WITH BROCK THOENE: Riders of the Silver Rim, 1990; The Man from Shadow Ridge, 1990; Writer to Writer, 1990; Sequoia Scout, 1991; Gold Rush Prodigal, 1991; A Thousand Shall Fall, 1992; Cannons of the Comstock, 1992; The Year of the Grizzly, 1992; Shooting Star, 1993; The Twilight of Courage, 1994; Shiloh Autumn, 1996; Only the River Runs Free, 1997; Winds of Promise, 1997; Of Men and of Angels, 1998; To Gather the Wind, 1998; Ashes of Remembrance, 1999; Winds of the Cumberland, 1999; Thunder from Jerusalem, 2000; All Rivers to the Sea, 2000; Jerusalem Vigil, 2000; The Jerusalem Scrolls, 2001; Jerusalem's Heart, 2001; Jerusalem's Hope, 2002; Stones of Jerusalem, 2002; First Light,

2003; Second Touch, 2004; Third Watch, 2004; Dunkirk Crescendo, 2005; Fourth Dawn, 2005; London Refrain, 2005; Paris Encore, 2005; Fifth Sea, 2006; Say to this Mountain, 2006; Why a Manager?, 2006; Legends of the West, 2007; Why a Shepherd?, 2007; Why a Crown?, 2007; Sixth Covenant, 2007; Seventh Day, 2007; Ninth Witness, 2007; Eighth Shepherd, 2008; Tenth Stone, 2008; Why a Star?, 2008; Eleventh Guest, 2009; The Gathering Storm, 2010; Twelfth Prophecy, 2011; Against the Wind, 2011; Beyond the Farthest Star, 2012. **Address:** c/o Author Mail, Tyndale House Publishers Inc., 351 Executive Dr., Carol Stream, IL 60188, U.S.A.

THOENE, (William) Brock. American (born United States), b. 1952?. **Genres:** Westerns/Adventure, Novels, Romance/Historical. **Career:** Novelist. **Publications:** AS WILLIAM BROCK THOENE: Protecting Your Income and Your Family's Future, 1989. AS BROCK THOENE: The Legend of Storey County, 1995; Delta Passage, 1997; Hope Valley War, 1997; The Listening Hills, 1997. SAGA OF THE SIERRAS SERIES WITH B. THOENE: The Man from Shadow Ridge, 1990; Riders of the Silver Rim, 1990; Gold Rush Prodigal, 1991; Sequoia Scout, 1991; Cannons of the Comstock, 1992; The Year of the Grizzly, 1992; Shooting Star, 1993; Flames on the Barbary Coast, 1994. ZION CHRONICLES SERIES WITH B. THOENE: The Gates of Zion, 1998; A Daughter of Zion, 1998; Jerusalem's Crown, 2001; The Return to Zion, 2006; A Light to Zion, 2006; The Key to Zion, 2006. ZION LEGACY SERIES WITH B. THOENE: Jerusalem Vigil, 2000; Thunder from Jerusalem, 2000; Jerusalem's Heart, 2001; The Jerusalem Scrolls, 2001; Stones of Jerusalem, 2002; Jerusalem's Hope, 2002. AS BROCK THOENE WITH B. THOENE: Writer to Writer, 1990; The Twilight of Courage, 1994; Shiloh Autumn, 1996; Only the River Runs Free, 1997; Winds of Promise, 1997; To Gather the Wind, 1998; Of Men and of Angels: A Novel, 1998; A New Frontier: Saga of the Sierras, 1998; Ashes of Remembrance: A Novel, 1999; Winds of the Cumberland, 1999; All Rivers to the Sea: A Novel, 2000; A Land without Law: Saga of the Sierras, 2000; A Light in Zion, 2006; Why a Star?, 2008; Twelfth Prophecy, 2011. A.D. CHRONICLES WITH B. THOENE: First Light, 2003; Second Touch, 2004; Third Watch, 2004; Fourth Dawn, 2005; Fifth Seal, 2006; Sixth Covenant, 2007; Seventh Day, 2007; Eighth Shepherd, 2008; Ninth Witness, 2008; Tenth Stone, 2009; Eleventh Guest, 2009. SHILOH LEGACY SERIES: (as Brock Thoene with B. Thoene) In My Father's House, 1993; A Thousand Shall Fall, 2006; Say to This Mountain, 2006. ZION COVENANT SERIES WITH B. THOENE: Vienna Prelude, 2005; Prague Counterpoint, 2005; Munich Signature, 2005; Jerusalem Interlude, 2005; Danzig Passage, 2005; Warsaw Requiem, 2005; London Refrain, 2005; Paris Encore, 2005; Dunkirk Crescendo, 2005. ZION MEMOIRS SERIES WITH B. THOENE: Evensong, 2010; Serenade, 2010. ZION DIARIES SERIES WITH B. THOENE: The Gathering Storm, 2010. THE LITTLE BOOKS OF WHY SERIES WITH B. THOENE: Why a Manager?, 2006; Why a Shepherd?, 2007; Why a Crown?, 2007. **Address:** Thomas Nelson Inc., 501 Nelson Pl., Elm Hill Pke., PO Box 141000, Nashville, TN 37214-1000, U.S.A.

THOLFSEN, Trygve R(ainone). American (born United States), b. 1924. **Genres:** History, Politics/Government, Social Sciences. **Career:** University of California, instructor, assistant professor of history, 1952-59; Louisiana State University, associate professor of history and chairman of department, 1959-62; Columbia University, Teachers College, associate professor, 1962-67, professor of modern European and English history, 1967-, now professor emeritus of history and education. Writer. **Publications:** Historical Thinking: An Introduction, 1967; (ed. and intro.) Sir James Kay-Shuttleworth on Popular Education in England, 1974; Working Class Radicalism in Mid-Victorian England, 1976; Ideology and Revolution in Modern Europe: An Essay on the Role of Ideas in History, 1984. Contributor to journals. **Address:** Department of History & Education, Teachers College, Columbia University, 334 Horace Mann, 525 W 120th St., New York, NY 10027, U.S.A.

THOM, James Alexander. American (born United States), b. 1933. **Genres:** Novels, Area Studies, History, Local History/Rural Topics. **Career:** Indianapolis Star, business editor and columnist, 1961-67; Saturday Evening Post Co., senior editor, 1967-94; Indiana State Trade Association, communications director, 1971-73; freelance writer, 1973-; Indiana University, lecturer, 1977-81, professor of journalism. **Publications:** Let the SunShine In, 1976; Spectator Sport, 1978; Long Knife, 1979; Follow the River, 1981; From Sea to Shining Sea, 1984; Staying Out of Hell, 1985; Panther in the Sky, 1989; The Children of First Man, 1994; The Spirit of the Place: Indiana Hill Country, 1995; Indiana II, 1996; The Red Heart, 1997; Sign-Talker: The Adventure of George Drouillard on the Lewis and Clark Expedition, 2000; (D.R. Thom)

Warrior Woman: The Exceptional Life Story of Nonhelema, Shawnee Indian Woman Chief, 2003; Saint Patrick's Battalion: A Novel, 2006; Art and Craft of Writing Historical Fiction, 2010. Contributor to periodicals. **Address:** 6276 W Stogsdill Rd., Bloomington, IN 47404, U.S.A.

THOM, Paul. Australian (born Australia), b. 1941. **Genres:** Philosophy, Music, Theatre. **Career:** University of Sydney, lecturer in philosophy, 1964-65, honorary visiting professor, 2007-; Australian National University, lecturer, 1967-74, senior lecturer, 1975-91, head of department, 1989-, reader in philosophy, 1992-96, professor, 1997-, dean of arts, 1998-2000; harpsichordist with Capella Corelli, 1977-86; freelance opera director, 1985-88; Southern Cross University, executive dean of Arts, 2001-07. Writer. **Publications:** The Syllogism, 1981; For an Audience: A Philosophy of the Performing Arts, 1993; The Logic of Essentialism: An Interpretation of Aristotle's Modal Syllogistic, 1996; Making Sense: A Theory of Interpretation, 2000; Medieval Modal Systems, 2004; The Musician as Interpreter, 2007; Logic and Ontology in the Syllogistic of Robert Kilwardby, 2007; The Logic of the Trinity: Augustine to Ockham, 2011. Contributor to philosophy journals. **Address:** Department of Philosophy, School of Philosophical & Historical Inquiry, University of Sydney, A14 Quadrangle Bldg., Sydney, NW NSW 2006, Australia. **Online address:** thm_pl@yahoo.com.au

THOMAS, Abigail. American (born United States), b. 1941?. **Genres:** Children's Fiction, Novels, Novellas/Short Stories, Social Sciences, Biography, Autobiography/Memoirs. **Career:** Viking Press, literary agent and editor; writer, 1988-. Educator. **Publications:** FOR CHILDREN: Wake up, Wilson Street, 1993; Pearl Paints, 1994; Lily, 1994. ADULT FICTION: Getting over Tom: Stories, 1994; An Actual Life (novel), 1996; Herb's Pajamas (short stories), 1998; Safekeeping: Some True Stories from a Life, 2000; (with P. Willis) Digging Up Deep Time: Fossils, Dinosaurs and Megabeasts from Australia's Distant Past, 2005; Three Dog Life, 2006; Thinking about Memoir, 2008. Contributor to magazines and journals. **Address:** c/o Chuck Verrill, Darhansoff, Verrill, Feldman, 236 W 26th St., Ste. 802, New York, NY 10001, U.S.A. **Online address:** abigailthomas@verizon.net

THOMAS, Adrian. American (born United States), b. 1947?. **Genres:** Music, Biography, Autobiography/Memoirs, History. **Career:** Queen's University, staff, 1973-96, senior lecturer, 1982, Hamilton Hardy professor of music, 1985-96; University of California, visiting lecturer, 1983-84; Cardiff University, professor of music, 1996-, now professor emeritus, School of Music's Central European Music Research Centre, founder and director; Gresham College, chair of music, 2003-06; Gresham College, fellow, 2006-09. Writer, academic and musicologist. **Publications:** Graziyna Bacewicz: Chamber and Orchestral Music, 1985; Gorecki, 1997; Polish Music since Szymanowski, 2005; Witold Lutoslawski: Cello Concerto (The Eighteenth Century), 2009. **Address:** Cardiff School of Music, Cardiff University, Rm.2.02, 33 Corbett Rd., Cardiff, CF10 3EB, Wales. **Online address:** thomasat@cardiff.ac.uk

THOMAS, A. M. Indian/Tanzanian (born Tanzania, United Republic of), b. 1960. **Genres:** International Relations/Current Affairs. **Career:** Institute of Management in Government, research assistant, 1983-84; Mahatma Gandhi University, lecturer, 1985-94, senior lecturer, 1994-98, reader in international relations, 1998-, School of International Relations and Politics, professor; Centre for Indian Diaspora Studies, chairman; South India American Studies Network, founding member; Mahatma Gandhi University Teachers Association, secretary and treasurer; Agrarian Economy of India, co-coordinator. Writer. **Publications:** The American Predicament: Apartheid and United States Foreign Policy, 1997. **Address:** School of International Relations & Politics, Mahatma Gandhi University, Priyadarshini Hills PO, Kottayam, KE 686560, India. **Online address:** amthomas@satyam.net.in

THOMAS, (Antony) Charles. (Percy Trevelyan). British (born England), b. 1928. **Genres:** Archaeology/Antiquities, History, Language/Linguistics, Military/Defense/Arms Control, Biography. **Career:** University of Edinburgh, lecturer in archaeology, 1957-67; Cornish Archaeology, editor, 1961-78; University of Leicester, professor of archaeology, 1967-71; Royal Institution of Cornwall, director, honorary librarian, president, 1970-71; Council for British Archaeology, president, 1970-73; University of Exeter, professor of Cornish studies, 1972-91, Institute of Cornish Studies, director, 1971-91, emeritus professor, 1993-; Cornish Studies, editor, 1973-90; BBC South West Regional Advisory Council, chairman, 1975-80, Department of the Environment, Cornwall and Devon, 1975-79, rescue archaeology, 1976-88; Royal Commission on Historical Monuments, director, 1983-97, acting chairman, 1988-89, vice

chairman, 1991-97; Cornwall Archaeological Society, president, 1984-88; Society for Medieval Archaeology, president, 1986-89; University of Oxford, Sir John Rhys fellow, 1985-86; Jesus College, visiting senior research fellow, 1985-86; Society for Landscape Studies, president, 1993-; Cornish Methodist Historical Association, president, 1993; Society for Church Archaeology, chairman, 1995-98. Writer. **Publications:** Christian Antiquities in Camborne, 1967; Britain and Ireland in Early Christian Times, 1971; The Early Christian Archaeology of North Britain, 1971; (with A. Small and D.M. Wilson) St. Ninian's Isle and Its Treasure, 2 vols., 1973; (with D.E. Ivall) Military Insignia of Cornwall, 1974; (as Percy Trevelyan) Mr. Holmes in Cornwall, 1980; Christianity in Roman Britain to A.D. 500, 1981; Exploration of a Drowned Landscape, 1985; Celtic Britain, 1986; Views and Likenesses: Early Photographers in Cornwall and Scilly, 1988; Whithorn's Christian Beginnings, 1992; Tintagel, Arthur and Archaeology, 1993; The Place-Names of Causse Mejean, 1994; And Shall These Mute Stones Speak? Post-Roman Inscriptions in Western Britain, 1994; Christian Celts: Messages and Images, 1998; Silent in the Shroud, 1999; Whispering Reeds, the Anglesey Catamanus Inscription Stript Bare: A Detective Story, 2002; Vita Sancti Paterni, 2003. EDITOR: Rural Settlement in Roman Britain, 1966; The Iron Age in the Irish Sea Province, 1972; Research Objectives in British Archaeology, 1983. **Address:** Institute of Cornish Studies, University of Exeter, Cornwall Campus, Trevenson House, Penryn, CW TR10 9EZ, England.

THOMAS, Audrey (Grace). Canadian/American (born United States), b. 1935. **Genres:** Novels, Novellas/Short Stories, Plays/Screenplays, inspirational/Motivational Literature, Literary Criticism And History, Young Adult Fiction. **Career:** Concordia University, visiting assistant professor of creative writing, 1978, visiting professor, 1989-90; University of Victoria, visiting professor of creative writing, 1978-79, writer-in-residence; Simon Fraser University, writer-in-residence, 1981-82; University of Ottawa, writer-in-residence, 1987; University of Toronto, writer-in-residence, 1993; Dartmouth College, visiting professor, 1994, 1996; University of British Columbia, writer-in-residence; David Thompson University Centre, writer-in-residence; Writers' Union of Canada, chair, 2000-01. **Publications:** NOVELS: Mrs. Blood, 1970; Munchmeyer and Prospero on the Island, 1972; Songs My Mother Taught Me, 1973; Blown Figures, 1974; Latakia, 1979; Intertidal Life, 1984; Graven Images, 1993; Coming Down from Wa, 1995; Isobel Gunn, 1999; Tattycoram, 2005. SHORT STORY COLLECTIONS: Ten Green Bottles, 1967; Ladies & Escorts, 1977; Two in the Bush and Other Stories, 1981; Real Mothers, 1981; Goodbye Harold, Good Luck, 1987; Wild Blue Yonder, 1990; The Path of Totality, 2001. Works appear in anthologies. Contributor to periodicals. **Address:** Writers' Union of Canada, 90 Richmond St. E, Ste. 200, Toronto, ON M5C 1P1, Canada.

THOMAS, Barbara L(ee). American (born United States), b. 1939. **Genres:** Human Relations/Parenting, Psychology, Social Sciences, Young Adult Nonfiction, Medicine/Health. **Career:** Episcopal Church, adult education coordinator, 1978-82; Diocesan Child Guidance Center, family therapist, 1986-87; independent personal growth educator, 1992-. Writer. **Publications:** (Contrib. with J.F. Vickers) No More Frogs, No More Princes, 1993; (with J.F. Vickers) Men on Midlife: Eighteen Men Talk about Making New Choices in Careers, Relationships, and What Really Matters in the Second Half of Live, 1996. **Address:** 465 Olenwood Ave., Worthington, OH 43085, U.S.A.

THOMAS, Brook. American (born United States), b. 1947. **Genres:** Literary Criticism And History. **Career:** University of Hawaii at Manoa, assistant professor, associate professor of English, 1976-85; University of Constance, visiting professor, 1976, 1984; University of Massachusetts at Amherst, associate professor of English, 1985-88; University of California, professor of English, 1988-, chancellor's professor, chair; Free University of Berlin, visiting professor, 1991. Writer. **Publications:** James Joyce's Ulysses: A Book of Many Happy Returns, 1982; Cross-Examinations of Law and Literature: Cooper, Hawthorne, Stowe and Melville, 1987; The New Historicism and Other Old-Fashioned Topics, 1991; American Literary Realism and the Failed Promise of Contract, 1997; (ed. and intro.) Plessy v. Ferguson: A Brief History with Documents, 1997; (ed.) Literature and the Nation, 1998; (ed.) Law and Literature, 2002; Civic Myths: A Law-and-Literature Approach to Citizenship, 2007. **Address:** Department of English and Comparative Literature, University of California, 162 Murray Krieger Hall, 435 Humanities Instructional Bldg., PO Box 2650, Irvine, CA 92697-2650, U.S.A. **Online address:** bthomas@uci.edu

THOMAS, Bruce. British (born England), b. 1948. **Genres:** Paranormal,

Philosophy, Autobiography/Memoirs, Biography, Sports/Fitness. **Career:** The Attraction Band, bassist. Freelance musician and writer. **Publications:** The Big Wheel, 1990; The Body of Time, 1991; Bruce Lee: Fighting Spirit: A Biography, 1994; (with K. Baumann) User Interface Design of Electronic Appliances, 2000; Bruce Lee: Fighting Words, 2005; Immortal Combat: Portrait of a True Warrior, 2007. **Address:** c/o Julian Alexander, Lucas Alexander Whitley, 14 Vernon St., London, GL W14 0RJ, England.

THOMAS, Chantal. French (born France), b. 1945?. **Genres:** Communications/Media, Literary Criticism And History. **Career:** Centre National de la Recherche Scientifique, director of research. Writer, educator, historian and researcher. **Publications:** Sade, l'oeil de la lettre, 1978, 2nd ed., 1994; Casanova: Un Voyage Libertin, 1985; (with C. Bonnange) Don Juan ou Pavlov: Essai Sur La Communication Publicitaire, 1987; La Reine Scélérate: Marie-Antoinette Dans Les Pamphlets, 1989; Thomas Bernhard, 1990; Sade, 1994; La Vie Réele Des Petites Filles, 1995; (with J. Abgrall) Healing or Stealing? Medical Charlatans in the New Age, 2000; Lettres de Madame du Deffand, 2002; Les Adieux á La Reine: Roman (novel), 2002; La Lectrice-adjointe: Suivi de Marie-Antoinette de le Théâtre, 2003; (co-author) Le Régent: Entre Fable Et Histoire, 2003; Chemins De Sable, 2006; Jardinière Arlequin, 2006; Cafés de la Mémoire: Récit, 2008; Le Testament d'Olympe, 2010. **Address:** c/o Author Mail, George Braziller Inc., 171 Madison Ave., New York, NY 10016-5110, U.S.A.

THOMAS, Clara McCandless. Canadian (born Canada), b. 1919. **Genres:** Literary Criticism And History, Autobiography/Memoirs, Biography, History. **Career:** University of Western Ontario, part-time lecturer in English, 1947-61; University of Toronto, part-time lecturer, 1958-61; York University, Department of English, instructor, 1961-84, professor, 1969-84, professor emeritus, 1984-, York University Libraries, Canadian Studies, research fellow, 1984. Writer. **Publications:** Canadian Novelists, 1920-1945, 1946; The Clear Spirit, 1966; Love and Work Enough: The Life of Anna Jameson, 1967; Ryerson of Upper Canada, 1969; Margaret Laurence (literary criticism), 1969; Our Nature, Our Voices: A Guidebook to English-Canadian Literature, 1972; Read Canadian, 1972; The Manawaka World of Margaret Laurence, 1975; (with J. Lennox) William Arthur Deacon: A Canadian Literary Life, 1982; All My Sisters: Essays on the Work of Canadian Women Writers, 1994; Chapters in a Lucky Life (memoir), 1999; Strathroy Lives, 2001. AUTHOR OF INTRODUCTION: Winter Studies and Summer Rambles in Canada, 1965; Typee Airmont, 1965; The Backwoods of Canada, 1966; Romeo and Juliet Ryerson, 1966; Henry V Ryerson, 1967; The Canadian Settler's Guide NCL, 1969; The Tomorrow-Tamer Knopf, 1970. Contributor to journals. **Address:** York University Libraries, York University, 4700 Keele St., Toronto, ON M3J 1P3, Canada.

THOMAS, Claudia E. American (born United States), b. 1956?. **Genres:** Novels, Young Adult Non-fiction. **Career:** Writer. **Publications:** Irish Hearts: Caress across the Ocean (novel), 1998. Contributor to newspapers. **Address:** 710 Lewis St., Apt. AO, Havre de Grace, MD 21078-3448, U.S.A. **Online address:** siochain7@aol.com

THOMAS, Cornell. American (born United States), b. 1955. **Genres:** Self Help, Sports/Fitness, Education, Young Adult Non-fiction, Reference. **Career:** Texas Christian University, Educational Administration, Curriculum and Instruction, assistant professor, associate professor, assistant; Oklahoma State University, institutional diversity, vice-president, 2001, adjunct professor of educational studies; Jarvis Christian College, faculty, president, 2009-. Writer. **Publications:** (Contrib.) Texas Public School Organization and Administration, 1991; (contrib.) Understanding the Many Faces of the Culture of Higher Education, 1993; You Can Only Be As Great As You Think You Are, 1994; It's All in the Way We Look at Things-Is it?, 1996; Educational Equality and Excellence, 1996; The Fruits of the Spirit in Teaching, 1998; (with P. Fitzhugh and P.T. Jefferies) We Can Have Better Urban Schools, 2000; (with J. Butler, C. Hernandez) Promoting Inclusion in Higher Education: The Challenge for Universities in the 21st Century, 2008. Works appear in anthologies. Contributor to education journals. **Address:** Jarvis Christian College, Hwy. 80 E, Private Rd. 7631, PO Box 1470, Hawkins, TX 75765, U.S.A. **Online address:** c.thomas@jarvis.edu

THOMAS, David H(urst). American (born United States), b. 1945. **Genres:** Anthropology/Ethnology, Archaeology/Antiquities. **Career:** City University of New York, City College, assistant professor of anthropology and chairman of department, 1971-72; American Museum of Natural History, Department of Anthropology, assistant curator, 1972-76, associate curator, 1977-82, curator, 1982-; Florida Museum of Natural History, Department of Anthropology, adjunct curator, 1987-; Columbia University, adjunct professor, 1991-. Writer. **Publications:** Predicting the Past: An Introduction to Anthropological Archaeology, 1974; (with E.H. McKee) Aboriginal Rock Alignment in the Toiyabe Range, Central Nevada, 1974; Figuring Anthropology: First Principles of Probability and Statistics, 1976; (with R.L. Bettinger) Prehistoric Piñon Ecotone Settlements of the Upper Reese River Valley, Central Nevada, 1976; (with S. South and C.S. Larsen) Rich Man, Poor Men: Observations on Three Antebellum Burials from the Georgia Coast, 1977; (ed.) Anthropology of St. Catherines Island, 1978; (with T.N. Layton) Archaeology of Silent Snake Springs, Humboldt County, Nevada, 1979; Archaeology, 1979, (with R.L. Kelly) 5th ed., 2010; (ed. with S. Koyama) Affluent Foragers: Pacific Coasts East and West, 1981; Archaeology of Monitor Valley, 1983; (with L.S.A. Pendleton) Fort Sage Drift Fence, Washoe County, Nevada, 1983; (ed. with intro.) Great Basin Shoshonean Source Book, 1986; (ed. with intro.) Blackfoot Source Book: Papers, 1986; Refiguring Anthropology, 1986; St. Catherines: An Island in Time, 1988; (ed.) Archaeological and Historical Perspectives on the Spanish Borderlands West, 1989; (ed.) Spanish Borderlands in Pan-American Perspective, 1991; (ed. with intro.) Missions of Spanish Florida, 1991; (ed. with intro.) Ethnology of the Indians of Spanish Florida, 1991; The Illustrated History of Humankind, vol. V, 1993-94; The Native Americans: An Illustrated History, 1993; Exploring Ancient Native America: An Archaeological Guide, 1994; (ed. with L. Pendleton) Native Americans, 1995; Archaeology: Down to Earth, 1999, 4th ed., 2011; Native North America, 2000; Skull Wars: Kennewick Man, Archaeology and the Battle for Native American Identity, 2000; Exploring Native North America, 2010. Contributor to periodicals. **Address:** Department of Anthropology, American Museum of Natural History, Central Park W, 79th St., New York, NY 10024-5192, U.S.A.

THOMAS, David St. John. British (born England), b. 1929. **Genres:** Transportation, Writing/Journalism, Animals/Pets, Novellas/Short Stories, History, Young Adult Non-fiction. **Career:** David & Charles Publishing Group, founder and chairman, 1960-90; David St. John Thomas Publishers, chairman, 1989-94; Writers News, chairman, 1989-99; David St John Thomas Charitable Trust, founder, 2001-. Writer. **Publications:** Great Moments with Trains, 1959; A Regional History of the Railways of Great Britain: vol. I: The West Country, 1960, 6th ed., 1987, as West Country Railway History, 1974, rev. ed., 1989; Lake District Transport Report: The Findings of the Lake District Transport Enquiry, 1961; Trains Work Like This, 1961; The Motor Revolution, 1961; (with G. Thomas) Double-Headed: Two Generations of Railway Enthusiasm, 1963; The Rural Transport Problem, 1963; North Devon Railway Report: The Findings of the North Devon Railway Enquiry, 1963; North East England, 1965; (with S.R. Smith) Summer Saturdays in the West, 1973; Non-Fiction: A Guide to Writing and Publishing, 1970; (with H. Bermont) Getting Published, 1973; The Great Way West: The History and Romance of the Great Western Railway's Route from Paddington to Penzance, 1975; The Country Railway, 1976; The Breakfast Book, 1980; (with P. Whitehouse) The Great Western Railway: 150 Glorious Years, 1984; (with P. Whitehouse) The Great Days of the Country Railway, 1986; (with P. Whitehouse) LMS: A Century and a Half of Progress, 1987; (with P. Whitehouse) LMS: 150: The London Midland & Scottish Railway: A Century and a Half of Progress, 1987; (with P. Whitehouse) SR 150: A Century and a Half of the Southern Railway, 1988, rev. ed., 2002; (with P. Whitehouse) A Passion for Steam, 1989; (with P. Whitehouse) LNER150, 1989; (with P. Whitehouse) The Great Days of Express Trains, 1990; The Cunard Book of Cruising, 1990; (with P. Whitehouse) BR in the Eighties, 1990; (with P. Whitehouse) The Great Days of the GWR, 1991; (with P. Whitehouse) The Great Days of the Southern Railway, 1992; (with P. Whitehouse) The Romance of Scotland's Railways, 1993; (with P. Whitehouse) The Trains We Loved, 1994; Journey through Britain: Landscape, People and Books, 2004; For the Love of a Cat: A Publisher's Story, 2007, 2nd ed., 2010. **Address:** David St John Thomas Charitable Trust, PO Box 6055, Nairn, IV12 4YB, Scotland. **Online address:** dsjtcharitynairn@fsmail.net

THOMAS, D(onald) M(ichael). British (born England), b. 1935. **Genres:** Novels, Poetry, Autobiography/Memoirs, Translations, Young Adult Non-fiction, Novellas/Short Stories, Literary Criticism And History, Music, Music. **Career:** English teacher, 1959-64; Hereford College of Education, lecturer, 1963-66, senior lecturer in English, 1966-78, head of department, 1977-78; Hamline University, visiting lecturer, 1967. Writer and translator. **Publications:** POETRY: Personal and Possessive, 1964; (with D.M. Black and P. Redgrove) Modern Poets II, 1968; Two Voices, 1968; The Lover's Horoscope:

Kinetic Poem, 1970; Logan Stone, 1971; The Shaft, 1973; Lilith-Prints; 1974; Symphony in Moscow, 1974; Love and Other Deaths, 1975; Orpheus in Hell, 1977; In the Fair Field, 1978; The Honeymoon Voyage, 1978; Dreaming in Bronze, 1981; Selected Poems, 1983; (with S. Kantaris) News from the Front, 1983; The Puberty Tree, 1992; Dear Shadows, 2004; Not Saying Everything: Poems of a Relationship, 1965-, 2006; Flight and Smoke, 2009. PROSE: The Devil and the Floral Dance, 1978; The Flute-Player, 1979; Birthstone, 1980; The White Hotel, 1981; Memories and Hallucinations, 1988; Lying Together, 1990; Flying into Love, 1992; Pictures at an Exhibition, 1993; Eating Pavlova, 1994; Lady with a Laptop, 1996; Charlotte, 2001; Bleak Hotel, 2007; Freud: Off the Record, 2010. RUSSIAN NIGHTS SERIES: Ararat, 1983; Swallow, 1984; Sphinx, 1986; Summit, 1988. BIOGRAPHY: Alexander Solzhenitsyn: A Century in His Life, 1998. TRANSLATIONS: A.A. Akhmatova, Requiem, and Poem without A Hero, 1976; A.A. Akhmatova, Way of All the Earth, 1979; (and intro.) A.S. Pushkin, The Bronze Horseman: Selected Poems of Alexander Pushkin, 1982; Y. Yevtushenko, A Dove in Santiago, 1982; A.A. Akhmatova, You Will Hear Thunder, 1985; A.A. Akhmatova, Selected Poems, 1988, new ed., 2006; A. Pushkin, Onegin, 2011. EDITOR: The Granite Kingdom: Poems of Cornwall, 1970; (and intro.) Songs from the Earth: Selected Poems of John Harris, Cornish Miner 1820-84, 1977. OTHERS: (comp.) Poetry in Crosslight, 1975; Flying in to Love, 1992; Two Countries, 2011. Works appear in anthologies. Contributor to journals. **Address:** John Johnson Ltd., Clerkenwell House, 45-47 Clerkenwell Green, London, GL EC1R 0HT, England.

THOMAS, Edmund Barrington. *See* Obituaries.

THOMAS, Evan. American (born United States), b. 1951. **Genres:** Biography, Social Sciences. **Career:** Time, writer and editor, 1977-86; Newsweek, Washington bureau chief, 1986-96, assistant managing editor, 1991-2006, editor-at-large, 2006-; Princeton University, visiting professor, 2003-07, Mathey College, faculty-in-residence, professor, Ferris professor of journalism, 2007-, Council of the Humanities, lecturer; Harvard University, visiting professor, 2004-05. **Publications:** (With W. Isaacson) The Wise Men: Six Friends and the World They Made, 1986; The Man to See: Edward Bennett Williams, the Ultimate Insider: Legendary Trial Lawyer, 1991; The Very Best Men: Four Who Dared: The Early Years of the CIA, 1995; (co-author) Back from the Dead: How Clinton Survived The Republican Revolution, 1997; Robert Kennedy: His Life, 2000; John Paul Jones: Sailor, Hero, Father of The American Navy, 2003; (co-author) Election 2004: How Bush Won and What You Can Expect in the Future, 2005; Sea of Thunder: Four Commanders and The Last Great Naval Campaign, 1941-1945, 2006; (with V. Goldberg and N. Mailer) RFK, 2008; Long Time Coming: The Inspiring, Combative 2008 Campaign and The Historic Election of Barack Obama, 2009; The War Lovers: Roosevelt, Lodge, Hearst and the Rush to Empire, 1898, 2010. **Address:** Mathey College, Princeton University, Hamilton Hall, 2nd Fl., Princeton, NJ 08544, U.S.A. **Online address:** evan.thomas@newsweek.com

THOMAS, G(regory) Scott. American (born United States), b. 1955. **Genres:** Urban Studies, Essays, Politics/Government, History, Business/Trade/Industry. **Career:** WMRA-Radio, news director, 1977-78; WXXI-Radio, news director, 1978-82; National Public Radio, newscaster, 1982-83; Virginia News Network, producer and reporter, 1983-85; WEBR-Radio, anchor and producer, 1985-87; United Way of Buffalo and Erie County, media relations director, 1989-90; Business First, projects editor, 1990-. **Publications:** The Pursuit of the White House, 1987; The Rating Guide to Life in America's Small Cities, 1990; Where to Make Money, 1993; The Rating Guide to Life in America's Fifty States, 1994; (contrib.) The New Rating Guide to Life in America's Small Cities, 1997; The United States of Suburbia, 1998; Leveling The Field: An Encyclopedia of Baseball's All-time Great Performances as Revealed Through Scientifically Adjusted Statistics, 2002; Advice From The Presidents: The Student's Guide to Reaching The Top in Business and Politics, 2008. Contributor to magazines and newspapers. **Address:** Business First, 465 Main St., Buffalo, NY 14203-1793, U.S.A.

THOMAS, Hedley. Australian (born Australia), b. 1967?. **Genres:** Medicine/Health. **Career:** Courier Mail, staff, 1988-, junior reporter, foreign correspondent; Queensland Gas Co., communications officer. Writer. **Publications:** Sick to Death: A Manipulative Surgeon and a Health System in Crisis'A Disaster Waiting to Happen, 2007. **Address:** Brookfield, QL , Australia.

THOMAS, H(ubert) Nigel. Canadian (born Canada), b. 1947. **Genres:** Novels, Novellas/Short Stories, Poetry, Literary Criticism And History, Mythol-

ogy/Folklore, History. **Career:** Protestant School Board of Greater Montreal, high school teacher of English and teacher of French, 1976-88; Universite Laval, assistant professor of U.S. literature, professor of American literature, 1988-2005, retired, 2006. Writer. **Publications:** From Folklore to Fiction: A Study of Folk Heroes and Rituals in the Black American Novel (monograph), 1988; (with M. Laroche and E. Figueiredo) Juan Bobo, Jan Sòt, Ti Jan et Bad John: Figures Littéraires de la Caraïbe, 1991; Spirits in the Dark (novel), 1993; How Loud Can the Village Cock Crow? (short stories), 1996; Moving through Darkness (poetry), 1999; Behind the Face of Winter (novel), 2001; (ed.) Why We Write: Conversations with African Canadian Poets and Novelists, 2006; Return to Arcadia: A Novel, 2007; Lives: Whole and Otherwise, 2010. **Address:** Department of Literature, Universite Laval, Quebec City, QC G1K 7P4, Canada. **Online address:** hnigelthomas@hotmail.ca

THOMAS, Hugh. British (born England), b. 1931. **Genres:** Novels, History, Biography. **Career:** Royal Military Academy, lecturer in politics and government, 1957; United Nations Association of Great Britain, adviser, 1960-61; United Nations Association of London, adviser, 1960-61; United Nations Association of Northern Ireland, adviser, 1960-61; University of Reading, professor of history and chairman of graduate school of contemporary European studies, 1966-75; Centre for Policy Studies, director, 1979-91. Writer. **Publications:** The World's Game (novel), 1957; (ed.) Establishment: Asymposium, 1959; Assault at Arms, 1960; The Spanish Civil War, 1961, 4th rev. ed., 2003; The Story of Sandhurst, 1961; Spain, 1962; The Suez Affair, 1967; Cuba, or, Pursuit of Freedom, 1971, rev. ed., 2002; Boadilla, 1971; Goya and the Third of May 1808, 1972; John Strachey, 1973; Europe, the Radical Challenge, 1973; Spanish Civil War, 1977; An Unfinished History of the World, 1979, rev. ed., 1982; The Case for the Round Reading Room, 1983; Revolution on Balance, 1983; Havannah (novel), 1984; (with G.A. Fauriol and J.C. Weiss) Cuban Revolution, 25 Years Later, 1984; Armed Truce: The Beginnings of the Cold War, 1945-46, 1986; Central America: Can Europe Play a Part?, 1987; Klara (novel), 1988; Madrid: A Traveller's Companion, 1988; Real Discovery of America: Mexico, November 8, 1519, 1992; Conquest: Montezuma, Cortés, and the Fall of Old Mexico, 1993; World History: The Story of Mankind from Prehistory to the Present, 1996; The Slave Trade: The Story of the Atlantic Slave Trade: 1440-1870, 1997; (co-author) La Revolución cubana, 1998; Who's Who of the Conquistadors, 2000; Rivers of Gold, the Prize of the Spanish Empire, 2003; Beaumarchais in Seville: An Intermezzo, 2006; Eduardo Barreiros and the Recovery of Spain, 2009; The Golden Age, 2010; Golden Empire: Spain, Charles V, and the Creation of America, 2011. EDITOR: The Selected Writings of Jose Antonio Primo de Rivera, 1972. **Address:** Curtis Brown Ltd., 1 Craven Hill, London, GL W2 3EW, England.

THOMAS, John Clayton. American (born United States), b. 1944. **Genres:** Public/Social Administration, Urban Studies, Politics/Government. **Career:** University of Minnesota, General College Department of Psychology, teaching and research assistant, 1965-67; University of Illinois, Department of Political Science, teaching and research assistant, 1968-70; Northwestern University, Department of Political Science, teaching assistant, 1969-70; University of Iowa, Institute of Public Affairs, urban affairs specialist, 1970-74; University of Cincinnati, assistant professor and research associate of Institute of Governmental Research, 1974-79; Texas Christian University, assistant professor and director of graduate program in public affairs and administration, 1979-81; University of Missouri, associate professor of public administration, 1981-87, director and professor of public administration, 1987-93; Georgia State University, Department of Public Administration and Urban Studies, department chair, 1993-2001, professor of public administration and urban studies, 1993-; National Conference of the American Society for Public Administration, program co-chair, 1994. **Publications:** Decline of Ideology in Western Political Parties: A Study of Changing Policy Orientations, 1975; Between Citizen and City: Neighborhood Organizations and Urban Politics in Cincinnati, 1986; (ed. with H.V. Savitch) Big City Politics in Transition, 1991; Public Participation in Public Decisions: New Skills and Strategies for Public Managers, 1995; Citizen, Customer, Partner: Engaging the Public in Public Management. **Address:** Department of Public Management and Policy, Andrew Young School of Policy Studies, Georgia State University, PO Box 3992, Atlanta, GA 30303-4992, U.S.A. **Online address:** jcthomas@gsu.edu

THOMAS, John Heywood. Welsh/British (born England), b. 1926. **Genres:** Philosophy, Theology/Religion, Writing/Journalism, Young Adult Fiction. **Career:** University of Manchester, lecturer in philosophy of religion, 1957-65; University of Durham, reader in divinity, 1965-74, dean of divinity, 1970-

72; University of Nottingham, professor of theology, 1974-92, pro-vice-chancellor, 1979-84, dean of arts, 1985-88; University of Bangor, honorary professor, 1993-. Writer. **Publications:** Subjectivity and Paradox, 1957, rev. ed., 1993; Paul Tillich: An Appraisal, 1963; Philosophy of Religion in Kierkegaard's Writings, 1994; Tillich, 2000; Models in Theology, 2003. **Address:** 1 Village Farm, Vale of Glamorgan, WG CF5 6TY, Wales.

THOMAS, Julian (Stewart). British (born England), b. 1959. **Genres:** Anthropology/Ethnology, Archaeology/Antiquities, Philosophy, Social Sciences. **Career:** University of Wales, St. David's University College, lecturer in archaeology, 1987-93; University of Southampton, lecturer in archaeology, 1994-96, senior lecturer, 1996-2000; Manchester University, chair and professor of archaeology, 2000-. Writer. **Publications:** Rethinking the Neolithic, 1991; Time, Culture and Identity: An Interpretive Archaeology, 1996; Understanding the Neolithic, 1999; Archaeology and Modernity, 2004; Place and Memory: Excavations at the Pict's Knowe, 2007. EDITOR AND CONTRIBUTOR: (with F. Baker) Writing the Past in the Present, 1990; (with T. Darvill) Neolithic Houses in Northwest Europe and Beyond, 1996; Interpretive Archaeology: A Reader, 2000; (with T. Darvill) Neolithic Enclosures in Atlantic Northwest Europe, 2000; (with R. Layton and P. Stone) Destruction and Conservation of Cultural Property, 2001; Place and Memory: Excavations at the Pict's Knowe, Holywood and Holm, 2007; (with V. Jorge) Overcoming the Modern Conception of Material Culture, 2007; Handbook of Landscape Archaeology, 2008; (with V. Jorge) Archaeology and the Politics of Vision, 2009; (with H. Anderson-Whymark) Regional Perspectives on Neolithic Pit Deposition, 2011. Works appear in anthologies. Contributor of articles to journals. **Address:** Archaeology Program, School of Arts, Histories and Cultures, Manchester University, Mansfield Cooper Bldg., Oxford Rd., Manchester, GM M13 9PL, England. **Online address:** julian.thomas@manchester.ac.uk

THOMAS, June Manning. American (born United States), b. 1950. **Genres:** Race Relations, Regional/Urban Planning, Urban Studies. **Career:** Voter Education Project, coordinator, 1968; Michigan State University, Office of Black Affairs (student council organization), co-director, 1970, Center for Urban Affairs, research assistant, 1971, Department of Urban and Metropolitan Studies, instructor, 1976-77, Department of Urban and Metropolitan Studies and Urban Planning, assistant professor, 1977-81, Urban Planning and Urban Affairs Programs, associate professor, 1982-95, Michigan Department of Commerce, special assistant and program evaluator, 1985-86, Urban and Regional Planning Program, director, 1996-2000; Cleveland State University, associate professor, 1981-82; Michigan State University Extension, Urban and Regional Planning Program, professor, 1995-2007, Urban Collaborators Program, director, 1999-2001, Urban Collaborators Program, co-director, 2001-07, Urban and Regional Planning Program, centennial professor, 2007-; Community Development Service Inc., consultant, 1993-94. Writer. **Publications:** (Co-author) Discrimination and the Welfare of Urban Minorities, 1981; (with J. Darden, R.C. Hill and R.W. Thomas) Detroit: Race and Uneven Development, 1987; Redevelopment and Race: Planning a Finer City in Postwar Detroit, 1997; Planning Progress: Lessons form Shaghi Effendi, 1999. CONTRIBUTOR: Rebuilding America's Cities: Roads to Recovery, 1984; Unequal Partnerships, 1989; Revitalizing Urban Neighborhoods, 1996; (ed. with M. Ritzdorf) Urban Planning and the African American Community: In the Shadows, 1997; The Inner City: Urban Poverty and Economic Development in the Next Century, 1997; Making the Invisible Visible: A Multicultural Planning History, 1998; (ed. with M. Dewar) The City After Abandonment, 2012. Contributor to journals and books. **Address:** Urban & Regional Planning Program, Taubman College of Architecture and Urban Planning, Michigan State University, Rm. 2208C, 2000 Bonisteel Blvd., Ann Arbor, MI 48109-2069, U.S.A. **Online address:** thomasju@umich.edu

THOMAS, Keith (Vivian). British/Welsh (born Wales), b. 1933. **Genres:** History, Intellectual History, Literary Criticism And History, Theology/Religion, Cultural/Ethnic Topics. **Career:** Oxford University, All Souls College, fellow, 1955-57, distinguished fellow, 2001-, St. John's College, fellow, 1957-86, honorary fellow, 1986-, tutor, 1957-78, reader, 1978-85, professor of modern history, 1986-, Corpus Christi College, president, 1986-2000; Royal Historical Society, joint literary director, 1970-74, vice president, 1980-84, honorable vice-president, 2001; Oxford University Press, delegate, 1980-2000, pro vice-chancellor, 1988-2000; Balliol College, honorary fellow, 1984. **Publications:** Religion and the Decline of Magic: Studies in Popular Beliefs in Sixteenth and Seventeenth Century England, 1971; Rule and Misrule in the Schools of Early Modern England, 1976; Age and Authority in Early Modern England, 1977; (ed. with D. Pennington) Puritans and Revo-

lutionaries: Essays in Seventeenth-Century History Presented to Christopher Hill, 1978; Man and the Natural World: A History of the Modern Sensibility, 1983; Perception of the Past in Early Modern England: The Creighton Trust Lecture 1983, 1983; Delivered Before the University of London on Monday 21 November 1983, 1983; History and Literature, 1989; (ed.) Dictionary of National Biography, 1986-1990: With an Index Covering the Years 1901-1990 in One Alphabetical Series, 1996; Man and the Natural World: Changing Attitudes in England, 1500-1800, 1996; (ed.) The Oxford Book of Work, 1999; Civil Histories: Essays Presented to Sir Keith Thomas, 2000; (ed. with A. Adonis) Roy Jenkins: A Retrospective, 2004; Changing Conceptions of National Biography: The Oxford DNB in Historical Perspective, 2005; Ends of Life: Roads to Fulfilment in Early Modern England, 2009. Contributor to books. **Address:** All Souls College, 27 High St., City Centre, Oxford, OX OX1 4AL, England. **Online address:** keith.thomas@all-souls.oxford.ac.uk

THOMAS, Laurence (Mordekhai). American (born United States), b. 1949. **Genres:** Social Sciences. **Career:** University of Notre Dame, instructor, 1975-76, assistant professor of philosophy, 1977-78; University of Pittsburgh, visiting assistant professor of philosophy, 1976-77; University of Maryland, assistant professor, 1978-80; Harvard University, Andrew Mellon faculty fellow, 1978-79; National Humanities Center, fellow, 1982-83; University of North Carolina, associate professor; Oberlin College, faculty; University of Rochester, professor of philosophy and political science; Syracuse University, professor of philosophy, Department of Political Science, professor, 1989; University of South Carolina, lecture. Writer. **Publications:** Living Morally: A Psychology of Moral Character, 1989; Vessels of Evil: American Slavery and the Holocaust, 1993; (with M.E. Levin) Sexual Orientation and Human Rights, 1999; The Family and the Political Self, 2006; (ed.) Contemporary Debates in Social Philosophy, 2008. Contributor to periodicals. **Address:** Department of Political Science, Syracuse University, 535 Hall of Languages, Syracuse, NY 13244-0001, U.S.A. **Online address:** lthomas@maxwell.syr.edu

THOMAS, Lee. See **PENDLETON, Thomas.**

THOMAS, Leslie (John). British/Welsh (born Wales), b. 1931. **Genres:** Novels, Travel/Exploration, Autobiography/Memoirs, Adult Non-fiction, Reference. **Career:** London Evening News, feature writer, 1956-67, chief feature writer, and special correspondent; Arlington Books, freelance writer and director. **Publications:** This Time Next Week, 1964; The Virgin Soldiers, 1966; Orange Wednesday, 1967; The Love Beach, 1968; Some Lovely Islands, 1968; Come to the War, 1969; His Lordship, 1970; Onward Virgin Soldiers, 1971; Arthur McCann and All His Women, 1972; The Man with The Power, 1973; Tropic of Ruislip, 1974; Stand Up Virgin Soldiers, 1975; Dangerous Davies: The Last Detective, 1976; Bedtimes, 1976; Bare Nell, 1977; Ormerod's Landing, 1978; Midnight Clear, 1978; That Old Gang of Mine, 1979; The Magic Army, 1981; The Hidden Places of Britain, 1981; A World of Islands, 1983; The Dearest and the Best: A Novel of 1940, 1984; In My Wildest Dreams (autobiography), 1984; The Adventures of Goodnight and Loving, 1986; Dangerous in Love, 1987; Orders for New York, 1989; Evening News Short Stories, 1990; The Loves and Journeys of Revolving Jones, 1991; (intro.) Evening News Collection, 1991; Arrivals and Departures: A Novel, 1992; Dangerous by Moonlight, 1993; Running Away, 1994; Kensington Heights, 1996; Chloe's Song, 1997; Dangerous Davies and the Lonely Heart, 1998; Other Times, 2000; Waiting for the Day, 2003; Dover Beach: Love, Life and Death in Wartime England, 2005; Soldiers and Lovers, 2008; Almost Heaven: True and Almost True Tales About a Cathedral, 2010. **Address:** c/o Desmond Elliott, Arlington Books, 3 Clifford St., London, GL W1, England.

THOMAS, Lyn. British (born England), b. 1953?. **Genres:** Women's Studies And Issues, Literary Criticism And History, Theology/Religion, Communications/Media. **Career:** Teacher, through 1989; University of North London, senior lecturer in French; London Metropolitan University, principal lecturer in French, Faculty of Humanities, research director, Institute for the Study of European Transformations, deputy director, professor of cultural studies. Writer. **Publications:** Annie Ernaux: An Introduction to the Writer and Her Audience, 1999; Fans, Feminisms, and Quality Media, 2002; (ed. with K. Soper and M. Ryle) Politics and Pleasures of Consuming Differently, 2009; (ed.) Religion, Consumerism and Sustainability: Paradise Lost?, 2011. **Address:** Institute for the Study of European, Transformations, London Metropolitan University, Tower Bldg., 166-220 Holloway Rd., London, GL N7 8DB, England. **Online address:** l.thomas@londonmet.ac.uk

THOMAS, Marin. *See* **BEAGLEY, Brenda E.**

THOMAS, Michael A. American (born United States), b. 1946?. **Genres:** Westerns/Adventure, Novels, Young Adult Fiction. **Career:** University of New Mexico, lecturer, professor of anthropology, UHP Conexiones Program, coordinator. Anthropologist and author. **Publications:** Crosswinds: A Darkly Comic Modern Western, 1987; Ostrich, 2000; Hat Dance, 2004. **Address:** University Honors Program, University of New Mexico, Rm. 21, Student Health Center Bldg., MSC 06 3890, 1 University of New Mexico, Albuquerque, NM 87131-0001, U.S.A. **Online address:** mthomas@unm.edu

THOMAS, Rob. American (born United States), b. 1965. **Genres:** Young Adult Fiction, Plays/Screenplays, Songs/Lyrics And Libretti, Young Adult Non-fiction, Novels, Humor/Satire. **Career:** ABC Television Series Cupid, executive producer and creator; UPN's Veronica Mars, executive producer and creator; Teacher, 1988-94; Channel One, staff, 1993-95; Dawson's Creek television Series, script writer, 1997. Writer. **Publications:** FOR YOUNG ADULTS: Rats Saw God, 1996; Doing Time: Notes from the Undergrad, 1997; Slave Day, 1997; Satellite Down, 1998; Green Thumb, 1999; (as E. Owens) Regeneration: A Novelization, 1999; Bent, 2000; (ed. with L. Wilson) Neptune Noir: Unauthorized Investigations into Veronica Mars, 2006. Contributor to magazines. **Address:** c/o Ari Greenburg, Endeavor Agency, 9701 Wilshire Blvd., 10th Fl., Beverly Hills, CA 90212, U.S.A. **Online address:** dartskeith@aol.com

THOMAS, Rosalind. British (born England), b. 1959. **Genres:** Classics, History. **Career:** University of London, Royal Holloway, Bedford New College, Egham, professor of ancient Greek history, 1987-; University of Oxford, director of ancient history, Balliol College, senior faculty, professor of Greek history and tutorial fellow in ancient history. Writer. **Publications:** Oral Tradition and Written Record in Classical Athens, 1989; Literacy and Orality in Ancient Greece, 1992; Herodotus in Context: Ethnography, Science and the Art of Persuasion, 2000. Contributor to books and periodicals. **Address:** Humanities Divisional Office, University of Oxford, 37a St Giles, Oxford, OX OX1 3LD, England. **Online address:** rosalind.thomas@classics.ox.ac.uk

THOMAS, Rosanne Daryl. (Prince Charming). American (born United States), b. 1956. **Genres:** Novels, Autobiography/Memoirs, Humor/Satire. **Career:** University of Massachsetts, Honors College, dean's book instructor. Writer. **Publications:** NOVELS: (as Prince Charming) Complications, 1988; The Angel Carver, 1993; Awaiting Grace, 1999. SELF-ILLUSTRATED: Coffee: The Bean of My Existence (humor), 1995. OTHER: Beeing: Life, Motherhood, and 180,000 Honeybees (memoir), 2002. Contributor to periodicals. **Address:** Emma Sweeney Agency, 280 Riverside Dr., Ste. 12E, New York, NY 10025, U.S.A.

THOMAS, Sue. British (born England), b. 1951. **Genres:** Novels, Novellas/Short Stories, Plays/Screenplays, History, Travel/Exploration, Young Adult Fiction. **Career:** Nottingham Trent University, part-time lecturer in English, 1988-94, module leader, 1990-93, senior lecturer in English, 1994-97, principal lecturer and artistic director, 1997-2003, reader in new media, 2003-04, Trace Online Writing Centre, founder, 1997-, artistic director, 2003-04; Manvers Pierrepont School, writer-in-residence, 1992; Greenwood Dale School, writer-in-residence, 1993; University of Massachusetts, visiting faculty in English, 1998; De Montfort University, Institute of Creative Technologies, faculty of humanities and research professor of new media, 2005-. Writer. **Publications:** Women at War, 1990; Correspondence (novel), 1993; (comp.) Elizabeth Robins, 1862-1952: A Bibliography, 1994; Water (novel), 1994; (ed.) Wild Woman: Contemporary Short Stories by Women Celebrating Women, 1994; (ed. with E.A. Cook and C. Wilcox) The Year of the Woman: Myths and Realities, 1994; (co-author) Creative Writing: A Handbook for Workshop Leaders, 1995; (ed. with Wilcox) Women and Elective Office: Past, Present, and Future, 1998; (ed. with Hoskin) The Noon Quilt, 1999; (with A. Blake and L. Gandhi) England through Colonial Eyes in Twentieth-Century Fiction, 2001; Essaying Virtuality, 2004; Hello World: Travels in Virtuality, 2004; Nature and Cyberspace: The Wild Surmise, 2012. Contributor to books and periodicals. **Address:** Faculty of Humanities, Institute of Creative Technologies, De Montfort University, The Gateway, Leicester, LE LE1 9BH, England. **Online address:** sue.thomas@dmu.ac.uk

THOMAS, Velma Maia. American (born United States), b. 1955. **Genres:** inspirational/Motivational Literature, History. **Career:** Black Holocaust Exhibit, creator and curator; Pan-African Orthodox Christian Church, minister.

Writer, historian and genealogist. **Publications:** Lest We Forget: The Passage from Africa to Slavery and Emancipation, 1997; Freedom's Children: The Journey from Emancipation into the Twentieth Century, 2000; No Man Can Hinder Me: The Journey from Slavery to Emancipation through Song, 2001; We Shall Not Be Moved: The Passage from the Great Migration to the Million Man March, 2002. **Address:** c/o Author Mail, Crown Publishing Group/Random House, 1745 Broadway, New York, NY 10019-4305, U.S.A. **Online address:** vmaiathomas@hotmail.com

THOMAS, Victoria. *See* **DEWEESE, Gene.**

THOMAS, Will. American (born United States), b. 1958. **Genres:** Novels, Mystery/Crime/Suspense. **Career:** Novelist, librarian and instructor. **Publications:** Some Danger Involved: A Novel, 2004; To Kingdom Come, 2005; The Limehouse Text, 2006; The Hellfire Conspiracy, 2007; The Black Hand: A Barker & Llewelyn Novel, 2008. Contributor to periodicals. **Address:** c/o Author Mail, Maria Carvainis, 1270 Ave. of the Americas, Ste. 2320, New York, NY 10020, U.S.A. **Online address:** feedback@willthomasauthor.com

THOMAS, William J. Canadian (born Canada), b. 1946. **Genres:** Humor/Satire, Young Adult Fiction, Animals/Pets. **Career:** Alive and Well, editor and feature writer; What's Up Niagara, editor; Canadian Broadcasting Corp., television writer. Humorist speaker. **Publications:** HUMOR: Malcolm and Me: Life in the Litterbox, 1993; Hey! Is That Guy Dead or Is He the Skip-: And Other Stories I Wish I'd Never Written, 1994; Guys: Not Real Bright-And Damn Proud of It!, 1996; Margaret and Me: All Humour Needs a Victim and Your Mother Should Come First!, 1998; Never Hitchhike on the Road Less Traveled, 2002; The Dog Rules: Damn Near Everything!, 2003; The Cat Rules Everything, Including the Dog, 2008; The True Story of Wainfleet. Contributor to periodicals. **Address:** RR 2, Port Colborne, ON L3K 5V4, Canada. **Online address:** williamjthomas@gmail.com

THOMAS-GRAHAM, Pamela (Borders). American (born United States), b. 1963. **Genres:** Mystery/Crime/Suspense. **Career:** Goldman, Sachs & Co., associate; McKinsey & Co., management consultant, partner, 1989-; CNBC.com, president, chief executive officer; CNBC Television, president and chief executive officer, 2001-05, chairman, CNBC Intl., director; Liz Claiborne, group president, 2005-; Harvard Law Review, editor; NBC, executive vice president; Idenix Pharmaceuticals Inc., director; Angelo, Gordon & Co., managing director; Credit Suisse Inc., chief talent, branding and communications officer, 2010-, senior executive. Writer. **Publications:** IVY LEAGUE MYSTERY SERIES: A Darker Shade of Crimson: An Ivy League Mystery, 1998; Blue Blood: An Ivy League Mystery, 1999; Orange Crushed: An Ivy League Mystery, 2004. Contributor to periodicals. **Address:** Credit Suisse Inc., 11 Madison Ave., New York, NY 10010-3629, U.S.A.

THOMASMA, Kenneth R. American (born United States), b. 1930. **Genres:** Children's Fiction, Young Adult Fiction, Novellas/Short Stories, History, Travel/Exploration. **Career:** Grand Rapids Public Schools, teacher administrator, 1953-77; Teton County Public Schools, teacher, 1977-87. Writer. **Publications:** Naya Nuki: Girl Who Ran, 1983 as Naya Nuki: Shoshoni Girl Who Ran, 1992; Soun Tetoken: Nez Perce Boy, 1984 as Soun Tetoken: Nez Perce Boy Tames a Stallion, 1989; Om-kas-toe of the Blackfeet, 1986; Om-kas-toe: Blackfeet Twin Captures an Elkdog, 1986; Kunu: Escape on the Missouri, 1989 as Kunu: Winnebago Boy Escapes, 1992; Pathki Nana: Kooentai Girl, 1991 as Pathki Nana: Kooentai Girl Solves a Mystery, 1991; Moho Wat: A Sheepeater Boy Attempts a Rescue, 1994; Amee-nah: Zuni Boy Runs the Race of His Life, 1995; The Truth about Sacajawea, 1997; Doe Sia: Bannock Girl and the Handcart Pioneers, 1999; Takini: Lakota Boy Alerts Sitting Bull, 2003. **Address:** Grandview Publishing, PO Box 2863, Jackson, WY 83001-2863, U.S.A. **Online address:** kenthomasma@blissnet.com

THOMASSIE, Tynia. American (born United States), b. 1959. **Genres:** Children's Fiction, Animals/Pets. **Career:** Home Box Office Inc., manager and program researcher, 1987-. Writer and lecturer. **Publications:** Feliciana Feydra LeRoux: A Cajun Tall Tale, 1995; Mi's Tutu, 1996; Feliciana Meets d'Loup Garou: A Cajun Tall Tale, 1998; Cajun Through and Through, 2000. **Address:** West Orange High School, 51 Conforti Ave., West Orange, NJ 07052, U.S.A. **Online address:** tthomassie@aol.com

THOMPSON, Alexander. American (born United States), b. 1972. **Genres:** History, Communications/Media. **Career:** Ohio State University, assistant professor, 2001-09, associate professor of political science, 2009-. Writer. **Pub-**

lications: Channels of Power: The UN Security Council and U.S. Statecraft in Iraq, 2009. Contributor to books and periodicals. **Address:** Department of Political Science, Ohio State University, 2140 Derby Hall, 154 N Oval Mall, Columbus, OH 43210, U.S.A. **Online address:** thompson.1191@osu.edu

THOMPSON, Augustine. American (born United States), b. 1954. **Genres:** Law. **Career:** Roman Catholic priest, 1985; University of Oregon, Department of Religious Studies, teacher, 1989-99, chair, 1995-99; University of Virginia, professor of religious studies and history, 2006-. **Publications:** Revival Preachers and Politics in Thirteenth-Century Italy: The Great Devotion of 1233, 1992; (trans.) Gratian, The Treatise on Laws: (Decretum DD. 1-20), 1993; Cities of God: The Religion of the Italian Communes, 1125-1325, 2005. Contributor to periodicals and journals. **Address:** Department of Religious Studies, University of Virginia, PO Box 400126, Charlottesville, VA 22904-4126, U.S.A. **Online address:** at3p@virginia.edu

THOMPSON, Charles Edward. *See* **THOMPSON, Charles P.**

THOMPSON, Charles P. (Charles Edward Thompson). American (born United States), b. 1933. **Genres:** Psychology, Biography. **Career:** University of Wyoming, assistant professor of psychology, 1962-65; Kansas State University, associate professor, 1965-72, professor of psychology, 1972-professor emeritus. Writer. **Publications:** (With T.M. Cowan and J. Frieman) Memory Search by a Memorist, 1993; (co-author) Autobiographical Memory: Remembering What and Remembering When, 1996; (ed.) Eyewitness Memory: Theoretical and Applied Perspectives, 1998; (ed.) Autobiographical memory: Theoretical and Applied Perspectives, 1998. **Address:** Department of Psychology, Kansas State University, 1100 Mid Campus Dr., Manhattan, KS 66506, U.S.A.

THOMPSON, Christina. American (born United States), b. 1959. **Genres:** Biography, Autobiography/Memoirs, History. **Career:** Harvard Review, editor. **Publications:** Come on Shore and We Will Kill and Eat You All: A New Zealand Story, 2008. Contributor to periodicals. **Address:** c/o Brettne Bloom, Kneerim & Williams at Fish & Richardson, Citigroup Ctr., 153 E 53rd St. 52nd Fl., New York, NY 10022-4633, U.S.A. **Online address:** christina@comeonshore.com

THOMPSON, Chuck. American (born United States) **Genres:** History, Theatre, Travel/Exploration. **Career:** Travelocity magazine, inaugural editor-in-chief; American Way, senior travel editor, through 1997, contributing editor. Alaska House of Representatives, ESL instructor, disc jockey, assistant sergeant of arms. Journalist and travel writer. **Publications:** (ed.) The Fun Also Rises Travel Guide North America: The Most Fun Places to Be at the Right Time, 1999; The 25 Best World War II Sites: Pacific Theater: The Ultimate Traveler's Guide to Battlefields, Monuments and Museums, 2002; (ed.) The Fun Seeker's North America: The Ultimate Travel Guide to the Most Fun Events & Destinations, 2nd ed., 2003; The 25 Best World War II Sites: European Theater: The Ultimate Traveler's Guide to Battlefields, Monuments and Museums, 2004, 2nd ed., 2007; Smile When You're Lying: Confessions of a Rogue Travel Writer, 2007. Contributor to periodicals. **Online address:** chuckthompsonbooks@gmail.com

THOMPSON, Claudia G(reig). American (born United States), b. 1953. **Genres:** Environmental Sciences/Ecology, Politics/Government, Art/Art History, Photography. **Career:** U.S. House of Representatives, congressional staff, 1975; high school teacher of sciences, natural history, and the arts, 1975-77; graphic designer, 1979-84; Claudia Thompson Consulting, founding principal, 1986-, operations manager, executive director, program director; Harvard University, John F. Kennedy School of Government, teaching fellow, 1996-98. Writer. **Publications:** Pneuma, 1985; Crosscurrents, 1985; Recycled Papers: The Essential Guide, 1992. **Address:** Claudia Thompson Consulting, 206 Lakeview Ave., Cambridge, MA 02138, U.S.A.

THOMPSON, Damian. British (born England), b. 1962?. **Genres:** History, Theology/Religion. **Career:** Catholic Herald, editor-in-chief; Scottish Catholic Observer, editor-in-chief; London Telegraph, editor and leader writer; Counterknowledge.com, editor-in-chief. **Publications:** The End of Time: Faith and Fear in the Shadow of the Millennium, 1996; (ed.) Loose Canon: A Portrait of Brian Brindley, 2004; Waiting for Antichrist: Charisma and Apocalypse in a Pentecostal Church, 2005; Counterknowledge: How We Surrendered to Conspiracy Theories, Quack Medicine, Bogus Science, and Fake History, 2008; Books Make a Home: Elegant Ideas for Storing and Displaying Books,

2011. **Address:** Ryland Peters & Small, 20-21 Jockey's Fields, London, GL WC1R 4BW, England. **Online address:** damian.thompson@telegraph.co.uk

THOMPSON, David C. American (born United States), b. 1979. **Genres:** Information Science/Computers, Technology. **Career:** Reputation.com Inc. (formerly ReputationDefender), general counsel and chief privacy officer; Munger Tolles & Olson LLP, corporate associate. Writer. **Publications:** (With M. Fertik) Wild West 2.0: How to Protect and Restore Your Online Reputation on the Untamed Social Frontier, 2010. Contributor to books. **Address:** Reputation.com Inc., Bldg. C, 2688 Middlefield Rd., Redwood City, CA 94063, U.S.A. **Online address:** david.c.thompson@gmail.com

THOMPSON, Deanna A. American (born United States), b. 1966. **Genres:** Theology/Religion. **Career:** Hamline University, professor of religion. Writer, theologian and educator. **Publications:** Crossing the Divide: Luther, Feminism and the Cross, 2004. **Address:** Hamline University, 1536 Hewitt Ave., St. Paul, MN 55104-1284, U.S.A.

THOMPSON, Donald N. (Donald Neil Thompson). Canadian (born Canada), b. 1939?. **Genres:** Economics, Marketing, Young Adult Non-fiction. **Career:** University of Alberta, associate professor, 1967; Harvard Business School, visiting professor, 1971-72; York University, professor of administrative studies, 1973-, Nabisco Brands Professor of Marketing and Strategy, 1992-; London School of Economics, visiting professor, 1978-79; Bilkent University, visiting professor, 2003-06; University College, visiting professor, 2007-08. Writer. **Publications:** NONFICTION: Franchise Operations and Antitrust, 1971; The Economics of Environmental Protection, 1973; (ed. with D.S.R. Leighton) Canadian Marketing: Problems and Prospects, 1973; (ed.) Problems in Canadian Marketing, 1977; (with D.J. Lecraw) Conglomerate Mergers in Canada, 1978; (ed.) Macromarketing: A Canadian Perspective, 1980; Challenges in Turkish Marketing, 2007; The $12 Million Stuffed Shark: The Curious Economics of Contemporary Art, 2008. **Address:** Lavin Agency Speaker's Bureau, 222 3rd St., Ste. 1130, Cambridge, MA 02142-1188, U.S.A. **Online address:** dthompson@schulich.yorku.ca

THOMPSON, Donald Neil. *See* **THOMPSON, Donald N.**

THOMPSON, E(rnest) V(ictor). British (born England), b. 1931. **Genres:** Novellas/Short Stories, Romance/Historical, Transportation. **Career:** Royal Navy, telegraphist, 1947-56; Bristol City Police, police officer, 1956-63; B.O.A.C., security investigator, 1963-64; Civil Aviation, chief of security, 1964-70; Mayfair Hotel, chief of security, 1970-72; freelance writer, 1973-. **Publications:** HISTORICAL ROMANCE NOVELS: Chase the Wind, 1977; Cornwall, 1978; Harvest of the Sun, 1979; The Music Makers, 1979; Ben Retallick, 1980; The Dream Traders, 1981; Singing Spears, 1982; The Restless Sea, 1983; Cry Once Alone, 1984 in US as Republic, 1985; Polrudden, 1985; The Stricken Land, 1986; Becky, 1988; God's Highlander, 1989; Lottie Trago, 1991; Cassie, 1991; Wychwood, 1991; Blue Dress Girl, 1992; Mistress of Polrudden, 1993; The Tolpuddle Woman, 1994; Ruddlemoor, 1995; Lewin's Mead, 1996; Moontide, 1996; Cast No Shadows, 1997; Mud Huts and Missionaries, 1997; Fires of Evening, 1998; Here, There and Yesterday, 1999; Somewhere a Bird is Singing, 1999; Homeland, 1999; Winds of Fortune, 2000; Seek a New Dawn, 2001. OTHER: Discovering Bodmin Moor, 1980; Discovering Cornwall's South Coast, 1982; Sea Stories of Devon, 1984; E.V. Thompson's West Country, 1986; Here, There and Yesterday, 2000; The Lost Years, 2002; Paths of Destiny, 2003; Tomorrow Is for Ever, 2004; The Vagrant King, 2005; Brothers in War, 2006; Though the Heavens May Fall, 2007; Though the Heavens May Fall, 2007; No Less Than the Journey, 2009; Churchyard and Hawke, 2009; Beyond the Storm, 2010. **Address:** Parc Franton, Pentewan, St. Austell, CW PL26 6EH, England. **Online address:** thompsoner@hotmail.com

THOMPSON, Francis George. Scottish (born Scotland), b. 1931. **Genres:** Engineering, Geography, Paranormal, Technology, History. **Career:** Associated Electrical Industries, technical author, 1957-59; Bruce Peebles Ltd., assistant publicity manager, 1959-63; Inverness Technical College, lecturer in electrical engineering, 1963-77; Sruth Newspaper, co-editor, 1966-70; Lews Castle College, senior lecturer, 1977-, now retired. **Publications:** History of Chatsworth, Being a Supplement to the Sixth Duke of Devnoshire's Handbook, 1949; Chatsworth, a Short History with a Tour of the House and Gardens, 1951; Electrical Installation and Workshop Technology, 3 vols., 1968-69, 1987; Problems in Electrical Installation: Craft, Theory and Practice, 1968; Harris and Lewis: Outer Hebrides, 1968, rev. ed., 1973; Harris

Tweed: The Story of a Hebridean Industry, 1969; Our Community at Work, 1969; St. Kilda and Other Hebridean Outliers, 1970; Highland Smugglers, 1972; Highland Waterway: The Caledonian Canal, 1972; The Ghosts, Spirits and Spectres of Scotland, 1973; (ed.) Highland Ways and Byways, 1973; The Highlands and Islands, 1974; The Uists and Barra, 1974, 2nd ed., 1999; Void-Air Aite Falamh: A Poem Sequence from The Memory-Books of Donald MacLeod on the Highland Clearances, 1975; Victorian and Edwardian Highlands from Old Photographs, 1976; Supernatural Highlands, 1976; Murder and Mystery in the Highlands, 1977; Scottish Bestiary: The Lore and Literature of Scottish Beasts, 1978; The Highlands and Islands Advisory Panel: A Review of Its Activities and Influence, 1946-64, 1979; Portrait of the Spey, 1979; The National Mod, 1979; Crofting Years, 1984; Shell Guide to Northern Scotland and the Islands, 1987; The Scottish Yules, 1987; The Western Isles of Scotland, 1988; Discovering Speyside, 1990; Lewis & Harris, 1999. **Address:** c/o Am Fasgadh, 5 Rathad na Muilne, Stornoway, Isle of Lewis, WI HS1 2TZ, Scotland.

THOMPSON, Gabriel. American (born United States), b. 1979?. **Genres:** Business/Trade/Industry. **Career:** Freelance journalist and writer. **Publications:** Calling All Radicals: How Grassroots Organizers Can Save Our Democracy, 2007; There's No José Here: Following the Hidden Lives of Mexican Immigrants, 2007; Working in the Shadows: A Year of Doing the Jobs (Most) Americans Won't Do, 2010. Contributor to periodicals. **Address:** Brooklyn, NY , U.S.A. **Online address:** thompson.gabriel@gmail.com

THOMPSON, Gregory Lee. American (born United States), b. 1946. **Genres:** Transportation, Industrial Relations. **Career:** Edmonton Transit System, transit planner, 1970-72; Canadian Transport Commission, Research Branch, senior systems analyst, 1972-73; City Planning Department, Berkeley Coordinated Transit Development Project, project coordinator, 1973-74; Integrated Planning Office and Department of Transportation, senior transportation planner, 1974-77; San Diego Metropolitan Transit Development Board, senior transportation planner, 1974-80; University of California, School of Social Science, teaching and research assistant, 1981-86; Hagley Museum and Library, advanced research fellow, 1987-88; Florida State University, Department of Urban and Regional Planning, assistant professor, 1988-94, associate professor, 1994-2003, professor, 2003-, Doctoral Program, director, 1999-2006. Writer. **Publications:** The Passenger Train in the Motor Age: California's Rail and Bus Industries, 1910-1941, 1993. **Address:** Department of Urban and Regional Planning, Florida State University, 330 Bellamy Bldg., Tallahassee, FL 32306-2280, U.S.A. **Online address:** gthompsn@coss.fsu.edu

THOMPSON, Harry F. American (born United States), b. 1953. **Genres:** Humanities. **Career:** University of Rochester, instructor, 1980-81; Winthrop College, instructor, 1981-82; Augustana College, Center for Western Studies, director of research collections and publications, 1984-2009, instructor, 1984-87, executive director, 2009-; University of Nebraska, Center for Great Plains Studies, associate fellow. Writer. **Publications:** (Ed.) The Archives and Manuscripts Collections of the Center for Western Studies, 1984; Guide to the Archives of the South Dakota Conference of the United Church of Christ, Center for Western Studies, 1986; (co-ed.) A Common Land, a Diverse People: Ethnic Identity on the Prairie Plains, 1987; Guide to Collections Relating to South Dakota Norwegian-Americans, 1991; (ed.) Impressions of Tribal Life, 2007; (ed.) A New South Dakota History, 2005, 2nd ed., 2009. Contributor to periodicals. **Address:** Center for Western Studies, Augustana College, 2001 S Summit Ave., Sioux Falls, SD 57197, U.S.A. **Online address:** harry.thompson@augie.edu

THOMPSON, Helen M. American (born United States), b. 1950. **Genres:** Librarianship, Education. **Career:** Library media specialist, 1973-74; language arts teacher and library media specialist, 1975-76; Haut Gap Middle School, library media specialist, 1994-. Writer. **Publications:** (With S.A. Henley) Fostering Information Literacy: Connecting National Standards, Goals 2000, and the SCANS Report, 2000. Contributor to periodicals. **Address:** Haut Gap Middle School, 1861 Bohicket Rd., Johns Island, SC 29455-3303, U.S.A. **Online address:** thompsonh@charleston.net

THOMPSON, Janet A(nn). American/Panamanian (born Panama), b. 1944. **Genres:** History, Psychology, Women's Studies And Issues. **Career:** Ohio Historical Society, Archives-Library Division, reference librarian, 1984-85; University of New Mexico, assistant head of special collections, 1986-88; Southwest Texas State University, assistant professor, 1988-90; Tallahassee Community College, professor of history, 1990-; University of Cincinnati, Department of British and European History, faculty. Writer. **Publications:** Wives, Widows, Witches & Bitches: Women in Seventeenth-Century Devon (history), 1993. Contributor of articles to periodicals. Works appear in anthologies. **Address:** Department of History, Tallahassee Community College, 444 Appleyard Dr., Tallahassee, FL 32304-2815, U.S.A. **Online address:** thompsja@tcc.fl.edu

THOMPSON, Jean. American (born United States), b. 1950. **Genres:** Novels, Novellas/Short Stories. **Career:** University of Illinois, professor of creative writing and rhetoric, 1973-2004, professor emeritus of English, 2004-; Reed College, teacher of creative writing; Northwestern University, teacher of creative writing. Writer. **Publications:** The Gasoline Wars: Stories, 1979; My Wisdom: A Novel, 1982; Little Face and Other Stories, 1984; The Woman Driver, 1985; Who Do You Love: Stories, 1999; Wide Blue Yonder: A Novel, 2002; City Boy: A Novel, 2004; Throw Like A Girl: Stories, 2007; Do Not Deny Me: Stories, 2009; The Year We Left Home, 2011. Contributor to periodicals. **Address:** Department of English, University of Illinois, Rm. 337, 608 S Wright St., Urbana, IL 61801, U.S.A. **Online address:** jlthomp@uiuc.edu

THOMPSON, Jerry Don. American (born United States), b. 1942. **Genres:** History, Writing/Journalism. **Career:** Menaul High School, teacher, 1965-66; University of New Mexico, Department of History, graduate assistant, 1966-68; Laredo Junior College, instructor, 1968-78, Division of Behavioral and Social Sciences, chair, 1978-83, Honors Program, director, 1983-85; Laredo State University, associate professor, 1985-91; Texas A&M International University, professor, 1991-95, College of Arts and Humanities, faculty, 1995-2002, dean, regents professor, 2001-04. Writer. **Publications:** Colonel John Robert Baylor: Texas Indian Fighter and Confederate Soldier, 1971; Laredo: A Pictorial History, 1986; Mexican Texans in the Union Army, 1986; Henry Hopkins Sibley: Confederate General of the West, 1987 as Confederate General of the West: Henry Hopkins Sibley, 1996; (ed. and intro.) Westward Texans: The Civil War Journal of Private William Randolph Howell, 1990; (ed. and intro.) Westward the Texans, 1990; (intro. and contrib.) Morgan Wolfe Merrick, From Desert to Bayou: The Civil War Journal and Sketches of Morgan Wolfe Merrick, 1991; Desert Tiger: Captain Paddy Graydon and the Civil War in the Far Southwest, 1992; (ed. and intro.) Juan Cortina and the Texas-Mexico Frontier, 1859-1877, 1994; (ed. and intro.) George Wythe Baylor, Into the Far, Wild Country: True Tales of the Old Southwest, 1996; A Wild and Vivid Land: An Illustrated History of the South Texas Border, 1997; (ed. and intro.) Fifty Miles and a Fight: Major Samuel Peter Heintzelman's Journal of Texas and the Cortina War, 1998; (with A.J. McGraw and E. Garner) Campfires and Coal Dust on the Rio Grande: The Archaeology and History of the Laredo-Colombia Solidarity International Bridge Site, Nuevo Leon, Mexico & Webb County, Texas, 1998; Vaqueros in Blue & Gray, 2000; (ed. and intro.) Texas and New Mexico on the Eve of the Civil War: The Mansfield and Johnston Inspections, 1859-1861, 2001; Civil War in the Southwest: Recollections of the Sibley Brigade, 2001; Palo Alto Battlefield National Historic Site, 2001; (ed. and intro., with J.P. Wilson) Henry Hopkins Sibley, The Civil War in West Texas and New Mexico: The Lost Letterbook of Brigadier General Henry Hopkins Sibley, 2001; (with L.T. Jones III) Civil War and Revolution on the Rio Grande Frontier: A Narrative and Photographic History, 2004; Civil War to the Bloody End: The Life & Times of Major General Samuel P. Heintzelman, 2006; Cortina: Defending the Mexican Name in Texas, 2007; (ed. and intro.) New Mexico Territory during the Civil War: Wallen and Evans Inspection Reports, 1862-1863, 2008. **Address:** Texas A&M International University, LBVSC 324 E, 5201 University Blvd., Laredo, TX 78041-1900, U.S.A. **Online address:** jthompson@tamiu.edu

THOMPSON, Jewel Taylor. American (born United States), b. 1935. **Genres:** Music, Biography, Art/Art History. **Career:** Virginia State University, assistant professor of music, 1960-62; West Virginia State College, Institute, assistant professor of music, 1967-68; West Virginia Institute of Technology, assistant professor of music, 1968-72; City University of New York, Hunter College, adjunct lecturer, 1972-75, adjunct assistant professor, 1975-85, assistant professor, 1985-91, associate professor, 1992-96, professor of music, 1996-. Writer. **Publications:** Samuel Coleridge-Taylor: The Development of his Compositional Style, 1994; (contrib.) International Dictionary of Black Composers, 1999. **Address:** Department of Music, Hunter College, City University of New York, Rm. 400e Hunter N, 695 Park Ave., New York, NY 10021, U.S.A. **Online address:** jewel.thompson@hunter.cuny.edu

THOMPSON, Judith (Clare Francesca). Canadian (born Canada), b. 1954. **Genres:** Plays/Screenplays, Film. **Career:** University of Guelph, professor of drama; playwright, 1979-80. **Publications:** The Crackwalker: A Play, 1981; The Other Side of the Dark: Four Plays, 1989; Lion in the Streets, 1992; Sled: A Play, 1997; Perfect Pie, 2000; Habitat, 2001; Late 20th Century Plays, 1980-2000, 2002; (comp. and ed.) She Speaks: Monologues for Women, 2004, rev. ed. 2006; Capture Me, 2006; Enoch Arden in the Hope Shelter, 2006; Palace of the End, 2007. (co-auth.) Body & Soul, 2011. Contributor to periodicals. **Address:** 16 Yarmouth Rd., Toronto, ON MOG 1W6, Canada.

THOMPSON, Kate. British (born England), b. 1956?. **Genres:** Children's Fiction, Young Adult Fiction, Novels, Poetry. **Career:** Writer. **Publications:** There is Something, 1992; Down among the Gods, 1997; Thin Air, 1999; An Act of Worship, 2000; The Alchemist's Apprentice, 2001; The Beguilers, 2001. SWITCHERS TRILOGY: Switchers, 1997; Midnight's Choice, 1998; Wild Blood, 1999; The Switchers Trilogy, 2004. MISSING LINK TRILOGY: The Missing Link, 2000 as Fourth World, 2005; Only Human, 2001; Origins, 2003; Annan Water, 2004; The New Policeman, 2005; The Fourth Horseman, 2006; The Last of the High Kings, 2007; Creature of the Night, 2008; Highway Robbery, 2008; The White Horse Trick, 2009; Wanted!, 2009; Most Wanted, 2010. **Address:** c/o Sophie Hicks, Ed Victor Ltd., 6 Bayley St., Bedford Sq., London, WC1B 3HE, United Kingdom.

THOMPSON, Kenneth W(infred). American (born United States), b. 1921. **Genres:** International Relations/Current Affairs, Philosophy, Business/Trade/Industry, Economics. **Career:** University of Chicago, lecturer in social sciences, 1948, assistant professor, 1951-53; Northwestern University, instructor and assistant professor, 1948-51, associate professor, 1953-55; The Rockefeller Foundation, consultant in international relations, 1953-55, assistant director for social sciences, 1955-57, associate director for social sciences, 1957-60, director for social sciences, 1960-61, vice president, 1961-74; Twelve Donor Agency Review of Higher Education in Africa, Asia and Latin America, director, 1974-75; Institute for the Study of World Politics, director, 1974-; University of Virginia, Commonwealth professor of government and foreign affairs, 1975-78, White Burkett Miller professor of government and foreign affairs, 1978-86, professor of religious studies, 1978-, J. Wilson Newman professor of government and foreign affairs, 1986-, White Burkett Miller Center of Public Affairs, director, 1978-98, Forum Program, head, 1998-2004, Woodrow Wilson Department of Politics, professor emeritus, Miller Center of Public Affairs, director emeritus. Writer. **Publications:** (With K. de Schweinitz) Man and Modern Society: Conflict and Choice in the Industrial Era, 1953; Ethics and National Purpose, 1957; Christian Ethics and the Dilemmas of Foreign Policy, 1959; Political Realism and the Crisis of World Politics: An American Approach to Foreign Policy, 1960; (with I.D. Duchacek) Conflict and Cooperation among Nations, 1960; America Diplomacy and Emergent Patterns, 1962; The Moral Issue in Statecraft: Twentieth-Century Approaches and Problems, 1966; (with H.J. Morgenthau and J.C. Brauer) U.S. Policy in the Far East: Ideology, Religion and Superstition, 1968; Foreign Assistance: A View from the Private Sector, 1972; Higher Education for National Development, 1972; Reconstituting the Human Community, 1972; Understanding World Politics, 1975; (with J. Rosenau and G. Boyd) World Politics, 1976; Interpreters and Critics of the Cold War, 1978; Ethics, Functionalism and Power in International Politics: Crisis in Values, 1979; Masters of International Thought, 1980; The Moral Imperatives of Human Rights: A World Survey, 1980; Morality and Foreign Policy, 1980; Cold War Theories, vol. I: World Polarization, 1943-53, 1981; The President and the Public Philosophy, 1981; American Diplomacy and Emergent Patterns, 1983; Winston Churchill's World-View, 1983; Toynbee's Philosophy of History and Politics, 1985; Moralism and Morality in Politics and Diplomacy, 1985; Theory and Practice in International Relations, 1987; Traditions and Values in Politics and Diplomacy, 1989; Fathers of International Thought: The Legacy of Political Theory, 1994; Schools of Thought in International Relations: Interpreters, Issues, and Morality, 1996; (with H.J. Morgenthau and W.D. Clinton) Politics among Nations: The Struggle for Power and Peace, 7th ed., 2006. EDITOR: (with H.J. Morgenthau) Principles and Problems of International Politics: Selected Readings, 1950, rev. ed., 1982; (with J.E. Black and contrib.) Foreign Policies in a World of Change, 1963; (with B.R. Fogel) Higher Education and Social Change: Promising Experiments in Developing Countries, vol. I-II, 1976; (with R.J. Myers) Truth and Tragedy: A Tribute to Hans J. Morgenthau, 1977; (with L.J. Halle) Foreign Policy and the Democratic Process: The Geneva Papers, 1978; (with H. Butterfield) The Ethics of History and Politics, 1979; Papers on Presidential Disability and the Twenty-fifth Amendment by Six Medical, Legal and Political Authorities, 1988; Presidency and a World in

Change, 1991; Negotiating Arms Control: Missed Opportunities and Limited Successes, 1991; Twenty Years of Papers On The Presidency, 1995; Korea, A World In Change, 1996; NATO And The Changing World Order: An Appraisal By Scholars and Policymakers, 1996. SERIES EDITOR: The Virginia Papers on the Presidency: The White Burkett Miller Center Forums, vol. I-XXVII, 1979-96; American Values Projected Abroad, vol. I-XX, 1980-83; The American Presidency: Principles and Problems, vol. I-III, 1982-84; The Credibility of Institutions, Policies and Leadership, vol. I-XX, 1983-86; The Presidential Nominating Process, vol. I-IV, 1983-86; The Presidency and the Press, vol. I-VI, 1983-86; Portraits of American Presidents, vol. I-XI, 1983-92; Ethics and Foreign Policy, vol. I-II, 1984-85; The American Presidency: Perspectives from Abroad, vol. I-II, 1986; Presidential Transitions and Foreign Policy, vol. I-IX, 1986-95; The Presidency and Science Advising, vol. I-VII, 1986-88; Rhetoric and Political Discourse, vol. I-XX, 1987-88; Arms Control, vol. I-XIII, 1987-88; The Presidency and Arms Control, vol. I-III, 1990-96; Statesmen Who Were Never President, 1996; The Budget Deficit and the National Debt, 1997; Conflict and Its Resolution in Contemporary Africa, 1997; The Presidency and Foreign Policy, 1997; The Presidency and Governance in Poland: Yesterday and Today, 1997; The Reagan Presidency: Ten Intimate Perspectives of Ronald Reagan, 1997; The Bush Presidency: Ten Intimate Perspectives of George Bush, 2 vols., 1997-98; China, Taiwan, Japan, the United States, and the World, 1997; (with L. Graybill) Africa's Second Wave of Freedom: Development, Democracy, and Rights, 1998; NATO Expansion, 1998. Contributor of articles to periodicals. **Address:** Miller Center of Public Affairs, University of Virginia, PO Box 400406, Charlottesville, VA 22904-4406, U.S.A. **Online address:** kwt8b@virginia.edu

THOMPSON, Marilyn W. American (born United States), b. 1952. **Genres:** Biography, Politics/Government, Engineering, Technology. **Career:** Columbia Record, governmental affairs and investigative reporter; Philadelphis Daily News, general assignment and investigative reporter, 1982-86; New York Daily News, 1986-87, general assignment reporter, 1987-88, assistant city editor for investigations, 1988-90, Washington bureau correspondent; Washington Post, reporter, 1990-91, government reporter, 1991-92, metropolitan projects editor, 1992-99, deputy national editor for domestic coverage and then investigations editor, 1999-2003, assistant managing editor for investigations, accountability editor; Lexington Herald-Leader, executive editor, 2003-06. **Publications:** Feeding the Beast: How Wedtech Became the Most Corrupt Little Company in America, 1990; (with J. Bass) Ol' Strom: An Unauthorized Biography of Strom Thurmond, 1998; The Killer Strain: Anthrax and a Government Exposed, 2003; (with J. Bass) Strom: The Complicated Personal and Political Life of Strom Thurmond, 2005. **Address:** The Washington Post, 1150 15th St. NW, Washington, DC 20071, U.S.A.

THOMPSON, Mark. American (born United States), b. 1952. **Genres:** Gay And Lesbian Issues. **Career:** Advocate, senior editor, 1975-94. **Publications:** Gay Spirit: Myth and Meaning, 1987; (ed.) Leatherfolk: Radical Sex, People, Politics and Practice, 1991, 2nd ed., 2001; Gay Soul: Finding the Heart of Gay Spirit and Nature with Sixteen Writers, Healers, Teachers, Visionaries, 1994; (ed.) Long Road to Freedom: The Advocate History of the Gay and Lesbian Movement, 1994; Gay Body: A Journey through Shadow to Self, 1997; The White War: Life and Death on the Italian Front, 1915-1919, 2008; Advocate Days and Other Stories, 2009; Motocross and Off-Road Motorcycle Setup Guide (Motorbooks Workshop), 2010; (ed. with D. Kilhefner, R. Neely and B. Young) Dancing in the Moonlight, 2010; (ed. with R. Neely and B. Young) The Fire in Moonlight: Stories from the Radical Faeries: 1975-2010, 2011. Contributor to periodicals. **Address:** c/o Author Mail, St. Martin's Press, 175 5th Ave., New York, NY 10010-7703, U.S.A. **Online address:** info@markthompsongayspirit.com

THOMPSON, Mark L. American (born United States), b. 1945. **Genres:** Business/Trade/Industry, Marine Sciences/Oceanography, Transportation, Young Adult Non-fiction. **Career:** Michigan House of Representatives, state representative, 1973-74; Lake Superior State College, instructor, 1979-81; Western Michigan University, regional consultant and education director, 1981-83; Great Lakes Maritime Academy, assistant to superintendent, 1983-85; U.S. Maritime Administration, marine consultant, 1984-87; Ford Motor Co., marine consultant, 1984-87; Cleveland-Cliffs Iron Co., marine consultant, 1984-87; Interlake Steamship Co., merchant seaman, 1989-94; USS Great Lakes Fleet, merchant marine officer, 1995-. Writer. **Publications:** Steamboats and Sailors of the Great Lakes, 1991; Queen of the Lakes, 1994; A Sailor's Logbook: A Season Aboard Great Lakes Freighters, 1999; Graveyard of the Lakes, 2000. Contributor to maritime periodicals. **Address:** Wayne

State University Press, The Leonard N. Simons Bldg., 4809 Woodward Ave., Detroit, MI 48201-1309, U.S.A. **Online address:** mltsailor@george.lhi.net

THOMPSON, Nancy Robards. (Elizabeth Robards). American (born United States), b. 1964?. **Genres:** Young Adult Fiction. **Career:** Writer. **Publications:** Reinventing Olivia, 2003; Out with the Old, in with the New, 2005; (as Elizabeth Robards) With Violets, 2005; Sisters, 2006; True Confessions of the Stratford Park PTA, 2006; What Happens in Paris: (Stays in Paris?), 2006; Beauty Shop Tales, 2007; Accidental Princess, 2008; Accidental Cinderella, 2009; An Angel in Provence, 2009; The Family They Chose, 2010. **Address:** FL , U.S.A. **Online address:** nancy@nancyrobardsthompson.com

THOMPSON, Nicholas. American (born United States), b. 1975. **Genres:** History. **Career:** Fox News, commentator; MSNBC, commentator; CNBC, commentator; American Broadcasting Companies Inc. (ABC), commentator; Columbia Broadcasting System Inc. (CBS), commentator; National Public Radio (NPR), commentator; Wired, senior editor; Washington Monthly, editor; Legal Affairs, editor; Bloomberg Television, contributing editor. Journalist and broadcaster. **Publications:** (With S. Thompson) The Baobab and the Mango Tree: Lessons about Development: African and Asian Contrasts, 2000; The Hawk and the Dove: Paul Nitze, George Kennan, and the History of the Cold War, 2009. Contributor to periodicals and newspapers. **Address:** U.S.A. **Online address:** thompson@newamerica.net

THOMPSON, Richard. Canadian (born Canada), b. 1951. **Genres:** Children's Fiction, Illustrations, Literary Criticism And History. **Career:** Preschool teacher, 1980-89. Writer. **Publications:** SELF-ILLUSTRATED: Draw-and-Tell, 1988; Frog's Riddle: And Other Draw-and-Tell Stories, 1990. OTHERS: I Have to See This, 1988; The Last Story, the First Story, 1988; Effie's Bath, 1989; Gurgle, Bubble, Splash, 1989; Foo, 1990, 2nd ed., 2000; Jenny's Neighbours, 1990; Zoe and the Mysterious X, 1990; Sky Full of Babies, 1990; Jesse on the Night Train, 1990; Maggee and the Lake Minder, 1991; The Gas Tank of My Heart, 1991; Jill and the Jogero, 1992; Tell Me One Good Thing, 1992; Thistle Broth, 1992; Don't Be Scared, Eleven, 1993; Who, 1993; The Ice Cream Bucket Effect, 1993; Cold Night, Brittle Light, 1994; Fishes in the Ocean, 1998; Then and Now, 1999; There is Music in a Pussycat, 1999; Fishes in the Ocean, 2000; The Follower, 2000; (with M. Spicer) We'll All Go Sailing, 2000; (with M. Spicer) We'll All Go Flying, 2002; The Night Walker, 2002; (with M. Spicer) We'll All Go Exploring, 2003; When They are Up, 2003; Zoo I.Q., forthcoming. **Address:** Fitzhenry & Whiteside Ltd., 195 Allstate Pkwy., Markham, ON L3R 4T8, Canada.

THOMPSON, Richard A. American (born United States), b. 1942?. **Genres:** Novels. **Career:** Writer. **Publications:** NOVELS: Fiddle Game, 2008; Frag Box, 2009. **Address:** St. Paul, MN , U.S.A. **Online address:** rich@fiddlegame.com

THOMPSON, Richard A. American (born United States), b. 1942. **Genres:** Communications/Media, Technology. **Career:** University of Pittsburgh, School of Information Sciences, professor of telecommunications, 1989-, Telecommunications Program, chair; Bell Labs, staff; Litton Industries, staff. Writer. **Publications:** Telephone Switching Systems, 2000; (co-author) The Physical Layer of Communications Systems, 2006. **Address:** School of Information Sciences, University of Pittsburgh, 717A IS Bldg., 135 N Bellefield Ave., Pittsburgh, PA 15260, U.S.A. **Online address:** rat@tele.pitt.edu

THOMPSON, Robert Bruce. New Zealander (born New Zealand), b. 1920. **Genres:** Poetry, Young Adult Fiction. **Career:** Image Magazine, editor, 1958-61; industrial chemist, now retired. Writer. **Publications:** Cast on the Doting Sea, 1955; (co-ed.) Poems by Several Hands, 1976; Northern Aspects, 1976. **Address:** Kawakawa, PO Box 79, Bay of Islands, Northland, 9479, New Zealand.

THOMPSON, Robert Farris. American (born United States), b. 1932. **Genres:** Art/Art History, History, Biography, Autobiography/Memoirs. **Career:** Yale University, acting instructor, 1964-65, instructor, 1965-66, assistant professor, 1966-69, associate professor, 1969-75, professor of art history, 1975-, Colonel John Trumbull professor of the history of art; University of California, Museum of Ethnic Arts, visiting curator, 1970. Writer. **Publications:** (Trans.) F. da Costa, The Antiquity of the Art of Painting, 1967; Black Gods and Kings: Yoruba Art at UCLA, 1971; African Art in Motion: Icon and Art in the Collection of Katerine Coryton White, 1974; The Grand Detroit N'Kondi, 1978; (with J. Cornet) The Four Moments of the Sun: Kongo

Art in Two Worlds, 1981; Flash of the Spirit: African and Afro-American Art and Philosophy, 1983; Painting from a Single Heart: Preliminary Remarks on Bark-Cloth Designs of the Mbute Women of Haut-Zaire, 1983; Soundings: An Exhibition of Sculpture by Ed Love, 1986; Rediscovered Masterpieces, 1987; Pygmées, 1990; (with S. Bahuchet) Pygmees': Peintures sur ecorce battue des mbuti (Haut-Zaire), 1991; Face of the Gods, 1993; (with G. Meurant) Mbuti Design, 1996; Resonance from the Past: African Sculpture from the New Orleans Museum of Art, 2005; Tango: The Art History of Love, 2005; Aesthetic of the Cool: Afro-Atlantic Art and Music, 2008. **Address:** 100 York St., Apt. 9N, New Haven, CT 06511, U.S.A. **Online address:** robert.thompson@yale.edu

THOMPSON, Thomas L. Danish/American (born United States), b. 1939. **Genres:** Anthropology/Ethnology, Archaeology/Antiquities, Intellectual History, Theology/Religion, History, Social Sciences. **Career:** University of Dayton, instructor of theology, 1964-65; University of Detroit, assistant professor of theology, 1967-69; University of Tubingen, research associate, 1969-77; handyman and housepainter, 1977-87; Brady High School, teacher, 1980-82; Ecole Biblique, annual professor of Old Testament, 1985, visiting professor, 1985-86; Lawrence University, associate professor of religion, 1988-89; Marquette University, associate professor of theology, 1989-93; University of Copenhagen, professor and chair of Old Testament, 1993-2009, professor emeritus, 2009-. Writer. **Publications:** The Historicity of the Patriarchal Narratives: The Quest for the Historical Abraham, 1974; The Settlement of Sinai and the Negev in the Bronze Age, 1975; The Settlement of Palestine in the Bronze Age, 1979; The Origin Tradition of Ancient Israel, 1987; (with F.J. Gonçalves and J.M. van Cangh) Toponymie palestinienne: plaine de St Jean d'Acre et corridor de Jérusalem, 1988; Early History of the Israelite People: From the Written and Archaeological Sources, 1992; (ed. with F.H. Cryer) Qumran between the Old and New Testaments, 1998; The Bible in History: How Writers Create a Past, 1999; Mythic Past: Biblical Archaeology and the Myth of Israel, 1999; (ed.) Jerusalem in Ancient History and Tradition, 2003; The Messiah Myth: The Near Eastern Background of Jesus and David, 2005; (ed. with T. Verenna) Is This Not The Carpenter?, 2011. Contributor of articles. **Address:** University of Copenhagen, Norregade 10, PO Box 2177, Copenhagen, DK-1017, Denmark. **Online address:** tlt@teol.ku.dk

THOMPSON, Tracy. American (born United States), b. 1955. **Genres:** Medicine/Health, Adult Non-fiction, Psychology. **Career:** Constitution, investigative reporter and staff writer, 1981-89; Washington Post, investigative reporter and staff writer, 1989-96, part-time writer; Tracy Thompson Enterprises, freelance writer, 1996-. **Publications:** The Beast: A Reckoning with Depression, 1995; The Beast: A Journey Through Depression, 1996; The Ghost in the House: Motherhood, Raising Children, and Struggling with Depression, 2006. Works appear in anthologies. Contributor to periodicals. **Address:** c/o Beth Vesel, The Beth Vesel Literary Agency, 80 5th Ave., Ste. 1101, New York, NY 10011-8011, U.S.A. **Online address:** tracythompson@fastmail.fm

THOMPSON, Vicki Lewis. Also writes as Corey Keaton, Cory Kenyon. American (born United States) **Genres:** Novels. **Career:** Full-time writer, 1984. Educator. **Publications:** Promise Me Sunshine, 1985; Impractical Passion, 1986; When Angels Dance, 1986; Butterflies in the Sun, 1987; As Time Goes By, 1987; Flip Side, 1988; Impulse, 1988; Be Mine Valentine, 1989; Full Coverage, 1989; Your Place or Mine, 1991; It Happened One Weekend, 1991; Anything Goes, 1992; Fools Rush In, 1993; The Bounty Hunter, 1994; Loverboy, 1994; The Drifter, 1995; The Lawman, 1995; The Trailblazer, 1995; Holding out for a Hero, 1996; The Heart Breaker, 1997; Operation Gigolo, 1998; Mr. Valentine, 1998; Pure Temptation, 1999; Bringing Up Baby New Year, 2000; The Colorado Kid, 2000; Two in the Saddle, 2000; Boone's Bounty, 2000; That's My Baby!, 2000; Notorious, 2001; Truly, Madly, Deeply, 2002; Nerd in Shining Armor, 2003; Drive Me Wild, 2003; After Hours, 2003; Old Enough to Know Better, 2004; (with S. Bond and J. Arnold) Fool for Love, 2004; Killer Cowboy Charm, 2004; The Nerd Who Loved Me, 2004; Tis the Season, 2004; Every Woman's Fantasy, 2004; (with K. O'Reilly) The Longest Night, 2004; (with L. Kelly) Reading between the Lines, 2004; Nerd Gone Wild, 2005; Gone with Nerd, 2005; Gone with the Nerd, 2005; Talking about Sex.., 2005; (with J.E. Leto and J. LaBrecque) Getting Real, 2005; Forever Mine, Valentine, 2006; Talk Nerdy to Me, 2006; Nerds Like It Hot, 2006; My Nerdy Valentine, 2007; Over Hexed, 2007; Wild & Hexy, 2008; (with J. Shalvis and R. Nelson) Better Naughty than Nice, 2009; Casual Hex, 2009; (with J. Lee and A. DeStefano) Winter Heat, 2009; Blonde with a Wand, 2010; Chick with a Charm: A Babes on Brooms Novel, 2010; Wanted!, 2010; (with N. Warren and D. Kelly) Racing Hearts,

2010; Claimed!, 2010; Ambushed!, 2010; Cupid Cats, 2010; A Werewolf in Manhattan, 2011; A Werewolf in the North Woods, 2011; Should've Been a Cowboy, 2011; Cowboy Up, 2011; Cowboys Like Us, 2011; Holiday Hideout, 2011; Merry Christmas, Baby, 2011; Werewolf in Seattle, 2012. AS CORY KENYON: Sheer Delight, 1986; Ruffled Feathers, 1986; Fortune Hunter, 1986; The Quintessential Woman, 1987; Fancy Footwork, 1987. AS COREY KEATON: The Nesting Instinct, 1987. **Address:** Harlequin.com, PO Box 5190, Buffalo, NY 14240-5190, U.S.A. **Online address:** vltauthor@aol.com

THOMPSON, Victoria. American (born United States), b. 1948?. **Genres:** Mystery/Crime/Suspense, Romance/Historical, Novels. **Career:** Novelists Inc., founding member and president; Pennwriters, co-founder and president; Romance Writers of America, director; New Jersey Romance Writers, co-founder and president; Penn State University, faculty; Seton Hill University, Master's Degree program, faculty. Writer. **Publications:** Texas Treasure, 1985; Texas Vixen, 1986; Texas Blonde, 1987; Texas Triumph, 1987; Angel Heart, 1988; Rogue's Lady, 1988; Beloved Outcast, 1989; Bold Texas Embrace, 1989; Fortune's Lady, 1989; Playing With Fire, 1990; Wild Texas Promise, 1990; Sweet Texas Surrender, 1991; Blazing Texas Nights, 1992; Wild Texas Wind, 1992; Winds of Promise, 1993; Winds of Destiny, 1994; Winds of Fortune, 1995; Cry Wolf, 1995; Winds of Fortune, 1995; Wings of Morning, 1996; From This Day Forward, 1997; Losing Alexandria: A Memoir, 1998; Reading Medieval Studies, 1999; Michael Patrick, 2000. GASLIGHT MYSTERY SERIES: Murder on Astor Place, 1999; Murder on St. Mark's Place, 2000; Murder on Gramercy Park, 2001; Murder on Washington Square, 2002; Murder on Mulberry Bend, 2003; Murder on Marble Row, 2004; Murder on Lenox Hill, 2005; Murder in Little Italy, 2006; Murder in Chinatown, 2007; Murder on Bank Street, 2008; Murder on Waverly Place, 2009; Murder on Lexington Avenue, 2010; Murder on Sisters Row, 2011; Murder on Fifth Avenue, 2012. **Address:** c/o Author Mail, Penguin Group, 375 Hudson St., New York, NY 10014, U.S.A. **Online address:** vestinpa@aol.com

THOMPSON, W. Grant. Canadian (born Canada), b. 1935. **Genres:** Medicine/Health. **Career:** Toronto General Hospital, junior intern, 1960-61; general practice of medicine, 1961-62; Montreal General Hospital, junior assistant resident to senior assistant resident in medicine, 1962-66, resident in gastroenterology, 1966-67; Vancouver General Hospital, assistant resident in pathology, 1964-65; Royal Postgraduate Medical School, Hammersmith Hospital, research fellow, 1967-68; University of Ottawa, lecturer, 1968-71, assistant professor, 1971-74, associate professor, 1974-79, professor of medicine, 1979-97, professor emeritus of medicine, 1997-; Ottawa Civic Hospital, physician, 1969-99, chief of division of gastroenterology, 1979-99, University of Bristol, fellow, 1977-78, visiting professor, 1994-95, professor emeritus of medicine, 1999-; Coeliac Ottawa, honorary adviser, 1980-86; Victoria University of Manchester, visiting professor, 1994-95; Proctor & Gamble, consultant; Roche Pharmaceuticals, consultant; U.S. National Institutes of Health, consultant. Writer. **Publications:** The Irritable Gut: Functional Disorders of the Alimentary Canal, 1979; Gut Reactions: Understanding Symptoms of the Digestive Tract, 1989; The Angry Gut: Coping with Colitis and Crohn's Disease, 1993; (co-author) Functional Gastrointestinal Disorders, 1994, 2nd ed., 2000; The Ulcer Story: The Authoritative Guide to Ulcers, Dyspepsia and Heartburn, 1996; (co-author) The Irritable Bowel, 1999, 2nd ed., 2003; (with B.B. Bolen) Breaking the Bonds of Irritable Bowel Syndrome: A Psychological Approach to Regaining Control of Your Life, 2000; Placebo Effect and Health: Combining Science and Compassionate Care, 2005; Understanding the Irritable Gut: The Functional Gastrointestinal Disorders, 2008; The Upper Gut, forthcoming. Contributor to journals. **Address:** University of Ottawa, 550 Cumberland St., Ottawa, ON K1N 6N5, Canada. **Online address:** wgthompson@rogers.com

THOMPSON, William Irwin. American (born United States), b. 1938. **Genres:** Novels, Poetry, History, Intellectual History, Essays, Cultural/Ethnic Topics. **Career:** Cornell University, teaching assistant of English, 1962-64; Massachusetts Institute of Technology, instructor of humanities, 1965-66, assistant professor of humanities, 1966-67, associate professor of humanities, 1968-; York University, associate professor of humanities, 1968-72, professor of humanities, 1973-; The Lindisfarne Association, founder and president, 1972-97; Syracuse University, visiting professor of religion, 1973-; University of Toronto, Saint Michael's College, visiting professor of Celtic studies, 1984-; University of Hawaii at Manoa, Department of Political Science, visiting professor of political science, 1985-; Western Behavioral Sciences Institute, adjunct faculty, 1987-; California Institute of Integral Studies, Rockefeller Faculty, 1993-95; Ross School, curriculum designer and consultant,

1995-2005. Writer. **Publications:** The Imagination of an Insurrection: Dublin, Easter 1916, 1967; At the Edge of History, 1971; Passages about Earth: An Exploration of the New Planetary Culture, 1974; Evil and World Order, 1976; Darkness and Scattered Light: Four Talks on the Future, 1978; The Time Falling Bodies Take to Light: Mythology, Sexuality and the Origins of Culture, 1981; From Nation to Emanation: Planetary Culture and World Governance, 1982; (contrib.) The Celtic Consciousness, 1982; Blue Jade from the Morning Star: An Essay and a Cycle of Poems on Quetzalcoatl, 1983; Pacific Shift, 1985; Islands Out of Time: A Memoir of the Last Days of Atlantis: A Metafiction, 1985; (ed.) Gaia, a Way of Knowing: Political Implications of the New Biology, 1987; Poems, Selections, Selected Poems, 1959-1989, 1989; Imaginary Landscape: Making Worlds of Myths and Science, 1989; (ed.) Gaia Two: Emergence: The New Science of Becoming, 1991; (with D. Spangler) Reimagination of the World: A Critique of the New Age, Science and Popular Culture, 1991; The American Replacement of Nature: The Everyday Acts and Outrageous Evolution of Economic Life, 1991; Coming into Being: Artifacts and Texts in the Evolution of Consciousness, 1996; Worlds Interpenetrating and Apart: Collected Poems 1959-1996, 1997; Transforming History: A Curriculum for Cultural Evolution, 2001; Self and Society: Studies in the Evolution of Consciousness, 2004; A Diary of Sorts and Streets, 2007; Transforming History: A New Curriculum for a Planetary Culture, 2009; Still Travels: Three Long Poems, 2009. Contributor to periodicals. **Address:** Imprint Academic, PO Box 7147, Charlottesville, VA 22906-7147, U.S.A.

THOMPSON, William J. American/New Zealander (born New Zealand), b. 1939?. **Genres:** Mathematics/Statistics, Sciences, Information Science/Computers. **Career:** University of North Carolina, faculty, 1969-, professor of physics, 1978-, professor emeritus; Computers in Physics, contributing and associate editor. **Publications:** Computing in Applied Science, 1984; (ed. with B.W. Carney and H.J. Karwowski) Primordial Nucleosynthesis, 1990; Computing for Scientists and Engineers: A Workbook of Analysis, Numerics and Applications, 1992; Angular Momentum: An Illustrated Guide to Rotational Symmetries for Physical Systems, 1994; Atlas for Computing Mathematical Functions: An Illustrated Guide for Practitioners with Programs in Fortran 90 and Mathematica, 1997; Atlas for Computing Mathematical Functions: An Illustrated Guide for Practitioners with Programs in C and Mathematica, 1997. **Address:** Department of Physics & Astronomy, University of North Carolina, CB 3255, Phillips Hall, Chapel Hill, NC 27599-3255, U.S.A. **Online address:** wmjthompson@msn.com

THOMPSON-CANNINO, Jennifer. American (born United States), b. 1962?. **Genres:** Autobiography/Memoirs, Mystery/Crime/Suspense. **Career:** Writer. **Publications:** (With R. Cotton and E. Torneo) Picking Cotton: Our Memoir of Injustice and Redemption, 2009. Contributor to magazines and journals. **Address:** St. Martin's Press, 175 5th Ave., New York, NY 10010, U.S.A. **Online address:** info@pickingcottonbook.com

THOMSON, Alistair. Australian (born Australia), b. 1960. **Genres:** Education, History. **Career:** Queenspark Books, administrator, 1986-89; Federation of Worker Writers and Community Publishers, national development worker, 1989-91; University of Sussex, lecturer, 1992-99, senior lecturer in continuing education, 1999-2007; Monash University, School of Philosophical, Historical and International Studies, Department of History, professor of history, 2007-, head; Institute for Public History, director. Writer. **Publications:** Anzac Memories: Living with the Legend, 1994; (ed. with P. Coare) Engaging with Difference: The Other in Adult Education, 1995; (ed. with M. Stuart) Through the Joy of Learning: Diary of a Thousand Adult Learners, 1996; (ed. with R. Perks) The Oral History Reader, 1998, 2nd ed., 2006; (with A.J. Hammerton) Ten Pound Poms: Australia's Invisible Migrants: A Life History of British Postwar Emigration to Australia, 2005. **Address:** School of Philosophical, Historical and, International Studies, Monash University, Bldg. 11, Menzies Bldg., 6th Fl., Clayton, VI 3800, Australia. **Online address:** alistair.thomson@monash.edu

THOMSON, Andrew. New Zealander/American (born United States), b. 1963?. **Genres:** Autobiography/Memoirs, Sex, History. **Career:** United Nations Medical Services Division, physician, 1993-2004. senate medical officer and writer. **Publications:** (With J.C. McLennan) On the Bunsen Flame Spectra of Metallic Vapours, 1917; Margaret Thatcher: The Woman Within, 1989; (with K. Cain and H. Postlewait) Emergency Sex and Other Desperate Measures: A True Story from Hell on Earth, 2004. **Address:** c/o Hyperion Editorial Deparment, Miramax Books, 77 W 66th St., 11th Fl., New York, NY 10023, U.S.A.

THOMSON, Celia. *See* **BRASWELL, Elizabeth.**

THOMSON, D(aisy) H(icks). British/Scottish (born Scotland), b. 1918?. **Genres:** Novels, Young Adult Fiction, Romance/Historical. **Career:** Bute County Council, assistant welfare officer, assistant registrar of births, 1939-45; writer, 1947-. **Publications:** Prelude to Love, 1963; To Love and Honour, 1964; Jealous Love, 1964; Love for a Stranger, 1966; A Truce for Love, 1967; Be Love Betrayed, 1967; Journey to Love, 1967; Be My Love, 1968; My Only Love, 1969; The Italian for Love, 1970; Summons to Love, 1971; Woman in Love, 1973; Hello My Love, 1974; Portrait of My Love, 1974; The Beginning of Love, 1975; The Summer of Love, 1976; My One and Only Love, 1976; From Solitude with Love, 1976; The Voice of Love, 1977; Myrtle for My Love, 1977; A Time for Love, 1977; In Love, in Vienna, 1978; Suddenly It Was Love, 1978; A Nightingale for Love, 1978; Love at Leisure, 1979; The Face of Love, 1979; The Web of Love, 1979; The Island of Love, 1980; I Love Your Julie, 1980; To Love and Be Wise, 1980; The Eve of Love, 1981; The Talisman of Love, 1982; Kiss Your Love Again, 1983; Inheritance of Love, 1983; The Colour of Love, 1983; Champagne for My Love, 1984; Quicksands of Love, 1984; Never Doubt My Love, 1985. **Address:** 28 Clover Ct., Church Rd., Haywards Health, WS RH16 3UP, England.

THOMSON, Derick S(mith). (Ruaraidh MacThòmais). Scottish (born Scotland), b. 1921. **Genres:** Poetry, Literary Criticism And History, Translations, Songs/Lyrics And Libretti. **Career:** University of Edinburgh, assistant in Celtic, 1948-49; University of Glasgow, lecturer in Welsh, 1949-56, professor of Celtic, 1963-91; Gairm Quarterly, editor, 1952-2002; Gaelic Magazine, founder and editor, 1952-; University of Aberdeen, reader in Celtic, 1956-63; Scottish Gaelic Studies, editor, 1961-75; Scottish Gaelic Texts Society, president, 1964-97; Gaelic Books Council, chairman, 1968-91. Writer. **Publications:** An Dealbh Briste, 1951; The Gaelic Sources of MacPherson's Ossian, 1952, new ed., 1973; (ed.) Branwen uerch Lyr: The Second of the Four Branches of the Mabinogi, 1961; (with J.L. Campbell) Edward Lhuyd in the Scottish Highlands, 1699-1700, 1963; (with I. Grimble) The Future of the Highlands, 1968; The Far Road and Other Poems, 1971; An Introduction to Gaelic Poetry, 1974, new ed., 1989; The New Verse in Scottish Gaelic: A Structural Analysis, 1974; Ossian Prize, 1974; The New English-Gaelic Dictionary, 1981, new ed., 1994; Creachadh na clarsaich: cruinneachadh debhardach, 1940-1980, 1982; (ed.) Companion to Gaelic Scotland, 1983, rev. ed., 1994; Why Gaelic Matters, 1986; European Poetry in Gaelic Translation, 1990; (ed.) MacDiarmid MS Anthology: Poems and Songs Mainly Anonymous from the Collection Dated 1770, 1992; Gaelic Poetry in the Eighteenth Century, 1994. AS RUARAIDH MacTHOMAIS: An Dealbh Briste, 1951; Eadar Samhradh is Foghar, 1967; An Rathad Cian, 1970; Saorsa Agus an Iolaire, 1977; Smeur anDochais, 1992; Meall Garbh, 1995. OTHER: Gaelic in Scotland: Gaidhlig annan Albainn: A Blueprint for Official and Private Initiatives, 1976; (trans.) R.MacLeod, Bith-eolas, 1976; Saorsa agus an Iolaire, 1977; Bardsand Makars: Scottish Language and Literature: Medieval and Renaissance, 1977; (ed.) Minority Languages Today: A Selection from the Papers Read at the First International Conference on Minority Languages held at Glasgow University from 8 to 13 September 1980, 1981; Gaelic Learners' Handbook: A Compendium of Vocabulary, Phrases, Sentences and Passages, Arranged under Subject-headings, with Glossary, 1989; (ed.) Gaelic and Scots in Harmony: Proceedings of the 2nd International Conference on the Languages of Scotland, University of Glasgow, 1988, 1990; Bardachd na Roinn-Eorpa an Gaidhlig: European Poetry in Gaelic, 1990; Appendix to Dwelly's Gaelic-English Dictionary, 1991; Bramble of Hope: Poems, 1991; (ed.) The MacDiarmid MS Anthology: Poems and Songs Mainly Anonymous From the Collection Dated 1770, 1992; (ed.) Gaelic Poetry in the Eighteenth Century: A Bilingual Anthology, 1993; (ed.) Selected Poems, 1999; (with I.C. Smith and A. Mitchell) Taking You home: Poems and Conversation, 2006; Suil air fàire: dain ura/le Ruaraidh MacThomais=Surveying the Horizon: Recent Poems, 2007. Contributor to periodicals. **Address:** Saint Margaret's, Taybridge Rd. S, Aberfeldy, TY PH15 2BH, Scotland.

THOMSON, George Henry. Canadian (born Canada), b. 1924. **Genres:** Literary Criticism And History, History, Theology/Religion, Autobiography/Memoirs, Humanities, Politics/Government. **Career:** Mount Allison University, lecturer to associate professor of English, 1953-66; Wayne State University, visiting professor of English, 1966-67; University of Ottawa, professor of English literature, 1969-89. Writer. **Publications:** The Fiction of E.M. Forster, 1967; (contrib.) Aspects of E.M. Forster, 1969; (ed. and intro.) Albergo Empedocle, and Other Writings: Uncollected Writings, 1900-1915, 1971; A Reader's Guide to Dorothy Richardson's Pilgrimage, 1996; Notes on Pilgrim-

age: Dorothy Richardson Annotated, 1999; (with D.F. Thomson) The Editions of Dorothy Richardson's Pilgrimage: A Comparison of Texts, 2001. Contributor of critical articles and reviews. **Address:** 655 Echo Dr., Ottawa, ON K1S 1P2, Canada. **Online address:** gthomson@uottawa.ca

THOMSON, Hugh. British (born England), b. 1960?. **Genres:** Adult Nonfiction. **Career:** Expedition leader, documentary filmmaker and producer; Sheffield International Documentary Film Festival, co-founder. Writer. **Publications:** (Ed.) Essentially Eton (lectures), 1978; The White Rock: An Exploration of the Inca Heartland, 2001; (intro.) Lost City of the Incas: The Story of Machu Picchu and Its Builders, 2002; Nanda Devi: A Journey to the Last Sanctuary, 2004; Cochineal Red: Travels through Ancient Peru, 2006 as A Sacred Landscape: The Search for Ancient Peru, 2007; 50 Wonders of the World, 2009; Tequila Oil: Getting Lost in Mexico, 2010. **Address:** c/o Elizabeth Allen, The Orion Publishing Group, 5 Upper St Martins Ln., London, GL WC2H 9EA, England. **Online address:** hugh@thomson.clara.co.uk

THOMSON, James Miln. Australian (born Australia), b. 1921. **Genres:** Marine Sciences/Oceanography, Zoology, Mathematics/Statistics, Sciences. **Career:** Commonwealth Scientific and Industrial Research Organization, Division of Fisheries, research officer, 1945-53, senior research officer, 1953-57, principal research officer, 1957-63; Marineland Oceanarium, scientific director, 1963-65; University of Queensland, senior lecturer, 1965-66, reader, 1967, professor of zoology, 1968-, professor emeritus of zoology, 1986-, director of applied ecology, 1973-81; Emmanuel College, head of department, vice-principal and dean of faculty of science; Australian Institute of Marine Science, Queensland director, 1981-. Writer. **Publications:** Synopsis of Biological Data on the Grey Mullet Mugil Cephalis Linnaeus 1758, 1963; A Bibliography of Systematic References to the Grey Mullets (Mugilidae), 1964; The Great Barrier Reef, 1966; (co-author) Zoology for Senior Forms, 1967, rev. ed., 1968; (with N. Taylor and E. Orr) Exploration of the Pacific, 1968; Ecological Backlash-Nature Versus Man, 1970; Fish of the Ocean & Shore, 1974; A Field Guide to the Common Sea & Estuary Fishes of Non-tropical Australia, 1978; The Mugilidae of the World, 1997; The Making of the Northern Territory University, 1998. Contributor to periodicals. **Address:** Emmanuel College, Sir William MacGregor Dr., St. Lucia, Brisbane, QL 4067, Australia. **Online address:** dijim@bigpond.ocm.au

THOMSON, Jennifer A. Kenyan/South African (born South Africa), b. 1947?. **Genres:** Genealogy/Heraldry, Medicine/Health. **Career:** University of Witwatersrand, Department of Genetics, lecturer, senior lecturer, associate professor of genetics; Council for Scientific and Industrial Research, founder, Laboratory for Molecular and Cell Biology, director; University of Cape Town, Department of Microbiology, professor of microbiology, head, deputy dean of science, now professor emeritus; South African Women in Science and Engineering, co-founder and chair; Academy of Science of South Africa, vice-president; International Service for the Acquisition of Agribiotech Applications (ISAAA), director; European Action Group on Life Sciences (EAGLES), director; African Agriculture Technology Foundation, board chair emeritus; Harvard Medical School, post-doctoral fellow. Writer. **Publications:** (Ed.) Recombinant DNA and Bacterial Fermentation, 1988; Genes for Africa: Genetically Modified Crops in the Developing World, 2002; GM Crops: The Impact and the Potential, 2006; Seeds for the Future: The Impact of Genetically Modified Crops on the Environment, 2007. Contributor to books. **Address:** African Agricultural Technology Foundation, PO Box 30709, Nairobi, 00100, Kenya. **Online address:** jennifer.thomson@uct.ac.za

THOMSON, June. British (born England), b. 1930. **Genres:** Mystery/Crime/Suspense, Novellas/Short Stories, Novels, Young Adult Fiction. **Career:** Teacher, 1953-73; writer, 1978-. **Publications:** Not One of Us, 1971; The Long Revenge, 1974; Case Closed, 1977; A Question of Identity, 1977; Death Cap, 1977; The Habit of Loving, 1979; Alibi in Time, 1980; Shadow of a Doubt, 1982; To Make a Killing, 1982; Portrait of Lilith, 1983; Sound Evidence, 1985; A Dying Fall, 1986; The Dark Stream, 1986; No Flowers by Request, 1987; Rosemary for Remembrance, 1988; The Spoils of Time, 1989; Past Reckoning, 1990; The Secret Files of Sherlock Holmes, 1990; Foul Play, 1991; Flowers for the Dead (short stories), 1992; The Secret Journals of Sherlock Holmes, 1993; The Secret Chronicles of Sherlock Holmes, 1994, new ed. 1999; Holmes and Watson: A Study in Friendship, 1995; Burden of Innocence, 1996; The Unquiet Grave, 2000; Going Home, 2006. **Address:** Constable & Robinson Ltd., 55-56 Russell Sq., London, GL WC1B 4HP, England.

THOMSON, Keith Stewart. American/British (born England), b. 1938.

Genres: Sciences. **Career:** University College, temporary lecturer in zoology, 1963-65; Yale University, assistant curator of zoology, 1965-70, assistant professor, 1965-70, associate professor, 1970-76, associate curator of vertebrate zoology, 1970-76, professor of biology, 1976-87, curator of vertebrate zoology, 1976-87, Peabody Museum of Natural History, director, 1977-79, Graduate School of Arts and Sciences, dean, 1979-86; Wetlands Institute, board member and trustee, 1975-93; Sears Foundation for Marine Research and Oceanographic History, director, 1977-88; Woods Hole Oceanographic Institute, 1981-; Academy of Natural Sciences, president, 1987-95; Wistar Institution, staff, 1987-95; Central Philadelphia Development Corp., 1987-95; New School for Social Research, distinguished scientist-in-residence, 1996-98; Charles Darwin Trust, staff, 1998-; University of Oxford, professor of natural history and director of Museum of Natural History, 1998-2003, professor emeritus, 2003-, Kellogg College, fellow, 1998-2003, emeritus fellow, 2003-; American Philosophical Society, senior research fellow, 2003-; International Center for Jefferson Studies, visiting fellow, 2008-. Writer. **Publications:** The Comparative Anatomy of the Snout in Rhipidistian Fishes, 1964; Revised Generic Diagnoses of the Fossil Fishes Megalichthys and Ectosteorhachis, 1964; (ed.) The Origin of Terrestrial Vertebrates, 1968; (with W.H. Weed and A.G. Taruski) Saltwater Fishes of Connecticut, 1971, 2nd ed., State Geological and Natural History Survey of Connecticut, 1978; (with K.S.W. Campbell) The Structure and Relationships of the Primitive Devonian Lungfish-Dipnorhynchus sussmilch, 1971; On the Biology of Cosmine, 1975; (with J.S. Rackoff and J.S. Darling) Specialized Scales in the Cloacal Region of Two Paleozoic Fishes, 1976; An Early Triassic Hybodont Shark from Northern Madagascar, 1982; Morphogenesis and Evolution, 1988; (as Keith S. Thomson) Living Fossil: The Story of the Coelacanth, 1991; The Common but Less Frequent Loon and Other Essays, 1993; (as Keith S. Thomson) HMS Beagle: The Story of Darwin's Ship, 1995 in UK as HMS Beagle: The Ship That Changed the Course of History, 2003; (as Keith S. Thomson) Treasures on Earth: Museums, Collections and Paradoxes, 2002; (as Keith Thomson) Before Darwin: Reconciling God and Nature, 2005 in UK as The Watch on the Heath: Science and Religion before Darwin, 2005; (as Keith Thomson) Fossils: A Very Short Introduction, 2005; (as Keith Thomson) The Legacy of the Mastodon: The Golden Age of Fossils in America, 2008; A Passion for Nature: Thomas Jefferson and Natural History, 2008; The Young Charles Darwin, 2009. Contributor to periodicals. **Address:** Kellogg College, University of Oxford, Banbury Rd., Oxford, OX2 6PN, England. **Online address:** keith.thomson@oum.ox.ac.uk

THOMSON, Pat. British (born England), b. 1939. **Genres:** Children's Fiction, Children's Non-fiction, Picture/Board Books, Literary Criticism And History. **Career:** University College of Northampton, education librarian, 1975-. Writer. **Publications:** (Ed.) Rhymes Around the Day, 1983; Trouble in the Cupboard, 1987; Family Gathering: A Collection of Family Stories, 1988; Strange Exchange, 1991; Beware of the Aunts!, 1991; Tales Told after Lights Out, 1993; A Ghost Light in the Attic, 1995; Superpooch, 1995; Superpooch and the Missing Sausages, 1996; The Silkworm Mystery: The Life of Louis Pasteur, 1998; Superpooch and the Garden Ghosts, 1999; Ghoul School, 2001; The Squeaky, Creaky Bed, 2003; Drat That Fat Cat, 2003; Cat Baby, 2007; The Badcat Game, 2007; It's So Unfair!, 2007; Badcat Gang, 2007; SHARE-A-STORY SERIES: The Treasure Sock, 1986; One of Those Days, 1986; Can You Hear Me, Grandad?, 1986; My Friend Mr. Morris, 1987; Thank You for the Tadpole, 1987; Good Girl Granny, 1987; Dial D for Disaster, 1990; No Trouble at All, 1990; Best Pest, 1990; The Best Thing of All, 1990. JETS SERIES: Jacko, 1989; Rhyming Russell, 1991; Messages, 1992; The Man in Shades, 1994; Lost Property, 1995; Talking Pictures, 1997. EDITOR: A Basket of Stories for Seven Year Olds, 1990; A Sackful of Stories for Eight Year Olds, 1990; A Bucketful of Stories for Six Year Olds, 1991; A Chest of Stories for Nine Year Olds, 1991; A Pocketful of Stories for Five Year Olds, 1992; A Satchel of School Stories, 1992; A Stocking Full of Christmas Stories, 1992; A Bus Full of Stories for Four Year Olds, 1994; A Cracker Full of Christmas Stories, 1994; A Band of Joining-in Stories, 1995; A Barrel of Stories for Seven Year Olds, 1995; A Crate Full of Stories for Eight Year Olds, 1997; A Box Full of Stories for Six Year Olds, 1997; A Bed Full of Night-time Stories, 1998; A Parcel Full of Stories for Five Year Olds, 1999; A Cauldron of Magical Stories, 2000. Contributor to periodicals. **Address:** Laura Cecil, 17 Alwyne Villas, Boughton Green Rd., London, GL N1 2HG, England. **Online address:** pthomson@onetel.com

THOMSON, Peter. American (born United States) **Genres:** Travel/Exploration. **Career:** National Public Radio's Living on Earth news program, founding producer and senior editor; Rockefeller Foundation's center, fellow.

Radio producer and environmental journalist. **Publications:** Sacred Sea: A Journey to Lake Baikal, 2007. **Address:** Boston, MA , U.S.A. **Online address:** sacredsea@earthlink.net

THOMSON, Peter (William). British (born England), b. 1938. **Genres:** Literary Criticism And History, Theatre, Biography, History, Essays. **Career:** Jesus College, reader in English, 1958-61; Victoria University of Manchester, lecturer in drama, 1964-71; University of Wales, lecturer in drama, 1971-74; University of Exeter, professor of drama, 1974-2001, professor emeritus of drama, 2001-. Writer. **Publications:** Notes on Julius Caesar, 1971; (with C. Goodhead) Ideas in Action, 1973; The Action to the Word: An Inaugural Lecture Delivered in the University of Exeter on 7 February, 1975, 1975; (with J. Needle) Bertolt Brecht, 1980; Shakespeare's Theatre, 1983, 2nd ed., 1992; (with G. Salgado) The Everyman Companion to the Theatre, 1985; Shakespeare's Professional Career, 1992; Brecht: Mother Courage and Her Children, 1997; On Actors and Acting, 2000; (foreword) Contemporary Shakespeare: Exploring a Living Theatre for the 21st Century, 2003; Extraordinary Actors: Essays on Popular Performers: Studies in Honor of Peter Thomson, 2004; The Cambridge Introduction to English Theatre, 1660-1900, 2006. EDITOR: Julius Caesar, 1968; (with K. Richards) Essays on Nineteenth Century British Theatre: The Proceedings of a Symposium, Sponsored by the Manchester University Department of Drama, 1970; (with K. Richards) Essays on Eighteenth-Century English Stage: The Proceedings of a Symposium Sponsored by the Manchester University Department of Drama, 1972; (intro. and contrib.) Plays, 1984; The Cambridge Guide to World Theatre, 1988; (with G. Sacks) The Cambridge Companion to Brecht, 1994, 2nd ed., 2006; The Cambridge History of British Theatre, 3 vols., 2004; The Erratics: Fifty Not Out, forthcoming; The Glory Decade, forthcoming; (co-ed.) New Dictionary of National Biography, forthcoming. **Address:** Department of Drama, University of Exeter, Alexander Bldg., New N Rd., Exeter, DN EX4 4LA, England. **Online address:** p.w.thomson@exeter.ac.uk

THOMSON, Richard. British/Scottish (born Scotland), b. 1953?. **Genres:** Art/Art History. **Career:** University of Edinburgh, Watson Gordon professor of fine art, 1996-; Visual Arts Research Institute, founding director, 1999-2004; National Galleries of Scotland, trustee. Writer. **Publications:** Toulouse-Lautrec, 1977; Harold Gilman, 1876-1919, Arts Council of Great Britain, 1981; Seurat, 1985; Impressionist Drawings: From British Public and Private Collections, 1986; The Private Degas, 1987; Degas: The Nudes, 1988; Camille Pissarro: Impressionism, Landscape, and Rural Labour, 1990; Edgar Degas: Waiting, 1995; (co-author) Seurat and the Bathers, 1997; (ed.) Framing France: The Representation of Landscape in France, 1870-1914, 1998; (with C. Stolwijk) Theo Van Gogh, 1857-1891: Art Dealer, Collector, and Brother of Vincent, 1999; (with P. Dennis Cate and G.B. Murray) Prints Abound: Paris in the 1890s: From the Collections of Virginia and Ira Jackson and the National Gallery of Art, 2000; (with M. Clarke) Monet: The Seine and the Sea, 1878-1883, 2003; (ed. with F. Fowle) Soil and Stone: Impressionism, Urbanism, Environment, 2003; The Troubled Republic: Visual Culture and Social Debate in France, 1889-1900, 2004; (with P.D. Cate, M.W. Chapin and F.E. Coman) Toulouse-Lautrec and Montmartre, 2005; Vincent Van Gogh: The Starry Nigh, 2008. Contributor to books. **Address:** University of Edinburgh, School of Arts, Culture & Environment, 20 Chambers St., Edinburgh, EH1 1JZ, Scotland. **Online address:** r.thomson@ed.ac.uk

THOMSON, Rodney M(alcolm). Australian (born Australia), b. 1946?. **Genres:** Adult Non-fiction, Translations, Essays. **Career:** Australian Academy of Humanities, fellow, 1992-; University of Tasmania, senior research fellow, professor of history, 1975-98, emeritus professor of history, 1998-. Writer. **Publications:** (Ed., trans. and intro.) Tractatus Garsiae or, The Translation of the Relics of SS. Gold and Silver, 1973; (ed. and trans.) The Chronicle of the Election of Hugh, Abbot of Bury St. Edmunds and Later Bishop of Ely, 1974; (ed.) The Life of Gundulf, Bishop of Rochester, 1977; (ed.) The Archives of the Abbey of Bury St. Edmunds, 1980; Manuscripts from St. Albans Abbey, 1066-1235, 1982; William of Malmesbury, 1987, rev. ed., 2003; (ed.) Speculum Speculationum, 1988; Catalogue of the Manuscripts of Lincoln Cathedral Chapter Library, 1989; (ed. with R.A.B. Mynors) Catalogue of the Manuscripts of Hereford Cathedral Library, 1993; The Cambridge History of the Book in Britain: 1100-1400, 1998; England and the 12th-Century Renaissance, 1998; (with M. Winterbottom) Gesta regum Anglorum: The History of the English Kings, 1998-99; The Bury Bible, 2001; A Descriptive Catalogue of the Medieval Manuscripts in Worcester Cathedral Library, 2001; (ed. with M. Winterbottom) Saints' Lives: Lives of S.S. Wulfstan, Dunstan, Patrick, Benignus and Indract, 2002; (ed. with C.J. Mews and C.J. Nederman) Rhetoric and Renewal in the Latin West 1100-1540: Essays in Honour of John O. Ward, 2003; (contrib.) Gesta Pontificum Anglorum/The History of the English Bishops, 2007. Contributor to journals. **Address:** School of History and Classics, University of Tasmania, 439 Humanities Bldg., Sandybay Campus, PO Box 81 Hobart, Hobart, AC 7001, Australia. **Online address:** rod.thomson@utas.edu.au

THOMSON, William. American (born United States), b. 1927. **Genres:** Music, Reference. **Career:** Sul Ross State College, faculty, 1951-60; Ford Foundation, composer in residence, 1960-61; Indiana University, professor of music, 1961-69; Case Western Reserve University, Kulas professor of music, 1969-73; University of Arizona, director of graduate studies, 1973-75; State University of New York-Buffalo, Department of Music, Ziegle professor and chairman, 1975-80; University of Southern California, School of Music, dean and professor, 1980-92, now professor emeritus. Writer. **Publications:** The Materials and Structure of Music, 1965; Introduction to Music Reading: Concepts and Applications, 1966; (with R.P. DeLone) Introduction to Ear Training, 1967; Transformations, for Orchestra, 1968; Advanced Music Reading, 1969; Introduction to Music as Structure, 1971; Music for Listeners, 1978; Introduction to Music Reading: Concepts and Applications, 1981; Schoenberg's Error, 1991; (trans.) T. Lipps, Consonance and Dissonance in Music, 1995; Tonality in Music: A General Theory, 1999; MetaMusic Versus the Sound of Music, 2010. **Address:** Thornton School of Music, University of Southern California, Los Angeles, CA 90089-0851, U.S.A. **Online address:** sansptom@aol.com

THON, Melanie Rae. American (born United States), b. 1957. **Genres:** Novels, Novellas/Short Stories, Adult Non-fiction. **Career:** Boston University, teaching fellow for creative writing, 1981; Emerson College, instructor in literature, 1986-92; Wheelock College, instructor in writing, 1986-87; Ploughshares, editorial assistant, 1987; University of Massachusetts, instructor in writing and history, 1987-90, research consultant, 1987; Emerson College, instructor, 1987-; Harvard University, instructor in writing, 1989-93; Syracuse University, assistant professor of writing and literature, 1993-96; Ohio State University, associate professor of writing and literature, 1996-2000; University of Utah, professor of creative writing and literature, 2000-, professor of English, 2001-; Vermont Studio Center, writer-in-residence, 2000; University of Idaho, distinguished visiting writer, 2000. **Publications:** NOVELS: Meteors in August, 1990; Iona Moon, 1993; Sweet Hearts, 2001. STORIES: Girls in the Grass, 1991; First Body, 1997; The Voice of the River, 2011; In This Light: New and Selected Stories, 2011. Contributor of stories and nonfiction to periodicals. Works appear in anthology. **Address:** Department of English, University of Utah, English Languages & Communication Bldg., Rm. 3500, 255 S Central Campus Dr., Salt Lake City, UT 84112-0494, U.S.A. **Online address:** melanie.thon@english.utah.edu

THONDUP, Tulku. American/Tibetan (born Tibet), b. 1939?. **Genres:** Theology/Religion, Cultural/Ethnic Topics, Translations, History, Psychology. **Career:** Lucknow University, lecturer of Tibetan and Tibetan literature, 1967-76; Visva-Bharati University, reader, 1976-80; Buddhayana Foundation, presiding officer, 1983-. Writer. **Publications:** (Trans.) The Assemblage of Vidhyadharas, 1980, 2nd ed., 1992; (trans.) Jig-me ling-pa, The Long-chen nying-thig ngon-dro, 1982; (trans.) Jig-meling-pa, The Glorious Blissful Garland, The Root Sadhana of the Dakini, The Queen of Great Bliss from Long-chen Nyingthig, 1983; The Tantric Tradition of the Nyingmapa: The Origin of Buddhism in Tibet, 1984; Hidden Teachings of Tibet: An Explanation of the Terma Tradition of the NyingmaSchool of Buddhism, 1986; Buddhist Civilization in Tibet, 1987; (trans. and intro.) The Practice of Dzogchen, 1989, 3rd ed., 2002; Buddha Mind: An Anthology of Longchen Rabjam's Writings on Dzogpa Chenpo, 1989; The Dzogchen Innermost Essence Library of Tibetan Preliminary Practice, 2nd ed., 1989; (trans.) Enlightened Living: Teachings of Tibetan Buddhist Masters, 1990, 2nd ed., 1997; (trans.) The Queen of Great Bliss, 2nd ed., 1992; Enlightened Journey: Buddhist Practice as Daily Life, 1995; The Healing Power of Mind: Simple Meditation Exercises for Health, Well-Being and Enlightenment, 1996; Masters of Meditation and Miracles: The Longchen Nyingthig Lineage of Tibetan Buddhism, 1996; (trans.) Hidden Teachings of Tibet: An Explanation of the Terma Tradition of Tibetan Buddhism, 2nd ed., 1997; Healing Meditations: Simple Exercises for Health, Peace and Well-Being, 1998; Boundless Healing: Meditation Exercises to Enlighten the Mind and Heal the Body, 2000; (trans.) Praise of the Twenty-One Taras, 2000; (trans.) The King of Noble Prayer Aspiring to the Deeds of the Excellent, 2000; Peaceful Death, Joyful Rebirth: A Tibetan Buddhist Guidebook, 2005; (trans.) T. Tshulthrim, Boundless Vision: Translation of a Com-

mentary on Boundless Vision of Dzogchen; (trans. with P. Richman) Thugje Chenpo Dugngal Rangdrol, Natural Liberation from Suffering of Long-Chen Nying-Thig, 2006; Incarnation: The History and Mysticism of the Tulku Tradition of Tibet, 2011. INTRODUCTION: Perfect Conduct: Ascertaining the Three Vows, 1996; Jiucheng Cidi, 1997; Yeshe Lama, 1998; Ningmapai Cidi Chan, 1998; The Warrior Song of King Gesar, 1996; The Precious Treasury of the Way of Abiding 1998; Liu Zhongyou Zijietuo Daoyin, 1999; A Treasure Trove of Scriptural Transmission, A Commentary on The Precious Treasury of the Basis Space of Phenomena, 2001; Secret of the Vajra World: The Tantric Buddhism of Tibet, 2001; A Treasure Trove of Blessing and Protection: The Seven Chapter Prayer of the Great Teacher Padmasambhava, 2005; The Precious Treasury of Pith Instructions, 2006; A Cascading Waterfall of Nectar, 2006. **Address:** Buddhayana Foundation, 202 Spring St., Marion, MA 02738, U.S.A.

THONE, Ruth Raymond. American (born United States), b. 1931. **Genres:** Cultural/Ethnic Topics, Women's Studies And Issues, Psychology. **Career:** Gathering Place, co-founder; Friends of Loren Eiseley, co-founder. Writer. **Publications:** Women and Aging: Celebrating Ourselves, 1992; Being Home (essays), 1993; Fat: A Fate Worse Than Death: Women, Weight and Appearance, 1997. Contributor to journals. **Address:** 3045 Woodsdale Blvd., Lincoln, NE 68502-5053, U.S.A.

THOR, Brad. American (born United States), b. 1970?. **Genres:** Mystery/Crime/Suspense. **Career:** Thor Entertainment Inc., president. Writer and host. **Publications:** The Lions of Lucerne, 2002; Path of the Assassin, 2003; State of the Union: A Thriller, 2004; Blowback: A Thriller, 2005; Takedown: A Thriller, 2006; First Commandment: A Thriller, 2007; Last Patriot: A Thriller, 2008; Apostle: A Thriller, 2009; Athena Project: A Thriller, 2010; Foreign Influence: A Thriller, 2010; Full Black, 2011. Contributor to periodicals. **Address:** c/o Author Mail, Pocket Books/Simon & Schuster, 1230 Ave. of the Americas, New York, NY 10020, U.S.A. **Online address:** author@bradthor.com

THORBURN, Doug. American (born United States), b. 1953. **Genres:** Medicine/Health, Money/Finance. **Career:** Writer and educator. **Publications:** Drunks, Drugs and Debits: How to Recognize Addicts and Avoid Financial Abuse, 2000; Get Out of the Way! How to Identify and Avoid a Driver under the Influence, 2002; How to Spot Hidden Alcoholics: Using Behavioral Clues to Recognize Addiction in Its Early Stages, 2004; Alcoholism Myths and Realities: Removing the Stigma of Society's Most Destructive Disease, 2005; (with House) Arm Action, Arm Path, and the Perfect Pitch: Building a Million-Dollar Arm, 2008. Contributor to periodicals. **Address:** PO Box 7301, Van Nuys, CA 91409, U.S.A. **Online address:** dougthorburn@preventragedy.com

THORINGTON, Richard W. American (born United States), b. 1937. **Genres:** Biology, Animals/Pets. **Career:** Harvard University, Regional Primate Center, primatologist, 1964-69; National Museum of Natural History, Smithsonian Institution, curator of mammals, 1969-. Writer and biologist. **Publications:** Proportions and Allometry in the Gray Squirrel, Sciurus Carolinensis, 1972; (ed. with P.G. Heltne) Neotropical Primates: Field Studies and Conservation: Proceedings of a Symposium on the Distribution and Abundance of Neotropical Primates, 1976; (with R.J. Emry) Descriptive and Comparative Osteology of the Oldest Fossil Squirrel Protosciurus, 1982; (with K. Ferrell) Squirrels: The Animal Answer Guide, 2006; Squirrels of the World, 2012; (with S. M. Jackson) Gliding Mammals: Taxonomy of Living and Extinct Species, 2012. Contributor to journals. **Address:** National Museum of Natural History, Smithsonian Institution, MRC 108, 10th and Constitution Ave. NW, PO Box 37012, Washington, DC 20560-0108, U.S.A. **Online address:** thoringtonr@si.edu

THORMÄHLEN, Marianne. Swedish (born Sweden), b. 1949. **Genres:** Literary Criticism And History, Translations. **Career:** University of Lund, reader, 1979-86, acting professor, 1986-89, senior lecturer in English literature, 1986-96, professor of English literature, 1996-, chair of English literature, dean of research in the humanities and theology. Writer. **Publications:** The Waste Land: A Fragmentary Wholeness, 1978; Eliot's Animals, 1984; Rochester: The Poems in Context, 1993; (ed.) T.S. Eliot at the Turn of the Century, 1994; The Brontës and Religion, 1999; (ed.) Rethinking Modernism, 2003; The Brontës and Education, 2007; (trans.) A Happy Man and Other Stories, or/oder, Der Glückliche und andere Erzählungen, 2008; (ed.) English Now: Selected Papers From the 20th IAUPE Conference in Lund 2007, 2008; (trans.) H. Kushner, When Bad Things Happen to Good People. Contributor to journals. **Address:** Department of English, Lund University, Helgonaback-en 14, Lund, S-22362, Sweden.

THORNE, Barrie. American (born United States), b. 1942. **Genres:** Sociology, Women's Studies And Issues. **Career:** The American Anthropologist, editorial assistant, 1963-64; Boston College, Department of Sociology, research associate, 1969-71; Michigan State University, sociology faculty, 1971-85, assistant professor, professor of sociology, 1971-87, professor of sociology, 1984-87; University of California-Santa Cruz, visiting assistant professor of sociology, 1976-77, visiting associate professor of sociology, 1980-81; University of California-Berkeley, professor of sociology and of gender and women's studies, 1995-, co-director, 1998-2002, Center for Working Families, director, 2001-02, Gender and Women's Studies Department, chair, 2003-08; Stanford University, visiting associate professor of sociology and feminist studies, 1981-82; University of Southern California, Streisand professor women's studies and sociology, professor of sociology, 1987-95, Program for the Study of Women and Men in Society, chair, 1992-95; American Sociological Association, vice president, 1993-94; University of Oslo, Centre for Gender Research, professor II, 2009-10. **Publications:** (Co-author) Education for the Professions of Medicine, Law, Theology, and Social Welfare, 1973; Gender Play: Girls and Boys in School, 1993. EDITOR: (with N. Henley) Language and Sex: Difference and Dominance, 1975; (comp. with N. Henley) She Said/He Said: An Annotated Bibliography of Sex Difference in Language, Speech, and Nonverbal Communication, 1975; (with M. Yalom) Rethinking the Family: Some Feminist Questions, 1982, rev. ed. 1992; (with C. Kramarae and N. Henley) Language, Gender and Society, 1983; (with B. Laslett) Feminist Sociology: Life Histories of a Movement, 1997. **Address:** Department of Sociology, University of California, 410 Barrows Hall, Berkeley, CA 94720-1980, U.S.A. **Online address:** bthorne@berkeley.edu

THORNE, Ian. *See* **MAY, Julian.**

THORNE, Jean Wright. *See* **MAY, Julian.**

THORNE, Kip S. American (born United States), b. 1940. **Genres:** Astronomy, Physics, Sciences, Air/Space Topics. **Career:** Princeton University, postdoctoral fellow in physics, 1965-66; California Institute of Technology, Department of Physics, research fellow in physics, 1966-67, associate professor of theoretical physics, 1967-70, professor of theoretical physics, 1970-91, The William R. Kenan, Jr., professor, 1981-91, Richard P. Feynman professor of theoretical physics, 1991-2009, Richard P. Feynman professor emeritus of theoretical physics, 2009-; University of Utah, adjunct professor of physics, 1971-98; Cornell University, Andrew D. White professor-at-large, 1986-92. Writer. **Publications:** (With B.K. Harrison, M. Wakano and J.A. Wheeler) Gravitation Theory and Gravitational Collapse, 1965; (with A.G.W. Cameron) High Energy Astrophysics, vol. III, 1967; (C.W. Misner and J.A. Wheeler) Gravitation, 1973; Black Holes and Time Warps: Einstein's Outrageous Legacy, 1994. EDITOR: (R.H. Price and D.A Macdonald) Black Holes: The Membrane Paradigm, 1986; (with W.D. Arnett) Relativistic Astrophysics, vol. I: Stars and Relativity, 1970, rev. ed., 1996; (with C. Eller) Systems with Small Dissipation, 1985; Quantum Measurement, 1992. Contributor to journals and magazines. **Address:** Department of Physics, California Institute of Technology, 1200 E California Blvd., PO Box 130-33, Pasadena, CA 91125, U.S.A. **Online address:** kip@tapir.caltech.edu

THORNE, Nicola. *See* **ELLERBECK, Rosemary.**

THORNE-SMITH, Courtney. American (born United States), b. 1967. **Genres:** Novels, Young Adult Fiction, Literary Criticism And History. **Career:** Trimark Pictures, board chairman, 1998; Susan G. Komen Cancer Foundation, Race for the Cure, spokesperson; Almay cosmetics, spokesperson, 1999. Actor and writer. **Publications:** Outside In (novel), 2007. Contributor to periodicals. **Address:** c/o Paradigm, 10100 Santa Monica Blvd., Ste. 2500, Los Angeles, CA 90067, U.S.A.

THORNLEY, Stew. American (born United States), b. 1955. **Genres:** Children's Non-fiction, Sports/Fitness, Biography, Recreation, History. **Career:** KHAD-Radio, announcer and sportscaster, 1975; KMSR-FM Radio, staff announcer and sports director, 1976; North Hennepin Community College, basketball public address announcer, 1980-82; Minneapolis Community College, basketball public address announcer, 1982-95; On-Line Intl., manufacturer's representative, 1983-84; Chapin Publishing Co., field editor, 1988-90; Lerner Publications Co., publicity director, 1991-92; Minnesota Department

of Health Minneapolis, health educator, 1993-; Major League Baseball, official scorer for Minnesota Twins games, 2007-. Writer. **Publications:** FOR ADULTS: On to Nicollet: The Glory and Fame of the Minneapolis Millers, 1988; Basketball's Original Dynasty: The History of the Lakers: Basketball's Original Dynasty, 1989; Holy Cow! The Life and Times of Halsey Hall, 1991; (with R. Christensen) Golden Memories, 1993; (with H. Carneal) Hi Everybody!, 1995; Land of the Giants: New York's Polo Grounds, 2000; Six Feet Under: A Graveyard Guide to Minnesota, 2004; Baseball in Minnesota: The Definitive History, 2006; (with M. Hugunin) Minnesota Hoops: Basketball in the North Star State, 2006. FOR YOUNG READERS: Cal Ripken, Jr.: Oriole Ironman, 1992; Deion Sanders: Prime Time Player, 1993, rev. ed., 1997; (with B.L. Himrich) Electrifying Medicine: How Electricity Sparked a Medical Revolution (children's book), 1995; Top 10 Football Receivers, 1995; Sports Great Dennis Rodman, 1996; Sports Great Reggie Miller, 1996; Sports Great Greg Maddux, 1996; Emmitt Smith: Relentless Rusher, 1996; Frank Thomas: Baseball's Big Hurt, 1997; Jerry Rice: Star Wide Receiver, 1998; Shawn Kemp: Star Forward, 1998; Alex Rodriguez: Slugging Shortstop, 1998; Roberto Alomar: Star Second Baseman, 1999; Grant Hill: Star Forward, 1999; Mark McGwire: Star Home Run Hitter, 1999; Allen Iverson: Star Guard, 2001; Hits, Hankies, and Homers: The Story of the Minnesota Twins, 2001; Super Sports Star Kevin Garnett, 2001; Super Sports Star Kobe Bryant, 2001; Super Sports Star Tim Duncan, 2001; Super Sports Star Chris Webber, 2002; Super Sports Star Jason Kidd, 2002; Super Sports Star Vince Carter, 2002; Super Sports Star Randy Moss, 2003; Super Sports Star Daunte Culpepper, 2003; Super Sports Star Eddie George, 2003; Super Sports Star Brett Favre, 2003; Derek Jeter: Daring to Dream, 2004; Super Sports Star Ken Griffey, Jr., 2004; Super Sports Star Chipper Jones, 2004; Super Sports Star Barry Bonds, 2004; Roberto Clemente, 2007; (ed.) Minnesotans In Baseball, 2009; Sports Jokes to Tickle Your Funny Bone, 2011; Kobe Bryant: Champion Basketball Star, 2013; Tim Duncan: Champion Basketball Star, 2013; Kevin Garnett: Champion Basketball Star, 2013. **Address:** 1082 Lovell Ave., Roseville, MN 55113-4419, U.S.A. **Online address:** stew@stewthornley.net

THORNTON, Arland. American (born United States), b. 1944. **Genres:** Social Sciences. **Career:** University of Michigan, Survey Research Center, Institute for Social Research, assistant research scientist to research professor, 1975-, Department of Sociology, lecturer, professor, 1977-, associate chair, 1986-87, Population Studies Center, research affiliate to research professor, 1983-, associate director, 1995-97, acting director, 1997-98, director, 2003-08, Center for Chinese Studies, faculty associate, 2005-, department of Sociology, executive committee member, 1985-87, 1994-95, 1997-99, 2007-08; Child Well-Being Research Network, member, 1993-99. Academic and writer. **Publications:** (co-author) Social Change and the Family in Taiwan, 1994; (co-ed.) Ties That Bind: Perspectives on Marriage and Cohabitation, 2000; (ed.) The Well-Being of Children and Families: Research and Data Needs, 2001; Reading History Sideways: The Fallacy and Enduring Impact of the Developmental Paradigm on Family Life, 2005; (with W.G. Axinn and Y. Xie) Marriage and Cohabitation, 2007; (ed. with R. Jayakody and W. Axinn) International Family Change: Ideational Perspectives, 2008. **Address:** Institute for Social Research, University of Michigan, 426 Thompson St., Ann Arbor, MI 48106-1248, U.S.A. **Online address:** arlandt@umich.edu

THORNTON, Bruce S. American (born United States), b. 1953. **Genres:** Classics, Humanities, History. **Career:** University of California, teaching associate, 1980-82; California State University, part-time lecturer, 1982-85, lecturer, 1985-89, assistant professor, 1989-91, associate professor, 1991-96, professor of classics and humanities, 1996-, chairman, 1996-2000, Interdisciplinary Humanities Program, coordinator, 2000-; Reedley Community College, Department of English, lecturer, 1983-85; Kings River Community College, lecturer, 1983-85; Stanford University, Hoover Institution, W. Glenn Campbell and Rita Ricardo-Campbell national fellow, 2009-, research fellow. Writer. **Publications:** Eros the Killer: The Myth of Ancient Greek Sexuality, 1997; Plagues of the Mind: The New Epidemic of False Knowledge, 1999; Humanities Handbook, 2000; Greek Ways: How the Greeks Created Western Civilization, 2000; (with V.D. Hanson and J. Heath) The Bonfire of the Humanities, 2001; Searching for Joaquin: Myth, Murieta, and History in California, 2003; A Student's Guide to the Classics, 2003; Decline and Fall: Europe's Slow-Motion Suicide, 2007; The Wages of Appeasement: Ancient Athens, Munich, and Obama's America, 2011. Contributor of articles to periodicals. **Address:** Department of Modern and Classical Languages, and Literatures, California State University, 2320 E San Ramon Ave., Fresno, CA 93740-8030, U.S.A. **Online address:** brucet@csufresno.edu

THORNTON, Margaret Rose. Australian (born Australia) **Genres:** Law, Women's Studies And Issues. **Career:** Macquarie University, lecturer, senior lecturer in law, 1980-90; La Trobe University, professor of law and legal studies, Law Program, foundation head, Richard McGarvie chair of socio-legal studies 1990-2006; Australian National University, professor of law, 2006-. Writer and academic. **Publications:** The Liberal Promise: Anti-Discrimination Legislation in Australia, 1990; Portia Lost in the Groves of Academe Wondering What to do about Legal Education, 1991; Dissonance and Distrust: Women in the Legal Profession, 1996. EDITOR: Public and Private: Feminist Legal Debates, 1995; Romancing the Tomes, 2002; Sex Discrimination in Uncertain Times, 2010. **Address:** ANU College of Law, Australian National University, Fellows Rd., Canberra, AC 0200, Australia. **Online address:** margaret.thornton@anu.edu.au

THORNTON, Mark. American (born United States), b. 1960. **Genres:** Economics, Social Sciences. **Career:** Alabama Libertarian Party, vice-chair, 1985; Auburn University, assistant professor of economic, 1988-94, graduate faculty, 1991-99, adjunct faculty, 1994-97, 1999, 2006, adjunct professor of economics, 1997-99; State Banking Department of Alabama, assistant superintendent of banking and economic adviser, 1997-99; Columbus State University, graduate faculty, 1992-2002, associate professor, 1999-2002; Free Market, contributing editor; Quarterly Journal of Austrian Economics, book review editor; Ludwig von Mises Institute, senior fellow, 2002-. **Publications:** Folk Psychology, 1989; Do We Have Free Will?, 1989; Alcohol Prohibition Was a Failure (monograph), 1991; The Economics of Prohibition, 1991; (with R.B. Ekelund, Jr.) Tariffs, Blockades, and Inflation: The Economics of the Civil War, 2004; (ed.) The Quotable Mises, 2005; Meditation in a New York Minute: Super Calm for the Super Busy, 2006; (ed.) The Bastiat Collection, 2007; (ed.) An Essay on Economic Theory, 2010. **Address:** Ludwig von Mises Institute, 518 W Magnolia Ave., Auburn, AL 36832-4528, U.S.A. **Online address:** mthornton@prodigy.net

THORNTON, Naoko Fuwa. Japanese (born Japan), b. 1943. **Genres:** Translations, Adult Non-fiction, Language/Linguistics, Social Sciences. **Career:** Indiana University-Bloomington, visiting lecturer in Japanese, 1972-73; Bunkyou Women's Junior College, adjunct instructor, 1975-83; Japan Women's University, lecturer, 1978-83, assistant professor, 1983-87, associate professor, 1987-92, professor of English, 1992-. Writer. **Publications:** (Trans.) The Voice of the Writer 1984, 1986; Yuudora ueruteino sekai: jozetu to chinmoku no shinwa, 1988; Strange Felicity: EudoraWelty's Subtexts on Fiction and Society, 2003; Authorship: An Ideology, forthcoming. **Address:** Japan Women's University, 2-8-1 Mejirodai, Bunkyo-ku, Tokyo, 112- 8681, Japan. **Online address:** thornton@aurora.ocn.ne.jp

THORNTON, Robert J(ames). American (born United States), b. 1949. **Genres:** Anthropology/Ethnology, Social Sciences, History. **Career:** Rubaga Girls Secondary School, instructor in geography and science, 1969-71; University of Chicago, lecturer in social sciences, 1977-78; University of Cape Town, Department of Anthropology, lecturer, 1979-82, senior lecturer, 1983-86, associate professor, 1987-90; Imagenesis, co-founder and co-owner, 1983-89; Institute for Advanced Study, Catherine T. and John D. MacArthur fellow, 1989-90; Rutgers University, Center for Historical Analysis, senior fellow, 1990-91, Raoul Wallenberg associate professor of human rights, 1991; Thornton Consulting, computer software creator and consultant, 1991-; University of the Witwatersrand, associate professor of anthropology, 1996-, head of department, 1992, 1996, 1999-2001, professor of anthropology; Exceptional African Experiences Ltd., director. Writer. **Publications:** Space, Time, and Culture Among the Iraqw of Tanzania, 1980; (ed. with P. Skalník) The Early Writings of Bronislaw Malinowski, 1993; Unimagined Community: Sex, Networks, and AIDS in Uganda and South Africa, 2008. Contributor to journals. **Address:** Department of Anthropology, University of the Witwatersrand, PO Box 3, Johannesburg, 2050, South Africa. **Online address:** robert.thornton@wits.ac.za

THORNTON, Sylvia. See GATHORNE-HARDY, Jonathan.

THORNTON, Yvonne S. American (born United States), b. 1947. **Genres:** Medicine/Health, Autobiography/Memoirs, Young Adult Non-fiction, Women's Studies And Issues. **Career:** Roosevelt Hospital, resident in obstetrics and gynecology, 1973-77; Columbia-Presbyterian Medical Center, fellow in maternal-fetal medicine, 1977-79; Uniformed Services University of Health Sciences, assistant professor of obstetrics and gynecology, 1979-82; Cornell University, Medical College, assistant professor, 1982-89, assistant attend-

ing, 1982-89, associate professor of obstetrics and gynecology, 1989-92; New York Lying-in Hospital, assistant, 1982-89, associate attending of obstetrics and gynecology, 1989-92; New York Hospital-Cornell Medical Center, Department of Obstetrics and Gynecology, director of clinical services, 1982-88, Chorionic Villus Sampling Program, director, 1984-92; Rockefeller University Hospital, visiting associate physician, 1986-96; Morristown Memorial Hospital, Perinatal Diagnostic Testing Center, director, 1992-2000; Columbia University, College of Physicians and Surgeons, associate clinical professor, 1995-2000; St. Luke's-Roosevelt Hospital, senior perinatologist, 2000-02; Jamaica Hospital Medical Center, vice-chair, professor of clinical obstetrics and gynecology, director of maternal-fetal medicine, 2002-05; consultant, 2006-; Westchester Medical Center, perinatal preceptor, 2007-; New York Medical College, clinical professor of obstetrics and gynecology, 2008-. Writer. **Publications:** (With J. Coudert) The Ditchdigger's Daughters: A Black Family's Astonishing Success Story, 1995; (with J. Coudert) Woman to Woman: A Leading Gynecologist Tells You All You Need to Know about Your Body and Your Health, 1997; (ed.) Primary Care for the Obstetrician and Gynecologist, 1997; (with A. Bartholomew) Something To Prove: A Daughter's Journey to Fulfill a Father's Legacy, 2010; Inside Information for Women: Answers to the Mysteries of the Female Body and Her Health, 2010. **Address:** Department of Obstetrics and Gynecology, Westchester Medical Center, Munger Pavilion, Ste. 617, Valhalla, NY 10595, U.S.A. **Online address:** doctorthornton@gmail.com

THORPE, Helen. American/British (born England), b. 1965?. **Genres:** Social Sciences. **Career:** New York Observer, staff writer, 1989-92; Texas Monthly, staff writer, 1994-. Producer. **Publications:** Just Like Us: The True Story of Four Mexican Girls Coming of Age in America, 2009. Contributor to periodicals. **Address:** c/o Denise Shannon, Shannon Literary Agency Inc., 20 W 22nd St., Ste. 1603, New York, NY 10010, U.S.A.

THORSON, John E. American (born United States), b. 1946. **Genres:** Environmental Sciences/Ecology, Law, Social Sciences, History. **Career:** Council of State Governments, attorney, 1980-84; Doney & Thorson, partner, 1986-90; Northern Lights Institute, Missouri River Management Project, director, 1988-90, president, 1992-2001; Arizona Supreme Court, Arizona General Stream Adjudication, special master, 1990-2000; attorney-at-law, 2000-; Water, Law & Policy, attorney and consultant, 2000-03; California Public Utilities Commission, administrative law judge, 2003-; Water Alternative Dispute Resolution Adjudication, assistant chief judge, 2007-; Montana Mental Health Association, public policy director; Bernalillo County Labor Relations Board, chairman; Contra Costa County Legal Services Foundation, vice president and treasurer; Richmond Art Center, board director, treasurer and president. **Publications:** (With M. O'Keefe and D. Snow) Boundaries Carved in Water: An Analysis of River and Water Management in the Upper Missouri Basin, 1986; (with G.D. Weatherford and T.O. Miller) The Salty Colorado, 1986; (ed.) Federal Lands, 1986; River of Promise, River of Peril: The Politics of Managing the Missouri River, 1994; (with B.G. Colby and S. Britton) Negotiating Tribal Water Rights: Fulfilling Promises in the Arid West, 2005; (ed. with B.G. Colby and S. Britton) Tribal Water Rights: Essays in Contemporary Law, Policy, and Economics, 2006. Contributor to journals. **Address:** 6625 Exeter Dr., Oakland, CA 94611-1642, U.S.A. **Online address:** johnethorson@earthlink.net

THORSSON, örnólfur. Icelander (born Iceland), b. 1953?. **Genres:** Adult Non-fiction, Ghost Writer, Literary Criticism And History, Novellas/Short Stories, Young Adult Fiction. **Career:** Leifur Eiriksson Publishing Ltd., editor. **Publications:** íslendinga Sögur, 1985; Brennu-Njáls Saga: Med Formala, Skýringum og Eftirmála Umíslendiga Sögur, K, 1991; Grettis Saga: Med Formála, Vidbti, Skýringum og Skrám, 1994; (ed.) The Sagas of the Icelanders, 2000. **Address:** Leifur Eiriksson Publishing Ltd., Flokagata 65, Reykjavík, 65-105, Iceland.

THRAILKILL, Jane. American (born United States), b. 1963. **Genres:** Literary Criticism And History. **Career:** Field School, teacher, 1987-90; Sidwell Friends School, teacher, 1990-92; University of North Carolina, assistant professor of English, 2000-06, associate professor of English and comparative literature, 2006-. Writer. **Publications:** Affecting Fictions: Mind, Body, and Emotion in American Literary Realism, 2007. Contributor to books and periodicals. **Address:** Department of English and Comparative Literature, University of North Carolina, 411 Greenlaw Hall, Chapel Hill, NC 27599, U.S.A. **Online address:** tkill@email.unc.edu

THRASHER, Peter Adam. British (born England), b. 1923?. **Genres:** Urban Studies, Biography, History, Autobiography/Memoirs. **Career:** Greater London Council, Department of Planning and Transportation, chartered civil engineer, 1966-. Writer. **Publications:** Pasquale Paoli: An Enlightened Hero 1725-1807, 1970; (with K.A.J. Crawford) Standard Statistical Sectors for Greater London, 1971. **Address:** 1b Denbridge Rd., Bickley, Bromley, KT BR1 2AG, England.

THRIBB, E. J. See **FANTONI, Barry (Ernest).**

THRICE, M. See **GILMAN, Owen W(inslow).**

THRIFT, Nigel. (Nigel John Thrift). British (born England), b. 1949. **Genres:** Geography, Economics, Politics/Government. **Career:** University of Oxford, visiting professor, Division of Life and Environmental Sciences, head, 2003, pro-vice-chancellor for research, 2005; University of Warwick, vice-chancellor, 2006-; University of Bristol, now professor emeritus. Writer. **Publications:** (As N.J. Thrift) Mathematical Dynamic Models in Geography: The Outlook, 1973; An Introduction to Time Geography, 1977; (ed. with T. Carlstein and D. Parkes) Human Activity and Time Geography, 1978; (ed. with T. Carlstein and D. Parkes) Making Sense of Time, 1978; (ed. with T. Carlstein and D. Parkes) Time and Regional Dynamics, 1978; (ed. as N.J. Thrift with R.L. Martin and R.J. Bennett) Towards the Dynamic Analysis of Spatial Systems, 1978; (with D. Parkes) Times, Spaces, and Places: A Chronogeographic Perspective, 1980; (ed. with M. Taylor) The Geography of Multinationals: Studies in the Spatial Development and Economic Consequences of Multinational Corporations, 1982; (ed. with M. Taylor) Multinationals and the Restructuring of the World Economy, 1986; (ed. with P. Williams) Class and Space: The Making of Urban Society, 1987; (ed. with D. Forbes) The Socialist Third World: Urban Development and Territorial Planning, 1987; (ed. with S. Corbridge and R. Martin) Money, Power, and Space, 1994; (ed. with A. Amin) Globalization, Institutions, and Regional Development in Europe, 1994; (ed. with S. Pile) Mapping the Subject: Geographies of Cultural Transformation, 1995; Spatial Formations, 1996; (with A. Leyshon) Money/Space: Geographies of Monetary Transformation, 1997; (ed. with M. Crang) Thinking Space, 2000; (ed. with S. Pile) City A-Z, 2000; (ed. with J. May) TimeSpace: Geographies of Temporality, 2001; (ed. with S. Whatmore) Cultural Geography: Critical Concepts in the Social Sciences, 2004; (ed. with A. Amin) The Blackwell Cultural Economy Reader, 2004; (ed. with M. Featherstone and J. Urry) Automobilities, 2005; Knowing Capitalism, 2005; Non-Representational Theory: Space, Politics, Affect, 2008; (with P. Glennie) Shaping the Day: A History of Timekeeping in England and Wales 1300-1800, 2009. **Address:** Vice Chancellor's Office, University of Warwick, University House, Coventry, WM CV4 8UW, England. **Online address:** vc@warwick.ac.uk

THRIFT, Nigel John. See **THRIFT, Nigel.**

THRUSH, Coll. Canadian (born Canada), b. 1970. **Genres:** History. **Career:** University of British Columbia, assistant professor of history. Writer. **Publications:** Native Seattle: Histories from the Crossing-Over Place, 2007. Contributor to books and journals. **Address:** Canada. **Online address:** cthrush@interchange.ubc.ca

THUBRON, Colin Gerald Dryden. British (born England), b. 1939. **Genres:** Novels, History, Travel/Exploration, Young Adult Fiction. **Career:** Hutchinson & Company Ltd., editorial staff, 1959-62; British Broadcasting Corp., Television, freelance filmmaker in Turkey, Morocco, Japan, 1963, 1965; Macmillan Co., editorial staff, 1965-66. **Publications:** Mirror to Damascus, 1968; The Hills of Adonis: A Quest in Lebanon, 1968 as The Hills of Adonis: A Journey in Lebanon, 1990; Jerusalem 1969; Journey into Cyprus, 1975; (co-ed.) Jerusalem, 1976; God in the Mountain, 1977; Emperor, 1978; (co-ed.) Istanbul, 1978; (co-ed.) The Venetians, 1980; (co-ed.) The Ancient Mariners, 1981; The Royal Opera House, Covent Garden, 1982; Among the Russians, 1983; Where Nights Are Longest: Travels by Car through Western Russia, 1984; A Cruel Madness, 1984; Behind The Wall: A Journey Through China, 1987; The Silk Road: Beyond the Celestial Kingdom, 1989; Falling, 1989; Turning Back the Sun, 1994; The Lost Heart of Asia, 1994; Distance, 1996; In Siberia, 1999; To the Last City, 2002; Shadow of the Silk Road, 2007; To a Mountain in Tibet, 2011. **Address:** Aitken Alexander Associates Ltd., 18-21 Cavaye Pl., London, GL SW10 9PT, England.

THUMANN, Albert. American (born United States), b. 1942. **Genres:** Engineering, Education, Sciences. **Career:** Bechtel, project engineer, 1964-77; Association of Energy Engineers, founder and executive director, 1977-; University of Louisville, adjunct professor. Writer. **Publications:** (With R.K. Miller) Secrets of Noise Control, 1974, 2nd ed., 1976; Plant Engineers and Managers Guide to Energy Conservation, 1977, (with S. Dunning) 10th ed., 2010; Biorhythms and Industrial Safety, 1977; Electrical Design, Safety and Energy Conservation, 1978; How to Patent without a Lawyer, 1978; Handbook of Energy Audits, 1979, (with W.J. Younger and T. Niehus) 8th ed., 2010; (comp. and ed.) The Emerging Synthetic Fuel Industry, 1981; (comp. and ed.) Energy Audit Sourcebook, 1983; (with R.J. Goldstick) The Waste Heat Recovery Handbook, 1983; Fundamentals of Energy Engineering, 1984; (comp. and ed.) Energy Management Systems Sourcebook, 1985; (with S. Ayraud) Introduction to Efficient Electrical Systems Design, 1985, 2nd ed., 1991; (with R.J. Goldstick) Principles of Waste Heat Recovery, 1986; (with R.K. Miller) Fundamentals of Noise Control Engineering, 1986, 2nd ed., 1990; (comp.) Optimizing HVAC Systems, 1988; (ed.) Guide to Improving Efficiency in Combustion Systems, 1988; (comp. and ed.) Lighting Efficiency Applications, 1989, 2nd ed., 1992; (with J. Bent) Project Management for Engineering and Construction, 1989, 2nd ed., 1993; (with D.P. Mehta) Handbook of Energy Engineering, 1989, 6th ed., 2008; (ed.) Energy Conservation in Existing Buildings Deskbook, 1992; (ed. with R. Hoshide) Energy Management Guide in Government Buildings, 1994; (with R.C. Hsu) Guide to Self Patenting, 1997; Efficient HVAC Systems Deskbook, 1997; (with F. Wainwright) Financing Energy Projects Deskbook, 1997; (comp. and ed.) Customer Choice: Purchasing Energy in a Deregulated Market, 1999; (with K.L. Petrocelly) Facilities Evaluation Handbook: Safety, Fire Protection and Environmental Compliance, 2000; (comp. and ed. with R.B. Fowler) The Market Survey of the Energy Industry 2000/2001, 2000; (with B. Benator) Project Management and Leadership Skills for Engineering and Construction Projects, 2003; (with E.A. Woodroof) Handbook of Financing Energy Projects, 2005; (with H. Franz) Efficient Electrical Systems Design Handbook, 2009; (E.A. Woodroof) Energy Project Financing: Resources and Strategies for Success, 2009. **Address:** Association of Energy Engineers, 4025 Pleasantdale Rd., Ste. 420, Atlanta, GA 30340, U.S.A. **Online address:** al@aeecenter.org

THURLEY, Simon. British (born England), b. 1962. **Genres:** Architecture, Art/Art History, Photography. **Career:** English Heritage, inspector, 1988-90, chief executive, 2002-; Historical Royal Palaces Agency, chief curator, 1990-97; Museum of London, director, 1998-2002; Royal Holloway College, visiting professor; Gresham College, visiting professor. Writer. **Publications:** The Royal Palaces of Tudor England: Architecture and court life, 1993; (with C. Lloyd) Henry VIII: Images of a Tudor King, 1995; The Privy Garden: The King's Privy Garden at Hampton Court Palace, 1995; The Whitehall Palace Plan of 1670, 1998; The Lost Palace of Whitehall, 1998; Whitehall Palace: An Architectural History of the Royal Apartments, 1240-1698, 1999; Hampton Court: A Social and Architectural History, 2004; Lost Buildings of Britain, 2004; Somerset House, 2009; Whitehall Palace: The Official History, 2009; (with R. Poulton and A. Cook) Oatlands Palace; History of English Architecture, forthcoming. **Address:** English Heritage, 1 Waterhouse Sq., 138-142 Holborn, London, GL EC1N 2ST, England. **Online address:** simon@kingstaithe.com

THURLO, Aimee. Also writes as Aimee Martel, Aimee Duvall. American/Cuban (born Cuba) **Genres:** Romance/Historical, Horror, Mystery/Crime/Suspense. **Career:** Writer. **Publications:** WITH D. THURLO: Ariel's Desire, 1987; The Right Combination, 1988; Expiration Date, 1989; Black Mesa, 1990; Suitable For Framing, 1990; Strangers Who Linger, 1991; Night Wind, 1991; Breach Of Faith, 1992; Shadow Of the Wolf, 1993; Spirit Warrior, 1993; Second Shadow, 1993; Timewalker, 1994; Bearing Gifts, 1994; Fatal Charm, 1995; Blackening Song, 1995; Cisco's Woman, 1996; Death Walker, 1996; Bad Medicine, 1997; Enemy Way, 1998; Redhawk's Heart, 1999; Redhawk's Return, 1999; Christmas Witness, 1999; Black Raven's Pride, 2000; Shooting Chant, 2000; Red Mesa, 2001; Bad Faith, 2002; Changing Woman, 2002; Second Sunrise, 2002; Plant Them Deep, 2003; Tracking Bear, 2003; Time Walker, 2003; Thief in Retreat, 2004; Spirit Line, 2004; Wind Spirit, 2004; Blood Retribution, 2004; Pale Death, 2005; White Thunder, 2005; Surrogate Evil, 2006; Prey For a Miracle, 2006; Mourning Dove, 2006; Turquoise Girl, 2007; False Witness, 2007; Council of Fire, 2007; Restless Wind, 2007; Stargazer's Woman, 2008; Coyote's Wife, 2008; Prodigal Nun, 2008; Bad Samaritan, 2009; Navajo Courage, 2009; Brotherhood of Warriors, 2009; Earthway, 2009; Never-ending-snake, 2010; Alpha Warrior, 2010; Twilight Warrior, 2011. FOUR WINDS TRILOGY: Her Destiny, 1997; Her Hope,

1997; Her Shadow, 1997. AS AIMEE MARTEL: Secrets Not Shared, 1981; The Fires Within, 1984; Hero At Large, 1984. AS AIMEE DUVALL: Too Near the Sun, 1982; Halfway There, 1982; Lover in Blue, 1982; The Loving Touch, 1983; After the Rain, 1984; One More Tomorrow, 1984; Brief Encounters, 1985; Spring Madness, 1985; Kid at Heart, 1986; Made for Each Other, 1987; To Tame a Heart, 1988; Wings Of Angels, 1989. Contributor to periodicals. **Address:** PO Box 2747, Corrales, NM 87048, U.S.A. **Online address:** adthurlo@aol.com

THURM, Marian. American (born United States), b. 1952?. **Genres:** Novels, Novellas/Short Stories. **Career:** Columbia University, adjunct associate professor of creative writing, Barnard College, faculty; Yale University, faculty; Sarah Lawrence College, instructor. Novelist. **Publications:** NOVELS: Floating, 1984; Walking Distance, 1987; Henry in Love, 1990; The Way We Live Now, 1991; The Clairvoyant, 1997. SHORT STORY COLLECTIONS: These Things Happen, 1988; What's Come Over You?: Stories, 2001. Contributor to magazines and journals. **Address:** Department of English, Barnard College, Columbia University, 417 Barnard Hall, 3009 Broadway, New York, NY 10027-6598, U.S.A.

THURMAN, Mark (Gordon Ian). Canadian (born Canada), b. 1948. **Genres:** Children's Fiction. **Career:** Bril-Light Neon Signs, designer and hand letterer, 1966-67; Guest Group, animation painter, 1967-68; Robert Simpson Co., designer and illustrator in display department, 1969-73; Display Arts, art director, designer and illustrator, 1973-76; writer and illustrator, 1976-; Toronto School of Art, teacher of design and illustration, life drawing/anatomy, 1981-91; Ontario Arts Council, teaching staff, 1982-90; Royal Ontario Museum, faculty, 1983-89; Claude Watson School for the Arts, faculty, 1985-86; Georgian College of Applied Arts and Technology, faculty, 1990; Central Technical School, staff, 1993-2000; Avenue Road Arts School, teaching faculty, 1999-2002; Sheridan College, Department of Classical Animation, faculty, 2003-, BAA Animation Program, instructor. **Publications:** FOR CHILDREN SELF-ILLUSTRATED: The Elephants Gold, 1979, rev. ed., 1985; The Elephant's New Bicycle, 1980, rev. ed., 1985; (with E. Hearn) The Mighty Mites in Dinosaur Land, 1981; The Birthday Party, 1981; The Lie That Grew and Grew, 1981; Belinda's Ball, 1981; Who Needs Me, 1981; Two Pals on an Adventure, 1982; City Scrapes, 1983; You Bug Me, 1985; Old Friends New Friends, 1985; Two Stupid Dummies, 1986; Some Sumo, 1988; Cabbage Town Gang, 1987; (with E. Hearn) Draw and Write Your Own Picture Book, Helping Kids Create Picture Books, and Illustration Ideas for Creating Picture Books, 1990; Funtastic Collages, 1992; How to Plan Your Drawings, 1992; One Two Many, 1993; Gimme A Break Rattlesnake, 1994. Illustrator of books by others. **Address:** 14 Washington Ave., Toronto, ON M5S 1L2, Canada. **Online address:** info@markthurman.ca

THUROW, Lester (Carl). American (born United States), b. 1938. **Genres:** Economics, Business/Trade/Industry, Politics/Government, Money/Finance. **Career:** Harvard University, assistant professor, 1965-68, Kennedy School of Government, research associate, 1968-; Massachusetts Institute of Technology, professor of economics, 1968-87, Solan School of Management, dean, 1987-93, now dean emeritus, Jerome and Dorothy Lemelson professor of management and economics, now Jerome and Dorothy Lemelson professor of management and economics emeritus, Asia-Pacific Initiatives, coordinator; WGBH-TV, Weekly commentator, 1969-75. Writer. **Publications:** (Ed. and contrib.) American Fiscal Policy: Experiment for Prosperity, 1967; Poverty and Discrimination, 1969; Investment in Human Capital, 1970; The Impact of Taxes on the American Economy, 1971; Activities by Various Central Banks to Promote Economic and Social Welfare Programs, 1971; (with R.E.B. Lucas) The American Distribution of Income, 1972; Foreign Experience with Monetary Policies to Promote Economic and Social Priority Programs, 1972; The Economics of Poverty and Racial Discrimination, 1972; (with R.L. Heilbroner) The Economic Problem, 1974, 7th ed., 1984; (with R.L. Heilbroner) Understanding Microeconomics, 1975, 6th ed., 1984; Generating Inequality: The Distributional Mechanisms of the U.S. Economy, 1975; The Political Economy of Income Redistribution Policies, 1977; Youth Unemployment: A Conference at the Rockefeller Foundation, 1977; The Zero-Sum Society: Distribution and the Possibilities for Economic Change, 1980; (with R.L Heilbroner) Five Economic Challenges, 1981; (with A. Packer and H.J. Samuels) Strengthening the Economy: Studies in Productivity, 1981; The Zero-sum Society, 1981; (intro.) Operating Internationally: A Sourcebook of Assistance of Associations, Business, Professionals, and Plain Citizens, 1981; (with R.L. Heilbroner) Economics Explained, 1982, rev. ed. as Economics Explained: Everything You Need to Know about How the Economy Works

and Where It's Going, 1994; Dangerous Currents: The State of Economics, 1983; (intro.) Military Expansion, Expansion, Economic Decline: The Impact of Military Spending on U.S. Economic Performance, 1983; The Case for Industrial Policies, 1984; (with D. Bell) The Deficits: How Big? How Long? How Dangerous?, 1985; (ed.) The Management Challenge: Japanese Views, 1985; The Zero Sum Solution: Building a World-Class American Economy, 1985; Amerika keizai no tenbōto keizai seisaku no arikata, 1986; The Zero-sum Solution: The Route to Economic Growth, 1987; Toward a High-Wage, High-Productivity Sector, 1989; (intro.) Regular Economic Cycles: Money, Inflation, Regulation and Depressions, 1989; Perspectives of U.S. Economic Policy Under the New Government, 1992; Head to Head: The Coming Economic Battle among Japan, Europe, and America, Morrow, 1992; al-Mutanāiūn: Al-marakah al-iqtiādīyah al-qādimah bayna al-Yabanwa-ūrūbbā wa-Amrīkā, 1996; The Future of Capitalism: How Today's Economic Forces Shape Tomorrow's World, 1997; Zi ben zhu yi diwei lai: jin ri di jing ji li shi zao ming ri di shi jie, 1998; Building Wealth: The New Rules for Individuals, Companies, and Nations in a Knowledge-Based Economy, 1999; The Age of Economic Exploration, 1999; Head to Head: The Economic Battle Among Japan, Europe, and America, 2003; Fortune Favors the Bold: What We Must Do to Build a New and Lasting Global Prosperity, 2003; al-Niẓām al-iqtiṣ ādīal-ālamī al-jadīd: al-jarah wa-al-mukhāṭarah ṭarīq ilá al-tharwah, 2006. **Address:** Sloan School of Management, Massachusetts Institute of Technology, Rm. E62-527, 77 Massachusetts Ave., Cambridge, MA 02139-4307, U.S.A. **Online address:** lthurow@mit.edu

THURSTON, H. D(avid). American (born United States), b. 1927. **Genres:** Agriculture/Forestry. **Career:** Rockefeller Foundation, Ministry of Agriculture, assistant plant pathologist, 1954-56, plant pathologist, 1958-67, Instituto Colombiano Agropecuario, director of plant pathology program, 1958-66, Department of Plant Sciences, director, 1965-67; University of Minnesota, Department of Plant Pathology, instructor, 1956-57, research fellow, 1957-58; Rockefeller Potato Program, director, 1963; Colombian Agricultural Institute, director of plant science; Cornell University, International Agriculture and Plant Pathology, Department of Plant Pathology, professor of plant pathology and international agriculture, 1967-96, professor emeritus, 1996-; Consortium for International Crop Protection, chairman and director, 1985-90; Cornell Institute for Food, Agriculture and Development, chairman, 1990-91; American Phytopathological Society, fellow. Writer. **Publications:** Tropical Plant Diseases, 1984, 2nd ed., 1998; Enfermedades de Cultivos en el Tropico, 1989; Sustainable Practices for Plant Disease Management in Traditional Farming Systems, 1992; (co-ed.) Los Sistemas de Siembra con Cobertura: Tapado, 1993; Slash/Mulch Systems: Sustainable Methods for Tropical Agriculture, 1997. **Address:** Department of Plant Pathology, Cornell University, 334 Plant Science, Day Hall Lobby, Ithaca, NY 14853, U.S.A. **Online address:** hdt1@cornell.edu

THURSTON, Robert (Donald). American (born United States), b. 1936. **Genres:** Science Fiction/Fantasy. **Career:** Union-Sun Journal, reporter, 1959-60; Alliance College, assistant professor, 1967-68; Bergen Community College, adjunct lecturer, 1988-92; New Jersey City University, coordinator of instructional services, 1992-. Writer. **Publications:** Alicia II, 1978; A Set of Wheels, 1983; Q Colony, 1985; For the Silverfish, 1985; Robot Jox, 1989; Robot City No. 9: Intruder, 1990; 1492: Conquest of Paradise, 1992. LEGEND OF THE JADE PHOENIX SERIES: No.1: Way of the Clans, 1991; No.2: Bloodname, 1991; No.3: Falcon Guard, 1991; I Am Jade Falcon, 1995; Freebirth, 1998; Falcon Rising, 1999. BATTLESTAR GALACTICA SERIES: (with G.A. Larson) Battlestar Galactica, 1978; No.2: The Cylon Death Machine, 1979; No.3: The Tombs of Kobol, 1979; No.4: The Young Warriors, 1980; No.11: The Nightmare Machine, 1985; No.12: Die, Chameleon!, 1986; No.13: Apollo's War, 1987; No.14: Surrender the Galactica, 1988. **Address:** 2039 Kennedy Blvd., Jersey City, NJ 07305, U.S.A. **Online address:** rthurston1@njcu.edu

THURSTON, Robert W. American (born United States), b. 1949. **Genres:** History, Social Sciences, Politics/Government. **Career:** University of Vermont, visiting assistant professor, 1980-81; University of California, visiting assistant professor, 1981-83; University of Texas, assistant professor, 1983-87; Miami University, assistant professor, 1987-90, associate professor, 1990-96, professor of history, 1996-2004, Phillip R. Shriver professor of history, 2004-. Writer. **Publications:** (With W.G. Rosenberg) Russian History and Politics: Selected Reference Works, 1978; Liberal City, Conservative State: Moscow and Russia's Urban Crisis 1906-1914, 1987; Life and Terror in Stalins Russia 1934-1941, 1996; (ed. with B. Bonwetsch) The People's War:

Responses to World War II in the Soviet Union, 2000; Witch Wicce Mother Goose: The Rise and Fall of the Witch Hunts in Europe and North America, 2001; The Witch Hunts: A History of the Witch Persecutions in Europe and North America, 2007; Lynching: American Mob Murder in Global Perspective, 2010; The Social, Moral and Economic Life of Coffee, forthcoming; A Cultural History of Coffee: Impact and Images in the West, 1600 to the Present, forthcoming. Contributor to books and periodicals. **Address:** Department of History, Miami University, Rm. 273, Upham Hall, 501 E High St., Oxford, OH 45056, U.S.A. **Online address:** thurstrw@muohio.edu

THWAITE, Ann (Barbara). British/New Zealander (born New Zealand), b. 1932. **Genres:** Children's Fiction, Biography, Young Adult Fiction. **Career:** Tokyo Joshi Daigaku, part-time lecturer in English literature, 1956-57, visiting professor, 1985-86, 2005; Cricket magazine, contributing editor, 1974-77; Toronto Public Library, Helen Stubbs memorial lecturer, 1990; St. Mary's Middle School, governor, 1990-2002; University of Southern Mississippi, Ezra Jack Keats memorial Llecturer, 1992; Hapton VC Primary School, governor, 1995-; Skidmore College, Fox-Adler lecturer, 2004. **Publications:** The Young Traveller in Japan, 1958; The House in Turner Square, 1960; Toby Stays with Jane, 1962; Toby Moves House, 1965; Jane and Toby Start School, 1965; Home and Away, 1967; The Travelling Tooth, 1968; The Holiday Map, 1969; The Day with the Duke, 1969; The Camelthorn Papers, 1969; The Only Treasure, 1970; Waiting for the Party: The Life of Frances Hodgson Burnett, 1849-1924, 1974; The Poor Pigeon, 1976; Rose in the River, 1976; Horrible Boy, 1976; The Chatterbox, 1978; Tracks, 1978; (reteller) A Piece of Parkin: A True Story from the Autobiography of Frances Hodgson Burnett, 1980; My Hat, 1983; Edmund Gosse: A Literary Landscape, 1984; Pennies for the Dog, 1985; Gilbert and the Birthday Cake, 1986; Amy and the Night-Time Visit, 1987; A.A. Milne: The Man behind Winnie-the-Pooh in UK as A.A. Milne: His Life, 1990; The Brilliant Career of Winnie-the-Pooh, 1992; The Ashton Affair, 1995; The Horse at Hilly Fields, 1996; Emily Tennyson: The Poet's Wife, 1996; Glimpses of the Wonderful: The Life of Philip Henry Gosse, 2002. EDITOR: All Sorts 1-7, 1968-75; My Oxford, 1977 as My Oxford, My Cambridge: Memories of University Life by Twenty-Four Distinguished Graduates, 1979, rev. ed. as My Oxford, 1986; All Sorts of Poems, 1978; (and intro.) Portraits from Life, 1991; Passageways, 2009. **Address:** c/o Camilla Hornby, Curtis Brown Group Ltd., 28-29 Haymarket, London, GL SW1Y 4SP, England.

THWAITE, Anthony (Simon). British (born England), b. 1930. **Genres:** Poetry, Literary Criticism And History, Travel/Exploration. **Career:** Tokyo University, visiting lecturer in English literature, 1955-57; BBC, radio producer, 1957-62; Listener, literary editor, 1962-65; University of Libya, assistant professor of English, 1965-67; New Statesman, literary editor, 1968-72; Encounter, co-editor, 1973-85; Andre Deutsch Ltd., editorial director, 1986-92, editorial consultant, 1992-95; Vanderbilt University, poet-in-residence, 1992. **Publications:** Poems, 1953; Home Truths, 1957; Essays on Contemporary English Poetry, 1957, rev. ed. as Contemporary English Poetry, 1959; The Owl in the Tree: Poems, 1963; The Stones of Emptiness: Poems 1963-66, 1967; (with R. Beny) Japan in Colour, 1967; The Deserts of Hesperides, 1969; (with A. Alvarez and Roy Fuller) Penguin Modern Poets 18, 1970; Points, 1972; Inscriptions, 1973; Poetry Today 1960-1973, 1973; New Confessions, 1974; (with R. Beny and P. Porter) Roloff Beny in Italy, 1974; Beyond the Inhabited World, 1976; A Portion for Foxes, 1977; Twentieth Century English Poetry, 1978; Victorian Voices, 1980; (with R. Beny) Odyssey: Mirror of the Mediterranean, 1981; Poems 1953-1983, 1984; Six Centuries of Verse, 1984; Letter from Tokyo, 1987; Poems 1953-1988, 1989; The Dust of the World, 1994; Selected Poems 1956-1996, 1997; A Different Country, 2000; A Move in the Weather: Poems 1994-2002, 2003; (ed. and intro.) Further Requirements: Interviews, Broadcasts, Statements, and Book Reviews, 1952-85, 2004; Collected Poems, 2004; Late Poems, 2010. EDITOR: (with H. Corke and W. Plomer) New Poems 1961, 1961; (and trans. with G. Bownas) The Penguin Book of Japanese Verse, 1964, rev. ed., 1998; (with P. Porter) The English Poets, 1974; (with F. Adock) New Poetry 4, 1978; Larkin at Sixty, 1982; Collected Poems, 1988; Selected Letters of Philip Larkin, 1992; Longfellow: Selected Poems, 1993; P. Larkin, Further Requirements (prose), 2001; (ed.) Ruins of Time: Antiquarian and Archaeological Poems, 2006; Letters to Monica, 2010. **Address:** Enitharmon Press, 26B Caversham Rd., London, GL NW5 2DU, England.

THWE, Pascal Khoo. British/Myanmar (born Myanmar), b. 1967?. **Genres:** Autobiography/Memoirs, History, Biography. **Career:** Writer and political activist. **Publications:** From the Land of Green Ghosts: A Burmese Odyssey

(memoir), 2002. Contributor to periodicals. **Address:** c/o Author Mail, HarperCollins, 10 E 53rd St., 7th Fl., New York, NY 10023, U.S.A.

THYBONY, Scott. American (born United States), b. 1948. **Genres:** Travel/Exploration, History, Sciences. **Career:** National Geographic Traveler, columnist. Archaeologist, teacher and writer. **Publications:** A Guide to Hiking the Inner Canyon, 1981; (with R.G. Rosenberg and E.M. Rosenberg) The Medicine Bows: Wyoming's Mountain Country, 1985; Fire and Stone: A Road Guide to Wupatki and Sunset Crater National Monuments, 1987; Walnut Canyon, 1988; Grand Canyon Trail Guide: Hermit, 1989; Grand Canyon Trail Guide: Havasu, 1989; Arizona, 1990; Portrait of Arizona, 1990; Fort Davis: The Men of Troop H, 1990; (with J. Babbitt) Grand Canyon Trail Guide: South and North Bass, 1991; Aztec Ruins National Monument, 1992; Canyon Country Parklands: Treasures of the Great Plateau, 1993; Rock Art of the American Southwest, 1994; The Official Guide to Hiking the Grand Canyon, 1994; Burntwater, 1995, new ed., 1997; The Rockies: Pillars of a Continent, 1996; Walnut Canyon National Monument, 2nd ed., 1996; Canyon de Chelly National Monument, 1997; The Hogan, 1998; Dry Rivers and Standing Rocks: A Word Finder for the American West, 2000; Phantom Ranch, 2001; Wildfire, 2002; The Painted Desert: Land of Wind and Stone, 2006; The Incredible Grand Canyon: Cliffhangers and Curiosities from America's Greatest Canyon, 2007; The Earthlodge, 2007; Kelso Depot: A Fully Restored Spanish Revival Railroad Depot in Mojave National Preserve, 2008. Contributor to magazines and newspapers. **Address:** PO Box 1381, Flagstaff, AZ 86002, U.S.A. **Online address:** scott@scott-thybony.com

THYNN, Alexander (George). British (born England), b. 1932. **Genres:** Novels, Poetry, Autobiography/Memoirs, Essays. **Career:** Longleat Enterprises, director, now retired; Wessex Regionalist Party, founder. Artist and writer. **Publications:** Lord Weymouth's Murals, 1973; A Regionalist Manifesto, 1975; The New World Order of Alexander Thynn (essays), 2000; Strictly Private to Public Exposure, 2002. AUTOBIOGRAPHY: A Plateful of Privilege, vol. I: The Early Years, vol. II: Top Hat and Tails, vol. III: Two Bites of the Apple. NOVELS: The Carry-Cot, 1972; The King Is Dead, 1976; Pillars of the Establishment, 1980; Some Sonnets, 2011. **Address:** Longleat House, Warminster, WT BA12 7NN, England. **Online address:** lordbath@btinternet.com

TIAN, Hao Jiang. American/Chinese (born China), b. 1954. **Genres:** Biography. **Career:** Writer and musician. **Publications:** Along the Roaring River: My Wild Ride from Mao to the Met, 2008. **Address:** Zemsky/Green Artists Management Inc., 104 W 73rd St., Ste. 1, New York, NY 10023, U.S.A. **Online address:** marthaliao@gmail.com

TIANDONG, Xue. See HSUEH, Tien tung.

TIBBER, Robert. See FRIEDMAN, Rosemary.

TIBBER, Rosemary. See FRIEDMAN, Rosemary.

TIBBETTS, Orlando L. American (born United States), b. 1919. **Genres:** Novels, Theology/Religion, Biography, Travel/Exploration, Cultural/Ethnic Topics. **Career:** Baptist Church, ordained minister, 1943-; Baptist Seminary, founder and president, 1947-53; pastor, 1953-63; Boston Baptist City Mission Society, executive minister, 1963-68; Massachusetts Council of Churches, Metropolitan Boston Commission, executive minister, 1968-70; American Baptist Churches of Connecticut, executive minister, 1971-81; Eastern Baptist Theological Seminary, adjunct professor, 1982, now retired; First Baptist Church in America, senior minister, 1983-; Home for Unwed Mothers, chaplain; Boston Industrial Mission, treasurer. Writer. **Publications:** Man of Salamanca, 1996; The Reconciling Community, 1969; Sidewalk Prayers, 1971; More Sidewalk Prayers, 1973; The Work of the Church Trustee, 1979; How to Keep Useful Church Records, 1983; The Minister's Handbook, 1986; The Spiritual Journey of J.C. Penney, 1999; My Spiritual Journey: Reaching Inward for Higher Thoughts, 2001. **Address:** 4410 Lewis Ave., Penney Farms, FL 32079, U.S.A. **Online address:** ottprc@aol.com

TIDWELL, John Edgar. American (born United States), b. 1945. **Genres:** Biography, Language/Linguistics, Poetry. **Career:** Maur Hill Catholic College, Department of English, instructor, 1968-70; Atchison Neighborhood Center, director, 1969-70; Creighton University, New Careers Program, instructor, 1970-71, Department of English, lecturer in English, 1971-73; University of Nebraska, Department of Black Studies, instructor, 1971-73, acting chairman, 1972-73, Department of English, instructor, 1971-73; St. Olaf College, Department of English, instructor in English, 1973-77, American Minority Studies, director, 1973-74; University of Minnesota II, teaching associate, 1975-78; University of Kentucky, Department of English, assistant professor, 1981-87; Yale University, visiting fellow, 1985-86; Miami University, Department of English, assistant professor, 1987-92, associate professor, 1993-99; University of Kansas, Department of English, associate professor, 1999-, professor of English; Harvard University, W.E.B. Du Bois Institute for Afro-American Research, non-resident fellow, 2003-04. Writer. **Publications:** (Ed. and intro.) Livin' the Blues: Memoirs of a Black Journalist and Poet, 1992; (ed.) Black Moods: Collected Poems, 2002; (ed. with M.A. Sanders) Sterling A. Brown's A Negro Looks at the South, 2007; (ed. with C.R. Ragar) Montage of a Dream: The Art and Life of Langston Hughes, 2007; (ed. and intro.) Writings of Frank Marshall Davis: A Voice of the Black Press, 2007; (ed. with S.C. Tracy) After Winter: The Art and Life of Sterling A. Brown, 2009. **Address:** Department of English, University of Kansas, Rm. 3001, 3027 Wescoe Hall, 1445 Jayhawk Blvd., Lawrence, KS 66045-7594, U.S.A. **Online address:** tidwelje@ku.edu

TIDWELL, Mike. American (born United States) **Genres:** Technology, Engineering, History, Information Science/Computers. **Career:** Chesapeake Climate Action Network, founder and director, 2002-; U.S. Climate Emergency Council, founder and director. Writer and documentary film maker. **Publications:** The Ponds of Kalambayi: An African Sojourn, 1990; In the Shadow of the White House: Drugs, Death and Redemption on the Streets of the Nation's Capital, 1992; Amazon Stranger: A Rainforest Chief Battles Big Oil, 1996; In the Mountains of Heaven: Tales of Adventure on Six Continents, 2000; Bayou Farewell: The Rich Life and Tragic Death of Louisiana's Cajun Coast, 2003; The Ravaging Tide: Strange Weather, Future Katrinas and the Coming Death of America's Coastal Cities, 2006; (with L. Pardew) Autodesk Maya and Autodesk 3ds Max Side-by-Side, 2006. **Address:** Chesapeake Climate Action Network, PO Box 11138, Takoma Park, MD 20912, U.S.A. **Online address:** mtidwell@chesapeakeclimate.org

TIERNEY, Kevin. American/British (born England), b. 1942. **Genres:** Law, Biography, History. **Career:** Donovan, Leisure, Newton & Irvine, associate lawyer, 1969-70; Wayne State University, Law School, associate professor, 1971-75, professor, 1975-79; University of California, Hastings College of the Law, visiting professor, 1979-80, professor of law, 1980-. Writer. **Publications:** Courtroom Testimony: A Policeman's Guide, 1970; How to Be a Witness, 1971; Darrow, 1979; (contrib.) University Club of San Francisco: Centennial History, 1890-1990, 1990. Contributor of articles to journals. **Address:** Hastings College of the Law, University of California, 200 McAllister St., San Francisco, CA 94102-4978, U.S.A. **Online address:** tierneyk@uchastings.edu

TIERNO, Michael. American (born United States) **Genres:** Art/Art History, Philosophy, History. **Career:** Miramax Films, Development Office, story analyst. Film editor, director and writer. **Publications:** Aristotle's Poetics for Screenwriters: Storytelling Secrets from the Greatest Mind in Western Civilization, 2002. **Address:** c/o Author Mail, Hyperion Books, 114 5th Ave., New York, NY 10011-5604, U.S.A. **Online address:** mtierno@nyc.rr.com

TIERNO, Philip M(ario). American (born United States), b. 1943. **Genres:** Medicine/Health, Sciences. **Career:** Lutheran Medical Center, microbiologist, 1965-66; Veterans Administration Hospital, Hemodialysis Unit, chief research microbiologist, 1966-70; New York University, Goldwater Memorial Hospital, Langone Medical Center, director of microbiology, 1970-81, director of clinical microbiology and immunology, Tisch Memorial Hospital, Department of Microbiology, director, 1981-, associate professor of microbiology and pathology, 1981-, School of Medicine, Department of Pathology, clinical professor, College of Dentistry, Department of Microbiology, associate professor; Maimonides Medical Center, associate, microbiologist, 1970-79, City University of New York, adjunct assistant professor, 1974-76; Bloomfield College, adjunct assistant professor, 1975-82; Foundation for Scientific Research in the Public Interest, founder, 1985; State University of New York, School of Optometry, lecturer. Writer. **Publications:** The Secret Life of Germs: Observations and Lessons from a Microbe Hunter, 2001; Protect Yourself against Bioterrorism, 2002; (with M.E. Byrnes and D.A. King) Nuclear, Chemical, and Biological Terrorism: Emergency Response and Public Protection, 2003; Secret Life of Germs: What They are, Why We Need Them, and How We can Protect Ourselves against Them, 2004. Contributor of articles to books, journals and periodicals. **Address:** Department of Microbiol-

ogy, School of Medicine, New York University, Rm. 374, Medical Science Bldg., 550 1st Ave., New York, NY 10016-6402, U.S.A. **Online address:** philip.tierno@nyumc.org

TIETENBERG, T(homas) H(arry). American (born United States), b. 1942. **Genres:** Economics, Institutions/Organizations. **Career:** Williams College, assistant professor of economics, 1971-77; Federal Energy Administration, Macroeconomic Impact Division, director, 1974-75; Colby College, Department of Economics, associate professor, 1977-84, professor of economics, 1984-, chairman, 1986-88, 1993-95, C.A. Johnson Distinguished Teaching Professor, 1990-93, Mitchell Family Professor of Economics, 1993-2008, Mitchell Family Emeritus Professor of Economics, 2008-, Environmental Studies Program, director, 1999-2004; Association of Environmental and Resource Economists, president, 1987-88; Efficiency Maine Trust, director, 2009-. Writer. **Publications:** (Co-author) The Automobile and the Regulation of Its Impact on the Environment, 1975; Energy Planning and Policy: The Political Economy of Project Independence, 1976; Environmental and Natural Resource Economics, 1984, (with L. Lewis) 9th ed., 2012; Emissions Trading: An Exercise in Reforming Pollution Policy, 1985, 2nd ed. as Emissions Trading: Principles and Practice, 2006; (ed.) Innovation in Environmental Policy: Economic and Legal Aspects of Recent Developments in Liability and Enforcement, 1992; Environmental Economics and Policy, 1994, (with L. Lewis) 6th ed., 2010; (ed.) The Economics of Global Warming, 1997; (ed. with H. Folmer) International Yearbook of Environmental and Resource Economics, 1997 as International Review of Environmental and Resource Economics, 2007; (ed. with K.J. Button and P. Nijkamp) Environmental Instruments and Institutions, 1999; (co-author) Toward a National Policy on Individual Fishing Quotas, 1999; (ed.) Emissions Trading Programs, 2001. Works appear in anthologies. Contributor of articles to journals. **Address:** Department of Economics, Colby College, 5242 Mayflower Hill, Waterville, ME 04901-8852, U.S.A. **Online address:** thtieten@colby.edu

TIFFANY, Grace. American (born United States), b. 1958?. **Genres:** Novels. **Career:** University of Notre Dame, instructor, 1985-89; Fordham University, visiting assistant professor, 1989-90; University of New Orleans, assistant professor, 1990-95; Western Michigan University, faculty, 1995-2003, professor of English, 2003-. Educator and writer. **Publications:** Erotic Beasts and Social Monsters: Shakespeare, Jonson and Comic Androgyny, 1995; (ed.) Reformations: Religion, Rulership and the Sixteenth-Century Stage, 1998; My Father Had a Daughter: Judith Shakespeare's Tale (novel), 2003; Will (novel), 2004; Ariel, 2005; Turquoise Ring, 2005; Love's Pilgrimage: The Holy Journey in English Renaissance Literature, 2006; (ed.) The Tempest, 2011. Contributor to books. **Address:** Department of English, Western Michigan University, Kalamazoo, MI 49008, U.S.A. **Online address:** grace.tiffany@wmich.edu

TIGER, Lionel. American (born United States), b. 1937. **Genres:** Anthropology/Ethnology, Food And Wine, Institutions/Organizations, Military/Defense/Arms Control, Social Commentary. **Career:** University of Ghana, lecturer, 1961; University of British Columbia, lecturer in political sociology, 1963, assistant professor of sociology, 1963-69; Western Washington State College, visiting lecturer, 1963; Rutgers University, Livingston College, associate professor of anthropology, 1969-72, Graduate School, associate professor of anthropology, 1970-72, Douglass College, professor of anthropology, 1972-90, professor emeritus of anthropology, 1990-, director of graduate programs in anthropology, 1970-72, Charles Darwin professor of anthropology, 1990-, now Charles Darwin professor emeritus of anthropology; Harry Frank Guggenheim Foundation, research director, 1972-84; Aspen Institute, Rockefeller fellow, 1979; U.S. News and World Report, Board of Social Scientists, chairman, 1986-88. Writer. **Publications:** (Co-author) Discipline and Discovery, 1966; Men in Groups, 1969, rev. ed., 2005; (with R. Fox) The Imperial Animal, 1971; (with J. Shepher) Women in the Kibbutz, 1975; Nashim ba-kibuts, 1976; Optimism: The Biology of Hope, 1979; (with R. Wolf) Chinas Food: A Photographic Journey, 1985; The Manufacture of Evil: Ethics, Evolution and the Industrial System, 1987; America Worked: The Photographs of Dan Weiner, 1989; The Pursuit of Pleasure, 1992; The Decline of Males, 1999; The Apes of New York, 2003; (with M. McGuire) God's Brain, 2010. EDITOR: Female Hierarchies, 1978; (with M.H. Robinson) Man & Beast Revisited, 1991. Contributor to books and journals. **Address:** Department of Anthropology, Rutgers University, Rm. 310, Ruth Adams Bldg., 131 George St., New Brunswick, NJ 08901-1414, U.S.A. **Online address:** ltiger@rci.rutgers.edu

TIGERMAN, Stanley. American (born United States), b. 1930. **Genres:** Architecture, History. **Career:** Archeworks, co-founder and director; Stanley Tigerman and Associates (now Tigerman McCurry Architects), principal, 1964-82; Cardiff College, visiting lecturer, 1965; University of Bangladesh, visiting lecturer, 1967; University of Illinois, professor of architecture, 1967-71, School of Architecture, director, 1985-93; University of California, visiting lecturer, 1968; Yale Arts Association, president, 1969-70; Cooper Union, visiting lecturer, 1970; Yale University, visiting lecturer, 1974; Cornell University, visiting lecturer, 1974; Tigerman Fugman McCurry, partner, 1982-88; American Institute of Architects, fellow. Writer. **Publications:** (Contrib.) Beyond Scale: Two Projects for the Physically Handicapped, 1978; (Comp.) Late Entries to the Chicago Tribune Tower Competition, 1980; Versus: An American Architect's Alternatives, 1982; (with S.G. Lewin) The California Condition: A Pregnant Architecture, 1982; (intro.) Architecture of Rome: A Nineteenth-Century Itinerary, 1986; The Architecture of Exile, 1988; Stanley Tigerman: Buildings and Projects 1966-1989, 1989; (intro.) Houses: The Architecture of Nagle, Hartray, Danker, Kagan, McKay, Penney, 2005; Schlepping Through Ambivalence: Essays on an American Architectural Condition, 2011. Contributor to periodicals. **Address:** Tigerman McCurry Architects, 444 N Wells St., Ste. 206, Chicago, IL 60654, U.S.A. **Online address:** tma@tigerman-mccurry.com

TIGHE, Carl. British/Irish (born Ireland), b. 1950?. **Genres:** Novels, History, Young Adult Non-fiction. **Career:** Derby University, professor of creative writing and head of creative writing department, Creative Writing Programme, senior lecturer. Writer. **Publications:** Gdańsk: National Identity in the Polish-German Borderlands, 1990; Rejoice!, 1992; The Politics of Literature: Poland, 1945-1989, 1999; Pax: Variations, 2000; Burning Worm, 2001; Writing and Responsibility, 2005; Druids Hill, 2008. Contributor to periodicals. **Address:** University of Derby, E708 Kedleston Rd., Derby, DB DE22 1GB, England. **Online address:** c.tighe@derby.ac.uk

TIHANYI, Eva. Canadian (born Canada), b. 1956. **Genres:** Poetry, Young Adult Fiction, Business/Trade/Industry, Novellas/Short Stories. **Career:** University of Windsor, teaching assistant, 1976-78, faculty, 1980-81; St. Clair College, Adult Retraining Program, faculty, 1978-80; Niagara College, professor of post-secondary English, 1978-; George Brown College and Humber College, faculty, 1981-86; Seneca College, faculty, 1981-86, professor of English, 1986-89; Books in Canada, columnist, 1994-99. Writer. **Publications:** (With H. Buckley) Canadian Policies for Rural Adjustment: A Study of the Economic Impact of ARDA, PFRA, and MMRA, 1967; A Sequence of the Blood, 1983; Prophecies: Near the Speed of Light, 1984; Saved by the Telling, 1995; Restoring the Wickedness, 2000; Wresting the Grace of the World, 2005; Truth and Other Fictions: Stories, 2009; In the Key of Red, 2010. **Address:** Niagara College of Applied Arts and Technology, 300 Woodlawn Rd., PO Box 1005, Welland, ON L3C 6Z7, Canada. **Online address:** eva@evatihanyi.com

TIKHOMIROV, Vladimir I. Australian/Russian (born Russia), b. 1959. **Genres:** International Relations/Current Affairs, History, Politics/Government, Adult Non-fiction, Theology/Religion. **Career:** Russian Academy of Sciences, Studies Research Institute, director, 1988-92; Moscow Independent University, associate professor of finance, 1992-93; University of Melbourne, senior research fellow, 1993-97, Contemporary Europe Research Centre, acting director, 1995-97, deputy director, 1997-. Writer. **Publications:** Partiia aparteida, 1987; The Party of Apartheid, 1987; The Church and the Political Struggle in South Africa, 1990; T. Serkov' i politicheskaia borba v Iuzhnoĭ Afrike, 1990; Razvitie politicheskoĭ mysli v Iuzhnoĭ Afrike, 1948-1988, 1991; States in Transition: Russia and South Africa, 1992; The Development of Political Thought in South Africa, 1948-1988, 1992; (ed.) Anatomy of the 1998 Russian Crisis, 1999; The Political Economy of Post-Soviet Russia, 2000; (ed.) Russia After Yeltsin, 2001; (co-ed.) Mathematical Events of the Twentieth Century, 2005. Contributor to periodicals. **Address:** Contemporary Europe Research Centre, University of Melbourne, Level 2, 234 Queensberry St., Carlton, VI 3010, Australia. **Online address:** v.tikhomirov@cerc.unimelb.edu.au

TILGHMAN, Benjamin R(oss). American (born United States), b. 1927. **Genres:** Art/Art History, Philosophy, Social Sciences, Cultural/Ethnic Topics. **Career:** Reed College, instructor in philosophy, 1956-57; Western State College of Colorado, assistant professor of philosophy, 1957-60; University of Wyoming, associate professor of philosophy and head of department, 1960-67; Kansas State University, professor of philosophy, 1967-94, head of department, 1967-80, now professor emeritus. Writer. **Publications:** The Expression of Emotion in the Visual Arts: A Philosophical Inquiry, 1970; (comp. with J.R. Hamilton and C.E. Reagan) Readings for an Introduction to Philosophy, 1976; But Is It Art?: The Value of Art and the Temptation of Theory, 1984; Wittgenstein, Ethics and Aesthetics: The View from Eternity, 1991; An Introduction to the Philosophy of Religion, 1994; Reflections on Aesthetic Judgment and Other Essays, 2006. EDITOR: Language and Aesthetic: Contributions to the Philosophy of Art, 1973. **Address:** 1602 Brandon Woods Ct., Lawrence, KS 66047-1985, U.S.A. **Online address:** b-mtil@sunflower.com

TILL, Barry Dorn. British (born England), b. 1923. **Genres:** History, Theology/Religion, Art/Art History. **Career:** Church of England, ordained priest, 1950; Parish Church, curate, 1950-53; Cambridge University, Jesus College, fellow, 1953-60, dean, 1956-60, tutor, 1957-60; St. John's Cathedral, dean, 1960-64; Morley College, principal, 1965-86; British Institute of Recorded Sound, governor and vice-chairman, 1967-73. Writer. **Publications:** Change and Exchange: Mutual Responsibility and the Church of England, 1965; Changing Frontiers in the Mission of the Church, 1965; The Churches Search for Unity, 1972; York Against Dunham: The Guardianship of the Spiritualities in the Diocese of Durham sede Vacante, 1993; Land of Morning Calm: Arts and Folkcrafts of Korea, 1998; Land of the Rising Sun: Arts of Japan, 1998; Shin Hanga: The New Print Movement of Japan, 2007; (with J. Patt and M. Warkentyne) Haiku, 2010. Contributor of articles to journals. **Address:** 44 Canonbury Sq., London, GL N1 2AW, England.

TILL, Nicholas. British (born England), b. 1955. **Genres:** Music, History, Humanities, Theatre. **Career:** Wimbledon School of Art, London, senior lecturer in art and performance, 1993-2004; Centre for Research in Opera and Music Theatre, director, 1998-; University of Sussex, Department of Music, professor of opera and music theatre, 2004-, director of doctoral studies; Royal College of Music, teacher; Britten-Pears School Aldeburgh, teacher; Stanford University, teacher. Writer. **Publications:** Rossini: His Life and Times, 1983; Mozart and the Enlightenment: Truth, Virtue and Beauty in Mozart's Operas, 1992. Contributor to journals. **Address:** Department of Music, University of Sussex, Silverstone Edb 216, Arts B B159, Falmer, Brighton, ES BN1 9QN, England. **Online address:** n.till@sussex.ac.uk

TILLEY, Patrick. British (born England), b. 1928. **Genres:** Novels, Science Fiction/Fantasy, Plays/Screenplays, Communications/Media. **Career:** Graphic designer, illustrator and consultant, 1954-68; scriptwriter, 1968-. **Publications:** NOVELS: Fade-Out, 1975; Mission, 1981; Xan, 1986; Star Wartz, 1995. THE AMTRAK WARS SERIES: Cloud Warrior, 1983; First Family, 1985; Iron Master, 1987; Blood River, 1988; Death Bringer, 1989; Earth-Thunder, 1990. **Address:** c/o Michael Sissons, Peters, Fraser & Dunlop Group Ltd., Drury House, 34-43 Russell St., London, GL WC2B 5HA, England. **Online address:** patrick.tilley@btinternet.com

TILLINGHAST, Richard. (Richard Williford Tillinghast). American (born United States), b. 1940. **Genres:** Poetry, Writing/Journalism, Adult Non-fiction, Travel/Exploration. **Career:** University of California, assistant professor of English, 1968-73; University of the South, visiting assistant professor, 1979-80; Harvard University, Briggs-Copeland lecturer, 1980-83; University of Michigan, Department of English, associate professor, 1983-92, professor, 1992-2005, professor emeritus, 2005-; Michigan Institute for the Humanities, associate, 1989-90, 1993-94. Writer. **Publications:** The Keeper, 1968; Sleep Watch, 1969, 2nd ed., 1983; The Knife and Other Poems, 1980; Sewanee in Ruins, 1981; Fossils, Metal, and the Blue Limit, 1982; Our Flag Was Still There, 1984; A Quiet Pint in Kinvara, 1991; The Stonecutter's Hand, 1995; Robert Lowell's Life and Work: Damaged Grandeur, 1995; Today in the Café Trieste, 1997; (ed. and intro.) A Visit to the Gallery: The University of Michigan Museum of Art, 1997; Six Mile Mountain, 2000; (contrib.) Rhyme: (2001): For Baritone Voice and Piano, 2001; Poetry and What is Real, 2004; The New Life, 2008; Finding Ireland: A Poet's Explorations of Irish Literature and Culture, 2008; Sewanee Poems, 2009; (as Richard Williford Tillinghast) Selected Poems, 2009. Contributor to newspapers and periodicals. **Address:** Department of English Language and Literature, University of Michigan, 3187 Angell Hall, 435 S State St., Ann Arbor, MI 48109-1003, U.S.A. **Online address:** richardtillinghast@eircom.net

TILLINGHAST, Richard Williford. See **TILLINGHAST, Richard.**

TILLIS, Steve. American (born United States) **Genres:** Theatre. **Career:**

University of California, lecturer in theater arts, 1996-98; Stanford University, fellow in humanities, 1998-2001; St. Mary's College, lecturer, 2001-. Writer. **Publications:** Toward an Aesthetics of the Puppet: Puppetry as a Theatrical Art, 1992; Rethinking Folk Drama, 1999. Contributor to periodicals. **Address:** School of Liberal Arts, St. Mary's College of California, 207B Galileo Hall, PO Box 515, Moraga, CA 94575, U.S.A. **Online address:** stillis@stmarys-ca.edu

TILLMAN, Deborah Lindsay. American (born United States), b. 1953. **Genres:** Poetry, Adult Non-fiction, Business/Trade/Industry, Human Relations/Parenting. **Career:** Allegheny General Hospital, financial representative, 1985-98; Shadyside Hospital, out patient registrar, 2000-01; Hillman Cancer Center, oncology coordinator, 2001-. Freelance writer and artist. **Publications:** Come Inside, 2003; Stepping Out on Faith: How to Open a Quality Childcare Center, 2005; Not Just Any Woman, forthcoming; Ode to Life, forthcoming. **Address:** c/o Author Mail, Harobed Publishing Creations, PO Box 8195, Pittsburgh, PA 15217-0195, U.S.A. **Online address:** dctlmn@att.net

TILLMAN, Lynne. American (born United States), b. 1947. **Genres:** Novellas/Short Stories. **Career:** State University of New York, University at Albany, associate professor of English, writer-in-residence; Fence magazine, fiction editor, 2003-; Yale University School of Art, critic in sculpture, 2011-. **Publications:** NOVELS: Haunted Houses, 1987; Absence Makes the Heart, 1990; Motion Sickness, 1991; Cast in Doubt, 1992; No Lease on Life, 1998; Love Sentence (chapbook), 1999; This Is Not It: Stories, 2002. STORIES: The Madame Realism Complex, 1992. NON-FICTION: Living with Contradictions, 1984; (with B. Schwabsky and L. Cooke) Jessica Stockholder, 1995; The Velvet Years: Warhol's Factory 1965-1967, 1995; The Broad Picture: Essays, 1997; Bookstore: The Life and Times of Jeannette Watson and Books & Co., 1999; Stephen Shore: Uncommon Places: The Complete Works, 2004; American Genius: A Comedy, 2006; Someday This Will be Funny, 2011. Contributor to periodicals. **Address:** Department of English, University at Albany, State University of New York, Rm. 333 Humanities, 1400 Washington Ave., Albany, NY 12222, U.S.A.

TILLSON, Albert H. American (born United States), b. 1948. **Genres:** History, Local History/Rural Topics, Politics/Government. **Career:** Northern Virginia Community College, part-time lecturer in history, 1975-76, 1985; St. Norbert College, instructor in history, 1984-85; Pan American University, instructor in history, 1986; University of Tampa, assistant professor, 1986-92, associate professor of history, 1992, professor of history. Writer. **Publications:** Gentry and Common Folk: Political Culture on a Virginia Frontier, 1740-1789, 1991; Accommodating Revolutions: Virginia's Northern Neck in an Era of Transformations, 1760-1810, 2010. Contributor to history journals. **Address:** Department of History, University of Tampa, Rm. SC 201, 401 W Kennedy Blvd., PO Box 2F, Tampa, FL 33606-1490, U.S.A. **Online address:** atillson@ut.edu

TILLY, Chris. (Brendan Rosis). American (born United States), b. 1955. **Genres:** Business/Trade/Industry, Economics, Sociology. **Career:** Massachusetts Institute of Technology, Department of Economics, instructor, 1986-87; Dollars and Sense, editor, 1986-2006; University of Massachusetts, Department of Economics, instructor and assistant professor, 1988-90, Department of Policy and Planning, assistant professor, 1991-94, associate professor, 1994-97, Department of Regional Economic and Social Development, associate professor, 1997-99, university professor, 1999-2006, professor, 2006-; University of California, Institute for Research on Labor and Employment, director; Contemporary Sociology, editor, 2003-06; American Sociological Association, editor, 2006-. **Publications:** (With Y.C. Freixas) Fifteen Years of Community-Based Development: An Annotated Bibliography, 1968-1983, 1985; Short Hours, Short Shrift: Causes and Consequences of Part-Time Work, 1990; (with R. Albelda) It'll Take More Than a Miracle: Income in Single-Mother Families in Massachusetts, 1979-1987, 1992; (with B. Bluestone and M.H. Stevenson) Public Policy Alternatives for Dealing with the Labor Market Problems of Central City Young Adults: Implications from Current Labor Market Research, 1994; Half a Job: Bad and Good Part-Time Jobs in a Changing Labor Market, 1996; (with R. Albelda) Glass Ceilings and Bottomless Pits: Women's Work, Women's Poverty, 1997; (with C. Tilly) Work under Capitalism, 1998; (ed. with A. O'Connor and L. Bobo) Urban Inequality: Evidence from Four Cities, 2001; (with P. Moss) Stories Employers Tell: Race, Skills and Hiring in America, 2001. **Address:** Department of Regional, Economic and Social Development, University of Massachusetts, Rm. 500 O, 61

Wilder St., Lowell, MA 01854, U.S.A. **Online address:** chris_tilly@uml.edu

TILLYARD, S. K. See **TILLYARD, Stella.**

TILLYARD, Stella. (S. K. Tillyard). British (born England), b. 1957. **Genres:** Biography. **Career:** Harvard University, Knox Fellow; University of California, faculty; University of London, faculty; Centre for Editing Lives and Letters, teacher. Writer. **Publications:** (As S.K. Tillyard) Impact of Modernism, 1900-1920: Early Modernism and the Arts and Crafts Movement in Edwardian England, 1988; Early Modernism and The Arts and Crafts Movement in Edwardian England, 1988; Aristocrats: Caroline, Emily, Louisa and Sara Lennox, 1740-1832, 1994; Citizen Lord: Edward Fitzgerald, 1763-1798, 1998; Aristocrats: The Illustrated Companion To The Television Series, 1999; (contrib.) Joshua Reynolds: The Creation of Celebrity, 2005; Royal Affair: George III and His Scandalous Siblings, 2006; Tides of War: A Novel, 2011. Contributor to periodicals. **Address:** Chatto/Random House UK Ltd., Random House, 20 Vauxhall Bridge Rd., London, GL SW1V 2SA, England. **Online address:** tillyard@waitrose.com

TILMAN, Leo M. American (born United States), b. 1971. **Genres:** Money/Finance, Business/Trade/Industry. **Career:** Bear Stearns, chief institutional strategist and senior managing director, 2001-08; L.M. Tilman & Co., president and chief executive officer, 2008-; BlackRock, staff; Columbia University, adjunct lecturer, lecturer; Journal of Risk Finance, contributing editor; Atlantic Partnership, board director. Consultant. **Publications:** (With B.W. Golub) Risk Management: Approaches for Fixed Income Markets, 2000; Financial Darwinism: Create Value or Self-destruct in a World of Risk, 2009. **Address:** Department of Industrial Engineering and, Operations Research, Columbia University, 590 Madison Ave., 21st Fl., New York, NY 10022, U.S.A. **Online address:** lmt13@columbia.edu

TIMBERLAKE, Richard Henry. American (born United States), b. 1922. **Genres:** Economics, Money/Finance. **Career:** Muhlenberg College, instructor in economics, 1948-51; Norwich University, assistant professor of economics, 1953-55; Florida State University, associate professor of economics, 1958-63; University of Georgia, professor of economics, 1964-90, Terry College, now business professor emeritus and libertarian economist; Federal Reserve Bank of Richmond, research consultant, 1970-71; University of Virginia, faculty; Rensselaer Polytechnic Institute, faculty; Texas A&M University, faculty; Southern Economic Association, vice president. Writer. **Publications:** Money, Banking and Central Banking, 1965; (with E.B. Selby) Money and Banking, 1972; The Origins of Central Banking in the United States, 1978; Gold, Greenbacks, and the Constitution, 1991; Monetary Policy in the United States, an Institutional and Intellectual History, 1993; (ed. with K. Dowd) Money and the Nation State: The Financial Revolution, Government, and the World Monetary System, 1998; They Never Saw Me Then, 2001. Contributor to journals. **Address:** Terry College of Business, University of Georgia, Brooks Hall, 5th Fl., Athens, GA 30602-6254, U.S.A. **Online address:** rightim@earthlink.net

TIMBRELL, Charles. American (born United States), b. 1942. **Genres:** Music. **Career:** American University, instructor of music, 1975-86; Howard University, Department of Music, associate professor of piano, 1986-98, professor, 1998-, coordinator of keyboard studies; Ecole Normale de Musique, lecturer; Universite de Paris, lecturer. Writer. **Publications:** French Pianism: An Historical Perspective: Including Interviews with Contemporary Performers, 1992, 2nd ed., 1999; Prince of Virtuosos: A Life of Walter Rummel, American Pianist, 2005. Contributor to journals. **Address:** Department of Music, Howard University, Rm. LVC 3025, 2455 6th St., Washington, DC 20059, U.S.A. **Online address:** ctimbrell@aol.com

TIMMERMAN, Kelsey. American (born United States), b. 1979. **Genres:** Travel/Exploration. **Career:** Travel writer. **Publications:** Where Am I Wearing?: A Global Tour to the Countries, Factories, and People That Make Our Clothes, 2008. Contributor to periodicals. **Address:** John Wiley & Sons Inc., 111 River St., Hoboken, NJ 07030-5774, U.S.A. **Online address:** hi@kelseytimmerman.com

TIMMERMANS, Tricia. Canadian/Australian (born Australia), b. 1946. **Genres:** Photography, Travel/Exploration, Writing/Journalism, Reference. **Career:** School for the Deaf, teacher, 1966-70; teacher, 1972-73, 1974-76; Atlantic Provinces Resource Centre for the Hearing Handicapped, teacher, 1979-80; Child Development Centre, teacher of the deaf, 1980, chairperson,

1982-85; Consumers Association of Canada, area director, 1983-84; CPR Yukon, volunteer bookkeeper, 1990-93; Canadian International Development Association, English teacher, 1991; Victoria International Development Education Association, office worker and data processor, 1994; Youth Challenge Intl., group leader, 1994-95; photojournalist, 1995-; Photo-J Inc., president. **Publications:** British Columbia: Off the Beaten Path, 1998, 5th ed., 2005. **Address:** Photo-J Inc., 106-2768 Satellite Pl., Victoria, BC V8S 5G8, Canada. **Online address:** photo-j@shaw.ca

TIMMS, Edward. British (born England), b. 1937. **Genres:** Adult Non-fiction, Psychology, Regional/Urban Planning, Biography, Essays. **Career:** University of Sussex, lecturer in European studies, 1963-65, research professor in German Studies, professor, 1992-, life fellow, Center for German-Jewish Studies, director; University of Cambridge, lecturer in German, 1965-91, Gonville and Caius College, life fellow, 1965-, 1992-2011; German Research Colloquium, coordinator, 1992-. Writer. **Publications:** Karl Kraus, Apocalyptic Satirist: Culture and Catastrophe in Habsburg Vienna (nonfiction), 1986; (with S. Göksu) Romantic Communist: The Life and Work of Nazim Hikmet, 1999; Karl Kraus und Die Fackel: Aufsätze zur Rezeptionsgeschichte (title means: 'Reading Karl Kraus: Essays on the Reception of Die Fackel'), 2001; Writing after Hitler, 2001; Jugend auf der Flucht: dieTagebücher von Ernst und Julie Stock, 2004; Karl Kraus, Apocalyptic Satirist: The Post-War Crisis and the Rise of the Swastika, 2005; Taking Up the Torch: English Institutions, German Dialectics and Multicultural Commitments, 2011. EDITOR: (with D. Kelley) Unreal City: Urban Experience in Modern European Literature and Art (essays), 1985; (with P. Scheichl) Karl Kraus in Neuer Sicht (title means: 'Karl Kraus in a New Perspective') (nonfiction), 1986; (with P. Collier) Visions and Blueprints: Avant-Garde Culture and Radical Politics in Early Twentieth-Century Europe (essays), 1988; (with N. Segal) Freud in Exile: Psychoanalysis and its Vicissitudes (essays), 1988; (with R. Robertson) Vienna 1900: From Altenberg to Wittgenstein (essays), 1990; (with R. Robertson) The Austrian Enlightenment and Its Aftermath (essays), 1991; (with R. Robertson) Psychoanalysis in its Cultural Context, 1992; (with R. Robertson) Theatre and Performance in Austria: From Mozart to Jelinek, 1993; (with R. Robertson) Habsburg Legacy: National Identity in Historical Perspective, 1994; (and intro.) Freud and the Child Woman: The Memoirs of Fritz Wittels, 1995; (with R. Robertson) Austrian Exodus: The Creative Achievements of Refugees from National Socialism, 1995; (with R. Robertson) Gender and Politics in Austrian Fiction, 1996; (with R. Robertson) Theodor Herzl and the Origins of Zionism, 1997; (with A. Hammel) German-Jewish Dilemma: From the Enlightenment to the Shoah, 1999, (ed. with J. Hughes) Intellectual Migration and Cultural Transformation: Refugees from National Socialism in the English-Speaking World, 2003; Nationalist Myths and Modern Media: Contested Identities in the Age of Globalization, 2006; (ed. with D. Schultz) Arnold Daghani's Memories of Mikhailowka: The Illustrated Diary of a Slave Labour Camp Survivor, 2009. Contributor to periodicals. **Address:** University of Sussex, Sussex House, Brighton, BN1 9RH, England. **Online address:** e.timms@sussex.ac.uk

TINDALL, Gillian (Elizabeth). British (born England), b. 1938. **Genres:** Literary Criticism And History, Urban Studies, Biography, Novels, Novellas/Short Stories, History, Autobiography/Memoirs, Young Adult Fiction, Young Adult Fiction. **Career:** Writer. **Publications:** No Name in the Street, 1959 in US as When We Had Other Names, 1960; The Water and the Sound, 1961; The Edge of the Paper, 1963; The Israeli Twins, 1963; A Handbook on Witchcraft, 1966; The Youngest, 1967; Someone Else, 1969; Fly Away Home, 1971; Dances of Death: Short Stories on a Theme, 1973; The Born Exile: George Gissing, 1974; The Traveller and His Child, 1975; The Fields Beneath: The History of One London Village, 1977, rev. ed., 2002; The Intruder, 1979; The China Egg and Other Stories, 1981; City of Gold: The Biography of Bombay, 1982; Looking Forward, 1983; Rosamond Lehmann: An Appreciation, 1985; A Little Touch of Death, 1985; To the City, 1987; Give Them All My Love, 1989; Journey of a Lifetime and other Stories, 1990; Countries of the Mind: The Meaning of Place to Writers, 1991; Spirit Weddings, 1992; Célestine: Voices from a French Village, 1995; The Night House, 1997; The Journey of Martin Nadaud: A Life and Turbulent Times, 1999; Man Who Drew London: Wenceslaus Hollar in Reality and Imagination, 2003; The House by the Thames: And the People who Lived There, 2006; Footprints in Paris: A Few Streets, A Few Lives, 2009. Contributor to periodicals. **Address:** c/o Curtis Brown, Curtis Brown Group Ltd., Haymarket House, 28-29 Haymarket, London, GL SW1Y 4SP, England.

TING, Windsor. American/Chinese (born China), b. 1953. **Genres:** Scienc-es, Medicine/Health, How-to Books, Psychiatry, Psychology, E-books. **Career:** Columbia University, Columbia Presbyterian Medical Center, general surgery resident, 1979-85, cardiac surgery fellow, 1985-87, Department of Cardiothoracic Surgery, faculty, 1987-, College of Physicians and Surgeons, assistant professor; The Mount Sinai Hospital, Mount Sinai Medical Center, assistant professor. Writer. **Publications:** (With G. Fricchione) The Heart-Mind Connection: How Emotions Contribute to Heart Disease and What to Do about It, 2006. **Address:** 5 East 98th St., Division of Vascular Surgery, Mt Sinai Medical School, New York, NY 10019, U.S.A. **Online address:** windsor.ting@mountsinai.org

TINGLE, Tim. American (born United States) **Genres:** Children's Fiction, Biography. **Career:** New Canaan Farms, co-owner and operator, 1979-97; Story Tribe Publishing, founder and publisher. Writer and musician. **Publications:** Walking the Choctaw Road, 2003; (with D. Moore) Texas Ghost Stories: Fifty Favorites for the Telling, 2004; (with D. Moore) Spooky Texas Tales, 2005; Crossing Bok Chitto, 2006; When Turtle Grew Feathers: A Folktale From The Choctaw Nation, 2007; Saltypie: A Choctaw Journey From Darkness Into Light, 2010; (with D. Moore) More Spooky Texas Tales, 2010; Riding the Red Dirt Road, forthcoming. **Address:** StoryTribe Publishing, 4417 Morningside Way, Canyon Lake, TX 78133-4085, U.S.A. **Online address:** timtingle@hotmail.com

TINGUM, Janice. American (born United States), b. 1958. **Genres:** Children's Non-fiction, Literary Criticism And History, Biography, Children's Fiction. **Career:** Grand Forks Abstract, title examiner, 1984-99; lawyer in private practice, 1984-97; Caldis Tingum and Tingum Ltd., lawyer, 2000-. Freelance writer. **Publications:** E.B. White: The Elements of a Writer, 1995. Contributor to periodicals. **Address:** 1317 Chestnut St., Grand Forks, ND 58201, U.S.A. **Online address:** janice@janicetingum.com

TINKLE, Theresa L. (Theresa Lynn Tinkle). American (born United States), b. 1954. **Genres:** Literary Criticism And History. **Career:** University of Michigan, English Language and Literature Department, Arthur F. Thurneau professor, associate professor, 1989-, professor, director of academic programs, 1995-99, Gayle Morris Sweetland Writing Center and English Composition Board, director, 1998-99. Writer. **Publications:** (As Theresa Lynn Tinkle) Medieval Venuses and Cupids: Sexuality, Hermeneutics and English Poetry, 1996; (ed. with G. Bornstein) The Iconic Page in Manuscript, Print and Digital Culture, 1998; (ed. with D. Minkova) Chaucer and the Challenges of Medievalism: Studies in Honor of H A. Kelly, 2003; Gender and Power in Medieval Exegesis, 2010. Contributor to publications. **Address:** Department of English, University of Michigan, 3224 AH, 435 S State St., Ann Arbor, MI 48109-1003, U.S.A. **Online address:** tinkle@umich.edu

TINKLE, Theresa Lynn. *See* **TINKLE, Theresa L.**

TINNISWOOD, Adrian. British (born England), b. 1954?. **Genres:** Homes/Gardens, Architecture, History, Cultural/Ethnic Topics. **Career:** The National Trust, architectural historian. Writer, lecturer and broadcaster. **Publications:** A History of Country House Visiting: Five Centuries of Tourism and Taste, 1989; Cross Currents: A Coastal Studies Handbook for Teachers, 1990; Historic Houses of the National Trust, 1991; The National Trust: Historic Houses of Britain, 1992; Country Houses from the Air, 1994; Life in the English Country Cottage, 1995; Visions of Power: Ambition and Architecture from Ancient Times to the Present, 1998; The Polite Tourist: Four Centuries of Country House Visiting, 1998; Arts & Crafts House, 1999; His Invention So Fertile: A Life of Christopher Wren, 2001; Art Deco House: Avant-garde Houses of the 1920s and 1930s, 2002; By Permission of Heaven: The Story of the Great Fire of London, 2004; The Verneys: A True Story of Love, War and Madness in Seventeenth-Century England, 2007; Pirates of Barbary: Corsairs, Conquests and Captivity in the Seventeenth-century Mediterranean, 2010. **Address:** Knight Ayton Management, 114 St. Martin's Ln., London, GL WC2N 4BE, England. **Online address:** adriantinniswood@hotmail.com

TINSLEY, Kevin (M.). American (born United States) **Genres:** Cartoons, Novels, Graphic Novels. **Career:** Marvel Entertainment Group, senior cover coordinator, 1990-96; Merkley and Partners, senior graphic artist, 2006-. Writer, colorist and publisher. **Publications:** Digital Prepress for Comic Books: The Definitive Desktop Production Guide, 1999; Homebrew: The Festering Season (graphic novel), 2002; (with P. Singer) Stonehaven: Milk Cartons and Dog Biscuits, 2004; Stonehaven: Subterranean Hearts, 2006; Stonehaven: Fruit of the Poisonous Vine, 2008; Digital Prepress for

Comic Books: Revised, Updated and Expanded, 2009. **Address:** Stickman Graphics, 141 16th St., Brooklyn, NY 11215, U.S.A. **Online address:** stckmngrphcs@stickmangraphics.com

TIPLER, Frank J(ennings). American (born United States), b. 1947. **Genres:** Physics, Anthropology/Ethnology. **Career:** University of California, research mathematician, 1976-79; Oxford University, senior research fellow, 1979; University of Texas, research associate, 1979-81; Tulane University, associate professor of mathematics, professor, 1981-87; University of Sussex, visiting fellow, 1987; University of Liége, Institut d'Astrophysique, visiting professor, 1988; Universität Bern, visiting professor, 1989. Writer. **Publications:** (Ed.) Essays in General Relativity: A Festschrift for Abraham Taub, 1980; (with J.D. Barrow and M.O. Monchicourt) L'Homme et le cosmos: Le Principe anthropique en astrophysique moderne (title means: 'Man and the Cosmos: The Anthropic Principle in Modern Astrophysics'), 1984; (with J.D. Barrow) The Anthropic Cosmological Principle, 1986; The Physics of Immortality: Modern Cosmology, God and the Resurrection of the Dead, 1994; The Physics of Christianity, 2007. Contributor to periodicals. **Address:** Department of Mathematics and Physics, Tulane University, 305 Gibson Hall, 6823 St. Charles Ave., New Orleans, LA 70118, U.S.A. **Online address:** tipler@tulane.edu

TIPPETS, John M. American (born United States), b. 1941?. **Genres:** Biography, Autobiography/Memoirs. **Career:** American Airlines, staff, American Airlines Federal Credit Union, chief executive officer, 1966-2008. Writer. **Publications:** Hearts of Courage: The Gillam Plane Crash and the Amazing True Story of Survival in the Frozen Wilderness of Alaska, 2008. **Address:** Colleyville, TX , U.S.A. **Online address:** johntippets@yahoo.com

TIPTON, David. British (born England), b. 1934. **Genres:** Novels, Novellas/Short Stories, Poetry, Travel/Exploration, Biography, Translations. **Career:** Educator, 1960-70; Rivelin Press, owner; Tedbeck Press, owner; Blue Bridge Press, owner. Writer. **Publications:** Poems in Transit, 1960; City of Kings and Other Poems, 1967; Millstone Grit, 1972; Pachacamac, 1974; Atahualpa, 1975; Graph of Love, 1976; Nomads and Settlers, 1980; Moving House, 1982; Sexual Disturbances, 1983; Wars of the Roses, 1984; Freak Summer, 1984; Sea Urchins and Other Poems, 1989; Green and Purple, 1993; Millstone Grit and Other Poems, 1993; Crossing the Rimac, 1995; Family Chronicle, 1997; Amulet Against the Evil Eye and other Poems, 1997; Paradise of Exiles (novel), 1999; Medal for Malaya (novel), 2002; Nordic Barbarians (short stories), 2002; A Sword in the Air (travel), 2003; (with S. Tipton) Star Trek, Klingons: Blood Will Tell, 2007. TRANSLATOR: (and ed.) Peru the New Poetry: 12 Peruvian Poets, 1970; (with M. Ahern and W. Rowe) The Spider Hangs Too Far from the Ground, 1970; Common Grave, 1973; (cotrans.) A. Cisneros, At Night the Cats, 1985; (co-trans.) A. Cisneros, Land of Angels, 1985; (with C.A. de Lomellini and ed.) J. Watanabe, Path through the Canefields, 1997; (with C.A. de Lomellini) T. Mora, A Mountain Crowned by a Cemetery, 2001. **Address:** Redbeck Press, 24 Aireville Rd., Frizinghall, Bradford, WY BD9 4HH, England.

TIPTON, James. American (born United States), b. 1952. **Genres:** Novels, History. **Career:** College of Marin, professor of English; University of California, instructor in English and creative writing; University of Bordeaux, instructor. Writer. **Publications:** Annette Vallon: A Novel of the French Revolution, 2007. **Address:** Kentfield Campus, College of Marin, 835 College Ave., Kentfield, CA 94904, U.S.A. **Online address:** james.tipton@marin.edu

TIRION, Wil. Dutch (born Netherlands), b. 1943. **Genres:** Astronomy, Natural History, Sciences. **Career:** Graphic artist and designer, 1966-68; lithographer, 1968-83; freelance sky cartographer, 1983-. Writer. **Publications:** Sky Atlas 2000.0, Desk, Field and Deluxe Editions, 1981, (with R.W. Sinnott) 2nd ed., 1998; Atlas of the Night Sky, 1984; (with I. Ridpath) Stars and Planets, 1984, 4th ed., 2007; B.A.A. Chart of the Heavens, 1985; (with I. Ridpath) Gem Guide: The Night Sky, 1985; (with B. Rappaport and G. Lovi) Uranometria 2000.0, 2nd ed., 2001; (with I. Ridpath) The Monthly Sky Guide, 1987, 6th ed., 2003; Bright Star Atlas 2000.0, 1989; (with G. Lovi) Men, Monsters, and the Modern Universe, 1989; Cambridge Star Atlas, 1991, 4th ed., 2010; (with C. Crossen) Binocular Astronomy, 1992, 2nd ed., 2008; (with D. Ellyard) The Southern Sky Guide, 1993, 3rd ed., 2008; (with M.D. Heifetz) A Walk through the Heavens, 1996, 3rd ed., 2004; Gem Guide: Stars, 1999; (with M.D. Heifetz) A Walk through the Southern Sky, 1999, 2nd ed., 2007; (with S. Dunlop) Collins Wild Guide: Night Sky, 1999; Wild Guide Night Sky: Star Finder, 2000; (with R. Burnham) Exploring the Starry Sky,

2003; (with S. Dunlop) Firefly Planisphere Deluxe, 2003; (with J. Mullaney) Cambridge Double Star Atlas, 2009; (with J. Mullaney) Cambridge Atlas of Herschel Objects, 2010. Contributor to books and journals. **Address:** Wisselspoor 221, Capelle aan de IJssel, 2908 AD, Netherlands. **Online address:** wil.tirion@mac.com

TIRMAN, John. American (born United States), b. 1949. **Genres:** Business/Trade/Industry, Economics, Politics/Government, Military/Defense/Arms Control, Social Sciences. **Career:** TIME magazine, researcher-reporter, 1977-79; New England Regional Commission, senior adviser, energy and the environment, 1980-82; Union of Concerned Scientists, senior editor and director of communications, 1982-86; Winston Foundation for World Peace, executive director, 1986-99; Social Science Research Council, program director, 2000-04, Washington office director, 2001-04; Massachusetts Institute of Technology, Center for International Studies, executive director and principal research scientist, 2004-. Writer. **Publications:** (Ed.) The Fallacy of Star Wars, 1984; (ed.) The Militarization of High Technology, 1984; (ed.) Empty Promise: The Growing Case against Star Wars, 1986; Sovereign Acts: American Unilateralism and Global Security, 1989; Spoils of War: The Human Cost of America's Arms Trade, 1997; Making the Money Sing: Private Wealth and Public Power in the Search for Peace, 2000; (ed.) The Maze of Fear: Security and Migration after 9/11, 2004; (ed. with R. Thakur and E. Newman) Multilateralism under Challenge?: Power, International Order and Structural Change, 2006; 100 Ways America is Screwing Up the World, 2006; (ed. with M. Heiberg and B. O'Leary) Terror, Insurgencies and States: Breaking the Cycles of Protracted Violence, 2007; (with S.F. Martin) Women, Migration and Conflict: Breaking a Deadly Cycle, 2009; The Deaths of Others: The Fate of Civilians in America's Wars, 2011. **Address:** Center for International Studies, Massachusetts Institute of Technology, Bldg. E40-447, 1 Amherst St., Cambridge, MA 02139, U.S.A. **Online address:** tirman@mit.edu

TIRTHA, Swami Sadashiva. American (born United States) **Genres:** Medicine/Health, Reference, Theology/Religion. **Career:** Ayurveda Holistic Center, owner, teacher and practitioner, 1988-, International Vedic Institute, founder; monk, 1990-; yoga teacher, 2003-. Writer. **Publications:** The Ayurveda Encyclopedia: Natural Secrets to Healing, Prevention & Longevity, 1998; Ayurveda Primer, 2000; Bhagavad Gita for Modern Times: Secrets to Attaining Inner Peace and Harmony, 2007. Contributor to periodicals. **Address:** Ayurveda Holistic Center, 132 Wilbur Hill Rd., Unadilla, NY 13849, U.S.A. **Online address:** pnp@peaceandparadise.com

TISCHAUSER, Leslie V. American (born United States), b. 1942. **Genres:** Local History/Rural Topics, Social Sciences, History, Politics/Government. **Career:** Prairie State College, Department of Social Sciences, professor, 1982-, chair. **Publications:** A History of Chicago, 1983; Burden of Ethnicity: The German Question in Chicago, 1914-1941, 1990; The German Question in Chicago, 1992; Black/White Relations in American History: An Annotated Bibliography, 1998; Black History for White People, 1999; The Changing Nature of Racial and Ethnic Conflict in United Sates History: 1492 to the Present, 2002; A College for All People: Prairie State College, 1981-, 2005; Race Relations in the United States, 1920-1940, 2008. Contributor to books. **Address:** Department of Social Sciences, Prairie State College, Rm. 2151, 202 S Halsted St.,, Chicago Heights, IL 60411, U.S.A. **Online address:** ltischauser@prairiestate.edu

TISDALE, Sallie. American (born United States), b. 1957. **Genres:** Adult Non-fiction, Biography, Theology/Religion, History. **Career:** Nurse, 1983-90; University of Portland, Schoenfeldt distinguished writer, 1992; University of California, visiting writer, 1992; University of Montana, visiting writer, 1994; Salon, columnist; Harper, editor. **Publications:** The Sorcerer's Apprentice: Tales of the Modern Hospital, 1986; Harvest Moon: Portrait of a Nursing Home, 1987; Lot's Wife: Salt and the Human Condition, 1988; Sorcerer's Apprentice: Medical Miracles and Other Disasters, 1988; Stepping Westward: The Long Search for Home in the Pacific Northwest, 1991; Talk Dirty to Me: An Intimate Philosophy of Sex, 1994; (contrib.) Portland from the Air, 2000; The Best Thing I Ever Tasted: The Secret of Food, 2000; Women of the Way: Discovering 2,500 Years of Buddhist Wisdom, 2006. Contributor to periodicals. **Address:** Witherspoon & Associates Inc., 1000 W Weatherford St., Fort Worth, TX 76102, U.S.A.

TISDELL, Clement Allan. Australian (born Australia), b. 1939. **Genres:**

Economics, Environmental Sciences/Ecology, Local History/Rural Topics. **Career:** Australian National University, lecturer in economics, 1966, senior lecturer in economics, 1967, reader in economics, 1967-72, Faculty of Economics, sub-dean, 1968-70; University of Newcastle, Department of Economics, professor of economics, 1972-89, head, 1975-79, 1983-86, Faculty of Commerce and Economics, dean, 1977-78; Institute of Industrial Economics, acting director, 1977-79; University of Queensland, Department of Economics, professor of economics, 1989-2004, professor emeritus, 2004-, head, 1989-98, Business, Economics and Law Faculty, acting executive dean, 1998. Writer. **Publications:** Countries: Experiences, Obstacles and Sustainability in Global Perspective 1991; (with Y. Toyama) Japan-Australia Economic Relations in the 1990s, 1991; (with K. Roy and R. Sen) Economic Development and Environment, 1992; Giant Clams in the Sustainable Development of the South Pacific, 1992; (co-author) Economic Development and Women in the World Community, 1996; (co-author) Environment and Sustainable Agricultural Development, 1996; (co-author) China and the Asia Pacific Economy, 1997; (with J. Chai) China's Economic Growth and Transition, 1997; (co-author) World Trade and Development, 1997; (with K. Roy) Tourism and Development, 1998; (with K. Roy) Tourism in India and India's Economic Development, 1998; (with K.C. Roy and H.C. Blomqvist) Economic Development and Women in The World Community, 1999; (with A.K. Dragun) Sustainable Agriculture and Environment: Globalisation and the Impact of Trade Liberalisation, 1999; (with W. Lakshman) Facets of Development of Sri Lanka Since Independence: Socio Political Economics Scientific and Cultural, 1999; (with W. Lakshman) Sri Lanka's Development Since Independence, 2000; The Economics of Tourism, 2000; (with A.K. Dragun) Sustainable Agriculture and Environment, 2001; (with R.K. Sen) Economic Globalisation: Social Conflicts, Labour and Environmental Issues, 2004; Globalisation and World Economic Policies: Effects and Policy Responses of Nations and their Groupings, 2005; (with J.M. Aurifeille and S. Svizzero) Leading Economic and Managerial Issues Involving Globalisation, 2006; Economics of Leisure, 2006; Poverty, Poverty Alleviation and Social Disadvantage, 2007; (with J.M. Aurifeille and S. Svizzero) Globalization and Partnerships: Features of Business Alliances and International Cooperation, 2007; (with K. Hartley) Microeconomic Policy: A New Perspective, 2008; Resource and Environmental Economics, 2009; (with T. Kiriti) Gender Inequality in Agricultural Households in Kenya: Economic Analysis, 2010; (with R. Bandara) Economic Management and Evaluation of Human-Elephant Conflict: Sri Lankan Empirical Evidence and Analysis, 2010; (with Z. Gao) Technology Transfer and China's Industrial Development: Consequences, Policy Reforms, Significant Case Studies, 2010; (with P. Moepeng) The Pattern of Livelihoods in a Typical Rural Village: The Importance of Subjective Poverty and Inequality Measures in Botswana: New Perspectives, 2010; (co-ed.) Globalisation, Governance and Ethics: New Managerial and Economic Insights, 2011. **Address:** School of Economics, University of Queensland, 618 Colin Clark Bldg., St. Lucia, Brisbane, QL 4072, Australia. **Online address:** c.tisdell@economics.uq.edu.au

TISMANEANU, Vladimir. American/Romanian (born Romania), b. 1951. **Genres:** Politics/Government. **Career:** Institute Typified Buildings Design, Department of Urban Sociology, sociologist, 1974-81; Foreign Policy Research Institute, faculty, 1983-90; University of Pennsylvania, faculty, 1985-90; University of Maryland, professor of government, Center for the Study of Post-Communist Societies, director, 1990-; East European Politics and Societies, editor, 1998-2004; Presidential Commission for the Study of the Communist Dictatorship in Romania, head; Institute for People's Studies, academic council chairman, 2009; Institute for the Investigation of Communist Crimes, president of the scientific council; Institut für die Wissenschaften vom Menschen, fellow, 2002; New York University, fellow, 2002; The Inter-American Institute, distinguished senior fellow in political science. **Publications:** Noua Stîngă și școala de la Frankfurt, 1976; The Crisis of Marxist Ideology in Eastern Europe: The Poverty of Utopia, 1988; (with M. Radu) Latin American Revolutionaries: Groups, Goals, Methods, 1990; Reinventing Politics: Eastern Europe from Stalin to Havel, 1992; Irepetabilul trecut, 1994; Noaptea totalitară: crepusculul ideologiilor radicale în Europa de Est, 1995; Fantoma lui Gheorghiu-Dej, 1995; Balul mascat: un dialog cu Mircea Mihăieș, 1996; Vecinii lui Franz Kafka: romanul unei nevroze, 1998; Fantasies of Salvation: Democracy, Nationalism and Myth in Post-Communist Europe, 1998; (with M. Mihăieș) Incet, spre Europa, 2000; Spectrele Europei Centrale, 2001; Ghilotina de scrum, 2002; Scrisori din Washington: reflecții despre secolul douăzeci, 2002; Stalinism pentru eternitate: o istorie politică a comunismului românesc, 2003, trans. as Stalinism for All Seasons: A Political History of Romanian Communism, 2003; (contrib.) The Great Shock at the End of a Short Century, 2004; Conversations with ion iliescu, 2004;

Scopul și mijloacele: eseuri despre ideologie, tiranie și mit, 2004; (with M. Mihăieș) Schelete în dulap, 2004; (contrib.) Marele soc din finalul unui secol scurt, 2004; (with D. Jela) Ungaria 1956, 2006; Democratie și memorie, 2006; (with M. Mihăieș) Cortina de ceață, 2007; Refuzul de a uita: articole și comentarii politice, 2006-2007, 2007; (with) Perfectul Acrobat, 2008; (with C. Vasile) Perfectul Acrobat, 2008. EDITOR: In Search of Civil Society: Independent Peace Movements in the Soviet Bloc, 1990; (with J. Shapiro) Debates on the Future of Communism, 1991; (with P. Clawson) Uprooting Leninism, Cultivating Liberty, 1992; Political Culture and Civil Society in Russia and the New States of Eurasia, 1995; The Revolutions of 1989, 1999; (with S. Antohi) Between Past and Future: The Revolutions of 1989 and their Aftermath, 2000; (with M.M. Howard and R. Sil) World Order after Leninism, 2006; (with D. Dobrincu and C. Vasile) Raport final, 2007; Stalinism Revisited: The Establishment of Communist Regimes in East-Central Europe, 2009; Promises of 1968, 2011. **Address:** Center for the Study of Post-Communist Societies, Department of Government & Politics, University of Maryland, 3140 Tydings Hall, College Park, MD 20742, U.S.A. **Online address:** vtisman@gvpt.umd.edu

TITCHKOSKY, Tanya. Canadian (born Canada), b. 1966?. **Genres:** Social Sciences, Self Help. **Career:** St. Francis Xavier University, professor, 1997-2006; University of Toronto, Ontario Institute for Studies in Education, assistant professor. Writer. **Publications:** Disability, Self, and Society, 2003; Reading and Writing Disability Differently: The Textured Life of Embodiment, 2007; (ed. with R. Michalko) Rethinking Normalcy: A Disability Studies Reader, 2009. Contributor to books and periodicals. **Address:** Ontario Institute for Studies in Education, University of Toronto, 252 Bloor St. W, 12th Fl., Toronto, ON M5S 1V6, Canada. **Online address:** tanyatitchkosky@oise.utoronto.ca

TITLE, Elise. (Alison Tyler). American (born United States) **Genres:** Romance/Historical, Novels, Mystery/Crime/Suspense, Novellas/Short Stories. **Career:** Psychotherapist and novelist. **Publications:** (With J. Title and J. Title) Loving Smart: Putting Your Cards on the Table, 1993. ROMANCE NOVELS: Business before Pleasure, 1984; Too Good to Be True, 1984; Tender Awakening, 1984; A Daring Alliance, 1984; Playing It Safe, 1984; Tamed Spirit, 1984; Pulling the Strings, 1985; A Matter of Style, 1985; Free and Easy, 1985; Lost in Love, 1985; A Question of Honor, 1985; How Many Tomorrows?, 1985; Perfect Charade, 1985; Today and Always, 1986; Take-Charge Lady, 1986; King of Seduction, 1986; Runaway Lover, 1987; Tempting Angel, 1987; Wild Surrender, 1987; Pink Satin Lady, 1987; Restless Yearning, 1987; Love Letters, 1988; Baby, It's You!, 1988; Circle of Deception, 1988; McNamara and Hall, 1989; All through the Night, 1989; Out of the Blue, 1989; Too Many Husbands, 1990; The Face in the Mirror, 1990; Trouble in Eden, 1991; Making It, 1991; Shadow of the Moon, 1991; Jack and Jill, 1991; Till the End of Time, 1991; Nearly Paradise, 1991; Stage Whispers, 1992; No Right Turn, 1992; Just the Way You Are, 1993; You Were Meant for Me, 1993; Who Is Deborah?, 1993; Body Heat, 1994; (with B. Bretton and L. Small) Love and Laughter, 1994; Meg and the Mystery Man, 1994; Hot Property, 1994; Romeo in UK as Bleeding Heart, 1996; Chain Reaction, 1998; Naughty or Nerdy? (romantic comedy), 2002. FORTUNE BOYS SERIES: Adam and Eve, 1992; For the Love of Pete, 1992; True Love, 1992; Taylor Made, 1992. HART GIRLS SERIES: Dangerous at Heart, 1994; Heartstruck, 1994; Heart to Heart, 1994. NATALIE PRICE SERIES: Killing Time, 2002; Inside Out, 2003; Conviction, 2004. AS ALISON TYLER: Daring Alliance, 1984; Business Before Pleasure, 1984; Question of Honor, 1985; Matter of Style, 1985; Lost in Love, 1985; How Many Tomorrows?, 1985; Glimmer of Trust, 1985; Free and Easy, 1985; Take-Charge Lady, 1986; Perfect Charade, 1986; King of Seduction, 1986; Bitter with the Sweet: A Candlelight Ecstasy Romance, 1986; Tempting Angel, 1987; Runaway Lover, 1987; Restless Yearning, 1987; Double Masquerade, 1987; Chase the Wind, 1987; Blue Rose, 1995; Virgin, 1996; Dial L for Loveless, 1996; Blue Sky Sideways and Other Stories, 1996; Venus Online, 1997; (with D. Davidson) Bondage on a Budget: A Frugal Lover's A-to-Z Guide to Kinky Sex, 1997; (ed.) Come Quickly: For Girls On the Go, 1997; (ed.) Best Bondage Erotica, 2003; (ed.) Three-Way: Erotic Stories, 2004; (ed.) Heat Wave: Sizzling Sex Stories, 2004; (ed.) Merry XXXmas Book of Erotica, 2005; Exposed: The Erotic Fiction of Alison Tyler, 2006; (ed.) Slave to Love: Sexy Tales of Erotic Restraint, 2006; (ed.) Red Hot Erotica, 2006; (ed.) Luscious: Stories of Anal Eroticism, 2006; (ed.) Happy Birthday Book of Erotica, 2006; (ed. with R.K. Bussel) Caught Looking, 2006; (ed.) F is for Fetish, 2007; (ed.) E is for Exotic, 2007; (ed.) D is for Dress-Up, 2007; (ed.) C is for Coeds, 2007; (ed.) B is for Bondage, 2007; (ed.) A is for Amour, 2007; (ed.) Naughty or Nice?: Christmas Erotica,

2007; (ed.) Love at First Sting: Sexy Tales of Erotic Restraint, 2007; (ed.) Got a Minute?: Sixty-Second Erotica, 2007; (ed.) G is for Games, 2007; (ed.) Never Have the Same Sex Twice, 2008; (ed.) L is for Leather, 2008; (ed.) K is for Kinky, 2008; (ed.) Hurts so Good, 2008; (ed.) J is for Jealousy, 2008; (ed.) I is for Indecent, 2008; (ed.) Pleasure Bound, 2009; (ed.) Playing with Fire, 2009; (ed.) Afternoon Delight, 2009. Address: c/o Helen Rees, Helen Rees Literary Agency, 123 N Washington St., Boston, MA 02114-2113, U.S.A. Online address: elise_title@hotmail.com

TJARDES, Tamara J. American (born United States), b. 1961. Genres: Art/Art History, Literary Criticism And History, Mythology/Folklore. Career: Museum of International Folk Art, curator of Asian and Middle Eastern collections. Writer. Publications: One Hundred Aspects of the Moon: Japanese Woodblock Prints by Yoshitoshi, 2003. Address: Museum of New Mexico Press, PO Box 2087, Santa Fe, NM 87504, U.S.A. Online address: ttjardes@moifa.org

TOBIAS, Michael (Charles). American (born United States), b. 1951. Genres: Novels, Biography, Anthropology/Ethnology, Art/Art History, Environmental Sciences/Ecology, History, Poetry, Physics, Sciences, Theology/Religion, Animals/Pets, Travel/Exploration, Intellectual History, Military/Defense/Arms Control. Career: Dartmouth College, assistant professor of environmental studies and adjunct assistant professor of English and the humanities, 1978-80; California State University, visiting associate professor of humanities, 1983-85, associate professor of humanities; KQED-PBS, science and current affairs producer, 1985-87; Maryland Public Broadcasting, executive producer for national and international productions, 1987-97; JMT Productions, president, director, writer, producer and executive producer, 1989-; Dancing Star Foundation, president and chief executive officer, 1999-; University of New Mexico, Garrey Carruthers chair of honors and distinguished visiting professor; University of California, distinguished visiting professor of environmental studies, 2001, Regents lecturer. Writer. Publications: Tsa, 1972; Dhaula Girideon, 1973; Biography of Self-Consciousness, 1977; Ice Bird, 1984; After Eden: History, Ecology & Conscience, 1985; One Earth, 1990; Life Force: The World of Jainism, 1991; Environmental Meditation, 1993; Felham's War, 1993; Rage and Reason, 1993; Naked Man, 1994; World War III: Population and the Biosphere at the End of the Millennium, 1994, 2nd ed., 1998; (with R. Rai) India 24 Hours, 1995; Vision of Nature: Traces of the Original World, 1995; A Day in the Life of India, 1996; Jan and Catharina, 1997; Nature's Keepers: On the Front Lines of the Fight to Save Wildlife in America, 1998; Voices from the Underground: For the Love of Animals, 1999; (with J.G. Morrison) Donkey: The Mystique of Equus Asinus, 2006; (with J.G. Morrison) Sanctuary: Global Oases of Innocence, 2008. NOVELS: Déva, 1982; Voice of the Planet, 1990; Fatal Exposure, 1991; (with W. Shatner) Believe, 1992; Mahavira, 1993; Felham's War, 1993; Rage and Reason, 1993; (with C. Traub) Twimc, 2003; The Adventures of Mr. Marigold, 2005; Chateau beyond Time, 2008. EDITOR: (with H. Drasdo) Mountain Spirit, 1979; Deep Ecology, 1985; Mountain People, 1986; (with G. Cowan) Soul of Nature: Visions of a Living Earth, 1994; (with J. Morrison and B. Gray) Parliament of Souls: In Search of Global Spirituality: Interviews With 28 Spiritual Leaders from Around the World, 1995; (with G. Cowan) Soul of Nature: Celebrating the Spirit of the Earth, 1996; (with G. Cowan) The Soul of Nature: Celebrating the Spirit of the Earth, 1996; Search for Reality: The Art of Documentary Filmmaking, 1998; (with K. Solisti-Mattelon) Kinship with the Animals, 1998; (with J.P. Fitzgerald and D. Rothenberg) Parliament of Minds: Philosophy for a New Millennium, 2000; (with T. Timmers and G. Wright) A Parliament of Science: Science for the 21st Century, 2003; (co-ed. and intro.) No Vacancy: Global Responses to the Human Population Explosion, 2005; (with K. Solisti) Kinship with Animals, 2006. Contributor to periodicals. Address: c/o Julie Castiglia, Castiglia Literary Agency, 1155 Camino Del Mar, Ste. 510, Del Mar, CA 92014-2605, U.S.A.

TOBIN, Betsy. British/American (born United States), b. 1961. Genres: Novels. Career: Writer. Publications: NOVELS: Bone House, 2000; The Bounce, 2002; Ice Land, 2008; Crimson China, 2010. Address: London, GL, England. Online address: betsy@icelandthebook.com

TOBIN, Michael R. Canadian (born Canada), b. 1953?. Genres: Art/Art History, Theology/Religion. Career: University of Saskatchewan, St. Thomas More College, associate professor. Writer. Publications: Georges Bernanos: The Theological Source of His Art, 2007. Contributor to periodicals. Address: Canada. Online address: michael.tobin@usask.ca

TOBIN, Richard J. American (born United States), b. 1946. Genres: Environmental Sciences/Ecology. Career: Pennsylvania State University, Center for the Study of Environmental Policy, faculty, 1973-75; State University of New York, professor of political science, 1975-93; Beijing College of Economics, lecturer, 1985; Institute for International Research, director of environmental programs, 1992-; Cornell University, lecturer; University of Hawaii, lecturer; University of Florida, lecturer; Oberlin College, lecturer; University of Malaya, lecturer; Trent University, lecturer; Brock University, lecturer; Winrock International Institute for Agricultural Development, consultant; Brunei's Department of Fisheries, consultant; Los Alamos National Laboratory, consultant; U.S. Environmental Protection Agency, consultant. Writer. Publications: The Social Gamble: Determining Acceptable Levels of Air Quality, 1979; The Expendable Future: U.S. Politics and the Protection of Biological Diversity, 1990. Works appear in anthologies. Contributor to journals. Address: 203 Cottonwood Dr., Williamsville, NY 14221, U.S.A.

TOBIN, Sheldon S(idney). American (born United States), b. 1931. Genres: Gerontology/Senior Issues, Social Sciences. Career: Michael Reese Hospital, intern in clinical psychology, 1961-62; University of Chicago, School of Social Service Administration, research associate in human development, 1962-63, instructor, 1963-65, assistant professor, 1966-73, associate professor of gerontology and psychology, 1973-82; State University of New York, professor of social welfare and public affairs and policy, 1982-, Ringel Institute of Gerontology, director, 1982-90; Albany Medical College, adjunct professor, 1985-; The Gerontologist, editor-in-chief, 1985-88. Publications: (With M.A. Lieberman) Last Home for the Aged: Critical Implications of Institutionalization, 1976; (with S.M. Davidson and A. Sack) Effective Social Services for Older Americans, 1976; (with M.A. Lieberman) The Experience of Old Age: Stress, Coping and Survival, 1983; (with J.W. Ellor and S.M. Anderson-Ray) Enabling the Elderly: Religious Institutions within the Community Service System, 1986; Personhood in Advanced Old Age: Implications for Practice, 1991; Preservation of the Self in the Oldest Years: With Implications for Practice, 1999. EDITOR: Current Gerontology: Long-Term Care, 1982; (with R.A. Ward) Health in Aging: Sociological Issues and Policy Directions, 1987; Personhood in Advanced Old Age: Implications for Practice, 1991; (with G. Smith, E. Robertson-Tehibo and P. Powers) Strengthening Aging Families: Diversity in Practise and Policy, 1995. Address: School of Social Welfare, State University of New York, 135 Western Ave., Albany, NY 12222, U.S.A.

TOCH, Thomas. American (born United States), b. 1954. Genres: Education. Career: Harvard Graduate School of Education, faculty; National Center on Education and the Economy, writer-in-residence; Carnegie Foundation for the Advancement of Teaching, writer-in-residence; U.S. News and World Report, senior editor, 1989-99, contributing editor, 1999, senior education correspondent-; Choate Rosemary Hall, faculty; Education Sector, co-founder and co-director, 2005; Independent Education, executive director. Publications: In the Name of Excellence: The Struggle to Reform the Nation's Schools and Why It's Failing and What Should Be Done, 1991; High Schools and Human Scale: How Small Schools Can Transform American Education, 2003. Address: Education Sector, 1201 Connecticut Ave. NW, Ste. 850, Washington, DC 20036, U.S.A. Online address: ttoch@educationsector.org

TOCHER, Michelle. Canadian (born Canada), b. 1956. Genres: Novels, Mythology/Folklore, Adult Non-fiction, Biography. Career: Creative Premises Ltd. (communications, health promotion and public education company), president, 1985-98; Storytelling School of Toronto, member; author, storyteller and facilitator, 1998; Mood Disorders Association, staff; Gilda's Club Greater Toronto, artist-in-residence, 2005; Casey House, artist-in-residence. Public speaker and writer. Publications: The Broad Mind, 1995; (with A. Simon) Brave Work: A Guide to the Hero's Journey at Work, 1998; A Seeker's Storybook: Stories for the Working Soul, 2000; How to Ride a Dragon: Women with Breast Cancer Tell Their Stories, 2002; The Tower Princess: A Fairy Tale Lived, 2005; The May Queen, 2008. Address: 19 Poplar Plains Rd., Toronto, ON M4V 2M7, Canada. Online address: michelle@michelletocher.com

TODD, Emmanuel. French (born France), b. 1951. Genres: Novels. Career: National Institute of Demographic Studies (INED), anthropologist, demographer, sociologist, political scientist and researcher. Writer. Publications: La Chute Finale: Essai Sur La Décomposition De La Sphère Soviétique, 1976; Le Fou Et Le Prolétaire, 1979; (with H.L. Bras) L'Invention De La France: Atlas Anthropologique Et Politique, 1981; La Troisiéme Planéte: Structures Familiales Et Systèmes Idéologiques, 1983; L'Enfance Du Monde: Structures familiales Et Développeme, 1984; La Nouvelle France, 1988; L'invention De l'Europe, 1990; Le Destin Des Immigrés: AssimilationEet Ségrégation Dans Les Démocraties Occidentales, 1994; L'illusion économique: Essai Sur La Stagnation Des Sociétés Développées, 1998; La Diversité Du Monde: Structures Familiales Et Modernité, 1999; Après L'empire: Essai Sur La Décomposition Du Système Amricain, 2002; (with Y. Courbage) Le Rendez-vous Des Civilisations, 2007; Après La Démocratie, 2008; (with Y. Courbage) Convergence of Civilizations: The Transformation of Muslim Societies Around the World, 2011. **Address:** Institut National déetudes Demographiques, 133 bd Davout, Paris, 75980, France.

TODD, Olivier. French (born France), b. 1929. **Genres:** Novels, Biography, Literary Criticism And History. **Career:** Lycee International de Shape, teacher, 1956-62; University of Saint-Cloud, university assistant, 1962-64; Le Nouvel Observateur, reporter, 1964-69, assistant editor 1970-77, editor, columnist; BBC, reporter, 1964-69; TV Programme Panorama, editor, 1969-70; L'Express, managing editor and columnist, through 1981, reporter. **Publications:** Traversée de la Manche, 1960; Des trous dans le jardin, 1969; Annee du Crabe, 1972; Les Paumes, 1973; Les Canards de Ca Mao, 1975; Year of the Crab, 1975; La Marelle de Giscard, 1926-1974, 1977; Un Fils Rebelle: récit, 1981; Un Cannibale Trés Convenable, 1982; Une Légère Guele de Bois, 1982; Jacques Brel: Une Vie, 1984; La Balade de Chômeur, 1985; Cruel Avril: 1975, La Chute de Saigon, 1987; La Sanglière, 1992; Albert Camus: Une Vie, 1996; Corrigez-Moi Si Je Me Trompe: Roman, 1998; André Malraux: une vie, 2001; Carte d'identités: souvenirs, 2005; Malraux: A Life, 2005; J'ai vécu en ces temps: roman, 2011. Contributor to periodicals. **Address:** 21 rue de l'Odeon, Paris, 75006, France.

TODD, Pamela A. American/British (born England), b. 1950. **Genres:** Children's Fiction, Novels, Literary Criticism And History. **Career:** Creative writing teacher; Punch Magazine, art exhibit and restaurant reviewer. Writer. **Publications:** (With D. Fordham) Private Tucker's Boer War Diary: The Transvaal War of 1899, 1900, 1901 and 1902 with Natal Field Forces, 1980; Forget-Me-Not: A Floral Treasury: Sentiments and Plant Lore from the Language of Flowers, 1993; The Little Book of Daffodils: A Garden of Poetry, History, Lore, and Floriculture, 1994; The Little Book of Tulips: A Garden of Poetry, History, Lore, and Floriculture, 1994; Celebrating the Impressionist Table: A Celebration of Regional French Foods through the Palettes of the Great Impressionists, 1997; Pig and the Shrink (young adult novel), 1999; Bloomsbury at Home, 1999; Pre-Raphaelites at Home, 2001; The Arts and Crafts Companion, 2004; William Morris and the Arts and Crafts Home, 2005; Impressionists at Home, 2005; Impressionists at Leisure, 2007; Blind Faith Hotel, 2008. EDITOR: The Sweet Days Die, 1996; Trailing Clouds of Glory, 1996; Heaven's Embroidered Cloths: Poems by W.B. Yeats, 1996. Contributor to periodicals. **Address:** c/o Erin Malone, William Morris Agency, 1325 Ave. of the Americas, New York, NY 10014-4403, U.S.A. **Online address:** pam@pamelatodd.com

TODD, Paul. *See* **POSNER, Richard.**

TOEWS, Miriam. Canadian (born Canada), b. 1964?. **Genres:** Novels, Young Adult Non-fiction, Literary Criticism And History. **Career:** Journalist. **Publications:** Summer of My Amazing Luck: A Novel, 1996; A Boy of Good Breeding: A Novel, 1998; Swing Low: A Life, 2000; A Complicated Kindness: A Novel, 2004; The Flying Troutmans: A Novel, 2008; Small Bird, Beating Heart, 2011; Irma Voth: A Novel, 2011. Contributor to periodicals. **Address:** Random House of Canada Ltd., 1 Toronto St., Ste. 300, Toronto, ON M5C 2V6, Canada.

TOEWS, Rita Y. Canadian (born Canada), b. 1949. **Genres:** Novels, Children's Fiction, Novellas/Short Stories. **Career:** Writer. **Publications:** The Bully: A Discussion and Activity Story, 2004, 2nd ed., 2005; (with A. Domokos) Body Traffic, 2005. **Address:** c/o Author Mail, Birds Hill Publishing, 9 Esker Pl., East St. Paul, MB R2E 0K2, Canada. **Online address:** r.toews@shaw.ca

TOFEL, Richard J. American (born United States), b. 1957. **Genres:** History, Politics/Government, Speech/Rhetoric, Sports/Fitness, Biography. **Career:** The Wall Street Journal, assistant general counsel, 1989-92, assistant managing editor, 1992-95, director of international development, 1995-97, assistant, 2000-02, assistant publisher; Dow Jones & Co., assistant general counsel, 1989-92, vice president of corporate communications, 1997-2000; The International Freedom Center, president and chief operating officer; Rockefeller

Foundation, vice president, general counsel and secretary; ProPublica, general manager. **Publications:** A Legend in the Making: The New York Yankees in 1939, 2002; Vanishing Point: The Disappearance of Judge Crater and the New York He Left Behind, 2004; Sounding the Trumpet: The Making of John F. Kennedy's Inaugural Address, 2005; Restless Genius: Barney Kilgore, The Wall Street Journal, and the Invention of Modern Journalism, 2009; Eight Weeks in Washington, 1861: Abraham Lincoln and the Hazards of Transition, 2011. **Address:** ProPublica, 1 Exchange Plz., 55 Broadway, 23rd Fl., New York, NY 10006, U.S.A. **Online address:** dick.tofel@propublica.org

TOFFLER, Alvin. American (born United States), b. 1928. **Genres:** Social Commentary, Politics/Government, Cultural/Ethnic Topics, Art/Art History, Social Sciences, Young Adult Non-fiction. **Career:** Correspondent, 1957-59; Fortune Magazine, associate editor, 1959-61; freelance writer, 1961-; New School for Social Research, faculty, 1965-67; Cornell University, visiting professor, 1969; Toffler Associates, co-founder. Consultant. **Publications:** The Culture Consumers: A Study of Art and Affluence in America, 1964; Future Shock, 1970; The Eco-Spasm Report, 1975; The Third Wave, 1980; Shashin de miru daisan no nami, 1982; Previews and Premises: An Interview with the Author of Future Shock and the Third Wave, 1983; (foreword) Order Out of Chaos: Man's New Dialogue with Nature, 1984; The Adaptive Corporation, 1985; Powershift: Knowledge, Wealth and Violence at the Edge of the 21st Century, 1990; (with H. Toffler) War and Anti-war: Survival at the Dawn of the 21st Century, 1993; (with K. Yūji) Jamerika no kiki, 1994; (with H. Toffler) Creating a New Civilization: The Politics of the Third Wave, 1994; (with H. Toffler) Revolutionary Wealth: Shaping Tomorrow's Way of Life, 2006. EDITOR: (and intro.) The Schoolhouse in the City, 1968; (and intro.) The Futurists, 1972; Learning for Tomorrow: The Role of Future in Education, 1974. Works appear in anthologies. Contributor to books and periodicals. **Address:** Toffler Associates, 302 Harbor's Point, 40 Beach St., Manchester, MA 01944-1468, U.S.A.

TOFFLER, Heidi. American (born United States), b. 1929. **Genres:** Environmental Sciences/Ecology, Politics/Government, Military/Defense/Arms Control, Social Sciences. **Career:** Toffler Associates Inc., co-founder, 1996-; National Defense University, Institute for National Strategic Studies, adjunct professor. Writer. **Publications:** WITH A. TOFFLER: Future Shock, 1970; The Eco-Spasm Report, 1975; The Third Wave, 1980; Powershift, 1990; War and Anti-War: Survival at the Dawn of the 21st Century, 1993; Creating a New Civilization: The Politics of the Third Wave, 1994; Revolutionary Wealth: Shaping Tomorrow's Way of Life, 2006. **Address:** Toffler Associates Inc., 1775 Wiehle Ave., Reston, VA 20190, U.S.A.

TOFTS, Darren (John). Australian (born Australia), b. 1960. **Genres:** Information Science/Computers, Art/Art History, Technology. **Career:** Swinburne University of Technology, senior lecturer, 1986-, associate professor, Media and Communications, professor, chairperson; 21C magazine, editorial correspondent. **Publications:** (With M. McKeich) Memory Trade: A Prehistory of Cyberculture, 1997; Parallax: Essays on Art, Culture, and Technology, 2000; (ed.) Prefiguring Cyberculture: An Intellectual History, 2002; Remembering It for You Wholesale: The New Ecology of Memory Work; Interzone: Media Arts in Australia, 2005; Illogic of Sense, 2007. Contributor to periodicals. **Address:** Department of Media Literature and Film, Swinburne University of Technology, AS421, PO Box 218, Hawthorn, VI 3122, Australia. **Online address:** dtofts@swin.edu.au

TÓIBÍN, Colm. Irish (born Ireland), b. 1955. **Genres:** Novels, Travel/Exploration, Documentaries/Reportage, Politics/Government, Essays, Novellas/Short Stories. **Career:** London Review, essayist; In Dublin, features editor, 1981; Hibernia, writer; Sunday Tribune, writer; Magill, editor, 1982-85; Dublin Sunday Independent, journalist and columnist; Dublin School of English, teacher; Dublin Review, contributor; Stanford University, Stein Visiting Writer; University of Texas, Michener Center, visiting writer; Princeton University, Leonard Milberg Lecturer. **Publications:** Walking along the Border (travelogue), 1987; Martyrs and Metaphors, 1987; The South (novel), 1990; Homage to Barcelona (travelogue), 1990; The Trial of the Generals: Selected Journalism, 1980-1990, 1990; Dubliners (travelogue), 1990; The Heather Blazing (novel), 1992; Homage to Barcelona, 1992; Bad Blood, 1994; The Sign of the Cross: Travels in Catholic Europe (travelogue), 1994; The Story of the Night (novel), 1996; The Blackwater Lightship (novel), 1999; Irish Famine, 1999; (with C. Callil) Modern Library: The Two Hundred Best Novels in English since 1950, 1999; Lady Gregory's Toothbrush, 2002; Love in a Dark Time: Gay Lives from Wilde to Almodóvar, 2002; Love in a Dark Time: And

Other Explorations of Gay Lives and Literature, 2002; (intro.) Ireland: On the Edge of Europe, 2003; Master, 2004; Beauty in a Broken Place, 2004; Mothers and Sons, 2006; Brooklyn: A Novel, 2009; The Empty Family: Stories, 2010; All a Novelist Needs, 2010; (intro.) Art of the Novel: Critical Prefaces, 2011. EDITOR: Seeing Is Believing: Moving Statues in Ireland, 1985; Soho Square Six: New Writing from Ireland, 1993; Kilfenora Teaboy: A Study of Paul Durcan, 1996; (and intro.) The Penguin Book of Irish Fiction, 1999; Synge: A Celebration, 2005; (and intro.) New York Stories of Henry James, 2006; (with C. Rafferty and intro.) Enniscorthy: A History, 2010. Contributor to periodicals. **Address:** A.P. Watt Ltd., 20 John St., London, GL WC1N 2DR, England. **Online address:** ourage@hotmail.com

TOKARCZYK, Michelle M. American (born United States), b. 1953. **Genres:** Poetry, Literary Criticism And History, Women's Studies And Issues, Art/Art History, Education, Bibliography, Young Adult Fiction. **Career:** Goucher College, Department of English, assistant professor, associate professor, professor, 1989-, chair; Educational Testing Service, reader and consultant. Writer. **Publications:** E.L. Doctorow: An Annotated Bibliography, 1988; The House I'm Running From (poetry), 1989; (ed. with E.A. Fay) Working-Class Women in the Academy: Laborers in the Knowledge Factory (non-fiction anthology), 1993; For a Living: Poetry of Work, 1995; E.L. Doctorow's Skeptical Commitment (literary criticism), 2000; (ed. with I. Papoulis) Teaching Composition/Teaching Literature: Crossing Great Divides, 2003; Class Definitions: On the Lives and Writings of Maxine Hong Kingston, Sandra Cisneros and Dorothy Allison, 2008; (ed.) Critical Approaches to American Working-Class Literature, 2011. **Address:** English Department, Goucher College, 1021 Dulaney Valley Rd., Van Meter G48, Baltimore, MD 21204, U.S.A. **Online address:** mtokarcz@goucher.edu

TOKER, Leona. Israeli/Lithuanian (born Lithuania), b. 1950. **Genres:** Intellectual History, Literary Criticism And History, Autobiography/Memoirs, History, Novels, Novellas/Short Stories, Education, Ethics, Essays. **Career:** School teacher, 1974-78; Hebrew University of Jeruslam, Department of English, instructor, 1978-80, lecturer, 1982-88, senior lecturer, 1988-94, associate professor, 1994-2000, department chair, 1994-96, 2011-, professor of English, 2000-, Partial Answers: Journal of Literature and the History of Ideas, editor, 2003-. **Publications:** Nabokov: The Mystery of Literary Structures, 1989; Eloquent Reticence: Withholding Information in Fictional Narrative, 1993; (ed.) Commitment in Reflection: Essays in Literature and Moral Philosophy, 1994; (ed. with S. Rimmon-Kenan and S. Barzilai) Rereading Texts, Rethinking Critical Presuppositions: Essays in Honour of H.M. Daleski, 1997; Return from the Archipelago: Narratives of Gulag Survivors, 2000; Towards the Ethics of Form in Fiction: Narratives of Cultural Remission, 2010. **Address:** Department of English, Hebrew University of Jerusalem, Rm. 7824, Mt. Scopus, Jerusalem, 91905, Israel. **Online address:** toker@mscc.huji.ac.il

TOKSVIG, Sandi. British/Danish (born Denmark), b. 1958. **Genres:** Children's Fiction, Novels, Young Adult Fiction, Travel/Exploration, Humor/Satire. **Career:** Nottingham Repertory Theatre, performer and playwright, 1980-81; New Shakespeare Co., actor, 1981; Comedy Store Players, actor and playwright, 1987-93. **Publications:** CHILDREN'S BOOKS: If I Didn't Have Elbows...: The Alternative Body Book, 1996; Unusual Boy, 1996; Supersaver Mouse, 1998; Supersaver Mouse to the Rescue, 1999; Whistling for the Elephants, 1999; The Troublesome Tooth Fairy, 2000; Hitler's Canary, 2007; OTHERS: (with E. Brewer) The Pocket Dream, 1992; (with J. McCarthy) Island Race: An Improbable Voyage round the Coast of Britain, 1995; Flying under Bridges (novel), 2001; The Gladys Society: A Personal American Journey, 2002; (with S. Nightingale) The Travels of Lady Bulldog Burton (humor), 2002; Gladys Reunited: A Personal American Journey, 2003; Melted into Air (novel), 2008; (intro.) Gay Icons, 2009. **Address:** Peters Fraser & Dunlop, Drury House, 34-43 Russell St., London, GL WC2B 5HA, England.

TOLBERT, Steve. Australian/American (born United States), b. 1944. **Genres:** Young Adult Fiction, Children's Fiction, Novels. **Career:** High school teacher, 1970-2001; author, 1991-. **Publications:** Channeary, 1991; Settling South, 1995; Eyeing Everest, 1996; Stepping Back, 1996; Escape to Kalimantan, 1998; Tracking the Dalai Lama, 2001; Dreaming Australia, 2005; Surfing for Wayan and Other Stories, 2006; Packing Smack, Talking Wombats, 2007; O'Leary, JI Terrorist Hunter, 2010. Contributor to periodicals. **Address:** 3 Honeywood Dr., Sandford, TA 7020, Australia. **Online address:** stolbert@southcom.com.au

TOLCHIN, Susan J(ane). American (born United States), b. 1941. **Genres:** Public/Social Administration, Politics/Government. **Career:** City College of New York, lecturer in political science, 1963-65; City University of New York, Brooklyn College, lecturer of political science, 1965-71; Seton Hall University, adjunct assistant professor, 1971-73; Drew University, assistant professor, 1974-75; Mount Vernon College, associate professor of Political Science, 1975-78, Institute for Women and Politics, director, 1975-78; George Washington University, professor of public administration, 1978-98; National War College, distinguished visiting lecturer, 1994; George Mason University, professor of public policy, 1998-2007, university professor of public policy, 2007- . Writer. **Publications:** The Angry American: How Voter Rage is Changing the Nation, 1996, 2nd ed., 1999. WITH M. TOLCHIN: To the Victor: Political Patronage from the Clubhouse to the White House, 1971; Clout: Womanpower and Politics, 1974; Women in the U.S. Congress, 1976; Dismantling America: The Rush to Deregulate, 1983; Buying into America: How Foreign Money is Changing the Face of our Nation, 1988, rev. ed., 1993; Selling Our Security: The Erosion of America's Assets, 1992; Glass Houses: Congressional Ethics and The Politics of Venom, 2001; A World Ignited: How Apostles of Ethnic, Religious, and Racial Hatred Torch the Globe, 2006; Global Anger: How Religious Hatreds, Ethnic Rivalries, and Political Struggles Undermine Peace and Freedom, 2006; Pinstripe Patronage: Political Favoritism from the Clubhouse to the White House and Beyond, 2011. **Address:** George Mason School of Public Policy, George Mason University, 3401 Fairfax Dr., PO Box 3B1, Arlington, VA 22201, U.S.A. **Online address:** tolchin@gmu.edu

TOLINS, Robert B. American (born United States), b. 1952. **Genres:** Novels. **Career:** Assistant district attorney, 1978-80; Public Housing Authority, litigation supervisor, 1984-90; civil and criminal lawyer, 1990-98; writer, 1998-; Willowgate Press, managing editor and publisher. **Publications:** NOVEL: Unhealthy Boundaries: A Story of Murder & the Internet, 2000. Works appear in anthologies. Contributor to magazines. **Address:** Willowgate Press, PO Box 6529, Holliston, MA 01746-6529, U.S.A. **Online address:** rtolins610@aol.com

TOLKIN, Michael. (Michael L. Tolkin). American (born United States), b. 1950. **Genres:** Novels, Plays/Screenplays, Theology/Religion, Art/Art History, Young Adult Fiction. **Career:** Journalist and director. **Publications:** NOVELS: The Player: A Novel, 1988; Among the Dead, 1993; Under Radar, 2002; The Return of the Player, 2006. OTHERS: Gleaming the Cube, 1989; The Rapture, 1991; (with H. Bean) Deep Cover, 1992; The New Age, 1994; (contrib. with F. Paul) Steven Pippin, 1995. **Address:** Sterling Lord Literistic Inc., 65 Bleecker St., New York, NY 10012-2420, U.S.A.

TOLKIN, Michael L. See **TOLKIN, Michael.**

TOLL, Emily. See **CANNON, Eileen E(mily).**

TOLL, Robert Charles. American (born United States), b. 1938. **Genres:** Art/Art History, History, Theatre, Photography. **Career:** Institute for the Study of Community and Race Relations, research associate, 1971-72; St. Mary's College, lecturer, 1974; University of California, lecturer in history, 1975-76. Writer. **Publications:** Blacking Up: The Minstrel Show in Nineteenth Century America, 1974; (ed.) Old Slack's Reminiscences and Pocket History of the Colored Profession, 1974; On with the Show: The First Century of Show Business in America, 1976; The Entertainment Machine: American Show Business in the Twentieth Century, 1982; Simply Eloquent: The Arviat Tradition of Inuit Art, 2007. **Address:** 3900 Harrison St., Apt. 301, Oakland, CA 94611, U.S.A. **Online address:** jandbtoll@aol.com

TOLLEFSEN, Christopher. American (born United States), b. 1968. **Genres:** Law, Theology/Religion. **Career:** Princeton University, Department of Politics, visiting associate professor, 2004-05; University of South Carolina, Department of Philosophy, associate professor, professor, 2009-, Graduate Placement, director. Writer. **Publications:** Biomedical Research and Beyond: Expanding the Ethics of Inquiry, 2008; (with R.P. George) Embryo: A Defense of Human Life, 2008. EDITOR: (with O. Tollefsen) Foundationalism Defended: Essays on Epistemology, Ethics and Aesthetics, 1995; John Paul II's Contribution to Catholic Bioethics, 2004; Artificial Nutrition and Hydration: The New Catholic Debate, 2008. **Address:** Department of Philosophy, University of South Carolina, 420 Byrnes, 902 Sumter St., Columbia, SC 29208, U.S.A. **Online address:** tollefsen@sc.edu

TOLLEFSON, James. *See* **TOLLEFSON, James W(illiam).**

TOLLEFSON, James W(illiam). (James Tollefson). American (born United States), b. 1950. **Genres:** Adult Non-fiction, Social Commentary, History, Language/Linguistics, Education, Social Sciences. **Career:** San Jose State University, lecturer, 1979-80; University of Washington, professor, 1980-2004, professor emeritus, 2004-; International Christian University-Tokyo, professor, 2001-11; University of Hong Kong, professor. Writer. **Publications:** The Language Situation and Language Policy in Slovenia, 1981; Alien Winds: The Reeducation of America's Indochinese Refugees, 1989; Planning Language, Planning Inequality: Language Policy in the Community, 1991; The Strength Not to Fight: An Oral History of Conscientious Objectors of the Vietnam War, 1993; (ed.) Power and Inequality in Language Education, 1995; The Strength Not to Fight: Conscientious Objectors of the Vietnam War-In Their Own Words, 2000; (ed.) Language Policies in Education: Critical Issues, 2002; (ed. with A.B.M. Tsui) Medium of Instruction Policies: Which Agenda? Whose Agenda?, 2004; (ed. with A.B.M. Tsui) Language Policy, Culture and Identity in Asian contexts, 2007; (ed.) Language Policies in Education, 2nd edition, 2012. Contributor to periodicals. **Address:** University of Hong Kong, Faculty of Education, Pokfulam Rd., Hong Kong, Hong Kong. **Online address:** tollefso@u.washington.edu

TOLSON, Jay. American (born United States), b. 1948. **Genres:** Biography, Autobiography/Memoirs, Literary Criticism And History, Young Adult Fiction. **Career:** Wilson Quarterly, editor, 1981-98; U.S. News & World Report, senior writer, 1999-; Washington Post, contributor; Wall Street Journal, contributor. **Publications:** Pilgrim in the Ruins: A Life of Walker Percy, 1992; (ed.) The Correspondence of Shelby Foote & Walker Percy, 1996. **Address:** Georges Borchardt Inc., 136 E 57th St., New York, NY 10022, U.S.A.

TOLTZ, Steve. Australian (born Australia), b. 1972. **Genres:** Novels. **Career:** Educator and writer. **Publications:** A Fraction of the Whole (novel), 2008. **Address:** Sydney, NW , Australia. **Online address:** mail@stevetoltz.com

TOMAJCZYK, S. F. (Stephen F. Tomajczyk). American (born United States), b. 1960. **Genres:** Military/Defense/Arms Control, Reference, Poetry, Novels, Adult Non-fiction. **Career:** CW Communications, new products editor, 1982-83; Soft Side Publications, senior editor and associate publisher, 1983-84; Ultimate Press, marketing communications director, 1984-88; Franklin Pierce University, senior lecturer, 1985-88; Rivier College, senior lecturer, 1988-91; New Hampshire Division of Public Health Services, public information officer, 1988-96; National Public Health Information Coalition, regional representative, 1993-96, vice-president, 1994-95, president, 1995-96; American Journal of Health Communications, founder and managing editor, 1995-2001; Turning Point Communications, president, 1996-; DisasterMagazine.com, editor-in-chief, 2001-03; New Hampshire Department of Health and Human Services, Homeland Security and Emergency Preparedness Coordinator, 2003-10. **Publications:** Eyes on the Gold: An Advanced Training Manual for Running Events, 1986; The Children's Writers' Marketplace, 1987; Dictionary of the Modern United States Military, 1996; US Elite Counter-terrorist Forces, 1997; Bomb Squad, 1999; 101 Ways to Survive the Y2K Crisis, 1999; Carrier Battle Group, 2000; Modern U.S. Navy Destroyers, 2001; U.S. Counterterrorist Forces, 2002; Black Hawk, 2003; To Be a U.S. Marine, 2004. Contributor to magazines and newspapers. **Address:** PO Box 7070, Loudon, NH 03307-7070, U.S.A. **Online address:** trnpnt@comcast.net

TOMAJCZYK, Stephen F. *See* **TOMAJCZYK, S. F.**

TOMALIN, Claire. British (born England), b. 1933. **Genres:** History, Literary Criticism And History, Social Commentary, Biography, Adult Non-fiction, Autobiography/Memoirs. **Career:** Reader and editor, 1955-67; Evening Standard, staff, 1967-68; New Statesman, assistant literary editor, 1968-74, literary editor, 1974-77; The Sunday Times, reviewer, 1977-79, literary editor, 1980-86. **Publications:** The Life and Death of Mary Wollstonecraft, 1974, rev. ed., 1992; Shelley and His World, 1980; (comp.) Parents and Children, 1981; Katherine Mansfield: A Secret Life, 1988; The Invisible Woman: The Story of Nelly Ternan and Charles Dickens, 1991; The Winter Wife, 1991; Mrs. Jordan's Profession: The Actress and the Prince, 1995; Jane Austen: A Life, 1997; (ed. and intro.) Maurice, or, the Fisher's Cot: A Tale, 1998; (contrib.) Quotations of a Body, 1998; Several Strangers: Writing from Three Decades, 1999; Samuel Pepys: The Unequalled Self, 2002; Thomas Hardy: The Time-Torn Man, 2006; (ed.) The Poems of Thomas Hardy, 2007; (ed.) The Poems of John Milton, 2008; (intro.) Unexpected Elegies: Poems of 1912-13,

and Other Poems about Emma, 2010; Charles Dickens: A Life, 2011. Contributor to periodicals. **Address:** David Godwin Associates, 55 Monmouth St., London, GL WC2H 9DG, England.

TOMALIN, Ruth. British/Irish (born Ireland), b. 1919?. **Genres:** Novels, Novellas/Short Stories, Children's Fiction, Poetry, Natural History, Biography, Young Adult Fiction. **Career:** London Law Court, freelance press reporter, 1966-74; reporter, 1942-65. **Publications:** Threnody for Dormice, 1946; The Day of the Rose, 1947; (as Ruth Leaver) Green Ink, 1951; Deer's Cry, 1952; All Souls, 1952; W.H. Hudson, 1954; (as Ruth Leaver) The Sound of Pens, 1955; The Daffodil Bird, 1959; The Sea Mice, 1962; The Garden House, 1964, new ed., 2002; The Spring House, 1968, new ed., 2004; (ed. and intro.) Best Country Stories, 1969; Away to the West, 1972; A Green Wishbone, 1975; A Stranger Thing, 1975; The Snake Crook, 1976; Gone Away, 1979; Little Nasty, 1985; A Summer Ghost, 1986; Another Day, 1988; Long Since, 1989; Garden House Diaries, 2003; Dormice Again: Collected Poems, 2004; The Orchard House, 2009. Works appear in anthologies. **Address:** 10 Pegasus Ct., 29 St. Leonard, Eastbourne, ES BN21 3UP, England.

TOMASELLI, Sylvana. British/Canadian (born Canada), b. 1957. **Genres:** History, Literary Criticism And History, Philosophy, Social Sciences, Essays, Translations, Politics/Government. **Career:** Cambridge University, Newnham College, Sarah Smithson research fellow, 1985-88; Hughes Hall, fellow, 1997-2002; St. John's College, college lecturer and director of studies, 2000-03, history faculty; European Centre for the Philosophy of Gender, founding member, 2005-. Writer. **Publications:** EDITOR: (with R. Porter and contrib.) Rape, 1986 as Rape: An Historical and Social Enquiry, 1989; (with R. Porter) The Dialectics of Friendship, 1989; Mary Wollstonecraft, Vindication of the Rights of Men, Vindication of the Rights of Woman and Hints, 1995; (with G.A.J. Rogers) The Philosophical Canon in the 17th and 18th Centuries: Essays in Honour of John W. Yolton, 1996. TRANSLATOR: Jacques Lacan, Le Seminaire II: Le Moidans la theorie de Freud et dans la technique de la psychoanalyse, 1988. OTHER: Rousseau, 2008. Contributor of articles to periodicals. Works appear in anthologies. **Address:** Department of History, St. John's College, University of Cambridge, Cambridge, CM CB2 1TP, England. **Online address:** st240@cam.ac.uk

TOMASULO, Daniel J. American (born United States), b. 1951. **Genres:** Medicine/Health, Autobiography/Memoirs. **Career:** Association for Retarded Citizens, Work Activity Training Center, director, grant writer, 1974-79; Young Adult Institute, group home manager, 1979-80; Brookdale College, professor, 1980-2001, Colleges Human Service Program, co-director; Riverview Medical Center, staff psychologist/group psychodramatist, 1984-86; Red Bank, psychologist, 1986-; YAI, National Institute for People with Disabilities, consultant, 1990-; Monmouth University, adjunct professor, 1998-2004; Princeton University, visiting professor, 1998-99; New Jersey City University, associate professor, 2001-. Writer and psychologist. **Publications:** Action Methods in Group Psychotherapy: Practical Aspects, 1998; (with N.J. Razza) Healing Trauma: The Power of Group Treatment for People with Intellectual Disabilities, 2005; Confessions of a Former Child: A Therapist's Memoir, 2008. Contributor to books and journals. **Address:** The Courts of Red Bank, 130 Maple Ave., Bldg. 9, Ste. 9, Red Bank, NJ 07701-1633, U.S.A. **Online address:** dtomasulo@gmail.com

TOMBS, Robert P. British/French (born France), b. 1949. **Genres:** Politics/Government, History, Biography, Autobiography/Memoirs, Military/Defense/Arms Control. **Career:** University of Cambridge, St. John's College, professor of French history and fellow. Writer. **Publications:** The War against Paris, 1871, 1981; (with J.P.T. Bury) Thiers, 1797-1877: A Political Life, 1986; (ed.) Nationhood and Nationalism in France: From Boulangism to the Great War, 1889-1918, 1991; France, 1814-1914, 1996; The Paris Commune, 1871, 1999; (with I. Tombs) That Sweet Enemy: The French and the British from the Sun King to the Present, 2006; (with M. Va ïisse) Histoire coloniale en débat en France et en Grande-Bretagne, 2010; (co-ed.) A la recherche de Winston Churchill, 2011. **Address:** St. John's College, University of Cambridge, Cambridge, CB CB2 1TP, England. **Online address:** rpt1000@cam.ac.uk

TOMEY, Ingrid. American (born United States), b. 1943. **Genres:** Novels, Poetry, Natural History, Young Adult Fiction. **Career:** Michigan Literacy Program, instructor, 1986-89. Writer. **Publications:** Neptune Princess, 1992; Grandfather's Day, 1992; Savage Carrot, 1993; The Queen of Dreamland,

1993; Nobody Else Has to Know, 1999; Loss Events (novel); Baby in a Tree (poem); Where the Skies are Not Cloudy (poem). Contributor to magazines, newspapers and periodicals. **Address:** 1725 N Dayton St., Ste. A, Chicago, IL 60614-5511, U.S.A.

TOMINE, Adrian. American (born United States), b. 1974. **Genres:** Graphic Novels. **Career:** Writer. **Publications:** GRAPHIC NOVELS: 32 Stories: The Complete Optic Nerve Mini-Comics, 1995; Sleepwalk and Other Stories, 1997; Summer Blonde, 2002; Scrapbook: Uncollected Work: 1990-2004, 2004; Optic Nerve: 30 Postcards, 2005; Shortcomings, 2007; (Designer) A Drifting Life, 2009. EDITOR: (Y. Tatsumi) The Push Man and Other Stories, 2005; (Y. Tatsumi) Abandon the Old in Tokyo, 2006; (Y. Tatsumi) Goodbye, 2008. **Address:** PO Box 94, Prince Sta., New York, NY 10012, U.S.A.

TOMKINS, Adam. Scottish/British (born England) **Genres:** Law, Politics/ Government. **Career:** King's College London, School of Law, senior lecturer in law, 1991-2000; University of Oxford, St. Catherine's College, fellow and tutor in law, 2000-03; University of Glasgow, School of Law, John Millar Professor of Public Law and John Millar Chair in Public Law, 2003-; Scottish Public Law Group, founding member. Writer and lawyer. **Publications:** (Ed. with C. Gearty) Understanding Human Rights, 1996; The Constitution after Scott: Government Unwrapped, 1998; (ed. with T. Campbell and K.D. Ewing) Sceptical Essays on Human Rights, 2001; Public Law, 2003; (with A. Gray) How We Should Rule Ourselves, 2005; Our Republican Constitution, 2005; (ed. with P. Craig) The Executive and Public Law: Power and Accountability in Comparative Perspective, 2005; (with D. Chalmers, C. Hadjiemmanuil and G. Monti) European Union Law, 2006; (with C. Turpin) British Government and the Constitution: Text and Materials, 6th ed., 2007, (with C. Turpin) 7th ed., 2011; (with D. Chalmers) European Union Public Law: Text and Materials, 2007; (ed. with T. Campbell and K.D. Ewing) Legal Protection of Human Rights: Sceptical Essays, 2011. Contributor to periodicals. **Address:** School of Law, University of Glasgow, 5-9 Stair Bldg., The Sq., Glasgow, G12 8QQ, Scotland. **Online address:** adam.tomkins@glasgow.ac.uk

TOMKINS, Calvin. American (born United States), b. 1925. **Genres:** Novels, Art/Art History, Biography, Young Adult Non-fiction, Autobiography/ Memoirs. **Career:** Radio Free Europe, reporter, 1953-57; Newsweek, associate editor, 1955, general editor, 1957-59, writer and editor, 1957-61; New Yorker, staff writer, 1960-, art critic, 1980-86, columnist, 1980-88. **Publications:** Intermission (novel), 1951; The Bride and the Bachelors: The Heretical Courtship in Modern, 1965; The Lewis and Clark Trail, 1965; The World of Marcel Duchamp, 1966, 2nd ed., 1977; Ahead of the Game: Four Versions of Avant-garde, 1968; Eric Hoffer: An American Odyssey, 1968; Merchants and Masterpieces: The Story of the Metropolitan Museum of Art, 1970, rev. ed., 1989; (contrib.) Andy Warhol, 1970; Living Well Is the Best Revenge, 1971; (with J. Tomkins) The Other Hampton, 1974; The Scene: Reports on Post-Modern Art, 1976; (with D. Bourdon) Christo, Running Fence: Sonoma and Marin Counties, California, 1972-1976, 1978; Off the Wall: Robert Rauschenberg and the Art World of Our Time, 1980; (with M. Goldwater and R. Smith) Jennifer Bartlett, 1985; Roy Lichtenstein: Mural with Blue Brushstroke, 1988; Post-to-Neo: The Art World of the 1980s, 1988; (contrib.) Robert Rauschenberg: The Silkscreen Paintings, 1962-64, 1990; (with D. Kazanjian) Alex: The Life of Alexander Liberman, 1993; Duchamp: A Biography, 1996; Omaggio a Leo Castelli: Da Rauschenberg a Warhol, Da Flavin a Judd: 20 Artisti a New York Negli anni Sessanta, 1996; Lives of the Artists, 2008. **Address:** The New Yorker, 4 Times Sq., New York, NY 10036, U.S.A.

TOMKINS, Jasper. American (born United States), b. 1946. **Genres:** Children's Fiction, Picture/Board Books, Animals/Pets, Illustrations. **Career:** Bantam Books Inc., staff artist, 1971-74; Great Northwest Publications, art director, 1974-78; freelance writer and artist, 1978-. **Publications:** SELF ILLUSTRATED: The Catalog, 1981; Nimby: An Extraordinary Cloud Who Meets a Remarkable Friend, 1982; The Hole in the Ocean!: A Daring Journey, 1984; The Sky Jumps into Your Shoes at Night, 1986; When a Bear Bakes a Cake, 1987; The Mountains Crack Up!, 1987; Bear Sleep Soup, 1989; My Secret Sunrise, 1989; My Cousin Has Eight Legs!, 1992; Catwalk, 2004; The Camelback Dogs, 2004. **Address:** Sasquatch Books, 119 S Main St., Ste. 400, Seattle, WA 98104-1006, U.S.A. **Online address:** jasper@jaspertomkins.com

TOMKINS, Stephen. British (born England), b. 1968?. **Genres:** Biography, History, Theology/Religion. **Career:** Third Way Magazine, deputy editor; Popular Ship of Fools, freelance writer and contributing editor. **Publications:** My Ministry Manual, 2002; John Wesley: A Biography, 2003; Paul

and His World, 2004; A Short History of Christianity, 2006; William Wilberforce: A Biography, 2007. **Address:** Eerdmans Publishing Co., 2140 Oak Industrial Dr. NE, Grand Rapids, MI 49505-6014, U.S.A. **Online address:** stevetom@btinternet.com

TOMLAN, Michael A. American (born United States), b. 1947. **Genres:** Cultural/Ethnic Topics, History, Illustrations. **Career:** Panto-Machine Engraving Inc., vice-president, 1975-90, president, 1990-; Cornell University, instructor in architecture, 1976-77, instructor, 1979-83, assistant professor, 1983-91, associate professor of city and regional planning, 1991-, professor, Historic Preservation Planning Program, director, Clarence S. Stein Institute for Urban and Landscape Studies, director; Ball State University, associate professor of architecture and planning, 1977-79; Cultural Resources Inventory of Richmond, co-director, 1978-83; City of Ithaca, board of zoning appeals, 1982-91, chair of board, 1985-91; House Museum and Center for the Arts, vice president and board directors, 1985-87; Tompkins County Public Library, board directors, 1987-89; Heritage Coalition, president, 1988-90; Historic Urban Plans Inc., president, 1992-; Global Heritage Fund, chair and senior board of advisor. Writer. **Publications:** Tinged with Gold: Hop Culture in the United States, 1992; (ed.) Preservation of What, For Whom?, 1997; (with M.R. Tomlan) Richmond, Indiana: Its Physical Development and Aesthetic Heritage to 1920, 2003; Historic Preservation: Caring for Our Expanding Legacy, 2009. Illustrator of works by J.A. Patrick. Works appear in anthologies. Contributor to journals. **Address:** Department of City & Regional Planning, College of Architecture, Art & Planning, Cornell University, 207 W Sibley Hall, 129 Sibley Dome, Ithaca, NY 14853, U.S.A. **Online address:** mat4@cornell.edu

TOMLINSON, (Alfred) Charles. British (born England), b. 1927. **Genres:** Poetry, Literary Criticism And History. **Career:** University of Bristol, lecturer, 1957-68, reader in English poetry, 1968-82, professor of English, 1982-92, Southey Lecturer, 1982, senior research fellow, emeritus professor of English poetry, 1992-; University of New Mexico, visiting professor, 1962-63, Witter Bynner lecturer, 1976; Colgate University, O'Connor professor of English, 1967-68; Princeton University, visiting professor, 1981; Cambridge University, Clark Lecturer, 1982; University of Liverpool, Kenneth Allott lecturer, 1983; Union College, Lamont professor of English, 1987; McMaster University, visiting professor, 1987; University of Keele, honorary professor, 1989; National Translation Centre, St. Jerome lecture on translation, 1995. Writer. **Publications:** Relations and Contraries, 1951; The Necklace, 1955; Seeing Is Believing, 1958; A Peopled Landscape: Poems, 1963; (with T. Connor and A. Clarke) Poems: A Selection, 1964; American Scenes and Other Poems, 1966; The Poems as Initiation, 1967; The Matachines, 1968; To Be Engraved on the Skull of a Cormorant, 1968; (with A. Brownjohn and M. Hamburger) Penguin Modern Poets 14, 1969; The Way of a World, 1969; America West Southwest, 1969; Renga, 1971, 4th ed., 1983; Words and Images, 1972; Written on Water, 1972; The Way In, 1974; In Black and White: Graphics, 1975; The Shaft, 1978; Selected Poems, 1978; The Flood, 1981; Some Americans, 1981; Airborn, 1981, 5th ed., 1991; Isaac Rosenberg of Bristol, 1982; Poetry and Metamorphosis (lectures), 1983; The Sense of the Past: 3 20th-Century Poets, 1983; Translations, 1983; Notes from New York and Other Poems, 1984; Collected Poems, 1985; Eden, 1985; The Return, 1987; Annunciations, 1989; Selected Poems, 1989; The Door in the Wall, 1992; Jubilation, 1995; Selected Poems: 1955-1997, 1997; The Vineyard above the Sea, 1999; American Essays, 2001; Skywriting, 2003; Metamorphoses: Poetry and Translation, 2003; Cracks in the Universe, 2006; New Collected Poems, 2009. TRANSLATOR: (with H. Gifford) Versions from Fyodor Tyutchev 1803-1873, 1960; (with H. Gifford) Castilian Ilexes: Versions from Antonio Machado, 1963; (with H. Gifford) C. Vallejo, Ten Versions from Trilce, 1970. EDITOR: Marianne Moore: A Collection of Critical Essays, 1970; William Carlos Williams: A Collection of Critical Essays, 1972; William Carlos Williams: Selected Poems, 1976, rev. ed., 1985; (and trans.) O. Paz, Selected Poems, 1979; The Oxford Book of Verse in English Translation, 1981; Selected Poems of George Oppen, 1990; Eros English'd: Classical Erotic Poetry in Translation from Golding to Hardy, 1992; (and trans.) A. Bertolucci, Selected Poems, 1993; John Dryden: Poems Selected by Charles Tomlinson, 2003. **Address:** University of Bristol, Senate House, Tyndall Ave., Bristol, BS8 1TH, England. **Online address:** egact@bristol.ac.uk

TOMLINSON, Harry. British (born England), b. 1943. **Genres:** Homes/ Gardens, Horticulture, Education, Young Adult Non-fiction. **Career:** Her Majesty's Land Registry, executive, 1960-80; bonsai artist, teacher and demonstrator, 1980-. Writer. **Publications:** The Complete Book of Bonsai, 1990;

Pocket Encyclopedia of Bonsai, 1994; (with P. Goff) The Bonsai Year Book, 1994; 101 Essentials Tips-Bonsai, 1996; Bonsai, 2003; Educational Leadership: Personal Growth for Professional Development, 2004. Contributor to periodicals. **Address:** Greenwood Bonsai Studio, Ollerton Rd., Arnold, NT NG5 8PR, England. **Online address:** harry@bonsai.co.uk

TOMLINSON, Heather. American (born United States) **Genres:** Novels. **Career:** Writer. **Publications:** NOVELS: The Swan Maiden, 2007; Aurelie: A Faerie Tale, 2008; Toads and Diamonds, 2010. **Address:** Southern, CA , U.S.A. **Online address:** heather@tomlinson.com

TOMLINSON, Stephen. American (born United States), b. 1954?. **Genres:** Social Sciences, Education. **Career:** Rydens School (high school), instructor in mathematics, 1978-80; University of Florida, Department of Mathematics, teaching assistant, 1980-85, teaching associate, 1985-91; Santa Fe Community College, instructor in mathematics, 1983-89; University of Alabama, assistant professor, 1991-97, associate professor, 1997-2005, professor of the social foundations of education, 2005-, coordinator of programs in educational foundations and educational leadership, 2000-03, chair of educational leadership, policy and technology studies, 2003-. Writer. **Publications:** Head Masters: Phrenology, Secular Education and Nineteenth-Century Social Thought, 2005. Contributor to periodicals. **Address:** Department of Education Leadership, Policy and, Technology Studies, University of Alabama, 301C Graves Hall, PO Box 870302, Tuscaloosa, AL 35487-0302, U.S.A. **Online address:** stomlins@bamaed.ua.edu

TOMLINSON, Theresa. British (born England), b. 1946. **Genres:** Young Adult Fiction, Mystery/Crime/Suspense, Romance/Historical, Novels. **Career:** Author, 1987-. **Publications:** YOUNG ADULT FICTION: The Flither Pickers, 1987; The Water Cat, 1988; Summer Witches, 1989; Riding the Waves, 1990; The Secret Place, 1990; The Rope Carrier, 1991; The Forestwife Trilogy, 1993; The Herring Girls, 1994; The Cellar Lad, 1995; Haunted House Blues, 1996; Dancing through the Shadows, 1997; Meet Me by the Steelmen, 1997; Little Stowaway, 1997; Child of the May, 1998; Ironstone Valley, 1998; The Path of the She Wolf, 2000; Beneath Burning Mountain, 2001; The Moon Riders, 2002; Errand Lass, 2003. CHILDREN'S FICTION: Night of the Red Devil, 2000; The Voyage of the Silver Bream, 2001; Scavenger Boy, 2003; Blitz Baby, 2004; Voyage of the Snake Lady, 2004; Wolf Girl, 2006. **Address:** c/o Caroline Walsh, David Higham Associates, 5-8 Lower John St., Golden Sq., London, GL W1R 4HA, England. **Online address:** theresatomlinson@talk21.com

TOMMASINI, Anthony. American (born United States), b. 1948?. **Genres:** Music, Biography, Classics. **Career:** New York Times, music critic, 1997-, senior music critic, chief classical music critic, 2000-; Boston Globe, music critic; Emerson College, assistant professor. Writer. **Publications:** Virgil Thomson's Musical Portrait, 1986; Virgil Thomson: Composer on the Aisle, 1997; Opera: A Critic's Guide to the 100 Most Important Works and the Best Recordings, 2004. Contributor to periodicals. **Address:** The New York Times, 620 8th Ave., New York, NY 10018-1618, U.S.A.

TOMPKINS, Ptolemy (Christian). American (born United States), b. 1962?. **Genres:** Art/Art History, Adult Non-fiction, Young Adult Fiction, Autobiography/Memoirs, Social Sciences. **Career:** Guideposts Magazine, senior editor; Angels on Earth Magazine, contributing editor; Beliefnet.com, columnist. Illustrator. **Publications:** This Tree Grows Out of Hell: Mesoamerica and the Search for the Magical Body, 1990, rev. ed., 2008; Color the Ancient Forest (juvenile), 1991; (ed.) Gardens in Central Europe, 1991; The Monkey in Art, 1994; (with N. Sapieha) A Dog Lover's Collection, 1995; Paradise Fever: Growing Up in the Shadow of the New Age (autobiography), 1997; The Beaten Path: Field Notes on Getting Wise in a Wisdom-Crazy World, 2001; Divine Life of Animals, 2010; Modern Book of the Dead, 2012. **Address:** Avon Books, 1350 Ave. of the Americas, New York, NY 10019, U.S.A.

TONE, John Lawrence. American (born United States), b. 1959. **Genres:** Adult Non-fiction, History. **Career:** Georgia Institute of Technology, Ivan Allen College, School of History, Technology, and Society, assistant professor, 1990-96, associate professor, 1996-2007, professor, 2007-, associate dean, 2008-; International Napoleonic Society, life fellow. Writer. **Publications:** The Fatal Knot: The Guerrilla War in Navarre and the Defeat of Napoleon in Spain, 1994; La Gguerrilla Espan˜ola y la Derrota de Napoleón (nonfiction), 1999; War and Genocide in Cuba, 1895-1898, 2006. **Address:** School of History, Technology and Society, Ivan Allen College, Georgia Institute of Technology, Rm. G17, Old Civil Engineering Bldg., Atlanta, GA 30332-0525, U.S.A. **Online address:** john.tone@hts.gatech.edu

TONG, Gary S. American/Hungarian (born Hungary), b. 1942. **Genres:** Crafts, Art/Art History, How-to Books, Children's Fiction, Illustrations. **Career:** Freelance illustrator and writer, 1970-. **Publications:** SELF-ILLUSTRATED: Modeling with Self-Hardening Clay, 1976; Gary Tong's Crazy Cut-Outs, 1979; Gary Tong's More Crazy Cut-Outs, 1980; (with M.F. Weisenfeld) The Runners Repair Manual, 1981; Gary Tong's Crazy Cut-Outs from Outer Space, 1982; Gary Tong's Crazy Cut-Out Tricks and Puzzles, 1983; Gary Tong's Crazy Pop-Ups, 1988. Illustrator of books by others. **Address:** 156 E 37th St., New York, NY 10016, U.S.A.

TONG, Raymond. British (born England), b. 1922. **Genres:** Poetry, Travel/Exploration, History, Young Adult Fiction. **Career:** British Overseas Education Service, education officer, 1949-53, senior education officer, 1953-56, Government Teacher Training College, principal, 1956-58, Secondary School, inspector, 1958-61; British Council (cultural relations), British Institute, director, 1961-65, Centre of English Studies, director, 1965-67, assistant representative-India, 1967-70, regional director-southwest England, 1971-75, representative-Kuwait, 1975-78, regional director-eastern England, 1978-82. Freelance writer. **Publications:** Requiem for the War Dead, and Other Poems, 1942; Today the Sun, 1947; Angry Decade, 1950; African Episodes, 1955; (comp.) African Helicon: A Poetry Anthology for African Schools, 1955, 2nd ed., 1975; Figures in Ebony: Past and Present in a West African City, 1958; English Comprehension Exercises, 1958; Tunde in Trouble (junior novel), 1959; Fabled City, 1960; A Matter of History, 1976; Crossing the Border, 1978; Observing the English, 1991; Selected Poems, 1994; Returning Home: Poems, 1996; Necessary Words, 2006. EDITOR: African Tales, 1956; African Adventure, 1956. Contributor to periodicals. **Address:** 1 Beaufort Rd., Clifton, Bristol, SY BS8 2JT, England.

TONG, Su. *See* **TONG, Zhong Gui.**

TONG, Zhong Gui. (Su Tong). Chinese (born China), b. 1963. **Genres:** Novellas/Short Stories, Novels, Translations, Young Adult Fiction. **Career:** Zhong Shan, editor, 1986-92. **Publications:** IN ENGLISH AS SU TONG: Raise the Red Lantern: Three Novellas, 1993; Rice, 2004; My Life as Emperor, 2005; Binu and the Great Wall, 2007; Mad Woman On the Bridge: And Other Stories, 2008; Tatoo, 2010; Boat to Redemption, 2010. IN CHINESE AS SU TONG: Shang Xin De Wu Dao, Yuan-Liou, 1991; Hong Fen, Yuan-Liou, 1991; Mi, YuanLiou, 1991; Qi Qie cheng gun, 1991; Nan Fang De Duo Luo, Yuan-Liou, 1992; Shi jie liang ce, 1993; Shao nian xie, 1993; Li hun zhi nan, 1993; Su Tong xiao shuo jing pin, 1993; Hun yin ji jing, 1993; Ci qing shi dai, 1993; Mo dai ai qing, 1994; Hou gong, 1994; Li hun zhi nan, 1995; Pu sa man, 1999; Pian duan pin jie, 2000; Qi qie cheng qun: Su Tong dai biao zuo, 2002; Ling yi zhong fu nu sheng huo, 2003; Su Tong Wang Hongtu dui hua lu, 2003; Si yan, 2006; Su Tong: hua fan qian xun, 2008; Sang yuan liu nian, 2008. OTHERS: Shao nian xue, 1993; (contrib.) Rouge, 1996; Wo de di wang sheng ya, 2009; Mi, 2009; Feng yang shu shan ge, 2011. **Address:** 10 Hu Nan Rd., Sheng Zojia Xie Hui, Nanjing, 21002, China.

TONKIN, Elizabeth. Irish/British (born England), b. 1934. **Genres:** Anthropology/Ethnology, Area Studies, History, Cultural/Ethnic Topics, Social Sciences. **Career:** British Civil Service, English teacher; Ahmadu Bello University, lecturer in English, 1963-66; University of Birmingham, Center of West African Studies, lecturer, senior lecturer in social anthropology, 1970-91; Queen's University of Belfast, professor of anthropology, 1991-99, professor emeritus, 1999-. Writer. **Publications:** Masking And Masquerading, with Examples from West Africa, 1979; (ed. with M. McDonald and M. Chapman) History and Ethnicity, 1989; Narrating Our Pasts: Social Construction of Oral History, 1992. **Address:** School of Anthropological Studies, Queen's University of Belfast, 15 University Sq., Belfast, BT7 1NN, Northern Ireland. **Online address:** etonkin@clio.arts.qub.ac.uk

TONKIN, Peter Francis. British/Irish (born Ireland), b. 1950. **Genres:** Novels, Mystery/Crime/Suspense, Young Adult Fiction. **Career:** Inner London Education Authority, teacher, 1975-80, 1987-89; Kent County Council, assistant headmaster, 1990-; writer, 1979-. **Publications:** Killer, 1979; The Journal of Edwin Underhill, 1981; The Coffin Ship, 1989; The Fire Ship, 1990; The Leper Ship, 1992; The Bomb Ship, 1993; The Iceberg, 1994; The Pirate Ship, 1995; Melt Down, 1996; The Action, 1996; Tiger Island, 1997; The Zero Option, 1997; Hell Gate, 1998; Power Down, 1999; High Water, 2000;

Thunder Bay, 2001; Titan 10, 2004; Wolf Rock, 2005; Resolution Burning, 2006; Cape Farewell, 2006; The Ship Breakers, 2007; High Wind in Java, 2007; Benin Light, 2008; River of Ghosts, 2009; Volcano Roads, 2009; The Red River, 2010; The Prison Ship, 2010; The Ice Station, 2011. THE MASTER OF DEFENCE SERIES: Point of Death, 2002; One Head Too Many, 2002; The Hound of the Borders, 2003; The Silent Woman, 2003. **Address:** 4 Mountfield Gardens, Royal Tunbridge Wells, KT TN1 1SJ, England. **Online address:** petertonkin@tesco.net

TOOBIN, Jeffrey (Ross). American (born United States), b. 1960. **Genres:** Law, Social Commentary, Politics/Government. **Career:** Harvard Law Review, editor, 1986; The New Republic, freelancer; Honorable J. Edward Lumbard, law clerk, 1986-87; Independent Counsel Lawrence Walsh, associate counsel, 1987-89; Eastern District New York, assistant U.S. attorney, 1990-93; The New Yorker, staff writer, 1993-, legal analyst; ABC News, legal analyst, 1994-2002; Cable News Network-TV, senior analyst and legal analyst, 2002-, senior legal analyst. **Publications:** Opening Arguments: A Young Lawyer's First Case-United States v Oliver North, 1991, rev. ed., 1992; The Run of His Life: The People v O.J. Simpson, 1996, rev. ed., 1997; Vast Conspiracy: The Real Story of the Sex Scandal the Nearly Brought down a President, 1999; Too Close to Call: The Thirty-Six-Day Battle to Decide the 2000 Election, 2001; The Nine: Inside the Secret World of the Supreme Court, 2007. **Address:** The New Yorker, 20 W 43rd St., New York, NY 10036-7400, U.S.A.

TOOZE, J. Adam. British (born England) **Genres:** History, Business/Trade/Industry, Economics. **Career:** University of Cambridge, Centre for History and Economics, research fellow, 1995-96, Jesus College, senior lecturer in modern European economic history, Gurnee Hart fellow in history and director of studies. Writer. **Publications:** Statistics and the German State, 1900-1945: The Making of Modern Economic Knowledge, 2001; The Wages of Destruction: The Making and Breaking of the Nazi Economy, 2006. Contributor to books and periodicals. **Address:** Jesus College, University of Cambridge, Cambridge, CB CB5 8BL, England. **Online address:** jat27@cam.ac.uk

TOPE, Rebecca. British (born England), b. 1948?. **Genres:** Mystery/Crime/Suspense, Literary Criticism And History, Young Adult Fiction. **Career:** Praxis Books, founder, 1992-. Writer and instructor. **Publications:** DEN COOPER SERIES: A Dirty Death, 1999; Death of a Friend, 2000; A Death to Record, 2001. DREW SLOCOMBE SERIES: Dark Undertakings, 1999; Grave Concerns, 2000; The Sting of Death, 2002; A Market for Murder, 2003. THEA OSBORNE SERIES: A Cotswold Killing, 2004; A Cotswold Ordeal, 2005; Death in the Cotswolds, 2006; A Cotswold Mystery, 2007; Blood in the Cotswolds, 2008; Slaughter in the Cotswolds, 2009; Fear in the Cotswolds, 2009; A Grave in the Cotswolds, 2010. OTHER: Memory of Water, 2006; (ed. with L. Ashford) Strange Days Indeed: Autobiographical Stories about Motherhood by Women from Wales, 2007. **Address:** Allison and Busby Ltd., 13 Charlotte Mews, London, GL W1T 4EJ, England. **Online address:** author@rebeccatope.fsnet.co.uk

TOPEK, Susan Remick. American (born United States), b. 1955. **Genres:** Children's Non-fiction, Theology/Religion, Children's Fiction, Picture/Board Books, inspirational/Motivational Literature. **Career:** Jewish Community Center, group social worker, 1977-79; Temple Isaiah, Sunday and supplemental Hebrew teacher, 1985-; North Shore Jewish Center Pre-School, camp director and teacher, 1986-95; Suffolk-Jewish Community Center, preschool teacher, 1995-; Suffolk Association for Jewish Educational Services (now The Jewish Education Project), story teller and early childhood consultant, 1996-, Department of Early Childhood and Library Services, director, Department of Early Childhood Education and Family Engagement, associate director. Writer. **Publications:** (With S.R. Topek) Israel Is, 1988; A Holiday for Noah, 1990; Ten Good Rules, 1991; A Turn for Noah, a Hanukkah Story, 1992; A Taste for Noah, 1993; A Costume for Noah: A Purim Story, 1995; Shalom Shabbat: A Book for Havdalah, 1997; Ten Good Rules: A Ten Commandments Counting Book, 2007. **Address:** The Jewish Education Project, 777 Larkfield Rd., Ste. 118, Commack, NY 11725, U.S.A. **Online address:** srtopek@thejewisheducationproject.org

TOPPING, Keith A. British (born England), b. 1963. **Genres:** Novels, Adult Non-fiction, Film, Young Adult Fiction. **Career:** Department of Employment, administrative officer, 1983-2001; full-time writer, 2001-. **Publications:** (With P. Cornell and M. Day) The Guinness Book of Classic British TV, 1993; (with P. Cornell and M. Day) The Avengers Programme Guide, 1994; (with P. Cornell and M. Day) The Doctor Who Discontinuity Guide, 1995; Hollywood Vampire: The Unofficial Guide to Angel, 2000; Slayer: The Totally Cool Unofficial Guide to Buffy, 2000; High Times: The Unofficial and Unauthorized Guide to Roswell High, 2001; Byzantium: A First Doctor, Ian Chesterton, Barbara Wright and Vicki Novel, 2002; Ghost Ship, 2002; The Inside Bartlet's White House, 2002; Doctor Who: Ghost Ship, 2002; Slayer: An Unofficial and Unauthorised Guide to Season Six of Buffy the Vampire Slayer, 2003; A Day in the Life: The Unofficial and Unauthorized Guide to 24, 2003; All That and The Pirates Song; A Vault of Horror, forthcoming; The Scourge and The Man in the Closet, forthcoming. NON FICTION: (with M. Day) Shut It!: A Fan's Guide to 70's Cops on the Box, 1999; Roswell, High Times: An Unofficial and Unauthorized Guide, 2001; Inside Bartlet's White House: An Unauthorised and Unofficial Guide to The West Wing, 2002; A Day in the Life: The Unofficial and Unauthorised Guide to 24, 2003; The Complete Clash, 2003; A Vault of Horror: A Book of 80 Great British Horror Movies from 1956-1974, 2004. Contributor to periodicals. **Address:** Campbell Thomson & McLaughlin Ltd., 1 Kings Mews, London, GL WC1N 2JA, England. **Online address:** keith@tooon.demon.xo.uk

TORGOVNICK, Kate. American (born United States) **Genres:** Education. **Career:** Jane magazine, associate editor; Dame magazine, editor. **Publications:** Cheer! Three Teams on a Quest for College Cheerleading's Ultimate Prize, 2008. Contributor to periodicals. **Address:** New York, NY , U.S.A. **Online address:** cheerbook@gmail.com

TORIYAMA, Akira. Japanese (born Japan), b. 1955. **Genres:** Novels, Children's Fiction, Graphic Novels. **Career:** Manga artist and writer, 1978-. **Publications:** World Special Akira Toriyama, 1994; Dragon Ball, vol. I, 2003, vol. IX, 2003. Contributor to periodicals. **Address:** c/o Author Mail, Viz Comics L.L.C., PO Box 77010, San Francisco, CA 94107, U.S.A.

TORNABENE, Wanda. Italian (born Italy) **Genres:** Food And Wine, Cultural/Ethnic Topics. **Career:** Writer. **Publications:** (With G. Tornabene and M. Evans) La cucina Siciliana di Gangivecchio, 1996; (with G. Tornabene and and M. Evans) La cucina Siciliana della casa, 2001; (with G. Tronabene and C. Carreño) 100 Ways to Be Pasta: Perfect Pasta Recipes from Gangivecchio, 2005. **Address:** Alfred Knopf Publishing Group, 1745 Broadway, New York, NY 10019, U.S.A.

TÖRNQVIST, Egil. Swedish (born Sweden), b. 1932. **Genres:** Plays/Screenplays, Film, Theatre, Translations, Cultural/Ethnic Topics. **Career:** Harvard University, lecturer in Swedish, 1957-58; Uppsala Universitet, Division for Drama Research, research assistant, 1965-69; University of Amsterdam, professor of Scandinavian studies, 1969-97, professor emeritus, 1997-; Tijdschrift voor Skandinavistiek, initiator, 1980. Writer. **Publications:** (Ed.) Drama och teater, 1968; A Drama of Souls, Studies in O'Neill's Super-Naturalistic Technique, 1968; (ed.) Ibsens dramatik, 1971; Svenska dramastrukturer, 1973; Bergman och Strindberg: Spöksonaten-drama och iscensättning, 1973; (with B. Jacobs) Strindberg's Miss Julie: A Play and Its Transpositions, 1988; Transposing Drama: Studies in Representation, 1991; Filmdiktaren Ingmar Bergman, 1993; Ibsen: A Doll's House, 1995; Between Stage and Screen: Ingmar Bergman Directs, 1995; Ibsen, Strindberg, and the Intimate Theatre: Studies in TV Presentation, 1999; Strindberg's The Ghost Sonata: From Text to Performance, 2000; Det talade ordet: Om Strindbergs dramadialog, 2001; Bergman's Muses: Aesthetic Versatility in Film, Theatre, Television, and Radio, 2003; Strindberg som TV-dramatiker, 2004; Eugene O'Neill: A Playwright's Theatre, 2004; Ibsen-byggmästaren, 2006; (trans. and ed. with B. Steene) Strindberg on Drama and Theatre: A Source Book, 2007; I Bergmans regi, 2008; Strindberg: The Master Weaver, 2010; Strindbergs dramatiska bildspråk, 2011. Contributor of articles to journals. **Address:** University of Amsterdam, Spuistraat 134, Amsterdam, 1012 VB, Netherlands. **Online address:** p.e.tornqvist@gmail.com

TORRANCE, Lee. British (born England), b. 1920?. **Genres:** Novels, Plays/Screenplays, Literary Criticism And History. **Career:** Teacher and writer, 1949-. **Publications:** NOVEL: Only on Friday, 1980. **Address:** Pimp Barn, Withyham, Hartfield, Sussex, ES TN7 4BB, England.

TORRES, Gerald. American (born United States), b. 1952?. **Genres:** Law, History, Politics/Government, Social Sciences. **Career:** Children's Defense Fund, staff attorney, 1977-78; University of Pittsburgh, Law School, assistant professor, 1980; University of Texas, School of Law, professor, 1993-,

Bryant Smith chair in law, visiting professor, vice provost and H. O. Head centennial professor in real property law; Harvard University, Law School, visiting professor; Vermont Law School, visiting professor; University of Minnesota, Law School, professor and associate dean; U.S. Department of Justice, Environment and Natural Resources Division, deputy assistant attorncy general. Writer. **Publications:** Farming and Groundwater: An Introduction, 1988; (with L. Guinier) The Miner's Canary: Enlisting Race, Resisting Power, Transforming Democracy, 2002. Contributor of articles to periodicals and books. **Address:** School of Law, University of Texas, 727 E Dean Keeton St., Rm. 3266, Austin, TX 78705, U.S.A. **Online address:** gtorres@mail.law.utexas.edu

TORRES, John A(lbert). American (born United States), b. 1965. **Genres:** Young Adult Non-fiction, Sports/Fitness, Illustrations, History. **Career:** Writer. **Publications:** FOR YOUNG PEOPLE: (with M.J. Sullivan) Sports Great Darry l Strawberry, 1990; Sports Reports: Hakeem Olajuwon: Star Center, 1997; Greg Maddux, Ace!, 1997; Sports Great Jason Kidd, 1998; Top 10 Basketball Three-Point Shooters, 1999; Sports Great Oscar De la Hoya, 1999; Tino Martinez, 1999; Bobby Bonilla, 1999; Kevin Garnett: Da Kid, 2000; Mia Hamm, 2000; Michelle Kwan, 2000; Sports Great Dikembe Mutombo, 2000; Top 10 NBA Finals Most Valuable Players, 2000; Top 10 Baseball Legends, 2000; Kobe Bryant, 2001; Fitness Stars of Bodybuilding: Featuring Profiles of Arnold Schwarzenegger, Lou Ferrigno, Ronnie Coleman and Lenda Murray, 2001; Kobe Bryant, 2001; Derek Jeter, 2001; Fitness Stars of Pro Football: Featuring Profiles of Deion Sanders, Shannon Sharpe, Darrell Green and Wayne Chrebet, 2001; Sports Great Grant Hill, 2001; Marc Anthony, 2001; (with S. Zannos) Careers in the Music Industry, 2002; Sports Great Tim Duncan, 2002; Sheryl Swoopes, 2002; Tiger Woods, 2002; Sports Great Sammy Sosa, 2003; Vince Carter: Slam Dunk Artist, 2004; The African Elephant, 2004; Shaquille O'Neal: Gentle Giant, 2004; The Manatee, 2004; Allen Iverson: Never Give Up, 2004; P. Diddy, 2005; Disaster in the Indian Ocean, Tsunami 2004, 2005; Clay Aiken, 2005; Tsunami Disaster in Indonesia, 2004, 2006; Usher, 2006; Texas Fight for Independence, from the Alamo to San Jacinto, 2006; The Cherokee Trail of Tears and the Forced March of a People, 2006; Hurricane Katrina and the Devastation of New Orleans, 2005, 2006; Hurricane Katrina, 2005, 2007; Ancient Mystery of Easter Island, 2007; Meet Our New Student from Nicaragua, 2009; Threat to Haiti, 2009; Timbaland, 2009; Lil Wayne, 2010; Hong Kong, 2010. SELF-ILLUSTRATED: Home-Run Hitters: Heroes of the Four Home-Run Game, 1995. OTHERS: (with M.J. Sullivan) Sports Great Darryl Strawberry, 1990; Meet our New Student from Zambia, 2010; We visit the Dominican Republic, 2010; We Visit Puerto Rico, 2011; The Battle of Midway, 2011; Top 25 Football Skills, Tips and Tricks, 2012; Top 25 Basketball Skills, Tips and Tricks, 2012. **Address:** c/o Author Mail, Enslow Publishers Inc., 40 Industrial Rd., Department F 61, PO Box 398, Berkeley Heights, NJ 07922-0398, U.S.A. **Online address:** johnalberttorres@aol.com

TORRES, Laura. American (born United States), b. 1967. **Genres:** Crafts, Art/Art History, How-to Books. **Career:** American Girl Magazine, editor; Klutz Press, senior editor; freelance writer, 1990-; creative consultant, 1995-. **Publications:** (With S. Haab) The Incredible Clay Book: How to Make and Bake a Million and One Clay Creations, 1994; Beads: A Book of Ideas and Instruction, 1996; Friendship Bracelets, 1996; The Sticker Book, 1996; (with M. Sherman) Pipe Cleaners Gone Crazy, 1996; Fantastic Foam Book, 1998; (with S. Haab) Create Anything with Clay, 1999; Pom Poms Gone Crazy, 1999; Clay Modeling with Pooh, 1999; November Ever After, 1999; Disney's Ten-Minute Crafts for Preschooler, 2000; Don't Eat Pete, 2000; (with S. Haab) Wire-o-Mania, 2000; Disney Princess Crafts, 2001; Paper Punch Art, 2001; Salt Dough!, 2001; Crossing Montana, 2002; Best Friends Forever!: 199 Projects to Make and Share, 2004; Rock Your Wardrobe, 2010; Rock Your Room, 2011; School Stuff, 2011; Party, 2011; Room, 2011; Wardrobe, 2011. Contributor to periodicals. **Address:** 1643 N 1100 W, Mapleton, UT 84664-3349, U.S.A. **Online address:** laura@lauratorres.com

TORRES, Steven. American (born United States), b. 1969?. **Genres:** Mystery/Crime/Suspense, Novels, Novellas/Short Stories, Young Adult Fiction, Literary Criticism And History. **Career:** New York Public Library, part-time staff; Bronx Community College, English instructor; Yeshiva College, English instructor; Utica College, assistant professor of English, 2002-04; Manchester Community College, instructor in English, 2004-. Writer. **Publications:** Precinct Puerto Rico, 2002; Death in Precinct Puerto Rico: Book Two, 2003; Burning Precinct Puerto Rico: Book Three, 2004; Missing in Precinct Puerto Rico: Book Four, 2006; The Concrete Maze, 2007; Blackout in Pre-

cinct Puerto Rico, 2010. Contributor to periodicals. **Address:** Public Relations, St. Martins Press, 175 5th Ave., New York, NY 10010, U.S.A.

TORSNEY, Cheryl B. American (born United States), b. 1955. **Genres:** Literary Criticism And History, Language/Linguistics, Autobiography/Memoirs, Humanities. **Career:** Universite de Savoie, Fulbright visiting lecturer, 1982-83; Delta State University, assistant professor of English, 1983-85; West Virginia University, assistant professor, 1985-89, associate professor of English, 1989-, professor of English, associate provost for academic programs; University of Utrecht, Fulbright lecturer, 1989. Writer. **Publications:** Constance Fenimore Woolson: The Grief of Artistry, 1989; (ed.)Critical Essays on Constance Fenimore Woolson, 1992; (ed. with J. Elsley) Quilt Culture: Tracing the Pattern, 1994; (ed.) The Wings of the Dove, 1997. Contributor of articles to journals. **Address:** Department of English, West Virginia University, 100 Colson Hall, 1503 University Ave., PO Box 6296, Morgantown, WV 26506-6296, U.S.A. **Online address:** cheryl.torsney@mail.wvu.edu

TŌSHOIN NO SEIHŌ *See* **Sullivan, M(ichael) J(ustin).**

TOSICS, Ivan. Hungarian (born Hungary), b. 1952. **Genres:** Regional/Urban Planning, Social Sciences, Politics/Government, Public/Social Administration, Sociology. **Career:** Planning Institute for Budapest, sociologist in research group, 1975-83; Institute for Building Economy and Organization, sociological researcher, 1983-89; Technical University of Budapest, teacher of sociology, 1989-90; Hungarian Academy of Sciences, Institute of Sociology, affiliate, 1989-91; Metropolitan Research Institute, co-founder, 1989, sociologist and managing director, 1989-; European Network for Housing Research, vice chair 2008-, Journal Urban Research and Practice, policy editor, 2008-. Writer. **Publications:** (With J. Hegedus and R.J. Struyk) Integrating State Rental Housing with the Private Market: Designing Housing Allowances for Hungary, 1991. EDITOR AND CONTRIBUTOR: (with J. Hegedus and B. Turner) The Reform of Housing in Eastern Europe and the Soviet Union, 1992; (with D. Clapham, J. Hegedus and K. Kintrea) Housing Privatization in Eastern Europe, 1996; (with R.V. Kempen, K. Dekker and S. Hall) Restructing Large Housing Estates in Europe, 2005; (with A. Piorr and J. Ravetz) Peri-urbanisation in Europe: Towards a European Policy to Sustain Urban-Rural Futures, 2011. Works appear in anthologies. Contributor to books and periodicals. **Address:** Metropolitan Research Institute, Lonyay utca 34, Budapest, 1093, Hungary. **Online address:** tosics@mri.hu

TOTANI, Yuma. American (born United States), b. 1972. **Genres:** History, Law. **Career:** University of Nevada, assistant professor. Writer. **Publications:** The Tokyo War Crimes Trial: The Pursuit of Justice in the Wake of World War II, 2008. **Address:** U.S.A. **Online address:** yuma.totani@unlv.edu

TOTEN, Teresa. Canadian/Croatian (born Croatia), b. 1955. **Genres:** Young Adult Fiction, Novels, Picture/Board Books. **Career:** Radio Canada, freelance writer and broadcaster, 1980; Royal Commission on Conditions of Foreign Service, senior analyst, 1982; Canada Museum Construction Corp., assistant to the chairman, 1982-84; Canadian Institute for International Peace and Security, corporate secretary, 1984-85; freelance book reviewer, 1996-. **Publications:** The Onlyhouse, 1995; The Game, 2001; Bright Red Kisses, 2005; Better than Blonde, 2007; Me and the Blondes, 2009; (ed.) Piece By Piece, 2010; Beyond Blonde, 2011; (with E. Walters) The Taming, 2012. **Address:** Penguin Books, 90 Eglinton Ave. E, Ste. 700, Toronto, ON M4P 2Y3, Canada. **Online address:** teresa@teresatoten.com

TOTH, Jennifer. American (born United States), b. 1967. **Genres:** Documentaries/Reportage, Social Sciences. **Career:** Los Angeles Times, journalist, 1990-92; News and Observer, journalist, 1994. **Publications:** The Mole People: Life in the Tunnels Under NYC, 1993; Orphans of the Living: America's Foster Care Crisis, 1997; What Happened to Johnnie Jordan: The Story of a Child Turning Violent, 2002. Contributor to periodicals. **Address:** c/o Keith Korman, Raines & Raines, 71 Park Ave., New York, NY 10016, U.S.A.

TOTTEN, Mark D. (Mark Douglas Totten). Canadian (born Canada), b. 1962. **Genres:** Adult Non-fiction, Social Sciences, Children's Fiction, Biography. **Career:** Children's Aid Society of Ottawa-Carleton, protection social worker, 1986-88; Carleton University, research assistant, 1985-86, teaching assistant, 1986; School of Continuing Education, Business Section Algonquin College, lecturer, 1987; Totten and Associates, consultant, 1997-; Youth Services Bureau of Ottawa, director of research, 1987-2007, coordinator, 1988-90, supervisor, 1990-93, director of service delivery, 1993-95, Community

Reintegration Project, director, 2000-01; University Research Project, Social Sciences and Humanities Research Council of Canada Community, director, 2000-03; National Gang Crime Prevention Center, Journal of Gang Research, reviewing editor, 2001-; Canadian Public Health Association, Youth Literacy and Violence Prevention Project, principal researcher, 2001-02, Anti-bullying Program Evaluation and Best Practices Project, principal researcher, 2003-04; Canadian Parks and Recreation Association, researcher, 2003-04. **Publications:** Guys, Gangs and Girlfriend Abuse, 2000; (with K. Kelly) When Children Kill: A Social-Psychological Study of Youth Homicide, 2002; (with K. Kelly) Restorative Justice: Working with Youth, 2003. Contributor of articles to periodicals. **Address:** Totten and Associates Inc., 392 Eastcastle Pl., London, ON N6G 3W5, Canada. **Online address:** mtotten@ysb.on.ca

TOTTEN, Mark Douglas. *See* **TOTTEN, Mark D.**

TOUB, Micah. Canadian/American (born United States), b. 1976?. **Genres:** Autobiography/Memoirs. **Career:** Abbeville Press, publicist; Art on Paper, editor; Toro, associate editor; Toronto Globe and Mail, editor. **Publications:** Growing Up Jung: Coming of Age As the Son of Two Shrinks (memoir), 2010. Contributor to periodicals. **Address:** c/o Doug Stewart, Sterling Lord Literistic Inc., 65 Bleecker St., New York, NY 10012, U.S.A. **Online address:** micah@micahtoub.com

TOUCHSTONE, Kathleen. American (born United States), b. 1950. **Genres:** Economics, Business/Trade/Industry. **Career:** Bureau of Labor Statistics, economist, 1978-80; Wofford College, assistant professor of economics, 1980-82; U.S. Department of the Navy, operation research and management analyst, 1983-94; Troy University-Atlantic Region, graduate faculty, 1994-2006; Troy University-Montgomery, Sorrell College of Business, assistant professor of economics, 2007-. Writer. **Publications:** Then Athena Said: Unilateral Transfers and the Transformation of Objectivist Ethics, 2006. Contributor to journals and periodicals. **Address:** Sorrell College of Business, Troy University Montgomery, Rm. 130, 206 McCartha Hall, 136 Catoma St., PO Box 4419, Montgomery, AL 36013, U.S.A. **Online address:** ktouchstone@troy.edu

TOULMIN, Vanessa Elizabeth. British (born England), b. 1967. **Genres:** Art/Art History, Literary Criticism And History, Photography. **Career:** Archaeologist, 1988-90; Antiquarian bookshop, assistant manager, 1990-92; University of Sheffield, National Fairground Archive, founder, assistant director, 1995-99, research director, 2000-05, director, 2005, chair in Early Film and Popular Entertainment; Yale University, visiting lecturer; University of Chicago, visiting lecturer; Utrecht University, visiting lecturer. Researcher, consultant and writer. **Publications:** Randall Williams: King of Showmen, 1998; (ed. with S. Popple) Visual Delights: The Popular and Projected Image in the Nineteenth Century, 2000; Pleasurelands, 2003; (with S. Popple and P. Russell) The Lost World of Mitchell & Kenyon: Edwardian Britain on Film, 2004; (ed. with S. Popple) Visual Delights Two: Exhibition and Reception, 2005; Electric Edwardians: The Story of the Mitchell & Kenyon Collection, 2006. Contributor to periodicals. **Address:** School of English Literaturer, Language and Linguistics, University of Sheffield, Western Bank, Sheffield, SY S10 2TN, England. **Online address:** v.toulmin@shef.ac.uk

TOURÉ. American (born United States), b. 1971. **Genres:** Novels, Novellas/Short Stories, Essays, Biography. **Career:** Black Entertainment Television (BET), writer, host, correspondent and consulting producer, 2005-08; MSNBC, contributor, 2008-. **Publications:** The Portable Promised Land: Stories, 2002; Soul City: A Novel, 2004; Never Drank the Kool Aid: Essays, 2006; Who's Afraid of Post-Blackness?: What It Means to be Black Now, 2011. Contributor to periodicals. **Address:** MSNBC, 30 Rockefeller Plz., New York, NY 10112, U.S.A.

TOURNEY, Leonard D(on). American (born United States), b. 1942. **Genres:** Mystery/Crime/Suspense, Novels, Novellas/Short Stories, History, Young Adult Fiction. **Career:** Western Illinois University, instructor in English, 1966-68; University of Tulsa, associate professor of English, 1970-85; University of California, lecturer in the writing program, 1985-; Brigham Young University, Department of English, associate professor, 2006-. Writer. **Publications:** Joseph Hall, 1979; Time's Fool: A Mystery of Shakespeare, 2004. CONSTABLE STOCK SERIES: The Players' Boy Is Dead, 1980; Low Treason, 1982; Familiar Spirits, 1984; The Bartholomew Fair Murders, 1986; Old Saxon Blood, 1988; Knaves Templar, 1991; Witness of Bones, 1992; Frobisher's Savage, 1994. Contributor to articles. **Address:** Department of

English, Brigham Young University, 4104 JFSB, 1 N University Ave., Provo, UT 84602, U.S.A. **Online address:** tourney@byu.edu

TOWER, S. D. *See* **JONES, (R.) Dennis.**

TOWERS, Frank. American (born United States), b. 1964?. **Genres:** History, Civil Liberties/Human Rights. **Career:** Clarion University of Pennsylvania, assistant professor of history, 1993-97; Bilkent University, assistant professor of history, 1997-99; Colorado State University, assistant professor, 1999-2002, associate professor of history, 2002-04; University of Calgary, associate professor of history, 2004-, professor. Writer and educator. **Publications:** The Urban South and the Coming of the Civil War, 2004; (ed. with L.D. Barnes and B. Schoen) Old South's Modern Worlds: Slavery, Region and Nation in The Age of Progress, 2011. CONTRIBUTOR: Encyclopedia of the War of 1812, 1997; From Mobtown to Charm City: New Perspectives on Baltimore Past, 2002; The Oxford Encyclopedia of African American History: The Early Republic, 2005; Another Look at Inevitability: The Upper South and the Limits of Compromise in the Secession Crisis, 2011; (ed. with D. Quigley) The Southern City Before 1900, 2012; (ed. with S.P. Adams) American Whigs, 2012. Contributor to periodicals and journals. **Address:** Department of History, University of Calgary, 2500 University Dr. NW, Calgary, AB T2N 1N4, Canada. **Online address:** ftowers@ucalgary.ca

TOWNE, Marian K(leinsasser). American (born United States), b. 1933. **Genres:** Romance/Historical, Food And Wine, Local History/Rural Topics, Theatre, Theology/Religion, Women's Studies And Issues, Autobiography/Memoirs, History, History, Literary Criticism And History, Biography. **Career:** Moundridge High School, faculty, 1955-57; Roosevelt University, part-time instructor in English, 1958-62; Findlay College (now University), part-time instructor in English, 1962-68, assistant professor of English, 1968-70; Indiana University-Purdue University, part-time instructor, faculty in speech communication, 1984-94; Butler University, part-time instructor; Bluffton College, part-time instructor; Caring Community Inc., founding director; Hoosiers Concerned About Gun Violence, founding director; Center for Church and Community Ministries, consultant; McCormick Theological Seminary, consultant. Writer. **Publications:** Bread of Life: Diaries and Memories of a Dakota Family, 1936-1945, 1994; The Onliest One Alive: Surviving Jonestown, Guyana, 1995; A Midwest Gardener's Cookbook, 1996; Dreaming the Impossible Dream: The First Thirty Years of the Edyvean Repertory Theatre at Christian Theological Seminary, Indianapolis, Indiana, 1996; That All May Be One: Centennial History of Church Women United in Indianapolis, 1898-1998, 1998; Celebrating the Journey: The Diamond Anniversary of Fairview Presbyterian Church, 1924-1999, 1999; Jacob Hutter's Friends: Twelve Narrative Voices from Switzerland to South Dakota over Four Centuries, 1999; Fiftieth Anniversary of Freeman Academy Class of 1951, 2001. **Address:** 5129 N Illinois St., Indianapolis, IN 46208-2613, U.S.A. **Online address:** edmarian@aol.com

TOWNEND, Paul A. American (born United States), b. 1967. **Genres:** Biography. **Career:** Colgate University, research assistant, 1987-98; University of Chicago, Office of Student Housing, assistant director, 1998-2000; Villanova University, Arthur Ennis fellow, 2000-01; University of North Carolina, Department of History, assistant professor, 2001-05, undergraduate coordinator, 2004-, associate professor, 2005-, chair. Writer. **Publications:** Father Mathew, Temperance and Irish Identity, 2002; (contrib.) The Written Word and Irish Historical Memory, 1870-1922, 2003. **Address:** Department of History, University of North Carolina Wilmington, Morton Hall 232, 601 S College Rd., Wilmington, NC 28403, U.S.A. **Online address:** townendp@uncw.edu

TOWNLEY, Wyatt. American (born United States) **Genres:** Poetry, Medicine/Health, Humanities. **Career:** Yoganetics, Shawnee Mission, founder and yoga instructor, 1977. Poet and freelance writer. **Publications:** Perfectly Normal (poetry), 1990; The Breathing Field: Meditations on Yoga (poetry), 2002; Yoganetics: Be Fit, Healthy and Relaxed One Breath at a Time, 2003; Kansas City Ballet: The First 50 Years, 2007; The Afterlife of Trees, 2010. Contributor of articles to periodicals. **Address:** c/o Sandy Choron, March Tenth Inc., 4 Myrtle St., Haworth, NJ 07641, U.S.A. **Online address:** wt@yoganetics.com

TOWNSEND, Ann. American (born United States), b. 1962. **Genres:** Poetry, Essays. **Career:** Denison University, associate professor of English, Dominick Consolo professor of English and director of creative writing, 1992-, professor of English; Carlow University, Master of Fine Arts in creative writing, faculty, 2007-. Writer. **Publications:** POETRY: Modern Love,

1995; (with D. Baker) Holding Katherine, 1996; The Braille Woods, 1997; Dime Store Erotics, 1998; The Coronary Garden, 2005. ESSAYS: (ed. with D. Baker) Radiant Lyre: Essays on Lyric Poetry, 2007. Contributor of articles to periodicals. **Address:** Departmentof English, Denison University, 201 Barney-Davis, 100 W College St., Granville, OH 43023-1100, U.S.A. **Online address:** townsend@denison.edu

TOWNSEND, Brad W. American (born United States), b. 1962. **Genres:** Biography, Adult Non-fiction, Sports/Fitness, Children's Non-fiction. **Career:** San Antonio Light, sports reporter, 1984-93; Houston Chronicle, copy editor, 1993-94; Dallas Morning News, staff writer, sports reporter, 1994-, national pro golf writer, 1997-2001. Sports projects/features writer. **Publications:** Shaquille O'Neal: Center of Attention, 1994, rev. ed., 1998; Anfernee Hardaway, Basketball's Lucky Penny, 1997; (with S. Humphries) Two Steps to a Perfect Golf Swing, 2004. **Address:** 508 Young St., Dallas, TX 75202-4808, U.S.A. **Online address:** btownsend@dallasnews.com

TOWNSEND, Craig D. American (born United States), b. 1955. **Genres:** Theology/Religion, History, Social Sciences. **Career:** Saint James Church, associate rector for education, senior associate vicar. Writer and theologian. **Publications:** Faith in Their Own Color: Black Episcopalians in Antebellum New York City, 2005. **Address:** New York, NY , U.S.A. **Online address:** cdt@craigdtownsend.com

TOWNSEND, Elizabeth A. Canadian (born Canada), b. 1945. **Genres:** Adult Non-fiction. **Career:** Dalhousie University, School of Occupational Therapy, professor and director, 1982-, professor emerita. Writer and occupational therapist. **Publications:** (Ed.) Enabling Occupation: An Occupational Therapy Perspective, 1997; Good Intentions Overruled: A Critique of Empowerment in the Routine Organization of Mental Health Services, 1998; (intro.) Sociology and Occupational Therapy Edinburgh: Churchill Livingstone, 1998; (ed.) Interdisciplinary Seminar on Occupation, 1998; (co-author) Spirituality in Enabling Occupation: A Learner-Centred Workbook, 1999; (with G. Morgan, J. Fingard and L.B. Morgan) A Sentinel on the Street: St. Matthew's United Church, 1749-1999, 1999; (ed. with C.H. Christiansen) Introduction to Occupation: The Art and Science of Living, 2004, 2nd ed., 2010. **Address:** School of Occupational Therapy, Dalhousie University, Rm. 215, Forrest Bldg., 5869 University Ave., Halifax, NS B3H 3J5, Canada. **Online address:** liz.townsend@dal.ca

TOWNSEND, John Rowe. British (born England), b. 1922. **Genres:** Young Adult Fiction, Children's Fiction, Literary Criticism And History, Novels, Young Adult Non-fiction, Essays, Children's Non-fiction, Biography, Biography. **Career:** Yorkshire Post, journalist, 1946; Evening Standard, journalist, 1949; Manchester Guardian, sub-editor, 1949-54, art editor, 1954-55, editor, 1955-59, children's book editor (part-time), 1968-78, columnist, 1968-81; University of Pennsylvania, visiting lecturer, 1965; University of Washington, visiting lecturer, 1969, 1971; writer, 1969-; New York Public Library, May Hill Arbuthnot honor lecturer, 1971; Library of Congress, Whittall lecturer, 1976; Simmons College, Center for Children's Literature, visiting faculty, 1978-84. **Publications:** FOR CHILDREN: Gumble's Yard, 1961, rev. ed. as Trouble in the Jungle, 1969; Widdershins Crescent, 1965, rev. ed. as Goodbye to the Jungle, 1967; Pirate's Island, 1968; A Wish for Wings, 1972; Top of the World, 1976; Clever Dick: The Diary of a Dreadful Child, 1982; Dan Alone, 1983; Gone to the Dogs, 1984; Tom Tiddler's Ground, 1986; The Persuading Stick, 1986. FOR YOUNG ADULTS: The Hallersage Sound, 1966; Hell's Edge, 1969; The Intruder, 1969; Goodnight, Prof, Love, 1970 as Goodnight, Prof, Dear, 1971; (ed.) Modern Poetry: A Selection for Young People, 1971; The Summer People, 1972; Forest of the Night, 1974; Noah's Castle, 1975; The Xanadu Manuscript, 1977; The Runaways, 1979; King Creature Come, as The Creatures, 1980; The Islanders, 1981; A Foreign Affair, as Kate And The Revolution, 1982; Cloudy-Bright: A Novel, 1984, as Sam and Jenny, 1992; Downstream: A Novel, 1987; Rob's Place, 1988; The Golden Journey, 1989, as The Fortunate Isles: A Novel, 1989; The Invaders, 1992. OTHERS: Written for Children: An Outline of English-language Children's Literature, 1965, 6th ed., 1996; A Sense of Story: Essays On Contemporary Writers For Children, 1971; 25 Years of British Children's Books, 1977; Visitors, 1977; A Sounding of Storytellers: New and Revised Essays on Contemporary Children's Writers, 1979; Cranford Revisited, 1990; John Newbery and His Books: Trade and Plumb-cake For Ever, Huzza!, 1994. Contributor of articles to books and periodicals. **Address:** 72 Water Ln., Histon, Cambridge, CB CB4 4LR, England. **Online address:** jrt@greenbay.clara.net

TOWNSEND, Lindsay. British (born England), b. 1960. **Genres:** Novels. **Career:** Writer, 1992-. **Publications:** NOVELS: Voices in the Dark, 1995; Night of the Storm, 1996; Chasing Rachel, 1999; A Secret Treasure, 2003; The English Daughter, 2004; A Knight's Vow, 2008; Flavia's Secret, 2008; Blue Gold, 2009; Bronze Lightning, 2009; A Knight's Captive, 2009; A Knight's Enchantment, 2010. **Address:** c/o Teresa Chris, Teresa Chris Literary Agency, 43 Musard Rd., London, GL W6 8NR, England. **Online address:** lindsaytownsend@yahoo.co.uk

TOWNSEND, Richard (Fraser). American (born United States), b. 1938. **Genres:** Art/Art History, History. **Career:** University of Nebraska, instructor in art history, 1967-69; University of Texas, assistant professor of art, 1974-79; Art Institute of Chicago, Department of Africa, Oceania and the Americas, curator, 1982-, Department of African Art and Indian Art of the Americas, chairman. Writer. **Publications:** State and Cosmos in the Art of Tenochtitlan, 1979; Art of Tribes and Early Kingdoms: Selections from Chicago Collections, 1983; The Aztecs, 1992, 2nd ed., 2000; (with K. Kokrda and B.L. Moulard) Casas Grandes and the Ceramic Art of the Ancient Southwest, 2005. EDITOR AND CONTRIBUTOR: The Ancient Americas: Art from Sacred Landscapes, 1992; Ancient West Mexico: Art and Archaeology of the Unknown Past, 1998; Hero, Hawk and Open Hand: American Indian Art of the Ancient Midwest and South, 2004. Contributor to periodicals. **Address:** Department of African Art and Indian Art of the Am, Art Institute of Chicago, 111 S Michigan Ave., Chicago, IL 60603-6110, U.S.A. **Online address:** rtownsend@artic.edu

TOWNSEND, Sue. British (born England), b. 1946. **Genres:** Novels, Plays/Screenplays, Young Adult Non-fiction, inspirational/Motivational Literature, Biography. **Career:** Phoenix Theatre, writer-in-residence. **Publications:** The Secret Diary of Adrian Mole, Aged 13 3/4, 1982; Bazaar and Rummage; Groping for Words & Womberang, 1984; Great Celestial Cow, 1984; The Growing Pains of Adrian Mole, 1984; The Adrian Mole Diaries (collection), 1986; Rebuilding Coventry: A Tale of Two Cities, 1988; Mr. Bevan's Dream, 1989; The True Confessions of Adrian Albert Mole, 1989; Ten Tiny Fingers, Nine Tiny Toes, 1990; The Queen and I, 1991; Adrian Mole: From Minor to Major, 1992; Adrian Mole: The Wilderness Years, 1993 in US as Adrian Mole: The Lost Years, 1994; Ghost Children, 1997; Adrian Mole: The Cappuccino Years, 1999; The Public Confessions of a Middle-aged Woman Aged 55 3/4, 2001; Number Ten, 2002; Adrian Mole and the Weapons of Mass Destruction, 2004; The Queen in Hell Close, 2005; Queen Camilla, 2006; The Lost Diaries of Adrian Mole, 1999-2001, 2008; Adrian Mole: The Prostrate Years, 2009; The Woman Who Went to Bed for a Year, 2012. Contributor to periodicals. **Address:** Sheil Land Associates, 52 Doughty St., London, GL WC1N 2LS, England.

TOWNSEND, Wendy. American (born United States), b. 1962?. **Genres:** Novels, Young Adult Non-fiction, Science Fiction/Fantasy, Travel/Exploration. **Career:** Empire State College, Summer Weekend Intensive Workshops, leader, 2004-; Sarah Lawrence College, The Writing Institute, faculty. Writer. **Publications:** (With F.L. Frye) Iguanas: A Guide to Their Biology and Captive Care, 1993; Lizard Love (young adult novel), 2008; Sundown rule, 2010. Contributor of articles to periodicals. **Address:** Namelos L.L.C., 910 Church St., Honesdale, PA 18431, U.S.A. **Online address:** contact@wendytownsend.com

TOWNSEND HALL, Brenda P. French/American (born United States) **Genres:** Novellas/Short Stories, Young Adult Fiction, Novels. **Career:** Writer and editor. **Publications:** Necklace of Warm Snow, 2002. **Address:** Au Village, Ansan, 32270, France. **Online address:** brendahall@compuserve.com

TOWSE, Ruth. British/Dutch (born Netherlands), b. 1943. **Genres:** Marketing, Economics, Law. **Career:** Middlesex University, lecturer, senior lecturer, 1966-83; Thammasat University, visiting professor, 1969-70; University of London, Institute of Education, research officer, 1983-84, 1987-88; City University, Department of Arts Policy and Management, visiting lecturer, 1986-88; London School of Economics, Department of Economics, research fellow, 1988-90; University of Exeter, Department of Economics, lecturer in economics, 1990-99; Erasmus University, Faculty of History and Arts, senior lecturer in cultural industries, 1999-2002, reader, 2002-; Association for Cultural Economics Intl., president; Society for Economic Research in Copyright Issues, president, 2004-06; Bournemouth University, professor of economics of creative industries, 2006-, Economics of Creative Industries, chair, 2006-. Writer. **Publications:** (Ed. with A. Khakee) Cultural Economics, 1992; Singers in the Marketplace: The Economics of the Singing Profession, 1993; Economics of Culture: Arts, Heritage, and the Media Industries, 1996; (ed.) Baumol's Cost Disease: The Arts and Other Victims, 1997; Creativity, Incentive, and Reward: An Economic Analysis of Copyright and Culture in the Information Age, 2001; (ed.) Copyright in the Cultural Industries, 2002; (ed. with R. Holzhauer) Economics of Intellectual Property, 2002; (ed. with I. Rizzo) Economics of Heritage: A Study in the Political Economy of Culture in Sicily, 2002; (ed.) Handbook of Cultural Economics, 2003; (ed. with L.N. Takeyama and W.J. Gordon) Developments in the Economics of Copyright: Research and Analysis, 2005; (ed.) Recent Developments in Cultural Economics, 2007; (ed. with R. Watt) Recent Trends in the Economics of Copyright, 2008; Textbook of Cultural Economics, 2010; Economics, Law and Intellectual Property, forthcoming. Contributor of articles to books and periodicals. **Address:** Bournemouth University, 89 Holdenhurst Rd., Bournemouth, DS BH8 8EB, England. **Online address:** ruth.towse@googlemail.com

TOYNBEE, Polly. British (born England), b. 1946. **Genres:** Novels, Documentaries/Reportage. **Career:** Observer, journalist, 1968-70, feature writer, 1973-77; Washington Monthly, news reporter, 1970-71, co-editor; The Guardian, columnist, 1977-88, 1997-; BBC TV and Radio, social affairs editor, 1988-95; The Independent, associate editor and columnist, 1995-97; Social Policy Association, president; Fabian Society, deputy treasurer; British Humanist Association, president. **Publications:** Leftovers, 1966; A Working Life, 1970; Hospital, 1977 in US as Patients, 1977; The Way We Live Now, 1982; Lost Children: The Story of Adopted Children Searching for Their Mothers, 1985; The Future of Care for Older People: Facing Up to Society's Choices, 1996; (with D. Walker) Did Things Get Better?, 2001; Hard Work: Life in Low Pay Britain, 2003; (with D. Walker) Better or Worse?: Has Labour Delivered, 2005; Rank, 2009; (with D. Walker) The Verdict: Did Labour Change Britain?, 2010. **Address:** The Guardian, 119 Farringdon Rd., London, GL EC1R 3ER, England. **Online address:** polly.toynbee@guardian.co.uk

TRACEY, Grant. American/Canadian (born Canada), b. 1960?. **Genres:** Popular Culture, Film, Novellas/Short Stories, Social Sciences, History. **Career:** University of Northern Iowa, Department of English, assistant professor, associate professor, professor, coordinator of creative writing, 1996-; United News of India, coordinator of creative writing; North American Review, editor, 2000-. **Publications:** Filmography of American History, 2002; Parallel Lines and the Hockey Universe, 2003; (ed. with S. Cawelti and R. Sandvik) Notes from the Flyover: Celebrating the Life and Works of Barbara Lounsberry, 2006; Playing Mac: A Novella in Two Acts, and Other Scenes, 2006; The Best Years of Our Lives, forthcoming. Contributor to periodicals. **Address:** Department of English Language and Literature, University of Northern Iowa, 128 Baker Hall, 1227 W 27th St., Cedar Falls, IA 50614-0502, U.S.A. **Online address:** grant.tracey@uni.edu

TRACHTENBERG, Peter. American (born United States), b. 1953. **Genres:** Women's Studies And Issues, Education. **Career:** Writer. **Publications:** The Casanova Complex: Compulsive Lovers and Their Women, 1988; 7 Tattoos: A Memoir in the Flesh, 1997; The Book of Calamities: Five Questions about Suffering and Its Meaning, 2008. Contributor to periodicals and magazines. **Address:** c/o Kathleen Anderson, Anderson Literary Management, 12 W 19th St., 2nd Fl., New York, NY 10011, U.S.A.

TRACHTENBERG, Stephen Joel. American (born United States), b. 1937?. **Genres:** Education, Institutions/Organizations. **Career:** U.S. Atomic Energy Commission, attorney; Department of Health, Education and Welfare, U.S. Education Commissioner, special assistant; Boston University, vice president for academic services and dean of the College of Liberal Arts, 1969-77; University of Hartford, president, 1977-88; George Washington University, professor of public service, president, 1988-2007, president emeritus, 2007-. Writer. **Publications:** (Ed. with R.H. Stein) The Art of Hiring in America's Colleges and Universities, 1993; Speaking His Mind, 1994; Thinking Out Loud, 1998; Reflections on Higher Education, 2002; Write Me a Letter!: The Wit and Wisdom of Stephen Joel Trachtenberg, President of the George Washington University, 2006; (with T.H. Blumer) Big Man on Campus: A University President Speaks Out on Higher Education, 2008. **Address:** George Washington University, 805 21st St. NW, Ste. 600, Washington, DC 20052, U.S.A. **Online address:** trachtenberg@gwu.edu

TRACY, James. American (born United States), b. 1961. **Genres:** History. **Career:** The Hotchkiss School, history instructor, 1993; Yale University, Department of History, visiting fellow, 1994-95; Institute for Writing and

Thinking, Bard College, associate, 1995; University of Massachusetts, adjunct professor, 1999-; Boston University Academy, headmaster, 2000-06; BU Chancellor John Silber, assistant. Writer. **Publications:** Direct Action: Radical Pacifism from the Union Eight to the Chicago Seven, 1996; (ed. with R. Horsley) Christmas Unwrapped: Consumerism, Christ, and Culture, 2001; (ed.) The Civil Disobedience Handbook: A Brief History and Practical Advice for the Politically Disenchanted, 2002; (co-author) Molotov Mouths: Explosive New Writing, 2003. Contributor to periodicals. **Address:** Trinity Press Intl., 4775 Linglestown Rd., Harrisburg, PA 17112, U.S.A.

TRACY, (John) Nicholas. Canadian (born Canada) **Genres:** Military/Defense/Arms Control, Travel/Exploration, History. **Career:** Acadia University, research associate in political science, 1973; Dalhousie University, research associate in political science, 1974-79; University of New Brunswick, assistant professor of history, 1981, 1983, adjunct professor, 1993-, Gregg Centre, associate; St. Thomas University, assistant professor of history, 1982; National University of Singapore, associate professor and senior visiting fellow, 1984-86; freelance researcher and writer, 1987-; University of London, Institute of Commonwealth Studies, visiting fellow. **Publications:** Navies, Deterrence and American Independence: Britain and Sea Power in the 1760s and 1770s, 1988; (ed.) Naval Warfare in the Age of Sail: The Evolution of Fighting Tactics, 1680-1815, 1990; Attack on Maritime Trade, 1991; A Cruising Guide to the Bay of Fundy and the St. John River Including Passamaquoddy Bay and the Southwestern Shore of Nova Scotia, 1992; Canada's Naval Strategy: Rooted in Experience, 1995; Manila Ransomed: The British Expedition to the Philippines in the Seven Years War, 1995; Nelson's Battles: The Art of Victory in the Age of Sail, 1996, rev. ed. as Nelson's Battles: The Triumph of British Seapower, 2008; (ed.) The Collective Naval Defence of the Empire: 1900 to 1940, 1997; The Naval Chronicle, Consolidated Edition, 5vols., 1998-99; (ed.) Sea Power and the Control of Trade: Belligerent Rights from the Russian War to the Beira Patrol: 1854-1970, 2005; Who's Who in Nelson's Navy: 200 Naval Heroes, 2006; Britannia's Palette: The Arts of Naval Victory, 2007; The Battle of Quiberon Bay, 1759: Admiral Hawke and the Defeat of the French Invasion, 2010; Master and Madman, the Spectacular Rise and Disastrous Fall of the Hon. Anthony Lockwood, RN, forthcoming; A Two-Edged Sword: The Navy as an Instrument of Canadian Policy, forthcoming. Contributor to periodicals. **Address:** Department of History, University of New Brunswick, 120 Tilley Hall, 9 Macaulay Ln., Fredericton, NB E3B 5A3, Canada. **Online address:** tracyn@unb.ca

TRACY, Kathleen. American (born United States) **Genres:** Novels, Biography, Picture/Board Books, Young Adult Non-fiction. **Career:** Stirling Publications, new media correspondent. Journalist and photographer. **Publications:** (With E. Greenwood) The Boy Who Would Be King, 1990; (with E. Greenwood) Elvis-Top Secret: The Untold Story of Elvis Presley's Secret FBI Files, 1991; (with J. Rovin) Ellen DeGeneres Up Close: The Unauthorized Biography of the Hot New Star of ABC's Ellen, 1994; (with J. Rovin and D. Perrell) Kelsey Grammer: The True Story, 1995; Antonio Banderas, 1997; (with J. Rovin) The Essential Jackie Chan Sourcebook, 1997; Home Brewed: The Drew Carey Story, 1997; The Girl's Got Bite: An Unofficial Guide to Buffy's World, 1998; Matt Damon, 1998; Jerry Seinfeld: The Entire Domain, 1998; Imus: America's Cowboy, 1999; Ricky Martin: Red-Hot and on the Rise!, 1999; Ellen: The Real Story of Ellen DeGeneres, 1999; Neve Campbell, 2000; Daytime Divas: The Dish on Dozens of Daytime TVs Great Ladies, 2000; Jennifer Lopez, 2000; Regis!: The Unauthorized Biography, 2001; Angelina Jolie, 2001; Barbara McClintock: Pioneering Geneticist, 2002; Marc Andreessen and the Development of the Web Browser, 2002; It Shouldn't Happen to a Journalist, 2002; The Complete Idiots Guide to Portrait Photography, 2002; The Secret Story of Polygamy, 2002; Willem Kolff and the Invention of the Dialysis Machine, 2003; William Hewlett: Pioneer of the Computer Age, 2003; Mariano Guadalupe Vallejo, 2003; Lorenzo de Zavala, 2003; Mary-Kate and Ashley Olsen, 2003; Clay Aiken: From Second Place to the Top of the Charts, 2004; Cesar Chavez, 2004; Welcome to the Dixie Chicks Photo Biography, 2004; Diana Rigg: The Biography, 2004; The Life and Times of Confucius, 2005; The Fall of the Berlin Wall, 2005; John Steinbeck, 2005; Top Secret: The Story of the Manhattan Project, 2005; The Life and Times of Constantine, 2005; The Life and Times of Homer, 2005; Henry Bessemer: Making Steel from Iron, 2005; Friedrich Miescher and the Story of Nucleic Acid, 2005; Queen Latifah, 2005; Robert Koch and the Study of Anthrax, 2005; Mario, 2005; Justin Berfield, 2005; Lindsay Lohan, 2005; Beyoncé, 2005; Avril Lavigne, 2005; Pierre and Marie Curie and the Discovery of Radium, 2005; Judy Blume, 2005; Carrie Underwood, 2006; Friedrich Miescher and the Story of Nucleic Acid, 2006; Henry Bessemer:

Making Steel from Iron, 2006; Unkindness of Ravens, 2006; Mario, 2006; Morgan Freeman: A Biography, 2006; Top Secret: The Story of the Manhattan Project, 2006; Sacha Baron Cohen: The Unauthorized Biography: From Cambridge to Kazakhstan, 2007; Tennessee Williams, 2007; Watergate Scandal, 2007; Elvis Presley: A Biography, 2007; Gwen Stefani, 2007; Kelly Clarkson, 2007; Life and Times of Cicero, 2007; Life and Times of Nathan Hale, 2007; Mariah Carey, 2007; Matt Christopher, 2007; Plymouth Colony: The Pilgrims Settle in New England, 2007; The Everything: Jacqueline Kennedy Onassis Book, 2008; Paul Cézanne, 2008; Theseus, 2008; Zac Efron, 2008; Aly and AJ, 2008; Angelina Jolie: A Biography, 2008; Chris Brown, 2008; Chris Daughtry, 2008; Jennifer Lopez: A Biography, 2008; Johnny Depp, 2008; Judy Blume: A Biography, 2008; Justin Timberlake, 2008; Historic Fight for the 2008 Democratic Presidential Nomination: The Clinton View, 2009; Leonardo da Vinci, 2009; Life and Times of Rosa Parks, 2009; Remembering Adelia: Quilts Inspired by Her Diary, 2009; Odysseus, 2009; Edouard Manet, 2009; The Story of September 11, 2001, 2009; Demi Lovato, 2009; Class Trip San Diego, 2009; We Visit Cuba, 2010; We Visit Brazil, 2010; Megan Fox, 2010; Emma Watson, 2010; Class trip Chicago, 2010; Orianthi, 2010; Medusa, 2010; Justin Bieber, 2010; Cerberus, 2010; Teen Icons of the 21st Century, 2010; (with B. Hinman) Your Land and My Land Set, 2010; Mark Sanchez, 2011; Prince William of Wales, 2011; We Visit Kuwait, 2011; We Visit Saudi Arabia, 2011; Troy Polamalu, 2011; The Civil War Sewing Circle, 2011; What it's Like to be Mark Sánchez, 2011; (with J. Rasemas) Day by Day with Eli Manning, 2011. Contributor to periodicals. **Address:** Stirling Publications, 14014 Milbank St., Sherman Oaks, CA 91423-2982, U.S.A. **Online address:** zrunt@aol.com

TRACY, Kristen. American (born United States), b. 1972?. **Genres:** Children's Fiction, Mystery/Crime/Suspense, Women's Studies And Issues, Young Adult Non-fiction. **Career:** Hawthorne High School, teacher; Brigham Young University, Johnson State College, instructor; Western Michigan University, instructor. Writer. **Publications:** Lost It, 2007; Crimes of the Sarahs, 2008; Camille McPhee Fell Under the Bus, 2009; A Field Guide for Heartbreakers, 2010; The Reinvention of Bessica Lefter, 2011; Sharks & Boys, 2011. Contributor to periodicals. **Address:** c/o Meg O'Brien, Delacorte Books for Young Readers, 1745 Broadway, 10th Fl., New York, NY 10019, U.S.A. **Online address:** tracy.kristen@gmail.com

TRACY, Lorna. British/American (born United States), b. 1934. **Genres:** Novellas/Short Stories, Writing/Journalism, Literary Criticism And History. **Career:** Oak Park Public Library, reader's adviser, 1957-58, Reference Department, head, 1959-60; Association of Junior Leagues of America, librarian, 1960-62; Long Island University, assistant reference librarian, 1962-64; University of Iowa, assistant acquisitions librarian, 1966-68; Stand Magazine, founding editor, fiction editor, 1969-; Cleveland State University, visiting writer-in-residence, 1986. **Publications:** (Co-author) Introduction Five, 1974; Amateur Passions, 1981; Passion Fruit, 1986; New Writing 5, 1996; New Writing 6, 1997. CO-EDITOR: (with M. Blackburn and J. Silkin) Stand One: Winners of the Stand Magazine Short Story Competition, 1984; (with J. Silkin and J. Wardle) Best Short Stories from Stand Magazine, 1988. Contributor to journals and peridoicals. **Address:** Stand Magazine Ltd., 179 Wingrove Rd., Newcastle upon Tyne, NM NE4 9DA, England.

TRACY, Margaret. See KLAVAN, Andrew.

TRACY, Sarah W. American (born United States), b. 1963. **Genres:** History, Food And Wine. **Career:** University of Oklahoma, associate professor, Honors College, adjunct assistant professor of the history of science. Writer. **Publications:** (ed. with C.J. Acker) Altering American Consciousness: The History of Alcohol and Drug Use in the United States, 1800-2000, 2004; Alcoholism in America: From Reconstruction to Prohibition, 2005. **Address:** Oklahoma City, ME , U.S.A. **Online address:** swtracy@ou.edu

TRACY, Thomas F. American (born United States), b. 1948. **Genres:** Philosophy, Theology/Religion. **Career:** Bates College, Department of Philosophy and Religion, instructor, 1976-80, assistant professor, 1980-83, associate professor, 1983-89, professor of religion, 1989-, chairperson of department, 1991-99, Phillips professor of religion, 1999-, Division of the Humanities, chairperson, 1985-89; Maine Humanities Council, board director, 1985-97, chair, 1991-92; University of California, visiting professor of religious thought, 1989-90. Writer and consultant. **Publications:** God, Action and Embodiment, 1984; (ed. and contrib.) The God Who Acts: Philosophical and Theological Explorations, 1994. Contributor to books. Contributor of periodi-

cals. **Address:** Department of Philosophy and Religion, Bates College, Rm. 306, Hedge Hall, 73-75 Campus Ave., 2 Andrews Rd., Lewiston, ME 04240-6028, U.S.A. **Online address:** ttracy@bates.edu

TRAIG, Jennifer. American (born United States) **Genres:** How-to Books, Biography, Crafts, Novels, History, Medicine/Health. **Career:** Writer. **Publications:** (With J. Balmain) Beauty: Things to Make and Do, 2001; (with J. Balmain) Cool Stuff: Things to Make and Do, 2001; Fun and Games: Things to Make and Do, 2001; Accessories: Things to Make and Do, 2002; (with V. Traig) Judaikitsch: Tchotchkes Schmattes and Nosherei, 2002; Slumber Parties: Things to Make and Do, 2002; Makeup: Things to Make and Do, 2003; Devil in the Details: Scenes from an Obsessive Girlhood, 2004; Hair: Things to Make and Do, 2004; (with V. Traig) Retox: Booze, Use and Snooze Your Way to Personal Fulfillment, 2006; (with S. Colón) What would Wonder Woman Do?: An Amazon's Guide to the Working World, 2007; (ed.) The Autobiographer's Handbook: The 826 National Guide to Writing your Memoir, 2008; Well Enough Alone: A Cultural History of My Hypochondria, 2008; Don't Forget to Write, 2011. **Address:** Little Brown & Co., 1271 Ave. of the Americas, New York, NY 10020, U.S.A. **Online address:** jtraig@hotmail.com

TRAINOR, Bernard E. American (born United States), b. 1928. **Genres:** Military/Defense/Arms Control. **Career:** New York Times, military correspondent, 1985-90; Harvard University, National Security Program, director; John F. Kennedy School of Government, adjunct lecturer in public policy, 1990-96; Council on Foreign Relations, senior fellow 1998-; NBC Television, military analyst, 1993-; World Affairs Counci, board director; Marine Toys for Tots Foundation, board director; American Broadcasting Co., military analyst. Writer. **Publications:** Military Perspectives on Humanitarian Intervention and Military-Media Relations (Chester W. Nimitz Memorial Lectures in National Security), 1995; (with M.R. Gordon) The General's War: The Inside Story of the Conflict in the Gulf, 1995; (with M.R. Gordon) Cobra II: The Inside Story of the Invasion and Occupation of Iraq, 2006. Contributor to books. **Address:** 80 Potter Pond, Lexington, MA 02421, U.S.A. **Online address:** mc151run@aol.com

TRANEL, Virginia. American (born United States) **Genres:** Adult Non-fiction, Essays, Biography. **Career:** Writer. **Publications:** Ten Circles Upon the Pond: Reflections of a Prodigal Mother (memoir), 2003; Amazing Disgrace, 2010. Works appear in anthologies. Contributor to periodicals. **Address:** c/o Author Mail, Knopf Publishing, 1745 Broadway, New York, NY 10019, U.S.A.

TRANG, Corinne. American/French (born France), b. 1967. **Genres:** Food And Wine. **Career:** Meigher Communications, producing editor of magazines and cookbooks, 1996-98, director of Saveur test kitchen, 1997-98; Drexel University, Department of Hospitality Management, adjunct associate professor, 2000-; Institute of Culinary Education, culinary instructor, 2003-; Casa Malaparte Foundation, lecturer; Massachusetts Museum of Contemporary Art, lecturer; California College of Arts and Crafts, lecturer; University of the Arts, lecturer; Rhode Island School of Design, lecturer; University of Applied Sciences, lecturer; New York University, lecturer, adjunct professor; Harvard Medical School, Center for Health and the Global Environment, lecturer; University of Texas, faculty. Food writer, food stylist, chef, food consultant, critic and travel photographer. **Publications:** Authentic Vietnamese Cooking: Food from a Family Table, 1999; Essentials of Asian Cuisine: Fundamentals and Favorite Recipes, 2003; (co-author) Curry Cuisine, 2006; Asian Grill: Great Recipes, Bold Flavors, 2006; A Food Lover's Collection: Vietnamese, 2007; Noodles Every Day: Delicious Asian Recipes from Ramen to Rice Sticks, 2009; Asian Flavors Diabetes Cookbook: Simple, Fresh Meals Perfect for Every Day, 2012. Contributor to books and periodicals. **Address:** Beth Shepard Communications L.L.C., 32 Franklin Rd., Gill, MA 01354, U.S.A. **Online address:** ct@corinnetrang.com

TRANSUE, Emily R. American (born United States), b. 1971?. **Genres:** Autobiography/Memoirs, Medicine/Health. **Career:** University of Washington, chief resident, through 2000, Department of Medicine, clinical assistant professor; Polyclinic, general internist, 2000-. Writer. **Publications:** On Call: A Doctor's Days and Nights in Residency, 2004; Patient by Patient: Lessons in Love, Loss, Hope, and Healing from a Doctor's Practice, 2008. **Address:** Department of Medicine, University of Washington, RR-512, Health Sciences Bldg., PO Box 356420, Seattle, WA 98195-6420, U.S.A.

TRANTER, John (Ernest). Australian (born Australia), b. 1943. **Genres:** Poetry, Mythology/Folklore. **Career:** Australian Broadcasting Commission, technician, 1967-68, script editor, 1970-74, radio scriptwriter, 1974-80, Radio Helicon Arts Program, coordinator, 1987-88; Angus and Robertson, publishers, senior editor, 1971-73; Special Broadcasting Service Multicultural TV, sub-editor, 1981-86; Bulletin, poetry editor, 1990-93; Rollins College, writer-in-residence, 1992; Cambridge University, writer-in-residence, 2001; Australian Literary Management, founder, co-director, 2004; Jacket, editor; Sydney College, creative writing teacher. **Publications:** POETRY: Parallax, 1970; Red Movie and Other Poems, 1973; The Blast Area, 1973; The Alphabet Murders: Notes from a Work in Progress, 1976; Crying in Early Infancy: 100 Sonnets, 1977; Dazed in the Ladies Lounge, 1979; Selected Poems, 1982; Under Berlin, 1988; The Floor of Heaven, 1992; Days in the Capital, 1992; At the Florida, 1993; Gasoline Kisses, 1997; Different Hands, 1998; Late Night Radio, 1998; Blackout, 2000; Ultra, 2001; Heart Print, 2001; Borrowed Voices, 2002; Studio Moon, 2003; Urban Myths: 210 Poems: New and Selected, 2006; Starlight: 150 Poems, 2010. EDITOR: The New Australian Poetry, 1979; The Tin Was Dish (poetry), 1989; (with P. Mead) Penguin Book of Modern Australian Poetry, 1992 in UK as Bloodaxe Book of Modern Australian Poetry, 1995; Martin Johnston-Selected Poems and Prose, 1993. **Address:** Australian Literary Management, 2-A Booth St., Balmain, NW 2041, Australia. **Online address:** delta@johntranter.com

TRAPIDO, Barbara. British/South African (born South Africa), b. 1941. **Genres:** Novels, Sex. **Career:** Secondary School, English teacher, 1964-70; Writer, 1980-. **Publications:** Brother of the More Famous Jack, 1982; Noah's Ark: A Novel, 1985; Temples of Delight, 1991; Juggling, 1994; The Travelling Hornplayer, 1998; Frankie and Stankie, 2003; Sex and Stravinsky, 2010. **Address:** c/o Victoria Hobbs, A.M. Heath & Company Ltd., 6 Warwick Ct., Holborn, GL WC1R 5DJ, England. **Online address:** barbaratrapido@hotmail.com

TRAPP, Kenneth R. American (born United States), b. 1943. **Genres:** Art/Art History, Literary Criticism And History, Reference. **Career:** Smithsonian Institution, Renwick Gallery, curator-in-charge, 1995-2003. Writer. **Publications:** (With C. Macht and D.D. Long) The Ladies, God Bless 'em: The Women's Art Movement in Cincinnati in the Nineteenth Century: Cincinnati Art Museum, February 19-April 18, 1976, 1976; Ode to Nature: Flowers and Landscapes of the Rookwood Pottery, 1880-1940, April 15-June 30, 1980, 1980; (ed.) Celebrate Cincinnati Art, 1982; (contrib.) Toward the Modern Style: Rookwood Pottery, The Later Years 1915-1950, 1983; (ed.) The Arts and Crafts Movement in California: Living the Good Life, 1993; (with P.J. Fidler) Art With a Mission: Objects of the Arts and Crafts Movement, 1993; (with H. Risatti and R. Gallery) Skilled Work: American Craft in the Renwick Gallery, National Museum of American Art, 1998; (contrib.) Larry Kirkland: Twenty-Five Years, 1999; Masters of Their Craft, 2003; (contrib.) The Art of Arthur and Lucia Mathews, 2006; (foreward) A Theory of Craft: Function and Aesthetic Expression, 2007. **Address:** University of North Carolina Press, 116 S Boundary St., Chapel Hill, NC 27514-3808, U.S.A.

TRAPP, Stefan (Alfred Josef). German (born Germany), b. 1962. **Genres:** Environmental Sciences/Ecology, Chemistry, Engineering, Earth Sciences. **Career:** National Center for Environmental Protection, staff, 1987-92; University of Osnabrueck, research assistant in mathematics and computer science, 1992-; Technical University, Institute of Environment and Resources, Department of Environmental Engineering, associate professor. Writer. **Publications:** (Ed. with C. McFarlane and contrib.) Plant Contamination: The Modeling and Simulation of Organic Chemical Processes, 1996; (with M. Matthies) Dynamikvon Schadstoffen: Umweltmodellierung mit CemoS. Eine Einfuehrung, 1996; (with M. Matthies) Chemodynamics and Environmental Modeling: An Introduction, 1998. Contributor to books and scientific journals. **Address:** Department of Environmental Engineering, Institute of Environmental Science and Engineering, Technical University, Rm. 048, Lyngby Bldg. 115, Kongens Lyngby, DK-2800, Denmark. **Online address:** sttr@env.dtu.dk

TRATTNER, Walter I. American (born United States), b. 1936. **Genres:** History, Social Commentary, Bibliography, Social Sciences. **Career:** Northern Illinois University, assistant professor of history, 1963-65; University of Wisconsin, assistant professor, 1965-67, associate professor, 1967-71, professor, 1971-98, emeritus professor of history, 1998-. Writer. **Publications:**

Homer Folks: Pioneer in Social Welfare, 1968; Crusade for the Children: A History of the National Child Labor Committee and Child Labor Reform in America, 1970; From Poor Law to Welfare State: A History of Social Welfare in America, 1974, 6th ed., 1999; (ed.) Social Welfare or Social Control?: Some Historical Reflections on Regulating the Poor, 1983; (ed. with W.A. Achenbaum) Social Welfare in America: An Annotated Bibliography, 1983; (ed.) Biographical Dictionary of Social Welfare in America, 1986. **Address:** Department of History, University of Wisconsin-Milwaukee, 2200 E Kenwood Blvd., PO Box 413, Milwaukee, WI 53201, U.S.A.

TRAUB, Charles (Henry). American (born United States), b. 1945. **Genres:** Art/Art History, Photography, Literary Criticism And History. **Career:** Columbia College, Department of Photography, instructor in photography, 1971-75, chairman, 1975-78; Center for Contemporary Photography, founder and chairman, 1975-78; Light Gallery, director, 1978-80; International Center of Photography, visiting lecturer, 1978-; School of Visual Arts, Master of Fine Arts Degree Program, chair, Photography and Related Media Department, chair; Charles H. Traub Photography, principal. Writer. **Publications:** Beach, 1978; (ed.) The New Vision: Forty Years of Photography at the Institute of Design, 1982; New York City Youth: An Intimate Portrait, Summer Jobs, 1987; (with L. Ballerini) Italy Observed in Photography and Literature, 1988; An Angler's Album: Fishing in Photography and Literature, 1990; Italy Observed: Photographs, 1991; Here is New York: A Democracy of Photographs, 2002; (with J. Lipkin) In the Realm of the Circuit: Computers, Art and Culture, 2004; (ed. with S. Heller and A.B. Bell) The Education of a Photographer, 2006. **Address:** School of Visual Arts, 209 E 23 St., New York, NY 10001-3994, U.S.A. **Online address:** ctraub@sva.edu

TRAUTMANN, Thomas R. See **TRAUTMANN, Thomas R(oger).**

TRAUTMANN, Thomas R(oger). (Thomas R. Trautmann). American (born United States), b. 1940. **Genres:** Anthropology/Ethnology, Area Studies, History, Language/Linguistics. **Career:** University of London, School of Oriental and African Studies, lecturer in the early history of South Asia, 1965-68; University of Michigan, Department of History, assistant professor, 1968-71, associate professor, 1971-77, professor of history, 1977-, Marshall Sahlins Collegiate professor of history, Department of Anthropology, professor of anthropology, 1984-, now professor emeritus of anthropology. Writer. **Publications:** (Contrib.) Man and His Gods, 1971; Kautilya and the Arthaśāstra: A Statistical Investigation of the Authorship and Evolution of the Text, 1971; (ed.) Kinship and History in South Asia, 1974; Dravidian Kinship, 1981; Lewis Henry Morgan and the Invention of Kinship, 1987, rev. ed., 2008; (with K.S. Kabelac) The Library of Lewis Henry Morgan, 1994; (ed. with D.O. Hughes) Time: Histories and Ethnologies, 1995; Aryans and British India, 1995; (ed. with M. Godelier and F.E. Tjon Sie Fat) Transformations of Kinship, 1998; The Aryan Debate in India, 2005; Languages and Nations: The Dravidian Proof in Colonial Madras, 2006; (ed.) The Madras School of Orientalism: Producing Knowledge in Colonial South India, 2009; Clash of Chronologies: Ancient India in the Modern World, 2009; India: Brief History of A Civilization, 2010; (ed. with P.M. Whiteley) Crow-Omaha: New Light On A Classic Problem of Kinship Analysis, 2012; Does India have History? Does History have India?, forthcoming. Contributor to journals and periodicals. **Address:** Department of history, University of Michigan, 1029 Tisch Hall, Ann Arbor, MI 48109-1003, U.S.A. **Online address:** ttraut@umich.edu

TRAVERS, Paul J(oseph). American (born United States), b. 1951. **Genres:** Young Adult Fiction, History, Literary Criticism And History, Reference. **Career:** U.S. Postal Service, management specialist, 1978-79; Maryland Park Service, park historian and ranger, 1979-84; U.S. Department of the Army, security analyst, 1984-. Writer. **Publications:** The Patapsco: Baltimore's River of History, 1990; Eyewitness to Infamy: An Oral History of Pearl Harbor, 1991; The Flight of the Shadow Drummer, 1998; The Cowgirl and The Colts, 2007. Contributor to periodicals. **Address:** 3 Apple Wood Ct., PO Box 555, Parkton, MD 21120-0555, U.S.A. **Online address:** paul@paultravers.com

TRAVERS, Phil. American (born United States), b. 1972. **Genres:** Psychology, Education. **Career:** Family Violence Prevention Services Inc., clinical director, 1997-. Writer. **Publications:** Counseling the Rainbow: Effectively Meeting the Needs of Gay and Lesbian Clients, 2001; The Counselor's Helpdesk, 2002. **Address:** Family Violence Prevention Services Inc., 7911 Broadway, San Antonio, TX 78209, U.S.A. **Online address:** phil.travers@fvps.org

TRAVERS, Robert. American (born United States), b. 1972. **Genres:** History. **Career:** Cornell University, faculty. Writer. **Publications:** Ideology and Empire in Eighteenth Century India: The British in Bengal, 2007. **Address:** Department of History, Cornell University, 345 McGraw Hall, Ithaca, NY 14853-4601, U.S.A. **Online address:** trt5@cornell.edu

TRAVIS, Aaron. *See* SAYLOR, Steven W(arren).

TRAVIS, Anthony S(tewart). British (born England), b. 1943. **Genres:** Chemistry, History, Technology, Environmental Sciences/Ecology, Transportation, Travel/Exploration. **Career:** D. Bishop Ltd. (textiles and printing company), director, 1961-80; Preston Manor High School, high school teacher and curriculum developer in science, 1980-85; Ort School of Chemical Technology, teacher of technical English and chemistry; Hebrew University of Jerusalem, Sidney M. Edelstein Center for the History and Philosophy of Science, Technology and Medicine, deputy director, 1988-, senior researcher in the history of technology, 1992-; Leo Baeck Institute, London, senior research fellow, 2005-; Ben-Gurion University of the Negev, Jacques Loeb Centre for the History and Philosophy of the Life Sciences, deputy director, 2007-10. Writer. **Publications:** The Channel Tunnel, 1802-1967, 1967; The Rainbow Makers: The Origins of the Synthetic Dyestuffs Industry in Western Europe, 1993; From Turkey Red to Tyrian Purple: Textile Colours for the Industrial Revolution, 1993; (co-editor) Chemical Industry in Europe, 1850-1914: Industrial Growth, Pollution and Professionalization, 1998; (co-editor) Determinants in the Evolution of the European Chemical Industry, 1900-1936: New Technologies, Political Frameworks, Markets and Companies, 1998; (with C. Reinhardt) Heinrich Caro and the Creation of Modern Chemical Industry, 2000; Dyes Made in America, 1915-1980: The Calco Chemical Company, American Cyanamid and the Raritan River, 2004; On Chariots with Horses of Fire and Iron: The Excursionists and the Narrow Gauge Railroad from Jaffa to Jerusalem, 2009; Planning for Tourism, Leisure and Sustainability: International Case Studies, 2011. Contributor to magazines. **Address:** Sidney M. Edelstein Center, Hebrew University of Jerusalem, Edmond Safra Campus, Givat Ram, Jerusalem, 91904, Israel. **Online address:** travis@cc.huji.ac.il

TRAVIS, Frederick F. American (born United States), b. 1942. **Genres:** History, Travel/Exploration. **Career:** Delta State University, instructor in mathematics, 1966-67; Georgia State University, instructor, 1967-68; Virginia Military Institute, assistant professor of history, 1970-72; Wilbraham and Monson Academy, instructor, 1974-77, department of history and the social sciences, chairperson, 1976-77; Fordham University, assistant professor, 1977-84, associate professor of history, 1984-88, assistant chair, 1979-81, freshman interdisciplinary program, director, 1981-83, College at Lincoln Center, Division of Social Sciences, chair, 1984-87; John Carroll University, associate professor, 1988-92, professor of history, 1992-2006, professor emeritus, 2006-, College of Arts and Sciences, dean, 1988-94, academic vice president, 1994-96, interim president, 1995-96, provost, 1996-2001; Seton Hall University, provost, 2006-08, professor of history, 2006-08; Assumption College, interim provost and academic vice president, 2008-. Writer. **Publications:** George Kennan and the American-Russian Relationship, 1865-1924, 1990. **Address:** John Carroll University, University Heights, OH 44118, U.S.A.

TRAVIS, Jack. American (born United States), b. 1952. **Genres:** Architecture, Design, Art/Art History. **Career:** Whisler-Patrri, designer/architect, 1978; Pacific Gas and Electric, draughtsman/architect, 1978-79; Eyes Group Design, designer/draughtsman/architect, 1979-80; Skidmore Owings and Merrill, designer/interior architect, space planner, 1980-82; Switzer Group Inc., interior architect, 1982-84; Sydney Philip Gilbert Associates, designer/interior architect, 1984; National Broadcasting Company Inc. (NBC-TV), designer/interior architect, 1985; Jack Travis Architect, owner and principal, 1985-; Fashion Institute of Technology, adjunct professor of interior design, 1991-93, adjunct assistant professor; Pratt Institute School of Interior Design, adjunct professor; Parsons School of Design, adjunct professor, City University of New York, City College, adjunct professor. Writer. **Publications:** (Ed.) African American Architects: In Current Practice (monograph), 1991; Black Interior Designer's Directory; The Children's Book. Contributor to journals. **Address:** Studio of Jack Travis Architect, 432 Austin Pl., Fl. 2, Bronx, NY 10455-5006, U.S.A. **Online address:** jta@jacktravis.net

TRAVIS, Lucille. American (born United States), b. 1931?. **Genres:** Children's Non-fiction, Travel/Exploration, Mystery/Crime/Suspense. **Career:** Educator and writer. **Publications:** FOR CHILDREN: A Summer's Growth, 1982; Tirzah, 1991; Jeanmarie and the Runaways, 2000; Jeanmarie and the FBI, 2000; Jeanmarie and the Missing Ring, 2001; Jeanmarie, with Love,

2001; Railroad Fever and Wolfhunt, forthcoming; The Mice of Fleur Gardens, forthcoming. BEN AND ZACK SERIES: Captured by a Spy, 1995; Thief from Five Points, 1995; Redheaded Orphan, 1995; Union Army Black, 1995. OTHERS: Timna, 2009; Far Journey, 2009. **Address:** 3638 Snelling Ave., Arden Hills, MN 55112, U.S.A.

TRAVISANO, Thomas (J.). American (born United States), b. 1951. **Genres:** Literary Criticism And History, Theology/Religion. **Career:** College of William and Mary, assistant professor of English, 1980-82; Hartwick College, assistant professor, 1982-88, associate professor, 1988-93, professor, 1993-96, 2007-, Cora A. Babcock professor of English, 1996-99, 2004-07, Department of English and Theatre Arts, chair, 2009-; National Endowment for the Humanities, American Century Project, director, 1995-97; Elizabeth Bishop Society, co-founder and president. Writer. **Publications:** Elizabeth Bishop: Her Artistic Development, 1988; Midcentury Quartet: Bishop, Lowell, Jarrell, Berryman, and the Making of a Postmodern Aesthetic, 1999. EDITOR: (with M. Dickie) Gendered Modernisms: American Women Poets and Their Readers, 1996; (with S.G. Axelrod and C. Roman) The New Anthology of American Poetry, vol. I: Traditions and Revolutions, Beginnings to 1900, 2003, vol. II: Modernisms, 1900-1950, 2005; (with S. Hamilton) Words in Air: The Complete Correspondence between Elizabeth Bishop and Robert Lowell, 2008. Contributor of articles to books and periodicals. **Address:** Department of English, Hartwick College, Clark 218, 1 Hartwick Dr., PO Box 4020, Oneonta, NY 13820, U.S.A. **Online address:** travisanot@hartwick.edu

TRAWICK, Leonard M. American (born United States), b. 1933. **Genres:** Poetry, Songs/Lyrics And Libretti, Literary Criticism And History, inspirational/Motivational Literature. **Career:** Columbia University, assistant professor of English, 1961-69; Cleveland State University, associate professor, 1969-71, professor of English and editor for poetry center, 1971-98, director of poetry center, 1990-91, professor emeritus, 1998-. Writer. **Publications:** (Ed.) Backgrounds of Romanticism: English Philosophical Prose of the Eighteenth Century, 1967; Beast Forms (poetry), 1971; Severed Parts, 1981; (ed.) World, Self, Poem: Essays on Contemporary Poetry from the Jubliation of Poets, 1990; Mary Stuart: A Queen Betrayed (opera libretto), 1991; (trans. and co-ed.) Beast morfs, 1992; (ed. and trans. with K.P. Hinze) An Anthology of German Literature of the Romantic Era and Age of Goethe, 1993; Leonard Trawick: Greatest Hits, 2001. Works appear in anthologies. Contributor to periodicals. **Address:** Department of English, Cleveland State University, 1983 E 24th St., RT 1820, 2121 Euclid Ave., Cleveland, OH 44115, U.S.A. **Online address:** l.trawick@csuohio.edu

TRAXEL, David Stephens. American (born United States), b. 1942?. **Genres:** History, Military/Defense/Arms Control. **Career:** University of the Sciences, faculty, 1992-, associate professor, through 2007, professor of history, 2007-. Writer. **Publications:** An American Saga: The Life and Times of Rockwell Kent, 1980; 1898: The Birth of the American Century, 1998; Crusader Nation: The United States in Peace and the Great War, 1898-1920, 2006. Contributor to periodicals. **Address:** Department of Humanities, University of the Sciences, 600 S 43rd St., Philadelphia, PA 19104, U.S.A. **Online address:** d.traxel@usp.edu

TRAXLER, Patricia. American (born United States), b. 1947. **Genres:** Novels, Novellas/Short Stories, Poetry. **Career:** Radcliffe University, Bunting Poet, 1990-92; University of Montana, Hugo Poet, 1996; Ohio State University, Thurber Poet, 1997. **Publications:** POETRY: Blood Calendar, 1975; The Glass Woman, 1983; Forbidden Words, 1994. OTHER: Blood (novel), 2001. Contributor of periodicals. Work appears in anthologies. **Address:** c/o Gail Hochman, Brandt & Hochman Literary Agents, 1501 Broadway, Ste. 2310, New York, NY 10036, U.S.A. **Online address:** ptdunne@swbell.net

TREAT, James. American (born United States), b. 1962. **Genres:** Theology/Religion, Environmental Sciences/Ecology, Humanities, Race Relations. **Career:** University of California, Department of American Studies, assistant professor of American studies, 1992-95, Center for Cultural Studies, research associate, Department of Community Studies, affiliate faculty; University of New Mexico, Department of American Studies, assistant professor of American studies, 1996-2000, Native American Studies Center, assistant director, Religious Studies Program, affiliate faculty; University of Oklahoma, Honors College, Reach for Excellence assistant professor, 2000-03, Reach for Excellence associate professor, 2003-05, Graduate College, graduate faculty, Religious Studies Program, core faculty, Native American Studies Program, affiliate faculty, School of International and Area Studies, affiliate faculty;

University of Illinois, Department of Religion, associate professor of religion, 2005-, affirmative action officer, Department of Natural Resources and Environmental Sciences, affiliate faculty, Department of Anthropology, affiliate faculty, Unit for Criticism and Interpretive Theory, affiliate faculty, Campus Honors Program, affiliate faculty, American Indian Studies Program, affiliate faculty and affirmative action officer, Graduate College, graduate faculty. Writer. **Publications:** (Ed.) Native and Christian: Indigenous Voices on Religious Identity in the United States and Canada, 1996; (ed. and intro.) For This Land: Writings on Religion in America, 1999; Around the Sacred Fire: Native Religious Activism in the Red Power Era, 2003; (ed.) Writing the Cross Culture: Native Fiction on the White Man's Religion, 2006. **Address:** Department of Religion, University of Illinois, 3023 Foreign Language Bldg.,, 707 S Mathews Ave., PO Box 166, Urbana, IL 61801, U.S.A. **Online address:** treaty@illinois.edu

TREBAY, Guy. American (born United States), b. 1952. **Genres:** Adult Non-fiction, Travel/Exploration. **Career:** Village Voice, staff writer and senior editor, 1980-. **Publications:** In the Place to Be: Guy Trebay's New York, 1992. Contributor to books and magazine. **Address:** The Village Voice, 36 Cooper Sq., New York, NY 10003-7118, U.S.A.

TREBILCO, Paul R. New Zealander (born New Zealand) **Genres:** Theology/Religion. **Career:** University of Otago, professor of theology & head of theology and religious studies. Academic and writer. **Publications:** Jewish Communities in Asia Minor, 1991; (ed.) Considering Orthodoxy: Foundations for Faith Today, 2006; The Early Christians in Ephesus from Paul to Ignatius, 2004; (with S. Rae) 1 Timothy, 2007. Contributor to periodicals and journals. **Address:** Department of Theology & Religious Studies, University of Otago, PO Box 56, Dunedin, 9054, New Zealand. **Online address:** paul.trebilco@otago.ac.nz

TRECKER, Jamie. American (born United States) **Genres:** Sports/Fitness. **Career:** Fox Sports, senior soccer writer. Journalist and sports writer. **Publications:** Love and Blood: At the World Cup with the Footballers, Fans and Freaks, 2007. Contributor to periodicals. **Address:** Chicago, IL , U.S.A. **Online address:** jamie.trecker@gmail.com

TREDELL, Nicolas (Samuel). British (born England), b. 1950. **Genres:** Film, Literary Criticism And History. **Career:** PN Review, contributing editor, 1983-89; Palgrave Macmillan Readers' Guides to Essential Criticism, consultant editor, 2002-. **Publications:** The Novels of Colin Wilson, 1982, rev. ed., 2004; Uncancelled Challenge: The Work of Raymond Williams, 1990; The Critical Decade: Culture in Crisis, 1993; Conversations with Critics, 1994; Caute's Confrontations: A Study of the Novels of David Caute, 1994; Fighting Fictions: The Novels of B.S. Johnson, 2000, rev. ed., 2010; The Palgrave Guide to Essential Criticism of Macbeth, 2006; Fitzgerald's The Great Gatsby: A Continuum Reader's Guide, 2007; The Palgrave Guide to Essential Criticism of A Midsummer Night's Dream, 2010; F. Scott Fitzgerald: The Great Gatsby/Tender is the Night: Analysing Texts, 2011. EDITOR: The Palgrave Guide to Essential Criticism of The Great Gatsby, 1997; The Palgrave Guide to Essential Criticism of Great Expectations, 1998; The Palgrave Guide to Essential Criticism of Heart of Darkness, 1998; The Palgrave Guide to Essential Criticism of The Sound and the Fury/As I Lay Dying, 1999; The Palgrave Guide to Essential Criticism of the Fiction of Martin Amis, 2000; Cinemas of the Mind: A Critical History of Film Theory, 2002. Contributor of articles to books and periodicals. **Address:** 9 Dymchurch Close, Seaford, ES BN25 3JX, England. **Online address:** nicolastredell@hotmail.com

TREFFERT, Darold A(llen). American (born United States), b. 1933. **Genres:** Medicine/Health, Psychiatry. **Career:** Sacred Heart General Hospital, intern, 1958-59; University of Wisconsin-Madison, Medical School, associate clinical professor, clinical professor; University of Wisconsin-Milwaukee, clinical professor, University Hospital, resident in psychiatry, 1959-62; Winnebago Mental Health Institute, staff psychiatrist and creator of Child-Adolescent Unit, 1962-64, superintendent, 1964-79; Board of Wisconsin, chairman of the controlled substances, 1970-82, 2004; State Medical Society, president, 1979-80, board chairman, 1981-87; Wisconsin Psychiatric Association, president; American Association of Psychiatric Administrators, president; Fond du Lac County Health Care Center, executive director; Saint Agnes Hospital, Adolescent and Adult Alcoholism Treatment Unit, medical director, through 1991; Medical Examining Board, staff, chairman, 2002; Savant Syndrome, researcher. Writer. **Publications:** Mellowing: An Alternative to Coping, 1983; Extraordinary People: Understanding Idiot Savants, 1989;

Extraordinary People: Understanding Savant Syndrome, 2000, new ed. 2006; Islands of Genius: The Bountiful Mind of the Autistic, Acquired and Sudden Savant, 2010. **Address:** W4065 Maplewood Ln., Fond du Lac, WI 54937, U.S.A. **Online address:** daroldt@charter.net

TREFIL, James. American (born United States), b. 1938. **Genres:** Sciences, Astronomy, Physics, Astronomy. **Career:** Stanford Linear Accelerator Center, fellow, 1966; European Center for Nuclear Research, fellow, 1966-67; Massachusetts Institute of Technology, Laboratory for Nuclear Science, fellow, 1967-68; University of Illinois, assistant professor of physics, 1968-70; University of Virginia, Center for Advanced Studies, fellow and associate professor, 1970-75, professor of physics, 1975-88; George Mason University, Clarence J. Robinson professor of physics, 1988-. Writer. **Publications:** Introduction to the Physics of Fluids and Solids, 1975; Physics as a Liberal Art, 1978; From Atoms to Quarks: An Introduction to the Strange World of Particle Physics, 1980; (with R.T. Rood) Are We Alone?: The Possibility of Extraterrestrial Civilizations, 1981; Living in Space, 1981; Extraterrestrial Civilizations, 1981; Colonies in Space, 1981; The Moment of Creation: Big Bang Physics from Before the First Millisecond to the Present Universe, 1983; The Unexpected Vista: A Physicist's View of Nature, 1983; A Scientist at the Seashore, 1984; Space, Time, Infinity: The Smithsonian Views the Universe, 1985; Meditations at 10, 000 Feet: A Scientist in the Mountains, 1986; Meditations at Sunset: A Scientist Looks at the Sky, 1987; Cultural Literacy: What Every American Needs to Know, 1987; The Dark Side of the Universe: A Scientist Explores the Mysteries of the Cosmos, 1988; (with E.D. Hirsch, Jr. and J.F. Kett) The Dictionary of Cultural Literacy, 1988, 3rd ed. as The New Dictionary of Cultural Literacy, 2002; Reading the Mind of God: In Search of the Principle of Universality, 1989; (with R.M. Hazen) Science Matters: Achieving Scientific Literacy, 1991; 1001 Things Everyone Should Know about Science, 1992; (with H.J. Morowitz) Facts of Life: Science and the Abortion Controversy, 1992; Sharks Have No Bones: 1001 Things You Should Know About Science, 1993; (with R.M. Hazen) Sciences: An Integrated Approach, 1994, 6th ed., 2010; A Scientist in the City, 1994; (with R.M. Hazen) Physical Sciences: An Integrated Approach, 1996; The Edge of the Unknown: 101 Things You don't Know About Science and No One Else Does Either, 1996; Are We Unique?: A Scientist Explores the Unparalleled Intelligence of the Human Mind, 1997; Other Worlds: The Solar System and Beyond, 1999; Other Worlds: Images of the Cosmos from Earth and Space, 1999; (ed. with H. Morowitz and P. Ceruzzi) Encyclopedia of Science and Technology, 2001; Cassell's Laws of Nature, 2002; (with M.H. Hazen) Good Seeing: A Century of Science at the Carnegie Institution of Washington, 2002; The Nature of Science: An A-Z Guide to the Laws and Principles Governing Our Universe, 2003; Human Nature: A Blueprint for Managing the Earth-By People, For People, 2004; Physics Matters: An Introduction to Conceptual Physics, 2004; Why Science?, 2008; Science in World History, 2012. Contributor to periodicals. **Address:** Department of Physics, George Mason University, Rm. 303, Science and Technology I, MSN 1D6, 207F E Bldg., 4400 University Dr., Fairfax, VA 22030-4422, U.S.A. **Online address:** jtrefil@gmu.edu

TREHEARNE, Elizabeth. *See* **MAXWELL, Patricia Anne.**

TREHUB, Arnold. American (born United States), b. 1923. **Genres:** Psychology, Sciences, Medicine/Health. **Career:** Massachusetts General Hospital, research psychologist, 1953-54; Northampton Veterans Administration Medical Center, Psychology Research Laboratory, coordinator of research and director, 1954-82; University of Massachusetts, adjunct professor of psychology, 1972-. Writer. **Publications:** The Cognitive Brain, 1991. Contributor to journals. **Address:** Department of Psychology, University of Massachusetts, Division 2 Cog, 441 Tobin Hall, 135 Hicks Way, Amherst, MA 01003-9271, U.S.A. **Online address:** trehub@psych.umass.edu

TREIER, Daniel J. American (born United States), b. 1972. **Genres:** Theology/Religion, inspirational/Motivational Literature, Adult Non-fiction, Institutions/Organizations. **Career:** Institute of Theological Studies, director of curriculum, 1996-99; Cornerstone University, part-time instructor, 1998-98; Trinity Evangelical Divinity School, instructor in biblical and systematic theology, 2000-01; Wheaton College, assistant professor, 2001-06, associate professor of theology, 2006-, coordinator of interdisciplinary studies program, 2004-05. Writer. **Publications:** (Ed. with M. Husbands) Justification: What's at Stake in the Current Debates, 2004; (ed. with M. Husbands) The Community of the Word: Toward an Evangelical Ecclesiology, 2005; (ed. with K.J. Vanhoozer, C.G. Bartholomew and N.T. Wright) Dictionary for Theological

Interpretation of the Bible, 2005; Virtue and the Voice of God: Toward Theology as Wisdom, 2006; (ed. with M. Husbands and R. Lundin) The Beauty of God: Theology and the Arts, 2007; (ed. with T. Larsen) The Cambridge Companion to Evangelical Theology, 2007; Introducing Theological Interpretation of Scripture: Recovering a Christian Practice, 2008; (ed.) Theological interpretation of the New Testament: A Book-by-Book Survey, 2008; (ed. with K.J. Vanhoozer and N.T. Wright) Theological Interpretation of the Old Testament, 2009; (ed. with D. Lauber) Trinitarian Theology for the Church: Scripture, Community, Worship, 2009; (ed. with J.C. Laansma) Christology and Hermeneutics: Hebrews as an Interdisciplinary Case Study, 2011; Proverbs & Ecclesiastes, 2011. **Address:** Department of Theology, Wheaton College, BGC 286, 501 College Ave., Wheaton, IL 60187, U.S.A. **Online address:** daniel.treier@wheaton.edu

TREITEL, G. H. See **TREITEL, Guenter.**

TREITEL, Guenter. Also writes as G. H. Treitel, Guenter Heinz Treitel. British/German (born Germany), b. 1928. **Genres:** Law, History. **Career:** London School of Economics, assistant lecturer, 1951-53; Oxford University, All Souls College, lecturer, 1953-54, all souls reader in English law, 1964-79, chair and fellow, 1979, Vinerian professor of English law, 1979-96, now retired; Magdalen College, fellow, 1954-79, reader, 1964-79; University of Chicago, visiting lecturer, 1963-64, visiting professor, 1968-69, 1971-72; University of Western Australia, visiting professor, 1976; University of Houston, visiting professor, 1977; Southern Methodist University, visiting professor, 1978, 1988-89; University of Virginia, visiting professor, 1978-79, 1983-84; University of Santa Clara, visiting professor, 1981. Writer. **Publications:** (As G.H. Treitel) The Law of Contract, 1962, 11th ed., 2003; (as G.H. Treitel) An Outline of the Law of Contract, 1975, 6th ed., 2004; (as G.H. Treitel) Remedies for Breach of Contract: A Comparative Account, 1988; (as G.H. Treitel) Unmöglichkeit, Impracticability und Frustration im anglo-amerikanischen Recht, 1991; (as G.H. Treitel) Frustration and Force Majeure, 1994, 2nd ed., 2004; (with F.M.B. Reynolds) Carver on Bills of Lading, 2001, 2nd ed., 2005; Some Landmarks of Twentieth Century Contract Law, 2002. CO-EDITOR: Dicey's Conflict of Laws, 7th ed., 1958, as Dicey and Morris: Conflict of Laws, 8th ed., 1967; Chitty on Contracts, 23rd ed., 1968, 29th ed., 2004; Benjamin's Sale of Goods, 1974, 6th ed., 2002. Works appear in anthologies. **Address:** All Souls College, Oxford University, High St., Oxford, OX OX1 4AL, England.

TREITEL, Guenter Heinz. See **TREITEL, Guenter.**

TRELA, D(ale) J(ohn). American (born United States), b. 1958. **Genres:** History, Literary Criticism And History, Bibliography. **Career:** University of Texas, Pan American, teacher of English, 1985-87; De Paul University, teacher of composition and rhetoric, 1987-89; University of St. Francis (then College of St. Francis), teacher, 1988-89; University of California, Norman and Charlotte Strouse lecturer, 1989; Roosevelt University, Department of English, assistant professor, 1989-94, associate professor, 1994-97, professor, 1997-99, department head and chair, 1990-93, senate, 1990-99, vice chair of the senate, 1994-96, senate secretary, 1997-99, School of Liberal Studies, interim director, 1993-94, assistant director, 1993, director, 1994-99; University of Michigan, professor of English, 1999-, College of Arts and Sciences, dean, 1999-. Writer. **Publications:** A History of Carlyle's Oliver Cromwell's Letters and Speeches, 1992; (contrib.) Past and Present, 2005. EDITOR: Margaret Oliphant: Critical Essays on a Gentle Subversive, 1995; (with D.N. Mancoff) Victorian Urban Settings: Essays on the Nineteenth-Century City and Its Contexts, 1996; (with J.S. Clarke) Margaret Oliphant A Descriptive Bibliography, 1996; (with R.L. Tarr) Critical Response to Thomas Carlyle's Major Works, 1997. Contributor to books and journals. **Address:** Office of the Dean, University of Michigan, 516 French Hall, 303 E Kearsley St., Flint, MI 48502-1950, U.S.A. **Online address:** djtrela@umflint.edu

TREMAIN, Rose. British (born England), b. 1943. **Genres:** Novels, Children's Fiction, Women's Studies And Issues, Biography, Novellas/Short Stories. **Career:** Teacher, 1967-68; British Printing Corporation Publications, editor, 1970-71; writer, 1970-; University of East Anglia, part-time lecturer, 1988-95. **Publications:** NON-FICTION: The Fight for Freedom for Women, 1973; Stalin: An Illustrated Biography, 1975. NOVELS: Sadler's Birthday, 1976; Letter to Sister Benedicta, 1978; The Cupboard, 1981; The Swimming Pool Season, 1985; Journey to the Volcano, 1985; Restoration: A Novel of Seventeenth-Century England, 1989; Sacred Country, 1992; The Way I Found Her, 1997; Music and Silence, 1999; The Colour, 2003; The Road Home,

2007; Trespass, 2010; A Man of His Time, 2011. SHORT STORIES: The Colonel's Daughter and Other Stories, 1984; (contrib.) Seven Deadly Sins, 1985; The Garden of the Villa Mollini and Other Stories, 1987; Evangelista's Fan and Other Stories, 1994; Collected Short Stories, 1996; The Darkness of Wallis Simpson and Other Stories, 2005; (co-author) Great Escapes, 2006; (co-author) Ox-Tales: Earth, 2009; Wildtrack, 2010. OTHERS: The Kite Flyer, 1996; Knife Skills, 1999. Works appear in anthologies. **Address:** c/o Vivien Green, Sheil Land Associates Ltd., 52 Doughty St., London, GL WC1N 2LS, England.

TREMAYNE, Peter. See **ELLIS, Peter Berresford.**

TREMBATH, Don. Canadian (born Canada), b. 1963. **Genres:** Young Adult Fiction, Mystery/Crime/Suspense, Language/Linguistics. **Career:** The Morinville Mirror, reporter, photographer and editor, 1988-90; freelance writer, 1990-; MacEwan College, teacher in writing. **Publications:** HARPER WINSLOW SERIES: The Tuesday Cafe, 1996; A Fly Named Alfred, 1997; A Beautiful Place on Yonge Street, 1998; Lefty Carmichael has a Fit, 1999; The Popsicle Journal, 2001. BLACK BELT SERIES: Frog Face and the Three Boys, 2001; One Missing Finger, 2001; The Bachelors, 2002; The Big Show, 2003. OTHER: Lefty Carmichael Has a Fit, 1999; Rooster, 2005; Emville Confidential, 2007; Hypnotized, 2007. **Address:** 10011-104th St., Morinville, AB T8R 1A5, Canada.

TREMBLAY, Florent A. Canadian (born Canada), b. 1933. **Genres:** Language/Linguistics, History, Education, Bibliography. **Career:** Immigration-Quebec, director of language programs, 1968-71; Université Laval, professor of applied linguistics, 1968-72; Bureau des Langues, coordinator of French as a second language, 1972-73; CND NATO Schools in Europe, coordinator, 1973-77; Royal Military College of Canada, professor of French language and literature, 1977-2002, head of the language department, 1986-95, now retired; Royal Military College, program director, 1977-95; McGill University, applied linguistics, 1978-82; CFB-Europe, coordinator of second language teaching. Writer. **Publications:** La Méthode situationnelle en Français-langue d'usage, 1972; Bibliotheca Lexicologiae Medii Aevi, vol. I: Classics and Education in the Middle Ages, vol. II-III: Lexicons in the Middle Ages, vol. IV: Grammars in the Middle Ages, vol. V: The Rise of Vernacular Languages, vol. VI: The Influence of Vulgar Latin, vol. VII-VIII: Lexicographical Manuscripts, vol. IX-X: Author, Geographical, Abbreviation, Title, Chronological and Incipits Index, 1989-90; Mélanges offerts en hommage aurévérend père Rodrigue LaRue, OFM, 1991; Bibliotheca grammaticorum, vol. I: Antiquity: Circa 2000 ante Christum-circa 200 ante Christum, 2 books, vol. II: The Classical Period: Circa 200 ante Christum-circa 200 post Christum, 2 books, vol. III: Roman Decadence: Circa 100 post Christum-circa 500 post Christum, 2 books, vol. IV: The Middle Ages: Circa 6th to the End of the 15th Century, 2 books, vol. V: The Renaissance: ca. 1450-ca. 1790, 2 books, vol. VI: The Modern Period: Circa 1790-Year 2000, 3 books, vol. VII, book 1: Index of Titles: Ca. 2000 ante Christum-ca. 1990 post Christum, vol. VII, book 2: Index of Authors: Ca. 2000 ante Christum-ca. 1990 post Christum, 1996; Repertorium siglorum: Acronyms and Abbreviations in Philology and Related Subjects: Sigles et abréviations en études anciennes et dans les sujets connexes, 2002; A Medieval Latin-English Dictionary, 2005; A Medieval English-Latin Dictionary: Based on a Set of Unpublished 15th Century Manuscripts, Medulla Grammaticae-Marrow of Grammar Kept in the British Museum, 2009. Contributor to journals. **Address:** College Militaire Royal St. Jean, Chercheur en Residence, PO Box 100, Sta. Main, St. Jean-sur-Richelieu, QC J0J 1R0, Canada. **Online address:** florent_tremblay@hotmail.com

TREMBLAY, Paul G. American (born United States), b. 1971. **Genres:** Novellas/Short Stories, Novels. **Career:** ChiZine, fiction editor; Fantasy Magazine, co-editor. Educator. **Publications:** Compositions for the Young and Old (stories), 2004; City Pier: Above and Below, 2007; The Little Sleep: A Novel, 2009; The Harlequin & The Train, 2008; No Sleep Till Wonderland: A Novel, 2010; In the Mean Time, 2010; (ed. with J. Langan) Creatures: Thirty Years of Monsters, 2011. Contributor to books. **Address:** c/o Author Mail, Prime Books, PO Box 83464, Gaithersburg, MD 20883, U.S.A. **Online address:** pnuke33@comcast.net

TREMENS, Del. See **MACDONALD, Amy.**

TREMLETT, George (William). British (born England), b. 1939. **Genres:** History, Politics/Government, Social Commentary, Biography, Autobiography/Memoirs. **Career:** Corran Books Ltd., director, 1981-; One London Group Ltd., founder and chair, 1985-; Richmond-upon-Thames, councillor. Writer. **Publications:** ROCK STARS SERIES: The Gary Glitter Story, 1974; The Rolling Stones Story, 1974; The David Essex Story, 1974; The Mark Bolan Story, 1975; The Paul McCartney Story, 1975; The Slade Story, 1975; The Cliff Richard Story, 1975; The Osmond Story, 1975; The Who, 1975; The David Bowie Story, 1975; The Rod Stewart Story, 1976; Slik, 1976; The Alvin Stardust Story, 1976; David Bowie, Living on the Brink, 1997. OTHER: The First Century, 1962; Living Cities, 1979; (with C. Thomas) Caitlin: A Warring Absence, 1986 in US as Caitlin: Life with Dylan Thomas, 1987; Clubmen: The History of the Working Men's Club and Institute Union, 1987; Dylan Thomas: In the Mercy of His Means, 1993; Gadaffi: The Desert Mystic, 1993; (with J. Nashold) Death of Dylan Thomas, 1997. **Address:** St. Martin's Press, 175 5th Ave., New York, NY 10010, U.S.A.

TREMLETT, Giles. British/Spanish (born Spain) **Genres:** History. **Career:** Guardian newspaper, Madrid correspondent. Writer. **Publications:** Ghosts of Spain: Travels through a Country's Hidden Past, 2006; Catherine of Aragon, 2008. Contributor to periodicals. **Address:** Guardian Newspaper, Kings Pl., 90 York Way, London, GL N1 9GU, England. **Online address:** giles.tremlett@guardian.co.uk

TRENERRY, Walter N. (Otis Hearn). American (born United States), b. 1917. **Genres:** Criminology/True Crime, Biography, History, Military/Defense/Arms Control. **Career:** Attorney-at-law, 1946-77, now retired; Minnesota Museum of Art, chair, 1965-72. Writer. **Publications:** Murder in Minnesota: A Collection of True Cases, 1962; (with W.J. Schutz) Abandoned by Lincoln: A Military Biography of General John Pope, 1990. Contributor to journals. **Address:** PO Box 18277, W, Saint Paul, FL 55118-0277, U.S.A.

TRENGOVE, Alan. See **TRENGOVE**, Alan Thomas.

TRENGOVE, Alan Thomas. (Alan Trengove). Australian/British (born England), b. 1929. **Genres:** History, Sports/Fitness, Biography. **Career:** West London Gazette, reporter, 1946-49; Wagga Wagga Advertiser, reporter, 1950-52; Australian Broadcasting Commission, reporter, 1952-53; Argus, reporter, 1953-55; Herald and Weekly Times, feature writer and columnist, 1955-75; Tennis Australia Ltd., Australian Tennis Magazine, founder and publisher, 1976-. **Publications:** (With H. Elliott) The Golden Mile, 1961; The Herb Elliott Story, 1961; (co-author and ed.) The Art of Tennis, 1964 in US as How to Play Tennis the Professional Way, 1964; The Unforgiving Minute, 1966; (ed.) Living with Arthritis, 1969; John Grey Gorton: An Informal Biography, 1969; (ed.) Geoff Hunt on Squash, 1974, rev. ed., 1977; (comp. and ed. with D. Ballantine) The Australasian Book of Thoroughbred Racing, 1974; (with K. Stackpole) Not Just for Openers, 1974; What's Good for Australia..!: The Story of BHP, 1975; Adventure in Iron: Hamersley's First Decade, 1976; Menzies: A Pictorial Biography, 1978; Discovery: Stories of Modern Mineral Exploration, 1979; The Story of the Davis Cup, 1985, rev. ed., 1991; Australia and the Davis Cup: A Centenary History, 2000; Advantage Australia, 2003. **Address:** 31 Trafalgar St., Mont Albert, VI 3127, Australia.

TRENHAILE, John Stevens. British (born England), b. 1949. **Genres:** Novels, Mystery/Crime/Suspense, Horror, Young Adult Fiction. **Career:** Barrister, 1973-76. Writer. **Publications:** Kyril: A Novel of Espionage, 1981 in US as The Man Called Kyril, 1983; A View from the Square, 1983; Nocturne for the General, 1985; The Mah-Jongg Spies, 1986; The Gates of Exquisite View, 1987; The Scroll of Benevolence, 1988; Krysalis, 1989; Acts of Betrayal, 1990; Blood Rules, 1991; The Tiger of Desire, 1992; A Means to Evil, 1993; Against All Reason, 1994. **Address:** c/o Julian Friedmann, Blake Friedmann Literary, Film & TV Agency, 122 Arlington Rd., London, GL NW1 7HP, England.

TRENTON, Gail. See **GRANT**, Neil.

TRESILLIAN, Richard. See **ELLIS**, Royston.

TRETHEWEY, Natasha. American (born United States), b. 1966?. **Genres:** Poetry. **Career:** Duke University, Documentary and American Studies, Lehman Brady joint chair professor, 2005-06; University of North Carolina-Chapel Hill, Lehman Brady joint chair professor of documentary and American studies, 2005-06; Auburn University, assistant professor of English; Emory University, assistant professor of English, Phillis Wheatley cistinguished chair and professor of poetry, Charles Howard Candler professor of English and creative writing; Yale University, Beinecke Library, James Weldon Johnson fellow in African American studies, 2009. Writer. **Publications:** Domestic Work: Poems, 2000; Bellocq's Ophelia: Poems, 2002; Native Guard, 2006; Beyond Katrina: A Meditation on the Mississippi Gulf Coast, 2010; Thrall, 2012. Contributor to periodicals. **Address:** Department of English, Emory University, N 302 Callaway Ctr., 537 Kilgo Cir., Atlanta, GA 30322, U.S.A.

TRETHEWEY, Rachel. American (born United States), b. 1967. **Genres:** Art/Art History, Biography, History. **Career:** Daily Express, features writer, 1989-92; Daily Mail, features writer, 1993-96; freelance journalist, 1996-; East Devon and Cornwall Liberal Democrats, chair, health spokesperson. **Publications:** Mistress of the Arts: The Passionate Life of Georgina, 2002. Contributor to periodicals. **Address:** c/o Author Mail, Hodder Headline, 338 Euston Rd., London, GL NW1 3BH, England.

TREUER, David. American (born United States), b. 1970. **Genres:** Novels, Young Adult Non-fiction. **Career:** University of Minnesota, instructor in creative writing, 1996, visiting professor of English, 1997-, assistant professor of English, 1999-2006, associate professor of English, 2006-; University of Wisconsin, lecturer in English, 1998-99. Writer. **Publications:** Little, 1995; The Hiawatha, 1999; Native American Fiction: A User's Manual (nonfiction), 2006; The Translation of Dr. Apelles: A Love Story, 2006. Contributor to periodicals. **Address:** Department of English, University of Minnesota, 207 Lind Hall, 207 Church St. SE, Minneapolis, MN 55455, U.S.A. **Online address:** treue003@umn.edu

TREVELYAN, Percy. See **THOMAS**, (Antony) Charles.

TREVELYAN, Raleigh. American/Indian (born India), b. 1923. **Genres:** Novels, History, Autobiography/Memoirs, Biography, Translations, Young Adult Fiction, Military/Defense/Arms Control. **Career:** Samuel Montagu, trainee, 1947-48; William Collins Sons and Company Ltd., editor, 1948-58; Hutchinson and Company Ltd., editor and director, 1958-61; Arrow Books Ltd., editor and director, 1958-61; New Authors Ltd., editor and director, 1958-61; Penguin Books Ltd., editor, 1961-62; Michael Joseph Ltd., editorial director, 1962-73; Hamish Hamilton Ltd., director, 1974-80; Jonathan Cape Ltd., literary advisor, 1980-86; Bloomsbury Publishers, literary advisor, 1986-88. **Publications:** The Fortress: A Diary of Anzio and After, 1956; A Hermit Disclosed, 1960; (trans.) G. Paladino, Peace at Alamein, 1962; The Big Tomato, 1966; (trans.) The Outlaws, 1966; Princes under the Volcano, 1972; The Shadow of Vesuvius, 1976; A Pre-Raphaelite Circle, 1978; Rome '44: The Battle for the Eternal City, 1981; Shades of the Alhambra, 1984; The Golden Oriole: Childhood Family and Friends in India, 1987; La Storia dei Whitaker, 1988; Grand Dukes and Diamonds: The Wernhers of Luton Hoo, 1991; The Companion Guide to Sicily, 1996; Princes under the volcano, 2002; Sir Walter Raleigh, 2002; Danton, 2009. EDITOR: Italian Short Stories: Penguin Parallel Texts, 1965; Italian Writing Today, 1967; A Clear Premonition: Letters of Tim Lloyd, 1995. Contributor to periodicals. **Address:** Brandt Literary Agency, 1501 Broadway, Ste. 2310, New York, NY 10036, U.S.A. **Online address:** raleigh@rtrevelyan.fsnet.co.uk

TREVINO, Roberto R. American (born United States) **Genres:** Theology/Religion. **Career:** University of Texas, associate professor of history & assistant director. Writer, historian and educator. **Publications:** The Church in the Barrio: Mexican American Ethno-Catholicism in Houston, 2006; (ed. with R.V. Francaviglia) Catholicism in the American West: A Rosary of Hidden Voices, 2007. **Online address:** trevino@uta.edu

TREVISAN, João Silvério. Brazilian (born Brazil), b. 1944. **Genres:** Gay And Lesbian Issues, Romance/Historical. **Career:** University of Texas, writer-in-residence, 2001. Director and translator. **Publications:** Testamento de Jônatas deixado a David, 1976; Asincríveis aventuras de El Condor (juvenile), 1982; En nome do desejo: romance, 1983; Vagas notícias de Melinha Marchiotti, 1984; Devassos no paraíso, 1986; (with I.A. Caruso) A separacao dos amantes: umafenomenologia da morte, 1989; O livro do avesso: romance, 1992; Ana emVeneza, 1994; O amor com olhos de adeus, 1995; Troços and destroços: contos, 1997; Seis balas numburaco só: a crise do masculino, 1998; Pedaço de mim, 2002; Rei do cheiro: romance, 2009. **Address:** c/o Author Mail, Editora Record, Rua Argentina 171, Rio de Janeiro, RJ 20921380, Brazil.

TREVOR, Douglas. American (born United States), b. 1969?. **Genres:** Literary Criticism And History, Young Adult Fiction. **Career:** University of

Iowa, Department of English, assistant professor, associate professor, faculty advisor to the general education program, 1999-2002, associate chair for undergraduate programs, 2005-; University of Michigan, Department of English Language and Literature, associate professor, 2007. Writer. **Publications:** (Ed. with C. Mazzio) Historicism, Psychoanalysis and Early Modern Culture, 2000; The Poetics of Melancholy in Early Modern England, 2004; The Thin Tear in the Fabric of Space, 2005. **Address:** Department of English, University of Michigan, 3219C Angell Hall, 435 S State St., Ann Arbor, MI 48109, U.S.A. **Online address:** dtrevor@umich.edu

TREVOR, Penelope. Australian (born Australia), b. 1960?. **Genres:** Novels, Young Adult Fiction. **Career:** The Melbourne Weekly Magazine, editorial assistant. Actress and writer. **Publications:** Listening for Small Sounds, 1996; Another Man's Office, 2000. Contributor of articles to periodicals. **Address:** Allen & Unwin Ltd., 8 Napier St., North Sydney, NW 2059, Australia.

TREVOR, William. British/Irish (born Ireland), b. 1928. **Genres:** Novels, Plays/Screenplays, Novellas/Short Stories, Young Adult Non-fiction, Literary Criticism And History, Young Adult Fiction. **Career:** Teacher, 1952-59; Notley's, advertising copywriter, 1960-65; writer, 1965-. **Publications:** A Standard of Behaviour, 1958; The Old Boys, 1964; The Boarding-House, 1965; The Love Department, 1966; Girl, 1968; Mrs. Eckdorf in O'Neill's Hotel, 1969; Miss Gomez and the Brethren, 1971; Going Home, 1972; A Night with Mrs. Da Tanka, 1972; Elizabeth Alone, 1973; Last Lunch of the Season, 1973; Marriages, 1974; The Children of Dynmouth, 1976; Old Schools Ties, 1976; Other People's Worlds, 1981; Scenes from an Album, 1981; Fools of Fortune, 1983; A Writer's Ireland: Landscape in Literature, 1984; Nights at the Alexandra, 1987; The Silence in the Garden, 1988; (ed.) The Oxford Book of Irish Short Stories, 1989; Two Lives, 1991; Felicia's Journey, 1994; Juliet's Story, 1994; Excursions in the Real World: Autobiographical Essays, 1994; The Silence in the Garden, 1996; Old Boys, 1996; Death in Summer, 1998; Personal Essays, 1999; Three Early Novels, 2000; The Story of Lucy Gault, 2002; My House in Umbria, 2003; The Dressmaker's Child, 2005. STORIES: The Day We Got Drunk on Cake, and Other Stories, 1967; The Ballroom of Romance, and Other Stories, 1972; Angles at the Ritz, and Other Stories, 1975; Lovers of Their Time and Other Stories, 1978; The Distant Past and Other Stories, 1979; Beyond the Pale & Other Stories, 1982; The Stories of William Trevor, 1983; The News from Ireland, and Other Stories, 1986; Family Sins, and Other Stories, 1989; Collected Stories, 1992; (co-author) Deadly Sins, 1993; Outside Ireland: Selected Stories, 1995; Marrying Damian, 1995; Cocktails at Doney's and Other Stories, 1996; After Rain: Stories, 1996; Ireland: Selected Stories, 1998; The Hill Bachelors, 2000; A Bit on the Side, 2004; Cheating at Canasta, 2007; Bodily Secrets, 2007; Love and Summer, 2009; The Mark-2 Wife, 2011; Selected Stories, 2011. **Address:** Peters Fraser & Dunlop Group Ltd., Drury House, 34-43 Russell St., London, GL WC2B 5HA, England.

TREYZ, Russell. American (born United States), b. 1940. **Genres:** Plays/Screenplays, Music. **Career:** Interlochen Arts Academy, Department of Drama, head, 1965-66; Ashtabula Playhouse, artistic director, 1966-68; Theatre by the Sea, artistic director and resident director, 1975-79; WNET-TV, broadcaster. Writer. **Publications:** (With T. Key) Cotton Patch Gospel (play), 1982. **Address:** 107 Bedford St., New York, NY 10014, U.S.A.

TRIBE, Laurence H. American/Chinese (born China), b. 1941. **Genres:** Law, Politics/Government. **Career:** Harvard Law School, assistant professor, 1968-72, professor of law, 1972-82, Ralph S. Tyler, Jr., professor of constitutional law, 1982-2004, Carl M. Loeb university professor, 2004-; United States Department of Justice, senior counselor for access to justice. Writer. **Publications:** Channeling Technology through Law, 1973; (ed. with C.S. Schelling and J. Voss) When Values Conflict: Essays on Environmental Analysis, Discourse, and Decision, 1976; American Constitutional Law, 1978, 3rd ed., 2000; The Supreme Court, Trends and Developments: An Edited Transcript of the ... Annual Supreme Court Review and Constitutional Law Symposium, 1979; Constitutional Choices, 1985; God Save This Honorable Court: How the Choice of Supreme Court Justices Shapes Our History, 1985; (with M.W. McConnell and P.D. Gewirtz) The Senate, the Courts, and the Constitution: A Debate, 1986; Abortion: The Clash of Absolutes, 1990, new ed., 1992; (with M.C. Dorf) On Reading the Constitution, 1991; The Invisible Constitution, 2008. **Address:** Senior Counsel for Access to Justice, United States Department of Justice, 950 Pennsylvania Ave., Washington, DC 20530, U.S.A. **Online address:** larry@tribelaw.com

TRIBE, Laurence H(enry). American/Chinese (born China), b. 1941.

Genres: Law, Politics/Government, Civil Liberties/Human Rights, Young Adult Non-fiction. **Career:** California Supreme Court, law clerk, 1966-67; U.S. Supreme Court, law clerk, 1967-68; National Academy of Sciences, Technology Assessment Panel, executive director, 1968-69; Harvard University, assistant professor of law, 1968-72, professor, 1972-82, Ralph S. Tyler, Jr. professor of constitutional law, 1982-2004, Carl M. Loeb University professor, 2004-; Marshall Islands Government, constitutional consultant, 1978-79; California Nuclear Litigation (California Energy Commission), chief appellate counselor, 1978-83; Marshall Islands Judicial Service Commission, chairman, 1979-80; Citizens for the Constitution, co-founder, 1979; National Endowment for the Humanities, consultant; National Science Foundation, consultant; American Constitution Society, co-founder. Writer. **Publications:** Criminal Law Enforcement and the Constitution, 1967; Channeling Technology through Law, 1973; (ed. with C.S. Schelling and J. Voss) When Values Conflict: Essays on Environmental Analysis, Discourse, and Decision, 1976; The Constitutional Protection of Individual Rights, 1978; American Constitutional Law (textbook), 1978, 3rd ed., 2000; The Constitutional Structure of American Government, 1978; (co-ed.) The Supreme Court: Trends and Developments, vol. I, 1979; Constitutional Choices, 1985; God Save This Honorable Court, 1985; (with M.W. McConnell) The Senate, the Courts, and the Constitution, 1986; (co-author) The Tanner Lectures on Human Values, 1988; Abortion: The Clash of Absolutes, 1990; (with M.C. Dorf) On Reading the Constitution, 1991; Invisible Constitution, 2008. Contributor to books and journals. **Address:** Harvard Law School, 420 Hauser Hall, 1525 Massachusetts Ave., Cambridge, MA 02138-2903, U.S.A. **Online address:** tribe@law.harvard.edu

TRIBLE, Phyllis. American (born United States), b. 1932. **Genres:** Theology/Religion, Women's Studies And Issues, History. **Career:** Masters School, teacher, 1960-63; Wake Forest University, School of Divinity, assistant professor, associate professor of religion, 1963-71, professor of biblical studies, 1998-2002, university professor of biblical studies, 2002-; Andover Newton Theological School, associate professor, professor of Old Testament, 1975-79; Union Theological Seminary, professor of Old Testament, 1979-81, Baldwin professor of sacred literature, 1981-98; Vancouver School of Theology, visiting professor; Iliff School of Theology, visiting professor; Seinan Gakuin University, visiting professor; University of Virginia, visiting professor; Boston University, visiting professor; Brown University, visiting professor; St. John's University, visiting professor; University of Notre Dame, visiting professor. Writer. **Publications:** God and the Rhetoric of Sexuality, 1978; Texts of Terror: Literary-Feminist Readings of Biblical Narratives, 1984, Rhetorical Criticism: Context, Method, and the Book of Jonah, 1994; (co-author) Feminist Approaches to the Bible: Symposium at the Smithsonian Institution, September 24, 1994, 1995; The New Interpreter's Bible, vol. VII: The Book of Jonah: Introduction, Commentary, and Reflections, 1996; (ed. with L.M. Russell) Hagar, Sarah, and Their Children: Jewish, Christian, and Muslim Perspectives, 2006. Contributor to periodicals. **Address:** School of Divinity, Wake Forest University, 1834 Wake Forest Rd., Winston-Salem, NC 27109-6000, U.S.A. **Online address:** triblep@wfu.edu

TRIBUS, Myron. American (born United States), b. 1921. **Genres:** Education, Engineering, Environmental Sciences/Ecology, Sciences, Technology, Physics. **Career:** University of California, Department of Engineering, instructor and assistant professor, 1946-50, associate professor and professor, 1953-61; General Electric Co., Jet Engine Division, engineer, 1950-51; University of Michigan, Aircraft Icing Research Project, director, 1951-53, visiting professor, 1951-53; Dartmouth College, Thayer School of Engineering, dean, 1961-69; United States Department of Commerce, assistant secretary of commerce for science and technology, 1969-70; Xerox Corp., senior vice-president for research and engineering, 1970-74; Massachusetts Institute of Technology, Center for Advanced Engineering Study, director, 1974-86; Exergy Inc., co-founder and director, 1986-; CASEE Founding, senior fellow. Writer. **Publications:** Introductory Heat Transfer, 1950; Thermodynamics in an Engineering Curriculum, 1951; Thermostatics and Thermodynamics: An Introduction to Energy, Information and States of Matter, with Engineering Applications, 1959; (co-author) Thermodynamic and Economic Considerations in the Preparation of Fresh Water from the Sea, 1960; (with R. Evans) Thermo-Economics of Sea-Water Conversion, 1963; On the Design of the Thermodynamics Stem in an Engineering Curriculum, 1968; Rational Descriptions, Decisions, and Designs, 1969; Three Faces of Technology and the Challenge to Engineering Education, 1975; (ed. with R.D. Levine) The Maximum Entropy Formalism: A Conference Held at the Massachusetts Institute of Technology on May 2-4, 1978, 1979; Perspective: Myron Tribus on Quality, 1995. **Address:** 4318 Whiteleaf Ct., Pensacola, FL 32504, U.S.A. **Online address:** mtribus@earthlink.net

TRICE, Dawn Turner. American (born United States) **Genres:** Novels, Psychology, Young Adult Fiction. **Career:** Chicago Tribune, editor, 1988-, columnist; Public Library Association, panelist, 1998. **Publications:** Only Twice I've Wished for Heaven, 1997; An Eighth of August, 2000. **Address:** Chicago Tribune, 435 N Michigan Ave., Chicago, IL 60611-4041, U.S.A. **Online address:** dtrice@tribune.com

TRIFKOVIC, Serge. (Srdja Trifkovic). American/Yugoslav (born United States), b. 1954. **Genres:** History, Politics/Government, Theology/Religion. **Career:** The Lord Byron Foundation for Balkan Studies, co-founder and executive director; BBC World Service, producer, 1980-86; Voice of America, broadcaster, 1986-87; University of St. Thomas, Department of International Studies, professor, 1996-98; Chronicles, foreign affairs editor, 1998-; University of Banja Luka, visiting professor of politics and international relations; Geopolitika Magazine, associate editor, columnist and U.S. correspondent; Rockford Institute, Center for International Affairs, director. Journalist and historian. **Publications:** (As Srdja Trifkovic) Ustasa: Croatian Separatism and European Politics, 1929-1945, 1998; The Sword of the Prophet: Islam: History, Theology, Impact on the World, 2002; (ed.) Peace in the Promised Land: A Realist Scenario, 2006. OTHERS: (intro.) The Kosovo Dossier, 1999; Defeating Jihad: How the War on Terrorism May Yet Be Won, In Spite of Ourselves, 2006. **Address:** Chronicles, 928 N Main St., Rockford, IL 61103, U.S.A.

TRIFKOVIC, Srdja. See **TRIFKOVIC, Serge.**

TRIGGER, David S. Australian (born Australia), b. 1953. **Genres:** Race Relations, Social Sciences. **Career:** University of Western Australia, senior lecturer, 1986, chair, director and Winthrop professor of anthropology and sociology; University of Queensland, professor of anthropology. Writer. **Publications:** Whitefella Comin': Aboriginal Responses to Colonialism in Northern Australia, 1992; (co-ed.) Disputed Territories: Land, Culture and Identity in Settler Societies, 2003. **Address:** Department of Anthropology and Sociology, University of Western Australia, M255, 35 Stirling Hwy., Crawley, WA 6009, Australia. **Online address:** david.trigger@uwa.edu.au

TRIGGS, Tony D. British (born England), b. 1946?. **Genres:** Children's Fiction, Poetry, Education, History, Biography, Translations, Music. **Career:** School teacher, 1969-71; lecturer, 1972-80; Sunshine Books, writer and private music teacher, series editor, Tristan Song Project, founder and director. **Publications:** FICTION: The Gibleteers, 1986; Once Upon an Island, 1987; To David and Rosie, 1988. NONFICTION: Ancient Britons, 1981; Founders of Religion, 1981; The Saxons, 1982; People in British History, 1985; Ancient Egyptians, 1985; The Black Death and the Peasants' Revolt, 1985; Inside Story, 3 books, 1986-87; Boom and Slump in Inter-War America, 1987; A History of Medicine, 1988; Saxon Britain, 1990; Viking Britain, 1990; Norman Britain, 1990; Tudor Britain, 1990; Victorian Britain, 1990; Viking Warriors, 1990; Transport from 1750, 1990; Germany between the Wars, 1991; Explorations and Encounters, 1992; The Victorians, 1992; Tudor Times, 1995; Fishbourne-A Day in a Roman Palace, 1997. OTHER: Janus (poetry), 1976; (trans.) The Book of Margery Kempe, 1995; (ed.) Rockhopper Penguins and Other Songs (music), 2010. **Address:** Mere House, Brewery Rd., Trunch, North Walsham, NF NR28 0PU, England. **Online address:** tkrtriggs@yahoo.co.uk

TRILLIN, Calvin. American (born United States), b. 1935. **Genres:** Social Commentary, Novellas/Short Stories, Novels, Young Adult Non-fiction, Civil Liberties/Human Rights, Humor/Satire. **Career:** Time Magazine, reporter, staff writer, 1960-63, columnist, 1996-2001; The New Yorker, staff writer, 1963-; The Nation, columnist, 1978-85; King Features, syndicated columnist, 1986-95. Writer. **Publications:** NONFICTION: Alice, Let's Eat: Further Adventures of a Happy Eater, 1964; An Education in Georgia, 1964; Barnett Frummer Is an Unbloomed Flower and Other Adventures of Barnett Frummer, Rosalie Mondle, Roland Magruder, and Their Friends, 1969; U.S. Journal, 1971; American Fried: Adventures of a Happy Eater, 1974; Runestruck, 1977; Floater, 1980; Uncivil Liberties, 1982; Third Helpings, 1983; Killings, 1984; With All Disrespect, 1985; If You Can't Say Something Nice, 1987; Travels with Alice, 1989; Enough's Enough (And Other Rules of Life), 1990; American Stories, 1991; Remembering Denny, 1993; The Tummy Trilogy, 1994; Deadline Poet, or, My Life as a Doggerelist, 1994; Too Soon to

Tell, 1995; Messages from My Father, 1996; Family Man, 1998; Tepper Isn't Going Out, 2001; Feeding a Yen: Savoring Local Specialties, from Kansas City to Cuzco, 2003; Obliviously On He Sails: The Bush Administration in Rhyme, 2004; About Alice, 2006; Regards: The Selected Nonfiction of John Gregory Dunne, 2006. OTHERS: Heckuva Job: More of the Bush Administration in Rhyme, 2006; Deciding the Next Decider: The 2008 Presidential Race in Rhyme, 2008; Companionship in Grief: Love and Loss in the Memoirs of C.S. Lewis, John Bayley, Donald Hall, Joan Didion, and Calvin Trillin, 2010; Quite Enough of Calvin Trillin, 2011; Trillin on Texas, 2011; Eating with the Pilgrims and Other Pieces, 2011. Contributor to periodicals. **Address:** The New Yorker, 4 Times Sq., New York, NY 10036-6522, U.S.A.

TRIMBERGER, E. Kay. (Ellen Kay Trimberger). American (born United States), b. 1940?. **Genres:** Women's Studies And Issues. **Career:** Sonoma State University, faculty, 1975, coordinator, Women's Studies Program, 1981-2000, Department of Women's and Gender Studies, now professor emeritus; Columbia University, faculty; Barnard College, faculty; City University of New York, Queens College, faculty; University of California, faculty; San Jose State University, faculty. Writer. **Publications:** Revolution from Above: Military Bureaucrats and Development in Japan, Turkey, Egypt, and Peru, 1978; (ed. with N. Boyce and H. Hapgood) Intimate Warriors: Portraits of a Modern Marriage, 1899-1944, 1991; The New Single Woman, 2005. Contributor of articles to journals. **Address:** Women & Gender Studies Department, Sonoma University, Rachel Carson Hall 18, 1801 E Cotati Ave., Rohnert Park, CA 94928, U.S.A. **Online address:** ktrim@berkeley.edu

TRIMBERGER, Ellen Kay. See **TRIMBERGER, E. Kay.**

TRIMBLE, Michael R. (M. R. Trimble). British (born England), b. 1946. **Genres:** Medicine/Health, Sciences. **Career:** University of London, Institute of Neurology, National Hospital for Neurology and Neurosurgery, consultant physician, 1976-2004, senior lecturer, professor of behavioral neurology, 1994-2004, chair of behavioral neurology, 1994-, professor emeritus, 2004-; Royal College of Physicians, fellow; Royal College of Psychiatrists, fellow; Royal Society of Medicine, vice president, 1995-98; International League Against Epilepsy, chairman, 1998-2001; British Association of Neuropsychiatry, chairman, 2001-03; World Federation of the Societies of Biological Psychiatry, chair, 2001-05, vice president, 2006; Psychiatrist and writer. **Publications:** (Ed. with E.H. Reynolds) Epilepsy and Psychiatry, 1981; Neuropsychiatry, 1981; Post-traumatic Neurosis: From Railway Spine to Whiplash, 1981; (ed. with W.P. Koella) Temporal Lobe Epilepsy, Mania, Schizophrenia and the Limbic System, 1982; (ed.) Benzodiazepines Divided: A Multidisciplinary Review, 1983; (ed.) Psychopharmacology of the Limbic System, 1984; (ed.) The Psychopharmacology of Epilepsy, 1985; (ed.) New Brain Imaging Techniques and Psychopharmacology, 1985; (ed.) Interface between Neurology and Psychiatry, 1985; (ed. with T.G. Bolwig) Aspects of Epilepsy and Psychiatry, 1986; (ed. with E.H. Reynolds) What Is Epilepsy? The Clinical and Scientific Basis of Epilepsy, 1987; Biological Psychiatry, 1988, 3rd ed., 2010; (ed.) Epilepsy, Behaviour and Cognitive Function, 1988; Chronic Epilepsy: Its Prognosis and Management, 1989; (ed. with E.H. Reynolds) The Bridge between Neurology and Psychiatry, 1989; (ed. with T.G. Bolwig) The Clinical Relevance of Kindling, 1989; (with R.M. Post and C.E. Pippenger) Clinical Use of Anticonvulsants in Psychiatric Disorders, 1989; (ed.) Women and Epilepsy, 1991; (ed. with D.B. Smith and D.M. Treiman) Neurobehavioral Problems in Epilepsy, 1991; The Psychoses of Epilepsy, 1991; (ed. with T.G. Bolwig) The Temporal Lobes and the Limbic System, 1992; (ed. with W.E. Dodson) Epilepsy and Quality of Life, 1994; (ed.) New Anticonvulsants: Advances in the Treatment of Epilepsy, 1994; (with J.L. Cummings) Concise Guide to Neuropsychiatry and Behavioral Neurology, 1995, 2nd ed., 2001; (ed. with J.L. Cummings) Contemporary Behavioral Neurology, 1996; (ed. with B. Schmitz) Forced Normalization and Alternative Psychoses of Epilepsy, 1998; (ed. with I. Hindmarch) Benzodiazepines, 2000; (ed. with B. Schmitz) The Neuropsychiatry of Epilepsy, 2002, 2nd ed., 2011; (ed. with S.B. Seizures) Affective Disorders and Anticonvulsant Drugs, 2002; (ed.) Learning disability and Function, 2003; Somatoform Disorders: A Medicolegal Guide, 2004; The Soul in the Brain: The Cerebral Basis of Language, Art, and Belief, 2007; (ed.) Seizure Freedom, 2007. **Address:** Department of Clinical Neurology, Institute of Neurology, University College London, Queen Sq., London, GL WC1N 3BG, England. **Online address:** m.trimble@ionucl.ac.uk

TRIMBLE, M. R. See **TRIMBLE, Michael R.**

TRIMBLE, Stephen. American (born United States), b. 1950. **Genres:** Adult Non-fiction, Photography. **Career:** Freelance writer and photographer, 1970-; National Park Service, seasonal ranger and naturalist, 1972-75; Museum of Northern Arizona Press, contributing editor, 1979-80, editor and publisher, 1980-81; University of Utah, Stegner fellow, Honors College, instructor, 2008-11; Westminster College, Department of English, instructor, 2011. **Publications:** Great Sand Dunes: The Shape of the Wind, 1970; The Bright Edge: A Guide to the National Parks of the Colorado Plateau, 1979; Longs Peak: A Rocky Mountain Chronicle, 1984; (ed.) Blessed By Light: Visions of the Colorado Plateau, 1986; Canyon Country, 1986; Talking With the Clay: The Art of Pueblo Pottery in the 21st Century, 1987, rev. ed., 2007; Rim of Time, 1988; (ed. and intro.) Words From the Land: Encounters with Natural History Writing, 1988; The Sagebrush Ocean: A Natural History of the Great Basin, 1989; Portrait of Canyon County, 1990; The People: Indians of the American Southwest, 1993; (with G.P. Nabhan) The Geography of Childhood: Why Children Need Wild Places, 1994; Lasting Light: 125 Years of Grand Canyon Photography, 2006; Bargaining for Eden: The Fight for the Last Open Spaces in America, 2008. Contributor to periodicals. **Address:** 779 4th Ave., Salt Lake City, UT 84103, U.S.A. **Online address:** steve@stephentrimble.net

TRIMBLE, William F. American (born United States), b. 1947. **Genres:** History, Air/Space Topics. **Career:** Auburn University, Department of History, professor of history, chair, 2000-06. Writer. **Publications:** High Frontier: A History of aeronautics in Pennsylvania, 1982; (with W.D. Lewis) The Airway to Everywhere: A History of All American Aviation, 1937-1953, 1988; Wings for the Navy: A History of the Naval Aircraft Factory, 1917-1956, 1990; Admiral William A. Moffett: Architect of Naval Aviation, 1994; (ed. with W.M. Leary) From Airships to Airbus: The History of Civil and Commercial Aviation, 1995; Jerome C. Hunsaker and the Rise of American Aeronautics, 2002; Attack from the Sea: A History of the U.S. Navy's Seaplane Striking Force, 2005. **Address:** Department of History, Auburn University, 309 Thach Hall, Auburn, AL 36849, U.S.A. **Online address:** trimbwf@auburn.edu

TRIMIEW, Darryl M. American (born United States), b. 1952. **Genres:** Theology/Religion, Economics, Social Sciences. **Career:** Irvington Neighborhood Development Corp., director, 1978; Rahway State Prison, counselor, 1978-79; City Colleges of Chicago, teacher, 1982-84; Chicago Christian College, lecturer, 1984; Fund for Theological Education, fellow, 1985-86, 1988-89; Texas Christian University, Brite Divinity School, lecturer, 1988-90, assistant professor of church in society, 1990-; Racial Justice Task Force of Georgia Sea Islands, activist and workshop leader, 1990; Community Christian Church, associate minister, 1991-; Christian Church (Disciples of Christ), ordained minister, 1991; Society of Christian Ethics, board director, 1993-97, president; Crozer Divinity School, Black Church Studies, dean, 1998-2004, Christian Social Ethics, John Price Crozer chair; City University of New York, Medgar Evers College, Department of Philosophy and Religion, chair. Writer. **Publications:** Voices of the Silenced: The Responsible Self in a Marginalized Community, 1993; (ed.) Out of Mighty Waters: Sermons from African American Disciples of Christ, 1994; God Bless the Child That's Got Its Own: The Economic Rights Debate, 1995; (ed. with F.E. Glennon and G.S. Hauk) Living Responsibly in Community, 1997; The Problem of Social Sin for Disciples of Christ in the 21st Century, 2008. Contributor of articles and reviews to periodicals. **Address:** Department of Philosophy & Religion, Medgar Evans College, City University of New York, B-1007P, PO Box 5633, New York, NY 10024, U.S.A. **Online address:** dtrimiew@mec.cuny.edu

TRIMPEY, Jack. See **TRIMPEY, John P.**

TRIMPEY, John P. Also writes as Oscar Region, Jack Trimpey. American (born United States), b. 1941. **Genres:** Novels, Education, Medicine/Health, Psychology, Politics/Government, Self Help, Social Sciences, Literary Criticism And History, Literary Criticism And History. **Career:** Institute for Rational-Emotive Therapy, associate, 1968-; Journal of Rational Recovery, editor, 1988-; Rational Recovery Systems, founder, 1986-, president and executive director, Rational Recovery Self-Help Network, director. Writer. **Publications:** (As Oscar Region) The Tales of Atavan, 1985; (as Jack Trimpey) The Small Book: A Revolutionary Alternative for Overcoming Alcohol and Drug Dependence, 1992; The Final Fix: Addictive Voice Recognition Technique, 1994; (as Jack Trimpey with L. Trimpey) Taming the Feast Beast: How to Recognize the Voice of Fatness and End Your Struggle with Food Forever, 1995; (as Jack Trimpey) Rational Recovery: The New Cure for Substance Addiction, 1996. **Address:** Rational Recovery Systems, PO Box 800, Lotus, CA 95651, U.S.A. **Online address:** rr@rational.org

TRINCHIERI, Camilla. See **CRESPI, Camilla T.**

TRINH, T. Min-Ha. American/Vietnamese (born Vietnam), b. 1952?. **Genres:** Women's Studies And Issues, Plays/Screenplays. **Career:** University of California, faculty, 1994-, Chancellor's distinguished professor of women's studies, professor of rhetoric and of gender and women's studies, 1997-; San Francisco State University, associate professor of cinema; Harvard University, faculty; Smith University, faculty; Cornell University, faculty; University of Illinois, faculty; Ochanomizu University, faculty; National Conservatory of Music, faculty. **Publications:** Un Art sans oeuvre, 1981; (with J. Bourdier) African Spaces: Designs for Living in Upper Volta, 1985; En minuscules (poetry collection), 1987; Women, Native, Other: Writing Postcoloniality and Feminism, 1989; (ed. with R. Ferguson, M. Gever and C. West) Out There: Marginalization in Contemporary Culture, 1990; When the Moon Waxes Red: Representation, Gender and Cultural Politics, 1991; Framer Framed: Film Scripts and Interviews, 1992; (with J. Bourdier) Drawn from African Dwellings, 1996; Cinema Interval, 1999; (contrib.) The Dream of the Audience: Theresa Hak Kyung Cha (1951-1982), 2001; The Digital Film Event, 2005; (with J. Bourdier) Habiter un monde: architectures de l'Afrique de l'ouest, 2005; (with J. Bourdier) Vernacular Architecture of West Africa: A World in Dwelling, 2011; Elsewhere, Within Here: Immigration, Refugeeism and the Boundary Event, 2011. Contributor to periodicals. **Address:** Dept. of Gender & Women's Studies & of Rhetoric, University of California, 3326 Dwinelle Hall, Ste. 1070, Berkeley, CA 94720, U.S.A. **Online address:** trinh@berkeley.edu

TRINKUNAS, Harold A. American (born United States) **Genres:** Social Commentary, Politics/Government, Civil Liberties/Human Rights, Young Adult Non-fiction. **Career:** Naval Postgraduate School, National Security Affairs, associate professor, chair of department; Carter Center, field officer and electoral observer, 1998-, Academic Affairs of the Center for Civil Military Relations, deputy director. Editor. **Publications:** Crafting Civilian Control of the Military in Venezuela: A Comparative Perspective, 2005; (ed. with J.K. Giraldo) Terrorism Financing and State Responses: A Comparative Perspective, 2007; (ed. with T. Bruneau) Global Politics of Defense Reform, 2008; (ed. with A.L. Clunan) Ungoverned Spaces: Alternatives To State Authority In An Era of Softened Sovereignty, 2010. **Address:** Public Affairs Office, Naval Postgraduate School, Code 004, 1 University Cir., Monterey, CA 93943, U.S.A. **Online address:** hatrinku@nps.edu

TRIPLEHORN, Charles A(lbert). American (born United States), b. 1927. **Genres:** Sciences, Zoology, Natural History, Zoology. **Career:** University of Delaware, assistant professor of entomology, 1952-54; Cornell University, teaching assistant, 1954-57; Ohio Agricultural Research and Development Center, assistant professor of entomology, 1957-61; Ohio State University, professor of entomology, 1961-92, emeritus professor, 1992-. Writer. **Publications:** Review of the Genus Zopherus of the World (Coleoptera: Tenebrionidae), 1972; (with D.J. Borror and D.M. DeLong) Introduction to the Study of Insects, 6th ed., 1989; The Eleoes of Baja California (Coleopters: Terebrionida), 1994; (with N.F. Johnson) Introduction to the Study of Insects, 2005. **Address:** Museum of Biological Diversity, Ohio State University, 1315 Kinnear Rd., Columbus, OH 43212-1192, U.S.A. **Online address:** triplehorn.1@osu.edu

TRIPODI, Tony. American (born United States), b. 1932. **Genres:** Administration/Management, Education, Psychology, Social Work, Sociology, Biography, Social Sciences, Young Adult Non-fiction, Young Adult Non-fiction. **Career:** California Department of Mental Hygiene, research technician, 1958-59; California Youth Authority, research analyst, 1959-60; Columbia University, research assistant, 1962-65; Brooklyn College, research associate, 1963-65; University of California, assistant professor, 1965-66; University of Michigan, associate professor, professor of social work, 1966-87; University of Pittsburgh, School of Social Work, associate dean and professor of social work, 1987-92; Florida International University, associate director, coordinator, professor of social work, 1992-94; Ohio State University, College of Social Work, acting dean and professor of social work, 1995-2005, dean, now professor emeritus, Hunter College, now visiting Moses professor of social work. Writer. **Publications:** (Co-author) Clinical and Social Judgment, 1966; (with P. Fellin and H. Meyer) The Assessment of Social Research: Guidelines for the Use of Research in Social Work and Social Science, 1969, 2nd ed., 1983; (co-author and contrib.) Thought and Personality, 1970; (with I. Epstein and P. Fellin) Social Program Evaluation: Guidelines for Health, Education and Welfare Administrators, 1971; (co-author) Advances in Behavioral

Theory, vol. IV, 1973; Uses & Abuses of Social Research in Social Work, 1974; (with I. Epstein) Research Techniques for Program Planning, Monitoring and Evaluation, 1977; (P. Fellin and I. Epstein) Differential Social Program Evaluation, 1978; (with I. Epstein) Research Techniques for Clinical Social Workers, 1980, (with M.E. Vonk and I. Epstein) 2nd ed., 2007; (with L. Bernadi) Metodi di Valutazione di Programmi Sociali, 1981; Evaluative Research for Social Workers, 1983; (with B.J. Blythe) Measurement in Direct Social Work Practice, 1989; (with L. Bernardi) Metodi di Misurazione Nelle Attivita di Servizio Sociale a Contatto Diretto con L'Utenza, 1993; A Primer on Single-Subject Design for Clinical Social Workers, 1994; (with A. Ivanoff and B.J. Blythe) Involuntary Clients in Social Work Practice: A Research-Based Approach, 1994; (with B. Blythe and S. Briar) Direct Practice Research in Human Service Agencies, 1994; Requiem for Torchy: The Life Story of a Gambler, 2003. CO-EDITOR: (with P. Fellin and H.J. Meyer) Exemplars of Social Research, 1969; Social Workers at Work: An Introduction to Social Work Practice, 1972, 2nd ed., 1977. OTHERS: (with M. Potocky-Tripodi) New Directions for Social Work Practice Research, 1999; (with M. Potocky-Tripodi) International Social Work Research: Issues and Prospects, 2007; (with J.D. Noia) Single-Case Design for Clinical Social Workers, 2008. **Address:** College of Social Work, Ohio State University, Rm. 325D, 300 Stillman Hall, 1947 College Rd., Columbus, OH 43210-1162, U.S.A. **Online address:** tripodi.5@osu.edu

TRIPP, Charles R(ees) H(oward). British (born England), b. 1952. **Genres:** History, Politics/Government, Area Studies, Local History/Rural Topics, International Relations/Current Affairs, Adult Non-fiction. **Career:** Imperial War Museum, interviewer, 1979-80; International Institute for Strategic Studies, research associate, 1981-83; Graduate Institute of International Studies, Program for Strategic and International Security Studies, assistant director, 1983-86; University of London, London School of Oriental and African Studies, lecturer, 1986-92, senior lecturer in politics, 1992-, professor of politics, Centre for the International Politics of Conflict, Rights and Justice, faculty, London Middle East Institute, faculty. Writer. **Publications:** (Ed.) Regional Security in the Middle East, 1984; Just Mole, 1987; (with C. Shahram) Iran and Iraq at War, 1988; (with A. Ehteshami and G. Nonneman) War and Peace In The Gulf: Domestic Politics and Regional Relations into the 1990s, 1991; (with C. Shahram) Iran-Saudi Arabia Relations and Regional Order: Iran and Saudi Arabia in The Balance of Power In The Gulf, 1996; A History of Iraq, 2000, 3rd ed., 2007; Irak: Een Geschiedenis, 2002; Historia de Iraq, 2003; Storia dell'Iraq, 2003; Historia do Iraque, 2003; Islam and the Moral Economy: The Challenge Of Capitalism, 2006; Power and the People: Paths of Resistance in the Middle East, 2012. CONTRIBUTOR: Superpower Competition and Security in the Third World, 1988; (ed. with R. Owen) Egypt under Mubarak, 1989; The Iran-Iraq War: Impact and Implications, 1989; (ed.) Contemporary Egypt: Through Egyptian Eyes: Essays in Honour of Professor P.J. Vatikiotis, 1993; Iraq: Power and Society, 1993; (ed. with W. Danspeckgruber) The Iraqi Aggression against Kuwait: Strategic Lessons and Implications for Europe, 1996; The Cold War and the Middle East, 1997. Contributor to books and journals. **Address:** Department of Political Studies, London School of Oriental and African Studies, University of London, Russell Sq., Thornhaugh St., College Bldg. Office 214, London, GL WC1H 0XG, England. **Online address:** ct2@soas.ac.uk

TRIPP, David. American (born United States), b. 1951. **Genres:** History, Mystery/Crime/Suspense, Business/Trade/Industry. **Career:** British School, archaeologist and photographer, 1969-71; Sotheby Parke Bernet, director of coins and medals, 1973-75, assistant vice president and director of coins, tapestries and musical instruments, 1976-79, Baltimore representative, 1979-80. Writer, consultant and cartoonist. **Publications:** Illegal Tender: Gold, Greed, and the Mystery of the Lost 1933 Double Eagle, 2004. Contributor to periodicals. **Address:** PO Box G, Stuyvesant, NY 12173, U.S.A.

TRIPP, Dawn Clifton. American (born United States), b. 1968?. **Genres:** Music, Novels. **Career:** Writer. **Publications:** Moon Tide, 2003; The Season of Open Water, 2005; Game of Secrets: A Novel, 2011. Contributor to periodicals. **Address:** c/o Author Mail, Random House, 299 Park Ave., New York, NY 10171-0002, U.S.A.

TRIPP, Elise Forbes. American (born United States), b. 1942?. **Genres:** Novels, History, Military/Defense/Arms Control. **Career:** World Bank, international relations counselor for United Nations affairs; Holyoke Community College, adjunct professor of American history, professor. Writer and historian. **Publications:** Surviving Iraq: Soldiers' Stories, 2008; American Veterans

on War, 2011. **Address:** Holyoke Community College, 303 Homestead Ave., Holyoke, MA 01041, U.S.A.

TRIPP, Nathaniel. American (born United States), b. 1944. **Genres:** Young Adult Non-fiction, Autobiography/Memoirs, Politics/Government, History. **Career:** Writer and producer. **Publications:** Thunderstorm! (juvenile), 1994; Father, Soldier, Son: Memoir of a Platoon Leader in Vietnam, 1996; (foreword) Barns and Outbuildings: And How to Build Them, 2000; Snow Comes to the Farm, 2001; Confluence: A River, the Environment, Politics & the Fate of All Humanity, 2005. **Address:** Steerforth Press, 25 Lebanon St., Hanover, NH 03755-2143, U.S.A.

TRIPP, Valerie. American (born United States), b. 1951. **Genres:** Children's Fiction, Young Adult Non-fiction. **Career:** Little, Brown and Co., staff, 1973; Addison-Wesley, writer in language arts program, 1974-80; freelance writer, 1981-. **Publications:** AMERICAN GIRLS COLLECTION SERIES: Meet Molly: An American Girl, 1986; Molly Learns a Lesson: A School Story, 1986; Molly's Surprise: A Christmas Story, 1986; Happy Birthday, Molly!: A Springtime Story, 1987; Happy Birthday Samantha!: A Springtime Story, 1987; Changes for Samantha: A Winter Story, 1988; Changes for Molly: A Winter Story, 1988; Molly Saves the Day: A Summer Story, 1988; Samantha Saves the Day: A Summer Story, 1988; Felicity's Surprise: A Christmas Story, 1991; Felicity Learns a Lesson: A School Story, 1991; Meet Felicity: An American Girl, 1991; Changes for Felicity: A Winter Story, 1992; Felicity Saves the Day: A Summer Story, 1992; Happy Birthday Felicity!: A Springtime Story, 1992; Así es Josefina, una niña americana, 1997; Josefina aprende una lección: un cuento de la escuela, 1997; Sorpresa para Josefina: un cuento de Navidad, 1997; Meet Josefina, An American Girl, 1997; Josefina Learns A Lesson: A School Story, 1997; Josefina's Surprise: A Christmas Story, 1997; Feliz cumpleaños, Josefina!: un cuento de primavera, 1998; Happy Birthday, Josefina, 1998; Josefina Saves the Day, 1998; Changes for Josefina: A Winter Story, 1998; Felicity's New Sister, 1999; Molly Takes Flight, 1999; Samantha's Winter Party, 1999; Reward for Josefina, 1999; Meet Kit, An American Girl, 2000; Kit Learns a Lesson: A School Story, 2000; Molly and the Movie Star, 2000; Samantha Saves the Wedding, 2000; Kit's Surprise: A Christmas Story, 2000; Again, Josefina!, 2000; Felicity's Dancing Shoes, 2000; Happy Birthday, Kit, 2001; Kit Saves the Day, 2001; Changes for Kit, 2001; (with S.S. Adler and M.R. Schur) Samantha's Story Collection, 2001; Felicity Takes a Dare, 2001; Josefina's Song, 2001; Molly Marches On, 2001; Samantha and the Missing Pearls, 2001; Felicity Discovers a Secret, 2002; Just Josefina, 2002; Kit's Home Run, 2002; Molly's A-plus Partner, 2002; Samantha's Blue Bicycle, 2002; Bright, Shiny Skylar, 2003; Hallie's Horrible Handwriting, 2003; Kit's Tree House, 2003; Molly's Puppy Tale, 2003; Thank You, Logan!, 2003; Thanks to Josefina, 2003; Good Sport Gwen, 2004; (contrib.) Samantha: An American Girl Holiday, 2004; Teasing Trouble, 2004; Fair-Share Pair, 2005; Lindy's Happy Ending, 2005; One and Only Delaney, 2005; Kirsten's Short Story Collection, 2006; (with S.M. Buckey) Samantha's Short Story Collection, 2006; Kit's Short Story Collection, 2006; Molly's Short Story Collection, 2006; Josefina's Short Story Collection, 2006; Felicity's Short Story Collection, 2006. JUST ONE MORE STORIES SERIES: The Singing Dog, 1986; Baby Koala Finds a Home, 1987; The Penguins Paint, 1987; Squirrel's Thanksgiving Surprise, 1988; Sillyhen's Big Surprise, 1989; Happy, Happy Mother's Day!, 1989. OTHERS: An Introduction to Williamsburg (nonfiction), 1985; Actions Speak Louder Than Words: A Play about Samantha, 1994; Molly's A+ Partner, 2002; Very funny, Elizabeth!, 2005. **Address:** Pleasant Co., 8400 Fairway Pl., Middleton, WI 53562, U.S.A.

TRITES, Roberta Seelinger. American (born United States), b. 1962. **Genres:** Literary Criticism And History. **Career:** Central Texas College, instructor in communication, 1988-89; Austin Community College, instructor in English, 1989; Illinois State University, Department of English, assistant professor, 1991-97, associate professor, 1997-2001, professor of English, 2001-, College of Arts and Sciences, associate dean, 1998-2002, Center for the Advancement of Teaching, faculty associate, 1998, acting dean, 2002-04, director of graduate studies, 2005-; Midwest Modern Language Association, chair, 1998; Children's Literature Association, vice president, 2005-06, president, 2006-08; Louisa May Alcott Society, board director, 2008-11. Writer. **Publications:** Waking Sleeping Beauty: Feminist Voices in Children's Novels, 1997; Disturbing the Universe: Power and Repression in Adolescent Literature, 2000; Twain, Alcott, and the Birth of the Adolescent Reform Novel, 2007; (ed. with B. Hearne) A Narrative Compass: Stories that Guide Women's Lives, 2009. Contributor to books and journals. **Address:** Department of Eng-

'ish, Illinois State University, 207 Stevenson Hall, PO Box 4240, Normal, IL 61790-4240, U.S.A. **Online address:** seeling@ilstu.edu

TRIVIZA, Eugeniou. *See* **TRIVIZAS, Eugene.**

TRIVIZAS, Eugene. Also writes as Eugeniou Triviza, Eugenios Trivizas. British/Greek (born Greece), b. 1946. **Genres:** Children's Fiction, Young Adult Fiction, Humor/Satire. **Career:** University of Reading, Department of Sociology, lecturer in international and comparative criminology, 1978-88, director of criminal justice studies, 1988-2002, visiting professor, 2002-08, senior research fellow, honorary fellow, 2008-; Polytechnic of Central London, part-time lecturer, 1983-84; London School of Economics, part-time lecturer, 1983-84; Panteion University, visiting professor in criminology and penology, 1992-. Writer. **Publications:** IN ENGLISH: The Three Little Wolves and the Big Bad Pig, 1993; A Swallow in Europe, 2003; The Last Black Cat, 2004. IN GREEK: (as Eugeniou Triviza) Krokodeilos pou pege ston odontogiatro, 1984; (as Eugeniou Triviza) To oneiro tou skiachtrou: to theatro me te mise aulaia, 1984; (as Eugenios Trivizas) Ho Erōteumenos Pyrosvestes, 1992; (as Eugenios Trivizas) He zōgraphia tes Christinas: to vivlio pou den to diavaze kaneis, 1993; (as Eugenios Trivizas) Hoi peirates tes Kaminadas, 1993; (as Eugeniou Triviza) Teleutaia maure gata, 2001; Fruitopia (50 vols.), 2004. Contributor to periodicals. **Address:** Department of Sociology, University of Reading, 293 Faculty of Life Sciences, Whiteknights, PO Box 218, Reading, BR RG6 6AA, England. **Online address:** e.trivizas@reading.ac.uk

TRIVIZAS, Eugenios. *See* **TRIVIZAS, Eugene.**

TROESKEN, Werner. American (born United States), b. 1963. **Genres:** Medicine/Health, Economics. **Career:** University of Pittsburgh, professor; George Mason University, professor; National Bureau of Economic Research, research associate; University of Chicago, Center for Population Economics, senior investigator & project leader. Historian and writer. **Publications:** Why Regulate Utilities? The New Institutional Economics and the Chicago Gas Industry, 1849- 1924, 1996; Water, Race and Disease, 2004; Death and the City: Chicago's Mortality Transition, 1850-1925, 2005; The Great Lead Water Pipe Disaster, 2006; (with K. Clay and M. Haines) Lead Pipes and Child Mortality, 2006. **Address:** College of Humanities & Social Sciences, George Mason University, 4400 University Dr., Ste. 3A3, Fairfax, VA 22030, U.S.A. **Online address:** wtroeske@gmu.edu

TROFIMUK, Thomas. Canadian (born Canada), b. 1958?. **Genres:** Novels. **Career:** Isabella Communications, president, 2008; Government of Alberta, Municipal Affairs Office, business planning analyst. Writer and educator. **Publications:** The Fifty-Second Poem: A Novel, 2002; Doubting Yourself to the Bone: A Novel, 2006; Waiting for Columbus (novel), 2009. Contributor to periodicals. **Address:** Municipal Affairs, Commerce Pl., 10155 102 St., 18th Fl., Edmonton, AB T5J 4L4, Canada. **Online address:** thomas.trofimuk@gov.ab.ca

TROLLIP, Stanley R. South African (born South Africa), b. 1947. **Genres:** History, Archaeology/Antiquities, Criminology/True Crime, Mystery/Crime/Suspense, Novels. **Career:** University of Minnesota, assistant professor, 1983-87; Capella University, faculty, 1976-2003, director of learning strategies, 1997-2003; full-time writer, 2003-. **Publications:** (With S.M. Alessi) Computer-Based Instruction: Methods and Development, 1985, 3rd ed. as Multimedia for Learning: Methods and Development, 2001; (with R.S. Jensen) Human Factors for General Aviation, 1991; Recent Archaeological Discoveries on National Road Schemes, 2004: Proceedings of a Seminar for the Public, Dublin, September 2004, 2005; Settlement, Industry and Ritual: Proceedings of a Public Seminar on Archaeological Discoveries on National Road Schemes, September 2005, 2006; New Routes to the Past: Proceedings of a Public Seminar on Archaeological Discoveries on National Road Schemes, August 2006, 2007. WITH M. SEARS AS MICHAEL STANLEY: The Swiss Conspiracy, 1976; Famous Dubliners: W.B. Yeats, James Joyce, Jonathan Swift, Wolfe Tone, Oscar Wilde, Edward Carson, 1996; A Carrion Death, 2008; The Second Death of Goodluck Tinubu, 2009; (ed. with P. Luckraft) Thomas Houseago, 2010; (ed. with S. Conran and E. Danaher) Past Times, Changing Fortunes, 2011; The Death of the Mantis, 2011. **Address:** HarperCollins Publishers, 10 E 53rd St., New York, NY 10022, U.S.A.

TROLLOPE, Joanna. Also writes as Caroline Curteis, Caroline Harvey. British (born England), b. 1943. **Genres:** Novels, Romance/Historical. **Career:** Writer, 1993-; County of Gloucestershire, deputy lieutenant, 2009; patron, 2002-08; National Portrait Gallery Fund Raising Gala, chair. **Publications:** Eliza Stanhope, 1978; Parson Harding's Daughter, 1979 in US as Mistaken Virtues, 1980; Leaves from the Valley, 1980; The City of Gems, 1981; The Steps of the Sun, 1983; Britannia's Daughters: A Study of Women in the British Empire, 1983; The Taverners' Place, 1986; The Choir, 1988; A Village Affair, 1989; A Passionate Man, 1990; The Rector's Wife, 1991; The Men and The Girls, 1992; A Spanish Lover, 1992; The Best of Friends, 1992; The Country Habbit (anthology), 1993; Next of Kin, 1996; Other People's Children, 1998; Marrying the Mistress, 2000; Girl from the South, 2002; Brother and Sister, 2004; Second Honeymoon, 2005; Friday Nights, 2007; The Other Family, 2010; Daughters in Law, 2011. AS CAROLINE HARVEY: Legacy of Love, 1992; A Second Legacy, 1993; The Brass Dolphin, 1997. **Address:** c/o Author Mail, United Artists, 12-26 Lexington St., 34-43 Russell St., London, GL W1F 0LE, England. **Online address:** joanna@joannatrollope.com

TROMBLEY, Laura Skandera. (Laura Elise Skandera-Trombley). American (born United States), b. 1961?. **Genres:** History, Poetry. **Career:** State University of New York, assistant, director of teaching, assistant provost and associate professor of English; Coe College, vice president for academic affairs and dean of the faculty, 1997-2002; Pitzer College, president, 2003-. Writer. **Publications:** Poetry and Epistemology: Turning Points in the History of Poetic Knowledge: Papers from the International Poetry Symposium, Eichstätt, 1983, 1986; (as Laura E. Skandera-Trombley) Mark Twain in the Company of Women, 1994; (ed. as Laura E. Skandera-Trombley) Critical Essays on Maxine Hong Kingston, 1998; (ed. and intro. with M.J. Kiskis) Constructing Mark Twain: New Directions in Scholarship, 2001; Mark Twain's Other Woman: The Hidden Story of His Final Years, 2010. Contributor to periodicals and journals. **Address:** Claremont, CA , U.S.A. **Online address:** laura@lauratrombley.org

TROOP, Alan F. American (born United States), b. 1945?. **Genres:** Essays, Novellas/Short Stories, Young Adult Fiction. **Career:** Shake-a-Leg, founder. Novelist. **Publications:** The Dragon DelaSangre, 2002; Dragon Moon, 2003; The Seadragons Daughter, 2004; A Host of Dragons, 2006; Goldenheart, forthcoming. **Address:** c/o dragonnovels.com, 1140 NW 159th Dr., Miami, FL 33169, U.S.A.

TROPMAN, John E. American (born United States), b. 1939?. **Genres:** Sociology, inspirational/Motivational Literature, Administration/Management, Business/Trade/Industry. **Career:** University of Michigan, instructor in sociology, 1966, School of Social Work, lecturer and instructor, 1965-68, assistant professor, 1968-70, associate professor, 1970-76, professor, 1976-, Program in American Culture, faculty associate, 1977-, School of Business, visiting professor and adjunct professor in organizational behavior and human resources management, 1986-, Journalism Fellows Program, faculty associate, 1990-, Honors College, College of Literature, Science and the Arts, professor, 1990-, External Relations, assistant, 2003-, associate dean for faculty affairs, interim dean, special counsel to the dean. Writer. **Publications:** (Co-ed.) Strategic Perspectives on Social Policy, 1976; Essentials of Committee Management, 1979; Effective Meetings: Improving Group Decision-Making, 1980, 2nd ed., 1996; (with R.M. Lind) New Strategic Perspectives on Social Policy, 1981; Policy Management in the Human Services, 1984; Meetings, How to Make Them Work for You, 1985; Conflict in Culture: Permissions Versus Controls and Alcohol Use in American Society, 1986; American Values on Social Welfare: Cultural Contradictions in the Welfare State, 1986; Public Policy Opinion and the Elderly, 1952-1978: A Kaleidoscope of Culture, 1987; (with G. Morningstar) Entrepreneurial systems for the 1990s: Their Creation, Structure and Management, 1989; American Values and Social Welfare, 1989; (with C.D. Garvin) Social Work in Contemporary Society, 1992, 2nd ed., 1998; (with H.R. Johnson and E.J. Tropman) Committee Management in Human Services, 2nd ed., 1992; The Catholic Ethic in American Society: An Exploration of Values, 1995; Making Meetings Work: Achieving High Quality Group Decisions, 1996, 2nd ed., 2003; Successful Leadership: A Skills Guide for Volunteers and Professionals, 1997; Does America Hate the Poor?: The Other American Dilemma, 1998; The Management of Ideas in the Creating Organization, 1998; (with E.J. Tropman) Nonprofit Boards: What to Do and How to Do It, 1999; (ed. with S.B. Ransom and W.W. Pinsky) Enhancing Physician Performance: Advanced Principles of Medical Management, 2000; The Compensation Solution: How to Develop an Employee-driven Rewards System, 2001; (ed. with J.L. Erlich and J. Rothman) Tactics and Techniques of Community Intervention, 4th ed., 2001; Strategies of Community Intervention, 2001; The Catholic Ethic and the Spirit of Community, 2002; Making Meetings Work: Achieving High Quality Group Decisions, 2003; Supervision and Management in Nonprofits and Human Services: How Not to Become the Administrator you Always Hated, 2006; (ed. with J. Rothman and J.L. Elrich) Strategies of Community Intervention, 2008; (with T.J. Harvey) Nonprofit Governance: The Why, What and How of Nonprofit Boardship, 2009; The Maestro Manager: Tips for CEOs, forthcoming; The Leadership Guide: Aids for Community Leaders, forthcoming. **Address:** School of Social Work, University of Michigan, Rm. 3734 SSWB, 1080 S University Ave., Ann Arbor, MI 48109-1106, U.S.A. **Online address:** tropman@umich.edu

TROST, Jennifer Ann. American (born United States) **Genres:** Social Sciences, History, Law. **Career:** Carnegie Mellon University, instructor, 1990-93, visiting assistant professor, 1997-98; Sweet Briar college, visiting assistant professor, 1998-99; Hiram College, visiting assistant professor, 1999-2000; Saint Leo University, assistant professor, 2000-05, associate professor of history, 2005-06; Muskingum College, instructor, 2006-; Utica College, executive director of economic crime and justice studies and associate professor of criminal justice. Writer and historian. **Publications:** Gateway to Justice: The Juvenile Court and Progressive Child Welfare in a Southern City, 2005. Contributor to periodicals and journals. **Online address:** jtrost@muskingum.edu

TROTMAN-DICKENSON, A. F. See **TROTMAN-DICKENSON, Aubrey Fiennes.**

TROTMAN-DICKENSON, Aubrey Fiennes. (A. F. Trotman-Dickenson). British (born England), b. 1926. **Genres:** Chemistry. **Career:** Manchester University, assistant lecturer, 1950-53; EI Pont de Nemours, technical officer, 1953-54; University of Edinburgh, lecturer, 1954-60; University of Wales, professor of chemistry, 1960-68, Institute of Science and Technology, principal, 1968-88, vice-chancellor, 1975-77, 1983-85, 1991, College of Cardiff, principal, 1987-93; Aberystwyth University, chair of chemistry, 1968; Cardiff University, vice-chancellor, 1988-93. Writer. **Publications:** Gas Kinetics; An Introduction to the Kinetics of Homogeneous Gas Reactions, 1955; Free Radicals: An Introduction, 1959; Chemical Kinetics, 1966; (with G.S. Milne) Tables of Bimolecular Gas Reactions, 1967; (ed.) Comprehensive Inorganic Chemistry, 1973. **Address:** Syston Ct., Bristol, BS16 9LU, England.

TROTT, Barry. American (born United States), b. 1961. **Genres:** Criminology/True Crime, Young Adult Fiction. **Career:** Williamsburg Regional Library, adult services director. Writer. **Publications:** (With J.L. Crowther) Partnering with Purpose: A Guide to Strategic Partnership Development for Libraries and Other Organizations, 2007; (ed.) Read On Fantasy Fiction: Reading Lists for Every Taste, 2007; (ed.) Read On Crime Fiction: Reading Lists for Every Taste, 2008; Read On Life Fiction: Reading Lists for Every Taste, 2009. Contributor to periodicals. **Address:** Williamsburg Regional Library, 7770 Croaker Rd., Williamsburg, VA 23188, U.S.A. **Online address:** btrott@mail.wrl.org

TROTT, Betty. (Betty J. Trott). American (born United States), b. 1933. **Genres:** Children's Fiction. **Career:** Bought Hills Grade School, third grade teacher, 1956-58; Center of Science and Industry (COSI), director, 1973; Merle Norman, beauty consultant, 1978-80; Fashion Academy, personal image consultant and teacher, 1980-90; Grandview Children's Musical, director, 1994; Griswald Players Play, director, 1995. Writer. **Publications:** Breathe on Me Butterflies, 1994. **Address:** 8808 Renfrew St., Powell, OH 43065, U.S.A.

TROTT, Betty J. See **TROTT, Betty.**

TROTTER, Bill. See **TROTTER, William R.**

TROTTER, David. British (born England), b. 1951. **Genres:** History. **Career:** University of Cambridge, King Edward VII professor of English literature. Writer. **Publications:** The Poetry of Abraham Cowley, 1979; The Making of the Reader: Language and Subjectivity in Modern American, English and Irish Poetry, 1984; Circulation: Defoe, Dickens and the Economies of the Novel, 1988; The English Novel in History, 1895-1920, 1993; (ed. and intro.) Sons and Lovers, 2009; (with S. Kemp and C. Mitchell) Edwardian Fiction: An Oxford Companion, 1997; (ed. and intro.) The Riddle of the Sands: A Record of Secret Service, 1998; Cooking with Mud: The Idea of Mess in Nineteenth-Century Art and Fiction, 2000; Paranoid Modernism: Literary Experiment, Psychosis and the Professionalization of English Society, 2001; Cinema and Modernism, 2007. **Address:** Cambridge, CB , England. **Online address:** wdt21@cam.ac.uk

TROTTER, Michael H(amilton). American (born United States), b. 1936 **Genres:** Law, Social Sciences. **Career:** Alston, Miller & Gaines, associate, 1962-67, partner, 1967-77; Good Government Atlanta, founder and president 1966-; Citizens and Southern Realty Investors, director, 1972-81; Research Atlanta, president, 1974-75; Trotter, Bondurant, Miller & Hishon, partner, 1977-82; Trotter Smith & Jacobs, president, 1982-92; Kilpatrick Stockton LLP, partner, 1992-; Emory University Law School, faculty securities regulation. Writer. **Publications:** Repelling Corporate Takeovers: Course Manual, 1978; (as G.A. Clay with S.S. Trotter) The Return of Brer Rabbit, 1995; Profit and the Practice of Law: What's Happened to the Legal Profession, 1997. **Address:** Kilpatrick Stockton L.L.P., 1100 Peachtree St., Ste. 2800, Atlanta, GA 30309-4530, U.S.A. **Online address:** mtrotter@kilstock.com

TROTTER, William R. (Bill Trotter). American (born United States), b. 1943. **Genres:** Novels, Music, Technology, History. **Career:** The Film Makers' Cooperative, archivist/production assistant, 1966-69; The Charlotte Observer, editorial writer, 1969-71; First Union National Bank, technical publications editor, 1971-73; World Film Productions, writer and director, 1973-77; Greensboro Sun, associate editor, 1975-81; City of Greensboro, Springfest Arts Festival, director, 1977-78; Peaches Records, Classical Section, head buyer and assistant manager, 1978-81; Northstate Reader, associate editor, 1980-83; Walden Books, bookseller, 1981-83, sales associate, 1983-85; Platterpus Records, manager, 1983-85; Successful Meetings Magazine, contributing editor, 1984-88; Spectator Magazine, music critic and feature writer, 1984-87; writer and editor, 1985-88; Carolina Piedmont, contributing editor, 1985-88; Military History Magazine, contributing editor, 1987-91; Imagine Media, senior writer, 1988-; Signal Research Corp., senior writer, 1988-92; Carolina Piedmont Magazine, contributing editor, 1988-89; Greensboro Sun, associate editor, 1975-81; Encyclopedia of Personal Computing, contributing editor, 1995; Triad Style Magazine, columnist, 1996-2000; Virginia Military Institute, visiting lecturer, 1999; Wildacres Writers Retreat, workshop leader, 2000; Viking Press, senior editor. **Publications:** (With T.J. Anderson) Word Processing, 1974; Life Begins at Forte: The Conductor as Musical Hobo, 1982-83; (with R.W. Newsom) Deadly Kin: A True Story of Mass Family Murder, 1988; The Darkest Thirst, 1998; The Civil War in North Carolina, vol. I: Silk Flags and Cold Steel, 1988, vol. II: Bushwhackers!, 1991, vol. III: Ironclads and Columbiads, 1991; A Frozen Hell: The Story of the Russo-Finnish War of 1939-1940, 1991; Winter Fire (novel), 1993; Priest of Music: The Life of Dimitri Mitropoulous, 1995; (with G. Meredith and S. Bateman) Ascendancy: The Official Strategy Guide, 1995; Close Combat, 1996; Microsoft Close Combat: A Bridge Too Far, 1998; Sands of Pride, 2002; The Fires of Pride, 2003; Warrener's Beastie, 2006. Contributor to magazines and newspapers. **Address:** TrotterBooks and Records, PO Box 14752, Greensboro, NC 27401, U.S.A.

TROTTIER, Maxine. Canadian (born Canada), b. 1950. **Genres:** Children's Fiction, Children's Non-fiction, Novels, Picture/Board Books, Crafts. **Career:** Writer and teacher. **Publications:** FICTION FOR CHILDREN: Alison's House, 1993; The Voyage of Wood Duck, 1995; The Tiny Kite of Eddie Wing, 1995; Loon Rock, 1996; Pavlova's Gift, 1996; A Safe Place, 1997; Heartsong, 1997; Prairie Willow, 1998; Walking Stick, 1998; Claire's Gift, 1999; Dreamstones, 1999; Flags, 1999; One is Canada, 1999; A Circle of Silver, 1999; The By the Standing Stone, 2000; Laura: A Childhood Tale of Laura Second, 2000; Little Dog Moon, 2000; Storm at Batoche, 2000; Native Crafts: Inspired by North America's First Peoples, 2000; There Have Always Been Foxes, 2001; Under a Shooting Star, 2001; Dear Canada: Alone in an Untamed Land the filles du Roi Diary of Hélène St. Onge, 2003; (with S. East) The Paint Box, 2003; Sister to the Wolf, 2004; Dear Canada: The Death of my Country the Plains of Abraham Diary of Geneviéve Aubuchon, 2005; The Long White Scarf, 2005; Three Songs for Courage, 2006; Dear Canada: A Season for Miracles, 2006; Forget-Me-Not, 2008; Dear Canada: Blood Upon Our Land: The North West Resistance Diary of Josephine Bouvier, 2009. JUVENILE NON-FICTION: Our Canadian Flag, 2004; Terry Fox: A Story of Hope, 2005. SCHOLASTIC CANADA BIOGRAPHIES SERIES: Canadian Greats, 2003; Canadian Inventors, 2004; Canadian Stars, 2004; Canadian Pioneers, 2004; Canadian Leaders, 2004; Canadian Artists, 2005; Canadian Explorers, 2005; Canadian Heroes, 2007. OTHERS: Migrant, 2012. Contributor to books. **Address:** Transatlantic Literary Agency, 72 Glengowan Rd., Toronto, ON M4N 1G4, Canada. **Online address:** maxine@maxinetrottier.com

TROUT, Robert J(ay). American (born United States), b. 1947. **Genres:** Children's Fiction, History, Biography, Autobiography/Memoirs, Military/Defense/Arms Control, Young Adult Fiction. **Career:** Eastern Lebanon

County School District, elementary school teacher, 1969-2002, now retired; Southern Cavalry Review, editor. **Publications:** They Followed the Plume: The Story of J.E.B. Stuart and His Staff, 1993; (ed.) Riding with Stuart: Memoirs of an Aide-de-Camp, 1993; (ed.) With Pen and Saber: The Letters and Diaries of J.E.B. Stuart's Staff Officers, 1995; In the Saddle with Stuart: The Story of Frank Smith Robertson of Jeb Stuart's Staff, 1998; Galloping Thunder: The Stuart Horse Artillery Battalion, 2002; The Hoss: Officer Biographies and Rosters of the Stuart Horse Artillery Battalion, 2003; (ed.) Memoirs of the Stuart Horse Artillery Battalion: Moorman's and Hart's Batteries, 2008. FICTION FOR CHILDREN: Drumbeat: The Story of a Civil War Drummer Boy, 2007. **Address:** 119 N Railroad St., Myerstown, PA 17067, U.S.A.

TROUT, Steven. American (born United States), b. 1963. **Genres:** Education. **Career:** Fort Hays State University, assistant professor of English, 1993-98, associate professor of English, 1998-2004, professor of English, 2004-, director of composition, 2004-06, chair, 2009-, Graduate Studies and Research, interim dean, 2006-07, Teacher-Scholar Journal, editor-in-chief; Hays Area Children's Center, board director, 1999-2003; Shenandoah University, Willa Cather Institute Lecturer, 2004; Center for Great Plains Research, associate fellow; Willa Cather Society Newsletter and Review, editor; University of South Carolina Press, advisory editor. **Publications:** (Ed. with P.J. Quinn) The Literature of the Great War Reconsidered: Beyond Modern Memory, 2001; Memorial Fictions: Willa Cather and the First World War, 2002; American Prose Writers of First World War: An Illustrated Chronicle, 2005; (ed.) American Prose Writers of World War I, 2005; (ed. and contrib.) Cather Studies 6: History, Memory and War, 2006; (ed.) Good-bye to All That and Other Great War Writings, 2007; On the Battlefield of Memory: The First World War and American Remembrance, 1919-1941, 2010; (ed.) No Hard Feelings!, 2011; (ed. with S. Paul and G. Sinclair) War and Ink, forthcoming. **Address:** Department of English, Fort Hays State University, 370 Rarick Hall, 600 Park St., Hays, KS 67601, U.S.A. **Online address:** strout@fhsu.edu

TROUTT, David Dante. American (born United States) **Genres:** Young Adult Fiction, Novels. **Career:** Rutgers Law School, faculty, 1995, professor of law. Writer. **Publications:** The Monkey Suit, and Other Short Fiction on African Americans and Justice, 1998; (ed.) After the Storm: Black Intellectuals Explore the Meaning of Hurricane Katrina, 2006; The Importance of Being Dangerous (novel), 2007. **Address:** Rutgers School of Law, 123 Washington St., Newark, NJ 07102, U.S.A. **Online address:** dtroutt@kinoy.rutgers.edu

TROY, Aidan. Irish (born Ireland), b. 1945. **Genres:** History, Theology/Religion. **Career:** Crossgar Co, vocations director, 1971-74; Mount Argus, preaching ministry and provincial counselor, 1974-80, 1989-94; St. Patricks Province of Passionists, provincial superior, 1980-86; Passionist Generalate, general counselor, 1994-2000; Holy Cross Church, rector, 2001-. Writer. **Publications:** Holy Cross: A Personal Experience, 2005; Out of the Shadow: Responding to Suicide, 2009. **Address:** Holy Cross Church, 432 Crumlin Rd., Belfast, AT BT14 7GE, Northern Ireland. **Online address:** atroy@compuserve.com

TROY, Judy. American (born United States), b. 1951. **Genres:** Novels, Novellas/Short Stories, Young Adult Fiction, Literary Criticism And History. **Career:** Auburn University, assistant professor, 1991-, associate professor of English, professor and alumni-writer-in residence; Crazyhorse (literary periodical), fiction editor, 1991-96. **Publications:** Mourning Doves: Stories, 1993; West of Venus, 1997; From the Black Hills, 1999. Contributor to periodicals. **Address:** Department of English, Auburn University, 9060 Haley Ctr., Auburn, AL 36849, U.S.A. **Online address:** troyjud@auburn.edu

TROY, Tevi David. American (born United States), b. 1967. **Genres:** Administration/Management. **Career:** Senator John Ashcroft, policy director, 1996-98; White House, deputy cabinet secretary, Domestic Policy Council, special adviser; Department of Policy, deputy assistant secretary; George Bush Administration, deputy assistant domestic policy for president; United States Department of Health and Human Services, deputy secretary, 2007-; Hudson Institute, visiting senior fellow; Potomac Institute, senior fellow; American Enterprise Institute, researcher; Department of Labor, deputy assistant secretary for policy. Writer. **Publications:** Intellectuals and the American Presidency: Philosophers, Jesters, or Technicians?, 2002. Contributor to periodicals. **Address:** c/o Author Mail, Rowman & Littlefield Publishing Group Inc., 4501 Forbes Blvd., Ste. 200, Lanham, MD 20706-4346, U.S.A.

TRUDEAU, Garretson Beekman. See **TRUDEAU, Garry (B.).**

TRUDEAU, Garry (B.). (Garretson Beekman Trudeau). American (born United States), b. 1948. **Genres:** Humor/Satire, Young Adult Fiction, Graphic Novels. **Career:** Yale Daily News, cartoonist, 1969-70. Writer. **Publications:** Still a Few Bugs in the System, 1972; The President Is a Lot Smarter Than You Think 1973; Doonesbury, 1973; But This War Had Such Promise, 1973; (with N. Hoffman) Fireside Watergate, 1973; Call Me When You Find America, 1973; Don't Ever Change, Boopsie, 1974; Guilty, Guilty, Guilty, 1974; Even Revolutionaries Like Chocolate Chip Cookies, 1974; Joanie, 1974; Dare to Be Great, Ms. Caucus, 1975; I Have No Son, 1975; What Do We Have for the Witnesses, Johnnie, 1975; Wouldn't a Gremlin Have Been More Sensible?, 1975; (with N. von Hoffman) We'll Take It from Here, Sarge, 1975; The Doonesbury Chronicles, 1975; (with N. Hoffman) Tales From the Margaret Mead Taproom, 1976; (with D. Leventhal) Hitler Moves East, 1977; As the Kid Goes for Broke, 1977; Any Grooming Hints for Your Fans, Rollie?, 1978; Doonesbury Greatest Hits, 1978; You're Never Too Old for Nuts and Berries, 1978; But the Pension Fund Was Just Sitting There, 1979; We're Not Out of the Woods Yet, 1979; And That's My Final Offer, 1980; A Tad Overweight, But Violet Eyes to Die For, 1980; He's Never Heard of You, Either, 1981; In Search of Reagan's Brain, 1981; The People's Doonesbury, 1981; Adjectives Will Cost You Extra, 1982; Ask for May, Settle for June, 1982; Gotta Run, My Government Is Collapsing, 1982; Unfortunately She Was Also Wired for Sound, 1982; The Wreck of the Rusty Nail, 1983; You Give Great Meeting, Sid, 1983; Doonesbury Dossier, 1984; Dressed for Failure, I See, 1984; Sir, I'm Worried about Your Mood Swings, 1984; Doonesbury: A Musical Comedy, 1984; Check Your Egos at the Door, 1985; That's Doctor Sinatra, You Little Bimbo!, 1986; Rap Master Ronnie, 1986; Doonesbury Deluxe, 1987; Downtown Doonesbury, 1987; Talkin' about My G-G-Generation, 1988; We're Eating More Beets!, 1988; Give Them Nymphs Some Hooters!, 1989; Read My Lips, Make My Day, Eat Quiche, and Die!, 1989; Recycled Doonesbury: Second Thoughts on a Guilded Age, 1990; You're Smokin' Now, Mr. Butts!, 1990; I'd Go with the Helmet, 1991; Action Figure!, 1992, 2nd ed., 2001; What Is It, Tink, Is Pan in Trouble?, 1992; Quality Time On Highway 1, 1993; The Portable Doonesbury, 1993; In Search of Cigarette Holder Man, 1994; Washed Out Bridges and Other Disasters, 1994; Flashbacks: Twenty-Five Years of Doonesbury, 1995; Doonesbury Nation, 1995; Virtual Doonesbury, 1996; Planet Doonesbury, 1997; The Bundled Doonesbury, 1998; Buck Wild Doonesbury, 1999; Duke 2000: Whatever It Takes, 2000; The Revolt of the English Majors, 2001; Peace Out, Dawg!: Tales from Ground Zero, 2002; (contrib.) Tribute to Sparky, 2003; Got War?, 2003; Doonesbury Redux, 2004; Talk to the Hand, 2004; The Long Road Home: One Step at a Time, 2005; Dude: The Big Book of Zonker, 2005; Doonesbury, the War Years, 2006; War Within: One Step at a Time, 2006; Heckuva Job, Bushie!, 2006; Welcome to the Nerd Farm!, 2007; (intro.) Doonesbury.com's The Sandbox: Dispatches from Troops in Iraq and Afghanistan, 2007; (intro.) Doonesbury.com's The War in Quotes, 2008; My Shorts R Bunching. Thoughts?: The Tweets of Roland Hedley, 2009. **Address:** Slate's, 395 Hudson St., 4th Fl., New York, NY 10014, U.S.A.

TRUDEAU, Noah Andre. American (born United States), b. 1949. **Genres:** History, Music, Biography, Autobiography/Memoirs, Military/Defense/Arms Control, Social Sciences. **Career:** WMHT-FM Radio, program producer, 1973-77; National Public Radio, producer of cultural programs, 1977-, executive producer for cultural programs. Writer. **Publications:** Bloody Roads South: The Wilderness to Cold Harbour, May-June, 1864, 1989; The Last Citadel: The Siege of Petersburg, Virginia, June 1864-April 1865, 1991; Out of the Storm: The End of the Civil War, 1994; Campaign to Appomattox, 1995; (contrib.) The Siege of Petersburg, 1995; Like Men of War: Black Troops in the Civil War, 1862-1865, 1998; Gettysburg: A Testing of Courage, 2002; Southern Storm: Sherman's March to the Sea, 2008; Robert E. Lee: Lessons in Leadership, 2009. Contributor to magazines. **Address:** National Public Radio, 635 Massachusetts Ave. NW, Washington, DC 20001-3753, U.S.A.

TRUEBLOOD, Kathryn. American (born United States), b. 1960. **Genres:** Novels. **Career:** Western Washington University, associate professor; Random House, editorial assistant; Shameless Hussy Press, editorial assistant; Columbus Foundation, director. **Publications:** (Ed. with I. Reed and S. Wong) The Before Columbus Foundation Fiction Anthology: Selections from the American Book Awards, 1980-1990, 1992; (ed. with L. Stovall) Home Ground, 1996; The Sperm Donor's Daughter and Other Tales of Modern Family, 1998; The Baby Lottery: A Novel, 2007. **Address:** Department of English, Western Washington University, MS 9055, 516 High St., Bellingham, WA 98225, U.S.A. **Online address:** kathryn.trueblood@wwu.edu

TRUEIT, Trudi Strain. American (born United States) **Genres:** Animals/Pets, Children's Fiction. **Career:** KAPP-TV, news reporter and weather forecaster, 1985-86; KREM-TV, news reporter and weather forecaster, 1986-89; Trueit Media, president and chief executive officer, 1990-. **Publications:** Octopuses, Squids and Cuttlefish, 2002; Storm Chasers, 2002; The Water Cycle, 2002; Rain, Hail and Snow, 2002; Clouds, 2002; Earthquakes, 2003; Volcanoes, 2003; Fossils, 2003; Rocks, Gems and Minerals, 2003; Lizards, 2003; Snakes, 2003; Turtles, 2003; Alligators and Crocodiles, 2003; Eating Disorders, 2003; ADHD, 2004; Dreams and Sleep, 2004; Keeping a Journal, 2004; Gunpowder, 2005; The Boston Tea Party, 2005; Julep O'Toole: Confessions of a Middle Child, 2005; Julep O'Toole: Miss Independent, 2006; The Camera, 2006; Surviving Divorce: Teens Talk about What Helps and What Hurts, 2006; Divorce: Homes Sweet Homes, 2006; Diwali, 2006; Valentine's Day, 2007; Christmas, 2007; Utah, 2007; Earth Day, 2007; Chanukah, 2007; Thanksgiving, 2007; Mississippi, 2007; Kwanzaa, 2007; Halloween, 2007; Independence Day, 2007; Martin Luther King, Jr., Day, 2007; Massachusetts, 2008; Easter, 2008; Presidents' Day, 2008; Hanukkah, 2008; Memorial Day, 2008; Windy Days, 2009; Worms, 2009; Mom, There's a Dinosaur in Beeson's Lake, 2009; No Girls Allowed, 2009; Sea Turtles, 2009; Sharks, 2009; Spiders, 2009; Starfish, 2009; Sunny Days, 2009; Video Gaming, 2009; (with R. Bjoklund) Kansas, 2009; Animation, 2009; Ants, 2009; Caterpillars, 2009; Grasshoppers, 2009; Stormy Days, 2010; Thomas Jefferson, 2010; Beetles, 2010; Cloudy Days, 2010; Jellyfish, 2010; Octopuses, 2010; Rainy Days, 2010; Sea Horses, 2010; Snowy Days, 2010; Caterpillars and Butterflies, 2011; Scab for Treasurer?, 2011; Squirrels, 2011; Birds, 2012; Vikings, 2012; Frogs and Toads, 2012; Dragonflies, 2013. **Address:** c/o Rosemary Stimola, Stimola Literary Studio, 308 Livingston Ct., Edgewater, NJ 07020, U.S.A. **Online address:** trumedia@verizon.net

TRUEMAN, Terry. American (born United States), b. 1947. **Genres:** Poetry, Education, Novels, Children's Fiction, Literary Criticism And History. **Career:** White Hills Technical Schools, English and social studies teacher, 1972-74; Spokane Community Mental Health Center, therapist, 1975-80; Escuela International Sanpedrana, secondary school counselor, 1981-82; Eastern Washington University, teaching fellow in English, 1983-85; Spokane Falls Community College, instructor in communications department, 1985-91; Spokane Public Schools, substance abuse intervention specialist, 1991-93; KPBX-FM, film, video and media critic. Novelist. **Publications:** POETRY CHAPBOOKS: The Chinese Painting Poems, 1990; Black Lipstick, 1991; Sheehan: Heartbreak and Redemption, 1992; Love on the Rack, 1995. NOVELS: Stuck in Neutral, 2000; Inside Out, 2003; Swallowing the Sun, 2003; Cruise Control, 2004; No Right Turn, 2005; 7 Days at the Hot Corner, 2007. OTHERS: (with M. Gurian) What Stories Does My Son Need?: A Guide to Books and Movies That Build Character in Boys, 2000; (with M. Gurian and P. Henley) Boys and Girls Learn Differently: A Guide for Teachers and Parents, 2001; Lay Ups and Long Shot, 2005; Hurricane, 2008. Contributor to periodicals. **Address:** HarperCollins, 1350 Ave. of the Americas, 3410 W Fort George Wright Dr., New York, NY 10019-4703, U.S.A. **Online address:** ttrueman1215@msn.com

TRUITT, Sam. American (born United States), b. 1960?. **Genres:** Poetry. **Career:** State University of New York, faculty; Bard College, faculty. Writer. **Publications:** POETRY: Anamorphosis Eisenhower, 1998; Vertical Elegies 5: The Section; Sonnets, 2003; Vertical Elegies: Three Works, 2008; Vertical Elegies 6: Street Mete, 2010. Works appear in anthologies. Contributor to journals. **Address:** NY , U.S.A. **Online address:** samtruitt@yahoo.com

TRUMAN, Ruth. (Ruth Dixon Truman). American (born United States), b. 1931. **Genres:** Novels, Young Adult Fiction, Science Fiction/Fantasy, Poetry, Education, How-to Books, Paranormal, Self Help, Theology/Religion, Women's Studies And Issues, Autobiography/Memoirs, E-books, Humor/Satire, Human Relations/Parenting, inspirational/Motivational Literature, Popular Culture, Songs/Lyrics And Libretti. **Career:** Teacher, 1954-55; Home Ec Teacher, 1955-56; Citrus College, counselor, 1966-67, instructor, 1967-68; San Antonio College, Women's Center, director, 1969; California Lutheran College, director of counseling, 1970-74; Bureau of Higher and Continuing Education, intern, 1978; Cancer Information Service of California, director, 1983-86; California State University, Extended Education for Program Services, director, 1986-92, acting associate vice president for research and external programs, 1990-92, now retired. Writer. **Publications:** Underground Manual for Minister's Wives, 1974; The Mission of the Church College, 1978; How to Be a Liberated Christian, 1981; Spaghetti from the Chandelier, 1984; Not of This Fold, 2001; The Day the Mountain Died, 2002; To Life!:

A Book of Poetry and Songs, 2008; No Safe College, 2008. Contributor to books and periodicals. **Address:** 2259 Barbara Dr., Santa Rosa Valley, CA 93012-9379, U.S.A. **Online address:** rtruman896@gmail.com

TRUMAN, Ruth Dixon. *See* **TRUMAN, Ruth.**

TRUMP, Donald J. American (born United States), b. 1946. **Genres:** Autobiography/Memoirs, Money/Finance, Education, Business/Trade/Industry. **Career:** The Trump Organization-Queens, staff, 1968-73; The Trump Organization-New York, president, chairman and chief executive officer. Writer. **Publications:** (With T. Schwartz) Trump: The Art of the Deal, 1987; (with C. Leerhsen) Trump: Surviving at the Top, 1990; (with K. Bohner) Trump: The Art of the Comeback, 1997; (with D. Shiflett) The America We Deserve, 2000; (with M. McIver) Trump: How to Get Rich, 2004; (with M. McIver) Trump: Think Like a Billionaire, 2004; (comp.) Way to the top, 2004; Trump: The Way to the Top, 2004; Trump: The Best Golf Advice I Ever Received, 2005; World According to Trump: An Unauthorized Portrait in His Own Words, 2005; Trump: The Best Real Estate Advice I Ever Received: 100 Top Experts Share their Strategies, 2006; (foreword) Trump University marketing 101, 2006; (with B. Zanker) Think Big and Kick Ass in Business and Life, 2007; (with M. McIver) Trump 101: The Way to Success, 2007; (ed.) Trump University Wealth Building 101: Your First 90 Days on the Path to Prosperity, 2007; (with M. McIver) Trump Never Give Up: How I Turned My Biggest Challenges into Success, 2008; (with M. McIver) Think Like a Champion: An Informal Education in Business and Life, 2009; (foreword) Trump University Entrepreneurship 101, 2nd ed., 2010; Time to Get Tough, 2011; (with J. Robinson) Trump Tower, 2011. **Address:** The Trump Organization, 725 5th Ave., New York, NY 10022-2519, U.S.A.

TRUNDLE, Robert C(hristner). American (born United States), b. 1943. **Genres:** Philosophy. **Career:** Toledo Public Schools, part-time teacher, 1972-74; University of Colorado, instructor, 1982-84; Regis College, adjunct assistant professor, 1982-86; Northern Kentucky University, associate professor, professor, 1987-. Writer. **Publications:** (With R. Puligandla) Beyond Absurdity: The Philosophy of Albert Camus, 1986; Ancient Greek Philosophy: Its Development and Relevance to Our Time, 1994; Medieval Modal Logic and Science: Augustine on Necessary Truth and Thomas on Its Impossibility without a First Cause, 1999; From Physics to Politics: The Metaphysical Foundations of Modern Philosophy, 1999; UFOs: Politics, God and Science: Philosophy on a Taboo Topic, 2000; Camus' Answer: No to the Western Pharisees Who Impose Reason on Reality, 2002; Is ET Here?: No Politically But Yes Scientifically and Theologically, 2005; A Theology of Science: From Science to Ethics to an Ethical Politics, 2007. Contributor to journals. **Address:** Department of Social Sciences and Philosophy, Northern Kentucky University, LA 228, Highland Heights, KY 41099, U.S.A. **Online address:** trundle@nku.edu

TRUPP, Claudia. American (born United States), b. 1968?. **Genres:** Law. **Career:** Lawyer, through 1997; Center for Appellate Litigation, senior appellate counsel, 1997-. Writer. **Publications:** Hard Time & Nursery Rhymes: A Mother's Tales of Law and Disorder, 2009. **Address:** NJ , U.S.A. **Online address:** ctrupp@claudiatrupp.com

TRUSCOTT, Peter. British (born England), b. 1959. **Genres:** Administration/Management. **Career:** Labour Party, organizer, 1986-89; Colchester Borough Council, councilor, 1988-92; European Parliament, representative, 1994-99; Life peer, 2004-; Department of Trade and Industry, parliamentary under-secretary of state for energy, 2006-07; Institute for Public Policy Research, visiting research fellow; Royal United Services Institute for Defence and Security Studies, associate fellow; Russian Federation, Parliamentary British council ambassador; mining consultant. Writer. **Publications:** Russia First: Breaking with the West, 1997; European Defence: Meeting the Strategic Challenge, 2000; Kursk: Russia's Lost Pride, 2002; Putin's Progress: A Biography of Russia's Enigmatic President, Vladimir Putin, 2004; The Ascendency of Political Risk Management and Its Implications for Global Security and Business Investment, 2006; European Energy Security, forthcoming. Contributor to periodicals. **Address:** Artillery Mansions, 75 Victoria St., Ste. 31, London, GL SW1H 0HZ, England.

TRZEBINSKI, Errol. Kenyan/British (born England), b. 1936. **Genres:** Documentaries/Reportage, Food And Wine, Autobiography/Memoirs, Biography, Literary Criticism And History, Criminology/True Crime. **Career:** Writer, 1977-. **Publications:** Silence Will Speak: A Study of the Life of Denys Finch Hatton and His Relationship with Karen Blixen, 1977; The Kenya Pioneers, 1985; The Lives of Beryl Markham: Out of Africa's Hidden Spirit and Denys Finch Hatton's Last Great Love, 1993, rev. ed. as The Lives of Beryl Markham: Out of Africa's Hidden Seductress: Denys Finch Hatton's Last Great Love, 1993; The Life and Death of Lord Erroll: The Truth behind the Happy Valley Murder, 2000; Barefoot at Shanzu, 2002. Contributor to books. Works appear in anthologies. **Address:** PO Box 84045, Mombasa, 485550, Kenya.

TRZYNADLOWSKI, Andrzej M. American/Polish (born Poland), b. 1941. **Genres:** Engineering, Technology. **Career:** Technical University of Wroclaw, staff, 1966-79; University of Salahuddin, visiting professor, 1980-82; University of Texas, visiting professor, 1983-84; University of Wyoming, assistant professor of electrical engineering, 1984-87; University of Nevada, Department of Electrical and Biomedical Engineering, associate professor, professor of electrical and biomedical engineering, 1987-, Industrial Assessment Center, assistant director, 1993-97; Aalborg University, Danfoss visiting professor, 1997; Naval Surface Warfare Center, summer faculty research fellow, 1998. Author. **Publications:** (With R. Naukowi, F. Andrzejewski and T. Kurowski) Naped elektryczny urzadzeń przewijakowych: 15-17 IX 1977, 1977; The Field Orientation Principle in Control of Induction Motors, 1994; Introduction to Modern Power Electronics, 1998, 2nd ed., 2010; Control of Induction Motors, 2001. Contributor to journals. **Address:** University of Nevada, 332 Scrugham Engineering/Mines Bldg., PO Box 260, Reno, NV 89557-0260, U.S.A. **Online address:** chin@engr.unr.edu

TSADIK, Daniel. American (born United States), b. 1969?. **Genres:** History. **Career:** Yeshiva University, assistant professor of Sephardic and Iranian studies; Hebrew University of Jerusalem, lecturer; Tel-Aviv University, Dayan Center for the Research of Islam and the Middle East, fellow; University of Pennsylvania, Center for Advanced Judaic Studies, fellow; Yale University, visiting assistant professor. Writer. **Publications:** Between Foreigners and Shi'is: Nineteenth-Century Iran and Its Jewish Minority, 2007. **Address:** Yeshiva University, 500 W 185th St., New York, NY 10033, U.S.A. **Online address:** tsadikim@yahoo.com

TSAI, Kellee S. American (born United States), b. 1968. **Genres:** Politics/Government, Economics. **Career:** Morgan Stanley & Company Inc., financial analyst, 1990-92; Women's World Banking, consultant, 1992-97; Emory University, assistant professor of political science, 1999-2000; World Bank, consultant, 2000-; Johns Hopkins University, assistant professor, 2001-06, associate professor, 2006-07, professor of political science, 2007-. Writer. **Publications:** Back-Alley Banking: Private Entrepreneurs in China, 2002; (ed. with S.M. Pekkanen) Japan and China in the World Political Economy, 2005; Capitalism without Democracy: The Private Sector in Contemporary China, 2007. Contributor of articles to journals and periodicals. **Address:** Department of Political Science, Johns Hopkins University, 3400 N Charles St., Baltimore, MD 21218, U.S.A. **Online address:** ktsai@jhu.edu

TSALOUMAS, Dimitris. Australian/Greek (born Greece), b. 1921. **Genres:** Poetry, Translations. **Career:** Department of Victoria Education (Australia), teacher of English and modern languages, 1958-82, retired, 1982; Oxford University, writer-in-residence, 1989; University of Melbourne, writer-in-residence; La Trobe University, writer-in-residence; University of Queensland, writer-in-residence. **Publications:** (Ed. and trans.) Contemporary Australian Poetry, 1986; (ed. and intro.) Selected Poems, 1972-1986, 1987; Falcon Drinking; The English Poems, 1988; Portrait of a Dog and Other Classical Bagatelles, 1991; Observatory, 1991; The Barge, 1993; Taxidi: 1963-1992, 1995; Six Improvisations on the River, 1995; The Harbour, 1998; Stoneland Harvest, 1999; New and Selected Poems, 2000; Helen of Troy: And Other Poems, 2007. **Address:** 72 Glenhuntly Rd., Elwood, VI 3184, Australia.

TSETSKHLADZE, Gocha R(evazi). British (born England), b. 1963. **Genres:** Archaeology/Antiquities, Classics. **Career:** Research Institute, research assistant, 1988; British Broadcasting Corp., Russian Service of World Service, special correspondent, 1991-92; University of London, Royal Holloway and Bedford New College, academic staff, 1994-2004, Jubilee fellow, 1994-95, British Academy Institution, research fellow, 1996-2000, lecturer in classical studies and archaeology, 2000-01, reader in classical archaeology, 2002-04; British Excavation, director, 1995-2001; International Congress on Black Sea Antiquities, Pontic Congress, secretary general, 1994-; Colloquia Pontica, series editor, 1995-2006; University of Copenhagen, Institute of Archaeology and Ethnology, visiting professor, 1998; Ancient West & East

(journal), editor-in-chief, 2002-; University of Melbourne, Centre for Classics and Archaeology, faculty, 2004-, associate professor and reader in classical archaeology; University of Melbourne Excavation, director, 2008-; University of Oxford, Institute of Archaeology, visiting senior research fellow; University of British Columbia, visiting professor, 2006; University of Chicago, visiting professor, 2006; University of Pennsylvania, visiting professor, 2006; University of Texas, visiting professor, 2006; Javakhishvili Tbilisi State University, visiting professor, 2009-. **Publications:** Die Griechen in der Kolchis: Historisch-archäologischer Abris, 1998; Pichvnari and Its Environs: 6th c. BC-4th c. AD, 1999; Karadeniz'in Tarih Ve Arkeolojisi Uzerine, 2005; The Eastern Edge of the Ancient Known World: A Brief Introduction to Black Sea Archaeology and History, 2007. EDITOR: (with F. De Angelis) The Archaeology of Greek Colonisation: Essays Dedicated to Sir John Boardman, 1994; New Studies on the Black Sea Littoral, 1996; Greek Colonisation of the Black Sea Area: Historical Interpretation of Archaeology, 1998; Ancient Greeks West and East, 1999; (with J. Boardman and intro.) S.L. Solovyov, Ancient Berezan: The Architecture, History and Culture of the First Greek Colony in the Northern Black Sea, 1999; (with A.J.N.W. Prag and A.M. Snodgrass) Periplous: Papers on Classical Art and Archaeology Presented to Sir John Boardman, 2000; North Pontic Archaeology: Recent Discoveries and Studies, 2001; (with A.M. Snodgrass) Greek Settlements in the Eastern Mediterranean and the Black Sea, 2001; Greek Pottery from the Iberian Peninsula, 2001; (with J. Boardman and S.L. Solovyov) Northern Pontic Antiquities in the State Hermitage Museum, 2001; (with J. de Boer) The Black Sea in the Greek, Roman and Byzantine Periods, 2002; Attic Fine Pottery of the Archaic to Hellenistic Periods in Phanagoria, 2004; Greek Colonisation: An Account of Greek Colonies and Other Settlements Overseas, vol. I, 2006, vol. II, 2008; The Black Sea, Greece, Anatolia and Europe in the First Millennium BC, 2011. **Address:** Center for Classics & Archaeology, University of Melbourne, Rm. 128, Old Quadrangle, Melbourne, VI 3010, Australia. **Online address:** g.tsetskhladze@unimelb.edu.au

TSIPENYUK, Yuri M. Russian/Ukranian (born Ukraine), b. 1938. **Genres:** Physics. **Career:** Russian Academy of Science, P. L. Kapitza Institute for Physical Problems, research assistant, research associate, research, senior research, advanced research fellow, 1962-; Moscow Institute of Physics and Technology, Soros professor, 1997. Writer. **Publications:** Principles and Methods of Nuclear Physics, 1993; The Physical Background of Superconductivity, 1996; Nuclear Methods in Science and Technology, 1997; The Microtron: Development and Applications, 2002; Fundamental nye i prikladnye issledovaniiana mikrotone, 2009. Contributor to journals. **Address:** P.L. Kapitza Institute for Physical Problems, Russian Academy of Science, Kosygina 2, Moscow, 117334, Russia. **Online address:** tsip@kapitza.ras.ru

TSOMO, Karma Lekshe. American (born United States), b. 1944?. **Genres:** Adult Non-fiction, Cultural/Ethnic Topics, Theology/Religion, Women's Studies And Issues, Humanities, Philosophy. **Career:** Jamyang Choling Institute of Buddhist Studies, director, 1988-; University of Hawaii, Buddhist Studies Program, researcher, 1991-95; East-West Center, fellow in cultural studies, 1993-2000; Antioch University, instructor, 1995-96; Chaminade University, instructor, 1996-2000; University of San Diego, Department of Theology and Religious Studies, assistant professor, 2000-, associate professor; Sakyadhita, International Association of Buddhist Women, president. Writer. **Publications:** (Trans.) Jorcho: Preparatory Practices, 1994; Sisters in Solitude: Two Traditions of Buddhist Monastic Ethics for Women, 1996; Into the Jaws of Yama, Lord of Death: Buddhism, Bioethics, and Death, 2006; Buddhist Women in a Global Multicultural Community, 2009. EDITOR: Sakyadhītā: Daughters of the Buddha, 1988; Buddhism through American Women's Eyes, 1995; Sisters in Solitude: Two Traditions of Buddhist Monastic Ethics for Women: A Comparative Analysis of the Chinese Dharmagupta and the Tibetan Mūlāsarvāstivada Bhikṣuṇī Prātimokṣa Sūtras, 1996; Buddhist Women across Cultures: Realizations, 1999; Innovative Buddhist Women Swimming against the Stream, 2000; Buddhist Women and Social Justice: Ideals, Challenges, and Achievements, 2004; Discipline and Practice of Buddhist Women Past and Present, 2004; Bridging Worlds: Buddhist Women's Voices across Generations, 2004; Out of the Shadows: Socially Engaged Buddhist Women, 2006. **Address:** Department of Theology and Religious Studies, University of San Diego, 5998 Alcala Pk., Maher 295, San Diego, CA 92110-2492, U.S.A. **Online address:** ktsomo@sandiego.edu

TSUI, Bonnie. American (born United States), b. 1977. **Genres:** History, Women's Studies And Issues. **Career:** Let's Go Inc., travel writer-Greece, 1999; Advertising Age, trends and features reporter, 2000-01; Blue, contributing editor, 2000-01; Travel + Leisure, associate editor, 2001-03. **Publications:** She Went to the Field: Women Soldiers of the Civil War, 2003; (ed.) A Leaky Tent Is a Piece of Paradise: Twenty Young Writers on Finding a Place in the Natural World, 2007; American Chinatown: A People's History of Five Neighborhoods, 2009. Contributor to books and periodicals. **Address:** c/o William Clark, Wm. Clark Associates, 186 5th Ave., New York, NY 10010, U.S.A. **Online address:** bonnie@bonnietsui.com

TSUJI, Shinichi. *See* **OIWA**, Keibo.

TSUSHIMA, Satoko. (Yūko Tsushima). Japanese (born Japan), b. 1947. **Genres:** Novels, Novellas/Short Stories, Literary Criticism And History. **Career:** University of Paris, Institute of Occidental Languages, lecturer in Japanese literature, 1991-92. Writer. **Publications:** NOVELS: Doji no Kage, 1973; Ikimono no Atsumaru Ie, 1973; Choji, 1978, trans. as Child of Fortune, 1983; Hikari no Ryobun, 1979; Moeru Kaze, 1980; Yama o Hashiru Onna, 1980; Hi no Kawa no Hotori de, 1983; Yoru no Hikari ni Owarete, 1986; Mahiru e, 1988; Oinatu Yumeyo, Hikariyo, 1991; Woman Running in the Mountains, 1991; Kaze yo, Sora Kakeru Kaze yo, 1995; Hino YamaYamazanuki, 1999; Watai Ookami, 2000. SHORT STORIES: Shanikusai, 1971; Danmariichi, 1974; Waga Chichitachi, 1975; Mugura no Haha, Kawaide Shobo, 1975; Kusa no Fushido, Kodansha, 1977; Yorokobi no Shima, 1978; Saigo no Shuryo, 1979; Hyogen, 1979; Suifu, 1982; Oma Monogatari, 1984; The Shooting Gallery, 1986; Yume no Kiroku, 1988; Kagayaku Mizu no jidai, 1994; Watashi, 1999. OTHER: Tomei Kukan ga Mieru Toki, 1977; Yoru no Tii Paati, 1979; Nani ga Seikaku o Tsukuruka, 1979; Yoru to Asa no Tegami, 1980; Watakushi no Jikan, 1982; Shosetsu no Naka no Fukei, 1982; Osanaki Hibi e, 1986; Hon no Naka no Shojotachi, 1989; Kusamura, 1989; Ise Monogatari, 1990; (contrib.) Margaret Drabble in Tokyo, 1991; Izumi Kyōka, 1992; (intro.) Tombent, tombent les gouttes d'argen, 1996; Shitto, 1997; Watashi no Ain, watashi na yame, 1999; (contrib.) Pour un autre roman japonais, 2005; (contrib.) San i innūn chip umul i innūn chip, 2007; Laughing Wolf, 2011. Contributor to periodicals. **Address:** Eneterprise Publishers, 1-7-12 Kanda-Jinmbocho, Chiyoda-ku, Tokyo, 101-0051, Japan. **Online address:** tatemi-sakai@ma.neweb.ne.jp

TSUSHIMA, Yūko. *See* **TSUSHIMA**, Satoko.

TSUTSUI, William M. American (born United States), b. 1963. **Genres:** History, Humanities, Area Studies, Film. **Career:** Hitotsubashi University, visiting researcher, 1991-92; University of Kansas, Department of History, assistant professor, 1993-99, associate professor of history, 1999-2006, professor of history, 2006-10, chair, 2007-08, Center for East Asian Studies, acting director, 1999-2001, 2004, College of Liberal Arts and Sciences, associate dean for international studies, 2008-10; Southern Methodist University, professor of history, 2010-, Dedman College of Humanities and Sciences, dean, 2010-. Writer. **Publications:** Banking Policy in Japan: American Efforts at Reform during the Occupation, 1988, rev. ed., 2010; Manufacturing Ideology: Scientific Management in Twentieth-Century Japan, 1998; (ed. and intro.) Banking in Japan, 1999; Godzilla on My Mind: Fifty Years of the King of Monsters, 2004; (ed. with M. Ito) In Godzilla's Footsteps: Japanese Pop Culture Icons on the Global Stage, 2006; (ed. and intro.) A Companion to Japanese History, 2007; Japanese Popular Culture and Globalization, 2010; (ed. with M. Baskett) The East Asian Olympiads: Building Bodies and Nations in Japan, Korea, and China, 2010. **Address:** Dedman College of Humanities and Sciences, Southern Methodist University, PO Box 750235, Dallas, TX 75275, U.S.A. **Online address:** btsutsui@smu.edu

TUAOLO, Esera. American (born United States), b. 1968. **Genres:** Autobiography/Memoirs, Sports/Fitness, Young Adult Non-fiction. **Career:** Writer. **Publications:** (With J. Rosengren) Alone in the Trenches: My Life As a Gay Man in the NFL (autobiography), 2006. **Address:** c/o Author Mail, Sourcebooks Inc., 1935 Brookdale Rd., Ste. 139, Naperville, IL 60563, U.S.A.

TUBB, Jonathan N. British (born England), b. 1951?. **Genres:** Archaeology/Antiquities. **Career:** Tell Nebi Mend, assistant director, 1976-82; British Museum, project director, 1984-, Tell es-Sa'idiyeh (ancient Zarethan) Jordan, director of museum's excavations, 1985-, Department of Western Asiatic, Syria-Palestine Section, curator, Department of the Middle East, assistant keeper. Writer. **Publications:** (Ed.) Palestine in the Bronze and Iron Ages: Papers in Honour of Olga Tufnell, 1985; Archeology and the Bible, 1990; Excavations at the Early Bronze Age Cemetery of Tiwal esh-Sharqi, 1990; Bible Lands, 1991; Canaanites, 1998, rev. ed., 2006. Contributor to journals. **Address:** Department of the Middle East, British Museum, London, GL WC1B 3DG, England. **Online address:** jtubb@thebritishmuseum.ac.uk

TUBB, Kristin O'Donnell. American (born United States), b. 1971. **Genres:** Children's Fiction, Art/Art History. **Career:** Author. **Publications:** The Bill of Rights: Freedom from Cruel and Unusual Punishment, 2005; Sunny Days, 2006; Craft Corner Art Studio, 2007; Autumn Winifred Oliver Does Things Different, 2008; Selling Hope, 2010; The 13th Sign, 2013. **Address:** Franklin, TN , U.S.A. **Online address:** ktubb@comcast.net

TUBE, Henry. *See* **SPURLING**, John.

TUCCILLO, Liz. American (born United States), b. 1963?. **Genres:** Novels, Self Help. **Career:** Home Box Office, executive story editor. Actress. **Publications:** (With G. Behrendt) He's Just Not That into You: The No-Excuses Truth to Understanding Guys (self-help book), 2004; (with G. Behrendt) He's Just Not That into You: Your Daily Wake-Up Call, 2005; How to be Single: A Novel, 2008. Contributor to periodicals. **Address:** c/o Author Mail, Simon Spotlight Publicity Department, Simon and Schuster Inc., 1230 Ave. of the Americas, New York, NY 10020, U.S.A.

TUCK, Lily. American/French (born France), b. 1938. **Genres:** Novels, Young Adult Non-fiction. **Career:** Writer. **Publications:** NOVELS: Interviewing Matisse; or, The Woman Who Died Standing Up, 1991; Woman Who Walked on Water, 1996; Siam, or, The Woman Who Shot a Man, 1999; The News from Paraguay, 2004. COLLECTION: Limbo, and Other Places I have Lived: Stories, 2002. NON FICTION: Woman of Rome: A Life of Elsa Morante, 2008; I Married You for Happiness, 2011. Contributor to periodicals. **Address:** Georges Borchardt Inc., 136 E 57th St., 14th Fl., New York, NY 10022-2940, U.S.A.

TUCKER, (Allan) James. Also writes as Judith Jones, David Craig, Bill James. Welsh (born Wales), b. 1929. **Genres:** Novels, Literary Criticism And History, Mystery/Crime/Suspense. **Career:** Western Mail, leader writer, 1954-56; Daily Mirror, reporter, 1956-58. Educator. **Publications:** Equal Partners, 1960; The Righthand Man, 1961; Burster, 1966; Honourable Estates, 1966; The Novels of Anthony Powell, 1976; Blaze of Riot, 1979; The King's Friend, 1982. AS DAVID CRAIG: The Alias Man, 1968; Message Ends, 1969; Contact Lost, 1970; Young Men May Die, 1970; A Walk at Night, 1971; Up from the Grave, 1971; Double Take, 1972; Bolthole, 1973; Knifeman, 1973; The Squeeze, 1974; Whose Little Girl Are You?, 1974; A Dead Liberty, 1974; The Albion Case, 1975; Faith, Hope and Death, 1976; Forget It, 1995; The Tattooed Detective, 1998; Torch, 1999; Bay City, 2000; Hear Me Talking to You, 2005. AS BILL JAMES: You'd Better Believe It, 1985; The Lolita Man, 1986; Halo Parade, 1987; Protection, 1988; Come Clean, 1989; Take, 1990; Club, 1991; Astride a Grave, 1991; Roses, Roses, 1993; In Good Hands, 1994; The Detective Is Dead, 1995; Top Banana, 1996; Panicking Ralph, 1997; Gospel, 1997; The Last Enemy, 1997; Lovely Mover, 1999; Eton Crop, 1999; Kill Me, 2000; Pay Days, 2001; Split, 2001; Double Jeopardy, 2001; Middleman, 2002; Naked at the Window, 2002; Between Lives, 2003; The Girl with the Long Back, 2003; Man's Enemies, 2003; Easy Streets, 2005; Wolves of Memory, 2005; The Sixth Man and Other Stories, 2006; Making Stuff Up, 2006; Letters from Carthage, 2007; Girls, 2007; Pix, 2007; Off-street Parking, 2008. AS JUDITH JONES: Baby Talk, 1998; After Melissa, 1999. **Address:** Curtis Brown Group Ltd., 28-29 Haymarket House, 5th Fl., London, GL SW1Y 4SP, England.

TUCKER, Cynthia Grant. American (born United States), b. 1941. **Genres:** Women's Studies And Issues, Biography, History, Autobiography/Memoirs. **Career:** University of Memphis, assistant professor, 1967-75, director of program in comparative literature, 1971-75, 1980-82, associate professor, 1975-81, professor of English, 1981-, director of graduate studies in English, 1988-90. Writer. **Publications:** Kate Freeman Clark: A Painter Rediscovered, 1981; A Woman's Ministry: Mary Collson's Search for Reform as a Unitarian Minister, Hull House Social Worker and Christian Science Practitioner, 1984; Prophetic Sisterhood: Liberal Women Ministers of the Frontier, 1880-1930, 1990; A Guide for Group Discussion or Independent Study of Prophetic Sisterhood: Liberal Women Ministers of the Frontier, 1880-1930, 1990; Right Relationships: Right Remembering: A Talk, 1990; Prophetic Sisterhood: A Study Guide, 1993; Healer in Harm's Way: Mary Collson, A Clergywoman in Christian Science, 1994; Spirited Threads: A Fabric Artist's Passion for Life: The Art and Writings of Patricia Roberts Cline, 1997;

No Silent Witness: The Eliot Parsonage Women and Their Unitarian World, 2010. **Address:** Department of English, University of Memphis, Patterson 423, 467 Patterson Hall, Memphis, TN 38152-3530, U.S.A. **Online address:** cgtucker@nosilentwitness.org

TUCKER, Ernest S. American (born United States), b. 1961. **Genres:** History, Translations. **Career:** U.S. Naval Academy, professor of Middle Eastern and Central Asian history. Writer. **Publications:** (Ed. and trans. with T. Sanders and G. Hamburg) Russian-Muslim Confrontation in the Caucasus: Alternative Visions of the Conflict between Imam Shamil and the Russians, 1830-1859, 2004; Nadir Shah's Quest for Legitimacy in Post-Safavid Iran, 2006; Middle East in Modern World History, 2011. Contributor to periodicals. **Address:** Department of History, U.S. Naval Academy, Sampson Hall, 101 Cooper Rd., Annapolis, MD 21402-5027, U.S.A. **Online address:** tucker@usna.edu

TUCKER, Helen. American (born United States), b. 1926. **Genres:** Novels, Novellas/Short Stories, Human Relations/Parenting, Romance/Historical. **Career:** Times-News, reporter, 1946-49; Statesman, reporter, 1950-51; Radio KDYL, copywriter, 1951-52; Radio WPTF, continuity supervisor, 1953-55; Raleigh Times, reporter, 1955-57; Columbia University Press, editorial assistant, 1959-60; North Carolina Museum of Art, director of publicity and publications, 1967-70. **Publications:** Remembrance, 1951; The Sound of Summer Voices, 1969; The Sound of Summer Glory, 1969; The Guilt of August Fielding, 1971; Horch, die Stimmen des Sommers, 1971; No Need of Glory, 1972; The Virgin of Lontano, 1973; A Strange and Ill-Starred Marriage, 1978; A Reason for Rivalry, 1979; A Mistress to the Regent, 1980; An Infamous Attachment, 1980; The Halverton Scandal, 1980; A Wedding Day Deception, 1981; The Double Dealers, 1982; Season of Dishonor, 1982; Ardent Vows, 1983; Bound by Honor, 1984; The Lady's Fancy, 1991; Bold Impostor, 1991. Contributor to periodicals and magazines. **Address:** Curtis Brown Ltd., 10 Astor Pl., New York, NY 10003, U.S.A.

TUCKER, Jennifer. American (born United States), b. 1965?. **Genres:** Art/Art History, Photography. **Career:** Wesleyan University, Department of History, assistant professor, associate professor of history, of science in society and of feminist, gender and sexuality studies, chair of feminist, gender and sexuality studies. Writer. **Publications:** Nature Exposed: Photography as Eyewitness in Victorian Science, 2005. **Address:** Science in Society Program, Wesleyan University, Middletown, CT 06459-0029, U.S.A. **Online address:** jtucker@wesleyan.edu

TUCKER, Judy H. (Judy Hall Tucker). American (born United States), b. 1939. **Genres:** Plays/Screenplays, Novellas/Short Stories, Literary Criticism And History, Theology/Religion, Autobiography/Memoirs. **Career:** Writer. **Publications:** PLAYS: (ed. and contrib. with W. Waters and C.R. McCord) Christmas Stories from Mississippi, 2001; (ed. with C.R. McCord) A Very Southern Christmas: Stories for the Holidays, 2003; (ed. with C.R. McCord) Christmas in the South, 2004; (ed. with W. Waters and C.R. McCord) Dixie Christmas, 2005; (ed. with C.R. McCord) Growing up in Mississippi, 2008; (ed. with C.R. McCord) Christmas Stories from the South's Best Writers, 2008; (ed. with C.R. McCord) Christmas Memories from Mississippi, 2010. Contributor of articles to periodicals. **Address:** 6019 Lake Trace Cir., Jackson, MS 39211, U.S.A. **Online address:** dtucker3@jam.rr.com

TUCKER, Judy Hall. *See* **TUCKER, Judy H.**

TUCKER, Karen. American (born United States), b. 1952. **Genres:** Astronomy, Sciences, Social Sciences. **Career:** Writer. **Publications:** WITH W.H. TUCKER: The Cosmic Inquirers: Modern Telescopes and Their Makers, 1986; The Dark Matter: Contemporary Science's Quest for the Mass Hidden in Our Universe, 1988; Revealing the Universe: The Making of the Chandra X-ray Observatory, 2001. **Address:** PO Box 266, Bonsall, CA 92003, U.S.A.

TUCKER, Lisa. American (born United States) **Genres:** Novels. **Career:** Bryn Mawr College, writing instructor and math teacher; University of Pennsylvania, faculty of creative writing; University of California, faculty of creative writing. Writer. **Publications:** NOVELS: The Song Reader, 2003; Shout Down the Moon, 2004; Once upon a Day, 2006; The Cure for Modern Life, 2008; The Promised World, 2009; The Winters in Bloom, 2011. Contributor to books and periodicals. **Address:** c/o Marly Rusoff, Marly Rusoff & Associates Inc., 811 Palmer Rd., Ste. AA, PO Box 524, Bronxville, NY 10708, U.S.A. **Online address:** lisa.tucker.mail@gmail.com

TUCKER, Martin. American (born United States), b. 1928. **Genres:** Poetry, Literary Criticism And History, Essays, Writing/Journalism, History, Bibliography. **Career:** Transradio Press, radio newswriter, 1950-51; Associated Press, radio newswriter, 1955; Long Island University, assistant professor, 1962-66, associate professor, 1966-68, professor of English, 1968-, now professor emeritus, Confrontation Magazine, co-founding editor, editor-in-chief. **Publications:** (Contrib.) Vocabularies in Special Fields, 1966; Africa in Modern Literature: A Survey of Contemporary Writing in English, 1967; (intro.) James Ngugi, 1969; (intro.) Olive Schreiner, 1972; (intro.) Undine, 1972; Joseph Conrad, 1976; Homes of Locks and Mysteries (poetry), 1982; Literary Exile in the Twentieth Century, 1991; Sam Shepard, 1992; Attention Spans (poetry), 1996; While there is Time: Penultimate Poems, 2005; Plenty of Exits, 2008; (with A. Russo) Boundaries of Exile, Conditions of Hope, 2009. EDITOR: (with R.Z. Temple) A Library of Literary Criticism: Modern British Literature, 3 vols., 1966, vol. IV (with R. Stein), 1974, (with J. Ferres) vol. V, 1975; Moulton's Library of Literary Criticism, 4 vols., 1968; (with R.Z. Temple) A Bibliography of Modern British Literature, 1968; Twentieth-Century Criticism of English and American Literature, 3 vols., 1971; The Critical Temper: A Survey of Modern Criticism on English and American Literature from the Beginnings to the Twentieth Century, 4 vols., 1979, vol. V, 1989; (comp. with J. Ferres) Modern Commonwealth Literature, 1977; Literary Exile in the Twentieth Century: An Analysis and Biographical Dictionary, 1991; Modern American Literature, 1998. **Address:** Confrontation Magazine, Long Island University, 720 Northern Blvd., Brookville, NY 11548-1300, U.S.A. **Online address:** mtucker277@aol.com

TUCKER, Michael. American (born United States), b. 1944. **Genres:** Food And Wine, Autobiography/Memoirs, Human Relations/Parenting, Biography. **Career:** Writer. **Publications:** I Never Forget a Meal: An Indulgent Reminiscence, 1995; Living in a Foreign Language: A Memoir of Food, Wine, and Love in Italy, 2007; Family Meals: Coming Together to Care for an Aging Parent, 2009. Contributor to periodicals. **Address:** Stone Manners Agency, 900 Broadway, Ste. 803, New York, NY 10003-1229, U.S.A.

TUCKER, Neely. American (born United States), b. 1963. **Genres:** Autobiography/Memoirs, Human Relations/Parenting. **Career:** Oxford Eagle, journalist; Miami Herald, journalist; Detroit Free Press, foreign correspondent; Washington Post, staff writer, 2000-. **Publications:** Love in the Driest Season: A Family Memoir, 2004. **Address:** c/o Washington Post, 1150 15th St. NW, Washington, DC 20071, U.S.A.

TUCKER, Spencer C. American (born United States), b. 1937. **Genres:** History, Military/Defense/Arms Control. **Career:** University of North Carolina, part-time instructor in history, 1962-65; Wake Forest University, instructor in history, 1965; University of Maryland, assistant professorial lecturer in history, 1966-67; Texas Christian University, assistant professor, associate professor, 1967-90, professor of history, 1990-97, department head, 1992-97; Smithsonian Institution, visiting research associate, 1969-70; Virginia Military Institute, John Biggs professor and chair of military history, 1997-2003, professor emeritus, 2003-; ABC-CLIO, senior fellow of military history. Writer. **Publications:** Arming the Fleet: U.S. Naval Ordnance in the Muzzle-Loading Era, 1989; The Jeffersonian Gunboat Navy, 1993; (with F. Reuter) Injured Honor: The Chesapeake-Leopard Affair, 1996; Raphael Semmes and the Alabama, 1996; (with E. Olmstead and W. Stark) The Big Guns: Heavy Civil War Ordnance, 1997; The Great War, 1914-18, 1998; Vietnam, 1999; Andrew Foote: Civil War Admiral on Western Waters, 2000; Handbook of 19th Century Naval Warfare, 2000; Unconditional Surrender: The Capture of Forts Henry and Donelson, February 1862, 2001; Who's Who in 20th-Century Warfare, 2001; A Short History of the Civil War at Sea, 2002; Brigadier General John D. Imloden: Confederate Commander in the Shenandoah, 2003; Second World War, 2004; Tanks: An Illustrated History of Their Impact, 2004; Stephen Decatur: A Life most Bold and Daring, 2005; Blue & Gray Navies: The Civil War Afloat, 2006; Rise and Fight Again: The Life of Nathanael Greene, 2009. EDITOR and CONTRIBUTOR: The European Powers in the First World War: An Encyclopedia, 1996; Encyclopedia of the Vietnam War, 3 vols., 1998, 2nd ed., 2011; Encyclopedia of the Korean War, 3 vols., 2000, 2nd ed., 2010; Naval Warfare: An International Encyclopedia, 3 vols., 2002; Encyclopedia of American Military History, 2003; World War I: Encyclopedia, 2005; World War II: Student Encyclopedia, 2005; Encyclopedia of World War II: A Political, Social, and Military History, 2005; World War I: Student Encyclopedia, 2006; Encyclopedia of the Cold War: A Political, Social, and Military History, 2007; Encyclopedia of the Arab-Israeli Conflict: A Political, Social, and Military History, 2008; Cold War: A Student Encyclopedia,

2008; Encyclopedia of North American Colonial Conflicts to 1775: A Political, Social, and Military History, 2008; U.S. Leadership in Wartime: Clashes, Controversy and Compromise, 2009; Encyclopedia of the Spanish-American and Philippine-American Wars: A Political, Social and Military History, 2009; Battles That Changed History: An Encyclopedia of World Conflict, 2010; Encyclopedia Of Middle East Wars: The United States in the Persian Gulf, Afghanistan and Iraq Conflicts, 2010; Global Chronology of Conflict: From the Ancient World to the Modern Middle East, 2010; Civil War Naval Encyclopedia, 2011; The Encyclopedia of North American Indian Wars, 1607-1890, 2011. Works appear in anthologies. Contributor of articles to journals. **Address:** Department of History, Virginia Military Institute, 536 Scott Shipp Hall, Lexington, VA 24450, U.S.A. **Online address:** tuckersc@vmi.edu

TUCKER, William. American (born United States), b. 1942. **Genres:** Documentaries/Reportage, Social Sciences. **Career:** Rockland Journal-News, reporter, 1971-73; Bergen Evening Record, reporter, 1973-75; Rockland County Times, reporter, 1975-76; Harper's, contributing editor, 1978-81. **Publications:** Progress and Privilege: America in the Age of Environmentalism, 1982; Vigilante, The Backlash Against Crime in America, 1985; The Excluded Americans: Homelessness and Housing Policies, 1990; Zoning, Rent Control and Affordable Housing, 1991; (ed.) Sources of Indoor Air Contaminants: Characterizing Emissions and Health Impacts, 1992; (with N. Gingrich) To Renew America, 1995; Terrestrial Energy: How a Nuclear-Solar Alliance Can Rescue the Planet, 2007. Contributor to periodicals. **Address:** 498 13th St., Brooklyn, NY 11215, U.S.A. **Online address:** source@terrestrialenergy.org

TUCKER, William Edward. American (born United States), b. 1932. **Genres:** Theology/Religion, Biography. **Career:** Atlantic Christian College, associate professor, 1959-63, chairman of department of religion and philosophy, 1962-66, professor of religion, 1963-66; Barton College, Department of Religion and Philosophy, professor, 1959-66, chairman, 1961-66; Texas Christian University, assistant dean, 1966-69, associate dean, 1969-71, dean and professor of church history, 1971-76, Brite Divinity School, chancellor, 1979-98, chancellor emeritus, 1998-; Bethany College, president, 1976-79. Writer. **Publications:** J.H. Garrison and Disciples of Christ, 1964; (with L.G. McAllister) Journey in Faith: History of the Christian Church (Disciples of Christ), 1975. CONTRIBUTOR: The Word We Preach, 1970; The Westminster Dictionary of Church History, 1971; Dictionary of American Biography, Supplement Three, 1941-45, 1973; The Encyclopedia of Southern History, 1979. **Address:** Brite Divinity School, 2855 S University Dr., Fort Worth, TX 76129, U.S.A.

TUCKMAN, Bruce Wayne. American (born United States), b. 1938. **Genres:** Education, Psychology. **Career:** University of Maryland, University College, adjunct professor, 1963-65; Naval Medical Research Institute, research psychologist, 1963-65; American Association for the Advancement of Science, curriculum developer, 1965-67; Rutgers University, associate professor, 1965-70, professor of education, 1970-78, director of educational research, 1975-78; City University of New York, Bernard M. Baruch College, School of Education, dean and professor of education, 1978-82, Graduate School, University Center, senior research fellow, 1982-83; Florida State University, professor of education, 1983-98; Ohio State University, Walter E. Dennis Learning Center, professor of education and founding director of academic learning lab, 1998-, Faculty and TA Development, interim director, 1999-2000. Writer. **Publications:** (Ed. with J.L. O'Brien) Preparing to Teach the Disadvantaged: Approaches to Teacher Education, 1969; Conducting Educational Research, 1972, 5th ed., 1999; Measuring Educational Outcomes: Fundamentals of Testing, 1975; Analyzing and Designing Educational Research, 1979; Evaluating Instructional Programs, 1979, 2nd ed., 1985; (with F.C. Johnson) Effective College Management: The Outcome Approach, 1987; Testing for Teachers, 1988; Long Road to Boston, 1988; Educational Psychology: From Theory to Application, 1992; (with D.A. Abry and D.R. Smith) Learning and Motivation Strategies: Your Guide to Success, 2002, 2nd ed., 2008; Student Study Skills, 2004; (with D.M. Monetti) Educational Psychology, 2011. Contributor to journals. **Address:** Ohio State University, 250B Younkin Success Ctr., 1640 Neil Ave., Columbus, OH 43201-2333, U.S.A. **Online address:** tuckman.5@osu.edu

TUDGE, Colin. British (born England), b. 1943. **Genres:** Environmental Sciences/Ecology, Sciences, Animals/Pets. **Career:** New Scientist, features editor, 1980-85; BBC-Radio, Science Unit, presenter, 1985-90; freelance writer, 1990-; London Zoo Reform Group, co-founder, 1991; University of London, visiting research fellow, London School of Economics, Centre for the Philosophy of the Natural and Social Sciences, visiting research fellow, 1995-2005. **Publications:** The Famine Business, 1977; (with M. Allaby) Home Farm: Complete Food Self-Sufficiency, 1977; Future Cook, 1980; Future Food: Politics, Philosophy and Recipes for the 21st Century, 1980; The Food Connection, 1985; Food Crops for the Future: The Development of Plant Resources, 1988; (ed.) The Environment of Life, 1988; Global Ecology, 1991; Last Animals at the Zoo: How Mass Extinction Can Be Stopped, 1992; The Engineer in the Garden: Genes and Genetics: From the Idea of Heredity to the Creation of Life, 1993; The Day Before Yesterday, 1995; The Time before History: 5 Million Years of Human Impact, 1996; Neanderthals, Bandits and Farmers: How Agriculture Really Began, 1999; (with I. Wilmut and K. Campbell) The Second Creation: Dolly and the Age of Biological Control, 2000; The Variety of Life: A Survey and a Celebration of all the Creatures that Have Ever Lived, 2000; In Mendel's Footnotes: An Introduction to the Science and Technologies of Genes and Genetics From the Nineteenth Century to the Twenty-Second, 2000; The Impact of the Gene: From Mendel's Peas to Designer Babies, 2001; Food for the Future, 2002; So Shall We Reap, 2003; Secret Life of Trees, 2005; Tree: A Natural History of What Trees are, How They Live and Why They Matter, 2006; Feeding People is Easy, 2007; Bird, 2008; Consider the Birds: Who They are and What They Do, 2008; (with J. Young) The Link: Uncovering Our Earliest Ancestor, 2009. Contributor to magazines and newspapers. **Address:** Magdalen Cottage, High St., Hook Norton, OX OX15 5NH, England. **Online address:** colintudge@supanet.com

TUDOR, Andrew. British/Scottish (born Scotland), b. 1942. **Genres:** Film, Sociology, History, Social Sciences, Adult Non-fiction. **Career:** Loughton College of Further Education, lecturer in sociology, 1965-66; University of Essex, research officer, 1966-68, lecturer in sociology, 1968-70; University of York, lecturer, 1970-75, senior lecturer in sociology, 1975-90, head of department, 1988-95, reader in sociology 1991-2004, professor of sociology 2004-06, professor of theatre, film and television 2006-, now retired, part-time professor. Writer. **Publications:** Theories of Film, 1974; Image and Influence: Studies in the Sociology of Film, 1974; Beyond Empiricism: Philosophy of Science in Sociology, 1982; Monsters and Mad Scientists: A Cultural History of the Horror Movie, 1989; Decoding Culture: Theory and Method in Cultural Studies, 1999. **Address:** Department of Theatre, Film & Television, University of York, Baird Ln., Heslington, York, YO10 5DD, England. **Online address:** aft1@york.ac.uk

TUGENDHAT, Christopher (Samuel). British (born England), b. 1937. **Genres:** Business/Trade/Industry, Politics/Government, Social Sciences. **Career:** Financial Times, editorial writer, 1960-70; British Parliament, member of cities of London and Westminster, 1970-76; Sunningdale, board director, 1971-76; Phillips Petroleum International Ltd., staff, 1972-76; Commission of the European Communities, staff, 1977-; National Westminser Bank and BOC Group, director, 1985-; Civil Aviation Authority, chairman, 1986-91; Rio Tinto Ltd., staff, 1997-; University of Bath, chancellor, 1998-; Lehman Brothers Europe Ltd., chairman, 2002-. **Publications:** Oil: The Biggest Business, 1968, rev. ed., 1975; The Multinationals, 1971; Britain, Europe, and the Third World, 1976; Conservatives in Europe: A Personal View, 1979; Making Sense of Europe, 1986; (with W. Wallace) Options for British Foreign Policy in the 1990s, 1988; (contrib.) Roy Jenkins A Retrospective, 2004. **Address:** University of Bath, 25 Bank St., 30th Fl., Bath, BA2 7AY, United Kingdom.

TUGENDHAT, Julia. (Julia Dobson). British (born England), b. 1941. **Genres:** Children's Fiction, Children's Non-fiction, Novels, History, Romance/Historical. **Career:** Grey Coat School for Girls, history teacher, 1963-64; Peckham Manor School for Boys, history teacher, 1964-65; Time, secretary, 1965-66; Town, general writer, 1966-67; Glendower Primary School, teacher, 1967-71; writer, 1971-. Family therapist. **Publications:** (As Julia Dobson) The Children of Charles I (history), 1975; The Smallest Man in England (historical novel), 1977; Children of the Tower (history), 1978; They Were at Waterloo (history), 1979; The Ivory Poachers: A Crisp Twins Adventure (novel), 1981; The Tomb Robbers (novel), 1981; (as Julia Dobson) Mountbatten, Sailor Hero (history), 1982; The Wreck Finders (novel), 1982; The Animal Rescuers (novel), 1982; Danger In the Magic Kingdom (novel), 1983; The Chinese Puzzle (novel), 1984; (as Julia Dobson) Hélène Cixous and the Theatre, 2002. NON-FICTION: What Teenagers Can Tell Us About Divorce and Stepfamilies, 1990; The Adoption Triangle, 1992. **Address:** 1 Caroline Terr., London, GL SW1W 8JT, England.

TULCHIN, Joseph S. American (born United States), b. 1939. **Genres:** Area Studies, History, International Relations/Current Affairs, Politics/Government. **Career:** Cambridge University, visiting fellow, 1959-60; Harvard University, teaching assistant, 1962-64, David Rockefeller Center for Latin American Studies, visiting fellow, 2010-; Yale University, assistant professor of history, 1964-71; Universidad del Salvador, visiting lecturer, 1969-70; University of North Carolina, associate professor, professor of history, 1971-90, Office of International Programs, director, 1982-90; Woodrow Wilson International Center, Latin American Program, director, 1990-2006; Instituto Universitario Jose Ortega y Gasset, visiting professor, 1990-92; Georgetown University, School of Foreign Service, adjunct professor, 1990-92; Johns Hopkins University, School of Advanced International Studies, adjunct professor, 1992-96. Writer. **Publications:** The Aftermath of War, 1971; Argentina and the United States: A Conflicted Relationship, 1990. EDITOR: (with D.J. Danielski) The Autobiographical Notes of Charles Evans Hughes, 1972; Problems in Latin American History, 1972; Latin America in the Year 2000, 1975; Hemispheric Perspectives on the United States, 1978; (with H. Munoz) Latin American Nations in World Politics, 1984, 2nd ed., 1996; Habitat, Health and Development: A New Way of Looking at Cities in the Third World, 1986; Spain's Entry into NATO: Conflicting Political and Strategic Perspectives, 1988; Argentina and the United States: A Conflicted Relationship, 1990; (with R. Hernandez) Cuba and the United States: Will the Cold War in the Caribbean End?, 1991; (with A. Varas) From Dictatorship to Democracy: Rebuilding Political Consensus in Chile, 1991; (with M. Grow and W.P. Glade) Scholar's Guide to Washington, DC, for Latin Americana and Caribbean Studies, 1992; (with W. Baer) Brazil and the Challenge of Economic Reform, 1993; (with G. Bland) Venezuela in the Wake of Radical Reform, 1993; (with W. Baer) Brazil and the Challenge of Economic Reform, 1993; (with W. Baer) Brazil and the Challenge of Economic Reform, 1993; (with G. Bland) Venezuela in the Wake of Radical Reform, 1993; (with G. Bland) Peru in Crisis: Dictatorship or Democracy?, 1994; (with A. Serbín) El Caribe y Cuba en la posguerra fría, 1994; (with J.C. Chasteen) Problems in Modern Latin American History: A Reader, 1994; (with J.C. Chasteen) Problems in Modern Latin American History, 1994; (with F. Rojas) Strategic Balance and Confidence Building Measures in the Americas, 1998; (with A. Garland) Argentina: The Challenges of Modernization, 1998; (with M. Naim) Competition Policy, Deregulation and Modernization in Latin America, 1999; (with B. Romero) The Consolidation of Democracy in Latin America, 1995; (with A. Servin and R. Hernandez) Cuba and the Caribbean: Regional Issues and Trends in the Post-Cold War Era, 1997; (with A.M. Garland) Argentina: The Challenges of Modernization, 1998; (with M. Naim) Competition Policy, Deregulation and Modernization in Latin America, 1999; (with M. Naim) Competition Policy, Deregulation, and Modernization in Latin America, 1999; (with R.H. Espach) Security in the Caribbean Basin: The Challenge of Regional Cooperation, 1999; (with R. Espach) Latin America in the New International System, 2000; (with R.H. Espach) Combatting Corruption in Latin America, 2000; (with A.M. Garland) Social Development in Latin America: The Politics of Reform, 2000; (with C. Rosan and B.A. Ruble) Urbanization, Population, Environment, and Security; (with R.H. Espach) Latin America in the New International System, 2001; (with A. Brown) Democratic Governance and Social Inequality, 2002; (with A. Brown) Democratic Governance and Social Inequality, 2002; Citizen Security in Latin America, 2002; (with R.H. Espach and H.A. Golding) Paths to Regional Integration, 2002; (with A.D. Selee) Mexico's Politics and Society in Transition, 2003; (with H Frühling and H.A. Golding) Crime and Violence in Latin America, 2003; (co-ed.) Decentralization and Democratic Governance in Latin America, 2004; (with P. Oxhorn and A.D. Selee) Decentralization, democratic Governance, and Civil Society in Comparative Perspective, 2004; (with V.K. Aggarwal and R. Espach) The Strategic Dynamics of Latin American Trade, 2004; (with G. Bland) Getting Globalization Right, 2005; (with E. Bryan) Changes in Cuban Society Since The Nineties, 2005; (with M. Ruthenburg) Toward A Society Under Law, 2006; (with R.B. Manaut and R. Diamint) El rompecabezas, 2006; (with M. Ruthenburg) Citizenship in Latin America, 2007. **Address:** Latin American Program, Woodrow Wilson Ctr., 1 Woodrow Wilson Plz., 1300 Pennsylvania Ave. NW, Washington, DC 20004-3027, U.S.A. **Online address:** joseph.tulchin@wilsoncenter.org

TULGAN, Bruce L. American (born United States), b. 1967. **Genres:** Administration/Management, Economics. **Career:** RainmakerThinking Inc., founder, 1993-. Writer and lawyer. **Publications:** Managing Generation X: How to Bring Out the Best in Young Talent, 1995, rev. ed., 2000; The Manager's Pocket Guide to Generation X, 1997; (with J. Coombs) Strategic Employee Polls: The Step-by-Step Guide to Discovering What Your Employees Are Really Thinking, 1998; Work This Way: How 1000 Young People Designed Their Own Careers in the New Workplace and How You Can Too, 1998; (with C.A. Martin) Managing Generation Y: Global Citizens Born in the Late Seventies and Early Eighties, 2001; Winning the Talent Wars: How to Manage and Compete in the High-Tech, High-Speed, Knowledge-Based Superfluid Economy, 2001; (with C.A. Martin) Managing the Generation Mix: From Collision to Collaboration, 2002, 2nd ed. as Managing the Generation Mix: From Urgency to Opportunity, 2006; (with H.W. Sormaz) Performance under Pressure: Managing Stress in the Workplace, 2003; (with C.A. Martin) The Customer Service Intervention: Bottom-Line Tactics for Front-line Managers, 2003; It's Okay to Be the Boss: The Step-by-Step Guide to Becoming the Manager Your Employees Need, 2007; Not Everyone Gets a Trophy, 2009; It's Okay to Manage Your Boss, 2010. **Address:** RainmakerThinking Inc., 125 Lawrence St., New Haven, CT 06511-2543, U.S.A. **Online address:** bruce@rainmakerthinking.com

TULLOCH, Richard (George). Australian (born Australia), b. 1949. **Genres:** Plays/Screenplays, Children's Fiction. **Career:** National Theatre, associate director, 1979-80; Toe Truck Theatre, artistic director, 1981-83. Writer. **Publications:** PLAYS: Year 9 Are Animals, 1983; Face to Face, 1987; Hating Alison Ashley: The Play, 1988; Space Demons: The Play, 1990; The Cocky of Bungaree, 1991; Could Do Better, 1992; Stagefright, 1996. CHILDREN'S BOOKS: Stories from Our House, 1987; Stories from Our Street, 1989; Rain for Christmas, 1989; The Strongest Man in Gundiwallanup, 1990; The Brown Felt Hat, 1990; Danny in the Toybox, 1990; Being Bad for the Babysitter, 1991; Barry the Burglar's Last Job, 1992; Our New Old House, 1992; (with S. Hopkinson) Adventures with Bananas in Pajamas, 1996; (with S. Hopkinson) Magic Mystery, 1996; (with K. Wyld) Wishes and Dreams, 1996; Mr. Biffey's Battle, 1997. OTHERS: Awesome Stuff, 2005; Weird Stuff, 2006; Freaky Stuff, 2007; Talking to Grandma While the World Goes By. **Address:** Cameron's Management, 163 Brougham St., Woolloomooloo, NW 2011, Australia. **Online address:** richardtulloch@hotmail.com

TULLOS, Allen E. American (born United States), b. 1950. **Genres:** Area Studies, Social Commentary, Race Relations, Essays, Art/Art History, Music, Technology. **Career:** Smithsonian Festival of American Folklife, regional America fieldwork coordinator, 1975; Yale University, American art history, teaching assistant, 1977-79, American folklore, teaching assistant, 1979-80; University of North Carolina, Chapel Hill, project coordinator and research associate, 1978-80; Southern Changes, editor, 1982-2003, Graduate Certificate Program in Digital Scholarship and Media Studies, co-director; Emory University, assistant professor of American studies, 1986-92, associate professor, 1992-; Southern Spaces, senior editor, 2003-. **Publications:** (Ed. and contrib.) Long Journey Home: Folklife in the South, 1977; (contrib.) Growing Up Southern, 1981; The Habits of Industry: White Culture and the Transformation of the Carolina Piedmont, 1989; (contrib.) Lewis Mumford, Public Intellectual, 1990; (contrib.) Christenberry Reconstruction: The Art of William Christenberry, 1996; (contrib.) The New Regionalism, 1998; (contrib.) Blackwell Companion to Post-1945 America, 2002; Alabama Getaway: The Political Imaginary and the Heart of Dixie, 2010. Contributor to books. **Address:** Graduate Institute of the Liberal Arts, Emory University, S407-Callaway, 537 Kilgo Cir., Atlanta, GA 30322, U.S.A. **Online address:** allenet@aol.com

TULLSON, Diane. Canadian (born Canada), b. 1958?. **Genres:** Novels. **Career:** Canadian Living Magazine, writer; Westworld Magazine, writer. **Publications:** Saving Jasey, 2002; Edge, 2002; Blue Highway, 2004; Red Sea, 2005; Zero, 2006; The Darwin Expedition, 2007; Lockdown, 2008; Riley Park, 2009; Sea Change, 2010; Riot Act, 2012. **Address:** Fitzhenry & Whiteside Ltd., 195 Allstate Pkwy., Markham, ON L3R 4T8, Canada. **Online address:** diane@dianetullson.com

TULLY, Anthony P. American (born United States), b. 1961. **Genres:** History. **Career:** Information technology and support. Writer. **Publications:** (with J.B. Parshall) Shattered Sword: The Untold Story of the Battle of Midway, 2005. Contributor of articles to periodicals. **Address:** Dallas, TX , U.S.A. **Online address:** aptully@aol.com

TULLY, Paul. See GARDNER, Jerome.

TULLY, (William) Mark. Indian (born India), b. 1935. **Genres:** Travel/Exploration, Biography, Documentaries/Reportage, Young Adult Fiction, Theology/Religion. **Career:** British Broadcasting Corporation (BBC), personnel department staff, 1964-65, assistant representative, 1965-69, Eastern service, 1969-71, bureau chief, 1972-93, South Asia correspondent, 1993-94. Writer, freelance journalist and broadcaster. **Publications:** (With S. Jacob) Amritsar: Mrs. Gandhi's Last Battle, 1985; (with Z. Masani) From Raj to Rajiv, 1988;

(with Z. Masani) India: Forty Years of Independence, 1988; No Full Stops in India, 1991; The Defeat of a Congressman: And Other Parables of Modern India, 1992; (co-author) Great Railway Journeys, 1994; The Heart of India, 1995; An Investigation into the Lives of Jesus: God, Jew, Rebel, the Hidden Jesus, 1996; Four Faces: A Journey in Search of Jesus the Divine, the Jew, the Rebel, the Sage, 1997; (with G. Wright) India in Slow Motion, 2002; India's Unending Journey: Finding Balance in a Time of Change, 2007; India: The Road Ahead, 2011. **Address:** c/o Anand and Anand B-41, 1, Nizamuddin East, New Delhi, DH 110 013, India. **Online address:** tulwri@ndf.vsnl.net.in

TUMAN, Myron C(hester). American (born United States), b. 1946. **Genres:** Writing/Journalism, Humanities. **Career:** University of New Orleans, instructor, 1978-81; West Virginia University, assistant professor, 1981-85; University of Alabama, associate professor, 1985-92, professor, 1992-2003; Nicholls State University, professor of English, 2003-, Belle L. and Leonard J. Toups endowed chair in writing, 2003-06. Writer. **Publications:** MONOGRAPHS: A Preface to Literacy: An Inquiry into Pedagogy, Practice and Progress, 1987; Word Perfect: Literacy in the Computer Age, 1992; Language and Limits: Resisting Reform in English Studies, 1998; CriticalThinking.com: A Guide to Deep Thinking in a Shallow Age, 2002; Melville's Gay Father and the Knot of Filicidal Desire: On Men and Their Demons, 2006; Don Juan and His Daughter: The Incestuous Father in the Female Literary Imagination, 2009. EDITOR: Literacy Online: The Promise (and Peril) of Reading and Writing with Computers, 1992; Crossfire Reader, 1993; Visions: Readings for a Changing World, 2000. TEXTS AND SOFTWARE: Writing with Norton Textra: A Guide for Composing Online, 1991; (with D. Rodrigues) Writing Essentials, 1996, 2nd ed. 1999; (with D. Rodrigues) A Norton Pocket Guide to Grammar and Punctuation, 2006; CourseDocs Cloud Computing for College Composition, 2011. **Address:** Institutional Advancement, Nicholls State University, Picciolla Hall, PO Box 2066, Thibodaux, LA 70310, U.S.A. **Online address:** mtuman@sprynet.com

TUNGATE, Mark. French (born France), b. 1967. **Genres:** Communications/Media, Fash Ion/Costume, History. **Career:** Worth Global Style Network, Paris correspondent; Campaign Magazine, Paris correspondent; Parsons Paris School of Art and Design, lecturer. Freelance writer. **Publications:** The Best of European Advertising, 2004; Media Monoliths: How Great Media Brands Thrive and Survive, 2004; Fashion Brands: Branding Style from Armani to Zara, 2005; Fifty: The Amazing World of Renzo Rosso and Diesel, 2006; Adland: A Global History of Advertising, 2007; Branded Male: Marketing to Men, 2008; Luxury World: The Past, Present and Future of Luxury Brands, 2009. Contributor to periodicals. **Address:** Kogan Page, 1518 Walnut St., Philadelphia, 19102, France. **Online address:** tungateinparis@hotmail.com

TUNNELL, Michael O('Grady). American (born United States), b. 1950. **Genres:** Children's Fiction, Young Adult Fiction, Children's Non-fiction, Education, Literary Criticism And History, Young Adult Non-fiction, Picture/Board Books. **Career:** Uintah School District, sixth-grade teacher, 1973-75; Utah State University, Department of Instructional Media, graduate assistant, 1975-76; Wasatch School District, teacher and library and media specialist, 1976-83; Arkansas State University, assistant professor of elementary education, 1985-87; Northern Illinois University, assistant professor of language arts and children's literature, 1987-92, associate professor, 1992; Brigham Young University, associate professor, 1992-97, professor of children's literature, 1997-; writer, 1993-. **Publications:** FOR CHILDREN: The Prydain Companion: A Reference Guide to Lloyd Alexander's Prydain Chronicles, 1989; Chinook!, 1993; The Joke's on George, 1993; Beauty and the Beastly Children, 1993; (with G.W. Chilcoat) The Children of Topaz: The Story of a Japanese-American Internment Camp: Based on a Classroom Diary, 1996; Mailing May, 1997; School Spirits, 1997; Halloween Pie, 1999; Brothers in Valor: A Story of Resistance, 2001; Wishing Moon, 2004; Moon Without Magic, 2007; Candy Bomber: The Story of the Berlin Airlift's Chocolate Pilot, 2010. OTHERS: (with J.S. Jacobs) Lloyd Alexander: A Bio-Bibliography, 1991; (ed. with R. Ammon) The Story of Ourselves: Teaching History through Children's Literature, 1993; Children's Literature Database: A Resource for Teachers, Parents and Media Specialists, 1996, rev. ed., 2008; (with J.S. Jacobs) Children's Literature, Briefly, 1996, 4th ed., 2008; (with D.L. Darigan and J.S. Jacobs) Children's Literature: Engaging Children and Teachers in Good Books, 2002. Contributor to books, magazines and journals. **Address:** Department of Teacher Education, Brigham Young University, 201-K McKay Bldg., Provo, UT 84602, U.S.A. **Online address:** motunnell@msn.com

TUNSTALL, C. Jeremy. British (born England), b. 1934. **Genres:** Communications/Media, Sociology, Politics/Government, Technology. **Career:** London School of Economics, research officer, 1962-65; University of Essex, research fellow, 1965-69; Open University, senior lecturer in sociology, 1969-74; City University, professor of sociology, 1974-; Royal Commission on the Press, consultant, 1975-76. Writer. **Publications:** The Fishermen, 1962; The Advertising Man in London Advertising Agencies, 1964; Old and Alone: A Sociological Study of Old People, 1966; Fish: An Antiquated Industry, 1968; The Westminster Lobby Correspondents: A Sociological Study of National Political Journalism, 1970; (ed.) Media Sociology: A Reader, 1970; (ed. with K. Thompson and F.G. Castles) Sociological Perspectives: Selected Readings, 1971, 2nd ed., 1972; Journalists at Work: Special Correspondents, 1971; (with F.S. Brooman) Economy and Society, 1971; (with Brooman) Money, Wealth and Class, 1971; Stability, Change and Conflict, 1971; (ed.) The Open University Opens, 1974; The Media Are American: Anglo-American Media in the World, 1977; (with O. Boyd-Barrett and C. Seymour-Ure) Studies on the Press, 1977; (with D. Walker) Media Made in California: News, Politics, the New Hollywood, 1981; The Media in Britain, 1983; Communications Deregulation: The Unleashing of America's Communications Industry, 1986; (with M. Palmer) Liberating Communications: Policy-Making in France and Britain, 1990; (with M. Palmer) Media Moguls, 1991; Television Producers, 1993; Newspaper Power: The New National Press in Britain, 1996; (with D. Machin) The Anglo-American Media Connection, 1999; (ed.) Media Occupations and Professions: A Reader, 2001; The Media Were American: U.S. Mass Media in Decline, 2008. **Address:** 19 S Villas, Camden Sq., London, GL NW1 9BS, England.

TURAN, Kenneth. American (born United States), b. 1946. **Genres:** Film, Biography, Photography. **Career:** Fremont News-Register, general assignment reporter, 1968-69; Washington Post, sports writer, 1969-72, staff writer, Sunday Magazine, staff writer, 1972-75, Style Section, general cultural critic and feature writer, 1975-78; New West/California, book review editor, 1978-86, film critic, 1980-86; National Public Radio, film critic, 1982-86, Morning Edition, freelance film critic; Entertainment Coast-to-Coast, Columbia Broadcasting System Inc., Radio, film critic, 1984-86; TV Guide, staff writer, 1984-86; Gentleman's Quarterly, film critic and contributing editor, 1985-90; Los Angeles Times, book review editor, 1990-91, film critic, 1991-, director, 1993-; Monitor Radio, film critic, 1992-; University of Southern California, Master of Professional Writing Program, lecturer. **Publications:** (With W. Gildea) The Future is Now; George Allen, Pro Football's Most Controversial Coach, 1972; (with S. Wright and W. Gildea) I'd rather be Wright; Memoirs of an Itinerant Tackle, 1974. (with S.F. Zito) Sinema: American Pornographic Films and the People Who Make Them, 1974; (with P. Duke) Call Me Anna: The Autobiography of Patty Duke, 1987; Sundance to Sarajevo: Film Festivals and the World they Made, 2002; Never Coming to a Theater near You: A Celebration of a Certain Kind of Movie, 2004; Now in Theaters Everywhere: A Celebration of a Certain Kind of Blockbuster, 2006; (with J. Papp) Free for All: Joe Papp, the Public and the Greatest Theater Story Ever Told, 2009. Contributor to books. **Address:** c/o Kathy Robbins, Robbins Office Inc., 405 Park Ave., 9th Fl., New York, NY 10022, U.S.A. **Online address:** kturan@usc.edu

TURBET, Richard. British (born England), b. 1948. **Genres:** Music. **Career:** University of Calgary, research assistant, 1971-72; National Central Library, assistant librarian, 1972-74; Prison Service Staff College, librarian, 1974-77; University of Aberdeen, special collections cataloguer and music librarian, 1977-2009, retired, 2009, honorary research fellow, 2009-; Academy of Saint Cecilia, fellow, 2011. Writer. **Publications:** (With A. Morrisson) The Organ and Organists of St. Andrew's Cathedral, Aberdeen, 1981, 2nd ed., 1988; William Byrd: A Guide to Research, 1987, 2nd ed., 2006; (contrib.) Magnificat and Nunc Dimittis: From the Short Service, 1989; (contrib.) Venite, Te Deum & Benedictus: With the Responses to the Commandments: From the Short Service, 1989; William Byrd (1540-1623): Lincoln's Greatest Musician, 1993, 2nd ed., 1999; Tudor Music: A Research and Information Guide, 1993, 2nd ed., 2006. EDITOR: (with M. Walsh) Creed from the Short Service, 1989; (with A. Brown) Byrd Studies, 1992; Music Librarianship in the United Kingdom: Fifty Years of the British Branch of the International Association of Music Libraries, Archives and Documentation Centres, 2003. Contributor of articles to periodicals and journals. **Address:** 24 Cley Rd., Holt, NF NR25 6JG, England. **Online address:** r.turbet@abdn.ac.uk

TURCHIN, Peter. American/Russian (born Russia), b. 1957. **Genres:** Social Sciences, Sciences, History, Mathematics/Statistics. **Career:** Duke University, Department of Zoology, teaching assistant, 1983-85; University of

Washington, Department of Zoology, postdoctoral research associate, 1985-88, lecturer, 1988; Forest Service Research, Southern Forest Experiment Station, ecologist, 1988-90, supervisory ecologist, 1990-94; University of Connecticut, College of Liberal Arts and Sciences, Department of Ecology and Evolutionary Biology, assistant professor, 1994-97, associate professor, 1997-2002, professor, 2002-, Department of Mathematics, adjunct faculty; Ecology Letters, associate editor, 1998-2000; Santa Fe Institute, visiting professor, 2007-08. Ecologist. **Publications:** Quantitative Analysis of Movement: Measuring and Modeling Population Redistribution in Animals and Plants, 1998; Historical Dynamics: Why States Rise and Fall, 2003; Complex Population Dynamics: A Theoretical/Empirical Synthesis, 2003; War and Peace and War: The Life Cycles of Imperial Nations, 2006; (co-ed.) History & Mathematics: Historical Dynamics and Development of Complex Societies, 2006; (with S.A. Nefedov) Secular Cycles, 2009. **Address:** Department of Ecology and Evolutionary Biology, University of Connecticut, 462 TLS, 75 N Eagleville Rd., Ste. 3043, Storrs, CT 06269-3043, U.S.A. **Online address:** peter.turchin@uconn.edu

TURCK, Mary C. American (born United States), b. 1950. **Genres:** Children's Non-fiction, Young Adult Non-fiction, Social Sciences, History. **Career:** West Town Legal Services, founder and director, 1975-76, 1979-80; University of Minnesota, University Student Legal Services, director, 1980-83; Twin Cities Daily Planet, editor, 2007-; freelance editor and curriculum developer. **Publications:** Facts about Alcohol and Tobacco, 1988; Facts about AIDS, 1988; Chicago, Illinois, 1989; Washington, DC, 1989; Jewish Holidays, 1990; Facts about Crack and Cocaine, 1990; Acid Rain, 1990; A Parent's Guide to the Best Children's Videos and Where to Find Them, 1994; The Mexican War of Independence, 1997; Haiti: Land of Inequality, 1999; (with N.J. Black) Guatemala: Land of the Maya, 1999; (with N.J. Black) Honduras: Hunger and Hope, 1999; Blizzard!: Snowstorm Fury, 2000; The Civil Rights Movement for Kids: A History with Twenty-One Activities, 2000; Healthy Snack and Fast-Food Choices, 2001; Food and Emotions, 2001; Healthy Eating for Weight Management, 2001; The War at Home: The United States in 1968, 2002; The Dirty Thirties: The United States from 1929-1941, 2002; A Country on the Move: The United States from 1900-1929, 2002; Mexico and Central America, A Fiesta of Crafts, Celebrations and Activities for Ages 8-12, 2004; (with R. Salzberger) Reparations for Slavery: A Reader, 2004; Freedom Song: Young Voices and the Struggle for Civil Rights, 2008. Contributor to books and periodicals. **Address:** 2212 St. Anthony Ave., St. Paul, MN 55104, U.S.A. **Online address:** maryturck@visi.com

TURCO, Lewis (Putnam). (Wesli Court). American (born United States), b. 1934. **Genres:** Children's Fiction, Poetry, Songs/Lyrics And Libretti, Literary Criticism And History, Essays, Reference, Young Adult Fiction. **Career:** University of Connecticut, faculty, 1959; Yaddo resident fellow, 1959; University of Iowa, faculty, 1959-60; Cleveland State University, Fenn College, instructor in English, 1960-64, Cleveland Poetry Center, founding director, 1961-64; Hillsdale College, assistant professor of English, 1964-65; State University of New York, assistant professor, 1965-68, associate professor, 1968-71, professor of English, 1971-96, Program in Writing Arts, founder and director, 1969-95, poet-in-residence, 1995-96, English Writing Arts, now professor emeritus; State University of New York, visiting professor, 1968-69; University of Louisville, poet-in-residence, 1982-; Ashland University, writer-in-residence, 1991-; Mathom Bookshop, owner. **Publications:** First Poems, 1960; While the Spider Slept, 1965; Awaken, Bells Falling: Poems 1959-1967, 1968; New Book of Forms: A Handbook of Poetics, 1968, 3rd ed., 2000; The Literature of New York: A Selective Bibliography of Colonial and Native New York State Authors, 1970; The Inhabitant, 1970; The Pocoangelini: A Fantography and Other Poems, 1971; Poetry: An Introduction Through Writing, 1973; The Weed Garden: Poems, 1973; Seasons of Blood: Poems, 1980; American Still Lifes: Poems, 1981; (ed.) That Band from Indiana, 1982; The Compleat Melancholick: Being a Sequence of Found, Composite, and Composed Poems, Based Largely upon Robert Burtons the Anatomy of Melancholy, 1985; The New Book of Forms: A Handbook of Poetics, 1986; Visions and Revisions: Of American Poetry, 1986; Dialogue: A Socratic Dialogue on the Art of Writing Dialogue in Fiction, 1989; The Shifting Web: New and Selected Poems, 1989; (with W. Hekster) The Fog: A Chamber Opera in One Act: 1987, 1990; A Family Album: Poems, 1990; The Public Poet, 1991; (ed.) Emily Dickinson, Woman of Letters: Poems and Centos from Lines in Emily Dickinsons Letters, 1993; (with A. Dibell and O.S. Card) How to Write a Million, 1995; (with G. OConnell) Bordello, 1996; Shaking the Family Tree: A Remembrance, 1998; (ed. and intro.) The Life and Poetry if Manoah Bodman: Bard of the Berkshires, 1999; The Book of Literary Terms: The Genres of Fiction,

Drama, Nonfiction, Literary Criticism, and Scholarship, 1999; The Green Maces of Autumn, 2002; A Sheaf of Leaves: Literary Memoirs, 2004; The Collected Lyrics of Lewis Turco/Wesli Court, 1953-2004, 2004; The Book of Dialogue: How to Write Effective Conversation in Fiction, Screenplays, Drama, and Poetry, 2004; Fantaseers: A Book of Memories, 2005; Museum of Ordinary People: And Other Stories, 2007; Fearful Pleasures: The Complete Poems, 1959-2007, 2007; Satans Scourge: A Narrative of the Age of Witchcraft In England and New England, 1580-1697, 2009; La Famiglia=The Family, 2009. AS WESLI COURT: Courses in Laments: Poems, 1977; Curses and Laments, 1978; Murgatroyd and Mabel, 1978; The Airs of Wales, 1981. Contributor to books and periodicals. **Address:** Mathom Bookshop and Bindery, 40 Blinn Hill Rd., PO Box 161, Dresden, ME 04342-0161, U.S.A. **Online address:** turco@oswego.edu

TURCO, Richard P. See **TURCO, Richard (Peter).**

TURCO, Richard (Peter). (Richard P. Turco). American (born United States), b. 1943. **Genres:** Earth Sciences, Environmental Sciences/Ecology. **Career:** National Aeronautics and Space Administration, Ames Research Center, research fellow, 1971; R and D Associates, senior research scientist and program manager, 1971-88; University of California, Department of Atmospheric Sciences, founding director, professor, 1988-, chair, 1993-96, Institute of the Environment, director, 1995-; United States Department of Defense, Department of Energy and Environmental Protection Agency, consultant. Writer. **Publications:** Environmental Consequences of Nuclear War, 1986; (with C. Sagan) A Path Where No Man Thought: Nuclear Winter and the End of the Arms Race, 1990; Earth Under Siege: From Air Pollution to Global Change, 1997, 2nd ed., 2002. Contributor of articles to journals. **Address:** Department of Atmospheric Sciences, University of California, 25000 Cannonero Ct., Tehachapi, CA 93561-9691, U.S.A. **Online address:** turco@ucla.edu

TURGEON, Pierre. Canadian (born Canada), b. 1947. **Genres:** Novels, Young Adult Fiction, Sciences. **Career:** Outlook, journalist, 1968-75; Editions Quinze, editor-in-chief, Fondateur, founder and president, 1975-78; University Press of Montréal, assistant director, 1978; Publishing Group Sogides, chief executive officer and publisher, 1979-85; News, literary journalist and columnist, 1985; Liberty Journal, 1987; full time writer and novelist, 1988-; Editions Primeur, publisher. **Publications:** NOVELS: Faire sa Mort Comme Faire l'amour, 1969; Coming Soon: Two Novels, 1983; Un, deux, trois, 1970; Prochainement sur Cetécran: Roman, 1973; La Première Personne: Roman, 1980; Le Bateau d'Hitler, 1988; Les Torrents de l'espoir, 1995; Jour de feu: Roman, 1998; (with D. Gillmor) Canada, vol. I: A People's History, 2000, vol. II, 2001. OTHERS: (contrib. with J. Godbout) L'interview, 1973; La Radissonie: Le pays de la Baie James (nonfiction), 1992. **Address:** Editions du Boreal Express, 4447 Rue St-Denis, Montreal, QC H2J 2L2, Canada.

TURK, Midge. See **RICHARDSON, Midge Turk.**

TURKEL, William J. Canadian (born Canada), b. 1967?. **Genres:** Young Adult Non-fiction. **Career:** University of Western Ontario, associate professor of history. Writer. **Publications:** NONFICTION: The Archive of Place: Unearthing the Pasts of the Chilcotin Plateau, 2007; (ed. with A. MacEachern) Method and Meaning in Canadian Environmental History, 2009. Contributor to journals. **Address:** Department of History, University of Western Ontario, Rm. 4087, Social Science Ctr., London, ON N6A 5C2, Canada. **Online address:** wturkel@uwo.ca

TURNBULL, Peter (John). British (born England), b. 1950. **Genres:** Mystery/Crime/Suspense, Novels. **Career:** Strathclyde Regional Council, social worker, 1978-95; Leeds City Council, social worker; writer, 1995-. **Publications:** P DIVISION SERIES: Deep and Crisp and Even, 1981; Dead Knock, 1982; Fair Friday, 1983; Big Money, 1984; Two Way Cut, 1988; Condition Purple, 1989; And Did Murder Him, 1991; Long Day Monday, 1992; The Killing Floor, 1994; The Man With No Face, 1998. HENNESSEY AND YELLICH SERIES: Fear of Drowning, 1999; Deathtrap, 2000; Perils and Dangers, 2001; The Return, 2001; After the Flood, 2002; Dark Secrets, 2002; All Roads Leadeth, 2003; The Dance Master, 2004; Hopes and Fears, 2004; The Chill Factor, 2005; The Legacy, 2005; False Knight, 2006; Fire Burn, 2006; Chelsea Smile, 2007; Once a Biker, 2007; No Stone Unturned, 2008; Turning Point, 2008. NOVELS: The Claws of the Gryphon, 1986; The Justice Game, 1990; Embracing Skeletons, 1996; Treasure Trove, 2003; Reality Checkpoint, 2004; The Trophy Wife, 2005; Sweet Humphrey, 2006; Informed

Consent, 2009; Aftermath, 2010; Improving the Silence, 2010; Deliver Us from Evil, 2010; Deep Cover, 2011. **Address:** Peters, Fraser & Dunlop, Drury House, 34-43 Russell St., London, GL WC2B 5HA, England. **Online address:** shroggs49@hotmail.com

TURNBULL, Stephen (Richard). British (born England), b. 1948. **Genres:** Anthropology/Ethnology, History, Theology/Religion, Military/Defense/Arms Control, Cultural/Ethnic Topics. **Career:** Health education officer in Leeds, 1979-; University of Leeds, research fellow, 1990-96, visiting lecturer in Southeast Asian religious studies; Picture Library and Consultancy, director of Japan archive; Adviser to the Royal Armouries; Akita International University, visiting professor of Japanese studies, 2008; Creative Assembly, consultant. Freelance writer. **Publications:** The Samurai: A Military History, 1977, rev. ed., 1996; Samurai Armies 1550-1615, 1979; Warlords of Japan, 1979; The Mongols, 1980; The Book of the Samurai: The Warrior Class of Japan, 1982; The Book of the Medieval Knight, 1985; Samurai Warriors, 1987; Battles of the Samurai, 1987; Samurai Warlords: The Book of The Daimyō, 1989; The Lone Samurai and the Martial Arts, 1990; Ninja: The True Story of Japan's Secret Warrior Cult, 1991; Devotion to Mary, 1993; Samurai the Warrior Tradition, 1996; The Kakure Kirishitan of Japan: A Study of Their Development, Beliefs and Rituals to the Present Day, 1998; The Samurai Sourcebook, 1998; Nagashino, 2000; Ashigaru, 2000; Siege Weapons I, 2001, II, 2001; The Knight Triumphant: The High Middle Ages, 1314-1485, 2001; Samurai Heraldry, 2002; War in Japan 1467-1615, 2002; Samurai Warfare, 2002; Samurai Invasion: Japan's Korean War, 1592-98, 2002; Fighting Ships of the Far East 1, China and Southeast Asia 202 BC-AD 1419, 2002; Ninja, 2003; Japanese Castles, 2003; Warrior Monks, 2003; Tannenberg, 1410: Disaster for the Teutonic Knights, 2003; Genghis Khan & the Mongol Conquests, 1190-1400, 2003; Ottoman Empire, 1326-1699, 2003; Teutonic Castles I, 2003; Samurai: The World of the Warrior, 2003; Kawanakajima, 2003; Mongol Warrior, 2003; Kawanakajima 1553-64: Samurai Power Struggle, 2005; Nagashino 1575: Slaughter at the Barricades, 2005; Warriors of Medieval Japan, 2005; Osaka 1615: The Last Battle of the Samurai, 2006; The Samurai and the Sacred, 2006; The Fall of Constantinople: The Ottoman Conquest of Byzantium, 2007; The Great Wall of China, 221 BC-AD 1644, 2007; Pirate of the Far East 811-1639, 2007; Japanese Castles in Korea, 1592-98, 2007; The Samurai Swordsman, 2008; Samurai Armies, 1467-1649, 2008; Japanese Castles, AD 250-1540, 2008; Samurai Invasion of Korea, 1592-98, 2008; Real Ninja: Over 20 True Stories of Japan's Secret Assassins, 2008; Samurai Capture a King: Okinawa 1609, 2009; Strongholds of the Samurai: Japanese Castles 250-1877, 2009; Chinese Walled Cities 221 BC-AD 1644, 2009; Mongol Invasions of Japan, 1274 and 1281, 2010; Katana, 2010; Samurai Women, 1184-1877, 2010; Toyotomi Hideyoshi: Leadership, Strategy, Conflict, 2010; Hatamoto: Samurai Horse and Foot Guards, 1540-1724, 2010; Most Daring Raid of the Samurai, 2011; Samurai: The Japanese Warrior's, 2012. **Address:** Department of Theology and Religious Studies, University of Leeds, Woodhouse Ln. Leeds, Leeds, WY LS2 9JT, England. **Online address:** stephenturnbull@ntlworld.com

TURNER, Amédée (Edward). British (born England), b. 1929. **Genres:** Business/Trade/Industry, Law. **Career:** Kenyon & Kenyon, patent barrister, associate, 1957-60; Macedonian Parliament, adviser on parliamentary democracy, 2001-02; CJA Consultants Ltd., director, 1999-2004, chairman, 2004-. Writer. **Publications:** The Law of Trade Secrets, 1962; The Law of the New European Patent, 1979; (co-author) Intellectual Property of the Single Market, 1996. **Address:** CJA Consultants Ltd., 37 Heol St. Denys, Lisvane, Cardiff, SG CF14 0RU, Wales. **Online address:** amedee.turner@btinternet.com

TURNER, Ann (Warren). American (born United States), b. 1945. **Genres:** Children's Fiction, Young Adult Fiction, Poetry, Children's Non-fiction, Autobiography/Memoirs, Picture/Board Books, Young Adult Non-fiction. **Career:** High school English teacher, 1968-69; Writer, 1969-; Antioch University, assistant director, 1978-80; affiliated with Friends of Meekins Library, 1986-87; University of Massachusetts, instructor of writing, 1987-90. **Publications:** FOR CHILDREN. FICTION: Rituals of Birth: From Prehistory to the Present, 1978; A Hunter Comes Home, 1980; The Way Home, 1982; Third Girl from the Left, 1986; Time of the Bison, 1987; Nettie's Trip South, 1987; Hedgehog for Breakfast, 1989; Grasshopper Summer, 1989; Heron Street, 1989; Through Moon and Stars and Night Skies, 1990; Rosemary's Witch, 1991; Stars forSarah, 1991; Katie's Trunk, 1992; Apple Valley Year, 1993; A Moon for Seasons, 1994; Sewing Quilts, 1994; One Brave Summer, 1995; Dust for Dinner, 1995; Elf song, 1995; Finding Walter, 1997; Drummer Boy: Marching to the Civil War, 1998; Angel Hide & Seek, 1998; Let's Be Ani-

mals, 1998; The Girl Who Chased Away Sorrow: The Diary of Sarah Nita, A Navajo Girl, 1999; Love Thy Neighbor, 2003; Sitting Bull Remembers, 2007; Father of Lies, 2011. POETRY: Dakota Dugout, 1985; Tickle a Pickle, 1986; Street Talk, 1986; Rainflowers, 1992; Grass Songs: Poems, 1993; The Christmas House, 1994; Mississippi Mud: 3 Prairie Journals, 1997; A Lion's Hunger: Poems of First Love, 1998; Learning to Swim, 2000; Secrets from the Dollhouse, 2000; What Did I Know of Freedom, 2000; In the Heart, 2001; Shaker Hearts, 2002; Pumpkin Cat, 2004; Maïa of Thebes: 1463 B.C., 2005; Hard Hit, 2006. NONFICTION: Vultures, 1973; Houses for the Dead, 1976. PICTURE/BOARDBOOKS: Red Flower Goes West, 1999; Abe Lincoln Remembers, 2001; When Mr. Jefferson Came to Philadelphia: What I Learned of Freedom, 1776, 2003. **Address:** Harper Collins Junior Books, 1350 Ave. of the Americas, New York, NY 10019, U.S.A. **Online address:** annwturner@aol.com

TURNER, Barry. British (born England), b. 1937. **Genres:** History, Social Sciences. **Career:** History Today and London Times, editor of country, 1995-2000; London Observer, journalist; Birmingham City University, Department of English, visiting lecturer; National Academy of Writing, founder and chair; The Writer's Handbook, founding editor; Macmillan, staff. **Publications:** NONFICTION: (with W. van der Eyken) Adventures in Education, 1969; Free Trade and Protection, 1971; A Place in the Country, 1972; Sweden, 1976; (with I. Lyche) Nordic Cultural Cooperation, 1981; (with G. Nordquist) The Other European Community: Integration and Cooperation in Nordic Europe, 1982; (with G. Jenkins) Richard Burton, My Brother, 1988; And the Policeman Smiled: 10,000 Children Escape from Nazi Europe, 1991; (with S. Elliott) Denholm Elliott: Quest for Love, 1994; (with T. Rennell) When Daddy Came Home: How Family Life Changed Forever in 1945, 1996; One Small Suitcase, 2003; Countdown to Victory: The Final European Campaigns of World War II, 2004; Suez, 1956: The Inside Story of the First Oil War, 2006; Suez 1956: the Inside Story of the First Oil War, 2006; The Connected Screenwrite, 2009; Outpost of Occupation: How the Channel Islands Survived Nazi Rule 1940-1945, 2010. EDITOR: NONFICTION: Raising the School Leaving Age: A Seminar, Encyclopaedia, 1971; Education and the Urban Crisis, 1972; Discipline in Schools, 1973; Equality for Some: The Story of Girls' Education, 1974; Truancy, 1974; The Writer's Handbook, 1988, rev. ed., 2008; The Statesman's Yearbook: The Politics, Cultures and Economies of the World, 1997, rev. ed., 2008; China Profiled: Essential Facts on Society, Business, and Politics in China, 1999; France Profiled: Essential Facts on Society, Business and Politics in France, 1999; Germany Profiled: Essential Facts on Society, Business, and Politics in Germany, 1999; Italy Profiled: Essential Facts on Society, Business, and Politics in Italy, 1999; The Statesman's Yearbook Centenary Collection, 1999; Central Europe Profiled: Essential Facts on Society, Business and Politics in Central Europe, 2000; Latin America Profiled: Essential Facts on Society, Business and Politics in Latin America, 2000; Scandinavia Profiled: Essential Facts on Society, Business and Politics in Scandinavia, 2000; Southern Africa Profiled: Essential Facts on Society, Business and Politics in Southern Africa, 2000; The World Today, 2000: Essential Facts in an Ever Changing World, 2000; U.K. Today: Essential Facts in an Ever Changing World, 2000; The World Today, 2001: The Writer's Handbook Guide to Crime Writing, 2003; The Writer's Handbook Guide to Writing for Stage and Screen, 2003; The Writer's Handbook Guide to Travel Writing, 2004; The Writer's Handbook Guide to Writing for Children, 2004; The Screenwriter's Handbook: The Essential Companion for All Screenwriters, 2007. Contributor to periodicals. **Address:** Michael Alcock, Johnson & Alcock, Clerkenwell House, 45-47 Clerkenwell Green, London, GL EC1R 0HT, England.

TURNER, B. L. American (born United States), b. 1945. **Genres:** Geography, Environmental Sciences/Ecology, Archaeology/Antiquities. **Career:** University of Maryland, assistant professor, 1974-76; University of Oklahoma, research associate, 1975-76, assistant professor of geography, 1976-79; Clark University, assistant professor, 1980-81, associate professor, 1981-84, Graduate School of Geography, director, 1983-88, 1997-98, 2004-08, professor of geography, 1985-2008, George Perkins Marsh Institute, director, 1991-97, Milton P. & Alice C. Higgins professor of environment and society, 1995-2008, research professor, 2008-; Arizona State University, School of Geographical Sciences, Gilbert F. White professor of environment and society, 2008-09, School of Sustainability, affiliate professor, 2008-09, School of the Geographical Sciences and Urban Planning and School of Sustainability, Gilbert F. White professor of environment and society, 2009-. Writer. **Publications:** Agricultural Livelihoods in Eastern Africa, 1980; Once Beneath the Forest: Prehistoric Terracing in the Rio Bec Region of the Maya Lowlands,

1983; (with T. Whitmore) Cultivated Landscapes of Native Middle America on the Eve of Conquest, 2001; (co-author) Global Change and the Earth System: A Planet under Pressure, 2004. EDITOR: (with P.D. Harrison) Pre-Hispanic Maya Agriculture, 1978; (with P.D. Harrison) Pulltrouser Swamp: Ancient Maya Habitat, Agriculture, and Settlement in Northern Belize, 1983; (with S.B. Brush) Comparative Farming Systems, 1987; (co-editor) The Earth as Transformed by Human Action, 1990; (with G. Hyden and R.W. Kates) Population Growth and Agricultural Change in Africa, 1993; (with J.X. Kasperson and R.E. Kasperson) Regions at Risk, 1995; (with W.B. Meyer) Changes in Land Use and Land Cover, 1994; (with A.G. Sal, F.G. Bernaldez and F. di Castri) Global Land-Use Change: A Perspective from the Columbian Encounter, 1995; (with J. Geoghegan and D. Foster) Integrated Land-Change Science and Tropical Deforestation in the Southern Yucatan, 2003; (co-author) Land Change Science: Observation, Monitoring and Understanding Trajectories of Change on the Earth's Surface, 2004. **Address:** School of Geographical Sciences & Urban Planning, Arizona State University, 975 S Myrtle Ave., COOR 5628, PO Box 875302, Tempe, AZ 85287-5302, U.S.A. **Online address:** billie.l.turner@asu.edu

TURNER, Brian (Lindsay). New Zealander (born New Zealand), b. 1944?. **Genres:** Poetry, Recreation, Travel/Exploration, Autobiography/Memoirs, Biography, Sports/Fitness, Literary Criticism And History. **Career:** New Zealand Customs Department, customs officer, 1962-66; Oxford University Press, trade and university sales representative and editor, 1968-74; Radio Otago, radio journalist, 1974; John McIndoe Ltd., managing editor, 1975-83, 1985-86, journalist; University of Otago, Robert Burns fellow, 1984; University of Canterbury, writer-in-residence, 1997. **Publications:** POETRY: Ladders of Rain, 1978; Ancestors, 1981; Listening to the River, 1983; Bones, 1985; All That Blue Can Be, 1989; Beyond, 1992; (with G. Sydney and O. Marshall) Timeless Land, 1995; Taking Off, 2001. OTHERS: Images of Coastal Otago, 1982; (with G. Roberts) New Zealand High Country: Four Seasons, 1983; (with G. Turner) Opening Up, 1987; The Last River's Song, 1989, (ed.) The Guide to Trout Fishing in Otago, 1994; (with G. Turner) Lifting the Covers, 1998; (with J. Kronfeld) On the Loose, 1999; (with S. Freeman) New Zealand Photographs, 2000; Meads, 2002; Somebodies and Nobodies, 2002; (with A. Oliver) Inside, 2005; Footfall, 2005; Into The Wider World: A Back Country Miscellany, 2008; Just This, 2009. **Address:** 3363 Ida Valley, Omakau Rd., Central Otago, 9339, New Zealand. **Online address:** blturner@xtra.co.nz

TURNER, Charles C. American (born United States) **Genres:** History, Politics/Government, Humanities. **Career:** New College of California, learning options supervisor, 1996; Jon and Lillian Lovelace, fellow, 1996-97; Claremont Graduate University, research assistant in politics and policy, 1997-98; McNair Scholars Program, writing instructor, 1998, 1999, Writing Center, assistant director, 1999; Woodbury University, adjunct instructor, 1998-99; Mount San Antonio College, adjunct instructor, 1999; Truman State University, visiting assistant professor, 1999-2000; California State University, assistant professor, 2000-05, associate professor of political science, 2005-, department vice chair, 2004-, department chair; Junior Statesmen Foundation, California symposium on leadership and politics, academic advisor, 2003-06. Writer. **Publications:** The Politics of Minor Concerns: American Indian Policy and Congressional Dynamics, 2005. Contributor to periodicals and journals. **Address:** Department of Political Science, California State University, Rm. 741A, Butte Hall, 400 W 1st St., Chico, CA 95929-0455, U.S.A. **Online address:** ccturner@csuchico.edu

TURNER, David M. Welsh (born Wales), b. 1972?. **Genres:** Social Sciences, Sex. **Career:** University of Glamorgan, lecturer, principal lecturer in history, 1999-2004, history field leader, 2003-04, professor; Swansea University, senior lecturer in history, 2005-, Centre for Research into Gender in Culture and Society, associate director. Writer. **Publications:** Fashioning Adultery: Gender, Sex and Civility in England, 1660-1740, 2002; (ed. with K. Stagg) Social Histories of Disability and Deformity, 2006, Disability in Eighteenth-century England: Imagining Physical Impairment, 2012. CONTRIBUTOR: English Masculinities, 1660-1800, 1999; Contexts of Conscience in Early Modern Europe, 1500-1700, 2004; The Kiss in History, 2005. Contributor to periodicals. **Address:** Department of History, Swansea University, James Callaghan Rm. 104, Singleton Pk., Swansea, WG SA2 8PP, Wales. **Online address:** d.m.turner@swansea.ac.uk

TURNER, Elizabeth. See OUST, Gail.

TURNER, Frederick C. (Frederick Clair Turner). American (born United States), b. 1938. **Genres:** International Relations/Current Affairs, Politics/Government, Social Sciences. **Career:** University of Connecticut, assistant professor, 1965-68, associate professor, 1968-70, professor of political science, 1970-97, emeritus professor, 1997-; Yale University, Department of Political Science, visiting lecturer, 1967-69; Roper Public Opinion Research Center, Latin American representative, 1972-74; World Association for Public Opinion Research, president, 1988-90; Universidad de San Andres, profesor de ciencia politica, 1997-. Writer. **Publications:** The Dynamic of Mexican Nationalism, 1968; Catholicism and Political Development in Latin America, 1971; Responsible Parenthood: The Politics of Mexico's New Population Policies, 1974; (ed. with J.E. Miguens) Juan Perón and the Reshaping of Argentina, 1983; (ed. with J.E. Miguens and C. Buchrucker) Racionalidad del peronismo, 1988; (ed.) Social Mobility and Political Attitudes: Comparative Perspectives, 1992; (ed. with F.J. Welsch) Opinión pública y elecciones an América, 2000; Transformación de las funciones del estado, 2003. **Address:** Department of Political Science, University of Connecticut, U-1024, 341 Mansfield Rd., Storrs, CT 06269-1024, U.S.A.

TURNER, Frederick Clair. See TURNER, Frederick C.

TURNER, Jack Scott. American (born United States), b. 1942. **Genres:** Travel/Exploration. **Career:** University of Illinois at Urbana-Champaign, teacher of philosophy; Exum Mountain Guides, guide, 1970-, director, corporate president; Grand Teton National Park, teacher; Cornell University, Woodrow Wilson national fellow. Writer. **Publications:** The Abstract Wild, 1996; Teewinot: A Year in the Teton Range, 2000; Teewinot: Climbing and Contemplating the Teton Range, 2001; Travels in the Greater Yellowstone, 2008. **Address:** Exum Mountain Guides, Grand Teton National Pk., S Jenny Lake, PO Box 56, Moose, WY 83012, U.S.A.

TURNER, John Christopher. New Zealander/British (born England), b. 1928. **Genres:** Mathematics/Statistics, Sciences. **Career:** Armaments Research Development Establishment, Mathematics Division, scientific officer, 1954-56; Mombasa Institute of Muslim Education, Tutor in mathematics physics, 1956-60; Nottingham College of Technology, lecturer in mathematics, 1960-62; University of Sierra Leone, lecturer in applied mathematics, 1962-65; Huddersfield Polytechnic, senior lecturer in statistics, 1965-67; Leeds Polytechnic, principal lecturer in statistics, 1967-70, Department of Mathematics and Computer Science, head, 1967-70; University of Waikato, faculty, 1970-, reader, 1970-86, acting director of computing services, 1971-73, School of Computing and Mathematical Sciences, dean, 1986-90, associate professor of mathematics, 1986-94, now retired; Hamilton New Zealand Statistical Society, area convenor, 1973-79; Hang-Gliding Society, founder and president, 1976, 1977; Classical Guitar Society, president, 1977, 1978, 1979, treasurer, 1983, 1984, 1985.Writer. **Publications:** Modern Applied Mathematics, 1970; (with R. Hosking and D. Joyce) First Steps in Numerical Analysis, 1978; Probability and Statistics, 1980; (with A. Schaake and D. Sedgwick) Braiding: Regular Knots, 1988; A New Chapter for Pythagorean Triples, 1989; Braiding: Regular Fiador Knots, 1990; (with with A.G. Schaake) Generalizing Euclid's Algorithm, Via the Regular and Moebius Knot Trees, Order-N Arithmetics, 1990; (with A.G. Schaake) Number Trees for Pythagoras, Plato, Euler, and The Modular Group, 1990; (with A.G. Schaake and D.A. Sedgwick) Edge Lacing: The Double Cordovan Stitch, 1991; Braiding: Standard Herringbone Pineapple Knots, 1991; (with A.G. Schaake and D.A. Sedgwick) Braiding Application: Horse Halter, 1991; (with A.G. Schaake) Introduction to Flat Braids, 1991; (with A.G. Schaake) Regular Knot Tree and Enlargement Processes, 1991; Braiding: Standard Herringbone Knots, 1992; (with A.G. Schaake) Braiding of Row-Coded Regular Knots, 1993; (ed. with P.V.D. Griend) History and Science of Knots, 1996. **Address:** 6 Hardley St., Hamilton, 3200, New Zealand. **Online address:** jct@thenet.net.nz

TURNER, John Frayn. British (born England), b. 1923. **Genres:** History, Biography, Military/Defense/Arms Control, Poetry. **Career:** Ideal Home, feature writer, 1951-55; House Beautiful, editor, 1956-57; News Chronicle, columnist, 1958-59; Weekend Magazine, feature writer, 1962-63; Royal Air Force, Publicity Branch, editor, 1963-73; Central Office of Information, senior editor, 1973-84. **Publications:** Service Most Silent: The Navy's Fight Against Enemy Mines, 1955; V.C.s of the Royal Navy, 1956; Prisoner at Large, 1957; Hovering Angels: The Record of the Royal Navy's Helicopters, 1957; Periscope Patrol: The Saga of Malta Submarines, 1957; Invasion '44: The Full Story of D-Day in Normandy, 1959; V.C.s of the Air, 1960; Battle Stations: The U.S. Navy's War, 1960; Highly Explosive: The Exploits of Major Bill Hartely, 1961; The Blinding Flash: The Remarkable Story of Ken Revise and His Struggle to Overcome Blindness, 1962; V.C.s of the Army, 1939-51, 1962; A Girl Called Johnnie: Three Weeks in an Open Boat, 1963, 2nd ed., 1967; Famous Air Battles, 1963; British Aircraft of World War II, 1975; Destination Berchtesgaden: The U.S. Seventh Army Story, 1975; Famous Flights, 1978; American Aircraft of World War II, 1979; The Bader Wing, 1981; (ed. with E.R.W. Hale) The Yanks are Coming, 1983; Frank Sinatra: A Personal Portrait, 1983; The Bader Tapes, 1986; The Good Spy Guide, 1988; Rupert Brooke: The Splendour and the Pain, 1992; Douglas Bader: A Biography of the Legendary World War II Fighter Pilot, 1995, 2nd ed., 2001; The Battle of Britain, 1998; Fight for the Air, 2000; Fight for the Sea: Naval Adventures from World War II, 2001; Heroic Flights, 2003; V.C.s of the Second World War, 2004; Life and Selected Works of Rupert Brooke, 2004; Awards of the George Cross, 1940-2005, 2006. **Address:** 16 Church St., Leatherhead, SR KT23 3PD, England.

TURNER, Judith. Also writes as Judy Turner, Lydia Balmain, Judith Arden, Katie Flynn, Judith Saxton. Welsh/British (born England), b. 1936. **Genres:** Romance/Historical. **Career:** Writer. **Publications:** Feather Light, Diamond Bright, 1974; Child of Passion, 1978; Merry Jade, 1978; White City: International Style Architecture in Israel, 1984; Tokio Marine Plaza Building, Osaka, 1991; Near Sitings: Photographs 1975-1995, 1995; Hidden World of Birthdays, 1999; Hidden World of Relationships, 2001; The Modern Wing: Renzo Piano and the Art Institute of Chicago, 2009. AS JUDY TURNER: Ralegh's Fair Bess, 1972; Cousin to the Queen: The Story of Lettice Knollys, 1972; Ralegh's Fair Bess, 1974; Sherida, 1981, as The Winyard Fortune, 1999; Gift for Pamela, 1981; Arcade, 1990; Harbour Hill, 1991. AS JUDITH SAXTON: The Bright Day Is Done: The Story of Amy Robsart, 1976; Princess in Waiting, 1976; Winter Queen, 1976; The Pride, 1981; The Glory, 1982; The Splendour, 1983; Full Circle, 1984; Sophie, 1985; Family Feeling, 1986; All My Fortunes, 1987; Jenny Alone, 1987; Chasing Rainbows, 1988; Summer in the Lakes, 1988; A Family Affair, 1989; Crock of Gold, 1990; Nobody's Children, 1991; This Royal Breed, 1992; First Love, Last Love, 1993; The Blue and Distant Hills, 1993; Someone Special, 1995; Harvest Moon, 1995; Still Waters, 1998; Waterloo Sunset, 1997; You Are My Sunshine, 2000. AS KATIE FLYNN: A Liverpool Lass, 1993; The Girl from Penny Lane, 1993; Liverpool Taffy, 1994; The Mersey Girls, 1994; Strawberry Fields, 1995; Rainbow's End, 1997; From Clare to Here, 1997; Rose of Tralee, 1998; No Silver Spoon, 1999; Polly's Angel, 2000; The Girl from Seaforth Sands, 2001; The Liverpool Rose, 2001; Poor Little Rich Girl, 2002; The Bad Penny, 2002; Down Daisy Street, 2003; A Kiss and a Promise, 2003; A Long and Lonely Road, 2004; Two Penn'orth of Sky, 2004; Darkest Before Dawn, 2005; The Cuckoo Child, 2005; Orphans of the Storm, 2005; Little Girl Lost, 2006; Beyond the Blue Hills, 2006; Forgotten Dreams, 2007; Sunshine and Shadows, 2008; Such Sweet Sorrow, 2008; A Mother's Hope, 2009; In Time for Christmas, 2009; Heading Home, 2010; A Mistletoe Kiss, 2010; The Lost Days of Summer, 2011; Christmas Wishes, 2011. AS JUDITH ARDEN: Golden Chains, Macdonald, 1980; Golden Promises, 1981. AS LYDIA BALMAIN: Caribbean Nurse, 1981; Ice Venture Nurse, 1983; Italian Nurse, 1984; Surgeon in the Snow, 1985; Theatre of Love, 1987; Hometown Hospital, 1991. AS JENNY FELIX: Masquerade, 1982; Prisoner in Peking, 1982; Overland Trail, 1983. **Address:** Caroline Sheldon Literary Agency, 71 Hillgate Pl., London, GL W8 7SS, England.

TURNER, Judy. See **TURNER, Judith.**

TURNER, Kathleen. American (born United States), b. 1954. **Genres:** Novels, Biography. **Career:** Planned Parenthood Federation of America Board of Advocates, chair. Writer. **Publications:** (With G. Feldt) Send Yourself Roses: Thoughts on My Life, Love and Leading Roles, 2008. **Address:** c/o Chris Andrews, International Creative Management, 8942 Wilshire Blvd., Beverly Hills, CA 90211-1934, U.S.A.

TURNER, Kathleen J. American (born United States), b. 1952. **Genres:** Communications/Media, Biography, History, Cultural/Ethnic Topics. **Career:** Purdue University, university fellow, teaching assistant, 1976-78; Denison University, assistant professor of communication, 1978-79; University of Notre Dame, assistant professor of communication, 1979-85; University of Tulsa, visiting associate professor of communication, 1985-86; Tulane University, Department of Communication, associate professor of communication, 1986-2000, chair, 1992-95, Newcomb College, Newcomb fellow, 1989-2000; Queens University, Department of Communication, professor, 2000-04, chair, 2000-04, Knight-Crane Professor of Communication, 2001-04, Davidson College, professor of communication studies and director of

oral communication, 2004-. Writer and consultant. **Publications:** Mass Media and Popular Culture, 1984; Lyndon Johnson's Dual War: Vietnam and the Press, 1985; (ed.) Doing Rhetorical History: Concepts and Cases, 1998; Comic Creations, forthcoming. **Address:** Communication Studies, Davidson College, 2268 Chambers, PO Box 7066, Davidson, NC 28035-7134, U.S.A. **Online address:** katurner@davidson.edu

TURNER, Lowell. (Lowell Ralph Turner). American (born United States), b. 1947. **Genres:** Organized Labor, Industrial Relations, Politics/Government. **Career:** Perpetual Motors, automotive mechanic and service manager, 1970-75; San Francisco Institute for Automotive Ecology, instructor, technical writer and president, 1972-75; U.S. Postal Service, letter carrier, parcel post driver and elected union representative, 1977-84; National Association of Letter Carriers, chief steward, newspaper editor, 1979-84; University of California, faculty; Cornell University, International and Comparative Labor and Collective Bargaining, assistant professor, 1990-94, associate professor, 1994-99, professor, 1999-, Industrial and Labor Relations School (ILR), associate director, 1992-94, Academic Integrity Board, chair, 1992, Department of International and Comparative Labor, chair, 2005-08, coordinator, 2005-10, Center for International Studies, director, 1994-96, Comparative Labor Movement Revitalization research project, organizer and coordinator, 2000-04, Global Democracy Research Group, director, 2002-05, Student Coalition Advocating Labor Education, faculty advisor, 2003-05, co-convener and organizer, 2002-10, faculty senate, 2007-08. **Publications:** (With H.L. Wilensky) Democratic Corporatism and Policy Linkages: The Interdependence of Industrial, Labor-market, Incomes, and Social Policies in Eight Countries, 1987; Democracy at Work: Changing World Markets and the Future of Labor Unions, 1991; (with H.C. Katz and S. Kuruvilla) Trade Unions and Collective Bargaining, 1993; (ed. with K.S. Wever) The Comparative Political Economy of Industrial Relations, 1995; (ed.) Negotiating the New Germany: Can Social Partnership Survive?, 1997; (with K. Thelen) German Codetermination in Comparative Perspective: Expertise für das Projekt Mitbestimmung und neue Unternehmenskulturen der Bertelsmann-Stiftung und der Hans-Böckler-Stiftung, 1997; Fighting for Partnership: Labor and Politics in Unified Germany, 1998; (ed. with M.E. Gordon) Transnational Cooperation Among Labor Unions, 2000; (with H.C. Katz and R.W. Hurd) Rekindling the Movement: Labor's Quest for Relevance in the Twenty-First Century, 2001; (ed. with D.B. Cornfield) Labor in the New Urban Battlegrounds: Local Solidarity in a Global Economy, 2007. **Address:** ILR School, Cornell University, 358 ILR Faculty Bldg., Ithaca, NY 14853-3901, U.S.A. **Online address:** lrt4@cornell.edu

TURNER, Lowell Ralph. See **TURNER, Lowell.**

TURNER, Marjorie Shepherd. American (born United States), b. 1921. **Genres:** Women's Studies And Issues, Economics, History, Intellectual History, Recreation, Travel/Exploration, Biography, Autobiography/Memoirs, Autobiography/Memoirs. **Career:** University of Texas, instructor in economics, 1947-52; University of Arizona, instructor in economics, 1952-54; San Diego State University, associate dean, 1954-56, professor of economics faculty, 1956-76, department head, 1967-69, professor emeritus, 1976-, Institute of Labor Economics, director, 1970-74. Writer. **Publications:** Women & Work, 1964; Early American Labor Conspiracy Cases, Their Place in Labor Law: A Reinterpretation, 1967; (with R. Floren, Jr. and J.W Leasure) Public Benefits Associated with Public Expenditures in Education: A Demographic Approach, 1969; (with J.W. Leasure) Prices, Profit, and Production: How Much Is Enough?, 1974; Joan Robinson and the Americans, 1989; Nicholas Kaldor and the Real World, 1993; The Sailing Life, 2003; Log of the Last Harrah, forthcoming; Louisa Mae and Lena Fay, forthcoming. **Address:** San Diego State University, 5500 Campanile Dr., San Diego, CA 92182-6060, U.S.A.

TURNER, Mark. American (born United States), b. 1954?. **Genres:** Literary Criticism And History, Sciences, Medicine/Health. **Career:** University of Chicago, assistant professor of English, 1983-90; National Endowment for the Humanities, fellow, 1986-87; National Humanities Center, fellow, 1989-90; University of Maryland, Department of English Language and Literature, associate professor, 1990-91, professor, 1992-2001, distinguished university professor, 2001-04; Center for Advanced Study in the Behavioral Sciences, fellow, 1994-95, 2001-02, associate director, 2002-04; Krasnow Institute for Advanced Study, external research professor, 1997-; New England Institute for Cognitive Science and Evolutionary Psychology, distinguished fellow, 2001-; Case Western Reserve University, College of Arts and Sciences, dean,

2004-06, Department of Cognitive Science, institute professor and professor of cognitive science, chair of cognitive science, 2007-09, Myrifield Institute for Cognition and the Arts, founding president, 2007-; Cleveland Museum of Natural History, research associate, 2004-08; Norwegian Academy of Science and Letters, Centre for Advanced Study, fellow, 2011-12; Cognitive Science Network, founding director. Writer. **Publications:** Death Is the Mother of Beauty: Mind, Metaphor, Criticism, 1987; (with G. Lakoff) More than Cool Reason: A Field Guide to Poetic Metaphor, 1989; Reading Minds: The Study of English in the Age of Cognitive Science, 1991; (with F. Thomas) Clear and Simple as the Truth: Writing Classic Prose, 1994, 2nd ed., 2010; The Literary Mind, 1996; (co-author) Figurative Language and Thought, 1998; (with G. Fauconnier) Amalgami: Introduzione ai Network di Integrazione Concettuale, 2001; Cognitive Dimensions of Social Science, 2001; (with G. Fauconnier) The Way We Think: Conceptual Blending and the Mind's Hidden Complexities, 2002; (ed.) The Artful Mind: Cognitive Science and the Riddle of Human Creativity, 2006; (ed. with F. Parrill and V. Tobin) Meaning, Form, and Body, 2009. Contributor to books and periodicals. **Address:** Department of Cognitive Science, Case Western Reserve University, 10900 Euclid Ave., Cleveland, OH 44106, U.S.A. **Online address:** turner@case.edu

TURNER, Martin. British (born England), b. 1948. **Genres:** Poetry, Translations, Education. **Career:** Educational psychologist, 1976-84; senior educational psychologist, 1984-91; Dyslexia Institute, head of psychology, 1991-2003. Writer. **Publications:** Trespasses (poems), 1992; Psychological Assessment of Dyslexia, 1997; (ed. with J. Townend) Dyslexia in Practice: A Guide for Teachers, 2000; (ed. with J.P. Rack) Study of Dyslexia, 2004; The Deer of Tamnies (poems), 2006. Contributor to periodicals. **Address:** Brocksett Cottage, Kennel Ln., Windlesham, SR GU20 6AA, England. **Online address:** mvlturner@clara.co.uk

TURNER, Megan Whalen. American (born United States), b. 1965. **Genres:** Novels, Young Adult Fiction, Novellas/Short Stories, Science Fiction/Fantasy, Children's Fiction, Literary Criticism And History. **Career:** Harper Court Bookstore, children's book buyer, 1988-89; Bick's Books, children's book buyer, 1991-92. Writer. **Publications:** COLLECTION: Instead of Three Wishes (young adult), 1995. ATTOLIA SERIES: The Thief, 1996; The Queen of Attolia, 2000; King of Attolia, 2006; A Conspiracy of Kings, 2010. Works appear in anthologies. **Address:** Greenwillow Books, Harpercollins Publishers, 10 E 53rd St., 23rd Fl., New York, NY 10022-5073, U.S.A. **Online address:** meganwhalenturner@harpercollins.com

TURNER, Nancy J. Canadian/American (born United States), b. 1947. **Genres:** Botany, Food And Wine. **Career:** University of British Columbia, The Botanical Garden, research assistant, 1970-71, Department of Botany, teaching assistant, 1970-74, adjunct professor, 1986-2000; Royal British Columbia Museum, Botany Division, research associate, 1974-; University of Victoria, University Extension, lecturer, 1975-93, School of Environmental Studies, Department of Biology, sessional lecturer, 1987, 1988, Environmental Studies Program, sessional lecturer, 1990-91, assistant professor, 1991-93, professor of environmental studies, 1993-2004, distinguished professor, 2004-, acting director, 2004-07; National Museum of Natural Sciences (now The Canadian Museum of Nature), writer, 1977-80; Nuxalk Food and Nutrition Program, ethnobotanical advisor, 1981-86; Simon Fraser University, adjunct professor, 1990-91; Society of Ethnobiology, president, 1997-; University of Manitoba, Natural Resources Institute, Clayton H. Riddell Faculty of Environment, Earth and Resources, adjunct professor, 2006-09. Writer. **Publications:** Food Plants of British Columbia Indians, 1975; (with A.F. Szczawinski) Edible Wild Plants of Canada, vol. I: Edible Garden Weeds of Canada, 1978, vol. II: Wild Coffee and Tea Substitutes of Canada, 1978, vol. III: Edible Wild Fruits and Nuts of Canada, 1979, vol. IV: Wild Green Vegetables of Canada, 1980; Plants in British Columbia Indian Technology, 1979; (with B.S. Efrat) Ethnobotany of the Hesquiat Indians of Vancouver Island, 1982; (co-ed.) Ethnobotany of the Nitinaht Indians of Vancouver Island, 1983; Wild Harvest Exhibit Background Information (exhibit manual), 1983; (co-author) Thompson Ethnobotany: Knowledge and Usage of Plants by the Thompson Indians of British Columbia, 1990; (with A.F. Szczawinski) Common Poisonous Plants and Mushrooms of North America, 1991; (with H.V. Kuhnlein) Traditional Plant Foods of Canadian Indigenous Peoples: Nutrition, Botany, and Use, 1991; Food Plants of Coastal First Peoples, 1995; Food Plants of Interior First Peoples, 1997; Plant Technology of First Peoples in British Columbia, 1998; (with R. Halter) Native Trees of British Columbia, 2003; Plants of Haida Gwaii, 2004; Earth's Blanket: Traditional Teachings for Sustainable Living, 2005; (ed. with D. Deur) Keeping it Living: Traditions of Plant Use

and Cultivation on the Northwest Coast of North America, 2005; (ed. with C.C. Parrish and S.M. Solberg) Resetting the Kitchen Table: Food Security, Culture, Health and Resilience in Coastal Communities, 2007; (with P. von Aderkas) North American Guide to Common Poisonous Plants and Mushrooms, 2009; (ed. with T.K. Mukherjee) Biocultural Knowledge Systems of Tribes of Eastern Himalayas, 2010; (co-ed.) Ethnobiology, 2011. Works appear in anthologies. Contributor to journals. **Address:** School of Environmental Studies, University of Victoria, B260, Social Sciences & Math Bldg., 3800 Finnerty Rd., PO Box 3060, Victoria, BC V8P 5C2, Canada. **Online address:** nturner@uvic.ca

TURNER, Ralph (Herbert). American (born United States), b. 1919. **Genres:** Sociology, Geography, Psychology, Natural History. **Career:** American Council on Race Relations, research associate, 1947-48; University of California, Department of Sociology, faculty, 1948-59, professor, 1959-90, chair, 1963-68, professor emeritus, 1990-, vice-chair of statewide academic senate, 1982-83, chair, 1983-84; University of Washington, visiting professor, 1960; University of Hawaii, visiting professor, 1962; National Institutes of Health, chair, 1963-64; Social Science Research Council, director-at-large, 1965-66; Foundations Fund for Research in Psychiatry, director, 1970-73; National Academy of Sciences, chair, 1974-75; University of Georgia, visiting professor, 1975; Annual Review of Sociology, editor, 1980-86. **Publications:** (With L.M. Killian) Collective Behavior, 1957, 3rd ed., 1987; The Social Context of Ambition: A Study of High-School Seniors in Los Angeles, 1964; (with T.M. Newcomb and P.E. Converse) Social Psychology: The Study of Human Interaction, 1965; (ed. and intro.) On Social Control and Collective Behavior, 1967; Family Interaction, 1970; Earthquake Prediction and Public Policy, 1975; (co-author) Earthquake Threat: The Human Response in Southern California, 1979; (ed. with M. Rosenberg) Social Psychology: Sociological Perspectives, 1981; (with J.M. Nigg and D.H. Paz) Waiting for Disaster: Earthquake Watch in California, 1986. Contributor to journals. **Address:** Department of Sociology, University of California, 264 Haines Hall, 375 Portola Plz., PO Box 951551, Los Angeles, CA 90095-1551, U.S.A. **Online address:** rht@soc.ucla.edu

TURNER, Richard Brent. American (born United States), b. 1951. **Genres:** Theology/Religion. **Career:** Boston College, tutor in religion, 1976; Boston Public Schools, teacher, 1977-80, 1984-86, Northeastern University, tutor, 1977-79; University of California, assistant professor of black studies, 1986-96; Harvard University, W.E.B. DuBois Institute for African and African American Research, fellow, 1988-89; Carleton College, Dana Lecturer, 1989; Xavier University, Department of Theology, assistant professor, 1996-99; Union Theological Seminary, African Americans and the Bible: An Interdisciplinary Research Project, associate, 1998-99; DePaul University, Department of Religious Studies, associate professor, 1999-2001; University of Iowa, Department of Religious Studies, associate professor, 2001-10, professor, 2010-, African American Studies, associate professor, 2001-10, professor, 2010-, coordinator, 2005-06; University of Louisville, lecturer; University of Massachusetts, lecturer; Georgia State University, lecturer; Fairfield University, lecturer; Gettysburg College, lecturer. **Publications:** Islam in the African-American Experience, 1997, 2nd ed., 2003; Jazz Religion, the Second Line, and Black New Orleans, 2009. Contributor of articles to periodicals. **Address:** Department of Religious Studies, University of Iowa, 310 Gilmore Hall, Iowa City, IA 52242-1320, U.S.A. **Online address:** richard-turner@uiowa.edu

TURNER, Robyn. (Robyn Montana Turner). American (born United States), b. 1947. **Genres:** Art/Art History, Biography, Children's Fiction. **Career:** Amarillo Community Center, visual arts coordinator and teacher, 1974-78; Campbell Elementary, Austin Independent School District, teacher, 1979-85; Holt, Rinehart and Winston, senior editor, 1985-89, script writer and editor of video programs, 1987-88, School Division, national marketing manager, 1989-90; Women and Their Work, consultant, 1989-90; Harcourt Brace Jovanovich, consultant, 1988-89, 1990; Davis Publishing Co., consultant, 1991; St. Edward's University, adjunct professor, 1991-; Robyn Turner and Associates, owner and manager, 1991-; Houston Museum of Fine Arts, consultant, 1992; McGraw-Hill Publishing Co., consultant, 1992. **Publications:** AS ROBYN MONTANA TURNER: Rosa Bonheur, 1991; Georgia O'Keeffe, 1991; Mary Cassatt, 1992; Frida Kahlo, 1993; Faith Ringgold, 1993; Dorothea Lange, 1994; Texas Traditions: The Culture of the Lone Star State, 1996. OTHERS: Austin Originals: Chats with Colorful Characters, 1982. Contributor to books and periodicals. **Address:** 3408 Werner Ave., Austin, TX 78722-2248, U.S.A.

TURNER, Robyn Montana. *See* **TURNER, Robyn.**

TURNER, Thomas Coleman. American (born United States), b. 1927. **Genres:** Novels, Young Adult Fiction. **Career:** U.S. Government, information and editorial supervisor unclassified material, 1951-52; Turner Dairies Inc., laboratory technician, 1953-54; Modern Masonry Materials Inc., executive vice-president, 1960-61; Phoenix Trading Co. (real estate developers), president, 1961-; Merrimac Corp. (real estate developers), secretary, treasurer, 1962-; Anniston Library, trustee, 1963. Writer. **Publications:** Buttermilk Road, 1963. Contributor of stories and articles. **Address:** 12 Sunset Dr., Anniston, AL 36207, U.S.A. **Online address:** zoeturner@earthlink.net

TURNER, Tom. American (born United States), b. 1942. **Genres:** Environmental Sciences/Ecology, Adult Non-fiction, Law, Economics. **Career:** Sierra Club, editor and administrative assistant, 1968-69, Legal Defense Fund, staff writer, 1986-; Friends of the Earth, editor, 1969-86; Earth justice, senior editor, 1986-. **Publications:** (Contrib.) Wild by Law: The Sierra Club Legal Defense Fund and the Places It Has Saved, 1990; Sierra Club: 100 Years of Protecting Nature, 1991; Landscape Planning and Environmental Impach Design, 1998; (co-author) The Spirit of the Road: One Hundred Years of the Californian State Automobile Association, 2000; Justice on Earth-Earth justice and the People It Has Served, 2002; Roadless Rules: The Struggle For The Last Wild Forests, 2009. **Address:** Earthjustice, 426 17th St., 6th Fl., Oakland, CA 94612-2820, U.S.A. **Online address:** tturner@earthjustice.org

TURNER, William Weyand. American (born United States), b. 1927. **Genres:** Criminology/True Crime, Law, Politics/Government, Social Sciences, Military/Defense/Arms Control, History. **Career:** Federal Bureau of Investigation, special agent, 1951-61; freelance writer, 1963-; Ramparts (magazine), senior editor, 1967, staff writer. Investigator and consultant. **Publications:** (Ed.) Case Investigation, 1965; (ed.) Criminalistics, 1965; (ed.) Drugs and Poisons, 1965; (ed.) Traffic Investigation, 1965; The Police Establishment, 1968; Invisible Witness: The Use and Abuse of the New Technology of Crime Investigation, 1968; Hoover's FBI: The Men and the Myth, 1970; Power on the Right, 1971; How to Avoid Electronic Eavesdropping and Privacy Invasion, 1972; (with E. Asinof and W. Hinckle) The 10-Second Jailbreak: The Helicopter Escape of Joel David Kaplan, 1973; (contrib.) Investigating the FBI, 1973; (with J.G. Christian) The Assassination of Robert F. Kennedy: A Searching Look at the Conspiracy and Cover-up, 1968-1978, 1978; (with W. Hinckle) The Fish Is Red: The Story of the Secret War Against Castro, 1981; (with W. Hinckle) Deadly Secrets: The CIA-Mafia War Against Castro and The Assassination of J.F.K., 1992; Rearview Mirror: Looking Back at the FBI, the CIA, and Other Tails, 2001; (co-author) Mission Not Accomplished: How George Bush Lost the War on Terrorism, 2004. **Address:** HarperCollins Publishers, 10 E 53rd St., New York, NY 10022, U.S.A. **Online address:** fanofjfk@aol.com

TURNEY, Denise. *See* **CAMPBELL, Rhonda.**

TURNEY, Jon. British (born England) **Genres:** Technology, Sciences, Adult Non-fiction, Medicine/Health. **Career:** Times Higher Education Supplement, science editor; University College London, senior lecturer in science communication; University of London, staff; City University, staff; Imperial College, educator and course leader of creative non-fiction; Penguin Press, editorial director, 2003-, consulting editor; Doctor, staff. **Publications:** (Ed.) Sci-Tech Report: Everything You Need to Know about Science and Technology in the 80s, 1984; Frankenstein's Footsteps: Science, Genetics and Popular Culture, 1998; (contrib.) Medicine and Health Science, 2001; (ed.) Science, not Art: Ten Scientists' Diaries, 2003; Lovelock and Gaia: Signs of Life, 2003; The Rough Guide to Genes & Cloning, 2007; Technology: Ethical Debates about the Application of Science, 2009; The Rough Guide to the Future, 2010; (ed. with B. Bryson) Seeing Further: The Story of Science & the Royal Society in US as Seeing Further: The Story of Science, Discovery, and the Genius of the Royal Society, 2010. **Address:** Pantheon Books, 1745 Broadway, New York, NY 10019, U.S.A. **Online address:** jonturney@gmail.com

TURNILL, Reginald. British (born England), b. 1915. **Genres:** Air/Space Topics, Engineering. **Career:** Press Association, reporter, 1930-56; BBC, industrial correspondent, 1956-58, aerospace/defense correspondent, 1958-76. Writer, 1976-. **Publications:** Moonslaught: The Story of Man's Race to the Moon, 1969; The Language of Space: A Dictionary of Astronautics, 1970; Observer's Book of Manned Spaceflight 1972, 3rd ed., 1978; Observer's Book of Unmanned Spaceflight, 1974; Spaceflight Directory, 1978; Space Age, 1980; (with A. Reed) Farnborough: The Story of RAE, 1980; Jane's Spaceflight Directory, 1984, 4th ed., 1988; Space Technology International,

1989; Celebrating Concorde: 25 Supersonic Years, 1994; The Moonlandings: An Eye Witness Account, 2003. **Address:** Somerville Lodge, Hillside, Sandgate, KT CT20 3DB, England.

TURNIPSEED, Erica Simone. American (born United States), b. 1971. **Genres:** Cultural/Ethnic Topics, Novels, Romance/Historical. **Career:** Twenty-First Century Foundation, director of development; Yale University, Afro-American Cultural Center, Five Years for the House Initiative, founder and co-chair. Writer. **Publications:** A Love Noire: A Novel, 2003; Hunger, 2006. Contributor to books. **Address:** c/o Author Mail, HarperCollins Publishers Inc., 10 E 53rd St., 17th Fl., New York, NY 10022-5244, U.S.A. **Online address:** erica@ericasimoneturnipseed.com

TUROK, Neil. British (born England), b. 1958?. **Genres:** Sciences, Mathematics/Statistics. **Career:** Cambridge University, professor of mathematical physics, chair of mathematical physics, 1997-, Centre for Theoretical Cosmology, director; Fermilab, associate scientist; Princeton University, associate professor of physics, professor of physics, 1994; African Institute for Mathematical Sciences, founder; Perimeter Institute for Theoretical Physics, director, 2008-. Writer. **Publications:** (Ed. with R.G. Crittenden) Structure Formation in the Universe, 2001; (with P.J. Steinhardt) Endless Universe: Beyond the Big Bang, 2007. Contributor to books. **Address:** Centre for Mathematical Sciences, Cambridge University, Cambridge, CB CB3 OWA, England. **Online address:** n.g.turok@damtp.cam.ac.uk

TUROW, (L.) Scott. (Scott F. Turow). American (born United States), b. 1949. **Genres:** Novels, Law, Mystery/Crime/Suspense, Young Adult Fiction, Biography, Young Adult Non-fiction. **Career:** Stanford University, Creative Writing Center, Edith Mirrielees fellow, 1970-72, E.H. Jones lecturer, 1972-75; Writer 1972-; Suffolk County District Attorney, clerk, 1977-78; U.S. District Court, assistant U.S. attorney, 1978-86; Sonnenschein, Nath and Rosenthal, partner, 1986-; Authors Guild, president, 1997-98; Amherst College, trustee; Illinois Executive Ethics Commission, chair. **Publications:** One L: An Inside Account of Life in the First Year at Harvard Law School, 1977. NOVELS: Presumed Innocent, 1987; The Burden of Proof, 1990; Pleading Guilty, 1993; The Laws of Our Fathers, 1996; Personal Injuries, 1999; Reversible Errors, 2002; Ultimate Punishment: A Lawyer's Reflections on Dealing with the Death Penalty, 2003; Ordinary Heroes, 2005; (with O. Penzler) The Best American Mystery Stories, 2006; Limitations, 2006; Innocent, 2010. Contributor to journals and newspapers. **Address:** Sonnenschein, Nath and Rosenthal, Sears Twr., 233 S Wacker Dr., Ste. 7800, Chicago, IL 60606-6404, U.S.A. **Online address:** scott@scottturow.com

TUROW, Scott F. *See* **TUROW, (L.) Scott.**

TURPIN, Jennifer. American (born United States), b. 1961. **Genres:** Sociology, Social Sciences, History, Anthropology/Ethnology. **Career:** University of California, Institute on Global Conflict and Cooperation, Seminar on Global Conflict and Arms Control, fellow, 1989; Chapman College, instructor in sociology, 1990; California State University, lecturer in sociology, 1990-91; University of San Francisco, Department of Sociology, associate professor of sociology, 1991-, professor of sociology, chair, Women's Studies Program, founder, head and coordinator, 1992-97, College of Arts and Sciences, associate dean, 1998-2003, dean, 2003-10, Academic Affairs, vice president and provost, 2010-; European University, Center for Peace Studies, associated faculty, 1992-; Universistat Jaume I, associated faculty member, 1998-; American Sociological Association, Section on Peace, War and Social Conflict, chairman; Peace and Justice Studies Association, chairman. Writer. **Publications:** (With R.D. Benford and L.R. Kurtz) Nuclear Cage, 1988; Reinventing the Soviet Self: Media and Social Change in the Former Soviet Union, 1995. EDITOR AND CONTRIBUTOR: (with R. Elias) Rethinking Peace, 1994; (with L.A. Lorentzen) The Gendered New World Order: Militarism, Development, and the Environment, 1996; (with L.R. Kurtz) The Web of Violence: From Interpersonal to Global, 1997; (with L.A. Lorentzen) The Women and War Reader, 1998; (with L.R. Kurtz) The Encyclopedia of Violence, Peace, and Conflict, 3 vols., 1999. Contributor of articles to books, journals and periodicals. **Address:** Department of Sociology, University of San Francisco, 420 Lone Mountain Rossi Wing, 2130 Fulton St., San Francisco, CA 94117-1080, U.S.A. **Online address:** turpinj@usfca.edu

TURPIN, Tom. American (born United States), b. 1943. **Genres:** Novellas/Short Stories, Sciences, Animals/Pets. **Career:** Purdue University, Center for Instructional Excellence, professor of entomology and instruction development specialist. Writer. **Publications:** Flies in the Face of Fashion, Mites Make Right, and Other Bugdacious Tales, 2006; What's Buggin' You Now?: Bee's Knees, Bug Lites and Beetles, 2009. **Address:** Department of Entomology, Purdue University, 901 W State St., West Lafayette, IN 47907-2089, U.S.A. **Online address:** turpin@purdue.edu

TURRILL, David A. American (born United States) **Genres:** Novels, Natural History. **Career:** Writer and educator. **Publications:** Michilimackinac: A Tale of the Straits, 1989; Bridge to Eden, 2001; An Apology for Autumn, 2004; Long in the Tooth, 2006. Contributor to periodicals. **Address:** c/o Author Mail, Toby Press, PO Box 8531, New Milford, CT 06776-8531, U.S.A.

TURSE, Nicholas Anthony. *See* **TURSE, Nick.**

TURSE, Nick. (Nicholas Anthony Turse). American (born United States), b. 1975?. **Genres:** Military/Defense/Arms Control, History. **Career:** Tomdispatch.com, associate editor and research director. **Publications:** The Complex: How the Military Invades Our Everyday Lives, 2008. Contributor to periodicals. **Address:** Melissa Flashman, Trident Media Group L.L.C., 41 Madison Ave., 36th Fl., New York, NY 10010-2257, U.S.A.

TURTELTAUB, H. N. *See* **TURTLEDOVE, Harry (Norman).**

TURTLEDOVE, Harry (Norman). Also writes as Eric Chernenko, Dan Chernenko, Eric G. Iverson, H. N. Turteltaub. American (born United States), b. 1949. **Genres:** Novels, Novellas/Short Stories, Science Fiction/Fantasy, Young Adult Non-fiction. **Career:** Los Angeles County Office of Education, technical writer, 1970-91. **Publications:** NOVELS: Agent of Byzantium, 1987; A Different Flesh, 1988; Noninterference, 1988; A World of Difference, 1990; Kaleidoscope, 1990; Earthgrip, 1991; The Guns of the South: A Novel of the Civil War, 1992; Departures, 1993; The Case of the Toxic Spell Dump, 1994; (with R. Dreyfuss) The Two Georges: The Novel of an Alternate America, 1995; Thessalonica, 1997; Between the Rivers, 1998; (with J. Tarr) Household Gods, 1999; Down in the Bottomlands: And Other Places, 1999; Wisdom of the Fox: The Man Who Wouldn't Be King, 1999; Tale of the Fox, 2000; Ruled Britannia, 2002; Counting Up, Counting Down, 2002; Conan of Venarium, 2003; In the Presence of Mine Enemies, 2003; Homeward Bound, 2004; Every Inch a King, 2005; Fort Pillow, 2006; Opening Atlantis, 2007; The Man with the Iron Heart, 2008; After the Downfall, 2008; Appeasement, 2008; The United States of Atlantis, 2008; Give Me Back My Legions!, 2009; Liberating Atlantis, 2009; Reincarnations, 2009; Forty, Counting Down & Twenty-One, Counting Up, 2009; Atlantis and Other Places, 2010. FANTASY NOVELS VIDESSOS CYCLE: The Misplaced Legion, 1987; An Emperor for the Legion, 1987; The Legion of Videssos, 1987; Swords of the Legion, 1987; Bridge of the Separator, 2005. RISPOS: Krispos Rising, 1991; Krispos of Videssos, 1991; Krispos the Emperor, 1994; The Tale of Krispos, 2007. SCIENCE-FICTION NOVELS WORLDWAR SERIES: In the Balance, 1994; Tilting the Balance, 1995; Upsetting the Balance, 1996; Striking the Balance, 1996. GERIN THE FOX: (as Eric G. Iverson) Were Blood, 1979; (as Eric G. Iverson) Werenight, 1979; Prince of the North, 1994; King of the North, 1996; Fox and Empire, 1997. TIME OF TROUBLES: The Stolen Throne, 1995; Hammer and Anvil, 1996; The Thousand Cities, 1997; Videssos Besieged, 1998. GREAT WAR: How Few Remain, 1997; The American Front, 1998; The Great War: Walk in Hell, 1999; Breakthroughs, 2000. DARKNESS: Into the Darkness, 1998; Darkness Descending, 2000; Through the Darkness, 2001; Rulers of the Darkness, 2002; Jaws of Darkness, 2003; Out of the Darkness, 2004. COLONISATION: Second Contact, 1999; Down to Earth, 2000; Aftershocks, 2001. WAR BETWEEN THE PROVINCES: Sentry Peak, 2000; Marching Through Peachtree, 2001; Advance and Retreat, 2002. AMERICAN EMPIRE: Blood and Iron, 2001; The Center Cannot Hold, 2002; The Victorious Opposition, 2003. CROSSTIME TRAFFIC: Gunpowder Empire, 2003; Curious Notions, 2004; In High Places, 2005; The Disunited States of America, 2006; The Gladiator, 2007; The Valley-Westside War, 2008. SETTLING ACCOUNTS: Return Engagement, 2004; Drive to the East, 2005; The Grapple, 2006; In At the Death, 2007. PACIFIC WAR: Days of Infamy, 2004; End of the Beginning, 2005. GAP SERIES: Beyond the Gap, 2007; The Breath of God, 2008; The Golden Shrine, 2009. WAR THAT CAME EARLY SERIES: Hitler's War, 2009; West and East, 2010. OTHERS: (trans.) The Chronicle of Theophanes: An English Translation of Anni Mundi 60959305 (A.D. 602-813), 1982; 3 x T, 2004; (ed. with N. Doyle) The First Heroes: New Tales of the Bronze Age, 2004; (with S.M. Stirling, M. Gentle, W.J. Williams) Worlds that Weren't, 2005; The Time of Troubles I, 2005; The Time of Troubles II, 2005; (ed. with R.J. Green) Alternate Generals III, 2005;

(ed. with M.H. Greenberg) The Best Time Travel Stories of the 20th Century, 2005; The Big Switch: The War that came Early, 2011; Supervolcano: vol. I: Eruption, 2012; vol. II, 2013; vol. III, 2014. AS DAN CHERNENKO: The Bastard King, 2003; The Chernagor Pirates, 2004; The Scepter's Return, 2005. AS H.N. TURTELTAUB: Justinian, 1998; Over the Wine-Dark Sea, 2001; The Gryphon's Skull, 2002; The Sacred Land, 2003; Owl to Athens, 2004. **Address:** Baen Books, PO Box 1403, New York, NY 10163, U.S.A.

TURVEY, Roger. Welsh (born Wales), b. 1961. **Genres:** History, Biography, Autobiography/Memoirs. **Career:** Institute of Educational Assessors, associate; Journal of the Pembrokeshire Historical Society, editor; Amman Valley School, Department of History, head. **Publications:** The Lord Rhys: Prince of Deheubarth, 1997; (ed. and intro.) A Critical Edition of Sir James Perrot's The Life, Deedes and Death of Sir John Perrott, Knight, 2002; The Welsh Princes: The Native Rulers of Wales, 1063-1283, 2002; The Treason and Trial of Sir John Perrot, 2005; Llywelyn the Great: Prince of Gwynedd, 2007; (with K. Randell) Henry VIII to Mary I: Government and Religion, 1509-58, 2008; (with N. Heard) Change and Protest, 1536-88: Mid-Tudor Crises?, 4th ed., 2009. Contributor to journals. **Address:** Department of History, Amman Valley School, Margaret St., Ammanford, SA18 2NW, Wales.

TUSAN, Michelle Elizabeth. American (born United States), b. 1971. **Genres:** Writing/Journalism, Women's Studies And Issues, History, Writing/Journalism. **Career:** University of Nevada, associate professor of history, 2001-. Writer. **Publications:** Women Making News: Gender and Journalism in Modern Britain, 2005. **Address:** Department of History, University of Nevada, Rm. A 318, Wright Hall, 4505 Maryland Pkwy., PO Box 455020, Las Vegas, NV 89154-5020, U.S.A. **Online address:** michelle.tusan@unlv.edu

TUTTLE, Lisa. British/American (born United States), b. 1952. **Genres:** Mystery/Crime/Suspense, Science Fiction/Fantasy, Children's Fiction, Women's Studies And Issues, Young Adult Fiction, Novellas/Short Stories, Novels. **Career:** Mathom Fan Magazine, editor, 1968-70; Austin American Statesman, television columnist, 1976-79; London University, City Literary College, teacher of courses in science fiction for extramural department, 1984-88; Women's Press, editor, 1987-. **Publications:** (With G.R.R. Martin) Windhaven (science fiction), 1981; Catwitch (juvenile), 1983; Angela's Rainbow (fantasy), 1983; Familiar Spirit (suspense), 1983; (with R. Ashe) Children's Literary Houses: Famous Dwellings in Children's Fiction (juvenile), 1984; A Nest of Nightmares (short stories), 1986; Encyclopedia of Feminism, 1986; Gabriel (suspense), 1987; (contrib.) Night Visions, 1987; A Spaceship Built of Stone (short stories), 1987; Heroines: Women Inspired by Women, 1988; (ed.) Skin of the Soul: New Horror Stories by Women, 1990; Mark Harrison's Dreamlands, 1990; Lost Futures (science fiction), 1992; Memories of the Body: Tales of Desire and Transformation (short stories), 1992; The Pillow Friend (novel), 1996; Panther in Argyll (juvenile), 1996; Love on Line (juvenile), 1998; Ghosts and Other Lovers, 2001; My Pathology, 2001; Writing Fantasy and Science Fiction, 2001; My Death, 2004; The Mysteries, 2005; The Silver Bough, 2006; (contrib.) Songs of Love & Death: All-Original Tales of Star-Crossed Love, 2010. Contributor to periodicals. **Address:** Howard Morhaim Literary Agency, Rm. 407, 11 John St., New York, NY 10038-4067, U.S.A. **Online address:** lisa@lisatuttle.com

TUTTLE, William McCullough. American (born United States), b. 1937. **Genres:** History, Race Relations, Biography, Politics/Government, Humanities. **Career:** University of Wisconsin, Department of History, research assistant, 1963-65; Educational Testing Service, historian for recent U.S. history, 1965-67; University of Kansas, assistant professor, 1967-70, associate professor, 1970-75, professor of history, 1975-2000, director of graduate studies in history, 1979-81, intra-university professor, 1982-83, courtesy professor of African and African-American studies, 1991-2008, professor of American studies, 2000-08, courtesy professor of history, 2000-08, professor emeritus, 2008-; Johns Hopkins University, Southern and Negro history, senior fellow, 1969-70; Harvard University, Warren Center, research fellow, 1972-73; University of Wisconsin, G. Gordon Fox lecturer in American institutions, 1978; University of South Carolina, visiting professor, 1980; Stanford University, Stanford Humanities Center, associate fellow, 1983-84; University of California, Institute of Human Development, research associate, 1986-88; Lake Forest College, Ruth Winters convocation lecturer, 1995; Stephen F. Austin University, Robert S. Maxwell lecturer, 1995; Kansas University Athletics Corp., vice chairperson, 1998-99; Radboud University, John Adams distinguished Fulbright chair in American history, 2007; University of Texas, lecturer; University of Maine, lecturer. Writer. **Publications:** (Contrib.) Black America:

Confrontation and Accommodation in the Twentieth Century, 1969; (contrib.) Afro-American History: Primary Sources, 1970; (contrib.) Black Labor in America, 1970; Race Riot: Chicago in the Red Summer of 1919, 1970; Black Workers and Organized Labor, 1971; (contrib.) American History: Urban Perspective, 1971; (contrib.) Civil Strife in America, 1972; W.E.B. Du Bois, 1973; (contrib.) Many Pasts, 1973; (contrib.) The Underside of American History, 1978; (ed. and intro. with D.M. Katzman) Plain Folk: The Life Stories of Undistinguished Americans, 1982; (co-author) A People and a Nation: A History of the United States, 1982, 7th ed., 2005; The Way We Lived: Essays and Documents in American Social History, 1988, 2nd ed., 1992; Childhood and Adolescence in America, 1992; Daddy's Gone to War: The Second World War in the Lives of America's Children, 1993; Children in Time and Place: Developmental and Historical Insights, 1993; A History of Child Welfare, 1996; (co-author) World War II and the American Home Front, 2007. Contributor to books. Works appear in anthologies. **Address:** American Studies Program, University of Kansas, 213, Bailey Hall, 1440 Jayhawk Blvd., Lawrence, KS 66045, U.S.A. **Online address:** tuttle@ku.edu

TUTU, Desmond M(pilo). South African (born South Africa), b. 1931. **Genres:** Race Relations, Essays, Theology/Religion, Young Adult Non-fiction, History, Regional/Urban Planning. **Career:** Teacher at high schools in Johannesburg, 1954-55; teacher at Krugersdorp, 1955-58; ordained deacon, 1960; Anglican priest, 1961; St. Alban's Churchin, curate, 1961-62; Federal Theological Seminary, lecturer, 1967-69; University of Fort Hare, chaplain, 1967-69; University of Botswana, staff, 1970-72; World Council of Churches' Theological Educational Fund, associate director, 1972-75; St. Augustine's Church, curate, 1972-75; Johannesburg Diocese, dean, 1975-76; Lesotho Diocese, bishop, 1976-78; South African Council of Churches, staff, 1978-85; assistant Anglican bishop of Johannesburg, 1978-85, bishop, 1984-86; St. Augustine's Parish, rector, 1981-85; General Theological Seminary, visiting professor, 1984; University of the Witwatersrand, Richard Feetham Academic Freedom Lecture, 1985; Anglican Church of Southern Africa, archbishop of Cape Town, 1986-96, archbishop emeritus of Cape Town, 1996-; All Africa Conference of Churches, president, 1987-; University of the Western Cape, chancellor, 1988-, chaplain, 1988-. Writer. **Publications:** The Divine Intention: Presentation, 1982; Crying in the Wilderness: The Struggle for Justice in South Africa, 1982; Hope and Suffering: Sermons and Speeches, 1983; (foreword) South Africa: The Cordoned Heart, 1986; (foreword) The War against Children: South Africas Youngest Victims, 1986; (contrib.) Hammering Swords Into Ploughshares: Essays in Honor of Archbisop Mpilo Desmond Tutu, 1987; Esperanza y Sufrimiento: Sermones y Discursos, 1988; (with F. England and T. Paterson) Bounty in Bondage: The Anglican Church in Southern Africa, Essays in Honor of Edward Iing, Dean of Cape Town, 1989; (with N. Tutu) The Words of Desmond Tutu, 1989; (foreword) Christianity Amidst Apartheid: Selected Perspectives on the Church in South Africa, 1990; (contrib.) Filtering People: Understanding and Confronting Our Prejudices, 1990; (with S. Williamson) Resistance Art in South Africa, 1990; (with J. Allen) The Rainbow People of God: The Making of a Peaceful Revolution, 1994; (intro.) An African Prayer Book, 1995; (with V. Havel and A.S.S. Kyi) Freedom from Fear: And Other Writings, 1995; Some Evidence of Things Seen: Children of South Africa, 1997; (with M.J. Battle) Reconciliation: The Ubuntu Theology of Desmond Tutu, 1997; (with G.W. Ashby) Go Out and Meet God: A Commentary on the Book of Exodus, 1998; (with R.D. Enright and J. North) Exploring Forgiveness, 1998; (with L. Boadt) The Hebrew Prophets: Visionaries of the Ancient World, 1999; No Future without Forgiveness, 1999; (with M. McAleese) Love in Chaos: Spiritual Growth and the Search for Peace in Northern Ireland, 2000; (with W. Vugt and G.D. Cloete) Race and Reconciliation in South Africa, 2000; (with T.R.H. Davenport and C. Saunders) South Africa: A Modern History, 2000; (co-author) At the Side of Torture Survivors: Treating a Terrible Assault on Human Dignity, 2001; (with K.E. Luckman) Place of Compassion, 2001; (with S. Rees) Passion for Peace: Exercising Power Creatively, 2002; (with B. Naidoo) Out of Bounds, 2003; (with C. Gregorowski and N. Daly) Fly, Eagle, Fly, 2003; (with V. Baird and G. Perry) Sex, Love and Homophobia: Lesbian, Gay, Bisexual and Transgender Lives, 2004; (with G. Gutierrez and M.H. Ellis) Toward a Jewish Theology of Liberation, 2004; (with H. McCullum) Radical Compassion: The Life and Times of Archbishop Ted Scott, 2004; Open Window, 2004; (with D. Abrams) God Has a Dream: A Vision of Hope for Our Time, 2004; (with T. MacDonald) Third World Health: Hostage to First World Wealth, 2005; (with R. Williams) Where God Happens: Discovering Christ in One Another and Other Lessons from the Desert Fathers, 2005; Threat to the Peace: A Call for the UN Security Council to Act in Burma, 2005; (with M. Ramose and T.H. MacDonald) Health, Trade and Human Rights, 2006; (co-author) The Soul of a New Cuisine: A Discovery of the Foods and Flavors of Africa, 2006; (intro.) Believe: The Words and Inspiration of Desmond Tutu, 2007; (intro.) Words For Silence: A Year of Contemplative Meditations, 2008; (with D.C. Abrams) Gods Dream, 2008; (foreword) Jesus Beyond Christianity: The Classic Texts, 2010; (reteller) Children of God Storybook Bible, 2010; (with M.A. Tutu) Made for Goodness: And Why This Makes all the Difference, 2010; (foreword) Dignity: The Essential Role it Plays in Resolving Conflict, 2011; God is not a Christian: And Other Provocations, 2011; (foreword) Season of Rains: Africa in the World, 2012. **Address:** Milnerton, PO Box 1092, Cape Town, 7435, South Africa.

TWADDELL, Kristie. See **MILLER, Kristie.**

TWEED, Stephen C. American (born United States), b. 1949. **Genres:** Administration/Management, Economics. **Career:** Joy Manufacturing Co., Customer Training Center, manager, 1971-78; Dana Corp., manager of education, 1978-79; Tweed Corp., president, 1979-90; Tweed-Weber Inc., principal, 1991-96; Tweed Jeffries L.L.C., principal, 1996-; Visiting Nurse Association, interim president, 1999-2000; Erie Tri-State American Society, founder and president; National Speakers Association, Consultants Professional Emphasis Group, editor; Southeast Outlook, contributing writer. **Publications:** Strategic Focus: A Game Plan for Developing Competitive Advantage, 1990; Strategic Focus: How Corporate Managers Gain the Competitive Advantage in Today's Marketplace, 1999. CO-AUTHOR: Get Ready, Get Set, Go-Go-Go: A Marketing Primer for Home Health Care Professionals, 1997; Strategic Recruiting: How to Find the Employees You Need in Home Health Care, 1999. **Address:** Tweed Jeffries L.L.C., 909 Tamarisk Ct., PO Box 24475, Louisville, KY 40223, U.S.A. **Online address:** stephen@tatsweedjeffries.com

TWEED, Thomas A. American (born United States), b. 1954. **Genres:** History, Human Relations/Parenting, Autobiography/Memoirs. **Career:** University of Miami, assistant professor of religious studies and American studies, 1988-93, professor of religious studies and American studies, Hecht Residential College, fellow, 1988-91, Honors Students Association, faculty fellow, 1990-93, Eaton Residential College, faculty associate, 1991-93; Indiana University, Center for the Study of Religion and American Culture, fellow, 1992-93; University of North Carolina, assistant professor, 1993-96, associate professor, adjunct associate professor of American studies, 1996-2000, College of Arts and Sciences, founding director, 1999-2000, Undergraduate Curriculum, associate dean, 1999-2004, Department of Religious Studies, associate professor, 1996-2000, professor, 2000-01, Zachary Smith distinguished professor of religious studies, 2002-06, Curriculum in American Studies, adjunct professor, 2000-01, Department of Religious Studies, chair, 2006-08; University of Texas-Austin, Department of Religious Studies, Gwyn Shive, Anita Nordan Lindsay and Joe and Cherry Gray professor of the history of Christianity, 2008-; American Society for the Study of Religion, vice president, 2008, program coordinator, 2009, president, 2011. Writer. **Publications:** (Intro.) A Dictionary of all Religions and Religious Denominations, 1992; The American Encounter with Buddhism, 1844-1912: Victorian Culture and the Limits of Dissent, 1992; Our Lady of the Exile, 1997; Crossing and Dwelling: A Theory of Religion, 2006; America's Church, 2011. EDITOR: Retelling U.S. Religious History, 1997; (with Prothero) Asian Religions in America, 1999; Crossing and Dwelling: A Theory of Religion, 2006. **Address:** Department of Religious Studies, University of Texas, BUR 422, PO Box A3700, 1 University Sta., Austin, TX 78712-6000, U.S.A. **Online address:** tomtweed@austin.utexas.edu

TWEIT, Susan J(oan). American (born United States), b. 1956. **Genres:** Homes/Gardens, Children's Non-fiction, Natural History, Young Adult Non-fiction, Autobiography/Memoirs, Essays, Writing/Journalism, Horticulture, Horticulture. **Career:** National Park Service, Yellowstone National Park, biological aide, 1976-77; U.S. Forest Service, Shoshone National Forest, biological technician, 1977-78, vegetation ecologist, 1978-81; University of Wyoming, Women's Resource Center, director, 1982-83; Washington State Department of Natural Resources, coordinating editor, 1984-87; KRWG-FM, radio commentator, 1991-98; Sun News, columnist, 1992-98; Mountain Mail, columnist, 1997-2010; Denver Post, columnist, 2000, 2004; KHEN-FM, radio commentator, 2003-. **Publications:** NONFICTION: Grassland and Shrubland Habitat Types of the Shoshone National Forest, 1980; Writers Handbook, 1987; Pieces of Light: A Year on Colorado's Front Range, 1990; The Great Southwest Nature Factbook: A Guide to the Region's Remarkable Animals, Plants and Natural Features, 1992; Meet the Wild Southwest: Land of Hoodoos and Gila Monsters (juvenile), 1995; Barren, Wild and Worthless:

Living in the Chihuahuan Desert, 1995; City Foxes (juvenile), 1997; Seasons in the Desert: A Naturalist's Notebook, 1998; Seasons on the Pacific Coast: A Naturalist's Notebook, 1999; The Rocky Mountain Garden Survival Guide, 2004; The San Luis Valley: Sand Dunes and Sandhill Cranes, 2005; Walking Nature Home: A Life's Journey, 2009. Contributor to periodicals. Works appear in anthologies. **Address:** PO Box 578, Salida, CO 81201-0578, U.S.A. **Online address:** info@susanjtweit.com

TWINE, France Winddance. American (born United States) **Genres:** Sociology, Women's Studies And Issues, Popular Culture, Cultural/Ethnic Topics, Area Studies, Race Relations. **Career:** Northwestern Memorial Hospital, Institute of Psychiatry, clinical specialist, 1982-86; University of Washington, Henry M. Jackson School of International Studies, assistant professor, 1994-97, associate professor of international studies and women studies, 1998-2000; University of California, Department of Sociology, assistant professor, 1997-98, associate professor of sociology, 1998-2002, professor, 2002-; Duke University, professor of sociology, 2003-05; London School of Economics and Political Science, visiting professor of sociology, 2007, The Gender Institute, visiting professor, 2007; Stanford University, Center for Advanced Study in the Behavioral Sciences, research fellow, 2008-09. Writer. **Publications:** (With J. Warren and F. Ferrandiz) Just Black? Multiracial Identity, 1991; (contrib.) The Multiracial Experience: Racial Borders as the New Frontier, 1995; Racism in a Racial Democracy: The Maintenance of White Supremacy in Brazil, 1998; (contrib.) Everyday Inequalities: Critical Inquiries, 1998; The White Mother, 1998; (contrib.) Dis-Placing Whiteness: Essays in Social and Cultural Criticism, 1998; (ed. with J.W. Warren) Racing Research, Researching Race: Methodological Dilemmas in Critical Race Studies, 2000; (ed. with H. Ragoné) Ideologies and Technologies of Motherhood: Race, Class, Sexuality, Nationalism, 2000; (ed. with K.M. Blee) Feminism and Antiracism: International Struggles for Justice, 2001; A White Side of Black Britain: Interracial Intimacy and Racial Literacy, 2010; Outsourcing the Womb: Race, Class and Gestational Surrogacy in a Global Market, 2011. Contributor to books and periodicals. **Address:** Department of Sociology, University of California, 3020 Social Sciences and Media Studies Bldg., Santa Barbara, CA 93106, U.S.A. **Online address:** winddance@soc.ucsb.edu

TWINGLEY, Jonathan. American (born United States), b. 1973. **Genres:** Illustrations. **Career:** University of the Arts, senior lecturer, 2007-. Writer and illustrator. **Publications:** SELF-ILLUSTRATED: The Badlands Saloon: A Novel, 2009. Contributor to periodicals. **Address:** New York, NY , U.S.A. **Online address:** twingley@verizon.net

TY-CASPER, Linda. American/Filipino (born Philippines), b. 1931. **Genres:** Novels, Novellas/Short Stories, Essays, Young Adult Fiction. **Career:** Silliman University, fellow, 1963; Radcliffe Institute, fellow, 1974-75; Ateneo de Manila University, lecturer in creative writing, 1980; University of the Philippines Creative Writing Center, writer-in-residence, 1980, 1982; The Boston Authors Club, officer. Writer. **Publications:** SHORT STORIES: The Transparent Sun, 1963; The Secret-Runner, 1974; Common Continent, 1991. NOVELS: The Peninsulars, 1964; The Three-Cornered Sun, 1979; Dread Empire, 1980; Hazards of Distance, 1981; Fortress in the Plaza, 1985; Awaiting Trespass, 1985; Wings of Stone, 1986; Ten Thousand Seeds, 1987; A Small Party in a Garden, 1988; Kulasyon: Uninterrupted Vigils, 1995; Dream Eden, 1996; The Stranded Whale, 2002. Works appear in anthologies. **Address:** c/o Bonnie Crown, International Literature & Arts Agency, 50 E 10th St., New York, NY 10003, U.S.A.

TYDEMAN, William (Marcus). Welsh/British (born England), b. 1935. **Genres:** Literary Criticism And History, Theatre, Young Adult Fiction. **Career:** Bangor University assistant lecturer, 1961-64, lecturer, 1964-70, senior lecturer, 1970-83, university reader, 1983-86, professor of English, 1986-97, head department, 1986-92, professor emeritus, 1997-. Writer. **Publications:** (Ed. and intro.) English Poetry, 1400-1580, 1970; (ed. and trans. with M.J. Heeath) Six Christmas plays, 1971; (ed. with A.R. Jones) Wordsworth: Lyrical Ballads, 1972; (ed. with A.R. Jones) Coleridge: The Ancient Mariner and Other Poems, 1973; The Theatre in the Middle Ages: Western European Stage Conditions, Circa 800-1576, 1978; (ed. with A.R. Jones) A Pedestrian Tour through Wales, 1979; (ed. with A.R. Jones) A Pedestrian Tour through North Wales, in a Series of Letters, 1979; (ed. and into.) Plays by Tom Robertson, 1982; (ed.) Wilde: Comedies, 1982; Dr. Faustus: Text and Performance, 1984; (ed. and intro.) Four Tudor Comedies: Jacke Jugeler, Roister Doister, Gammer Gurton's Needle, 1984; (ed. and contrib.) The Welsh Connections, 1985; English Medieval Theatre, 1986; Henry V, 1987; T.S. Eliot: Murder in the

Cathedral and The Cocktail Party, 1988; (with V. Thomas) The State of the Art: Christopher Marlowe: A Guide through the Critical Maze, 1989; (ed. and intro.) Two Tudor Tragedies, 1992; (ed. with V. Thomas) Christopher Marlow: The Plays and Their Sources, 1994; The Medieval European Stage, 500-1550, 1994; The Bancrofts at the Prince of Wales's Theatre, 1996; (with S. Price) Oscar Wilde: Salome, 1996; (with S. Price) Wilde-Salome, 1996; (ed.) The Medieval European Stage, 500-1550, 2001. Contributor to periodicals. **Address:** School of English, Bangor University, Ysgol Saesneg Prifysgol Cymru, Bangor, GY LL57 2DG, Wales.

TYE, Michael. British/American (born United States), b. 1950. **Genres:** Philosophy, Literary Criticism And History. **Career:** Haverford College, assistant professor, 1975-76; Oxford University, visiting fellow, 1984; Northern Illinois University, assistant professor, 1976-82, associate professor, 1982-87; University of California, associate professor, 1987-88; Temple University, associate professor, 1988-91, professor of philosophy, 1991-; King's College, professor of philosophy, 1991-, visiting professor; University of St. Andrews, chair in philosophy, 1996-; University of Texas, TACA centennial professor in liberal arts, Department of Philosophy, professor, philosopher. Writer. **Publications:** The Metaphysics of Mind, 1989; The Imagery Debate, 1991; Ten Problems of Consciousness: A Representational Theory of the Phenomenal Mind, 1995; Consciousness, Color and Content, 2000; Consciousness and Persons: Unity and Identity, 2003; Consciousness Revisited: Materialism Without Phenomenal Concepts, 2009; (with M. Sainsbury) Seven Puzzles of Thought, forthcoming. Contributor of articles to periodicals and journals. **Address:** Department of Philosophy, The University of Texas at Austin, WAG 425, PO Box C3500, 1 University Sta., Austin, TX 78712, U.S.A. **Online address:** mtye@mail.utexas.edu

TYERMAN, Christopher. British (born England), b. 1953. **Genres:** History, Social Sciences, Humanities. **Career:** University of Oxford, Hertford College, lecturer in modern history, senior research fellow, tutor in history; New College, lecturer in medical history. Writer. **Publications:** England and the Crusades, 1095-1588, 1988; Who's Who in Early Medieval England, 1066-1272, 1996; The Invention of the Crusades, 1998; A History of Harrow School, 1324-1991, 2000; Eyewitnesses to the Crusades, 2004; Fighting for Christendom: Holy War and the Crusades, 2004; Crusades: A Very Short Introduction, 2005; God's War: A New History of the Crusades, 2006; (ed. with P. Coss) Soldiers, Nobles and Gentlemen: Essays in Honour of Maurice Keen, 2009. Contributor of articles to journals. **Address:** Faculty of Modern History, Hertford College, University of Oxford, Catte St., Oxford, OX OX1 3BW, England. **Online address:** christopher.tyerman@hertford.ox.ac.uk

TYLDESLEY, Joyce (Ann). British (born England), b. 1960. **Genres:** Archaeology/Antiquities, Anthropology/Ethnology, Mythology/Folklore. **Career:** University of Liverpool, lecturer in archaeology of the eastern mediterranean, 1986-87, Institute of Prehistoric Science and Archaeology, research fellow, 1987-93, School of Archaeology, Classics, and Egyptology, honorary research fellow, 1993-; University of Manchester, KNH Centre for Biomedical Egyptology, teaching fellow in egyptology. Writer. **Publications:** The Wolvercote Channel Handaxe Assemblage: A Comparative Study, 1986; The Bout Coupe Handaxe: A Typological Problem, 1987; (with S.R. Snape) Nazlet Tuna: An Archaeological Survey in Middle Egypt, 1988; Daughters of Isis: Women of Ancient Egypt, 1994; Hatchepsut: The Female Pharaoh, 1998; Nefertiti: Egypt's Sun Queen, 1998; The Mummy: Unwrap The Ancient Secrets of The Mummies' Tombs, 1999 as The Ancient Egyptian Mummy, 2006; Judgement of the Pharaoh: Crime and Punishment in Ancient Egypt, 2000; Ramesses: Egypt's Greatest Pharaoh, 2000; The Private Lives of the Pharaoh, 2000; Pyramids: The Real Story Behind Egypt's Most Ancient Monuments, 2003; Tales from Ancient Egypt, 2004; Egypt: How a Lost Civilization was Rediscovered, 2005; Chronicle of the Queens of Egypt: From Early Dynastic Times to The Death of Cleopatra, 2006, Egyptian Games and Sports, 2007; Egypt, 2007; Cleopatra: Last Queen of Egypt, 2008; The Pharaohs, 2009; Myths and Legends of Ancient Egypt, 2010. Contributor of articles to journals and magazines. **Address:** School of Archaeology, Classics and Egyptology, University of Liverpool, Liverpool, MS L69 3BX, England. **Online address:** joyce.tyldesley@manchester.ac.uk

TYLER, Alison. *See* TITLE, Elise.

TYLER, Anne. American (born United States), b. 1941. **Genres:** Novels, Novellas/Short Stories, Literary Criticism And History, Mystery/Crime/Suspense. **Career:** Duke University Library, Russian bibliographer, 1962-63;

McGill University Law Library, assistant, 1964-65. Writer. **Publications:** If Morning Ever Comes, 1964; The Tin Can Tree, 1965; A Slipping-Down Life, 1969; The Clock Winder, 1972; Celestial Navigation, 1974; Searching for Caleb, 1976; Earthly Possessions, 1977, Morgan's Passing, 1980; Dinner at the Homesick Restaurant, 1982; (ed. and intro. with S. Ravenel) The Best American Short Stories 1983, 1983; The Accidental Tourist, 1985; Breathing Lessons, 1988; Anne Tyler: Four Complete Novels 1990; Anne Tyler: A New Collection, 1991; Saint Maybe, 1991; Tumble Tower (juvenile), 1993; Ladder of Years, 1995; (ed. and intro. with S. Ravenel) Best of the South: From Ten Years of New Stories from the South, 1996; A Patchwork Planet, 1998; Back When We Were Grownups, 2001; Anne Tyler: Three Complete Novels, 2001; The Amateur Marriage, 2004; Timothy Tugbottom Says No!, 2005; (ed. and intro. with S. Ravenel) Best of the South: From the Second Decade of New Stories from the South, 2005; Digging to America: A Novel, 2006; Noah's Compass: A Novel, 2009; The Beginner's Goodbye, 2012. Contributor of articles to periodicals. **Address:** Russell & Volkening Inc., 50 W 29th St., Ste. 7E, New York, NY 10001-4227, U.S.A.

TYLER, Ben. See **JORDAN, Richard Tyler.**

TYLER, C. American (born United States), b. 1951. **Genres:** Science Fiction/Fantasy, Graphic Novels. **Career:** Tennessee Arts Commission, artist-in-residence, 1979; Olympic Winter Games, Children's Art Program, program coordinator, 1979-80; Syracuse University, honors fellow, 1982-83; Vorpal Gallery, gallery assistant, 1983-85; Davis Art Center, comics teacher, 1986-89; Sacramento History Museum, exhibit curator, 1988; University of Cincinnati, School of Art, adjunct professor; Ohio Arts Council, Arts Learning Program, residency artist. Writer and comic artist. **Publications:** The Job Thing: Stories about Shitty Jobs, 1993; Late Bloomer, 2005; You'll Never Know, vol. I: A Good & Decent Man, 2009, vol. II: Collateral Damage, 2010. Contributor to periodicals, books and journals. **Address:** College of Design, Architecture, Art, and Planning, University of Cincinnati, 5470 Aronoff Ctr., PO Box 210016, Cincinnati, OH 45221-0016, U.S.A. **Online address:** bloomerlandinfo@fuse.net

TYLER, Sandra. American (born United States), b. 1963. **Genres:** Novels, Young Adult Fiction, Literary Criticism And History. **Career:** Montauk Light, feature writer and reporter, 1985-86; Ploughshares, assistant editor, 1986-88; Columbia: A Magazine of Poetry and Prose, editorial assistant, 1988; Seventeen, book reviewer, 1989-90; Paris Review, editorial assistant, 1989-90; Manhattanville College, adjunct professor of creative writing, 1994-95; Columbia University, adjunct professor of creative writing, 1994-95; Wesleyan University, adjunct professor of creative writing, 1994-; Southampton College of LIU, adjunct professor of creative writing, 1994-; Nassau Community College, teacher of writing. **Publications:** NOVELS: Blue Glass, 1992; After Lydia, 1995. Contributor to periodicals. **Address:** Nassau Community College, Bradley Hall- WW, 1 Education Dr., Garden City, NY 11530-6793, U.S.A.

TYLER, Stephen Albert. American (born United States), b. 1932. **Genres:** Anthropology/Ethnology, Language/Linguistics. **Career:** University of California-Davis, assistant professor of anthropology, 1964-67; University of California-Berkeley, 1966; Tulane University, associate professor of anthropology, 1967-70; Rice University, Department of of anthropology and linguistics, professor, 1970-90, chairman, 1971-73, Herbert S. Autrey professor of anthropology and linguistics, 1990-, now Herbert S. Autrey professor emeritus of anthropology and linguistics; University of New Mexico, Department of Anthropology, Journal of Anthropological Research, associate editor, 1980-; Annual Review Inc., American Ethnologist, associate editor. **Publications:** Koya: An Outline of Grammar, 1969; Concepts and Assumptions in Contemporary Anthropology, 1969; (ed.) Cognitive Anthropology, 1969; India: An Anthropological Perspective, 1973; The Said and the Unsaid: Mind, Meaning, and, Culture, 1978; The Unspeakable: Discourse, Dialogue and Rhetoric in the Post-Modern World, 1987; (ed. with I. Strecker) Culture & Rhetoric, 2009. Contributor to journals. **Address:** Department of Anthropology, Rice University, MS-20, PO Box 1892, Houston, TX 77251-1892, U.S.A. **Online address:** styler@rice.edu

TYNAN, Ronan. Irish (born Ireland), b. 1960. **Genres:** Education, Autobiography/Memoirs. **Career:** Irish Tenors, musician, 1998-2004. Physician, orthopedist and writer. **Publications:** Halfway Home: My Life 'Til Now, 2002. Contributor to periodicals. **Address:** c/o Author Mail, Simon & Schuster Inc., 1230 Ave. of the Americas, New York, NY 10020, U.S.A. **Online address:** ronannotes@hotmail.com

TYRE, Peg. American (born United States), b. 1960. **Genres:** Novels, Mystery/Crime/Suspense. **Career:** Newsday, law enforcement journalist, 1989; CNN News, correspondent, 1995-98; Newsweek, general editor, 2001-. **Publications:** Strangers in the Night, 1994; (co-author) Two Seconds Under the World, 1994; In the Midnight Hour, 1995; The trouble with Boys: A Surprising Report Card on Our Sons, Their Problems at School, and What Parents and Educators Must Do, 2008. **Address:** c/o Richard Pine, Inkwell Management, 521 5th Ave., 26th Fl., New York, NY 10175, U.S.A. **Online address:** pegtyre@pegtyre.com

TYRRELL, Ian. See **TYRRELL, Ian R(obert).**

TYRRELL, Ian R(obert). (Ian Tyrrell). Australian (born Australia), b. 1947. **Genres:** History, Women's Studies And Issues, Humanities. **Career:** University of New South Wales, lecturer, associate professor of history, 1975-2001, professor, 2001-06, School of History and Philosophy, scientia professor of history, 2007-; Australasian Journal of American Studies, editor, 1991-96; Australian Academy of the Humanities, fellow, 2001; University of Sydney, Australian and New Zealand American Studies Association, president, 2002-06; Ecole des Hautes Etudes en Sciences Sociales, visiting professor; University of Oxford, Harold Vyvyan Harmsworth Professor of American History, 2010-11; Queens College, professorial fellow. **Publications:** Sobering Up, 1979; The Absent Marx, 1986; Woman's World/Woman's Empire: The Woman's Christian Temperance Union in International Perspective, 1991; True Gardens of the Gods, 1999; (co-ed.) Alcohol and Temperance in Modern History, 2003; Historians in Public: The Practice of American History, 1890-1970, 2005; Transnational Nation: United States History in Global Perspective since 1789, 2007; Reforming the World, 2010. Contributor to periodicals. **Address:** School of History and Philosophy, University of New South Wales, Rm. 352, Morven Brown Bldg., Sydney, NW 2052, Australia. **Online address:** i.tyrrell@unsw.edu.au

TYSDAHL, Bjorn Johan. Norwegian (born Norway), b. 1933. **Genres:** Literary Criticism And History, Autobiography/Memoirs, Humanities. **Career:** University of Oslo, lecturer, 1965-72, reader in English literature, 1972-84, professor of English literature, 1985-2002, professor emeritus, 2002-; University of Sussex, visiting lecturer, 1970. Writer. **Publications:** Joyce and Ibsen: A Study of Literary Influence, 1968; William Godwin as Novelist, 1981; Maurits Hansens fortellerkunst, 1988; (ed. with L.Bliksrud) Literature and Ethics: Proceedings from the Symposium SkjØnn Litteratur Og Etikk, Held at the Norwegian Academy of Science and Letters, Oslo, 23-24 April 1992, 1992; (ed. with I. Ewbank and O. Lausund) Anglo-Scandinavian Cross-Currents, 1999; (ed.) English and Nordic Modernisms, 2002; James Joyce: Liv Og Diktning, 2003. **Address:** Department of English, University of Oslo, PO Box 1003, Oslo, 0315 OSLO, Norway. **Online address:** bjorn.tysdahl@ilos.uio.no

TYSON, Ann Scott. American (born United States), b. 1959. **Genres:** Documentaries/Reportage, History. **Career:** Christian Science Monitor, senior writer, staff correspondent, congressional correspondent, pentagon correspondent 1987-. **Publications:** (With J.L. Tyson, Jr.) Chinese Awakenings: Life Stories from the Unofficial China, 1995. **Address:** Christian Science Monitor, 910 16th St. NW, Washington, DC 20006, U.S.A. **Online address:** tysona@csps.com

TYSON, Joseph B. American (born United States), b. 1928. **Genres:** History, Theology/Religion. **Career:** Southern Methodist University, Department of Religious Studies, instructor, 1958-60, assistant professor, 1960-65, associate professor, 1965-74, chair, 1965-75, 1986-93, professor, 1974-98, professor emeritus of religious studies, 1998-. Writer. **Publications:** Study of Early Christianity, 1973; (with T.R.W. Longstaff, E.A. Tipper and L.M. Guier) Synoptic Abstract, 1978; The New Testament and Early Christianity, 1984; The Death of Jesus in Luke-Acts, 1986; Images of Judaism in Luke-Acts, 1992; Luke, Judaism, and the Scholars: Critical Approaches to Luke-Acts, 1999; Marcion and Luke-Acts: A Defining Struggle, 2006. EDITOR: (and intro. with A.J. Bellinzoni, Jr. and W.O. Walker, Jr.) The Two Source Hypothesis: A Critical Appraisal, 1985; Luke-Acts and the Jewish People: Eight Critical Perspectives, 1988; (with M.C. Parsons) Cadbury, Knox, and Talbert: American Contributions to the Study of Acts, 1992. **Address:** Department of Religious Studies, Southern Methodist University, Hyer Hall, 6424 Robert S.

Hyer Ln., Ste. 300, PO Box 750202, Dallas, TX 75275-0202, U.S.A. **Online address:** jtyson@mail.smu.edu

TYSON, Lois (M.). American (born United States), b. 1950?. **Genres:** Literary Criticism And History, Philosophy, Young Adult Fiction, Humanities. **Career:** Grand Valley State University, assistant professor, 1989-95, associate professor, 1995-2002, professor of English, 2002-, faculty development coordinator. Writer. **Publications:** Psychological Politics of the American Dream: The Commodification of Subjectivity in Twentieth-Century American Literature, 1994; Critical Theory Today: A User-Friendly Guide, 1999; Learning for a Diverse World: Using Critical Theory to Read and Write about Literature, 2001; Critical Theory Today: A User-Friendly Guide, 2006; Using Critical Theory: How to Read and Write About Literature, 2011. Contributor to books and journals. **Address:** Department of English, Grand Valley State University, 226 Lake Huron Hall, Allendale, MI 49401, U.S.A. **Online address:** tysonl@gvsu.edu

TYSON, Neil deGrasse. American (born United States), b. 1958. **Genres:** Astronomy, Sciences, Air/Space Topics. **Career:** University of Maryland, Department of Astronomy, lecturer, 1987; Princeton University, Department of Astrophysics, postdoctoral research associate, 1991-94, visiting research scientist and lecturer, 1994-2003; American Museum of Natural History, Hayden Planetarium, staff scientist, 1994-95, acting director, 1995-96, astrophysicist and Frederick P. Rose director, 1996-, Department of Astrophysics, founder and chair, 1997-99, research associate, 2003-, Rose Center for Earth and Space, project scientist, 1997-2000. Writer. **Publications:** Merlin's Tour of the Universe, 1989 as Merlin's Tour of the Universe: A Skywatcher's Guide to Everything from Mars and Quasars to Comets, Planets, Blue Moons, and Werewolves, 1997; Universe down to Earth, 1994; Just Visiting This Planet: Merlin Answers More Questions about Everything under the Sun, Moon, and Stars, 1998; (with C. Liu and R. Irion) One Universe: At Home in the Cosmos, 2000; The Sky Is Not the Limit: Adventures of an Urban Astrophysicist, 2000; (ed. with S. Soter) Cosmic Horizons: Astronomy at the Cutting Edge, 2001; (with D. Goldsmith) Origins: Fourteen Billion Years of Cosmic Evolution, 2004; Death by Black Hole: And Other Cosmic Quandaries, 2007; Pluto Files: The Rise and Fall of America's Favorite Planet, 2009; Space Chronicles: Facing the Ultimate Frontier, 2012. **Address:** Department of Astrophysics, American Museum of Natural History, 79th St., Central Pk. W, New York, NY 10024-5192, U.S.A. **Online address:** tyson@amnh.org

TYSON, Salinda. American (born United States), b. 1952?. **Genres:** Adult Non-fiction, Science Fiction/Fantasy, Literary Criticism And History. **Career:** San Francisco Bay Area, freelance graphic artist, 1980-90; Bay City News Service, reporter and editor, 1991-99; San Francisco Chronicle Library, editorial assistant, 1999-. **Publications:** Wheel of Dreams, 1996. **Address:** Richard Curtis Associates Inc., 171 E 74th St., Fl. 2, New York, NY 10021, U.S.A. **Online address:** styson@sfchronicle.com

TZOULIADIS, Tim. British/Greek (born Greece), b. 1968?. **Genres:** History, Politics/Government. **Career:** Writer and film producer. **Publications:** The Forsaken: An American Tragedy in Stalin's Russia in UK as The Forsaken: From the Great Depression to the Gulags: Hope and Betrayal in Stalin's Russia, 2008. Contributor to periodicals. **Address:** Conville & Walsh Ltd., 2 Ganton St., Westminster, London, GL W1F 7QL, England

U

UBELAKER, Douglas H. American (born United States), b. 1946. **Genres:** Anthropology/Ethnology, Archaeology/Antiquities. **Career:** Federal Bureau of Investigation Laboratory, consultant in forensic anthropology, 1978-; Smithsonian Institution, National Museum of Natural History, Department of Anthropology, chairman, 1980-85, assistant director, 1988, curator of anthropology, Museum of Man Planning Group, chairman, 1980-85, Division of Physical Anthropology, head, 1989-92, senior scientist; George Washington University, Department of Anatomy, professorial lecturer in anatomy and anthropology, 1986-; American Board of Forensic Anthropology, president, 1995-98; Forensic Sciences Foundation Inc., American Academy of Forensic Sciences, vice president, 2007-08; Michigan State University, Department of Anatomy, professor, 2009-. Writer. **Publications:** (With W.M. Bass) A Review of Human Origins, 1969, (with W.M. Bass, R.L. Jantz and F.H. Smith) 6th ed., 1990; Reconstruction of Demographic Profiles from Ossuary Skeletal Samples, 1974; Human Skeletal Remains: Excavation, Analysis, Interpretation, 1978, 3rd ed., 1999; Human Bones and Archeology, 1980; The Ayalan Cemetery: A Late Integration Period Burial Site on the South Coast of Ecuador, 1981; (ed. with H.J. Viola) Plains Indian Studies: A Collection of Essays in Honor of John C. Ewers and Waldo R. Wedel, 1982; (with H. Scammell) Bones: A Forensic Detective's Casebook, 1992; (ed. with J.W. Verano) Disease and Demography in the Americas, 1992; (ed. with J.E. Buikstra and D. Aftandilian) Standards for Data Collection from Human Skeletal Remains, 1994; Skeletal Biology of Human Remains from La Tolita, Esmeraldas Province, Ecuador, 1997; (with C.E. Ripley) The Ossuary of San Francisco Church, Quito, Ecuador: Human Skeletal Biology, 1999; Human Remains from La Florida, Quito, Ecuador, 2000; (with G.A. Grisbaum) An Analysis of Forensic Anthropology Cases Submitted to the Smithsonian Institution by the Federal Bureau of Investigation from 1962 to 1994, 2001; (ed. with E.B. Jones and D.B. Landers) Human Remains from Voegtly Cemetery, Pittsburgh, Pennsylvania, 2003; (ed. with S. Blau) Handbook of Forensic Anthropology and Archaeology, 2009. Contributor of articles to books and journals. **Address:** Department of Anthropology, National Museum of Natural History, Smithsonian Institution, MRC 112, 10th and Constitution Ave. NW, Washington, DC 20560, U.S.A. **Online address:** ubelaked@si.edu

UCKO, Barbara. American (born United States), b. 1945. **Genres:** Novels, Novellas/Short Stories. **Career:** Cambridge University Press, copywriter, 1972-74; Bantam Books, copywriter, 1974-75; Pocket Books, promotional director of school and college division, 1975-76; Antioch Press, promotional director, 1977. Writer. **Publications:** NOVELS: Family Trappings, 1985; Scarlett Greene, 1987. Contributor to periodicals. **Address:** 2528 Queen Anne's Ln. NW, Washington, DC 20037-2148, U.S.A. **Online address:** barbara.ucko@verizon.net

UDALL, Brady. American (born United States), b. 1957?. **Genres:** Novels, Young Adult Fiction. **Career:** University of Idaho, lecturer, 1998-; Franklin and Marshall College, faculty, 1998-; Southern Illinois University, faculty; Boise State University, associate professor of English, professor. Writer. **Publications:** Letting Loose the Hounds: Stories, 1997; The Miracle Life of Edgar Mint: A Novel, 2001; Lonely Polygamist: A Novel, 2010. Contributor to periodicals. **Address:** Department of English, Boise State University, Rm. G-118, 228 Liberal Arts Bldg., 1910 University Dr., Boise, ID 83725-1525, U.S.A. **Online address:** bradenudall@boisestate.edu

UDJO, Eric O. (Eric Ogheneriobororue Udjo). South African/Nigerian (born Nigeria), b. 1954. **Genres:** Social Sciences. **Career:** Ogbavweni Grammar School, teacher, 1973-75; University of Maiduguri, graduate assistant, senior lecturer, 1979-90; Population Council of America, postdoctoral fellow, 1990-92; University of Botswana, 1992-96; Botswana Sukokai Karate School, assistant instructor, 1994-96; Statistics South Africa, senior lecturer & director of Analysis and Statistical Consulting, 1997-; University of Pretoria, Center for Population Studies, 1998; Human Sciences Research Council, HIV/AIDS and Health Programme, research director; University of South Africa, Bureau of Market Research, research professor. Administrator, academic and writer. **Publications:** (ed. with T. Zuberi and A. Sibanda) The Demography of South Africa, 2005. **Address:** Bureau of Market Research, University of South Africa, PO Box 392, Pretoria, UNISA 003, South Africa. **Online address:** bororue@yahoo.com

UDJO, Eric Ogheneriobororue. See **UDJO, Eric O.**

UEDA, Makoto. American/Japanese (born Japan), b. 1931. **Genres:** Literary Criticism And History, Poetry, Translations, Novellas/Short Stories, Essays, Young Adult Fiction. **Career:** University of Toronto, lecturer, 1961-62, assistant professor, 1962-64, associate professor, 1965-67, professor, 1968-71; Stanford University, professor of Japanese and comparative literature, 1971-96, now professor emeritus. Writer. **Publications:** (Trans.) The Old Pine Tree and Other Noh Plays, 1962; Zeami, Bashō, Yeats, Pound: A Study in Japanese and English Poetics, 1965; Literary and Art Theories in Japan, 1967; Matsuo Bashō, 1970; (trans., comp. and intro.) Modern Japanese Haiku: An Anthology, 1976; Modern Japanese Writers and the Nature of Literature, 1976; Modern Japanese Poets and the Nature of Literature, 1983; (with Y.M. Hen) Owari no bigaku: Nihon bungaku ni okeru shūketsu, 1990; (trans., comp. and intro.) Bashō and His Interpreters: Selected Hokku with Commentary, 1991; The Path of Flowering Thorn: The Life and Poetry of Yosa Buson, 1998; (trans., comp. and intro.) Light Verse from the Floating World: An Anthology of Premodern Japanese Senryu, 1999; (trans., comp. and intro.) Far Beyond the Field: Haiku by Japanese Women: An Anthology, 2003; Dew On the Grass: The Life and poetry of Kobayashi Issa, 2004. EDITOR: The Mother of Dreams and Other Short Stories: Portrayals of Women in Modern Japanese Fiction, 1986; Explorations: Essays in Comparative Literature, 1986; (and trans.) Modern Japanese Tanka: An Anthology, 1996. **Address:** Department of East Asian Languages and Cultures, Stanford University, 450 Serra Mall Bldg. 250, Main Quad, Stanford, CA 94305-2000, U.S.A.

UEKERT, Brenda K. American (born United States), b. 1963. **Genres:** Race Relations, How-to Books. **Career:** Syracuse University, instructor and teaching associate, 1986-89; University of California, senior research analyst, 1990-94; University of Wisconsin-Green Bay, Lakeland College, adjunct instructor, 1995-96; Atlanta Police Department, crime analyst, 1997-98; Institute for Law and Justice, senior research associate, 1998-2001; National Center for State Courts, senior research associate, 2001-; Family Violence Community of Practice/Children and Families Initiative, chair, 2001-06; Avalon, board director, 2004; Elder Abuse and the Courts Working Group, chair, 2005-; National Guardianship Network, representative, 2008-. Writer. **Publications:** Rivers of Blood: A Comparative Study of Government Massacres, 1995; 10 Steps to Successful International Adoption: A Guide Workbook for Prospective Parents, 2007. **Address:** National Center for State Courts, 300 Newport Ave., Williamsburg, VA 23185, U.S.A. **Online address:** buekert@ncsc.org

UGEL, Edward. American (born United States) **Genres:** Autobiography/Memoirs, Biography. **Career:** Freelance writer. **Publications:** Money for Nothing: One Man's Journey through the Dark Side of Lottery Millions (memoir), 2007; I'm with Fatty: Losing Fifty Pounds in Fifty Miserable Weeks, 2010. Contributor to journals. **Address:** c/o Farley Chase, The Waxman Literary Agency, 80 5th Ave., Ste. 1101, New York, NY 10011, U.S.A. **Online address:** ed@edwardugel.com

UGWUEGBU, Denis Chima E. American/Nigerian (born Nigeria), b. 1942. **Genres:** Education, Psychology. **Career:** University of Ibadan, lecturer, 1973-77, senior lecturer, 1978-82, professor of psychology and department chair, 1982-2004; University of Waterloo, visiting professor, 1982-83; University of Michigan, visiting professor, 1999-2003. Writer. **Publications:** (With G. Siann) Educational Psychology in a Changing World, 1980; (ed. with S.O. Onwumere) Social Research and Information Gathering, 1987; (ed.) National Orientation Movement, 1989; (ed.) Youth and Pornography, 1991; The Psychology of Management in African Organizations, 2001; The Shifting Tides of Value Orientation: A Case for National Development, 2004; Social Psychology and Social Change in Nigeria, 2011. Contributor to books and journals. **Address:** iUniverse Inc., 1663 Liberty Dr., Bloomington, IN 47403, U.S.A. **Online address:** profugw42@yahoo.com

UHER, Lorna. See **CROZIER, Lorna.**

UHLENBECK, Karen (Keskulla). American (born United States), b. 1942. **Genres:** Mathematics/Statistics, Education, Sciences. **Career:** Massachusetts Institute of Technology, math instructor, 1968-69; University of California-Berkeley, lecturer, 1969-71, chancellor's distinguished visiting professor, 1979; University of Illinois-Urbana-Champaign, assistant professor, associate professor, 1971-76; Northwestern University, visiting associate professor, 1976; University of Illinois-Chicago, associate professor, professor, 1977-83; Princeton University, Institute of Advanced Studies, Albert Einstein fellow, 1979-80; Harvard University, visiting professor, 1983; University of Chicago, professor, 1983-88; Max-Planck-Institute, visiting professor, 1985; University of California-San Diego, visiting professor, 1986; University of Texas, Department of Mathematics, Sid W. Richardson Foundation regents chair in mathematics and visiting professor, 1987-88, professor; Institute for Advanced Study, distinguished visiting professor, 1997-98. Writer. **Publications:** (With D.S. Freed) Instantons and Four-Manifold Topology, 1984; (ed.) Global Analysis in Modern Mathematics: A Symposium in Honor of Richard Palais Sixtieth Birthday, 1993; (ed. with D.S. Freed) Geometry and Quantum Field Theory, 1995. Contributor of articles to journals. **Address:** Department of Mathematics, University of Texas, 9.160 Robert Lee Moore Hall, 2515 Speedway, 1 University Sta., C1200, Austin, TX 78712-0257, U.S.A. **Online address:** uhlen@math.utexas.edu

UHLIG, Richard. (Richard Allen Uhlig). American (born United States), b. 1970?. **Genres:** Novels, Young Adult Fiction. **Career:** Wilkes University, College of Graduate and Professional Studies, faculty; Gotham Writer's Workshop, staff. Writer. **Publications:** NOVELS: Last Dance at the Frosty Queen, 2007; Boy Minus Girl, 2008. **Address:** College of Graduate and Professional Studies, Wilkes University, 245 S. River St., Wilkes-Barre, PA 18766, U.S.A. **Online address:** author@richarduhlig.com

UHLIG, Richard Allen. See **UHLIG, Richard.**

ULANSKI, Stan L. American (born United States), b. 1946. **Genres:** Environmental Sciences/Ecology. **Career:** James Madison University, Department of Geology and Environmental Science, professor of meteorology. Writer. **Publications:** The Science of Fly-fishing, 2003; The Gulf Stream: Tiny Plankton, Giant Bluefin, and the Amazing Story of the Powerful River in the Atlantic, 2008. Contributor to journals. **Address:** Department of Geology and Environmental Science, James Madison University, 7105C Memorial Hall, Harrisonburg, VA 22807, U.S.A. **Online address:** ulansksl@jmu.edu

ULDRICH, Jack. American (born United States), b. 1964?. **Genres:** Novels, Business/Trade/Industry, Economics, History, Military/Defense/Arms Control. **Career:** Pentagon, policy analyst; NanoVeritas Group, president; Foresight Institute, senior associate; Minnesota Office of Strategic and Long-range Planning, deputy director. Writer. **Publications:** (And ed.) Gibraltar Conspir-

acy, 2000; (with D. Newberry) The Next Big Thing is Really Small: How Nanotechnology Will Change the Future of Your Business, 2003; Into the Unknown: Leadership Lessons from Lewis and Clark's Daring Westward Adventure, 2004; Soldier, Statesman, Peacemaker: Leadership Lessons from George C. Marshall, 2005; Investing in Nanotechnology: Profiles Over 100 Leading Nonotechnology Companies, 2006; Jump the Curve, 2008; Green Investing: A Guide to Making Money Through Environment-Friendly Stocks, 2008. Contributor to Periodicals. **Address:** Amacom Books, 600 Ama Way, New York, NY 10019-7420, U.S.A. **Online address:** jack.uldrich@state.mn.us

ULITSKAYA, Ludmila. Russian (born Russia), b. 1943. **Genres:** Novels, Novellas/Short Stories. **Career:** Institute of Genetics, scientist; Hebrew Theatre of Moscow, repertory director and scriptwriter. Writer. **Publications:** Bednye rodstvenniki, 1994; Medeia i ee deti: povesti, 1996; Veselye pokhorony: povest i rasskazy, 1998; Kazus Kukotskogo, 2000; Pikovaia Dama i drugie: rasskazy, 2001; Devochki, 2002; Skvoznaia liniia: povest, rasskazy, 2002; Iskrenne vash Shurik: roman, 2004; Istoriia o starike Kulebiakine, plaksivoĭ kobyle Mile i zherebenke Ravkine, 2004; Istoriia pro kotalgnasiia, trubochista Fediu i Odinokuiu Mysh, 2004; Liudi nashego tsaria, 2005; Daniel Shtaĭn, perevodchik, 2006; Chelovek popal v bol'nitsu, 2009; Tri povesti, 2009; khochu zhit! Dnevnik sovetskoĭ shkol'nitsy, 2010; Zelenyĭ shater, 2011. **Address:** c/o Author Mail, Schocken Books, Random House, 1745 Broadway, New York, NY 10019-4368, U.S.A.

ULLMAN, Ellen. American (born United States), b. 1950?. **Genres:** Novels, Autobiography/Memoirs, Psychology. **Career:** Computer programmer, 1978-. Freelance consultant and writer. **Publications:** Close to the Machine: Technophilia and Its Discontents: A Memoir, 1997; The Bug: A Novel, 2003; (intro.) Yehudhith, 2004. Contributor to periodicals, books and anthologies. **Address:** c/o Author Mail, Nan A. Talese, Doubleday Broadway Group, 1540 Broadway, New York, NY 10036, U.S.A.

ULLMANN, Owen. American (born United States), b. 1947. **Genres:** Documentaries/Reportage, Biography, Autobiography/Memoirs. **Career:** Elizabeth Daily Journal, reporter, 1969-73; Associated Press, automotive correspondent, 1973-77, labor writer, 1978-81, chief economics correspondent, 1981-83; Knight-Ridder Newspapers, economics correspondent, 1983-84, White House correspondent, 1984-90, State Department correspondent, 1991-93; Business Week, economics correspondent, 1993-94, news editor, 1994-98; USA Today, economics correspondent, 1999-2000, Washington editor, 2000-02, deputy editorial page editor, 2002-04, deputy managing editor, 2004-, senior correspondent, news editor; The International Economy, managing editor; Washingtonian Magazine, contributing editor. **Publications:** Stockman: The Man, The Myth, The Future, 1986. Contributor of articles to periodicals. **Address:** USA Today, 7950 Jones Branch Dr., McLean, VA 22102-3302, U.S.A.

ULLMANN-MARGALIT, Edna. Israeli (born Israel), b. 1946. **Genres:** Sciences. **Career:** Hebrew University of Jerusalem, lecturer in philosophy. Writer. **Publications:** The Emergence of Norms, 1977; (ed.) The Prism of Science, 1986; (ed.) The Kaleidoscope of Science, 1986; (ed. with A. Margalit) Isaiah Berlin: A Celebration, 1991; (ed.) The Scientific Enterprise, 1992; (ed.) Reasoning Practically, 2000; Out of the Cave: A Philosophical Inquiry into the Dead Sea Scrolls Research, 2006. **Online address:** ednaum@math.huji.ac.il

ULMER, Gregory L(eland). American (born United States), b. 1944. **Genres:** Literary Criticism And History, Communications/Media, Education, Film. **Career:** University of Florida, Department of Humanities, assistant professor, 1972-77, associate professor, 1977-85, Department of English, professor, 1985-, Film Studies Program, 1986-89; Lilly Foundation, postdoctoral teaching fellow, 1979-80; Institute for European & Comparative Studies, co-director, 1987-90; European Graduate School, Joseph Beuys chair, professor of electronic languages and cybermedia. Writer. **Publications:** The Legend of Herostratus: Existential Envy in Rousseau and Unamuno, 1977; Applied Grammatology: Post(e)-Pedagogy from Jacques Derrida to Joseph Beuys, 1985; (with R. Scholes and N.R. Comley) Text Book: An Introduction to Literary Language, 1988, 2nd ed., 1995; Teletheory: Grammatology in the Age of Video, Routledge, 1989; Heuretics: The Logic of Invention, 1994; (with R. Scholes and N.R. Comley) Text Book: Writing through Literature, 2002; Internet Invention: From Literacy to Electracy, 2003; Electronic Monuments, 2005. Contributor to books. **Address:** Department of English, University of Florida, 4221 Turlington Hall, PO Box 117310, Gainesville, FL 32611-7310, U.S.A. **Online address:** gulmer@english.ufl.edu

ULRICH, Larry. American (born United States) **Genres:** Environmental Sciences/Ecology, Photography. **Career:** Larry Ulrich Stock Photography Inc., co-founder, 1972-. Writer and photographer. **Publications:** SELF-ILLUSTRATED: Arizona: Magnificent Wilderness, 1987. OTHER: (with W. Clay) Northern California, 1986; Wildflowers of the Rocky Mountains, forthcoming. **Address:** Larry Ulrich Stock Photography Inc., 220 Raven Ridge Rd., PO Box 178, Trinidad, CA 95570-0178, U.S.A. **Online address:** lustock@reninet.com

ULRICH, Laurel. *See* **ULRICH, Laurel Thatcher.**

ULRICH, Laurel Thatcher. (Laurel Ulrich). American (born United States), b. 1938. **Genres:** History, Adult Non-fiction. **Career:** University of New Hampshire, assistant professor humanities program, 1980-84, assistant professor history, 1985-88, associate professor history, 1988-92; Harvard University, James Duncan Phillips professor of early American history and professor of women's studies, 1995-2006, 300th Anniversary University professor, 2006-. Writer. **Publications:** (Co-author) A Beginner's Boston, 1970; Good Wives: Image and Reality in the Lives of Women in Northern New England, 1650-1750, 1982; A Midwife's Tale: The Life of Martha Ballard, Based on Her Diary, 1785-1812, 1990; (with E.L. Thayne) All God's Critters Got a Place in the Choir, 1995; The Age of Homespun: Objects and Stories in the Creation of an American Myth, 2001; Yards and Gates: Gender in Harvard and Radcliffe History, 2004; Well-behaved Women Seldom Make History, 2007. Contributor to periodicals. **Address:** Department of History, Harvard University, Robinson Hall, Rm. 121, 35 Quincy St., Cambridge, MA 02138, U.S.A. **Online address:** ulrich@fas.harvard.edu

ULRICH, Maureen. Canadian (born Canada), b. 1958?. **Genres:** Novels. **Career:** Teacher, 1980-. Author and playwright. **Publications:** Power Plays, 2007; Sam Spud: Private Eye, 2009. **Address:** Lampman, SK , Canada. **Online address:** maureen.ulrich@sasktel.net

UMAN, Myron F. American (born United States), b. 1939. **Genres:** Sciences, Physics, Environmental Sciences/Ecology, Engineering. **Career:** University of California, assistant professor, 1968-73; National Academy of Sciences, associate executive officer, 1973-, project officer and editor; Johns Hopkins University, visiting fellow; George Mason University, adjunct lecturer. Writer. **Publications:** Introduction to the Physics of Electronics, 1974; Issues in the Assessment of the Environmental Impact of Oil and Gas Production in the OCS, 1974; Research and Development in the U.S. EPA, 1977; The Potential for Increasing Production of Natural Gas From Existing Fields in the Near Term, 1978; Controlling Airborne Particles, 1980; On Prevention of Significant Deterioration of Air Quality, 1981; Electric Power From Orbit: A Critique of a Satellite Power System, 1981; Causes and Effects of Stratospheric Ozone Reduction: An Update, 1982; Acid Deposition: Atmospheric Processes in Eastern North America, 1983; Causes and Effects of Changes in Stratospheric Ozone: Update 1983, 1984; Prospectus for an Evaluation of Critical Aspects of the National Pollution Control Program, 1984; (contrib.) Acid Rain: How Serious and What to Do, 1986; The Nuclear Weapons Complex: Management for Health, Safety and the Environment, 1989; (ed.) Keeping Pace With Science and Engineering: Case Studies in Environmental Regulation, 1993; Technical Bases for Yucca Mountain Standards, 1995. Contributor to books and periodicals. **Address:** National Academy of Sciences, 2101 Constitution Ave. NW, Washington, DC 20418, U.S.A. **Online address:** muman@nas.edu

UMLAND, Samuel J(oseph). American (born United States), b. 1954. **Genres:** Film, Biography, Autobiography/Memoirs, Literary Criticism And History, Young Adult Fiction. **Career:** University of Nebraska-Lincoln, instructor, 1982-86, lecturer, 1987-88; University of Nebraska, assistant professor, 1988-91, associate professor, 1991-97, professor of English, 1997-, College of Fine Arts and Humanities, associate dean, 1994-97, interim dean, 1997-98, Museum of Nebraska Art, director, 1998-99, director of film studies program, 1999-. Writer. **Publications:** (Ed. and contrib.) Philip K. Dick: Contemporary Critical Interpretations, 1995; (with R.A. Umland) The Use of Arthurian Legend in Hollywood Film: From Connecticut Yankees to Fisher Kings, 1996; Donald Cammell: A Life on the Wild Side, 2006. Contributor to books and periodicals. **Address:** Department of English, University of Nebraska, Thomas 203B, Kearney, NE 68849, U.S.A. **Online address:** umlands@unk.edu

UMSTATTER, Jack. American (born United States), b. 1950. **Genres:** Education, Language/Linguistics, Young Adult Non-fiction, Art/Art History, Reference. **Career:** West Islip Public Schools, English teacher, 1972-94; Dowling College, adjunct assistant professor of education, 1990-, professor; Cold Spring Harbor School District, English teacher, 1994-, co-chair of department, 2000-, now retired. Writer. **Publications:** Hooked on Literature!: Ready-to-Use Activities and Materials to Spark Students' Interest in Literature, Grades 9 & Up, 1994; 201 Ready-to-Use Word Games for the English Classroom, 1994; Brain Games!: Ready-to-Use Activities That Make Thinking Fun for Grades 6-12, 1996; Hooked on English!: Ready-to-Use Activities for the English Curriculum, Grades 7-12, 1997; Writing Skills Curriculum Library, 1999; Ready-to-Use Sentence Activities, 1999; Ready-to-Use Paragraph Writing Activities, 1999; Ready-to-Use Prewriting & Organization Activities, 1999; Ready-to-Use Revision & Proofreading Activities, 1999; Ready-to-Use Portfolio Development Activities, 1999; Grammar Grabbers, 2001; Hands-on English!: Ready-to-Use Games and Activities that Make Language Skills Practice Fun, 2002; Where Words Come From, 2002; English Brain Stormers!, 2002; Words, Words, Words: Ready-to-Use Games and Activities for Vocabulary Building, Grades 7-12, 2004; Readers at Risk: 160 Activities to Develop Language Arts Skills in the Inclusive Classroom, 2005; Got Grammar?: Ready-to-use Lessons & Activities that Make Grammar Fun, 2007. **Address:** Dowling College, 150 Idle Hour Blvd., Oakdale, NY 11769-1999, U.S.A. **Online address:** jumstatter@aol.com

UNDERDAHL, S. T. American (born United States), b. 1964?. **Genres:** Children's Fiction, Novels. **Career:** Writer and neuropsychologist. **Publications:** The Other Sister, 2007; Remember this, 2008; Summer on Lake Tulaby, 2011; No Man's Land, 2012; The Lost Life of Astrid Jones, forthcoming. **Address:** Adams Literary, Quinlan Lee, 7845 Colony Rd., C4 Ste.215, Charlotte, NC 28226, U.S.A. **Online address:** sjtu1964@aol.com

UNDERHILL, Charles. *See* **HILL, Reginald (Charles).**

UNDERHILL, Lois Beachy. American (born United States), b. 1935?. **Genres:** Biography, Adult Non-fiction. **Career:** Compton Advertising, executive; Saatchi and Saatchi (advertising agency), senior vice president, Cadwell Davis Partners Division, group account director; Sag Harbor Express, columnist. Educator. **Publications:** The Woman Who Ran for President: The Many Lives of Victoria Woodhull, 1995. **Address:** 68 Bay St., PO Box 1645, Sag Harbor, NY 11963, U.S.A. **Online address:** loisunderhill@hotmail.com

UNDERWOOD, Blair. American (born United States), b. 1964. **Genres:** Novels, Mystery/Crime/Suspense. **Career:** Artists for a New South Africa, co-founder, 1989; Intrepid Inc., co-founder. Writer, actor, film director and producer. **Publications:** Before I Got Here: The Wondrous Things We Hear When We Listen to the Souls of Our Children, 2005; (with T. Due and S. Barnes) Casanegra: A Tennyson Hardwick Novel, 2007; (with T. Due and S. Barnes) In the Night of the Heat: A Tennyson Hardwick Novel, 2008; (with T. Due and S. Barnes) From Cape Town with Love: A Tennyson Hardwick Novel, 2010. **Address:** Media Relations, National Broadcasting Company Inc., 30 Rockefeller Plz., New York, NY 10112-0015, U.S.A.

UNDERWOOD, Deborah. American (born United States), b. 1962?. **Genres:** Picture/Board Books, Young Adult Non-fiction. **Career:** Writer and singer. **Publications:** The Northern Lights, 2004; Librarian, 2005; The Easter Island Statues, 2005; Pirate Mom, 2006; Watching Giraffes in Africa, 2006; Watching Orangutans in Africa, 2006; Where Are Your Manners?, 2006; Has a Cow Saved Your Life?, 2007; Colorful Peacocks, 2007; Africa, 2007; Nat Love (biography), 2008; Animal Secrets, 2008; Mexico or Bust, 2008; Safari Adventure, 2008; Australia, Hawaii, and the Pacific, 2008; Graphing the Universe, 2009; Graphing Transportation, 2009; Staging a Play, 2010; Granny Gomez & Jigsaw, 2010; Ballroom Dancing, 2010; The Quiet Book, 2010; A Balloon for Isabel, 2010; (W. Goldberg) Terrible Terrel, 2010; (W. Goldberg) Sugar Plums to the Rescue!, 2011; 101 Ways to Organize Your Life, 2011; Hiding in Forests, 2011; Hiding in Grasslands, 2011; Hiding in Mountains, 2011; Hiding in Oceans, 2011; Hiding in Rain Forests, 2011; Hiding in the Polar Regions, 2011; Hiding in Wetlands, 2011; Loud Book!, 2011; Hiding in Deserts, 2011; Part-time Princess, 2012; Christmas Quiet Book, 2012; (W. Goldberg) Dancing Diva, 2012. SUGAR PLUM BALLERINAS SERIES: (with W. Goldberg) Plum Fantastic, 2008; (with W. Goldberg) Toeshoe Trouble, 2009; (with W. Goldberg) Perfectly Prima, 2010. Contributor to periodicals. **Address:** U.S.A. **Online address:** mail@deborahunderwoodbooks.com

UNDERWOOD, Elizabeth Ann. American (born United States), b. 1961?. **Genres:** Social Sciences. **Career:** Eastern Kentucky University, assistant professor of sociology; University of Illinois, Department of Consumer and Family Sciences, research data analyst, 1992-95. Writer, sociologist and missionary. **Publications:** Challenged Identities: North American Missionaries in Korea, 1884-1934, 2003. Contributor to periodicals and journals. **Address:** Dept. of Anthropology, Sociology & Social Work, Eastern Kentucky University, Keith Hall, Richmond, KY 40475, U.S.A. **Online address:** elizabeth. underwood@eku.edu

UNDERWOOD, Judy K. American (born United States), b. 1946. **Genres:** Trivia/Facts, Medicine/Health. **Career:** University of Northern Colorado, professor; Blue Spruce Associates, psychotherapist, 1982-, life coach, 1999-; Death, Dying and Legacy, co-leader; Centennial Center for Human Services, counselor. Author and speaker. **Publications:** Dying: Finding Comfort and Guidance in a Story of a Peaceful Passing, 2008. **Address:** 515 S Sherwood St., Fort Collins, CO 80521, U.S.A. **Online address:** drunderwood@passingpeacefully.com

UNDERWOOD, Marion K. American/Lebanese (born Lebanon), b. 1964. **Genres:** Sociology. **Career:** State University of New York, Health Science Center, clinical assistant instructor and intern in clinical child psychology, 1990-91; Reed College, assistant professor, 1991-96, associate professor of psychology, 1996-98; University of Texas, School of Behavioral and Brain Sciences, associate professor of psychology, 1998-2005, professor, 2005-, program head, Ashbel Smith professor, Center for Children and Families, interim director, 2008-09, core faculty. Writer. **Publications:** Social Aggression among Girls, 2003; (ed. with L.H. Rosen) Social Development, 2011. Contributor to books and journals. **Address:** School of Behavioral and Brain Sciences, University of Texas, GR 4.118, 800 W Campbell Rd., PO Box 830688, Richardson, TX 75080-3021, U.S.A. **Online address:** undrwd@utdallas.edu

UNDERWOOD, Peter. British (born England), b. 1923. **Genres:** Novellas/Short Stories, Film, Paranormal, Autobiography/Memoirs, Biography, Reference. **Career:** J.M. Dent & Sons, staff, 1945-71, production manager, 1966-71; Society for Psychical Research, research officer, president, 1960-; Constitutional Club, honorary librarian, 1968-74; Unitarian Society for Psychical Studies, vice-president, 1969-; Savage Club, honorary librarian, 1974-79; Ghost Club Society, president; Unitarian Society for Psychical Studies, president. Writer. **Publications:** A Gazetteer of British Ghosts, 1971; Into the Occult, 1972; Horror Man: The Life of Boris Karloff, 1972; Karloff: The Life of Boris Karloff, 1972; A Gazetteer of Scottish and Irish Ghosts, 1973 as Gazetteer of Scottish Ghosts, 1974; A Host of Hauntings, a Shuddersome Book of Ghosts and Ghostly Adventures, 1973; (with P. Tabori) The Ghosts of Borley, Annals of the Haunted Rectory, 1973; Haunted London, 1973; Life's A Drag: A Biography of Danny La Rue, 1974; The Vampire's Bedside Companion: The Amazing World of Vampires in Fact and Fiction, 1975; (with L. Wilder) Lives to Remember: A Case Book on Reincarnation, 1975; Deeper into the Occult, 1975; Hauntings: New Light on the Greatest True Ghost Stories of the World, 1977; Ghosts of North West England, 1978; Dictionary of the Supernatural: An A to Z of Hauntings, Possession, Witchcraft Demonology and Other Occult Phenomena, 1978; Ghosts of Wales, 1978; The Complete Book of Dowsing and Divining, 1980; A Ghost Hunter's Handbook, 1980; Ghosts of Devon, 1982; Ghosts of Hampshire and the Isle of Wight, 1983; Ghosts of Cornwall, 1983; No Common Task: The Autobiography of a Ghost Hunter, 1983; This Haunted Isle: The Ghosts and Legends of Britain's Historic Buildings, 1984; Ghosts of Kent: Authentic Ghost Stories from the Garden of England, 1984; The Ghost Hunters: Who They are and What They Do, 1985; Ghosts of Somerset, 1985; West Country Hauntings, 1986; The Ghost Hunter's Guide, 1986; Queen Victoria's Other World, 1986; Jack the Ripper: 100 Years of Mystery, 1987; Mysterious Places, 1988; Ghosts of Dorset, 1988; Ghosts of Wiltshire, 1989; Exorcism!, 1990; Ghostly Encounters, 1992; The A-Z of British Ghosts, 1992; Death in Hollywood, 1992; Ghosts and How to See Them, 1993; Ghosts and Phantoms of the West, 1993; Ghosts: And How to See Them, 1993; Nights in Haunted Houses, 1994; Peter Underwood's Guide to Ghosts and Haunted Places, 1996; Ghosts of North Devon, 1999; Favourite Tales of the Fantastical, 2000; Borley Postscript, 2002; A-Z British Ghosts, 2002; Ghostly Encounters in the South West, 2003; The Murder Club (novel), 2004; Borley Rectory Companion, 2009; Haunted Gardens, 2009; Haunted Wales, 2010; The Ghost Club - A History, 2010; (with P. Adams and E. Brazil) Shadows in the Nave, 2011. EDITOR: Thirteen Famous Ghost Stories, 1977; Peter Underwood's Favourite Tale of the Fantastical,

2001. Contributor to periodicals. **Address:** c/o Andrew Hewson, John Johnson, Clerkenwell House, 45- 47 Clerkenwell Green, London, GL EC1R 0HT, England.

UNG, Loung. American/Cambodian (born Cambodia), b. 1970. **Genres:** Autobiography/Memoirs, History. **Career:** Vietnam Veterans of America Foundation, staff, 1997-2003. Writer. **Publications:** First They Killed My Father: A Daughter of Cambodia Remembers, 2000; Lucky Child: A Daughter of Cambodia Reunites with the Sister She Left Behind, 2005; After They Killed Our Father: A Daughter from the Killing Fields Reunites with the Sister She Left Behind, 2007. Contributor to periodicals. **Address:** Loung Ung c/o Author Mail, HarperCollins Publishers Inc., 10 E 53rd St., New York, NY 10022, U.S.A. **Online address:** info@loungung.com

UNGAR, Sanford J. American (born United States), b. 1945. **Genres:** Civil Liberties/Human Rights, Law, Politics/Government. **Career:** United Press Intl., correspondent, 1967-69; Washington Post, staff writer, 1969-74; Economist, special correspondent, 1973-86; Atlantic Magazine (formerly Atlantic Monthly), Washington editor, 1975-77, contributor editor, 1977-91; Foreign Policy, managing editor, 1977-80; National Public Radio, program host, 1979-83; American University, School of Communication, dean, 1986-99; Voice of America, director, 1999-2001; Goucher College, president, Department of Communications and Media Studies, professor of communication, professor of history, 2001-; Newsweek, correspondent. **Publications:** (With A.A. Priaulx) The Almost Revolution: France, 1968, 1969; FBI: An Uncensored Look behind the Walls, 1976; Africa: The People and Politics of an Emerging Continent, 1985, rev. ed., 1989; (ed. and intro.) Estrangement: America and the World, 1985; The Papers & the Papers: An Account of the Legal and Political Battle over the Pentagon Papers, 1989; Fresh Blood: The New American Immigrants, 1995. CONTRIBUTOR: In the Name of Profit: Profiles in Corporate Irresponsibility, 1972; Valium Zum Beispiel: Die Multinationalen Konzerne d. Pharmazeut Industrie, 1974; Stop the Presses, I Want to Get Off!, 1975; Great Decisions, 1980, 3rd ed., 1982; The American People and South Africa, 1981; Subject to Solution: Problems in Cuban-U.S. Relations, 1988. **Address:** President's Office, Goucher College, 1021 Dulaney Valley Rd., Baltimore, MD 21204-2794, U.S.A. **Online address:** sandy.ungar@goucher.edu

UNGER, Harlow Giles. American (born United States), b. 1931. **Genres:** Education, History, How-to Books, Self Help, Biography, Reference. **Career:** New York Herald Tribune Overseas News Service, editor, 1956-60; freelance journalist, 1960-; Canadian Broadcasting Corp., radio commentator, 1964-80; Sponsors for Educational Opportunity, vice president, 1965-75; London Times, U.S. correspondent, 1966-72; Sunday Times, U.S. correspondent, 1966-72; Briarcliff College, associate professor of journalism and chair of department, 1975-77; Sarah Lawrence College, Journalism Certificate Program, director, 1976-77; Yale University, Class of 1953 Bequest and Endowment Program, chair, 1985-. **Publications:** A Student's Guide to College Admissions: Everything Your Guidance Counselor Has No Time to Tell You, 1986, (with R.D. Potier) 3rd ed., 1995; What Did You Learn in School Today?: A Parent's Guide for Evaluating Your Child's School, 1991; But What if I Don't Want to Go to College?: A Guide to Success through Alternative Education, 1992, 3rd ed., 2006; How to Pick a Perfect Private School, 1993, rev. ed., 1999; Teachers and Educators, 1994; Encyclopedia of American Education, 1996, 3rd ed., 2007; Learning Disabilities Trap: How to Save Your Child from the Perils of Special Education, 1997; Noah Webster: The Life and Times of an American Patriot, 1998; School Choice: How to Select the Best Schools for Your Children, 1999; John Hancock: Merchant King and American Patriot, 2000; Lafayette, 2002; French War Against America: How a Trusted Ally Betrayed Washington and the Founding Fathers, 2005; Unexpected George Washington: His Private Life, 2006; America's Second Revolution: How George Washington Defeated Patrick Henry and Saved the Nation, 2007; Last Founding Father: James Monroe and a Nation's Call to Greatness, 2009; Lion of Liberty: Patrick Henry and the Call to a New Nation, 2010; Improbable Patriot, 2011; American Tempest, 2011. Contributor of articles to periodicals. **Address:** 200 E 66th St., Apt. E1505, New York, NY 10021-9194, U.S.A.

UNGER, Peter K(enneth). American (born United States), b. 1942. **Genres:** Philosophy, Ethics, Humanities, Politics/Government. **Career:** University of Wisconsin, instructor, 1965-66, assistant professor, 1966-70, associate professor of philosophy, 1970-72; New York University, visiting associate professor, 1971-72, associate professor, 1972-75, professor of philosophy, 1975-. Writer. **Publications:** (Ed. with M.K. Munitz) Semantics and Philosophy,

1974; Ignorance: A Case for Scepticism, 1975, rev. ed., 2002; Philosophical Relativity, 1984; Identity, Consciousness, and Value, 1990; Living High and Letting Die: Our Illusion of Innocence, 1996; All the Power in the World, 2005; Philosophical Papers, vol, I-II, 2006. Contributor to journals. **Address:** Department of Philosophy, New York University, 5 Washington Pl., New York, NY 10003-6611, U.S.A. **Online address:** peter.unger@nyu.edu

UNGER, Roberto Mangabeira. American/Brazilian (born Brazil), b. 1947?. **Genres:** Novels, Economics, Essays. **Career:** Harvard University, faculty, 1969-, assistant professor, 1971-, professor of law, 1976-2000, Roscoe Pound professor of law, 2000; Brazilian Government, minister, 2007-09. Writer. **Publications:** Knowledge & Politics, 1975; Law in Modern Society: Toward a Criticism of Social Theory, 1976; Participação, salário e voto: um projeto de democracia para o Brasil, 1978; Passion: An Essay on Personality, 1984; The Critical Legal Studies Movement, 1986; False Necessity-Anti-necessitarian Social Theory in the Service of Radical Democracy, 1987; Plasticity into Power: Comparative-Historical Studies of the Institutional Conditions of Economic and Military Success, 1987; Politics: A Work in Constructive Social Theory, 1987; Social Theory, Its Situation and Its Task, 1987; A alternativa transformadora: como democratizar o Brasil, 1990; (with C. Gomes) O proximo passo: uma alternativa prstica ao neoliberalismo, 1996; What Should Legal Analysis Become?, 1996; Politics the Central Texts: Theory against Fate, 1997; Democracy Realized: The Progressive Alternative, 1998; (with C. West) The Future of American Progressivism: An Initiative for Political and Economic Reform, 1998; Respuestas al neoliberalismo, 1999; Xian dai she hui de fa lü, 2000; A segunda via: presente e futuro do Brasil, 2001; Politics, 2004; What Should the Left Propose?, 2005; Free Trade Reimagined: The World Division of Labor and the Method of Economics, 2007; The Self Awakened: Pragmatism Unbound, 2007; Left Alternative, 2009. **Address:** Harvard Law School, Harvard University, 226 Areeda, 1563 Massachusetts Ave., Cambridge, MA 02138-2996, U.S.A. **Online address:** unger@law.harvard.edu

UNGERER, Miriam. American (born United States), b. 1929. **Genres:** Food And Wine, Young Adult Fiction. **Career:** U.S. Information Services, U.S. Air Force in Europe, reporter, 1953-57; Women's Wear Daily, sportswear editor, 1958-60; New York Journal-American, fashion and features reporter, 1960-62; New York Herald Tribune, women's features, contributing editor, 1962-64, design research and publicity, 1965-68; freelance writer, 1968-; East Hampton Star, food columnist, 1980-2005. **Publications:** (With T. Ungerer) Come into My Parlor (juvenile), 1963; The Too Hot to Cookbook, 1966; Good Cheap Food, 1973, rev. ed., 1996; Country Food: A Seasonal Journal, 1983; Summertime Food, 1989. Contributor to magazines. **Address:** c/o Robert Lescher, Lescher & Lescher Ltd., 155 E 71st St., New York, NY 10021, U.S.A. **Online address:** goulier@sprynet.com

UNGLAUB, Jonathan. American (born United States) **Genres:** Art/Art History, Literary Criticism And History, Photography. **Career:** Brandeis University, assistant professor of fine arts, 2001-, associate professor of fine arts, chair of medieval and renaissance studies; Columbia University, lecturer; Washington University, lecturer. Writer and art historian. **Publications:** Poussin and the Poetics of Painting: Pictorial Narrative and the Legacy of Tasso, 2006. Contributor to periodicals and journals. **Address:** Department of Fine Arts, Brandeis University, 415 South St., Waltham, MA 02453, U.S.A. **Online address:** unglaub@brandeis.edu

UNRUE, Darlene Harbour. American (born United States), b. 1938. **Genres:** Literary Criticism And History, Biography. **Career:** The Ohio State University, Department of English, instructor, 1965-66, teaching, research assistant, research associate, 1966-70; University of Nevada, assistant professor of English, 1972-76, associate professor of English, 1976-85, professor of English, 1985-96, distinguished professor of English, 1996-; The Katherine Anne Porter Society, president, 1994-97. **Publications:** Truth and Vision in Katherine Anne Porter's Fiction, 1985; Understanding Katherine Anne Porter, 1988; (ed. with intro.) This Strange, Old World and Other Book Reviews, 1991; (ed. with intro.) Katherine Anne Porter's Poetry, 1996; (ed. with intro.) Critical Essays on Katherine Anne Porter, 1997; Katherine Anne Porter: The Life of an Artist, 2005; (ed.) Collected Stories and Other Writings, 2008; (ed. with intro.) Katherine Anne Porter Remembered, 2010. **Address:** Department of English, University of Nevada, Rm. FDH 635, 4505 Maryland Pkwy., Las Vegas, NV 89154-5011, U.S.A. **Online address:** unrued@unlv.nevada.edu

UNRUH, James A(rlen). American (born United States), b. 1941. **Genres:**

Business/Trade/Industry, Economics. **Career:** Fairchild Camera and Instrument, director of corporate planning and analysis, 1974-76, vice president of treasury and corporate development, 1976-79, vice president of finance, 1979-80; Memorex Corp., vice president of finance, 1980-82; Burroughs Corp. (later Unisys Corp.), vice president of finance, 1982-84, senior vice president of finance, 1984-86, executive vice president of finance, 1986, executive vice president, 1986-89, president and chief operating officer, 1989-90, president and chief executive officer, 1990-91, chair and chief executive officer, 1991-; Alerion Capital Group L.L.C., principal, 1998-; Greater Philadelphia First Foundation, vice chair; Franklin Institute, chair; Ameritech Corp., director; Prudential Insurance Co. of America, director. Writer. **Publications:** Customers Mean Business: Six Steps to Building Relationships That Last, 1996. **Address:** 5426 E Morrison Ln., Paradise Valley, AZ 85253-3017, U.S.A.

UNSWORTH, Barry (Forster). Italian/British (born England), b. 1930. **Genres:** Novels, Plays/Screenplays, Young Adult Fiction, Romance/Historical. **Career:** Norwood Technical College, lecturer in English, 1960, 1963-65; University of Athens, lecturer in English for British council, 1960-63; Istanbul University, lecturer in English for British council, 1965-; Liverpool University, writer-in-residence, 1984-85; Lund University, writer-in-residence, 1988; University of Iowa, Writers' Workshop, teacher, 1999, visiting professor; Kenyon College, faculty; Durham University, visiting literary fellow; University of Newcastle, visiting literary fellow. **Publications:** The Partnership, 1966; The Greeks Have a Word for It, 1967; The Hide, 1970; Mooncranker's Gift, 1973; The Big Day, 1976; Pascali's Island, 1980 in US as Idol Hunter, 1980; (with J.L. Cook and A. Gethin) The Student's Book of English: A Complete Coursebook and Grammar to Advanced Intermediate Level, 1981; The Rage of the Vulture, 1982; Stone Virgin, 1986; Sugar and Rum, 1988; Sacred Hunger, 1992; Novels and Novelists in the 1990s, 1993; Morality Play, 1995; After Hannibal, 1997; Losing Nelson: A Novel, 1999; The Songs of the Kings, 2003; Crete, 2004; The Ruby in Her Navel: A Novel of Love and Intrigue in the Twelfth Cenury, 2006; Land of Marvels: A Novel, 2009; The Quality of Mercy, 2011. **Address:** c/o Vivien Green, Sheil Land Associates, 52 Doughty St., London, GL WC1N 2LS, England.

UNTERBERGER, Betty Miller. American/Scottish (born Scotland), b. 1922. **Genres:** History, Military/Defense/Arms Control. **Career:** East Carolina University, assistant professor of history, 1948-50; Whittier College, lecturer, 1950-54, associate professor and director of liberal arts center for adults, 1954-61; California State University, associate professor, 1961-65, professor of history and chairman of graduate studies, 1965-68; Texas A&M University, professor of history, 1968-91, Patricia and Bookman Peters professor of history, 1991-2000, regents professor, 2000-04, professor emeritus, 2004-. Writer. **Publications:** America's Siberian Expedition, 1918-1920: A Study of National Policy, 1956; American Intervention in the Russian Civil War, 1969; American Views of Mohammed Ali Jinnah and the Pakistan Liberation Movement, 1981; Woodrow Wilson and the Russian Revolution, 1982; The United States, Revolutionary Russia, and the Rise of Czechoslovakia, 1989. Contributor to journals. **Address:** Department of History, Texas A&M University, Rm. 101, Melbern G. Glasscock Bldg., PO Box 4236, College Station, TX 77843-4236, U.S.A. **Online address:** bettymu@tamu.edu

UNWIN, Peter. Canadian/British (born England), b. 1956?. **Genres:** Novels, Novellas/Short Stories, History, Young Adult Fiction. **Career:** Writer. **Publications:** The Rock Farmers (short stories), 1994; Nine Bells for a Man (novel), 2000; The Wolf's Head (literary nonfiction), 2002; Hard Surface: In Search of the Canadian Road (literary nonfiction), 2009; Written in Stone, forthcoming. Contributor to magazines. **Address:** Westwood Creative Arts, 94 Harbord St., Toronto, ON M5S 1G6, Canada. **Online address:** dclipper@yorku.ca

UPCHURCH, Charles. American (born United States), b. 1969. **Genres:** Gay And Lesbian Issues. **Career:** Florida State University, associate professor of history. Writer. **Publications:** Before Wilde: Sex between Men in Britain's Age of Reform, 2009. **Address:** Department of History, Florida State University, 401 Bellamy Bldg., Tallahassee, FL 32306, U.S.A. **Online address:** cupchurch@fsu.edu

UPCHURCH, Michael. American (born United States), b. 1954. **Genres:** Novels, Young Adult Fiction. **Career:** Novelist and freelance writer, 1989-; Seattle Times, author, 1989-92, book critic, 1998-. **Publications:** NOVELS: Jamboree, 1981; Air, 1986; The Flame Forest, 1989; Passive Intruder, 1995. Contributor of book and periodicals. **Address:** Susan Golomb, 35 E 9th St., New York, NY 10003-6303, U.S.A. **Online address:** michaelupchurch@comcast.net

UPTON, Martin. British (born England), b. 1933. **Genres:** Agriculture/Forestry, Economics, Business/Trade/Industry, Technology, Money/Finance. **Career:** University of Reading, research agriculturist, 1957-60, lecturer, 1967-78, reader, 1978-88, professor, 1988-, now professor emeritus; University of Ibadan, lecturer in agricultural economics, 1960-66; Queen's University, Belfast, Ministry of Agriculture, economist, 1966-67. **Publications:** (With Q.B.O. Anthonio) Farming as a Business, 1965; Agriculture in South-West Nigeria: A Study of the Relationship between Production and Social Characteristics in Selected Villages, 1967; A Report on the Economic Potential for Irrigation in Botswana, 1969; (with R.S. Cook) Phasing of Milk Production for Maximum Profitability, 1971; Farm Management in Africa: The Principles of Production and Farming, 1973; (with J.I. Wittenberg) Demand for Butter in the Netherlands, 1974; Agricultural Production Economics and Resource-Use, 1976; Success in Farming, 1984; (with D.J. Ansell and C. Bishop) Part-time Farming in Cyprus, 1984; African Farm Management, 1987; (ed. with J.M. Dixon) Methods of Micro-Level Analysis for Agricultural Programmes and Policies: A Guideline for Policy Analysts, 1994; The Economics of Tropical Farming Systems, 1996; (ed. with J. Rutterford and D. Kodwani) Financial Strategy, 2006. **Address:** Department of Agricultural and Food Economics, University of Reading, Rm. 314, New Agriculture Bldg., Reading, BR RG6 6AR, England. **Online address:** m.upton@reading.ac.uk

URAKAMI, Hiroko. Japanese (born Japan), b. 1937. **Genres:** Food And Wine. **Career:** Tsuji Cooking School, instructor and editor of a cooking publication, 1970-73; Teahouse Management School, cooking instructor, 1973-78; Yomiuri Culture Center, cooking instructor, 1979-; University of California, instructor, 1991-92. NHK (Japanese national television and radio network) Culture Center, cooking instructor, 1988-91; Radio Pacific Japan, cooking instructor, 1991-92; Japan Milk Association, consultant. **Publications:** Japanese Family-Style Recipes, 1992. Contributor to newspapers. **Address:** 307 4-30-24 Tokumaru, Itabashi-ku, Tokyo, 175, Japan.

URBAINCZYK, Theresa. Irish (born Ireland), b. 1960. **Genres:** History, Young Adult Non-fiction. **Career:** Blackwell Publishing, staff; University College Dublin, School of Classics, lecturer, senior lecturer, 1992-. Writer. **Publications:** NONFICTION: (ed.) Classics Ireland, vol. I-VII, 1994 -2000; Socrates of Constantinople: Historian of Church and State, 1997; Theodoret of Cyrrhus: The Bishop and the Holy Man, 2002; Spartacus, 2004; Slave Revolts in Antiquity, 2008. Contributor to books and journals. **Address:** School of Classics, University College Dublin, Newman Bldg., Belfield, DU 4, Ireland. **Online address:** urbain@ucd.ie

URBAN, Mark. British (born England), b. 1961. **Genres:** International Relations/Current Affairs, Politics/Government. **Career:** British Broadcasting Corp., assistant producer, 1983, Two's Newsnight, general reporter, diplomatic and defence editor, News, Middle East correspondent, 1993-94; The Independent, defence correspondent, 1986-90. **Publications:** Soviet Land Power, 1985; War in Afghanistan, 1988, 2nd ed., 1990; Big Boys' Rules: The Secret Struggle Against the IRA, 1993; U.K. Eyes Alpha: Inside British Intelligence, 1996; The Man Who Broke Napoleon's Codes: The Story of George Scovell, 2001; Rifles: Six Years with Wellington's Legendary Sharpshooters, 2003; Wellington's Rifles: Six Years to Waterloo with England's Legendary Sharpshooters, 2004; Generals: Ten British Commanders Who Shaped the World, 2005; Fusiliers: The Saga of a British Redcoat Regiment in the American Revolution, 2007; Task Force Black, 2010. **Address:** British Broadcasting Corp., PO Box 1922, Darlington, DU DL3 0UR, England.

URBINATI, Nadia. American (born United States), b. 1955. **Genres:** Philosophy, Politics/Government. **Career:** Columbia University, Department of Political Science, Nell and Herbert M. Singer professor of contemporary civilization, Kyriakos Tsakopoulos professor of political theory and Hellenic studies; New York University, visiting professor; University of Pennsylvania, visiting professor; Scuola Superiore di Studi Universitari e Perfezionamento Sant'Anna of Pisa, visiting professor; Princeton University, faculty, University Center for Human Values, Laurance S. Rockefeller visiting fellow, 2006-07; University UNICAMP, faculty; University of Turin, Department of Political Studies, faculty. Writer. **Publications:** (Co-author) Studi sulla cultura filosofica italiana fra Ottocento e Novecento, 2nd ed., 1982; Le civili libertà: positivismo e liberalismo nell'Italia unita, 1990; (with M. Sabella) Quale fed-

eralismo? Interviste sull'Italia del futuro, 1994; (ed.) Liberal Socialism, 1994; Individualismo democratico: Emerson, Dewey e la cultura politica americana, 1997; (ed. and intro.) On Liberal Revolution, 2000; Mill on Democracy: From the Athenian Polis to Representative Government, 2002; (ed. with M. Canto-Sperber) Le socialisme libéral: Une anthologie: Europe-Etats-Unis, 2003; Representative Democracy: Principles and Genealogy, 2006; Ai confini della democrazia: Opportunità e rischi dell'universalismo democratico, 2007; (ed. with A. Zakaras) J.S. Mill's Political Thought: A Bicentennial Reassessment, 2007; (ed. and intro. with S. Recchia) A Cosmopolitanism of Nations, 2009; Liberi e uguali, 2011. Contributor of articles to periodicals. **Address:** Department of Political Science, Columbia University, 719 International Affairs Bldg., 420 W 118th St., PO Box 3320, New York, NY 10027, U.S.A. **Online address:** nu15@columbia.edu

URCH, Elizabeth. (Elise Brogan). Scottish/Irish (born Ireland), b. 1921. **Genres:** Autobiography/Memoirs, inspirational/Motivational Literature, Theology/Religion. **Career:** Ministry of Aircraft Production, aeronautical inspector, 1941-43; Moyle School, assistant teacher, 1959-66; Larne Grammar School, assistant teacher, 1966-69; Newbigging School, head teacher, 1969-72; Logierait School, Tayside education authority, staff, 1972-86. Writer. **Publications:** (As Elise Brogan) Queen of the Manse: The Musing of a Parson's Wife, 1957; Be Still My Soul, 1964; For God's Sake Watch Your Language, 1977; (ed.) Ladders Up to Heaven, vol. I: Friendship, 1980, vol. III: Sorrow, 1981, vol. IV: Worship, 1981, vol. V: Odds and Ends, 1982; Just Listen to This, 1997; I Forgot to Tell You, 2000. **Address:** Lochalsh, 11 Tomna-Moan Rd., Pitlochry, PH16 5HL, Scotland.

URE, Jean. (Sara McCulloch). British (born England), b. 1943. **Genres:** Romance/Historical, Children's Fiction, Young Adult Fiction, Translations, Novels, Social Sciences, Young Adult Non-fiction. **Career:** Writer, translator, television production assistant. **Publications:** Dance for Two in US as Ballet Dance for Two, 1960; The Other Theatre, 1965; The Text of Love, 1968; If You Speak Love, 1972; Farther Off from England, 1972; Daybreak, 1974; All Thy Love, 1975; Marriage of True Minds, 1975; Had We But World Enough and Time, 1976; Hear No Evil, 1976; No Precious Time, 1976; All in a Summer Season, 1977; Early Stages, 1977; Bid Time Return, 1978; Curtain Fall, 1978; Dress Rehearsal, 1978; A Girl Like That, 1979; Masquerade, 1979; See You Thursday, 1981; If It Weren't for Sebastian, 1982; Proper Little Nooryeff in US as What if They Saw Me Now?, 1982; Hi There, Supermouse!, 1983 in US as Supermouse, 1984; You Two, 1984; You Win Some, You Lose Some, 1984; After Thursday, 1985; Megastar, 1985; Nicola Mimosa, 1985 in US as The Most Important Thing, 1986; A Bottled Cherry Angel, 1986; Brenda the Bold, 1986; The Other Side of the Fence, 1986; Swings and Roundabouts, 1986; The Fright, 1987; One Green Leaf, 1987; Tea-Leaf on the Roof, 1987; War with Old Mouldy!, 1987; Who's Talking?, 1987; Frankie's Dad, 1988; Soppy Birthday, 1988; Trouble with Vanessa, 1988; Loud Mouth, 1988; A Muddy Kind of Magic, 1988; There's Always Danny, 1988; Two Men in a Boat, 1988; Plague 99, 1989; Who's for the Zoo?, 1989; King of Spuds, 1989; Say Goodbye, 1990; Jo in the Middle, 1990; Play Nimrod for Him, 1990; Cool Simon, 1991; Plague, 1991; Bossy Boots, 1991; Dreaming of Larry, 1991; Fat Lollipop, 1991; William in Love, 1991; The Wizard in Woods, 1992; Come Lucky April, 1992; Jam Today, 1992; The Matchmakers, 1992; Star Turn, 1993; Wizard in Wonderland, 1993; The Watchers at the Shrine, 1994; Help It's Harriet, 1994; A Dream Come True, 1994; The Wizard and the Witch, 1995; Fandango!, 1995; Comets Pack: 1, 1995; Harriet Strikes Again, 1996; Comets Pack: 2, 1996; The Great Safe Blag, 1996; Whatever Happened to Katy-Jane, 1996; Has Anyone Seen This Girl?, 1996; Gools, 1996; (ed.) Collins Book of Ballet and Dance Stories, 1996; Children Next Door, 1996; Skinny Melon and Me, 1996; Whistle and I'll Come, 1997; Lucky, 1997; Girl in the Blue Tunic, 1997; Becky Bananas: This Is Your Life!, 1997; Danny Dynamite, 1998; Brave Warrior, 1998; Lucky Pup, 1998; Fruit and Nutcase, 1998; Love Is Forever, 1998; Puppy Present, 1998; Muddy Four Paws, 1998; Foxglove, 1998; Daffy Down Donkey, 1998; Snow Kittens, 1998; Just 16, 1999; A Christmas Tree of Stories, 1999; Secret Life of Sally Tomato, 1999; Honey Bun, 1999; Big Tom, 2000; A Twist in Time, 2000; Chums, 2000; (co-author) The Animals' Bedtime Storybook, 2000; Family Fan Club, 2000; Monster in the Mirror, 2000; Get a Life, 2000; Boys on the Brain, 2001; Shrinking Violet, 2002; Pumpkin Pie, 2002; Daisy May, 2002; Passion Flower, 2003; Dazzling Danny, 2003; Bad Alice, 2003; Dazzling Danny, 2003; Is Anybody There?: Seeing is Believing, 2004; Family Fan Club, 2004; Secret Meeting, 2004; Boys Beware, 2005; Sugar and Spice, 2005; Over the Moon, 2006; Gone Missing, 2007; Hunky Dory, 2007; Friends Forever Collection, 2007; Just Sixteen, 2008; Star Crazy, 2008; Love and Kisses, 2009; Fortune

Cookie, 2009; Ice Lolly, 2010; Galaxy Patrol, 2010; Frankie Foster: Fizzy-pop, 2011. SANDY SIMMONS SERIES: Sandy Simmons and the Spotlight Spook, 1998; Sandy Simmons Star Struck, 1998; Sandy Simmons Saves the Day, 1999; Sandy Simmons Show Stealer, 1999; Sandy Simmons Superstar!, 1999; Sandy Simmons Sweet Success, 1999. FOSTER FAMILY SERIES: Foster Family, 1999; Here Comes Ellen, 1999; Meet the Radish, 1999; My Sister Sam, 1999; Secret Simon, 1999; Babycakes, 2000; Little Miss Perfect!, 2000. GIRLFRIENDS SERIES: Boys Are OK!, 2002; Girls Are Groovy!, 2002; Girls Stick Together!, 2002; Pink Knickers Aren't Cool, 2002; Boys R Us, 2009; Boys Will be Boys, 2009; Boys are Back, 2010; Boys Behaving Badly, 2010. STREETWISE SERIES: Prince Pantyhose, 2003. STEVIE SILVER SERIES: Stage Struck, 2006; Star Light, 2006. GEORGIAN RO-MANCES AS SARAH McCULLOCH: Not Quite a Lady, 1980; A Lady for Ludovic, 1981; A Most Insistent Lady, 1981; Merely a Gentleman, 1982; A Perfect Gentleman, 1982. FRANKIE FOSTER SERIES: Fizzypop!, 2011; Pick 'n' Mix, 2011. TRANSLATOR: (and ed.) Pacala and Tandala, And Other Rumanian Folk Tales, 1960; H. Vernes, City of a Thousand Drums, 1966; H. Vernes, The Dinosaur Hunters, 1966; H. Vernes, The Yellow Shadow, 1966; J. Bruce, Cold Spell, 1967; J. Bruce, Top Secret, 1967; H. Vernes, Treasure of the Golcondas, 1967; H. Vernes, The White Gorilla, 1967; H. Vernes, Op-eration Parrot, 1968; J. Bruce, Strip Tease, 1968; S. Hassel, March Battal-ion, 1970; S. Hassel, Assignment Gestapo, 1971; L. Havas, Hitler's Plot to Kill the Big Three, 1971; S. Hassel, SS General, 1972; S. Hassel, Reign of Hell, 1973; S. Hassel, Liquidate Paris, 2004. Works appear in anthologies. Contributor of articles to periodicals. **Address:** Caroline Sheldon Literary Agency, 71 Hillgate Pl., London, GL W8 7SS, England. **Online address:** jeanure@talktalk.net

URE, John (Burns). British (born England), b. 1931. **Genres:** History, Trav-el/Exploration, Biography. **Career:** Ernest Benn publisher, staff, 1951-53; British Foreign Service, staff, 1956-91, third secretary and private secretary to the ambassador, 1957-59, second secretary in Leopoldville, 1962-63, first secretary in Santiago, 1967-70; Foreign and Commonwealth Office, head of South America department, 1977-79, assistant under-secretary of state, 1981-84; ambassador to Cuba, 1979-81, ambassador to Brazil, 1984-87; ambassa-dor to Sweden, 1987-91; Thomas Cook Group, director, 1991-99; Sotheby's Scandinavia, director, 1991-99; CSE Aviation, director, 1992-94. Writer. **Publications:** Cucumber Sandwiches in the Andes, 1973; Prince Henry the Navigator, 1977; The Trail of Tamerlane, 1980; The Quest for Captain Morgan, 1983; Trespassers on the Amazon, 1986; A Bird on the Wing: Bon-nie Prince Charlie's Flight from Culloden Retraced, 1992; (ed.) Diplomatic Bag: An Anthology of Diplomatic Incidents and Anecdotes from the Renais-sance to the Gulf War, 1994; The Cossacks: An Illustrated History, 1999; In Search of Nomads: An Anglo-American Obsession from Hester Stanhope to Bruce Chatwin, 2003; Pilgrimage: The Great Adventure of the Middle Ages, 2006. Contributor to newspapers. **Address:** Netters Hall, Hawkhurst, KT TN18 5AS, England.

U'REN, Andrea. American (born United States), b. 1968. **Genres:** Chil-dren's Fiction, Translations, Illustrations, How-to Books, History, Picture/Board Books. **Career:** The New Museum of American Art, assistant librarian, 1989; Thread Waxing Space, gallery assistant, 1992-93; Whitney Museum of American Art, office and program manager, 1993-94. Writer. **Publications:** SELF-ILLUSTRATED FOR CHILDREN: White Water Kayaking, 1990; The Canoe Handbook, 1992; Pugdog, 2001; Mary Smith, 2003. Illustrator of books by others. **Address:** Farrar, Straus and Giroux, 175 5th Ave., New York, NY 10010, U.S.A. **Online address:** andreauren@gmail.com

URENECK, Lou. American (born United States), b. 1950?. **Genres:** Auto-biography/Memoirs, Biography. **Career:** Boston University, Department of Journalism, chair; Portland Press Herald, editor and vice president; Phila-delphia Inquirer, assistant and deputy managing editor; Harvard University, Neiman Foundation, editor-in-residence. Journalist. **Publications:** Backcast: Fatherhood, Fly-Fishing and a River Journey through the Heart of Alaska (memoir), 2007; Cabin: Two Brothers, a Dream, and Five Acres in Maine, 2011. Contributor to periodicals. **Address:** University of Boston, College of Communication, 640 Commonwealth Ave., Boston, MA 02215, U.S.A. **On-line address:** lureneck@bu.edu

URQUHART, Brian Edward. American/British (born England), b. 1919. **Genres:** International Relations/Current Affairs, Biography, Social Sciences, Autobiography/Memoirs, Politics/Government. **Career:** United Nations, Preparatory Commission, personal assistant to executive secretary, 1945-46,

personal assistant to secretary-general, 1945-49, Collective Measures Com-mittee, secretary, 1951-53, executive secretary, 1955, 1958, Preparatory Com-mission of International Atomic Energy Agency, deputy executive secretary, 1957, assistant to special representative, 1960, representative, 1961-62, assis-tant secretary-general, 1972-74, undersecretary-general for special political affairs, 1974-86; International Peace Academy, director, advisor; Internation-al Peacekeeping, editorial advisor; Center for UN Reform Education, trustee. Writer. **Publications:** Hammarskjold, 1972; A Life in Peace and War, 1987; Decolonization and World Peace, 1989; (with E. Childers) A World in Need of Leadership: Tomorrow's United Nations, 1990; (with E. Childers) Towards a More Effective United Nations, 1991; Ralph Bunche: An American Life, 1993; (with E. Childers) Renewing the United Nations System, 1994; (with E. Childers) A World in Need of Leadership: A Fresh Appraisal, 1996. Con-tributor to magazines. **Address:** 50 W 29th St., New York, NY 10001, U.S.A.

URRY, James. British/New Zealander (born New Zealand), b. 1949. **Genres:** Anthropology/Ethnology, History. **Career:** British Crown depen-dency, teacher; Australian Institute of Aboriginal Studies, faculty member; Australian National University, senior tutor, 1978-82; Victoria University of Wellington, lecturer, senior lecturer, reader, 1983-; Siberian Mennonite Re-search Initiative, member. Historian, educator and writer. **Publications:** None but Saints: The Transformation of Mennonite Life in Russia, 1789-1889, 1989; Before Social Anthropology: Essays on the History of British Anthro-pology, 1993; Mennonites, Politics and Peoplehood: Europe, Russia, Canada, 1525-1980, 2006. Contributor to books and periodicals. **Address:** Victoria University of Wellington, PO Box 600, Wellington, 6140, New Zealand. **On-line address:** james.urry@vuw.ac.nz

URSANO, Robert J. American (born United States), b. 1947. **Genres:** Medicine/Health, Sports/Fitness. **Career:** Wilford Hall U.S. Air Force Medi-cal Center, intern, 1973-74, resident in psychiatry, 1974-75; Yale University, Yale Psychiatric Institute, postdoctoral fellow, 1975-77; University of Texas Health Sciences Center, clinical assistant professor, 1977-79; Uniformed Ser-vices University of Health Sciences, assistant professor, 1979-81, associate professor, 1981-86, professor of psychiatry and neuroscience, 1987-, head of department, 1992-, Department of Psychiatry, chairman, Center for the Study of Traumatic Stress, director; Georgetown University, National Naval Medi-cal Center, assistant professor, 1980-84, associate professor, 1984-90, pro-fessor, 1990-; Washington Psychoanalytic Institute, Psychoanalytic Psycho-therapy Program, supervisor, 1985-90, teaching analyst, 1989-; Psychiatry, editor. **Publications:** (With S.M. Sonnenberg and S.G. Lazar) Concise Guide to Psychodynamic Psychotherapy: Principles and Techniques in the Era of Managed Care, 1991, 3rd ed., 2007; (with S.M. Sonnenberg and S.G. Lazar) Concise Guide to Psychodynamic Psychotherapy: Principles and Techniques of Brief, Intermittent and Long-Term Psychodynamic Psychotherapy, 2004. EDITOR: (with B.G. McCaughey and C.S. Fullerton) and contrib.) Individual and Community Responses to Trauma and Disaster: The Structure of Human Chaos, 1994; (with C.S. Fullerton) Groups and Organizations in War, Disas-ters and Trauma, 1988; (with Fullerton) Performance and Operations in Toxic Environments, 1988; (with Fullerton) Exposure to Death, Disasters and Bod-ies, 1988; (with Fullerton) Individual and Group Behavior in Toxic and Con-tained Environments, 1988; (with Fullerton, K.M. Wright and J.E. McCarroll) Trauma, Disasters and Recovery, 1990; (co-author) 1992; (co-author) Stress and Coping with War, 1992; (co-author) Stress and Coping with War, 1992; (with Fullerton and B. McCaughey and contrib.) Individual and Community Responses to Trauma and Disaster: The Structure of Human Chaos, 1994; (co-author) Responses to Disasters, Natural and Man-Made and Interventions with Social Supports, 1994; (with A.E. Norwood and contrib.) The Emotional Aftermath of the Persian Gulf War: Veterans, Families, Communities and Na-tions, 1996; (with C.S. Fullerton) Post-Traumatic Stress Disorder: Acute and Long-Term Responses to Trauma and Disaster, 1997; (with C.S. Fullerton and A.E. Norwood) Terrorism and Disaster: Individual and Community Mental Health Interventions, 2003; (with A.E. Norwood) Trauma and Disaster Re-sponses and Management, 2003; (with A.E. Norwood and C.S. Fullerton) Bioterrorism: Psychological and Public Health Interventions, 2004; (co-ed.) Textbook of Disaster Psychiatry, 2007; (ed. with M. Blumenfield) Interven-tion and Resilience after Mass Trauma, 2008. Contributor of articles to books and journals. **Address:** Department of Psychiatry, Uniformed Svcs University of the Health Sciences, 4301 Jones Bridge Rd., Bethesda, MD 20814-4799, U.S.A. **Online address:** rursano@usuhs.mil

URSELL, Geoffrey. Canadian (born Canada), b. 1943. **Genres:** Poetry, Novels, Novellas/Short Stories, Plays/Screenplays. **Career:** University of

Regina, lecturer, 1975-79, special assistant professor in English, 1980-81, 1982-83, instructor of Canadian literature and creative writing; Saskatchewan Writers' Guild, founder, chairman, 1975-76, president, 1976-77; Saskatoon Public Library, writer-in-residence, 1984-85. **Publications:** The Running of the Deer: A Play, 1981; Trap Lines (poetry), 1982; Perdue, or, How the West Was Lost (novel), 1984; Sky High: Stories fom Saskatchewan, 1988; Way Out West! (short stories), 1989; The Look-Out Tower (poetry), 1989; Prairie Jungle (childrens book); Saskatoon Pie!, 1992. EDITOR: (co-ed.) Number One Northern: Poetry from Saskatchewan, 1977; Saskatchewan Gold (short stories), 1982; More Saskatchewan Gold, 1984; (with G. Hyland and B. Sapergia) 200-percent Cracked Wheat, 1992; (with W. Tefs and A. Van Herk) Due West, 1996. Works appear in anthologies. Contributor to periodicals. **Address:** 2226 MacTavish St., Regina, SK S4T 3X2, Canada.

URSU, Liliana. Romanian (born Romania), b. 1949. **Genres:** Novels. **Career:** Pennsylvania State University, Fulbright fellow, 1992, 1997; Bucknell University, Stadler Center for Poetry, poet-in-residence, 2003; University of Louisville, creative writing professor; University of Bucharest, creative writing professor; Romania Culturala, radio producer; University of Texas, professor of literature. **Publications:** Viata Deasupra Oraşului: Versuri, 1977; Ordinea Clipelor: Versuri, 1978; Piata Aurarilor: Poezii, 1980; (ed. and trans.) 15 Young Romanian Poets: An Anthology of Verse, 1982; La jumătatea drumului: proză scurtă, 1986; Corali: Versuri, 1987; (trans. with A.J. Sorkin) Focuri pe apa: 7 Poeti Din Sibiu: Poezii, 1992; Visul, 1995; (trans. with A.J. Sorkin and T. Gallagher) The Sky Behind the Forest: Selected Poems, 1997; (trans. with B. Weigl) Angel Riding a Beast: Poems, 1998; Goldsmith Market, 2003; Lightwall: Zidul de lumină, 2009; Port Angeles, forthcoming. **Address:** c/o Author Mail, Northwestern University Press, 629 Noyes St., Evanston, IL 60208, U.S.A.

URTON, Gary. American (born United States), b. 1946. **Genres:** Mythology/Folklore. **Career:** Colgate University, staff member, 1978-2002; Picker research fellow, 1987; Cornell University, Latin American Studies, research fellow, 1989; Social Science Research Council fellow, 1993; National Endowment for the Humanities fellow, 1994, 2000; MacArthur fellow, 2001-05; Harvard University, Dumbarton Oaks professor of pre-Columbian studies, 2002-. Academic, archaeologist and writer. **Publications:** At the Crossroads of the Earth and the Sky: An Andean Cosmology, 1981; (ed. with A.F. Aveni) Ethnoastronomy and Archaeoastronomy in the American Tropics, 1982; (ed.) Animal Myths and Metaphors in South America, 1985; The History of a Myth: Pacariqtambo and the Origin of the Inkas, 1990; (with P.N. Llanos) The Social Life of Numbers: A Quechua Ontology of Numbers and Philosophy of Arithmetic, 1997; Inca Myths, 1999; (ed. with J. Quilter) Narrative Threads: Accounting and Recounting in Andean Khipu, 2002; Quipu: Knotting Account in the Inka Empire: ExposiciOn, Julio 2003-Abril 2004, 2003; Signs of the Inka Khipu: Binary Coding in the Andean Knotted-String Records, 2003; (comp. and author of intro.) Carlos Radicati di Primeglio, Estudios Sobre Los Quipus, 2006; (ed. with C. Ruggles) Skywatching in the Ancient World: New Perspectives in Cultural Astronomy Studies in Honor of Anthony F. Aveni, 2007. Contributor to periodicals and journals. **Address:** Department of Anthropology, Peabody Museum, Harvard University, 11 Divinity Ave., Cambridge, MA 02138, U.S.A. **Online address:** gurton@fas.harvard.edu

URUBURU, Paula. (Paula M. Uruburu). American (born United States), b. 1957. **Genres:** Literary Criticism And History, Biography, Autobiography/Memoirs, Mystery/Crime/Suspense. **Career:** Hofstra University, associate professor of English, department chair, School for University Studies, vice dean; Arts and Entertainment, consultant; Public Broadcasting Service, consultant; History Channel, consultant; Smithsonian Channel, consultant. Writer. **Publications:** (as Paula M. Uruburu) The Gruesome Doorway: An Analysis of the American Grotesque, 1987; American Eve: Evelyn Nesbit, Stanford White, the Birth of the It Girl, and the Crime of the Century, 2008. **Address:** Department of English, Hofstra University, 204 Mason Hall, Hempstead, NY 11549, U.S.A. **Online address:** paula.m.uruburu@hofstra.edu

URUBURU, Paula M. See **URUBURU, Paula.**

URWIN, Derek W(illiam). Scottish/British (born England), b. 1939. **Genres:** History, Politics/Government, International Relations/Current Affairs, Social Sciences. **Career:** University of Strathclyde, lecturer in politics, 1963-72; Yale University, visiting research fellow, 1969-70; University of Bergen, associate professor of comparative politics, 1972-80; University of Warwick, professor of politics, 1981-90; McGill University, visiting professor, 1973;

University of Mannheim, visiting research professor, 1990; University of Aberdeen, professor of politics and international relations, 1990-, now retired. Writer. **Publications:** (With I. Budge) Scottish Political Behaviour: A Case Study in British Homogeneity, 1966; Western Europe Since 1945, 1968, 5th ed. as A Political History of Western Europe since 1945, 1997; (ed.) Elections in Western Nations, 1945-1968, 1970; (with R. Rose) Regional Differentiation and Political Unity in Western Nations, 1975; From Ploughshare to Ballotbox: The Politics of Agrarian Defence in Europe, 1980; (ed. with S. Rokkan) The Politics of Territorial Identity, 1982; (with S. Rokkan) Economy, Territory, Identity, 1983; (co-author) Centre-Periphery Structures in Europe, 1987; (ed. with W.E. Paterson) Politics in Western Europe Today, 1990; The Community of Europe, 1991, 2nd ed., 1995; Historical Dictionary of European Organizations, 1994; Dictionary of European History and Politics, 1945-1995, 1996; (ed. with P. Flora and S. Kuhnle) State Formation, Nation-building, and Mass Politics in Europe, 1999. **Address:** Oxford University Press, 198 Madison Ave., New York, NY 10016-4314, U.S.A.

URY, Allen B. American (born United States), b. 1954. **Genres:** Children's Fiction, Plays/Screenplays, Novellas/Short Stories, Communications/Media, Film, Horror, Novels. **Career:** Public relations account executive, 1977-88; screenwriter, 1985-; The Writers Network, screenplay analyst and lecturer, 1993-; Fade In Magazine, staff writer, 1995-; The Peterson Group, senior copywriter, 1996-2009; Fantastic Plastic Models, owner; Corinthian Colleges, internet content writer, 2009-. **Publications:** Bites: The Hunt & More Fright with a Bite, 1996; The Hunt and More Fright with a Bite, 1996; Bites: A Fate Worse Than Death & More Fright with a Bite, 1996; Lost in Horror Valley: Novel, 1996; The Living Ghost: A Novel, 1996; Scary Stories for When You're Home Alone, 1996; More Scary Stories for When You're Home Alone, 1996; More Scary Mysteries for Sleep-Overs, 1996; Duh!: Heir Head & Other Stories Even Dumber than Dumb and Dumber, 1996; Fangs!, 1997; Duh!: Brain, Brain Go Away & Other Stories Even Dumber Than Dumb and Dumber, 1997; Crawlers: Home Ick-o-Nomics and Other Tasty Tales, 1997; Still More Scary Stories for When You're Home Alone, 1997; Still More Scary Mysteries for Sleep-Overs, 1997; Even More Scary Mysteries for Sleep-Overs, 1997; Crawlers: The Roaches' Revenge, 1997; Scary Stories for Sleep-Overs: Tomb of Eternity, 1997; Worm Meal, 1998; Grizzly!: Real-Life Animal Attacks, 1998; Scary Stories for Stormy Nights, 1998; Squirmburgers & Other Tasty Tales, 1998; Cobra!: Real-Life Animal Attacks, 1999; Secrets of the Screen Trade: From Concept to Trade, 2005. **Address:** 625 Rhine Ln., Costa Mesa, CA 92626, U.S.A. **Online address:** abu625@aol.com

USABIAGA (IBÁÑEZ), Carlos. Spanish (born Spain), b. 1965. **Genres:** Economics, Adult Non-fiction, Business/Trade/Industry. **Career:** University of Seville, assistant professor, 1989-95, faculty of economics, 1993-94, associate professor of economics, 1995-98, vice dean; Universidad Pablo de Olavide, associate professor, 1998-2003, professor of applied economics, 2003, head of the department, director. Writer. **Publications:** La Nueva Macroeconomia Clasica: el Debate Sobre la Proposicion de Inefectividad, 1993; (with J.M. O'Kean) La Nueva Macroeconomia Clasica: Una Aproximacion Metodologica al Pensamiento Economico, 1994; The Current State of Macroeconomics: Leading Thinkers in Conversation, 1999; (ed. with J.A. Herce and J.F. Jimeno) La Economia Andaluza: Diagnostico y Orientaciones Estrategicas al Inicio del S.CCI, 2001; El Diferencial deDesempleo Andaluz: Analisis Macroeconomico del Mercado de Trabajo Andaluzen Comparacion con el Resto de Espana (1980-2000), 2004; (ed.) Comparacion Entre las Technicas de Simulacion y Prevision Mediante Vectores Autorregresivos y Dinamica de Sistemas, forthcoming. Contributor to books and journals. **Address:** Departamento de Economia y Empresa, Universityersidad Pablo de Olavide, Carretera de Utrera Km. 1, Seville, 41013, Spain. **Online address:** cusaiba@dee.upo.es

USBORNE, Cornelie. British/German (born Germany), b. 1942. **Genres:** History, Women's Studies And Issues, Adult Non-fiction, Politics/Government. **Career:** Open University, tutor and counselor, 1986-89; Roehampton University of Surrey, reader in European history, 1989-95, professor of history, 1995-, now professor emeritus; University of London, Institute of Historical Research, senior research fellow. Writer. **Publications:** The Politics of the Body in Weimar Germany: Women's Reproductive Rights and Duties, 1992, trans. as Frauenkoerper-Volkskoerper: Geburtenkontrolleund Bevoelkerungspolitik in der Weimarer Republik, 1994; Cultures of Abortion in Weimar Germany, 2007; Women under Nazism: Agents and Victims, 2008. EDITOR: (with M. Arnot) Gender and Crime in Modern Europe, 1999; (with W. de Blecourt) Cultural Approaches to the History of Medicine: Mediating Medicine in Early Modern and Modern Europe, 2003; Women under Nazism: Agents and Victims, 2004; Cultures of Abortion in Weimar Germany: The Strategy of Tension and The Politics of Non-reconciliation, 2007. Contributor to books and journals. **Address:** School of Humanities & Cultural Studies, Roehampton University of Surrey, Erasmus House, Roehampton Ln., London, GL SW15 5PH, England. **Online address:** c.usborne@roehampton.ac.uk

USRY, Becky (S.). (Becky Walden). American (born United States), b. 1949. **Genres:** Women's Studies And Issues, Biography. **Career:** Northern Commercial Co., collection manager, 1970-72; Open Door Clinic, administrative director, 1972-73; Mary Magdalene Ministries, executive director, 1980-87; Case Conference, director, 1995-96; Advocates for Victims of Violence, direct services coordinator, 2002-; Prince William Sound Community College, adjunct professor, 2002-; National Hotline for Juvenile Prostitutes, trainer; sociologist. Writer. **Publications:** Sisterhood of the Night: A True Story, 1995. **Address:** c/o Kier & Cottle, Cine-Lit Representations, 7415 181st Pl. SW, PO Box 802918, Edmonds, WA 98020, U.S.A.

USSHER, Jane M. Australian/British (born England), b. 1961. **Genres:** Psychology, Women's Studies And Issues, Medicine/Health, Psychiatry, Sex. **Career:** University of Sussex, lecturer, 1989-91; University College, senior lecturer, 1991-; University of Western Sydney, School of Psychology, Department Health Services and Outcomes Research Group, professor, Women's Health Psychology, chair, 2002-, director of gender, culture and health. Writer. **Publications:** The Psychology of the Female Body, 1989; Women's Madness: Misogyny or Mental Illness?, 1992; (ed. with P. Nicolson) Gender Issues in Clinical Psychology, 1992; (with P. Nicolson) The Psychology of Women's Health and Health Care, 1992; (ed. with C.D. Baker) Psychological Perspectives on Sexual Problems: New Directions in Theory and Practice, 1993; Fantasies of Feminity: Reframing the Boundaries of Sex, 1997; (ed.) Body Talk: The Material and Discursive Regulation of Sexuality, Madness and Reproduction, 1997; (ed.) Women's Health: Contemporary International Perspectives, 2000; The Ongoing Silencing of Women in Families: An Analysis and Rethinking of Premenstrual Syndrome and Therapy, 2003; Premenstrual Syndrome and Self-policing: Ruptures in Self-Silencing Leading to Increased Self-Surveillance and Blaming of the Body, 2004; (ed.) Blaming the Body for Distress: Premenstrual Dysphoric Disorder and the Subjectification of Women, 2004; Managing the Monstrous Feminine: Regulating the Reproductive Body, 2006; The Madness of Women: Myth and Experience, 2011. **Address:** School of Psychology, University of Western Sydney, Bankstown Campus, Rm. 24.3.23, 24 Psychology Bldg., PO Box 1797, Penrith South DC, NW 2751, Australia. **Online address:** j.ussher@uws.edu.au

UTLEY, Robert M(arshall). American (born United States), b. 1929. **Genres:** History, Autobiography/Memoirs. **Career:** U.S. Department of Defense, Joint Chiefs of Staff, historian, 1954-57; U.S. Department of Interior, National Park Service, southwest regional historian, 1957-62, chief historian, 1964-70, assistant director, 1973-77, Office of Archeology and Historic Preservation, director 1970-73; Advisory Council on Historic Preservation, deputy executive director, 1977-80, retired, 1980; freelance writer and consultant, 1980-. **Publications:** Custer and the Great Controversy: Origin and Development of a Legend, 1962; The Last Days of the Sioux Nation, 1963, rev. ed., 2004; (ed.) Battlefield and Classroom: Four Decades with the American Indian, 1867-1904, 1963, rev. ed., 2004; Frontiersmen in Blue: The U.S. Army and the Indian, 1848-65, 1967; Frontier Regulars: The U.S. Army and the Indian, 1866-91, 1973 in UK as Bluecoats and Redskins, 1973; (ed.) Life in Custer's Cavalry: Diaries and Letters of Albert and Jennie Barnitz 1867-68, 1977; (with W.E. Washburn) American Heritage History of the Indian Wars, 1977; The Indian Frontier of the American West 1846-1891, 1984, rev. ed., 2003; High Noon in Lincoln: Violence on the Western Frontier, 1987; Cavalier in Buckskin: George Armstrong Custer and the Western Military Frontier, 1988, rev. ed. as Custer: Cavalier in Buckskin, 2001; Billy the Kid: A Short and Violent Life, 1989; Fort Union and the Santa Fe Trail, 1989; The Lance and the Shield: The Life and Times of Sitting Bull, 1993; (ed.) Encyclopedia of the American West, 1997; A Life Wild and Perilous: Mountain Men and Paths to the Pacific, 1997 as After Lewis and Clark, 2004; Lone Star Justice: The First Century of the Texas Rangers, 2002; (ed.) Story of the West, 2003; Custer and Me: A Historian's Memoir, 2004; Lone Star Lawmen: The Second Century of the Texas Rangers, 2007. **Address:** 7501 E Thompson Peak Pkwy., Ste. 420, Scottsdale, AZ 85255-4537, U.S.A. **Online address:** old.bison@ymail.com

UTTER, Glenn H. American (born United States), b. 1945?. **Genres:** The-

ology/Religion, Politics/Government, Popular Culture. **Career:** Lamar University, instructor, 1969-71, 1972-74, assistant professor, 1974-77, associate professor, 1977-88, professor of political science, 1988-, chair of department, 1992-2010. Writer. **Publications:** (With C. Lockhart) American Political Scientists: A Dictionary, 1993, 2nd. ed., 2002; (with J.W. Storey) The Religious Right: A Reference Handbook, 1995, 3rd ed., 2007; (with R.A. Strickland) Campaign and Election Reform: A Reference Handbook, 1997, 2nd ed., 2008; Encyclopedia of Gun Control and Gun Rights, 2000, 2nd ed., 2011; (with J.W. Storey) Religion and Politics: A Reference Handbook, 2002; (with J.L. True) Conservative Christians and Political Participation: A Reference Handbook, 2004; Mainline Christians and U.S. Public Policy: A Reference Handbook, 2007; Culture Wars in America: A Documentary and Reference Guide, 2010; Youth and Political Participation: A Reference Handbook, 2012. **Address:** Department of Political Science, Lamar University, PO Box 10030, Beaumont, TX 77710, U.S.A. **Online address:** glenn.utter@lamar.edu

UVALIĆ, Milica. Italian (born Italy), b. 1952. **Genres:** Economics, Business/Trade/Industry, Politics/Government, Social Sciences. **Career:** Institute of International Politics and Economics, research fellow and research assistant, 1978-82; European University Institute, Department of Economics, researcher, 1984-88, research fellow, 1989-90, library assistant, 1989-92; University of Perugia, Faculty of Political Sciences, Department of Economics, Finance and Statistics, associate professor of economics, 1992-2002, professor of economics, 2002-, Institute of Economic Sciences, director, 1993-97. Writer. **Publications:** Shareholding in Yugoslav Theory and Practice, 1988; Investment and Property Rights in Yugoslavia: The Long Transition to a Market Economy, 1992; Serbia's Transition: Towards a Better Future, 2010. EDITOR: (with E. Espa and J. Lorentzen) Impediments to the Transition in Eastern Europe, 1993; (with D. Vaughan-Whitehead) Privatization Surprises in Transition Economies: Employee Ownership in Central and Eastern Europe, 1997; (with S. Bianchini) The Balkans and the Challenge of Economic Integration: Regional and European Perspectives, 1997; (with V. Franičević) Equality, Participation, Transition: Essays in Honour of Branko Horvat, 2000; (with D.M. Nuti) Post-communist Transition to a Market Economy: Lessons and Challenges, 2003; (with S. Estrin and G.W. Kolodko) Transition and Beyond: Essays in Honour of Mario Nuti, 2007; (with P.D. Posta and A. Verdun) Globalization, Development, and Integration: A European Perspective, 2008. Contributor to books and journals. **Address:** Faculty of Political Science, University of Perugia, Via Pascoli 20, Perugia, 06123, Italy. **Online address:** uvalic@unipg.it

UVILLER, Daphne. American (born United States), b. 1972?. **Genres:** Novels. **Career:** Time Out New York, books/poetry editor. **Publications:** (Ed. with D. Siegel) Only Child: Writers on the Singular Joys and Solitary Sorrows of Growing Up Solo, 2006; Super in the City (novel), 2009. Contributor to periodicals. **Address:** New York, NY , U.S.A. **Online address:** daphneuviller@gmail.com

UYS, Errol Lincoln. American/South African (born South Africa), b. 1943. **Genres:** Novels, Romance/Historical, History, Politics/Government. **Career:** The Star, reporter and special features writer, 1963-66; The Post, regional editor and chief reporter, 1967-68; Mercury, chief reporter and deputy news editor, 1968-69; Reader's Digest, associate editor, 1969-72, editor-in-chief, 1972-77; writer, 1981-. **Publications:** Brazil, 1986, trans. as La Forteresse Verte, 1987, rev. ed., 2007; Riding the Rails: Teenagers on the Move during the Great Depression, 2000. **Address:** 27 Range Rd., Dorchester, MA 02124, U.S.A. **Online address:** errol1@erroluys.com

UZENDOSKI, Michael. (Michael A. Uzendoski). American (born United States), b. 1968. **Genres:** History. **Career:** Weber High School, Spanish teacher, 1991; University of Virginia, teaching assistant for introduction to anthropology, 1992, Department of Anthropology, teaching assistant for social organization, 1993, grader, 1995, instructor of English, 1993, Department of Academic Affairs, academic tutor, 1999; Nebraska Department of Labor, unemployment claims deputy, 1995-96; Cox Communications, customer care specialist, 1998; Redmond University, instructor, 2000; Florida State University, Department of Anthropology, assistant professor, 2000-06, associate professor of anthropology, 2006-08, Department of Modern Languages and Linguistics, associate professor, 2008-. Writer. **Publications:** The Napo Runa of Amazonian Ecuador, 2005; (with E.F. Calapucha-Tapuy as Michael A. Uzendoski) The Ecology of the Spoken Word: Amazonian Storytelling and Shamanism among the Napo Runa, 2012. Contributor to books and journals. **Address:** Department of Modern Languages and Linguistics, Florida State

University, 308 Diffenbaugh Bldg., 625 University Way, PO 3061540, Tallahassee, FL 32306-1540, U.S.A. **Online address:** muzendoski@fsu.edu

UZENDOSKI, Michael A. *See* **UZENDOSKI**, **Michael.**

UZZI, **Brian.** American (born United States), b. 1960. **Genres:** Novels, Economics. **Career:** Northwestern University, associate professor of sociology management, 1993-, Kellogg School of Management, Richard L. Thomas professor of leadership and organizational change, Richard L. Thomas distinguished chair, McCormick School of Engineering, professor of industrial engineering and management sciences, Weinberg College of Arts & Sciences, professor of sociology, Northwestern Institute on Complex Systems and Network Science, co-director; University of California, Warren E. and Carol Spieker professor, 2008; Administrative Science Quarterly, board director and consulting editor; American Journal of Sociology, board director and consulting editor; American Sociological Review, board director and consulting editor. **Publications:** (Co-author) Athena Unbound: The Advancement of Women in Science and Technology, 2000; (ed. with R. Tzeng) Embeddedness & Corporate Change in a Global Economy, 2000. **Address:** Department of Management & Organizations, Kellogg School of Management, Northwestern University, Rm. 355, Leverone Hall, Evanston, IL 60208-2011, U.S.A. **Online address:** uzzi@northwestern.edu